THE WORLD FACTBOOK

The Central Intelligence Agency (CIA) publishes *The World Factbook* in printed and Internet versions and has placed it in the public domain. In general, information available as of January 10, 2006 was used in the preparation of this edition.

2006 Barnes & Noble Publishing

ISBN-13: 978-07607-8302-3
ISBN-10: 0-7607-8302-0

Printed in Singapore

1 3 5 7 9 10 8 6 4 2

THE WORLD FACTBOOK

STATISTICS AND ANALYSIS FOR EVERY COUNTRY ON THE PLANET

PREPARED BY THE CENTRAL INTELLIGENCE AGENCY

BARNES & NOBLE
NEW YORK

TABLE OF CONTENTS

INTRODUCTION

The World Factbook is prepared by the Central Intelligence Agency for the use of US Government officials, and the style, format, coverage, and content are designed to meet their specific requirements. Information is provided by Antarctic Information Program (National Science Foundation), Bureau of the Census (Department of Commerce), Bureau of Labor Statistics (Department of Labor), Central Intelligence Agency, Council of Managers of National Antarctic Programs, Defense Intelligence Agency (Department of Defense), Department of State, Fish and Wildlife Service (Department of the Interior), National Geospatial-Intelligence Agency (Department of Defense), Naval Facilities Engineering Command (Department of Defense), Office of Insular Affairs (Department of the Interior), US Board on Geographic Names (Department of the Interior), and other public and private sources.

The *Factbook* is in the public domain. Accordingly, it may be copied freely without permission of the Central Intelligence Agency (CIA). The official seal of the CIA, however, may **NOT** be copied without permission as required by the CIA Act of 1949 (50 U.S.C. section 403m). Misuse of the official seal of the CIA could result in civil and criminal penalties.

Comments and queries are welcome and may be addressed to:

Central Intelligence Agency
Attn.: Office of Public Affairs
Washington, DC 20505
Hours: Monday-Friday 8:00 AM-4:30 PM Eastern Standard Time
Telephone: [1] (703) 482-0623
FAX: [1] (703) 482-1739

A BRIEF HISTORY OF BASIC INTELLIGENCE AND *THE WORLD FACTBOOK*

The Intelligence Cycle is the process by which information is acquired, converted into intelligence, and made available to policymakers. ***Information*** *is raw data from any source, data that may be fragmentary, contradictory, unreliable, ambiguous, deceptive, or wrong.* ***Intelligence*** *is information that has been collected, integrated, evaluated, analyzed, and interpreted.* ***Finished intelligence*** *is the final product of the Intelligence Cycle ready to be delivered to the policymaker.*

The three types of finished intelligence are: basic, current, and estimative. Basic intelligence provides the fundamental and factual reference material on a country or issue. Current intelligence reports on new developments. Estimative intelligence judges probable outcomes. The three are mutually supportive: basic intelligence is the foundation on which the other two are constructed; current intelligence continually updates the inventory of knowledge; and estimative intelligence revises overall interpretations of country and issue prospects for guidance of basic and current intelligence. *The World Factbook, The President's Daily Brief,* and the *National Intelligence Estimates* are examples of the three types of finished intelligence.

The United States has carried on foreign intelligence activities since the days of George Washington but only since World War II have they been coordinated on a government-wide basis. Three programs have highlighted the development of coordinated basic intelligence since that time: (1) *the Joint Army Navy Intelligence Studies* (JANIS), (2) *the National Intelligence Survey* (NIS), and (3) *The World Factbook.*

During World War II, intelligence consumers realized that the production of basic intelligence by different components of the US Government resulted in a great duplication of effort and conflicting information. The Japanese attack on Pearl Harbor in 1941 brought home to leaders in Congress and the executive branch the need for integrating departmental reports to national policymakers. Detailed and coordinated information was needed not only on such major powers as Germany and Japan, but also on places of little previous interest. In the Pacific Theater, for example, the Navy and Marines had to launch amphibious operations against many islands about which information was unconfirmed or nonexistent. Intelligence authorities resolved that the United States should never again be caught unprepared.

In 1943, Gen. George B. Strong (G-2), Adm. H. C. Train (Office of Naval Intelligence – ONI), and Gen. William J. Donovan (Director of the Office of Strategic Services – OSS) decided that a joint effort should be initiated. A steering committee was appointed on April 27, 1943 that recommended the formation of a Joint Intelligence Study Publishing Board to assemble, edit, coordinate, and publish the *Joint Army Navy Intelligence Studies* (JANIS). JANIS was the first interdepartmental basic intelligence program to fulfill the needs of the US Government for an authoritative and coordinated appraisal of strategic basic intelligence. Between April 1943 and July 1947, the board published 34 JANIS studies. JANIS performed well in the war effort, and numerous letters of commendation were received, including a statement from Adm. Forrest Sherman, Chief of Staff, Pacific Ocean Areas, which said, "JANIS has become the indispensable reference work for the shore-based planners."

The need for more comprehensive basic intelligence in the postwar world was well expressed in 1946 by George S. Pettee, a noted author on national security. He wrote in *The Future of American Secret Intelligence* (Infantry Journal Press, 1946, page 46) that world leadership in peace requires even more elaborate intelligence than in war. "The conduct of peace involves all countries, all human activities – not just the enemy and his war production."

The Central Intelligence Agency was established on July 26, 1947 and officially began operating on September 18, 1947. Effective October 1, 1947, the Director of Central Intelligence assumed operational responsibility for JANIS. On January 13, 1948, the National Security Council issued Intelligence Directive (NSCID) No. 3, which authorized the *National Intelligence Survey* (NIS) program as a peacetime replacement for the wartime JANIS program. Before adequate NIS country sections could be produced, government agencies had to develop more comprehensive gazetteers and better maps. The US Board on Geographic Names (BGN) compiled the names; the Department of the Interior produced the gazetteers; and CIA produced the maps.

The Hoover Commission's Clark Committee, set up in 1954 to study the structure and administration of the CIA, reported to Congress in 1955 that: "The National Intelligence Survey is an invaluable publication which provides the essential elements of basic intelligence on all areas of the world. There will always be a continuing requirement for keeping the Survey up-to-date." The *Factbook* was created as an annual summary and update to the encyclopedic NIS studies. The first classified *Factbook* was published in August 1962, and the first unclassified version was published in June 1971. The NIS program was terminated in 1973 except for the *Factbook*, map, and gazetteer components. The 1975 *Factbook* was the first to be made available to the public with sales through the US Government Printing Office (GPO). The year 2006 marks the 59th anniversary of the establishment of the Central Intelligence Agency and the 63rd year of continuous basic intelligence support to the US Government by *The World Factbook* and its two predecessor programs.

NOTES AND DEFINITIONS

Abbreviations This information is included in **Appendix A: Abbreviations,** which includes all abbreviations and acronyms used in the *Factbook,* with their expansions.

Acronyms An acronym is an abbreviation coined from the initial letter of each successive word in a term or phrase. In general, an acronym made up solely from the first letter of the major words in the expanded form is rendered in all capital letters (NATO from North Atlantic Treaty Organization; an exception would be ASEAN for Association of Southeast Asian Nations). In general, an acronym made up of more than the first letter of the major words in the expanded form is rendered with only an initial capital letter (Comsat from Communications Satellite Corporation; an exception would be NAM from Nonaligned Movement). Hybrid forms are sometimes used to distinguish between initially identical terms (WTO: WTrO for World Trade Organization and WToO for World Tourism Organization.)

Administrative divisions This entry generally gives the numbers, designatory terms, and first-order administrative divisions as approved by the US Board on Geographic Names (BGN). Changes that have been reported but not yet acted on by BGN are noted.

Age structure This entry provides the distribution of the population according to age. Information is included by sex and age group (*0-14 years, 15-64 years, 65 years and over*). The age structure of a population affects a nation's key socioeconomic issues. Countries with young populations (high percentage under age 15) need to invest more in schools, while countries with older populations (high percentage ages 65 and over) need to invest more in the health sector. The age structure can also be used to help predict potential political issues. For example, the rapid growth of a young adult population unable to find employment can lead to unrest.

Agriculture – products This entry is an ordered listing of major crops and products starting with the most important.

Airports This entry gives the total number of airports. The runway(s) may be paved (concrete or asphalt surfaces) or unpaved (grass, dirt, sand, or gravel surfaces), but must be usable. Not all airports have facilities for refueling, maintenance, or air traffic control.

Airports - with paved runways This entry gives the total number of airports with paved runways (concrete or asphalt surfaces) by length. For airports with more than one runway, only the longest runway is included according to the following five groups - (1) *over 3,047 m,* (2) *2,438 to 3,047 m,* (3) *1,524 to 2,437 m,* (4) *914 to 1,523 m,* and (5) *under 914 m.* Only airports with usable runways are included in this listing. Not all airports have facilities for refueling, maintenance, or air traffic control.

Airports - with unpaved runways This entry gives the total number of airports with unpaved runways (grass, dirt, sand, or gravel surfaces) by length. For airports with more than one runway, only the longest runway is included according to the following five groups - (1) *over 3,047 m,* (2) *2,438 to 3,047 m,* (3) *1,524 to 2,437 m,* (4) *914 to 1,523 m,* and (5) *under 914 m.* Only airports with usable runways are included in this listing. Not all airports have facilities for refueling, maintenance, or air traffic control.

Appendixes This section includes *Factbook*-related material by topic.

Area This entry includes three subfields. *Total area* is the sum of all land and water areas delimited by international boundaries and/or coastlines. *Land area* is the aggregate of all surfaces delimited by international boundaries and/or coastlines, excluding inland water bodies (lakes, reservoirs, rivers). *Water area* is the sum of all water surfaces delimited by international boundaries and/or coastlines, including inland water bodies (lakes, reservoirs, rivers).

Area – comparative This entry provides an area comparison based on total area equivalents. Most entities are compared with the entire US or one of the 50 states based on area measurements (1990 revised) provided by the US Bureau of the Census. The smaller entities are compared with Washington, DC (178 sq km, 69 sq mi) or The Mall in Washington, DC (0.59 sq km, 0.23 sq mi, 146 acres).

Background This entry usually highlights major historic events and current issues and may include a statement about one or two key future trends.

Birth rate This entry gives the average annual number of births during a year per 1,000 persons in the population at midyear; also known as crude birth rate. The birth rate is usually the dominant factor in determining the rate of population growth. It depends on both the level of fertility and the age structure of the population.

Budget This entry includes *revenues, total expenditures,* and capital expenditures. These figures are calculated on an exchange rate basis, i.e., not in purchasing power parity (PPP) terms.

Capital This entry gives the location of the seat of government.

Climate This entry includes a brief description of typical weather regimes throughout the year.

Coastline This entry gives the total length of the boundary between the land area (including islands) and the sea.
Communications This category deals with the means of exchanging information and includes the telephone, radio, television, and Internet host entries.
Communications - note This entry includes miscellaneous communications information of significance not included elsewhere.
Constitution This entry includes the dates of adoption, revisions, and major amendments.
Country data codes see **Data codes**
Country map Most versions of the *Factbook* provide a country map in color. The maps were produced from the best information available at the time of preparation. Names and/or boundaries may have changed subsequently.
Country name This entry includes all forms of the country's name approved by the US Board on Geographic Names (Italy is used as an example): *conventional long form* (Italian Republic), *conventional short form* (Italy), *local long form* (Repubblica Italiana), *local short form* (Italia), *former* (Kingdom of Italy), as well as the *abbreviation*. Also see the **Terminology** note.
Crude oil See entry for oil.
Currency (code) This entry identifies the national medium of exchange and, in parenthesis, gives the International Organization for Standardization (ISO) 4217 alphabetic currency code for each country.
Current account balance This entry records a country's net trade in goods and services, plus net earnings from rents, interest, profits, and dividends, and net transfer payments (such as pension funds and worker remittances) to and from the rest of the world during the period specified. These figures are calculated on an exchange rate basis, i.e., not in purchasing power parity (PPP) terms.
Data codes This information is presented in **Appendix D: Cross-Reference List of Country Data Codes and Appendix E: Cross-Reference List of Hydrographic Data Codes.**
Date of information In general, information available as of January 1, 2006, was used in the preparation of this edition.
Death rate This entry gives the average annual number of deaths during a year per 1,000 population at midyear; also known as crude death rate. The death rate, while only a rough indicator of the mortality situation in a country, accurately indicates the current mortality impact on population growth. This indicator is significantly affected by age distribution, and most countries will eventually show a rise in the overall death rate, in spite of continued decline in mortality at all ages, as declining fertility results in an aging population.
Debt - external This entry gives the total public and private debt owed to nonresidents repayable in foreign currency, goods, or services. These figures are calculated on an exchange rate basis, i.e., not in purchasing power parity (PPP) terms.
Dependency status This entry describes the formal relationship between a particular nonindependent entity and an independent state.
Dependent areas This entry contains an alphabetical listing of all nonindependent entities associated in some way with a particular independent state.
Diplomatic representation The US Government has diplomatic relations with 187 independent states, including 186 of the 191 UN members (excluded UN members are Bhutan, Cuba, Iran, North Korea, and the US itself). In addition, the US has diplomatic relations with 1 independent state that is not in the UN - the Holy See, as well as with the EU.
Diplomatic representation from the US This entry includes the *chief of mission, embassy address, mailing address, telephone* number, *FAX* number, *branch office* locations, *consulate general* locations, and *consulate* locations.
Diplomatic representation in the US This entry includes the chief of mission, chancery, telephone, FAX, consulate general locations, and consulate locations.
Disputes - international This entry includes a wide variety of situations that range from traditional bilateral boundary disputes to unilateral claims of one sort or another. Information regarding disputes over international terrestrial and maritime boundaries has been reviewed by the US Department of State. References to other situations involving borders or frontiers may also be included, such as resource disputes, geopolitical questions, or irredentist issues; however, inclusion does not necessarily constitute official acceptance or recognition by the US Government.
Distribution of family income - Gini index This index measures the degree of inequality in the distribution of family income in a country. The index is calculated from the Lorenz curve, in which cumulative family income is plotted against the number of families arranged from the poorest to the richest. The index is the ratio of (a) the area between a country's Lorenz curve and the 45 degree helping line to (b) the entire triangular area under the 45 degree line. The more nearly equal a country's income distribution, the closer its Lorenz curve to the 45 degree line and the lower its Gini index, e.g., a Scandinavian country with an index of 25. The more unequal a country's income distribution, the farther its Lorenz curve from the 45 degree line and the higher its Gini index, e.g., a Sub-Saharan country with an index of 50. If income were distributed with perfect equality, the

Lorenz curve would coincide with the 45 degree line and the index would be zero; if income were distributed with perfect inequality, the Lorenz curve would coincide with the horizontal axis and the right vertical axis and the index would be 100.

Economic aid – donor This entry refers to net official development assistance (ODA) from Organization for Economic Cooperation and Development (OECD) nations to developing countries and multilateral organizations. ODA is defined as financial assistance that is concessional in character, has the main objective to promote economic development and welfare of the less developed countries (LDCs), and contains a grant element of at least 25%. The entry does not cover other official flows (OOF) or private flows. These figures are calculated on an exchange rate basis, i.e., not in purchasing power parity (PPP) terms.

Economic aid – recipient This entry, which is subject to major problems of definition and statistical coverage, refers to the net inflow of Official Development Finance (ODF) to recipient countries. The figure includes assistance from the World Bank, the IMF, and other international organizations and from individual nation donors. Formal commitments of aid are included in the data. Omitted from the data are grants by private organizations. Aid comes in various forms including outright grants and loans. The entry thus is the difference between new inflows and repayments. These figures are calculated on an exchange rate basis, i.e., not in purchasing power parity (PPP) terms.

Economy This category includes the entries dealing with the size, development, and management of productive resources, i.e., land, labor, and capital.

Economy – overview This entry briefly describes the type of economy, including the degree of market orientation, the level of economic development, the most important natural resources, and the unique areas of specialization. It also characterizes major economic events and policy changes in the most recent 12 months and may include a statement about one or two key future macroeconomic trends.

Electricity – consumption This entry consists of total electricity generated annually plus imports and minus exports, expressed in kilowatt-hours. The discrepancy between the amount of electricity generated and/or imported and the amount consumed and/or exported is accounted for as loss in transmission and distribution.

Electricity – exports This entry is the total exported electricity in kilowatt-hours.

Electricity – imports This entry is the total imported electricity in kilowatt-hours.

Electricity – production This entry is the annual electricity generated expressed in kilowatt-hours. The discrepancy between the amount of electricity generated and/or imported and the amount consumed and/or exported is accounted for as loss in transmission and distribution.

Elevation extremes This entry includes both the highest point and the lowest point.

Entities Some of the independent states, dependencies, areas of special sovereignty, and governments included in this publication are not independent, and others are not officially recognized by the US Government. "Independent state" refers to a people politically organized into a sovereign state with a definite territory. "Dependencies" and "areas of special sovereignty" refer to a broad category of political entities that are associated in some way with an independent state. "Country" names used in the table of contents or for page headings are usually the short-form names as approved by the US Board on Geographic Names and may include independent states, dependencies, and areas of special sovereignty, or other geographic entities. There are a total of 271 separate geographic entities in *The World Factbook* that may be categorized as follows:

INDEPENDENT STATES

(192) Afghanistan, Albania, Algeria, Andorra, Angola, Antigua and Barbuda, Argentina, Armenia, Australia, Austria, Azerbaijan, The Bahamas, Bahrain, Bangladesh, Barbados, Belarus, Belgium, Belize, Benin, Bhutan, Bolivia, Bosnia and Herzegovina, Botswana, Brazil, Brunei, Bulgaria, Burkina Faso, Burma, Burundi, Cambodia, Cameroon, Canada, Cape Verde, Central African Republic, Chad, Chile, China, Colombia, Comoros, Democratic Republic of the Congo, Republic of the Congo, Costa Rica, Cote d'Ivoire, Croatia, Cuba, Cyprus, Czech Republic, Denmark, Djibouti, Dominica, Dominican Republic, East Timor, Ecuador, Egypt, El Salvador, Equatorial Guinea, Eritrea, Estonia, Ethiopia, Fiji, Finland, France, Gabon, The Gambia, Georgia, Germany, Ghana, Greece,Grenada, Guatemala, Guinea, Guinea-Bissau, Guyana, Haiti, Holy See, Honduras, Hungary, Iceland, India, Indonesia, Iran, Iraq, Ireland, Israel, Italy, Jamaica, Japan, Jordan, Kazakhstan, Kenya, Kiribati, North Korea, South Korea, Kuwait, Kyrgyzstan, Laos, Latvia, Lebanon, Lesotho, Liberia, Libya, Liechtenstein, Lithuania, Luxembourg, Macedonia, Madagascar, Malawi, Malaysia, Maldives, Mali, Malta, Marshall Islands, Mauritania, Mauritius, Mexico, Federated States of Micronesia, Moldova, Monaco, Mongolia, Morocco, Mozambique, Namibia, Nauru, Nepal, Netherlands, NZ, Nicaragua, Niger, Nigeria,

Norway, Oman, Pakistan, Palau, Panama, Papua New Guinea, Paraguay, Peru, Philippines, Poland, Portugal, Qatar, Romania, Russia, Rwanda, Saint Kitts and Nevis, Saint Lucia, Saint Vincent and the Grenadines, Samoa, San Marino, Sao Tome and Principe, Saudi Arabia, Senegal, Serbia and Montenegro, Seychelles, Sierra Leone, Singapore, Slovakia, Slovenia, Solomon Islands, Somalia, South Africa, Spain, Sri Lanka, Sudan, Suriname, Swaziland, Sweden, Switzerland, Syria, Tajikistan, Tanzania, Thailand, Togo, Tonga, Trinidad and Tobago, Tunisia, Turkey, Turkmenistan, Tuvalu, Uganda, Ukraine, UAE, UK, US, Uruguay, Uzbekistan, Vanuatu, Venezuela, Vietnam, Yemen, Zambia, Zimbabwe

OTHER

(2) Taiwan, European Union

DEPENDENCIES AND AREAS OF SPECIAL SOVEREIGNTY

(6) Australia - Ashmore and Cartier Islands, Christmas Island, Cocos (Keeling) Islands, Coral Sea Islands, Heard Island and McDonald Islands, Norfolk Island

(2) China - Hong Kong, Macau

(2) Denmark - Faroe Islands, Greenland

(16) France - Bassas da India, Clipperton Island, Europa Island, French Guiana, French Polynesia, French Southern and Antarctic Lands, Glorioso Islands, Guadeloupe, Juan de Nova Island, Martinique, Mayotte, New Caledonia, Reunion, Saint Pierre and Miquelon, Tromelin Island, Wallis and Futuna

(2) Netherlands - Aruba, Netherlands Antilles

(3) New Zealand - Cook Islands, Niue, Tokelau

(3) Norway - Bouvet Island, Jan Mayen, Svalbard

(17) UK - Akrotiri, Anguilla, Bermuda, British Indian Ocean Territory, British Virgin Islands, Cayman Islands, Dhekelia, Falkland Islands, Gibraltar, Guernsey, Jersey, Isle of Man, Montserrat, Pitcairn Islands, Saint Helena, South Georgia and the South Sandwich Islands, Turks and Caicos Islands

(14) US - American Samoa, Baker Island, Guam, Howland Island, Jarvis Island, Johnston Atoll, Kingman Reef, Midway Islands, Navassa Island, Northern Mariana Islands, Palmyra Atoll, Puerto Rico, Virgin Islands, Wake Island

MISCELLANEOUS

(6) Antarctica, Gaza Strip, Paracel Islands, Spratly Islands, West Bank, Western Sahara

OTHER ENTITIES

(5) oceans - Arctic Ocean, Atlantic Ocean, Indian Ocean, Pacific Ocean, Southern Ocean

(1) World

271 total

Environment - current issues This entry lists the most pressing and important environmental problems. The following terms and abbreviations are used throughout the entry:

acidification - the lowering of soil and water pH due to acid precipitation and deposition usually through precipitation; this process disrupts ecosystem nutrient flows and may kill freshwater fish and plants dependent on more neutral or alkaline conditions (see acid rain).

acid rain - characterized as containing harmful levels of sulfur dioxide or nitrogen oxide; acid rain is damaging and potentially deadly to the earth's fragile ecosystems; acidity is measured using the pH scale where 7 is neutral, values greater than 7 are considered alkaline, and values below 5.6 are considered acid precipitation; note - a pH of 2.4 (the acidity of vinegar) has been measured in rainfall in New England.

aerosol - a collection of airborne particles dispersed in a gas, smoke, or fog.

afforestation - converting a bare or agricultural space by planting trees and plants; reforestation involves replanting trees on areas that have been cut or destroyed by fire.

asbestos - a naturally occurring soft fibrous mineral commonly used in fireproofing materials and considered to be highly carcinogenic in particulate form.

biodiversity - also biological diversity; the relative number of species, diverse in form and function, at the genetic, organism, community, and ecosystem level; loss of biodiversity reduces an ecosystem's ability to recover from natural or man-induced disruption.

bio-indicators - a plant or animal species whose presence, abundance, and health reveal the general condition of its habitat.

biomass - the total weight or volume of living matter in a given area or volume.

carbon cycle - the term used to describe the exchange of carbon (in various forms, e.g., as carbon dioxide) between the atmosphere, ocean, terrestrial biosphere, and geological deposits.

catchments - assemblages used to capture and retain rainwater and runoff; an important water management technique in areas with limited freshwater resources, such as Gibraltar.

DDT (dichloro-diphenyl-trichloro-ethane) - a colorless, odorless insecticide that has toxic effects on most animals; the use of DDT was banned in the US in 1972.

defoliants - chemicals which cause plants to lose their leaves artificially; often used in agricultural practices

for weed control, and may have detrimental impacts on human and ecosystem health.
deforestation - the destruction of vast areas of forest (e.g., unsustainable forestry practices, agricultural and range land clearing, and the over exploitation of wood products for use as fuel) without planting new growth.
desertification - the spread of desert-like conditions in arid or semi-arid areas, due to overgrazing, loss of agriculturally productive soils, or climate change.
dredging - the practice of deepening an existing waterway; also, a technique used for collecting bottom-dwelling marine organisms (e.g., shellfish) or harvesting coral, often causing significant destruction of reef and ocean-floor ecosystems.
drift-net fishing - done with a net, miles in extent, that is generally anchored to a boat and left to float with the tide; often results in an over harvesting and waste of large populations of non-commercial marine species (by-catch) by its effect of "sweeping the ocean clean".
ecosystems - ecological units comprised of complex communities of organisms and their specific environments.
effluents - waste materials, such as smoke, sewage, or industrial waste which are released into the environment, subsequently polluting it.
endangered species - a species that is threatened with extinction either by direct hunting or habitat destruction.
freshwater - water with very low soluble mineral content; sources include lakes, streams, rivers, glaciers, and underground aquifers.
greenhouse gas - a gas that "traps" infrared radiation in the lower atmosphere causing surface warming; water vapor, carbon dioxide, nitrous oxide, methane, hydrofluorocarbons, and ozone are the primary greenhouse gases in the Earth's atmosphere.
groundwater - water sources found below the surface of the earth often in naturally occurring reservoirs in permeable rock strata; the source for wells and natural springs.
Highlands Water Project - a series of dams constructed jointly by Lesotho and South Africa to redirect Lesotho's abundant water supply into a rapidly growing area in South Africa; while it is the largest infrastructure project in southern Africa, it is also the most costly and controversial; objections to the project include claims that it forces people from their homes, submerges farmlands, and squanders economic resources.
Inuit Circumpolar Conference (ICC) - represents the 145,000 Inuits of Russia, Alaska, Canada, and Greenland in international environmental issues; a General Assembly convenes every three years to determine the focus of the ICC; the most current concerns are long-range transport of pollutants, sustainable development, and climate change.
metallurgical plants - industries which specialize in the science, technology, and processing of metals; these plants produce highly concentrated and toxic wastes which can contribute to pollution of ground water and air when not properly disposed.
noxious substances - injurious, very harmful to living beings.
overgrazing - the grazing of animals on plant material faster than it can naturally regrow leading to the permanent loss of plant cover, a common effect of too many animals grazing limited range land.
ozone shield - a layer of the atmosphere composed of ozone gas (O3) that resides approximately 25 miles above the Earth's surface and absorbs solar ultraviolet radiation that can be harmful to living organisms.
poaching - the illegal killing of animals or fish, a great concern with respect to endangered or threatened species.
pollution - the contamination of a healthy environment by man-made waste.
potable water - water that is drinkable, safe to be consumed.
salination - the process through which fresh (drinkable) water becomes salt (undrinkable) water; hence, desalination is the reverse process; also involves the accumulation of salts in topsoil caused by evaporation of excessive irrigation water, a process that can eventually render soil incapable of supporting crops.
siltation - occurs when water channels and reservoirs become clotted with silt and mud, a side effect of deforestation and soil erosion.
slash-and-burn agriculture - a rotating cultivation technique in which trees are cut down and burned in order to clear land for temporary agriculture; the land is used until its productivity declines at which point a new plot is selected and the process repeats; this practice is sustainable while population levels are low and time is permitted for regrowth of natural vegetation; conversely, where these conditions do not exist, the practice can have disastrous consequences for the environment.
soil degradation - damage to the land's productive capacity because of poor agricultural practices such as the excessive use of pesticides or fertilizers, soil compaction from heavy equipment, or erosion of topsoil, eventually resulting in reduced ability to produce agricultural products.

soil erosion - the removal of soil by the action of water or wind, compounded by poor agricultural practices, deforestation, overgrazing, and desertification.
ultraviolet (UV) radiation - a portion of the electromagnetic energy emitted by the sun and naturally filtered in the upper atmosphere by the ozone layer; UV radiation can be harmful to living organisms and has been linked to increasing rates of skin cancer in humans.
water-born diseases - those in which bacteria survive in, and are transmitted through, water; always a serious threat in areas with an untreated water supply.

Environment - international agreements This entry separates country participation in international environmental agreements into two levels - *party to* and *signed, but not ratified*. Agreements are listed in alphabetical order by the abbreviated form of the full name.

Environmental agreements This information is presented in **Appendix C: Selected International Environmental Agreements**, which includes the name, abbreviation, date opened for signature, date entered into force, objective, and parties by category.

Ethnic groups This entry provides an ordered listing of ethnic groups starting with the largest and normally includes the percent of total population.

Exchange rates This entry provides the official value of a country's monetary unit at a given date or over a given period of time, as expressed in units of local currency per US dollar and as determined by international market forces or official fiat.

Executive branch This entry includes several subfields. *Chief of state* includes the name and title of the titular leader of the country who represents the state at official and ceremonial functions but may not be involved with the day-to-day activities of the government. *Head of government* includes the name and title of the top administrative leader who is designated to manage the day-to-day activities of the government. For example, in the UK, the monarch is the chief of state, and the prime minister is the head of government. In the US, the president is both the chief of state and the head of government. *Cabinet* includes the official name for this body of high-ranking advisers and the method for selection of members. *Elections* includes the nature of election process or accession to power, date of the last election, and date of the next election. *Election results* includes the percent of vote for each candidate in the last election.

Exports This entry provides the total US dollar amount of merchandise exports on an f.o.b. (free on board) basis. These figures are calculated on an exchange rate basis, i.e., not in purchasing power parity (PPP) terms.

Exports – commodities This entry provides a rank ordering of exported products starting with the most important; it sometimes includes the percent of total dollar value.

Exports – partners This entry provides a rank ordering of trading partners starting with the most important; it sometimes includes the percent of total dollar value.

Fiscal year This entry identifies the beginning and ending months for a country's accounting period of 12 months, which often is the calendar year but which may begin in any month. All yearly references are for the calendar year (CY) unless indicated as a noncalendar fiscal year (FY).

Flag description This entry provides a written flag description produced from actual flags or the best information available at the time the entry was written. The flags of independent states are used by their dependencies unless there is an officially recognized local flag. Some disputed and other areas do not have flags.

Flag graphic Most versions of the *Factbook* include a color flag at the beginning of the country profile. The flag graphics were produced from actual flags or the best information available at the time of preparation. The flags of independent states are used by their dependencies unless there is an officially recognized local flag. Some disputed and other areas do not have flags.

GDP (purchasing power parity) This entry gives the gross domestic product (GDP) or value of all final goods and services produced within a nation in a given year. GDP dollar estimates in the *Factbook* are derived from purchasing power parity (PPP) calculations. See the note on **GDP methodology** for more information.

GDP - composition by sector This entry gives the percentage contribution of *agriculture*, *industry*, and *services* to total GDP. The distribution will total less than 100 percent if the data are incomplete.

GDP - per capita This entry shows GDP on a purchasing power parity basis divided by population as of July 1 for the same year.

GDP - real growth rate This entry gives GDP growth on an annual basis adjusted for inflation and expressed as a percent.

GDP methodology In the **Economy** category, GDP dollar estimates for all countries are derived from purchasing power parity (PPP) calculations rather than from conversions at official currency exchange rates. The PPP method involves the use of standardized international dollar price weights, which are applied to the quantities of final goods and services produced in a given economy. The data derived from the PPP method provide the best available starting point for comparisons of economic strength and well-being between countries. The division of a GDP estimate in domestic currency by the corresponding PPP estimate in dollars gives the PPP conversion rate. Whereas PPP estimates for OECD countries are quite reliable, PPP estimates for developing countries are often rough approximations. Most of the GDP estimates are based on extrapolation of PPP numbers published by the UN International Comparison Program (UNICP) and by Professors Robert Summers and Alan Heston of the University of Pennsylvania and their colleagues. In contrast, the currency exchange rate method involves a variety of international and domestic financial forces that often have little relation to domestic output. In developing countries with weak currencies the exchange rate estimate of GDP in dollars is typically one-fourth to one-half the PPP estimate. Furthermore, exchange rates may suddenly go up or down by 10% or more because of market forces or official fiat whereas real output has remained unchanged. On 12 January 1994, for example, the 14 countries of the African Financial Community (whose currencies are tied to the French franc) devalued their currencies by 50%. This move, of course, did not cut the real output of these countries by half. One important caution: the proportion of, say, defense expenditures as a percentage of GDP in local currency accounts may differ substantially from the proportion when GDP accounts are expressed in PPP terms, as, for example, when an observer tries to estimate the dollar level of Russian or Japanese military expenditures. Note: the numbers for GDP and other economic data cannot be chained together from successive volumes of the *Factbook* because of changes in the US dollar measuring rod, revisions of data by statistical agencies, use of new or different sources of information, and changes in national statistical methods and practices.

GNP Gross national product (GNP) is the value of all final goods and services produced within a nation in a given year, plus income earned by its citizens abroad, minus income earned by foreigners from domestic production. The *Factbook*, following current practice, uses GDP rather than GNP to measure national production. However, the user must realize that in certain countries net remittances from citizens working abroad may be important to national well-being.

GWP This entry gives the gross world product (GWP) or aggregate value of all final goods and services produced worldwide in a given year.

Geographic coordinates This entry includes rounded latitude and longitude figures for the purpose of finding the approximate geographic center of an entity and is based on the Gazetteer of Conventional Names, Third Edition, August 1988, US Board on Geographic Names and on other sources.

Geographic names This information is presented in **Appendix F: Cross-Reference List of Geographic Names.** It includes a listing of various alternate names, former names, local names, and regional names referenced to one or more related *Factbook* entries. Spellings are normally, but not always, those approved by the US Board on Geographic Names (BGN). Alternate names and additional information are included in parentheses.

Geography This category includes the entries dealing with the natural environment and the effects of human activity.

Geography – note This entry includes miscellaneous geographic information of significance not included elsewhere.

Gini index See entry for **Distribution of family income - Gini index**

Government This category includes the entries dealing with the system for the adoption and administration of public policy.

Government – note This entry includes miscellaneous government information of significance not included elsewhere.

Government type This entry gives the basic form of government. Definitions of the major governmental terms are as follows:

Anarchy - a condition of lawlessness or political disorder brought about by the absence of governmental authority.

Commonwealth - a nation, state, or other political entity founded on law and united by a compact of the people for the common good.

Communism - a system of government in which the state plans and controls the economy and a single - often authoritarian - party holds power; state controls are imposed with the elimination of private ownership of property or capital while claiming to make progress toward a higher social order in which all goods are equally shared by the people (i.e., a classless society).

Confederacy (Confederation) - a union by compact or treaty between states, provinces, or territories, that creates a central government with limited powers; the constituent entities retain supreme authority over all matters except those delegated to the central government.

Constitutional - a government by or operating under an authoritative document (constitution) that sets forth the system of fundamental laws and principles that determines the nature, functions, and limits of that government.

Constitutional democracy - a form of government in which the sovereign power of the people is spelled out in a governing constitution.

Constitutional monarchy - a system of government in which a monarch is guided by a constitution whereby his/her rights, duties, and responsibilities are spelled out in written law or by custom.
Democracy - a form of government in which the supreme power is retained by the people, but which is usually exercised indirectly through a system of representation and delegated authority periodically renewed.
Democratic republic - a state in which the supreme power rests in the body of citizens entitled to vote for officers and representatives responsible to them.
Dictatorship - a form of government in which a ruler or small clique wield absolute power (not restricted by a constitution or laws).
Ecclesiastical - a government administrated by a church.
Federal (Federative) - a form of government in which sovereign power is formally divided - usually by means of a constitution - between a central authority and a number of constituent regions (states, colonies, or provinces) so that each region retains some management of its internal affairs; differs from a confederacy in that the central government exerts influence directly upon both individuals as well as upon the regional units.
Federal republic - a state in which the powers of the central government are restricted and in which the component parts (states, colonies, or provinces) retain a degree of self-government; ultimate sovereign power rests with the voters who chose their governmental representatives.
Maoism - the theory and practice of Marxism-Leninism developed in China by Mao Zedong (Mao Tse-tung), which states that a continuous revolution is necessary if the leaders of a communist state are to keep in touch with the people.
Marxism - the political, economic, and social principles espoused by 19th century economist Karl Marx; he viewed the struggle of workers as a progression of historical forces that would proceed from a class struggle of the proletariat (workers) exploited by capitalists (business owners), to a socialist "dictatorship of the proletariat," to, finally, a classless society - communism.
Marxism-Leninism - an expanded form of communism developed by Lenin from doctrines of Karl Marx; Lenin saw imperialism as the final stage of capitalism and shifted the focus of workers' struggle from developed to underdeveloped countries.
Monarchy - a government in which the supreme power is lodged in the hands of a monarch who reigns over a state or territory, usually for life and by hereditary right; the monarch may be either a sole absolute ruler or a sovereign - such as a king, queen, or prince - with constitutionally limited authority.
Oligarchy - a government in which control is exercised by a small group of individuals whose authority generally is based on wealth or power.
Parliamentary democracy - a political system in which the legislature (parliament) selects the government - a prime minister, premier, or chancellor along with the cabinet ministers - according to party strength as expressed in elections; by this system, the government acquires a dual responsibility: to the people as well as to the parliament.
Parliamentary government (Cabinet-Parliamentary government) - a government in which members of an executive branch (the cabinet and its leader - a prime minister, premier, or chancellor) are nominated to their positions by a legislature or parliament, and are directly responsible to it; this type of government can be dissolved at will by the parliament (legislature) by means of a no confidence vote or the leader of the cabinet may dissolve the parliament if it can no longer function.
Parliamentary monarchy - a state headed by a monarch who is not actively involved in policy formation or implementation (i.e., the exercise of sovereign powers by a monarch in a ceremonial capacity); true governmental leadership is carried out by a cabinet and its head - a prime minister, premier, or chancellor - who are drawn from a legislature (parliament).
Republic - a representative democracy in which the people's elected deputies (representatives), not the people themselves, vote on legislation.
Socialism - a government in which the means of planning, producing, and distributing goods is controlled by a central government that theoretically seeks a more just and equitable distribution of property and labor; in actuality, most socialist governments have ended up being no more than dictatorships over workers by a ruling elite.
Sultanate - similar to a monarchy, but a government in which the supreme power is in the hands of a sultan (the head of a Muslim state); the sultan may be an absolute ruler or a sovereign with constitutionally limited authority.
Theocracy - a form of government in which a Deity is recognized as the supreme civil ruler, but the Deity's laws are interpreted by ecclesiastical authorities (bishops, mullahs, etc.); a government subject to religious authority.
Totalitarian - a government that seeks to subordinate the individual to the state by controlling not only all political and economic matters, but also the attitudes, values, and beliefs of its population.

Gross domestic product see **GDP**
Gross national product see **GNP**
Gross world product see **GWP**
HIV/AIDS - adult prevalence rate This entry gives an estimate of the percentage of adults (aged 15-49) living with HIV/AIDS. The adult prevalence rate is calculated by dividing the estimated number of adults living with HIV/AIDS at yearend by the total adult population at yearend.
HIV/AIDS – deaths This entry gives an estimate of the number of adults and children who died of AIDS during a given calendar year.
HIV/AIDS - people living with HIV/AIDS This entry gives an estimate of all people (adults and children) alive at yearend with HIV infection, whether or not they have developed symptoms of AIDS.
Heliports This entry gives the total number of heliports with hard-surface runways, helipads, or landing areas that support routine sustained helicopter operations exclusively and have support facilities including one or more of the following facilities: lighting, fuel, passenger handling, or maintenance. It includes former airports used exclusively for helicopter operations but excludes heliports limited to day operations and natural clearings that could support helicopter landings and takeoffs.
Highways This entry states the total length of the highway system and the length of the paved and unpaved parts.
Household income or consumption by percentage share Data on household income or consumption come from household surveys, the results adjusted for household size. Nations use different standards and procedures in collecting and adjusting the data. Surveys based on income will normally show a more unequal distribution than surveys based on consumption. The quality of surveys is improving with time, yet caution is still necessary in making inter-country comparisons.
Hydrographic data codes see **Data codes**
Illicit drugs This entry gives information on the five categories of illicit drugs - narcotics, stimulants, depressants (sedatives), hallucinogens, and cannabis. These categories include many drugs legally produced and prescribed by doctors as well as those illegally produced and sold outside of medical channels.

Cannabis (Cannabis sativa) is the common hemp plant, which provides hallucinogens with some sedative properties, and includes marijuana (pot, Acapulco gold, grass, reefer), tetrahydrocannabinol (THC, Marinol), hashish (hash), and hashish oil (hash oil).

Coca (mostly Erythroxylum coca) is a bush with leaves that contain the stimulant used to make cocaine. Coca is not to be confused with cocoa, which comes from cacao seeds and is used in making chocolate, cocoa, and cocoa butter.

Cocaine is a stimulant derived from the leaves of the coca bush.

Depressants (sedatives) are drugs that reduce tension and anxiety and include chloral hydrate, barbiturates (Amytal, Nembutal, Seconal, phenobarbital), benzodiazepines (Librium, Valium), methaqualone (Quaalude), glutethimide (Doriden), and others (Equanil, Placidyl, Valmid).

Drugs are any chemical substances that effect a physical, mental, emotional, or behavioral change in an individual.

Drug abuse is the use of any licit or illicit chemical substance that results in physical, mental, emotional, or behavioral impairment in an individual.

Hallucinogens are drugs that affect sensation, thinking, self-awareness, and emotion. Hallucinogens include LSD (acid, microdot), mescaline and peyote (mexc, buttons, cactus), amphetamine variants (PMA, STP, DOB), phencyclidine (PCP, angel dust, hog), phencyclidine analogues (PCE, PCPy, TCP), and others (psilocybin, psilocyn).

Hashish is the resinous exudate of the cannabis or hemp plant (Cannabis sativa).

Heroin is a semisynthetic derivative of morphine.

Mandrax is a trade name for methaqualone, a pharmaceutical depressant.

Marijuana is the dried leaf of the cannabis or hemp plant (Cannabis sativa).

Methaqualone is a pharmaceutical depressant, referred to as mandrax in Southwest Asia and Africa.

Narcotics are drugs that relieve pain, often induce sleep, and refer to opium, opium derivatives, and synthetic substitutes. Natural narcotics include opium (paregoric, parepectolin), morphine (MS-Contin, Roxanol), codeine (Tylenol with codeine, Empirin with codeine, Robitussan AC), and thebaine. Semisynthetic narcotics include heroin (horse, smack), and hydromorphone (Dilaudid). Synthetic *narcotics* include meperidine or Pethidine (Demerol, Mepergan), methadone (Dolophine, Methadose), and others (Darvon, Lomotil).

Opium is the brown, gummy exudate of the incised, unripe seedpod of the opium poppy.

Opium poppy (Papaver somniferum) is the source for the natural and semisynthetic narcotics.

Poppy straw is the entire cut and dried opium poppy-plant material, other than the seeds. Opium is extracted from poppy straw in commercial operations that produce the drug for medical use.

Qat (kat, khat) is a stimulant from the buds or leaves of Catha edulis that is chewed or drunk as tea.

Quaaludes is the North American slang term for methaqualone, a pharmaceutical depressant.

Stimulants are drugs that relieve mild depression, increase energy and activity, and include cocaine (coke, snow, crack), amphetamines (Desoxyn, Dexedrine), ephedrine, ecstasy (clarity, essence, doctor, Adam), phenmetrazine (Preludin), methylphenidate (Ritalin), and others (Cylert, Sanorex, Tenuate).

Imports This entry provides the total US dollar amount of merchandise imports on a c.i.f. (cost, insurance, and freight) or f.o.b. (free on board) basis. These figures are calculated on an exchange rate basis, i.e., not in purchasing power parity (PPP) terms.

Imports - commodities This entry provides a rank ordering of imported products starting with the most important; it sometimes includes the percent of total dollar value.

Imports - partners This entry provides a rank ordering of trading partners starting with the most important; it sometimes includes the percent of total dollar value.

Independence For most countries, this entry gives the date that sovereignty was achieved and from which nation, empire, or trusteeship. For the other countries, the date given may not represent "independence" in the strict sense, but rather some significant nationhood event such as the traditional founding date or the date of unification, federation, confederation, establishment, fundamental change in the form of government, or state succession. Dependent areas include the notation "none" followed by the nature of their dependency status. Also see the **Terminology** note.

Industrial production growth rate This entry gives the annual percentage increase in industrial production (includes manufacturing, mining, and construction).

Industries This entry provides a rank ordering of industries starting with the largest by value of annual output.

Infant mortality rate This entry gives the number of deaths of infants under one year old in a given year per 1,000 live births in the same year; included is the total death rate, and deaths by sex, *male* and *female*. This rate is often used as an indicator of the level of health in a country.

Inflation rate (consumer prices) This entry furnishes the annual percent change in consumer prices compared with the previous year's consumer prices.

International disputes see **Disputes - international**

International organization participation This entry lists in alphabetical order by abbreviation those international organizations in which the subject country is a member or participates in some other way.

International organizations This information is presented in **Appendix B: International Organizations and Groups** which includes the name, abbreviation, date established, aim, and members by category.

Internet country code This entry includes the two-letter codes maintained by the International Organization for Standardization (ISO) in the ISO 3166 Alpha-2 list and used by the Internet Assigned Numbers Authority (IANA) to establish country-coded top-level domains (ccTLDs).

Internet hosts This entry lists the number of Internet hosts available within a country. An Internet host is a computer connected directly to the Internet; normally an Internet Service Provider's (ISP) computer is a host. Internet users may use either a hard-wired terminal, at an institution with a mainframe computer connected directly to the Internet, or may connect remotely by way of a modem via telephone line, cable, or satellite to the Internet Service Provider's host computer. The number of hosts is one indicator of the extent of Internet connectivity.

Internet users This entry gives the number of users within a country that access the Internet. Statistics vary from country to country and may include users who access the Internet at least several times a week to those who access it only once within a period of several months.

Introduction This category includes one entry, **Background.**

Investment (gross fixed) This entry records total business spending on fixed assets, such as factories, machinery, equipment, dwellings, and inventories of raw materials, which provide the basis for future production. It is measured gross of the depreciation of the assets, i.e., it includes investment that merely replaces worn-out or scrapped capital.

Irrigated land This entry gives the number of square kilometers of land area that is artificially supplied with water.

Judicial branch This entry contains the name(s) of the highest court(s) and a brief description of the selection process for members.

Labor force This entry contains the total labor force figure.

Labor force - by occupation This entry lists the percentage distribution of the labor force by occupation. The distribution will total less than 100 percent if the data are incomplete.

Land boundaries This entry contains the *total* length of all land boundaries and the individual lengths for each of the contiguous *border countries*.

Land use This entry contains the percentage shares of total land area for three different types of land use: *arable land* - land cultivated for crops like wheat, maize, and rice that are replanted after each harvest; *permanent crops* - land cultivated for crops like citrus, coffee, and rubber that are not replanted after each harvest; includes land under flowering shrubs, fruit trees, nut trees, and vines, but excludes land under trees grown for wood or timber; *other* - any land not arable or under permanent crops; includes permanent meadows and pastures, forests and woodlands, built-on areas, roads, barren land, etc.

Languages This entry provides a rank ordering of languages starting with the largest and sometimes includes the percent of total population speaking that language.

Legal system This entry contains a brief description of the legal system's historical roots, role in government, and acceptance of International Court of Justice (ICJ) jurisdiction.

Legislative branch This entry contains information on the structure (unicameral, bicameral, tricameral), formal name, number of seats, and term of office. *Elections* includes the nature of election process or accession to power, date of the last election, and date of the next election. *Election results* includes the percent of vote and/or number of seats held by each party in the last election.

Life expectancy at birth This entry contains the average number of years to be lived by a group of people born in the same year, if mortality at each age remains constant in the future. The entry includes *total population* as well as the *male* and *female* components. Life expectancy at birth is also a measure of overall quality of life in a country and summarizes the mortality at all ages. It can also be thought of as indicating the potential return on investment in human capital and is necessary for the calculation of various actuarial measures.

Literacy This entry includes a *definition* of literacy and Census Bureau percentages for the *total population, males,* and *females*. There are no universal definitions and standards of literacy. Unless otherwise specified, all rates are based on the most common definition - the ability to read and write at a specified age. Detailing the standards that individual countries use to assess the ability to read and write is beyond the scope of the *Factbook*. Information on literacy, while not a perfect measure of educational results, is probably the most easily available and valid for international comparisons. Low levels of literacy, and education in general, can impede the economic development of a country in the current rapidly changing, technology-driven world.

Location This entry identifies the country's regional location, neighboring countries, and adjacent bodies of water.

Major infectious diseases This entry lists major infectious diseases likely to be encountered in countries where the risk of such diseases is assessed to be very high as compared to the United States. These infectious diseases represent risks to US government personnel traveling to the specified country for a period of less than three years. The **degree of risk** is assessed by considering the foreign nature of these infectious diseases, their severity, and the probability of being affected by the diseases present. The diseases listed do not necessarily represent the total disease burden experienced by the local population. The risk to an individual traveler varies considerably by the specific location, visit duration, type of activities, type of accommodations, time of year, and other factors. Consultation with a travel medicine physician is needed to evaluate individual risk and recommend appropriate preventive measures such as vaccines. Diseases are organized into the following six exposure categories shown in bold *and listed in typical descending order of risk*. Note - The sequence of exposure categories listed in individual country entries may vary according to local conditions.

food or waterborne diseases acquired through eating or drinking on the local economy:

Hepatitis A - viral disease that interferes with the functioning of the liver; spread through consumption of food or water contaminated with fecal matter, principally in areas of poor sanitation; victims exhibit fever, jaundice, and diarrhea; 15% of victims will experience prolonged symptoms over 6-9 months; vaccine available.

Hepatitis E - water-borne viral disease that interferes with the functioning of the liver; most commonly spread through fecal contamination of drinking water; victims exhibit jaundice, fatigue, abdominal pain, and dark colored urine.

Typhoid fever - bacterial disease spread through contact with food or water contaminated by fecal matter or sewage; victims exhibit sustained high fevers; left untreated, mortality rates can reach 20%.

vectorborne diseases acquired through the bite of an infected arthropod:

Malaria - caused by single-cell parasitic protozoa *Plasmodium*; transmitted to humans via the bite of the female Anopheles mosquito; parasites multiply in the liver attacking red blood cells resulting in cycles of fever, chills, and sweats accompanied by anemia; death due to damage to vital organs and interruption of blood supply to the brain; endemic in 100, mostly tropical, countries with 90% of cases and the majority of 1.5-2.5 million estimated annual deaths occurring in sub-Saharan Africa.

Dengue fever - mosquito-borne (*Aedes aegypti*) viral disease associated with urban environments; manifests as sudden onset of fever and severe headache; occasionally produces shock and hemorrhage leading to death in 5% of cases.

Yellow fever - mosquito-borne viral disease; severity ranges from influenza-like symptoms to severe hepatitis and hemorrhagic fever; occurs only in tropical South America and sub-Saharan Africa, where most cases are reported; fatality rate is less than 20%.

Japanese Encephalitis - mosquito-borne (*Culex tritaeniorhynchus*) viral disease associated with rural areas in Asia; acute encephalitis can progress to paralysis, coma, and death; fatality rates 30%.

African Trypanosomiasis - caused by the parasitic protozoa *Trypanosoma*; transmitted to humans via the bite of bloodsucking Tsetse flies; infection leads to malaise and irregular fevers and, in advanced cases when the parasites invade the central nervous system, coma and death; endemic in 36 countries of sub-Saharan Africa; cattle and wild animals act as reservoir hosts for the parasites.

Cutaneous Leishmaniasis - caused by the parasitic protozoa *leishmania*; transmitted to humans via the bite of sandflies; results in skin lesions that may become chronic; endemic in 88 countries; 90% of cases occur in Iran, Afghanistan, Syria, Saudi Arabia, Brazil, and Peru; wild and domesticated animals as well as humans can act as reservoirs of infection.

Plague - bacterial disease transmitted by fleas normally associated with rats; person-to-person airborne transmission also possible; recent plague epidemics occurred in areas of Asia, Africa, and South America associated with rural areas or small towns and villages; manifests as fever, headache, and painfully swollen lymph nodes; disease progresses rapidly and without antibiotic treatment leads to pneumonic form with a death rate in excess of 50%.

Crimean-Congo hemorrhagic fever - tick-borne viral disease; infection may also result from exposure to infected animal blood or tissue; geographic distribution includes Africa, Asia, the Middle East, and Eastern Europe; sudden onset of fever, headache, and muscle aches followed by hemorrhaging in the bowels, urine, nose, and gums; mortality rate is approximately 30%.

Rift Valley fever - viral disease affecting domesticated animals and humans; transmission is by mosquito and other biting insects; infection may also occur through handling of infected meat or contact with blood; geographic distribution includes eastern and southern Africa where cattle and sheep are raised; symptoms are generally mild with fever and some liver abnormalities, but the disease may progress to hemorrhagic fever, encephalitis, or ocular disease; fatality rates are low at about 1% of cases.

Chikungunya - mosquito-borne (*Aedes aegypti*) viral disease associated with urban environments, similar to Dengue Fever; characterized by sudden onset of fever, rash, and severe joint pain usually lasting 3-7 days, some cases result in persistent arthritis.

water contact diseases acquired through swimming or wading in freshwater lakes, streams, and rivers:

Leptospirosis - bacterial disease that affects animals and humans; infection occurs through contact with water, food, or soil contaminated by animal urine; symptoms include high fever, severe headache, vomiting, jaundice, and diarrhea; untreated, the disease can result in kidney damage, liver failure, meningitis, or respiratory distress; fatality rates are low but left untreated recovery can take months.

Schistosomiasis - caused by parasitic trematode flatworm Schistosoma; fresh water snails act as intermediate host and release larval form of parasite that penetrates the skin of people exposed to contaminated water; worms mature and reproduce in the blood vessels, liver, kidneys, and intestines releasing eggs, which become trapped in tissues triggering an immune response; may manifest as either urinary or intestinal disease resulting in decreased work or learning capacity; mortality, while generally low, may occur in advanced cases usually due to bladder cancer; endemic in 74 developing countries with 80% of infected people living in sub-Saharan Africa; humans act as the reservoir for this parasite.

aerosolized dust or soil contact disease acquired through inhalation of aerosols contaminated with rodent urine:

Lassa fever - viral disease carried by rats of the genus Mastomys; endemic in portions of West Africa; infection occurs through direct contact with or consumption of food contaminated by rodent urine or fecal matter containing virus particles; fatality rate can reach 50% in epidemic outbreaks.

respiratory disease acquired through close contact with an infectious person:

Meningococcal meningitis - bacterial disease causing an inflammation of the lining of the brain and spinal cord; one of the most important bacterial pathogens is Neisseria meningitidis because of its potential to cause epidemics; symptoms include stiff neck, high fever, headaches, and vomiting; bacteria are transmitted from person to person by respiratory droplets and facilitated by close and prolonged contact resulting from crowded living conditions, often with a seasonal distribution; death occurs in 5-15% of cases, typically within 24-48 hours of onset of symptoms; highest burden of meningococcal disease occurs in the hyperendemic region of sub-Saharan Africa known as the "Meningitis Belt" which stretches from Senegal east to Ethiopia.

animal contact disease acquired through direct contact with local animals:

Rabies - viral disease of mammals usually transmitted through the bite of an infected animal, most commonly dogs; virus affects the central nervous system causing brain alteration and death; symptoms initially are non-specific fever and headache progressing to neurological symptoms; death occurs within days of the onset of symptoms.

Manpower available for military service This entry gives the total numbers of males and females age 15-49 and assumes that every individual is fit to serve.

Manpower fit for military service This entry gives the number of males and females age 15-49 fit for military service. This is a more refined measure of potential military manpower availability which tries to account for the health situation in the country and reduces the maximum potential number to a more realistic estimate of the actual number fit to serve.

Manpower reaching military service age annually This entry gives the number of draft-age males and females entering the military manpower pool in any given year and is a measure of the availability of draft-age young adults.

Map references This entry includes the name of the *Factbook* reference map on which a country may be found. The entry on **Geographic coordinates** may be helpful in finding some smaller countries.

Maritime claims This entry includes the following claims, the definitions of which are excerpted from the United Nations Convention on the Law of the Sea (UNCLOS), which alone contains the full and definitive descriptions:

territorial sea - the sovereignty of a coastal state extends beyond its land territory and internal waters to an adjacent belt of sea, described as the territorial sea in the UNCLOS (Part II); this sovereignty extends to the air space over the territorial sea as well as its underlying seabed and subsoil; every state has the right to establish the breadth of its territorial sea up to a limit not exceeding 12 nautical miles; the normal baseline for measuring the breadth of the territorial sea is the low-water line along the coast as marked on large-scale charts officially recognized by the coastal state; the UNCLOS describes specific rules for archipelagic states.

contiguous zone - according to the UNCLOS (Article 33), this is a zone contiguous to a coastal state's territorial sea, over which it may exercise the control necessary to: prevent infringement of its customs, fiscal, immigration, or sanitary laws and regulations within its territory or territorial sea; punish infringement of the above laws and regulations committed within its territory or territorial sea; the contiguous zone may not extend beyond 24 nautical miles from the baselines from which the breadth of the territorial sea is measured (e.g. the US has claimed a 12-nautical mile contiguous zone in addition to its 12-nautical mile territorial sea).

exclusive economic zone (EEZ) - the UNCLOS (Part V) defines the EEZ as a zone beyond and adjacent to the territorial sea in which a coastal state has: sovereign rights for the purpose of exploring and exploiting, conserving and managing the natural resources, whether living or non-living, of the waters superjacent to the seabed and of the seabed and its subsoil, and with regard to other activities for the economic exploitation and exploration of the zone, such as the production of energy from the water, currents, and winds; jurisdiction with regard to the establishment and use of artificial islands, installations, and structures; marine scientific research; the protection and preservation of the marine environment; the outer limit of the exclusive economic zone shall not exceed 200 nautical miles from the baselines from which the breadth of the territorial sea is measured.

continental shelf - the UNCLOS (Article 76) defines the continental shelf of a coastal state as comprising the seabed and subsoil of the submarine areas that extend beyond its territorial sea throughout the natural prolongation of its land territory to the outer edge of the continental margin, or to a distance of 200 nautical miles from the baselines from which the breadth of the territorial sea is measured where the outer edge of the continental margin does not extend up to that distance; the continental margin comprises the submerged prolongation of the landmass of the coastal state, and consists of the seabed and subsoil of the shelf, the slope and the rise; wherever the continental margin extends beyond 200 nautical miles from the baseline, coastal states may extend their claim to a distance not to exceed 350 nautical miles from the baseline or 100 nautical miles from the 2500 meter isobath; it does not include the deep ocean floor with its oceanic ridges or the subsoil thereof.

exclusive fishing zone - while this term is not used in the UNCLOS, some states (e.g. the United Kingdom) have chosen not to claim an EEZ, but rather to claim jurisdiction over the living resources off their coast; in such cases, the term exclusive fishing zone is often used; the breadth of this zone is normally the same as the EEZ or 200 nautical miles.

Median age This entry is the age that divides a population into two numerically equal groups; that is, half the people are younger than this age and half are older. It is a single index that summarizes the age distribution of a population. Currently, the median age ranges from a low of about 15 in Uganda and Gaza Strip to 40 or more in several European countries and Japan. See the entry for "Age structure" for the importance of a young versus an older age structure and, by implication, a low versus a higher median age.

Merchant marine Merchant marine may be defined as all ships engaged in the carriage of goods; or all commercial vessels (as opposed to all nonmilitary ships), which excludes tugs, fishing vessels, offshore oil rigs, etc. This entry contains information in four fields - *total*, ships *by type*, *foreign-owned*, and *registered in other countries*.

Total includes the number of ships (1,000 GRT or over), total DWT for those ships, and total GRT for those ships. DWT or dead weight tonnage is the total weight of cargo, plus bunkers, stores, etc., that a ship can carry when immersed to the appropriate load line. GRT or gross register tonnage is a figure obtained by measuring the entire sheltered volume of a ship available for cargo and passengers and converting it to tons on the basis of 100 cubic feet per ton; there is no stable relationship between GRT and DWT.

by type includes a listing of barge carriers, bulk cargo ships, cargo ships, chemical tankers, combination bulk carriers, combination ore/oil carriers, container ships, liquefied gas tankers, livestock carriers, multifunctional large-load carriers, petroleum tankers, passenger ships, passenger/cargo ships, railcar carriers, refrigerated cargo ships, roll-on/roll-off cargo ships, short-sea passenger ships, specialized tankers, and vehicle carriers.

Foreign-owned are ships that fly the flag of one country but belong to owners in another.

Registered in other countries are ships that belong to owners in one country but fly the flag of another.

Military This category includes the entries dealing with a country's military structure, manpower, and expenditures.

Military – note This entry includes miscellaneous military information of significance not included elsewhere.

Military branches This entry lists the names of the ground, naval, air, marine, and other defense or security forces.

Military expenditures - dollar figure This entry gives current military expenditures in US dollars; the figure is calculated by multiplying the estimated defense spending in percentage terms by the gross domestic product (GDP) calculated on an exchange rate basis, not purchasing power parity (PPP) terms. Dollar figures for military expenditures should be treated with caution because of different price patterns and accounting methods among nations, as well as wide variations in the strength of their currencies.

Military expenditures - percent of GDP This entry gives current military expenditures as an estimated percent of gross domestic product (GDP). These figures are calculated on an exchange rate basis, i.e., not in purchasing power parity (PPP) terms.

Military service age and obligation This entry gives the minimum age at which an individual may volunteer for military service or be subject to conscription.

Money figures All money figures are expressed in contemporaneous US dollars unless otherwise indicated.

National holiday This entry gives the primary national day of celebration - usually independence day.

Nationality This entry provides the identifying terms for citizens - *noun* and *adjective*.

Natural gas – consumption This entry is the total natural gas consumed in cubic meters (cu m). The discrepancy between the amount of natural gas produced and/or imported and the amount consumed and/or exported is due to the omission of stock changes and other complicating factors.

Natural gas – exports This entry is the total natural gas exported in cubic meters (cu m).

Natural gas – imports This entry is the total natural gas imported in cubic meters (cu m).

Natural gas – production This entry is the total natural gas produced in cubic meters (cu m). The discrepancy between the amount of natural gas produced and/or imported and the amount consumed and/or exported is due to the omission of stock changes and other complicating factors.

Natural gas - proved reserves This entry is the stock of proved reserves of natural gas in cubic meters (cu m). Proved reserves are those quantities of natural gas, which, by analysis of geological and engineering data, can be estimated with a high degree of confidence to be commercially recoverable from a given date forward, from known reservoirs and under current economic conditions.

Natural hazards This entry lists potential natural disasters.

Natural resources This entry lists a country's mineral, petroleum, hydropower, and other resources of commercial importance.

Net migration rate This entry includes the figure for the difference between the number of persons entering and leaving a country during the year per 1,000 persons (based on midyear population). An excess of persons entering the country is referred to as net immigration (e.g., 3.56 migrants/1,000 population); an excess of persons leaving the country as net emigration (e.g., -9.26 migrants/1,000 population). The net migration rate indicates the contribution of migration to the overall level of population change. High levels of migration can cause problems such as increasing unemployment and potential ethnic strife (if people are coming in) or a reduction in the labor force, perhaps in certain key sectors (if people are leaving).

Oil – consumption This entry is the total oil consumed in barrels per day (bbl/day). The discrepancy between the amount of oil produced and/or imported and the amount consumed and/or exported is due to the omission of stock changes, refinery gains, and other complicating factors.

Oil – exports This entry is the total oil exported in barrels per day (bbl/day), including both crude oil and oil products.

Oil – imports This entry is the total oil imported in barrels per day (bbl/day), including both crude oil and oil products.

Oil – production This entry is the total oil produced in barrels per day (bbl/day). The discrepancy between the amount of oil produced and/or imported and the amount consumed and/or exported is due to the omission of stock changes, refinery gains, and other complicating factors.

Oil - proved reserves This entry is the stock of proved reserves of crude oil in barrels (bbl). Proved reserves are those quantities of petroleum which, by analysis of geological and engineering data, can be estimated with a high degree of confidence to be commercially recoverable from a given date forward, from known reservoirs and under current economic conditions.

People This category includes the entries dealing with the characteristics of the people and their society.

People – note: This entry includes miscellaneous demographic information of significance not included elsewhere.

Personal Names – Capitalization The *Factbook* capitalizes the surname or family name of individuals for the convenience of our users who are faced with a world of different cultures and naming conventions. The need for capitalization, bold type, underlining, italics, or some other indicator of the individual's surname is apparent in the following examples: MAO Zedong, Fidel CASTRO Ruz, George W. BUSH, and TUNKU SALAHUDDIN Abdul Aziz Shah ibni Al-Marhum Sultan Hisammuddin Alam Shah. By knowing the surname, a short form without all capital letters can be used with confidence as in President Castro, Chairman Mao, President Bush, or Sultan Tunku Salahuddin. The same system of capitalization is extended to the names of leaders with surnames that are not commonly used such as Queen ELIZABETH II.

Personal Names – Spelling The romanization of personal names in the *Factbook* normally follows the same transliteration system used by the US Board on Geographic Names for spelling place names. At times, however, a foreign leader expressly indicates a preference for, or the media or official documents regularly use, a romanized spelling that differs from the transliteration derived from the US Government standard. In such cases, the *Factbook* uses the alternative spelling.

Personal Names – Titles The *Factbook* capitalizes any valid title (or short form of it) immediately preceding a person's name. A title standing alone is not capitalized. Examples: President PUTIN and President BUSH are chiefs of state. In Russia, the president is chief of state and the premier is the head of the government, while in the US, the president is both chief of state and head of government.

Petroleum See entry for "oil."

Petroleum products See entry for "oil."

Pipelines This entry gives the lengths and types of pipelines for transporting products like natural gas, crude oil, or petroleum products.

Political parties and leaders This entry includes a listing of significant political organizations and their leaders.

Political pressure groups and leaders This entry includes a listing of organizations with leaders involved in politics, but not standing for legislative election.

Population This entry gives an estimate from the US Bureau of the Census based on statistics from population censuses, vital statistics registration systems, or sample surveys pertaining to the recent past and on assumptions about future trends. The total population presents one overall measure of the potential impact of the country on the world and within its region. Note: starting with the 1993 *Factbook*, demographic estimates for some countries (mostly African) have explicitly taken into account the effects of the growing impact of the HIV/AIDS epidemic. These countries are currently: The Bahamas, Benin, Botswana, Brazil, Burkina Faso, Burma, Burundi, Cambodia, Cameroon, Central African Republic, Democratic Republic of the Congo, Republic of the Congo, Cote d'Ivoire, Ethiopia, Gabon, Ghana, Guyana, Haiti, Honduras, Kenya, Lesotho, Malawi,

Mozambique, Namibia, Nigeria, Rwanda, South Africa, Swaziland, Tanzania, Thailand, Togo, Uganda, Zambia, and Zimbabwe.

Population below poverty line National estimates of the percentage of the population falling below the poverty line are based on surveys of sub-groups, with the results weighted by the number of people in each group. Definitions of poverty vary considerably among nations. For example, rich nations generally employ more generous standards of poverty than poor nations.

Population growth rate The average annual percent change in the population, resulting from a surplus (or deficit) of births over deaths and the balance of migrants entering and leaving a country. The rate may be positive or negative. The growth rate is a factor in determining how great a burden would be imposed on a country by the changing needs of its people for infrastructure (e.g., schools, hospitals, housing, roads), resources (e.g., food, water, electricity), and jobs. Rapid population growth can be seen as threatening by neighboring countries.

Ports and harbors This entry lists the major ports and harbors selected on the basis of overall importance to each country. This is determined by evaluating a number of factors (e.g., dollar value of goods handled, gross tonnage, facilities, military significance).

Public debt This entry records the cumulative total of all government borrowings less repayments that are denominated in a country's home currency. Public debt should not be confused with external debt, which reflects the foreign currency liabilities of both the private and public sector and must be financed out of foreign exchange earnings.

Radio broadcast stations This entry includes the total number of AM, FM, and shortwave broadcast stations.

Railways This entry states the total route length of the railway network and of its component parts by gauge: *broad, standard, narrow,* and *dual.* Other gauges are listed under *note.*

Reference maps This section includes world and regional maps.

Refugees and internally displaced persons This entry includes those persons residing in a country as *refugees* or internally displaced persons (*IDPs*). The definition of a refugee according to a United Nations Convention is "a person who is outside his/her country of nationality or habitual residence; has a well-founded fear of persecution because of his/her race, religion, nationality, membership in a particular social group or political opinion; and is unable or unwilling to avail himself/herself of the protection of that country, or to return there, for fear of persecution." The UN established the Office of the UN High Commissioner for Refugees (UNHCR) in 1950 to handle refugee matters worldwide. The UN Relief and Works Agency for Palestine Refugees in the Near East (UNRWA) has a different, operational definition for a Palestinian refugee: "a person whose normal place of residence was Palestine during the period 1 June 1946 to 15 May 1948 and who lost both home and means of livelihood as a result of the 1948 conflict." However, UNHCR also assists some 400,000 Palestinian refugees not covered under the UNRWA definition. The term "internally displaced person" is not specifically covered in the UN Convention; it is used to describe people who have fled their homes for reasons similar to refugees, but who remain within their own national territory and are subject to the laws of that state.

Religions This entry is an ordered listing of religions by adherents starting with the largest group and sometimes includes the percent of total population.

Reserves of foreign exchange and gold This entry gives the dollar value for the stock of all financial assets that are available to the central monetary authority for use in meeting a country's balance of payments needs as of the end-date of the period specified. This category includes not only foreign currency and gold, but also a country's holdings of Special Drawing Rights in the International Monetary Fund, and its reserve position in the Fund.

Roadways This entry gives the total length of the road network and includes the length of the *paved* and *unpaved* portions.

Sex ratio This entry includes the number of males for each female in five age groups - *at birth, under 15 years, 15-64 years, 65 years and over,* and for the *total population.* Sex ratio at birth has recently emerged as an indicator of certain kinds of sex discrimination in some countries. For instance, high sex ratios at birth in some Asian countries are now attributed to sex-selective abortion and infanticide due to a strong preference for sons. This will affect future marriage patterns and fertility patterns. Eventually, it could cause unrest among young adult males who are unable to find partners.

Suffrage This entry gives the age at enfranchisement and whether the right to vote is universal or restricted.

Telephone numbers All telephone numbers in the *Factbook* consist of the country code in brackets, the city or area code (where required) in parentheses, and the local number. The one component that is not presented is the international access code, which varies from country to country. For example, an international direct dial telephone call placed from the US to Madrid, Spain, would be as follows: 011 [34] (1) 577-xxxx, where 011 is the international access code for station-to-station calls;

01 is for calls other than station-to-station calls, [34] is the country code for Spain, (1) is the city code for Madrid, 577 is the local exchange, and xxxx is the local telephone number. An international direct dial telephone call placed from another country to the US would be as follows: international access code + [1] (202) 939-xxxx, where [1] is the country code for the US, (202) is the area code for Washington, DC, 939 is the local exchange, and xxxx is the local telephone number.

Telephone system This entry includes a brief general assessment of the system with details on the domestic and international components. The following terms and abbreviations are used throughout the entry:

Africa ONE - a fiber-optic submarine cable link encircling the continent of Africa.

Arabsat - Arab Satellite Communications Organization (Riyadh, Saudi Arabia).

Autodin - Automatic Digital Network (US Department of Defense).

CB - citizen's band mobile radio communications.

cellular telephone system - the telephones in this system are radio transceivers, with each instrument having its own private radio frequency and sufficient radiated power to reach the booster station in its area (cell), from which the telephone signal is fed to a telephone exchange.

Central American Microwave System - a trunk microwave radio relay system that links the countries of Central America and Mexico with each other.

coaxial cable - a multichannel communication cable consisting of a central conducting wire, surrounded by and insulated from a cylindrical conducting shell; a large number of telephone channels can be made available within the insulated space by the use of a large number of carrier frequencies.

Comsat - Communications Satellite Corporation (US).

DSN - Defense Switched Network (formerly Automatic Voice Network or Autovon); basic general-purpose, switched voice network of the Defense Communications System (US Department of Defense).

Eutelsat - European Telecommunications Satellite Organization (Paris).

fiber-optic cable - a multichannel communications cable using a thread of optical glass fibers as a transmission medium in which the signal (voice, video, etc.) is in the form of a coded pulse of light.

GSM - a global system for mobile (cellular) communications devised by the Groupe Special Mobile of the pan-European standardization organization, Conference Europeanne des Posts et Telecommunications (CEPT) in 1982.

HF - high frequency; any radio frequency in the 3,000- to 30,000-kHz range.

Inmarsat - International Maritime Satellite Organization (London); provider of global mobile satellite communications for commercial, distress, and safety applications at sea, in the air, and on land.

Intelsat - International Telecommunications Satellite Organization (Washington, DC).

Intersputnik - International Organization of Space Communications (Moscow); first established in the former Soviet Union and the East European countries, it is now marketing its services worldwide with earth stations in North America, Africa, and East Asia.

landline - communication wire or cable of any sort that is installed on poles or buried in the ground.

Marecs - Maritime European Communications Satellite used in the Inmarsat system on lease from the European Space Agency.

Marisat - satellites of the Comsat Corporation that participate in the Inmarsat system.

Medarabtel - the Middle East Telecommunications Project of the International Telecommunications Union (ITU) providing a modern telecommunications network, primarily by microwave radio relay, linking Algeria, Djibouti, Egypt, Jordan, Libya, Morocco, Saudi Arabia, Somalia, Sudan, Syria, Tunisia, and Yemen; it was initially started in Morocco in 1970 by the Arab Telecommunications Union (ATU) and was known at that time as the Middle East Mediterranean Telecommunications Network.

microwave radio relay - transmission of long distance telephone calls and television programs by highly directional radio microwaves that are received and sent on from one booster station to another on an optical path.

NMT - Nordic Mobile Telephone; an analog cellular telephone system that was developed jointly by the national telecommunications authorities of the Nordic countries (Denmark, Finland, Iceland, Norway, and Sweden).

Orbita - a Russian television service; also the trade name of a packet-switched digital telephone network.

radiotelephone communications - the two-way transmission and reception of sounds by broadcast radio on authorized frequencies using telephone handsets.

PanAmSat - PanAmSat Corporation (Greenwich, CT).

SAFE - South African Far East Cable

satellite communication system - a communication system

consisting of two or more earth stations and at least one satellite that provide long distance transmission of voice, data, and television; the system usually serves as a trunk connection between telephone exchanges; if the earth stations are in the same country, it is a domestic system.

satellite earth station - a communications facility with a microwave radio transmitting and receiving antenna and required receiving and transmitting equipment for communicating with satellites.

satellite link - a radio connection between a satellite and an earth station permitting communication between them, either one-way (down link from satellite to earth station - television receive-only transmission) or two-way (telephone channels).

SHF - super high frequency; any radio frequency in the 3,000- to 30,000-MHz range.

shortwave - radio frequencies (from 1.605 to 30 MHz) that fall above the commercial broadcast band and are used for communication over long distances.

Solidaridad - geosynchronous satellites in Mexico's system of international telecommunications in the Western Hemisphere.

Statsionar - Russia's geostationary system for satellite telecommunications.

submarine cable - a cable designed for service under water.

TAT - Trans-Atlantic Telephone; any of a number of high-capacity submarine coaxial telephone cables linking Europe with North America.

telefax - facsimile service between subscriber stations via the public switched telephone network or the international Datel network.

telegraph - a telecommunications system designed for unmodulated electric impulse transmission.

telex - a communication service involving teletypewriters connected by wire through automatic exchanges.

tropospheric scatter - a form of microwave radio transmission in which the troposphere is used to scatter and reflect a fraction of the incident radio waves back to earth; powerful, highly directional antennas are used to transmit and receive the microwave signals; reliable over-the-horizon communications are realized for distances up to 600 miles in a single hop; additional hops can extend the range of this system for very long distances. trunk network - a network of switching centers, connected by multichannel trunk lines.

UHF - ultra high frequency; any radio frequency in the 300- to 3,000-MHz range.

VHF - very high frequency; any radio frequency in the 30- to 300-MHz range.

Telephones - main lines in use This entry gives the total number of main telephone lines in use.

Telephones - mobile cellular This entry gives the total number of mobile cellular telephones in use.

Television broadcast stations This entry gives the total number of separate broadcast stations plus any repeater stations.

Terminology Due to the highly structured nature of the *Factbook* database, some collective generic terms have to be used. For example, the word **Country** in the **Country name** entry refers to a wide variety of dependencies, areas of special sovereignty, uninhabited islands, and other entities in addition to the traditional countries or independent states. **Military** is also used as an umbrella term for various civil defense, security, and defense activities in many entries. The **Independence** entry includes the usual colonial independence dates and former ruling states as well as other significant nationhood dates such as the traditional founding date or the date of unification, federation, confederation, establishment, or state succession that are not strictly independence dates. Dependent areas have the nature of their dependency status noted in this same entry.

Terrain This entry contains a brief description of the topography.

Total fertility rate This entry gives a figure for the average number of children that would be born per woman if all women lived to the end of their childbearing years and bore children according to a given fertility rate at each age. The total fertility rate (TFR) is a more direct measure of the level of fertility than the crude birth rate, since it refers to births per woman. This indicator shows the potential for population change in the country. A rate of two children per woman is considered the replacement rate for a population, resulting in relative stability in terms of total numbers. Rates above two children indicate populations growing in size and whose median age is declining. Higher rates may also indicate difficulties for families, in some situations, to feed and educate their children and for women to enter the labor force. Rates below two children indicate populations decreasing in size and growing older. Global fertility rates are in general decline and this trend is most pronounced in industrialized countries, especially Western Europe, where populations are projected to decline dramatically over the next 50 years.

Transnational issues This category includes three entries - **Disputes - international, Refugees and internally displaced persons**, and **Illicit drugs** - that deal with current issues going beyond national boundaries.

Transportation This category includes the entries deal-

ing with the means for movement of people and goods.
Transportation - note This entry includes miscellaneous transportation information of significance not included elsewhere.
Unemployment rate This entry contains the percent of the labor force that is without jobs. Substantial underemployment might be noted.
Waterways This entry gives the total length of navigable rivers, canals, and other inland bodies of water.
Years All year references are for the calendar year (CY) unless indicated as fiscal year (FY). The calendar year is an accounting period of 12 months from January 1 to December 31. The fiscal year is an accounting period of 12 months other than January 1 to December 31.

Note: Information for the US and US dependencies was compiled from material in the public domain and does not represent Intelligence Community estimates.

GUIDE TO COUNTRY PROFILES

INTRODUCTION

Background

GEOGRAPHY

Location
Geographic coordinates
Map references
Area
total
land
water
Area - comparative
Land boundaries
total
border countries
Coastline
Maritime claims
contiguous zone
exclusive fishing zone
continental shelf
exclusive economic zone
extended fishing zone
territorial sea
Climate
Terrain
Elevation extremes
lowest point
highest point
Natural resources
Land use
arable land
permanent crops
other
Irrigated land
Natural hazards
Environment - current issues
Environment - international agreements
party to
signed, but not ratified
Geography - note

PEOPLE

Population
Age structure
0-14 years
15-64 years
65 years and over
Median Age
total
male
female
Population growth rate
Birth rate
Death rate
Net migration rate
Sex ratio
at birth
under 15 years
15-64 years
65 years and over
total population
Infant mortality rate
Life expectancy at birth
total population
male
female
Total fertility rate
HIV/AIDS - adult prevalence rate
HIV/AIDS - people living with HIV/AIDS
HIV/AIDS - deaths
Major infectious diseases
Nationality
noun
adjective
Ethnic groups
Religions
Languages
Literacy
definition
total population
male
female
People - note

GOVERNMENT

Country name
conventional long form
conventional short form
local long form
local short form
former
abbreviation
Dependency status
Government type
Capital
Administrative divisions
Dependent areas
Independence
National holiday
Constitution
Legal system
Suffrage
Executive branch
chief of state
head of government
cabinet
elections
election results
Legislative branch
elections
election results
Judicial branch
Political parties and leaders
Political pressure groups and leaders
International organization participation
Diplomatic representation in the US
chief of mission
chancery
telephone
FAX
consulate(s) general
consulate(s)
Diplomatic representation from the US
chief of mission
embassy
mailing address
telephone
FAX
consulate(s) general
consulate(s)
branch office(s)
Flag description
Government - note

ECONOMY

Economy - overview
GDP (purchasing power parity)
GDP - real growth rate
GDP - per capita
GDP - composition by sector
agriculture
industry
services
Investment (gross fixed)
Population below poverty line
Household income or consumption by percentage share
lowest 10%
highest 10%
Distribution of family income - Gini index
Inflation rate (consumer prices)
Labor force
Labor force - by occupation
Unemployment rate
Budget
revenues
expenditures
Public debt
Agriculture - products
Industries
Industrial production growth rate
Electricity - production
Electricity - consumption
Electricity - exports
Electricity - imports
Oil - production
Oil - consumption
Oil - exports
Oil - imports
Oil - proved reserves
Natural Gas - production
Natural Gas - consumption
Natural Gas - exports
Natural Gas - imports
Natural Gas - proved reserves
Current account balance
Exports
Exports - commodities
Exports - partners
Imports

Imports - commodities
Imports - partners
Reserves of foreign exchange and gold
Debt - external
Economic aid - donor
Economic aid - recipient
Currency (code)
Exchange rates
Fiscal year

COMMUNICATIONS

Telephones - main lines in use
Telephones - mobile cellular
Telephone system
general assessment
domestic
international
Radio broadcast stations
Television broadcast stations
Internet country code
Internet hosts
Internet users
Communications - note

TRANSPORTATION

Railways
total
broad gauge
standard gauge
narrow gauge
dual gauge
Highways
total
paved
unpaved
Waterways
Pipelines
Ports and harbors
Merchant marine
total
ships by type
foreign-owned
registered in other countries
Airports
Airports - with paved runways
total
over 3,047 m
2,438 to 3,047 m
1,524 to 2,437 m
914 to 1,523 m
under 914 m
Airports - with unpaved runways
total
over 3,047 m
2,438 to 3,047 m
1,524 to 2,437 m
914 to 1,523 m
under 914 m
Heliports
Transportation - note

MILITARY

Military branches
Military service age and obligation
Manpower available for military service
males age 15-49
females age 15-49
Manpower fit for military service
males age 15-49
females age 15-49
Manpower reaching military service age annually
males
females
Military expenditures - dollar figure
Military expenditures - percent of GDP
Military - note

TRANSNATIONAL ISSUES

Disputes - international
Refugees and internally displaced persons
Illicit drugs

AFGHANISTAN

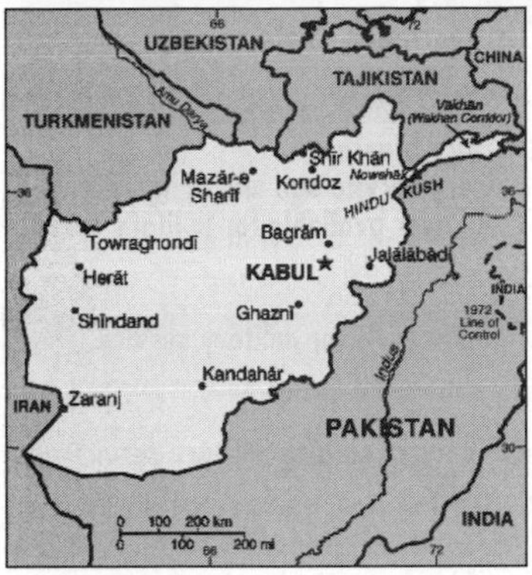

INTRODUCTION

Background: Ahmad Shah DURRANI unified the Pashtun tribes and founded Afghanistan in 1747. The country served as a buffer between the British and Russian empires until it won independence from notional British control in 1919. A brief experiment in democracy ended in a 1973 coup and a 1978 Communist counter-coup. The Soviet Union invaded in 1979 to support the tottering Afghan Communist regime, but withdrew 10 years later under relentless pressure by internationally supported anti-Communist mujahedin rebels. A civil war between mujahedin factions erupted following the 1992 fall of the Communist regime. The Taliban, a hard-line Pakistani-sponsored movement that emerged in 1994 to end the country's civil war and anarchy, seized Kabul in 1996 and most of the country outside of opposition Northern Alliance strongholds by 1998. Following the 11 September 2001 terrorist attacks, a US, Allied, and Northern Alliance military action toppled the Taliban for sheltering Osama BIN LADIN. In late 2001, a conference in Bonn, Germany, established a process for political reconstruction that included the adoption of a new constitution in 2003, a presidential election in 2004, and National Assembly elections in 2005. On 9 October 2004, Hamid KARZAI became the first democratically elected president of Afghanistan. The National Assembly was inaugurated on 19 December 2005.

GEOGRAPHY

Location: Southern Asia, north and west of Pakistan, east of Iran
Geographic coordinates: 33 00 N, 65 00 E
Map references: Asia
Area:
total: 647,500 sq km
land: 647,500 sq km
water: 0 sq km
Area - comparative: slightly smaller than Texas
Land boundaries:
total: 5,529 km
border countries: China 76 km, Iran 936 km, Pakistan 2,430 km, Tajikistan 1,206 km, Turkmenistan 744 km, Uzbekistan 137 km
Coastline: 0 km (landlocked)
Maritime claims: none (landlocked)
Climate: arid to semiarid; cold winters and hot summers
Terrain: mostly rugged mountains; plains in north and southwest
Elevation extremes:
lowest point: Amu Darya 258 m
highest point: Nowshak 7,485 m
Natural resources: natural gas, petroleum, coal, copper, chromite, talc, barites, sulfur, lead, zinc, iron ore, salt, precious and semiprecious stones
Land use:
arable land: 12.13%
permanent crops: 0.22%
other: 87.65% (2001)
Irrigated land: 23,860 sq km (1998 est.)
Natural hazards: damaging earthquakes occur in Hindu Kush mountains; flooding; droughts
Environment - current issues: limited natural fresh water resources; inadequate supplies of potable water; soil degradation; overgrazing; deforestation (much of the remaining forests are being cut down for fuel and building materials); desertification; air and water pollution
Environment - international agreements:
party to: Biodiversity, Desertification, Endangered Species, Environmental Modification, Marine Dumping
signed, but not ratified: Climate Change, Hazardous Wastes, Law of the Sea, Marine Life Conservation
Geography - note: landlocked; the Hindu Kush mountains that run northeast to southwest divide the northern provinces from the rest of the country; the highest peaks are in the northern Vakhan (Wakhan Corridor)

PEOPLE

Population: 29,928,987 (July 2005 est.)
Age structure:
0-14 years: 44.7% (male 6,842,857/female 6,524,485)
15-64 years: 52.9% (male 8,124,077/female 7,713,603)
65 years and over: 2.4% (male 353,193/female 370,772) (2005 est.)
Median age:
total: 17.56 years
male: 17.55 years
female: 17.57 years (2005 est.)
Population growth rate: 4.77%
note: this rate does not take into consideration the recent war and its continuing impact (2005 est.)
Birth rate: 47.02 births/1,000 population (2005 est.)
Death rate: 20.75 deaths/1,000 population (2005 est.)
Net migration rate: 21.43 migrant(s)/1,000 population (2005 est.)
Sex ratio:
at birth: 1.05 male(s)/female
under 15 years: 1.05 male(s)/female
15-64 years: 1.05 male(s)/female
65 years and over: 0.95 male(s)/female
total population: 1.05 male(s)/female (2005 est.)
Infant mortality rate:
total: 163.07 deaths/1,000 live births
male: 167.79 deaths/1,000 live births
female: 158.12 deaths/1,000 live births (2005 est.)
Life expectancy at birth:
total population: 42.9 years
male: 42.71 years
female: 43.1 years (2005 est.)
Total fertility rate: 6.75 children born/woman (2005 est.)
HIV/AIDS - adult prevalence rate: 0.01% (2001 est.)
HIV/AIDS - people living with HIV/AIDS: NA
HIV/AIDS - deaths: NA
Major infectious diseases:
degree of risk: high
food or waterborne diseases: bacterial and protozoal diarrhea, hepatitis A, and typhoid fever
vectorborne disease: malaria is a high risk countrywide below 2,000 meters from March through November
animal contact disease: rabies (2004)
Nationality:
noun: Afghan(s)
adjective: Afghan
Ethnic groups: Pashtun 42%, Tajik 27%, Hazara 9%, Uzbek 9%, Aimak 4%, Turkmen 3%, Baloch 2%, other 4%
Religions: Sunni Muslim 80%, Shi'a Muslim 19%, other 1%
Languages: Pashtu (official) 35%, Afghan Persian (Dari) 50%, Turkic languages (primarily Uzbek and Turkmen) 11%, 30 minor languages (primarily Balochi and Pashai) 4%, much bilingualism
Literacy:
definition: age 15 and over can read and write
total population: 36%
male: 51%
female: 21% (1999 est.)

People - note: of the estimated 4 million refugees in October 2001, 2.3 million have returned

GOVERNMENT

Country name:
conventional long form: Islamic Republic of Afghanistan
conventional short form: Afghanistan
local long form: Dowlat-e Eslami-ye Afghanestan
local short form: Afghanestan
former: Republic of Afghanistan
Government type: Islamic republic
Capital: Kabul
Administrative divisions: 34 provinces (velayat, singular - velayat); Badakhshan, Badghis, Baghlan, Balkh, Bamian, Daykondi, Farah, Faryab, Ghazni, Ghowr, Helmand, Herat, Jowzjan, Kabol, Kandahar, Kapisa, Khowst, Konar, Kondoz, Laghman, Lowgar, Nangarhar, Nimruz, Nurestan, Oruzgan, Paktia, Paktika, Panjshir, Parvan, Samangan, Sar-e Pol, Takhar, Vardak, and Zabol
Independence: 19 August 1919 (from UK control over Afghan foreign affairs)
National holiday: Independence Day, 19 August (1919)
Constitution: new constitution drafted 14 December 2003 - 4 January 2004; signed 16 January 2004
Legal system: according to the new constitution, no law should be "contrary to Islam"; the state is obliged to create a prosperous and progressive society based on social justice, protection of human dignity, protection of human rights, realization of democracy, and to ensure national unity and equality among all ethnic groups and tribes; the state shall abide by the UN charter, international treaties, international conventions that Afghanistan signed, and the Universal Declaration of Human Rights
Suffrage: 18 years of age; universal
Executive branch:
chief of state: President of the Islamic Republic of Afghanistan, Hamid KARZAI (since 7 December 2004); note - the president is both the chief of state and head of government; former King ZAHIR Shah holds the honorific, "Father of the Country," and presides symbolically over certain occasions, but lacks any governing authority; the honorific is not hereditary
head of government: President of the Islamic Republic of Afghanistan, Hamid KARZAI (since 7 December 2004); note - the president is both chief of state and head of government
cabinet: 27 ministers; note - under the new constitution, ministers are appointed by the president and approved by the National Assembly
elections: the president and two vice presidents are elected by direct vote for a five-year term; if no candidate receives 50% or more of the vote in the first round of voting, the two candidates with the most votes will participate in a second round; a president can only be elected for two terms; election last held 9 October 2004 (next to be held in 2009)
election results: Hamid KARZAI elected president; percent of vote - Hamid KARZAI - 55.4%, Yunus QANOONI - 16.3%, Mohammad MOHAQEQ - 11.6%, Abdul Rashid DOSTAM 10.0%, Abdul Latif PEDRAM - 1.4%, Masooda JALAL - 1.2%
Legislative branch: the bicameral National Assembly consists of the Wolesi Jirga or House of People (no more than 249 seats), directly elected for five-year terms, and the Meshrano Jirga or House of Elders (102 seats, one third elected from provincial councils for four-year terms, one third elected from local district councils for three-year terms - provincial councils elected temporary members to fill these seats until district councils are formed, and one third presidential appointees for five-year terms; the presidential appointees will include two representatives of Kuchis and two representatives of the disabled; half of the presidential appointees will be women)
note: on rare occasions the government may convene a Loya Jirga (Grand Council) on issues of independence, national sovereignty, and territorial integrity; it can amend the provisions of the constitution and prosecute the president; it is made up of members of the National Assembly and chairpersons of the provincial and district councils
elections: last held 18 September 2005; next to be held for the Wolesi Jirga by September 2009; next to be held for the provincial councils to the Meshrano Jirga by September 2008
election results: the single non-transferable vote (SNTV) system used in the election did not make use of political party slates; most candidates ran as independents
Judicial branch: the new constitution establishes a nine-member Stera Mahkama or Supreme Court (its nine justices are appointed for 10-year terms by the president with approval of the Wolesi Jirga) and subordinate High Courts and Appeals Courts; there is also a Minister of Justice; a separate Afghan Independent Human Rights Commission established by the Bonn Agreement is charged with investigating human rights abuses and war crimes
Political parties and leaders: note - includes only political parties approved by the Ministry of Justice: Afghan Millat [Anwarul Haq AHADI]; De Afghanistan De Solay Ghorzang Gond [Shahnawaz TANAI]; De Afghanistan De Solay Mili Islami Gond [Shah Mahmood Polal ZAI]; Harakat-e-Islami Afghanistan [Mohammad Asif MOHSINEE]; Hezb-e-Aarman-e-Mardum-e-Afghanistan [Iihaj Saraj-u-din ZAFAREE]; Hezb-e-Aazadee Afghanistan [Abdul MALIK]; Hezb-e-Adalat-e-Islami Afghanistan [Mohammad Kabeer MARZBAN]; Hezb-e-Afghanistan-e-Wahid [Mohammad Wasil RAHEEMEE]; Hezb-e-Afghan Watan Islami Gond [leader NA]; Hezb-e-Congra-e-Mili Afghanistan [Latif PEDRAM]; Hezb-e-Falah-e-Mardum-e-Afghanistan [Mohammad ZAREEF]; Hezb-e-Libral-e-Aazadee Khwa-e-Mardum-e-Afghanistan [Ajmal SOHAIL]; Hezb-e-Hambastagee Mili Jawanan-e-Afghanistan [Mohammad Jamil KARZAI]; Hezb-e-Hamnbatagee-e-Afghanistan [Abdul Khaleq NEMAT]; Hezb-e-Harakat-e-Mili Wahdat-e-Afghanistan [Mohammad Nadir AATASH]; Hezb-e-Harak-e-Islami Mardum-e-Afghanistan [Ilhaj Said Hssain ANWARY]; Hezb-e-Ifazat Az Uqoq-e-Bashar Wa Inkishaf-e-Afghanistan [Baryalai NASRATEE]; Hezb-e-Istiqlal-e-Afghanistan [Dr. Gh. Farooq NIJZRABEE]; Hezb-e-Jamhoree Khwahan [Sibghatullah SANJAR]; Hezb-e-Kar Wa Tawsiha-e-Afghanistan [Zulfiar OMID]; Hezb-e-Mili Afghanistan [Abdul Rasheed AARYAN]; Hezb-e-Mili Wahdat-e-Aqwam-e-Islami Afghanistan [Mohammad Shah KHOGYANEE]; Hezb-e-Nuhzhat-e-Mili Afghanistan [Ahmad Wali MASOUD]; Hezb-e-Paiwand-e-Mili Afghanistan [Said Mansoor NADIRI]; Hezb-e-Rastakhaiz-e-Islami Mardum-e-Afghanistan [Said ZAHIR]; Hezb-e-Refah-e-Mardum-e-Afghanistan [Mia Gul WASEEQ]; Hezb-e-Risalat-e-Mardum-e-Afghanistan [Noor Aqa ROEEN]; Hezb-e-Sahadat-e-Mardum-e-Afghanistan [Mohammad Zubair PAIROZ]; Hezb-e-Sahadat-e-Mili Wa Islami Afghanistan [Mohammad Usman SALIGZADA]; Hezb-e-Sulh-e-Mili Islami Aqwam-e-Afghanistan [Abdul Qahir SHARYATEE]; Hezb-e-Sulh Wa Wahdat-e-Mili Afghanistan [Abdul Qadir IMAMEE]; Hezb-e-Tafahum-e-Wa Democracy Afghanistan [Ahamad SHAHEEN]; Hezb-e-Wahdat-e-Islami Afghanistan [Mohammad Karim

KHALILI]; Hezb-e-Wahdat-e-Islami Mardum-e-Afghanistan [Ustad Mohammad MOHAQQEQ]; Hezb-e-Wahdat-e-Mili Afghanistan [Abdul Rasheed Jalili]; Jamahat-ul-Dahwat ilal Qurhan-wa-Sunat-ul-Afghanistan [Mawlawee Samiullah NAJEEBEE]; Jombesh-e Milli [Abdul Rashid DOSTAM]; Mahaz-e-Mili Islami Afghanistan [Said Ahmad GAILANEE]; Majmah-e-Mili Fahaleen-e-Sulh-e-Afghanistan [Shams ul Haq Noor SHAMS]; Nuhzat-e-Aazadee Wa democracy Afghanistan [Abdul Raqeeb Jawid KUHISTANEE]; Nuhzat-e-Hambastagee Mili Afghanistan [Peer Said Ishaq GAILANEE]; Sazman-e-Islami Afghanistan-e-Jawan [Siad Jawad HUSSAINEE]; Tahreek Wahdat-e-Mili [Sultan Mahmood DHAZI] (30 Sep 2004)

Political pressure groups and leaders: Jamiat-e Islami (Society of Islam), [former President Burhanuddin RABBANI]; Ittihad-e Islami (Islamic Union for the Liberation of Afghanistan), [Abdul Rasul Sayyaf]; there are also small monarchist, communist, and democratic groups

International organization participation: AsDB, CP, ECO, FAO, G-77, GUUAM, IAEA, IBRD, ICAO, ICCt, ICRM, IDA, IDB, IFAD, IFC, IFRCS, ILO, IMF, Interpol, IOC, IOM, ITU, MIGA, NAM, NATO, OIC, OPCW, OSCE, SACEP, UN, UNCTAD, UNESCO, UNIDO, UPU, WCO, WFTU, WHO, WMO, WTO (observer), WToO

Diplomatic representation in the US:
chief of mission: Ambassador Said Tayeb JAWAD
chancery: 2118 Kalorama Road NW, Washington, DC 20008
telephone: [1] 202-483-6410
FAX: [1] 202-483-6488
consulate(s) general: New York

Diplomatic representation from the US:
chief of mission: Ambassador Ronald E. NEUMANN
embassy: The Great Masood Road, Kabul
mailing address: 6180 Kabul Place, Dulles, VA 20189-6180
telephone: [00] (2) 230-0436
FAX: [0093] (2) 230-1364

Flag description: three equal vertical bands of black (hoist), red, and green, with a gold emblem centered on the red band; the emblem features a temple-like structure encircled by a wreath on the left and right and by a bold Islamic inscription above

ECONOMY

Economy - overview: Afghanistan's economic outlook has improved significantly since the fall of the Taliban regime in 2001 because of the infusion of over $4 billion in international assistance, recovery of the agricultural sector and growth of the service sector, and the reestablishment of market institutions. Real GDP growth is estimated to have slowed last fiscal year primarily because adverse weather conditions cut agricultural production, but is expected to rebound over 2005-06 because of foreign donor reconstruction and service sector growth. Despite the progress of the past few years, Afghanistan remains extremely poor, landlocked, and highly dependent on foreign aid, farming, and trade with neighboring countries. It will probably take the remainder of the decade and continuing donor aid and attention to significantly raise Afghanistan's living standards from its current status, among the lowest in the world. Much of the population continues to suffer from shortages of housing, clean water, electricity, medical care, and jobs, but the Afghan government and international donors remain committed to improving access to these basic necessities by prioritizing infrastructure development, education, housing development, jobs programs, and economic reform over the next year. Growing political stability and continued international commitment to Afghan reconstruction create an optimistic outlook for continuing improvements in the Afghan economy in 2006. Expanding poppy cultivation and a growing opium trade may account for one-third of GDP and looms as one of Kabul's most serious policy challenges.

GDP: purchasing power parity - $21.5 billion (2004 est.)

GDP - real growth rate: 8% (2005 est.)

GDP - per capita: purchasing power parity - $800 (2004 est.)

GDP - composition by sector:
agriculture: 38%
industry: 24%
services: 38% (2005 est.)

Labor force: 15 million (2004 est.)

Labor force - by occupation: agriculture 80%, industry 10%, services 10% (2004 est.)

Unemployment rate: 40% NA (2005 est.)

Population below poverty line: 53% (2003)

Household income or consumption by percentage share:
lowest 10%: NA
highest 10%: NA

Inflation rate (consumer prices): 16.3% (2005 est.)

Budget:
revenues: $269 million
expenditures: $561 million, including capital expenditures of $41.7 million NA (FY04-05 budget)

Agriculture - products: opium, wheat, fruits, nuts, wool, mutton, sheepskins, lambskins

Industries: small-scale production of textiles, soap, furniture, shoes, fertilizer, cement; handwoven carpets; natural gas, coal, copper

Industrial production growth rate: NA

Electricity - production: 905 million kWh (2003)

Electricity - production by source:
fossil fuel: 36.3%
hydro: 63.7%
nuclear: 0%
other: 0% (2001)

Electricity - consumption: 1.042 billion kWh (2003)

Electricity - exports: 0 kWh (2003)

Electricity - imports: 200 million kWh (2003)

Oil - production: 0 bbl/day (2003 est.)

Oil - consumption: 5,000 bbl/day (2003 est.)

Oil - exports: NA (2005)

Oil - imports: NA (2005)

Oil - proved reserves: 0 bbl (1 January 2002)

Natural gas - production: 220 million cu m (2001 est.)

Natural gas - consumption: 220 million cu m (2001 est.)

Natural gas - exports: 0 cu m (2001 est.)

Natural gas - imports: 0 cu m (2001 est.)

Natural gas - proved reserves: 49.98 billion cu m (1 January 2002)

Exports: $471 million (not including illicit exports or reexports) (2005 est.)

Exports - partners: Pakistan 24%, India 21.3%, US 12.4%, Germany 5.5% (2004)

Imports: $3.87 billion (2005 est.)

Imports - partners: Pakistan 25.5%, US 8.7%, India 8.5%, Germany 6.5%, Turkmenistan 5.3%, Kenya 4.7%, South Korea 4.2%, Russia 4.2% (2004)

Debt - external: $8 billion in bilateral debt, mostly to Russia; Afghanistan has $500 million in debt to Multilateral Development Banks (2004)

Economic aid - recipient: international pledges made by more than 60 countries and international financial institutions at the Berlin Donors Conference for Afghan reconstruction in March 2004 reached $8.9 billion for 2004-09

Currency: afghani (AFA)

Currency code: AFA

Exchange rates: afghanis per US dollar - NA (2005), 50 (2004), 50 (2003), 3,000 (2002), 3,000 (2001)
note: in 2002, the afghani was revalued and the currency stabilized at about 50 afghanis to the dollar; before 2002, the market rate varied widely from the official rate

Fiscal year: 21 March - 20 March

COMMUNICATIONS

Telephones - main lines in use: 33,100 (2002)
Telephones - mobile cellular: 15,000 (2002)
Telephone system:
general assessment: very limited telephone and telegraph service
domestic: telephone service is improving with the establishment of two mobile phone operators by 2003; telephone main lines remain weak with only .1 line per 10 people
international: country code - 93; five VSAT's installed in Kabul, Herat, Mazar-e-Sharif, Kandahar, and Jalalabad provide international and domestic voice and data connectivity
Radio broadcast stations: AM 21, FM 23, shortwave 1 (broadcasts in Pashtu, Afghan Persian (Dari), Urdu, and English) (2003)
Television broadcast stations: at least 10 (one government-run central television station in Kabul and regional stations in nine of the 32 provinces; the regional stations operate on a reduced schedule; also, in 1997, there was a station in Mazar-e Sharif reaching four northern Afghanistan provinces) (1998)
Internet country code: .af
Internet users: 1,000 (2002)
Communications - note: in March 2003 "af" was established as Afghanistan's domain name; Internet access is growing through Internet cafes as well as public "telekiosks" in Kabul that are part of a nationwide network proposed by the Transitional Authority for Internet access (2002)

TRANSPORTATION

Airports: 47 (2004 est.)
Airports - with paved runways:
total: 10
over 3,047 m: 3
2,438 to 3,047 m: 4
1,524 to 2,437 m: 2
under 914 m: 1 (2005 est.)
Airports - with unpaved runways:
total: 36
over 3,047 m: 1
2,438 to 3,047 m: 5
1,524 to 2,437 m: 17
914 to 1,523 m: 4
under 914 m: 9 (2005 est.)
Heliports: 9 (2005 est.)
Pipelines: gas 387 km (2004)
Roadways:
total: 34,789 km
paved: 8,231 km
unpaved: 26,558 km (2003)
Waterways: 1,200 km
note: chiefly Amu Darya, which handles vessels up to 500 DWT (2004)
Ports and terminals: Kheyrabad, Shir Khan

MILITARY

Military branches: Afghan National Army (includes Afghan Air Force), Afghan Militia Force (AMF) (2005)
Military service and obligation: 22 years of age; inductees are contracted into service for a 4-year term (2005)
Manpower available for military service: *males 22-49:* 4,952,812 (2005 est.)
Manpower fit for military service: *males 22-49:* 2,662,946 (2005 est.)
Manpower reaching military age annually: *males:* 275,362 (2005 est.)
Military expenditures - dollar figure: $188.4 million (2004)
Military expenditures - percent of GDP: 2.6% (2004)

TRANSNATIONAL ISSUES

Disputes - international: the UN has been able to repatriate over two million Afghan refugees but several million more continue to reside in Iran and Pakistan in camps and elsewhere, many at their own choosing; Coalition and Pakistani forces continue to patrol remote tribal areas to control the borders and stem organized terrorist and other illegal cross-border activities; regular meetings between Pakistani and Coalition allies aim to resolve periodic claims of boundary encroachments; occasional conflicts over water-sharing arrangements with Amu Darya and Helmand River states
Refugees and internally displaced persons: *IDPs:* 167,000 - 200,000 (mostly Pashtuns and Kuchis displaced in south and west due to drought and instability) (2004)
Illicit drugs: world's largest producer of opium; cultivation of opium poppy reached unprecedented level of 206,700 hectares in 2004; counterdrug efforts largely unsuccessful; potential opium production of 4,950 metric tons; potential heroin production of 582 metric tons if all opium was processed; source of hashish; many narcotics-processing labs throughout the country; drug trade source of instability and some antigovernment groups profit from the trade; 80-90% of the heroin consumed in Europe comes from Afghan opium; vulnerable to narcotics money laundering through informal financial networks

AKROTIRI

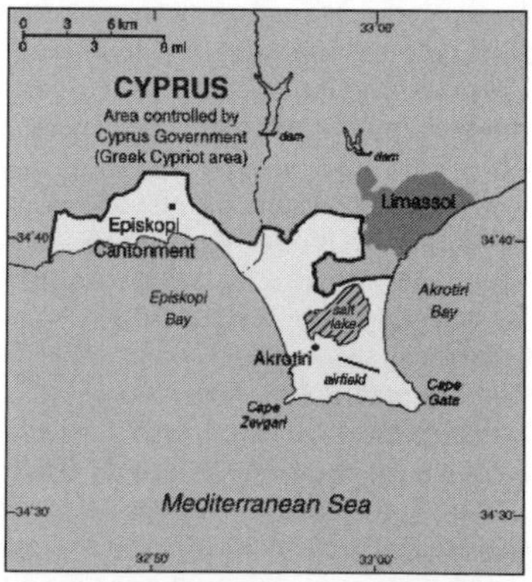

INTRODUCTION

Background: By terms of the 1960 Treaty of Establishment that created the independent Republic of Cyprus, the UK retained full sovereignty and jurisdiction over two areas of almost 254 square kilometers in total: Akrotiri and Dhekelia. The southernmost and smallest of these is the Akrotiri Sovereign Base Area, which is also referred to as the Western Sovereign Base Area.

GEOGRAPHY

Location: peninsula on the southwest coast of Cyprus
Geographic coordinates: 34 37 N, 32 58 E
Map references: Middle East
Area:
total: 123 sq km
note: includes a salt lake and wetlands
Area - comparative: about 0.7 times the size of Washington, DC
Land boundaries:
total: 47.4 km
border countries: Cyprus 47.4 km
Coastline: 56.3 km
Climate: temperate; Mediterranean with hot, dry summers and cool winters
Environment - current issues: shooting around the salt lake; note - breeding place for loggerhead and green turtles; only remaining colony of griffon vultures is on the base
Geography - note: British extraterritorial rights also extended to several small off-post sites scattered across Cyprus

PEOPLE

Population: no indigenous inhabitants
note: approximately 1,300 military per-

sonnel are on the base; there are another 5,000 British citizens who are families of military personnel or civilian staff on both Akrotiri and Dhekelia; Cyprus citizens work on the base, but do not live there
Languages: English, Greek

GOVERNMENT

Country name:
conventional long form: Akrotiri Sovereign Base Area
conventional short form: Akrotiri
Dependency status: overseas territory of UK; administered by an administrator who is also the Commander, British Forces Cyprus
Capital: Episkopi Cantonment; also serves as capital of Dhekelia
Legal system: the laws of the UK, where applicable, apply
Executive branch:
chief of state: Queen ELIZABETH II (since 6 February 1952)
head of government: Administrator Maj. Gen. Peter Thomas Clayton PEARSON (since 9 May 2003); note - reports to the British Ministry of Defence
elections: none; the monarch is hereditary; the administrator is appointed by the monarch
Diplomatic representation in the US: none (overseas territory of the UK)
Diplomatic representation from the US: none (overseas territory of the UK)
Flag description: the flag of the UK is used

ECONOMY

Economy - overview: Economic activity is limited to providing services to the military and their families located in Akrotiri. All food and manufactured goods must be imported.

MILITARY

Military - note: Akrotiri has a full RAF base, Headquarters for British Forces on Cyprus, and Episkopi Support Unit

ALBANIA

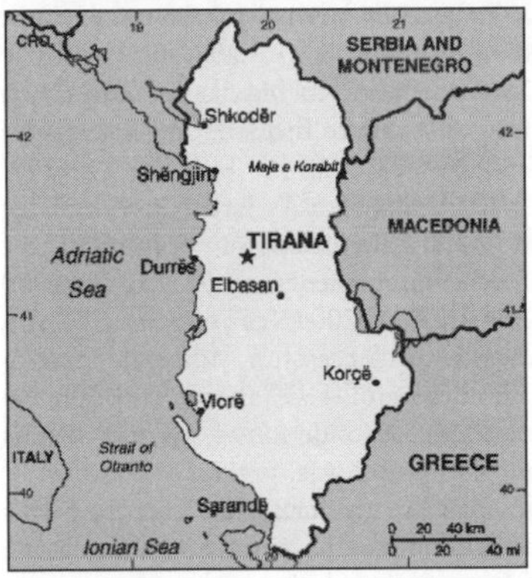

INTRODUCTION

Background: Between 1990 and 1992 Albania ended 46 years of xenophobic Communist rule and established a multiparty democracy. The transition has proven difficult as successive governments have tried to deal with high unemployment, widespread corruption, a dilapidated infrastructure, powerful organized crime networks with links to government officials, and disruptive political opponents. Albania has made incremental progress in its democratic development since first holding multiparty elections in 1991, but deficiencies remain - particularly in regard to the rule of law. Despite some lingering problems, international observers have judged elections to be largely free and fair since the restoration of political stability following the collapse of pyramid schemes in 1997. In the 2005 general elections, the Democratic Party and its allies won a decisive victory on pledges of reducing crime and corruption, promoting economic growth, and decreasing the size of government. Although Albania's economy continues to grow, the country is still one of the poorest in Europe, hampered by a large informal economy, large public debt, and an inadequate energy and transportation infrastructure. Albania has played a largely helpful role in managing inter-ethnic tensions in southeastern Europe, and is continuing to work toward joining NATO and the EU.

GEOGRAPHY

Location: Southeastern Europe, bordering the Adriatic Sea and Ionian Sea, between Greece and Serbia and Montenegro
Geographic coordinates: 41 00 N, 20 00 E
Map references: Europe
Area:
total: 28,748 sq km
land: 27,398 sq km
water: 1,350 sq km
Area - comparative: slightly smaller than Maryland
Land boundaries:
total: 720 km
border countries: Greece 282 km, Macedonia 151 km, Serbia and Montenegro 287 km
Coastline: 362 km
Maritime claims:
territorial sea: 12 nm
continental shelf: 200-m depth or to the depth of exploitation
Climate: mild temperate; cool, cloudy, wet winters; hot, clear, dry summers; interior is cooler and wetter
Terrain: mostly mountains and hills; small plains along coast
Elevation extremes:
lowest point: Adriatic Sea 0 m
highest point: Maja e Korabit (Golem Korab) 2,764 m
Natural resources: petroleum, natural gas, coal, bauxite, chromite, copper, iron ore, nickel, salt, timber, hydropower
Land use:
arable land: 21.09%
permanent crops: 4.42%
other: 74.49% (2001)
Irrigated land: 3,400 sq km (1998 est.)
Natural hazards: destructive earthquakes; tsunamis occur along southwestern coast; floods; drought
Environment - current issues: deforestation; soil erosion; water pollution from industrial and domestic effluents
Environment - international agreements:
party to: Biodiversity, Climate Change, Desertification, Endangered Species, Hazardous Wastes, Law of the Sea, Ozone Layer Protection, Wetlands
signed, but not ratified: none of the selected agreements
Geography - note: strategic location along Strait of Otranto (links Adriatic Sea to Ionian Sea and Mediterranean Sea)

PEOPLE

Population: 3,563,112 (July 2005 est.)
Age structure:
0-14 years: 25.6% (male 476,989/female 434,298)
15-64 years: 65.8% (male 1,199,964/female 1,144,886)
65 years and over: 8.6% (male 141,559/female 165,416) (2005 est.)
Median age:
total: 28.52 years
male: 27.95 years
female: 29.1 years (2004 est.)
Population growth rate: 0.52% (2005 est.)
Birth rate: 15.08 births/1,000 population (2005 est.)
Death rate: 5.12 deaths/1,000 population (2005 est.)
Net migration rate: -4.8 migrant(s)/

1,000 population (2005 est.)
Sex ratio:
at birth: 1.1 male(s)/female
under 15 years: 1.1 male(s)/female
15-64 years: 1.05 male(s)/female
65 years and over: 0.86 male(s)/female
total population: 1.04 male(s)/female (2005 est.)
Infant mortality rate:
total: 21.52 deaths/1,000 live births
male: 21.96 deaths/1,000 live births
female: 21.03 deaths/1,000 live births (2005 est.)
Life expectancy at birth:
total population: 77.24 years
male: 74.6 years
female: 80.15 years (2005 est.)
Total fertility rate: 2.04 children born/woman (2005 est.)
HIV/AIDS - adult prevalence rate: NA%
HIV/AIDS - people living with HIV/AIDS: NA
HIV/AIDS - deaths: NA
Nationality:
noun: Albanian(s)
adjective: Albanian
Ethnic groups: Albanian 95%, Greek 3%, other 2% (Vlach, Roma (Gypsy), Serb, Macedonian, Bulgarian) (1989 est.)
note: in 1989, other estimates of the Greek population ranged from 1% (official Albanian statistics) to 12% (from a Greek organization)
Religions: Muslim 70%, Albanian Orthodox 20%, Roman Catholic 10%
note: percentages are estimates; there are no available current statistics on religious affiliation; all mosques and churches were closed in 1967 and religious observances prohibited; in November 1990, Albania began allowing private religious practice
Languages: Albanian (official - derived from Tosk dialect), Greek, Vlach, Romani, Slavic dialects
Literacy:
definition: age 9 and over can read and write
total population: 86.5%
male: 93.3%
female: 79.5% (2003 est.)

GOVERNMENT

Country name:
conventional long form: Republic of Albania
conventional short form: Albania
local long form: Republika e Shqiperise
local short form: Shqiperia
former: People's Socialist Republic of Albania
Government type: emerging democracy
Capital: Tirana
Administrative divisions: 12 counties (qarqe, singular - qark); Qarku i Beratit, Qarku I Dibres, Qarku i Durresit, Qarku i Elbasanit, Qarku i Fierit, Qarku i Gjirokastres, Qarku i Korces, Qarku i Kukesit, Qarku i Lezhes, Qarku i Shkodres, Qarku i Tiranes, Qarku i Vlores
Independence: 28 November 1912 (from Ottoman Empire)
National holiday: Independence Day, 28 November (1912)
Constitution: adopted by popular referendum on 28 November 1998
Legal system: has a civil law system; has not accepted compulsory ICJ jurisdiction; has accepted jurisdiction of the International Criminal Court for its citizens
Suffrage: 18 years of age; universal
Executive branch:
chief of state: President of the Republic Alfred MOISIU (since 24 July 2002)
head of government: Prime Minister Sali BERISHA (since 10 September 2005)
cabinet: Council of Ministers proposed by the prime minister, nominated by the president, and approved by parliament
elections: president elected by the People's Assembly for a five-year term; election last held 24 June 2002 (next to be held June 2007); prime minister appointed by the president
election results: Alfred MOISIU elected president; People's Assembly vote by number - total votes 116, for 97, against 19
Legislative branch: unicameral People's Assembly or Kuvendi Popullor (140 seats; 100 are elected by direct popular vote and 40 by proportional vote for four-year terms)
elections: last held 4 July 2005 (next to be held July 2009)
election results: percent of vote by party - NA%; seats by party - PD 55, PS 40, PR 11, PSD 7, LSI 5, other 22
Judicial branch: Constitutional Court, Supreme Court (chairman is elected by the People's Assembly for a four-year term), and multiple appeals and district courts
Political parties and leaders: Agrarian Environmentalist Party or PAA [Lufter XHUVELI]; Christian Democratic Party or PDK [Nikolle LESI]; Communist Party of Albania or PKSH [Hysni MILLOSHI]; Democratic Alliance Party or PAD [Neritan CEKA]; Democratic Party or PD [Sali BERISHA]; Legality Movement Party or PLL [Ekrem SPAHIU]; Liberal Union Party or PBL [Arjan STAROVA]; National Front Party (Balli KOMBETAR) or PBK [Adriatik ALIMAGHI]; New Democratic Party or PDR [Genc POLLO]; Party of National Unity or PUK [Idajet BEQIRI]; Renewed Democratic Party or PDR [Dashamir SHEHI]; Republican Party or PR [Fatmir MEDIU]; Social Democracy Party or PDS [Paskal MILO]; Social Democratic Party or PSD [Skender GJINUSHI]; Socialist Movement for Integration or LSI [Ilir META]; Socialist Party or PS (formerly the Albanian Party of Labor) [Fatos NANO]; Union for Human Rights Party or PBDNJ [Vangjel DULE]
Political pressure groups and leaders: Confederation of Trade Unions of Albania or KSSH [Kastriot MUCO]; Front for Albanian National Unification or FBKSH [Gafur ADILI]; Omonia [Jani JANI]; Union of Independent Trade Unions of Albania or BSPSH [Gezim KALAJA]
International organization participation: ACCT, BSEC, CE, CEI, EAPC, EBRD, FAO, IAEA, IBRD, ICAO, ICCt, ICFTU, ICRM, IDA, IDB, IFAD, IFC, IFRCS, ILO, IMF, IMO, Interpol, IOC, IOM, ISO (correspondent), ITU, MIGA, OIC, OPCW, OSCE, PFP, UN, UNCTAD, UNESCO, UNIDO, UNOMIG, UPU, WCO, WFTU, WHO, WIPO, WMO, WToO, WTO
Diplomatic representation in the US:
chief of mission: Acting Ambassador Kreshink COLLAKU
chancery: 2100 S Street NW, Washington, DC 20008
telephone: [1] (202) 223-4942
FAX: [1] (202) 628-7342
Diplomatic representation from the US:
chief of mission: Ambassador Marcie B. RIES
embassy: Rruga Elbasanit, Labinoti #103, Tirana
mailing address: U. S. Department of State, 9510 Tirana Place, Dulles, VA 20189-9510
telephone: [355] (4) 247285
FAX: [355] (4) 374957 and [355] (4) 232222
Flag description: red with a black two-headed eagle in the center

ECONOMY

Economy - overview: Lagging behind its Balkan neighbors, Albania is making the difficult transition to a more modern open-market economy. The government has taken measures to curb violent crime and to spur economic activity and trade. The economy is bolstered by annual remittances from abroad of $600-$800 million, mostly from Greece and Italy; this helps offset the towering trade deficit. Agriculture, which accounts for about one-quarter of GDP, is held back because of frequent drought and the need to modernize equipment, to clarify property rights, and to consolidate small plots of land. Energy shortages and antiquated and inad-

equate infrastructure contribute to Albania's poor business environment, which make it difficult to attract and sustain foreign investment. The planned construction of a new thermal power plant near Vlore and improved transmission and distribution facilities will help relieve the energy shortages. Also, the government is moving slowly to improve the poor national road and rail network, a long-standing barrier to sustained economic growth. On the positive side: growth was strong in 2003-05 and inflation is not a problem.
GDP: purchasing power parity - $18.05 billion
note: Albania has a large gray economy that may be as large as 50 percent of official GDP. (2005 est.)
GDP (official exchange rate): $8.741 billion (2005 est.)
GDP - real growth rate: 6% (2005 est.)
GDP - per capita: purchasing power parity - $4,900 (2004 est.)
GDP - composition by sector:
agriculture: 23.6%
industry: 20.5%
services: 55.9% (2005 est.)
Labor force: 1.09 million (not including 352,000 emigrant workers) (2004 est.)
Labor force - by occupation: agriculture 57%, non-agricultural private sector 20%, public sector 23% (2004 est.)
Unemployment rate: 14.8% officially; may be as high as 30% (2001 est.)
Population below poverty line: 25% (2004 est.)
Household income or consumption by percentage share:
lowest 10%: NA
highest 10%: NA
Inflation rate (consumer prices): 2.5% (2005 est.)
Investment (gross fixed): 22.6% of GDP (2005 est.)
Budget:
revenues: $1.96 billion
expenditures: $2.377 billion, including capital expenditures of $500 million (2005 est.)
Agriculture - products: wheat, corn, potatoes, vegetables, fruits, sugar beets, grapes; meat, dairy products
Industries: food processing, textiles and clothing; lumber, oil, cement, chemicals, mining, basic metals, hydropower
Industrial production growth rate: 3.1% (2004 est.)
Electricity - production: 5.68 billion kWh (2004)
Electricity – production by source:
fossil fuel: 2.9%
hydro: 97.1%
nuclear: 0%
other: 0% (2001)
Electricity - consumption: 6.76 billion kWh (2004)
Electricity - exports: 200 million kWh (2003)
Electricity - imports: 1.08 billion kWh (2004 est.)
Oil - production: 2,000 bbl/day (2004 est.)
Oil - consumption: 7,500 bbl/day (2004 est.)
Oil - exports: 0 bbl/day (2004 est.)
Oil - imports: 5,500 bbl/day (2004 est.)
Oil - proved reserves: 185.5 million bbl (1 January 2002)
Natural gas - production: 30 million cu m (2001 est.)
Natural gas - consumption: 30 million cu m (2001 est.)
Natural gas - exports: 0 cu m (2001 est.)
Natural gas - imports: 0 cu m (2001 est.)
Natural gas - proved reserves: 3.316 billion cu m (1 January 2002)
Current account balance: $-475 million (2005 est.)
Exports: $708.8 million f.o.b. (2005 est.)
Exports - commodities: textiles and footwear; asphalt, metals and metallic ores, crude oil; vegetables, fruits, tobacco
Exports - partners: Italy 71.7%, Canada 4.3%, Germany 4.3% (2004)
Imports: $2.473 billion f.o.b. (2005 est.)
Imports - commodities: machinery and equipment, foodstuffs, textiles, chemicals
Imports - partners: Italy 34.8%, Greece 19.8%, Turkey 7.7%, Germany 5.3% (2004)
Reserves of foreign exchange and gold: $1.45 billion (2005 est.)
Debt - external: $1.41 billion (2003)
Economic aid - recipient: ODA: $315 million (top donors were Italy, EU, Germany) (2000 est.)
Currency: lek (ALL)
Currency code: ALL
Exchange rates: leke per US dollar - 103.07 (2005), 102.649 (2004), 121.863 (2003), 140.155 (2002), 143.485 (2001), 143.709 (2000)
Fiscal year: calendar year

COMMUNICATIONS

Telephones - main lines in use: 255,000 (2003)
Telephones - mobile cellular: 1.1 million (2003)
Telephone system:
general assessment: despite new investment in fixed lines, the density of main lines remains the lowest in Europe with roughly 8 lines per 100 people; however, cellular telephone use is widespread and generally effective
domestic: offsetting the shortage of fixed line capacity, mobile phone service has been available since 1996; by 2003 two companies were providing mobile services at a greater density than some of Albania's Balkan neighbors
international: country code - 355; inadequate fixed main lines; adequate cellular connections; international traffic carried by microwave radio relay from the Tirana exchange to Italy and Greece (2003)
Radio broadcast stations: AM 13, FM 4, shortwave 2 (2001)
Radios: 1 million (2001)
Television broadcast stations: 3 (plus 58 repeaters) (2001)
Televisions: 700,000 (2001)
Internet country code: .al
Internet hosts: 455 (2004)
Internet Service Providers (ISPs): 10 (2001)
Internet users: 30,000 (2003)

TRANSPORTATION

Airports: 11 (2004 est.)
Airports - with paved runways:
total: 3
2,438 to 3,047 m: 3 (2005 est.)
Airports - with unpaved runways:
total: 8
over 3,047 m: 1
1,524 to 2,437 m: 2
914 to 1,523 m: 1
under 914 m: 4 (2005 est.)
Heliports: 1 (2005 est.)
Pipelines: gas 339 km; oil 207 km (2004)
Railways:
total: 447 km
standard gauge: 447 km 1.435-m gauge (2004)
Roadways:
total: 18,000 km
paved: 5,400 km
unpaved: 12,600 km (2002)
Waterways: 43 km (2004)
Merchant marine:
total: 25 ships (1,000 GRT or over) 40,878 GRT/62,676 DWT
by type: cargo 24, roll on/roll off 1
foreign-owned: 2 (Denmark 1, Turkey 1)
registered in other countries: 1 (2005)
Ports and terminals: Durres, Sarande, Shengjin, Vlore

MILITARY

Military branches: General Staff Headquarters, Land Forces Command (Army), Naval Forces Command, Air Defense Command, Logistics Command, Training and Doctrine Command
Military service age and obligation: 19 years of age (2004)
Manpower available for military service: *males age 19-49:* 809,524 (2005 est.)
Manpower fit for military service: *males age 19-49:* 668,526 (2005 est.)
Manpower reaching military service age annually: *males:* 37,407 (2005 est.)
Military expenditures - dollar figure: $56.5 million (FY02)
Military expenditures - percent of GDP: 1.49% (FY02)

TRANSNATIONAL ISSUES

Disputes - international: the Albanian Government calls for the protection of the rights of ethnic Albanians in neighboring countries, and the peaceful resolution of interethnic disputes; some ethnic Albanian groups in neighboring countries advocate for a "greater Albania," but the idea has little appeal among Albanian nationals; thousands of unemployed Albanians emigrate annually to nearby Italy and other developed countries
Illicit drugs: increasingly active transshipment point for Southwest Asian opiates, hashish, and cannabis transiting the Balkan route and - to a far lesser extent - cocaine from South America destined for Western Europe; limited opium and growing cannabis production; ethnic Albanian narcotrafficking organizations active and expanding in Europe; vulnerable to money laundering associated with regional trafficking in narcotics, arms, contraband, and illegal aliens

ALGERIA

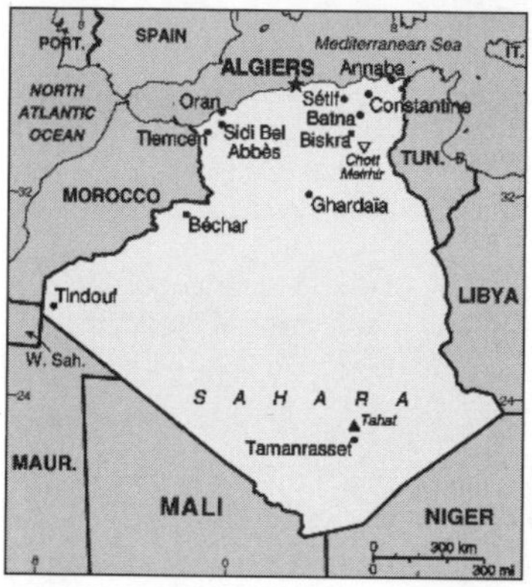

INTRODUCTION

Background: After more than a century of rule by France, Algerians fought through much of the 1950s to achieve independence in 1962. Algeria's primary political party, the National Liberation Front (FLN), has dominated politics ever since. Many Algerians in the subsequent generation were not satisfied, however, and moved to counter the FLN's centrality in Algerian politics. The surprising first round success of the Islamic Salvation Front (FIS) in the December 1991 balloting spurred the Algerian army to intervene and postpone the second round of elections to prevent what the secular elite feared would be an extremist-led government from assuming power. The army began a crack down on the FIS that spurred FIS supporters to begin attacking government targets. The government later allowed elections featuring pro-government and moderate religious-based parties, but did not appease the activists who progressively widened their attacks. The fighting escalated into an insurgency, which saw intense fighting between 1992-98 and which resulted in over 100,000 deaths - many attributed to indiscriminate massacres of villagers by extremists. The government gained the upper hand by the late-1990s and FIS's armed wing, the Islamic Salvation Army, disbanded in January 2000. However, small numbers of armed militants persist in confronting government forces and conducting ambushes and occasional attacks on villages. The army placed Abdelaziz BOUTEFLIKA in the presidency in 1999 in a fraudulent election but claimed neutrality in his 2004 landslide reelection victory. Longstanding problems continue to face BOUTEFLIKA in his second term, including the ethnic minority Berbers' ongoing autonomy campaign, large-scale unemployment, a shortage of housing, unreliable electrical and water supplies, government inefficiencies and corruption, and the continuing - although significantly degraded - activities of extremist militants. Algeria must also diversify its petroleum-based economy, which has yielded a large cash reserve but which has not been used to redress Algeria's many social and infrastructure problems. Algeria assumed a two-year seat on the UN Security Council in January 2004.

GEOGRAPHY

Location: Northern Africa, bordering the Mediterranean Sea, between Morocco and Tunisia
Geographic coordinates: 28 00 N, 3 00 E
Map references: Africa
Area:
total: 2,381,740 sq km
land: 2,381,740 sq km
water: 0 sq km
Area - comparative: slightly less than 3.5 times the size of Texas
Land boundaries:
total: 6,343 km
border countries: Libya 982 km, Mali 1,376 km, Mauritania 463 km, Morocco 1,559 km, Niger 956 km, Tunisia 965 km, Western Sahara 42 km
Coastline: 998 km
Maritime claims:
territorial sea: 12 nm
exclusive fishing zone: 32-52 nm
Climate: arid to semiarid; mild, wet winters with hot, dry summers along coast; drier with cold winters and hot summers on high plateau; sirocco is a hot, dust/sand-laden wind especially common in summer
Terrain: mostly high plateau and desert; some mountains; narrow, discontinuous coastal plain
Elevation extremes:
lowest point: Chott Melrhir -40 m
highest point: Tahat 3,003 m
Natural resources: petroleum, natural gas, iron ore, phosphates, uranium, lead, zinc
Land use:
arable land: 3.22%
permanent crops: 0.25%
other: 96.53% (2001)
Irrigated land: 5,600 sq km (1998 est.)
Natural hazards: mountainous areas subject to severe earthquakes; mudslides and floods in rainy season
Environment - current issues: soil erosion from overgrazing and other poor farming practices; desertification; dumping of raw sewage, petroleum refining wastes, and other industrial effluents is leading to the pollution of rivers and coastal waters; Mediterranean Sea, in particular, becoming polluted from oil wastes, soil erosion, and fertilizer runoff; inadequate supplies of potable water
Environment - international agreements:
party to: Biodiversity, Climate Change, Climate Change-Kyoto Protocol, Desertification, Endangered Species, Environmental Modification, Hazardous Wastes, Law of the Sea, Ozone Layer Protection, Ship Pollution, Wetlands
signed, but not ratified: none of the selected agreements
Geography - note: second-largest country in Africa (after Sudan)

PEOPLE

Population: 32,531,853 (July 2005 est.)
Age structure:
0-14 years: 29% (male 4,811,086/female 4,626,271)
15-64 years: 66.3% (male 10,861,862/female 10,701,459)
65 years and over: 4.7% (male 719,460/female 811,715) (2005 est.)
Median age:
total: 24.36 years
male: 24.18 years
female: 24.53 years (2005 est.)

Population growth rate: 1.22% (2005 est.)
Birth rate: 17.13 births/1,000 population (2005 est.)
Death rate: 4.6 deaths/1,000 population (2005 est.)
Net migration rate: -0.37 migrant(s)/1,000 population (2005 est.)
Sex ratio:
at birth: 1.05 male(s)/female
under 15 years: 1.04 male(s)/female
15-64 years: 1.02 male(s)/female
65 years and over: 0.89 male(s)/female
total population: 1.02 male(s)/female (2005 est.)
Infant mortality rate:
total: 31 deaths/1,000 live births
male: 34.83 deaths/1,000 live births
female: 26.98 deaths/1,000 live births (2005 est.)
Life expectancy at birth:
total population: 73 years
male: 71.45 years
female: 74.63 years (2005 est.)
Total fertility rate: 1.92 children born/woman (2005 est.)
HIV/AIDS - adult prevalence rate: 0.1% ; note - no country specific models provided (2001 est.)
HIV/AIDS - people living with HIV/AIDS: 9,100 (2003 est.)
HIV/AIDS - deaths: less than 500 (2003 est.)
Major infectious diseases:
degree of risk: intermediate
food or waterborne diseases: bacterial diarrhea, hepatitis A, and typhoid fever
vectorborne disease: cutaneous leishmaniasis is a high risk in some locations (2004)
Nationality:
noun: Algerian(s)
adjective: Algerian
Ethnic groups: Arab-Berber 99%, European less than 1%
note: almost all Algerians are Berber in origin, not Arab; the minority who identify themselves as Berber live mostly in the mountainous region of Kabylie east of Algiers; the Berbers are also Muslim but identify with their Berber rather than Arab cultural heritage; Berbers have long agitated, sometimes violently, for autonomy; the government is unlikely to grant autonomy but has offered to begin sponsoring teaching Berber language in schools
Religions: Sunni Muslim (state religion) 99%, Christian and Jewish 1%
Languages: Arabic (official), French, Berber dialects
Literacy:
definition: age 15 and over can read and write
total population: 70%
male: 78.8%
female: 61% (2003 est.)

GOVERNMENT

Country name:
conventional long form: People's Democratic Republic of Algeria
conventional short form: Algeria
local long form: Al Jumhuriyah al Jaza'iriyah ad Dimuqratiyah ash Sha'biyah
local short form: Al Jaza'ir
Government type: republic
Capital: Algiers
Administrative divisions: 48 provinces (wilayas, singular - wilaya); Adrar, Ain Defla, Ain Temouchent, Alger, Annaba, Batna, Bechar, Bejaia, Biskra, Blida, Bordj Bou Arreridj, Bouira, Boumerdes, Chlef, Constantine, Djelfa, El Bayadh, El Oued, El Tarf, Ghardaia, Guelma, Illizi, Jijel, Khenchela, Laghouat, Mascara, Medea, Mila, Mostaganem, M'Sila, Naama, Oran, Ouargla, Oum el Bouaghi, Relizane, Saida, Setif, Sidi Bel Abbes, Skikda, Souk Ahras, Tamanghasset, Tebessa, Tiaret, Tindouf, Tipaza, Tissemsilt, Tizi Ouzou, Tlemcen
Independence: 5 July 1962 (from France)
National holiday: Revolution Day, 1 November (1954)
Constitution: 19 November 1976, effective 22 November 1976; revised 3 November 1988, 23 February 1989, and 28 November 1996
Legal system: socialist, based on French and Islamic law; judicial review of legislative acts in ad hoc Constitutional Council composed of various public officials, including several Supreme Court justices; has not accepted compulsory ICJ jurisdiction
Suffrage: 18 years of age; universal
Executive branch:
chief of state: President Abdelaziz BOUTEFLIKA (since 28 April 1999)
head of government: Prime Minister Ahmed OUYAHIA (since 9 May 2003)
cabinet: Cabinet of Ministers appointed by the president
elections: president elected by popular vote for a five-year term; election last held 8 April 2004 (next to be held NA April 2009); prime minister appointed by the president
election results: Abdelaziz BOUTEFLIKA reelected president for second term; percent of vote - Abdelaziz BOUTEFLIKA 85%, Ali BENFLIS 6.4%, Abdellah DJABALLAH 5%
Legislative branch: bicameral Parliament consists of the National People's Assembly or Al-Majlis Ech-Chaabi Al-Watani (389 seats - changed from 380 seats in the 2002 elections; members elected by popular vote to serve five-year terms) and the Council of Nations (Senate) (144 seats; one-third of the members appointed by the president, two-thirds elected by indirect vote; members serve six-year terms; the constitution requires half the council to be renewed every three years)
elections: National People's Assembly - last held 30 May 2002 (next to be held NA 2007); Council of Nations (Senate) - last held 30 December 2003 (next to be held NA 2006)
election results: National People's Assembly - percent of vote by party - NA%; seats by party - FLN 199, RND 48, Islah 43, MSP 38, PT 21, FNA 8, EnNahda 1, PRA 1, MEN 1, independents 29; Council of Nations - percent of vote by party - NA%; seats by party NA%
Judicial branch: Supreme Court or Court Supreme
Political parties and leaders: Algerian National Front or FNA [Moussa TOUATI]; Democratic National Rally or RND [Ahmed OUYAHIA, chairman]; Islamic Salvation Front or FIS (outlawed April 1992) [Ali BELHADJ and Dr. Abassi MADANI, Rabeh KEBIR (self-exiled in Germany)]; National Entente Movement or MEN [Ali BOUKHAZNA]; National Liberation Front or FLN [Abdelaziz BELKHADEM, secretary general (also serves as Minister of State and Special Representative of the Head of State)]; National Reform Movement or Islah (formerly MRN) [Abdellah DJABALLAH]; National Renewal Party or PRA [Yacine TERKMANE]; Progressive Republican Party [Khadir DRISS]; Rally for Culture and Democracy or RCD [Said SAADI, secretary general]; Renaissance Movement or EnNahda Movement [Fatah RABEI]; Socialist Forces Front or FFS [Hocine Ait AHMED, secretary general (self-exiled in Switzerland)]; Social Liberal Party or PSL [Ahmed KHELIL]; Society of Peace Movement or MSP [Boujerra SOLTANI]; Workers Party or PT [Louisa HANOUN]
note: a law banning political parties based on religion was enacted in March 1997
Political pressure groups and leaders: The Algerian Human Rights League or LADH or LADDH [Yahia Ali ABDENOUR]; SOS Disparus [Nacera DUTOUR]; Somoud [Ali MERABET]
International organization participation: ABEDA, AfDB, AFESD, AMF, AMU, AU, BIS, FAO, G-15, G-24, G-77, IAEA, IBRD, ICAO, ICC, ICCt (signatory), ICFTU, ICRM, IDA, IDB, IFAD, IFC, IFRCS, IHO, ILO, IMF, IMO, Interpol, IOC, IOM, ISO, ITU, LAS, MIGA, MONUC, NAM, OAPEC,

OAS (observer), OIC, OPCW, OPEC, OSCE (partner), UN, UN Security Council (temporary), UNCTAD, UNESCO, UNHCR, UNIDO, UNMEE, UPU, WCO, WHO, WIPO, WMO, WToO, WTO (observer)
Diplomatic representation in the US:
chief of mission: Ambassador Amine KHERBI
chancery: 2137 Wyoming Ave NW, Washington, DC 20008
telephone: [1] (202) 265-2800
FAX: [1] (202) 667-2174
Diplomatic representation from the US:
chief of mission: Ambassador Richard W. ERDMAN
embassy: 4 Chemin Cheikh Bachir El-Ibrahimi, Algiers
mailing address: B. P. 408, Alger-Gare, 16030 Algiers
telephone: [213] (21) 691-425/255/186
FAX: [213] (21) 69-39-79
Flag description: two equal vertical bands of green (hoist side) and white; a red, five-pointed star within a red crescent centered over the two-color boundary; the crescent, star, and color green are traditional symbols of Islam (the state religion)

ECONOMY

Economy - overview: The hydrocarbons sector is the backbone of the economy, accounting for roughly 60% of budget revenues, 30% of GDP, and over 95% of export earnings. Algeria has the seventh-largest reserves of natural gas in the world and is the second-largest gas exporter; it ranks 14th in oil reserves. Sustained high oil prices in recent years, along with macroeconomic policy reforms supported by the IMF, have helped improve Algeria's financial and macroeconomic indicators. Algeria is running substantial trade surpluses and building up record foreign exchange reserves. Real GDP has risen due to higher oil output and increased government spending. The government's continued efforts to diversify the economy by attracting foreign and domestic investment outside the energy sector, however, has had little success in reducing high unemployment and improving living standards. Structural reform within the economy moves ahead slowly.
GDP: purchasing power parity - $237 billion (2005 est.)
GDP: official exchange rate - $88.86 billion (2005 est.)
GDP - real growth rate: 7.1% (2005 est.)
GDP - per capita: purchasing power parity - $7,300 (2005 est.)
GDP - composition by sector:
agriculture: 10%
industry: 59.5%
services: 30.5% (2005 est.)
Labor force: 10.15 million (2005 est.)
Labor force - by occupation: agriculture 14%, industry 13.4%, construction and public works 10%, trade 14.6%, government 32%, other 16% (2003 est.)
Unemployment rate: 22.5% (2005 est.)
Population below poverty line: 23% (1999 est.)
Household income or consumption by percentage share:
lowest 10%: 2.8%
highest 10%: 26.8% (1995)
Distribution of family income - Gini index: 35.3 (1995)
Inflation rate (consumer prices): 4.7% (2005 est.)
Investment (gross fixed): 22.8% of GDP
Budget:
revenues: $42.05 billion
expenditures: $30.75 billion, including capital expenditures of $5.8 billion (2005 est.)
Public debt: 14.8% of GDP (2005 est.)
Agriculture - products: wheat, barley, oats, grapes, olives, citrus, fruits; sheep, cattle
Industries: petroleum, natural gas, light industries, mining, electrical, petrochemical, food processing
Industrial production growth rate: 25.5% (2005 est.)
Electricity - production: 26.99 billion kWh (2003)
Electricity – production by source:
fossil fuel: 99.7%
hydro: 0.3%
nuclear: 0%
other: 0% (2001)
Electricity - consumption: 24.9 billion kWh (2003)
Electricity - exports: 400 million kWh (2003)
Electricity - imports: 200 million kWh (2003)
Oil - production: 1.373 million bbl/day (2005 est.)
Oil - consumption: 232,000 bbl/day (2003 est.)
Oil - exports: NA (2001)
Oil - imports: NA (2001)
Oil - proved reserves: 12.46 billion bbl (2005 est.)
Natural gas - production: 80.3 billion cu m (2001 est.)
Natural gas - consumption: 22.32 billion cu m (2001 est.)
Natural gas - exports: 57.98 billion cu m (2001 est.)
Natural gas - imports: 0 cu m (2001 est.)
Natural gas - proved reserves: 4.739 trillion cu m (2005)
Current account balance: $21.83 billion (2005 est.)
Exports: $49.59 billion f.o.b. (2005 est.)
Exports - partners: US 22.6%, Italy 17.2%, France 11.4%, Spain 10.1%, Canada 7.5%, Brazil 6.1%, Belgium 4.6% (2004)
Imports: $22.53 billion f.o.b. (2005 est.)
Imports - partners: France 30.3%, Italy 8.2%, Germany 6.5%, Spain 5.5%, US 5.2%, China 5.1%, Turkey 4.3% (2004)
Reserves of foreign exchange and gold: $61.01 billion (2005 est.)
Debt - external: $21.54 billion (2005 est.)
Economic aid - recipient: $122.8 million (2002 est.)
Currency: Algerian dinar (DZD)
Currency code: DZD
Exchange rates: Algerian dinars per US dollar - 71.67 (2005), Algerian dinars per US dollar - 72.061 (2004), 77.395 (2003), 79.682 (2002), 77.215 (2001), 75.26 (2000)
Fiscal year: calendar year

COMMUNICATIONS

Telephones - main lines in use: 2,199,600 (2003)
Telephones - mobile cellular: 1,447,310 (2003)
Telephone system:
general assessment: telephone density in Algeria is very low, not exceeding five telephones per 100 persons; the number of fixed main lines increased in the last few years to a little more than 2,000,000, but only about two-thirds of these have subscribers; much of the infrastructure is outdated and inefficient
domestic: good service in north but sparse in south; domestic satellite system with 12 earth stations (20 additional domestic earth stations are planned)
international: country code - 213; submarine cables - 5; microwave radio relay to Italy, France, Spain, Morocco, and Tunisia; coaxial cable to Morocco and Tunisia; participant in Medarabtel; satellite earth stations - 51 (Intelsat, Intersputnik, and Arabsat) (2005)
Radio broadcast stations: AM 25, FM 1, shortwave 8 (1999)
Radios: 7.1 million (1997)
Television broadcast stations: 46 (plus 216 repeaters) (1995)
Televisions: 3.1 million (1997)
Internet country code: .dz
Internet hosts: 897 (2004)
Internet Service Providers (ISPs): 2 (2000)
Internet users: 500,000 (2002)

TRANSPORTATION

Airports: 137 (2004 est.)
Airports - with paved runways:
total: 52
over 3,047 m: 10
2,438 to 3,047 m: 27
1,524 to 2,437 m: 10

914 to 1,523 m: 4
under 914 m: 1 (2005 est.)
Airports - with unpaved runways:
total: 85
2,438 to 3,047 m: 2
1,524 to 2,437 m: 26
914 to 1,523 m: 38
under 914 m: 19 (2005 est.)
Heliports: 1 (2005 est.)
Pipelines: condensate 1,344 km; gas 85,946 km; liquid petroleum gas 2,213 km; oil 6,496 km (2004)
Railways:
total: 3,973 km
standard gauge: 2,888 km 1.435-m gauge (283 km electrified)
narrow gauge: 1,085 km 1.055-m gauge (2004)
Roadways:
total: 104,000 km
paved: 71,656 km (including 640 km of expressways)
unpaved: 32,344 km (1999)
Merchant marine:
total: 56 ships (1,000 GRT or over) 837,676 GRT/929,847 DWT
by type: bulk carrier 9, cargo 14, chemical tanker 4, liquefied gas 10, passenger/cargo 4, petroleum tanker 6, roll on/roll off 9
foreign-owned: 3 (United Kingdom 3)
registered in other countries: 1 (2005)
Ports and terminals: Algiers, Annaba, Arzew, Bejaia, Djendjene, Jijel, Mostaganem, Oran, Skikda

MILITARY

Military branches: People's National Army (ANP; includes Land Forces), Algerian National Navy (MRA), Air Force (QJJ), Territorial Air Defense Force (2005)
Military service age and obligation: 19-30 years of age for compulsory military service; conscript service obligation - 18 months (October 2003)
Manpower available for military service:
males age 19-49: 8,033,049 (2005 est.)
Manpower fit for military service: *males age 19-49:* 6,590,079 (2005 est.)
Manpower reaching military age annually: *males:* 374,639 (2005 est.)
Military expenditures - dollar figure: $2.48 billion (2004)
Military expenditures - percent of GDP: 3.2% (2004)

TRANSNATIONAL ISSUES

Disputes - international: Algeria supports the exiled Sahrawi Polisario Front and rejects Moroccan administration of Western Sahara; Algeria's border with Morocco remains an irritant to bilateral relations, each nation has accused the other of harboring militants and arms smuggling; in an attempt to improve relations after unilaterally imposing a visa requirement on Algerians in the early 1990s, Morocco lifted the requirement in mid-2004 - a gesture not reciprocated by Algeria; Algeria remains concerned about armed bandits operating throughout the Sahel who sometimes destabilize southern Algerian towns; dormant disputes include Libyan claims of about 32,000 sq km still reflected on its maps of southeastern Algeria and the FLN's assertions of a claim to Chirac Pastures in southeastern Morocco
Refugees and internally displaced persons:
refugees (country of origin): 165,000 (Western Saharan Sahrawi, mostly living in Algerian-sponsored camps in the southwestern Algerian town of Tindouf)
IDPs: 100,000 - 200,000 (conflict between government forces, Islamic insurgents) (2004)

AMERICAN SAMOA

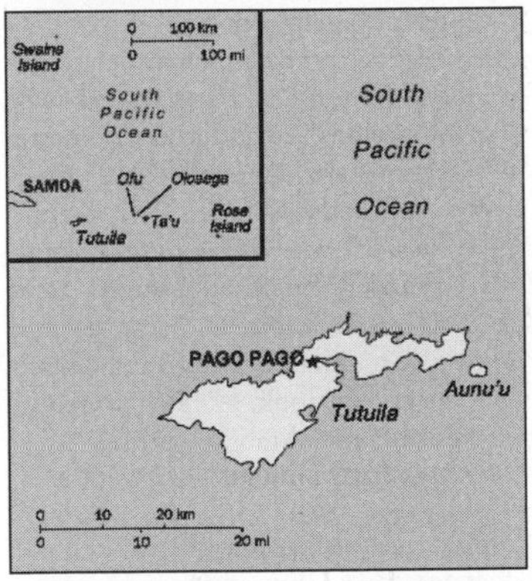

INTRODUCTION

Background: Settled as early as 1000 B.C., Samoa was "discovered" by European explorers in the 18th century. International rivalries in the latter half of the 19th century were settled by an 1899 treaty in which Germany and the US divided the Samoan archipelago. The US formally occupied its portion - a smaller group of eastern islands with the excellent harbor of Pago Pago - the following year.

GEOGRAPHY

Location: Oceania, group of islands in the South Pacific Ocean, about half way between Hawaii and New Zealand
Geographic coordinates: 14 20 S, 170 00 W
Map references: Oceania
Area:
total: 199 sq km
land: 199 sq km
water: 0 sq km
note: includes Rose Island and Swains Island
Area - comparative: slightly larger than Washington, DC
Land boundaries: 0 km
Coastline: 116 km
Maritime claims:
territorial sea: 12 nm
exclusive economic zone: 200 nm
Climate: tropical marine, moderated by southeast trade winds; annual rainfall averages about 3 m; rainy season from November to April, dry season from May to October; little seasonal temperature variation
Terrain: five volcanic islands with rugged peaks and limited coastal plains, two coral atolls (Rose Island, Swains Island)
Elevation extremes:
lowest point: Pacific Ocean 0 m
highest point: Lata 966 m
Natural resources: pumice, pumicite
Land use:
arable land: 10%
permanent crops: 15%
other: 75% (2001)
Irrigated land: NA sq km
Natural hazards: typhoons common from December to March
Environment - current issues: limited natural fresh water resources; the water division of the government has spent substantial funds in the past few years to improve water catchments and pipelines
Geography - note: Pago Pago has one of the best natural deepwater harbors in the South Pacific Ocean, sheltered by shape from rough seas and protected by peripheral mountains from high winds; strategic location in the South Pacific Ocean

PEOPLE

Population: 57,881 (July 2005 est.)
Age structure:
0-14 years: 35.7% (male 10,705/female 9,956)
15-64 years: 61.3% (male 18,351/female 17,125)
65 years and over: 3% (male 664/female 1,080) (2005 est.)

Median age:
total: 22.76 years
male: 22.5 years
female: 23.05 years (2005 est.)
Population growth rate: -0.11% (2005 est.)
Birth rate: 23.13 births/1,000 population (2005 est.)
Death rate: 3.33 deaths/1,000 population (2005 est.)
Net migration rate: -20.89 migrant(s)/1,000 population (2005 est.)
Sex ratio:
at birth: 1.06 male(s)/female
under 15 years: 1.08 male(s)/female
15-64 years: 1.07 male(s)/female
65 years and over: 0.62 male(s)/female
total population: 1.06 male(s)/female (2005 est.)
Infant mortality rate:
total: 9.27 deaths/1,000 live births
male: 9.85 deaths/1,000 live births
female: 8.65 deaths/1,000 live births (2005 est.)
Life expectancy at birth:
total population: 75.84 years
male: 72.27 years
female: 79.62 years (2005 est.)
Total fertility rate: 3.25 children born/woman (2005 est.)
HIV/AIDS - adult prevalence rate: NA%
HIV/AIDS - people living with HIV/AIDS: NA
HIV/AIDS - deaths: NA
Nationality:
noun: American Samoan(s)
adjective: American Samoan
Ethnic groups: native Pacific islander 92.9%, Asian 2.9%, white 1.2%, mixed 2.8%, other 0.2% (2000 census)
Religions: Christian Congregationalist 50%, Roman Catholic 20%, Protestant and other 30%
Languages: Samoan 90.6% (closely related to Hawaiian and other Polynesian languages), English 2.9%, Tongan 2.4%, other Pacific islander 2.1%, other 2%
note: most people are bilingual (2000 census)
Literacy:
definition: age 15 and over can read and write
total population: 97%
male: 98%
female: 97% (1980 est.)

GOVERNMENT

Country name:
conventional long form: Territory of American Samoa
conventional short form: American Samoa
abbreviation: AS
Dependency status: unincorporated and unorganized territory of the US; administered by the Office of Insular Affairs, US Department of the Interior
Government type: NA
Capital: Pago Pago
Administrative divisions: none (territory of the US); there are no first-order administrative divisions as defined by the US Government, but there are three districts and two islands* at the second order; Eastern, Manu'a, Rose Island*, Swains Island*, Western
Independence: none (territory of the US)
National holiday: Flag Day, 17 April (1900)
Constitution: ratified 2 June 1966, effective 1 July 1967
Legal system: NA
Suffrage: 18 years of age; universal
Executive branch:
chief of state: President George W. BUSH of the US (since 20 January 2001) and Vice President Richard B. CHENEY (since 20 January 2001)
head of government: Governor Togiola TULAFONO (since 7 April 2003)
cabinet: cabinet made up of 12 department directors
elections: US president and vice president elected on the same ticket for four-year terms; governor and lieutenant governor elected on the same ticket by popular vote for four-year terms; election last held 2 and 16 November 2004 (next to be held November 2008)
election results: Togiola TULAFONO elected governor; percent of vote - Togiola TULAFONO 55.7%, Afoa Moega LUTU 44.3%
Legislative branch: bicameral Fono or Legislative Assembly consists of the House of Representatives (21 seats - 20 of which are elected by popular vote and 1 is an appointed, nonvoting delegate from Swains Island; members serve two-year terms) and the Senate (18 seats; members are elected from local chiefs and serve four-year terms)
elections: House of Representatives - last held 2 November 2004 (next to be held November 2006); Senate - last held 2 November 2004 (next to be held November 2008)
election results: House of Representatives - percent of vote by party - NA%; seats by party - NA; Senate - percent of vote by party - NA%; seats by party - independents 18
note: American Samoa elects one nonvoting representative to the US House of Representatives; election last held 2 November 2004 (next to be held November 2006); results - Eni F. H. FALEOMAVAEGA (Democrat) reelected as delegate
Judicial branch: High Court (chief justice and associate justices are appointed by the US Secretary of the Interior)
Political parties and leaders: Democratic Party [Oreta M. TOGAFAU]; Republican Party [Tautai A. F. FAALEVAO]
Political pressure groups and leaders: NA
International organization participation: Interpol (subbureau), IOC, UPU
Diplomatic representation in the US: none (territory of the US)
Diplomatic representation from the US: none (territory of the US)
Flag description: blue, with a white triangle edged in red that is based on the outer side and extends to the hoist side; a brown and white American bald eagle flying toward the hoist side is carrying two traditional Samoan symbols of authority, a staff and a war club

ECONOMY

Economy - overview: This is a traditional Polynesian economy in which more than 90% of the land is communally owned. Economic activity is strongly linked to the US, with which American Samoa conducts most of its foreign trade. Tuna fishing and tuna processing plants are the backbone of the private sector, with canned tuna the primary export. Transfers from the US Government add substantially to American Samoa's economic well-being. Attempts by the government to develop a larger and broader economy are restrained by Samoa's remote location, its limited transportation, and its devastating hurricanes. Tourism is a promising developing sector.
GDP: purchasing power parity - $500 million (2000 est.)
GDP (official exchange rate): NA
GDP - real growth rate: NA
GDP - per capita: purchasing power parity - $8,000 (2000 est.)
GDP - composition by sector:
agriculture: NA%
industry: NA%
services: NA%
Inflation rate (consumer prices): NA%
Labor force: 14,000 (1996)
Labor force - by occupation: tuna canneries 34%, government 33%, other 33% (1990)
Unemployment rate: 6% (2000)
Population below poverty line: NA
Household income or consumption by percentage share:
lowest 10%: NA
highest 10%: NA
Budget:
revenues: $121 million (37% in local revenue and 63% in US grants)
expenditures: $127 million, including capital expenditures of NA (FY96/97)

Agriculture - products: bananas, coconuts, vegetables, taro, breadfruit, yams, copra, pineapples, papayas; dairy products, livestock
Industries: tuna canneries (largely supplied by foreign fishing vessels), handicrafts
Industrial production growth rate: NA%
Electricity - production: 130 million kWh (2003)
Electricity - production by source:
fossil fuel: 100%
hydro: 0%
nuclear: 0%
other: 0% (2001)
Electricity - consumption: 120.9 million kWh (2003)
Electricity - exports: 0 kWh (2003)
Electricity - imports: 0 kWh (2003)
Oil - production: 0 bbl/day (2003 est.)
Oil - consumption: 4,000 bbl/day (2003 est.)
Oil - exports: NA (2001)
Oil - imports: NA (2001)
Exports: $10 million (2004)
Exports - partners: Samoa 39.8%, Australia 19.9%, Japan 15.1%, New Zealand 10.5% (2004)
Imports: $105 million (2004 est.)
Imports - partners: Japan 31.4%, New Zealand 27.9%, Germany 17.1%, Australia 8.9% (2004)
Debt - external: $NA
Economic aid - recipient: important financial support from the US, more than $40 million in 1994
Currency: US dollar (USD)
Currency code: USD
Exchange rates: the US dollar is used
Fiscal year: 1 October - 30 September

COMMUNICATIONS

Telephones - main lines in use: 15,000 (2001)
Telephones - mobile cellular: 2,377 (1999)
Telephone system:
general assessment: NA
domestic: good telex, telegraph, facsimile and cellular telephone services; domestic satellite system with 1 Comsat earth station
international: country code - 1-684; satellite earth station - 1 Intelsat (Pacific Ocean)
Radio broadcast stations: AM 3, FM 4, shortwave 1 (2004)
Radios: 57,000 (1997)
Television broadcast stations: 1; note - one cable TV station (2004)
Televisions: 14,000 (1997)
Internet country code: .as
Internet Service Providers (ISPs): 1 (2000)
Internet users: NA

TRANSPORTATION

Airports: 3 (2004 est.)
Airports - with paved runways:
total: 2
2,438 to 3,047 m: 1
under 914 m: 1 (2005 est.)
Airports - with unpaved runways:
total: 1
under 914 m: 1 (2005 est.)
Roadways:
total: 185 km
paved: 185 km
unpaved: 0 km (2004)
Ports and terminals: Pago Pago

MILITARY

Military — note: defense is the responsibility of the US

TRANSNATIONAL ISSUES

Disputes - international: none

ANDORRA

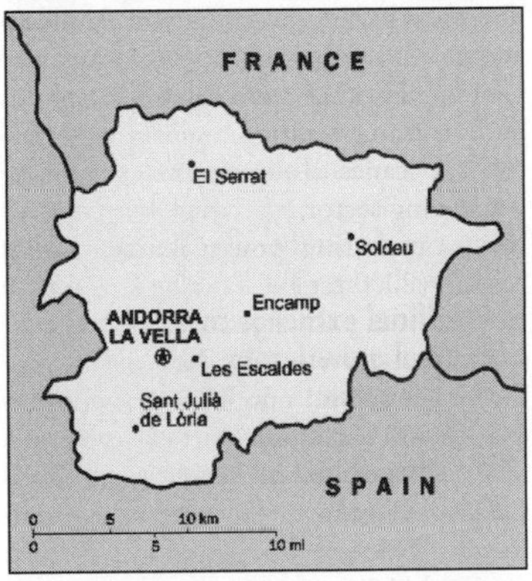

INTRODUCTION

Background: For 715 years, from 1278 to 1993, Andorrans lived under a unique co-principality, ruled by French and Spanish leaders (from 1607 onward, the French chief of state and the Spanish bishop of Urgel). In 1993, this feudal system was modified with the titular heads of state retained, but the government transformed into a parliamentary democracy. Long isolated and impoverished, mountainous Andorra achieved considerable prosperity since World War II through its tourist industry. Many immigrants (legal and illegal) are attracted to the thriving economy with its lack of income taxes.

GEOGRAPHY

Location: Southwestern Europe, between France and Spain
Geographic coordinates: 42 30 N, 1 30 E
Map references: Europe
Area:
total: 468 sq km
land: 468 sq km
water: 0 sq km
Area - comparative: 2.5 times the size of Washington, DC
Land boundaries:
total: 120.3 km
border countries: France 56.6 km, Spain 63.7 km
Coastline: 0 km (landlocked)
Maritime claims: none (landlocked)
Climate: temperate; snowy, cold winters and warm, dry summers
Terrain: rugged mountains dissected by narrow valleys
Elevation extremes:
lowest point: Riu Runer 840 m
highest point: Coma Pedrosa 2,946 m
Natural resources: hydropower, mineral water, timber, iron ore, lead
Land use:
arable land: 2.22%
permanent crops: 0%
other: 97.78% (2001)
Irrigated land: NA sq km
Natural hazards: avalanches
Environment - current issues: deforestation; overgrazing of mountain meadows contributes to soil erosion; air pollution; wastewater treatment and solid waste disposal
Environment - international agreements:
party to: Hazardous Wastes
signed, but not ratified: none of the selected agreements
Geography - note: landlocked; straddles a number of important crossroads in the Pyrenees

PEOPLE

Population: 70,549 (July 2005 est.)
Age structure:
0-14 years: 14.8% (male 5,471/female 4,995)
15-64 years: 71.5% (male 26,463/female 23,977)
65 years and over: 13.7% (male 4,780/female 4,863) (2005 est.)
Median age:
total: 40.34 years
male: 40.63 years
female: 40.02 years (2005 est.)
Population growth rate: 0.95% (2005 est.)
Birth rate: 9 births/1,000 population (2005 est.)
Death rate: 6.07 deaths/1,000 population (2005 est.)
Net migration rate: 6.53 migrant(s)/1,000 population (2005 est.)

Sex ratio:
at birth: 1.07 male(s)/female
under 15 years: 1.1 male(s)/female
15-64 years: 1.1 male(s)/female
65 years and over: 0.98 male(s)/female
total population: 1.08 male(s)/female (2005 est.)
Infant mortality rate:
total: 4.05 deaths/1,000 live births
male: 4.38 deaths/1,000 live births
female: 3.69 deaths/1,000 live births (2005 est.)
Life expectancy at birth:
total population: 83.51 years
male: 80.6 years
female: 86.6 years (2005 est.)
Total fertility rate: 1.29 children born/woman (2005 est.)
HIV/AIDS - adult prevalence rate: NA%
HIV/AIDS - people living with HIV/AIDS: NA
HIV/AIDS - deaths: NA
Nationality:
noun: Andorran(s)
adjective: Andorran
Ethnic groups: Spanish 43%, Andorran 33%, Portuguese 11%, French 7%, other 6% (1998)
Religions: Roman Catholic (predominant)
Languages: Catalan (official), French, Castilian, Portuguese
Literacy:
definition: NA
total population: 100%
male: NA%
female: NA%

GOVERNMENT

Country name:
conventional long form: Principality of Andorra
conventional short form: Andorra
local long form: Principat d'Andorra
local short form: Andorra
Government type: parliamentary democracy (since March 1993) that retains as its chiefs of state a coprincipality; the two princes are the president of France and bishop of Seo de Urgel, Spain, who are represented locally by coprinces' representatives
Capital: Andorra la Vella
Administrative divisions: 7 parishes (parroquies, singular - parroquia); Andorra la Vella, Canillo, Encamp, La Massana, Escaldes-Engordany, Ordino, Sant Julia de Loria
Independence: 1278 (was formed under the joint suzerainty of the French count of Foix and the Spanish bishop of Urgel)
National holiday: Our Lady of Meritxell Day, 8 September (1278)
Constitution: Andorra's first written constitution was drafted in 1991, approved by referendum 14 March 1993, effective 4 May 1993
Legal system: based on French and Spanish civil codes; no judicial review of legislative acts; has not accepted compulsory ICJ jurisdiction
Suffrage: 18 years of age; universal
Executive branch:
chief of state: French Coprince Jacques CHIRAC (since 17 May 1995), represented by Philippe MASSONI (since 26 July 2002); Spanish Coprince Bishop Joan Enric VIVES i SICILIA (since 12 May 2003), represented by Nemesi MARQUES i OSTE (since NA)
head of government: Executive Council President Albert PINTAT SANTOLARIA (since 27 May 2005)
cabinet: Executive Council or Govern designated by the Executive Council president
elections: Executive Council president elected by the General Council and formally appointed by the coprinces for a four-year term; election last held 4 March 2001 (next to be held April-May 2005)
election results: Marc FORNE MOLNE elected executive council president; percent of General Council vote - NA%
Legislative branch: unicameral General Council of the Valleys or Consell General de las Valls (28 seats; members are elected by direct popular vote, 14 from a single national constituency and 14 to represent each of the 7 parishes; members serve four-year terms)
elections: last held 24 April 2005 (next to be held March-April 2009)
election results: percent of vote by party - PLA 41.2%, PS 38.1%, CDA 11%, other 9.7%; seats by party - PLA 14, PS 12, CDA 2
Judicial branch: Tribunal of Judges or Tribunal de Batlles; Tribunal of the Courts or Tribunal de Corts; Supreme Court of Justice of Andorra or Tribunal Superior de Justicia d'Andorra; Supreme Council of Justice or Consell Superior de la Justicia; Fiscal Ministry or Ministeri Fiscal; Constitutional Tribunal or Tribunal Constitucional
Political parties and leaders: Andorran Democratic Center Party or CDA (formerly Democratic Party or PD) [leader NA]; Liberal Party of Andorra or PLA (formerly Liberal Union or UL) [Albert PINTAT]; Social Democratic Party or PS (formerly part of National Democratic Group or AND) [Mariona GONZALEZ REOLIT]
Political pressure groups and leaders: NA
International organization participation: CE, ICAO, ICCt, ICRM, IFRCS, Interpol, IOC, ITU, OPCW, OSCE, UN, UNESCO, WCO, WHO, WIPO, WToO, WTO (observer)
Diplomatic representation in the US:
chief of mission: Ambassador (vacant); Charge d'Affaires Jelena V. PIA-COMELLA
chancery: 2 United Nations Plaza, 25th Floor, New York, NY 10017
telephone: [1] (212) 750-8064
FAX: [1] (212) 750-6630
Diplomatic representation from the US: the US does not have an embassy in Andorra; the US Ambassador to Spain is accredited to Andorra; US interests in Andorra are represented by the Consulate General's office in Barcelona (Spain)
mailing address: Paseo Reina Elisenda, 23, 08034 Barcelona, Spain
telephone: [34] (93) 280-2227
FAX: [34] (93) 280-6175
Flag description: three equal vertical bands of blue (hoist side), yellow, and red with the national coat of arms centered in the yellow band; the coat of arms features a quartered shield; similar to the flags of Chad and Romania, which do not have a national coat of arms in the center, and the flag of Moldova, which does bear a national emblem

ECONOMY

Economy - overview: Tourism, the mainstay of Andorra's tiny, well-to-do economy, accounts for roughly 80% of GDP. An estimated 9 million tourists visit annually, attracted by Andorra's duty-free status and by its summer and winter resorts. Andorra's comparative advantage has recently eroded as the economies of neighboring France and Spain have been opened up, providing broader availability of goods and lower tariffs. The banking sector, with its "tax haven" status, also contributes substantially to the economy. Agricultural production is limited - only 2% of the land is arable - and most food has to be imported. The principal livestock activity is sheep raising. Manufacturing output consists mainly of cigarettes, cigars, and furniture. Andorra is a member of the EU Customs Union and is treated as an EU member for trade in manufactured goods (no tariffs) and as a non-EU member for agricultural products.
GDP: purchasing power parity - $1.9 billion (2003 est.)
GDP - official exchange rate: NA
GDP - real growth rate: 2% (2003 est.)
GDP - per capita: purchasing power parity - $26,800 (2003 est.)
GDP - composition by sector:
agriculture: NA%
industry: NA%
services: NA%
Labor force: 33,000 (2001 est.)
Labor force - by occupation: agriculture 1%, industry 21%, services 78% (2000 est.)

Unemployment rate: 0% (1996 est.)
Population below poverty line: NA
Household income or consumption by percentage share:
lowest 10%: NA%
highest 10%: NA%
Inflation rate (consumer prices): 4.3% (2000)
Budget:
revenues: $385 million
expenditures: $342 million, including capital expenditures of NA (1997)
Agriculture - products: small quantities of rye, wheat, barley, oats, vegetables; sheep
Industries: tourism (particularly skiing), cattle raising, timber, banking
Industrial production growth rate: NA
Electricity - production: NA kWh
Electricity - consumption: NA kWh
Electricity - exports: 0 kWh (2002)
Electricity - imports: NA kWh; note - most electricity supplied by Spain and France; Andorra generates a small amount of hydropower
Exports: $58 million f.o.b. (1998)
Exports - commodities: tobacco products, furniture
Exports - partners: Spain 58%, France 34% (2000)
Imports: $1.077 billion (1998)
Imports - commodities: consumer goods, food, electricity
Imports - partners: Spain 48%, France 35%, US 2.3% (2004)
Debt - external: $NA
Economic aid - recipient: none
Currency: euro (EUR)
Currency code: EUR
Exchange rates: euros per US dollar - 0.79697 (2005), 0.8054 (2004), 0.886 (2003), 1.0626 (2002), 1.1175 (2001), 1.0854 (2000)
Fiscal year: calendar year

COMMUNICATIONS

Telephones - main lines in use: 35,000 (2001)
Telephones - mobile cellular: 23,500 (2001)
Telephone system:
general assessment: NA
domestic: modern system with microwave radio relay connections between exchanges
international: country code - 376; landline circuits to France and Spain
Radio broadcast stations: AM 0, FM 15, shortwave 0 (1998)
Television broadcast stations: 0 (1997)
Internet country code: .ad
Internet hosts: 4,144 (2004)
Internet users: 24,500 (2001)

TRANSPORTATION

Airports: none (2004 est.)
Roadways:
total: 269 km
paved: 198 km
unpaved: 71 km
Waterways: 1,200 km
Merchant marine:
registered in other countries: 1

MILITARY

Military branches: no regular military forces, Police Service of Andorra; note: defense is the responsibility of France and Spain

TRANSNATIONAL ISSUES

Disputes - international: none

ANGOLA

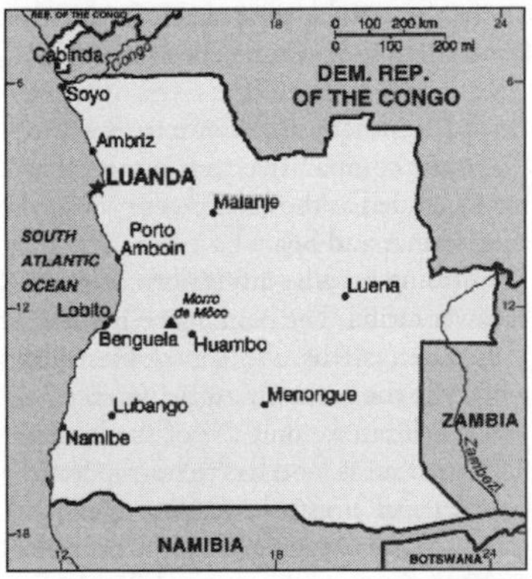

INTRODUCTION

Background: Angola is slowly rebuilding its country after the end of a 27-year civil war in 2002. Fighting between the Popular Movement for the Liberation of Angola (MPLA), led by Jose Eduardo DOS SANTOS, and the National Union for the Total Independence of Angola (UNITA), led by Jonas SAVIMBI, followed independence from Portugal in 1975. Peace seemed imminent in 1992 when Angola held national elections, but UNITA renewed fighting after being beaten by the MPLA at the polls. Up to 1.5 million lives may have been lost - and 4 million people displaced - in the quarter century of fighting. SAVIMBI's death in 2002 ended UNITA's insurgency and strengthened the MPLA's hold on power. DOS SANTOS has pledged to hold legislative elections in 2006.

GEOGRAPHY

Location: Southern Africa, bordering the South Atlantic Ocean, between Namibia and Democratic Republic of the Congo
Geographic coordinates: 12 30 S, 18 30 E
Map references: Africa
Area:
total: 1,246,700 sq km
land: 1,246,700 sq km
water: 0 sq km
Area - comparative: slightly less than twice the size of Texas
Land boundaries:
total: 5,198 km
border countries: Democratic Republic of the Congo 2,511 km (of which 225 km is the boundary of discontiguous Cabinda Province), Republic of the Congo 201 km, Namibia 1,376 km, Zambia 1,110 km
Coastline: 1,600 km
Maritime claims:
territorial sea: 12 nm
contiguous zone: 24 nm
exclusive economic zone: 200 nm
Climate: semiarid in south and along coast to Luanda; north has cool, dry season (May to October) and hot, rainy season (November to April)
Terrain: narrow coastal plain rises abruptly to vast interior plateau
Elevation extremes:
lowest point: Atlantic Ocean 0 m
highest point: Morro de Moco 2,620 m
Natural resources: petroleum, diamonds, iron ore, phosphates, copper, feldspar, gold, bauxite, uranium
Land use:
arable land: 2.41%
permanent crops: 0.24%
other: 97.35% (2001)
Irrigated land: 750 sq km (1998 est.)
Natural hazards: locally heavy rainfall causes periodic flooding on the plateau
Environment - current issues: overuse of pastures and subsequent soil erosion attributable to population pressures; desertification; deforestation of tropical rain forest, in response to both international demand for tropical timber and to domestic use as fuel, resulting in loss of biodiversity; soil erosion contributing to water pollution and siltation of rivers and dams; inadequate supplies of potable water
Environment - international agreements:
party to: Biodiversity, Climate Change, Desertification, Law of the Sea, Ozone Layer Protection, Ship Pollution
signed, but not ratified: none of the selected agreements
Geography - note: the province of Cabinda is an exclave, separated from the

rest of the country by the Democratic Republic of the Congo

PEOPLE

Population: 11,190,786 (July 2005 est.)
Age structure:
0-14 years: 43.4% (male 2,454,209/female 2,407,083)
15-64 years: 53.7% (male 3,059,339/female 2,955,060)
65 years and over: 2.8% (male 139,961/female 175,134) (2005 est.)
Median age:
total: 18.12 years
male: 18.12 years
female: 18.11 years (2005 est.)
Population growth rate: 1.9% (2005 est.)
Birth rate: 44.64 births/1,000 population (2005 est.)
Death rate: 25.9 deaths/1,000 population (2005 est.)
Net migration rate: 0.28 migrant(s)/1,000 population (2005 est.)
Sex ratio:
at birth: 1.05 male(s)/female
under 15 years: 1.02 male(s)/female
15-64 years: 1.04 male(s)/female
65 years and over: 0.8 male(s)/female
total population: 1.02 male(s)/female (2005 est.)
Infant mortality rate:
total: 191.19 deaths/1,000 live births
male: 203.68 deaths/1,000 live births
female: 178.07 deaths/1,000 live births (2005 est.)
Life expectancy at birth:
total population: 38.43 years
male: 37.28 years
female: 39.64 years (2005 est.)
Total fertility rate: 6.27 children born/woman (2005 est.)
HIV/AIDS - adult prevalence rate: 3.9% (2003 est.)
HIV/AIDS - people living with HIV/AIDS: 240,000 (2003 est.)
HIV/AIDS - deaths: 21,000 (2003 est.)
Major infectious diseases:
degree of risk: very high
food or waterborne diseases: bacterial and protozoal diarrhea, hepatitis A, typhoid fever
vectorborne diseases: malaria, African trypanosomiasis (sleeping sickness) are high risks in some locations
respiratory disease: meningococcal meningitis
water contact disease: schistosomiasis (2004)
Nationality:
noun: Angolan(s)
adjective: Angolan
Ethnic groups: Ovimbundu 37%, Kimbundu 25%, Bakongo 13%, mestico (mixed European and native African) 2%, European 1%, other 22%
Religions: indigenous beliefs 47%, Roman Catholic 38%, Protestant 15% (1998 est.)
Languages: Portuguese (official), Bantu and other African languages
Literacy:
definition: age 15 and over can read and write
total population: 66.8%
male: 82.1%
female: 53.8% (2001 est.)

GOVERNMENT

Country name:
conventional long form: Republic of Angola
conventional short form: Angola
local long form: Republica de Angola
local short form: Angola
former: People's Republic of Angola
Government type: republic, nominally a multiparty democracy with a strong presidential system
Capital: Luanda
Administrative divisions: 18 provinces (provincias, singular - provincia); Bengo, Benguela, Bie, Cabinda, Cuando Cubango, Cuanza Norte, Cuanza Sul, Cunene, Huambo, Huila, Luanda, Lunda Norte, Lunda Sul, Malanje, Moxico, Namibe, Uige, Zaire
Independence: 11 November 1975 (from Portugal)
National holiday: Independence Day, 11 November (1975)
Constitution: 11 November 1975; revised 7 January 1978, 11 August 1980, 6 March 1991, and 26 August 1992; note - new constitution has not yet been approved
Legal system: based on Portuguese civil law system and customary law; recently modified to accommodate political pluralism and increased use of free markets
Suffrage: 18 years of age; universal
Executive branch:
chief of state: President Jose Eduardo DOS SANTOS (since 21 September 1979); note - the president is both chief of state and head of government
head of government: President Jose Eduardo DOS SANTOS (since 21 September 1979); note - the president is both chief of state and head of government; Fernando de Piedade Dias DOS SANTOS was appointed Prime Minister on 6 December 2002, but this is not a position of real power
cabinet: Council of Ministers appointed by the president
elections: president elected by universal ballot for a five-year term; President DOS SANTOS originally elected (in 1979) without opposition under a one-party system and stood for reelection in Angola's first multiparty elections 29-30 September 1992 (next to be held September 2006)
election results: DOS SANTOS 49.6%, Jonas SAVIMBI 40.1%, making a run-off election necessary; the run-off was not held and SAVIMBI's National Union for the Total Independence of Angola (UNITA) repudiated the results of the first election; the civil war resumed
Legislative branch: unicameral National Assembly or Assembleia Nacional (220 seats; members elected by proportional vote to serve four-year terms)
elections: last held 29-30 September 1992 (next to be held September 2006)
election results: percent of vote by party - MPLA 54%, UNITA 34%, others 12%; seats by party - MPLA 129, UNITA 70, PRS 6, FNLA 5, PLD 3, others 7
Judicial branch: Supreme Court or Tribunal da Relacao (judges are appointed by the president)
Political parties and leaders: Liberal Democratic Party or PLD [Analia de Victoria PEREIRA]; National Front for the Liberation of Angola or FNLA [disputed leadership: Lucas NGONDA, Holden ROBERTO]; National Union for the Total Independence of Angola or UNITA [Isaias SAMAKUVA], largest opposition party has engaged in years of armed resistance; Popular Movement for the Liberation of Angola or MPLA [Jose Eduardo DOS SANTOS], ruling party in power since 1975; Social Renewal Party or PRS [disputed leadership: Eduardo KUANGANA, Antonio MUACHICUNGO]
note: about a dozen minor parties participated in the 1992 elections but only won a few seats and have little influence in the National Assembly
Political pressure groups and leaders: Front for the Liberation of the Enclave of Cabinda or FLEC [N'zita Henriques TIAGO, Antonio Bento BEMBE]
note: FLEC is waging a small-scale, highly factionalized, armed struggle for the independence of Cabinda Province
International organization participation: ACP, AfDB, AU, FAO, G-77, IAEA, IBRD, ICAO, ICCt (signatory), ICFTU, ICRM, IDA, IFAD, IFC, IFRCS, ILO, IMF, IMO, Interpol, IOC, IOM, ISO (correspondent), ITU, MIGA, NAM, OAS (observer), SADC, UN, UNCTAD, UNESCO, UNIDO, UPU, WCO, WFTU, WHO, WIPO, WMO, WToO, WTO
Diplomatic representation in the US:
chief of mission: Ambassador Josefina Perpetua Pitra DIAKIDI
chancery: 2108 16th Street NW, Washington, DC 20009
telephone: [1] (202) 785-1156
FAX: [1] (202) 785-1258
consulate(s) general: Houston and New York

Diplomatic representation from the US:
chief of mission: Ambassador Cynthia EFFIRD
embassy: number 32 Rua Houari Boumedienne (in the Miramar area of Luanda), Luanda
mailing address: international mail: Caixa Postal 6468, Luanda; pouch: American Embassy Luanda, Department of State, Washington, DC 20521-2550
telephone: [244] (2) 445-481, 447-028, 446-224
FAX: [244] (2) 446-924
Flag description: two equal horizontal bands of red (top) and black with a centered yellow emblem consisting of a five-pointed star within half a cogwheel crossed by a machete (in the style of a hammer and sickle)

ECONOMY

Economy - overview: Angola's high growth rate is driven by its oil sector, but record oil prices and rising petroleum production have occurred without improved performance in other parts of the economy. Oil production and its supporting activities, contribute about 45% to GDP and more than half of exports, and much of the country's infrastructure is still damaged or undeveloped from the 22 year-long civil war. Remnants of the conflict such as widespread land mines still mar the countryside even though an apparently durable peace has been established after the death of rebel leader Jonas SAVIMBI in February 2002. Subsistence agriculture provides the main livelihood for 85% of the population, but much of the country's food must still be imported. In 2005, the government started using a $2 billion line of credit from China to rebuild Angola's public infrastructure, and several large-scale projects are scheduled for completion by 2006. The central bank in 2003 implemented an exchange rate stabilization program using foreign exchange reserves to buy kwanzas out of circulation, a policy that was more sustainable in 2005 because of strong oil export earnings, and has significantly reduced inflation. Consumer inflation declined from 325% in 2000 to about 18% in 2005, but the stabilization policy places pressure on international net liquidity. To fully take advantage of its rich national resources - gold, diamonds, extensive forests, Atlantic fisheries, and large oil deposits - Angola will need to continue reforming government policies and to reduce corruption. The government has made sufficient progress on reforms recommended by the IMF, such as promoting greater transparency in government spending, and continues to be without a formal monitoring agreement with the institution. Increased oil production supported 12% growth in 2004 and 14% growth in 2005.
GDP: purchasing power parity - $27.66 billion (2005 est.)
GDP: official exchange rate - $24.13 billion (2005 est.)
GDP - real growth rate: 14.1% (2005 est.)
GDP - per capita: purchasing power parity - $2,500 (2005 est.)
GDP - composition by sector:
agriculture: 8%
industry: 67%
services: 25% (2001 est.)
Labor force: 5.58 million (2005 est.)
Labor force - by occupation: agriculture 85%, industry and services 15% (2003 est.)
Unemployment rate: extensive unemployment and underemployment affecting more than half the population (2001 est.)
Population below poverty line: 70% (2003 est.)
Household income or consumption by percentage share:
lowest 10%: NA
highest 10%: NA
Inflation rate (consumer prices): 17.7% (2005 est.)
Investment (gross fixed): 30.6% of GDP (2005 est.)
Budget:
revenues: $8.5 billion
expenditures: $ 10 billion, including capital expenditures of $963 million (2005 est.)
Public debt: 40.9% of GDP (2005 est.)
Agriculture - products: bananas, sugarcane, coffee, sisal, corn, cotton, manioc (tapioca), tobacco, vegetables, plantains; livestock; forest products; fish
Industries: petroleum; diamonds, iron ore, phosphates, feldspar, bauxite, uranium, and gold; cement; basic metal products; fish processing; food processing; brewing; tobacco products; sugar; textiles, ship repair
Industrial production growth rate: 1% (2000)
Electricity - production: 1.916 billion kWh (2003)
Electricity – production by source:
fossil fuel: 36.4%
hydro: 63.6%
nuclear: 0%
other: 0% (2001)
Electricity - consumption: 1.782 billion kWh (2003)
Electricity - exports: 0 kWh (2003)
Electricity - imports: 0 kWh (2003)
Oil - production: 1.6 million bbl/day (2005 est.)
Oil - consumption: 46,000 bbl/day (2003 est.)
Oil - exports: NA
Oil - imports: NA
Oil - proved reserves: 25 billion bbl (2005 est.)
Natural gas - production: 530 million cu m (2001 est.)
Natural gas - consumption: 530 million cu m (2001 est.)
Natural gas - exports: 0 cu m (2001 est.)
Natural gas - imports: 0 cu m (2001 est.)
Natural gas - proved reserves: 79.57 billion cu m (2005)
Current account balance: $4.484 billion (2005 est.)
Exports: $26.8 billion f.o.b. (2005 est.)
Exports - partners: US 37.7%, China 35.6%, Taiwan 6.7%, France 6.4% (2004)
Imports: $4.896 billion f.o.b. (2004 est.)
Imports - commodities: machinery and electrical equipment, vehicles and spare parts; medicines, food, textiles, military goods
Imports - partners: South Korea 28.3%, Portugal 13.1%, US 9.3%, South Africa 7.4%, Brazil 5.6%, Japan 4.8%, France 4.4% (2004)
Reserves of foreign exchange and gold: $2.425 billion (2005 est.)
Debt - external: $9.879 billion (2005 est.)
Economic aid - recipient: $383.5 million (1999)
Currency: kwanza (AOA)
Currency code: AOA
Exchange rates: kwanza per US dollar – 88.6 (2005), 83.541 (2004), 74.606 (2003), 43.53 (2002), 22.058 (2001), 10.041 (2000)
Fiscal year: calendar year

COMMUNICATIONS

Telephones - main lines in use: 96,300 (2003)
Telephones - mobile cellular: 130,000 (2002)
Telephone system:
general assessment: telephone service limited mostly to government and business use; HF radiotelephone used extensively for military links
domestic: limited system of wire, microwave radio relay, and tropospheric scatter
international: country code - 244; satellite earth stations - 29; fiber optic submarine cable (SAT-3/WASC) provides connectivity to Europe and Asia (2005)
Radio broadcast stations: AM 21, FM 6, shortwave 7 (2000)
Radios: 815,000 (2000)
Television broadcast stations: 6 (2000)
Televisions: 196,000 (2000)
Internet country code: .ao
Internet hosts: 17 (2003)
Internet Service Providers (ISPs): 1 (2000)
Internet users: 41,000 (2002)

TRANSPORTATION

Airports: 243 (2004 est.)
Airports - with paved runways:
total: 31
over 3,047 m: 5
2,438 to 3,047 m: 8
1,524 to 2,437 m: 12
914 to 1,523 m: 5
under 914 m: 1 (2005 est.)
Airports - with unpaved runways:
total: 212
over 3,047 m: 2
2,438 to 3,047 m: 5
1,524 to 2,437 m: 30
914 to 1,523 m: 95
under 914 m: 80 (2005 est.)
Pipelines: gas 214 km; liquid natural gas 14 km; liquid petroleum gas 30 km; oil 837 km; refined products 56 km (2004)
Railways:
total: 2,761 km
narrow gauge: 2,638 km 1.067-m gauge; 123 km 0.600-m gauge (2004)
Roadways:
total: 51,429 km
paved: 5,328 km
unpaved: 46,101 km (2001)
Waterways: 1,300 km (2004)
Merchant marine:
total: 4 ships (1,000 GRT or over) 26,123 GRT/42,879 DWT
by type: cargo 1, passenger/cargo 2, petroleum tanker 1
registered in other countries: 4 (2005)
Ports and terminals: Cabinda, Luanda, Soyo

MILITARY

Military branches: Army, Navy (Marinha de Guerra, MdG), Air and Air Defense Forces (FANA)
Military service age and obligation: 17 years of age for compulsory military service; conscript service obligation - 2 years plus time for training (2001)
Manpower available for military service: *males age 17-49:* 2,423,221 (2005 est.)
Manpower fit for military service: *males age 17-49:* 1,174,548 (2005 est.)
Manpower reaching military age annually: *males:* 121,254 (2005 est.)
Military expenditures - dollar figure: $183.58 million (2004)
Military expenditures - percent of GDP: 10.6% (2004)

TRANSNATIONAL ISSUES

Disputes - international: 90,000 Angolan refugees were repatriated by 2004, the remaining refugees in the Democratic Republic of the Congo and Zambia are expected to return in 2005; many Cabinda exclave secessionists have sought shelter in neighboring states
Refugees and internally displaced persons: *IDPs:* 40,000-60,000 (27-year civil war ending in 2002; 4 million IDPs already have returned) (2004)
Illicit drugs: used as a transshipment point for cocaine destined for Western Europe and other African states

ANGUILLA

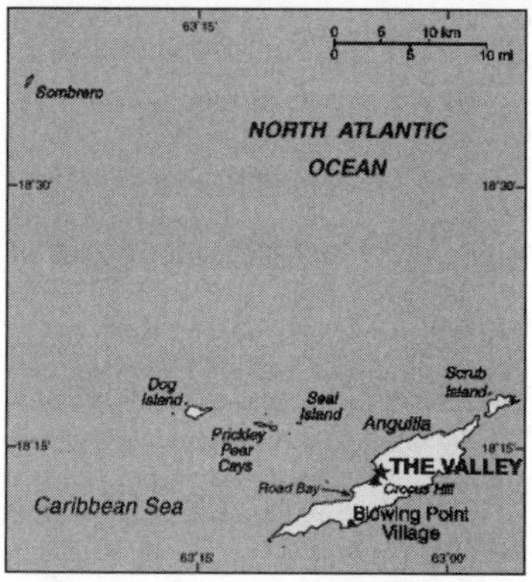

INTRODUCTION

Background: Colonized by English settlers from Saint Kitts in 1650, Anguilla was administered by Great Britain until the early 19th century, when the island - against the wishes of the inhabitants - was incorporated into a single British dependency, along with Saint Kitts and Nevis. Several attempts at separation failed. In 1971, two years after a revolt, Anguilla was finally allowed to secede; this arrangement was formally recognized in 1980, with Anguilla becoming a separate British dependency.

GEOGRAPHY

Location: Caribbean, islands between the Caribbean Sea and North Atlantic Ocean, east of Puerto Rico
Geographic coordinates: 18 15 N, 63 10 W
Map references: Central America and the Caribbean
Area:
total: 102 sq km
land: 102 sq km
water: 0 sq km
Area - comparative: about half the size of Washington, DC
Land boundaries: 0 km
Coastline: 61 km
Maritime claims:
territorial sea: 3 nm
exclusive fishing zone: 200 nm
Climate: tropical; moderated by northeast trade winds
Terrain: flat and low-lying island of coral and limestone
Elevation extremes:
lowest point: Caribbean Sea 0 m
highest point: Crocus Hill 65 m
Natural resources: salt, fish, lobster
Land use:
arable land: 0%
permanent crops: 0%
other: 100% (mostly rock with sparse scrub oak, few trees, some commercial salt ponds) (2001)
Irrigated land: NA
Natural hazards: frequent hurricanes and other tropical storms (July to October)
Environment - current issues: supplies of potable water sometimes cannot meet increasing demand largely because of poor distribution system
Geography - note: the most northerly of the Leeward Islands in the Lesser Antilles

PEOPLE

Population: 13,254 (July 2005 est.)
Age structure:
0-14 years: 23.2% (male 1,561/female 1,517)
15-64 years: 69.9% (male 4,767/female 4,501)
65 years and over: 6.9% (male 405/female 503) (2005 est.)
Median age:
total: 30.76 years
male: 30.81 years
female: 30.7 years (2005 est.)
Population growth rate: 1.77% (2005 est.)
Birth rate: 14.26 births/1,000 population (2005 est.)
Death rate: 5.43 deaths/1,000 population (2005 est.)
Net migration rate: 8.83 migrant(s)/1,000 population (2005 est.)
Sex ratio:
at birth: 1.03 male(s)/female
under 15 years: 1.03 male(s)/female
15-64 years: 1.06 male(s)/female
65 years and over: 0.8 male(s)/female
total population: 1.03 male(s)/female (2005 est.)
Infant mortality rate:
total: 21.03 deaths/1,000 live births
male: 27.59 deaths/1,000 live births
female: 14.27 deaths/1,000 live births (2005 est.)
Life expectancy at birth:
total population: 77.11 years
male: 74.18 years

female: 80.12 years (2005 est.)
Total fertility rate: 1.73 children born/woman (2005 est.)
HIV/AIDS - adult prevalence rate: NA%
HIV/AIDS - people living with HIV/AIDS: NA
HIV/AIDS - deaths: NA
Nationality:
noun: Anguillan(s)
adjective: Anguillan
Ethnic groups: black (predominant) 90.1%, mixed, mulatto 4.6%, white 3.7%, other 1.6% (2001 Census)
Religions: Anglican 29%, Methodist 23.9%, other Protestant 30.2%, Roman Catholic 5.7%, other Christian 1.7%, other 5.2%, none or unspecified 4.3% (2001 Census)
Languages: English (official)
Literacy:
definition: age 12 and over can read and write
total population: 95%
male: 95%
female: 95% (1984 est.)

GOVERNMENT

Country name:
conventional long form: none
conventional short form: Anguilla
Dependency Status: overseas territory of the UK
Government type: NA
Capital: The Valley
Administrative divisions: none (overseas territory of the UK)
Independence: none (overseas territory of the UK)
National holiday: Anguilla Day, 30 May
Constitution: Anguilla Constitutional Order 1 April 1982; amended 1990
Legal system: based on English common law
Suffrage: 18 years of age; universal
Executive branch:
chief of state: Queen ELIZABETH II (since 6 February 1952); represented by Governor Alan Eden HUCKLE (since 28 May 2004)
head of government: Chief Minister Osbourne FLEMING (since 3 March 2000)
cabinet: Executive Council appointed by the governor from among the elected members of the House of Assembly
elections: none; the monarch is hereditary; governor appointed by the monarch; following legislative elections, the leader of the majority party or the leader of the majority coalition is usually appointed chief minister by the governor
Legislative branch: unicameral House of Assembly (11 seats total, 7 elected by direct popular vote, 2 ex officio members, and 2 appointed; members serve five-year terms)
elections: last held 21 February 2005 (next to be held 2010)
election results: percent of vote by party - AUF 38.9%, ANSA 19.2%, AUM 19.4%, APP 9.5 %, independents 13%; seats by party - AUF 4, ANSA 2, AUM 1
Judicial branch: High Court (judge provided by Eastern Caribbean Supreme Court)
Political parties and leaders: Anguilla United Movement or AUM [Hubert HUGHES]; The Anguilla United Front or AUF [Osbourne FLEMING, Victor BANKS], a coalition of the Anguilla Democratic Party or ADP and the Anguilla National Alliance or ANA; Anguilla Progressive Party or APP [Roy ROGERS]; Anguilla Strategic Alternative or ANSA [Edison BAIRD]
Political pressure groups and leaders: NA
International organization participation: Caricom (associate), CDB, Interpol (subbureau), OECS (associate), UPU
Diplomatic representation in the US: none (overseas territory of the UK)
Diplomatic representation from the US: none (overseas territory of the UK)
Flag description: blue, with the flag of the UK in the upper hoist-side quadrant and the Anguillan coat of arms centered in the outer half of the flag; the coat of arms depicts three orange dolphins in an interlocking circular design on a white background with blue wavy water below

ECONOMY

Economy - overview: Anguilla has few natural resources, and the economy depends heavily on luxury tourism, offshore banking, lobster fishing, and remittances from emigrants. Increased activity in the tourism industry, which has spurred the growth of the construction sector, has contributed to economic growth. Anguillan officials have put substantial effort into developing the offshore financial sector, which is small, but growing. In the medium term, prospects for the economy will depend largely on the tourism sector and, therefore, on revived income growth in the industrialized nations as well as on favorable weather conditions.
GDP: purchasing power parity - $112 million (2002 est.)
GDP - real growth rate: 2.8% (2001 est.)
GDP - per capita: purchasing power parity - $7,500 (2002 est.)
GDP - composition by sector:
agriculture: 4%
industry: 18%
services: 78% (2002 est.)
Labor force: 6,049 (2001)
Labor force - by occupation: agriculture/fishing/forestry/mining 4%, manufacturing 3%, construction 18%, transportation and utilities 10%, commerce 36%, services 29% (2000 est.)
Unemployment rate: 8% (2002)
Population below poverty line: 23% (2002)
Household income or consumption by percentage share:
lowest 10%: NA
highest 10%: NA
Inflation rate (consumer prices): 2.3%
Budget:
revenues: $22.8 million
expenditures: $22.5 million, including capital expenditures of NA (2000 est.)
Agriculture - products: small quantities of tobacco, vegetables; cattle raising
Industries: tourism, boat building, offshore financial services
Industrial production growth rate: 3.1% (1997 est.)
Electricity - production: NA
Electricity – production by source:
fossil fuel: NA
hydro: NA
nuclear: NA
other: NA
Electricity - consumption: 42.6 million kWh
Exports: $2.6 million (1999)
Exports - partners: UK, US, Puerto Rico, Saint-Martin (2004)
Imports: $80.9 million (1999)
Imports - partners: US, Puerto Rico, UK (2004)
Debt - external: $8.8 million (1998)
Economic aid - recipient: $9 million (2004 est.)
Currency: East Caribbean dollar (XCD)
Currency code: XCD
Exchange rates: East Caribbean dollars per US dollar – NA (2005), 2.7 (2004), 2.7 (2003), 2.7 (2002), 2.7 (2001), 2.7 (2000)
note: fixed rate since 1976
Fiscal year: 1 April - 31 March

COMMUNICATIONS

Telephones - main lines in use: 6,200 (2002)
Telephones - mobile cellular: 1,800 (2002)
Telephone system:
general assessment: NA
domestic: modern internal telephone system
international: country code - 1-264; microwave radio relay to island of Saint Martin (Guadeloupe and Netherlands Antilles)
Radio broadcast stations: AM 2, FM 7, shortwave 0 (2004)
Radios: 3,000 (1997)
Television broadcast stations: 1 (1997)
Televisions: 1,000 (1997)
Internet country code: .ai
Internet Service Providers (ISPs): 16 (2000)
Internet users: 3,000 (2002)

TRANSPORTATION

Airports: 3 (2004 est.)
Airports - with paved runways:
total: 1
914 to 1,523 m: 1 (2004 est.)
Airports - with unpaved runways:
total: 2
under 914 m: 2 (2004 est.)
Roadways:
total: 105 km
paved: 65 km
unpaved: 40 km (1997)
Ports and terminals: Blowing Point, Road Bay

MILITARY

Military - note: defense is the responsibility of the UK

TRANSNATIONAL ISSUES

Disputes - international: none
Illicit drugs: transshipment point for South American narcotics destined for the US and Europe

ANTARCTICA

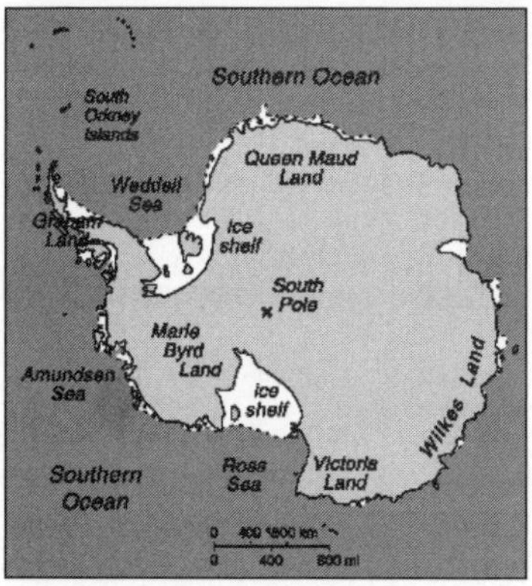

INTRODUCTION

Background: Speculation over the existence of a "southern land" was not confirmed until the early 1820s when British and American commercial operators and British and Russian national expeditions began exploring the Antarctic Peninsula region and other areas south of the Antarctic Circle. Not until 1840 was it established that Antarctica was indeed a continent and not just a group of islands. Several exploration "firsts" were achieved in the early 20th century. Following World War II, there was an upsurge in scientific research on the continent. A number of countries have set up year-round research stations on Antarctica. Seven have made territorial claims, but not all countries recognize these claims. In order to form a legal framework for the activities of nations on the continent, an Antarctic Treaty was negotiated that neither denies nor gives recognition to existing territorial claims; signed in 1959, it entered into force in 1961.

GEOGRAPHY

Location: continent mostly south of the Antarctic Circle
Geographic coordinates: 90 00 S, 0 00 E
Map references: Antarctic Region
Area:
total: 14 million sq km
land: 14 million sq km (280,000 sq km ice-free, 13.72 million sq km ice-covered) (est.)
note: fifth-largest continent, following Asia, Africa, North America, and South America, but larger than Australia and the subcontinent of Europe
Area - comparative: slightly less than 1.5 times the size of the US
Land boundaries: 0 km
note: see entry on Disputes - international
Coastline: 17,968 km
Maritime claims: Australia, Chile, and Argentina claim Exclusive Economic Zone (EEZ) rights or similar over 200 nm extensions seaward from their continental claims, but like the claims themselves, these zones are not accepted by other countries; 20 of 27 Antarctic consultative nations have made no claims to Antarctic territory (although Russia and the US have reserved the right to do so) and do not recognize the claims of the other nations; also see the Disputes - international entry
Climate: severe low temperatures vary with latitude, elevation, and distance from the ocean; East Antarctica is colder than West Antarctica because of its higher elevation; Antarctic Peninsula has the most moderate climate; higher temperatures occur in January along the coast and average slightly below freezing
Terrain: about 98% thick continental ice sheet and 2% barren rock, with average elevations between 2,000 and 4,000 meters; mountain ranges up to nearly 5,000 meters; ice-free coastal areas include parts of southern Victoria Land, Wilkes Land, the Antarctic Peninsula area, and parts of Ross Island on McMurdo Sound; glaciers form ice shelves along about half of the coastline, and floating ice shelves constitute 11% of the area of the continent
Elevation extremes:
lowest point: Bentley Subglacial Trench -2,555 m
highest point: Vinson Massif 4,897 m
note: the lowest known land point in Antarctica is hidden in the Bentley Subglacial Trench; at its surface is the deepest ice yet discovered and the world's lowest elevation not under seawater
Natural resources: iron ore, chromium, copper, gold, nickel, platinum and other minerals, and coal and hydrocarbons have been found in small uncommercial quantities; none presently exploited; krill, finfish, and crab have been taken by commercial fisheries
Land use:
arable land: 0%
permanent crops: 0%
other: 100% (ice 98%, barren rock 2%) (2001)
Irrigated land: 0 sq km
Natural hazards: katabatic (gravity-driven) winds blow coastward from the high interior; frequent blizzards form near the foot of the plateau; cyclonic storms form over the ocean and move clockwise along the coast; volcanism on Deception Island and isolated areas of West Antarctica; other seismic activity rare and weak; large icebergs may calve from ice shelf
Environment - current issues: in 1998, NASA satellite data showed that the antarctic ozone hole was the largest on record, covering 27 million square kilometers; researchers in 1997 found that increased ultraviolet light passing through the hole damages the DNA of icefish, an antarctic fish lacking hemoglobin; ozone depletion earlier was shown to harm one-celled antarctic marine plants; in 2002, significant areas of ice shelves disintegrated in response to regional warming
Geography - note: the coldest, windiest, highest (on average), and driest continent; during summer, more solar radiation reaches the surface at the South Pole than is received at the Equator in an equivalent period; mostly uninhabitable

PEOPLE

Population: no indigenous inhabitants, but there are both permanent and summer-only staffed research stations
note: 26 nations, all signatory to the Antarctic Treaty, operate seasonal (summer) and year-round research stations on the continent and in its surrounding oceans; the population of persons doing and supporting science on the continent

and its nearby islands south of 60 degrees south latitude (the region covered by the Antarctic Treaty) varies from approximately 4,000 in summer to 1,000 in winter; in addition, approximately 1,000 personnel including ship's crew and scientists doing onboard research are present in the waters of the treaty region; summer (January) population - 3,687 total; Argentina 302, Australia 201, Belgium 13, Brazil 80, Bulgaria 16, Chile 352, China 70, Finland 11, France 100, Germany 51, India 60, Italy 106, Japan 136, South Korea 14, Netherlands 10, NZ 60, Norway 40, Peru 28, Poland 70, Russia 254, South Africa 80, Spain 43, Sweden 20, UK 192, US 1,378 (1998-99); winter (July) population - 964 total; Argentina 165, Australia 75, Brazil 12, Chile 129, China 33, France 33, Germany 9, India 25, Japan 40, South Korea 14, NZ 10, Poland 20, Russia 102, South Africa 10, UK 39, US 248 (1998-99); research stations operated within the Antarctic Treaty area (south of 60 degrees south) by members of the Council of Managers of National Antarctic Programs (COMNAP): year-round stations - 38 total; Argentina 6, Australia 3, Brazil 1, Chile 4, China 2, France 1, Germany 1, India 1, Japan 1, South Korea 1, NZ 1, Poland 1, Russia 6, South Africa 1, Ukraine 1, UK 2, US 3, Uruguay 1, Italy and France jointly 1 (2005); summer-only stations - 34 total; Argentina 8, Australia 2, Bulgaria 1, Chile 5, Ecuador 1, Finland 1, Germany 2, Italy 1, Japan 3, Norway 2, Peru 1, Russia 2, South Africa 1, Spain 2, Sweden 1, UK 1 (2004-2005); in addition, during the austral summer some nations have numerous occupied locations such as tent camps, summer-long temporary facilities, and mobile traverses in support of research

GOVERNMENT

Country name:
conventional long form: none
conventional short form: Antarctica

Government type: Antarctic Treaty Summary - the Antarctic Treaty, signed on 1 December 1959 and entered into force on 23 June 1961, establishes the legal framework for the management of Antarctica; the 27th Antarctic Treaty Consultative Meeting was held in Cape Town, South Africa in May-June 2004; at these periodic meetings, decisions are made by consensus (not by vote) of all consultative member nations; at the end of 2003, there were 45 treaty member nations: 28 consultative and 17 non-consultative; consultative (decision-making) members include the seven nations that claim portions of Antarctica as national territory (some claims overlap) and 21 non-claimant nations; the US and Russia have reserved the right to make claims; the US does not recognize the claims of others; Antarctica is administered through meetings of the consultative member nations; decisions from these meetings are carried out by these member nations (with respect to their own nationals and operations) in accordance with their own national laws; the year in parentheses indicates when an acceding nation was accepted as a consultative member, while no date indicates the country was an original 1959 treaty signatory; claimant nations are - Argentina, Australia, Chile, France, New Zealand, Norway, and the UK. Nonclaimant consultative nations are - Belgium, Brazil (1983), Bulgaria (1998) China (1985), Ecuador (1990), Finland (1989), Germany (1981), India (1983), Italy (1987), Japan, South Korea (1989), Netherlands (1990), Peru (1989), Poland (1977), Russia, South Africa, Spain (1988), Sweden (1988), Ukraine (1992), Uruguay (1985), and the US; non-consultative members, with year of accession in parentheses, are - Austria (1987), Canada (1988), Colombia (1989), Cuba (1984), Czech Republic (1993), Denmark (1965), Estonia (2001), Greece (1987), Guatemala (1991), Hungary (1984), North Korea (1987), Papua New Guinea (1981), Romania (1971), Slovakia (1993), Switzerland (1990), Turkey (1995), and Venezuela (1999); Article 1 - area to be used for peaceful purposes only; military activity, such as weapons testing, is prohibited, but military personnel and equipment may be used for scientific research or any other peaceful purpose; Article 2 - freedom of scientific investigation and cooperation shall continue; Article 3 - free exchange of information and personnel, cooperation with the UN and other international agencies; Article 4 - does not recognize, dispute, or establish territorial claims and no new claims shall be asserted while the treaty is in force; Article 5 - prohibits nuclear explosions or disposal of radioactive wastes; Article 6 - includes under the treaty all land and ice shelves south of 60 degrees 00 minutes south and reserves high seas rights; Article 7 - treaty-state observers have free access, including aerial observation, to any area and may inspect all stations, installations, and equipment; advance notice of all expeditions and of the introduction of military personnel must be given; Article 8 - allows for jurisdiction over observers and scientists by their own states; Article 9 - frequent consultative meetings take place among member nations; Article 10 - treaty states will discourage activities by any country in Antarctica that are contrary to the treaty; Article 11 - disputes to be settled peacefully by the parties concerned or, ultimately, by the ICJ; Articles 12, 13, 14 - deal with upholding, interpreting, and amending the treaty among involved nations; other agreements - some 200 recommendations adopted at treaty consultative meetings and ratified by governments include - Agreed Measures for Fauna and Flora (1964) which were later incorporated into the Environmental Protocol; Convention for the Conservation of Antarctic Seals (1972); Convention on the Conservation of Antarctic Marine Living Resources (1980); a mineral resources agreement was signed in 1988 but remains unratified; the Protocol on Environmental Protection to the Antarctic Treaty was signed 4 October 1991 and entered into force 14 January 1998; this agreement provides for the protection of the Antarctic environment through five specific annexes: 1) environmental impact assessment, 2) conservation of Antarctic fauna and flora, 3) waste disposal and waste management, 4) prevention of marine pollution, and 5) area protection and management; it prohibits all activities relating to mineral resources except scientific research; a permanent Antarctic Treaty Secretariat was established in 2004 in Buenos Aires, Argentina

Legal system: Antarctica is administered through meetings of the consultative member nations; decisions from these meetings are carried out by these member nations (with respect to their own nationals and operations) in accordance with their own national laws; US law, including certain criminal offenses by or against US nationals, such as murder, may apply extra-territorially; some US laws directly apply to Antarctica; for example, the Antarctic Conservation Act, 16 U.S.C. section 2401 et seq., provides civil and criminal penalties for the following activities, unless authorized by regulation of statute: the taking of native mammals or birds; the introduction of nonindigenous plants and animals; entry into specially protected areas; the discharge or disposal of pollutants; and the importation into the US of certain items from Antarctica; violation of the Antarctic Conservation Act carries penalties of up to $10,000 in fines and one year in prison; the National Science Foundation and Department of Justice share enforcement responsibilities;

Public Law 95-541, the US Antarctic Conservation Act of 1978, as amended in 1996, requires expeditions from the US to Antarctica to notify, in advance, the Office of Oceans, Room 5805, Department of State, Washington, DC 20520, which reports such plans to other nations as required by the Antarctic Treaty; for more information, contact Permit Office, Office of Polar Programs, National Science Foundation, Arlington, Virginia 22230; telephone: (703) 292-8030, or visit their website at www.nsf.gov; more generally, access to the Antarctic Treaty area, that is to all areas between 60 and 90 degrees latitude South, is subject to a number of relevant legal instruments and authorization procedures adopted by the states party to the Antarctic Treaty.

ECONOMY

Economy - overview: Fishing off the coast and tourism, both based abroad, account for the limited economic activity. Antarctic fisheries in 2000-01 (1 July-30 June) reported landing 112,934 metric tons. Unregulated fishing, particularly of Patagonian toothfish, is a serious problem. The Convention on the Conservation of Antarctic Marine Living Resources determines the recommended catch limits for marine species. A total of 13,571 tourists visited in the 2002-03 antarctic summer, up from the 11,588 visitors the previous year. Nearly all of them were passengers on commercial (nongovernmental) ships and several yachts that make trips during the summer. Most tourist trips last approximately two weeks.

COMMUNICATIONS

Telephones - main lines in use: 0
note: information for US bases only (2001)
Telephones - mobile cellular: NA
Telephone system:
general assessment: local systems at some research stations
domestic: NA
international: country code - 672; via satellite (mobile Inmarsat and Iridium system) from some research stations
Radio broadcast stations: AM NA, FM 2, shortwave 1
note: information for US bases only (2002)
Radios: NA
Television broadcast stations: 1 (cable system with six channels; American Forces Antarctic Network-McMurdo)
note: information for US bases only (2002)
Televisions: several hundred at McMurdo Station (US)
note: information for US bases only (2001)
Internet country code: .aq
Internet hosts: 455 (2004)
Internet Service Providers (ISPs): NA

TRANSPORTATION

Ports and harbors: there are no developed ports and harbors in Antarctica; most coastal stations have offshore anchorages, and supplies are transferred from ship to shore by small boats, barges, and helicopters; a few stations have a basic wharf facility; US coastal stations include McMurdo (77 51 S, 166 40 E), Palmer (64 43 S, 64 03 W); government use only except by permit (see Permit Office under "Legal System"); all ships at port are subject to inspection in accordance with Article 7, Antarctic Treaty; offshore anchorage is sparse and intermittent; relevant legal instruments and authorization procedures adopted by the states party to the Antarctic Treaty regulating access to the Antarctic Treaty area, to all areas between 60 and 90 degrees of latitude South, have to be complied with (see "Legal System") (2004)
Airports: there are no developed public access airports or landing facilities; 30 stations, operated by 16 national governments party to the Antarctic Treaty, have restricted aircraft landing facilities for either helicopters or fixed-wing aircraft; commercial enterprises operate two additional aircraft landing facilities; helicopter pads are available at 27 stations; runways at 15 locations are gravel, sea-ice, blue-ice, or compacted snow suitable for landing wheeled, fixed-wing aircraft; of these, one is greater than 3 km in length, six are between 2 km and 3 km in length, three are between 1 km and 2 km in length, three are less than 1 km in length, and two are of unknown length; snow surface skiways, limited to use by ski-equipped, fixed-wing aircraft, are available at another 15 locations; of these, four are greater than 3 km in length, three are between 2 km and 3 km in length, two are between 1 km and 2 km in length, two are less than 1 km in length, and four are of unknown length; aircraft landing facilities generally subject to severe restrictions and limitations resulting from extreme seasonal and geographic conditions; aircraft landing facilities do not meet ICAO standards; advance approval from the respective governmental or nongovernmental operating organization required for using their facilities; landed aircraft are subject to inspection in accordance with Article 7, Antarctic Treaty; guidelines for the operation of aircraft near concentrations of birds in Antarctica were adopted in 2004; relevant legal instruments and authorization procedures adopted by states party to the Antarctic Treaty regulating access to the Antarctic Treaty area, that is to all areas between 60 and 90 degrees of latitude South, have to be complied with (see information under "Legal System"); an Antarctic Flight Information Manual (AFIM) providing up-to-date details of Antarctic air facilities and procedures is maintained and published by the Council of Managers of National Antarctic Programs (2004 est.)
Airports - with unpaved runways:
total: 20
over 3,047 m: 6
2,438 to 3,047 m: 3
1,524 to 2,437 m: 1
914 to 1,523 m: 4
under 914 m: 6 (2005 est.)
Heliports: 27 stations have restricted helicopter landing facilities (helipads) (2005 est.)

MILITARY

Military - note: the Antarctic Treaty prohibits any measures of a military nature, such as the establishment of military bases and fortifications, the carrying out of military maneuvers, or the testing of any type of weapon; it permits the use of military personnel or equipment for scientific research or for any other peaceful purposes

TRANSNATIONAL ISSUES

Disputes - international: Antarctic Treaty freezes claims (see Antarctic Treaty Summary in Government type entry); Argentina, Australia, Chile, France, NZ, Norway, and UK claim land and maritime sectors (some overlapping) for a large portion of the continent; the US and many other states do not recognize these territorial claims and have made no claims themselves (the US and Russia reserve the right to do so); no claims have been made in the sector between 90 degrees west and 150 degrees west; several states with territorial claims in Antarctica have expressed their intention to submit data to the UN Commission on the Limits of the Continental Shelf to extend their continental shelf claims to adjoining undersea ridges

ANTIGUA AND BARBUDA

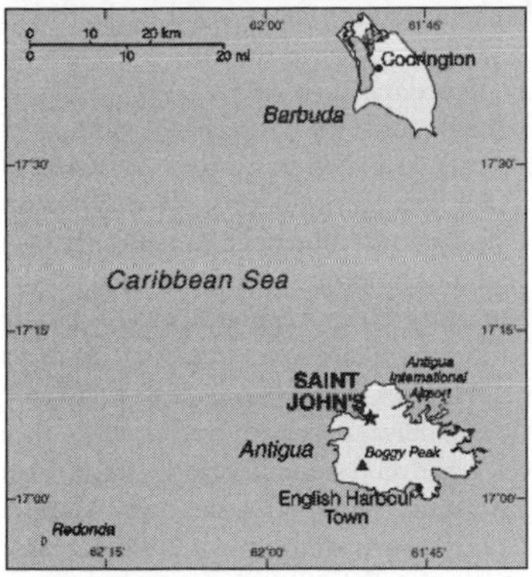

INTRODUCTION

Background: The Siboney were the first to inhabit the islands of Antigua and Barbuda in 2400 B.C., but Arawak and Carib Indians populated the islands when Columbus landed on his second voyage in 1493. Early settlements by the Spanish and French were succeeded by the English who formed a colony in 1667. Slavery, established to run the sugar plantations on Antigua, was abolished in 1834. The islands became an independent state within the British Commonwealth of Nations in 1981.

GEOGRAPHY

Location: Caribbean, islands between the Caribbean Sea and the North Atlantic Ocean, east-southeast of Puerto Rico
Geographic coordinates: 17 03 N, 61 48 W
Map references: Central America and the Caribbean
Area:
total: 442.6 sq km (Antigua 280 sq km; Barbuda 161 sq km)
land: 442.6 sq km
water: 0 sq km
note: includes Redonda, 1.6 sq km
Area - comparative: 2.5 times the size of Washington, DC
Land boundaries: 0 km
Coastline: 153 km
Maritime claims:
territorial sea: 12 nm
contiguous zone: 24 nm
exclusive economic zone: 200 nm
continental shelf: 200 nm or to the edge of the continental margin
Climate: tropical maritime; little seasonal temperature variation
Terrain: mostly low-lying limestone and coral islands, with some higher volcanic areas
Elevation extremes:
lowest point: Caribbean Sea 0 m
highest point: Boggy Peak 402 m
Natural resources: NEGL; pleasant climate fosters tourism
Land use:
arable land: 18.18%
permanent crops: 4.55%
other: 77.27% (2001)
Irrigated land: NA
Natural hazards: hurricanes and tropical storms (July to October); periodic droughts
Environment - current issues: water management - a major concern because of limited natural fresh water resources - is further hampered by the clearing of trees to increase crop production, causing rainfall to run off quickly
Environment - international agreements:
party to: Biodiversity, Climate Change, Climate Change-Kyoto Protocol, Desertification, Endangered Species, Environmental Modification, Hazardous Wastes, Law of the Sea, Marine Dumping, Ozone Layer Protection, Ship Pollution, Whaling
signed, but not ratified: none of the selected agreements
Geography - note: Antigua has a deeply indented shoreline with many natural harbors and beaches; Barbuda has a very large western harbor

PEOPLE

Population: 68,722 (July 2005 est.)
Age structure:
0-14 years: 27.9% (male 9,767/female 9,427)
15-64 years: 68% (male 23,466/female 23,250)
65 years and over: 4.1% (male 1,085/female 1,727) (2005 est.)
Median age:
total: 29.67 years
male: 29.19 years
female: 30.15 years (2005 est.)
Population growth rate: 0.57% (2005 est.)
Birth rate: 17.26 births/1,000 population (2005 est.)
Death rate: 5.44 deaths/1,000 population (2005 est.)
Net migration rate: -6.11 migrant(s)/1,000 population (2005 est.)
Sex ratio:
at birth: 1.05 male(s)/female
under 15 years: 1.04 male(s)/female
15-64 years: 1.01 male(s)/female
65 years and over: 0.63 male(s)/female
total population: 1 male(s)/female (2005 est.)
Infant mortality rate:
total: 19.46 deaths/1,000 live births
male: 23.43 deaths/1,000 live births
female: 15.29 deaths/1,000 live births (2005 est.)
Life expectancy at birth:
total population: 71.9 years
male: 69.53 years
female: 74.38 years (2005 est.)
Total fertility rate: 2.26 children born/woman (2005 est.)
HIV/AIDS - adult prevalence rate: NA%
HIV/AIDS - people living with HIV/AIDS: NA
HIV/AIDS - deaths: NA
Nationality:
noun: Antiguan(s), Barbudan(s)
adjective: Antiguan, Barbudan
Ethnic groups: black, British, Portuguese, Lebanese, Syrian
Religions: Christian, (predominantly Anglican with other Protestant, and some Roman Catholic)
Languages: English (official), local dialects
Literacy:
definition: age 15 and over has completed five or more years of schooling
total population: 89%
male: 90%
female: 88% (1960 est.)

GOVERNMENT

Country name:
conventional long form: none
conventional short form: Antigua and Barbuda
Government type: constitutional monarchy with UK-style parliament
Capital: Saint John's (Antigua)
Administrative divisions: 6 parishes and 2 dependencies*; Barbuda*, Redonda*, Saint George, Saint John, Saint Mary, Saint Paul, Saint Peter, Saint Philip
Independence: 1 November 1981 (from UK)
National holiday: Independence Day (National Day), 1 November (1981)
Constitution: 1 November 1981
Legal system: based on English common law
Suffrage: 18 years of age; universal
Executive branch:
chief of state: Queen ELIZABETH II (since 6 February 1952), represented by Governor General Sir James B. CARLISLE (since 10 June 1993)
head of government: Prime Minister Winston Baldwin SPENCER (since 24 March 2004)
cabinet: Council of Ministers appointed by the governor general on the advice of the prime minister
elections: none; the monarch is hereditary; governor general chosen by the monarch on the advice of the prime minister; following legislative elections, the leader of the majority party or the leader of the majority coalition is usually appointed

prime minister by the governor general
Legislative branch: bicameral Parliament consists of the Senate (17-member body appointed by the governor general) and the House of Representatives (17 seats; members are elected by proportional representation to serve five-year terms)
elections: House of Representatives - last held 23 March 2004 (next to be held NA 2009)
election results: percent of vote by party - NA%; seats by party - ALP 4, UPP 13
Judicial branch: Eastern Caribbean Supreme Court (based in Saint Lucia; one judge of the Supreme Court is a resident of the islands and presides over the Court of Summary Jurisdiction)
Political parties and leaders: Antigua Labor Party or ALP [Lester Bryant BIRD]; Barbuda People's Movement or BPM [Thomas H. FRANK]; United Progressive Party or UPP [Baldwin SPENCER] (a coalition of three opposition parties - United National Democratic Party or UNDP, Antigua Caribbean Liberation Movement or ACLM, and Progressive Labor Movement or PLM)
Political pressure groups and leaders: Antigua Trades and Labor Union or ATLU [William ROBINSON]; People's Democratic Movement or PDM [Hugh MARSHALL]
International organization participation: ACP, C, Caricom, CDB, FAO, G-77, IBRD, ICAO, ICCt, ICFTU, ICRM, IFAD, IFC, IFRCS, ILO, IMF, IMO, Interpol, IOC, ISO (subscriber), ITU, OAS, OECS, OPANAL, UN, UNCTAD, UNESCO, UPU, WCL, WFTU, WHO, WIPO, WMO, WTO
Diplomatic representation in the US:
chief of mission: Ambassador Lionel A. HURST
chancery: 3216 New Mexico Avenue NW, Washington, DC 20016
telephone: [1] (202) 362-5122
FAX: [1] (202) 362-5225
consulate(s) general: Miami
Diplomatic representation from the US: the US does not have an embassy in Antigua and Barbuda (embassy closed 30 June 1994); the US Ambassador to Barbados is accredited to Antigua and Barbuda
Flag description: red, with an inverted isosceles triangle based on the top edge of the flag; the triangle contains three horizontal bands of black (top), light blue, and white, with a yellow rising sun in the black band

ECONOMY

Economy - overview: Tourism continues to dominate the economy, accounting for more than half of GDP. Weak tourist arrival numbers since early 2000 have slowed the economy, however, and pressed the government into a tight fiscal corner. The dual-island nation's agricultural production is focused on the domestic market and constrained by a limited water supply and a labor shortage stemming from the lure of higher wages in tourism and construction. Manufacturing comprises enclave-type assembly for export with major products being bedding, handicrafts, and electronic components. Prospects for economic growth in the medium term will continue to depend on income growth in the industrialized world, especially in the US, which accounts for slightly more than one-third of tourist arrivals.
GDP: purchasing power parity - $750 million (2002 est.)
GDP: official exchange rate - NA
GDP - real growth rate: 3% (2002 est.)
GDP - per capita: purchasing power parity - $11,000 (2002 est.)
GDP - composition by sector:
agriculture: 3.9%
industry: 19.2%
services: 76.8% (2002)
Labor force: 30,000
Labor force - by occupation: agriculture 7%, industry 11%, services 82% (1983)
Unemployment rate: 11% (2001 est.)
Population below poverty line: NA
Household income or consumption by percentage share:
lowest 10%: NA
highest 10%: NA
Inflation rate (consumer prices): 0.4% (2000 est.)
Budget:
revenues: $123.7 million
expenditures: $145.9 million, including capital expenditures of NA (2000 est.)
Agriculture - products: cotton, fruits, vegetables, bananas, coconuts, cucumbers, mangoes, sugarcane; livestock
Industries: tourism, construction, light manufacturing (clothing, alcohol, household appliances)
Industrial production growth rate: 6% (1997 est.)
Electricity - production: 100 million kWh (2003)
Electricity - production by source:
fossil fuel: 100%
hydro: 0%
nuclear: 0%
other: 0% (2001)
Electricity - consumption: 93 million kWh (2003)
Electricity - exports: 0 kWh (2003)
Electricity - imports: 0 kWh (2003)
Oil - production: 0 bbl/day (2003 est.)
Oil - consumption: 3,600 bbl/day (2003 est.)
Oil - exports: NA
Oil - imports: NA
Exports: $214 million (2004 est.)
Exports - partners: Poland 47.8%, UK 24.6%, Germany 8.7% (2004)
Imports: $735 million (2004 est.)
Imports - partners: China 19.5%, US 18.7%, Singapore 14.8%, Poland 8.5%, Trinidad and Tobago 4.7% (2004)
Debt - external: $231 million (1999)
Economic aid - recipient: $2.3 million (1995)
Currency: East Caribbean dollar (XCD)
Currency code: XCD
Exchange rates: East Caribbean dollars per US dollar – NA (2005), 2.7 (2004), 2.7 (2003), 2.7 (2002), 2.7 (2001), 2.7 (2000)
note: fixed rate since 1976
Fiscal year: 1 April - 31 March

COMMUNICATIONS

Telephones - main lines in use: 38,000 (2002)
Telephones - mobile cellular: 38,200 (2002)
Telephone system:
general assessment: NA
domestic: good automatic telephone system
international: country code - 1-268; 1 coaxial submarine cable; satellite earth station - 1 Intelsat (Atlantic Ocean); tropospheric scatter to Saba (Netherlands Antilles) and Guadeloupe
Radio broadcast stations: AM 4, FM 2, shortwave 0 (1998)
Radios: 36,000 (1997)
Television broadcast stations: 2 (1997)
Televisions: 31,000 (1997)
Internet country code: .ag
Internet hosts: 1,665 (2003)
Internet Service Providers (ISPs): 16 (2000)
Internet users: 10,000 (2002)

TRANSPORTATION

Airports: 3 (2004 est.)
Airports - with paved runways:
total: 2
2,438 to 3,047 m: 1
under 914 m: 1 (2005 est.)
Airports - with unpaved runways:
total: 1
under 914 m: 1 (2005 est.)
Roadways:
total: 1,165 km
paved: 384 km
unpaved: 781 km (2002)
Merchant marine:
total: 980 ships (1,000 GRT or over) 5,873,626 GRT/7,683,143 DWT
by type: bulk carrier 33, cargo 630, chemical tanker 9, container 272, liquefied gas 9, petroleum tanker 1, refrigerated cargo 8, roll on/roll off 17, vehicle carrier 1

foreign-owned: 923 (Australia 2, Bangladesh 4, Belgium 4, Colombia 2, Denmark 8, Estonia 2, Germany 849, Iceland 5, Latvia 5, Lebanon 2, Lithuania 1, Netherlands 11, Norway 3, Philippines 1, Russia 1, Slovenia 5, Sweden 1, Switzerland 5, Turkey 4, United Kingdom 1, United States 7) (2005)
Ports and terminals: Saint John's

MILITARY

Military branches: Royal Antigua and Barbuda Defense Force: Infantry, Coast Guard (2004)
Military manpower - military age and obligation: 18 years of age (est.); no conscript military service (2001)
Military expenditures - dollar figure: NA
Military expenditures - percent of GDP: NA

TRANSNATIONAL ISSUES

Disputes - international: none
Illicit drugs: considered a minor transshipment point for narcotics bound for the US and Europe; more significant as an offshore financial center

ARCTIC OCEAN

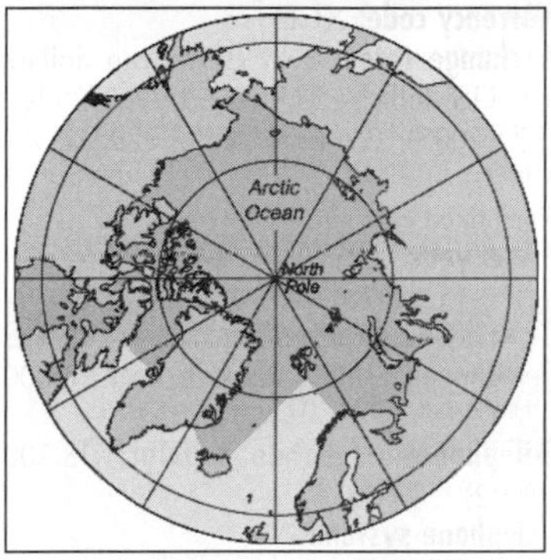

INTRODUCTION

Background: The Arctic Ocean is the smallest of the world's five oceans (after the Pacific Ocean, Atlantic Ocean, Indian Ocean, and the recently delimited Southern Ocean). The Northwest Passage (US and Canada) and Northern Sea Route (Norway and Russia) are two important seasonal waterways. A sparse network of air, ocean, river, and land routes circumscribes the Arctic Ocean.

GEOGRAPHY

Location: body of water between Europe, Asia, and North America, mostly north of the Arctic Circle
Geographic coordinates: 90 00 N, 0 00 E
Map references: Arctic Region
Area:
total: 14.056 million sq km
note: includes Baffin Bay, Barents Sea, Beaufort Sea, Chukchi Sea, East Siberian Sea, Greenland Sea, Hudson Bay, Hudson Strait, Kara Sea, Laptev Sea, Northwest Passage, and other tributary water bodies
Area - comparative: slightly less than 1.5 times the size of the US
Coastline: 45,389 km
Climate: polar climate characterized by persistent cold and relatively narrow annual temperature ranges; winters characterized by continuous darkness, cold and stable weather conditions, and clear skies; summers characterized by continuous daylight, damp and foggy weather, and weak cyclones with rain or snow
Terrain: central surface covered by a perennial drifting polar icepack that, on average, is about 3 meters thick, although pressure ridges may be three times that thickness; clockwise drift pattern in the Beaufort Gyral Stream, but nearly straight-line movement from the New Siberian Islands (Russia) to Denmark Strait (between Greenland and Iceland); the icepack is surrounded by open seas during the summer, but more than doubles in size during the winter and extends to the encircling landmasses; the ocean floor is about 50% continental shelf (highest percentage of any ocean) with the remainder a central basin interrupted by three submarine ridges (Alpha Cordillera, Nansen Cordillera, and Lomonosov Ridge)
Elevation extremes:
lowest point: Fram Basin -4,665 m
highest point: sea level 0 m
Natural resources: sand and gravel aggregates, placer deposits, polymetallic nodules, oil and gas fields, fish, marine mammals (seals and whales)
Natural hazards: ice islands occasionally break away from northern Ellesmere Island; icebergs calved from glaciers in western Greenland and extreme northeastern Canada; permafrost in islands; virtually ice locked from October to June; ships subject to superstructure icing from October to May
Environment - current issues: endangered marine species include walruses and whales; fragile ecosystem slow to change and slow to recover from disruptions or damage; thinning polar icepack
Geography - note: major chokepoint is the southern Chukchi Sea (northern access to the Pacific Ocean via the Bering Strait); strategic location between North America and Russia; shortest marine link between the extremes of eastern and western Russia; floating research stations operated by the US and Russia; maximum snow cover in March or April about 20 to 50 centimeters over the frozen ocean; snow cover lasts about 10 months

ECONOMY

Economy - overview: Economic activity is limited to the exploitation of natural resources, including petroleum, natural gas, fish, and seals.

TRANSPORTATION

Ports and terminals: Churchill (Canada), Murmansk (Russia), Prudhoe Bay (US)
Transportation - note: sparse network of air, ocean, river, and land routes; the Northwest Passage (North America) and Northern Sea Route (Eurasia) are important seasonal waterways

TRANSNATIONAL ISSUES

Disputes - international: some maritime disputes (see littoral states)

ARGENTINA

INTRODUCTION

Background: Following independence from Spain in 1816, Argentina experienced periods of internal political conflict between conservatives and liberals and between civilian and military factions. After World War II, a long period of Peronist authoritarian rule and interference in subsequent governments was followed by a military junta that took power in 1976. Democracy returned in 1983, and has persisted despite numerous challenges, the most formidable of which was a severe economic crisis in 2001-02 that led to violent public protests and the resignation of several interim presidents.

GEOGRAPHY

Location: Southern South America, bor-

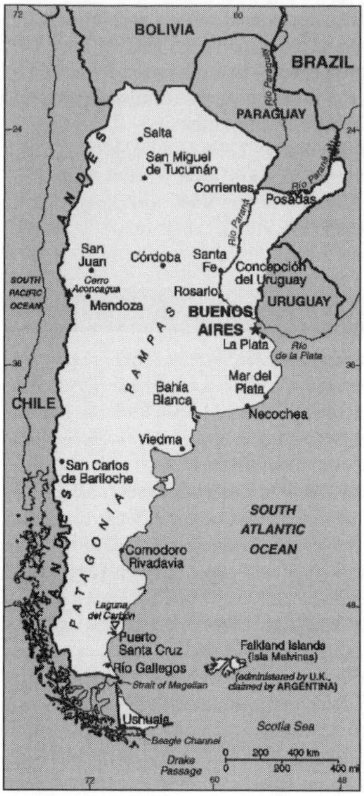

dering the South Atlantic Ocean, between Chile and Uruguay
Geographic coordinates: 34 00 S, 64 00 W
Map references: South America
Area:
total: 2,766,890 sq km
land: 2,736,690 sq km
water: 30,200 sq km
Area - comparative: slightly less than three-tenths the size of the US
Land boundaries:
total: 9,665 km
border countries: Bolivia 832 km, Brazil 1,224 km, Chile 5,150 km, Paraguay 1,880 km, Uruguay 579 km
Coastline: 4,989 km
Maritime claims:
territorial sea: 12 nm
contiguous zone: 24 nm
exclusive economic zone: 200 nm
continental shelf: 200 nm or to the edge of the continental margin
Climate: mostly temperate; arid in southeast; subantarctic in southwest
Terrain: rich plains of the Pampas in northern half, flat to rolling plateau of Patagonia in south, rugged Andes along western border
Elevation extremes:
lowest point: Laguna del Carbon -105 m (located between Puerto San Julian and Comandante Luis Piedra Buena in the province of Santa Cruz)
highest point: Cerro Aconcagua 6,960 m (located in the northwestern corner of the province of Mendoza)
Natural resources: fertile plains of the pampas, lead, zinc, tin, copper, iron ore, manganese, petroleum, uranium
Land use:
arable land: 12.31%
permanent crops: 0.48%
other: 87.21% (2001)
Irrigated land: 15,610 sq km (1998 est.)
Natural hazards: San Miguel de Tucuman and Mendoza areas in the Andes subject to earthquakes; pamperos are violent windstorms that can strike the pampas and northeast; heavy flooding
Environment - current issues: environmental problems (urban and rural) typical of an industrializing economy such as deforestation, soil degradation, desertification, air pollution, and water pollution
note: Argentina is a world leader in setting voluntary greenhouse gas targets
Environment - international agreements:
party to: Antarctic-Environmental Protocol, Antarctic-Marine Living Resources, Antarctic Seals, Antarctic Treaty, Biodiversity, Climate Change, Climate Change-Kyoto Protocol, Desertification, Endangered Species, Environmental Modification, Hazardous Wastes, Law of the Sea, Marine Dumping, Ozone Layer Protection, Ship Pollution, Wetlands, Whaling
signed, but not ratified: Marine Life Conservation
Geography - note: second-largest country in South America (after Brazil); strategic location relative to sea lanes between the South Atlantic and the South Pacific Oceans (Strait of Magellan, Beagle Channel, Drake Passage); Cerro Aconcagua is South America's tallest mountain, while Laguna del Carbon is the lowest point in the Western Hemisphere

PEOPLE

Population: 39,537,943 (July 2005 est.)
Age structure:
0-14 years: 25.6% (male 5,170,721/female 4,938,171)
15-64 years: 63.9% (male 12,626,711/female 12,627,026)
65 years and over: 10.6% (male 1,712,117/female 2,463,197) (2005 est.)
Median age:
total: 29.42 years
male: 28.52 years
female: 30.4 years (2005 est.)
Population growth rate: 0.98% (2005 est.)
Birth rate: 16.9 births/1,000 population (2005 est.)
Death rate: 7.56 deaths/1,000 population (2005 est.)
Net migration rate: 0.4 migrant(s)/1,000 population (2005 est.)
Sex ratio:
at birth: 1.05 male(s)/female
under 15 years: 1.05 male(s)/female
15-64 years: 1 male(s)/female
65 years and over: 0.7 male(s)/female
total population: 0.97 male(s)/female (2005 est.)
Infant mortality rate:
total: 15.18 deaths/1,000 live births
male: 17.07 deaths/1,000 live births
female: 13.19 deaths/1,000 live births (2005 est.)
Life expectancy at birth:
total population: 75.91 years
male: 72.17 years
female: 79.85 years (2005 est.)
Total fertility rate: 2.19 children born/woman (2005 est.)
HIV/AIDS - adult prevalence rate: 0.7% (2001 est.)
HIV/AIDS - people living with HIV/AIDS: 130,000 (2001 est.)
HIV/AIDS - deaths: 1,500 (2003 est.)
Nationality:
noun: Argentine(s)
adjective: Argentine
Ethnic groups: white (mostly Spanish and Italian) 97%, mestizo (mixed white and Amerindian ancestry), Amerindian, or other non-white groups 3%
Religions: nominally Roman Catholic 92% (less than 20% practicing), Protestant 2%, Jewish 2%, other 4%
Languages: Spanish (official), English, Italian, German, French
Literacy:
definition: age 15 and over can read and write
total population: 97.1%
male: 97.1%
female: 97.1% (2003 est.)

GOVERNMENT

Country name:
conventional long form: Argentine Republic
conventional short form: Argentina
local long form: Republica Argentina
local short form: Argentina
Government type: republic
Capital: Buenos Aires
Administrative divisions: 23 provinces (provincias, singular - provincia), and 1 autonomous city* (distrito federal); Buenos Aires, Buenos Aires Capital Federal*, Catamarca, Chaco, Chubut, Cordoba, Corrientes, Entre Rios, Formosa, Jujuy, La Pampa, La Rioja, Mendoza, Misiones, Neuquen, Rio Negro, Salta, San Juan, San Luis, Santa Cruz, Santa Fe, Santiago del Estero, Tierra del Fuego - Antartida e Islas del Atlantico Sur, Tucuman
note: the US does not recognize any claims to Antarctica

Independence: 9 July 1816 (from Spain)
National holiday: Revolution Day, 25 May (1810)
Constitution: 1 May 1853; revised August 1994
Legal system: mixture of US and West European legal systems; has not accepted compulsory ICJ jurisdiction
Suffrage: 18 years of age; universal and compulsory
Executive branch:
chief of state: President Nestor KIRCHNER (since 25 May 2003); Vice President Daniel SCIOLI (since 25 May 2003); note - the president is both the chief of state and head of government
head of government: President Nestor KIRCHNER (since 25 May 2003); Vice President Daniel SCIOLI (since 25 May 2003); note - the president is both the chief of state and head of government
cabinet: Cabinet appointed by the president
elections: president and vice president elected on the same ticket by popular vote for four-year terms; election last held 27 April 2003 (next election to be held NA 2007)
election results: results of the presidential election of 27 April 2003: Carlos Saul MENEM 24.3%, Nestor KIRCHNER 22%, Ricardo Lopez MURPHY 16.4%, Adolfo Rodriguez SAA 14.4%, Elisa CARRIO 14.2%, other 8.7%; the subsequent runoff election slated for 25 May 2003 was awarded to KIRCHNER by default after MENEM withdrew his candidacy on the eve of the election
Legislative branch: bicameral National Congress or Congreso Nacional consists of the Senate (72 seats; members are elected by direct vote; presently one-third of the members elected every two years to a six-year term) and the Chamber of Deputies (257 seats; members are elected by direct vote; one-half of the members elected every two years to a four-year term)
elections: Senate - last held intermittently by province during the 2nd half of 2003 (next to be held NA 2005); Chamber of Deputies - last held intermittently by province during the 2nd half of 2003 (next to be held NA 2005)
election results: Senate - percent of vote by bloc or party - NA%; seats by bloc or party - PJ 41, UCR 16, provincial parties 15; Chamber of Deputies - percent of vote by bloc or party - NA%; seats by bloc or party - PJ 133, UCR 46, IF 23, ARI 11, Socialist 6, other/provincial parties 38
Judicial branch: Supreme Court or Corte Suprema (the nine Supreme Court judges are appointed by the president with approval by the Senate)
Political parties and leaders: Alternative for a Republic of Equals or ARI [Elisa CARRIO]; Front for Victory or FV [Nestor KIRCHNER]; Interbloque Federal or IF (a broad coalition of approximately 12 parties including RECREAR) [leader NA]; Justicialist Party or PJ (Peronist umbrella political organization) [leader NA]; Justicialist Front or FJ [Eduardo DUHALDE]; Radical Civic Union or UCR [Roberto IGLESIAS]; Republican Initiative Alliance or PRO (including Federal Recreate Movement or RECREAR [Ricardo LOPEZ MURPHY] and Commitment for Change or CPC [Mauricio MACRI]); Socialist Party or PS [Ruben GIUSTINIANI]; Union For All [Patricia BULLRICH]; several provincial parties
Political pressure groups and leaders: Argentine Association of Pharmaceutical Labs (CILFA); Argentine Industrial Union (manufacturers' association); Argentine Rural Society (large landowners' association); business organizations; Central of Argentine Workers or CTA (a radical union for employed and unemployed workers); General Confederation of Labor or CGT (Peronist-leaning umbrella labor organization); Peronist-dominated labor movement; Roman Catholic Church; students
International organization participation: AfDB, Australia Group, BCIE, BIS, CSN, FAO, G-6, G-15, G-24, G-77, IADB, IAEA, IBRD, ICAO, ICC, ICCt, ICFTU, ICRM, IDA, IFAD, IFC, IFRCS, IHO, ILO, IMF, IMO, Interpol, IOC, IOM, ISO, ITU, LAES, LAIA, Mercosur, MIGA, MINURSO, MINUSTAH, NSG, OAS, OPANAL, OPCW, PCA, RG, UN, UN Security Council (temporary), UNCTAD, UNESCO, UNFICYP, UNHCR, UNIDO, UNMIK, UNMOVIC, UNTSO, UPU, WCL, WCO, WFTU, WHO, WIPO, WMO, WToO, WTO, ZC
Diplomatic representation in the US:
chief of mission: Ambassador Jose Octavio BORDON
chancery: 1600 New Hampshire Avenue NW, Washington, DC 20009
telephone: [1] (202) 238-6400
FAX: [1] (202) 332-3171
consulate(s) general: Atlanta, Chicago, Houston, Los Angeles, Miami, New York
Diplomatic representation from the US:
chief of mission: Ambassador Lino GUTIERREZ
embassy: Avenida Colombia 4300, C1425GMN Buenos Aires
mailing address: international mail: use street address; APO address: Unit 4334, APO AA 34034
telephone: [54] (11) 5777-4533
FAX: [54] (11) 5777-4240
Flag description: three equal horizontal bands of light blue (top), white, and light blue; centered in the white band is a radiant yellow sun with a human face known as the Sun of May

ECONOMY

Economy - overview: Argentina benefits from rich natural resources, a highly literate population, an export-oriented agricultural sector, and a diversified industrial base. Over the past decade, however, the country has suffered problems of inflation, external debt, capital flight, and budget deficits. Growth in 2000 was a negative 0.8%, as both domestic and foreign investors remained skeptical of the government's ability to pay debts and maintain the peso's fixed exchange rate with the US dollar. The economic situation worsened in 2001 with the widening of spreads on Argentine bonds, massive withdrawals from the banks, and a further decline in consumer and investor confidence. Government efforts to achieve a "zero deficit," to stabilize the banking system, and to restore economic growth proved inadequate in the face of the mounting economic problems. The peso's peg to the dollar was abandoned in January 2002, and the peso was floated in February; the exchange rate plunged and real GDP fell by 10.9% in 2002, but by mid-year the economy had stabilized, albeit at a lower level. GDP expanded by about 8% per year from 2003 to 2005. Growth is being led by a revival in domestic demand, solid exports, and favorable external conditions. The government boosted spending ahead of the October 2005 midterm congressional elections, but strong revenue performance will allow Argentina to exceed its primary budget surplus target for this year of 3.2 percent of GDP. Inflation has been rising steadily and is expected to reach 11.8 percent this year.
GDP: purchasing power parity - $537.2 billion (2005 est.)
GDP - official exchange rate: $182 billion (2005 est.)
GDP - real growth rate: 8.2% (2005 est.)
GDP - per capita: purchasing power parity - $13,600 (2005 est.)
GDP - composition by sector:
agriculture: 10.5%
industry: 35.8%
services: 53.7% (2004 est.)
Labor force: 15.34 million (2005 est.)
Labor force - by occupation: agriculture NA%, industry NA%, services NA%
Unemployment rate: 11.1% (September 2005)
Population below poverty line: 38.5% (June 2005)

Household income or consumption by percentage share:
lowest 10%: NA%
highest 10%: NA%
Distribution of family income – Gini index: 52.2 (2001)
Inflation rate (consumer prices): 11.8% (2005 est.)
Investment (gross fixed): 21.4% of GDP (2005 est.)
Budget:
revenues: $42.63 billion
expenditures: $39.98 billion, including capital expenditures of NA (2005 est.)
Public debt: 69.7% of GDP (June 2005)
Agriculture - products: sunflower seeds, lemons, soybeans, grapes, corn, tobacco, peanuts, tea, wheat; livestock
Industries: food processing, motor vehicles, consumer durables, textiles, chemicals and petrochemicals, printing, metallurgy, steel
Industrial production growth rate: 7.5% (2005 est.)
Electricity - production: 83.29 billion kWh (2003)
Electricity – production by source:
fossil fuel: 52.2%
hydro: 40.8%
nuclear: 6.7%
other: 0.2% (2001)
Electricity - consumption: 83.31 billion kWh (2003)
Electricity - exports: 2.443 billion kWh (2003)
Electricity - imports: 8.3 billion kWh (2003)
Oil - production: 745,000 bbl/day (2005 est.)
Oil - consumption: 450,000 bbl/day (2001 est.)
Oil - exports: NA
Oil - imports: NA
Oil - proved reserves: 2.95 billion bbl (2005 est.)
Natural gas - production: 37.15 billion cu m (2001 est.)
Natural gas - consumption: 31.1 billion cu m (2001 est.)
Natural gas - exports: 6.05 billion cu m (2001 est.)
Natural gas - imports: 0 cu m (2001 est.)
Natural gas - proved reserves: 768 billion cu m (2004)
Current Account Balance: $1.908 billion (2005 est.)
Exports: $40 billion f.o.b. (2005 est.)
Exports - partners: Brazil 15.4%, Chile 10.4%, US 10.2%, China 8.7%, Spain 4.4% (2004)
Imports - partners: Brazil 36.2%, US 16.6%, Germany 5.7%, China 4.3% (2004)
Reserves of foreign exchange and gold: $26.37 billion (2005 est.)
Debt - external: $119 billion (June 2005 est.)
Economic aid - recipient: $10 billion (2001 est.)
Currency: Argentine peso (ARS)
Currency code: ARS
Exchange rates: Argentine pesos per US dollar – 2.88 (2005), 2.9233 (2004), 2.9006 (2003), 3.0633 (2002), 0.9995 (2001), 0.9995 (2000)
Fiscal year: calendar year

COMMUNICATIONS

Telephones - main lines in use: 8,009,400 (2002)
Telephones - mobile cellular: 6.5 million (2002)
Telephone system:
general assessment: by opening the telecommunications market to competition and foreign investment with the "Telecommunications Liberalization Plan of 1998," Argentina encouraged the growth of modern telecommunication technology; fiber-optic cable trunk lines are being installed between all major cities; the major networks are entirely digital and the availability of telephone service is being improved; however, telephone density is presently minimal, and making telephone service universally available will take time
domestic: microwave radio relay, fiber-optic cable, and a domestic satellite system with 40 earth stations serve the trunk network; more than 110,000 pay telephones are installed and mobile telephone use is rapidly expanding
international: country code - 54; satellite earth stations - 8 Intelsat (Atlantic Ocean); Atlantis II and Unisur submarine cables; two international gateways near Buenos Aires (1999)
Radio broadcast stations: AM 260 (including 10 inactive stations), FM NA (probably more than 1,000, mostly unlicensed), shortwave 6 (1998)
Radios: 24.3 million (1997)
Television broadcast stations: 42 (plus 444 repeaters) (1997)
Televisions: 7.95 million (1997)
Internet country code: .ar
Internet users: 4.1 million (2002)
Internet Hosts: 742,358 (2003)
Internet Service Providers (ISPs): 33 (2000)

TRANSPORTATION

Airports: 1,334 (2004 est.)
Airports - with paved runways:
total: 144
over 3,047 m: 4
2,438 to 3,047 m: 26
1,524 to 2,437 m: 62
914 to 1,523 m: 44
under 914 m: 8 (2005 est.)
Airports - with unpaved runways:
total: 1,189
over 3,047 m: 2
2,438 to 3,047 m: 2
1,524 to 2,437 m: 50
914 to 1,523 m: 569
under 914 m: 566 (2005 est.)
Pipelines: gas 27,166 km; liquid petroleum gas 41 km; oil 3,668 km; refined products 2,945 km; unknown (oil/water) 13 km (2004)
Railways:
total: 34,091 km (167 km electrified)
broad gauge: 20,594 km 1.676-m gauge (141 km electrified)
standard gauge: 2,885 km 1.435-m gauge (26 km electrified)
narrow gauge: 10,375 km 1.000-m gauge; 237 km 0.750-m gauge (2004)
Roadways:
total: 215,471 km
paved: 63,348 km (including 734 km of expressways)
unpaved: 152,123 km (1999)
Waterways: 11,000 km (2004)
Merchant marine:
total: 26 ships (1,000 GRT or over) 149,007 GRT/212,620 DWT
by type: bulk carrier 2, cargo 9, chemical tanker 1, passenger 1, passenger/cargo 3, petroleum tanker 7, refrigerated cargo 2, roll on/roll off 1
foreign-owned: 2 (Chile 1, Uruguay 1)
registered in other countries: 23 (2005)
Ports and terminals: Bahia Blanca, Buenos Aires, Concepcion del Uruguay, La Plata, Punta Colorada, Rosario, San Lorenzo-San Martin, San Nicolas

MILITARY

Military branches: Argentine Army, Navy of the Argentine Republic (includes Naval Aviation and Marines), Argentine Air Force (Fuerza Aerea Argentina, FAA)
Military service age and obligation: 18 years of age for voluntary military service; no conscription (2001)
Manpower available for military service:
males age 18-49: 8,981,886 (2005 est.)
Manpower fit for military service: *males age 18-49:* 7,316,038 (2005 est.)
Manpower reaching military age annually: *males:* 344,575 (2005 est.)
Military expenditures - dollar figure: $4.3 billion (FY99)
Military expenditures - percent of GDP: 1.3% (FY00)
Military note: the Argentine military is a well-organized force constrained by the country's prolonged economic hardship; the country has recently experienced a strong recovery, and the military is now

implementing "Plan 2000," aimed at making the ground forces lighter and more responsive (2005)

TRANSNATIONAL ISSUES

Disputes - international: Argentina claims the UK-administered Falkland Islands (Islas Malvinas) and South Georgia and the South Sandwich Islands in its constitution; it briefly occupied the Falklands in 1982, but in 1995 agreed no longer to seek settlement by force; territorial claim in Antarctica partially overlaps UK and Chilean claims (see Antarctic disputes); unruly region at convergence of Argentina-Brazil-Paraguay borders is locus of money laundering, smuggling, arms and illegal narcotics trafficking, and fundraising for extremist organizations; uncontested dispute between Brazil and Uruguay over Braziliera Island in the Quarai/Cuareim River leaves the tripoint with Argentina in question
Illicit drugs: used as a transshipment country for cocaine headed for Europe and the US; some money-laundering activity, especially in the Tri-Border Area; domestic consumption of drugs in urban centers is increasing

ARMENIA

INTRODUCTION

Background: Armenia prides itself on being the first nation to formally adopt Christianity (early 4th century). Despite periods of autonomy, over the centuries Armenia came under the sway of various empires including the Roman, Byzantine, Arab, Persian, and Ottoman. It was incorporated into Russia in 1828 and the USSR in 1920. Armenian leaders remain preoccupied by the long conflict with Muslim Azerbaijan over Nagorno-Karabakh, a primarily Armenian-populated region, assigned to Soviet Azerbaijan in the 1920s by Moscow. Armenia and Azerbaijan began fighting over the area in 1988; the struggle escalated after both countries attained independence from the Soviet Union in 1991. By May 1994, when a cease-fire took hold, Armenian forces held not only Nagorno-Karabakh but also a significant portion of Azerbaijan proper. The economies of both sides have been hurt by their inability to make substantial progress toward a peaceful resolution. Turkey imposed an economic blockade on Armenia and closed the common border because of the Armenian occupation of Nagorno-Karabakh and surrounding areas.

GEOGRAPHY

Location: Southwestern Asia, east of Turkey
Geographic coordinates: 40 00 N, 45 00 E
Map references: Asia
Area:
total: 29,800 sq km
land: 28,400 sq km
water: 1,400 sq km
Area - comparative: slightly smaller than Maryland
Land boundaries:
total: 1,254 km
border countries: Azerbaijan-proper 566 km, Azerbaijan-Naxcivan exclave 221 km, Georgia 164 km, Iran 35 km, Turkey 268 km
Coastline: 0 km (landlocked)
Maritime claims: none (landlocked)
Climate: highland continental, hot summers, cold winters
Terrain: Armenian Highland with mountains; little forest land; fast flowing rivers; good soil in Aras River valley
Elevation extremes:
lowest point: Debed River 400 m
highest point: Aragats Lerrnagagat' 4,090 m
Natural resources: small deposits of gold, copper, molybdenum, zinc, alumina
Land use:
arable land: 17.55%
permanent crops: 2.3%
other: 80.15% (2001)
Irrigated land: 2,870 sq km (1998 est.)
Natural hazards: occasionally severe earthquakes; droughts
Environment - current issues: soil pollution from toxic chemicals such as DDT; the energy crisis of the 1990s led to deforestation when citizens scavenged for firewood; pollution of Hrazdan (Razdan) and Aras Rivers; the draining of Sevana Lich (Lake Sevan), a result of its use as a source for hydropower, threatens drinking water supplies; restart of Metsamor nuclear power plant in spite of its location in a seismically active zone
Environment - international agreements:
party to: Air Pollution, Biodiversity, Climate Change, Climate Change-Kyoto Protocol, Desertification, Hazardous Wastes, Law of the Sea, Ozone Layer Protection, Wetlands
signed, but not ratified: Air Pollution-Persistent Organic Pollutants
Geography - note: landlocked in the Lesser Caucasus Mountains; Sevana Lich (Lake Sevan) is the largest lake in this mountain range

PEOPLE

Population: 2,982,904 (July 2005 est.)
Age structure:
0-14 years: 21.6% (male 339,453/female 305,214)
15-64 years: 67.5% (male 938,734/female 1,074,240)
65 years and over: 10.9% (male 131,519/female 193,744) (2005 est.)
Median age:
total: 30.07 years
male: 27.45 years
female: 32.84 years (2005 est.)
Population growth rate: -0.25% (2005 est.)
Birth rate: 11.76 births/1,000 population (2005 est.)
Death rate: 8.16 deaths/1,000 population (2005 est.)
Net migration rate: -6.1 migrant(s)/1,000 population (2005 est.)
Sex ratio:
at birth: 1.17 male(s)/female
under 15 years: 1.11 male(s)/female
15-64 years: 0.87 male(s)/female
65 years and over: 0.68 male(s)/female
total population: 0.9 male(s)/female (2005 est.)
Infant mortality rate:
total: 23.28 deaths/1,000 live births
male: 28.51 deaths/1,000 live births
female: 17.13 deaths/1,000 live births (2005 est.)
Life expectancy at birth:
total population: 71.55 years
male: 67.97 years
female: 75.75 years (2005 est.)
Total fertility rate: 1.32 children born/woman (2005 est.)
HIV/AIDS - adult prevalence rate: 0.1% (2003 est.)
HIV/AIDS - people living with HIV/AIDS: 2,600 (2003 est.)
HIV/AIDS - deaths: less than 200 (2003 est.)
Nationality:
noun: Armenian(s)
adjective: Armenian

Ethnic groups: Armenian 97.9%, Yezidi (Kurd) 1.3%, Russian 0.5%, other 0.3% (2001 census)
Religions: Armenian Apostolic 94.7%, other Christian 4%, Yezidi (monotheist with elements of nature worship) 1.3%
Languages: Armenian 97.7%, Yezidi 1%, Russian 0.9%, other 0.4% (2001 census)
Literacy:
definition: age 15 and over can read and write
total population: 98.6%
male: 99.4%
female: 98% (2003 est.)

GOVERNMENT

Country name:
conventional long form: Republic of Armenia
conventional short form: Armenia
local long form: Hayastani Hanrapetut'yun
local short form: Hayastan
former: Armenian Soviet Socialist Republic; Armenian Republic
Government type: republic
Capital: Yerevan
Administrative divisions: 11 provinces (marzer, singular - marz); Aragatsotn, Ararat, Armavir, Geghark'unik', Kotayk', Lorri, Shirak, Syunik', Tavush, Vayots' Dzor, Yerevan
Independence: 21 September 1991 (from Soviet Union)
National holiday: Independence Day, 21 September (1991)
Constitution: adopted by nationwide referendum 5 July 1995
Legal system: based on civil law system
Suffrage: 18 years of age; universal
Executive branch:
chief of state: President Robert KOCHARIAN (since 30 March 1998)
head of government: Prime Minister Andranik MARGARYAN (since 12 May 2000)
cabinet: Council of Ministers appointed by the prime minister
elections: president elected by popular vote for a five-year term; election last held 19 February and 5 March 2003 (next to be held NA 2008); prime minister appointed by the president and confirmed with the majority support of the National Assembly; the prime minister and Council of Ministers must resign if the National Assembly refuses to accept their program
election results: Robert KOCHARIAN reelected president; percent of vote - Robert KOCHARIAN 67.5%, Stepan DEMIRCHYAN 32.5%
Legislative branch: unicameral National Assembly (Parliament) or Azgayin Zhoghov (131 seats; members elected by popular vote to serve four-year terms; 75 members elected by party list, 56 by direct vote)
elections: last held 25 May 2003 (next to be held in the spring of 2007)
note: percent of vote by party - Republican Party 23.5%, Justice Bloc 13.6%, Rule of Law 12.3%, ARF (Dashnak) 11.4%, National Unity Party 8.8%, United Labor Party 5.7%; seats by party - Republican Party 23, Justice Bloc 14, Rule of Law 12, ARF (Dashnak) 11, National Unity 9, United Labor 6; note - seats by party change frequently as deputies switch parties or announce themselves independent
Judicial branch: Constitutional Court; Court of Cassation (Appeals Court)
Political parties and leaders: Agro-Industrial Party [Vladimir BADALYAN]; Armenia Party [Myasnik MALKHASYAN]; Armenian National Movement or ANM [Alex ARZUMANYAN, chairman]; Armenian Ramkavar Liberal Party or HRAK [Harutyun MIRZAKHANYAN, chairman]; Armenian Revolutionary Federation ("Dashnak" Party) or ARF [Vahan HOVHANISSIAN]; Democratic Party [Aram SARKISYAN]; Justice Bloc (comprised of the Democratic Party, National Democratic Party, National Democratic Union, the People's Party, and the Republic Party) [Stepan DEMIRCHYAN]; National Democratic Party [Shavarsh KOCHARIAN]; National Democratic Union or NDU [Vazgen MANUKIAN]; National Revival Party [Albert BAZEYAN]; National Unity Party [Artashes GEGAMIAN, chairman]; People's Party of Armenia [Stepan DEMIRCHYAN]; Republic Party [Aram SARKISYAN, chairman]; Republican Party or RPA [Andranik MARKARYAN]; Rule of Law Party [Artur BAGHDASARYAN, chairman]; Union of Constitutional Rights [Hrant KHACHATURYAN]; United Labor Party [Gurgen ARSENYAN]
Political pressure groups and leaders: Yerkrapah Union [Manvel GRIGORIAN]
International organization participation: BSEC, CE, CIS, EAPC, EBRD, FAO, IAEA, IBRD, ICAO, ICCt (signatory), ICRM, IDA, IFAD, IFC, IFRCS, ILO, IMF, Interpol, IOC, IOM, ISO, ITU, MIGA, NAM (observer), OAS (observer), OPCW, OSCE, PFP, UN, UNCTAD, UNESCO, UNIDO, UPU, WCO, WFTU, WHO, WIPO, WMO, WToO, WTO
Diplomatic representation in the US:
chief of mission: Ambassador Tatoul MARKARIAN
chancery: 2225 R Street NW, Washington, DC 20008
telephone: [1] (202) 319-1976
FAX: [1] (202) 319-2982
consulate(s) general: Los Angeles
Diplomatic representation from the US:
chief of mission: Ambassador John M. EVANS
embassy: 18 Baghramyan Ave., Yerevan 375019
mailing address: American Embassy Yerevan, Department of State, 7020 Yerevan Place, Washington, DC 20521-7020
telephone: [374](1) 521-611, 520-791, 542-117, 542-132, 524-661, 527-001, 524-840
FAX: [374](1) 520-800
Flag description: three equal horizontal bands of red (top), blue, and orange

ECONOMY

Economy - overview: Under the old Soviet central planning system, Armenia had developed a modern industrial sector, supplying machine tools, textiles, and other manufactured goods to sister republics in exchange for raw materials and energy. Since the implosion of the USSR in December 1991, Armenia has switched to small-scale agriculture away from the large agroindustrial complexes of the Soviet era. The agricultural sector has long-term needs for more investment and updated technology. The privatization of industry has been at a slower pace, but has been given renewed emphasis by the current administration. Armenia is a food importer, and its mineral deposits (copper, gold, bauxite) are small. The ongoing conflict with Azerbaijan over the ethnic Armenian-dominated region of Nagorno-Karabakh and the breakup of the centrally directed economic system of the former Soviet Union contributed to a severe economic decline in the early 1990s. By 1994, however, the Armenian Government had launched an ambitious IMF-sponsored economic liberalization program that resulted in positive growth rates in 1995-2005. Armenia joined the WTO in January 2003. Armenia also has managed to slash inflation, stabilize the local currency (the dram), and privatize most small- and medium-sized enterprises. Armenia's unemployment rate, however, remains high, despite strong economic growth. The chronic energy shortages Armenia suffered in the early and mid-1990s have been offset by the energy supplied by one of its nuclear power plants at Metsamor. Armenia is now a net energy exporter, although it does not have sufficient generating capacity to replace Metsamor, which is under international pressure to close. The elec-

tricity distribution system was privatized in 2002. Armenia's severe trade imbalance has been offset somewhat by international aid, remittances from Armenians working abroad, and foreign direct investment. Economic ties with Russia remain close, especially in the energy sector. The government made some improvements in tax and customs administration in 2005, but anti-corruption measures will be more difficult to implement. Investment in the construction and industrial sectors is expected to continue in 2006 and will help to ensure annual average real GDP growth of about 7.5%.
GDP - purchasing power parity: $15.27 billion (2005 est.)
GDP - official exchange rate: $3.426 billion (2005 est.)
GDP - real growth rate: 8% (2005 est.)
GDP - per capita: purchasing power parity - $5,100 (2005 est.)
GDP - composition by sector:
agriculture: 22.9%
industry: 36.1%
services: 41.1% (2004 est.)
Labor force: 1.2 million (2004)
Labor force - by occupation: agriculture 45%, industry 25%, services 30% (2002 est.)
Unemployment rate: 30% (2003 est.)
Population below poverty line: 43% (2003 est.)
Household income or consumption by percentage share:
lowest 10%: 2.3%
highest 10%: 46.2% (1999)
Distribution of family income - Gini index: 44.4 (1996)
Inflation rate (consumer prices): 2.4% (2005 est.)
Investment (gross fixed): 23% of GDP (2005 est.)
Budget:
revenues: $786.1 million
expenditures: $930.7 million, including capital expenditures of NA (2005 est.)
Agriculture - products: fruit (especially grapes), vegetables; livestock
Industries: diamond-processing, metal-cutting machine tools, forging-pressing machines, electric motors, tires, knitted wear, hosiery, shoes, silk fabric, chemicals, trucks, instruments, microelectronics, jewelry manufacturing, software development, food processing, brandy
Industrial production growth rate: 15% (2002 est.)
Electricity - production: 4.954 billion kWh (2003)
Electricity – production by source:
fossil fuel: 42.3%
hydro: 27%
nuclear: 30.7%
other: 0% (2001)
Electricity - consumption: 4.42 billion kWh (2003)
Electricity - exports: 650 million kWh; note - exports an unknown quantity to Georgia; includes exports to Nagorno-Karabakh region in Azerbaijan (2003)
Electricity - imports: 463 million kWh; note - imports an unknown quantity from Iran (2003)
Oil - production: 0 bbl/day (2003 est.)
Oil - consumption: 40,000 bbl/day (2003 est.)
Oil - exports: NA (2001)
Oil - imports: NA (2001)
Natural gas - production: 0 cu m (2001 est.)
Natural gas - consumption: 1.4 billion cu m (2001 est.)
Natural gas - exports: 0 cu m (2001 est.)
Natural gas - imports: 1.4 billion cu m (2001 est.)
Current account balance: $-237.7 million (2005 est.)
Exports: $800 million f.o.b. (2005 est.)
Exports - partners: Belgium 18%, Israel 15.3%, Germany 13.3%, Russia 12.5%, US 8.1%, Netherlands 7.2%, Iran 5.5%, Georgia 4.3%, UAE 4% (2004)
Imports: $1.5 billion f.o.b. (2005 est.)
Imports - partners: Russia 11.3%, Belgium 10.1%, Israel 8.4%, US 7.6%, Iran 7.1%, UAE 6.1%, Ukraine 5.9%, Italy 5.5%, Germany 5.2%, Georgia 4.6%, France 4.5% (2004)
Reserves of foreign exchange and gold: $625.6 million (2005 est.)
Debt - external: $1.868 billion (31 December 2004)
Economic aid - recipient: ODA $170 million (2000)
Currency: dram (AMD)
Currency code: AMD
Exchange rates: drams per US dollar – 445 (2005), 533.45 (2004), 578.76 (2003), 573.35 (2002), 555.08 (2001), 539.53 (2000)
Fiscal year: calendar year

COMMUNICATIONS

Telephones - main lines in use: 562,600 (2003)
Telephones - mobile cellular: 114,400 (2003)
Telephone system:
general assessment: system inadequate; now 90% privately owned and undergoing modernization and expansion
domestic: the majority of subscribers and the most modern equipment are in Yerevan (this includes paging and mobile cellular service)
international: country code - 374; Yerevan is connected to the Trans-Asia-Europe fiber-optic cable through Iran; additional international service is available by microwave radio relay and landline connections to the other countries of the Commonwealth of Independent States and through the Moscow international switch and by satellite to the rest of the world; satellite earth stations - 3 (2005)
Radio broadcast stations: AM 9, FM 6, shortwave 1 (1998)
Radios: 850,000 (1997)
Television broadcast stations: 3 (plus an unknown number of repeaters); (1998)
Televisions: 825,000 (1997)
Internet country code: . am
Internet hosts: 2,206 (2004)
Internet Service Providers (ISPs): 9 (2001)
Internet users: 150,000 (2003)

TRANSPORTATION

Airports: 16 (2004 est.)
Airports - with paved runways:
total: 11
over 3,047 m: 2
2,438 to 3,047 m: 2
1,524 to 2,437 m: 4
914 to 1,523 m: 3 (2005 est.)
Airports - with unpaved runways:
total: 5
1,524 to 2,437 m: 2
914 to 1,523 m: 2
under 914 m: 1 (2005 est.)
Railways:
total: 845 km
broad gauge: 845 km 1.520-m gauge (828 km electrified)
note: some lines are out of service (2004)
Roadways:
total: 7,633 km
paved: 7,633 km (includes 1,561 km of expressways) (2003)
Pipelines: gas 1,871 km (2004)

MILITARY

Military branches: Army, Air Force, Air Defense Force
Military service age and obligation: 18-27 years of age for compulsory military service, conscript service obligation - 12 months; 18 years of age for voluntary military service (May 2004)
Manpower available for military service: *males age 18-49:* 722,836 (2005 est.)
Manpower fit for military service: *males age 18-49:* 551,938 (2005 est.)
Manpower reaching military age annually: *males:* 31,774 (2005 est.)
Military expenditures - dollar figure: $135 million (FY01)
Military expenditures - percent of GDP: 6.5% (FY01)

TRANSNATIONAL ISSUES

Disputes - international: Armenia supports ethnic Armenian secessionists in Nagorno-Karabakh and since the early 1990s, has militarily occupied 16% of Azerbaijan - Organization for Security and Cooperation in Europe (OSCE) continues to mediate dispute; over 800,000 mostly ethnic Azerbaijanis were driven from the occupied lands and Armenia; about 230,000 ethnic Armenians were driven from their homes in Azerbaijan into Armenia; Azerbaijan seeks transit route through Armenia to connect to Naxcivan exclave; border with Turkey remains closed over Nagorno-Karabakh dispute; ethnic Armenian groups in Javakheti region of Georgia seek greater autonomy; tens of thousands of Armenians emigrate, primarily to Russia, to seek employment

Refugees and internally displaced persons:
refugees (country of origin): 236,306 (Azerbaijan)
IDPs: 50,000 (conflict with Azerbaijan over Nagorno-Karabakh) (2004)

Illicit drugs: illicit cultivation of small amount of cannabis for domestic consumption; used as a transit point for illicit drugs - mostly opium and hashish - moving from Southwest Asia to Russia and to a lesser extent the rest of Europe

ARUBA

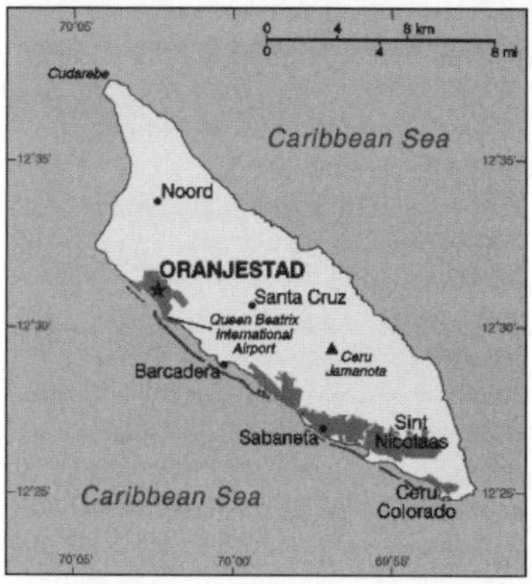

INTRODUCTION

Background: Discovered and claimed for Spain in 1499, Aruba was acquired by the Dutch in 1636. The island's economy has been dominated by three main industries. A 19th century gold rush was followed by prosperity brought on by the opening in 1924 of an oil refinery. The last decades of the 20th century saw a boom in the tourism industry. Aruba seceded from the Netherlands Antilles in 1986 and became a separate, autonomous member of the Kingdom of the Netherlands. Movement toward full independence was halted at Aruba's request in 1990.

GEOGRAPHY

Location: Caribbean, island in the Caribbean Sea, north of Venezuela
Geographic coordinates: 12 30 N, 69 58 W
Map references: Central America and the Caribbean
Area:
total: 193 sq km
land: 193 sq km
water: 0 sq km
Area - comparative: slightly larger than Washington, DC
Land boundaries: 0 km
Coastline: 68.5 km
Maritime claims:
territorial sea: 12 nm
Climate: tropical marine; little seasonal temperature variation
Terrain: flat with a few hills; scant vegetation
Elevation extremes:
lowest point: Caribbean Sea 0 m
highest point: Mount Jamanota 188 m
Natural resources: NEGL; white sandy beaches
Land use:
arable land: 10.53% (including aloe 0.01%)
permanent crops: 0%
other: 89.47% (2001)
Irrigated land: 0.01 sq km (1998 est.)
Natural hazards: lies outside the Caribbean hurricane belt
Environment - current issues: NA
Geography - note: a flat, riverless island renowned for its white sand beaches; its tropical climate is moderated by constant trade winds from the Atlantic Ocean; the temperature is almost constant at about 27 degrees Celsius (81 degrees Fahrenheit)

PEOPLE

Population: 71,566 (July 2005 est.)
Age structure:
0-14 years: 19.9% (male 7,308/female 6,960)
15-64 years: 68.2% (male 23,736/female 25,068)
65 years and over: 11.9% (male 3,486/female 5,008) (2005 est.)
Median age:
total: 38 years
male: 36.07 years
female: 39.7 years (2005 est.)
Population growth rate: 0.47% (2005 est.)
Birth rate: 11.26 births/1,000 population (2005 est.)
Death rate: 6.57 deaths/1,000 population (2005 est.)
Net migration rate: 0 migrant(s)/1,000 population (2005 est.)
Sex ratio:
at birth: 1.05 male(s)/female
under 15 years: 1.05 male(s)/female
15-64 years: 0.95 male(s)/female
65 years and over: 0.7 male(s)/female
total population: 0.93 male(s)/female (2005 est.)
Infant mortality rate:
total: 5.89 deaths/1,000 live births
male: 6.71 deaths/1,000 live births
female: 5.03 deaths/1,000 live births (2005 est.)
Life expectancy at birth:
total population: 79.14 years
male: 75.8 years
female: 82.65 years (2005 est.)
Total fertility rate: 1.79 children born/woman (2005 est.)
HIV/AIDS - adult prevalence rate: NA%
HIV/AIDS - people living with HIV/AIDS: NA
HIV/AIDS - deaths: NA
Nationality:
noun: Aruban(s)
adjective: Aruban; Dutch
Ethnic groups: mixed white/Caribbean Amerindian 80%
Religions: Roman Catholic 82%, Protestant 8%, Hindu, Muslim, Confucian, Jewish
Languages: Dutch (official), Papiamento (a Spanish, Portuguese, Dutch, English dialect), English (widely spoken), Spanish
Literacy:
definition:
total population: 97%
male: NA%
female: NA%

GOVERNMENT

Country name:
conventional long form: none
conventional short form: Aruba
Dependency Status: part of the Kingdom of the Netherlands; full autonomy in internal affairs obtained in 1986 upon separation from the Netherlands Antilles; Dutch Government responsible for defense and foreign affairs
Government type: parliamentary democracy
Capital: Oranjestad
Administrative divisions: none (part of the Kingdom of the Netherlands)
Independence: none (part of the Kingdom of the Netherlands)
National holiday: Flag Day, 18 March
Constitution: 1 January 1986
Legal system: based on Dutch civil law system, with some English common law influence
Suffrage: 18 years of age; universal

Executive branch:
chief of state: Queen BEATRIX of the Netherlands (since 30 April 1980), represented by Governor General Fredis REFUNJOL (since 11 May 2004)
head of government: Prime Minister Nelson O. ODUBER (since 30 October 2001)
cabinet: Council of Ministers (elected by the Staten)
elections: the monarch is hereditary; governor general appointed for a six-year term by the monarch; prime minister and deputy prime minister elected by the Staten for four-year terms; election last held 28 September 2001 (next to be held by December 2005)
election results: Nelson O. ODUBER elected prime minister; percent of legislative vote – NA
Judicial branch: Common Court of Justice of Aruba (judges are appointed by the monarch)
Political parties and leaders: Aliansa/Aruban Social Movement or MSA [Robert WEVER]; Aruban Liberal Organization or OLA [Glenbert CROES]; Aruban Patriotic Movement or MPA [Monica ARENDS-KOCK]; Aruban Patriotic Party or PPA [Benny NISBET]; Aruban People's Party or AVP [Mike EMAN]; People's Electoral Movement Party or MEP [Nelson O. ODUBER]; Real Democracy or PDR [Andin BIKKER]; RED [Rudy LAMPE]; Workers Political Platform or PTT [Gregorio WOLFF]
Political pressure groups and leaders: NA
International organization participation: ILO, IMF, Interpol, IOC, UNESCO (associate), UPU, WCL, WToO (associate)
Diplomatic representation in the US: none (represented by the Kingdom of the Netherlands); note - Mr. Henry Baarh, Minister Plenipotentiary for Aruba at the Embassy of the Kingdom of the Netherlands
Diplomatic representation from the US: the US does not have an embassy in Aruba; the Consul General to Netherlands Antilles is accredited to Aruba
Flag description: blue, with two narrow, horizontal, yellow stripes across the lower portion and a red, four-pointed star outlined in white in the upper hoist-side corner

ECONOMY

Economy - overview: Tourism is the mainstay of the small, open Aruban economy, with offshore banking and oil refining and storage also important. The rapid growth of the tourism sector over the last decade has resulted in a substantial expansion of other activities. Construction has boomed, with hotel capacity five times the 1985 level. In addition, the reopening of the country's oil refinery in 1993, a major source of employment and foreign exchange earnings, has further spurred growth. Aruba's small labor force and exceptionally low unemployment rate have led to a large number of unfilled job vacancies, despite sharp rises in wage rates in recent years. Tourist arrivals have declined in the aftermath of the 11 September 2001 terrorist attacks on the US. The government now must deal with a budget deficit and a negative trade balance.
GDP: purchasing power parity - $1.94 billion (2002 est.)
GDP: official exchange rate - NA
GDP - real growth rate: -1.5% (2002 est.)
GDP - per capita: purchasing power parity - $28,000 (2002 est.)
GDP - composition by sector:
agriculture: NA%
industry: NA%
services: NA%
Labor force: 41,500 (1997 est.)
Labor force - by occupation: most employment is in wholesale and retail trade and repair, followed by hotels and restaurants; oil refining
Unemployment rate: 0.6% (2003 est.)
Population below poverty line: NA
Household income or consumption by percentage share:
lowest 10%: NA
highest 10%: NA
Inflation rate (consumer prices): 3.2% (2002 est.)
Budget:
revenues: $135.8 million
expenditures: $147 million, including capital expenditures of NA (2000)
Agriculture - products: aloes; livestock; fish
Industries: tourism, transshipment facilities, oil refining
Industrial production growth rate: NA%
Electricity - production: 770 million kWh (2003)
Electricity – production by source:
fossil fuel: 100%
hydro: 0%
nuclear: 0%
other: 0% (2001)
Electricity - consumption: 716.1 million kWh (2003)
Electricity - exports: 0 kWh (2003)
Electricity - imports: 0 kWh (2003)
Oil - production: 2,363 bbl/day (2003)
Oil - consumption: 6,500 bbl/day (2003 est.)
Oil - exports: NA
Oil - imports: NA
Exports: $80 million f.o.b. (including oil reexports) (2004 est.)
Exports - partners: Netherlands 28.5%, Panama 17.5%, Venezuela 14.7%, Netherlands Antilles 11.2%, Colombia 10.7%, US 10.4% (2004)
Imports: $875 million f.o.b. (2004 est.)
Imports - partners: US 55.5%, Netherlands 14.1%, Venezuela 3.3% (2004)
Debt - external: $285 million (1996)
Economic aid - recipient: $26 million (1995); note - the Netherlands provided a $127 million aid package to Aruba and Suriname in 1996
Currency: Aruban guilder/florin (AWG)
Currency code: AWG
Exchange rates: Aruban guilders/florins per US dollar – NA (2005), 1.79 (2004), 1.79 (2003), 1.79 (2002), 1.79 (2001), 1.79 (2000)
Fiscal year: calendar year

COMMUNICATIONS

Telephones - main lines in use: 37,100 (2002)
Telephones - mobile cellular: 53,000 (2001)
Telephone system:
general assessment: modern fully automatic telecommunications system
domestic: increased competition through privatization; 3 wireless service providers are now licensed
international: country code - 297; 1 submarine cable to Sint Maarten (Netherlands Antilles); extensive interisland microwave radio relay links
Radio broadcast stations: AM 2, FM 16, shortwave 0 (2004)
Radios: 50,000 (1997)
Television broadcast stations: 1 (1997)
Televisions: 20,000 (1997)
Internet country code: .aw
Internet hosts: 923 (2001)
Internet Service Providers (ISPs): NA
Internet users: 24,000 (2002)

TRANSPORTATION

Airports: 1 (2004 est.)
Airports - with paved runways:
total: 1
2,438 to 3,047 m: 1 (2005 est.)
Ports and terminals: Barcadera, Oranjestad, Sint Nicolaas

MILITARY

Military branches: no regular indigenous military forces; Royal Dutch Navy and Marines, Coast Guard
Military - note: defense is the responsibility of the Kingdom of the Netherlands

TRANSNATIONAL ISSUES

Disputes - international: none
Illicit drugs: transit point for US- and Europe-bound narcotics with some accompanying money-laundering activity

ASHMORE AND CARTIER ISLANDS

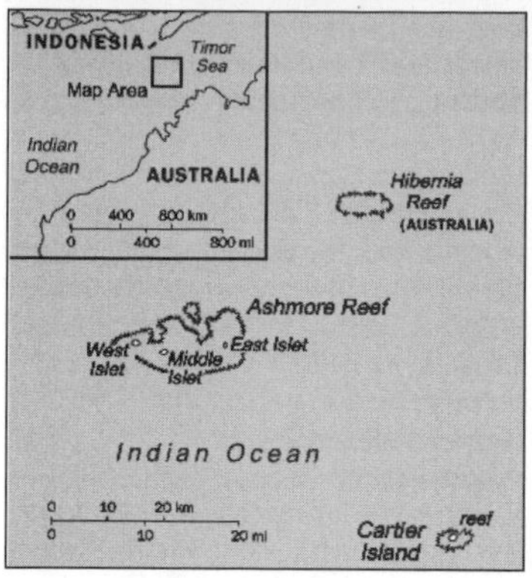

INTRODUCTION

Background: These uninhabited islands came under Australian authority in 1931; formal administration began two years later. Ashmore Reef supports a rich and diverse avian and marine habitat; in 1983, it became a National Nature Reserve. Cartier Island, a former bombing range, is now a marine reserve.

GEOGRAPHY

Location: Southeastern Asia, islands in the Indian Ocean, midway between northwestern Australia and Timor island
Geographic coordinates: 12 14 S, 123 05 E
Map references: Southeast Asia
Area:
total: 5 sq km
land: 5 sq km
water: 0 sq km
note: includes Ashmore Reef (West, Middle, and East Islets) and Cartier Island
Area - comparative: about eight times the size of The Mall in Washington, DC
Land boundaries: 0 km
Coastline: 74.1 km
Maritime claims:
territorial sea: 12 nm
contiguous zone: 12 nm
continental shelf: 200-m depth or to the depth of exploitation
exclusive fishing zone: 200 nm
Climate: tropical
Terrain: low with sand and coral
Elevation extremes:
lowest point: Indian Ocean 0 m
highest point: unnamed location 3 m
Natural resources: fish
Land use:
arable land: 0%
permanent crops: 0%
other: 100% (all grass and sand) (2001)
Irrigated land: 0 sq km (1998 est.)
Natural hazards: surrounded by shoals and reefs that can pose maritime hazards
Environment - current issues: NA
Geography - note: Ashmore Reef National Nature Reserve established in August 1983

PEOPLE

Population: no indigenous inhabitants
note: Indonesian fishermen are allowed access to the lagoon and fresh water at Ashmore Reef's West Island (July 2005 est.)
People - note: the landing of illegal immigrants from Indonesia's Rote Island has become an ongoing problem

GOVERNMENT

Country name:
conventional long form: Territory of Ashmore and Cartier Islands
conventional short form: Ashmore and Cartier Islands
Dependency Status: territory of Australia; administered by the Australian Department of Transport and Regional Services
Legal system: the laws of the Commonwealth of Australia and the laws of the Northern Territory of Australia, where applicable, apply
Diplomatic representation in the US: none (territory of Australia)
Diplomatic representation from the US: none (territory of Australia)
Flag description: the flag of Australia is used

ECONOMY

Economy - overview: no economic activity

TRANSPORTATION

Ports and harbors: none; offshore anchorage only

MILITARY

Military - note: defense is the responsibility of Australia; periodic visits by the Royal Australian Navy and Royal Australian Air Force

TRANSNATIONAL ISSUES

Disputes - international: Indonesian groups challenge Australia's claim to Ashmore Reef; Australia closed the surrounding waters to Indonesian traditional fishing and created a national park in the region while continuing to prospect for hydrocarbons in the vicinity

ATLANTIC OCEAN

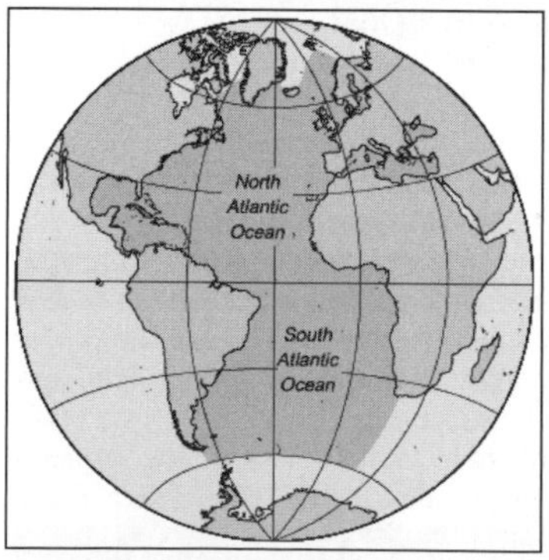

INTRODUCTION

Background: The Atlantic Ocean is the second largest of the world's five oceans (after the Pacific Ocean, but larger than the Indian Ocean, Southern Ocean, and Arctic Ocean). The Kiel Canal (Germany), Oresund (Denmark-Sweden), Bosporus (Turkey), Strait of Gibraltar (Morocco-Spain), and the Saint Lawrence Seaway (Canada-US) are important strategic access waterways. The decision by the International Hydrographic Organization in the spring of 2000 to delimit a fifth world ocean, the Southern Ocean, removed the portion of the Atlantic Ocean south of 60 degrees south.

GEOGRAPHY

Location: body of water between Africa, Europe, the Southern Ocean, and the Western Hemisphere
Geographic coordinates: 0 00 N, 25 00 W
Map references: Political Map of the World
Area:
total: 76.762 million sq km
note: includes Baltic Sea, Black Sea, Caribbean Sea, Davis Strait, Denmark Strait, part of the Drake Passage, Gulf of Mexico, Labrador Sea, Mediterranean Sea, North Sea, Norwegian Sea, almost all of the Scotia Sea, and other tributary water bodies
Area - comparative: slightly less than 6.5 times the size of the US
Coastline: 111,866 km
Climate: tropical cyclones (hurricanes) develop off the coast of Africa near Cape Verde and move westward into the Caribbean Sea; hurricanes can occur

from May to December, but are most frequent from August to November
Terrain: surface usually covered with sea ice in Labrador Sea, Denmark Strait, and coastal portions of the Baltic Sea from October to June; clockwise warm-water gyre (broad, circular system of currents) in the northern Atlantic, counterclockwise warm-water gyre in the southern Atlantic; the ocean floor is dominated by the Mid-Atlantic Ridge, a rugged north-south centerline for the entire Atlantic basin
Elevation extremes:
lowest point: Milwaukee Deep in the Puerto Rico Trench -8,605 m
highest point: sea level 0 m
Natural resources: oil and gas fields, fish, marine mammals (seals and whales), sand and gravel aggregates, placer deposits, polymetallic nodules, precious stones
Natural hazards: icebergs common in Davis Strait, Denmark Strait, and the northwestern Atlantic Ocean from February to August and have been spotted as far south as Bermuda and the Madeira Islands; ships subject to superstructure icing in extreme northern Atlantic from October to May; persistent fog can be a maritime hazard from May to September; hurricanes (May to December)
Environment - current issues: endangered marine species include the manatee, seals, sea lions, turtles, and whales; drift net fishing is hastening the decline of fish stocks and contributing to international disputes; municipal sludge pollution off eastern US, southern Brazil, and eastern Argentina; oil pollution in Caribbean Sea, Gulf of Mexico, Lake Maracaibo, Mediterranean Sea, and North Sea; industrial waste and municipal sewage pollution in Baltic Sea, North Sea, and Mediterranean Sea
Geography - note: major chokepoints include the Dardanelles, Strait of Gibraltar, access to the Panama and Suez Canals; strategic straits include the Strait of Dover, Straits of Florida, Mona Passage, The Sound (Oresund), and Windward Passage; the Equator divides the Atlantic Ocean into the North Atlantic Ocean and South Atlantic Ocean

ECONOMY

Economy - overview: The Atlantic Ocean provides some of the world's most heavily trafficked sea routes, between and within the Eastern and Western Hemispheres. Other economic activity includes the exploitation of natural resources, e.g., fishing, dredging of aragonite sands (The Bahamas), and production of crude oil and natural gas (Caribbean Sea, Gulf of Mexico, and North Sea).

TRANSPORTATION

Ports and terminals: Alexandria (Egypt), Algiers (Algeria), Antwerp (Belgium), Barcelona (Spain), Buenos Aires (Argentina), Casablanca (Morocco), Colon (Panama), Copenhagen (Denmark), Dakar (Senegal), Gdansk (Poland), Hamburg (Germany), Helsinki (Finland), Las Palmas (Canary Islands, Spain), Le Havre (France), Lisbon (Portugal), London (UK), Marseille (France), Montevideo (Uruguay), Montreal (Canada), Naples (Italy), New Orleans (US), New York (US), Oran (Algeria), Oslo (Norway), Peiraiefs or Piraeus (Greece), Rio de Janeiro (Brazil), Rotterdam (Netherlands), Saint Petersburg (Russia), Stockholm (Sweden)
Transportation - note: Kiel Canal and Saint Lawrence Seaway are two important waterways; significant domestic commercial and recreational use of Intracoastal Waterway on central and south Atlantic seaboard and Gulf of Mexico coast of US

TRANSNATIONAL ISSUES

Disputes - international: some maritime disputes (see littoral states)

AUSTRALIA

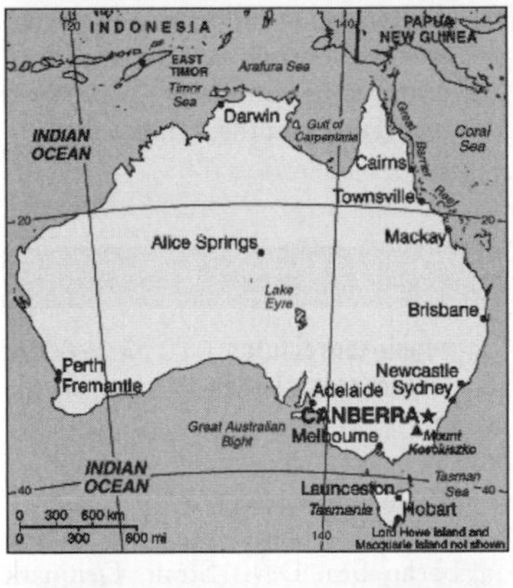

INTRODUCTION

Background: Aboriginal settlers arrived on the continent from Southeast Asia about 40,000 years before the first Europeans began exploration in the 17th century. No formal territorial claims were made until 1770, when Capt. James COOK took possession in the name of Great Britain. Six colonies were created in the late 18th and 19th centuries; they federated and became the Commonwealth of Australia in 1901. The new country took advantage of its natural resources to rapidly develop its agricultural and manufacturing industries and to make a major contribution to the British effort in World Wars I and II. In recent decades, Australia has transformed itself into an internationally competitive, advanced market economy. It boasted one of the OECD's fastest growing economies during the 1990's, a performance due in large part to economic reforms adopted in the 1980's. Long-term concerns include pollution, particularly depletion of the ozone layer, and management and conservation of coastal areas, especially the Great Barrier Reef.

GEOGRAPHY

Location: Oceania, continent between the Indian Ocean and the South Pacific Ocean
Geographic coordinates: 27 00 S, 133 00 E
Map references: Oceania
Area:
total: 7,686,850 sq km
land: 7,617,930 sq km
water: 68,920 sq km
note: includes Lord Howe Island and Macquarie Island
Area - comparative: slightly smaller than the US contiguous 48 states
Land boundaries: 0 km
Coastline: 25,760 km
Maritime claims:
territorial sea: 12 nm
contiguous zone: 24 nm
exclusive economic zone: 200 nm
continental shelf: 200 nm or to the edge of the continental margin
Climate: generally arid to semiarid; temperate in south and east; tropical in north
Terrain: mostly low plateau with deserts; fertile plain in southeast
Elevation extremes:
lowest point: Lake Eyre -15 m
highest point: Mount Kosciuszko 2,229 m
Natural resources: bauxite, coal, iron ore, copper, tin, gold, silver, uranium, nickel, tungsten, mineral sands, lead, zinc, diamonds, natural gas, petroleum
Land use:
arable land: 6.55% (includes about 27 million hectares of cultivated grassland)
permanent crops: 0.04%
other: 93.41% (2001)
Irrigated land: 24,000 sq km (1998 est.)

Natural hazards: cyclones along the coast; severe droughts; forest fires
Environment - current issues: soil erosion from overgrazing, industrial development, urbanization, and poor farming practices; soil salinity rising due to the use of poor quality water; desertification; clearing for agricultural purposes threatens the natural habitat of many unique animal and plant species; the Great Barrier Reef off the northeast coast, the largest coral reef in the world, is threatened by increased shipping and its popularity as a tourist site; limited natural fresh water resources
Environment - international agreements:
party to: Antarctic-Environmental Protocol, Antarctic-Marine Living Resources, Antarctic Seals, Antarctic Treaty, Biodiversity, Climate Change, Desertification, Endangered Species, Environmental Modification, Hazardous Wastes, Law of the Sea, Marine Dumping, Marine Life Conservation, Ozone Layer Protection, Ship Pollution, Tropical Timber 83, Tropical Timber 94, Wetlands, Whaling
signed, but not ratified: Climate Change-Kyoto Protocol
Geography - note: world's smallest continent but sixth-largest country; population concentrated along the eastern and southeastern coasts; the invigorating tropical sea breeze known as the "Fremantle Doctor" affects the city of Perth on the west coast, and is one of the most consistent winds in the world

PEOPLE

Population: 20,090,437 (July 2005 est.)
Age structure:
0-14 years: 19.8% (male 2,038,809/female 1,943,563)
15-64 years: 67.2% (male 6,815,600/ female 6,695,189)
65 years and over: 12.9% (male 1,145,274/ female 1,452,002) (2005 est.)
Median age:
total: 36.56 years
male: 35.74 years
female: 37.4 years (2005 est.)
Population growth rate: 0.87% (2005 est.)
Birth rate: 12.26 births/1,000 population (2005 est.)
Death rate: 7.44 deaths/1,000 population (2005 est.)
Net migration rate: 3.91 migrant(s)/ 1,000 population (2005 est.)
Sex ratio:
at birth: 1.05 male(s)/female
under 15 years: 1.05 male(s)/female
15-64 years: 1.02 male(s)/female
65 years and over: 0.79 male(s)/female
total population: 0.99 male(s)/female (2005 est.)
Infant mortality rate:
total: 4.69 deaths/1,000 live births
male: 5.08 deaths/1,000 live births
female: 4.27 deaths/1,000 live births (2005 est.)
Life expectancy at birth:
total population: 80.39 years
male: 77.52 years
female: 83.4 years (2005 est.)
Total fertility rate: 1.76 children born/woman (2005 est.)
HIV/AIDS - adult prevalence rate: 0.1% (2003 est.)
HIV/AIDS - people living with HIV/AIDS: 14,000 (2003 est.)
HIV/AIDS - deaths: less than 200 (2003 est.)
Nationality:
noun: Australian(s)
adjective: Australian
Ethnic groups: Caucasian 92%, Asian 7%, aboriginal and other 1%
Religions: Catholic 26.4%, Anglican 20.5%, other Christian 20.5%, Buddhist 1.9%, Muslim 1.5%, other 1.2%, unspecified 12.7%, none 15.3% (2001 Census)
Languages: English 79.1%, Chinese 2.1%, Italian 1.9%, other 11.1%, unspecified 5.8% (2001 Census)
Literacy:
definition: age 15 and over can read and write
total population: 100%
male: 100%
female: 100% (1980 est.)

GOVERNMENT

Country name:
conventional long form: Commonwealth of Australia
conventional short form: Australia
Government type: democratic, federal-state system recognizing the British monarch as sovereign
Capital: Canberra
Administrative divisions: 6 states and 2 territories*; Australian Capital Territory*, New South Wales, Northern Territory*, Queensland, South Australia, Tasmania, Victoria, Western Australia
Dependent areas: Ashmore and Cartier Islands, Christmas Island, Cocos (Keeling) Islands, Coral Sea Islands, Heard Island and McDonald Islands, Norfolk Island, Macquarie Island
Independence: 1 January 1901 (federation of UK colonies)
National holiday: Australia Day, 26 January (1788)
Constitution: 9 July 1900, effective 1 January 1901
Legal system: based on English common law; accepts compulsory ICJ jurisdiction, with reservations
Suffrage: 18 years of age; universal and compulsory
Executive branch:
chief of state: Queen of Australia ELIZABETH II (since 6 February 1952), represented by Governor General Maj. Gen. (Ret.) Michael JEFFERY (since 11 August 2003)
head of government: Prime Minister John Winston HOWARD (since 11 March 1996); Deputy Prime Minister Mark VAILE (since 6 July 2005)
cabinet: Prime Minister nominates, from among members of Parliament, candidates who are subsequently sworn in by the Governor General to serve as government ministers
elections: none; the monarch is hereditary; governor general appointed by the monarch on the recommendation of the prime minister; following legislative elections, the leader of the majority party or leader of a majority coalition is sworn in as prime minister by the governor general
note: government coalition - Liberal Party and National Party
Legislative branch: bicameral Federal Parliament consists of the Senate (76 seats - 12 from each of the six states and two from each of the two mainland territories; one-half of state members are elected every three years by popular vote to serve six-year terms while all territory members are elected every three years) and the House of Representatives (150 seats; members elected by popular preferential voting to serve terms of up to three-years; no state can have fewer than five representatives)
elections: Senate - last held 9 October 2004 (next to be held no later than June 2008); House of Representatives - last held 9 October 2004 (next to be called no later than November 2007)
election results: Senate - percent of vote by party - NA%; seats by party (for session beginning on 1 July 2005) - Liberal Party-National Party coalition 39, Australian Labor Party 28, Democrats 4, Australian Greens 4, Family First Party 1; House of Representatives - percent of vote by party - NA%; seats by party - Liberal Party-National Party coalition 87, Australian Labor Party 60, independents 3
Judicial branch: High Court (the chief justice and six other justices are appointed by the governor general)
Political parties and leaders Australian Democrats [Lyn ALLISON]; Australian Labor Party [Kim BEAZLEY]; Australian Progressive Alliance [Meg LEES]; Australian Greens [Bob BROWN]; Liberal Party [John Winston HOWARD]; The Nationals [Mark VAILE]; One Nation Party [Len HARRIS]; Family First Party [Steve FIELDING]

International organization participation: ANZUS, APEC, ARF, AsDB, ASEAN (dialogue partner), Australia Group, BIS, C, CP, EBRD, FAO, IAEA, IBRD, ICAO, ICC, ICCt, ICFTU, ICRM, IDA, IEA, IFAD, IFC, IFRCS, IHO, ILO, IMF, IMO, Interpol, IOC, IOM, ISO, ITU, MIGA, NAM (guest), NEA, NSG, OECD, OPCW, Paris Club, PCA, PIF, Sparteca, UN, UNCTAD, UNESCO, UNHCR, UNMEE, UNMISET, UNTSO, UPU, WCO, WFTU, WHO, WIPO, WMO, WTO, WToO, ZC
Diplomatic representation in the US:
chief of mission: Ambassador Michael J. THAWLEY
chancery: 1601 Massachusetts Avenue NW, Washington, DC 20036
telephone: [1] (202) 797-3000
FAX: [1] (202) 797-3168
consulate(s) general: Atlanta, Chicago, Honolulu, Los Angeles, New York, and San Francisco
Diplomatic representation from the US:
chief of mission: William A. STANTON, Charge d'Affaires ad interim
embassy: Moonah Place, Yarralumla, Canberra, Australian Capital Territory 2600
mailing address: APO AP 96549
telephone: [61] (02) 6214-5600
FAX: [61] (02) 6214-5970
consulate(s) general: Melbourne, Perth, Sydney
Flag description: blue with the flag of the UK in the upper hoist-side quadrant and a large seven-pointed star in the lower hoist-side quadrant known as the Commonwealth Star, representing the federation of the colonies of Australia in 1901; the star depicts one point for each of the six original states and one representing all of Australia's internal and external territories; the remaining half is a representation of the Southern Cross constellation in white with one small five-pointed star and four larger, seven-pointed stars

ECONOMY

Economy - overview: Australia has an enviable Western-style capitalist economy, with a per capita GDP on par with the four dominant West European economies. Rising output in the domestic economy, robust business and consumer confidence, and rising exports of raw materials and agricultural products are fueling the economy. Australia's emphasis on reforms, low inflation, and growing ties with China are other key factors behind the economy's strength. The impact of drought, weak foreign demand, and strong import demand pushed the trade deficit up from $8 billion in 2002, to $18 billion in 2003, and to $13 billion in 2004. One other concern is the rapid increase in domestic housing prices, which have raised the prospect that interest rates will need to be raised to prevent a speculative bubble. Conservative fiscal policies have kept Australia's budget in surplus from 2002 to 2005.
GDP: purchasing power parity - $642.7 billion (2005 est.)
GDP: official exchange rate - $649.9 billion (2005 est.)
GDP - real growth rate: 2.7% (2005 est.)
GDP - per capita: purchasing power parity - $32,000 (2005 est.)
GDP - composition by sector:
agriculture: 4%
industry: 26.4%
services: 69.6% (2004 est.)
Labor force: 10.42 million (2005 est.)
Labor force - by occupation: agriculture 3.6%, industry 26.4%, services 70% (2004 est.)
Unemployment rate: 5.2% (2005 est.)
Population below poverty line: NA
Household income or consumption by percentage share:
lowest 10%: 2%
highest 10%: 25.4% (1994)
Distribution of family income - Gini index: 35.2 (1994)
Inflation rate (consumer prices): 2.7% (2005 est.)
Investment (gross fixed): 24.8% of GDP (2005 est.)
Budget:
revenues: $249.8 billion
expenditures: $240.2 billion, including capital expenditures of NA (2005 est.)
Public Debt: 17.4% of GDP (2004 est.)
Agriculture - products: wheat, barley, sugarcane, fruits; cattle, sheep, poultry
Industries: mining, industrial and transportation equipment, food processing, chemicals, steel
Industrial production growth rate: 1.6% (2005 est.)
Electricity – production: 215.8 billion kWh (2003)
Electricity – production by source:
fossil fuel: 90.8%
hydro: 8.3%
nuclear: 0%
other: 0.9% (2001)
Electricity - consumption: 200.7 billion kWh (2003)
Electricity - exports: 0 kWh (2003)
Electricity - imports: 0 kWh (2003)
Oil - production: 530,000 bbl/day (2005 est.)
Oil - consumption: 875,600 bbl/day (2003 est.)
Oil - exports: 523,400 bbl/day (2001)
Oil - imports: 530,800 bbl/day (2001)
Oil - proved reserves: 3.664 billion bbl (1 January 2002)
Natural gas - production: 33.08 billion cu m (2001 est.)
Natural gas - consumption: 23.33 billion cu m (2001 est.)
Natural gas - exports: 9.744 billion cu m (2001 est.)
Natural gas - imports: 0 cu m (2001 est.)
Natural gas - proved reserves: 2.407 trillion cu m (1 January 2002)
Current Account Balance: $-41.1 billion (2005 est.)
Exports: $103 billion (2005 est.)
Exports - partners: Japan 18.6%, China 9.2%, US 8.1%, South Korea 7.7%, New Zealand 7.4%, India 4.6%, UK 4.2% (2004)
Imports: $119.6 billion (2005 est.)
Imports - partners: US 14.8%, China 12.7%, Japan 11.8%, Germany 5.8%, Singapore 4.4%, UK 4.1% (2004)
Reserves of foreign exchange and gold: $39.03 billion (2005 est.)
Debt - external: $509.6 billion (30 June 2005 est.)
Economic aid - donor: ODA, $894 million (FY99/00)
Currency: Australian dollar (AUD)
Currency code: AUD
Exchange rates: Australian dollars per US dollar – 1.31 (2005), 1.3598 (2004), 1.5419 (2003), 1.8406 (2002), 1.9334 (2001), 1.7248 (2000)
Fiscal year: 1 July - 30 June

COMMUNICATIONS

Telephones - main lines in use: 10.815 million (2003)
Telephones - mobile cellular: 14.347 million (2003)
Telephone system:
general assessment: excellent domestic and international service
domestic: domestic satellite system; much use of radiotelephone in areas of low population density; rapid growth of mobile cellular telephones
international: country code - 61; submarine cables to New Zealand, Papua New Guinea, and Indonesia; satellite earth stations - 19 (10 Intelsat - 4 Indian Ocean and 6 Pacific Ocean, 2 Inmarsat - Indian and Pacific Ocean regions, 2 Globalstar, 5 other) (2005)
Radio broadcast stations: AM 262, FM 345, shortwave 1 (1998)
Radios: 25.5 million (1997)
Television broadcast stations: 104 (1997)
Televisions: 10.15 million (1997)
Internet country code: . au
Internet users: 9.472 million (2002)
Internet Hosts: 2,847,763 (2003)
Internet Service Providers (ISPs): 571 (2002)

TRANSPORTATION

Airports: 448 (2004 est.)
Airports - with paved runways:
total: 308
over 3,047 m: 10
2,438 to 3,047 m: 12
1,524 to 2,437 m: 133
914 to 1,523 m: 140
under 914 m: 13 (2005 est.)
Airports - with unpaved runways:
total: 142
1,524 to 2,437 m: 18
914 to 1,523 m: 110
under 914 m: 14 (2005 est.)
Heliports: 1 (2005 est.)
Pipelines: condensate/gas 492 km; gas 28,680 km; liquid petroleum gas 240 km; oil 4,773 km; oil/gas/water 110 km (2004)
Railways:
total: 54,439 km (3859 km electrified)
broad gauge: 5,434 km 1.600-m gauge
standard gauge: 34,110 km 1.435-m gauge (1,397 km electrified)
narrow gauge: 14,895 km 1.067-m gauge (2,462 km electrified)
dual gauge: 213 km dual gauge (2004)
Roadways:
total: 811,601 km
paved: 316,524 km
unpaved: 495,077 km (2002)
Waterways: 2,000 km (mainly used for recreation on Murray and Murray-Darling river systems) (2004)
Merchant marine:
total: 55 ships (1,000 GRT or over) 1,531,461 GRT/1,999,409 DWT
by type: bulk carrier 16, cargo 7, chemical tanker 3, container 1, liquefied gas 4, passenger 5, passenger/cargo 6, petroleum tanker 8, roll on/roll off 5
foreign-owned: 16 (France 1, Germany 3, Japan 1, Philippines 1, Saudi Arabia 1, United Kingdom 2, United States 7)
registered in other countries: 35 (2005)
Ports and terminals: Brisbane, Dampier, Fremantle, Gladstone, Hay Point, Melbourne, Newcastle, Port Hedland, Port Kembla, Port Walcott, Sydney

MILITARY

Military branches: Australian Defense Force (ADF): Australian Army, Royal Australian Navy, Royal Australian Air Force, Special Operations Command
Military service age and obligation: 16 years of age for voluntary service (2001)
Manpower available for military service: *males age 16-49:* 4,943,676 (2005 est.)
Manpower fit for military service: *males age 16-49:* 4,092,717 (2005 est.)
Manpower reaching military age annually: *males:* 142,158 (2005 est.)
Military expenditures - dollar figure: $16.65 billion (2004)
Military expenditures - percent of GDP: 2.7% (2004)

TRANSNATIONAL ISSUES

Disputes - international: East Timor and Australia continue to meet but disagree over how to delimit a permanent maritime boundary and share unexploited petroleum resources that fall outside the Joint Petroleum Development Area covered by the 2002 Timor Sea Treaty; East Timor dispute hampers creation of a revised maritime boundary with Indonesia (see also Ashmore and Cartier Islands dispute); regional states express concern over Australia's 2004 declaration of a 1,000-nautical mile-wide maritime identification zone; Australia asserts land and maritime claims to Antarctica (see Antarctica); in 2004 Australia submitted claims to UNCLOS to extend its continental margin from both its mainland and Antarctic claims
Illicit drugs: Tasmania is one of the world's major suppliers of licit opiate products; government maintains strict controls over areas of opium poppy cultivation and output of poppy straw concentrate

AUSTRIA

INTRODUCTION

Background: Once the center of power for the large Austro-Hungarian Empire, Austria was reduced to a small republic after its defeat in World War I. Following annexation by Nazi Germany in 1938 and subsequent occupation by the victorious Allies in 1945, Austria's status remained unclear for a decade. A State Treaty signed in 1955 ended the occupation, recognized Austria's independence, and forbade unification with Germany. A constitutional law that same year declared the country's "perpetual neutrality" as a condition for Soviet military withdrawal. Following the Soviet Union's collapse in 1991 and Austria's entry into the European Union in 1995, some Austrians have called into question this neutrality. A prosperous, democratic country, Austria entered the Economic and Monetary Union in 1999.

GEOGRAPHY

Location: Central Europe, north of Italy and Slovenia
Geographic coordinates: 47 20 N, 13 20 E
Map references: Europe
Area:
total: 83,870 sq km
land: 82,444 sq km
water: 1,426 sq km
Area - comparative: slightly smaller than Maine
Land boundaries:
total: 2,562 km
border countries: Czech Republic 362 km, Germany 784 km, Hungary 366 km, Italy 430 km, Liechtenstein 35 km, Slovakia 91 km, Slovenia 330 km, Switzerland 164 km
Coastline: 0 km (landlocked)
Maritime claims: 0 km (landlocked)
Climate: temperate; continental, cloudy; cold winters with frequent rain and some snow in lowlands and snow in mountains; moderate summers with occasional showers
Terrain: in the west and south mostly mountains (Alps); along the eastern and northern margins mostly flat or gently sloping
Elevation extremes:
lowest point: Neusiedler See 115 m
highest point: Grossglockner 3,798 m
Natural resources: oil, coal, lignite, timber, iron ore, copper, zinc, antimony, magnesite, tungsten, graphite, salt, hydropower
Land use:
arable land: 16.91%
permanent crops: 0.86%
other: 82.23% (2001)
Irrigated land: 457 sq km (2000 est.)
Natural hazards: landslides; avalanches; earthquakes
Environment - current issues: some forest degradation caused by air and soil pollution; soil pollution results from the use of agricultural chemicals; air pollution

results from emissions by coal- and oil-fired power stations and industrial plants and from trucks transiting Austria between northern and southern Europe
Environment - international agreements:
party to: Air Pollution, Air Pollution-Nitrogen Oxides, Air Pollution-Persistent Organic Pollutants, Air Pollution-Sulfur 85, Air Pollution-Sulphur 94, Air Pollution-Volatile Organic Compounds, Antarctic Treaty, Biodiversity, Climate Change, Climate Change-Kyoto Protocol, Desertification, Endangered Species, Environmental Modification, Hazardous Wastes, Law of the Sea, Ozone Layer Protection, Ship Pollution, Tropical Timber 83, Tropical Timber 94, Wetlands, Whaling
signed, but not ratified: none of the selected agreements
Geography - note: landlocked; strategic location at the crossroads of central Europe with many easily traversable Alpine passes and valleys; major river is the Danube; population is concentrated on eastern lowlands because of steep slopes, poor soils, and low temperatures elsewhere

PEOPLE

Population: 8,184,691 (July 2005 est.)
Age structure:
0-14 years: 15.6% (male 656,058/female 624,574)
15-64 years: 67.8% (male 2,790,673/female 2,756,612)
65 years and over: 16.6% (male 543,626/female 813,148) (2005 est.)
Median age:
total: 40.44 years
male: 39.3 years
female: 41.61 years (2005 est.)
Population growth rate: 0.11% (2005 est.)
Birth rate: 8.81 births/1,000 population (2005 est.)
Death rate: 9.7 deaths/1,000 population (2005 est.)
Net migration rate: 1.97 migrant(s)/1,000 population (2005 est.)
Sex ratio:
at birth: 1.05 male(s)/female
under 15 years: 1.05 male(s)/female
15-64 years: 1.01 male(s)/female
65 years and over: 0.67 male(s)/female
total population: 0.95 male(s)/female (2005 est.)
Infant mortality rate:
total: 4.66 deaths/1,000 live births
male: 5.74 deaths/1,000 live births
female: 3.53 deaths/1,000 live births (2005 est.)
Life expectancy at birth:
total population: 78.92 years
male: 76.03 years
female: 81.96 years (2005 est.)
Total fertility rate: 1.36 children born/woman (2005 est.)
HIV/AIDS - adult prevalence rate: 0.3% (2003 est.)
HIV/AIDS - people living with HIV/AIDS: 10,000 (2003 est.)
HIV/AIDS - deaths: less than 100 (2003 est.)
Nationality:
noun: Austrian(s)
adjective: Austrian
Ethnic groups: Austrians 91.1%, former Yugoslavs 4% (includes Croatians, Slovenes, Serbs, and Bosniaks), Turks 1.6%, German 0.9%, other or unspecified 2.4% (2001 census)
Religions: Roman Catholic 73.6%, Protestant 4.7%, Muslim 4.2%, other 3.5%, unspecified 2%, none 12% (2001 census)
Languages: German (official nationwide), Slovene (official in Carinthia), Croatian (official in Burgenland), Hungarian (official in Burgenland)
Literacy:
definition: age 15 and over can read and write
total population: 98%
male: NA%
female: NA%

GOVERNMENT

Country name:
conventional long form: Republic of Austria
conventional short form: Austria
local long form: Republik Oesterreich
local short form: Oesterreich
Government type: federal republic
Capital: Vienna
Administrative divisions: 9 states (Bundeslaender, singular - Bundesland); Burgenland, Kaernten, Niederoesterreich, Oberoesterreich, Salzburg, Steiermark, Tirol, Vorarlberg, Wien (Vienna)
Independence: 1156 (Duchy of Austria founded); 12 November 1918 (republic proclaimed)
National holiday: National Day, 26 October (1955); note - commemorates the State Treaty restoring national sovereignty and the end of occupation and the passage of the law on permanent neutrality
Constitution: 1920; revised 1929 (reinstated 1 May 1945)
Legal system: civil law system with Roman law origin; judicial review of legislative acts by the Constitutional Court; separate administrative and civil/penal supreme courts; accepts compulsory ICJ jurisdiction
Suffrage: 18 years of age; universal; compulsory for presidential elections
Executive branch:
chief of state: President Heinz FISCHER (since 8 July 2004)
head of government: Chancellor Wolfgang SCHUESSEL (OeVP) (since 4 February 2000); Vice Chancellor Hubert GORBACH (since 21 October 2003)
cabinet: Council of Ministers chosen by the president on the advice of the chancellor
elections: president elected by direct popular vote for a six-year term; presidential election last held 25 April 2004 (next to be held April 2010); chancellor traditionally chosen by the president from the plurality party in the National Council; vice chancellor chosen by the president on the advice of the chancellor
election results: Heinz FISCHER elected president; percent of vote - Heinz FISCHER (SPOe) 52.4%, Benita FERRERO-WALDNER (OeVP) 47.6%
note: government coalition - OeVP and FPOe
Legislative branch: bicameral Federal Assembly or Bundesversammlung consists of Federal Council or Bundesrat (62 members; members represent each of the states on the basis of population, but with each state having at least three representatives; members serve a five- or six-year term) and the National Council or Nationalrat (183 seats; members elected by direct popular vote to serve four-year terms)
elections: National Council - last held 24 November 2002 (next to be held in the fall of 2006)
election results: National Council - percent of vote by party - OeVP 42.3%, SPOe 36.5%, FPOe 10.0%, Greens 9.5%; seats by party - OeVP 79, SPOe 69, FPOe 18, Greens 17; seating as of May 2005 after split within the Freedom Party: OeVP 79, SPOe 69, Greens 17, BZOe 11, FPOe 7
Judicial branch: Supreme Judicial Court or Oberster Gerichtshof; Administrative Court or Verwaltungsgerichtshof; Constitutional Court or Verfassungsgerichtshof
Political parties and leaders: Alliance for the Future of Austria or BZOe [Joerg HAIDER]; Austrian People's Party or OeVP [Wolfgang SCHUESSEL]; Freedom Party of Austria or FPOe [Heinz Christian STRACHE]; Social Democratic Party of Austria or SPOe [Alfred GUSENBAUER]; The Greens [Alexander VAN DER BELLEN]
Political pressure groups and leaders: Austrian Trade Union Federation (nominally independent but primarily Socialist) or OeGB; Federal Economic Chamber; OeVP-oriented League of Austrian Industrialists or VOeI; Roman Catholic Church, including its chief lay organization, Catholic Action; three composite leagues of the Austrian People's Party or OeVP representing business, labor, and farmers and other

non-government organizations in the areas of environment and human rights
International organization participation: AfDB, AsDB, Australia Group, BIS, BSEC (observer), CE, CEI, CERN, EAPC, EBRD, EIB, EMU, ESA, EU, FAO, G- 9, IADB, IAEA, IBRD, ICAO, ICC, ICCt, ICFTU, ICRM, IDA, IEA, IFAD, IFC, IFRCS, ILO, IMF, IMO, Interpol, IOC, IOM, ISO, ITU, MIGA, MINURSO, NAM (guest), NEA, NSG, OAS (observer), OECD, OPCW, OSCE, Paris Club, PCA, PFP, UN, UNCTAD, UNDOF, UNESCO, UNFICYP, UNHCR, UNIDO, UNITAR, UNMEE, UNMIK, UNOMIG, UNTSO, UPU, WCL, WCO, WEU (observer), WFTU, WHO, WIPO, WMO, WToO, WTO, ZC
Diplomatic representation in the US:
chief of mission: Ambassador Eva NOWOTNY
chancery: 3524 International Court NW, Washington, DC 20008-3035
telephone: [1] (202) 895-6700
FAX: [1] (202) 895-6750
consulate(s) general: Chicago, Los Angeles, and New York
Diplomatic representation from the US:
chief of mission: Ambassador Susan R. McCAW
embassy: Boltzmanngasse 16, A-1090, Vienna
mailing address: use embassy street address
telephone: [43] (1) 31339-0, 31375, 31335
FAX: [43] (1) 3100682
Flag description: three equal horizontal bands of red (top), white, and red

ECONOMY

Economy - overview: Austria, with its well-developed market economy and high standard of living, is closely tied to other EU economies, especially Germany's. The economy features up-to-date industrial and agricultural sectors. Timber is a key industry, 47% of the land area being forested. Membership in the EU has drawn an influx of foreign investors attracted by Austria's access to the single European market and proximity to the new EU economies. Slow growth in Europe has held the economy to 0.7% growth in 2001, 1.4% in 2002, 0.8% in 2003, and 1.9% in 2004. To meet increased competition from both EU and Central European countries, particularly the new EU members, Austria will need to emphasize knowledge-based sectors of the economy, continue to deregulate the service sector, and encourage much greater participation in the labor market by its aging population. The aging phenomenon, together with already high health and pension costs, poses fundamental problems in tax and welfare policies.
GDP - purchasing power parity: - $269.4 billion (2005 est.)
GDP - official exchange rate: - $302.7 billion (2005 est.)
GDP - real growth rate: 1.9% (2005 est.)
GDP - per capita: purchasing power parity - $32,900 (2005 est.)
GDP - composition by sector:
agriculture: 2.3%
industry: 30.8%
services: 66.9% (2004 est.)
Labor force: 3.49 million (2005 est.)
Labor force - by occupation: agriculture and forestry 4%, industry and crafts 29%, services 67% (2001 est.)
Unemployment rate: 5.1% (2005 est.)
Population below poverty line: 3.9% (1999)
Household income or consumption by percentage share:
lowest 10%: 2.5%
highest 10%: 22.5% (1995)
Distribution of family income - Gini index: 30 (1997)
Inflation rate (consumer prices): 2.3% (2005 est.)
Investment (gross fixed): 21.1% of GDP (2005 est.)
Budget:
revenues: $148.6 billion
expenditures: $154.5 billion, including capital expenditures of NA (2005 est.)
Public debt: 64.5% of GDP (2005 est.)
Agriculture - products: grains, potatoes, sugar beets, wine, fruit; dairy products, cattle, pigs, poultry; lumber
Industries: construction, machinery, vehicles and parts, food, metals, chemicals, lumber and wood processing, paper and paperboard, communications equipment, tourism
Industrial production growth rate: 3.2% (2005 est.)
Electricity - production: 55.75 billion kWh (2003)
Electricity – production by source:
fossil fuel: 29.3%
hydro: 67.2%
nuclear: 0%
other: 3.5% (2001)
Electricity - consumption: 57.45 billion kWh (2003)
Electricity - exports: 13.4 billion kWh (2003)
Electricity - imports: 19 billion kWh (2003)
Oil - production: 25,650 bbl/day (2003)
Oil - consumption: 286,200 bbl/day (2003 est.)
Oil - exports: 35,470 bbl/day (2001)
Oil - imports: 262,000 bbl/day (2001)
Oil - proved reserves: 85.69 million bbl (1 January 2002)
Natural gas - production: 1.731 billion cu m (2001 est.)
Natural gas - consumption: 7.81 billion cu m (2001 est.)
Natural gas - exports: 403 million cu m (2001 est.)
Natural gas - imports: 6.033 billion cu m (2001 est.)
Natural gas - proved reserves: 24.9 billion cu m (1 January 2002)
Current account balance: $1.755 billion (2005 est.)
Exports: $122.5 billion f.o.b. (2005 est.)
Exports - partners: Germany 32%, Italy 8.9%, US 6%, Switzerland 4.8%, France 4.2%, UK 4.2% (2004)
Imports: $118.8 billion f.o.b. (2005 est.)
Imports - partners: Germany 46.3%, Italy 6.8%, Switzerland 4.3% (2004)
Reserves of foreign exchange and gold: $12.19 billion (2004 est.)
Debt - external: $510.6 billion (30 June 2005 est.)
Economic aid - donor: ODA, $520 million (2002)
Currency: euro (EUR)
note: on 1 January 1999, the European Monetary Union introduced the euro as a common currency to be used by the financial institutions of member countries; as of 1 January 2002, the euro became the only legal tender in EMU member countries, including Austria
Currency code: EUR
Exchange rates: euros per US dollar - 0.79697 (2005), 0.8054 (2004), 0.886 (2003), 1.0626 (2002), 1.1175 (2001), 1.0854 (2000)
Fiscal year: calendar year

COMMUNICATIONS

Telephones - main lines in use: 3.881 million (2003)
Telephones - mobile cellular: 7,094,500 (2003)
Telephone system:
general assessment: highly developed and efficient
domestic: there are 48 main lines for every 100 persons; the fiber optic net is very extensive; all telephone applications and Internet services are available
international: country code - 43; satellite earth stations - 2 Intelsat (1 Atlantic Ocean and 1 Indian Ocean) and 1 Eutelsat; in addition, there are about 600 VSAT (very small aperture terminals) (2002)
Radio broadcast stations: AM 2, FM 65 (plus several hundred repeaters), shortwave 1 (2001)
Radios: 6.08 million (1997)
Television broadcast stations: 10 (plus more than 1,000 repeaters) (2001)
Televisions: 4.25 million (1997)
Internet country code: .at
Internet hosts: 387,006 (2004)

Internet Service Providers (ISPs): 37 (2000)
Internet users: 3.73 million (2003)

TRANSPORTATION

Airports: 55 (2004 est.)
Airports - with paved runways:
total: 24
over 3,047 m: 1
2,438 to 3,047 m: 5
1,524 to 2,437 m: 1
914 to 1,523 m: 3
under 914 m: 14 (2005 est.)
Airports - with unpaved runways:
total: 31
1,524 to 2,437 m: 1
914 to 1,523 m: 3
under 914 m: 27 (2005 est.)
Heliports: 1 (2005 est.)
Pipelines: gas 2,722 km; oil 663 km; refined products 149 km (2004)
Railways:
total: 6,021 km (3,552 km electrified)
standard gauge: 5,565 km 1.435-m gauge (3,430 km electrified)
narrow gauge: 34 km 1.000-m gauge (28 km electrified); 422 km 0.760-m gauge (94 km electrified) (2004)
Roadways:
total: 133,718 km
paved: 133,718 km (including 1,677 km of expressways) (2003)
Waterways: 358 km (2003)
Merchant marine:
total: 8 ships (1,000 GRT or over) 29,624 GRT/37,425 DWT
by type: cargo 6, container 2
foreign-owned: 2 (Netherlands 2)
registered in other countries: 19 (2005)
Ports and terminals: Enns, Krems, Linz, Vienna

MILITARY

Military branches: Land Forces (KdoLdSK), Air Forces (KdoLuSK)
Military service age and obligation: 18 years of age for compulsory military service; 16 years of age for voluntary service; from 2007, at the earliest, compulsory military service obligation will be reduced from 8 months to 6 (2005)
Manpower available for military service:
males age 18-49: 1,914,800 (2005 est.)
Manpower fit for military service: *males age 18-49:* 1,550,441 (2005 est.)
Manpower reaching military age annually: *males:* 48,967 (2005 est.)
Military expenditures - dollar figure: $1.497 billion (FY01/02)
Military expenditures - percent of GDP: 0.9% (2004)

TRANSNATIONAL ISSUES

Disputes - international: none
Illicit drugs: transshipment point for Southwest Asian heroin and South American cocaine destined for Western Europe

AZERBAIJAN

INTRODUCTION

Background: Azerbaijan - a nation with a Turkic and majority-Muslim population - regained its independence after the collapse of the Soviet Union in 1991. Despite a 1994 cease-fire, Azerbaijan has yet to resolve its conflict with Armenia over the Azerbaijani Nagorno-Karabakh enclave (largely Armenian populated). Azerbaijan has lost 16% of its territory and must support some 571,000 internally displaced persons as a result of the conflict. Corruption is ubiquitous and the promise of widespread wealth from Azerbaijan's undeveloped petroleum resources remains largely unfulfilled.

GEOGRAPHY

Location: Southwestern Asia, bordering the Caspian Sea, between Iran and Russia, with a small European portion north of the Caucasus range
Geographic coordinates: 40 30 N, 47 30 E
Map references: Asia
Area:
total: 86,600 sq km
land: 86,100 sq km
water: 500 sq km
note: includes the exclave of Naxcivan Autonomous Republic and the Nagorno-Karabakh region; the region's autonomy was abolished by Azerbaijani Supreme Soviet on 26 November 1991
Area - comparative: slightly smaller than Maine
Land boundaries:
total: 2,013 km
border countries: Armenia (with Azerbaijan-proper) 566 km, Armenia (with Azerbaijan-Naxcivan exclave) 221 km, Georgia 322 km, Iran (with Azerbaijan-proper) 432 km, Iran (with Azerbaijan-Naxcivan exclave) 179 km, Russia 284 km, Turkey 9 km
Coastline: 0 km (landlocked); note - Azerbaijan borders the Caspian Sea (800 km, est.)
Maritime claims: none (landlocked)
Climate: dry, semiarid steppe
Terrain: large, flat Kur-Araz Ovaligi (Kura-Araks Lowland) (much of it below sea level) with Great Caucasus Mountains to the north, Qarabag Yaylasi (Karabakh Upland) in west; Baku lies on Abseron Yasaqligi (Apsheron Peninsula) that juts into Caspian Sea
Elevation extremes:
lowest point: Caspian Sea -28 m
highest point: Bazarduzu Dagi 4,485 m
Natural resources: petroleum, natural gas, iron ore, nonferrous metals, alumina
Land use:
arable land: 19.63%
permanent crops: 2.71%
other: 77.66% (2001)
Irrigated land: 14,550 sq km (1998 est.)
Natural hazards: droughts
Environment - current issues: local scientists consider the Abseron Yasaqligi (Apsheron Peninsula) (including Baku and Sumqayit) and the Caspian Sea to be the ecologically most devastated area in the world because of severe air, soil, and water pollution; soil pollution results from oil spills, from the use of DDT as a pesticide, and from toxic defoliants used in the production of cotton
Environment - international agreements:
party to: Air Pollution, Biodiversity, Climate Change, Climate Change-Kyoto Protocol, Desertification, Endangered Species, Hazardous Wastes, Marine Dumping, Ozone Layer Protection, Wetlands
signed, but not ratified: none of the selected agreements
Geography - note: both the main area of the country and the Naxcivan exclave are landlocked

PEOPLE

Population: 7,911,974 (July 2005 est.)
Age structure:
0-14 years: 26.4% (male 1,063,731/female 1,028,684)
15-64 years: 65.7% (male 2,533,762/female 2,665,381)

65 years and over: 7.8% (male 245,758/ female 374,658) (2005 est.)
Median age:
total: 27.53 years
male: 26.09 years
female: 29 years (2005 est.)
Population growth rate: 0.59% (2005 est.)
Birth rate: 20.4 births/1,000 population (2005 est.)
Death rate: 9.86 deaths/1,000 population (2005 est.)
Net migration rate: -4.64 migrant(s)/ 1,000 population (2005 est.)
Sex ratio:
at birth: 1.05 male(s)/female
under 15 years: 1.03 male(s)/female
15-64 years: 0.95 male(s)/female
65 years and over: 0.66 male(s)/female
total population: 0.94 male(s)/female (2005 est.)
Infant mortality rate:
total: 81.74 deaths/1,000 live births
male: 83.58 deaths/1,000 live births
female: 79.8 deaths/1,000 live births (2005 est.)
Life expectancy at birth:
total population: 63.35 years
male: 59.24 years
female: 67.66 years (2005 est.)
Total fertility rate: 2.44 children born/ woman (2005 est.)
HIV/AIDS - adult prevalence rate: less than 0.1% (2003 est.)
HIV/AIDS - people living with HIV/AIDS: 1,400 (2003 est.)
HIV/AIDS - deaths: less than 100 (2001 est.)
Nationality:
noun: Azerbaijani(s)
adjective: Azerbaijani
Ethnic groups: Azeri 90.6%, Dagestani 2.2%, Russian 1.8%, Armenian 1.5%, other 3.9% (1999 census)
note: almost all Armenians live in the separatist Nagorno-Karabakh region
Religions: Muslim 93.4%, Russian Orthodox 2.5%, Armenian Orthodox 2.3%, other 1.8% (1995 est.)
note: religious affiliation is still nominal in Azerbaijan; percentages for actual practicing adherents are much lower
Languages: Azerbaijani (Azeri) 89%, Russian 3%, Armenian 2%, other 6% (1995 est.)
Literacy:
definition: age 15 and over can read and write
total population: 98.8%
male: 99.5%
female: 98.2% (1999 est.)

GOVERNMENT

Country name:
conventional long form: Republic of Azerbaijan
conventional short form: Azerbaijan
local long form: Azarbaycan Respublikasi
local short form: none
former: Azerbaijan Soviet Socialist Republic
Government type: republic
Capital: Baku (Baki)
Administrative divisions: 59 rayons (rayonlar; rayon - singular), 11 cities* (saharlar; sahar - singular), 1 autonomous republic** (muxtar respublika)
: rayons: Abseron Rayonu, Agcabadi Rayonu, Agdam Rayonu, Agdas Rayonu, Agstafa Rayonu, Agsu Rayonu, Astara Rayonu, Balakan Rayonu, Barda Rayonu, Beylaqan Rayonu, Bilasuvar Rayonu, Cabrayil Rayonu, Calilabad Rayonu, Daskasan Rayonu, Davaci Rayonu, Fuzuli Rayonu, Gadabay Rayonu, Goranboy Rayonu, Goycay Rayonu, Haciqabul Rayonu, Imisli Rayonu, Ismayilli Rayonu, Kalbacar Rayonu, Kurdamir Rayonu, Lacin Rayonu, Lankaran Rayonu, Lerik Rayonu, Masalli Rayonu, Neftcala Rayonu, Oguz Rayonu, Qabala Rayonu, Qax Rayonu, Qazax Rayonu, Qobustan Rayonu, Quba Rayonu, Qubadli Rayonu, Qusar Rayonu, Saatli Rayonu, Sabirabad Rayonu, Saki Rayonu, Salyan Rayonu, Samaxi Rayonu, Samkir Rayonu, Samux Rayonu, Siyazan Rayonu, Susa Rayonu, Tartar Rayonu, Tovuz Rayonu, Ucar Rayonu, Xacmaz Rayonu, Xanlar Rayonu, Xizi Rayonu, Xocali Rayonu, Xocavand Rayonu, Yardimli Rayonu, Yevlax Rayonu, Zangilan Rayonu, Zaqatala Rayonu, Zardab Rayonu
: cities: Ali Bayramli Sahari, Baki Sahari, Ganca Sahari, Lankaran Sahari, Mingacevir Sahari, Naftalan Sahari, Saki Sahari, Sumqayit Sahari, Susa Sahari, Xankandi Sahari, Yevlax Sahari
: autonomous republic: Naxcivan Muxtar Respublikasi
Independence: 30 August 1991 (from Soviet Union)
National holiday: Founding of the Democratic Republic of Azerbaijan, 28 May (1918)
Constitution: adopted 12 November 1995
Legal system: based on civil law system
Suffrage: 18 years of age; universal
Executive branch:
chief of state: President Ilham ALIYEV (since 31 October 2003)
head of government: Prime Minister Artur RASIZADE (since 4 November 2003); First Deputy Prime Minister Abbas ABBASOV (since 10 November 2003)
cabinet: Council of Ministers appointed by the president and confirmed by the National Assembly
elections: president elected by popular vote to a five-year term; election last held 15 October 2003 (next to be held October 2008); prime minister and first deputy prime ministers appointed by the president and confirmed by the National Assembly
election results: Ilham ALIYEV elected president; percent of vote - Ilham ALIYEV 76.8%, Isa GAMBAR 14%
Legislative branch: unicameral National Assembly or Milli Mejlis (125 seats; members elected by popular vote to serve five-year terms)
elections: last held 6 November 2005 (next to be held in November 2010)
election results: percent of vote by party - NA%; seats by party - NAP 58. Azadliq coalition 8, CSP 2, YES 2, Motherland 2, other parties with single seats 7, independents 42, undetermined 4
Judicial branch: Supreme Court
Political parties and leaders: Azerbaijan Popular Front or APF [Ali KARIMLI, leader of "Reform" faction; Mirmahmud MIRALI-OGLU, leader of "Classic" faction]; Civic Solidarity Party or CSP [Sabir RUSTAMKHANLY]; Civic Union Party [Ayaz MUTALIBOV]; Communist Party of Azerbaijan or CPA [Ramiz AHMADOV]; Compatriot Party [Mais SAFARLI]; Democratic Party for Azerbaijan or DPA [Rasul QULIYEV, chairman]; Justice Party [Ilyas ISMAILOV]; Liberal Party of Azerbaijan [Lala Shovkat HACIYEVA]; Musavat [Isa GAMBAR, chairman]; New Azerbaijan Party or NAP [vacant]; Party for National Independence of Azerbaijan or PNIA [Etibar MAMMADLI, chairman]; Social Democratic Party of Azerbaijan or SDP [Araz ALIZADE and Ayaz MUTALIBOV]
note: opposition parties regularly factionalize and form new parties
Political pressure groups and leaders: Sadval, Lezgin movement; self-proclaimed Armenian Nagorno-Karabakh Republic; Talysh independence movement; Union of Pro-Azerbaijani Forces (UPAF)
International organization participation: AsDB, BSEC, CE, CIS, EAPC, EBRD, ECO, FAO, GUUAM, IAEA, IBRD, ICAO, ICFTU, ICRM, IDA, IDB, IFAD, IFC, IFRCS, ILO, IMF, IMO, Interpol, IOC, IOM, ISO, ITU, MIGA, OAS (observer), OIC, OPCW, OSCE, PFP, UN, UNCTAD, UNESCO, UNIDO, UPU, WCO, WFTU, WHO, WIPO, WMO, WToO, WTO (observer)
Diplomatic representation in the US:
chief of mission: Ambassador Hafiz PASHAYEV
chancery: 2741 34th Street NW, Washington, DC 20008
telephone: [1] (202) 337-3500

FAX: [1] (202) 337-5911
Diplomatic representation from the US:
chief of mission: Ambassador Reno L. HARNISH III
embassy: 83 Azadlyg Prospecti, Baku AZ1007
mailing address: American Embassy Baku, Department of State, 7050 Baku Place, Washington, DC 20521-7050
telephone: [9] (9412) 98-03-35, 36, 37
FAX: [9] (9412) 656-671
Flag description: three equal horizontal bands of blue (top), red, and green; a crescent and eight-pointed star in white are centered in red band

ECONOMY

Economy - overview: Azerbaijan's number one export is oil. Azerbaijan's oil production declined through 1997 but has registered an increase every year since. Negotiation of production-sharing arrangements (PSAs) with foreign firms, which have thus far committed $60 billion to long-term oilfield development, should generate the funds needed to spur future industrial development. Oil production under the first of these PSAs, with the Azerbaijan International Operating Company, began in November 1997. Azerbaijan shares all the formidable problems of the former Soviet republics in making the transition from a command to a market economy, but its considerable energy resources brighten its long-term prospects. Baku has only recently begun making progress on economic reform, and old economic ties and structures are slowly being replaced. One obstacle to economic progress is the need for stepped up foreign investment in the non-energy sector. A second obstacle is the continuing conflict with Armenia over the Nagorno-Karabakh region. Trade with Russia and the other former Soviet republics is declining in importance while trade is building with Turkey and the nations of Europe. Long-term prospects will depend on world oil prices, the location of new pipelines in the region, and Azerbaijan's ability to manage its oil wealth.
GDP: purchasing power parity - $36.53 billion (2005 est.)
GDP: official exchange rate - $10.81 billion (2005 est.)
GDP - real growth rate: 18.3% (2005 est.)
GDP - per capita: purchasing power parity - $4,600 (2005 est.)
GDP - composition by sector:
agriculture: 14.1%
industry: 45.7%
services: 40.2% (2002 est.)
Labor force: 5.45 million (2005 est.)
Labor force - by occupation: agriculture and forestry 41%, industry 7%, services 52% (2001)
Unemployment rate: 1.2% (official rate) (2005 est.)
Population below poverty line: 49% (2002 est.)
Household income or consumption by percentage share:
lowest 10%: 2.8%
highest 10%: 27.8% (1995)
Distribution of family income - Gini index: 36.5 (2001)
Inflation rate (consumer prices): 12% (2005 est.)
Investment (gross fixed): 57.4% of GDP (2005 est.)
Budget:
revenues: $3.18 billion
expenditures: $2.986 billion, including capital expenditures of NA (2005 est.)
Public debt: 13.9% of GDP (2005 est.)
Agriculture - products: cotton, grain, rice, grapes, fruit, vegetables, tea, tobacco; cattle, pigs, sheep, goats
Industries: petroleum and natural gas, petroleum products, oilfield equipment; steel, iron ore, cement; chemicals and petrochemicals; textiles
Industrial production growth rate: 25% (2005 est.)
Electricity - production: 20 billion kWh (2003)
Electricity - production by source:
fossil fuel: 89.7%
hydro: 10.3%
nuclear: 0%
other: 0% (2001)
Electricity - consumption: 20.25 billion kWh (2003)
Electricity - exports: 700 million kWh (2003)
Electricity - imports: 2.35 billion kWh (2003)
Oil - production: 477,000 bbl/day (2005 est.)
Oil - consumption: 123,000 bbl/day (2003 est.)
Oil - exports: NA (2001)
Oil - imports: NA (2001)
Oil - proved reserves: 589 million bbl (1 January 2002)
Natural gas - production: 5.72 billion cu m (2001 est.)
Natural gas - consumption: 6.72 billion cu m (2001 est.)
Natural gas - exports: 0 cu m (2001 est.)
Natural gas - imports: 1 billion cu m (2001 est.)
Natural gas - proved reserves: 62.3 billion cu m (1 January 2002)
Current account balance: $-1.53 billion (2005 est.)
Exports: $6.117 billion f.o.b. (2005 est.)
Exports - partners: Italy 26.6%, Czech Republic 11.9%, Germany 8.1%, Indonesia 6.4%, Romania 6.2%, Georgia 6%, Russia 5.3%, Turkey 5.2%, France 4.1% (2004)
Imports: $4.656 billion f.o.b. (2005 est.)
Imports - partners: Russia 16.1%, UK 12.5%, Turkey 10.5%, Germany 7.8%, Ukraine 5.6%, Netherlands 4.9%, US 4.1%, Italy 4% (2004)
Reserves of foreign exchange and gold: $1.2 billion (2005 est.)
Debt - external: $2.253 billion (2005 est.)
Economic aid - recipient: ODA, $140 million (2000 est.)
Currency: Azerbaijani manat (AZM)
Currency code: AZM
Exchange rates: Azerbaijani manats per US dollar - 4,794.15 (2005), 4,913.48 (2004), 4,910.73 (2003), 4,860.82 (2002), 4,656.58 (2001), 4,474.15 (2000)
Fiscal year: calendar year

COMMUNICATIONS

Telephones - main lines in use: 923,800 (2002)
Telephones - mobile cellular: 870,000 (2002)
Telephone system:
general assessment: inadequate; requires considerable expansion and modernization; teledensity of 10 main lines per 100 persons is low (2002)
domestic: the majority of telephones are in Baku and other industrial centers - about 700 villages still without public telephone service; satellite service connects Baku to a modern switch in its exclave of Naxcivan
international: country code - 994; the old Soviet system of cable and microwave is still serviceable; satellite earth stations - 2 (2005)
Radio broadcast stations: AM 10, FM 17, shortwave 1 (1998)
Radios: 175,000 (1997)
Television broadcast stations: 2 (1997)
Televisions: 170,000 (1997)
Internet country code: .az
Internet hosts: 586 (2004)
Internet Service Providers (ISPs): 2 (2000)
Internet users: 300,000 (2002)

TRANSPORTATION

Airports: 50 (2004 est.)
Airports - with paved runways:
total: 27
over 3,047 m: 2
2,438 to 3,047 m: 6
1,524 to 2,437 m: 15
914 to 1,523 m: 3
under 914 m: 1 (2005 est.)
Airports - with unpaved runways:
total: 19
914 to 1,523 m: 3
under 914 m: 15 (2005 est.)
Heliports: 2 (2005 est.)

Pipelines: gas 4,451 km; oil 1,518 km (2004)

Railways:
total: 2,957 km
broad gauge: 2,957 km 1.520-m gauge (1,278 km electrified) (2004)

Roadways:
total: 27,016 km
paved: 12,698 km (including 128 km of expressways)
unpaved: 14,318 km (2003)

Merchant marine:
total: 81 ships (1,000 GRT or over) 253,004 GRT/318,922 DWT
by type: cargo 26, passenger 2, passenger/cargo 8, petroleum tanker 41, roll on/roll off 2, specialized tanker 2
registered in other countries: 3 (2005)

Ports and terminals: Baku (Baki)

MILITARY

Military branches: Army, Navy, Air and Air Defense Forces

Military service age and obligation: 18 years of age for compulsory and voluntary military service; law passed December 2001 raises maximum conscription age from 28 to 35 (December 2001)

Manpower available for military service:
males age 18-49: 1,961,973 (2005 est.)

Manpower fit for military service: *males age 18-49:* 1,314,955 (2005 est.)

Manpower reaching military age annually: *males: males:* 82,358 (2005 est.)

Military expenditures - dollar figure: $121 million (FY99)

Military expenditures - percent of GDP: 2.6% (FY99)

TRANSNATIONAL ISSUES

Disputes - international: Armenia supports ethnic Armenian secessionists in Nagorno-Karabakh and since the early 1990s has militarily occupied 16% of Azerbaijan - Organization for Security and Cooperation in Europe (OSCE) continues to mediate dispute; over 800,000 mostly ethnic Azerbaijanis were driven from the occupied lands and Armenia; about 230,000 ethnic Armenians were driven from their homes in Azerbaijan into Armenia; Azerbaijan seeks transit route through Armenia to connect to Naxcivan exclave; Azerbaijan, Kazakhstan, and Russia ratify Caspian seabed delimitation treaties based on equidistance, while Iran continues to insist on an even one-fifth allocation and challenges Azerbaijan's hydrocarbon exploration in disputed waters; bilateral talks continue with Turkmenistan on dividing the seabed and contested oilfields in the middle of the Caspian; Azerbaijan and Georgia cannot resolve the alignment of their boundary at certain crossing areas

Refugees and internally displaced persons:
IDPs: 571,000 (conflict with Armenia over Nagorno-Karabakh) (2004)

Illicit drugs: limited illicit cultivation of cannabis and opium poppy, mostly for CIS consumption; small government eradication program; transit point for Southwest Asian opiates bound for Russia and to a lesser extent the rest of Europe

BAHAMAS, THE

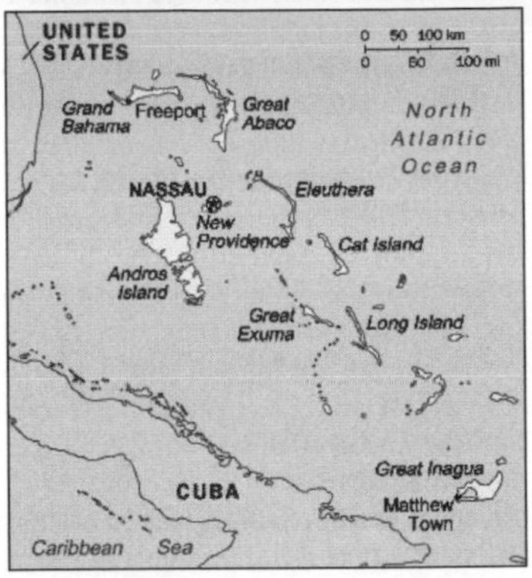

INTRODUCTION

Background: Arawak Indians inhabited the islands when Christopher Columbus first set foot in the New World on San Salvador in 1492. British settlement of the islands began in 1647; the islands became a colony in 1783. Since attaining independence from the UK in 1973, The Bahamas have prospered through tourism and international banking and investment management. Because of its geography, the country is a major transshipment point for illegal drugs, particularly shipments to the US, and its territory is used for smuggling illegal migrants into the US.

GEOGRAPHY

Location: Caribbean, chain of islands in the North Atlantic Ocean, southeast of Florida, northeast of Cuba
Geographic coordinates: 24 15 N, 76 00 W
Map references: Central America and the Caribbean
Area:
total: 13,940 sq km
land: 10,070 sq km
water: 3,870 sq km
Area - comparative: slightly smaller than Connecticut
Land boundaries: 0 km
Coastline: 3,542 km
Maritime claims:
territorial sea: 12 nm
exclusive economic zone: 200 nm
Climate: tropical marine; moderated by warm waters of Gulf Stream
Terrain: long, flat coral formations with some low rounded hills
Elevation extremes:
lowest point: Atlantic Ocean 0 m
highest point: Mount Alvernia, on Cat Island 63 m
Natural resources: salt, aragonite, timber, arable land
Land use:
arable land: 0.8%
permanent crops: 0.4%
other: 98.8% (2001)
Irrigated land: NA
Natural hazards: hurricanes and other tropical storms cause extensive flood and wind damage
Environment - current issues: coral reef decay; solid waste disposal
Environment - international agreements:
party to: Biodiversity, Climate Change, Climate Change-Kyoto Protocol, Desertification, Endangered Species, Hazardous Wastes, Law of the Sea, Ozone Layer Protection, Ship Pollution, Wetlands
signed, but not ratified: none of the selected agreements
Geography - note: strategic location adjacent to US and Cuba; extensive island chain of which 30 are inhabited

PEOPLE

Population: 301,790
note: estimates for this country explicitly take into account the effects of excess mortality due to AIDS; this can result in lower life expectancy, higher infant mortality and death rates, lower population and growth rates, and changes in the distribution of population by age and sex than would otherwise be expected (July 2005 est.)
Age structure:
0-14 years: 27.9% (male 42,142/female 42,096)
15-64 years: 65.9% (male 97,865/female 101,047)
65 years and over: 6.2% (male 7,616/ female 11,024) (2005 est.)
Median age:
total: 27.55 years
male: 26.78 years
female: 28.34 years (2005 est.)
Population growth rate: 0.67% (2005 est.)
Birth rate: 17.87 births/1,000 population (2005 est.)
Death rate: 8.97 deaths/1,000 population (2005 est.)
Net migration rate: -2.18 migrant(s)/ 1,000 population (2005 est.)
Sex ratio:
at birth: 1.02 male(s)/female
under 15 years: 1 male(s)/female
15-64 years: 0.97 male(s)/female
65 years and over: 0.69 male(s)/female
total population: 0.96 male(s)/female (2005 est.)
Infant mortality rate:
total: 25.21 deaths/1,000 live births
male: 31.02 deaths/1,000 live births
female: 19.28 deaths/1,000 live births (2005 est.)
Life expectancy at birth:
total population: 65.54 years
male: 62.11 years
female: 69.04 years (2005 est.)
Total fertility rate: 2.2 children born/ woman (2005 est.)
HIV/AIDS - adult prevalence rate: 3% (2003 est.)
HIV/AIDS - people living with HIV/AIDS: 5,600 (2003 est.)
HIV/AIDS - deaths: less than 200 (2003 est.)
Nationality:
noun: Bahamian(s)
adjective: Bahamian
Ethnic groups: black 85%, white 12%, Asian and Hispanic 3%
Religions: Baptist 35.4%, Anglican 15.1%, Roman Catholic 13.5%, Pentecostal 8.1%, Church of God 4.8%, Methodist 4.2%, other Christian 15.2%, none or unspecified 2.9%, other 0.8% (2000 census)
Languages: English (official), Creole (among Haitian immigrants)
Literacy:
definition: age 15 and over can read and write
total population: 95.6%
male: 94.7%
female: 96.5% (2003 est.)

GOVERNMENT

Country name:
conventional long form: Commonwealth of The Bahamas
conventional short form: The Bahamas
Government type: constitutional parliamentary democracy
Capital: Nassau
Administrative divisions: 21 districts; Acklins and Crooked Islands, Bimini, Cat Island, Exuma, Freeport, Fresh Creek, Governor's Harbour, Green Turtle Cay, Harbour Island, High Rock, Inagua, Kemps Bay, Long Island, Marsh Harbour, Mayaguana, New Providence, Nichollstown and Berry Islands, Ragged Island, Rock Sound, Sandy Point, San Salvador and Rum Cay
Independence: 10 July 1973 (from UK)
National holiday: Independence Day, 10 July (1973)
Constitution: 10 July 1973
Legal system: based on English common law
Suffrage: 18 years of age; universal
Executive branch:
chief of state: Queen ELIZABETH II (since 6 February 1952), represented by Governor General Dame Ivy DUMONT (since NA May 2002)
head of government: Prime Minister Perry CHRISTIE (since 3 May 2002) and Deputy Prime Minister Cynthia PRATT (since 7 May 2002)

cabinet: Cabinet appointed by the governor general on the prime minister's recommendation
elections: none; the monarch is hereditary; governor general appointed by the monarch; following legislative elections, the leader of the majority party or the leader of the majority coalition is usually appointed prime minister by the governor general; the prime minister recommends the deputy prime minister
Legislative branch: bicameral Parliament consists of the Senate (16-member body appointed by the governor general upon the advice of the prime minister and the opposition leader for five-year terms) and the House of Assembly (40 seats; members elected by direct popular vote to serve five-year terms); the government may dissolve the parliament and call elections at any time
elections: last held 1 May 2002 (next to be held by May 2007)
election results: percent of vote by party - PLP 50.8%, FNM 41.1%, independents 5.2%; seats by party - PLP 29, FNM 7, independents 4
Judicial branch: Supreme Court; Court of Appeal; magistrates courts
Political parties and leaders: Free National Movement or FNM [Tommy TURNQUEST]; Progressive Liberal Party or PLP [Perry CHRISTIE]
Political pressure groups and leaders: NA
International organization participation: ACP, C, Caricom, CDB, FAO, G-77, IADB, IBRD, ICAO, ICCt (signatory), ICFTU, ICRM, IFC, IFRCS, ILO, IMF, IMO, Interpol, IOM, IOC, ITU, LAES, MIGA, NAM, OAS, OPANAL, OPCW (signatory), UN, UNCTAD, UNESCO, UNIDO, UPU, WCO, WHO, WIPO, WMO, WTO (observer)
Diplomatic representation in the US:
chief of mission: Ambassador Joshua SEARS
chancery: 2220 Massachusetts Avenue NW, Washington, DC 20008
telephone: [1] (202) 319-2660
FAX: [1] (202) 319-2668
consulate(s) general: Miami and New York
Diplomatic representation from the US:
chief of mission: Ambassador John D. ROOD
embassy: 42 Queen Street, Nassau
mailing address: local or express mail address: P. O. Box N-8197, Nassau; Department of State, 3370 Nassau Place, Washington, DC 20521-3370
telephone: [1] (242) 322-1181, 328-2206 (after hours)
FAX: [1] (242) 356-0222
Flag description: three equal horizontal bands of aquamarine (top), gold, and aquamarine, with a black equilateral triangle based on the hoist side

ECONOMY

Economy - overview: The Bahamas is a stable, developing nation with an economy heavily dependent on tourism and offshore banking. Tourism alone accounts for more than 60% of GDP and directly or indirectly employs half of the archipelago's labor force. Steady growth in tourism receipts and a boom in construction of new hotels, resorts, and residences had led to solid GDP growth in recent years, but the slowdown in the US economy and the attacks of 11 September 2001 held back growth in these sectors in 2001-03. Financial services constitute the second-most important sector of the Bahamian economy, accounting for about 15% of GDP. However, since December 2000, when the government enacted new regulations on the financial sector, many international businesses have left The Bahamas. Manufacturing and agriculture together contribute approximately a tenth of GDP and show little growth, despite government incentives aimed at those sectors. Overall growth prospects in the short run rest heavily on the fortunes of the tourism sector, which depends on growth in the US, the source of more than 80% of the visitors. In addition to tourism and banking, the government supports the development of a "third pillar," e-commerce.
GDP: purchasing power parity - $5.685 billion (2005 est.)
GDP (official exchange rate): $5.924 billion (2005 est.)
GDP - real growth rate: 3% (2005 est.)
GDP - per capita: purchasing power parity - $18,800 (2005 est.)
GDP - composition by sector:
agriculture: 3%
industry: 7%
services: 90% (2001 est.)
Labor force: 156,000 (1999)
Labor force - by occupation: agriculture 5%, industry 5%, tourism 50%, other services 40% (1999 est.)
Unemployment rate: 10.2% (2004 est.)
Population below poverty line: NA
Household income or consumption by percentage share:
lowest 10%: NA
highest 10%: 27% (2000)
Inflation rate (consumer prices): 1.2% (Year ending September 2004) (Year ending September 2004)
Budget:
revenues: $1 billion
expenditures: $1 billion, including capital expenditures of $106.7 million (FY03/04)
Agriculture - products: citrus, vegetables; poultry
Industries: tourism, banking, cement, oil transshipment, salt, rum, aragonite, pharmaceuticals, spiral-welded steel pipe
Industrial production growth rate: NA
Electricity - production: 1.81 billion kWh (2003)
Electricity – production by source:
fossil fuel: 100%
hydro: 0%
nuclear: 0%
other: 0% (2001)
Electricity - consumption: 1.683 billion kWh (2003)
Electricity - exports: 0 kWh (2003)
Electricity - imports: 0 kWh (2003)
Oil - production: 0 bbl/day (2003 est.)
Oil - consumption: 23,000 bbl/day (2003 est.)
Oil - exports: transhipments of 29,000 bbl/day (2003)
Oil - imports: NA (2001)
Exports: $1.507 billion (2004 est.)
Exports - partners: US 40.3%, Poland 13.3%, Spain 11.7%, Germany 5.9%, France 4.3% (2004)
Imports: $5.806 billion (2004 est.)
Imports - partners: US 22.4%, South Korea 18.9%, Brazil 9.2%, Japan 7.9%, Italy 7.8%, Venezuela 6.6% (2004)
Debt - external: $308.5 million (2002)
Economic aid - recipient: $9.8 million (1995)
Currency: Bahamian dollar (BSD)
Currency code: BSD
Exchange rates: Bahamian dollars per US dollar - NA (2005), 1 (2004), 1 (2003), 1 (2002), 1 (2001)
Fiscal year: 1 July - 30 June

COMMUNICATIONS

Telephones - main lines in use: 131,700 (2003)
Telephones - mobile cellular: 121,800 (2002)
Telephone system:
general assessment: modern facilities
domestic: totally automatic system; highly developed
international: country code - 1-242; tropospheric scatter and submarine cable to Florida; 3 coaxial submarine cables; satellite earth station - 2 (2005)
Radio broadcast stations: AM 3, FM 5, shortwave 0 (2004)
Radios: 215,000 (1997)
Television broadcast stations: 2 (2004)
Televisions: 67,000 (1997)
Internet country code: .bs
Internet hosts: 302 (2003)
Internet Service Providers (ISPs): 19 (2000)
Internet users: 84,000 (2003)

TRANSPORTATION

Airports: 63 (2004 est.)
Airports - with paved runways:
total: 30

over 3,047 m: 2
2,438 to 3,047 m: 3
1,524 to 2,437 m: 14
914 to 1,523 m: 10
under 914 m: 1 (2005 est.)
Airports - with unpaved runways:
total: 34
1,524 to 2,437 m: 3
914 to 1,523 m: 9
under 914 m: 22 (2005 est.)
Heliports: 1 (2005 est.)
Roadways:
total: 2,693 km
paved: 1,546 km
unpaved: 1,147 km (1999)
Merchant marine:
total: 1,119
by type: barge carrier 2, bulk carrier 183, cargo 259, chemical tanker 54, combination ore/oil 17, container 74, liquefied gas 28, livestock carrier 2, passenger 116, passenger/cargo 40, petroleum tanker 168, refrigerated cargo 130, roll on/roll off 20, specialized tanker 2, vehicle carrier 24
foreign-owned: 968 (Angola 4, Australia 4, Belgium 17, Canada 9, China 3, Croatia 1, Cuba 1, Cyprus 13, Denmark 18, Estonia 1, Finland 7, France 28, Germany 15, Greece 194, Hong Kong 11, Indonesia 2, Ireland 1, Israel 1, Italy 7, Japan 49, Jordan 2, Kenya 1, Latvia 1, Malaysia 12, Monaco 15, Netherlands 24, New Zealand 1, Nigeria 2, Norway 229, Poland 13, Reunion 1, Russia 2, Saudi Arabia 12, Serbia & Montenegro 2, Singapore 11, Slovenia 1, South Korea 1, Spain 6, Sweden 9, Switzerland 4, Thailand 1, Trinidad & Tobago 2, Turkey 7, UAE 12, United Kingdom 55, United States 154, Uruguay 2)
registered in other countries: 35 (2005)
Ports and terminals: Freeport, Nassau, South Riding Point

MILITARY

Military branches: Royal Bahamaian Defense Force (naval forces) (2004)
Military manpower - military age and obligation: 18 years of age (est.); no conscription (2001)
Military expenditures - dollar figure: NA
Military expenditures - percent of GDP: NA

TRANSNATIONAL ISSUES

Disputes - international: have not been able to agree on the alignment of a maritime boundary with the US; continues to monitor and interdict Haitian refugees fleeing economic privation and political instability
Illicit drugs: transshipment point for cocaine and marijuana bound for US and Europe; offshore financial center

BAHRAIN

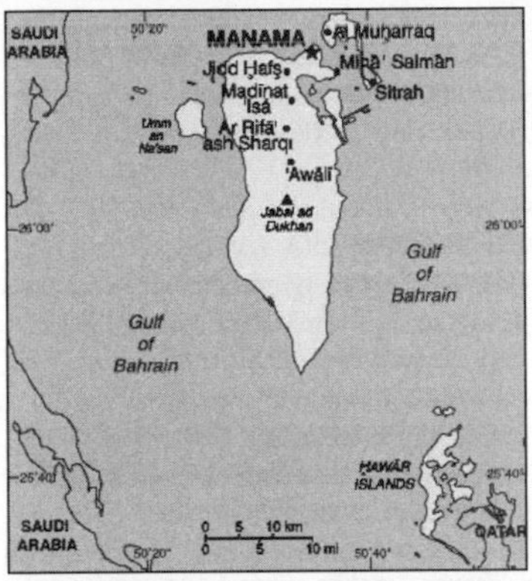

INTRODUCTION

Background: Bahrain's small size and central location among Persian Gulf countries require it to play a delicate balancing act in foreign affairs among its larger neighbors. Facing declining oil reserves, Bahrain has turned to petroleum processing and refining and has transformed itself into an international banking center. The amir, installed in 1999, has pushed economic and political reforms and has worked to improve relations with the Shi'a community. In February 2001, Bahraini voters approved a referendum on the National Action Charter - the centerpiece of the amir's political liberalization program. In February 2002, Amir HAMAD bin Isa Al Khalifa proclaimed himself king. In October 2002, Bahrainis elected members of the lower house of Bahrain's reconstituted bicameral legislature, the National Assembly.

GEOGRAPHY

Location: Middle East, archipelago in the Persian Gulf, east of Saudi Arabia
Geographic coordinates: 26 00 N, 50 33 E
Map references: Middle East
Area:
total: 665 sq km
land: 665 sq km
water: 0 sq km
Area - comparative: 3.5 times the size of Washington, DC
Land boundaries: 0 km
Coastline: 161 km
Maritime claims:
territorial sea: 12 nm
contiguous zone: 24 nm
continental shelf: extending to boundaries to be determined
Climate: arid; mild, pleasant winters; very hot, humid summers
Terrain: mostly low desert plain rising gently to low central escarpment
Elevation extremes:
lowest point: Persian Gulf 0 m
highest point: Jabal ad Dukhan 122 m
Natural resources: oil, associated and nonassociated natural gas, fish, pearls
Land use:
arable land: 2.82%
permanent crops: 5.63%
other: 91.55% (2001)
Irrigated land: 50 sq km (1998 est.)
Natural hazards: periodic droughts; dust storms
Environment - current issues: desertification resulting from the degradation of limited arable land, periods of drought, and dust storms; coastal degradation (damage to coastlines, coral reefs, and sea vegetation) resulting from oil spills and other discharges from large tankers, oil refineries, and distribution stations; lack of freshwater resources, groundwater and seawater are the only sources for all water needs
Environment - international agreements:
party to: Biodiversity, Climate Change, Desertification, Hazardous Wastes, Law of the Sea, Ozone Layer Protection, Wetlands
signed, but not ratified: none of the selected agreements
Geography - note: close to primary Middle Eastern petroleum sources; strategic location in Persian Gulf, through which much of the Western world's petroleum must transit to reach open ocean

PEOPLE

Population: 688,345
note: includes 235,108 non-nationals (July 2005 est.)
Age structure:
0-14 years: 27.8% (male 96,807/female 94,863)
15-64 years: 68.7% (male 275,792/female 197,424)
65 years and over: 3.4% (male 12,078/female 11,381) (2005 est.)
Median age:
total: 29.19 years
male: 32.16 years
female: 25.54 years (2005 est.)
Population growth rate: 1.51% (2005 est.)
Birth rate: 18.1 births/1,000 population (2005 est.)
Death rate: 4.08 deaths/1,000 population (2005 est.)

Net migration rate: 1.04 migrant(s)/1,000 population (2005 est.)
Sex ratio:
at birth: 1.03 male(s)/female
under 15 years: 1.02 male(s)/female
15-64 years: 1.4 male(s)/female
65 years and over: 1.06 male(s)/female
total population: 1.27 male(s)/female (2005 est.)
Infant mortality rate:
total: 17.27 deaths/1,000 live births
male: 20.17 deaths/1,000 live births
female: 14.28 deaths/1,000 live births (2005 est.)
Life expectancy at birth:
total population: 74.23 years
male: 71.76 years
female: 76.78 years (2005 est.)
Total fertility rate: 2.63 children born/woman (2005 est.)
HIV/AIDS - adult prevalence rate: 0.2% (2001 est.)
HIV/AIDS - people living with HIV/AIDS: less than 600 (2003 est.)
HIV/AIDS - deaths: less than 200 (2003 est.)
Nationality:
noun: Bahraini(s)
adjective: Bahraini
Ethnic groups: Bahraini 62.4%, non-Bahraini 37.6% (2001 census)
Religions: Muslim (Shi'a and Sunni) 81.2%, Christian 9%, other 9.8% (2001 census)
Languages: Arabic, English, Farsi, Urdu
Literacy:
definition: age 15 and over can read and write
total population: 89.1%
male: 91.9%
female: 85% (2003 est.)

GOVERNMENT

Country name:
conventional long form: Kingdom of Bahrain
conventional short form: Bahrain
local long form: Mamlakat al Bahrayn
local short form: Al Bahrayn
former: Dilmun
Government type: constitutional hereditary monarchy
Capital: Manama
Administrative divisions: 12 municipalities (manatiq, singular - mintaqah); Al Hadd, Al Manamah, Al Mintaqah al Gharbiyah, Al Mintaqah al Wusta, Al Mintaqah ash Shamaliyah, Al Muharraq, Ar Rifa' wa al Mintaqah al Janubiyah, Jidd Hafs, Madinat Hamad, Madinat 'Isa, Juzur Hawar, Sitrah
note: all municipalities administered from Manama
Independence: 15 August 1971 (from UK)
National holiday: National Day, 16 December (1971); note - 15 August 1971 is the date of independence from the UK, 16 December 1971 is the date of independence from British protection
Constitution: new constitution 14 February 2002
Legal system: based on Islamic law and English common law
Suffrage: 18 years of age; universal
Executive branch:
chief of state: King HAMAD bin Isa al-Khalifa (since 6 March 1999); Heir Apparent Crown Prince SALMAN bin Hamad (son of the monarch, born 21 October 1969)
head of government: Prime Minister KHALIFA bin Salman al-Khalifa (since NA 1971)
cabinet: Cabinet appointed by the monarch
elections: none; the monarchy is hereditary; prime minister appointed by the monarch
Legislative branch: bicameral Parliament consists of Shura Council (40 members appointed by the King) and House of Deputies (40 members directly elected to serve four-year terms)
elections: House of Deputies - last held 31 October 2002 (next election to be held in 2006)
election results: House of Deputies - percent of vote by party - NA; seats by party - independents 21, Sunni Islamists 9, other 10
note: first elections since 7 December 1973; unicameral National Assembly dissolved 26 August 1975; National Action Charter created bicameral legislature on 23 December 2000; approved by referendum 14 February 2001; first legislative session of Parliament held on 25 December 2002
Judicial branch: High Civil Appeals Court
Political parties and leaders: political parties prohibited but politically oriented societies are allowed
Political pressure groups and leaders: Shi'a activists fomented unrest sporadically in 1994-97 and have recently engaged in peaceful protests and marches, demanding the return of an elected National Assembly and an end to unemployment; several small, clandestine leftist and Islamic fundamentalist groups are active
International organization participation: ABEDA, AFESD, AMF, FAO, G-77, GCC, IBRD, ICAO, ICC, ICCt (signatory), ICFTU, ICRM, IDB, IFC, IFRCS, IHO, ILO, IMF, IMO, Interpol, IOC, ISO, ITU, LAS, MIGA, NAM, OAPEC, OIC, OPCW, UN, UNCTAD, UNESCO, UNIDO, UPU, WCO, WFTU, WHO, WIPO, WMO, WToO, WTO
Diplomatic representation in the US:
chief of mission: Ambassador Nasir al-BALUSHI
chancery: 3502 International Drive NW, Washington, DC 20008
telephone: [1] (202) 342-1111
FAX: [1] (202) 362-2192
consulate(s) general: New York
Diplomatic representation from the US:
chief of mission: Ambassador William T. MONROE
embassy: Building #979, Road 3119 (next to Al-Ahli Sports Club), Block 331, Zinj District, Manama
mailing address: American Embassy Manama, PSC 451, FPO AE 09834-5100; international mail: American Embassy, Box 26431, Manama
telephone: [973] 1724-2700
FAX: [973] 1727-0547 (consular)
Flag description: red, the traditional color for flags of Persian Gulf states, with a white serrated band (five white points) on the hoist side; the five points represent the five pillars of Islam

ECONOMY

Economy - overview: Petroleum production and refining account for about 60% of Bahrain's export receipts, 60% of government revenues, and 30% of GDP. With its highly developed communication and transport facilities, Bahrain is home to numerous multinational firms with business in the Gulf. A large share of exports consists of petroleum products made from refining imported crude. Construction proceeds on several major industrial projects. Unemployment, especially among the young, and the depletion of oil and underground water resources are major long-term economic problems. In September 2004 Bahrain signed a Free Trade Agreement (FTA) with the United States - the first such agreement undertaken by a Gulf state. Both countries must ratify the FTA before it is enforced.
GDP: purchasing power parity - $14.08 billion (2005 est.)
GDP (official exchange rate): $11.58 billion (2005 est.)
GDP - real growth rate: 5.9% (2005 est.)
GDP - per capita: purchasing power parity - $20,500 (2005 est.)
GDP - composition by sector:
agriculture: 0.6%
industry: 42.5%
services: 56.9% (2005 est.)
Labor force: 380,000
note: 44% of the population in the 15-64 age group is non-national (2005 est.)
Labor force - by occupation: agriculture 1%, industry, commerce, and services 79%, government 20% (1997 est.)

Unemployment rate: 15% (1998 est.)
Population below poverty line: NA
Household income or consumption by percentage share:
lowest 10%: NA
highest 10%: NA
Inflation rate (consumer prices): 2.7% (2005 est.)
Investment (gross fixed): 14.7% of GDP (2005 est.)
Budget:
revenues: $4.662 billion
expenditures: $3.447 billion, including capital expenditures of $700 million (2005 est.)
Public debt: 51.5% of GDP (2005 est.)
Agriculture - products: fruit, vegetables; poultry, dairy products; shrimp, fish
Industries: petroleum processing and refining, aluminum smelting, iron pelletization, fertilizers, offshore banking, ship repairing; tourism
Industrial production growth rate: 2% (2000 est.)
Electricity - production: 7.345 billion kWh (2003)
Electricity – production by source:
fossil fuel: 100%
hydro: 0%
nuclear: 0%
other: 0% (2001)
Electricity - consumption: 6.83 billion kWh (2003)
Electricity - exports: 0 kWh (2003)
Electricity - imports: 0 kWh (2003)
Oil - production: 188,300 bbl/day (2005 est.)
Oil - consumption: 26,000 bbl/day (2003 est.)
Oil - exports: NA (2001)
Oil - imports: NA (2001)
Oil - proved reserves: 124 million bbl (2005 est.)
Natural gas - production: 32.7 billion cu m (2002 est.)
Natural gas - consumption: 32.7 billion cu m (2002 est.)
Natural gas - exports: 0 cu m (2002 est.)
Natural gas - imports: 0 cu m (2002 est.)
Natural gas - proved reserves: 46 billion cu m (2005)
Current account balance: $1.569 billion (2005 est.)
Exports: $11.17 billion (2005 est.)
Exports - partners: Saudi Arabia 3%, US 2.9%, UAE 2.2% (2004)
Imports: $7.83 billion (2005 est.)
Imports - partners: Saudi Arabia 32.4%, Japan 7.3%, Germany 6.1%, US 5.6%, UK 5.4%, France 4.8% (2004)
Reserves of foreign exchange and gold: $2.433 billion (2005 est.)
Debt - external: $6.831 billion (2005 est.)
Economic aid - recipient: $150 million; note - $50 million annually since 1992 from each of Saudi Arabia, UAE, and Kuwait (2002)
Currency: Bahraini dinar (BHD)
Currency code: BHD
Exchange rates: Bahraini dinars per US dollar - 0.38 (2005), 0.376 (2004), 0.376 (2003), 0.376 (2002), 0.376 (2001)
Fiscal year: calendar year

COMMUNICATIONS

Telephones - main lines in use: 185,800 (2003)
Telephones - mobile cellular: 443,100 (2003)
Telephone system:
general assessment: modern system
domestic: modern fiber-optic integrated services; digital network with rapidly growing use of mobile cellular telephones
international: country code - 973; tropospheric scatter to Qatar and UAE; microwave radio relay to Saudi Arabia; submarine cable to Qatar, UAE, and Saudi Arabia; satellite earth stations - 1 (1997)
Radio broadcast stations: AM 2, FM 3, shortwave 0 (1998)
Radios: 338,000 (1997)
Television broadcast stations: 4 (1997)
Televisions: 275,000 (1997)
Internet country code: .bh
Internet hosts: 1,334 (2003)
Internet Service Providers (ISPs): 1 (2000)
Internet users: 195,700 (2003)

TRANSPORTATION

Airports: 4 (2004 est.)
Airports - with paved runways:
total: 3
over 3,047 m: 2
1,524 to 2,437 m: 1 (2005 est.)
Heliports: 1 (2005 est.)
Pipelines: gas 20 km; oil 53 km (2004)
Roadways:
total: 3,498 km
paved: 2,768 km
unpaved: 730 km (2003)
Merchant marine:
total: 8 ships (1,000 GRT or over) 219,083 GRT/312,638 DWT
by type: bulk carrier 3, cargo 2, container 2, petroleum tanker 1
foreign-owned: 2 (Kuwait 2) (2005)
Ports and terminals: Mina' Salman, Sitrah

MILITARY

Military branches: Bahrain Defense Forces (BDF): Ground Force (includes Air Defense), Navy, Air Force, National Guard
Military manpower - military age and obligation: 18 years of age for voluntary military service (2001)
Manpower available for military service:
males age 18-49: 202,126 (2005 est.)
Manpower fit for military service: *males age 18-49:* 161,372 (2005 est.)
Manpower reaching military service age annually: *males:* 6,013 (2005 est.)
Military expenditures - dollar figure: $628.9 million (2004)
Military expenditures - percent of GDP: 6.3% (2004)

TRANSNATIONAL ISSUES

Disputes - international: none

BAKER ISLAND

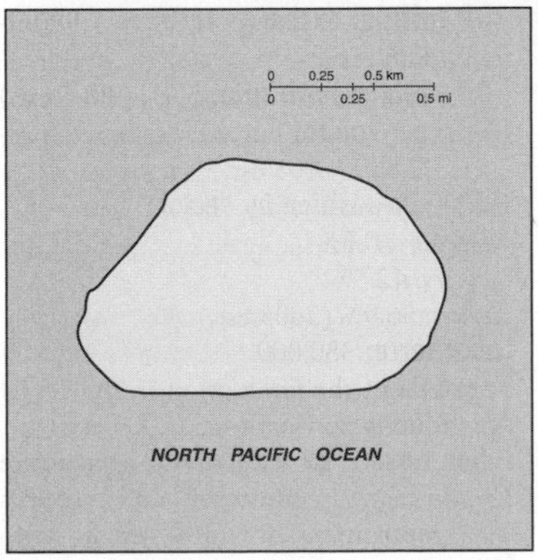

INTRODUCTION

Background: The US took possession of the island in 1857, and its guano deposits were mined by US and British companies during the second half of the 19th century. In 1935, a short-lived attempt at colonization was begun on this island - as well as on nearby Howland Island - but was disrupted by World War II and thereafter abandoned. Presently the island is a National Wildlife Refuge run by the US Department of the Interior; a day beacon is situated near the middle of the west coast.

GEOGRAPHY

Location: Oceania, atoll in the North Pacific Ocean, about half way between Hawaii and Australia
Geographic coordinates: 0 13 N, 176 28 W
Map references: Oceania
Area:
total: 1.4 sq km
land: 1.4 sq km
water: 0 sq km
Area - comparative: about 2.5 times the size of The Mall in Washington, DC
Land boundaries: 0 km
Coastline: 4.8 km

Maritime claims:
territorial sea: 12 nm
exclusive economic zone: 200 nm
Climate: equatorial; scant rainfall, constant wind, burning sun
Terrain: low, nearly level coral island surrounded by a narrow fringing reef
Elevation extremes:
lowest point: Pacific Ocean 0 m
highest point: unnamed location 8 m
Natural resources: guano (deposits worked until 1891), terrestrial and aquatic wildlife
Land use:
arable land: 0%
permanent crops: 0%
other: 100% (2001)
Irrigated land: 0 sq km (1998 est.)
Natural hazards: the narrow fringing reef surrounding the island can be a maritime hazard
Environment - current issues: no natural fresh water resources
Geography - note: treeless, sparse, and scattered vegetation consisting of grasses, prostrate vines, and low growing shrubs; primarily a nesting, roosting, and foraging habitat for seabirds, shorebirds, and marine wildlife

PEOPLE

Population: uninhabited
note: American civilians evacuated in 1942 after Japanese air and naval attacks during World War II; occupied by US military during World War II, but abandoned after the war; public entry is by special-use permit from US Fish and Wildlife Service only and generally restricted to scientists and educators; a cemetery and remnants of structures from early settlement are located near the middle of the west coast; visited annually by US Fish and Wildlife Service (2005 est.)

GOVERNMENT

Country name:
conventional long form: none
conventional short form: Baker Island
Dependency Status: unincorporated territory of the US; administered from Washington, DC, by the Fish and Wildlife Service of the US Department of the Interior as part of the National Wildlife Refuge system
Legal system: the laws of the US, where applicable, apply
Flag description: the flag of the US is used

ECONOMY

Economy - overview: no economic activity

TRANSPORTATION

Airports: 1 abandoned World War II runway of 1,665 m, completely covered with vegetation and unusable (2004 est.)
Ports and terminals: none; offshore anchorage only; note - there is one small boat landing area along the middle of the west coast
Transportation – note: there is a day beacon near the middle of the west coast

MILITARY

Military – note: defense is the responsibility of the US; visited annually by the US Coast Guard

TRANSNATIONAL ISSUES

Disputes - international: none

BANGLADESH

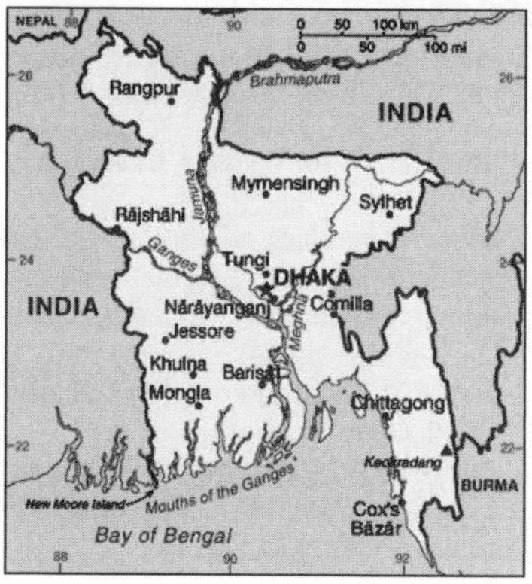

INTRODUCTION

Background: Bangladesh came into existence in 1971 when Bengali East Pakistan seceded from its union with West Pakistan. About a third of this extremely poor country floods annually during the monsoon rainy season, hampering economic development.

GEOGRAPHY

Location: Southern Asia, bordering the Bay of Bengal, between Burma and India
Geographic coordinates: 24 00 N, 90 00 E
Map references: Asia
Area:
total: 144,000 sq km
land: 133,910 sq km
water: 10,090 sq km
Area - comparative: slightly smaller than Iowa
Land boundaries:
total: 4,246 km
border countries: Burma 193 km, India 4,053 km
Coastline: 580 km
Maritime claims:
territorial sea: 12 nm
contiguous zone: 18 nm
exclusive economic zone: 200 nm
continental shelf: up to the outer limits of the continental margin
Climate: tropical; mild winter (October to March); hot, humid summer (March to June); humid, warm rainy monsoon (June to October)
Terrain: mostly flat alluvial plain; hilly in southeast
Elevation extremes:
lowest point: Indian Ocean 0 m
highest point: Keokradong 1,230 m
Natural resources: natural gas, arable land, timber, coal
Land use:
arable land: 62.11%
permanent crops: 3.07%
other: 34.82% (2001)
Irrigated land: 38,440 sq km (1998 est.)
Natural hazards: droughts, cyclones; much of the country routinely inundated during the summer monsoon season
Environment - current issues: many people are landless and forced to live on and cultivate flood-prone land; water-borne diseases prevalent in surface water; water pollution, especially of fishing areas, results from the use of commercial pesticides; ground water contaminated by naturally occurring arsenic; intermittent water shortages because of falling water tables in the northern and central parts of the country; soil degradation and erosion; deforestation; severe overpopulation
Environment - international agreements:
party to: Biodiversity, Climate Change, Climate Change-Kyoto Protocol, Desertification, Endangered Species, Environmental Modification, Hazardous Wastes, Law of the Sea, Ozone Layer Protection, Wetlands
signed, but not ratified: none of the selected agreements
Geography - note: most of the country is situated on deltas of large rivers flowing from the Himalayas: the Ganges unites with the Jamuna (main channel of the Brahmaputra) and later joins the Meghna to eventually empty into the Bay of Bengal

PEOPLE

Population: 144,319,628 (July 2005 est.)
Age structure:
0-14 years: 33.1% (male 24,590,207/female 23,162,420)
15-64 years: 63.5% (male 46,764,824/

female 44,868,733)
65 years and over: 3.4% (male 2,650,683/female 2,282,761) (2005 est.)
Median age:
total: 21.87 years
male: 21.88 years
female: 21.85 years (2005 est.)
Population growth rate: 2.09% (2005 est.)
Birth rate: 30.01 births/1,000 population (2005 est.)
Death rate: 8.4 deaths/1,000 population (2005 est.)
Net migration rate: -0.69 migrant(s)/1,000 population (2005 est.)
Sex ratio:
at birth: 1.06 male(s)/female
under 15 years: 1.06 male(s)/female
15-64 years: 1.04 male(s)/female
65 years and over: 1.16 male(s)/female
total population: 1.05 male(s)/female (2005 est.)
Infant mortality rate:
total: 62.6 deaths/1,000 live births
male: 63.65 deaths/1,000 live births
female: 61.48 deaths/1,000 live births (2005 est.)
Life expectancy at birth:
total population: 62.08 years
male: 62.13 years
female: 62.02 years (2005 est.)
Total fertility rate: 3.13 children born/woman (2005 est.)
HIV/AIDS - adult prevalence rate: less than 0.1% (2001 est.)
HIV/AIDS - people living with HIV/AIDS: 13,000 (2001 est.)
HIV/AIDS - deaths: 650 (2001 est.)
Major infectious diseases:
degree of risk: high
food or waterborne diseases: bacterial diarrhea, hepatitis A and E, and typhoid fever
vectorborne diseases: dengue fever and malaria are high risks in some locations
water contact disease: leptospirosis
animal contact disease: rabies (2004)
Nationality:
noun: Bangladeshi(s)
adjective: Bangladeshi
Ethnic groups: Bengali 98%, tribal groups, non-Bengali Muslims (1998)
Religions: Muslim 83%, Hindu 16%, other 1% (1998)
Languages: Bangla (official, also known as Bengali), English
Literacy:
definition: age 15 and over can read and write
total population: 43.1%
male: 53.9%
female: 31.8% (2003 est.)

GOVERNMENT

Country name:
conventional long form: People's Republic of Bangladesh
conventional short form: Bangladesh
former: East Pakistan
Government type: parliamentary democracy
Capital: Dhaka
Administrative divisions: 6 divisions; Barisal, Chittagong, Dhaka, Khulna, Rajshahi, and Sylhet
Independence: 16 December 1971 (from West Pakistan); note - 26 March 1971 is the date of independence from West Pakistan, 16 December 1971 is known as Victory Day and commemorates the official creation of the state of Bangladesh
National holiday: Independence Day, 26 March (1971); note - 26 March 1971 is the date of independence from West Pakistan, 16 December 1971 is Victory Day and commemorates the official creation of the state of Bangladesh
Constitution: 4 November 1972, effective 16 December 1972; suspended following coup of 24 March 1982, restored 10 November 1986; amended many times
Legal system: based on English common law
Suffrage: 18 years of age; universal
Executive branch:
chief of state: President Iajuddin AHMED (since 6 September 2002); note - the president's duties are normally ceremonial, but with the 13th amendment to the constitution ("Caretaker Government Amendment"), the president's role becomes significant at times when Parliament is dissolved and a caretaker government is installed - at presidential direction - to supervise the elections
head of government: Prime Minister Khaleda ZIA (since 10 October 2001)
cabinet: Cabinet selected by the prime minister and appointed by the president
elections: president elected by National Parliament for a five-year term; election scheduled for 16 September 2002 was not held since Iajuddin AHMED was the only presidential candidate; he was sworn in on 6 September 2002 (next election to be held by NA 2007); following legislative elections, the leader of the party that wins the most seats is usually appointed prime minister by the president
election results: Iajuddin AHMED declared by the Election Commission elected unopposed as president; percent of National Parliament vote - NA
Legislative branch: unicameral National Parliament or Jatiya Sangsad; 300 seats elected by popular vote from single territorial constituencies (the constitutional amendment reserving 30 seats for women over and above the 300 regular parliament seats expired in May 2001); members serve five-year terms
elections: last held 1 October 2001 (next to be held no later than January 2007)
election results: percent of vote by party - BNP and alliance partners 41%, AL 40%; seats by party - BNP 193, AL 58, JI 17, JP (Ershad faction) 14, IOJ 2, JP (Manzur) 4, other 8; note - the election of October 2001 brought a majority BNP government aligned with three other smaller parties - Jamaat-e-Islami, Islami Oikya Jote, and Jatiya Party (Manzur)
Judicial branch: Supreme Court (the chief justices and other judges are appointed by the president)
Political parties and leaders: Awami League or AL [Sheikh HASINA]; Bangladesh Communist Party or BCP [Saifuddin Ahmed MANIK]; Bangladesh Nationalist Party or BNP [Khaleda ZIA]; Islami Oikya Jote or IOJ [Mufti Fazlul Haq AMINI]; Jamaat-e-Islami or JI [Motiur Rahman NIZAMI]; Jatiya Party or JP (Ershad faction) [Hussain Mohammad ERSHAD]; Jatiya Party (Manzur faction) [Naziur Rahman MANZUR]
Political pressure groups and leaders: NA
International organization participation: AsDB, C, CP, FAO, G-77, IAEA, IBRD, ICAO, ICC, ICCt (signatory), ICFTU, ICRM, IDA, IDB, IFAD, IFC, IFRCS, IHO, ILO, IMF, IMO, Interpol, IOC, IOM, ISO, ITU, MIGA, MINURSO, MONUC, NAM, OIC, ONUB, OPCW, SAARC, SACEP, UN, UNAMSIL, UNCTAD, UNESCO, UNHCR, UNIDO, UNMEE, UNMIL, UNMIS, UNOCI, UNOMIG, UPU, WCL, WCO, WFTU, WHO, WIPO, WMO, WToO, WTO
Diplomatic representation in the US:
chief of mission: Ambassador Shamsher Mobin CHOWDHURY
chancery: 3510 International Drive NW, Washington, DC 20008
telephone: [1] (202) 244-0183
FAX: [1] (202) 244-5366
consulate(s) general: Los Angeles and New York
Diplomatic representation from the US:
chief of mission: Charge d'Affaires Ms. Judith CHAMMAS
embassy: Madani Avenue, Baridhara, Dhaka 1212
mailing address: G. P. O. Box 323, Dhaka 1000
telephone: [880] (2) 885-5500
FAX: [880] (2) 882-3744
Flag description: green with a large red disk slightly to the hoist side of center; the red sun of freedom represents the blood shed to achieve independence; the green field symbolizes the lush countryside, and secondarily, the traditional color of Islam

ECONOMY

Economy - overview: Despite sustained domestic and international efforts to improve economic and demographic prospects, Bangladesh remains a poor, overpopulated, and ill-governed nation. Although half of GDP is generated through the service sector, nearly two-thirds of Bangladeshis are employed in the agriculture sector, with rice as the single-most-important product. Major impediments to growth include frequent cyclones and floods, inefficient state-owned enterprises, inadequate port facilities, a rapidly growing labor force that cannot be absorbed by agriculture, delays in exploiting energy resources (natural gas), insufficient power supplies, and slow implementation of economic reforms. Economic reform is stalled in many instances by political infighting and corruption at all levels of government. Progress also has been blocked by opposition from the bureaucracy, public sector unions, and other vested interest groups. The BNP government, led by Prime Minister Khaleda ZIA, has the parliamentary strength to push through needed reforms, but the party's political will to do so has been lacking in key areas. One encouraging note: growth has been a steady 5% for the past several years.
GDP: purchasing power parity - $299.9 billion (2005 est.)
GDP (official exchange rate): $64.85 billion (2005 est.)
GDP - real growth rate: 5.2% (2005 est.)
GDP - per capita: purchasing power parity - $2,100 (2005 est.)
GDP - composition by sector:
agriculture: 20.5%
industry: 26.7%
services: 52.8% (2004 est.)
Labor force: 66.6 million
note: extensive export of labor to Saudi Arabia, Kuwait, UAE, Oman, Qatar, and Malaysia; workers' remittances estimated at $1.71 billion in 1998-99 (2005 est.)
Labor force - by occupation: agriculture 63%, industry 11%, services 26% (FY95/96)
Unemployment rate: 2.5% (includes underemployment) (2005 est.)
Population below poverty line: 45% (2004 est.)
Household income or consumption by percentage share:
lowest 10%: 3.9%
highest 10%: 28.6% (1995-96 est.)
Distribution of family income - Gini index: 31.8 (2000)
Inflation rate (consumer prices): 6.7% (2005 est.)
Investment (gross fixed): 24.6% of GDP (2005 est.)
Budget:
revenues: $5.993 billion
expenditures: $8.598 billion, including capital expenditures of NA (2005 est.)
Public debt: 46.1% of GDP (2005 est.)
Agriculture - products: rice, jute, tea, wheat, sugarcane, potatoes, tobacco, pulses, oilseeds, spices, fruit; beef, milk, poultry
Industries: cotton textiles, jute, garments, tea processing, paper newsprint, cement, chemical fertilizer, light engineering, sugar
Industrial production growth rate: 6.7% (2005 est.)
Electricity - production: 17.42 billion kWh (2003)
Electricity – production by source:
fossil fuel: 93.7%
hydro: 6.3%
nuclear: 0%
other: 0% (2001)
Electricity - consumption: 16.2 billion kWh (2003)
Electricity - exports: 0 kWh (2003)
Electricity - imports: 0 kWh (2003)
Oil - production: 6,825 bbl/day (2003)
Oil - consumption: 84,000 bbl/day (2003 est.)
Oil - exports: NA (2001)
Oil - imports: NA (2001)
Oil - proved reserves: 28.45 million bbl (1 January 2002)
Natural gas - production: 9.9 billion cu m (2001 est.)
Natural gas - consumption: 9.9 billion cu m (2001 est.)
Natural gas - exports: 0 cu m (2001 est.)
Natural gas - imports: 0 cu m (2001 est.)
Natural gas - proved reserves: 150.3 billion cu m (1 January 2002)
Current account balance: $-591 million (2005 est.)
Exports: $9.372 billion (2005 est.)
Exports - partners: US 22.4%, Germany 14.5%, UK 11.2%, France 6.9%, Italy 4% (2004)
Imports: $12.97 billion (2005 est.)
Imports - partners: India 15.1%, China 12.5%, Singapore 7.5%, Kuwait 5.5%, Japan 5.3%, Hong Kong 4.5% (2004)
Reserves of foreign exchange and gold: $3.45 billion (2005 est.)
Debt - external: $21.25 billion (2005 est.)
Economic aid - recipient: $1.575 billion (2000 est.)
Currency: taka (BDT)
Currency code: BDT
Exchange rates: taka per US dollar - 64.26 (2005), 59.513 (2004), 58.15 (2003), 57.888 (2002), 55.807 (2001)
Fiscal year: 1 July - 30 June

COMMUNICATIONS

Telephones - main lines in use: 740,000 (2003)
Telephones - mobile cellular: 1.365 million (2003)
Telephone system:
general assessment: totally inadequate for a modern country
domestic: modernizing; introducing digital systems; trunk systems include VHF and UHF microwave radio relay links, and some fiber-optic cable in cities
international: country code - 880; satellite earth stations - 6; international radiotelephone communications and landline service to neighboring countries (2005)
Radio broadcast stations: AM 12, FM 12, shortwave 2 (1999)
Radios: 6.15 million (1997)
Television broadcast stations: 15 (1999)
Televisions: 770,000 (1997)
Internet country code: .bd
Internet hosts: 1 (2003)
Internet Service Providers (ISPs): 10 (2000)
Internet users: 243,000 (2003)

TRANSPORTATION

Airports: 16 (2004 est.)
Airports - with paved runways:
total: 15
over 3,047 m: 1
2,438 to 3,047 m: 4
1,524 to 2,437 m: 4
914 to 1,523 m: 1
under 914 m: 5 (2005 est.)
Airports - with unpaved runways:
total: 1
1,524 to 2,437 m: 1 (2005 est.)
Pipelines: gas 2,012 km (2004)
Railways:
total: 2,706 km
broad gauge: 884 km 1.676-m gauge
narrow gauge: 1,822 km 1.000-m gauge (2004)
Roadways:
total: 239,226 km
paved: 22,726 km
unpaved: 216,500 km (2003)
Waterways: 8,372 km
note: includes 2,575 km main cargo routes (2004)
Merchant marine:
total: 41 ships (1,000 GRT or over) 319,897 GRT/440,575 DWT
by type: bulk carrier 2, cargo 28, container 6, passenger/cargo 1, petroleum tanker 4
foreign-owned: 10 (China 1, Singapore 9)
registered in other countries: 14 (2005)
Ports and terminals: Chittagong, Mongla Port

MILITARY

Military branches: Army, Navy, Air Force
Military service age and obligation: 18 years of age for voluntary military service; no conscription (2005)
Manpower available for military service:
males age 18-49: 35,170,019 (2005 est.)
Manpower fit for military service: *males*

age 18-49: 26,841,255 (2005 est.)
Military expenditures - dollar figure: $995.3 million (2004)
Military expenditures - percent of GDP: 1.8% (2004)

TRANSNATIONAL ISSUES

Disputes - international: discussions with India remain stalled to delimit a small section of river boundary, exchange 162 miniscule enclaves in both countries, allocate divided villages, and stop illegal cross-border trade, migration, violence, and transit of terrorists through the porous border; Bangladesh protests India's attempts to fence off high-traffic sections of the porous boundary; a joint Bangladesh-India boundary inspection in 2005 revealed 92 pillars are missing; dispute with India over New Moore/South Talpatty/Purbasha Island in the Bay of Bengal deters maritime boundary delimitation; Burmese Muslim refugees strain Bangladesh's meager resources
Refugees and internally displaced persons: *IDPs:* 61,000 (land conflicts, religious persecution) (2004)
Illicit drugs: transit country for illegal drugs produced in neighboring countries

BARBADOS

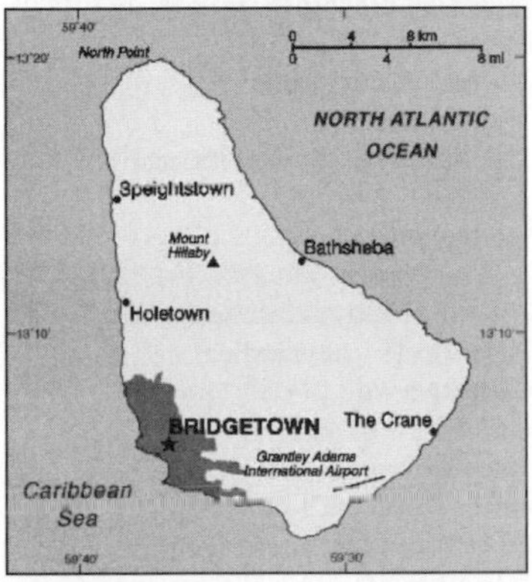

INTRODUCTION

Background: The island was uninhabited when first settled by the British in 1627. Slaves worked the sugar plantations established on the island until 1834 when slavery was abolished. The economy remained heavily dependent on sugar, rum, and molasses production through most of the 20th century. The gradual introduction of social and political reforms in the 1940s and 1950s led to complete independence from the UK in 1966. In the 1990s, tourism and manufacturing surpassed the sugar industry in economic importance.

GEOGRAPHY

Location: Caribbean, island in the North Atlantic Ocean, northeast of Venezuela
Geographic coordinates: 13 10 N, 59 32 W
Map references: Central America and the Caribbean
Area:
total: 431 sq km
land: 431 sq km
water: 0 sq km
Area - comparative: 2.5 times the size of Washington, DC
Land boundaries: 0 km
Coastline: 97 km
Maritime claims:
territorial sea: 12 nm
exclusive economic zone: 200 nm
Climate: tropical; rainy season (June to October)
Terrain: relatively flat; rises gently to central highland region
Elevation extremes:
lowest point: Atlantic Ocean 0 m
highest point: Mount Hillaby 336 m
Natural resources: petroleum, fish, natural gas
Land use:
arable land: 37.21%
permanent crops: 2.33%
other: 60.46% (2001)
Irrigated land: 10 sq km (1998 est.)
Natural hazards: infrequent hurricanes; periodic landslides
Environment - current issues: pollution of coastal waters from waste disposal by ships; soil erosion; illegal solid waste disposal threatens contamination of aquifers
Environment - international agreements:
party to: Biodiversity, Climate Change, Climate Change-Kyoto Protocol, Desertification, Endangered Species, Hazardous Wastes, Law of the Sea, Marine Dumping, Ozone Layer Protection, Ship Pollution
signed, but not ratified: none of the selected agreements
Geography - note: easternmost Caribbean island

PEOPLE

Population: 279,254 (July 2005 est.)
Age structure:
0-14 years: 20.6% (male 28,813/female 28,634)
15-64 years: 70.6% (male 96,590/female 100,622)
65 years and over: 8.8% (male 9,432/female 15,163) (2005 est.)
Median age:
total: 34.15 years
male: 32.99 years
female: 35.28 years (2005 est.)
Population growth rate: 0.33% (2005 est.)
Birth rate: 12.83 births/1,000 population (2005 est.)
Death rate: 9.17 deaths/1,000 population (2005 est.)
Net migration rate: -0.31 migrant(s)/1,000 population (2005 est.)
Sex ratio:
at birth: 1.01 male(s)/female
under 15 years: 1.01 male(s)/female
15-64 years: 0.96 male(s)/female
65 years and over: 0.62 male(s)/female
total population: 0.93 male(s)/female (2005 est.)
Infant mortality rate:
total: 12.5 deaths/1,000 live births
male: 14.14 deaths/1,000 live births
female: 10.83 deaths/1,000 live births (2005 est.)
Life expectancy at birth:
total population: 72.59 years
male: 70.6 years
female: 74.6 years (2005 est.)
Total fertility rate: 1.65 children born/woman (2005 est.)
HIV/AIDS - adult prevalence rate: 1.5% (2003 est.)
HIV/AIDS - people living with HIV/AIDS: 2,500 (2003 est.)
HIV/AIDS - deaths: less than 200 (2003 est.)
Nationality:
noun: Barbadian(s) or Bajan (colloquial)
adjective: Barbadian or Bajan (colloquial)
Ethnic groups: black 90%, white 4%, Asian and mixed 6%
Religions: Protestant 67% (Anglican 40%, Pentecostal 8%, Methodist 7%, other 12%), Roman Catholic 4%, none 17%, other 12%
Languages: English
Literacy:
definition: age 15 and over has ever attended school
total population: 99.7%
male: 99.7%
female: 99.7% (2002 est.)

GOVERNMENT

Country name:
conventional long form: none
conventional short form: Barbados
Government type: parliamentary democracy; independent sovereign state within the Commonwealth
Capital: Bridgetown
Administrative divisions: 11 parishes; Christ Church, Saint Andrew, Saint George, Saint James, Saint John, Saint

Joseph, Saint Lucy, Saint Michael, Saint Peter, Saint Philip, Saint Thomas; note - the city of Bridgetown may be given parish status
Independence: 30 November 1966 (from UK)
National holiday: Independence Day, 30 November (1966)
Constitution: 30 November 1966
Legal system: English common law; no judicial review of legislative acts
Suffrage: 18 years of age; universal
Executive branch:
chief of state: Queen ELIZABETH II (since 6 February 1952), represented by Governor General Sir Clifford Straughn HUSBANDS (since 1 June 1996)
head of government: Prime Minister Owen Seymour ARTHUR (since 7 September 1994); Deputy Prime Minister Mia MOTTLEY (since 26 May 2003)
cabinet: Cabinet appointed by the governor general on the advice of the prime minister
elections: none; the monarch is hereditary; governor general appointed by the monarch; following legislative elections, the leader of the majority party or the leader of the majority coalition is usually appointed prime minister by the governor general; the prime minister recommends the deputy prime minister
Legislative branch: bicameral Parliament consists of the Senate (21-member body appointed by the governor general) and the House of Assembly (30 seats; members are elected by direct popular vote to serve five-year terms)
elections: House of Assembly - last held 21 May 2003 (next to be held by May 2008)
election results: House of Assembly - percent of vote by party - NA%; seats by party - BLP 23, DLP 7
Judicial branch: Supreme Court of Judicature (judges are appointed by the Service Commissions for the Judicial and Legal Services)
Political parties and leaders: Barbados Labor Party or BLP [Owen ARTHUR]; Democratic Labor Party or DLP [Clyde MASCOLL]
Political pressure groups and leaders: Barbados Workers Union [Leroy TROTMAN]; Clement Payne Labor Union [David COMMISSIONG]; People's Progressive Movement [Eric SEALY]; Worker's Party of Barbados [Dr. George BELLE]
International organization participation: ACP, C, Caricom, CDB, FAO, G-77, IADB, IBRD, ICAO, ICCt, ICFTU, ICRM, IDA, IFAD, IFC, IFRCS, ILO, IMF, IMO, Interpol, IOC, ISO, ITU, LAES, MIGA, NAM, OAS, OPANAL, UN, UNCTAD, UNESCO, UNIDO, UPU, WCO, WFTU, WHO, WIPO, WMO, WTO
Diplomatic representation in the US:
chief of mission: Ambassador Michael Ian KING
chancery: 2144 Wyoming Avenue NW, Washington, DC 20008
telephone: [1] (202) 939-9200
FAX: [1] (202) 332-7467
consulate(s) general: Miami and New York
consulate(s): Los Angeles
Diplomatic representation from the US:
chief of mission: Ambassador Mary E. KRAMER
embassy: Canadian Imperial Bank of Commerce Building, Broad Street, Bridgetown; (courier) ALICO Building-Cheapside, Bridgetown
mailing address: P. O. Box 302, Bridgetown; CMR 1014, APO AA 34055
telephone: [1] (246) 436-4950
FAX: [1] (246) 429-5246, 429-3379
Flag description: three equal vertical bands of blue (hoist side), gold, and blue with the head of a black trident centered on the gold band; the trident head represents independence and a break with the past (the colonial coat of arms contained a complete trident)

ECONOMY

Economy - overview: Historically, the Barbadian economy had been dependent on sugarcane cultivation and related activities, but production in recent years has diversified into light industry and tourism. Offshore finance and information services are important foreign exchange earners. The government continues its efforts to reduce unemployment, to encourage direct foreign investment, and to privatize remaining state-owned enterprises. The economy contracted in 2002-03 mainly due to a decline in tourism. Growth was positive in 2005, as economic conditions in the US and Europe moderately improved.
GDP: purchasing power parity - $4.831 billion (2005 est.)
GDP (official exchange rate): $3.051 billion (2005 est.)
GDP - real growth rate: 2.5% (2005 est.)
GDP - per capita: purchasing power parity - $17,300 (2005 est.)
GDP - composition by sector:
agriculture: 6%
industry: 16%
services: 78% (2000 est.)
Labor force: 128,500 (2001 est.)
Labor force - by occupation: agriculture 10%, industry 15%, services 75% (1996 est.)
Unemployment rate: 10.7% (2003 est.)
Population below poverty line: NA
Household income or consumption by percentage share:
lowest 10%: NA
highest 10%: NA
Inflation rate (consumer prices): -0.5% (2003 est.)
Budget:
revenues: $847 million (including grants)
expenditures: $886 million, including capital expenditures of NA (2000 est.)
Agriculture - products: sugarcane, vegetables, cotton
Industries: tourism, sugar, light manufacturing, component assembly for export
Industrial production growth rate: -3.2% (2000 est.)
Electricity - production: 819 million kWh (2003)
Electricity – production by source:
fossil fuel: 100%
hydro: 0%
nuclear: 0%
other: 0% (2001)
Electricity - consumption: 761.7 million kWh (2003)
Electricity - exports: 0 kWh (2003)
Electricity - imports: 0 kWh (2003)
Oil - production: 1,000 bbl/day (2003)
Oil - consumption: 10,000 bbl/day (2003 est.)
Oil - exports: NA (2001)
Oil - imports: NA (2001)
Oil - proved reserves: 1.254 million bbl (1 January 2002)
Natural gas - production: 29.17 million cu m (2001 est.)
Natural gas - consumption: 29.17 million cu m (2001 est.)
Natural gas - exports: 0 cu m (2001 est.)
Natural gas - imports: 0 cu m (2001 est.)
Natural gas - proved reserves: 70.79 million cu m (1 January 2002)
Exports: $209 million (2004 est.)
Exports - partners: US 20.6%, UK 14.5%, Trinidad and Tobago 13.9%, Saint Lucia 6.9%, Jamaica 6.6%, Saint Vincent and the Grenadines 5.1% (2004)
Imports: $1.476 billion (2004 est.)
Imports - partners: US 35.2%, Trinidad and Tobago 20%, UK 5.6%, Japan 4.3% (2004)
Debt - external: $668 million (2003)
Economic aid - recipient: $9.1 million (1995)
Currency: Barbadian dollar (BBD)
Currency code: BBD
Exchange rates: Barbadian dollars per US dollar - NA (2005), 2 (2004), 2 (2003), 2 (2002), 2 (2001)
Fiscal year: 1 April - 31 March

COMMUNICATIONS

Telephones - main lines in use: 134,000 (2003)
Telephones - mobile cellular: 140,000 (2003)

Telephone system:
general assessment: NA
domestic: island-wide automatic telephone system
international: country code - 1-246; satellite earth stations - 1 (Intelsat -Atlantic Ocean); tropospheric scatter to Trinidad and Saint Lucia
Radio broadcast stations: AM 2, FM 6, shortwave 0 (2004)
Radios: 237,000 (1997)
Television broadcast stations: 1 (plus two cable channels) (2004)
Televisions: 76,000 (1997)
Internet country code: .bb
Internet hosts: 204 (2003)
Internet Service Providers (ISPs): 19 (2000)
Internet users: 100,000 (2003)

TRANSPORTATION

Airports: 1 (2004 est.)
Airports - with paved runways:
total: 1
over 3,047 m: 1 (2005 est.)
Roadways:
total: 1,600 km
paved: 1,600 km (2003)
Merchant marine:
total: 58 ships (1,000 GRT or over) 427,465 GRT/668,195 DWT
by type: bulk carrier 14, cargo 31, chemical tanker 6, passenger/cargo 1, petroleum tanker 3, roll on/roll off 2, specialized tanker 1
foreign-owned: 53 (Bahamas 1, Bangladesh 1, Canada 12, Greece 11, Lebanon 2, Netherlands 1, Norway 17, UAE 1, United Kingdom 7)
registered in other countries: 1 (2005)
Ports and terminals: Bridgetown

MILITARY

Military branches: Royal Barbados Defense Force: Troops Command and Coast Guard (2005)
Military service age and obligation: 18 years of age for voluntary military service; volunteers at earlier age with parental consent; no conscription (2001)
Manpower available for military service:
males age 18-49: 71,330 (2005 est.)
Manpower fit for military service: *males age 18-49:* 51,298 (2005 est.)
Military expenditures - dollar figure: NA
Military expenditures - percent of GDP: NA
Military - note: the Royal Barbados Defense Force includes a land-based Troop Command and a small Coast Guard; the primary role of the land element is to defend the island against external aggression; the Command consists of a single, part-time battalion with a small regular cadre that is deployed throughout the island; it increasingly supports the police in patrolling the coastline to prevent smuggling and other illicit activities (2005)

TRANSNATIONAL ISSUES

Disputes - international: in 2005, Barbados and Trinidad and Tobago agreed to compulsory international arbitration that will result in a binding award challenging whether the northern limit of Trinidad and Tobago's and Venezuela's maritime boundary extends into Barbadian waters and the southern limit of Barbadian traditional fishing; joins other Caribbean states to counter Venezuela's claim that Aves Island sustains human habitation, a criterion under UNCLOS, which permits Venezuela to extend its EEZ/continental shelf over a large portion of the Caribbean Sea
Illicit drugs: one of many Caribbean transshipment points for narcotics bound for Europe and the US; offshore financial center

BASSAS DA INDIA

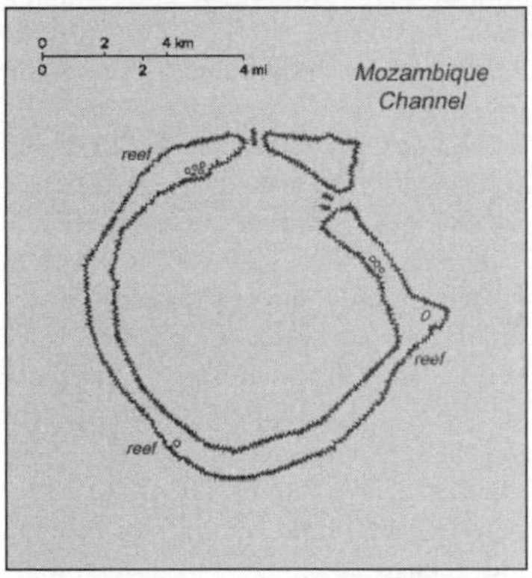

INTRODUCTION

Background: This atoll is a volcanic rock surrounded by reefs and is awash at high tide. A French possession since 1897, it was placed under the administration of a commissioner residing in Reunion in 1968.

GEOGRAPHY

Location: Southern Africa, islands in the southern Mozambique Channel, about one-half of the way from Madagascar to Mozambique
Geographic coordinates: 21 30 S, 39 50 E
Map references: Africa
Area:
total: 0.2 sq km
land: 0.2 sq km
water: 0 sq km
Area - comparative: about one-third the size of The Mall in Washington, DC
Land boundaries: 0 km
Coastline: 35.2 km
Maritime claims:
territorial sea: 12 nm
exclusive economic zone: 200 nm
Climate: tropical
Terrain: volcanic rock
Elevation extremes:
lowest point: Indian Ocean 0 m
highest point: unnamed location 2.4 m
Natural resources: none
Land use:
arable land: 0%
permanent crops: 0%
other: 100% (all rock) (2001)
Irrigated land: 0 sq km (1998 est.)
Natural hazards: maritime hazard since it is usually under water during high tide and surrounded by reefs; subject to periodic cyclones
Environment - current issues: NA
Geography - note: the islands emerge from a circular reef that sits atop a long-extinct, submerged volcano

PEOPLE

Population: uninhabited (July 2005 est.)

GOVERNMENT

Country name:
conventional long form: none
conventional short form: Bassas da India
Dependency Status: possession of France; administered by the Administrateur Superieur of the French Southern and Antarctic Lands
Legal system: the laws of France, where applicable, apply
Flag description: the flag of France is used

ECONOMY

Economy - overview: no economic activity

TRANSPORTATION

Ports and terminals: none; offshore anchorage only

MILITARY

Military – note: defense is the responsibility of France

TRANSNATIONAL ISSUES

Disputes - international: claimed by Madagascar

BELARUS

INTRODUCTION

Background: After seven decades as a constituent republic of the USSR, Belarus attained its independence in 1991. It has retained closer political and economic ties to Russia than any of the other former Soviet republics. Belarus and Russia signed a treaty on a two-state union on 8 December 1999 envisioning greater political and economic integration. Although Belarus agreed to a framework to carry out the accord, serious implementation has yet to take place. Since his election in July 1995 as the country's first president, Alexander LUKASHENKO has steadily consolidated his power through authoritarian means. Government restrictions on freedom of speech and the press, peaceful assembly, and religion continue.

GEOGRAPHY

Location: Eastern Europe, east of Poland
Geographic coordinates: 53 00 N, 28 00 E
Map references: Europe
Area:
total: 207,600 sq km
land: 207,600 sq km
water: 0 sq km
Area - comparative: slightly smaller than Kansas
Land boundaries:
total: 2,900 km
border countries: Latvia 141 km, Lithuania 502 km, Poland 407 km, Russia 959 km, Ukraine 891 km
Coastline: 0 km (landlocked)
Maritime claims: none (landlocked)
Climate: cold winters, cool and moist summers; transitional between continental and maritime
Terrain: generally flat and contains much marshland
Elevation extremes:
lowest point: Nyoman River 90 m
highest point: Dzyarzhynskaya Hara 346 m
Natural resources: forests, peat deposits, small quantities of oil and natural gas, granite, dolomitic limestone, marl, chalk, sand, gravel, clay
Land use:
arable land: 29.55%
permanent crops: 0.6%
other: 69.85% (2001)
Irrigated land: 1,150 sq km (1998 est.)
Natural hazards: NA
Environment - current issues: soil pollution from pesticide use; southern part of the country contaminated with fallout from 1986 nuclear reactor accident at Chornobyl' in northern Ukraine
Environment - international agreements:
party to: Air Pollution, Air Pollution-Nitrogen Oxides, Air Pollution-Sulfur 85, Biodiversity, Climate Change, Desertification, Endangered Species, Environmental Modification, Hazardous Wastes, Marine Dumping, Ozone Layer Protection, Ship Pollution, Wetlands
signed, but not ratified: Law of the Sea
Geography - note: landlocked; glacial scouring accounts for the flatness of Belarusian terrain and for its 11,000 lakes; the country is geologically well endowed with extensive deposits of granite, dolomitic limestone, marl, chalk, sand, gravel, and clay

PEOPLE

Population: 10,300,483 (July 2005 est.)
Age structure:
0-14 years: 16% (male 839,292/female 804,738)
15-64 years: 69.5% (male 3,481,432/female 3,672,991)
65 years and over: 14.6% (male 498,717/female 1,003,313) (2005 est.)
Median age:
total: 37.03 years
male: 34.32 years
female: 39.7 years (2005 est.)
Population growth rate: -0.09% (2005 est.)
Birth rate: 10.83 births/1,000 population (2005 est.)
Death rate: 14.15 deaths/1,000 population (2005 est.)
Net migration rate: 2.42 migrant(s)/1,000 population (2005 est.)
Sex ratio:
at birth: 1.05 male(s)/female
under 15 years: 1.04 male(s)/female
15-64 years: 0.95 male(s)/female
65 years and over: 0.5 male(s)/female
total population: 0.88 male(s)/female (2005 est.)
Infant mortality rate:
total: 13.37 deaths/1,000 live births
male: 14.3 deaths/1,000 live births
female: 12.39 deaths/1,000 live births (2005 est.)
Life expectancy at birth:
total population: 68.72 years
male: 63.03 years
female: 74.69 years (2005 est.)
Total fertility rate: 1.39 children born/woman (2005 est.)
HIV/AIDS - adult prevalence rate: 0.3% (2001 est.)
HIV/AIDS - people living with HIV/AIDS: 15,000 (2001 est.)
HIV/AIDS - deaths: 1,000 (2001 est.)
Nationality:
noun: Belarusian(s)
adjective: Belarusian
Ethnic groups: Belarusian 81.2%, Russian 11.4%, Polish 3.9%, Ukrainian 2.4%, other 1.1% (1999 census)
Religions: Eastern Orthodox 80%, other (including Roman Catholic, Protestant, Jewish, and Muslim) 20% (1997 est.)
Languages: Belarusian, Russian, other
Literacy:
definition: age 15 and over can read and write
total population: 99.6%
male: 99.8%
female: 99.5% (2003 est.)

GOVERNMENT

Country name:
conventional long form: Republic of Belarus
conventional short form: Belarus
local long form: Respublika Byelarus'
local short form: none
former: Belorussian (Byelorussian) Soviet Socialist Republic
Government type: republic in name, although in fact a dictatorship
Capital: Minsk
Administrative divisions: 6 provinces (voblastsi, singular - voblasts') and 1 municipality* (horad); Brest, Homyel', Horad Minsk*, Hrodna, Mahilyow, Minsk, Vitsyebsk
note: administrative divisions have the same names as their administrative centers
Independence: 25 August 1991 (from Soviet Union)
National holiday: Independence Day, 3 July (1944); note - 3 July 1944 was the date Minsk was liberated from German troops, 25 August 1991 was the date of independence from the Soviet Union
Constitution: 15 March 1994; revised by national referendum of 24 November 1996 giving the presidency greatly expanded powers and became effective 27 November 1996; revised again 17 October 2004 removing presidential term limits
Legal system: based on civil law system
Suffrage: 18 years of age; universal

Executive branch:
chief of state: President Aleksandr LUKASHENKO (since 20 July 1994)
head of government: Prime Minister Sergei SIDORSKY (since 19 December 2003); First Deputy Prime Minister Vladimir SEMASHKO (since December 2003)
cabinet: Council of Ministers
elections: president elected by popular vote for a five-year term; first election took place 23 June and 10 July 1994; according to the 1994 constitution, the next election should have been held in 1999, however LUKASHENKO extended his term to 2001 via a November 1996 referendum; new election held 9 September 2001; October 2004 referendum ended presidential term limits allowing president to run for a third term in September 2006; prime minister and deputy prime ministers appointed by the president
election results: Aleksandr LUKASHENKO reelected president; percent of vote - Aleksandr LUKASHENKO 75.6%, Vladimir GONCHARIK 15.4%

Legislative branch: bicameral National Assembly or Natsionalnoye Sobranie consists of the Council of the Republic or Soviet Respubliki (64 seats; 56 members elected by regional councils and 8 members appointed by the president, all for 4-year terms) and the Chamber of Representatives or Palata Predstaviteley (110 seats; members elected by universal adult suffrage to serve 4-year terms)
elections: last held 18 March and 1 April 2001 and 17 and 31 October 2004; international observers widely denounced the October 2004 elections as flawed and undemocratic, based on massive government falsification; pro-Lukashenko candidates won every seat, after many opposition candidates were disqualified for technical reasons
election results: Soviet Respubliki - percent of vote by party - NA%; seats by party - NA; Palata Predstaviteley - percent of vote by party - NA%; seats by party - NA

Judicial branch: Supreme Court (judges are appointed by the president); Constitutional Court (half of the judges appointed by the president and half appointed by the Chamber of Representatives)

Political parties and leaders: Pro-government parties: Agrarian Party or AP [leader NA]; Belarusian Communist Party or KPB [leader NA]; Belarusian Patriotic Movement (Belarusian Patriotic Party) or BPR [Anatoliy BARANKEVICH, chairman]; Liberal Democratic Party of Belarus [Sergei GAYDUKEVICH]; Social-Sports Party [leader NA]; Opposition parties: 10 Plus Coalition [Alyaksandr MILINKEVICH], includes: Belarusian Party of Communists or PKB [Syarhey KALYAKIN]; Belarusian Party of Labor (unregistered) [Aleksandr BUKHVOSTOV, Leonid LEMESHONAK]; Belarusian Popular Front or BPF [Vintsyuk VYACHORKA]; Belarusian Social-Democratic Party Narodnaya HROMADA or BSDP NH [Alyaksandr KOZULIN, chairman]; Green Party [Alyaksandr SYKALA]; United Civic Party or UCP [Anatol LYABEDSKA]; Party of Freedom and Progress (unregistered) [Vladimir NOVOSYAD]; Women's Party "Nadezhda" [Valentina MATUSEVICH, chairperson]

Political pressure groups and leaders: Belarusian Congress of Democratic Trade Unions [Alyaksandr YAROSHUK]; Perspektiva kiosk watchdog NGO [Anatol SHUMCHENKO]; Lenin Communist Union of Youth (youth wing of the Belarusian Party of Communists or PKB); National Strike Committee of Entrepreneurs [Aleksandr VASILYEV, Valery LEVONEVSKY]; Partnership NGO [Nikolay ASTREYKA]; Young Belarus [multiple leaders]; Youth Front (Malady Front) [Dzmitryy DASHKEVICH, Syarhey BAKHUN]; Zubr youth group [Vladimir KOBETS]

International organization participation: CEI, CIS, EAPC, EBRD, IAEA, IBRD, ICAO, ICFTU, ICRM, IFC, IFRCS, ILO, IMF, Interpol, IOC, IOM (observer), ISO, ITU, MIGA, NAM, NSG, OPCW, OSCE, PCA, PFP, UN, UNCTAD, UNESCO, UNIDO, UPU, WCO, WFTU, WHO, WIPO, WMO, WToO, WTO (observer)

Diplomatic representation in the US:
chief of mission: Ambassador Mikhail KHVOSTOV
chancery: 1619 New Hampshire Avenue NW, Washington, DC 20009
telephone: [1] (202) 986-1604
FAX: [1] (202) 986-1805
consulate(s) general: New York

Diplomatic representation from the US:
chief of mission: Ambassador George A. KROL
embassy: 46 Starovilenskaya St., Minsk 220002
mailing address: PSC 78, Box B Minsk, APO 09723
telephone: [375] (17) 210-12-83, 217-7347, 217-7348
FAX: [375] (17) 234-7853

Flag description: red horizontal band (top) and green horizontal band one-half the width of the red band; a white vertical stripe on the hoist side bears Belarusian national ornamention in red

ECONOMY

Economy - overview: Belarus's economy in 2004-05 posted 6.4% and 7.8% growth. Still, the economy continues to be hampered by high inflation, persistent trade deficits, and ongoing rocky relations with Russia, Belarus' largest trading partner and energy supplier. Belarus has seen little structural reform since 1995, when President LUKASHENKO launched the country on the path of "market socialism." In keeping with this policy, LUKASHENKO reimposed administrative controls over prices and currency exchange rates and expanded the state's right to intervene in the management of private enterprises. In addition, businesses have been subject to pressure on the part of central and local governments, e.g., arbitrary changes in regulations, numerous rigorous inspections, retroactive application of new business regulations, and arrests of "disruptive" businessmen and factory owners. A wide range of redistributive policies has helped those at the bottom of the ladder; the Gini coefficient is among the lowest in the world. For the time being, Belarus remains self-isolated from the West and its open-market economies. Growth has been strong in recent years, despite the roadblocks in a tough, centrally directed economy and the high, but decreasing, rate of inflation. Growth has been buoyed by increased Russian demand for generally noncompetitive Belarusian goods.

GDP: purchasing power parity - $77.77 billion (2005 est.)

GDP (official exchange rate): $23.94 billion (2005 est.)

GDP - real growth rate: 7.8% (2005 est.)

GDP - per capita: purchasing power parity - $7,600 (2005 est.)

GDP - composition by sector:
agriculture: 11.1%
industry: 38.4%
services: 50.4% (2004 est.)

Labor force: 4.305 million (31 December 2003)

Labor force - by occupation: agriculture 14%, industry 34.7%, services 51.3% (2003 est.)

Unemployment rate: 2% officially registered unemployed; large number of underemployed workers (2004)

Population below poverty line: 27.1% (2003 est.)

Household income or consumption by percentage share:
lowest 10%: 5.1%
highest 10%: 20% (1998)

Distribution of family income - Gini index: 30.4 (2000)

Inflation rate (consumer prices): 11.5% (2005 est.)

Investment (gross fixed): 24.2% of GDP (2005 est.)
Budget:
revenues: $5.903 billion
expenditures: $6.343 billion, including capital expenditures of $180 million (2005 est.)
Agriculture - products: grain, potatoes, vegetables, sugar beets, flax; beef, milk
Industries: metal-cutting machine tools, tractors, trucks, earthmovers, motorcycles, televisions, chemical fibers, fertilizer, textiles, radios, refrigerators
Industrial production growth rate: 4% (2004 est.)
Electricity - production: 30 billion kWh (2004)
Electricity – production by source:
fossil fuel: 99.5%
hydro: 0.1%
nuclear: 0%
other: 0.4% (2001)
Electricity - consumption: 34.3 billion kWh (2004)
Electricity - exports: 800 million kWh (2004)
Electricity - imports: 7 billion kWh (2003)
Oil - production: 36,000 bbl/day (2004 est.)
Oil - consumption: 252,000 bbl/day (2003 est.)
Oil - exports: 14,500 bbl/day (2003 est.)
Oil - imports: 360,000 bbl/day (2004 est.)
Natural gas - production: 250 million cu m (2004 est.)
Natural gas - consumption: 18.8 billion cu m (2004 est.)
Natural gas - exports: 0 cu m (2004 est.)
Natural gas - imports: 18.5 billion cu m (2004 est.)
Current account balance: $312.4 million (2005 est.)
Exports: $16.14 billion f.o.b. (2005 est.)
Exports - partners: Russia 47%, UK 8.3%, Netherlands 6.7%, Poland 5.3% (2004)
Imports: $16.94 billion f.o.b. (2005 est.)
Imports - partners: Russia 68.2%, Germany 6.6%, Ukraine 3.3% (2004)
Reserves of foreign exchange and gold: $835.4 million (2005 est.)
Debt - external: $4.662 billion (30 June 2005 est.)
Economic aid - recipient: $194.3 million (1995)
Currency: Belarusian ruble (BYB/BYR)
Currency code: BYB/BYR
Exchange rates: Belarusian rubles per US dollar - 2,140 (2005), 2,160.26 (2004), 2,051.27 (2003), 1,790.92 (2002), 1,390 (2001)
Fiscal year: calendar year

COMMUNICATIONS

Telephones - main lines in use: 3,071,300 (2003)
Telephones - mobile cellular: 1.118 million (2003)
Telephone system:
general assessment: the Ministry of Telecommunications controls all telecommunications through its carrier (a joint stock company) Beltelcom which is a monopoly
domestic: local - Minsk has a digital metropolitan network and a cellular NMT-450 network; waiting lists for telephones are long; local service outside Minsk is neglected and poor; intercity - Belarus has a partly developed fiber-optic backbone system presently serving at least 13 major cities (1998); Belarus' fiber optics form synchronous digital hierarchy rings through other countries' systems; an inadequate analog system remains operational
international: country code - 375; Belarus is a member of the Trans-European Line (TEL), Trans-Asia-Europe (TAE) fiber-optic line, and has access to the Trans-Siberia Line (TSL); three fiber-optic segments provide connectivity to Latvia, Poland, Russia, and Ukraine; worldwide service is available to Belarus through this infrastructure; additional analog lines to Russia; Intelsat, Eutelsat, and Intersputnik earth stations
Radio broadcast stations: AM 28, FM 37, shortwave 11 (1998)
Radios: 3.02 million (1997)
Television broadcast stations: 47 (plus 27 repeaters) (1995)
Televisions: 2.52 million (1997)
Internet country code: .by
Internet hosts: 5,308 (2004)
Internet Service Providers (ISPs): 23 (2002)
Internet users: 1,391,900 (2003)

TRANSPORTATION

Airports: 133 (2004 est.)
Airports - with paved runways:
total: 44
over 3,047 m: 2
2,438 to 3,047 m: 22
1,524 to 2,437 m: 4
914 to 1,523 m: 1
under 914 m: 15 (2005 est.)
Airports - with unpaved runways:
total: 57
over 3,047 m: 2
2,438 to 3,047 m: 1
1,524 to 2,437 m: 5
914 to 1,523 m: 7
under 914 m: 42 (2005 est.)
Heliports: 1 (2005 est.)
Pipelines: gas 5,223 km; oil 2,443 km; refined products 1,686 km (2004)
Railways:
total: 5,512 km
broad gauge: 5,497 km 1.520-m gauge (874 km electrified)
standard gauge: 15 km 1.435-m (2004)
Roadways:
total: 93,055 km
paved: 93,055 km (2003)
Waterways: 2,500 km (use limited by location on perimeter of country and by shallowness) (2003)
Ports and terminals: Mazyr

MILITARY

Military branches: Army, Air and Air Defense Force
Military service age and obligation: 18-27 years of age for compulsory military service; conscript service obligation - 18 months (2005)
Manpower available for military service: *males age 18-49:* 2,520,644 (2005 est.)
Manpower fit for military service: *males age 18-49:* 1,657,984 (2005 est.)
Manpower reaching military service age annually: *males:* 85,202 (2005 est.)
Military expenditures - dollar figure: $176.1 million (FY02)
Military expenditures - percent of GDP: 1.4% (FY02)

TRANSNATIONAL ISSUES

Disputes - international: 1997 boundary treaty with Ukraine remains unratified over unresolved financial claims, preventing demarcation and diminishing border security; boundary with Latvia remains undemarcated but a third of the border with Lithuania was demarcated in 2004
Illicit drugs: limited cultivation of opium poppy and cannabis, mostly for the domestic market; transshipment point for illicit drugs to and via Russia, and to the Baltics and Western Europe; a small and lightly regulated financial center; new anti-money-laundering legislation does not meet international standards; few investigations or prosecutions of money-laundering activities

BELGIUM

INTRODUCTION

Background: Belgium became independent from the Netherlands in 1830 and was occupied by Germany during World Wars I and II. It has prospered in the past half century as a modern, technologically advanced European state and member of NATO and the EU. Tensions between the Dutch-speaking Flemings of the north and the French-speaking Walloons of the south have led in recent years to constitutional amendments granting these regions formal recognition and autonomy.

GEOGRAPHY

Location: Western Europe, bordering the North Sea, between France and the Netherlands
Geographic coordinates: 50 50 N, 4 00 E
Map references: Europe
Area:
total: 30,528 sq km
land: 30,278 sq km
water: 250 sq km
Area - comparative: about the size of Maryland
Land boundaries:
total: 1,385 km
border countries: France 620 km, Germany 167 km, Luxembourg 148 km, Netherlands 450 km
Coastline: 66.5 km
Maritime claims:
territorial sea: 12 nm
exclusive economic zone: geographic coordinates define outer limit
continental shelf: median line with neighbors
Climate: temperate; mild winters, cool summers; rainy, humid, cloudy
Terrain: flat coastal plains in northwest, central rolling hills, rugged mountains of Ardennes Forest in southeast
Elevation extremes:
lowest point: North Sea 0 m
highest point: Signal de Botrange 694 m
Natural resources: construction materials, silica sand, carbonates
Land use:
arable land: 23.28%
permanent crops: 0.4%
other: 76.32%
note: includes Luxembourg (2001)
Irrigated land: 40 sq km (includes Luxembourg) (1998 est.)
Natural hazards: flooding is a threat along rivers and in areas of reclaimed coastal land, protected from the sea by concrete dikes
Environment - current issues: the environment is exposed to intense pressures from human activities: urbanization, dense transportation network, industry, extensive animal breeding and crop cultivation; air and water pollution also have repercussions for neighboring countries; uncertainties regarding federal and regional responsibilities (now resolved) have slowed progress in tackling environmental challenges
Environment - international agreements:
party to: Air Pollution, Air Pollution-Nitrogen Oxides, Air Pollution-Sulfur 85, Air Pollution-Sulfur 94, Air Pollution-Volatile Organic Compounds, Antarctic-Environmental Protocol, Antarctic-Marine Living Resources, Antarctic Seals, Antarctic Treaty, Biodiversity, Climate Change, Climate Change-Kyoto Protocol, Desertification, Endangered Species, Environmental Modification, Hazardous Wastes, Law of the Sea, Marine Dumping, Marine Life Conservation, Ozone Layer Protection, Ship Pollution, Tropical Timber 83, Tropical Timber 94, Wetlands
signed, but not ratified: Air Pollution-Persistent Organic Pollutants
Geography - note: crossroads of Western Europe; majority of West European capitals within 1,000 km of Brussels, the seat of both the European Union and NATO

PEOPLE

Population: 10,364,388 (July 2005 est.)
Age structure:
0-14 years: 16.9% (male 892,995/female 855,177)
15-64 years: 65.7% (male 3,435,282/female 3,373,917)
65 years and over: 17.4% (male 745,178/female 1,061,839) (2005 est.)
Median age:
total: 40.55 years
male: 39.29 years
female: 41.81 years (2005 est.)
Population growth rate: 0.15% (2005 est.)
Birth rate: 10.48 births/1,000 population (2005 est.)
Death rate: 10.22 deaths/1,000 population (2005 est.)
Net migration rate: 1.23 migrant(s)/1,000 population (2005 est.)
Sex ratio:
at birth: 1.04 male(s)/female
under 15 years: 1.04 male(s)/female
15-64 years: 1.02 male(s)/female
65 years and over: 0.7 male(s)/female
total population: 0.96 male(s)/female (2005 est.)
Infant mortality rate:
total: 4.68 deaths/1,000 live births
male: 5.27 deaths/1,000 live births
female: 4.06 deaths/1,000 live births (2005 est.)
Life expectancy at birth:
total population: 78.62 years
male: 75.44 years
female: 81.94 years (2005 est.)
Total fertility rate: 1.64 children born/woman (2005 est.)
HIV/AIDS - adult prevalence rate: 0.2% (2003 est.)
HIV/AIDS - people living with HIV/AIDS: 10,000 (2003 est.)
HIV/AIDS - deaths: less than 100 (2003 est.)
Nationality:
noun: Belgian(s)
adjective: Belgian
Ethnic groups: Fleming 58%, Walloon 31%, mixed or other 11%
Religions: Roman Catholic 75%, Protestant or other 25%
Languages: Dutch (official) 60%, French (official) 40%, German (official) less than 1%, legally bilingual (Dutch and French)
Literacy:
definition: age 15 and over can read and write
total population: 98%
male: NA%
female: NA%

GOVERNMENT

Country name:
conventional long form: Kingdom of Belgium
conventional short form: Belgium
local long form: Royaume de Belgique/Koninkrijk Belgie
local short form: Belgique/Belgie
Government type: federal parliamentary democracy under a constitutional monarch
Capital: Brussels
Administrative divisions: 10 provinces (French: provinces, singular - province; Dutch: provincies, singular - provincie) and 3 regions* (French: regions; Dutch: gewesten); Antwerpen, Brabant Wallon, Brussels* (Bruxelles), Flanders*, Hainaut, Liege, Limburg, Luxembourg,

Namur, Oost-Vlaanderen, Vlaams-Brabant, Wallonia*, West-Vlaanderen
note: as a result of the 1993 constitutional revision that furthered devolution into a federal state, there are now three levels of government (federal, regional, and linguistic community) with a complex division of responsibilities
Independence: 4 October 1830 (a provisional government declares independence from the Netherlands); 21 July 1831 (King Leopold I ascends to the throne)
National holiday: 21 July (1831) ascension to the Throne of King Leopold I
Constitution: 7 February 1831; amended many times; revised 14 July 1993 to create a federal state
Legal system: civil law system influenced by English constitutional theory; judicial review of legislative acts; accepts compulsory ICJ jurisdiction, with reservations
Suffrage: 18 years of age; universal and compulsory
Executive branch:
chief of state: King ALBERT II (since 9 August 1993); Heir Apparent Prince PHILIPPE, son of the monarch
head of government: Prime Minister Guy VERHOFSTADT (since 13 July 1999)
cabinet: Council of Ministers formally appointed by the monarch
elections: none; the monarchy is hereditary; following legislative elections, the leader of the majority party or the leader of the majority coalition is usually appointed prime minister by the monarch and then approved by parliament
note: government coalition - VLD, MR, PS, SP.A-Spirit
Legislative branch: bicameral Parliament consists of a Senate or Senaat in Dutch, Senat in French (71 seats; 40 members are directly elected by popular vote, 31 are indirectly elected; members serve four-year terms) and a Chamber of Deputies or Kamer van Volksvertegenwoordigers in Dutch, Chambre des Representants in French (150 seats; members are directly elected by popular vote on the basis of proportional representation to serve four-year terms)
elections: Senate and Chamber of Deputies - last held 18 May 2003 (next to be held no later than May 2007)
election results: Senate - percent of vote by party - SP.A-Spirit 15.5%, VLD 15.4%, CD & V 12.7%, PS 12.8%, MR 12.1%, VB 9.4%, CDH 5.6%; seats by party - SP.A-Spirit 7, VLD 7, CD & V 6, PS 6, MR 5, VB 5, CDH 2, other 2 (note - there are also 31 indirectly elected senators); Chamber of Deputies - percent of vote by party - VLD 15.4%, SP.A-Spirit 14.9%, CD & V 13.3%, PS 13.0%, VB 11.6%, MR 11.4%, CDH 5.5%, Ecolo 3.1%; seats by party - VLD 25, SP.A-Spirit 23, CD & V 21, PS 25, VB 18, MR 24, CDH 8 Ecolo 4, other 2
note: as a result of the 1993 constitutional revision that furthered devolution into a federal state, there are now three levels of government (federal, regional, and linguistic community) with a complex division of responsibilities; this reality leaves six governments each with its own legislative assembly
Judicial branch: Supreme Court of Justice or Hof van Cassatie (in Dutch) or Cour de Cassation (in French) (judges are appointed for life by the Government; candidacies have to be submitted by the High Justice Council)
Political parties and leaders: *Flemish parties:* Christian Democrats and Flemish or CD & V [Jo VANDEURZEN]; Flemish Liberal Democrats or VLD [Bart SOMERS]; GROEN! (formerly AGALEV, Flemish Greens) [Vera DUA]; New Flemish Alliance or NVA [Bart DE WEVER]; Socialist Party.Alternative or SP.A [Caroline GENNEZ]; Spirit [Geert LAMBERT] (new party now associated with SP.A); Vlaams Belang (Flemish Interest) or VB [Frank VANHECKE]
Francophone parties: Ecolo (Francophone Greens) [Jean-Michel JAVAUX, Evelyne HUYTEBROECK, Claude BROUIR]; Humanist and Democratic Center of CDH [Joelle MILQUET]; National Front or FN [Daniel FERET]; Reformist Movement or MR [Didier REYNDERS]; Socialist Party or PS [Elio DI RUPO]; other minor parties
Political pressure groups and leaders: Christian, Socialist, and Liberal Trade Unions; Federation of Belgian Industries; numerous other associations representing bankers, manufacturers, middle-class artisans, and the legal and medical professions; various organizations represent the cultural interests of Flanders and Wallonia; various peace groups such as Pax Christi and groups representing immigrants
International organization participation: ACCT, AfDB, AsDB, Australia Group, Benelux, BIS, CE, CERN, EAPC, EBRD, EIB, EMU, ESA, EU, FAO, G-9, G-10, IADB, IAEA, IBRD, ICAO, ICC, ICCt, ICFTU, ICRM, IDA, IEA, IFAD, IFC, IFRCS, IHO, ILO, IMF, IMO, Interpol, IOC, IOM, ISO, ITU, MIGA, MONUC, NATO, NEA, NSG, OAS (observer), OECD, ONUB, OPCW, OSCE, Paris Club, PCA, UN, UNCTAD, UNESCO, UNHCR, UNIDO, UNITAR, UNMOGIP, UNRWA, UNTSO, UPU, WADB (nonregional), WCL, WCO, WEU, WHO, WIPO, WMO, WTO, ZC
Diplomatic representation in the US:
chief of mission: Ambassador Franciskus VAN DAELE
chancery: 3330 Garfield Street NW, Washington, DC 20008
telephone: [1] (202) 333-6900
FAX: [1] (202) 333-3079
consulate(s) general: Atlanta, Los Angeles, and New York
Diplomatic representation from the US:
chief of mission: Ambassador Tom C. KOROLOGOS
embassy: Regentlaan 27 Boulevard du Regent, B-1000 Brussels
mailing address: PSC 82, Box 002, APO AE 09710
telephone: [32] (2) 508-2111
FAX: [32] (2) 511-2725
Flag description: three equal vertical bands of black (hoist side), yellow, and red; the design was based on the flag of France

ECONOMY

Economy - overview: This modern private enterprise economy has capitalized on its central geographic location, highly developed transport network, and diversified industrial and commercial base. Industry is concentrated mainly in the populous Flemish area in the north. With few natural resources, Belgium must import substantial quantities of raw materials and export a large volume of manufactures, making its economy unusually dependent on the state of world markets. Roughly three-quarters of its trade is with other EU countries. Public debt is nearly 100% of GDP. On the positive side, the government has succeeded in balancing its budget, and income distribution is relatively equal. Belgium began circulating the euro currency in January 2002. Economic growth in 2001-03 dropped sharply because of the global economic slowdown, with moderate recovery in 2004-05.
GDP: purchasing power parity - $329.3 billion (2005 est.)
GDP (official exchange rate): $361.4 billion (2005 est.)
GDP - real growth rate: 1.5% (2005 est.)
GDP - per capita: purchasing power parity - $31,800 (2005 est.)
GDP - composition by sector:
agriculture: 1.3%
industry: 24.7%
services: 74% (2004 est.)
Labor force: 4.77 million (2005 est.)
Labor force - by occupation: agriculture 1.3%, industry 24.5%, services 74.2% (2003 est.)
Unemployment rate: 7.6% (2005 est.)
Population below poverty line: 4% (1989 est.)

Household income or consumption by percentage share:
lowest 10%: 3.2%
highest 10%: 23% (1996)
Distribution of family income - Gini index: 25 (1996)
Inflation rate (consumer prices): 2.7% (2005 est.)
Investment (gross fixed): 18.4% of GDP (2005 est.)
Budget:
revenues: $180.4 billion
expenditures: $180.5 billion, including capital expenditures of $1.56 billion (2005 est.)
Public debt: 93.6% of GDP (2005 est.)
Agriculture - products: sugar beets, fresh vegetables, fruits, grain, tobacco; beef, veal, pork, milk
Industries: engineering and metal products, motor vehicle assembly, transportation equipment, scientific instruments, processed food and beverages, chemicals, basic metals, textiles, glass, petroleum
Industrial production growth rate: 1.1% (2005 est.)
Electricity - production: 78.77 billion kWh (2003)
Electricity – production by source:
fossil fuel: 38.4%
hydro: 0.6%
nuclear: 59.3%
other: 1.8% (2001)
Electricity - consumption: 79.66 billion kWh (2003)
Electricity - exports: 8.3 billion kWh (2003)
Electricity - imports: 14.7 billion kWh (2003)
Oil - production: 13,060 bbl/day (2003)
Oil - consumption: 624,200 bbl/day (2003 est.)
Oil - exports: 450,000 bbl/day (2001)
Oil - imports: 1.042 million bbl/day (2001)
Natural gas - production: 0 cu m (2001 est.)
Natural gas - consumption: 15.5 billion cu m (2001 est.)
Natural gas - exports: 0 cu m (2001 est.)
Natural gas - imports: 15.4 billion cu m (2001 est.)
Current account balance: $6.983 billion (2005 est.)
Exports: $269.6 billion f.o.b. (2005 est.)
Exports - partners: Germany 19.9%, France 17.2%, Netherlands 11.8%, UK 8.6%, US 6.5%, Italy 5.2% (2004)
Imports: $264.5 billion f.o.b. (2005 est.)
Imports - partners: Germany 18.4%, Netherlands 17%, France 12.5%, UK 6.8%, Ireland 6.3%, US 5.5% (2004)
Reserves of foreign exchange and gold: $13.99 billion (2004 est.)
Debt - external: $980.1 billion (30 June 2005 est.)
Economic aid - donor: ODA, $1.072 billion (2002)
Currency: euro (EUR)
note: on 1 January 1999, the European Monetary Union introduced the euro as a common currency to be used by financial institutions of member countries; on 1 January 2002, the euro became the sole currency for everyday transactions within the member countries
Currency code: EUR
Exchange rates: euros per US dollar - 0.79697 (2005), 0.8054 (2004), 0.886 (2003), 1.0626 (2002), 1.1175 (2001)
Fiscal year: calendar year

COMMUNICATIONS

Telephones - main lines in use: 5,120,400 (2002)
Telephones - mobile cellular: 8,135,500 (2002)
Telephone system:
general assessment: highly developed, technologically advanced, and completely automated domestic and international telephone and telegraph facilities
domestic: nationwide cellular telephone system; extensive cable network; limited microwave radio relay network
international: country code - 32; submarine cables - 5; satellite earth stations - 7 (Intelsat - 3) (2005)
Radio broadcast stations: FM 79, AM 7, shortwave 1 (1998)
Radios: 8.075 million (1997)
Television broadcast stations: 25 (plus 10 repeaters) (1997)
Televisions: 4.72 million (1997)
Internet country code: .be
Internet hosts: 166,799 (2004)
Internet Service Providers (ISPs): 61 (2000)
Internet users: 3.4 million (2002)

TRANSPORTATION

Airports: 43 (2004 est.)
Airports - with paved runways:
total: 25
over 3,047 m: 6
2,438 to 3,047 m: 7
1,524 to 2,437 m: 3
914 to 1,523 m: 2
under 914 m: 7 (2005 est.)
Airports - with unpaved runways:
total: 18
914 to 1,523 m: 2
under 914 m: 16 (2005 est.)
Heliports: 1 (2005 est.)
Pipelines: gas 1,485 km; oil 158 km; refined products 535 km (2004)
Railways:
total: 3,521 km
standard gauge: 3,521 km 1.435-m gauge (2,927 km electrified) (2004)
Roadways:
total: 149,757 km
paved: 117,110 km (including 1,747 km of expressways)
unpaved: 32,647 km (2003)
Waterways: 2,043 km (1,528 km in regular commercial use) (2003)
Merchant marine:
total: 53 ships (1,000 GRT or over) 1,146,301 GRT/1,588,184 DWT
by type: bulk carrier 15, cargo 2, chemical tanker 2, container 8, liquefied gas 17, petroleum tanker 9
foreign-owned: 12 (Denmark 4, France 4, Greece 4)
registered in other countries: 101 (2005)
Ports and terminals: Antwerp, Brussels, Gent, Liege, Oostende, Zeebrugge

MILITARY

Military branches: Land, Naval, and Air Components (2005)
Military service age and obligation: 16 years of age for voluntary military service; women comprise some 7% of the Belgian armed forces (2001)
Manpower available for military service:
males age 16-49: 2,436,736 (2005 est.)
Manpower fit for military service: *males age 16-49:* 1,998,003 (2005 est.)
Manpower reaching military service age annually: *males:* 64,263 (2005 est.)
Military expenditures - dollar figure: $3.999 billion (2003)
Military expenditures - percent of GDP: 1.3% (2003)

TRANSNATIONAL ISSUES

Disputes - international: none
Illicit drugs: growing producer of synthetic drugs; transit point for US-bound ecstasy; source of precursor chemicals for South American cocaine processors; transshipment point for cocaine, heroin, hashish, and marijuana entering Western Europe; despite a strengthening of legislation, the country remains vulnerable to money laundering related to narcotics, automobiles, alcohol, and tobacco

BELIZE

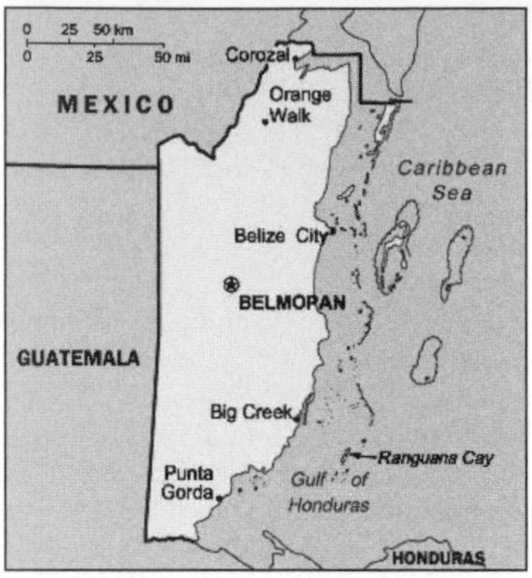

INTRODUCTION

Background: Territorial disputes between the UK and Guatemala delayed the independence of Belize (formerly British Honduras) until 1981. Guatemala refused to recognize the new nation until 1992. Tourism has become the mainstay of the economy. The country remains plagued by high unemployment, growing involvement in the South American drug trade, and increasing urban crime.

GEOGRAPHY

Location: Central America, bordering the Caribbean Sea, between Guatemala and Mexico
Geographic coordinates: 17 15 N, 88 45 W
Map references: Central America and the Caribbean
Area:
total: 22,966 sq km
land: 22,806 sq km
water: 160 sq km
Area - comparative: slightly smaller than Massachusetts
Land boundaries:
total: 516 km
border countries: Guatemala 266 km, Mexico 250 km
Coastline: 386 km
Maritime claims:
territorial sea: 12 nm in the north, 3 nm in the south; note - from the mouth of the Sarstoon River to Ranguana Cay, Belize's territorial sea is 3 nm; according to Belize's Maritime Areas Act, 1992, the purpose of this limitation is to provide a framework for negotiating a definitive agreement on territorial differences with Guatemala
exclusive economic zone: 200 nm
Climate: tropical; very hot and humid; rainy season (May to November); dry season (February to May)
Terrain: flat, swampy coastal plain; low mountains in south
Elevation extremes:
lowest point: Caribbean Sea 0 m
highest point: Victoria Peak 1,160 m
Natural resources: arable land potential, timber, fish, hydropower
Land use:
arable land: 2.85%
permanent crops: 1.71%
other: 95.44% (2001)
Irrigated land: 30 sq km (1998 est.)
Natural hazards: frequent, devastating hurricanes (June to November) and coastal flooding (especially in south)
Environment - current issues: deforestation; water pollution from sewage, industrial effluents, agricultural runoff; solid and sewage waste disposal
Environment - international agreements:
party to: Biodiversity, Climate Change, Climate Change-Kyoto Protocol, Desertification, Endangered Species, Hazardous Wastes, Law of the Sea, Ozone Layer Protection, Ship Pollution, Wetlands
signed, but not ratified: none of the selected agreements
Geography - note: only country in Central America without a coastline on the North Pacific Ocean

PEOPLE

Population: 279,457 (July 2005 est.)
Age structure:
0-14 years: 40.1% (male 57,114/female 54,877)
15-64 years: 56.4% (male 79,694/female 77,881)
65 years and over: 3.5% (male 4,768/female 5,123) (2005 est.)
Median age:
total: 19.35 years
male: 19.21 years
female: 19.49 years (2005 est.)
Population growth rate: 2.33% (2005 est.)
Birth rate: 29.34 births/1,000 population (2005 est.)
Death rate: 6.04 deaths/1,000 population (2005 est.)
Net migration rate: 0 migrant(s)/1,000 population (2005 est.)
Sex ratio:
at birth: 1.05 male(s)/female
under 15 years: 1.04 male(s)/female
15-64 years: 1.02 male(s)/female
65 years and over: 0.93 male(s)/female
total population: 1.03 male(s)/female (2005 est.)
Infant mortality rate:
total: 25.69 deaths/1,000 live births
male: 28.97 deaths/1,000 live births
female: 22.25 deaths/1,000 live births (2005 est.)
Life expectancy at birth:
total population: 68.44 years
male: 66.54 years
female: 70.44 years (2005 est.)
Total fertility rate: 3.68 children born/woman (2005 est.)
HIV/AIDS - adult prevalence rate: 2.4% (2003 est.)
HIV/AIDS - people living with HIV/AIDS: 3,600 (2003 est.)
HIV/AIDS - deaths: less than 200 (2003 est.)
Nationality:
noun: Belizean(s)
adjective: Belizean
Ethnic groups: mestizo 48.7%, Creole 24.9%, Maya 10.6%, Garifuna 6.1%, other 9.7%
Religions: Roman Catholic 49.6%, Protestant 27% (Pentecostal 7.4%, Anglican 5.3%, Seventh-Day Adventist 5.2%, Mennonite 4.1%, Methodist 3.5%, Jehovah's Witnesses 1.5%), other 14%, none 9.4% (2000)
Languages: English (official), Spanish, Mayan, Garifuna (Carib), Creole
Literacy:
definition: age 15 and over can read and write
total population: 94.1%
male: 94.1%
female: 94.1% (2003 est.)

GOVERNMENT

Country name:
conventional long form: none
conventional short form: Belize
former: British Honduras
Government type: parliamentary democracy
Capital: Belmopan
Administrative divisions: 6 districts; Belize, Cayo, Corozal, Orange Walk, Stann Creek, Toledo
Independence: 21 September 1981 (from UK)
National holiday: Independence Day, 21 September (1981)
Constitution: 21 September 1981
Legal system: English law
Suffrage: 18 years of age; universal
Executive branch:
chief of state: Queen ELIZABETH II (since 6 February 1952), represented by Governor General Sir Colville YOUNG, Sr. (since 17 November 1993)
head of government: Prime Minister Said Wilbert MUSA (since 28 August 1998); Deputy Prime Minister John BRICENO (since 1 September 1998)
cabinet: Cabinet appointed by the governor general on the advice of the prime minister
elections: none; the monarch is hereditary; governor general appointed by the monarch; following legislative elections, the leader of the majority party or the

leader of the majority coalition is usually appointed prime minister by the governor general; prime minister recommends the deputy prime minister

Legislative branch: bicameral National Assembly consists of the Senate (12 members appointed by the governor general - six on the advice of the prime minister, three on the advice of the leader of the opposition, and one each on the advice of the Belize Council of Churches and Evangelical Association of Churches, the Belize Chamber of Commerce and Industry and the Belize Better Business Bureau, and the National Trade Union Congress and the Civil Society Steering Committee; members are appointed for five-year terms) and the House of Representatives (29 seats; members are elected by direct popular vote to serve five-year terms)

elections: House of Representatives - last held 5 March 2003 (next to be held March 2008)

election results: percent of vote by party - NA%; seats by party - PUP 21, UDP 8

Judicial branch: Supreme Court (the chief justice is appointed by the governor general on the advice of the prime minister)

Political parties and leaders: People's United Party or PUP [Said MUSA]; United Democratic Party or UDP [Dean BARROW, party leader; Douglas SINGH, party chairman]

Political pressure groups and leaders: Society for the Promotion of Education and Research or SPEAR [Adele CATZIM]

International organization participation: ACP, C, Caricom, CDB, FAO, G-77, IADB, IBRD, ICAO, ICCt, ICFTU, ICRM, IDA, IFAD, IFC, IFRCS, ILO, IMF, IMO, Interpol, IOC, IOM, ITU, LAES, MIGA, NAM, OAS, OPANAL, OPCW, PCA, UN, UNCTAD, UNESCO, UNIDO, UPU, WCL, WHO, WIPO, WMO, WTO

Diplomatic representation in the US:

chief of mission: Ambassador Lisa M. SHOMAN

chancery: 2535 Massachusetts Avenue NW, Washington, DC 20008

telephone: [1] (202) 332-9636

FAX: [1] (202) 332-6888

consulate(s) general: Los Angeles

Diplomatic representation from the US:

chief of mission: Ambassador Robert J. DIETER

embassy: 29 Gabourel Lane, Belize City

mailing address: P. O. Box 286, Belize City

telephone: [501] 227-7161 through 7163

FAX: [501] 2-30802

Flag description: blue with a narrow red stripe along the top and the bottom edges; centered is a large white disk bearing the coat of arms; the coat of arms features a shield flanked by two workers in front of a mahogany tree with the related motto SUB UMBRA FLOREO (I Flourish in the Shade) on a scroll at the bottom, all encircled by a green garland

ECONOMY

Economy - overview: In this small, essentially private enterprise economy the tourism industry is the number one foreign exchange earner followed by marine products, citrus, cane sugar, bananas, and garments. The government's expansionary monetary and fiscal policies, initiated in September 1998, led to sturdy GDP growth averaging nearly 5% in 1999-2005. Major concerns continue to be the sizable trade deficit and foreign debt. A key short-term objective remains the reduction of poverty with the help of international donors.

GDP: purchasing power parity - $1.778 billion (2004 est.)

GDP (official exchange rate): $908 million (2005 est.)

GDP - real growth rate: 3.8% (2005 est.)

GDP - per capita: purchasing power parity - $6,800 (2005 est.)

GDP - composition by sector:

agriculture: 22.5%

industry: 23%

services: 54.5% (2004 est.)

Population below poverty line: 33% (1999 est.)

Household income or consumption by percentage share:

lowest 10%: NA

highest 10%: NA

Inflation rate (consumer prices): 3% (2005 est.)

Labor force: 90,000

note: shortage of skilled labor and all types of technical personnel (2001 est.)

Labor force - by occupation: agriculture 27%, industry 18%, services 55% (2001 est.)

Unemployment rate: 12.9% (2003)

Investment (gross fixed): 35.4% of GDP (2005 est.)

Budget:

revenues: $262 million

expenditures: $329 million, including capital expenditures of $70 million (2005 est.)

Agriculture - products: bananas, coca, citrus, sugar; fish, cultured shrimp; lumber; garments

Industries: garment production, food processing, tourism, construction

Industrial production growth rate: 4.6% (1999)

Electricity - production: 120 million kWh (2003)

Electricity - production by source:

fossil fuel: 59.9%

hydro: 40.1%

nuclear: 0%

other: 0% (2001)

Electricity - consumption: 111.6 million kWh (2003)

Electricity - exports: 0 kWh (2003)

Electricity - imports: 0 kWh (2003)

Oil - production: 0 bbl/day (2003)

Oil - consumption: 6,000 bbl/day (2003 est.)

Oil - exports: NA (2001)

Oil - imports: NA (2001)

Current account balance: $-200.1 million (2005 est.)

Exports: $349.9 million f.o.b. (2005 est.)

Exports - partners: US 37.2%, UK 26.8%, Jamaica 4.6% (2004)

Imports: $622.4 million f.o.b. (2005 est.)

Imports - partners: US 30.1%, Mexico 12%, Guatemala 7.4%, Cuba 7.2%, China 4.2%, Japan 4.1% (2004)

Reserves of foreign exchange and gold: $90.45 million (2005 est.)

Debt - external: $1.362 billion (June 2004 est.)

Economic aid - recipient: NA

Currency: Belizean dollar (BZD)

Currency code: BZD

Exchange rates: Belizean dollars per US dollar - 2 (2005), 2 (2004), 2 (2003), 2 (2002), 2 (2001)

Fiscal year: 1 April - 31 March

COMMUNICATIONS

Telephones - main lines in use: 33,300 (2003)

Telephones - mobile cellular: 60,400 (2003)

Telephone system:

general assessment: above-average system

domestic: trunk network depends primarily on microwave radio relay

international: country code - 501; satellite earth station - 8 (Intelsat - 2, unknown - 6) (2005)

Radio broadcast stations: AM 1, FM 12, shortwave 0 (1998)

Radios: 133,000 (1997)

Television broadcast stations: 2 (1997)

Televisions: 41,000 (1997)

Internet country code: .bz

Internet hosts: 2,613 (2003)

Internet Service Providers (ISPs): 2 (2000)

Internet users: 30,000 (2002)

TRANSPORTATION

Airports: 43 (2004 est.)

Airports - with paved runways:

total: 5

1,524 to 2,437 m: 1

914 to 1,523 m: 2

under 914 m: 2 (2005 est.)

Airports - with unpaved runways:

total: 38

2,438 to 3,047 m: 1

914 to 1,523 m: 11

under 914 m: 26 (2005 est.)

Roadways:
total: 2,872 km
paved: 488 km
unpaved: 2,384 km (1999)
Waterways: 825 km (navigable only by small craft) (2004)
Merchant marine:
total: 295 ships (1,000 GRT or over) 1,015,270 GRT/1,336,890 DWT
by type: bulk carrier 25, cargo 207, chemical tanker 9, container 6, passenger/cargo 6, petroleum tanker 20, refrigerated cargo 17, roll on/roll off 5
foreign-owned: 142 (Australia 2, Belgium 1, China 50, Cuba 1, Cyprus 1, Estonia 9, Germany 4, Hong Kong 6, Indonesia 3, Italy 2, Japan 5, Latvia 4, Malaysia 1, Nigeria 1, Pakistan 1, Poland 2, Russia 23, Singapore 5, South Korea 6, Spain 3, Switzerland 1, Turkey 2, Ukraine 4, UAE 3, United States 2) (2005)
Ports and terminals: Belize City

MILITARY

Military branches: Belize Defense Force (BDF): Army, Maritime Wing, Air Wing, and Volunteer Guard
Military service age and obligation: 18 years of age for voluntary military service; laws allow for conscription only if volunteers are insufficient; conscription has never been implemented; volunteers typically outnumber available positions by 3:1 (2001)
Manpower available for military service: *males age 18-49:* 60,750 (2005 est.)
Manpower fit for military service: *males age 18-49:* 41,368 (2005 est.)
Manpower reaching military service age annually: *males:* 3,209 (2005 est.)
Military expenditures - dollar figure: $18 million (2003)
Military expenditures - percent of GDP: 2% (2003)

TRANSNATIONAL ISSUES

Disputes - international: Guatemalan squatters continue to settle in the largely uninhabited rain forests of Belize's border region; OAS is attempting to revive the 2002 failed Differendum that created a small adjustment to land boundary, a Guatemalan maritime corridor in Caribbean, joint ecological park for disputed Sapodilla Cays, and substantial US-UK financial package
Illicit drugs: major transshipment point for cocaine; small-scale illicit producer of cannabis for the international drug trade; money-laundering activity related to narcotics trafficking and offshore sector

BENIN

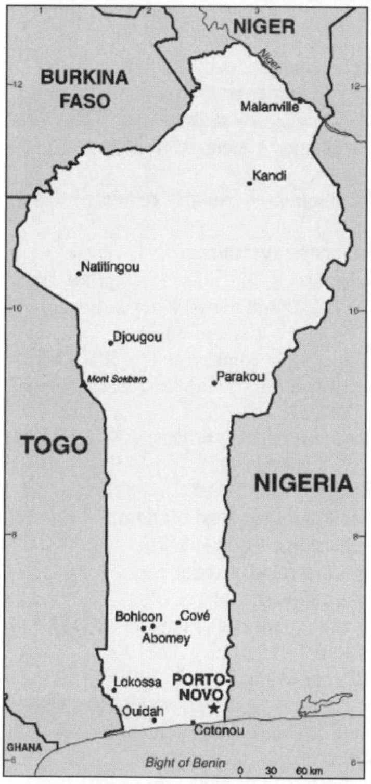

INTRODUCTION

Background: Present day Benin was the site of Dahomey, a prominent West African kingdom that rose in the 15th century. The territory became a French Colony in 1872 and achieved independence on 1 August 1960, as the Republic of Benin. A succession of military governments ended in 1972 with the rise to power of Mathieu KEREKOU and the establishment of a government based on Marxist-Leninist principles. A move to representative government began in 1989. Two years later, free elections ushered in former Prime Minister Nicephore SOGLO as president, marking the first successful transfer of power in Africa from a dictatorship to a democracy. KEREKOU was returned to power by elections held in 1996 and 2001, though some irregularities were alleged.

GEOGRAPHY

Location: Western Africa, bordering the Bight of Benin, between Nigeria and Togo
Geographic coordinates: 9 30 N, 2 15 E
Map references: Africa
Area:
total: 112,620 sq km
land: 110,620 sq km
water: 2,000 sq km
Area - comparative: slightly smaller than Pennsylvania
Land boundaries:
total: 1,989 km
border countries: Burkina Faso 306 km, Niger 266 km, Nigeria 773 km, Togo 644 km
Coastline: 121 km
Maritime claims:
territorial sea: 200 nm
Climate: tropical; hot, humid in south; semiarid in north
Terrain: mostly flat to undulating plain; some hills and low mountains
Elevation extremes:
lowest point: Atlantic Ocean 0 m
highest point: Mont Sokbaro 658 m
Natural resources: small offshore oil deposits, limestone, marble, timber
Land use:
arable land: 18.08%
permanent crops: 2.4%
other: 79.52% (2001)
Irrigated land: 120 sq km (1998 est.)
Natural hazards: hot, dry, dusty harmattan wind may affect north from December to March
Environment - current issues: inadequate supplies of potable water; poaching threatens wildlife populations; deforestation; desertification
Environment - international agreements:
party to: Biodiversity, Climate Change, Climate Change-Kyoto Protocol, Desertification, Endangered Species, Environmental Modification, Hazardous Wastes, Law of the Sea, Ozone Layer Protection, Ship Pollution, Wetlands
signed, but not ratified: none of the selected agreements
Geography - note: sandbanks create difficult access to a coast with no natural harbors, river mouths, or islands

PEOPLE

Population: 7,460,025
note: estimates for this country explicitly take into account the effects of excess mortality due to AIDS; this can result in lower life expectancy, higher infant mortality and death rates, lower population and growth rates, and changes in the distribution of population by age and sex than would otherwise be expected (July 2005 est.)

Age structure:
0-14 years: 46.5% (male 1,752,243/female 1,719,458)
15-64 years: 51.2% (male 1,868,630/female 1,948,610)
65 years and over: 2.3% (male 70,367/female 100,717) (2005 est.)
Median age:
total: 16.56 years
male: 16.12 years
female: 17.01 years (2005 est.)
Population growth rate: 2.82% (2005 est.)
Birth rate: 41.99 births/1,000 population (2005 est.)
Death rate: 13.76 deaths/1,000 population (2005 est.)
Net migration rate: 0 migrant(s)/1,000 population (2005 est.)
Sex ratio:
at birth: 1.03 male(s)/female
under 15 years: 1.02 male(s)/female
15-64 years: 0.96 male(s)/female
65 years and over: 0.7 male(s)/female
total population: 0.98 male(s)/female (2005 est.)
Infant mortality rate:
total: 85 deaths/1,000 live births
male: 90 deaths/1,000 live births
female: 79.86 deaths/1,000 live births (2005 est.)
Life expectancy at birth:
total population: 52.66 years
male: 51.53 years
female: 53.82 years (2005 est.)
Total fertility rate: 5.86 children born/woman (2005 est.)
HIV/AIDS - adult prevalence rate: 1.9% (2003 est.)
HIV/AIDS - people living with HIV/AIDS: 68,000 (2003 est.)
HIV/AIDS - deaths: 5,800 (2003 est.)
Major infectious diseases:
degree of risk: very high
food or waterborne diseases: bacterial and protozoal diarrhea, hepatitis A, and typhoid fever
vectorborne diseases: malaria, yellow fever, and others are high risks in some locations
respiratory disease: meningococcal meningitis (2004)
Nationality:
noun: Beninese (singular and plural)
adjective: Beninese
Ethnic groups: African 99% (42 ethnic groups, most important being Fon, Adja, Yoruba, Bariba), Europeans 5,500
Religions: indigenous beliefs 50%, Christian 30%, Muslim 20%
Languages: French (official), Fon and Yoruba (most common vernaculars in south), tribal languages (at least six major ones in north)
Literacy:
definition: age 15 and over can read and write
total population: 33.6%
male: 46.4%
female: 22.6% (2002 est.)

GOVERNMENT

Country name:
conventional long form: Republic of Benin
conventional short form: Benin
local long form: Republique du Benin
local short form: Benin
former: Dahomey
Government type: republic under multiparty democratic rule; dropped Marxism-Leninism December 1989
Capital: Porto-Novo is the official capital; Cotonou is the seat of government
Administrative divisions: 12 departments; Alibori, Atakora, Atlantique, Borgou, Collines, Kouffo, Donga, Littoral, Mono, Oueme, Plateau, Zou
Independence: 1 August 1960 (from France)
National holiday: National Day, 1 August (1960)
Constitution: December 1990
Legal system: based on French civil law and customary law; has not accepted compulsory ICJ jurisdiction
Suffrage: 18 years of age; universal
Executive branch:
chief of state: President Mathieu KEREKOU (since 4 April 1996); note - the president is both the chief of state and head of government
head of government: President Mathieu KEREKOU (since 4 April 1996); note - the president is both the chief of state and head of government
cabinet: Council of Ministers appointed by the president
elections: president reelected by popular vote for a five-year term; runoff election held 22 March 2001 (next to be held March 2006)
election results: Mathieu KEREKOU reelected president; percent of vote - Mathieu KEREKOU 84.1%, Bruno AMOUSSOU 15.9%
note: the four top-ranking contenders following the first-round presidential elections were: Mathieu KEREKOU (incumbent) 45.4%, Nicephore SOGLO (former president) 27.1%, Adrien HOUNGBEDJI (National Assembly Speaker) 12.6%, and Bruno AMOUSSOU (Minister of State) 8.6%; the second-round balloting, originally scheduled for 18 March 2001, was postponed four days because both SOGLO and HOUNGBEDJI withdrew alleging electoral fraud; this left KEREKOU to run against his own Minister of State, AMOUSSOU, in what was termed a "friendly match"
Legislative branch: unicameral National Assembly or Assemblee Nationale (83 seats; members are elected by direct popular vote to serve four-year terms)
elections: last held 30 March 2003 (next to be held March 2007)
election results: percent of vote by party - NA%; seats by party - Presidential Movement 52, opposition (PRB, PRD, E'toile, and 5 other small parties) 31
Judicial branch: Constitutional Court or Cour Constitutionnelle; Supreme Court or Cour Supreme; High Court of Justice
Political parties and leaders: African Congress for Renewal or DUNYA [Saka SALEY]; African Movement for Democracy and Progress or MADEP [Sefou FAGBOHOUN]; Alliance of the Social Democratic Party or PSD [Bruno AMOUSSOU]; Coalition of Democratic Forces [Gatien HOUNGBEDJI]; Democratic Renewal Party or PRD [Adrien HOUNGBEDJI]; Front for Renewal and Development or FARD-ALAFIA [Jerome Sakia KINA]; Impulse for Progress and Democracy or IPD [Bertin BORNA]; Key Force or FC [leader NA]; Presidential Movement (UBF, MADEP, FC, IDP, and four small parties), Renaissance Party du Benin or PRB [Nicephore SOGLO]; The Star Alliance (Alliance E'toile) [Sacca Lafia]; Union of Tomorrow's Benin or UBF [Bruno AMOUSSOU]
note: approximately 20 additional minor parties
Political pressure groups and leaders: NA
International organization participation: ACCT, ACP, AfDB, AU, CEMAC, ECOWAS, Entente, FAO, FZ, G-77, IAEA, IBRD, ICAO, ICCt, ICFTU, ICRM, IDA, IDB, IFAD, IFC, IFRCS, ILO, IMF, IMO, Interpol, IOC, IOM, ISO (correspondent), ITU, MIGA, MINUSTAH, MONUC, NAM, OIC, ONUB, OPCW, UN, UN Security Council (temporary), UNCTAD, UNESCO, UNIDO, UNMIL, UNMIS, UNOCI, UPU, WADB (regional), WAEMU, WCL, WCO, WFTU, WHO, WIPO, WMO, WToO, WTO
Diplomatic representation in the US:
chief of mission: Ambassador Cyrille Segbe OGUIN
chancery: 2124 Kalorama Road NW, Washington, DC 20008
telephone: [1] (202) 232-6656
FAX: [1] (202) 265-1996
Diplomatic representation from the US:
chief of mission: Ambassador Wayne NEILL
embassy: Rue Caporal Bernard Anani, Cotonou
mailing address: 01 B. P. 2012, Cotonou

telephone: [229] 30-06-50
FAX: [229] 30-06-70
Flag description: two equal horizontal bands of yellow (top) and red (bottom) with a vertical green band on the hoist side

ECONOMY

Economy - overview: The economy of Benin remains underdeveloped and dependent on subsistence agriculture, cotton production, and regional trade. Growth in real output has averaged around 5% in the past six years, but rapid population growth has offset much of this increase. Inflation has subsided over the past several years. In order to raise growth still further, Benin plans to attract more foreign investment, place more emphasis on tourism, facilitate the development of new food processing systems and agricultural products, and encourage new information and communication technology. Many of these proposals are included in Benin's application to receive Millennium Challenge Account funding - for which it was a finalist in 2004-05. The 2001 privatization policy continues in telecommunications, water, electricity, and agriculture in spite of government reluctance. The Paris Club and bilateral creditors have eased the external debt situation, with Benin benefiting from a G8 debt reduction announced in July 2005, while pressing for more rapid structural reforms. Benin continues to be hurt by Nigerian trade protection that bans imports of a growing list of products from Benin and elsewhere, which has resulted in increased smuggling and criminality in the border region.
GDP: purchasing power parity - $8.676 billion (2005 est.)
GDP (official exchange rate): $4.433 billion (2005 est.)
GDP - real growth rate: 4.2% (2005 est.)
GDP - per capita: purchasing power parity - $1,200 (2005 est.)
GDP - composition by sector:
agriculture: 33.9%
industry: 13.6%
services: 52.5% (2004 est.)
Labor force: NA (1996)
Unemployment rate: NA
Population below poverty line: 33% (2001 est.)
Household income or consumption by percentage share:
lowest 10%: NA
highest 10%: NA
Inflation rate (consumer prices): 3.2% (2005 est.)
Investment (gross fixed): 20.1% of GDP (2005 est.)
Budget:
revenues: $766.8 million
expenditures: $1.017 billion, including capital expenditures of NA (2005 est.)
Agriculture - products: cotton, corn, cassava (tapioca), yams, beans, palm oil, peanuts, livestock (2001)
Industries: textiles, food processing, construction materials, cement (2001)
Industrial production growth rate: 8.3% (2001 est.)
Electricity - production: 69 million kWh (2003)
Electricity - production by source:
fossil fuel: 14.2%
hydro: 85.8%
nuclear: 0%
other: 0% (2001)
Electricity - consumption: 538.2 million kWh (2003)
Electricity - exports: 0 kWh (2003)
Electricity - imports: 474 million kWh (2003)
Oil - production: 400 bbl/day (2003)
Oil - consumption: 12,000 bbl/day (2003 est.)
Oil - exports: NA (2001)
Oil - imports: NA (2001)
Oil - proved reserves: 4.105 million bbl (1 January 2002)
Natural gas - proved reserves: 608.8 million cu m (1 January 2002)
Current account balance: $-155.1 million (2005 est.)
Exports: $826.9 million f.o.b. (2005 est.)
Exports - partners: China 29.5%, India 18.8%, Ghana 6.4%, Niger 6%, Indonesia 4.3%, Nigeria 4.3% (2004)
Imports: $1.043 billion f.o.b. (2005 est.)
Imports - partners: China 32.2%, France 13%, Thailand 6.7%, Cote d"Ivoire 5.3% (2004)
Reserves of foreign exchange and gold: $523.7 million (2005 est.)
Debt - external: $1.6 billion (2000)
Economic aid - recipient: $342.6 million (2000)
Currency: Communaute Financiere Africaine franc (XOF); note - responsible authority is the Central Bank of the West African States
Currency code: XOF
Exchange rates: Communaute Financiere Africaine francs (XOF) per US dollar - 480.56 (2005), 528.29 (2004), 581.2 (2003), 696.99 (2002), 733.04 (2001)
Fiscal year: calendar year

COMMUNICATIONS

Telephones - main lines in use: 66,500 (2003)
Telephones - mobile cellular: 236,200 (2003)
Telephone system:
general assessment: NA
domestic: fair system of open-wire, microwave radio relay, and cellular connections
international: country code - 229; satellite earth station - 7 (Intelsat-Atlantic Ocean); fiber optic submarine cable (SAT-3/WASC) provides connectivity to Europe and Asia (2005)
Radio broadcast stations: AM 2, FM 9, shortwave 4 (2000)
Radios: 660,000 (2000)
Television broadcast stations: 1 (2001)
Televisions: 66,000 (2000)
Internet country code: .bj
Internet hosts: 879 (2004)
Internet Service Providers (ISPs): 4 (2002)
Internet users: 70,000 (2003)

TRANSPORTATION

Airports: 5 (2004 est.)
Airports - with paved runways:
total: 1
1,524 to 2,437 m: 1 (2005 est.)
Airports - with unpaved runways:
total: 4
2,438 to 3,047 m: 1
1,524 to 2,437 m: 1
914 to 1,523 m: 2 (2005 est.)
Railways:
total: 578 km
narrow gauge: 578 km 1.000-m gauge (2004)
Roadways:
total: 6,787 km
paved: 1,357 km
unpaved: 5,430 km (1999)
Waterways: 150 km (on River Niger along northern border) (2004)
Ports and terminals: Cotonou

MILITARY

Military branches: Army, Navy, Air Force
Military service age and obligation: 21 years of age for compulsory and voluntary military service; in practice, volunteers may be taken at the age of 18; both sexes are eligible for military service; conscript tour of duty - 18 months (2004)
Manpower available for military service:
males age 21-49: 1,207,071
females age 21-49: 1,216,180 (2005 est.)
Manpower fit for military service:
males age 21-49: 670,170
females age 21-49: 630,078 (2005 est.)
Manpower reaching military service age annually:
males: 72,841
females: 71,428 (2005 est.)
Military expenditures - dollar figure: $96.5 million (2004)
Military expenditures - percent of GDP: 2.4% (2004)

TRANSNATIONAL ISSUES

Disputes - international: two villages remain in dispute along the border with Burkina Faso; accuses Burkina Faso of moving boundary pillars; much of Benin-Niger boundary, including tripoint with Nigeria, remains undemarcated, and the states expect a ruling in 2005 from the ICJ over the disputed Niger and Mekrou River islands; a joint task force was established in 2004 that resolved disputes over and redrew the maritime and the 870-km land boundary with Nigeria, including the sovereignty over seven villages along the Okpara River; a joint boundary commission continues to resurvey the boundary with Togo to verify Benin's claim that Togo moved boundary stones

Illicit drugs: transshipment point for narcotics associated with Nigerian trafficking organizations and most commonly destined for Western Europe and the US; vulnerable to money laundering due to a poorly regulated financial infrastructure

BERMUDA

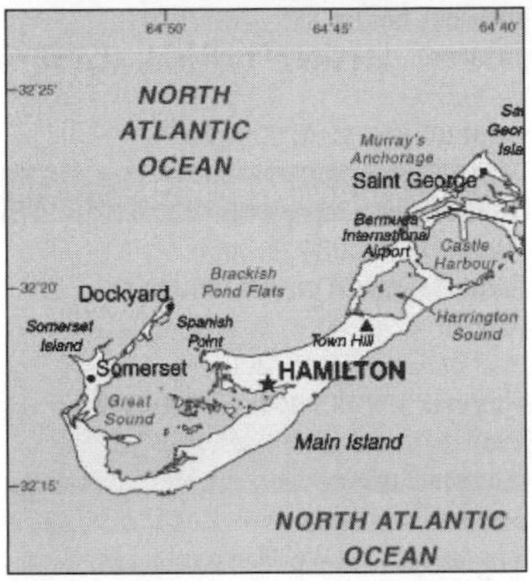

INTRODUCTION

Background: Bermuda was first settled in 1609 by shipwrecked English colonists headed for Virginia. Tourism to the island to escape North American winters first developed in Victorian times. Tourism continues to be important to the island's economy, although international business has overtaken it in recent years. Bermuda has developed into a highly successful offshore financial center. A referendum on independence was soundly defeated in 1995.

GEOGRAPHY

Location: North America, group of islands in the North Atlantic Ocean, east of South Carolina (US)
Geographic coordinates: 32 20 N, 64 45 W
Map references: North America
Area:
total: 53.3 sq km
land: 53.3 sq km
water: 0 sq km
Area - comparative: about one-third the size of Washington, DC
Land boundaries: 0 km
Coastline: 103 km
Maritime claims:
territorial sea: 12 nm
exclusive fishing zone: 200 nm
Climate: subtropical; mild, humid; gales, strong winds common in winter
Terrain: low hills separated by fertile depressions
Elevation extremes:
lowest point: Atlantic Ocean 0 m
highest point: Town Hill 76 m
Natural resources: limestone, pleasant climate fostering tourism
Land use:
arable land: 20%
permanent crops: 0%
other: 80% (55% developed, 45% rural/open space) (2001)
Irrigated land: NA
Natural hazards: hurricanes (June to November)
Environment - current issues: asbestos disposal; water pollution; preservation of open space; sustainable development
Geography - note: consists of about 138 coral islands and islets with ample rainfall, but no rivers or freshwater lakes; some land was leased by US Government from 1941 to 1995

PEOPLE

Population: 65,365 (July 2005 est.)
Age structure:
0-14 years: 18.9% (male 6,177/female 6,154)
15-64 years: 69.2% (male 22,422/female 22,828)
65 years and over: 11.9% (male 3,378/female 4,406) (2005 est.)
Median age:
total: 39.76 years
male: 38.78 years
female: 40.58 years (2005 est.)
Population growth rate: 0.64% (2005 est.)
Birth rate: 11.6 births/1,000 population (2005 est.)
Death rate: 7.63 deaths/1,000 population (2005 est.)
Net migration rate: 2.45 migrant(s)/1,000 population (2005 est.)
Sex ratio:
at birth: 1.02 male(s)/female
under 15 years: 1 male(s)/female
15-64 years: 0.98 male(s)/female
65 years and over: 0.77 male(s)/female
total population: 0.96 male(s)/female (2005 est.)
Infant mortality rate:
total: 8.53 deaths/1,000 live births
male: 10.14 deaths/1,000 live births
female: 6.9 deaths/1,000 live births (2005 est.)
Life expectancy at birth:
total population: 77.79 years
male: 75.7 years
female: 79.91 years (2005 est.)
Total fertility rate: 1.89 children born/woman (2005 est.)
HIV/AIDS - adult prevalence rate: NA
HIV/AIDS - people living with HIV/AIDS: NA
HIV/AIDS - deaths: NA
Nationality:
noun: Bermudian(s)
adjective: Bermudian
Ethnic groups: black 54.8%, white 34.1%, mixed 6.4%, other races 4.3%, unspecified 0.4% (2000 census)
Religions: Anglican 23%, Roman Catholic 15%, African Methodist Episcopal 11%, other Protestant 18%, other 12%, unaffiliated 6%, unspecified 1%, none 14% (2000 census)
Languages: English (official), Portuguese
Literacy:
definition: age 15 and over can read and write
total population: 98%
male: 98%
female: 99% (1970 est.)

GOVERNMENT

Country name:
conventional long form: none
conventional short form: Bermuda
former: Somers Islands
Dependency status: overseas territory of the UK
Government type: parliamentary British overseas territory with internal self-government
Capital: Hamilton
Administrative divisions: 9 parishes and 2 municipalities*; Devonshire, Hamilton, Hamilton*, Paget, Pembroke, Saint George*, Saint George's, Sandys, Smith's, Southampton, Warwick
Independence: none (overseas territory of the UK)
National holiday: Bermuda Day, 24 May
Constitution: 8 June 1968; amended 1989 and 2003
Legal system: English law
Suffrage: 18 years of age; universal
Executive branch:
chief of state: Queen ELIZABETH II (since 6 February 1952), represented by Governor Sir John VEREKER (since 11 April 2002)

head of government: Premier William Alexander SCOTT (since 24 July 2003); Deputy Premier Ewart BROWN
cabinet: Cabinet nominated by the premier, appointed by the governor
elections: none; the monarch is hereditary; governor appointed by the monarch; following legislative elections, the leader of the majority party or the leader of the majority coalition is usually appointed premier by the governor
Legislative branch: bicameral Parliament consists of the Senate (an 11-member body appointed by the governor, the premier, and the opposition) and the House of Assembly (36 seats; members are elected by popular vote to serve up to five-year terms)
elections: last general election held 24 July 2003 (next to be held July 2008)
election results: percent of vote by party - PLP 51.7%, UBP 48%; seats by party - PLP 22, UBP 14
Judicial branch: Supreme Court; Court of Appeal; Magistrate Courts
Political parties and leaders: Progressive Labor Party or PLP [William Alexander SCOTT]; United Bermuda Party or UBP [Grant GIBBONS]
Political pressure groups and leaders: Bermuda Employer's Union [Eddie SAINTS]; Bermuda Industrial Union or BIU [Derrick BURGESS]; Bermuda Public Services Union or BPSU [Ed BALL]; Bermuda Union of Teachers [Michael CHARLES]
International organization participation: Caricom (associate), ICFTU, Interpol (subbureau), IOC, UPU, WCO
Diplomatic representation in the US: none (overseas territory of the UK)
Diplomatic representation from the US:
chief of mission: Deputy Chief of Mission Antoinette BOECKER
consulate(s) general: Crown Hill, 16 Middle Road, Devonshire DVO3
mailing address: P. O. Box HM325, Hamilton HMBX; American Consulate General Hamilton, Department of State, 5300 Hamilton Place, Washington, DC 20520-5300
telephone: [1] (441) 295-1342
FAX: [1] (441) 295-1592, [1] (441) 296-9233
Flag description: red, with the flag of the UK in the upper hoist-side quadrant and the Bermudian coat of arms (white and green shield with a red lion holding a scrolled shield showing the sinking of the ship Sea Venture off Bermuda in 1609) centered on the outer half of the flag

ECONOMY

Economy - overview: Bermuda enjoys one of the highest per capita incomes in the world, nearly equal to that of the US. Its economy is primarily based on providing financial services for international business and luxury facilities for tourists. The effects of 11 September 2001 have had both positive and negative ramifications for Bermuda. On the positive side, a number of new reinsurance companies have located on the island, contributing to the expansion of an already robust international business sector. On the negative side, Bermuda's tourism industry - which derives over 80% of its visitors from the US - was severely hit as American tourists chose not to travel. Tourism rebounded in 2002-05. Most capital equipment and food must be imported. Bermuda's industrial sector is small, although construction continues to be important; the average cost of a house in June 2003 had risen to $976,000. Agriculture is limited, only 20% of the land being arable.
GDP: purchasing power parity - $2.33 billion (2003 est.)
GDP (official exchange rate): NA
GDP - real growth rate: 2% (2003 est.)
GDP - per capita: purchasing power parity - $36,000 (2003 est.)
GDP - composition by sector:
agriculture: 1%
industry: 10%
services: 89% (2002 est.)
Labor force: 37,470 (2000)
Labor force - by occupation: agriculture and fishing 3%, laborers 17%, clerical 22%, professional and technical 17%, administrative and managerial 13%, sales 8%, services 20% (2000 est.)
Unemployment rate: 5% (2002 est.)
Population below poverty line: 19% (2000)
Household income or consumption by percentage share:
lowest 10%: NA
highest 10%: NA
Inflation rate (consumer prices): 3.3% (mid-2003 est.)
Budget:
revenues: $671.1 million
expenditures: $594.6 million, including capital expenditures of $55 million (FY03/04)
Agriculture - products: bananas, vegetables, citrus, flowers; dairy products
Industries: tourism, international business, light manufacturing
Industrial production growth rate: NA%
Electricity - production: 624 million kWh (2003)
Electricity - production by source:
fossil fuel: 100%
hydro: 0%
nuclear: 0%
other: 0% (2001)
Electricity - consumption: 580.3 million kWh (2003)
Electricity - exports: 0 kWh (2003)
Electricity - imports: 0 kWh (2003)
Oil - production: 0 bbl/day (2003)
Oil - consumption: 4,000 bbl/day (2003 est.)
Oil - exports: NA (2001)
Oil - imports: NA (2001)
Exports: $1.469 billion (2004 est.)
Exports - partners: France 73.2%, UK 6.2%, Spain 2.4% (2004)
Imports: $8.078 billion (2004 est.)
Imports - partners: Kazakhstan 39.2%, France 16.2%, Japan 13.1%, Italy 9.2%, South Korea 8.8%, US 6.4% (2004)
Debt - external: $160 million (FY99/00)
Economic aid - recipient: NA
Currency: Bermudian dollar (BMD)
Currency code: BMD
Exchange rates: Bermudian dollar per US dollar - 1.0000 (fixed rate pegged to the US dollar)
Fiscal year: 1 April - 31 March

COMMUNICATIONS

Telephones - main lines in use: 56,000 (2002)
Telephones - mobile cellular: 37,873 (2003)
Telephone system:
general assessment: good
domestic: fully automatic digital telephone system; fiber optic trunk lines
international: country code - 1-441; submarine cables - 3 (fiber optic); satellite earth stations - 3 (2005)
Radio broadcast stations: AM 5, FM 3, shortwave 0 (2004)
Radios: 82,000 (1997)
Television broadcast stations: 4 (2004)
Televisions: 66,000 (1997)
Internet country code: .bm
Internet hosts: 5,161 (2001)
Internet Service Providers (ISPs): 20 (2000)
Internet users: 34,500 (2003)

TRANSPORTATION

Airports: 1 (2004 est.)
Airports - with paved runways:
total: 1
2,438 to 3,047 m: 1 (2005 est.)
Roadways:
total: 447 km
paved: 447 km
note: public roads - 225 km; private roads - 222 km (2002)
Merchant marine:
total: 108 ships (1,000 GRT or over) 4,845,326 GRT/6,501,782 DWT
by type: bulk carrier 22, cargo 6, container 22, liquefied gas 13, passenger 13, passenger/cargo 6, petroleum tanker 8, refrigerated cargo 11, roll on/roll off 7
foreign-owned: 103 (Australia 2, Canada

20, Finland 2, Germany 1, Greece 1, Hong Kong 5, Indonesia 1, Nigeria 8, Norway 5, Sweden 9, Switzerland 2, United Kingdom 27, United States 20)
registered in other countries: 1 (2005)
Ports and terminals: Hamilton, Saint George

MILITARY

Military branches: Bermuda Regiment
Military expenditures - dollar figure: $4.03 million (2001)
Military expenditures - percent of GDP: 0.11% (FY00/01)
Military - note: defense is the responsibility of the UK

TRANSNATIONAL ISSUES

Disputes - international: none

BHUTAN

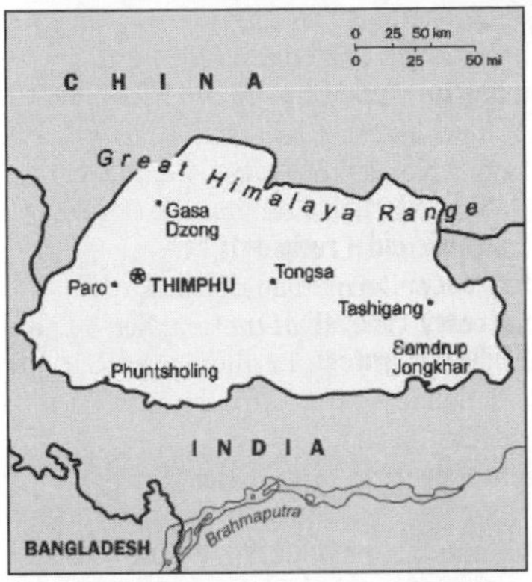

INTRODUCTION

Background: In 1865, Britain and Bhutan signed the Treaty of Sinchulu, under which Bhutan would receive an annual subsidy in exchange for ceding some border land. Under British influence, a monarchy was set up in 1907; three years later, a treaty was signed whereby the British agreed not to interfere in Bhutanese internal affairs and Bhutan allowed Britain to direct its foreign affairs. This role was assumed by independent India after 1947. Two years later, a formal Indo-Bhutanese accord returned the areas of Bhutan annexed by the British, formalized the annual subsidies the country received, and defined India's responsibilities in defense and foreign relations. A refugee issue of some 100,000 Bhutanese in Nepal remains unresolved; 90% of the refugees are housed in seven United Nations Office of the High Commissioner for Refugees (UNHCR) camps. In March 2005, King WANGCHUCK unveiled the government's draft constitution - which would introduce major democratic reforms - and pledged to hold a national referendum for its approval. A referendum date has yet to be named.

GEOGRAPHY

Location: Southern Asia, between China and India
Geographic coordinates: 27 30 N, 90 30 E
Map references: Asia
Area:
total: 47,000 sq km
land: 47,000 sq km
water: 0 sq km
Area - comparative: about half the size of Indiana
Land boundaries:
total: 1,075 km
border countries: China 470 km, India 605 km
Coastline: 0 km (landlocked)
Maritime claims: none (landlocked)
Climate: varies; tropical in southern plains; cool winters and hot summers in central valleys; severe winters and cool summers in Himalayas
Terrain: mostly mountainous with some fertile valleys and savanna
Elevation extremes:
lowest point: Drangme Chhu 97 m
highest point: Kula Kangri 7,553 m
Natural resources: timber, hydropower, gypsum, calcium carbonate
Land use:
arable land: 3.09%
permanent crops: 0.43%
other: 96.48% (2001)
Irrigated land: 400 sq km (1998 est.)
Natural hazards: violent storms from the Himalayas are the source of the country's name which translates as Land of the Thunder Dragon; frequent landslides during the rainy season
Environment - current issues: soil erosion; limited access to potable water
Environment - international agreements:
party to: Biodiversity, Climate Change, Climate Change-Kyoto Protocol, Endangered Species, Hazardous Wastes
signed, but not ratified: Law of the Sea
Geography - note: landlocked; strategic location between China and India; controls several key Himalayan mountain passes

PEOPLE

Population: 2,232,291
note: other estimates range as low as 810,000 (July 2005 est.)
Age structure:
0-14 years: 39.1% (male 452,213/female 420,675)
15-64 years: 56.9% (male 654,109/female 615,431)
65 years and over: 4% (male 45,281/female 44,582) (2005 est.)
Median age:
total: 20.27 years
male: 20.11 years
female: 20.44 years (2005 est.)
Population growth rate: 2.11% (2005 est.)
Birth rate: 34.03 births/1,000 population (2005 est.)
Death rate: 12.94 deaths/1,000 population (2005 est.)
Net migration rate: 0 migrant(s)/1,000 population (2005 est.)
Sex ratio:
at birth: 1.05 male(s)/female
under 15 years: 1.08 male(s)/female
15-64 years: 1.06 male(s)/female
65 years and over: 1.02 male(s)/female
total population: 1.07 male(s)/female (2005 est.)
Infant mortality rate:
total: 100.44 deaths/1,000 live births
male: 98.19 deaths/1,000 live births
female: 102.81 deaths/1,000 live births (2005 est.)
Life expectancy at birth:
total population: 54.39 years
male: 54.65 years
female: 54.11 years (2005 est.)
Total fertility rate: 4.81 children born/woman (2005 est.)
HIV/AIDS - adult prevalence rate: less than 0.1% (2001 est.)
HIV/AIDS - people living with HIV/AIDS: less than 100 (1999 est.)
HIV/AIDS - deaths: NA
Nationality:
noun: Bhutanese (singular and plural)
adjective: Bhutanese
Ethnic groups: Bhote 50%, ethnic Nepalese 35% (includes Lhotsampas - one of several Nepalese ethnic groups), indigenous or migrant tribes 15%
Religions: Lamaistic Buddhist 75%, Indian- and Nepalese-influenced Hinduism 25%
Languages: Dzongkha (official), Bhotes speak various Tibetan dialects, Nepalese speak various Nepalese dialects
Literacy:
definition: age 15 and over can read and write
total population: 42.2%
male: 56.2%
female: 28.1% (1995 est.)

GOVERNMENT

Country name:
conventional long form: Kingdom of Bhutan

conventional short form: Bhutan
Government type: monarchy; special treaty relationship with India
Capital: Thimphu
Administrative divisions: 18 districts (dzongkhag, singular and plural); Bumthang, Chhukha, Chirang, Dagana, Geylegphug, Ha, Lhuntshi, Mongar, Paro, Pemagatsel, Punakha, Samchi, Samdrup Jongkhar, Shemgang, Tashigang, Thimphu, Tongsa, Wangdi Phodrang
note: there may be two new districts named Gasa and Yangtse
Independence: 8 August 1949 (from India)
National holiday: National Day (Ugyen WANGCHUCK became first hereditary king), 17 December (1907)
Constitution: no written constitution or bill of rights; note - in 2001 the King commissioned the drafting of a constitution, and in March 2005 publicly unveiled it; now awaiting referendum
Legal system: based on Indian law and English common law; has not accepted compulsory ICJ jurisdiction
Suffrage: each family has one vote in village-level elections; note - in late 2003 Bhutan's legislature passed a new election law
Executive branch:
chief of state: King Jigme Singye WANGCHUCK (since 24 July 1972)
head of government: Chairman of the Council of Ministers Sangay NGEDUP (since 5 September 2005)
cabinet: Council of Ministers (Lhengye SHUNGTSOG) nominated by the monarch, approved by the National Assembly; members serve fixed, five-year terms; note - there is also a Royal Advisory Council (Lodoi Tsokde), members nominated by the monarch
elections: none; the monarch is hereditary, but democratic reforms in July 1998 grant the National Assembly authority to remove the monarch with two-thirds vote
Legislative branch: unicameral National Assembly or Tshogdu (150 seats; 105 elected from village constituencies, 10 represent religious bodies, and 35 are designated by the monarch to represent government and other secular interests; members serve three-year terms)
elections: local elections last held November 2002 (next to be held NA 2005)
election results: NA
Judicial branch: Supreme Court of Appeal (the monarch); High Court (judges appointed by the monarch)
Political parties and leaders: no legal parties
Political pressure groups and leaders: Buddhist clergy; ethnic Nepalese organizations leading militant antigovernment campaign; Indian merchant community; United Front for Democracy (exiled)
International organization participation: AsDB, CP, FAO, G-77, IBRD, ICAO, IDA, IFAD, IFC, IMF, Interpol, IOC, IOM (observer), ISO (correspondent), ITU, NAM, OPCW, SAARC, SACEP, UN, UNCTAD, UNESCO, UNIDO, UPU, WCO, WHO, WIPO, WMO, WToO, WTO (observer)
Diplomatic representation in the US: none; note - Bhutan has a Permanent Mission to the UN; address: 2 United Nations Plaza, 27th Floor, New York, NY 10017; telephone [1] (212) 826-1919; FAX [1] (212) 826-2998; the Bhutanese mission to the UN has consular jurisdiction in the US
consulate(s) general: New York
Diplomatic representation from the US: the US and Bhutan have no formal diplomatic relations, although informal contact is maintained between the Bhutanese and US Embassy in New Delhi (India)
Flag description: divided diagonally from the lower hoist side corner; the upper triangle is yellow and the lower triangle is orange; centered along the dividing line is a large black and white dragon facing away from the hoist side

ECONOMY

Economy - overview: The economy, one of the world's smallest and least developed, is based on agriculture and forestry, which provide the main livelihood for more than 90% of the population. Agriculture consists largely of subsistence farming and animal husbandry. Rugged mountains dominate the terrain and make the building of roads and other infrastructure difficult and expensive. The economy is closely aligned with India's through strong trade and monetary links and dependence on India's financial assistance. The industrial sector is technologically backward, with most production of the cottage industry type. Most development projects, such as road construction, rely on Indian migrant labor. Bhutan's hydropower potential and its attraction for tourists are key resources. Model education, social, and environment programs are underway with support from multilateral development organizations. Each economic program takes into account the government's desire to protect the country's environment and cultural traditions. For example, the government, in its cautious expansion of the tourist sector, encourages visits by upscale, environmentally conscientious tourists. Detailed controls and uncertain policies in areas like industrial licensing, trade, labor, and finance continue to hamper foreign investment.
GDP: purchasing power parity - $2.9 billion (2003 est.)
GDP (official exchange rate): NA
GDP - real growth rate: 5.3% (2003 est.)
GDP - per capita: purchasing power parity - $1,400 (2003 est.)
GDP - composition by sector:
agriculture: 45%
industry: 10%
services: 45% (2002 est.)
Labor force: NA
note: massive lack of skilled labor
Labor force - by occupation: agriculture 93%, industry and commerce 2%, services 5%
Unemployment rate: NA
Population below poverty line: NA
Household income or consumption by percentage share:
lowest 10%: NA
highest 10%: NA
Inflation rate (consumer prices): 3% (2002 est.)
Budget:
revenues: $146 million
expenditures: $152 million, including capital expenditures of NA
note: the government of India finances nearly three-fifths of Bhutan's budget expenditures (FY95/96 est.)
Agriculture - products: rice, corn, root crops, citrus, foodgrains; dairy products, eggs
Industries: cement, wood products, processed fruits, alcoholic beverages, calcium carbide
Industrial production growth rate: 9.3% (1996 est.)
Electricity - production: 1.882 billion kWh (2003)
Electricity - production by source:
fossil fuel: 0.1%
hydro: 99.9%
nuclear: 0%
other: 0% (2001)
Electricity - consumption: 250.3 million kWh (2003)
Electricity - exports: 1.51 billion kWh (2003)
Electricity - imports: 10 million kWh (2003)
Oil - production: 0 bbl/day (2003)
Oil - consumption: 1,100 bbl/day (2003 est.)
Oil - exports: NA (2001)
Oil - imports: NA (2001)
Exports: $154 million f.o.b. (2000 est.)
Exports - partners: India 85.6%, Bangladesh 6.7%, Japan 4.3% (2004)
Imports: $196 million c.i.f. (2000 est.)
Imports - partners: Germany 41.8%, India 35.5%, Japan 9.2%, Austria 4.3% (2004)
Debt - external: $245 million (2000)
Economic aid - recipient: substantial aid from India and other nations

Currency: ngultrum (BTN); Indian rupee (INR)
Currency code: BTN; INR
Exchange rates: ngultrum per US dollar - NA (2005), 45.317 (2004), 46.583 (2003), 48.61 (2002), 47.186 (2001)
Fiscal year: 1 July - 30 June

COMMUNICATIONS

Telephones - main lines in use: 25,200 (2003)
Telephones - mobile cellular: 22,000 (2005)
Telephone system:
general assessment: telecommunications facilities are poor
domestic: very low tele-density; domestic service is very poor especially in rural areas; wireless service available since 2003
international: country code - 975; international telephone and telegraph service via landline and microwave relay through India; satellite earth station - 1 (2005)
Radio broadcast stations: AM 0, FM 1, shortwave 1 (2004)
Radios: 37,000 (1997)
Television broadcast stations: 1 (2005)
Televisions: 11,000 (1997)
Internet country code: .bt
Internet hosts: 985 (2003)
Internet Service Providers (ISPs): NA
Internet users: 15,000 (2003)

TRANSPORTATION

Airports: 2 (2004 est.)
Airports - with paved runways:
total: 1
1,524 to 2,437 m: 1 (2005 est.)
Airports - with unpaved runways:
total: 1
914 to 1,523 m: 1 (2005 est.)
Roadways:
total: 8,050 km
paved: 4,991 km
unpaved: 3,059 km (2003)

MILITARY

Military branches: Royal Bhutan Army (includes Royal Bodyguard and Royal Bhutan Police) (2005)
Military service age and obligation: 18 years of age for voluntary military service; no conscription (2001)
Manpower available for military service: *males age 18-49:* 483,860 (2005 est.)
Manpower fit for military service: *males age 18-49:* 314,975 (2005 est.)
Manpower reaching military service age annually: *males:* 23,939 (2005 est.)
Military expenditures - dollar figure: $13.7 million (2004)
Military expenditures - percent of GDP: 1.8% (2004)

TRANSNATIONAL ISSUES

Disputes - international: approximately 104,000 Bhutanese refugees live in Nepal, 90% of whom reside in seven UN Office of the High Commissioner for Refugees camps; Bhutan cooperates with India to expel Indian separatists

BOLIVIA

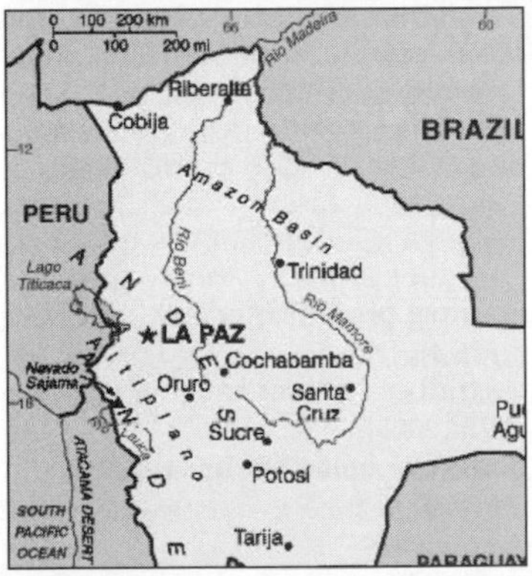

INTRODUCTION

Background: Bolivia, named after independence fighter Simon BOLIVAR, broke away from Spanish rule in 1825; much of its subsequent history has consisted of a series of nearly 200 coups and counter-coups. Comparatively democratic civilian rule was established in 1982, but leaders have faced difficult problems of deep-seated poverty, social unrest, and illegal drug production. In December 2005, Bolivians elected Movement Toward Socialism leader Evo MORALES president - by the widest margin of any leader since the restoration of civilian rule in 1982 - after he ran on a promise to change the country's traditional political class and empower the nation's poor majority.

GEOGRAPHY

Location: Central South America, southwest of Brazil
Geographic coordinates: 17 00 S, 65 00 W
Map references: South America
Area:
total: 1,098,580 sq km
land: 1,084,390 sq km
water: 14,190 sq km
Area - comparative: slightly less than three times the size of Montana
Land boundaries:
total: 6,743 km
border countries: Argentina 832 km, Brazil 3,400 km, Chile 861 km, Paraguay 750 km, Peru 900 km
Coastline: 0 km (landlocked)
Maritime claims: none (landlocked)
Climate: varies with altitude; humid and tropical to cold and semiarid
Terrain: rugged Andes Mountains with a highland plateau (Altiplano), hills, lowland plains of the Amazon Basin
Elevation extremes:
lowest point: Rio Paraguay 90 m
highest point: Nevado Sajama 6,542 m
Natural resources: tin, natural gas, petroleum, zinc, tungsten, antimony, silver, iron, lead, gold, timber, hydropower
Land use:
arable land: 2.67%
permanent crops: 0.19%
other: 97.14% (2001)
Irrigated land: 1,280 sq km (1998 est.)
Natural hazards: flooding in the northeast (March-April)
Environment - current issues: the clearing of land for agricultural purposes and the international demand for tropical timber are contributing to deforestation; soil erosion from overgrazing and poor cultivation methods (including slash-and-burn agriculture); desertification; loss of biodiversity; industrial pollution of water supplies used for drinking and irrigation
Environment - international agreements:
party to: Biodiversity, Climate Change, Climate Change-Kyoto Protocol, Desertification, Endangered Species, Hazardous Wastes, Law of the Sea, Marine Dumping, Ozone Layer Protection, Ship Pollution, Tropical Timber 83, Tropical Timber 94, Wetlands
signed, but not ratified: Environmental Modification, Marine Life Conservation, Ozone Layer Protection
Geography - note: landlocked; shares control of Lago Titicaca, world's highest navigable lake (elevation 3,805 m), with Peru

PEOPLE

Population: 8,857,870 (July 2005 est.)
Age structure:
0-14 years: 35.7% (male 1,613,049/female 1,551,023)
15-64 years: 59.8% (male 2,591,328/female 2,701,892)
65 years and over: 4.5% (male 178,486/female 222,092) (2005 est.)
Median age:
total: 21.47 years

male: 20.79 years
female: 22.17 years (2005 est.)
Population growth rate: 1.49% (2005 est.)
Birth rate: 23.76 births/1,000 population (2005 est.)
Death rate: 7.64 deaths/1,000 population (2005 est.)
Net migration rate: -1.27 migrant(s)/1,000 population (2005 est.)
Sex ratio:
at birth: 1.05 male(s)/female
under 15 years: 1.04 male(s)/female
15-64 years: 0.96 male(s)/female
65 years and over: 0.8 male(s)/female
total population: 0.98 male(s)/female (2005 est.)
Infant mortality rate:
total: 53.11 deaths/1,000 live births
male: 56.7 deaths/1,000 live births
female: 49.33 deaths/1,000 live births (2005 est.)
Life expectancy at birth:
total population: 65.5 years
male: 62.89 years
female: 68.25 years (2005 est.)
Total fertility rate: 2.94 children born/woman (2005 est.)
HIV/AIDS - adult prevalence rate: 0.1% (2003 est.)
HIV/AIDS - people living with HIV/AIDS: 4,900 (2003 est.)
HIV/AIDS - deaths: less than 500 (2003 est.)
Nationality:
noun: Bolivian(s)
adjective: Bolivian
Ethnic groups: Quechua 30%, mestizo (mixed white and Amerindian ancestry) 30%, Aymara 25%, white 15%
Religions: Roman Catholic 95%, Protestant (Evangelical Methodist) 5%
Languages: Spanish (official), Quechua (official), Aymara (official)
Literacy:
definition: age 15 and over can read and write
total population: 87.2%
male: 93.1%
female: 81.6% (2003 est.)

GOVERNMENT

Country name:
conventional long form: Republic of Bolivia
conventional short form: Bolivia
local long form: Republica de Bolivia
local short form: Bolivia
Government type: republic
Capital: La Paz (seat of government); Sucre (legal capital and seat of judiciary)
Administrative divisions: 9 departments (departamentos, singular - departamento); Chuquisaca, Cochabamba, Beni, La Paz, Oruro, Pando, Potosi, Santa Cruz, Tarija
Independence: 6 August 1825 (from Spain)
National holiday: Independence Day, 6 August (1825)
Constitution: 2 February 1967; revised in August 1994
Legal system: based on Spanish law and Napoleonic Code; has not accepted compulsory ICJ jurisdiction
Suffrage: 18 years of age, universal and compulsory (married); 21 years of age, universal and compulsory (single)
Executive branch:
chief of state: President Eduardo RODRIGUEZ Veltze (since 9 June 2005); Vice President (vacant); note - the president is both chief of state and head of government
head of government: President Eduardo RODRIGUEZ Veltze (since 9 June 2005); Vice President (vacant); note - the president is both chief of state and head of government
cabinet: Cabinet appointed by the president
elections: president and vice president elected on the same ticket by popular vote for five-year terms; election last held 18 December 2005 (next to be held NA 2010)
election results: Juan Evo MORALES Ayma elected president; percent of vote - Juan Evo MORALES Ayma 53.7%; Jorge Fernando QUIROGA Ramirez 28.6%; Samuel DORIA MEDINA Arana 7.8%; Michiaki NAGATANI Morishit 6.5%; Felipe QUISPE Huanca 2.2% Guildo ANGULA Cabrera 0.7%; Eliseo RODRIGUEZ 0.3%; Nestor GARCIA Rojas 0.3%; note - Juan Evo MORALES Ayma will assume the presidency on 22 January 2006
Legislative branch: bicameral National Congress or Congreso Nacional consists of Chamber of Senators or Camara de Senadores (27 seats; members are elected by proportional representation from party lists to serve five-year terms) and Chamber of Deputies or Camara de Diputados (130 seats; 69 are directly elected from their districts and 61 are elected by proportional representation from party lists to serve five-year terms)
elections: Chamber of Senators and Chamber of Deputies - last held 18 December 2005 (next to be held NA 2010)
election results: Chamber of Senators - percent of vote by party - NA%; seats by party - PODEMOS 13, MAS 12, UN 1, MNR 1; Chamber of Deputies - percent of vote by party - NA%; seats by party - MAS 73, PODEMOS 43, UN 8, MNR 6
Judicial branch: Supreme Court or Corte Suprema (judges appointed for 10-year terms by National Congress); District Courts (one in each department); provincial and local courts (to try minor cases)
Political parties and leaders: Bolivian Socialist Falange or FSB [Romel PANTOJA]; Civic Solidarity Union or UCS [Johnny FERNANDEZ]; Free Bolivia Movement or MBL [Franz BARRIOS]; Marshal of Ayacucho Institutional Vanguard or VIMA [Freddy ZABALA]; Movement of the Revolutionary Left or MIR [Jaime PAZ Zamora]; Movement Toward Socialism or MAS [Juan Evo MORALES Ayma]; Movement Without Fear or MSM [Juan DEL GRANADO]; Poder Democratico Nacional or PODEMOS [Jorge Fernando QUIROGA Ramirez]; New Republican Force or NFR [Manfred REYES-VILLA]; Pachakuti Indigenous Movement or MIP [Felipe QUISPE Huanca]; Poder Democratico Nacional or PODEMOS [Jorge Fernando QUIROGA Ramirez]; Socialist Party or PS [Jeres JUSTINIANO]
Political pressure groups and leaders: Cocalero groups; indigenous organizations; labor unions; Sole Confederation of Campesino Workers of Bolivia or CSUTCB [Roman LOAYZA]
International organization participation: CAN, CSN, FAO, G-77, IADB, IAEA, IBRD, ICAO, ICCt, ICRM, IDA, IFAD, IFC, IFRCS, ILO, IMF, IMO, Interpol, IOC, IOM, ISO (correspondent), ITU, LAES, LAIA, Mercosur (associate), MIGA, MINUSTAH, MONUC, NAM, OAS, ONUB, OPANAL, OPCW, PCA, RG, UN, UNCTAD, UNESCO, UNIDO, UNMIL, UNMISET, UNOCI, UPU, WCL, WCO, WFTU, WHO, WIPO, WMO, WToO, WTO
Diplomatic representation in the US:
chief of mission: Ambassador Jaime Aparicio OTERO
chancery: 3014 Massachusetts Avenue NW, Washington, DC 20008
telephone: [1] (202) 483-4410
FAX: [1] (202) 328-3712
consulate(s) general: Miami, New York, and San Francisco
Diplomatic representation from the US:
chief of mission: Ambassador David N. GREENLEE
embassy: Avenida Arce 2780, San Jorge, La Paz
mailing address: P. O. Box 425, La Paz; APO AA 34032
telephone: [591] (2) 216-8000
FAX: [591] (2) 216-8111
Flag description: three equal horizontal bands of red (top), yellow, and green with the coat of arms centered on the yellow band; similar to the flag of Ghana, which has a large black five-pointed star centered in the yellow band

ECONOMY

Economy - overview: Bolivia, long one of the poorest and least developed Latin American countries, reformed its economy after suffering a disastrous economic crisis in the early 1980s. The reforms spurred real GDP growth, which averaged 4 percent in the 1990s, and poverty rates fell. Economic growth, however, lagged again beginning in 1999 because of a global slowdown and homegrown factors such as political turmoil, civil unrest, and soaring fiscal deficits, all of which hurt investor confidence. In 2003, violent protests against the pro-foreign investment economic policies of President SANCHEZ DE LOZADA led to his resignation and the cancellation of plans to export Bolivia's newly discovered natural gas reserves to large northern hemisphere markets. Foreign investment dried up as companies adopted a wait-and-see attitude regarding new President Carlos MESA's willingness to protect investor rights in the face of increased demands by radical groups that the government expropriate foreign-owned assets. Real GDP growth in 2003-05 - helped by increased demand for natural gas in neighboring Brazil - was positive, but still below the levels seen during the 1990s. Bolivia remains dependent on foreign aid from multilateral lenders and foreign governments.
GDP: purchasing power parity - $23.59 billion (2005 est.)
GDP (official exchange rate): $10.06 billion (2005 est.)
GDP - real growth rate: 3% (2005 est.)
GDP - per capita: purchasing power parity - $2,700 (2005 est.)
GDP - composition by sector:
agriculture: 12.6%
industry: 35%
services: 52.4% (2005 est.)
Labor force: 4.22 million (2005 est.)
Labor force - by occupation: agriculture NA%, industry NA%, services NA%
Unemployment rate: 8% in urban areas
note: widespread underemployment (2005 est.)
Population below poverty line: 64% (2004 est.)
Household income or consumption by percentage share:
lowest 10%: 1.3%
highest 10%: 32% (1999)
Distribution of family income - Gini index: 44.7 (1999)
Inflation rate (consumer prices): 5.4% (2005 est.)
Investment (gross fixed): 12.5% of GDP (2005 est.)
Budget:
revenues: $2.931 billion
expenditures: $3.453 billion, including capital expenditures of $741 million (2005 est.)
Agriculture - products: soybeans, coffee, coca, cotton, corn, sugarcane, rice, potatoes; timber
Industries: mining, smelting, petroleum, food and beverages, tobacco, handicrafts, clothing
Industrial production growth rate: 5.7% (2004 est.)
Electricity - production: 4.25 billion kWh (2003)
Electricity - production by source:
fossil fuel: 44.4%
hydro: 54%
nuclear: 0%
other: 1.5% (2001)
Electricity - consumption: 3.963 billion kWh (2003)
Electricity - exports: 0 kWh (2003)
Electricity - imports: 10 million kWh (2003)
Oil - production: 42,000 bbl/day (2005 est.)
Oil - consumption: 48,000 bbl/day (2003 est.)
Oil - exports: NA (2001)
Oil - imports: NA (2001)
Oil - proved reserves: 458.8 million bbl (1 January 2002)
Natural gas - production: 8.44 billion cu m (2004 est.)
Natural gas - consumption: 1.15 billion cu m (2001 est.)
Natural gas - exports: 2.9 billion cu m (2001 est.)
Natural gas - imports: 0 cu m (2001 est.)
Natural gas - proved reserves: 727.2 billion cu m (1 January 2002)
Current account balance: $376 million (2005 est.)
Exports: $2.371 billion f.o.b. (2005 est.)
Exports - partners: Brazil 40%, US 13.9%, Colombia 8.7%, Peru 6.3%, Japan 4.5% (2004)
Imports: $1.845 billion f.o.b. (2005 est.)
Imports - partners: Brazil 29.7%, Argentina 17.6%, US 10.8%, Chile 7.7%, Peru 7.3% (2004)
Reserves of foreign exchange and gold: $1.342 billion (2005 est.)
Debt - external: $6.43 billion (2005 est.)
Economic aid - recipient: $681 million (2002)
Currency: boliviano (BOB)
Currency code: BOB
Exchange rates: bolivianos per US dollar - 8.11 (2005), 7.9363 (2004), 7.6592 (2003), 7.17 (2002), 6.6069 (2001)
Fiscal year: calendar year

COMMUNICATIONS

Telephones - main lines in use: 600,100 (2003)
Telephones - mobile cellular: 1,401,500 (2003)
Telephone system:
general assessment: new subscribers face bureaucratic difficulties; most telephones are concentrated in La Paz and other cities; mobile cellular telephone use expanding rapidly
domestic: primary trunk system, which is being expanded, employs digital microwave radio relay; some areas are served by fiber-optic cable; mobile cellular systems are being expanded
international: country code - 591; satellite earth station - 1 Intelsat (Atlantic Ocean)
Radio broadcast stations: AM 171, FM 73, shortwave 77 (1999)
Radios: 5.25 million (1997)
Television broadcast stations: 48 (1997)
Televisions: 900,000 (1997)
Internet country code: .bo
Internet hosts: 7,080 (2003)
Internet Service Providers (ISPs): 9 (2000)
Internet users: 270,000 (2002)

TRANSPORTATION

Airports: 1,065 (2004 est.)
Airports - with paved runways:
total: 16
over 3,047 m: 4
2,438 to 3,047 m: 4
1,524 to 2,437 m: 5
914 to 1,523 m: 3 (2005 est.)
Airports - with unpaved runways:
total: 1,051
over 3,047 m: 1
2,438 to 3,047 m: 3
1,524 to 2,437 m: 60
914 to 1,523 m: 207
under 914 m: 780 (2005 est.)
Pipelines: gas 4,860 km; liquid petroleum gas 47 km; oil 2,457 km; refined products 1,589 km; unknown (oil/water) 247 km (2004)
Railways:
total: 3,519 km
narrow gauge: 3,519 km 1.000-m gauge (2004)
Roadways:
total: 8,050 km
paved: 4,991 km
unpaved: 3,059 km (2003)
Waterways: 10,000 km (commercially navigable) (2004)
Merchant marine: *total:* 32 ships (1,000 GRT or over) 413,407 GRT/699,901 DWT
by type: bulk carrier 2, cargo 16, chemical tanker 1, container 1, passenger/cargo 2, petroleum tanker 9, refrigerated cargo 1
foreign-owned: 11 (Argentina 1, Egypt 2, Eritrea 1, Germany 1, Iran 1, Singapore 2, United Kingdom 1, United States 2) (2005)
Ports and terminals: Puerto Aguirre (on the Paraguay/Parana waterway, at the

Bolivia/Brazil border); also, Bolivia has free port privileges in maritime ports in Argentina, Brazil, Chile, and Paraguay

MILITARY

Military branches: Army (Ejercito Boliviano), Navy (Fuerza Naval; includes Marines), Air Force (Fuerza Aerea Boliviana) (2004)
Military service age and obligation: 18 years of age for voluntary military service; when annual number of volunteers falls short of goal, compulsory recruitment is effected, including conscription of boys as young as 14; one estimate holds that 40% of the armed forces are under the age of 18, with 50% of those under the age of 16; conscript tour of duty - 12 months (2002)
Manpower available for military service:
males age 18-49: 1,923,234 (2005 est.)
Manpower fit for military service: *males age 18-49:* 1,311,414 (2005 est.)
Manpower reaching military service age annually: *males:* 101,101 (2005 est.)
Military expenditures - dollar figure: $132.2 million (2004)
Military expenditures - percent of GDP: 1.6% (2004)

TRANSNATIONAL ISSUES

Disputes - international: Chile rebuffs Bolivia's reactivated claim to restore the Atacama corridor, ceded to Chile in 1884, offering instead unrestricted but not sovereign maritime access through Chile for Bolivian natural gas and other commodities
Illicit drugs: world's third-largest cultivator of coca (after Colombia and Peru) with an estimated 28,450 hectares under cultivation in June 2003, a 23% increase from June 2002; intermediate coca products and cocaine exported mostly to or through Brazil, Argentina, and Chile to European and US drug markets; eradication and alternative crop programs under the MESA administration have been unable to keep pace with farmers' attempts to increase cultivation; money-laundering activity related to narcotics trade, especially along the borders with Brazil and Paraguay

BOSNIA AND HERZEGOVINA

INTRODUCTION

Background: Bosnia and Herzegovina's declaration of sovereignty in October 1991, was followed by a declaration of independence from the former Yugoslavia on 3 March 1992 after a referendum boycotted by ethnic Serbs. The Bosnian Serbs - supported by neighboring Serbia and Montenegro - responded with armed resistance aimed at partitioning the republic along ethnic lines and joining Serb-held areas to form a "Greater Serbia." In March 1994, Bosniaks and Croats reduced the number of warring factions from three to two by signing an agreement creating a joint Bosniak/Croat Federation of Bosnia and Herzegovina. On 21 November 1995, in Dayton, Ohio, the warring parties initialed a peace agreement that brought to a halt three years of interethnic civil strife (the final agreement was signed in Paris on 14 December 1995). The Dayton Peace Accords retained Bosnia and Herzegovina's international boundaries and created a joint multi-ethnic and democratic government charged with conducting foreign, diplomatic, and fiscal policy. Also recognized was a second tier of government comprised of two entities roughly equal in size: the Bosniak/Croat Federation of Bosnia and Herzegovina and the Bosnian Serb-led Republika Srpska (RS). The Federation and RS governments were charged with overseeing most government functions. The Office of the High Representative (OHR) was established to oversee the implementation of the civilian aspects of the agreement. In 1995-96, a NATO-led international peacekeeping force (IFOR) of 60,000 troops served in Bosnia to implement and monitor the military aspects of the agreement. IFOR was succeeded by a smaller, NATO-led Stabilization Force (SFOR) whose mission was to deter renewed hostilities. European Union peacekeeping troops (EUFOR) replaced SFOR in December 2004; their mission is to maintain peace and stability throughout the country.

GEOGRAPHY

Location: Southeastern Europe, bordering the Adriatic Sea and Croatia
Geographic coordinates: 44 00 N, 18 00 E
Map references: Europe
Area:
total: 51,129 sq km
land: 51,129 sq km
water: 0 sq km
Area - comparative: slightly smaller than West Virginia
Land boundaries:
total: 1,459 km
border countries: Croatia 932 km, Serbia and Montenegro 527 km
Coastline: 20 km
Maritime claims: no data available
Climate: hot summers and cold winters; areas of high elevation have short, cool summers and long, severe winters; mild, rainy winters along coast
Terrain: mountains and valleys
Elevation extremes:
lowest point: Adriatic Sea 0 m
highest point: Maglic 2,386 m
Natural resources: coal, iron ore, bauxite, copper, lead, zinc, chromite, cobalt, manganese, nickel, clay, gypsum, salt, sand, forests, hydropower
Land use:
arable land: 13.6%
permanent crops: 2.96%
other: 83.44% (2001)
Irrigated land: 20 sq km (1998 est.)
Natural hazards: destructive earthquakes
Environment - current issues: air pollution from metallurgical plants; sites for disposing of urban waste are limited; water shortages and destruction of infrastructure because of the 1992-95 civil strife; deforestation
Environment - international agreements:
party to: Biodiversity, Climate Change, Climate Change-Kyoto Protocol, Desertification, *party to:* Air Pollution, Biodiversity, Climate Change, Hazardous Wastes, Law of the Sea, Marine Life Conservation, Ozone Layer Protection, Wetlands
signed, but not ratified: none of the selected agreements
Geography - note: within Bosnia and Herzegovina's recognized borders, the country is divided into a joint Bosniak/Croat Federation (about 51% of the territory) and the Bosnian Serb-led Republika Srpska or RS (about 49% of the territory); the region called Herzegovina is contiguous to Croatia and Serbia and Montenegro (Montenegro), and traditionally has been settled by an ethnic Croat majority in the west and an ethnic Serb majority in the east

PEOPLE

Population: 4,025,476 (July 2005 est.)
Age structure:
0-14 years: 18.3% (male 378,784/female 358,784)
15-64 years: 70.7% (male 1,458,405/female 1,388,793)
65 years and over: 10.9% (male 188,741/female 251,969) (2005 est.)
Median age:
total: 36.21 years
male: 35.81 years
female: 36.63 years (2005 est.)
Population growth rate: 0.44% (2005 est.)
Birth rate: 12.49 births/1,000 population (2005 est.)
Death rate: 8.44 deaths/1,000 population (2005 est.)
Net migration rate: 0.3 migrant(s)/1,000 population (2005 est.)
Sex ratio:
at birth: 1.07 male(s)/female
under 15 years: 1.06 male(s)/female
15-64 years: 1.05 male(s)/female
65 years and over: 0.75 male(s)/female
total population: 1.01 male(s)/female (2005 est.)
Infant mortality rate:
total: 21.05 deaths/1,000 live births
male: 23.62 deaths/1,000 live births
female: 18.31 deaths/1,000 live births (2005 est.)
Life expectancy at birth:
total population: 77.83 years
male: 74.21 years
female: 81.72 years (2005 est.)
Total fertility rate: 1.71 children born/woman (2005 est.)
HIV/AIDS - adult prevalence rate: less than 0.1% (2001 est.)
HIV/AIDS - people living with HIV/AIDS: 900 (2003 est.)
HIV/AIDS - deaths: 100 (2001 est.)
Nationality:
noun: Bosnian(s), Herzegovinian(s)
adjective: Bosnian, Herzegovinian
Ethnic groups: Serb 37.1%, Bosniak 48%, Croat 14.3%, other 0.6% (2000)
note: Bosniak has replaced Muslim as an ethnic term in part to avoid confusion with the religious term Muslim - an adherent of Islam
Religions: Muslim 40%, Orthodox 31%, Roman Catholic 15%, other 14%
Languages: Bosnian, Croatian, Serbian
Literacy:
definition: age 15 and over can read and write
total population: 94.6%
male: 98.4%
female: 91.1% (2000 est.)

GOVERNMENT

Country name:
conventional long form: none
conventional short form: Bosnia and Herzegovina
local long form: none
local short form: Bosna i Hercegovina
former: People's Republic of Bosnia and Herzegovina, Socialist Republic of Bosnia and Herzegovina
Government type: emerging federal democratic republic
Capital: Sarajevo
Administrative divisions: 2 first-order administrative divisions and 1 internationally supervised district* - Brcko district (Brcko Distrikt)*, the Bosniak/Croat Federation of Bosnia and Herzegovina (Federacija Bosna i Hercegovina) and the Bosnian Serb-led Republika Srpska; note - Brcko district is in northeastern Bosnia and is an administrative unit under the sovereignty of Bosnia and Herzegovina; the district remains under international supervision
Independence: 1 March 1992 (from Yugoslavia; referendum for independence was completed 1 March 1992; independence was declared 3 March 1992)
National holiday: National Day, 25 November (1943)
Constitution: the Dayton Agreement, signed 14 December 1995, included a new constitution now in force; note - each of the entities also has its own constitution
Legal system: based on civil law system
Suffrage: 18 years of age, universal
Executive branch:
chief of state: Chairman of the Presidency Ivo Miro JOVIC (since 28 June 2005; presidency member since 9 May 2005 - Croat; note - Dragan COVIC was sacked by High Representative Paddy ASHDOWN on 29 Mar 2005); other members of the three-member rotating (every eight months) presidency: Borislav PARAVEC (since 10 April 2003 - Serb); and Sulejman TIHIC (since 5 October 2002 - Bosniak)
head of government: Chairman of the Council of Ministers Adnan TERZIC (since 20 December 2002)
cabinet: Council of Ministers nominated by the council chairman; approved by the National House of Representatives
elections: the three members of the presidency (one Bosniak, one Croat, one Serb) are elected by popular vote for a four-year term; the member with the most votes becomes the chairman unless he or she was the incumbent chairman at the time of the election, but the chairmanship rotates every eight months; election last held 5 October 2002 (next to be held NA 2006); the chairman of the Council of Ministers is appointed by the presidency and confirmed by the National House of Representatives
election results: percent of vote - Mirko SAROVIC with 35.5% of the Serb vote was elected chairman of the collective presidency for the first eight months (note - SAROVIC resigned in April 2003); Dragan COVIC received 61.5% of the Croat vote; Sulejman TIHIC received 37% of the Bosniak vote
note: President of the Federation of Bosnia and Herzegovina: Niko LOZANCIC (since 27 January 2003); Vice Presidents Sahbaz DZIHANOVIC (since NA 2003) and Desnica RADIVOJEVIC (since NA 2003); President of the Republika Srpska: Dragan CAVIC (since 28 November 2002)
Legislative branch: bicameral Parliamentary Assembly or Skupstina consists of the national House of Representatives or Predstavnicki Dom (42 seats - elected by proportional representation, 28 seats allocated from the Federation of Bosnia and Herzegovina and 14 seats from the Republika Srpska; members elected by popular vote to serve four-year terms); and the House of Peoples or Dom Naroda (15 seats - 5 Bosniak, 5 Croat, 5 Serb; members elected by the Bosniak/Croat Federation's House of Representatives and the Republika Srpska's National Assembly to serve four-year terms); note - Bosnia's election law specifies four-year terms for the state and first-order administrative division entity legislatures
elections: national House of Representatives - elections last held 5 October 2002 (next to be held in NA 2006); House of Peoples - last constituted NA January 2003 (next to be constituted in 2007)
election results: national House of Representatives - percent of vote by party/coalition - SDA 21.9%, SDS 14.0%, SBiH 10.5%, SDP 10.4%, SNSD 9.8%, HDZ 9.5%, PDP 4.6%, others 19.3%; seats by party/coalition - SDA 10, SDS 5, SBiH 6, SDP 4, SNSD 3, HDZ 5, PDP 2, others 7; House of Peoples - percent of vote by party/coalition - NA%; seats by party/coalition - NA
note: the Bosniak/Croat Federation has a bicameral legislature that consists of a House of Representatives (98 seats; members elected by popular vote to serve four-year terms); elections last held 5 October 2002 (next to be held NA October 2006); percent of vote by party - NA%; seats by party/coalition - SDA 32, HDZ-BiH 16, SDP 15, SBiH 15, other 20; and a House of Peoples (60 seats - 30 Bosniak, 30 Croat); last constituted

December 2002; the Republika Srpska has a National Assembly (83 seats; members elected by popular vote to serve four-year terms); elections last held 5 October 2002 (next to be held in the fall of 2006); percent of vote by party - NA%; seats by party/coalition - SDS 26, SNSD 19, PDP 9, SDA 6, SRS 4, SPRS 3, DNZ 3, SBiH 4, SDP 3, others 6; as a result of the 2002 constitutional reform process, a 28-member Republika Srpska Council of Peoples (COP) was established in the Republika Srpska National Assembly including 8 Croats, 8 Bosniaks, 8 Serbs, and 4 members of the smaller communities

Judicial branch: BiH Constitutional Court (consists of nine members: four members are selected by the Bosniak/Croat Federation's House of Representatives, two members by the Republika Srpska's National Assembly, and three non-Bosnian members by the president of the European Court of Human Rights); BiH State Court (consists of nine judges and three divisions - Administrative, Appellate and Criminal - having jurisdiction over cases related to state-level law and appellate jurisdiction over cases initiated in the entities; note - a War Crimes Chamber opened in March 2005

note: the entities each have a Supreme Court; each entity also has a number of lower courts; there are 10 cantonal courts in the Federation, plus a number of municipal courts; the Republika Srpska has five municipal courts

Political parties and leaders: Alliance of Independent Social Democrats or SNSD [Milorad DODIK]; Bosnian Party or BOSS [Mirnes AJANOVIC]; Civic Democratic Party or GDS [Ibrahim SPAHIC]; Croat Christian Democratic Union of Bosnia and Herzegovina or HKDU [Marin TOPIC]; Croat Party of Rights or HSP [Zvonko JURISIC]; Croat Peasants Party or HSS [Marko TADIC]; Croatian Democratic Union of Bosnia and Herzegovina or HDZ-BH [Dragan COVIC]; Croatian Peoples Union [Milenko BRKIC]; Democratic National Union or DNZ [Rifet DOLIC]; Democratic Peoples Alliance [Marko PAVIC]; Liberal Democratic Party or LDS [Rasim KADIC]; New Croat Initiative or NHI [Kresimir ZUBAK]; Party for Bosnia and Herzegovina or SBiH [Safet HALILOVIC]; Party for Democratic Action or SDA [Sulejman TIHIC]; Party of Democratic Progress or PDP [Mladen IVANIC]; Serb Democratic Party or SDS [Dragan CAVIC]; Serb Radical Party of the Republika Srpska or SRS-RS [Milanko MIHAJLICA]; Serb Radical Party-Dr. Vojislav Seselj or SRS-VS [Radislav KANJERIC]; Social Democratic Party of BIH or SDP [Zlatko LAGUMDZIJA]; Social Democratic Union or SDU [Sejfudin TOKIC]; Socialist Party of Republika Srpska or SPRS [Petar DJOKIC]

Political pressure groups and leaders: NA

International organization participation: BIS, CE, CEI, EBRD, FAO, G-77, IAEA, IBRD, ICAO, ICCt, ICFTU, ICRM, IDA, IFAD, IFC, IFRCS, ILO, IMF, IMO, Interpol, IOC, IOM, ISO, ITU, MIGA, MONUC, NAM (guest), OAS (observer), OIC (observer), OPCW, OSCE, UN, UNCTAD, UNESCO, UNIDO, UNMEE, UPU, WHO, WIPO, WMO, WToO, WTO (observer)

Diplomatic representation in the US:
chief of mission: Ambassador Bisera TURKOVIC
chancery: 2109 E Street NW, Washington, DC 20037
telephone: [1] (202) 337-1500
FAX: [1] (202) 337-1502
consulate(s) general: Chicago, New York

Diplomatic representation from the US:
chief of mission: Ambassador Douglas L. McELHANEY
embassy: Alipasina 43, 71000 Sarajevo
mailing address: use street address
telephone: [387] (33) 445-700
FAX: [387] (33) 659-722
branch office(s): Banja Luka, Mostar

Flag description: a wide medium blue vertical band on the fly side with a yellow isosceles triangle abutting the band and the top of the flag; the remainder of the flag is medium blue with seven full five-pointed white stars and two half stars top and bottom along the hypotenuse of the triangle

ECONOMY

Economy - overview: Bosnia and Herzegovina ranked next to Macedonia as the poorest republic in the old Yugoslav federation. Although agriculture is almost all in private hands, farms are small and inefficient, and the republic traditionally is a net importer of food. Industry has been greatly overstaffed, one reflection of the socialist economic structure of Yugoslavia. TITO had pushed the development of military industries in the republic with the result that Bosnia was saddled with a host of industrial firms with little commercial potential. The interethnic warfare in Bosnia caused production to plummet by 80% from 1992 to 1995 and unemployment to soar. With an uneasy peace in place, output recovered in 1996-99 at high percentage rates from a low base; but output growth slowed in 2000-02. Part of the lag in output was made up in 2003-05. National-level statistics are limited and do not capture the large share of black market activity. The konvertibilna marka (convertible mark or BAM)- the national currency introduced in 1998 - is pegged to the euro, and confidence in the currency and the banking sector has increased. Implementation of privatization, however, has been slow, and local entities only reluctantly support national-level institutions. Banking reform accelerated in 2001 as all the Communist-era payments bureaus were shut down; foreign banks, primarily from Western Europe, now control most of the banking sector. A sizeable current account deficit and high unemployment rate remain the two most serious economic problems. The country receives substantial amounts of reconstruction assistance and humanitarian aid from the international community but will have to prepare for an era of declining assistance.

GDP: purchasing power parity - $28.26 billion
note: Bosnia has a large informal sector that could also be as much as 50 percent of official GDP. (2005 est.)

GDP (official exchange rate): $8.889 billion (2005 est.)

GDP - real growth rate: 5.2% (2005 est.)

GDP - per capita: purchasing power parity - $6,800 (2005 est.)

GDP - composition by sector:
agriculture: 14.2%
industry: 30.8%
services: 55% (2002)

Labor force: 1.026 million (2001)

Labor force - by occupation: agriculture NA, industry NA, services NA

Unemployment rate: 45.5% officially; however, grey economy may reduce actual unemployment to between 25 and 30% (31 December 2004 est.)

Population below poverty line: 25% (2004 est.)

Household income or consumption by percentage share:
lowest 10%: NA%
highest 10%: NA%

Inflation rate (consumer prices): 1.4% (2005 est.)

Budget:
revenues: $4.373 billion
expenditures: $4.401 billion, including capital expenditures of NA (2005 est.)

Agriculture - products: wheat, corn, fruits, vegetables; livestock

Industries: steel, coal, iron ore, lead, zinc, manganese, bauxite, vehicle assembly, textiles, tobacco products, wooden furniture, tank and aircraft assembly, domestic appliances, oil refining (2001)

Industrial production growth rate: 5.5% (2003 est.)

Electricity - production: 10.51 billion kWh (2003)
Electricity - production by source:
fossil fuel: 53.5%
hydro: 46.5%
nuclear: 0%
other: 0% (2001)
Electricity - consumption: 8.849 billion kWh (2003)
Electricity - exports: 3.2 billion kWh (2003)
Electricity - imports: 2.271 billion kWh (2003)
Oil - production: 0 bbl/day (2003)
Oil - consumption: 21,000 bbl/day (2003 est.)
Oil - exports: NA (2001)
Oil - imports: NA (2001)
Natural gas - production: 0 cu m (2001 est.)
Natural gas - consumption: 300 million cu m (2001 est.)
Natural gas - exports: 0 cu m (2001 est.)
Natural gas - imports: 300 million cu m (2001 est.)
Current account balance: $-2.375 billion (2005 est.)
Exports: $2.7 billion f.o.b. (2005 est.)
Exports - partners: Italy 22.3%, Croatia 21.1%, Germany 20.8%, Austria 7.4%, Slovenia 7.1%, Hungary 4.8% (2004)
Imports: $6.8 billion f.o.b. (2005 est.)
Imports - partners: Croatia 23.8%, Slovenia 15.8%, Germany 14.8%, Italy 11.4%, Austria 6.6%, Hungary 6.1% (2004)
Reserves of foreign exchange and gold: $3 billion (2005 est.)
Debt - external: $3.1 billion (2005 est.)
Economic aid - recipient: $650 million (2001 est.)
Currency: marka (BAM)
Currency code: BAM
Exchange rates: marka per US dollar - 1.43 (2005), 1.5752 (2004), 1.7329 (2003), 2.0782 (2002), 2.1857 (2001)
note: the marka is pegged to the euro
Fiscal year: calendar year

COMMUNICATIONS

Telephones - main lines in use: 938,000 (2003)
Telephones - mobile cellular: 1.05 million (2003)
Telephone system:
general assessment: telephone and telegraph network needs modernization and expansion; many urban areas are below average as contrasted with services in other former Yugoslav republics
domestic: NA
international: country code - 387; no satellite earth stations
Radio broadcast stations: AM 8, FM 16, shortwave 1 (1998)
Radios: 940,000 (1997)
Television broadcast stations: 33 (plus 277 repeaters) (September 1995)
Televisions: NA
Internet country code: .ba
Internet hosts: 6,994 (2004)
Internet Service Providers (ISPs): 3 (2000)
Internet users: 100,000 (2002)

TRANSPORTATION

Airports: 27 (2004 est.)
Airports - with paved runways:
total: 8
2,438 to 3,047 m: 4
1,524 to 2,437 m: 1
under 914 m: 3 (2005 est.)
Airports - with unpaved runways:
total: 19
1,524 to 2,437 m: 1
914 to 1,523 m: 7
under 914 m: 11 (2005 est.)
Heliports: 5 (2005 est.)
Railways:
total: 1,021 km (795 km electrified)
standard gauge: 1,021 km 1.435-m gauge (2004)
Roadways:
total: 21,846 km
paved: 11,425 km
unpaved: 10,421 km (1999)
Waterways: Sava River (northern border) open to shipping but use limited because of no agreement with neighboring countries (2004)
foreign-owned: 11 (Argentina 1, Egypt 2, Eritrea 1, Germany 1, Iran 1, Singapore 2, United Kingdom 1, United States 2) (2005)
Ports and terminals: Bosanska Gradiska, Bosanski Brod, Bosanski Samac, and Brcko (all inland waterway ports on the Sava), Orasje

MILITARY

Military branches: VF Army (the air and air defense forces are subordinate commands within the Army), VRS Army (the air and air defense forces are subordinate commands within the Army)
Military service age and obligation: 18 years of age for compulsory military service in the Federation of Bosnia and Herzegovina; 16 years of age in times of war; 18 years of age for Republika Srpska; 17 years of age for voluntary military service in the Federation and in the Republika Srpska; by law, military obligations cover all healthy men between the ages of 18 and 60, and all women between the ages of 18 and 55; service obligation is 4 months (July 2004)
Manpower available for military service: *males age 18-49:* 1,034,367 (2005 est.)
Manpower fit for military service: *males age 18-49:* 829,530 (2005 est.)
Manpower reaching military service age annually: *males:* 31,264 (2005 est.)
Military expenditures - dollar figure: $234.3 million (FY02)
Military expenditures - percent of GDP: 4.5% (FY02)

TRANSNATIONAL ISSUES

Disputes - international: Bosnia and Herzegovina and Serbia and Montenegro have delimited most of their boundary, but sections along the Drina River remain in dispute; discussions continue with Croatia on several small disputed sections of the boundary
Refugees and internally displaced persons: *IDPs:* 327,200 (Bosnian Croats, Serbs, and Muslims displaced in 1992-95 war) (2004)
Illicit drugs: minor transit point for marijuana and opiate trafficking routes to Western Europe; remains highly vulnerable to money-laundering activity given a primarily cash-based and unregulated economy, weak law enforcement and instances of corruption

BOTSWANA

INTRODUCTION

Background: Formerly the British protectorate of Bechuanaland, Botswana adopted its new name upon independence in 1966. Four decades of uninterrupted civilian leadership, progressive social policies, and significant capital investment have created one of the most dynamic economies in Africa. Mineral extraction, principally diamond mining, dominates economic activity, though tourism is a growing sector due to the country's conservation practices and extensive nature preserves. Botswana has one of the world's highest known rates of HIV/AIDS infection, but also one of Africa's most progressive and comprehensive programs for dealing with the disease.

GEOGRAPHY

Location: Southern Africa, north of South Africa
Geographic coordinates: 22 00 S, 24 00 E
Map references: Africa
Area:
total: 600,370 sq km
land: 585,370 sq km
water: 15,000 sq km

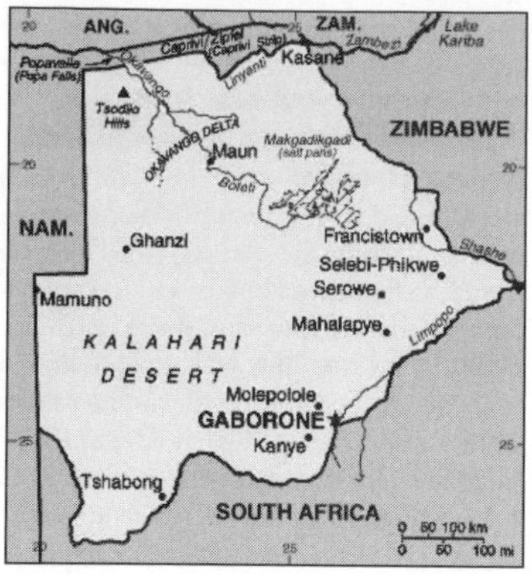

Area - comparative: slightly smaller than Texas
Land boundaries:
total: 4,013 km
border countries: Namibia 1,360 km, South Africa 1,840 km, Zimbabwe 813 km
Coastline: 0 km (landlocked)
Maritime claims: none (landlocked)
Climate: semiarid; warm winters and hot summers
Terrain: predominantly flat to gently rolling tableland; Kalahari Desert in southwest
Elevation extremes:
lowest point: junction of the Limpopo and Shashe Rivers 513 m
highest point: Tsodilo Hills 1,489 m
Natural resources: diamonds, copper, nickel, salt, soda ash, potash, coal, iron ore, silver
Land use:
arable land: 0.65%
permanent crops: 0.01%
other: 99.34% (2001)
Irrigated land: 10 sq km (1998 est.)
Natural hazards: periodic droughts; seasonal August winds blow from the west, carrying sand and dust across the country, which can obscure visibility
Environment - current issues: overgrazing; desertification; limited fresh water resources
Environment - international agreements:
party to: Biodiversity, Climate Change, Climate Change-Kyoto Protocol, Desertification, Endangered Species, Hazardous Wastes, Law of the Sea, Ozone Layer Protection, Wetlands
signed, but not ratified: none of the selected agreements
Geography - note: landlocked; population concentrated in eastern part of the country

PEOPLE

Population: 1,640,115
note: estimates for this country explicitly take into account the effects of excess mortality due to AIDS; this can result in lower life expectancy, higher infant mortality and death rates, lower population and growth rates, and changes in the distribution of population by age and sex than would otherwise be expected (July 2005 est.)
Age structure:
0-14 years: 38.8% (male 322,916/female 312,735)
15-64 years: 57.5% (male 455,183/female 487,236)
65 years and over: 3.8% (male 23,914/female 38,131) (2005 est.)
Median age:
total: 19.29 years
male: 18.64 years
female: 19.93 years (2005 est.)
Population growth rate: 0% (2005 est.)
Birth rate: 23.33 births/1,000 population (2005 est.)
Death rate: 29.36 deaths/1,000 population (2005 est.)
Net migration rate: 6.07 migrant(s)/1,000 population (2005 est.)
Sex ratio:
at birth: 1.03 male(s)/female
under 15 years: 1.03 male(s)/female
15-64 years: 0.93 male(s)/female
65 years and over: 0.63 male(s)/female
total population: 0.96 male(s)/female (2005 est.)
Infant mortality rate:
total: 54.58 deaths/1,000 live births
male: 55.97 deaths/1,000 live births
female: 53.14 deaths/1,000 live births (2005 est.)
Life expectancy at birth:
total population: 33.87 years
male: 33.89 years
female: 33.84 years (2005 est.)
Total fertility rate: 2.85 children born/woman (2005 est.)
HIV/AIDS - adult prevalence rate: 37.3% (2003 est.)
HIV/AIDS - people living with HIV/AIDS: 350,000 (2003 est.)
HIV/AIDS - deaths: 33,000 (2003 est.)
Major infectious diseases:
degree of risk: high
food or waterborne diseases: bacterial diarrhea, hepatitis A, and typhoid fever
vectorborne disease: malaria (2004)
Nationality:
noun: Motswana (singular), Batswana (plural)
adjective: Motswana (singular), Batswana (plural)
Ethnic groups: Tswana (or Setswana) 79%, Kalanga 11%, Basarwa 3%, other, including Kgalagadi and white 7%
Religions: Christian 71.6%, Badimo 6%, other 1.4%, unspecified 0.4%, none 20.6% (2001 census)
Languages: Setswana 78.2%, Kalanga 7.9%, Sekgalagadi 2.8%, English 2.1% (official), other 8.6%, unspecified 0.4% (2001 census)
Literacy:
definition: age 15 and over can read and write
total population: 79.8%
male: 76.9%
female: 82.4% (2003 est.)

GOVERNMENT

Country name:
conventional long form: Republic of Botswana
conventional short form: Botswana
former: Bechuanaland
Government type: parliamentary republic
Capital: Gaborone
Administrative divisions: 9 districts and 5 town councils*; Central, Francistown*, Gaborone*, Ghanzi, Jwaneng*, Kgalagadi, Kgatleng, Kweneng, Lobatse*, Northwest, Northeast, Selebi-Pikwe*, Southeast, Southern
Independence: 30 September 1966 (from UK)
National holiday: Independence Day (Botswana Day), 30 September (1966)
Constitution: March 1965, effective 30 September 1966
Legal system: based on Roman-Dutch law and local customary law; judicial review limited to matters of interpretation; has not accepted compulsory ICJ jurisdiction
Suffrage: 18 years of age; universal
Executive branch:
chief of state: President Festus G. MOGAE (since 1 April 1998) and Vice President Seretse Ian KHAMA (since 13 July 1998); note - the president is both the chief of state and head of government
head of government: President Festus G. MOGAE (since 1 April 1998) and Vice President Seretse Ian KHAMA (since 13 July 1998); note - the president is both the chief of state and head of government
cabinet: Cabinet appointed by the president
elections: president indirectly elected for a five-year term; election last held 20 October 2004 (next to be held NA 2009); vice president appointed by the president
election results: Festus G. MOGAE elected president; percent of National Assembly vote - 52%
Legislative branch: bicameral Parliament consists of the House of Chiefs (a largely advisory 15-member body consisting of the chiefs of the eight principal tribes, four elected subchiefs, and three members selected by the other 12 members) and the National Assembly (61 seats, 57 members are directly elected by popular vote and four are appointed by the majority party; members serve five-year terms)
elections: National Assembly elections last held 30 October 2004 (next to be held October 2009)

election results: percent of vote by party - BDP 52%, BNF 26%, BCP 17%, other 5%; seats by party - BDP 44, BNF 12, BCP 1
Judicial branch: High Court; Court of Appeal; Magistrates' Courts (one in each district)
Political parties and leaders: Botswana Democratic Party or BDP [Festus G. MOGAE]; Botswana National Front or BNF [Otswoletse MOUPO]; Botswana Congress Party or BCP [Otlaadisa KOOSALETSE]; Botswana Alliance Movement or BAM [Ephraim Lepetu SETSHWAELO]
note: a number of minor parties joined forces in 1999 to form the BAM but did not capture any parliamentary seats; the BAM parties are: the United Action Party [Ephraim Lepetu SETSHWAELO]; the Independence Freedom Party or IFP [Motsamai MPHO]; and the Botswana Progressive Union [D. K. KWELE]
Political pressure groups and leaders: NA
International organization participation: ACP, AfDB, AU, C, FAO, G-77, IAEA, IBRD, ICAO, ICCt, ICFTU, ICRM, IDA, IFAD, IFC, IFRCS, ILO, IMF, Interpol, IOC, ISO, ITU, MIGA, NAM, OPCW, SACU, SADC, UN, UNCTAD, UNESCO, UNIDO, UPU, WCO, WFTU, WHO, WIPO, WMO, WToO, WTO
Diplomatic representation in the US:
chief of mission: Ambassador Lapologang Caesar LEKOA
chancery: 1531-1533 New Hampshire Avenue NW, Washington, DC 20036
telephone: [1] (202) 244-4990
FAX: [1] (202) 244-4164
Diplomatic representation from the US:
chief of mission: Ambassador Joseph HUGGINS
embassy: address NA, Gaborone
mailing address: Embassy Enclave, P. O. Box 90, Gaborone
telephone: [267] 353982
FAX: [267] 312782
Flag description: light blue with a horizontal white-edged black stripe in the center

ECONOMY

Economy - overview: Botswana has maintained one of the world's highest economic growth rates since independence in 1966. Through fiscal discipline and sound management, Botswana has transformed itself from one of the poorest countries in the world to a middle-income country with a per capita GDP of $10,100 in 2005. Two major investment services rank Botswana as the best credit risk in Africa. Diamond mining has fueled much of the expansion and currently accounts for more than one-third of GDP and for 70-80% of export earnings. Tourism, financial services, subsistence farming, and cattle raising are other key sectors. On the downside, the government must deal with high rates of unemployment and poverty. Unemployment officially is 23.8%, but unofficial estimates place it closer to 40%. HIV/AIDS infection rates are the second highest in the world and threaten Botswana's impressive economic gains. An expected leveling off in diamond mining production overshadow long-term prospects.
GDP: purchasing power parity - $16.64 billion (2005 est.)
GDP (official exchange rate): $9.594 billion (2005 est.)
GDP - real growth rate: 4.5% (2005 est.)
GDP - per capita: purchasing power parity - $10,100 (2005 est.)
GDP - composition by sector:
agriculture: 2.4%
industry: 46.9% (including 36% mining)
services: 50.7% (2003 est.)
Labor force: 288,400 formal sector employees (2004)
Labor force - by occupation: NA
Unemployment rate: 23.8% (2004)
Population below poverty line: 47% (2003)
Household income or consumption by percentage share:
lowest 10%: NA
highest 10%: NA
Inflation rate (consumer prices): 8.3% (2005 est.)
Investment (gross fixed): 23.6% of GDP (2005 est.)
Budget:
revenues: $3.766 billion
expenditures: $3.767 billion, including capital expenditures of NA (2005 est.)
Public debt: 7.3% of GDP (2005 est.)
Agriculture - products: livestock, sorghum, maize, millet, beans, sunflowers, groundnuts
Industries: diamonds, copper, nickel, salt, soda ash, potash; livestock processing; textiles
Industrial production growth rate: 3.4% (2005 est.)
Electricity - production: 891 million kWh (2004)
Electricity - production by source:
fossil fuel: 100%
hydro: 0%
nuclear: 0%
other: 0% (2001)
Electricity - consumption: 2.641 billion kWh (2004)
Electricity - exports: 0 kWh (2002)
Electricity - imports: 1.39 billion kWh (2002)
Oil - production: 0 bbl/day (2003)
Oil - consumption: 12,000 bbl/day (2003 est.)
Oil - exports: NA (2001)
Oil - imports: 16,000 bbl/day NA (2001)
Current account balance: $562 million (2005 est.)
Exports: $3.68 billion f.o.b. (2005 est.)
Exports - partners: European Free Trade Association (EFTA) 87%, Southern African Customs Union (SACU) 7%, Zimbabwe 4% (2004)
Imports: $3.37 billion f.o.b. (2005 est.)
Imports - partners: Southern African Customs Union (SACU) 74%, EFTA 17%, Zimbabwe 4% (2004)
Reserves of foreign exchange and gold: $6.12 billion (2005 est.)
Debt - external: $556 million (2005 est.)
Economic aid - recipient: $73 million (1995)
Currency: pula (BWP)
Currency code: BWP
Exchange rates: pulas per US dollar - 5.16 (2005), 4.6929 (2004), 4.9499 (2003), 6.3278 (2002), 5.8412 (2001)
Fiscal year: 1 April - 31 March

COMMUNICATIONS

Telephones - main lines in use: 142,400 (2002)
Telephones - mobile cellular: 435,000 (2002)
Telephone system:
general assessment: the system is expanding with the growth of mobile cellular service and participation in regional development
domestic: small system of open-wire lines, microwave radio relay links, and a few radiotelephone communication stations; mobile cellular service is growing fast
international: country code - 267; two international exchanges; digital microwave radio relay links to Namibia, Zambia, Zimbabwe, and South Africa; satellite earth station - 1 Intelsat (Indian Ocean)
Radio broadcast stations: AM 8, FM 13, shortwave 4 (2001)
Radios: 252,720 (2000)
Television broadcast stations: 1 (2001)
Televisions: 31,000 (1997)
Internet country code: .bw
Internet hosts: 1,920 (2003)
Internet Service Providers (ISPs): 11 (2001)
Internet users: 60,000 (2002)

TRANSPORTATION

Airports: 85 (2004 est.)
Airports - with paved runways:
total: 10
2,438 to 3,047 m: 2
1,524 to 2,437 m: 7
914 to 1,523 m: 1 (2005 est.)
Airports - with unpaved runways:
total: 75
1,524 to 2,437 m: 3
914 to 1,523 m: 55
under 914 m: 17 (2005 est.)
Railways:
total: 888 km

narrow gauge: 888 km 1.067-m gauge (2004)
Roadways:
total: 25,233 km
paved: 8,867 km
unpaved: 16,366 km (2003)

MILITARY

Military branches: Botswana Defense Force (includes an Air Wing)
Military service age and obligation: 18 is the apparent age of voluntary military service; the official qualifications for determining minimum age are unknown (2001)
Manpower available for military service: *males age 18-49:* 350,649 (2005 est.)
Manpower fit for military service: *males age 18-49:* 136,322 (2005 est.)
Manpower reaching military service age annually: *males:* 21,103 (2005 est.)
Military expenditures - dollar figure: $338.5 million (2004)
Military expenditures - percent of GDP: 3.9% (2004)

TRANSNATIONAL ISSUES

Disputes - international: commission established with Namibia has yet to resolve small residual disputes along the Caprivi Strip, including the Situngu marshlands along the Linyanti River; downstream Botswana residents protest Namibia's planned construction of the Okavango hydroelectric dam at Popavalle (Popa Falls); Botswana has built electric fences to stem the thousands of Zimbabweans who flee to find work and escape political persecution; Namibia has long supported and in 2004 Zimbabwe dropped objections to plans between Botswana and Zambia to build a bridge over the Zambezi River, thereby de facto recognizing their short, but not clearly delimited Botswana-Zambia boundary

BOUVET ISLAND

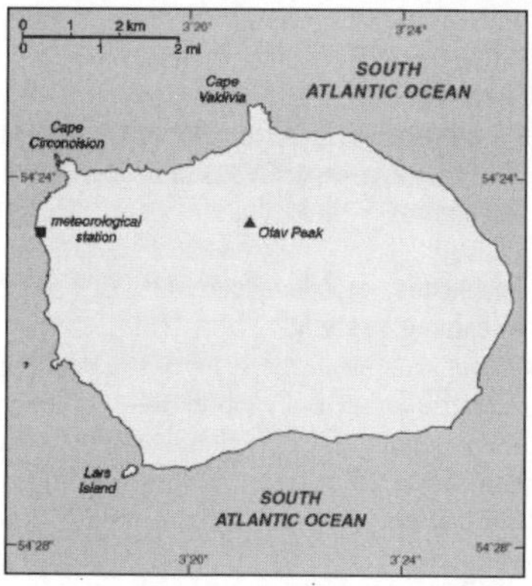

INTRODUCTION

Background: This uninhabited volcanic island is almost entirely covered by glaciers and is difficult to approach. It was discovered in 1739 by a French naval officer after whom the island was named. No claim was made until 1825, when the British flag was raised. In 1928, the UK waived its claim in favor of Norway, which had occupied the island the previous year. In 1971, Bouvet Island and the adjacent territorial waters were designated a nature reserve. Since 1977, Norway has run an automated meteorological station on the island.

GEOGRAPHY

Location: island in the South Atlantic Ocean, southwest of the Cape of Good Hope (South Africa)
Geographic coordinates: 54 26 S, 3 24 E
Map references: Antarctic Region
Area:
total: 58.5 sq km
land: 58.5 sq km
water: 0 sq km
Area - comparative: about 0.3 times the size of Washington, DC
Land boundaries: 0 km
Coastline: 29.6 km
Maritime claims:
territorial sea: 4 nm
Climate: antarctic
Terrain: volcanic; coast is mostly inaccessible
Elevation extremes:
lowest point: South Atlantic Ocean 0 m
highest point: Olav Peak 935 m
Natural resources: none
Land use:
arable land: 0%
permanent crops: 0%
other: 100% (93% ice) (2001)
Irrigated land: 0 sq km (1998 est.)
Natural hazards: NA
Environment - current issues: NA
Geography - note: covered by glacial ice; declared a nature reserve

PEOPLE

Population: uninhabited (July 2005 est.)

GOVERNMENT

Country name:
conventional long form: none
conventional short form: Bouvet Island
Dependency Status: territory of Norway; administered by the Polar Department of the Ministry of Justice and Police from Oslo
Legal system: the laws of Norway, where applicable, apply
Flag description: the flag of Norway is used

ECONOMY

Economy - overview: no economic activity; declared a nature reserve

COMMUNICATIONS

Internet country code: .bv
Communications – note: automatic meteorological station

TRANSPORTATION

Ports and terminals: none; offshore anchorage only

MILITARY

Military – note: defense is the responsibility of Norway

TRANSNATIONAL ISSUES

Disputes - international: none

BRAZIL

INTRODUCTION

Background: Following three centuries under the rule of Portugal, Brazil became an independent nation in 1822. By far the largest and most populous country in South America, Brazil overcame more than half a century of military intervention in the governance of the country when in 1985 the military regime peacefully ceded power to civilian rulers. Brazil continues to pursue industrial and agricultural growth and development of its interior. Exploiting vast natural resources and a large labor pool, it is today South America's leading economic power and a regional leader. Highly unequal income distribution remains a pressing problem.

GEOGRAPHY

Location: Eastern South America, bordering the Atlantic Ocean
Geographic coordinates: 10 00 S, 55 00 W
Map references: South America
Area:
total: 8,511,965 sq km
land: 8,456,510 sq km
water: 55,455 sq km
note: includes Arquipelago de Fernando de Noronha, Atol das Rocas, Ilha da Trindade, Ilhas Martin Vaz, and Penedos de Sao Pedro e Sao Paulo
Area - comparative: slightly smaller than the US
Land boundaries:
total: 14,691 km
border countries: Argentina 1,224 km, Bolivia 3,400 km, Colombia 1,643 km, French Guiana 673 km, Guyana 1,119 km, Paraguay 1,290 km, Peru 1,560 km, Suriname 597 km, Uruguay 985 km, Venezuela 2,200 km
Coastline: 7,491 km
Maritime claims:
territorial sea: 12 nm
contiguous zone: 24 nm
exclusive economic zone: 200 nm
continental shelf: 200 nm or to edge of the continental margin
Climate: mostly tropical, but temperate in south
Terrain: mostly flat to rolling lowlands in north; some plains, hills, mountains, and narrow coastal belt
Elevation extremes:
lowest point: Atlantic Ocean 0 m
highest point: Pico da Neblina 3,014 m
Natural resources: bauxite, gold, iron ore, manganese, nickel, phosphates, platinum, tin, uranium, petroleum, hydropower, timber
Land use:
arable land: 6.96%
permanent crops: 0.9%
other: 92.15% (2001)
Irrigated land: 26,560 sq km (1998 est.)
Natural hazards: recurring droughts in northeast; floods and occasional frost in south
Environment - current issues: deforestation in Amazon Basin destroys the habitat and endangers a multitude of plant and animal species indigenous to the area; there is a lucrative illegal wildlife trade; air and water pollution in Rio de Janeiro, Sao Paulo, and several other large cities; land degradation and water pollution caused by improper mining activities; wetland degradation; severe oil spills
Environment - international agreements:
party to: Antarctic-Environmental Protocol, Antarctic-Marine Living Resources, Antarctic Seals, Antarctic Treaty, Biodiversity, Climate Change, Climate Change-Kyoto Protocol, Desertification, Endangered Species, Environmental Modification, Hazardous Wastes, Law of the Sea, Marine Dumping, Ozone Layer Protection, Ship Pollution, Tropical Timber 83, Tropical Timber 94, Wetlands, Whaling
signed, but not ratified: none of the selected agreements
Geography - note: largest country in South America; shares common boundaries with every South American country except Chile and Ecuador

PEOPLE

Population: 186,112,794
note: Brazil took a count in August 2000, which reported a population of 169,799,170; that figure was about 3.3% lower than projections by the US Census Bureau, and is close to the implied underenumeration of 4.6% for the 1991 census; estimates for this country explicitly take into account the effects of excess mortality due to AIDS; this can result in lower life expectancy, higher infant mortality and death rates, lower population and growth rates, and changes in the distribution of population by age and sex than would otherwise be expected (July 2005 est.)
Age structure:
0-14 years: 26.1% (male 24,789,495/female 23,842,715)
15-64 years: 67.9% (male 62,669,392/female 63,719,631)
65 years and over: 6% (male 4,549,552/female 6,542,009) (2005 est.)
Median age:
total: 27.81 years
male: 27.06 years
female: 28.57 years (2005 est.)
Population growth rate: 1.06% (2005 est.)
Birth rate: 16.83 births/1,000 population (2005 est.)
Death rate: 6.15 deaths/1,000 population (2005 est.)
Net migration rate: -0.03 migrant(s)/1,000 population (2005 est.)
Sex ratio:
at birth: 1.05 male(s)/female
under 15 years: 1.04 male(s)/female
15-64 years: 0.98 male(s)/female
65 years and over: 0.7 male(s)/female
total population: 0.98 male(s)/female (2005 est.)
Infant mortality rate:
total: 29.61 deaths/1,000 live births
male: 33.37 deaths/1,000 live births
female: 25.66 deaths/1,000 live births (2005 est.)
Life expectancy at birth:
total population: 71.69 years
male: 67.74 years
female: 75.85 years (2005 est.)
Total fertility rate: 1.93 children born/woman (2005 est.)
HIV/AIDS - adult prevalence rate: 0.7% (2003 est.)
HIV/AIDS - people living with HIV/AIDS: 660,000 (2003 est.)
HIV/AIDS - deaths: 15,000 (2003 est.)
Nationality:
noun: Brazilian(s)
adjective: Brazilian
Ethnic groups: white 53.7%, mulatto (mixed white and black) 38.5%, black 6.2%, other (includes Japanese, Arab, Amerindian) 0.9%, unspecified 0.7% (2000 census)
Religions: Roman Catholic (nominal) 73.6%, Protestant 15.4%, Spriritualist 1.3%, Bantu/voodoo 0.3%, other 1.8%, unspecified 0.2%, none 7.4% (2000 census)
Languages: Portuguese (official), Spanish, English, French
Literacy:
definition: age 15 and over can read and write
total population: 86.4%

male: 86.1%
female: 86.6% (2003 est.)

GOVERNMENT

Country name:
conventional long form: Federative Republic of Brazil
conventional short form: Brazil
local long form: Republica Federativa do Brasil
local short form: Brasil
Government type: federative republic
Capital: Brasilia
Administrative divisions: 26 states (estados, singular - estado) and 1 federal district* (distrito federal); Acre, Alagoas, Amapa, Amazonas, Bahia, Ceara, Distrito Federal*, Espirito Santo, Goias, Maranhao, Mato Grosso, Mato Grosso do Sul, Minas Gerais, Para, Paraiba, Parana, Pernambuco, Piaui, Rio de Janeiro, Rio Grande do Norte, Rio Grande do Sul, Rondonia, Roraima, Santa Catarina, Sao Paulo, Sergipe, Tocantins
Independence: 7 September 1822 (from Portugal)
National holiday: Independence Day, 7 September (1822)
Constitution: 5 October 1988
Legal system: based on Roman codes; has not accepted compulsory ICJ jurisdiction
Suffrage: voluntary between 16 and 18 years of age and over 70; compulsory over 18 and under 70 years of age; note - military conscripts do not vote
Executive branch:
chief of state: President Luiz Inacio LULA DA SILVA (since 1 January 2003); Vice President Jose ALENCAR (since 1 January 2003); note - the president is both the chief of state and head of government
head of government: President Luiz Inacio LULA DA SILVA (since 1 January 2003); Vice President Jose ALENCAR (since 1 January 2003); note - the president is both the chief of state and head of government
cabinet: Cabinet appointed by the president
elections: president and vice president elected on the same ticket by popular vote for four-year terms; election last held 6 October 2002 (next to be held 1 October 2006, with a runoff on 29 October 2006 if necessary); runoff election held 27 October 2002
election results: in runoff election 27 October 2002, Luiz Inacio LULA DA SILVA (PT) elected with 61.3% of the vote; Jose SERRA (PSDB) 38.7%
Legislative branch: bicameral National Congress or Congresso Nacional consists of the Federal Senate or Senado Federal (81 seats; three members from each state and federal district elected according to the principle of majority to serve eight-year terms; one-third elected after a four-year period, two-thirds elected after the next four-year period) and the Chamber of Deputies or Camara dos Deputados (513 seats; members are elected by proportional representation to serve four-year terms)
elections: Federal Senate - last held 6 October 2002 for two-thirds of the Senate (next to be held October 2006 for one-third of the Senate); Chamber of Deputies - last held 6 October 2002 (next to be held October 2006)
election results: Federal Senate - percent of vote by party - NA%; seats by party - PMBD 19, PFL 19, PT 14, PSDB 11, PDT 5, PSB 4, PL 3, PTB 3, PPS 1, PSD 1, PP 1; Chamber of Deputies - percent of vote by party - NA%; seats by party - PT 91, PFL 84, PMDB 74, PSDB 71, PP 49, PL 26, PTB 26, PSB 22, PDT 21, PPS 15, PCdoB 12, PRONA 6, PV 5, other 11; note - many congressmen have changed party affiliation since the most recent election
Judicial branch: Supreme Federal Tribunal (11 ministers are appointed for life by the president and confirmed by the Senate); Higher Tribunal of Justice; Regional Federal Tribunals (judges are appointed for life); note - though appointed "for life," judges, like all federal employees, have a mandatory retirement age of 70
Political parties and leaders: Brazilian Democratic Movement Party or PMDB [Federal Deputy Michel TEMER]; Brazilian Labor Party or PTB [Federal Deputy Roberto JEFFERSON]; Brazilian Social Democracy Party or PSDB [Senator Tasso JEREISSATI]; Brazilian Socialist Party or PSB [Federal Deputy Eduardo CAMPOS]; Communist Party of Brazil or PCdoB [Renato RABELO]; Democratic Labor Party or PDT [Carlos LUPI]; Democratic Socialist Party or PSD [Luis Marques MENDES]; Green Party or PV [Jose Luiz de Franca PENNA]; Liberal Front Party or PFL [Senator Jorge BORNHAUSEN]; Liberal Party or PL [Federal Deputy Valdemar Costa NETO]; National Order Reconstruction Party or PRONA [Federal Deputy Dr. Eneas CARNEIRO]; Partido Municipalista Renovador or PMR [Pastor Vitor Paulo ARAUJO DOS SANTOS]; Popular Socialist Party or PPS [Federal Deputy Roberto FREIRE]; Progressive Party or PP [Federal Deputy Pedro CORREA]; Social Christian Party or PSC [Vitor Jorge Abdala NOSSEIS]; Worker's Party or PT [Ricardo BERZOIN]
Political pressure groups and leaders: Landless Worker's Movement; labor unions and federations; large farmers' associations; religious groups including evangelical Christian churches and the Catholic Church
International organization participation: AfDB, BIS, CSN, FAO, G-15, G-24, G-77, IADB, IAEA, IBRD, ICAO, ICC, ICCt, ICFTU, ICRM, IDA, IFAD, IFC, IFRCS, IHO, ILO, IMF, IMO, Interpol, IOC, IOM, ISO, ITU, LAES, LAIA, Mercosur, MIGA, MINUSTAH, NAM (observer), NSG, OAS, OPANAL, OPCW, PCA, RG, UN, UN Security Council (temporary), UNCTAD, UNESCO, UNHCR, UNIDO, UNITAR, UNMIL, UNMIS, UNMOVIC, UNOCI, UPU, WCL, WCO, WFTU, WHO, WIPO, WMO, WToO, WTO
Diplomatic representation in the US:
chief of mission: Ambassador Roberto ABDENUR
chancery: 3006 Massachusetts Avenue NW, Washington, DC 20008
telephone: [1] (202) 238-2700
FAX: [1] (202) 238-2827
consulate(s) general: Boston, Chicago, Houston, Los Angeles, Miami, New York, and San Francisco
Diplomatic representation from the US:
chief of mission: Ambassador John DANILOVICH
embassy: Avenida das Nacoes, Quadra 801, Lote 3, Distrito Federal Cep 70403-900, Brasilia
mailing address: Unit 3500, APO AA 34030
telephone: [55] (61) 3312-7000
FAX: [55] (61) 3225-9136
consulate(s) general: Rio de Janeiro, Sao Paulo
consulate(s): Recife
Flag description: green with a large yellow diamond in the center bearing a blue celestial globe with 27 white five-pointed stars (one for each state and the Federal District) arranged in the same pattern as the night sky over Brazil; the globe has a white equatorial band with the motto ORDEM E PROGRESSO (Order and Progress)

ECONOMY

Economy - overview: Characterized by large and well-developed agricultural, mining, manufacturing, and service sectors, Brazil's economy outweighs that of all other South American countries and is expanding its presence in world markets. From 2001-03 real wages fell and Brazil's economy grew, on average, only 2.2% per year, as the country absorbed a series of

domestic and international economic shocks. That Brazil absorbed these shocks without financial collapse is a tribute to the resiliency of the Brazilian economy and the economic program put in place by former President CARDOSO and strengthened by President LULA DA SILVA. In 2004, Brazil enjoyed more robust growth that yielded increases in employment and real wages. The three pillars of the economic program are a floating exchange rate, an inflation-targeting regime, and tight fiscal policy, all reinforced by a series of IMF programs. The currency depreciated sharply in 2001 and 2002, which contributed to a dramatic current account adjustment; in 2003 to 2005, Brazil ran record trade surpluses and recorded its first current account surpluses since 1992. Productivity gains - particularly in agriculture - also contributed to the surge in exports, and Brazil in 2005 surpassed the previous year's record export level. While economic management has been good, there remain important economic vulnerabilities. The most significant are debt-related: the government's largely domestic debt increased steadily from 1994 to 2003 - straining government finances - before falling as a percentage of GDP in 2005, while Brazil's foreign debt (a mix of private and public debt) is large in relation to Brazil's small (but growing) export base. Another challenge is maintaining economic growth over a period of time to generate employment and make the government debt burden more manageable.
GDP: purchasing power parity - $1.58 trillion (2005 est.)
GDP (official exchange rate): $605.6 billion (2005 est.)
GDP - real growth rate: 2.6% (2005 est.)
GDP - per capita: purchasing power parity - $8,500 (2005 est.)
GDP - composition by sector:
agriculture: 10%
industry: 39.4%
services: 50.6% (2005 est.)
Labor force: 90.41 million (2005 est.)
Labor force - by occupation: agriculture 20%, industry 14%, services 66% (2003 est.)
Unemployment rate: 9.9% (2005 est.)
Population below poverty line: 22% (1998 est.)
Household income or consumption by percentage share:
lowest 10%: 0.7%
highest 10%: 48% (1998)
Distribution of family income - Gini index: 59.7 (2004)
Inflation rate (consumer prices): 6.8% (2005 est.)
Investment (gross fixed): 19.8% of GDP (2005 est.)
Budget:
revenues: $140.6 billion
expenditures: $172.4 billion, including capital expenditures of NA (2004)
Public debt: 50.2% of GDP (2005 est.)
Agriculture - products: coffee, soybeans, wheat, rice, corn, sugarcane, cocoa, citrus; beef
Industries: textiles, shoes, chemicals, cement, lumber, iron ore, tin, steel, aircraft, motor vehicles and parts, other machinery and equipment
Industrial production growth rate: 4.7% (2005 est.)
Electricity - production: 359.2 billion kWh (2003)
Electricity - production by source:
fossil fuel: 8.3%
hydro: 82.7%
nuclear: 4.4%
other: 4.6% (2001)
Electricity - consumption: 371.4 billion kWh (2003)
Electricity - exports: 6 million kWh (2003)
Electricity - imports: 37.4 billion kWh; note - supplied by Paraguay (2003)
Oil - production: 2.01 million bbl/day (2005 est.)
Oil - consumption: 2.1 million bbl/day (2001 est.)
Oil - exports: NA (2001)
Oil - imports: NA (2001)
Oil - proved reserves: 15.12 billion bbl (2005 est.)
Natural gas - production: 5.95 billion cu m (2001 est.)
Natural gas - consumption: 9.59 billion cu m (2001 est.)
Natural gas - exports: 0 cu m (2001 est.)
Natural gas - imports: 3.64 billion cu m (2001 est.)
Natural gas - proved reserves: 221.7 billion cu m (2005)
Current account balance: $10.42 billion (2005 est.)
Exports: $115.1 billion f.o.b. (2005 est.)
Exports - partners: US 20.8%, Argentina 7.5%, Netherlands 6.1%, China 5.6%, Germany 4.1%, Mexico 4% (2004)
Imports: $78.02 billion f.o.b. (2005 est.)
Imports - partners: US 18.3%, Argentina 8.9%, Germany 8.1%, China 5.9%, Nigeria 5.6%, Japan 4.6% (2004)
Reserves of foreign exchange and gold: $69.28 billion (2005 est.)
Debt - external: $211.4 billion (30 June 2005 est.)
Economic aid - recipient: $30 billion (2002)
Currency: real (BRL)
Currency code: BRL
Exchange rates: reals per US dollar - 2.49 (2005), 2.9251 (2004), 3.0771 (2003), 2.9208 (2002), 2.3577 (2001)
Fiscal year: calendar year

COMMUNICATIONS

Telephones - main lines in use: 38.81 million (2002)
Telephones - mobile cellular: 46,373,300 (2003)
Telephone system:
general assessment: good working system
domestic: extensive microwave radio relay system and a domestic satellite system with 64 earth stations
international: country code - 55; 3 coaxial submarine cables; satellite earth stations - 3 Intelsat (Atlantic Ocean), 1 Inmarsat (Atlantic Ocean region east), connected by microwave relay system to Mercosur Brazilsat B3 satellite earth station
Radio broadcast stations: AM 1,365, FM 296, shortwave 161 (of which 91 are collocated with AM stations) (1999)
Radios: 71 million (1997)
Television broadcast stations: 138 (1997)
Televisions: 36.5 million (1997)
Internet country code: .br
Internet hosts: 3,163,349 (2003)
Internet Service Providers (ISPs): 50 (2000)
Internet users: 14.3 million (2002)

TRANSPORTATION

Airports: 4,136 (2004 est.)
Airports - with paved runways:
total: 709
over 3,047 m: 8
2,438 to 3,047 m: 24
1,524 to 2,437 m: 162
914 to 1,523 m: 463
under 914 m: 52 (2005 est.)
Airports - with unpaved runways:
total: 3,514
over 3,047 m: 2
1,524 to 2,437 m: 79
914 to 1,523 m: 1,609
under 914 m: 1,824 (2005 est.)
Heliports: 417 (2005 est.)
Pipelines: condensate/gas 244 km; gas 10,739 km; liquid petroleum gas 341 km; oil 5,212 km; refined products 4,755 km (2004)
Railways:
total: 29,412 km (1,567 km electrified)
broad gauge: 4,907 km 1.600-m gauge (908 km electrified)
standard gauge: 194 km 1.440-m gauge
narrow gauge: 23,915 km 1.000-m gauge (581 km electrified)
dual gauge: 396 km 1.000-m and 1.600-m gauges (three rails) (78 km electrified) (2004)
Roadways:
total: 1,724,929 km
paved: 94,871 km
unpaved: 1,630,058 km (2000)
Waterways: 50,000 km (most in areas remote from industry and population) (2004)

Merchant marine:
total: 150 ships (1,000 GRT or over) 2,961,431 GRT/4,725,267 DWT
by type: bulk carrier 28, cargo 25, chemical tanker 7, combination ore/oil 2, container 7, liquefied gas 12, passenger/cargo 12, petroleum tanker 48, roll on/roll off 9
foreign-owned: 17 (Chile 2, Germany 7, Norway 1, Spain 7)
registered in other countries: 8 (2005)
Ports and terminals: Gebig, Itaqui, Rio de Janeiro, Rio Grande, San Sebasttiao, Santos, Sepetiba Terminal, Tubarao, Vitoria

MILITARY

Military branches: Brazilian Army, Brazilian Navy (includes Naval Air and Marines), Brazilian Air Force (FAB)
Military service age and obligation: 19 years of age for compulsory military service, conscript service obligation - 12 months; 17 years of age for voluntary service (2001)
Manpower available for military service: *males age 19-49:* 45,586,036 (2005 est.)
Manpower fit for military service: *males age 19-49:* 33,119,098 (2005 est.)
Manpower reaching military service age annually: *males:* 1,785,930 (2005 est.)
Military expenditures - dollar figure: $11 billion (2004)
Military expenditures - percent of GDP: 1.8% (2004)

TRANSNATIONAL ISSUES

Disputes - international: unruly region at convergence of Argentina-Brazil-Paraguay borders is locus of money laundering, smuggling, arms and illegal narcotics trafficking, and fundraising for extremist organizations; uncontested dispute with Uruguay over certain islands in the Quarai/Cuareim and Invernada boundary streams and the resulting tripoint with Argentina; in 2004 Brazil submitted its claims to UNCLOS to extend its maritime continental margin
Illicit drugs: illicit producer of cannabis; minor coca cultivation in the Amazon region, used for domestic consumption; government has a large-scale eradication program to control cannabis; important transshipment country for Bolivian, Colombian, and Peruvian cocaine headed for Europe and the US; also used by traffickers as a way station for narcotics air transshipments between Peru and Colombia; upsurge in drug-related violence and weapons smuggling; important market for Colombian, Bolivian, and Peruvian cocaine; illicit narcotics proceeds earned in Brazil are often laundered through the financial system; significant illicit financial activity in the Tri-Border Area

BRITISH INDIAN OCEAN TERRITORY

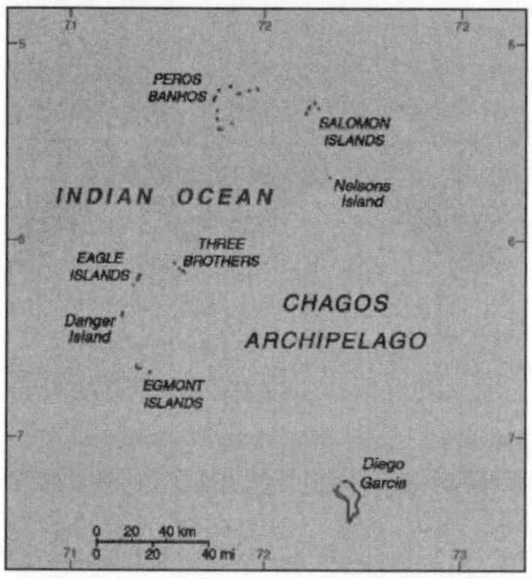

INTRODUCTION

Background: Established as a territory of the UK in 1965, a number of the British Indian Ocean Territory (BIOT) islands were transferred to the Seychelles when it attained independence in 1976. Subsequently, BIOT has consisted only of the six main island groups comprising the Chagos Archipelago. The largest and most southerly of the islands, Diego Garcia, contains a joint UK-US naval support facility. All of the remaining islands are uninhabited. Former agricultural workers, earlier residents in the islands, were relocated primarily to Mauritius but also to the Seychelles, between 1967 and 1973. In 2000, a British High Court ruling invalidated the local immigration order that had excluded them from the archipelago, but upheld the special military status of Diego Garcia.

GEOGRAPHY

Location: archipelago in the Indian Ocean, south of India, about one-half the way from Africa to Indonesia
Geographic coordinates: 6 00 S, 71 30 E
Map references: Political Map of the World
Area:
total: 60 sq km
land: 60 sq km
water: 0 sq km
note: includes the entire Chagos Archipelago
Area - comparative: about 0.3 times the size of Washington, DC
Land boundaries: 0 km
Coastline: 698 km
Maritime claims:
territorial sea: 3 nm
exclusive fishing zone: 200 nm
Climate: tropical marine; hot, humid, moderated by trade winds
Terrain: flat and low (most areas do not exceed four meters in elevation)
Elevation extremes:
lowest point: Indian Ocean 0 m
highest point: unnamed location on Diego Garcia 15 m
Natural resources: coconuts, fish, sugarcane
Land use:
arable land: 0%
permanent crops: 0%
other: 100% (2001)
Irrigated land: 0 sq km (1998 est.)
Natural hazards: NA
Environment - current issues: NA
Geography - note: archipelago of 2,300 islands; Diego Garcia, largest and southernmost island, occupies strategic location in central Indian Ocean; island is site of joint US-UK military facility

PEOPLE

Population: no indigenous inhabitants
note: approximately 1,200 former agricultural workers resident in the Chagos Archipelago, often referred to as Chagossians or Ilois, were relocated to Mauritius and the Seychelles in the 1960s and 1970s, in November 2000 they were granted the right of return by a British High Court ruling, though no timetable has been set; in 2001, there were approximately 1,500 UK and US military personnel and 2,000 civilian contractors living on the island of Diego Garcia (July 2005 est.)

GOVERNMENT

Country name:
conventional long form: British Indian Ocean Territory
conventional short form: none
abbreviation: BIOT
Dependency Status: overseas territory of the UK; administered by a commissioner, resident in the Foreign and Commonwealth Office in London
Legal system: the laws of the UK, where applicable, apply
Executive branch:
chief of state: Queen ELIZABETH II (since 6 February 1952)
head of government: Commissioner Tony CROMBIE (since January 2004); Administrator Tony HUMPHRIES

(since February 2005); note - both reside in the UK
cabinet: NA
elections: none; the monarch is hereditary; commissioner and administrator appointed by the monarch
Diplomatic representation in the US: none (overseas territory of the UK)
Diplomatic representation from the US: none (overseas territory of the UK)
Flag description: white with six blue wavy horizontal stripes; the flag of the UK is in the upper hoist-side quadrant; the striped section bears a palm tree and yellow crown centered on the outer half of the flag

ECONOMY

Economy - overview: All economic activity is concentrated on the largest island of Diego Garcia, where joint UK-US defense facilities are located. Construction projects and various services needed to support the military installations are done by military and contract employees from the UK, Mauritius, the Philippines, and the US. There are no industrial or agricultural activities on the islands. When the Ilois return, they plan to reestablish sugarcane production and fishing.
Electricity - production: NA kWh; note - electricity supplied by the US military
Electricity - consumption: NA kWh

COMMUNICATIONS

Telephones - main lines in use: NA
Telephone system:
general assessment: separate facilities for military and public needs are available
domestic: all commercial telephone services are available, including connection to the Internet
international: international telephone service is carried by satellite (2000)
Radio broadcast stations: AM 1, FM 2, shortwave 0 (1998)
Radios: NA
Television broadcast stations: 1 (1997)
Televisions: NA
Internet country code: .io
Internet Service Providers (ISPs): 1 (2000)

TRANSPORTATION

Airports: 1 (2004 est.)
Airports - with paved runways:
total: 1
over 3,047 m: 1 (2005 est.)
Ports and terminals: Diego Garcia

MILITARY

Military – note: defense is the responsibility of the UK; the US lease on Diego Garcia expires in 2016

TRANSNATIONAL ISSUES

Disputes - international: Mauritius and Seychelles claim the Chagos Archipelago and its former inhabitants, who reside chiefly in Mauritius, but in 2001 were granted UK citizenship and the right to repatriation since eviction in 1965; the UK resists the Chagossians' demand for an immediate return to the islands; repatriation is complicated by the exclusive US military lease of Diego Garcia that restricts access to the largest island in the chain

BRITISH VIRGIN ISLANDS

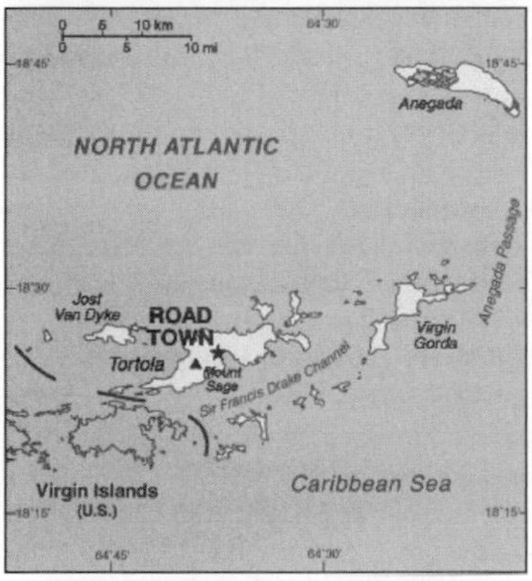

INTRODUCTION

Background: First settled by the Dutch in 1648, the islands were annexed in 1672 by the English. The economy is closely tied to the larger and more populous US Virgin Islands to the west; the US dollar is the legal currency.

GEOGRAPHY

Location: Caribbean, between the Caribbean Sea and the North Atlantic Ocean, east of Puerto Rico
Geographic coordinates: 18 30 N, 64 30 W
Map references: Central America and the Caribbean
Area:
total: 153 sq km
land: 153 sq km
water: 0 sq km
note: comprised of 16 inhabited and more than 20 uninhabited islands; includes the island of Anegada
Area - comparative: about 0.9 times the size of Washington, DC
Land boundaries: 0 km
Coastline: 80 km
Maritime claims:
territorial sea: 3 nm
exclusive fishing zone: 200 nm
Climate: subtropical; humid; temperatures moderated by trade winds
Terrain: coral islands relatively flat; volcanic islands steep, hilly
Elevation extremes:
lowest point: Caribbean Sea 0 m
highest point: Mount Sage 521 m
Natural resources: NEGL
Land use:
arable land: 20%
permanent crops: 6.67%
other: 73.33% (2001)
Irrigated land: NA
Natural hazards: hurricanes and tropical storms (July to October)
Environment - current issues: limited natural fresh water resources (except for a few seasonal streams and springs on Tortola, most of the islands' water supply comes from wells and rainwater catchments)
Geography - note: strong ties to nearby US Virgin Islands and Puerto Rico

PEOPLE

Population: 22,643 (July 2005 est.)
Age structure:
0-14 years: 21% (male 2,400/female 2,358)
15-64 years: 73.9% (male 8,607/female 8,115)
65 years and over: 5.1% (male 614/female 549) (2005 est.)
Median age:
total: 30.9 years
male: 31.1 years
female: 30.7 years (2005 est.)
Population growth rate: 2.06% (2005 est.)
Birth rate: 14.96 births/1,000 population (2005 est.)
Death rate: 4.42 deaths/1,000 population (2005 est.)
Net migration rate: 10.01 migrant(s)/1,000 population (2005 est.)
Sex ratio:
at birth: 1.02 male(s)/female
under 15 years: 1.02 male(s)/female
15-64 years: 1.06 male(s)/female
65 years and over: 1.12 male(s)/female
total population: 1.05 male(s)/female (2005 est.)
Infant mortality rate:
total: 18.05 deaths/1,000 live births
male: 21.02 deaths/1,000 live births
female: 14.95 deaths/1,000 live births (2005 est.)

Life expectancy at birth:
total population: 76.49 years
male: 75.41 years
female: 77.62 years (2005 est.)
Total fertility rate: 1.72 children born/woman (2005 est.)
HIV/AIDS - adult prevalence rate: NA
HIV/AIDS - people living with HIV/AIDS: NA
HIV/AIDS - deaths: NA
Nationality:
noun: British Virgin Islander(s)
adjective: British Virgin Islander
Ethnic groups: black 83%, white, Indian, Asian and mixed
Religions: Protestant 86% (Methodist 33%, Anglican 17%, Church of God 9%, Seventh-Day Adventist 6%, Baptist 4%, Jehovah's Witnesses 2%, other 15%), Roman Catholic 10%, none 2%, other 2% (1991)
Languages: English (official)
Literacy:
definition: age 15 and over can read and write
total population: 97.8% (1991 est.)
male: NA%
female: NA%

GOVERNMENT

Country name:
conventional long form: none
conventional short form: British Virgin Islands
abbreviation: BVI
Dependency status: overseas territory of the UK; internal self-governing
Government type: NA
Capital: Road Town
Administrative divisions: none (overseas territory of the UK)
Independence: none (overseas territory of the UK)
National holiday: Territory Day, 1 July
Constitution: 1 June 1977
Legal system: English law
Suffrage: 18 years of age, universal
Executive branch:
chief of state: Queen ELIZABETH II (since 6 February 1952), represented by Governor Tom MACAN (since 14 October 2002)
head of government: Chief Minister Orlando D. SMITH (since 17 June 2003)
cabinet: Executive Council appointed by the governor from members of the Legislative Council
elections: none; the monarch is hereditary; governor appointed by the monarch; following legislative elections, the leader of the majority party or the leader of the majority coalition is usually appointed chief minister by the governor
Legislative branch: unicameral Legislative Council (13 seats; members are elected by direct popular vote, one member from each of 9 electoral districts, four at-large members; members serve four-year terms)
elections: last held 16 May 2003 (next to be held NA 2007)
election results: percent of vote by party - NA%; seats by party - NDP 8, VIP 5
Judicial branch: Eastern Caribbean Supreme Court, consisting of the High Court of Justice and the Court of Appeal (one judge of the Supreme Court is a resident of the islands and presides over the High Court); Magistrate's Court; Juvenile Court; Court of Summary Jurisdiction
Political parties and leaders: Concerned Citizens Movement or CCM [Ethlyn SMITH]; National Democratic Party or NDP [Orlando SMITH]; United Party or UP [Gregory MADURO]; Virgin Islands Party or VIP [Ralph T. O'NEAL]
Political pressure groups and leaders: NA
International organization participation: Caricom (associate), CDB, Interpol (subbureau), IOC, OECS (associate), UNESCO (associate), UPU
Diplomatic representation in the US: none (overseas territory of the UK)
Diplomatic representation from the US: none (overseas territory of the UK)
Flag description: blue, with the flag of the UK in the upper hoist-side quadrant and the Virgin Islander coat of arms centered in the outer half of the flag; the coat of arms depicts a woman flanked on either side by a vertical column of six oil lamps above a scroll bearing the Latin word VIGILATE (Be Watchful)

ECONOMY

Economy - overview: The economy, one of the most stable and prosperous in the Caribbean, is highly dependent on tourism, generating an estimated 45% of the national income. An estimated 350,000 tourists, mainly from the US, visited the islands in 1998. Tourism suffered in 2002 because of the lackluster US economy. In the mid-1980s, the government began offering offshore registration to companies wishing to incorporate in the islands, and incorporation fees now generate substantial revenues. Roughly 400,000 companies were on the offshore registry by yearend 2000. The adoption of a comprehensive insurance law in late 1994, which provides a blanket of confidentiality with regulated statutory gateways for investigation of criminal offenses, is expected to make the British Virgin Islands even more attractive to international business. Livestock raising is the most important agricultural activity; poor soils limit the islands' ability to meet domestic food requirements. Because of traditionally close links with the US Virgin Islands, the British Virgin Islands has used the dollar as its currency since 1959.
GDP: purchasing power parity - $2.498 billion (2004 est.)
GDP (official exchange rate): NA
GDP - real growth rate: 1% NA (2002 est.)
GDP - per capita: purchasing power parity - $38,500 (2004 est.)
GDP - composition by sector:
agriculture: 1.8%
industry: 6.2%
services: 92% (1996 est.)
Labor force: 12,770 (2004)
Labor force - by occupation: agriculture NA%, industry NA%, services NA%
Unemployment rate: 3% (1995)
Population below poverty line: NA
Household income or consumption by percentage share:
lowest 10%: NA%
highest 10%: NA%
Inflation rate (consumer prices): 2.5% (2003)
Budget:
revenues: $121.5 million
expenditures: $115.5 million, including capital expenditures of NA (1997)
Agriculture - products: fruits, vegetables; livestock, poultry; fish
Industries: tourism, light industry, construction, rum, concrete block, offshore financial center
Industrial production growth rate: NA%
Electricity - production: 34.55 million kWh (2003)
Electricity - production by source:
fossil fuel: 100%
hydro: 0%
nuclear: 0%
other: 0% (2001)
Electricity - consumption: 32.13 million kWh (2003)
Electricity - exports: 0 kWh (2003)
Electricity - imports: 0 kWh (2003)
Oil - production: 0 bbl/day (2003)
Oil - consumption: 410 bbl/day (2003 est.)
Oil - exports: NA (2001)
Oil - imports: NA (2001)
Exports: $25.3 million (2002)
Exports - partners: Virgin Islands (US), Puerto Rico, US (2004)
Imports: $187 million (2002 est.)
Imports - partners: Virgin Islands (US), Puerto Rico, US (2004)
Debt - external: $36.1 million (1997)
Economic aid - recipient: NA
Currency: US dollar (USD)
Currency code: USD
Exchange rates: the US dollar is used

Fiscal year: 1 April - 31 March

COMMUNICATIONS

Telephones - main lines in use: 11,700 (2002)
Telephones - mobile cellular: 8,000 (2002)
Telephone system:
general assessment: worldwide telephone service
domestic: NA
international: country code - 1-284; submarine cable to Bermuda
Radio broadcast stations: AM 1, FM 5, shortwave 0 (2004)
Radios: 9,000 (1997)
Television broadcast stations: 1 (plus one cable company) (1997)
Televisions: 4,000 (1997)
Internet country code: .vg
Internet Service Providers (ISPs): 16 (2000)
Internet users: 4,000 (2002)

TRANSPORTATION

Airports: 3 (2004 est.)
Airports - with paved runways:
total: 2
914 to 1,523 m: 1
under 914 m: 1 (2005 est.)
Airports - with unpaved runways:
total: 1
914 to 1,523 m: 1 (2005 est.)
Roadways:
total: 177 km
paved: 177 km (2002)
Merchant marine:
total: 1 ships (1,000 GRT or over) 83,825 GRT/155,909 DWT
by type: cargo 1
registered in other countries: 7 (2005)
Ports and terminals: Road Town

MILITARY

Military - note: defense is the responsibility of the UK

TRANSNATIONAL ISSUES

Disputes - international: none
Illicit drugs: transshipment point for South American narcotics destined for the US and Europe; large offshore financial center makes it vulnerable to money laundering

BRUNEI

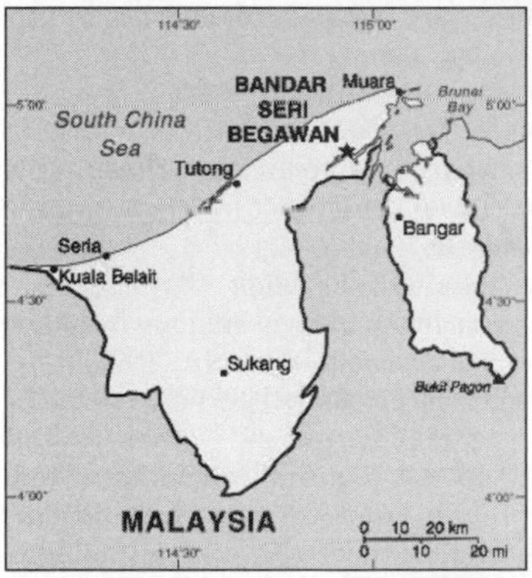

INTRODUCTION

Background: The Sultanate of Brunei's influence peaked between the 15th and 17th centuries when its control extended over coastal areas of northwest Borneo and the southern Philippines. Brunei subsequently entered a period of decline brought on by internal strife over royal succession, colonial expansion of European powers, and piracy. In 1888, Brunei became a British protectorate; independence was achieved in 1984. The same family has ruled Brunei for over six centuries. Brunei benefits from extensive petroleum and natural gas fields, the source of one of the highest per capita GDPs in the developing world.

GEOGRAPHY

Location: Southeastern Asia, bordering the South China Sea and Malaysia
Geographic coordinates: 4 30 N, 114 40 E
Map references: Southeast Asia
Area:
total: 5,770 sq km
land: 5,270 sq km
water: 500 sq km
Area - comparative: slightly smaller than Delaware
Land boundaries:
total: 381 km
border countries: Malaysia 381 km
Coastline: 161 km
Maritime claims:
territorial sea: 12 nm
exclusive economic zone: 200 nm or to median line
Climate: tropical; hot, humid, rainy
Terrain: flat coastal plain rises to mountains in east; hilly lowland in west
Elevation extremes:
lowest point: South China Sea 0 m
highest point: Bukit Pagon 1,850 m
Natural resources: petroleum, natural gas, timber
Land use:
arable land: 0.57%
permanent crops: 0.76%
other: 98.67% (2001)
Irrigated land: 10 sq km (1998 est.)
Natural hazards: typhoons, earthquakes, and severe flooding are rare
Environment - current issues: seasonal smoke/haze resulting from forest fires in Indonesia
Environment - international agreements:
party to: Endangered Species, Hazardous Wastes, Law of the Sea, Ozone Layer Protection, Ship Pollution
signed, but not ratified: none of the selected agreements
Geography - note: close to vital sea lanes through South China Sea linking Indian and Pacific Oceans; two parts physically separated by Malaysia; almost an enclave of Malaysia

PEOPLE

Population: 372,361 (July 2005 est.)
Age structure:
0-14 years: 28.6% (male 54,342/female 52,084)
15-64 years: 68.4% (male 134,908/female 119,814)
65 years and over: 3% (male 5,301/female 5,912) (2005 est.)
Median age:
total: 27.04 years
male: 27.63 years
female: 26.4 years (2005 est.)
Population growth rate: 1.9% (2005 est.)
Birth rate: 19.01 births/1,000 population (2005 est.)
Death rate: 3.42 deaths/1,000 population (2005 est.)
Net migration rate: 3.45 migrant(s)/1,000 population (2005 est.)
Sex ratio:
at birth: 1.06 male(s)/female
under 15 years: 1.04 male(s)/female
15-64 years: 1.13 male(s)/female
65 years and over: 0.9 male(s)/female
total population: 1.09 male(s)/female (2005 est.)
Infant mortality rate:
total: 12.61 deaths/1,000 live births
male: 15.93 deaths/1,000 live births
female: 9.1 deaths/1,000 live births (2005 est.)
Life expectancy at birth:
total population: 74.8 years
male: 72.36 years
female: 77.36 years (2005 est.)
Total fertility rate: 2.3 children born/woman (2005 est.)
HIV/AIDS - adult prevalence rate: less than 0.1% (2003 est.)
HIV/AIDS - people living with HIV/AIDS: less than 200 (2003 est.)
HIV/AIDS - deaths: less than 200 (2003 est.)
Nationality:
noun: Bruneian(s)
adjective: Bruneian

Ethnic groups: Malay 67%, Chinese 15%, indigenous 6%, other 12%
Religions: Muslim (official) 67%, Buddhist 13%, Christian 10%, indigenous beliefs and other 10%
Languages: Malay (official), English, Chinese
Literacy:
definition: age 15 and over can read and write
total population: 93.9%
male: 96.3%
female: 91.4% (2002)

GOVERNMENT

Country name:
conventional long form: Negara Brunei Darussalam
conventional short form: Brunei
Government type: constitutional sultanate
Capital: Bandar Seri Begawan
Administrative divisions: 4 districts (daerah-daerah, singular - daerah); Belait, Brunei and Muara, Temburong, Tutong
Independence: 1 January 1984 (from UK)
National holiday: National Day, 23 February (1984); note - 1 January 1984 was the date of independence from the UK, 23 February 1984 was the date of independence from British protection
Constitution: 29 September 1959 (some provisions suspended under a State of Emergency since December 1962, others since independence on 1 January 1984)
Legal system: based on English common law; for Muslims, Islamic Shari'a law supersedes civil law in a number of areas
Suffrage: none
Executive branch:
chief of state: Sultan and Prime Minister Sir HASSANAL Bolkiah (since 5 October 1967); note - the monarch is both the chief of state and head of government
head of government: Sultan and Prime Minister Sir HASSANL Bolkiah (since 5 October 1967); note - the monarch is both the chief of state and head of government
cabinet: Council of Cabinet Ministers appointed and presided over by the monarch; deals with executive matters; note - there is also a Religious Council (members appointed by the monarch) that advises on religious matters, a Privy Council (members appointed by the monarch) that deals with constitutional matters, and the Council of Succession (members appointed by the monarch) that determines the succession to the throne if the need arises
elections: none; the monarch is hereditary
Legislative branch: Legislative Council met on 25 September 2004 for first time in 20 years with 21 members appointed by the Sultan; passed constitutional amendments calling for a 45-seat council with 15 elected members; Sultan dissolved council on 1 September 2005 and appointed a new council with 29 members as of 2 September 2005
elections: last held in March 1962 (date of next election NA)
Judicial branch: Supreme Court (chief justice and judges are sworn in by the monarch for three-year terms)
Political parties and leaders: National Development Party (NDP) [YASSIN Affendi]; National Unity Party of Brunei (PPKB) [Haji Mohd HATTA bin Haji Zainal Abidin]; People's Awareness Party (PAKAR) [Awang Haji MAIDIN bin Haji Ahmad]
note: parties are small and inactive (2005)
Political pressure groups and leaders: NA
International organization participation: APEC, APT, ARF, ASEAN, C, EAS, G-77, IBRD, ICAO, ICRM, IDB, IFRCS, IMF, IMO, Interpol, IOC, ISO (correspondent), ITU, NAM, OIC, OPCW, UN, UNCTAD, UPU, WCO, WHO, WIPO, WMO, WTO
Diplomatic representation in the US:
chief of mission: Ambassador Pengiran Anak Dato PUTEH
chancery: 3520 International Court NW, Washington, DC 20008
telephone: [1] (202) 237-1838
FAX: [1] (202) 885-0560
Diplomatic representation from the US:
chief of mission: Ambassador Emil SKODON
embassy: Third Floor, Teck Guan Plaza, Jalan Sultan, Bandar Seri Begawan, BS8811
mailing address: PSC 470 (BSB), FPO AP 96507
telephone: [673] (2) 220-384
FAX: [673] (2) 225-293
Flag description: yellow with two diagonal bands of white (top, almost double width) and black starting from the upper hoist side; the national emblem in red is superimposed at the center; the emblem includes a swallow-tailed flag on top of a winged column within an upturned crescent above a scroll and flanked by two upraised hands

ECONOMY

Economy - overview: This small, well-to-do economy encompasses a mixture of foreign and domestic entrepreneurship, government regulation, welfare measures, and village tradition. Crude oil and natural gas production account for nearly half of GDP. Per capita GDP is far above most other Third World countries, and substantial income from overseas investment supplements income from domestic production. The government provides for all medical services and free education through the university level and subsidizes rice and housing. Brunei's leaders are concerned that steadily increased integration in the world economy will undermine internal social cohesion, although it became a more prominent player by serving as chairman for the 2000 APEC (Asian Pacific Economic Cooperation) forum. Plans for the future include upgrading the labor force, reducing unemployment, strengthening the banking and tourist sectors, and, in general, further widening the economic base beyond oil and gas.
GDP: purchasing power parity - $6.842 billion (2003 est.)
GDP (official exchange rate): NA
GDP - real growth rate: 3.2% (2003 est.)
GDP - per capita: purchasing power parity - $23,600 (2003 est.)
GDP - composition by sector:
agriculture: 5%
industry: 45%
services: 50% (2001 est.)
Labor force: 158,000
note: includes foreign workers and military personnel; temporary residents make up about 40% of labor force (2002 est.)
Labor force - by occupation: agriculture, forestry, and fishing 10%, production of oil, natural gas, services, and construction 42%, government 48% (1999 est.)
Unemployment rate: 3.2% (2002 est.)
Population below poverty line: NA
Household income or consumption by percentage share:
lowest 10%: NA
highest 10%: NA
Inflation rate (consumer prices): 0.3% (2003 est.)
Budget:
revenues: $4.9 billion
expenditures: $4.2 billion, including capital expenditures of $1.35 billion (2003 est.)
Agriculture - products: rice, vegetables, fruits, chickens, water buffalo
Industries: petroleum, petroleum refining, liquefied natural gas, construction
Industrial production growth rate: 5% (2002 est.)
Electricity - production: 2.659 billion kWh (2003)
Electricity - production by source:
fossil fuel: 100%
hydro: 0%
nuclear: 0%
other: 0% (2001)
Electricity - consumption: 2.473 billion kWh (2003)
Electricity - exports: 0 kWh (2003)
Electricity - imports: 0 kWh (2003)

Oil - production: 196,400 bbl/day (2003)
Oil - consumption: 12,000 bbl/day (2003 est.)
Oil - exports: 199,000 bbl/day (2003)
Oil - imports: NA (2003)
Oil - proved reserves: 1.255 billion bbl (1 January 2002)
Natural gas - production: 10.35 billion cu m (2001 est.)
Natural gas - consumption: 1.35 billion cu m (2001 est.)
Natural gas - exports: 9 billion cu m (2001 est.)
Natural gas - imports: 0 cu m (2001 est.)
Natural gas - proved reserves: 315 billion cu m (1 January 2002)
Exports: $4.514 billion f.o.b. (2004 est.)
Exports - partners: Japan 38.1%, South Korea 14%, Australia 11.2%, US 8.6%, Thailand 7.9%, Indonesia 5.9%, China 4.5% (2004)
Imports: $1.641 billion c.i.f. (2004 est.)
Imports - partners: Singapore 32.7%, Malaysia 21.2%, UK 8.3%, Japan 7.2% (2004)
Debt - eternal: $0
Economic aid - recipient: NA $4.3 million (1995)
Currency: Bruneian dollar (BND)
Currency code: BND
Exchange rates: Bruneian dollars per US dollar - NA (2005), 1.6902 (2004), 1.7422 (2003), 1.7906 (2002), 1.7917 (2001)
Fiscal year: calendar year

COMMUNICATIONS

Telephones - main lines in use: 90,000 (2002)
Telephones - mobile cellular: 137,000 (2002)
Telephone system:
general assessment: service throughout the country is excellent; international service is good to East Asia, Europe, and the US
domestic: every service available
international: country code - 673; satellite earth stations - 2 Intelsat (1 Indian Ocean and 1 Pacific Ocean); digital submarine cable links to Malaysia, the Philippines, and Singapore (2001)
Radio broadcast stations: AM 3, FM 10, shortwave 0 (1998)
Radios: 329,000 (1998)
Television broadcast stations: 2 (1997)
Televisions: 201,900 (1998)
Internet country code: .bn
Internet hosts: 6,409 (2003)
Internet Service Providers (ISPs): 2 (2000)
Internet users: 35,000 (2002)

TRANSPORTATION

Airports: 2 (2004 est.)
Airports - with paved runways:
total: 1
over 3,047 m: 1 (2005 est.)
Airports - with unpaved runways:
total: 1
914 to 1,523 m: 1 (2005 est.)
Heliports: 3 (2005 est.)
Pipelines: gas 665 km; oil 439 km (2004)
Roadways:
total: 1,150 km
paved: 399 km
unpaved: 751 km (1999)
Waterways: 209 km (navigable by craft drawing less than 1.2 m) (2004)
Merchant marine:
total: 8 ships (1,000 GRT or over) 465,937 GRT/413,393 DWT
by type: liquefied gas 8
foreign-owned: 8 (United Kingdom 8) (2005)
Ports and terminals: Lumut, Muara, Seria

MILITARY

Military branches: Royal Brunei Armed Forces: Royal Brunei Land Forces, Royal Brunei Navy, Royal Brunei Air Force
Military service age and obligation: 18 years of age (est.) (2004)
Manpower available for military service:
males age 18-49: 103,885 (2005 est.)
Manpower fit for military service: *males age 18-49:* approx. 85,045 (2005 est.)
Manpower reaching military service age annually: *males:* 3,478 (2005 est.)
Military expenditures - dollar figure: $290.7 million (2004)
Military expenditures - percent of GDP: 5.1% (2004)

TRANSNATIONAL ISSUES

Disputes - international: in 2003 Brunei and Malaysia ceased gas and oil exploration in their disputed offshore and deepwater seabeds and negotiations have stalemated prompting consideration of international legal adjudication; Malaysia's land boundary with Brunei around Limbang is in dispute; Brunei established an exclusive economic fishing zone encompassing Louisa Reef in southern Spratly Islands in 1984 but makes no public territorial claim to the offshore reefs; the 2002 "Declaration on the Conduct of Parties in the South China Sea" has eased tensions in the Spratly Islands but falls short of a legally binding "code of conduct" desired by several of the disputants
Illicit drugs: drug trafficking and illegally importing controlled substances are serious offenses in Brunei and carry a mandatory death penalty

BULGARIA

INTRODUCTION

Background: The Bulgars, a Central Asian Turkic tribe, merged with the local Slavic inhabitants in the late 7th century to form the first Bulgarian state. In succeeding centuries, Bulgaria struggled with the Byzantine Empire to assert its place in the Balkans, but by the end of the 14th century the country was overrun by the Ottoman Turks. Northern Bulgaria attained autonomy in 1878 and all of Bulgaria became independent in 1908. Having fought on the losing side in both World Wars, Bulgaria fell within the Soviet sphere of influence and became a People's Republic in 1946. Communist domination ended in 1990, when Bulgaria held its first multiparty election since World War II and began the contentious process of moving toward political democracy and a market economy while combating inflation, unemployment, corruption, and crime. Today, reforms and democratization keep Bulgaria on a path toward eventual integration into the EU. The country joined NATO in 2004.

GEOGRAPHY

Location: Southeastern Europe, bordering the Black Sea, between Romania and Turkey
Geographic coordinates: 43 00 N, 25 00 E
Map references: Europe

Area:
total: 110,910 sq km
land: 110,550 sq km
water: 360 sq km
Area - comparative: slightly larger than Tennessee
Land boundaries:
total: 1,808 km
border countries: Greece 494 km, Macedonia 148 km, Romania 608 km, Serbia and Montenegro 318 km, Turkey 240 km
Coastline: 354 km
Maritime claims:
territorial sea: 12 nm
contiguous zone: 24 nm
exclusive economic zone: 200 nm
Climate: temperate; cold, damp winters; hot, dry summers
Terrain: mostly mountains with lowlands in north and southeast
Elevation extremes:
lowest point: Black Sea 0 m
highest point: Musala 2,925 m
Natural resources: bauxite, copper, lead, zinc, coal, timber, arable land
Land use:
arable land: 40.02%
permanent crops: 1.92%
other: 58.06% (2001)
Irrigated land: 8,000 sq km (1998 est.)
Natural hazards: earthquakes, landslides
Environment - current issues: air pollution from industrial emissions; rivers polluted from raw sewage, heavy metals, detergents; deforestation; forest damage from air pollution and resulting acid rain; soil contamination from heavy metals from metallurgical plants and industrial wastes
Environment - international agreements:
party to: Air Pollution, Air Pollution-Nitrogen Oxides, Air Pollution-Persistent Organic Pollutants, Air Pollution-Sulfur 85, Air Pollution-Volatile Organic Compounds, Antarctic-Environmental Protocol, Antarctic-Marine Living Resources, Antarctic Treaty, Biodiversity, Climate Change, Climate Change-Kyoto Protocol, Desertification, Endangered Species, Environmental Modification, Hazardous Wastes, Law of the Sea, Ozone Layer Protection, Ship Pollution, Wetlands
signed, but not ratified: Air Pollution-Sulfur 94
Geography - note: strategic location near Turkish Straits; controls key land routes from Europe to Middle East and Asia

PEOPLE

Population: 7,450,349 (July 2005 est.)
Age structure:
0-14 years: 14.1% (male 539,005/female 512,762)
15-64 years: 68.7% (male 2,516,368/female 2,599,524)
65 years and over: 17.2% (male 531,008/female 751,682) (2005 est.)
Median age:
total: 40.66 years
male: 38.59 years
female: 42.66 years (2005 est.)
Population growth rate: -0.89% (2005 est.)
Birth rate: 9.66 births/1,000 population (2005 est.)
Death rate: 14.26 deaths/1,000 population (2005 est.)
Net migration rate: -4.3 migrant(s)/1,000 population (2005 est.)
Sex ratio:
at birth: 1.06 male(s)/female
under 15 years: 1.05 male(s)/female
15-64 years: 0.97 male(s)/female
65 years and over: 0.71 male(s)/female
total population: 0.93 male(s)/female (2005 est.)
Infant mortality rate:
total: 20.55 deaths/1,000 live births
male: 24.31 deaths/1,000 live births
female: 16.56 deaths/1,000 live births (2005 est.)
Life expectancy at birth:
total population: 72.03 years
male: 68.41 years
female: 75.87 years (2005 est.)
Total fertility rate: 1.38 children born/woman (2005 est.)
HIV/AIDS - adult prevalence rate: less than 0.1% - note - no country specific models provided (2001 est.)
HIV/AIDS - people living with HIV/AIDS: 346 (2001 est.)
HIV/AIDS - deaths: 100 (2001 est.)
Nationality:
noun: Bulgarian(s)
adjective: Bulgarian
Ethnic groups: Bulgarian 83.9%, Turk 9.4%, Roma 4.7%, other 2% (including Macedonian, Armenian, Tatar, Circassian) (2001 census)
Religions: Bulgarian Orthodox 82.6%, Muslim 12.2%, other Christian 1.2%, other 4% (2001 census)
Languages: Bulgarian 84.5%, Turkish 9.6%, Roma 4.1%, other and unspecified 1.8% (2001 census)
Literacy:
definition: age 15 and over can read and write
total population: 98.6%
male: 99.1%
female: 98.2% (2003 est.)

GOVERNMENT

Country name:
conventional long form: Republic of Bulgaria
conventional short form: Bulgaria
Government type: parliamentary democracy
Capital: Sofia
Administrative divisions: 28 provinces (oblasti, singular - oblast); Blagoevgrad, Burgas, Dobrich, Gabrovo, Khaskovo, Kurdzhali, Kyustendil, Lovech, Montana, Pazardzhik, Pernik, Pleven, Plovdiv, Razgrad, Ruse, Shumen, Silistra, Sliven, Smolyan, Sofiya, Sofiya-Grad, Stara Zagora, Turgovishte, Varna, Veliko Turnovo, Vidin, Vratsa, Yambol
Independence: 3 March 1878 (as an autonomous principality within the Ottoman Empire); 22 September 1908 (complete independence from the Ottoman Empire)
National holiday: Liberation Day, 3 March (1878)
Constitution: adopted 12 July 1991
Legal system: civil law and criminal law based on Roman law; accepts compulsory ICJ jurisdiction
Suffrage: 18 years of age; universal
Executive branch:
chief of state: President Georgi PURVANOV (since 22 January 2002); Vice President Angel MARIN (since 22 January 2002)
head of government: Prime Minister Sergei STANISHEV (since 16 August 2005); Deputy Prime Ministers Ivaylo KALFIN, Daniel VULCHEV, and Emel ETEM (since 16 August 2005)
cabinet: Council of Ministers nominated by the prime minister and elected by the National Assembly
elections: president and vice president elected on the same ticket by popular vote for five-year terms; election last held 11 and 18 November 2001 (next to be held NA 2006); chairman of the Council of Ministers (prime minister) nominated by the president and elected by the National Assembly; deputy prime ministers nominated by the prime minister and elected by the National Assembly
election results: Georgi Purvanov elected president; percent of vote - Georgi PURVANOV 54.13%, Petar Stoyanov 45.87%; Sergei STANISHEV elected prime minister, result of legislative vote - 168 to 67
Legislative branch: unicameral National Assembly or Narodno Sobranie (240 seats; members elected by popular vote to serve four-year terms)
elections: last held 25 June 2005 (next to be held June 2009)
election results: percent of vote by party - CfB 31.1%, NMS2 19.9%, MRF 12.7%, ATAKA 8.2%, UDF 7.7%, DSB 6.5%, BPU 5.2%; seats by party - CfB 83, NMS2 53, MRF 33, UDF 20, ATAKA 17, DSB 17, BPU 13, independents 4
Judicial branch: Supreme Administrative Court; Supreme Court of Cassation; Constitutional Court (12 justices

appointed or elected for nine-year terms); Supreme Judicial Council (consists of the chairmen of the two Supreme Courts, the Chief Prosecutor, and 22 other members; responsible for appointing the justices, prosecutors, and investigating magistrates in the justice system; members of the Supreme Judicial Council elected for five-year terms, 11 elected by the National Assembly and 11 by bodies of the judiciary)
Political parties and leaders: Attack National Union [Volen Siderov]; ATAKA (Attack Coalition) (coalition of parties headed by the Attack National Union); Bulgarian Agrarian National Union-People's Union or BANU [Anastasia MOZER]; Bulgarian People's Union or BPU (coalition of UFD, IMRO, and BANU); Bulgarian Socialist Party or BSP [Sergei STANISHEV]; Coalition for Bulgaria or CfB (coalition of parties dominated by BSP) [Sergei STANISHEV]; Democrats for a Strong Bulgaria or DSB [Ivan KOSTOV]; Internal Macedonian Revolutionary Organization or IMRO [Krasimir KARAKACHANOV]; Movement for Rights and Freedoms or MRF [Ahmed DOGAN]; National Movement for Simeon II or NMS2 [Simeon SAXE-COBURG-GOTHA]; New Time [Emil KOSHLUKOV]; Union of Democratic Forces or UDF [Petur STOYANOV]; Union of Free Democrats or UFD [Stefan SOFIYANSKI]; United Democratic Forces or UtDF (a coalition of center-right parties dominated by UDF)
Political pressure groups and leaders: Confederation of Independent Trade Unions of Bulgaria or CITUB; Podkrepa Labor Confederation; numerous regional, ethnic, and national interest groups with various agendas
International organization participation: ACCT, Australia Group, BIS, BSEC, CE, CEI, CERN, EAPC, EBRD, EU (applicant), FAO, G- 9, IAEA, IBRD, ICAO, ICCt, ICFTU, ICRM, IFC, IFRCS, ILO, IMF, IMO, Interpol, IOC, IOM, ISO, ITU, MIGA, NAM (guest), NATO, NSG, OAS (observer), OPCW, OSCE, PCA, UN, UNCTAD, UNESCO, UNIDO, UNMEE, UNMIL, UPU, WCL, WCO, WEU (associate affiliate), WFTU, WHO, WIPO, WMO, WToO, WTO, ZC
Diplomatic representation in the US:
chief of mission: Ambassador Elena B. POPTODOROVA
chancery: 1621 22nd Street NW, Washington, DC 20008
telephone: [1] (202) 387-0174
FAX: [1] (202) 234-7973
consulate(s) general: Chicago and New York
consulate(s): Los Angeles
Diplomatic representation from the US:
chief of mission: Ambassador John Ross BEYRLE
embassy: 16 Kozyak Street, Sofia 1407
mailing address: American Embassy Sofia, Department of State, 5740 Sofia Place, Washington, DC 20521-5740
telephone: [359] (2) 937-5100
FAX: [359] (2) 937-5230
Flag description: three equal horizontal bands of white (top), green, and red; note - the national emblem, formerly on the hoist side of the white stripe, has been removed

ECONOMY

Economy - overview: Bulgaria, a former communist country striving to enter the European Union, has experienced macroeconomic stability and strong growth since a major economic downturn in 1996 led to the fall of the then socialist government. As a result, the government became committed to economic reform and responsible fiscal planning. Minerals, including coal, copper, and zinc play an important role in industry. In 1997, macroeconomic stability was reinforced by the imposition of a fixed exchange rate of the lev against the German D-mark and the negotiation of an IMF standby agreement. Low inflation and steady progress on structural reforms improved the business environment; Bulgaria has averaged 4% growth since 2000 and has begun to attract significant amounts of foreign direct investment. Corruption in the public administration, a weak judiciary, and the presence of organized crime remain the largest challenges for Bulgaria.
GDP: purchasing power parity - $66.96 billion (2005 est.)
GDP (official exchange rate): $26.32 billion (2005 est.)
GDP - real growth rate: 5.4% (2005 est.)
GDP - per capita: purchasing power parity - $9,000 (2005 est.)
GDP - composition by sector:
agriculture: 10.1%
industry: 30.2%
services: 59.7% (2005 est.)
Labor force: 3.34 million (2005 est.)
Labor force - by occupation: agriculture 11%, industry 32.7%, services 56.3% (3rd quarter 2004 est.)
Unemployment rate: 11.5% (2005 est.)
Population below poverty line: 13.4% (2002 est.)
Household income or consumption by percentage share:
lowest 10%: 4.5%
highest 10%: 22.8% (1997)
Distribution of family income - Gini index: 31.9 (2001)
Inflation rate (consumer prices): 4.5% (2005 est.)
Investment (gross fixed): 22.1% of GDP (2005 est.)
Budget:
revenues: $11.18 billion
expenditures: $10.9 billion, including capital expenditures of NA (2005 est.)
Public debt: 32.4% of GDP (2005 est.)
Agriculture - products: vegetables, fruits, tobacco, livestock, wine, wheat, barley, sunflowers, sugar beets
Industries: electricity, gas and water; food, beverages and tobacco; machinery and equipment, base metals, chemical products, coke, refined petroleum, nuclear fuel
Industrial production growth rate: 7% (2005 est.)
Electricity - production: 38.07 billion kWh (2003)
Electricity - production by source:
fossil fuel: 47.8%
hydro: 8.1%
nuclear: 44.1%
other: 0% (2001)
Electricity - consumption: 31.75 billion kWh (2003)
Electricity - exports: 5.449 billion kWh (2003)
Electricity - imports: 1.8 billion kWh (2003)
Oil - production: 2,908 bbl/day (2003)
Oil - consumption: 107,000 bbl/day (2003 est.)
Oil - exports: NA (2001)
Oil - imports: NA (2001)
Oil - proved reserves: 8.1 million bbl (1 January 2002)
Natural gas - production: 4 million cu m (2001 est.)
Natural gas - consumption: 5.804 billion cu m (2001 est.)
Natural gas - exports: 0 cu m (2001 est.)
Natural gas - imports: 5.8 billion cu m (2001 est.)
Natural gas - proved reserves: 3.724 billion cu m (1 January 2002)
Current account balance: $-2.741 billion (2005 est.)
Exports: $11.67 billion f.o.b. (2005 est.)
Exports - partners: Italy 13.1%, Germany 11.6%, Turkey 9.3%, Belgium 6.1%, Greece 5.6%, US 5.3%, France 4.9% (2004)
Imports: $15.9 billion f.o.b. (2005 est.)
Imports - partners: Germany 15.1%, Italy 10.2%, Russia 7.9%, Greece 7.5%, Turkey 6.9%, France 4.4% (2004)
Reserves of foreign exchange and gold: $9.707 billion (2005 est.)
Debt - external: $15.46 billion (2005 est.)
Economic aid - recipient: $300 million (2000 est.)
Currency: lev (BGL)
Currency code: BGL

Exchange rates: leva per US dollar - 1.56 (2005), 1.5751 (2004), 1.7327 (2003), 2.077 (2002), 2.1847 (2001)
note: on 5 July 1999, the lev was redenominated; the post-5 July 1999 lev is equal to 1,000 of the pre-5 July 1999 lev
Fiscal year: calendar year

COMMUNICATIONS

Telephones - main lines in use: 2,868,200 (2002)
Telephones - mobile cellular: 2,597,500 (2002)
Telephone system:
general assessment: extensive but antiquated
domestic: more than two-thirds of the lines are residential; telephone service is available in most villages; a fairly modern digital cable trunk line now connects switching centers in most of the regions, the others are connected by digital microwave radio relay
international: country code - 359; direct dialing to 58 countries; satellite earth stations - 1 Intersputnik (Atlantic Ocean region); 2 Intelsat (Atlantic and Indian Ocean regions)
Radio broadcast stations: AM 31, FM 63, shortwave 2 (2001)
Radios: 4.51 million (1997)
Television broadcast stations: 39 (plus 1,242 repeaters) (2001)
Televisions: 3.31 million (1997)
Internet country code: .bg
Internet hosts: 53,421 (2004)
Internet Service Providers (ISPs): 200 (2001)
Internet users: 630,000 (2002)

TRANSPORTATION

Airports: 213 (2004 est.)
Airports - with paved runways:
total: 128
over 3,047 m: 1
2,438 to 3,047 m: 19
1,524 to 2,437 m: 15
914 to 1,523 m: 1
under 914 m: 92 (2005 est.)
Airports - with unpaved runways:
total: 85
1,524 to 2,437 m: 2
914 to 1,523 m: 11
under 914 m: 72 (2005 est.)
Heliports: 1 (2005 est.)
Pipelines: gas 2,425 km; oil 339 km; refined products 156 km (2004)
Railways:
total: 4,294 km
standard gauge: 4,049 km 1.435-m gauge (2,710 km electrified)
narrow gauge: 245 km 0.760-m gauge (2004)
Roadways:
total: 102,016 km
paved: 93,855 km (including 328 km of expressways)
unpaved: 8,161 km (2003)
Waterways: 470 km (2004)
Merchant marine:
total: 64 ships (1,000 GRT or over) 757,972 GRT/1,115,238 DWT
by type: bulk carrier 34, cargo 13, chemical tanker 4, container 6, passenger/cargo 1, petroleum tanker 3, roll on/roll off 3
registered in other countries: 45 (2005)
Ports and terminals: Burgas, Varna

MILITARY

Military branches: Ground Forces, Naval Forces, Air and Air Defense Forces
Military service age and obligation: 18 years of age for compulsory and voluntary military service; conscript service obligation - 9 months; plans call for fully professionalizing the army by the end of 2007 when conscription will terminate; air force and navy will become fully professional by the end of 2006 (2005)
Manpower available for military service: *males age 18-49:* 1,661,211 (2005 est.)
Manpower fit for military service: *males age 18-49:* 1,302,037 (2005 est.)
Manpower reaching military service age annually: *males:* 51,023 (2005 est.)
Military expenditures - dollar figure: $356 million (FY02)
Military expenditures - percent of GDP: 2.6% (2003)

TRANSNATIONAL ISSUES

Disputes - international: none
Illicit drugs: major European transshipment point for Southwest Asian heroin and, to a lesser degree, South American cocaine for the European market; limited producer of precursor chemicals; some money laundering of drug-related proceeds through financial institutions

BURKINA FASO

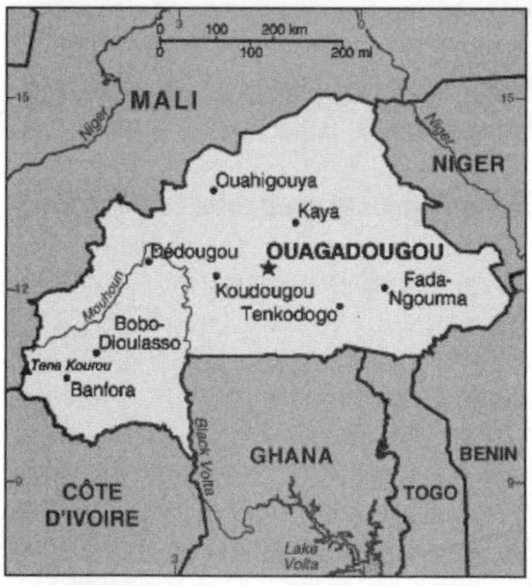

INTRODUCTION

Background: Burkina Faso (formerly Upper Volta) achieved independence from France in 1960. Repeated military coups during the 1970s and 1980s were followed by multiparty elections in the early 1990s. Burkina Faso's high population density and limited natural resources result in poor economic prospects for the majority of its citizens. Recent unrest in Cote d'Ivoire and northern Ghana has hindered the ability of several hundred thousand seasonal Burkinabe farm workers to find employment in neighboring countries.

GEOGRAPHY

Location: Western Africa, north of Ghana
Geographic coordinates: 13 00 N, 2 00 W
Map references: Africa
Area:
total: 274,200 sq km
land: 273,800 sq km
water: 400 sq km
Area - comparative: slightly larger than Colorado
Land boundaries:
total: 3,193 km
border countries: Benin 306 km, Cote d'Ivoire 584 km, Ghana 549 km, Mali 1,000 km, Niger 628 km, Togo 126 km
Coastline: 0 km (landlocked)
Maritime claims: none (landlocked)
Climate: tropical; warm, dry winters; hot, wet summers
Terrain: mostly flat to dissected, undulating plains; hills in west and southeast
Elevation extremes:
lowest point: Mouhoun (Black Volta) River 200 m
highest point: Tena Kourou 749 m
Natural resources: manganese, limestone, marble; small deposits of gold, phosphates, pumice, salt
Land use:
arable land: 14.43%
permanent crops: 0.19%
other: 85.38% (2001)
Irrigated land: 250 sq km (1998 est.)
Natural hazards: recurring droughts
Environment - current issues: recent droughts and desertification severely affecting agricultural activities, population distribution, and the economy; overgrazing; soil degradation; deforestation
Environment - international agreements:
party to: Biodiversity, Climate Change,

Desertification, Endangered Species, Hazardous Wastes, Law of the Sea, Marine Life Conservation, Ozone Layer Protection, Wetlands
signed, but not ratified: none of the selected agreements
Geography - note: landlocked savanna cut by the three principal rivers of the Black, Red, and White Voltas

PEOPLE

Population: 13,925,313
note: estimates for this country explicitly take into account the effects of excess mortality due to AIDS; this can result in lower life expectancy, higher infant mortality and death rates, lower population and growth rates, and changes in the distribution of population by age and sex than would otherwise be expected (July 2005 est.)
Age structure:
0-14 years: 46% (male 3,213,436/female 3,193,253)
15-64 years: 51.2% (male 3,487,201/ female 3,635,673)
65 years and over: 2.8% (male 164,418/ female 231,332) (2005 est.)
Median age:
total: 16.82 years
male: 16.43 years
female: 17.22 years (2005 est.)
Population growth rate: 2.53% (2005 est.)
Birth rate: 44.17 births/1,000 population (2005 est.)
Death rate: 18.86 deaths/1,000 population (2005 est.)
Net migration rate: 0 migrant(s)/1,000 population (2005 est.)
Sex ratio:
at birth: 1.03 male(s)/female
under 15 years: 1.01 male(s)/female
15-64 years: 0.96 male(s)/female
65 years and over: 0.71 male(s)/female
total population: 0.97 male(s)/female (2005 est.)
Infant mortality rate:
total: 97.57 deaths/1,000 live births
male: 105.55 deaths/1,000 live births
female: 89.34 deaths/1,000 live births (2005 est.)
Life expectancy at birth:
total population: 48.45 years
male: 46.96 years
female: 49.99 years (2005 est.)
Total fertility rate: 6.23 children born/woman (2005 est.)
HIV/AIDS - adult prevalence rate: 4.2% (2003 est.)
HIV/AIDS - people living with HIV/AIDS: 300,000 (2003 est.)
HIV/AIDS - deaths: 29,000 (2003 est.)
Major infectious diseases:
degree of risk: very high
food or waterborne diseases: bacterial and protozoal diarrhea, hepatitis A, and typhoid fever
vectorborne disease: malaria is a high risk in some locations
water contact disease: schistosomiasis
respiratory disease: meningococcal meningitis (2004)
Nationality:
noun: Burkinabe (singular and plural)
adjective: Burkinabe
Ethnic groups: Mossi over 40%, Gurunsi, Senufo, Lobi, Bobo, Mande, Fulani
Religions: indigenous beliefs 40%, Muslim 50%, Christian (mainly Roman Catholic) 10%
Languages: French (official), native African languages belonging to Sudanic family spoken by 90% of the population
Literacy:
definition: age 15 and over can read and write
total population: 26.6%
male: 36.9%
female: 16.6% (2003 est.)

GOVERNMENT

Country name:
conventional long form: none
conventional short form: Burkina Faso
former: Upper Volta, Republic of Upper Vo
Government type: parliamentary republic
Capital: Ouagadougou
Administrative divisions: 45 provinces; Bale, Bam, Banwa, Bazega, Bougouriba, Boulgou, Boulkiemde, Comoe, Ganzourgou, Gnagna, Gourma, Houet, Ioba, Kadiogo, Kenedougou, Komondjari, Kompienga, Kossi, Koulpelogo, Kouritenga, Kourweogo, Leraba, Loroum, Mouhoun, Namentenga, Nahouri, Nayala, Noumbiel, Oubritenga, Oudalan, Passore, Poni, Sanguie, Sanmatenga, Seno, Sissili, Soum, Sourou, Tapoa, Tuy, Yagha, Yatenga, Ziro, Zondoma, Zoundweogo
Independence: 5 August 1960 (from France)
National holiday: Republic Day, 11 December (1958)
Constitution: 2 June 1991 approved by referendum, 11 June 1991 formally adopted; amended April 2000
Legal system: based on French civil law system and customary law
Suffrage: universal
Executive branch:
chief of state: President Blaise COMPAORE (since 15 October 1987)
head of government: Prime Minister Ernest Paramanga YONLI (since 6 November 2000)
cabinet: Council of Ministers appointed by the president on the recommendation of the prime minister
elections: president elected by popular vote for a five-year term; election last held 13 November 2005 (next to be held NA 2010); in April 2000, the constitution was amended reducing the presidential term from seven to five years, enforceable as of 2005, and allowing the president to be reelected only once; prime minister appointed by the president with the consent of the legislature
election results: Blaise Compaore reelected president; percent of popular vote - Blaise COMPAORE 80.3%, Benewende Stanislas SANKARA 4.9%
Legislative branch: unicameral National Assembly or Assemblee Nationale (111 seats; members are elected by popular vote to serve five-year terms)
elections: National Assembly election last held 5 May 2002 (next to be held May 2007)
election results: percent of vote by party - NA%; seats by party - CDP 57, RDA-ADF 17, PDP/PS 10, CFD 5, PAI 5, others 17
Judicial branch: Supreme Court; Appeals Court
Political parties and leaders: African Democratic Rally-Alliance for Democracy and Federation or RDA-ADF [Herman YAMEOGO]; Confederation for Federation and Democracy or CFD [Amadou Diemdioda DICKO]; Congress for Democracy and Progress or CDP [Roch Marc-Christian KABORE]; Movement for Tolerance and Progress or MTP [Nayabtigungou Congo KABORE]; Party for African Independence or PAI [Philippe OUEDRAOGO]; Party for Democracy and Progress or PDP [Joseph KI-ZERBO]; Socialist Party or PS [leader NA]; Union of Greens for the Development of Burkina Faso or UVDB [Ram OVEDRAGO]
Political pressure groups and leaders: Burkinabe General Confederation of Labor or CGTB; Burkinabe Movement for Human Rights or MBDHP; Group of 14 February; National Confederation of Burkinabe Workers or CNTB; National Organization of Free Unions or ONSL; watchdog/political action groups throughout the country in both organizations and communities
International organization participation: ACCT, ACP, AfDB, AU, CEMAC, ECOWAS, Entente, FAO, FZ, G-77, IAEA, IBRD, ICAO, ICC, ICCt, ICFTU, ICRM, IDA, IDB, IFAD, IFC, IFRCS, ILO, IMF, Interpol, IOC, IOM, ISO (correspondent), ITU, MIGA, MONUC, NAM, OIC, ONUB, OPCW, PCA, UN, UNCTAD, UNESCO, UNIDO, UNOCI, UPU,

WADB (regional), WAEMU, WCL, WCO, WFTU, WHO, WIPO, WMO, WToO, WTO
Diplomatic representation in the US:
chief of mission: Ambassador Tertius ZONGO
chancery: 2340 Massachusetts Avenue NW, Washington, DC 20008
telephone: [1] (202) 332-5577
FAX: [1] (202) 667-1882
Diplomatic representation from the US:
chief of mission: (vacant)
embassy: 602 Avenue Raoul Follereau, Koulouba, Secteur 4
mailing address: 01 B. P. 35, Ouagadougou 01; pouch mail - U. S. Department of State, 2440 Ouagadougou Place, Washington, DC 20521-2440
telephone: [226] 306723
FAX: [226] 303890
Flag description: two equal horizontal bands of red (top) and green with a yellow five-pointed star in the center; uses the popular pan-African colors of Ethiopia

ECONOMY

Economy - overview: One of the poorest countries in the world, landlocked Burkina Faso has few natural resources and a weak industrial base. About 90% of the population is engaged in subsistence agriculture, which is vulnerable to harsh climatic conditions. Cotton is the key crop and the government has joined with other cotton producing countries in the region to lobby for improved access to Western markets. GDP growth has largely been driven by increases in world cotton prices. Industry remains dominated by unprofitable government-controlled corporations. Following the CFA franc currency devaluation in January 1994 the government updated its development program in conjunction with international agencies; exports and economic growth have increased. The government devolved macroeconomic policy and inflation targeting to the West African regional central bank (BCEAO), but maintains control over fiscal and microeconomic policies, including implementing reforms to encourage private investment. The bitter internal crisis in neighboring Cote d'Ivoire continues to hurt trade and industrial prospects and deepens the need for international assistance.
GDP: purchasing power parity - $16.94 billion (2005 est.)
GDP (official exchange rate): $5.555 billion (2005 est.)
GDP - real growth rate: 5% (2005 est.)
GDP - per capita: purchasing power parity - $1,200 (2005 est.)
GDP - composition by sector:
agriculture: 39.5%
industry: 19.3%
services: 41.3% (2004 est.)
Labor force: 5 million
note: a large part of the male labor force migrates annually to neighboring countries for seasonal employment (2003)
Labor force - by occupation: agriculture 90% (2000 est.)
Unemployment rate: NA%
Population below poverty line: 45% (2003 est.)
Household income or consumption by percentage share:
lowest 10%: 2%
highest 10%: 46.8% (1994)
Distribution of family income - Gini index: 48.2 (1998)
Inflation rate (consumer prices): 3% (2005 est.)
Investment (gross fixed): 20.3% of GDP (2005 est.)
Budget:
revenues: $1.033 billion
expenditures: $1.382 billion, including capital expenditures of NA (2005 est.)
Agriculture - products: cotton, peanuts, shea nuts, sesame, sorghum, millet, corn, rice; livestock
Industries: cotton lint, beverages, agricultural processing, soap, cigarettes, textiles, gold
Industrial production growth rate: 14% (2001 est.)
Electricity - production: 375.6 million kWh (2003)
Electricity - production by source:
fossil fuel: 69.9%
hydro: 30.1%
nuclear: 0%
other: 0% (2001)
Electricity - consumption: 349.3 million kWh (2003)
Electricity - exports: 0 kWh (2003)
Electricity - imports: 0 kWh (2003)
Oil - production: 0 bbl/day (2003)
Oil - consumption: 8,000 bbl/day (2003 est.)
Oil - exports: NA
Oil - imports: NA
Current account balance: $-562 million (2005 est.)
Exports: $395 million f.o.b. (2005 est.)
Exports - partners: China 31.9%, Singapore 11.5%, Ghana 4.7%, Bangladesh 4.3% (2004)
Imports: $992 million f.o.b. (2005 est.)
Imports - partners: France 29.3%, Cote d'Ivoire 16%, Togo 9.8% (2004)
Reserves of foreign exchange and gold: $791 million (2005 est.)
Debt - eternal: $1.85 billion (2003)
Economic aid - recipient: $468.4 million (2003)
Currency: Communaute Financiere Africaine franc (XOF); note - responsible authority is the Central Bank of the West African States
Currency code: XOF
Exchange rates: Communaute Financiere Africaine francs (XOF) per US dollar - 518.65 (2005), 528.29 (2004), 581.2 (2003), 696.99 (2002), 733.04 (2001)
Fiscal year: calendar year

COMMUNICATIONS

Telephones - main lines in use: 65,400 (2003)
Telephones - mobile cellular: 227,000 (2003)
Telephone system:
general assessment: all services only fair
domestic: microwave radio relay, open-wire, and radiotelephone communication stations
international: country code - 226; satellite earth station - 1 Intelsat (Atlantic Ocean)
Radio broadcast stations: AM 3, FM 17, shortwave 3 (2002)
Radios: 394,020 (2000)
Television broadcast stations: 1 (2002)
Televisions: 131,340 (2002)
Internet country code: .bf
Internet hosts: 442 (2003)
Internet Service Providers (ISPs): 1 (2002)
Internet users: 48,000 (2003)

TRANSPORTATION

Airports: 33 (2004 est.)
Airports - with paved runways:
total: 2
over 3,047 m: 1
2,438 to 3,047 m: 1 (2005 est.)
Airports - with unpaved runways:
total: 31
1,524 to 2,437 m: 3
914 to 1,523 m: 11
under 914 m: 17 (2005 est.)
Railways:
total: 622 km
narrow gauge: 622 km 1.000-m gauge
note: another 660 km of this railway extends into Cote D'Ivoire (2004)
Roadways:
total: 12,506 km
paved: 2,001 km
unpaved: 10,505 km (1999)

MILITARY

Military branches: Army, Air Force, National Gendarmerie (2005)
Military service age and obligation: 18 years of age for compulsory military service; 20 years of age for voluntary military service (2001)
Manpower available for military service:
males age 18-49: 2,664,572 (2005 est.)

Manpower fit for military service: *males age 18-49:* 1,323,548 (2005 est.)
Military expenditures - dollar figure: $64.2 million (2004)
Military expenditures - percent of GDP: 1.3% (2004)

TRANSNATIONAL ISSUES

Disputes - international: two villages are in dispute along the border with Benin; Benin accuses Burkina Faso of moving boundary pillars; Burkina Faso border regions remain a staging area for Liberia and Cote d'Ivoire rebels and an asylum for refugees caught in local fighting; the Ivoirian Government accuses Burkina Faso of sheltering Ivoirian rebels

BURMA

INTRODUCTION

Background: Britain conquered Burma over a period of 62 years (1824-1886) and incorporated it into its Indian Empire. Burma was administered as a province of India until 1937 when it became a separate, self-governing colony; independence from the Commonwealth was attained in 1948. Gen. NE WIN dominated the government from 1962 to 1988, first as military ruler, then as self-appointed president, and later as political kingpin. Despite multiparty legislative elections in 1990 that resulted in the main opposition party - the National League for Democracy (NLD) - winning a landslide victory, the ruling junta refused to hand over power. NLD leader and Nobel Peace Prize recipient AUNG SAN SUU KYI, who was under house arrest from 1989 to 1995 and 2000 to 2002, was imprisoned in May 2003 and is currently under house arrest. In November 2005, the junta announced it was extending her detention for at least another six months. Her supporters, as well as all those who promote democracy and improved human rights, are routinely harassed or jailed.

GEOGRAPHY

Location: Southeastern Asia, bordering the Andaman Sea and the Bay of Bengal, between Bangladesh and Thailand
Geographic coordinates: 22 00 N, 98 00 E
Map references: Southeast Asia
Area:
total: 678,500 sq km
land: 657,740 sq km
water: 20,760 sq km
Area - comparative: slightly smaller than Texas
Land boundaries:
total: 5,876 km
border countries: Bangladesh 193 km, China 2,185 km, India 1,463 km, Laos 235 km, Thailand 1,800 km
Coastline: 1,930 km
Maritime claims:
territorial sea: 12 nm
contiguous zone: 24 nm
exclusive economic zone: 200 nm
continental shelf: 200 nm or to the edge of the continental margin
Climate: tropical monsoon; cloudy, rainy, hot, humid summers (southwest monsoon, June to September); less cloudy, scant rainfall, mild temperatures, lower humidity during winter (northeast monsoon, December to April)
Terrain: central lowlands ringed by steep, rugged highlands
Elevation extremes:
lowest point: Andaman Sea 0 m
highest point: Hkakabo Razi 5,881 m
Natural resources: petroleum, timber, tin, antimony, zinc, copper, tungsten, lead, coal, some marble, limestone, precious stones, natural gas, hydropower
Land use:
arable land: 15.19%
permanent crops: 0.97%
other: 83.84% (2001)
Irrigated land: 15,920 sq km (1998 est.)
Natural hazards: destructive earthquakes and cyclones; flooding and landslides common during rainy season (June to September); periodic droughts
Environment - current issues: deforestation; industrial pollution of air, soil, and water; inadequate sanitation and water treatment contribute to disease
Environment - international agreements:
party to: Biodiversity, Climate Change, Climate Change-Kyoto Protocol, Desertification, Endangered Species, Law of the Sea, Ozone Layer Protection, Ship Pollution, Tropical Timber 83, Tropical Timber 94
signed, but not ratified: none of the selected agreements
Geography - note: strategic location near major Indian Ocean shipping lanes

PEOPLE

Population: 42,909,464
note: estimates for this country take into account the effects of excess mortality due to AIDS; this can result in lower life expectancy, higher infant mortality and death rates, lower population growth rates, and changes in the distribution of population by age and sex than would otherwise be expected (July 2005 est.)
Age structure:
0-14 years: 27.2% (male 5,967,487/female 5,717,795)
15-64 years: 67.8% (male 14,448,887/female 14,641,419)
65 years and over: 5% (male 939,092/female 1,194,784) (2005 est.)
Median age:
total: 26.14 years
male: 25.57 years
female: 26.72 years (2005 est.)
Population growth rate: 0.42% (2005 est.)
Birth rate: 18.11 births/1,000 population (2005 est.)
Death rate: 12.15 deaths/1,000 population (2005 est.)
Net migration rate: -1.8 migrant(s)/1,000 population (2005 est.)
Sex ratio:
at birth: 1.06 male(s)/female
under 15 years: 1.04 male(s)/female
15-64 years: 0.99 male(s)/female
65 years and over: 0.79 male(s)/female
total population: 0.99 male(s)/female (2005 est.)
Infant mortality rate:
total: 67.24 deaths/1,000 live births
male: 73.11 deaths/1,000 live births
female: 61.03 deaths/1,000 live births (2005 est.)

Life expectancy at birth:
total population: 60.7 years
male: 57.8 years
female: 63.78 years (2005 est.)
Total fertility rate: 2.01 children born/woman (2005 est.)
HIV/AIDS - adult prevalence rate: 1.2% (2003 est.)
HIV/AIDS - people living with HIV/AIDS: 330,000 (2003 est.)
HIV/AIDS - deaths: 20,000 (2003 est.)
Major infectious diseases:
degree of risk: very high
food or waterborne diseases: bacterial and protozoal diarrhea, hepatitis A, and typhoid fever
vectorborne diseases: dengue fever and malaria are high risks in some locations (2004)
Nationality:
noun: Burmese (singular and plural)
adjective: Burmese
Ethnic groups: Burman 68%, Shan 9%, Karen 7%, Rakhine 4%, Chinese 3%, Indian 2%, Mon 2%, other 5%
Religions: Buddhist 89%, Christian 4% (Baptist 3%, Roman Catholic 1%), Muslim 4%, animist 1%, other 2%
Languages: Burmese, minority ethnic groups have their own languages
Literacy:
definition: age 15 and over can read and write
total population: 85.3%
male: 89.2%
female: 81.4% (2002)

GOVERNMENT

Country name:
conventional long form: Union of Burma
conventional short form: Burma
local long form: Pyidaungzu Myanma Naingngandaw (translated by the US Government as Union of Myanma and by the Burmese as Union of Myanmar)
local short form: Myanma Naingngandaw
former: Socialist Republic of the Union of Burma
note: since 1989 the military authorities in Burma have promoted the name Myanmar as a conventional name for their state; this decision was not approved by any sitting legislature in Burma, and the US Government did not adopt the name, which is a derivative of the Burmese short-form name Myanma Naingngandaw
Government type: military junta
Capital: Rangoon (government refers to capital as Yangon)
note: junta began shifting seat of government to Pyinmana area of central Burma in November 2005
Administrative divisions: 7 divisions (taing-myar, singular - taing) and 7 states (pyi ne-myar, singular - pyi ne)
: divisions: Ayeyarwady, Bago, Magway, Mandalay, Sagaing, Tanintharyi, Yangon
: states: Chin State, Kachin State, Kayin State, Kayah State, Mon State, Rakhine State, Shan State
Independence: 4 January 1948 (from UK)
National holiday: Independence Day, 4 January (1948); Union Day, 12 February (1947)
Constitution: 3 January 1974; suspended since 18 September 1988; national convention convened in 1993 to draft a new constitution but collapsed in 1996; reconvened in 2004 but does not include participation of democratic opposition
Legal system: has not accepted compulsory ICJ jurisdiction
Suffrage: 18 years of age; universal
Executive branch:
chief of state: Chairman of the State Peace and Development Council Sr. Gen. THAN SHWE (since 23 April 1992)
head of government: Prime Minister, Gen SOE WIN (since 19 October 2004)
cabinet: State Peace and Development Council (SPDC); military junta, so named 15 November 1997, which initially assumed power 18 September 1988 under the name State Law and Order Restoration Council (SLORC); the SPDC oversees the cabinet
elections: none
Legislative branch: unicameral People's Assembly or Pyithu Hluttaw (485 seats; members elected by popular vote to serve four-year terms)
elections: last held 27 May 1990, but Assembly never allowed by junta to convene
election results: percent of vote by party - NA%; seats by party - NLD 392 (opposition), SNLD 23 (opposition), NUP 10 (pro-government), other 60
Judicial branch: remnants of the British-era legal system are in place, but there is no guarantee of a fair public trial; the judiciary is not independent of the executive
Political parties and leaders: National League for Democracy or NLD [AUNG SHWE, chairman, AUNG SAN SUU KYI, general secretary]; National Unity Party or NUP (pro-regime) [THA KYAW] (at last report); Shan Nationalities League for Democracy or SNLD [KHUN HTUN OO]; and other smaller parties
Political pressure groups and leaders: National Coalition Government of the Union of Burma or NCGUB (self-proclaimed government in exile) ["Prime Minister" Dr. SEIN WIN] consists of individuals, some legitimately elected to the People's Assembly in 1990 (the group fled to a border area and joined insurgents in December 1990 to form parallel government in exile); Kachin Independence Army or KIA; Karen National Union or KNU; several Shan factions; United Wa State Army or UWSA; Union Solidarity and Development Association or USDA (pro-regime, a social and political organization) [HTAY OO, general secretary]
International organization participation: APT, ARF, AsDB, ASEAN, CP, EAS, FAO, G-77, IAEA, IBRD, ICAO, ICRM, IDA, IFAD, IFC, IFRCS, IHO, ILO, IMF, IMO, Interpol, IOC, ISO (correspondent), ITU, NAM, OPCW (signatory), UN, UNCTAD, UNESCO, UNIDO, UPU, WCO, WHO, WIPO, WMO, WTO
Diplomatic representation in the US:
chief of mission: Linn MYAING
chancery: 2300 S Street NW, Washington, DC 20008
telephone: [1] (202) 332-9044
FAX: [1] (202) 332-9046
consulate(s) general: New York
Diplomatic representation from the US:
chief of mission: Charge d'Affaires Shari VILLAROSA
embassy: 581 Merchant Street, Rangoon (GPO 521)
mailing address: Box B, APO AP 96546
telephone: [95] (1) 379-880, 379-881
FAX: [95] (1) 256-018
Flag description: red with a blue rectangle in the upper hoist-side corner bearing, 14 white five-pointed stars encircling a cogwheel containing a stalk of rice; the 14 stars represent the 7 administrative divisions and 7 states

ECONOMY

Economy - overview: Burma is a resource-rich country that suffers from government controls, inefficient economic policies, and abject rural poverty. The junta took steps in the early 1990s to liberalize the economy after decades of failure under the "Burmese Way to Socialism", but those efforts stalled and some of the liberalization measures were rescinded. Burma has been unable to achieve monetary or fiscal stability, resulting in an economy that suffers from serious macroeconomic imbalances - including inflation, multiple official exchange rates that overvalue the Burmese kyat, and a distorted interest rate regime. Most overseas development assistance ceased after the junta began to suppress the democracy movement in 1988 and subsequently ignored the results of the 1990 legislative elections. Economic sanctions against Burma by the United States - including a ban on imports of Burmese products and a ban on provision of financial services by US persons in response to the government of Burma's attack in May 2003 on AUNG SAN SUU KYI and her convoy - further slowed the inflow of foreign exchange. Oil and gas development will drive growth in the next few years. Other areas, however, are struggling. In February 2003, a major banking crisis hit the country's 20 private banks, shutting them down and disrupting the economy. As of December 2005, the largest private banks remained moribund, leaving the private sector with little formal access to credit. Official statistics are inaccurate. Published statistics on foreign trade are greatly understated because of the size of the black market and unofficial border trade - often estimated to be one to two times the size of the official economy. Burma's trade with Thailand, China, and India is rising. Though the Burmese government has good economic relations with its neighbors, a better investment climate and an improved political situation are needed to promote foreign investment, exports, and tourism.

GDP: purchasing power parity - $76.2 billion (2005 est.)

GDP (official exchange rate): $8.243 billion (2005 est.)

GDP - real growth rate: 1.5% (2005 est.)

GDP - per capita: purchasing power parity - $1,800 (2005 est.)

GDP - composition by sector:
agriculture: 54.6%
industry: 13%
services: 32.4% (2005 est.)

Labor force: 27.75 million (2005 est.)

Labor force - by occupation: agriculture 70%, industry 7%, services 23% (2001 est.)

Unemployment rate: 5% (2005 est.)

Population below poverty line: 25% (2000 est.)

Household income or consumption by percentage share:
lowest 10%: 2.8%
highest 10%: 32.4% (1998)

Inflation rate (consumer prices): 18% (2005 est.)

Investment (gross fixed): 11.5% of GDP (2005 est.)

Budget:
revenues: $523.5 million
expenditures: $769.3 million, including capital expenditures of $5.7 billion (2005 est.)

Agriculture - products: rice, pulses, beans, sesame, groundnuts, sugarcane; hardwood; fish and fish products

Industries: agricultural processing; knit and woven apparel; wood and wood products; copper, tin, tungsten, iron; construction materials; pharmaceuticals; fertilizer; cement; natural gas

Industrial production growth rate: NA

Electricity - production: 7.393 billion kWh (2003)

Electricity - production by source:
fossil fuel: 44.5%
hydro: 43.4%
nuclear: 0%
other: 12.1% (2002)

Electricity - consumption: 6.875 billion kWh (2003)

Electricity - exports: 0 kWh (2003)

Electricity - imports: 0 kWh (2004)

Oil - production: 18,500 bbl/day (2005 est.)

Oil - consumption: 32,000 bbl/day (2003 est.)

Oil - exports: 3,356 bbl/day (2003)

Oil - imports: 49,230 bbl/day (2003)

Oil - proved reserves: 3.2 billion bbl (2003)

Natural gas - production: 9.98 billion cu m (2003 est.)

Natural gas - consumption: 1.569 billion cu m (2003 est.)

Natural gas - exports: 8.424 billion cu m (2003 est.)

Natural gas - imports: 0 cu m (2003 est.)

Natural gas - proved reserves: 2.46 trillion cu m (2003)

Current account balance: $-215 million (2005 est.)

Exports: $2.514 billion f.o.b.
note: official export figures are grossly underestimated due to the value of timber, gems, narcotics, rice, and other products smuggled to Thailand, China, and Bangladesh (2005 est.)

Exports - partners: Thailand 38.9%, India 11.5%, China 5.9%, Japan 5.2% (2004)

Imports: $2.183 billion f.o.b.
note: import figures are grossly underestimated due to the value of consumer goods, diesel fuel, and other products smuggled in from Thailand, China, Malaysia, and India (2005 est.)

Imports - partners: China 29.8%, Singapore 20.8%, Thailand 19.3%, South Korea 5.2%, Malaysia 4.8% (2004)

Reserves of foreign exchange and gold: $721.1 million (June 2005)

Debt - eternal: $6.967 billion (2005 est.)

Economic aid - recipient: $127 million (2001 est.)

Currency: kyat (MMK)

Currency code: MMK

Exchange rates: kyats per US dollar - 5.82 (2005), 5.7459 (2004), 6.0764 (2003), 6.5734 (2002), 6.6841 (2001)
note: these are official exchange rates; unofficial exchange rates ranged in 2004 from 815 kyat/US dollar to nearly 970 kyat/US dollar, and by year-end 2005, the unofficial exchange rate was 1,075 kyat/US dollar

Fiscal year: 1 April - 31 March

COMMUNICATIONS

Telephones - main lines in use: 357,300 (2003)

Telephones - mobile cellular: 66,500 (2003)

Telephone system:
general assessment: barely meets minimum requirements for local and intercity service for business and government; international service is fair
domestic: NA
international: country code - 95; satellite earth station - 2, Intelsat (Indian Ocean), and ShinSat

Radio broadcast stations: AM 1, FM 1 (2004)

Radios: 4.2 million (1997)

Television broadcast stations: 2 (2004)

Televisions: 320,000 (2000)

Internet country code: .mm

Internet hosts: 3 (2003)

Internet Service Providers (ISPs): 1
note: as of September 2000, Internet connections were legal only for the government, tourist offices, and a few large businesses (2000)

Internet users: 28,000 (2003)

TRANSPORTATION

Airports: 78 (2004 est.)

Airports - with paved runways:
total: 19
over 3,047 m: 6
2,438 to 3,047 m: 10
1,524 to 2,437 m: 3 (2005 est.)

Airports - with unpaved runways:
total: 65
1,524 to 2,437 m: 14
914 to 1,523 m: 19
under 914 m: 32 (2005 est.)

Heliports: 1 (2005 est.)

Pipelines: gas 2,056 km; oil 558 km (2004)

Railways:
total: 3,955 km
narrow gauge: 3,955 km 1.000-m gauge (2004)

Roadways:
total: 30,000 km

Waterways: 12,800 km (2004)

Merchant marine:
total: 37 ships (1,000 GRT or over) 429,144 GRT/659,622 DWT
by type: bulk carrier 8, cargo 19, passenger 3, passenger/cargo 3, roll on/roll off 3, specialized tanker 1
foreign-owned: 10 (Germany 4, Japan 5, United Kingdom 1) (2005)

Ports and terminals: Moulmein, Rangoon, Sittwe

MILITARY

Military branches: Myanmar Armed Forces (Tatmadaw): Army, Navy, Air

Force (2005)

Military service age and obligation: 18 years of age for voluntary military service for both sexes (May 2002)

Manpower available for military service:
males age 18-49: 11,254,374
females age 18-49: 11,303,100 (2005 est.)

Manpower fit for military service: *males age 18-49:* 6,512,923
females age 18-49: 6,789,720 (2005 est.)

Manpower reaching military service age annually: *males:* 440,914
females: 427,382 (2005 est.)

Military expenditures - dollar figure: $39 million (FY97)

Military expenditures - percent of GDP: 2.1% (FY97)

TRANSNATIONAL ISSUES

Disputes - international: over half of Burma's population consists of diverse ethnic groups with substantial numbers of kin beyond its borders; despite continuing border committee talks, significant differences remain with Thailand over boundary alignment and the handling of ethnic rebels, refugees, and illegal cross-border activities; ethnic Karens flee into Thailand to escape fighting between Karen rebels and Burmese troops, in 2004 Thailand sheltered about 118,000 Burmese refugees; Karens also protest Thai support for a Burmese hydroelectric dam on the Salween River near the border; environmentalists in Burma and Thailand continue to voice concern over China's construction of hydroelectric dams upstream on the Nujiang/Salween River in Yunnan Province; India seeks cooperation from Burma to keep Indian Nagaland separatists from hiding in remote Burmese uplands

Refugees and internally displaced persons: *IDPs:* 600,000 - 1,000,000 (government offensives against ethnic insurgent groups near borders; most IDPs are ethnic Karen, Karenni, Shan, and Mon) (2004)

Illicit drugs: remains world's second largest producer of illicit opium (estimated production in 2004 - 292 metric tons, down 40% from 2003 due to eradication efforts and drought; cultivation in 2004 - 30,900 hectares, a 34% decline from 2003); lack of government will and ability to take on major narcotrafficking groups and lack of serious commitment against money laundering continues to hinder the overall antidrug effort; major source of methamphetamine and heroin for regional consumption; currently under Financial Action Task Force countermeasures due to continued failure to address its inadequate money-laundering controls (2005)

BURUNDI

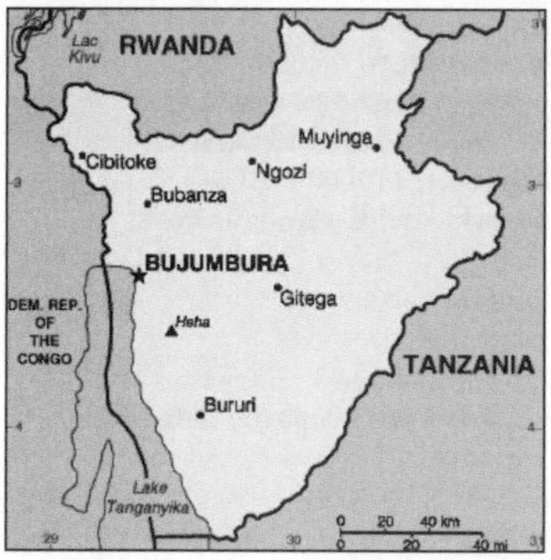

INTRODUCTION

Background: Burundi's first democratically elected president was assassinated in October 1993 after only one hundred days in office, triggering widespread ethnic violence between Hutu and Tutsi factions. Over 200,000 Burundians perished during the conflict that spanned almost a dozen years. Hundreds of thousands of Burundians were internally displaced or became refugees in neighboring countries. An internationally brokered power-sharing agreement between the Tutsi-dominated government and the Hutu rebels in 2003 paved the way for a transition process that led to an integrated defense force, established a new constitution in October 2004, and elected a majority Hutu government in 2005. The new government, led by President Pierre NKURUNZIZA, faces many challenges, particularly from the country's last rebel group who remains outside of the peace process and continue attacks in the western provinces of Burundi.

GEOGRAPHY

Location: Central Africa, east of Democratic Republic of the Congo

Geographic coordinates: 3 30 S, 30 00 E

Map references: Africa

Area:
total: 27,830 sq km
land: 25,650 sq km
water: 2,180 sq km

Area - comparative: slightly smaller than Maryland

Land boundaries:
total: 974 km
border countries: Democratic Republic of the Congo 233 km, Rwanda 290 km, Tanzania 451 km

Coastline: 0 km (landlocked)

Maritime claims: none (landlocked)

Climate: equatorial; high plateau with considerable altitude variation (772 m to 2,670 m above sea level); average annual temperature varies with altitude from 23 to 17 degrees centigrade but is generally moderate as the average altitude is about 1,700 m; average annual rainfall is about 150 cm; wet seasons from February to May and September to November, and dry seasons from June to August and December to January

Terrain: hilly and mountainous, dropping to a plateau in east, some plains

Elevation extremes:
lowest point: Lake Tanganyika 772 m
highest point: Heha 2,670 m

Natural resources: nickel, uranium, rare earth oxides, peat, cobalt, copper, platinum, vanadium, arable land, hydropower, niobium, tantalum, gold, tin, tungsten, kaolin, limestone

Land use:
arable land: 35.05%
permanent crops: 14.02%
other: 50.93% (2001)

Irrigated land: 740 sq km (1998 est.)

Natural hazards: flooding, landslides, drought

Environment - current issues: soil erosion as a result of overgrazing and the expansion of agriculture into marginal lands; deforestation (little forested land remains because of uncontrolled cutting of trees for fuel); habitat loss threatens wildlife populations

Environment - international agreements:
party to: Biodiversity, Climate Change, Climate Change-Kyoto Protocol, Desertification, Endangered Species, Hazardous Wastes, Ozone Layer Protection
signed, but not ratified: Law of the Sea

Geography - note: landlocked; straddles crest of the Nile-Congo watershed; the Kagera, which drains into Lake Victoria, is the most remote headstream of the White Nile

PEOPLE

Population: 6,370,609
note: estimates for this country explicitly take into account the effects of excess mortality due to AIDS; this can result in lower life expectancy, higher infant mortality and death rates, lower population and growth rates, and changes in the distribution of population by age and sex

than would otherwise be expected (July 2005 est.)

Age structure:
0-14 years: 46% (male 1,479,941/female 1,450,808)
15-64 years: 51.3% (male 1,617,864/ female 1,653,331)
65 years and over: 2.6% (male 66,199/ female 102,466) (2005 est.)

Median age:
total: 16.6 years
male: 16.27 years
female: 16.95 years (2005 est.)

Population growth rate: 2.22% (2005 est.)

Birth rate: 39.66 births/1,000 population (2005 est.)

Death rate: 17.43 deaths/1,000 population (2005 est.)

Net migration rate: 0 migrant(s)/1,000 population (2005 est.)

Sex ratio:
at birth: 1.03 male(s)/female
under 15 years: 1.02 male(s)/female
15-64 years: 0.98 male(s)/female
65 years and over: 0.65 male(s)/female
total population: 0.99 male(s)/female (2005 est.)

Infant mortality rate:
total: 69.29 deaths/1,000 live births
male: 75.87 deaths/1,000 live births
female: 62.5 deaths/1,000 live births (2005 est.)

Life expectancy at birth:
total population: 50.29 years
male: 49.61 years
female: 50.99 years (2005 est.)

Total fertility rate: 5.81 children born/woman (2005 est.)

HIV/AIDS - adult prevalence rate: 6% (2003 est.)

HIV/AIDS - people living with HIV/AIDS: 250,000 (2003 est.)

HIV/AIDS - deaths: 25,000 (2003 est.)

Major infectious diseases:
degree of risk: very high
food or waterborne diseases: bacterial diarrhea, hepatitis A, and typhoid fever
vectorborne disease: malaria (2004)

Nationality:
noun: Burundian(s)
adjective: Burundian

Ethnic groups: Hutu (Bantu) 85%, Tutsi (Hamitic) 14%, Twa (Pygmy) 1%, Europeans 3,000, South Asians 2,000

Religions: Christian 67% (Roman Catholic 62%, Protestant 5%), indigenous beliefs 23%, Muslim 10%

Languages: Kirundi (official), French (official), Swahili (along Lake Tanganyika and in the Bujumbura area)

Literacy:
definition: age 15 and over can read and write
total population: 51.6%
male: 58.5%
female: 45.2% (2003 est.)

GOVERNMENT

Country name:
conventional long form: Republic of Burundi
conventional short form: Burundi
local long form: Republika y'u Burundi
local short form: Burundi
former: Urundi

Government type: republic

Capital: Bujumbura

Administrative divisions: 16 provinces; Bubanza, Bujumbura, Bururi, Cankuzo, Cibitoke, Gitega, Karuzi, Kayanza, Kirundo, Makamba, Muramvya, Muyinga, Mwaro, Ngozi, Rutana, Ruyigi

Independence: 1 July 1962 (from UN trusteeship under Belgian administration)

National holiday: Independence Day, 1 July (1962)

Constitution: 28 February 2005; ratified by popular referendum

Legal system: based on German and Belgian civil codes and customary law; has not accepted compulsory ICJ jurisdiction

Suffrage: NA years of age; universal adult

Executive branch:
chief of state: President Pierre NKURUNZIZA (since 26 August 2005); Vice President Martin NDUWIMANA (since 26 August 2005)
head of government: President Pierre NKURUNZIZA (since 26 August 2005); Vice President Martin NDUWIMANA (since 26 August 2005)
cabinet: Council of Ministers appointed by president
elections: the president is elected by popular vote to a five year term; elections (by the legislature) last held 19 August 2005 (next to be held NA 2010); note - the constitution adopted in February 2005 permits the post-transition president to be elected by a two-thirds majority of the legislature
election results: Pierre NKURUNZIZA was elected president by the legislature by a vote of 151 to 9; note - the constitution adopted in February 2005 permits the post-transition president to be elected by a two-thirds majority of the legislature

Legislative branch: bicameral, consists of a National Assembly or Assemblee Nationale (minimum 100 seats; additional seats appointed by a National Independent Electoral Commission to ensure ethnic representation; members are elected by popular vote to serve five-year terms) and a Senate (54 seats; 34 by indirect vote to serve five year terms, with remaining seats assigned to ethnic groups and former chiefs of state)
elections: last held 4 July 2005 (next to be held in 2010)
election results: percent of vote by party - CNDD-FDD 58.6%, FRODEBU 21.7%, UPRONA 7.2%, CNDD 4.1%, MRC-Rurenzangemero 2.1%, others 6.2%; seats by party - CNDD-FDD 59, FRODEBU 25, UPRONA 10, CNDD 4, MRC-Rurenzangemero 2

Judicial branch: Supreme Court or Cour Supreme; Constitutional Court; Courts of Appeal (there are three in separate locations); Tribunals of First Instance (17 at the province level and 123 small local tribunals)

Political parties and leaders: the three national, mainstream, governing parties are: Unity for National Progress or UPRONA [Jean-Baptiste MANWANGARI, secretary general]; Burundi Democratic Front or FRODEBU [Leonce NGENDAKUMANA, president]; National Council for the Defense of Democracy, Front for the Defense of Democracy of CNDD-FDD [Hussein RADJABU, president]
note: a multiparty system was introduced after 1998, included are: National Resistance Movement for the Rehabilitation of the Citizen or MRC-Rurenzangemero [Epitace BANYAGANAKANDI]; Party for National Redress or PARENA [Jean-Baptiste BAGAZA]

Political pressure groups and leaders: Party for the Liberation of the Hutu People - National Liberation Front (Palipehutu - FNL); note - as of December 2005, the only insurgent group still fighting the government

International organization participation: ACCT, ACP, AfDB, AU, CEPGL, COMESA, FAO, G-77, IBRD, ICAO, ICCt, ICFTU, ICRM, IDA, IFAD, IFC, IFRCS, ILO, IMF, Interpol, IOC, IOM (observer), ISO (subscriber), ITU, MIGA, NAM, OPCW, UN, UNCTAD, UNESCO, UNIDO, UPU, WCO, WHO, WIPO, WMO, WToO, WTO

Diplomatic representation in the US:
chief of mission: Ambassador Antoine NTAMOBWA
chancery: Suite 212, 2233 Wisconsin Avenue NW, Washington, DC 20007
telephone: [1] (202) 342-2574
FAX: [1] (202) 342-2578

Diplomatic representation from the US:
chief of mission: Ambassador (vacant, as of 20 December 2005)
embassy: Avenue des Etats-Unis, Bujumbura
mailing address: B. P. 1720, Bujumbura
telephone: [257] 223454
FAX: [257] 222926

Flag description: divided by a white diagonal cross into red panels (top and bottom) and green panels (hoist side and outer side) with a white disk superimposed at the center bearing three red six-pointed stars outlined in green arranged in a triangular design (one star above, two stars below)

ECONOMY

Economy - overview: Burundi is a landlocked, resource-poor country with an underdeveloped manufacturing sector. The economy is predominantly agricultural with more than 90% of the population dependent on subsistence agriculture. Economic growth depends on coffee and tea exports, which account for 90% of foreign exchange earnings. The ability to pay for imports, therefore, rests primarily on weather conditions and international coffee and tea prices. The Tutsi minority, 14% of the population, dominates the government and the coffee trade at the expense of the Hutu majority, 85% of the population. Since October 1993 an ethnic-based war has resulted in more than 200,000 deaths, forced 450,000 refugees into Tanzania, and displaced 140,000 others internally. Only one in two children go to school, and approximately one in ten adults has HIV/AIDS. Food, medicine, and electricity remain in short supply. Political stability and the end of the civil war have improved aid flows and economic activity has increased, but underlying weaknesses - a high poverty rate, poor education rates, a weak legal system, and low administrative capacity - risk undermining planned economic reforms.
GDP: purchasing power parity - $4.432 billion (2005 est.)
GDP (official exchange rate): $739.5 million (2005 est.)
GDP - real growth rate: 5.5% (2005 est.)
GDP - per capita: purchasing power parity - purchasing power parity - $700 (2005 est.)
GDP - composition by sector:
agriculture: 45.6%
industry: 20.8%
services: 33.6% (2005 est.)
Labor force: 2.99 million (2002)
Labor force - by occupation: agriculture 93.6%, industry 2.3%, services 4.1% (2002 est.)
Unemployment rate: NA
Population below poverty line: 68% (2002 est.)
Household income or consumption by percentage share:
lowest 10%: 1.8%
highest 10%: 32.9% (1998)
Distribution of family income - Gini index: 33.3 (1998)
Inflation rate (consumer prices): 14% (2005 est.)
Investment (gross fixed): 11.5% of GDP (2005 est.)
Budget:
revenues: $215.4 million
expenditures: $278 million, including capital expenditures of NA (2005 est.)
Agriculture - products: coffee, cotton, tea, corn, sorghum, sweet potatoes, bananas, manioc (tapioca); beef, milk, hides
Industries: light consumer goods such as blankets, shoes, soap; assembly of imported components; public works construction; food processing
Industrial production growth rate: 18% (2001)
Electricity - production: 141.3 million kWh (2003)
Electricity - production by source:
fossil fuel: 0.6%
hydro: 99.4%
nuclear: 0%
other: 0% (2001)
Electricity - consumption: 141.4 million kWh (2003)
Electricity - exports: 0 kWh (2003)
Electricity - imports: 10 million kWh; note - supplied by the Democratic Republic of the Congo (2003)
Oil - production: 0 bbl/day (2003)
Oil - consumption: 3,000 bbl/day (2003 est.)
Oil - exports: NA (2001)
Oil - imports: NA (2001)
Current account balance: $-55 million (2005 est.)
Exports: $52 million f.o.b. (2005 est.)
Exports - partners: Germany 20.7%, Belgium 8.6%, Pakistan 7%, US 5.9%, Rwanda 5.9% (2004)
Imports: $200 million f.o.b. (2005 est.)
Imports - partners: Kenya 13.6%, Tanzania 11.1%, US 8.8%, Belgium 8.5%, France 8.3%, Italy 5.9%, Uganda 5.6%, Japan 4.6%, Germany 4.4% (2004)
Reserves of foreign exchange and gold: $76 million (2005 est.)
Debt - eternal: $1.2 billion (2003)
Economic aid - recipient: $105.5 million (2003)
Currency: Burundi franc (BIF)
Currency code: BIF
Exchange rates: Burundi francs per US dollar - 1,138 (2005), 1,100.91 (2004), 1,082.62 (2003), 930.75 (2002), 830.35 (2001)
Fiscal year: calendar year

COMMUNICATIONS

Telephones - main lines in use: 23,900 (2003)
Telephones - mobile cellular: 64,000 (2003)
Telephone system:
general assessment: primitive system
domestic: sparse system of open-wire, radiotelephone communications, and low-capacity microwave radio relay
international: country code - 257; satellite earth station - 1 Intelsat (Indian Ocean)
Radio broadcast stations: AM 0, FM 4, shortwave 1 (2001)
Radios: 440,000 (2001)
Television broadcast stations: 1 (2001)
Televisions: 25,000 (1997)
Internet country code: .bi
Internet hosts: 22 (2003)
Internet Service Providers (ISPs): 1 (2000)
Internet users: 14,000 (2003)

TRANSPORTATION

Airports: 8 (2004 est.)
Airports - with paved runways:
total: 1
over 3,047 m: 1 (2005 est.)
Airports - with unpaved runways:
total: 7
914 to 1,523 m: 4
under 914 m: 3 (2005 est.)
Roadways:
total: 14,480 km
paved: 1,028 km
unpaved: 13,452 km (1999)
Waterways: mainly on Lake Tanganyika (2004)
Ports and terminals: Bujumbura

MILITARY

Military branches: National Defense Force (Forces de Defense Nationales, FDN): Army (includes Naval Detachment and Air Wing), National Gendarmerie (disbanding begun in 2004) (2005)
Military service age and obligation: 16 years of age for compulsory and voluntary military service (2001)
Manpower available for military service:
males age 16-49: 1,379,793 (2005 est.)
Manpower fit for military service: *males age 16-49:* 693,956 (2005 est.)
Manpower reaching military service age annually: *males:* 84,597 (2005 est.)
Military expenditures - dollar figure: $38.7 million (2004)
Military expenditures - percent of GDP: 6% (2004)

TRANSNATIONAL ISSUES

Disputes - international: Tutsi, Hutu, other conflicting ethnic groups, associated political rebels, armed gangs, and various government forces continue fighting in the Great Lakes region, transcending the boundaries of Burundi, Democratic Republic of the Congo, Rwanda, and Uganda in an effort to gain control over populated and natural resource areas; government heads pledge to end conflict, but localized violence continues despite the presence of about

6,000 peacekeepers from the UN Operation in Burundi (ONUB) since 2004; although some 150,000 Burundian refugees have been repatriated, as of February 2005, Burundian refugees still reside in camps in western Tanzania as well as the Democratic Republic of the Congo

Refugees and internally displaced persons: *refugees (country of origin)*: 60,288 (Democratic Republic of the Congo)
IDPs: 140,000 (armed conflict between government and rebels; most IDPs in northern and western Burundi) (2004)

CAMBODIA

INTRODUCTION

Background: Most Cambodians consider themselves to be Khmers, descendants of the Angkor Empire that extended over much of Southeast Asia and reached its zenith between the 10th and 13th centuries. Attacks by the Thai and Cham (from present-day Vietnam) weakened the empire ushering in a long period of decline. The king placed the country under French protection in 1863. Cambodia became part of French Indochina in 1887. Following Japanese occupation in World War II, Cambodia gained full independence from France in 1953. In April 1975, after a five-year struggle, Communist Khmer Rouge forces captured Phnom Penh and evacuated all cities and towns. At least 1.5 million Cambodians died from execution, forced hardships, or starvation during the Khmer Rouge regime under POL POT. A December 1978 Vietnamese invasion drove the Khmer Rouge into the countryside, began a 10-year Vietnamese occupation, and touched off almost 13 years of civil war. The 1991 Paris Peace Accords mandated democratic elections and a ceasefire, which was not fully respected by the Khmer Rouge. UN-sponsored elections in 1993 helped restore some semblance of normalcy under a coalition government. Factional fighting in 1997 ended the first coalition government, but a second round of national elections in 1998 led to the formation of another coalition government and renewed political stability. The remaining elements of the Khmer Rouge surrendered in early 1999. Some of the remaining leaders are awaiting trial by a UN-sponsored tribunal for crimes against humanity. Elections in July 2003 were relatively peaceful, but it took one year of negotiations between contending political parties before a coalition government was formed.

GEOGRAPHY

Location: Southeastern Asia, bordering the Gulf of Thailand, between Thailand, Vietnam, and Laos

Geographic coordinates: 13 00 N, 105 00 E

Map references: Southeast Asia

Area:
total: 181,040 sq km
land: 176,520 sq km
water: 4,520 sq km

Area - comparative: slightly smaller than Oklahoma

Land boundaries:
total: 2,572 km
border countries: Laos 541 km, Thailand 803 km, Vietnam 1,228 km

Coastline: 443 km

Maritime claims:
territorial sea: 12 nm
contiguous zone: 24 nm
exclusive economic zone: 200 nm
continental shelf: 200 nm

Climate: tropical; rainy, monsoon season (May to November); dry season (December to April); little seasonal temperature variation

Terrain: mostly low, flat plains; mountains in southwest and north

Elevation extremes:
lowest point: Gulf of Thailand 0 m
highest point: Phnum Aoral 1,810 m

Natural resources: oil and gas, timber, gemstones, some iron ore, manganese, phosphates, hydropower potential

Land use:
arable land: 20.96%
permanent crops: 0.61%
other: 78.43% (2001)

Irrigated land: 2,700 sq km (1998 est.)

Natural hazards: monsoonal rains (June to November); flooding; occasional droughts

Environment - current issues: illegal logging activities throughout the country and strip mining for gems in the western region along the border with Thailand have resulted in habitat loss and declining biodiversity (in particular, destruction of mangrove swamps threatens natural fisheries); soil erosion; in rural areas, most of the population does not have access to potable water; declining fish stocks because of illegal fishing and overfishing

Environment - international agreements:
party to: Biodiversity, Climate Change, Climate Change-Kyoto Protocol, Desertification, Endangered Species, Hazardous Wastes, Marine Life Conservation, Ozone Layer Protection, Ship Pollution, Tropical Timber 94, Wetlands
signed, but not ratified: Law of the Sea

Geography - note: a land of paddies and forests dominated by the Mekong River and Tonle Sap

PEOPLE

Population: 13,607,069
note: estimates for this country take into account the effects of excess mortality due to AIDS; this can result in lower life expectancy, higher infant mortality and death rates, lower population growth rates, and changes in the distribution of population by age and sex than would otherwise be expected (July 2005 est.)

Age structure:
0-14 years: 37.3% (male 2,559,734/female 2,510,235)
15-64 years: 59.7% (male 3,887,642/female 4,232,313)
65 years and over: 3.1% (male 150,862/female 266,283) (2005 est.)

Median age:
total: 19.91 years
male: 19.16 years
female: 20.79 years (2005 est.)

Population growth rate: 1.81% (2005 est.)

Birth rate: 27.08 births/1,000 population (2005 est.)

Death rate: 8.97 deaths/1,000 population (2005 est.)

Net migration rate: 0 migrant(s)/1,000 population (2005 est.)

Sex ratio:
at birth: 1.05 male(s)/female
under 15 years: 1.02 male(s)/female
15-64 years: 0.92 male(s)/female
65 years and over: 0.57 male(s)/female
total population: 0.94 male(s)/female (2005 est.)

Infant mortality rate:
total: 71.48 deaths/1,000 live births
male: 80.13 deaths/1,000 live births
female: 62.43 deaths/1,000 live births (2005 est.)

Life expectancy at birth:
total population: 58.92 years
male: 56.98 years
female: 60.95 years (2005 est.)

Total fertility rate: 3.44 children born/woman (2005 est.)

HIV/AIDS - adult prevalence rate: 2.6% (2003 est.)

HIV/AIDS - people living with HIV/AIDS: 170,000 (2003 est.)

HIV/AIDS - deaths: 15,000 (2003 est.)

Major infectious diseases:
degree of risk: very high
food or waterborne diseases: bacterial and protozoal diarrhea, hepatitis A, and typhoid fever
vectorborne diseases: dengue fever, malaria,

and Japanese encephalitis are high risks in some locations
note: at present, H5N1 avian influenza poses a minimal risk; during outbreaks among birds, rare cases could occur among US personnel who have close contact with infected birds or poultry (2005)
Nationality:
noun: Cambodian(s)
adjective: Cambodian
Ethnic groups: Khmer 90%, Vietnamese 5%, Chinese 1%, other 4%
Religions: Theravada Buddhist 95%, other 5%
Languages: Khmer (official) 95%, French, English
Literacy:
definition: age 15 and over can read and write
total population: 73.6%
male: 84.7%
female: 64.1% (2004 est.)

GOVERNMENT

Country name:
conventional long form: Kingdom of Cambodia
conventional short form: Cambodia
local long form: Preahreacheanacha Kampuchea (phonetic pronunciation)
local short form: Kampuchea
former: Kingdom of Cambodia, Khmer Republic, Democratic Kampuchea, People's Republic of Kampuchea, State of Cambodia
Government type: multiparty democracy under a constitutional monarchy established in September 1993
Capital: Phnom Penh
Administrative divisions: 20 provinces (khaitt, singular and plural) and 4 municipalities (krong, singular and plural)
: provinces: Banteay Mean Chey, Batdambang, Kampong Cham, Kampong Chhnang, Kampong Spoe, Kampong Thum, Kampot, Kandal, Koh Kong, Kracheh, Mondol Kiri, Otdar Mean Chey, Pouthisat, Preah Vihear, Prey Veng, Rotanakir, Siem Reab, Stoeng Treng, Svay Rieng, Takao
: municipalities: Keb, Pailin, Phnom Penh, Preah Seihanu
Independence: 9 November 1953 (from France)
National holiday: Independence Day, 9 November (1953)
Constitution: promulgated 21 September 1993
Legal system: primarily a civil law mixture of French-influenced codes from the United Nations Transitional Authority in Cambodia (UNTAC) period, royal decrees, and acts of the legislature, with influences of customary law and remnants of communist legal theory; increasing influence of common law in recent years
Suffrage: 18 years of age; universal
Executive branch:
chief of state: King Norodom SIHAMONI (since 29 October 2004)
head of government: Prime Minister HUN SEN (since 14 January 1985) and Deputy Prime Ministers SAR KHENG (since 3 February 1992), Norodom SIRIVUDH, SOK AN, LU LAY SRENG, TEA BANH, HOR NAMHONG, NHEK BUNCHHAY (since 16 July 2004)
cabinet: Council of Ministers in theory appointed by the monarch; in practice named by the prime minister
elections: none; the monarch is chosen by a Royal Throne Council; following legislative elections, a member of the majority party or majority coalition is named prime minister by the Chairman of the National Assembly and appointed by the king
Legislative branch: bicameral, consists of the National Assembly (123 seats; members elected by popular vote to serve five year terms) and the Senate (61 seats; two members appointed by the monarch, two elected by the National Assembly, and 57 elected by "functional constituencies"; members serve five-year terms)
elections: National Assembly - last held 27 July 2003 (next to be held in July 2008); Senate - last held 2 March 1999 (next to be held in January 2006)
election results: National Assembly - percent of vote by party - CPP 47%, SRP 22%, FUNCINPEC 21%, other 10%; seats by party - CPP 73, FUNCINPEC 26, SRP 24; Senate - percent of vote by party - NA%; seats by party - CPP 31, FUNCINPEC 21, SRP 7, other 2 (July 2003)
Judicial branch: Supreme Council of the Magistracy (provided for in the constitution and formed in December 1997); Supreme Court (and lower courts) exercises judicial authority
Political parties and leaders: Cambodian Pracheachon Party (Cambodian People's Party) or CPP [CHEA SIM]; National United Front for an Independent, Neutral, Peaceful, and Cooperative Cambodia or FUNCINPEC [Prince Norodam RANARIDDH]; Sam Rangsi Party or SRP [Sam RANGSI]
Political pressure groups and leaders: NA
International organization participation: ACCT, APT, ARF, AsDB, ASEAN, EAS, FAO, G-77, IBRD, ICAO, ICCt, ICRM, IDA, IFAD, IFC, IFRCS, ILO, IMF, IMO, Interpol, IOC, IOM, ISO (subscriber), ITU, MIGA, NAM, OPCW, PCA, UN, UNCTAD, UNESCO, UNIDO, UNMIS, UPU, WCO, WFTU, WHO, WIPO, WMO, WToO, WTO
Diplomatic representation in the US:
chief of mission: Ambassador EK SEREYWATH
chancery: 4530 16th Street NW, Washington, DC 20011
telephone: [1] (202) 726-7742
FAX: [1] (202) 726-8381
Diplomatic representation from the US:
chief of mission: Ambassador Joseph A. MUSSOMELI
embassy: 1, Street 96, Sangkat Wat Phnom, Phnom Penh
mailing address: Box P, APO AP 96546
telephone: [855] (23) 728-000
FAX: [855] (23) 216-437/811
Flag description: three horizontal bands of blue (top), red (double width), and blue with a white three-towered temple representing Angkor Wat outlined in black in the center of the red band; only national flag to incorporate a building in its design

ECONOMY

Economy - overview: In 1999, the first full year of peace in 30 years, the government made progress on economic reforms. The United States and Cambodia signed a Bilateral Textile Agreement, which gave Cambodia a guaranteed quota of US textile imports and established a bonus for improving working conditions and enforcing Cambodian labor laws and international labor standards in the industry. From 2001 to 2004, the economy grew at an average rate of 6.4%, driven largely by an expansion in the garment sector and tourism. With the January 2005 expiration of a WTO Agreement on Textiles and Clothing, Cambodia-based textile producers were forced to compete directly with lower priced producing countries such as China and India. Economic growth slowed to an estimated 3.8% in 2005, due to sharply higher competitive pressures in the garment industry and early droughts in 14 of 24 provinces. Faced with the possibility that that its vibrant garment industry, with more than 200,000 jobs, could be in serious danger, the Cambodian government has committed itself to a policy of continued support for high labor standards in an attempt to maintain favor with buyers. The tourism industry continues to grow rapidly, with foreign visitors surpassing one million for the year by September 2005. The long-term development of the economy remains a daunting challenge. The Cambodian government continues to work with bilateral and multilateral donors, including the World Bank and IMF, to address the country's many pressing needs. In December 2004, official donors pledged $504 million in aid for 2005 on the condition that the Cambodian government implement steps to reduce corruption. The major economic challenge for Cambodia over the next decade will be fashioning an economic environment in which the private sector can create enough jobs to handle Cambodia's demographic imbalance. More than 50% of the population is 20 years or younger. The population lacks education and productive skills, particularly in the poverty-ridden countryside, which suffers from an almost total lack of basic infrastructure. Fully 75% of the population remains engaged in subsistence farming.

GDP (purchasing power parity): $28.71 billion (2005 est.)
GDP (official exchange rate): $4.92 billion (2005 est.)
GDP - real growth rate: 4% (2005 est.)
GDP - per capita: purchasing power parity - $2,100 (2005 est.)
GDP – composition by sector: *agriculture:* 32.9%
industry: 29.2%
services: 37.9% (2004)
Labor force: 7 million (2003 est.)
Labor force - by occupation: agriculture 75% (2004 est.)
Unemployment rate: 2.5% (2000 est.)
Population below poverty line: 40% (2004 est.)
Household income or consumption by percentage share:
lowest 10%: 2.9%
highest 10%: 33.8% (1997)
Distribution of family income - Gini index: 40 (2004 est.)
Inflation rate (consumer prices): 4.3% (2005 est.)
Investment (gross fixed): 22.8% of GDP (2005 est.)
Budget:
revenues: $559.4 million
expenditures: $772 million (2005 est.)
Agriculture - products: rice, rubber, corn, vegetables, cashews, tapioca
Industries: tourism, garments, rice milling, fishing, wood and wood products, rubber, cement, gem mining, textiles
Industrial production growth rate: 22% (2002 est.)
Electricity - production: 123.7 million kWh (2003)
Electricity - production by source:
fossil fuel: 65%
hydro: 35%
nuclear: 0%
other: 0% (2001)
Electricity - consumption: 115 million kWh (2003)
Electricity - exports: 0 kWh (2003)
Electricity - imports: 0 kWh (2003)
Oil - production: 0 bbl/day (2003)
Oil - consumption: 3,700 bbl/day (2003 est.)
Oil - exports: NA (2001)
Oil - imports: NA (2001)
Current account balance: $-269 million (2005 est.)
Exports: $2.663 billion f.o.b. (2005 est.)
Exports - partners: US 55.9%, Germany 11.7%, UK 6.9%, Vietnam 4.4%, Canada 4.2% (2004)
Imports: $3.538 billion f.o.b. (2005 est.)
Imports - partners: Thailand 22.5%, Hong Kong 14.1%, China 13.6%, Vietnam 10.9%, Singapore 10.8%, Taiwan 8.4% (2004)
Reserves of foreign exchange and gold: $1.1 billion (2005 est.)
Debt - external: $800 million (2003 est.)
Economic aid - recipient: $504 million pledged in grants and concessional loans for 2005 by international donors
Currency (code): riel (KHR)
Currency code: KHR
Exchange rates: riels per US dollar - 4,098 (2005), 4,016.25 (2004), 3,973.33 (2003), 3,912.08 (2002), 3,916.33 (2001)
Fiscal year: calendar year

COMMUNICATION

Telephones - main lines in use: 35,400 (2002)
Telephones - mobile cellular: 380,000 (2002)
Telephone system:
general assessment: adequate landline and/or cellular service in Phnom Penh and other provincial cities; mobile phone coverage is rapidly expanding in rural areas
domestic: NA
international: country code - 855; adequate but expensive landline and cellular service available to all countries from Phnom Penh and major provincial cities; satellite earth station - 1 Intersputnik (Indian Ocean region)
Radio broadcast stations: AM 2, FM 17, (2003)
Radios: 1.34 million (1997)
Television broadcast stations: 7 (2003)
Televisions: 94,000 (1997)
Internet country code: .kh
Internet hosts: 818 (2003)
Internet Service Providers (ISPs): 2 (2000)
Internet users: 30,000 (2002)

TRANSPORTATION

Airports: 20 (2004 est.)
Airports - with paved runways:
total: 6
2,438 to 3,047 m: 2
1,524 to 2,437 m: 2
914 to 1,523 m: 2 (2005 est.)
Airports - with unpaved runways:
total: 14
1,524 to 2,437 m: 2
914 to 1,523 m: 11
under 914 m: 1 (2005 est.)
Heliports: 2 (2005 est.)
Railways:
total: 602 km
narrow gauge: 602 km 1.000-m gauge (2004)
Roadways:
total: 12,323 km
paved: 1,996 km
unpaved: 10,327 km (2000)
Waterways: 2,400 km (mainly on Mekong River) (2004)
Merchant marine:
total: 479 ships (1,000 GRT or over) 1,913,910 GRT/2,713,967 DWT
by type: bulk carrier 34, cargo 396, chemical tanker 9, container 6, livestock carrier 3, passenger/cargo 3, petroleum tanker 11, refrigerated cargo 11, roll on/roll off 5, specialized tanker 1
foreign-owned: 193 (Canada 4, China 39, China 2, Cyprus 4, Egypt 5, Estonia 2, France 1, Germany 1, Greece 6, Honduras 1, Hong Kong 3, Indonesia 1, Isle of Man 1, Israel 1, Italy 1, Japan 1, Lebanon 1, Nigeria 2, Norway 1, Russia 58, Singapore 5, South Korea 23, Syria 8, Turkey 7, Ukraine 6, UAE 1, United States 7, Yemen 1) (2005)
Ports and terminals: Phnom Penh

MILITARY

Military branches: Royal Cambodian Armed Forces: Army, Royal Khmer Navy, Royal Cambodian Air Force (2005)
Military service age and obligation: 18-30 years of age for compulsory military service for all males; conscription law passed September 2004; service obligation is 18 months (September 2004)
Manpower available for military service: *males age 18-49:* 2,981,823 (2005 est.)
Manpower fit for military service: *males age 18-49:* 1,844,144 (2005 est.)
Manpower reaching military service age annually: *males:* 175,305 (2005 est.)
Military expenditures - dollar figure: $112 million (FY01 est.)
Military expenditures - percent of GDP: 3% (FY01 est.)

TRANSNATIONAL ISSUES

Disputes - international: Southeast Asian states have enhanced border surveillance to check the spread of avian flu;

Cambodia and Thailand dispute sections of boundary with missing boundary markers and Thai encroachments into Cambodian territory; maritime boundary with Vietnam is hampered by unresolved dispute over offshore islands; Cambodia accuses Thailand of obstructing access to Preah Vihear temple ruins awarded to Cambodia by ICJ decision in 1962; in 2004 Cambodian-Laotian and Laotian-Vietnamese boundary commissions reerect missing markers completing most of their demarcations
Illicit drugs: narcotics-related corruption reportedly involving some in the government, military, and police; possible small-scale opium, heroin, and amphetamine production; large producer of cannabis for the international market; vulnerable to money laundering due to its cash-based economy and porous borders

CAMEROON

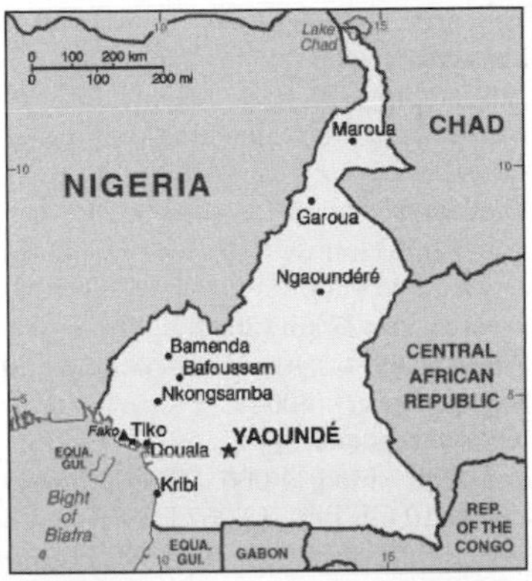

INTRODUCTION

Background: The former French Cameroon and part of British Cameroon merged in 1961 to form the present country. Cameroon has generally enjoyed stability, which has permitted the development of agriculture, roads, and railways, as well as a petroleum industry. Despite a slow movement toward democratic reform, political power remains firmly in the hands of an ethnic oligarchy headed by President Paul BIYA.

GEOGRAPHY

Location: Western Africa, bordering the Bight of Biafra, between Equatorial Guinea and Nigeria
Geographic coordinates: 6 00 N, 12 00 E
Map references: Africa
Area:
total: 475,440 sq km
land: 469,440 sq km
water: 6,000 sq km
Area - comparative: slightly larger than California
Land boundaries:
total: 4,591 km
border countries: Central African Republic 797 km, Chad 1,094 km, Republic of the Congo 523 km, Equatorial Guinea 189 km, Gabon 298 km, Nigeria 1,690 km
Coastline: 402 km
Maritime claims: *territorial sea:* 50 nm
Climate: varies with terrain, from tropical along coast to semiarid and hot in north
Terrain: diverse, with coastal plain in southwest, dissected plateau in center, mountains in west, plains in north
Elevation extremes:
lowest point: Atlantic Ocean 0 m
highest point: Fako (on Mount Cameroon) 4,095 m
Natural resources: petroleum, bauxite, iron ore, timber, hydropower
Land use:
arable land: 12.81%
permanent crops: 2.58%
other: 84.61% (2001)
Irrigated land: 330 sq km (1998 est.)
Natural hazards: volcanic activity with periodic releases of poisonous gases from Lake Nyos and Lake Monoun volcanoes
Environment - current issues: waterborne diseases are prevalent; deforestation; overgrazing; desertification; poaching; overfishing
Environment - international agreements:
party to: Biodiversity, Climate Change, Climate Change-Kyoto Protocol, Desertification, Endangered Species, Hazardous Wastes, Law of the Sea, Ozone Layer Protection, Tropical Timber 83, Tropical Timber 94
signed, but not ratified: none of the selected agreements
Geography - note: sometimes referred to as the hinge of Africa; throughout the country there are areas of thermal springs and indications of current or prior volcanic activity; Mount Cameroon, the highest mountain in Sub-Saharan west Africa, is an active volcano

PEOPLE

Population: 16,380,005
note: estimates for this country explicitly take into account the effects of excess mortality due to AIDS; this can result in lower life expectancy, higher infant mortality and death rates, lower population and growth rates, and changes in the distribution of population by age and sex than would otherwise be expected (July 2005 est.)
Age structure:
0-14 years: 41.7% (male 3,457,180/female 3,375,668)
15-64 years: 55% (male 4,537,281/female 4,477,163)
65 years and over: 3.3% (male 239,634/female 293,079) (2005 est.)
Median age:
total: 18.6 years
male: 18.45 years
female: 18.76 years (2005 est.)
Population growth rate: 1.93% (2005 est.)
Birth rate: 34.67 births/1,000 population (2005 est.)
Death rate: 15.4 deaths/1,000 population (2005 est.)
Net migration rate: 0 migrant(s)/1,000 population (2005 est.)
Sex ratio:
at birth: 1.03 male(s)/female
under 15 years: 1.02 male(s)/female
15-64 years: 1.01 male(s)/female
65 years and over: 0.82 male(s)/female
total population: 1.01 male(s)/female (2005 est.)
Infant mortality rate:
total: 68.26 deaths/1,000 live births
male: 72.14 deaths/1,000 live births
female: 64.27 deaths/1,000 live births (2005 est.)
Life expectancy at birth:
total population: 50.89 years
male: 50.71 years
female: 51.08 years (2005 est.)
Total fertility rate: 4.47 children born/woman (2005 est.)
HIV/AIDS - adult prevalence rate: 6.9% (2003 est.)
HIV/AIDS - people living with HIV/AIDS: 560,000 (2003 est.)
HIV/AIDS - deaths: 49,000 (2003 est.)
Major infectious diseases:
degree of risk: very high
food or waterborne diseases: bacterial diarrhea, hepatitis A, and typhoid fever
vectorborne diseases: malaria and yellow fever are high risks in some locations
water contact disease: schistosomiasis
respiratory disease: meningococcal meningitis (2004)
Nationality:
noun: Cameroonian(s)
adjective: Cameroonian
Ethnic groups: Cameroon Highlanders 31%, Equatorial Bantu 19%, Kirdi 11%, Fulani 10%, Northwestern Bantu 8%, Eastern Nigritic 7%, other African 13%, non-African less than 1%
Religions: indigenous beliefs 40%, Christian 40%, Muslim 20%
Languages: 24 major African language groups, English (official), French (official)
Literacy:
definition: age 15 and over can read and write

total population: 79%
male: 84.7%
female: 73.4% (2003 est.)

GOVERNMENT

Country name:
conventional long form: Republic of Cameroon
conventional short form: Cameroon
former: French Cameroon
Government type: unitary republic; multiparty presidential regime (opposition parties legalized in 1990)
note: preponderance of power remains with the president
Capital: Yaounde
Administrative divisions: 10 provinces; Adamaoua, Centre, Est, Extreme-Nord, Littoral, Nord, Nord-Ouest, Ouest, Sud, Sud-Ouest
Independence: 1 January 1960 (from French-administered UN trusteeship)
National holiday: Republic Day (National Day), 20 May (1972)
Constitution: 20 May 1972 approved by referendum, 2 June 1972 formally adopted; revised January 1996
Legal system: based on French civil law system, with common law influence; has not accepted compulsory ICJ jurisdiction
Suffrage: 20 years of age; universal
Executive branch:
chief of state: President Paul BIYA (since 6 November 1982)
head of government: Prime Minister Ephraim INONI (since 8 Dec 2004)
cabinet: Cabinet appointed by the president from proposals submitted by the prime minister
elections: president elected by popular vote for a seven-year term; election last held 11 October 2004 (next to be held NA October 2011); prime minister appointed by the president
election results: President Paul BIYA reelected; percent of vote - Paul BIYA 70.9%, John FRUNDI 17.4%, Adamou Ndam NJOYA 4.5%, Garga Haman ADJI 3.7%
Legislative branch: unicameral National Assembly or Assemblee Nationale (180 seats; members are elected by direct popular vote to serve five-year terms; note - the president can either lengthen or shorten the term of the legislature)
elections: last held 23 June 2002 (next to be held NA 2007)
election results: percent of vote by party - NA%; seats by party - RDCP 133, SDF 21, UDC 5, other 21
note: the constitution calls for an upper chamber for the legislature, to be called a Senate, but it has yet to be established
Judicial branch: Supreme Court (judges are appointed by the president); High Court of Justice (consists of 9 judges and 6 substitute judges, elected by the National Assembly)
Political parties and leaders: Cameroonian Democratic Union or UDC [Adamou NDAM NJOYA]; Democratic Rally of the Cameroon People or RDCP [Paul BIYA]; Movement for the Defense of the Republic or MDR [Dakole DAISSALA]; Movement for the Liberation and Development of Cameroon or MLDC [leader Marcel YONDO]; Movement for the Youth of Cameroon or MYC [Dieudonne TINA]; National Union for Democracy and Progress or UNDP [Maigari Bello BOUBA]; Social Democratic Front or SDF [John Fru NDI]; Union of Cameroonian Populations or UPC [Augustin Frederic KODOCK]
Political pressure groups and leaders: Southern Cameroon National Council [Ayamba Ette OTUN]; Human Rights Defense Group [Albert MUKONG, president]
International organization participation: ACCT, ACP, AfDB, AU, BDEAC, C, CEMAC, FAO, FZ, G-77, IAEA, IBRD, ICAO, ICC, ICCt (signatory), ICFTU, ICRM, IDA, IDB, IFAD, IFC, IFRCS, ILO, IMF, IMO, Interpol, IOC, ITU, MIGA, MONUC, NAM, OIC, OPCW, PCA, UN, UNCTAD, UNESCO, UNIDO, UPU, WCL, WCO, WFTU, WHO, WIPO, WMO, WToO, WTO
Diplomatic representation in the US:
chief of mission: Ambassador Jerome MENDOUGA
chancery: 2349 Massachusetts Avenue NW, Washington, DC 20008
telephone: [1] (202) 265-8790
FAX: [1] (202) 387-3826
Diplomatic representation from the US:
chief of mission: Ambassador Niels MARQUADT
embassy: Rue Nachtigal, Yaounde
mailing address: P. O. Box 817, Yaounde; pouch: American Embassy, Department of State, Washington, DC 20521-2520
telephone: [237] 223-05-12, 222-25-89, 222-17-94, 223-40-14
FAX: [237] 223-07-53
branch office(s): Douala
Flag description: three equal vertical bands of green (hoist side), red, and yellow with a yellow five-pointed star centered in the red band; uses the popular pan-African colors of Ethiopia

ECONOMY

Economy - overview: Because of its oil resources and favorable agricultural conditions, Cameroon has one of the best-endowed primary commodity economies in sub-Saharan Africa. Still, it faces many of the serious problems facing other underdeveloped countries, such as a top-heavy civil service and a generally unfavorable climate for business enterprise. Since 1990, the government has embarked on various IMF and World Bank programs designed to spur business investment, increase efficiency in agriculture, improve trade, and recapitalize the nation's banks. In June 2000, the government completed an IMF-sponsored, three-year structural adjustment program; however, the IMF is pressing for more reforms, including increased budget transparency, privatization, and poverty reduction programs. International oil and cocoa prices have considerable impact on the economy.
GDP (purchasing power parity): $32.35 billion (2005 est.)
GDP (official exchange rate): $15.91 billion (2005 est.)
GDP - real growth rate: 5% (2005 est.)
GDP - per capita: purchasing power parity - $2,000 (2005 est.)
GDP - composition by sector:
agriculture: 44.8%
industry: 17.3%
services: 37.9% (2005 est.)
Labor force: 6.86 million (2005 est.)
Labor force - by occupation: agriculture 70%, industry and commerce 13%, other 17%
Unemployment rate: 30% (2001 est.)
Population below poverty line: 48% (2000 est.)
Household income or consumption by percentage share:
lowest 10%: 1.9%
highest 10%: 36.6% (1996)
Distribution of family income - Gini index: 44.6 (2001)
Inflation rate (consumer prices): 1.5% (2005 est.)
Investment (gross fixed): 17.3% of GDP (2005 est.)
Budget:
revenues: $3.263 billion
expenditures: $2.705 billion, including capital expenditures of NA (2005 est.)
Public debt: 64.8% of GDP (2005 est.)
Agriculture - products: coffee, cocoa, cotton, rubber, bananas, oilseed, grains, root starches; livestock; timber
Industries: petroleum production and refining, aluminum production, food processing, light consumer goods, textiles, lumber, ship repair
Industrial production growth rate: 4.2% (1999 est.)

Electricity - production: 2.988 billion kWh (2003)
Electricity - production by source:
fossil fuel: 2.7%
hydro: 97.3%
nuclear: 0%
other: 0% (2001)
Electricity - consumption: 2.779 billion kWh (2003)
Electricity - exports: 0 kWh (2003)
Electricity - imports: 0 kWh (2003)
Oil - production: 82,300 bbl/day (2005 est.)
Oil - consumption: 23,000 bbl/day (2001 est.)
Oil - exports: NA (2001)
Oil - imports: NA (2001)
Oil - proved reserves: 85 million bbl (2005 est.)
Natural gas - production: 0 cu m (2001 est.)
Natural gas - consumption: 0 cu m (2001 est.)
Natural gas - exports: 0 cu m (2001 est.)
Natural gas - imports: 0 cu m (2001 est.)
Natural gas - proved reserves: 55.22 billion cu m (2005)
Current account balance: $159 million (2005 est.)
Exports: $3.236 billion f.o.b. (2005 est.)
Exports - partners: Spain 15.2%, Italy 12.3%, UK 10.2%, France 9.2%, US 8.8%, South Korea 7.1%, Netherlands 4.3% (2004)
Imports: $2.514 billion f.o.b. (2005 est.)
Imports - partners: France 28.2%, Nigeria 9.9%, Belgium 7.6%, US 4.9%, China 4.8%, Germany 4.6%, Italy 4.1% (2004)
Reserves of foreign exchange and gold: $1.092 billion (2005 est.)
Debt - external: $9.223 billion (2005 est.)
Economic aid - recipient: on 23 January 2001, the Paris Club agreed to reduce Cameroon's debt of $1.3 billion by $900 million; debt relief now totals $1.26 billion
Currency (code): Communaute Financiere Africaine franc (XAF); note - responsible authority is the Bank of the Central African States
Currency code: XAF
Exchange rates: Communaute Financiere Africaine francs (XAF) per US dollar - 521.74 (2005), 528.29 (2004), 581.2 (2003), 696.99 (2002), 733.04 (2001)
Fiscal year: 1 July - 30 June

COMMUNICATION

Telephones - main lines in use: 110,900 (2002)
Telephones - mobile cellular: 1.077 million (2003)
Telephone system:
general assessment: available only to business and government
domestic: cable, microwave radio relay, and tropospheric scatter
international: country code - 237; satellite earth stations - 2 Intelsat (Atlantic Ocean); fiber optic submarine cable (SAT-3/WASC) provides connectivity to Europe and Asia
Radio broadcast stations: AM 2, FM 9, shortwave 3 (2002)
Radios: 2.27 million (1997)
Television broadcast stations: 1 (2002)
Televisions: 450,000 (1997)
Internet country code: .cm
Internet hosts: 479 (2004)
Internet Service Providers (ISPs): 1 (2002)
Internet users: 60,000 (2002)
note: Cameroon also had more than 100 cyber-cafes in 2001

TRANSPORTATION

Airports: 47 (2004 est.)
Airports - with paved runways:
total: 11
over 3,047 m: 2
2,438 to 3,047 m: 4
1,524 to 2,437 m: 3
914 to 1,523 m: 1
under 914 m: 1 (2005 est.)
Airports - with unpaved runways:
total: 36
1,524 to 2,437 m: 7
914 to 1,523 m: 20
under 914 m: 9 (2005 est.)
Pipelines: gas 90 km; liquid petroleum gas 9 km; oil 1,120 km (2004)
Railways:
total: 1,008 km
narrow gauge: 1,008 km 1.000-m gauge (2004)
Roadways:
total: 80,932 km
paved: 5,398 km
unpaved: 75,534 km (2002)
Waterways: navigation mainly on Benue River; limited during rainy season (2004)
Merchant marine:
total: 1 ships (1,000 GRT or over) 169,593 GRT/357,023 DWT
by type: petroleum tanker 1 (2005)
Ports and terminals: Douala, Limboh Terminal

MILITARY

Military branches: Cameroon Armed Forces: Army, Navy (includes Naval Infantry), Air Force
Military service age and obligation: 18 years of age for voluntary military service; no conscription (1999)
Manpower available for military service: *males age 18-49:* 3,410,440 (2005 est.)
Manpower fit for military service: *males age 18-49:* 1,720,385 (2005 est.)
Manpower reaching military service age annually: *males:* 188,662 (2005 est.)
Military expenditures - dollar figure: $221.1 million (2004)
Military expenditures - percent of GDP: 1.6% (2004)

TRANSNATIONAL ISSUES

Disputes - international: ICJ ruled in 2002 on the entire Cameroon-Nigeria land and maritime boundary but the parties formed a Joint Border Commission, which continues to meet regularly to resolve differences bilaterally and have commenced with demarcation in less-contested sections of the boundary, starting in Lake Chad in the north; implementation of the ICJ ruling on the Cameroon-Equatorial Guinea-Nigeria maritime boundary in the Gulf of Guinea is impeded by imprecisely defined coordinates, the unresolved Bakassi allocation, and a sovereignty dispute between Equatorial Guinea and Cameroon over an island at the mouth of the Ntem River; Nigeria initially rejected cession of the Bakasi Peninsula, then agreed, but has yet to withdraw its forces while much of the indigenous population opposes cession; only Nigeria and Cameroon have heeded the Lake Chad Commission's admonition to ratify the delimitation treaty which also includes Chad and Niger
Refugees and internally displaced persons: *refugees (country of origin):* 39,261 (Chad) 16,983 (Nigeria) 9,634 (Cote d'Ivoire) (2004)

CANADA

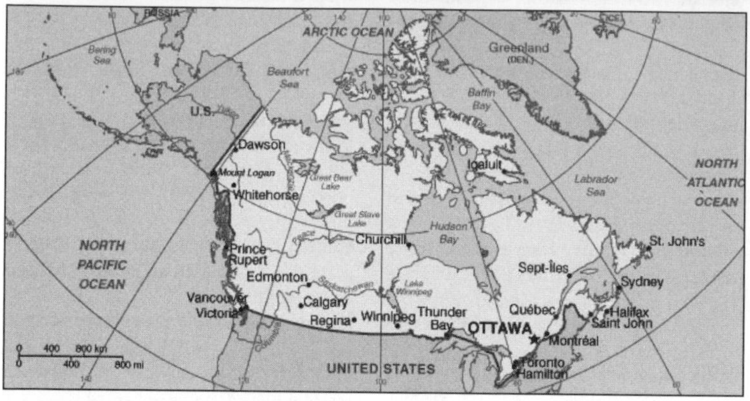

INTRODUCTION

Background: A land of vast distances and rich natural resources, Canada became a self-governing dominion in 1867 while retaining ties to the British crown. Economically and technologically the nation has developed in parallel with the US, its neighbor to the south across an unfortified border. Canada's paramount political problem is meeting public demands for quality improvements in health care and education services after a decade of budget cuts. Canada also faces questions about integrity in government following revelations regarding a corruption scandal in the federal government which has helped revive the fortunes of separatists in predominantly francophone Quebec.

GEOGRAPHY

Location: Northern North America, bordering the North Atlantic Ocean on the east, North Pacific Ocean on the west, and the Arctic Ocean on the north, north of the conterminous US
Geographic coordinates: 60 00 N, 95 00 W
Map references: North America
Area:
total: 9,984,670 sq km
land: 9,093,507 sq km
water: 891,163 sq km
Area - comparative: somewhat larger than the US
Land boundaries:
total: 8,893 km
border countries: US 8,893 km (includes 2,477 km with Alaska)
Coastline: 202,080 km
Maritime claims:
territorial sea: 12 nm
contiguous zone: 24 nm
exclusive economic zone: 200 nm
continental shelf: 200 nm or to the edge of the continental margin
Climate: varies from temperate in south to subarctic and arctic in north
Terrain: mostly plains with mountains in west and lowlands in southeast
Elevation extremes:
lowest point: Atlantic Ocean 0 m
highest point: Mount Logan 5,959 m
Natural resources: iron ore, nickel, zinc, copper, gold, lead, molybdenum, potash, diamonds, silver, fish, timber, wildlife, coal, petroleum, natural gas, hydropower
Land use:
arable land: 4.96%
permanent crops: 0.02%
other: 95.02% (2001)
Irrigated land: 7,200 sq km (1998 est.)
Natural hazards: continuous permafrost in north is a serious obstacle to development; cyclonic storms form east of the Rocky Mountains, a result of the mixing of air masses from the Arctic, Pacific, and North American interior, and produce most of the country's rain and snow east of the mountains
Environment - current issues: air pollution and resulting acid rain severely affecting lakes and damaging forests; metal smelting, coal-burning utilities, and vehicle emissions impacting on agricultural and forest productivity; ocean waters becoming contaminated due to agricultural, industrial, mining, and forestry activities
Environment - international agreements:
party to: Air Pollution, Air Pollution-Nitrogen Oxides, Air Pollution-Persistent Organic Pollutants, Air Pollution-Sulfur 85, Air Pollution-Sulfur 94, Antarctic-Environmental Protocol, Antarctic-Marine Living Resources, Antarctic Seals, Antarctic Treaty, Biodiversity, Climate Change, Climate Change-Kyoto Protocol, Desertification, Endangered Species, Environmental Modification, Hazardous Wastes, Law of the Sea, Marine Dumping, Ozone Layer Protection, Ship Pollution, Tropical Timber 83, Tropical Timber 94, Wetlands
signed, but not ratified: Air Pollution-Volatile Organic Compounds, Marine Life Conservation
Geography - note: second-largest country in world (after Russia); strategic location between Russia and US via north polar route; approximately 90% of the population is concentrated within 160 km of the US border

PEOPLE

Population: 32,805,041 (July 2005 est.)
Age structure:
0-14 years: 17.9% (male 3,016,032/female 2,869,244)
15-64 years: 68.9% (male 11,357,425/female 11,244,356)
65 years and over: 13.2% (male 1,842,496/female 2,475,488) (2005 est.)
Median age:
total: 38.54 years
male: 37.54 years
female: 39.56 years (2005 est.)
Population growth rate: 0.9% (2005 est.)
Birth rate: 10.84 births/1,000 population (2005 est.)
Death rate: 7.73 deaths/1,000 population (2005 est.)
Net migration rate: 5.9 migrant(s)/1,000 population (2005 est.)
Sex ratio:
at birth: 1.05 male(s)/female
under 15 years: 1.05 male(s)/female
15-64 years: 1.01 male(s)/female
65 years and over: 0.74 male(s)/female
total population: 0.98 male(s)/female (2005 est.)
Infant mortality rate:
total: 4.75 deaths/1,000 live births
male: 5.21 deaths/1,000 live births
female: 4.27 deaths/1,000 live births (2005 est.)
Life expectancy at birth:
total population: 80.1 years
male: 76.73 years
female: 83.63 years (2005 est.)
Total fertility rate: 1.61 children born/woman (2005 est.)
HIV/AIDS - adult prevalence rate: 0.3% (2003 est.)
HIV/AIDS - people living with HIV/AIDS: 56,000 (2003 est.)
HIV/AIDS - deaths: 1,500 (2003 est.)
Nationality:
noun: Canadian(s)
adjective: Canadian
Ethnic groups: British Isles origin 28%, French origin 23%, other European 15%, Amerindian 2%, other, mostly Asian, African, Arab 6%, mixed background 26%
Religions: Roman Catholic 42.6%,

Protestant 23.3% (including United Church 9.5%, Anglican 6.8%, Baptist 2.4%, Lutheran 2%), other Christian 4.4%, Muslim 1.9%, other and unspecified 11.8%, none 16% (2001 census)
Languages: English (official) 59.3%, French (official) 23.2%, other 17.5%
Literacy:
definition: age 15 and over can read and write
total population: 97% (1986 est.)
male: NA%
female: NA%

GOVERNMENT

Country name:
conventional long form: none
conventional short form: Canada
Government type: a constitutional monarchy that is also a parliamentary democracy and a federation
Capital: Ottawa
Administrative divisions: 10 provinces and 3 territories*; Alberta, British Columbia, Manitoba, New Brunswick, Newfoundland and Labrador, Northwest Territories*, Nova Scotia, Nunavut*, Ontario, Prince Edward Island, Quebec, Saskatchewan, Yukon Territory*
Independence: 1 July 1867 (union of British North American colonies); 11 December 1931 (independence recognized)
National holiday: Canada Day, 1 July (1867)
Constitution: made up of unwritten and written acts, customs, judicial decisions, and traditions; the written part of the constitution consists of the Constitution Act of 29 March 1867, which created a federation of four provinces, and the Constitution Act of 17 April 1982, which transferred formal control over the constitution from Britain to Canada, and added a Canadian Charter of Rights and Freedoms as well as procedures for constitutional amendments
Legal system: based on English common law, except in Quebec, where civil law system based on French law prevails; accepts compulsory ICJ jurisdiction, with reservations
Suffrage: 18 years of age; universal
Executive branch:
chief of state: Queen ELIZABETH II (since 6 February 1952), represented by Governor General Michaelle JEAN (since 27 September 2005)
head of government: Prime Minister Paul MARTIN (since 12 December 2003); Deputy Prime Minister Anne McLELLAN (since 12 December 2003)
cabinet: Federal Ministry chosen by the prime minister usually from among the members of his own party sitting in Parliament
elections: none; the monarchy is hereditary; governor general appointed by the monarch on the advice of the prime minister for a five-year term; following legislative elections, the leader of the majority party or the leader of the majority coalition in the House of Commons is automatically designated prime minister by the governor general
Legislative branch: bicameral Parliament or Parlement consists of the Senate or Senat (members appointed by the governor general with the advice of the prime minister and serve until reaching 75 years of age; its normal limit is 105 senators) and the House of Commons or Chambre des Communes (308 seats; members elected by direct, popular vote to serve for up to five-year terms)
elections: House of Commons - last held 28 June 2004 (next to be held 23 January 2006)
election results: House of Commons - percent of vote by party - Liberal Party 36.7%, Conservative Party 29.6%, New Democratic Party 15.7%, Bloc Quebecois 12.4%, Greens 4.3%, independents 0.4%, other 0.9%; seats by party - Liberal Party 134, Conservative Party 99, Bloc Quebecois 54, New Democratic Party 19, independent 2
Judicial branch: Supreme Court of Canada (judges are appointed by the prime minister through the governor general); Federal Court of Canada; Federal Court of Appeal; Provincial Courts (these are named variously Court of Appeal, Court of Queens Bench, Superior Court, Supreme Court, and Court of Justice)
Political parties and leaders: Bloc Quebecois [Gilles DUCEPPE]; Conservative Party of Canada (a merger of the Canadian Alliance and the Progressive Conservative Party) [Stephen HARPER]; Green Party [Jim HARRIS]; Liberal Party [Paul MARTIN]; New Democratic Party [Jack LAYTON]
Political pressure groups and leaders: NA
International organization participation: ACCT, AfDB, APEC, ARF, AsDB, ASEAN (dialogue partner), Australia Group, BIS, C, CDB, CE (observer), EAPC, EBRD, ESA (cooperating state), FAO, G-7, G-8, G-10, IADB, IAEA, IBRD, ICAO, ICC, ICCt, ICFTU, ICRM, IDA, IEA, IFAD, IFC, IFRCS, IHO, ILO, IMF, IMO, Interpol, IOC, IOM, ISO, ITU, MIGA, MINUSTAH, MONUC, NAFTA, NAM (guest), NATO, NEA, NSG, OAS, OECD, OPCW, OSCE, Paris Club, PCA, PIF (partner), UN, UNAMSIL, UNCTAD, UNDOF, UNESCO, UNFICYP, UNHCR, UNMOVIC, UNTSO, UPU, WCL, WCO, WFTU, WHO, WIPO, WMO, WToO, WTO, ZC
Diplomatic representation in the US:
chief of mission: Ambassador Francis Joseph McKENNA
chancery: 501 Pennsylvania Avenue NW, Washington, DC 20001
telephone: [1] (202) 682-1740
FAX: [1] (202) 682-7726
consulate(s) general: Atlanta, Boston, Buffalo, Chicago, Dallas, Denver, Detroit, Los Angeles, Miami, Minneapolis, New York, Phoenix, San Diego, and Seattle
consulate(s): Anchorage, Houston, Philadelphia, Princeton, Raleigh, San Francisco, and San Jose
Diplomatic representation from the US:
chief of mission: Ambassador David H. WILKINS
embassy: 490 Sussex Drive, Ottawa, Ontario K1N 1G8
mailing address: P. O. Box 5000, Ogdensburgh, NY 13669-0430
telephone: [1] (613) 238-5335, 4470
FAX: [1] (613) 688-3082
consulate(s) general: Calgary, Halifax, Montreal, Quebec, Toronto, Vancouver, Winnipeg
Flag description: two vertical bands of red (hoist and fly side, half width), with white square between them; an 11-pointed red maple leaf is centered in the white square; the official colors of Canada are red and white

ECONOMY

Economy - overview: As an affluent, high-tech industrial society, in the trillion dollar class, Canada closely resembles the US in its market-oriented economic system, pattern of production, and affluent living standards. Since World War II, the impressive growth of the manufacturing, mining, and service sectors has transformed the nation from a largely rural economy into one primarily industrial and urban. The 1989 US-Canada Free Trade Agreement (FTA) and the 1994 North American Free Trade Agreement (NAFTA) (which includes Mexico) touched off a dramatic increase in trade and economic integration with the US. Given its great natural resources, skilled labor force, and modern capital plant Canada enjoys solid economic prospects. Solid fiscal management has produced a balanced budget, although public debate continues over how to manage the rising cost of the publicly funded healthcare system. Exports account for roughly a third of GDP. Canada enjoys a substantial trade surplus with its principal trading partner, the United States, which

absorbs more than 85% of Canadian exports.
GDP (purchasing power parity): $1.077 trillion (2005 est.)
GDP (official exchange rate): $1.047 trillion (2005 est.)
GDP - real growth rate: 2.8% (2005 est.)
GDP - per capita: purchasing power parity - $32,800 (2005 est.)
GDP - composition by sector:
agriculture: 2.2%
industry: 29.1%
services: 68.7% (2005 est.)
Labor force: 17.35 million (2005 est.)
Labor force - by occupation: agriculture 2%, manufacturing 14%, construction 5%, services 75%, other 3% (2004)
Unemployment rate: 6.8% (2005 est.)
Population below poverty line: 15.9% (2003)
Household income or consumption by percentage share:
lowest 10%: 2.8%
highest 10%: 23.8% (1994)
Distribution of family income - Gini index: 33.1 (1998)
Inflation rate (consumer prices): 2.3% (2005 est.)
Investment (gross fixed): 20.2% of GDP (2005 est.)
Budget:
revenues: $159.6 billion
expenditures: $152.6 billion, including capital expenditures of NA (2004 est.)
Public debt: 68.2% of GDP NA (2005 est.)
Agriculture - products: wheat, barley, oilseed, tobacco, fruits, vegetables; dairy products; forest products; fish
Industries: transportation equipment, chemicals, processed and unprocessed minerals, food products; wood and paper products; fish products, petroleum and natural gas
Industrial production growth rate: 2.9% (2005 est.)
Electricity - production: 566.3 billion kWh (2003)
Electricity - production by source:
fossil fuel: 28%
hydro: 57.9%
nuclear: 12.9%
other: 1.3% (2001)
Electricity - consumption: 520.9 billion kWh (2003)
Electricity - exports: 29.32 billion kWh (2003)
Electricity - imports: 23.58 billion kWh (2003)
Oil - production: 3.07 million bbl/day (2005 est.)
Oil - consumption: 2.193 million bbl/day (2003 est.)
Oil - exports: 1.37 million bbl/day (2004)
Oil - imports: 987,000 bbl/day (2004)
Oil - proved reserves: 178.9 billion bbl including shale oil (2004 est.)
Natural gas - production: 165.8 billion cu m (2003 est.)
Natural gas - consumption: 55.8 billion cu m (2003 est.)
Natural gas - exports: 91.52 billion cu m (2003 est.)
Natural gas - imports: 8.73 billion cu m (2003 est.)
Natural gas - proved reserves: 1.691 trillion cu m (2004)
Current account balance: $16.89 billion (2005 est.)
Exports: $364.8 billion f.o.b. (2005 est.)
Exports - partners: US 85.1%, Japan 2.1%, UK 1.6% (2004)
Imports: $317.7 billion f.o.b. (2005 est.)
Imports - partners: US 58.9%, China 6.8%, Mexico 3.8% (2004)
Reserves of foreign exchange and gold: $34.48 billion (2004 est.)
Debt - external: $600.7 billion (30 June 2005)
Economic aid - donor: ODA, $2.6 billion (2004)
Currency (code): Canadian dollar (CAD)
Currency code: CAD
Exchange rates: Canadian dollars per US dollar - 1.21 (2005), 1.301 (2004), 1.4011 (2003), 1.5693 (2002), 1.5488 (2001)
Fiscal year: 1 April - 31 March

COMMUNICATION

Telephones - main lines in use: 19,950,900 (2003)
Telephones - mobile cellular: 13,221,800 (2003)
Telephone system:
general assessment: excellent service provided by modern technology
domestic: domestic satellite system with about 300 earth stations
international: country code - 1-xxx; 5 coaxial submarine cables; satellite earth stations - 5 Intelsat (4 Atlantic Ocean and 1 Pacific Ocean) and 2 Intersputnik (Atlantic Ocean region)
Radio broadcast stations: AM 245, FM 582, shortwave 6 (2004)
Radios: 32.3 million (1997)
Television broadcast stations: 80 (plus many repeaters) (1997)
Televisions: 21.5 million (1997)
Internet country code: .ca
Internet hosts: 3,210,081 (2003)
Internet Service Providers (ISPs): 760 (2000 est.)
Internet users: 16.11 million (2002)

TRANSPORTATION

Airports: 1,326 (2004 est.)
Airports - with paved runways:
total: 508
over 3,047 m: 18
2,438 to 3,047 m: 15
1,524 to 2,437 m: 151
914 to 1,523 m: 247
under 914 m: 77 (2005 est.)
Airports - with unpaved runways:
total: 823
1,524 to 2,437 m: 66
914 to 1,523 m: 351
under 914 m: 406 (2005 est.)
Heliports: 319 (2005 est.)
Pipelines: crude and refined oil 23,564 km; liquid petroleum gas 74,980 km (2003)
Railways:
total: 48,683 km
standard gauge: 48,683 km 1.435-m gauge (2004)
Roadways:
total: 1,408,800 km
paved: 493,080 km (including 16,906 km of expressways)
unpaved: 915,720 km (2002)
Waterways: 631 km
note: Saint Lawrence Seaway of 3,769 km, including the Saint Lawrence River of 3,058 km, shared with United States (2003)
Merchant marine:
total: 169 ships (1,000 GRT or over) 1,784,229 GRT/2,657,499 DWT
by type: bulk carrier 22, cargo 49, chemical tanker 6, combination ore/oil 1, container 1, passenger 6, passenger/cargo 65, petroleum tanker 13, roll on/roll off 6
foreign-owned: 6 (France 1, Germany 3, United States 2)
registered in other countries: 112 (2005)
Ports and terminals: Fraser River Port, Goderich, Halifax, Montreal, Port Cartier, Quebec, Saint John's (Newfoundland), Sept Isles, Vancouver

MILITARY

Military branches: Canadian Armed Forces: Land Forces Command, Maritime Command, Air Command, Canada Command (homeland security) to be operational in early 2006 (2005)
Military service age and obligation: 16 years of age for voluntary military service; women comprise some 11% of Canada's armed forces (2001)
Manpower available for military service: *males age 16-49:* 8,216,510 (2005 est.)
Manpower fit for military service: *males age 16-49:* 6,740,490 (2005 est.)
Manpower reaching military service age annually: *males:* 223,821 (2005 est.)
Military expenditures - dollar figure: $9,801.7 million (2003)
Military expenditures - percent of GDP: 1.1% (2003)

TRANSNATIONAL ISSUES

Disputes - international: managed maritime boundary disputes with the US at

Dixon Entrance, Beaufort Sea, Strait of Juan de Fuca, and around the disputed Machias Seal Island and North Rock; working toward greater cooperation with US in monitoring people and commodities crossing the border; uncontested sovereignty dispute with Denmark over Hans Island in the Kennedy Channel between Ellesmere Island and Greenland
Illicit drugs: illicit producer of cannabis for the domestic drug market and export to US; use of hydroponics technology permits growers to plant large quantities of high-quality marijuana indoors; transit point for heroin and cocaine entering the US market; vulnerable to narcotics money laundering because of its mature financial services sector

CAPE VERDE

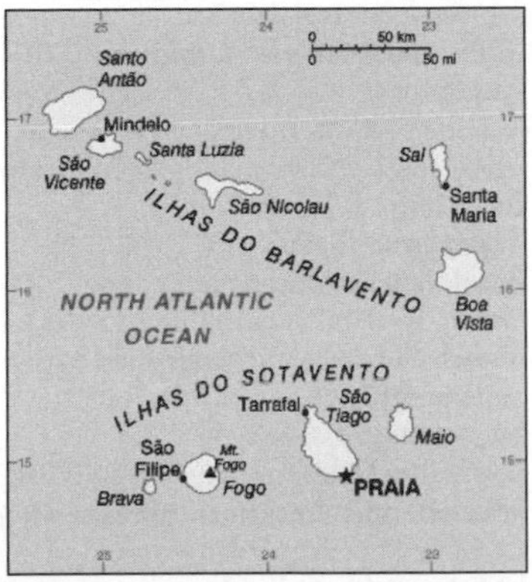

INTRODUCTION

Background: The uninhabited islands were discovered and colonized by the Portuguese in the 15th century; Cape Verde subsequently became a trading center for African slaves and later an important coaling and resupply stop for whaling and transatlantic shipping. Following independence in 1975, and a tentative interest in unification with Guinea-Bissau, a one-party system was established and maintained until multi-party elections were held in 1990. Cape Verde continues to exhibit one of Africa's most stable democratic governments. Repeated droughts during the second half of the 20th century caused significant hardship and prompted heavy emigration. As a result, Cape Verde's expatriate population is greater than its domestic one. Most Cape Verdeans have both African and Portuguese antecedents.

GEOGRAPHY

Location: Western Africa, group of islands in the North Atlantic Ocean, west of Senegal
Geographic coordinates: 16 00 N, 24 00 W
Map references: Political Map of the World
Area:
total: 4,033 sq km
land: 4,033 sq km
water: 0 sq km
Area - comparative: slightly larger than Rhode Island
Land boundaries: 0 km
Coastline: 965 km
Maritime claims:
measured from claimed archipelagic baselines
territorial sea: 12 nm
contiguous zone: 24 nm
exclusive economic zone: 200 nm
Climate: temperate; warm, dry summer; precipitation meager and very erratic
Terrain: steep, rugged, rocky, volcanic
Elevation extremes:
lowest point: Atlantic Ocean 0 m
highest point: Mt. Fogo 2,829 m (a volcano on Fogo Island)
Natural resources: salt, basalt rock, limestone, kaolin, fish, clay, gypsum
Land use:
arable land: 9.68%
permanent crops: 0.5%
other: 89.82% (2001)
Irrigated land: 30 sq km (1998 est.)
Natural hazards: prolonged droughts; seasonal harmattan wind produces obscuring dust; volcanically and seismically active
Environment - current issues: soil erosion; deforestation due to demand for wood used as fuel; desertification; environmental damage has threatened several species of birds and reptiles; illegal beach sand extraction; overfishing
Environment - international agreements:
party to: Biodiversity, Climate Change, Desertification, Environmental Modification, Hazardous Wastes, Law of the Sea, Marine Dumping, Ozone Layer Protection
signed, but not ratified: none of the selected agreements
Geography - note: strategic location 500 km from west coast of Africa near major north-south sea routes; important communications station; important sea and air refueling site

PEOPLE

Population: 418,224 (July 2005 est.)
Age structure:
0-14 years: 39% (male 82,249/female 80,752)
15-64 years: 54.3% (male 110,119/female 116,816)
65 years and over: 6.8% (male 10,599/female 17,689) (2005 est.)
Median age:
total: 19.4 years
male: 18.62 years
female: 20.25 years (2005 est.)
Population growth rate: 0.67% (2005 est.)
Birth rate: 25.33 births/1,000 population (2005 est.)
Death rate: 6.62 deaths/1,000 population (2005 est.)
Net migration rate: -11.99 migrant(s)/1,000 population (2005 est.)
Sex ratio:
at birth: 1.03 male(s)/female
under 15 years: 1.02 male(s)/female
15-64 years: 0.94 male(s)/female
65 years and over: 0.6 male(s)/female
total population: 0.94 male(s)/female (2005 est.)
Infant mortality rate:
total: 47.77 deaths/1,000 live births
male: 52.95 deaths/1,000 live births
female: 42.44 deaths/1,000 live births (2005 est.)
Life expectancy at birth:
total population: 70.45 years
male: 67.13 years
female: 73.86 years (2005 est.)
Total fertility rate: 3.48 children born/woman (2005 est.)
HIV/AIDS - adult prevalence rate: 0.035% (2001 est.)
HIV/AIDS - people living with HIV/AIDS: 775 (2001)
HIV/AIDS - deaths: 225 (as of 2001)
Nationality:
noun: Cape Verdean(s)
adjective: Cape Verdean
Ethnic groups: Creole (mulatto) 71%, African 28%, European 1%
Religions: Roman Catholic (infused with indigenous beliefs); Protestant (mostly Church of the Nazarene)
Languages: Portuguese, Crioulo (a blend of Portuguese and West African words)
Literacy:
definition: age 15 and over can read and write
total population: 76.6%
male: 85.8%
female: 69.2% (2003 est.)

GOVERNMENT

Country name:
conventional long form: Republic of Cape Verde
conventional short form: Cape Verde
local long form: Republica de Cabo Verde

local short form: Cabo Verde
Government type: republic
Capital: Praia
Administrative divisions: 17 municipalities (concelhos, singular - concelho); Boa Vista, Brava, Maio, Mosteiros, Paul, Praia, Porto Novo, Ribeira Grande, Sal, Santa Catarina, Santa Cruz, Sao Domingos, Sao Filipe, Sao Miguel, Sao Nicolau, Sao Vicente, Tarrafal
Independence: 5 July 1975 (from Portugal)
National holiday: Independence Day, 5 July (1975)
Constitution: new constitution came into force 25 September 1992; underwent a major revision on 23 November 1995, substantially increasing the powers of the president, and a further revision in 1999, to create the position of national ombudsman (Provedor de Justica)
Legal system: derived from the legal system of Portugal
Suffrage: 18 years of age; universal
Executive branch:
chief of state: President Pedro Verona PIRES (since 22 March 2001)
head of government: Prime Minister Jose Maria Pereira NEVES (since 1 February 2001)
cabinet: Council of Ministers appointed by the president on the recommendation of the prime minister
elections: president elected by popular vote for a five-year term; election last held 11 and 25 February 2001 (next to be held 12 February 2006); prime minister nominated by the National Assembly and appointed by the president
election results: Pedro PIRES elected president; percent of vote - Pedro PIRES (PAICV) 49.43%, Carlos VIEGA (MPD) 49.42%; note - the election was won by only twelve votes
Legislative branch: unicameral National Assembly or Assembleia Nacional (72 seats; members are elected by popular vote to serve five-year terms)
elections: last held 14 January 2001 (next to be held 22 January 2006)
election results: percent of vote by party - PAICV 47.3%, MPD 39.8%, ADM 6%, other 6.9%; seats by party - PAICV 40, MPD 30, ADM 2
Judicial branch: Supreme Tribunal of Justice or Supremo Tribunal de Justia
Political parties and leaders: African Party for Independence of Cape Verde or PAICV [Jose Maria Pereira NEVES, chairman]; Democratic Alliance for Change or ADM [Dr. Eurico MONTEIRO] (a coalition of PCD, PTS, and UCID); Democratic Christian Party or PDC [Manuel RODRIGUES, chairman]; Democratic Renovation Party or PRD [Victor FIDALGO, president]; Movement for Democracy or MPD [Agostinho LOPES, president]; Party for Democratic Convergence or PCD [Dr. Eurico MONTEIRO, president]; Party of Work and Solidarity or PTS [Isaias RODRIGUES, president]; Social Democratic Party or PSD [Joao ALEM, president]
Political pressure groups and leaders: NA
International organization participation: ACCT, ACP, AfDB, AU, ECOWAS, FAO, G-77, IBRD, ICAO, ICCt (signatory), ICFTU, ICRM, IDA, IFAD, IFC, IFRCS, ILO, IMF, IMO, Interpol, IOC, IOM, ITU, MIGA, NAM, OPCW, UN, UNCTAD, UNESCO, UNIDO, UPU, WCO, WHO, WIPO, WMO, WToO, WTO (observer)
Diplomatic representation in the US:
chief of mission: Ambassador Jose BRITO
chancery: 3415 Massachusetts Avenue NW, Washington, DC 20007
telephone: [1] (202) 965-6820
FAX: [1] (202) 965-1207
consulate(s) general: Boston
Diplomatic representation from the US:
chief of mission: Ambassador Roger D. PIERCE
embassy: Rua Abilio m. Macedo 81, Praia
mailing address: C. P. 201, Praia
telephone: [238] 261 56 16, 261 56 17
FAX: [238] 261 13 55
Flag description: three horizontal bands of light blue (top, double width), white (with a horizontal red stripe in the middle third), and light blue; a circle of 10 yellow five-pointed stars is centered on the hoist end of the red stripe and extends into the upper and lower blue bands

ECONOMY

Economy - overview: This island economy suffers from a poor natural resource base, including serious water shortages exacerbated by cycles of long-term drought. The economy is service-oriented, with commerce, transport, tourism, and public services accounting for 72% of GDP. Although nearly 70% of the population lives in rural areas, the share of agriculture in GDP in 2004 was only 12%, of which fishing accounted for 1.5%. About 82% of food must be imported. The fishing potential, mostly lobster and tuna, is not fully exploited. Cape Verde annually runs a high trade deficit, financed by foreign aid and remittances from emigrants; remittances supplement GDP by more than 20%. Economic reforms are aimed at developing the private sector and attracting foreign investment to diversify the economy. Future prospects depend heavily on the maintenance of aid flows, the encouragement of tourism, remittances, and the momentum of the government's development program.
GDP (purchasing power parity): $2.99 billion (2005 est.)
GDP (official exchange rate): $1.128 billion (2005 est.)
GDP - real growth rate: 5.5% (2005 est.)
GDP - per capita: purchasing power parity - $6,200 (2005 est.)
GDP - composition by sector:
agriculture: 12.1%
industry: 21.9%
services: 66% (2004 est.)
Labor force: NA
Unemployment rate: 21% (2000 est.)
Population below poverty line: 30% (2000)
Household income or consumption by percentage share:
lowest 10%: NA
highest 10%: NA
Inflation rate (consumer prices): 1.8% (2005 est.)
Investment (gross fixed): 26.4% of GDP (2005 est.)
Budget:
revenues: $328.1 million
expenditures: $393.1 million, including capital expenditures of NA (2005 est.)
Agriculture - products: bananas, corn, beans, sweet potatoes, sugarcane, coffee, peanuts; fish
Industries: food and beverages, fish processing, shoes and garments, salt mining, ship repair
Industrial production growth rate: NA
Electricity - production: 44.15 million kWh (2003)
Electricity - production by source:
fossil fuel: 100%
hydro: 0%
nuclear: 0%
other: 0% (2001)
Electricity - consumption: 41.06 million kWh (2003)
Electricity - exports: 0 kWh (2003)
Electricity - imports: 0 kWh (2003)
Oil - production: 0 bbl/day (2003)
Oil - consumption: 1,200 bbl/day (2003 est.)
Oil - exports: NA (2001)
Oil - imports: NA (2001)
Current account balance: $-147.7 million (2005 est.)
Exports: $73.35 million f.o.b. (2005 est.)
Exports - partners: Portugal 57.6%, US 16.7%, UK 11% (2004)
Imports: $500 million f.o.b. (2005 est.)
Imports - partners: Portugal 41.8%, US 12.3%, Netherlands 8.4%, Spain 5.2%, Italy 4.2%, Brazil 4% (2004)
Reserves of foreign exchange and gold: $152.2 million (2005 est.)
Debt - external: $325 million (2002)

Economic aid - recipient: $136 million (1999)
Currency (code): Cape Verdean escudo (CVE)
Currency code: CVE
Exchange rates: Cape Verdean escudos (CVE) per US dollar - 80.78 (2005), 88.808 (2004), 97.703 (2003), 117.168 (2002), 123.228 (2001)
Fiscal year: calendar year

COMMUNICATION

Telephones - main lines in use: 71,700 (2003)
Telephones - mobile cellular: 53,300 (2003)
Telephone system:
general assessment: effective system, extensive modernization from 1996-2000 following partial privatization in 1995
domestic: major service provider is Cabo Verde Telecom (CVT); fiber optic ring, completed in 2001, links all islands providing Internet access and ISDN services; cellular service introduced in 1998
international: country code - 238; 2 coaxial submarine cables; HF radiotelephone to Senegal and Guinea-Bissau; satellite earth station - 1 Intelsat (Atlantic Ocean)
Radio broadcast stations: AM 0, FM 22 (and 12 low power repeaters), shortwave 0 (2002)
Radios: 100,000 (2002 est.)
Television broadcast stations: 1 (and 7 repeaters) (2002)
Televisions: 15,000 (2002 est.)
Internet country code: .cv
Internet hosts: 118 (2004)
Internet Service Providers (ISPs): 1 (2002)
Internet users: 20,400 (2003)

TRANSPORTATION

Airports: 7 *note:* 3 airorts are reported to be nonoperational (2004 est.)
Airports - with paved runways:
total: 6
over 3,047 m: 1
914 to 1,523 m: 5 (2005 est.)
Airports - with unpaved runways:
total: 1
under 914 m: 1 (2005 est.)
Roadways:
total: 1,350 km
paved: 1,053 km
unpaved: 297 km (2002)
Merchant marine:
total: 5 ships (1,000 GRT or over) 5,395 GRT/6,614 DWT
by type: cargo 2, chemical tanker 1, passenger/cargo 2
foreign-owned: 1 (United Kingdom 1) (2005)
Ports and terminals: Mindelo, Praia, Tarrafal

MILITARY

Military branches: People's Revolutionary Armed Forces (FARP): Army, Coast Guard (includes maritime air wing)
Manpower available for military service: *males age 18-49:* 84,641 (2005 est.)
Manpower fit for military service: *males age 18-49:* 65,614 (2005 est.)
Military expenditures - dollar figure: $14.1 million (2004)
Military expenditures - percent of GDP: 1.5% (2004)

TRANSNATIONAL ISSUES

Disputes - international: none
Illicit drugs: used as a transshipment point for illicit drugs moving from Latin America and Asia destined for Western Europe; the lack of a well-developed financial system limits the country's utility as a money-laundering center

CAYMAN ISLANDS

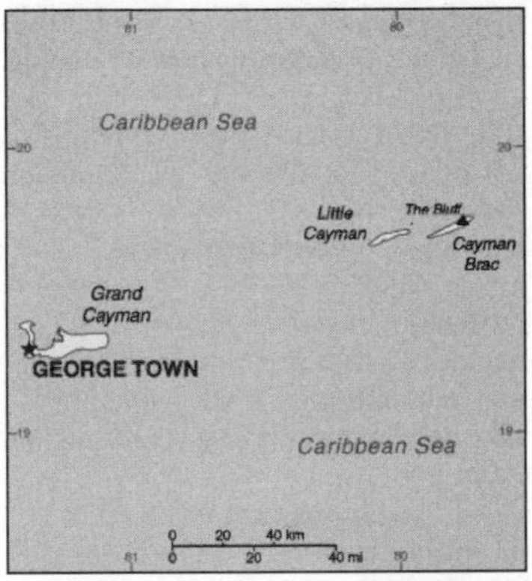

INTRODUCTION

Background: The Cayman Islands were colonized from Jamaica by the British during the 18th and 19th centuries. Administered by Jamaica since 1863, they remained a British dependency after 1962 when the former became independent.

GEOGRAPHY

Location: Caribbean, island group in Caribbean Sea, nearly one-half of the way from Cuba to Honduras
Geographic coordinates: 19 30 N, 80 30 W
Map references: Central America and the Caribbean
Area:
total: 262 sq km
land: 262 sq km
water: 0 sq km
Area - comparative: 1.5 times the size of Washington, DC
Land boundaries: 0 km
Coastline: 160 km
Maritime claims:
territorial sea: 12 nm
exclusive fishing zone: 200 nm
Climate: tropical marine; warm, rainy summers (May to October) and cool, relatively dry winters (November to April)
Terrain: low-lying limestone base surrounded by coral reefs
Elevation extremes:
lowest point: Caribbean Sea 0 m
highest point: The Bluff 43 m
Natural resources: fish, climate and beaches that foster tourism
Land use:
arable land: 3.85%
permanent crops: 0%
other: 96.15% (2001)
Irrigated land: NA sq km
Natural hazards: hurricanes (July to November)
Environment - current issues: no natural fresh water resources; drinking water supplies must be met by rainwater catchments
Geography - note: important location between Cuba and Central America

PEOPLE

Population: 44,270 (July 2005 est.)
Age structure:
0-14 years: 21.1% (male 4,658/female 4,662)
15-64 years: 70.8% (male 15,284/female 16,050)
65 years and over: 8.2% (male 1,699/female 1,917) (2005 est.)
Median age:
total: 36.83 years
male: 36.48 years
female: 37.18 years (2005 est.)
Population growth rate: 2.64% (2005 est.)
Birth rate: 12.92 births/1,000 population (2005 est.)
Death rate: 4.81 deaths/1,000 population (2005 est.)
Net migration rate:
18.25 migrant(s)/1,000 population
note: major destination for Cubans trying to migrate to the US (2005 est.)
Sex ratio:
at birth: 1.02 male(s)/female
under 15 years: 1 male(s)/female

15-64 years: 0.95 male(s)/female
65 years and over: 0.89 male(s)/female
total population: 0.96 male(s)/female (2005 est.)
Infant mortality rate:
total: 8.19 deaths/1,000 live births
male: 9.39 deaths/1,000 live births
female: 6.97 deaths/1,000 live births (2005 est.)
Life expectancy at birth:
total population: 79.95 years
male: 77.33 years
female: 82.6 years (2005 est.)
Total fertility rate: 1.9 children born/woman (2005 est.)
HIV/AIDS - adult prevalence rate: NA
HIV/AIDS - people living with HIV/AIDS: NA
HIV/AIDS - deaths: NA
Nationality:
noun: Caymanian(s)
adjective: Caymanian
Ethnic groups: mixed 40%, white 20%, black 20%, expatriates of various ethnic groups 20%
Religions: United Church (Presbyterian and Congregational), Anglican, Baptist, Church of God, other Protestant, Roman Catholic
Languages: English
Literacy:
definition: age 15 and over has ever attended school
total population: 98%
male: 98%
female: 98% (1970 est.)

GOVERNMENT

Country name:
conventional long form: none
conventional short form: Cayman Islands
Dependency status: overseas territory of the UK
Government type: British crown colony
Capital: George Town
Administrative divisions: 8 districts; Creek, Eastern, Midland, South Town, Spot Bay, Stake Bay, West End, Western
Independence: none (overseas territory of the UK)
National holiday: Constitution Day, first Monday in July
Constitution: 1959; revised 1972 and 1992
Legal system: British common law and local statutes
Suffrage: 18 years of age; universal
Executive branch:
chief of state: Queen ELIZABETH II (since 6 February 1952); Governor Stuart JACK (since 23 November 2005)
head of government: Leader of Government Business Kurt TIBBETTS (since 18 May 2005)
cabinet: Executive Council (three members appointed by the governor, four members elected by the Legislative Assembly)
elections: none; the monarch is hereditary; the governor is appointed by the monarch; following legislative elections, the leader of the majority party or coalition is appointed by the governor Leader of Government Business
Legislative branch: unicameral Legislative Assembly (18 seats, three appointed members from the Executive Council and 15 elected by popular vote; members serve four-year terms)
elections: last held 11 May 2005 (next to be held 2009)
election results: percent of vote - NA%; seats - PPM 9, UDP 5, independent 1
Judicial branch: Summary Court; Grand Court; Cayman Islands Court of Appeal
Political parties and leaders: no national teams (loose groupings of political organizations) were formed for the 2000 elections; United Democratic Party or UDP [leader McKeeva BUSH]; People's Progressive Movement or PPM [leader Kurt TIBBETS]
Political pressure groups and leaders: NA
International organization participation: Caricom (associate), CDB, Interpol (subbureau), IOC, UNESCO (associate), UPU
Diplomatic representation in the US: none (overseas territory of the UK)
Diplomatic representation from the US: none (overseas territory of the UK)
Flag description: blue, with the flag of the UK in the upper hoist-side quadrant and the Caymanian coat of arms centered on the outer half of the flag; the coat of arms includes a pineapple and turtle above a shield with three stars (representing the three islands) and a scroll at the bottom bearing the motto HE HATH FOUNDED IT UPON THE SEAS

ECONOMY

Economy - overview: With no direct taxation, the islands are a thriving offshore financial center. More than 40,000 companies were registered in the Cayman Islands as of 1998, including almost 600 banks and trust companies; banking assets exceed $500 billion. A stock exchange was opened in 1997. Tourism is also a mainstay, accounting for about 70% of GDP and 75% of foreign currency earnings. The tourist industry is aimed at the luxury market and caters mainly to visitors from North America. Total tourist arrivals exceeded 1.2 million in 1997, with 600,000 from the US. About 90% of the islands' food and consumer goods must be imported. The Caymanians enjoy one of the highest outputs per capita and one of the highest standards of living in the world.
GDP (purchasing power parity): $1.391 billion (2004 est.)
GDP (official exchange rate): NA
GDP - real growth rate: 1.7% (2002 est.)
GDP - per capita: purchasing power parity - $32,300 (2004 est.)
GDP - composition by sector:
agriculture: 1.4%
industry: 3.2%
services: 95.4% (1994 est.)
Labor force: 19,820 (1995)
Labor force - by occupation: agriculture 1.4%, industry 12.6%, services 86% (1995)
Unemployment rate: 4.1% (1997)
Population below poverty line: NA
Household income or consumption by percentage share:
lowest 10%: NA
highest 10%: NA
Inflation rate (consumer prices): 2.8% (2002)
Budget:
revenues: $265.2 million
expenditures: $248.9 million, including capital expenditures of NA (1997)
Agriculture - products: vegetables, fruit; livestock, turtle farming
Industries: tourism, banking, insurance and finance, construction, construction materials, furniture
Industrial production growth rate: NA%
Electricity - production: 441.9 million kWh (2003)
Electricity - production by source:
fossil fuel: 100%
hydro: 0%
nuclear: 0%
other: 0% (2001)
Electricity - consumption: 411 million kWh (2003)
Electricity - exports: 0 kWh (2003)
Electricity - imports: 0 kWh (2003)
Oil - production: 0 bbl/day (2003)
Oil - consumption: 2,450 bbl/day (2003 est.)
Oil - exports: NA (2001)
Oil - imports: NA (2001)
Exports: $1.2 million (1999)
Exports - partners: mostly US (2004)
Imports: $457.4 million (1999)
Imports - partners: US, Trinidad and Tobago, UK, Netherlands Antilles, Japan (2004)
Debt - external: $70 million (1996)
Economic aid - recipient: NA
Currency (code): Caymanian dollar (KYD)
Currency code: KYD
Exchange rates: Caymanian dollars per US dollar - 0.82 (29 October 2001), 0.83 (3 November 1995), 0.85 (22 November 1993)
Fiscal year: 1 April - 31 March

COMMUNICATION

Telephones - main lines in use: 38,000 (2002)
Telephones - mobile cellular: 17,000 (2002)
Telephone system:
general assessment: reasonably good system
domestic: liberalization of telecom market in 2003 reflected in falling prices and improving services
international: country code - 1-345; 2 submarine fiber optic cables (Maya-1, Cayman-Jamaica); satellite earth station - 1 Intelsat (Atlantic Ocean)
Radio broadcast stations: AM 1, FM 4, shortwave 0 (2004)
Radios: 36,000 (1997)
Television broadcast stations: 4 with cable system (2004)
Televisions: 7,000 (1997)
Internet country code: .ky
Internet Service Providers (ISPs): 16 (2000)
Internet users: 9,909 (2003)

TRANSPORTATION

Airports: 3 (2004 est.)
Airports - with paved runways:
total: 2
1,524 to 2,437 m: 2 (2005 est.)
Airports - with unpaved runways:
total: 1
914 to 1,523 m: 1 (2005 est.)
Roadways:
total: 785 km
paved: 785 km (2002)
Merchant marine:
total: 129 ships (1,000 GRT or over) 2,827,837 GRT/4,555,974 DWT
by type: bulk carrier 29, cargo 12, chemical tanker 39, liquefied gas 1, petroleum tanker 17, refrigerated cargo 28, roll on/roll off 3
foreign-owned: 126 (Denmark 1, Germany 14, Greece 20, Italy 12, Norway 1, Philippines 1, Sweden 13, Switzerland 11, United Kingdom 9, United States 44) (2005)
Ports and terminals: Cayman Brac, George Town

MILITARY

Military branches: no regular military forces; Royal Cayman Islands Police Force
Military - note: defense is the responsibility of the UK

TRANSNATIONAL ISSUES

Disputes - international: none
Illicit drugs: offshore financial center; vulnerable to drug transshipment to the US and Europe

CENTRAL AFRICAN REPUBLIC

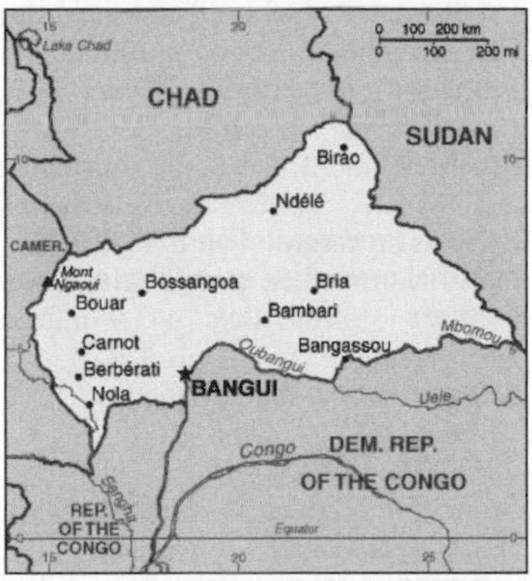

INTRODUCTION

Background: The former French colony of Ubangi-Shari became the Central African Republic upon independence in 1960. After three tumultuous decades of misrule - mostly by military governments - civilian rule was established in 1993 and lasted for one decade. President Ange-Felix PATASSE'S civilian government was plagued by unrest, and in March 2003 he was deposed in a military coup led by General Francois BOZIZE, who has since established a transitional government. Though the government has the tacit support of civil society groups and the main parties, a wide field of affiliated and independent candidates will contest the municipal, legislative, and presidential elections scheduled for February 2005. The government still does not fully control the countryside, where pockets of lawlessness persist.

GEOGRAPHY

Location: Central Africa, north of Democratic Republic of the Congo
Geographic coordinates: 7 00 N, 21 00 E
Map references: Africa
Area:
total: 622,984 sq km
land: 622,984 sq km
water: 0 sq km
Area - comparative: slightly smaller than Texas
Land boundaries:
total: 5,203 km
border countries: Cameroon 797 km, Chad 1,197 km, Democratic Republic of the Congo 1,577 km, Republic of the Congo 467 km, Sudan 1,165 km
Coastline: 0 km (landlocked)
Maritime claims: none (landlocked)
Climate: tropical; hot, dry winters; mild to hot, wet summers
Terrain: vast, flat to rolling, monotonous plateau; scattered hills in northeast and southwest
Elevation extremes:
lowest point: Oubangui River 335 m
highest point: Mont Ngaoui 1,420 m
Natural resources: diamonds, uranium, timber, gold, oil, hydropower
Land use:
arable land: 3.1%
permanent crops: 0.14%
other: 96.76% (2001)
Irrigated land: NA sq km
Natural hazards: hot, dry, dusty harmattan winds affect northern areas; floods are common
Environment - current issues: tap water is not potable; poaching has diminished the country's reputation as one of the last great wildlife refuges; desertification; deforestation
Environment - international agreements:
party to: Biodiversity, Climate Change, Desertification, Endangered Species, Ozone Layer Protection, Tropical Timber 94
signed, but not ratified: Law of the Sea
Geography - note: landlocked; almost the precise center of Africa

PEOPLE

Population: 3,799,897
note: estimates for this country explicitly take into account the effects of excess mortality due to AIDS; this can result in lower life expectancy, higher infant mortality and death rates, lower population and growth rates, and changes in the distribution of population by age and sex than would otherwise be expected (July 2005 est.)
Age structure:
0-14 years: 42.5% (male 813,596/female 802,728)
15-64 years: 54% (male 1,010,696/female 1,041,903)
65 years and over: 3.4% (male 54,345/female 76,629) (2005 est.)
Median age:
total: 18.12 years
male: 17.75 years
female: 18.5 years (2005 est.)
Population growth rate: 1.49% (2005 est.)
Birth rate: 35.17 births/1,000 population (2005 est.)
Death rate: 20.27 deaths/1,000 population (2005 est.)
Net migration rate: 0 migrant(s)/1,000

population (2005 est.)
Sex ratio:
at birth: 1.03 male(s)/female
under 15 years: 1.01 male(s)/female
15-64 years: 0.97 male(s)/female
65 years and over: 0.71 male(s)/female
total population: 0.98 male(s)/female (2005 est.)
Infant mortality rate:
total: 91 deaths/1,000 live births
male: 97.84 deaths/1,000 live births
female: 83.96 deaths/1,000 live births (2005 est.)
Life expectancy at birth:
total population: 43.39 years
male: 43.27 years
female: 43.52 years (2005 est.)
Total fertility rate: 4.5 children born/woman (2005 est.)
HIV/AIDS - adult prevalence rate: 13.5% (2003 est.)
HIV/AIDS - people living with HIV/AIDS: 260,000 (2003 est.)
HIV/AIDS - deaths: 23,000 (2003 est.)
Major infectious diseases:
degree of risk: very high
food or waterborne diseases: bacterial diarrhea, hepatitis A, and typhoid fever
vectorborne disease: malaria
respiratory disease: meningococcal meningitis (2004)
Nationality:
noun: Central African(s)
adjective: Central African
Ethnic groups: Baya 33%, Banda 27%, Mandjia 13%, Sara 10%, Mboum 7%, M'Baka 4%, Yakoma 4%, other 2%
Religions: indigenous beliefs 35%, Protestant 25%, Roman Catholic 25%, Muslim 15%
note: animistic beliefs and practices strongly influence the Christian majority
Languages: French (official), Sangho (lingua franca and national language), tribal languages
Literacy:
definition: age 15 and over can read and write
total population: 51%
male: 63.3%
female: 39.9% (2003 est.)

GOVERNMENT

Country name:
conventional long form: Central African Republic
conventional short form: none
local long form: Republique Centrafricaine
local short form: none
former: Ubangi-Shari, Central African Empire
abbreviation: CAR
Government type: republic
Capital: Bangui
Administrative divisions: 14 prefectures (prefectures, singular - prefecture), 2 economic prefectures* (prefectures economiques, singular - prefecture economique), and 1 commune**; Bamingui-Bangoran, Bangui**, Basse-Kotto, Haute-Kotto, Haut-Mbomou, Kemo, Lobaye, Mambere-Kadei, Mbomou, Nana-Grebizi*, Nana-Mambere, Ombella-Mpoko, Ouaka, Ouham, Ouham-Pende, Sangha-Mbaere*, Vakaga
Independence: 13 August 1960 (from France)
National holiday: Republic Day, 1 December (1958)
Constitution: 5 December 2004; ratified by popular referendum
Legal system: based on French law
Suffrage: 21 years of age; universal
Executive branch:
chief of state: President Francois BOZIZE (since 15 March 2003 coup)
head of government: Prime Minister Elie DOTE (since 13 June 2005) note - Celestin GAOMBALET resigned 11 June 2005
cabinet: Council of Ministers
elections: president elected to five year term with a two-term limit; next presidential elections scheduled for 10 April 2005; prime minister appointed by the political party with a parliamentary majority
Legislative branch: unicameral National Assembly or Assemblee Nationale (109 seats; members are elected by popular vote to serve five-year terms)
elections: last held 13 March 2005 and 8 May 2005 (next to be held NA 2010)
election results: percent of vote by party - MLPC 43%, RDC 18%, MDD 9%, FPP 6%, PSD 5%, ADP 4%, PUN 3%, FODEM 2%, PLD 2%, UPR 1%, FC 1%, independents 6%; seats by party - MLPC 47, RDC 20, MDD 8, FPP 7, PSD 6, ADP 5, PUN 3, FODEM 2, PLD 2, UPR 1, FC 1, independents 7
Judicial branch: Supreme Court or Cour Supreme; Constitutional Court (3 judges appointed by the president, 3 by the president of the National Assembly, and 3 by fellow judges); Court of Appeal; Criminal Courts; Inferior Courts
Political parties and leaders: Alliance for Democracy and Progress or ADP [Jacques MBOLIEDAS]; Central African Democratic Assembly or RDC [Andre KOLINGBA]; Civic Forum or FC [Gen. Timothee MALENDOMA]; Democratic Forum for Modernity or FODEM [Charles MASSI]; Liberal Democratic Party or PLD [Nestor KOMBO-NAGUEMON]; Movement for Democracy and Development or MDD [David DACKO]; Movement for the Liberation of the Central African People or MLPC [the party of deposed president, Ange-Felix PATASSE]; Patriotic Front for Progress or FPP [Abel GOUMBA]; People's Union for the Republic or UPR [Pierre Sammy MAKFOY]; National Unity Party or PUN [Jean-Paul NGOUPANDE]; Social Democratic Party or PSD [Enoch LAKOUE]
Political pressure groups and leaders: NA
International organization participation: ACCT, ACP, AfDB, AU, BDEAC, CEMAC, FAO, FZ, G-77, IAEA, IBRD, ICAO, ICCt, ICFTU, ICRM, IDA, IFAD, IFC, IFRCS, ILO, IMF, Interpol, IOC, ITU, MIGA, NAM, OIC (observer), OPCW (signatory), UN, UNCTAD, UNESCO, UNIDO, UPU, WCL, WCO, WHO, WIPO, WMO, WToO, WTO
Diplomatic representation in the US:
chief of mission: Ambassador Emmanuel TOUABOY
chancery: 1618 22nd Street NW, Washington, DC 20008
telephone: [1] (202) 483-7800
FAX: [1] (202) 332-9893
Diplomatic representation from the US:
chief of mission: Charge d'Affaires James PANOS
embassy: Avenue David Dacko, Bangui
mailing address: B. P. 924, Bangui
telephone: [236] 61 02 00
FAX: [236] 61 44 94
note: the embassy is currently operating with a minimal staff
Flag description: four equal horizontal bands of blue (top), white, green, and yellow with a vertical red band in center; there is a yellow five-pointed star on the hoist side of the blue band

ECONOMY

Economy - overview: Subsistence agriculture, together with forestry, remains the backbone of the economy of the Central African Republic (CAR), with more than 70% of the population living in outlying areas. The agricultural sector generates half of GDP. Timber has accounted for about 16% of export earnings and the diamond industry, for 40%. Important constraints to economic development include the CAR's landlocked position, a poor transportation system, a largely unskilled work force, and a legacy of misdirected macroeconomic policies. Factional fighting between the government and its opponents remains a drag on economic revitalization, with GDP

growth at only 0.5% in 2004 and 2.5% in 2005. Distribution of income is extraordinarily unequal. Grants from France and the international community can only partially meet humanitarian needs.
GDP (purchasing power parity): $4.47 billion (2005 est.)
GDP (official exchange rate): $1.467 billion (2005 est.)
GDP - real growth rate: 2.5% (2005 est.)
GDP - per capita: purchasing power parity - $1,200 (2005 est.)
GDP - composition by sector:
agriculture: 55%
industry: 20%
services: 25% (2001 est.)
Labor force: NA
Unemployment rate: 8% (23% for Bangui) (2001 est.)
Population below poverty line: NA
Household income or consumption by percentage share:
lowest 10%: 0.7%
highest 10%: 47.7% (1993)
Distribution of family income - Gini index: 61.3 (1993)
Inflation rate (consumer prices): 3.6% (2001 est.)
Budget:
revenues: NA
expenditures: NA, including capital expenditures of NA
Agriculture - products: cotton, coffee, tobacco, manioc (tapioca), yams, millet, corn, bananas; timber
Industries: gold and diamond mining, logging, brewing, textiles, footwear, assembly of bicycles and motorcycles
Industrial production growth rate: 3% (2002)
Electricity - production: 106 million kWh (2003)
Electricity - production by source:
fossil fuel: 19.8%
hydro: 80.2%
nuclear: 0%
other: 0% (2001)
Electricity - consumption: 98.58 million kWh (2003)
Electricity - exports: 0 kWh (2003)
Electricity - imports: 0 kWh (2003)
Oil - production: 0 bbl/day (2003)
Oil - consumption: 2,400 bbl/day (2003 est.)
Oil - exports: NA
Oil - imports: NA
Exports: $131 million f.o.b. (2004 est.)
Exports - partners: Belgium 39.6%, Italy 8.7%, Spain 8%, US 6.2%, France 6.1%, Indonesia 5.9%, China 4.9% (2004)
Imports: $203 million f.o.b. (2004 est.)
Imports - partners: France 17.6%, US 16.3%, Cameroon 9.3%, Belgium 5% (2004)
Debt - external: $1.06 billion (2002 est.)
Economic aid - recipient: ODA $59.8 million; note - traditional budget subsidies from France (2002 est.)
Currency (code): Communaute Financiere Africaine franc (XAF); note - responsible authority is the Bank of the Central African States
Currency code: XAF
Exchange rates: Communaute Financiere Africaine francs (XAF) per US dollar - 528.28 (2005), 528.29 (2004), 581.2 (2003), 696.99 (2002), 733.04 (2001)
Fiscal year: calendar year

COMMUNICATION

Telephones main lines in use: 9,000 (2002)
Telephones - mobile cellular: 13,000 (2003)
Telephone system:
general assessment: fair system
domestic: network consists principally of microwave radio relay and low-capacity, low-powered radiotelephone communication
international: country code - 236; satellite earth station - 1 Intelsat (Atlantic Ocean)
Radio broadcast stations: AM 1, FM 5, shortwave 1 (2002)
Radios: 283,000 (1997)
Television broadcast stations: 1 (2001)
Televisions: 18,000 (1997)
Internet country code: .cf
Internet hosts: 6 (2002)
Internet Service Providers (ISPs): 1 (2002)
Internet users: 5,000 (2002)

TRANSPORTATION

Airports: 50 (2004 est.)
Airports - with paved runways:
total: 3
2,438 to 3,047 m: 1
1,524 to 2,437 m: 2 (2005 est.)
Airports - with unpaved runways:
total: 47
2,438 to 3,047 m: 1
1,524 to 2,437 m: 10
914 to 1,523 m: 23
under 914 m: 13 (2005 est.)
Roadways: *total:* 23,810 km (1999)
Waterways: 2,800 km (primarily on the Oubangui and Sangha rivers) (2004)
Ports and terminals: Bangui, Nola, Salo, Nzinga

MILITARY

Military branches: Central African Armed Forces (FACA): Ground Forces, Air Force; General Directorate of Gendarmerie Inspection (DGIG), Republican Guard (2004)
Military service age and obligation: 18 years of age for voluntary and compulsory military service; conscript service obligation is two years (2005)
Manpower available for military service:
males age 18-49: 758,103 (2005 est.)
Manpower fit for military service: *males age 18-49:* 330,255 (2005 est.)
Military expenditures - dollar figure: $15.5 million (2004)
Military expenditures - percent of GDP: 1% (2004)

TRANSNATIONAL ISSUES

Disputes - international: about 30,000 refugees fleeing the 2002 civil conflict in the CAR still reside in southern Chad; periodic skirmishes over water and grazing rights among related pastoral populations along the border with southern Sudan persist
Refugees and internally displaced persons:
refugees (country of origin): 36,479 (Sudan) 1,864 (Chad) 6,484 (Democratic Republic of the Congo)
IDPs: 200,000 (unrest following coup in 2003) (2004)

CHAD

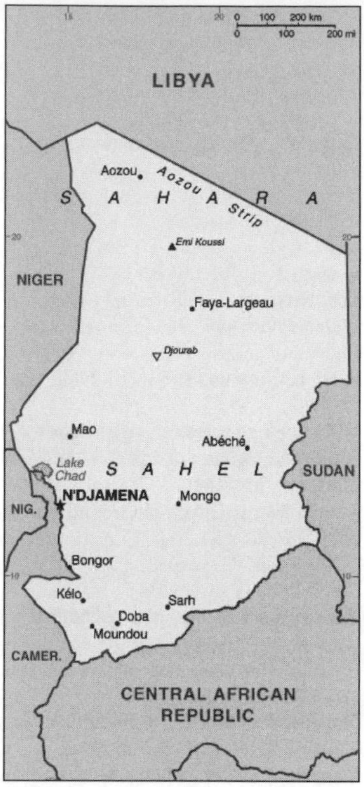

INTRODUCTION

Background: Chad, part of France's African holdings until 1960, endured three decades of civil warfare as well as invasions by Libya before a semblance of peace was finally restored in 1990. The government eventually drafted a democratic constitution, and held flawed presidential elections in 1996 and 2001. In 1998, a rebellion broke out in northern Chad, which sporadically flares up despite several peace agreements between the government and the rebels. In 2005 new rebel groups emerged in western Sudan and have made probing attacks into eastern Chad. Power remains in the hands of an ethnic minority. In June 2005, President Idriss DEBY held a referendum successfully removing constitutional term limits.

GEOGRAPHY

Location: Central Africa, south of Libya
Geographic coordinates: 15 00 N, 19 00 E
Map references: Africa
Area:
total: 1.284 million sq km
land: 1,259,200 sq km
water: 24,800 sq km
Area - comparative: slightly more than three times the size of California
Land boundaries:
total: 5,968 km
border countries: Cameroon 1,094 km, Central African Republic 1,197 km, Libya 1,055 km, Niger 1,175 km, Nigeria 87 km, Sudan 1,360 km
Coastline: 0 km (landlocked)
Maritime claims: none (landlocked)
Climate: tropical in south, desert in north
Terrain: broad, arid plains in center, desert in north, mountains in northwest, lowlands in south
Elevation extremes:
lowest point: Djourab Depression 160 m
highest point: Emi Koussi 3,415 m
Natural resources: petroleum, uranium, natron, kaolin, fish (Lake Chad), gold, limestone, sand and gravel, salt
Land use:
arable land: 2.86%
permanent crops: 0.02%
other: 97.12% (2001)
Irrigated land: 200 sq km (1998 est.)
Natural hazards: hot, dry, dusty harmattan winds occur in north; periodic droughts; locust plagues
Environment - current issues: inadequate supplies of potable water; improper waste disposal in rural areas contributes to soil and water pollution; desertification
Environment - international agreements:
party to: Biodiversity, Climate Change, Desertification, Endangered Species, Ozone Layer Protection, Wetlands
signed, but not ratified: Law of the Sea, Marine Dumping
Geography - note: landlocked; Lake Chad is the most significant water body in the Sahel

PEOPLE

Population: 9,826,419 (July 2005 est.)
Age structure:
0-14 years: 47.9% (male 2,365,277/female 2,337,388)
15-64 years: 49.4% (male 2,323,110/female 2,528,086)
65 years and over: 2.8% (male 109,535/female 163,023) (2005 est.)
Median age:
total: 16.02 years
male: 15.32 years
female: 16.71 years (2005 est.)
Population growth rate: 2.95% (2005 est.)
Birth rate: 45.98 births/1,000 population (2005 est.)
Death rate: 16.41 deaths/1,000 population (2005 est.)
Net migration rate: -0.11 migrant(s)/1,000 population (2005 est.)
Sex ratio:
at birth: 1.04 male(s)/female
under 15 years: 1.01 male(s)/female
15-64 years: 0.92 male(s)/female
65 years and over: 0.67 male(s)/female
total population: 0.95 male(s)/female (2005 est.)
Infant mortality rate:
total: 93.82 deaths/1,000 live births
male: 103.03 deaths/1,000 live births
female: 84.24 deaths/1,000 live births (2005 est.)
Life expectancy at birth:
total population: 47.18 years
male: 45.55 years
female: 48.87 years (2005 est.)
Total fertility rate: 6.32 children born/woman (2005 est.)
HIV/AIDS - adult prevalence rate: 4.8% (2003 est.)
HIV/AIDS - people living with HIV/AIDS: 200,000 (2003 est.)
HIV/AIDS - deaths: 18,000 (2003 est.)
Major infectious diseases:
degree of risk: very high
food or waterborne diseases: bacterial and protozoal diarrhea, hepatitis A, and typhoid fever
vectorborne disease: malaria
water contact disease: schistosomiasis
respiratory disease: meningococcal meningitis (2004)
Nationality:
noun: Chadian(s)
adjective: Chadian
Ethnic groups: 200 distinct groups; in the north and center: Arabs, Gorane (Toubou, Daza, Kreda), Zaghawa, Kanembou, Ouaddai, Baguirmi, Hadjerai, Fulbe, Kotoko, Hausa, Boulala, and Maba, most of whom are Muslim; in the south: Sara (Ngambaye, Mbaye, Goulaye), Moundang, Moussei, Massa, most of whom are Christian or animist; about 1,000 French citizens live in Chad
Religions: Muslim 51%, Christian 35%, animist 7%, other 7%
Languages: French (official), Arabic (official), Sara (in south), more than 120 different languages and dialects
Literacy:
definition: age 15 and over can read and write French or Arabic
total population: 47.5%
male: 56%
female: 39.3% (2003 est.)

GOVERNMENT

Country name:
conventional long form: Republic of Chad
conventional short form: Chad
local long form: Republique du Tchad
local short form: Tchad
Government type: republic
Capital: N'Djamena
Administrative divisions: 14 prefectures

(prefectures, singular - prefecture); Batha, Biltine, Borkou-Ennedi-Tibesti, Chari-Baguirmi, Guera, Kanem, Lac, Logone Occidental, Logone Oriental, Mayo-Kebbi, Moyen-Chari, Ouaddai, Salamat, Tandjile
note: instead of 14 prefectures, there may be a new administrative structure of 28 departments (departments, singular - department), and 1 city*; Assongha, Baguirmi, Bahr El Gazal, Bahr Koh, Batha Oriental, Batha Occidental, Biltine, Borkou, Dababa, Ennedi, Guera, Hadjer Lamis, Kabia, Kanem, Lac, Lac Iro, Logone Occidental, Logone Oriental, Mandoul, Mayo-Boneye, Mayo-Dallah, Monts de Lam, N'Djamena*, Ouaddai, Salamat, Sila, Tandjile Oriental, Tandjile Occidental, Tibesti
Independence: 11 August 1960 (from France)
National holiday: Independence Day, 11 August (1960)
Constitution: passed by referendum 31 March 1996
Legal system: based on French civil law system and Chadian customary law; has not accepted compulsory ICJ jurisdiction
Suffrage: 18 years of age; universal
Executive branch:
chief of state: President Lt. Gen. Idriss DEBY (since 4 December 1990)
head of government: Prime Minister Pascal YOADIMNADJI (since 3 February 2005)
cabinet: Council of State, members appointed by the president on the recommendation of the prime minister
elections: president elected by popular vote to serve five-year term; if no candidate receives at least 50% of the total vote, the two candidates receiving the most votes must stand for a second round of voting; last held 20 May 2001 (next to be held NA 2006); prime minister appointed by the president
election results: Lt. Gen. Idriss DEBY reelected president; percent of vote - Lt. Gen. Idriss DEBY 63%, Ngarlegy YORONGAR 16%, Saleh KEBZABO 7%
Legislative branch: bicameral according to constitution, consists of a National Assembly (155 seats; members elected by popular vote to serve four-year terms) and a Senate (not yet created and size unspecified, members to serve six-year terms, one-third of membership renewable every two years)
elections: National Assembly - last held 21 April 2002 (next to be held in April 2006)
election results: percent of vote by party - NA%; seats by party - MPS 110, RDP 12, FAR 9, RNDP 5, URD 5, UNDR 3, others 11
Judicial branch: Supreme Court; Court of Appeal; Criminal Courts; Magistrate Courts
Political parties and leaders: Federation Action for the Republic or FAR [Ngarlejy YORONGAR]; National Union for Democracy and Renewal or UNDR [Saleh KEBZABO]; Party for Liberty and Development or PLD [Ibni Oumar Mahamat SALEH]; Patriotic Salvation Movement or MPS [Mahamat Saleh AHMAT, chairman]; Rally for Democracy and Progress or RDP [Lol Mahamat CHOUA]; Union for Democracy and Republic or UDR [Jean ALINGUE]; Union for Renewal and Democracy or URD [Gen. Wadal Abdelkader KAMOUGUE]; Viva Rally for Development and Progress or Viva RNDP [Delwa Kassire COUMAKOYE]
Political pressure groups and leaders: NA
International organization participation: ACCT, ACP, AfDB, AU, BDEAC, CEMAC, FAO, FZ, G-77, IAEA, IBRD, ICAO, ICCt (signatory), ICFTU, ICRM, IDA, IDB, IFAD, IFC, IFRCS, ILO, IMF, Interpol, IOC, ITU, MIGA, NAM, OIC, ONUB, OPCW, UN, UNCTAD, UNESCO, UNIDO, UNOCI, UPU, WCL, WCO, WHO, WIPO, WMO, WToO, WTO
Diplomatic representation in the US:
chief of mission: Ambassador Mahamat Adam BECHIR
chancery: 2002 R Street NW, Washington, DC 20009
telephone: [1] (202) 462-4009
FAX: [1] (202) 265-1937
Diplomatic representation from the US:
chief of mission: Ambassador Marc WALL
embassy: Avenue Felix Eboue, N'Djamena
mailing address: B. P. 413, N'Djamena
telephone: [235] (51) 70-09
FAX: [235] (51) 56-54
Flag description: three equal vertical bands of blue (hoist side), yellow, and red; similar to the flag of Romania; also similar to the flags of Andorra and Moldova, both of which have a national coat of arms centered in the yellow band; design was based on the flag of France

ECONOMY

Economy - overview: Chad's primarily agricultural economy will continue to be boosted by major foreign direct investment projects in the oil sector that began in 2000. Over 80% of Chad's population relies on subsistence farming and livestock raising for its livelihood. Chad's economy has long been handicapped by its landlocked position, high energy costs, and a history of instability. Chad relies on foreign assistance and foreign capital for most public and private sector investment projects. A consortium led by two US companies has been investing $3.7 billion to develop oil reserves, estimated at 1 billion barrels, in southern Chad. The nation's total oil reserves have been estimated to be 2 billion barrels. Oil production came on stream in late 2003. Chad began to export oil in 2004. Cotton, cattle, and gum arabic provide the bulk of Chad's non-oil export earnings.
GDP (purchasing power parity): $18.3 billion (2005 est.)
GDP (official exchange rate): $4.988 billion (2005 est.)
GDP - real growth rate: 14% (2005 est.)
GDP - per capita: purchasing power parity - $1,900 (2005 est.)
GDP - composition by sector:
agriculture: 23.7%
industry: 38.6%
services: 37.7% (2005 est.)
Labor force: NA
Labor force - by occupation: agriculture more than 80% (subsistence farming, herding, and fishing)
Unemployment rate: NA
Population below poverty line: 80% (2001 est.)
Household income or consumption by percentage share:
lowest 10%: NA
highest 10%: NA
Inflation rate (consumer prices): 5.5% (2005 est.)
Investment (gross fixed): 7.2% of GDP (2005 est.)
Budget:
revenues: $765.2 million
expenditures: $653.3 million, including capital expenditures of $146 million (2005 est.)
Agriculture - products: cotton, sorghum, millet, peanuts, rice, potatoes, manioc (tapioca); cattle, sheep, goats, camels
Industries: oil, cotton textiles, meatpacking, beer brewing, natron (sodium carbonate), soap, cigarettes, construction materials
Industrial production growth rate: 5% (1995)
Electricity - production: 120 million kWh (2003)
Electricity - production by source:
fossil fuel: 100%
hydro: 0%
nuclear: 0%
other: 0% (2001)
Electricity - consumption: 111.6 million kWh (2003)
Electricity - exports: 0 kWh (2003)
Electricity - imports: 0 kWh (2003)

Oil - production: 225,000 bbl/day (2005 est.)
Oil - consumption: 1,450 bbl/day (2003 est.)
Oil - exports: NA
Oil - imports: NA
Current account balance: $663.3 million (2005 est.)
Exports: $3.016 billion f.o.b. (2005 est.)
Exports - partners: US 67.7%, China 21.5%, Portugal 4.3% (2004)
Imports: $749.1 million f.o.b. (2005 est.)
Imports - partners: France 21.9%, Cameroon 16.1%, US 10.8%, Portugal 10.4%, Germany 6.4%, Belgium 4.6% (2004)
Reserves of foreign exchange and gold: $881.8 million (2005 est.)
Debt - external: $1.5 billion (2003 est.)
Economic aid - recipient: $238.3 million received; note - $125 million committed by Taiwan (August 1997); $30 million committed by African Development Bank; ODA $246.9 million (2003 est.)
Currency (code): Communaute Financiere Africaine franc (XAF); note - responsible authority is the Bank of the Central African States
Currency code: XAF
Exchange rates: Communaute Financiere Africaine francs (XAF) per US dollar - 516.5 (2005), 528.29 (2004), 581.2 (2003), 696.99 (2002), 733.04 (2001)
Fiscal year: calendar year

COMMUNICATION

Telephones - main lines in use: 11,800 (2002)
Telephones - mobile cellular: 65,000 (2003)
Telephone system:
general assessment: primitive system
domestic: fair system of radiotelephone communication stations
international: country code - 235; satellite earth station - 1 Intelsat (Atlantic Ocean)
Radio broadcast stations: AM 2, FM 4, shortwave 5 (2002)
Radios: 1.67 million (1997)
Television broadcast stations: 1 (2002)
Televisions: 10,000 (1997)
Internet country code: .td
Internet hosts: 8 (2004)
Internet Service Providers (ISPs): 1 (2002)
Internet users: 15,000 (2002)

TRANSPORTATION

Airports: 50 (2004 est.)
Airports - with paved runways:
total: 7
over 3,047 m: 2
2,438 to 3,047 m: 3
1,524 to 2,437 m: 1
under 914 m: 1 (2005 est.)
Airports - with unpaved runways:
total: 44
1,524 to 2,437 m: 14
914 to 1,523 m: 21
under 914 m: 9 (2005 est.)
Pipelines: oil 205 km (2004)
Roadways:
total: 33,400 km
paved: 267 km
unpaved: 33,133 km (1999)
Waterways: Chari and Legone rivers are navigable only in wet season (2002)

MILITARY

Military branches: Chadian National Army (Armee Nationale Tchadienne, ANT), Air Force, Gendarmerie (2004)
Military service age and obligation: 20 years of age for conscripts, with 3-year service obligation; 18 years of age for volunteers; no minimum age restriction for volunteers with consent from a guardian (2004)
Manpower available for military service: *males age 20-49:* 1,559,382 (2005 est.)
Manpower fit for military service: *males age 20-49:* 834,695 (2005 est.)
Manpower reaching military service age annually: *males:* 95,228 (2005 est.)
Military expenditures - dollar figure: $101.3 million (2004)
Military expenditures - percent of GDP: 2.1% (2004)

TRANSNATIONAL ISSUES

Disputes - international: since 2003, Janjawid armed militia and Sudanese military have driven about 200,000 Darfur region refugees into eastern Chad; Chad remains an important mediator in the Sudanese civil conflict; Chadian Aozou rebels reside in southern Libya; only Nigeria and Cameroon have heeded the Lake Chad Commission's admonition to ratify the delimitation treaty which also includes Chad and Niger
Refugees and internally displaced persons: *refugees (country of origin):* 200,000 (Sudan) 30,000 (Central African Republic) (2004)

CHILE

INTRODUCTION

Background: Prior to the coming of the Spanish in the 16th century, northern Chile was under Inca rule while Araucanian Indians inhabited central and southern Chile; the latter were not completely subjugated until the early 1880s. Although Chile declared its independence in 1810, decisive victory over the Spanish was not achieved until 1818. In the War of the Pacific (1879-84), Chile defeated Peru and Bolivia and won its present northern lands. A three-year-old Marxist government of Salvador ALLENDE was overthrown in 1973 by a dictatorial military regime led by Augusto PINOCHET, who ruled until a freely elected president was installed in 1990. Sound economic policies, maintained consistently since the 1980s, have contributed to steady growth and have helped secure the country's commitment to democratic and representative government. Chile has increasingly assumed regional and international leadership roles befitting its status as a stable, democratic nation.

GEOGRAPHY

Location: Southern South America, bordering the South Pacific Ocean, between Argentina and Peru
Geographic coordinates: 30 00 S, 71 00 W
Map references: South America
Area:
total: 756,950 sq km
land: 748,800 sq km
water: 8,150 sq km
note: includes Easter Island (Isla de Pascua) and Isla Sala y Gomez
Area - comparative: slightly smaller than twice the size of Montana
Land boundaries:
total: 6,171 km
border countries: Argentina 5,150 km, Bolivia 861 km, Peru 160 km
Coastline: 6,435 km
Maritime claims:
territorial sea: 12 nm
contiguous zone: 24 nm
exclusive economic zone: 200 nm
continental shelf: 200/350 nm
Climate: temperate; desert in north; Mediterranean in central region; cool and damp in south
Terrain: low coastal mountains; fertile central valley; rugged Andes in east
Elevation extremes:
lowest point: Pacific Ocean 0 m
highest point: Nevado Ojos del Salado 6,880 m
Natural resources: copper, timber, iron ore, nitrates, precious metals, molybdenum, hydropower

Land use:
arable land: 2.65%
permanent crops: 0.42%
other: 96.93% (2001)
Irrigated land: 18,000 sq km (1998 est.)
Natural hazards: severe earthquakes; active volcanism; tsunamis
Environment - current issues: widespread deforestation and mining threaten natural resources; air pollution from industrial and vehicle emissions; water pollution from raw sewage
Environment - international agreements:
party to: Antarctic-Environmental Protocol, Antarctic-Marine Living Resources, Antarctic Seals, Antarctic Treaty, Biodiversity, Climate Change, Climate Change-Kyoto Protocol, Desertification, Endangered Species, Environmental Modification, Hazardous Wastes, Law of the Sea, Marine Dumping, Ozone Layer Protection, Ship Pollution, Wetlands, Whaling
signed, but not ratified: none of the selected agreements
Geography - note: strategic location relative to sea lanes between Atlantic and Pacific Oceans (Strait of Magellan, Beagle Channel, Drake Passage); Atacama Desert is one of world's driest regions

PEOPLE

Population: 15,980,912 (July 2005 est.)
Age structure:
0-14 years: 25.2% (male 2,062,735/female 1,970,913)
15-64 years: 66.7% (male 5,320,870/female 5,342,771)
65 years and over: 8% (male 534,737/female 748,886) (2005 est.)
Median age:
total: 30.07 years
male: 29.17 years
female: 31.05 years (2005 est.)
Population growth rate: 0.97% (2005 est.)
Birth rate: 15.44 births/1,000 population (2005 est.)
Death rate: 5.76 deaths/1,000 population (2005 est.)
Net migration rate: 0 migrant(s)/1,000 population (2005 est.)
Sex ratio:
at birth: 1.05 male(s)/female
under 15 years: 1.05 male(s)/female
15-64 years: 1 male(s)/female
65 years and over: 0.71 male(s)/female
total population: 0.98 male(s)/female (2005 est.)
Infant mortality rate:
total: 8.8 deaths/1,000 live births
male: 9.55 deaths/1,000 live births
female: 8.01 deaths/1,000 live births (2005 est.)
Life expectancy at birth:
total population: 76.58 years
male: 73.3 years
female: 80.03 years (2005 est.)
Total fertility rate: 2.02 children born/woman (2005 est.)
HIV/AIDS - adult prevalence rate: 0.3% (2003 est.)
HIV/AIDS - people living with HIV/AIDS: 26,000 (2003 est.)
HIV/AIDS - deaths: 1,400 (2003 est.)
Nationality:
noun: Chilean(s)
adjective: Chilean
Ethnic groups: white and white-Amerindian 95%, Amerindian 3%, other 2%
Religions: Roman Catholic 89%, Protestant 11%, Jewish NEGL%
Languages: Spanish
Literacy:
definition: age 15 and over can read and write
total population: 96.2%
male: 96.4%
female: 96.1% (2003 est.)

GOVERNMENT

Country name:
conventional long form: Republic of Chile
conventional short form: Chile
local long form: Republica de Chile
local short form: Chile
Government type: republic
Capital: Santiago
Administrative divisions: 13 regions (regiones, singular - region); Aisen del General Carlos Ibanez del Campo, Antofagasta, Araucania, Atacama, Bio-Bio, Coquimbo, Libertador General Bernardo O'Higgins, Los Lagos, Magallanes y de la Antartica Chilena, Maule, Region Metropolitana (Santiago), Tarapaca, Valparaiso
note: the US does not recognize claims to Antarctica
Independence: 18 September 1810 (from Spain)
National holiday: Independence Day, 18 September (1810)
Constitution: 11 September 1980, effective 11 March 1981; amended 1989, 1991, 1997, 1999, 2000, 2003, and 2005
Legal system: based on Code of 1857 derived from Spanish law and subsequent codes influenced by French and Austrian law; judicial review of legislative acts in the Supreme Court; has not accepted compulsory ICJ jurisdiction
note: Chile is in the process of completely overhauling its criminal justice system; a new, US-style adversarial system is being gradually implemented throughout the country, and the final stage of implementation in the Santiago metropolitan region began in June 2005
Suffrage: 18 years of age; universal and compulsory
Executive branch:
chief of state: President Ricardo LAGOS Escobar (since 11 March 2000); note - the president is both the chief of state and head of government
head of government: President Ricardo LAGOS Escobar (since 11 March 2000); note - the president is both the chief of state and head of government
cabinet: Cabinet appointed by the president
elections: president elected by popular vote for a four-year term; election last held 11 December 2005, with runoff election to be held 15 January 2006 (next to be held December 2009)
election results: Ricardo LAGOS Escobar elected president; percent of vote - Ricardo LAGOS Escobar 51.32%, Joaquin LAVIN 48.68%
Legislative branch: bicameral National Congress or Congreso Nacional consists of the Senate or Senado (38 seats elected by popular vote); elected members serve eight-year terms (one-half elected every four years) and the Chamber of Deputies or Camara de Diputados (120 seats; members are elected by popular vote to serve four-year terms)
elections: Senate - last held 11 December 2005 (next to be held December 2009); Chamber of Deputies - last held 11

December 2005 (next to be held December 2009)
election results: Senate - percent of vote by party - NA%; seats by party - CPD 20 (PDC 6, PS 8, PPD 3, PRSD 3), APC 17 (UDI 9, RN 8), independent 1; Chamber of Deputies - percent of vote by party - NA%; seats by party - CPD 65 (PDC 21, PPD 22, PS 15, PRSD 7), APC 54 (UDI 34, RN 20, independent 1)
Judicial branch: Supreme Court or Corte Suprema (judges are appointed by the president and ratified by the Senate from lists of candidates provided by the court itself; the president of the Supreme Court is elected every three years by the 20-member court); Constitutional Tribunal
Political parties and leaders: Alliance for Chile ("Alianza") or APC (including National Renewal or RN [Sergio DIEZ Urzia] and Independent Democratic Union or UDI [Jovino NOVOA Vasquez]); Coalition of Parties for Democracy ("Concertacion") or CPD (including Christian Democratic Party or PDC [Adolfo ZALDIVAR Larrain], Socialist Party or PS [Ricardo NUNEZ], Party for Democracy or PPD [Victor BARRUETO], Radical Social Democratic Party or PRSD [Jose Antonio Gomez URRUTIA]); Communist Party or PC [Guillermo TEILLIER]
Political pressure groups and leaders: revitalized university student federations at all major universities; Roman Catholic Church; United Labor Central or CUT includes trade unionists from the country's five largest labor confederations
International organization participation: APEC, BIS, CSN, FAO, G-15, G-77, IADB, IAEA, IBRD, ICAO, ICC, ICCt (signatory), ICFTU, ICRM, IDA, IFAD, IFC, IFRCS, IHO, ILO, IMF, IMO, Interpol, IOC, IOM, ISO, ITU, LAES, LAIA, Mercosur (associate), MIGA, MINUSTAH, NAM, OAS, OPANAL, OPCW, PCA, RG, UN, UNCTAD, UNESCO, UNHCR, UNIDO, UNMOGIP, UNTSO, UPU, WCL, WCO, WFTU, WHO, WIPO, WMO, WToO, WTO
Diplomatic representation in the US:
chief of mission: Ambassador Andres BIANCHI
chancery: 1732 Massachusetts Avenue NW, Washington, DC 20036
telephone: [1] (202) 785-1746
FAX: [1] (202) 887-5579
consulate(s) general: Chicago, Houston, Los Angeles, Miami, New York, Philadelphia, San Francisco, and San Juan (Puerto Rico)
Diplomatic representation from the US:
chief of mission: Ambassador Craig A. KELLY
embassy: Avenida Andres Bello 2800, Las Condes, Santiago
mailing address: APO AA 34033
telephone: [56] (2) 232-2600
FAX: [56] (2) 330-3710
Flag description: two equal horizontal bands of white (top) and red; there is a blue square the same height as the white band at the hoist-side end of the white band; the square bears a white five-pointed star in the center representing a guide to progress and honor; blue symbolizes the sky, white is for the snow-covered Andes, and red stands for the blood spilled to achieve independence; design was influenced by the US flag

ECONOMY

Economy - overview: Chile has a market-oriented economy characterized by a high level of foreign trade. During the early 1990s, Chile's reputation as a role model for economic reform was strengthened when the democratic government of Patricio AYLWIN - which took over from the military in 1990 - deepened the economic reform initiated by the military government. Growth in real GDP averaged 8% during 1991-97, but fell to half that level in 1998 because of tight monetary policies implemented to keep the current account deficit in check and because of lower export earnings - the latter a product of the global financial crisis. A severe drought exacerbated the recession in 1999, reducing crop yields and causing hydroelectric shortfalls and electricity rationing, and Chile experienced negative economic growth for the first time in more than 15 years. Despite the effects of the recession, Chile maintained its reputation for strong financial institutions and sound policy that have given it the strongest sovereign bond rating in South America. By the end of 1999, exports and economic activity had begun to recover, and growth rebounded to 4.2% in 2000. Growth fell back to 3.1% in 2001 and 2.1% in 2002, largely due to lackluster global growth and the devaluation of the Argentine peso. Chile's economy began a slow recovery in 2003, growing 3.2%, and accelerated to 6.1% in 2004-05, while Chile maintained a low rate of inflation. GDP growth benefited from high copper prices, solid export earnings (particularly forestry, fishing, and mining), and stepped-up foreign direct investment. Unemployment, however, remains stubbornly high. Chile deepened its long-standing commitment to trade liberalization with the signing of a free trade agreement with the US, which took effect on 1 January 2004. Chile signed a free trade agreement with China in November 2005. Record-high copper prices strengthened the peso to a 5½-year high, as of December 2005, and will boost GDP in 2006.
GDP (purchasing power parity): $180.6 billion (2005 est.)
GDP (official exchange rate): $97 billion (2005 est.)
GDP - real growth rate: 5.9% (2005 est.)
GDP - per capita: purchasing power parity - $11,300 (2005 est.)
GDP - composition by sector:
agriculture: 6.2%
industry: 46.5%
services: 47.3% (2005 est.)
Labor force: 6.3 million (2005 est.)
Labor force - by occupation: agriculture 13.6%, industry 23.4%, services 63% (2003)
Unemployment rate: 7.4% (2005 est.)
Population below poverty line: 20.6% (2000)
Household income or consumption by percentage share:
lowest 10%: 1.2%
highest 10%: 47% (2000)
Distribution of family income - Gini index: 57.1 (2000)
Inflation rate (consumer prices): 4% (2005 est.)
Investment (gross fixed): 23.2% of GDP (2005 est.)
Budget:
revenues: $29.2 billion
expenditures: $24.75 billion, including capital expenditures of $3.33 billion (2005 est.)
Public debt: 8.1% of GDP (2005 est.)
Agriculture - products: grapes, apples, pears, onions, wheat, corn, oats, peaches, garlic, asparagus, beans, beef, poultry, wool; fish; timber
Industries: copper, other minerals, foodstuffs, fish processing, iron and steel, wood and wood products, transport equipment, cement, textiles
Industrial production growth rate: 6% (2005 est.)
Electricity - production: 45.3 billion kWh (2003)
Electricity - production by source:
fossil fuel: 47%
hydro: 51.5%
nuclear: 0%
other: 1.4% (2001)
Electricity - consumption: 44.13 billion kWh (2003)
Electricity - exports: 0 kWh (2003)
Electricity - imports: 2 billion kWh (2003)
Oil - production: 4,000 bbl/day (2005 est.)

Oil - consumption: 228,000 bbl/day (2003 est.)
Oil - exports: 0 bbl/day (2003)
Oil - imports: 221,500 bbl/day (2003 est.)
Oil - proved reserves: 150 million bbl (1 January 2004)
Natural gas - production: 1.18 billion cu m (2002 est.)
Natural gas - consumption: 6.517 billion cu m (2002 est.)
Natural gas - exports: 0 cu m (2002)
Natural gas - imports: 5.337 billion cu m (2002 est.)
Natural gas - proved reserves: 99.05 billion cu m (1 January 2004)
Current account balance: $309 million (2005 est.)
Exports: $38.03 billion f.o.b. (2005 est.)
Exports - partners: US 14%, Japan 11.4%, China 9.9%, South Korea 5.5%, Netherlands 5.1%, Brazil 4.3%, Italy 4.1%, Mexico 4% (2004)
Imports: $30.09 billion f.o.b. (2005 est.)
Imports - partners: Argentina 16.8%, US 13.7%, Brazil 11.2%, China 7.5% (2004)
Reserves of foreign exchange and gold: $16.03 billion (November 2005 est.)
Debt - external: $44.8 billion (31 October 2005 est.)
Economic aid - recipient: ODA, $0 (2002)
Currency (code): Chilean peso (CLP)
Currency code: CLP
Exchange rates: Chilean pesos per US dollar - 511.45 (2005), 609.37 (2004), 691.43 (2003), 688.94 (2002), 634.94 (2001)
Fiscal year: calendar year

COMMUNICATION

Telephones - main lines in use: 3.467 million (2002)
Telephones - mobile cellular: 6,445,700 (2002)
Telephone system:
general assessment: modern system based on extensive microwave radio relay facilities
domestic: extensive microwave radio relay links; domestic satellite system with 3 earth stations
international: country code - 56; satellite earth stations - 2 Intelsat (Atlantic Ocean)
Radio broadcast stations: AM 180 (eight inactive), FM 64, shortwave 17 (one inactive) (1998)
Radios: 5.18 million (1997)
Television broadcast stations: 63 (plus 121 repeaters) (1997)
Televisions: 3.15 million (1997)
Internet country code: .cl
Internet hosts: 202,429 (2003)
Internet Service Providers (ISPs): 7 (2000)
Internet users: 3.575 million (2002)

TRANSPORTATION

Airports: 364 (2004 est.)
Airports - with paved runways:
total: 72
over 3,047 m: 5
2,438 to 3,047 m: 7
1,524 to 2,437 m: 22
914 to 1,523 m: 21
under 914 m: 17 (2005 est.)
Airports - with unpaved runways:
total: 291
over 3,047 m: 1
2,438 to 3,047 m: 4
1,524 to 2,437 m: 11
914 to 1,523 m: 59
under 914 m: 216 (2005 est.)
Pipelines: gas 2,583 km; gas/lpg 42 km; liquid petroleum gas 539 km; oil 1,003 km; refined products 757 km (2004)
Railways:
total: 6,585 km
broad gauge: 2,831 km 1.676-m gauge (1,317 km electrified)
narrow gauge: 3,754 km 1.000-m gauge (2004)
Roadways:
total: 79,605 km
paved: 16,080 km (including 407 km of expressways)
unpaved: 63,525 km (2001)
Merchant marine:
total: 47 ships (1,000 GRT or over) 725,216 GRT/954,519 DWT
by type: bulk carrier 10, cargo 6, chemical tanker 9, container 1, liquefied gas 3, passenger 3, passenger/cargo 2, petroleum tanker 8, roll on/roll off 1, vehicle carrier 4
registered in other countries: 21 (2005)
Ports and terminals: Antofagasta, Arica, Huasco, Iquique, Lirquen, San Antonio, San Vicente, Valparaiso

MILITARY

Military branches: Army of the Nation, National Navy (includes naval air, Coast Guard, and Marine Corps), Chilean Air Force, Chilean Carabineros (National Police)
Military service age and obligation: 18 years of age for compulsory military service; all citizens 18-45 are obligated to perform military service; conscript service obligation - 12 months for Army, 24 months for Navy and Air Force (2004)
Manpower available for military service: *males age 18-49:* 3,815,761 (2005 est.)
Manpower fit for military service: *males age 18-49:* 3,123,281 (2005 est.)
Manpower reaching military service age annually: *males:* 140,084 (2005 est.)
Military expenditures - dollar figure: $3.42 billion (2004)
Military expenditures - percent of GDP: 3.8% (2004)

TRANSNATIONAL ISSUES

Disputes - international: Chile rebuffs Bolivia's reactivated claim to restore the Atacama corridor, ceded to Chile in 1884, offering instead unrestricted but not sovereign maritime access through Chile to Bolivian gas and other commodities; Peru proposes changing its latitudinal maritime boundary with Chile to an equidistance line with a southwestern axis; territorial claim in Antarctica (Chilean Antarctic Territory) partially overlaps Argentine and British claims
Illicit drugs: important transshipment country for cocaine destined for Europe and the US; economic prosperity and increasing trade have made Chile more attractive to traffickers seeking to launder drug profits, especially through the Iquique Free Trade Zone, but a new anti-money-laundering law improves controls; imported precursors passed on to Bolivia; domestic cocaine consumption is rising

CHINA

INTRODUCTION

Background: For centuries China stood as a leading civilization, outpacing the rest of the world in the arts and sciences, but in the 19th and early 20th centuries, the country was beset by civil unrest, major famines, military defeats, and foreign occupation. After World War II, the Communists under MAO Zedong established an autocratic socialist system that, while ensuring China's sovereignty, imposed strict controls over everyday life and cost the lives of tens of millions of people. After 1978, his successor DENG Xiaoping and other leaders focused on market-oriented economic development and by 2000 output had quadrupled. For much of the population, living standards have improved dramatically and the room for personal choice has expanded, yet political controls remain tight.

GEOGRAPHY

Location: Eastern Asia, bordering the East China Sea, Korea Bay, Yellow Sea, and South China Sea, between North Korea and Vietnam
Geographic coordinates: 35 00 N, 105 00 E
Map references: Asia
Area:
total: 9,596,960 sq km
land: 9,326,410 sq km
water: 270,550 sq km
Area - comparative: slightly smaller than the US
Land boundaries:
total: 22,117 km
border countries: Afghanistan 76 km, Bhutan 470 km, Burma 2,185 km, India 3,380 km, Kazakhstan 1,533 km, North Korea 1,416 km, Kyrgyzstan 858 km, Laos 423 km, Mongolia 4,677 km, Nepal 1,236 km, Pakistan 523 km, Russia (northeast) 3,605 km, Russia (northwest) 40 km, Tajikistan 414 km, Vietnam 1,281 km
regional borders: Hong Kong 30 km, Macau 0.34 km
Coastline: 14,500 km
Maritime claims:
territorial sea: 12 nm
contiguous zone: 24 nm
exclusive economic zone: 200 nm
continental shelf: 200 nm or to the edge of the continental margin
Climate: extremely diverse; tropical in south to subarctic in north
Terrain: mostly mountains, high plateaus, deserts in west; plains, deltas, and hills in east
Elevation extremes:
lowest point: Turpan Pendi -154 m
highest point: Mount Everest 8,850 m
Natural resources: coal, iron ore, petroleum, natural gas, mercury, tin, tungsten, antimony, manganese, molybdenum, vanadium, magnetite, aluminum, lead, zinc, uranium, hydropower potential (world's largest)
Land use:
arable land: 15.4%
permanent crops: 1.25%
other: 83.35% (2001)
Irrigated land: 525,800 sq km (1998 est.)
Natural hazards: frequent typhoons (about five per year along southern and eastern coasts); damaging floods; tsunamis; earthquakes; droughts; land subsidence
Environment - current issues: air pollution (greenhouse gases, sulfur dioxide particulates) from reliance on coal produces acid rain; water shortages, particularly in the north; water pollution from untreated wastes; deforestation; estimated loss of one-fifth of agricultural land since 1949 to soil erosion and economic development; desertification; trade in endangered species
Environment - international agreements:
party to: Antarctic-Environmental Protocol, Antarctic Treaty, Biodiversity, Climate Change, Climate Change-Kyoto Protocol, Desertification, Endangered Species, Hazardous Wastes, Law of the Sea, Marine Dumping, Ozone Layer Protection, Ship Pollution, Tropical Timber 83, Tropical Timber 94, Wetlands, Whaling
signed, but not ratified: none of the selected agreements
Geography - note: world's fourth largest country (after Russia, Canada, and US); Mount Everest on the border with Nepal is the world's tallest peak

PEOPLE

Population: 1,306,313,812 (July 2005 est.)
Age structure:
0-14 years: 21.4% (male 148,134,928/female 131,045,415)
15-64 years: 71% (male 477,182,072/female 450,664,933)
65 years and over: 7.6% (male 47,400,282/female 51,886,182) (2005 est.)
Median age:
total: 32.26 years
male: 31.87 years
female: 32.67 years (2005 est.)
Population growth rate: 0.58% (2005 est.)
Birth rate: 13.14 births/1,000 population (2005 est.)
Death rate: 6.94 deaths/1,000 population (2005 est.)
Net migration rate: -0.4 migrant(s)/1,000 population (2005 est.)
Sex ratio:
at birth: 1.12 male(s)/female
under 15 years: 1.13 male(s)/female
15-64 years: 1.06 male(s)/female
65 years and over: 0.91 male(s)/female
total population: 1.06 male(s)/female (2005 est.)
Infant mortality rate:
total: 24.18 deaths/1,000 live births
male: 21.21 deaths/1,000 live births
female: 27.5 deaths/1,000 live births (2005 est.)
Life expectancy at birth:
total population: 72.27 years
male: 70.65 years
female: 74.09 years (2005 est.)
Total fertility rate: 1.72 children born/woman (2005 est.)
HIV/AIDS - adult prevalence rate: 0.1% (2003 est.)
HIV/AIDS - people living with HIV/AIDS: 840,000 (2003 est.)
HIV/AIDS - deaths: 44,000 (2003 est.)
Nationality:
noun: Chinese (singular and plural)
adjective: Chinese
Ethnic groups: Han Chinese 91.9%, Zhuang, Uygur, Hui, Yi, Tibetan, Miao, Manchu, Mongol, Buyi, Korean, and other nationalities 8.1%

Religions: Daoist (Taoist), Buddhist, Muslim 1%-2%, Christian 3%-4%
note: officially atheist (2002 est.)
Languages: Standard Chinese or Mandarin (Putonghua, based on the Beijing dialect), Yue (Cantonese), Wu (Shanghaiese), Minbei (Fuzhou), Minnan (Hokkien-Taiwanese), Xiang, Gan, Hakka dialects, minority languages (see Ethnic groups entry)
Literacy:
definition: age 15 and over can read and write
total population: 90.9%
male: 95.1%
female: 86.5% (2002)

GOVERNMENT

Country name:
conventional long form: People's Republic of China
conventional short form: China
local long form: Zhonghua Renmin Gongheguo
local short form: Zhongguo
abbreviation: PRC
Government type: Communist state
Capital: Beijing
Administrative divisions: 23 provinces (sheng, singular and plural), 5 autonomous regions (zizhiqu, singular and plural), and 4 municipalities (shi, singular and plural)
: provinces: Anhui, Fujian, Gansu, Guangdong, Guizhou, Hainan, Hebei, Heilongjiang, Henan, Hubei, Hunan, Jiangsu, Jiangxi, Jilin, Liaoning, Qinghai, Shaanxi, Shandong, Shanxi, Sichuan, Yunnan, Zhejiang
: autonomous regions: Guangxi, Nei Mongol, Ningxia, Xinjiang, Xizang (Tibet)
: municipalities: Beijing, Chongqing, Shanghai, Tianjin
note: China considers Taiwan its 23rd province; see separate entries for the special administrative regions of Hong Kong and Macau
Independence: 221 BC (unification under the Qin or Ch'in Dynasty); 1 January 1912 (Manchu Dynasty replaced by a Republic); 1 October 1949 (People's Republic established)
National holiday: Anniversary of the Founding of the People's Republic of China, 1 October (1949)
Constitution: most recent promulgation 4 December 1982
Legal system: based on civil law system; derived from Soviet and continental civil code legal principles; legislature retains power to interpret statutes; constitution ambiguous on judicial review of legislation; has not accepted compulsory ICJ jurisdiction.
Suffrage: 18 years of age; universal
Executive branch:
chief of state: President HU Jintao (since 15 March 2003) and Vice President ZENG Qinghong (since 15 March 2003)
head of government: Premier WEN Jiabao (since 16 March 2003); Vice Premiers HUANG Ju (since 17 March 2003), WU Yi (17 March 2003), ZENG Peiyan (since 17 March 2003), and HUI Liangyu (since 17 March 2003)
cabinet: State Council appointed by the National People's Congress (NPC)
elections: president and vice president elected by the National People's Congress for five-year terms; elections last held 15-17 March 2003 (next to be held mid-March 2008); premier nominated by the president, confirmed by the National People's Congress
election results: HU Jintao elected president by the Tenth National People's Congress with a total of 2,937 votes (four delegates voted against him, four abstained, and 38 did not vote); ZENG Qinghong elected vice president by the Tenth National People's Congress with a total of 2,578 votes (177 delegates voted against him, 190 abstained, and 38 did not vote); two seats were vacant
Legislative branch: unicameral National People's Congress or Quanguo Renmin Daibiao Dahui (2,985 seats; members elected by municipal, regional, and provincial people's congresses to serve five-year terms)
elections: last held December 2002-February 2003 (next to be held late 2007-February 2008)
election results: percent of vote - NA%; seats - NA
Judicial branch: Supreme People's Court (judges appointed by the National People's Congress); Local Peoples Courts (comprise higher, intermediate and local courts); Special Peoples Courts (primarily military, maritime, and railway transport courts)
Political parties and leaders: Chinese Communist Party or CCP [HU Jintao, General Secretary of the Central Committee]; eight registered small parties controlled by CCP
Political pressure groups and leaders: no substantial political opposition groups exist, although the government has identified the Falungong spiritual movement and the China Democracy Party as subversive groups
International organization participation: AfDB, APEC, APT, ARF, AsDB, ASEAN (dialogue partner), BCIE, BIS, CDB, EAS, FAO, G-77, IAEA, IBRD, ICAO, ICC, ICRM, IDA, IFAD, IFC, IFRCS, IHO, ILO, IMF, IMO, Interpol, IOC, IOM (observer), ISO, ITU, LAIA (observer), MIGA, MINURSO, MONUC, NAM (observer), NSG, OAS (observer), ONUB, OPCW, PCA, PIF (partner), SAARC (observer), SCO, UN, UN Security Council, UNAMSIL, UNCTAD, UNESCO, UNHCR, UNIDO, UNITAR, UNMEE, UNMIL, UNMIS, UNMOVIC, UNOCI, UNTSO, UPU, WCO, WHO, WIPO, WMO, WToO, WTO, ZC
Diplomatic representation in the US:
chief of mission: Ambassador ZHOU Wenzhong
chancery: 2300 Connecticut Avenue NW, Washington, DC 20008
telephone: [1] (202) 328-2500
FAX: [1] (202) 328-2582
consulate(s) general: Chicago, Houston, Los Angeles, New York, and San Francisco
consulate(s): Los Angeles
Diplomatic representation from the US:
chief of mission: Ambassador Clark T. RANDT, Jr.
embassy: Xiu Shui Bei Jie 3, 100600 Beijing
mailing address: PSC 461, Box 50, FPO AP 96521-0002
telephone: [86] (10) 6532-3831
FAX: [86] (10) 6532-3178
consulate(s) general: Chengdu, Guangzhou, Hong Kong and Macau, Shanghai, Shenyang
Flag description: red with a large yellow five-pointed star and four smaller yellow five-pointed stars (arranged in a vertical arc toward the middle of the flag) in the upper hoist-side corner

ECONOMY

Economy - overview: China's economy during the last quarter-century has changed from a centrally planned system that was largely closed to international trade to a more market-oriented economy that has a rapidly growing private sector and is a major player in the global economy. Reforms started in the late 1970s with the phasing out of collectivized agriculture, and expanded to include the gradual liberalization of prices, fiscal decentralization, increased autonomy for state enterprises, the foundation of a diversified banking system, the development of stock markets, the rapid growth of the non-state sector, and the opening to foreign trade and investment. China has generally implemented reforms in a gradualist or piecemeal fashion. The process continues with key moves in 2005 including the sale of equity in China's largest state banks to foreign investors and refinements in foreign exchange and bond markets. The restructuring of the economy and resulting efficiency gains have contributed to a more than ten-fold increase in GDP since 1978. Measured on a purchasing power parity (PPP) basis, China in 2005 stood as the second-largest economy in the world after the US, although in per capita terms the country is still lower middle-income and 150 million Chinese fall below international poverty lines. Economic development has generally been more rapid in coastal provinces than in the interior and there are large disparities in per capita income between regions. The government has struggled to (a) sustain adequate jobs growth for tens of millions of workers laid off from state-owned enterprises, migrants, and new entrants to the work force; (b) reduce corruption and other economic crimes; and (c) contain environmental damage and social strife related to the economy's rapid transformation. From 100 to 150 million surplus rural workers are adrift between the villages and the cities, many subsisting through part-time, low-paying jobs. One demographic consequence of the "one child" policy is that China is now one of the most rapidly aging countries in the world. Another long-term threat to growth is the deterioration in the environment - notably air pollution, soil erosion, and the steady fall of the water table especially in the north. China continues to lose arable land because of erosion and economic development. China has benefited from a huge expansion in computer Internet use, with more than 100 million users at the end of 2005. Foreign investment remains a strong element in China's remarkable expansion in world trade and has been an important factor in growth of urban jobs. On 21 July 2005 China revalued its currency by 2.1 percent against the US dollar and moved to an exchange rate system that references a basket of currencies. Reports of shortages of electric power in the summer of 2005 in southern China receded by September-October and did not have a substantial impact on China's economy. More power generating capacity is scheduled to come on line in 2006 as large scale investments are completed. The Central Committee of the Chinese Communist Party in October 2005 approved the draft 11th Five-Year Plan and the National People's Congress is expected to give final approval in March 2006. The plan calls for a 20 percent reduction in energy consumption per unit of GDP by 2010 and an estimated 45 percent increase in GDP by 2010. The plan states that conserving resources and protecting the environment are basic goals but it lacks details on the policies and reforms necessary to achieve these goals.

GDP (purchasing power parity): $8.158 trillion (2005 est.)
GDP (official exchange rate): $1.833 trillion (2005 est.)
GDP - real growth rate: 9.2% (official data) (2005 est.)
GDP - per capita: purchasing power parity - $6,200 (2005 est.)
GDP - composition by sector:
agriculture: 14.4%
industry and construction: 53.1%
services: 32.5% (2005 est.)
Labor force: 791.4 million (2005 est.)
Labor force - by occupation: agriculture 49%, industry 22%, services 29% (2003 est.)
Unemployment rate: 4.2% official registered unemployment in urban areas in 2004; substantial unemployment and underemployment in rural areas; an official Chinese journal estimated overall unemployment (including rural areas) for 2003 at 20% (2004)
Population below poverty line: 10% (2001 est.)
Household income or consumption by percentage share:
lowest 10%: 2.4%
highest 10%: 30.4% (1998)
Distribution of family income - Gini index: 44 (2002)
Inflation rate (consumer prices): 1.9% (2005 est.)
Investment (gross fixed): 43.6% of GDP (2005 est.)
Budget:
revenues: $392.1 billion
expenditures: $424.3 billion, including capital expenditures of NA (2005 est.)
Public debt: 28.8% of GDP (2005 est.)
Agriculture - products: rice, wheat, potatoes, corn, peanuts, tea, millet, barley, apples, cotton, oilseed, pork, fish
Industries: mining and ore processing, iron, steel, aluminum, and other metals; coal; machine building; armaments; textiles and apparel; petroleum; cement; chemicals; fertilizers; consumer products, including footwear, toys, and electronics; food processing; transportation equipment, including automobiles, rail cars and locomotives, ships, and aircraft; telecommunications equipment, commercial space launch vehicles and satellites
Industrial production growth rate: 27.7% (2005 est.)
Electricity - production: 2.19 trillion kWh (2004)
Electricity - production by source:
fossil fuel: 80.2%
hydro: 18.5%
nuclear: 1.2%
other: 0.1% (2001)
Electricity - consumption: 2.17 trillion kWh (2004)
Electricity - exports: 10.6 billion kWh (2003)
Electricity - imports: 1.546 billion kWh (2003)
Oil - production: 3.504 million bbl/day (2004)
Oil - consumption: 6.391 million bbl/day (2004)
Oil - exports: 340,300 bbl/day (2004)
Oil - imports: 3.226 million bbl/day (2004)
Oil - proved reserves: 18.26 billion bbl (2004)
Natural gas - production: 35.02 billion cu m (2003)
Natural gas - consumption:33.91 billion cu m (2003)
Natural gas - exports: 2.79 billion cu m (2004)
Natural gas - imports: 0 cu m (2004)
Natural gas - proved reserves: 2.53 trillion cu m (2004)
Current account balance: $129.1 billion (2005 est.)
Exports: $752.2 billion f.o.b. (2005 est.)
Exports - partners: US 21.1%, Hong Kong 17%, Japan 12.4%, South Korea 4.7%, Germany 4% (2004)
Imports: $631.8 billion f.o.b. (2005 est.)
Imports - partners: Japan 16.8%, Taiwan 11.4%, South Korea 11.1%, US 8%, Germany 5.4% (2004)
Reserves of foreign exchange and gold: $795.1 billion (2005 est.)
Debt - external: $242 billion (2005 est.)
Economic aid - recipient: NA
Currency (code): yuan (CNY)
note:: also referred to as the Renminbi (RMB)
Currency code: CNY
Exchange rates: yuan per US dollar - 8.19 (2005), 8.2768 (2004), 8.277 (2003), 8.277 (2002), 8.2771 (2001)
Fiscal year: calendar year

COMMUNICATION

Telephones - main lines in use: 263 million (2003)
Telephones - mobile cellular: 269 million (2003)
Telephone system:
general assessment: domestic and international services are increasingly available for private use; unevenly distributed domestic system serves principal cities, industrial centers, and many towns
domestic: interprovincial fiber-optic trunk

lines and cellular telephone systems have been installed; a domestic satellite system with 55 earth stations is in place
international: country code - 86; satellite earth stations - 5 Intelsat (4 Pacific Ocean and 1 Indian Ocean), 1 Intersputnik (Indian Ocean region) and 1 Inmarsat (Pacific and Indian Ocean regions); several international fiber-optic links to Japan, South Korea, Hong Kong, Russia, and Germany (2000)
Radio broadcast stations: AM 369, FM 259, shortwave 45 (1998)
Radios: 417 million (1997)
Television broadcast stations: 3,240 (of which 209 are operated by China Central Television, 31 are provincial TV stations and nearly 3,000 are local city stations) (1997)
Televisions: 400 million (1997)
Internet country code: .cn
Internet hosts: 160,421 (2003)
Internet Service Providers (ISPs): 3 (2000)
Internet users: 94 million (2004)

TRANSPORTATION

Airports: 472 (2004 est.)
Airports - with paved runways:
total: 389
over 3,047 m: 54
2,438 to 3,047 m: 120
1,524 to 2,437 m: 139
914 to 1,523 m: 23
under 914 m: 53 (2005 est.)
Airports - with unpaved runways:
total: 117
over 3,047 m: 4
2,438 to 3,047 m: 5
1,524 to 2,437 m: 15
914 to 1,523 m: 29
under 914 m: 36 (2005 est.)
Heliports: 30 (2005 est.)
Pipelines: gas 15,890 km; oil 14,478 km; refined products 3,280 km (2004)
Railways:
total: 71,898 km
standard gauge: 71,898 km 1.435-m gauge (18,115 km electrified)
dual gauge: 23,945 km (multiple track not included in total) (2002)
Roadways:
total: 1,809,829 km
paved: 1,447,682 km (with at least 29,745 km of expressways)
unpaved: 362,147 km (2003)
Waterways: 121,557 km (2002)
Merchant marine:
total: 1,649 ships (1,000 GRT or over) 18,724,653 GRT/27,749,784 DWT
by type: barge carrier 2, bulk carrier 362, cargo 696, chemical tanker 38, combination ore/oil 1, container 135, liquefied gas 30, passenger 7, passenger/cargo 81, petroleum tanker 246, refrigerated cargo 30, roll on/roll off 11, vehicle carrier 10
foreign-owned: 9 (Hong Kong 4, Japan 2, South Korea 2, United States 1)
registered in other countries: 872 (2005)
Ports and terminals: Dalian, Guangzhou, Nanjing, Ningbo, Qingdao, Qinhuangdao, Shanghai

MILITARY

Military branches: People's Liberation Army (PLA): Ground Forces, Navy (includes marines and naval aviation), Air Force (includes Airborne Forces), and II Artillery Corps (strategic missile force); People's Armed Police Force (internal security troops considered to be an adjunct to the PLA); Militia (2003)
Military service age and obligation: 18-22 years of age for compulsory military service, with 24-month service obligation; no minimum age for voluntary service; 17 years of age for women who meet requirements for specific military jobs (2004)
Manpower available for military service:
males age 18-49: 342,956,265 (2005 est.)
Manpower fit for military service: *males age 18-49:* 281,240,272 (2005 est.)
Manpower reaching military service age annually: *males:* 13,186,433 (2005 est.)
Military expenditures - dollar figure: $67.49 billion (2004)
Military expenditures - percent of GDP: 4.3% (2004)

TRANSNATIONAL ISSUES

Disputes - international: in 2005, China and India initiate drafting principles to resolve all aspects of their extensive boundary and territorial disputes together with a security and foreign policy dialogue to consolidate discussions related to the boundary, regional nuclear proliferation, and other matters; recent talks and confidence-building measures have begun to defuse tensions over Kashmir, site of the world's largest and most militarized territorial dispute with portions under the de facto administration of China (Aksai Chin), India (Jammu and Kashmir), and Pakistan (Azad Kashmir and Northern Areas); India does not recognize Pakistan's ceding historic Kashmir lands to China in 1964; about 90,000 ethnic Tibetan exiles reside primarily in India as well as Nepal and Bhutan; China asserts sovereignty over the Spratly Islands together with Malaysia, Philippines, Taiwan, Vietnam, and possibly Brunei; the 2002 "Declaration on the Conduct of Parties in the South China Sea" has eased tensions in the Spratlys but is not the legally binding "code of conduct" sought by some parties; in March 2005, the national oil companies of China, the Philippines, and Vietnam signed a joint accord on marine seismic activities in the Spratly Islands; China occupies some of the Paracel Islands also claimed by Vietnam and Taiwan; China and Taiwan have become more vocal in rejecting both Japan's claims to the uninhabited islands of Senkaku-shoto (Diaoyu Tai) and Japan's unilaterally declared exclusive economic zone in the East China Sea, the site of intensive hydrocarbon prospecting; certain islands in the Yalu and Tumen rivers are in an uncontested dispute with North Korea and a section of boundary around Mount Paektu is considered indefinite; China seeks to stem illegal migration of tens of thousands of North Koreans; in 2004, China and Russia divided up the islands in the Amur, Ussuri, and Argun Rivers, ending a century-old border dispute; demarcation of the China-Vietnam boundary proceeds slowly and although the maritime boundary delimitation and fisheries agreements were ratified in June 2004, implementation has been delayed; environmentalists in Burma and Thailand remain concerned about China's construction of hydroelectric dams upstream on the Nujiang/Salween River in Yunnan Province
Refugees and internally displaced persons: *refugees (country of origin):* 299,287 (Vietnam) estimated 30,000-50,000 (North Korea) (2004)
Illicit drugs: major transshipment point for heroin produced in the Golden Triangle; growing domestic drug abuse problem; source country for chemical precursors and methamphetamine

CHRISTMAS ISLAND

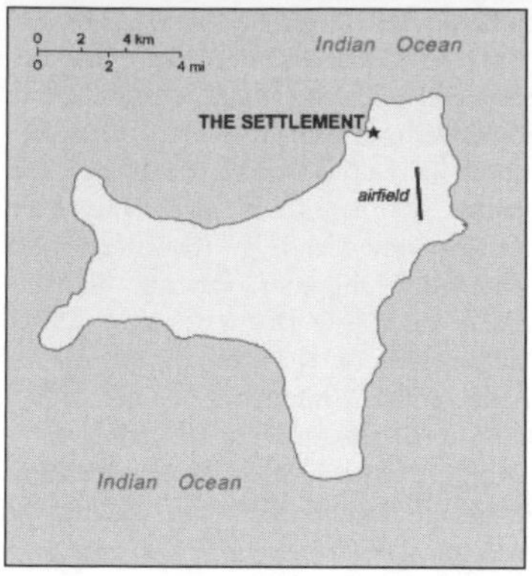

INTRODUCTION

Background: Named in 1643 for the day of its discovery, the island was annexed and settlement was begun by the UK in 1888. Phosphate mining began in the 1890s. The UK transferred sovereignty to Australia in 1958. Almost two-thirds of the island has been declared a national park.

GEOGRAPHY

Location: Southeastern Asia, island in the Indian Ocean, south of Indonesia
Geographic coordinates: 10 30 S, 105 40 E
Map references: Southeast Asia
Area:
total: 135 sq km
land: 135 sq km
water: 0 sq km
Area - comparative: about three-quarters the size of Washington, DC
Land boundaries: 0 km
Coastline: 138.9 km
Maritime claims:
territorial sea: 12 nm
contiguous zone: 12 nm
exclusive fishing zone: 200 nm
Climate: tropical with a wet and dry season; heat and humidity moderated by trade winds; wet season December to April
Terrain: steep cliffs along coast rise abruptly to central plateau
Elevation extremes:
lowest point: Indian Ocean 0 m
highest point: Murray Hill 361 m
Natural resources: phosphate, beaches
Land use:
arable land: 0%
permanent crops: 0%
other: 100%
note: mainly tropical rainforest; 63% of the island is a national park (2001)
Irrigated land: NA sq km
Natural hazards: the narrow fringing reef surrounding the island can be a maritime hazard
Environment - current issues: NA
Geography - note: located along major sea lanes of Indian Ocean

PEOPLE

Population: 361 (July 2005 est.)
Age structure:
0-14 years: NA
15-64 years: NA
65 years and over: NA
Population growth rate: 0% (2005 est.)
Birth rate: NA
Death rate: NA
Net migration rate: NA
Sex ratio: NA
Infant mortality rate:
total: NA
male: NA
female: NA
Life expectancy at birth:
total population: NA
male: NA
female: NA
Total fertility rate: NA
HIV/AIDS - adult prevalence rate: NA
HIV/AIDS - people living with HIV/AIDS: NA
HIV/AIDS - deaths: NA
Nationality:
noun: Christmas Islander(s)
adjective: Christmas Island
Ethnic groups:
Chinese 70%, European 20%, Malay 10%
note: no indigenous population (2001)
Religions: Buddhist 36%, Muslim 25%, Christian 18%, other 21% (1997)
Languages: English (official), Chinese, Malay
Literacy: NA
People - note: the Australian Bureau of Statistics reports a population of 1,508 as of the 2001 Census

GOVERNMENT

Country name:
conventional long form: Territory of Christmas Island
conventional short form: Christmas Island
Dependency status: territory of Australia; administered by the Australian Department of Transport and Regional Services
Government type: NA
Capital: The Settlement
Administrative divisions: none (territory of Australia)
Independence: none (territory of Australia)
National holiday: Australia Day, 26 January (1788)
Constitution: Christmas Island Act of 1958-59 (1 October 1958)
Legal system: under the authority of the governor general of Australia and Australian law
Executive branch:
chief of state: Queen ELIZABETH II (since 6 February 1952), represented by the Australian governor general
head of government: Administrator Evan WILLIAMS (since 1 November 2003)
elections: none; the monarch is hereditary; administrator appointed by the governor general of Australia and represents the monarch and Australia
Legislative branch: unicameral Christmas Island Shire Council (9 seats; members elected by popular vote to serve four-year terms)
elections: held every two years with half the members standing for election; last held 3 May 2003 (next to be held in 2005)
election results: percent of vote - NA%; seats - independents 9
Judicial branch: Supreme Court; District Court; Magistrate's Court
Political parties and leaders: none
Political pressure groups and leaders: none
International organization participation: none
Diplomatic representation in the US: none (territory of Australia)
Diplomatic representation from the US: none (territory of Australia)
Flag description: the flag of Australia is used; note - in early 1986, the Christmas Island Assembly held a design competition for an island flag, however, the winning design has never been formally adopted as the official flag of the territory

ECONOMY

Economy - overview: Phosphate mining had been the only significant economic activity, but in December 1987 the Australian Government closed the mine. In 1991, the mine was reopened. With the support of the government, a $34 million casino opened in 1993. The casino closed in 1998. The Australian Government in 2001 agreed to support the creation of a commercial space-launching site on the island, projected to begin operations in the near future
GDP (purchasing power parity): NA
GDP (official exchange rate): NA
GDP - real growth rate: NA
GDP - composition by sector:
agriculture: NA
industry: NA
services: NA
Labor force: NA
Labor force - by occupation: NA

Budget:
revenues: NA
expenditures: NA, including capital expenditures of NA
Agriculture - products: NA
Industries: tourism, phosphate extraction (near depletion)
Electricity - production by source:
fossil fuel: NA
hydro: NA
nuclear: NA
other: NA
Exports: NA
Exports - partners: Australia, NZ (2004)
Imports: NA
Imports - partners: principally Australia (2004)
Economic aid - recipient: NA
Currency (code): Australian dollar (AUD)
Currency code: AUD
Exchange rates: Australian dollars per US dollar - 1.38 (2005), 1.3598 (2004), 1.5419 (2003), 1.8406 (2002), 1.9334 (2001)
Fiscal year: 1 July - 30 June

COMMUNICATION

Telephones - main lines in use: NA
Telephones - mobile cellular: NA
Telephone system:
general assessment: service provided by the Australian network
domestic: GSM mobile telephone service replaced older analog system in February 2005
international: country code - 61-891; satellite earth stations - one INTELSAT earth station provides telephone and telex service (2005)
Radio broadcast stations: AM 1, FM 1, shortwave 0 (2004)
Radios: 1,000 (1997)
Television broadcast stations: NA
Televisions: 600 (1997)
Internet country code: .cx
Internet Service Providers (ISPs): 2 (2000)
Internet users: NA

TRANSPORTATION

Airports: 1 (2004 est.)
Airports - with paved runways:
total: 1
1,524 to 2,437 m: 1 (2005 est.)
Roadways:
total: 140 km
paved: 30 km
unpaved: 110 km (2002)
Ports and terminals: Flying Fish Cove

MILITARY

Military - note: defense is the responsibility of Australia

TRANSNATIONAL ISSUES

Disputes - international: none

CLIPPERTON ISLAND

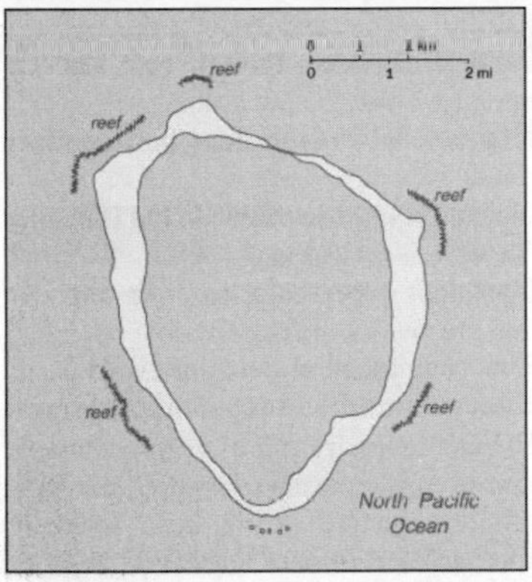

INTRODUCTION

Background: This isolated island was named for John CLIPPERTON, a pirate who made it his hideout early in the 18th century. Annexed by France in 1855, it was seized by Mexico in 1897. Arbitration eventually awarded the island to France, which took possession in 1935.

GEOGRAPHY

Location: Middle America, atoll in the North Pacific Ocean, 1,120 km southwest of Mexico
Geographic coordinates: 10 17 N, 109 13 W
Map references: Political Map of the World
Area:
total: 6 sq km
land: 6 sq km
water: 0 sq km
Area - comparative: about 12 times the size of The Mall in Washington, DC
Land boundaries: 0 km
Coastline: 11.1 km
Maritime claims:
territorial sea: 12 nm
exclusive economic zone: 200 nm
Climate: tropical; humid, average temperature 20-32 degrees C, rains May-October
Terrain: coral atoll
Elevation extremes:
lowest point: Pacific Ocean 0 m
highest point: Rocher Clipperton 29 m
Natural resources: fish
Land use:
arable land: 0%
permanent crops: 0%
other: 100% (all coral) (2001)
Irrigated land: 0 sq km (1998 est.)
Natural hazards: NA
Environment - current issues: NA
Geography - note: reef 12 km in circumference

PEOPLE

Population: uninhabited (July 2005 est.)

GOVERNMENT

Country name:
conventional long form: none
conventional short form: Clipperton Island
local long form: none
local short form: Ile Clipperton
former: sometimes called Ile de la Passion
Dependency status: possession of France; administered by France from French Polynesia by a high commissioner of the Republic
Legal system: the laws of France, where applicable, apply
Flag description: the flag of France is used

ECONOMY

Economy - overview: Although 115 species of fish have been identified in the territorial waters of Clipperton Island, the only economic activity is tuna fishing.

TRANSPORTATION

Ports and terminals: none; offshore anchorage only

MILITARY

Military - note: defense is the responsibility of France

CTRANSNATIONAL ISSUES

Disputes - international: none

COCOS (KEELING) ISLANDS

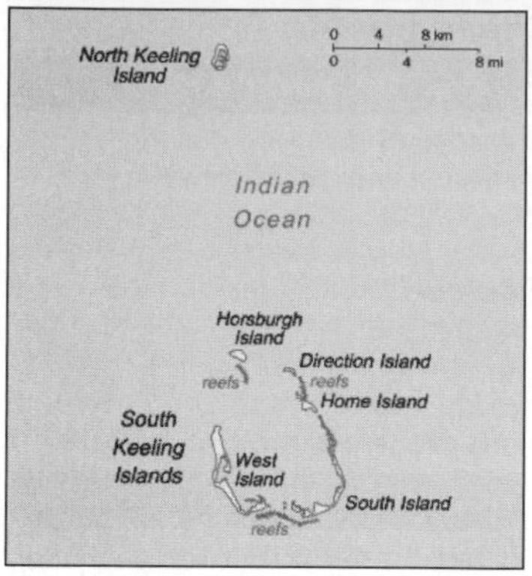

INTRODUCTION

Background: There are 27 coral islands in the group. Captain William KEELING discovered the islands in 1609, but they remained uninhabited until the 19th century. Annexed by the UK in 1857, they were transferred to the Australian Government in 1955. The population on the two inhabited islands generally is split between the ethnic Europeans on West Island and the ethnic Malays on Home Island.

GEOGRAPHY

Location: Southeastern Asia, group of islands in the Indian Ocean, southwest of Indonesia, about halfway from Australia to Sri Lanka
Geographic coordinates: 12 30 S, 96 50 E
Map references: Southeast Asia
Area:
total: 14 sq km
land: 14 sq km
water: 0 sq km
note: includes the two main islands of West Island and Home Island
Area - comparative: about 24 times the size of The Mall in Washington, DC
Land boundaries: 0 km
Coastline: 26 km
Maritime claims:
territorial sea: 12 nm
exclusive fishing zone: 200 nm
Climate: tropical with high humidity, moderated by the southeast trade winds for about nine months of the year
Terrain: flat, low-lying coral atolls
Elevation extremes:
lowest point: Indian Ocean 0 m
highest point: unnamed location 5 m
Natural resources: fish
Land use:
arable land: 0%
permanent crops: 0%
other: 100% (2001)
Irrigated land: NA sq km
Natural hazards: cyclone season is October to April
Environment - current issues: fresh water resources are limited to rainwater accumulations in natural underground reservoirs
Geography - note: islands are thickly covered with coconut palms and other vegetation

PEOPLE

Population: 628 (July 2005 est.)
Age structure:
0-14 years: NA
15-64 years: NA
65 years and over: NA
Population growth rate: 0% (2005 est.)
Birth rate: NA
Death rate: NA
Net migration rate: NA
Infant mortality rate:
total: NA
male: NA
female: NA
Life expectancy at birth:
total population: NA
male: NA
female: NA
Total fertility rate: NA
HIV/AIDS - adult prevalence rate: NA
HIV/AIDS - people living with HIV/AIDS: NA
HIV/AIDS - deaths: NA
Nationality:
noun: Cocos Islander(s)
adjective: Cocos Islander
Ethnic groups: Europeans, Cocos Malays
Religions: Sunni Muslim 80%, other 20% (2002 est.)
Languages: Malay (Cocos dialect), English

GOVERNMENT

Country name:
conventional long form: Territory of Cocos (Keeling) Islands
conventional short form: Cocos (Keeling) Islands
Dependency status: territory of Australia; administered from Canberra by the Australian Department of Transport and Regional Services
Government type: NA
Capital: West Island
Administrative divisions: none (territory of Australia)
Independence: none (territory of Australia)
National holiday: Australia Day, 26 January (1788)
Constitution: Cocos (Keeling) Islands Act of 1955 (23 November 1953)
Legal system: based upon the laws of Australia and local laws
Suffrage: NA
Executive branch:
chief of state: Queen ELIZABETH II (since 6 February 1952), represented by the Australian governor general
head of government: Administrator (non-resident) Evan WILLIAMS (since 1 November 2003)
cabinet: NA
elections: none; the monarch is hereditary; administrator appointed by the governor general of Australia and represents the monarch and Australia
Legislative branch: unicameral Cocos (Keeling) Islands Shire Council (7 seats)
elections: held every two years with half the members standing for election; last held NA
Judicial branch: Supreme Court; Magistrate's Court
Political parties and leaders: none
Political pressure groups and leaders: none
International organization participation: none
Diplomatic representation in the US: none (territory of Australia)
Diplomatic representation from the US: none (territory of Australia)
Flag description: the flag of Australia is used

ECONOMY

Economy - overview: Grown throughout the islands, coconuts are the sole cash crop. Small local gardens and fishing contribute to the food supply, but additional food and most other necessities must be imported from Australia. There is a small tourist industry.
GDP (purchasing power parity): NA
GDP (official exchange rate): NA
GDP - real growth rate: NA%
GDP - composition by sector:
agriculture: NA%
industry: NA%
services: NA%
Labor force: NA
Labor force - by occupation: the Cocos Islands Cooperative Society Ltd. employs construction workers, stevedores, and lighterage workers; tourism employs others
Unemployment rate: 60% (2000 est.)
Budget:
revenues: NA
expenditures: NA
Agriculture - products: vegetables, bananas, pawpaws, coconuts
Industries: copra products and tourism
Electricity - production by source:
fossil fuel: NA
hydro: NA
nuclear: NA

other: NA
Exports: NA
Exports - partners: Australia (2004)
Imports: NA
Imports - partners: Australia (2004)
Economic aid - recipient: NA
Currency (code): Australian dollar (AUD)
Currency code: AUD
Exchange rates: Australian dollars per US dollar - 1.38 (2005), 1.3598 (2004), 1.5419 (2003), 1.8406 (2002), 1.9334 (2001)
Fiscal year: 1 July - 30 June

COMMUNICATION

Telephones - main lines in use: 287 (1992)
Telephones - mobile cellular: note - analog cellular service available
Telephone system:
general assessment: connected within Australia's telecommunication system
domestic: NA
international: country code - 61-891; telephone, telex, and facsimile communications with Australia and elsewhere via satellite; 1 INTELSAT satellite earth station (2005)
Radio broadcast stations: AM 1, FM 2, shortwave 0 (2004)
Radios: 300 (1992)
Television broadcast stations: NA
Televisions: NA
Internet country code: .cc
Internet Service Providers (ISPs): 2 (2000)
Internet users: NA

TRANSPORTATION

Airports: 1 (2004 est.)
Airports - with paved runways:
total: 1
1,524 to 2,437 m: 1 (2005 est.)
Roadways: *total:* 15 km (2005)
Ports and terminals: Port Refuge

MILITARY

Military - note: defense is the responsibility of Australia; the territory does have a five-person police force

TRANSNATIONAL ISSUES

Disputes - international: none

COLOMBIA

INTRODUCTION

Background: Colombia was one of the three countries that emerged from the collapse of Gran Colombia in 1830 (the others are Ecuador and Venezuela). A 40-year conflict between government forces and anti-government insurgent groups and illegal paramilitary groups - both heavily funded by the drug trade - escalated during the 1990s. The insurgents lack the military or popular support necessary to overthrow the government and violence has been decreasing since about 2002, but insurgents continue attacks against civilians and large swaths of the countryside are under guerrilla influence. Paramilitary groups challenge the insurgents for control of territory and the drug trade, and also the government's ability to exert its dominion over rural areas. Although several thousand paramilitary members have demobilized since 2002 in an ongoing peace process, their commitment to ceasing illicit activity is unclear. While Bogota steps up efforts to reassert government control throughout the country, neighboring countries worry about the violence spilling over their borders.

GEOGRAPHY

Location: Northern South America, bordering the Caribbean Sea, between Panama and Venezuela, and bordering the North Pacific Ocean, between Ecuador and Panama
Geographic coordinates: 4 00 N, 72 00 W
Map references: South America
Area:
total: 1,138,910 sq km
land: 1,038,700 sq km
water: 100,210 sq km
note: includes Isla de Malpelo, Roncador Cay, Serrana Bank, and Serranilla Bank
Area - comparative: slightly less than three times the size of Montana
Land boundaries:
total: 6,004 km
border countries: Brazil 1,643 km, Ecuador 590 km, Panama 225 km, Peru 1,496 km (est.), Venezuela 2,050 km
Coastline: 3,208 km (Caribbean Sea 1,760 km, North Pacific Ocean 1,448 km)
Maritime claims:
territorial sea: 12 nm
exclusive economic zone: 200 nm
continental shelf: 200-m depth or to the depth of exploitation
Climate: tropical along coast and eastern plains; cooler in highlands
Terrain: flat coastal lowlands, central highlands, high Andes Mountains, eastern lowland plains
Elevation extremes:
lowest point: Pacific Ocean 0 m
highest point: Pico Cristobal Colon 5,775 m
note: nearby Pico Simon Bolivar also has the same elevation
Natural resources: petroleum, natural gas, coal, iron ore, nickel, gold, copper, emeralds, hydropower
Land use:
arable land: 2.42%
permanent crops: 1.67%
other: 95.91% (2001)
Irrigated land: 8,500 sq km (1998 est.)
Natural hazards: highlands subject to volcanic eruptions; occasional earthquakes; periodic droughts
Environment - current issues: deforestation; soil and water quality damage from overuse of pesticides; air pollution, especially in Bogota, from vehicle emissions
Environment - international agreements:
party to: Antarctic Treaty, Biodiversity, Climate Change, Climate Change-Kyoto Protocol, Desertification, Endangered Species, Hazardous Wastes, Marine Life Conservation, Ozone Layer Protection, Ship Pollution, Tropical Timber 83, Tropical Timber 94, Wetlands
signed, but not ratified: Law of the Sea
Geography - note: only South American country with coastlines on both the North Pacific Ocean and Caribbean Sea

PEOPLE

Population: 42,954,279 (July 2005 est.)
Age structure:
0-14 years: 30.7% (male 6,670,950/female 6,516,371)
15-64 years: 64.2% (male 13,424,433/female 14,142,825)
65 years and over: 5.1% (male 968,127/female 1,231,573) (2005 est.)
Median age:
total: 26.04 years
male: 25.14 years
female: 26.93 years (2005 est.)
Population growth rate: 1.49% (2005 est.)
Birth rate: 20.82 births/1,000 population (2005 est.)

Death rate: 5.59 deaths/1,000 population (2005 est.)
Net migration rate: -0.31 migrant(s)/1,000 population (2005 est.)
Sex ratio:
at birth: 1.03 male(s)/female
under 15 years: 1.02 male(s)/female
15-64 years: 0.95 male(s)/female
65 years and over: 0.79 male(s)/female
total population: 0.96 male(s)/female (2005 est.)
Infant mortality rate:
total: 20.97 deaths/1,000 live births
male: 24.92 deaths/1,000 live births
female: 16.89 deaths/1,000 live births (2005 est.)
Life expectancy at birth:
total population: 71.72 years
male: 67.88 years
female: 75.7 years (2005 est.)
Total fertility rate: 2.56 children born/woman (2005 est.)
HIV/AIDS - adult prevalence rate: 0.7% (2003 est.)
HIV/AIDS - people living with HIV/AIDS: 190,000 (2003 est.)
HIV/AIDS - deaths: 3,600 (2003 est.)
Nationality:
noun: Colombian(s)
adjective: Colombian
Ethnic groups: mestizo 58%, white 20%, mulatto 14%, black 4%, mixed black-Amerindian 3%, Amerindian 1%
Religions: Roman Catholic 90%, other 10%
Languages: Spanish
Literacy:
definition: age 15 and over can read and write
total population: 92.5%
male: 92.4%
female: 92.6% (2003 est.)

GOVERNMENT

Country name:
conventional long form: Republic of Colombia
conventional short form: Colombia
local long form: Republica de Colombia
local short form: Colombia
Government type: republic; executive branch dominates government structure
Capital: Bogota
Administrative divisions: 32 departments (departamentos, singular - departamento) and 1 capital district* (distrito capital); Amazonas, Antioquia, Arauca, Atlantico, Distrito Capital de Bogota*, Bolivar, Boyaca, Caldas, Caqueta, Casanare, Cauca, Cesar, Choco, Cordoba, Cundinamarca, Guainia, Guaviare, Huila, La Guajira, Magdalena, Meta, Narino, Norte de Santander, Putumayo, Quindio, Risaralda, San Andres y Providencia, Santander, Sucre, Tolima, Valle del Cauca, Vaupes, Vichada
Independence: 20 July 1810 (from Spain)
National holiday: Independence Day, 20 July (1810)
Constitution: 5 July 1991
Legal system: based on Spanish law; a new criminal code modeled after US procedures was enacted into law in 2004 and is gradually being implemented; judicial review of executive and legislative acts; accepts compulsory ICJ jurisdiction, with reservations
Suffrage: 18 years of age; universal
Executive branch:
chief of state: President Alvaro URIBE Velez (since 7 August 2002); Vice President Francisco SANTOS (since 7 August 2002); note - the president is both the chief of state and head of government
head of government: President Alvaro URIBE Velez (since 7 August 2002); Vice President Francisco SANTOS (since 7 August 2002); note - the president is both the chief of state and head of government
cabinet: Cabinet consists of a coalition of the two dominant parties - the PL and PSC - and independents
elections: president and vice president elected by popular vote for a four-year term; election last held 26 May 2002 (next to be held May 2006)
election results: President Alvaro URIBE Velez received 53% of the vote; Vice President Francisco SANTOS was elected on the same ticket
Legislative branch: bicameral Congress or Congreso consists of the Senate or Senado (102 seats; members are elected by popular vote to serve four-year terms) and the House of Representatives or Camara de Representantes (166 seats; members are elected by popular vote to serve four-year terms)
elections: Senate - last held 10 March 2002 (next to be held March 2006); House of Representatives - last held 10 March 2002 (next to be held March 2006)
election results: Senate - percent of vote by party - NA%; seats by party - PL 28, PSC 13, independents and smaller parties (many aligned with conservatives) 61; House of Representatives - percent of vote by party - NA%; seats by party - PL 54, PSC 21, independents and other parties 91
Judicial branch: four roughly coequal, supreme judicial organs; Supreme Court of Justice or Corte Suprema de Justicia (highest court of criminal law; judges are selected by their peers from the nominees of the Superior Judicial Council for eight-year terms); Council of State (highest court of administrative law; judges are selected from the nominees of the Superior Judicial Council for eight-year terms); Constitutional Court (guards integrity and supremacy of the constitution; rules on constitutionality of laws, amendments to the constitution, and international treaties); Superior Judicial Council (administers and disciplines the civilian judiciary; resolves jurisdictional conflicts arising between other courts; members are elected by three sister courts and Congress for eight-year terms)
Political parties and leaders: Colombian Communist Party or PCC [Jaime CAICEDO]; Conservative Party or PSC [Carlos HOLGUIN Sardi]; Democratic Pole or PDI [Samuel MORENO Rojas]; Liberal Party or PL [Cesar GAVIRIA]
note: Colombia has about 60 formally recognized political parties, most of which do not have a presence in either house of Congress
Political pressure groups and leaders: two largest insurgent groups active in Colombia - Revolutionary Armed Forces of Colombia or FARC and National Liberation Army or ELN; largest illegal paramilitary group, a roughly organized umbrella group of disparate paramilitary forces, is United Self-Defense Groups of Colombia or AUC
International organization participation: BCIE, CAN, CDB, CSN, FAO, G-3, G-15, G-24, G-77, IADB, IAEA, IBRD, ICAO, ICC, ICCt, ICFTU, ICRM, IDA, IFAD, IFC, IFRCS, IHO, ILO, IMF, IMO, Interpol, IOC, IOM, ISO, ITU, LAES, LAIA, Mercosur (associate), MIGA, NAM, OAS, OPANAL, OPCW, PCA, RG, UN, UNCTAD, UNESCO, UNHCR, UNIDO, UPU, WCL, WCO, WFTU, WHO, WIPO, WMO, WToO, WTO
Diplomatic representation in the US:
chief of mission: Ambassador Andres PASTRANA
chancery: 2118 Leroy Place NW, Washington, DC 20008
telephone: [1] (202) 387-8338
FAX: [1] (202) 232-8643
consulate(s) general: Atlanta, Beverly Hills, Boston, Chicago, Houston, Miami, New Orleans, New York, San Francisco, San Juan (Puerto Rico), and Washington, DC
Diplomatic representation from the US:
chief of mission: Ambassador William B. WOOD
embassy: Calle 22D-BIS, numbers 47-51, Apartado Aereo 3831
mailing address: Carrera 45 #22D-45, Bogota, D.C., APO AA 34038
telephone: [57] (1) 315-0811
FAX: [57] (1) 315-2197

Flag description: three horizontal bands of yellow (top, double-width), blue, and red; similar to the flag of Ecuador, which is longer and bears the Ecuadorian coat of arms superimposed in the center

ECONOMY

Economy - overview: Colombia's economy has been on a recovery trend during the past two years despite a serious armed conflict. The economy continues to improve thanks to austere government budgets, focused efforts to reduce public debt levels, and an export-oriented growth focus. Ongoing economic problems facing President URIBE range from reforming the pension system to reducing high unemployment. New exploration is needed to offset declining oil production. On the positive side, several international financial institutions have praised the economic reforms introduced by URIBE, succeeded in reducing the public-sector deficit below 1.5% of GDP. The government's economic policy and democratic security strategy have engendered a growing sense of confidence in the economy, particularly within the business sector. Coffee prices have recovered from previous lows as the Colombian coffee industry pursues greater market shares in developed countries such as the United States.
GDP (purchasing power parity): $303.1 billion (2005 est.)
GDP (official exchange rate): $100.9 billion (2005 est.)
GDP - real growth rate: 4.3% (2005 est.)
GDP - per capita: purchasing power parity - $7,100 (2005 est.)
GDP - composition by sector:
agriculture: 12.5%
industry: 34.3%
services: 53.3% (2005 est.)
Labor force: 20.52 million (2005 est.)
Labor force - by occupation: agriculture 22.7%, industry 18.7%, services 58.5% (2000 est.)
Unemployment rate: 11.8% (2005 est.)
Population below poverty line: 59% (2001 est.)
Household income or consumption by percentage share:
lowest 10%: 1%
highest 10%: 44% (1999)
Distribution of family income - Gini index: 57.1 (2003 est.)
Inflation rate (consumer prices): 5% (2005 est.)
Investment (gross fixed): 20.2% of GDP (2005 est.)
Budget:
revenues: $46.82 billion
expenditures: $48.77 billion, including capital expenditures of NA (2005 est.)
Public debt: 44.2% of GDP (2005 est.)
Agriculture - products: coffee, cut flowers, bananas, rice, tobacco, corn, sugarcane, cocoa beans, oilseed, vegetables; forest products; shrimp
Industries: textiles, food processing, oil, clothing and footwear, beverages, chemicals, cement; gold, coal, emeralds
Industrial production growth rate: 4.5% (2005 est.)
Electricity - production: 47.14 billion kWh (2003)
Electricity - production by source:
fossil fuel: 26%
hydro: 72.7%
nuclear: 0%
other: 1.3% (2001)
Electricity - consumption: 42.85 billion kWh (2003)
Electricity - exports: 1.082 billion kWh (2003)
Electricity - imports: 100 million kWh (2003)
Oil - production: 512,400 bbl/day (2005 est.)
Oil - consumption: 270,000 bbl/day (2003 est.)
Oil - exports: NA (2003)
Oil - imports: NA (2003)
Oil - proved reserves: 1.436 billion bbl (2005 est.)
Natural gas - production: 6.354 billion cu m (2004 est.)
Natural gas - consumption: 6.219 billion cu m (2004 est.)
Natural gas - exports: 0 cu m (2004 est.)
Natural gas - imports: 0 cu m (2004 est.)
Natural gas - proved reserves: 127.4 billion cu m (2005)
Current account balance: $-917 million (2005 est.)
Exports: $23.06 billion f.o.b. (2005 est.)
Exports - partners: US 42.1%, Venezuela 9.7%, Ecuador 6% (2004)
Imports: $20.42 billion f.o.b. (2005 est.)
Imports - partners: US 29.1%, Venezuela 6.5%, China 6.4%, Mexico 6.2%, Brazil 5.8% (2004)
Reserves of foreign exchange and gold: $14.18 billion (2005 est.)
Debt - external: $37.06 billion (30 June 2005 est.)
Economic aid - recipient: NA
Currency (code): Colombian peso (COP)
Currency code: COP
Exchange rates: Colombian pesos per US dollar - 2,324.08 (2005), 2,628.61 (2004), 2,877.65 (2003), 2,504.24 (2002), 2,299.63 (2001)
Fiscal year: calendar year

COMMUNICATION

Telephones - main lines in use: 8,768,100 (2003)
Telephones - mobile cellular: 6,186,200 (2003)
Telephone system:
general assessment: modern system in many respects
domestic: nationwide microwave radio relay system; domestic satellite system with 41 earth stations; fiber-optic network linking 50 cities
international: country code - 57; satellite earth stations - 6 Intelsat, 1 Inmarsat; 3 fully digitalized international switching centers; 8 submarine cables
Radio broadcast stations: AM 454, FM 34, shortwave 27 (1999)
Radios: 21 million (1997)
Television broadcast stations: 60 (includes seven low-power stations) (1997)
Televisions: 4.59 million (1997)
Internet country code: .co
Internet hosts: 115,158 (2003)
Internet Service Providers (ISPs): 18 (2000)
Internet users: 2,732,200 (2003)

TRANSPORTATION

Airports: 980 (2004 est.)
Airports - with paved runways:
total: 100
over 3,047 m: 2
2,438 to 3,047 m: 9
1,524 to 2,437 m: 38
914 to 1,523 m: 40
under 914 m: 11 (2005 est.)
Airports - with unpaved runways:
total: 881
over 3,047 m: 1
1,524 to 2,437 m: 35
914 to 1,523 m: 273
under 914 m: 572 (2005 est.)
Heliports: 2 (2005 est.)
Pipelines: gas 4,360 km; oil 6,134 km; refined products 3,140 km (2004)
Railways:
total: 3,304 km
standard gauge: 150 km 1.435-m gauge
narrow gauge: 3,154 km 0.914-m gauge (2004)
Roadways:
total: 112,998 km
paved: 26,000 km
unpaved: 84,000 km (2000)
Waterways: 9,187 km (2004)
Merchant marine:
total: 15 ships (1,000 GRT or over) 35,427 GRT/46,301 DWT
by type: bulk carrier 1, cargo 11, liquefied gas 1, petroleum tanker 2
registered in other countries: 7 (2005)
Ports and terminals: Barranquilla, Buenaventura, Cartagena, Muelles El Bosque, Puerto Bolivar, Santa Marta, Turbo

MILITARY

Military branches: Army (Ejercito Nacional), Navy (Armada Nacional,

includes Naval Aviation, Marines, and Coast Guard), Air Force (Fuerza Aerea Colombiana)
Military service age and obligation: 18 years of age for compulsory and voluntary military service; conscript service obligation - 24 months (2004)
Manpower available for military service: *males age 18-49:* 10,212,456 (2005 est.)
Manpower fit for military service: *males age 18-49:* 6,986,228 (2005 est.)
Manpower reaching military service age annually: *males:* 389,735 (2005 est.)
Military expenditures - dollar figure: $3.3 billion (FY01)
Military expenditures - percent of GDP: 3.4% (FY01)

TRANSNATIONAL ISSUES

Disputes - international: Nicaragua filed a claim against Honduras in 1999 and against Colombia in 2001 at the ICJ over disputed maritime boundary involving 50,000 sq km in the Caribbean Sea, including the Archipelago de San Andres y Providencia and Quita Sueno Bank; dispute with Venezuela over maritime boundary and Los Monjes Islands near the Gulf of Venezuela; Colombian-organized illegal narcotics, guerrilla, and paramilitary activities penetrate all of its neighbors' borders and have created a serious refugee crisis with over 300,000 persons having fled the country, mostly into neighboring states
Refugees and internally displaced persons: *IDPs:* 2,730,000 - 3,100,000 (conflict between government and FARC; drug wars) (2004)
Illicit drugs: illicit producer of coca, opium poppy, and cannabis; world's leading coca cultivator (cultivation of coca in 2002 was 144,450 hectares, a 15% decline since 2001); potential production of opium between 2001 and 2002 declined by 25% to 91 metric tons; potential production of heroin declined to 11.3 metric tons; the world's largest processor of coca derivatives into cocaine; supplier of about 90% of the cocaine to the US market and the great majority of cocaine to other international drug markets; important supplier of heroin to the US market; active aerial eradication program; a significant portion of non-US narcotics proceeds are either laundered or invested in Colombia through the black market peso exchange

COMOROS

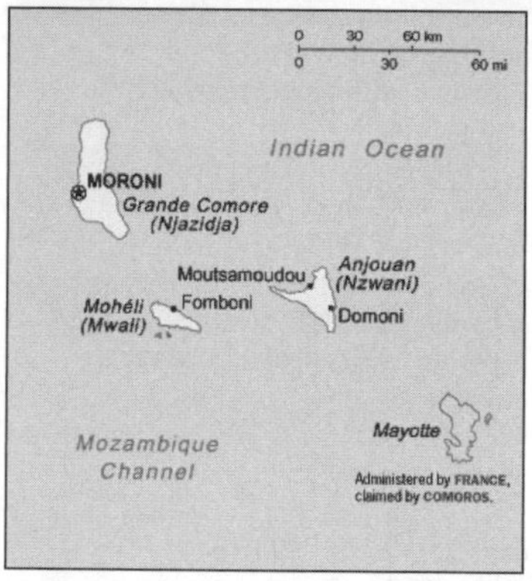

INTRODUCTION

Background: Unstable Comoros has endured 19 coups or attempted coups since gaining independence from France in 1975. In 1997, the islands of Anjouan and Moheli declared their independence from Comoros. In 1999, military chief Col. AZALI seized power. He pledged to resolve the secessionist crisis through a confederal arrangement named the 2000 Fomboni Accord. In December 2001, voters approved a new constitution and presidential elections took place in the spring of 2002. Each island in the archipelago elected its own president and a new union president took office in May of 2002.

GEOGRAPHY

Location: Southern Africa, group of islands at the northern mouth of the Mozambique Channel, about two-thirds of the way between northern Madagascar and northern Mozambique
Geographic coordinates: 12 10 S, 44 15 E
Map references: Africa
Area:
total: 2,170 sq km
land: 2,170 sq km
water: 0 sq km
Area - comparative: slightly more than 12 times the size of Washington, DC
Land boundaries: 0 km
Coastline: 340 km
Maritime claims:
territorial sea: 12 nm
exclusive economic zone: 200 nm
Climate: tropical marine; rainy season (November to May)
Terrain: volcanic islands, interiors vary from steep mountains to low hills
Elevation extremes:
lowest point: Indian Ocean 0 m
highest point: Le Kartala 2,360 m
Natural resources: NEGL
Land use:
arable land: 35.87%
permanent crops: 23.32%
other: 40.81% (2001)
Irrigated land: NA sq km
Natural hazards: cyclones possible during rainy season (December to April); Le Kartala on Grand Comore is an active volcano
Environment - current issues: soil degradation and erosion results from crop cultivation on slopes without proper terracing; deforestation
Environment - international agreements:
party to: Biodiversity, Climate Change, Desertification, Endangered Species, Hazardous Wastes, Law of the Sea, Ozone Layer Protection, Ship Pollution, Wetlands
signed, but not ratified: none of the selected agreements
Geography - note: important location at northern end of Mozambique Channel

PEOPLE

Population: 671,247 (July 2005 est.)
Age structure:
0-14 years: 42.8% (male 144,075/female 143,175)
15-64 years: 54.2% (male 179,541/female 184,488)
65 years and over: 3% (male 9,407/female 10,561) (2005 est.)
Median age:
total: 18.61 years
male: 18.35 years
female: 18.87 years (2005 est.)
Population growth rate: 2.91% (2005 est.)
Birth rate: 37.52 births/1,000 population (2005 est.)
Death rate: 8.4 deaths/1,000 population (2005 est.)
Net migration rate: 0 migrant(s)/1,000 population (2005 est.)
Sex ratio:
at birth: 1.03 male(s)/female
under 15 years: 1.01 male(s)/female
15-64 years: 0.97 male(s)/female
65 years and over: 0.89 male(s)/female
total population: 0.99 male(s)/female (2005 est.)
Infant mortality rate:
total: 74.93 deaths/1,000 live births
male: 83.48 deaths/1,000 live births
female: 66.13 deaths/1,000 live births (2005 est.)
Life expectancy at birth:
total population: 61.96 years
male: 59.65 years
female: 64.33 years (2005 est.)
Total fertility rate: 5.09 children born/woman (2005 est.)

HIV/AIDS - adult prevalence rate: 0.12% (2001 est.)
HIV/AIDS - people living with HIV/AIDS: NA
HIV/AIDS - deaths: NA
Nationality:
noun: Comoran(s)
adjective: Comoran
Ethnic groups: Antalote, Cafre, Makoa, Oimatsaha, Sakalava
Religions: Sunni Muslim 98%, Roman Catholic 2%
Languages: Arabic (official), French (official), Shikomoro (a blend of Swahili and Arabic)
Literacy:
definition: age 15 and over can read and write
total population: 56.5%
male: 63.6%
female: 49.3% (2003 est.)

GOVERNMENT

Country name:
conventional long form: Union of the Comoros
conventional short form: Comoros
local long form: Union des Comores
local short form: Comores
Government type: independent republic
Capital: Moroni
Administrative divisions: 3 islands; Grande Comore (Njazidja), Anjouan (Nzwani), and Moheli (Mwali); note - there are also four municipalities named Domoni, Fomboni, Moroni, and Moutsamoudou
Independence: 6 July 1975 (from France)
National holiday: Independence Day, 6 July (1975)
Constitution: 23 December 2001
Legal system: French and Sharia (Islamic) law in a new consolidated code
Suffrage: 18 years of age; universal
Executive branch:
chief of state: President AZALI Assoumani (since 26 May 2002); note - following a 1999 coup AZALI was appointed president; in January 2002 he resigned his position to run in the 14 April 2002 presidential elections; Prime Minister Hamada Madi BOLERO was appointed interim president until replaced again by AZALI in May 2002 when BOLERO was appointed Minister of External Defense and Territorial Security; the president is both the chief of state and the head of government
head of government: President AZALI Assoumani (since 26 May 2002); note - following a 1999 coup AZALI was appointed president; in January 2002 he resigned his position to run in the 14 April 2002 presidential elections; Prime Minister Hamada Madi BOLERO was appointed interim president until replaced again by Azali in May 2002 when BOLERO was appointed Minister of External Defense and Territorial Security; the president is both the chief of state and the head of government
cabinet: Council of Ministers appointed by the president
elections: as defined by the 2001 constitution, the presidency rotates every four years among the elected presidents from the three main islands in the Union; election last held 14 April 2002 (next to be held April 2006); prime minister appointed by the president; note - AZALI has not appointed a Prime Minister since he was sworn into office in May 2002
election results: President AZALI Assoumani elected president with 75% of the vote
Legislative branch: unicameral Assembly of the Union (33 seats; 15 deputies are selected by the individual islands' local assemblies and the 18 by universal suffrage; deputies serve for five years);
elections: last held 18 and 25 April 2004 (next to be held NA 2009)
election results: NA
Judicial branch: Supreme Court or Cour Supremes (two members appointed by the president, two members elected by the Federal Assembly, one elected by the Council of each island, and others are former presidents of the republic)
Political parties and leaders: Forces pour l'Action Republicaine or FAR [Col. Abdourazak ABDULHAMID]; Forum pour la Redressement National or FRN (alliance of 12 parties); Front Democratique or FD [Moustoifa Said CHEIKH]; Front National pour la Justice or FNJ (Islamic party in opposition) [Ahmed RACHID]; Movement des Citoyens pour la Republique or MCR [Mahamoud MRADABI]; Mouvement Populaire Anjouanais or MPA (Anjouan separatist movement) [leader NA]; Mouvement pour la Democratie et le Progress or MDP-NGDC [Abbas DJOUSSOUF]; Movement pour le Socialisme et la Democratie or MSD (splinter group of FD) [Abdou SOEFOU]; Parti Comorien pour la Democratie et le Progress or PCDP [Ali MROUDJAE]; Rassemblement National pour le Development or RND (party of the government) [Omar TAMOU, Abdoulhamid AFFRAITANTE]
Political pressure groups and leaders: NA
International organization participation: ACCT, ACP, AfDB, AMF, AU, COMESA, FAO, FZ, G-77, IBRD, ICAO, ICCt (signatory), ICRM, IDA, IDB, IFAD, IFC, IFRCS (observer), ILO, IMF, IMO, InOC, Interpol, IOC, ITU, LAS, NAM, OIC, OPCW (signatory), UN, UNCTAD, UNESCO, UNIDO, UPU, WCO, WHO, WIPO, WMO
Diplomatic representation in the US:
chief of mission: Ambassador Mahmoud M. ABOUD (ambassador to the US and Canada and permanent representative to the UN)
chancery: (temporary) care of the Permanent Mission of the Union of the Comoros to the United Nations, 420 East 50th Street, New York, NY 10022
telephone: [1] (212) 972-8010 and 223-2711
FAX: [1] (212) 983-4712 and 715-0699
Diplomatic representation from the US: the US does not have an embassy in Comoros; the ambassador to Mauritius is accredited to Comoros
Flag description: four equal horizontal bands of yellow (top), white, red, and blue with a green isosceles triangle based on the hoist; centered within the triangle is a white crescent with the convex side facing the hoist and four white, five-pointed stars placed vertically in a line between the points of the crescent; the horizontal bands and the four stars represent the four main islands of the archipelago - Mwali, Njazidja, Nzwani, and Mayotte (a territorial collectivity of France, but claimed by Comoros); the crescent, stars, and color green are traditional symbols of Islam

ECONOMY

Economy - overview: One of the world's poorest countries, Comoros is made up of three islands that have inadequate transportation links, a young and rapidly increasing population, and few natural resources. The low educational level of the labor force contributes to a subsistence level of economic activity, high unemployment, and a heavy dependence on foreign grants and technical assistance. Agriculture, including fishing, hunting, and forestry, contributes 40% to GDP, employs 80% of the labor force, and provides most of the exports. The country is not self-sufficient in food production; rice, the main staple, accounts for the bulk of imports. The government - which is hampered by internal political disputes - is struggling to upgrade education and technical training, privatize commercial and industrial enterprises, improve health services, diversify exports, promote tourism, and reduce the high population growth rate. Increased foreign support is essential if the goal of 4% annual GDP growth is to be met. Remittances from

150,000 Comorans abroad help supplement GDP.
GDP (purchasing power parity): $441 million (2002 est.)
GDP (official exchange rate): $402 million NA (2005 est.)
GDP - real growth rate: 3% (2005 est.)
GDP - per capita: purchasing power parity - $600 (2005 est.)
GDP - composition by sector:
agriculture: 40%
industry: 4%
services: 56% (2001 est.)
Labor force: 144,500 (1996 est.)
Labor force - by occupation: agriculture 80%
Unemployment rate: 20% (1996 est.)
Population below poverty line: 60% (2002 est.)
Household income or consumption by percentage share:
lowest 10%: NA
highest 10%: NA
Inflation rate (consumer prices): 3% (2005 est.)
Budget:
revenues: $27.6 million
expenditures: NA, including capital expenditures of NA (2001 est.)
Agriculture - products: vanilla, cloves, perfume essences, copra, coconuts, bananas, cassava (tapioca)
Industries: tourism, perfume distillation
Industrial production growth rate: -2% (1999 est.)
Electricity - production: 18 million kWh (2003)
Electricity - production by source:
fossil fuel: 90.6%
hydro: 9.4%
nuclear: 0%
other: 0% (2001)
Electricity - consumption: 16.74 million kWh (2003)
Electricity - exports: 0 kWh (2003)
Electricity - imports: 0 kWh (2003)
Oil - production: 0 bbl/day (2003)
Oil - consumption: 700 bbl/day (2003 est.)
Oil - exports: NA (2001)
Oil - imports: NA (2001)
Exports: $34 million f.o.b. (2004 est.)
Exports - partners: US 43.8%, France 18.6%, Singapore 16.5%, Turkey 4.8%, Germany 4.5% (2004)
Imports: $115 million f.o.b. (2004 est.)
Imports - partners: France 23.5%, South Africa 11%, Kenya 7.5%, UAE 7.2%, Italy 4.9%, Pakistan 4.7%, Mauritius 4.2%, Singapore 4.1% (2004)
Debt - external: $232 million (2000 est.)
Economic aid - recipient: $24 million (2003 est.)
Currency (code): Comoran franc (KMF)
Currency code: KMF
Exchange rates: Comoran francs (KMF) per US dollar - NA (2005), 396.21 (2004), 435.9 (2003), 522.74 (2002), 549.78 (2001)
note: the Comoran franc is pegged to the euro at a rate of 491.9677 Comoran francs per euro
Fiscal year: calendar year

COMMUNICATION

Telephones - main lines in use: 13,200 (2003)
Telephones - mobile cellular: 2,000 (2003)
Telephone system:
general assessment: sparse system of microwave radio relay and HF radiotelephone communication stations
domestic: HF radiotelephone communications and microwave radio relay
international: country code - 269; HF radiotelephone communications to Madagascar and Reunion
Radio broadcast stations: AM 1, FM 4, shortwave 1 (2001)
Radios: 90,000 (1997)
Television broadcast stations: NA
Televisions: 1,000 (1997)
Internet country code: .km
Internet hosts: 11 (2003)
Internet Service Providers (ISPs): 1 (2000)
Internet users: 5,000 (2003)

TRANSPORTATION

Airports: 4 (2004 est.)
Airports - with paved runways:
total: 4
2,438 to 3,047 m: 1
914 to 1,523 m: 3 (2005 est.)
Roadways:
total: 880 km
paved: 673 km
unpaved: 207 km (1999)
Merchant marine:
total: 79 ships (1,000 GRT or over) 452,801 GRT/681,343 DWT
by type: bulk carrier 9, cargo 55, chemical tanker 1, container 1, livestock carrier 1, passenger/cargo 1, petroleum tanker 5, refrigerated cargo 5, roll on/roll off 1
foreign-owned: 35 (Bulgaria 1, Germany 1, Greece 7, India 1, Jordan 1, Kenya 1, Lebanon 3, Nigeria 1, Norway 1, Pakistan 1, Philippines 1, Russia 2, Syria 3, Turkey 6, Ukraine 4, United Kingdom 1) (2005)
Ports and terminals: Mayotte, Moutsamoudou

MILITARY

Military branches: Comoran Security Force
Manpower available for military service:
males age 18-49: 138,940 (2005 est.)
Manpower fit for military service: *males age 18-49:* 98,792 (2005 est.)
Military expenditures - dollar figure: $11.6 million (2004)
Military expenditures - percent of GDP: 3% (2004)

TRANSNATIONAL ISSUES

Disputes - international: claims French-administered Mayotte

CONGO, DEMOCRATIC REPUBLIC OF THE

INTRODUCTION

Background: Established as a Belgian colony in 1908, the Republic of the Congo gained its independence in 1960, but its early years were marred by political and social instability. Col. Joseph MOBUTU seized power and declared himself president in a November 1965 coup. He subsequently changed his name - to MOBUTU Sese Seko - as well as that of the country - to Zaire. MOBUTU retained his position for 32 years through several subsequent sham elections as well as through the use of brutal force. Ethnic strife and civil war, touched off by a massive inflow of refugees in 1994 from fighting in Rwanda and Burundi, led in May 1997 to the toppling of the MOBUTU regime by a rebellion led by Laurent KABILA. He renamed the country the Democratic Republic of the Congo (DROC), but in August 1998 his regime was itself challenged by an insurrection backed by Rwanda and Uganda. Troops from Zimbabwe, Angola, Namibia, Chad, and Sudan intervened to support the Kinshasa regime. A cease-fire was signed in July 1999 by the DROC, Zimbabwe, Angola, Uganda, Namibia, Rwanda, and Congolese armed rebel groups, but sporadic fighting continued. Laurent KABILA was assassinated in January 2001 and his son Joseph KABILA was named head of state. In October 2002, the new president was successful in negotiating the withdrawal of Rwandan forces occupying eastern Congo; two months later, the Pretoria Accord was signed by all remaining warring parties to end the fighting and establish a government of

national unity. A transitional government was set up in July 2003; Joseph KABILA remains as president and is joined by four vice presidents representing the former government, former rebel groups, and the political opposition. The transitional government plans to hold a series of elections in 2006 to determine the presidency and National Assembly seats.

GEOGRAPHY

Location: Central Africa, northeast of Angola
Geographic coordinates: 0 00 N, 25 00 E
Map references: Africa
Area:
total: 2,345,410 sq km
land: 2,267,600 sq km
water: 77,810 sq km
Area - comparative: slightly less than one-fourth the size of the US
Land boundaries:
total: 10,730 km
border countries: Angola 2,511 km (of which 225 km is the boundary of Angola's discontiguous Cabinda Province), Burundi 233 km, Central African Republic 1,577 km, Republic of the Congo 2,410 km, Rwanda 217 km, Sudan 628 km, Tanzania 459 km, Uganda 765 km, Zambia 1,930 km
Coastline: 37 km
Maritime claims:
territorial sea: 12 nm
exclusive economic zone: boundaries with neighbors
Climate: tropical; hot and humid in equatorial river basin; cooler and drier in southern highlands; cooler and wetter in eastern highlands; north of Equator - wet season April to October, dry season December to February; south of Equator - wet season November to March, dry season April to October
Terrain: vast central basin is a low-lying plateau; mountains in east
Elevation extremes:
lowest point: Atlantic Ocean 0 m
highest point: Pic Marguerite on Mont Ngaliema (Mount Stanley) 5,110 m
Natural resources: cobalt, copper, niobium, tantalum, petroleum, industrial and gem diamonds, gold, silver, zinc, manganese, tin, uranium, coal, hydropower, timber
Land use:
arable land: 2.96%
permanent crops: 0.52%
other: 96.52% (2001)
Irrigated land: 110 sq km (1998 est.)
Natural hazards: periodic droughts in south; Congo River floods (seasonal); in the east, in the Great Rift Valley, there are active volcanoes
Environment - current issues: poaching threatens wildlife populations; water pollution; deforestation; refugees responsible for significant deforestation, soil erosion, and wildlife poaching; mining of minerals (coltan - a mineral used in creating capacitors, diamonds, and gold) causing environmental damage
Environment - international agreements:
party to: Biodiversity, Climate Change, Desertification, Endangered Species, Hazardous Wastes, Law of the Sea, Marine Dumping, Ozone Layer Protection, Tropical Timber 83, Tropical Timber 94, Wetlands
signed, but not ratified: Environmental Modification
Geography - note: straddles equator; has very narrow strip of land that controls the lower Congo River and is only outlet to South Atlantic Ocean; dense tropical rain forest in central river basin and eastern highlands

PEOPLE

Population: 60,085,804
note: estimates for this country explicitly take into account the effects of excess mortality due to AIDS; this can result in lower life expectancy, higher infant mortality and death rates, lower population and growth rates, and changes in the distribution of population by age and sex than would otherwise be expected (July 2005 est.)
Age structure:
0-14 years: 48.1% (male 14,513,779/female 14,396,952)
15-64 years: 49.4% (male 14,579,101/female 15,121,297)
65 years and over: 2.5% (male 597,776/female 876,099) (2005 est.)
Median age:
total: 15.8 years
male: 15.4 years
female: 16.2 years (2005 est.)
Population growth rate: 2.98% (2005 est.)
Birth rate: 44.38 births/1,000 population (2005 est.)
Death rate: 14.43 deaths/1,000 population (2005 est.)
Net migration rate:
-0.17 migrant(s)/1,000 population
note: fighting between the Congolese Government and Uganda- and Rwanda-backed Congolese rebels spawned a regional war in DROC in August 1998, which left 1.8 million Congolese internally displaced and caused 300,000 Congolese refugees to flee to surrounding countries (2005 est.)
Sex ratio:
at birth: 1.01 male(s)/female
under 15 years: 1.01 male(s)/female
15-64 years: 0.96 male(s)/female
65 years and over: 0.68 male(s)/female
total population: 0.98 male(s)/female (2005 est.)
Infant mortality rate:
total: 92.87 deaths/1,000 live births
male: 101.25 deaths/1,000 live births
female: 84.23 deaths/1,000 live births (2005 est.)
Life expectancy at birth:
total population: 51.1 years
male: 49.68 years
female: 52.56 years (2005 est.)
Total fertility rate: 6.54 children born/woman (2005 est.)
HIV/AIDS - adult prevalence rate: 4.2% (2003 est.)
HIV/AIDS - people living with HIV/AIDS: 1.1 million (2003 est.)
HIV/AIDS - deaths: 100,000 (2003 est.)
Major infectious diseases:
degree of risk: very high
food or waterborne diseases: bacterial and protozoal diarrhea, hepatitis A, and typhoid fever
vectorborne diseases: malaria, plague, and African trypanosomiasis (sleeping sickness) are high risks in some locations
water contact disease: schistosomiasis (2004)
Nationality:
noun: Congolese (singular and plural)
adjective: Congolese or Congo
Ethnic groups: over 200 African ethnic groups of which the majority are Bantu; the four largest tribes - Mongo, Luba, Kongo (all Bantu), and the Mangbetu-Azande (Hamitic) make up about 45% of the population
Religions: Roman Catholic 50%, Protestant 20%, Kimbanguist 10%, Muslim 10%, other syncretic sects and indigenous beliefs 10%
Languages: French (official), Lingala (a lingua franca trade language), Kingwana (a dialect of Kiswahili or Swahili), Kikongo, Tshiluba
Literacy:
definition: age 15 and over can read and

write French, Lingala, Kingwana, or Tshiluba
total population: 65.5%
male: 76.2%
female: 55.1% (2003 est.)

GOVERNMENT

Country name:
conventional long form: Democratic Republic of the Congo
conventional short form: none
local long form: Republique Democratique du Congo
local short form: none
former: Congo Free State, Belgian Congo, Congo/Leopoldville, Congo/Kinshasa, Zaire
abbreviation: DROC
Government type: dictatorship; presumably undergoing a transition to representative government
Capital: Kinshasa
Administrative divisions: 10 provinces (provinces, singular - province) and 1 city* (ville); Bandundu, Bas-Congo, Equateur, Kasai-Occidental, Kasai-Oriental, Katanga, Kinshasa*, Maniema, Nord-Kivu, Orientale, Sud-Kivu
Independence: 30 June 1960 (from Belgium)
National holiday: Independence Day, 30 June (1960)
Constitution: new constitution adopted 17 July 2003
Legal system: based on Belgian civil law system and tribal law; has not accepted compulsory ICJ jurisdiction
Suffrage: 18 years of age; universal and compulsory
Executive branch:
chief of state: President Joseph KABILA (since 26 January 2001); note - following the assassination of his father, Laurent Desire KABILA, on 16 January 2001, Joseph KABILA succeeded to the presidency; the president is both the chief of state and head of government
head of government: President Joseph KABILA (since 26 January 2001); note - following the assassination of his father, Laurent Desire KABILA, on 16 January 2001, Joseph KABILA succeeded to the presidency; the president is both the chief of state and head of government
cabinet: National Executive Council, appointed by the president
elections: prior to the overthrow of MOBUTU Sese Seko, the president was elected by popular vote for a seven-year term; election last held 29 July 1984 (next was scheduled to be held in May 1997); formerly, there was also a prime minister who was elected by the High Council of the Republic; note - a Transitional Government is finalizing a new constitution with free elections scheduled to be held in early 2006
election results: MOBUTU Sese Seko Kuku Ngbendu wa Za Banga reelected president in 1984 without opposition
note: Joseph KABILA succeeded his father, Laurent Desire KABILA, following the latter's assassination in January 2001, negotiations with rebel leaders led to the establishment of a transitional government in July 2003 with free elections scheduled to be held in early 2006
Legislative branch: a 500-member National Assembly and a 120-seat Senate established in June 2003
elections: NA; members of the National Assembly were appointed by leaders in the factions integrated into the new government
Judicial branch: Supreme Court or Cour Supreme
Political parties and leaders: Democratic Social Christian Party or PDSC [Andre BO-BOLIKO]; Forces for Renovation for Union and Solidarity or FONUS [Joseph OLENGHANKOY]; National Congolese Lumumbist Movement or MNC [Francois LUMUMBA]; Popular Movement of the Revolution or MPR (three factions: MPR-Fait Prive [Catherine NZUZI wa Mbombo]; MPR/Vunduawe [Felix VUNDUAWE]; MPR/Mananga [MANANGA Dintoka Mpholo]); Unified Lumumbast Party or PALU [Antoine GIZENGA]; Union for Democracy and Social Progress or UDPS [Etienne TSHISEKEDI wa Mulumba]; Union of Federalists and Independent Republicans or UFERI (two factions: UFERI [Lokambo OMOKOKO]; UFERI/OR [Adolph Kishwe MAYA])
Political pressure groups and leaders: NA
International organization participation: ACCT, ACP, AfDB, AU, CEPGL, COMESA, FAO, G-24, G-77, IAEA, IBRD, ICAO, ICCt, ICFTU, ICRM, IDA, IFAD, IFC, IFRCS, IHO, ILO, IMF, IMO, Interpol, IOC, IOM, ISO (correspondent), ITU, MIGA, NAM, OPCW, PCA, SADC, UN, UNCTAD, UNESCO, UNHCR, UNIDO, UPU, WCL, WCO, WFTU, WHO, WIPO, WMO, WToO, WTO
Diplomatic representation in the US:
chief of mission: Ambassador Faida MITIFU
chancery: 1800 New Hampshire Avenue NW, Washington, DC 20009: note - Consular Office at 1726 M Street, NW, Wasington, DC, 20036
telephone: [1] (202) 234-7690, 7691
FAX: [1] (202) 234-2609
Diplomatic representation from the US:
chief of mission: Ambassador Roger MEECE
embassy: 310 Avenue des Aviateurs, Kinshasa
mailing address: Unit 31550, APO AE 09828
telephone: [243] (88) 43608
FAX: [243] (88) 43467
Flag description: light blue with a large yellow five-pointed star in the center and a columnar arrangement of six small yellow five-pointed stars along the hoist side

ECONOMY

Economy - overview: The economy of the Democratic Republic of the Congo - a nation endowed with vast potential wealth - has declined drastically since the mid-1980s. The war, which began in August 1998, dramatically reduced national output and government revenue, increased external debt, and resulted in the deaths of perhaps 3.5 million people from war, famine, and disease. Foreign businesses curtailed operations due to uncertainty about the outcome of the conflict, lack of infrastructure, and the difficult operating environment. Conditions improved in late 2002 with the withdrawal of a large portion of the invading foreign troops. The transitional government has reopened relations with international financial institutions and international donors, with President Kabila implementing reforms. Much economic activity lies outside the GDP data. Economic stability improved in 2003-05, although an uncertain legal framework, corruption, and a lack of openness in government policy continues to hamper growth. In 2005, renewed activity in the mining sector, the source of most exports, boosted Kinshasa's fiscal position and GDP growth. Business and economic prospects are expected to improve once a new government is installed after elections.
GDP (purchasing power parity): $46.27 billion (2005 est.)
GDP (official exchange rate): $7.541 billion (2005 est.)
GDP - real growth rate: 6.5% (2005 est.)
GDP - per capita: purchasing power parity - $800 (2005 est.)
GDP - composition by sector:
agriculture: 55%
industry: 11%
services: 34% (2000 est.)
Labor force: 14.51 million (1993 est.)
Labor force - by occupation: NA
Unemployment rate: NA (2003 est.)
Population below poverty line: NA

Household income or consumption by percentage share:
lowest 10%: NA
highest 10%: NA
Inflation rate (consumer prices): 9% (2004 est.)
Budget:
revenues: $700 million
expenditures: $750 million, including capital expenditures of $24 million (2004)
Agriculture - products: coffee, sugar, palm oil, rubber, tea, quinine, cassava (tapioca), palm oil, bananas, root crops, corn, fruits; wood products
Industries: mining (diamonds, copper, zinc), mineral processing, consumer products (including textiles, footwear, cigarettes, processed foods and beverages), cement, commercial ship repair
Industrial production growth rate: NA
Electricity - production: 6.036 billion kWh (2003)
Electricity - production by source:
fossil fuel: 1.8%
hydro: 98.2%
nuclear: 0%
other: 0% (2001)
Electricity - consumption: 4.324 billion kWh (2003)
Electricity - exports: 1.3 billion kWh (2003)
Electricity - imports: 10 million kWh (2003)
Oil - production: 22,000 bbl/day (2003)
Oil - consumption: 8,300 bbl/day (2003 est.)
Oil - exports: NA (2001)
Oil - imports: NA (2001)
Oil - proved reserves: 1.538 billion bbl (1 January 2002)
Natural gas - proved reserves: 104.8 billion cu m (1 January 2002)
Exports: $1.108 billion f.o.b. (2004 est.)
Exports - partners: Belgium 47.5%, Finland 20.8%, US 10.9%, China 7.5% (2004)
Imports: $1.319 billion f.o.b. (2004 est.)
Imports - partners: South Africa 17.2%, Belgium 14.5%, France 10.1%, Zambia 8.5%, Kenya 5.9%, US 5.6%, Germany 5.5% (2004)
Debt - external: $10.6 billion (2003 est.)
Economic aid - recipient: $2.2 billion (FY03/04)
Currency (code): Congolese franc (CDF)
Currency code: CDF
Exchange rates: Congolese francs per US dollar - 437.86 (2005), 401.04 (2004), 405.34 (2003), 346.49 (2002), 206.62 (2001)
Fiscal year: calendar year

COMMUNICATION

Telephones - main lines in use: 10,000 (2002)
Telephones - mobile cellular: 1 million (2003)
Telephone system:
general assessment: poor
domestic: barely adequate wire and microwave radio relay service in and between urban areas; domestic satellite system with 14 earth stations
international: country code - 243; satellite earth station - 1 Intelsat (Atlantic Ocean)
Radio broadcast stations: AM 3, FM 11, shortwave 2 (2001)
Radios: 18.03 million (1997)
Television broadcast stations: 4 (2001)
Televisions: 6.478 million (1997)
Internet country code: .cd
Internet hosts: 153 (2003)
Internet Service Providers (ISPs): 1 (2001)
Internet users: 50,000 (2002)

TRANSPORTATION

Airports: 230 (2004 est.)
Airports - with paved runways:
total: 25
over 3,047 m: 4
2,438 to 3,047 m: 2
1,524 to 2,437 m: 16
914 to 1,523 m: 2
under 914 m: 1 (2005 est.)
Airports - with unpaved runways:
total: 207
1,524 to 2,437 m: 18
914 to 1,523 m: 92
under 914 m: 97 (2005 est.)
Pipelines: gas 54 km; oil 71 km (2004)
Railways:
total: 5,138 km
narrow gauge: 3,987 km 1.067-m gauge (858 km electrified); 125 km 1.000-m gauge; 1,026 km 0.600-m gauge (2004)
Roadways: *total:* 157,000 km (including 30 km of expressways) (1999)
Waterways: 15,000 km (navigation on the Congo curtailed by fighting) (2004)
Merchant marine: *registered in other countries:* 1
Ports and terminals: Banana, Boma, Bukavu, Bumba, Goma, Kalemie, Kindu, Kinshasa, Kisangani, Matadi, Mbandaka

MILITARY

Military branches: Army, Navy, Air Force
Manpower available for military service: *males age 18-49:* 11,052,696 (2005 est.)
Manpower fit for military service: *males age 18-49:* 5,851,292 (2005 est.)
Military expenditures - dollar figure: $93.5 million (2004)
Military expenditures - percent of GDP: 1.5% (2004)

TRANSNATIONAL ISSUES

Disputes - international: heads of the Great Lakes states and UN pledge to end conflict but unchecked tribal, rebel, and militia fighting continues unabated in the northeastern region of the Democratic Republic of the Congo, drawing in the neighboring states of Burundi, Rwanda and Uganda; the UN Organization Mission in the Democratic Republic of the Congo (MONUC) has maintained over 14,000 peacekeepers in the region since 1999; thousands of Ituri refugees from the Congo continue to flee the fighting primarily into Uganda; 90,000 Angolan refugees were repatriated by 2004 with the remainder in the Democratic Republic of the Congo expected to return in 2005; in 2005, DROC and Rwanda established a border verification mechanism to address accusations of Rwandan military supporting Congolese rebels and the DROC providing rebel Rwandan "Interhamwe" forces the means and bases to attack Rwandan forces; the location of the boundary in the broad Congo River with the Republic of the Congo is indefinite except in the Pool Malebo/Stanley Pool area
Refugees and internally displaced persons:
refugees (country of origin): 45,060 (Sudan) 100,000 (Angola) 19,552 (Burundi) 6,626 (Republic of Congo) 19,743 (Rwanda) 18,953 (Uganda)
IDPs: 2.33 million (fighting between government forces and rebels since mid-1990s; most IDPs are in eastern provinces) (2004)
Illicit drugs: illicit producer of cannabis, mostly for domestic consumption; while rampant corruption and inadequate supervision leaves the banking system vulnerable to money laundering, the lack of a well-developed financial system limits the country's utility as a money-laundering center

CONGO, REPUBLIC OF THE

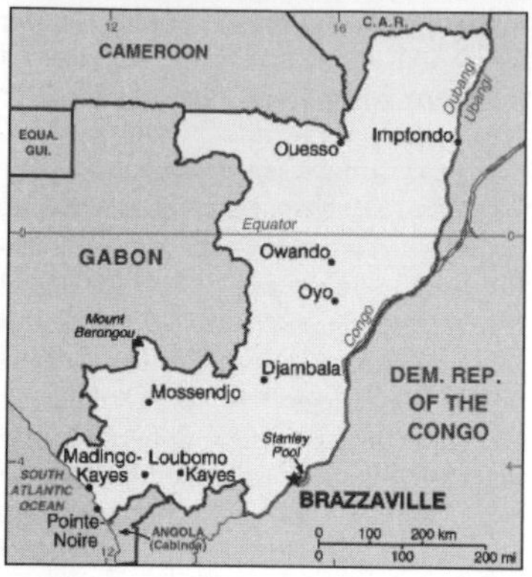

INTRODUCTION

Background: Upon independence in 1960, the former French region of Middle Congo became the Republic of the Congo. A quarter century of experimentation with Marxism was abandoned in 1990 and a democratically elected government took office in 1992. A brief civil war in 1997 restored former Marxist President Denis SASSOU-NGUESSO, but ushered in a period of ethnic and political unrest. Southern-based rebel groups agreed to a final peace accord in March 2003, but the calm is tenuous and refugees continue to present a humanitarian crisis. The Republic of Congo was once one of Africa's largest petroleum producers, but with declining production it will need to hope for new offshore oil finds to sustain its oil earnings over the long-term.

GEOGRAPHY

Location: Western Africa, bordering the South Atlantic Ocean, between Angola and Gabon

Geographic coordinates: 1 00 S, 15 00 E

Map references: Africa

Area:
total: 342,000 sq km
land: 341,500 sq km
water: 500 sq km

Area - comparative: slightly smaller than Montana

Land boundaries:
total: 5,504 km
border countries: Angola 201 km, Cameroon 523 km, Central African Republic 467 km, Democratic Republic of the Congo 2,410 km, Gabon 1,903 km

Coastline: 169 km

Maritime claims: *territorial sea:* 200 nm

Climate: tropical; rainy season (March to June); dry season (June to October); constantly high temperatures and humidity; particularly enervating climate astride the Equator

Terrain: coastal plain, southern basin, central plateau, northern basin

Elevation extremes:
lowest point: Atlantic Ocean 0 m
highest point: Mount Berongou 903 m

Natural resources: petroleum, timber, potash, lead, zinc, uranium, copper, phosphates, gold, magnesium, natural gas, hydropower

Land use:
arable land: 0.51%
permanent crops: 0.13%
other: 99.36% (2001)

Irrigated land: 10 sq km (1998 est.)

Natural hazards: seasonal flooding

Environment - current issues: air pollution from vehicle emissions; water pollution from the dumping of raw sewage; tap water is not potable; deforestation

Environment - international agreements:
party to: Biodiversity, Climate Change, Desertification, Endangered Species, Ozone Layer Protection, Tropical Timber 83, Tropical Timber 94, Wetlands
signed, but not ratified: Law of the Sea

Geography - note: about 70% of the population lives in Brazzaville, Pointe-Noire, or along the railroad between them

PEOPLE

Population: 3,039,126
note: estimates for this country explicitly take into account the effects of excess mortality due to AIDS; this can result in lower life expectancy, higher infant mortality and death rates, lower population and growth rates, and changes in the distribution of population by age and sex than would otherwise be expected (July 2005 est.)

Age structure:
0-14 years: 37.3% (male 571,011/female 563,414)
15-64 years: 59% (male 886,297/female 907,348)
65 years and over: 3.7% (male 45,799/female 65,257) (2005 est.)

Median age:
total: 20.7 years
male: 20.2 years
female: 21.1 years (2005 est.)

Population growth rate: 1.31% (2005 est.)

Birth rate: 27.88 births/1,000 population (2005 est.)

Death rate: 14.82 deaths/1,000 population (2005 est.)

Net migration rate: 0 migrant(s)/1,000 population (2005 est.)

Sex ratio:
at birth: 1.01 male(s)/female
under 15 years: 1.01 male(s)/female
15-64 years: 0.98 male(s)/female
65 years and over: 0.7 male(s)/female
total population: 0.98 male(s)/female (2005 est.)

Infant mortality rate:
total: 92.41 deaths/1,000 live births
male: 98.48 deaths/1,000 live births
female: 86.16 deaths/1,000 live births (2005 est.)

Life expectancy at birth:
total population: 52.26 years
male: 51.17 years
female: 53.39 years (2005 est.)

Total fertility rate: 3.54 children born/woman (2005 est.)

HIV/AIDS - adult prevalence rate: 4.9% (2003 est.)

HIV/AIDS - people living with HIV/AIDS: 90,000 (2003 est.)

HIV/AIDS - deaths: 9,700 (2003 est.)

Major infectious diseases:
degree of risk: very high
food or waterborne diseases: bacterial diarrhea, hepatitis A, and typhoid fever
vectorborne disease: malaria (2004)

Nationality:
noun: Congolese (singular and plural)
adjective: Congolese or Congo

Ethnic groups:
Kongo 48%, Sangha 20%, M'Bochi 12%, Teke 17%, Europeans and other 3%
note: Europeans estimated at 8,500, mostly French, before the 1997 civil war; may be half that in 1998, following the widespread destruction of foreign businesses in 1997

Religions: Christian 50%, animist 48%, Muslim 2%

Languages: French (official), Lingala and Monokutuba (lingua franca trade languages), many local languages and dialects (of which Kikongo is the most widespread)

Literacy:
definition: age 15 and over can read and write
total population: 83.8%
male: 89.6%
female: 78.4% (2003 est.)

GOVERNMENT

Country name:
conventional long form: Republic of the Congo
conventional short form: Congo (Brazzaville)
local long form: Republique du Congo
local short form: none
former: Middle Congo, Congo/Brazzaville, Congo

Government type: republic

Capital: Brazzaville

Administrative divisions: 10 regions (regions, singular - region) and 1 com-

mune*; Bouenza, Brazzaville*, Cuvette, Cuvette-Ouest, Kouilou, Lekoumou, Likouala, Niari, Plateaux, Pool, Sangha
Independence: 15 August 1960 (from France)
National holiday: Independence Day, 15 August (1960)
Constitution: approved by referendum 20 January 2002
Legal system: based on French civil law system and customary law
Suffrage: 18 years of age; universal
Executive branch:
chief of state: President Denis SASSOU-NGUESSO (since 25 October 1997, following the civil war in which he toppled elected president Pascal LISSOUBA); note - the president is both the chief of state and head of government
head of government: President Denis SASSOU-NGUESSO (since 25 October 1997, following the civil war in which he toppled elected president Pascal LISSOUBA); note - the president is both the chief of state and head of government
cabinet: Council of Ministers appointed by the president
elections: president elected by popular vote for a seven-year term (eligible for a second seven-year term); election last held 10 March 2002 (next to be held NA 2009)
election results: Denis SASSOU-NGUESSO reelected president; percent of vote - Denis SASSOU-NGUESSO 89.4%, Joseph Kignoumbi Kia MBOUNGOU 2.7%
Legislative branch: bicameral Parliament consists of the Senate (66 seats; members are elected by popular vote to serve five-year terms) and the National Assembly (137 seats; members are elected by popular vote to serve five-year terms)
elections: Senate - last held 11 July 2002 (next to be held July 2007); National Assembly - last held 27 May and 26 June 2002 (next to be held by NA May 2007)
election results: Senate - percent of vote by party - NA%; seats by party - FDP 56, other 10; National Assembly - percent of vote by party - NA%; seats by party - FDP 83, UDR 6, UPADS 3, other 45
Judicial branch: Supreme Court or Cour Supreme
Political parties and leaders: the most important of the many parties are the Democratic and Patriotic Forces or FDP (an alliance of Convention for Alternative Democracy, Congolese Labor Party or PCT, Liberal Republican Party, National Union for Democracy and Progress, Patriotic Union for the National Reconstruction, and Union for the National Renewal) [Denis SASSOU-NGUESSO, president]; Congolese Movement for Democracy and Integral Development or MCDDI [Michel MAMPOUYA]; Pan-African Union for Social Development or UPADS [Martin MBERI]; Rally for Democracy and Social Progress or RDPS [Jean-Pierre Thystere TCHICAYA, president]; Rally for Democracy and the Republic or RDR [Raymond Damasge NGOLLO]; Union for Democracy and Republic or UDR [leader NA]; Union of Democratic Forces or UFD [Sebastian EABO]
Political pressure groups and leaders: Congolese Trade Union Congress or CSC; General Union of Congolese Pupils and Students or UGEEC; Revolutionary Union of Congolese Women or URFC; Union of Congolese Socialist Youth or UJSC
International organization participation: ACCT, ACP, AfDB, AU, BDEAC, CEMAC, FAO, FZ, G-77, IBRD, ICAO, ICCt, ICFTU, ICRM, IDA, IFAD, IFC, IFRCS, ILO, IMF, IMO, Interpol, IOC, IOM, ITU, MIGA, NAM, OPCW (signatory), UN, UNCTAD, UNESCO, UNIDO, UNOCI, UPU, WCL, WCO, WFTU, WHO, WIPO, WMO, WToO, WTO
Diplomatic representation in the US:
chief of mission: Ambassador Serge MOMBOULI
chancery: 4891 Colorado Avenue NW, Washington, DC 20011
telephone: [1] (202) 726-5500
FAX: [1] (202) 726-1860
Diplomatic representation from the US:
chief of mission: Ambassador (vacant); Charge d'Affaires Mark BIEDLINGMAIER
embassy: NA
mailing address: NA
telephone: [243] (88) 43608
note: the embassy is temporarily collocated with the US Embassy in the Democratic Republic of the Congo (US Embassy Kinshasa, 310 Avenue des Aviateurs, Kinshasa)
Flag description: divided diagonally from the lower hoist side by a yellow band; the upper triangle (hoist side) is green and the lower triangle is red; uses the popular pan-African colors of Ethiopia

ECONOMY

Economy - overview: The economy is a mixture of village agriculture and handicrafts, an industrial sector based largely on oil, support services, and a government characterized by budget problems and overstaffing. Oil has supplanted forestry as the mainstay of the economy, providing a major share of government revenues and exports. In the early 1980s, rapidly rising oil revenues enabled the government to finance large-scale development projects with GDP growth averaging 5% annually, one of the highest rates in Africa. The government has mortgaged a substantial portion of its oil earnings through oil-backed loans that has contributed to a growing debt burden and chronic revenue shortfalls. Economic reform efforts have been undertaken with the support of international organizations, notably the World Bank and the IMF. However, the reform program came to a halt in June 1997 when civil war erupted. Denis SASSOU-NGUESSO, who returned to power when the war ended in October 1997, publicly expressed interest in moving forward on economic reforms and privatization and in renewing cooperation with international financial institutions. Economic progress was badly hurt by slumping oil prices and the resumption of armed conflict in December 1998, which worsened the republic's budget deficit. The current administration presides over an uneasy internal peace and faces difficult economic challenges of stimulating recovery and reducing poverty. Recovery of oil prices has boosted the economy's GDP and near term prospects. The Republic of Congo may be eligible for an IMF-World Bank heavily indebted poor countries (HIPC) initiative in early 2006, provided it meets the strict fiscal and monetary targets set out for it under a new three-year PRGF with the IMF.
GDP (purchasing power parity): $2.52 billion (2005 est.)
GDP (official exchange rate): $4.798 billion (2005 est.)
GDP - real growth rate: 5.5% (2005 est.)
GDP - per capita: purchasing power parity - $800 (2005 est.)
GDP - composition by sector:
agriculture: 6.7%
industry: 62.4%
services: 30.9% (2005 est.)
Labor force: NA
Unemployment rate: NA (2003)
Population below poverty line: NA
Household income or consumption by percentage share:
lowest 10%: NA
highest 10%: NA
Inflation rate (consumer prices): 2% (2005 est.)
Investment (gross fixed): 28.9% of GDP (2005 est.)
Budget:
revenues: $1.328 billion
expenditures: $1.065 billion, including capital expenditures of NA (2005 est.)
Agriculture - products: cassava (tapioca), sugar, rice, corn, peanuts, vegetables, cof-

fee, cocoa; forest products
Industries: petroleum extraction, cement, lumber, brewing, sugar, palm oil, soap, flour, cigarettes
Industrial production growth rate: 0% (2002 est.)
Electricity - production: 343 million kWh (2003)
Electricity - production by source:
fossil fuel: 0.3%
hydro: 99.7%
nuclear: 0%
other: 0% (2001)
Electricity - consumption: 619 million kWh (2003)
Electricity - exports: 0 kWh (2003)
Electricity - imports: 300 million kWh (2003)
Oil - production: 267,100 bbl/day (2005 est.)
Oil - consumption: 5,200 bbl/day (2003 est.)
Oil - exports: NA (2001)
Oil - imports: NA (2001)
Oil - proved reserves: 93.5 million bbl (1 January 2002)
Natural gas - production: 0 cu m (2001 est.)
Natural gas - consumption: 0 cu m (2001 est.)
Natural gas - exports: 0 cu m (2001 est.)
Natural gas - imports: 0 cu m (2001 est.)
Natural gas - proved reserves: 495.5 million cu m (1 January 2002)
Current account balance: $195.6 million (2005 est.)
Exports: $2.209 billion f.o.b. (2005 est.)
Exports - partners: China 26.8%, Taiwan 19.2%, North Korea 8.4%, US 7.3%, France 5.5%, South Korea 4.8% (2004)
Imports: $806.5 million f.o.b. (2005 est.)
Imports - partners: France 32.7%, US 10.1%, Germany 6.2%, Italy 6%, China 5.2%, Netherlands 4.5% (2004)
Reserves of foreign exchange and gold: $102.2 million (2005 est.)
Debt - external: $5 billion (2000 est.)
Economic aid - recipient: $159.1 million (1995)
Currency (code): Communaute Financiere Africaine franc (XAF); note - responsible authority is the Bank of the Central African States
Currency code: XAF
Exchange rates: Communaute Financiere Africaine francs (XAF) per US dollar - 480.56 (2005), 528.29 (2004), 581.2 (2003), 696.99 (2002), 733.04 (2001)
Fiscal year: calendar year

COMMUNICATION

Telephones - main lines in use: 7,000 (2003)
Telephones - mobile cellular: 330,000 (2003)
Telephone system:
general assessment: services barely adequate for government use; key exchanges are in Brazzaville, Pointe-Noire, and Loubomo; intercity lines frequently out of order
domestic: primary network consists of microwave radio relay and coaxial cable
international: country code - 242; satellite earth station - 1 Intelsat (Atlantic Ocean)
Radio broadcast stations: AM 1, FM 5, shortwave 3 (2001)
Radios: 341,000 (1997)
Television broadcast stations: 1 (2002)
Televisions: 33,000 (1997)
Internet country code: .cg
Internet hosts: 46 (2003)
Internet Service Providers (ISPs): 1 (2000)
Internet users: 15,000 (2003)

TRANSPORTATION

Airports: 32 (2004 est.)
Airports - with paved runways:
total: 4
over 3,047 m: 1
2,438 to 3,047 m: 1
1,524 to 2,437 m: 2 (2005 est.)
Airports - with unpaved runways:
total: 28
1,524 to 2,437 m: 6
914 to 1,523 m: 11
under 914 m: 11 (2005 est.)
Pipelines: gas 53 km; oil 646 km (2004)
Railways:
total: 894 km
narrow gauge: 894 km 1.067-m gauge (2004)
Roadways:
total: 12,800 km
paved: 1,242 km
unpaved: 11,558 km (1999)
Waterways: 4,385 km (on Congo and Oubanqui rivers) (2004)
Ports and terminals: Brazzaville, Djeno, Impfondo, Ouesso, Oyo, Pointe-Noire

MILITARY

Military branches: Congolese Armed Forces (FAC): Army, Air Force (Armee de l'Air Congolaise), Navy, Gendarmerie, Republican Guard (2005)
Military service age and obligation: 18 years of age for voluntary military service (2001)
Manpower available for military service: *males age 18-49:* 686,123 (2005 est.)
Manpower fit for military service: *males age 18-49:* 360,492 (2005 est.)
Manpower reaching military service age annually: *males:* 34,281 (2005 est.)
Military expenditures - dollar figure: $126.5 million (2004)
Military expenditures - percent of GDP: 2.8% (2004)

TRANSNATIONAL ISSUES

Disputes - international: about 7,000 Congolese refugees fleeing internal civil conflicts since the mid-1990s still reside in the Democratic Republic of the Congo; the location of the boundary in the broad Congo River with the Democratic Republic of the Congo is indefinite except in the Pool Malebo/Stanley Pool area
Refugees and internally displaced persons: *IDPs:* 60,000 (multiple civil wars since 1992; most IDPs are ethnic Lari) (2004)

COOK ISLANDS

INTRODUCTION

Background: Named after Captain COOK, who sighted them in 1770, the islands became a British protectorate in 1888. By 1900, administrative control was transferred to New Zealand; in 1965 residents chose self-government in free association with New Zealand. The emigration of skilled workers to New Zealand and government deficits are continuing problems.

GEOGRAPHY

Location: Oceania, group of islands in the South Pacific Ocean, about one-half of the way from Hawaii to New Zealand
Geographic coordinates: 21 14 S, 159 46 W
Map references: Oceania
Area:
total: 240 sq km
land: 240 sq km
water: 0 sq km
Area - comparative: 1.3 times the size of Washington, DC
Land boundaries: 0 km
Coastline: 120 km
Maritime claims:
territorial sea: 12 nm
exclusive economic zone: 200 nm
continental shelf: 200 nm or to the edge of the continental margin
Climate: tropical; moderated by trade winds
Terrain: low coral atolls in north; volcanic, hilly islands in south
Elevation extremes:
lowest point: Pacific Ocean 0 m
highest point: Te Manga 652 m

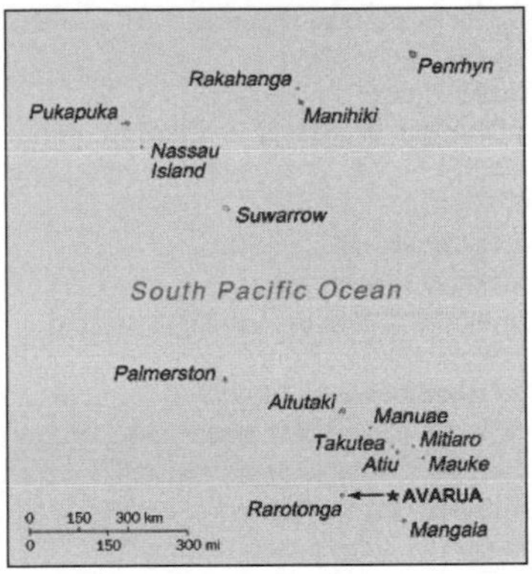

Natural resources: NEGL
Land use:
arable land: 17.39%
permanent crops: 13.04%
other: 69.57% (2001)
Irrigated land: NA
Natural hazards: typhoons (November to March)
Environment - current issues: NA
Environment - international agreements:
party to: Biodiversity, Climate Change, Climate Change-Kyoto Protocol, Desertification, Law of the Sea
signed, but not ratified: none of the selected agreements
Geography - note: the northern Cook Islands are seven low-lying, sparsely populated, coral atolls; the southern Cook Islands consist of eight elevated, fertile, volcanic isles where most of the populace lives

PEOPLE

Population: 21,388 (July 2005 est.)
Age structure:
0-14 years: NA
15-64 years: NA
65 years and over: NA
Population growth rate: NA
Birth rate: NA
Death rate: NA
Sex ratio: NA
Infant mortality rate:
total: NA
male: NA
female: NA
Life expectancy at birth:
total population: NA
male: NA
female: NA
Total fertility rate: NA children born/woman (2005 est.)
HIV/AIDS - adult prevalence rate: NA
HIV/AIDS - people living with HIV/AIDS: NA
HIV/AIDS - deaths: NA
Nationality:
noun: Cook Islander(s)
adjective: Cook Islander
Ethnic groups: Cook Island Maori (Polynesian) 87.7%, part Cook Island Maori 5.8%, other 6.5% (2001 census)
Religions: Cook Islands Christian Church 55.9%, Roman Catholic 16.8%, Seventh-Day Adventists 7.9%, Church of Latter Day Saints 3.8%, other Protestant 5.8%, other 4.2%, unspecified 2.6%, none 3% (2001 census)
Languages: English (official), Maori
Literacy:
definition: NA
total population: 95%
male: NA%
female: NA%

GOVERNMENT

Country name:
conventional long form: none
conventional short form: Cook Islands
former: Harvey Islands
Dependency status: self-governing in free association with New Zealand; Cook Islands is fully responsible for internal affairs; New Zealand retains responsibility for external affairs and defense, in consultation with the Cook Islands
Government type: self-governing parliamentary democracy
Capital: Avarua
Administrative divisions: none
Independence: none (became self-governing in free association with New Zealand on 4 August 1965 and has the right at any time to move to full independence by unilateral action)
National holiday: Constitution Day, first Monday in August (1965)
Constitution: 4 August 1965
Legal system: based on New Zealand law and English common law
Suffrage: NA years of age; universal adult
Executive branch:
chief of state: Queen ELIZABETH II (since 6 February 1952), represented by Frederick GOODWIN (since 9 February 2001); New Zealand High Commissioner Kurt MEYER (since July 2001), representative of New Zealand
head of government: Prime Minister Jim MARURAI (since 14 December 2004); Deputy Prime Minister Terepai MAOATE (since 9 August 2005)
cabinet: Cabinet chosen by the prime minister; collectively responsible to Parliament
elections: none; the monarch is hereditary; the UK representative is appointed by the monarch; the New Zealand high commissioner is appointed by the New Zealand Government; following legislative elections, the leader of the majority party or the leader of the majority coalition usually becomes prime minister
Legislative branch: unicameral Parliament (25 seats; members elected by popular vote to serve five-year terms)
elections: last held 7 September 2004 (next to be held by 2009)
election results: percent of vote by party - NA%; seats by party - CIP 10, DAP 9, Demo Tumu 4, independent 1; note - one seat undecided pending by-election
note: the House of Ariki (chiefs) advises on traditional matters and maintains considerable influence, but has no legislative powers
Judicial branch: High Court
Political parties and leaders: Cook Islands People's Party or CIP [Geoffrey HENRY]; Democratic Alliance Party or DAP [Terepai MAOATE]; New Alliance Party or NAP [Norman GEORGE]; Cook Islands National Party or CIN [Teariki HEATHER]; Demo Party Tumu [Robert WOONTON]
Political pressure groups and leaders: NA
International organization participation: ACP, AsDB, FAO, ICAO, ICFTU, ICRM, IFAD, IFRCS, IOC, OPCW, PIF, Sparteca, SPC, UNESCO, UPU, WHO, WMO
Diplomatic representation in the US: none (self-governing in free association with New Zealand)
Diplomatic representation from the US: none (self-governing in free association with New Zealand)
Flag description: blue, with the flag of the UK in the upper hoist-side quadrant and a large circle of 15 white five-pointed stars (one for every island) centered in the outer half of the flag

ECONOMY

Economy - overview: Like many other South Pacific island nations, the Cook Islands' economic development is hindered by the isolation of the country from foreign markets, the limited size of domestic markets, lack of natural resources, periodic devastation from natural disasters, and inadequate infrastructure. Agriculture provides the economic base with major exports made up of copra and citrus fruit. Manufacturing activities are limited to fruit processing, clothing, and handicrafts. Trade deficits are offset by remittances from emigrants and by foreign aid, overwhelmingly from New Zealand. In the 1980s and 1990s, the country lived beyond its means, maintaining a bloated public service and accumulating a large foreign debt. Subsequent reforms, including the sale of state assets, the strengthening of economic management, the encouragement of tourism, and a debt restructuring

agreement, have rekindled investment and growth.
GDP (purchasing power parity): $105 million (2001 est.)
GDP (official exchange rate): NA
GDP - real growth rate: 7.1% (2001 est.)
GDP - per capita: purchasing power parity - $5,000 (2001 est.)
GDP - composition by sector:
agriculture: 17%
industry: 7.8%
services: 75.2% (2000 est.)
Labor force: 8,000 (1996)
Labor force - by occupation: agriculture 29%, industry 15%, services 56%
note: shortage of skilled labor (1995)
Unemployment rate: 13% (1996)
Population below poverty line: NA
Household income or consumption by percentage share:
lowest 10%: NA
highest 10%: NA
Inflation rate (consumer prices): 3.2% (2000 est.)
Budget:
revenues: $28 million
expenditures: $27 million, including capital expenditures of $3.3 million (FY00/01 est.)
Agriculture - products: copra, citrus, pineapples, tomatoes, beans, pawpaws, bananas, yams, taro, coffee; pigs, poultry
Industries: fruit processing, tourism, fishing, clothing, handicrafts
Industrial production growth rate: 1% (2002)
Electricity - production: 28 million kWh (2003)
Electricity - production by source:
fossil fuel: 100%
hydro: 0%
nuclear: 0%
other: 0% (2001)
Electricity - consumption: 26.04 million kWh (2003)
Electricity - exports: 0 kWh (2003)
Electricity - imports: 0 kWh (2003)
Oil - production: 0 bbl/day (2003)
Oil - consumption: 400 bbl/day (2003 est.)
Oil - exports: NA (2001)
Oil - imports: NA (2001)
Exports: $9.1 million (2000)
Exports - partners: Australia 34%, Japan 27%, New Zealand 25%, US 8% (2004)
Imports: $50.7 million (2000)
Imports - partners: New Zealand 61%, Fiji 19%, US 9%, Australia 6%, Japan 2% (2004)
Debt - external: $141 million (1996 est.)
Economic aid - recipient: $13.1 million; note - New Zealand continues to furnish the greater part (1995)
Currency (code): New Zealand dollar (NZD)
Currency code: NZD
Exchange rates: New Zealand dollars per US dollar - 1.53 (2005), 1.5087 (2004), 1.7221 (2003), 2.1622 (2002), 2.3788 (2001)
Fiscal year: 1 April - 31 March

COMMUNICATION

Telephones - main lines in use: 6,200 (2002)
Telephones - mobile cellular: 1,500 (2002)
Telephone system:
general assessment: Telecom Cook Islands offers international direct dialing, Internet, email, fax, and Telex
domestic: the individual islands are connected by a combination of satellite earth stations, microwave systems, and VHF and HF radiotelephone; within the islands, service is provided by small exchanges connected to subscribers by open-wire, cable, and fiber-optic cable
international: country code - 682; satellite earth station - 1 Intelsat (Pacific Ocean)
Radio broadcast stations: AM 1, FM 1, shortwave 0 (2004)
Radios: 14,000 (1997)
Television broadcast stations: 1 (outer islands receive satellite broadcasts) (2004)
Televisions: 4,000 (1997)
Internet country code: .ck
Internet Service Providers (ISPs): 3 (2000)
Internet users: 3,600 (2002)

TRANSPORTATION

Airports: 9 (2004 est.)
Airports - with paved runways:
total: 2
1,524 to 2,437 m: 2 (2005 est.)
Airports - with unpaved runways:
total: 7
1,524 to 2,437 m: 2
914 to 1,523 m: 4
under 914 m: 1 (2005 est.)
Roadways:
total: 320 km
paved: 33 km
unpaved: 287 km (2003)
Merchant marine:
total: 1 ships (1,000 GRT or over) 4,074 GRT/7,520 DWT
by type: petroleum tanker 1 (2005)
Ports and terminals: Avatiu

MILITARY

Military branches: no regular military forces; Ministry of Police and Disaster Management (2004)
Military - note: defense is the responsibility of New Zealand, in consultation with the Cook Islands and at its request

TRANSNATIONAL ISSUES

Disputes - international: none

CORAL SEA ISLANDS

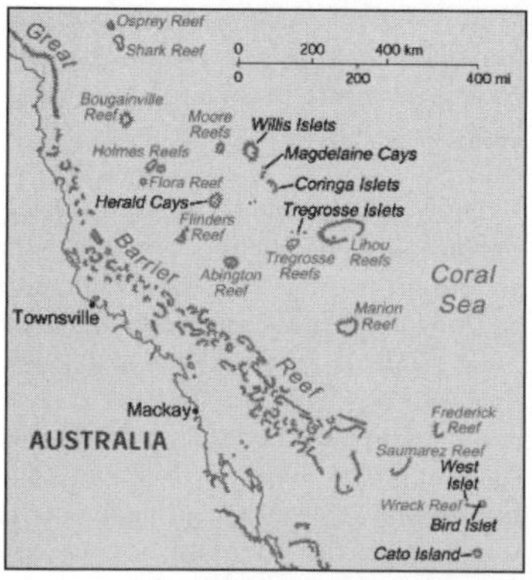

INTRODUCTION

Background: Scattered over some 1 million square kilometers of ocean, the Coral Sea Islands were declared a territory of Australia in 1969. They are uninhabited except for a small meteorological staff on the Willis Islets. Automated weather stations, beacons, and a lighthouse occupy many other islands and reefs.

GEOGRAPHY

Location: Oceania, islands in the Coral Sea, northeast of Australia
Geographic coordinates: 18 00 S, 152 00 E
Map references: Oceania
Area:
total: less than 3 sq km
land: less than 3 sq km
water: 0 sq km
note: includes numerous small islands and reefs scattered over a sea area of about 780,000 sq km, with the Willis Islets the most important
Area - comparative: NA
Land boundaries: 0 km
Coastline: 3,095 km
Maritime claims:
territorial sea: 3 nm
exclusive fishing zone: 200 nm
Climate: tropical
Terrain: sand and coral reefs and islands (or cays)

Elevation extremes:
lowest point: Pacific Ocean 0 m
highest point: unnamed location on Cato Island 6 m
Natural resources: NEGL
Land use:
arable land: 0%
permanent crops: 0%
other: 100% (mostly grass or scrub cover) (2001)
Irrigated land: 0 sq km
Natural hazards: occasional tropical cyclones
Environment - current issues: no permanent fresh water resources
Geography - note: important nesting area for birds and turtles

PEOPLE

Population: no indigenous inhabitants
note: there is a staff of three to four at the meteorological station (2005 est.)

GOVERNMENT

Country name:
conventional long form: Coral Sea Islands Territory
conventional short form: Coral Sea Islands
Dependency status: territory of Australia; administered from Canberra by the Department of the Environment, Sport, and Territories
Legal system: the laws of Australia, where applicable, apply
Executive branch: administered from Canberra by the Department of the Environment, Sport, and Territories
Diplomatic representation in the US: none (territory of Australia)
Diplomatic representation from the US: none (territory of Australia)
Flag description: the flag of Australia is used

ECONOMY

Economy - overview: no economic activity

COMMUNICATION

Communications - note: there are automatic weather stations on many of the isles and reefs relaying data to the mainland

TRANSPORTATION

Ports and terminals: none; offshore anchorage only

MILITARY

Military - note: defense is the responsibility of Australia; visited regularly by the Royal Australian Navy; Australia has control over the activities of visitors

TRANSNATIONAL ISSUES

Disputes - international: none

COSTA RICA

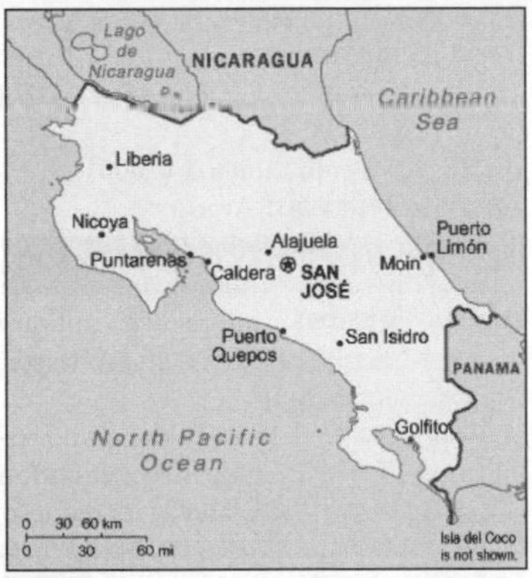

INTRODUCTION

Background: Costa Rica is a Central American success story: since the late 19th century, only two brief periods of violence have marred its democratic development. Although still a largely agricultural country, it has expanded its economy to include strong technology and tourism sectors. The standard of living is relatively high. Land ownership is widespread.

GEOGRAPHY

Location: Central America, bordering both the Caribbean Sea and the North Pacific Ocean, between Nicaragua and Panama
Geographic coordinates: 10 00 N, 84 00 W
Map references: Central America and the Caribbean
Area:
total: 51,100 sq km
land: 50,660 sq km
water: 440 sq km
note: includes Isla del Coco
Area - comparative: slightly smaller than West Virginia
Land boundaries:
total: 639 km
border countries: Nicaragua 309 km, Panama 330 km
Coastline: 1,290 km
Maritime claims:
territorial sea: 12 nm
exclusive economic zone: 200 nm
continental shelf: 200 nm
Climate: tropical and subtropical; dry season (December to April); rainy season (May to November); cooler in highlands
Terrain: coastal plains separated by rugged mountains including over 100 volcanic cones, of which several are major volcanoes
Elevation extremes:
lowest point: Pacific Ocean 0 m
highest point: Cerro Chirripo 3,810 m
Natural resources: hydropower
Land use:
arable land: 4.41%
permanent crops: 5.88%
other: 89.71% (2001)
Irrigated land: 1,260 sq km (1998 est.)
Natural hazards: occasional earthquakes, hurricanes along Atlantic coast; frequent flooding of lowlands at onset of rainy season and landslides; active volcanoes
Environment - current issues: deforestation and land use change, largely a result of the clearing of land for cattle ranching and agriculture; soil erosion; coastal marine pollution; fisheries protection; solid waste management; air pollution
Environment - international agreements:
party to: Biodiversity, Climate Change, Climate Change-Kyoto Protocol, Desertification, Endangered Species, Environmental Modification, Hazardous Wastes, Law of the Sea, Marine Dumping, Ozone Layer Protection, Wetlands, Whaling
signed, but not ratified: Marine Life Conservation
Geography - note: four volcanoes, two of them active, rise near the capital of San Jose in the center of the country; one of the volcanoes, Irazu, erupted destructively in 1963-65

PEOPLE

Population: 4,016,173 (July 2005 est.)
Age structure:
0-14 years: 28.9% (male 593,540/female 566,361)
15-64 years: 65.5% (male 1,330,481/female 1,300,664)
65 years and over: 5.6% (male 104,564/female 120,563) (2005 est.)
Median age:
total: 26.03 years
male: 25.59 years
female: 26.5 years (2005 est.)
Population growth rate: 1.48% (2005 est.)
Birth rate: 18.6 births/1,000 population (2005 est.)
Death rate: 4.33 deaths/1,000 population (2005 est.)
Net migration rate: 0.5 migrant(s)/1,000 population (2005 est.)
Sex ratio:
at birth: 1.05 male(s)/female
under 15 years: 1.05 male(s)/female
15-64 years: 1.02 male(s)/female

65 years and over: 0.87 male(s)/female
total population: 1.02 male(s)/female (2005 est.)
Infant mortality rate:
total: 9.95 deaths/1,000 live births
male: 10.85 deaths/1,000 live births
female: 9 deaths/1,000 live births (2005 est.)
Life expectancy at birth:
total population: 76.84 years
male: 74.26 years
female: 79.55 years (2005 est.)
Total fertility rate: 2.28 children born/woman (2005 est.)
HIV/AIDS - adult prevalence rate: 0.6% (2003 est.)
HIV/AIDS - people living with HIV/AIDS: 12,000 (2003 est.)
HIV/AIDS - deaths: 900 (2003 est.)
Nationality:
noun: Costa Rican(s)
adjective: Costa Rican
Ethnic groups: white (including mestizo) 94%, black 3%, Amerindian 1%, Chinese 1%, other 1%
Religions: Roman Catholic 76.3%, Evangelical 13.7%, Jehovah's Witnesses 1.3%, other Protestant 0.7%, other 4.8%, none 3.2%
Languages: Spanish (official), English
Literacy:
definition: age 15 and over can read and write
total population: 96%
male: 95.9%
female: 96.1% (2003 est.)

GOVERNMENT

Country name:
conventional long form: Republic of Costa Rica
conventional short form: Costa Rica
local long form: Republica de Costa Rica
local short form: Costa Rica
Government type: democratic republic
Capital: San Jose
Administrative divisions: 7 provinces (provincias, singular - provincia); Alajuela, Cartago, Guanacaste, Heredia, Limon, Puntarenas, San Jose
Independence: 15 September 1821 (from Spain)
National holiday: Independence Day, 15 September (1821)
Constitution: 7 November 1949
Legal system: based on Spanish civil law system; judicial review of legislative acts in the Supreme Court; has accepted compulsory ICJ jurisdiction
Suffrage: 18 years of age; universal and compulsory
Executive branch:
chief of state: President Abel PACHECO (since 8 May 2002); First Vice President Lineth SABORIO (since 8 May 2002); Second Vice President (vacant); note - the president is both the chief of state and head of government
head of government: President Abel PACHECO (since 8 May 2002); First Vice President Lineth SABORIO (since 8 May 2002); Second Vice President (vacant); note - the president is both the chief of state and head of government
cabinet: Cabinet selected by the president
elections: president and vice presidents elected on the same ticket by popular vote for four-year terms; election last held 3 February 2002; run-off election held 7 April 2002 (next to be held 5 February 2006)
election results: Abel PACHECO elected president; percent of vote - Abel PACHECO (PUSC) 58%; Rolando ARAYA (PLN) 42%
Legislative branch: unicameral Legislative Assembly or Asamblea Legislativa (57 seats; members are elected by direct, popular vote to serve four-year terms)
elections: last held 3 February 2002 (next to be held 5 February 2006)
election results: percent of vote by party - NA%; seats by party - PUSC 19, PLN 17, PAC 14, PML 6, PRC 1; note - seats by party as of January 2005 - PUSC 19, PLN 16, PAC 8, PML 5, PRC 1, Patriotic Union 3, Homeland First 1, Authentic Member from Heredia 1, Democratic National Alliance 1, independent 2
Judicial branch: Supreme Court or Corte Suprema (22 justices are elected for eight-year terms by the Legislative Assembly)
Political parties and leaders: Authentic Member from Heredia [Jose SALAS]; Citizen Action Party or PAC [Otton SOLIS]; Costa Rican Renovation Party or PRC [Gerardo Justo OROZCO Alvarez]; Democratic Force Party or PFD [Vladimir DE LA CRUZ]; General Union Party or PUGEN [Carlos Alberto FERNANDEZ Vega]; Homeland First or PP [Juan Jose VARGAS Fallas]; Independent Worker Party or PIO [Jose Alberto CUBERO Carmona]; Libertarian Movement Party or PML [Otto GUEVARA Guth]; National Christian Alliance Party or ANC [Juan Carlos CHAVEZ Mora]; National Integration Party or PIN [Walter MUNOZ Cespedes]; National Liberation Party or PLN [Francisco Antonio PACHECO]; National Patriotic Party or PPN [Daniel Enrique Reynolds VARGAS]; National Restoration Party or PRN [Carlos AVENDANO]; Nationalist Democratic Alliance or ADN [Jose Miguel VILLALOBOS Umana]; Patriotic Union or UP [Humberto ARCE Salas]; Social Christian Unity Party or PUSC [Lorena VASQUEZ Badilla]; Union for Change Party or UPC [Antonio ALVAREZ Desanti]; United Leftist Coalition or IU [Humberto VARGAS Carbonel]
Political pressure groups and leaders: Authentic Confederation of Democratic Workers or CATD (Communist Party affiliate); Chamber of Coffee Growers; Confederated Union of Workers or CUT (Communist Party affiliate); Costa Rican Confederation of Democratic Workers or CCTD (Liberation Party affiliate); Federation of Public Service Workers or FTSP; National Association for Economic Development or ANFE; National Association of Educators or ANDE; Rerum Novarum or CTRN (PLN affiliate) [Gilbert Brown]
International organization participation: BCIE, CACM, FAO, G-77, IADB, IAEA, IBRD, ICAO, ICC, ICCt, ICFTU, ICRM, IDA, IFAD, IFC, IFRCS, ILO, IMF, IMO, Interpol, IOC, IOM, ISO, ITU, LAES, LAIA (observer), MIGA, NAM (observer), OAS, OPANAL, OPCW, PCA, RG, UN, UNCTAD, UNESCO, UNIDO, UPU, WCL, WCO, WFTU, WHO, WIPO, WMO, WToO, WTO
Diplomatic representation in the US:
chief of mission: Ambassador Tomas DUENAS
chancery: 2114 S Street NW, Washington, DC 20008
telephone: [1] (202) 234-2945
FAX: [1] (202) 265-4795
consulate(s) general: Atlanta, Chicago, Hammond (temporary location in Louisiana), Houston, Los Angeles, Miami, New York, San Juan (Puerto Rico), Tampa (temporarily closed), and Washington DC
consulate(s): San Francisco
Diplomatic representation from the US:
chief of mission: Ambassador Mark LANGDALE
embassy: Calle 120 Avenida O, Pavas, San Jose
mailing address: APO AA 34020
telephone: [506] 519-2000
FAX: [506] 519-2305
Flag description: five horizontal bands of blue (top), white, red (double width), white, and blue, with the coat of arms in a white elliptical disk on the hoist side of the red band; above the coat of arms a light blue ribbon contains the words, AMERICA CENTRAL, and just below it near the top of the coat of arms is a white ribbon with the words, REPUBLICA COSTA RICA

ECONOMY

Economy - overview: Costa Rica's basically stable economy depends on tourism, agriculture, and electronics exports. Poverty has been substantially reduced over the past 15 years, and a strong social safety net has been put into place. Foreign investors remain attracted by the country's political stability and high education levels, and tourism continues to bring in foreign exchange. Low prices for coffee and bananas have hurt the agricultural sector. The government continues to grapple with its large internal and external deficits and sizable internal debt. The reduction of inflation remains a difficult problem because of rises in the price of imports, labor market rigidities, and fiscal deficits. The country also needs to reform its tax system and its pattern of public expenditure. Costa Rica is the only signatory to the US-Central American Free Trade Agreement (CAFTA) that has not ratified it. CAFTA implementation would result in economic reforms and an improved investment climate.
GDP (purchasing power parity): $40.32 billion (2005 est.)
GDP (official exchange rate): $19.81 billion (2005 est.)
GDP - real growth rate: 3.2% (2005 est.)
GDP - per capita: purchasing power parity - $10,000 (2005 est.)
GDP - composition by sector:
agriculture: 8.6%
industry: 28.3%
services: 63.1% (2005 est.)
Labor force: 1.82 million (2005 est.)
Labor force - by occupation: agriculture 20%, industry 22%, services 58% (1999 est.)
Unemployment rate: 6.6% (2005 est.)
Population below poverty line: 18% (2004 est.)
Household income or consumption by percentage share:
lowest 10%: 1.1%
highest 10%: 36.8% (2002)
Distribution of family income - Gini index: 46.5 (2000)
Inflation rate (consumer prices): 13.8% (2005 est.)
Investment (gross fixed): 18% of GDP (2005 est.)
Budget:
revenues: $2.722 billion
expenditures: $3.195 billion, including capital expenditures of NA (2005 est.)
Public debt: 56.2% of GDP (2005 est.)
Agriculture - products: coffee, pineapples, bananas, sugar, corn, rice, beans, potatoes; beef; timber
Industries: microprocessors, food processing, textiles and clothing, construction materials, fertilizer, plastic products
Industrial production growth rate: 2.6% (2005 est.)
Electricity - production: 7.726 billion kWh (2003)
Electricity - production by source:
fossil fuel: 1.5%
hydro: 81.9%
nuclear: 0%
other: 16.6% (2001)
Electricity - consumption: 7.12 billion kWh (2003)
Electricity - exports: 115 million kWh (2003)
Electricity - imports: 50 million kWh (2003)
Oil - production: 0 bbl/day (2003)
Oil - consumption: 40,000 bbl/day (2003 est.)
Oil - exports: NA (2001)
Oil - imports: NA (2001)
Current account balance: $-1.179 billion (2005 est.)
Exports: $7.005 billion (2005 est.)
Exports - partners: US 46.9%, Netherlands 5.3%, Guatemala 4.4% (2004)
Imports: $9.69 billion (2005 est.)
Imports - partners: US 46.1%, Japan 5.9%, Mexico 5.1%, Brazil 4.2% (2004)
Reserves of foreign exchange and gold: $2.208 billion (2005 est.)
Debt - external: $3.633 billion (30 June 2005 est.)
Currency (code): Costa Rican colon (CRC)
Currency code: CRC
Exchange rates: Costa Rican colones per US dollar - 479.28 (2005), 437.91 (2004), 398.66 (2003), 359.82 (2002), 328.87 (2001)
Fiscal year: calendar year

COMMUNICATION

Telephones - main lines in use: 1.132 million (2002)
Telephones - mobile cellular: 528,047 (2002)
Telephone system:
general assessment: good domestic telephone service in terms of breadth of coverage; restricted cellular telephone service
domestic: point-to-point and point-to-multi-point microwave, fiber-optic, and coaxial cable link rural areas; Internet service is available
international: country code - 506; connected to Central American Microwave System; satellite earth stations - 2 Intelsat (Atlantic Ocean); two submarine cables (1999)
Radio broadcast stations: AM 65, FM 51, shortwave 19 (2002)
Radios: 980,000 (1997)
Television broadcast stations: 20 (plus 43 repeaters) (2002)
Televisions: 525,000 (1997)
Internet country code: .cr
Internet hosts: 10,826 (2003)
Internet Service Providers (ISPs): 3 (of which only one is legal) (2000)
Internet users: 800,000 (2002)

TRANSPORTATION

Airports: 149 (2004 est.)
Airports - with paved runways:
total: 31
2,438 to 3,047 m: 2
1,524 to 2,437 m: 2
914 to 1,523 m: 18
under 914 m: 9 (2005 est.)
Airports - with unpaved runways:
total: 125
914 to 1,523 m: 25
under 914 m: 100 (2005 est.)
Pipelines: refined products 242 km (2004)
Railways:
total: 278 km
narrow gauge: 278 km 1.067-m gauge (2004)
Roadways:
total: 35,889 km
paved: 8,075 km
unpaved: 27,814 km (2003)
Waterways: 730 km (seasonally navigable by small craft) (2004)
Merchant marine:
total: 2 ships (1,000 GRT or over) 1,716 GRT/ DWT
by type: passenger/cargo 2 (2005)
Ports and terminals: Caldera, Puerto Limon

MILITARY

Military branches: no regular military forces; Ministry of Public Security, Government, and Police
Military service age and obligation: 18 years of age (2004)
Manpower available for military service: *males age 18-49:* 997,690 (2005 est.)
Manpower fit for military service: *males age 18-49:* 829,874 (2005 est.)
Manpower reaching military service age annually: *males:* 41,097 (2005 est.)
Military expenditures - dollar figure: $64.2 million (2004)
Military expenditures - percent of GDP: 0.4% (2003)

TRANSNATIONAL ISSUES

Disputes - international: legal dispute over navigational rights of Rio San Juan on the border with Nicaragua remains unresolved
Illicit drugs: transshipment country for cocaine and heroin from South America; illicit production of cannabis on small, scattered plots; domestic cocaine consumption, particularly crack cocaine, is rising.

COTE D'IVOIRE

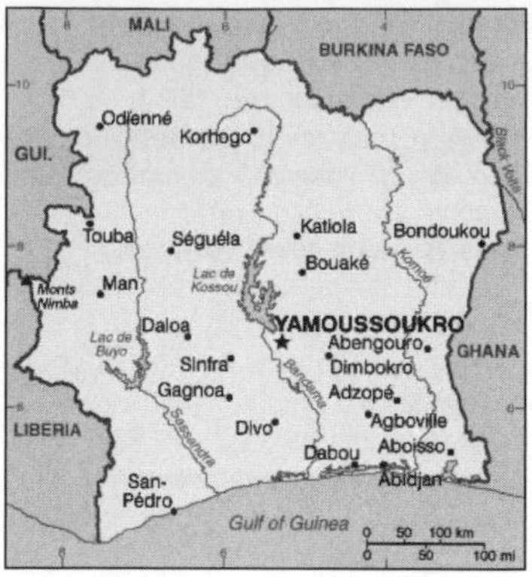

INTRODUCTION

Background: Close ties to France since independence in 1960, the development of cocoa production for export, and foreign investment made Cote d'Ivoire one of the most prosperous of the tropical African states, but did not protect it from political turmoil. On 25 December 1999, a military coup - the first ever in Cote d'Ivoire's history - overthrew the government led by President Henri Konan BEDIE. Junta leader Robert GUEI held elections in late 2000, but excluded prominent opposition leader Alassane OUATTARA, blatantly rigged the polling results, and declared himself winner. Popular protest forced GUEI to step aside and brought runner-up Laurent GBAGBO into power. Ivorian dissidents and disaffected members of the military launched a failed coup attempt in September 2002. Rebel forces claimed the northern half of the country and in January 2003 were granted ministerial positions in a unity government under the auspices of the Linas-Marcoussis Peace Accord. President GBAGBO and rebel forces resumed implementation of the peace accord in December 2003 after a three-month stalemate, but issues that sparked the civil war, such as land reform and grounds for nationality remain unresolved. The central government has yet to exert control over the northern regions and tensions remain high between GBAGBO and opposition leaders. Several thousand French and West African troops remain in Cote d'Ivoire to maintain peace and facilitate the disarmament, demobilization, and rehabilitation process.

GEOGRAPHY

Location: Western Africa, bordering the North Atlantic Ocean, between Ghana and Liberia
Geographic coordinates: 8 00 N, 5 00 W
Map references: Africa
Area:
total: 322,460 sq km
land: 318,000 sq km
water: 4,460 sq km
Area - comparative: slightly larger than New Mexico
Land boundaries:
total: 3,110 km
border countries: Burkina Faso 584 km, Ghana 668 km, Guinea 610 km, Liberia 716 km, Mali 532 km
Coastline: 515 km
Maritime claims:
territorial sea: 12 nm
exclusive economic zone: 200 nm
continental shelf: 200 nm
Climate: tropical along coast, semiarid in far north; three seasons - warm and dry (November to March), hot and dry (March to May), hot and wet (June to October)
Terrain: mostly flat to undulating plains; mountains in northwest
Elevation extremes:
lowest point: Gulf of Guinea 0 m
highest point: Mont Nimba 1,752 m
Natural resources: petroleum, natural gas, diamonds, manganese, iron ore, cobalt, bauxite, copper, gold, nickel, tantalum, silica sand, clay, cocoa beans, coffee, palm oil, hydropower
Land use:
arable land: 9.75%
permanent crops: 13.84%
other: 76.41% (2001)
Irrigated land: 730 sq km (1998 est.)
Natural hazards: coast has heavy surf and no natural harbors; during the rainy season torrential flooding is possible
Environment - current issues: deforestation (most of the country's forests - once the largest in West Africa - have been heavily logged); water pollution from sewage and industrial and agricultural effluents
Environment - international agreements:
party to: Biodiversity, Climate Change, Desertification, Endangered Species, Hazardous Wastes, Law of the Sea, Marine Dumping, Ozone Layer Protection, Ship Pollution, Tropical Timber 83, Tropical Timber 94, Wetlands
signed, but not ratified: none of the selected agreements
Geography - note: most of the inhabitants live along the sandy coastal region; apart from the capital area, the forested interior is sparsely populated

PEOPLE

Population: 17,298,040
note: estimates for this country explicitly take into account the effects of excess mortality due to AIDS; this can result in lower life expectancy, higher infant mortality and death rates, lower population and growth rates, and changes in the distribution of population by age and sex than would otherwise be expected (July 2005 est.)
Age structure:
0-14 years: 41% (male 3,490,536/female 3,596,208)
15-64 years: 56.3% (male 4,920,726/female 4,820,326)
65 years and over: 2.7% (male 231,514/female 238,730) (2005 est.)
Median age:
total: 19.05 years
male: 19.36 years
female: 18.76 years (2005 est.)
Population growth rate: 2.06% (2005 est.)
Birth rate: 35.51 births/1,000 population (2005 est.)
Death rate: 14.94 deaths/1,000 population (2005 est.)
Net migration rate: 0 migrant(s)/1,000 population (2005 est.)
Sex ratio:
at birth: 1.03 male(s)/female
under 15 years: 0.97 male(s)/female
15-64 years: 1.02 male(s)/female
65 years and over: 0.97 male(s)/female
total population: 1 male(s)/female (2005 est.)
Infant mortality rate:
total: 90.83 deaths/1,000 live births
male: 107.64 deaths/1,000 live births
female: 73.52 deaths/1,000 live births (2005 est.)
Life expectancy at birth:
total population: 48.62 years
male: 46.05 years
female: 51.27 years (2005 est.)
Total fertility rate: 4.58 children born/woman (2005 est.)
HIV/AIDS - adult prevalence rate: 7% (2003 est.)
HIV/AIDS - people living with HIV/AIDS: 570,000 (2003 est.)
HIV/AIDS - deaths: 47,000 (2003 est.)
Major infectious diseases:
degree of risk: very high
food or waterborne diseases: bacterial diarrhea, hepatitis A, and typhoid fever
vectorborne diseases: malaria, yellow fever, and others are high risks in some locations
water contact: schistosomiasis (2004)
Nationality:
noun: Ivoirian(s)
adjective: Ivoirian
Ethnic groups: Akan 42.1%, Voltaiques or Gur 17.6%, Northern Mandes 16.5%, Krous 11%, Southern Mandes 10%, other 2.8% (includes 130,000 Lebanese and 14,000 French) (1998)
Religions: Christian 20-30%, Muslim 35-

40%, indigenous 25-40% (2001)
note: the majority of foreigners (migratory workers) are Muslim (70%) and Christian (20%)
Languages: French (official), 60 native dialects with Dioula the most widely spoken
Literacy:
definition: age 15 and over can read and write
total population: 50.9%
male: 57.9%
female: 43.6% (2003 est.)

GOVERNMENT

Country name:
conventional long form: Republic of Cote d'Ivoire
conventional short form: Cote d'Ivoire
local long form: Republique de Cote d'Ivoire
local short form: Cote d'Ivoire
former: Ivory Coast
Government type: republic; multiparty presidential regime established 1960
Capital: Yamoussoukro; note - although Yamoussoukro has been the official capital since 1983, Abidjan remains the commercial and administrative center; the US, like other countries, maintains its Embassy in Abidjan
Administrative divisions: 19 regions; Agneby, Bafing, Bas-Sassandra, Denguele, Dix-Huit Montagnes, Fromager, Haut-Sassandra, Lacs, Lagunes, Marahoue, Moyen-Cavally, Moyen-Comoe, N'zi-Comoe, Savanes, Sud-Bandama, Sud-Comoe, Vallee du Bandama, Worodougou, Zanzan
Independence: 7 August 1960 (from France)
National holiday: Independence Day, 7 August (1960)
Constitution: new constitution adopted 4 August 2000
Legal system: based on French civil law system and customary law; judicial review in the Constitutional Chamber of the Supreme Court; has not accepted compulsory ICJ jurisdiction
Suffrage: 18 years of age; universal
Executive branch:
chief of state: President Laurent GBAGBO (since 26 October 2000)
head of government: Transitional Prime Minister Charles Konan BANNY (since 7 December 2005)
cabinet: Council of Ministers appointed by the president
elections: president elected by popular vote for a five-year term; election last held 26 October 2000 (next to be held by October 2006); prime minister appointed by the president
election results: Laurent GBAGBO elected president; percent of vote - Laurent GBAGBO 59.4%, Robert GUEI 32.7%, Francis WODIE 5.7%, other 2.2%
Legislative branch: unicameral National Assembly or Assemblee Nationale (225 seats; members are elected in single- and multi-district elections by direct popular vote to serve five-year terms)
elections: elections last held 10 December 2000 with by-elections on 14 January 2001 (next to be held by October 2006)
election results: percent of vote by party - NA%; seats by party - FPI 96, PDCI-RDA 94, RDR 5, PIT 4, other 2, independents 22, vacant 2
note: a Senate is scheduled to be created in the next full election in 2005
Judicial branch: Supreme Court or Cour Supreme consists of four chambers: Judicial Chamber for criminal cases, Audit Chamber for financial cases, Constitutional Chamber for judicial review cases, and Administrative Chamber for civil cases; there is no legal limit to the number of members
Political parties and leaders: Citizen's Democratic Union or UDCY [Eg Theodore MEL]; Democratic Party of Cote d'Ivoire-African Democratic Rally or PDCI-RDA [Henri Konan BEDIE]; Ivorian Popular Front or FPI [Laurent GBAGBO]; Ivorian Worker's Party or PIT [Francis WODIE]; Rally of the Republicans or RDR [Alassane OUATTARA]; Union for Democracy and Peace or UDPCI [Paul Akoto YAO]; over 20 smaller parties
Political pressure groups and leaders: NA
International organization participation: ACCT, ACP, AfDB, AU, CEMAC, ECOWAS, Entente, FAO, FZ, G-24, G-77, IAEA, IBRD, ICAO, ICCt (signatory), ICFTU, ICRM, IDA, IDB, IFAD, IFC, IFRCS, ILO, IMF, IMO, Interpol, IOC, IOM, ITU, MIGA, NAM, OIC, OPCW, UN, UNCTAD, UNESCO, UNHCR, UNIDO, UPU, WADB (regional), WAEMU, WCL, WCO, WFTU, WHO, WIPO, WMO, WToO, WTO
Diplomatic representation in the US:
chief of mission: Ambassador Daouda DIABATE
chancery: 3421 Massachusetts Avenue NW, Washington, DC 20007
telephone: [1] (202) 797-0300
FAX: [1] (202) 462-9444
Diplomatic representation from the US:
chief of mission: Ambassador Aubrey HOOKS
embassy: Riviera Golf 01, Abidjan
mailing address: B. P. 1866, Abidjan 01
telephone: [225] 20 21 09 79
FAX: [225] 20 22 32 59
Flag description: three equal vertical bands of orange (hoist side), white, and green; similar to the flag of Ireland, which is longer and has the colors reversed - green (hoist side), white, and orange; also similar to the flag of Italy, which is green (hoist side), white, and red; design was based on the flag of France

ECONOMY

Economy - overview: Cote d'Ivoire is among the world's largest producers and exporters of coffee, cocoa beans, and palm oil. Consequently, the economy is highly sensitive to fluctuations in international prices for these products and weather conditions. Despite government attempts to diversify the economy, it is still heavily dependent on agriculture and related activities, engaging roughly 68% of the population. Growth was negative in 2000-03 because of the difficulty of meeting the conditions of international donors, continued low prices of key exports, and severe civil war. In November 2004 the situation deteriorated when President GBAGBO's troops attacked and killed nine French peacekeeping forces, and the UN imposed an arms embargo. Political turmoil damaged the economy in 2005, with fear among Ivorians spreading, foreign investment shriveling, French businesses and expats fleeing, travel within the country falling, and criminal elements that traffic in weapons and diamonds gaining ground. The Government will continue to survive financially off of the sale of cocoa, which represents 40% of GDP and 90% of foreign exchange earning. Though the 2005 harvest has been largely unaffected by past fighting, the Government will likely lose between 10% and 20% of its cocoa harvest to northern rebels who smuggle the cocoa they control to neighboring countries where cocoa prices are higher. The Government remains hopeful that ongoing exploration of Cote d'Ivoire's offshore oil reserves will result in signifcant production that could boost daily crude output from roughly 33,000 barrels per day (b/d) to over 200,000 b/d by the end of the decade.
GDP (purchasing power parity): $24.81 billion (2005 est.)
GDP (official exchange rate): $16.17 billion (2005 est.)
GDP - real growth rate: -1.5% (2005 est.)
GDP - per capita: purchasing power parity - $1,400 (2005 est.)
GDP - composition by sector:
agriculture: 27.7%
industry: 16.7%
services: 55.6% (2005 est.)
Labor force: 6.95 million (68% agricul-

tural) (2005 est.)
Unemployment rate: 13% in urban areas (1998)
Population below poverty line: 37% (1995)
Household income or consumption by percentage share:
lowest 10%: 3.1%
highest 10%: 28.8% (1995)
Distribution of family income - Gini index: 45.2 (1998)
Inflation rate (consumer prices): 2% (2005 est.)
Investment (gross fixed): 8.7% of GDP (2005 est.)
Budget:
revenues: $2.434 billion
expenditures: $2.83 billion, including capital expenditures of $420 million (2005 est.)
Public debt: 70.4% of GDP (2005 est.)
Agriculture - products: coffee, cocoa beans, bananas, palm kernels, corn, rice, manioc (tapioca), sweet potatoes, sugar, cotton, rubber; timber
Industries: foodstuffs, beverages; wood products, oil refining, truck and bus assembly, textiles, fertilizer, building materials, electricity, ship construction and repair
Industrial production growth rate: 15% (1998 est.)
Electricity - production: 5.127 billion kWh (2003)
Electricity - production by source:
fossil fuel: 61.9%
hydro: 38.1%
nuclear: 0%
other: 0% (2001)
Electricity - consumption: 3.418 billion kWh (2003)
Electricity - exports: 1.35 billion kWh (2003)
Electricity - imports: 0 kWh (2003)
Oil - production: 32,900 bbl/day (2005 est.)
Oil - consumption: 20,000 bbl/day (2003 est.)
Oil - exports: NA (2001)
Oil - imports: NA (2001)
Oil - proved reserves: 220 million bbl (2005 est.)
Natural gas - production: 1.35 billion cu m (2001 est.)
Natural gas - consumption: 1.35 billion cu m (2001 est.)
Natural gas - exports: 0 cu m (2001 est.)
Natural gas - imports: 0 cu m (2001 est.)
Natural gas - proved reserves: 14.87 billion cu m (2005)
Current account balance: $-289 million (2005 est.)
Exports: $6.49 billion f.o.b. (2005 est.)
Exports - partners: US 11.6%, Netherlands 10.2%, France 9.5%, Italy 5.5%, Belgium 4.7%, Germany 4.7% (2004)
Imports: $4.759 billion f.o.b. (2005 est.)
Imports - partners: France 24.3%, Nigeria 19.2%, UK 4% (2004)
Reserves of foreign exchange and gold: $1.95 billion (2005 est.)
Debt - external: $13.26 billion (2005 est.)
Economic aid - recipient: ODA, $1 billion (1996 est.)
Currency (code): Communaute Financiere Africaine franc (XOF); note - responsible authority is the Central Bank of the West African States
Currency code: XOF
Exchange rates: Communaute Financiere Africaine francs (XOF) per US dollar - 521.74 (2005), 528.29 (2004), 581.2 (2003), 696.99 (2002), 733.04 (2001)
Fiscal year: calendar year

COMMUNICATION

Telephones - main lines in use: 328,000 (2003)
Telephones - mobile cellular: 1.236 million (2003)
Telephone system:
general assessment: well developed by African standards but operating well below capacity
domestic: open-wire lines and microwave radio relay; 90% digitalized
international: country code - 225; satellite earth stations - 2 Intelsat (1 Atlantic Ocean and 1 Indian Ocean); 2 submarine cables (June 1999)
Radio broadcast stations: AM 2, FM 9, shortwave 3 (1998)
Radios: 2.26 million (1997)
Television broadcast stations: 14 (1999)
Televisions: 1.09 million (2000)
Internet country code: .ci
Internet hosts: 3,795 (2004)
Internet Service Providers (ISPs): 5 (2001)
Internet users: 90,000 (2002)

TRANSPORTATION

Airports: 37 (2004 est.)
Airports - with paved runways:
total: 7
over 3,047 m: 1
2,438 to 3,047 m: 2
1,524 to 2,437 m: 4 (2005 est.)
Airports - with unpaved runways:
total: 28
1,524 to 2,437 m: 8
914 to 1,523 m: 15
under 914 m: 5 (2005 est.)
Pipelines: condensate 107 km; gas 223 km; oil 104 km (2004)
Railways:
total: 660 km
narrow gauge: 660 km 1.000-meter gauge
note: an additional 622 km of this railroad extends into Burkina Faso (2004)
Roadways:
total: 50,400 km
paved: 4,889 km
unpaved: 45,511 km (1999)
Waterways: 980 km (navigable rivers, canals, and numerous coastal lagoons) (2003)
Ports and terminals: Abidjan, Aboisso, Dabou, San-Pedro

MILITARY

Military branches: Army, Navy, Air Force
Military service age and obligation: 18 years of age for compulsory and voluntary military service; conscript service obligation - 18 months (2004)
Manpower available for military service: *males age 18-49:* 3,696,106 (2005 est.)
Manpower fit for military service: *males age 18-49:* 1,973,265 (2005 est.)
Manpower reaching military service age annually: *males:* 189,354 (2005 est.)
Military expenditures - dollar figure: $180.2 million (2004)
Military expenditures - percent of GDP: 1.2% (2004)

TRANSNATIONAL ISSUES

Disputes - international: rebel and ethnic fighting against the central government in 2002 has spilled into neighboring states, driven out foreign cocoa workers from nearby countries, and, in 2004, resulted in 6,000 peacekeepers deployed as part of UN Operation in Cote d'Ivoire (UNOCI) assisting 4,000 French troops already in-country; the Ivorian Government accuses Burkina Faso and Liberia of supporting Ivorian rebels
Refugees and internally displaced persons: *refugees (country of origin):* 71,711 (Liberia)
IDPs: 500,000 (2002 coup; most IDPs are in western regions) (2004)
Illicit drugs: illicit producer of cannabis, mostly for local consumption; transshipment point for Southwest and Southeast Asian heroin to Europe and occasionally to the US, and for Latin American cocaine destined for Europe and South Africa; while rampant corruption and inadequate supervision leave the banking system vulnerable to money laundering, the lack of a developed financial system limits the country's utility as a major money-laundering center

CROATIA

INTRODUCTION

Background: The lands that today comprise Croatia were part of the Austro-Hungarian Empire until the close of World War I. In 1918, the Croats, Serbs, and Slovenes formed a kingdom known after 1929 as Yugoslavia. Following World War II, Yugoslavia became a federal independent Communist state under the strong hand of Marshal TITO. Although Croatia declared its independence from Yugoslavia in 1991, it took four years of sporadic, but often bitter, fighting before occupying Serb armies were mostly cleared from Croatian lands. Under UN supervision, the last Serb-held enclave in eastern Slavonia was returned to Croatia in 1998.

GEOGRAPHY

Location: Southeastern Europe, bordering the Adriatic Sea, between Bosnia and Herzegovina and Slovenia

Geographic coordinates: 45 10 N, 15 30 E

Map references: Europe

Area:
total: 56,542 sq km
land: 56,414 sq km
water: 128 sq km

Area - comparative: slightly smaller than West Virginia

Land boundaries:
total: 2,197 km
border countries: Bosnia and Herzegovina 932 km, Hungary 329 km, Serbia and Montenegro (north) 241 km, Serbia and Montenegro (south) 25 km, Slovenia 670 km

Coastline: 5,835 km (mainland 1,777 km, islands 4,058 km)

Maritime claims:
territorial sea: 12 nm
continental shelf: 200-m depth or to the depth of exploitation

Climate: Mediterranean and continental; continental climate predominant with hot summers and cold winters; mild winters, dry summers along coast

Terrain: geographically diverse; flat plains along Hungarian border, low mountains and highlands near Adriatic coastline and islands

Elevation extremes:
lowest point: Adriatic Sea 0 m
highest point: Dinara 1,830 m

Natural resources: oil, some coal, bauxite, low-grade iron ore, calcium, gypsum, natural asphalt, silica, mica, clays, salt, hydropower

Land use:
arable land: 26.09%
permanent crops: 2.27%
other: 71.65% (2001)

Irrigated land: 30 sq km (1998 est.)

Natural hazards: destructive earthquakes

Environment - current issues: air pollution (from metallurgical plants) and resulting acid rain is damaging the forests; coastal pollution from industrial and domestic waste; landmine removal and reconstruction of infrastructure consequent to 1992-95 civil strife

Environment - international agreements:
party to: Air Pollution, Air Pollution-Sulfur 94, Biodiversity, Climate Change, Desertification, Endangered Species, Hazardous Wastes, Law of the Sea, Marine Dumping, Ozone Layer Protection, Ship Pollution, Wetlands
signed, but not ratified: Air Pollution-Persistent Organic Pollutants, Climate Change-Kyoto Protocol

Geography - note: controls most land routes from Western Europe to Aegean Sea and Turkish Straits

PEOPLE

Population: 4,495,904 (July 2005 est.)

Age structure:
0-14 years: 16.4% (male 378,615/female 359,231)
15-64 years: 67% (male 1,497,355/female 1,514,993)
65 years and over: 16.6% (male 283,460/female 462,250) (2005 est.)

Median age:
total: 39.97 years
male: 38.01 years
female: 41.76 years (2005 est.)

Population growth rate:-0.02% (2005 est.)

Birth rate: 9.57 births/1,000 population (2005 est.)

Death rate: 11.38 deaths/1,000 population (2005 est.)

Net migration rate: 1.58 migrant(s)/1,000 population (2005 est.)

Sex ratio:
at birth: 1.06 male(s)/female
under 15 years: 1.05 male(s)/female
15-64 years: 0.99 male(s)/female
65 years and over: 0.61 male(s)/female
total population: 0.92 male(s)/female (2005 est.)

Infant mortality rate:
total: 6.84 deaths/1,000 live births
male: 6.79 deaths/1,000 live births
female: 6.88 deaths/1,000 live births (2005 est.)

Life expectancy at birth:
total population: 74.45 years
male: 70.79 years
female: 78.31 years (2005 est.)

Total fertility rate: 1.39 children born/woman (2005 est.)

HIV/AIDS - adult prevalence rate: less than 0.1% (2001 est.)

HIV/AIDS - people living with HIV/AIDS: 200 (2001 est.)

HIV/AIDS - deaths: less than 10 (2001 est.)

Nationality:
noun: Croat(s), Croatian(s)
adjective: Croatian

Ethnic groups: Croat 89.6%, Serb 4.5%, other 5.9% (including Bosniak, Hungarian, Slovene, Czech, and Roma) (2001 census)

Religions: Roman Catholic 87.8%, Orthodox 4.4%, other Christian 0.4%, Muslim 1.3%, other and unspecified 0.9%, none 5.2% (2001 census)

Languages: Croatian 96.1%, Serbian 1%, other and undesignated 2.9% (including Italian, Hungarian, Czech, Slovak, and German) (2001 census)

Literacy:
definition: age 15 and over can read and write
total population: 98.5%
male: 99.4%
female: 97.8% (2003 est.)

GOVERNMENT

Country name:
conventional long form: Republic of Croatia
conventional short form: Croatia
local long form: Republika Hrvatska
local short form: Hrvatska
former: People's Republic of Croatia, Socialist Republic of Croatia

Government type: presidential/parliamentary democracy

Capital: Zagreb

Administrative divisions: 20 counties (zupanije, zupanija - singular) and 1 city* (grad - singular); Bjelovarsko-Bilogorska Zupanija, Brodsko-Posavska Zupanija, Dubrovacko-Neretvanska Zupanija, Istarska Zupanija,

Karlovacka Zupanija, Koprivnicko-Krizevacka Zupanija, Krapinsko-Zagorska Zupanija, Licko-Senjska Zupanija, Medimurska Zupanija, Osjecko-Baranjska Zupanija, Pozesko-Slavonska Zupanija, Primorsko-Goranska Zupanija, Sibensko-Kninska Zupanija, Sisacko-Moslavacka Zupanija, Splitsko-Dalmatinska Zupanija, Varazdinska Zupanija, Viroviticko-Podravska Zupanija, Vukovarsko-Srijemska Zupanija, Zadarska Zupanija, Zagreb*, Zagrebacka Zupanija

Independence: 25 June 1991 (from Yugoslavia)

National holiday: Independence Day, 8 October (1991); note - 25 June 1991 is the day the Croatian Parliament voted for independence; following a 3-month moratorium to allow the European Community to solve the Yugoslav crisis peacefully, Parliament adopted a decision on 8 October 1991 to sever constitutional relations with Yugoslavia

Constitution: adopted on 22 December 1990; revised 2000, 2001

Legal system: based on civil law system

Suffrage: 18 years of age; universal (16 years of age, if employed)

Executive branch:
chief of state: President Stjepan (Stipe) MESIC (since 18 February 2000)
head of government: Prime Minister Ivo SANADER (since 9 December 2003); Deputy Prime Ministers Jadranka KOSOR (since 23 December 2003) and Damir POLANCEC (since NA February 2005)
cabinet: Council of Ministers named by the prime minister and approved by the parliamentary Assembly
elections: president elected by popular vote for a five-year term; election last held 16 January 2005 (next to be held January 2010); the leader of the majority party or the leader of the majority coalition is usually appointed prime minister by the president and then approved by the Assembly
election results: Stjepan Mesic reelected president; percent of vote - Stjepan MESIC 66%, Jadranka KOSOR (HDZ) 34% in the second round

Legislative branch: unicameral Assembly or Sabor (152 seats; note - one seat was added in the November 2003 parliamentary elections; members elected from party lists by popular vote to serve four-year terms)
elections: Assembly - last held 23 November 2003 (next to be held in 2007)
election results: Assembly - percent of vote by party - NA%; number of seats by party - HDZ 66, SDP 34, HSS 10, HNS 10, HSP 8, IDS 4, Libra 3, HSU 3, SDSS 3, other 11
note: minority government coalition - HDZ, DC, HSLS, HSU, SDSS

Judicial branch: Supreme Court; Constitutional Court; judges for both courts appointed for eight-year terms by the Judicial Council of the Republic, which is elected by the Assembly

Political parties and leaders: Croatian Bloc or HB [Ivic PASALIC]; Croatian Christian Democratic Union or HKDU [Anto KOVACEVIC]; Croatian Democratic Union or HDZ [Ivo SANADER]; Croatian Party of Rights or HSP [Anto DJAPIC]; Croatian Peasant Party or HSS [Josip FRISCIC]; Croatian Pensioner Party or HSU [Vladimir JORDAN]; Croatian People's Party or HNS [Vesna PUSIC] (in 2005 party merged with Libra to become Croatian People's Party-Liberal Democrats or NS-LD [Vesna PUSIC]); Croatian Social Liberal Party or HSLS [Ivan CEHOK]; Croatian True Revival Party or HIP [Miroslav TUDJMAN]; Democratic Centre or DC [Vesna SKARE-OZBOLT]; Independent Democratic Serb Party or SDSS [Vojislav STANIMIROVIC]; Istrian Democratic Forum or IDF [Luciano DELBIANCO]; Liberal Party or LS [Zlatko BENASIC]; Social Democratic Party of Croatia or SDP [Ivica RACAN]

Political pressure groups and leaders: NA

International organization participation: ACCT (observer), BIS, CE, CEI, EAPC, EBRD, FAO, IADB, IAEA, IBRD, ICAO, ICC, ICCt, ICFTU, ICRM, IDA, IFAD, IFC, IFRCS, IHO, ILO, IMF, IMO, Interpol, IOC, IOM, ISO, ITU, MIGA, MINURSO, MINUSTAH, NAM (observer), OAS (observer), OPCW, OSCE, PCA, PFP, UN, UNAMSIL, UNCTAD, UNESCO, UNFICYP, UNIDO, UNMEE, UNMIL, UNMIS, UNMOGIP, UNOCI, UNOMIG, UPU, WCO, WHO, WIPO, WMO, WToO, WTO

Diplomatic representation in the US:
chief of mission: Ambassador Neven JURICA
chancery: 2343 Massachusetts Avenue NW, Washington, DC 20008
telephone: [1] (202) 588-5899
FAX: [1] (202) 588-8936
consulate(s) general: Chicago, Los Angeles, New York

Diplomatic representation from the US:
chief of mission: Ambassador Ralph FRANK
embassy: 2 Thomas Jefferson, 10010 Zagreb
mailing address: use street address
telephone: [385] (1) 661-2200
FAX: [385] (1) 661-2373

Flag description: red, white, and blue horizontal bands with Croatian coat of arms (red and white checkered)

ECONOMY

Economy - overview: Before the dissolution of Yugoslavia, the Republic of Croatia, after Slovenia, was the most prosperous and industrialized area, with a per capita output perhaps one-third above the Yugoslav average. The economy emerged from a mild recession in 2000 with tourism, banking, and public investments leading the way. Unemployment remains high, at about 18 percent, with structural factors slowing its decline. While macroeconomic stabilization has largely been achieved, structural reforms lag because of deep resistance on the part of the public and lack of strong support from politicians. Growth, while impressively about 3% to 4% for the last several years, has been stimulated, in part, through high fiscal deficits and rapid credit growth. The EU accession process should accelerate fiscal and structural reform.

GDP (purchasing power parity): $53.29 billion (2005 est.)

GDP (official exchange rate): $35.77 billion (2005 est.)

GDP - real growth rate: 3.2% (2005 est.)

GDP - per capita: purchasing power parity - $11,600 (2005 est.)

GDP - composition by sector:
agriculture: 8.1%
industry: 31%
services: 60.8% (2005 est.)

Labor force: 1.71 million (2005 est.)

Labor force - by occupation: agriculture 2.7%, industry 32.8%, services 64.5% (2004)

Unemployment rate: 18.7% official rate; labor force surveys indicate unemployment around 14% (December 2004 est.)

Population below poverty line: 11% (2003)

Household income or consumption by percentage share:
lowest 10%: 3.4%
highest 10%: 24.5% (2003 est.)

Distribution of family income - Gini index: 29 (2001)

Inflation rate (consumer prices): 3.2% (2005 est.)

Investment (gross fixed): 28.1% of GDP (2005 est.)

Budget:
revenues: $17.69 billion
expenditures: $19.35 billion, including capital expenditures of NA (2005 est.)

Public debt: 52.1% of GDP (2005 est.)
Agriculture - products: wheat, corn, sugar beets, sunflower seed, barley, alfalfa, clover, olives, citrus, grapes, soybeans, potatoes; livestock, dairy products
Industries: chemicals and plastics, machine tools, fabricated metal, electronics, pig iron and rolled steel products, aluminum, paper, wood products, construction materials, textiles, shipbuilding, petroleum and petroleum refining, food and beverages; tourism
Industrial production growth rate: 4.5% (2005 est.)
Electricity - production: 11.15 billion kWh (2003)
Electricity - production by source:
fossil fuel: 33.6%
hydro: 66%
nuclear: 0%
other: 0.4% (2001)
Electricity - consumption: 15.81 billion kWh (2003)
Electricity - exports: 550 million kWh (2003)
Electricity - imports: 5.99 billion kWh (2003)
Oil - production: 20,500 bbl/day (2005 est.)
Oil - consumption: 90,000 bbl/day (2003 est.)
Oil - exports: NA (2001)
Oil - imports: NA (2001)
Oil - proved reserves: 93.6 million bbl (1 January 2002)
Natural gas - production: 1.76 billion cu m (2001 est.)
Natural gas - consumption: 2.84 billion cu m (2001 est.)
Natural gas - exports: 0 cu m (2001 est.)
Natural gas - imports: 1.08 billion cu m (2001 est.)
Natural gas - proved reserves: 34.36 billion cu m (1 January 2002)
Current account balance: $-1.79 billion (2005 est.)
Exports: $10.3 billion f.o.b. (2005 est.)
Exports - partners: Italy 23%, Bosnia and Herzegovina 13.4%, Germany 11.4%, Austria 9.6%, Slovenia 7.6% (2004)
Imports: $18.93 billion f.o.b. (2005 est.)
Imports - partners: Italy 17.1%, Germany 15.5%, Russia 7.3%, Slovenia 7.1%, Austria 6.9%, France 4.4% (2004)
Reserves of foreign exchange and gold: $8.811 billion (2005 est.)
Debt - external: $29.28 billion (30 June 2005 est.)
Economic aid - recipient: ODA $166.5 million (2002)
Currency (code): kuna (HRK)
Currency code: HRK
Exchange rates: kuna per US dollar - 5.92 (2005), 6.0358 (2004), 6.7035 (2003), 7.8687 (2002), 8.34 (2001)
Fiscal year: calendar year

COMMUNICATION

Telephones - main lines in use: 1.825 million (2002)
Telephones - mobile cellular: 2.553 million (2003)
Telephone system:
general assessment: NA
domestic: reconstruction plan calls for replacement of all analog circuits with digital and enlarging the network; a backup will be included in the plan for the main trunk
international: country code - 385; digital international service is provided through the main switch in Zagreb; Croatia participates in the Trans-Asia-Europe (TEL) fiber-optic project, which consists of two fiber-optic trunk connections with Slovenia and a fiber-optic trunk line from Rijeka to Split and Dubrovnik; Croatia is also investing in ADRIA 1, a joint fiber-optic project with Germany, Albania, and Greece (2000)
Radio broadcast stations: AM 16, FM 98, shortwave 5 (1999)
Radios: 1.51 million (1997)
Television broadcast stations: 36 (plus 321 repeaters) (September 1995)
Televisions: 1.22 million (1997)
Internet country code: .hr
Internet hosts: 29,644 (2004)
Internet Service Providers (ISPs): 9 (2000)
Internet users: 1.014 million (2003)

TRANSPORTATION

Airports: 68 (2004 est.)
Airports - with paved runways:
total: 23
over 3,047 m: 2
2,438 to 3,047 m: 6
1,524 to 2,437 m: 2
914 to 1,523 m: 4
under 914 m: 9 (2005 est.)
Airports - with unpaved runways:
total: 45
1,524 to 2,437 m: 1
914 to 1,523 m: 7
under 914 m: 37 (2005 est.)
Heliports: 1 (2005 est.)
Pipelines: gas 1,340 km; oil 583 km (2004)
Railways:
total: 2,726 km
standard gauge: 2,726 km 1.435-m gauge (984 km electrified) (2004)
Roadways:
total: 28,588 km
paved: 24,186 km (including 583 km of expressways)
unpaved: 4,402 km (2003)
Waterways: 785 km (2004)
Merchant marine:
total: 73 ships (1,000 GRT or over) 750,579 GRT/1,178,786 DWT
by type: bulk carrier 25, cargo 12, chemical tanker 2, passenger/cargo 25, petroleum tanker 4, refrigerated cargo 1, roll on/roll off 4
foreign-owned: 1 (Denmark 1)
registered in other countries: 31 (2005)
Ports and terminals: Omisalj, Ploce, Rijeka, Sibenik, Vukovar (on Danube)

MILITARY

Military branches: Ground Forces (Hrvatska Vojska, HKoV), Naval Forces (Hrvatska Ratna Mornarica, HRM), Air and Air Defense Forces (Hrvatsko Ratno Zrakoplovstvo i Protuzrakoplovna Obrana, HRZiPZO)
Military service age and obligation: 18 years of age for compulsory military service, with 6-month service obligation; 16 years of age with consent for voluntary service; Croatian Military Police planning to end conscription in 2005 (December 2004)
Manpower available for military service: *males age 18-49:* 1,005,058 (2005 est.)
Manpower fit for military service: *males age 18-49:* 725,914 (2005 est.)
Manpower reaching military service age annually: *males:* 29,020 (2005 est.)
Military expenditures - dollar figure: $620 million (2004)
Military expenditures - percent of GDP: 2.39% (2002 est.)

TRANSNATIONAL ISSUES

Disputes - international: discussions continue with Bosnia and Herzegovina over several small disputed sections of the boundary; the Croatia-Slovenia land and maritime boundary agreement, which would have ceded most of Pirin Bay and maritime access to Slovenia and several villages to Croatia, remains un-ratified and in dispute; as a European Union peripheral state, neighboring Slovenia must conform to the strict Schengen border rules to curb illegal migration and commerce through southeastern Europe while encouraging close cross-border ties with Croatia
Refugees and internally displaced persons: *IDPs:* 12,600 (Croats and Serbs displaced in 1992-1995 war) (2004)
Illicit drugs: transit point along the Balkan route for Southwest Asian heroin to Western Europe; has been used as a transit point for maritime shipments of South American cocaine bound for Western Europe

CUBA

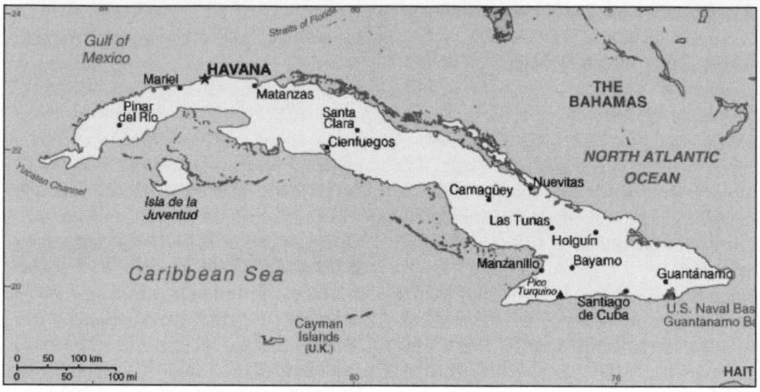

INTRODUCTION

Background: The native Amerindian population of Cuba began to decline after the European discovery of the island by Christopher COLUMBUS in 1492 and following its development as a Spanish colony during the next several centuries. Large numbers of African slaves were imported to work the coffee and sugar plantations and Havana became the launching point for the annual treasure fleets bound for Spain from Mexico and Peru. Spanish rule, marked initially by neglect, became increasingly repressive, provoking an independence movement and occasional rebellions which were harshly suppressed. It was US intervention during the Spanish-American War in 1898 that finally overthrew Spanish rule. The subsequent Treaty of Paris established Cuban independence, which was granted in 1902 after a three-year transition period. Fidel CASTRO led a rebel army to victory in 1959; his iron rule has held the regime together since then. Cuba's Communist regime, with Soviet support, attempted to export its revolution throughout Latin America and Africa during the 1960s, 1970s, and 1980s. The country is now slowly recovering from a severe economic recession in 1990, following the withdrawal of former Soviet subsidies, worth $4 billion to $6 billion annually. Cuba portrays its difficulties as the result of the US embargo in place since 1961. Illicit migration to the US - using homemade rafts, alien smugglers, air flights, or via the southwest border - is a continuing problem. The US Coast Guard intercepted 2,712 individuals attempting to cross the Straits of Florida in fiscal year 2005.

GEOGRAPHY

Location: Caribbean, island between the Caribbean Sea and the North Atlantic Ocean, 150 km south of Key West, Florida
Geographic coordinates: 21 30 N, 80 00 W
Map references: Central America and the Caribbean
Area:
total: 110,860 sq km
land: 110,860 sq km
water: 0 sq km
Area - comparative: slightly smaller than Pennsylvania
Land boundaries:
total: 29 km
border countries: US Naval Base at Guantanamo Bay 29 km
note: Guantanamo Naval Base is leased by the US and thus remains part of Cuba
Coastline: 3,735 km
Maritime claims:
territorial sea: 12 nm
exclusive economic zone: 200 nm
Climate: tropical; moderated by trade winds; dry season (November to April); rainy season (May to October)
Terrain: mostly flat to rolling plains, with rugged hills and mountains in the southeast
Elevation extremes:
lowest point: Caribbean Sea 0 m
highest point: Pico Turquino 2,005 m
Natural resources: cobalt, nickel, iron ore, chromium, copper, salt, timber, silica, petroleum, arable land
Land use:
arable land: 33.05%
permanent crops: 7.6%
other: 59.35% (2001)
Irrigated land: 870 sq km (1998 est.)
Natural hazards: the east coast is subject to hurricanes from August to November (in general, the country averages about one hurricane every other year); droughts are common
Environment - current issues: air and water pollution; biodiversity loss; deforestation
Environment - international agreements:
party to: Antarctic Treaty, Biodiversity, Climate Change, Climate Change-Kyoto Protocol, Desertification, Endangered Species, Environmental Modification, Hazardous Wastes, Law of the Sea, Marine Dumping, Ozone Layer Protection, Ship Pollution, Wetlands
signed, but not ratified: Marine Life Conservation
Geography - note: largest country in Caribbean and westernmost island of the Greater Antilles

PEOPLE

Population: 11,346,670 (July 2005 est.)
Age structure:
0-14 years: 19.6% (male 1,139,644/female 1,079,412)
15-64 years: 70.1% (male 3,977,110/female 3,975,818)
65 years and over: 10.4% (male 540,720/female 633,966) (2005 est.)
Median age:
total: 35.36 years
male: 34.73 years
female: 35.98 years (2005 est.)
Population growth rate: 0.33% (2005 est.)
Birth rate: 12.03 births/1,000 population (2005 est.)
Death rate: 7.19 deaths/1,000 population (2005 est.)
Net migration rate: -1.58 migrant(s)/1,000 population (2005 est.)
Sex ratio:
at birth: 1.06 male(s)/female
under 15 years: 1.06 male(s)/female
15-64 years: 1 male(s)/female
65 years and over: 0.85 male(s)/female
total population: 0.99 male(s)/female (2005 est.)
Infant mortality rate:
total: 6.33 deaths/1,000 live births
male: 7.11 deaths/1,000 live births
female: 5.5 deaths/1,000 live births (2005 est.)
Life expectancy at birth:
total population: 77.23 years
male: 74.94 years
female: 79.65 years (2005 est.)
Total fertility rate: 1.66 children born/woman (2005 est.)
HIV/AIDS - adult prevalence rate: less than 0.1% (2003 est.)
HIV/AIDS - people living with HIV/AIDS: 3,300 (2003 est.)
HIV/AIDS - deaths: less than 200 (2003 est.)
Nationality:
noun: Cuban(s)
adjective: Cuban
Ethnic groups: mulatto 51%, white 37%, black 11%, Chinese 1%
Religions: nominally 85% Roman Catholic prior to CASTRO assuming power; Protestants, Jehovah's Witnesses, Jews, and Santeria are also represented
Languages: Spanish

Literacy:
definition: age 15 and over can read and write
total population: 97%
male: 97.2%
female: 96.9% (2003 est.)
People - note: illicit migration is a continuing problem; Cubans attempt to depart the island and enter the US using homemade rafts, alien smugglers, direct flights, or falsified visas; Cubans also use non-maritime routes to enter the US including direct flights to Miami and overland via the southwest border

GOVERNMENT

Country name:
conventional long form: Republic of Cuba
conventional short form: Cuba
local long form: Republica de Cuba
local short form: Cuba
Government type: Communist state
Capital: Havana
Administrative divisions: 14 provinces (provincias, singular - provincia) and 1 special municipality* (municipio especial); Camaguey, Ciego de Avila, Cienfuegos, Ciudad de La Habana, Granma, Guantanamo, Holguin, Isla de la Juventud*, La Habana, Las Tunas, Matanzas, Pinar del Rio, Sancti Spiritus, Santiago de Cuba, Villa Clara
Independence: 20 May 1902 (from Spain 10 December 1898; administered by the US from 1898 to 1902)
National holiday: Independence Day, 10 December (1898); note - 10 December 1898 is the date of independence from Spain, 20 May 1902 is the date of independence from US administration; Rebellion Day, 26 July (1953)
Constitution: 24 February 1976; amended July 1992 and June 2002
Legal system: based on Spanish and American law, with large elements of Communist legal theory; has not accepted compulsory ICJ jurisdiction
Suffrage: 16 years of age; universal
Executive branch:
chief of state: President of the Council of State and President of the Council of Ministers Fidel CASTRO Ruz (prime minister from February 1959 until 24 February 1976 when office was abolished; president since 2 December 1976); First Vice President of the Council of State and First Vice President of the Council of Ministers Gen. Raul CASTRO Ruz (since 2 December 1976); note - the president is both the chief of state and head of government
head of government: President of the Council of State and President of the Council of Ministers Fidel CASTRO Ruz (prime minister from February 1959 until 24 February 1976 when office was abolished; president since 2 December 1976); First Vice President of the Council of State and First Vice President of the Council of Ministers Gen. Raul CASTRO Ruz (since 2 December 1976); note - the president is both the chief of state and head of government
cabinet: Council of Ministers proposed by the president of the Council of State and appointed by the National Assembly or the 31-member Council of State, elected by the Assembly to act on its behalf when it is not in session
elections: president and vice presidents elected by the National Assembly for a term of five years; election last held 6 March 2003 (next to be held in 2008)
election results: Fidel CASTRO Ruz reelected president; percent of legislative vote - 100%; Raul CASTRO Ruz elected vice president; percent of legislative vote - 100%
Legislative branch: unicameral National Assembly of People's Power or Asemblea Nacional del Poder Popular (609 seats, elected directly from slates approved by special candidacy commissions; members serve five-year terms)
elections: last held 19 January 2003 (next to be held in NA 2008)
election results: percent of vote - PCC 97.6%; seats - PCC 609
Judicial branch: People's Supreme Court or Tribunal Supremo Popular (president, vice president, and other judges are elected by the National Assembly)
Political parties and leaders: only party - Cuban Communist Party or PCC [Fidel CASTRO Ruz, first secretary]
Political pressure groups and leaders: NA
International organization participation: ACP, FAO, G-77, IAEA, ICAO, ICC, ICRM, IFAD, IFRCS, IHO, ILO, IMO, Interpol, IOC, IOM (observer), ISO, ITU, LAES, LAIA, NAM, OAS (excluded from formal participation since 1962), OPANAL, OPCW, PCA, UN, UNCTAD, UNESCO, UNIDO, UPU, WCL, WCO, WFTU, WHO, WIPO, WMO, WToO, WTO
Diplomatic representation in the US: none; note - Cuba has an Interests Section in the Swiss Embassy, headed by Principal Officer Dagoberto RODRIGUEZ Barrera; address: Cuban Interests Section, Swiss Embassy, 2630 16th Street NW, Washington, DC 20009; telephone: [1] (202) 797-8518
Diplomatic representation from the US: none; note - the US has an Interests Section in the Swiss Embassy, headed by Principal Officer Michael E. PARMLY; address: USINT, Swiss Embassy, Calzada between L and M Streets, Vedado, Havana; telephone: [53] (7) 833-3551 through 3559 (operator assistance required); FAX: [53] (7) 833-3700; protecting power in Cuba is Switzerland
Flag description: five equal horizontal bands of blue (top, center, and bottom) alternating with white; a red equilateral triangle based on the hoist side bears a white, five-pointed star in the center

ECONOMY

Economy - overview: The government continues to balance the need for economic loosening against a desire for firm political control. It has rolled back limited reforms undertaken in the 1990s to increase enterprise efficiency and alleviate serious shortages of food, consumer goods, and services. The average Cuban's standard of living remains at a lower level than before the downturn of the 1990s, which was caused by the loss of Soviet aid and domestic inefficiencies. The government in 2005 strengthened its controls over dollars coming into the economy from tourism, remittances, and trade. External financing has helped growth in the mining, oil, construction, and tourism sectors.
GDP (purchasing power parity): $37.05 billion (2005 est.)
GDP (official exchange rate): NA
GDP - real growth rate: 5.2% (2005 est.)
GDP - per capita: purchasing power parity - $3,300 (2005 est.)
GDP - composition by sector:
agriculture: 5.5%
industry: 26.1%
services: 68.4% (2005 est.)
Labor force: 4.6 million
note: state sector 78%, non-state sector 22% (2005 est.)
Labor force - by occupation: agriculture 21.2%, industry 14.4%, services 64.4% (2004)
Unemployment rate: 1.9% (2005 est.)
Population below poverty line: NA
Household income or consumption by percentage share:
lowest 10%: NA
highest 10%: NA
Inflation rate (consumer prices): 4.2% (2005 est.)
Investment (gross fixed): 9.8% of GDP (2005 est.)
Budget:
revenues: $22.11 billion
expenditures: $23.65 billion, including capital expenditures of NA (2005 est.)
Agriculture - products: sugar, tobacco, citrus, coffee, rice, potatoes, beans; livestock
Industries: sugar, petroleum, tobacco, construction, nickel, steel, cement, agricultural machinery, pharmaceuticals
Industrial production growth rate: 3.5% (2005 est.)

Electricity - production: 15.65 billion kWh (2004)
Electricity - production by source:
fossil fuel: 93.9%
hydro: 0.6%
nuclear: 0%
other: 5.4% (2001)
Electricity - consumption: 14.62 billion kWh (2003)
Electricity - exports: 0 kWh (2003)
Electricity - imports: 0 kWh (2003)
Oil - production: 72,000 bbl/day (2005 est.)
Oil - consumption: 205,000 bbl/day (2003 est.)
Oil - exports: NA (2001)
Oil - imports: NA (2001)
Oil - proved reserves: 532 million bbl (1 January 2002)
Natural gas - production: 704 million cu m (2004)
Natural gas - consumption: 704 million cu m (2004)
Natural gas - exports: 0 cu m (2004)
Natural gas - imports: 0 cu m (2004)
Natural gas - proved reserves: 42.62 billion cu m (1 January 2002)
Current account balance: $-748 million (2005 est.)
Exports: $2.388 billion f.o.b. (2005 est.)
Exports - partners: Netherlands 22.7%, Canada 20.6%, China 7.7%, Russia 7.5%, Spain 6.4%, Venezuela 4.4% (2004)
Imports: $6.916 billion f.o.b. (2005 est.)
Imports - partners: Spain 14.7%, Venezuela 13.5%, US 11%, China 8.9%, Canada 6.4%, Italy 6.2%, Mexico 4.9% (2004)
Reserves of foreign exchange and gold: $2.518 billion (2005 est.)
Debt - external: $13.1 billion (convertible currency); another $15-20 billion owed to Russia (2005 est.)
Economic aid - recipient: $68.2 million (1997 est.)
Currency (code): Cuban peso (CUP) and Convertible peso (CUC)
Currency code: CUP (nonconvertible Cuban peso) and CUC (convertible Cuban peso)
Exchange rates: Convertible pesos per US dollar - 0.93
note: Cuba has three currencies in circulation: the Cuban peso (CUP), the convertible peso (CUC), and the US dollar (USD), although the dollar is being withdrawn from circulation; in April 2005 the official exchange rate changed from $1 per CUC to $1.08 per CUC (0.93 CUC per $1), both for individuals and enterprises; individuals can buy 24 Cuban pesos (CUP) for each CUC sold, or sell 25 Cuban pesos for each CUC bought; enterprises, however, must exchange CUP and CUC at a 1:1 ratio.
Fiscal year: calendar year

COMMUNICATION

Telephones - main lines in use: 574,400 (2002)
Telephones - mobile cellular: 17,900 (2002)
Telephone system:
general assessment: greater investment beginning in 1994 and the establishment of a new Ministry of Information Technology and Communications in 2000 has resulted in improvements in the system; wireless service is expensive and remains restricted to foreigners and regime elites, many Cubans procure wireless service illegally with the help of foreigners
domestic: national fiber-optic system under development; 85% of switches digitized by end of 2004; telephone line density remains low, at 10 per 100 inhabitants; domestic cellular service expanding
international: country code - 53; fiber-optic cable laid to but not linked to US network; satellite earth station - 1 Intersputnik (Atlantic Ocean region)
Radio broadcast stations: AM 169, FM 55, shortwave 1 (1998)
Radios: 3.9 million (1997)
Television broadcast stations: 58 (1997)
Televisions: 2.64 million (1997)
Internet country code: .cu
Internet hosts: 1,529 (2003)
Internet Service Providers (ISPs): 5 (2001)
Internet users: 120,000
note: private citizens are prohibited from buying computers or accessing the Internet without special authorization; foreigners may access the Internet in large hotels, but are subject to firewalls; some Cubans buy illegal passwords on the black market, or take advantage of public outlets to access limited email and the government-controlled "intranet" (2004)

TRANSPORTATION

Airports: 170 (2004 est.)
Airports - with paved runways:
total: 78
over 3,047 m: 7
2,438 to 3,047 m: 9
1,524 to 2,437 m: 18
914 to 1,523 m: 7
under 914 m: 37 (2005 est.)
Airports - with unpaved runways:
total: 92
1,524 to 2,437 m: 1
914 to 1,523 m: 29
under 914 m: 62 (2005 est.)
Pipelines: gas 49 km; oil 230 km (2004)
Railways:
total: 4,226 km
standard gauge: 4,226 km 1.435-m gauge (140 km electrified)
note: an additional 7,742 km of track is used by sugar plantations; about 65% of this track is standard gauge; the rest is narrow gauge (2004)
Roadways:
total: 60,858 km
paved: 29,820 km (including 638 km of expressway)
unpaved: 31,038 km (1999)
Waterways: 240 km (2004)
Merchant marine:
total: 15 ships (1,000 GRT or over) 54,818 GRT/81,850 DWT
by type: bulk carrier 2, cargo 4, chemical tanker 1, passenger 2, petroleum tanker 4, refrigerated cargo 2
foreign-owned: 1 (Spain 1)
registered in other countries: 20 (2005)
Ports and terminals: Cienfuegos, Havana, Matanzas

MILITARY

Military branches: Revolutionary Armed Forces (FAR): Revolutionary Army (ER), Revolutionary Navy (MGR), Air and Air Defense Force (DAAFAR), Territorial Militia Troops (MTT), Youth Labor Army (EJT)
Military service age and obligation: 17 years of age; both sexes are eligible for military service (2004)
Manpower available for military service:
males age 17-49: 2,967,865
females age 17-49: 2,913,559 (2005 est.)
Manpower fit for military service:
males age 17-49: 2,441,927
females age 17-49: 2,396,741 (2005 est.)
Manpower reaching military service age annually: *males:* 91,901
females: 87,500 (2005 est.)
Military expenditures - dollar figure: $572.3 million (2003)
Military expenditures - percent of GDP: 1.8% (2003)
Military - note: Moscow, for decades the key military supporter and supplier of Cuba, cut off almost all military aid by 1993

TRANSNATIONAL ISSUES

Disputes - international: US Naval Base at Guantanamo Bay is leased to US and only mutual agreement or US abandonment of the area can terminate the lease
Illicit drugs: territorial waters and air space serve as transshipment zone primarily for marijuana bound for North America; established the death penalty for certain drug-related crimes in 1999

CYPRUS

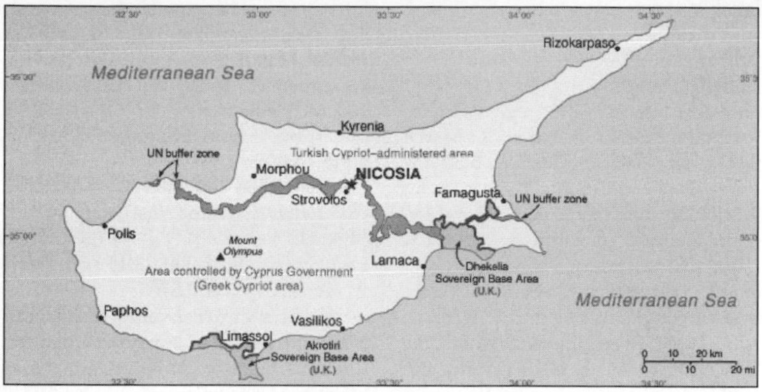

INTRODUCTION

Background: A former British colony, Cyprus received independence in 1960 following years of resistance to British rule. Tensions between the Greek Cypriot majority and Turkish Cypriot minority came to a head in December 1963, when violence broke out in the capital of Nicosia. Despite the deployment of UN peacekeepers in 1964, sporadic intercommunal violence continued forcing most Turkish Cypriots into enclaves throughout the island. In 1974, a Greek-sponsored attempt to seize the government was met by military intervention from Turkey, which soon controlled more than a third of the island. In 1983, the Turkish-held area declared itself the "Turkish Republic of Northern Cyprus," but it is recognized only by Turkey. The latest two-year round of UN-brokered direct talks - between the leaders of the Greek Cypriot and Turkish Cypriot communities to reach an agreement to reunite the divided island - ended when the Greek Cypriots rejected the UN settlement plan in an April 2004 referendum. The entire island entered the EU on 1 May 2004, although the EU acquis - the body of common rights and obligations - applies only to the areas under direct Republic of Cyprus control. At present, every Cypriot carrying a Cyprus passport has the status of a European citizen; however, EU laws do not apply to north Cyprus. Nicosia continues to oppose EU efforts to establish direct trade and economic links to north Cyprus as a way of encouraging the Turkish Cypriot community to continue to support reunification.

GEOGRAPHY

Location: Middle East, island in the Mediterranean Sea, south of Turkey
Geographic coordinates: 35 00 N, 33 00 E
Map references: Middle East
Area:
total: 9,250 sq km (of which 3,355 sq km are in north Cyprus)
land: 9,240 sq km
water: 10 sq km
Area - comparative: about 0.6 times the size of Connecticut
Land boundaries:
total: NA; note - boundary with Dhekelia is being resurveyed
border countries: Akrotiri 47.4 km, Dhekelia NA
Coastline: 648 km
Maritime claims:
territorial sea: 12 nm
continental shelf: 200-m depth or to the depth of exploitation
Climate: temperate; Mediterranean with hot, dry summers and cool winters
Terrain: central plain with mountains to north and south; scattered but significant plains along southern coast
Elevation extremes:
lowest point: Mediterranean Sea 0 m
highest point: Mount Olympus 1,951 m
Natural resources: copper, pyrites, asbestos, gypsum, timber, salt, marble, clay earth pigment
Land use:
arable land: 7.79%
permanent crops: 4.44%
other: 87.77% (2001)
Irrigated land: 382 sq km (2001 est.)
Natural hazards: moderate earthquake activity; droughts
Environment - current issues: water resource problems (no natural reservoir catchments, seasonal disparity in rainfall, sea water intrusion to island's largest aquifer, increased salination in the north); water pollution from sewage and industrial wastes; coastal degradation; loss of wildlife habitats from urbanization
Environment - international agreements:
party to: Air Pollution, Air Pollution-Persistent Organic Pollutants, Biodiversity, Climate Change, Climate Change-Kyoto Protocol, Desertification, Endangered Species, Environmental Modification, Hazardous Wastes, Law of the Sea, Marine Dumping, Ozone Layer Protection, Ship Pollution
signed, but not ratified: none of the selected agreements
Geography - note: the third largest island in the Mediterranean Sea (after Sicily and Sardinia)

PEOPLE

Population: 780,133 (July 2005 est.)
Age structure:
0-14 years: 20.9% (male 83,256/female 79,701)
15-64 years: 67.7% (male 267,446/female 260,846)
65 years and over: 11.4% (male 38,766/female 50,118) (2005 est.)
Median age:
total: 34.68 years
male: 33.64 years
female: 35.7 years (2005 est.)
Population growth rate: 0.54% (2005 est.)
Birth rate: 12.57 births/1,000 population (2005 est.)
Death rate: 7.64 deaths/1,000 population (2005 est.)
Net migration rate: 0.43 migrant(s)/1,000 population (2005 est.)
Sex ratio:
at birth: 1.05 male(s)/female
under 15 years: 1.05 male(s)/female
15-64 years: 1.03 male(s)/female
65 years and over: 0.77 male(s)/female
total population: 1 male(s)/female (2005 est.)
Infant mortality rate:
total: 7.18 deaths/1,000 live births
male: 8.94 deaths/1,000 live births
female: 5.33 deaths/1,000 live births (2005 est.)
Life expectancy at birth:
total population: 77.65 years
male: 75.29 years
female: 80.13 years (2005 est.)
Total fertility rate: 1.83 children born/woman (2005 est.)
HIV/AIDS - adult prevalence rate: 0.1% (2003 est.)
HIV/AIDS - people living with HIV/AIDS: less than 1,000 (1999 est.)
HIV/AIDS - deaths: NA
Nationality:
noun: Cypriot(s)
adjective: Cypriot
Ethnic groups: Greek 77%, Turkish 18%, other 5% (2001)
Religions: Greek Orthodox 78%, Muslim 18%, Maronite, Armenian Apostolic, and other 4%
Languages: Greek, Turkish, English

Literacy:
definition: age 15 and over can read and write
total population: 97.6%
male: 98.9%
female: 96.3% (2003 est.)

GOVERNMENT

Country name:
conventional long form: Republic of Cyprus
conventional short form: Cyprus
note: the Turkish Cypriot community (north Cyprus) refers to itself as the "Turkish Republic of Northern Cyprus" (TRNC)

Government type: republic
note: a separation of the two ethnic communities inhabiting the island began following the outbreak of communal strife in 1963; this separation was further solidified after the Turkish intervention in July 1974 that followed a Greek junta-supported coup attempt gave the Turkish Cypriots de facto control in the north; Greek Cypriots control the only internationally recognized government; on 15 November 1983 Turkish Cypriot "President" Rauf DENKTASH declared independence and the formation of a "Turkish Republic of Northern Cyprus" (TRNC), recognized only by Turkey

Capital: Nicosia

Administrative divisions: 6 districts; Famagusta, Kyrenia, Larnaca, Limassol, Nicosia, Paphos; note - Turkish Cypriot area's administrative divisions include Kyrenia, all but a small part of Famagusta, and small parts of Lefkosia (Nicosia) and Larnaca

Independence: 16 August 1960 (from UK); note - Turkish Cypriots proclaimed self-rule on 13 February 1975 and independence in 1983, but these proclamations are only recognized by Turkey

National holiday: Independence Day, 1 October (1960); note - Turkish Cypriots celebrate 15 November (1983) as Independence Day

Constitution: 16 August 1960; from December 1963, the Turkish Cypriots no longer participated in the government; negotiations to create the basis for a new or revised constitution to govern the island and for better relations between Greek and Turkish Cypriots have been held intermittently since the mid-1960s; in 1975, following the 1974 Turkish intervention, Turkish Cypriots created their own constitution and governing bodies within the "Turkish Federated State of Cyprus," which became the "Turkish Republic of Northern Cyprus" when the Turkish Cypriots declared their independence in 1983; a new constitution for the "TRNC" passed by referendum on 5 May 1985

Legal system: based on common law, with civil law modifications

Suffrage: 18 years of age; universal

Executive branch:
chief of state: President Tassos PAPADAPOULOS (since 1 March 2003); note - the president is both the chief of state and head of government; post of vice president is currently vacant; under the 1960 constitution, the post is reserved for a Turkish Cypriot
head of government: President Tassos PAPADAPOULOS (since 1 March 2003); note - the president is both the chief of state and head of government; post of vice president is currently vacant; under the 1960 constitution, the post is reserved for a Turkish Cypriot
cabinet: Council of Ministers appointed jointly by the president and vice president
elections: president elected by popular vote for a five-year term; election last held 16 February 2003 (next to be held February 2008)
election results: Tassos PAPADAPOULOS elected president; percent of vote - Tassos PAPADAPOULOS 51.5%, Glafkos KLIRDIS 38.8%, Alekos MARKIDIS 6.6%
note: Mehmet Ali TALAT becomes "president" of north Cyprus, 24 April 2005, after "presidential" elections on 17 April 2005; results - Mehmet Ali TALAT 55.6%, Dervis EROGLU 22.7%; Ferdi Sabit SOYER is "prime minister"; there is a Council of Ministers (cabinet) in north Cyprus, appointed by the "prime minister"

Legislative branch: unicameral - Republic of Cyprus: House of Representatives or Vouli ANTIPROSOPON (80 seats; 56 assigned to the Greek Cypriots, 24 to Turkish Cypriots; note - only those assigned to Greek Cypriots are filled; members are elected by popular vote to serve five-year terms); north Cyprus: Assembly of the Republic or Cumhuriyet Meclisi (50 seats; members are elected by popular vote to serve five-year terms)
elections: Republic of Cyprus: last held 27 May 2001 (next to be held May 2006); north Cyprus: last held 14 December 2003 (next to be held NA 2008)
election results: Republic of Cyprus: House of Representatives - percent of vote by party - AKEL 34.71%, DISY 34%, DIKO 14.84%, KISOS 6.51%, others 9.94%; seats by party - AKEL (Communist) 20, DISY 19, DIKO 9, KISOS 4, others 4; north Cyprus: Assembly of the Republic - percent of vote by party - CTP 35.8%, UBP 32.3%, Peace and Democratic Movement 13.4%, DP 12.3%; seats by party - CTP 19, UBP 18, Peace and Democratic Movement 6, DP 7

Judicial branch: Supreme Court (judges are appointed jointly by the president and vice president)
note: there is also a Supreme Court in north Cyprus

Political parties and leaders: Republic of Cyprus: Democratic Party or DIKO [Tassos PAPADAPOULOS]; Democratic Rally or DISY [Nikos ANASTASIADHIS]; Fighting Democratic Movement or ADIK [Dinos MIKHAILIDIS]; Green Party of Cyprus [George PERDIKIS]; New Horizons [Nikolaus KOUSTOU]; Restorative Party of the Working People or AKEL (Communist Party) [Dimitrios CHRISTOFIAS]; Social Democratic Party or EDEK (formerly United Democratic Union of Cyprus) [Yiannakis OMIROU]; United Democrats Movement or EDE [George VASSILIOU]; north Cyprus: Democratic Party or DP [Serder DENKTASH]; National Birth Party or UDP [Enver EMIN]; National Unity Party or UBP [Dervis EROGLU]; Our Party or BP [Okyay SADIKOGLU]; Patriotic Unity Movement or YBH [Alpay DURDURAN]; Peace and Democratic Movement [Mustafa AKINCI]; Republican Turkish Party or CTP [Mehmet Ali TALAT]

Political pressure groups and leaders: Confederation of Cypriot Workers or SEK (pro-West); Confederation of Revolutionary Labor Unions or Dev-Is; Federation of Turkish Cypriot Labor Unions or Turk-Sen; Pan-Cyprian Labor Federation or PEO (Communist controlled)

International organization participation: Australia Group, C, CE, EBRD, EIB, EU (new member), FAO, IAEA, IBRD, ICAO, ICC, ICCt, ICFTU, IDA, IFAD, IFC, IHO, ILO, IMF, IMO, Interpol, IOC, IOM, ISO, ITU, MIGA, NAM, NSG, OAS (observer), OPCW, OSCE, PCA, UN, UNCTAD, UNESCO, UNHCR, UNIDO, UPU, WCL, WCO, WFTU, WHO, WIPO, WMO, WToO, WTO

Diplomatic representation in the US:
chief of mission: Ambassador Euripides L. EVRIVIADES
chancery: 2211 R Street NW, Washington, DC 20008
telephone: [1] (202) 462-5772
FAX: [1] (202) 483-6710
consulate(s) general: New York
note: representative of the Turkish Cypriot community in the US is Osman

ERTUG; office at 1667 K Street NW, Washington, DC; telephone [1] (202) 887-6198

Diplomatic representation from the US:
chief of mission: Ambassador Ronasld B. SCHLICHER
embassy: corner of Metochiou and Ploutarchou Streets, Engomi, 2407 Nicosia
mailing address: P. O. Box 24536, 1385 Nikosia
telephone: [357] (22) 393939
FAX: [357] (22) 780944

Flag description: white with a copper-colored silhouette of the island (the name Cyprus is derived from the Greek word for copper) above two green crossed olive branches in the center of the flag; the branches symbolize the hope for peace and reconciliation between the Greek and Turkish communities
note: the "Turkish Republic of Northern Cyprus" flag has a horizontal red stripe at the top and bottom between which is a red crescent and red star on a white field

ECONOMY

Economy - overview: The Republic of Cyprus has a capitalist economy dominated by the service sector, which accounts for 76% of GDP. Tourism and financial services are the most important sectors; erratic growth rates over the past decade reflect the economy's reliance on tourism, which often fluctuates with political instability in the region and economic conditions in Western Europe. Cyprus joined the European Exchange Rate Mechanism (ERM2) in May 2005 and could adopt the euro within the next two years. Although sluggish tourism and poor fiscal management have resulted in high budget deficits since 2001, the government is pursuing reforms to trim the deficit. As in the Turkish sector, water shortages are a perennial problem; a few desalination plants are now on-line. After 10 years of drought, the country received substantial rainfall from 2001-03, alleviating immediate concerns. The Turkish Cypriot economy has roughly one-third of the per capita GDP of the south, and economic growth tends to be volatile, given north Cyprus's relative isolation, bloated public sector, reliance on the Turkish lira, and small market size. The Turkish Cypriot economy grew 15.4% in 2004, fueled by growth in the construction and education sectors as well as increased employment of Turkish Cypriots in the Republic of Cyprus. The Turkish Cypriots are heavily dependent on transfers from the Turkish government. Under the 2003-06 economic protocol, Ankara plans to provide around $550 million to the "TRNC." Agriculture and services, together, employ more than half of the work force, especially with tourism growth and the easing of border restrictions with the Greek Cypriots since April 2003.

GDP (purchasing power parity):
Republic of Cyprus: $16.82 billion; north Cyprus: $4.54 billion (2005 est.)

GDP (official exchange rate): Republic of Cyprus: $15.83 billion (2005 est.)

GDP - real growth rate:
Republic of Cyprus: 3.8% (2005 est.); north Cyprus: 15.4% (2004 est.)

GDP - per capita:
Republic of Cyprus: purchasing power parity - $21,600 (2005 est.); north Cyprus: purchasing power parity - $7,135 (2004 est.)

GDP - composition by sector:
Republic of Cyprus: agriculture 3.8%; industry 20%; services 76.2% (2005 est.)
north Cyprus: agriculture 10.6%; industry 20.5%; services 68.9% (2003 est.)

Labor force: Republic of Cyprus: 370,000, north Cyprus: 95,025 (2005 est.)

Labor force - by occupation:
Republic of Cyprus: 7.4%, agriculture 7.4%, industry 38.2%, services 54.4% (2004 est.)
north Cyprus: agriculture 14.5%, industry 29%, services 56.5%

Unemployment rate:
Republic of Cyprus: 3.5% (2005 est.); north Cyprus: 5.6% (2004 est.)

Population below poverty line: NA

Household income or consumption by percentage share:
lowest 10%: NA%
highest 10%: NA%

Inflation rate (consumer prices):
Republic of Cyprus: 2.3% (2005 est.); north Cyprus: 9.1% (2004 est.)

Investment (gross fixed): Republic of Cyprus: 18.9% of GDP (2005 est.)

Budget:
revenues: Republic of Cyprus - $6.698 billion (2005 est.), north Cyprus - $231.3 million (2003 est.)
expenditures: Republic of Cyprus - $7.122 billion (2005 est.), north Cyprus - $432.8 million (2003 est.)

Public debt: Republic of Cyprus: 72% of GDP (2005 est.)

Agriculture - products: citrus, vegetables, barley, grapes, olives, vegetables, poultry, pork, lamb, kids, dairy, cheese

Industries: tourism, food and beverage processing; cement and gypsum production; ship repair and refurbishment; textiles; light chemicals; metal products; wood, paper, stone, and clay products

Industrial production growth rate:
Republic of Cyprus: 3.7% (2005 est); north Cyprus: -0.3% (2002 est.) (2005 est.)

Electricity - production:
Republic of Cyprus: 3.801 billion kWh; north Cyprus: NA (2003)

Electricity - production by source:
fossil fuel: 100%
hydro: 0%
nuclear: 0%
other: 0% (2001)

Electricity - consumption:
Republic of Cyprus: 3.535 billion kWh (2004); north Cyprus: NA (2003)

Electricity - exports: 0 kWh (2003)

Electricity - imports: 0 kWh (2003)

Oil - production: Republic of Cyprus: 300 bbl/day (2005 est.)

Oil - consumption: Republic of Cyprus: 52,000 bbl/day (2003 est.)

Oil - exports: NA (2001)

Oil - imports: Republic of Cyprus: NA (2001)

Current account balance: Republic of Cyprus: $-849 million (2005 est.)

Exports:
Republic of Cyprus: $1.237 billion f.o.b. north Cyprus: $49.3 million f.o.b. (2005 est.)

Exports - partners: UK 27.2%, Greece 11.9%, Germany 5%, UAE 4.8% (2004)

Imports:
Republic of Cyprus: $5.552 billion f.o.b. north Cyprus: $415.2 million f.o.b. (2005 est.)

Imports - partners: Greece 15.2%, Italy 10.5%, Germany 8.9%, UK 8.6%, France 6.3%, Japan 4.7%, Israel 4.4%, China 4% (2004)

Reserves of foreign exchange and gold:
Republic of Cyprus: $3.989 billion $3.989 billion
north Cyprus: NA (2005 est.)

Debt - external:
Republic of Cyprus: $7.803 billion; north Cyprus: $NA (2005 est.)

Economic aid - recipient:
Republic of Cyprus - NA; north Cyprus - $700 million from Turkey in grants and loans, which are usually forgiven (2003-06)

Currency (code): Greek Cypriot area: Cypriot pound (CYP); Turkish Cypriot area: Turkish New lira (YTL)

Currency code: CYP; TRL

Exchange rates: Cypriot pounds per US dollar - 0.47 (2005), 0.4686 (2004), 0.5174 (2003), 0.6107 (2002), 0.6431 (2001), Turkish new lira per US dollar 1.426 million (2005), 1.426 million (2004), 1.501 million (2003), 1.507 million (2002), 1.226 million (2001)

Fiscal year: calendar year

COMMUNICATION

Telephones - main lines in use: Republic of Cyprus: 427,400 (2002); north Cyprus: 86,228 (2002)

Telephones - mobile cellular: Republic of Cyprus: 417,900 (2002); north Cyprus: 143,178 (2002)

Telephone system:
general assessment: excellent in both Republic of Cyprus and north Cyprus areas
domestic: open-wire, fiber-optic cable, and microwave radio relay
international: country code - 357; tropospheric scatter; 3 coaxial and 5 fiber-optic submarine cables; satellite earth stations - 3 Intelsat (1 Atlantic Ocean and 2 Indian Ocean), 2 Eutelsat, 2 Intersputnik, and 1 Arabsat
Radio broadcast stations: Republic of Cyprus: AM 7, FM 60, shortwave 1 (1998); north Cyprus: AM 3, FM 11, shortwave 1 (1998)
Radios: Greek Cypriot area: 310,000 (1997); Turkish Cypriot area: 56,450 (1994)
Television broadcast stations: Republic of Cyprus: 4 (plus 225 low-power repeaters) (September 1995); north Cyprus: 4 (plus 5 repeaters) (September 1995)
Televisions: Greek Cypriot area: 248,000 (1997); Turkish Cypriot area: 52,300 (1994)
Internet country code: .cy
Internet hosts: 5,901 (2004)
Internet Service Providers (ISPs): 6 (2000)
Internet users: 210,000 (2002)

TRANSPORTATION

Airports: 17 (2004 est.)
Airports - with paved runways:
total: 13
2,438 to 3,047 m: 7
1,524 to 2,437 m: 2
914 to 1,523 m: 3
under 914 m: 1 (2005 est.)
Airports - with unpaved runways:
total: 3
1,524 to 2,437 m: 1
under 914 m: 2 (2005 est.)
Heliports: 10 (2005 est.)
Roadways:
total: 14,110 km (Republic of Cyprus: 11,760 km; north Cyprus: 2,350 km)
paved: Republic of Cyprus: 7,403 km (including 268 km of expressways); north Cyprus: 1,370 km
unpaved: Republic of Cyprus: 4,357 km; north Cyprus: 980 km (2003/1996 est.)
Merchant marine:
total: 972 ships (1,000 GRT or over) 22,016,374 GRT/35,760,004 DWT
by type: bulk carrier 384, cargo 248, chemical tanker 45, container 125, liquefied gas 4, passenger 8, passenger/cargo 19, petroleum tanker 103, refrigerated cargo 19, roll on/roll off 12, vehicle carrier 5
foreign-owned: 899 (Austria 2, Belgium 1, Canada 10, China 8, Croatia 3, Cuba 5, Egypt 1, Estonia 3, France 1, Germany 236, Greece 396, Hong Kong 2, India 2, Iran 2, Israel 3, Japan 18, Latvia 7, Monaco 1, Netherlands 12, Norway 14, Philippines 1, Poland 20, Portugal 2, Russia 56, Singapore 2, Slovenia 4, South Korea 1, Spain 4, Sweden 6, Switzerland 4, Syria 2, Ukraine 3, UAE 11, United Kingdom 24, United States 31, Vietnam 1)
registered in other countries: 54 (2005)
Ports and terminals: Famagusta, Kyrenia, Larnaca, Limassol, Vasilikos

MILITARY

Military branches:
Republic of Cyprus: Greek Cypriot National Guard (GCNG; includes air and naval elements)
north Cyprus: Turkish Cypriot Security Force (GKK)
Military service age and obligation: 18 years of age (2004)
Manpower available for military service:
males age 18-49: 184,352 (2005 est.)
Manpower fit for military service:
males age 18-49: 150,750 (2005 est.)
Manpower reaching military service age annually: *males:* 6,578 (2005 est.)
Military expenditures - dollar figure: $384 million (FY02)
Military expenditures - percent of GDP: 3.8% (FY02)

TRANSNATIONAL ISSUES

Disputes - international: hostilities in 1974 divided the island into two de facto autonomous entities, the internationally recognized Cypriot Government and a Turkish-Cypriot community (north Cyprus); the 1,000-strong UN Peacekeeping Force in Cyprus (UNFICYP) has served in Cyprus since 1964 and maintains the buffer zone between north and south; March 2003 reunification talks failed, but Turkish-Cypriots later opened their borders to temporary visits by Greek Cypriots; on 24 April 2004, the Greek Cypriot and Turkish Cypriot communities voted in simultaneous and parallel referenda on whether to approve the UN-brokered Annan Plan that would have ended the thirty-year division of the island by establishing a new "United Cyprus Republic," a majority of Greek Cypriots voted "no"; on 1 May 2004, Cyprus entered the European Union still divided, with the EU's body of legislation and standards (acquis communitaire) suspended in the north
Refugees and internally displaced persons:
IDPs: 265,000 (both Turkish and Greek Cypriots; many displaced for over 30 years) (2004)
Illicit drugs: minor transit point for heroin and hashish via air routes and container traffic to Europe, especially from Lebanon and Turkey; some cocaine transits as well; despite a strengthening of anti-money-laundering legislation, remains highly vulnerable to money laundering; identification of benefiting owners and reporting of suspicious transactions by nonresident-controlled companies in offshore sector remains weak

CZECH REPUBLIC

INTRODUCTION

Background: Following the First World War, the closely related Czechs and Slovaks of the former Austro-Hungarian Empire merged to form Czechoslovakia. During the interwar years, the new country's leaders were frequently preoccupied with meeting the demands of other ethnic minorities within the republic, most notably the Sudeten Germans and the Ruthenians (Ukrainians). After World War II, a truncated Czechoslovakia fell within the Soviet sphere of influence. In 1968, an invasion by Warsaw Pact troops ended the efforts of the country's leaders to liberalize Communist party rule and create "socialism with a human face." Anti-Soviet demonstrations the following year ushered in a period of harsh repression. With the collapse of Soviet authority in 1989, Czechoslovakia regained its freedom through a peaceful "Velvet Revolution." On 1 January 1993, the country underwent a "velvet divorce" into its two national components, the Czech Republic and Slovakia. The Czech Republic joined NATO in 1999 and the European Union in 2004.

GEOGRAPHY

Location: Central Europe, southeast of Germany
Geographic coordinates: 49 45 N, 15 30 E
Map references: Europe
Area:
total: 78,866 sq km
land: 77,276 sq km
water: 1,590 sq km
Area - comparative: slightly smaller than South Carolina
Land boundaries:
total: 1,881 km
border countries: Austria 362 km, Germany

646 km, Poland 658 km, Slovakia 215 km
Coastline: 0 km (landlocked)
Maritime claims: none (landlocked)
Climate: temperate; cool summers; cold, cloudy, humid winters
Terrain: Bohemia in the west consists of rolling plains, hills, and plateaus surrounded by low mountains; Moravia in the east consists of very hilly country
Elevation extremes:
lowest point: Elbe River 115 m
highest point: Snezka 1,602 m
Natural resources: hard coal, soft coal, kaolin, clay, graphite, timber
Land use:
arable land: 39.8%
permanent crops: 3.05%
other: 57.15% (2001)
Irrigated land: 240 sq km (1998 est.)
Natural hazards: flooding
Environment - current issues: air and water pollution in areas of northwest Bohemia and in northern Moravia around Ostrava present health risks; acid rain damaging forests; efforts to bring industry up to EU code should improve domestic pollution
Environment - international agreements:
party to: Air Pollution, Air Pollution-Nitrogen Oxides, Air Pollution-Persistent Organic Pollutants, Air Pollution-Sulfur 85, Air Pollution-Sulfur 94, Air Pollution-Volatile Organic Compounds, Antarctic Treaty, Biodiversity, Climate Change, Climate Change-Kyoto Protocol, Desertification, Endangered Species, Environmental Modification, Hazardous Wastes, Law of the Sea, Ozone Layer Protection, Ship Pollution, Wetlands
signed, but not ratified: none of the selected agreements
Geography - note: landlocked; strategically located astride some of oldest and most significant land routes in Europe; Moravian Gate is a traditional military corridor between the North European Plain and the Danube in central Europe

PEOPLE

Population: 10,241,138 (July 2005 est.)
Age structure:
0-14 years: 14.7% (male 773,028/female 731,833)
15-64 years: 71.1% (male 3,651,018/female 3,627,006)
65 years and over: 14.2% (male 565,374/female 892,879) (2005 est.)
Median age:
total: 38.97 years
male: 37.2 years
female: 40.82 years (2005 est.)
Population growth rate: -0.05% (2005 est.)
Birth rate: 9.07 births/1,000 population (2005 est.)
Death rate: 10.54 deaths/1,000 population (2005 est.)
Net migration rate: 0.97 migrant(s)/1,000 population (2005 est.)
Sex ratio:
at birth: 1.06 male(s)/female
under 15 years: 1.06 male(s)/female
15-64 years: 1.01 male(s)/female
65 years and over: 0.63 male(s)/female
total population: 0.95 male(s)/female (2005 est.)
Infant mortality rate:
total: 3.93 deaths/1,000 live births
male: 4.28 deaths/1,000 live births
female: 3.55 deaths/1,000 live births (2005 est.)
Life expectancy at birth:
total population: 76.02 years
male: 72.74 years
female: 79.49 years (2005 est.)
Total fertility rate: 1.2 children born/woman (2005 est.)
HIV/AIDS - adult prevalence rate: less than 0.1% (2001 est.)
HIV/AIDS - people living with HIV/AIDS: 2,500 (2001 est.)
HIV/AIDS - deaths: less than 10 (2001 est.)
Nationality:
noun: Czech(s)
adjective: Czech
Ethnic groups: Czech 90.4%, Moravian 3.7%, Slovak 1.9%, other 4% (2001 census)
Religions: Roman Catholic 26.8%, Protestant 2.1%, other 3.3%, unspecified 8.8%, unaffiliated 59% (2001 census)
Languages: Czech
Literacy:
definition: NA
total population: 99.9% (1999 est.)
male: NA%
female: NA%

GOVERNMENT

Country name:
conventional long form: Czech Republic
conventional short form: Czech Republic
local long form: Ceska Republika
local short form: Ceska Republika
Government type: parliamentary democracy
Capital: Prague
Administrative divisions: 13 regions (kraje, singular - kraj) and 1 capital city* (hlavni mesto); Jihocesky Kraj, Jihomoravsky Kraj, Karlovarsky Kraj, Kralovehradecky Kraj, Liberecky Kraj, Moravskoslezsky Kraj, Olomoucky Kraj, Pardubicky Kraj, Plzensky Kraj, Praha (Prague)*, Stredocesky Kraj, Ustecky Kraj, Vysocina, Zlinsky Kraj
Independence: 1 January 1993 (Czechoslovakia split into the Czech Republic and Slovakia)
National holiday: Czech Founding Day, 28 October (1918)
Constitution: ratified 16 December 1992, effective 1 January 1993
Legal system: civil law system based on Austro-Hungarian codes; has not accepted compulsory ICJ jurisdiction; legal code modified to bring it in line with Organization on Security and Cooperation in Europe (OSCE) obligations and to expunge Marxist-Leninist legal theory
Suffrage: 18 years of age; universal
Executive branch:
chief of state: President Vaclav KLAUS (since 7 March 2003)
note: the Czech Republic's first president Vaclav HAVEL stepped down from office on 2 February 2003 having served exactly 10 years; parliament finally elected a successor on 28 February 2003 after two inconclusive elections in January 2003
head of government: Prime Minister Jiri PAROUBEK (since 25 April 2005), Deputy Prime Ministers Zdenek SKROMACH (since 4 August 2004), Martin JAHN (since 4 August 2004), Pavel NEMEC (since 4 August 2004), Milan SIMONOVSKY (since 4 August 2004)
cabinet: Cabinet appointed by the president on the recommendation of the prime minister
elections: president elected by Parliament for a five-year term; last successful election held 28 February 2003 (after earlier elections held 15 and 24 January 2003 were inconclusive; next election to be held January 2008); prime minister appointed by the president
election results: Vaclav KLAUS elected president on 28 February 2003; Vaclav KLAUS 142 votes, Jan SOKOL 124 votes (third round; combined votes of both chambers of parliament)
Legislative branch: bicameral Parliament or Parlament consists of the Senate or Senat (81 seats; members are elected by popular vote to serve six-year terms; one-

third elected every two years) and the Chamber of Deputies or Poslanecka Snemovna (200 seats; members are elected by popular vote to serve four-year terms)
elections: Senate - last held in two rounds 5-6 November and 12-13 November 2004 (next to be held November 2006); Chamber of Deputies - last held 14-15 June 2002 (next to be held by June 2006)
election results: Senate - percent of vote by party - NA%; seats by party - ODS 37, KDU-CSL 14, Open Democracy 13, CSSD 7, Caucus Open Democracy 7, independents 3; Chamber of Deputies - percent of vote by party - CSSD 30.2%, ODS 24.5%, KSCM 18.5%, KDU-CSL & US-DEU coalition 14.3%, other minor 12.5%; seats by party - CSSD 70, ODS 57, KSCM 41, KDU-CSL 21, US-DEU 10, independent 1
Judicial branch: Supreme Court; Constitutional Court; chairman and deputy chairmen are appointed by the president for a 10-year term
Political parties and leaders: Caucus SNK [Josef ZOSER]; Christian and Democratic Union-Czechoslovak People's Party or KDU-CSL [Miroslav KALOUSEK, chairman]; Civic Democratic Alliance or ODA [Jirina NOVAKOVA, chairwoman]; Civic Democratic Party or ODS [Mirek TOPOLANEK, chairman]; Communist Party of Bohemia and Moravia or KSCM [Miroslav GREBENICEK, chairman]; Communist Party of Czechoslovakia or KSC [Miroslav STEPAN, chairman]; Czech National Social Party of CSNS [Jaroslav ROVNY, chairman]; Czech Social Democratic Party or CSSD [Stanislav GROSS, acting chairman]; European Democrats [Jan Kasl]; Freedom Union-Democratic Union or US-DEU [Hana MARVANOVA, chairwoman]; Open Democracy [Sona PAUKRTOVA, chairwoman]
Political pressure groups and leaders: Bohemian and Moravian Trade Union Confederation [Milan STECH]
International organization participation: ACCT (observer), Australia Group, BIS, CE, CEI, CERN, EAPC, EBRD, EIB, ESA (cooperating state), EU (new member), FAO, IAEA, IBRD, ICAO, ICC, ICCt (signatory), ICFTU, ICRM, IDA, IEA, IFC, IFRCS, ILO, IMF, IMO, Interpol, IOC, IOM, ISO, ITU, MIGA, MONUC, NAM (guest), NATO, NEA, NSG, OAS (observer), OECD, OPCW, OSCE, PCA, UN, UNAMSIL, UNCTAD, UNESCO, UNIDO, UNITAR, UNMEE, UNMIL, UNOMIG, UPU, WCL, WCO, WEU (associate), WFTU, WHO, WIPO, WMO, WToO, WTO, ZC
Diplomatic representation in the US:
chief of mission: Ambassador Martin PALOUS
chancery: 3900 Spring of Freedom Street NW, Washington, DC 20008
telephone: [1] (202) 274-9100
FAX: [1] (202) 966-8540
consulate(s) general: Los Angeles and New York
Diplomatic representation from the US:
chief of mission: Ambassador William J. CABANISS
embassy: Trziste 15, 11801 Prague 1
mailing address: use embassy street address
telephone: [420] (2) 5753-0663
FAX: [420] (2) 5753-0920
Flag description: two equal horizontal bands of white (top) and red with a blue isosceles triangle based on the hoist side (identical to the flag of the former Czechoslovakia)

ECONOMY

Economy - overview: The Czech Republic is one of the most stable and prosperous of the post-Communist states of Central and Eastern Europe. Growth in 2000-05 was supported by exports to the EU, primarily to Germany, and a strong recovery of foreign and domestic investment. Domestic demand is playing an ever more important role in underpinning growth as interest rates drop and the availability of credit cards and mortgages increases. Current account deficits of around 5% of GDP are beginning to decline as demand for Czech products in the European Union increases. Inflation is under control. Recent accession to the EU gives further impetus and direction to structural reform. In early 2004 the government passed increases in the Value Added Tax (VAT) and tightened eligibility for social benefits with the intention to bring the public finance gap down to 4% of GDP by 2006, but more difficult pension and healthcare reforms will have to wait until after the next elections. Privatization of the state-owned telecommunications firm Cesky Telecom took place in 2005. Intensified restructuring among large enterprises, improvements in the financial sector, and effective use of available EU funds should strengthen output growth.
GDP (purchasing power parity): $184.9 billion (2005 est.)
GDP (official exchange rate): $112.8 billion (2005 est.)
GDP - real growth rate: 4.6% (2005 est.)
GDP - per capita: purchasing power parity - $18,100 (2005 est.)
GDP - composition by sector:
agriculture: 3.4%
industry: 39.3%
services: 57.3% (2004 est.)
Labor force: 5.27 million (2005 est.)
Labor force - by occupation: agriculture 4%, industry 38%, services 58% (2002 est.)
Unemployment rate: 9.1% (2005 est.)
Population below poverty line: NA
Household income or consumption by percentage share:
lowest 10%: 4.3%
highest 10%: 22.4% (1996)
Distribution of family income - Gini index: 25.4 (1996)
Inflation rate (consumer prices): 2% (2005 est.)
Investment (gross fixed): 26.2% of GDP (2005 est.)
Budget:
revenues: $48.16 billion
expenditures: $53.04 billion, including capital expenditures of NA (2005 est.)
Public debt: 33.1% of GDP (2005 est.)
Agriculture - products: wheat, potatoes, sugar beets, hops, fruit; pigs, poultry
Industries: metallurgy, machinery and equipment, motor vehicles, glass, armaments
Industrial production growth rate: 6% (2005 est.)
Electricity - production: 78.18 billion kWh (2003)
Electricity - production by source:
fossil fuel: 76.1%
hydro: 2.9%
nuclear: 20%
other: 1% (2001)
Electricity - consumption: 56.5 billion kWh (2003)
Electricity - exports: 26.3 billion kWh (2003)
Electricity - imports: 10.1 billion kWh (2003)
Oil - production: 12,380 bbl/day (2003)
Oil - consumption: 185,200 bbl/day (2003 est.)
Oil - exports: 26,670 bbl/day (2001)
Oil - imports: 192,300 bbl/day (2001)
Oil - proved reserves: 17.25 million bbl (1 January 2002)
Natural gas - production: 160 million cu m (2001 est.)
Natural gas - consumption: 9.892 billion cu m (2001 est.)
Natural gas - exports: 1 million cu m (2001 est.)
Natural gas - imports: 9.521 billion cu m (2001 est.)
Natural gas - proved reserves: 3.057 billion cu m (1 January 2002)
Current account balance: $-3.523 billion (2005 est.)
Exports: $78.37 billion f.o.b. (2005 est.)

Exports - partners: Germany 36.2%, Slovakia 8.5%, Austria 6%, Poland 5.3%, UK 4.7%, France 4.6%, Italy 4.3%, Netherlands 4.3% (2004)
Imports: $76.59 billion f.o.b. (2005 est.)
Imports - partners: Germany 31.7%, Slovakia 5.4%, Italy 5.3%, China 5.2%, Poland 4.8%, France 4.7%, Russia 4.1%, Austria 4% (2004)
Reserves of foreign exchange and gold: $30.49 billion (2005 est.)
Debt - external: $43.2 billion (30 June 2005 est.)
Economic aid - recipient: $2.4 billion in available EU structural adjustment and cohesion funds (2004-06)
Currency (code): Czech koruna (CZK)
Currency code: CZK
Exchange rates: koruny per US dollar - 23.72 (2005), 25.7 (2004), 28.209 (2003), 32.739 (2002), 38.035 (2001)
Fiscal year: calendar year

COMMUNICATION

Telephones - main lines in use: 3.626 million (2003)
Telephones - mobile cellular: 9,708,700 (2003)
Telephone system:
general assessment: privatization and modernization of the Czech telecommunication system got a late start but is advancing steadily; growth in the use of mobile cellular telephones is particularly vigorous
domestic: 86% of exchanges now digital; existing copper subscriber systems now being enhanced with Asymmetric Digital Subscriber Line (ADSL) equipment to accommodate Internet and other digital signals; trunk systems include fiber-optic cable and microwave radio relay
international: country code - 420; satellite earth stations - 2 Intersputnik (Atlantic and Indian Ocean regions), 1 Intelsat, 1 Eutelsat, 1 Inmarsat, 1 Globalstar
Radio broadcast stations: AM 31, FM 304, shortwave 17 (2000)
Radios: 3,159,134 (December 2000)
Television broadcast stations: 150 (plus 1,434 repeaters) (2000)
Televisions: 3,405,834 (December 2000)
Internet country code: .cz
Internet hosts: 295,677 (2004)
Internet Service Providers (ISPs): more than 300 (2000)
Internet users: 2.7 million (2003)

TRANSPORTATION

Airports: 120 (2004 est.)
Airports - with paved runways:
total: 44
over 3,047 m: 2
2,438 to 3,047 m: 9
1,524 to 2,437 m: 14
914 to 1,523 m: 2
under 914 m: 17 (2005 est.)
Airports - with unpaved runways:
total: 77
914 to 1,523 m: 28
under 914 m: 49 (2005 est.)
Heliports: 2 (2005 est.)
Pipelines: gas 7,020 km; oil 547 km; refined products 94 km (2004)
Railways:
total: 9,543 km
standard gauge: 9,421 km 1.435-m gauge (2,893 km electrified)
narrow gauge: 122 km 0.760-m gauge (23 km electrified) (2004)
Roadways:
total: 127,672 km
paved: 127,672 km (including 518 km of expressways) (2002)
Waterways: 664 km (on Elbe, Vltava, and Oder rivers) (2004)
Merchant marine: *registered in other countries:* 3
Ports and terminals: Decin, Prague, Usti nad Labem

MILITARY

Military branches: Army of the Czech Republic (ACR): Joint Forces Command, Support and Training Forces Command (2005)
Military service age and obligation: 18-50 years of age for voluntary military service; on-going transformation of military service into a fully professional, all-volunteer force no longer dependent on conscription began in January 2004 and is scheduled to be completed by 2007 (2005)
Manpower available for military service: *males age 18-49:* 2,414,728 (2005 est.)
Manpower fit for military service: *males age 18-49:* 1,996,631 (2005 est.)
Manpower reaching military service age annually: *males:* 66,583 (2005 est.)
Military expenditures - dollar figure: $2.17 billion (2004)
Military expenditures - percent of GDP: 1.81% FY05 (2005)

TRANSNATIONAL ISSUES

Disputes - international: in February 2005, the ICJ refused to rule on the restitution of Liechtenstein's land and property assets in the Czech Republic confiscated in 1945 as German property; individual Sudeten Germans seek restitution for property confiscated in connection with their expulsion after World War II
Illicit drugs: transshipment point for Southwest Asian heroin and minor transit point for Latin American cocaine to Western Europe; producer of synthetic drugs for local and regional markets; susceptible to money laundering related to drug trafficking, organized crime

DENMARK

INTRODUCTION

Background: Once the seat of Viking raiders and later a major north European power, Denmark has evolved into a modern, prosperous nation that is participating in the general political and economic integration of Europe. It joined NATO in 1949 and the EEC (now the EU) in 1973. However, the country has opted out of certain elements of the European Union's Maastricht Treaty, including the European Economic and Monetary Union (EMU), European defense cooperation, and issues concerning certain justice and home affairs.

GEOGRAPHY

Location: Northern Europe, bordering the Baltic Sea and the North Sea, on a peninsula north of Grmany (Jutland); also includes two major islands (Sjaelland and Fyn)
Geographic coordinates: 56 00 N, 10 00 E
Map references: Europe
Area:
total: 43,094 sq km
land: 42,394 sq km
water: 700 sq km
note: includes the island of Bornholm in the Baltic Sea and the rest of metropolitan Denmark (the Jutland Peninsula, and the major islands of Sjaelland and Fyn), but excludes the Faroe Islands and Greenland
Area - comparative: slightly less than twice the size of Massachusetts
Land boundaries:
total: 68 km
border countries: Germany 68 km
Coastline: 7,314 km
Maritime claims:
territorial sea: 12 nm
exclusive economic zone: 200 nm
continental shelf: 200-m depth or to the depth of exploitation
Climate: temperate; humid and overcast; mild, windy winters and cool summers
Terrain: low and flat to gently rolling plains
Elevation extremes:
lowest point: Lammefjord -7 m
highest point: Yding Skovhoej 173 m
Natural resources: petroleum, natural gas, fish, salt, limestone, chalk, stone, gravel and sand
Land use:
arable land: 54.02%
permanent crops: 0.19%
other: 45.79% (2001)
Irrigated land: 4,760 sq km (1998 est.)
Natural hazards: flooding is a threat in some areas of the country (e.g., parts of Jutland, along the southern coast of the island of Lolland) that are protected from the sea by a system of dikes
Environment - current issues: air pollution, principally from vehicle and power plant emissions; nitrogen and phosphorus pollution of the North Sea; drinking and surface water becoming polluted from animal wastes and pesticides
Environment - international agreements:
party to: Air Pollution, Air Pollution-Nitrogen Oxides, Air Pollution-Persistent Organic Pollutants, Air Pollution-Sulfur 85, Air Pollution-Sulfur 94, Air Pollution-Volatile Organic Compounds, Antarctic Treaty, Biodiversity, Climate Change, Climate Change-Kyoto Protocol, Desertification, Endangered Species, Environmental Modification, Hazardous Wastes, Law of the Sea, Marine Dumping, Marine Life Conservation, Ozone Layer Protection, Ship Pollution, Tropical Timber 83, Tropical Timber 94, Wetlands, Whaling
signed, but not ratified: none of the selected agreements
Geography - note: controls Danish Straits (Skagerrak and Kattegat) linking Baltic and North Seas; about one-quarter of the population lives in greater Copenhagen

PEOPLE

Population: 5,432,335 (July 2005 est.)
Age structure:
0-14 years: 18.8% (male 524,250/female 497,683)
15-64 years: 66.1% (male 1,811,787/female 1,780,907)
65 years and over: 15.1% (male 349,458/female 468,250) (2005 est.)
Median age:
total: 39.47 years
male: 38.55 years
female: 40.4 years (2005 est.)
Population growth rate: 0.34% (2005 est.)
Birth rate: 11.36 births/1,000 population (2005 est.)
Death rate: 10.43 deaths/1,000 population (2005 est.)
Net migration rate: 2.53 migrant(s)/1,000 population (2005 est.)
Sex ratio:
at birth: 1.06 male(s)/female
under 15 years: 1.05 male(s)/female
15-64 years: 1.02 male(s)/female
65 years and over: 0.75 male(s)/female
total population: 0.98 male(s)/female (2005 est.)
Infant mortality rate:
total: 4.56 deaths/1,000 live births
male: 4.59 deaths/1,000 live births
female: 4.53 deaths/1,000 live births (2005 est.)
Life expectancy at birth:
total population: 77.62 years
male: 75.34 years
female: 80.03 years (2005 est.)
Total fertility rate: 1.74 children born/woman (2005 est.)
HIV/AIDS - adult prevalence rate: 0.2% (2003 est.)
HIV/AIDS - people living with HIV/AIDS: 5,000 (2003 est.)
HIV/AIDS - deaths: less than 100 (2003 est.)
Nationality:
noun: Dane(s)
adjective: Danish
Ethnic groups: Scandinavian, Inuit, Faroese, German, Turkish, Iranian, Somali
Religions: Evangelical Lutheran 95%, other Protestant and Roman Catholic 3%, Muslim 2%
Languages: Danish, Faroese, Greenlandic (an Inuit dialect), German (small minority)
note: English is the predominant second language
Literacy:
definition: age 15 and over can read and write
total population: 100%
male: 100%
female: 100%

GOVERNMENT

Country name:
conventional long form: Kingdom of Denmark
conventional short form: Denmark
local long form: Kongeriget Danmark
local short form: Danmark
Government type: constitutional monarchy
Capital: Copenhagen
Administrative divisions: metropolitan Denmark - 14 counties (amter, singular - amt) and 2 boroughs* (amtskommuner, singular - amtskommune); Arhus, Bornholm, Frederiksberg*, Frederiksborg, Fyn, Kobenhavn, Kobenhavn

(Copenhagen)*, Nordjylland, Ribe, Ringkobing, Roskilde, Sonderjylland, Storstrom, Vejle, Vestsjalland, Viborg
note: since 2005 Bornholm may have become a borough; in the future the counties may be replaced by regions; see separate entries for the Faroe Islands and Greenland, which are part of the Kingdom of Denmark and are self-governing overseas administrative divisions
Independence: first organized as a unified state in 10th century; in 1849 became a constitutional monarchy
National holiday: none designated; Constitution Day, 5 June (1849) is generally viewed as the National Day
Constitution: 5 June 1849 adoption of original constitution; a major overhaul of 5 June 1953 allowed for a unicameral legislature and a female chief of state
Legal system: civil law system; judicial review of legislative acts; accepts compulsory ICJ jurisdiction, with reservations
Suffrage: 18 years of age; universal
Executive branch:
chief of state: Queen MARGRETHE II (since 14 January1972); Heir Apparent Crown Prince FREDERIK, elder son of the monarch (born 26 May 1968)
head of government: Prime Minister Anders Fogh RASMUSSEN (since 27 November 2001)
cabinet: Cabinet appointed by the prime minister and approved by parliament
elections: none; the monarch is hereditary; following legislative elections, the leader of the majority party or the leader of the majority coalition is usually appointed prime minister by the monarch
Legislative branch: unicameral People's Assembly or Folketinget (179 seats, including 2 from Greenland and 2 from the Faroe Islands; members are elected by popular vote on the basis of proportional representation to serve four-year terms)
elections: last held 8 February 2005 (next to be held February 2009)
election results: percent of vote by party - Liberal Party 29%, Social Democrats 25.9%, Danish People's Party 13.2%, Conservative Party 10.3%, Social Liberal Party 9.2%, Socialist People's Party 6%, Unity List 3.4%; seats by party - Liberal Party 52, Social Democrats 47, Danish People's Party 24, Conservative Party 18, Social Liberal Party 17, Socialist People's Party 11, Unity List 6; note - does not include the 2 seats from Greenland and the 2 seats from the Faroe Islands
Judicial branch: Supreme Court (judges are appointed by the monarch for life)
Political parties and leaders: Center Democratic Party [Mimi JAKOBSEN]; Christian Democrats (was Christian People's Party) [Marianne KARLSMOSE]; Conservative Party (sometimes known as Conservative People's Party) [Bendt BENDTSEN]; Danish People's Party [Pia KJAERSGAARD]; Liberal Party [Anders Fogh RASMUSSEN]; Social Democratic Party [Helle THORNING-SCHMIDT]; Social Liberal Party (sometimes called the Radical Left) [Marianne JELVED, leader; Soren BALD, chairman]; Socialist People's Party [Villy SOEVNDAL]; Red-Green Unity List (bloc includes Left Socialist Party, Communist Party of Denmark, Socialist Workers' Party) [collective leadership]
Political pressure groups and leaders: NA
International organization participation: AfDB, AsDB, Australia Group, BIS, CBSS, CE, CERN, EAPC, EBRD, EIB, ESA, EU, FAO, G- 9, IADB, IAEA, IBRD, ICAO, ICC, ICCt, ICFTU, ICRM, IDA, IEA, IFAD, IFC, IFRCS, IHO, ILO, IMF, IMO, Interpol, IOC, IOM, ISO, ITU, MIGA, MONUC, NATO, NC, NEA, NIB, NSG, OAS (observer), OECD, OPCW, OSCE, Paris Club, PCA, UN, UN Security Council (temporary), UNCTAD, UNESCO, UNHCR, UNIDO, UNMEE, UNMIL, UNMOGIP, UNOMIG, UNTSO, UPU, WCO, WEU (observer), WHO, WIPO, WMO, WTO, ZC
Diplomatic representation in the US:
chief of mission: Ambassador Friis PETERSEN
chancery: 3200 Whitehaven Street NW, Washington, DC 20008
telephone: [1] (202) 234-4300
FAX: [1] (202) 328-1470
consulate(s) general: Chicago and New York
Diplomatic representation from the US:
chief of mission: Ambassador James P. CAIN
embassy: Dag Hammarskjolds Alle 24, 2100 Copenhagen
mailing address: PSC 73, APO AE 09716
telephone: [45] 33 41 71 00
FAX: [45] 35 43 02 23
Flag description: red with a white cross that extends to the edges of the flag; the vertical part of the cross is shifted to the hoist side, and that design element of the Dannebrog (Danish flag) was subsequently adopted by the other Nordic countries of Finland, Iceland, Norway, and Sweden

ECONOMY

Economy - overview: This thoroughly modern market economy features high-tech agriculture, up-to-date small-scale and corporate industry, extensive government welfare measures, comfortable living standards, a stable currency, and high dependence on foreign trade. Denmark is a net exporter of food and energy and enjoys a comfortable balance of payments surplus. Government objectives include streamlining the bureaucracy and further privatization of state assets. The government has been successful in meeting, and even exceeding, the economic convergence criteria for participating in the third phase (a common European currency) of the European Economic and Monetary Union (EMU), but Denmark has decided not to join 12 other EU members in the euro; even so, the Danish krone remains pegged to the euro. Growth in 2005 was sluggish, yet above the scanty 0.3% of 2003. Because of high GDP per capita, welfare benefits, a low Gini index, and political stability, the Danish people enjoy living standards topped by no other nation. A major long-term issue will be the sharp decline in the ratio of workers to retirees.
GDP (purchasing power parity): $182.1 billion (2005 est.)
GDP (official exchange rate): $254.1 billion (2005 est.)
GDP - real growth rate: 2.2% (2005 est.)
GDP - per capita: purchasing power parity - $33,500 (2005 est.)
GDP - composition by sector:
agriculture: 2.2%
industry: 24%
services: 73.8% (2005 est.)
Labor force: 2.9 million (2005 est.)
Labor force - by occupation: agriculture 4%, industry 17%, services 79% (2002 est.)
Unemployment rate: 5.7% (2005 est.)
Population below poverty line: NA
Household income or consumption by percentage share:
lowest 10%: 2%
highest 10%: 24% (2000 est.)
Distribution of family income - Gini index: 24.7 (1997)
Inflation rate (consumer prices): 1.9% (2005 est.)
Investment (gross fixed): 19.5% of GDP (2005 est.)
Budget:
revenues: $148.8 billion
expenditures: $142.6 billion, including capital expenditures of $500 million (2005 est.)
Public debt: 40.4% of GDP (2005 est.)
Agriculture - products: barley, wheat, potatoes, sugar beets; pork, dairy products; fish
Industries: iron, steel, nonferrous metals, chemicals, food processing, machinery and transportation equipment, textiles

and clothing, electronics, construction, furniture and other wood products, shipbuilding and refurbishment, windmills
Industrial production growth rate: 4% (2005 est.)
Electricity - production: 43.32 billion kWh (2003)
Electricity - production by source:
fossil fuel: 82.7%
hydro: 0.1%
nuclear: 0%
other: 17.3% (2001)
Electricity - consumption: 31.68 billion kWh (2003)
Electricity - exports: 15.6 billion kWh (2003)
Electricity - imports: 7 billion kWh (2003)
Oil - production: 376,900 bbl/day (2003)
Oil - consumption: 188,300 bbl/day (2003 est.)
Oil - exports: 332,100 bbl/day (2001)
Oil - imports: 195,000 bbl/day (2001)
Oil - proved reserves: 1.23 billion bbl (1 January 2002)
Natural gas - production: 8.38 billion cu m (2001 est.)
Natural gas - consumption: 5.28 billion cu m (2001 est.)
Natural gas - exports: 3.1 billion cu m (2001 est.)
Natural gas - imports: 0 cu m (2001 est.)
Natural gas - proved reserves: 81.98 billion cu m (1 January 2002)
Current account balance: $7.019 billion (2005 est.)
Exports: $84.95 billion f.o.b. (2005 est.)
Exports - partners: Germany 18%, Sweden 13.2%, UK 8.7%, US 5.8%, Netherlands 5.5%, Norway 5.4%, France 5% (2004)
Imports: $74.69 billion f.o.b. (2005 est.)
Imports - partners: Germany 22.3%, Sweden 13.5%, Netherlands 6.8%, UK 6.1%, France 4.5%, Norway 4.5%, Italy 4.1%, China 4% (2004)
Reserves of foreign exchange and gold: $40.05 billion (2004 est.)
Debt - external: $352.9 billion (30 June 2005)
Economic aid - donor: ODA, $1.63 billion (1999)
Currency (code): Danish krone (DKK)
Currency code: DKK
Exchange rates: Danish kroner per US dollar - 5.93 (2005), 5.9911 (2004), 6.5877 (2003), 7.8947 (2002), 8.3228 (2001)
Fiscal year: calendar year

COMMUNICATIONS

Telephones - main lines in use: 3,610,100 (2003)
Telephones - mobile cellular: 4,785,300 (2003)
Telephone system:
general assessment: excellent telephone and telegraph services
domestic: buried and submarine cables and microwave radio relay form trunk network, 4 cellular mobile communications systems
international: country code - 45; 18 submarine fiber-optic cables linking Denmark with Canada, Faroe Islands, Germany, Iceland, Netherlands, Norway, Poland, Russia, Sweden, and UK; satellite earth stations - 6 Intelsat, 10 Eutelsat, 1 Orion, 1 Inmarsat (Blaavand-Atlantic-East); note - the Nordic countries (Denmark, Finland, Iceland, Norway, and Sweden) share the Danish earth station and the Eik, Norway, station for worldwide Inmarsat access (1997)
Radio broadcast stations: AM 2, FM 355, shortwave 0 (1998)
Radios: 6.02 million (1997)
Television broadcast stations: 26 (plus 51 repeaters) (1998)
Televisions: 3.121 million (1997)
Internet country code: .dk
Internet hosts: 1,219,925 (2004)
Internet Service Providers (ISPs): 13 (2000)
Internet users: 2.756 million (2002)

TRANSPORTATION

Airports: 97 (2004 est.)
Airports - with paved runways:
total: 28
over 3,047 m: 2
2,438 to 3,047 m: 7
1,524 to 2,437 m: 4
914 to 1,523 m: 12
under 914 m: 3 (2005 est.)
Airports - with unpaved runways:
total: 69
914 to 1,523 m: 6
under 914 m: 63 (2005 est.)
Pipelines: condensate 12 km; gas 3,892 km; oil 455 km; oil/gas/water 2 km; unknown (oil/water) 64 km (2004)
Railways:
total: 2,628 km
standard gauge: 2,628 km 1.435-m gauge (595 km electrified) (2004)
Roadways:
total: 71,847 km
paved: 71,847 km (including 920 km of expressways) (2002)
Waterways: 417 km (2001)
Merchant marine:
total: 287 ships (1,000 GRT or over) 6,952,473 GRT/9,030,444 DWT
by type: bulk carrier 2, cargo 67, chemical tanker 40, container 79, liquefied gas 10, livestock carrier 2, passenger 1, passenger/cargo 42, petroleum tanker 25, refrigerated cargo 7, roll on/roll off 8, specialized tanker 4
foreign-owned: 23 (Bahamas 14, France 1, Greece 1, Greenland 1, Norway 2, Sweden 2, UAE 1, Vietnam 1)
registered in other countries: 487 (2005)
Ports and terminals: Aalborg, Aarhus, Asnaesvaerkets, Copenhagen, Elsinore, Ensted, Esbjerg, Fredericia, Frederikshavn, Graasten, Kalundborg, Odense, Roenne

MILITARY

Military branches: Royal Danish Army, Royal Danish Navy (Sovaernet), Royal Danish Air Force, Home Guard (Hjemmevaernet) (2005)
Military service age and obligation: 18 years of age for compulsory and volunteer military service; conscripts serve an initial training period that varies from 4 to 12 months according to specialization; reservists are assigned to mobilization units following completion of their conscript service (2004)
Manpower available for military service: *males age 18-49:* 1,175,108 (2005 est.)
Manpower fit for military service: *males age 18-49:* 955,168 (2005 est.)
Manpower reaching military service age annually: *males:* 31,317 (2005 est.)
Military expenditures - dollar figure: $3,271.6 million (2003)
Military expenditures - percent of GDP: 1.5% (2004)

TRANSNATIONAL ISSUES

Disputes - international: Iceland disputes the Faroe Islands' fisheries median line; Iceland, the UK, and Ireland dispute Denmark's claim that the Faroe Islands' continental shelf extends beyond 200 nm; Faroese continue to study proposals for full independence; uncontested sovereignty dispute with Canada over Hans Island in the Kennedy Channel between Ellesmere Island and Greenland

DHEKELIA

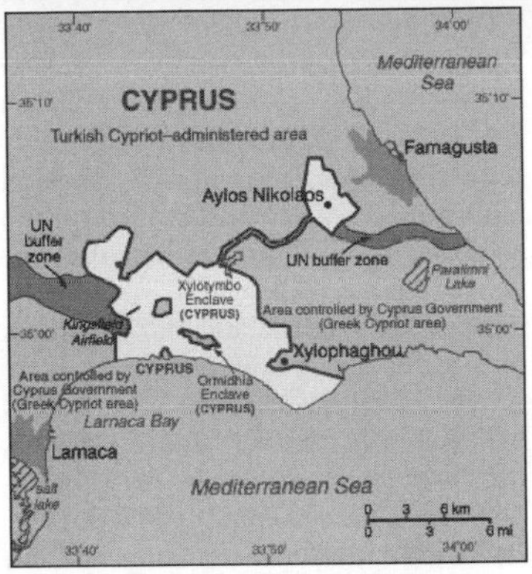

INTRODUCTION

Background: By terms of the 1960 Treaty of Establishment that created the independent Republic of Cyprus, the UK retained full sovereignty and jurisdiction over two areas of almost 254 square kilometers in total: Akrotiri and Dhekelia. The larger of these is the Dhekelia Sovereign Base Area, which is also referred to as the Eastern Sovereign Base Area.

GEOGRAPHY

Location: on the southeast coast of Cyprus near Famagusta
Geographic coordinates: 34 59 N, 33 45 E
Map references: Middle East
Area:
total: 130.8 sq km
note: area surrounds three Cypriot enclaves
Area - comparative: about three-quarters the size of Washington, DC
Land boundaries:
total: NA; note - boundary with Cyprus is being resurveyed
Coastline: 27.5 km
Climate: temperate; Mediterranean with hot, dry summers and cool winters
Environment - current issues: netting and trapping of small migrant songbirds in the spring and autumn
Geography - note: British extraterritorial rights also extended to several small off-post sites scattered across Cyprus

PEOPLE

Population: no indigenous personnel
note: approximately 2,200 military personnel are on the base; there are another 5,000 British citizens who are families of military personnel or civilian staff on both the bases of Akrotiri and Dhekelia; Cyprus citizens work on the base, but do not live there
Languages: English, Greek

GOVERNMENT

Country name:
conventional long form: Dhekelia Sovereign Base Area
conventional short form: Dhekelia
Dependency status: overseas territory of UK; administered by an administrator who is also the Commander, British Forces Cyprus
Capital: Episkopi Cantonment; located in Akrotiri
Legal system: the laws of the UK, where applicable, apply
Executive branch:
chief of state: Queen Elizabeth II (since 6 February1952)
head of government: Administrator Maj. Gen. Peter Tomas Clayton PEARSON (since 9 May 2003); note - reports to the British Ministry of Defence
elections: none; the monarch is hereditary; the administrator is appointed by the monarch
Diplomatic representation in the US: none (overseas territory of the UK)
Diplomatic representation from the US: none (overseas territory of the UK)
Flag description: the flag of the UK is used

ECONOMY

Economy - overview: Economic activity is limited to providing services to the military and their families located in Dhekelia. All food and manufactured goods must be imported.
Industries: none

MILITARY

Military - note: includes Dheklia Garrison and Ayios Nikolaos Station connected by a roadway

DJIBOUTI

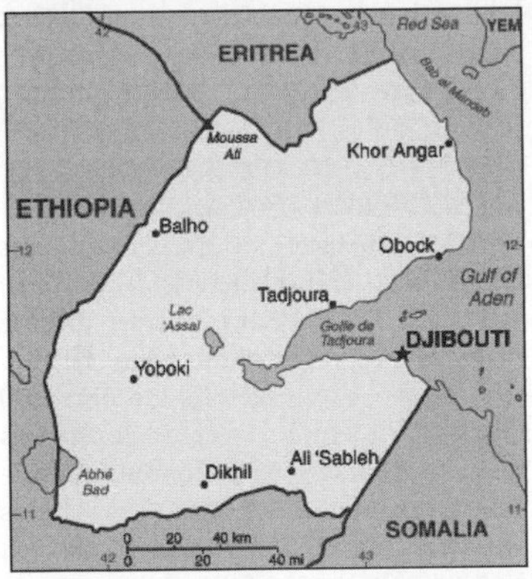

INTRODUCTION

Background: The French Territory of the Afars and the Issas became Djibouti in 1977. Hassan Gouled APTIDON installed an authoritarian one-party state and proceeded to serve as president until 1999. Unrest among the Afars minority during the 1990s led to a civil war that ended in 2001 following the conclusion of a peace accord between Afar rebels and the Issa-dominated government. Djibouti's first multi-party presidential elections in 1999 resulted in the election of Ismail Omar GUELLEH. Djibouti occupies a very strategic geographic location at the mouth of the Red Sea and serves as an important transshipment location for goods entering and leaving the east African highlands. The present leadership favors close ties to France, which maintains a significant military presence in the country, but has also developed increasingly stronger ties with the United States in recent years. Djibouti currently hosts the only United States military base in sub-Saharan Africa and is a front-line state in the global war on terrorism.

GEOGRAPHY

Location: Eastern Africa, bordering the Gulf of Aden and the Red Sea, between Eritrea and Somalia
Geographic coordinates: 11 30 N, 43 00 E
Map references: Africa
Area:
total: 23,000 sq km
land: 22,980 sq km
water: 20 sq km
Area - comparative: slightly smaller than Massachusetts
Land boundaries:
total: 516 km
border countries: Eritrea 109 km, Ethiopia 349 km, Somalia 58 km
Coastline: 314 km
Maritime claims:
territorial sea: 12 nm
contiguous zone: 24 nm
exclusive economic zone: 200 nm
Climate: desert; torrid, dry
Terrain: coastal plain and plateau separated by central mountains
Elevation extremes:
lowest point: Lac Assal -155 m

highest point: Moussa Ali 2,028 m
Natural resources: geothermal areas, gold, clay, granite, limestone, marble, salt, diatomite, gypsum, pumice, petroleum
Land use:
arable land: 0.04%
permanent crops: 0%
other: 99.96% (2001)
Irrigated land: 10 sq km (1998 est.)
Natural hazards: earthquakes; droughts; occasional cyclonic disturbances from the Indian Ocean bring heavy rains and flash floods
Environment - current issues: inadequate supplies of potable water; limited arable land; desertification; endangered species
Environment - international agreements:
party to: Biodiversity, Climate Change, Climate Change-Kyoto Protocol, Desertification, Endangered Species, Hazardous Wastes, Law of the Sea, Ozone Layer Protection, Ship Pollution
signed, but not ratified: none of the selected agreements
Geography - note: strategic location near world's busiest shipping lanes and close to Arabian oilfields; terminus of rail traffic into Ethiopia; mostly wasteland; Lac Assal (Lake Assal) is the lowest point in Africa

PEOPLE

Population: 476,703 (July 2005 est.)
Age structure:
0-14 years: 43.3% (male 103,516/female 102,860)
15-64 years: 53.5% (male 133,168/female 121,823)
65 years and over: 3.2% (male 7,748/female 7,588) (2005 est.)
Median age:
total: 18.23 years
male: 18.77 years
female: 17.69 years (2005 est.)
Population growth rate: 2.06% (2005 est.)
Birth rate: 39.98 births/1,000 population (2005 est.)
Death rate: 19.39 deaths/1,000 population (2005 est.)
Net migration rate: 0 migrant(s)/1,000 population (2005 est.)
Sex ratio:
at birth: 1.03 male(s)/female
under 15 years: 1.01 male(s)/female
15-64 years: 1.09 male(s)/female
65 years and over: 1.02 male(s)/female
total population: 1.05 male(s)/female (2005 est.)
Infant mortality rate:
total: 104.13 deaths/1,000 live births
male: 111.82 deaths/1,000 live births
female: 96.21 deaths/1,000 live births (2005 est.)
Life expectancy at birth:
total population: 43.1 years
male: 41.84 years
female: 44.39 years (2005 est.)
Total fertility rate: 5.4 children born/woman (2005 est.)
HIV/AIDS - adult prevalence rate: 2.9% (2003 est.)
HIV/AIDS - people living with HIV/AIDS: 9,100 (2003 est.)
HIV/AIDS - deaths: 690 (2003 est.)
Major infectious diseases:
degree of risk: high
food or waterborne diseases: bacterial and protozoal diarrhea, hepatitis A and E, and typhoid fever
vectorborne disease: malaria (2004)
Nationality:
noun: Djiboutian(s)
adjective: Djiboutian
Ethnic groups: Somali 60%, Afar 35%, French, Arab, Ethiopian, and Italian 5%
Religions: Muslim 94%, Christian 6%
Languages: French (official), Arabic (official), Somali, Afar
Literacy:
definition: age 15 and over can read and write
total population: 67.9%
male: 78%
female: 58.4% (2003 est.)

GOVERNMENT

Country name:
conventional long form: Republic of Djibouti
conventional short form: Djibouti
former: French Territory of the Afars and Issas, French Somaliland
Government type: republic
Capital: Djibouti
Administrative divisions: 5 districts (cercles, singular - cercle); 'Ali Sabih, Dikhil, Djibouti, Obock, Tadjoura
Independence: 27 June 1977 (from France)
National holiday: Independence Day, 27 June (1977)
Constitution: multiparty constitution approved by referendum 4 September 1992
Legal system: based on French civil law system, traditional practices, and Islamic law
Suffrage: 18 years of age; universal adult
Executive branch:
chief of state: President Ismail Omar GUELLEH (since 8 May 1999)
head of government: Prime Minister Mohamed Dileita DILEITA (since 4 March 2001)
cabinet: Council of Ministers responsible to the president
elections: president elected by popular vote for a six-year term; election last held 8 April 2005 (next to be held by April 2011); prime minister appointed by the president
election results: Ismail Omar GUELLEH reelected president; percent of vote - Ismail Omar GUELLEH 100%
Legislative branch: unicameral Chamber of Deputies or Chambre des Deputes (65 seats; members elected by popular vote for five-year terms)
elections: last held 10 January 2003 (next to be held January 2008)
election results: percent of vote - RPP 62.2%, FRUD 36.9%; seats - RPP 65, FRUD 0; note - RPP (the ruling party) dominated the election
Judicial branch: Supreme Court or Cour Supreme
Political parties and leaders: Democratic National Party or PND [ADEN Robleh Awaleh]; Democratic Renewal Party or PRD [Abdillahi HAMARITEH]; Djibouti Development Party or PDD [Mohamed Daoud CHEHEM]; Front pour la Restauration de l'Unite Democratique or FRUD [Ali Mohamed DAOUD]; People's Progress Assembly or RPP (governing party) [Ismail Omar GUELLEH]; Peoples Social Democratic Party or PPSD [Moumin Bahdon FARAH]; Republican Alliance for Democracy or ARD [Ahmed Dini AHMED]; Union for Democracy and Justice or UDJ [leader NA]
Political pressure groups and leaders: Union for Presidential Majority UMP (coalition includes RPP, FRUD, PPSD and PND); Union for Democratic Changeover or UAD (opposition coalition includes ARD, MRDD, UDJ, and PDD) [Ahmed Dini AHMED]
International organization participation: ACCT, ACP, AfDB, AFESD, AMF, AU, COMESA, FAO, G-77, IBRD, ICAO, ICCt, ICFTU, ICRM, IDA, IDB, IFAD, IFC, IFRCS, IGAD, ILO, IMF, IMO, Interpol, IOC, ITU, LAS, NAM, OIC, OPCW (signatory), UN, UNCTAD, UNESCO, UNIDO, UPU, WFTU, WHO, WIPO, WMO, WToO, WTO
Diplomatic representation in the US:
chief of mission: Ambassador ROBLE Olhaye
chancery: Suite 515, 1156 15th Street NW, Washington, DC 20005
telephone: [1] (202) 331-0270
FAX: [1] (202) 331-0302
Diplomatic representation from the US:
chief of mission: Ambassador Marguerita RAGSDALE
embassy: Plateau du Serpent, Boulevard Marechal Joffre, Djibouti
mailing address: B. P. 185, Djibouti
telephone: [253] 35 39 95
FAX: [253] 35 39 40

Flag description: two equal horizontal bands of light blue (top) and light green with a white isosceles triangle based on the hoist side bearing a red five-pointed star in the center

ECONOMY

Economy - overview: The economy is based on service activities connected with the country's strategic location and status as a free trade zone in northeast Africa. Two-thirds of the inhabitants live in the capital city, the remainder are mostly nomadic herders. Scanty rainfall limits crop production to fruits and vegetables, and most food must be imported. Djibouti provides services as both a transit port for the region and an international transshipment and refueling center. Djibouti has few natural resources and little industry. The nation is, therefore, heavily dependent on foreign assistance to help support its balance of payments and to finance development projects. An unemployment rate of at least 50% continues to be a major problem. While inflation is not a concern, due to the fixed tie of the Djiboutian franc to the US dollar, the artificially high value of the Djiboutian franc adversely affects Djibouti's balance of payments. Per capita consumption dropped an estimated 35% over the last seven years because of recession, civil war, and a high population growth rate (including immigrants and refugees). Faced with a multitude of economic difficulties, the government has fallen in arrears on long-term external debt and has been struggling to meet the stipulations of foreign aid donors.
GDP (purchasing power parity): $619 million (2002 est.)
GDP (official exchange rate): NA
GDP - real growth rate: 3.5% (2002 est.)
GDP - per capita: purchasing power parity - $1,300 (2002 est.)
GDP - composition by sector:
agriculture: 3.5%
industry: 15.8%
services: 80.7% (2001 est.)
Labor force: 282,000 (2000)
Labor force - by occupation: NA
Unemployment rate: 50% (2004 est.)
Population below poverty line: 50% (2001 est.)
Household income or consumption by percentage share:
lowest 10%: NA
highest 10%: NA
Inflation rate (consumer prices): 2% (2002 est.)
Budget:
revenues: $135 million
expenditures: $182 million, including capital expenditures of NA (1999 est.)
Agriculture - products: fruits, vegetables; goats, sheep, camels, animal hides
Industries: construction, agricultural processing, salt
Industrial production growth rate: 3% (1996 est.)
Electricity - production: 240 million kWh (2003)
Electricity - production by source:
fossil fuel: 100%
hydro: 0%
nuclear: 0%
other: 0% (2001)
Electricity - consumption: 223.2 million kWh (2003)
Electricity - exports: 0 kWh (2003)
Electricity - imports: 0 kWh (2003)
Oil - production: 0 bbl/day (2003)
Oil - consumption: 12,000 bbl/day (2003 est.)
Oil - exports: NA (2001)
Oil - imports: NA (2001)
Exports: $250 million f.o.b. (2004 est.)
Exports - partners: Somalia 63.8%, Yemen 22.6%, Ethiopia 5% (2004)
Imports: $987 million f.o.b. (2004 est.)
Imports - partners: Saudi Arabia 19.7%, India 12.4%, Ethiopia 11.8%, China 8.1%, France 5.6%, US 4.8% (2004)
Debt - external: $366 million (2002 est.)
Economic aid - recipient: $36 million (2001)
Currency (code): Djiboutian franc (DJF)
Currency code: DJF
Exchange rates: Djiboutian francs per US dollar - NA (2005), 177.72 (2004), 177.72 (2003), 177.72 (2002), 177.72 (2001)
Fiscal year: calendar year

COMMUNICATIONS

Telephones - main lines in use: 9,500 (2003)
Telephones - mobile cellular: 23,000 (2003)
Telephone system:
general assessment: telephone facilities in the city of Djibouti are adequate as are the microwave radio relay connections to outlying areas of the country
domestic: microwave radio relay network
international: country code - 253; submarine cable to Jiddah, Suez, Sicily, Marseilles, Colombo, and Singapore; satellite earth stations - 1 Intelsat (Indian Ocean) and 1 Arabsat; Medarabtel regional microwave radio relay telephone network
Radio broadcast stations: AM 1, FM 2, shortwave 0 (2001)
Radios: 52,000 (1997)
Television broadcast stations: 1 (2002)
Televisions: 28,000 (1997)
Internet country code: .dj
Internet hosts: 702 (2004)
Internet Service Providers (ISPs): 1 (2000)
Internet users: 6,500 (2003)

TRANSPORTATION

Airports: 13 (2004 est.)
Airports - with paved runways:
total: 3
over 3,047 m: 1
2,438 to 3,047 m: 1
1,524 to 2,437 m: 1 (2005 est.)
Airports - with unpaved runways:
total: 10
1,524 to 2,437 m: 2
914 to 1,523 m: 5
under 914 m: 3 (2005 est.)
Railways:
total: 100 km (Djibouti segment of the Addis Ababa-Djibouti railway)
narrow gauge: 100 km 1.000-m gauge
note: railway under joint control of Djibouti and Ethiopia (2004)
Roadways:
total: 2,890 km
paved: 364 km
unpaved: 2,526 km (1999)
Merchant marine:
total: 1 ships (1,000 GRT or over) 1,369 GRT/3,030 DWT
by type: cargo 1 (2005)
Ports and terminals: *Djibouti*

MILITARY

Military branches: Djibouti National Army (includes Navy and Air Force)
Military service age and obligation: 18 years of age (est.); no conscription (2001)
Manpower available for military service:
males age 18-49: 95,328 (2005 est.)
Manpower fit for military service: *males age 18-49:* 46,020 (2005 est.)
Military expenditures - dollar figure: $28.6 million (2004)
Military expenditures - percent of GDP: 4.4% (2004)

TRANSNATIONAL ISSUES

Disputes - international: Djibouti maintains economic ties and border accords with "Somaliland" leadership while maintaining some political ties to various factions in Somalia; although most of the 26,000 Somali refugees in Djibouti who fled civil unrest in the early 1990s have returned, several thousand still await repatriation in UNHCR camps
Refugees and internally displaced persons:
refugees (country of origin): 25,474 (Somalia) (2004)

DOMINICA

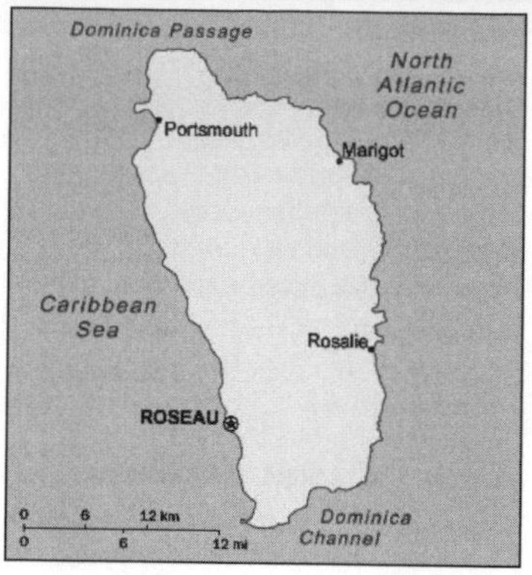

INTRODUCTION

Background: Dominica was the last of the Caribbean islands to be colonized by Europeans, due chiefly to the fierce resistance of the native Caribs. France ceded possession to Great Britain in 1763, which made the island a colony in 1805. In 1980, two years after independence, Dominica's fortunes improved when a corrupt and tyrannical administration was replaced by that of Mary Eugenia CHARLES, the first female prime minister in the Caribbean, who remained in office for 15 years. Some 3,000 Carib Indians still living on Dominica are the only pre-Columbian population remaining in the eastern Caribbean.

GEOGRAPHY

Location: Caribbean, island between the Caribbean Sea and the North Atlantic Ocean, about one-half of the way from Puerto Rico to Trinidad and Tobago
Geographic coordinates: 15 25 N, 61 20 W
Map references: Central America and the Caribbean
Area:
total: 754 sq km
land: 754 sq km
water: 0 sq km
Area - comparative: slightly more than four times the size of Washington, DC
Land boundaries: 0 km
Coastline: 148 km
Maritime claims:
territorial sea: 12 nm
contiguous zone: 24 nm
exclusive economic zone: 200 nm
Climate: tropical; moderated by northeast trade winds; heavy rainfall
Terrain: rugged mountains of volcanic origin
Elevation extremes:
lowest point: Caribbean Sea 0 m
highest point: Morne Diablatins 1,447 m
Natural resources: timber, hydropower, arable land
Land use:
arable land: 6.67%
permanent crops: 20%
other: 73.33% (2001)
Irrigated land: NA sq km
Natural hazards: flash floods are a constant threat; destructive hurricanes can be expected during the late summer months
Environment - current issues: NA
Environment - international agreements:
party to: Biodiversity, Climate Change, Climate Change-Kyoto Protocol, Desertification, Endangered Species, Environmental Modification, Hazardous Wastes, Law of the Sea, Ozone Layer Protection, Ship Pollution, Whaling
signed, but not ratified: none of the selected agreements
Geography - note: known as "The Nature Island of the Caribbean" due to its spectacular, lush, and varied flora and fauna, which are protected by an extensive natural park system; the most mountainous of the Lesser Antilles, its volcanic peaks are cones of lava craters and include Boiling Lake, the second-largest, thermally active lake in the world

PEOPLE

Population: 69,029 (July 2005 est.)
Age structure:
0-14 years: 26.7% (male 9,328/female 9,125)
15-64 years: 65.4% (male 23,225/female 21,900)
65 years and over: 7.9% (male 2,193/female 3,258) (2005 est.)
Median age:
total: 29.59 years
male: 29.26 years
female: 29.95 years (2005 est.)
Population growth rate: -0.27% (2005 est.)
Birth rate: 15.73 births/1,000 population (2005 est.)
Death rate: 6.81 deaths/1,000 population (2005 est.)
Net migration rate: -11.6 migrant(s)/1,000 population (2005 est.)
Sex ratio:
at birth: 1.05 male(s)/female
under 15 years: 1.02 male(s)/female
15-64 years: 1.06 male(s)/female
65 years and over: 0.67 male(s)/female
total population: 1.01 male(s)/female (2005 est.)
Infant mortality rate:
total: 14.15 deaths/1,000 live births
male: 18.68 deaths/1,000 live births
female: 9.38 deaths/1,000 live births (2005 est.)
Life expectancy at birth:
total population: 74.65 years
male: 71.73 years
female: 77.71 years (2005 est.)
Total fertility rate: 1.96 children born/woman (2005 est.)
HIV/AIDS - adult prevalence rate: NA
HIV/AIDS - people living with HIV/AIDS: NA
HIV/AIDS - deaths: NA
Nationality:
noun: Dominican(s)
adjective: Dominican
Ethnic groups: black, mixed black and European, European, Syrian, Carib Amerindian
Religions: Roman Catholic 77%, Protestant 15% (Methodist 5%, Pentecostal 3%, Seventh-Day Adventist 3%, Baptist 2%, other 2%), other 6%, none 2%
Languages: English (official), French patois
Literacy:
definition: age 15 and over has ever attended school
total population: 94%
male: 94%
female: 94% (2003 est.)

GOVERNMENT

Country name:
conventional long form: Commonwealth of Dominica
conventional short form: Dominica
Government type: parliamentary democracy; republic within the Commonwealth
Capital: Roseau
Administrative divisions: 10 parishes; Saint Andrew, Saint David, Saint George, Saint John, Saint Joseph, Saint Luke, Saint Mark, Saint Patrick, Saint Paul, Saint Peter
Independence: 3 November 1978 (from UK)
National holiday: Independence Day, 3 November (1978)
Constitution: 3 November 1978
Legal system: based on English common law
Suffrage: 18 years of age; universal
Executive branch:
chief of state: President Nicholas J. O. LIVERPOOL (since October 2003)
head of government: Prime Minister Roosevelt SKERRIT (since 8 January 2004); note - assumed post after death of Prime Minister Pierre CHARLES
cabinet: Cabinet appointed by the president on the advice of the prime minister
elections: president elected by the House of Assembly for a five-year term; election last held 1 October 2003 (next to be held October 2008); prime minister appoint-

ed by the president
election results: Nicholas LIVERPOOL elected president; percent of legislative vote - NA%
Legislative branch: unicameral House of Assembly (30 seats, 9 appointed senators, 21 elected by popular vote; members serve five-year terms)
elections: last held 5 May 2005 (next to be held by 5 August 2010); note - tradition dictates that the election will be held within five years of the last election, but technically it is five years from the first seating of parliament (12 May 2005) plus a 90-day grace period
election results: percent of vote by party - DLP 52.08%, UWP 43.6%, DFP 3.15%; seats by party - DLP 12, UWP 8, independent 1
Judicial branch: Eastern Caribbean Supreme Court, consisting of the Court of Appeal and the High Court (located in Saint Lucia; one of the six judges must reside in Dominica and preside over the Court of Summary Jurisdiction)
Political parties and leaders: Dominica Freedom Party or DFP [Charles SAVARIN]; Dominica Labor Party or DLP [Roosevelt SKERRIT]; United Workers Party or UWP [Edison JAMES]
Political pressure groups and leaders: Dominica Liberation Movement or DLM (a small leftist party)
International organization participation: ACCT, ACP, C, Caricom, CDB, FAO, G-77, IBRD, ICCt, ICFTU, ICRM, IDA, IFAD, IFC, IFRCS, ILO, IMF, IMO, Interpol, IOC, ISO (subscriber), ITU, MIGA, NAM (observer), OAS, OECS, OPANAL, OPCW, UN, UNCTAD, UNESCO, UNIDO, UPU, WCL, WHO, WIPO, WMO, WTO
Diplomatic representation in the US:
chief of mission: Ambassador Swinburne LESTRADE
chancery: 3216 New Mexico Avenue NW, Washington, DC 20016
telephone: [1] (202) 364-6781
FAX: [1] (202) 364-6791
consulate(s) general: New York
Diplomatic representation from the US: the US does not have an embassy in Dominica; the US Ambassador to Barbados is accredited to Dominica
Flag description: green, with a centered cross of three equal bands - the vertical part is yellow (hoist side), black, and white and the horizontal part is yellow (top), black, and white; superimposed in the center of the cross is a red disk bearing a sisserou parrot encircled by 10 green, five-pointed stars edged in yellow; the 10 stars represent the 10 administrative divisions (parishes)

ECONOMY

Economy - overview: The Dominican economy depends on agriculture, primarily bananas, and remains highly vulnerable to climatic conditions and international economic developments. Production of bananas dropped precipitously in 2003, a major reason for the 1% decline in GDP. Tourism increased in 2003 as the government sought to promote Dominica as an "ecotourism" destination. Development of the tourism industry remains difficult, however, because of the rugged coastline, lack of beaches, and the absence of an international airport. The government began a comprehensive restructuring of the economy in 2003 - including elimination of price controls, privatization of the state banana company, and tax increases - to address Dominica's economic crisis and to meet IMF targets. In order to diversify the island's production base the government is attempting to develop an offshore financial sector and is planning to construct an oil refinery on the eastern part of the island.
GDP (purchasing power parity): $384 million (2003 est.)
GDP (official exchange rate): NA
GDP - real growth rate: -1% (2003 est.)
GDP - per capita: purchasing power parity - $5,500 (2003 est.)
GDP - composition by sector:
agriculture: 18%
industry: 24%
services: 58% (2002 est.)
Labor force: 25,000 (1999 est.)
Labor force - by occupation: agriculture 40%, industry and commerce 32%, services 28%
Unemployment rate: 23% (2000 est.)
Population below poverty line: 30% (2002 est.)
Household income or consumption by percentage share:
lowest 10%: NA
highest 10%: NA
Inflation rate (consumer prices): 1% (2001 est.)
Budget:
revenues: $73.9 million
expenditures: $84.4 million, including capital expenditures of NA (2001)
Agriculture - products: bananas, citrus, mangoes, root crops, coconuts, cocoa; forest and fishery potential not exploited
Industries: soap, coconut oil, tourism, copra, furniture, cement blocks, shoes
Industrial production growth rate: -10% (1997 est.)
Electricity - production: 69.98 million kWh (2003)
Electricity - production by source:
fossil fuel: 47.1%
hydro: 52.9%
nuclear: 0%
other: 0% (2001)
Electricity - consumption: 65.09 million kWh (2003)
Electricity - exports: 0 kWh (2003)
Electricity - imports: 0 kWh (2003)
Oil - production: 0 bbl/day (2003)
Oil - consumption: 800 bbl/day (2003 est.)
Oil - exports: NA (2001)
Oil - imports: NA (2001)
Exports: $74 million f.o.b. (2004 est.)
Exports - partners: UK 21.6%, Jamaica 14.8%, Antigua and Barbuda 8.8%, Guyana 7.5%, Japan 5.4%, Trinidad and Tobago 4.8%, US 4.3%, Saint Lucia 4% (2004)
Imports: $234 million f.o.b. (2004 est.)
Imports - commodities: capital goods, food, textiles, petroleum products
Imports - partners: China 20.4%, US 16.8%, Trinidad and Tobago 12.3%, UK 6.9%, South Korea 4.6%, Japan 4.3% (2004)
Debt - external: $161.5 million (2001)
Economic aid - recipient: $22.8 million (2003 est.)
Currency (code): East Caribbean dollar (XCD)
Currency code: XCD
Exchange rates: East Caribbean dollars per US dollar - NA (2005), 2.7 (2004), 2.7 (2003), 2.7 (2002), 2.7 (2001)
Fiscal year: 1 July - 30 June

COMMUNICATIONS

Telephones - main lines in use: 23,700 (2002)
Telephones - mobile cellular: 9,400 (2002)
Telephone system:
general assessment: NA
domestic: fully automatic network
international: country code - 1-767; microwave radio relay and SHF radiotelephone links to Martinique and Guadeloupe; VHF and UHF radiotelephone links to Saint Lucia
Radio broadcast stations: AM 2, FM 4, shortwave 0 (2004)
Radios: 46,000 (1997)
Television broadcast stations: 1 (2004)
Televisions: 6,000 (1997)
Internet country code: .dm
Internet hosts: 681 (2003)
Internet Service Providers (ISPs): 16 (2000)
Internet users: 12,500 (2002)

TRANSPORTATION

Airports: 2 (2004 est.)
Airports - with paved runways:
total: 2
914 to 1,523 m: 2 (2005 est.)

Roadways:
total: 780 km
paved: 393 km
unpaved: 387 km (1999)
Merchant marine:
total: 32 ships (1,000 GRT or over) 13,771 GRT/19,736 DWT
by type: bulk carrier 2, cargo 19, chemical tanker 2, container 1, passenger/cargo 1, petroleum tanker 5, refrigerated cargo 1, roll on/roll off 1
foreign-owned: 21 (Estonia 6, Greece 3, Pakistan 1, Russia 2, Singapore 6, Syria 2, UAE 1) (2005)
Ports and terminals: Portsmouth, Roseau

MILITARY

Military branches: no regular military forces; Commonwealth of Dominica Police Force (includes Coast Guard)
Military expenditures - dollar figure: NA
Military expenditures - percent of GDP: NA

TRANSNATIONAL ISSUES

Disputes - international: joins other Caribbean states to counter Venezuela's claim that Aves Island sustains human habitation, a criterion under UNCLOS, which permits Venezuela to extend its EEZ/continental shelf over a large portion of the Caribbean Sea
Illicit drugs: transshipment point for narcotics bound for the US and Europe; minor cannabis producer; anti-money-laundering enforcement is weak, making the country particularly vulnerable to money laundering

DOMINICAN REPUBLIC

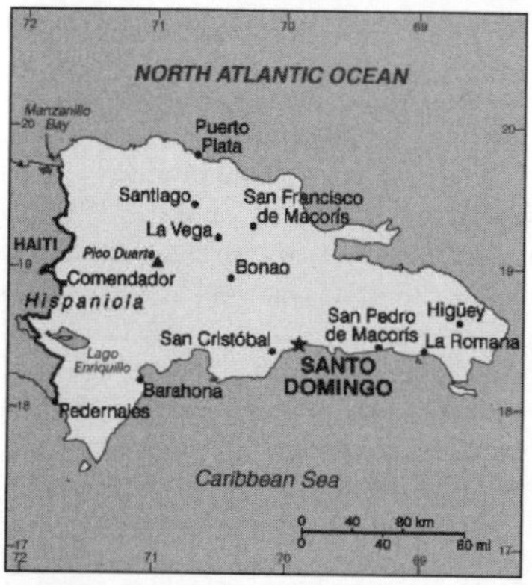

INTRODUCTION

Background: Explored and claimed by Columbus on his first voyage in 1492, the island of Hispaniola became a springboard for Spanish conquest of the Caribbean and the American mainland. In 1697, Spain recognized French dominion over the western third of the island, which in 1804 became Haiti. The remainder of the island, by then known as Santo Domingo, sought to gain its own independence in 1821, but was conquered and ruled by the Haitians for 22 years; it finally attained independence as the Dominican Republic in 1844. In 1861, the Dominicans voluntarily returned to the Spanish Empire, but two years later they launched a war that restored independence in 1865. A legacy of unsettled, mostly non-representative, rule for much of its subsequent history was brought to an end in 1966 when Joaquin BALAGUER became president. He maintained a tight grip on power for most of the next 30 years when international reaction to flawed elections forced him to curtail his term in 1996. Since then, regular competitive elections have been held in which opposition candidates have won the presidency. The Dominican economy has had one of the fastest growth rates in the hemisphere over the past decade.

GEOGRAPHY

Location: Caribbean, eastern two-thirds of the island of Hispaniola, between the Caribbean Sea and the North Atlantic Ocean, east of Haiti
Geographic coordinates: 19 00 N, 70 40 W
Map references: Central America and the Caribbean
Area:
total: 48,730 sq km
land: 48,380 sq km
water: 350 sq km
Area - comparative: slightly more than twice the size of New Hampshire
Land boundaries:
total: 360 km
border countries: Haiti 360 km
Coastline: 1,288 km
Maritime claims:
territorial sea: 6 nm
contiguous zone: 24 nm
exclusive economic zone: 200 nm
continental shelf: 200 nm or to the edge of the continental margin
Climate: tropical maritime; little seasonal temperature variation; seasonal variation in rainfall
Terrain: rugged highlands and mountains with fertile valleys interspersed
Elevation extremes:
lowest point: Lago Enriquillo -46 m
highest point: Pico Duarte 3,175 m
Natural resources: nickel, bauxite, gold, silver
Land use:
arable land: 22.65%
permanent crops: 10.33%
other: 67.02% (2001)
Irrigated land: 2,590 sq km (1998 est.)
Natural hazards: lies in the middle of the hurricane belt and subject to severe storms from June to October; occasional flooding; periodic droughts
Environment - current issues: water shortages; soil eroding into the sea damages coral reefs; deforestation
Environment - international agreements:
party to: Biodiversity, Climate Change, Climate Change-Kyoto Protocol, Desertification, Endangered Species, Hazardous Wastes, Marine Dumping, Marine Life Conservation, Ozone Layer Protection, Ship Pollution
signed, but not ratified: Law of the Sea
Geography - note: shares island of Hispaniola with Haiti

PEOPLE

Population: 8,950,034 (July 2005 est.)
Age structure:
0-14 years: 32.9% (male 1,505,964/female 1,438,809)
15-64 years: 61.7% (male 2,815,544/female 2,703,012)
65 years and over: 5.4% (male 226,372/female 260,333) (2005 est.)
Median age:
total: 23.88 years
male: 23.68 years
female: 24.09 years (2005 est.)
Population growth rate: 1.29% (2005 est.)
Birth rate: 23.28 births/1,000 population (2005 est.)
Death rate: 7.35 deaths/1,000 population (2005 est.)
Net migration rate: -3.02 migrant(s)/1,000 population (2005 est.)
Sex ratio:
at birth: 1.05 male(s)/female
under 15 years: 1.05 male(s)/female
15-64 years: 1.04 male(s)/female
65 years and over: 0.87 male(s)/female
total population: 1.03 male(s)/female (2005 est.)
Infant mortality rate:
total: 32.38 deaths/1,000 live births
male: 34.81 deaths/1,000 live births
female: 29.84 deaths/1,000 live births (2005 est.)
Life expectancy at birth:
total population: 71.44 years
male: 69.94 years
female: 73.03 years (2005 est.)
Total fertility rate: 2.86 children

born/woman (2005 est.)
HIV/AIDS - adult prevalence rate: 1.7% (2003 est.)
HIV/AIDS - people living with HIV/AIDS: 88,000 (2003 est.)
HIV/AIDS - deaths: 7,900 (2003 est.)
Nationality:
noun: Dominican(s)
adjective: Dominican
Ethnic groups: white 16%, black 11%, mixed 73%
Religions: Roman Catholic 95%
Languages: Spanish
Literacy:
definition: age 15 and over can read and write
total population: 84.7%
male: 84.6%
female: 84.8% (2003 est.)

GOVERNMENT

Country name:
conventional long form: Dominican Republic
conventional short form: The Dominican
local long form: Republica Dominicana
local short form: La Dominicana
Government type: representative democracy
Capital: Santo Domingo
Administrative divisions: 31 provinces (provincias, singular - provincia) and 1 district* (distrito); Azua, Baoruco, Barahona, Dajabon, Distrito Nacional*, Duarte, Elias Pina, El Seibo, Espaillat, Hato Mayor, Independencia, La Altagracia, La Romana, La Vega, Maria Trinidad Sanchez, Monsenor Nouel, Monte Cristi, Monte Plata, Pedernales, Peravia, Puerto Plata, Salcedo, Samana, Sanchez Ramirez, San Cristobal, San Jose de Ocoa, San Juan, San Pedro de Macoris, Santiago, Santiago Rodriguez, Santo Domingo, Valverde
Independence: 27 February 1844 (from Haiti)
National holiday: Independence Day, 27 February (1844)
Constitution: 28 November 1966; amended 25 July 2002
Legal system: based on French civil codes; undergoing modification in 2004 towards an accusatory system
Suffrage: 18 years of age, universal and compulsory; married persons regardless of age note: members of the armed forces and national police cannot vote
Executive branch:
chief of state: President Leonel FERNANDEZ Reyna (since 16 August 2004); Vice President Rafael ALBURQUERQUE de Castro (since 16 August 2004); note - the president is both the chief of state and head of government
head of government: President Leonel FERNANDEZ Reyna (since 16 August 2004); Vice President Rafael ALBURQUERQUE de Castro (since 16 August 2004); note - the president is both the chief of state and head of government
cabinet: Cabinet nominated by the president
elections: president and vice president elected on the same ticket by popular vote for four-year terms; election last held 16 May 2004 (next to be held in May 2008)
election results: Leonel FERNANDEZ elected president; percent of vote - Leonel FERNANDEZ (PLD) 57.1%, Rafael Hipolito MEJIA Dominguez (PRD) 33.7%, Eduardo ESTRELLA (PRSC) 8.7%
Legislative branch: bicameral National Congress or Congreso Nacional consists of the Senate or Senado (32 seats; members are elected by popular vote to serve four-year terms) and the Chamber of Deputies or Camara de Diputados (150 seats; members are elected by popular vote to serve four-year terms)
elections: Senate - last held 16 May 2002 (next to be held May 2006); Chamber of Deputies - last held 16 May 2002 (next to be held May 2006)
election results: Senate - percent of vote by party - NA%; seats by party - PRD 29, PLD 2, PRSC 1; Chamber of Deputies - percent of vote by party - NA%; seats by party - PRD 73, PLD 41, PRSC 36
Judicial branch: Supreme Court or Corte Suprema (judges are appointed by a the National Judicial Council comprised of the President, the leaders of both chambers of congress, the President of the Supreme Court, and an opposition or non-governing party member)
Political parties and leaders: Dominican Liberation Party or PLD [Leonel FERNANDEZ Reyna]; Dominican Revolutionary Party or PRD [Vicente Sanchez BARET]; Social Christian Reformist Party or PRSC [Enrique ATUN]
Political pressure groups and leaders: Collective of Popular Organizations or COP; Citizen Participation Group (Participacion Ciudadania); Foundation for Institution-Building (FINJUS)
International organization participation: ACP, FAO, G-77, IADB, IAEA, IBRD, ICAO, ICC, ICCt (signatory), ICFTU, ICRM, IDA, IFAD, IFC, IFRCS, IHO, ILO, IMF, IMO, Interpol, IOC, IOM, ISO (correspondent), ITU, LAES, LAIA (observer), MIGA, NAM, OAS, OPANAL, OPCW (signatory), PCA, RG, UN, UNCTAD, UNESCO, UNIDO, UNOCI, UPU, WCL, WCO, WFTU, WHO, WIPO, WMO, WToO, WTO
Diplomatic representation in the US:
chief of mission: Ambassador-designate Flavio Dario Espinal JACOBO
chancery: 1715 22nd Street NW, Washington, DC 20008
telephone: [1] (202) 332-6280
FAX: [1] (202) 265-8057
consulate(s) general: Boston, Chicago, Mayaguez (Puerto Rico), Miami, New Orleans, New York, Philadelphia, and San Juan (Puerto Rico)
Diplomatic representation from the US:
chief of mission: Ambassador Hans H. HERTELL
embassy: corner of Calle Cesar Nicolas Penson and Calle Leopoldo Navarro, Santo Domingo
mailing address: Unit 5500, APO AA 34041-5500
telephone: [1] (809) 221-5511
FAX: [1] (809) 686-7437
Flag description: a centered white cross that extends to the edges divides the flag into four rectangles - the top ones are blue (hoist side) and red, and the bottom ones are red (hoist side) and blue; a small coat of arms featuring a shield supported by an olive branch (left) and a palm branch (right) is at the center of the cross; above the shield a blue ribbon displays the motto, DIOS, PATRIA, LIBERTAD (God, Fatherland, Liberty), and below the shield, REPUBLICA DOMINICANA appears on a red ribbon

ECONOMY

Economy - overview: The Dominican Republic is a Caribbean representative democracy which enjoyed GDP growth of more than 7% in 1998-2000. Growth subsequently plummeted as part of the global economic slowdown. Although the country has long been viewed primarily as an exporter of sugar, coffee, and tobacco, in recent years the service sector has overtaken agriculture as the economy's largest employer, due to growth in tourism and free trade zones. The country suffers from marked income inequality; the poorest half of the population receives less than one-fifth of GNP, while the richest 10% enjoys nearly 40% of national income. Growth turned negative in 2003 with reduced tourism, a major bank fraud, and limited growth in the US economy (the source of about 85% of export revenues), but recovered in 2004 and 2005. Resumption of a badly needed IMF loan, slowed due to government repurchase of electrical power plants, is basic to the restoration of social and economic stability. Newly elected President FERNANDEZ in mid-2004 promised belt-tightening reform. His administration has passed tax reform and arranged a $600 million IMF standby

arrangement in March 20005 to ease the country's fiscal situation. Although the economy continues to grow at a respectable rate, inflation and unemployment remain the two biggest challenges.
GDP (purchasing power parity): $58.52 billion (2005 est.)
GDP (official exchange rate): $17.68 billion (2005 est.)
GDP - real growth rate: 4.1% (2005 est.)
GDP - per capita: purchasing power parity - $6,500 (2005 est.)
GDP - composition by sector:
agriculture: 10.7%
industry: 31.5%
services: 57.8% (2003)
Labor force: 2.3 million - 2.6 million (2000 est.)
Labor force - by occupation: agriculture 17%, industry 24.3%, services and government 58.7% (1998 est.)
Unemployment rate: 17% (2005 est.)
Population below poverty line: 25%
Household income or consumption by percentage share:
lowest 10%: 2.1%
highest 10%: 37.9% (1998)
Distribution of family income - Gini index: 47.4 (1998)
Inflation rate (consumer prices): 4.3% (2005 est.)
Investment (gross fixed): 25.4% of GDP (2005 est.)
Budget:
revenues: $5.322 billion
expenditures: $5.485 billion, including capital expenditures of $1.1 billion (2005 est.)
Public debt: 51.4% of GDP (2005 est.)
Agriculture - products: sugarcane, coffee, cotton, cocoa, tobacco, rice, beans, potatoes, corn, bananas; cattle, pigs, dairy products, beef, eggs
Industries: tourism, sugar processing, ferronickel and gold mining, textiles, cement, tobacco
Industrial production growth rate: 2% (2001 est.)
Electricity - production: 12.6 billion kWh (2003)
Electricity - production by source:
fossil fuel: 92%
hydro: 7.6%
nuclear: 0%
other: 0.4% (2001)
Electricity - consumption: 11.71 billion kWh (2003)
Electricity - exports: 0 kWh (2003)
Electricity - imports: 0 kWh (2003)
Oil - production: 0 bbl/day (2001 est.)
Oil - consumption: 128,000 bbl/day (2003 est.)
Oil - exports: NA (2001)
Oil - imports: 129,900 bbl/day (2003)
Current account balance: $-383 million (2005 est.)
Exports: $5.818 billion f.o.b. (2005 est.)
Exports - partners: US 80%, South Korea 2.1%, Canada 1.9% (2004)
Imports: $9.747 billion f.o.b. (2005 est.)
Imports - partners: US 48.1%, Venezuela 13.5%, Colombia 4.8%, Mexico 4.8% (2004)
Reserves of foreign exchange and gold: $1.379 billion (2005 est.)
Debt - external: $7.907 billion (2005 est.)
Economic aid - recipient: $239.6 million (1995)
Currency (code): Dominican peso (DOP)
Currency code: DOP
Exchange rates: Dominican pesos per US dollar - 30.42 (2005), 42.12 (2004), 30.831 (2003), 18.61 (2002), 16.952 (2001)
Fiscal year: calendar year

COMMUNICATIONS

Telephones - main lines in use: 901,800 (2003)
Telephones - mobile cellular: 2,120,400 (2003)
Telephone system:
general assessment: NA
domestic: relatively efficient system based on island-wide microwave radio relay network
international: country code - 1-809; 1 coaxial submarine cable; satellite earth station - 1 Intelsat (Atlantic Ocean)
Radio broadcast stations: AM 120, FM 56, shortwave 4 (1998)
Radios: 1.44 million (1997)
Television broadcast stations: 25 (2003)
Televisions: 770,000 (1997)
Internet country code: .do
Internet hosts: 64,197 (2003)
Internet Service Providers (ISPs): 24 (2000)
Internet users: 500,000 (2003)

TRANSPORTATION

Airports: 31 (2004 est.)
Airports - with paved runways:
total: 13
over 3,047 m: 3
2,438 to 3,047 m: 3
1,524 to 2,437 m: 3
914 to 1,523 m: 3
under 914 m: 1 (2005 est.)
Airports - with unpaved runways:
total: 19
1,524 to 2,437 m: 4
914 to 1,523 m: 5
under 914 m: 10 (2005 est.)
Railways:
total: 1,743 km
standard gauge: 375 km 1.435-m gauge
narrow gauge: 142 km 0.762-m gauge
note: additional 1,226 km operated by sugar companies in 1.076-m, 0.889-m, and 0.762-m gauges (2004)
Roadways:
total: 12,600 km
paved: 6,224 km
unpaved: 6,376 km (1999)
Merchant marine:
total: 3 ships (1,000 GRT or over) 11,230 GRT/17,011 DWT
by type: cargo 3 (2005)
Ports and terminals: Boca Chica, Puerto Plata, Rio Haina, Santo Domingo

MILITARY

Military branches: Army, Navy, Air Force
Military service age and obligation: 18 years of age for voluntary military service (2001)
Manpower available for military service: *males age 18-49:* 2,108,197 (2005 est.)
Manpower fit for military service: *males age 18-49:* 1,420,693 (2005 est.)
Manpower reaching military service age annually: *males:* 91,597 (2005 est.)
Military expenditures - dollar figure: $180 million (1998)
Military expenditures - percent of GDP: 1.1% (1998)

TRANSNATIONAL ISSUES

Disputes - international: increasing numbers of illegal migrants from the Dominican Republic cross the Mona Passage each year to Puerto Rico to find work
Illicit drugs: transshipment point for South American drugs destined for the US and Europe; has become a transshipment point for ecstasy from the Netherlands and Belgium destined for US and Canada; substantial money-laundering activity; Colombian narcotics traffickers favor the Dominican Republic for illicit financial transactions

EAST TIMOR

INTRODUCTION

Background: The Portuguese began to trade with the island of Timor in the early 16th century and colonized it in mid-century. Skirmishing with the Dutch in the region eventually resulted in an 1859 treaty in which Portugal ceded the western portion of the island. Imperial Japan occupied East Timor from 1942 to 1945, but Portugal resumed colonial authority after the Japanese defeat in World War II. East Timor declared itself independent from Portugal on 28 November 1975 and was invaded and occupied by Indonesian forces nine days later. It was incorporated into Indonesia in July 1976 as the province of East Timor. An unsuccessful campaign of pacification followed over the next two decades, during which an estimated 100,000 to 250,000 individuals lost their lives. On 30 August 1999, in a UN-supervised popular referendum, an overwhelming majority of the people of East Timor voted for independence from Indonesia. Between the referendum and the arrival of a multinational peacekeeping force in late September 1999, anti-independence Timorese militias - organized and supported by the Indonesian military - commenced a large-scale, scorched-earth campaign of retribution. The militias killed approximately 1,300 Timorese and forcibly pushed 300,000 people into West Timor as refugees. The majority of the country's infrastructure, including homes, irrigation systems, water supply systems, and schools, and nearly 100% of the country's electrical grid were destroyed. On 20 September 1999 the Australian-led peacekeeping troops of the International Force for East Timor (INTERFET) deployed to the country and brought the violence to an end. On 20 May 2002, East Timor was internationally recognized as an independent state.

GEOGRAPHY

Location: Southeastern Asia, northwest of Australia in the Lesser Sunda Islands at the eastern end of the Indonesian archipelago; note - East Timor includes the eastern half of the island of Timor, the Oecussi (Ambeno) region on the northwest portion of the island of Timor, and the islands of Pulau Atauro and Pulau Jaco
Geographic coordinates: 8 50 S, 125 55 E
Map references: Southeast Asia
Area:
total: 15,007 sq km
land: NA
water: NA
Area - comparative: slightly larger than Connecticut
Land boundaries:
total: 228 km
border countries: Indonesia 228 km
Coastline: 706 km
Maritime claims:
territorial sea: NA
exclusive economic zone: NA
continental shelf: NA
exclusive fishing zone: NA
Climate: tropical; hot, humid; distinct rainy and dry seasons
Terrain: mountainous
Elevation extremes:
lowest point: Timor Sea, Savu Sea, and Banda Sea 0 m
highest point: Foho Tatamailau 2,963 m
Natural resources: gold, petroleum, natural gas, manganese, marble
Land use:
arable land: 4.71%
permanent crops: 0.67%
other: 94.62% (2001)
Irrigated land: 1,065 sq km (est.)
Natural hazards: floods and landslides are common; earthquakes, tsunamis, tropical cyclones
Environment - current issues: widespread use of slash and burn agriculture has led to deforestation and soil erosion
Environment - international agreements: NA
Geography - note: Timor comes from the Malay word for "East"; the island of Timor is part of the Malay Archipelago and is the largest and easternmost of the Lesser Sunda Islands

PEOPLE

Population: 1,040,880
note: other estimates range as low as 800,000 (July 2005 est.)
Age structure:
0-14 years: 37.1% (male 196,108/female 189,753)
15-64 years: 59.9% (male 318,173/female 305,479)
65 years and over: 3% (male 15,353/female 16,014) (2005 est.)
Median age:
total: 20.41 years
male: 20.46 years
female: 20.35 years (2005 est.)
Population growth rate: 2.09% (2005 est.)
Birth rate: 27.19 births/1,000 population (2005 est.)
Death rate: 6.3 deaths/1,000 population (2005 est.)
Net migration rate: 0 migrant(s)/1,000 population (2005 est.)
Sex ratio:
at birth: 1.05 male(s)/female
under 15 years: 1.03 male(s)/female
15-64 years: 1.04 male(s)/female
65 years and over: 0.96 male(s)/female
total population: 1.04 male(s)/female (2005 est.)
Infant mortality rate:
total: 47.41 deaths/1,000 live births
male: 53.71 deaths/1,000 live births
female: 40.8 deaths/1,000 live births (2005 est.)
Life expectancy at birth:
total population: 65.9 years
male: 63.63 years
female: 68.29 years (2005 est.)
Total fertility rate: 3.61 children born/woman (2005 est.)
HIV/AIDS - adult prevalence rate: NA
HIV/AIDS - people living with HIV/AIDS: NA
HIV/AIDS - deaths: NA
Nationality:
noun: Timorese
adjective: Timorese
Ethnic groups: Austronesian (Malayo-Polynesian), Papuan, small Chinese minority
Religions: Roman Catholic 90%, Muslim 4%, Protestant 3%, Hindu 0.5%, Buddhist, Animist (1992 est.)
Languages: Tetum (official), Portuguese (official), Indonesian, English
note: there are about 16 indigenous languages; Tetum, Galole, Mambae, and Kemak are spoken by significant numbers of people
Literacy:
definition: age 15 and over can read and write
total population: 58.6% (2002)

GOVERNMENT

Country name:
conventional long form: Democratic Republic of Timor-Leste
conventional short form: East Timor
local long form: Republika Demokratika

Timor Lorosa'e [Tetum]; Republica Democratica de Timor-Leste [Portuguese]
local short form: Timor Lorosa'e [Tetum]; Timor-Leste [Portuguese]
former: Portuguese Timor
Government type: Republic
Capital: Dili
Administrative divisions: 13 administrative districts; Aileu, Ainaro, Baucau, Bobonaro (Maliana), Cova-Lima (Suai), Dili, Ermera, Lautem (Los Palos), Liquica, Manatuto, Manufahi (Same), Oecussi (Ambeno), Viqueque
Independence: 28 November 1975 (date of proclamation of independence from Portugal); note - 20 May 2002 is the official date of international recognition of East Timor's independence from Indonesia
National holiday: Independence Day, 28 November (1975)
Constitution: 22 March 2002 (based on the Portuguese model)
Legal system: UN-drafted legal system based on Indonesian law remains in place but will be replaced by civil and penal codes based on Portuguese law (2004)
Suffrage: 17 years of age; universal
Executive branch:
chief of state: President Kay Rala Xanana GUSMAO (since 20 May 2002); note - the president plays a largely symbolic role but is able to veto some legislation; he formerly used the name Jose Alexandre GUSMAO
head of government: Prime Minister Mari Bin Amude ALKATIRI (since 20 May 2002)
cabinet: Council of Ministers
elections: president elected by popular vote for a five-year term; election last held 14 April 2002 (next to be held in April 2007); after the legislature was sworn in, the leader of the majority party was appointed prime minister by the president, suggesting a precedent for the future
election results: Kay Rala Xanana GUSMAO elected president; percent of vote - Kay Rala Xanana GUSMAO 82.7%, Francisco Xavier do AMARAL 17.3%
Legislative branch: unicameral National Parliament (number of seats can vary, minimum requirement of 52 and a maximum of 65 seats; members elected by popular vote to serve five-year terms); note - for its first term of office, the National Parliament is comprised of 88 members on an exceptional basis
elections: (next to be held August 2006); direct elections for national parliament were never held; elected delegates to the national convention named themselves legislators instead of having elections; hence the exceptional numbers for this term of the national parliament.
election results: percent of vote by party - FRETILIN 57.37%, PD 8.72%, PSD 8.18%, ASDT 7.84%, UDT 2.36%, PNT 2.21%, KOTA 2.13%, PPT 2.01%, PDC 1.98%, PST 1.78%, independents/other 5.42%; seats by party - FRETILIN 55, PD 7, PSD 6, ASDT 6, PDC 2, UDT 2, KOTA 2, PNT 2, PPT 2, UDC/PDC 1, PST 1, PL 1, independent 1
Judicial branch: Supreme Court of Justice - constitution calls for one judge to be appointed by National Parliament and rest appointed by Superior Council for Judiciary; note - until Supreme Court is established, Court of Appeals is highest court
Political parties and leaders: Associacao Social-Democrata Timorense or ASDT [Francisco Xavier do AMARAL]; Christian Democratic Party of Timor or PDC [Antonio XIMENES]; Christian Democratic Union of Timor or UDC [Vicente da Silva GUTERRES]; Democratic Party or PD [Fernando de ARAUJO]; Liberal Party or PL [leader NA]; Maubere Democratic Party or PDM [leader NA]; People's Party of Timor or PPT [Jacob XAVIER]; Revolutionary Front of Independent East Timor or FRETILIN [Lu OLO]; Social Democrat Party of East Timor or PSD [Mario CARRASCALAO]; Socialist Party of Timor or PST [leader Avelino COELHO]; Sons of the Mountain Warriors (also known as Association of Timorese Heroes) or KOTA [Clementino dos Reis AMARAL]; Timor Democratic Union or UDT [Joao CARRASCALAO]; Timor Labor Party or PTT [Paulo Freitas DA SILVA]; Timorese Nationalist Party or PNT [Abilio ARAUJO]; Timorese Popular Democratic Association or APODETI [Frederico Almeida-Santos DA COSTA]
Political pressure groups and leaders: Popular Council for the Defense of the Democratic Republic of East Timor or CPD-RDTL [leader Antonio-Aitahan MATAK] is largest political pressure group; dissatisfied veterans of struggle against Indonesia, led by one-time government advisor Cornelio GAMA (also known as L-7), also play an important role in pressuring government
International organization participation: ACP, ARF, AsDB, FAO, G-77, IBRD, ICAO, ICCt, IDA, IFAD, IFC, IFRCS (observer), ILO, IMF, IMO, Interpol, IOC, MIGA, OPCW, PIF (observer), UN, UNCTAD, UNESCO, UNIDO, UPU, WCO, WHO
Diplomatic representation in the US:
chief of mission: Ambassador Jose Luis GUTERRES
chancery: 3415 Massachusetts Avenue, Washington, DC 20007
telephone: 202 965-1515
FAX: 202 965-1517
consulate(s) general: New York (the ambassador resides in New York) (2004)
Diplomatic representation from the US:
chief of mission: Ambassador Grover Joseph REES
embassy: Avenida de Portugal, Praia dos Conqueiros, Dili
mailing address: Department of State, 8250 Dili Place, Washington, DC 20521-8250
telephone: (670) 332-4684
FAX: (670) 331-3206
Flag description: red, with a black isosceles triangle (based on the hoist side) superimposed on a slightly longer yellow arrowhead that extends to the center of the flag; there is a white star in the center of the black triangle

ECONOMY

Economy - overview: In late 1999, about 70% of the economic infrastructure of East Timor was laid waste by Indonesian troops and anti-independence militias, and 300,000 people fled westward. Over the next three years, however, a massive international program, manned by 5,000 peacekeepers (8,000 at peak) and 1,300 police officers, led to substantial reconstruction in both urban and rural areas. By 2003, all but about 30,000 of the refugees had returned. Non-petroleum GDP growth was held back in 2003 by extensive drought and the gradual winding down of the international presence, but recovered somewhat in 2004. The country faces great challenges in continuing the rebuilding of infrastructure, strengthening the infant civil administration, and generating jobs for young people entering the workforce. The development of oil and gas resources in nearby waters has begun to supplement government revenues ahead of schedule and above expectations - the result of high petroleum prices - but the technology-intensive industry does little to create jobs for the unemployed. The Parliament in June 2005 unanimously approved the creation of a Petroleum Fund to serve as a repository for all petroleum revenues and preserve the value of East Timor's petroleum wealth for future generations.
GDP (purchasing power parity): $370 million (2004 est.)
GDP (official exchange rate): NA
GDP - real growth rate: 1% (2004 est.)
GDP - per capita: purchasing power parity - $400 (2004 est.)

GDP - composition by sector:
agriculture: 25.4%
industry: 17.2%
services: 57.4% (2001)
Labor force: NA
Labor force - by occupation: NA
Unemployment rate: 50%
note: unemployment in urban areas reached 20%; data do not include underemployed (2001)
Population below poverty line: 42% (2003 est.)
Household income or consumption by percentage share:
lowest 10%: NA
highest 10%: NA
Distribution of family income - Gini index: 38 (2002 est.)
Inflation rate (consumer prices): 1.8% (2004)
Budget:
revenues: $107.7 million
expenditures: $73 million, including capital expenditures of NA (2004)
Agriculture - products: coffee, rice, maize, cassava, sweet potatoes, soybeans, cabbage, mangoes, bananas, vanilla
Industries: printing, soap manufacturing, handicrafts, woven cloth
Industrial production growth rate: 8.5%
Electricity - production: NA kWh (2003)
Electricity - production by source:
fossil fuel: 100%
hydro: 0%
nuclear: 0%
other: 0% (2001)
Electricity - consumption: NA kWh (2003)
Electricity - exports: 0 kWh (2003)
Electricity - imports: 0 kWh (2003)
Exports: $10 million excluding oil (2005 est.)
Exports - partners: Indonesia 100% (2004)
Imports: $202 million (2004 est.)
Imports - partners: Indonesia, Australia, Singapore, Vietnam, Bangladesh (2004)
Debt - external: none
Economic aid - recipient: $2.2 billion (1999-2002 est.)
Currency (code): US dollar (USD)
Currency code: USD
Exchange rates: the US dollar is the legal tender
Fiscal year: 1 July - 30 June

COMMUNICATIONS

Telephones - main lines in use: NA
Telephones - mobile cellular: NA
Telephone system: NA
Radio broadcast stations: AM NA, FM NA, shortwave NA
Radios: NA
Television broadcast stations: NA
Televisions: NA
Internet country code: .tl; note - ICANN approved the change from .tp in January 2005
Internet Service Providers (ISPs): NA
Internet users: NA

TRANSPORTATION

Airports: 8 (2004 est.)
Airports - with paved runways:
total: 3
2,438 to 3,047 m: 1
1,524 to 2,437 m: 1
914 to 1,523 m: 1 (2005 est.)
Airports - with unpaved runways:
total: 5
914 to 1,523 m: 3
under 914 m: 2 (2005 est.)
Heliports: 9 (2005 est.)
Roadways:
total: 3,800 km
paved: 428 km
unpaved: 3,372 km (1995)
Ports and terminals: Dili

MILITARY

Military branches: East Timor Defense Force (Forcas de Defesa de Timor-L'este, FDTL): Army, Navy (Armada) (2005)
Military service age and obligation: 18 years of age for voluntary military service (2001)
Manpower available for military service: NA
Manpower fit for military service: *males age 18-49:* NA
Manpower reaching military service age annually: NA
Military expenditures - dollar figure: $4.4 million (FY03)
Military expenditures - percent of GDP: NA

TRANSNATIONAL ISSUES

Disputes - international: UN Mission of Support in East Timor (UNMISET) has maintained about a thousand peacekeepers in East Timor since 2002; East Timor-Indonesia Boundary Committee continues to meet, survey, and delimit the land boundary, but several sections of the boundary especially around the Oekussi enclave remain unresolved; Indonesia and East Timor contest the sovereignty of the uninhabited coral island of Palau Batek/Fatu Sinai, which prevents delimitation of the northern maritime boundaries; many of 28,000 East Timorese refugees still residing in Indonesia in 2003 have returned, but many continue to refuse repatriation; East Timor and Australia continue to meet but disagree over how to delimit a permanent maritime boundary and share unexploited potential petroleum resources that fall outside the Joint Petroleum Development Area covered by the 2002 Timor Sea Treaty; dispute with Australia also hampers creation of a southern maritime boundary with Indonesia
Illicit drugs: NA

ECUADOR

INTRODUCTION

Background: The "Republic of the Equator" was one of three countries that emerged from the collapse of Gran Colombia in 1830 (the others are Colombia and Venezuela). Between 1904 and 1942, Ecuador lost territories in a series of conflicts with its neighbors. A border war with Peru that flared in 1995 was resolved in 1999. Although Ecuador marked 25 years of civilian governance in 2004, the period has been marred by political instability. Seven presidents have governed Ecuador since 1996.

GEOGRAPHY

Location: Western South America, bordering the Pacific Ocean at the Equator, between Colombia and Peru
Geographic coordinates: 2 00 S, 77 30 W
Map references: South America
Area:
total: 283,560 sq km
land: 276,840 sq km
water: 6,720 sq km
note: includes Galapagos Islands
Area - comparative: slightly smaller than Nevada
Land boundaries:
total: 2,010 km

border countries: Colombia 590 km, Peru 1,420 km
Coastline: 2,237 km
Maritime claims:
territorial sea: 200 nm
continental shelf: 100 nm from 2,500 meter isobath
Climate: tropical along coast, becoming cooler inland at higher elevations; tropical in Amazonian jungle lowlands
Terrain: coastal plain (costa), inter-Andean central highlands (sierra), and flat to rolling eastern jungle (oriente)
Elevation extremes:
lowest point: Pacific Ocean 0 m
highest point: Chimborazo 6,267 m
Natural resources: petroleum, fish, timber, hydropower
Land use:
arable land: 5.85%
permanent crops: 4.93%
other: 89.22% (2001)
Irrigated land: 8,650 sq km (1998 est.)
Natural hazards: frequent earthquakes, landslides, volcanic activity; floods; periodic droughts
Environment - current issues: deforestation; soil erosion; desertification; water pollution; pollution from oil production wastes in ecologically sensitive areas of the Amazon Basin and Galapagos Islands
Environment - international agreements:
party to: Antarctic-Environmental Protocol, Antarctic Treaty, Biodiversity, Climate Change, Climate Change-Kyoto Protocol, Desertification, Endangered Species, Hazardous Wastes, Ozone Layer Protection, Ship Pollution, Tropical Timber 83, Tropical Timber 94, Wetlands
signed, but not ratified: none of the selected agreements
Geography - note: Cotopaxi in Andes is highest active volcano in world

PEOPLE

Population: 13,363,593 (July 2005 est.)
Age structure:
0-14 years: 33.5% (male 2,282,252/female 2,195,942)
15-64 years: 61.5% (male 4,094,146/female 4,130,096)
65 years and over: 4.9% (male 310,336/female 350,821) (2005 est.)
Median age:
total: 23.27 years
male: 22.82 years
female: 23.74 years (2005 est.)
Population growth rate: 1.24% (2005 est.)
Birth rate: 22.67 births/1,000 population (2005 est.)
Death rate: 4.24 deaths/1,000 population (2005 est.)
Net migration rate: -6.07 migrant(s)/1,000 population (2005 est.)
Sex ratio:
at birth: 1.05 male(s)/female
under 15 years: 1.04 male(s)/female
15-64 years: 0.99 male(s)/female
65 years and over: 0.88 male(s)/female
total population: 1 male(s)/female (2005 est.)
Infant mortality rate:
total: 23.66 deaths/1,000 live births
male: 28.36 deaths/1,000 live births
female: 18.72 deaths/1,000 live births (2005 est.)
Life expectancy at birth:
total population: 76.21 years
male: 73.35 years
female: 79.22 years (2005 est.)
Total fertility rate: 2.72 children born/woman (2005 est.)
HIV/AIDS - adult prevalence rate: 0.3% (2003 est.)
HIV/AIDS - people living with HIV/AIDS: 21,000 (2003 est.)
HIV/AIDS - deaths: 1,700 (2003 est.)
Nationality:
noun: Ecuadorian(s)
adjective: Ecuadorian
Ethnic groups: mestizo (mixed Amerindian and white) 65%, Amerindian 25%, Spanish and others 7%, black 3%
Religions: Roman Catholic 95%, other 5%
Languages: Spanish (official), Amerindian languages (especially Quechua)
Literacy:
definition: age 15 and over can read and write
total population: 92.5%
male: 94%
female: 91% (2003 est.)

GOVERNMENT

Country name:
conventional long form: Republic of Ecuador
conventional short form: Ecuador
local long form: Republica del Ecuador
local short form: Ecuador
Government type: republic
Capital: Quito
Administrative divisions: 22 provinces (provincias, singular - provincia); Azuay, Bolivar, Canar, Carchi, Chimborazo, Cotopaxi, El Oro, Esmeraldas, Galapagos, Guayas, Imbabura, Loja, Los Rios, Manabi, Morona-Santiago, Napo, Orellana, Pastaza, Pichincha, Sucumbios, Tungurahua, Zamora-Chinchipe
Independence: 24 May 1822 (from Spain)
National holiday: Independence Day (independence of Quito), 10 August (1809)
Constitution: 10 August 1998
Legal system: based on civil law system; has not accepted compulsory ICJ jurisdiction
Suffrage: 18 years of age; universal, compulsory for literate persons ages 18-65, optional for other eligible voters
Executive branch:
chief of state: President Alfredo PALACIO (since 20 April 2005); Vice President Nicanor Alejandro SERRANO Aguilar (since 5 May 2005); note - the president is both the chief of state and head of government; former President Lucio GUTIERREZ was removed from office by congress effective 20 April 2005
head of government: President Alfredo PALACIO (since 20 April 2005); Vice President Nicanor Alejandro SERRANO Aguilar (since 5 May 2005); note - the president is both the chief of state and head of government
cabinet: Cabinet appointed by the president elections: the president and vice president are elected on the same ticket by popular vote for a four-year term (no immediate reelection); election last held 20 October 2002; runoff election held 24 November 2002 (next to be held October 2006)
election results: results of the 24 November 2002 runoff election - Lucio GUTIERREZ elected president; percent of vote - Lucio GUTIERREZ 54.3%; Alvaro NOBOA 45.7%; note - Vice President Alfredo PALACIO assumed the presidency on 20 April 2005 after congress removed Lucio GUTIERREZ from office
Legislative branch: unicameral National Congress or Congreso Nacional (100 seats; members are popularly elected by province to serve four-year terms)
elections: last held 20 October 2002 (next to be held October 2006)
election results: percent of vote by party - NA%; seats by party - PSC 25, PRE 15, ID 16, PRIAN 10, PSP 9, Pachakutik Movement 6, MPD 5, DP 4, PS-FA 3, independents 7; note - defections by members of National Congress are commonplace, resulting in frequent changes in the numbers of seats held by the various parties
Judicial branch: Supreme Court or Corte Suprema (according to the Constitution, new justices are elected by the full Supreme Court; in December 2004, however, Congress successfully replaced the entire court via a simple-majority resolution)
Political parties and leaders: Concentration of Popular Forces or CFP [Averroes BUCARAM]; Democratic Left or ID [Guillermo LANDAZURI]; National Action Institutional Renewal

Party or PRIAN [Alvaro NOBOA]; Pachakutik Movement [Gilberto TALAHUA]; Patriotic Society Party or PSP [Lucio GUTIERREZ Borbua]; Popular Democracy or DP [Dr. Juan Manuel FUERTES]; Popular Democratic Movement or MPD [Gustavo TERAN Acosta]; Radical Alfarista Front or FRA [Fabian ALARCON, director]; Roldosist Party or PRE [Abdala BUCARAM Ortiz, director]; Social Christian Party or PSC [Leon FEBRES CORDERO]; Socialist Party - Broad Front or PS-FA [Victor GRANDA]

Political pressure groups and leaders: Confederation of Indigenous Nationalities of Ecuador or CONAIE [Luis MACAS, president]; Coordinator of Social Movements or CMS [F. Napoleon SANTOS]; Federation of Indigenous Evangelists of Ecuador or FEINE [Marco MURILLO, president]; National Federation of Indigenous Afro-Ecuatorianos and Peasants or FENOCIN [Pedro DE LA CRUZ, president]

International organization participation: CAN, CSN, FAO, G-77, IADB, IAEA, IBRD, ICAO, ICC, ICCt, ICFTU, ICRM, IDA, IFAD, IFC, IFRCS, IHO, ILO, IMF, IMO, Interpol, IOC, IOM, ISO, ITU, LAES, LAIA, Mercosur (associate), MIGA, MINUSTAH, NAM, OAS, OPANAL, OPCW, PCA, RG, UN, UNCTAD, UNESCO, UNHCR, UNIDO, UNMIL, UNOCI, UPU, WCL, WCO, WFTU, WHO, WIPO, WMO, WToO, WTO

Diplomatic representation in the US:
chief of mission: Ambassador Luis Benigno GALLEGOS Chiriboga
chancery: 2535 15th Street NW, Washington, DC 20009
telephone: [1] (202) 234-7200
FAX: [1] (202) 667-3482
consulate(s) general: Chicago, Houston, Jersey City (New Jersey), Los Angeles, Miami, New Orleans, New York, and San Francisco

Diplomatic representation from the US:
chief of mission: Ambassador Linda J. JEWELL
embassy: Avenida 12 de Octubre y Avenida Patria, Quito
mailing address: APO AA 34039
telephone: [593] (2) 256-2890
FAX: [593] (2) 250-2052
consulate(s) general: Guayaquil

Flag description: three horizontal bands of yellow (top, double width), blue, and red with the coat of arms superimposed at the center of the flag; similar to the flag of Colombia, which is shorter and does not bear a coat of arms

ECONOMY

Economy - overview: Ecuador has substantial petroleum resources, which have accounted for 40% of the country's export earnings and one-fourth of central government budget revenues in recent years. Consequently, fluctuations in world market prices can have a substantial domestic impact. In the late 1990s, Ecuador suffered its worst economic crisis, with natural disasters and sharp declines in world petroleum prices driving Ecuador's economy into free fall in 1999. Real GDP contracted by more than 6%, with poverty worsening significantly. The banking system also collapsed, and Ecuador defaulted on its external debt later that year. The currency depreciated by some 70% in 1999, and, on the brink of hyperinflation, the MAHAUD government announced it would dollarize the economy. A coup, however, ousted MAHAUD from office in January 2000, and after a short-lived junta failed to garner military support, Vice President Gustavo NOBOA took over the presidency. In March 2000, Congress approved a series of structural reforms that also provided the framework for the adoption of the US dollar as legal tender. Dollarization stabilized the economy, and growth returned to its pre-crisis levels in the years that followed. Under the administration of Lucio GUTIERREZ - January 2003 to April 2005 - Ecuador benefited from higher world petroleum prices, and the new government under Alfredo PALACIO has proposed economic reforms to reduce Ecuador's vulnerability to petroleum price swings and financial crises. High oil prices have kept the current account in surplus. PALACIO is committed to spending a part of the oil windfall on social projects.

GDP (purchasing power parity): $52.66 billion (2005 est.)

GDP (official exchange rate): $31.36 billion (2005 est.)

GDP - real growth rate: 3% (2005 est.)

GDP - per capita: purchasing power parity - $3,900 (2005 est.)

GDP - composition by sector:
agriculture: 7.4%
industry: 31.8%
services: 60.8% (2005 est.)

Labor force: 4.6 million (urban) (2005 est.)

Labor force - by occupation: agriculture 8%, industry 24%, services 68% (2001)

Unemployment rate: 11.2%; note - underemployment of 47% (2005 est.)

Population below poverty line: 45% (2001 est.)

Household income or consumption by percentage share:
lowest 10%: 2%
highest 10%: 32%
note: data for urban households only (October 2003)

Distribution of family income - Gini index: 42
note: data are for urban households (2003)

Inflation rate (consumer prices): 2% (2005 est.)

Investment (gross fixed): 22% of GDP (2005 est.)

Budget:
revenues: $8.822 billion
expenditures: planned $8.153 billion, including capital expenditures of $1.6 billion (2005 est.)

Public debt: 44.9% of GDP (2005 est.)

Agriculture - products: bananas, coffee, cocoa, rice, potatoes, manioc (tapioca), plantains, sugarcane; cattle, sheep, pigs, beef, pork, dairy products; balsa wood; fish, shrimp

Industries: petroleum, food processing, textiles, wood products, chemicals

Industrial production growth rate: 4.5% (2005 est.)

Electricity - production: 11.27 billion kWh (2003)

Electricity - production by source:
fossil fuel: 81%
hydro: 19%
nuclear: 0%
other: 0% (2001)

Electricity - consumption: 10.55 billion kWh (2003)

Electricity - exports: 65 million kWh (2003)

Electricity - imports: 140 million kWh (2003)

Oil - production: 493,200 bbl/day (2005 est.)

Oil - consumption: 155,000 bbl/day (2003 est.)

Oil - exports: 387,000 bbl/day (2004 est.)

Oil - imports: NA (2001)

Oil - proved reserves: 4.512 billion bbl (2005 est.)

Natural gas - production: 160 million cu m (2001 est.)

Natural gas - consumption: 160 million cu m (2001 est.)

Natural gas - exports: 0 cu m (2001 est.)

Natural gas - imports: 0 cu m (2001 est.)

Natural gas - proved reserves: 106.5 billion cu m (2005)

Current account balance: $58 million (2005 est.)

Exports: $9.224 billion (2005 est.)

Exports - partners: US 42.9%, Panama 14.3%, Peru 7.9%, Italy 4.6% (2004)

Imports: $8.436 billion (2005 est.)

Imports - partners: US 16.5%, Colombia 14.1%, China 9.2%, Venezuela 7.1%, Brazil 6.5%, Chile 4.6%, Japan 4.5%, Mexico 4.3% (2004)

Reserves of foreign exchange and gold: $1.618 billion (2005 est.)
Debt - external: $17.01 billion (31 December 2004 est.)
Economic aid - recipient: $216 million (2002)
Currency (code): US dollar (USD)
Currency code: USD
Exchange rates: 25,000 (2005), 25,000 (2004), 25,000 (2003), 25,000 (2002), 24,988 (2001)
Fiscal year: calendar year

COMMUNICATIONS

Telephones - main lines in use: 1.549 million (2003)
Telephones - mobile cellular: 2,394,400 (2003)
Telephone system:
general assessment: generally elementary but being expanded
domestic: facilities generally inadequate and unreliable
international: country code - 593; satellite earth station - 1 Intelsat (Atlantic Ocean)
Radio broadcast stations: AM 392, FM 35, shortwave 29 (2001)
Radios: 5 million (2001)
Television broadcast stations: 7 (plus 14 repeaters) (2001)
Televisions: 2.5 million (2001)
Internet country code: .ec
Internet hosts: 3,188 (2003)
Internet Service Providers (ISPs): 31 (2001)
Internet users: 569,700 (2003)

TRANSPORTATION

Airports: 205 (2004 est.)
Airports - with paved runways:
total: 85
over 3,047 m: 3
2,438 to 3,047 m: 4
1,524 to 2,437 m: 19
914 to 1,523 m: 30
under 914 m: 29 (2005 est.)
Airports - with unpaved runways:
total: 200
914 to 1,523 m: 31
under 914 m: 169 (2005 est.)
Heliports: 1 (2005 est.)
Pipelines: extra heavy crude 578 km; gas 71 km; oil 1,386 km; refined products 1,185 km (2004)
Railways:
total: 966 km
narrow gauge: 966 km 1.067-m gauge (2004)
Roadways:
total: 43,197 km
paved: 7,287 km
unpaved: 35,910 km (2003)
Waterways: 1,500 km (most inaccessible) (2003)
Merchant marine:
total: 31 ships (1,000 GRT or over) 241,403 GRT/391,898 DWT
by type: chemical tanker 2, liquefied gas 1, passenger 8, petroleum tanker 20
foreign-owned: 3 (Germany 1, Greece 1, Paraguay 1) (2005)
Ports and terminals: Esmeraldas, Guayaquil, La Libertad, Manta, Puerto Bolivar

MILITARY

Military branches: Army, Navy (includes Naval Infantry, Naval Aviation, Coast Guard), Air Force (Fuerza Aerea Ecuatoriana, FAE)
Military service age and obligation: 20 years of age for conscript military service; 12-month service obligation (2004)
Manpower available for military service: *males age 20-49*: 2,792,770 (2005 est.)
Manpower fit for military service: *males age 20-49*: 2,338,428 (2005 est.)
Manpower reaching military service age annually: *males*: 133,922 (2005 est.)
Military expenditures - dollar figure: $655 million (2004)
Military expenditures - percent of GDP: 2.2% (2004)

TRANSNATIONAL ISSUES

Disputes - international: organized illegal narcotics operations in Colombia penetrate across Ecuador's shared border and caused over 20,000 refugees to flee into Ecuador in 2004 Illicit drugs: significant transit country for cocaine originating in Colombia and Peru; importer of precursor chemicals used in production of illicit narcotics; attractive location for cash-placement by drug traffickers laundering money because of dollarization and weak anti-money-laundering regime, especially vulnerable along the border with Colombia; increased activity on the northern frontier by trafficking groups and Colombian insurgents

EGYPT

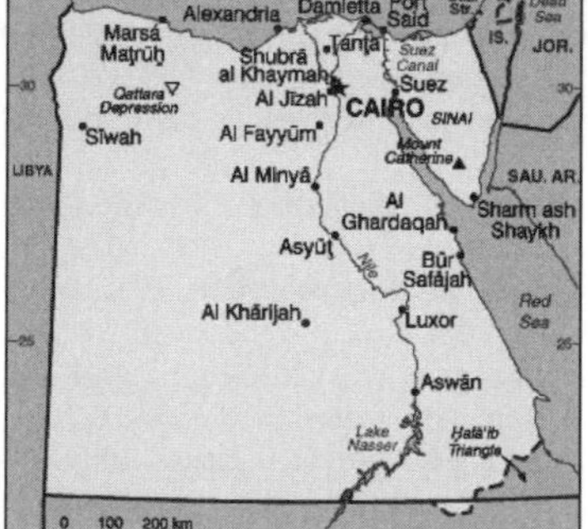

INTRODUCTION

Background: The regularity and richness of the annual Nile River flood, coupled with semi-isolation provided by deserts to the east and west, allowed for the development of one of the world's great civilizations. A unified kingdom arose circa 3200 B.C. and a series of dynasties ruled in Egypt for the next three millennia. The last native dynasty fell to the Persians in 341 B.C., who in turn were replaced by the Greeks, Romans, and Byzantines. It was the Arabs who introduced Islam and the Arabic language in the 7th century and who ruled for the next six centuries. A local military caste, the Mamluks took control about 1250 and continued to govern after the conquest of Egypt by the Ottoman Turks in 1517. Following the completion of the Suez Canal in 1869, Egypt became an important world transportation hub, but also fell heavily into debt. Ostensibly to protect its investments, Britain seized control of Egypt's government in 1882, but nominal allegiance to the Ottoman Empire continued until 1914. Partially independent from the UK in 1922, Egypt acquired full sovereignty following World War II. The completion of the Aswan High Dam in 1971 and the resultant Lake Nasser have altered the time-honored place of the Nile River in the agriculture and ecology of Egypt. A rapidly growing population (the largest in the Arab world), limited arable land, and dependence on the Nile all continue to overtax resources and stress society. The government has struggled to ready the economy for the new millennium through economic reform and massive investment in communications and physical infrastructure.

GEOGRAPHY

Location: Northern Africa, bordering the Mediterranean Sea, between Libya and the Gaza Strip, and the Red Sea north of Sudan, and includes the Asian Sinai Peninsula
Geographic coordinates: 27 00 N, 30 00 E
Map references: Africa
Area:
total: 1,001,450 sq km
land: 995,450 sq km

water: 6,000 sq km
Area - comparative: slightly more than three times the size of New Mexico
Land boundaries:
total: 2,665 km
border countries: Gaza Strip 11 km, Israel 266 km, Libya 1,115 km, Sudan 1,273 km
Coastline: 2,450 km
Maritime claims:
territorial sea: 12 nm
contiguous zone: 24 nm
exclusive economic zone: 200 nm
continental shelf: 200-m depth or to the depth of exploitation
Climate: desert; hot, dry summers with moderate winters
Terrain: vast desert plateau interrupted by Nile valley and delta
Elevation extremes:
lowest point: Qattara Depression -133 m
highest point: Mount Catherine 2,629 m
Natural resources: petroleum, natural gas, iron ore, phosphates, manganese, limestone, gypsum, talc, asbestos, lead, zinc
Land use:
arable land: 2.87%
permanent crops: 0.48%
other: 96.65% (2001)
Irrigated land: 33,000 sq km (1998 est.)
Natural hazards: periodic droughts; frequent earthquakes, flash floods, landslides; hot, driving windstorm called khamsin occurs in spring; dust storms, sandstorms
Environment - current issues: agricultural land being lost to urbanization and windblown sands; increasing soil salination below Aswan High Dam; desertification; oil pollution threatening coral reefs, beaches, and marine habitats; other water pollution from agricultural pesticides, raw sewage, and industrial effluents; very limited natural fresh water resources away from the Nile which is the only perennial water source; rapid growth in population overstraining the Nile and natural resources
Environment - international agreements:
party to: Biodiversity, Climate Change, Climate Change-Kyoto Protocol, Desertification, Endangered Species, Environmental Modification, Hazardous Wastes, Law of the Sea, Marine Dumping, Ozone Layer Protection, Ship Pollution, Tropical Timber 83, Tropical Timber 94, Wetlands
signed, but not ratified: none of the selected agreements
Geography - note: controls Sinai Peninsula, only land bridge between Africa and remainder of Eastern Hemisphere; controls Suez Canal, a sea link between Indian Ocean and Mediterranean Sea; size, and juxtaposition to Israel, establish its major role in Middle Eastern geopolitics; dependence on upstream neighbors; dominance of Nile basin issues; prone to influxes of refugees

PEOPLE

Population: 77,505,756 (July 2005 est.)
Age structure:
0-14 years: 33% (male 13,106,043/female 12,483,899)
15-64 years: 62.6% (male 24,531,266/female 23,972,216)
65 years and over: 4.4% (male 1,457,097/female 1,955,235) (2005 est.)
Median age:
total: 23.68 years
male: 23.31 years
female: 24.05 years (2005 est.)
Population growth rate: 1.78% (2005 est.)
Birth rate: 23.32 births/1,000 population (2005 est.)
Death rate: 5.26 deaths/1,000 population (2005 est.)
Net migration rate: -0.22 migrant(s)/1,000 population (2005 est.)
Sex ratio:
at birth: 1.05 male(s)/female
under 15 years: 1.05 male(s)/female
15-64 years: 1.02 male(s)/female
65 years and over: 0.74 male(s)/female
total population: 1.02 male(s)/female (2005 est.)
Infant mortality rate:
total: 32.59 deaths/1,000 live births
male: 33.31 deaths/1,000 live births
female: 31.83 deaths/1,000 live births (2005 est.)
Life expectancy at birth:
total population: 71 years
male: 68.5 years
female: 73.62 years (2005 est.)
Total fertility rate: 2.88 children born/woman (2005 est.)
HIV/AIDS - adult prevalence rate: less than 0.1% (2001 est.)
HIV/AIDS - people living with HIV/AIDS: 12,000 (2001 est.)
HIV/AIDS - deaths: 700 (2003 est.)
Nationality:
noun: Egyptian(s)
adjective: Egyptian
Ethnic groups: Eastern Hamitic stock (Egyptians, Bedouins, and Berbers) 99%, Greek, Nubian, Armenian, other European (primarily Italian and French) 1%
Religions: Muslim (mostly Sunni) 94%, Coptic Christian and other 6%
Languages: Arabic (official), English and French widely understood by educated classes
Literacy:
definition: age 15 and over can read and write
total population: 57.7%
male: 68.3%
female: 46.9% (2003 est.)

GOVERNMENT

Country name:
conventional long form: Arab Republic of Egypt
conventional short form: Egypt
local long form: Jumhuriyat Misr al-Arabiyah
local short form: Misr
former: United Arab Republic (with Syria)
Government type: republic
Capital: Cairo
Administrative divisions: 26 governorates (muhafazat, singular - muhafazah); Ad Daqahliyah, Al Bahr al Ahmar, Al Buhayrah, Al Fayyum, Al Gharbiyah, Al Iskandariyah, Al Isma'iliyah, Al Jizah, Al Minufiyah, Al Minya, Al Qahirah, Al Qalyubiyah, Al Wadi al Jadid, Ash Sharqiyah, As Suways, Aswan, Asyut, Bani Suwayf, Bur Sa'id, Dumyat, Janub Sina', Kafr ash Shaykh, Matruh, Qina, Shamal Sina', Suhaj
Independence: 28 February 1922 (from UK)
National holiday: Revolution Day, 23 July (1952)
Constitution: 11 September 1971; amended 22 May 1980
Legal system: based on English common law, Islamic law, and Napoleonic codes; judicial review by Supreme Court and Council of State (oversees validity of administrative decisions); accepts compulsory ICJ jurisdiction, with reservations
Suffrage: 18 years of age; universal and compulsory
Executive branch:
chief of state: President Mohammed Hosni MUBARAK (since 14 October 1981)
head of government: Prime Minister Ahmed NAZIF (since 9 July 2004)
cabinet: Cabinet appointed by the president
elections: president elected by popular vote for six-year term; note - a national referendum in May 2005 approved a constitutional amendment that changed the presidential election to a multicandidate popular vote; previously the president was nominated by the People's Assembly and the nomination was validated by a national, popular referendum; last referendum held 26 September 1999; first election under terms of constitutional amendment held 7 September 2005; next election scheduled for 2011
election results: Hosni MUBARAK reelected president; percent of vote - Hosni MUBARAK 88.6%, Ayman NOUR 7.6%, Noman GOMAA 2.9%
Legislative branch: bicameral system consists of the People's Assembly or Majlis

al-Sha'b (454 seats; 444 elected by popular vote, 10 appointed by the president; members serve five-year terms) and the Advisory Council or Majlis al-Shura - which functions only in a consultative role (264 seats; 176 elected by popular vote, 88 appointed by the president; members serve six-year terms; mid-term elections for half the members)
elections: People's Assembly - three-phase voting - last held 7 and 20 November, 1 December 2005;(next to be held November-December 2010); Advisory Council - last held May-June 2004 (next to be held May-June 2007)
election results: People's Assembly - percent of vote by party - NA; seats by party - NDP 311, NWP 6, Tagammu 2, Tomorrow Party 1, independents 112 (12 seats to be determined by rerun elections, 10 seats appointed by President); Advisory Council - percent of vote by party - NA; seats by party - NA
Judicial branch: Supreme Constitutional Court
Political parties and leaders: National Democratic Party or NDP [Mohammed Hosni MUBARAK (governing party)]; National Progressive Unionist Grouping or Tagammu [Rifaat EL-SAID]; New Wafd Party or NWP [No'man GOMAA]; Tomorrow Party [Ayman NOUR]
note: formation of political parties must be approved by the government
Political pressure groups and leaders: despite a constitutional ban against religious-based parties, the technically illegal Muslim Brotherhood constitutes MUBARAK's potentially most significant political opposition; MUBARAK tolerated limited political activity by the Brotherhood for his first two terms, but moved more aggressively since then to block its influence; civic society groups are sanctioned, but constrained in practical terms; trade unions and professional associations are officially sanctioned
International organization participation: ABEDA, ACCT, AfDB, AFESD, AMF, AU, BSEC (observer), CAEU, COMESA, EBRD, FAO, G-15, G-24, G-77, IAEA, IBRD, ICAO, ICC, ICCt (signatory), ICRM, IDA, IDB, IFAD, IFC, IFRCS, IHO, ILO, IMF, IMO, Interpol, IOC, IOM, ISO, ITU, LAS, MIGA, MINURSO, MONUC, NAM, OAPEC, OAS (observer), OIC, ONUB, OSCE (partner), PCA, UN, UNAMSIL, UNCTAD, UNESCO, UNHCR, UNIDO, UNITAR, UNMIL, UNMIS, UNOMIG, UNRWA, UPU, WCO, WFTU, WHO, WIPO, WMO, WToO, WTO
Diplomatic representation in the US:
chief of mission: Ambassador M. Nabil FAHMY
chancery: 3521 International Court NW, Washington, DC 20008
telephone: [1] (202) 895-5400
FAX: [1] (202) 244-5139
consulate(s) general: Chicago, Houston, New York, and San Francisco
Diplomatic representation from the US:
chief of mission: Ambassador designate Francis J. RICCIARDONE, Jr
embassy: 8 Kamal El Din Salah St., Garden City, Cairo
mailing address: Unit 64900, Box 15, APO AE 09839-4900
telephone: [20] (2) 797-3300
FAX: [20] (2) 797-3200
Flag description: three equal horizontal bands of red (top), white, and black; the national emblem (a gold Eagle of Saladin facing the hoist side with a shield superimposed on its chest above a scroll bearing the name of the country in Arabic) centered in the white band; design is based on the Arab Liberation flag and similar to the flag of Syria, which has two green stars, Iraq, which has three green stars (plus an Arabic inscription) in a horizontal line centered in the white band, and Yemen, which has a plain white band

ECONOMY

Economy - overview: Lack of substantial progress on economic reform since the mid 1990s has limited foreign direct investment in Egypt and kept annual GDP growth in the range of 2%-3% in 2001-03. However, in 2004 Egypt implemented several measures to boost foreign direct investment. In September 2004, Egypt pushed through custom reforms, proposed income and corporate tax reforms, reduced energy subsidies, and privatized several enterprises. The budget deficit rose to an estimated 8% of GDP in 2004 compared to 6.1% of GDP the previous year, in part as a result of these reforms. Monetary pressures on an overvalued Egyptian pound led the government to float the currency in January 2003, leading to a sharp drop in its value and consequent inflationary pressure. The development of an export market for natural gas is a bright spot for future growth prospects, but improvement in the capital-intensive hydrocarbons sector does little to reduce Egypt's persistent unemployment.
GDP (purchasing power parity): $337.9 billion (2005 est.)
GDP (official exchange rate): $81.47 billion (2005 est.)
GDP - real growth rate: 4.5% (2005 est.)
GDP - per capita: purchasing power parity - $4,400 (2005 est.)
GDP - composition by sector:
agriculture: 15%
industry: 36.7%
services: 48.4% (2005 est.)
Labor force: 21.34 million (2005 est.)
Labor force - by occupation: agriculture 32%, industry 17%, services 51% (2001 est.)
Unemployment rate: 10% (2005 est.)
Population below poverty line: 16.7% (2000 est.)
Household income or consumption by percentage share:
lowest 10%: 4.4%
highest 10%: 25% (1995)
Distribution of family income - Gini index: 34.4 (2001)
Inflation rate (consumer prices): 5.4% (2005 est.)
Investment (gross fixed): 16.2% of GDP (2005 est.)
Budget:
revenues: $18.03 billion
expenditures: $24.55 billion, including capital expenditures of $2.7 billion (2005 est.)
Public debt: 93.6% of GDP (2005 est.)
Agriculture - products: cotton, rice, corn, wheat, beans, fruits, vegetables; cattle, water buffalo, sheep, goats
Industries: textiles, food processing, tourism, chemicals, hydrocarbons, construction, cement, metals
Industrial production growth rate: 3.2% (2005 est.)
Electricity - production: 84.26 billion kWh (2003)
Electricity - production by source:
fossil fuel: 81%
hydro: 19%
nuclear: 0%
other: 0% (2001)
Electricity - consumption: 78.16 billion kWh (2003)
Electricity - exports: 450 million kWh (2003)
Electricity - imports: 250 million kWh (2003)
Oil - production: 700,000 bbl/day (2005 est.)
Oil - consumption: 566,000 bbl/day (2003 est.)
Oil - exports: NA (2001)
Oil - imports: NA (2001)
Oil - proved reserves: 2.7 billion bbl (2005 est.)
Natural gas - production: 21.2 billion cu m (2001 est.)
Natural gas - consumption: 21.2 billion cu m (2001 est.)
Natural gas - exports: 0 cu m (2001 est.)
Natural gas - imports: 0 cu m (2001 est.)
Natural gas - proved reserves: 1.264 trillion cu m (2005)
Current account balance: $2.928 billion (2005 est.)

Exports: $14.33 billion f.o.b. (2005 est.)
Exports - partners: Italy 11.9%, US 10.8%, UK 7%, Syria 6.2%, Germany 4.7%, Spain 4.2% (2004)
Imports: $24.1 billion f.o.b. (2005 est.)
Imports - partners: US 12.2%, Germany 7%, Italy 6.6%, France 5.7%, China 5.4%, UK 4.7%, Saudi Arabia 4.1% (2004)
Reserves of foreign exchange and gold: $20.31 billion (2005 est.)
Debt - external: $28.95 billion (30 June 2005 est.)
Economic aid - recipient: ODA, $1.12 billion (2002)
Currency (code): Egyptian pound (EGP)
Currency code: EGP
Exchange rates: Egyptian pounds per US dollar - 5.78 (2005), 6.1963 (2004), 5.8509 (2003), 4.4997 (2002), 3.973 (2001)
Fiscal year: 1 July - 30 June

COMMUNICATIONS

Telephones - main lines in use: 9.6 million (2005)
Telephones - mobile cellular: 8,583,940 (2005)
Telephone system:
general assessment: large system; underwent extensive upgrading during 1990s and is reasonably modern; Internet access and cellular service are available
domestic: principal centers at Alexandria, Cairo, Al Mansurah, Ismailia, Suez, and Tanta are connected by coaxial cable and microwave radio relay
international: country code - 20; satellite earth stations - 2 Intelsat (Atlantic Ocean and Indian Ocean), 1 Arabsat, and 1 Inmarsat; 5 coaxial submarine cables; tropospheric scatter to Sudan; microwave radio relay to Israel; a participant in Medarabtel
Radio broadcast stations: AM 42 (plus 15 repeaters), FM 14, shortwave 3 (1999)
Radios: 20.5 million (1997)
Television broadcast stations: 98 (September 1995)
Televisions: 7.7 million (1997)
Internet country code: .eg
Internet hosts: 3,401 (2004)
Internet Service Providers (ISPs): 50 (2000)
Internet users: 4.2 million (2005)

TRANSPORTATION

Airports: 87 (2004 est.)
Airports - with paved runways:
total: 72
over 3,047 m: 13
2,438 to 3,047 m: 38
1,524 to 2,437 m: 17
under 914 m: 4 (2005 est.)
Airports - with unpaved runways:
total: 15
2,438 to 3,047 m: 1
1,524 to 2,437 m: 2
914 to 1,523 m: 5
under 914 m: 7 (2005 est.)
Heliports: 2 (2005 est.)
Pipelines: condensate 289 km; condensate/gas 94 km; gas 6,115 km; liquid petroleum gas 852 km; oil 5,032 km; oil/gas/water 36 km; refined products 246 km (2004)
Railways:
total: 5,063 km
standard gauge: 5,063 km 1.435-m gauge (62 km electrified) (2004)
Roadways:
total: 64,000 km
paved: 49,984 km
unpaved: 14,016 km (1999)
Waterways: 3,500 km
note: includes Nile River, Lake Nasser, Alexandria-Cairo Waterway, and numerous smaller canals in delta; Suez Canal (193.5 km including approaches) navigable by oceangoing vessels drawing up to 17.68 m (2004)
Merchant marine:
total: 77 ships (1,000 GRT or over) 1,194,696 GRT/1,754,815 DWT
by type: bulk carrier 14, cargo 34, container 2, passenger/cargo 5, petroleum tanker 14, roll on/roll off 8
foreign-owned: 10 (Denmark 1, Greece 6, Lebanon 2, Turkey 1)
registered in other countries: 34 (2005)
Ports and terminals: Alexandria, Damietta, El Dekheila, Port Said, Suez, Zeit

MILITARY

Military branches: Army, Navy, Air Force, Air Defense Command
Military service age and obligation: 18 years of age for conscript military service; 3-year service obligation (2001)
Manpower available for military service: *males age 18-49*: 18,347,560 (2005 est.)
Manpower fit for military service: *males age 18-49*: 15,540,234 (2005 est.)
Manpower reaching military service age annually: *males*: 802,920 (2005 est.)
Military expenditures - dollar figure: $2.44 billion (2003)
Military expenditures - percent of GDP: 3.4% (2004)

TRANSNATIONAL ISSUES

Disputes - international: Egypt and Sudan retain claims to administer the two triangular areas that extend north and south of the 1899 Treaty boundary along the 22nd Parallel, but have withdrawn their military presence; Egypt is developing the Hala'ib Triangle north of the Treaty line; since the attack on Taba and other Egyptian resort towns on the Red Sea in October 2004, Egypt vigilantly monitors the Sinai and borders with Israel and the Gaza Strip; Egypt does not extend domestic asylum to some 70,000 persons who identify as Palestinians but who largely lack UNRWA assistance and, until recently, UNHCR recognition as refugees
Refugees and internally displaced persons:
refugees (country of origin): 70,215 (Palestinian Territories) (2004)
Illicit drugs: transit point for Southwest Asian and Southeast Asian heroin and opium moving to Europe, Africa, and the US; transit stop for Nigerian couriers; concern as money-laundering site due to lax financial regulations and enforcement

EL SALVADOR

INTRODUCTION

Background: El Salvador achieved independence from Spain in 1821 and from the Central American Federation in 1839. A 12-year civil war, which cost about 75,000 lives, was brought to a close in 1992 when the government and leftist rebels signed a treaty that provided for military and political reforms.

GEOGRAPHY

Location: Central America, bordering the North Pacific Ocean, between Guatemala and Honduras
Geographic coordinates: 13 50 N, 88 55 W
Map references: Central America and the Caribbean
Area:
total: 21,040 sq km
land: 20,720 sq km
water: 320 sq km
Area - comparative: slightly smaller than Massachusetts
Land boundaries:
total: 545 km
border countries: Guatemala 203 km, Honduras 342 km
Coastline: 307 km
Maritime claims:
territorial sea: 200 nm
Climate: tropical; rainy season (May to October); dry season (November to April); tropical on coast; temperate in uplands

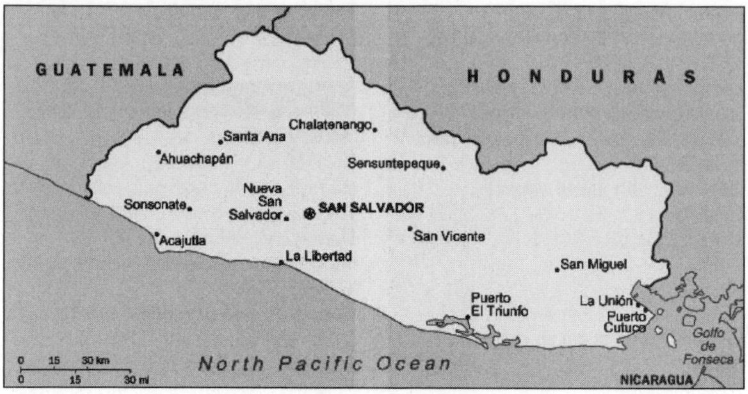

Terrain: mostly mountains with narrow coastal belt and central plateau
Elevation extremes:
lowest point: Pacific Ocean 0 m
highest point: Cerro El Pital 2,730 m
Natural resources: hydropower, geothermal power, petroleum, arable land
Land use:
arable land: 31.85%
permanent crops: 12.07%
other: 56.08% (2001)
Irrigated land: 360 sq km (1998 est.)
Natural hazards: known as the Land of Volcanoes; frequent and sometimes very destructive earthquakes and volcanic activity; extremely susceptible to hurricanes
Environment - current issues: deforestation; soil erosion; water pollution; contamination of soils from disposal of toxic wastes
Environment - international agreements:
party to: Biodiversity, Climate Change, Climate Change-Kyoto Protocol, Desertification, Endangered Species, Hazardous Wastes, Ozone Layer Protection, Wetlands
signed, but not ratified: Law of the Sea
Geography - note: smallest Central American country and only one without a coastline on Caribbean Sea

PEOPLE

Population: 6,704,932 (July 2005 est.)
Age structure:
0-14 years: 36.5% (male 1,250,901/female 1,198,589)
15-64 years: 58.3% (male 1,860,084/female 2,051,140)
65 years and over: 5.1% (male 153,133/female 191,085) (2005 est.)
Median age:
total: 21.57 years
male: 20.44 years
female: 22.69 years (2005 est.)
Population growth rate: 1.75% (2005 est.)
Birth rate: 27.04 births/1,000 population (2005 est.)
Death rate: 5.85 deaths/1,000 population (2005 est.)
Net migration rate: -3.67 migrant(s)/1,000 population (2005 est.)
Sex ratio:
at birth: 1.05 male(s)/female
under 15 years: 1.04 male(s)/female
15-64 years: 0.91 male(s)/female
65 years and over: 0.8 male(s)/female
total population: 0.95 male(s)/female (2005 est.)
Infant mortality rate:
total: 25.1 deaths/1,000 live births
male: 27.98 deaths/1,000 live births
female: 22.08 deaths/1,000 live births (2005 est.)
Life expectancy at birth:
total population: 71.22 years
male: 67.61 years
female: 75.01 years (2005 est.)
Total fertility rate: 3.16 children born/woman (2005 est.)
HIV/AIDS - adult prevalence rate: 0.7% (2003 est.)
HIV/AIDS - people living with HIV/AIDS: 29,000 (2003 est.)
HIV/AIDS - deaths: 2,200 (2003 est.)
Nationality:
noun: Salvadoran(s)
adjective: Salvadoran
Ethnic groups: mestizo 90%, white 9%, Amerindian 1%
Religions: Roman Catholic 83%, other 17%
note: there is extensive activity by Protestant groups throughout the country; by the end of 1992, there were an estimated 1 million Protestant evangelicals in El Salvador
Languages: Spanish, Nahua (among some Amerindians)
Literacy:
definition: age 10 and over can read and write
total population: 80.2%
male: 82.8%
female: 77.7% (2003 est.)

GOVERNMENT

Country name:
conventional long form: Republic of El Salvador
conventional short form: El Salvador
local long form: Republica de El Salvador
local short form: El Salvador
Government type: republic
Capital: San Salvador
Administrative divisions: 14 departments (departamentos, singular - departamento); Ahuachapan, Cabanas, Chalatenango, Cuscatlan, La Libertad, La Paz, La Union, Morazan, San Miguel, San Salvador, Santa Ana, San Vicente, Sonsonate, Usulutan
Independence: 15 September 1821 (from Spain)
National holiday: Independence Day, 15 September (1821)
Constitution: 23 December 1983
Legal system: based on civil and Roman law, with traces of common law; judicial review of legislative acts in the Supreme Court; accepts compulsory ICJ jurisdiction, with reservations
Suffrage: 18 years of age; universal
Executive branch:
chief of state: President Elias Antonio SACA Gonzalez (since 1 June 2004); Vice President Ana Vilma DE ESCOBAR (since 1 June 2004); note - the president is both the chief of state and head of government
head of government: President Elias Antonio SACA Gonzalez (since 1 June 2004); Vice President Ana Vilma DE ESCOBAR (since 1 June 2004); note - the president is both the chief of state and head of government
cabinet: Council of Ministers selected by the president
elections: president and vice president elected on the same ticket by popular vote for five-year terms; election last held 21 March 2004 (next to be held March 2009)
election results: Elias Antonio SACA Gonzalez elected president; percent of vote - Elias Antonio SACA Gonzalez (ARENA) 57.7%, Schafik HANDAL (FMLN) 35.6%, Hector SILVA (CDU-PDC) 3.9%, other 2.8%
Legislative branch: unicameral Legislative Assembly or Asamblea Legislativa (84 seats; members are elected by direct, popular vote to serve three-year terms)
elections: last held 16 March 2003 (next to be held March 2006)
election results: percent of vote by party - NA%; seats by party - FMLN 31, ARENA 28, PCN 15, PDC 5, CD 5
Judicial branch: Supreme Court or Corte Suprema (judges are selected by the Legislative Assembly)
Political parties and leaders: Christian Democratic Party or PDC [Rodolfo PARKER, secretary general]; Democratic Convergence or CD (for-

merly United Democratic Center or CDU) [Ruben ZAMORA, secretary general]; Democratic Party or PD [Jorge MELENDEZ]; Farabundo Marti National Liberation Front or FMLN [Medardo GONZALEZ, coordinator general]; Liberal Democratic Party or PLD [Kirio Waldo SALGADO, president]; National Action Party or PAN [Gustavo Rogelio SALINAS, secretary general]; National Conciliation Party or PCN [Ciro CRUZ ZEPEDA, president]; National Republican Alliance or ARENA [Elias Antonio SACA Gonzalez]; Popular Social Christian Party or PPSC [Rene AGUILUZ]; Revolutionary Democratic Front or FDR [Julio Cesar HERNANDEZ Carcamo, coordinator general]; Social Christian Union or USC (formed by the merger of Christian Social Renewal Party or PRSC and Unity Movement or MU) [Abraham RODRIGUEZ, president]; Social Democratic Party or PSD [Juan MEDRANO]

Political pressure groups and leaders: labor organizations - Electrical Industry Union of El Salvador or SIES; Federation of the Construction Industry, Similar Transport and other activities, or FESINCONTRANS; National Confederation of Salvadoran Workers or CNTS; National Union of Salvadoran Workers or UNTS; Port Industry Union of El Salvador or SIPES; Salvadoran Union of Ex-Petrolleros and Peasant Workers or USEPOC; Salvadoran Workers Central or CTS; Workers Union of Electrical Corporation or STCEL; business organizations - National Association of Small Enterprise or ANEP; Salvadoran Assembly Industry Association or ASIC; Salvadoran Industrial Association or ASI

International organization participation: BCIE, CACM, FAO, G-77, IADB, IAEA, IBRD, ICAO, ICC, ICFTU, ICRM, IDA, IFAD, IFC, IFRCS, ILO, IMF, IMO, Interpol, IOC, IOM, ISO (correspondent), ITU, MIGA, MINURSO, NAM (observer), OAS, OPANAL, OPCW, PCA, RG, UN, UNCTAD, UNESCO, UNIDO, UNMIL, UNMIS, UNOCI, UPU, WCL, WCO, WFTU, WHO, WIPO, WMO, WToO, WTO

Diplomatic representation in the US:
chief of mission: Ambassador Rene Antonio LEON Rodriguez
chancery: 2308 California Street NW, Washington, DC 20008
telephone: [1] (202) 265-9671
FAX: [1] (202) 234-3834
consulate(s) general: Chicago, Dallas, Houston, Las Vegas, Los Angeles, Miami, New York (2), San Francisco, and Washington, DC
consulate(s): Boston

Diplomatic representation from the US:
chief of mission: Ambassador H. Douglas BARCLAY
embassy: Final Boulevard Santa Elena Sur, Antiguo Cuscatlan, La Libertad, San Salvador
mailing address: Unit 3116, APO AA 34023
telephone: [503] 2278-4444
FAX: [503] 2278-5522

Flag description: three equal horizontal bands of blue (top), white, and blue with the national coat of arms centered in the white band; the coat of arms features a round emblem encircled by the words REPUBLICA DE EL SALVADOR EN LA AMERICA CENTRAL; similar to the flag of Nicaragua, which has a different coat of arms centered in the white band - it features a triangle encircled by the words REPUBLICA DE NICARAGUA on top and AMERICA CENTRAL on the bottom; also similar to the flag of Honduras, which has five blue stars arranged in an X pattern centered in the white band

ECONOMY

Economy - overview: The smallest country in Central America, El Salvador has the third largest economy, but growth has been minimal in recent years. Hoping to stimulate the sluggish economy, the government is striving to open new export markets, encourage foreign investment, and modernize the tax and healthcare systems. Implementation in 2006 of the Central America-Dominican Republic Free Trade Agreement, which El Salvador was the first to ratify, is viewed as a key policy to help achieve these objectives. The trade deficit has been offset by annual remittances from Salvadorans living abroad - 16% of GDP in 2004 - and external aid. With the adoption of the US dollar as its currency, El Salvador has lost control over monetary policy and must concentrate on maintaining a disciplined fiscal policy.

GDP (purchasing power parity): $33.89 billion (2005 est.)

GDP (official exchange rate): $16.52 billion (2005 est.)

GDP - real growth rate: 2% (2005 est.)

GDP - per capita: purchasing power parity - $5,100 (2005 est.)

GDP - composition by sector:
agriculture: 9.8%
industry: 30.3%
services: 60% (2005 est.)

Labor force: 2.81 million (2005 est.)

Labor force - by occupation: agriculture 17.1%, industry 17.1%, services 65.8% (2003 est.)

Unemployment rate: 6.5% - but the economy has much underemployment (2005 est.)

Population below poverty line: 36.1% (2003 est.)

Household income or consumption by percentage share:
lowest 10%: 1.4%
highest 10%: 39.3% (2001)

Distribution of family income - Gini index: 52.5 (2001)

Inflation rate (consumer prices): 4.7% (2005 est.)

Investment (gross fixed): 15.8% of GDP (2005 est.)

Budget:
revenues: $2.84 billion
expenditures: $3.167 billion, including capital expenditures of NA (2005 est.)

Public debt: 45.8% of GDP (2005 est.)

Agriculture - products: coffee, sugar, corn, rice, beans, oilseed, cotton, sorghum; shrimp; beef, dairy products

Industries: food processing, beverages, petroleum, chemicals, fertilizer, textiles, furniture, light metals

Industrial production growth rate: 0.3% (2005 est.)

Electricity - production: 4.158 billion kWh (2004)

Electricity - production by source:
fossil fuel: 44%
hydro: 30.9%
nuclear: 0%
other: 25.1% (2001)

Electricity - consumption: 4.45 billion kWh (2004)

Electricity - exports: 91 million kWh (2004)

Electricity - imports: 473 million kWh (2004)

Oil - production: 0 bbl/day (2003 est.)

Oil - consumption: 40,000 bbl/day (2003 est.)

Oil - exports: NA (2001)

Oil - imports: NA (2001)

Current account balance: $-858 million (2005 est.)

Exports: $3.586 billion (2005 est.)

Exports - partners: US 65.6%, Guatemala 11.8%, Honduras 6.3% (2004)

Imports: $6.678 billion (2005 est.)

Imports - partners: US 46.3%, Guatemala 8.1%, Mexico 6% (2004)

Reserves of foreign exchange and gold: $2.003 billion (2005 est.)

Debt - external: $8.273 billion (30 June 2005 est.)

Economic aid - recipient: $125 million of which, $53 million from US (2003)

Currency (code): US dollar (USD)

Currency code: USD

Exchange rates: the US dollar became El Salvador's currency in 2001

Fiscal year: calendar year

COMMUNICATIONS

Telephones - main lines in use: 752,600 (2003)
Telephones - mobile cellular: 1,149,800 (2003)
Telephone system:
general assessment: NA
domestic: nationwide microwave radio relay system
international: country code - 503; satellite earth station - 1 Intelsat (Atlantic Ocean); connected to Central American Microwave System
Radio broadcast stations: AM 61 (plus 24 repeaters), FM 30, shortwave 0 (1998)
Radios: 2.75 million (1997)
Television broadcast stations: 5 (1997)
Televisions: 600,000 (1990)
Internet country code: .sv
Internet hosts: 4,084 (2003)
Internet Service Providers (ISPs): 4 (2000)
Internet users: 550,000 (2003)

TRANSPORTATION

Airports: 73 (2004 est.)
Airports - with paved runways:
total: 4
over 3,047 m: 1
1,524 to 2,437 m: 1
914 to 1,523 m: 2 (2005 est.)
Airports - with unpaved runways:
total: 72
1,524 to 2,437 m: 1
914 to 1,523 m: 15
under 914 m: 56 (2005 est.)
Heliports: 1 (2005 est.)
Railways:
total: 283 km
narrow gauge: 283 km 0.914-m gauge
note: length of operational route reduced from 562 km to 283 km by disuse and lack of maintenance (2004)
Roadways:
total: 10,029 km
paved: 1,986 km
unpaved: 8,043 km (1999)
Waterways: Rio Lempa partially navigable (2004)
Ports and terminals: Acajutla, Puerto Cutuco

MILITARY

Military branches: Army, Navy (FNES), Air Force (FAS)
Military service age and obligation: 18 years of age for compulsory military service, with 12-month service obligation; 16 years of age for volunteers (2002)
Manpower available for military service: *males age 18-49*: 1,391,278 (2005 est.)
Manpower fit for military service: *males age 18-49*: 960,315 (2005 est.)
Manpower reaching military service age annually: *males*: 70,286 (2005 est.)
Military expenditures - dollar figure: $157 million (2003)
Military expenditures - percent of GDP: 1.1% (2003)

TRANSNATIONAL ISSUES

Disputes - international: in 1992, the ICJ ruled on the delimitation of "bolsones" (disputed areas) along the El Salvador-Honduras boundary, but despite OAS intervention and a further ICJ ruling in 2003, full demarcation of the border remains stalled; the 1992 ICJ ruling advised a tripartite resolution to a maritime boundary in the Gulf of Fonseca advocating Honduran access to the Pacific; El Salvador continues to claim tiny Conejo Island, not identified in the ICJ decision, off Honduras in the Gulf of Fonseca
Illicit drugs: transshipment point for cocaine; small amounts of marijuana produced for local consumption; domestic cocaine abuse on the rise

EQUATORIAL GUINEA

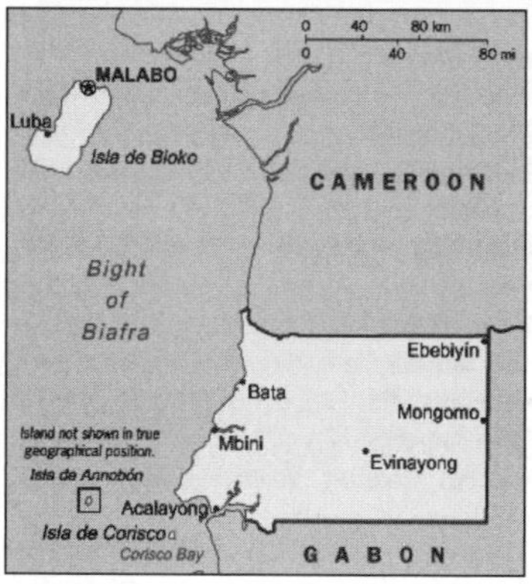

INTRODUCTION

Background: Equatorial Guinea gained independence in 1968 after 190 years of Spanish rule. This tiny country, composed of a mainland portion plus five inhabited islands, is one of the smallest on the African continent. President OBIANG NGUEMA MBASOGO has ruled the country for over two decades since seizing power from his uncle, then President MACIAS, in a 1979 coup. Although nominally a constitutional democracy since 1991, the 1996 and 2002 presidential elections - as well as the 1999 and 2004 legislative elections - were widely seen as flawed. The president exerts almost total control over the political system and has discouraged political opposition. Equatorial Guinea has also experienced rapid economic growth due to the discovery of large offshore oil reserves, and in the last decade has become Sub-Saharan Africa's third largest oil exporter. Despite the country's economic windfall from oil production resulting in a massive increase in government revenue in recent years, there have been few improvements in the population's living standards.

GEOGRAPHY

Location: Western Africa, bordering the Bight of Biafra, between Cameroon and Gabon
Geographic coordinates: 2 00 N, 10 00 E
Map references: Africa
Area:
total: 28,051 sq km
land: 28,051 sq km
water: 0 sq km
Area - comparative: slightly smaller than Maryland
Land boundaries:
total: 539 km
border countries: Cameroon 189 km, Gabon 350 km
Coastline: 296 km
Maritime claims:
territorial sea: 12 nm
exclusive economic zone: 200 nm
Climate: tropical; always hot, humid
Terrain: coastal plains rise to interior hills; islands are volcanic
Elevation extremes:
lowest point: Atlantic Ocean 0 m
highest point: Pico Basile 3,008 m
Natural resources: petroleum, natural gas, timber, gold, bauxite, diamonds, tantalum, sand and gravel, clay
Land use:
arable land: 4.63%
permanent crops: 3.57%
other: 91.8% (2001)
Irrigated land: NA sq km
Natural hazards: violent windstorms, flash floods
Environment - current issues: tap water is not potable; deforestation
Environment - international agreements:
party to: Biodiversity, Climate Change, Climate Change-Kyoto Protocol, Desertification, Endangered Species, Hazardous Wastes, Law of the Sea, Ship Pollution
signed, but not ratified: none of the selected agreements
Geography - note: insular and continen-

tal regions rather widely separated

PEOPLE

Population: 535,881 (July 2005 est.)
Age structure:
0-14 years: 41.7% (male 112,326/female 111,244)
15-64 years: 54.5% (male 140,568/female 151,500)
65 years and over: 3.8% (male 8,900/female 11,343) (2005 est.)
Median age:
total: 18.83 years
male: 18.2 years
female: 19.46 years (2005 est.)
Population growth rate: 2.42% (2005 est.)
Birth rate: 36.18 births/1,000 population (2005 est.)
Death rate: 12 deaths/1,000 population (2005 est.)
Net migration rate: 0 migrant(s)/1,000 population (2005 est.)
Sex ratio:
at birth: 1.03 male(s)/female
under 15 years: 1.01 male(s)/female
15-64 years: 0.93 male(s)/female
65 years and over: 0.78 male(s)/female
total population: 0.96 male(s)/female (2005 est.)
Infant mortality rate:
total: 85.13 deaths/1,000 live births
male: 91.28 deaths/1,000 live births
female: 78.8 deaths/1,000 live births (2005 est.)
Life expectancy at birth:
total population: 49.7 years
male: 48.01 years
female: 51.44 years (2005 est.)
Total fertility rate: 4.62 children born/woman (2005 est.)
HIV/AIDS - adult prevalence rate: 3.4% (2001 est.)
HIV/AIDS - people living with HIV/AIDS: 5,900 (2001 est.)
HIV/AIDS - deaths: 370 (2001 est.)
Major infectious diseases:
degree of risk: very high
food or waterborne diseases: bacterial diarrhea, hepatitis A, and typhoid fever
vectorborne disease: malaria (2004)
Nationality:
noun: Equatorial Guinean(s) or Equatoguinean(s)
adjective: Equatorial Guinean or Equatoguinean
Ethnic groups: Bioko (primarily Bubi, some Fernandinos), Rio Muni (primarily Fang), Europeans less than 1,000, mostly Spanish
Religions: nominally Christian and predominantly Roman Catholic, pagan practices
Languages: Spanish (official), French (official), pidgin English, Fang, Bubi, Ibo
Literacy:
definition: age 15 and over can read and write
total population: 85.7%
male: 93.3%
female: 78.4% (2003 est.)

GOVERNMENT

Country name:
conventional long form: Republic of Equatorial Guinea
conventional short form: Equatorial Guinea
local long form: Republica de Guinea Ecuatorial
local short form: Guinea Ecuatorial
former: Spanish Guinea
Government type: republic
Capital: Malabo
Administrative divisions: 7 provinces (provincias, singular - provincia); Annobon, Bioko Norte, Bioko Sur, Centro Sur, Kie-Ntem, Litoral, Wele-Nzas
Independence: 12 October 1968 (from Spain)
National holiday: Independence Day, 12 October (1968)
Constitution: approved by national referendum 17 November 1991; amended January 1995
Legal system: partly based on Spanish civil law and tribal custom
Suffrage: 18 years of age; universal adult
Executive branch:
chief of state: President Brig. Gen. (Ret.) Teodoro OBIANG NGUEMA MBASOGO (since 3 August 1979 when he seized power in a military coup)
head of government: Prime Minister Miguel Abia BITEO Borico (since 14 June 2004); First Deputy Prime Minister Mercelino Oyono NTUTUMU (since 15 June 2004); Deputy Prime Minister Ricardo Mangue Obama NFUBEA (since 15 June 2004)
cabinet: Council of Ministers appointed by the president
elections: president elected by popular vote for a seven-year term; election last held 15 December 2002 (next to be held December 2009); prime minister and deputy prime ministers appointed by the president
election results: Teodoro OBIANG NGUEMA MBASOGO reelected president; percent of vote - Teodoro OBIANG NGUEMA MBASOGO 97.1%, Celestino Bonifacio BACALE 2.2%; elections marred by widespread fraud
Legislative branch: unicameral House of People's Representatives or Camara de Representantes del Pueblo (80 seats; members directly elected by popular vote to serve five-year terms)
elections: last held 25 April 2004 (next to be held NA 2009)
election results: percent of vote by party - NA; seats by party - PDGE 98, NA 2
note: Parliament has little power since the constitution vests all executive authority in the president
Judicial branch: Supreme Tribunal
Political parties and leaders: Convergence Party for Social Democracy or CPDS [Placido MIKO Abogo]; Democratic Party for Equatorial Guinea or PDGE (ruling party) [Teodoro OBIANG NGUEMA MBASOGO]; Party for Progress of Equatorial Guinea or PPGE [Severo MOTO]; Popular Action of Equatorial Guinea or APGE [Miguel Esono EMAN]; Popular Union or UP [Andres Moises Bda ADA]; Progressive Democratic Alliance or ADP [Victorino Bolekia BONAY]; Union of Independent Democrats of UDI [Daniel OYONO]
Political pressure groups and leaders: NA
International organization participation: ACCT, ACP, AfDB, AU, BDEAC, CEMAC, FAO, FZ, G-77, IBRD, ICAO, ICRM, IDA, IFAD, IFC, IFRCS, ILO, IMF, IMO, Interpol, IOC, ITU, MIGA, NAM, OAS (observer), OPCW, UN, UNCTAD, UNESCO, UNIDO, UPU, WHO, WIPO, WToO, WTO (observer)
Diplomatic representation in the US:
chief of mission: Ambassador Purificacion ANGUE ONDO
chancery: 2020 16th Street NW, Washington, DC 20009
telephone: [1] (202) 518-5700
FAX: [1] (202) 518-5252
Diplomatic representation from the US:
chief of mission: the US ambassador to Cameroon is accredited to Equatorial Guinea
embassy: K-3, Carretera de Aeropuerto, Al lado de Restaurante El Paraiso, Malabo
telephone: [240] 098-895
FAX: [240] 098-894
Flag description: three equal horizontal bands of green (top), white, and red with a blue isosceles triangle based on the hoist side and the coat of arms centered in the white band; the coat of arms has six yellow six-pointed stars (representing the mainland and five offshore islands) above a gray shield bearing a silk-cotton tree and below which is a scroll with the motto UNIDAD, PAZ, JUSTICIA (Unity, Peace, Justice)

ECONOMY

Economy - overview: The discovery and exploitation of large oil reserves have con-

tributed to dramatic economic growth in recent years. Forestry, farming, and fishing are also major components of GDP. Subsistence farming predominates. Although pre-independence Equatorial Guinea counted on cocoa production for hard currency earnings, the neglect of the rural economy under successive regimes has diminished potential for agriculture-led growth (the government has stated its intention to reinvest some oil revenue into agriculture). A number of aid programs sponsored by the World Bank and the IMF have been cut off since 1993 because of corruption and mismanagement. No longer eligible for concessional financing because of large oil revenues, the government has been unsuccessfully trying to agree on a "shadow" fiscal management program with the World Bank and IMF. Businesses, for the most part, are owned by government officials and their family members. Undeveloped natural resources include titanium, iron ore, manganese, uranium, and alluvial gold. Growth remained strong in 2005, led by oil. Equatorial Guinea now has the second highest per capita income in the world, after Luxembourg.
GDP (purchasing power parity): $25.69 billion (2005 est.)
GDP (official exchange rate): $7.644 billion (2005 est.)
GDP - real growth rate: 18.6% (2005 est.)
GDP - per capita: purchasing power parity - $50,200 (2005 est.)
GDP - composition by sector:
agriculture: 2.4%
industry: 95.5%
services: 2.2% (2005 est.)
Labor force: NA
Unemployment rate: 30% (1998 est.)
Population below poverty line: NA
Household income or consumption by percentage share:
lowest 10%: NA
highest 10%: NA
Inflation rate (consumer prices): 5% (2005 est.)
Investment (gross fixed): 46.3% of GDP (2005 est.)
Budget:
revenues: $1.973 billion
expenditures: $711.5 million, including capital expenditures of NA (2005 est.)
Agriculture - products: coffee, cocoa, rice, yams, cassava (tapioca), bananas, palm oil nuts; livestock; timber
Industries: petroleum, fishing, sawmilling, natural gas
Industrial production growth rate: 30% (2002 est.)
Electricity - production: 29.43 million kWh (2003)
Electricity - production by source:
fossil fuel: 94.3%
hydro: 5.7%
nuclear: 0%
other: 0% (2001)
Electricity - consumption: 27.37 million kWh (2003)
Electricity - exports: 0 kWh (2003)
Electricity - imports: 0 kWh (2003)
Oil - production: 420,000 bbl/day (2005 est.)
Oil - consumption: 1,200 bbl/day (2003 est.)
Oil - exports: NA (2001)
Oil - imports: NA (2001)
Oil - proved reserves: 563.5 million bbl (1 January 2002)
Natural gas - production: 20 million cu m (2001 est.)
Natural gas - consumption: 20 million cu m (2001 est.)
Natural gas - exports: 0 cu m (2001 est.)
Natural gas - imports: 0 cu m (2001 est.)
Natural gas - proved reserves: 68.53 billion cu m (1 January 2002)
Current account balance: $1.364 billion (2005 est.)
Exports: $6.727 billion f.o.b. (2005 est.)
Exports - partners: US 29.3%, China 22.8%, Spain 16%, Taiwan 14.9%, Canada 6.8% (2004)
Imports: $1.864 billion f.o.b. (2005 est.)
Imports - partners: US 26.8%, Cote d'Ivoire 21.4%, Spain 13.6%, France 8.8%, UK 7.8%, Italy 4.4% (2004)
Reserves of foreign exchange and gold: $1.078 billion (2005 est.)
Debt - external: $248 million (2000 est.)
Economic aid - recipient: $33.8 million (1995)
Currency (code): Communaute Financiere Africaine franc (XAF); note - responsible authority is the Bank of the Central African States
Currency code: XAF
Exchange rates: Communaute Financiere Africaine francs (XAF) per US dollar - 480.56 (2005), 528.29 (2004), 581.2 (2003), 696.99 (2002), 733.04 (2001)
Fiscal year: 1 January - 31 December

COMMUNICATIONS

Telephones - main lines in use: 9,600 (2003)
Telephones - mobile cellular: 41,500 (2003)
Telephone system:
general assessment: poor system with adequate government services
domestic: NA
international: country code - 240; international communications from Bata and Malabo to African and European countries; satellite earth station - 1 Intelsat (Indian Ocean)
Radio broadcast stations: AM 0, FM 3, shortwave 5 (2002)
Radios: 180,000 (1997)
Television broadcast stations: 1 (2002)
Televisions: 4,000 (1997)
Internet country code: .gq
Internet hosts: 3 (2004)
Internet Service Providers (ISPs): 1 (2002)
Internet users: 1,800 (2002)

TRANSPORTATION

Airports: 4 (2004 est.)
Airports - with paved runways:
total: 3
2,438 to 3,047 m: 1
1,524 to 2,437 m: 1
under 914 m: 1 (2005 est.)
Airports - with unpaved runways:
total: 1
under 914 m: 1 (2005 est.)
Pipelines: condensate 37 km; gas 39 km; liquid natural gas 4 km; oil 24 km (2004)
Roadways:
total: 2,880 km (1999)
Merchant marine:
total: 1 ships (1,000 GRT or over) 6,556 GRT/9,704 DWT
by type: cargo 1 (2005)
Ports and terminals: Malabo

MILITARY

Military branches: Army, Navy, Air Force (2005)
Military service age and obligation: 18 years of age (est.) (2004)
Manpower available for military service:
males age 18-49: 106,571 (2005 est.)
Manpower fit for military service: *males age 18-49*: 66,379 (2005 est.)
Military expenditures - dollar figure: $126.2 million (2004)
Military expenditures - percent of GDP: 2.5% (2004)

TRANSNATIONAL ISSUES

Disputes - international: in 2002, ICJ ruled on an equidistance settlement of Cameroon-Equatorial Guinea-Nigeria maritime boundary in the Gulf of Guinea, but a dispute between Equatorial Guinea and Cameroon over an island at the mouth of the Ntem River, imprecisely defined maritime coordinates in the ICJ decision, and the unresolved Bakasi allocation contribute to the delay in implementation; UN has been pressing Equatorial Guinea and Gabon to pledge to resolve the sovereignty dispute over Gabon-occupied Mbane Island and create a maritime boundary in the hydrocarbon-rich Corisco Bay

ERITREA

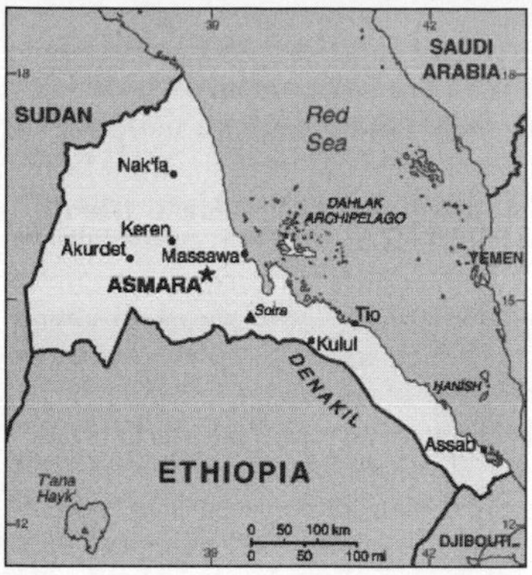

INTRODUCTION

Background: Eritrea was awarded to Ethiopia in 1952 as part of a federation. Ethiopia's annexation of Eritrea as a province 10 years later sparked a 30-year struggle for independence that ended in 1991 with Eritrean rebels defeating governmental forces; independence was overwhelmingly approved in a 1993 referendum. A two-and-a-half-year border war with Ethiopia that erupted in 1998 ended under UN auspices on 12 December 2000. Eritrea currently hosts a UN peacekeeping operation that is monitoring a 25 km-wide Temporary Security Zone on the border with Ethiopia. An international commission, organized to resolve the border dispute, posted its findings in 2002 but final demarcation is on hold due to Ethiopian objections.

GEOGRAPHY

Location: Eastern Africa, bordering the Red Sea, between Djibouti and Sudan
Geographic coordinates: 15 00 N, 39 00 E
Map references: Africa
Area:
total: 121,320 sq km
land: 121,320 sq km
water: 0 sq km
Area - comparative: slightly larger than Pennsylvania
Land boundaries:
total: 1,626 km
border countries: Djibouti 109 km, Ethiopia 912 km, Sudan 605 km
Coastline: 2,234 km total; mainland on Red Sea 1,151 km, islands in Red Sea 1,083 km
Maritime claims:
territorial sea: 12 nm
Climate: hot, dry desert strip along Red Sea coast; cooler and wetter in the central highlands (up to 61 cm of rainfall annually); semiarid in western hills and lowlands; rainfall heaviest during June-September except in coastal desert
Terrain: dominated by extension of Ethiopian north-south trending highlands, descending on the east to a coastal desert plain, on the northwest to hilly terrain and on the southwest to flat-to-rolling plains
Elevation extremes:
lowest point: near Kulul within the Denakil depression -75 m
highest point: Soira 3,018 m
Natural resources: gold, potash, zinc, copper, salt, possibly oil and natural gas, fish
Land use:
arable land: 4.95%
permanent crops: 0.03%
other: 95.02% (2001)
Irrigated land: 220 sq km (1998 est.)
Natural hazards: frequent droughts; locust swarms
Environment - current issues: deforestation; desertification; soil erosion; overgrazing; loss of infrastructure from civil warfare
Environment - international agreements:
party to: Biodiversity, Climate Change, Desertification, Endangered Species
signed, but not ratified: none of the selected agreements
Geography - note: strategic geopolitical position along world's busiest shipping lanes; Eritrea retained the entire coastline of Ethiopia along the Red Sea upon de jure independence from Ethiopia on 24 May 1993

PEOPLE

Population: 4,561,599 (July 2005 est.)
Age structure:
0-14 years: 44.8% (male 1,023,898/female 1,019,389)
15-64 years: 51.9% (male 1,170,823/female 1,194,741)
65 years and over: 3.3% (male 74,312/female 78,436) (2005 est.)
Median age:
total: 17.54 years
male: 17.35 years
female: 17.73 years (2005 est.)
Population growth rate: 2.51% (2005 est.)
Birth rate: 38.62 births/1,000 population (2005 est.)
Death rate: 13.53 deaths/1,000 population (2005 est.)
Net migration rate: 0 migrant(s)/1,000 population
note: UNHCR began repatriating about 150,000 Eritrean refugees from Sudan in 2001 following the restoration of diplomatic relations between the two countries in 2000 (2005 est.)
Sex ratio:
at birth: 1.03 male(s)/female
under 15 years: 1 male(s)/female
15-64 years: 0.98 male(s)/female
65 years and over: 0.95 male(s)/female
total population: 0.99 male(s)/female (2005 est.)
Infant mortality rate:
total: 74.87 deaths/1,000 live births
male: 82.28 deaths/1,000 live births
female: 67.24 deaths/1,000 live births (2005 est.)
Life expectancy at birth:
total population: 58.47 years
male: 56.96 years
female: 60.02 years (2005 est.)
Total fertility rate: 5.61 children born/woman (2005 est.)
HIV/AIDS - adult prevalence rate: 2.7% (2003 est.)
HIV/AIDS - people living with HIV/AIDS: 60,000 (2003 est.)
HIV/AIDS - deaths: 6,300 (2003 est.)
Major infectious diseases:
degree of risk: high
food or waterborne diseases: bacterial diarrhea, hepatitis A, and typhoid fever *vectorborne disease*: malaria is a high risk in some locations (2004)
Nationality:
noun: Eritrean(s)
adjective: Eritrean
Ethnic groups: ethnic Tigrinya 50%, Tigre and Kunama 40%, Afar 4%, Saho (Red Sea coast dwellers) 3%, other 3%
Religions: Muslim, Coptic Christian, Roman Catholic, Protestant
Languages: Afar, Arabic, Tigre and Kunama, Tigrinya, other Cushitic languages
Literacy:
definition: NA
total population: 58.6%
male: 69.9%
female: 47.6% (2003 est.)

GOVERNMENT

Country name:
conventional long form: State of Eritrea
conventional short form: Eritrea
local long form: Hagere Ertra
local short form: Ertra
former: Eritrea Autonomous Region in Ethiopia
Government type: transitional government
note: following a successful referendum on independence for the Autonomous Region of Eritrea on 23-25 April 1993, a National Assembly, composed entirely of the People's Front for Democracy and Justice or PFDJ, was established as a transitional legislature; a Constitutional Commission was also established to draft a constitution; ISAIAS Afworki was elected president by the transitional legislature; the constitution, ratified in May 1997, did not enter into effect, pending

parliamentary and presidential elections; parliamentary elections had been scheduled in December 2001, but were postponed indefinitely; currently the sole legal party is the People's Front for Democracy and Justice (PFDJ)

Capital: Asmara

Administrative divisions: 6 regions (zobatat, singular - zoba); Anseba, Debub (Southern), Debubawi K'eyih Bahri (Southern Red Sea), Gash Barka, Ma'akel (Central), Semenawi Keyih Bahri (Northern Red Sea)

Independence: 24 May 1993 (from Ethiopia)

National holiday: Independence Day, 24 May (1993)

Constitution: a transitional constitution, decreed on 19 May 1993, was replaced by a new constitution adopted on 23 May 1997, but not yet implemented

Legal system: primary basis is the Ethiopian legal code of 1957, with revisions; new civil, commercial, and penal codes have not yet been promulgated; also relies on customary and post-independence-enacted laws and, for civil cases involving Muslims, Sharia law

Suffrage: 18 years of age; universal

Executive branch:

chief of state: President ISAIAS Afworki (since 8 June 1993); note - the president is both the chief of state and head of government and is head of the State Council and National Assembly

head of government: President ISAIAS Afworki (since 8 June 1993); note - the president is both the chief of state and head of government and is head of the State Council and National Assembly

cabinet: State Council is the collective executive authority; members appointed by the president

elections: president elected by the National Assembly; election last held 8 June 1993 (next election date uncertain as the National Assembly did not hold a presidential election in December 2001 as anticipated)

election results: ISAIAS Afworki elected president; percent of National Assembly vote - ISAIAS Afworki 95%

Legislative branch: unicameral National Assembly (150 seats; term limits not established)

elections: in May 1997, following the adoption of the new constitution, 75 members of the PFDJ Central Committee (the old Central Committee of the EPLF), 60 members of the 527-member Constituent Assembly, that had been established in 1997 to discuss and ratify the new constitution, and 15 representatives of Eritreans living abroad were formed into a Transitional National Assembly to serve as the country's legislative body until countrywide elections to a National Assembly were held; although only 75 of 150 members of the Transitional National Assembly were elected, the constitution stipulates that once past the transition stage, all members of the National Assembly will be elected by secret ballot of all eligible voters; National Assembly elections scheduled for December 2001 were postponed indefinitely

Judicial branch: High Court - regional, subregional, and village courts; also have military and special courts

Political parties and leaders: People's Front for Democracy and Justice or PFDJ, the only party recognized by the government [ISAIAS Afworki]; note - a National Assembly committee drafted a law on political parties in January 2001, but the full National Assembly has not yet debated or voted on it

Political pressure groups and leaders: Eritrean Islamic Jihad or EIJ [leader NA] (also including Eritrean Islamic Jihad Movement or EIJM (also known as the Abu Sihel Movement) [leader NA]); Eritrean Islamic Salvation or EIS (also known as the Arafa Movement) [leader NA]; Eritrean Liberation Front or ELF [ABDULLAH Muhammed]; Eritrean National Alliance or ENA (a coalition including EIJ, EIS, ELF, and a number of ELF factions) [HERUY Tedla Biru]; Eritrean Public Forum or EPF [ARADOM Iyob]

International organization participation: ACP, AfDB, AU, COMESA, FAO, G-77, IAEA, IBRD, ICAO, ICCt (signatory), ICFTU, IDA, IFAD, IFC, IFRCS (observer), IGAD, ILO, IMF, IMO, Interpol, IOC, ISO (correspondent), ITU, MIGA, NAM, OPCW, PCA, UN, UNCTAD, UNESCO, UNIDO, UPU, WCO, WFTU, WHO, WIPO, WMO, WToO

Diplomatic representation in the US:

chief of mission: Ambassador GIRMA Asmerom

chancery: 1708 New Hampshire Avenue NW, Washington, DC 20009

telephone: [1] (202) 319-1991

FAX: [1] (202) 319-1304

consulate(s) general: Oakland (California)

Diplomatic representation from the US:

chief of mission: Ambassador Scott H. DELISI

embassy: Franklin D. Roosevelt Street, Asmara

mailing address: P. O. Box 211, Asmara

telephone: [291] (1) 120004

FAX: [291] (1) 127584

Flag description: red isosceles triangle (based on the hoist side) dividing the flag into two right triangles; the upper triangle is green, the lower one is blue; a gold wreath encircling a gold olive branch is centered on the hoist side of the red triangle

ECONOMY

Economy - overview: Since independence from Ethiopia on 24 May 1993, Eritrea has faced the economic problems of a small, desperately poor country. Like the economies of many African nations, the economy is largely based on subsistence agriculture, with 80% of the population involved in farming and herding. The Ethiopian-Eritrea war in 1998-2000 severely hurt Eritrea's economy. GDP growth fell to zero in 1999 and to -12.1% in 2000. The May 2000 Ethiopian offensive into northern Eritrea caused some $600 million in property damage and loss, including losses of $225 million in livestock and 55,000 homes. The attack prevented planting of crops in Eritrea's most productive region, causing food production to drop by 62%. Even during the war, Eritrea developed its transportation infrastructure, asphalting new roads, improving its ports, and repairing war damaged roads and bridges. Since the war ended, the government has maintained a firm grip on the economy, expanding the use of the military and party-owned businesses to complete Eritrea's development agenda. Erratic rainfall and the delayed demobilization of agriculturalists from the military kept cereal production well below normal, holding down growth in 2002-05. Eritrea's economic future depends upon its ability to master social problems such as illiteracy, unemployment, and low skills, and to open its economy to private enterprise so the diaspora's money and expertise can foster economic growth.

GDP (purchasing power parity): $4.471 billion (2005 est.)

GDP (official exchange rate): $1.244 billion (2005 est.)

GDP - real growth rate: 2% (2005 est.)

GDP - per capita: purchasing power parity - $1,000 (2005 est.)

GDP - composition by sector:

agriculture: 8.7%

industry: 26.3%

services: 65% (2005 est.)

Labor force: NA

Labor force - by occupation: agriculture 80%, industry and services 20%

Unemployment rate: NA (2003 est.)

Population below poverty line: 50% (2004 est.)

Household income or consumption by percentage share:

lowest 10%: NA

highest 10%: NA

Inflation rate (consumer prices): 15% (2005 est.)

Investment (gross fixed): 26.8% of GDP (2005 est.)
Budget:
revenues: $248.8 million
expenditures: $409.4 million, including capital expenditures of NA (2005 est.)
Agriculture - products: sorghum, lentils, vegetables, corn, cotton, tobacco, coffee, sisal; livestock, goats; fish
Industries: food processing, beverages, clothing and textiles, salt, cement, commercial ship repair
Industrial production growth rate: NA
Electricity - production: 270.9 million kWh (2003)
Electricity - production by source:
fossil fuel: 100%
hydro: 0%
nuclear: 0%
other: 0% (2001)
Electricity - consumption: 251.9 million kWh (2003)
Electricity - exports: 0 kWh (2003)
Electricity - imports: 0 kWh (2003)
Oil - production: 0 bbl/day (2003 est.)
Oil - consumption: 4,600 bbl/day (2003 est.)
Oil - exports: NA (2001)
Oil - imports: NA (2001)
Current account balance: $-278.7 million (2005 est.)
Exports: $33.58 million f.o.b. (2005 est.)
Exports - partners: Malaysia 21.4%, Italy 13.7%, Eqypt 8.3%, India 7.8%, Japan 6.4%, Germany 5.3%, China 4.1%, UK 4% (2004)
Imports: $676.5 million f.o.b. (2005 est.)
Imports - partners: Ireland 25.7%, US 17.9%, Italy 16%, Turkey 6.2% (2004)
Reserves of foreign exchange and gold: $32.6 million (2005 est.)
Debt - external: $311 million (2000 est.)
Economic aid - recipient: $77 million (1999)
Currency (code): nakfa (ERN)
Currency code: ERN
Exchange rates: nakfa (ERN) per US dollar - 14.5 (2005), 13.788 (2004), 13.878 (2003), 13.958 (2002), 11.31 (2001)
Fiscal year: calendar year

COMMUNICATIONS

Telephones - main lines in use: 38,100 (2003)
Telephones - mobile cellular: NA
Telephone system:
general assessment: inadequate
domestic: very inadequate; most telephones are in Asmara; government is seeking international tenders to improve the system (2002)
international: country code - 291; note - international connections exist
Radio broadcast stations: AM 2, FM NA, shortwave 2 (2000)
Radios: 345,000 (1997)
Television broadcast stations: 1 (2000)
Televisions: 1,000 (1997)
Internet country code: .er
Internet hosts: 1,047 (2004)
Internet Service Providers (ISPs): 5 (2001)
Internet users: 9,500 (2003)

TRANSPORTATION

Airports: 17 (2004 est.)
Airports - with paved runways:
total: 4
over 3,047 m: 2
2,438 to 3,047 m: 2 (2005 est.)
Airports - with unpaved runways:
total: 13
over 3,047 m: 1
2,438 to 3,047 m: 1
1,524 to 2,437 m: 5
914 to 1,523 m: 4
under 914 m: 2 (2005 est.)
Railways:
total: 306 km
narrow gauge: 306 km 0.950-m gauge (2004)
Roadways:
total: 4,010 km
paved: 874 km
unpaved: 3,136 km (1999)
Merchant marine:
total: 6 ships (1,000 GRT or over) 16,069 GRT/19,549 DWT
by type: cargo 3, liquefied gas 1, petroleum tanker 1, roll on/roll off 1
registered in other countries: 1 (2005)
Ports and terminals: Assab, Massawa

MILITARY

Military branches: Army, Navy, Air Force
Military service age and obligation: 18 years of age for voluntary and compulsory military service; conscript service obligation - 16 months (2004)
Manpower fit for military service: *males age 18-49*: NA (2005)
Military expenditures - dollar figure: $151 million (2004)
Military expenditures - percent of GDP: 13.4% (2004)

TRANSNATIONAL ISSUES

Disputes - international: Eritrea and Ethiopia agreed to abide by 2002 Ethiopia-Eritrea Boundary Commission's (EEBC) delimitation decision, but despite international intervention, mutual animosities, accusations and armed posturing prevail, preventing demarcation; Ethiopia refuses to withdraw to the delimited boundary until technical errors made by the EEBC that ignored "human geography" are addressed, including the award of Badme, the focus of the 1998-2000 war; Eritrea insists that the EEBC decision be implemented immediately without modifications; since 2000, the UN Peacekeeping Mission to Ethiopia and Eritrea (UNMEE) monitors the 25km-wide Temporary Security Zone in Eritrea until the demarcation; Sudan accuses Eritrea of supporting Sudanese rebel groups; Eritrea protests Yemeni fishing around the Hanish Islands awarded to Eritrea by the ICJ in 1999
Refugees and internally displaced persons: *IDPs*: 59,000 (border war with Ethiopia from 1998-2000; most IDPs are near the central border region) (2004)

ESTONIA

INTRODUCTION

Background: After centuries of Danish, Swedish, German, and Russian rule, Estonia attained independence in 1918. Forcibly incorporated into the USSR in 1940, it regained its freedom in 1991, with the collapse of the Soviet Union. Since the last Russian troops left in 1994, Estonia has been free to promote economic and political ties with Western Europe. It joined both NATO and the EU in the spring of 2004.

GEOGRAPHY

Location: Eastern Europe, bordering the Baltic Sea and Gulf of Finland, between Latvia and Russia
Geographic coordinates: 59 00 N, 26 00 E
Map references: Europe
Area:
total: 45,226 sq km
land: 43,211 sq km
water: 2,015 sq km
note: includes 1,520 islands in the Baltic Sea
Area - comparative: slightly smaller than New Hampshire and Vermont combined
Land boundaries:
total: 633 km
border countries: Latvia 339 km, Russia 294 km
Coastline: 3,794 km
Maritime claims:
territorial sea: 12 nm
exclusive economic zone: limits fixed in coordination with neighboring states
Climate: maritime, wet, moderate winters, cool summers
Terrain: marshy, lowlands; flat in the north, hilly in the south

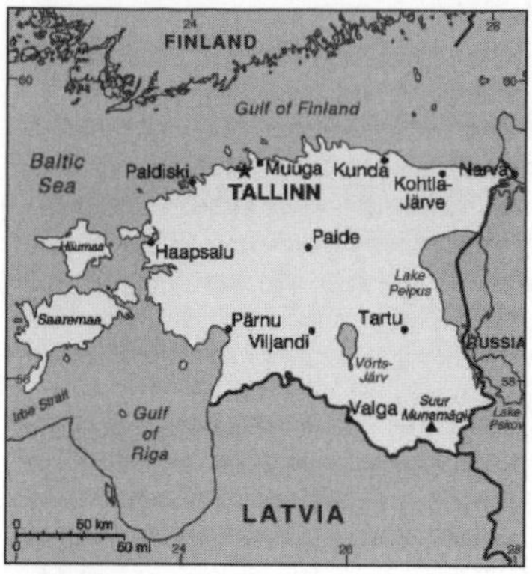

Elevation extremes:
lowest point: Baltic Sea 0 m
highest point: Suur Munamagi 318 m
Natural resources: oil shale, peat, phosphorite, clay, limestone, sand, dolomite, arable land, sea mud
Land use:
arable land: 16.04%
permanent crops: 0.45%
other: 83.51% (2001)
Irrigated land: 40 sq km (1998 est.)
Natural hazards: sometimes flooding occurs in the spring
Environment - current issues: air polluted with sulfur dioxide from oil-shale burning power plants in northeast; however, the amount of pollutants emitted to the air have fallen steadily, the emissions of 2000 were 80% less than in 1980; the amount of unpurified wastewater discharged to water bodies in 2000 was one twentieth the level of 1980; in connection with the start-up of new water purification plants, the pollution load of wastewater decreased; Estonia has more than 1,400 natural and manmade lakes, the smaller of which in agricultural areas need to be monitored; coastal seawater is polluted in certain locations
Environment - international agreements:
party to: Air Pollution, Air Pollution-Nitrogen Oxides, Air Pollution-Sulfur 85, Air Pollution-Volatile Organic Compounds, Antarctic Treaty, Biodiversity, Climate Change, Climate Change-Kyoto Protocol, Endangered Species, Hazardous Wastes, Ship Pollution, Ozone Layer Protection, Wetlands
signed, but not ratified: none of the selected agreements
Geography - note: the mainland terrain is flat, boggy, and partly wooded; offshore lie more than 1,500 islands

PEOPLE

Population: 1,332,893 (July 2005 est.)
Age structure:
0-14 years: 15.5% (male 106,300/female 100,446)
15-64 years: 67.7% (male 429,843/female 472,034)
65 years and over: 16.8% (male 74,037/female 150,233) (2005 est.)
Median age:
total: 39.06 years
male: 35.52 years
female: 42.35 years (2005 est.)
Population growth rate: -0.65% (2005 est.)
Birth rate: 9.91 births/1,000 population (2005 est.)
Death rate: 13.21 deaths/1,000 population (2005 est.)
Net migration rate: -3.18 migrant(s)/1,000 population (2005 est.)
Sex ratio:
at birth: 1.06 male(s)/female
under 15 years: 1.06 male(s)/female
15-64 years: 0.91 male(s)/female
65 years and over: 0.49 male(s)/female
total population: 0.84 male(s)/female (2005 est.)
Infant mortality rate:
total: 7.87 deaths/1,000 live births
male: 9.06 deaths/1,000 live births
female: 6.6 deaths/1,000 live births (2005 est.)
Life expectancy at birth:
total population: 71.77 years
male: 66.28 years
female: 77.6 years (2005 est.)
Total fertility rate: 1.39 children born/woman (2005 est.)
HIV/AIDS - adult prevalence rate: 1.1% (2001 est.)
HIV/AIDS - people living with HIV/AIDS: 7,800 (2003 est.)
HIV/AIDS - deaths: less than 200 (2003 est.)
Nationality:
noun: Estonian(s)
adjective: Estonian
Ethnic groups: Estonian 67.9%, Russian 25.6%, Ukrainian 2.1%, Belarusian 1.3%, Finn 0.9%, other 2.2% (2000 census)
Religions: Evangelical Lutheran 13.6%, Orthodox 12.8%, other Christian (including Methodist, Seventh-Day Adventist, Roman Catholic, Pentecostal) 1.4%, unaffiliated 34.1%, other and unspecified 32%, none 6.1% (2000 census)
Languages: Estonian (official) 67.3%, Russian 29.7%, other 2.3%, unknown 0.7% (2000 census)
Literacy:
definition: age 15 and over can read and write
total population: 99.8%
male: 99.8%
female: 99.8% (2003 est.)

GOVERNMENT

Country name:
conventional long form: Republic of Estonia
conventional short form: Estonia
local long form: Eesti Vabariik
local short form: Eesti
former: Estonian Soviet Socialist Republic
Government type: parliamentary republic
Capital: Tallinn
Administrative divisions: 15 counties (maakonnad, singular - maakond): Harjumaa (Tallinn), Hiiumaa (Kardla), Ida-Virumaa (Johvi), Jarvamaa (Paide), Jogevamaa (Jogeva), Laanemaa (Haapsalu), Laane-Virumaa (Rakvere), Parnumaa (Parnu), Polvamaa (Polva), Raplamaa (Rapla), Saaremaa (Kuressaare), Tartumaa (Tartu), Valgamaa (Valga), Viljandimaa (Viljandi), Vorumaa (Voru)
note: counties have the administrative center name following in parentheses
Independence: 20 August 1991 (from Soviet Union)
National holiday: Independence Day, 24 February (1918); note - 24 February 1918 is the date Estonia declared its independence from Soviet Russia; 20 August 1991 is the date it declared its independence from the Soviet Union
Constitution: adopted 28 June 1992
Legal system: based on civil law system; no judicial review of legislative acts
Suffrage: 18 years of age; universal for all Estonian citizens
Executive branch:
chief of state: President Arnold RUUTEL (since 8 October 2001)
head of government: Prime Minister Andrus ANSIP (since 12 April 2005)
cabinet: Council of Ministers appointed by the prime minister, approved by Parliament
elections: president elected by Parliament for a five-year term; if a candidate does not secure two-thirds of the votes after three rounds of balloting in the Parliament, then an electoral assembly (made up of Parliament plus members of local governments) elects the president, choosing between the two candidates with the largest percentage of votes; election last held 21 September 2001 (next to be held in the fall of 2006); prime minister nominated by the president and approved by Parliament
election results: Arnold RUUTEL elected president on 21 September 2001 by a 367-member electoral assembly that convened following Parliament's failure in August to elect then-President MERI's successor; on the second ballot of voting, RUUTEL received 186 votes to Parliament Speaker Toomas SAVI's 155; the remaining 26 ballots were either left blank or invalid
Legislative branch: unicameral Parliament or Riigikogu (101 seats; members are elected by popular vote to serve four-year terms)

elections: last held 2 March 2003 (next to be held NA March 2007)
election results: percent of vote by party - Center Party 25.4%, Res Publica 24.6%, Reform Party 17.7%, Estonian People's Union 13%, Pro Patria Union (Fatherland League) 7.3% People's Party Moodukad 7%; seats by party - Res Publica 26, Center Party 20, Reform Party 19, Estonian People's Union 13, Pro Patria Union 7, Social Democrats 6, non-affiliated (Social Liberals and independents) 10
Judicial branch: National Court (chairman appointed by Parliament for life)
Political parties and leaders: Center Party of Estonia (Keskerakond) [Edgar SAVISAAR, chairman]; Estonian People's Union (Rahvaliit) [Villu REILJAN, chairman]; Estonian Reform Party (Reformierakond) [Andrus ANSIP]; Estonian United Russian People's Party or EUVRP [Yevgeniy TOMBERG, chairman]; Pro Patria Union (Isamaaliit) [Tonis LUKAS, chairman]; Res Publica [Taavi VESKIMAGI, chairman]; Social Democratic Party (formerly People's Party Moodukad or Moderates) [Ivari PADAR, chairman]; Social Liberals (group of 8 parliamentarians, former Center Party members) [Peeter Kreitzberg]
Political pressure groups and leaders: NA
International organization participation: Australia Group, BIS, CBSS, CE, EAPC, EBRD, EIB, EU (new member), FAO, IAEA, IBRD, ICAO, ICCt, ICFTU, ICRM, IFC, IFRCS, IHO, ILO, IMF, IMO, Interpol, IOC, IOM, ISO (correspondent), ITU, MIGA, NATO, NIB, NSG, OAS (observer), OPCW, OSCE, PCA, UN, UNCTAD, UNESCO, UNTSO, UPU, WCO, WEU (associate partner), WHO, WIPO, WMO, WTO
Diplomatic representation in the US:
chief of mission: Ambassador Juri LUIK
chancery: 2131 Massachusetts Ave. NW, Washington, DC 20008
telephone: [1] (202) 588-0101
FAX: [1] (202) 588-0108
consulate(s) general: New York
Diplomatic representation from the US:
chief of mission: Ambassador Aldona Zofia WOS
embassy: Kentmanni 20, 15099 Tallinn
mailing address: use embassy street address
telephone: [372] 668-8100
FAX: [372] 668-8134
Flag description: pre-1940 flag restored by Supreme Soviet in May 1990 - three equal horizontal bands of blue (top), black, and white

ECONOMY

Economy - overview: Estonia, as a new member of the World Trade Organization and the European Union, has transitioned effectively to a modern market economy with strong ties to the West, including the pegging of its currency to the euro. The economy benefits from strong electronics and telecommunications sectors and is greatly influenced by developments in Finland, Sweden, and Germany, three major trading partners. The current account deficit remains high; however, the state budget is essentially in balance, and public debt is low.
GDP (purchasing power parity): $21.81 billion (2005 est.)
GDP (official exchange rate): $12.56 billion (2005 est.)
GDP - real growth rate: 7.1% (2005 est.)
GDP - per capita: purchasing power parity - $16,400 (2005 est.)
GDP - composition by sector:
agriculture: 4.1%
industry: 29.1%
services: 66.8% (2005 est.)
Labor force: 670,000 (2005 est.)
Labor force - by occupation: agriculture 11%, industry 20%, services 69% (1999 est.)
Unemployment rate: 9.2% (2005 est.)
Population below poverty line: NA (2000)
Household income or consumption by percentage share:
lowest 10%: 3%
highest 10%: 29.8% (1998)
Distribution of family income - Gini index: 37.2 (2000)
Inflation rate (consumer prices): 4% (2005 est.)
Investment (gross fixed): 27.6% of GDP (2005 est.)
Budget:
revenues: $5.126 billion
expenditures: $5.017 billion, including capital expenditures of NA (2005 est.)
Public debt: 3.8% of GDP (2005 est.)
Agriculture - products: potatoes, vegetables; livestock and dairy products; fish
Industries: engineering, electronics, wood and wood products, textile; information technology, telecommunications
Industrial production growth rate: 7.3% (2004 est.)
Electricity - production: 9.017 billion kWh (2003)
Electricity - production by source:
fossil fuel: 99.8%
hydro: 0.1%
nuclear: 0%
other: 0.2% (2001)
Electricity - consumption: 7.024 billion kWh (2003)
Electricity - exports: 1.562 billion kWh (2003)
Electricity - imports: 200 million kWh (2003)
Oil - production: 6,100 bbl/day (2003 est.)
Oil - consumption: 25,000 bbl/day (2003 est.)
Oil - exports: NA (2001)
Oil - imports: NA (2001)
Natural gas - production: 0 cu m (2001 est.)
Natural gas - consumption: 1.27 billion cu m (2001 est.)
Natural gas - exports: 0 cu m (2001 est.)
Natural gas - imports: 1.27 billion cu m (2001 est.)
Current account balance: $-1.403 billion (2005 est.)
Exports: $7.439 billion f.o.b. (2005 est.)
Exports - partners: Finland 23.1%, Sweden 15.3%, Germany 8.4%, Latvia 7.9%, Russia 5.7%, Lithuania 4.4% (2004)
Imports: $9.189 billion f.o.b. (2005 est.)
Imports - partners: Finland 22.1%, Germany 12.9%, Sweden 9.7%, Russia 9.2%, Lithuania 5.3%, Latvia 4.7% (2004)
Reserves of foreign exchange and gold: $1.852 billion (2005 est.)
Debt - external: $10.09 billion (30 June 2005 est.)
Economic aid - recipient: $108 million (2000)
Currency (code): Estonian kroon (EEK)
Currency code: EEK
Exchange rates: krooni per US dollar - 12.45 (2005), 12.596 (2004), 13.856 (2003), 16.612 (2002), 17.478 (2001)
Fiscal year: calendar year

COMMUNICATIONS

Telephones - main lines in use: 475,000 (2002)
Telephones - mobile cellular: 881,000 (2002)
Telephone system:
general assessment: foreign investment in the form of joint business ventures greatly improved telephone service; substantial fiber-optic cable systems carry telephone, TV, and radio traffic in the digital mode; Internet services are available throughout most of the country - only about 11,000 subscriber requests were unfilled by September 2000
domestic: a wide range of high quality voice, data, and Internet services is available throughout the country
international: country code - 372; fiber-optic cables to Finland, Sweden, Latvia, and Russia provide worldwide packet-switched service; two international switches are located in Tallinn (2001)
Radio broadcast stations: AM 0, FM 98, shortwave 0 (2001)
Radios: 1.01 million (1997)
Television broadcast stations: 3 (2001)
Televisions: 605,000 (1997)
Internet country code: .ee

Internet hosts: 82,142 (2004)
Internet Service Providers (ISPs): 38 (2001)
Internet users: 444,000 (2002)

TRANSPORTATION

Airports: 29 (2004 est.)
Airports - with paved runways:
total: 12
over 3,047 m: 1
2,438 to 3,047 m: 7
1,524 to 2,437 m: 1
914 to 1,523 m: 3 (2005 est.)
Airports - with unpaved runways:
total: 14
over 3,047 m: 1
2,438 to 3,047 m: 1
1,524 to 2,437 m: 2
914 to 1,523 m: 4
under 914 m: 6 (2005 est.)
Heliports: 1 (2005 est.)
Pipelines: gas 859 km (2004)
Railways:
total: 958 km
broad gauge: 958 km 1.520-m/1.524-m gauge (132 km electrified) (2004)
Roadways:
total: 56,849 km
paved: 13,303 km (including 99 km of expressways)
unpaved: 45,546 km (2003)
Waterways: 500 km (2003)
Merchant marine:
total: 43 ships (1,000 GRT or over) 212,998 GRT/177,488 DWT
by type: cargo 17, passenger/cargo 20, petroleum tanker 2, roll on/roll off 4
foreign-owned: 6 (Norway 6)
registered in other countries: 51 (2005)
Ports and terminals: Kopli, Kuivastu, Muuga, Tallinn, Virtsu

MILITARY

Military branches: Estonian Defense Forces: Ground Forces, Navy, Air Force and Air Defense Staff, Republic Security Forces (internal and border troops), Volunteer Defense League (Kaitseliit), Maritime Border Guard, Coast Guard
note: Border Guards and Ministry of Internal Affairs become part of the Estonian Defense Forces in wartime; the Coast Guard is subordinate to the Ministry of Defense in peacetime and the Estonian Navy in wartime
Military service age and obligation: 18 years of age for compulsory military service for all male citizens, with 8-month service obligation for conscripts and 11 months for sergeants and reserve officers; Estonia has committed to retaining conscription for men and women up to 2010 and, unlike Latvia and Lithuania, has no plan to transition to a contract armed forces; 17 years of age for volunteers; reserve commitment up to the age of 60 (2005)
Manpower available for military service:
males age 18-49: 291,696 (2005 est.)
Manpower fit for military service: *males age 18-49*: 200,382 (2005 est.): note - in 2004, 51% of the young men called up for service were determined to be unfit; main obstacles to conscription were psychiatric and behavioral
Manpower reaching military service age annually: *males*: 11,146 (2005 est.)
Military expenditures - dollar figure: $155 million (2002 est.)
Military expenditures - percent of GDP: 2% (2002 est.)

TRANSNATIONAL ISSUES

Disputes - international: in 1996, the Estonia-Russia technical border agreement was initialed but both states have been hesitant to sign and ratify it, with Russia asserting that Estonia needs to better assimilate Russian-speakers and Estonian groups pressing for realignment of the boundary based more closely on the 1920 Tartu Peace Treaty that would bring the now divided ethnic Setu people and parts of the Narva region within Estonia; as a member state that forms part of the EU's external border, Estonia must implement the strict Schengen border rules
Illicit drugs: transshipment point for opiates and cannabis from Southwest Asia and the Caucasus via Russia, cocaine from Latin America to Western Europe and Scandinavia, and synthetic drugs from Western Europe to Scandinavia; increasing domestic drug abuse problem; possible precursor manufacturing and/or trafficking; potential money laundering related to organized crime and drug trafficking is a concern as is possible use of the gambling sector to launder funds

ETHIOPIA

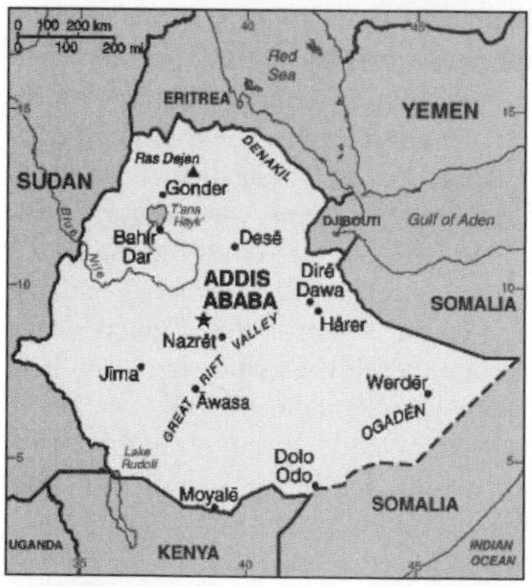

INTRODUCTION

Background: Unique among African countries, the ancient Ethiopian monarchy maintained its freedom from colonial rule, with the exception of the 1936-41 Italian occupation during World War II. In 1974 a military junta, the Derg, deposed Emperor Haile SELASSIE (who had ruled since 1930) and established a socialist state. Torn by bloody coups, uprisings, wide-scale drought, and massive refugee problems, the regime was finally toppled in 1991 by a coalition of rebel forces, the Ethiopian People's Revolutionary Democratic Front (EPRDF). A constitution was adopted in 1994 and Ethiopia's first multiparty elections were held in 1995. A two and a half year border war with Eritrea ended with a peace treaty on 12 December 2000. Final demarcation of the boundary is currently on hold due to Ethiopian objections to an international commission's finding requiring it to surrender sensitive territory.

GEOGRAPHY

Location: Eastern Africa, west of Somalia
Geographic coordinates: 8 00 N, 38 00 E
Map references: Africa
Area:
total: 1,127,127 sq km
land: 1,119,683 sq km
water: 7,444 sq km
Area - comparative: slightly less than twice the size of Texas
Land boundaries:
total: 5,328 km
border countries: Djibouti 349 km, Eritrea 912 km, Kenya 861 km, Somalia 1,600 km, Sudan 1,606 km
Coastline: 0 km (landlocked)
Maritime claims: none (landlocked)
Climate: tropical monsoon with wide topographic-induced variation
Terrain: high plateau with central mountain range divided by Great Rift Valley
Elevation extremes:
lowest point: Denakil Depression -125 m
highest point: Ras Dejen 4,620 m
Natural resources: small reserves of gold, platinum, copper, potash, natural gas, hydropower
Land use:
arable land: 10.71%
permanent crops: 0.75%
other: 88.54% (2001)
Irrigated land: 1,900 sq km (1998 est.)

Natural hazards: geologically active Great Rift Valley susceptible to earthquakes, volcanic eruptions; frequent droughts
Environment - current issues: deforestation; overgrazing; soil erosion; desertification; water shortages in some areas from water-intensive farming and poor management
Environment - international agreements:
party to: Biodiversity, Climate Change, Desertification, Endangered Species, Hazardous Wastes, Ozone Layer Protection
signed, but not ratified: Environmental Modification, Law of the Sea
Geography - note: landlocked - entire coastline along the Red Sea was lost with the de jure independence of Eritrea on 24 May 1993; the Blue Nile, the chief headstream of the Nile by water volume, rises in T'ana Hayk (Lake Tana) in northwest Ethiopia; three major crops are believed to have originated in Ethiopia: coffee, grain sorghum, and castor bean

PEOPLE

Population: 73,053,286
note: estimates for this country explicitly take into account the effects of excess mortality due to AIDS; this can result in lower life expectancy, higher infant mortality and death rates, lower population and growth rates, and changes in the distribution of population by age and sex than would otherwise be expected (July 2005 est.)
Age structure:
0-14 years: 43.9% (male 16,082,504/ female 15,999,602)
15-64 years: 53.4% (male 19,452,737/ female 19,525,746)
65 years and over: 2.7% (male 905,648/ female 1,087,049) (2005 est.)
Median age:
total: 17.75 years
male: 17.64 years
female: 17.85 years (2005 est.)
Population growth rate: 2.36% (2005 est.)
Birth rate: 38.61 births/1,000 population (2005 est.)
Death rate: 15.06 deaths/1,000 population (2005 est.)
Net migration rate: 0 migrant(s)/1,000 population
note: repatriation of Ethiopians who fled to Sudan for refuge from war and famine in earlier years is expected to continue for several years; some Sudanese and Somali refugees, who fled to Ethiopia from the fighting or famine in their own countries, continue to return to their homes (2005 est.)
Sex ratio:
at birth: 1.03 male(s)/female
under 15 years: 1.01 male(s)/female
15-64 years: 1 male(s)/female
65 years and over: 0.83 male(s)/female
total population: 1 male(s)/female (2005 est.)
Infant mortality rate:
total: 95.32 deaths/1,000 live births
male: 105.3 deaths/1,000 live births
female: 85.05 deaths/1,000 live births (2005 est.)
Life expectancy at birth:
total population: 48.83 years
male: 47.67 years
female: 50.03 years (2005 est.)
Total fertility rate: 5.33 children born/woman (2005 est.)
HIV/AIDS - adult prevalence rate: 4.4% (2003 est.)
HIV/AIDS - people living with HIV/AIDS: 1.5 million (2003 est.)
HIV/AIDS - deaths: 120,000 (2003 est.)
Major infectious diseases:
degree of risk: very high
food or waterborne diseases: bacterial and protozoal diarrhea, hepatitis A, typhoid fever, and hepatitis E
vectorborne diseases: malaria and cutaneous leishmaniasis are high risks in some locations
respiratory disease: meningococcal meningitis
animal contact disease: rabies
water contact disease: schistosomiasis (2004)
Nationality:
noun: Ethiopian(s)
adjective: Ethiopian
Ethnic groups: Oromo 40%, Amhara and Tigre 32%, Sidamo 9%, Shankella 6%, Somali 6%, Afar 4%, Gurage 2%, other 1%
Religions: Muslim 45%-50%, Ethiopian Orthodox 35%-40%, animist 12%, other 3%-8%
Languages: Amharic, Tigrinya, Oromigna, Guaragigna, Somali, Arabic, other local languages, English (major foreign language taught in schools)
Literacy:
definition: age 15 and over can read and write
total population: 42.7%
male: 50.3%
female: 35.1% (2003 est.)

GOVERNMENT

Country name:
conventional long form: Federal Democratic Republic of Ethiopia
conventional short form: Ethiopia
local long form: Ityop'iya Federalawi Demokrasiyawi Ripeblik
local short form: Ityop'iya
former: Abyssinia, Italian East Africa
abbreviation: FDRE
Government type: federal republic
Capital: Addis Ababa
Administrative divisions: 9 ethnically-based states (kililoch, singular - kilil) and 2 self-governing administrations* (astedaderoch, singular - astedader); Adis Abeba* (Addis Ababa), Afar, Amara (Amhara), Binshangul Gumuz, Dire Dawa*, Gambela Hizboch (Gambela Peoples), Hareri Hizb (Harari People), Oromiya (Oromia), Sumale (Somali), Tigray, Ye Debub Biheroch Bihereseboch na Hizboch (Southern Nations, Nationalities and Peoples)
Independence: oldest independent country in Africa and one of the oldest in the world - at least 2,000 years
National holiday: National Day (defeat of MENGISTU regime), 28 May (1991)
Constitution: ratified December 1994, effective 22 August 1995
Legal system: currently transitional mix of national and regional courts
Suffrage: 18 years of age; universal
Executive branch:
chief of state: President GIRMA Woldegiorgis (since 8 October 2001)
head of government: Prime Minister MELES Zenawi (since NA August 1995)
cabinet: Council of Ministers as provided for in the December 1994 constitution; ministers are selected by the prime minister and approved by the House of People's Representatives
elections: president elected by the House of People's Representatives for a six-year term; election last held 8 October 2001 (next to be held October 2007); prime minister designated by the party in power following legislative elections
election results: GIRMA Woldegiorgis elected president; percent of vote by the House of People's Representatives - 100%
Legislative branch: bicameral Parliament consists of the House of Federation or upper chamber (108 seats; members are chosen by state assemblies to serve five-year terms) and the House of People's Representatives or lower chamber (548 seats; members are directly elected by popular vote from single-member districts to serve five-year terms)
elections: last held 15 May 2005 (next to be held NA 2010)
election results: percent of vote - NA%; seats by party - OPDO 177, ANDM 134, TPLF 38, WGGPDO 27, EPRDF 19, SPDO 18, GNDM 15, KSPDO 10, ANDP 8, GPRDF 7, SOPDM 7, BGP-DUF 6, BMPDO 5, KAT 4, other regional political groupings 22, independents 8; note - 43 seats unconfirmed
note: irregularities and violence at some polling stations necessitated the rescheduling of voting in certain constituencies; voting postponed in Somali regional state because of severe drought
Judicial branch: Federal Supreme Court (the president and vice president of the

Federal Supreme Court are recommended by the prime minister and appointed by the House of People's Representatives; for other federal judges, the prime minister submits to the House of People's Representatives for appointment candidates selected by the Federal Judicial Administrative Council)
Political parties and leaders: Afar National Democratic Party or ANDP [leader NA]; Benishangul Gumuz People's Democratic Unity Front or BGPDUF [Mulualem BESSE]; Coalition for Unity and Democracy or CUD [HAILU Shawil]; Ethiopian People's Revolutionary Democratic Front or EPRDF [MELES Zenawi] (an alliance of ANDM, OPDO, SEPDF, and TPLF); Gurage Nationalities' Democratic Movement or GNDM [leader NA]; United Ethopian Democratic Forces or UEDF [MERARA Gudina]; dozens of small parties
Political pressure groups and leaders: Afar Revolutionary Democratic Union Front or ARDUF [leader NA]; Council of Alternative Forces for Peace and Democracy in Ethiopia or CAFPDE [BEYANE Petros]; Southern Ethiopia People's Democratic Coalition or SEPDC [BEYANE Petros]
International organization participation: ACP, AfDB, AU, COMESA, FAO, G-24, G-77, IAEA, IBRD, ICAO, ICFTU, ICRM, IDA, IFAD, IFC, IFRCS, IGAD, ILO, IMF, IMO, Interpol, IOC, IOM (observer), ISO, ITU, MIGA, NAM, ONUB, OPCW, PCA, UN, UNCTAD, UNESCO, UNHCR, UNIDO, UNMIL, UPU, WCO, WFTU, WHO, WIPO, WMO, WToO, WTO (observer)
Diplomatic representation in the US:
chief of mission: Ambassador KASSAHUN Ayele
chancery: 3506 International Drive NW, Washington, DC 20008
telephone: [1] (202) 364-1200
FAX: [1] (202) 686-9551
consulate(s) general: Los Angeles
consulate(s): New York
Diplomatic representation from the US:
chief of mission: Ambassador Aurelia A. BRAZEAL
embassy: Entoto Street, Addis Ababa
mailing address: P. O. Box 1014, Addis Ababa
telephone: [251] (1) 550666
FAX: [251] (1) 551328
Flag description: three equal horizontal bands of green (top), yellow, and red with a yellow pentagram and single yellow rays emanating from the angles between the points on a light blue disk centered on the three bands; Ethiopia is the oldest independent country in Africa, and the three main colors of her flag were so often adopted by other African countries upon independence that they became known as the pan-African colors

ECONOMY

Economy - overview: Ethiopia's poverty-stricken economy is based on agriculture, accounting for half of GDP, 60% of exports, and 80% of total employment. The agricultural sector suffers from frequent drought and poor cultivation practices. Coffee is critical to the Ethiopian economy with exports of some $156 million in 2002, but historically low prices have seen many farmers switching to qat to supplement income. The war with Eritrea in 1998-2000 and recurrent drought have buffeted the economy, in particular coffee production. In November 2001, Ethiopia qualified for debt relief from the Highly Indebted Poor Countries (HIPC) initiative. Under Ethiopia's land tenure system, the government owns all land and provides long-term leases to the tenants; the system continues to hamper growth in the industrial sector as entrepreneurs are unable to use land as collateral for loans. Drought struck again late in 2002, leading to a 2% decline in GDP in 2003. Normal weather patterns late in 2003 helped agricultural and GDP growth recover in 2004-05.
GDP (purchasing power parity): $59.93 billion (2005 est.)
GDP (official exchange rate): $9.034 billion (2005 est.)
GDP - real growth rate: 6.5% (2005 est.)
GDP - per capita: purchasing power parity - $800 (2005 est.)
GDP - composition by sector:
agriculture: 40.1%
industry: 12.7%
services: 47.2% (2005 est.)
Labor force: NA (2001 est.)
Labor force - by occupation: agriculture and animal husbandry 80%, industry and construction 8%, government and services 12% (1985)
Unemployment rate: NA (2002)
Population below poverty line: 50% (2004 est.)
Household income or consumption by percentage share:
lowest 10%: 3%
highest 10%: 33.7% (1995)
Distribution of family income - Gini index: 30 (2000)
Inflation rate (consumer prices): 6% (2005 est.)
Investment (gross fixed): 20.8% of GDP (2005 est.)
Budget:
revenues: $2.338 billion
expenditures: $2.88 billion, including capital expenditures of $788 million (2005 est.)
Agriculture - products: cereals, pulses, coffee, oilseed, sugarcane, potatoes, qat; hides, cattle, sheep, goats
Industries: food processing, beverages, textiles, chemicals, metals processing, cement
Industrial production growth rate: 6.7% (2001 est.)
Electricity - production: 2.058 billion kWh (2003)
Electricity - production by source:
fossil fuel: 1.3%
hydro: 97.6%
nuclear: 0%
other: 1.2% (2001)
Electricity - consumption: 1.914 billion kWh (2003)
Electricity - exports: 0 kWh (2003)
Electricity - imports: 0 kWh (2003)
Oil - production: 0 bbl/day (2003 est.)
Oil - consumption: 27,000 bbl/day (2003 est.)
Oil - exports: NA (2001)
Oil - imports: NA (2001)
Oil - proved reserves: 214,000 bbl (1 January 2002)
Natural gas - proved reserves: 12.46 billion cu m (1 January 2002)
Current account balance: $-1.023 billion (2005 est.)
Exports: $612 million f.o.b. (2005 est.)
Exports - partners: Djibouti 13.3%, Germany 10%, Japan 8.4%, Saudi Arabia 5.6%, US 5.2%, UAE 5%, Italy 4.6% (2004)
Imports: $2.722 billion f.o.b. (2005 est.)
Imports - partners: Saudi Arabia 25.3%, US 15.8%, China 6.6% (2004)
Reserves of foreign exchange and gold: $1.192 billion (2005 est.)
Debt - external: $2.9 billion (2001 est.)
Economic aid - recipient: $308 million (FY00/01)
Currency (code): birr (ETB)
Currency code: ETB
Exchange rates: birr per US dollar - 8.72 (2005), 8.68 (2004), 8.5997 (2003), 8.5678 (2002), 8.4575 (2001)
note: since 24 October 2001 exchange rates are determined on a daily basis via interbank transactions regulated by the Central Bank
Fiscal year: 8 July - 7 July

COMMUNICATIONS

Telephones - main lines in use: 435,000 (2003)
Telephones - mobile cellular: 97,800 (2003)
Telephone system:
general assessment: adequate for government use
domestic: open-wire; microwave radio relay; radio communication in the HF,

VHF, and UHF frequencies; two domestic satellites provide the national trunk service
international: country code - 251; open-wire to Sudan and Djibouti; microwave radio relay to Kenya and Djibouti; satellite earth stations - 3 Intelsat (1 Atlantic Ocean and 2 Pacific Ocean)
Radio broadcast stations: AM 8, FM 0, shortwave 1 (2001)
Radios: 15.2 million (2002)
Television broadcast stations: 1 plus 24 repeaters (2002)
Televisions: 682,000 (2002)
Internet country code: .et
Internet hosts: 9 (2003)
Internet Service Providers (ISPs): 1 (2002)
Internet users: 75,000 (2003)

TRANSPORTATION

Airports: 83 (2004 est.)
Airports - with paved runways:
total: 14
over 3,047 m: 3
2,438 to 3,047 m: 5
1,524 to 2,437 m: 5
914 to 1,523 m: 1 (2005 est.)
Airports - with unpaved runways:
total: 68
over 3,047 m: 3
2,438 to 3,047 m: 3
1,524 to 2,437 m: 13
914 to 1,523 m: 27
under 914 m: 22 (2005 est.)
Railways:
total: 681 km (Ethiopian segment of the Addis Ababa-Djibouti railroad)
narrow gauge: 681 km 1.000-m gauge
note: railway under joint control of Djibouti and Ethiopia (2004)
Roadways:
total: 33,856 km
paved: 4,367 km
unpaved: 29,489 km (2003)
Merchant marine:
total: 8 ships (1,000 GRT or over) 81,933 GRT/101,287 DWT
by type: cargo 6, roll on/roll off 2 (2005)
Ports and terminals: Ethiopia is landlocked and has used ports of Assab and Massawa in Eritrea and port of Djibouti

MILITARY

Military branches: Ethiopian National Defense Force (ENDF): Ground Forces, Air Force
note: Ethiopia is landlocked and has no navy; following the secession of Eritrea, Ethiopian naval facilities remained in Eritrean possession (2003)
Military service age and obligation: 18 years of age for compulsory and voluntary military service (2001)
Manpower available for military service:
males age 18-49: 14,568,277 (2005 est.)
Manpower fit for military service:
males age 18-49: 8,072,755 (2005 est.)
Manpower reaching military service age annually: *males*: 803,777 (2005 est.)
Military expenditures - dollar figure: $337.1 million (2004)
Military expenditures - percent of GDP: 4.6% (2004)

TRANSNATIONAL ISSUES

Disputes - international: Eritrea and Ethiopia agreed to abide by the 2002 Eritrea-Ethiopia Boundary Commission's (EEBC) delimitation decision, but despite international intervention, mutual animosities, accusations and armed posturing prevail, preventing demarcation; Ethiopia refuses to withdraw to the delimited boundary until technical errors made by the EEBC that ignored "human geography" are addressed, including the award of Badme, the focus of the 1998-2000 war; Eritrea insists that the EEBC decision be implemented immediately without modifications; Ethiopia has only an administrative line and no international border with the Oromo region of southern Somalia where it maintains alliances with local clans in opposition to the unrecognized Somali Interim Government in Mogadishu; "Somaliland" secessionists provide port facilities and trade ties to landlocked Ethiopia; the UNHCR expects most of the remaining 23,000 Somali refugees in Ethiopia to be repatriated in 2005; efforts to demarcate the porous boundary with Sudan have been delayed by civil war
Refugees and internally displaced persons:
refugees (country of origin): 93,032 (Sudan) 23,578 (Somalia)
IDPs: 132,000 (border war with Eritrea from 1998-2000 and ethnic clashes in Gambela; most IDPs are in Tigray and Gambela Provinces) (2004)
Illicit drugs: Transit hub for heroin originating in Southwest and Southeast Asia and destined for Europe and North America as well as cocaine destined for markets in southern Africa; cultivates qat (khat) for local use and regional export, principally to Djibouti and Somalia (legal in all three countries); the lack of a well-developed financial system limits the country's utility as a money-laundering center

EUROPA ISLAND

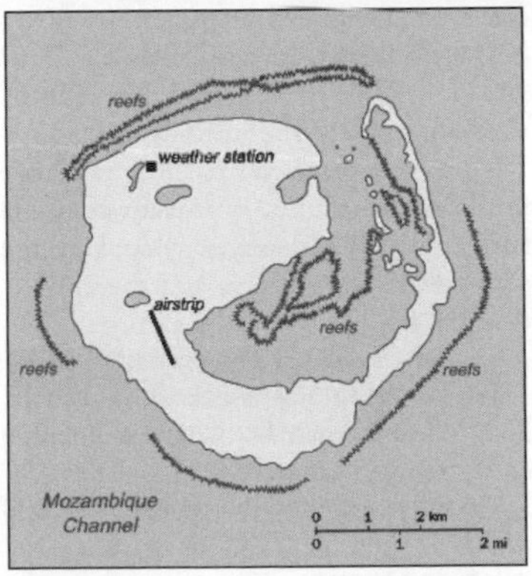

INTRODUCTION

Background: A French possession since 1897, the island is heavily wooded; it is the site of a small military garrison that staffs a weather station.

GEOGRAPHY

Location: Southern Africa, island in the Mozambique Channel, about half way between southern Madagascar and southern Mozambique
Geographic coordinates: 22 20 S, 40 22 E
Map references: Africa
Area:
total: 28 sq km
land: 28 sq km
water: 0 sq km
Area - comparative: about 0.16 times the size of Washington, DC
Land boundaries: 0 km
Coastline: 22.2 km
Maritime claims:
territorial sea: 12 nm
exclusive economic zone: 200 nm
Climate: tropical
Terrain: low and flat
Elevation extremes:
lowest point: Indian Ocean 0 m
highest point: unnamed location 24 m
Natural resources: NEGL
Land use:
arable land: 0%
permanent crops: 0%
other: 100% (mangrove forests and woodlands) (2001)
Irrigated land: 0 sq km (1998 est.)
Natural hazards: NA
Environment - current issues: NA
Geography - note: wildlife sanctuary

PEOPLE

Population: no indigenous inhabitants
note: there is a small French military gar-

rison and a few meteorologists; visited by scientists (July 2005 est.)

GOVERNMENT

Country name:
conventional long form: none
conventional short form: Europa Island
local long form: none
local short form: Ile Europa
Dependency status: possession of France; administered by the Administrateur Superieur of the French Southern and Antarctic Lands
Legal system: the laws of France, where applicable, apply
Flag description: the flag of France is used

ECONOMY

Economy - overview: no economic activity

COMMUNICATIONS

Communications - note: 1 meteorological station

TRANSPORTATION

Airports: 1 (2004 est.)
Airports - with unpaved runways:
total: 1
914 to 1,523 m: 1 (2005 est.)
Ports and terminals: none; offshore anchorage only

MILITARY

Military - note: defense is the responsibility of France

TRANSNATIONAL ISSUES

Disputes - international: claimed by Madagascar

EUROPEAN UNION

INTRODUCTION

Preliminary statement: The evolution of the European Union (EU) from a regional economic agreement among six neighboring states in 1951 to today's supranational organization of 25 countries across the European continent stands as an unprecedented phenomenon in the annals of history. Dynastic unions for territorial consolidation were long the norm in Europe. On a few occasions even country-level unions were arranged - the Polish-Lithuanian Commonwealth and the Austro-Hungarian Empire were examples - but for such a large number of nation-states to cede some of their sovereignty to an overarching entity is truly unique. Although the EU is not a federation in the strict sense, it is far more than a free-trade association such as ASEAN, NAFTA, or Mercosur, and it has many of the attributes associated with independent nations: its own flag, anthem, founding date, and currency, as well as an incipient common foreign and security policy in its dealings with other nations. In the future, many of these nation-like characteristics are likely to be expanded. Thus, inclusion of basic intelligence on the EU has been deemed appropriate as a new, separate entity in The World Factbook. However, because of the EU's special status, this description is placed after the regular country entries.
Background: Following the two devastating World Wars of the first half of the 20th century, a number of European leaders in the late 1940s became convinced that the only way to establish a lasting peace was to unite the two chief belligerent nations - France and Germany - both economically and politically. In 1950, the French Foreign Minister Robert SCHUMAN proposed an eventual union of all Europe, the first step of which would be the integration of the coal and steel industries of Western Europe. The following year the European Coal and Steel Community (ECSC) was set up when six members, Belgium, France, West Germany, Italy, Luxembourg, and the Netherlands, signed the Treaty of Paris. The ECSC was so successful that within a few years the decision was made to integrate other parts of the countries' economies. In 1957, the Treaties of Rome created the European Economic Community (EEC) and the European Atomic Energy Community (Euratom), and the six member states undertook to eliminate trade barriers among themselves by forming a common market. In 1967, the institutions of all three communities were formally merged into the European Community (EC), creating a single Commission, a single Council of Ministers, and the European Parliament. Members of the European Parliament were initially selected by national parliaments, but in 1979 the first direct elections were undertaken and they have been held every five years since. In 1973, the first enlargement of the EC took place with the addition of Denmark, Ireland, and the United Kingdom. The 1980s saw further membership expansion with Greece joining in 1981 and Spain and Portugal in 1986. The 1992 Treaty of Maastricht laid the basis for further forms of cooperation in foreign and defense policy, in judicial and internal affairs, and in the creation of an economic and monetary union - including a common currency. This further integration created the European Union (EU). In 1995, Austria, Finland, and Sweden joined the EU, raising the membership total to 15. A new currency, the euro, was launched in world money markets on 1 January 1999; it become the unit of exchange for all of the EU states except the United Kingdom, Sweden, and Denmark. In 2002, citizens of the 12 euro-area countries began using the euro banknotes and coins. Ten new countries joined the EU in 2004 - Cyprus, the Czech Republic, Estonia, Hungary, Latvia, Lithuania, Malta, Poland, Slovakia, and Slovenia - bringing the current membership to 25. In order to ensure that the EU can continue to function efficiently with an expanded membership, the 2003 Treaty of Nice set forth rules streamlining the size and procedures of EU institutions. An EU Constitutional Treaty, signed in Rome on 29 October 2004, gave member states two years to ratify the document before it was scheduled to take effect on 1 November 2006. Referenda held in France and the Netherlands in May-June 2005 that rejected the constitution suspended the ratification effort. Despite the expansion of membership and functions, "Eurosceptics" in various countries have raised questions about the erosion of national cultures and the imposition of a flood of regulations from the EU capital in Brussels. Failure by all member states to ratify the constitution or the inability of newcomer countries to meet euro currency standards might force a loosening of some EU agreements and perhaps lead to several levels of EU participation. These "tiers" might eventually range from an "inner" core of politically integrated countries to a looser "outer" economic association of members.

GEOGRAPHY

Location: Europe between Belarus, Ukraine, Russia, southeastern Europe, and the North Atlantic Ocean
Map references: Europe
Area: total: 3,976,372 sq km
Area - comparative: less than one-half the size of the US
Land boundaries:
total: 11,214.8 km
border countries: Albania 282 km, Andorra 120.3 km, Belarus 1,050 km, Bulgaria 494 km, Croatia 999 km, Holy See 3.2 km, Liechtenstein 34.9 km, Macedonia 246 km, Monaco 4.4 km, Norway 2,348 km, Romania 443 km, Russia 2,257 km, San Marino 39 km, Serbia and Montenegro 151 km, Switzerland 1,811 km, Turkey 206 km, Ukraine 726 km
note: data for European Continent only
Coastline: 65,413.9 km
Maritime claims: NA
Climate: cold temperate; potentially subarctic in the north to temperate; mild wet winters; hot dry summers in the south
Terrain: fairly flat along the Baltic and Atlantic coast; mountainous in the central and southern areas
Elevation extremes:
lowest point: Lammefjord, Denmark -7 m; Zuidplaspolder, Netherlands -7 m
highest point: Mont Blanc, France 4,807 m
Natural resources: iron ore, arable land, natural gas, petroleum, coal, copper, lead, zinc, hydropower, uranium, potash, fish
Land use:
arable land: NA%
permanent crops: NA%
other: NA%
Irrigated land: 115,807 sq km
Natural hazards: flooding along coasts; avalanches in mountainous area; earthquakes in the south; volcanic eruptions in Italy; periodic droughts in Spain; ice floes in the Baltic
Environment - current issues: NA
Environment - international agreements:
party to: Air Pollution, Air Pollution-Nitrogen Oxides, Air Pollution-Persistent Organic Pollutants, Air Pollution-Sulphur 94, Antarctic-Marine Living Resources, Biodiversity, Climate Change, Climate Change-Kyoto Protocol, Desertification, Hazardous Wastes, Law of the Sea, Ozone Layer Protection, Tropical Timber 82, Tropical Timber 94
signed but not ratified: Air Pollution-Volatile Organic Compounds

PEOPLE

Population: 456,953,258 (July 2005 est.)
Age structure:
0-14 years: 16.03% (male 37,608,010/female 35,632,351)
15-64 years: 67.17% (male 154,439,536/female 152,479,619)
65 years and over: 16.81% (male 31,515,921/female 45,277,821) (2005 est.)
Median age: NA
Population growth rate: 0.15% (July 2005 est.)
Birth rate: 10 births/1,000 population (July 2005 est.)
Death rate: 10.1 deaths/1,000 population (July 2005 est.)
Net migration rate: 1.5 migrant(s)/1,000 population (July 2005 est.)
Sex ratio:
at birth: NA
under 15 years: 1.06 male(s)/female
15-64 years: 1.01 male(s)/female
65 years and older: 0.69 male(s)/female
total population: 0.96 male(s)/female (July 2004 est.)
Infant mortality rate:
total: 5.1 deaths/1,000 live births
male: 5.6 deaths/1,000 live births
female: 4.5 deaths/1,000 live births (July 2005 est.)
Life expectancy at birth:
total population: 78.3 years
male: 75.1 years
female: 81.6 years (July 2005 est.)
Total fertility rate: 1.47 children born/woman (July 2005 est.)
HIV/AIDS - adult prevalence rate: NA%
HIV/AIDS - people living with HIV/AIDS: NA
HIV/AIDS - deaths: NA
Religions: Roman Catholic, Protestant, Orthodox, Muslim, Jewish
Languages: Czech, Danish, Dutch, English, Estonian, Finnish, French, German, Greek, Hungarian, Italian, Latvian, Lithuanian, Maltese, Polish, Portuguese, Slovak, Slovene, Spanish, Swedish; note - only official languages are listed; Irish (Gaelic) will become the twenty-first language on 1 January 2007

GOVERNMENT

Union name:
conventional long form: European Union
abbreviation: EU
Political structure: a hybrid intergovernmental and supranational organization
Capital: Brussels, Belgium
note: the Council of the European Union meets in Brussels, the European Parliament meets in Strasbourg, France, and the Court of Justice of the European Communities meets in Luxembourg
Member states: 25 countries: Austria, Belgium, Cyprus, Czech Republic, Denmark, Estonia, Finland, France, Germany, Greece, Hungary, Ireland, Italy, Latvia, Lithuania, Luxembourg, Malta, Netherlands, Poland, Portugal, Slovakia, Slovenia, Spain, Sweden, UK; note - Canary Islands (Spain), Azores and Madeira (Portugal), and French Guyana, Guadeloupe, Martinique, and Reunion (France) are sometimes listed separately even though they are legally a part of Spain, Portugal, and France; candidate countries: Bulgaria, Croatia, Romania, Turkey; note - the EC has recommended that Macedonia become a candidate country
Independence: 7 February 1992 (Maastricht Treaty signed establishing the EU); 1 November 1993 (Maastricht Treaty entered into force)
National holiday: Europe Day 9 May (1950); note - a Union-wide holiday, the day that Robert Schuman proposed the creation of an organized Europe
Constitution: based on a series of treaties: the Treaty of Paris, which set up the European Coal and Steel Community (ECSC) in 1951; the Treaties of Rome, which set up the European Economic Community (EEC) and the European Atomic Energy Community (Euratom) in 1957; the Single European Act in 1986; the Treaty on European Union (Maastricht) in 1992; the Treaty of Amsterdam in 1997; and the Treaty of Nice in 2001; note - a new draft Constitutional Treaty, signed on 29 October 2004 in Rome, gave member states two years for ratification either by parliamentary vote or national referendum before it was scheduled to take effect on 1 November 2006; defeat in French and Dutch referenda in May-June 2005 caused a suspension of the ratification process
Suffrage: 18 years of age; universal
Executive branch:
chief of union: President of the European Commission Jose Manuel DURAO BARROSO (since 22 November 2004)
cabinet: European Commission (composed of 25 members, one from each member country; each commissioner responsible for one or more policy areas)
elections: the president of the European Commission is designated by member governments; the president-designate then chooses the other Commission members; the European Parliament confirms the entire Commission for a five-year term; election last held 18 November 2004 (next to be held 2009)
election results: European Parliament approved the European Commission by an approval vote of 449 to 149 with 82 abstentions
note: the European Council brings together heads of state and government and the president of the European Commission and meets at least twice a year; its aim is to provide the impetus for the major political issues relating to European integration and to issue general policy guidelines

Legislative branch: Council of the European Union (25 member-state ministers having 321 votes; the number of votes is roughly proportional to member-states' population); note - the Council is the main decision-making body of the EU; European Parliament (732 seats; seats allocated among member states by proportion to population); members elected by direct universal suffrage for a five-year term
elections: last held 10-13 June 2004 (next to be held June 2009)
election results: percent of vote - NA%; seats by party - EPP-ED 268, PES 202, ALDE 88, Greens/EFA 42, EUL/NGL 41, IND/DEM 36, UEN 27, independents 28
Judicial branch: Court of Justice of the European Communities (ensures that the treaties are interpreted and applied correctly) - 25 justices (one from each member state) appointed for a six-year term; note - for the sake of efficiency, the court can sit with 11 justices known as the "Grand Chamber"; Court of First Instance - 25 justices appointed for a six-year term
Political parties and leaders: Group of the Alliance of Liberals and Democrats for Europe or ALDE [Graham R. WATSON]; Independence/Democracy Group or IND/DEM [Jens-Peter BONDE and Nigel FARAGE]; Group of Greens/European Free Alliance or Greens/EFA [Monica FRASSONI and Daniel Marc COHN-BENDIT]; Socialist Group in the European Parliament or PES [Martin SCHULZ]; Confederal Group of the European United Left-Nordic Green Left or EUL/NGL [Francis WURTZ]; European People's Party-European Democrats or EPP-ED [Hans-Gert POETTERING]; Union for Europe of the Nations Group or UEN [Brian CROWLEY and Cristiana MUSCARDINI]
International organization participation: European Union: ASEAN (dialogue member), ARF (dialogue member), EBRD, FAO, IDA, OAS (observer), OECD, UN (observer), WTO European Commission: Australian Group, CBSS, CERN, G-10, NSG (observer) European Central Bank: BIS European Investment Bank: EBRD, WADB (nonregional member)
Diplomatic representation in the US:
chief of mission: Ambassador John BRUTON
chancery: 2300 M Street, NW, Washington, D.C. 20037
telephone: [1] (202) 862-9500
FAX: [1] (202) 429-1766
Diplomatic representation from the US:
chief of mission: Ambassador (vacant); Charge d'Affaires P. Michael McKINLEY
embassy: 13 Zinnerstraat/Rue Zinner, B-1000 Brussels
mailing address: same as above
telephone: [32] (2) 508-2222
FAX: [32] (2) 512-5720
Flag description: on a blue field, 12 five-pointed gold stars arranged in a circle, representing the union of the peoples of Europe; the number of stars is fixed

ECONOMY

Economy - overview: Domestically, the European Union attempts to lower trade barriers, adopt a common currency, and move toward convergence of living standards. Internationally, the EU aims to bolster Europe's trade position and its political and economic power. Because of the great differences in per capita income (from $10,000 to $28,000) and historic national animosities, the European Community faces difficulties in devising and enforcing common policies. For example, both Germany and France since 2003 have flouted the member states' treaty obligation to prevent their national budgets from running more than a 3% deficit. In 2004, the EU admitted 10 central and eastern European countries that are, in general, less advanced technologically and economically than the existing 15. Twelve EU member states introduced the euro as their common currency on 1 January 1999. The UK, Sweden, and Denmark do not now participate; the 10 new member states may choose to adopt the euro when they meet the EU's fiscal and monetary criteria and the member states so agree.
GDP (purchasing power parity): $12.18 trillion (2005 est.)
GDP (official exchange rate): $13.31 trillion (2005 est.)
GDP - real growth rate: 1.7% (2005 est.)
GDP - per capita: purchasing power parity - $28,100 (2005 est.)
GDP - composition by sector:
agriculture: 2.2%
industry: 27.3%
services: 70.5% (2004 est.)
Labor force: 218.5 million (2005 est.)
Labor force - by occupation: agriculture 4.5%, industry 27.4%, services 66.9%
note: the remainder is in miscellaneous public and private sector industries and services (2002 est.)
Unemployment rate: 9.4% (2005 est.)
Population below poverty line: See individual country listings
Household income or consumption by percentage share:
lowest 10%: 2.8%
highest 10%: 25.5% (1995 est.)
Distribution of family income - Gini index: 32 (2003 est.)
Inflation rate (consumer prices): 2.2% (2005 est.)
Investment (gross fixed): percent of GDP - 19.6% of GDP (2005 est.)
Agriculture - products: wheat, barley, oilseeds, sugar beets, wine, grapes, dairy products, cattle, sheep, pigs, poultry, fish
Industries: among the world's largest and most technologically advanced, the European Union industrial base includes: ferrous and non-ferrous metal production and processing, metal products, petroleum, coal, cement, chemicals, pharmaceuticals, aerospace, rail transportation equipment, passenger and commercial vehicles, construction equipment, industrial equipment, shipbuilding, electrical power equipment, machine tools and automated manufacturing systems, electronics and telecommunications equipment, fishing, food and beverage processing, furniture, paper, textiles, tourism
Industrial production growth rate: 1.3% (2005 est.)
Electricity - production: 2.925 trillion kWh (2002 est.)
Electricity - consumption: 2.711 trillion kWh (2002 est.)
Electricity - exports: 282.6 billion kWh (2002)
Electricity - imports: 281.2 billion kWh (2002 est.)
Oil - production: 3.424 million bbl/day (2001)
Oil - consumption: 14.59 million bbl/day (2001)
Oil - exports: 5.322 million bbl/day (2001)
Oil - imports: 15.69 million bbl/day (2001)
Oil - proved reserves: 7.294 billion bbl (1 January 2002)
Natural gas - production: 239.2 billion cu m (2001)
Natural gas - consumption: 465.6 billion cu m (2001)
Natural gas - exports: 78.1 billion cu m (2001)
Natural gas - imports: 297.8 billion cu m (2001)
Natural gas - proved reserves: 3.256 trillion cu m (1 January 2002)
Current account balance: $NA
Exports: $1.318 trillion
note: external exports, excluding intra EU trade (2004)
Exports - partners: US 24.2%, Switzerland 7.7%, China 5%, Russia 4.7% (2004)
Imports: $1.402 trillion
note: external imports, excluding intra-EU trade (2004)

Imports - partners: US 15.3%, China 12.4%, Russia 7.8%, Japan 7.2% (2004)
Reserves of foreign exchange and gold: $NA
Currency (code): euro, British pound, Danish kroner, Swedish kroner, Cypriot pound, koruny (Czech Republic), krooni (Estonia), forint (Hungary), lati (Latvia), litai (Lithuania), Maltese liri, zloty (Poland), koruny (Slovakia), tolar (Slovenia)
Currency code: EUR
Exchange rates: euros per US dollar - 0.79697 (2005), 0.8054 (2004), 0.886 (2003), 1.0626 (2002), 1.1175 (2001)
Fiscal year: NA

COMMUNICATIONS

Telephones - main lines in use: 238,763,162 (2002)
Telephones - mobile cellular: 314,644,700 (2002)
Telephone system: note - see individual country entries of member states
Radio broadcast stations: AM 866, FM 13,396, shortwave 73 (1998); note - sum of individual country radio broadcast stations; there is also a European-wide station (Euroradio)
Television broadcast stations: 2,791 (1995); note - does not include repeaters; sum of individual country television broadcast stations; there is also a European-wide station (Eurovision)
Internet country code: .eu (effective 2005); note - see country entries of member states for individual country codes
Internet hosts: 22,000,414 (2004); note - sum of individual country Internet hosts
Internet users: 206,032,067 (September 2004)

TRANSPORTATION

Airports: 3,130 (2004 est.)
Airports - with paved runways: 1,852 (2005 est.)
Airports - with unpaved runways: 1,274 (2005 est.)
Heliports: 93 (2005 est.)
Railways:
total: 222,293 km
broad gauge: 28,438 km
standard gauge: 186,405 km
narrow gauge: 7,427 km
other: 23 km (2003)
Roadways:
total: 4,634,810 km (including 56,704 km of expressways)
paved: 4,161,318 km
unpaved: 473,492 km (1999-2000)
Waterways: 53,512 km
Ports and terminals: Antwerp (Belgium), Barcelona (Spain), Bremen (Germany), Copenhagen (Denmark), Gdansk (Poland), Hamburg (Germany), Helsinki (Finland), Las Palmas (Canary Islands, Spain), Le Havre (France), Lisbon (Portugal), London (UK), Marseille (France), Naples (Italy), Peiraiefs or Piraeus (Greece), Riga (Latvia), Rotterdam (Netherlands), Stockholm (Sweden), Talinn (Estonia)

MILITARY

Military - note: In November 2004, the European Union heads of government signed a "Treaty Establishing a Constitution for Europe" that offers possibilities - with some limits - for increased defense and security cooperation. If ratified, in a process that may take some two years, this treaty will in effect make operational the European Security and Defense Policy (ESDP) approved in the 2000 Nice Treaty. Despite limits of cooperation for some EU members, development of a European military planning unit is likely to continue. So is creation of a rapid-reaction military force and a humanitarian aid system, which the planning unit will support. France, Germany, Belgium, Netherlands, Luxembourg, and Italy continue to press for wider coordination. The five-nation Eurocorps - created in 1992 by France, Germany, Belgium, Spain, and Luxembourg - has already deployed troops and police on peacekeeping missions to Bosnia and Herzegovina, Macedonia, and the Democratic Republic of Congo and assumed command of the International Security Assistance Force (ISAF) in Afghanistan in August 2004. Eurocorps directly commands the 5,000-man Franco-German Brigade, the Multinational Command Support Brigade, and EUFOR, which took over from SFOR in Bosnia in December 2004. Other troop contributions are under national command - commitments to provide 67,100 troops were made at the Helsinki EU session in 2000. Some 56,000 EU troops were actually deployed in 2003. In August 2004, the new European Defense Agency, tasked with promoting cooperative European defense capabilities, began operations. In November 2004, the EU Council of Ministers formally committed to creating thirteen 1,500-man "battle groups" by the end of 2007, to respond to international crises on a rotating basis. Twenty-two of the EU's 25 nations have agreed to supply troops. France, Italy, and the UK are to form the first three battle groups in 2005, with Spain to follow. In May 2005, Norway, Sweden, and Finland agreed to establish one of the battle groups, possibly to include Estonian forces. The remaining groups are to be formed by 2007. (2005)

TRANSNATIONAL ISSUES

Disputes - international: the EU has no border disputes with neighboring countries; it has set up a Schengen area - consisting of 13 EU member states that have signed the convention implementing the Schengen agreements (1985 and 1990) on the free movement of persons and the harmonization of border controls in Europe; the Schengen agreements ("acquis") became incorporated into EU law with the implementation of the 1997 Treaty of Amsterdam on 1 May 1999; member states are: Austria, Belgium, Denmark, Finland, France, Germany, Greece, Italy, Luxembourg, Netherlands, Portugal, Spain, and Sweden; in addition, non-EU states Iceland and Norway (as part of the Nordic Union) have been included in the Schengen area since 1996 (full members in 2001), bringing the total current membership to 15; the UK (since 2000) and Ireland (since 2002) take part in some aspects of the Schengen area, especially with respect to police and criminal matters; the 10 new member states that joined the EU in 2004 eventually are expected to participate in Schengen, following a transition period to upgrade their border controls and procedures

FALKLAND ISLANDS (ISLAS MALVINAS)

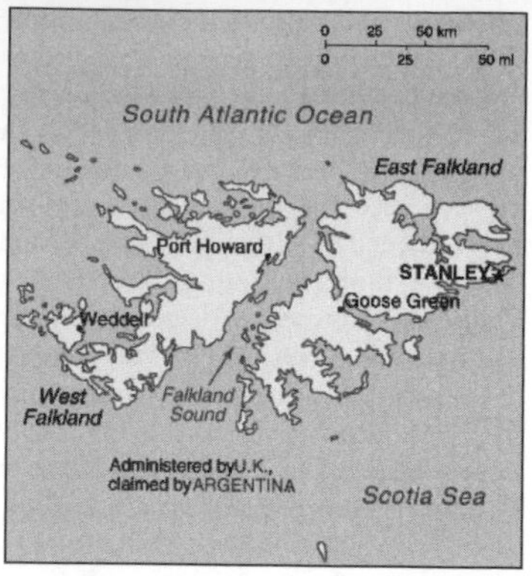

INTRODUCTION

Background: Although first sighted by an English navigator in 1592, the first landing (English) did not occur until almost a century later in 1690, and the first settlement (French) was not established until 1764. The colony was turned over to Spain two years later and the islands have since been the subject of a territorial dispute, first between Britain and Spain, then between Britain and Argentina. The UK asserted its claim to the islands by establishing a naval garrison there in 1833. Argentina invaded the islands on 2 April 1982. The British responded with an expeditionary force that landed seven weeks later and after fierce fighting forced Argentine surrender on 14 June 1982.

GEOGRAPHY

Location: Southern South America, islands in the South Atlantic Ocean, east of southern Argentina
Geographic coordinates: 51 45 S, 59 00 W
Map references: South America
Area:
total: 12,173 sq km
land: 12,173 sq km
water: 0 sq km
note: includes the two main islands of East and West Falkland and about 200 small islands
Area - comparative: slightly smaller than Connecticut
Land boundaries: 0 km
Coastline: 1,288 km
Maritime claims:
territorial sea: 12 nm
continental shelf: 200 nm
exclusive fishing zone: 200 nm
Climate: cold marine; strong westerly winds, cloudy, humid; rain occurs on more than half of days in year; average annual rainfall is 24 inches in Stanley; occasional snow all year, except in January and February, but does not accumulate
Terrain: rocky, hilly, mountainous with some boggy, undulating plains
Elevation extremes:
lowest point: Atlantic Ocean 0 m
highest point: Mount Usborne 705 m
Natural resources: fish, squid, wildlife, calcified seaweed, sphagnum moss
Land use:
arable land: 0%
permanent crops: 0%
other: 100% (99% permanent pastures, 1% other) (2001)
Irrigated land: NA sq km
Natural hazards: strong winds persist throughout the year
Environment - current issues: overfishing by unlicensed vessels is a problem; reindeer were introduced to the islands in 2001 for commercial reasons; this is the only commercial reindeer herd in the world unaffected by the Chernobyl disaster
Geography - note: deeply indented coast provides good natural harbors; short growing season

PEOPLE

Population: 2,967 (July 2005 est.)
Age structure:
0-14 years: NA
15-64 years: NA
65 years and over: NA (2005 est.)
Population growth rate: 2.44% (2005 est.)
Birth rate: NA births/1,000 population (2005 est.)
Death rate: NA deaths/1,000 population (2005 est.)
Net migration rate: NA migrant(s)/1,000 population (2005 est.)
Infant mortality rate:
total: NA
male: NA
female: NA (2005 est.)
Life expectancy at birth:
total population: NA years
male: NA years
female: NA years (2005 est.)
Total fertility rate: NA children born/woman (2005 est.)
HIV/AIDS - adult prevalence rate: NA
HIV/AIDS - people living with HIV/AIDS: NA
HIV/AIDS - deaths: NA
Nationality:
noun: Falkland Islander(s)
adjective: Falkland Island
Ethnic groups: British
Religions: primarily Anglican, Roman Catholic, United Free Church, Evangelist Church, Jehovah's Witnesses, Lutheran, Seventh-Day Adventist
Languages: English

GOVERNMENT

Country name:
conventional long form: none
conventional short form: Falkland Islands (Islas Malvinas)
Dependency status: overseas territory of the UK; also claimed by Argentina
Government type: NA
Capital: Stanley
Administrative divisions: none (overseas territory of the UK; also claimed by Argentina)
Independence: none (overseas territory of the UK; also claimed by
National holiday: Liberation Day, 14 June (1982)
Constitution: 3 October 1985; amended 1997 and 1998
Legal system: English common law
Suffrage: 18 years of age; universal
Executive branch:
chief of state: Queen ELIZABETH II (since 6 February 1952)
head of government: Governor Howard PEARCE (since 3 December 2002); Chief Executive Chris SIMPKINS (since NA March 2003); Financial Secretary Derek F. HOWATT (since NA)
cabinet: Executive Council; three members elected by the Legislative Council, two ex officio members (chief executive and the financial secretary), and the governor
elections: none; the monarchy is hereditary; governor appointed by the monarch
Legislative branch: unicameral Legislative Council (10 seats - 2 ex officio, 8 elected by popular vote, members serve four-year terms); presided over by the governor
elections: last held 22 November 2001 (next to be held November 2005)
election results: percent of vote - NA%; seats - independents 8; note - 71% voter turnout
Judicial branch: Supreme Court (chief justice is a nonresident); Magistrates Court (senior magistrate presides over civil and criminal divisions); Court of Summary Jurisdiction
Political parties and leaders: none; all independents
Political pressure groups and leaders: none
International organization participation: ICFTU, UPU
Diplomatic representation in the US: none (overseas territory of the UK; also claimed by Argentina)
Diplomatic representation from the US: none (overseas territory of the UK; also claimed by Argentina)
Flag description: blue with the flag of the UK in the upper hoist-side quadrant and

the Falkland Island coat of arms centered on the outer half of the flag; the coat of arms contains a white ram (sheep raising was once the major economic activity) above the sailing ship Desire (whose crew discovered the islands) with a scroll at the bottom bearing the motto DESIRE THE RIGHT

ECONOMY

Economy - overview: The economy was formerly based on agriculture, mainly sheep farming, but today fishing contributes the bulk of economic activity. In 1987 the government began selling fishing licenses to foreign trawlers operating within the Falklands exclusive fishing zone. These license fees total more than $40 million per year, which goes to support the island's health, education, and welfare system. Squid accounts for 75% of the fish taken. Dairy farming supports domestic consumption; crops furnish winter fodder. Exports feature shipments of high-grade wool to the UK and the sale of postage stamps and coins. The islands are now self-financing except for defense. The British Geological Survey announced a 200-mile oil exploration zone around the islands in 1993, and early seismic surveys suggest substantial reserves capable of producing 500,000 barrels per day; to date no exploitable site has been identified. An agreement between Argentina and the UK in 1995 seeks to defuse licensing and sovereignty conflicts that would dampen foreign interest in exploiting potential oil reserves. Tourism, especially eco-tourism, is increasing rapidly, with about 30,000 visitors in 2001. Another large source of income is interest paid on money the government has in the bank. The British military presence also provides a sizeable economic boost.
GDP (purchasing power parity): $75 million (2002 est.)
GDP (official exchange rate): NA
GDP - real growth rate: NA%
GDP - per capita: purchasing power parity - $25,000 (2002 est.)
GDP - composition by sector:
agriculture: NA%
industry: NA%
services: NA%
Labor force: 1,100 (est.)
Labor force - by occupation: agriculture 95% (mostly sheepherding and fishing)
Unemployment rate: full employment; labor shortage (2001)
Population below poverty line: NA
Household income or consumption by percentage share:
lowest 10%: NA%
highest 10%: NA%
Inflation rate (consumer prices): 3.6% (1998)
Budget:
revenues: $66.2 million
expenditures: $67.9 million, including capital expenditures of $23.2 million (FY98/99 est.)
Agriculture - products: fodder and vegetable crops; sheep, dairy products
Industries: fish and wool processing; tourism
Industrial production growth rate: NA%
Electricity - production: 22.23 million kWh (2003)
Electricity - production by source:
fossil fuel: 100%
hydro: 0%
nuclear: 0%
other: 0% (2001)
Electricity - consumption: 20.68 million kWh (2003)
Electricity - exports: 0 kWh (2003)
Electricity - imports: 0 kWh (2003)
Oil - production: 0 bbl/day (2003 est.)
Oil - consumption: 200 bbl/day (2003 est.)
Oil - exports: NA (2001)
Oil - imports: NA (2001)
Exports: $125 million (2004 est.)
Exports - partners: Spain 77.4%, UK 9.4%, US 4.9% (2004)
Imports: $90 million (2004 est.)
Imports - partners: UK 63.2%, Spain 30.3%, France 3.6% (2004)
Debt - external: $NA
Economic aid - recipient: $0 (1997 est.)
Currency (code): Falkland pound (FKP)
Currency code: FKP
Exchange rates: Falkland pounds per US dollar - 0.54 (2005), 0.5462 (2004), 0.6125 (2003), 0.6672 (2002), 0.6947 (2001)
note: the Falkland pound is at par with the British pound
Fiscal year: 1 April - 31 March

COMMUNICATIONS

Telephones - main lines in use: 2,400 (2002)
Telephones - mobile cellular: 0 (2001)
Telephone system:
general assessment: NA
domestic: government-operated radiotelephone and private VHF/CB radiotelephone networks provide effective service to almost all points on both islands
international: country code - 500; satellite earth station - 1 Intelsat (Atlantic Ocean) with links through London to other countries
Radio broadcast stations: AM 1, FM 7, shortwave 0 (1998)
Radios: 1,000 (1997)
Television broadcast stations: 2 (operated by the British Forces Broadcasting Service)
note: cable television is available in Stanley (2002)
Televisions: 1,000 (1997)
Internet country code: .fk
Internet Service Providers (ISPs): 2 (2000)
Internet users: NA; however one-half of all households are reported to have internet access (2002)

TRANSPORTATION

Airports: 5 (2004 est.)
Airports - with paved runways:
total: 2
2,438 to 3,047 m: 1
914 to 1,523 m: 1 (2005 est.)
Airports - with unpaved runways:
total: 3
under 914 m: 3 (2005 est.)
Roadways:
total: 440 km
paved: 50 km
unpaved: 390 km (2003)
Merchant marine: none
Ports and terminals: Stanley

MILITARY

Military branches: no regular military forces
Military expenditures - dollar figure: NA
Military expenditures - percent of GDP: NA
Military - note: defense is the responsibility of the UK

TRANSNATIONAL ISSUES

Disputes - international: Argentina, which claims the islands in its constitution and briefly occupied the islands by force in 1982, agreed in 1995 to no longer seek settlement by force; UK continues to reject Argentine requests for sovereignty talks

FAROE ISLANDS

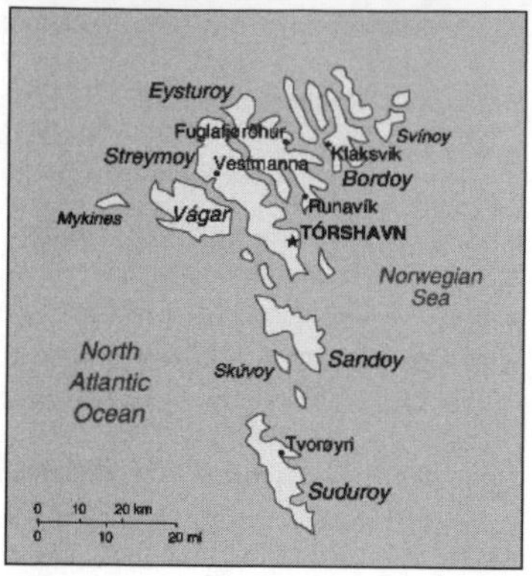

INTRODUCTION

Background: The population of the Faroe Islands is largely descended from Viking settlers who arrived in the 9th century. The islands have been connected politically to Denmark since the 14th century. A high degree of self-government was attained in 1948.

GEOGRAPHY

Location: Northern Europe, island group between the Norwegian Sea and the North Atlantic Ocean, about one-half of the way from Iceland to Norway
Geographic coordinates: 62 00 N, 7 00 W
Map references: Europe
Area:
total: 1,399 sq km
land: 1,399 sq km
water: 0 sq km (some lakes and streams)
Area - comparative: eight times the size of Washington, DC
Land boundaries: 0 km
Coastline: 1,117 km
Maritime claims:
territorial sea: 3 nm
continental shelf: 200 nm or agreed boundaries or median line
exclusive fishing zone: 200 nm or agreed boundaries or median line
Climate: mild winters, cool summers; usually overcast; foggy, windy
Terrain: rugged, rocky, some low peaks; cliffs along most of coast
Elevation extremes:
lowest point: Atlantic Ocean 0 m
highest point: Slaettaratindur 882 m
Natural resources: fish, whales, hydropower, possible oil and gas
Land use:
arable land: 2.14%
permanent crops: 0%
other: 97.86% (2001)
Irrigated land: 0 sq km (1998 est.)
Natural hazards: NA
Environment - current issues: NA
Geography - note: archipelago of 17 inhabited islands and one uninhabited island, and a few uninhabited islets; strategically located along important sea lanes in northeastern Atlantic; precipitous terrain limits habitation to small coastal lowlands

PEOPLE

Population: 46,962 (July 2005 est.)
Age structure:
0-14 years: 21.3% (male 4,997/female 4,999)
15-64 years: 64.9% (male 16,120/female 14,360)
65 years and over: 13.8% (male 2,923/female 3,563) (2005 est.)
Median age:
total: 35.11 years
male: 34.64 years
female: 35.68 years (2005 est.)
Population growth rate: 0.62% (2005 est.)
Birth rate: 13.97 births/1,000 population (2005 est.)
Death rate: 8.69 deaths/1,000 population (2005 est.)
Net migration rate: 0.94 migrant(s)/1,000 population (2005 est.)
Sex ratio:
at birth: 1 male(s)/female
under 15 years: 1 male(s)/female
15-64 years: 1.12 male(s)/female
65 years and over: 0.82 male(s)/female
total population: 1.05 male(s)/female (2005 est.)
Infant mortality rate:
total: 6.24 deaths/1,000 live births
male: 7.54 deaths/1,000 live births
female: 4.93 deaths/1,000 live births (2005 est.)
Life expectancy at birth:
total population: 79.21 years
male: 75.77 years
female: 82.67 years (2005 est.)
Total fertility rate: 2.2 children born/woman (2005 est.)
HIV/AIDS - adult prevalence rate: NA%
HIV/AIDS - people living with HIV/AIDS: NA
HIV/AIDS - deaths: NA
Nationality:
noun: Faroese (singular and plural)
adjective: Faroese
Ethnic groups: Scandinavian
Religions: Evangelical Lutheran
Languages: Faroese (derived from Old Norse), Danish
Literacy:
definition: NA
total population: NA%
male: NA%
female: NA%
note: probably the same as Denmark proper

GOVERNMENT

Country name:
conventional long form: none
conventional short form: Faroe Islands
local long form: none
local short form: Foroyar
Dependency status: part of the Kingdom of Denmark; self-governing overseas administrative division of Denmark since 1948
Government type: NA
Capital: Torshavn
Administrative divisions: none (part of the Kingdom of Denmark; self-governing overseas administrative division of Denmark); there are no first-order administrative divisions as defined by the US Government, but there are 49 municipalities
Independence: none (part of the Kingdom of Denmark; self-governing overseas administrative division of Denmark)
National holiday: Olaifest (Olavasoka), 29 July
Constitution: 5 June 1953 (Danish constitution)
Legal system: Danish
Suffrage: 18 years of age; universal
Executive branch:
chief of state: Queen MARGRETHE II of Denmark (since 14 January 1972), represented by High Commissioner Birgit KLEIS, chief administrative officer (since 1 November 2001)
head of government: Prime Minister Joannes EIDESGAARD (since 3 February 2004)
cabinet: Landsstyri appointed by the prime minister
elections: the monarch is hereditary; high commissioner appointed by the monarch; following legislative elections, the leader of the majority party or the leader of the majority coalition is usually elected prime minister by the Faroese Parliament; election last held 20 January 2004 (next to be held no later than January 2008)
election results: Joannes EIDESGAARD elected prime minister; percent of parliamentary vote - NA%
note: coalition of Social Democrats, Union Party, and People's Party
Legislative branch: unicameral Faroese Parliament or Logting (32 seats; members are elected by popular vote on a proportional basis from the seven constituencies to serve four-year terms)
elections: last held 20 January 2004 (next to be held no later than January 2008)
election results: percent of vote by party -

Union Party 23.7%, Social Democrats 21.8%, Republican Party 21.7%, People's Party 20.6%, Center Party 5.2%, Independence Party 4.6%; seats by party - Union Party 7, Social Democrats 7, Republican Party 8, People's Party 7, Center Party 2, Independence Party 1
note: election of 2 seats to the Danish Parliament was last held on 8 February 2005 (next to be held February 2009); results - percent of vote by party - NA; seats by party - Republican Party 1, People's Party 1
Judicial branch: none
Political parties and leaders: Center Party [Jenis A. RANA]; Independence Party [Kari P. HOJGAARD]; People's Party [Anfinn KALLSBERG]; Republican Party [Hogni HOYDAL]; Social Democratic Party [Joannes EIDESGAARD]; Union Party [Kaj Oeo JOHANNESEN]
Political pressure groups and leaders: NA
International organization participation: IMO (associate), NC, NIB, UPU
Diplomatic representation in the US: none (self-governing overseas administrative division of Denmark)
Diplomatic representation from the US: none (self-governing overseas administrative division of Denmark)
Flag description: white with a red cross outlined in blue extending to the edges of the flag; the vertical part of the cross is shifted toward the hoist side in the style of the Dannebrog (Danish flag)

ECONOMY

Economy - overview: The Faroese economy has had a strong performance since 1994, mostly as a result of increasing fish landings and high and stable export prices. Unemployment is minimal and there are signs of labor shortages in several sectors. The positive economic development has helped the Faroese Home Rule Government produce increasing budget surpluses, which in turn has helped to reduce the large public debt, most of it owed to Denmark. However, the total dependence on fishing makes the Faroese economy extremely vulnerable, and the present fishing efforts appear in excess of what is a sustainable level of fishing in the long term. Oil finds close to the Faroese area give hope for deposits in the immediate Faroese area, which may eventually lay the basis for a more diversified economy and thus lessen dependence on Danish economic assistance. Aided by a substantial annual subsidy (15% of GDP) from Denmark, the Faroese have a standard of living not far below the Danes and other Scandinavians.
GDP (purchasing power parity): $1 billion (2001 est.)
GDP (official exchange rate): NA
GDP - real growth rate: 10% (2001 est.)
GDP - per capita: purchasing power parity - $22,000 (2001 est.)
GDP - composition by sector:
agriculture: 27%
industry: 11%
services: 62% (1999)
Labor force: 24,250 (October 2000)
Labor force - by occupation: fishing, fish processing, and manufacturing 33%, construction and private services 33%, public services 34%
Unemployment rate: 1% (October 2000)
Population below poverty line: NA
Household income or consumption by percentage share:
lowest 10%: NA%
highest 10%: NA%
Inflation rate (consumer prices): 5.1% (1999)
Budget:
revenues: $488 million
expenditures: $484 million, including capital expenditures of $21 million (1999)
Agriculture - products: milk, potatoes, vegetables; sheep; salmon, other fish
Industries: fishing, fish processing, small ship repair and refurbishment, handicrafts
Industrial production growth rate: 8% (1999 est.)
Electricity - production: 260.2 million kWh (2003)
Electricity - production by source:
fossil fuel: 62.4%
hydro: 37.6%
nuclear: 0%
other: 0% (2001)
Electricity - consumption: 242 million kWh (2003)
Electricity - exports: 0 kWh (2003)
Electricity - imports: 0 kWh (2003)
Oil - production: 0 bbl/day (2003 est.)
Oil - consumption: 4,500 bbl/day (2003 est.)
Oil - exports: NA (2001)
Oil - imports: NA (2001)
Exports: $533 million f.o.b. (2004 est.)
Exports - partners: Denmark 33.5%, UK 29.7%, Norway 8.4%, Nigeria 7.1% (2004)
Imports: $639 million c.i.f. (2004 est.)
Imports - partners: Denmark 52.5%, Norway 18.2%, Iceland 5%, Sweden 4.2% (2004)
Debt - external: $64 million (1999)
Economic aid - recipient: $135 million (annual subsidy from Denmark) (1998)
Currency (code): Danish krone (DKK)
Currency code: DKK
Exchange rates: Danish kroner per US dollar - NA (2005), 5.9911 (2004), 6.5877 (2003), 7.8947 (2002), 8.3228 (2001)
Fiscal year: calendar year

COMMUNICATIONS

Telephones - main lines in use: 23,000 (2002)
Telephones - mobile cellular: 30,700 (2002)
Telephone system:
general assessment: good international communications; good domestic facilities
domestic: digitalization was completed in 1998; both NMT (analog) and GSM (digital) mobile telephone systems are installed
international: country code - 298; satellite earth stations - 1 Orion; 1 fiber-optic submarine cable to the Shetland Islands, linking the Faroe Islands with Denmark and Iceland; fiber-optic submarine cable connection to Canada-Europe cable
Radio broadcast stations: AM 1, FM 13, shortwave 0 (1998)
Radios: 26,000 (1997)
Television broadcast stations: 3 (plus 43 low-power repeaters) (September 1995)
Televisions: 15,000 (1997)
Internet country code: .fo
Internet Service Providers (ISPs): 2 (2000)
Internet users: 25,000 (2002)

TRANSPORTATION

Airports: 1 (2004 est.)
Airports - with paved runways:
total: 1
914 to 1,523 m: 1 (2005 est.)
Roadways:
total: 463 km
paved: 454 km
unpaved: 9 km (1999)
Merchant marine:
total: 14 ships (1,000 GRT or over) 24,051 GRT/11,998 DWT
by type: cargo 6, container 1, passenger/cargo 5, petroleum tanker 2
foreign-owned: 8 (Denmark 2, Germany 1, Iceland 2, Norway 2, United Kingdom 1) (2005)
Ports and terminals: Torshavn

MILITARY

Military branches: no regular military forces
Military expenditures - dollar figure: $NA
Military expenditures - percent of GDP: NA
Military - note: defense is the responsibility of Denmark

TRANSNATIONAL ISSUES

Disputes - international: because anticipated offshore hydrocarbon resources have not been realized, earlier Faroese proposals for full independence have been deferred; Iceland disputes the Faroe Islands' fisheries median line boundary; Iceland, the UK, and Ireland dispute Denmark's claim that the Faroe Islands' continental shelf extends beyond 200 nm

FIJI

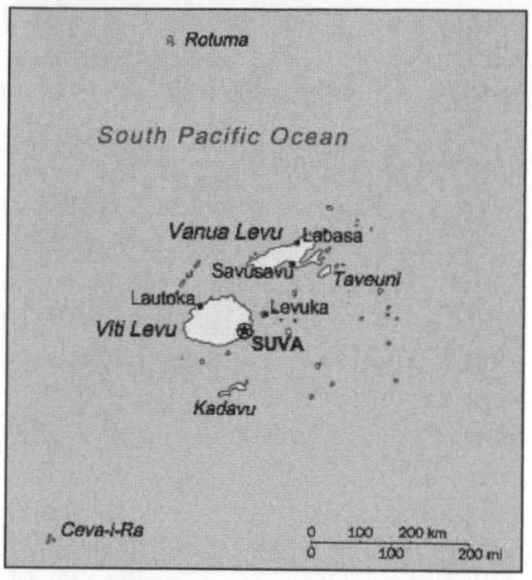

INTRODUCTION

Background: Fiji became independent in 1970, after nearly a century as a British colony. Democratic rule was interrupted by two military coups in 1987, caused by concern over a government perceived as dominated by the Indian community (descendants of contract laborers brought to the islands by the British in the 19th century). A 1990 constitution favored native Melanesian control of Fiji, but led to heavy Indian emigration; the population loss resulted in economic difficulties, but ensured that Melanesians became the majority. Amendments enacted in 1997 made the constitution more equitable. Free and peaceful elections in 1999 resulted in a government led by an Indo-Fijian, but a coup in May 2000 ushered in a prolonged period of political turmoil. Parliamentary elections held in August 2001 provided Fiji with a democratically elected government and gave a mandate to the government of Prime Minister Laisenia QARASE.

GEOGRAPHY

Location: Oceania, island group in the South Pacific Ocean, about two-thirds of the way from Hawaii to New Zealand
Geographic coordinates: 18 00 S, 175 00 E
Map references: Oceania
Area:
total: 18,270 sq km
land: 18,270 sq km
water: 0 sq km
Area - comparative: slightly smaller than New Jersey
Land boundaries: 0 km
Coastline: 1,129 km
Maritime claims: measured from claimed archipelagic straight baselines
territorial sea: 12 nm
exclusive economic zone: 200 nm
continental shelf: 200-m depth or to the depth of exploitation; rectilinear shelf claim added
Climate: tropical marine; only slight seasonal temperature variation
Terrain: mostly mountains of volcanic origin
Elevation extremes:
lowest point: Pacific Ocean 0 m
highest point: Tomanivi 1,324 m
Natural resources: timber, fish, gold, copper, offshore oil potential, hydropower
Land use:
arable land: 10.95%
permanent crops: 4.65%
other: 84.4% (2001)
Irrigated land: 30 sq km (1998 est.)
Natural hazards: cyclonic storms can occur from November to January
Environment - current issues: deforestation; soil erosion
Environment - international agreements:
party to: Biodiversity, Climate Change, Climate Change-Kyoto Protocol, Desertification, Endangered Species, Law of the Sea, Marine Life Conservation, Ozone Layer Protection, Tropical Timber 83, Tropical Timber 94
signed, but not ratified: none of the selected agreements
Geography - note: includes 332 islands of which approximately 110 are inhabited

PEOPLE

Population: 893,354 (July 2005 est.)
Age structure:
0-14 years: 31.4% (male 143,066/female 137,346)
15-64 years: 64.5% (male 288,434/female 287,720)
65 years and over: 4.1% (male 16,797/female 19,991) (2005 est.)
Median age:
total: 24.28 years
male: 23.84 years
female: 24.74 years (2005 est.)
Population growth rate: 1.4% (2005 est.)
Birth rate: 22.73 births/1,000 population (2005 est.)
Death rate: 5.65 deaths/1,000 population (2005 est.)
Net migration rate: -3.04 migrant(s)/1,000 population (2005 est.)
Sex ratio:
at birth: 1.05 male(s)/female
under 15 years: 1.04 male(s)/female
15-64 years: 1 male(s)/female
65 years and over: 0.84 male(s)/female
total population: 1.01 male(s)/female (2005 est.)
Infant mortality rate:
total: total: 12.62 deaths/1,000 live births
male: 13.97 deaths/1,000 live births
female: 11.2 deaths/1,000 live births (2005 est.)
Life expectancy at birth:
total population: 69.53 years
male: 67.05 years
female: 72.14 years (2005 est.)
Total fertility rate: 2.75 children born/woman (2005 est.)
HIV/AIDS - adult prevalence rate: 0.1% (2003 est.)
HIV/AIDS - people living with HIV/AIDS: 600 (2003 est.)
HIV/AIDS - deaths: less than 200 (2003 est.)
Nationality:
noun: Fijian(s)
adjective: Fijian
Ethnic groups: Fijian 51% (predominantly Melanesian with a Polynesian admixture), Indian 44%, European, other Pacific Islanders, overseas Chinese, and other 5% (1998 est.)
Religions: Christian 52% (Methodist 37%, Roman Catholic 9%), Hindu 38%, Muslim 8%, other 2%
note: Fijians are mainly Christian, Indians are Hindu, and there is a Muslim minority (1986)
Languages: English (official), Fijian, Hindustani
Literacy:
definition: age 15 and over can read and write
total population: 93.7%
male: 95.5%
female: 91.9% (2003 est.)

GOVERNMENT

Country name:
conventional long form: Republic of the Fiji Islands
conventional short form: Fiji
Government type: republic
note: military coup leader Maj. Gen. Sitiveni RABUKA formally declared Fiji a republic on 6 October 1987
Capital: Suva (Viti Levu)
Administrative divisions: 4 divisions and 1 dependency*; Central, Eastern, Northern, Rotuma*, Western
Independence: 10 October 1970 (from UK)

National holiday: Independence Day, second Monday of October (1970)
Constitution: promulgated on 25 July 1990; amended on 25 July 1997 to allow nonethnic Fijians greater say in government and to make multiparty government mandatory; effective 28 July 1998
Legal system: based on British system
Suffrage: 21 years of age; universal
Executive branch:
chief of state: President Ratu Josefa ILOILOVATU Uluivuda (since 18 July 2000)
head of government: Prime Minister Laisenia QARASE (since 10 September 2000)
cabinet: Cabinet appointed by the prime minister from among the members of Parliament and is responsible to Parliament; note - there is also a Presidential Council that advises the president on matters of national importance and a Great Council of Chiefs, which consists of the highest ranking members of the traditional chief system
elections: president elected by the Great Council of Chiefs for a five-year term; prime minister appointed by the president
election results: Ratu Josefa ILOILOVATU Uluivuda elected president by the Great Council of Chiefs; percent of vote - NA%
Legislative branch: bicameral Parliament consists of the Senate (34 seats; 24 appointed by the President on the advice of the Great Council of Chiefs, nine appointed by the president, and one appointed by the council of Rotuma) and the House of Representatives (71 seats; 23 reserved for ethnic Fijians, 19 reserved for ethnic Indians, three reserved for other ethnic groups, one reserved for the council of Rotuma constituency encompassing the whole of Fiji, and 25 open seats; members serve five-year terms)
elections: House of Representatives - last held 25 August through 1 September and 19 September 2001 (next to be held not later than September 2006)
election results: House of Representatives - percent of vote by party - FLP 26.5%, SDL 27.5%, NFP 1.2%, MV 4.2%, NLUP 1.3%, UGP .3%, independents 1.4%; seats by party - FLP 27, SDL 32, MV 6, NFP 1, NLUP 2, UGP 1, independents 2
Judicial branch: Supreme Court (judges are appointed by the president); Court of Appeal; High Court; Magistrates' Courts
Political parties and leaders: Bai Kei Viti Party or BKV [Ratu Tevita MOMOEDONU]; Conservative Alliance Party/Matanitu Vanua or CAMV [Ratu Rakuita VAKALALABURE]; Dodonu Ni Taukei Party or DNT [Fereti S. DEWA]; Fiji Democratic Party or FDP [Felipe BOLE] (a merger of the Christian Democrat Alliance or VLV [Poesci Waqalevu BUNE], Fijian Association Party or FAP [Adi Kuini SPEED], Fijian Political Party or SVT (primarily Fijian) [Felipe BOLE], and New Labor Unity Party or NLUP [Tupeni BABA]); Fiji Labor Party or FLP [Mahendra CHAUDHRY]; General Voters Party or GVP [leader NA] (became part of United General Party); Girmit Heritage Party or GHP [leader NA]; Justice and Freedom Party or AIM [leader NA]; Lio 'On Famor Rotuma Party or LFR [leader NA]; National Federation Party or NFP (primarily Indian) [Pramond RAE]; Nationalist Vanua Takolavo Party or NVTLP [Saula TELAWA]; Party of National Unity or PANU [Meli BOGILEKA]; Party of the Truth or POTT [leader NA]; United Fiji Party/Sogosogo Duavata ni Lewenivanua or SDL [Laisenia QARASE]; United General Party or UGP [Millis Mick BEDDOES]
Political pressure groups and leaders: NA
International organization participation: ACP, AsDB, C, CP, FAO, G-77, IBRD, ICAO, ICCt, ICFTU, ICRM, IDA, IFAD, IFC, IFRCS, IHO, ILO, IMF, IMO, Interpol, IOC, ISO (correspondent), ITU, MIGA, OPCW, PCA, PIF, Sparteca, SPC, UN, UNCTAD, UNESCO, UNIDO, UNMIS, UPU, WCO, WFTU, WHO, WIPO, WMO, WToO, WTO
Diplomatic representation in the US:
chief of mission: Mr. Paula NAVUNISARAVI (Charge D'Affaires ad Interim)
chancery: 2233 Wisconsin Avenue NW, Suite 240, Washington, DC 20007
telephone: [1] (202) 337-8320
FAX: [1] (202) 337-1996
Diplomatic representation from the US:
chief of mission: Ambassador Larry Miles DINGER
embassy: 31 Loftus Street, Suva
mailing address: P. O. Box 218, Suva
telephone: [679] 331-4466
FAX: [679] 330-0081
Flag description: light blue with the flag of the UK in the upper hoist-side quadrant and the Fijian shield centered on the outer half of the flag; the shield depicts a yellow lion above a white field quartered by the cross of Saint George featuring stalks of sugarcane, a palm tree, bananas, and a white dove

ECONOMY

Economy - overview: Fiji, endowed with forest, mineral, and fish resources, is one of the most developed of the Pacific island economies, though still with a large subsistence sector. Sugar exports and a growing tourist industry - with 300,000 to 400,000 tourists annually - are the major sources of foreign exchange. Fiji's sugar has special access to European Union markets, but will be harmed by the EU's decision to cut sugar subsidies. Sugar processing makes up one-third of industrial activity, but is not efficient. Long-term problems include low investment, uncertain land ownership rights, and the government's ability to manage its budget. Yet short-run economic prospects are good, provided tensions do not again erupt between indigenous Fijians and Indo-Fijians. Overseas remittances from Fijians working in Kuwait and Iraq have increased significantly.
GDP (purchasing power parity): $5.398 billion (2005 est.)
GDP (official exchange rate): $1.992 billion (2005 est.)
GDP - real growth rate: 2% (2005 est.)
GDP - per capita: purchasing power parity - $6,000 (2005 est.)
GDP - composition by sector:
agriculture: 16.6%
industry: 22.4%
services: 61% (2001 est.)
Labor force: 137,000 (1999)
Labor force - by occupation: agriculture, including subsistence agriculture 70% (2001 est.)
Unemployment rate: 7.6% (1999)
Population below poverty line: 25.5% (1990-91)
Household income or consumption by percentage share:
lowest 10%: NA
highest 10%: NA
Inflation rate (consumer prices): 1.6% (2002 est.)
Budget:
revenues: $427.9 million
expenditures: $531.4 million, including capital expenditures of NA (2000 est.)
Agriculture - products: sugarcane, coconuts, cassava (tapioca), rice, sweet potatoes, bananas; cattle, pigs, horses, goats; fish
Industries: tourism, sugar, clothing, copra, gold, silver, lumber, small cottage industries
Industrial production growth rate: NA
Electricity - production: 775.7 million kWh (2003)
Electricity - production by source:
fossil fuel: 18.5%
hydro: 81.5%
nuclear: 0%
other: 0% (2001)
Electricity - consumption: 721.4 million kWh (2003)

Electricity - exports: 0 kWh (2003)
Electricity - imports: 0 kWh (2003)
Oil - production: 0 bbl/day (2003 est.)
Oil - consumption: 10,000 bbl/day (2003 est.)
Oil - exports: NA (2001)
Oil - imports: NA (2001)
Exports: $862 million f.o.b. (2004 est.)
Exports - partners: US 24%, Australia 19%, UK 12.6%, Samoa 6.5%, Japan 4.1% (2004)
Imports: $1.235 billion c.i.f. (2004 est.)
Imports - partners: Australia 25.9%, Singapore 23.1%, New Zealand 21.1% (2004)
Debt - external: $188.1 million (2001 est.)
Economic aid - recipient: $40.3 million (1995)
Currency (code): Fijian dollar (FJD)
Currency code: FJD
Exchange rates: Fijian dollars per US dollar - NA (2005), 1.7331 (2004), 1.8958 (2003), 2.1869 (2002), 2.2766 (2001)
Fiscal year: calendar year

COMMUNICATIONS

Telephones - main lines in use: 102,000 (2003)
Telephones - mobile cellular: 109,900 (2003)
Telephone system:
general assessment: modern local, interisland, and international (wire/radio integrated) public and special-purpose telephone, telegraph, and teleprinter facilities; regional radio communications center
domestic: NA
international: country code - 679; access to important cable links between US and Canada as well as between NZ and Australia; 2 satellite earth stations - 2 INMARSAT (Pacific Ocean)
Radio broadcast stations: AM 13, FM 40, shortwave 0 (1998)
Radios: 541,476 (1999)
Television broadcast stations: NA
Televisions: 88,110 (1999)
Internet country code: .fj
Internet hosts: 493 (2003)
Internet Service Providers (ISPs): 2 (2000)
Internet users: 55,000 (2003)

TRANSPORTATION

Airports: 28 (2004 est.)
Airports - with paved runways:
total: 3
over 3,047 m: 1
1,524 to 2,437 m: 1
914 to 1,523 m: 1 (2005 est.)
Airports - with unpaved runways:
total: 25
914 to 1,523 m: 7
under 914 m: 18 (2005 est.)
Railways:
total: 597 km
narrow gauge: 597 km 0.600-m gauge
note: belongs to the government-owned Fiji Sugar Corporation; used to haul sugarcane during harvest season (May to December) (2003)
Roadways:
total: 3,440 km
paved: 1,692 km
unpaved: 1,748 km (1999)
Waterways: 203 km
note: 122 km navigable by motorized craft and 200-metric-ton barges (2004)
Merchant marine:
total: 7 ships (1,000 GRT or over) 6,372 GRT/7,453 DWT
by type: passenger 3, passenger/cargo 2, roll on/roll off 2
foreign-owned: 1 (Australia 1) (2005)
Ports and terminals: Lambasa, Lautoka, Suva

MILITARY

Military branches: Republic of Fiji Military Forces (RFMF): Land Forces, Naval Division (2005)
Military service age and obligation: 18 years of age for voluntary military service (2001)
Manpower available for military service: *males age 18-49:* 215,104 (2005 est.)
Manpower fit for military service: *males age 18-49:* 163,960 (2005 est.)
Manpower reaching military service age annually: *males:* 9,266 (2005 est.)
Military expenditures - dollar figure: $36 million (2004)
Military expenditures - percent of GDP: 2.2% (FY02)

TRANSNATIONAL ISSUES

Disputes - international: none

FINLAND

INTRODUCTION

Background: Finland was a province and then a grand duchy under Sweden from the 12th to the 19th centuries and an autonomous grand duchy of Russia after 1809. It won its complete independence in 1917. During World War II, it was able to successfully defend its freedom and resist invasions by the Soviet Union - albeit with some loss of territory. In the subsequent half century, the Finns made a remarkable transformation from a farm/forest economy to a diversified modern industrial economy; per capita income is now on par with Western Europe. As a member of the European Union, Finland was the only Nordic state to join the euro system at its initiation in January 1999.

GEOGRAPHY

Location: Northern Europe, bordering the Baltic Sea, Gulf of Bothnia, and Gulf of Finland, between Sweden and Russia
Geographic coordinates: 64 00 N, 26 00 E
Map references: Europe
Area:
total: 338,145 sq km
land: 304,473 sq km
water: 33,672 sq km
Area - comparative: slightly smaller than Montana
Land boundaries:
total: 2,681 km
border countries: Norway 727 km, Sweden 614 km, Russia 1,340 km
Coastline: 1,250 km
Maritime claims:
territorial sea: 12 nm (in the Gulf of Finland - 3 nm)
continental shelf: 200-m depth or to the depth of exploitation
exclusive fishing zone: 12 nm; extends to continental shelf boundary with Sweden
Climate: cold temperate; potentially subarctic but comparatively mild because of moderating influence of the North Atlantic Current, Baltic Sea, and more than 60,000 lakes
Terrain: mostly low, flat to rolling plains interspersed with lakes and low hills
Elevation extremes:
lowest point: Baltic Sea 0 m
highest point: Haltiatunturi 1,328 m
Natural resources: timber, iron ore, copper, lead, zinc, chromite, nickel, gold, silver, limestone
Land use:
arable land: 7.19%
permanent crops: 0.03%
other: 92.78% (2001)
Irrigated land: 640 sq km (1998 est.)
Natural hazards: NA
Environment - current issues: air pollution from manufacturing and power plants contributing to acid rain; water pollution from industrial wastes, agricultural chemicals; habitat loss threatens wildlife populations
Environment - international agreements:
party to: Air Pollution, Air Pollution-Nitrogen Oxides, Air Pollution-Persistent Organic Pollutants, Air Pollution-Sulfur 85, Air Pollution-Sulfur 94, Air Pollution-Volatile Organic

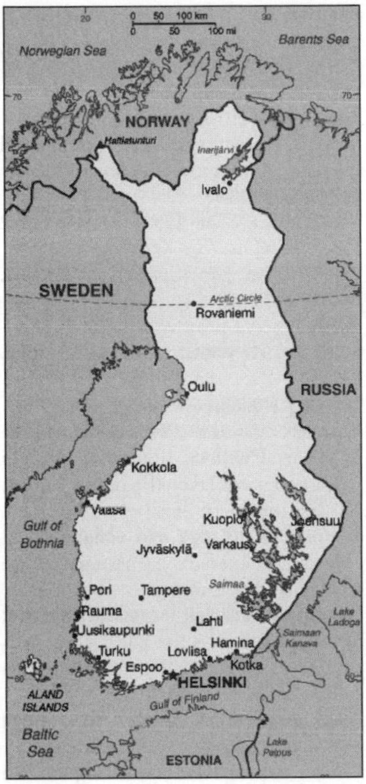

Compounds, Antarctic-Environmental Protocol, Antarctic-Marine Living Resources, Antarctic Treaty, Biodiversity, Climate Change, Climate Change-Kyoto Protocol, Desertification, Endangered Species, Environmental Modification, Hazardous Wastes, Law of the Sea, Marine Dumping, Marine Life Conservation, Ozone Layer Protection, Ship Pollution, Tropical Timber 83, Tropical Timber 94, Wetlands, Whaling
signed, but not ratified: none of the selected agreements
Geography - note: long boundary with Russia; Helsinki is northernmost national capital on European continent; population concentrated on small southwestern coastal plain

PEOPLE

Population: 5,223,442 (July 2005 est.)
Age structure:
0-14 years: 17.3% (male 460,977/female 443,859)
15-64 years: 66.8% (male 1,764,874/ female 1,723,385)
65 years and over: 15.9% (male 328,952/female 501,395) (2005 est.)
Median age:
total: 40.97 years
male: 39.43 years
female: 42.52 years (2005 est.)
Population growth rate: 0.16% (2005 est.)
Birth rate: 10.5 births/1,000 population (2005 est.)
Death rate: 9.79 deaths/1,000 population (2005 est.)
Net migration rate: 0.89 migrant(s)/ 1,000 population (2005 est.)
Sex ratio:
at birth: 1.04 male(s)/female
under 15 years: 1.04 male(s)/female
15-64 years: 1.02 male(s)/female
65 years and over: 0.66 male(s)/female
total population: 0.96 male(s)/female (2005 est.)
Infant mortality rate:
total: 3.57 deaths/1,000 live births
male: 3.89 deaths/1,000 live births
female: 3.24 deaths/1,000 live births (2005 est.)
Life expectancy at birth:
total population: 78.35 years
male: 74.82 years
female: 82.02 years (2005 est.)
Total fertility rate: 1.73 children born/ woman (2005 est.)
HIV/AIDS - adult prevalence rate: less than 0.1% (2003 est.)
HIV/AIDS - people living with HIV/AIDS: 1,500 (2003 est.)
HIV/AIDS - deaths: less than 100 (2003 est.)
Nationality:
noun: Finn(s)
adjective: Finnish
Ethnic groups: Finn 93.4%, Swede 5.7%, Russian 0.4%, Estonian 0.2%, Roma 0.2%, Sami 0.1%
Religions: Lutheran National Church 84.2%, Greek Orthodox in Finland 1.1%, other Christian 1.1%, other 0.1%, none 13.5% (2003)
Languages: Finnish 92% (official), Swedish 5.6% (official), other 2.4% (small Sami- and Russian-speaking minorities) (2003)
Literacy:
definition: age 15 and over can read and write
total population: 100%
male: 100%
female: 100%

GOVERNMENT

Country name:
conventional long form: Republic of Finland
conventional short form: Finland
local long form: Suomen Tasavalta
local short form: Suomi
Government type: republic
Capital: Helsinki
Administrative divisions: 6 provinces (laanit, singular - laani); Aland, Etela-Suomen Laani, Ita-Suomen Laani, Lansi-Suomen Laani, Lappi, Oulun Laani
Independence: 6 December 1917 (from Russia)
National holiday: Independence Day, 6 December (1917)
Constitution: 1 March 2000
Legal system: civil law system based on Swedish law; the president may request the Supreme Court to review laws; accepts compulsory ICJ jurisdiction, with reservations
Suffrage: 18 years of age; universal
Executive branch:
chief of state: President Tarja HALONEN (since 1 March 2000)
head of government: Prime Minister Matti VANHANEN (since 24 June 2003) and Deputy Prime Minister Eero HEINALUOMA (since 24 September 2005)
cabinet: Council of State or Valtioneuvosto appointed by the president, responsible to parliament
elections: president elected by popular vote for a six-year term; election last held 16 January 2000 and 6 February 2000 (next to be held February 2006); the president appoints the prime minister and deputy prime minister from the majority party or the majority coalition after parliamentary elections and the parliament must approve the appointment
election results: Tarja HALONEN elected president; percent of vote - Tarja HALONEN (SDP) 51.6%, Esko AHO (Kesk) 48.4%
note: government coalition - Kesk, SDP, and SFP
Legislative branch: unicameral Parliament or Eduskunta (200 seats; members are elected by popular vote on a proportional basis to serve four-year terms)
elections: last held 16 March 2003 (next to be held March 2007)
election results: percent of vote by party - Kesk 24.7%, SDP 24.5%, Kok 18.5%, VAS 9.9%, VIHR 8%, KD 5.3%, SFP 4.6%; seats by party - Kesk 55, SDP 53, Kok 40, VAS 19, VIHR 14, KD 7, SFP 8, others 4
Judicial branch: Supreme Court or Korkein Oikeus (judges appointed by the president)
Political parties and leaders: Center Party or Kesk [Matti VANHANEN]; Christian Democrats or KD [Paivi RASANEN]; Green League or VIHR [Tarja CRONBERG]; Left Alliance or VAS composed of People's Democratic League and Democratic Alternative [Suvi-Anne SIIMES]; National Coalition (conservative) Party or Kok [Jyrki KATAINEN]; Social Democratic Party or SDP [Eero HEINALUOMA]; Swedish People's Party or SFP [Jan-Erik ENESTAM]
International organization participation: AfDB, AsDB, Australia Group, BIS, CBSS, CE, CERN, EAPC, EBRD, EIB, EMU, ESA, EU, FAO, G- 9, IADB, IAEA, IBRD, ICAO, ICC, ICCt,

ICFTU, ICRM, IDA, IEA, IFAD, IFC, IFRCS, IHO, ILO, IMF, IMO, Interpol, IOC, IOM, ISO, ITU, MIGA, NAM (guest), NC, NEA, NIB, NSG, OAS (observer), OECD, OPCW, OSCE, Paris Club, PCA, PFP, UN, UNCTAD, UNESCO, UNFICYP, UNHCR, UNIDO, UNMEE, UNMIL, UNMIS, UNMOGIP, UNTSO, UPU, WCO, WEU (observer), WFTU, WHO, WIPO, WMO, WTO, ZC

Diplomatic representation in the US:
chief of mission: Ambassador Jukka Robert VALTASAARI
chancery: 3301 Massachusetts Avenue NW, Washington, DC 20008
telephone: [1] (202) 298-5800
FAX: [1] (202) 298-6030
consulate(s) general: Los Angeles and New York

Diplomatic representation from the US:
chief of mission: Ambassador (vacant); Charge d'Affaires Amy HYATT
embassy: Itainen Puistotie 14B, 00140 Helsinki
mailing address: APO AE 09723
telephone: [358] (9) 616250
FAX: [358] (9) 6162 5800

Flag description: white with a blue cross extending to the edges of the flag; the vertical part of the cross is shifted to the hoist side in the style of the Dannebrog (Danish flag)

ECONOMY

Economy - overview: Finland has a highly industrialized, largely free-market economy, with per capita output roughly that of the UK, France, Germany, and Italy. Its key economic sector is manufacturing - principally the wood, metals, engineering, telecommunications, and electronics industries. Trade is important, with exports equaling two-fifths of GDP. Finland excels in high-tech exports, e.g., mobile phones. Except for timber and several minerals, Finland depends on imports of raw materials, energy, and some components for manufactured goods. Because of the climate, agricultural development is limited to maintaining self-sufficiency in basic products. Forestry, an important export earner, provides a secondary occupation for the rural population. Rapidly increasing integration with Western Europe - Finland was one of the 12 countries joining the European Economic and Monetary Union (EMU) - will dominate the economic picture over the next several years. High unemployment remains a persistent problem.

GDP (purchasing power parity): $158.4 billion (2005 est.)

GDP (official exchange rate): $191.3 billion (2005 est.)

GDP - real growth rate: 1.7% (2005 est.)

GDP - per capita: purchasing power parity - $30,300 (2005 est.)

GDP - composition by sector:
agriculture: 3.1%
industry: 30.4%
services: 66.5% (2005 est.)

Labor force: 2.61 million (2005 est.)

Labor force - by occupation: agriculture and forestry 8%, industry 22%, construction 6%, commerce 14%, finance, insurance, and business services 10%, transport and communications 8%, public services 32%

Unemployment rate: 7.9% (2005 est.)

Population below poverty line: NA

Household income or consumption by percentage share:
lowest 10%: 4.2%
highest 10%: 21.6% (1991)

Distribution of family income - Gini index: 26.9 (2000)

Inflation rate (consumer prices): 1.2% (2005 est.)

Investment (gross fixed): 19.4% of GDP (2005 est.)

Budget:
revenues: $99.61 billion
expenditures: $97.14 billion, including capital expenditures of NA (2005 est.)

Public debt: 42% of GDP (2005 est.)

Agriculture - products: barley, wheat, sugar beets, potatoes; dairy cattle; fish

Industries: metals and metal products, electronics, machinery and scientific instruments, shipbuilding, pulp and paper, foodstuffs, chemicals, textiles, clothing

Industrial production growth rate: 3% (2005 est.)

Electricity - production: 79.61 billion kWh (2003)

Electricity - production by source:
fossil fuel: 39%
hydro: 18.7%
nuclear: 30.4%
other: 11.8% (2001)

Electricity - consumption: 78.94 billion kWh (2003)

Electricity - exports: 7 billion kWh (2003)

Electricity - imports: 11.9 billion kWh (2003)

Oil - production: 9,013 bbl/day (2003 est.)

Oil - consumption: 219,700 bbl/day (2003 est.)

Oil - exports: 101,000 bbl/day (2001)

Oil - imports: 318,300 bbl/day (2001)

Natural gas - production: 0 cu m (2001 est.)

Natural gas - consumption: 4.557 billion cu m (2001 est.)

Natural gas - exports: 0 cu m (2001 est.)

Natural gas - imports: 4.567 billion cu m (2001 est.)

Current account balance: $5.858 billion (2005 est.)

Exports: $67.88 billion f.o.b. (2005 est.)

Exports - partners: Sweden 11.1%, Germany 10.7%, Russia 8.9%, UK 7%, US 6.4%, Netherlands 5.1% (2004)

Imports: $56.45 billion f.o.b. (2005 est.)

Imports - partners: Germany 16.2%, Sweden 14.3%, Russia 12.8%, Netherlands 6.3%, Denmark 5.2%, UK 4.6%, France 4.3% (2004)

Reserves of foreign exchange and gold: $13.01 billion (2004 est.)

Debt - external: $211.7 billion (30 June 2005)

Economic aid - donor: ODA, $379 million (2001)

Currency (code): euro (EUR)
note: on 1 January 1999, the European Monetary Union introduced the euro as a common currency to be used by financial institutions of member countries; on 1 January 2002, the euro became the sole currency for everyday transactions within the member countries

Currency code: EUR

Exchange rates: euros per US dollar - 0.79697 (2005), 0.8054 (2004), 0.886 (2003), 1.0626 (2002), 1.1175 (2001)

Fiscal year: calendar year

COMMUNICATIONS

Telephones - main lines in use: 2.548 million (2003)

Telephones - mobile cellular: 4.7 million (2003)

Telephone system:
general assessment: modern system with excellent service
domestic: digital fiber-optic fixed-line network and an extensive cellular network provide domestic needs
international: country code - 358; 1 submarine cable (Finland Estonia Connection); satellite earth stations - access to Intelsat transmission service via a Swedish satellite earth station, 1 Inmarsat (Atlantic and Indian Ocean regions); note - Finland shares the Inmarsat earth station with the other Nordic countries (Denmark, Iceland, Norway, and Sweden)

Radio broadcast stations: AM 2, FM 186, shortwave 1 (1998)

Radios: 7.7 million (1997)

Television broadcast stations: 120 (plus 431 repeaters) (1999)

Televisions: 3.2 million (1997)

Internet country code: .fi

Internet hosts: 1,219,173 (2004)

Internet Service Providers (ISPs): 3 (2002)

Internet users: 2.65 million (2002)

TRANSPORTATION

Airports: 148 (2004 est.)

Airports - with paved runways:
total: 76

over 3,047 m: 2
2,438 to 3,047 m: 27
1,524 to 2,437 m: 10
914 to 1,523 m: 23
under 914 m: 14 (2005 est.)
Airports - with unpaved runways:
total: 72
914 to 1,523 m: 5
under 914 m: 67 (2005 est.)
Pipelines: gas 694 km (2004)
Railways:
total: 5,851 km
broad gauge: 5,851 km 1.524-m gauge (2,400 km electrified) (2004)
Roadways:
total: 78,168 km
paved: 50,616 km (including 653 km of expressways)
unpaved: 27,552 km (2004)
Waterways: 7,842 km
note: includes Saimaa Canal system of 3,577 km; southern part leased from Russia (2004)
Merchant marine:
total: 94 ships (1,000 GRT or over) 1,152,175 GRT/1,053,906 DWT
by type: bulk carrier 3, cargo 27, chemical tanker 6, container 1, passenger 5, passenger/cargo 20, petroleum tanker 7, roll on/roll off 25
foreign-owned: 2 (Norway 1, United States 1)
registered in other countries: 42 (2005)
Ports and terminals: Hamina, Hanko, Helsinki, Kotka, Naantali, Pori, Porvoo, Raahe, Rauma, Turku

MILITARY

Military branches: Finnish Defense Forces: Army, Navy (includes Coastal Defense Forces), Air Force (2003)
Military service age and obligation: 18 years of age for voluntary and compulsory military service (October 2004)
Manpower available for military service: *males age 18-49*: 1,121,275 (2005 est.)
Manpower fit for military service: *males age 18-49*: 913,617 (2005 est.)
Manpower reaching military service age annually: *males*: 32,040 (2005 est.)
Military expenditures - dollar figure: $1.8 billion (FY98/99)
Military expenditures - percent of GDP: 2% (FY98/99)

TRANSNATIONAL ISSUES

Disputes - international: various groups in Finland advocate restoration of Karelia and other areas ceded to the Soviet Union, but the Finnish Government asserts no territorial demands

FRANCE

INTRODUCTION

Background: Although ultimately a victor in World Wars I and II, France suffered extensive losses in its empire, wealth, manpower, and rank as a dominant nation-state. Nevertheless, France today is one of the most modern countries in the world and is a leader among European nations. Since 1958, it has constructed a presidential democracy resistant to the instabilities experienced in earlier parliamentary democracies. In recent years, its reconciliation and cooperation with Germany have proved central to the economic integration of Europe, including the introduction of a common exchange currency, the euro, in January 1999. At present, France is at the forefront of efforts to develop the EU's military capabilities to supplement progress toward an EU foreign policy.

GEOGRAPHY

Location: Western Europe, bordering the Bay of Biscay and English Channel, between Belgium and Spain, southeast of the UK; bordering the Mediterranean Sea, between Italy and Spain
Geographic coordinates: 46 00 N, 2 00 E
Map references: Europe
Area:
total: 547,030 sq km
land: 545,630 sq km
water: 1,400 sq km
note: includes only metropolitan France; excludes the overseas administrative divisions
Area - comparative: slightly less than twice the size of Colorado
Land boundaries:
total: 2,889 km
border countries: Andorra 56.6 km, Belgium 620 km, Germany 451 km, Italy 488 km, Luxembourg 73 km, Monaco 4.4 km, Spain 623 km, Switzerland 573 km
Coastline: 3,427 km
Maritime claims:
territorial sea: 12 nm
contiguous zone: 24 nm
exclusive economic zone: 200 nm (does not apply to the Mediterranean)
continental shelf: 200-m depth or to the depth of exploitation
Climate: generally cool winters and mild summers, but mild winters and hot summers along the Mediterranean; occasional strong, cold, dry, north-to-northwesterly wind known as mistral
Terrain: mostly flat plains or gently rolling hills in north and west; remainder is mountainous, especially Pyrenees in south, Alps in east
Elevation extremes:
lowest point: Rhone River delta -2 m
highest point: Mont Blanc 4,807 m
Natural resources: coal, iron ore, bauxite, zinc, uranium, antimony, arsenic, potash, feldspar, fluorospar, gypsum, timber, fish
Land use:
arable land: 33.53%
permanent crops: 2.07%
other: 64.4% (2001)
Irrigated land: 20,000 sq km (1998 est.)
Natural hazards: flooding; avalanches; midwinter windstorms; drought; forest fires in south near the Mediterranean
Environment - current issues: some forest damage from acid rain; air pollution from industrial and vehicle emissions; water pollution from urban wastes, agricultural runoff
Environment - international agreements:
party to: Air Pollution, Air Pollution-Nitrogen Oxides, Air Pollution-Persistent Organic Pollutants, Air Pollution-Sulfur 85, Air Pollution-Sulfur 94, Air Pollution-Volatile Organic Compounds, Antarctic-Environmental Protocol, Antarctic-Marine Living Resources, Antarctic Seals, Antarctic Treaty, Biodiversity, Climate Change, Climate Change-Kyoto Protocol, Desertification, Endangered Species, Hazardous Wastes, Law of the Sea, Marine Dumping, Marine Life Conservation, Ozone Layer Protection, Ship Pollution, Tropical Timber 83, Tropical Timber 94, Wetlands, Whaling
signed, but not ratified: none of the selected agreements
Geography - note: largest West European nation

PEOPLE

Population: 60,656,178 (July 2005 est.)
Age structure:
0-14 years: 18.4% (male 5,717,761/female 5,440,060)

15-64 years: 65.2% (male 19,784,749/female 19,752,432)
65 years and over: 16.4% (male 4,084,193/female 5,876,983) (2005 est.)
Median age:
total: 38.85 years
male: 37.3 years
female: 40.39 years (2005 est.)
Population growth rate: 0.37% (2005 est.)
Birth rate: 12.15 births/1,000 population (2005 est.)
Death rate: 9.08 deaths/1,000 population (2005 est.)
Net migration rate: 0.66 migrant(s)/1,000 population (2005 est.)
Sex ratio:
at birth: 1.05 male(s)/female
under 15 years: 1.05 male(s)/female
15-64 years: 1 male(s)/female
65 years and over: 0.7 male(s)/female
total population: 0.95 male(s)/female (2005 est.)
Infant mortality rate:
total: 4.26 deaths/1,000 live births
male: 4.76 deaths/1,000 live births
female: 3.73 deaths/1,000 live births (2005 est.)
Life expectancy at birth:
total population: 79.6 years
male: 75.96 year
female: 83.42 years (2005 est.)
Total fertility rate: 1.85 children born/woman (2005 est.)
HIV/AIDS - adult prevalence rate: 0.4% (2003 est.)
HIV/AIDS - people living with HIV/AIDS: 120,000 (2003 est.)
HIV/AIDS - deaths: less than 1,000 (2003 est.)
Nationality:
noun: Frenchman(men), Frenchwoman (women)
adjective: French
Ethnic groups: Celtic and Latin with Teutonic, Slavic, North African, Indochinese, Basque minorities
Religions: Roman Catholic 83%-88%, Protestant 2%, Jewish 1%, Muslim 5%-10%, unaffiliated 4%
Languages: French 100%, rapidly declining regional dialects and languages (Provencal, Breton, Alsatian, Corsican, Catalan, Basque, Flemish)
Literacy:
definition: age 15 and over can read and write
total population: 99%
male: 99%
female: 99% (1980 est.)

GOVERNMENT

Country name:
conventional long form: French Republic
conventional short form: France
local long form: Republique Francaise
local short form: France
Government type: republic
Capital: Paris
Administrative divisions: 22 regions (regions, singular - region); Alsace, Aquitaine, Auvergne, Basse-Normandie, Bourgogne, Bretagne, Centre, Champagne-Ardenne, Corse, Franche-Comte, Haute-Normandie, Ile-de-France, Languedoc-Roussillon, Limousin, Lorraine, Midi-Pyrenees, Nord-Pas-de-Calais, Pays de la Loire, Picardie, Poitou-Charentes, Provence-Alpes-Cote d'Azur, Rhone-Alpes
note: metropolitan France is divided into 22 regions (including the "territorial collectivity" of Corse or Corsica) and is subdivided into 96 departments; see separate entries for the overseas departments (French Guiana, Guadeloupe, Martinique, Reunion) and the overseas territorial collectivities (Mayotte, Saint Pierre and Miquelon)
Dependent areas: Bassas da India, Clipperton Island, Europa Island, French Polynesia, French Southern and Antarctic Lands, Glorioso Islands, Juan de Nova Island, New Caledonia, Tromelin Island, Wallis and Futuna
note: the US does not recognize claims to Antarctica
Independence: 486 (unified by Clovis)
National holiday: Bastille Day, 14 July (1789)
Constitution: adopted by referendum 28 September 1958, effective 4 October 1958; amended concerning election of president in 1962; amended to comply with provisions of 1992 EC Maastricht Treaty, 1996 Amsterdam Treaty, 2000 Treaty of Nice; amended to tighten immigration laws in 1993; amended in 2000 to change the seven-year presidential term to a five-year term
Legal system: civil law system with indigenous concepts; review of administrative but not legislative acts
Suffrage: 18 years of age; universal
Executive branch:
chief of state: President Jacques CHIRAC (since 17 May 1995)
head of government: Prime Minister Dominique DE VILLEPIN (since 31 May 2005)
cabinet: Council of Ministers appointed by the president on the suggestion of the prime minister
elections: president elected by popular vote for a five-year term (changed from seven-year term in October 2000); election last held 21 April and 5 May 2002 (next to be held, first round April 2007, second round May 2007); prime minister nominated by the National Assembly majority and appointed by the president
election results: Jacques CHIRAC reelected president; percent of vote, second ballot - Jacques CHIRAC (RPR) 81.96%, Jean-Marie LE PEN (FN) 18.04%
Legislative branch: bicameral Parliament or Parlement consists of the Senate or Senat (321 seats - 296 for metropolitan France, 13 for overseas departments and territories, and 12 for French nationals abroad; members are indirectly elected by an electoral college to serve nine-year terms; elected by thirds every three years); note - between now and 2010, 25 new seats will be added to the Senate for a total of 346 seats - 326 for metropolitan France and overseas departments, 2 for New Caledonia, 2 for Mayotte, 1 for Saint-Pierre and Miquelon, 3 for overseas territories, and 12 for French nationals abroad; members will be indirectly elected by an electoral college to serve six-year terms, with one-half the seats being renewed every three years; and the National Assembly or Assemblee Nationale (577 seats; members are elected by popular vote under a single-member majority system to serve five-year terms)
elections: Senate - last held 26 September 2004 (next to be held September 2007); National Assembly - last held 8-16 June 2002 (next to be held not later than June 2007)
election results: Senate - percent of vote by party - NA%; seats by party - UMP 156, PS 97, UDF 33, PCF 23, RDSE 15, other 7; National Assembly - percent of vote by party - NA%; seats by party - UMP 355, PS 140, UDF 29, PCF 21, Radical Party 7, Greens 3, other 22
Judicial branch: Supreme Court of Appeals or Cour de Cassation (judges are appointed by the president from nominations of the High Council of the Judiciary); Constitutional Council or Conseil Constitutionnel (three members appointed by the president, three appointed by the president of the National Assembly, and three appointed by the president of the Senate); Council of State or Conseil d'Etat
Political parties and leaders: Citizen and Republican Movement or MCR [Jean Pierre CHEVENEMENT]; Democratic and European Social Rally or RDSE (mainly Radical Republican and Socialist Parties, and PRG) [Jacques PELLETIER]; French Communist Party or PCF [Marie-George BUFFET]; Left Radical Party or PRG (previously Radical Socialist Party or PRS and the Left Radical Movement or MRG) [Jean-Michel BAYLET]; Movement for France or MPF Philippe DE VILLIERS]; National Front or NF [Jean-Marie LE PEN]; Rally for France or RPF [Charles

PASQUA]; Socialist Party or PS [Francois HOLLANDE]; Greens [Yann WEHRLING, national secretary]; Union for French Democracy or UDF [Francois BAYROU]; Union for a Popular Movement or UMP (including RPR, DL, and a part of UDF) [Nicolas SARKOZY]
Political pressure groups and leaders: historically-Communist labor union (Confederation Generale du Travail) or CGT, approximately 700,000 members (claimed); left-leaning labor union (Confederation Francaise Democratique du Travail) or CFDT, approximately 889,000 members (claimed); independent labor union (Confederation Generale du Travail - Force Ouvriere) or FO, 300,000 members (est.); independent white-collar union (Confederation Generale des Cadres) or CGC, 196,000 members (claimed); employers' union (Mouvement des Entreprises de France) or MEDEF, 750,000 companies as members (claimed)
International organization participation: ABEDA, ACCT, AfDB, AsDB, Australia Group, BDEAC, BIS, BSEC (observer), CBSS (observer), CE, CERN, EAPC, EBRD, EIB, EMU, ESA, EU, FAO, FZ, G-5, G-7, G-8, G-10, IADB, IAEA, IBRD, ICAO, ICC, ICCt, ICFTU, ICRM, IDA, IEA, IFAD, IFC, IFRCS, IHO, ILO, IMF, IMO, InOC, Interpol, IOC, IOM, ISO, ITU, MIGA, MINURSO, MINUSTAH, MONUC, NATO, NEA, NSG, OAS (observer), OECD, OPCW, OSCE, Paris Club, PCA, PIF (partner), SPC, UN, UN Security Council, UNCTAD, UNESCO, UNHCR, UNIDO, UNIFIL, UNITAR, UNMEE, UNMIL, UNMOVIC, UNOCI, UNOMIG, UNRWA, UNTSO, UPU, WADB (nonregional), WCL, WCO, WEU, WFTU, WHO, WIPO, WMO, WToO, WTO, ZC
Diplomatic representation in the US:
chief of mission: Ambassador Jean-David LEVITTE
chancery: 4101 Reservoir Road NW, Washington, DC 20007
telephone: [1] (202) 944-6000
FAX: [1] (202) 944-6166
consulate(s) general: Atlanta, Boston, Chicago, Houston, Los Angeles, Miami, New Orleans, New York, and San Francisco
Diplomatic representation from the US:
chief of mission: Ambassador Craig R. STAPLETON
embassy: 2 Avenue Gabriel, 75382 Paris Cedex 08
mailing address: PSC 116, APO AE 09777
telephone: [33] (1) 43-12-22-22
FAX: [33] (1) 42 66 97 83
consulate(s) general: Marseille, Strasbourg
Flag description: three equal vertical bands of blue (hoist side), white, and red; known as the "Le drapeau tricolore" (French Tricolor), the origin of the flag dates to 1790 and the French Revolution; the design and/or colors are similar to a number of other flags, including those of Belgium, Chad, Ireland, Cote d'Ivoire, Luxembourg, and Netherlands; the official flag for all French dependent areas

ECONOMY

Economy - overview: France is in the midst of transition, from a well-to-do modern economy that has featured extensive government ownership and intervention to one that relies more on market mechanisms. The government has partially or fully privatized many large companies, banks, and insurers. It retains controlling stakes in several leading firms, including Air France, France Telecom, Renault, and Thales, and is dominant in some sectors, particularly power, public transport, and defense industries. The telecommunications sector is gradually being opened to competition. France's leaders remain committed to a capitalism in which they maintain social equity by means of laws, tax policies, and social spending that reduce income disparity and the impact of free markets on public health and welfare. The government has lowered income taxes and introduced measures to boost employment and reform the pension system. In addition, it is focusing on the problems of the high cost of labor and labor market inflexibility resulting from the 35-hour workweek and restrictions on lay-offs. The tax burden remains one of the highest in Europe (nearly 50% of GDP in 2005). The lingering economic slowdown and inflexible budget items have pushed the budget deficit above the eurozone's 3%-of-GDP limit; unemployment stands at 10%.
GDP (purchasing power parity): $1.816 trillion (2005 est.)
GDP (official exchange rate): $2.118 trillion (2005 est.)
GDP - real growth rate: 1.5% (2005 est.)
GDP - per capita: purchasing power parity - $29,900 (2005 est.)
GDP - composition by sector:
agriculture: 2.5%
industry: 21.4%
services: 76.1% (2005 est.)
Labor force: 27.72 million (2005 est.)
Labor force - by occupation: agriculture 4.1%, industry 24.4%, services 71.5% (1999)
Unemployment rate: 10% (2005 est.)
Population below poverty line: 6.5% (2000)
Household income or consumption by percentage share:
lowest 10%: 2.8%
highest 10%: 25.1% (1995)
Distribution of family income - Gini index: 32.7 (1995)
Inflation rate (consumer prices): 1.9% (2005 est.)
Investment (gross fixed): 19.4% of GDP (2005 est.)
Budget:
revenues: $1.06 trillion
expenditures: $1.144 trillion, including capital expenditures of $23 billion (2005 est.)
Public debt: 66.5% of GDP (2005 est.)
Agriculture - products: wheat, cereals, sugar beets, potatoes, wine grapes; beef, dairy products; fish
Industries: machinery, chemicals, automobiles, metallurgy, aircraft, electronics; textiles, food processing; tourism
Industrial production growth rate: 0.3% (2005 est.)
Electricity - production: 536.9 billion kWh (2003)
Electricity - production by source:
fossil fuel: 8.2%
hydro: 14%
nuclear: 77.1%
other: 0.7% (2001)
Electricity - consumption: 433.3 billion kWh (2003)
Electricity - exports: 72.2 billion kWh (2003)
Electricity - imports: 6.2 billion kWh (2003)
Oil - production: 76,300 bbl/day (2003 est.)
Oil - consumption: 2.06 million bbl/day (2003 est.)
Oil - exports: 409,600 bbl/day (2001)
Oil - imports: 2.281 million bbl/day (2001)
Oil - proved reserves: 144.3 million bbl (1 January 2002)
Natural gas - production: 1.898 billion cu m (2001 est.)
Natural gas - consumption: 42.01 billion cu m (2001 est.)
Natural gas - exports: 1.725 billion cu m (2001 est.)
Natural gas - imports: 40.26 billion cu m (2001 est.)
Natural gas - proved reserves: 12.86 billion cu m (1 January 2002)
Current account balance: $-30.11 billion (2005 est.)
Exports: $443.4 billion f.o.b. (2005 est.)
Exports - partners: Germany 15%, Spain 9.5%, UK 9.3%, Italy 9%, Belgium 7.2%, US 6.7% (2004)
Imports: $473.3 billion f.o.b. (2005 est.)
Imports - partners: Germany 19.2%, Belgium 9.9%, Italy 8.8%, Spain 7.4%, UK 7%, Netherlands 6.7%, US 5.1% (2004)

Reserves of foreign exchange and gold: $77.35 billion (2004 est.)
Debt - external: $2.826 trillion (30 June 2005)
Economic aid - donor: ODA, $5.4 billion (2002)
Currency (code): euro (EUR)
note: on 1 January 1999, the European Monetary Union introduced the euro as a common currency to be used by financial institutions of member countries; on 1 January 2002, the euro became the sole currency for everyday transactions within the member countries
Currency code: EUR
Exchange rates: euros per US dollar - 0.79697 (2005), 0.8054 (2004), 0.886 (2003), 1.0626 (2002), 1.1175 (2001)
Fiscal year: calendar year

COMMUNICATIONS

Telephones - main lines in use: 33,905,400 (2003)
Telephones - mobile cellular: 41,683,100 (2003)
Telephone system:
general assessment: highly developed
domestic: extensive cable and microwave radio relay; extensive introduction of fiber-optic cable; domestic satellite system
international: country code - 33; satellite earth stations - 2 Intelsat (with total of 5 antennas - 2 for Indian Ocean and 3 for Atlantic Ocean), NA Eutelsat, 1 Inmarsat (Atlantic Ocean region); HF radiotelephone communications with more than 20 countries
Radio broadcast stations: AM 41, FM about 3,500 (this figure is an approximation and includes many repeaters), shortwave 2 (1998)
Radios: 55.3 million (1997)
Television broadcast stations: 584 (plus 9,676 repeaters) (1995)
Televisions: 34.8 million (1997)
Internet country code: .fr
Internet hosts: 2,396,761 (2004)
Internet Service Providers (ISPs): 62 (2000)
Internet users: 21.9 million (2003)

TRANSPORTATION

Airports: 478 (2004 est.)
Airports - with paved runways:
total: 288
over 3,047 m: 13
2,438 to 3,047 m: 28
1,524 to 2,437 m: 96
914 to 1,523 m: 82
under 914 m: 69 (2005 est.)
Airports - with unpaved runways:
total: 191
1,524 to 2,437 m: 3
914 to 1,523 m: 72
under 914 m: 116 (2005 est.)
Heliports: 3 (2005 est.)
Pipelines: gas 14,232 km; oil 3,024 km; refined products 4,889 km (2004)
Railways:
total: 29,519 km
standard gauge: 29,352 km 1.435-m gauge (14,481 km electrified)
narrow gauge: 167 km 1.000-m gauge (2004)
Roadways:
total: 891,290 km
paved: 891,290 km (including 10,390 km of expressways) (2003)
Waterways: 8,500 km (1,686 km accessible to craft of 3,000 metric tons) (2000)
Merchant marine:
total: 56 ships (1,000 GRT or over) 703,639 GRT/889,705 DWT
by type: cargo 4, chemical tanker 6, liquefied gas 4, passenger 3, passenger/cargo 30, petroleum tanker 8, roll on/roll off 1
foreign-owned: 6 (Sweden 5, Switzerland 1)
registered in other countries: 139 (2005)
Ports and terminals: Bordeaux, Calais, Dunkerque, La Pallice, Le Havre, Marseille, Nantes, Paris, Rouen, Strasbourg

MILITARY

Military branches: Army (includes Marines, Foreign Legion, Army Light Aviation), Navy (includes naval air), Air Force (includes Air Defense), National Gendarmerie
Military service age and obligation: 17 years of age with consent for voluntary military service (2001)
Manpower available for military service: *males age 17-49:* 13,676,509 (2005 est.)
Manpower fit for military service: *males age 17-49:* 11,262,661 (2005 est.)
Manpower reaching military service age annually: *males:* 389,204 (2005 est.)
Military expenditures - dollar figure: $45 billion FY06 (2005)
Military expenditures - percent of GDP: 2.6% FY06 (2005 est.)

TRANSNATIONAL ISSUES

Disputes - international: Madagascar claims Bassas da India, Europa Island, Glorioso Islands, and Juan de Nova Island; Comoros claims Mayotte; Mauritius claims Tromelin Island; territorial dispute between Suriname and the French overseas department of French Guiana; France asserts a territorial claim in Antarctica (Adelie Land); France and Vanuatu claim Matthew and Hunter Islands, east of New Caledonia
Illicit drugs: transshipment point for and consumer of South American cocaine, Southwest Asian heroin, and European synthetics

FRENCH GUIANA

INTRODUCTION

Background: First settled by the French in 1604, French Guiana was the site of notorious penal settlements until 1951. The European Space Agency launches its communication satellites from Kourou.

GEOGRAPHY

Location: Northern South America, bordering the North Atlantic Ocean, between Brazil and Suriname
Geographic coordinates: 4 00 N, 53 00 W
Map references: South America
Area:
total: 91,000 sq km
land: 89,150 sq km
water: 1,850 sq km
Area - comparative: slightly smaller than Indiana
Land boundaries:
total: 1,183 km
border countries: Brazil 673 km, Suriname 510 km
Coastline: 378 km
Maritime claims:
territorial sea: 12 nm
exclusive economic zone: 200 nm
Climate: tropical; hot, humid; little seasonal temperature variation
Terrain: low-lying coastal plains rising to hills and small mountains
Elevation extremes:
lowest point: Atlantic Ocean 0 m
highest point: Bellevue de l'Inini 851 m
Natural resources: bauxite, timber, gold

(widely scattered), petroleum, kaolin, fish, niobium, tantalum, clay

Land use:
arable land: 0.14%
permanent crops: 0.05%
other: 99.81% (90% forest, 10% other) (2001)

Irrigated land: 20 sq km (1998 est.)

Natural hazards: high frequency of heavy showers and severe thunderstorms; flooding

Environment - current issues: NA

Geography - note: mostly an unsettled wilderness; the only non-independent portion of the South American continent

PEOPLE

Population: 195,506 (July 2005 est.)

Age structure:
0-14 years: 29.3% (male 29,262/female 27,947)
15-64 years: 64.7% (male 67,895/female 58,534)
65 years and over: 6.1% (male 6,038/female 5,830) (2005 est.)

Median age:
total: 28.45 years
male: 29.19 years
female: 27.31 years (2005 est.)

Population growth rate: 2.1% (2005 est.)

Birth rate: 20.7 births/1,000 population (2005 est.)

Death rate: 4.85 deaths/1,000 population (2005 est.)

Net migration rate: 5.11 migrant(s)/1,000 population (2005 est.)

Sex ratio:
at birth: 1.05 male(s)/female
under 15 years: 1.05 male(s)/female
15-64 years: 1.16 male(s)/female
65 years and over: 1.04 male(s)/female
total population: 1.12 male(s)/female (2005 est.)

Infant mortality rate:
total: 12.07 deaths/1,000 live births
male: 12.91 deaths/1,000 live births
female: 11.2 deaths/1,000 live births (2005 est.)

Life expectancy at birth:
total population: 77.09 years
male: 73.77 years
female: 80.58 years (2005 est.)

Total fertility rate: 3.01 children born/woman (2005 est.)

HIV/AIDS - adult prevalence rate: NA%

HIV/AIDS - people living with HIV/AIDS: NA

HIV/AIDS - deaths: NA

Nationality:
noun: French Guianese (singular and plural)
adjective: French Guianese

Ethnic groups: black or mulatto 66%, white 12%, East Indian, Chinese, Amerindian 12%, other 10%

Religions: Roman Catholic

Languages: French

Literacy:
definition: age 15 and over can read and write
total population: 83%
male: 84%
female: 82% (1982 est.)

GOVERNMENT

Country name:
conventional long form: Department of Guiana
conventional short form: French Guiana
local long form: none
local short form: Guyane

Dependency status: overseas department of France

Government type: NA

Capital: Cayenne

Administrative divisions: none (overseas department of France)

Independence: none (overseas department of France)

National holiday: Bastille Day, 14 July (1789)

Constitution: 4 October 1958 (French Constitution)

Legal system: French legal system

Suffrage: 18 years of age, universal

Executive branch:
chief of state: President Jacques CHIRAC of France (since 17 May 1995), represented by Prefect Ange MANCINI (since 31 July 2002)
head of government: President of the General Council Joseph HO-TEN-YOU (since 26 March 2001); President of the Regional Council Antoine KARAM (since 22 March 1992)
cabinet: NA
elections: French president elected by popular vote for a five-year term; prefect appointed by the French president on the advice of the French Ministry of Interior; presidents of the General and Regional Councils are appointed by the members of those councils

Legislative branch: unicameral General Council or Conseil General (19 seats; members are elected by popular vote to serve six-year terms) and a unicameral Regional Council or Conseil Regional (31 seats; members are elected by popular vote to serve six-year terms)
elections: General Council - last held NA March 2000 (next to be held NA 2006); Regional Council - last held 15 March 1998 (next to be held NA 2004)
election results: General Council - percent of vote by party - NA%; seats by party - PSG 5, various left-wing parties 5, independents 7, other 2; Regional Council - percent of vote by party - PS 28.28%, various left parties 22.56%, RPR 15.91%, independents 8.6%, Walwari Committee 6%; seats by party - PS 11, various left parties 9, RPR 6, independents 3, Walwari Committee 2
note: one seat was elected to the French Senate on 27 September 1998 (next to be held September 2007); results - percent of vote by party - NA%; seats by party - NA; 2 seats were elected to the French National Assembly on 9 June-16 June 2002 (next to be held NA 2007); results - percent of vote by party - NA%; seats by party - UMP/RPR 1, Walwari Committee 1

Judicial branch: Court of Appeals or Cour d'Appel (highest local court based in Martinique with jurisdiction over Martinique, Guadeloupe, and French Guiana)

Political parties and leaders: Guyanese Democratic Action or ADG [Andre LECANTE]; Guyanese Socialist Party or PSG [Marie-Claude VERDAN]; Guyana Democratic Forces or FDG [Georges OTHILY]; Popular National Guyanese Party or PNPG [Jose DORCY]; Socialist Party or PS [Paul DEBRIETTE]; Union for a Popular Movement or UMP (includes RPR) [Muriel ICARE]; Walwari Committee (aligned with the PRG in France) [Christine TAUBIRA-DELANON]

Political pressure groups and leaders: NA

International organization participation: UPU, WCL, WFTU

Diplomatic representation in the US: none (overseas department of France)

Diplomatic representation from the US: none (overseas department of France)

Flag description: the flag of France is used

ECONOMY

Economy - overview: The economy is tied closely to the much larger French economy through subsidies and imports. Besides the French space center at Kourou (which accounts for 25% of GDP), fishing and forestry are the most important economic activities. Forest and woodland cover 90% of the country. The large reserves of tropical hardwoods, not fully exploited, support an expanding sawmill industry that provides sawn logs for export. Cultivation of crops is limited to the coastal area, where the population is largely concentrated; rice and manioc are the major crops. French Guiana is heavily dependent on imports of food and energy. Unemployment is a serious problem, particularly among younger workers.

GDP (purchasing power parity): $1.551 billion (2003 est.)

GDP (official exchange rate): NA

GDP - real growth rate: NA%

GDP - per capita: purchasing power par-

ity - $8,300 (2003 est.)
GDP - composition by sector:
agriculture: NA%
industry: NA%
services: NA% (2001 est.)
Labor force: 58,800 (1997)
Labor force - by occupation: agriculture 18.2%, industry 21.2%, services, government, and commerce 60.6% (1980)
Unemployment rate: 22% (2001)
Population below poverty line: NA
Household income or consumption by percentage share:
lowest 10%: NA%
highest 10%: NA%
Inflation rate (consumer prices): 1.5% (2002 est.)
Budget:
revenues: $225 million
expenditures: $390 million, including capital expenditures of $105 million (1996)
Agriculture - products: corn, rice, manioc (tapioca), sugar, cocoa, vegetables, bananas; cattle, pigs, poultry
Industries: construction, shrimp processing, forestry products, rum, gold mining
Industrial production growth rate: NA%
Electricity - production: 465.2 million kWh (2003)
Electricity - production by source:
fossil fuel: 100%
hydro: 0%
nuclear: 0%
other: 0% (2001)
Electricity - consumption: 432.6 million kWh (2003)
Electricity - exports: 0 kWh (2003)
Electricity - imports: 0 kWh (2003)
Oil - production: 0 bbl/day (2003 est.)
Oil - consumption: 6,600 bbl/day (2003 est.)
Oil - exports: NA (2001)
Oil - imports: NA (2001)
Exports: $155 million f.o.b. (2002 est.)
Exports - partners: France 62%, Switzerland 7%, US 2% (2004)
Imports: $625 million c.i.f. (2002 est.)
Imports - partners: France 63%, US, Trinidad and Tobago, Italy (2004)
Debt - external: $1.2 billion (1988)
Economic aid - recipient: NA
Currency (code): euro (EUR)
Currency code: EUR
Exchange rates: Euros per US dollar - NA (2005), 0.8054 (2004), 0.886 (2003), 1.0626 (2002), 1.1175 (2001)
Fiscal year: calendar year

COMMUNICATIONS

Telephones - main lines in use: 51,000 (2001)
Telephones - mobile cellular: 138,200 (2002)
Telephone system:
general assessment: NA
domestic: fair open-wire and microwave radio relay system
international: country code - 594; satellite earth station - 1 Intelsat (Atlantic Ocean)
Radio broadcast stations: AM 2, FM 14 (including 6 repeaters), shortwave 6 (including 5 repeaters) (1998)
Radios: 104,000 (1997)
Television broadcast stations: 3 (plus eight low-power repeaters) (1997)
Televisions: 30,000 (1997)
Internet country code: .gf
Internet Service Providers (ISPs): 2 (2000)
Internet users: 3,200 (2002)

TRANSPORTATION

Airports: 11 (2004 est.)
Airports - with paved runways:
total: 4
over 3,047 m: 1
914 to 1,523 m: 2
under 914 m: 1 (2005 est.)
Airports - with unpaved runways:
total: 7
914 to 1,523 m: 2
under 914 m: 5 (2005 est.)
Roadways:
total: 817 km (1998)
Waterways: 3,760 km
note: 460 km navigable by small oceangoing vessels and coastal and river steamers, 3,300 km by native craft (2004)
Merchant marine:
registered in other countries: 3
Ports and terminals: Degrad des Cannes

MILITARY

Military branches: no regular military forces; Gendarmerie
Manpower available for military service: *males age 18-49:* 47,809 (2005 est.)
Manpower fit for military service: *males age 18-49:* 38,676 (2005 est.)
Military expenditures - dollar figure: $NA
Military expenditures - percent of GDP: NA
Military - note: defense is the responsibility of France

TRANSNATIONAL ISSUES

Disputes - international: Suriname claims area between Riviere Litani and Riviere Marouini (both headwaters of the Lawa) in French Guiana
Illicit drugs: small amount of marijuana grown for local consumption; minor transshipment point to Europe

FRENCH POLYNESIA

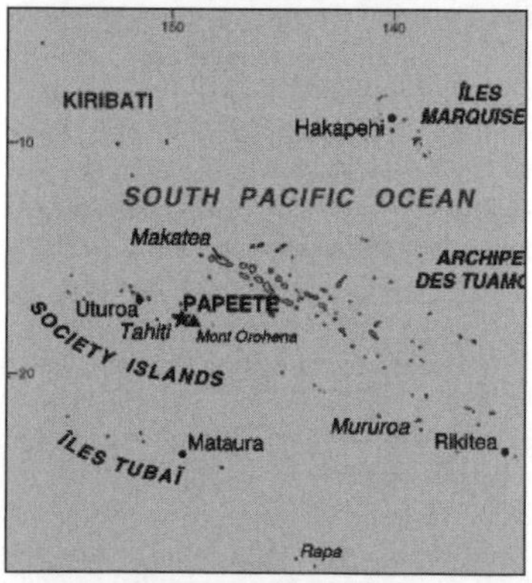

INTRODUCTION

Background: The French annexed various Polynesian island groups during the 19th century. In September 1995, France stirred up widespread protests by resuming nuclear testing on the Mururoa atoll after a three-year moratorium. The tests were suspended in January 1996.

GEOGRAPHY

Location: Oceania, archipelagoes in the South Pacific Ocean, about one-half of the way from South America to Australia
Geographic coordinates: 15 00 S, 140 00 W
Map references: Oceania
Area:
total: 4,167 sq km (118 islands and atolls)
land: 3,660 sq km
water: 507 sq km
Area - comparative: slightly less than one-third the size of Connecticut
Land boundaries: 0 km
Coastline: 2,525 km
Maritime claims:
territorial sea: 12 nm
exclusive economic zone: 200 nm
Climate: tropical, but moderate
Terrain: mixture of rugged high islands and low islands with reefs
Elevation extremes:
lowest point: Pacific Ocean 0 m
highest point: Mont Orohena 2,241 m
Natural resources: timber, fish, cobalt, hydropower
Land use:
arable land: 0.82%
permanent crops: 5.46%
other: 93.72% (2001)
Irrigated land: NA sq km
Natural hazards: occasional cyclonic storms in January
Environment - current issues: NA
Geography - note: includes five archipel-

agoes (4 volcanic, 1 coral); Makatea in French Polynesia is one of the three great phosphate rock islands in the Pacific Ocean - the others are Banaba (Ocean Island) in Kiribati and Nauru

PEOPLE

Population: 270,485 (July 2005 est.)
Age structure:
0-14 years: 26.7% (male 36,947/female 35,403)
15-64 years: 67.4% (male 94,710/female 87,546)
65 years and over: 5.9% (male 8,018/female 7,861) (2005 est.)
Median age:
total: 27.48 years
male: 27.84 years
female: 27.1 years (2005 est.)
Population growth rate: 1.52% (2005 est.)
Birth rate: 16.93 births/1,000 population (2005 est.)
Death rate: 4.63 deaths/1,000 population (2005 est.)
Net migration rate: 2.89 migrant(s)/1,000 population (2005 est.)
Sex ratio:
at birth: 1.05 male(s)/female
under 15 years: 1.04 male(s)/female
15-64 years: 1.08 male(s)/female
65 years and over: 1.02 male(s)/female
total population: 1.07 male(s)/female (2005 est.)
Infant mortality rate:
total: 8.44 deaths/1,000 live births
male: 9.73 deaths/1,000 live births
female: 7.09 deaths/1,000 live births (2005 est.)
Life expectancy at birth:
total population: 75.9 years
male: 73.5 years
female: 78.42 years (2005 est.)
Total fertility rate: 2.04 children born/woman (2005 est.)
HIV/AIDS - adult prevalence rate: NA%
HIV/AIDS - people living with HIV/AIDS: NA
HIV/AIDS - deaths: NA
Nationality:
noun: French Polynesian(s)
adjective: French Polynesian
Ethnic groups: Polynesian 78%, Chinese 12%, local French 6%, metropolitan French 4%
Religions: Protestant 54%, Roman Catholic 30%, other 10%, no religion 6%
Languages: French 61.1% (official), Polynesian 31.4% (official), Asian languages 1.2%, other 0.3%, unspecified 6% (2002 census)
Literacy:
definition: age 14 and over can read and write
total population: 98%
male: 98%
female: 98% (1977 est.)

GOVERNMENT

Country name:
conventional long form: Overseas Lands of French Polynesia
conventional short form: French Polynesia
local long form: Pays d'outre-mer de la Polynesie Francaise
local short form: Polynesie Francaise
former: French Colony of Oceania
Dependency status: overseas lands of France; overseas territory of France from 1946-2004
Government type: NA
Capital: Papeete
Administrative divisions: none (overseas lands of France); there are no first-order administrative divisions as defined by the US Government, but there are 5 archipelagic divisions named Archipel des Marquises, Archipel des Tuamotu, Archipel des Tubuai, Iles du Vent, and Iles Sous-le-Vent
note: Clipperton Island is administered by France from French Polynesia
Independence: none (overseas lands of France); note - the Australian government calls them "overseas entities"
National holiday: Bastille Day, 14 July (1789)
Constitution: 4 October 1958 (French Constitution)
Legal system: based on French system
Suffrage: 18 years of age; universal
Executive branch:
chief of state: President Jacques CHIRAC of France (since 17 May 1995), represented by High Commissioner of the Republic Anne BOQUET (since September 2005)
head of government: President of the Territorial Government of French Polynesia Oscar TEMARU (since 3 March 2005); President of the Territorial Assembly Antony GEROS (since 9 May 2004)
cabinet: Council of Ministers; president submits a list of members of the Territorial Assembly for approval by them to serve as ministers
elections: French president elected by popular vote for a five-year term; high commissioner appointed by the French president on the advice of the French Ministry of Interior; president of the Territorial Government and the president of the Territorial Assembly are elected by the members of the assembly
Legislative branch: unicameral Territorial Assembly or Assemblee Territoriale (57 seats - changed from 49 seats for May 2004 election; members are elected by popular vote to serve five-year terms)
elections: last held 23 May 2004 (next to be held May 2009)
election results: percent of vote by party - NA%; seats by party - People's Rally for the Republic (Gaullist) 28, Union for Democracy 27, New Star 1, This Country is Yours 1; after by-elections of 13 February 2005 seating was as follows: People's Rally for the Republic 27, Union for Democracy 27, and Alliance for a New Democracy 3
note: one seat was elected to the French Senate on 27 September 1998 (next to be held September 2007); results - percent of vote by party - NA%; seats by party - NA; two seats were elected to the French National Assembly on 9 June-16 June 2002 (next to be held NA 2007); results - percent of vote by party - NA%; seats by party - UMP/RPR 1, UMP 1
Judicial branch: Court of Appeal or Cour d'Appel; Court of the First Instance or Tribunal de Premiere Instance; Court of Administrative Law or Tribunal Administratif
Political parties and leaders: Alliance for a New Democracy or ADN [Nicole BOUTEAU]; Independent Front for the Liberation of Polynesia (Tavini Huiraatira) [Oscar TEMARU]; New Fatherland Party (Ai'a Api) [Emile VERNAUDON]; People's Rally for the Republic of Polynesia or RPR (Tahoeraa Huiraatira) [Gaston FLOSSE]; The New Star (Te Fetia Api) [Philippe SHYLE]; This Country is Yours (No Oe E Te Nunaa) [Nicle BOUTEAU]; Union for Democracy or UPD [Oscar TEMARU]
Political pressure groups and leaders: NA
International organization participation: FZ, ICFTU, PIF (observer), SPC, UPU, WMO
Diplomatic representation in the US: none (overseas lands of France)
Diplomatic representation from the US: none (overseas lands of France)
Flag description: two narrow red horizontal bands encase a wide white band; centered on the white band is a disk with blue and white wave pattern on the lower half and gold and white ray pattern on the upper half; a stylized red, blue and white ship rides on the wave pattern; the French flag is used for official occasions

ECONOMY

Economy - overview: Since 1962, when France stationed military personnel in the region, French Polynesia has changed from a subsistence agricultural economy to one in which a high proportion of the work force is either employed by the military or supports the tourist industry. With the halt of French nuclear testing in 1996, the military contribution to the economy fell sharply. Tourism accounts

for about one-fourth of GDP and is a primary source of hard currency earnings. Other sources of income are pearl farming and deep-sea commercial fishing. The small manufacturing sector primarily processes agricultural products. The territory benefits substantially from development agreements with France aimed principally at creating new businesses and strengthening social services.
GDP (purchasing power parity): $4.58 billion (2003 est.)
GDP (official exchange rate): NA
GDP - real growth rate: NA% (2001 est.)
GDP - per capita: purchasing power parity - $17,500 (2003 est.)
GDP - composition by sector:
agriculture: 6%
industry: 18%
services: 76% (2002)
Labor force: 70,000 (1996)
Labor force - by occupation: agriculture 13%, industry 19%, services 68% (2002)
Unemployment rate: 11.8% (1994)
Population below poverty line: NA
Household income or consumption by percentage share:
lowest 10%: NA%
highest 10%: NA%
Inflation rate (consumer prices): 1.5% (2002 est.)
Budget:
revenues: $1 billion
expenditures: $900 million, including capital expenditures of $185 million (1996)
Agriculture - products: coconuts, vanilla, vegetables, fruits; poultry, beef, dairy products, coffee
Industries: tourism, pearls, agricultural processing, handicrafts, phosphates
Industrial production growth rate: NA%
Electricity - production: 493.7 million kWh (2003)
Electricity - production by source:
fossil fuel: 60.7%
hydro: 39.3%
nuclear: 0%
other: 0% (2001)
Electricity - consumption: 459.2 million kWh (2003)
Electricity - exports: 0 kWh (2003)
Electricity - imports: 0 kWh (2003)
Oil - production: 0 bbl/day (2003 est.)
Oil - consumption: 4,800 bbl/day (2003 est.)
Oil - exports: NA (2001)
Oil - imports: NA (2001)
Exports: $385 million f.o.b. (2004 est.)
Exports - partners: France 36.6%, Japan 22.7%, US 16.1%, Niger 13%, Thailand 4.1% (2004)
Imports: $1.437 billion f.o.b. (2004 est.)
Imports - partners: France 47.6%, New Zealand 8.9%, Singapore 8.4%, Australia 8.4%, US 7.1% (2004)
Debt - external: NA
Economic aid - recipient: $367 million (1997)
Currency (code): Comptoirs Francais du Pacifique franc (XPF)
Currency code: XPF
Exchange rates: Comptoirs Francais du Pacifique francs (XPF) per US dollar - NA (2005), 96.04 (2004), 105.66 (2003), 126.71 (2002), 133.26 (2001)
note: pegged at the rate of 119.25 XPF to the euro
Fiscal year: calendar year

COMMUNICATIONS

Telephones - main lines in use: 52,500 (2002)
Telephones - mobile cellular: 90,000 (2002)
Telephone system:
general assessment: NA
domestic: NA
international: country code - 689; satellite earth station - 1 Intelsat (Pacific Ocean)
Radio broadcast stations: AM 2, FM 14, shortwave 2 (1998)
Radios: 128,000 (1997)
Television broadcast stations: 7 (plus 17 low-power repeaters) (1997)
Televisions: 40,000 (1997)
Internet country code: .pf
Internet hosts: 5,123 (2003)
Internet Service Providers (ISPs): 2 (2000)
Internet users: 35,000 (2002)

TRANSPORTATION

Airports: 50 (2004 est.)
Airports - with paved runways:
total: 37
over 3,047 m: 2
1,524 to 2,437 m: 5
914 to 1,523 m: 23
under 914 m: 7 (2005 est.)
Airports - with unpaved runways:
total: 13
914 to 1,523 m: 5
under 914 m: 8 (2005 est.)
Heliports: 1 (2005 est.)
Roadways:
total: 2,590 km
paved: 1,735 km
unpaved: 855 km (1999)
Merchant marine:
total: 15 ships (1,000 GRT or over) 17,537 GRT/15,150 DWT
by type: cargo 4, passenger 4, passenger/cargo 5, refrigerated cargo 1, roll on/roll off 1
foreign-owned: 1 (France 1) (2005)
Ports and terminals: Papeete

MILITARY

Military branches: no regular military forces; Gendarmerie and National Police Force
Military - note: defense is the responsibility of France

TRANSNATIONAL ISSUES

Disputes - international: none

FRENCH SOUTHERN AND ANTARCTIC LANDS

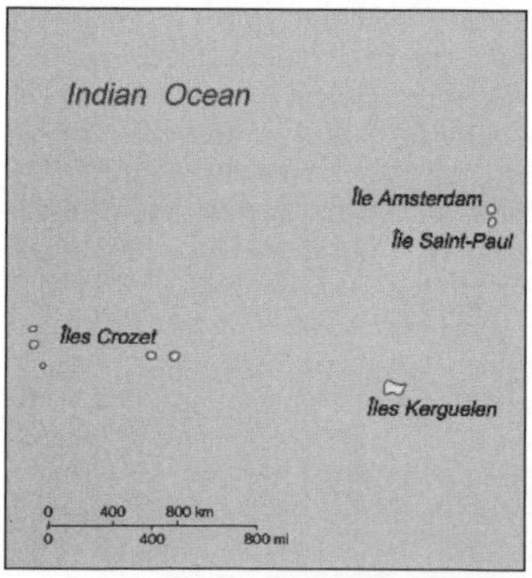

INTRODUCTION

Background: The Southern Lands consist of two archipelagos, Iles Crozet and Iles Kerguelen, and two volcanic islands, Ile Amsterdam and Ile Saint-Paul. They contain no permanent inhabitants and are visited only by researchers studying the native fauna. The Antarctic portion consists of "Adelie Land," a thin slice of the Antarctic continent discovered and claimed by the French in 1840.

GEOGRAPHY

Location: southeast of Africa, islands in the southern Indian Ocean, about equidistant between Africa, Antarctica, and Australia; note - French Southern and Antarctic Lands include Ile Amsterdam, Ile Saint-Paul, Iles Crozet, and Iles Kerguelen in the southern Indian Ocean, along with the French-claimed sector of Antarctica, "Adelie Land"; the US does not recognize the French claim to "Adelie Land"
Geographic coordinates: 43 00 S, 67 00 E
Map references: Antarctic Region
Area:
total: 7,829 sq km
land: 7,829 sq km
water: 0 sq km
note: includes Ile Amsterdam, Ile Saint-

Paul, Iles Crozet and Iles Kerguelen; excludes "Adelie Land" claim of about 500,000 sq km in Antarctica that is not recognized by the US
Area - comparative: slightly less than 1.3 times the size of Delaware
Land boundaries: 0 km
Coastline: 1,232 km
Maritime claims:
territorial sea: 12 nm
exclusive economic zone: 200 nm from Iles Kerguelen (does not include the rest of French Southern and Antarctic Lands)
Climate: antarctic
Terrain: volcanic
Elevation extremes:
lowest point: Indian Ocean 0 m
highest point: Mont Ross on Iles Kerguelen 1,850 m
Natural resources: fish, crayfish
Land use:
arable land: 0%
permanent crops: 0%
other: 100% (2001)
Irrigated land: 0 sq km (1998 est.)
Natural hazards: Ile Amsterdam and Ile Saint-Paul are extinct volcanoes
Environment - current issues: NA
Geography - note: islands component is widely scattered across remote locations in the southern Indian Ocean

PEOPLE

Population: no indigenous inhabitants (July 2005 est.)
note: in 2002, there were 145 researchers whose numbers vary from winter (July) to summer (January) (July 2005 est.)

GOVERNMENT

Country name:
conventional long form: Territory of the French Southern and Antarctic Lands
conventional short form: French Territoire des Terres Australes et Antarctiques Francaises
local short form: Terres Australes et Antarctiques Francaises
Dependency status: overseas territory of France since 1955; administered from Paris by Administrateur Superieur Michel CHAMPON (since 20 December 2004), assisted by Secretary General Jean-Yves HERMOSO (since NA)
Administrative divisions: none (overseas territory of France); there are no first-order administrative divisions as defined by the US Government, but there are 3 districts named Ile Crozet, Iles Kerguelen, and Iles Saint-Paul et Amsterdam; excludes "Adelie Land" claim in Antarctica that is not recognized by the US
Legal system: the laws of France, where applicable, apply
Diplomatic representation in the US: none (overseas territory of France)
Diplomatic representation from the US: none (overseas territory of France)
Flag description: the flag of France is used

ECONOMY

Economy - overview: Economic activity is limited to servicing meteorological and geophysical research stations and French and other fishing fleets. The fish catches landed on Iles Kerguelen by foreign ships are exported to France and Reunion.

COMMUNICATIONS

Internet country code: .tf

TRANSPORTATION

Airports: none (2004 est.)
Merchant marine:
total: 75 ships (1,000 GRT or over) 3,092,387 GRT/5,056,658 DWT
by type: bulk carrier 2, cargo 1, chemical tanker 21, container 19, liquefied gas 7, petroleum tanker 15, roll on/roll off 6, vehicle carrier 4
foreign-owned: 71 (Belgium 5, Denmark 2, France 45, Germany 2, Greece 2, Hong Kong 5, Japan 4, Saudi Arabia 1, Sweden 5) (2005)
Ports and terminals: none; offshore anchorage only

MILITARY

Military - note: defense is the responsibility of France

TRANSNATIONAL ISSUES

Disputes - international: French claim to "Adelie Land" in Antarctica is not recognized by the United States

G

GABON

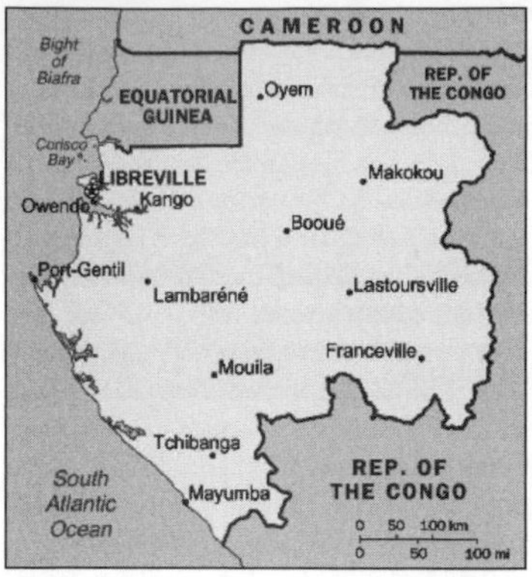

INTRODUCTION

Background: Only two autocratic presidents have ruled Gabon since independence from France in 1960. Gabon's current President, El Hadj Omar BONGO Ondimba - one of the longest-serving heads of state in the world - has dominated Gabon's political scene for almost four decades. President BONGO introduced a nominal multiparty system and a new constitution in the early 1990s. However, allegations of electoral fraud during local elections in 2002-03 and the presidential elections in 2005 have exposed the weaknesses of formal political structures in Gabon. Gabon's political opposition remains weak, divided, and financially dependent on the current regime. Despite political conditions, a small population, abundant natural resources, and considerable foreign support have helped make Gabon one of the more prosperous and stable African countries.

GEOGRAPHY

Location: Western Africa, bordering the Atlantic Ocean at the Equator, between Republic of the Congo and Equatorial Guinea
Geographic coordinates: 1 00 S, 11 45 E
Map references: Africa
Area:
total: 267,667 sq km
land: 257,667 sq km
water: 10,000 sq km
Area - comparative: slightly smaller than Colorado
Land boundaries:
total: 2,551 km
border countries: Cameroon 298 km, Republic of the Congo 1,903 km, Equatorial Guinea 350 km
Coastline: 885 km
Maritime claims:
territorial sea: 12 nm
contiguous zone: 24 nm
exclusive economic zone: 200 nm
Climate: tropical; always hot, humid
Terrain: narrow coastal plain; hilly interior; savanna in east and south
Elevation extremes:
lowest point: Atlantic Ocean 0 m
highest point: Mont Iboundji 1,575 m
Natural resources: petroleum, natural gas, diamond, niobium, manganese, uranium, gold, timber, iron ore, hydropower
Land use:
arable land: 1.26%
permanent crops: 0.66%
other: 98.08% (2001)
Irrigated land: 150 sq km (1998 est.)
Natural hazards: NA
Environment - current issues: deforestation; poaching
Environment - international agreements:
party to: Biodiversity, Climate Change, Desertification, Endangered Species, Law of the Sea, Marine Dumping, Ozone Layer Protection, Ship Pollution, Tropical Timber 83, Tropical Timber 94, Wetlands
signed, but not ratified: none of the selected agreements
Geography - note: a small population and oil and mineral reserves have helped Gabon become one of Africa's wealthier countries; in general, these circumstances have allowed the country to maintain and conserve its pristine rain forest and rich biodiversity

PEOPLE

Population: 1,389,201
note: estimates for this country explicitly take into account the effects of excess mortality due to AIDS; this can result in lower life expectancy, higher infant mortality and death rates, lower population and growth rates, and changes in the distribution of population by age and sex than would otherwise be expected (July 2005 est.)
Age structure:
0-14 years: 42.1% (male 293,668/female 291,816)
15-64 years: 53.8% (male 372,134/female 374,850)
65 years and over: 4.1% (male 23,551/female 33,182) (2005 est.)
Median age:
total: 18.57 years
male: 18.34 years
female: 18.8 years (2005 est.)
Population growth rate: 2.45% (2005 est.)
Birth rate: 36.24 births/1,000 population (2005 est.)
Death rate: 11.72 deaths/1,000 population (2005 est.)
Net migration rate: 0 migrant(s)/1,000 population (2005 est.)
Sex ratio:
at birth: 1.03 male(s)/female
under 15 years: 1.01 male(s)/female
15-64 years: 0.99 male(s)/female
65 years and over: 0.71 male(s)/female
total population: 0.99 male(s)/female (2005 est.)
Infant mortality rate:
total: 53.64 deaths/1,000 live births
male: 63.21 deaths/1,000 live births
female: 43.79 deaths/1,000 live births (2005 est.)
Life expectancy at birth:
total population: 55.02 years
male: 53.63 years
female: 56.45 years (2005 est.)
Total fertility rate: 4.77 children born/woman (2005 est.)
HIV/AIDS - adult prevalence rate: 8.1% (2003 est.)
HIV/AIDS - people living with HIV/AIDS: 48,000 (2003 est.)
HIV/AIDS - deaths: 3,000 (2003 est.)
Major infectious diseases:
degree of risk: very high
food or waterborne diseases: bacterial diarrhea, hepatitis A, and typhoid fever
vectorborne disease: malaria (2004)
Nationality:
noun: Gabonese (singular and plural)
adjective: Gabonese
Ethnic groups: Bantu tribes including four major tribal groupings (Fang, Bapounou, Nzebi, Obamba), other Africans and Europeans 154,000, including 10,700 French and 11,000 persons of dual nationality
Religions: Christian 55%-75%, animist, Muslim less than 1%
Languages: French (official), Fang, Myene, Nzebi, Bapounou/Eschira, Bandjabi
Literacy:
definition: age 15 and over can read and write
total population: 63.2%
male: 73.7%
female: 53.3% (1995 est.)

GOVERNMENT

Country name:
conventional long form: Gabonese Republic
conventional short form: Gabon
local long form: Republique Gabonaise
local short form: Gabon
Government type: republic; multiparty presidential regime (opposition parties legalized in 1990)
Capital: Libreville
Administrative divisions: 9 provinces; Estuaire, Haut-Ogooue, Moyen-Ogooue, Ngounie, Nyanga, Ogooue-Ivindo, Ogooue-Lolo, Ogooue-

Maritime, Woleu-Ntem
Independence: 17 August 1960 (from France)
National holiday: Founding of the Gabonese Democratic Party (PDG), 12 March (1968)
Constitution: adopted 14 March 1991
Legal system: based on French civil law system and customary law; judicial review of legislative acts in Constitutional Chamber of the Supreme Court; has not accepted compulsory ICJ jurisdiction
Suffrage: 21 years of age; universal
Executive branch:
chief of state: President El Hadj Omar BONGO Ondimba (since 2 December 1967)
head of government: Prime Minister Jean-Francois NTOUTOUME-EMANE (since 23 January 1999)
cabinet: Council of Ministers appointed by the prime minister in consultation with the president
elections: president elected by popular vote for a seven-year term; election last held 27 November 2005 (next to be held NA 2012); prime minister appointed by the president
election results: President El Hadj Omar BONGO Ondimba reelected; percent of vote - El Hadj Omar BONGO Ondimba 79.2%, Pierre MAMBOUNDOU 13.6%, Zacharie MYBOTO 6.6%
Legislative branch: bicameral legislature consists of the Senate (91 seats; members elected by members of municipal councils and departmental assemblies) and the National Assembly or Assemblee Nationale (120 seats; members are elected by direct, popular vote to serve five-year terms)
elections: National Assembly - last held 9 and 23 December 2001 (next to be held December 2006); Senate - last held 26 January and 9 February 2003 (next to be held by January 2009)
election results: National Assembly - percent of vote by party - NA%; seats by party - PDG 86, RNB-RPG 8, PGP 3, ADERE 3, CLR 2, PUP 1, PSD 1, independents 13, others 3; Senate - percent of vote by party - NA%; seats by party - PDG 53, RNB 20, PGP 4, ADERE 3, RDP 1, CLR 1, independents 9
Judicial branch: Supreme Court or Cour Supreme consisting of three chambers - Judicial, Administrative, and Accounts; Constitutional Court; Courts of Appeal; Court of State Security; County Courts
Political parties and leaders: Circle of Liberal Reformers or CLR [General Jean Boniface ASSELE]; Congress for Democracy and Justice or CDJ [Jules Aristide Bourdes OGOULIGUENDE]; Democratic and Republican Alliance or ADERE [Divungui-di-Ndinge DIDJOB]; Gabonese Democratic Party or PDG, former sole party [Simplice Nguedet MANZELA]; Gabonese Party for Progress or PGP [Pierre-Louis AGONDJO-OKAWE]; National Rally of Woodcutters-Rally for Gabon or RNB-RPG (Bucherons) [Fr. Paul M'BA-ABESSOLE]; People's Unity Party or PUP [Louis Gaston MAYILA]; Rally for Democracy and Progress or RDP [Pierre EMBONI]; Social Democratic Party or PSD [Pierre Claver MAGANGA-MOUSSAVOU]; Union for Democracy and Social Integration or UDIS [leader NA]; Union of Gabonese People or UPG [Pierre MAMBOUNDOU]
Political pressure groups and leaders: NA
International organization participation: ACCT, ACP, AfDB, AU, BDEAC, CEMAC, FAO, FZ, G-24, G-77, IAEA, IBRD, ICAO, ICCt, ICFTU, ICRM, IDA, IDB, IFAD, IFC, IFRCS, ILO, IMF, IMO, Interpol, IOC, IOM, ITU, MIGA, NAM, OIC, ONUB, OPCW, UN, UNCTAD, UNESCO, UNIDO, UPU, WCL, WCO, WHO, WIPO, WMO, WToO, WTO
Diplomatic representation in the US:
chief of mission: Ambassador Jules Marius OGOUEBANDJA
chancery: Suite 200, 2034 20th Street NW, Washington, DC 20009
telephone: [1] (202) 797-1000
FAX: [1] (202) 332-0668
consulate(s): New York
Diplomatic representation from the US:
chief of mission: Ambassador Barrie R. WALKLEY.
embassy: Boulevard du Bord de Mer, Libreville
mailing address: Centre Ville, B. P. 4000, Libreville
telephone: [241] 76 20 03 through 76 20 04, after hours - 74 34 92
FAX: [241] 74 55 07
Flag description: three equal horizontal bands of green (top), yellow, and blue

ECONOMY

Economy - overview: Gabon enjoys a per capita income four times that of most of sub-Saharan African nations. This has supported a sharp decline in extreme poverty; yet because of high income inequality a large proportion of the population remains poor. Gabon depended on timber and manganese until oil was discovered offshore in the early 1970s. The oil sector now accounts for 50% of GDP. Gabon continues to face fluctuating prices for its oil, timber, and manganese exports. Despite the abundance of natural wealth, poor fiscal management hobbles the economy. Devaluation of its currency by 50% in January 1994 sparked a one-time inflationary surge, to 35%; the rate dropped to 6% in 1996. The IMF provided a one-year standby arrangement in 1994-95, a three-year Enhanced Financing Facility (EFF) at near commercial rates beginning in late 1995, and stand-by credit of $119 million in October 2000. Those agreements mandated progress in privatization and fiscal discipline. France provided additional financial support in January 1997 after Gabon had met IMF targets for mid-1996. In 1997, an IMF mission to Gabon criticized the government for overspending on off-budget items, overborrowing from the central bank, and slipping on its schedule for privatization and administrative reform. The rebound of oil prices in 1999-2000 helped growth, but drops in production hampered Gabon from fully realizing potential gains. In December 2000, Gabon signed a new agreement with the Paris Club to reschedule its official debt. A follow-up bilateral repayment agreement with the US was signed in December 2001. Gabon signed a 14 month Stand-By Arrangement with the IMF in May 2004, and received Paris Club debt rescheduling later that year. Short-term progress depends on an upbeat world economy and fiscal and other adjustments in line with IMF policies.
GDP (purchasing power parity): $8.031 billion (2005 est.)
GDP (official exchange rate): $7.332 billion (2005 est.)
GDP - real growth rate: 2.1% (2005 est.)
GDP - per capita: purchasing power parity - $5,800 (2005 est.)
GDP - composition by sector:
agriculture: 6%
industry: 58.8%
services: 35.1% (2005 est.)
Labor force: 640,000 (2005 est.)
Labor force - by occupation: agriculture 60%, industry 15%, services 25%
Unemployment rate: 21% (1997 est.)
Population below poverty line: NA
Household income or consumption by percentage share:
lowest 10%: NA
highest 10%: NA
Inflation rate (consumer prices): 1.5% (2005 est.)
Investment (gross fixed): 24.5% of GDP (2005 est.)
Budget:
revenues: $2.463 billion
expenditures: $1.618 billion, including capital expenditures of $325 million (2005 est.)

Public debt: 29.5% of GDP (2005 est.)
Agriculture - products: cocoa, coffee, sugar, palm oil, rubber; cattle; okoume (a tropical softwood); fish
Industries: petroleum extraction and refining; manganese, and gold mining; chemicals; ship repair; food and beverage; textile; lumbering and plywood; cement
Industrial production growth rate: 1.6% (2002 est.)
Electricity - production: 1.487 billion kWh (2003)
Electricity - production by source:
fossil fuel: 34.5%
hydro: 65.5%
nuclear: 0%
other: 0% (2001)
Electricity - consumption: 1.383 billion kWh (2003)
Electricity - exports: 0 kWh (2003)
Electricity - imports: 0 kWh (2003)
Oil - production: 268,900 bbl/day (2005 est.)
Oil - consumption: 12,250 bbl/day (2003 est.)
Oil - exports: NA (2001)
Oil - imports: NA (2001)
Oil - proved reserves: 1.921 billion bbl (2005 est.)
Natural gas - production: 80 million cu m (2001 est.)
Natural gas - consumption: 80 million cu m (2001 est.)
Natural gas - exports: 0 cu m (2001 est.)
Natural gas - imports: 0 cu m (2001 est.)
Natural gas - proved reserves: 66.47 billion cu m (2005)
Current account balance: $1.11 billion (2005 est.)
Exports: $5.813 billion f.o.b. (2005 est.)
Exports - partners: US 52.9%, China 8.5%, France 7.3% (2004)
Imports: $1.533 billion f.o.b. (2005 est.)
Imports - partners: France 43.8%, US 6.3%, UK 5.9%, Netherlands 4% (2004)
Reserves of foreign exchange and gold: $525 million (2005 est.)
Debt - external: $3.857 billion (2005 est.)
Economic aid - recipient: $331 million (1995)
Currency (code): Communaute Financiere Africaine franc (XAF); note - responsible authority is the Bank of the Central African States
Currency code: XAF
Exchange rates: Communaute Financiere Africaine francs (XAF) per US dollar - 521.74 (2005), 528.29 (2004), 581.2 (2003), 696.99 (2002), 733.04 (2001)
Fiscal year: calendar year

COMMUNICATIONS

Telephones - main lines in use: 38,400 (2003)
Telephones - mobile cellular: 300,000 (2003)
Telephone system:
general assessment: adequate service by African standards and improving with the help of the growing mobile cell system
domestic: adequate system of cable, microwave radio relay, tropospheric scatter, radiotelephone communication stations, and a domestic satellite system with 12 earth stations
international: country code - 241; satellite earth stations - 3 Intelsat (Atlantic Ocean); fiber optic submarine cable (SAT-3/WASC) provides connectivity to Europe and Asia
Radio broadcast stations: AM 6, FM 7 (and 11 repeaters), shortwave 4 (2001)
Radios: 208,000 (1997)
Television broadcast stations: 4 (plus four low-power repeaters) (2001)
Televisions: 63,000 (1997)
Internet country code: .ga
Internet hosts: 93 (2004)
Internet Service Providers (ISPs): 1 (2001)
Internet users: 35,000 (2003)

TRANSPORTATION

Airports: 56 (2004 est.)
Airports - with paved runways:
total: 11
over 3,047 m: 1
2,438 to 3,047 m: 1
1,524 to 2,437 m: 8
914 to 1,523 m: 1 (2005 est.)
Airports - with unpaved runways:
total: 45
1,524 to 2,437 m: 7
914 to 1,523 m: 15
under 914 m: 23 (2005 est.)
Pipelines: gas 210 km; oil 1,385 km (2004)
Railways:
total: 814 km
standard gauge: 814 km 1.435-m gauge (2004)
Roadways:
total: 32,333 km
paved: 6,247 km
unpaved: 26,086 km (2003)
Waterways: 1,600 km (310 km on Ogooue River) (2003)
Ports and terminals: Gamba, Libreville, Lucinda, Owendo, Port-Gentil

MILITARY

Military branches: Army, Navy, Air Force, National Gendarmerie, National Police
Military service age and obligation: 18 years of age for compulsory and voluntary military service (2001)
Manpower available for military service: *males age 18-49:* 276,310 (2005 est.)
Manpower fit for military service: *males age 18-49:* 156,632 (2005 est.)
Manpower reaching military service age annually: *males:* 15,150 (2005 est.)
Military expenditures - dollar figure: $184.8 million (2004)
Military expenditures - percent of GDP: 2% (2004)

TRANSNATIONAL ISSUES

Disputes - international: UN presses Equatorial Guinea and Gabon to resolve the sovereignty dispute over Gabon-occupied Mbane Island and to establish a maritime boundary in hydrocarbon-rich Corisco Bay; only a few hundred out of the 20,000 Republic of the Congo refugees who fled militia fighting in 2000 remain in Gabon

GAMBIA, THE

INTRODUCTION

Background: The Gambia gained its independence from the UK in 1965; it formed a short-lived federation of Senegambia with Senegal between 1982 and 1989. In 1991 the two nations signed a friendship and cooperation treaty. A military coup in 1994 overthrew the president and banned political activity, but a 1996 constitution and presidential elections, followed by parliamentary balloting in 1997, completed a nominal return to civilian rule. The country undertook another round of presidential and legislative elections in late 2001 and early 2002. Yahya A. J. J. JAMMEH, the leader of the coup, has been elected president in all subsequent elections.

GEOGRAPHY

Location: Western Africa, bordering the North Atlantic Ocean and Senegal
Geographic coordinates: 13 28 N, 16 34 W
Map references: Africa
Area:
total: 11,300 sq km
land: 10,000 sq km
water: 1,300 sq km
Area - comparative: slightly less than twice the size of Delaware
Land boundaries:
total: 740 km
border countries: Senegal 740 km
Coastline: 80 km

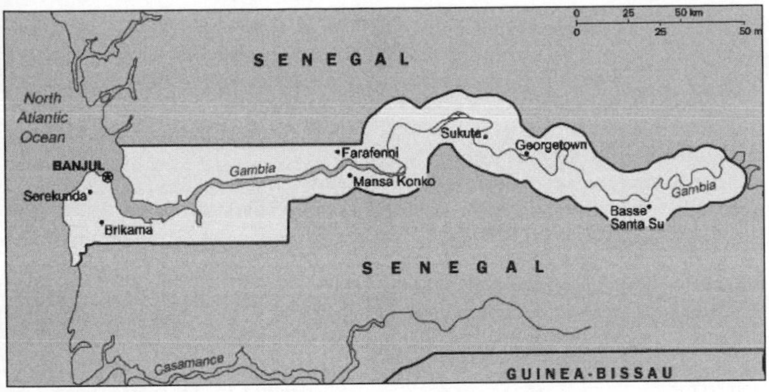

Maritime claims:
territorial sea: 12 nm
contiguous zone: 18 nm
continental shelf: not specified
exclusive fishing zone: 200 nm
Climate: tropical; hot, rainy season (June to November); cooler, dry season (November to May)
Terrain: flood plain of the Gambia River flanked by some low hills
Elevation extremes:
lowest point: Atlantic Ocean 0 m
highest point: unnamed location 53 m
Natural resources: fish, titanium (rutile and ilmenite), tin, zircon, silica sand, clay, petroleum
Land use:
arable land: 25%
permanent crops: 0.5%
other: 74.5% (2001)
Irrigated land: 20 sq km (1998 est.)
Natural hazards: drought (rainfall has dropped by 30% in the last 30 years)
Environment - current issues: deforestation; desertification; water-borne diseases prevalent
Environment - international agreements:
party to: Biodiversity, Climate Change, Climate Change-Kyoto Protocol, Desertification, Endangered Species, Hazardous Wastes, Law of the Sea, Ozone Layer Protection, Ship Pollution, Wetlands
signed, but not ratified: none of the selected agreements
Geography - note: almost an enclave of Senegal; smallest country on the continent of Africa

PEOPLE

Population: 1,593,256 (July 2005 est.)
Age structure:
0-14 years: 44.5% (male 356,079/female 352,894)
15-64 years: 52.8% (male 416,809/female 424,429)
65 years and over: 2.7% (male 22,111/female 20,934) (2005 est.)
Median age:
total: 17.59 years
male: 17.45 years
female: 17.74 years (2005 est.)
Population growth rate: 2.93% (2005 est.)
Birth rate: 39.86 births/1,000 population (2005 est.)
Death rate: 11.81 deaths/1,000 population (2005 est.)
Net migration rate: 1.27 migrant(s)/1,000 population (2005 est.)
Sex ratio:
at birth: 1.03 male(s)/female
under 15 years: 1.01 male(s)/female
15-64 years: 0.98 male(s)/female
65 years and over: 1.06 male(s)/female
total population: 1 male(s)/female (2005 est.)
Infant mortality rate:
total: 72.02 deaths/1,000 live births
male: 78.6 deaths/1,000 live births
female: 65.24 deaths/1,000 live births (2005 est.)
Life expectancy at birth:
total population: 53.75 years
male: 51.91 years
female: 55.64 years (2005 est.)
Total fertility rate: 5.38 children born/woman (2005 est.)
HIV/AIDS - adult prevalence rate: 1.2% (2003 est.)
HIV/AIDS - people living with HIV/AIDS: 6,800 (2003 est.)
HIV/AIDS - deaths: 600 (2003 est.)
Major infectious diseases:
degree of risk: very high
food or waterborne diseases: bacterial and protozoal diarrhea, hepatitis A, and typhoid fever
vectorborne diseases: dengue fever, malaria, Crimean-Congo hemorrhagic fever, yellow fever are high risks in some locations
water contact disease: schistosomiasis
respiratory disease: meningococcal meningitis (2004)
Nationality:
noun: Gambian(s)
adjective: Gambian
Ethnic groups: African 99% (Mandinka 42%, Fula 18%, Wolof 16%, Jola 10%, Serahuli 9%, other 4%), non-African 1%
Religions: Muslim 90%, Christian 9%, indigenous beliefs 1%
Languages: English (official), Mandinka, Wolof, Fula, other indigenous vernaculars
Literacy:
definition: age 15 and over can read and write
total population: 40.1%
male: 47.8%
female: 32.8% (2003 est.)

GOVERNMENT

Country name:
conventional long form: Republic of The Gambia
conventional short form: The Gambia
Government type: republic
Capital: Banjul
Administrative divisions: 5 divisions and 1 city*; Banjul*, Central River, Lower River, North Bank, Upper River, Western
Independence: 18 February 1965 (from UK)
National holiday: Independence Day, 18 February (1965)
Constitution: 24 April 1970; suspended July 1994; rewritten and approved by national referendum 8 August 1996; reestablished January 1997
Legal system: based on a composite of English common law, Koranic law, and customary law; accepts compulsory ICJ jurisdiction, with reservations
Suffrage: 18 years of age, universal
Executive branch:
chief of state: President Yahya A. J. J. JAMMEH (since 18 October 1996; note - from 1994 to 1996 he was Chairman of the Junta); Vice President Isatou Njie SAIDY (since 20 March 1997); note - the president is both the chief of state and head of government
head of government: President Yahya A. J. J. JAMMEH (since 18 October 1996; note - from 1994 to 1996 was he Chairman of the Junta); Vice President Isatou Njie SAIDY (since 20 March 1997); note - the president is both the chief of state and head of government
cabinet: Cabinet appointed by the president
elections: president elected by popular vote for a five-year term; election last held 18 October 2001 (next to be held October 2006)
election results: Yahya A. J. J. JAMMEH reelected president; percent of vote - Yahya A. J. J. JAMMEH 52.9%, Ousainou DARBOE 32.7%
Legislative branch: unicameral National Assembly (53 seats; 48 elected by popular vote, five appointed by the president; members serve five-year terms)
elections: last held 17 January 2002 (next to be held February 2007)
election results: percent of vote by party - NA%; seats by party - APRC 45, PDOIS 2, NRP 1

Judicial branch: Supreme Court
Political parties and leaders: Alliance for Patriotic Reorientation and Construction or APRC - the ruling party [Yahya A. J. J. JAMMEH]; Gambian People's Party-Progressive People's Party-United Democratic Party or GPP-PPP-UDP Coalition [Ousainou DARBOE]; National Convention Party or NCP [Sheriff DIBBA]; National Reconciliation Party or NRP [Hamat N. K. BAH]; People's Democratic Organization for Independence and Socialism or PDOIS [Sidia JATTA]
note: in August 2001, an independent electoral commission allowed the reregistration of the GPP, NCP, and PPP, three parties banned since 1996
Political pressure groups and leaders: NA
International organization participation: ACP, AfDB, AU, C, ECOWAS, FAO, G-77, IBRD, ICAO, ICCt, ICFTU, ICRM, IDA, IDB, IFAD, IFC, IFRCS, ILO, IMF, IMO, Interpol, IOC, IOM, ITU, MIGA, NAM, OIC, ONUB, OPCW, UN, UNAMSIL, UNCTAD, UNESCO, UNIDO, UNMEE, UNMIL, UNOCI, UPU, WCL, WCO, WFTU, WHO, WIPO, WMO, WToO, WTO
Diplomatic representation in the US:
chief of mission: Ambassador (vacant)
chancery: Suite 905, 1156 15th Street NW, Washington, DC 20005
telephone: [1] (202) 785-1379
FAX: [1] (202) 785-1430
Diplomatic representation from the US:
chief of mission: Ambassador Joseph D. STAFFORD, III
embassy: Kairaba Avenue, Fajara, Banjul
mailing address: P. M. B. No. 19, Banjul
telephone: [220] 392856, 392858, 391971
FAX: [220] 392475
Flag description: three equal horizontal bands of red (top), blue with white edges, and green

ECONOMY

Economy - overview: The Gambia has no significant mineral or natural resource deposits and has a limited agricultural base. About 75% of the population depends on crops and livestock for its livelihood. Small-scale manufacturing activity features the processing of peanuts, fish, and hides. Reexport trade normally constitutes a major segment of economic activity, but a 1999 government-imposed preshipment inspection plan, and instability of the Gambian dalasi (currency) have drawn some of the reexport trade away from The Gambia. The government's 1998 seizure of the private peanut firm Alimenta eliminated the largest purchaser of Gambian groundnuts. Despite an announced program to begin privatizing key parastatals, no plans have been made public that would indicate that the government intends to follow through on its promises. Unemployment and underemployment rates remain extremely high; short-run economic progress depends on sustained bilateral and multilateral aid, on responsible government economic management, on continued technical assistance from the IMF and bilateral donors, and on expected growth in the construction sector.
GDP (purchasing power parity): $3.094 billion (2005 est.)
GDP (official exchange rate): $443.7 million (2005 est.)
GDP - real growth rate: 7.1% (2005 est.)
GDP - per capita: purchasing power parity - $1,900 (2005 est.)
GDP - composition by sector:
agriculture: 35.5%
industry: 12.2%
services: 52.3% (2005 est.)
Labor force: 400,000 (1996)
Labor force - by occupation: agriculture 75%, industry, commerce, and services 19%, government 6%
Unemployment rate: NA
Population below poverty line: NA
Household income or consumption by percentage share:
lowest 10%: NA
highest 10%: NA
Inflation rate (consumer prices): 8.8% (2005 est.)
Investment (gross fixed): 25.8% of GDP (2005 est.)
Budget:
revenues: $46.63 million
expenditures: $62.66 million, including capital expenditures of $4.1 million (2005 est.)
Agriculture - products: rice, millet, sorghum, peanuts, corn, sesame, cassava (tapioca), palm kernels; cattle, sheep, goats
Industries: processing peanuts, fish, and hides; tourism; beverages; agricultural machinery assembly, woodworking, metalworking; clothing
Industrial production growth rate: NA
Electricity - production: 140 million kWh (2003)
Electricity - production by source:
fossil fuel: 100%
hydro: 0%
nuclear: 0%
other: 0% (2001)
Electricity - consumption: 130.2 million kWh (2003)
Electricity - exports: 0 kWh (2003)
Electricity - imports: 0 kWh (2003)
Oil - production: 0 bbl/day (2003 est.)
Oil - consumption: 2,000 bbl/day (2003 est.)
Oil - exports: NA (2001)
Oil - imports: NA (2001)
Current account balance: $-20.54 million (2005 est.)
Exports: $140.3 million f.o.b. (2005 est.)
Exports - partners: India 23.7%, UK 15.2%, France 14.2%, Germany 9.6%, Italy 8.3%, Thailand 5.9%, Malaysia 4.1% (2004)
Imports: $197 million f.o.b. (2005 est.)
Imports - partners: China 23.7%, Senegal 11.6%, Brazil 5.9%, UK 5.5%, Netherlands 4.5%, US 4.4% (2004)
Reserves of foreign exchange and gold: $81.55 million (2005 est.)
Debt - external: $628.8 million (2003 est.)
Economic aid - recipient: $59.8 million (2003)
Currency (code): dalasi (GMD)
Currency code: GMD
Exchange rates: dalasi per US dollar - NA (2005), 32.3 (2004), 27.306 (2004), 27.306 (2003), 19.918 (2002), 15.687 (2001)
Fiscal year: calendar year

COMMUNICATIONS

Telephones - main lines in use: 38,400 (2002)
Telephones - mobile cellular: 100,000 (2002)
Telephone system:
general assessment: adequate; a packet switched data network is available
domestic: adequate network of microwave radio relay and open-wire
international: country code - 220; microwave radio relay links to Senegal and Guinea-Bissau; satellite earth station - 1 Intelsat (Atlantic Ocean)
Radio broadcast stations: AM 3, FM 2, shortwave 0 (2001)
Radios: 196,000 (1997)
Television broadcast stations: 1 (government-owned) (1997)
Televisions: 5,000 (2000)
Internet country code: .gm
Internet hosts: 568 (2004)
Internet Service Providers (ISPs): 2 (2001)
Internet users: 25,000 (2002)

TRANSPORTATION

Airports: 1 (2004 est.)
Airports - with paved runways:
over 3,047 m: 1 (2005 est.)
Roadways:
total: 3,742 km
paved: 723 km
unpaved: 3,019 km (2003)
Waterways: 390 km (on River Gambia; small ocean-going vessels can reach 190 km) (2004)

Merchant marine:
total: 4 ships (1,000 GRT or over) 30,976 GRT/10,978 DWT
by type: passenger/cargo 3, petroleum tanker 1
foreign-owned: 1 (Switzerland 1) (2005)
Ports and terminals: Banjul

MILITARY

Military branches: Gambian National Army (GNA), Gambian Navy (GN), Presidential Guard, National Guard
Military service age and obligation: 18 years of age for voluntary military service; no conscription (2001)
Manpower available for military service: *males age 18-49:* 309,279 (2005 est.)
Manpower fit for military service: *males age 18-49:* 188,117 (2005 est.)
Military expenditures - dollar figure: $1 million (2004)
Military expenditures - percent of GDP: 0.3% (2004)

TRANSNATIONAL ISSUES

Disputes - international: attempts to stem refugees, cross-border raids, arms smuggling, and other illegal activities by separatists from southern Senegal's Casamance region as well as from conflicts in other west African states

GAZA STRIP

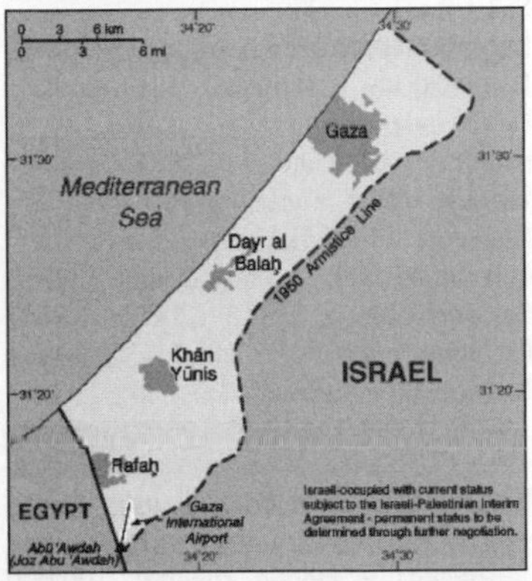

INTRODUCTION

Background: The Israel-PLO Declaration of Principles on Interim Self-Government Arrangements (the DOP), signed in Washington on 13 September 1993, provided for a transitional period not exceeding five years of Palestinian interim self-government in the Gaza Strip and the West Bank. Under the DOP, Israel agreed to transfer certain powers and responsibilities to the Palestinian Authority (PA) as part of the interim self-governing arrangements in the West Bank and Gaza Strip. A transfer of powers and responsibilities for the Gaza Strip and Jericho took place pursuant to the Israel-PLO 4 May 1994 Cairo Agreement on the Gaza Strip and the Jericho Area and in additional areas of the West Bank pursuant to the Israel-PLO 28 September 1995 Interim Agreement, the Israel-PLO 15 January 1997 Protocol Concerning Redeployment in Hebron, the Israel-PLO 23 October 1998 Wye River Memorandum, and the 4 September 1999 Sharm el-Sheikh Agreement. The DOP provides that Israel will retain responsibility during the transitional period for external and internal security and for public order of settlements and Israeli citizens. Direct negotiations to determine the permanent status of Gaza and West Bank began in September 1999 after a three-year hiatus, but were derailed by a second intifadah that broke out in September 2000. In June 2003 the Quartet (US, European Union, United Nations, and Russia) presented a roadmap to a final settlement of the conflict by 2005 based on reciprocal steps by the two parties leading to two states, Israel and a democratic Palestine. The proposed date for a permanent status agreement has been postponed indefinitely due to violence and accusations that both sides have not followed through on their commitments. Longtime Palestinian leader Yasir ARAFAT died in November 2004 and Mahmud ABBAS was elected PA President in January 2005, bringing hope of a turning point in the conflict. In February 2005 Israel and the PA agreed to the Sharm el-Sheikh Commitments, focused on security issues, in an effort to move the peace process forward. Progress has been slow because of different interpretations of the verbal agreement by the two sides. Israel in September 2005 withdrew all Israeli settlers and soldiers and dismantled its military facilities in the Gaza Strip. Nonetheless, Israel controls maritime, airspace, and most access to the Gaza Strip. An agreement signed by the PA and Israel in November 2005 authorized the reopening of the Rafah border crossing between the Gaza Strip and Egypt under joint PA and Egyptian control, with monitoring provided by the European Union. The future political status of the Gaza Strip has yet to be determined.

GEOGRAPHY

Location: Middle East, bordering the Mediterranean Sea, between Egypt and Israel
Geographic coordinates: 31 25 N, 34 20 E
Map references: Middle East
Area:
total: 360 sq km
land: 360 sq km
water: 0 sq km
Area - comparative: slightly more than twice the size of Washington, DC
Land boundaries:
total: 62 km
border countries: Egypt 11 km, Israel 51 km
Coastline: 40 km
Maritime claims: Israeli-occupied with current status subject to the Israeli-Palestinian Interim Agreement - permanent status to be determined through further negotiation
Climate: temperate, mild winters, dry and warm to hot summers
Terrain: flat to rolling, sand- and dune-covered coastal plain
Elevation extremes:
lowest point: Mediterranean Sea 0 m
highest point: Abu 'Awdah (Joz Abu 'Auda) 105 m
Natural resources: arable land, natural gas
Land use:
arable land: 28.95%
permanent crops: 21.05%
other: 50% (2001)
Irrigated land: 120 sq km (1998 est.)
Natural hazards: droughts
Environment - current issues: desertification; salination of fresh water; sewage treatment; water-borne disease; soil degradation; depletion and contamination of underground water resources
Geography - note: there are 25 Israeli settlements and civilian land use sites in the Gaza Strip (February 2002 est.)

PEOPLE

Population: 1,376,289
note: in addition, there are more than 5,000 Israeli settlers in the Gaza Strip (July 2005 est.)
Age structure:
0-14 years: 48.5% (male 342,186/female 325,899)
15-64 years: 48.8% (male 342,927/female 329,354)
65 years and over: 2.6% (male 15,036/

female 20,887) (2005 est.)
Median age:
total: 15.65 years
male: 15.5 years
female: 15.81 years (2005 est.)
Population growth rate: 3.77% (2005 est.)
Birth rate: 40.03 births/1,000 population (2005 est.)
Death rate: 3.87 deaths/1,000 population (2005 est.)
Net migration rate: 1.54 migrant(s)/1,000 population (2005 est.)
Sex ratio:
at birth: 1.05 male(s)/female
under 15 years: 1.05 male(s)/female
15-64 years: 1.04 male(s)/female
65 years and over: 0.72 male(s)/female
total population: 1.04 male(s)/female (2005 est.)
Infant mortality rate:
total: 22.93 deaths/1,000 live births
male: 24.05 deaths/1,000 live births
female: 21.76 deaths/1,000 live births (2005 est.)
Life expectancy at birth:
total population: 71.79 years
male: 70.5 years
female: 73.15 years (2005 est.)
Total fertility rate: 5.91 children born/woman (2005 est.)
HIV/AIDS - adult prevalence rate: NA
HIV/AIDS - people living with HIV/AIDS: NA
HIV/AIDS - deaths: NA
Nationality:
noun: NA
adjective: NA
Ethnic groups: Palestinian Arab and other 99.4%, Jewish 0.6%
Religions: Muslim (predominantly Sunni) 98.7%, Christian 0.7%, Jewish 0.6%
Languages: Arabic, Hebrew (spoken by Israeli settlers and many Palestinians), English (widely understood)
Literacy:
definition: age 15 and over can read and write
total population: 91.9%
male: 96.3%
female: 87.4% (2003 est.)

GOVERNMENT

Country name:
conventional long form: none
conventional short form: Gaza Strip
local long form: none
local short form: Qita Ghazzah

ECONOMY

Economy - overview: High population density, limited land access, and strict internal and external controls have kept economic conditions in the Gaza Strip - the smaller of the two areas under the Palestinian Authority - even more degraded than in the West Bank. The beginning of the second intifadah in September 2000 sparked an economic downturn, largely the result of Israeli closure policies; these policies, which were imposed in response to security interests in Israel, disrupted labor and commodity relationships with the Gaza Strip. In 2001, and even more severely in 2003, Israeli military measures in Palestinian Authority areas resulted in the destruction of much capital plant, the disruption of administrative structure, and widespread business closures. Including the West Bank, the UN estimates that more than 100,000 Palestinians out of the 125,000 who used to work in Israel or in joint industrial zones have lost their jobs. Unemployment has continued at half the labor force. Israeli withdrawal from the Gaza Strip in September 2005 offers some medium-term opportunities for economic growth, especially given the removal of restrictions on internal movement. In addition, recent agreements and continuing negotiations on the administration of Gaza's border crossings increase the prospects for trade.
GDP (purchasing power parity): $768 million (2003 est.)
GDP (official exchange rate): NA
GDP - real growth rate: 4.5% (2003 est.)
GDP - per capita: purchasing power parity - $600 (2003 est.)
GDP - composition by sector:
agriculture: 9%
industry: 28%
services: 63% (includes West Bank) (2002 est.)
Labor force: 278,000 (April-June 2005)
Labor force - by occupation: agriculture 11.9%, industry 18%, services 70.1% (April-June 2005)
Unemployment rate: 31% (includes West Bank) (January-September 2005 avg.)
Population below poverty line: 81% (2004 est.)
Household income or consumption by percentage share:
lowest 10%: NA
highest 10%: NA
Inflation rate (consumer prices): 3% (includes West Bank) (2004)
Budget:
revenues: $964 million
expenditures: $1.34 billion, including capital expenditures of NA; note - these budget data include West Bank (2004)
Agriculture - products: olives, citrus, vegetables; beef, dairy products
Industries: generally small family businesses that produce textiles, soap, olive-wood carvings, and mother-of-pearl souvenirs; the Israelis have established some small-scale modern industries in an industrial center, but operations ceased prior to Israel's evacuation of Gaza Strip settlements
Industrial production growth rate: NA
Electricity - production: NA kWh; note - electricity supplied by the Gaza Strip power plant and by an Israeli utility
Electricity - consumption: NA kWh
Electricity - exports: 0 kWh (2001)
Electricity - imports: NA kWh; note - some electricity supplied by an Israeli utility (2005)
Exports: $270 million f.o.b., includes West Bank (2003)
Exports - partners: Israel, Egypt, West Bank (2004)
Imports: $1.952 billion c.i.f., includes West Bank (2003)
Imports - partners: Israel, Egypt, West Bank (2004)
Debt - external: $0 (includes West Bank) (2002)
Economic aid - recipient: $2 billion (includes West Bank) (2004 est.)
Currency (code): new Israeli shekel (ILS)
Currency code: ILS
Exchange rates: new Israeli shekels per US dollar - 4.35 (2005), 4.482 (2004), 4.5541 (2003), 4.7378 (2002), 4.2057 (2001)
Fiscal year: calendar year

COMMUNICATIONS

Telephones - main lines in use: 95,729 (total for Gaza Strip and West Bank) (1997)
Telephones - mobile cellular: 320,000 (cellular subscribers in both Gaza Strip and West Bank) (2002)
Telephone system:
general assessment: NA
domestic: Israeli company BEZEK and the Palestinian company PALTEL are responsible for landline services in the Gaza Strip; the Palestinian JAWAL company provides cellular services
international: NA
Radio broadcast stations: AM 0, FM 8, shortwave 0 (2005)
Radios: NA; note - most Palestinian households have radios (1999)
Television broadcast stations: NA (2005)
Televisions: NA; note - most Palestinian households have televisions (1997)
Internet country code: .ps
Internet Service Providers (ISPs): 3 (1999)
Internet users: 60,000 (includes West Bank) (2001)

TRANSPORTATION

Airports: 2 (2001)
note: includes Gaza International Airport (GIA), inaugurated on 24 November 1998 as part of agreements stipulated in the September 1995 Oslo II Accord and

the 23 October 1998 Wye River Memorandum; GIA has been largely closed since October 2000 by Israeli orders and its runway was destroyed by the Israeli Defense Forces in December 2001 (2004 est.)
Airports - with paved runways:
total: 1
over 3,047 m: 1 (2005 est.)
Airports - with unpaved runways:
total: 1
under 914 m: 1 (2005 est.)
Heliports: 1 (2005 est.)
Roadways:
note: see entry for West Bank
Ports and terminals: Gaza

MILITARY

Military branches: in accordance with the peace agreement, the Palestinian Authority is not permitted conventional military forces; there are, however, public security forces (2002)
Military expenditures - dollar figure: NA
Military expenditures - percent of GDP: NA

TRANSNATIONAL ISSUES

Disputes - international: West Bank and Gaza Strip are Israeli-occupied with current status subject to the Israeli-Palestinian Interim Agreement - permanent status to be determined through further negotiation; Israel announced its intention to pull out settlers and withdraw from the Gaza Strip in 2005
Refugees and internally displaced persons:
refugees (country of origin): 922,674 (Palestinian Refugees (UNRWA)) (2004)

GEORGIA

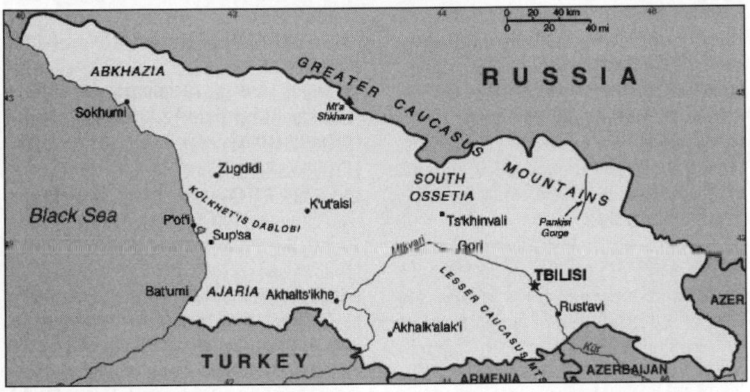

INTRODUCTION

Background: The region of present-day Georgia contained the ancient kingdoms of Colchis and Kartli-Iberia. The area came under Roman influence in the first centuries AD and Christianity became the state religion in the 330s. Domination by Persians, Arabs, and Turks was followed by a Georgian golden age (11th to the 13th centuries) that was cut short by the Mongol invasion of 1236. Subsequently, the Ottoman and Persian empires competed for influence in the region. Georgia was absorbed into the Russian Empire in the 19th century. Independent for three years (1918-1921) following the Russian revolution, it was forcibly incorporated into the USSR until the Soviet Union dissolved in 1991. Despite myriad problems, some progress on market reforms and democratization has been made since then. An attempt by the government to manipulate legislative elections in November 2003 touched off widespread protests that led to the resignation of Eduard SHEVARDNADZE, president since 1995. New elections in early 2004 swept Mikheil SAAKASHVILI into power along with his National Movement Party.

GEOGRAPHY

Location: Southwestern Asia, bordering the Black Sea, between Turkey and Russia
Geographic coordinates: 42 00 N, 43 30 E
Map references: Asia
Area:
total: 69,700 sq km
land: 69,700 sq km
water: 0 sq km
Area - comparative: slightly smaller than South Carolina
Land boundaries:
total: 1,461 km
border countries: Armenia 164 km, Azerbaijan 322 km, Russia 723 km, Turkey 252 km
Coastline: 310 km
Maritime claims: NA
Climate: warm and pleasant; Mediterranean-like on Black Sea coast
Terrain: largely mountainous with Great Caucasus Mountains in the north and Lesser Caucasus Mountains in the south; Kolkhet'is Dablobi (Kolkhida Lowland) opens to the Black Sea in the west; Mtkvari River Basin in the east; good soils in river valley flood plains, foothills of Kolkhida Lowland
Elevation extremes:
lowest point: Black Sea 0 m
highest point: Mt'a Shkhara 5,201 m
Natural resources: forests, hydropower, manganese deposits, iron ore, copper, minor coal and oil deposits; coastal climate and soils allow for important tea and citrus growth
Land use:
arable land: 11.44%
permanent crops: 3.86%
other: 84.7% (2001)
Irrigated land: 4,700 sq km (1998 est.)
Natural hazards: earthquakes
Environment - current issues: air pollution, particularly in Rust'avi; heavy pollution of Mtkvari River and the Black Sea; inadequate supplies of potable water; soil pollution from toxic chemicals
Environment - international agreements:
party to: Air Pollution, Biodiversity, Climate Change, Climate Change-Kyoto Protocol, Desertification, Endangered Species, Hazardous Wastes, Law of the Sea, Ozone Layer Protection, Ship Pollution, Wetlands
signed, but not ratified: none of the selected agreements
Geography - note: strategically located east of the Black Sea; Georgia controls much of the Caucasus Mountains and the routes through them

PEOPLE

Population: 4,677,401 (July 2005 est.)
Age structure:
0-14 years: 18% (male 444,779/female 398,162)
15-64 years: 65.9% (male 1,480,557/female 1,603,743)
65 years and over: 16% (male 300,859/female 449,301) (2005 est.)
Median age:
total: 37.36 years
male: 34.93 years
female: 39.7 years (2005 est.)
Population growth rate: -0.35% (2005 est.)

Birth rate: 10.25 births/1,000 population (2005 est.)
Death rate: 9.09 deaths/1,000 population (2005 est.)
Net migration rate: -4.62 migrant(s)/1,000 population (2005 est.)
Sex ratio:
at birth: 1.16 male(s)/female
under 15 years: 1.12 male(s)/female
15-64 years: 0.92 male(s)/female
65 years and over: 0.67 male(s)/female
total population: 0.91 male(s)/female (2005 est.)
Infant mortality rate:
total: 18.59 deaths/1,000 live births
male: 20.71 deaths/1,000 live births
female: 16.13 deaths/1,000 live births (2005 est.)
Life expectancy at birth:
total population: 75.88 years
male: 72.59 years
female: 79.67 years (2005 est.)
Total fertility rate: 1.41 children born/woman (2005 est.)
HIV/AIDS - adult prevalence rate: less than 0.1% (2001 est.)
HIV/AIDS - people living with HIV/AIDS: 3,000 (2003 est.)
HIV/AIDS - deaths: less than 200 (2003 est.)
Nationality:
noun: Georgian(s)
adjective: Georgian
Ethnic groups: Georgian 83.8%, Azeri 6.5%, Armenian 5.7%, Russian 1.5%, other 2.5% (2002 census)
Religions: Orthodox Christian 83.9%, Armenian-Gregorian 3.9%, Catholic 0.8%, Muslim 9.9%, other 0.8%, none 0.7% (2002 census)
Languages: Georgian 71% (official), Russian 9%, Armenian 7%, Azeri 6%, other 7%
note: Abkhaz is the official language in Abkhazia
Literacy:
definition: age 15 and over can read and write
total population: 99%
male: 100%
female: 98% (1999 est.)

GOVERNMENT

Country name:
conventional long form: none
conventional short form: Georgia
local long form: none
local short form: Sak'art'velo
former: Georgian Soviet Socialist Republic
Government type: republic
Capital: T'bilisi
Administrative divisions: 9 regions (mkharebi, singular - mkhare), 9 cities (k'alak'ebi, singular - k'alak'i), and 2 autonomous republics (avtomnoy respubliki, singular - avtom respublika)
regions: Guria, Imereti, Kakheti, Kvemo Kartli, Mtskheta-Mtianeti, Racha-Lechkhumi and Kvemo Svaneti, Samegrelo and Zemo Svaneti, Samtskhe-Javakheti, Shida Kartli
cities: Chiat'ura, Gori, K'ut'aisi, P'ot'i, Rust'avi, T'bilisi, Tqibuli, Tsqaltubo, Zugdidi
autonomous republics: Abkhazia or p'k-hazet'is Avtonomiuri Respublika (Sokhumi), Ajaria or Acharis Avtonomiuri Respublika (Bat'umi)
note: the administrative centers of the 2 autonomous republics are shown in parentheses
Independence: 9 April 1991 (from Soviet Union)
National holiday: Independence Day, 26 May (1918); note - 26 May 1918 is the date of independence from Soviet Russia, 9 April 1991 is the date of independence from the Soviet Union
Constitution: adopted 24 August 1995
Legal system: based on civil law system
Suffrage: 18 years of age, universal
Executive branch:
chief of state: President Mikheil SAAKASHVILI (since 25 January 2004); note - the president is both the chief of state and head of government for the power ministries: state security (includes interior) and defense
head of government: President Mikheil SAAKASHVILI (since 25 January 2004); Prime Minister Zurab NOGHAIDELI (since 17 February 2005); note - the president is the chief of state and head of government for the power ministries: state security (includes interior) and defense; the prime minister is head of the remaining ministries of government
cabinet: Cabinet of Ministers
elections: president elected by popular vote for a five-year term; election last held 4 January 2004 (next to be held NA 2009)
election results: Mikheil SAAKASHVILI elected president; percent of vote - Mikheil SAAKASHVILI 96.3%, Temur SHASHIASHVILI 1.9%
Legislative branch: unicameral Supreme Council (commonly referred to as Parliament) or Umaghiesi Sabcho (235 seats - 150 elected by party lists); members are elected by popular vote to serve four-year terms)
elections: last held 28 March 2004 (next to be held spring 2008)
election results: percent of vote by party - National Movement-Democrats 67.6%, Rightist Opposition 7.6%, all other parties received less than 7% each; seats by party - National Movement-Democrats 135, Rightist Opposition 15
Judicial branch: Supreme Court (judges elected by the Supreme Council on the president's recommendation); Constitutional Court; first and second instance courts
Political parties and leaders: Burjanadze-Democrats [Nino BURJANADZE]; Georgian People's Front [Nodar NATADZE]; Georgian United Communist Party or UCPG [Panteleimon GIORGADZE]; Greens [Giorgi GACHECHILADZE]; Industry Will Save Georgia (Industrialists) or IWSG [Georgi TOPADZE]; Labor Party [Shalva NATELASHVILI]; National Democratic Party or NDP [Bachuki KARDAVA]; National Movement Democratic Front [Mikheil SAAKASHVILI] bloc composed of National Movement and Burjanadze-Democrats; National Movement [Mikheil SAAKASHVILI]; New Right [David GAMKRELIDZE]; Republican Party [David BERDZENISHVILI]; Rightist Opposition [David GAMKRELIDZE] bloc composed of Industrialists and New Right Party; Socialist Party or SPG [Irakli MINDELI]; Traditionalists [Akaki ASATIANI]; Union of National Forces-Conservatives [Koba DAVITASHVILI and Zviad DZIDZIGURI]
Political pressure groups and leaders: Georgian independent deputies from Abkhaz government in exile; separatists in the breakaway regions of Abkhazia and South Ossetia; supporters of the late ousted President Zviad GAMSAKHURDYA
International organization participation: ACCT (observer), BSEC, CE, CIS, EAPC, EBRD, FAO, GUAM, IAEA, IBRD, ICAO, ICC, ICCt, ICFTU, ICRM, IDA, IFAD, IFC, IFRCS, ILO, IMF, IMO, Interpol, IOC, IOM, ITU, MIGA, OAS (observer), OPCW, OSCE, PFP, UN, UNCTAD, UNESCO, UNIDO, UPU, WCO, WHO, WIPO, WMO, WToO, WTO
Diplomatic representation in the US:
chief of mission: Ambassador Levan MIKELADZE
chancery: Suite 602, 1101 15th Street NW, Washington, DC 20005
telephone: [1] (202) 387-4537
FAX: [1] (202) 393-4537
Diplomatic representation from the US:
chief of mission: Ambassador John F. TEFFT
embassy: 11 George Balanchine St., T'bilisi 0131
mailing address: 7060 Tbilisi Place, Washington, DC 20521-7060
telephone: [995] (32) 27-70-00
FAX: [995] (32) 53-23-10

Flag description: white rectangle, in its central portion a red cross connecting all four sides of the flag; in each of the four corners is a small red bolnur-katskhuri cross; the five-cross flag appears to date back to the 14th century

ECONOMY

Economy - overview: Georgia's main economic activities include the cultivation of agricultural products such as citrus fruits, tea, hazelnuts, and grapes; mining of manganese and copper; and output of a small industrial sector producing alcoholic and nonalcoholic beverages, metals, machinery, and chemicals. The country imports the bulk of its energy needs, including natural gas and oil products. Its only sizable internal energy resource is hydropower. Despite the severe damage the economy has suffered due to civil strife, Georgia, with the help of the IMF and World Bank, has made substantial economic gains since 1995, achieving positive GDP growth and curtailing inflation. Georgia had suffered from a chronic failure to collect tax revenues, however, the new government is making progress in reforming the tax code, enforcing taxes, and cracking down on corruption. In addition, the privatisation process has taken off, permitting the government to boost expenditures on infrastructure, defence and poverty reduction. Smuggling is a perennial drain on the economy. Georgia also suffers from energy shortages; it privatized the T'bilisi electricity distribution network in 1998, but payment collection rates remain low, both in T'bilisi and throughout the regions. The country is pinning its hopes for long-term growth on its role as a transit state for pipelines and trade. The construction on the Baku-T'bilisi-Ceyhan oil pipeline and the Baku-T'bilisi-Erzerum gas pipeline have brought much-needed investment and job opportunities. Nevertheless, high energy prices in 2006 will compound the pressure on the country's inefficient energy sector. Restructuring the sector and finding energy supply alternatives to Russia remains a major challenge.
GDP (purchasing power parity): $16.13 billion (2005 est.)
GDP (official exchange rate): $5.135 billion (2005 est.)
GDP - real growth rate: 10% (2005 est.)
GDP - per capita: purchasing power parity - $3,400 (2005 est.)
GDP - composition by sector:
agriculture: 16%
industry: 26.8%
services: 57.2% (2005 est.)
Labor force: 2.1 million (2001 est.)
Labor force - by occupation: agriculture 40%, industry 20%, services 40% (1999 est.)
Unemployment rate: 17% (2001 est.)
Population below poverty line: 54% (2001 est.)
Household income or consumption by percentage share:
lowest 10%: 2.3%
highest 10%: 27.9% (1996)
Distribution of family income - Gini index: 36.9 (2001)
Inflation rate (consumer prices): 8% (2005 est.)
Investment (gross fixed): 24.6% of GDP (2005 est.)
Budget:
revenues: $872.5 million
expenditures: $1.097 billion, including capital expenditures of NA (2005 est.)
Agriculture - products: citrus, grapes, tea, hazelnuts, vegetables; livestock
Industries: steel, aircraft, machine tools, electrical appliances, mining (manganese and copper), chemicals, wood products, wine
Industrial production growth rate: 3% (2000)
Electricity - production: 8.634 billion kWh (2003)
Electricity - production by source:
fossil fuel: 19.7%
hydro: 80.3%
nuclear: 0%
other: 0% (2001)
Electricity - consumption: 8.63 billion kWh (2003)
Electricity - exports: 250 million kWh (2003)
Electricity - imports: 850 million kWh (2003)
Oil - production: 1,982 bbl/day (2003)
Oil - consumption: 13,000 bbl/day (2003 est.)
Oil - exports: NA (2001)
Oil - imports: NA (2001)
Natural gas - production: 60 million cu m (2001 est.)
Natural gas - consumption: 1.16 billion cu m (2001 est.)
Natural gas - exports: 0 cu m (2001 est.)
Natural gas - imports: 1.1 billion cu m (2001 est.)
Current account balance: $-439.3 million (2005 est.)
Exports: $1.4 billion (2005 est.)
Exports - partners: Turkey 18.3%, Turkmenistan 17.8%, Russia 16.2%, Armenia 8.4%, UK 4.9% (2004)
Imports: $2.5 billion (2005 est.)
Imports - partners: Russia 14%, Turkey 11%, UK 9.3%, Azerbaijan 8.5%, Germany 8.2%, Ukraine 7.7%, US 6% (2004)
Reserves of foreign exchange and gold: $350.1 million (2005 est.)
Debt - external: $1.9 billion (2003)
Economic aid - recipient: ODA $150 million (2000 est.)
Currency (code): lari (GEL)
Currency code: GEL
Exchange rates: lari per US dollar - 1.82 (2005), 1.9167 (2004), 2.1457 (2003), 2.1957 (2002), 2.073 (2001)
Fiscal year: calendar year

COMMUNICATIONS

Telephones - main lines in use: 650,500 (2003)
Telephones - mobile cellular: 522,300 (2003)
Telephone system:
general assessment: NA
domestic: local - T'bilisi and K'ut'aisi have cellular telephone networks; urban telephone density is about 20 per 100 people; rural telephone density is about 4 per 100 people; intercity facilities include a fiber-optic line between T'bilisi and K'ut'aisi; nationwide pager service is available
international: country code - 995; Georgia and Russia are working on a fiber-optic line between P'ot'i and Sochi (Russia); present international service is available by microwave, landline, and satellite through the Moscow switch; international electronic mail and telex service are available
Radio broadcast stations: AM 7, FM 12, shortwave 4 (1998)
Radios: 3.02 million (1997)
Television broadcast stations: 12 (plus repeaters) (1998)
Televisions: 2.57 million (1997)
Internet country code: .ge
Internet hosts: 5,160 (2004)
Internet Service Providers (ISPs): 6 (2000)
Internet users: 150,500 (2003)

TRANSPORTATION

Airports: 30 (2004 est.)
Airports - with paved runways:
total: 19
over 3,047 m: 1
2,438 to 3,047 m: 7
1,524 to 2,437 m: 5
914 to 1,523 m: 4
under 914 m: 2 (2005 est.)
Airports - with unpaved runways:
total: 6
1,524 to 2,437 m: 4
914 to 1,523 m: 1
under 914 m: 1 (2005 est.)
Heliports: 3 (2005 est.)
Pipelines: gas 1,697 km; oil 1,027 km; refined products 232 km (2004)
Railways:
total: 1,612 km (1,612 km electrified)
broad gauge: 1,575 km 1.520-m gauge (1,575 electrified)

narrow gauge: 37 km 0.912-m gauge (37 electrified) (2004)
Roadways:
total: 20,247 km
paved: 7,973 km
unpaved: 12,274 km (2003)
Merchant marine:
total: 175 ships (1,000 GRT or over) 855,908 GRT/1,288,812 DWT
by type: bulk carrier 22, cargo 133, container 3, liquefied gas 1, passenger 1, passenger/cargo 3, petroleum tanker 6, refrigerated cargo 4, roll on/roll off 1, specialized tanker 1
foreign-owned: 105 (Albania 1, Azerbaijan 2, Cyprus 2, Egypt 3, Estonia 1, Germany 1, Greece 4, Israel 1, Lebanon 3, Romania 6, Russia 8, Syria 27, Turkey 14, Ukraine 30, UAE 2)
registered in other countries: 1 (2005)
Ports and terminals: Bat'umi, P'ot'i
Transportation - note: transportation network is in poor condition resulting from ethnic conflict, criminal activities, and fuel shortages; network lacks maintenance and repair

MILITARY

Military branches: Ground Forces (includes National Guard), Air and Air Defense Forces, Maritime Defense Force, Interior Forces
Military service age and obligation: 18 to 34 years of age for compulsory and voluntary active duty military service; conscript service obligation - 18 months (2005)
Manpower available for military service: *males age 18-49:* 1,038,736 (2005 est.)
Manpower fit for military service: *males age 18-49:* 827,281 (2005 est.)
Manpower reaching military service age annually: *males:* 38,857 (2005 est.)
Military expenditures - dollar figure: $23 million (FY00)
Military expenditures - percent of GDP: 0.59% (FY00)
Military - note: a CIS peacekeeping force of Russian troops is deployed in the Abkhazia region of Georgia together with a UN military observer group; a Russian peacekeeping battalion is deployed in South Ossetia

TRANSNATIONAL ISSUES

Disputes - international: Russia and Georgia agree on delimiting 80% of their common border, leaving certain small, strategic segments and the maritime boundary unresolved; OSCE observers monitor volatile areas such as the Pankisi Gorge in the Akhmeti region and the Argun Gorge in Abkhazia; UN Observer Mission in Georgia has maintained a peacekeeping force in Georgia since 1993; Meshkheti Turks scattered throughout the former Soviet Union seek to return to Georgia; boundary with Armenia remains undemarcated; ethnic Armenian groups in Javakheti region of Georgia seek greater autonomy from the Georgian government; Azerbaijan and Georgia cannot resolve the alignment of their boundary at certain crossing areas
Refugees and internally displaced persons: *IDPs:* 260,000 (displaced from Abkhazia and South Ossetia) (2004)
Illicit drugs: limited cultivation of cannabis and opium poppy, mostly for domestic consumption; used as transshipment point for opiates via Central Asia to Western Europe and Russia

GERMANY

INTRODUCTION

Background: As Europe's largest economy and second most populous nation, Germany remains a key member of the continent's economic, political, and defense organizations. European power struggles immersed Germany in two devastating World Wars in the first half of the 20th century and left the country occupied by the victorious Allied powers of the US, UK, France, and the Soviet Union in 1945. With the advent of the Cold War, two German states were formed in 1949: the western Federal Republic of Germany (FRG) and the eastern German Democratic Republic (GDR). The democratic FRG embedded itself in key Western economic and security organizations, the EC, which became the EU, and NATO, while the Communist GDR was on the front line of the Soviet-led Warsaw Pact. The decline of the USSR and the end of the Cold War allowed for German unification in 1990. Since then, Germany has expended considerable funds to bring Eastern productivity and wages up to Western standards. In January 1999, Germany and 10 other EU countries introduced a common European exchange currency, the euro.

GEOGRAPHY

Location: Central Europe, bordering the Baltic Sea and the North Sea, between the Netherlands and Poland, south of Denmark
Geographic coordinates: 51 00 N, 9 00 E
Map references: Europe
Area:
total: 357,021 sq km
land: 349,223 sq km
water: 7,798 sq km
Area - comparative: slightly smaller than Montana
Land boundaries:
total: 3,621 km
border countries: Austria 784 km, Belgium 167 km, Czech Republic 646 km, Denmark 68 km, France 451 km, Luxembourg 138 km, Netherlands 577 km, Poland 456 km, Switzerland 334 km
Coastline: 2,389 km
Maritime claims:
territorial sea: 12 nm
exclusive economic zone: 200 nm
continental shelf: 200-m depth or to the depth of exploitation
Climate: temperate and marine; cool, cloudy, wet winters and summers; occasional warm mountain (foehn) wind
Terrain: lowlands in north, uplands in center, Bavarian Alps in south
Elevation extremes:
lowest point: Neuendorf bei Wilster -3.54 m
highest point: Zugspitze 2,963 m
Natural resources: coal, lignite, natural gas, iron ore, copper, nickel, uranium, potash, salt, construction materials, timber, arable land
Land use:
arable land: 33.85%
permanent crops: 0.59%
other: 65.56% (2001)
Irrigated land: 4,850 sq km (1998 est.)
Natural hazards: flooding
Environment - current issues: emissions from coal-burning utilities and industries contribute to air pollution; acid rain, resulting from sulfur dioxide emissions, is damaging forests; pollution in the Baltic Sea from raw sewage and industri-

al effluents from rivers in eastern Germany; hazardous waste disposal; government established a mechanism for ending the use of nuclear power over the next 15 years; government working to meet EU commitment to identify nature preservation areas in line with the EU's Flora, Fauna, and Habitat directive

Environment - international agreements:
party to: Air Pollution, Air Pollution-Nitrogen Oxides, Air Pollution-Persistent Organic Pollutants, Air Pollution-Sulfur 85, Air Pollution-Sulfur 94, Air Pollution-Volatile Organic Compounds, Antarctic-Environmental Protocol, Antarctic-Marine Living Resources, Antarctic Seals, Antarctic Treaty, Biodiversity, Climate Change, Climate Change-Kyoto Protocol, Desertification, Endangered Species, Environmental Modification, Hazardous Wastes, Law of the Sea, Marine Dumping, Ozone Layer Protection, Ship Pollution, Tropical Timber 83, Tropical Timber 94, Wetlands, Whaling
signed, but not ratified: none of the selected agreements

Geography - note: strategic location on North European Plain and along the entrance to the Baltic Sea

PEOPLE

Population: 82,431,390 (July 2005 est.)

Age structure:
0-14 years: 14.4% (male 6,078,885/female 5,766,065)
15-64 years: 66.7% (male 28,006,268/female 27,003,958)
65 years and over: 18.9% (male 6,359,776/female 9,216,438) (2005 est.)

Median age:
total: 42.16 years
male: 40.88 years
female: 43.53 years (2005 est.)

Population growth rate: 0% (2005 est.)

Birth rate: 8.33 births/1,000 population (2005 est.)

Death rate: 10.55 deaths/1,000 population (2005 est.)

Net migration rate: 2.18 migrant(s)/1,000 population (2005 est.)

Sex ratio:
at birth: 1.06 male(s)/female
under 15 years: 1.05 male(s)/female
15-64 years: 1.04 male(s)/female
65 years and over: 0.69 male(s)/female
total population: 0.96 male(s)/female (2005 est.)

Infant mortality rate:
total: 4.16 deaths/1,000 live births
male: 4.61 deaths/1,000 live births
female: 3.69 deaths/1,000 live births (2005 est.)

Life expectancy at birth:
total population: 78.65 years
male: 75.66 years
female: 81.81 years (2005 est.)

Total fertility rate: 1.39 children born/woman (2005 est.)

HIV/AIDS - adult prevalence rate: 0.1% (2001 est.)

HIV/AIDS - people living with HIV/AIDS: 43,000 (2001 est.)

HIV/AIDS - deaths: less than 1,000 (2003 est.)

Nationality:
noun: German(s)
adjective: German

Ethnic groups: German 91.5%, Turkish 2.4%, other 6.1% (made up largely of Greek, Italian, Polish, Russian, Serbo-Croatian, Spanish)

Religions: Protestant 34%, Roman Catholic 34%, Muslim 3.7%, unaffiliated or other 28.3%

Languages: German

Literacy:
definition: age 15 and over can read and write
total population: 99% (1997 est.)
male: NA%
female: NA%

GOVERNMENT

Country name:
conventional long form: Federal Republic of Germany
conventional short form: Germany
local long form: Bundesrepublik Deutschland
local short form: Deutschland
former: German Empire, German Republic, German Reich

Government type: federal republic

Capital: Berlin

Administrative divisions: 13 states (Laender, singular - Land) and 3 free states* (Freistaaten, singular - Freistaat); Baden-Wuerttemberg, Bayern*, Berlin, Brandenburg, Bremen, Hamburg, Hessen, Mecklenburg-Vorpommern, Niedersachsen, Nordrhein-Westfalen, Rheinland-Pfalz, Saarland, Sachsen*, Sachsen-Anhalt, Schleswig-Holstein, Thueringen*

Independence: 18 January 1871 (German Empire unification); divided into four zones of occupation (UK, US, USSR, and later, France) in 1945 following World War II; Federal Republic of Germany (FRG or West Germany) proclaimed 23 May 1949 and included the former UK, US, and French zones; German Democratic Republic (GDR or East Germany) proclaimed 7 October 1949 and included the former USSR zone; unification of West Germany and East Germany took place 3 October 1990; all four powers formally relinquished rights 15 March 1991

National holiday: Unity Day, 3 October (1990)

Constitution: 23 May 1949, known as Basic Law; became constitution of the united German people 3 October 1990

Legal system: civil law system with indigenous concepts; judicial review of legislative acts in the Federal Constitutional Court; has not accepted compulsory ICJ jurisdiction

Suffrage: 18 years of age, universal

Executive branch:
chief of state: President Horst KOEHLER (since 1 July 2004)
head of government: Chancellor Angela MERKEL (since 22 November 2005)
cabinet: Cabinet or Bundesminister (Federal Ministers) appointed by the president on the recommendation of the chancellor
elections: president elected for a five-year term by a Federal Convention including all members of the Federal Assembly and an equal number of delegates elected by the state parliaments; election last held 23 May 2004 (next to be held 23 May 2009); chancellor elected by an absolute majority of the Federal Assembly for a four-year term; election last held 22 November 2005 (next to be held November 2009)
election results: Horst KOEHLER elected president; received 604 votes of the Federal Convention against 589 for Gesine SCHWAN; Angela MERKEL elected chancellor; vote by Federal Assembly 397 to 202 with 12 abstentions

Legislative branch: bicameral Parliament or Parlament consists of the Federal Assembly or Bundestag (613 seats; elected by popular vote under a system combining direct and proportional representation; a party must win 5% of the national vote or three direct mandates to gain representation; members serve four-year terms) and the Federal Council or Bundesrat (69 votes; state governments are directly represented by votes; each has 3 to 6 votes depending on population and are required to vote as a block)
elections: Federal Assembly - last held 18 September 2005 (next to be held September 2009); note - there are no elections for the Bundesrat; composition is determined by the composition of the state-level governments; the composition of the Bundesrat has the potential to change any time one of the 16 states holds an election
election results: Federal Assembly - percent of vote by party - CDU/CSU 35.2%, SPD 34.3%, FDP 9.8%, Left 8.7%, Greens 8.1%; seats by party - CDU/CSU 225, SPD 222, FDP 61, Left 54, Greens 51; Federal Council - current composition - NA

Judicial branch: Federal Constitutional Court or Bundesverfassungsgericht (half the judges are elected by the Bundestag and half by the Bundesrat)

Political parties and leaders: Alliance '90/Greens [Angelika BEER and Reinhard BUETIKOFER]; Christian Democratic Union or CDU [Angela MERKEL]; Christian Social Union or CSU [Edmund STOIBER, chairman]; Free Democratic Party or FDP [Guido WESTERWELLE, chairman]; Left Party or PDS/WASG [Oskar LAFONTAINE and Gregor GYSI]; Party of Democratic Socialism or PDS [Lothar BISKY]; Social Democratic Party or SPD [Franz MUENTEFERING]

Political pressure groups and leaders: business associations, employers' organizations; expellee, refugee, trade unions, and veterans groups

International organization participation: AfDB, AsDB, Australia Group, BIS, BSEC (observer), CBSS, CDB, CE, CERN, EAPC, EBRD, EIB, EMU, ESA, EU, FAO, G- 5, G- 7, G- 8, G-10, IADB, IAEA, IBRD, ICAO, ICC, ICCt, ICFTU, ICRM, IDA, IEA, IFAD, IFC, IFRCS, IHO, ILO, IMF, IMO, Interpol, IOC, IOM, ISO, ITU, MIGA, NAM (guest), NATO, NEA, NSG, OAS (observer), OECD, OPCW, OSCE, Paris Club, PCA, UN, UNAMSIL, UNCTAD, UNESCO, UNHCR, UNIDO, UNMEE, UNMIS, UNMOVIC, UNOMIG, UPU, WADB (nonregional), WCO, WEU, WHO, WIPO, WMO, WToO, WTO, ZC

Diplomatic representation in the US:
chief of mission: Ambassador Wolfgang Friedrich ISCHINGER
chancery: 4645 Reservoir Road NW, Washington, DC 20007
telephone: [1] (202) 298-8140
FAX: [1] (202) 298-4249
consulate(s) general: Atlanta, Boston, Chicago, Houston, Los Angeles, Miami, New York, San Francisco

Diplomatic representation from the US:
chief of mission: Ambassador William R. TIMKEN, Jr.
embassy: Neustaedtische Kirchstrasse 4-5, 10117 Berlin; note - a new embassy will be built near the Brandenburg Gate in Berlin; ground was broken in October 2004 and completion is scheduled for 2008
mailing address: PSC 120, Box 1000, APO AE 09265
telephone: [49] (030) 2385 174
FAX: [49] (030) 8305-1215
consulate(s) general: Duesseldorf, Frankfurt am Main, Hamburg, Leipzig, Munich

Flag description: three equal horizontal bands of black (top), red, and gold

ECONOMY

Economy - overview: Germany's affluent and technologically powerful economy - the fifth largest in the world - has become one of the slowest growing economies in the euro zone. A quick turnaround is not in the offing in the foreseeable future. Growth in 2001-03 fell short of 1%, rising to 1.7% in 2004 before falling back to 0.8% in 2005. The modernization and integration of the eastern German economy continues to be a costly long-term process, with annual transfers from west to east amounting to roughly $70 billion. Germany's aging population, combined with high unemployment, has pushed social security outlays to a level exceeding contributions from workers. Structural rigidities in the labor market - including strict regulations on laying off workers and the setting of wages on a national basis - have made unemployment a chronic problem. Corporate restructuring and growing capital markets are setting the foundations that could allow Germany to meet the long-term challenges of European economic integration and globalization, particularly if labor market rigidities are further addressed. In the short run, however, the fall in government revenues and the rise in expenditures have raised the deficit above the EU's 3% debt limit.

GDP (purchasing power parity): $2.446 trillion (2005 est.)

GDP (official exchange rate): $2.83 trillion (2005 est.)

GDP - real growth rate: 0.8% (2005 est.)

GDP - per capita: purchasing power parity - $29,700 (2005 est.)

GDP - composition by sector:
agriculture: 1.1%
industry: 28.6%
services: 70.3% (2005 est.)

Labor force: 43.32 million (2005 est.)

Labor force - by occupation: agriculture 2.8%, industry 33.4%, services 63.8% (1999)

Unemployment rate: 11.6% (2005 est.)

Population below poverty line: NA

Household income or consumption by percentage share:
lowest 10%: 3.6%
highest 10%: 25.1% (1997)

Distribution of family income - Gini index: 28.3 (2000)

Inflation rate (consumer prices): 2% (2005 est.)

Investment (gross fixed): 17.1% of GDP (2005 est.)

Budget:
revenues: $1.249 trillion
expenditures: $1.362 trillion, including capital expenditures of NA (2005 est.)

Public debt: 68.1% of GDP (2005 est.)

Agriculture - products: potatoes, wheat, barley, sugar beets, fruit, cabbages; cattle, pigs, poultry

Industries: among the world's largest and most technologically advanced producers of iron, steel, coal, cement, chemicals, machinery, vehicles, machine tools, electronics, food and beverages; shipbuilding; textiles

Industrial production growth rate: 1.7% (2005 est.)

Electricity - production: 558.1 billion kWh (2003)

Electricity - production by source:
fossil fuel: 61.8%
hydro: 4.2%
nuclear: 29.9%
other: 4.1% (2001)

Electricity - consumption: 510.4 billion kWh (2003)

Electricity - exports: 54.1 billion kWh (2003)

Electricity - imports: 45.4 billion kWh (2003)

Oil - production: 158,700 bbl/day (2003)

Oil - consumption: 2.677 million bbl/day (2003)

Oil - exports: 12,990 bbl/day (2003)

Oil - imports: 2.135 million bbl/day (2003)

Oil - proved reserves: 395.8 million bbl (1 January 2004)

Natural gas - production: 21 billion cu m (2003)

Natural gas - consumption: 99.55 billion cu m (2003)

Natural gas - exports: 7.731 billion cu m (2003)

Natural gas - imports: 85.02 billion cu m (2003)

Natural gas - proved reserves: 293 billion cu m (1 January 2004)

Current account balance: $119.8 billion (2005 est.)

Exports: $1.016 trillion f.o.b. (2005 est.)

Exports - partners: France 10.3%, US 8.8%, UK 8.3%, Italy 7.2%, Netherlands 6.2%, Belgium 5.6%, Austria 5.4%, Spain 5% (2004)

Imports: $801 billion f.o.b. (2005 est.)

Imports - partners: France 9%, Netherlands 8.3%, US 7%, Italy 6.1%, UK 5.9%, China 5.6%, Belgium 4.9%, Austria 4.2% (2004)

Reserves of foreign exchange and gold: $97.17 billion (2004 est.)

Debt - external: $3.626 trillion (30 June 2005)

Economic aid - donor: ODA, $5.6 billion (1998)

Currency (code): euro (EUR)
note: on 1 January 1999, the European Monetary Union introduced the euro as a common currency to be used by finan-

cial institutions of member countries; on 1 January 2002, the euro became the sole currency for everyday transactions within the member countries
Currency code: EUR
Exchange rates: euros per US dollar - 0.79697 (2005), 0.8054 (2004), 0.886 (2003), 1.0626 (2002), 1.1175 (2001)
Fiscal year: calendar year

COMMUNICATIONS

Telephones - main lines in use: 54.35 million (2003)
Telephones - mobile cellular: 64.8 million (2003)
Telephone system:
general assessment: Germany has one of the world's most technologically advanced telecommunications systems; as a result of intensive capital expenditures since reunification, the formerly backward system of the eastern part of the country, dating back to World War II, has been modernized and integrated with that of the western part
domestic: Germany is served by an extensive system of automatic telephone exchanges connected by modern networks of fiber-optic cable, coaxial cable, microwave radio relay, and a domestic satellite system; cellular telephone service is widely available, expanding rapidly, and includes roaming service to many foreign countries
international: country code - 49; Germany's international service is excellent worldwide, consisting of extensive land and undersea cable facilities as well as earth stations in the Inmarsat, Intelsat, Eutelsat, and Intersputnik satellite systems (2001)
Radio broadcast stations: AM 51, FM 787, shortwave 4 (1998)
Radios: 77.8 million (1997)
Television broadcast stations: 373 (plus 8,042 repeaters) (1995)
Televisions: 51.4 million (1998)
Internet country code: .de
Internet hosts: 2,686,119 (2004)
Internet Service Providers (ISPs): 200 (2001)
Internet users: 39 million (2003)

TRANSPORTATION

Airports: 550 (2004 est.)
Airports - with paved runways:
total: 332
over 3,047 m: 12
2,438 to 3,047 m: 55
1,524 to 2,437 m: 58
914 to 1,523 m: 73
under 914 m: 134 (2005 est.)
Airports - with unpaved runways:
total: 220
2,438 to 3,047 m: 1
1,524 to 2,437 m: 3
914 to 1,523 m: 33
under 914 m: 183 (2005 est.)
Heliports: 33 (2005 est.)
Pipelines: condensate 325 km; gas 25,293 km; oil 3,540 km; refined products 3,827 km (2004)
Railways:
total: 46,142 km (20,100 km electrified)
standard gauge: 45,928 km 1.435-m gauge (20,084 km electrified)
narrow gauge: 214 km 1.000-m gauge (16 km electrified); 24 km 0.750-m gauge (2004)
Roadways:
total: 231,581 km
paved: 231,581 km (including 12,037 km of expressways) (2003)
Waterways: 7,300 km
note: Rhine River carries most goods; Main-Danube Canal links North Sea and Black Sea (2004)
Merchant marine:
total: 332 ships (1,000 GRT or over) 5,721,495 GRT/6,810,631 DWT
by type: cargo 69, chemical tanker 13, container 208, liquefied gas 3, passenger 7, passenger/cargo 25, petroleum tanker 3, roll on/roll off 4
foreign-owned: 5 (Finland 2, Netherlands 1, Switzerland 1, UAE 1)
registered in other countries: 2,289 (2005)
Ports and terminals: Bremen, Bremerhaven, Brunsbuttel, Duisburg, Frankfurt, Hamburg, Karlsruhe, Mainz, Rostock, Wilhemshaven

MILITARY

Military branches: Federal Armed Forces (Bundeswehr): Army (Heer), Navy (Deutsche Marine, includes naval air arm), Air Force (Luftwaffe), Joint Support Service, Central Medical Service
Military service age and obligation: 18 years of age (conscripts serve a nine-month tour of compulsory military service) (2004)
Manpower available for military service: *males age 18-49:* 18,917,537 (2005 est.)
Manpower fit for military service: *males age 18-49:* 15,250,931 (2005 est.)
Manpower reaching military service age annually: *males:* 497,048 (2005 est.)
Military expenditures - dollar figure: $35.063 billion (2003)
Military expenditures - percent of GDP: 1.5% (2003)

TRANSNATIONAL ISSUES

Disputes - international: none
Illicit drugs: source of precursor chemicals for South American cocaine processors; transshipment point for and consumer of Southwest Asian heroin, Latin American cocaine, and European-produced synthetic drugs; major financial center

GHANA

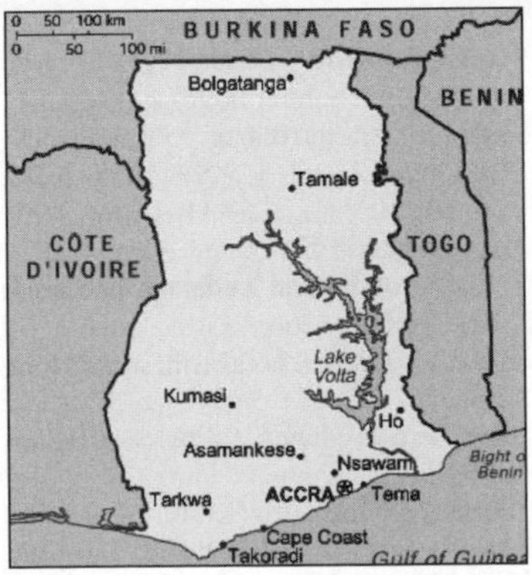

INTRODUCTION

Background: Formed from the merger of the British colony of the Gold Coast and the Togoland trust territory, Ghana in 1957 became the first sub-Saharan country in colonial Africa to gain its independence. A long series of coups resulted in the suspension of the constitution in 1981 and a ban on political parties. A new constitution, restoring multiparty politics, was approved in 1992. Lt. Jerry RAWLINGS, head of state since 1981, won presidential elections in 1992 and 1996, but was constitutionally prevented from running for a third term in 2000. John KUFUOR, who defeated former Vice President Atta MILLS in a free and fair election, succeeded him.

GEOGRAPHY

Location: Western Africa, bordering the Gulf of Guinea, between Cote d'Ivoire and Togo
Geographic coordinates: 8 00 N, 2 00 W
Map references: Africa
Area:
total: 239,460 sq km
land: 230,940 sq km
water: 8,520 sq km
Area - comparative: slightly smaller than Oregon
Land boundaries:
total: 2,094 km

border countries: Burkina Faso 549 km, Cote d'Ivoire 668 km, Togo 877 km
Coastline: 539 km
Maritime claims:
territorial sea: 12 nm
contiguous zone: 24 nm
exclusive economic zone: 200 nm
continental shelf: 200 nm
Climate: tropical; warm and comparatively dry along southeast coast; hot and humid in southwest; hot and dry in north
Terrain: mostly low plains with dissected plateau in south-central area
Elevation extremes:
lowest point: Atlantic Ocean 0 m
highest point: Mount Afadjato 880 m
Natural resources: gold, timber, industrial diamonds, bauxite, manganese, fish, rubber, hydropower, petroleum, silver, salt, limestone
Land use:
arable land: 16.26%
permanent crops: 9.67%
other: 74.07% (2001)
Irrigated land: 110 sq km (1998 est.)
Natural hazards: dry, dusty, northeastern harmattan winds occur from January to March; droughts
Environment - current issues: recurrent drought in north severely affects agricultural activities; deforestation; overgrazing; soil erosion; poaching and habitat destruction threatens wildlife populations; water pollution; inadequate supplies of potable water
Environment - international agreements:
party to: Biodiversity, Climate Change, Climate Change-Kyoto Protocol, Desertification, Endangered Species, Environmental Modification, Hazardous Wastes, Law of the Sea, Ozone Layer Protection, Ship Pollution, Tropical Timber 83, Tropical Timber 94, Wetlands
signed, but not ratified: Marine Life Conservation
Geography - note: Lake Volta is the world's largest artificial lake

PEOPLE

Population: 21,029,853
note: estimates for this country explicitly take into account the effects of excess mortality due to AIDS; this can result in lower life expectancy, higher infant mortality and death rates, lower population and growth rates, and changes in the distribution of population by age and sex than would otherwise be expected (July 2005 est.)
Age structure:
0-14 years: 37.1% (male 3,946,326/female 3,862,390)
15-64 years: 59.1% (male 6,203,035/ female 6,235,107)
65 years and over: 3.7% (male 366,472/ female 416,523) (2005 est.)
Median age:
total: 20.45 years
male: 20.2 years
female: 20.7 years (2005 est.)
Population growth rate: 1.25% (2005 est.)
Birth rate: 23.97 births/1,000 population (2005 est.)
Death rate: 10.84 deaths/1,000 population (2005 est.)
Net migration rate: -0.59 migrant(s)/1,000 population (2005 est.)
Sex ratio:
at birth: 1.03 male(s)/female
under 15 years: 1.02 male(s)/female
15-64 years: 1 male(s)/female
65 years and over: 0.88 male(s)/female
total population: 1 male(s)/female (2005 est.)
Infant mortality rate:
total: 51.43 deaths/1,000 live births
male: 54.25 deaths/1,000 live births
female: 48.53 deaths/1,000 live births (2005 est.)
Life expectancy at birth:
total population: 58.47 years
male: 57.7 years
female: 59.26 years (2005 est.)
Total fertility rate: 3.02 children born/woman (2005 est.)
HIV/AIDS - adult prevalence rate: 3.1% (2003 est.)
HIV/AIDS - people living with HIV/AIDS: 350,000 (2003 est.)
HIV/AIDS - deaths: 30,000 (2003 est.)
Major infectious diseases:
degree of risk: very high
food or waterborne diseases: bacterial and protozoal diarrhea, hepatitis A, and typhoid fever
vectorborne diseases: malaria and yellow fever are high risks in some locations
water contact disease: schistosomiasis
respiratory disease: meningococcal meningitis (2004)
Nationality:
noun: Ghanaian(s)
adjective: Ghanaian
Ethnic groups: black African 98.5% (major tribes - Akan 44%, Moshi-Dagomba 16%, Ewe 13%, Ga 8%, Gurma 3%, Yoruba 1%), European and other 1.5% (1998)
Religions: Christian 63%, Muslim 16%, indigenous beliefs 21%
Languages: English (official), African languages (including Akan, Moshi-Dagomba, Ewe, and Ga)
Literacy:
definition: age 15 and over can read and write
total population: 74.8%
male: 82.7%
female: 67.1% (2003 est.)

GOVERNMENT

Country name:
conventional long form: Republic of Ghana
conventional short form: Ghana
former: Gold Coast
Government type: constitutional democracy
Capital: Accra
Administrative divisions: 10 regions; Ashanti, Brong-Ahafo, Central, Eastern, Greater Accra, Northern, Upper East, Upper West, Volta, Western
Independence: 6 March 1957 (from UK)
National holiday: Independence Day, 6 March (1957)
Constitution: approved 28 April 1992
Legal system: based on English common law and customary law; has not accepted compulsory ICJ jurisdiction
Suffrage: 18 years of age, universal
Executive branch:
chief of state: President John Agyekum KUFUOR (since 7 January 2001); Vice President Alhaji Aliu MAHAMA (since 7 January 2001); note - the president is both the chief of state and head of government
head of government: President John Agyekum KUFUOR (since 7 January 2001); Vice President Alhaji Aliu MAHAMA (since 7 January 2001); note - the president is both the chief of state and head of government
cabinet: Council of Ministers; president nominates members subject to approval by Parliament
elections: president and vice president elected on the same ticket by popular vote for four-year terms; election last held 7 December 2004 (next to be held December 2008)
election results: John Agyekum KUFUOR reelected president in election; percent of vote - John KUFUOR 53.4%, John Atta MILLS 43.7%
Legislative branch: unicameral Parliament (230 seats; note - increased from 200 seats in last election; members are elected by direct, popular vote to serve four-year terms)
elections: last held 7 December 2004 (next to be held December 2008)
election results: percent of vote by party - NA%; seats by party - NPP 128, NDC 92, other 10
Judicial branch: Supreme Court
Political parties and leaders: Convention People's Party or CPP [Nii Noi DOWUONA, general secretary]; Every Ghanaian Living Everywhere or EGLE [Owuraku AMOFA, chairman]; Great Consolidated Popular Party or GCPP [Dan LARTY]; National Convention Party or NCP [Sarpong KUMA-KUMA]; National Democratic Congress or NDC [Dr. Huudu

YAHAYA, general secretary]; New Patriotic Party or NPP [Samuel Arthur ODOI-SYKES]; People's Convention Party or PCP [P. K. DONKOH-AYIFI, acting chairman]; People's Heritage Party or PHP [Emmanuel Alexander ERSKINE]; People's National Convention or PNC [Edward MAHAMA]; Reform Party [Kyeretwie OPUKU, general secretary]

Political pressure groups and leaders: NA

International organization participation: ACP, AfDB, AU, C, ECOWAS, FAO, G-24, G-77, IAEA, IBRD, ICAO, ICC, ICCt, ICFTU, ICRM, IDA, IFAD, IFC, IFRCS, ILO, IMF, IMO, Interpol, IOC, IOM (observer), ISO, ITU, MIGA, MINURSO, MONUC, NAM, OAS (observer), ONUB, OPCW, UN, UNAMSIL, UNCTAD, UNESCO, UNHCR, UNIDO, UNIFIL, UNITAR, UNMEE, UNMIL, UNOCI, UPU, WCL, WCO, WFTU, WHO, WIPO, WMO, WToO, WTO

Diplomatic representation in the US:
chief of mission: Ambassador Fritz Kwabena POKU
chancery: 3512 International Drive NW, Washington, DC 20008
telephone: [1] (202) 686-4520
FAX: [1] (202) 686-4527
consulate(s) general: New York

Diplomatic representation from the US:
chief of mission: Ambassador Mary Carlin YATES
embassy: 6th and 10th Lanes, 798/1 Osu, Accra
mailing address: P. O. Box 194, Accra
telephone: [233] (21) 775-347, 775-348
FAX: [233] (21) 701-813

Flag description: three equal horizontal bands of red (top), yellow, and green with a large black five-pointed star centered in the yellow band; uses the popular pan-African colors of Ethiopia; similar to the flag of Bolivia, which has a coat of arms centered in the yellow band

ECONOMY

Economy - overview: Well endowed with natural resources, Ghana has roughly twice the per capita output of the poorer countries in West Africa. Even so, Ghana remains heavily dependent on international financial and technical assistance. Gold, timber, and cocoa production are major sources of foreign exchange. The domestic economy continues to revolve around subsistence agriculture, which accounts for 34% of GDP and employs 60% of the work force, mainly small landholders. Ghana opted for debt relief under the Heavily Indebted Poor Country (HIPC) program in 2002, but was included in a G8 debt relief program decided upon at the Gleneagles Summit in July 2005. Priorities under its current $38 million PRGF include tighter monetary and fiscal policies, accelerated privatization, and improvement of social services. Receipts from the gold sector helped sustain GDP growth in 2005 along with record high prices for Ghana's largest cocoa crop to date. Inflation should ease, but remain a major internal problem. Ghana also remains a candidate country to benefit from Millennium Challenge Corporation (MCC) funding that could assist in transforming Ghana's agricultural export sector. A final decision on its MCC bid is expected for spring 2006.

GDP (purchasing power parity): $51.8 billion (2005 est.)

GDP (official exchange rate): $9.464 billion (2005 est.)

GDP - real growth rate: 4.3% (2005 est.)

GDP - per capita: purchasing power parity - $2,500 (2005 est.)

GDP - composition by sector:
agriculture: 35.5%
industry: 25.6%
services: 39% (2005 est.)

Labor force: 10.62 million (2005 est.)

Labor force - by occupation: agriculture 60%, industry 15%, services 25% (1999 est.)

Unemployment rate: 20% (1997 est.)

Population below poverty line: 31.4% (1992 est.)

Household income or consumption by percentage share:
lowest 10%: 2.2%
highest 10%: 30.1% (1999)

Distribution of family income - Gini index: 30 (1999)

Inflation rate (consumer prices): 15% (2005 est.)

Investment (gross fixed): 24.6% of GDP (2005 est.)

Budget:
revenues: $3.216 billion
expenditures: $3.506 billion, including capital expenditures of NA (2005 est.)

Public debt: 80.1% of GDP (2005 est.)

Agriculture - products: cocoa, rice, coffee, cassava (tapioca), peanuts, corn, shea nuts, bananas; timber

Industries: mining, lumbering, light manufacturing, aluminum smelting, food processing, cement, small commercial ship building

Industrial production growth rate: 3.8% (2000 est.)

Electricity - production: 5.356 billion kWh (2003)

Electricity - production by source:
fossil fuel: 5%
hydro: 95%
nuclear: 0%
other: 0% (2001)

Electricity - consumption: 5.081 billion kWh (2003)

Electricity - exports: 400 million kWh (2003)

Electricity - imports: 500 million kWh (2003)

Oil - production: 7,433 bbl/day (2003 est.)

Oil - consumption: 39,000 bbl/day (2003 est.)

Oil - exports: NA (2001)

Oil - imports: NA (2001)

Oil - proved reserves: 8.255 million bbl (1 January 2002)

Natural gas - proved reserves: 11.89 billion cu m (1 January 2002)

Current account balance: $57 million (2005 est.)

Exports: $2.911 billion f.o.b. (2005 est.)

Exports - partners: Netherlands 12.3%, UK 10%, France 6.9%, US 6.4%, Belgium 4.7%, Germany 4.6%, Japan 4.2% (2004)

Imports: $4.273 billion f.o.b. (2005 est.)

Imports - partners: Nigeria 12.6%, China 11.4%, UK 6.6%, US 6.4%, France 4.9%, Netherlands 4.2% (2004)

Reserves of foreign exchange and gold: $1.732 billion (2005 est.)

Debt - external: $7.084 billion (2005 est.)

Economic aid - recipient: $6.9 billion (1999)

Currency (code): cedi (GHC)

Currency code: GHC

Exchange rates: cedis per US dollar - 9,127.42 (2005), 9,004.6 (2004), 8,677.4 (2003), 7,932.7 (2002), 7,170.8 (2001)

Fiscal year: calendar year

COMMUNICATIONS

Telephones - main lines in use: 302,300 (2003)

Telephones - mobile cellular: 799,900 (2003)

Telephone system:
general assessment: poor to fair system; Internet accessible; many rural communities not yet connected; expansion of services is underway
domestic: primarily microwave radio relay; wireless local loop has been installed
international: country code - 233; satellite earth stations - 4 Intelsat (Atlantic Ocean); microwave radio relay link to Panaftel system connects Ghana to its neighbors; fiber optic submarine cable (SAT-3/WASC) provides connectivity to Europe and Asia

Radio broadcast stations: AM 0, FM 49, shortwave 3 (2001)

Radios: 12.5 million (2001)

Television broadcast stations: 10 (2001)

Televisions: 1.9 million (2001)

Internet country code: .gh

Internet hosts: 407 (2004)

Internet Service Providers (ISPs): 12 (2000)

Internet users: 170,000 (2002)

TRANSPORTATION

Airports: 12 (2004 est.)
Airports - with paved runways:
total: 7
over 3,047 m: 1
1,524 to 2,437 m: 4
914 to 1,523 m: 2 (2005 est.)
Airports - with unpaved runways:
total: 5
914 to 1,523 m: 3
under 914 m: 2 (2005 est.)
Pipelines: refined products 74 km (2004)
Railways:
total: 953 km
narrow gauge: 953 km 1.067-m gauge (2004)
Roadways:
total: 47,787 km
paved: 8,563 km
unpaved: 39,224 km (2003)
Waterways: 1,293 km
note: 168 km for launches and lighters on Volta, Ankobra, and Tano rivers; 1,125 km of arterial and feeder waterways on Lake Volta (2003)
Merchant marine:
total: 4 ships (1,000 GRT or over) 19,086 GRT/26,185 DWT
by type: petroleum tanker 1, refrigerated cargo 3
foreign-owned: 1 (Brazil 1) (2005)
Ports and terminals: Takoradi, Tema

MILITARY

Military branches: Army, Navy, Air Force
Military service age and obligation: 18 years of age for compulsory and volunteer military service (2001)
Manpower available for military service:
males age 18-49: 4,761,226 (2005 est.)
Manpower fit for military service: *males age 18-49:* 2,721,239 (2005 est.)
Manpower reaching military service age annually: *males:* 250,782 (2005 est.)
Military expenditures - dollar figure: $49.2 million (2004)
Military expenditures - percent of GDP: 0.6% (2004)

TRANSNATIONAL ISSUES

Disputes - international: Ghana struggles to accommodate returning nationals who worked in the cocoa plantations and escaped rebel fighting in Cote d'Ivoire
Refugees and internally displaced persons:
refugees (country of origin): 42,466 (Liberia) (2004)
Illicit drugs: illicit producer of cannabis for the international drug trade; major transit hub for Southwest and Southeast Asian heroin and, to a lesser extent, South American cocaine destined for Europe and the US; widespread crime and money laundering problem, but the lack of a well-developed financial infrastructure limits the country's utility as a money-laundering center

GIBRALTAR

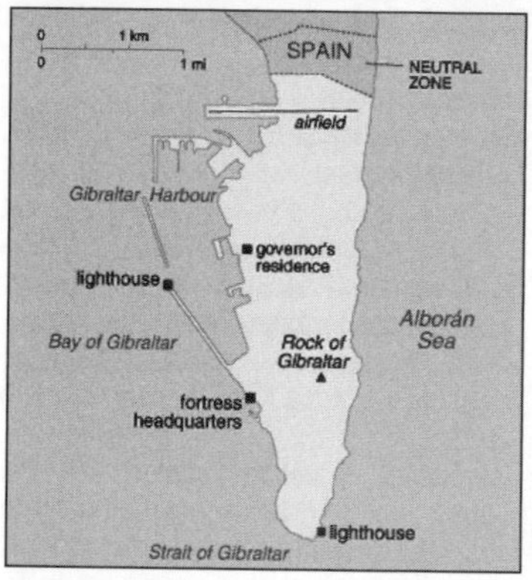

INTRODUCTION

Background: Strategically important, Gibraltar was ceded to Great Britain by Spain in the 1713 Treaty of Utrecht; the British garrison was formally declared a colony in 1830. In referendums held in 1967 and 2002, Gibraltarians ignored Spanish pressure and voted overwhelmingly to remain a British dependency.

GEOGRAPHY

Location: Southwestern Europe, bordering the Strait of Gibraltar, which links the Mediterranean Sea and the North Atlantic Ocean, on the southern coast of Spain
Geographic coordinates: 36 8 N, 5 21 W
Map references: Europe
Area:
total: 6.5 sq km
land: 6.5 sq km
water: 0 sq km
Area - comparative: about 11 times the size of The Mall in Washington, DC
Land boundaries:
total: 1.2 km
border countries: Spain 1.2 km
Coastline: 12 km
Maritime claims:
territorial sea: 3 nm
Climate: Mediterranean with mild winters and warm summers
Terrain: a narrow coastal lowland borders the Rock of Gibraltar
Elevation extremes:
lowest point: Mediterranean Sea 0 m
highest point: Rock of Gibraltar 426 m
Natural resources: none
Land use:
arable land: 0%
permanent crops: 0%
other: 100% (2001)
Irrigated land: NA sq km
Natural hazards: NA
Environment - current issues: limited natural freshwater resources: large concrete or natural rock water catchments collect rainwater (no longer used for drinking water) and adequate desalination plant
Geography - note: strategic location on Strait of Gibraltar that links the North Atlantic Ocean and Mediterranean Sea

PEOPLE

Population: 27,884 (July 2005 est.)
Age structure:
0-14 years: 17.8% (male 2,529/female 2,426)
15-64 years: 66% (male 9,442/female 8,970)
65 years and over: 16.2% (male 2,008/female 2,509) (2005 est.)
Median age:
total: 39.4 years
male: 39.12 years
female: 39.63 years (2005 est.)
Population growth rate: 0.17% (2005 est.)
Birth rate: 10.87 births/1,000 population (2005 est.)
Death rate: 9.18 deaths/1,000 population (2005 est.)
Net migration rate: 0 migrant(s)/1,000 population (2005 est.)
Sex ratio:
at birth: 1.05 male(s)/female
under 15 years: 1.04 male(s)/female
15-64 years: 1.05 male(s)/female
65 years and over: 0.8 male(s)/female
total population: 1.01 male(s)/female (2005 est.)
Infant mortality rate:
total: 5.13 deaths/1,000 live births
male: 5.71 deaths/1,000 live births
female: 4.52 deaths/1,000 live births (2005 est.)
Life expectancy at birth:
total population: 79.67 years
male: 76.8 years
female: 82.7 years (2005 est.)
Total fertility rate: 1.65 children born/woman (2005 est.)
HIV/AIDS - adult prevalence rate: NA%
HIV/AIDS - people living with HIV/AIDS: NA
HIV/AIDS - deaths: NA
Nationality:
noun: Gibraltarian(s)
adjective: Gibraltar

Ethnic groups: Spanish, Italian, English, Maltese, Portuguese, German, North Africans
Religions: Roman Catholic 78.1%, Church of England 7%, other Christian 3.2%, Muslim 4%, Jewish 2.1%, Hindu 1.8%, other or unspecified 0.9%, none 2.9% (2001 census)
Languages: English (used in schools and for official purposes), Spanish, Italian, Portuguese
Literacy:
definition: NA
total population: above 80%
male: NA%
female: NA%

GOVERNMENT

Country name:
conventional long form: none
conventional short form: Gibraltar
Dependency status: overseas territory of the UK
Government type: NA
Capital: Gibraltar
Administrative divisions: none (overseas territory of the UK)
Independence: none (overseas territory of the UK)
National holiday: National Day, 10 September (1967); note - day of the national referendum to decide whether to remain with the UK or go with Spain
Constitution: 30 May 1969
Legal system: English law
Suffrage: 18 years of age; universal, plus other British citizens who have been residents six months or more
Executive branch:
chief of state: Queen ELIZABETH II (since 6 February 1952), represented by Governor and Commander-in-Chief Sir Francis RICHARDS (since 27 May 2003)
head of government: Chief Minister Peter CARUANA (since 17 May 1996)
cabinet: Council of Ministers appointed from among the 15 elected members of the House of Assembly by the governor in consultation with the chief minister
elections: none; the monarch is hereditary; governor appointed by the monarch; following legislative elections, the leader of the majority party or the leader of the majority coalition is usually appointed chief minister by the governor
Legislative branch: unicameral House of Assembly (18 seats - 15 elected by popular vote, one appointed for the Speaker, and two ex officio members; members serve four-year terms)
elections: last held 27 November 2003 (next to be held not later than February 2008)
election results: percent of vote by party - GSD 58%, GSLP 41%; seats by party - GSD 8, GSLP 7
Judicial branch: Supreme Court; Court of Appeal
Political parties and leaders: Gibraltar Liberal Party [Joseph GARCIA]; Gibraltar Social Democrats or GSD [Peter CARUANA]; Gibraltar Socialist Labor Party or GSLP [Joseph John BOSSANO]
Political pressure groups and leaders: Chamber of Commerce; Gibraltar Representatives Organization; Women's Association
International organization participation: Interpol (subbureau), UPU
Diplomatic representation in the US: none (overseas territory of the UK)
Diplomatic representation from the US: none (overseas territory of the UK)
Flag description: two horizontal bands of white (top, double width) and red with a three-towered red castle in the center of the white band; hanging from the castle gate is a gold key centered in the red band

ECONOMY

Economy - overview: Self-sufficient Gibraltar benefits from an extensive shipping trade, offshore banking, and its position as an international conference center. The British military presence has been sharply reduced and now contributes about 7% to the local economy, compared with 60% in 1984. The financial sector, tourism (almost 5 million visitors in 1998), shipping services fees, and duties on consumer goods also generate revenue. The financial sector, the shipping sector, and tourism each contribute 25%-30% of GDP. Telecommunications accounts for another 10%. In recent years, Gibraltar has seen major structural change from a public to a private sector economy, but changes in government spending still have a major impact on the level of employment.
GDP (purchasing power parity): $769 million (2000 est.)
GDP (official exchange rate): NA
GDP - real growth rate: NA%
GDP - per capita: purchasing power parity - $27,900 (2000 est.)
GDP - composition by sector:
agriculture: NA%
industry: NA%
services: NA% (2002 est.)
Labor force: 14,800 (including non-Gibraltar laborers) (1999)
Labor force - by occupation: agriculture negligible, industry 40%, services 60%
Unemployment rate: 2% (2001 est.)
Population below poverty line: NA
Household income or consumption by percentage share:
lowest 10%: NA%
highest 10%: NA%
Inflation rate (consumer prices): 1.5% (1998)
Budget:
revenues: $307 million
expenditures: $284 million, including capital expenditures of NA (FY00/01 est.)
Agriculture - products: none
Industries: tourism, banking and finance, ship repairing, tobacco
Industrial production growth rate: NA%
Electricity - production: 106.1 million kWh (2003)
Electricity - production by source:
fossil fuel: 100%
hydro: 0%
nuclear: 0%
other: 0% (2001)
Electricity - consumption: 98.69 million kWh (2003)
Electricity - exports: 0 kWh (2003)
Electricity - imports: 0 kWh (2003)
Oil - production: 0 bbl/day (2003 est.)
Oil - consumption: 23,500 bbl/day (2003 est.)
Oil - exports: NA (2001)
Oil - imports: NA (2001)
Exports: $271 million f.o.b. (2004 est.)
Exports - partners: France 19.4%, Spain 14.1%, Turkmenistan 12.1%, Switzerland 11.7%, Germany 10.1%, UK 9.1%, Greece 6.8% (2004)
Imports: $2.967 billion c.i.f. (2004 est.)
Imports - partners: Spain 19.9%, Russia 18.4%, UK 10.8%, Italy 8.8%, Germany 7.5%, US 5.1%, Sweden 4.7%, France 4.2% (2004)
Debt - external: $NA (2000 est.)
Economic aid - recipient: $NA
Currency (code): Gibraltar pound (GIP)
Currency code: GIP
Exchange rates: Gibraltar pounds per US dollar - 0.54 (2005), 0.5462 (2004), 0.6125 (2003), 0.6672 (2002), 0.6947 (2001)
note: the Gibraltar pound is at par with the British pound
Fiscal year: 1 July - 30 June

COMMUNICATIONS

Telephones - main lines in use: 24,512 (2002)
Telephones - mobile cellular: 9,797 (2002)
Telephone system:
general assessment: adequate, automatic domestic system and adequate international facilities
domestic: automatic exchange facilities
international: country code - 350; radiotelephone; microwave radio relay; satellite earth station - 1 Intelsat (Atlantic Ocean)
Radio broadcast stations: AM 1, FM 5, shortwave 0 (1998)

Radios: 37,000 (1997)
Television broadcast stations: 1 (plus three low-power repeaters) (1997)
Televisions: 10,000 (1997)
Internet country code: .gi
Internet Service Providers (ISPs): 2 (2000)
Internet users: 6,200 (2002)

TRANSPORTATION

Airports: 1 (2004 est.)
Airports - with paved runways:
total: 1
1,524 to 2,437 m: 1 (2005 est.)
Roadways:
total: 29 km
paved: 29 km (2002)
Merchant marine:
total: 161 ships (1,000 GRT or over) 980,636 GRT/1,254,661 DWT
by type: barge carrier 3, bulk carrier 2, cargo 96, chemical tanker 21, container 22, passenger 3, passenger/cargo 1, petroleum tanker 11, roll on/roll off 2
foreign-owned: 142 (Belgium 1, Cyprus 1, Finland 1, France 1, Germany 105, Greece 12, Iceland 1, Ireland 1, Italy 1, Latvia 1, Norway 8, Sweden 2, Switzerland 1, Taiwan 1, United Kingdom 3, United States 2) (2005)
Ports and terminals: Gibraltar

MILITARY

Military branches: Royal Gibraltar Regiment
Military - note: defense is the responsibility of the UK; the last British regular infantry forces left Gibraltar in 1992, replaced by the Royal Gibraltar Regiment

TRANSNATIONAL ISSUES

Disputes - international: in 2003, Gibraltar residents voted overwhelmingly by referendum to remain a British colony and against a "total shared sovereignty" arrangement while demanding participation in talks between the UK and Spain; Spain disapproves of UK plans to grant Gibraltar even greater autonomy

GLORIOSO ISLANDS

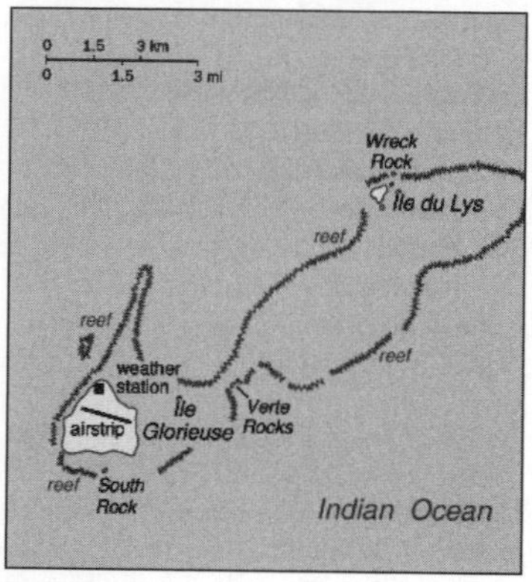

INTRODUCTION

Background: A French possession since 1892, the Glorioso Islands are composed of two lushly vegetated coral islands (Ile Glorieuse and Ile du Lys) and three rock islets. A military garrison operates a weather and radio station on Ile Glorieuse.

GEOGRAPHY

Location: Southern Africa, group of islands in the Indian Ocean, northwest of Madagascar
Geographic coordinates: 11 30 S, 47 20 E
Map references: Africa
Area:
total: 5 sq km
land: 5 sq km
water: 0 sq km
note: includes Ile Glorieuse, Ile du Lys, Verte Rocks, Wreck Rock, and South Rock
Area - comparative: about eight times the size of The Mall in Washington, DC
Land boundaries: 0 km
Coastline: 35.2 km
Maritime claims:
territorial sea: 12 nm
exclusive economic zone: 200 nm
Climate: tropical
Terrain: low and flat
Elevation extremes:
lowest point: Indian Ocean 0 m
highest point: unnamed location 12 m
Natural resources: guano, coconuts
Land use:
arable land: 0%
permanent crops: 0%
other: 100% (all lush vegetation and coconut palms) (2001)
Irrigated land: 0 sq km (1998 est.)
Natural hazards: periodic cyclones
Environment - current issues: NA
Geography - note: the islands and rocks are surrounded by an extensive reef system

PEOPLE

Population: no indigenous inhabitants
note: there is a small French military garrison along with a few meteorologists; visited by scientists (July 2005 est.)

GOVERNMENT

Country name:
conventional long form: none
conventional short form: Glorioso Islands
local long form: none
local short form: Iles Glorieuses
Dependency status: possession of France; administered by the Administrateur Superieur of the French Southern and Antarctic Lands
Legal system: the laws of France, where applicable, apply
Flag description: the flag of France is used

ECONOMY

Economy - overview: no economic activity

COMMUNICATIONS

Communications - note: 1 meteorological station

TRANSPORTATION

Airports: 1 (2004 est.)
Airports - with unpaved runways:
total: 1
914 to 1,523 m: 1 (2005 est.)
Ports and terminals: none; offshore anchorage only

MILITARY

Military - note: defense is the responsibility of France

TRANSNATIONAL ISSUES

Disputes - international: claimed by Madagascar

GREECE

INTRODUCTION

Background: Greece achieved its independence from the Ottoman Empire in 1829. During the second half of the 19th century and the first half of the 20th century, it gradually added neighboring islands and territories, most with Greek-speaking populations. In World War II, Greece was first invaded by Italy (1940) and subsequently occupied by Germany (1941-44); fighting endured in a protracted civil war between royalist supporters of the king and communist rebels. Following the latter's defeat in

1949, Greece was able to join NATO in 1952. A military dictatorship, which in 1967 suspended many political liberties and forced the king to flee the country, lasted seven years. The 1974 democratic elections and a referendum created a parliamentary republic and abolished the monarchy. Greece joined the European Community or EC in 1981 (which became the EU in 1992); it became the 12th member of the euro zone in 2001.

GEOGRAPHY

Location: Southern Europe, bordering the Aegean Sea, Ionian Sea, and the Mediterranean Sea, between Albania and Turkey
Geographic coordinates: 39 00 N, 22 00 E
Map references: Europe
Area:
total: 131,940 sq km
land: 130,800 sq km
water: 1,140 sq km
Area - comparative: slightly smaller than Alabama
Land boundaries:
total: 1,228 km
border countries: Albania 282 km, Bulgaria 494 km, Turkey 206 km, Macedonia 246 km
Coastline: 13,676 km
Maritime claims:
territorial sea: 12 nm
continental shelf: 200-m depth or to the depth of exploitation
Climate: temperate; mild, wet winters; hot, dry summers
Terrain: mostly mountains with ranges extending into the sea as peninsulas or chains of islands
Elevation extremes:
lowest point: Mediterranean Sea 0 m
highest point: Mount Olympus 2,917 m
Natural resources: lignite, petroleum, iron ore, bauxite, lead, zinc, nickel, magnesite, marble, salt, hydropower potential
Land use:
arable land: 21.1%
permanent crops: 8.78%
other: 70.12% (2001)
Irrigated land: 14,220 sq km (1998 est.)
Natural hazards: severe earthquakes
Environment - current issues: air pollution; water pollution
Environment - international agreements:
party to: Air Pollution, Air Pollution-Nitrogen Oxides, Air Pollution-Sulfur 94, Antarctic-Environmental Protocol, Antarctic-Marine Living Resources, Antarctic Treaty, Biodiversity, Climate Change, Climate Change-Kyoto Protocol, Desertification, Endangered Species, Environmental Modification, Hazardous Wastes, Law of the Sea, Marine Dumping, Ozone Layer Protection, Ship Pollution, Tropical Timber 83, Tropical Timber 94, Wetlands
signed, but not ratified: Air Pollution-Persistent Organic Pollutants, Air Pollution-Volatile Organic Compounds
Geography - note: strategic location dominating the Aegean Sea and southern approach to Turkish Straits; a peninsular country, possessing an archipelago of about 2,000 islands

PEOPLE

Population: 10,668,354 (July 2005 est.)
Age structure:
0-14 years: 14.4% (male 791,227/female 744,178)
15-64 years: 66.8% (male 3,561,689/female 3,564,675)
65 years and over: 18.8% (male 884,497/female 1,122,088) (2005 est.)
Median age:
total: 40.5 years
male: 39.39 years
female: 41.65 years (2005 est.)
Population growth rate: 0.19% (2005 est.)
Birth rate: 9.72 births/1,000 population (2005 est.)
Death rate: 10.15 deaths/1,000 population (2005 est.)
Net migration rate: 2.34 migrant(s)/1,000 population (2005 est.)
Sex ratio:
at birth: 1.06 male(s)/female
under 15 years: 1.06 male(s)/female
15-64 years: 1 male(s)/female
65 years and over: 0.79 male(s)/female
total population: 0.96 male(s)/female (2005 est.)
Infant mortality rate:
total: 5.53 deaths/1,000 live births
male: 6.08 deaths/1,000 live births
female: 4.94 deaths/1,000 live births (2005 est.)
Life expectancy at birth:
total population: 79.09 years
male: 76.59 years
female: 81.76 years (2005 est.)
Total fertility rate: 1.33 children born/woman (2005 est.)
HIV/AIDS - adult prevalence rate: 0.2% (2001 est.)
HIV/AIDS - people living with HIV/AIDS: 9,100 (2001 est.)
HIV/AIDS - deaths: less than 100 (2003 est.)
Nationality:
noun: Greek(s)
adjective: Greek
Ethnic groups: Greek 98%, other 2%
note: the Greek Government states there are no ethnic divisions in Greece
Religions: Greek Orthodox 98%, Muslim 1.3%, other 0.7%
Languages: Greek 99% (official), English, French
Literacy:
definition: age 15 and over can read and write
total population: 97.5%
male: 98.6%
female: 96.5% (2003 est.)
People - note: women, men, and children are trafficked to and within Greece for the purposes of sexual exploitation and forced labor

GOVERNMENT

Country name:
conventional long form: Hellenic Republic
conventional short form: Greece
local long form: Elliniki Dhimokratia
local short form: Ellas or Ellada
former: Kingdom of Greece
Government type: parliamentary republic; monarchy rejected by referendum 8 December 1974
Capital: Athens
Administrative divisions: 51 prefectures (nomoi, singular - nomos) and 1 autonomous region*; Agion Oros* (Mt. Athos), Achaia, Aitolia kai Akarmania, Argolis, Arkadia, Arta, Attiki, Chalkidiki, Chanion, Chios, Dodekanisos, Drama, Evros, Evrytania, Evvoia, Florina, Fokidos, Fthiotis, Grevena, Ileia, Imathia, Ioannina, Irakleion, Karditsa, Kastoria, Kavala, Kefallinia, Kerkyra, Kilkis, Korinthia, Kozani, Kyklades, Lakonia, Larisa, Lasithi, Lefkas, Lesvos, Magnisia, Messinia, Pella, Pieria, Preveza, Rethynnis, Rodopi, Samos, Serrai, Thesprotia, Thessaloniki, Trikala, Voiotia, Xanthi, Zakynthos
Independence: 1829 (from the Ottoman Empire)
National holiday: Independence Day, 25 March (1821)
Constitution: 11 June 1975; amended March 1986 and April 2001
Legal system: based on codified Roman law; judiciary divided into civil, criminal, and administrative courts

Suffrage: 18 years of age, universal and compulsory
Executive branch:
chief of state: President Karolos PAPOULIAS (since 12 March 2005)
head of government: Prime Minister Konstandinos KARAMANLIS (since 7 March 2004)
cabinet: Cabinet appointed by the president on the recommendation of the prime minister
elections: president elected by parliament for a five-year term; election last held 8 February 2005 (next to be held by February 2010); according to the Greek Constitution, presidents may only serve two terms; president appoints leader of the party securing plurality of vote in election to become prime minister and form a government
election results: Karolos PAPOULIAS elected president; number of parlimentary votes, 279 out of 300
Legislative branch: unicameral Parliament or Vouli ton Ellinon (300 seats; members are elected by direct popular vote to serve four-year terms)
elections: elections last held 7 March 2004 (next to be held by March 2008)
election results: percent of vote by party - ND 45.4%, PASOK 40.6%, KKE 5.9%, Synaspismos 3.3%; seats by party - ND 165, PASOK 117, KKE 12, Synaspismos 6
Judicial branch: Supreme Judicial Court; Special Supreme Tribunal; all judges appointed for life by the president after consultation with a judicial council
Political parties and leaders: Coalition of the Left and Progress (Synaspismos) [Alekos ALAVANOS]; Communist Party of Greece or KKE [Aleka PAPARIGA]; New Democracy or ND (conservative) [Konstandinos KARAMANLIS]; Panhellenic Socialist Movement or PASOK [Yiorgos PAPANDREOU]; Popular Orthodox Rally or LAOS [Yeoryios KARATZAFERIS]
Political pressure groups and leaders: General Confederation of Greek Workers or GSEE [Khristos POLYZOGOPOULOS]; Federation of Greek Industries or SEV [Odysseas KYRIAKOPOULOS]; Civil Servants Confederation or ADEDY [Spyros PAPASPYROS]
International organization participation: ACCT (associate), Australia Group, BIS, BSEC, CE, CERN, EAPC, EBRD, EIB, EMU, EU, FAO, G- 6, IAEA, IBRD, ICAO, ICC, ICCt, ICFTU, ICRM, IDA, IEA, IFAD, IFC, IFRCS, IHO, ILO, IMF, IMO, Interpol, IOC, IOM, ISO, ITU, MIGA, MINURSO, NAM (guest), NATO, NEA, NSG, OAS (observer), OECD, OPCW, OSCE, PCA, UN, UN Security Council (temporary), UNCTAD, UNESCO, UNHCR, UNIDO, UNMEE, UNMIS, UNOMIG, UPU, WCO, WEU, WFTU, WHO, WIPO, WMO, WToO, WTO, ZC
Diplomatic representation in the US:
chief of mission: Ambassador Alexandros MALLIAS
chancery: 2221 Massachusetts Avenue NW, Washington, DC 20008
telephone: [1] (202) 939-1300
FAX: [1] (202) 939-1324
consulate(s) general: Boston, Chicago, Los Angeles, New York, San Francisco, and Tampa
consulate(s): Atlanta, Houston, and New Orleans
Diplomatic representation from the US:
chief of mission: Ambassador Charles P. RIES
embassy: 91 Vasilissis Sophias Avenue, 10160 Athens
mailing address: PSC 108, APO AE 09842-0108
telephone: [30] (210) 721-2951
FAX: [30] (210) 645-6282
consulate(s) general: Thessaloniki
Flag description: nine equal horizontal stripes of blue alternating with white; there is a blue square in the upper hoist-side corner bearing a white cross; the cross symbolizes Greek Orthodoxy, the established religion of the country

ECONOMY

Economy - overview: Greece has a capitalist economy with the public sector accounting for about 40% of GDP and with per capita GDP 70% of the leading euro-zone economies. Tourism provides 15% of GDP. Immigrants make up nearly one-fifth of the work force, mainly in menial jobs. Greece is a major beneficiary of EU aid, equal to about 3.3% of annual GDP. The Greek economy grew by about 4.0% for the past three years, largely because of an investment boom and infrastructure upgrades for the 2004 Athens Olympic Games. Economic growth slowed to about 3% in 2005 and, Greece has not met the EU's Growth and Stability Pact budget deficit criteria of 3% of GDP since 2000. Public debt, inflation, and unemployment are above the eurozone average. To overcome these challenges, the Greek government is expected to continue cutting government spending, reducing the size of the public sector, and reforming the labor and pension systems.
GDP (purchasing power parity): $242.8 billion (2005 est.)
GDP (official exchange rate): $215.9 billion (2005 est.)
GDP - real growth rate: 3.3% (2005 est.)
GDP - per capita: purchasing power parity - $22,800 (2005 est.)
GDP - composition by sector:
agriculture: 6.2%
industry: 22.1%
services: 71.7% (2005 est.)
Labor force: 4.72 million (2005 est.)
Labor force - by occupation: agriculture 12%, industry 20%, services 68% (2004 est.)
Unemployment rate: 10.8% (2005 est.)
Population below poverty line: NA
Household income or consumption by percentage share:
lowest 10%: 3%
highest 10%: 28.3% (1998 est.)
Distribution of family income - Gini index: 35.1 (2003)
Inflation rate (consumer prices): 3.8% (2005 est.)
Investment (gross fixed): 25.3% of GDP (2005 est.)
Budget:
revenues: $94.13 billion
expenditures: $103.4 billion, including capital expenditures of NA (2005 est.)
Public debt: 108.9% of GDP (2005 est.)
Agriculture - products: wheat, corn, barley, sugar beets, olives, tomatoes, wine, tobacco, potatoes; beef, dairy products
Industries: tourism; food and tobacco processing, textiles; chemicals, metal products; mining, petroleum
Industrial production growth rate: 1.7% (2005 est.)
Electricity - production: 54.56 billion kWh (2003)
Electricity - production by source:
fossil fuel: 94.5%
hydro: 3.8%
nuclear: 0%
other: 1.7% (2001)
Electricity - consumption: 53.5 billion kWh (2005 est.)
Electricity - exports: 2.1 billion kWh (2002)
Electricity - imports: 4.2 billion kWh (2002)
Oil - production: 5,805 bbl/day (2003 est.)
Oil - consumption: 435,700 bbl/day (2005 est.)
Oil - exports: 84,720 bbl/day (2001)
Oil - imports: 468,300 bbl/day (2001)
Oil - proved reserves: 4.5 million bbl (1 January 2002)
Natural gas - production: 35 million cu m (2001 est.)
Natural gas - consumption: 2.34 billion cu m (2005 est.)
Natural gas - exports: 0 cu m (2001 est.)
Natural gas - imports: 2.018 billion cu m (2001 est.)
Natural gas - proved reserves: 254.9 million cu m (1 January 2002)

Current account balance: $-14.5 billion (2005 est.)
Exports: $18.54 billion f.o.b. (2005 est.)
Exports - partners: Germany 13.1%, Italy 10.3%, UK 7.5%, Bulgaria 6.3%, US 5.3%, Cyprus 4.6%, Turkey 4.5%, France 4.2% (2004)
Imports: $48.2 billion f.o.b. (2005 est.)
Imports - partners: Germany 13.3%, Italy 12.8%, France 6.4%, Netherlands 5.5%, Russia 5.5%, US 4.4%, UK 4.2%, South Korea 4.1% (2004)
Reserves of foreign exchange and gold: $2.3 billion (2005 est.)
Debt - external: $75.1 billion (2005 est.)
Economic aid - recipient: $8 billion from EU (2000-06)
Currency (code): euro (EUR)
note: on 1 January 1999, the European Monetary Union introduced the euro as a common currency to be used by financial institutions of member countries; on 1 January 2002, the euro became the sole currency for everyday transactions within the member countries
Currency code: EUR
Exchange rates: euros per US dollar - 0.79697 (2005), 0.8054 (2004), 0.886 (2003), 1.0626 (2002), 1.1175 (2001)
Fiscal year: calendar year

COMMUNICATIONS

Telephones - main lines in use: 5,205,100 (2003)
Telephones - mobile cellular: 8,936,200 (2003)
Telephone system:
general assessment: adequate, modern networks reach all areas; good mobile telephone and international service
domestic: microwave radio relay trunk system; extensive open-wire connections; submarine cable to offshore islands
international: country code - 30; tropospheric scatter; 8 submarine cables; satellite earth stations - 2 Intelsat (1 Atlantic Ocean and 1 Indian Ocean), 1 Eutelsat, and 1 Inmarsat (Indian Ocean region)
Radio broadcast stations: AM 26, FM 88, shortwave 4 (1998)
Radios: 5.02 million (1997)
Television broadcast stations: 36 (plus 1,341 low-power repeaters); also two stations in the US Armed Forces Radio and Television Service (1995)
Televisions: 2.54 million (1997)
Internet country code: .gr
Internet hosts: 208,977 (2004)
Internet Service Providers (ISPs): 27 (2000)
Internet users: 1,718,400 (2003)

TRANSPORTATION

Airports: 80 (2004 est.)
Airports - with paved runways:
total: 67
over 3,047 m: 5
2,438 to 3,047 m: 16
1,524 to 2,437 m: 19
914 to 1,523 m: 17
under 914 m: 10 (2005 est.)
Airports - with unpaved runways:
total: 15
914 to 1,523 m: 3
under 914 m: 12 (2005 est.)
Heliports: 8 (2005 est.)
Pipelines: gas 1,166 km; oil 94 km (2004)
Railways:
total: 2,571 km (764 km electrified)
standard gauge: 1,565 km 1.435-m gauge
narrow gauge: 961 km 1.000-m gauge; 22 km 0.750-m gauge
dual gauge: 23 km combined 1.435-m and 1.000-m gauges (three rail system) (2004)
Roadways:
total: 116,470 km
paved: 106,920 km (including 880 km of expressways)
unpaved: 9,550 km (1999)
Waterways: 6 km
note: Corinth Canal (6 km) crosses the Isthmus of Corinth; shortens sea voyage by 325 km (2004)
Merchant marine:
total: 861 ships (1,000 GRT or over) 30,186,624 GRT/52,943,968 DWT
by type: bulk carrier 296, cargo 65, chemical tanker 47, combination ore/oil 2, container 46, liquefied gas 2, passenger 13, passenger/cargo 121, petroleum tanker 252, roll on/roll off 17
foreign-owned: 25 (Chile 1, China 1, Cyprus 5, Norway 6, Sweden 1, United Kingdom 11)
registered in other countries: 2,208 (2005)
Ports and terminals: Agioitheodoroi, Aspropyrgos, Irakleion, Pachi, Peiraiefs, Thessaloniki

MILITARY

Military branches: Hellenic Army, Hellenic Navy, Hellenic Air Force (Polemiki Aeroporia, EPA)
Military service age and obligation: 18 years of age for compulsory military service; during wartime the law allows for recruitment after reaching January of the year of inductee's 18th birthday, thus including 17 year olds; 17 years of age for volunteers; conscript service obligation - 12 months for the Army and Air Force, 15 months for Navy (2005)
Manpower available for military service:
males age 18-49: 2,459,988 (2005 est.)
Manpower fit for military service: *males age 18-49:* 2,018,557 (2005 est.)
Manpower reaching military service age annually: *males:* 58,399 (2005 est.)
Military expenditures - dollar figure: $5.89 billion (2004)
Military expenditures - percent of GDP: 4.3% (2003)

TRANSNATIONAL ISSUES

Disputes - international: Greece and Turkey continue discussions to resolve their complex maritime, air, territorial, and boundary disputes in the Aegean Sea; Cyprus question with Turkey; Greece rejects the use of the name Macedonia or Republic of Macedonia
Illicit drugs: a gateway to Europe for traffickers smuggling cannabis and heroin from the Middle East and Southwest Asia to the West and precursor chemicals to the East; some South American cocaine transits or is consumed in Greece; money laundering related to drug trafficking and organized crime

GREENLAND

INTRODUCTION

Background: The world's largest island, Greenland is about 81% ice-capped. Vikings reached the island in the 10th century from Iceland; Danish colonization began in the 18th century and Greenland was made an integral part of Denmark in 1953. It joined the European Community (now the European Union) with Denmark in 1973 but withdrew in 1985 over a dispute over stringent fishing quotas. Greenland was granted self-government in 1979 by the Danish parliament. The law went into effect the following year. Denmark continues to exercise control of Greenland's foreign affairs.

GEOGRAPHY

Location: Northern North America, island between the Arctic Ocean and the North Atlantic Ocean, northeast of Canada
Geographic coordinates: 72 00 N, 40 00 W
Map references: Arctic Region
Area:
total: 2,166,086 sq km
land: 2,166,086 sq km (410,449 sq km ice-free, 1,755,637 sq km ice-covered) (2000 est.)
Area - comparative: slightly more than three times the size of Texas
Land boundaries: 0 km
Coastline: 44,087 km

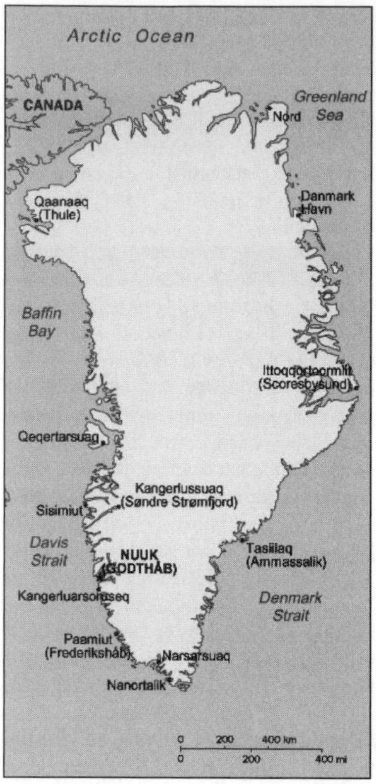

Maritime claims:
territorial sea: 3 nm
continental shelf: 200 nm or agreed boundaries or median line
exclusive fishing zone: 200 nm or agreed boundaries or median line
Climate: arctic to subarctic; cool summers, cold winters
Terrain: flat to gradually sloping icecap covers all but a narrow, mountainous, barren, rocky coast
Elevation extremes:
lowest point: Atlantic Ocean 0 m
highest point: Gunnbjorn 3,700 m
Natural resources: coal, iron ore, lead, zinc, molybdenum, gold, platinum, uranium, fish, seals, whales, hydropower, possible oil and gas
Land use:
arable land: 0%
permanent crops: 0%
other: 100% (2001)
Irrigated land: NA sq km
Natural hazards: continuous permafrost over northern two-thirds of the island
Environment - current issues: protection of the arctic environment; preservation of the Inuit traditional way of life, including whaling and seal hunting
Geography - note: dominates North Atlantic Ocean between North America and Europe; sparse population confined to small settlements along coast, but close to one-quarter of the population lives in the capital, Nuuk; world's second largest ice cap

PEOPLE

Population: 56,375 (July 2005 est.)
Age structure:
0-14 years: 25% (male 7,216/female 6,888)
15-64 years: 68.7% (male 20,897/female 17,823)
65 years and over: 6.3% (male 1,672/female 1,879) (2005 est.)
Median age:
total: 33.83 years
male: 35.15 years
female: 32.14 years (2005 est.)
Population growth rate: -0.02% (2005 est.)
Birth rate: 15.93 births/1,000 population (2005 est.)
Death rate: 7.77 deaths/1,000 population (2005 est.)
Net migration rate: -8.37 migrant(s)/1,000 population (2005 est.)
Sex ratio:
at birth: 1.02 male(s)/female
under 15 years: 1.05 male(s)/female
15-64 years: 1.17 male(s)/female
65 years and over: 0.89 male(s)/female
total population: 1.12 male(s)/female (2005 est.)
Infant mortality rate:
total: 15.82 deaths/1,000 live births
male: 17.15 deaths/1,000 live births
female: 14.45 deaths/1,000 live births (2005 est.)
Life expectancy at birth:
total population: 69.65 years
male: 66.07 years
female: 73.31 years (2005 est.)
Total fertility rate: 2.41 children born/woman (2005 est.)
HIV/AIDS - adult prevalence rate: NA%
HIV/AIDS - people living with HIV/AIDS: 100 (1999)
HIV/AIDS - deaths: NA
Nationality:
noun: Greenlander(s)
adjective: Greenlandic
Ethnic groups: Greenlander 88% (Inuit and Greenland-born whites), Danish and others 12% (January 2000)
Religions: Evangelical Lutheran
Languages: Greenlandic (East Inuit), Danish, English
Literacy:
definition: NA
total population: NA%
male: NA%
female: NA%
note: similar to Denmark proper

GOVERNMENT

Country name:
conventional long form: none
conventional short form: Greenland
local long form: none
local short form: Kalaallit Nunaat
Dependency status: part of the Kingdom of Denmark; self-governing overseas administrative division of Denmark since 1979
Government type: parliamentary democracy within a constitutional monarchy
Capital: Nuuk (Godthab)
Administrative divisions: 3 districts (landsdele); Avannaa (Nordgronland), Tunu (Ostgronland), Kitaa (Vestgronland)
note: there are 18 municipalities in Greenland
Independence: none (part of the Kingdom of Denmark; foreign affairs is the responsibility of Denmark, but Greenland actively participates in international agreements relating to Greenland)
National holiday: June 21 (longest day)
Constitution: 5 June 1953 (Danish constitution)
Legal system: Danish
Suffrage: 18 years of age; universal
Executive branch:
chief of state: Queen MARGRETHE II of Denmark (since 14 January 1972), represented by High Commissioner Peter LAURITEEN (since NA 2002)
head of government: Prime Minister Hans ENOKSEN (since 14 December 2002)
cabinet: Home Rule Government is elected by the parliament (Landstinget) on the basis of the strength of parties
elections: the monarchy is hereditary; high commissioner appointed by the monarch; prime minister is elected by parliament (usually the leader of the majority party); election last held 3 December 2002 (next to be held December 2006)
election results: Hans ENOKSEN elected prime minister
note: government coalition - Siumut and Inuit Ataqatigiit
Legislative branch: unicameral Parliament or Landstinget (31 seats; members are elected by popular vote on the basis of proportional representation to serve four-year terms)
elections: last held on 15 November 2005 (next to be held by December 2009)
election results: percent of vote by party - Siumut 30.8%, Demokratiit 23%, Inuit Ataqatigiit 22.7%, Atassut Party 19.2%; seats by party - Siumut 10, Demokratiit 7, Inuit Ataqatigiit 7, Atassut 6, other 1
note: two representatives were elected to the Danish Parliament or Folketing on 8 February 2005 (next to be held February 2009); percent of vote by party - NA%; seats by party - Siumut 1, Inuit Ataqatigiit 1
Judicial branch: High Court or Landsret (appeals can be made to the Ostre

Landsret or Eastern Division of the High Court or Supreme Court in Copenhagen)
Political parties and leaders: Atassut Party (Solidarity, a conservative party favoring continuing close relations with Denmark) [Augusta SALLING]; Demokratiit [Per BERTHELSEN]; Inuit Ataqatigiit or IA (Eskimo Brotherhood, a leftist party favoring complete independence from Denmark rather than home rule) [Josef MOTZFELDT]; Issituup (Polar Party) [Nicolai HEINRICH]; Kattusseqatigiit (Candidate List, an independent right-of-center party with no official platform [leader NA]; Siumut (Forward Party, a social democratic party advocating more distinct Greenlandic identity and greater autonomy from Denmark) [Hans ENOKSEN]
Political pressure groups and leaders: NA
International organization participation: NC, NIB, UPU
Diplomatic representation in the US: none (self-governing overseas administrative division of Denmark)
Diplomatic representation from the US: none (self-governing overseas administrative division of Denmark)
Flag description: two equal horizontal bands of white (top) and red with a large disk slightly to the hoist side of center - the top half of the disk is red, the bottom half is white

ECONOMY

Economy - overview: The economy remains critically dependent on exports of fish and substantial support from the Danish Government, which supplies about half of government revenues. The public sector, including publicly-owned enterprises and the municipalities, plays the dominant role in the economy. Despite several interesting hydrocarbon and minerals exploration activities, it will take several years before production can materialize. Tourism is the only sector offering any near-term potential, and even this is limited due to a short season and high costs.
GDP (purchasing power parity): $1.1 billion (2001 est.)
GDP (official exchange rate): NA
GDP - real growth rate: 1.8% (2001 est.)
GDP - per capita: purchasing power parity - $20,000 (2001 est.)
GDP - composition by sector:
agriculture: NA%
industry: NA%
services: NA%
Labor force: 24,500 (1999 est.)
Unemployment rate: 10% (2000 est.)
Population below poverty line: NA
Household income or consumption by percentage share:
lowest 10%: NA%
highest 10%: NA%
Inflation rate (consumer prices): 1.6% (1999 est.)
Budget:
revenues: $646 million
expenditures: $629 million, including capital expenditures of $85 million (1999)
Agriculture - products: forage crops, garden and greenhouse vegetables; sheep, reindeer; fish
Industries: fish processing (mainly shrimp and Greenland halibut); gold, niobium, tantalite, uranium, iron and diamond mining; handicrafts, hides and skins, small shipyards
Industrial production growth rate: NA%
Electricity - production: 242.2 million kWh (2003)
Electricity - production by source:
fossil fuel: 100%
hydro: 0%
nuclear: 0%
other: 0%
note: Greenland is shifting its electricity production from fossil fuel to hydropower production (2001)
Electricity - consumption: 225.3 million kWh (2003)
Electricity - exports: 0 kWh (2003)
Electricity - imports: 0 kWh (2003)
Oil - production: 0 bbl/day (2003 est.)
Oil - consumption: 3,850 bbl/day (2003 est.)
Oil - exports: NA (2001)
Oil - imports: NA (2001)
Exports: $480 million f.o.b. (2004 est.)
Exports - partners: Denmark 63.7%, Japan 12.6%, China 3.9% (2004)
Imports: $601 million c.i.f. (2004 est.)
Imports - partners: Denmark 78.4%, Sweden 11.9%, Norway 2.7% (2004)
Debt - external: $25 million (1999)
Economic aid - recipient: $380 million subsidy from Denmark (1997)
Currency (code): Danish krone (DKK)
Currency code: DKK
Exchange rates: Danish kroner per US dollar - NA (2005), 5.9911 (2004), 6.5877 (2003), 7.8947 (2002), 8.3228 (2001)
Fiscal year: calendar year

COMMUNICATIONS

Telephones - main lines in use: 26,000 (2001)
Telephones - mobile cellular: 16,747 (2001)
Telephone system:
general assessment: adequate domestic and international service provided by satellite, cables and microwave radio relay; totally digitalized in 1995
domestic: microwave radio relay and satellite
international: country code - 299; satellite earth stations - 12 Intelsat, 1 Eutelsat, 2 Americom GE-2 (all Atlantic Ocean)
Radio broadcast stations: AM 5, FM 12, shortwave 0 (1998)
Radios: 30,000 (1998 est.)
Television broadcast stations: 1 publicly-owned station, some local low-power stations, and three AFRTS (US Air Force) stations (1997)
Televisions: 30,000 (1998 est.)
Internet country code: .gl
Internet hosts: 2,642 (2004)
Internet Service Providers (ISPs): 1 (2000)
Internet users: 20,000 (2002)

TRANSPORTATION

Airports: 14 (2004 est.)
Airports - with paved runways:
total: 9
2,438 to 3,047 m: 2
1,524 to 2,437 m: 1
914 to 1,523 m: 1
under 914 m: 5 (2005 est.)
Airports - with unpaved runways:
total: 5
1,524 to 2,437 m: 1
914 to 1,523 m: 2
under 914 m: 2 (2005 est.)
Merchant marine:
total: 3 ships (1,000 GRT or over) 4,593 GRT/3,640 DWT
by type: cargo 1, passenger 2
foreign-owned: 1 (Denmark 1)
registered in other countries: 1 (2005)
Ports and terminals: Sisimiut

MILITARY

Military - note: defense is the responsibility of Denmark

TRANSNATIONAL ISSUES

Disputes - international: uncontested dispute between Canada and Denmark over Hans Island in the Kennedy Channel between Canada's Ellesmere Island and Greenland

GRENADA

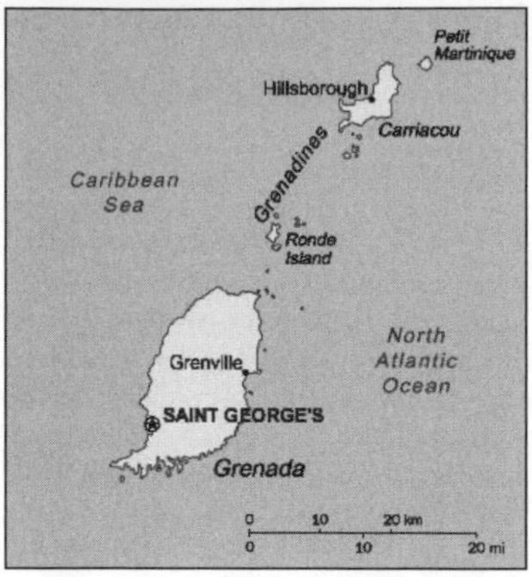

INTRODUCTION

Background: One of the smallest independent countries in the western hemisphere, Grenada was seized by a Marxist military council on 19 October 1983. Six days later the island was invaded by US forces and those of six other Caribbean nations, which quickly captured the ringleaders and their hundreds of Cuban advisers. Free elections were reinstituted the following year.

GEOGRAPHY

Location: Caribbean, island between the Caribbean Sea and Atlantic Ocean, north of Trinidad and Tobago
Geographic coordinates: 12 07 N, 61 40 W
Map references: Central America and the Caribbean
Area:
total: 344 sq km
land: 344 sq km
water: 0 sq km
Area - comparative: twice the size of Washington, DC
Land boundaries: 0 km
Coastline: 121 km
Maritime claims:
territorial sea: 12 nm
exclusive economic zone: 200 nm
Climate: tropical; tempered by northeast trade winds
Terrain: volcanic in origin with central mountains
Elevation extremes:
lowest point: Caribbean Sea 0 m
highest point: Mount Saint Catherine 840 m
Natural resources: timber, tropical fruit, deepwater harbors
Land use:
arable land: 5.88%
permanent crops: 29.41%
other: 64.71% (2001)
Irrigated land: NA sq km
Natural hazards: lies on edge of hurricane belt; hurricane season lasts from June to November
Environment - current issues: NA
Environment - international agreements:
party to: Biodiversity, Climate Change, Climate Change-Kyoto Protocol, Desertification, Endangered Species, Law of the Sea, Ozone Layer Protection, Whaling
signed, but not ratified: none of the selected agreements
Geography - note: the administration of the islands of the Grenadines group is divided between Saint Vincent and the Grenadines and Grenada

PEOPLE

Population: 89,502 (July 2005 est.)
Age structure:
0-14 years: 33.9% (male 15,329/female 14,997)
15-64 years: 62.7% (male 29,711/female 26,436)
65 years and over: 3.4% (male 1,431/female 1,598) (2005 est.)
Median age:
total: 21.26 years
male: 21.73 years
female: 20.76 years (2005 est.)
Population growth rate: 0.19% (2005 est.)
Birth rate: 22.3 births/1,000 population (2005 est.)
Death rate: 7.17 deaths/1,000 population (2005 est.)
Net migration rate: -13.25 migrant(s)/1,000 population (2005 est.)
Sex ratio:
at birth: 1 male(s)/female
under 15 years: 1.02 male(s)/female
15-64 years: 1.12 male(s)/female
65 years and over: 0.9 male(s)/female
total population: 1.08 male(s)/female (2005 est.)
Infant mortality rate:
total: 14.62 deaths/1,000 live births
male: 14.18 deaths/1,000 live births
female: 15.07 deaths/1,000 live births (2005 est.)
Life expectancy at birth:
total population: 64.53 years
male: 62.74 years
female: 66.31 years (2005 est.)
Total fertility rate: 2.37 children born/woman (2005 est.)
HIV/AIDS - adult prevalence rate: NA
HIV/AIDS - people living with HIV/AIDS: NA
HIV/AIDS - deaths: NA
Nationality:
noun: Grenadian(s)
adjective: Grenadian
Ethnic groups: black 82%, mixed black and European 13%, European and East Indian 5%, and trace of Arawak/Carib Amerindian
Religions: Roman Catholic 53%, Anglican 13.8%, other Protestant 33.2%
Languages: English (official), French patois
Literacy:
definition: age 15 and over can read and write
total population: 98%
male: 98%
female: 98% (1970 est.)

GOVERNMENT

Country name:
conventional long form: none
conventional short form: Grenada
Government type: constitutional monarchy with Westminster-style parliament
Capital: Saint George's
Administrative divisions: 6 parishes and 1 dependency*; Carriacou and Petit Martinique*, Saint Andrew, Saint David, Saint George, Saint John, Saint Mark, Saint Patrick
Independence: 7 February 1974 (from UK)
National holiday: Independence Day, 7 February (1974)
Constitution: 19 December 1973
Legal system: based on English common law
Suffrage: 18 years of age; universal
Executive branch:
chief of state: Queen ELIZABETH II (since 6 February 1952), represented by Governor General Daniel WILLIAMS (since 9 August 1996)
head of government: Prime Minister Keith MITCHELL (since 22 June 1995)
cabinet: Cabinet appointed by the governor general on the advice of the prime minister
elections: none; the monarch is hereditary; governor general appointed by the monarch; following legislative elections, the leader of the majority party or the leader of the majority coalition is usually appointed prime minister by the governor general
Legislative branch: bicameral Parliament consists of the Senate (a 13-member body, 10 appointed by the government and three by the leader of the opposition) and the House of Representatives (15 seats; members are elected by popular vote to serve five-year terms)
elections: last held on 27 November 2003 (next to be held by November 2008)
election results: House of Representatives - percent of vote by party - NA%; seats by party - NNP 8, NDC 7
Judicial branch: West Indies Associate States Supreme Court (an associate judge resides in Grenada)
Political parties and leaders: Grenada

United Labor Party or GULP [Gloria Payne BANFIELD]; National Democratic Congress or NDC [Tillman THOMAS]; New National Party or NNP [Keith MITCHELL]; People Labor Movement or PLM [Dr. Francis ALEXIS]
Political pressure groups and leaders: NA
International organization participation: ACP, C, Caricom, CDB, FAO, G-77, IBRD, ICAO, ICFTU, ICRM, IDA, IFAD, IFC, IFRCS, ILO, IMF, IMO, Interpol, IOC, ISO (subscriber), ITU, MIGA, NAM, OAS, OECS, OPANAL, OPCW, UN, UNCTAD, UNESCO, UNIDO, UPU, WHO, WIPO, WMO, WTO
Diplomatic representation in the US:
chief of mission: Ambassador Denis G. ANTOINE
chancery: 1701 New Hampshire Avenue NW, Washington, DC 20009
telephone: [1] (202) 265-2561
FAX: [1] (202) 265-2468
consulate(s) general: New York
Diplomatic representation from the US:
chief of mission: the US Ambassador to Barbados is accredited to Grenada
embassy: Lance-aux-Epines Stretch, Saint George's
mailing address: P. O. Box 54, Saint George's, Grenada, West Indies
telephone: [1] (473) 444-1173 through 1176
FAX: [1] (473) 444-4820
Flag description: a rectangle divided diagonally into yellow triangles (top and bottom) and green triangles (hoist side and outer side), with a red border around the flag; there are seven yellow, five-pointed stars with three centered in the top red border, three centered in the bottom red border, and one on a red disk superimposed at the center of the flag; there is also a symbolic nutmeg pod on the hoist-side triangle (Grenada is the world's second-largest producer of nutmeg, after Indonesia); the seven stars represent the seven administrative divisions

ECONOMY

Economy - overview: Grenada relies on tourism as its main source of foreign exchange, especially since the construction of an international airport in 1985. Strong performances in construction and manufacturing, together with the development of an offshore financial industry, have also contributed to growth in national output.
GDP (purchasing power parity): $440 million (2002 est.)
GDP (official exchange rate): NA
GDP - real growth rate: 2.5% (2002 est.)
GDP - per capita: purchasing power parity - $5,000 (2002 est.)
GDP - composition by sector:
agriculture: 7.7%
industry: 23.9%
services: 68.4% (2000)
Labor force: 42,300 (1996)
Labor force - by occupation: agriculture 24%, industry 14%, services 62% (1999 est.)
Unemployment rate: 12.5% (2000)
Population below poverty line: 32% (2000)
Household income or consumption by percentage share:
lowest 10%: NA
highest 10%: NA
Inflation rate (consumer prices): 2.8% (2001 est.)
Budget:
revenues: $85.8 million
expenditures: $102.1 million, including capital expenditures of $28 million (1997)
Agriculture - products: bananas, cocoa, nutmeg, mace, citrus, avocados, root crops, sugarcane, corn, vegetables
Industries: food and beverages, textiles, light assembly operations, tourism, construction
Industrial production growth rate: 0.7% (1997 est.)
Electricity - production: 159.8 million kWh (2003)
Electricity - production by source:
fossil fuel: 100%
hydro: 0%
nuclear: 0%
other: 0% (2001)
Electricity - consumption: 148.6 million kWh (2003)
Electricity - exports: 0 kWh (2003)
Electricity - imports: 0 kWh (2003)
Oil - production: 0 bbl/day (2003 est.)
Oil - consumption: 1,800 bbl/day (2003 est.)
Oil - exports: NA (2001)
Oil - imports: NA (2001)
Exports: $40 million (2004 est.)
Exports - partners: Saint Lucia 12.7%, US 12.2%, Antigua and Barbuda 8.7%, Netherlands 7.9%, Saint Kitts and Nevis 7.8%, Dominica 7.8%, Germany 7.1%, France 4.6% (2004)
Imports: $276 million (2004 est.)
Imports - partners: Trinidad and Tobago 29.6%, US 27.8%, UK 4.8% (2004)
Debt - external: $196 million (2000)
Economic aid - recipient: $8.3 million (1995)
Currency (code): East Caribbean dollar (XCD)
Currency code: XCD
Exchange rates: East Caribbean dollars per US dollar - NA (2005), 2.7 (2004), 2.7 (2003), 2.7 (2002), 2.7 (2001)
Fiscal year: calendar year

COMMUNICATIONS

Telephones - main lines in use: 33,500 (2002)
Telephones - mobile cellular: 7,600 (2002)
Telephone system:
general assessment: automatic, islandwide telephone system
domestic: interisland VHF and UHF radiotelephone links
international: country code - 1-473; new SHF radiotelephone links to Trinidad and Tobago and Saint Vincent; VHF and UHF radio links to Trinidad
Radio broadcast stations: AM 2, FM 13, shortwave 0 (1998)
Radios: 57,000 (1997)
Television broadcast stations: 2 (1997)
Televisions: 33,000 (1997)
Internet country code: .gd
Internet hosts: 18 (2003)
Internet Service Providers (ISPs): 14 (2000)
Internet users: 15,000 (2002)

TRANSPORTATION

Airports: 3 (2004 est.)
Airports - with paved runways:
total: 3
2,438 to 3,047 m: 1
1,524 to 2,437 m: 1
under 914 m: 1 (2005 est.)
Roadways:
total: 1,127 km
paved: 687 km
unpaved: 440 km (1999)
Ports and terminals: Saint George's

MILITARY

Military branches: no regular military forces; Royal Grenada Police Force
Military expenditures - dollar figure: NA
Military expenditures - percent of GDP: NA

TRANSNATIONAL ISSUES

Disputes - international: none
Illicit drugs: small-scale cannabis cultivation; lesser transshipment point for marijuana and cocaine to US

GUADELOUPE

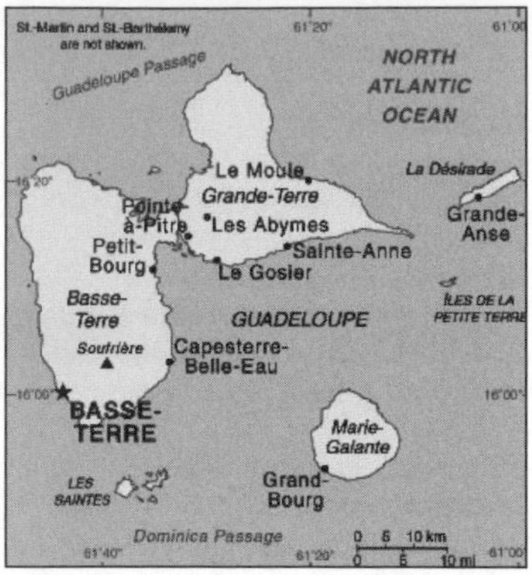

INTRODUCTION

Background: Guadeloupe has been a French possession since 1635. The island of Saint Martin is shared with the Netherlands; its southern portion is named Sint Maarten and is part of the Netherlands Antilles and its northern portion is named Saint-Martin and is part of Guadeloupe

GEOGRAPHY

Location: Caribbean, islands between the Caribbean Sea and the North Atlantic Ocean, southeast of Puerto Rico
Geographic coordinates: 16 15 N, 61 35 W
Map references: Central America and the Caribbean
Area:
total: 1,780 sq km
land: 1,706 sq km
water: 74 sq km
note: Guadeloupe is an archipelago of nine inhabited islands, including Basse-Terre, Grande-Terre, Marie-Galante, La Desirade, Iles des Saintes (2), Saint-Barthelemy, Iles de la Petite Terre, and Saint-Martin (French part of the island of Saint Martin)
Area - comparative: 10 times the size of Washington, DC
Land boundaries:
total: 10.2 km
border countries: Netherlands Antilles (Sint Maarten) 10.2 km
Coastline: 306 km
Maritime claims:
territorial sea: 12 nm
exclusive economic zone: 200 nm
Climate: subtropical tempered by trade winds; moderately high humidity
Terrain: Basse-Terre is volcanic in origin with interior mountains; Grande-Terre is low limestone formation; most of the seven other islands are volcanic in origin
Elevation extremes:
lowest point: Caribbean Sea 0 m
highest point: Soufriere 1,484 m
Natural resources: cultivable land, beaches and climate that foster tourism
Land use:
arable land: 11.24%
permanent crops: 3.55%
other: 85.21% (2001)
Irrigated land: 20 sq km (1998 est.)
Natural hazards: hurricanes (June to October); Soufriere de Guadeloupe is an active volcano
Environment - current issues: NA
Geography - note: a narrow channel, the Riviere Salee, divides Guadeloupe proper into two islands: the larger, western Basse-Terre and the smaller, eastern Grande-Terre

PEOPLE

Population: 448,713 (July 2005 est.)
Age structure:
0-14 years: 24% (male 55,072/female 52,677)
15-64 years: 66.9% (male 148,880/female 151,238)
65 years and over: 9.1% (male 17,032/female 23,814) (2005 est.)
Median age:
total: 31.81 years
male: 30.91 years
female: 32.73 years (2005 est.)
Population growth rate: 0.92% (2005 est.)
Birth rate: 15.42 births/1,000 population (2005 est.)
Death rate: 6.06 deaths/1,000 population (2005 est.)
Net migration rate: -0.15 migrant(s)/1,000 population (2005 est.)
Sex ratio:
at birth: 1.05 male(s)/female
under 15 years: 1.05 male(s)/female
15-64 years: 0.98 male(s)/female
65 years and over: 0.72 male(s)/female
total population: 0.97 male(s)/female (2005 est.)
Infant mortality rate:
total: 8.6 deaths/1,000 live births
male: 9.81 deaths/1,000 live births
female: 7.33 deaths/1,000 live births (2005 est.)
Life expectancy at birth:
total population: 77.9 years
male: 74.74 years
female: 81.21 years (2005 est.)
Total fertility rate: 1.91 children born/woman (2005 est.)
HIV/AIDS - adult prevalence rate: NA%
HIV/AIDS - people living with HIV/AIDS: NA
HIV/AIDS - deaths: NA
Nationality:
noun: Guadeloupian(s)
adjective: Guadeloupe
Ethnic groups: black or mulatto 90%, white 5%, East Indian, Lebanese, Chinese less than 5%
Religions: Roman Catholic 95%, Hindu and pagan African 4%, Protestant 1%
Languages: French (official) 99%, Creole patois
Literacy:
definition: age 15 and over can read and write
total population: 90%
male: 90%
female: 90% (1982 est.)

GOVERNMENT

Country name:
conventional long form: Department of Guadeloupe
conventional short form: Guadeloupe
local long form: Departement de la Guadeloupe
local short form: Guadeloupe
Dependency status: overseas department of France
Government type: NA
Capital: Basse-Terre
Administrative divisions: none (overseas department of France)
Independence: none (overseas department of France)
National holiday: Bastille Day, 14 July (1789)
Constitution: 4 October 1958 (French Constitution)
Legal system: French legal system
Suffrage: 18 years of age; universal
Executive branch:
chief of state: President Jacques CHIRAC of France (since 17 May 1995), represented by Prefect Paul GIROT DE LANGLADE (since 17 August 2004)
head of government: President of the General Council Jacques GILLOT (since 26 March 2001); President of the Regional Council Victorin LUREL (since 2 April 2004)
cabinet: NA
elections: French president elected by popular vote for a five-year term; prefect appointed by the French president on the advice of the French Ministry of Interior; the presidents of the General and Regional Councils are elected by the members of those councils
election results: NA
Legislative branch: unicameral General Council or Conseil General (42 seats; members are elected by popular vote to serve six-year terms) and the unicameral Regional Council or Conseil Regional (41 seats; members are elected by popular vote to serve six-year terms)
elections: General Council - last held

March 2004 (next to be held by NA 2010); Regional Council - last held 28 March 2004 (next to be held NA 2010)
election results: General Council - percent of vote by party - NA%; seats by party - left-wing candidates 11, PS 8, RPR 8, PPDG 6, right-wing candidates 5, PCG 3, UDF 1; Regional Council (second round) - percent of vote by party - PS 58.4%, UMP 41.6%; seats by party - PS 29, UMP 12
note: Guadeloupe elects two representatives to the French Senate; elections last held September 2004 (next to be held September 2013); percent of vote by party - NA%; seats by party - NA, Guadeloupe elects four representatives to the French National Assembly; elections last held 9 June-16 June 2002 (next to be held NA 2007); percent of vote by party - NA%; seats by party - RPR 2, PS 1, different right parties 1
Judicial branch: Court of Appeal or Cour d'Appel with jurisdiction over Guadeloupe, French Guiana, and Martinique
Political parties and leaders: Communist Party of Guadeloupe or PCG [Mona CADOCE]; FGPS [Dominique LARIFLA]; Left Radical Party or PRG [Flavien FERRANT]; Progressive Democratic Party or PPDG [Henri BANGOU]; Socialist Party or PS [Marlene MELISSE and Favrot DAVRAIN]; Union for French Democracy or UDF [Marcel ESDRAS]; Union for a Popular Movement or UMP (including RPR) [Robert JOYEUX]
Political pressure groups and leaders: Christian Movement for the Liberation of Guadeloupe or KLPG; General Federation of Guadeloupe Workers or CGT-G; General Union of Guadeloupe Workers or UGTG; Movement for Independent Guadeloupe or MPGI; The Socialist Renewal Movement
International organization participation: WCL, WFTU
Diplomatic representation in the US: none (overseas department of France)
Diplomatic representation from the US: none (overseas department of France)
Flag description: the flag of France is used

ECONOMY

Economy - overview: The Caribbean economy depends on agriculture, tourism, light industry, and services. It also depends on France for large subsidies and imports. Tourism is a key industry, with most tourists from the US; an increasingly large number of cruise ships visit the islands. The traditional sugarcane crop is slowly being replaced by other crops, such as bananas (which now supply about 50% of export earnings), eggplant, and flowers. Other vegetables and root crops are cultivated for local consumption, although Guadeloupe is still dependent on imported food, mainly from France. Light industry features sugar and rum production. Most manufactured goods and fuel are imported. Unemployment is especially high among the young. Hurricanes periodically devastate the economy.
GDP (purchasing power parity): $3.513 billion (2003 est.)
GDP (official exchange rate): NA
GDP - real growth rate: NA%
GDP - per capita: purchasing power parity - $7,900 (2003 est.)
GDP - composition by sector:
agriculture: 15%
industry: 17%
services: 68% (1997 est.)
Labor force: 125,900 (1997)
Labor force - by occupation: NA
Unemployment rate: 27.8% (1998)
Population below poverty line: NA
Household income or consumption by percentage share:
lowest 10%: NA%
highest 10%: NA%
Inflation rate (consumer prices): NA%
Budget:
revenues: $225 million
expenditures: $390 million, including capital expenditures of $105 million (1996)
Agriculture - products: bananas, sugarcane, tropical fruits and vegetables; cattle, pigs, goats
Industries: construction, cement, rum, sugar, tourism
Industrial production growth rate: NA%
Electricity - production: 1.165 billion kWh (2003)
Electricity - production by source:
fossil fuel: 100%
hydro: 0%
nuclear: 0%
other: 0% (2001)
Electricity - consumption: 1.084 billion kWh (2003)
Electricity - exports: 0 kWh (2003)
Electricity - imports: 0 kWh (2003)
Oil - production: 0 bbl/day (2003 est.)
Oil - consumption: 13,000 bbl/day (2003 est.)
Oil - exports: NA (2001)
Oil - imports: NA (2001)
Exports: $140 million f.o.b. (1997)
Exports - partners: France 60%, Martinique 18%, US 4% (2004)
Imports: $1.7 billion c.i.f. (1997)
Imports - partners: France 63%, Germany 4%, US 3%, Japan 2%, Netherlands Antilles 2% (2004)
Debt - external: $NA (yearend 2003 est.)
Economic aid - recipient: NA; note - substantial annual French subsidies (2004)
Currency (code): euro (EUR)
Currency code: EUR
Exchange rates: euros per US dollar - 0.79697 (2005), 0.8054 (2004), 0.886 (2003), 1.0626 (2002), 1.1175 j(2001)
Fiscal year: calendar year

COMMUNICATIONS

Telephones - main lines in use: 210,000 (2001)
Telephones - mobile cellular: 323,500 (2002)
Telephone system:
general assessment: domestic facilities inadequate
domestic: NA
international: country code - 590; satellite earth station - 1 Intelsat (Atlantic Ocean); microwave radio relay to Antigua and Barbuda, Dominica, and Martinique
Radio broadcast stations: AM 1, FM 17, shortwave 0 (1998)
Radios: 113,000 (1997)
Television broadcast stations: 5 (plus several low-power repeaters) (1997)
Televisions: 118,000 (1997)
Internet country code: .gp
Internet Service Providers (ISPs): 3 (2000)
Internet users: 20,000 (2002)

TRANSPORTATION

Airports: 9 (2004 est.)
Airports - with paved runways:
total: 8
over 3,047 m: 1
914 to 1,523 m: 2
under 914 m: 5 (2005 est.)
Airports - with unpaved runways:
total: 1
under 914 m: 1 (2005 est.)
Roadways:
total: 947 km (2002)
Merchant marine:
total: 1 ships (1,000 GRT or over) 1,240 GRT/109 DWT
by type: passenger 1
foreign-owned: 1 (France 1) (2005)
Ports and terminals: Basse-Terre, Gustavia, Pointe-a-Pitre

MILITARY

Military branches: no regular military forces
Military - note: defense is the responsibility of France

TRANSNATIONAL ISSUES

Disputes - international: none

GUAM

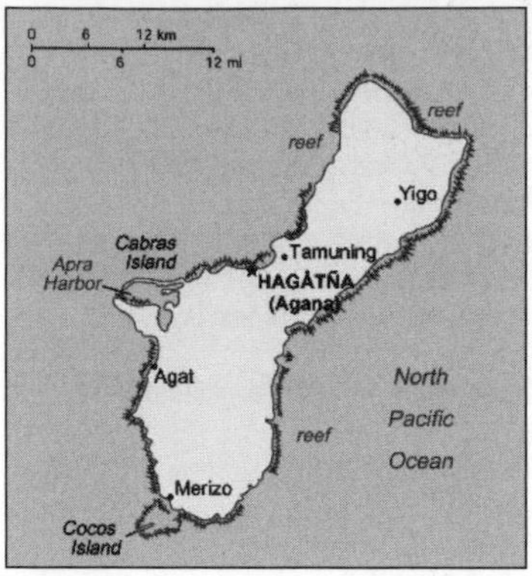

INTRODUCTION

Background: Guam was ceded to the US by Spain in 1898. Captured by the Japanese in 1941, it was retaken by the US three years later. The military installation on the island is one of the most strategically important US bases in the Pacific.

GEOGRAPHY

Location: Oceania, island in the North Pacific Ocean, about three-quarters of the way from Hawaii to the Philippines
Geographic coordinates: 13 28 N, 144 47 E
Map references: Oceania
Area:
total: 549 sq km
land: 549 sq km
water: 0 sq km
Area - comparative: three times the size of Washington, DC
Land boundaries: 0 km
Coastline: 125.5 km
Maritime claims:
territorial sea: 12 nm
exclusive economic zone: 200 nm
Climate: tropical marine; generally warm and humid, moderated by northeast trade winds; dry season from January to June, rainy season from July to December; little seasonal temperature variation
Terrain: volcanic origin, surrounded by coral reefs; relatively flat coralline limestone plateau (source of most fresh water), with steep coastal cliffs and narrow coastal plains in north, low hills in center, mountains in south
Elevation extremes:
lowest point: Pacific Ocean 0 m
highest point: Mount Lamlam 406 m
Natural resources: fishing (largely undeveloped), tourism (especially from Japan)
Land use:
arable land: 9.09%
permanent crops: 16.36%
other: 74.55% (2001)
Irrigated land: NA
Natural hazards: frequent squalls during rainy season; relatively rare, but potentially very destructive typhoons (June - December)
Environment - current issues: extirpation of native bird population by the rapid proliferation of the brown tree snake, an exotic, invasive species
Geography - note: largest and southernmost island in the Mariana Islands archipelago; strategic location in western North Pacific Ocean

PEOPLE

Population: 168,564 (July 2005 est.)
Age structure:
0-14 years: 29.4% (male 25,645/female 23,887)
15-64 years: 64.1% (male 55,115/female 52,935)
65 years and over: 6.5% (male 5,157/female 5,825) (2005 est.)
Median age:
total: 28.38 years
male: 28.16 years
female: 28.61 years (2005 est.)
Population growth rate: 1.46% (2005 est.)
Birth rate: 19.03 births/1,000 population (2005 est.)
Death rate: 4.41 deaths/1,000 population (2005 est.)
Net migration rate: 0 migrant(s)/1,000 population (2005 est.)
Sex ratio:
at birth: 1.06 male(s)/female
under 15 years: 1.07 male(s)/female
15-64 years: 1.04 male(s)/female
65 years and over: 0.88 male(s)/female
total population: 1.04 male(s)/female (2005 est.)
Infant mortality rate:
total: 6.94 deaths/1,000 live births
male: 7.61 deaths/1,000 live births
female: 6.24 deaths/1,000 live births (2005 est.)
Life expectancy at birth:
total population: 78.4 years
male: 75.34 years
female: 81.64 years (2005 est.)
Total fertility rate: 2.6 children born/woman (2005 est.)
HIV/AIDS - adult prevalence rate: NA
HIV/AIDS - people living with HIV/AIDS: NA
HIV/AIDS - deaths: NA
Nationality:
noun: Guamanian(s)
adjective: Guamanian
Ethnic groups: Chamorro 37.1%, Filipino 26.3%, other Pacific islander 11.3%, white 6.9%, other Asian 6.3%, other ethnic origin or race 2.3%, mixed 9.8% (2000 census)
Religions: Roman Catholic 85%, other 15% (1999 est.)
Languages: English 38.3%, Chamorro 22.2%, Philippine languages 22.2%, other Pacific island languages 6.8%, Asian languages 7%, other languages 3.5% (2000 census)
Literacy:
definition: age 15 and over can read and write
total population: 99%
male: 99%
female: 99% (1990 est.)

GOVERNMENT

Country name:
conventional long form: Territory of Guam
conventional short form: Guam
local long form: Guahan
Dependency status: organized, unincorporated territory of the US with policy relations between Guam and the US under the jurisdiction of the Office of Insular Affairs, US Department of the Interior
Government type: NA
Capital: Hagatna (Agana)
Administrative divisions: none (territory of the US)
Independence: none (territory of the US)
National holiday: Discovery Day, first Monday in March (1521)
Constitution: Organic Act of 1 August 1950
Legal system: modeled on US; US federal laws apply
Suffrage: 18 years of age; universal; US citizens, but do not vote in US presidential elections
Executive branch:
chief of state: President George W. BUSH of the US (since 20 January 2001); Vice President Richard B. CHENEY (since 20 January 2001)
head of government: Governor Felix P. P. CAMACHO (since 6 January 2003) and Lieutenant Governor Kaleo MOYLAN (since 6 January 2003)
cabinet: executive departments; heads appointed by the governor with the consent of the Guam legislature
elections: US president and vice president elected on the same ticket for a four-year term; governor and lieutenant governor elected on the same ticket by popular vote for four-year term; election last held 5 November 2002 (next to be held November 2006)
election results: Felix P. P. CAMACHO elected governor; percent of vote - Felix P. P. CAMACHO (Republican Party)

55.4%, Robert A. UNDERWOOD (Democratic Party) 44.6%

Legislative branch: unicameral Legislature (15 seats; members are elected by popular vote to serve two-year terms)
elections: last held 2 November 2004 (next to be held November 2006)
election results: percent of vote by party - NA%; seats by party - Democratic Party 6, Republican Party 9
note: Guam elects one nonvoting delegate to the US House of Representatives; election last held 2 November 2004 (next to be held November 2006); results - Madeleine BORDALLO (Democratic Party) was elected as delegate; percent of vote by party - Democratic Party 64.6%, Republican Party 35.4%; seats by party - Democratic Party 1

Judicial branch: Federal District Court (judge is appointed by the president); Territorial Superior Court (judges appointed for eight-year terms by the governor)

Political parties and leaders: Democratic Party [leader Michael PHILLIPS]; Republican Party (controls the legislature) [leader Philip J. FLORES]

Political pressure groups and leaders: NA

International organization participation: IOC, SPC, UPU

Diplomatic representation in the US: none (territory of the US)

Diplomatic representation from the US: none (territory of the US)

Flag description: territorial flag is dark blue with a narrow red border on all four sides; centered is a red-bordered, pointed, vertical ellipse containing a beach scene, outrigger canoe with sail, and a palm tree with the word GUAM superimposed in bold red letters; US flag is the national flag

ECONOMY

Economy - overview: The economy depends on US military spending, tourism, and the export of fish and handicrafts. Total US grants, wage payments, and procurement outlays amounted to $1 billion in 1998. Over the past 20 years, the tourist industry has grown rapidly, creating a construction boom for new hotels and the expansion of older ones. More than 1 million tourists visit Guam each year. The industry had recently suffered setbacks because of the continuing Japanese slowdown; the Japanese normally make up almost 90% of the tourists. Most food and industrial goods are imported. Guam faces the problem of building up the civilian economic sector to offset the impact of military downsizing.

GDP (purchasing power parity): $3.2 billion (2000 est.)

GDP (official exchange rate): NA

GDP - real growth rate: NA

GDP - per capita: purchasing power parity - $21,000 (2000 est.)

GDP - composition by sector:
agriculture: 7%
industry: 15%
services: 78% (2002 est.)

Labor force: 60,000 (2000 est.)

Labor force - by occupation: private 74% (industry 10%, trade 24%, other services 40%), federal and territorial government 26% (2000 est.)

Unemployment rate: 15% (2000 est.)

Population below poverty line: 23% (2001 est.)

Household income or consumption by percentage share:
lowest 10%: NA
highest 10%: NA

Inflation rate (consumer prices): 0% (1999 est.)

Budget:
revenues: $340 million
expenditures: $445 million, including capital expenditures of NA (2000 est.)

Agriculture - products: fruits, copra, vegetables; eggs, pork, poultry, beef

Industries: US military, tourism, construction, transshipment services, concrete products, printing and publishing, food processing, textiles

Industrial production growth rate: NA

Electricity - production: 840.1 million kWh (2003)

Electricity - production by source:
fossil fuel: 100%
hydro: 0%
nuclear: 0%
other: 0% (2001)

Electricity - consumption: 781.3 million kWh (2003)

Electricity - exports: 0 kWh (2003)

Electricity - imports: 0 kWh (2003)

Oil - production: 0 bbl/day (2003 est.)

Oil - consumption: 19,000 bbl/day (2003 est.)

Oil - exports: NA (2001)

Oil - imports: NA (2001)

Exports: $45 million f.o.b. (2004 est.)

Exports - partners: Japan 66.1%, South Korea 9.9%, Singapore 8.4% (2004)

Imports: $701 million f.o.b. (2004 est.)

Imports - partners: Singapore 39.5%, South Korea 20.8%, Japan 19%, Hong Kong 9%, Philippines 4.3% (2004)

Debt - external: NA

Economic aid - recipient: Guam receives large transfer payments from the US Federal Treasury ($143 million in 1997) into which Guamanians pay no income or excise taxes; under the provisions of a special law of Congress, the Guam Treasury, rather than the US Treasury, receives federal income taxes paid by military and civilian Federal employees stationed in Guam (2001 est.)

Currency (code): US dollar (USD)

Currency code: USD

Exchange rates: the US dollar is used

Fiscal year: 1 October - 30 September

COMMUNICATIONS

Telephones - main lines in use: 84,134 (2001)

Telephones - mobile cellular: 32,600 (2001)

Telephone system:
general assessment: modern system, integrated with US facilities for direct dialing, including free use of 800 numbers
domestic: modern digital system, including cellular mobile service and local access to the Internet
international: country code - 1-671; satellite earth stations - 2 Intelsat (Pacific Ocean); submarine cables to US and Japan (Guam is a trans-Pacific communications hub for MCI, Sprint, AT&T, IT&E, and GTE, linking the US and Asia)

Radio broadcast stations: AM 4, FM 7, shortwave 2 (2003)

Radios: 221,000 (1997)

Television broadcast stations: 3 (2004)

Televisions: 106,000 (1997)

Internet country code: .gu

Internet Service Providers (ISPs): 20 (2000)

Internet users: 50,000 (2002)

TRANSPORTATION

Airports: 5 (2004 est.)

Airports - with paved runways:
total: 4
over 3,047 m: 2
2,438 to 3,047 m: 1
914 to 1,523 m: 1 (2005 est.)

Airports - with unpaved runways:
total: 1
under 914 m: 1 (2005 est.)

Roadways:
total: 977 km
paved: 962 km
unpaved: 15 km (2004)

Ports and terminals: Apra Harbor

MILITARY

Military - note: defense is the responsibility of the US

TRANSNATIONAL ISSUES

Disputes - international: none

GUATEMALA

INTRODUCTION

Background: The Maya civilization flourished in Guatemala and surrounding regions during the first millennium A.D. After almost three centuries as a Spanish colony, Guatemala won its independence in 1821. During the second half of the 20th century, it experienced a variety of military and civilian governments as well as a 36-year guerrilla war. In 1996, the government signed a peace agreement formally ending the conflict, which had left more than 100,000 people dead and had created some 1 million refugees.

GEOGRAPHY

Location: Central America, bordering the North Pacific Ocean, between El Salvador and Mexico, and bordering the Gulf of Honduras (Caribbean Sea) between Honduras and Belize
Geographic coordinates: 15 30 N, 90 15 W
Map references: Central America and the Caribbean
Area:
total: 108,890 sq km
land: 108,430 sq km
water: 460 sq km
Area - comparative: slightly smaller than Tennessee
Land boundaries:
total: 1,687 km
border countries: Belize 266 km, El Salvador 203 km, Honduras 256 km, Mexico 962 km
Coastline: 400 km
Maritime claims:
territorial sea: 12 nm
exclusive economic zone: 200 nm
continental shelf: 200-m depth or to the depth of exploitation
Climate: tropical; hot, humid in lowlands; cooler in highlands
Terrain: mostly mountains with narrow coastal plains and rolling limestone plateau (Peten)
Elevation extremes:
lowest point: Pacific Ocean 0 m
highest point: Volcan Tajumulco 4,211 m
Natural resources: petroleum, nickel, rare woods, fish, chicle, hydropower
Land use:
arable land: 12.54%
permanent crops: 5.03%
other: 82.43% (2001)
Irrigated land: 1,250 sq km (1998 est.)
Natural hazards: numerous volcanoes in mountains, with occasional violent earthquakes; Caribbean coast extremely susceptible to hurricanes and other tropical storms
Environment - current issues: deforestation in the Peten rainforest; soil erosion; water pollution
Environment - international agreements:
party to: Antarctic Treaty, Biodiversity, Climate Change, Climate Change-Kyoto Protocol, Desertification, Endangered Species, Environmental Modification, Hazardous Wastes, Law of the Sea, Marine Dumping, Ozone Layer Protection, Ship Pollution, Wetlands
signed, but not ratified: none of the selected agreements
Geography - note: no natural harbors on west coast

PEOPLE

Population: 14,655,189 (July 2005 est.)
Age structure:
0-14 years: 42.4% (male 3,185,037/female 3,033,947)
15-64 years: 54.2% (male 4,019,052/female 3,928,984)
65 years and over: 3.3% (male 226,745/female 261,424) (2005 est.)
Median age:
total: 18.47 years
male: 18.25 years
female: 18.71 years (2005 est.)
Population growth rate: 2.57% (2005 est.)
Birth rate: 34.11 births/1,000 population (2005 est.)
Death rate: 6.81 deaths/1,000 population (2005 est.)
Net migration rate: -1.63 migrant(s)/1,000 population (2005 est.)
Sex ratio:
at birth: 1.05 male(s)/female
under 15 years: 1.05 male(s)/female
15-64 years: 1.02 male(s)/female
65 years and over: 0.87 male(s)/female
total population: 1.03 male(s)/female (2005 est.)
Infant mortality rate:
total: 35.93 deaths/1,000 live births
male: 36.74 deaths/1,000 live births
female: 35.09 deaths/1,000 live births (2005 est.)
Life expectancy at birth:
total population: 69.06 years
male: 67.37 years
female: 70.84 years (2005 est.)
Total fertility rate: 4.53 children born/woman (2005 est.)
HIV/AIDS - adult prevalence rate: 1.1% (2003 est.)
HIV/AIDS - people living with HIV/AIDS: 78,000 (2003 est.)
HIV/AIDS - deaths: 5,800 (2003 est.)
Nationality:
noun: Guatemalan(s)
adjective: Guatemalan
Ethnic groups: Mestizo (mixed Amerindian-Spanish - in local Spanish called Ladino) and European 59.4%, K'iche 9.1%, Kaqchikel 8.4%, Mam 7.9%, Q'eqchi 6.3%, other Mayan 8.6%, indigenous non-Mayan 0.2%, other 0.1% (2001 census)
Religions: Roman Catholic, Protestant, indigenous Mayan beliefs
Languages: Spanish 60%, Amerindian languages 40% (23 officially recognized Amerindian languages, including Quiche, Cakchiquel, Kekchi, Mam, Garifuna, and Xinca)
Literacy:
definition: age 15 and over can read and write
total population: 70.6%
male: 78%
female: 63.3% (2003 est.)

GOVERNMENT

Country name:
conventional long form: Republic of Guatemala
conventional short form: Guatemala
local long form: Republica de Guatemala
local short form: Guatemala
Government type: constitutional democratic republic
Capital: Guatemala
Administrative divisions: 22 departments (departamentos, singular - departamento); Alta Verapaz, Baja Verapaz, Chimaltenango, Chiquimula, El Progreso, Escuintla, Guatemala, Huehuetenango, Izabal, Jalapa, Jutiapa, Peten, Quetzaltenango, Quiche, Retalhuleu, Sacatepequez, San Marcos, Santa Rosa, Solola, Suchitepequez, Totonicapan, Zacapa
Independence: 15 September 1821 (from Spain)
National holiday: Independence Day, 15 September (1821)
Constitution: 31 May 1985, effective 14 January 1986; note - suspended 25 May 1993 by former President SERRANO; reinstated 5 June 1993 following ouster

of president; amended November 1993
Legal system: civil law system; judicial review of legislative acts; has not accepted compulsory ICJ jurisdiction
Suffrage: 18 years of age; universal (active duty members of the armed forces may not vote and are restricted to their barracks on election day)
Executive branch:
chief of state: President Oscar Jose Rafael BERGER Perdomo (since 14 January 2004); Vice President Eduardo STEIN Barillas (since 14 January 2004); note - the president is both the chief of state and head of government
head of government: President Oscar Jose Rafael BERGER Perdomo (since 14 January 2004); Vice President Eduardo STEIN Barillas (since 14 January 2004); note - the president is both the chief of state and head of government
cabinet: Council of Ministers appointed by the president
elections: president elected by popular vote for a four-year term; election last held 9 November 2003; runoff held 28 December 2003 (next to be held November 2007)
election results: Oscar BERGER Perdomo elected president; percent of vote - Oscar BERGER Perdomo (GANA) 54.1%, Alvarado COLOM (UNE) 45.9%
Legislative branch: unicameral Congress of the Republic or Congreso de la Republica (158 seats; members are elected by popular vote to serve four-year terms)
elections: last held 9 November 2003 (next to be held November 2007)
election results: percent of vote by party - NA%; seats by party - GANA 49, FRG 41, UNE 33, PAN 17, other 18
note: for the 9 November 2003 election, the number of congressional seats increased from 113 to 158
Judicial branch: Constitutional Court or Corte de Constitutcionalidad is Guatemala's highest court (five judges are elected for concurrent five-year terms by Congress, each serving one year as president of the Constitutional Court; one is elected by Congress, one elected by the Supreme Court of Justice, one appointed by the President, one elected by Superior Counsel of Universidad San Carlos de Guatemala, and one by Colegio de Abogados); Supreme Court of Justice or Corte Suprema de Justicia (13 members serve concurrent five-year terms and elect a president of the Court each year from among their number; the president of the Supreme Court of Justice also supervises trial judges around the country, who are named to five-year terms)
Political parties and leaders: Authentic Integral Development or DIA [Eduardo SUGER]; Grand National Alliance or GANA (an alliance of smaller parties) [Alfredo VILA Giron, secretary general]; Green Party or LOV [Rodolfo ROSALES Garcis-Salaz]; Guatemalan Christian Democracy or DCG [Vinicio CEREZO Arevalo]; Guatemalan National Revolutionary Unity or URNG [Alba ESTELA Maldonado, secretary general]; Guatemalan Republican Front or FRG [Efrain RIOS Montt]; Movement for Guatemalan Unity or MGU [Jacobo ARBENZ Villanueva]; Movement for Principals and Values or MPV [Francisco BIANCHI]; National Advancement Party or PAN [Leonel LOPEZ Rodas, secretary general]; National Unity for Hope or UNE [Alvarado COLOM Caballeros]; New Nation Alliance or ANN (formed by an alliance of DIA, URNG, and several splinter groups most of whom subsequently defected) [led by three co-equal partners - Nineth Varenca MONTENEGRO Cottom, Rodolfo BAUER Paiz, and Jorge Antonio BALSELLS TUT]; Patriot Party or PP [retired General Otto PEREZ Molina]; Progressive Liberator Party or PLP [Acisclo VALLADARES Molina]; Reform Movement or MR [Alfredo SKINNER-KLEE, secretary general]; Unionista Party [leader NA]
Political pressure groups and leaders: Agrarian Owners Group or UNAGRO; Alliance Against Impunity or AAI; Committee for Campesino Unity or CUC; Coordinating Committee of Agricultural, Commercial, Industrial, and Financial Associations or CACIF; Mutual Support Group or GAM
International organization participation: BCIE, CACM, FAO, G-24, G-77, IADB, IAEA, IBRD, ICAO, ICC, ICFTU, ICRM, IDA, IFAD, IFC, IFRCS, IHO, ILO, IMF, IMO, Interpol, IOC, IOM, ISO (correspondent), ITU, LAES, LAIA (observer), MIGA, MINUSTAH, MONUC, NAM, OAS, ONUB, OPANAL, OPCW, PCA, UN, UNCTAD, UNESCO, UNIDO, UNMIS, UNOCI, UPU, WCL, WCO, WFTU, WHO, WIPO, WMO, WToO, WTO
Diplomatic representation in the US:
chief of mission: Ambassador Guillermo CASTILLO
chancery: 2220 R Street NW, Washington, DC 20008
telephone: [1] (202) 745-4952
FAX: [1] (202) 745-1908
consulate(s) general: Chicago, Denver, Houston, Los Angeles, Miami, New York, and San Francisco
Diplomatic representation from the US:
chief of mission: Ambassador James M. DURHAM
embassy: 7-01 Avenida Reforma, Zone 10, Guatemala City
mailing address: APO AA 34024
telephone: [502] 2326-4000
FAX: [502] 2334-8477
Flag description: three equal vertical bands of light blue (hoist side), white, and light blue with the coat of arms centered in the white band; the coat of arms includes a green and red quetzal (the national bird) and a scroll bearing the inscription LIBERTAD 15 DE SEPTIEMBRE DE 1821 (the original date of independence from Spain) all superimposed on a pair of crossed rifles and a pair of crossed swords and framed by a wreath

ECONOMY

Economy - overview: Guatemala is the largest and most populous of the Central American countries with a GDP per capita roughly one-half that of Brazil, Argentina, and Chile. The agricultural sector accounts for about one-fourth of GDP, two-thirds of exports, and half of the labor force. Coffee, sugar, and bananas are the main products. The 1996 signing of peace accords, which ended 36 years of civil war, removed a major obstacle to foreign investment, but widespread political violence and corruption scandals continue to dampen investor confidence. The distribution of income remains highly unequal, with perhaps 75% of the population below the poverty line. Other ongoing challenges include increasing government revenues, negotiating further assistance from international donors, upgrading both government and private financial operations, curtailing drug trafficking, and narrowing the trade deficit.
GDP (purchasing power parity): $62.78 billion (2005 est.)
GDP (official exchange rate): $28.27 billion (2005 est.)
GDP - real growth rate: 3.1% (2005 est.)
GDP - per capita: purchasing power parity - $4,300 (2005 est.)
GDP - composition by sector:
agriculture: 22.8%
industry: 19.1%
services: 58.1% (2005 est.)
Labor force: 3.76 million (2005 est.)
Labor force - by occupation: agriculture 50%, industry 15%, services 35% (1999 est.)
Unemployment rate: 7.5% (2003 est.)
Population below poverty line: 75% (2004 est.)
Household income or consumption by percentage share:
lowest 10%: 1.6%
highest 10%: 46% (1998)
Distribution of family income - Gini index: 48.3 (2000)

Inflation rate (consumer prices): 9.1% (2005 est.)
Investment (gross fixed): 15.5% of GDP (2005 est.)
Budget:
revenues: $3.374 billion
expenditures: $4.041 billion, including capital expenditures of $750 million (2005 est.)
Public debt: 26.9% of GDP (2005 est.)
Agriculture - products: sugarcane, corn, bananas, coffee, beans, cardamom; cattle, sheep, pigs, chickens
Industries: sugar, textiles and clothing, furniture, chemicals, petroleum, metals, rubber, tourism
Industrial production growth rate: 4.1% (1999)
Electricity - production: 6.898 billion kWh (2003)
Electricity - production by source:
fossil fuel: 51.9%
hydro: 35.2%
nuclear: 0%
other: 12.9% (2001)
Electricity - consumption: 6.025 billion kWh (2003)
Electricity - exports: 425 million kWh (2003)
Electricity - imports: 35 million kWh (2003)
Oil - production: 22,300 bbl/day (2005 est.)
Oil - consumption: 66,000 bbl/day (2003 est.)
Oil - exports: 3,104 bbl/day (2003)
Oil - imports: NA (2001)
Oil - proved reserves: 263 million bbl (1 January 2002)
Natural gas - proved reserves: 1.543 billion cu m (1 January 2002)
Current account balance: $-1.236 billion (2005 est.)
Exports: $3.94 billion f.o.b. (2005 est.)
Exports - partners: US 53%, El Salvador 11.4%, Honduras 7.1%, Mexico 4.1% (2004)
Imports: $7.744 billion f.o.b. (2005 est.)
Imports - partners: US 34%, Mexico 8.1%, South Korea 6.8%, China 6.6%, Japan 4.4% (2004)
Reserves of foreign exchange and gold: $3.764 billion (2005 est.)
Debt - external: $5.503 billion (2005 est.)
Economic aid - recipient: $250 million (2000 est.)
Currency (code): quetzal (GTQ), US dollar (USD), others allowed
Currency code: GTQ; USD
Exchange rates: quetzales per US dollar - 7.65 (2005), 7.9465 (2004), 7.9409 (2003), 7.8216 (2002), 7.8586 (2001)
Fiscal year: calendar year

COMMUNICATIONS

Telephones - main lines in use: 846,000 (2002)
Telephones - mobile cellular: 1,577,100 (2002)
Telephone system:
general assessment: fairly modern network centered in the city of Guatemala
domestic: NA
international: country code - 502; connected to Central American Microwave System; satellite earth station - 1 Intelsat (Atlantic Ocean)
Radio broadcast stations: AM 130, FM 487, shortwave 15 (2000)
Radios: 835,000 (1997)
Television broadcast stations: 26 (plus 27 repeaters) (1997)
Televisions: 1.323 million (1997)
Internet country code: .gt
Internet hosts: 20,360 (2003)
Internet Service Providers (ISPs): 5 (2000)
Internet users: 400,000 (2002)

TRANSPORTATION

Airports: 452 (2004 est.)
Airports - with paved runways:
total: 11
2,438 to 3,047 m: 3
1,524 to 2,437 m: 2
914 to 1,523 m: 4
under 914 m: 2 (2005 est.)
Airports - with unpaved runways:
total: 438
2,438 to 3,047 m: 1
1,524 to 2,437 m: 8
914 to 1,523 m: 110
under 914 m: 319 (2005 est.)
Pipelines: oil 480 km (2004)
Railways:
total: 886 km
narrow gauge: 886 km 0.914-m gauge (2004)
Roadways:
total: 14,095 km
paved: 4,863 km (including 75 km of expressways)
unpaved: 9,232 km (1999)
Waterways: 990 km
note: 260 km navigable year round; additional 730 km navigable during high-water season (2004)
Ports and terminals: Puerto Quetzal, Santo Tomas de Castilla

MILITARY

Military branches: Army, Navy (includes Marines), Air Force
Military service age and obligation: all male citizens between the ages of 18 and 50 are liable for military service; conscript service obligation varies from 12 to 24 months (2005)
Manpower available for military service: *males age 18-49*: 3,020,292 (2005 est.)
Manpower fit for military service: *males age 18-49*: 2,106,847 (2005 est.)
Manpower reaching military service age annually: *males*: 161,964 (2005 est.)
Military expenditures - dollar figure: $201.9 million (2004)
Military expenditures - percent of GDP: 0.8% (2003)

TRANSNATIONAL ISSUES

Disputes - international: Guatemalan squatters continue to settle in the rain forests of Belize's border region; OAS is attempting to revive the 2002 failed Differendum that created a small adjustment to land boundary, a Guatemalan maritime corridor in Caribbean, a joint ecological park for the disputed Sapodilla Cays, and a substantial US-UK financial package; Guatemalans enter Mexico illegally seeking work or transit to the US
Refugees and internally displaced persons: *IDPs*: 250,000 (government's scorched-earth offensive in 1980s against indigenous people) (2004)
Illicit drugs: major transit country for cocaine and heroin; minor producer of illicit opium poppy and cannabis for mostly domestic consumption; proximity to Mexico makes Guatemala a major staging area for drugs (particularly for cocaine); money laundering is a serious problem; corruption is a major problem; remains on Financial Action Task Force Non-Cooperative Countries and Territories List for continued failure to address deficiencies in money-laundering control regime

GUERNSEY

INTRODUCTION

Background: The island of Guernsey and the other Channel Islands represent the last remnants of the medieval Dukedom of Normandy, which held sway in both France and England. The islands were the only British soil occupied by German troops in World War II.

GEOGRAPHY

Location: Western Europe, islands in the English Channel, northwest of France
Geographic coordinates: 49 28 N, 2 35 W
Map references: Europe
Area:
total: 78 sq km
land: 78 sq km

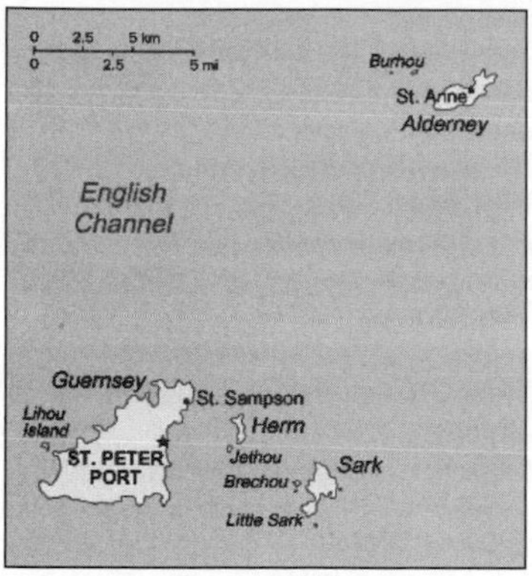

water: 0 sq km
note: includes Alderney, Guernsey, Herm, Sark, and some other smaller islands
Area - comparative: about one-half the size of Washington, DC
Land boundaries: 0 km
Coastline: 50 km
Maritime claims:
territorial sea: 3 nm
exclusive fishing zone: 12 nm
Climate: temperate with mild winters and cool summers; about 50% of days are overcast
Terrain: mostly level with low hills in southwest
Elevation extremes:
lowest point: Atlantic Ocean 0 m
highest point: unnamed location on Sark 114 m
Natural resources: cropland
Land use:
arable land: NA%
permanent crops: NA%
other: NA%
Irrigated land: NA sq km
Natural hazards: NA
Environment - current issues: NA
Geography - note: large, deepwater harbor at Saint Peter Port

PEOPLE

Population: 65,228 (July 2005 est.)
Age structure:
0-14 years: 15.4% (male 5,084/female 4,937)
15-64 years: 66.9% (male 21,611/female 22,002)
65 years and over: 17.8% (male 4,882/female 6,712) (2005 est.)
Median age:
total: 40.99 years
male: 40.03 years
female: 41.91 years (2005 est.)
Population growth rate: 0.29% (2005 est.)
Birth rate: 9.01 births/1,000 population (2005 est.)
Death rate: 9.95 deaths/1,000 population (2005 est.)
Net migration rate: 3.83 migrant(s)/1,000 population (2005 est.)
Sex ratio:
at birth: 1.03 male(s)/female
under 15 years: 1.03 male(s)/female
15-64 years: 0.98 male(s)/female
65 years and over: 0.73 male(s)/female
total population: 0.94 male(s)/female (2005 est.)
Infant mortality rate:
total: 4.71 deaths/1,000 live births
male: 5.26 deaths/1,000 live births
female: 4.13 deaths/1,000 live births (2005 est.)
Life expectancy at birth:
total population: 80.3 years
male: 77.3 years
female: 83.41 years (2005 est.)
Total fertility rate: 1.38 children born/woman (2005 est.)
HIV/AIDS - adult prevalence rate: NA%
HIV/AIDS - people living with HIV/AIDS: NA
HIV/AIDS - deaths: NA
Nationality:
noun: Channel Islander(s)
adjective: Channel Islander
Ethnic groups: UK and Norman-French descent with small percentages from other European countries
Religions: Anglican, Roman Catholic, Presbyterian, Baptist, Congregational, Methodist
Languages: English, French, Norman-French dialect spoken in country districts
Literacy:
definition: NA
total population: NA%
male: NA%
female: NA%

GOVERNMENT

Country name:
conventional long form: Bailiwick of Guernsey
conventional short form: Guernsey
Dependency status: British crown dependency
Government type: NA
Capital: Saint Peter Port
Administrative divisions: none (British crown dependency); there are no first-order administrative divisions as defined by the US Government, but there are 10 parishes including Saint Peter Port, Saint Sampson, Vale, Castel, Saint Saviour, Saint Pierre du Bois, Torteval, Forest, Saint Martin, Saint Andrew
Independence: none (British crown dependency)
National holiday: Liberation Day, 9 May (1945)
Constitution: unwritten; partly statutes, partly common law and practice
Legal system: English law and local statutes; justice is administered by the Royal Court
Suffrage: 18 years of age; universal
Executive branch:
chief of state: Queen ELIZABETH II (since 6 February 1952), represented by Lieutenant Governor Sir Fabian MALBON (since 28 October 2005)
head of government: Chief Minister Laurie MORGAN (since 1 May 2004)
cabinet: Policy Council elected by the States of Deliberation
elections: the monarch is hereditary; lieutenant governor appointed by the monarch; chief minister is elected by States of Delibertion
election results: Laurie MORGAN elected chief minister, percent of vote of the States of Deliberation NA%
Legislative branch: unicameral States of Deliberation (45 seats; members are elected by popular vote for 4 years); note - Alderney and Sark have their own parliaments
elections: last held 21 April 2004 (next to be held NA 2008)
election results: percent of vote - NA%; seats - all independents
Judicial branch: Royal Court
Political parties and leaders: none; all independents
Political pressure groups and leaders: none
International organization participation: UPU
Diplomatic representation in the US: none (British crown dependency)
Diplomatic representation from the US: none (British crown dependency)
Flag description: white with the red cross of Saint George (patron saint of England) extending to the edges of the flag and a yellow equal-armed cross of William the Conqueror superimposed on the Saint George cross

ECONOMY

Economy - overview: Financial services - banking, fund management, insurance - account for about 55% of total income in this tiny, prosperous Channel Island economy. Tourism, manufacturing, and horticulture, mainly tomatoes and cut flowers, have been declining. Light tax and death duties make Guernsey a popular tax haven. The evolving economic integration of the EU nations is changing the environment under which Guernsey operates.
GDP (purchasing power parity): $2.59 billion (2003 est.)
GDP (official exchange rate): NA
GDP - real growth rate: 3% (2003 est.)
GDP - per capita: purchasing power parity - $40,000 (2003 est.)
GDP - composition by sector:
agriculture: 3%
industry: 10%
services: 87% (2000)

Labor force: 32,290 (2001)
Unemployment rate: 0.5% (1999 est.)
Population below poverty line: NA
Household income or consumption by percentage share:
lowest 10%: NA%
highest 10%: NA%
Inflation rate (consumer prices): 4.9% (2004 est.)
Budget:
revenues: $539.2 million
expenditures: $448.3 million, including capital expenditures of NA (2002 est.)
Agriculture - products: tomatoes, greenhouse flowers, sweet peppers, eggplant, fruit; Guernsey cattle
Industries: tourism, banking
Industrial production growth rate: NA%
Electricity - production: NA kWh
Electricity - production by source:
fossil fuel: NA
hydro: NA
nuclear: NA
other: NA
Electricity - consumption: NA kWh
Electricity - exports: 0 kWh (2002)
Electricity - imports: 0 kWh (2002)
Exports: $NA
Exports - partners: UK (regarded as internal trade) (2004)
Imports: $NA
Imports - partners: UK (regarded as internal trade) (2004)
Debt - external: $NA
Economic aid - recipient: NA
Currency (code): British pound (GBP); note - there is also a Guernsey pound
Currency code: GBP
Exchange rates: Guernsey pounds per US dollar - 0.54 (2005), 0.5462 (2004), 0.6125 (2003), 0.6672 (2002), 0.6947 (2001)
note: the Guernsey pound is at par with the British pound
Fiscal year: calendar year

COMMUNICATIONS

Telephones - main lines in use: 55,000 (2001)
Telephones - mobile cellular: 31,500 (2001)
Telephone system:
general assessment: NA
domestic: NA
international: 1 submarine cable
Radio broadcast stations: AM 1, FM 1, shortwave 0 (1998)
Radios: NA
Television broadcast stations: 1 (1997)
Televisions: NA
Internet country code: .gg
Internet Service Providers (ISPs): NA
Internet users: NA

TRANSPORTATION

Airports: 2 (2004 est.)
Airports - with paved runways:
total: 2
914 to 1,523 m: 1
under 914 m: 1 (2005 est.)
Ports and terminals: Saint Peter Port, Saint Sampson

MILITARY

Military - note: defense is the responsibility of the UK

TRANSNATIONAL ISSUES

Disputes - international: none

GUINEA-BISSAU

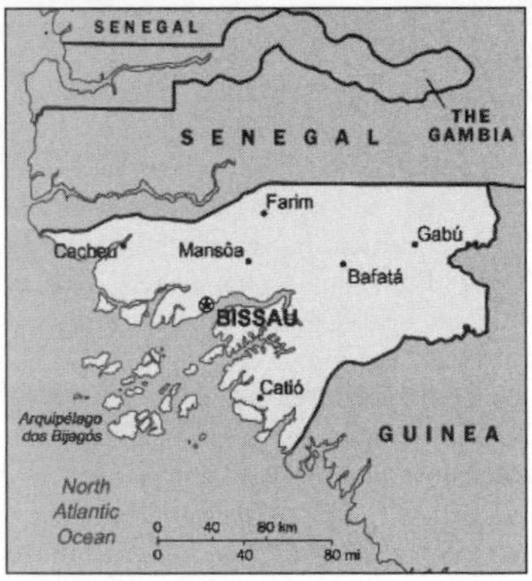

INTRODUCTION

Background: Since independence from Portugal in 1974, Guinea-Bissau has experienced considerable political and military upheaval. In 1980, a military coup established authoritarian dictator Joao Bernardo 'Nino' VIEIRA as president. Despite setting a path to a market economy and multiparty system, VIEIRA's regime was characterized by the suppression of political opposition and the purging of political rivals. Several coup attempts through the 1980s and early 1990s failed to unseat him and in 1994 VIEIRA was elected president in the country's first free elections. A military mutiny and resulting civil war in 1998 eventually led to VIEIRA's ouster in May 1999. In February 2000, a transitional government turned over power to opposition leader Kumba YALA after he was elected president in transparent polling. In September 2003, after only three years in office, YALA was ousted by the military in a bloodless coup and businessman Henrique ROSA was sworn in as interim President. In August 2005 former President VIEIRA was re-elected President in the second round of presidential polling. Since formally assuming office in October 2005, Vieira has pledged to pursue economic development and national reconciliation.

GEOGRAPHY

Location: Western Africa, bordering the North Atlantic Ocean, between Guinea and Senegal
Geographic coordinates: 12 00 N, 15 00 W
Map references: Africa
Area:
total: 36,120 sq km
land: 28,000 sq km
water: 8,120 sq km
Area - comparative: slightly less than three times the size of Connecticut
Land boundaries:
total: 724 km
border countries: Guinea 386 km, Senegal 338 km
Coastline: 350 km
Maritime claims:
territorial sea: 12 nm
exclusive economic zone: 200 nm
Climate: tropical; generally hot and humid; monsoonal-type rainy season (June to November) with southwesterly winds; dry season (December to May) with northeasterly harmattan winds
Terrain: mostly low coastal plain rising to savanna in east
Elevation extremes:
lowest point: Atlantic Ocean 0 m
highest point: unnamed location in the northeast corner of the country 300 m
Natural resources: fish, timber, phosphates, bauxite, clay, granite, limestone, unexploited deposits of petroleum
Land use:
arable land: 10.67%
permanent crops: 8.82%
other: 80.51% (2001)
Irrigated land: 170 sq km (1998 est.)
Natural hazards: hot, dry, dusty harmattan haze may reduce visibility during dry season; brush fires
Environment - current issues: deforestation; soil erosion; overgrazing; overfishing
Environment - international agreements:
party to: Biodiversity, Climate Change, Desertification, Endangered Species, Law of the Sea, Wetlands
signed, but not ratified: none of the selected agreements

Geography - note: this small country is swampy along its western coast and low-lying further inland

PEOPLE

Population: 1,416,027 (July 2005 est.)
Age structure:
0-14 years: 41.5% (male 293,280/female 294,483)
15-64 years: 55.5% (male 376,719/female 409,402)
65 years and over: 3% (male 17,865/female 24,278) (2005 est.)
Median age:
total: 18.97 years
male: 18.37 years
female: 19.57 years (2005 est.)
Population growth rate: 1.96% (2005 est.)
Birth rate: 37.65 births/1,000 population (2005 est.)
Death rate: 16.53 deaths/1,000 population (2005 est.)
Net migration rate: -1.54 migrant(s)/1,000 population (2005 est.)
Sex ratio:
at birth: 1.03 male(s)/female
under 15 years: 1 male(s)/female
15-64 years: 0.92 male(s)/female
65 years and over: 0.74 male(s)/female
total population: 0.94 male(s)/female (2005 est.)
Infant mortality rate:
total: 107.17 deaths/1,000 live births
male: 117.78 deaths/1,000 live births
female: 96.25 deaths/1,000 live births (2005 est.)
Life expectancy at birth:
total population: 46.61 years
male: 44.77 years
female: 48.52 years (2005 est.)
Total fertility rate: 4.93 children born/woman (2005 est.)
HIV/AIDS - adult prevalence rate: 10% (2003 est.)
HIV/AIDS - people living with HIV/AIDS: 17,000 (2001 est.)
HIV/AIDS - deaths: 1,200 (2001 est.)
Major infectious diseases:
degree of risk: very high
food or waterborne diseases: bacterial and protozoal diarrhea, hepatitis A, and typhoid fever
vectorborne diseases: malaria and yellow fever are high risks in some locations
water contact disease: schistosomiasis
respiratory disease: meningococcal meningitis (2004)
Nationality:
noun: Guinean(s)
adjective: Guinean
Ethnic groups: African 99% (Balanta 30%, Fula 20%, Manjaca 14%, Mandinga 13%, Papel 7%), European and mulatto less than 1%
Religions: indigenous beliefs 50%, Muslim 45%, Christian 5%
Languages: Portuguese (official), Crioulo, African languages
Literacy:
definition: age 15 and over can read and write
total population: 42.4%
male: 58.1%
female: 27.4% (2003 est.)

GOVERNMENT

Country name:
conventional long form: Republic of Guinea-Bissau
conventional short form: Guinea-Bissau
local long form: Republica da Guine-Bissau
local short form: Guine-Bissau
former: Portuguese Guinea
Government type: republic, multiparty since mid-1991
Capital: Bissau
Administrative divisions: 9 regions (regioes, singular - regiao); Bafata, Biombo, Bissau, Bolama, Cacheu, Gabu, Oio, Quinara, Tombali; note - Bolama may have been renamed Bolama/Bijagos
Independence: 24 September 1973 (unilaterally declared by Guinea-Bissau); 10 September 1974 (recognized by Portugal)
National holiday: Independence Day, 24 September (1973)
Constitution: 16 May 1984; amended 4 May 1991, 4 December 1991, 26 February 1993, 9 June 1993, and 1996
Legal system: NA
Suffrage: 18 years of age; universal
Executive branch:
chief of state: President Joao Bernardo "Nino" VIEIRA (since 1 October 2005)
head of government: Prime Minister Aristides GOMES (since 2 November 2005)
cabinet: NA
elections: president elected by popular vote for a five-year term; election last held 24 July 2005 (next to be held NA 2010); prime minister appointed by the president after consultation with party leaders in the legislature
election results: Joao Bernardo VIEIRA elected president; percent of vote, second ballot - Joao Bernardo VIEIRA 52.4%, Malan Bacai SANHA 47.6%
Legislative branch: unicameral National People's Assembly or Assembleia Nacional Popular (100 seats; members are elected by popular vote to serve a maximum of four years)
elections: last held 28 March 2004 (next to be held NA 2008)
election results: percent of vote by party - PAIGC 31.5%, PRS 24.8%, PUSD 16.1%, UE 4.1%, APU 1.3%, 13 other parties 22.2%; seats by party - PAIGC 45, PRS 35, PUSD 17, UE 2, APU 1
Judicial branch: Supreme Court or Supremo Tribunal da Justica (consists of nine justices appointed by the president and serve at his pleasure; final court of appeals in criminal and civil cases); Regional Courts (one in each of nine regions; first court of appeals for Sectoral Court decisions; hear all felony cases and civil cases valued at over $1,000); 24 Sectoral Courts (judges are not necessarily trained lawyers; they hear civil cases under $1,000 and misdemeanor criminal cases)
Political parties and leaders: African Party for the Independence of Guinea-Bissau and Cape Verde or PAIGC [Carlos GOMES Junior]; Front for the Liberation and Independence of Guinea or FLING [Francois MENDY]; Guinea-Bissau Resistance-Ba Fata Movement or RGB-MB [Helder Vaz LOPES]; Guinean Civic Forum or FCG [Antonieta Rosa GOMES]; International League for Ecological Protection or LIPE [Alhaje Bubacar DJALO, president]; National Union for Democracy and Progress or UNDP [Abubacer BALDE, secretary general]; Party for Democratic Convergence or PCD [Victor MANDINGA]; Social Renovation Party or PRS [Alberto NAMBEIA]; Union for Change or UM [Jorge MANDINGA, president, Dr. Anne SAAD, secretary general]; United Platform or UP [coalition formed by PCD, FDS, FLING, and RGB-MB]; United Social Democratic Party or PUSD [Francisco Jose FADUL]
Political pressure groups and leaders: NA
International organization participation: ACCT, ACP, AfDB, AU, CEMAC, ECOWAS, FAO, FZ, G-77, IBRD, ICAO, ICCt (signatory), ICFTU, ICRM, IDA,
IDB, IFAD, IFC, IFRCS, ILO, IMF, IMO, Interpol, IOC, IOM, ISO (correspondent), ITU, NAM, OIC, OPCW (signatory), UN, UNCTAD, UNESCO, UNIDO, UPU, WADB (regional), WAEMU, WFTU, WHO, WIPO, WMO, WToO, WTO
Diplomatic representation in the US:
chief of mission: Ambassador (vacant); Charge d'Affaires Henrique Adriano DA SILVA
chancery: 1511 K Street NW, Suite 519, Washington, DC 20005
telephone: [1] (202) 347-3950
FAX: [1] (202) 347-3954
Diplomatic representation from the US: the US Embassy suspended operations on 14 June 1998 in the midst of violent conflict between forces loyal to then President VIEIRA and military-led

junta; US embassy Dakar is responsible for covering Guinea-Bissau: telephone - [221] 823-4296; FAX - [221] 822-5903
Flag description: two equal horizontal bands of yellow (top) and green with a vertical red band on the hoist side; there is a black five-pointed star centered in the red band; uses the popular pan-African colors of Ethiopia

ECONOMY

Economy - overview: One of the 10 poorest countries in the world, Guinea-Bissau depends mainly on farming and fishing. Cashew crops have increased remarkably in recent years, and the country now ranks sixth in cashew production. Guinea-Bissau exports fish and seafood along with small amounts of peanuts, palm kernels, and timber. Rice is the major crop and staple food. However, intermittent fighting between Senegalese-backed government troops and a military junta destroyed much of the country's infrastructure and caused widespread damage to the economy in 1998; the civil war led to a 28% drop in GDP that year, with partial recovery in 1999-2002. Before the war, trade reform and price liberalization were the most successful part of the country's structural adjustment program under IMF sponsorship. The tightening of monetary policy and the development of the private sector had also begun to reinvigorate the economy. Because of high costs, the development of petroleum, phosphate, and other mineral resources is not a near-term prospect. However, offshore oil prospecting has begun and could lead to much-needed revenue in the long run. The inequality of income distribution is one of the most extreme in the world. The government and international donors continue to work out plans to forward economic development from a lamentably low base. In December 2003, the World Bank, IMF, and UNDP were forced to step in to provide emergency budgetary support in the amount of $107 million for 2004, representing over 80% of the total national budget. Government drift and indecision, however, have resulted in continued low growth in 2002-05.
GDP (purchasing power parity): $1.101 billion (2005 est.)
GDP (official exchange rate): $287.1 million (2005 est.)
GDP - real growth rate: 2.8% (2005 est.)
GDP - per capita: purchasing power parity - $800 (2005 est.)
GDP - composition by sector:
agriculture: 62%
industry: 12%
services: 26% (1999 est.)
Labor force: 480,000 (1999)
Labor force - by occupation: agriculture 82% (2000 est.)
Unemployment rate: NA (1998)
Population below poverty line: NA
Household income or consumption by percentage share:
lowest 10%: 0.5%
highest 10%: 42.4% (1991)
Inflation rate (consumer prices): 4% (2002 est.)
Budget:
revenues: NA
expenditures: NA, including capital expenditures of NA
Agriculture - products: rice, corn, beans, cassava (tapioca), cashew nuts, peanuts, palm kernels, cotton; timber; fish
Industries: agricultural products processing, beer, soft drinks
Industrial production growth rate: 4.7% (2003 est.)
Electricity - production: 56 million kWh (2003)
Electricity - production by source:
fossil fuel: 100%
hydro: 0%
nuclear: 0%
other: 0% (2001)
Electricity - consumption: 52.08 million kWh (2003)
Electricity - exports: 0 kWh (2003)
Electricity - imports: 0 kWh (2003)
Oil - production: 0 bbl/day (2003 est.)
Oil - consumption: 2,450 bbl/day (2003 est.)
Oil - exports: NA (2001)
Oil - imports: NA (2001)
Exports: $116 million f.o.b. (2004 est.)
Exports - partners: India 52.2%, US 22.2%, Nigeria 13.2% (2004)
Imports: $176 million f.o.b. (2004 est.)
Imports - partners: Senegal 44.6%, Portugal 13.8%, China 4.2% (2004)
Debt - external: $941.5 million (2000 est.)
Economic aid - recipient: $115.4 million (1995)
Currency (code): Communaute Financiere Africaine franc (XOF); note - responsible authority is the Central Bank of the West African States; previously the Guinea-Bissau peso (GWP) was used
Currency code: XOF; GWP
Exchange rates: Communaute Financiere Africaine francs (XOF) per US dollar - 528.28 (2005), 528.29 (2004), 581.2 (2003), 696.99 (2002), 733.04 (2001)
note: since 1 January 1999, the XOF franc is pegged to the euro at a rate of 655.957 XOF francs per euro
Fiscal year: calendar year

COMMUNICATIONS

Telephones - main lines in use: 10,600 (2003)
Telephones - mobile cellular: 1,300 (2003)
Telephone system:
general assessment: small system
domestic: combination of microwave radio relay, open-wire lines, radiotelephone, and cellular communications
international: country code - 245
Radio broadcast stations: AM 1 (transmitter out of service), FM 4, shortwave 0 (2002)
Radios: 49,000 (1997)
Television broadcast stations: NA (1997)
Televisions: NA
Internet country code: .gw
Internet hosts: 2 (2004)
Internet Service Providers (ISPs): 2 (2002)
Internet users: 19,000 (2003)

TRANSPORTATION

Airports: 28 (2004 est.)
Airports - with paved runways:
total: 3
over 3,047 m: 1
1,524 to 2,437 m: 1
914 to 1,523 m: 1 (2005 est.)
Airports - with unpaved runways:
total: 25
1,524 to 2,437 m: 1
914 to 1,523 m: 4
under 914 m: 20 (2005 est.)
Roadways:
total: 4,400 km
paved: 453 km
unpaved: 3,947 km (1999)
Waterways: 4 largest rivers are navigable for some distance; many inlets and creeks give shallow-water access to much of interior (2004)
Ports and terminals: Bissau, Buba, Cacheu, Farim

MILITARY

Military branches: People's Revolutionary Armed Force (FARP; includes Army, Navy, and Air Force), paramilitary force
Military service age and obligation: 18 years of age for compulsory military service (2001)
Manpower available for military service:
males age 18-49: 288,770 (2005 est.)
Manpower fit for military service: *males age 18-49*: 152,760 (2005 est.)
Military expenditures - dollar figure: $8.9 million (2004)
Military expenditures - percent of GDP: 3.1% (2004)

TRANSNATIONAL ISSUES

Disputes - international: attempts to stem refugees and cross-border raids, arms smuggling, and political instability from a separatist movement in Senegal's Casamance region

GUINEA

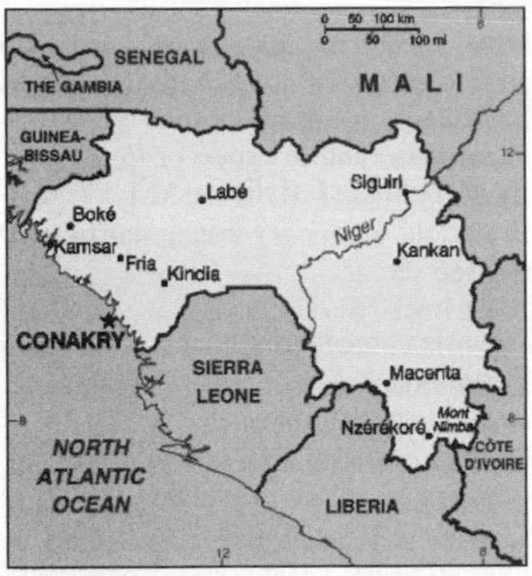

INTRODUCTION

Background: Guinea has had only two presidents since gaining its independence from France in 1958. Lansana CONTE came to power in 1984, when the military seized the government after the death of the first president, Sekou TOURE. Guinea did not hold democratic elections until 1993 when Gen. CONTE (head of the military government) was elected president of the civilian government. He was reelected in 1998 and again in 2003. Unrest in Sierra Leone and Liberia has spilled over into Guinea on several occasions over the past decade, threatening stability and creating humanitarian emergencies.

GEOGRAPHY

Location: Western Africa, bordering the North Atlantic Ocean, between Guinea-Bissau and Sierra Leone
Geographic coordinates: 11 00 N, 10 00 W
Map references: Africa
Area:
total: 245,857 sq km
land: 245,857 sq km
water: 0 sq km
Area - comparative: slightly smaller than Oregon
Land boundaries:
total: 3,399 km
border countries: Cote d'Ivoire 610 km, Guinea-Bissau 386 km, Liberia 563 km, Mali 858 km, Senegal 330 km, Sierra Leone 652 km
Coastline: 320 km
Maritime claims:
territorial sea: 12 nm
exclusive economic zone: 200 nm
Climate: generally hot and humid; monsoonal-type rainy season (June to November) with southwesterly winds; dry season (December to May) with northeasterly harmattan winds
Terrain: generally flat coastal plain, hilly to mountainous interior
Elevation extremes:
lowest point: Atlantic Ocean 0 m
highest point: Mont Nimba 1,752 m
Natural resources: bauxite, iron ore, diamonds, gold, uranium, hydropower, fish, salt
Land use:
arable land: 3.63%
permanent crops: 2.58%
other: 93.79% (2001)
Irrigated land: 950 sq km (1998 est.)
Natural hazards: hot, dry, dusty harmattan haze may reduce visibility during dry season
Environment - current issues: deforestation; inadequate supplies of potable water; desertification; soil contamination and erosion; overfishing, overpopulation in forest region; poor mining practices have led to environmental damage
Environment - international agreements:
party to: Biodiversity, Climate Change, Climate Change-Kyoto Protocol, Desertification, Endangered Species, Hazardous Wastes, Law of the Sea, Ozone Layer Protection, Wetlands, Whaling
signed, but not ratified: none of the selected agreements
Geography - note: the Niger and its important tributary the Milo have their sources in the Guinean highlands

PEOPLE

Population: 9,467,866 (July 2005 est.)
Age structure:
0-14 years: 44.4% (male 2,123,207/female 2,079,475)
15-64 years: 52.4% (male 2,478,820/female 2,486,300)
65 years and over: 3.2% (male 131,130/female 168,934) (2005 est.)
Median age:
total: 17.67 years
male: 17.42 years
female: 17.93 years (2005 est.)
Population growth rate: 2.37% (2005 est.)
Birth rate: 42.03 births/1,000 population (2005 est.)
Death rate: 15.38 deaths/1,000 population (2005 est.)
Net migration rate: -2.99 migrant(s)/1,000 population
note: as a result of conflict in neighboring countries, Guinea is host to approximately 150,000 Liberian and Sierra Leonean refugees (2005 est.)
Sex ratio:
at birth: 1.03 male(s)/female
under 15 years: 1.02 male(s)/female
15-64 years: 1 male(s)/female
65 years and over: 0.78 male(s)/female
total population: 1 male(s)/female (2005 est.)
Infant mortality rate:
total: 90.37 deaths/1,000 live births
male: 95.82 deaths/1,000 live births
female: 84.76 deaths/1,000 live births (2005 est.)
Life expectancy at birth:
total population: 49.36 years
male: 48.19 years
female: 50.57 years (2005 est.)
Total fertility rate: 5.83 children born/woman (2005 est.)
HIV/AIDS - adult prevalence rate: 3.2% (2003 est.)
HIV/AIDS - people living with HIV/AIDS: 140,000 (2003 est.)
HIV/AIDS - deaths: 9,000 (2003 est.)
Major infectious diseases:
degree of risk: very high
food or waterborne diseases: bacterial and protozoal diarrhea, hepatitis A, and typhoid fever
vectorborne diseases: malaria and yellow fever are high risks in some locations
water contact disease: schistosomiasis
respiratory disease: meningococcal meningitis
aerosolized dust or soil contact disease: Lassa fever (2004)
Nationality:
noun: Guinean(s)
adjective: Guinean
Ethnic groups: Peuhl 40%, Malinke 30%, Soussou 20%, smaller ethnic groups 10%
Religions: Muslim 85%, Christian 8%, indigenous beliefs 7%
Languages: French (official), each ethnic group has its own language
Literacy:
definition: age 15 and over can read and write
total population: 35.9%
male: 49.9%
female: 21.9% (1995 est.)

GOVERNMENT

Country name:
conventional long form: Republic of Guinea
conventional short form: Guinea
local long form: Republique de Guinee
local short form: Guinee
former: French Guinea
Government type: republic
Capital: Conakry
Administrative divisions: 33 prefectures and 1 special zone (zone special)*; Beyla, Boffa, Boke, Conakry*, Coyah, Dabola, Dalaba, Dinguiraye, Dubreka, Faranah, Forecariah, Fria, Gaoual, Gueckedou, Kankan, Kerouane, Kindia, Kissidougou, Koubia, Koundara, Kouroussa, Labe, Lelouma, Lola, Macenta, Mali, Mamou, Mandiana, Nzerekore, Pita, Siguiri,

Telimele, Tougue, Yomou
Independence: 2 October 1958 (from France)
National holiday: Independence Day, 2 October (1958)
Constitution: 23 December 1990 (Loi Fundamentale)
Legal system: based on French civil law system, customary law, and decree; legal codes currently being revised; has not accepted compulsory ICJ jurisdiction
Suffrage: 18 years of age; universal
Executive branch:
chief of state: President Lansana CONTE (head of military government since 5 April 1984, elected president 19 December 1993)
head of government: Prime Minister Cellou Dalein DIALLO (since 4 December 2004)
cabinet: Council of Ministers appointed by the president
elections: president elected by popular vote for a seven-year term; candidate must receive a majority of the votes cast to be elected president; election last held 21 December 2003 (next to be held December 2010); the prime minister is appointed by the president
election results: Lansana CONTE reelected president; percent of vote - Lansana CONTE (PUP) 95.3%, Mamadou Boye BARRY (UPR) 4.6%
Legislative branch: unicameral People's National Assembly or Assemblee Nationale Populaire (114 seats; members are elected by direct, popular vote to serve five-year terms)
elections: last held 30 June 2002 (next to be held NA 2007)
election results: percent of vote by party - PUP 61.6%, UPR 26.6%, other 11.8%; seats by party - PUP 85, UPR 20, other 9
Judicial branch: Court of Appeal or Cour d'Appel
Political parties and leaders: Democratic Party of Guinea-African Democratic Rally or PDG-RDA [El Hadj Ismael Mohamed Gassim GUSHEIN]; National Union for Progress or UPN [Mamadou Bhoye BARRY]; Party for Unity and Progress or PUP [Lansana CONTE] - the governing party; People's Party of Guinea or PPG [Pascal TOLNO]; Rally for the Guinean People or RPG [Alpha CONDE]; Union of Democratic Forces of Guinea or UFDG [Mamadou BA]; Union of Republican Forces or UFR [Sidya TOURE]; Union for Progress and Renewal or UPR [Ousmane BAH]; Union for Progress of Guinea or UPG [Jean-Marie DORE, secretary-general]
Political pressure groups and leaders: Student and teacher unions
International organization participation: ACCT, ACP, AfDB, AU, ECOWAS, FAO, G-77, IBRD, ICAO, ICCt, ICFTU, ICRM, IDA, IDB, IFAD, IFC, IFRCS, ILO, IMF, IMO, Interpol, IOC, IOM, ISO (correspondent), ITU, MIGA, MINURSO, NAM, OIC, ONUB, OPCW, UN, UNAMSIL, UNCTAD, UNESCO, UNHCR, UNIDO, UNOCI, UPU, WCL, WCO, WFTU, WHO, WIPO, WMO, WToO, WTO
Diplomatic representation in the US:
chief of mission: Ambassador Rafiou Alpha Oumar BARRY
chancery: 2112 Leroy Place NW, Washington, DC 20008
telephone: [1] (202) 986-4300
FAX: [1] (202) 478-3010
Diplomatic representation from the US:
chief of mission: Ambassador Jackson MCDONALD
embassy: Rue Ka 038, Conakry
mailing address: B. P. 603, Conakry
telephone: [224] 41 15 20, 41 15 21, 41 15 23
FAX: [224] 41 15 22
Flag description: three equal vertical bands of red (hoist side), yellow, and green; uses the popular pan-African colors of Ethiopia

ECONOMY

Economy - overview: Guinea possesses major mineral, hydropower, and agricultural resources, yet remains an underdeveloped nation. The country possesses almost half of the world's bauxite reserves and is the second-largest bauxite producer. The mining sector accounted for over 70% of exports in 2004. Long-run improvements in government fiscal arrangements, literacy, and the legal framework are needed if the country is to move out of poverty. Fighting along the Sierra Leonean and Liberian borders, as well as refugee movements, have caused major economic disruptions, aggravating a loss in investor confidence. Panic buying has created food shortages and inflation and caused riots in local markets. Guinea is not receiving multilateral aid. The IMF and World Bank cut off most assistance in 2003. Growth rose slightly in 2005, primarily due to increases in global demand and commodity prices on world markets.
GDP (purchasing power parity): $20.74 billion (2005 est.)
GDP (official exchange rate): $3.786 billion (2005 est.)
GDP - real growth rate: 2% (2005 est.)
GDP - per capita: purchasing power parity - $2,200 (2005 est.)
GDP - composition by sector:
agriculture: 23.7%
industry: 36.2%
services: 40.1% (2005 est.)
Labor force: 3 million (1999)
Labor force - by occupation: agriculture 80%, industry and services 20% (2000 est.)
Unemployment rate: NA
Population below poverty line: 40% (2003 est.)
Household income or consumption by percentage share:
lowest 10%: 2.6%
highest 10%: 32% (1994)
Distribution of family income - Gini index: 40.3 (1994)
Inflation rate (consumer prices): 25% (2005 est.)
Investment (gross fixed): 17.3% of GDP (2005 est.)
Budget:
revenues: $305.6 million
expenditures: $590.4 million, including capital expenditures of NA (2005 est.)
Agriculture - products: rice, coffee, pineapples, palm kernels, cassava (tapioca), bananas, sweet potatoes; cattle, sheep, goats; timber
Industries: bauxite, gold, diamonds; alumina refining; light manufacturing and agricultural processing industries
Industrial production growth rate: 3.2% (1994)
Electricity - production: 775 million kWh (2003)
Electricity - production by source:
fossil fuel: 45.5%
hydro: 54.5%
nuclear: 0%
other: 0% (2001)
Electricity - consumption: 720.8 million kWh (2003)
Electricity - exports: 0 kWh (2003)
Electricity - imports: 0 kWh (2003)
Oil - production: 0 bbl/day (2003 est.)
Oil - consumption: 8,400 bbl/day (2003 est.)
Oil - exports: NA (2001)
Oil - imports: NA (2001)
Current account balance: $-268.4 million (2005 est.)
Exports: $612.1 million f.o.b. (2005 est.)
Exports - partners: France 17.7%, Belgium 14.7%, UK 14.7%, Switzerland 12.8%, Ukraine 4.2% (2004)
Imports: $680 million f.o.b. (2005 est.)
Imports - partners: Cote d"Ivoire 15.5%, France 9%, Belgium 6.1%, China 6%, South Africa 4.8% (2004)
Reserves of foreign exchange and gold: $69.83 million (2005 est.)
Debt - external: $3.46 billion (2003 est.)
Economic aid - recipient: $237.5 million (2003)
Currency (code): Guinean franc (GNF)
Currency code: GNF
Exchange rates: Guinean francs per US dollar - 2,810 (2005), 2,550 (2004),

1,984.9 (2003), 1,975.8 (2002), 1,950.6 (2001)
Fiscal year: calendar year

COMMUNICATIONS

Telephones - main lines in use: 26,200 (2003)
Telephones - mobile cellular: 111,500 (2003)
Telephone system:
general assessment: poor to fair system of open-wire lines, small radiotelephone communication stations, and new microwave radio relay system
domestic: microwave radio relay and radiotelephone communication
international: country code - 224; satellite earth station - 1 Intelsat (Atlantic Ocean)
Radio broadcast stations: AM 4 (one station is inactive), FM 1 (plus 7 repeaters), shortwave 3 (2001)
Radios: 357,000 (1997)
Television broadcast stations: 6 low-power stations (2001)
Televisions: 85,000 (1997)
Internet country code: .gn
Internet hosts: 380 (2004)
Internet Service Providers (ISPs): 4 (2001)
Internet users: 40,000 (2003)

TRANSPORTATION

Airports: 16 (2004 est.)
Airports - with paved runways:
total: 5
over 3,047 m: 1
2,438 to 3,047 m: 1
1,524 to 2,437 m: 3 (2005 est.)
Airports - with unpaved runways:
total: 11
1,524 to 2,437 m: 6
914 to 1,523 m: 3
under 914 m: 2 (2005 est.)
Railways:
total: 837 km
standard gauge: 175 km 1.435-m gauge
narrow gauge: 662 km 1.000-m gauge (2004)
Roadways:
total: 44,348 km
paved: 4,342 km
unpaved: 40,006 km (2003)
Waterways: 1,295 km (navigable by shallow-draft native craft) (2003)
Ports and terminals: Kamsar

MILITARY

Military branches: Army (includes Presidential Guard, Republican Guard), Navy, Air Force, National Gendarmerie, General Directorate of National Police
Military service age and obligation: 18 years of age for compulsory military service; conscript service obligation - 2 years (2004)
Manpower available for military service: *males age 18-49*: 1,853,316 (2005 est.)
Manpower fit for military service: *males age 18-49*: 1,038,036 (2005 est.)
Military expenditures - dollar figure: $56.7 million (2004)
Military expenditures - percent of GDP: 1.7% (2004)

TRANSNATIONAL ISSUES

Disputes - international: conflicts among rebel groups, warlords, and youth gangs in neighboring states has spilled over into Guinea, resulting in domestic instability; Sierra Leone pressures Guinea to remove its forces from the town of Yenga occupied since 1998
Refugees and internally displaced persons:
refugees (country of origin): 133,175 (Liberia) 13,633 (Sierra Leone) 7,064 (Cote d'Ivoire)
IDPs: 100,000 (cross-border incursions from Liberia, Sierra Leone, Cote d'Ivoire) (2004)

GUYANA

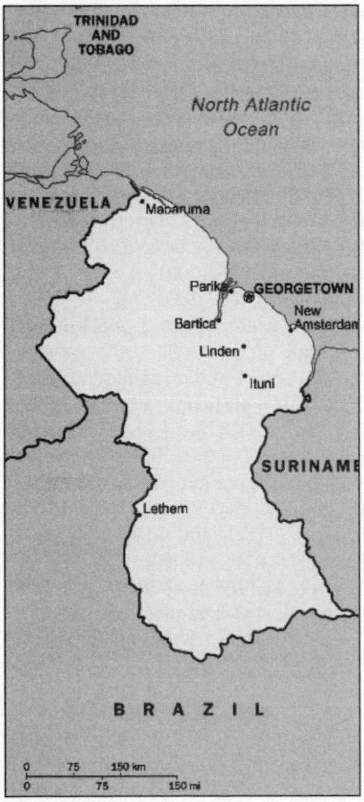

INTRODUCTION

Background: Originally a Dutch colony in the 17th century, by 1815 Guyana had become a British possession. The abolition of slavery led to black settlement of urban areas and the importation of indentured servants from India to work the sugar plantations. This ethnocultural divide has persisted and has led to turbulent politics. Guyana achieved independence from the UK in 1966, but until the early 1990s it was ruled mostly by socialist-oriented governments. In 1992, Cheddi JAGAN was elected president, in what is considered the country's first free and fair election since independence. Upon his death five years later, he was succeeded by his wife Janet, who resigned in 1999 due to poor health. Her successor, Bharrat JAGDEO, was reelected in 2001.

GEOGRAPHY

Location: Northern South America, bordering the North Atlantic Ocean, between Suriname and Venezuela
Geographic coordinates: 5 00 N, 59 00 W
Map references: South America
Area:
total: 214,970 sq km
land: 196,850 sq km
water: 18,120 sq km
Area - comparative: slightly smaller than Idaho
Land boundaries:
total: 2,462 km
border countries: Brazil 1,119 km, Suriname 600 km, Venezuela 743 km
Coastline: 459 km
Maritime claims:
territorial sea: 12 nm
exclusive economic zone: 200 nm
continental shelf: 200 nm or to the outer edge of the continental margin
Climate: tropical; hot, humid, moderated by northeast trade winds; two rainy seasons (May to mid-August, mid-November to mid-January)
Terrain: mostly rolling highlands; low coastal plain; savanna in south
Elevation extremes:
lowest point: Atlantic Ocean 0 m
highest point: Mount Roraima 2,835 m
Natural resources: bauxite, gold, diamonds, hardwood timber, shrimp, fish
Land use:
arable land: 2.44%
permanent crops: 0.15%
other: 97.41% (2001)
Irrigated land: 1,500 sq km (1998 est.)
Natural hazards: flash floods are a constant threat during rainy seasons

Environment - current issues: water pollution from sewage and agricultural and industrial chemicals; deforestation
Environment - international agreements:
party to: Biodiversity, Climate Change, Climate Change-Kyoto Protocol, Desertification, Endangered Species, Hazardous Wastes, Law of the Sea, Ozone Layer Protection, Ship Pollution, Tropical Timber 83, Tropical Timber 94
signed, but not ratified: none of the selected agreements
Geography - note: the third-smallest country in South America after Suriname and Uruguay; substantial portions of its western and eastern territories are claimed by Venezuela and Suriname respectively

PEOPLE

Population: 765,283
note: estimates for this country explicitly take into account the effects of excess mortality due to AIDS; this can result in lower life expectancy, higher infant mortality and death rates, lower population and growth rates, and changes in the distribution of population by age and sex than would otherwise be expected (July 2005 est.)
Age structure:
0-14 years: 26.4% (male 103,054/female 99,279)
15-64 years: 68.5% (male 263,953/female 260,000)
65 years and over: 5.1% (male 16,801/female 22,196) (2005 est.)
Median age:
total: 26.91 years
male: 26.44 years
female: 27.4 years (2005 est.)
Population growth rate: 0.26% (2005 est.)
Birth rate: 18.45 births/1,000 population (2005 est.)
Death rate: 8.32 deaths/1,000 population (2005 est.)
Net migration rate: -7.51 migrant(s)/1,000 population (2005 est.)
Sex ratio:
at birth: 1.05 male(s)/female
under 15 years: 1.04 male(s)/female
15-64 years: 1.02 male(s)/female
65 years and over: 0.76 male(s)/female
total population: 1.01 male(s)/female (2005 est.)
Infant mortality rate:
total: 33.26 deaths/1,000 live births
male: 36.94 deaths/1,000 live births
female: 29.38 deaths/1,000 live births (2005 est.)
Life expectancy at birth:
total population: 65.5 years
male: 62.86 years
female: 68.28 years (2005 est.)
Total fertility rate: 2.05 children born/woman (2005 est.)
HIV/AIDS - adult prevalence rate: 2.5% (2003 est.)
HIV/AIDS - people living with HIV/AIDS: 11,000 (2003 est.)
HIV/AIDS - deaths: 1,100 (2003 est.)
Nationality:
noun: Guyanese (singular and plural)
adjective: Guyanese
Ethnic groups: East Indian 50%, black 36%, Amerindian 7%, white, Chinese, and mixed 7%
Religions: Christian 50%, Hindu 35%, Muslim 10%, other 5%
Languages: English, Amerindian dialects, Creole, Hindi, Urdu
Literacy:
definition: age 15 and over has ever attended school
total population: 98.8%
male: 99.1%
female: 98.5% (2003 est.)

GOVERNMENT

Country name:
conventional long form: Co-operative Republic of Guyana
conventional short form: Guyana
former: British Guiana
Government type: republic within the Commonwealth
Capital: Georgetown
Administrative divisions: 10 regions; Barima-Waini, Cuyuni-Mazaruni, Demerara-Mahaica, East Berbice-Corentyne, Essequibo Islands-West Demerara, Mahaica-Berbice, Pomeroon-Supenaam, Potaro-Siparuni, Upper Demerara-Berbice, Upper Takutu-Upper Essequibo
Independence: 26 May 1966 (from UK)
National holiday: Republic Day, 23 February (1970)
Constitution: 6 October 1980
Legal system: based on English common law with certain admixtures of Roman-Dutch law; has not accepted compulsory ICJ jurisdiction
Suffrage: 18 years of age; universal
Executive branch:
chief of state: President Bharrat JAGDEO (since 11 August 1999); note - assumed presidency after resignation of President Janet JAGAN and reelected in 2001
head of government: Prime Minister Samuel HINDS (since December 1997)
cabinet: Cabinet of Ministers appointed by the president, responsible to the legislature
elections: president elected by the majority party in the National Assembly following legislative elections, which must be held at least every five years; elections last held 19 March 2001 (next to be called by March 2006); prime minister appointed by the president
election results: President Bharrat JAGDEO reelected; percent of legislative vote - NA%
Legislative branch: unicameral National Assembly (68 seats, 65 elected by popular vote, 1 elected Speaker of the National Assembly, and 2 nonvoting members appointed by the president; members serve five-year terms) elections: last held 19 March 2001 (next to be called by March 2006); note - national elections will likely take place in Summer 2006
election results: percent of vote by party - NA%; seats by party - PPP/C 34, PNC 27, GAP and WPA 2, ROAR 1, TUF 1
Judicial branch: Supreme Court of Judicature; Judicial Court of Appeal; High Court
Political parties and leaders: Alliance for Guyana or AFG (includes Guyana Labor Party or GLP and Working People's Alliance or WPA) [Rupert ROOPNARAINE]; Guyana Action Party or GAP [Paul HARDY]; Guyana Labor Party or GLP [leader NA]; People's National Congress or PNC [Robert Herman Orlando CORBIN]; People's Progressive Party/Civic or PPP/C [Bharrat JAGDEO]; Rise, Organize, and Rebuild or ROAR [Ravi DEV]; The United Force or TUF [Manzoor NADIR]; Working People's Alliance or WPA [Rupert ROOPNARAINE]
Political pressure groups and leaders: Civil Liberties Action Committee or CLAC; Guyana Council of Indian Organizations or GCIO; Trades Union Congress or TUC
note: the GCIO and the CLAC are small and active but not well organized
International organization participation: ACP, C, Caricom, CDB, CSN, FAO, G-77, IADB, IBRD, ICAO, ICCt, ICFTU, ICRM, IDA, IFAD, IFC, IFRCS, ILO, IMF, IMO, Interpol, IOC, IOM (observer), ISO (subscriber), ITU, LAES, MIGA, NAM, OAS, OIC, OPANAL, OPCW, PCA, UN, UNCTAD, UNESCO, UNIDO, UPU, WCL, WCO, WFTU, WHO, WIPO, WMO, WTO
Diplomatic representation in the US:
chief of mission: Ambassador Bayney KARRAN
chancery: 2490 Tracy Place NW, Washington, DC 20008
telephone: [1] (202) 265-6900
FAX: [1] (202) 232-1297
consulate(s) general: New York
Diplomatic representation from the US:
chief of mission: Ambassador Roland W. BULLEN
embassy: 100 Young and Duke Streets, Kingston, Georgetown
mailing address: P. O. Box 10507, Georgetown
telephone: [592] 225-4900 through 4909

FAX: [592] 225-8497
Flag description: green, with a red isosceles triangle (based on the hoist side) superimposed on a long, yellow arrowhead; there is a narrow, black border between the red and yellow, and a narrow, white border between the yellow and the green

ECONOMY

Economy - overview: The Guyanese economy exhibited moderate economic growth in 2001-02, based on expansion in the agricultural and mining sectors, a more favorable atmosphere for business initiatives, a more realistic exchange rate, fairly low inflation, and the continued support of international organizations. Growth then slowed in 2003 and came back gradually in 2004, buoyed largely by increased export earnings, and slowed again in 2005. Chronic problems include a shortage of skilled labor and a deficient infrastructure. The government is juggling a sizable external debt against the urgent need for expanded public investment. The bauxite mining sector should benefit in the near term from restructuring and partial privatization. Export earnings from agriculture and mining have fallen sharply, while the import bill has risen, driven by higher energy prices.
GDP (purchasing power parity): $3.002 billion (2005 est.)
GDP (official exchange rate): $822.4 million (2005 est.)
GDP - real growth rate: 0.5% (2005 est.)
GDP - per capita: purchasing power parity - $3,900 (2005 est.)
GDP - composition by sector:
agriculture: 36.8%
industry: 20.2%
services: 43% (2005 est.)
Labor force: 418,000 (2001 est.)
Labor force - by occupation: agriculture NA%, industry NA%, services NA%
Unemployment rate: 9.1% (understated) (2000)
Population below poverty line: NA
Household income or consumption by percentage share:
lowest 10%: NA
highest 10%: NA
Inflation rate (consumer prices): 5.5% (2005 est.)
Investment (gross fixed): 36.2% of GDP (2005 est.)
Budget:
revenues: $320.1 million
expenditures: $362.6 million, including capital expenditures of $93.4 million (2005 est.)
Agriculture - products: sugarcane, rice, wheat, vegetable oils; beef, pork, poultry, dairy products; fish, shrimp
Industries: bauxite, sugar, rice milling, timber, textiles, gold mining
Industrial production growth rate: NA
Electricity - production: 779 million kWh (2003)
Electricity - production by source:
fossil fuel: 99.4%
hydro: 0.6%
nuclear: 0%
other: 0% (2001)
Electricity - consumption: 724.5 million kWh (2003)
Electricity - exports: 0 kWh (2003)
Electricity - imports: 0 kWh (2003)
Oil - production: 0 bbl/day (2003 est.)
Oil - consumption: 11,300 bbl/day (2003 est.)
Oil - exports: NA (2001)
Oil - imports: NA (2001)
Current account balance: $-92.72 million (2005 est.)
Exports: $587.2 million f.o.b. (2005 est.)
Exports - partners: Canada 23.2%, US 19.2%, UK 10.9%, Portugal 9%, Belgium 6.4%, Jamaica 5.2% (2004)
Imports: $681.6 million f.o.b. (2005 est.)
Imports - partners: Trinidad and Tobago 24.8%, US 24.5%, Cuba 6.8%, UK 5.4% (2004)
Reserves of foreign exchange and gold: $248.8 million (2005 est.)
Debt - external: $1.2 billion (2002)
Economic aid - recipient: $84 million (1995), Heavily Indebted Poor Country Initiative (HIPC) $253 million (1997)
Currency (code): Guyanese dollar (GYD)
Currency code: GYD
Exchange rates: Guyanese dollars per US dollar - 200.79 (2005), 198.33 (2004), 193.88 (2003), 190.67 (2002), 187.32 (2001)
Fiscal year: calendar year

COMMUNICATIONS

Telephones - main lines in use: 80,400 (2002)
Telephones - mobile cellular: 87,300 (2002)
Telephone system:
general assessment: fair system for long-distance service
domestic: microwave radio relay network for trunk lines
international: country code - 592; tropospheric scatter to Trinidad; satellite earth station - 1 Intelsat (Atlantic Ocean)
Radio broadcast stations: AM 3, FM 3, shortwave 1 (1998)
Radios: 420,000 (1997)
Television broadcast stations: 3 (one public station; two private stations which relay US satellite services) (1997)
Televisions: 46,000 (1997)
Internet country code: .gy
Internet hosts: 613 (2003)
Internet Service Providers (ISPs): 3 (2000)
Internet users: 125,000 (2002)

TRANSPORTATION

Airports: 49 (2004 est.)
Airports - with paved runways:
total: 8
1,524 to 2,437 m: 3
under 914 m: 5 (2005 est.)
Airports - with unpaved runways:
total: 61
1,524 to 2,437 m: 2
914 to 1,523 m: 12
under 914 m: 47 (2005 est.)
Railways:
total: 187 km
standard gauge: 139 km 1.435-m gauge
narrow gauge: 48 km 0.914-m gauge
note: all dedicated to ore transport (2001 est.)
Roadways:
total: 7,970 km
paved: 590 km
unpaved: 7,380 km (1999)
Waterways: 1,077 km
note: Berbice, Demerara, and Essequibo rivers are navigable by oceangoing vessels for 150 km, 100 km, and 80 km respectively (2004)
Merchant marine:
total: 6 ships (1,000 GRT or over) 7,475 GRT/8,758 DWT
by type: cargo 5, refrigerated cargo 1
registered in other countries: 3 (2005)
Ports and terminals: Georgetown

MILITARY

Military branches: Guyana Defense Force: Ground Forces, Coast Guard, Air Corps, Guyana People's Militia
Manpower available for military service:
males age 18-49: 206,098 (2005 est.)
Manpower fit for military service: *males age 18-49*: 137,964 (2005 est.)
Military expenditures - dollar figure: $6.5 million (2003)
Military expenditures - percent of GDP: 0.9% (2004)

TRANSNATIONAL ISSUES

Disputes - international: all of the area west of the Essequibo (river) is claimed by Venezuela preventing any discussion of a maritime boundary; Guyana has expressed its intention to join Barbados in asserting claims before UNCLOS that Trinidad and Tobago's maritime boundary with Venezuela extends into their waters; Suriname claims a triangle of land between the New and Kutari/Koetari rivers in a historic dispute over the headwaters of the Courantyne; Guyana seeks UNCLOS arbitration to resolve the long-standing dispute with Suriname over the axis of the territorial sea boundary in potentially oil-rich waters
Illicit drugs: transshipment point for narcotics from South America - primarily Venezuela - to Europe and the US; producer of cannabis

H

HAITI

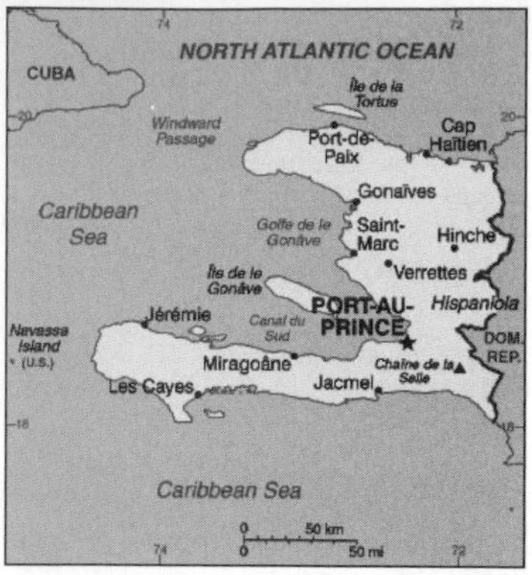

INTRODUCTION

Background: The native Arawak Amerindians - who inhabited the island of Hispaniola when it was discovered by Columbus in 1492 - were virtually annihilated by Spanish settlers within 25 years. In the early 17th century, the French established a presence on Hispaniola, and in 1697, Spain ceded to the French the western third of the island - Haiti. The French colony, based on forestry and sugar-related industries, became one of the wealthiest in the Caribbean, but only through the heavy importation of African slaves and considerable environmental degradation. In the late 18th century, Haiti's nearly half million slaves revolted under Toussaint L'OUVERTURE and after a prolonged struggle, became the first black republic to declare its independence in 1804. Haiti has been plagued by political violence for most of its history. It is the poorest country in the Western Hemisphere.

GEOGRAPHY

Location: Caribbean, western one-third of the island of Hispaniola, between the Caribbean Sea and the North Atlantic Ocean, west of the Dominican Republic
Geographic coordinates: 19 00 N, 72 25 W
Map references: Central America and the Caribbean
Area:
total: 27,750 sq km
land: 27,560 sq km
water: 190 sq km
Area - comparative: slightly smaller than Maryland
Land boundaries:
total: 360 km
border countries: Dominican Republic 360 km
Coastline: 1,771 km
Maritime claims:
territorial sea: 12 nm
contiguous zone: 24 nm
exclusive economic zone: 200 nm
continental shelf: to depth of exploitation
Climate: tropical; semiarid where mountains in east cut off trade winds
Terrain: mostly rough and mountainous
Elevation extremes:
lowest point: Caribbean Sea 0 m
highest point: Chaine de la Selle 2,680 m
Natural resources: bauxite, copper, calcium carbonate, gold, marble, hydropower
Land use:
arable land: 28.3%
permanent crops: 11.61%
other: 60.09% (2001)
Irrigated land: 750 sq km (1998 est.)
Natural hazards: lies in the middle of the hurricane belt and subject to severe storms from June to October; occasional flooding and earthquakes; periodic droughts
Environment - current issues: extensive deforestation (much of the remaining forested land is being cleared for agriculture and used as fuel); soil erosion; inadequate supplies of potable water
Environment - international agreements:
party to: Biodiversity, Climate Change, Desertification, Law of the Sea, Marine Dumping, Marine Life Conservation, Ozone Layer Protection
signed, but not ratified: Hazardous Wastes
Geography - note: shares island of Hispaniola with Dominican Republic (western one-third is Haiti, eastern two-thirds is the Dominican Republic)

PEOPLE

Population: 8,121,622
note: estimates for this country explicitly take into account the effects of excess mortality due to AIDS; this can result in lower life expectancy, higher infant mortality and death rates, lower population and growth rates, and changes in the distribution of population by age and sex than would otherwise be expected (July 2005 est.)
Age structure:
0-14 years: 42.6% (male 1,741,622/female 1,721,436)
15-64 years: 53.9% (male 2,137,225/female 2,242,639)
65 years and over: 3.4% (male 124,383/female 154,317) (2005 est.)
Median age:
total: 18.03 years
male: 17.63 years
female: 18.44 years (2005 est.)
Population growth rate: 2.26% (2005 est.)
Birth rate: 36.59 births/1,000 population (2005 est.)
Death rate: 12.34 deaths/1,000 population (2005 est.)
Net migration rate: -1.68 migrant(s)/1,000 population (2005 est.)
Sex ratio:
at birth: 1.03 male(s)/female
under 15 years: 1.01 male(s)/female
15-64 years: 0.95 male(s)/female
65 years and over: 0.81 male(s)/female
total population: 0.97 male(s)/female (2005 est.)
Infant mortality rate:
total: 73.45 deaths/1,000 live births
male: 79.92 deaths/1,000 live births
female: 66.79 deaths/1,000 live births (2005 est.)
Life expectancy at birth:
total population: 52.92 years
male: 51.58 years
female: 54.31 years (2005 est.)
Total fertility rate: 5.02 children born/woman (2005 est.)
HIV/AIDS - adult prevalence rate: 5.6% (2003 est.)
HIV/AIDS - people living with HIV/AIDS: 280,000 (2003 est.)
HIV/AIDS - deaths: 24,000 (2003 est.)
Nationality:
noun: Haitian(s)
adjective: Haitian
Ethnic groups: black 95%, mulatto and white 5%
Religions: Roman Catholic 80%, Protestant 16% (Baptist 10%, Pentecostal 4%, Adventist 1%, other 1%), none 1%, other 3% (1982)
note: roughly half of the population practices Voodoo
Languages: French (official), Creole (official)
Literacy:
definition: age 15 and over can read and write
total population: 52.9%
male: 54.8%
female: 51.2% (2003 est.)

GOVERNMENT

Country name:
conventional long form: Republic of Haiti
conventional short form: Haiti
local long form: Republique d'Haiti
local short form: Haiti
Government type: elected government
Capital: Port-au-Prince
Administrative divisions: 9 departments (departements, singular - departement); Artibonite, Centre, Grand 'Anse, Nord, Nord-Est, Nord-Ouest, Ouest, Sud, Sud-Est
Independence: 1 January 1804 (from France)
National holiday: Independence Day, 1 January (1804)
Constitution: approved March 1987; suspended June 1988 with most articles

reinstated March 1989; in October 1991 government claimed to be observing the constitution; returned to constitutional rule in October 1994

Legal system: based on Roman civil law system; accepts compulsory ICJ jurisdiction

Suffrage: 18 years of age; universal

Executive branch:

chief of state: Interim President Boniface ALEXANDRE (since 29 February 2004)

note: Jean-Bertrand ARISTIDE resigned as president on 29 February 2004; ALEXANDRE, as Chief of the Supreme Court, constitutionally succeeded Aristide

head of government: Interim Prime Minister Gerald LATORTUE (since 12 March 2004), chosen by extraconstitutional Council of Eminent Persons representing cross-section of political and civic interests

cabinet: Cabinet chosen by the prime minister in consultation with the president

elections: president elected by popular vote for a five-year term; election last held 26 November 2000 (next to be held in November 2005); prime minister appointed by the president, ratified by the National Assembly

election results: Jean-Bertrand ARISTIDE elected president; percent of vote - Jean-Bertrand ARISTIDE 92%

Legislative branch: bicameral National Assembly or Assemblee Nationale consists of the Senate (27 seats; members elected by popular vote to serve six-year terms; one-third elected every two years) and the Chamber of Deputies (83 seats; members are elected by popular vote to serve four-year terms); note - the National Assembly stopped functioning in January 2004 when the terms of all Deputies and two-thirds of sitting Senators expired; no replacements have been elected; the President is currently ruling by decree

elections: Senate - last held for two-thirds of seats 21 May 2000 with runoffs on 9 July boycotted by the opposition; seven seats still disputed; election for remaining one-third held on 26 November 2000 (next to be held in 2005); Chamber of Deputies - last held 21 May 2000 with runoffs on 30 July boycotted by the opposition; one vacant seat rerun 26 November 2000 (next to be held in November 2005)

election results: Senate - percent of vote by party - NA%; seats by party - FL 26, independent 1; Chamber of Deputies - percent of vote by party - NA%; seats by party - FL 73, MOCHRENA 3, PLB 2, OPL 1, vacant 1, other minor parties and independents 3

Judicial branch: Supreme Court or Cour de Cassation

Political parties and leaders: Alliance for the Liberation and Advancement of Haiti or ALAH [Reynold GEORGES]; Assembly of Progressive National Democrats or RDNP [Leslie MANIGAT]; Ayiti Kapab [Ernst VERDIEU]; Convention for Democratic Unity or KID [Evans PAUL]; National Congress of Democratic Movements or KONAKOM [Victor BENOIT]; Nationalist Progressive Revolutionary Party or PANPRA [Serge GILLES]; Democratic Movement for the Liberation of Haiti or MODELH [Francois LATORTUE]; Grand Center Right Front coalition (composed of MDN, MRN, and PDCH) [Hubert de RONCERAY, Jean BUTEAU, Osner FEVRY and Marie-Denise CLAUDE]; Haitian Christian Democratic Party or PDCH [Osner FEVRY and Marie-Denise CLAUDE]; Haitian Democratic Party or PADEMH [Clark PARENT]; Haitian Democratic and Reform Movement or MODEREH [Dany TOUSSAINT and Pierre Soncon PRINCE]; Heads Together [Dr. Gerard BLOT]; Lavalas Family or FL [leader NA]; Liberal Party of Haiti or PLH [Michael MADSEN]; Mobilization for National Development or MDN [Hubert DE RONCERAY]; Movement for National Reconstruction or MRN [Jean Henold BUTEAU]; Movement for the Installation of Democracy in Haiti or MIDH [Marc BAZIN]; National Front for the Reconstruction of Haiti or FRON [Guy PHILIPPE]; National Progressive Democratic Party or PNDPH [Turneb DELPE]; New Christian Movement for a New Haiti or MOCHRENA [Luc MESADIEU]; Open the Gate Party (Parti Louvri Bayre) or PLB [leader NA]; Popular Party for the Renewal of Haiti, or Generation 2000 [Claude ROMAIN and Daniel SUPPLICE]; Struggling People's Organization or OPL [Edgard LEBLANC]; MNP28 [Dejean BELIZAIRE]; KOMBA [Evans LESCOUFLAIR]

Political pressure groups and leaders: Autonomous Organizations of Haitian Workers or CATH [Fignole ST-CYR]; Confederation of Haitian Workers or CTH; Federation of Workers Trade Unions or FOS; Group of 184 Civil Society Organization, or G-184 [Andy APAID]; National Popular Assembly or APN; Papaye Peasants Movement or MPP [Chavannes JEAN-BAPTISTE]; Popular Organizations Gathering Power or PROP; Roman Catholic Church; Protestant Federation of Haiti

International organization participation: ACCT, ACP, Caricom, FAO, G-77, IADB, IAEA, IBRD, ICAO, ICCt (signatory), ICRM, IDA, IFAD, IFC, IFRCS, ILO, IMF, IMO, Interpol, IOC, IOM, ITU, LAES, MIGA, OAS, OPANAL, OPCW (signatory), PCA, UN, UNCTAD, UNESCO, UNIDO, UPU, WCL, WCO, WFTU, WHO, WIPO, WMO, WToO, WTO

Diplomatic representation in the US:

chief of mission: Charge d'Affaires Raymond JOSEPH (as of November 2004)

chancery: 2311 Massachusetts Avenue NW, Washington, DC 20008

telephone: [1] (202) 332-4090

FAX: [1] (202) 745-7215

consulate(s) general: Boston, Chicago, Miami, New York, and San Juan (Puerto Rico)

Diplomatic representation from the US:

chief of mission: Ambassador Timothy M. CARNEY

embassy: 5 Harry S Truman Boulevard, Port-au-Prince

mailing address: P. O. Box 1761, Port-au-Prince

telephone: [509] 222-0200

FAX: [509] 223-9038

Flag description: two equal horizontal bands of blue (top) and red with a centered white rectangle bearing the coat of arms, which contains a palm tree flanked by flags and two cannons above a scroll bearing the motto L'UNION FAIT LA FORCE (Union Makes Strength)

ECONOMY

Economy - overview: In this poorest country in the Western Hemisphere, 80% of the population lives in abject poverty, and natural disasters frequently sweep the nation. Two-thirds of all Haitians depend on the agriculture sector, which consists mainly of small-scale subsistence farming. Following legislative elections in May 2000, fraught with irregularities, international donors - including the US and EU - suspended almost all aid to Haiti. The economy grew 3.5% in 2005. Suspended aid and loan disbursements totaled more than $500 million at the start of 2003. Haiti suffers from rampant inflation, a lack of investment, and a severe trade deficit. Civil strife in 2004 combined with extensive damage from flooding in southern Haiti in May 2004 and Tropical Storm Jeanne in northwestern Haiti in September 2004 further impoverished Haiti. In early 2005 Haiti paid its arrears to the World Bank, paving the way to reengagement with the Bank. The resumption of aid flows from all donors

is alleviating but not ending the nation's bitter economic problems.
GDP (purchasing power parity): $12.94 billion (2005 est.)
GDP (official exchange rate): $5.191 billion (2005 est.)
GDP - real growth rate: 3.5% (2005 est.)
GDP - per capita: purchasing power parity - $1,600 (2005 est.)
GDP - composition by sector:
agriculture: 30%
industry: 20%
services: 50% (2001 est.)
Labor force: 3.6 million
note: shortage of skilled labor, unskilled labor abundant (1995)
Labor force - by occupation: agriculture 66%, industry 9%, services 25%
Unemployment rate: widespread unemployment and underemployment; more than two-thirds of the labor force do not have formal jobs (2002 est.)
Population below poverty line: 80% (2003 est.)
Household income or consumption by percentage share:
lowest 10%: NA
highest 10%: NA
Inflation rate (consumer prices): 13.3% (2005 est.)
Investment (gross fixed): 27.4% of GDP (2004 est.)
Budget:
revenues: $400 million
expenditures: $600.8 million, including capital expenditures of NA (2005 est.)
Agriculture - products: coffee, mangoes, sugarcane, rice, corn, sorghum, wood
Industries: sugar refining, flour milling, textiles, cement, light assembly industries based on imported parts
Industrial production growth rate: NA
Electricity - production: 546 million kWh (2003)
Electricity - production by source:
fossil fuel: 60.3%
hydro: 39.7%
nuclear: 0%
other: 0% (2001)
Electricity - consumption: 507.8 million kWh (2003)
Electricity - exports: 0 kWh (2003)
Electricity - imports: 0 kWh (2003)
Oil - production: 0 bbl/day (2003 est.)
Oil - consumption: 11,800 bbl/day (2003 est.)
Oil - exports: NA (2001)
Oil - imports: NA (2001)
Current account balance: $34.08 million (2005 est.)
Exports: $390.7 million f.o.b. (2005 est.)
Exports - partners: US 81.2%, Dominican Republic 7.3%, Canada 4.1% (2004)
Imports: $1.471 billion f.o.b. (2005 est.)
Imports - partners: US 34.8%, Netherlands Antilles 18%, Malaysia 5.1%, Colombia 4.7% (2004)
Reserves of foreign exchange and gold: $95.26 million (2005 est.)
Debt - external: $1.3 billion (2005 est.)
Economic aid - recipient: $150 million (FY04 est.)
Currency (code): gourde (HTG)
Currency code: HTG
Exchange rates: gourdes per US dollar - 39.14 (2005), 38.352 (2004), 42.367 (2003), 29.251 (2002), 24.429 (2001)
Fiscal year: 1 October - 30 September

COMMUNICATIONS

Telephones - main lines in use: 130,000 (2002)
Telephones - mobile cellular: 140,000 (2002)
Telephone system:
general assessment: domestic facilities barely adequate; international facilities slightly better
domestic: coaxial cable and microwave radio relay trunk service
international: country code - 509; satellite earth station - 1 Intelsat (Atlantic Ocean)
Radio broadcast stations: AM 41, FM 26, shortwave 0 (1999)
Radios: 415,000 (1997)
Television broadcast stations: 2 (plus a cable TV service) (1997)
Televisions: 38,000 (1997)
Internet country code: .ht
Internet hosts: NA
Internet Service Providers (ISPs): 3 (2000)
Internet users: 80,000 (2002)

TRANSPORTATION

Airports: 13 (2004 est.)
Airports - with paved runways:
total: 4
2,438 to 3,047 m: 1
914 to 1,523 m: 3 (2005 est.)
Airports - with unpaved runways:
total: 8
914 to 1,523 m: 1
under 914 m: 7 (2005 est.)
Roadways:
total: 4,160 km
paved: 1,011 km
unpaved: 3,149 km (1999)
Ports and terminals: Cap-Haitien

MILITARY

Military branches: the regular Haitian Armed Forces (FAdH) - Army, Navy, and Air Force - have been demobilized but still exist on paper until or unless they are constitutionally abolished
Military service age and obligation: 18 years of age for voluntary recruitment into the police force (2001)
Manpower available for military service:
males age 18-49: 1,626,491 (2005 est.)
Manpower fit for military service: *males age 18-49:* 948,320 (2005 est.)
Manpower reaching military service age annually: *males:* 98,554 (2005 est.)
Military expenditures - dollar figure: $26 million (2003)
Military expenditures - percent of GDP: 0.9% (2003)

TRANSNATIONAL ISSUES

Disputes - international: since 2004, about 8,000 peacekeepers from the UN Stabilization Mission in Haiti (MINUSTAH) maintain civil order in Haiti; despite efforts to control illegal migration, Haitians fleeing economic privation and civil unrest continue to cross into Dominican Republic and to sail to neighboring countries; Haiti claims US-administered Navassa Island
Illicit drugs: major Caribbean transshipment point for cocaine en route to the US and Europe; substantial money-laundering activity; Colombian narcotics traffickers favor Haiti for illicit financial transactions; pervasive corruption

HEARD ISLAND AND MCDONALD ISLANDS

INTRODUCTION

Background: These uninhabited, barren, sub-Antarctic islands were transferred from the UK to Australia in 1947. Populated by large numbers of seal and bird species, the islands have been designated a nature preserve.

GEOGRAPHY

Location: islands in the Indian Ocean, about two-thirds of the way from Madagascar to Antarctica
Geographic coordinates: 53 06 S, 72 31 E
Map references: Antarctic Region
Area:
total: 412 sq km
land: 412 sq km
water: 0 sq km
Area - comparative: slightly more than two times the size of Washington, DC
Land boundaries: 0 km
Coastline: 101.9 km

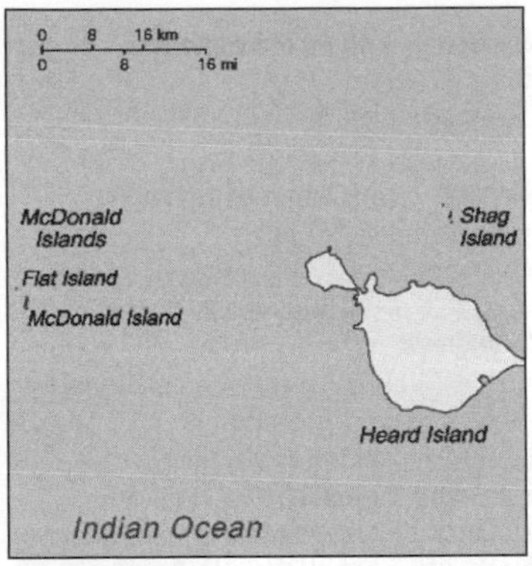

Maritime claims:
territorial sea: 12 nm
exclusive fishing zone: 200 nm
Climate: antarctic
Terrain: Heard Island - 80% ice-covered, bleak and mountainous, dominated by a large massif (Big Ben) and an active volcano (Mawson Peak); McDonald Islands - small and rocky
Elevation extremes:
lowest point: Indian Ocean 0 m
highest point: Mawson Peak, on Big Ben 2,745 m
Natural resources: fish
Land use:
arable land: 0%
permanent crops: 0%
other: 100% (2001)
Irrigated land: 0 sq km
Natural hazards: Mawson Peak, an active volcano, is on Heard Island
Environment - current issues: NA

PEOPLE

Population: uninhabited (July 2005 est.)

GOVERNMENT

Country name:
conventional long form: Territory of Heard Island and McDonald Islands
conventional short form: Heard Island and McDonald Islands
Dependency status: territory of Australia; administered from Canberra by the Australian Antarctic Division of the Department of the Environment and Heritage
Legal system: the laws of Australia, where applicable, apply
Diplomatic representation in the US: none (territory of Australia)
Diplomatic representation from the US: none (territory of Australia)
Flag description: the flag of Australia is used

ECONOMY

Economy - overview: No indigenous economic activity, but the Australian Government allows limited fishing around the islands.

COMMUNICATIONS

Internet country code: .hm

TRANSPORTATION

Ports and terminals: none; offshore anchorage only

MILITARY

Military - note: defense is the responsibility of Australia; Australia conducts fisheries patrols

TRANSNATIONAL ISSUES

Disputes - international: none

HOLY SEE (VATICAN CITY)

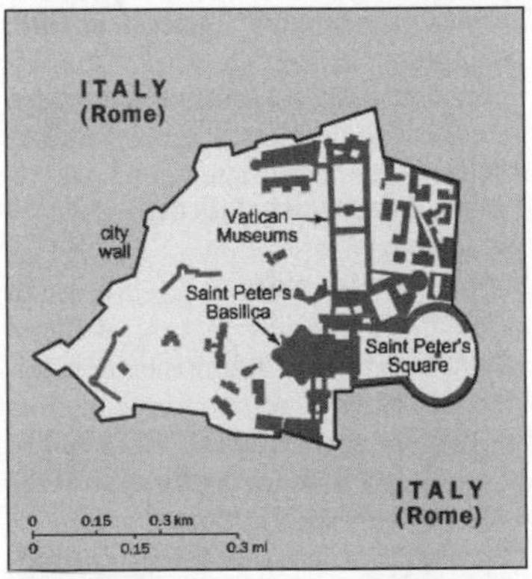

INTRODUCTION

Background: Popes in their secular role ruled portions of the Italian peninsula for more than a thousand years until the mid 19th century, when many of the Papal States were seized by the newly united Kingdom of Italy. In 1870, the pope's holdings were further circumscribed when Rome itself was annexed. Disputes between a series of "prisoner" popes and Italy were resolved in 1929 by three Lateran Treaties, which established the independent state of Vatican City and granted Roman Catholicism special status in Italy. In 1984, a concordat between the Holy See and Italy modified certain of the earlier treaty provisions, including the primacy of Roman Catholicism as the Italian state religion. Present concerns of the Holy See include religious freedom, international development, the Middle East, terrorism, interreligious dialogue and reconciliation, and the application of church doctrine in an era of rapid change and globalization. About 1 billion people worldwide profess the Catholic faith.

GEOGRAPHY

Location: Southern Europe, an enclave of Rome (Italy)
Geographic coordinates: 41 54 N, 12 27 E
Map references: Europe
Area:
total: 0.44 sq km
land: 0.44 sq km
water: 0 sq km
Area - comparative: about 0.7 times the size of The Mall in Washington, DC
Land boundaries:
total: 3.2 km
border countries: Italy 3.2 km
Coastline: 0 km (landlocked)
Maritime claims: none (landlocked)
Climate: temperate; mild, rainy winters (September to mid-May) with hot, dry summers (May to September)
Terrain: low hill
Elevation extremes:
lowest point: unnamed location 19 m
highest point: unnamed location 75 m
Natural resources: none
Land use:
arable land: 0%
permanent crops: 0%
other: 100% (urban area) (2001)
Irrigated land: 0 sq km (1998 est.)
Natural hazards: NA
Environment - current issues: NA
Environment - international agreements:
party to: none of the selected agreements
signed, but not ratified: Air Pollution, Environmental Modification
Geography - note: urban; landlocked; enclave in Rome, Italy; world's smallest state; outside the Vatican City, 13 buildings in Rome and Castel Gandolfo (the pope's summer residence) enjoy extraterritorial rights

PEOPLE

Population: 921 (July 2005 est.)
Population growth rate: 0.01% (2005 est.)
HIV/AIDS - adult prevalence rate: NA%
HIV/AIDS - people living with HIV/AIDS: NA
HIV/AIDS - deaths: NA
Nationality:
noun: none
adjective: none
Ethnic groups: Italians, Swiss, other
Religions: Roman Catholic
Languages: Italian, Latin, French, various other languages
Literacy:
definition: NA
total population: 100%

male: 100%
female: 100%

GOVERNMENT

Country name:
conventional long form: The Holy See (State of the Vatican City)
conventional short form: Holy See (Vatican City)
local long form: Santa Sede (Stato della Citta del Vaticano)
local short form: Santa Sede (Citta del Vaticano)
Government type: ecclesiastical
Capital: Vatican City
Administrative divisions: none
Independence: 11 February 1929 (from Italy); note - the three treaties signed with Italy on 11 February 1929 acknowledged, among other things, the full sovereignty of the Vatican and established its territorial extent; however, the origin of the Papal States, which over the years have varied considerably in extent, may be traced back to the 8th century
National holiday: Coronation Day of Pope BENEDICT XVI, 24 April (2005)
Constitution: new Fundamental Law promulgated by Pope JOHN PAUL II on 26 November 2000, effective 22 February 2001 (replaces the first Fundamental Law of 1929)
Legal system: based on Code of Canon Law and revisions to it
Suffrage: limited to cardinals less than 80 years old
Executive branch:
chief of state: Pope BENEDICT XVI (since 19 April 2005)
head of government: Secretary of State Cardinal Angelo SODANO (since 1 December 1990)
cabinet: Pontifical Commission appointed by the pope
elections: pope elected for life by the College of Cardinals; election last held 19 April 2005 (next to be held after the death of the current pope); secretary of state appointed by the pope
election results: Joseph RATZINGER elected Pope BENEDICT XVI
Legislative branch: unicameral Pontifical Commission
Judicial branch: there are three tribunals responsible for civil and criminal matters within Vatican City; three other tribunals rule on issues pertaining to the Holy See
note: judicial duties were established by the Motu Proprio of Pius XII on 1 May 1946
Political parties and leaders: none
Political pressure groups and leaders: none (exclusive of influence exercised by church officers)
International organization participation: CE (observer), IAEA, IOM (observer), ITU, NAM (guest), OAS (observer), OPCW, OSCE, UN (observer), UNCTAD, UNHCR, UPU, WIPO, WToO (observer), WTO (observer)
Diplomatic representation in the US:
chief of mission: Apostolic Nuncio Archbishop Gabriel MONTALVO
chancery: 3339 Massachusetts Avenue NW, Washington, DC 20008
telephone: [1] (202) 333-7121
FAX: [1] (202) 337-4036
Diplomatic representation from the US:
chief of mission: Ambassador Francis ROONEY
embassy: Villa Domiziana, Via delle Terme Deciane 26, 00153 Rome
mailing address: PSC 59, Box 66, APO AE 09624
telephone: [39] (06) 4674-3428
FAX: [39] (06) 575-8346
Flag description: two vertical bands of yellow (hoist side) and white with the crossed keys of Saint Peter and the papal miter centered in the white band

ECONOMY

Economy - overview: This unique, noncommercial economy is supported financially by an annual contribution from Roman Catholic dioceses throughout the world (known as Peter's Pence); by the sale of postage stamps, coins, medals, and tourist mementos; by fees for admission to museums; and by the sale of publications. Investments and real estate income also account for a sizable portion of revenue. The incomes and living standards of lay workers are comparable to those of counterparts who work in the city of Rome.
Labor force: NA
Labor force - by occupation: essentially services with a small amount of industry; note - dignitaries, priests, nuns, guards, and 3,000 lay workers live outside the Vatican
Population below poverty line: NA
Household income or consumption by percentage share:
lowest 10%: NA%
highest 10%: NA%
Budget:
revenues: $245.2 million
expenditures: $260.4 million, including capital expenditures of NA (2002)
Industries: printing; production of coins, medals, postage stamps; a small amount of mosaics and staff uniforms; worldwide banking and financial activities
Electricity - production: NA kWh
Electricity - consumption: NA kWh
Electricity - exports: 0 kWh
Electricity - imports: NA kWh; note - electricity supplied by Italy
Economic aid - recipient: none
Currency (code): euro (EUR)
Currency code: EUR
Exchange rates: euros per US dollar - 0.79697 (2005), 0.8054 (2004), 0.886 (2003), 1.0626 (2002), 1.1175 (2001)
Fiscal year: calendar year

COMMUNICATIONS

Telephones - main lines in use: NA
Telephones - mobile cellular: NA
Telephone system:
general assessment: automatic exchange
domestic: tied into Italian system
international: country code - 39; uses Italian system
Radio broadcast stations: AM 3, FM 4, shortwave 2 (1998)
Radios: NA
Television broadcast stations: 1 (1996)
Televisions: NA
Internet country code: .va
Internet hosts: 9 (2004)
Internet Service Providers (ISPs): NA
Internet users: NA

TRANSPORTATION

Airports: none (2004 est.)

MILITARY

Military branches: Pontifical Swiss Guard (Corpo della Guardia Svizzera Pontificia)
Military - note: defense is the responsibility of Italy; ceremonial and limited security duties performed by Pontifical Swiss Guard

TRANSNATIONAL ISSUES

Disputes - international: none

HONDURAS

INTRODUCTION

Background: Once part of Spain's vast empire in the New World, Honduras became an independent nation in 1821. After two and a half decades of mostly military rule, a freely elected civilian government came to power in 1982. During the 1980s, Honduras proved a haven for anti-Sandinista contras fighting the Marxist Nicaraguan Government and an ally to Salvadoran Government forces fighting leftist guerrillas. The country was devastated by Hurricane Mitch in 1998, which killed about 5,600 people and caused approximately $2 billion in damage.

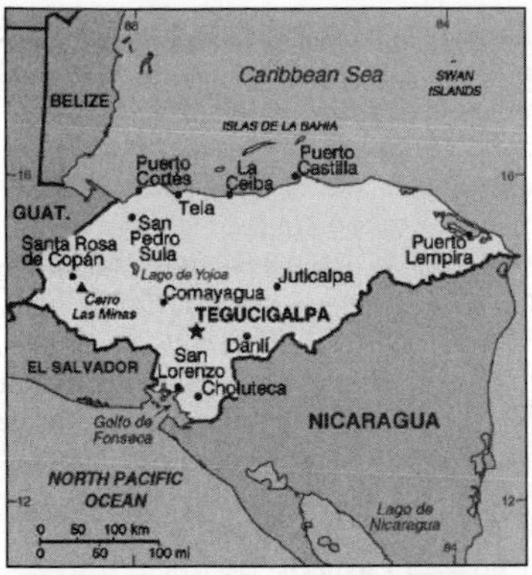

GEOGRAPHY

Location: Central America, bordering the Caribbean Sea, between Guatemala and Nicaragua and bordering the Gulf of Fonseca (North Pacific Ocean), between El Salvador and Nicaragua
Geographic coordinates: 15 00 N, 86 30 W
Map references: Central America and the Caribbean
Area:
total: 112,090 sq km
land: 111,890 sq km
water: 200 sq km
Area - comparative: slightly larger than Tennessee
Land boundaries:
total: 1,520 km
border countries: Guatemala 256 km, El Salvador 342 km, Nicaragua 922 km
Coastline: 820 km
Maritime claims:
territorial sea: 12 nm
contiguous zone: 24 nm
exclusive economic zone: 200 nm
continental shelf: natural extension of territory or to 200 nm
Climate: subtropical in lowlands, temperate in mountains
Terrain: mostly mountains in interior, narrow coastal plains
Elevation extremes:
lowest point: Caribbean Sea 0 m
highest point: Cerro Las Minas 2,870 m
Natural resources: timber, gold, silver, copper, lead, zinc, iron ore, antimony, coal, fish, hydropower
Land use:
arable land: 9.55%
permanent crops: 3.22%
other: 87.23% (2001)
Irrigated land: 760 sq km (1998 est.)
Natural hazards: frequent, but generally mild, earthquakes; extremely susceptible to damaging hurricanes and floods along the Caribbean coast
Environment - current issues: urban population expanding; deforestation results from logging and the clearing of land for agricultural purposes; further land degradation and soil erosion hastened by uncontrolled development and improper land use practices such as farming of marginal lands; mining activities polluting Lago de Yojoa (the country's largest source of fresh water), as well as several rivers and streams, with heavy metals
Environment - international agreements:
party to: Biodiversity, Climate Change, Climate Change-Kyoto Protocol, Desertification, Endangered Species, Hazardous Wastes, Law of the Sea, Marine Dumping, Ozone Layer Protection, Ship Pollution, Tropical Timber 83, Tropical Timber 94, Wetlands
signed, but not ratified: none of the selected agreements
Geography - note: has only a short Pacific coast but a long Caribbean shoreline, including the virtually uninhabited eastern Mosquito Coast

PEOPLE

Population: 6,975,204
note: estimates for this country explicitly take into account the effects of excess mortality due to AIDS; this can result in lower life expectancy, higher infant mortality and death rates, lower population and growth rates, and changes in the distribution of population by age and sex than would otherwise be expected (July 2005 est.)
Age structure:
0-14 years: 40.8% (male 1,452,646/female 1,393,271)
15-64 years: 55.5% (male 1,921,432/female 1,948,656)
65 years and over: 3.7% (male 122,146/female 137,053) (2005 est.)
Median age:
total: 19.15 years
male: 18.75 years
female: 19.56 years (2005 est.)
Population growth rate: 2.16% (2005 est.)
Birth rate: 30.38 births/1,000 population (2005 est.)
Death rate: 6.87 deaths/1,000 population (2005 est.)
Net migration rate: -1.95 migrant(s)/1,000 population (2005 est.)
Sex ratio:
at birth: 1.05 male(s)/female
under 15 years: 1.04 male(s)/female
15-64 years: 0.99 male(s)/female
65 years and over: 0.89 male(s)/female
total population: 1.01 male(s)/female (2005 est.)
Infant mortality rate:
total: 29.32 deaths/1,000 live births
male: 32.84 deaths/1,000 live births
female: 25.63 deaths/1,000 live births (2005 est.)
Life expectancy at birth:
total population: 69.3 years
male: 67.71 years
female: 70.97 years (2005 est.)
Total fertility rate: 3.87 children born/woman (2005 est.)
HIV/AIDS - adult prevalence rate: 1.8% (2003 est.)
HIV/AIDS - people living with HIV/AIDS: 63,000 (2003 est.)
HIV/AIDS - deaths: 4,100 (2003 est.)
Nationality:
noun: Honduran(s)
adjective: Honduran
Ethnic groups: mestizo (mixed Amerindian and European) 90%, Amerindian 7%, black 2%, white 1%
Religions: Roman Catholic 97%, Protestant 3%
Languages: Spanish, Amerindian dialects
Literacy:
definition: age 15 and over can read and write
total population: 76.2%
male: 76.1%
female: 76.3% (2003 est.)

GOVERNMENT

Country name:
conventional long form: Republic of Honduras
conventional short form: Honduras
local long form: Republica de Honduras
local short form: Honduras
Government type: democratic constitutional republic
Capital: Tegucigalpa
Administrative divisions: 18 departments (departamentos, singular - departamento); Atlantida, Choluteca, Colon, Comayagua, Copan, Cortes, El Paraiso, Francisco Morazan, Gracias a Dios, Intibuca, Islas de la Bahia, La Paz, Lempira, Ocotepeque, Olancho, Santa Barbara, Valle, Yoro
Independence: 15 September 1821 (from Spain)
National holiday: Independence Day, 15 September (1821)
Constitution: 11 January 1982, effective 20 January 1982; amended 1995
Legal system: rooted in Roman and Spanish civil law with increasing influence of English common law; recent judicial reforms include abandoning Napoleonic legal codes in favor of the oral adversarial system; accepts ICJ jurisdiction, with reservations
Suffrage: 18 years of age; universal and compulsory
Executive branch:
chief of state: President Ricardo (Joest) MADURO (since 27 January 2002); First Vice President Vicente WILLIAMS Agasse (since 27 January 2002); Second

Vice President Armida Villela Maria DE LOPEZ Contreras (since 27 January 2002); Third Vice President Alberto DIAZ Lobo (since 27 January 2002); note - the president is both the chief of state and head of government
head of government: President Ricardo (Joest) MADURO (since 27 January 2002); First Vice President Vicente WILLIAMS Agasse (since 27 January 2002); Second Vice President Armida Villela Maria DE LOPEZ Contreras (since 27 January 2002); Third Vice President Alberto DIAZ Lobo (since 27 January 2002); note - the president is both the chief of state and head of government
cabinet: Cabinet appointed by president
elections: president elected by popular vote for a four-year term; election last held 27 November 2005 (next to be held November 2009)
election results: Manuel "Mel" ZELAYA (PL) elected president - 49.8%, Porfirio "Pepe" LOBO Sosa (PN) 46.1%, others 4.1%; note - Manuel "Mel" ZELAYA will take office on 27 January 2006
Legislative branch: unicameral National Congress or Congreso Nacional (128 seats; members are elected proportionally to the number of votes their party's presidential candidate receives to serve four-year terms)
elections: last held 27 November 2005 (next to be held November 2009)
election results: percent of vote by party - NA%; seats by party - PL 62, PN 55, PUD 5, CD 4, PINU 2
Judicial branch: Supreme Court of Justice or Corte Suprema de Justicia (judges are elected for seven-year terms by the National Congress)
Political parties and leaders: Christian Democratic Party or PDC [Saul ESCOBAR Andrade]; Democratic Unification Party or PUD [Matias FUNES]; Liberal Party or PL [Patricia RODAS]; National Innovation and Unity Party or PINU [Olban F. VALLADARES]; National Party of Honduras or PN [Gilberto GOLDSTEIN]
Political pressure groups and leaders: Committee for the Defense of Human Rights in Honduras or CODEH; Confederation of Honduran Workers or CTH; Coordinating Committee of Popular Organizations or CCOP; General Workers Confederation or CGT; Honduran Council of Private Enterprise or COHEP; National Association of Honduran Campesinos or ANACH; National Union of Campesinos or UNC; Popular Bloc or BP; United Federation of Honduran Workers or FUTH
International organization participation: BCIE, CACM, FAO, G-77, IADB, IAEA, IBRD, ICAO, ICCt, ICFTU, ICRM, IDA, IFAD, IFC, IFRCS, ILO, IMF, IMO, Interpol, IOC, IOM, ISO (subscriber), ITU, LAES, LAIA (observer), MIGA, MINURSO, NAM, OAS, OPANAL, OPCW, PCA, RG, UN, UNCTAD, UNESCO, UNIDO, UPU, WCL, WFTU, WHO, WIPO, WMO, WToO, WTO
Diplomatic representation in the US:
chief of mission: Ambassador Norman GARCIA Paz
chancery: Suite 4-M, 3007 Tilden Street NW, Washington, DC 20008
telephone: [1] (202) 966-7702
FAX: [1] (202) 966-9751
consulate(s) general: Atlanta, Chicago, Houston, Los Angeles, Miami, New Orleans, New York, Phoenix, San Francisco
honorary consulate(s): Boston, Detroit, Jacksonville
Diplomatic representation from the US:
chief of mission: Ambassador Charles A. FORD
embassy: Avenida La Paz, Apartado Postal No. 3453, Tegucigalpa
mailing address: American Embassy, APO AA 34022, Tegucigalpa
telephone: [504] 236-9320
FAX: [504] 236-9037
Flag description: three equal horizontal bands of blue (top), white, and blue with five blue, five-pointed stars arranged in an X pattern centered in the white band; the stars represent the members of the former Federal Republic of Central America - Costa Rica, El Salvador, Guatemala, Honduras, and Nicaragua; similar to the flag of El Salvador, which features a round emblem encircled by the words REPUBLICA DE EL SALVADOR EN LA AMERICA CENTRAL centered in the white band; also similar to the flag of Nicaragua, which features a triangle encircled by the word REPUBLICA DE NICARAGUA on top and AMERICA CENTRAL on the bottom, centered in the white band

ECONOMY

Economy - overview: Honduras, one of the poorest countries in the Western Hemisphere with an extraordinarily unequal distribution of income and massive unemployment, is banking on expanded trade under the U.S.-Central America Free Trade Agreement (CAFTA) and on debt relief under the Heavily Indebted Poor Countries (HIPC) initiative. The country has met most of its macroeconomic targets, and began a three-year IMF Poverty Reduction and Growth Facility (PGRF) program in February 2004. Growth remains dependent on the economy of the US, its largest trading partner, on commodity prices, particularly coffee, and on reduction of the high crime rate.
GDP (purchasing power parity): $20.56 billion (2005 est.)
GDP (official exchange rate): $8.038 billion (2005 est.)
GDP - real growth rate: 4% (2005 est.)
GDP - per capita: purchasing power parity - $2,900 (2005 est.)
GDP - composition by sector:
agriculture: 12.7%
industry: 31.2%
services: 56.1% (2005 est.)
Labor force: 2.54 million (2005 est.)
Labor force - by occupation: agriculture 34%, industry 21%, services 45% (2001 est.)
Unemployment rate: 28% (2005 est.)
Population below poverty line: 53% (1993 est.)
Household income or consumption by percentage share:
lowest 10%: 0.6%
highest 10%: 42.7% (1998)
Distribution of family income - Gini index: 55 (1999)
Inflation rate (consumer prices): 9.2% (2005 est.)
Investment (gross fixed): 27% of GDP (2005 est.)
Budget:
revenues: $1.693 billion
expenditures: $1.938 billion, including capital expenditures of $106 million (2005 est.)
Public debt: 70.5% of GDP (2005 est.)
Agriculture - products: bananas, coffee, citrus; beef; timber; shrimp
Industries: sugar, coffee, textiles, clothing, wood products
Industrial production growth rate: 7.7% (2003 est.)
Electricity - production: 4.338 billion kWh (2003)
Electricity - production by source:
fossil fuel: 50.2%
hydro: 49.8%
nuclear: 0%
other: 0% (2001)
Electricity - consumption: 4.369 billion kWh (2003)
Electricity - exports: 0 kWh (2003)
Electricity - imports: 335 million kWh (2003)
Oil - production: 0 bbl/day (2003 est.)
Oil - consumption: 37,000 bbl/day (2003 est.)
Oil - exports: NA (2001)
Oil - imports: NA (2001)
Current account balance: $-456 million (2005 est.)
Exports: $1.726 billion f.o.b. (2005 est.)
Exports - partners: US 54.4%, El Salvador 8.1%, Germany 5.9%,

Guatemala 5.4% (2004)
Imports: $4.161 billion f.o.b. (2005 est.)
Imports - partners: US 37.5%, Guatemala 6.9%, Mexico 5.4%, Costa Rica 4.3%, El Salvador 4% (2004)
Reserves of foreign exchange and gold: $2.23 billion (2005 est.)
Debt - external: $4.675 billion (2005 est.)
Economic aid - recipient: $557.8 million (1999)
Currency (code): lempira (HNL)
Currency code: HNL
Exchange rates: lempiras per US dollar - 18.92 (2005), 18.206 (2004), 17.345 (2003), 16.433 (2002), 15.474 (2001)
Fiscal year: calendar year

COMMUNICATIONS

Telephones - main lines in use: 322,500 (2002)
Telephones - mobile cellular: 326,500 (2002)
Telephone system:
general assessment: inadequate system
domestic: NA
international: country code - 504; satellite earth stations - 2 Intelsat (Atlantic Ocean); connected to Central American Microwave System
Radio broadcast stations: AM 241, FM 53, shortwave 12 (1998)
Radios: 2.45 million (1997)
Television broadcast stations: 11 (plus 17 repeaters) (1997)
Televisions: 570,000 (1997)
Internet country code: .hn
Internet hosts: 1,944 (2003)
Internet Service Providers (ISPs): 8 (2000)
Internet users: 168,600 (2002)

TRANSPORTATION

Airports: 115 (2004 est.)
Airports - with paved runways:
total: 11
2,438 to 3,047 m: 3
1,524 to 2,437 m: 2
914 to 1,523 m: 3
under 914 m: 3 (2005 est.)
Airports - with unpaved runways:
total: 105
1,524 to 2,437 m: 2
914 to 1,523 m: 19
under 914 m: 84 (2005 est.)
Railways:
total: 699 km
narrow gauge: 279 km 1.067-m gauge; 420 km 0.914-m gauge (2004)
Roadways:
total: 13,603 km
paved: 2,775 km
unpaved: 10,828 km (1999)
Waterways: 465 km (most navigable only by small craft) (2004)
Merchant marine:
total: 137 ships (1,000 GRT or over) 598,600 GRT/616,158 DWT
by type: bulk carrier 10, cargo 67, chemical tanker 6, container 2, liquefied gas 1, livestock carrier 1, passenger 4, passenger/cargo 5, petroleum tanker 30, refrigerated cargo 9, roll on/roll off 1, specialized tanker 1
foreign-owned: 44 (Canada 1, China 3, Egypt 1, Greece 4, Hong Kong 2, Israel 1, Japan 4, Lebanon 1, Mexico 1, Singapore 12, South Korea 6, Taiwan 2, Tanzania 1, Turkey 1, United States 2, Vanuatu 1, Vietnam 1)
registered in other countries: 1 (2005)
Ports and terminals: Puerto Castilla, Puerto Cortes, San Lorenzo, Tela

MILITARY

Military branches: Army, Navy (includes Naval Infantry), Air Force
Military service age and obligation: 18 years of age for voluntary 2-3 year military service (2004)
Manpower available for military service:
males age 18-49: 1,448,369 (2005 est.)
Manpower fit for military service: *males age 18-49:* 955,019 (2005 est.)
Manpower reaching military service age annually: *males:* 77,399 (2005 est.)
Military expenditures - dollar figure: $100.6 million (2004)
Military expenditures - percent of GDP: 1.4% (2004)

TRANSNATIONAL ISSUES

Disputes - international: in 1992, ICJ ruled on the delimitation of "bolsones" (disputed areas) along the El Salvador-Honduras border, but despite OAS intervention and a further ICJ ruling in 2003, full demarcation of the border remains stalled; the 1992 ICJ ruling advised a tripartite resolution to a maritime boundary in the Gulf of Fonseca with consideration of Honduran access to the Pacific; El Salvador continues to claim tiny Conejo Island, not mentioned in the ICJ ruling, off Honduras in the Gulf of Fonseca; Honduras claims Sapodilla Cays off the coast of Belize, but agreed to creation of a joint ecological park and Guatemalan corridor in the Caribbean in the failed 2002 Belize-Guatemala Differendum, which the OAS is attempting to revive; Nicaragua filed a claim against Honduras in 1999 and against Colombia in 2001 at the ICJ over a complex dispute over islands and maritime boundaries in the Caribbean Sea
Illicit drugs: transshipment point for drugs and narcotics; illicit producer of cannabis, cultivated on small plots and used principally for local consumption; corruption is a major problem; some money-laundering activity

HONG KONG

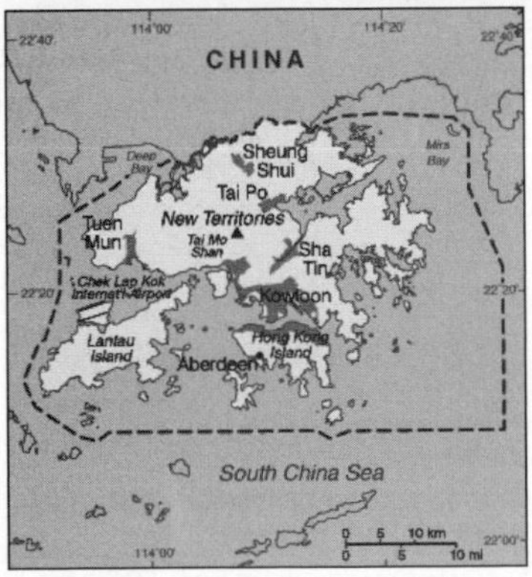

INTRODUCTION

Background: Occupied by the UK in 1841, Hong Kong was formally ceded by China the following year; various adjacent lands were added later in the 19th century. Pursuant to an agreement signed by China and the UK on 19 December 1984, Hong Kong became the Hong Kong Special Administrative Region (SAR) of China on 1 July 1997. In this agreement, China has promised that, under its "one country, two systems" formula, China's socialist economic system will not be imposed on Hong Kong and that Hong Kong will enjoy a high degree of autonomy in all matters except foreign and defense affairs for the next 50 years.

GEOGRAPHY

Location: Eastern Asia, bordering the South China Sea and China
Geographic coordinates: 22 15 N, 114 10 E
Map references: Southeast Asia
Area:
total: 1,092 sq km
land: 1,042 sq km
water: 50 sq km
Area - comparative: six times the size of Washington, DC
Land boundaries:
total: 30 km
regional border: China 30 km
Coastline: 733 km
Maritime claims: *territorial sea:* 3 nm
Climate: subtropical monsoon; cool and

humid in winter, hot and rainy from spring through summer, warm and sunny in fall
Terrain: hilly to mountainous with steep slopes; lowlands in north
Elevation extremes:
lowest point: South China Sea 0 m
highest point: Tai Mo Shan 958 m
Natural resources: outstanding deepwater harbor, feldspar
Land use:
arable land: 5.05%
permanent crops: 1.01%
other: 93.94% (2001)
Irrigated land: 20 sq km (1998 est.)
Natural hazards: occasional typhoons
Environment - current issues: air and water pollution from rapid urbanization
Environment - international agreements:
party to: Marine Dumping (associate member)
Geography - note: more than 200 islands

PEOPLE

Population: 6,898,686 (July 2005 est.)
Age structure:
0-14 years: 13.8% (male 498,771/female 454,252)
15-64 years: 73.5% (male 2,479,656/female 2,591,170)
65 years and over: 12.7% (male 404,308/female 470,529) (2005 est.)
Median age:
total: 39.4 years
male: 39.3 years
female: 39.6 years (2005 est.)
Population growth rate: 0.65% (2005 est.)
Birth rate: 7.23 births/1,000 population (2005 est.)
Death rate: 5.98 deaths/1,000 population (2005 est.)
Net migration rate: 5.24 migrant(s)/1,000 population (2005 est.)
Sex ratio:
at birth: 1.1 male(s)/female
under 15 years: 1.1 male(s)/female
15-64 years: 0.96 male(s)/female
65 years and over: 0.86 male(s)/female
total population: 0.96 male(s)/female (2005 est.)
Infant mortality rate:
total: 2.97 deaths/1,000 live births
male: 3.16 deaths/1,000 live births
female: 2.77 deaths/1,000 live births (2005 est.)
Life expectancy at birth:
total population: 81.5 years
male: 78.81 years
female: 84.41 years (2005 est.)
Total fertility rate: 0.91 children born/woman (2005 est.)
HIV/AIDS - adult prevalence rate: 0.1% (2003 est.)
HIV/AIDS - people living with HIV/AIDS: 2,600 (2003 est.)
HIV/AIDS - deaths: less than 200 (2003 est.)
Nationality:
noun: Chinese/Hong Konger
adjective: Chinese/Hong Kong
Ethnic groups: Chinese 95%, other 5%
Religions: eclectic mixture of local religions 90%, Christian 10%
Languages: Chinese (Cantonese), English; both are official
Literacy:
definition: age 15 and over has ever attended school
total population: 93.5%
male: 96.9%
female: 89.6% (2002)

GOVERNMENT

Country name:
conventional long form: Hong Kong Special Administrative Region
conventional short form: Hong Kong
local long form: Xianggang Tebie Xingzhengqu
local short form: Xianggang
abbreviation: HK
Dependency status: special administrative region of China
Government type: limited democracy
Administrative divisions: none (special administrative region of China)
Independence: none (special administrative region of China)
National holiday: National Day (Anniversary of the Founding of the People's Republic of China), 1 October (1949); note - 1 July 1997 is celebrated as Hong Kong Special Administrative Region Establishment Day
Constitution: Basic Law, approved in March 1990 by China's National People's Congress, is Hong Kong's "mini-constitution"
Legal system: based on English common law
Suffrage: direct election 18 years of age; universal for permanent residents living in the territory of Hong Kong for the past seven years; indirect election limited to about 200,000 members of functional constituencies and an 800-member election committee drawn from broad regional groupings, municipal organizations, and central government bodies
Executive branch:
chief of state: President of China HU Jintao (since 15 March 2003)
head of government: Chief Executive Donald TSANG (since 24 June 2005)
cabinet: Executive Council consists of four official members and 15 non-official members
elections: previous chief executive TUNG Chee-hwa was elected to second five-year term in March 2002 by 800-member election committee dominated by pro-Beijing forces, resignation accepted 12 March 2005; Donald TSANG acted as chief executive between 12 March 2005 and 25 May 2005; Henry TANG acted as chief executive between 25 May 2005 and 24 June 2005; TSANG was elected on 16 June 2005 to fill final two years of TUNG's term (next election to be held in March 2007)
Legislative branch: unicameral Legislative Council or LEGCO (60 seats; in 2004 30 seats indirectly elected by functional constituencies, 30 elected by popular vote; members serve four-year terms)
elections: last held 12 September 2004 (next to be held in September 2008)
election results: percent of vote by party - pro-democracy group 62%; seats by party - (pro-Beijing 34) DAB 12, Liberal Party 10, independents 11, FTU 1; (pro-democracy 25) independents 11, Democratic Party 9, CTU 2, ADPL 1, Frontier Party 1, NWSC 1; other 1
Judicial branch: Court of Final Appeal in the Hong Kong Special Administrative Region
Political parties and leaders: Association for Democracy and People's Livelihood or ADPL [Frederick FUNG Kin-kee, chairman]; Citizens Party [Alex CHAN Kai-chung]; Democratic Alliance for the Betterment and Progress of Hong Kong or DAB [MA Lik, chairman]; Democratic Party [LEE Wing-tat, chairman]; Frontier Party [Emily LAU Wai-hing, chairwoman]; Liberal Party [James TIEN Pei-chun, chairman]
note: political blocs include: pro-democracy - ADPL, Democratic Party, Frontier Party; pro-Beijing - DAB, Liberal Party
Political pressure groups and leaders: Chinese General Chamber of Commerce (pro-China); Chinese Manufacturers' Association of Hong Kong; Confederation of Trade Unions or CTU (pro-democracy) [Lau Chin-shek, president; Lee Cheuk-yan, general secretary]; Federation of Hong Kong Industries; Federation of Trade Unions or FTU (pro-China) [Cheng Yiu-tong, executive councilor]; Hong Kong Alliance in Support of the Patriotic Democratic Movement in China [Szeto Wah, chairman]; Hong Kong and Kowloon Trade Union Council (pro-Taiwan); Hong Kong General Chamber of Commerce; Hong Kong Professional Teachers' Union [Cheung Man-kwong, president]; Neighborhood and Workers' Service Center or NWSC (pro-democracy); The Alliance [Bernard Chan, exco member]
International organization participation: APEC, AsDB, BIS, ICC, ICFTU, IHO, IMF, IMO (associate), IOC, ISO (correspondent), UPU, WCL, WCO, WMO, WToO (associate), WTO

Diplomatic representation in the US: none (special administrative region of China)
Diplomatic representation from the US:
chief of mission: Consul General James B. CUNNINGHAM
consulate(s) general: 26 Garden Road, Hong Kong
mailing address: PSC 461, Box 1, FPO AP 96521-0006
telephone: [852] 2523-9011
FAX: [852] 2845-1598
Flag description: red with a stylized, white, five-petal bauhinia flower in the center

ECONOMY

Economy - overview: Hong Kong has a free market, entrepot economy, highly dependent on international trade. Natural resources are limited, and food and raw materials must be imported. Gross imports and exports (i.e., including reexports to and from third countries) each exceed GDP in dollar value. Even before Hong Kong reverted to Chinese administration on 1 July 1997, it had extensive trade and investment ties with China. Hong Kong has been further integrating its economy with China because China's growing openness to the world economy has made manufacturing in China much more cost effective. Hong Kong's reexport business to and from China is a major driver of growth. Per capita GDP is comparable to that of the four big economies of Western Europe. GDP growth averaged a strong 5% from 1989 to 2005, but Hong Kong suffered two recessions in the past eight years because of the Asian financial crisis in 1997-1998 and the global downturn in 2001-2002. Although the Severe Acute Respiratory Syndrome (SARS) outbreak also battered Hong Kong's economy, a solid rise in exports, a boom in tourism from the mainland because of China's easing of travel restrictions, and a return of consumer confidence resulted in the resumption of strong growth from late 2003 through 2005.
GDP (purchasing power parity): $254.2 billion (2005 est.)
GDP (official exchange rate): $181.6 billion (2005 est.)
GDP - real growth rate: 7% (2005 est.)
GDP - per capita: purchasing power parity - $36,800 (2005 est.)
GDP - composition by sector:
agriculture: 0.1%
industry: 10%
services: 89.9% (2005 est.)
Labor force: 3.58 million (October 2005)
Labor force - by occupation: manufacturing 7.5%, construction 2.9%, wholesale and retail trade, restaurants, and hotels 43.7%, financing, insurance, and real estate 19.2%, transport and communications 7.9%, community and social services 18.5%
note: above data exclude public sector (2004 est.)
Unemployment rate: 5.8% (October 2005)
Population below poverty line: NA
Household income or consumption by percentage share:
lowest 10%: NA
highest 10%: NA
Inflation rate (consumer prices): 0.9% (2005 est.)
Investment (gross fixed): 21.2% of GDP (2005 est.)
Budget:
revenues: $31.31 billion
expenditures: $32.3 billion, including capital expenditures of $5.9 billion (2005 est.)
Public debt: 1.8% of GDP (2005 est.)
Agriculture - products: fresh vegetables, poultry, fish, pork
Industries: textiles, clothing, tourism, banking, shipping, electronics, plastics, toys, watches, clocks
Industrial production growth rate: 1% (2005 est.)
Electricity - production: 33.38 billion kWh (2003)
Electricity - production by source:
fossil fuel: 100%
hydro: 0%
nuclear: 0%
other: 0% (2001)
Electricity - consumption: 38.43 billion kWh (2003)
Electricity - exports: 3.008 billion kWh (2003)
Electricity - imports: 10.4 billion kWh (2003)
Oil - production: 0 bbl/day (2003 est.)
Oil - consumption: 260,000 bbl/day (2003 est.)
Oil - exports: NA
Oil - imports: NA
Natural gas - production: NA (2001 est.)
Natural gas - consumption: 680.9 million cu m (2001 est.)
Natural gas - exports: 0 cu m (2001 est.)
Natural gas - imports: 680.9 million cu m (2001 est.)
Current account balance: $23.85 billion (2005 est.)
Exports: $286.3 billion f.o.b., including reexports (2005 est.)
Exports - partners: China 44%, US 17%, Japan 5.3% (2004)
Imports: $291.6 billion (2005 est.)
Imports - partners: China 43.5%, Japan 12.1%, Taiwan 7.3%, US 5.3%, Singapore 5.3%, South Korea 4.8% (2004)
Reserves of foreign exchange and gold: $122.3 billion (2005 est.)
Debt - external: $416.5 billion (30 June 2005 est.)
Currency (code): Hong Kong dollar (HKD)
Currency code: HKD
Exchange rates: Hong Kong dollars per US dollar - 7.79 (2005), 7.788 (2004), 7.7868 (2003), 7.7989 (2002), 7.7988 (2001)
Fiscal year: 1 April - 31 March

COMMUNICATIONS

Telephones - main lines in use: 3,801,300 (2003)
Telephones - mobile cellular: 7,241,400 (2003)
Telephone system:
general assessment: modern facilities provide excellent domestic and international services
domestic: microwave radio relay links and extensive fiber-optic network
international: country code - 852; satellite earth stations - 3 Intelsat (1 Pacific Ocean and 2 Indian Ocean); coaxial cable to Guangzhou, China; access to 5 international submarine cables providing connections to ASEAN member nations, Japan, Taiwan, Australia, Middle East, and Western Europe
Radio broadcast stations: AM 5, FM 9, shortwave 0 (2004)
Radios: 4.45 million (1997)
Television broadcast stations: 4 (2004)
Televisions: 1.84 million (1997)
Internet country code: .hk
Internet hosts: 591,993 (2003)
Internet Service Providers (ISPs): 17 (2000)
Internet users: 3,212,800 (2003)

TRANSPORTATION

Airports: 4 (2004 est.)
Airports - with paved runways:
total: 3
over 3,047 m: 1
1,524 to 2,437 m: 1
under 914 m: 1 (2005 est.)
Heliports: 3 (2005 est.)
Roadways:
total: 1,831 km
paved: 1,831 km (1999)
Merchant marine:
total: 837 ships (1,000 GRT or over) 20,478,042 GRT/34,554,455 DWT
by type: barge carrier 1, bulk carrier 446, cargo 119, chemical tanker 44, combination ore/oil 2, container 105, liquefied gas 20, passenger 6, passenger/cargo 6, petroleum tanker 75, roll on/roll off 5, vehicle carrier 8
foreign-owned: 453 (Australia 1, Bahamas 1, Belgium 3, Canada 9, China 246, Denmark 3, France 5, Germany 13, Greece 19, India 1, Indonesia 1, Israel 1, Japan 51, Norway 16, Philippines 13,

Singapore 17, South Korea 8, Taiwan 5, Thailand 4, UAE 1, United Kingdom 32, United States 3)
registered in other countries: 373 (2005)
Ports and terminals: Hong Kong

MILITARY

Military branches: no regular indigenous military forces; Hong Kong garrison of China's People's Liberation Army (PLA) includes elements of the PLA Ground Forces, PLA Navy, and PLA Air Force; these forces are under the direct leadership of the Central Military Commission in Beijing and under administrative control of the adjacent Guangzhou Military Region
Military service age and obligation: 18 years of age (2004)
Manpower available for military service: *males age 18-49:* 1,743,972 (2005 est.)
Manpower fit for military service: *males age 18-49:* 1,403,088 (2005 est.)
Manpower reaching military service age annually: *males:* 40,343 (2005 est.)
Military expenditures - dollar figure: Hong Kong garrison is funded by China; figures are NA
Military expenditures - percent of GDP: NA
Military - note: defense is the responsibility of China

TRANSNATIONAL ISSUES

Disputes - international: none
Illicit drugs: makes strenuous law enforcement efforts, but faces difficult challenges in controlling transit of heroin and methamphetamine to regional and world markets; modern banking system provides conduit for money laundering; rising indigenous use of synthetic drugs, especially among young people

HOWLAND ISLAND

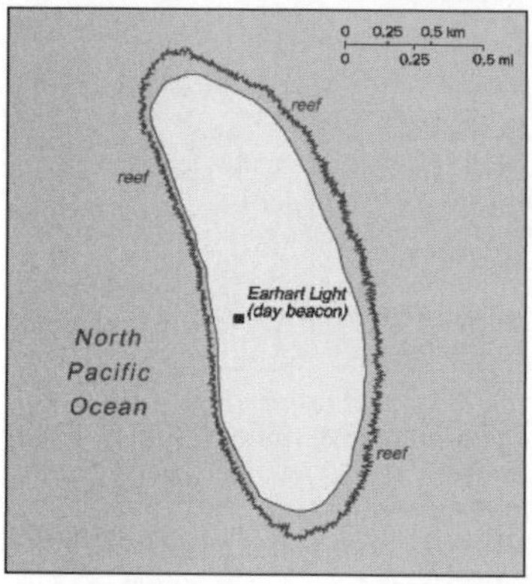

INTRODUCTION

Background: Discovered by the US early in the 19th century, the island was officially claimed by the US in 1857. Both US and British companies mined for guano until about 1890. Earhart Light is a day beacon near the middle of the west coast that was partially destroyed during World War II, but has since been rebuilt; it is named in memory of the famed aviatrix Amelia EARHART. The island is administered by the US Department of the Interior as a National Wildlife Refuge.

GEOGRAPHY

Location: Oceania, island in the North Pacific Ocean, about half way between Hawaii and Australia
Geographic coordinates: 0 48 N, 176 38 W
Map references: Oceania
Area:
total: 1.6 sq km
land: 1.6 sq km
water: 0 sq km
Area - comparative: about three times the size of The Mall in Washington, DC
Land boundaries: 0 km
Coastline: 6.4 km
Maritime claims:
territorial sea: 12 nm
exclusive economic zone: 200 nm
Climate: equatorial; scant rainfall, constant wind, burning sun
Terrain: low-lying, nearly level, sandy, coral island surrounded by a narrow fringing reef; depressed central area
Elevation extremes:
lowest point: Pacific Ocean 0 m
highest point: unnamed location 3 m
Natural resources: guano (deposits worked until late 1800s), terrestrial and aquatic wildlife
Land use:
arable land: 0%
permanent crops: 0%
other: 100% (2001)
Irrigated land: 0 sq km
Natural hazards: the narrow fringing reef surrounding the island can be a maritime hazard
Environment - current issues: no natural fresh water resources
Geography - note: almost totally covered with grasses, prostrate vines, and low-growing shrubs; small area of trees in the center; primarily a nesting, roosting, and foraging habitat for seabirds, shorebirds, and marine wildlife

PEOPLE

Population: uninhabited
note: American civilians evacuated in 1942 after Japanese air and naval attacks during World War II; occupied by US military during World War II, but abandoned after the war; public entry is by special-use permit from US Fish and Wildlife Service only and generally restricted to scientists and educators; visited annually by US Fish and Wildlife Service (July 2005 est.)

GOVERNMENT

Country name:
conventional long form: none
conventional short form: Howland Island
Dependency status: unincorporated territory of the US; administered from Washington, DC, by the Fish and Wildlife Service of the US Department of the Interior as part of the National Wildlife Refuge system
Legal system: the laws of the US, where applicable, apply
Flag description: the flag of the US is used

ECONOMY

Economy - overview: no economic activity

TRANSPORTATION

Airports: airstrip constructed in 1937 for scheduled refueling stop on the round-the-world flight of Amelia EARHART and Fred NOONAN - they left Lae, New Guinea, for Howland Island, but were never seen again; the airstrip is no longer serviceable (2004 est.)
Ports and terminals: none; offshore anchorage only; note - there is one small boat landing area along the middle of the west coast
Transportation - note: Earhart Light is a day beacon near the middle of the west coast that was partially destroyed during World War II, but has since been rebuilt; named in memory of famed aviatrix Amelia EARHART

MILITARY

Military - note: defense is the responsibility of the US; visited annually by the US Coast Guard

TRANSNATIONAL ISSUES

Disputes - international: none

HUNGARY

INTRODUCTION

Background: Hungary was part of the polyglot Austro-Hungarian Empire, which collapsed during World War I. The country fell under Communist rule following World War II. In 1956, a revolt and announced withdrawal from the Warsaw Pact were met with a massive military intervention by Moscow. Under the leadership of Janos KADAR in 1968, Hungary began liberalizing its economy, introducing so-called "Goulash Communism." Hungary held its first multiparty elections in 1990 and initiated a free market economy. It joined NATO in 1999 and the EU in 2004.

GEOGRAPHY

Location: Central Europe, northwest of Romania
Geographic coordinates: 47 00 N, 20 00 E
Map references: Europe
Area:
total: 93,030 sq km
land: 92,340 sq km
water: 690 sq km
Area - comparative: slightly smaller than Indiana
Land boundaries:
total: 2,171 km
border countries: Austria 366 km, Croatia 329 km, Romania 443 km, Serbia and Montenegro 151 km, Slovakia 677 km, Slovenia 102 km, Ukraine 103 km
Coastline: 0 km (landlocked)
Maritime claims: none (landlocked)
Climate:
temperate; cold, cloudy, humid winters; warm summers
Terrain: mostly flat to rolling plains; hills and low mountains on the Slovakian border
Elevation extremes:
lowest point: Tisza River 78 m
highest point: Kekes 1,014 m
Natural resources: bauxite, coal, natural gas, fertile soils, arable land
Land use:
arable land: 50.09%
permanent crops: 2.06%
other: 47.85% (2001)
Irrigated land: 2,100 sq km (1998 est.)
Environment - current issues: the upgrading of Hungary's standards in waste management, energy efficiency, and air, soil, and water pollution to meet EU requirements will require large investments
Environment - international agreements:
party to: Air Pollution, Air Pollution-Nitrogen Oxides, Air Pollution-Persistent Organic Pollutants, Air Pollution-Sulfur 85, Air Pollution-Volatile Organic Compounds, Antarctic Treaty, Biodiversity, Climate Change, Climate Change-Kyoto Protocol, Desertification, Endangered Species, Environmental Modification, Hazardous Wastes, Law of the Sea, Marine Dumping, Ozone Layer Protection, Ship Pollution, Wetlands
signed, but not ratified: Air Pollution-Sulfur 94
Geography - note: landlocked; strategic location astride main land routes between Western Europe and Balkan Peninsula as well as between Ukraine and Mediterranean basin; the north-south flowing Duna (Danube) and Tisza Rivers divide the country into three large regions

PEOPLE

Population: 10,006,835 (July 2005 est.)
Age structure:
0-14 years: 15.8% (male 813,203/female 769,687)
15-64 years: 69.1% (male 3,405,559/female 3,511,141)
65 years and over: 15.1% (male 547,323/female 959,922) (2005 est.)
Median age:
total: 38.57 years
male: 36.1 years
female: 41.24 years (2005 est.)
Population growth rate: -0.26% (2005 est.)
Birth rate: 9.76 births/1,000 population (2005 est.)
Death rate: 13.19 deaths/1,000 population (2005 est.)
Net migration rate: 0.86 migrant(s)/1,000 population (2005 est.)
Sex ratio:
at birth: 1.06 male(s)/female
under 15 years: 1.06 male(s)/female
15-64 years: 0.97 male(s)/female
65 years and over: 0.57 male(s)/female
total population: 0.91 male(s)/female (2005 est.)
Infant mortality rate:
total: 8.57 deaths/1,000 live births
male: 9.27 deaths/1,000 live births
female: 7.83 deaths/1,000 live births (2005 est.)
Life expectancy at birth:
total population: 72.4 years
male: 68.18 years
female: 76.89 years (2005 est.)
Total fertility rate: 1.32 children born/woman (2005 est.)
HIV/AIDS - adult prevalence rate: 0.1% (2001 est.)
HIV/AIDS - people living with HIV/AIDS: 2,800 (2001 est.)
HIV/AIDS - deaths: less than 100 (2001 est.)
Nationality:
noun: Hungarian(s)
adjective: Hungarian
Ethnic groups: Hungarian 92.3%, Roma 1.9%, other or unknown 5.8% (2001 census)
Religions: Roman Catholic 51.9%, Calvinist 15.9%, Lutheran 3%, Greek Catholic 2.6%, other Christian 1%, other or unspecified 11.1%, unaffiliated 14.5% (2001 census)
Languages: Hungarian 93.6%, other or unspecified 6.4% (2001 census)
Literacy:
definition: age 15 and over can read and write
total population: 99.4%
male: 99.5%
female: 99.3% (2003 est.)

GOVERNMENT

Country name:
conventional long form: Republic of Hungary
conventional short form: Hungary
local long form: Magyar Koztarsasag
local short form: Magyarorszag
Government type: parliamentary democracy
Capital: Budapest
Administrative divisions: 19 counties (megyek, singular - megye), 20 urban counties (singular - megyei varos), and 1 capital city (fovaros)

: counties: Bacs-Kiskun, Baranya, Bekes, Borsod-Abauj-Zemplen, Csongrad, Fejer, Gyor-Moson-Sopron, Hajdu-Bihar, Heves, Jasz-Nagykun-Szolnok, Komarom-Esztergom, Nograd, Pest, Somogy, Szabolcs-Szatmar-Bereg, Tolna, Vas, Veszprem, Zala
: urban counties: Bekescsaba, Debrecen, Dunaujvaros, Eger, Gyor, Hodmezovasarhely, Kaposvar, Kecskemet, Miskolc, Nagykanizsa, Nyiregyhaza, Pecs, Sopron, Szeged, Szekesfehervar, Szolnok, Szombathely, Tatabanya, Veszprem, Zalaegerszeg
: capital city: Budapest
Independence: 1001 (unification by King Stephen I)
National holiday: Saint Stephen's Day, 20 August
Constitution: 18 August 1949, effective 20 August 1949; revised 19 April 1972; 18 October 1989 revision ensured legal rights for individuals and constitutional checks on the authority of the prime minister and also established the principle of parliamentary oversight; 1997 amendment streamlined the judicial system
Legal system: rule of law based on Western model
Suffrage: 18 years of age; universal
Executive branch:
chief of state: Laszlo SOLYOM (since 5 August 2005)
head of government: Prime Minister Ferenc GYURCSANY (since 29 September 2004)
cabinet: Council of Ministers elected by the National Assembly on the recommendation of the president
elections: president elected by the National Assembly for a five-year term; election last held 6-7 June 2005 (next to be held by June 2010); prime minister elected by the National Assembly on the recommendation of the president; election last held 29 September 2004
election results: Laszlo SOLYOM elected president by a simple majority in the third round of voting, 185 to 182; Ferenc GYURCSANY elected prime minister; result of legislative vote - 197 to 12
note: to be elected, the president must win two-thirds of legislative vote in the first two rounds or a simple majority in the third round
Legislative branch: unicameral National Assembly or Orszaggyules (386 seats; members are elected by popular vote under a system of proportional and direct representation to serve four-year terms)
elections: last held 7 and 21 April 2002 (next to be held NA April 2006)
election results: percent of vote by party (5% or more of the vote required for parliamentary representation in the first round) - Fidesz/MDF 48.70%, MSzP 46.11%, SzDSz 4.92%, other 0.27%; seats by party - Fidesz 164, MSzP 178, MDF 24, SzDSz 20
Judicial branch: Constitutional Court (judges are elected by the National Assembly for nine-year terms)
Political parties and leaders: Alliance of Free Democrats or SzDSz [Gabor KUNCZE]; Hungarian Civic Alliance or Fidesz [Viktor ORBAN, chairman]; Hungarian Democratic Forum or MDF [Ibolya DAVID]; Hungarian Democratic People's Party or MDNP [Erzsebet PUSZTAI, chairman]; Hungarian Socialist Party or MSzP [Istvan HILLER, chairman]; Hungarian Workers' Party or MMP [Gyula THURMER, chairman]
Political pressure groups and leaders: NA
International organization participation: ACCT (observer), Australia Group, BIS, CE, CEI, CERN, EAPC, EBRD, EIB, ESA (cooperating state), EU (new member), FAO, G- 9, IAEA, IBRD, ICAO, ICC, ICCt, ICFTU, ICRM, IDA, IEA, IFC, IFRCS, ILO, IMF, IMO, Interpol, IOC, IOM, ISO, ITU, MIGA, MINURSO, NAM (guest), NATO, NEA, NSG, OAS (observer), OECD, OPCW, OSCE, PCA, UN, UNCTAD, UNESCO, UNFICYP, UNHCR, UNIDO, UNOMIG, UPU, WCL, WCO, WEU (associate), WFTU, WHO, WIPO, WMO, WToO, WTO, ZC
Diplomatic representation in the US:
chief of mission: Ambassador Andras SIMONYI
chancery: 3910 Shoemaker Street NW, Washington, DC 20008
telephone: [1] (202) 362-6730
FAX: [1] (202) 966-8135
consulate(s) general: Los Angeles and New York
Diplomatic representation from the US:
chief of mission: Ambassador George Herbert WALKER
embassy: Szabadsag ter 12, H-1054 Budapest
mailing address: pouch: American Embassy Budapest, 5270 Budapest Place, Department of State, Washington, DC 20521-5270
telephone: [36] (1) 475-4400
FAX: [36] (1) 475-4764
Flag description: three equal horizontal bands of red (top), white, and green

ECONOMY

Economy - overview: Hungary has made the transition from a centrally planned to a market economy, with a per capita income one-half that of the Big Four European nations. Hungary continues to demonstrate strong economic growth and acceded to the European Union in May 2004. The private sector accounts for over 80% of GDP. Foreign ownership of and investment in Hungarian firms are widespread, with cumulative foreign direct investment totaling more than $23 billion since 1989. Hungarian sovereign debt was upgraded in 2000 and together with the Czech Republic holds the highest rating among the Central European transition economies; however, ratings agencies have expressed concerns over Hungary's unsustainable budget and current account deficits. Inflation has declined from 14% in 1998 to 3.7% in 2005. Unemployment has persisted around the 6% level, but Hungary's labor force participation rate of 57% is one of the lowest in the OECD. Germany is by far Hungary's largest economic partner. Policy challenges include cutting the public sector deficit to 3% of GDP by 2008, from about 6.5% in 2005, and orchestrating an orderly interest rate reduction without sparking capital outflows.
GDP (purchasing power parity): $159 billion (2005 est.)
GDP (official exchange rate): $106.9 billion (2005 est.)
GDP - real growth rate: 3.7% (2005 est.)
GDP - per capita: purchasing power parity - $15,900 (2005 est.)
GDP - composition by sector:
agriculture: 3.9%
industry: 30.9%
services: 65.3% (2005 est.)
Labor force: 4.18 million (2005 est.)
Labor force - by occupation: agriculture 6.2%, industry 27.1%, services 66.7% (2002)
Unemployment rate: 7.1% (2005 est.)
Population below poverty line: 8.6% (1993 est.)
Household income or consumption by percentage share:
lowest 10%: 4.1%
highest 10%: 20.5% (1998)
Distribution of family income - Gini index: 24.4 (1999)
Inflation rate (consumer prices): 3.7% (2005 est.)
Investment (gross fixed): 23.1% of GDP (2005 est.)
Budget:
revenues: $51.4 billion
expenditures: $58.34 billion, including capital expenditures of NA (2005 est.)
Public debt: 60.9% of GDP (2005 est.)
Agriculture - products: wheat, corn, sunflower seed, potatoes, sugar beets; pigs, cattle, poultry, dairy products
Industries: mining, metallurgy, construction materials, processed foods, textiles,

chemicals (especially pharmaceuticals), motor vehicles
Industrial production growth rate: 7.5% (2005 est.)
Electricity - production: 32.21 billion kWh (2003)
Electricity - production by source:
fossil fuel: 60.1%
hydro: 0.5%
nuclear: 39%
other: 0.3% (2001)
Electricity - consumption: 36.96 billion kWh (2003)
Electricity - exports: 7.1 billion kWh (2003)
Electricity - imports: 14.1 billion kWh (2003)
Oil - production: 43,920 bbl/day (2003 est.)
Oil - consumption: 134,100 bbl/day (2003 est.)
Oil - exports: 47,180 bbl/day (2001)
Oil - imports: 136,600 bbl/day (2001)
Oil - proved reserves: 110.7 million bbl (1 January 2002)
Natural gas - production: 3.231 billion cu m (2001 est.)
Natural gas - consumption: 13.37 billion cu m (2001 est.)
Natural gas - exports: 4 million cu m (2001 est.)
Natural gas - imports: 9.587 billion cu m (2001 est.)
Natural gas - proved reserves: 50.45 billion cu m (1 January 2002)
Current account balance: $-8.667 billion (2005 est.)
Exports: $61.75 billion f.o.b. (2005 est.)
Exports - partners: Germany 31.4%, Austria 6.8%, France 5.7%, Italy 5.6%, UK 5.1% (2004)
Imports: $64.83 billion f.o.b. (2005 est.)
Imports - partners: Germany 29.2%, Austria 8.3%, Russia 5.7%, Italy 5.5%, Netherlands 4.9%, China 4.8%, France 4.7% (2004)
Reserves of foreign exchange and gold: $18.49 billion (2005 est.)
Debt - external: $76.23 billion (30 June 2005 est.)
Economic aid - recipient: $4.2 billion in available EU structural adjustment and cohesion funds (2004-06)
Currency (code): forint (HUF)
Currency code: HUF
Exchange rates: forints per US dollar - 196.83 (2005), 202.75 (2004), 224.31 (2003), 257.89 (2002), 286.49 (2001)
Fiscal year: calendar year

COMMUNICATIONS

Telephones - main lines in use: 3,666,400 (2002)
Telephones - mobile cellular: 6,862,800 (2002)
Telephone system:
general assessment: the telephone system has been modernized and is capable of satisfying all requests for telecommunication service
domestic: the system is digitalized and highly automated; trunk services are carried by fiber-optic cable and digital microwave radio relay; a program for fiber-optic subscriber connections was initiated in 1996; heavy use is made of mobile cellular telephones
international: country code - 36; Hungary has fiber-optic cable connections with all neighboring countries; the international switch is in Budapest; satellite earth stations - 2 Intelsat (Atlantic Ocean and Indian Ocean regions), 1 Inmarsat, 1 very small aperture terminal (VSAT) system of ground terminals
Radio broadcast stations: AM 17, FM 57, shortwave 3 (1998)
Radios: 7.01 million (1997)
Television broadcast stations: 35 (plus 161 low-power repeaters) (1995)
Televisions: 4.42 million (1997)
Internet country code: .hu
Internet hosts: 383,071 (2004)
Internet Service Providers (ISPs): 16 (2000)
Internet users: 1.6 million (2002)

TRANSPORTATION

Airports: 44 (2004 est.)
Airports - with paved runways:
total: 19
over 3,047 m: 2
2,438 to 3,047 m: 8
1,524 to 2,437 m: 4
914 to 1,523 m: 4
under 914 m: 1 (2005 est.)
Airports - with unpaved runways:
total: 25
2,438 to 3,047 m: 2
1,524 to 2,437 m: 3
914 to 1,523 m: 11
under 914 m: 9 (2005 est.)
Heliports: 5 (2005 est.)
Pipelines: gas 4,397 km; oil 990 km; refined products 335 km (2004)
Railways:
total: 7,937 km
broad gauge: 36 km 1.524-m gauge
standard gauge: 7,682 km 1.435-m gauge (2,628 km electrified)
narrow gauge: 219 km 0.760-m gauge (2004)
Roadways:
total: 159,568 km
paved: 70,050 km (including 527 km of expressways)
unpaved: 89,518 km (2002)
Waterways: 1,622 km (most on Danube River) (2004)
Ports and terminals: Budapest, Dunaujvaros, Gyor-Gonyu, Csepel, Baja, Mohacs (2003)

MILITARY

Military branches: Ground Forces, Air Forces
Military service age and obligation: 18 years of age for voluntary military service; conscription abolished in June 2004 (June 2004)
Manpower available for military service: *males age 18-49:* 2,303,116 (2005 est.)
Manpower fit for military service: *males age 18-49:* 1,780,513 (2005 est.)
Manpower reaching military service age annually: *males:* 63,847 (2005 est.)
Military expenditures - dollar figure: $1.08 billion (2002 est.)
Military expenditures - percent of GDP: 1.75% (2002 est.)

TRANSNATIONAL ISSUES

Disputes - international: in 2004, Hungary amended the status law extending special social and cultural benefits and voted down a referendum to extend dual citizenship to ethnic Hungarians living in neighboring states, which have objected to such measures; consultations continue between Slovakia and Hungary over Hungary's completion of its portion the Gabcikovo-Nagymaros hydroelectric dam project along the Danube; as a member state that forms part of the EU's external border, Hungary must implement the strict Schengen border rules
Illicit drugs: transshipment point for Southwest Asian heroin and cannabis and for South American cocaine destined for Western Europe; limited producer of precursor chemicals, particularly for amphetamine and methamphetamine; improving, but remains vulnerable to money laundering related to organized crime and drug trafficking

ICELAND

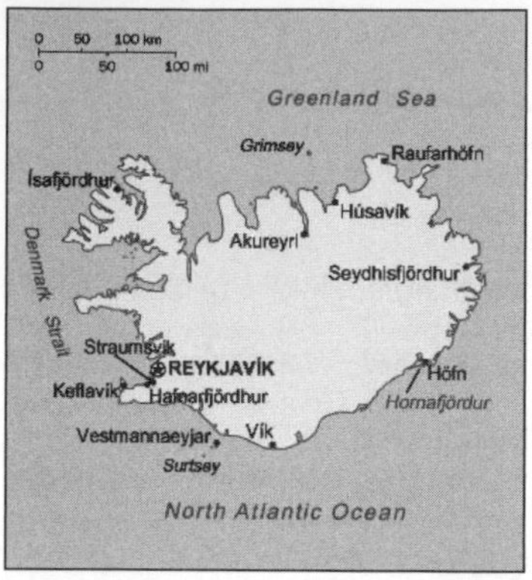

INTRODUCTION

Background: Settled by Norwegian and Celtic (Scottish and Irish) immigrants during the late 9th and 10th centuries A.D., Iceland boasts the world's oldest functioning legislative assembly, the Althing, established in 930. Independent for over 300 years, Iceland was subsequently ruled by Norway and Denmark. Fallout from the Askja volcano of 1875 devastated the Icelandic economy and caused widespread famine. Over the next quarter century, 20% of the island's population emigrated, mostly to Canada and the US. Limited home rule from Denmark was granted in 1874 and complete independence attained in 1944. Literacy, longevity, income, and social cohesion are first-rate by world standards.

GEOGRAPHY

Location: Northern Europe, island between the Greenland Sea and the North Atlantic Ocean, northwest of the UK
Geographic coordinates: 65 00 N, 18 00 W
Map references: Arctic Region
Area:
total: 103,000 sq km
land: 100,250 sq km
water: 2,750 sq km
Area - comparative: slightly smaller than Kentucky
Land boundaries: 0 km
Coastline: 4,970 km
Maritime claims:
territorial sea: 12 nm
exclusive economic zone: 200 nm
continental shelf: 200 nm or to the edge of the continental margin
Climate: temperate; moderated by North Atlantic Current; mild, windy winters; damp, cool summers
Terrain: mostly plateau interspersed with mountain peaks, icefields; coast deeply indented by bays and fiords
Elevation extremes:
lowest point: Atlantic Ocean 0 m
highest point: Hvannadalshnukur 2,110 m (at Vatnajokull glacier)
Natural resources: fish, hydropower, geothermal power, diatomite
Land use:
arable land: 0.07%
permanent crops: 0%
other: 99.93% (2001)
Irrigated land: NA sq km
Natural hazards: earthquakes and volcanic activity
Environment - current issues: water pollution from fertilizer runoff; inadequate wastewater treatment
Environment - international agreements:
party to: Air Pollution, Air Pollution-Persistent Organic Pollutants, Biodiversity, Climate Change,Climate Change-Kyoto Protocol, Desertification, Endangered Species, Hazardous Wastes, Kyoto Protocol, Law of the Sea, Marine Dumping, Ozone, Layer Protection, Ship Pollution, Transboundary Air Pollution, Wetlands
signed, but not ratified: Environmental Modification, Marine Life Conservation
Geography - note: strategic location between Greenland and Europe; westernmost European country; Reykjavik is the northernmost national capital in the world; more land covered by glaciers than in all of continental Europe

PEOPLE

Population: 296,737 (July 2005 est.)
Age structure:
0-14 years: 22.1% (male 33,302/female 32,257)
15-64 years: 66.2% (male 99,513/female 96,886)
65 years and over: 11.7% (male 15,723/female 19,056) (2005 est.)
Median age:
total: 34 years
male: 33.53 years
female: 34.49 years (2005 est.)
Population growth rate: 0.91% (2005 est.)
Birth rate: 13.73 births/1,000 population (2005 est.)
Death rate: 6.68 deaths/1,000 population (2005 est.)
Net migration rate: 2.06 migrant(s)/1,000 population (2005 est.)
Sex ratio:
at birth: 1.04 male(s)/female
under 15 years: 1.03 male(s)/female
15-64 years: 1.03 male(s)/female
65 years and over: 0.82 male(s)/female
total population: 1 male(s)/female (2005 est.)
Infant mortality rate:
total: 3.31 deaths/1,000 live births
male: 3.45 deaths/1,000 live births
female: 3.16 deaths/1,000 live births (2005 est.)
Life expectancy at birth:
total population: 80.19 years
male: 78.13 years
female: 82.34 years (2005 est.)
Total fertility rate: 1.92 children born/woman (2005 est.)
HIV/AIDS - adult prevalence rate: 0.2% (2001 est.)
HIV/AIDS - people living with HIV/AIDS: 220 (2001 est.)
HIV/AIDS - deaths: less than 100 (2003 est.)
Nationality:
noun: Icelander(s)
adjective: Icelandic
Ethnic groups: homogeneous mixture of descendants of Norse and Celts 94%, population of foreign origin 6%
Religions: Lutheran Church of Iceland 85.5%, Reykjavik Free Church 2.1%, Roman Catholic Church 2%, Hafnarfjorour Free Church 1.5%, other Christian 2.7%, other or unspecified 3.8%, unaffiliated 2.4% (2004)
Languages: Icelandic, English, Nordic languages, German widely spoken
Literacy:
definition: age 15 and over can read and write
total population: 99.9% (1997 est.)
male: NA%
female: NA%

GOVERNMENT

Country name:
conventional long form: Republic of Iceland
conventional short form: Iceland
local long form: Lydhveldidh Island
local short form: Island
Government type: constitutional republic
Capital: Reykjavik
Administrative divisions: 8 regions; Austurland, Hofudhborgarsvaedhi, Nordhurland Eystra, Nordhurland Vestra, Sudhurland, Sudhurnes, Vestfirdhir, Vesturland
Independence: 1 December 1918 (became a sovereign state under the Danish Crown); 17 June 1944 (from Denmark)
National holiday: Independence Day, 17 June (1944)
Constitution: 16 June 1944, effective 17 June 1944; amended many times
Legal system: civil law system based on Danish law; has not accepted compulsory ICJ jurisdiction
Suffrage: 18 years of age; universal
Executive branch:
chief of state: President Olafur Ragnar GRIMSSON (since 1 August 1996)
head of government: Prime Minister

Halldor ASGRIMSSON (since 15 September 2004); note - Former Prime Minister David ODDSSON switched positions with former Foreign Minister Halldor ASGRIMMSON
cabinet: Cabinet appointed by the prime minister and approved by parliament
elections: president, which is largely a ceremonial post, elected by popular vote for a four-year term; election last held 26 June 2004 (next to be held June 2008); following legislative elections, the leader of the majority party or the leader of the majority coalition is usually the prime minister
election results: Olafur Ragnar GRIMSSON wins with 85.6% of the vote, Baldur AGUSTSSON 12.5%, Astthor MAGNUSSON 1.9%
Legislative branch: unicameral Parliament or Althing (63 seats; members are elected by popular vote to serve four-year terms)
elections: last held 10 May 2003 (next to be held by May 2007)
election results: percent of vote by party - Independence Party 33.7%, Social Democratic Alliance 31.0%, Progressive Party 17.7%, Left-GreenAlliance 8.8%, Liberal Party 7.4%; seats by party - Independence Party 22, Social Democratic Alliance 20, Progressive Party 12, Left-Green Alliance 5, Liberal Party 4
Judicial branch: Supreme Court or Haestirettur (justices are appointed for life by the Minister of Justice); eight district courts (justices are appointed for life by the Minister of Justice)
Political parties and leaders: Independence Party or IP [David ODDSSON]; Left-Green Alliance or LGP [Steingrimur SIGFUSSON]; Liberal Party or LP [Gudjon KRISTJANSSON]; Progressive Party or PP [Halldor ASGRIMSSON]; Social Democratic Alliance (includes People's Alliance or PA, Social Democratic Party or SDP, Women's List) or SDA [Ingibjorg Solrun GISLADOTTIR]
Political pressure groups and leaders: NA
International organization participation: Australia Group, BIS, CBSS, CE, EAPC, EBRD, EFTA, FAO, IAEA, IBRD, ICAO, ICC, ICCt, ICFTU, ICRM, IDA, IFAD, IFC, IFRCS, IHO, ILO, IMF, IMO, Interpol, IOC, ISO, ITU, MIGA, NATO, NC, NEA, NIB, OECD, OPCW, OSCE, PCA, UN, UNCTAD, UNESCO, UPU, WCO, WEU (associate), WHO, WIPO, WMO, WTO
Diplomatic representation in the US:
chief of mission: Ambassador Helgi AGUSTSSON
chancery: Suite 1200, 1156 15th Street NW, Washington, DC 20005-1704
telephone: [1] (202) 265-6653
FAX: [1] (202) 265-6656
consulate(s) general: New York
Diplomatic representation from the US:
chief of mission: Ambassador-designate Carol VAN VOORST
embassy: Laufasvegur 21, 101 Reykjavik
mailing address: US Embassy, PSC 1003, Box 40, FPO AE 09728-0340
telephone: [354] 562-9100
FAX: [354] 562-9118
Flag description: blue with a red cross outlined in white extending to the edges of the flag; the vertical part of the cross is shifted to the hoist side in the style of the Dannebrog (Danish flag)

ECONOMY

Economy - overview: Iceland's Scandinavian-type economy is basically capitalistic, yet with an extensive welfare system (including generous housing subsidies), low unemployment, and remarkably even distribution of income. In the absence of other natural resources (except for abundant geothermal power), the economy depends heavily on the fishing industry, which provides 70% of export earnings and employs 8% of the work force. The economy remains sensitive to declining fish stocks as well as to fluctuations in world prices for its main exports: fish and fish products, aluminum, and ferrosilicon. Government policies include reducing the budget and current account deficits, limiting foreign borrowing, containing inflation, revising agricultural and fishing policies, diversifying the economy, and privatizing state-owned industries. The government remains opposed to EU membership, primarily because of Icelanders' concern about losing control over their fishing resources. Iceland's economy has been diversifying into manufacturing and service industries in the last decade, and new developments in software production, biotechnology, and financial services are taking place. The tourism sector is also expanding, with the recent trends in ecotourism and whale watching. Growth had been remarkably steady in 1996-2001 at 3%-5%, but could not be sustained in 2002 in an environment of global recession. Growth resumed in 2003, and estimates call for strong growth until 2007, slowly dropping until the end of the decade.
GDP (purchasing power parity): $10.26 billion (2005 est.)
GDP (official exchange rate): $13.64 billion (2005 est.)
GDP - real growth rate: 5.9% (2005 est.)
GDP - per capita: purchasing power parity - $34,600 (2005 est.)
GDP - composition by sector:
agriculture: 11.8%
industry: 22.3%
services: 65.9% (2005 est.)
Labor force: 160,000 (2005 est.)
Labor force - by occupation: agriculture, fishing and fish processing 10.3%, industry 18.3%, services 71.4% (2003)
Unemployment rate: 2.1% (2005 est.)
Population below poverty line: NA
Household income or consumption by percentage share:
lowest 10%: NA%
highest 10%: NA%
Inflation rate (consumer prices): 4.1% (2005 est.)
Investment (gross fixed): 27.1% of GDP (2005 est.)
Budget:
revenues: $6.995 billion
expenditures: $6.761 billion, including capital expenditures of $467 million (2005 est.)
Public debt: 34% of GDP (2005 est.)
Agriculture - products: potatoes, green vegetables, mutton, dairy products, fish
Industries: fish processing; aluminum smelting, ferrosilicon production, geothermal power; tourism
Industrial production growth rate: 14.2% (2005 est.)
Electricity - production: 8.354 billion kWh (2003)
Electricity - production by source:
fossil fuel: 0.1%
hydro: 82.5%
nuclear: 0%
other: 17.5% (geothermal) (2001)
Electricity - consumption: 7.769 billion kWh (2003)
Electricity - exports: 0 kWh (2003)
Electricity - imports: 0 kWh (2003)
Oil - production: 0 bbl/day (2003 est.)
Oil - consumption: 17,280 bbl/day (2003 est.)
Oil - exports: 0 bbl/day (2001)
Oil - imports: 15,470 bbl/day (2001)
Current account balance: $-2.009 billion (2005 est.)
Exports: $3.215 billion f.o.b. (2005 est.)
Exports - partners: UK 19.1%, Germany 17.3%, Netherlands 10.7%, US 9.3%, Spain 7%, Denmark 4.8%, France 4.1% (2004)
Imports: $4.582 billion (2005 est.)
Imports - partners: Germany 12.6%, US 10.1%, Norway 9.5%, Denmark 7.6%, UK 6.8%, Sweden 6.3%, Netherlands 5.7% (2004)
Reserves of foreign exchange and gold: $1.074 billion (2004 est.)
Debt - external: $3.073 billion (2002)
Economic aid - donor: $NA
Currency (code): Icelandic krona (ISK)
Currency code: ISK
Exchange rates: Icelandic kronur per US dollar - 63.65 (2005), 70.192 (2004),

76.709 (2003), 91.662 (2002), 97.425 (2001)
Fiscal year: calendar year

COMMUNICATIONS

Telephones - main lines in use: 190,700 (2003)
Telephones - mobile cellular: 279,100 (2003)
Telephone system:
general assessment: extensive domestic service
domestic: the trunk network consists of coaxial and fiber-optic cables and microwave radio relay links
international: country code - 354; satellite earth stations - 2 Intelsat (Atlantic Ocean), 1 Inmarsat (Atlantic and Indian Ocean regions); note - Iceland shares the Inmarsat earth station with the other Nordic countries (Denmark, Finland, Norway, and Sweden)
Radio broadcast stations: AM 3, FM about 70 (including repeaters), shortwave 1 (1998)
Radios: 260,000 (1997)
Television broadcast stations: 14 (plus 156 low-power repeaters) (1997)
Televisions: 98,000 (1997)
Internet country code: .is
Internet hosts: 122,175 (2004)
Internet Service Providers (ISPs): 20 (2001)
Internet users: 195,000 (2003)

TRANSPORTATION

Airports: 98 (2004 est.)
Airports - with paved runways:
total: 5
over 3,047 m: 1
1,524 to 2,437 m: 3
914 to 1,523 m: 1 (2005 est.)
Airports - with unpaved runways:
total: 92
1,524 to 2,437 m: 3
914 to 1,523 m: 29
under 914 m: 60 (2005 est.)
Roadways:
total: 13,004 km
paved/oiled gravel: 4,331 km
unpaved: 8,673 km (2004)
Merchant marine:
total: 3 ships (1,000 GRT or over) 4,341 GRT/6,019 DWT
by type: cargo 2, passenger/cargo 1
registered in other countries: 30 (2005)
Ports and terminals: Grundartangi, Hafnarfjordur, Hornafjordhur, Reykjavik, Seydhisfjordhur

MILITARY

Military branches: no regular armed forces; Icelandic National Police, Icelandic Coast Guard (Islenska Landhelgisgaeslan)
Manpower available for military service: *males age 18-49:* 69,038 (2005est.)
Manpower fit for military service: *males age 18-49:* 56,777 (2005 est.)
Military expenditures - dollar figure: 0
Military - note: defense is provided by the US-manned Icelandic Defense Force (IDF headquartered at Keflavik

TRANSNATIONAL ISSUES

Disputes - international: Iceland disputes Denmark's alignment of the Faroe Islands' fisheries median line; Iceland, the UK, and Ireland dispute Denmark's claim that the Faroe Islands' continental shelf extends beyond 200 nm

INDIA

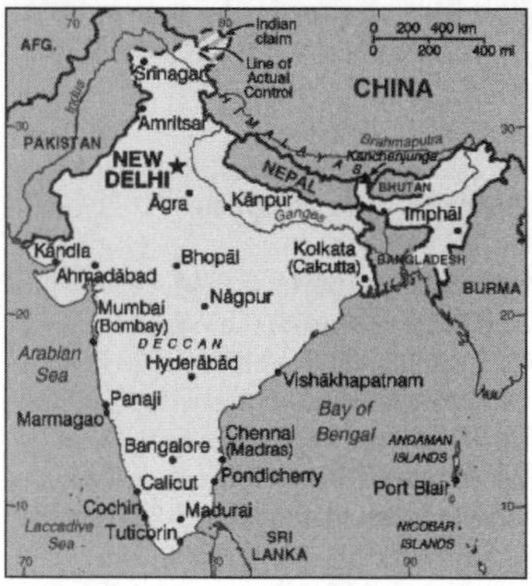

INTRODUCTION

Background: The Indus Valley civilization, one of the oldest in the world, dates back at least 5,000 years. Aryan tribes from the northwest invaded about 1500 B.C.; their merger with the earlier Dravidian inhabitants created the classical Indian culture. Arab incursions starting in the 8th century and Turkish in the 12th were followed by those of European traders, beginning in the late 15th century. By the 19th century, Britain had assumed political control of virtually all Indian lands. Indian armed forces in the British army played a vital role in both World Wars. Nonviolent resistance to British colonialism led by Mohandas GANDHI and Jawaharlal NEHRU brought independence in 1947. The subcontinent was divided into the secular state of India and the smaller Muslim state of Pakistan. A third war between the two countries in 1971 resulted in East Pakistan becoming the separate nation of Bangladesh. Despite impressive gains in economic investment and output, India faces pressing problems such as the ongoing dispute with Pakistan over Kashmir, massive overpopulation, environmental degradation, extensive poverty, and ethnic and religious strife.

GEOGRAPHY

Location: Southern Asia, bordering the Arabian Sea and the Bay of Bengal, between Burma and Pakistan
Geographic coordinates: 20 00 N, 77 00 E
Map references: Asia
Area:
total: 3,287,590 sq km
land: 2,973,190 sq km
water: 314,400 sq km
Area - comparative: slightly more than one-third the size of the US
Land boundaries:
total: 14,103 km
border countries: Bangladesh 4,053 km, Bhutan 605 km, Burma 1,463 km, China 3,380 km, Nepal 1,690 km, Pakistan 2,912 km
Coastline: 7,000 km
Maritime claims:
territorial sea: 12 nm
contiguous zone: 24 nm
exclusive economic zone: 200 nm
continental shelf: 200 nm or to the edge of the continental margin
Climate: varies from tropical monsoon in south to temperate in north
Terrain: upland plain (Deccan Plateau) in south, flat to rolling plain along the Ganges, deserts in west, Himalayas in north
Elevation extremes:
lowest point: Indian Ocean 0 m
highest point: Kanchenjunga 8,598 m
Natural resources: coal (fourth-largest reserves in the world), iron ore, manganese, mica, bauxite, titanium ore, chromite, natural gas, diamonds, petroleum, limestone, arable land
Land use:
arable land: 54.4%
permanent crops: 2.74%
other: 42.86% (2001)
Irrigated land: 590,000 sq km (1998 est.)
Natural hazards: droughts; flash floods, as well as widespread and destructive flooding from monsoonal rains; severe thunderstorms; earthquakes
Environment - current issues: deforestation; soil erosion; overgrazing; desertification; air pollution from industrial efflu-

ents and vehicle emissions; water pollution from raw sewage and runoff of agricultural pesticides; tap water is not potable throughout the country; huge and growing population is overstraining natural resources

Environment - international agreements:
party to: Antarctic-Environmental Protocol, Antarctic-Marine Living Resources, Antarctic Treaty, Biodiversity, Climate Change, Climate Change-Kyoto Protocol, Desertification, Endangered Species, Environmental Modification, Hazardous Wastes, Law of the Sea, Ozone Layer Protection, Ship Pollution, Tropical Timber 83, Tropical Timber 94, Wetlands, Whaling
signed, but not ratified: none of the selected agreements

Geography - note: dominates South Asian subcontinent; near important Indian Ocean trade routes

PEOPLE

Population: 1,080,264,388 (July 2005 est.)

Age structure:
0-14 years: 31.2% (male 173,634,432/ female 163,932,475)
15-64 years: 63.9% (male 356,932,082/ female 333,283,590)
65 years and over: 4.9% (male 26,542,025/ female 25,939,784) (2005 est.)

Median age:
total: 24.66 years
male: 24.64 years
female: 24.67 years (2005 est.)

Population growth rate: 1.4% (2005 est.)

Birth rate: 22.32 births/1,000 population (2005 est.)

Death rate: 8.28 deaths/1,000 population (2005 est.)

Net migration rate: -0.07 migrant(s)/ 1,000 population (2005 est.)

Sex ratio:
at birth: 1.05 male(s)/female
under 15 years: 1.06 male(s)/female
15-64 years: 1.07 male(s)/female
65 years and over: 1.02 male(s)/female
total population: 1.06 male(s)/female (2005 est.)

Infant mortality rate:
total: 56.29 deaths/1,000 live births
male: 56.86 deaths/1,000 live births
female: 55.69 deaths/1,000 live births (2005 est.)

Life expectancy at birth:
total population: 64.35 years
male: 63.57 years
female: 65.16 years (2005 est.)

Total fertility rate: 2.78 children born/ woman (2005 est.)

HIV/AIDS - adult prevalence rate: 0.9% (2001 est.)

HIV/AIDS - people living with HIV/AIDS: 5.1 million (2001 est.)

HIV/AIDS - deaths: 310,000 (2001 est.)

Major infectious diseases:
degree of risk: high
food or waterborne diseases: bacterial diarrhea, hepatitis A and E, and typhoid fever
vectorborne diseases: dengue fever, malaria, and Japanese encephalitis are high risks in some locations
animal contact disease: rabies (2004)

Nationality:
noun: Indian(s)
adjective: Indian

Ethnic groups: Indo-Aryan 72%, Dravidian 25%, Mongoloid and other 3% (2000)

Religions: Hindu 80.5%, Muslim 13.4%, Christian 2.3%, Sikh 1.9%, other 1.8%, unspecified 0.1% (2001 census)

Languages: English enjoys associate status but is the most important language for national, political, and commercial communication; Hindi is the national language and primary tongue of 30% of the people; there are 14 other official languages: Bengali, Telugu, Marathi, Tamil, Urdu, Gujarati, Malayalam, Kannada, Oriya, Punjabi, Assamese, Kashmiri, Sindhi, and Sanskrit; Hindustani is a popular variant of Hindi/Urdu spoken widely throughout northern India but is not an official language

Literacy:
definition: age 15 and over can read and write
total population: 59.5%
male: 70.2%
female: 48.3% (2003 est.)

GOVERNMENT

Country name:
conventional long form: Republic of India
conventional short form: India

Government type: federal republic

Capital: New Delhi

Administrative divisions: 28 states and 7 union territories*; Andaman and Nicobar Islands*, Andhra Pradesh, Arunachal Pradesh, Assam, Bihar, Chandigarh*, Chhattisgarh, Dadra and Nagar Haveli*, Daman and Diu*, Delhi*, Goa, Gujarat, Haryana, Himachal Pradesh, Jammu and Kashmir, Jharkhand, Karnataka, Kerala, Lakshadweep*, Madhya Pradesh, Maharashtra, Manipur, Meghalaya, Mizoram, Nagaland, Orissa, Pondicherry*, Punjab, Rajasthan, Sikkim, Tamil Nadu, Tripura, Uttaranchal, Uttar Pradesh, West Bengal

Independence: 15 August 1947 (from UK)

National holiday: Republic Day, 26 January (1950)

Constitution: 26 January 1950; amended many times

Legal system: based on English common law; limited judicial review of legislative acts; accepts compulsory ICJ jurisdiction, with reservations; separate personal law codes apply to Muslims, Christians, and Hindus

Suffrage: 18 years of age; universal

Executive branch:
chief of state: President A.P.J. Abdul KALAM (since 26
July 2002); Vice President Bhairon Singh SHEKHAWAT (since 19 August 2002)
head of government: Prime Minister Manmohan SINGH (since 22 May 2004)
cabinet: appointed by the president on the recommendation of the prime minister
elections: president elected by an electoral college consisting of elected members of both houses of Parliament and the legislatures of the states for a five-year term; election last held July 2002 (next to be held 18 July 2007); vice president elected by both houses of Parliament for a five-year term; election last held 12 August 2002 (next to be held August 2007), prime minister chosen by parliamentary members of the majority party following legislative elections; election last held April - May 2004 (next to be held May 2009)
election results: Abdul KALAM elected president; percent of electoral college vote - 89.6%; Bhairon Singh SHEKHAWAT elected vice president; percent of Parliament vote - 59.8%

Legislative branch: bicameral Parliament or Sansad consists of the Council of States or Rajya Sabha (a body consisting of not more than 250 members, up to 12 of whom are appointed by the president, the remainder are chosen by the elected members of the state and territorial assemblies; members serve six-year terms) and the People's Assembly or Lok Sabha (545 seats; 543 elected by popular vote, 2 appointed by the president; members serve five-year terms)
elections: People's Assembly - last held 20 April through 10 May 2004 (next must be held before May 2009)
election results: People's Assembly - percent of vote by party - NA%; seats by party - INC 145, BJP 138, CPI(M) 43, SP 36, RJD 24, BSP 19, DMK 16, SS 12, BJD 11, CPI 10, NCP 9, JDU 8, SAD 8, PMK 6, TDP 5, TRS 5, JMM 5, LJSP 4, MDMK 4, independents 5, other 30

Judicial branch: Supreme Court (one chief justice and 25 associate justices are appointed by the president and remain in office until they reach the age of 65 or are removed for "proved misbehavior")

Political parties and leaders: note - India has dozens of national and regional political parties; only parties with four or more seats in the People's Assembly are listed; Bahujan Samaj Party or BSP [MAYAWATI]; Bharatiya Janata Party or BJP [Lal Krishna ADVANI]; Biju Janata Dal or BJD [Naveen PATNAIK]; Communist Party of India or CPI [Ardhendu Bhushan BARDHAN]; Communist Party of India (Marxist) or CPI (M) [Prakash KARAT]; Dravida Munnetra Kazagham or DMK [M. KARUNANIDHI]; Eqtedar-e-Melli-Eslami (National Islamic Empowerment) [Ahmad Shah AHMADZAI]; Indian National Congress or INC [Sonia GANDHI]; Janata Dal (United) or JDU [George FERNANDEZ]; Jharkhand Mukti Morcha or JMM [Shibu SOREN]; Lok Jan Shakti Party or LJSP [Ram Vilas PASWAN]; Marumalarchi Dravida Munnetra Kazhagam or MDMK [VAIKO]; Nahzat-e-Faragir-e-Democracy Wa Taraqi-e-Afghanistan (Afghanistan's Democracy and Progress Movement) [Sher Mohammad BUZGAR]; Nationalist Congress Party or NCP [Sharad PAWAR]; Pattali Makkal Katchi or PMK [S. RAMADOSS]; Rashtriya Janata Dal or RJD [Laloo Prasad YADAV]; Samajwadi Party or SP [Mulayam Singh YADAV]; Shiromani Akali Dal or SAD [Prakash Singh BADAL]; Shiv Sena or SS [Bal THACKERAY]; Telangana Rashtra Samithi or TRS [K. Chandrashekar RAO]; Telugu Desam Party or TDP [Chandrababu NAIDU]

Political pressure groups and leaders: numerous religious or militant/chauvinistic organizations, including Vishwa Hindu Parishad, Bajrang Dal, and Rashtriya Swayamsevak Sangh; various separatist groups seeking greater communal and/or regional autonomy, including the All Parties Hurriyat Conference in the Kashmir Valley and the National Socialist Council of Nagaland in the Northeast

International organization participation: AfDB, ARF, AsDB, ASEAN (dialogue partner), BIS, C, CERN (observer), CP, EAS, FAO, G- 6, G-15, G-24, G-77, IAEA, IBRD, ICAO, ICC, ICFTU, ICRM, IDA, IFAD, IFC, IFRCS, IHO, ILO, IMF, IMO, Interpol, IOC, IOM (observer), ISO, ITU, MIGA, MONUC, NAM, OAS (observer), ONUB, OPCW, PCA, PIF (partner), SAARC, SACEP, SCO (observer), UN, UNCTAD, UNESCO, UNHCR, UNIDO, UNIFIL, UNMEE, UNMIS, UNMOVIC, UNOCI, UPU, WCL, WCO, WFTU, WHO, WIPO, WMO, WToO, WTO

Diplomatic representation in the US:
chief of mission: Ambassador Ranendra SEN
chancery: 2107 Massachusetts Avenue NW, Washington, DC 20008; note - Consular Wing located at 2536 Massachusetts Avenue NW, Washington, DC 20008
telephone: [1] (202) 939-7000
FAX: [1] (202) 265-4351
consulate(s) general: Chicago, Houston, New York, and San Francisco

Diplomatic representation from the US:
chief of mission: Ambassador David C. MULFORD
embassy: Shantipath, Chanakyapuri, New Delhi 110021
mailing address: use embassy street address
telephone: [91] (11) 2419-8000
FAX: [91] (11) 2419-0017
consulate(s) general: Chennai (Madras), Kolkata (Calcutta), Mumbai (Bombay)

Flag description: three equal horizontal bands of saffron (subdued orange) (top), white, and green with a blue chakra (24-spoked wheel) centered in the white band; similar to the flag of Niger, which has a small orange disk centered in the white band

ECONOMY

Economy - overview: India's diverse economy encompasses traditional village farming, modern agriculture, handicrafts, a wide range of modern industries, and a multitude of services. Services are the major source of economic growth, accounting for half of India's output with less than one quarter of its labor force. About two-thirds of the workforce is in agriculture, leading the UPA government to articulate an economic reform program that includes developing basic infrastructure to improve the lives of the rural poor and boost economic performance. Government controls on foreign trade and investment have been reduced in some areas, but high tariffs (averaging 20% on non-agricultural items in 2004) and limits on foreign direct investment are still in place. The government in 2005 liberalized investment in the civil aviation, telecom, and construction sectors. Privatization of government-owned industries essentially came to a halt in 2005, and continues to generate political debate; continued social, political, and economic rigidities hold back needed initiatives. The economy has posted an excellent average growth rate of more than 6.8% in the decade since 1994, reducing poverty by about 10 percentage points. India probably achieved greater than 7 percent GDP growth in 2005, significantly expanding manufacturing. India is capitalizing on its large numbers of well-educated people skilled in the English language to become a major exporter of software services and software workers. Despite strong growth, the World Bank and others worry about the combined state and federal budget deficit, running at approximately 9% of GDP. The huge and growing population is the fundamental social, economic, and environmental problem.

GDP (purchasing power parity): $3.678 trillion (2005 est.)

GDP (official exchange rate): $735.6 billion (2005 est.)

GDP - real growth rate: 7.1% (2005 est.)

GDP - per capita: purchasing power parity - $3,400 (2005 est.)

GDP - composition by sector:
agriculture: 20.6%
industry: 28.1%
services: 51.4% (2005 est.)

Labor force: 496.4 million (2005 est.)

Labor force - by occupation: agriculture 60%, industry 17%, services 23% (1999)

Unemployment rate: 9% (2005 est.)

Population below poverty line: 25% (2002 est.)

Household income or consumption by percentage share:
lowest 10%: 3.5%
highest 10%: 33.5% (1997)

Distribution of family income - Gini index: 32.5 (2000)

Inflation rate (consumer prices): 4.4% (2005 est.)

Investment (gross fixed): 24.8% of GDP (2005 est.)

Budget:
revenues: $111.2 billion
expenditures: $135.8 billion, including capital expenditures of $15 billion (2005 est.)

Public debt: 82% of GDP (federal and state debt combined) (2005 est.)

Agriculture - products: rice, wheat, oilseed, cotton, jute, tea, sugarcane, potatoes; cattle, water buffalo, sheep, goats, poultry; fish

Industries: textiles, chemicals, food processing, steel, transportation equipment, cement, mining, petroleum, machinery, software

Industrial production growth rate: 8.2% (2005 est.)

Electricity - production: 556.8 billion kWh (2003)

Electricity - production by source:
fossil fuel: 81.7%
hydro: 14.5%
nuclear: 3.4%
other: 0.3% (2001)

Electricity - consumption: 519 billion kWh (2003)

Electricity - exports: 87 million kWh (2003)

Electricity - imports: 1.4 billion kWh (2003)

Oil - production: 785,000 bbl/day (2005 est.)

Oil - consumption: 2.32 million bbl/day (2003 est.)
Oil - exports: 350,000 bbl/day NA (2005 est.)
Oil - imports: 2.09 million bbl/day NA (2005 est.)
Oil - proved reserves: 5.7 billion bbl (2005 est.)
Natural gas - production: 22.75 billion cu m (2001 est.)
Natural gas - consumption: 22.75 billion cu m (2001 est.)
Natural gas - exports: 0 cu m (2001 est.)
Natural gas - imports: 0 cu m (2001 est.)
Natural gas - proved reserves: 542.4 billion cu m (2005)
Current account balance: $-13.19 billion (2005 est.)
Exports: $76.23 billion f.o.b. (2005 est.)
Exports - partners: US 17%, UAE 8.8%, China 5.5%, Hong Kong 4.7%, UK 4.5%, Singapore 4.5% (2004)
Imports: $113.1 billion f.o.b. (2005 est.)
Imports - partners: China 6.1%, US 6%, Switzerland 5.2%, Belgium 4.4% (2004)
Reserves of foreign exchange and gold: $145 billion (2005 est.)
Debt - external: $119.7 billion (2005 est.)
Economic aid - recipient: $2.9 billion (FY98/99)
Currency (code): Indian rupee (INR)
Currency code: INR
Exchange rates: Indian rupees per US dollar - 43.6 (2005), 45.317 (2004), 46.583 (2003), 48.61 (2002), 47.186 (2001)
Fiscal year: 1 April - 31 March

COMMUNICATIONS

Telephones - main lines in use: 48.917 million (2003)
Telephones - mobile cellular: 26,154,400 (2003)
Telephone system:
general assessment: recent deregulation and liberalization of telecommunications laws and policies have prompted rapid change; local and long distance service provided throughout all regions of the country, with services primarily concentrated in the urban areas; steady improvement is taking place with the recent admission of private and private-public investors, but telephone density remains low at about seven for each 100 persons nationwide but only one per 100 persons in rural areas and a national waiting list of over 1.7 million; fastest growth is in cellular service with modest growth in fixed lines
domestic: expansion of domestic service, although still weak in rural areas, resulted from increased competition and dramatic reductions in price led in large part by wireless service; mobile cellular service (both CDMA and GSM) introduced in 1994 and organized nationwide into four metropolitan cities and 19 telecom circles each with about three private service providers and one state-owned service provider; in recent years significant trunk capacity added in the form of fiber-optic cable and one of the world's largest domestic satellite systems, the Indian National Satellite system (INSAT), with five satellites supporting 33,000 very small aperture terminals (VSAT) international: country code - 91; satellite earth stations - 8 Intelsat (Indian Ocean) and 1 Inmarsat (Indian Ocean region); nine gateway exchanges operating from Mumbai (Bombay), New Delhi, Kolkata (Calcutta), Chennai (Madras), Jalandhar, Kanpur, Gandhinagar, Hyderabad, and Ernakulam; 5 submarine cables, including Sea-Me-We-3 with landing sites at Cochin and Mumbai (Bombay), Fiber-Optic Link Around the Globe (FLAG) with landing site at Mumbai (Bombay), South Africa Far East (SAFE) with landing site at Cochin, i2icn linking to Singapore with landing sites at Mumbai (Bombay) and Chennai (Madras), and Tata Indicom linking Singapore and Chennai (Madras), provide a significant increase in the bandwidth available for both voice and data traffic (2004)
Radio broadcast stations: AM 153, FM 91, shortwave 68 (1998)
Radios: 116 million (1997)
Television broadcast stations: 562 (of which 82 stations have 1 kW or greater power and 480 stations have less than 1 kW of power) (1997)
Televisions: 63 million (1997)
Internet country code: .in
Internet hosts: 86,871 (2003)
Internet Service Providers (ISPs): 43 (2000)
Internet users: 18.481 million (2003)

TRANSPORTATION

Airports: 333 (2004 est.)
Airports - with paved runways:
total: 239
over 3,047 m: 17
2,438 to 3,047 m: 48
1,524 to 2,437 m: 75
914 to 1,523 m: 79
under 914 m: 20 (2005 est.)
Airports - with unpaved runways:
total: 95
2,438 to 3,047 m: 2
1,524 to 2,437 m: 6
914 to 1,523 m: 39
under 914 m: 48 (2005 est.)
Heliports: 27 (2005 est.)
Pipelines: gas 6,171 km; liquid petroleum gas 1,195 km; oil 5,613 km; refined products 5,567 km (2004)
Railways:
total: 63,230 km (16,693 km electrified)
broad gauge: 45,718 km 1.676-m gauge
narrow gauge: 14,406 km 1.000-m gauge; 3,106 km 0.762-m gauge and 0.610-m gauge (2004)
Roadways:
total: 3,851,440 km
paved: 2,411,001 km
unpaved: 1,440,439 km (2002)
Waterways: 14,500 km
note: 5,200 km on major rivers and 485 km on canals suitable for mechanized vessels (2004)
Merchant marine:
total: 299 ships (1,000 GRT or over) 6,555,507
GRT/11,069,791 DWT
by type: bulk carrier 85, cargo 75, chemical tanker 13, combination ore/oil 1, container 7, liquefied gas 14, passenger 3, passenger/cargo 9,petroleum tanker 91, roll on/roll off 1
foreign-owned: 10 (Australia 1, China 1, Greece 1, UAE 6, United Kingdom 1)
registered in other countries: 30 (2005)
Ports and terminals: Chennai, Haldia, Jawaharal Nehru, Kandla, Kolkata (Calcutta), Mumbai (Bombay), New Mangalore, Vishakhapatnam

MILITARY

Military branches: Army, Navy (includes naval air arm), Air Force, Coast Guard, various security or paramilitary forces (includes Border Security Force, Assam Rifles, National Security Guards, Indo-Tibetan Border Police, Special Frontier Force, Central Reserve Police Force, Central Industrial Security Force, Railway Protection Force, and Defense Security Corps)
Military service age and obligation: 16 years of age for voluntary military service (2001)
Manpower available for military service:
males age 16-49: 287,551,111 (2005 est.)
Manpower fit for military service: *males age 16-49:* 219,471,999 (2005 est.)
Manpower reaching military service age annually: *males:* 11,446,452 (2005 est.)
Military expenditures - dollar figure: $18.86 billion (2005)
Military expenditures - percent of GDP: 2.93% (2005/06)

TRANSNATIONAL ISSUES

Disputes - international: China and India launched a security and foreign policy dialogue in 2005, consolidating discussions related to the dispute over most of their rugged, militarized boundary, regional nuclear proliferation, Indian claims that China transferred missiles to Pakistan, and other matters; recent talks and confidence-building measures have begun to defuse tensions over Kashmir, site of the world's largest and most militarized territorial dispute with portions under the de facto administration of China (Aksai Chin), India (Jammu and Kashmir), and Pakistan (Azad Kashmir and Northern Areas); in 2004, India and Pakistan instituted a cease fire in the Kashmir and in 2005, restored bus service across the highly militarized Line of Control; Pakistan has taken its dispute on the impact and benefits of India's building the Baglihar dam on the Chenab River in Jammu and Kashmir to the World Bank for arbitration; UN Military Observer Group in India and Pakistan (UNMOGIP) has maintained a small group of peacekeepers since 1949; India does not recognize Pakistan's ceding historic Kashmir lands to China in 1964; disputes persist with Pakistan over Indus River water sharing; to defuse tensions and prepare for discussions on a maritime boundary, in 2004, India and Pakistan resurveyed a portion of the disputed boundary in Sir Creek estuary at the mouth of the Rann of Kutch; Pakistani maps continue to show Junagadh claim in Indian Gujarat State; discussions with Bangladesh remain stalled to delimit a small section of river boundary, to exchange 162 miniscule enclaves in both countries, to allocate divided villages, and to stop illegal cross-border trade, migration, violence, and transit of terrorists through the porous border; Bangladesh protests India's attempts to fence off high-traffic sections; dispute with Bangladesh over New Moore/South Talpatty/Purbasha Island in the Bay of Bengal deters maritime boundary delimitation; India seeks cooperation from Bhutan and Burma to keep Indian Nagaland and Assam separatists from hiding in remote areas along the borders; Joint Border Committee with Nepal continues to demarcate minor disputed boundary sections; India has instituted a stricter border regime to keep out Maoist insurgents and control illegal cross-border activities from Nepal

Refugees and internally displaced persons: *refugees (country of origin):* 92,394 (Tibet/China) 60,922 (Sri Lanka)
IDPs: 650,000 (Jammu and Kashmir conflicts; most IDPs are Kashmiri Hindus); 113,000 (resulting from 26 December 2004 tsunami) (2004)

Illicit drugs: world's largest producer of licit opium for the pharmaceutical trade, but an undetermined quantity of opium is diverted to illicit international drug markets; transit point for illicit narcotics produced in neighboring countries; illicit producer of methaqualone; vulnerable to narcotics money laundering through the hawala system

INDIAN OCEAN

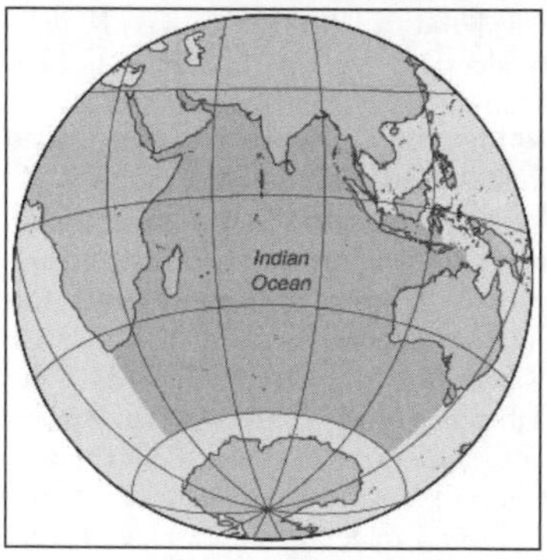

INTRODUCTION

Background: The Indian Ocean is the third largest of the world's five oceans (after the Pacific Ocean and Atlantic Ocean, but larger than the Southern Ocean and Arctic Ocean). Four critically important access waterways are the Suez Canal (Egypt), Bab el Mandeb (Djibouti-Yemen), Strait of Hormuz (Iran-Oman), and Strait of Malacca (Indonesia-Malaysia). The decision by the International Hydrographic Organization in the spring of 2000 to delimit a fifth ocean, the Southern Ocean, removed the portion of the Indian Ocean south of 60 degrees south.

GEOGRAPHY

Location: body of water between Africa, the Southern Ocean, Asia, and Australia

Geographic coordinates: 20 00 S, 80 00 E

Map references: Political Map of the World

Area:
total: 68.556 million sq km
note: includes Andaman Sea, Arabian Sea, Bay of Bengal, Flores Sea, Great Australian Bight, Gulf of Aden, Gulf of Oman, Java Sea, Mozambique Channel, Persian Gulf, Red Sea, Savu Sea, Strait of Malacca, Timor Sea, and other tributary water bodies

Area - comparative: about 5.5 times the size of the US

Coastline: 66,526 km

Climate: northeast monsoon (December to April), southwest monsoon (June to October); tropical cyclones occur during May/June and October/November in the northern Indian Ocean and January/February in the southern Indian Ocean

Terrain: surface dominated by counterclockwise gyre (broad, circular system of currents) in the southern Indian Ocean; unique reversal of surface currents in the northern Indian Ocean; low atmospheric pressure over southwest Asia from hot, rising, summer air results in the southwest monsoon and southwest-to-northeast winds and currents, while high pressure over northern Asia from cold, falling, winter air results in the northeast monsoon and northeast-to-southwest winds and currents; ocean floor is dominated by the Mid-Indian Ocean Ridge and subdivided by the Southeast Indian Ocean Ridge, Southwest Indian Ocean Ridge, and Ninetyeast Ridge

Elevation extremes:
lowest point: Java Trench -7,258 m
highest point: sea level 0 m

Natural resources: oil and gas fields, fish, shrimp, sand and gravel aggregates, placer deposits, polymetallic nodules

Natural hazards: occasional icebergs pose navigational hazard in southern reaches

Environment - current issues: endangered marine species include the dugong, seals, turtles, and whales; oil pollution in the Arabian Sea, Persian Gulf, and Red Sea

Geography - note: major chokepoints include Bab el Mandeb, Strait of Hormuz, Strait of Malacca, southern access to the Suez Canal, and the Lombok Strait

ECONOMY

Economy - overview: The Indian Ocean provides major sea routes connecting the Middle East, Africa, and East Asia with Europe and the Americas. It carries a particularly heavy traffic of petroleum and petroleum products from the oilfields of the Persian Gulf and Indonesia. Its fish are of great and growing importance to the bordering countries for domestic consumption and export. Fishing fleets from Russia, Japan, South Korea, and Taiwan also exploit the Indian Ocean, mainly for shrimp and tuna. Large reserves of hydrocarbons are being tapped in the offshore areas of Saudi Arabia, Iran, India, and western Australia. An estimated 40% of the world's offshore oil production comes from the Indian Ocean. Beach sands rich in heavy minerals and offshore placer deposits are actively exploited by bordering countries, particularly India, South Africa, Indonesia, Sri Lanka, and Thailand.

TRANSPORTATION

Ports and terminals: Chennai (Madras; India), Colombo (Sri Lanka), Durban (South Africa), Jakarta (Indonesia), Kolkata (Calcutta; India) Melbourne (Australia), Mumbai (Bombay; India), Richards Bay (South Africa)

TRANSNATIONAL ISSUES

Disputes - international: some maritime disputes (see littoral states)

INDONESIA

INTRODUCTION

Background: The Dutch began to colonize Indonesia in the early 17th century; the islands were occupied by Japan from 1942 to 1945. Indonesia declared its independence after Japan's surrender, but it required four years of intermittent negotiations, recurring hostilities, and UN mediation before the Netherlands agreed to relinquish its colony. Indonesia is the world's largest archipelagic state. Current issues include: alleviating widespread poverty, preventing terrorism, continuing the transition to popularly-elected governments after four decades of authoritarianism, implementing reforms of the banking sector, addressing charges of cronyism and corruption, and holding the military and police accountable for human rights violations. Indonesia has been dealing with armed separatist movements in Aceh and in Papua.

GEOGRAPHY

Location: Southeastern Asia, archipelago between the Indian Ocean and the Pacific Ocean
Geographic coordinates: 5 00 S, 120 00 E
Map references: Southeast Asia
Area:
total: 1,919,440 sq km
land: 1,826,440 sq km
water: 93,000 sq km
Area - comparative: slightly less than three times the size of Texas
Land boundaries:
total: 2,830 km
border countries: East Timor 228 km, Malaysia 1,782 km, Papua New Guinea 820 km
Coastline: 54,716 km
Maritime claims: measured from claimed archipelagic straight baselines
territorial sea: 12 nm
exclusive economic zone: 200 nm
Climate: tropical; hot, humid; more moderate in highlands
Terrain: mostly coastal lowlands; larger islands have interior mountains
Elevation extremes:
lowest point: Indian Ocean 0 m
highest point: Puncak Jaya 5,030 m
Natural resources: petroleum, tin, natural gas, nickel, timber, bauxite, copper, fertile soils, coal, gold, silver
Land use:
arable land: 11.32%
permanent crops: 7.23%
other: 81.45% (2001)
Irrigated land: 48,150 sq km (1998 est.)
Natural hazards: occasional floods, severe droughts, tsunamis, earthquakes, volcanoes, forest fires
Environment - current issues: deforestation; water pollution from industrial wastes, sewage; air pollution in urban areas; smoke and haze from forest fires
Environment - international agreements:
party to: Biodiversity, Climate Change, Climate Change-Kyoto Protocol, Desertification, Endangered Species, Hazardous Wastes, Law of the Sea, Ozone Layer Protection, Ship Pollution, Tropical Timber 83, Tropical Timber 94, Wetlands
signed, but not ratified: Marine Life Conservation
Geography - note: archipelago of 17,508 islands (6,000 inhabited); straddles equator; strategic location astride or along major sea lanes from Indian Ocean to Pacific Ocean

PEOPLE

Population: 241,973,879 (July 2005 est.)
Age structure:
0-14 years: 29.1% (male 35,823,456/female 34,590,631)
15-64 years: 65.7% (male 79,447,560/female 79,449,399)
65 years and over: 5.2% (male 5,526,389/female 7,136,444) (2005 est.)
Median age:
total: 26.48 years
male: 26.05 years
female: 26.93 years (2005 est.)
Population growth rate: 1.45% (2005 est.)
Birth rate: 20.71 births/1,000 population (2005 est.)
Death rate: 6.25 deaths/1,000 population (2005 est.)
Net migration rate: 0 migrant(s)/1,000 population (2005 est.)
Sex ratio:
at birth: 1.05 male(s)/female
under 15 years: 1.04 male(s)/female
15-64 years: 1 male(s)/female
65 years and over: 0.77 male(s)/female
total population: 1 male(s)/female (2005 est.)
Infant mortality rate:
total: 35.6 deaths/1,000 live births
male: 40.72 deaths/1,000 live births
female: 30.22 deaths/1,000 live births (2005 est.)
Life expectancy at birth:
total population: 69.57 years
male: 67.13 years
female: 72.13 years (2005 est.)
Total fertility rate: 2.44 children born/woman (2005 est.)
HIV/AIDS - adult prevalence rate: 0.1% (2003 est.)
HIV/AIDS - people living with HIV/AIDS: 110,000 (2003 est.)
HIV/AIDS - deaths: 2,400 (2003 est.)
Major infectious diseases:
degree of risk: high
food or waterborne diseases: bacterial and protozoal diarrhea, hepatitis A and E, and typhoid fever
vectorborne diseases: dengue fever, malaria, and chikungunya are high risks in some locations
note: at present, H5N1 avian influenza poses a minimal risk; during outbreaks

among birds, rare cases could occur among US personnel who have close contact with infected birds or poultry (2005)

Nationality:
noun: Indonesian(s)
adjective: Indonesian

Ethnic groups: Javanese 45%, Sundanese 14%, Madurese 7.5%, coastal Malays 7.5%, other 26%

Religions: Muslim 88%, Protestant 5%, Roman Catholic 3%, Hindu 2%, Buddhist 1%, other 1% (1998)

Languages: Bahasa Indonesia (official, modified form of Malay), English, Dutch, local dialects, the most widely spoken of which is Javanese

Literacy:
definition: age 15 and over can read and write
total population: 87.9%
male: 92.5%
female: 83.4% (2002 est.)

GOVERNMENT

Country name:
conventional long form: Republic of Indonesia
conventional short form: Indonesia
local long form: Republik Indonesia
local short form: Indonesia
former: Netherlands East Indies; Dutch East Indies

Government type: republic

Capital: Jakarta

Administrative divisions: 30 provinces (propinsi-propinsi, singular -propinsi), 2 special regions* (daerah-daerah istimewa, singular - daerah istimewa), and 1 special capital city district** (daerah khusus ibukota); Aceh*, Bali, Banten, Bengkulu, Gorontalo, Irian Jaya Barat, Jakarta Raya**, Jambi, Jawa Barat, Jawa Tengah, Jawa Timur, Kalimantan Barat, Kalimantan Selatan, Kalimantan Tengah, Kalimantan Timur, Kepulauan Bangka Belitung, Kepulauan Riau, Lampung, Maluku, Maluku Utara, Nusa Tenggara Barat, Nusa Tenggara Timur, Papua, Riau, Sulawesi Barat, Sulawesi Selatan, Sulawesi Tengah, Sulawesi Tenggara, Sulawesi Utara, Sumatera Barat, Sumatera Selatan, Sumatera Utara, Yogyakarta*; note - with the implementation of decentralization on 1 January 2001, the 357 districts or regencies became the key administrative units responsible for providing most government services

Independence: 17 August 1945 (independence proclaimed); 27 December 1949 (Netherlands recognizes Indonesian independence)

National holiday: Independence Day, 17 August (1945)

Constitution: August 1945; abrogated by Federal Constitution of 1949 and Provisional Constitution of 1950, restored 5 July 1959

Legal system: based on Roman-Dutch law, substantially modified by indigenous concepts and by new criminal procedures and election codes; has not accepted compulsory ICJ jurisdiction

Suffrage: 17 years of age; universal and married persons regardless of age

Executive branch:
chief of state: President Susilo Bambang YUDHOYONO (since 20 October 2004) and Vice President Muhammad Yusuf KALLA (since 20 October 2004); note- the president is both the chief of state and head of government
head of government: President Susilo Bambang YUDHOYONO (since 20 October 2004) and Vice President Muhammad Yusuf KALLA (since 20 October 2004);
cabinet: Cabinet appointed by the president
elections: president and vice president were elected for five-year terms by direct vote of the citizenry; last held 20 September 2004 (next to be held in September 2009)
election results: Susilo Bambang YUDHOYONO elected president receiving 60.6% of vote; MEGAWATI Sukarnoputri received 39.4%

Legislative branch: unicameral House of Representatives or Dewan Perwakilan Rakyat (DPR) (550 seats; members elected to serve five-year terms); House of Regional Representatives (Dewan Perwakilan Daerah or DPD), constitutionally mandated role includes providing legislative input to DPR on issues affecting regions; People's Consultative Assembly (Majelis Permusyawaratan Rakyat or MPR) has role in inaugurating and impeaching President and in amending constitution; consists of popularly-elected members in DPR and DPD; MPR does not formulate national policy
elections: last held 5 April 2004 (next to be held in April 2009)
election results: percent of vote by party - Golkar 21.6%, PDI-P 18.5%, PKB 10.6%, PPP 8.2%, PD 7.5%, PKS 7.3%, PAN 6.4%, others 19.9%; seats by party - Golkar 128, PDI-P 109, PPP 58, PD 55, PAN 53, PKB 52, PKS 45, others 50
note: because of election rules, the number of seats won does not always follow the number of votes received by parties

Judicial branch: Supreme Court or Mahkamah Agung (justices appointed by the president from a list of candidates approved by the legislature); a separate Constitutional Court or Makhama Konstitusi was invested by the president on 16 August 2003; in March 2004 the Supreme Court assumed administrative and financial responsibility for the lower court system from the Ministry of Justice and Human Rights

Political parties and leaders: Crescent Moon and Star Party or PBB [Yusril Ihza MAHENDRA, chairman]; Democratic Party or PD [Subur BUDHISANTOSO, chairman]; Functional Groups Party or Golkar [Yusuf KALLA, chairman]; Indonesia Democratic Party-Struggle or PDI-P [MEGAWATI Sukarnoputri,chairperson]; National Awakening Party or PKB [Alwi SHIHAB, chairman]; National Mandate Party or PAN [Sutrisno BACHIR, chairman]; Prosperous Justice Party or PKS [Tifatul SEMBIRING, chairman]; United Development Party or PPP [Hamzah HAZ, chairman]

Political pressure groups and leaders: NA

International organization participation: APEC, APT, ARF, AsDB, ASEAN, BIS, CP, EAS, FAO, G-15, G-77, IAEA, IBRD, ICAO, ICC, ICFTU, ICRM, IDA, IDB, IFAD, IFC, IFRCS, IHO, ILO, IMF, IMO, Interpol, IOC, IOM (observer), ISO, ITU, MIGA, MONUC, NAM, OIC, OPCW, OPEC, PIF (partner), UN, UNAMSIL, UNCTAD, UNESCO, UNIDO, UNMIL, UNOMIG, UPU, WCL, WCO, WFTU, WHO, WIPO, WMO, WToO, WTO

Diplomatic representation in the US:
chief of mission: Charge Andri HADI
chancery: 2020 Massachusetts Avenue NW, Washington, DC 20036
telephone: [1] (202) 775-5200
FAX: [1] (202) 775-5365
consulate(s) general: Chicago, Houston, Los Angeles, New York, and San Francisco

Diplomatic representation from the US:
chief of mission: Ambassador B. Lynn PASCOE
embassy: Jalan 1 Medan Merdeka Selatan 4-5, Jakarta 10110
mailing address: Unit 8129, Box 1, FPO AP 96520
telephone: [62] (21) 3435-9000
FAX: [62] (21) 3435-9922
consulate(s) general: Surabaya

Flag description: two equal horizontal bands of red (top) and white; similar to the flag of Monaco, which is shorter; also similar to the flag of Poland, which is white (top) and red

ECONOMY

Economy - overview: Indonesia, a vast polyglot nation, has struggled to overcome the Asian financial crisis, and still grapples with high unemployment, a fragile banking sector, endemic corrup-

tion, inadequate infrastructure, a poor investment climate, and unequal resource distribution among regions. Indonesia became a net oil importer in 2004 because of declining production and lack of new exploration investment. The cost of subsidizing domestic fuel placed increasing strain on the budget in 2005, and combined with indecisive monetary policy, contributed to a run on the currency in August, prompting the government to enact a 126% average fuel price hike in October. The resulting inflation and interest rate hikes will dampen growth prospects in 2006. Keys to future growth remain internal reform, building up the confidence of international and domestic investors, and strong global economic growth. In late December 2004, the Indian Ocean tsunami took 131,000 lives with another 37,000 missing, left some 570,000 displaced persons, and caused an estimated $4.5 billion in damages and losses. Terrorist incidents in 2005 have slowed tourist arrivals. Indonesia experienced several human cases of avian influenza in late 2005, sparking concerns of a pandemic.
GDP (purchasing power parity): $899 billion (2005 est.)
GDP (official exchange rate): $245.3 billion (2005 est.)
GDP - real growth rate: 5.3% (2005 est.)
GDP - per capita: purchasing power parity - $3,700 (2005 est.)
GDP - composition by sector:
agriculture: 15.1%
industry: 44.5%
services: 40.4% (2005 est.)
Labor force: 110.4 million (2005 est.)
Labor force - by occupation: agriculture 45%, industry 16%, services 39% (1999 est.)
Unemployment rate: 10% (2005 est.)
Population below poverty line: 15.2% (2004)
Household income or consumption by percentage share:
lowest 10%: 3.6%
highest 10%: 28.5% (2002)
Distribution of family income - Gini index: 34.3 (2002)
Inflation rate (consumer prices): 9.3% (2005 est.)
Investment (gross fixed): 21.5% of GDP (2005 est.)
Budget:
revenues: $56.13 billion
expenditures: $58.72 billion, including capital expenditures of NA (2005 est.)
Public debt: 52.6% of GDP (2005 est.)
Agriculture - products: rice, cassava (tapioca), peanuts, rubber, cocoa, coffee, palm oil, copra, poultry, beef, pork, eggs
Industries: petroleum and natural gas, textiles, apparel, footwear, mining, cement, chemical fertilizers, plywood, rubber, food, tourism
Industrial production growth rate: 2.1% (2005 est.)
Electricity - production: 109.5 billion kWh (2003)
Electricity - production by source:
fossil fuel: 86.9%
hydro: 10.5%
nuclear: 0%
other: 2.6% (2001)
Electricity - consumption: 101.8 billion kWh (2003)
Electricity - exports: 0 kWh (2003)
Electricity - imports: 0 kWh (2003)
Oil - production: 1.094 million bbl/day (2004)
Oil - consumption: 1.155 million bbl/day (2003)
Oil - exports: 556,200 bbl/day (2004)
Oil - imports: 606,200 bbl/day (2004)
Oil - proved reserves: 4.6 billion bbl (2005 est.)
Natural gas - production: 77.6 billion cu m (2003 est.)
Natural gas - consumption: 55.3 billion cu m (2003 est.)
Natural gas - exports: 39.7 billion cu m (2003 est.)
Natural gas - imports: 0 cu m (2003 est.)
Natural gas - proved reserves: 2.549 trillion cu m (2005)
Current account balance: $3.899 billion (2005 est.)
Exports: $83.64 billion f.o.b. (2005 est.)
Exports - partners: Japan 22.3%, US 12.3%, Singapore 8.4%, South Korea 6.8%, China 6.4%, Malaysia 4.2% (2004)
Imports: $62.02 billion f.o.b. (2005 est.)
Imports - partners: Singapore 13.1%, Japan 13.1%, China 8.8%, US 7%, Thailand 6%, Australia 4.8%, Saudi Arabia 4.2%, South Korea 4.2% (2004)
Reserves of foreign exchange and gold: $33.58 billion (2005 est.)
Debt - external: $140.6 billion (2005 est.)
Economic aid - recipient: $43 billion
note: Indonesia finished its IMF program in December 2003 but still receives bilateral aid through the Consultative Group on Indonesia (CGI), which pledged $2.8 billion in grants and loans for 2004 and again in 2005; nearly $5 billion in aid money pledged by a variety bilateral, multilateral and NGO donors following the 2004 tsunami; money is slated for use in relief and rebuilding efforts in Aceh.
Currency (code): Indonesian rupiah (IDR)
Currency code: IDR
Exchange rates: Indonesian rupiahs per US dollar - 9,739.35 (2005), 8,938.9 (2004), 8,577.1 (2003), 9,311.2 (2002), 10,260.8 (2001)
Fiscal year: calendar year; note - previously was 1 April - 31 March, but starting with 2001, has been changed to calendar year

COMMUNICATIONS

Telephones - main lines in use: 7.75 million (2002)
Telephones - mobile cellular: 11.7 million (2002)
Telephone system:
general assessment: domestic service fair, international service good
domestic: interisland microwave system and HF radio police net; domestic satellite communications system
international: country code - 62; satellite earth stations - 2 Intelsat (1 Indian Ocean and 1 Pacific Ocean)
Radio broadcast stations: AM 678, FM 43, shortwave 82 (1998)
Radios: 31.5 million (1997)
Television broadcast stations: 41 (1999)
Televisions: 13.75 million (1997)
Internet country code: .id
Internet hosts: 62,036 (2003)
Internet Service Providers (ISPs): 24 (2000)
Internet users: 8 million (2002)

TRANSPORTATION

Airports: 667 (2004 est.)
Airports - with paved runways:
total: 161
over 3,047 m: 4
2,438 to 3,047 m: 15
1,524 to 2,437 m: 48
914 to 1,523 m: 51
under 914 m: 43 (2005 est.)
Airports - with unpaved runways:
total: 507
1,524 to 2,437 m: 6
914 to 1,523 m: 26
under 914 m: 475 (2005 est.)
Heliports: 23 (2005 est.)
Pipelines: condensate 850 km; condensate/gas 128 km; gas 8,506 km; oil 7,472 km; oil/gas/water 66 km; refined products 1,329 km (2004)
Railways:
total: 6,458 km
narrow gauge: 5,961 km 1.067-m gauge (125 km electrified); 497 km 0.750-m gauge (2004)
Roadways: total: 368,360 km
paved: 213,648 km
unpaved: 154,711 km (2002)
Waterways: 21,579 km
note: Sumatra 5,471 km, Java and Madura 820 km, Kalimantan 10,460 km, Sulawesi (Celebes) 241 km, Irian Jaya 4,587 km (2004)
Merchant marine:
total: 728 ships (1,000 GRT or over) 3,192,847
GRT/4,319,739 DWT

by type: bulk carrier 35, cargo 409, chemical tanker 19, container 36, liquefied gas 7, livestock carrier 1, passenger 41, passenger/cargo 36, petroleum tanker 125, refrigerated cargo 2, roll on/roll off 13, specialized tanker 2, vehicle carrier 2
foreign-owned: 19 (France 1, Japan 3, Philippines 1, Singapore 11, Switzerland 1, United Kingdom 2)
registered in other countries: 113 (2005)
Ports and terminals: Banjarmasin, Belawan, Ciwandan, Krueg Geukueh, Palembang, Panjang, Sungai Pakning, Tanjung Perak, Tanjung Priok

MILITARY

Military branches: Indonesia Armed Forces (TNI): Army (TNI-AD), Navy (TNI-AL, includes Marines, Naval Air arm), Air Force (TNI-AU)
Military service age and obligation: 18 years of age for compulsory and voluntary military service; conscript service obligation - 2 years (2002)
Manpower available for military service: *males age 18-49:* 60,543,028 (2005 est.)
Manpower fit for military service: *males age 18-49:* 48,687,234 (2005 est.)
Manpower reaching military service age annually: *males:* 2,201,047 (2005 est.)
Military expenditures - dollar figure: $1.3 billion (2004)
Military expenditures - percent of GDP: 3% (2004)

TRANSNATIONAL ISSUES

Disputes - international: East Timor-Indonesia Boundary Committee continues to meet, survey and delimit land boundary, but several sections of the boundary remain unresolved; Indonesia and East Timor contest the sovereignty of the uninhabited coral island of Palau Batek/Fatu Sinai, which hinders a decision on a northern maritime boundary; a 1997 treaty between Indonesia and Australia settled some parts of their maritime boundary but outstanding issues remain; ICJ's award of Sipadan and Ligitan islands to Malaysia in 2002 left maritime boundary in the hydrocarbon-rich Celebes Sea in dispute, culminating in hostile confrontations in March 2005 over concessions to the Ambalat oil block; the ICJ decision has prompted Indonesia to assert claims to and to establish a presence on its smaller outer islands; Indonesia and Singapore pledged in 2005 to finalize their 1973 maritime boundary agreement by defining unresolved areas north of Batam Island; Indonesian secessionists, squatters, and illegal migrants create repatriation problems for Papua New Guinea; piracy remains a problem in the Malacca Strait
Refugees and internally displaced persons: *IDPs:* 535,000 (government offensives against rebels in Aceh; most IDPs in Aceh, Central Kalimantan, Maluku, and Central Sulawesi Provinces); 441,000 (resulting from 26 December 2004 tsunami) (2004)
Illicit drugs: illicit producer of cannabis largely for domestic use; possible growing role as transshipment point for Golden Triangle heroin

IRAN

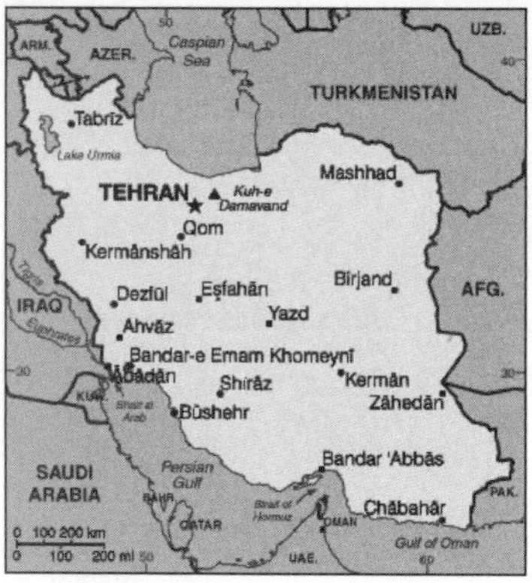

INTRODUCTION

Background: Known as Persia until 1935, Iran became an Islamic republic in 1979 after the ruling monarchy was overthrown and the shah was forced into exile. Conservative clerical forces established a theocratic system of government with ultimate political authority nominally vested in a learned religious scholar. Iranian-US relations have been strained since a group of Iranian students seized the US Embassy in Tehran on 4 November 1979 and held it until 20 January 1981. During 1980-88, Iran fought a bloody, indecisive war with Iraq that eventually expanded into the Persian Gulf and led to clashes between US Navy and Iranian military forces between 1987-1988. Iran has been designated a state sponsor of terrorism for its activities in Lebanon and elsewhere in the world and remains subject to US economic sanctions and export controls because of its continued involvement. Following the elections of a reformist president and Majlis in the late 1990s, attempts to foster political reform in response to popular dissatisfaction floundered as conservative politicians prevented reform measures from being enacted, increased repressive measures, and made electoral gains against reformers. Parliamentary elections in 2004 and the August 2005 inauguration of a conservative stalwart as president, completed the reconsolidation of conservative power in Iran's government.

GEOGRAPHY

Location: Middle East, bordering the Gulf of Oman, the Persian Gulf, and the Caspian Sea, between Iraq and Pakistan
Geographic coordinates: 32 00 N, 53 00 E
Map references: Middle East
Area:
total: 1.648 million sq km
land: 1.636 million sq km
water: 12,000 sq km
Area - comparative: slightly larger than Alaska
Land boundaries:
total: 5,440 km
border countries: Afghanistan 936 km, Armenia 35 km, Azerbaijan-proper 432 km, Azerbaijan-Naxcivan exclave 179 km, Iraq 1,458 km, Pakistan 909 km, Turkey 499 km, Turkmenistan 992 km
Coastline: 2,440 km; note - Iran also borders the Caspian Sea (740 km)
Maritime claims:
territorial sea: 12 nm
contiguous zone: 24 nm
exclusive economic zone: bilateral agreements or median lines in the Persian Gulf
continental shelf: natural prolongation
Climate: mostly arid or semiarid, subtropical along Caspian coast
Terrain: rugged, mountainous rim; high, central basin with deserts, mountains; small, discontinuous plains along both coasts
Elevation extremes:
lowest point: Caspian Sea -28 m
highest point: Kuh-e Damavand 5,671 m
Natural resources: petroleum, natural gas, coal, chromium, copper, iron ore, lead, manganese, zinc, sulfur
Land use:
arable land: 8.72%
permanent crops: 1.39%
other: 89.89% (2001)
Irrigated land:75,620 sq km (1998 est.)
Natural hazards: periodic droughts, floods; dust storms, sandstorms; earthquakes
Environment - current issues: air pollution, especially in urban areas, from vehicle emissions, refinery operations, and industrial effluents; deforestation; overgrazing; desertification; oil pollution in

the Persian Gulf; wetland losses from drought; soil degradation (salination); inadequate supplies of potable water; water pollution from raw sewage and industrial waste; urbanization

Environment - international agreements:
party to: Biodiversity, Climate Change, Desertification, Endangered Species, Hazardous Wastes, Marine Dumping, Ozone Layer Protection, Wetlands
signed, but not ratified: Environmental Modification, Law of the Sea, Marine Life Conservation

Geography - note: strategic location on the Persian Gulf and Strait of Hormuz, which are vital maritime pathways for crude oil transport

PEOPLE

Population: 68,017,860 (July 2005 est.)

Age structure:
0-14 years: 27.1% (male 9,465,475/female 8,973,828)
15-64 years: 68% (male 23,556,970/female 22,701,065)
65 years and over: 4.9% (male 1,637,512/female 1,683,010) (2005 est.)

Median age:
total: 24.23 years
male: 24.03 years
female: 24.44 years (2005 est.)

Population growth rate: 0.86% (2005 est.)

Birth rate:16.83 births/1,000 population (2005 est.)

Death rate: 5.55 deaths/1,000 population (2005 est.)

Net migration rate: -2.64 migrant(s)/ 1,000 population (2005 est.)

Sex ratio:
at birth: 1.05 male(s)/female
under 15 years: 1.06 male(s)/female
15-64 years: 1.04 male(s)/female
65 years and over: 0.97 male(s)/female
total population: 1.04 male(s)/female (2005 est.)

Infant mortality rate:
total: 41.58 deaths/1,000 live births
male: 41.75 deaths/1,000 live births
female: 41.41 deaths/1,000 live births (2005 est.)

Life expectancy at birth:
total population: 69.96 years
male: 68.58 years
female: 71.4 years (2005 est.)

Total fertility rate: 1.82 children born/ woman (2005 est.)

HIV/AIDS - adult prevalence rate: less than 0.1% (2001 est.)

HIV/AIDS - people living with HIV/AIDS: 31,000 (2001 est.)

HIV/AIDS - deaths: 800 (2003 est.)

Nationality:
noun: Iranian(s)
adjective: Iranian

Ethnic groups: Persian 51%, Azeri 24%, Gilaki and Mazandarani 8%, Kurd 7%, Arab 3%, Lur 2%, Baloch 2%, Turkmen 2%, other 1%

Religions: Shi'a Muslim 89%, Sunni Muslim 9%, Zoroastrian, Jewish, Christian, and Baha'i 2%

Languages: Persian and Persian dialects 58%, Turkic and Turkic dialects 26%, Kurdish 9%, Luri 2%, Balochi 1%, Arabic 1%, Turkish 1%, other 2%

Literacy:
definition: age 15 and over can read and write
total population: 79.4%
male: 85.6%
female: 73% (2003 est.)

GOVERNMENT

Country name:
conventional long form: Islamic Republic of Iran
conventional short form: Iran
local long form: Jomhuri-ye Eslami-ye Iran
local short form: Iran
former: Persia

Government type: theocratic republic

Capital: Tehran

Administrative divisions: 30 provinces (ostanha, singular - ostan); Ardabil, Azarbayjan-e Gharbi, Azarbayjan-e Sharqi, Bushehr, Chahar Mahall va Bakhtiari, Esfahan, Fars, Gilan, Golestan, Hamadan, Hormozgan, Ilam, Kerman, Kermanshah, Khorasan-e Janubi, Khorasan-e Razavi, Khorasan-e Shemali, Khuzestan, Kohgiluyeh va Buyer Ahmad, Kordestan, Lorestan, Markazi, Mazandaran, Qazvin, Qom, Semnan, Sistan va Baluchestan, Tehran, Yazd, Zanjan

Independence: 1 April 1979 (Islamic Republic of Iran proclaimed)

National holiday: Republic Day, 1 April (1979) note: additional holidays celebrated widely in Iran include Revolution Day, 11 February (1979); Noruz (New Year's Day), 21 March; Constitutional Monarchy Day, 5 August (1925); and various Islamic observances which change in accordance with the lunar-based hejira calendar

Constitution: 2-3 December 1979; revised 1989 to expand powers of the presidency and eliminate the prime ministership

Legal system: the Constitution codifies Islamic principles of government

Suffrage: 15 years of age; universal

Executive branch:
chief of state: Supreme Leader Ayatollah Ali Hoseini-KHAMENEI (since 4 June 1989)
head of government: President Mahmud AHMADI-NEJAD (since 3 August 2005) First Vice President Parviz DAVUDI (since 11 September 2005)
cabinet: Council of Ministers selected by the president with legislative approval; the Supreme Leader has some control over appointments to the more sensitive ministries
elections: leader of the Islamic Revolution appointed for life by the Assembly of Experts; president elected by popular vote for a four-year term; election last held 17 June 2005 with a two-candidate runoff on 24 June 2005 (next to be held NA 2009)
election results: Mahmud AHMADI-NEJAD elected president; percent of vote - Mahmud AHMADI-NEJAD 62%, Ali Akbar Hashemi RAFSANJANI 36%; note - 2% of ballots spoiled

Legislative branch: unicameral Islamic Consultative Assembly or Majles-e-Shura-ye-Eslami (290 seats, note - changed from 270 seats with the 18 February 2000 election; members elected by popular vote to serve four-year terms)
elections: last held 20 February 2004 with a runoff held 7 May 2004 (next to be held February 2008)
election results: percent of vote - NA%; seats by party -conservatives/Islamists 190, reformers 50, independents 43, religious minorities 5, and 2 seats unaccounted for

Judicial branch: Supreme Court - above a special clerical court, a revolutionary court, and a special administrative court

Political parties and leaders: formal political parties are a relatively new phenomenon in Iran and most conservatives still prefer to work through political pressure groups rather than parties; a loose pro-reform coalition called the 2nd Khordad front, which includes political parties as well as less formal pressure groups and organizations, achieved considerable success at elections to the sixth Majles in early 2000; groups in the coalition include: Islamic Iran Participation Front (IIPF); Executives of Construction Party (Kargozaran); Solidarity Party; Islamic Labor Party; Mardom Salari; Mojahedin of the Islamic Revolution Organization(MIRO); and Militant Clerics Society (Ruhaniyun); the coalition participated in the seventh Majles elections in early 2004; a new apparently conservative group, the Builders of Islamic Iran, took aleading position in the new Majles after winning a majority of the seats in February 2004

Political pressure groups and leaders: political pressure groups conduct most of Iran's political activities; groups that generally support the Islamic Republic include Ansar-e Hizballah, Muslim Students Following the Line of the

Imam, Tehran Militant Clergy Association (Ruhaniyat), Islamic Coalition Party (Motalefeh), and Islamic Engineers Society; active pro-reform student groups include the Organization for Strengthening Unity; opposition groups include Freedom Movement of Iran, the National Front, Marz-e Por Gohar, and various ethnic and Monarchist organizations; armed political groups that have been almost completely repressed by the government include Mujahidin-e Khalq Organization (MEK), People's Fedayeen, Democratic Party of Iranian Kurdistan, and Komala
International organization participation: ABEDA, CP, ECO, FAO, G-15, G-24, G-77, IAEA, IBRD, ICAO, ICC, ICCt (signatory), ICRM, IDA, IDB, IFAD, IFC, IFRCS, IHO, ILO, IMF, IMO, Interpol, IOC, IOM, ISO, ITU, MIGA, NAM, OIC, OPCW, OPEC, PCA, SCO (observer), UN, UNCTAD, UNESCO, UNHCR, UNIDO, UNMEE, UPU, WCL, WCO, WFTU, WHO, WIPO, WMO, WToO, WTO (observer)
Diplomatic representation in the US: none; note - Iran has an Interests Section in the Pakistani Embassy; address: Iranian Interests Section, Pakistani Embassy, 2209 Wisconsin Avenue NW, Washington, DC 20007; telephone: [1] (202) 965-4990; FAX [1] (202) 965-1073
Diplomatic representation from the US: none; note - protecting power in Iran is Switzerland
Flag description: three equal horizontal bands of green (top), white, and red; the national emblem (a stylized representation of the word Allah in the shape of a tulip, a symbol of martyrdom) in red is centered in the white band; ALLAH AKBAR (God is Great) in white Arabic script is repeated 11 times along the bottom edge of the green band and 11 times along the top edge of the red band

ECONOMY

Economy - overview: Iran's economy is marked by a bloated, inefficient state sector, over reliance on the oil sector, and statist policies that create major distortions throughout. Most economic activity is controlled by the state. Private sector activity is typically small-scale - workshops, farming, and services. President KHATAMI has continued to follow the market reform plans of former President RAFSANJANI, with limited progress. Relatively high oil prices in recent years have enabled Iran to amass some $40 billion in foreign exchange reserves, but have not eased economic hardships such as high unemployment and inflation. The proportion of the economy devoted to the development of weapons of mass destruction remains a contentious issue with leading Western nations.
GDP (purchasing power parity): $551.6 billion (2005 est.)
GDP (official exchange rate): $182.5 billion (2005 est.)
GDP - real growth rate: 4.8% (2005 est.)
GDP - per capita: purchasing power parity - $8,100 (2005 est.)
GDP - composition by sector: agriculture: 11.8%
industry: 43.3%
services: 44.9% (2005 est.)
Labor force:23.68 million
note: shortage of skilled labor (2005 est.)
Labor force - by occupation: agriculture 30%, industry 25%, services 45%
(2001 est.)
Unemployment rate:11.2% (2004 est.) 40% (2002 est.)
Household income or consumption by percentage share:
lowest 10%: NA
highest 10%: NA
Inflation rate (consumer prices):16% (2005 est.)
Investment (gross fixed): 30.5% of GDP (2005 est.)
Budget:
revenues: $48.82 billion
expenditures: $60.4 billion, including capital expenditures of $7.6 billion (2005 est.)
Public debt: 27.5% of GDP (2005 est.)
Agriculture - products: wheat, rice, other grains, sugar beets, fruits, nuts, cotton; dairy products, wool; caviar
Industries: petroleum, petrochemicals, textiles, cement and other construction materials, food processing (particularly sugar refining and vegetable oil production), metal fabrication, armaments
Industrial production growth rate: 3% excluding oil (2005 est.)
Electricity - production: 142.3 billion kWh (2003)
Electricity - production by source:
fossil fuel: 97.1%
hydro: 2.9%
nuclear: 0%
other: 0% (2001)
Electricity - consumption: 132.1 billion kWh (2003)
Electricity - exports: 840 million kWh (2003)
Electricity - imports: 600 million kWh (2003)
Oil - production: 3.979 million bbl/day (2005 est.)
Oil - consumption: 1.425 million bbl/day (2003 est.)
Oil - exports: 2.5 million bbl/day (2004 est.)
Oil - imports: NA (2001)
Oil - proved reserves: 133.3 billion bbl (2005 est.)
Natural gas - production: 79 billion cu m (2003 est.)
Natural gas - consumption: 72.4 billion cu m (2003 est.)
Natural gas - exports: 3.4 billion cu m (2003 est.)
Natural gas - imports: 4.92 billion cu m (2003 est.)
Natural gas - proved reserves: 26.7 trillion cu m (2005)
Current account balance: $8.179 billion (2005 est.)
Exports: $55.42 billion f.o.b. (2005 est.)
Exports - partners: Japan 18.4%, China 9.7%, Italy 6%, South Africa 5.8%, South Korea 5.4%, Taiwan 4.6%, Turkey 4.4%, Netherlands 4% (2004)
Imports: $42.5 billion f.o.b. (2005 est.)
Imports - partners: Germany 12.8%, France 8.3%, Italy 7.7%, China 7.2%, UAE 7.2%, South Korea 6.1%, Russia 5.4% (2004)
Reserves of foreign exchange and gold: $40.06 billion (2005 est.)
Debt - external: $16.94 billion (2005 est.)
Economic aid - recipient: $408 million (2002 est.)
Currency (code): Iranian rial (IRR)
Currency code: IRR
Exchange rates: rials per US dollar - 9,040.26 (2005), 8,614 (2004), 8,193.9 (2003), 6,907 (2002), 1,753.6 (2001) note: Iran has been using a managed floating exchange rate regime since unifying multiple exchange rates in March 2002
Fiscal year: 21 March - 20 March

COMMUNICATIONS

Telephones - main lines in use: 14,571,100 (2003)
Telephones - mobile cellular: 3,376,500 (2003)
Telephone system:
general assessment: inadequate but currently being modernized and expanded with the goal of not only improving the efficiency and increasing the volume of the urban service but also bringing telephone service to several thousand villages, not presently connected
domestic: as a result of heavy investing in the telephone system since 1994, the number of long-distance channels in the microwave radio relay trunk has grown substantially; many villages have been brought into the net; the number of main lines in the urban systems has approximately doubled; and thousands of mobile cellular subscribers are being served; moreover, the technical level of the system has been raised by the installation of thousands of digital switches

international: country code - 98; HF radio and microwave radio relay to Turkey, Azerbaijan, Pakistan, Afghanistan, Turkmenistan, Syria, Kuwait, Tajikistan, and Uzbekistan; submarine fiber-optic cable to UAE with access to Fiber-Optic Link Around the Globe (FLAG); Trans-Asia-Europe (TAE) fiber-optic line runs from Azerbaijan through the northern portion of Iran to Turkmenistan with expansion to Georgia and Azerbaijan; satellite earth stations - 9 Intelsat and 4 Inmarsat

Radio broadcast stations: AM 72, FM 5, shortwave 5 (1998)

Radios: 17 million (1997)

Television broadcast stations: 28 (plus 450 low-power repeaters) (1997)

Televisions: 4.61 million (1997)

Internet country code: .ir

Internet hosts: 5,269 (2004)

Internet Service Providers (ISPs): 100 (2002)

Internet users: 4.3 million (2003)

TRANSPORTATION

Airports: 305 (2004 est.)

Airports - with paved runways:

total: 129

over 3,047 m: 40

2,438 to 3,047 m: 26

1,524 to 2,437 m: 25

914 to 1,523 m: 33

under 914 m: 5 (2005 est.)

Airports - with unpaved runways:

total: 181

over 3,047 m: 1

1,524 to 2,437 m: 8

914 to 1,523 m: 130

under 914 m: 42 (2005 est.)

Heliports :15 (2005 est.)

Pipelines: condensate/gas 212 km; gas 16,998 km; liquid petroleum gas 570 km; oil 8,256 km; refined products 7,808 km (2004)

Railways:

total: 7,203 km

broad gauge: 94 km 1.676-m gauge

standard gauge: 7,109 km 1.435-m gauge (189 km electrified) (2004)

Roadways: total: 178,152 km

paved: 118,115 km (including 751 km of expressways)

unpaved: 60,037 km (2002)

Waterways: 850 km (on Karun River and Lake Urmia) (2004)

Merchant marine:

total: 144 ships (1,000 GRT or over) 4,715,242 GRT/8,240,069 DWT

by type: bulk carrier 38, cargo 49, chemical tanker 4, container 14, liquefied gas 1, passenger 1, passenger/cargo 5, petroleum tanker 30, roll on/roll off 2

foreign-owned: 1 (UAE 1)

registered in other countries: 8 (2005)

Ports and terminals: Assaluyeh, Bushehr

MILITARY

Military branches:

Islamic Republic of Iran Regular Forces (Artesh): Ground Forces, Navy, Air Force (includes Air Defense)

Islamic Revolutionary Guard Corps (Sepah-e Pasdaran-e Enqelab-e Eslami, IRGC): Ground Forces, Navy, Air Force, Qods Force (special operations), and Basij Force (Popular Mobilization Army)

Law Enforcement Forces: (2004)

Military service age and obligation: 18 years of age for compulsory military service; 16 years of age for volunteers; soldiers as young as 9 were recruited extensively during the Iran-Iraq War; conscript service obligation - 18 months (2004)

Manpower available for military service: *males age 18-49:* 18,319,545 (2005 est.)

Manpower fit for military service: *males age 18-49:* 15,665,725 (2005 est.)

Manpower reaching military service age annually: *males:* 862,056 (2005 est.)

Military expenditures - dollar figure: $4.3 billion (2003 est.)

Military expenditures - percent of GDP: 3.3% (2003 est.)

TRANSNATIONAL ISSUES

Disputes - international: Iran protests Afghanistan's limiting flow of dammed tributaries to the Helmand River in periods of drought; Iraq's lack of a maritime boundary with Iran prompts jurisdiction disputes beyond the mouth of the Shatt al Arab in the Persian Gulf; Iran and UAE engage in direct talks and solicit Arab League support to resolve disputes over Iran's occupation of Tunb Islands and Abu Musa Island; Iran stands alone among littoral states in insisting upon a division of the Caspian Sea into five equal sectors

Refugees and internally displaced persons: *refugees (country of origin):* 1,223,823 (Afghanistan) 124,014 (Iraq) (2004)

Illicit drugs: despite substantial interdiction efforts, Iran remains a key transshipment point for Southwest Asian heroin to Europe; domestic narcotics consumption remains a persistent problem and according to official Iranian statistics there are at least two million drug users in the country; lax anti-money-laundering regulations

IRAQ

INTRODUCTION

Background: Formerly part of the Ottoman Empire, Iraq was occupied by Britain during the course of World War I; in 1920, it was declared a League of Nations mandate under UK administration. In stages over the next dozen years, Iraq attained its independence as a kingdom in 1932. A "republic" was proclaimed in 1958, but in actuality a series of military strongmen ruled the country, the latest was SADDAM Husayn. Territorial disputes with Iran led to an inconclusive and costly eight-year war (1980-88). In August 1990, Iraq seized Kuwait, but was expelled by US-led, UN coalition forces during the Gulf War of January-February 1991. Following Kuwait's liberation, the UN Security Council (UNSC) required Iraq to scrap all weapons of mass destruction and long-range missiles and to allow UN verification inspections. Continued Iraqi noncompliance with UNSC resolutions over a period of 12 years resulted in the US-led invasion of Iraq in March 2003 and the ouster of the SADDAM Husayn regime. Coalition forces remain in Iraq, helping to restore degraded infrastructure and facilitating the establishment of a freely elected government, while simultaneously dealing with a robust insurgency. The Coalition Provisional Authority transferred sovereignty to the Iraqi Interim Government (IG) in June 2004. Iraqis voted on 30 January 2005 to elect a 275-member Transitional National Assembly and voted on 15 December 2005 to elect a 275-member Council of Representatives that will finalize a permanent constitution.

GEOGRAPHY

Location: Middle East, bordering the Persian Gulf, between Iran and Kuwait
Geographic coordinates: 33 00 N, 44 00 E
Map references: Middle East
Area:
total: 437,072 sq km
land: 432,162 sq km
water: 4,910 sq km
Area - comparative: slightly more than twice the size of Idaho
Land boundaries: total: 3,650 km
border countries: Iran 1,458 km, Jordan 181 km, Kuwait 240 km, Saudi Arabia 814 km, Syria 605 km, Turkey 352 km
Coastline: 58 km
Maritime claims:
territorial sea: 12 nm
continental shelf: not specified
Climate: mostly desert; mild to cool winters with dry, hot, cloudless summers; northern mountainous regions along Iranian and Turkish borders experience cold winters with occasionally heavy snows that melt in early spring, sometimes causing extensive flooding in central and southern Iraq
Terrain: mostly broad plains; reedy marshes along Iranian border in south with large flooded areas; mountains along borders with Iran and Turkey
Elevation extremes:
lowest point: Persian Gulf 0 m
highest point: unnamed peak; 3,611 m; note - this peak is not Gundah Zhur 3,607 m or Kuh-e Hajji-Ebrahim 3,595 m
Natural resources: petroleum, natural gas, phosphates, sulfur
Land use:
arable land: 13.15%
permanent crops: 0.78%
other: 86.07% (2001)
Irrigated land: 35,250 sq km (1998 est.)
Natural hazards: dust storms, sandstorms, floods
Environment - current issues: government water control projects have drained most of the inhabited marsh areas east of An Nasiriyah by drying up or diverting the feeder streams and rivers; a once sizable population of Marsh Arabs, who inhabited these areas for thousands of years, has been displaced; furthermore, the destruction of the natural habitat poses serious threats to the area's wildlife populations; inadequate supplies of potable water; development of the Tigris and Euphrates rivers system contingent upon agreements with upstream riparian Turkey; air and water pollution; soil degradation (salination) and erosion; desertification
Environment - international agreements:
party to: Law of the Sea
signed, but not ratified: Environmental Modification
Geography - note: strategic location on Shatt al Arab waterway and at the head of the Persian Gulf

PEOPLE

Population: 26,074,906 (July 2005 est.)
Age structure:
0-14 years: 40% (male 5,293,709/female 5,130,826)
15-64 years: 57% (male 7,530,619/female 7,338,109)
65 years and over: 3% (male 367,832/female 413,811) (2005 est.)
Median age:
total: 19.43 years
male: 19.35 years
female: 19.51 years (2005 est.)
Population growth rate: 2.7% (2005 est.)
Birth rate: 32.5 births/1,000 population (2005 est.)
Death rate: 5.49 deaths/1,000 population (2005 est.)
Net migration rate: 0 migrant(s)/1,000 population (2005 est.)
Sex ratio:
at birth: 1.05 male(s)/female
under 15 years: 1.03 male(s)/female
15-64 years: 1.03 male(s)/female
65 years and over: 0.89 male(s)/female
total population: 1.02 male(s)/female (2005 est.)
Infant mortality rate:
total: 50.25 deaths/1,000 live births
male: 56.06 deaths/1,000 live births
female: 44.14 deaths/1,000 live births (2005 est.)
Life expectancy at birth:
total population: 68.7 years
male: 67.49 years
female: 69.97 years (2005 est.)
Total fertility rate: 4.28 children born/woman (2005 est.)
HIV/AIDS - adult prevalence rate: less than 0.1% (2001 est.)
HIV/AIDS - people living with HIV/AIDS: less than 500 (2003 est.)
HIV/AIDS - deaths: NA
Nationality:
noun: Iraqi(s)
adjective: Iraqi
Ethnic groups: Arab 75%-80%, Kurdish 15%-20%, Turkoman, Assyrian or other 5%
Religions: Muslim 97% (Shi'a 60%-65%, Sunni 32%-37%), Christian or other 3%
Languages: Arabic, Kurdish (official in Kurdish regions), Assyrian, Armenian
Literacy:
definition: age 15 and over can read and write
total population: 40.4%
male: 55.9%
female: 24.4% (2003 est.)

GOVERNMENT

Country name:
conventional long form: Republic of Iraq
conventional short form: Iraq
local long form: Al Jumhuriyah al Iraqiyah
local short form: Al Iraq
Government type: none; note - the Iraqi Transitional Government (ITG) was elected on 30 January 2005
Capital: Baghdad
Administrative divisions: 18 governorates (muhafazat, singular - muhafazah); Al Anbar, Al Basrah, Al Muthanna, Al Qadisiyah, An Najaf, Arbil, As Sulaymaniyah, At Ta'mim, Babil, Baghdad, Dahuk, Dhi Qar, Diyala, Karbala', Maysan, Ninawa, Salah ad Din, Wasit
Independence: 3 October 1932 (from League of Nations mandate under British administration); note - on 28 June 2004 the Coalition Provisional Authority transferred sovereignty to the Iraqi Interim Government
National holiday: Revolution Day, 17 July (1968); note - this holiday was celebrated under the SADDAM Husayn regime but the Iraqi Interim Government has yet to declare a new national holiday
Constitution: interim constitution signed 8 March 2004; note – the Transitional Administrative Law (TAL) was enacted 8 March 2004 to govern the country until an elected Iraqi Government can finalize a new constitution in 2006
Legal system: based on civil and Islamic law under the Iraqi Interim
Government (IG) and Transitional Administrative Law (TAL)
Suffrage: formerly 18 years of age; universal
Executive branch:
chief of state: Iraqi Transitional Government (ITG) President Jalal TALABANI (since 6 April 2005); Deputy Presidents Adil Abd AL-MAHDI and Ghazi al-Ujayl al-YAWR (since 6 April 2005); note – the President and Deputy Presidents comprise the Presidency Council)
head of government: Iraqi Transitional Government (ITG) Prime Minister Ibrahim al-JAFARI (since April 2005); Deputy Prime Ministers Rowsch SHAWAYS, Ahmad CHALABI, and Abid al-Mutlaq al-JABBURI (since May 2005) cabinet: 32 ministers appointed by the Presidency Council, plus Prime Minister Ibrahim al-JAFARI, Deputy Prime Ministers Rowsch SHAWAYS, Ahmad CHALABI, and Abid al-Mutlaq al-JABBURI
elections: held 15 December 2005 to elect a 275-member Council of Representatives that will finalize a permanent constitution

Legislative branch: unicameral Council of Representatives or Mejlis Watani (consisting of 275 members elected by a closed-list, proportional-representation system)
elections: held 15 December 2005 to elect a 275-member Council of Representatives that will finalize a permanent constitution
election results: Council of Representatives - percent of vote by party - NA; number of seats by party - NA
Judicial branch: Supreme Court appointed by the Prime Minister, confirmed by the Presidency Council
Political parties and leaders: Al-Sadr Movement [Muqtada Al-SADR]; Assyrian Democratic Movement [Yunadim KANNA]; Conference of Iraqi People [Adnan al-DULAYMI]; Constitutional Monarchy Movement or CMM [Sharif Ali Bin al-HUSAYN]; Da'wa Party [Ibrahim al-JA'FARI]; Independent Iraqi Alliance or IIA [Falah al-NAQIB]; Iraqi Communist Party [Hamid al-MUSA]; Iraqi Hizballah [Karim Mahud al-MUHAMMADAWI]; Iraqi Independent Democrats or IID [Adnan PACHACHI, Mahdi al-HAFIZ]; Iraqi Islamic Party or IIP [Muhsin Abdal-HAMID, Hajim al-HASSANI]; Iraqi National Accord or INA [Ayad ALLAWI]; Iraqi National Congress or INC [Ahmad CHALABI]; Iraqi National Council for Dialogue or INCD [Khalaf Ulayan al-Khalifawi al-DULAYMI]; Iraqi National Unity Movement or INUM [Ahmad al-KUBAYSI, chairman]; Islamic Action Organization or IAO [Ayatollah Muhammad al-MUDARRISI]; Jama'at al Fadilah or JAF [Ayatollah Muhammad ' Ali al-YAQUBI]; Kurdistan Democratic Party or KDP [Masud BARZANI]; Muslim Ulama Council or MUC [Harith Sulayman al-DARI, secretary general]; National Iraqi Front [Salih al-MUTLAQ]; National Reconciliation and Liberation Party [Mishan al-JABBURI]; Patriotic Union of Kurdistan or PUK [Jalal TALABANI]; Supreme Council for the Islamic Revolution in Iraq or SCIRI [Abd al-Aziz al-HAKIM] note: the Kurdish Alliance, the National Iraqi List, the Iraqi Consensus Front, the Iraqi Front for National Dialogue, and the United Iraqi Alliance were only electoral slates consisting of the representatives from the various Iraqi political parties
Political pressure groups and leaders: an insurgency against the Iraqi Transitional Government and Coalition forces is primarily concentrated in Baghdad and in areas west and north of the capital; the diverse, multigroup insurgency is led principally by Sunni Arabs whose only common denominator is a shared desire to oust the Coalition and end US influence in Iraq
International organization participation: ABEDA, AFESD, AMF, CAEU, FAO, G-77, IAEA, IBRD, ICAO, ICRM, IDA, IDB, IFAD, IFC, IFRCS, ILO, IMF, IMO, Interpol, IOC, ISO, ITU, LAS, NAM, OAPEC, OIC, OPEC, PCA, UN, UNCTAD, UNESCO, UNIDO, UPU, WCO, WFTU, WHO, WIPO, WMO, WToO, WTO (observer)
Diplomatic representation in the US:
chief of mission: Ambassador (vacant)
chancery: 1801 P Street, NW, Washington, D.C. 20036
telephone: [1] (202) 483-7500
FAX: [1] (202) 462-5066
Diplomatic representation from the US:
chief of mission: Ambassador Zalmay KHALILZAD; Deputy Chief of Mission David M. SATTERFIELD
embassy: Baghdad
mailing address: APO AE 09316
telephone: 00-1-240-553-0584 ext. 5340 OR 5635; note - Consular Section
FAX: NA
Flag description: three equal horizontal bands of red (top), white, and black with three green five-pointed stars in a horizontal line centered in the white band; the phrase ALLAHU AKBAR (God is Great) in green Arabic script - Allahu to the right of the middle star and Akbar to the left of the middle star - was added in January 1991 during the Persian Gulf crisis; similar to the flag of Syria, which has two stars but no script, Yemen, which has a plain white band, and that of Egypt which has a gold Eagle of Saladin centered in the white band; design is based upon the Arab Liberation colors

ECONOMY

Economy - overview: Iraq's economy is dominated by the oil sector, which has traditionally provided about 95% of foreign exchange earnings. Iraq's seizure of Kuwait in August 1990, subsequent international economic sanctions, and damage from military action by an international coalition beginning in January 1991 drastically reduced economic activity. Although government policies supporting large military and internal security forces and allocating resources to key supporters of the regime hurt the economy, implementation of the UN's oil-for-food program beginning in December 1996 helped improve conditions for the average Iraqi citizen. Iraq was allowed to export limited amounts of oil in exchange for food, medicine, and some infrastructure spare parts. In December 1999, the UN Security Council authorized Iraq to export under the program as much oil as required to meet humanitarian needs. Per capita food imports increased significantly, while medical supplies and health care services steadily improved. Per capita output and living standards were still well below the pre-1991 level, but any estimates have a wide range of error. The military victory of the US-led coalition in March-April 2003 resulted in the shutdown of much of the central economic administrative structure. Although a comparatively small amount of capital plant was damaged during the hostilities, looting, insurgent attacks and sabotage have undermined efforts to rebuild the economy. Attacks on key economic facilities - especially oil pipelines and infrastructure - have prevented Iraq from reaching projected export volumes, but total government revenues have been higher than anticipated due to high oil prices. Despite political uncertainty, Iraq has established the institutions needed to implement economic policy, has successfully concluded a three-stage debt reduction agreement with the Paris Club, and is working toward a Standby Arrangement with the IMF. The Standby Arrangement would clear the way for continued debt relief from the Paris Club.
GDP (purchasing power parity): $94.1 billion (2005 est.)
GDP (official exchange rate): $46.5 billion (2005 est.)
GDP - real growth rate: 2.4% (2005 est.)
GDP - per capita: purchasing power parity - $3,400 (2005 est.)
GDP - composition by sector:
agriculture: 7.3%
industry: 66.6%
services: 26.1% (2004 est.)
Labor force: 7.4 million (2004 est.)
Labor force - by occupation: agriculture NA, industry NA, services NA
Unemployment rate: 25% to 30% (2005 est.)
Population below poverty line: NA
Household income or consumption by percentage share:
lowest 10%: NA
highest 10%: NA
Inflation rate (consumer prices): 40% (2005 est.)
Budget:
revenues: $19.3 billion
expenditures: $24 billion, including capital expenditures of $5 billion (2005 budget)
Agriculture - products: wheat, barley, rice, vegetables, dates, cotton; cattle, sheep, poultry
Industries: petroleum, chemicals, textiles, construction materials, food processing, fertilizer, metal fabrication/processing

Industrial production growth rate: NA
Electricity - production: 31.7 billion kWh (2005)
Electricity - production by source:
fossil fuel: 98.4%
hydro: 1.6%
nuclear: 0%
other: 0% (2001)
Electricity - consumption: 33.3 billion kWh (2005)
Electricity - exports: 0 kWh (2005)
Electricity - imports: 2.02 billion kWh (2005)
Oil - production: 2.093 million bbl/day (2004 est.); note - prewar production (in 2002) was 2.03 million bbl/day (2005 est.)
Oil - consumption: 351,500 bbl/day (2005 est.)
Oil - exports: 1.42 million bbl/day (2005 est.)
Oil - imports: NA (2005)
Oil - proved reserves: 112.5 billion bbl (2005 est.)
Natural gas - production: 2.35 billion cu m (2002 est.)
Natural gas – consumption: 2.35 billion cu m (2002 est.)
Natural gas - exports: 0 cu m (2004 est.)
Natural gas - imports: 0 cu m (2004 est.)
Natural gas - proved reserves: 3.149 trillion cu m (2005)
Current account balance: $-9.447 billion (2004 est.)
Exports: $17.78 billion f.o.b. (2004)
Exports - partners: US 51.9%, Spain 7.3%, Japan 6.6%, Italy 5.7%, Canada 5.2% (2004)
Imports: $19.57 billion f.o.b. (2004)
Imports - partners: Syria 22.9%, Turkey 19.5%, US 9.2%, Jordan 6.7%,Germany 4.9% (2004)
Reserves of foreign exchange and gold: $8.4 billion (2005 est.)
Debt - external: $82.1 billion (2005 est.)
Economic aid - recipient: more than $33 billion in foreign aid pledged for 2004-07 (2004)
Currency (code): New Iraqi dinar (NID) as of 22 January 2004
Currency code: NID, IQD prior to 22 January 2004
Exchange rates: New Iraqi dinars per US dollar - 1,475 (2005), 1,890 (second half, 2003), 0.3109 (2002), 0.3109 (2001)
Fiscal year: calendar year

COMMUNICATIONS

Telephones - main lines in use: 675,000; note - an unknown number of telephone lines were damaged or destroyed during the March-April 2003 war (2003)
Telephones - mobile cellular: 20,000 (2002)
Telephone system:
general assessment: the 2003 war severely disrupted telecommunications throughout Iraq including international connections; USAID is overseeing the repair of switching capability and the construction of mobile and satellite communication facilities
domestic: repairs to switches and lines destroyed in the recent fighting continue, but sabotage remains a problem; cellular service is expected to be in place within two years
international: country code - 964; satellite earth stations - 2 Intelsat (1 Atlantic Ocean and 1 Indian Ocean), 1 Intersputnik (Atlantic Ocean region), and 1 Arabsat (inoperative); coaxial cable and microwave radiorelay to Jordan, Kuwait, Syria, and Turkey; Kuwait line is probably nonoperational
Radio broadcast stations: after 17 months of unregulated media growth, there are approximately 80 radio stations on the air inside Iraq (2004)
Radios: 4.85 million (1997)
Television broadcast stations: 21 (2004)
Televisions: 1.75 million (1997)
Internet country code: .iq
Internet Service Providers (ISPs): 1 (2000)
Internet users: 25,000 (2002)

TRANSPORTATION

Airports: 111; note - unknown number were damaged during the March-April 2003 war (2004 est.)
Airports - with paved runways:
total: 78
over 3,047 m: 20
2,438 to 3,047 m: 37
1,524 to 2,437 m: 5
914 to 1,523 m: 7
under 914 m: 9 (2005 est.)
Airports - with unpaved runways:
total: 33
over 3,047 m: 2
2,438 to 3,047 m: 4
1,524 to 2,437 m: 5
914 to 1,523 m: 12
under 914 m: 10 (2005 est.)
Heliports: 8 (2005 est.)
Pipelines: gas 1,739 km; oil 5,418 km; refined products 1,343 km (2004)
Railways:
total: 2,200 km
standard gauge: 2,200 km 1.435-m gauge (2004)
Roadways:
total: 45,550 km
paved: 38,399 km
unpaved: 7,151 km (1999)
Waterways: 5,275 km (not all navigable)
note: Euphrates River (2,815 km), Tigris River (1,895 km), and Third River (565 km) are principal waterways (2004)
Merchant marine:
total: 14 ships (1,000 GRT or over) 83,221 GRT/125,255 DWT
by type: cargo 11, petroleum tanker 3 (2005)
Ports and terminals: Al Basrah, Khawr az Zubayr, Umm Qasr

MILITARY

Military branches:
Iraqi Armed Forces: Iraqi Regular Army (includes Iraqi Special Operations Force, Iraqi Intervention Force), Iraqi Navy (former Iraqi Coastal Defense Force), Iraqi Air Force (former Iraqi Army Air Corps) (2005)
Military service age and obligation: 18 years of age; the Iraqi Interim Government is creating a new professional Iraqi military force of men aged 18 to 40 to defend Iraq from external threats and the current insurgency (2004)
Manpower available for military service:
males age 18-49: 5,870,640 (2005 est.)
Manpower fit for military service: *males age 18-49:* 4,930,074 (2005 est.)
Manpower reaching military service age annually: *males:* 298,518 (2005 est.)
Military expenditures - dollar figure: $1.3 billion (FY00)
Military expenditures - percent of GDP: NA

TRANSNATIONAL ISSUES

Disputes - international: coalition forces assist Iraqis in monitoring boundary security; Iraq's lack of a maritime boundary with Iran prompts jurisdiction disputes beyond the mouth of the Shatt al Arab in the Persian Gulf; Turkey has expressed concern over the status of Kurds in Iraq
Refugees and internally displaced persons:
refugees (country of origin): 150,000 (Palestinian Territories)
IDPs: 1,340,280 (ongoing US-led war and Kurds' subsequent return) (2004)

IRELAND

INTRODUCTION

Background: Celtic tribes arrived on the island between 600-150 B.C. Invasions by Norsemen that began in the late 8th century were finally ended when King Brian BORU defeated the Danes in 1014. English invasions began in the 12th century and set off more than seven centuries of Anglo-Irish struggle marked by fierce rebellions and harsh repressions. A failed 1916 Easter Monday Rebellion touched off several years of guerrilla warfare that in 1921 resulted in independence from the UK for 26 southern counties; six northern (Ulster) counties remained part of the United Kingdom. In 1948 Ireland withdrew from the British Commonwealth; it joined the European Community in 1973. Irish governments have sought the peaceful unification of Ireland and have cooperated with Britain against terrorist groups. A peace settlement for Northern Ireland, known as the Good Friday Agreement and approved in 1998, is being implemented with some difficulties.

GEOGRAPHY

Location: Western Europe, occupying five-sixths of the island of Ireland in the North Atlantic Ocean, west of Great Britain
Geographic coordinates: 53 00 N, 8 00 W
Map references: Europe
Area:
total: 70,280 sq km
land: 68,890 sq km
water: 1,390 sq km
Area - comparative: slightly larger than West Virginia
Land boundaries:
total: 360 km
border countries: UK 360 km
Coastline: 1,448 km
Maritime claims:
territorial sea: 12 nm
exclusive fishing zone: 200 nm
Climate: temperate maritime; modified by North Atlantic Current; mild winters, cool summers; consistently humid; overcast about half the time
Terrain: mostly level to rolling interior plain surrounded by rugged hills and low mountains; sea cliffs on west coast
Elevation extremes:
lowest point: Atlantic Ocean 0 m
highest point: Carrauntoohil 1,041 m
Natural resources: natural gas, peat, copper, lead, zinc, silver, barite, gypsum, limestone, dolomite
Land use:
arable land: 15.2%
permanent crops: 0.03%
other: 84.77% (2001)
Irrigated land: NA sq km
Natural hazards: NA
Environment - current issues: water pollution, especially of lakes, from agricultural runoff
Environment - international agreements:
party to: Air Pollution, Air Pollution-Nitrogen Oxides, Air Pollution-Sulfur 94, Biodiversity, Climate Change, Climate Change-Kyoto Protocol, Desertification, Endangered Species, Environmental Modification, Hazardous Wastes, Law of the Sea, Marine Dumping, Ozone Layer Protection, Ship Pollution, Tropical Timber83, Tropical Timber 94, Wetlands, Whaling
signed, but not ratified: Air Pollution-Persistent Organic Pollutants, Marine Life Conservation
Geography - note: strategic location on major air and sea routes between North America and northern Europe; over 40% of the population resides within 100 km of Dublin

PEOPLE

Population: 4,015,676 (July 2005 est.)
Age structure:
0-14 years: 20.9% (male 434,225/female 406,730)
15-64 years: 67.5% (male 1,358,086/female 1,354,148)
65 years and over: 11.5% (male 203,614/female 258,873) (2005 est.)
Median age:
total: 33.7 years
male: 32.9 years
female: 34.49 years (2005 est.)
Population growth rate: 1.16% (2005 est.)
Birth rate: 14.47 births/1,000 population (2005 est.)
Death rate: 7.85 deaths/1,000 population (2005 est.)
Net migration rate: 4.93 migrant(s)/1,000 population (2005 est.)
Sex ratio:
at birth: 1.07 male(s)/female
under 15 years: 1.07 male(s)/female
15-64 years: 1 male(s)/female
65 years and over: 0.79 male(s)/female
total population: 0.99 male(s)/female (2005 est.)
Infant mortality rate:
total: 5.39 deaths/1,000 live births
male: 5.91 deaths/1,000 live births
female: 4.84 deaths/1,000 live births (2005 est.)
Life expectancy at birth:
total population: 77.56 years
male: 74.95 years
female: 80.34 years (2005 est.)
Total fertility rate: 1.87 children born/woman (2005 est.)
HIV/AIDS - adult prevalence rate: 0.1% (2001 est.)
HIV/AIDS - people living with HIV/AID: 2,800 (2001 est.)
HIV/AIDS - deaths: less than 100 (2003 est.)
Nationality:
noun: Irishman (men), Irishwoman (women), Irish (collective plural)
adjective: Irish
Ethnic groups: Celtic, English
Religions: Roman Catholic 88.4%, Church of Ireland 3%, other Christian 1.6%, other 1.5%, unspecified 2%, none 3.5% (2002 census)
Languages: English (official) is the language generally used, Irish (official) (Gaelic or Gaeilge) spoken mainly in areas located along the western seaboard
Literacy:
definition: age 15 and over can read and write
total population: 98% (1981 est.)
male: NA%
female: NA%

GOVERNMENT

Country name:
conventional long form: none
conventional short form: Ireland
local long form: none
local short form: Eire
Government type: parliamentary democracy
Capital: Dublin
Administrative divisions: 26 counties; Carlow, Cavan, Clare, Cork, Donegal, Dublin, Galway, Kerry, Kildare, Kilkenny, Laois, Leitrim, Limerick, Longford, Louth, Mayo, Meath, Monaghan, Offaly, Roscommon, Sligo, Tipperary, Waterford, Westmeath, Wexford, Wicklow note: Cavan, Donegal, and Monaghan are part of Ulster Province
Independence: 6 December 1921 (from UK by treaty)

National holiday: Saint Patrick's Day, 17 March
Constitution: adopted 1 July 1937 by plebiscite; effective 29 December 1937
Legal system: based on English common law, substantially modified by indigenous concepts; judicial review of legislative acts in Supreme Court; has not accepted compulsory ICJ jurisdiction
Suffrage: 18 years of age; universal
Executive branch:
chief of state: President Mary MCALEESE (since 11 November 1997)
head of government: Prime Minister Bertie AHERN (since 26 June 1997)
cabinet: Cabinet appointed by the president with previous nomination by the prime minister and approval of the House of Representatives
elections: president elected by popular vote for a seven-year term; election last held 31 October 1997 (next scheduled for October 2011); note - Mary MCALEESE appointed to a second term when no other candidate qualified for the 2004 presidential election; prime minister nominated by the House of Representatives and appointed by the president
election results: Mary MCALEESE elected president; percent of vote – Mar MCALEESE 44.8%, Mary BANOTTI 29.6%
note: government coalition - Fianna Fail and the Progressive Democrats
Legislative branch: bicameral Parliament or Oireachtas consists of the Senate or Seanad Eireann (60 seats - 49 elected by the universities and from candidates put forward by five vocational panels, 11 are nominated by the prime minister; members serve five-year terms) and the House of Representatives or Dail Eireann (166 seats; members are elected by popular vote on the basis of proportional representation to serve five-year terms)
elections: Senate - last held 16 and 17 July 2002 (next to be held by July 2007); House of Representatives - last held 17 May 2002 (next to be held by May 2007)
election results: Senate - percent of vote by party - NA%; seats by party - Fianna Fail 30, Fine Gael 15, Labor Party 5, Progressive Democrats 4, independents and others 6; House of Representatives - percent of vote by party - Fianna Fail 41.5%, Fine Gael 22.5%, Labor Party 10.8%, Sinn Fein 6.5%, Progressive Democrats 4.0%, Green Party 3.8%, others 10.9%; seats by party - Fianna Fail 81, Fine Gael 31, Labor Party 21, Progressive Democrats 8, Green Party 6, Sinn Fein 5, others 14
Judicial branch: Supreme Court (judges appointed by the president on the advice of the prime minister and cabinet)
Political parties and leaders: Fianna Fail [Bertie AHERN]; Fine Gael [Enda KENNY]; Green Party [Trevor SARGENT]; Labor Party [Pat RABITTE]; Progressive Democrats [Mary HARNEY]; Sinn Fein [Gerry ADAMS]; Socialist Party [Joe HIGGINS]; The Workers' Party [Sean GARLAND]
Political pressure groups and leaders: NA
International organization participation: Australia Group, BIS, CE, EAPC, EBRD, EIB, EMU, ESA, EU, FAO, IAEA, IBRD, ICAO, ICC, ICCt, ICRM, IDA, IEA, IFAD, IFC, IFRCS, ILO, IMF, IMO, Interpol, IOC, IOM, ISO, ITU, MIGA, MINURSO, MONUC, NEA, NSG, OAS (observer), OECD, OPCW, OSCE, Paris Club, PCA, PFP, UN, UNCTAD, UNESCO, UNHCR, UNIDO, UNIFIL, UNMIL, UNMOVIC, UNOCI, UNTSO, UPU, WCO, WEU (observer), WHO, WIPO, WMO, WTO, ZC
Diplomatic representation in the US:
chief of mission: Ambassador Noel FAHEY
chancery: 2234 Massachusetts Avenue NW, Washington, DC 20008
telephone: [1] (202) 462-3939
FAX: [1] (202) 232-5993
consulate(s) general: Boston, Chicago, New York, and San Francisco
Diplomatic representation from the US:
chief of mission: Ambassador James C. KENNY
embassy: 42 Elgin Road, Ballsbridge, Dublin 4
mailing address: use embassy street address
telephone: [353] (1) 668-8777
FAX: [353] (1) 668-9946
Flag description: three equal vertical bands of green (hoist side), white, and orange; similar to the flag of Cote d'Ivoire, which is shorter and has the colors reversed - orange (hoist side), white, and green; also similar to the flag of Italy, which is shorter and has colors of green (hoist side), white, and red

ECONOMY

Economy - overview: Ireland is a small, modern, trade-dependent economy with growth averaging a robust 7% in 1995-2004. Agriculture, once the most important sector, is now dwarfed by industry and services. Industry accounts for 46% of GDP, about 80% of exports, and 29% of the labor force. Although exports remain the primary engine for Ireland's growth, the economy has also benefited from a rise in consumer spending, construction, and business investment. Per capita GDP is 10% above that of the four big European economies and the second highest in the EU behind Luxembourg. Over the past decade, the Irish Government has implemented a series of national economic programs designed to curb price and wage inflation, reduce government spending, increase labor force skills, and promote foreign investment. Ireland joined in circulating the euro on 1 January 2002 along with 11 other EU nations.
GDP (purchasing power parity): $136.9 billion (2005 est.)
GDP (official exchange rate): $194.2 billion (2005 est.)
GDP - real growth rate: 4.9% (2005 est.)
GDP - per capita: purchasing power parity - $34,100 (2005 est.)
GDP - composition by sector:
agriculture: 5%
industry: 46%
services: 49% (2002 est.)
Labor force: 2.03 million (2005 est.)
Labor force - by occupation: agriculture 8%, industry 29%, services 64% (2002 est.)
Unemployment rate: 4.2% (2005 est.)
Population below poverty line: 10% (1997 est.)
Household income or consumption by percentage share:
lowest 10%: 2%
highest 10%: 27.3% (1997)
Distribution of family income - Gini index: 35.9 (1996)
Inflation rate (consumer prices): 2.7% (2005 est.)
Investment (gross fixed): 25.6% of GDP (2005 est.)
Budget:
revenues: $70.46 billion
expenditures: $69.4 billion, including capital expenditures of $5.5 billion (2005 est.)
Public debt: 27.5% of GDP (2005 est.)
Agriculture - products: turnips, barley, potatoes, sugar beets, wheat; beef, dairy products
Industries: steel, lead, zinc, silver, aluminum, barite, and gypsum mining processing; food products, brewing, textiles, clothing; chemicals, pharmaceuticals; machinery, rail transportation equipment, passenger and commercial vehicles, ship construction and refurbishment; glass and crystal; software, tourism
Industrial production growth rate: 3% (2005 est.)
Electricity - production: 23.41 billion kWh (2003)
Electricity - production by source:
fossil fuel: 95.9%
hydro: 2.3%
nuclear: 0%
other: 1.7% (2001)
Electricity - consumption: 22.97 billion kWh (2003)
Electricity - exports: 0 kWh (2003)
Electricity - imports: 1.2 billion kWh (2003)
Oil - production: 0 bbl/day (2003 est.)

Oil - consumption: 175,600 bbl/day (2003 est.)
Oil - exports: 27,450 bbl/day (2001)
Oil - imports: 178,600 bbl/day (2001)
Oil - proved reserves: 0 bbl (1 January 2002)
Natural gas - production: 815 million cu m (2001 est.)
Natural gas - consumption: 4.199 billion cu m (2001 est.)
Natural gas - exports: 0 cu m (2001 est.)
Natural gas - imports: 3.384 billion cu m (2001 est.)
Natural gas - proved reserves: 9.911 billion cu m (1 January 2002)
Current account balance: $-5.19 billion (2005 est.)
Exports: $102 billion f.o.b. (2005 est.)
Exports - partners: US 19.7%, UK 17.7%, Belgium 14.7%, Germany 7.7%, France 6%, Netherlands 4.6%, Italy 4.5% (2004)
Imports: $65.47 billion f.o.b. (2005 est.)
Imports - partners: UK 35.7%, US 13.8%, Germany 9%, Netherlands 4.3%, France 4.2% (2004)
Reserves of foreign exchange and gold: $2.908 billion (2004 est.)
Debt - external: $1.049 trillion (30 June 2005)
Economic aid - donor: ODA, $607 million (2004)
Currency (code): euro (EUR)
note: on 1 January 1999, the European Monetary Union introduced the euro as a common currency to be used by financial institutions of member countries; on 1 January 2002, the euro became the sole currency for everyday transactions within the member countries
Currency code: EUR
Exchange rates: euros per US dollar - 0.79697 (2005), 0.8054 (2004), 0.886 (2003), 1.0626 (2002), 1.1175 (2001)
Fiscal year: calendar year

COMMUNICATIONS

Telephones - main lines in use: 1.955 million (2003)
Telephones - mobile cellular: 3.4 million (2003)
Telephone system:
general assessment: modern digital system using cable and microwave radio relay
domestic: microwave radio relay
international: country code - 353; satellite earth station - 1 Intelsat (Atlantic Ocean)
Radio broadcast stations: AM 9, FM 106, shortwave 0 (1998)
Radios: 2.55 million (1997)
Television broadcast stations: 4 (many low-power repeaters) (2001)
Televisions: 1.82 million (2001)
Internet country code: .ie
Internet hosts: 162,228 (2004)
Internet Service Providers (ISPs):22 (2000)
Internet users: 1.26 million (2003)

TRANSPORTATION

Airports: 36 (2004 est.)
Airports - with paved runways:
total: 15
over 3,047 m: 1
2,438 to 3,047 m: 1
1,524 to 2,437 m: 4
914 to 1,523 m: 3
under 914 m: 6 (2005 est.)
Airports - with unpaved runways:
total: 21
914 to 1,523 m: 4
under 914 m: 17 (2005 est.)
Pipelines: gas 1,795 km (2004)
Railways:
total: 3,312 km
broad gauge: 1,947 km 1.600-m gauge (46 km electrified)
narrow gauge: 1,365 km 0.914-m gauge (operated by the Irish Peat Board to transport peat to power stations and briquetting plants) (2004)
Roadways:
total: 95,736 km
paved: 95,736 km (including 125 km of expressways) (2002)
Waterways: 753 km (pleasure craft only) (2004)
Merchant marine:
total: 39
by type: bulk carrier 4, cargo 27, chemical tanker 1, container 1, passenger/cargo 4, roll on/roll off 2
foreign-owned: 11 (Germany 3, Italy 3, Norway 1, Switzerland 1, United Kingdom 3)
registered in other countries: 18 (2005)
Ports and terminals: Cork, Dublin, New Ross, Shannon Foynes, Waterford

MILITARY

Military branches: Army (includes Naval Service and Air Corps)
Military service age and obligation: 17 years of age for voluntary military service; enlistees under the age of 17 can be recruited for specialist positions (2001)
Manpower available for military service:
males age 17-49: 977,092 (2005 est.)
Manpower fit for military service: *males age 17-49:* 814,768 (2005 est.)
Manpower reaching military service age annually: *males:* 29,327 (2005 est.)
Military expenditures - dollar figure: $700 million (FY00/01)
Military expenditures - percent of GDP: 0.9% (FY00/01)

TRANSNATIONAL ISSUES

Disputes - international: Ireland, Iceland, and the UK dispute Denmark's claim that the Faroe Islands' continental shelf extends beyond 200 nm
Illicit drugs: transshipment point for and consumer of hashish from North Africa to the UK and Netherlands and of European-produced synthetic drugs; minor transshipment point for heroin and cocaine destined for Western Europe; despite recent legislation, narcotics-related money laundering using bureaux de change, trusts, and shell companies involving the offshore financial community remains a concern

ISLE OF MAN

INTRODUCTION

Background: Part of the Norwegian Kingdom of the Hebrides until the 13th century when it was ceded to Scotland, the isle came under the British crown in 1765. Current concerns include reviving the almost extinct Manx Gaelic language.

GEOGRAPHY

Location: Western Europe, island in the Irish Sea, between Great Britain and Ireland
Geographic coordinates: 54 15 N, 4 30 W
Map references: Europe
Area:
total: 572 sq km
land: 572 sq km
water: 0 sq km
Area - comparative: slightly more than three times the size of Washington, DC
Land boundaries: 0 km
Coastline: 160 km
Maritime claims:
territorial sea: 12 nm
exclusive fishing zone: 12 nm
Climate: temperate; cool summers and mild winters; overcast about one-third of the time
Terrain: hills in north and south bisected by central valley
Elevation extremes:
lowest point: Irish Sea 0 m
highest point: Snaefell 621 m
Natural resources: none
Land use:
arable land: 9%
permanent crops: 0%
other: 91% (permanent pastures, forests,

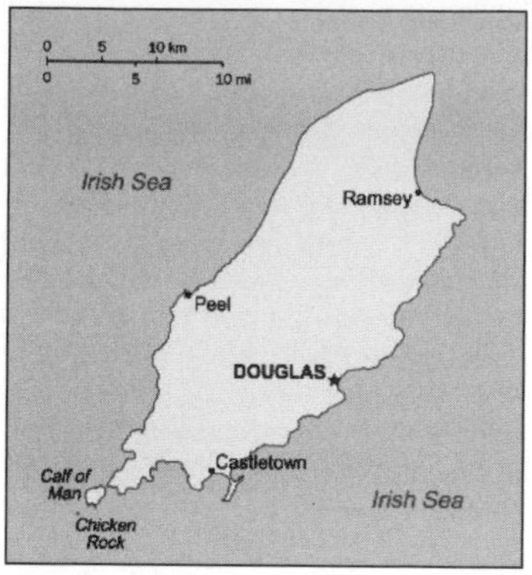

mountain, and heathland) (2002)
Irrigated land: 0 sq km (1998 est.)
Natural hazards: NA
Environment - current issues: waste disposal (both household and industrial); transboundary air pollution
Geography - note: one small islet, the Calf of Man, lies to the southwest, and is a bird sanctuary

PEOPLE

Population: 75,049 (July 2005 est.)
Age structure:
0-14 years: 17.4% (male 6,681/female 6,365)
15-64 years: 65.5% (male 24,693/female 24,482)
65 years and over: 17.1% (male 5,163/female 7,665) (2005 est.)
Median age:
total: 39.48 years
male: 38.16 years
female: 40.89 years (2005 est.)
Population growth rate: 0.52% (2005 est.)
Birth rate: 11.18 births/1,000 population (2005 est.)
Death rate: 11.26 deaths/1,000 population (2005 est.)
Net migration rate: 5.33 migrant(s)/1,000 population (2005 est.)
Sex ratio:
at birth: 1.05 male(s)/female
under 15 years: 1.05 male(s)/female
15-64 years: 1.01 male(s)/female
65 years and over: 0.67 male(s)/female
total population: 0.95 male(s)/female (2005 est.)
Infant mortality rate:
total: 5.93 deaths/1,000 live births
male: 6.93 deaths/1,000 live births
female: 4.87 deaths/1,000 live births (2005 est.)
Life expectancy at birth:
total population: 78.34 years
male: 74.98 years
female: 81.87 years (2005 est.)
Total fertility rate: 1.65 children born/woman (2005 est.)
HIV/AIDS - adult prevalence rate: NA%
HIV/AIDS - people living with HIV/AIDS: NA
HIV/AIDS - deaths: NA
Nationality:
noun: Manxman (men), Manxwoman (women)
adjective: Manx
Ethnic groups: Manx (Norse-Celtic descent), Briton
Religions: Anglican, Roman Catholic, Methodist, Baptist, Presbyterian, Society of Friends
Languages: English, Manx Gaelic
Literacy:
definition: NA
total population: NA%
male: NA%
female: NA%

GOVERNMENT

Country name:
conventional long form: none
conventional short form: Isle of Man
Dependency status: British crown dependency
Government type: parliamentary democracy
Capital: Douglas
Administrative divisions: none; there are no first-order administrative divisions as defined by the US Government, but there are 24 local authorities each with its own elections
Independence: none (British crown dependency)
National holiday: Tynwald Day, 5 July
Constitution: unwritten; note - The Isle of Man Constitution Act of 1961 does not embody the unwritten Manx Constitution
Legal system: English common law and Manx statute
Suffrage: 18 years of age; universal
Executive branch:
chief of state: Lord of Mann Queen ELIZABETH II (since 6 February 1952), represented by Lieutenant Governor Ian MACFADYEN (since 26 October 2002)
head of government: Chief Minister Donald GELLING (since 14 December 2004)
cabinet: Council of Ministers
elections: the monarch is hereditary; lieutenant governor appointed by the monarch for a five-year term; the Chief Minister is elected by the Tynwald; election last held 14 December 2004 (next to be held December 2006)
election results: Donald GELLING elected chief minister by the Tynwald; note - Richard CORKILL resigned 2 December 2004
Legislative branch: bicameral Tynwald consists of the Legislative Council (an 11-member body composed of the President of Tynwald, the Lord Bishop of Sodor and Man, a nonvoting attorney general, and 8 others named by the House of Keys) and the House of Keys (24 seats; members are elected by popular vote to serve five-year terms)
elections: House of Keys - last held 22 November 2001 (next to be held November 2006)
election results: House of Keys - percent of vote by party - Man Labor Party 17.3%, Alliance for Progressive Government 14.6%; seats by party - Man Labor Party 2, Alliance for Progressive Government 3, independents 19
Judicial branch: High Court of Justice (justices are appointed by the Lord Chancellor of England on the nomination of the lieutenant governor)
Political parties and leaders: Man Labor Party [leader NA]; Alliance for Progressive Government [leader NA]; Man Nationalist Party [leader NA] note: most members sit as independents
Political pressure groups and leaders: none
International organization participation: UPU
Diplomatic representation in the US: none (British crown dependency)
Diplomatic representation from the US: none (British crown dependency) red with the Three Legs of Man emblem (Trinacria), in the center; the three legs are joined at the thigh and bent at the knee; in order to have the toes pointing clockwise on both sides of the flag, a two-sided emblem is used

ECONOMY

Economy - overview: Offshore banking, manufacturing, and tourism are key sectors of the economy. The government's policy of offering incentives to high-technology companies and financial institutions to locate on the island has paid off in expanding employment opportunities in high-income industries. As a result, agriculture and fishing, once the mainstays of the economy, have declined in their shares of GDP. Trade is mostly with the UK. The Isle of Man enjoys free access to EU markets.
GDP (purchasing power parity): $2.113 billion (2003 est.)
GDP (official exchange rate): NA
GDP - real growth rate: NA%
GDP - per capita: purchasing power parity - $28,500 (2003 est.)
GDP - composition by sector:
agriculture: 1%
industry: 13%
services: 86% (2000 est.)
Labor force: 39,690 (2001)
Labor force - by occupation: agriculture,

forestry and fishing 3%, manufacturing 11%, construction 10%, transport and communication 8%, wholesale and retail distribution 11%, professional and scientific services 18%, public administration 6%, banking and finance 18%, tourism 2%, entertainment and catering 3%, miscellaneous services 10%
Unemployment rate: 0.6% (2004 est.)
Population below poverty line: NA
Household income or consumption by percentage share:
lowest 10%: NA%
highest 10%: NA%
Inflation rate (consumer prices): 3.6% (March 2003 est.)
Budget:
revenues: $485 million
expenditures: $463 million, including capital expenditures of NA (FY00/01 est.)
Agriculture - products: cereals, vegetables; cattle, sheep, pigs, poultry
Industries: financial services, light manufacturing, tourism
Industrial production growth rate: 3.2% (FY96/97)
Exports: $NA
Exports - partners: UK (2004)
Imports: $NA
Imports - partners: UK (2004)
Debt - external: $NA
Economic aid - recipient: NA
Currency (code): British pound (GBP); note - there is also a Manx pound
Currency code: GBP
Exchange rates: Manx pounds per US dollar - 0.54 (2005), 0.5462 (2004), 0.6125 (2003), 0.6672 (2002), 0.6947 (2001)
Fiscal year: 1 April - 31 March

COMMUNICATIONS

Telephones - main lines in use: 51,000 (1999)
Telephones - mobile cellular: NA
Telephone system:
general assessment: NA
domestic: landline, telefax, mobile cellular telephone system
international: fiber-optic cable, microwave radio relay, satellite earth station, submarine cable
Radio broadcast stations: AM 1, FM 1, shortwave 0 (1998)
Radios: NA
Television broadcast stations: 0 (receives broadcasts from the UK and satellite) (1999)
Televisions: 27,490 (1999)
Internet country code: .im
Internet Service Providers (ISPs): NA
Internet users: NA

TRANSPORTATION

Airports: 1 (2004 est.)
Airports - with paved runways:
total: 1
1,524 to 2,437 m: 1 (2005 est.)
Railways:
total: 61 km (35 km electrified) (2003)
Roadways:
total: 800 km
paved: 800 km
unpaved: 0 km (1999)
Merchant marine:
total: 267 ships (1,000 GRT or over) 6,834,626 GRT/11,354,689 DWT
by type: bulk carrier 31, cargo 54, chemical tanker 45, combination ore/oil 1, container 15, liquefied gas 46, passenger/cargo 2, petroleum tanker 53, refrigerated cargo 4, roll on/roll off 10, specialized tanker 1, vehicle carrier 5
foreign-owned: 253 (Australia 1, Bahamas 8, Denmark 39, France 2, Germany 55, Greece 20, Hong Kong 3, Italy 7, Japan 4, Netherlands 2, New Zealand 1, Norway 18, Singapore 2, Sweden 1, Turkey 2, United Kingdom 86, United States 2)
registered in other countries: 9 (2005)
Ports and terminals: Castletown, Douglas, Ramsey

MILITARY

Military - note: defense is the responsibility of the UK

TRANSNATIONAL ISSUES

Disputes - international: none

ISRAEL

INTRODUCTION

Background: Following World War II, the British withdrew from their mandate of Palestine, and the UN partitioned the area into Arab and Jewish states, an arrangement rejected by the Arabs. Subsequently, the Israelis defeated the Arabs in a series of wars without ending the deep tensions between the two sides. The territories occupied by Israel since the 1967 war are not included in the Israel country profile, unless otherwise noted. On 25 April 1982, Israel withdrew from the Sinai pursuant to the 1979 Israel-Egypt Peace Treaty. Israel and Palestinian officials signed on 13 September 1993 a Declaration of Principles (also known as the "Oslo accords") guiding an interim period of Palestinian self-rule. Outstanding territorial and other disputes with Jordan were resolved in the 26 October 1994 Israel-Jordan Treaty of Peace. In addition, on 25 May 2000, Israel withdrew unilaterally from southern Lebanon, which it had occupied since 1982. In keeping with the framework established at the Madrid Conference in October 1991, bilateral negotiations were conducted between Israel and Palestinian representatives and Syria to achieve a permanent settlement. On 24 June 2002, US President BUSH laid out a "road map" for resolving the Israeli-Palestinian conflict, which envisions a two-state solution. However, progress toward a permanent status agreement was undermined by Palestinian-Israeli violence between September 2000 and February 2005. An agreement reached at Sharm al-Sheikh in February 2005 significantly reduced the violence. The election in January 2005 of Mahmud ABBAS as the new Palestinian leader following the November 2004 death of Yasir ARAFAT, the formation of a Likud-Labor-United Torah Judaism coalition government in January 2005, and the successful Israeli disengagement from the Gaza Strip (August-September 2005), presented an opportunity for a renewed peace effort. However, internal Israeli political events between October and December 2005 have destabilized the political situation and forced early elections, scheduled for March 2006.

GEOGRAPHY

Location: Middle East, bordering the Mediterranean Sea, between Egypt and Lebanon
Geographic coordinates: 31 30 N, 34 45 E
Map references: Middle East
Area:
total: 20,770 sq km
land: 20,330 sq km
water: 440 sq km
Area - comparative: slightly smaller than New Jersey
Land boundaries:
total: 1,017 km
border countries: Egypt 266 km, Gaza Strip 51 km, Jordan 238 km, Lebanon 79 km, Syria 76 km, West Bank 307 km
Coastline: 273 km
Maritime claims:
territorial sea: 12 nm
continental shelf: to depth of exploitation
Climate: temperate; hot and dry in southern and eastern desert areas

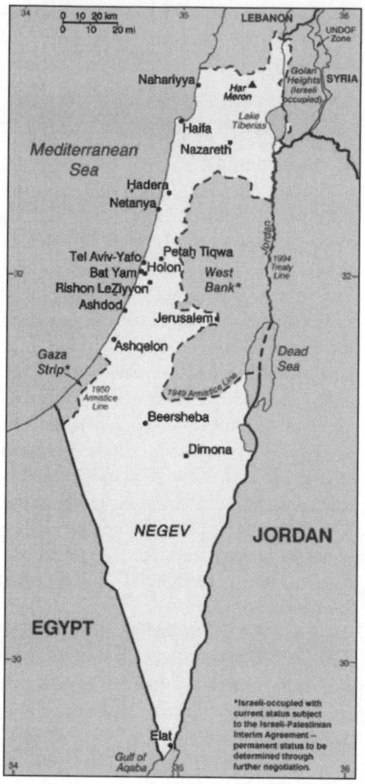

Terrain: Negev desert in the south; low coastal plain; central mountains; Jordan Rift Valley

Elevation extremes:
lowest point: Dead Sea -408 m
highest point: Har Meron 1,208 m

Natural resources: timber, potash, copper ore, natural gas, phosphate rock, magnesium bromide, clays, sand

Land use:
arable land: 16.39%
permanent crops: 4.17%
other: 79.44% (2001)

Irrigated land: 1,990 sq km (1998 est.)

Natural hazards: sandstorms may occur during spring and summer; droughts; periodic earthquakes

Environment - current issues: limited arable land and natural fresh water resources pose serious constraints; desertification; air pollution from industrial and vehicle emissions; groundwater pollution from industrial and domestic waste, chemical fertilizers, and pesticides

Environment - international agreements:
party to: Biodiversity, Climate Change, Climate Change-Kyoto Protocol, Desertification, Endangered Species, Hazardous Wastes, Ozone Layer Protection, Ship Pollution, Wetlands
signed, but not ratified: Marine Life Conservation

Geography - note: there are 242 Israeli settlements and civilian land use sites in the West Bank, 42 in the Israeli-occupied Golan Heights, 0 in the Gaza Strip, and 29 in East Jerusalem (August 2005 est.); Sea of Galilee is an important freshwater source

PEOPLE

Population: 6,276,883
note: includes about 187,000 Israeli settlers in the West Bank, about 20,000 in the Israeli-occupied Golan Heights, more than 5,000 in the Gaza Strip, and fewer than 177,000 in East Jerusalem (July 2005 est.)

Age structure:
0-14 years: 26.5% (male 851,415/female 812,095)
15-64 years: 63.7% (male 2,010,888/female 1,986,256)
65 years and over: 9.8% (male 264,708/female 351,521) (2005 est.)

Median age:
total: 29.39 years
male: 28.58 years
female: 30.27 years (2005 est.)

Population growth rate: 1.2% (2005 est.)

Birth rate: 18.21 births/1,000 population (2005 est.)

Death rate: 6.18 deaths/1,000 population (2005 est.)

Net migration rate: 0 migrant(s)/1,000 population (2005 est.)

Sex ratio:
at birth: 1.05 male(s)/female
under 15 years: 1.05 male(s)/female
15-64 years: 1.01 male(s)/female
65 years and over: 0.75 male(s)/female
total population: 0.99 male(s)/female (2005 est.)

Infant mortality rate:
total: 7.03 deaths/1,000 live births
male: 7.77 deaths/1,000 live births
female: 6.26 deaths/1,000 live births (2005 est.)

Life expectancy at birth:
total population: 79.32 years
male: 77.21 years
female: 81.55 years (2005 est.)
Total fertility rate: 2.44 children born/woman (2005 est.)

HIV/AIDS - adult prevalence rate: 0.1% (2001 est.)

HIV/AIDS - people living with HIV/AIDS: 3,000 (1999 est.)

HIV/AIDS - deaths: 100 (2001 est.)

Nationality:
noun: Israeli(s)
adjective: Israeli

Ethnic groups: Jewish 80.1% (Europe/America-born 32.1%, Israel-born 20.8%, Africa-born 14.6%, Asia-born 12.6%), non-Jewish 19.9% (mostly Arab) (1996est.)

Religions: Jewish 76.5%, Muslim 15.9%, Arab Christians 1.7%, other Christian 0.4%, Druze 1.6%, unspecified 3.9% (2003)

Languages: Hebrew (official), Arabic used officially for Arab minority, English most commonly used foreign language

Literacy:
definition: age 15 and over can read and write
total population: 95.4%
male: 97.3%
female: 93.6% (2003 est.)

GOVERNMENT

Country name:
conventional long form: State of Israel
conventional short form: Israel
local long form: Medinat Yisra'el
local short form: Yisra'el

Government type: parliamentary democracy

Capital: Jerusalem; note - Israel proclaimed Jerusalem as its capital in 1950, but the US, like nearly all other countries, maintains its Embassy in Tel Aviv

Administrative divisions: 6 districts (mehozot, singular - mehoz); Central, Haifa, Jerusalem, Northern, Southern, Tel Aviv

Independence: 14 May 1948 (from League of Nations mandate under British administration)

National holiday: Independence Day, 14 May (1948); note - Israel declared independence on 14 May 1948, but the Jewish calendar is lunar and the holiday may occur in April or May

Constitution: no formal constitution; some of the functions of a constitution are filled by the Declaration of Establishment (1948), the Basic Laws of the parliament (Knesset), and the Israeli citizenship law

Legal system: mixture of English common law, British Mandate regulations, and, in personal matters, Jewish, Christian, and Muslim legal systems; in December 1985, Israel informed the UN Secretariat that it would no longer accept compulsory ICJ jurisdiction

Suffrage: 18 years of age; universal

Executive branch:
chief of state: President Moshe KATZAV (since 31 July 2000)
head of government: Prime Minister (Acting) Ehud OLMERT
cabinet: Cabinet selected by prime minister and approved by the Knesset
elections: president is largely a ceremonial role and is elected by the Knesset for a seven-year term; election last held 31 July 2000 (next to be held mid-2007); following legislative elections, the president assigns a Knesset member - traditionally the leader of the largest party - the task of forming a governing coalition; election last held 28 January 2003 (next scheduled to be held March 2006)
election results: Moshe KATZAV elected

president by the 120-member Knesset with a total of 60 votes, other candidate, Shimon PERES, received 57 votes (there were three abstentions); Ariel SHARON continued as prime minister after Likud Party victory in January 2003 Knesset elections; Likud won 38 seats and then formed coalition government with Shinui, the National Religious Party, and the National Union; controversy surrounding SHARON's disengagement plan ultimately led to the formation of a Likud-Labor-United Torah Judaism (UTJ) coalition government in January 2005

Legislative branch: unicameral Knesset (120 seats; members elected by popular vote to serve four-year terms)
elections: last held 28 January 2003 (next scheduled to be held March 2006)
election results: percent of vote by party - Likud Party 29.4%, Labor 14.5%, Shinui 12.3%, Shas 8.2%, National Union 5.5%, Meretz 5.2%, United Torah Judaism 4.3%, National Religious Party 4.2%, Democratic Front for Peace and Equality 3.0%, One Nation 2.8%, National Democratic Assembly 2.3%, Yisra'el Ba'Aliya (YBA) 2.2%, United Arab List 2.1%, Green Leaf Party 1.2%, Herut 1.2%, other 1.6%; seats by party - Likud 38, Labor 19, Shinui 15, Shas 11, National Union 7, Meretz 6, National Religious Party 6, United Torah Judaism 5, Democratic Front for Peace and Equality 3, One Nation 3, National Democratic Assembly 3, YBA 2, United Arab List 2

Judicial branch: Supreme Court (justices appointed for life by the president)

Political parties and leaders: Democratic Front for Peace and Equality (Hadash) [Muhammad BARAKA]; Green Leaf Party (no longer active) [Boaz WACHTEL and Shlomi SANDAK]; Herut (no longer active) [Michael KLEINER]; Kadima (formed in November 2005) [Ariel SHARON]; Labor Party [Amir PERETZ]; Likud Party [leader NA]; Meretz (merged with YAHAD) [Zahava GALON]; National Democratic Assembly (Balad) [Azmi BISHARA]; National Religious Party [Ephraim "Efie" EITAM]; National Union (Haichud Haleumi) [Avigdor LIBERMAN] (includes Tekuma Moledet and Yisra'el Beiteinu); One Nation [David TAL]; Shas [Eliyahu YISHAI]; Shinui [Yosef "Tommy" LAPID]; Tzalash (Zionism, Liberty, and Equality) [Joseph PARITZKY]; United Arab List [Abd al-Malik DAHAMSHAH]; United Torah Judaism [Yaakov LITZMAN]; YAHAD [Yossi BEILIN]; Yisra'el Ba'Aliya or YBA (merged with Likud) [Natan SHARANSKY]

Political pressure groups and leaders: Israeli nationalists advocating Jewish settlement on the West Bank and Gaza Strip; Peace Now supports territorial concessions in the West Bank and Gaza Strip; Yesha (settler) Council promotes settler interests and opposes territorial compromise; B'Tselem monitors human rights abuses

International organization participation: BIS, BSEC (observer), CE (observer), CERN (observer), EBRD, FAO, IADB, IAEA, IBRD, ICAO, ICC, ICCt (signatory), ICFTU, IDA, IFAD, IFC, IFRCS (observer), ILO, IMF, IMO, Interpol, IOC, IOM, ISO, ITU, MIGA, OAS (observer), OPCW (signatory), OSCE (partner), PCA, UN, UNCTAD, UNESCO, UNHCR, UNIDO, UPU, WCO, WHO, WIPO, WMO, WToO, WTO

Diplomatic representation in the US:
chief of mission: Ambassador Daniel AYALON
chancery: 3514 International Drive NW, Washington, DC 20008
telephone: [1] (202) 364-5500
FAX: [1] (202) 364-5560
consulate(s) general: Atlanta, Boston, Chicago, Houston, Los Angeles, Miami, New York, Philadelphia, and San Francisco

Diplomatic representation from the US:
chief of mission: Ambassador Richard H. JONES
embassy: 71 Hayarkon Street, Tel Aviv 63903
mailing address: PSC 98, Box 29, APO AE 09830
telephone: [972] (3) 519-7369/7453/7454/7457/7458/7551/7575
FAX: [972] (3) 516-4390
consulate(s) general: Jerusalem; note - an independent US mission, established in 1928, whose members are not accredited to a foreign government

Flag description: white with a blue hexagram (six-pointed linear star) known as the Magen David (Shield of David) centered between two equal horizontal blue bands near the top and bottom edges of the flag

ECONOMY

Economy - overview: Israel has a technologically advanced market economy with substantial government participation. It depends on imports of crude oil, grains, raw materials, and military equipment. Despite limited natural resources, Israel has intensively developed its agricultural and industrial sectors over the past 20 years. Israel imports substantial quantities of grain, but is largely self-sufficient in other agricultural products. Cut diamonds, high-technology equipment, and agricultural products (fruits and vegetables) are the leading exports. Israel usually posts sizable current account deficits, which are covered by large transfer payments from abroad and by foreign loans. Roughly half of the government's external debt is owed to the US, which is its major source of economic and military aid. The bitter Israeli-Palestinian conflict; difficulties in the high-technology, construction, and tourist sectors; and fiscal austerity in the face of growing inflation led to small declines in GDP in 2001 and 2002. The economy rebounded in 2003 and 2004, growing at a 4% rate each year, as the government tightened fiscal policy and implemented structural reforms to boost competition and efficiency in the markets. In 2005, rising consumer confidence, tourism and foreign direct investment - as well as higher demand for Israeli exports – boosted GDP by 4.3%.

GDP (purchasing power parity): $139.2 billion (2005 est.)

GDP (official exchange rate): $123.7 billion (2005 est.)

GDP - real growth rate: 4.3% (2005 est.)

GDP - per capita: purchasing power parity - $22,200 (2005 est.)

GDP - composition by sector:
agriculture: 2.8%
industry: 37.7%
services: 59.5% (2003 est.)

Labor force: 2.42 million (2005 est.)

Labor force - by occupation: agriculture, forestry, and fishing 2.6%, manufacturing 20.2%, construction 7.5%, commerce 12.8%, transport, storage, and communications 6.2%, finance and business 13.1%, personal and other services 6.4%, public services 31.2% (1996)

Unemployment rate: 8.9% (2005 est.)

Population below poverty line: 21% (2005)

Household income or consumption by percentage share:
lowest 10%: 2.4%
highest 10%: 28.3% (1997)

Distribution of family income - Gini index: 34 (2005)

Inflation rate (consumer prices): 1.3% (2005 est.)

Investment (gross fixed): 17.5% of GDP (2005 est.)

Budget:
revenues: $43.82 billion
expenditures: $58.04 billion, including capital expenditures of NA (2005 est.)

Public debt: 101% of GDP (2005 est.)

Agriculture - products: citrus, vegetables, cotton; beef, poultry, dairy products

Industries: high-technology projects

(including aviation, communications, computer-aided design and manufactures, medical electronics, fiber optics), wood and paper products, potash and phosphates, food, beverages, and tobacco, caustic soda, cement, construction, metals products, chemical products, plastics, diamond cutting, textiles and footwear
Industrial production growth rate: 4.8% (2005 est.)
Electricity - production: 44.24 billion kWh (2003)
Electricity - production by source:
fossil fuel: 99.9%
hydro: 0.1%
nuclear: 0%
other: 0% (2001)
Electricity - consumption: 39.67 billion kWh (2003)
Electricity - exports: 1.47 billion kWh (2003)
Electricity - imports: 0 kWh (2003)
Oil - production: 2,740 bbl/day (2003 est.)
Oil - consumption: 270,100 bbl/day (2003 est.)
Oil - exports: NA (2001)
Oil - imports: NA (2001)
Oil - proved reserves: 1.92 million bbl (1 January 2002)
Natural gas - production: 10 million cu m (2001 est.)
Natural gas - consumption: 10 million cu m (2001 est.)
Natural gas - exports: 0 cu m (2001 est.)
Natural gas - imports: 0 cu m (2001 est.)
Natural gas - proved reserves: 20.81 billion cu m (1 January 2002)
Current account balance: $500 million (2005 est.)
Exports: $40.14 billion f.o.b. (2005 est.)
Exports - partners: US 36.8%, Belgium 7.5%, Hong Kong 4.9% (2004)
Imports: $43.19 billion f.o.b. (2005 est.)
Imports - partners: US 15%, Belgium 10.1%, Germany 7.5%, Switzerland 6.5%, UK 6.1% (2004)
Reserves of foreign exchange and gold: $29.69 billion (2005 est.)
Debt - external: $73.87 billion (30 June 2005 est.)
Economic aid - recipient: $662 million from US (2003 est.)
Currency (code): new Israeli shekel (ILS); note - NIS is the currency abbreviation; ILS is the International Organization for Standardization (ISO) code for the NIS
Currency code: ILS
Exchange rates: new Israeli shekels per US dollar - 4.46 (2005), 4.482 (2004), 4.5541 (2003), 4.7378 (2002), 4.2057 (2001)
Fiscal year: calendar year

COMMUNICATIONS

Telephones - main lines in use: 3.006 million (2002)
Telephones - mobile cellular: 6.334 million (2002)
Telephone system:
general assessment: most highly developed system in the Middle East although not the largest
domestic: good system of coaxial cable and microwave radio relay; all systems are digital
international: country code - 972; 3 submarine cables; satellite earth stations - 3 Intelsat (2 Atlantic Ocean and 1 Indian Ocean)
Radio broadcast stations: AM 23, FM 15, shortwave 2 (1998)
Radios: 3.07 million (1997)
Television broadcast stations: 17 (plus 36 low-power repeaters) (1995)
Televisions: 1.69 million (1997)
Internet country code: .il
Internet hosts: 437,516 (2004)
Internet Service Providers (ISPs): 21 (2000)
Internet users: 2 million (2002)

TRANSPORTATION

Airports: 51 (2004 est.)
Airports - with paved runways:
total: 28
over 3,047 m: 2
2,438 to 3,047 m: 4
1,524 to 2,437 m: 8
914 to 1,523 m: 10
under 914 m: 4 (2005 est.)
Airports - with unpaved runways:
total: 23
1,524 to 2,437 m: 1
914 to 1,523 m: 2
under 914 m: 20 (2005 est.)
Heliports: 3 (2005 est.)
Pipelines: gas 140 km; oil 1,509 km (2004)
Railways:
total: 640 km
standard gauge: 640 km 1.435-m gauge (2004)
Roadways:
total: 17,237 km
paved: 17,237 km (including 126 km of expressways) (2002)
Merchant marine:
total: 17 ships (1,000 GRT or over) 752,873 GRT/881,711 DWT
by type: cargo 1, container 16
registered in other countries: 48 (2005)
Ports and terminals: Ashdod, Elat (Eilat), Hadera, Haifa

MILITARY

Military branches: Israel Defense Forces (IDF): Ground Corps, Navy, Air and Space Force (includes Air Defense Forces); historically there have been no separate Israeli military services
Military service age and obligation: 17 years of age for compulsory (Jews, Druzes) and voluntary (Christians, Muslims, Circassians) military service; both sexes are eligible for military service; conscript service obligation - 36 months for men, 21 months for women (2004)
Manpower available for military service:
males age 17-49: 1,492,125
females age 17-49: 1,443,916 (2005 est.)
Manpower fit for military service: *males age 17-49:* 1,255,902
females age 17-49: 1,212,394 (2005 est.)
Manpower reaching military service age annually:
males: 53,760
females: 51,293 (2005 est.)
Military expenditures - dollar figure: $9.11 billion (FY03)
Military expenditures - percent of GDP: 8.7% (FY02)

TRANSNATIONAL ISSUES

Disputes - international: West Bank and Gaza Strip are Israeli-occupied with current status subject to the Israeli-Palestinian Interim Agreement - permanent status to be determined through further negotiation; Israel continues construction of a "seam line" separation barrier along parts of the Green Line and within the West Bank; Israel announced its intention to pull out Israeli settlers and withdraw from the Gaza Strip and four settlements in the northern West Bank in 2005; Golan Heights is Israeli-occupied (Lebanon claims the Shab'a Farms area of Golan Heights); since 1948, about 350 peacekeepers from the UN Truce Supervision Organization (UNTSO) headquartered in Jerusalem monitor ceasefires, supervise armistice agreements, prevent isolated incidents from escalating, and assist other UN personnel in the region
Refugees and internally displaced persons: *IDPs:* 276,000 (Arab villagers displaced from homes in northern Israel) (2004)
Illicit drugs: increasingly concerned about cocaine and heroin abuse; drugs arrive in country from Lebanon and, increasingly, from Jordan; money-laundering center

ITALY

INTRODUCTION

Background: Italy became a nation-state in 1861 when the city-states of the peninsula, along with Sardinia and Sicily, were united under King Victor EMMANUEL II. An era of parliamentary government came to a close in the early 1920s when Benito MUSSOLINI established a Fascist dictatorship. His disastrous alliance with Nazi Germany led to Italy's defeat in World War II. A democratic republic replaced the monarchy in 1946 and economic revival followed. Italy was a charter member of NATO and the European Economic Community (EEC). It has been at the forefront of European economic and political unification, joining the Economic and Monetary Union in 1999. Persistent problems include illegal immigration, organized crime, corruption, high unemployment, sluggish economic growth, and the low incomes and technical standards of southern Italy compared with the prosperous north.

GEOGRAPHY

Location: Southern Europe, a peninsula extending into the central Mediterranean Sea, northeast of Tunisia
Geographic coordinates: 42 50 N, 12 50 E
Map references: Europe
Area:
total: 301,230 sq km
land: 294,020 sq km
water: 7,210 sq km
note: includes Sardinia and Sicily
Area - comparative: slightly larger than Arizona
Land boundaries:
total: 1,932.2 km
border countries: Austria 430 km, France 488 km, Holy See (Vatican City) 3.2 km, San Marino 39 km, Slovenia 232 km, Switzerland 740 km
Coastline: 7,600 km
Maritime claims:
territorial sea: 12 nm
continental shelf: 200-m depth or to the depth of exploitation
Climate: predominantly Mediterranean; Alpine in far north; hot, dry in south
Terrain: mostly rugged and mountainous; some plains, coastal lowlands
Elevation extremes:
lowest point: Mediterranean Sea 0 m
highest point: Mont Blanc (Monte Bianco) de Courmayeur 4,748 m (a secondary peak of Mont Blanc)
Natural resources: coal, mercury, zinc, potash, marble, barite, asbestos, pumice, fluorospar, feldspar, pyrite (sulfur), natural gas and crude oil reserves, fish, arable land
Land use:
arable land: 27.79%
permanent crops: 9.53%
other: 62.68% (2001)
Irrigated land: 26,980 sq km (1998 est.)
Natural hazards: regional risks include landslides, mudflows, avalanches, earthquakes, volcanic eruptions, flooding; land subsidence in Venice
Environment - current issues: air pollution from industrial emissions such as sulfur dioxide; coastal and inland rivers polluted from industrial and agricultural effluents; acid rain damaging lakes; inadequate industrial waste treatment and disposal facilities
Environment - international agreements:
party to: Air Pollution, Air Pollution-Nitrogen Oxides, Air Pollution-Sulfur 85, Air Pollution-Sulfur 94, Air Pollution-Volatile Organic Compounds, Antarctic-Environmental Protocol, Antarctic-Marine Living Resources, Antarctic Seals, Antarctic Treaty, Biodiversity, Climate Change, Climate Change-Kyoto Protocol, Desertification, Endangered Species, Environmental Modification, Hazardous Wastes, Law of the Sea, Marine Dumping, Ozone Layer Protection, Ship Pollution, Tropical Timber 83, Tropical Timber 94, Wetlands, Whaling
signed, but not ratified: Air Pollution-Persistent Organic Pollutants
Geography - note: strategic location dominating central Mediterranean as well as southern sea and air approaches to Western Europe

PEOPLE

Population: 58,103,033 (July 2005 est.)
Age structure:
0-14 years: 13.9% (male 4,166,213/female 3,919,288)
15-64 years: 66.7% (male 19,554,416/female 19,174,629)
65 years and over: 19.4% (male 4,698,441/female 6,590,046) (2005 est.)
Median age:
total: 41.77 years
male: 40.24 years
female: 43.35 years (2005 est.)
Population growth rate: 0.07% (2005 est.)
Birth rate: 8.89 births/1,000 population (2005 est.)
Death rate: 10.3 deaths/1,000 population (2005 est.)
Net migration rate: 2.07 migrant(s)/1,000 population (2005 est.)
Sex ratio:
at birth: 1.07 male(s)/female
under 15 years: 1.06 male(s)/female
15-64 years: 1.02 male(s)/female
65 years and over: 0.71 male(s)/female
total population: 0.96 male(s)/female (2005 est.)
Infant mortality rate:
total: 5.94 deaths/1,000 live births
male: 6.55 deaths/1,000 live births
female: 5.29 deaths/1,000 live births (2005 est.)
Life expectancy at birth:
total population: 79.68 years
male: 76.75 years
female: 82.81 years (2005 est.)
Total fertility rate: 1.28 children born/woman (2005 est.)
HIV/AIDS - adult prevalence rate: 0.5% (2001 est.)
HIV/AIDS - people living with HIV/AIDS: 140,000 (2001 est.)
HIV/AIDS - deaths: less than 1,000 (2003 est.)
Nationality:
noun: Italian(s)
adjective: Italian
Ethnic groups: Italian (includes small clusters of German-, French-, and Slovene-Italians in the north and Albanian-Italians and Greek-Italians in the south)
Religions: predominately Roman Catholic with mature Protestant and Jewish communities and a growing Muslim immigrant community
Languages: Italian (official), German (parts of Trentino-Alto Adige region are predominantly German speaking), French (small French-speaking minority in Valle d'Aosta region), Slovene (Slovene-speaking minority in the Trieste-Gorizia area)
Literacy:
definition: age 15 and over can read and write
total population: 98.6%
male: 99%
female: 98.3% (2003 est.)

GOVERNMENT

Country name:
conventional long form: Italian Republic
conventional short form: Italy
local long form: Repubblica Italiana
local short form: Italia
former: Kingdom of Italy
Government type: republic
Capital: Rome
Administrative divisions: 16 regions (regioni, singular - regione) and 5 autonomous regions* (regioni autonome, singular - regione autonoma); Abruzzo, Basilicata, Calabria, Campania, Emilia-Romagna, Friuli-Venezia Giulia*, Lazio, Liguria, Lombardia, Marche, Molise, Piemonte, Puglia, Sardegna*, Sicilia*, Toscana, Trentino-Alto Adige*, Umbria, Valle d'Aosta*, Veneto
Independence: 17 March 1861 (Kingdom of Italy proclaimed; Italy was not finally unified until 1870)
National holiday: Republic Day, 2 June (1946)
Constitution: passed 11 December 1947, effective 1 January 1948; amended many times
Legal system: based on civil law system; appeals treated as new trials; judicial review under certain conditions in Constitutional Court; has not accepted compulsory ICJ jurisdiction
Suffrage: 18 years of age; universal (except in senatorial elections, where minimum age is 25)
Executive branch:
chief of state: President Carlo Azeglio CIAMPI (since 13 May 1999)
head of government: Prime Minister (referred to in Italy as the president of the Council of Ministers) Silvio BERLUSCONI (since 10 June 2001)
cabinet: Council of Ministers nominated by the prime minister and approved by the president
elections: president elected by an electoral college consisting of both houses of parliament and 58 regional representatives for a seven-year term; election last held 13 May 1999 (next to be held May 2006); prime minister appointed by the president and confirmed by parliament
election results: Carlo Azeglio CIAMPI elected president; percent of electoral college vote - 70% note: a four-party government coalition includes Forza Italia, National Alliance, Northern League, and Union of Christian Democrats and Center Democrats
Legislative branch: bicameral Parliament or Parlamento consists of the Senate or Senato della Repubblica (315 seats elected by popular vote of which 232 are directly elected and 83 are elected by regional proportional representation; in addition, there are a small number of senators-for-life including former presidents of the republic; members serve five-year terms) and the Chamber of Deputies or Camera dei Deputati (630 seats; 475 are directly elected, 155 by regional proportional representation; members serve five-year terms)
elections: Senate - last held 13 May 2001 (next to be held 2006); Chamber of Deputies - last held 13 May 2001 (next to be held May 2006)
election results: Senate - percent of vote by party - NA%; seats by party - House of Liberties 172 (Forza Italia 77, National Alliance 47, UDC 31, Lega Padana 17), Olive Tree 108 (Democrats of the Left 63, Daisy Alliance 35, Greens 10), Per le Autonomie 10, other 25; Chamber of Deputies - percent of vote by party - NA%; seats by party - House of Liberties 337 (Forza Italia 176, National Alliance 97, UDC 36, Northern League 28), Olive Tree 214 (Democrats of the Left 135, Daisy Alliance 79), Rifondazione Communista (Italian Communist Party) 11, other 68
Judicial branch: Constitutional Court or Corte Costituzionale (composed of 15 judges: one-third appointed by the president, one-third elected by parliament, one-third elected by the ordinary and administrative Supreme Courts)
Political parties and leaders: Center-Left Olive Tree Coalition [Francesco RUTELLI] - Democrats of the Left, Daisy Alliance (including Italian Popular Party, Italian Renewal, Union of Democrats for Europe, The Democrats), Sunflower Alliance (including Green Federation, Italian Democratic Socialists), Italian Communist Party; Center-Right Freedom House Coalition [Silvio BERLUSCONI] (formerly House of Liberties and Freedom Alliance) - Forza Italia, National Alliance, The Whiteflower Alliance (includes Christian Democratic Center, United Christian Democrats), Northern League; Democrats of the Left or DS [Piero FASSINO]; Forza Italia or FI [Silvio BERLUSCONI]; Green Federation [Alfonso Pecoraro SCANIO]; Italian Communist Party or PdCI [Armando COSSUTTA]; Italian Renewal or RI [Lamberto DINI]; merged with PPI and I Democratici to form La Margherita (or The Daisy Alliance); Italian Social Democrats or SDI [Enrico BOSELLI]; Lega Padana [Roberto BERNARDELLI]; National Alliance or AN [Gianfranco FINI]; Northern League or NL [Umberto BOSSI]; Per le Autonomie [leader NA]; Socialist Movement-Tricolor Flame or MS-Fiamma [Luca ROMAGNOLI]; South Tyrol People's Party or SVP (German speakers) [Elmar Pichler ROLLE]; Sunflower Alliance (includes Green Federation, Italian Social Democrats); The Daisy Alliance (includes Italian Popular Party, Italian Renewal, Union of Democrats for Europe, The Democrats) [Francesco RUTELLI]; The Democrats [Arturo PARISI]; The Radicals (formerly Pannella Reformers and Autonomous List) [Marco PANNELLA]; Union of Democrats for Europe or UDEUR [Clemente MASTELLA]; Union of Christian and Center Democrats or UDC [Marco FOLLINI]
Political pressure groups and leaders: Italian manufacturers and merchants associations (Confindustria, Confcommercio); organized farm groups Confcoltivatori, Confagricoltura); Roman Catholic Church; three major trade union confederations (Confederazione Generale Italiana del Lavoro or CGIL [Guglielmo EPIFANI] which is left wing, Confederazione Italiana dei Sindacati Lavoratori or CISL [Savino PEZZOTTA], which is Roman Catholic centrist, and Unione Italiana del Lavoro or UIL [Luigi ANGELETTI] which is lay centrist)
International organization participation: AfDB, AsDB, Australia Group, BIS, BSEC (observer), CBSS (observer), CDB, CE, CEI, CERN, EAPC, EBRD, EIB, EMU, ESA, EU, FAO, G- 7, G- 8, G-10, IADB, IAEA, IBRD, ICAO, ICC, ICCt, ICFTU, ICRM, IDA, IEA, IFAD, IFC, IFRCS, IHO, ILO, IMF, IMO, Interpol, IOC, IOM, ISO, ITU, LAIA (observer), MIGA, MINURSO, NAM (guest), NATO, NEA, NSG, OAS (observer), OECD, OPCW, OSCE, Paris Club, PCA, UN, UNCTAD, UNESCO, UNHCR, UNIDO, UNIFIL, UNMEE, UNMIS, UNMOGIP, UNTSO, UPU, WCL, WCO, WEU, WHO, WIPO, WMO, WToO, WTO, ZC
Diplomatic representation in the US:
chief of mission: Ambassador Giovanni CASTELLANETA
chancery: 3000 Whitehaven Street NW, Washington, DC 20008
telephone: [1] (202) 612-4400
FAX: [1] (202) 518-2151
consulate(s) general: Boston, Chicago, Houston, Miami, New York, Los Angeles, Philadelphia, and San Francisco
consulate(s): Detroit and San Francisco
Diplomatic representation from the US:
chief of mission: Ambassador Ronald P. SPOGLI

embassy: Via Vittorio Veneto 121, 00187-Rome
mailing address: PSC 59, Box 100, APO AE 09624
telephone: [39] (06) 46741
FAX: [39] (06) 488-2672, 4674-2356
consulate(s) general: Florence, Milan, Naples
Flag description: three equal vertical bands of green (hoist side), white, and red; similar to the flag of Ireland, which is longer and is green (hoist side), white, and orange; also similar to the flag of the Cote d'Ivoire, which has the colors reversed - orange (hoist side), white, and green
note: inspired by the French flag brought to Italy by Napoleon in 1797

ECONOMY

Economy - overview: Italy has a diversified industrial economy with roughly the same total and per capita output as France and the UK. This capitalistic economy remains divided into a developed industrial north, dominated by private companies, and a less developed, welfare-dependent agricultural south, with 20% unemployment. Most raw materials needed by industry and more than 75% of energy requirements are imported. Over the past decade, Italy has pursued a tight fiscal policy in order to meet the requirements of the Economic and Monetary Unions and has benefited from lower interest and inflation rates. The current government has enacted numerous short-term reforms aimed at improving competitiveness and long-term growth. Italy has moved slowly, however, on implementing needed structural reforms, such as lightening the high tax burden and overhauling Italy's rigid labor market and over-generous pension system, because of the current economic slowdown and opposition from labor unions. But the leadership faces a severe economic constraint: the budget deficit has breached the 3% EU ceiling. The economy experienced no growth in 2005, and unemployment remained at a high level.
GDP (purchasing power parity): $1.645 trillion (2005 est.)
GDP (official exchange rate): $1.733 trillion (2005 est.)
GDP - real growth rate: 0% (2005 est.)
GDP - per capita: purchasing power parity - $28,300 (2005 est.)
GDP - composition by sector:
agriculture: 2.1%
industry: 28.8%
services: 69.1% (2005 est.)
Labor force: 24.49 million (2005 est.)
Labor force - by occupation: agriculture 5%, industry 32%, services 63% (2001)
Unemployment rate: 7.9% (2005 est.)
Population below poverty line: NA
Household income or consumption by percentage share:
lowest 10%: 2.1%
highest 10%: 26.6% (2000)
Distribution of family income - Gini index: 36 (2000)
Inflation rate (consumer prices): 1.9% (2005 est.)
Investment (gross fixed): 19.3% of GDP (2005 est.)
Budget:
revenues: $785.7 billion
expenditures: $861.5 billion, including capital expenditures of NA (2005 est.)
Public debt: 107.3% of GDP (2005 est.)
Agriculture - products: fruits, vegetables, grapes, potatoes, sugar beets, soybeans, grain, olives; beef, dairy products; fish
Industries: tourism, machinery, iron and steel, chemicals, food processing, textiles, motor vehicles, clothing, footwear, ceramics
Industrial production growth rate: -1.5% (2005 est.)
Electricity - production: 270.1 billion kWh (2003)
Electricity - production by source:
fossil fuel: 78.6%
hydro: 18.4%
nuclear: 0%
other: 3% (2001)
Electricity - consumption: 302.2 billion kWh (2003)
Electricity - exports: 500 million kWh (2003)
Electricity - imports: 51.5 billion kWh (2003)
Oil - production: 136,200 bbl/day (2003 est.)
Oil - consumption: 1.874 million bbl/day (2003 est.)
Oil - exports: 456,600 bbl/day (2001)
Oil - imports: 2.158 million bbl/day (2001)
Oil - proved reserves: 586.6 million bbl (1 January 2002)
Natural gas - production: 15.49 billion cu m (2001 est.)
Natural gas - consumption: 71.18 billion cu m (2001 est.)
Natural gas - exports: 61 million cu m (2001 est.)
Natural gas - imports: 54.78 billion cu m (2001 est.)
Natural gas - proved reserves: 209.7 billion cu m (1 January 2002)
Current account balance: $-27.62 billion (2005 est.)
Exports: $371.9 billion f.o.b. (2005 est.)
Exports - partners: Germany 13.6%, France 12.3%, US 8%, Spain 7.2%, UK 6.9%, Switzerland 4.2% (2004)
Imports: $369.2 billion f.o.b. (2005 est.)
Imports - partners: Germany 18%, France 10.9%, Netherlands 5.9%, Spain 4.6%, Belgium 4.4%, UK 4.3%, China 4.2% (2004)
Reserves of foreign exchange and gold: $60 billion (2005 est.)
Debt - external: $1.682 trillion (30 June 2005 est.)
Economic aid - donor: ODA, $1 billion (2002 est.)
Currency (code): euro (EUR)
note: on 1 January 1999, the European Monetary Union introduced the euro as a common currency to be used by financial institutions of member countries; on 1 January 2002, the euro became the sole currency for everyday transactions within the member countries
Currency code: EUR
Exchange rates: euros per US dollar - 0.79697 (2005), 0.8054 (2004), 0.886 (2003), 1.0626 (2002), 1.1175 (2001)
Fiscal year: calendar year

COMMUNICATIONS

Telephones - main lines in use: 26.596 million (2003)
Telephones - mobile cellular: 55.918 million (2003)
Telephone system:
general assessment: modern, well developed, fast; fully automated telephone, telex, and data services
domestic: high-capacity cable and microwave radio relay trunks
international: country code - 39; satellite earth stations - 3 Intelsat (with a total of 5 antennas - 3 for Atlantic Ocean and 2 for Indian Ocean), 1 Inmarsat (Atlantic Ocean region), and NA Eutelsat; 21 submarine cables
Radio broadcast stations: AM about 100, FM about 4,600, shortwave 9 (1998)
Radios: 50.5 million (1997)
Television broadcast stations: 358 (plus 4,728 repeaters) (1995)
Televisions: 30.3 million (1997)
Internet country code: .it
Internet hosts: 1,437,511 (2004)
Internet Service Providers (ISPs): 93 (Italy and Holy See) (2000)
Internet users: 18.5 million (2003)

TRANSPORTATION

Airports: 134 (2004 est.)
Airports - with paved runways:
total: 98
over 3,047 m: 7
2,438 to 3,047 m: 30
1,524 to 2,437 m: 16
914 to 1,523 m: 31
under 914 m: 14 (2005 est.)
Airports - with unpaved runways:
total: 37
1,524 to 2,437 m: 2
914 to 1,523 m: 16

under 914 m: 19 (2005 est.)
Heliports: 3 (2005 est.)
Pipelines: gas 17,335 km; oil 1,136 km (2004)
Railways:
total: 19,319 km (11,613 km electrified)
standard gauge: 18,001 km 1.435-m gauge (11,333 km electrified)
narrow gauge: 123 km 1.000-m gauge (122 km electrified); 1,195 km 0.950-m gauge (158 km electrified) (2004)
Roadways:
total: 479,688 km
paved: 479,688 km (including 6,620 km of expressways) (1999)
Waterways: 2,400 km
note: used for commercial traffic; of limited overall value compared to road and rail (2004)
Merchant marine:
total: 565 ships (1,000 GRT or over) 8,970,017 GRT/10,354,685 DWT
by type: bulk carrier 38, cargo 43, chemical tanker 128, combination ore/oil 1, container 19, liquefied gas 38, livestock carrier 2, passenger 16, passenger/cargo 152, petroleum tanker 53, refrigerated cargo 4, roll on/roll off 34, specialized tanker 11, vehicle carrier 26
foreign-owned: 47 (France 3, Greece 7, Monaco 2, Switzerland 5, Taiwan 8, Turkey 2, United Kingdom 5, United States 15)
registered in other countries: 125 (2005)
Ports and terminals: Augusta, Genoa, Livorno, Melilli Oil Terminal, Ravenna, Taranto, Trieste, Venice

MILITARY

Military branches: Army (Esercito Italiano, EI), Navy (Marina Militare Italiana, MMI), Air Force (Aeronautica Militare Italiana, AMI), Carabinieri Corps (Corpo dei Carabinieri, CC) (2005)
Military service age and obligation: 18 years of age (2004)
Manpower available for military service: *males age 18-49:* 13,491,260 (2005 est.)
Manpower fit for military service: *males age 18-49:* 10,963,513 (2005 est.)
Manpower reaching military service age annually: *males:* 286,344 (2005 est.)
Military expenditures - dollar figure: $28,182.8 million (2003)
Military expenditures - percent of GDP: 1.8% (2004)

TRANSNATIONAL ISSUES

Disputes - international: Italy's long coastline and developed economy entices tens of thousands of illegal immigrants from southeastern Europe and northern Africa
Illicit drugs: important gateway for and consumer of Latin American cocaine and Southwest Asian heroin entering the European market; money laundering by organized crime and from smuggling

JAMAICA

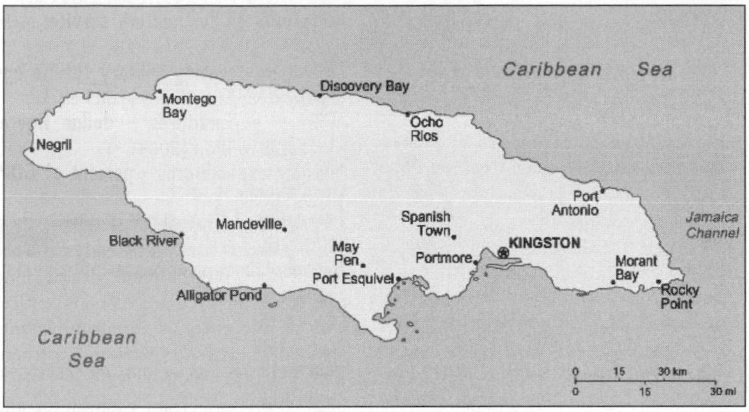

INTRODUCTION

Background: Jamaica gained full independence within the British Commonwealth in 1962. Deteriorating economic conditions during the 1970s led to recurrent violence and a drop off in tourism. Elections in 1980 saw the democratic socialists voted out of office. Political violence marred elections during the 1990s.

GEOGRAPHY

Location: Caribbean, island in the Caribbean Sea, south of Cuba
Geographic coordinates: 18 15 N, 77 30 W
Map references: Central America and the Caribbean
Area:
total: 10,991 sq km
land: 10,831 sq km
water: 160 sq km
Area - comparative: slightly smaller than Connecticut
Land boundaries: 0 km
Coastline: 1,022 km
Maritime claims:
measured from claimed archipelagic straight baselines
territorial sea: 12 nm
contiguous zone: 24 nm
exclusive economic zone: 200 nm
continental shelf: 200 nm or to edge of the continental margin
Climate: tropical; hot, humid; temperate interior
Terrain: mostly mountains, with narrow, discontinuous coastal plain
Elevation extremes:
lowest point: Caribbean Sea 0 m
highest point: Blue Mountain Peak 2,256 m
Natural resources: bauxite, gypsum, limestone
Land use:
arable land: 16.07%
permanent crops: 10.16%
other: 73.77% (2001)
Irrigated land: 250 sq km (1998 est.)
Natural hazards: hurricanes (especially July to November)
Environment - current issues: heavy rates of deforestation; coastal waters polluted by industrial waste, sewage, and oil spills; damage to coral reefs; air pollution in Kingston results from vehicle emissions
Environment - international agreements:
party to: Biodiversity, Climate Change, Climate Change-Kyoto Protocol, Desertification, Endangered Species, Hazardous Wastes, Law of the Sea, Marine Dumping, Marine Life Conservation, Ozone Layer Protection, Ship Pollution, Wetlands
signed, but not ratified: none of the selected agreements
Geography - note: strategic location between Cayman Trench and Jamaica Channel, the main sea lanes for the Panama Canal

PEOPLE

Population: 2,731,832 (July 2005 est.)
Age structure:
0-14 years: 27.5% (male 385,099/female 367,398)
15-64 years: 65.6% (male 897,953/female 893,509)
65 years and over: 6.9% (male 83,632/female 104,241) (2005 est.)
Median age:
total: 27.25 years
male: 26.55 years
female: 27.97 years (2005 est.)
Population growth rate: 0.71% (2005 est.)
Birth rate: 16.56 births/1,000 population (2005 est.)
Death rate: 5.37 deaths/1,000 population (2005 est.)
Net migration rate: -4.07 migrant(s)/1,000 population (2005 est.)
Sex ratio:
at birth: 1.05 male(s)/female
under 15 years: 1.05 male(s)/female
15-64 years: 1.01 male(s)/female
65 years and over: 0.8 male(s)/female
total population: 1 male(s)/female (2005 est.)
Infant mortality rate:
total: 12.36 deaths/1,000 live births
male: 13.35 deaths/1,000 live births
female: 11.32 deaths/1,000 live births (2005 est.)
Life expectancy at birth:
total population: 73.33 years
male: 71.63 years
female: 75.12 years (2005 est.)
Total fertility rate: 1.95 children born/woman (2005 est.)
HIV/AIDS - adult prevalence rate: 1.2% (2003 est.)
HIV/AIDS - people living with HIV/AIDS: 22,000 (2003 est.)
HIV/AIDS - deaths: 900 (2003 est.)
Nationality:
noun: Jamaican(s)
adjective: Jamaican
Ethnic groups: black 90.9%, East Indian 1.3%, white 0.2%, Chinese 0.2%, mixed 7.3%, other 0.1%
Religions: Protestant 61.3% (Church of God 21.2%, Baptist 8.8%, Anglican 5.5%, Seventh-Day Adventist 9%, Pentecostal 7.6%, Methodist 2.7%, United Church 2.7%, Brethren 1.1%, Jehovah's Witness 1.6%, Moravian 1.1%), Roman Catholic 4%, other including some spiritual cults 34.7%
Languages: English, patois English
Literacy:
definition: age 15 and over has ever attended school
total population: 87.9%
male: 84.1%
female: 91.6% (2003 est.)

GOVERNMENT

Country name:
conventional long form: none
conventional short form: Jamaica
Government type: constitutional parliamentary democracy
Capital: Kingston
Administrative divisions: 14 parishes; Clarendon, Hanover, Kingston, Manchester, Portland, Saint Andrew, Saint Ann, Saint Catherine, Saint Elizabeth, Saint James, Saint Mary, Saint Thomas, Trelawny, Westmoreland
note: for local government purposes, Kingston and Saint Andrew were amalgamated in 1923 into the present single corporate body known as the Kingston and Saint Andrew Corporation
Independence: 6 August 1962 (from UK)
National holiday: Independence Day, 6 August (1962)
Constitution: 6 August 1962

Legal system: based on English common law; has not accepted compulsory ICJ jurisdiction
Suffrage: 18 years of age; universal
Executive branch:
chief of state: Queen ELIZABETH II (since 6 February 1952), represented by Governor General Sir Howard Felix COOKE (since 1 August 1991)
head of government: Prime Minister Percival James PATTERSON (since 30 March 1992)
cabinet: Cabinet appointed by the governor general on the advice of the prime minister
elections: none; the monarch is hereditary; governor general appointed by the monarch on the recommendation of the prime minister; following legislative elections, the leader of the majority party or the leader of the majority coalition in the House of Representatives is appointed prime minister by the governor general; the deputy prime minister is recommended by the prime minister
Legislative branch: bicameral Parliament consists of the Senate (a 21-member body appointed by the governor general on the recommendations of the prime minister and the leader of the opposition; ruling party is allocated 13 seats, and the opposition is allocated eight seats) and the House of Representatives (60 seats; members are elected by popular vote to serve five-year terms)
elections: last held 16 October 2002 (next to be held in October 2007)
election results: percent of vote by party - PNP 52%, JLP 47.3%; seats by party - PNP 34, JLP 26
Judicial branch: Supreme Court (judges appointed by the governor general on the advice of the prime minister); Court of Appeal
Political parties and leaders: Jamaica Labor Party or JLP [Bruce GOLDING]; National Democratic Movement or NDM [Hyacinth BENNETT]; People's National Party or PNP [Percival James PATTERSON]
Political pressure groups and leaders: New Beginnings Movement or NBM; Rastafarians (black religious/racial cultists, pan-Africanists)
International organization participation: ACP, C, Caricom, CDB, FAO, G-15, G-77, IADB, IAEA, IBRD, ICAO, ICCt (signatory), ICFTU, ICRM, IFAD, IFC, IFRCS, IHO, ILO, IMF, IMO, Interpol, IOC, IOM, ISO, ITU, LAES, MIGA, NAM, OAS, OPANAL, OPCW, UN, UNCTAD, UNESCO, UNIDO, UPU, WCO, WFTU, WHO, WIPO, WMO, WToO, WTO
Diplomatic representation in the US:
chief of mission: Ambassador Gordon SHIRLEY
chancery: 1520 New Hampshire Avenue NW, Washington, DC 20036
telephone: [1] (202) 452-0660
FAX: [1] (202) 452-0081
consulate(s) general: Miami and New York
Diplomatic representation from the US:
chief of mission: Ambassador Brenda LaGrange JOHNSON
embassy: Jamaica Mutual Life Center, 2 Oxford Road, 3rd floor, Kingston 5
mailing address: use embassy street address
telephone: [1] (876) 929-4850 through 4859
FAX: [1] (876) 935-6001
Flag description: diagonal yellow cross divides the flag into four triangles - green (top and bottom) and black (hoist side and outer side)

ECONOMY

Economy - overview: The Jamaican economy is heavily dependent on services, which now account for 60% of GDP. The country continues to derive most of its foreign exchange from tourism, remittances, and bauxite/alumina. The global economic slowdown, particularly after the terrorist attacks in the US on 11 September 2001, stunted economic growth; the economy rebounded moderately in 2003-04, with brisk tourist seasons. But the economy faces serious long-term problems: high interest rates; increased foreign competition; a pressured, sometimes sliding, exchange rate; a sizable merchandise trade deficit; large-scale unemployment; and a growing internal debt, the result of government bailouts to ailing sectors of the economy. The ratio of debt to GDP is more than 125%. Inflation, previously a bright spot, is expected to remain in the double digits. Uncertain economic conditions have led to increased civil unrest, including gang violence fueled by the drug trade. In 2004, the government faced the difficult prospect of having to achieve fiscal discipline in order to maintain debt payments while simultaneously attacking a serious and growing crime problem which is hampering economic growth. Attempts at deficit control were derailed by Hurricane Ivan in September 2004, which required substantial government spending to repair the damage. Despite the hurricane, tourism looks set to enjoy solid growth for the foreseeable future.
GDP (purchasing power parity): $11.69 billion (2005 est.)
GDP (official exchange rate): $8.704 billion (2005 est.)
GDP - real growth rate: 3.2% (2005 est.)
GDP - per capita: purchasing power parity - $4,300 (2005 est.)
GDP - composition by sector:
agriculture: 4.9%
industry: 33.8%
services: 61.3% (2005 est.)
Labor force: 1.2 million (2005 est.)
Labor force - by occupation: agriculture 20.1%, industry 16.6%, services 63.4% (2003)
Unemployment rate: 11.5% (2005 est.)
Population below poverty line: 19.7% (2002 est.)
Household income or consumption by percentage share:
lowest 10%: 2.7%
highest 10%: 30.3% (2000)
Distribution of family income - Gini index: 37.9 (2000)
Inflation rate (consumer prices): 14.9% (2005 est.)
Investment (gross fixed): 32.4% of GDP (2005 est.)
Budget:
revenues: $3.224 billion
expenditures: $3.329 billion, including capital expenditures of $236 million (2005 est.)
Public debt: 127.5% of GDP (2005 est.)
Agriculture - products: sugarcane, bananas, coffee, citrus, yams, vegetables, poultry, goats, milk, crustaceans, and mollusks
Industries: tourism, bauxite/alumina, textiles, agro processing, wearing apparel, light manufactures, rum, cement, metal, paper, chemical products, telecommunications
Industrial production growth rate: -2% (2000 est.)
Electricity - production: 6.585 billion kWh (2003)
Electricity - production by source:
fossil fuel: 96.8%
hydro: 1.8%
nuclear: 0%
other: 1.4% (2001)
Electricity - consumption: 6.124 billion kWh (2003)
Electricity - exports: 0 kWh (2003)
Electricity - imports: 0 kWh (2003)
Oil - production: 0 bbl/day (2001 est.)
Oil - consumption: 69,000 bbl/day (2003 est.)
Oil - exports: NA (2001)
Oil - imports: NA (2001)
Current account balance: $-1.186 billion (2005 est.)
Exports: $1.593 billion f.o.b. (2005 est.)
Exports - partners: US 17.4%, Canada 14.8%, France 13%, China 10.5%, UK 8.7%, Netherlands 7.5%, Norway 6%, Germany 5.9% (2004)
Imports: $4.144 billion f.o.b. (2005 est.)
Imports - partners: US 38.7%, Trinidad and Tobago 13.2%, France 5.6%, Japan 4.7% (2004)
Reserves of foreign exchange and gold: $1.9 billion (2005 est.)

Debt - external: $6.792 billion (2005 est.)
Economic aid - recipient: $16 million (2003)
Currency (code): Jamaican dollar (JMD)
Currency code: JMD
Exchange rates: Jamaican dollars per US dollar - 62.04 (2005), 61.197 (2004), 57.741 (2003), 48.416 (2002), 45.996 (2001)
Fiscal year: 1 April - 31 March

COMMUNICATIONS

Telephones - main lines in use: 444,400 (2002)
Telephones - mobile cellular: 1.4 million (2002)
Telephone system:
general assessment: fully automatic domestic telephone network
domestic: NA
international: country code - 1-876; satellite earth stations - 2 Intelsat (Atlantic Ocean); 3 coaxial submarine cables
Radio broadcast stations: AM 10, FM 13, shortwave 0 (1998)
Radios: 1.215 million (1997)
Television broadcast stations: 7 (1997)
Televisions: 460,000 (1997)
Internet country code: .jm
Internet hosts: 1,480 (2003)
Internet Service Providers (ISPs): 21 (2000)
Internet users: 600,000 (2002)

TRANSPORTATION

Airports: 35 (2004 est.)
Airports - with paved runways:
total: 11
2,438 to 3,047 m: 2
914 to 1,523 m: 4
under 914 m: 5 (2005 est.)
Airports - with unpaved runways:
total: 24
914 to 1,523 m: 2
under 914 m: 22 (2005 est.)
Railways:
total: 272 km
standard gauge: 272 km 1.435-m gauge
note: 207 of these km belonging to the Jamaica Railway Corporation had been in common carrier service until 1992 but are no longer operational; 57 km of the remaining track is privately owned and used by ALCAN to transport bauxite (2003)
Roadways:
total: 18,700 km
paved: 13,909 km
unpaved: 5,610 km (1999)
Merchant marine:
total: 9 ships (1,000 GRT or over) 74,881 GRT/100,682 DWT
by type: bulk carrier 5, petroleum tanker 1, roll on/roll off 3
foreign-owned: 8 (Germany 2, Greece 5, UAE 1) (2005)
Ports and terminals: Kingston, Port Esquivel, Port Kaiser, Port Rhoades, Rocky Point

MILITARY

Military branches: Jamaica Defense Force: Ground Forces, Coast Guard, Air Wing
Military service age and obligation: 18 years of age for voluntary military service; younger recruits may be conscripted with parental consent (2001)
Manpower available for military service: *males age 18-49:* 696,900 (2005 est.)
Manpower fit for military service: *males age 18-49:* 587,006 (2005 est.)
Manpower reaching military service age annually: *males:* 26,080 (2005 est.)
Military expenditures - dollar figure: $31.2 million (2003)
Military expenditures - percent of GDP: 0.4% (2003)

TRANSNATIONAL ISSUES

Disputes - international: none
Illicit drugs: major transshipment point for cocaine from South America to North America and Europe; illicit cultivation of cannabis; government has an active manual cannabis eradication program; corruption is a major concern; substantial money-laundering activity; Colombian narcotics traffickers favor Jamaica for illicit financial transactions

JAN MAYEN

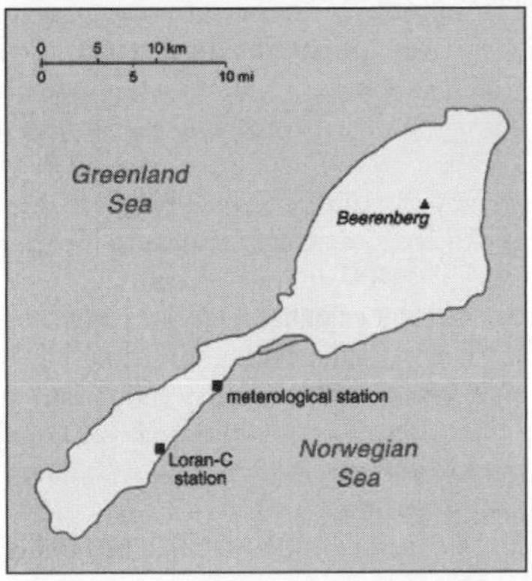

INTRODUCTION

Background: This desolate, mountainous island was named after a Dutch whaling captain who indisputably discovered it in 1614 (earlier claims are inconclusive). Visited only occasionally by seal hunters and trappers over the following centuries, the island came under Norwegian sovereignty in 1929. The long dormant Haakon VII Toppen/Beerenberg volcano resumed activity in 1970; it is the northernmost active volcano on earth.

GEOGRAPHY

Location: Northern Europe, island between the Greenland Sea and the Norwegian Sea, northeast of Iceland
Geographic coordinates: 71 00 N, 8 00 W
Map references: Arctic Region
Area:
total: 373 sq km
land: 373 sq km
water: 0 sq km
Area - comparative: slightly more than twice the size of Washington, DC
Land boundaries: 0 km
Coastline: 124.1 km
Maritime claims:
territorial sea: 4 nm
contiguous zone: 10 nm
exclusive economic zone: 200 nm
continental shelf: 200-m depth or to the depth of exploitation
Climate: arctic maritime with frequent storms and persistent fog
Terrain: volcanic island, partly covered by glaciers
Elevation extremes:
lowest point: Norwegian Sea 0 m
highest point: Haakon VII Toppen/ Beerenberg 2,277 m
Natural resources: none
Land use:
arable land: 0%
permanent crops: 0%
other: 100% (2001)
Irrigated land: 0 sq km (1998 est.)
Natural hazards: dominated by the volcano Haakon VII Toppen/Beerenberg; volcanic activity resumed in 1970
Environment - current issues: NA
Geography - note: barren volcanic island with some moss and grass

PEOPLE

Population: no indigenous inhabitants
note: personnel operate the Long Range Navigation (Loran-C) base and the weather and coastal services radio station (July 2005 est.)

GOVERNMENT

Country name:
conventional long form: none

conventional short form: Jan Mayen
Dependency status: territory of Norway; since August 1994, administered from Oslo through the county governor (fylkesmann) of Nordland; however, authority has been delegated to a station commander of the Norwegian Defense Communication Service
Legal system: the laws of Norway, where applicable, apply
Flag description: the flag of Norway is used

ECONOMY

Economy - overview: Jan Mayen is a volcanic island with no exploitable natural resources. Economic activity is limited to providing services for employees of Norway's radio and meteorological stations on the island.

COMMUNICATIONS

Radio broadcast stations: AM NA, FM NA, shortwave NA
note: there is one radio and meteorological station (1998)
Internet Service Providers (ISPs): 13 (Jan Mayen and Svalbard) (2000)

TRANSPORTATION

Airports: 1 (2004 est.)
Airports - with unpaved runways:
total: 1
1,524 to 2,437 m: 1 (2005 est.)
Ports and terminals: none; offshore anchorage only

MILITARY

Military - note: defense is the responsibility of Norway

TRANSNATIONAL ISSUES

Disputes - international: none

JAPAN

INTRODUCTION

Background: In 1603, a Tokugawa shogunate (military dictatorship) ushered in a long period of isolation from foreign influence in order to secure its power. For 250 years this policy enabled Japan to enjoy stability and a flowering of its indigenous culture. Following the Treaty of Kanagawa with the United States in 1854, Japan opened its ports and began to intensively modernize and industrialize. During the late 19th and early 20th centuries, Japan became a regional power that was able to defeat the forces of both China and Russia. It occupied Korea, Formosa (Taiwan), and southern Sakhalin Island. In 1933 Japan occupied Manchuria and in 1937 it launched a full-scale invasion of China. Japan attacked US forces in 1941 - triggering America's entry into World War II - and soon occupied much of East and Southeast Asia. After its defeat in World War II, Japan recovered to become an economic power and a staunch ally of the US. While the emperor retains his throne as a symbol of national unity, actual power rests in networks of powerful politicians, bureaucrats, and business executives. The economy experienced a major slowdown starting in the 1990s following three decades of unprecedented growth, but Japan still remains a major economic power, both in Asia and globally. In 2005, Japan began a two-year term as a non-permanent member of the UN Security Council.

GEOGRAPHY

Location: Eastern Asia, island chain between the North Pacific Ocean and the Sea of Japan, east of the Korean Peninsula
Geographic coordinates: 36 00 N, 138 00 E
Map references: Asia
Area:
total: 377,835 sq km
land: 374,744 sq km
water: 3,091 sq km
note: includes Bonin Islands (Ogasawara-gunto), Daito-shoto, Minami-jima, Okino-tori-shima, Ryukyu Islands (Nansei-shoto), and Volcano Islands (Kazan-retto)
Area - comparative: slightly smaller than California
Land boundaries: 0 km
Coastline: 29,751 km
Maritime claims:
territorial sea: 12 nm; between 3 nm and 12 nm in the international straits - La Perouse or Soya, Tsugaru, Osumi, and Eastern and Western Channels of the Korea or Tsushima Strait
contiguous zone: 24 nm
exclusive economic zone: 200 nm
Climate: varies from tropical in south to cool temperate in north
Terrain: mostly rugged and mountainous
Elevation extremes:
lowest point: Hachiro-gata -4 m
highest point: Mount Fuji 3,776 m
Natural resources: negligible mineral resources, fish
Land use:
arable land: 12.19%
permanent crops: 0.96%
other: 86.85% (2001)
Irrigated land: 26,790 sq km (1998 est.)
Natural hazards: many dormant and some active volcanoes; about 1,500 seismic occurrences (mostly tremors) every year; tsunamis; typhoons
Environment - current issues: air pollution from power plant emissions results in acid rain; acidification of lakes and reservoirs degrading water quality and threatening aquatic life; Japan is one of the largest consumers of fish and tropical timber, contributing to the depletion of these resources in Asia and elsewhere
Environment - international agreements:
party to: Antarctic-Environmental Protocol, Antarctic-Marine Living Resources, Antarctic Seals, Antarctic Treaty, Biodiversity, Climate Change, Climate Change-Kyoto Protocol, Desertification, Endangered Species, Environmental Modification, Hazardous Wastes, Law of the Sea, Marine Dumping, Ozone Layer Protection, Ship Pollution, Tropical Timber 83, Tropical Timber 94, Wetlands, Whaling
Geography - note: strategic location in northeast Asia

PEOPLE

Population: 127,417,244 (July 2005 est.)
Age structure:
0-14 years: 14.3% (male 9,328,584/female 8,866,772)
15-64 years: 66.2% (male 42,462,533/female 41,942,835)
65 years and over: 19.5% (male 10,435,284/female 14,381,236) (2005 est.)
Median age:
total: 42.64 years
male: 40.87 years
female: 44.44 years (2005 est.)
Population growth rate: 0.05% (2005 est.)
Birth rate: 9.47 births/1,000 population (2005 est.)

Death rate: 8.95 deaths/1,000 population (2005 est.)
Net migration rate: 0 migrant(s)/1,000 population (2005 est.)
Sex ratio:
at birth: 1.05 male(s)/female
under 15 years: 1.05 male(s)/female
15-64 years: 1.01 male(s)/female
65 years and over: 0.73 male(s)/female
total population: 0.96 male(s)/female (2005 est.)
Infant mortality rate:
total: 3.26 deaths/1,000 live births
male: 3.52 deaths/1,000 live births
female: 2.99 deaths/1,000 live births (2005 est.)
Life expectancy at birth:
total population: 81.15 years
male: 77.86 years
female: 84.61 years (2005 est.)
Total fertility rate: 1.39 children born/woman (2005 est.)
HIV/AIDS - adult prevalence rate: less than 0.1% (2003 est.)
HIV/AIDS - people living with HIV/AIDS: 12,000 (2003 est.)
HIV/AIDS - deaths: 500 (2003 est.)
Nationality:
noun: Japanese (singular and plural)
adjective: Japanese
Ethnic groups: Japanese 99%, others 1% (Korean 511,262, Chinese 244,241, Brazilian 182,232, Filipino 89,851, other 237,914)
note: up to 230,000 Brazilians of Japanese origin migrated to Japan in the 1990s to work in industries; some have returned to Brazil (2004)
Religions: observe both Shinto and Buddhist 84%, other 16% (including Christian 0.7%)
Languages: Japanese
Literacy:
definition: age 15 and over can read and write
total population: 99%
male: 99%
female: 99% (2002)

GOVERNMENT

Country name:
conventional long form: none
conventional short form: Japan
Government type: constitutional monarchy with a parliamentary government
Capital: Tokyo
Administrative divisions: 47 prefectures; Aichi, Akita, Aomori, Chiba, Ehime, Fukui, Fukuoka, Fukushima, Gifu, Gunma, Hiroshima, Hokkaido, Hyogo, Ibaraki, Ishikawa, Iwate, Kagawa, Kagoshima, Kanagawa, Kochi, Kumamoto, Kyoto, Mie, Miyagi, Miyazaki, Nagano, Nagasaki, Nara, Niigata, Oita, Okayama, Okinawa, Osaka, Saga, Saitama, Shiga, Shimane, Shizuoka, Tochigi, Tokushima, Tokyo, Tottori, Toyama, Wakayama, Yamagata, Yamaguchi, Yamanashi
Independence: 660 BC (traditional founding by Emperor JIMMU)
National holiday: Birthday of Emperor AKIHITO, 23 December (1933)
Constitution: 3 May 1947
Legal system: modeled after European civil law system with English-American influence; judicial review of legislative acts in the Supreme Court; accepts compulsory ICJ jurisdiction with reservations
Suffrage: 20 years of age; universal
Executive branch:
chief of state: Emperor AKIHITO (since 7 January 1989)
head of government: Prime Minister Junichiro KOIZUMI (since 26 April 2001)
cabinet: Cabinet appointed by the prime minister
elections: Diet designates prime minister; constitution requires that prime minister commands parliamentary majority; following legislative elections, leader of majority party or leader of majority coalition in House of Representatives usually becomes prime minister; KOIZUMI's term as leader of the LDP is scheduled to end in September 2006; a new prime minister may be chosen at that time; monarch is hereditary
Legislative branch: bicameral Diet or Kokkai consists of the House of Councillors or Sangi-in (242 seats - members elected for six-year terms; half reelected every three years; 146 members in multi-seat constituencies and 96 by proportional representation) and the House of Representatives or Shugi-in (480 seats - members elected for four-year terms; 300 in single-seat constituencies; 180 members by proportional representation in 11 regional blocs)
elections: House of Councillors - last held 11 July 2004 (next to be held in July 2007); House of Representatives - last held 11 September 2005 (next election by September 2009)
election results: House of Councillors - percent of vote by party - NA; seats by party - LDP 115, DPJ 82, Komeito 24, JCP 9, SDP 5, others 7; distribution of seats as of December 2004 - LDP 113, DPJ 83, Komeito 24, JCP 9, SDP 6, others 6
: House of Representatives - percent of vote by party - LDP 47.8%, DPJ 36.4%, others 15.8%; seats by party - LDP 296, DPJ 113, Komeito 31, JCP 9, SDP 7, others 24; distribution of seats as of December 2005 - LDP 296, DPJ 112, Komeito 31, JCP 9, SDP 7, others 25 (2005)
Judicial branch: Supreme Court (chief justice is appointed by the monarch after designation by the cabinet; all other justices are appointed by the cabinet)
Political parties and leaders: Democratic Party of Japan or DPJ [Seiji MAEHARA, president; Yukio HATOYAMA, secretary general]; Japan Communist Party or JCP [Kazuo SHII, chairman; Tadayoshi ICHIDA, head of secretariat]; Komeito [Takenori KANZAKI, chief representative; Tetsuzo FUYUSHIBA, secretary general]; Liberal Democratic Party or LDP [Junichiro KOIZUMI, president; Tsutomu TAKEBE, secretary general]; Social Democratic Party or SDP [Mizuho FUKUSHIMA, chairperson; Seiji MATAICHI, secretary general]
Political pressure groups and leaders: NA
International organization participation: AfDB, APEC, APT, ARF, AsDB, ASEAN (dialogue partner), Australia Group, BIS, CE (observer), CERN (observer), CP, EAS, EBRD, FAO, G-5, G-7, G-8, G-10, IADB, IAEA, IBRD, ICAO, ICC, ICFTU, ICRM, IDA, IEA, IFAD, IFC, IFRCS, IHO, ILO, IMF, IMO, Interpol, IOC, IOM, ISO, ITU, LAIA, MIGA, NAM (guest), NEA, NSG, OAS (observer), OECD, OPCW, OSCE (partner), Paris Club, PCA, PIF (partner), SAARC (observer), UN, UN Security Council (temporary), UNCTAD, UNDOF, UNESCO, UNHCR, UNIDO, UNITAR, UNMOVIC, UNRWA, UPU, WCL, WCO, WFTU, WHO, WIPO, WMO, WToO, WTO, ZC
Diplomatic representation in the US:
chief of mission: Ambassador Ryozo KATO
chancery: 2520 Massachusetts Avenue NW, Washington, DC 20008
telephone: [1] (202) 238-6700
FAX: [1] (202) 328-2187
consulate(s) general: Anchorage, Atlanta, Boston, Chicago, Denver, Detroit, Agana (Guam), Honolulu, Houston, Los Angeles, Miami, New Orleans, New York, Portland (Oregon), San Francisco, and Seattle
consulate(s): Saipan (Northern Mariana Islands)
Diplomatic representation from the US:
chief of mission: Ambassador J. Thomas SCHIEFFER
embassy: 1-10-5 Akasaka, Minato-ku, Tokyo 107-8420
mailing address: Unit 45004, Box 258, APO AP 96337-5004
telephone: [81] (03) 3224-5000
FAX: [81] (03) 3505-1862
consulate(s) general: Naha (Okinawa), Osaka-Kobe, Sapporo

consulate(s): Fukuoka, Nagoya
Flag description: white with a large red disk (representing the sun without rays) in the center

ECONOMY

Economy - overview: Government-industry cooperation, a strong work ethic, mastery of high technology, and a comparatively small defense allocation (1% of GDP) helped Japan advance with extraordinary rapidity to the rank of third largest economy in the world after the US and China, measured on a purchasing power parity (PPP) basis. Japan is the second largest economy, measured on an exchange rate basis. One notable characteristic of the economy is the working together of manufacturers, suppliers, and distributors in closely-knit groups called keiretsu. A second basic feature has been the guarantee of lifetime employment for a substantial portion of the urban labor force. Both features are now eroding. Japan's industrial sector is heavily dependent on imported raw materials and fuels. The tiny agricultural sector is highly subsidized and protected, with crop yields among the highest in the world. Usually self sufficient in rice, Japan must import about 50% of its requirements of other grain and fodder crops. Japan maintains one of the world's largest fishing fleets and accounts for nearly 15% of the global catch. For three decades, overall real economic growth had been spectacular: a 10% average in the 1960s, a 5% average in the 1970s, and a 4% average in the 1980s. Growth slowed markedly in the 1990s, averaging just 1.7%, largely because of the after effects of overinvestment during the late 1980s and contractionary domestic policies intended to wring speculative excesses from the stock and real estate markets and to force a restructuring of the economy. From 2000 to 2003, government efforts to revive economic growth met with little success and were further hampered by the slowing of the US, European, and Asian economies. In 2004 and 2005, growth improved and the lingering fears of deflation in prices and economic activity lessened. Japan's huge government debt, which totals 170% of GDP, and the aging of the population are two major long-run problems. A rise in taxes could be viewed as endangering the revival of growth. Internal conflict over the proper way to reform the financial system will continue as Japan Post's banking, insurance, and delivery services undergo privatization between 2007 and 2017.
GDP (purchasing power parity): $3.867 trillion (2005 est.)
GDP (official exchange rate): $4.955 trillion (2005 est.)
GDP - real growth rate: 2.1% (2005 est.)
GDP - per capita: purchasing power parity - $30,400 (2005 est.)
GDP - composition by sector:
agriculture: 1.3%
industry: 25.3%
services: 73.5% (2005 est.)
Labor force: 66.4 million (2005 est.)
Labor force - by occupation: agriculture 4.6%, industry 27.8%, services 67.7% (2004)
Unemployment rate: 4.3% (2005 est.)
Population below poverty line: NA
Household income or consumption by percentage share:
lowest 10%: 4.8%
highest 10%: 21.7% (1993)
Distribution of family income - Gini index: 37.9 (2000)
Inflation rate (consumer prices): -0.2% (2005 est.)
Investment (gross fixed): 24.4% of GDP (2005 est.)
Budget:
revenues: $1.429 trillion
expenditures: $1.775 trillion, including capital expenditures (public works only) of about $71 billion (2005 est.)
Public debt: 170% of GDP (2005 est.)
Agriculture - products: rice, sugar beets, vegetables, fruit, pork, poultry, dairy products, eggs, fish
Industries: among world's largest and technologically advanced producers of motor vehicles, electronic equipment, machine tools, steel and nonferrous metals, ships, chemicals, textiles, processed foods
Industrial production growth rate: 1.3% (2005 est.)
Electricity - production: 1.017 trillion kWh (2003)
Electricity - production by source:
fossil fuel: 60%
hydro: 8.4%
nuclear: 29.8%
other: 1.8% (2001)
Electricity - consumption: 946.3 billion kWh (2003)
Electricity - exports: 0 kWh (2003)
Electricity - imports: 0 kWh (2003)
Oil - production: 120,700 bbl/day (2003 est.)
Oil - consumption: 5.578 million bbl/day (2003 est.)
Oil - exports: 93,360 bbl/day (2001)
Oil - imports: 5.449 million bbl/day (2001)
Oil - proved reserves: 29.29 million bbl (1 January 2002)
Natural gas - production: 2.519 billion cu m (2001 est.)
Natural gas - consumption: 80.42 billion cu m (2001 est.)
Natural gas - exports: 0 cu m (2001 est.)
Natural gas - imports: 77.73 billion cu m (2001 est.)
Natural gas - proved reserves: 20.02 billion cu m (1 January 2002)
Current account balance: $158.3 billion (2005 est.)
Exports: $550.5 billion f.o.b. (2005 est.)
Exports - partners: US 22.7%, China 13.1%, South Korea 7.8%, Taiwan 7.4%, Hong Kong 6.3% (2004)
Imports: $451.1 billion f.o.b. (2005 est.)
Imports - partners: China 20.7%, US 14%, South Korea 4.9%, Australia 4.3%, Indonesia 4.1%, Saudi Arabia 4.1%, UAE 4% (2004)
Reserves of foreign exchange and gold: $845 billion (2004)
Debt - external: $1.545 trillion (31 December 2004)
Economic aid - donor: ODA, $8.9 billion (2004)
Currency (code): yen (JPY)
Currency code: JPY
Exchange rates: yen per US dollar - 109 (2005), 108.19 (2004), 115.93 (2003), 125.39 (2002), 121.53 (2001)
Fiscal year: 1 April - 31 March

COMMUNICATIONS

Telephones - main lines in use: 71.149 million (2002)
Telephones - mobile cellular: 86,658,600 (2003)
Telephone system:
general assessment: excellent domestic and international service
domestic: high level of modern technology and excellent service of every kind
international: country code - 81; satellite earth stations - 5 Intelsat (4 Pacific Ocean and 1 Indian Ocean), 1 Intersputnik (Indian Ocean region), and 1 Inmarsat (Pacific and Indian Ocean regions); submarine cables to China, Philippines, Russia, and US (via Guam) (1999)
Radio broadcast stations: AM 215 plus 370 repeaters, FM 89 plus 485 repeaters, shortwave 21 (2001)
Radios: 120.5 million (1997)
Television broadcast stations: 211 plus 7,341 repeaters
note: in addition, US Forces are served by 3 TV stations and 2 TV cable services (1999)
Televisions: 86.5 million (1997)
Internet country code: .jp
Internet hosts: 12,962,065 (2003)
Internet Service Providers (ISPs): 73 (2000)
Internet users: 57.2 million (2002)

TRANSPORTATION

Airports: 174 (2004 est.)

Airports - with paved runways:
total: 142
over 3,047 m: 7
2,438 to 3,047 m: 39
1,524 to 2,437 m: 37
914 to 1,523 m: 29
under 914 m: 30 (2005 est.)
Airports - with unpaved runways:
total: 31
over 3,047 m: 1
914 to 1,523 m: 4
under 914 m: 26 (2005 est.)
Heliports: 15 (2005 est.)
Pipelines: gas 2,719 km; oil 170 km; oil/gas/water 60 km (2004)
Railways:
total: 23,577 km (16,519 km electrified)
standard gauge: 3,204 km 1.435-m gauge (3,204 km electrified)
narrow gauge: 77 km 1.372-m gauge (77 km electrified); 20,265 km 1.067-m gauge (13,227 km electrified); 11 km 0.762-m gauge (11 km electrified) (2004)
Roadways:
total: 1,177,278 km
paved: 914,745 km (including 6,946 km of expressways)
unpaved: 262,533 km (2002)
Waterways: 1,770 km (seagoing vessels use inland seas) (2004)
Merchant marine:
total: 702 ships (1,000 GRT or over) 10,149,196 GRT/12,680,544 DWT
by type: bulk carrier 136, cargo 29, chemical tanker 23, container 13, liquefied gas 53, passenger 16, passenger/cargo 157, petroleum tanker 160, refrigerated cargo 4, roll on/roll off 52, vehicle carrier 59
registered in other countries: 2,233 (2005)
Ports and terminals: Chiba, Kawasaki, Kiire, Kisarazu, Kobe, Mizushima, Nagoya, Osaka, Tokyo, Yohohama

MILITARY

Military branches: Ground Self-Defense Force (Army), Maritime Self-Defense Force (Navy), Air Self-Defense Force (Air Force)
Military service age and obligation: 18 years of age for voluntary military service (2001)
Manpower available for military service: *males age 18-49:* 27,003,112 (2005 est.)
Manpower fit for military service: *males age 18-49:* 22,234,663 (2005 est.)
Manpower reaching military service age annually: *males:* 683,147 (2005 est.)
Military expenditures - dollar figure: $45.841 billion (2004)
Military expenditures - percent of GDP: 1% (2004)

TRANSNATIONAL ISSUES

Disputes - international: the sovereignty dispute over the islands of Etorofu, Kunashiri, and Shikotan, and the Habomai group, known in Japan as the "Northern Territories" and in Russia as the"Southern Kuril Islands", occupied by the Soviet Union in 1945, now administered by Russia and claimed by Japan, remains the primary sticking point to signing a peace treaty formally ending World War II hostilities; Japan and South Korea claim Liancourt Rocks (Take-shima/Tok-do), occupied by South Korea since 1954; China and Taiwan dispute both Japan's claims to the uninhabited islands of the Senkaku-shoto (Diaoyu Tai) and Japan's unilaterally declared exclusive economic zone in the East China Sea, the site of intensive hydrocarbon prospecting

JARVIS ISLAND

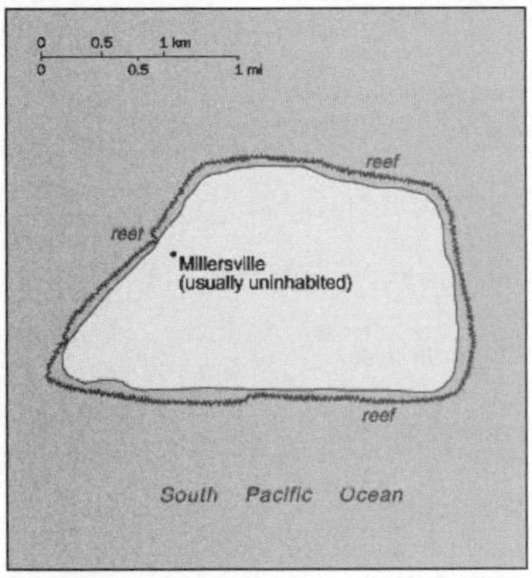

INTRODUCTION

Background: First discovered by the British in 1821, the uninhabited island was annexed by the US in 1858, but abandoned in 1879 after tons of guano had been removed. The UK annexed the island in 1889, but never carried out plans for further exploitation. The US occupied and reclaimed the island in 1935. Abandoned after World War II, the island is currently a National Wildlife Refuge administered by the US Department of the Interior.

GEOGRAPHY

Location: Oceania, island in the South Pacific Ocean, about half way between Hawaii and the Cook Islands
Geographic coordinates: 0 23 S, 160 01 W
Map references: Oceania
Area:
total: 4.5 sq km
land: 4.5 sq km
water: 0 sq km
Area - comparative: about eight times the size of The Mall in Washington, DC
Land boundaries: 0 km
Coastline: 8 km
Maritime claims:
territorial sea: 12 nm
exclusive economic zone: 200 nm
Climate: tropical; scant rainfall, constant wind, burning sun
Terrain: sandy, coral island surrounded by a narrow fringing reef
Elevation extremes:
lowest point: Pacific Ocean 0 m
highest point: unnamed location 7 m
Natural resources: guano (deposits worked until late 1800s), terrestrial and aquatic wildlife
Land use:
arable land: 0%
permanent crops: 0%
other: 100% (2001)
Irrigated land: 0 sq km (1998 est.)
Natural hazards: the narrow fringing reef surrounding the island poses a maritime hazard
Environment - current issues: no natural fresh water resources
Geography - note: sparse bunch grass, prostrate vines, and low-growing shrubs; primarily a nesting, roosting, and foraging habitat for seabirds, shorebirds, and marine wildlife

PEOPLE

Population: uninhabited
note: Millersville settlement on western side of island occasionally used as a weather station from 1935 until World War II, when it was abandoned; reoccupied in 1957 during the International Geophysical Year by scientists who left in 1958; public entry is by special-use permit from US Fish and Wildlife Service only and generally restricted to scientists and educators; visited annually by US Fish and Wildlife Service (July 2005 est.)

GOVERNMENT

Country name:
conventional long form: none
conventional short form: Jarvis Island
Dependency status: unincorporated territory of the US; administered from Washington, DC, by the Fish and Wildlife Service of the US Department of the Interior as part of the National Wildlife Refuge system
Legal system: the laws of the US, where

applicable, apply
Flag description: the flag of the US is used

ECONOMY

Economy - overview: no economic activity

TRANSPORTATION

Ports and terminals: none; offshore anchorage only; note - there is one small boat landing area in the middle of the west coast and another near the southwest corner of the island
Transportation - note: there is a day beacon near the middle of the west coast

MILITARY

Military - note: defense is the responsibility of the US; visited annually by the US Coast Guard

TRANSNATIONAL ISSUES

Disputes - international: none

JERSEY

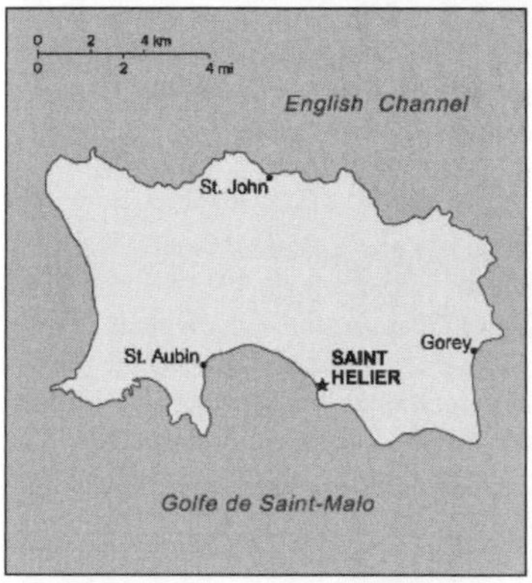

INTRODUCTION

Background: The island of Jersey and the other Channel Islands represent the last remnants of the medieval Dukedom of Normandy that held sway in both France and England. These islands were the only British soil occupied by German troops in World War II.

GEOGRAPHY

Location: Western Europe, island in the English Channel, northwest of France
Geographic coordinates: 49 15 N, 2 10 W
Map references: Europe
Area:
total: 116 sq km
land: 116 sq km
water: 0 sq km
Area - comparative: about two-thirds the size of Washington, DC
Land boundaries: 0 km
Coastline: 70 km
Maritime claims:
territorial sea: 3 nm
exclusive fishing zone: 12 nm
Climate: temperate; mild winters and cool summers
Terrain: gently rolling plain with low, rugged hills along north coast
Elevation extremes:
lowest point: Atlantic Ocean 0 m
highest point: unnamed location 143 m
Natural resources: arable land
Land use:
arable land: 0%
permanent crops: 0%
other: 100% (2001)
Irrigated land: NA sq km
Natural hazards: NA
Environment - current issues: NA
Geography - note: largest and southernmost of Channel Islands; about 30% of population concentrated in Saint Helier

PEOPLE

Population: 90,812 (July 2005 est.)
Age structure:
0-14 years: 17.5% (male 8,222/female 7,658)
15-64 years: 67% (male 30,296/female 30,561)
65 years and over: 15.5% (male 6,176/female 7,899) (2005 est.)
Median age:
total: 40.89 years
male: 40.13 years
female: 41.63 years (2005 est.)
Population growth rate: 0.32% (2005 est.)
Birth rate: 9.66 births/1,000 population (2005 est.)
Death rate: 9.19 deaths/1,000 population (2005 est.)
Net migration rate: 2.75 migrant(s)/1,000 population (2005 est.)
Sex ratio:
at birth: 1.08 male(s)/female
under 15 years: 1.07 male(s)/female
15-64 years: 0.99 male(s)/female
65 years and over: 0.78 male(s)/female
total population: 0.97 male(s)/female (2005 est.)
Infant mortality rate:
total: 5.24 deaths/1,000 live births
male: 5.6 deaths/1,000 live births
female: 4.85 deaths/1,000 live births (2005 est.)
Life expectancy at birth:
total population: 79.24 years
male: 76.77 years
female: 81.91 years (2005 est.)
Total fertility rate: 1.57 children born/woman (2005 est.)
HIV/AIDS - adult prevalence rate: NA%
HIV/AIDS - people living with HIV/AIDS: NA
HIV/AIDS - deaths: NA
Nationality:
noun: Channel Islander(s)
adjective: Channel Islander
Ethnic groups: Jersey 51.1%, British 34.8%, Irish, French, and other white 6.6%, Portuguese/Madeiran 6.4%, other 1.1% (2001 census)
Religions: Anglican, Roman Catholic, Baptist, Congregational New Church, Methodist, Presbyterian
Languages: English 94.5% (official), Portuguese 4.6%, other 0.9% (2001 census)
Literacy:
definition: NA
total population: NA%
male: NA%
female: NA%

GOVERNMENT

Country name:
conventional long form: Bailiwick of Jersey
conventional short form: Jersey
Dependency status: British crown dependency
Government type: NA
Capital: Saint Helier
Administrative divisions: none (British crown dependency)
Independence: none (British crown dependency)
National holiday: Liberation Day, 9 May (1945)
Constitution: unwritten; partly statutes, partly common law and practice
Legal system: English law and local statute; justice is administered by the Royal Court
Suffrage: NA years of age; universal adult
Executive branch:
chief of state: Queen ELIZABETH II (since 6 February 1952)
head of government: Lieutenant Governor and Commander in Chief Air Chief Marshall Sir John CHESHIRE (since 24 January 2001) and Bailiff Philip Martin BAILHACHE (since NA February 1995)
cabinet: committees appointed by the Assembly of the States
elections: none; the monarch is hereditary; lieutenant governor and bailiff appointed by the monarch

Legislative branch: unicameral Assembly of the States (55 voting members - 12 senators (elected for 6-year terms), 12 constables or heads of parishes (elected for 3-year terms), 29 deputies (elected for 3-year terms); the bailiff and the deputy bailiff; and 3 non-voting members - the Dean of Jersey, the Attorney General, and the Solicitor General all appointed by the monarch)
elections: last held NA (next to be held NA); note - on 23 November 2005, 29 deputies, independents were elected
election results: percent of vote - NA%; seats - independents 53
Judicial branch: Royal Court (judges elected by an electoral college and the bailiff)
Political parties and leaders: none; all independents
Political pressure groups and leaders: none
Diplomatic representation in the US: none (British crown dependency)
Diplomatic representation from the US: none (British crown dependency)
Flag description: white with a diagonal red cross extending to the corners of the flag; in the upper quadrant, surmounted by a yellow crown, a red shield with the three lions of England in yellow

ECONOMY

Economy - overview: The Channel Island economy is based on international financial services, agriculture, and tourism. In 1996 the finance sector accounted for about 60% of the island's output. Potatoes, cauliflower, tomatoes, and especially flowers are important export crops, shipped mostly to the UK. The Jersey breed of dairy cattle is known worldwide and represents an important export income earner. Milk products go to the UK and other EU countries. Tourism accounts for 24% of GDP. In recent years, the government has encouraged light industry to locate in Jersey, with the result that an electronics industry has developed alongside the traditional manufacturing of knitwear. All raw material and energy requirements are imported, as well as a large share of Jersey's food needs. Light taxes and death duties make the island a popular tax haven. Living standards come close to those of the UK.
GDP (purchasing power parity): $3.6 billion (2003 est.)
GDP (official exchange rate): NA
GDP - real growth rate: NA%
GDP - per capita: purchasing power parity - $40,000 (2003 est.)
GDP - composition by sector:
agriculture: 5%
industry: 2%
services: 93% (1996)
Labor force: 52,790 (2004)
Unemployment rate: 0.9% (2004 est.)
Population below poverty line: NA
Household income or consumption by percentage share:
lowest 10%: NA%
highest 10%: NA%
Inflation rate (consumer prices): 5.3% (2004)
Budget:
revenues: $601 million
expenditures: $588 million, including capital expenditures of $98 million (2000 est.)
Agriculture - products: potatoes, cauliflower, tomatoes; beef, dairy products
Industries: tourism, banking and finance, dairy
Industrial production growth rate: NA%
Electricity - consumption: 630.1 million kWh (2004 est.)
Electricity - imports: NA kWh; note - electricity supplied by France
Exports: $NA
Exports - partners: UK (2004)
Imports: $NA
Imports - partners: UK (2004)
Debt - external: none
Economic aid - recipient: none
Currency (code): British pound (GBP); note - there is also a Jersey pound
Currency code: GBP
Exchange rates: Jersey pounds per US dollar - 0.54 (2005), 0.5462 (2004), 0.6125 (2003), 0.6672 (2002), 0.6947 (2001)
note: the Jersey pound is at par with the British pound
Fiscal year: 1 April - 31 March

COMMUNICATIONS

Telephones - main lines in use: 73,900 (2001)
Telephones - mobile cellular: 61,400 (2001)
Telephone system:
general assessment: NA
domestic: NA
international: 3 submarine cables
Radio broadcast stations: AM NA, FM 1, shortwave 0 (1998)
Radios: NA
Television broadcast stations: 2 (1997)
Televisions: NA
Internet country code: .je
Internet Service Providers (ISPs): NA
Internet users: NA

TRANSPORTATION

Airports: 1 (2004 est.)
Airports - with paved runways:
total: 1
1,524 to 2,437 m: 1 (2005 est.)
Ports and terminals: Gorey, Saint Aubin, Saint Helier

MILITARY

Military - note: defense is the responsibility of the UK

TRANSNATIONAL ISSUES

Disputes - international: none

JOHNSTON ATOLL

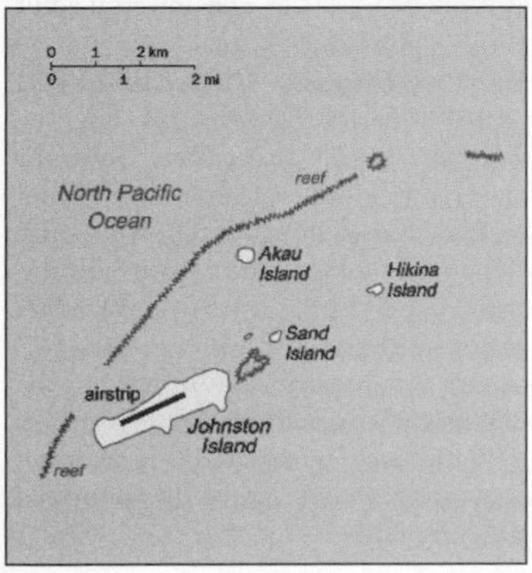

INTRODUCTION

Background: Both the US and the Kingdom of Hawaii annexed Johnston Atoll in 1858, but it was the US that mined the guano deposits until the late 1880s. Johnston and Sand Islands were designated wildlife refuges in 1926. The US Navy took over the atoll in 1934, and subsequently the US Air Force assumed control in 1948. The site was used for high-altitude nuclear tests in the 1950s and 1960s, and until late in 2000 the atoll was maintained as a storage and disposal site for chemical weapons. Munitions destruction is now complete. Cleanup and closure of the facility was completed by May 2005.

GEOGRAPHY

Location: Oceania, atoll in the North Pacific Ocean 717 nm (1328 km) southwest of Honolulu, Hawaii, about one-third of the way from Hawaii to the Marshall Islands
Geographic coordinates: 16 45 N, 169 31 W
Map references: Oceania
Area:
total: 2.63 sq km
land: 2.63 sq km

water: 0 sq km
Area - comparative: about 4.7 times the size of The Mall in Washington, DC
Land boundaries: 0 km
Coastline: 34 km
Maritime claims:
territorial sea: 12 nm
exclusive economic zone: 200 nm
Climate: tropical, but generally dry; consistent northeast trade winds with little seasonal temperature variation
Terrain: mostly flat
Elevation extremes:
lowest point: Pacific Ocean 0 m
highest point: Summit Peak 5 m
Natural resources: guano deposits worked until depletion about 1890, terrestrial and aquatic wildlife
Land use:
arable land: 0%
permanent crops: 0%
other: 100% (2001)
Irrigated land: 0 sq km (1998 est.)
Natural hazards: NA
Environment - current issues: no natural fresh water resources
Geography - note: strategic location in the North Pacific Ocean; Johnston Island and Sand Island are natural islands, which have been expanded by coral dredging; North Island (Akau) and East Island (Hikina) are manmade islands formed from coral dredging; the egg-shaped reef is 34 km in circumference; closed to the public; a former US nuclear weapons test site; site of now-closed Johnston Atoll Chemical Agent Disposal System (JACADS); most facilities dismantled and cleanup complete in 2004; some low-growing vegetation

PEOPLE

Population: uninhabited
note: in previous years, there was an average of 1,100 US military and civilian contractor personnel present; as of September 2001, population had decreased significantly when US Army Chemical Activity Pacific (USACAP) departed; as of May 2005 all US government personnel had left the island (July 2005 est.)

GOVERNMENT

Country name:
conventional long form: none
conventional short form: Johnston Atoll
Dependency status: unincorporated territory of the US; administered from Honolulu, HI, by Pacific Air Forces, Hickam Air Force Base, and the Fish and Wildlife Service of the US Department of the Interior as part of the National Wildlife Refuge system
Legal system: the laws of the US, where applicable, apply
Flag description: the flag of the US is used

ECONOMY

Economy - overview: no economic activity

COMMUNICATIONS

Internet Service Providers (ISPs): 1 256 KB circuit to US Department of Defense-run Nonsecure Internet Protocol Router Network (NIPRNET) (2002)

TRANSPORTATION

Airports: 1
note: non-operational (2005)
Airports - with paved runways:
total: 1
2,438 to 3,047 m: 1 (2005 est.)
Ports and terminals: Johnston Island

MILITARY

Military - note: defense is the responsibility of the US

TRANSNATIONAL ISSUES

Disputes - international: none

JORDAN

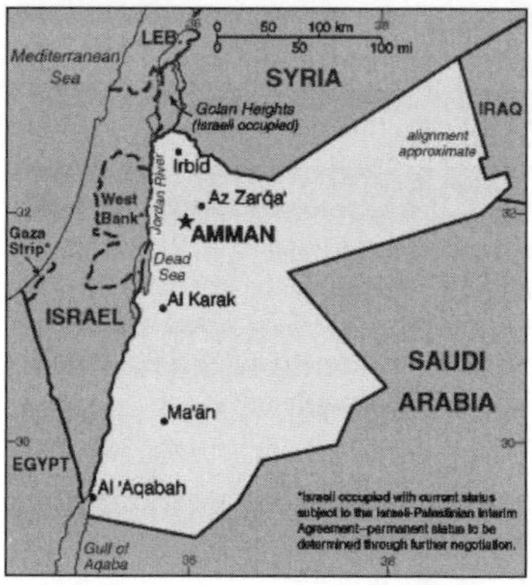

INTRODUCTION

Background: For most of its history since independence from British administration in 1946, Jordan was ruled by King HUSSEIN (1953-99). A pragmatic ruler, he successfully navigated competing pressures from the major powers (US, USSR, and UK), various Arab states, Israel, and a large internal Palestinian population, despite several wars and coup attempts. In 1989 he reinstituted parliamentary elections and gradual political liberalization; in 1994 he signed a peace treaty with Israel. King ABDALLAH II, the son of King HUSSEIN, assumed the throne following his father's death in February 1999. Since then, he has consolidated his power and undertaken an aggressive economic reform program. Jordan acceded to the World Trade Organization in 2000, and began to participate in the European Free Trade Association in 2001. After a two-year delay, parliamentary and municipal elections took place in the summer of 2003. The prime minister appointed in December 2005 said the government would focus on political reforms, improving conditions for the poor, and fighting corruption.

GEOGRAPHY

Location: Middle East, northwest of Saudi Arabia
Geographic coordinates: 31 00 N, 36 00 E
Map references: Middle East
Area:
total: 92,300 sq km
land: 91,971 sq km
water: 329 sq km
Area - comparative: slightly smaller than Indiana
Land boundaries:
total: 1,635 km
border countries: Iraq 181 km, Israel 238 km, Saudi Arabia 744 km, Syria 375 km, West Bank 97 km
Coastline: 26 km
Maritime claims:
territorial sea: 3 nm
Climate: mostly arid desert; rainy season in west (November to April)
Terrain: mostly desert plateau in east, highland area in west; Great Rift Valley separates East and West Banks of the Jordan River
Elevation extremes:
lowest point: Dead Sea -408 m
highest point: Jabal Ram 1,734 m
Natural resources: phosphates, potash, shale oil
Land use:
arable land: 2.67%
permanent crops: 1.83%
other: 95.5% (2001)
Irrigated land: 750 sq km (1998 est.)
Natural hazards: droughts; periodic earthquakes
Environment - current issues: limited natural fresh water resources; deforestation; overgrazing; soil erosion; desertification

Environment - international agreements:
party to: Biodiversity, Climate Change, Climate Change-Kyoto Protocol, Desertification, Endangered Species, Hazardous Wastes, Law of the Sea, Marine Dumping, Ozone Layer Protection, Wetlands
signed, but not ratified: none of the selected agreements
Geography - note: strategic location at the head of the Gulf of Aqaba and as the Arab country that shares the longest border with Israel and the occupied West Bank

PEOPLE

Population: 5,759,732 (July 2005 est.)
Age structure:
0-14 years: 34.5% (male 1,015,084/female 973,220)
15-64 years: 61.7% (male 1,897,643/ female 1,656,570)
65 years and over: 3.8% (male 106,168/ female 111,047) (2005 est.)
Median age:
total: 22.62 years
male: 23.25 years
female: 21.94 years (2005 est.)
Population growth rate: 2.56% (2005 est.)
Birth rate: 21.76 births/1,000 population (2005 est.)
Death rate: 2.63 deaths/1,000 population (2005 est.)
Net migration rate: 6.42 migrant(s)/ 1,000 population (2005 est.)
Sex ratio:
at birth: 1.06 male(s)/female
under 15 years: 1.04 male(s)/female
15-64 years: 1.15 male(s)/female
65 years and over: 0.96 male(s)/female
total population: 1.1 male(s)/female (2005 est.)
Infant mortality rate:
total: 17.35 deaths/1,000 live births
male: 20.75 deaths/1,000 live births
female: 13.75 deaths/1,000 live births (2005 est.)
Life expectancy at birth:
total population: 78.24 years
male: 75.75 years
female: 80.88 years (2005 est.)
Total fertility rate: 2.71 children born/woman (2005 est.)
HIV/AIDS - adult prevalence rate: less than 0.1% (2001 est.)
HIV/AIDS - people living with HIV/AIDS: 600 (2003 est.)
HIV/AIDS - deaths: less than 500 (2003 est.)
Nationality:
noun: Jordanian(s)
adjective: Jordanian
Ethnic groups: Arab 98%, Circassian 1%, Armenian 1%
Religions: Sunni Muslim 92%, Christian 6% (majority Greek Orthodox, but some Greek and Roman Catholics, Syrian Orthodox, Coptic Orthodox, Armenian Orthodox, and Protestant denominations), other 2% (several small Shi'a Muslim and Druze populations) (2001 est.)
Languages: Arabic (official), English widely understood among upper and middle classes
Literacy:
definition: age 15 and over can read and write
total population: 91.3%
male: 95.9%
female: 86.3% (2003 est.)

GOVERNMENT

Country name:
conventional long form: Hashemite Kingdom of Jordan
conventional short form: Jordan
local long form: Al Mamlakah al Urduniyah al Hashimiyah
local short form: Al Urdun
former: Transjordan
Government type: constitutional monarchy
Capital: 'Amman
Administrative divisions: 12 governorates (muhafazat, singular - muhafazah); Ajlun, Al 'Aqabah, Al Balqa', Al Karak, Al Mafraq, 'Amman, At Tafilah, Az Zarqa', Irbid, Jarash, Ma'an, Madaba
Independence: 25 May 1946 (from League of Nations mandate under British administration)
National holiday: Independence Day, 25 May (1946)
Constitution: 1 January 1952; amended 1954, 1955, 1958, 1960, 1965, 1973, 1974, 1976, 1984
Legal system: based on Islamic law and French codes; judicial review of legislative acts in a specially provided High Tribunal; has not accepted compulsory ICJ jurisdiction
Suffrage: 18 years of age; universal
Executive branch:
chief of state: King ABDALLAH II (since 7 February 1999); Prince HUSSEIN (born 1994), eldest son of King ABDALLAH, is first in line to inherit the throne
head of government: Prime Minister Marouf al-BAKHIT(since 24 November 2005); Deputy Prime Minister Ziad FARIZ (since 24 November 2005)
cabinet: Cabinet appointed by the prime minister in consultation with the monarch
elections: none; the monarch is hereditary; prime minister appointed by the monarch
Legislative branch: bicameral National Assembly or Majlis al-'Umma consists of the Senate, also called the House of Notables (Majlis al-Ayan) (55 seats; members appointed by the monarch from designated categories of public figures; members serve four-year terms) and the House of Representatives, also called the House of Deputies (Majlis al-Nuwaab) (110 seats; members elected by popular vote on the basis of proportional representation to serve four-year terms; note - six seats are reserved for women and are allocated by a special electoral panel if no women are elected)
elections: House of Representatives - last held 17 June 2003 (next to be held NA 2007)
election results: House of Representatives - percent of vote by party - independents and others 89.6%, Islamic Action Front (IAF) 10.4%; seats by party - independents and others 92, Islamic Action Front 18; note - one of the six quota seats was given to a female IAF candidate
note: the House of Representatives has been convened and dissolved by the monarch several times since 1974; in November 1989, the first parliamentary elections in 22 years were held; political parties were not legalized until 1992; King ABDALLAH delayed the 2001 elections until 2003
Judicial branch: Court of Cassation; Supreme Court (court of final appeal)
Political parties and leaders: Al-Ajyal [Muhammad KHALAYLEH, secretary general]; Al-Umma (Nation) Party [Ahmad al-HANANDEH, secretary general]; Arab Land Party [Dr. Ayishah Salih HIJAZAYN, secretary general]; Ba'th Arab Progressive Party [Fu'ad DABBUR, secretary general]; Communist Party [Munir HAMARINAH, secretary general]; Constitutional National Party [Ahmad al-SHUNNAQ, secretary general; Democratic Arab Islamic Movement [Yusuf ABU BAKR, president]; Green Party [Muhammad BATAYNEH, secretary general]; Islamic Action Front [Hazma MANSOUR, secretary general]; Islamic al-Walsat Party [Marwan al-FAURI], secretary general; Jordanian Democratic Left Party [Musa MA'AYTEH, secretary general]; Jordanian Democratic Popular Unity Party [Sa'id Dhiyab Ali MUSTAFA, secretary general]; Jordanian People's Democratic (Hashd) Party [Ahmad YUSUF, secretary general]; Jordanian Progressive Party [Fawwaz al-ZUBI, secretary general]; Labor Party [Dr. Mazin Sulayman Jiryis HANNA, secretary general]; Muslim Centrist Party [leader NA]; National Action (Haqq) Party [Tariq al-KAYYALI, secretary general]; National Constitutional Party [Abdul Hadi MAJALI, secretary general]; National Movement for Direct Democracy [Mahmud al-NUWAYHI, secretary general]; Pan-Arab

(Democratic) Movement [Mahmud al-NUWAYHI, secretary general]; (Arab) Socialist Ba'th Party [Taysir al-HIMSI, secretary general]
Political pressure groups and leaders: Anti-Normalization Committee [Ali Abu SUKKAR, president vice chairman]; Jordanian Bar Association [Saleh ARMOUTI, president]; Jordanian Press Association [Sayf al-SHARIF, president]; Muslim Brotherhood [Abd-al-Majid DHUNAYBAT, secretary general]
International organization participation: ABEDA, AFESD, AMF, CAEU, FAO, G-77, IAEA, IBRD, ICAO, ICC, ICCt, ICFTU, ICRM, IDA, IDB, IFAD, IFC, IFRCS, ILO, IMF, IMO, Interpol, IOC, IOM, ISO, ITU, LAS, MIGA, MINUSTAH, MONUC, NAM, OIC, ONUB, OPCW, OSCE (partner), PCA, UN, UNAMSIL, UNCTAD, UNESCO, UNIDO, UNMEE, UNMIL, UNMIS, UNOCI, UNOMIG, UNRWA, UPU, WCO, WFTU, WHO, WIPO, WMO, WToO, WTO
Diplomatic representation in the US:
chief of mission: Ambassador Karim Tawfiq KAWAR
chancery: 3504 International Drive NW, Washington, DC 20008
telephone: [1] (202) 966-2664
FAX: [1] (202) 966-3110
Diplomatic representation from the US:
chief of mission: Ambassador David M. HALE
embassy: Abdoun, Amman
mailing address: P. O. Box 354, Amman 11118 Jordan; Unit 70200, Box 5, APO AE 09892-0200
telephone: [962] (6) 590-6000
FAX: [962] (6) 592-0121
Flag description: three equal horizontal bands of black (top), representing the Abbassid Caliphate, white, representing the Ummayyad Caliphate, and green, representing the Fatimid Caliphate; a red isosceles triangle on the hoist side, representing the Great Arab Revolt of 1916, and bearing a small white seven-pointed star symbolizing the seven verses of the opening Sura (Al-Fatiha) of the Holy Koran; the seven points on the star represent faith in One God, humanity, national spirit, humility, social justice, virtue, and aspirations; design is based on the Arab Revolt flag of World War I

ECONOMY

Economy - overview: Jordan is a small Arab country with inadequate supplies of water and other natural resources such as oil. Debt, poverty, and unemployment are fundamental problems, but King ABDALLAH, since assuming the throne in 1999, has undertaken some broad economic reforms in a long-term effort to improve living standards. Amman in the past three years has worked closely with the IMF, practiced careful monetary policy, and made substantial headway with privatization. The government also has liberalized the trade regime sufficiently to secure Jordan's membership in the WTO (2000), a free trade accord with the US (2001), and an association agreement with the EU (2001). These measures have helped improve productivity and have put Jordan on the foreign investment map. Jordan imported most of its oil from Iraq, but the US-led war in Iraq in 2003 made Jordan more dependent on oil from other Gulf nations forcing the Jordanian government to raise retail petroleum product prices and the sales tax base. Jordan's export market, which is heavily dependent on exports to Iraq, was also affected by the war but recovered quickly while contributing to the Iraq recovery effort. The main challenges facing Jordan are reducing dependence on foreign grants, reducing the budget deficit, and creating investment incentives to promote job creation.
GDP (purchasing power parity): $27.7 billion (2005 est.)
GDP (official exchange rate): $11.86 billion (2005 est.)
GDP - real growth rate: 5.5% (2005 est.)
GDP - per capita: purchasing power parity - $4,800 (2005 est.)
GDP - composition by sector:
agriculture: 3.5%
industry: 29.9%
services: 66.7% (2005 est.)
Labor force: 1.46 million (2005 est.)
Labor force - by occupation: agriculture 5%, industry 12.5%, services 82.5% (2001 est.)
Unemployment rate: 15% official rate; unofficial rate is approximately 30% (2004 est.)
Population below poverty line: 30% (2001 est.)
Household income or consumption by percentage share:
lowest 10%: 3.3%
highest 10%: 29.8% (1997)
Distribution of family income - Gini index: 36.4 (1997)
Inflation rate (consumer prices): 3.9% (2005 est.)
Investment (gross fixed): 20.9% of GDP (2005 est.)
Budget:
revenues: $3.68 billion
expenditures: $4.688 billion, including capital expenditures of $782 million (2005 est.)
Public debt: 77.7% of GDP (2005 est.)
Agriculture - products: wheat, barley, citrus, tomatoes, melons, olives; sheep, goats, poultry
Industries: phosphate mining, pharmaceuticals, petroleum refining, cement, potash, inorganic chemicals, light manufacturing, tourism
Industrial production growth rate: 7.5% (2005 est.)
Electricity - production: 7.517 billion kWh (2003)
Electricity - production by source:
fossil fuel: 99.4%
hydro: 0.6%
nuclear: 0%
other: 0% (2001)
Electricity - consumption: 7.959 billion kWh (2003)
Electricity - exports: 4 million kWh (2003)
Electricity - imports: 972 million kWh (2003)
Oil - production: 40 bbl/day (2004 est.)
Oil - consumption: 103,000 bbl/day (2004 est.)
Oil - exports: 0 bbl/day (2004 est.)
Oil - imports: 100,000 bbl/day (2004 est.)
Oil - proved reserves: 445,000 bbl (1 January 2002)
Natural gas - production: 290 million cu m (2001 est.)
Natural gas - consumption: 290 million cu m (2001 est.)
Natural gas - exports: 0 cu m (2001 est.)
Natural gas - imports: 0 cu m (2001 est.)
Natural gas - proved reserves: 3.256 billion cu m (1 January 2002)
Current account balance: $-1.08 billion (2005 est.)
Exports: $4.226 billion f.o.b. (2005 est.)
Exports - partners: US 28.9%, Iraq 17.6%, India 7.1%, Saudi Arabia 5.6% (2004)
Imports: $8.681 billion f.o.b. (2005 est.)
Imports - partners: Saudi Arabia 19.8%, China 8.4%, Germany 6.8%, US 6.8% (2004)
Reserves of foreign exchange and gold: $5.509 billion (2005 est.)
Debt - external: $8.459 billion (2005 est.)
Economic aid - recipient: ODA, $500 million (2004 est.)
Currency (code): Jordanian dinar (JOD)
Currency code: JOD
Exchange rates: Jordanian dinars per US dollar - 0.71 (2005), 0.709 (2004), 0.709 (2003), 0.709 (2002), 0.709 (2001)
Fiscal year: calendar year

COMMUNICATIONS

Telephones - main lines in use: 622,600 (2003)
Telephones - mobile cellular: 1,325,300 (2003)
Telephone system:
general assessment: service has improved recently with increased use of digital switching equipment, but better access to

the telephone system is needed in the rural areas and easier access to pay telephones is needed by the urban public
domestic: microwave radio relay transmission and coaxial and fiber-optic cable are employed on trunk lines; considerable use of mobile cellular systems; Internet service is available
international: country code - 962; satellite earth stations - 3 Intelsat, 1 Arabsat, and 29 land and maritime Inmarsat terminals; fiber-optic cable to Saudi Arabia and microwave radio relay link with Egypt and Syria; connection to international submarine cable FLAG (Fiber-Optic Link Around the Globe); participant in MEDARABTEL; international links total about 4,000
Radio broadcast stations: AM 6, FM 5, shortwave 1 (1999)
Radios: 1.66 million (1997)
Television broadcast stations: 20 (plus 96 repeaters) (1995)
Televisions: 500,000 (1997)
Internet country code: .jo
Internet hosts: 3,160 (2004)
Internet Service Providers (ISPs): 5 (2000)
Internet users: 457,000 (2003)

TRANSPORTATION

Airports: 17 (2004 est.)
Airports - with paved runways:
total: 15
over 3,047 m: 7
2,438 to 3,047 m: 6
914 to 1,523 m: 1
under 914 m: 1 (2005 est.)
Airports - with unpaved runways:
total: 2
under 914 m: 2 (2005 est.)
Heliports: 1 (2005 est.)
Pipelines: gas 10 km; oil 743 km (2004)
Railways:
total: 505 km
narrow gauge: 505 km 1.050-m gauge (2004)
Roadways:
total: 7,364 km
paved: 7,364 km (2003)
Merchant marine:
total: 20 ships (1,000 GRT or over) 78,814 GRT/92,695 DWT
by type: bulk carrier 2, cargo 7, container 2, passenger/cargo 5, roll on/roll off 4
foreign-owned: 12 (Greece 3, UAE 9)
registered in other countries: 14 (2005)
Ports and terminals: Al 'Aqabah

MILITARY

Military branches: Jordanian Armed Forces (JAF): Royal Jordanian Land Force, Royal Jordanian Navy, Royal Jordanian Air Force, and Special Operations Command (SOCOM); note - Public Security Directorate normally falls under Ministry of Interior but comes under JAF in wartime or crisis situations
Military service age and obligation: 17 years of age for voluntary military service; conscription at age 18 was suspended in 1999, although all males under age 37 are required to register (2004)
Manpower available for military service: *males age 17-49:* 1,573,995 (2005 est.)
Manpower fit for military service: *males age 17-49:* 1,348,076 (2005 est.)
Manpower reaching military service age annually: *males:* 60,625 (2005 est.)
Military expenditures - dollar figure: $1.46 billion (2004)
Military expenditures - percent of GDP: 14.6% (2004)

TRANSNATIONAL ISSUES

Disputes - international: 2004 Agreement settles border dispute with Syria pending demarcation
Refugees and internally displaced persons: *refugees (country of origin):* 1,740,170 (Palestinian Refugees (UNRWA))
IDPs: 800,000 (1967 Arab-Israeli War) (2004)

JUAN DE NOVA ISLAND

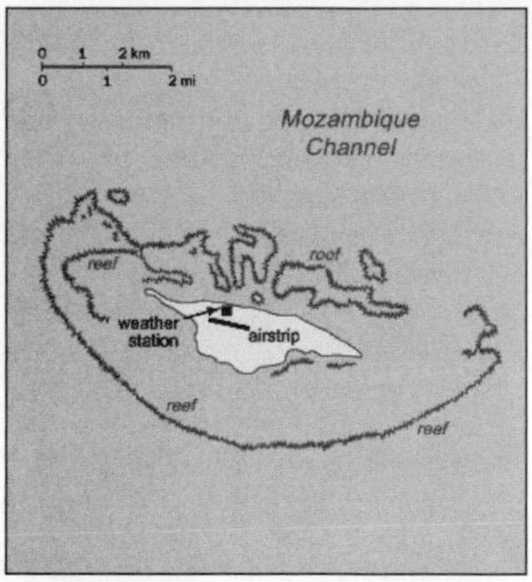

INTRODUCTION

Background: Named after a famous 15th century Spanish navigator and explorer, the island has been a French possession since 1897. It has been exploited for its guano and phosphate. Presently a small military garrison oversees a meteorological station.

GEOGRAPHY

Location: Southern Africa, island in the Mozambique Channel, about one-third of the way between Madagascar and Mozambique
Geographic coordinates: 17 03 S, 42 45 E
Map references: Africa
Area:
total: 4.4 sq km
land: 4.4 sq km
water: 0 sq km
Area - comparative: about seven times the size of The Mall in Washington, DC
Land boundaries: 0 km
Coastline: 24.1 km
Maritime claims:
territorial sea: 12 nm
exclusive economic zone: 200 nm
continental shelf: 200-m depth or to the depth of exploitation
Climate: tropical
Terrain: low and flat
Elevation extremes:
lowest point: Indian Ocean 0 m
highest point: unnamed location 10 m
Natural resources: guano deposits and other fertilizers
Land use:
arable land: 0%
permanent crops: 0%
other: 100% (90% forest) (2001)
Irrigated land: 0 sq km (1998 est.)
Natural hazards: periodic cyclones
Environment - current issues: NA
Geography - note: wildlife sanctuary

PEOPLE

Population: no indigenous inhabitants
note: there is a small French military garrison along with a few meteorologists; occasionally visited by scientists (July 2005 est.)

GOVERNMENT

Country name:
conventional long form: none
conventional short form: Juan de Nova Island
local long form: none
local short form: Ile Juan de Nova
Dependency status: possession of France; administered by the Administrateur Superieur of the French Southern and Antarctic Lands
Legal system: the laws of France, where applicable, apply
Flag description: the flag of France is used

ECONOMY

Economy - overview: Up to 12,000 tons of guano are mined per year.

COMMUNICATIONS

Communications - note: 1 meteorological station

TRANSPORTATION

Airports: 1 (2004 est.)
Airports - with unpaved runways:
total: 1
914 to 1,523 m: 1 (2005 est.)

Ports and terminals: none; offshore anchorage only

MILITARY

Military - note: defense is the responsibility of France

TRANSNATIONAL ISSUES

Disputes - international: claimed by Madagascar

KAZAKHSTAN

INTRODUCTION

Background: Native Kazakhs, a mix of Turkic and Mongol nomadic tribes who migrated into the region in the 13th century, were rarely united as a single nation. The area was conquered by Russia in the 18th century and Kazakhstan became a Soviet Republic in 1936. During the 1950s and 1960s agricultural "Virgin Lands" program, Soviet citizens were encouraged to help cultivate Kazakhstan's northern pastures. This influx of immigrants (mostly Russians, but also some other deported nationalities) skewed the ethnic mixture and enabled non-Kazakhs to outnumber natives. Independence in 1991 caused many of these newcomers to emigrate. Current issues include: developing a cohesive national identity; expanding the development of the country's vast energy resources and exporting them to world markets; achieving a sustainable economic growth outside the oil, gas, and mining sectors; and strengthening relations with neighboring states and other foreign powers.

GEOGRAPHY

Location: Central Asia, northwest of China; a small portion west of the Ural River in eastern-most Europe
Geographic coordinates: 48 00 N, 68 00 E
Map references: Asia
Area:
total: 2,717,300 sq km
land: 2,669,800 sq km
water: 47,500 sq km
Area - comparative: slightly less than four times the size of Texas
Land boundaries:
total: 12,012 km
border countries: China 1,533 km, Kyrgyzstan 1,051 km, Russia 6,846 km, Turkmenistan 379 km, Uzbekistan 2,203 km
Coastline: 0 km (landlocked); note - Kazakhstan borders the Aral Sea, now split into two bodies of water (1,070 km), and the Caspian Sea (1,894 km)
Maritime claims: none (landlocked)
Climate: continental, cold winters and hot summers, arid and semiarid
Terrain: extends from the Volga to the Altai Mountains and from the plains in western Siberia to oases and desert in Central Asia
Elevation extremes:
lowest point: Vpadina Kaundy -132 m
highest point: Khan Tangiri Shyngy (Pik Khan-Tengri) 6,995 m
Natural resources: major deposits of petroleum, natural gas, coal, iron ore, manganese, chrome ore, nickel, cobalt, copper, molybdenum, lead, zinc, bauxite, gold, uranium
Land use:
arable land: 7.98%
permanent crops: 0.05%
other: 91.97% (2001)
Irrigated land: 23,320 sq km (1998 est.)
Natural hazards: earthquakes in the south, mudslides around Almaty
Environment - current issues: radioactive or toxic chemical sites associated with former defense industries and test ranges scattered throughout the country pose health risks for humans and animals; industrial pollution is severe in some cities; because the two main rivers which flowed into the Aral Sea have been diverted for irrigation, it is drying up and leaving behind a harmful layer of chemical pesticides and natural salts; these substances are then picked up by the wind and blown into noxious dust storms; pollution in the Caspian Sea; soil pollution from overuse of agricultural chemicals and salination from poor infrastructure and wasteful irrigation practices
Environment - international agreements:
party to: Air Pollution, Biodiversity, Climate Change, Desertification, Endangered Species, Hazardous Wastes, Ozone Layer Protection, Ship Pollution
signed, but not ratified: Climate Change-Kyoto Protocol
Geography - note: landlocked; Russia leases approximately 6,000 sq km of territory enclosing the Baykonur Cosmodrome; in January 2004, Kazakhstan and Russia extended the lease to 2050

PEOPLE

Population: 15,185,844 (July 2005 est.)
Age structure:
0-14 years: 23.7% (male 1,834,535/female 1,758,988)
15-64 years: 68.4% (male 5,075,243/female 5,312,536)
65 years and over: 7.9% (male 424,341/female 780,201) (2005 est.)
Median age:
total: 28.52 years
male: 26.92 years
female: 30.25 years (2005 est.)
Population growth rate: 0.3% (2005 est.)
Birth rate: 15.78 births/1,000 population (2005 est.)
Death rate: 9.46 deaths/1,000 population (2005 est.)
Net migration rate: -3.34 migrant(s)/1,000 population (2005 est.)
Sex ratio:
at birth: 1.06 male(s)/female
under 15 years: 1.04 male(s)/female
15-64 years: 0.96 male(s)/female
65 years and over: 0.54 male(s)/female
total population: 0.93 male(s)/female (2005 est.)
Infant mortality rate:
total: 29.21 deaths/1,000 live births
male: 33.85 deaths/1,000 live births
female: 24.3 deaths/1,000 live births (2005 est.)
Life expectancy at birth:
total population: 66.55 years
male: 61.21 years
female: 72.2 years (2005 est.)
Total fertility rate: 1.89 children born/woman (2005 est.)
HIV/AIDS - adult prevalence rate: 0.2% (2001 est.)
HIV/AIDS - people living with HIV/AIDS: 16,500 (2001 est.)
HIV/AIDS - deaths: less than 200 (2003 est.)
Nationality:
noun: Kazakhstani(s)
adjective: Kazakhstani
Ethnic groups: Kazakh (Qazaq) 53.4%, Russian 30%, Ukrainian 3.7%, Uzbek 2.5%, German 2.4%, Tatar 1.7%, Uygur 1.4%, other 4.9% (1999 census)
Religions: Muslim 47%, Russian Orthodox 44%, Protestant 2%, other 7%

Languages: Kazakh (Qazaq, state language) 64.4%, Russian (official, used in everyday business, designated the "language of interethnic communication") 95% (2001 est.)

Literacy:
definition: age 15 and over can read and write
total population: 98.4%
male: 99.1%
female: 97.7% (1999 est.)

GOVERNMENT

Country name:
conventional long form: Republic of Kazakhstan
conventional short form: Kazakhstan
local long form: Qazaqstan Respublikasy
local short form: none
former: Kazakh Soviet Socialist Republic

Government type: republic; authoritarian presidential rule, with little power outside the executive branch

Capital: Astana; note - the government moved from Almaty to Astana in December 1998

Administrative divisions: 14 provinces (oblystar, singular - oblys) and 3 cities* (qala, singular - qalasy); Almaty Oblysy, Almaty Qalasy*, Aqmola Oblysy (Astana), Aqtobe Oblysy, Astana Qalasy*, Atyrau Oblysy, Batys Qazaqstan Oblysy (Oral), Bayqongyr Qalasy*, Mangghystau Oblysy (Aqtau), Ongtustik Qazaqstan Oblysy (Shymkent), Pavlodar Oblysy, Qaraghandy Oblysy, Qostanay Oblysy, Qyzylorda Oblysy, Shyghys Qazaqstan Oblysy (Oskemen), Soltustik Qazaqstan Oblysy (Petropavlovsk), Zhambyl Oblysy (Taraz)
note: administrative divisions have the same names as their administrative centers (exceptions have the administrative center name following in parentheses); in 1995, the Governments of Kazakhstan and Russia entered into an agreement whereby Russia would lease for a period of 20 years an area of 6,000 sq km enclosing the Baykonur space launch facilities and the city of Bayqongyr (Baykonur, formerly Leninsk); in 2004, a new agreement extended the lease to 2050

Independence: 16 December 1991 (from the Soviet Union)

National holiday: Independence Day, 16 December (1991)

Constitution: first post-independence constitution adopted 28 January 1993; new constitution adopted by national referendum 30 August 1995

Legal system: based on civil law system

Suffrage: 18 years of age, universal

Executive branch:
chief of state: President Nursultan A. NAZARBAYEV (chairman of the Supreme Soviet from 22 February 1990, elected president 1 December 1991)
head of government: Prime Minister Daniyal AKHMETOV (since 13 June 2003); First Deputy Prime Minister Akhmetzhan YESIMOV (since 14 May 2004)
cabinet: Council of Ministers appointed by the president
elections: president elected by popular vote for a seven-year term; election last held 4 December 2005 (next to be held NA 2012); prime minister and first deputy prime minister appointed by the president
election results: Nursultan A. NAZARBAYEV reelected president; percent of vote - Nursultan A. NAZARBAYEV 91.1%, Zharmakhan A. TUYAKBAI 6.6%, Alikhan M. BAIMENOV 1.6%
note: President NAZARBAYEV arranged a referendum in 1995 that extended his term of office and expanded his presidential powers: only he can initiate constitutional amendments, appoint and dismiss the government, dissolve Parliament, call referenda at his discretion, and appoint administrative heads of regions and cities

Legislative branch: bicameral Parliament consists of the Senate (39 seats; 7 senators are appointed by the president; other members are elected by local government bodies, two from each of the 14 oblasts, the capital of Astana, and the city of Almaty, to serve six-year terms; note - formerly composed of 47 seats) and the Mazhilis (77 seats; 10 out of the 77 Mazhilis members are elected from the winning party's lists; members are popularly elected to serve five-year terms)
elections: Senate - (indirect) last held 17 September 1999 (next to be held December 2005); Mazhilis - last held 19 September and 3 October 2004 (next to be held September 2009)
election results: Senate - percent of vote by party - NA%; seats by party - NA; candidates nominated by local councils; Mazhilis - percent of vote by party - NA%; seats by party - Otan 42, AIST 11, ASAR (All Together) 4, Aq Zhol (Bright Path) 1, Democratic Party 1 (party refused to take the seat due to criticism of the election's conduct, and seat remained unoccupied), independent 18; note - most independent candidates are affiliated with parastatal enterprises and other pro-government institutions

Judicial branch: Supreme Court (44 members); Constitutional Council (7 members)

Political parties and leaders: Agrarian Party [Romin MADINOV, chairman]; Aq Zhol Party "Bright Path" [Alikhan BAYMENOV, chairman]; ASAR "All Together" [Dariga NAZARBAYEVA, chairwoman]; AUL "Village" [Gani KALIYEV, chairman]; Civic Party [Azat PERUASHEV, first secretary]; Communist Party of Kazakhstan or KPK [Serikbolsyn ABDILDIN, first secretary]; Communist People's Party of Kazakhstan [Vladislav KOSAREV, first secretary]; Democratic Party of Kazakhstan [Maksut NARIKBAEV, chairman]; Otan "Fatherland" [Bakhytzhan ZHUMAGULOV, executor]; Patriots' Party [Gani KASYMOV, chairman]; Rukhaniyat [Altynshash ZHAGANOVA, chairwoman]

Political pressure groups and leaders: Adil-Soz [Tamara KALEYEVA]; Almaty Helsinki Group [Ninel FOKINA]; Confederation of Free Trade Unions [Sergei BELKIN]; For a Just Kazakhstan [Bolat ABILOV, Altynbek SARSENBAYEV]; For Fair Elections [Yevgeniy ZHOVTIS, Sabit ZHUSUPOV, Sergey DUVANOV, Ibrash NUSUPBAYEV]; Kazakhstan International Bureau on Human Rights [Yevgeniy ZHOVTIS, executive director]; Pensioners Movement or Pokoleniye [Irina SAVOSTINA, chairwoman]; Republican Network of International Monitors [Dos KUSHIM]; Transparency International [Sergei ZLOTNIKOV]

International organization participation: AsDB, CIS, EAPC, EBRD, ECO, FAO, IAEA, IBRD, ICAO, ICRM, IDA, IDB, IFAD, IFC, IFRCS, ILO, IMF, IMO, Interpol, IOC, IOM, ISO, ITU, MIGA, NAM (observer), NSG, OAS (observer), OIC, OPCW, OSCE, PFP, SCO, UN, UNCTAD, UNESCO, UNIDO, UPU, WCL, WCO, WFTU, WHO, WIPO, WMO, WToO, WTO (observer)

Diplomatic representation in the US:
chief of mission: Ambassador Kanat B. SAUDABAYEV
chancery: 1401 16th Street NW, Washington, DC 20036
telephone: [1] (202) 232-5488
FAX: [1] (202) 232-5845
consulate(s): New York

Diplomatic representation from the US:
chief of mission: Ambassador John M. ORDWAY
embassy: 97 Zholdasbekova, Samal-2, Almaty, 480099
mailing address: use embassy street address
telephone: [7] (3272) 50-48-02
FAX: [7] (3272) 50-48-84

Flag description: sky blue background representing the endless sky and a gold sun with 32 rays soaring above a golden steppe eagle in the center; on the hoist side is a "national ornamentation" in gold

ECONOMY

Economy - overview: Kazakhstan, the largest of the former Soviet republics in territory, excluding Russia, possesses enormous fossil fuel reserves as well as plentiful supplies of other minerals and metals. It also has a large agricultural sector featuring livestock and grain. Kazakhstan's industrial sector rests on the extraction and processing of these natural resources and also on a growing machine-building sector specializing in construction equipment, tractors, agricultural machinery, and some defense items. The breakup of the USSR in December 1991 and the collapse in demand for Kazakhstan's traditional heavy industry products resulted in a short-term contraction of the economy, with the steepest annual decline occurring in 1994. In 1995-97, the pace of the government program of economic reform and privatization quickened, resulting in a substantial shifting of assets into the private sector. Kazakhstan enjoyed double-digit growth in 2000-01 - and more than 9% per year in 2002-05 - thanks largely to its booming energy sector, but also to economic reform, good harvests, and foreign investment. The opening of the Caspian Consortium pipeline in 2001, from western Kazakhstan's Tengiz oilfield to the Black Sea, substantially raised export capacity. Kazakhstan also has begun work on an ambitious cooperative construction effort with China to build an oil pipeline that will extend from the country's Caspian coast eastward to the Chinese border. The country has embarked upon an industrial policy designed to diversify the economy away from overdependence on the oil sector, by developing light industry. The policy aims to reduce the influence of foreign investment and foreign personnel; the government has engaged in several disputes with foreign oil companies over the terms of production agreements, and tensions continue. Upward pressure on the local currency continued in 2005 due to massive oil-related foreign-exchange inflows.
GDP (purchasing power parity): $132.7 billion (2005 est.)
GDP (official exchange rate): $43.82 billion (2005 est.)
GDP - real growth rate: 9% (2005 est.)
GDP - per capita: purchasing power parity - $8,700 (2005 est.)
GDP - composition by sector:
agriculture: 7.8%
industry: 40.4%
services: 51.8% (2005 est.)
Labor force: 7.85 million (2005 est.)
Labor force - by occupation: agriculture 20%, industry 30%, services 50% (2002 est.)
Unemployment rate: 7.6% (2005 est.)
Population below poverty line: 19% (2004 est.)
Household income or consumption by percentage share:
lowest 10%: 3.3%
highest 10%: 26.5% (2004 est.)
Distribution of family income - Gini index: 31.5 (2003)
Inflation rate (consumer prices): 7.4% (2005 est.)
Investment (gross fixed): 22% of GDP (2005 est.)
Budget:
revenues: $12.19 billion
expenditures: $12.44 billion, including capital expenditures of NA (2005 est.)
Public debt: 9.8% of GDP (2005 est.)
Agriculture - products: grain (mostly spring wheat), cotton; livestock
Industries: oil, coal, iron ore, manganese, chromite, lead, zinc, copper, titanium, bauxite, gold, silver, phosphates, sulfur, iron and steel; tractors and other agricultural machinery, electric motors, construction materials
Industrial production growth rate: 10.7% (2005 est.)
Electricity - production: 60.33 billion kWh (2003)
Electricity - production by source:
fossil fuel: 84.3%
hydro: 15.7%
nuclear: 0%
other: 0% (2001)
Electricity - consumption: 52.55 billion kWh (2003)
Electricity - exports: 6 billion kWh (2003)
Electricity - imports: 2.45 billion kWh (2003)
Oil - production: 1.3 million bbl/day (2005 est.)
Oil - consumption: 221,000 bbl/day (2003 est.)
Oil - exports: 890,000 bbl/day (2003)
Oil - imports: 47,000 bbl/day (2003)
Oil - proved reserves: 26 billion bbl (1 January 2004)
Natural gas - production: 18.5 billion cu m (2004 est.)
Natural gas - consumption: 15.2 billion cu m (2004 est.)
Natural gas - exports: 4.1 billion cu m (2004 est.)
Natural gas - imports: 4.1 billion cu m (2004 est.)
Natural gas - proved reserves: 3 trillion cu m (1 January 2004)
Current account balance: $3.343 billion (2005 est.)
Exports: $30.09 billion f.o.b. (2005 est.)
Exports - partners: Russia 15.1%, Bermuda 13.8%, Germany 11%, China 9.9%, France 6.6%, Italy 4% (2004)
Imports: $17.51 billion f.o.b. (2005 est.)
Imports - partners: Russia 34.6%, China 15.4%, Germany 8.2%, France 5.7%, Ukraine 4.6% (2004)
Reserves of foreign exchange and gold: $11.13 billion (2005 est.)
Debt - external: $32.7 billion (2005 est.)
Economic aid - recipient: $74.2 million in US assistance programs, 1992-2000 (FY2004)
Currency (code): tenge (KZT)
Currency code: KZT
Exchange rates: tenge per US dollar - 133.44 (2005), 136.04 (2004), 149.58 (2003), 153.28 (2002), 146.74 (2001)
Fiscal year: calendar year

COMMUNICATIONS

Telephones - main lines in use: 2,081,900 (2002)
Telephones - mobile cellular: 1.027 million (2002)
Telephone system:
general assessment: service is poor; equipment antiquated
domestic: intercity by landline and microwave radio relay; mobile cellular systems are available in most of Kazakhstan
international: country code - 7; international traffic with other former Soviet republics and China carried by landline and microwave radio relay and with other countries by satellite and by the Trans-Asia-Europe (TAE) fiber-optic cable; satellite earth stations - 2 Intelsat
Radio broadcast stations: AM 60, FM 17, shortwave 9 (1998)
Radios: 6.47 million (1997)
Television broadcast stations: 12 (plus nine repeaters) (1998)
Televisions: 3.88 million (1997)
Internet country code: .kz
Internet hosts: 21,984 (2004))
Internet Service Providers (ISPs): 10 (with their own international channels) (2001)
Internet users: 250,000 (2002)

TRANSPORTATION

Airports: 314 (2004 est.)
Airports - with paved runways:
total: 66
over 3,047 m: 9
2,438 to 3,047 m: 26
1,524 to 2,437 m: 17
914 to 1,523 m: 4
under 914 m: 10 (2005 est.)
Airports - with unpaved runways:
total: 94
over 3,047 m: 6
2,438 to 3,047 m: 6
1,524 to 2,437 m: 12

914 to 1,523 m: 12
under 914 m: 58 (2005 est.)
Heliports: 4 (2005 est.)
Pipelines: condensate 18 km; gas 10,370 km; oil 10,158 km; refined products 1,187 km (2004)
Railways:
total: 13,700 km
broad gauge: 13,700 km 1.520-m gauge (3,700 km electrified) (2004)
Roadways:
total: 258,029 km
paved: 247,347 km
unpaved: 106,824 km (2003)
Waterways: 4,000 km
note: on the Syr Darya (Syrdariya) and Ertis (Irtysh) rivers (2004)
Merchant marine:
total: 3 ships (1,000 GRT or over) 1,064 GRT/646 DWT
by type: cargo 2, refrigerated cargo 1
foreign-owned: 2 (United Kingdom 2) (2005)
Ports and terminals: Aqtau (Shevchenko), Atyrau (Gur'yev), Oskemen (Ust-Kamenogorsk), Pavlodar, Semey (Semipalatinsk)

MILITARY

Military branches: Ground Forces, Air and Air Defense Forces, Naval Force, Republican Guard
Military service age and obligation: 18 years of age for compulsory military service; conscript service obligation - 2 years; minimum age for volunteers NA (2004)
Manpower available for military service:
males age 18-49: 3,758,255 (2005 est.)
Manpower fit for military service: *males age 18-49*: 2,473,529 (2005 est.)
Manpower reaching military service age annually: *males*: 173,129 (2005 est.)
Military expenditures - dollar figure: $221.8 million (Ministry of Defense expenditures) (FY02)
Military expenditures - percent of GDP: 0.9% (Ministry of Defense expenditures) (FY02)

TRANSNATIONAL ISSUES

Disputes - international: in 2005, Kazakhstan agreed with Russia, Turkmenistan, and Uzbekistan to commence demarcating their boundaries; delimitation with Kyrgyzstan is complete; creation of a seabed boundary with Turkmenistan in the Caspian Sea remains unresolved; equidistant seabed treaties have been ratified with Azerbaijan and Russia in the Caspian Sea, but no resolution has been made on dividing the water column among any of the littoral states
Illicit drugs: significant illicit cultivation of cannabis for CIS markets, as well as limited cultivation of opium poppy and ephedra (for the drug ephedrine); limited government eradication of illicit crops; transit point for Southwest Asian narcotics bound for Russia and the rest of Europe

KENYA

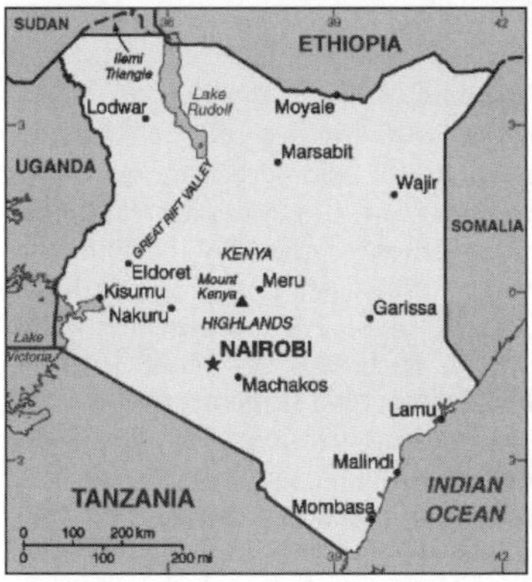

INTRODUCTION

Background: Founding president and liberation struggle icon Jomo KENYATTA led Kenya from independence until his death in 1978, when President Daniel Toroitich arap MOI took power in a constitutional succession. The country was a de facto one-party state from 1969 until 1982 when the ruling Kenya African National Union (KANU) made itself the sole legal party in Kenya. MOI acceded to internal and external pressure for political liberalization in late 1991. The ethnically fractured opposition failed to dislodge KANU from power in elections in 1992 and 1997, which were marred by violence and fraud, but are viewed as having generally reflected the will of the Kenyan people. President MOI stepped down in December of 2002 following fair and peaceful elections. Mwai KIBAKI, running as the candidate of the multiethnic, united opposition group, the National Rainbow Coalition, defeated KANU candidate Uhuru KENYATTA and assumed the presidency following a campaign centered on an anticorruption platform.

GEOGRAPHY

Location: Eastern Africa, bordering the Indian Ocean, between Somalia and Tanzania
Geographic coordinates: 1 00 N, 38 00 E
Map references: Africa
Area:
total: 582,650 sq km
land: 569,250 sq km
water: 13,400 sq km
Area - comparative: slightly more than twice the size of Nevada
Land boundaries:
total: 3,477 km
border countries: Ethiopia 861 km, Somalia 682 km, Sudan 232 km, Tanzania 769 km, Uganda 933 km
Coastline: 536 km
Maritime claims:
territorial sea: 12 nm
exclusive economic zone: 200 nm
continental shelf: 200-m depth or to the depth of exploitation
Climate: varies from tropical along coast to arid in interior
Terrain: low plains rise to central highlands bisected by Great Rift Valley; fertile plateau in west
Elevation extremes:
lowest point: Indian Ocean 0 m
highest point: Mount Kenya 5,199 m
Natural resources: limestone, soda ash, salt, gemstones, fluorspar, zinc, diatomite, gypsum, wildlife, hydropower
Land use:
arable land: 8.08%
permanent crops: 0.98%
other: 90.94% (2001)
Irrigated land: 670 sq km (1998 est.)
Natural hazards: recurring drought; flooding during rainy seasons
Environment - current issues: water pollution from urban and industrial wastes; degradation of water quality from increased use of pesticides and fertilizers; water hyacinth infestation in Lake Victoria; deforestation; soil erosion; desertification; poaching
Environment - international agreements:
party to: Biodiversity, Climate Change, Climate Change-Kyoto Protocol, Desertification, Endangered Species, Hazardous Wastes, Law of the Sea, Marine Dumping, Marine Life Conservation, Ozone Layer Protection, Ship Pollution, Wetlands, Whaling
signed, but not ratified: none of the selected agreements
Geography - note: the Kenyan Highlands comprise one of the most successful agricultural production regions in Africa; glaciers are found on Mount Kenya, Africa's second highest peak; unique physiography supports abundant and varied wildlife of scientific and economic value

PEOPLE

Population: 33,829,590
note: estimates for this country explicitly take into account the effects of excess mortality due to AIDS; this can result in lower life expectancy, higher infant mortality and death rates, lower population and growth rates, and changes in the distribution of population by age and sex than would otherwise be expected (July 2005 est.)
Age structure:
0-14 years: 42.5% (male 7,252,075/female 7,124,034)
15-64 years: 55.2% (male 9,378,428/female 9,295,471)
65 years and over: 2.3% (male 356,116/female 423,466) (2005 est.)
Median age:
total: 18.19 years
male: 18.08 years
female: 18.3 years (2005 est.)
Population growth rate: 2.56% (2005 est.)
Birth rate: 40.13 births/1,000 population (2005 est.)
Death rate: 14.65 deaths/1,000 population (2005 est.)
Net migration rate: 0.08 migrant(s)/1,000 population
note: according to UNHCR, by the end of 2001 Kenya was host to 220,000 refugees from neighboring countries, including: Somalia 145,000 and Sudan 68,000 (2005 est.)
Sex ratio:
at birth: 1.02 male(s)/female
under 15 years: 1.02 male(s)/female
15-64 years: 1.01 male(s)/female
65 years and over: 0.84 male(s)/female
total population: 1.01 male(s)/female (2005 est.)
Infant mortality rate:
total: 61.47 deaths/1,000 live births
male: 64.26 deaths/1,000 live births
female: 58.62 deaths/1,000 live births (2005 est.)
Life expectancy at birth:
total population: 47.99 years
male: 48.87 years
female: 47.09 years (2005 est.)
Total fertility rate: 4.96 children born/woman (2005 est.)
HIV/AIDS - adult prevalence rate: 6.7% (2003 est.)
HIV/AIDS - people living with HIV/AIDS: 1.2 million (2003 est.)
HIV/AIDS - deaths: 150,000 (2003 est.)
Major infectious diseases:
degree of risk: very high
food or waterborne diseases: bacterial and protozoal diarrhea, hepatitis A, and typhoid fever
vectorborne disease: malaria is a high risk in some locations
water contact disease: schistosomiasis (2004)
Nationality:
noun: Kenyan(s)
adjective: Kenyan
Ethnic groups: Kikuyu 22%, Luhya 14%, Luo 13%, Kalenjin 12%, Kamba 11%, Kisii 6%, Meru 6%, other African 15%, non-African (Asian, European, and Arab) 1%
Religions: Protestant 45%, Roman Catholic 33%, indigenous beliefs 10%, Muslim 10%, other 2%
note: a large majority of Kenyans are Christian, but estimates for the percentage of the population that adheres to Islam or indigenous beliefs vary widely
Languages: English (official), Kiswahili (official), numerous indigenous languages
Literacy:
definition: age 15 and over can read and write
total population: 85.1%
male: 90.6%
female: 79.7% (2003 est.)

GOVERNMENT

Country name:
conventional long form: Republic of Kenya
conventional short form: Kenya
former: British East Africa
Government type: republic
Capital: Nairobi
Administrative divisions: 7 provinces and 1 area*; Central, Coast, Eastern, Nairobi Area*, North Eastern, Nyanza, Rift Valley, Western
Independence: 12 December 1963 (from UK)
National holiday: Independence Day, 12 December (1963)
Constitution: 12 December 1963; amended as a republic 1964; reissued with amendments 1979, 1982, 1986, 1988, 1991, 1992, 1997, and 2001
Legal system: based on Kenyan statutory law, Kenyan and English common law, tribal law, and Islamic law; judicial review in High Court; accepts compulsory ICJ jurisdiction, with reservations; constitutional amendment of 1982 making Kenya a de jure one-party state repealed in 1991
Suffrage: 18 years of age, universal
Executive branch:
chief of state: President Mwai KIBAKI (since 30 December 2002) and Vice President Moody AWORI (since 25 September 2003); note - the president is both the chief of state and head of government
head of government: President Mwai KIBAKI (since 30 December 2002) and Vice President Moody AWORI (since 25 September 2003); note - the president is both the chief of state and head of government
cabinet: Cabinet appointed by the president
elections: president elected by popular vote for a five-year term; in addition to receiving the largest number of votes in absolute terms, the presidential candidate must also win 25% or more of the vote in at least five of Kenya's seven provinces and one area to avoid a runoff; election last held 27 December 2002 (next to be held December 2007); vice president appointed by the president
election results: President Mwai KIBAKI elected; percent of vote - Mwai KIBAKI 63%, Uhuru KENYATTA 30%
Legislative branch: unicameral National Assembly or Bunge (224 seats; 210 members elected by popular vote to serve five-year terms, 12 so-called "nominated" members who are appointed by the president but selected by the parties in proportion to their parliamentary vote totals, 2 ex-officio members)
elections: last held 27 December 2002 (next to be held by early 2007)
election results: percent of vote by party - NA%; seats by party - NARC 125, KANU 64, FORD-P 14, other 7; ex-officio 2; seats appointed by the president - NARC 7, KANU 4, FORD-P 1
Judicial branch: Court of Appeal (chief justice is appointed by the president); High Court
Political parties and leaders: Forum for the Restoration of Democracy-People or FORD-People [Kimaniwa NYOIKE, chairman]; Kenya African National Union or KANU [Uhuru KENYATTA]; National Rainbow Coalition or NARC [Mwai KIBAKI] - the governing party
Political pressure groups and leaders: human rights groups; labor unions; Muslim organizations; National Convention Executive Council or NCEC, a proreform coalition of political parties and nongovernment organizations [Kivutha KIBWANA]; Protestant National Council of Churches of Kenya or NCCK [Mutava MUSYIMI]; Roman Catholic and other Christian churches; Supreme Council of Kenya Muslims or SUPKEM [Shaykh Abdul Gafur al-BUSAIDY]
International organization participation: ACP, AfDB, AU, C, COMESA, EADB, FAO, G-15, G-77, IAEA, IBRD, ICAO, ICCt, ICFTU, ICRM, IDA, IFAD, IFC, IFRCS, IGAD, ILO, IMF, IMO, Interpol, IOC, IOM, ISO, ITU, MIGA, MINURSO, MONUC, NAM, ONUB, OPCW, UN, UNAMSIL, UNCTAD, UNESCO, UNHCR, UNIDO, UNMEE, UNMIL, UNMIS, UNOCI, UPU, WCO, WHO, WIPO, WMO, WToO, WTO

Diplomatic representation in the US:
chief of mission: Ambassador Leonard NGAITHE
chancery: 2249 R Street NW, Washington, DC 20008
telephone: [1] (202) 387-6101
FAX: [1] (202) 462-3829
consulate(s) general: Los Angeles
Diplomatic representation from the US:
chief of mission: Ambassador William M. BELLAMY
embassy: US Embassy, United Nations Ave., Gigiri; P. O. Box 606 Village Market Nairobi
mailing address: Box 21A, Unit 64100, APO AE 09831
telephone: [254] (20) 537-800
FAX: [254] (20) 537-810
Flag description: three equal horizontal bands of black (top), red, and green; the red band is edged in white; a large warrior's shield covering crossed spears is superimposed at the center

ECONOMY

Economy - overview: The regional hub for trade and finance in East Africa, Kenya has been hampered by corruption and by reliance upon several primary goods whose prices have remained low. In 1997, the IMF suspended Kenya's Enhanced Structural Adjustment Program due to the government's failure to maintain reforms and curb corruption. A severe drought from 1999 to 2000 compounded Kenya's problems, causing water and energy rationing and reducing agricultural output. As a result, GDP contracted by 0.2% in 2000. The IMF, which had resumed loans in 2000 to help Kenya through the drought, again halted lending in 2001 when the government failed to institute several anticorruption measures. Despite the return of strong rains in 2001, weak commodity prices, endemic corruption, and low investment limited Kenya's economic growth to 1.2%. Growth lagged at 1.1% in 2002 because of erratic rains, low investor confidence, meager donor support, and political infighting up to the elections. In the key 27 December 2002 elections, Daniel Arap MOI's 24-year-old reign ended, and a new opposition government took on the formidable economic problems facing the nation. In 2003, progress was made in rooting out corruption and encouraging donor support. GDP grew 5% in 2005.
GDP (purchasing power parity): $39.45 billion (2005 est.)
GDP (official exchange rate): $16.63 billion (2005 est.)
GDP - real growth rate: 5% (2005 est.)
GDP - per capita: purchasing power parity - $1,200 (2005 est.)
GDP - composition by sector:
agriculture: 16.3%
industry: 18.8%
services: 65.1% (2004 est.)
Labor force: 11.85 million (2005 est.)
Labor force - by occupation: agriculture 75% (2003 est.)
Unemployment rate: 40% (2001 est.)
Population below poverty line: 50% (2000 est.)
Household income or consumption by percentage share:
lowest 10%: 2%
highest 10%: 37.2% (2000)
Distribution of family income - Gini index: 44.5 (1997)
Inflation rate (consumer prices): 12% (2005 est.)
Investment (gross fixed): 17.2% of GDP (2005 est.)
Budget:
revenues: $3.715 billion
expenditures: $3.88 billion, including capital expenditures of NA (2005 est.)
Public debt: 67.4% of GDP (2005 est.)
Agriculture - products: tea, coffee, corn, wheat, sugarcane, fruit, vegetables; dairy products, beef, pork, poultry, eggs
Industries: small-scale consumer goods (plastic, furniture, batteries, textiles, soap, cigarettes, flour), agricultural products; oil refining, aluminum, steel, lead, cement; commercial ship repair, tourism
Industrial production growth rate: 4.6% (2005 est.)
Electricity - production: 4.342 billion kWh (2003)
Electricity - production by source:
fossil fuel: 17.7%
hydro: 71%
nuclear: 0%
other: 11.3% (2001)
Electricity - consumption: 4.238 billion kWh (2003)
Electricity - exports: 0 kWh (2003)
Electricity - imports: 200 million kWh (2003)
Oil - production: 0 bbl/day (2003 est.)
Oil - consumption: 52,000 bbl/day (2003 est.)
Oil - exports: NA (2001)
Oil - imports: NA (2001)
Current account balance: $-694 million (2005 est.)
Exports: $3.173 billion f.o.b. (2005 est.)
Exports - partners: Uganda 13.2%, UK 11.3%, US 10.5%, Netherlands 8.1%, Egypt 4.8%, Tanzania 4.4%, Pakistan 4.3% (2004)
Imports: $5.126 billion f.o.b. (2005 est.)
Imports - partners: UAE 12.5%, Saudi Arabia 9.1%, South Africa 8.7%, US 7.7%, India 7.2%, UK 6.7%, China 6.4%, Japan 5% (2004)
Reserves of foreign exchange and gold: $1.67 billion (2005 est.)
Debt - external: $7.349 billion (2005 est.)
Economic aid - recipient: $453 million (1997)
Currency (code): Kenyan shilling (KES)
Currency code: KES
Exchange rates: Kenyan shillings per US dollar - 76.38 (2005), 79.174 (2004), 75.936 (2003), 78.749 (2002), 78.563 (2001)
Fiscal year: 1 July - 30 June

COMMUNICATIONS

Telephones - main lines in use: 328,400 (2003)
Telephones - mobile cellular: 1,590,800 (2003)
Telephone system:
general assessment: unreliable; little attempt to modernize except for service to business
domestic: trunks are primarily microwave radio relay; business data commonly transferred by a very small aperture terminal (VSAT) system
international: country code - 254; satellite earth stations - 4 Intelsat
Radio broadcast stations: AM 24, FM 18, shortwave 6 (2001)
Radios: 3.07 million (1997)
Television broadcast stations: 8 (2002)
Televisions: 730,000 (1997)
Internet country code: .ke
Internet hosts: 8,325 (2003)
Internet Service Providers (ISPs): 65 (2001)
Internet users: 400,000 (2002)

TRANSPORTATION

Airports: 221 (2004 est.)
Airports - with paved runways:
total: 15
over 3,047 m: 4
2,438 to 3,047 m: 1
1,524 to 2,437 m: 4
914 to 1,523 m: 5
under 914 m: 1 (2005 est.)
Airports - with unpaved runways:
total: 209
1,524 to 2,437 m: 11
914 to 1,523 m: 114
under 914 m: 84 (2005 est.)
Pipelines: refined products 752 km (2004)
Railways:
total: 2,778 km
narrow gauge: 2,778 km 1.000-m gauge (2004)
Roadways:
total: 63,942 km
paved: 7,737 km
unpaved: 56,205 km (2000)
Waterways: part of Lake Victoria system is within boundaries of Kenya (2004)
Merchant marine:
total: 3 ships (1,000 GRT or over) 6,049 GRT/7,082 DWT

by type: cargo 2, petroleum tanker 1
registered in other countries: 6 (2005)
Ports and terminals: Mombasa

MILITARY

Military branches: Army, Navy, Air Force
Military service age and obligation: 18 years of age (est.) (2004)
Manpower available for military service: *males age 18-49:* 7,303,153 (2005 est.)
Manpower fit for military service: *males age 18-49:* 3,963,532 (2005 est.)
Military expenditures - dollar figure: $177.1 million (2004)
Military expenditures - percent of GDP: 1.3% (2004)

TRANSNATIONAL ISSUES

Disputes - international: Kenya served as an important mediator in brokering Sudan's north-south separation in February 2005; Kenya provides shelter to approximately a quarter of a million refugees including Ugandans who flee across the border periodically to seek protection from Lord's Resistance Army (LRA) rebels; Kenya's administrative limits extend beyond the treaty border into the Sudan, creating the Ilemi Triangle
Refugees and internally displaced persons: *refugees (country of origin):* 154,272 (Somalia) 11,139 (Ethiopia) 63,197 (Sudan)
IDPs: 350,000 (KANU attacks on opposition tribal groups in 1990s) (2004)
Illicit drugs: widespread harvesting of small plots of marijuana; transit country for South Asian heroin destined for Europe and North America; Indian methaqualone also transits on way to South Africa; significant potential for money-laundering activity given the country's status as a regional financial center; massive corruption, and relatively high levels of narcotics-associated activities

KINGMAN REEF

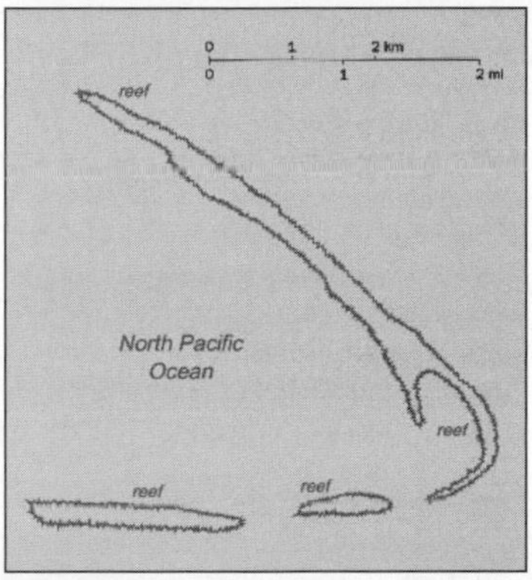

INTRODUCTION

Background: The US annexed the reef in 1922. Its sheltered lagoon served as a way station for flying boats on Hawaii-to-American Samoa flights during the late 1930s. There are no terrestrial plants on the reef, which is frequently awash, but it does support abundant and diverse marine fauna and flora. In 2001, the waters surrounding the reef out to 12 nm were designated a US National Wildlife Refuge.

GEOGRAPHY

Location: Oceania, reef in the North Pacific Ocean, about half way between Hawaii and American Samoa
Geographic coordinates: 6 23 N, 162 25 W
Map references: Oceania
Area:
total: 1 sq km
land: 1 sq km
water: 0 sq km
Area - comparative: about 1.7 times the size of The Mall in Washington, DC
Land boundaries: 0 km
Coastline: 3 km
Maritime claims:
territorial sea: 12 nm
exclusive economic zone: 200 nm
Climate: tropical; moderated by prevailing winds
Terrain: low and nearly level
Elevation extremes:
lowest point: Pacific Ocean 0 m
highest point: unnamed location 1 m
Natural resources: terrestrial and aquatic wildlife
Land use:
arable land: 0%
permanent crops: 0%
other: 100% (2001)
Irrigated land: 0 sq km (1998 est.)
Natural hazards: wet or awash most of the time, maximum elevation of about 1 meter makes Kingman Reef a maritime hazard
Environment - current issues: none
Geography - note: barren coral atoll with deep interior lagoon; closed to the public

PEOPLE

Population: uninhabited (July 2005 est.)

GOVERNMENT

Country name:
conventional long form: none
conventional short form: Kingman Reef
Dependency status: unincorporated territory of the US; administered from Washington, DC, by the US Fish and Wildlife Service of the Department of the Interior
note: on 1 September 2000, the Department of the Interior accepted restoration of its administrative jurisdiction over Kingman Reef from the Department of the Navy; Executive Order 3223 signed 18 January 2001 established Kingman Reef National Wildlife Refuge to be administered by the Director, US Fish and Wildlife Service; this refuge is managed to protect the terrestrial and aquatic wildlife of Kingman Reef out to the 12-nautical-mile territorial sea limit
Legal system: the laws of the US, where applicable, apply
Flag description: the flag of the US is used

ECONOMY

Economy - overview: no economic activity

TRANSPORTATION

Airports: lagoon was used as a halfway station between Hawaii and American Samoa by Pan American Airways for flying boats in 1937 and 1938 (2004 est.)
Ports and terminals: none; offshore anchorage only

MILITARY

Military - note: defense is the responsibility of the US

TRANSNATIONAL ISSUES

Disputes - international: none

KIRIBATI

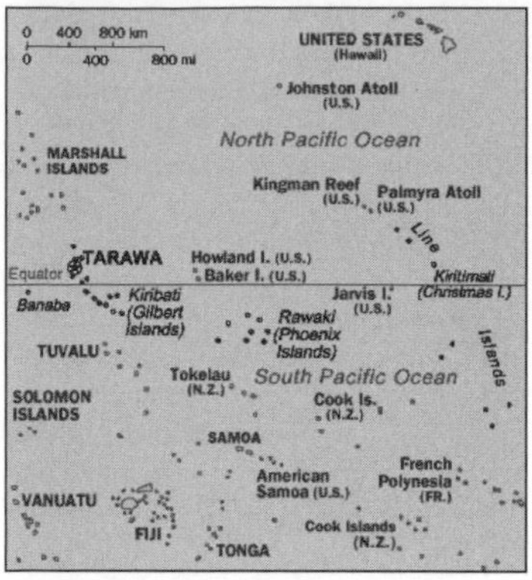

INTRODUCTION

Background: The Gilbert Islands were granted self-rule by the UK in 1971 and complete independence in 1979 under the new name of Kiribati. The US relinquished all claims to the sparsely inhabited Phoenix and Line Island groups in a 1979 treaty of friendship with Kiribati.

GEOGRAPHY

Location: Oceania, group of 33 coral atolls in the Pacific Ocean, straddling the equator; the capital Tarawa is about one-half of the way from Hawaii to Australia; note - on 1 January 1995, Kiribati proclaimed that all of its territory lies in the same time zone as its Gilbert Islands group (GMT +12) even though the Phoenix Islands and the Line Islands under its jurisdiction lie on the other side of the International Date Line

Geographic coordinates: 1 25 N, 173 00 E

Map references: Oceania

Area:
total: 811 sq km
land: 811 sq km
water: 0 sq km
note: includes three island groups - Gilbert Islands, Line Islands, Phoenix Islands

Area - comparative: four times the size of Washington, DC

Land boundaries: 0 km

Coastline: 1,143 km

Maritime claims:
territorial sea: 12 nm
exclusive economic zone: 200 nm

Climate: tropical; marine, hot and humid, moderated by trade winds

Terrain: mostly low-lying coral atolls surrounded by extensive reefs

Elevation extremes:
lowest point: Pacific Ocean 0 m
highest point: unnamed location on Banaba 81 m

Natural resources: phosphate (production discontinued in 1979)

Land use:
arable land: 2.74%
permanent crops: 50.68%
other: 46.58% (2001)

Irrigated land: NA

Natural hazards: typhoons can occur any time, but usually November to March; occasional tornadoes; low level of some of the islands make them very sensitive to changes in sea level

Environment - current issues: heavy pollution in lagoon of south Tarawa atoll due to heavy migration mixed with traditional practices such as lagoon latrines and open-pit dumping; ground water at risk

Environment - international agreements:
party to: Biodiversity, Climate Change, Climate Change-Kyoto Protocol, Desertification, Hazardous Wastes, Law of the Sea, Marine Dumping, Ozone Layer Protection
signed, but not ratified: none of the selected agreements

Geography - note: 21 of the 33 islands are inhabited; Banaba (Ocean Island) in Kiribati is one of the three great phosphate rock islands in the Pacific Ocean - the others are Makatea in French Polynesia, and Nauru

PEOPLE

Population: 103,092 (July 2005 est.)

Age structure:
0-14 years: 38.9% (male 20,342/female 19,806)
15-64 years: 57.7% (male 29,362/female 30,136)
65 years and over: 3.3% (male 1,477/female 1,969) (2005 est.)

Median age:
total: 20.05 years
male: 19.61 years
female: 20.58 years (2005 est.)

Population growth rate: 2.25% (2005 est.)

Birth rate: 30.86 births/1,000 population (2005 est.)

Death rate: 8.37 deaths/1,000 population (2005 est.)

Net migration rate: 0 migrant(s)/1,000 population (2005 est.)

Sex ratio:
at birth: 1.05 male(s)/female
under 15 years: 1.03 male(s)/female
15-64 years: 0.97 male(s)/female
65 years and over: 0.75 male(s)/female
total population: 0.99 male(s)/female (2005 est.)

Infant mortality rate:
total: 48.52 deaths/1,000 live births
male: 53.64 deaths/1,000 live births
female: 43.16 deaths/1,000 live births (2005 est.)

Life expectancy at birth:
total population: 61.71 years
male: 58.71 years
female: 64.86 years (2005 est.)

Total fertility rate: 4.2 children born/woman (2005 est.)

HIV/AIDS - adult prevalence rate: NA

HIV/AIDS - people living with HIV/AIDS: NA

HIV/AIDS - deaths: NA

Nationality:
noun: I-Kiribati (singular and plural)
adjective: I-Kiribati

Ethnic groups: Micronesian 98.8%, other 1.2% (2000 census)

Religions: Roman Catholic 52%, Protestant (Congregational) 40%, some Seventh-Day Adventist, Muslim, Baha'i, Latter-day Saints, and Church of God (1999)

Languages: I-Kiribati, English (official)

Literacy:
definition: NA
total population: NA%
male: NA%
female: NA%

GOVERNMENT

Country name:
conventional long form: Republic of Kiribati
conventional short form: Kiribati
note: pronounced keer-ree-bahss
former: Gilbert Islands

Government type: republic

Capital: Tarawa

Administrative divisions: 3 units; Gilbert Islands, Line Islands, Phoenix Islands; note - in addition, there are 6 districts (Banaba, Central Gilberts, Line Islands, Northern Gilberts, Southern Gilberts, Tarawa) and 21 island councils - one for each of the inhabited islands (Abaiang, Abemama, Aranuka, Arorae, Banaba, Beru, Butaritari, Kanton, Kiritimati, Kuria, Maiana, Makin, Marakei, Nikunau, Nonouti, Onotoa, Tabiteuea, Tabuaeran, Tamana, Tarawa, Teraina)

Independence: 12 July 1979 (from UK)

National holiday: Independence Day, 12 July (1979)

Constitution: 12 July 1979

Legal system: NA

Suffrage: 18 years of age, universal

Executive branch:
chief of state: President Anote TONG (since 10 July 2003); Vice President Teima ONORIO; note - the president is both the chief of state and head of government
head of government: President Anote TONG (since 10 July 2003); Vice President Teima ONORIO; note - the president is both the chief of state and head of government

cabinet: 12-member Cabinet appointed by the president from among the members of the House of Parliament
elections: the House of Parliament chooses the presidential candidates from among its members and then those candidates compete in a general election; president is elected by popular vote for a four-year term; election last held 4 July 2003 (next to be held not later than July 2007); vice president appointed by the president
election results: Anote TONG 47.4%, Harry TONG 43.5%, Banuera BERINA 9.1%
Legislative branch: unicameral House of Parliament or Maneaba Ni Maungatabu (42 seats; 39 elected by popular vote, one ex officio member - the attorney general, one appointed to represent Banaba, and one other; members serve four-year terms)
elections: first round elections last held 29 November 2002; second round elections held 6 December 2002 (next to be held by November 2006)
election results: percent of vote by party - NA%; seats by party - BTK 17, MTM 16, independents 7, other 2 (includes attorney general) note: legislative elections were held in two rounds - the first round on 9 May 2003 and the second round on 14 May 2003
Judicial branch: Court of Appeal; High Court; 26 Magistrates' courts; judges at all levels are appointed by the president
Political parties and leaders: Boutokaan Te Koaua Party or BTK [Taberannang TIMEON]; Maneaban Te Mauri Party or MTM [Teburoro TITO]; Maurin Kiribati Pati or MKP [leader NA]; National Progressive Party or NPP [Dr. Harry TONG]
note: there is no tradition of formally organized political parties in Kiribati; they more closely resemble factions or interest groups because they have no party headquarters, formal platforms, or party structures
Political pressure groups and leaders: NA
International organization participation: ACP, AsDB, C, FAO, IBRD, ICAO, ICFTU, ICRM, IDA, IFAD, IFC, IFRCS, ILO, IMF, IMO, IOC, ITU, OPCW, PIF, Sparteca, SPC, UN, UNCTAD, UNESCO, UPU, WHO, WMO
Diplomatic representation in the US: Kiribati does not have an embassy in the US; there is an honorary consulate in Honolulu
Diplomatic representation from the US: the US does not have an embassy in Kiribati; the ambassador to Fiji is accredited to Kiribati
Flag description: the upper half is red with a yellow frigate bird flying over a yellow rising sun, and the lower half is blue with three horizontal wavy white stripes to represent the ocean

ECONOMY

Economy - overview: A remote country of 33 scattered coral atolls, Kiribati has few natural resources. Commercially viable phosphate deposits were exhausted at the time of independence from the UK in 1979. Copra and fish now represent the bulk of production and exports. The economy has fluctuated widely in recent years. Economic development is constrained by a shortage of skilled workers, weak infrastructure, and remoteness from international markets. Tourism provides more than one-fifth of GDP. The financial sector is at an early stage of development as is the expansion of private sector initiatives. Foreign financial aid from UK, Japan, Australia, New Zealand, and China equals 25%-50% of GDP. Remittances from workers abroad account for more than $5 million each year.
GDP (purchasing power parity): $79 million - supplemented by a nearly equal amount from external sources (2001 est.)
GDP (official exchange rate): NA
GDP - real growth rate: 1.5% (2001 est.)
GDP - per capita: purchasing power parity - $800 (2001 est.)
GDP - composition by sector:
agriculture: 30%
industry: 7%
services: 63% (1998 est.)
Labor force: 7,870 economically active, not including subsistence farmers (2001 est.)
Unemployment rate: 2%
note: underemployment 70% (1992 est.)
Population below poverty line: NA
Household income or consumption by percentage share:
lowest 10%: NA
highest 10%: NA
Inflation rate (consumer prices): 2.5% (2001 est.)
Budget:
revenues: $28.4 million
expenditures: $37.2 million, including capital expenditures of NA (2000 est.)
Agriculture - products: copra, taro, breadfruit, sweet potatoes, vegetables; fish
Industries: fishing, handicrafts
Industrial production growth rate: 0.7% (1991 est.)
Electricity - production: 12 million kWh (2003)
Electricity - production by source:
fossil fuel: 100%
hydro: 0%
nuclear: 0%
other: 0% (2001)
Electricity - consumption: 11.16 million kWh (2003)
Electricity - exports: 0 kWh (2003)
Electricity - imports: 0 kWh (2003)
Oil - production: 0 bbl/day (2003 est.)
Oil - consumption: 200 bbl/day (2003 est.)
Oil - exports: NA (2001)
Oil - imports: NA (2001)
Oil - proved reserves: 395.8 million bbl (1 January 2004)
Exports: $17 million f.o.b. (2004 est.)
Exports - partners: France 45.7%, Japan 29.2%, US 9.1%, Thailand 5.4% (2004)
Imports: $62 million c.i.f. (2004 est.)
Imports - partners: Australia 33.6%, Fiji 29.8%, Japan 10.3%, New Zealand 6.9%, France 4.1% (2004)
Debt - external: $10 million (1999 est.)
Economic aid - recipient: $15.5 million largely from UK and Japan (2001 est.)
Currency (code): Australian dollar (AUD)
Currency code: AUD
Exchange rates: Australian dollars per US dollar - 1.31 (2005), 1.3598 (2004), 1.5419 (2003), 1.8406 (2002), 1.9334 (2001)
Fiscal year: NA

COMMUNICATIONS

Telephones - main lines in use: 4,500 (2002)
Telephones - mobile cellular: 500 (2002)
Telephone system:
general assessment: generally good quality national and international service
domestic: wire line service available on Tarawa and Kiritimati; connections to outer islands by HF/VHF radiotelephone; wireless service available in Tarawa since 1999
international: country code - 686; Kiribati is being linked to the Pacific Ocean Cooperative Telecommunications Network, which should improve telephone service; satellite earth station - 1 Intelsat (Pacific Ocean)
Radio broadcast stations: AM 1, FM 2, shortwave 1
note: the shortwave station may be inactive (2002)
Radios: 17,000 (1997)
Television broadcast stations: 1 (not reported to be active) (2002)
Televisions: 1,000 (1997)
Internet country code: .ki
Internet Service Providers (ISPs): 1 (2000)
Internet users: 2,000 (2002)

TRANSPORTATION

Airports: 20 (2004 est.)
Airports - with paved runways:
total: 3
1,524 to 2,437 m: 3 (2005 est.)
Airports - with unpaved runways:
total: 16

1,524 to 2,437 m: 1
914 to 1,523 m: 11
under 914 m: 4 (2005 est.)
Roadways:
total: 670 km (1999)
Waterways: 5 km (small network of canals in Line Islands) (2003)
Merchant marine:
total: 1 ships (1,000 GRT or over) 1,291 GRT/1,295 DWT
by type: passenger/cargo 1 (2005)
Ports and terminals: Betio

MILITARY

Military branches: no regular military forces; Police Force (carries out law enforcement functions and paramilitary duties; small police posts are on all islands)
Military expenditures - dollar figure: NA
Military expenditures - percent of GDP: NA
Military - note: Kiribati does not have military forces; defense assistance is provided by Australia and NZ

TRANSNATIONAL ISSUES

Disputes - international: none

KOREA, NORTH

INTRODUCTION

Background: An independent kingdom for much of the past millennium, Korea was occupied by Japan in 1905 following the Russo-Japanese War; five years later, Japan formally annexed the entire peninsula. Following World War II, Korea was split with the northern half coming under Soviet-sponsored Communist domination. After failing in the Korean War (1950-53) to conquer the US-backed republic in the southern portion by force, North Korea, under its founder President KIM Il-so'ng, adopted a policy of ostensible diplomatic and economic "self-reliance" as a check against excessive Soviet or Communist Chinese influence. It molded political, economic, and military policies around the core ideological objective of eventual unification of Korea under Pyongyang's control. KIM's son, the current ruler KIM Jong Il, was officially designated as KIM's successor in 1980 and assumed a growing political and managerial role until his father's death in 1994. He assumed full power without opposition. After decades of economic mismanagement and resource misallocation, the North since the mid-1990s has relied heavily on international aid to feed its population while continuing to expend resources to maintain an army of about 1 million. North Korea's long-range missile development and research into nuclear, chemical, and biological weapons and massive conventional armed forces are of major concern to the international community. In December 2002, following revelations it was pursuing a nuclear weapons program based on enriched uranium in violation of a 1994 agreement with the United States to freeze and ultimately dismantle its existing plutonium-based program, North Korea expelled monitors from the International Atomic Energy Agency (IAEA). In January 2003, it declared its withdrawal from the international Non-Proliferation Treaty. In mid-2003 Pyongyang announced it had completed the reprocessing of spent nuclear fuel rods (to extract weapons-grade plutonium) and was developing a "nuclear deterrent." From August 2003, North Korea has participated on and off in six-party talks with the China, Japan, Russia, South Korea, and the United States to resolve the stalemate over its nuclear programs.

GEOGRAPHY

Location: Eastern Asia, northern half of the Korean Peninsula bordering the Korea Bay and the Sea of Japan, between China and South Korea
Geographic coordinates: 40 00 N, 127 00 E
Map references: Asia
Area:
total: 120,540 sq km
land: 120,410 sq km
water: 130 sq km
Area - comparative: slightly smaller than Mississippi
Land boundaries:
total: 1,673 km
border countries: China 1,416 km, South Korea 238 km, Russia 19 km
Coastline: 2,495 km
Maritime claims:
territorial sea: 12 nm
exclusive economic zone: 200 nm
note: military boundary line 50 nm in the Sea of Japan and the exclusive economic zone limit in the Yellow Sea where all foreign vessels and aircraft without permission are banned
Climate: temperate with rainfall concentrated in summer
Terrain: mostly hills and mountains separated by deep, narrow valleys; coastal plains wide in west, discontinuous in east
Elevation extremes:
lowest point: Sea of Japan 0 m
highest point: Paektu-san 2,744 m
Natural resources: coal, lead, tungsten, zinc, graphite, magnesite, iron ore, copper, gold, pyrites, salt, fluorspar, hydropower
Land use:
arable land: 20.76%
permanent crops: 2.49%
other: 76.75% (2001)
Irrigated land: 14,600 sq km (1998 est.)
Natural hazards: late spring droughts often followed by severe flooding; occasional typhoons during the early fall
Environment - current issues: water pollution; inadequate supplies of potable water; waterborne disease; deforestation; soil erosion and degradation
Environment - international agreements:
party to: Antarctic Treaty, Biodiversity, Climate Change, Environmental Modification, Ozone Layer Protection, Ship Pollution
signed, but not ratified: Law of the Sea
Geography - note: strategic location bordering China, South Korea, and Russia; mountainous interior is isolated and sparsely populated

PEOPLE

Population: 22,912,177 (July 2005 est.)
Age structure:
0-14 years: 24.2% (male 2,816,844/female 2,735,478)
15-64 years: 67.9% (male 7,668,581/female 7,883,267)
65 years and over: 7.9% (male 625,819/female 1,182,188) (2005 est.)
Median age:
total: 31.74 years
male: 30.47 years
female: 33 years (2005 est.)
Population growth rate: 0.9% (2005 est.)
Birth rate: 16.09 births/1,000 population (2005 est.)

Death rate: 7.05 deaths/1,000 population (2005 est.)
Net migration rate: 0 migrant(s)/1,000 population (2005 est.)
Sex ratio:
at birth: 1.05 male(s)/female
under 15 years: 1.03 male(s)/female
15-64 years: 0.97 male(s)/female
65 years and over: 0.53 male(s)/female
total population: 0.94 male(s)/female (2005 est.)
Infant mortality rate:
total: 24.04 deaths/1,000 live births
male: 25.77 deaths/1,000 live births
female: 22.23 deaths/1,000 live births (2005 est.)
Life expectancy at birth:
total population: 71.37 years
male: 68.65 years
female: 74.22 years (2005 est.)
Total fertility rate: 2.15 children born/woman (2005 est.)
HIV/AIDS - adult prevalence rate: NA
HIV/AIDS - people living with HIV/AIDS: NA
HIV/AIDS - deaths: NA
Nationality:
noun: Korean(s)
adjective: Korean
Ethnic groups: racially homogeneous; there is a small Chinese community and a few ethnic Japanese
Religions: traditionally Buddhist and Confucianist, some Christian and syncretic Chondogyo (Religion of the Heavenly Way)
note: autonomous religious activities now almost nonexistent; government-sponsored religious groups exist to provide illusion of religious freedom
Languages: Korean
Literacy:
definition: age 15 and over can read and write
total population: 99%
male: 99%
female: 99%

GOVERNMENT

Country name:
conventional long form: Democratic People's Republic of Korea
conventional short form: North Korea
local long form: Choson-minjujuui-inmin-konghwaguk
local short form: none
note: the North Koreans generally use the term "Choson" to refer to their country
abbreviation: DPRK
Government type: Communist state one-man dictatorship
Capital: Pyongyang
Administrative divisions: 9 provinces (do, singular and plural) and 4 municipalities (si, singular and plural)
provinces: Chagang-do (Chagang), Hamgyong-bukto (North Hamgyong), Hamgyong-namdo (South Hamgyong), Hwanghae-bukto (North Hwanghae), Hwanghae-namdo (South Hwanghae), Kangwon-do (Kangwon), P'yongan-bukto (North P'yongan), P'yongan-namdo (South P'yongan), Yanggang-do (Yanggang)
municipalites: Kaesong-si (Kaesong), Najin Sonbong-si (Najin), Namp'o-si (Namp'o), P'yongyang-si (Pyongyang)
Independence: 15 August 1945 (from Japan)
National holiday: Founding of the Democratic People's Republic of Korea (DPRK), 9 September (1948)
Constitution: adopted 1948; completely revised 27 December 1972, revised again in April 1992, and September 1998
Legal system: based on German civil law system with Japanese influences and Communist legal theory; no judicial review of legislative acts; has not accepted compulsory ICJ jurisdiction
Suffrage: 17 years of age, universal
Executive branch:
chief of state: KIM Jong Il (since July 1994); note - on 3 September 2003, rubberstamp Supreme People's Assembly (SPA) reelected KIM Jong Il Chairman of the National Defense Commission, a position accorded nation's "highest administrative authority"; SPA reelected KIM Yong Nam President of its Presidium also with responsibility of representing state and receiving diplomatic credentials; SPA appointed PAK Pong Ju Premier
head of government: Premier PAK Pong Ju (since 3 September 2003); Vice Premiers KWAK Pom Gi (since 5 September 1998), JON Sung Hun (since 3 September 2003), RO Tu Chol (since 3 September 2003)
cabinet: Cabinet (Naegak), members, except for the Minister of People's Armed Forces, are appointed by the SPA
elections: election last held in September 2003 (next to be held in September 2008)
election results: KIM Jong Il and KIM Yong Nam were only nominees for positions and ran unopposed
Legislative branch: unicameral Supreme People's Assembly or Ch'oego Inmin Hoeui (687 seats; members elected by popular vote to serve five-year terms)
elections: last held 3 August 2003 (next to be held in August 2008)
election results: percent of vote by party - NA; seats by party - NA; ruling party approves a list of candidates who are elected without opposition; some seats are held by minor parties
Judicial branch: Central Court (judges are elected by the Supreme People's Assembly)
Political parties and leaders: major party - Korean Workers' Party or KWP [KIM Jong Il, general secretary]; minor parties - Chondoist Chongu Party [RYU Mi Yong, chairwoman] (under KWP control); Social Democratic Party [KIM Yong Dae, chairman] (under KWP control)
Political pressure groups and leaders: none
International organization participation: ARF, FAO, G-77, ICAO, ICRM, IFAD, IFRCS, IHO, IMO, IOC, ISO, ITU, NAM, UN, UNCTAD, UNESCO, UNIDO, UPU, WFTU, WHO, WIPO, WMO, WToO
Diplomatic representation in the US: none; North Korea has a Permanent Mission to the UN in New York
Diplomatic representation from the US: none (Swedish Embassy in Pyongyang represents the US as consular protecting power)
Flag description: three horizontal bands of blue (top), red (triple width), and blue; the red band is edged in white; on the hoist side of the red band is a white disk with a red five-pointed star

ECONOMY

Economy - overview: North Korea, one of the world's most centrally planned and isolated economies, faces desperate economic conditions. Industrial capital stock is nearly beyond repair as a result of years of underinvestment and spare parts shortages. Industrial and power output have declined in parallel. Despite an increased harvest this year due to more stable weather conditions, fertilizer assistance from South Korea, and an extraordinary mobilization of the population to help with agricultural production, the nation has suffered its eleventh year of food shortages due to on-going systemic problems, including a lack of arable land, collective farming practices, and chronic shortages of inputs such as tractors and fuel. Massive international food aid deliveries have allowed the regime to escape mass starvation since 1995, but the population remains the victim of prolonged malnutrition and deteriorating living conditions. Large-scale military spending eats up resources needed for investment and civilian consumption. In 2004, the regime allowed private markets to sell a wider range of goods and permitted private farming on an experimental basis in an effort to boost agricultural output but in October 2005 retracted some of those policies by forbidding the sale of grains in markets.

The regime also revitalized its food rationing system in October, an apparent backtrack on earlier reforms. Black market prices have continued to rise, leaving some vulnerable groups, such as the elderly and unemployed, less able to buy goods. As of December 2005, the regime intended to expel all nongovernmental organizations by year-end and tightly restrict the activity of governmental and international organization aid organizations such as the World Food Program. Firm political control remains the Communist government's overriding concern, which will constrain any further loosening of economic regulations.
GDP (purchasing power parity): $40 billion (2005 est.)
GDP (official exchange rate): NA
GDP - real growth rate: 1% (2005 est.)
GDP - per capita: purchasing power parity - $1,800 (2005 est.)
GDP - composition by sector:
agriculture: 30%
industry: 34%
services: 36% (2002 est.)
Labor force: 9.6 million
Labor force - by occupation: agricultural 36%, nonagricultural 64%
Unemployment rate: NA (2003)
Population below poverty line: NA
Household income or consumption by percentage share:
lowest 10%: NA
highest 10%: NA
Inflation rate (consumer prices): NA (2003 est.)
Budget:
revenues: NA
expenditures: NA, including capital expenditures of NA
Agriculture - products: rice, corn, potatoes, soybeans, pulses; cattle, pigs, pork, eggs
Industries: military products; machine building, electric power, chemicals; mining (coal, iron ore, magnesite, graphite, copper, zinc, lead, and precious metals), metallurgy; textiles, food processing; tourism
Industrial production growth rate: NA
Electricity - production: 18.75 billion kWh (2003)
Electricity - production by source:
fossil fuel: 29%
hydro: 71%
nuclear: 0%
other: 0% (2001)
Electricity - consumption: 17.43 billion kWh (2003)
Electricity - exports: 0 kWh (2003)
Electricity - imports: 0 kWh (2003)
Oil - production: 0 bbl/day (2004 est.)
Oil - consumption: 25,000 bbl/day NA (2003)
Oil - exports: NA (2004)
Oil - imports: 22,000 bbl/day (2004 est.)
Exports: $1.275 billion f.o.b. (2004 est.)
Exports - partners: China 45.6%, South Korea 20.2%, Japan 12.9% (2004)
Imports: $2.819 billion c.i.f. (2004 est.)
Imports - partners: China 32.9%, Thailand 10.7%, Japan 4.8% (2004)
Debt - external: $12 billion (1996 est.)
Economic aid - recipient: NA; note - approximately 350,000 metric tons, worth approximately $118 million, in food aid through the World Food Program appeal in 2004 plus additional aid from bilateral donors and non-governmental organizations
Currency (code): North Korean won (KPW)
Currency code: KPW
Exchange rates: official: North Korean won per US dollar - 170 (December 2004), 150 (December 2002), 2.15 (December 2001); market: North Korean won per US dollar - 300-600 (December 2002)
Fiscal year: calendar year

COMMUNICATIONS

Telephones - main lines in use: 1.1 million (2001)
Telephones - mobile cellular: NA
Telephone system:
general assessment: NA
domestic: NA
international: country code - 850; satellite earth stations - 1 Intelsat (Indian Ocean) and 1 Russian (Indian Ocean region); other international connections through Moscow and Beijing
Radio broadcast stations: AM 17 (including 11 stations of Korean Central Broadcasting Station), FM 14, shortwave 14 (2003)
Radios: 3.36 million (1997)
Television broadcast stations: 4 (includes Korean Central Television, Mansudae Television, Korean Educational and Cultural Network, and Kaesong Television targeting South Korea) (2003)
Televisions: 1.2 million (1997)
Internet country code: .kp
Internet Service Providers (ISPs): 1 (2000)
Internet users: NA

TRANSPORTATION

Airports: 78 (2004 est.)
Airports - with paved runways:
total: 35
over 3,047 m: 2
2,438 to 3,047 m: 22
1,524 to 2,437 m: 7
914 to 1,523 m: 1
under 914 m: 3 (2005 est.)
Airports - with unpaved runways:
total: 44
2,438 to 3,047 m: 1
1,524 to 2,437 m: 21
914 to 1,523 m: 14
under 914 m: 8 (2005 est.)
Heliports: 20 (2005 est.)
Pipelines: oil 154 km (2004)
Railways:
total: 5,214 km
standard gauge: 5,214 km 1.435-m gauge (3,500 km electrified) (2004)
Roadways:
total: 31,200 km
paved: 1,997 km
unpaved: 29,203 km (1999 est.)
Waterways: 2,250 km
note: most navigable only by small craft (2004)
Merchant marine:
total: 238 ships (1,000 GRT or over) 985,108 GRT/1,389,389 DWT
by type: bulk carrier 13, cargo 191, container 2, livestock carrier 4, passenger/cargo 5, petroleum tanker 13, refrigerated cargo 5, roll on/roll off 5
foreign-owned: 52 (China 1, Denmark 2, France 1, Greece 4, Italy 1, Lebanon 4, Lithuania 1, Netherlands 1, Pakistan 2, Romania 10, Russia 2, Singapore 2, South Korea 2, Syria 9, Turkey 6, Ukraine 1, UAE 3) (2005)
Ports and terminals: Ch'ongjin, Haeju, Hungnam (Hamhung), Kimch'aek, Kosong, Najin, Namp'o, Sinuiju, Songnim, Sonbong (formerly Unggi), Ungsang, Wonsan

MILITARY

Military branches: North Korean People's Army: Ground Force, Navy, Air Force; Civil Security Forces (2005)
Military service age and obligation: 17 years of age (2004)
Manpower available for military service: *males age 17-49:* 5,851,801 (2005 est.)
Manpower fit for military service: *males age 17-49:* 4,810,831 (2005 est.)
Manpower reaching military service age annually: *males:* 194,605 (2005 est.)
Military expenditures - dollar figure: $5,217.4 million (FY02)
Military expenditures - percent of GDP: NA

TRANSNATIONAL ISSUES

Disputes - international: China seeks to stem illegal migration of tens of thousands of North Koreans escaping famine, economic privation, and political oppression; North Korea and China dispute the sovereignty of certain islands in Yalu and Tumen rivers and a section of boundary around Paektu-san (mountain) is indefinite; Military Demarcation Line within

the 4-km wide Demilitarized Zone has separated North from South Korea since 1953; periodic maritime disputes with South over the Northern Limit Line; North Korea supports South Korea in rejecting Japan's claim to Liancourt Rocks (Tok-do/Take-shima)
Refugees and internally displaced persons:
IDPs: 50,000-250,000 (government repression and famine) (2004)
Illicit drugs: for years, from the 1970's into the 2000's, citizens of the Democratic People's Republic of (North) Korea (DPRK), many of them diplomatic employees of the government, were apprehended abroad while trafficking in narcotics, including two in Turkey in December 2004; in recent years, police investigations in Taiwan and Japan have linked North Korea to large illicit shipments of heroin and methamphetamine, including an attempt by the North Korean merchant ship Pong Su to deliver 150 kg of heroin to Australia in April 2003; all indications point to North Korea emerging as an important regional source of illicit drugs targeting markets in Japan, Taiwan, the Russian Far East, and China

KOREA, SOUTH

INTRODUCTION

Background: Korea was an independent kingdom for much of the past millennium. Following its victory in the Russo-Japanese War in 1905, Japan occupied Korea; five years later it formally annexed the entire peninsula. After World War II, a republic was set up in the southern half of the Korean Peninsula while a Communist-style government was installed in the north. During the Korean War (1950-53), US and other UN forces intervened to defend South Korea from North Korean attacks supported by the Chinese. An armistice was signed in 1953, splitting the peninsula along a demilitarized zone at about the 38th parallel. Thereafter, South Korea achieved rapid economic growth with per capita income rising to roughly 14 times the level of North Korea. In 1993, KIM Yo'ng-sam became South Korea's first civilian president following 32 years of military rule. South Korea today is a fully functioning modern democracy. In June 2000, a historic first North-South summit took place between the South's President KIM Tae-chung and the North's leader KIM Jong Il.

GEOGRAPHY

Location: Eastern Asia, southern half of the Korean Peninsula bordering the Sea of Japan and the Yellow Sea
Geographic coordinates: 37 00 N, 127 30 E
Map references: Asia
Area:
total: 98,480 sq km
land: 98,190 sq km
water: 290 sq km
Area - comparative: slightly larger than Indiana
Land boundaries:
total: 238 km
border countries: North Korea 238 km
Coastline: 2,413 km
Maritime claims:
territorial sea: 12 nm; between 3 nm and 12 nm in the Korea Strait
contiguous zone: 24 nm
exclusive economic zone: 200 nm
continental shelf: not specified
Climate: temperate, with rainfall heavier in summer than winter
Terrain: mostly hills and mountains; wide coastal plains in west and south
Elevation extremes:
lowest point: Sea of Japan 0 m
highest point: Halla-san 1,950 m
Natural resources: coal, tungsten, graphite, molybdenum, lead, hydropower potential
Land use:
arable land: 17.18%
permanent crops: 1.95%
other: 80.87% (2001)
Irrigated land: 11,590 sq km (1998 est.)
Natural hazards: occasional typhoons bring high winds and floods; low-level seismic activity common in southwest
Environment - current issues: air pollution in large cities; acid rain; water pollution from the discharge of sewage and industrial effluents; drift net fishing
Environment - international agreements:
party to: Antarctic-Environmental Protocol, Antarctic-Marine Living Resources, Antarctic Treaty, Biodiversity, Climate Change, Climate Change-Kyoto Protocol, Desertification, Endangered Species, Environmental Modification, Hazardous Wastes, Law of the Sea, Marine Dumping, Ozone Layer Protection, Ship Pollution, Tropical Timber 83, Tropical Timber 94, Wetlands, Whaling
signed, but not ratified: none of the selected agreements
Geography - note: strategic location on Korea Strait

PEOPLE

Population: 48,422,644 (July 2005 est.)
Age structure:
0-14 years: 19.4% (male 4,952,177/female 4,450,821)
15-64 years: 72% (male 17,715,267/female 17,147,808)
65 years and over: 8.6% (male 1,670,971/female 2,485,600) (2005 est.)
Median age:
total: 34.51 years
male: 33.53 years
female: 35.53 years (2005 est.)
Population growth rate: 0.38% (2005 est.)
Birth rate: 10.08 births/1,000 population (2005 est.)
Death rate: 6.26 deaths/1,000 population (2005 est.)
Net migration rate: 0 migrant(s)/1,000 population (2005 est.)
Sex ratio:
at birth: 1.08 male(s)/female
under 15 years: 1.11 male(s)/female
15-64 years: 1.03 male(s)/female
65 years and over: 0.67 male(s)/female
total population: 1.01 male(s)/female (2005 est.)
Infant mortality rate:
total: 7.05 deaths/1,000 live births
male: 7.5 deaths/1,000 live births
female: 6.57 deaths/1,000 live births (2005 est.)
Life expectancy at birth:
total population: 76.85 years
male: 73.42 years
female: 80.57 years (2005 est.)
Total fertility rate: 1.26 children born/woman (2005 est.)
HIV/AIDS - adult prevalence rate: less than 0.1% (2003 est.)
HIV/AIDS - people living with HIV/AIDS: 8,300 (2003 est.)
HIV/AIDS - deaths: less than 200 (2003 est.)
Nationality:
noun: Korean(s)

adjective: Korean
Ethnic groups: homogeneous (except for about 20,000 Chinese)
Religions: no affiliation 46%, Christian 26%, Buddhist 26%, Confucianist 1%, other 1%
Languages: Korean, English widely taught in junior high and high school
Literacy:
definition: age 15 and over can read and write
total population: 97.9%
male: 99.2%
female: 96.6% (2002)

GOVERNMENT

Country name:
conventional long form: Republic of Korea
conventional short form: South Korea
local long form: Taehan-min'guk
local short form: none
note: the South Koreans generally use the term "Han'guk" to refer to their country
abbreviation: ROK
Government type: republic
Capital: Seoul
Administrative divisions: 9 provinces (do, singular and plural) and 7 metropolitan cities (gwangyoksi, singular and plural)
provinces: Cheju-do, Cholla-bukto (North Cholla), Cholla-namdo (South Cholla), Ch'ungch'ong-bukto (North Ch'ungch'ong), Ch'ungch'ong-namdo (South Ch'ungch'ong), Kangwon-do, Kyonggi-do, Kyongsang-bukto (North Kyongsang), Kyongsang-namdo (South Kyongsang)
metropolitan cities: Inch'on-gwangyoksi (Inch'on), Kwangju-gwangyoksi (Kwangju), Pusan-gwangyoksi (Pusan), Soul-t'ukpyolsi (Seoul), Taegu-gwangyoksi (Taegu), Taejon-gwangyoksi (Taejon), Ulsan-gwangyoksi (Ulsan)
Independence: 15 August 1945 (from Japan)
National holiday: Liberation Day, 15 August (1945)
Constitution: 17 July 1948
Legal system: combines elements of continental European civil law systems, Anglo-American law, and Chinese classical thought
Suffrage: 19 years of age, universal
Executive branch:
chief of state: President ROH Moo-hyun (since 25 February 2003)
head of government: Prime Minister LEE Hae-chan (since 25 May 2004); Deputy Prime Ministers HAN Duck-soo (14 March 2005), KIM Jin-pyo (since 28 January 2005), and OH Myung (since 18 October 2004)
cabinet: State Council appointed by the president on the prime minister's recommendation
elections: president elected by popular vote for single five-year term; election last held 19 December 2002 (next to be held in December 2007); prime minister appointed by president with consent of National Assembly; deputy prime ministers appointed by president on prime minister's recommendation
election results: results of the 19 December 2002 election - ROH Moo-hyun elected president; percent of vote - ROH Moo-hyun (MDP) 48.9%; LEE Hoi-chang (GNP) 46.6%; other 4.5%
Legislative branch: unicameral National Assembly or Kukhoe (299 seats - members elected for four-year terms; 243 in single-seat constituencies, 56 by proportional representation
elections: last held 15 April 2004 (next to be held in April 2008; byelections held on 30 April 2005 and on 26 October 2005)
election results: percent of vote by party - Uri 51%, GNP 41%, DLP 3%, DP 3%, others 2%; seats by party - Uri 144, GNP 127, DP 11, DLP 9, ULD 3, independents 5
note: percent of vote is for 2004 general election; seats by party reflect results of April and October 2005 byelections involving six and four seats respectively; MDP became DP in May 2005 (2005)
Judicial branch: Supreme Court (justices appointed by president with consent of National Assembly); Constitutional Court (justices appointed by president based partly on nominations by National Assembly and Chief Justice of the court)
Political parties and leaders: Democratic Labor Party or DLP [KWON Young-ghil, interim chairman]; Democratic Party or DP [HAHN Hwa-kap, chairman]; Grand National Party or GNP [PARK Geun-hye, chairwoman]; People-Centered Party or PCP [SHIM Dae-pyong, chairman]; United Liberal Democrats or ULD [KIM Hak-won, chairman]; Uri Party [CHUNG Sye-kyun, interim chairman]
Political pressure groups and leaders: Federation of Korean Industries; Federation of Korean Trade Unions; Korean Confederation of Trade Unions; Korean National Council of Churches; Korean Traders Association; Korean Veterans' Association; National Council of Labor Unions; National Democratic Alliance of Korea; National Federation of Farmers' Associations; National Federation of Student Associations
International organization participation: AfDB, APEC, APT, ARF, AsDB, ASEAN (dialogue partner), Australia Group, BIS, CP, EAS, EBRD, FAO, IAEA, IBRD, ICAO, ICC, ICCt, ICFTU, ICRM, IDA, IEA, IFAD, IFC, IFRCS, IHO, ILO, IMF, IMO, Interpol, IOC, IOM, ISO, ITU, LAIA, MIGA, MINURSO, NAM (guest), NEA, NSG, OAS (observer), OECD, ONUB, OPCW, OSCE (partner), PCA, PIF (partner), UN, UNCTAD, UNESCO, UNHCR, UNIDO, UNMIL, UNMOGIP, UNOMIG, UPU, WCL, WCO, WHO, WIPO, WMO, WToO, WTO, ZC
Diplomatic representation in the US:
chief of mission: Ambassador Lee Tae-sik
chancery: 2450 Massachusetts Avenue NW, Washington, DC 20008
telephone: [1] (202) 939-5600
FAX: [1] (202) 387-0205
consulate(s) general: Atlanta, Boston, Chicago, Honolulu, Houston, Los Angeles, New York, San Francisco, and Seattle
consulate(s): Agana (Guam) and New York
Diplomatic representation from the US:
chief of mission: Ambassador Alexander VERSHBOW
embassy: 32 Sejong-no, Jongno-gu, Seoul 110-710
mailing address: American Embassy Seoul, Unit 15550, APO AP 96205-5550
telephone: [82] (2) 397-4114
FAX: [82] (2) 738-8845
Flag description: white with a red (top) and blue yin-yang symbol in the center; there is a different black trigram from the ancient I Ching (Book of Changes) in each corner of the white field

ECONOMY

Economy - overview: Since the early 1960s, South Korea has achieved an incredible record of growth and integration into the high-tech modern world economy. Four decades ago, GDP per capita was comparable with levels in the poorer countries of Africa and Asia. In 2004, South Korea joined he trillion dollar club of world economies. Today its GDP per capita is equal to the lesser economies of the European Union. This success through the late 1980s was achieved by a system of close government/business ties, including directed credit, import restrictions, sponsorship of specific industries, and a strong labor effort. The government promoted the import of raw materials and technology at the expense of consumer goods and encouraged savings and investment over consumption. The Asian financial crisis of 1997-99 exposed longstanding weaknesses in South Korea's development model, including high debt/equity ratios, massive foreign borrowing, and an undisciplined financial sector. Growth plunged to a negative 6.9% in 1998, then strongly

recovered to 9.5% in 1999, and 8.5% in 2000. Growth fell back to 3.3% in 2001 because of the slowing global economy, falling exports, and the perception that much-needed corporate and financial reforms had stalled. Led by consumer spending and exports, growth in 2002 was an impressive 7.0%, despite anemic global growth. Between 2003 and 2005, growth moderated to about 4%. A downturn in consumer spending was offset by rapid export growth. In 2005, the government proposed labor reform legislation and a corporate pension scheme to help make the labor market more flexible, and new real estate policies to cool property speculation. Moderate inflation, low unemployment, an export surplus, and fairly equal distribution of income characterize this solid economy.
GDP (purchasing power parity): $983.3 billion (2005 est.)
GDP (official exchange rate): $726.5 billion (2005 est.)
GDP - real growth rate: 3.7% (2005 est.)
GDP - per capita: purchasing power parity - $20,300 (2005 est.)
GDP - composition by sector:
agriculture: 3.8%
industry: 41.4%
services: 54.8% (2005 est.)
Labor force: 23.65 million (2005 est.)
Labor force - by occupation: agriculture 8%, industry 19%, services 73% (2004 est.)
Unemployment rate: 3.7% (2005 est.)
Population below poverty line: 4% (2001 est.)
Household income or consumption by percentage share:
lowest 10%: 2.9%
highest 10%: 22.5% (1999 est.)
Distribution of family income - Gini index: 35.8 (2000)
Inflation rate (consumer prices): 2.8% (2005 est.)
Investment (gross fixed): 31.4% of GDP (2005 est.)
Budget:
revenues: $184 billion
expenditures: $187.4 billion, including capital expenditures of NA (2005)
Public debt: 20.5% of GDP (2005 est.)
Agriculture - products: rice, root crops, barley, vegetables, fruit; cattle, pigs, chickens, milk, eggs; fish
Industries: electronics, telecommunications, automobile production, chemicals, shipbuilding, steel
Industrial production growth rate: 3.9% (2005 est.)
Electricity - production: 326.2 billion kWh (2003)
Electricity - production by source:
fossil fuel: 62.4%
hydro: 0.8%
nuclear: 36.6%
other: 0.2% (2001)
Electricity - consumption: 303.3 billion kWh (2003)
Electricity - exports: 0 kWh (2003)
Electricity - imports: 0 kWh (2003)
Oil - production: 0 bbl/day (2004 est.)
Oil - consumption: 2.168 million bbl/day (2003 est.)
Oil - exports: 630,100 bbl/day (2003)
Oil - imports: 2.263 million bbl/day (2003)
Natural gas - production: 0 cu m (2003 est.)
Natural gas - consumption: 20.92 billion cu m (2003 est.)
Natural gas - exports: 0 cu m (2003 est.)
Natural gas - imports: 21.11 billion cu m (2003 est.)
Current account balance: $14.32 billion (2005 est.)
Exports: $277.6 billion f.o.b. (2005 est.)
Exports - partners: China 19.7%, US 17%, Japan 8.6%, Hong Kong 7.2% (2004)
Imports: $248.4 billion f.o.b. (2005 est.)
Imports - partners: Japan 20.6%, China 13.2%, US 12.9%, Saudi Arabia 5.3% (2004)
Reserves of foreign exchange and gold: $220.1 billion (2005 est.)
Debt - external: $188.4 billion (30 June 2005 est.)
Economic aid - donor: ODA $334 million (2003)
Currency (code): South Korean won (KRW)
Currency code: KRW
Exchange rates: South Korean won per US dollar - 1,015 (2005), 1,145.3 (2004), 1,191.6 (2003), 1,251.1 (2002), 1,291 (2001)
Fiscal year: calendar year

COMMUNICATIONS

Telephones - main lines in use: 22.877 million (2003)
Telephones - mobile cellular: 33,591,800 (2003)
Telephone system:
general assessment: excellent domestic and international services
domestic: NA
international: country code - 82; fiber-optic submarine cable to China; the Russia-Korea-Japan submarine cable; satellite earth stations - 3 Intelsat (2 Pacific Ocean and 1 Indian Ocean) and 1 Inmarsat (Pacific Ocean region)
Radio broadcast stations: AM 58, FM 150, shortwave 2 (2004)
Radios: 47.5 million (2000)
Television broadcast stations: 64 (additionally 119 Cable Operators; 239 Relay Cable Operators) (2004)
Televisions: 15.9 million (1997)
Internet country code: .kr
Internet hosts: 694,206 (2001)
Internet Service Providers (ISPs): 11 (2000)
Internet users: 29.22 million (2003)

TRANSPORTATION

Airports: 179 (2004 est.)
Airports - with paved runways:
total: 70
over 3,047 m: 3
2,438 to 3,047 m: 21
1,524 to 2,437 m: 14
914 to 1,523 m: 11
under 914 m: 21 (2005 est.)
Airports - with unpaved runways:
total: 38
914 to 1,523 m: 3
under 914 m: 35 (2005 est.)
Heliports: 537 (2005 est.)
Pipelines: gas 1,433 km; refined products 827 km (2004)
Railways:
total: 3,472 km
standard gauge: 3,472 km 1.435-m gauge (1,342 km electrified) (2004)
Roadways:
total: 97,252 km
paved: 74,641 km (including 2,778 km of expressways)
unpaved: 22,611 km (2003)
Waterways: 1,608 km
note: most navigable only by small craft (2004)
Merchant marine:
total: 601 ships (1,000 GRT or over) 6,992,656 GRT/11,081,142 DWT
by type: bulk carrier 125, cargo 196, chemical tanker 88, container 71, liquefied gas 20, passenger 5, passenger/cargo 22, petroleum tanker 51, refrigerated cargo 15, roll on/roll off 5, vehicle carrier 3
foreign-owned: 2 (Germany 1, United Kingdom 1)
registered in other countries: 366 (2005)
Ports and terminals: Inch'on, Masan, P'ohang, Pusan, Ulsan

MILITARY

Military branches: Army, Navy, Air Force, Marine Corps, National Maritime Police (Coast Guard)
Military service age and obligation: 20-30 years of age for compulsory military service; conscript service obligation - 24-28 months, depending on the military branch involved; 18 years of age for voluntary military service; some 4,000 women serve as commissioned and noncommissioned officers, approx. 2.3% of all officers; women, in service since 1950, are admitted to seven service branches, including infantry; excluded from artillery, armor, anti-air, and chaplaincy corps (2005)

Manpower available for military service: *males age 20-49:* 12,458,257 (2005 est.)
Manpower fit for military service: *males age 20-49:* 9,932,026 (2005 est.)
Manpower reaching military service age annually: *males:* 344,723 (2005 est.)
Military expenditures - dollar figure: $20 billion FY05 (2005)
Military expenditures - percent of GDP: 2.5% FY05 (2005)

TRANSNATIONAL ISSUES

Disputes - international: Military Demarcation Line within the 4-km wide Demilitarized Zone has separated North from South Korea since 1953; periodic maritime disputes with North Korea over the Northern Limit Line; South Korea and Japan claim Liancourt Rocks (Tok-do/Take-shima), occupied by South Korea since 1954

KUWAIT

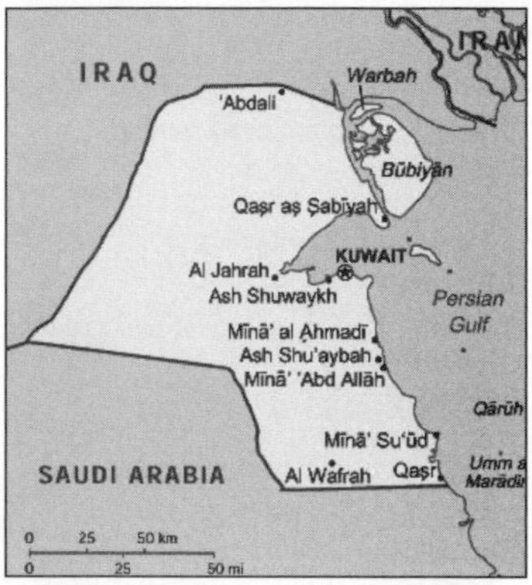

INTRODUCTION

Background: Britain oversaw foreign relations and defense for the ruling Kuwaiti AL-SABAH dynasty from 1899 until independence in 1961. Kuwait was attacked and overrun by Iraq on 2 August 1990. Following several weeks of aerial bombardment, a US-led, UN coalition began a ground assault on 23 February 1991 that liberated Kuwait in four days. Kuwait spent more than $5 billion to repair oil infrastructure damaged during 1990-91.

GEOGRAPHY

Location: Middle East, bordering the Persian Gulf, between Iraq and Saudi Arabia
Geographic coordinates: 29 30 N, 45 45 E
Map references: Middle East
Area:
total: 17,820 sq km
land: 17,820 sq km
water: 0 sq km
Area - comparative: slightly smaller than New Jersey
Land boundaries:
total: 462 km
border countries: Iraq 240 km, Saudi Arabia 222 km
Coastline: 499 km
Maritime claims:
territorial sea: 12 nm
Climate: dry desert; intensely hot summers; short, cool winters
Terrain: flat to slightly undulating desert plain
Elevation extremes:
lowest point: Persian Gulf 0 m
highest point: unnamed location 306 m
Natural resources: petroleum, fish, shrimp, natural gas
Land use:
arable land: 0.73%
permanent crops: 0.11%
other: 99.16% (2001)
Irrigated land: 60 sq km (1998 est.)
Natural hazards: sudden cloudbursts are common from October to April and bring heavy rain, which can damage roads and houses; sandstorms and dust storms occur throughout the year, but are most common between March and August
Environment - current issues: limited natural fresh water resources; some of world's largest and most sophisticated desalination facilities provide much of the water; air and water pollution; desertification
Environment - international agreements:
party to: Biodiversity, Climate Change, Desertification, Endangered Species, Environmental Modification, Hazardous Wastes, Law of the Sea, Ozone Layer Protection
signed, but not ratified: Marine Dumping
Geography - note: strategic location at head of Persian Gulf

PEOPLE

Population: 2,335,648
note: includes 1,291,354 non-nationals (July 2005 est.)
Age structure:
0-14 years: 27.2% (male 323,382/female 311,700)
15-64 years: 70.1% (male 1,045,589/ female 591,243)
65 years and over: 2.7% (male 40,439/ female 23,295) (2005 est.)
Median age:
total: 25.86 years
male: 28.05 years
female: 22.12 years (2005 est.)
Population growth rate: 3.44%
note: this rate reflects a return to pre-Gulf crisis immigration of expatriates (2005 est.)
Birth rate: 21.88 births/1,000 population (2005 est.)
Death rate: 2.42 deaths/1,000 population (2005 est.)
Net migration rate: 14.96 migrant(s)/ 1,000 population (2005 est.)
Sex ratio:
at birth: 1.04 male(s)/female
under 15 years: 1.04 male(s)/female
15-64 years: 1.77 male(s)/female
65 years and over: 1.74 male(s)/female
total population: 1.52 male(s)/female (2005 est.)
Infant mortality rate:
total: 9.95 deaths/1,000 live births
male: 10.96 deaths/1,000 live births
female: 8.9 deaths/1,000 live births (2005 est.)
Life expectancy at birth:
total population: 77.03 years
male: 76.01 years
female: 78.1 years (2005 est.)
Total fertility rate: 2.97 children born/woman (2005 est.)
HIV/AIDS - adult prevalence rate: 0.12% (2001 est.)
HIV/AIDS - people living with HIV/AIDS: NA
HIV/AIDS - deaths: NA
Nationality:
noun: Kuwaiti(s)
adjective: Kuwaiti
Ethnic groups: Kuwaiti 45%, other Arab 35%, South Asian 9%, Iranian 4%, other 7%
Religions: Muslim 85% (Sunni 70%, Shi'a 30%), Christian, Hindu, Parsi, and other 15%
Languages: Arabic (official), English widely spoken
Literacy:
definition: age 15 and over can read and write
total population: 83.5%
male: 85.1%
female: 81.7% (2003 est.)

GOVERNMENT

Country name:
conventional long form: State of Kuwait
conventional short form: Kuwait
local long form: Dawlat al Kuwayt
local short form: Al Kuwayt
Government type: nominal constitutional monarchy
Capital: Kuwait
Administrative divisions: 5 governorates (muhafazat, singular - muhafazah); Al Ahmadi, Al Farwaniyah, Al 'Asimah, Al Jahra', Hawalli

Independence: 19 June 1961 (from UK)
National holiday: National Day, 25 February (1950)
Constitution: approved and promulgated 11 November 1962
Legal system: civil law system with Islamic law significant in personal matters; has not accepted compulsory ICJ jurisdiction
Suffrage: adult males who have been naturalized for 30 years or more or have resided in Kuwait since before 1920 and their male descendants at age 21
note: only 10% of all citizens are eligible to vote; in 1996, naturalized citizens who do not meet the pre-1920 qualification but have been naturalized for 30 years were eligible to vote for the first time
Executive branch:
chief of state: Amir JABIR al-Ahmad al-Jabir al-Sabah (since 31 December 1977); Crown Prince SAAD al-Abdullah al-Salim al-Sabah
head of government: Prime Minister SABAH al-Ahmad al-Jabir al-Sabah (since 13 July 2003); First Deputy Prime Minister and Minister of the Interior NAWWAF al-Ahmad al-Sabah (since 2003); Deputy Prime Ministers JABIR MUBARAK al-Hamad al-Sabah (since 2001) and Muhammad Dhayfallah SHARAR (since 2003)
cabinet: Council of Ministers appointed by the prime minister and approved by the Amir
elections: none; the Amir is hereditary; prime minister and deputy prime ministers appointed by the Amir
Legislative branch: unicameral National Assembly or Majlis al-Umma (50 seats; members elected by popular vote to serve four-year terms)
elections: last held 6 July 2003 (next to be held NA 2007)
election results: percent of vote - NA%; seats - Islamists 21, government supporters 14, liberals 3, and independents 12; note - all cabinet ministers are also ex officio members of the National Assembly
Judicial branch: High Court of Appeal
Political parties and leaders: none; formation of political parties is illegal
Political pressure groups and leaders: several political groups act as de facto parties with legislative blocs in the Assembly: Bedouins, merchants, Sunni and Shi'a activists, and secular leftists and nationalists
International organization participation: ABEDA, AfDB, AFESD, AMF, BDEAC, CAEU, FAO, G-77, GCC, IAEA, IBRD, ICAO, ICC, ICCt (signatory), ICRM, IDA, IDB, IFAD, IFC, IFRCS, IHO, ILO, IMF, IMO, Interpol, IOC, ISO, ITU, LAS, MIGA, NAM, OAPEC, OIC, OPCW, OPEC, PCA, UN, UNCTAD, UNESCO, UNIDO, UNITAR, UPU, WCO, WFTU, WHO, WIPO, WMO, WToO, WTO
Diplomatic representation in the US:
chief of mission: Ambassador SALIM Abdallah al-Jabir al-Sabah
chancery: 2940 Tilden Street NW, Washington, DC 20008
telephone: [1] (202) 966-0702
FAX: [1] (202) 364-2868
Diplomatic representation from the US:
chief of mission: Ambassador Richard LEBARON
embassy: Bayan 36302, Area 14, Al-Masjed Al-Aqsa Street (near the Bayan palace), Kuwait City
mailing address: P. O. Box 77 Safat 13001 Kuwait; or PSC 1280 APO AE 09880-9000
telephone: [965] 259-1001, 259-1002
FAX: [965] 259-1438, 538-0282
Flag description: three equal horizontal bands of green (top), white, and red with a black trapezoid based on the hoist side; design, which dates to 1961, based on the Arab revolt flag of World War I

ECONOMY

Economy - overview: Kuwait is a small, rich, relatively open economy with proved crude oil reserves of about 96 billion barrels - 10% of world reserves. Petroleum accounts for nearly half of GDP, 95% of export revenues, and 80% of government income. Kuwait's climate limits agricultural development. Consequently, with the exception of fish, it depends almost wholly on food imports. About 75% of potable water must be distilled or imported. Kuwait continues its discussions with foreign oil companies to develop fields in the northern part of the country.
GDP (purchasing power parity): $51.62 billion (2005 est.)
GDP (official exchange rate): $56.62 billion (2005 est.)
GDP - real growth rate: 4.5% (2005 est.)
GDP - per capita: purchasing power parity - $22,100 (2005 est.)
GDP - composition by sector:
agriculture: 0.5%
industry: 52.1%
services: 47.4% (2005 est.)
Labor force: 1.67 million
note: non-Kuwaitis represent about 80% of the labor force (2005 est.)
Labor force - by occupation: agriculture NA, industries NA, services NA
Unemployment rate: 2.2% (2004 est.)
Population below poverty line: NA
Household income or consumption by percentage share:
lowest 10%: NA
highest 10%: NA
Inflation rate (consumer prices): 3.5% (2005 est.)
Investment (gross fixed): 6.6% of GDP (2005 est.)
Budget:
revenues: $47.21 billion
expenditures: $20.77 billion, including capital expenditures of NA (2005 est.)
Public debt: 17.6% of GDP (2005 est.)
Agriculture - products: practically no crops; fish
Industries: petroleum, petrochemicals, cement, shipbuilding and repair, desalination, food processing, construction materials
Industrial production growth rate: -5% (2002 est.)
Electricity - production: 38.19 billion kWh (2003)
Electricity - production by source:
fossil fuel: 100%
hydro: 0%
nuclear: 0%
other: 0% (2001)
Electricity - consumption: 35.52 billion kWh (2003)
Electricity - exports: 0 kWh (2003)
Electricity - imports: 0 kWh (2003)
Oil - production: 2.418 million bbl/day (2005 est.)
Oil - consumption: 305,000 bbl/day (2003 est.)
Oil - exports: 1.97 million bbl/day (2003)
Oil - imports: NA (2003)
Oil - proved reserves: 96.5 billion bbl (2005 est.)
Natural gas - production: 8.7 billion cu m (2002 est.)
Natural gas - consumption: 8.7 billion cu m (2002 est.)
Natural gas - exports: 0 cu m (2002 est.)
Natural gas - imports: 0 cu m (2002 est.)
Natural gas - proved reserves: 1.548 trillion cu m (2005)
Current account balance: $31.51 billion (2005 est.)
Exports: $44.43 billion f.o.b. (2005 est.)
Exports - partners: Japan 20.5%, South Korea 13.7%, US 12.4%, Singapore 11.3%, Taiwan 9.9% (2004)
Imports: $12.23 billion f.o.b. (2005 est.)
Imports - partners: US 12.9%, Germany 11.9%, Japan 7.9%, UK 5.5%, Saudi Arabia 5.5%, Italy 5%, France 4.5%, China 4.1% (2004)
Reserves of foreign exchange and gold: $9.296 billion (2005 est.)
Debt - external: $14.93 billion (2005 est.)
Economic aid - recipient: NA (2001)
Currency (code): Kuwaiti dinar (KD)

Currency code: KWD
Exchange rates: Kuwaiti dinars per US dollar - 0.29 (2005), 0.2947 (2004), 0.298 (2003), 0.3039 (2002), 0.3067 (2001)
Fiscal year: 1 April - 31 March

COMMUNICATIONS

Telephones - main lines in use: 486,900 (2003)
Telephones - mobile cellular: 1.42 million (2003)
Telephone system:
general assessment: the quality of service is excellent
domestic: new telephone exchanges provide a large capacity for new subscribers; trunk traffic is carried by microwave radio relay, coaxial cable, and open-wire and fiber-optic cable; a cellular telephone system operates throughout Kuwait, and the country is well supplied with pay telephones
international: country code - 965; coaxial cable and microwave radio relay to Saudi Arabia; linked to Bahrain, Qatar, UAE via the Fiber-Optic Gulf (FOG) cable; satellite earth stations - 3 Intelsat (1 Atlantic Ocean, 2 Indian Ocean), 1 Inmarsat (Atlantic Ocean), and 2 Arabsat
Radio broadcast stations: AM 6, FM 11, shortwave 1 (1998)
Radios: 1.175 million (1997)
Television broadcast stations: 13 (plus several satellite channels) (1997)
Televisions: 875,000 (1997)
Internet country code: .kw
Internet hosts: 3,437 (2001)
Internet Service Providers (ISPs): 3 (2000)
Internet users: 567,000 (2003)

TRANSPORTATION

Airports: 7 (2004 est.)
Airports - with paved runways:
total: 4
over 3,047 m: 1
2,438 to 3,047 m: 2
1,524 to 2,437 m: 1 (2005 est.)
Airports - with unpaved runways:
total: 3
1,524 to 2,437 m: 1
under 914 m: 2 (2005 est.)
Heliports: 4 (2005 est.)
Pipelines: gas 169 km; oil 540 km; refined products 57 km (2004)
Roadways:
total: 4,450 km
paved: 3,587 km
unpaved: 863 km (1999)
Merchant marine:
total: 39 ships (1,000 GRT or over) 2,319,082 GRT/3,768,828 DWT
by type: bulk carrier 3, container 6, liquefied gas 5, livestock carrier 5, petroleum tanker 20
registered in other countries: 19 (2005)
Ports and terminals: Ash Shu'aybah, Ash Shuwaykh, Mina' 'Abd Allah, Mina' al Ahmadi, Mina' Su'ud

MILITARY

Military branches: Land Forces, Navy, Air Force (includes Air Defense Force), National Guard (2002)
Military service age and obligation: 18 years of age for compulsory and voluntary military service (2001)
Manpower available for military service:
males age 18-49: 864,745 (2005 est.)
Manpower fit for military service: *males age 18-49:* 737,292 (2005 est.)
Manpower reaching military service age annually: *males:* 18,743 (2005 est.)
Military expenditures - dollar figure: $2,584.5 million (2004)
Military expenditures - percent of GDP: 5.3% (2004)

TRANSNATIONAL ISSUES

Disputes - international: Kuwait and Saudi Arabia continue negotiating a joint maritime boundary with Iran; no maritime boundary exists with Iraq in the Persian Gulf

KYRGYZSTAN

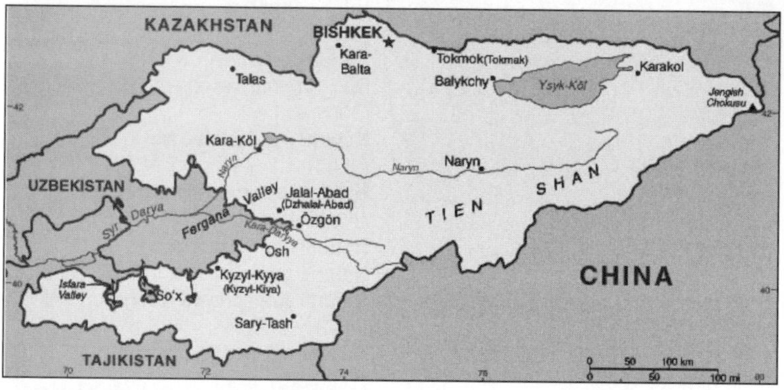

INTRODUCTION

Background: A Central Asian country of incredible natural beauty and proud nomadic traditions, Kyrgyzstan was annexed by Russia in 1864; it achieved independence from the Soviet Union in 1991. Nation-wide demonstrations in the spring of 2005 resulted in the ouster of President Askar AKAYEV, who had run the country since 1990. Subsequent presidential elections in July of 2005 were won overwhelmingly by former prime minister Kurmanbek BAKIYEV. Current concerns include: privatization of state-owned enterprises, expansion of democracy and political freedoms, reduction of corruption, improving interethnic relations, and combating terrorism.

GEOGRAPHY

Location: Central Asia, west of China
Geographic coordinates: 41 00 N, 75 00 E
Map references: Asia
Area:
total: 198,500 sq km
land: 191,300 sq km
water: 7,200 sq km
Area - comparative: slightly smaller than South Dakota
Land boundaries:
total: 3,878 km
border countries: China 858 km, Kazakhstan 1,051 km, Tajikistan 870 km, Uzbekistan 1,099 km
Coastline: 0 km (landlocked)
Maritime claims: none (landlocked)
Climate: dry continental to polar in high Tien Shan; subtropical in southwest (Fergana Valley); temperate in northern foothill zone
Terrain: peaks of Tien Shan and associated valleys and basins encompass entire nation
Elevation extremes:
lowest point: Kara-Daryya (Karadar'ya) 132 m
highest point: Jengish Chokusu (Pik Pobedy) 7,439 m
Natural resources: abundant hydropower; significant deposits of gold and rare earth metals; locally exploitable coal, oil, and natural gas; other deposits of nepheline, mercury, bismuth, lead, and zinc
Land use:
arable land: 7.3%
permanent crops: 0.35%

other: 92.35%
note: Kyrgyzstan has the world's largest natural growth walnut forest (2001)
Irrigated land: 10,740 sq km (1998 est.)
Natural hazards: NA
Environment - current issues: water pollution; many people get their water directly from contaminated streams and wells; as a result, water-borne diseases are prevalent; increasing soil salinity from faulty irrigation practices
Environment - international agreements:
party to: Air Pollution, Biodiversity, Climate Change, Climate Change-Kyoto Protocol, Desertification, Hazardous Wastes, Ozone Layer Protection
signed, but not ratified: none of the selected agreements
Geography - note: landlocked; entirely mountainous, dominated by the Tien Shan range; many tall peaks, glaciers, and high-altitude lakes

PEOPLE

Population: 5,146,281 (July 2005 est.)
Age structure:
0-14 years: 31.6% (male 827,751/female 796,029)
15-64 years: 62.3% (male 1,571,476/female 1,632,506)
65 years and over: 6.2% (male 123,992/female 194,527) (2005 est.)
Median age:
total: 23.39 years
male: 22.52 years
female: 24.27 years (2005 est.)
Population growth rate: 1.29% (2005 est.)
Birth rate: 22.48 births/1,000 population (2005 est.)
Death rate: 7.13 deaths/1,000 population (2005 est.)
Net migration rate: -2.47 migrant(s)/1,000 population (2005 est.)
Sex ratio:
at birth: 1.05 male(s)/female
under 15 years: 1.04 male(s)/female
15-64 years: 0.96 male(s)/female
65 years and over: 0.64 male(s)/female
total population: 0.96 male(s)/female (2005 est.)
Infant mortality rate:
total: 35.64 deaths/1,000 live births
male: 40.97 deaths/1,000 live births
female: 30.03 deaths/1,000 live births (2005 est.)
Life expectancy at birth:
total population: 68.16 years
male: 64.16 years
female: 72.38 years (2005 est.)
Total fertility rate: 2.7 children born/woman (2005 est.)
HIV/AIDS - adult prevalence rate: less than 0.1% (2001 est.)
HIV/AIDS - people living with HIV/AIDS: 3,900 (2003 est.)
HIV/AIDS - deaths: less than 200 (2003 est.)
Nationality:
noun: Kyrgyzstani(s)
adjective: Kyrgyzstani
Ethnic groups: Kyrgyz 64.9%, Uzbek 13.8%, Russian 12.5%, Dungan 1.1%, Ukrainian 1%, Uygur 1%, other 5.7% (1999 census)
Religions: Muslim 75%, Russian Orthodox 20%, other 5%
Languages: Kyrgyz (official), Russian (official)
Literacy:
definition: age 15 and over can read and write
total population: 98.7%
male: 99.3%
female: 98.1% (1999 est.)

GOVERNMENT

Country name:
conventional long form: Kyrgyz Republic
conventional short form: Kyrgyzstan
local long form: Kyrgyz Respublikasy
local short form: none
former: Kirghiz Soviet Socialist Republic
Government type: republic
Capital: Bishkek
Administrative divisions: 7 provinces (oblastlar, singular - oblasty) and 1 city* (shaar); Batken Oblasty, Bishkek Shaary*, Chuy Oblasty (Bishkek), Jalal-Abad Oblasty, Naryn Oblasty, Osh Oblasty, Talas Oblasty, Ysyk-Kol Oblasty (Karakol)
note: administrative divisions have the same names as their administrative centers (exceptions have the administrative center name following in parentheses)
Independence: 31 August 1991 (from Soviet Union)
National holiday: Independence Day, 31 August (1991)
Constitution: adopted 5 May 1993; note - amendment proposed by President AKAYEV and passed in a national referendum on 2 February 2003 significantly expands the powers of the president at the expense of the legislature; following the spring 2005 demonstrations, a new Constitutional Council was appointed and the reform process is ongoing
Legal system: based on civil law system
Suffrage: 18 years of age, universal
Executive branch:
chief of state: President Kurmanbek BAKIYEV (since 14 August 2005); note - former President Askar AKAYEV resigned effective 11 April 2005 following widespread protests that forced him to flee the country on 24 March 2005
head of government: Prime Minister Feliks KULOV (since 1 September 2005); First Deputy Prime Minister Medetbek KERIMKULOV (since 2 December 2005)
cabinet: Cabinet of Ministers appointed by the president on the recommendation of the prime minister
elections: Kurmanbek BAKIYEV elected by popular vote for a five-year term; election last held 10 July 2005 (next scheduled for NA 2010); prime minister nominated by the president for approval by Parliament)
election results: Kurmanbek BAKIYEV elected president; percent of vote - Kurmanbek BAKIYEV 88.6%, Tursunbai BAKIR-UULU 3.9%, other candidates 7.5%; Feliks KULOV approved as prime minister 55-8
Legislative branch: unicameral Supreme Council or Jorgorku Kenesh (75 seats; members are elected by popular vote to serve five year terms)
elections: elections for the new unicameral body or Jorgorku Kenesh were held 27 February 2005, but the vast majority of positions remained undecided and were contested in a runoff election on 13 March 2005; election irregularities caused widespread protests that resulted in the president being forced to flee the country
election results: Supreme Council - percent of vote by party - NA%; seats by party - NA
Judicial branch: Supreme Court (judges are appointed for 10-year terms by the Supreme Council on the recommendation of the president); Constitutional Court; Higher Court of Arbitration
Political parties and leaders: Adilet (Justice) Party [Toychubek KASYMOV]; Agrarian Labor Party of Kyrgyzstan [Uson SYDYKOV]; Agrarian Party of Kyrgyzstan [Erkin ALIYEV]; Alga, Kyrgyzstan (Forward, Kyrgyzstan) [Bolot BEGALIYEV]; Ar-Namys (Dignity) Party [Emil ALIYEV]; Asaba (Banner National Revival Party) [Azimbek BEKNAZAROV]; Ata-Meken (Fatherland) [Omurbek TEKEBAYEV]; Communist Party of Kyrgyzstan [Klara ADZHIBEKOVA]; Democratic Movement of Kyrgyzstan or DDK [Jypar JEKSHEYEV]; Erkin Kyrgyzstan Progressive and Democratic Party [Bektur ASANOV]; Erkindik (Freedom) Party [Topchubek TURGUNALIYEV]; Future of Kyrgyzstan [Balbak TULEBAYEV]; Jany Kyrgyzstan (New Kyrgyzstan) [Dosbol NUR UULU]; Kairan El [Dooronbek SADYKOV]; Kyrgyz National Party [Bakyt BESHIMOV]; Kyrgyzstan Kelechegi [Ruslan CHYNYBAYEV]; Manas El (Party of Spiritual Restoration) [Chingiz AITMATOV]; Moya Strana (My Country Party of

Action) [Joomart OTORBAYEV]; Party of Communists of Kyrgyzstan or KCP [Bakytbek BEKBOYEV]; Party of Justice and Progress [Muratbek IMANALIEV]; Party of Peasants [Esengul ISAKOV]

Political pressure groups and leaders: Council of Free Trade Unions; Kyrgyz Committee on Human Rights [Ramazan DYRYLDAYEV]; National Unity Democratic Movement; Union of Entrepreneurs

International organization participation: AsDB, CIS, EAPC, EBRD, ECO, FAO, IAEA, IBRD, ICAO, ICCt (signatory), ICRM, IDA, IDB, IFAD, IFC, IFRCS, ILO, IMF, Interpol, IOC, IOM, ISO (correspondent), ITU, MIGA, NAM (observer), OIC, ONUB, OPCW, OSCE, PCA, PFP, SCO, UN, UNAMSIL, UNCTAD, UNESCO, UNIDO, UNMIL, UNMIS, UPU, WCO, WFTU, WHO, WIPO, WMO, WToO, WTO

Diplomatic representation in the US:
chief of mission: Ambassador Zamira SYDYKOVA
chancery: 1732 Wisconsin Avenue NW, Washington, DC 20007
telephone: [1] (202) 338-5141
FAX: [1] (202) 338-5139
consulate(s): New York

Diplomatic representation from the US:
chief of mission: Ambassador Marie L. YOVANOVITCH
embassy: 171 Prospect Mira, Bishkek 720016
mailing address: use embassy street address
telephone: [996] (312) 551-241, (517) 777-217
FAX: [996] (312) 551-264

Flag description: red field with a yellow sun in the center having 40 rays representing the 40 Kyrgyz tribes; on the obverse side the rays run counterclockwise, on the reverse, clockwise; in the center of the sun is a red ring crossed by two sets of three lines, a stylized representation of the roof of the traditional Kyrgyz yurt

ECONOMY

Economy - overview: Kyrgyzstan is a poor, mountainous country with a predominantly agricultural economy. Cotton, tobacco, wool, and meat are the main agricultural products, although only tobacco and cotton are exported in any quantity. Industrial exports include gold, mercury, uranium, and natural gas and electricity. Kyrgyzstan has been fairly progressive in carrying out market reforms, such as an improved regulatory system and land reform. Kyrgyzstan was the first CIS country to be accepted into the World Trade Organization. Much of the government's stock in enterprises has been sold. Drops in production had been severe after the breakup of the Soviet Union in December 1991, but by mid-1995 production began to recover and exports began to increase. Kyrgyzstan has distinguished itself by adopting relatively liberal economic policies. The drop in output at the Kumtor gold mine sparked a 0.5% decline in GDP in 2002, but GDP growth bounced back to nearly 6% in 2003-05. The government has made steady strides in controlling its substantial fiscal deficit and reduced the deficit to 1% of GDP in 2005. The government and the international financial institutions have been engaged in a comprehensive medium-term poverty reduction and economic growth strategy, and in 2005 agreed to pursue much-needed tax reform. Progress fighting corruption, further restructuring of domestic industry, and success in attracting foreign investment are keys to future growth.

GDP (purchasing power parity): $9.324 billion (2005 est.)

GDP (official exchange rate): $2.162 billion (2005 est.)

GDP - real growth rate: 2% (2005 est.)

GDP - per capita: purchasing power parity - $1,800 (2005 est.)

GDP - composition by sector:
agriculture: 37.1%
industry: 21.9%
services: 41% (2005 est.)

Labor force: 2.7 million (2000)

Labor force - by occupation: agriculture 55%, industry 15%, services 30% (2000 est.)

Unemployment rate: 18% (2004 est.)

Population below poverty line: 40% (2004 est.)

Household income or consumption by percentage share:
lowest 10%: 3.9%
highest 10%: 23.3% (2001)

Distribution of family income - Gini index: 29 (2001)

Inflation rate (consumer prices): 4.2% (2005 est.)

Investment (gross fixed): 15% of GDP (2005 est.)

Budget:
revenues: $516.3 million
expenditures: $539.9 million, including capital expenditures of NA (2005 est.)

Agriculture - products: tobacco, cotton, potatoes, vegetables, grapes, fruits and berries; sheep, goats, cattle, wool

Industries: small machinery, textiles, food processing, cement, shoes, sawn logs, refrigerators, furniture, electric motors, gold, rare earth metals

Industrial production growth rate: 7.1% (2004 est.)

Electricity - production: 13.77 billion kWh (2003)

Electricity - production by source:
fossil fuel: 7.6%
hydro: 92.4%
nuclear: 0%
other: 0% (2001)

Electricity - consumption: 8.783 billion kWh (2003)

Electricity - exports: 4.13 billion kWh (2003)

Electricity - imports: 108 million kWh (2003)

Oil - production: 1,990 bbl/day (2003)

Oil - consumption: 11,000 bbl/day (2003 est.)

Oil - exports: NA (2001)

Oil - imports: NA (2001)

Natural gas - production: 0 cu m (2004 est.)

Natural gas - consumption: 1.5 billion cu m (2004 est.)

Natural gas - exports: 0 cu m (2004 est.)

Natural gas - imports: 1.5 billion cu m (2004 est.)

Current account balance: $-77.02 million (2005 est.)

Exports: $759 million f.o.b. (2005 est.)

Exports - partners: UAE 28.2%, Russia 19.1%, China 12%, Kazakhstan 11.1%, Switzerland 6.3% (2004)

Imports: $937.4 million f.o.b. (2005 est.)

Imports - partners: China 26.3%, Russia 22.3%, Kazakhstan 17.1%, Turkey 5.4% (2004)

Reserves of foreign exchange and gold: $593.2 million (2005 est.)

Debt - external: $2.428 billion (31 December 2004 est.)

Economic aid - recipient: $50 million from the US (2001)

Currency (code):

Currency code: KGS

Exchange rates: soms per US dollar - 40.13 (2005), 42.65 (2004), 43.648 (2003), 46.937 (2002), 48.378 (2001)

Fiscal year: calendar year

COMMUNICATIONS

Telephones - main lines in use: 394,800 (2002)

Telephones - mobile cellular: 53,100 (2002)

Telephone system:
general assessment: poorly developed; about 100,000 unsatisfied applications for household telephones
domestic: principally microwave radio relay; two cellular providers, probably limited to Bishkek region
international: country code - 996; connections with other CIS countries by landline or microwave radio relay and with other countries by leased connections with Moscow international gateway switch and by satellite; satellite earth stations - 1 Intersputnik and 1 Intelsat; connected internationally by the Trans-Asia-

Europe (TAE) fiber-optic line
Radio broadcast stations: AM 12 (plus 10 repeater stations), FM 14, shortwave 2 (1998)
Radios: 520,000 (1997)
Television broadcast stations: NA (repeater stations throughout the country relay programs from Russia, Uzbekistan, Kazakhstan, and Turkey) (1997)
Televisions: 210,000 (1997)
Internet country code: .kg
Internet hosts: 12,299 (2004)
Internet Service Providers (ISPs): NA
Internet users: 152,000 (2002)

TRANSPORTATION

Airports: 52 (2004 est.)
Airports - with paved runways:
total: 18
over 3,047 m: 1
2,438 to 3,047 m: 3
1,524 to 2,437 m: 11
under 914 m: 3 (2005 est.)
Airports - with unpaved runways:
total: 19
1,524 to 2,437 m: 2
914 to 1,523 m: 1
under 914 m: 16 (2005 est.)
Pipelines: gas 367 km; oil 13 km (2004)
Railways:
total: 470 km
broad gauge: 470 km 1.520-m gauge (2004)
Roadways:
total: 18,500 km
paved: 16,854 km
unpaved: 1,646 km (1999)
Waterways: 600 km (2004)
Ports and terminals: Balykchy (Ysyk-Kol or Rybach'ye)

MILITARY

Military branches: Army, Air Force, National Guard (2004)
Military service age and obligation: 18 years of age for compulsory military service (2001)
Manpower available for military service: *males age 18-49:* 1,193,529 (2005 est.)
Manpower fit for military service: *males age 18-49:* 871,493 (2005 est.)
Manpower reaching military service age annually: *males:* 61,091 (2005 est.)
Military expenditures - dollar figure: $19.2 million (FY01)
Military expenditures - percent of GDP: 1.4% (FY01)

TRANSNATIONAL ISSUES

Disputes - international: delimitation with Kazakhstan is complete; disputes in Isfara Valley delay completion of delimitation with Tajikistan; delimitation is underway with Uzbekistan but serious disputes around enclaves and elsewhere continue to mar progress for some 130 km of border
Illicit drugs: limited illicit cultivation of cannabis and opium poppy for CIS markets; limited government eradication of illicit crops; transit point for Southwest Asian narcotics bound for Russia and the rest of Europe

L

LAOS

INTRODUCTION

Background: Modern-day Laos has its roots in the ancient Lao kingdom of Lan Xang, established in the 14th Century under King FA NGUM. For three hundred years Lan Xang included large parts of present-day Cambodia and Thailand, as well as all of what is now Laos. After centuries of gradual decline, Laos came under the control of Siam (Thailand) from the late 18th century until the late 19th century when it became part of French Indochina. The Franco-Siamese Treaty of 1907 defined the current Lao border with Thailand. In 1975, the Communist Pathet Lao took control of the government ending a six-century-old monarchy and instituting a strict socialist regime closely aligned to Vietnam. A gradual return to private enterprise and the liberalization of foreign investment laws began in 1986. Laos became a member of ASEAN in 1997.

GEOGRAPHY

Location: Southeastern Asia, northeast of Thailand, west of Vietnam
Geographic coordinates: 18 00 N, 105 00 E
Map references: Southeast Asia
Area:
total: 236,800 sq km
land: 230,800 sq km
water: 6,000 sq km
Area - comparative: slightly larger than Utah
Land boundaries:
total: 5,083 km
border countries: Burma 235 km, Cambodia 541 km, China 423 km, Thailand 1,754 km, Vietnam 2,130 km
Coastline: 0 km (landlocked)
Maritime claims: none (landlocked)
Climate: tropical monsoon; rainy season (May to November); dry season (December to April)
Terrain: mostly rugged mountains; some plains and plateaus
Elevation extremes:
lowest point: Mekong River 70 m
highest point: Phou Bia 2,817 m
Natural resources: timber, hydropower, gypsum, tin, gold, gemstones
Land use:
arable land: 3.8%
permanent crops: 0.35%
other: 95.85% (2001)
Irrigated land: 1,640 sq km
note: rainy season irrigation - 2,169 sq km; dry season irrigation - 750 sq km (1998 est.)
Natural hazards: floods, droughts
Environment - current issues: unexploded ordnance; deforestation; soil erosion; most of the population does not have access to potable water
Environment - international agreements:
party to: Biodiversity, Climate Change, Climate Change-Kyoto Protocol, Desertification, Endangered Species, Environmental Modification, Law of the Sea, Ozone Layer Protection
signed, but not ratified: none of the selected agreements
Geography - note: landlocked; most of the country is mountainous and thickly forested; the Mekong River forms a large part of the western boundary with Thailand

PEOPLE

Population: 6,217,141 (July 2005 est.)
Age structure:
0-14 years: 41.6% (male 1,300,094/female 1,289,227)
15-64 years: 55.2% (male 1,693,494/female 1,737,196)
65 years and over: 3.2% (male 88,744/female 108,386) (2005 est.)
Median age:
total: 18.74 years
male: 18.42 years
female: 19.08 years (2005 est.)
Population growth rate: 2.42% (2005 est.)
Birth rate: 35.99 births/1,000 population (2005 est.)
Death rate: 11.83 deaths/1,000 population (2005 est.)
Net migration rate: 0 migrant(s)/1,000 population (2005 est.)
Sex ratio:
at birth: 1.04 male(s)/female
under 15 years: 1.01 male(s)/female
15-64 years: 0.98 male(s)/female
65 years and over: 0.82 male(s)/female
total population: 0.98 male(s)/female (2005 est.)
Infant mortality rate:
total: 85.22 deaths/1,000 live births
male: 95.04 deaths/1,000 live births
female: 75.01 deaths/1,000 live births (2005 est.)
Life expectancy at birth:
total population: 55.08 years
male: 53.07 years
female: 57.17 years (2005 est.)
Total fertility rate: 4.77 children born/woman (2005 est.)
HIV/AIDS - adult prevalence rate: 0.1% (2003 est.)
HIV/AIDS - people living with HIV/AIDS: 1,700 (2003 est.)
HIV/AIDS - deaths: less than 200 (2003 est.)
Nationality:
noun: Lao(s) or Laotian(s)
adjective: Lao or Laotian
Ethnic groups: Lao Loum (lowland) 68%, Lao Theung (upland) 22%, Lao Soung (highland) including the Hmong and the Yao 9%, ethnic Vietnamese/Chinese 1%
Religions: Buddhist 60%, animist and other 40% (including various Christian denominations 1.5%)
Languages: Lao (official), French, English, and various ethnic languages
Literacy:
definition: age 15 and over can read and write
total population: 66.4%
male: 77.4%
female: 55.5% (2002)

GOVERNMENT

Country name:
conventional long form: Lao People's Democratic Republic
conventional short form: Laos PDR or Laos
local long form: Sathalanalat Paxathipatai Paxaxon Lao
local short form: none
Government type: Communist state
Capital: Vientiane
Administrative divisions: 16 provinces (khoueng, singular and plural), 1 municipality* (kampheng nakhon, singular and plural), and 1 special zone** (khetphiset, singular and plural); Attapu, Bokeo, Bolikhamxai, Champasak, Houaphan, Khammouan, Louangnamtha, Louangphrabang, Oudomxai, Phongsali, Salavan, Savannakhet, Viangchan (Vientiane)*, Viangchan, Xaignabouli, Xaisomboun**, Xekong, Xiangkhoang
Independence: 19 July 1949 (from France)
National holiday: Republic Day, 2 December (1975)
Constitution: promulgated 14 August 1991
Legal system: based on traditional customs, French legal norms and procedures, and socialist practice
Suffrage: 18 years of age; universal

Executive branch:
chief of state: President Gen. KHAMTAI Siphadon (since 26 February 1998) and Vice President Lt. Gen. CHOUMMALI Saignason (since 27 March 2001)
head of government: Prime Minister BOUNGNANG Volachit (since 27 March 2001); First Deputy Prime Minister Bouasone BOUPHAVANH (since 3 October 2003) Deputy Prime Minister Maj. Gen. ASANG Laoli (since May 2002), Deputy Prime Minister THONGLOUN Sisolit (since 27 March 2001), and Deputy Prime Minister SOMSAVAT Lengsavat (since 26 February 1998)
cabinet: Council of Ministers appointed by the president, approved by the National Assembly
elections: president elected by the National Assembly for a five-year term; election last held 24 February 2002 (next to be held in 2007); prime minister appointed by the president with the approval of the National Assembly for a five-year term
election results: KHAMTAI Siphadon elected president; percent of National Assembly vote - NA%

Legislative branch: unicameral National Assembly (109 seats; members elected by popular vote to serve five-year terms; note - total number of seats increased from 99 to 109 for the 2002 election)
elections: last held 24 February 2002 (next to be held in 2007)
election results: percent of vote by party - NA%; seats by party - LPRP or LPRP-approved (independent, non-party members) 109

Judicial branch: People's Supreme Court (the president of the People's Supreme Court is elected by the National Assembly on the recommendation of the National Assembly Standing Committee; the vice president of the People's Supreme Court and the judges are appointed by the National Assembly Standing Committee)

Political parties and leaders: Lao People's Revolutionary Party or LPRP [KHAMTAI Siphadon, party president]; other parties proscribed

Political pressure groups and leaders: noncommunist political groups proscribed; most opposition leaders fled the country in 1975

International organization participation: ACCT, APT, ARF, AsDB, ASEAN, CP, EAS, FAO, G-77, IBRD, ICAO, ICRM, IDA, IFAD, IFC, IFRCS, ILO, IMF, Interpol, IOC, ITU, MIGA, NAM, OPCW, PCA, UN, UNCTAD, UNESCO, UNIDO, UPU, WFTU, WHO, WIPO, WMO, WToO, WTO (observer)

Diplomatic representation in the US:
chief of mission: Ambassador PHANTHONG Phommahaxay
chancery: 2222 S Street NW, Washington, DC 20008
telephone: [1] (202) 332-6416
FAX: [1] (202) 332-4923

Diplomatic representation from the US:
chief of mission: Ambassador Patricia M. HASLACH
embassy: 19 Rue Bartholonie, That Dam Road, B. P. 114, Vientiane
mailing address: American Embassy Vientiane, Box V, APO AP 96546
telephone: [856] (21) 267000
FAX: [856] (21) 267190

Flag description: three horizontal bands of red (top), blue (double width), and red with a large white disk centered in the blue band

ECONOMY

Economy - overview: The government of Laos, one of the few remaining official Communist states, began decentralizing control and encouraging private enterprise in 1986. The results, starting from an extremely low base, were striking - growth averaged 6% in 1988-2004 except during the short-lived drop caused by the Asian financial crisis beginning in 1997. Despite this high growth rate, Laos remains a country with a primitive infrastructure. It has no railroads, a rudimentary road system, and limited external and internal telecommunications, though the government is sponsoring major improvements in the road system with possible support from Japan. Electricity is available in only a few urban areas. Subsistence agriculture, dominated by rice, accounts for half of GDP and provides 80% of total employment. The economy will continue to benefit from aid from the IMF and other international sources and from new foreign investment in food processing and mining. Construction will be another strong economic driver, especially as hydroelectric dam and road projects gain steam. In late 2004, Laos gained Normal Trade Relations status with the US, allowing Laos-based producers to face lower tariffs on exports. This may help spur growth. In addition, the European Union has agreed to provide $1 million to the Lao government for technical assistance in preparations for WTO membership. If the avian flu worsens and spreads in the region, however, prospects for tourism could dim.

GDP (purchasing power parity): $11.92 billion (2005 est.)

GDP (official exchange rate): $2.598 billion (2005 est.)

GDP - real growth rate: 7.2% (2005 est.)

GDP - per capita: purchasing power parity - $1,900 (2005 est.)

GDP - composition by sector:
agriculture: 48.6%
industry: 25.9%
services: 25.5% (2005 est.)

Labor force: 2.8 million (2002 est.)

Labor force - by occupation: agriculture 80% (1997 est.)

Unemployment rate: 5.7% (1997 est.)

Population below poverty line: 40% (2002 est.)

Household income or consumption by percentage share:
lowest 10%: 3.2%
highest 10%: 30.6% (1997)

Distribution of family income - Gini index: 37 (1997)

Inflation rate (consumer prices): 9.4% (2005 est.)

Budget:
revenues: $319.3 million
expenditures: $434.6 million, including capital expenditures of NA (2005 est.)

Agriculture - products: sweet potatoes, vegetables, corn, coffee, sugarcane, tobacco, cotton, tea, peanuts, rice, water buffalo, pigs, cattle, poultry

Industries: copper, tin, and gypsum mining, timber, electric power, agricultural processing, construction, garments, tourism, cement

Industrial production growth rate: 13% (2005 est.)

Electricity - production: 3.767 billion kWh (2003)

Electricity - production by source:
fossil fuel: 1.4%
hydro: 98.6%
nuclear: 0%
other: 0% (2001)

Electricity - consumption: 3.298 billion kWh (2003)

Electricity - exports: 435 million kWh (2003)

Electricity - imports: 230 million kWh (2003)

Oil - production: 0 bbl/day (2003 est.)

Oil - consumption: 2,950 bbl/day (2003 est.)

Oil - exports: NA (2001)

Oil - imports: NA (2001)

Current account balance: $-58.35 million (2005 est.)

Exports: $379 million (2005 est.)

Exports - partners: Thailand 19.3%, Vietnam 13.4%, France 8%, Germany 5.3%, UK 5% (2004)

Imports: $541 million f.o.b. (2005 est.)

Imports - partners: Thailand 60.5%, China 10.3%, Vietnam 7.1%, Singapore 4% (2004)

Reserves of foreign exchange and gold: $217 million (August 2005)

Debt - external: $2.49 billion (2001)

Economic aid - recipient: $243 million (2001 est.)
Currency (code): kip (LAK)
Currency code: LAK
Exchange rates: kips per US dollar - 10,751 (2005), 10,820 (2004), 10,569 (2003), 10,056.3 (2002), 8,954.6 (2001)
Fiscal year: 1 October - 30 September

COMMUNICATIONS

Telephones - main lines in use: 61,900 (2002)
Telephones - mobile cellular: 55,200 (2002)
Telephone system:
general assessment: service to general public is poor but improving with over 20,000 telephones currently in service and an additional 48,000 expected by 2001; the government relies on a radiotelephone network to communicate with remote areas
domestic: radiotelephone communications
international: country code - 856; satellite earth station - 1 Intersputnik (Indian Ocean region)
Radio broadcast stations: AM 12, FM 1, shortwave 4 (1998)
Radios: 730,000 (1997)
Television broadcast stations: 4 (1999)
Televisions: 52,000 (1997)
Internet country code: .la
Internet hosts: 937 (2003)
Internet Service Providers (ISPs): 1 (2000)
Internet users: 15,000 (2002)

TRANSPORTATION

Airports: 44 (2004 est.)
Airports - with paved runways:
total: 9
2,438 to 3,047 m: 1
1,524 to 2,437 m: 5
914 to 1,523 m: 3 (2005 est.)
Airports - with unpaved runways:
total: 35
1,524 to 2,437 m: 1
914 to 1,523 m: 13
under 914 m: 21 (2005 est.)
Pipelines: refined products 540 km (2004)
Roadways:
total: 32,620 km
paved: 4,590 km
unpaved: 28,030 km (2002)
Waterways: 4,600 km
note: primarily Mekong and tributaries; 2,897 additional km are intermittently navigable by craft drawing less than 0.5 m (2003)
Merchant marine:
total: 1 ship (1,000 GRT or over) 2,370 GRT/3,110 DWT
by type: cargo 1 (2005)

MILITARY

Military branches: Lao People's Army (LPA; includes Riverine Force), Air Force
Military service age and obligation: 15 years of age for compulsory military service; conscript service obligation - minimum 18 months (2004)
Manpower available for military service: *males age 15-49:* 1,500,625 (2005 est.)
Manpower fit for military service: *males age 15-49:* 954,816 (2005 est.)
Manpower reaching military service age annually: *males:* 73,167 (2005 est.)
Military expenditures - dollar figure: $10.7 million (2004)
Military expenditures - percent of GDP: 0.5% (2004)
Military - note: Laos is one of the world's least developed countries; the Lao People's Armed Forces are small, poorly funded, and ineffectively resourced; there is little political will to allocate sparse funding to the military, and the armed forces' gradual degradation is likely to continue; the massive drug production and trafficking industry centered in the Golden Triangle makes Laos an important narcotics transit country, and armed Wa and Chinese smugglers are active on the Lao-Burma border (2005)

TRANSNATIONAL ISSUES

Disputes - international: Southeast Asian states have enhanced border surveillance to check the spread of avian flu; Laos and Thailand pledge to complete demarcation of boundaries in 2005, while ongoing disputes over squatters and boundary encroachment by Thailand including Mekong River islets persist; in 2004 Cambodian-Laotian boundary commission agrees to re-erect missing markers in two adjoining provinces; concern among Mekong Commission members that China's construction of dams on the Mekong River will affect water levels
Illicit drugs: estimated cultivation in 2004 - 10,000 hectares, a 45% decrease from 2003; estimated potential production in 2004 - 49 metric tons, a significant decrease from 200 metric tons in 2003 (2005)

LATVIA

INTRODUCTION

Background: After a brief period of independence between the two World Wars, Latvia was annexed by the USSR in 1940. It reestablished its independence in 1991 following the breakup of the Soviet Union. Although the last Russian troops left in 1994, the status of the Russian minority (some 30% of the population) remains of concern to Moscow. Latvia joined both NATO and the EU in the spring of 2004.

GEOGRAPHY

Location: Eastern Europe, bordering the Baltic Sea, between Estonia and Lithuania
Geographic coordinates: 57 00 N, 25 00 E
Map references: Europe
Area:
total: 64,589 sq km
land: 63,589 sq km
water: 1,000 sq km
Area - comparative: slightly larger than West Virginia
Land boundaries:
total: 1,150 km
border countries: Belarus 141 km, Estonia 339 km, Lithuania 453 km, Russia 217 km
Coastline: 531 km
Maritime claims:
territorial sea: 12 nm
exclusive economic zone: 200 nm
continental shelf: 200-m depth or to the depth of exploitation

Climate: maritime; wet, moderate winters
Terrain: low plain
Elevation extremes:
lowest point: Baltic Sea 0 m
highest point: Gaizinkalns 312 m
Natural resources: peat, limestone, dolomite, amber, hydropower, wood, arable land
Land use:
arable land: 29.67%
permanent crops: 0.47%
other: 69.86% (2001)
Irrigated land: 200 sq km
note: land in Latvia is often too wet, and in need of drainage, not irrigation; approximately 16,000 sq km or 85% of agricultural land has been improved by drainage (1998 est.)
Natural hazards: NA
Environment - current issues: Latvia's environment has benefited from a shift to service industries after the country regained independence; the main environmental priorities are improvement of drinking water quality and sewage system, household, and hazardous waste management, as well as reduction of air pollution; in 2001, Latvia closed the EU accession negotiation chapter on environment committing to full enforcement of EU environmental directives by 2010
Environment - international agreements:
party to: Air Pollution, Air Pollution-Persistent Organic Pollutants, Biodiversity, Climate Change, Climate Change-Kyoto Protocol, Endangered Species, Hazardous Wastes, Law of the Sea, Ozone Layer Protection, Ship Pollution, Wetlands
signed, but not ratified: none of the selected agreements
Geography - note: most of the country is composed of fertile, low-lying plains, with some hills in the east

PEOPLE

Population: 2,290,237 (July 2005 est.)
Age structure:
0-14 years: 14.4% (male 169,284/female 161,648)
15-64 years: 69.4% (male 770,839/female 819,309)
65 years and over: 16.1% (male 120,306/female 248,851) (2005 est.)
Median age:
total: 39.12 years
male: 35.95 years
female: 42.15 years (2005 est.)
Population growth rate: -0.69% (2005 est.)
Birth rate: 9.04 births/1,000 population (2005 est.)
Death rate: 13.7 deaths/1,000 population (2005 est.)
Net migration rate: -2.24 migrant(s)/1,000 population (2005 est.)
Sex ratio:
at birth: 1.05 male(s)/female
under 15 years: 1.05 male(s)/female
15-64 years: 0.94 male(s)/female
65 years and over: 0.48 male(s)/female
total population: 0.86 male(s)/female (2005 est.)
Infant mortality rate:
total: 9.55 deaths/1,000 live births
male: 11.55 deaths/1,000 live births
female: 7.45 deaths/1,000 live births (2005 est.)
Life expectancy at birth:
total population: 71.05 years
male: 65.78 years
female: 76.6 years (2005 est.)
Total fertility rate: 1.26 children born/woman (2005 est.)
HIV/AIDS - adult prevalence rate: 0.6% (2001 est.)
HIV/AIDS - people living with HIV/AIDS: 7,600 (2001 est.)
HIV/AIDS - deaths: less than 500 (2003 est.)
Nationality:
noun: Latvian(s)
adjective: Latvian
Ethnic groups: Latvian 57.7%, Russian 29.6%, Belarusian 4.1%, Ukrainian 2.7%, Polish 2.5%, Lithuanian 1.4%, other 2% (2002)
Religions: Lutheran, Roman Catholic, Russian Orthodox
Languages: Latvian (official) 58.2%, Russian 37.5%, Lithuanian and other 4.3% (2000 census)
Literacy:
definition: age 15 and over can read and write
total population: 99.8%
male: 99.8%
female: 99.8% (2003 est.)

GOVERNMENT

Country name:
conventional long form: Republic of Latvia
conventional short form: Latvia
local long form: Latvijas Republika
local short form: Latvija
former: Latvian Soviet Socialist Republic
Government type: parliamentary democracy
Capital: Riga
Administrative divisions: 26 counties (singular - rajons) and 7 municipalities*: Aizkraukles Rajons, Aluksnes Rajons, Balvu Rajons, Bauskas Rajons, Cesu Rajons, Daugavpils*, Daugavpils Rajons, Dobeles Rajons, Gulbenes Rajons, Jekabpils Rajons, Jelgava*, Jelgavas Rajons, Jurmala*, Kraslavas Rajons, Kuldigas Rajons, Liepaja*, Liepajas Rajons, Limbazu Rajons, Ludzas Rajons, Madonas Rajons, Ogres Rajons, Preilu Rajons, Rezekne*, Rezeknes Rajons, Riga*, Rigas Rajons, Saldus Rajons, Talsu Rajons, Tukuma Rajons, Valkas Rajons, Valmieras Rajons, Ventspils*, Ventspils Rajons
Independence: 21 August 1991 (from Soviet Union)
National holiday: Independence Day, 18 November (1918); note - 18 November 1918 is the date Latvia declared itself independent from Soviet Russia; 4 May 1990 is when it declared the renewal of independence; 21 August 1991 is the date of de facto independence from the Soviet Union
Constitution: 15 February 1922; an October 1998 amendment on Fundamental Human Rights replaced the 1991 Constitutional Law, which had supplemented the constitution
Legal system: based on civil law system
Suffrage: 18 years of age; universal for Latvian citizens
Executive branch:
chief of state: President Vaira VIKE-FREIBERGA (since 8 July 1999)
head of government: Prime Minister Aigars KALVITIS (since 2 December 2004)
cabinet: Council of Ministers nominated by the prime minister and appointed by the Parliament
elections: president reelected by Parliament for a four-year term; election last held 20 June 2003 (next to be held by June 2007); prime minister appointed by the president
election results: Vaira VIKE-FREIBERGA reelected president; parliamentary vote - Vaira VIKE-FREIBERGA 88 of 94 votes cast
Legislative branch: unicameral Parliament or Saeima (100 seats; members are elected by direct, popular vote to serve four-year terms)
elections: last held 5 October 2002 (next to be held 7 October 2006)
election results: percent of vote by party - JL 23.9%, PCTVL 18.9%, TP 16.7%, ZZS 9.5%, First Party 7.6%, LNNK 5.4%; seats by party - JL 24, TP 20, LPP 14, ZZS 12, TSP 8, TB/LNNK 7, PCTVL 6, LSP 5, independents 4
Judicial branch: Supreme Court (judges' appointments are confirmed by Parliament)
Political parties and leaders: First Party of Latvia or LPP [Juris LUJANS]; For Human Rights in a United Latvia or PCTVL [Tatjana ZDANOKA, Jakovs PLINERS]; For the Fatherland and Freedom/Latvian National Independence Movement or TB/LNNK [Janis STRAUME]; Harmony Center or SC [Sergejs DOLGOPOLOVS]; Latvian Green Party or ZZS [Indulis EMSIS, Viesturs SILENIEKS, Raimonds VEJONIS]; Latvian Farmer's Union or LZS [Augusts BRIG-

MANIS]; Latvian Social Democratic Workers Party (Social Democrats) or LSDSP [Juris BOJARS]; Latvian Socialist Party or LSP [Alfreds RUBIKS]; Latvia's Way or LC [Ivars GODMANIS]; New Democrats or JD [Maris GULBIS]; New Era Party or JL [Einars REPSE]; People's Harmony Party or TSP [Aivars DATAVS]; People's Party or TP [Atis SLAKTERIS]; Social Democratic Union or SDS [Egils BALDZENS]
Political pressure groups and leaders: Headquarters for the Protection of Russian Schools (SHTAB) [Aleksandr KAZAKOV]
International organization participation: Australia Group, BIS, CBSS, CE, EAPC, EBRD, EIB, EU (new member), FAO, IAEA, IBRD, ICAO, ICCt, ICFTU, ICRM, IDA, IFC, IFRCS, IHO, ILO, IMF, IMO, Interpol, IOC, IOM, ISO (correspondent), ITU, MIGA, NATO, NIB, NSG, OAS (observer), OPCW, OSCE, PCA, UN, UNCTAD, UNESCO, UPU, WCO, WEU (associate partner), WHO, WIPO, WMO, WToO, WTO
Diplomatic representation in the US:
chief of mission: Ambassador Maris RIEKSTINS
chancery: 4325 17th Street NW, Washington, DC 20011
telephone: [1] (202) 726-8213, 8214
FAX: [1] (202) 726-6785
Diplomatic representation from the US:
chief of mission: Ambassador Catherine TODD-BAILEY
embassy: 7 Raina Boulevard, Riga LV-1510
mailing address: American Embassy Riga, PSC 78, Box Riga, APO AE 09723
telephone: [371] 703-6200
FAX: [371] 782-0047
Flag description: three horizontal bands of maroon (top), white (half-width), and maroon

ECONOMY

Economy - overview: Latvia's transitional economy recovered from the 1998 Russian financial crisis, largely due to the government's budget stringency and a gradual reorientation of exports toward EU countries, lessening Latvia's trade dependency on Russia. The majority of companies, banks, and real estate have been privatized, although the state still holds sizable stakes in a few large enterprises. Latvia officially joined the World Trade Organization in February 1999. EU membership, a top foreign policy goal, came in May 2004. The current account and internal government deficits remain major concerns, but the government's efforts to increase efficiency in revenue collection may lessen the budget deficit. A growing perception that many of Latvia's banks facilitate illicit activity could damage the country's vibrant financial sector.
GDP (purchasing power parity): $29.42 billion (2005 est.)
GDP (official exchange rate): $14.94 billion (2005 est.)
GDP - real growth rate: 7.8% (2005 est.)
GDP - per capita: purchasing power parity - $12,800 (2005 est.)
GDP - composition by sector:
agriculture: 4.1%
industry: 26%
services: 69.9% (2005 est.)
Labor force: 1.11 million (2005 est.)
Labor force - by occupation: agriculture 15%, industry 25%, services 60% (2000 est.)
Unemployment rate: 8.8% (2005 est.)
Population below poverty line: NA
Household income or consumption by percentage share:
lowest 10%: 2.9%
highest 10%: 25.9% (1998)
Distribution of family income - Gini index: 32 (1999)
Inflation rate (consumer prices): 5.9% (2005 est.)
Investment (gross fixed): 29.9% of GDP (2005 est.)
Budget:
revenues: $5.646 billion
expenditures: $5.889 billion, including capital expenditures of NA (2005 est.)
Public debt: 12% of GDP (2005 est.)
Agriculture - products: grain, sugar beets, potatoes, vegetables; beef, pork, milk, eggs; fish
Industries: buses, vans, street and railroad cars, synthetic fibers, agricultural machinery, fertilizers, washing machines, radios, electronics, pharmaceuticals, processed foods, textiles; note - dependent on imports for energy and raw materials
Industrial production growth rate: 8.5% (2005 est.)
Electricity - production: 3.573 billion kWh (2003)
Electricity - production by source:
fossil fuel: 29.1%
hydro: 70.9%
nuclear: 0%
other: 0% (2001)
Electricity - consumption: 5.839 billion kWh (2003)
Electricity - exports: 300 million kWh (2003)
Electricity - imports: 2.816 billion kWh (2003)
Oil - production: 0 bbl/day (2003 est.)
Oil - consumption: 29,000 bbl/day (2003 est.)
Oil - exports: NA (2001)
Oil - imports: NA (2001)
Natural gas - production: 0 cu m (2001 est.)
Natural gas - consumption: 1.7 billion cu m (2001 est.)
Natural gas - exports: 0 cu m (2001 est.)
Natural gas - imports: 1.7 billion cu m (2001 est.)
Current account balance: $-1.392 billion (2005 est.)
Exports: $5.749 billion f.o.b. (2005 est.)
Exports - partners: UK 12.8%, Germany 12%, Sweden 10%, Lithuania 9.1%, Estonia 8%, Russia 6.4%, Denmark 5.4% (2004)
Imports: $8.559 billion f.o.b. (2005 est.)
Imports - partners: Germany 13.9%, Lithuania 12.2%, Russia 8.7%, Estonia 7%, Finland 6.3%, Sweden 6.1%, Poland 5.4%, Belarus 4.8% (2004)
Reserves of foreign exchange and gold: $2.2 billion (2005 est.)
Debt - external: $13.2 billion (30 June 2005 est.)
Economic aid - recipient: $96.2 million (1995)
Currency (code): Latvian lat (LVL)
Currency code: LVL
Exchange rates: lati per US dollar - 0.56 (2005), 0.5402 (2004), 0.5715 (2003), 0.6182 (2002), 0.6279 (2001)
Fiscal year: calendar year

COMMUNICATIONS

Telephones - main lines in use: 653,900 (2003)
Telephones - mobile cellular: 1,219,600 (2003)
Telephone system:
general assessment: inadequate, but is being modernized to provide an international capability independent of the Moscow international switch; more facilities are being installed for individual use
domestic: expansion underway in intercity trunk line connections, rural exchanges, and mobile systems; still many unsatisfied subscriber applications
international: country code - 371; international connections are now available via cable and a satellite earth station at Riga, enabling direct connections for most calls (1998)
Radio broadcast stations: AM 8, FM 56, shortwave 1 (1998)
Radios: 1.76 million (1997)
Television broadcast stations: 44 (plus 31 repeaters) (1995)
Televisions: 1.22 million (1997)
Internet country code: .lv
Internet hosts: 51,758 (2004)
Internet Service Providers (ISPs): 41 (2001)
Internet users: 936,000 (2003)

TRANSPORTATION

Airports: 50 (2004 est.)

Airports - with paved runways:
total: 23
2,438 to 3,047 m: 7
1,524 to 2,437 m: 2
914 to 1,523 m: 1
under 914 m: 13 (2005 est.)
Airports - with unpaved runways:
total: 24
2,438 to 3,047 m: 1
1,524 to 2,437 m: 2
914 to 1,523 m: 2
under 914 m: 19 (2005 est.)
Pipelines: gas 1,097 km; oil 409 km; refined products 415 km (2004)
Railways:
total: 2,303 km
broad gauge: 2,270 km 1.520-m gauge (257 km electrified)
narrow gauge: 33 km 0.750-m gauge (2004)
Roadways:
total: 69,919 km
paved: 69,919 km (2003)
Waterways: 300 km (2004)
Merchant marine:
total: 19 ships (1,000 GRT or over) 53,153 GRT/37,414 DWT
by type: cargo 7, chemical tanker 1, liquefied gas 2, passenger/cargo 3, petroleum tanker 5, roll on/roll off 1
registered in other countries: 86 (2005)
Ports and terminals: Riga, Ventspils

MILITARY

Military branches: Latvian Republic Defense Force: Ground Forces, Navy, Air Force, Border Guard, Home Guard (Zemessardze) (2005)
Military service age and obligation: 19 years of age for compulsory military service, conscript service obligation - 12 months; 18 years of age for volunteers; Latvia plans to phase out conscription, tentatively moving to an all-professional force by 2007 (August 2004)
Manpower available for military service: *males age 19-49:* 517,713 (2005 est.)
Manpower fit for military service: *males age 19-49:* 361,098 (2005 est.)
Manpower reaching military service age annually: *males:* 19,137 (2005 est.)
Military expenditures - dollar figure: $87 million (FY01)
Military expenditures - percent of GDP: 1.2% (FY01)

TRANSNATIONAL ISSUES

Disputes - international: the Latvian-Russian boundary treaty of 1997 remains unsigned and unratified with Russia linking it to better Latvian treatment of ethnic Russians and Latvian politicians demanding Russian agreement to a declaration that admits Soviet aggression during the Second World War and other issues; the Latvian parliament has not ratified its 1998 maritime boundary treaty with Lithuania, primarily due to concerns over oil exploration rights; as a member state that forms part of the EU's external border, Latvia must implement the strict Schengen border rules
Illicit drugs: transshipment point for opiates and cannabis from Central and Southwest Asia to Western Europe and Scandinavia and Latin American cocaine and some synthetics from Western Europe to CIS; vulnerable to money laundering despite improved legislation due to nascent enforcement capabilities and comparatively weak regulation of offshore companies and the gaming industry; organized crime (including counterfeiting, corruption, extortion, stolen cars, and prostitution) accounts for most laundered proceeds

LEBANON

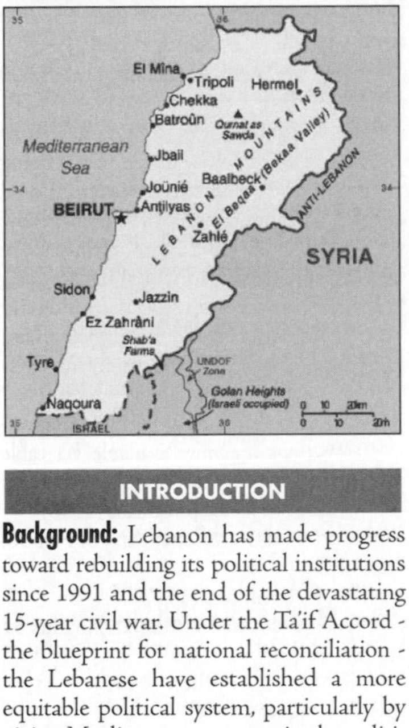

INTRODUCTION

Background: Lebanon has made progress toward rebuilding its political institutions since 1991 and the end of the devastating 15-year civil war. Under the Ta'if Accord - the blueprint for national reconciliation - the Lebanese have established a more equitable political system, particularly by giving Muslims a greater say in the political process while institutionalizing sectarian divisions in the government. Since the end of the war, the Lebanese have conducted several successful elections, most of the militias have been weakened or disbanded, and the Lebanese Armed Forces (LAF) have extended central government authority over about two-thirds of the country. Hizballah, a radical Shia organization, retains its weapons. During Lebanon's civil war, the Arab League legitimized in the Ta'if Accord Syria's troop deployment, numbering about 16,000 based mainly east of Beirut and in the Bekaa Valley. Damascus justified its continued military presence in Lebanon by citing Beirut's requests and the failure of the Lebanese Government to implement all of the constitutional reforms in the Ta'if Accord. Israel's withdrawal from southern Lebanon in May 2000, however, encouraged some Lebanese groups to demand that Syria withdraw its forces as well. The passage of UNSCR 1559 in early October 2004 - a resolution calling for Syria to withdraw from Lebanon and end its interference in Lebanese affairs - further emboldened Lebanese groups opposed to Syria's presence in Lebanon. Syria finally withdrew the remainder of its forces from Lebanon in April of 2005. In May-June 2005, Lebanon held its first legislative elections since the end of the civil war that were free of the Syrian presence.

GEOGRAPHY

Location: Middle East, bordering the Mediterranean Sea, between Israel and Syria
Geographic coordinates: 33 50 N, 35 50 E
Map references: Middle East
Area:
total: 10,400 sq km
land: 10,230 sq km
water: 170 sq km
Area - comparative: about 0.7 times the size of Connecticut
Land boundaries:
total: 454 km
border countries: Israel 79 km, Syria 375 km
Coastline: 225 km
Maritime claims: *territorial sea:* 12 nm
Climate: Mediterranean; mild to cool, wet winters with hot, dry summers; Lebanon mountains experience heavy winter snows
Terrain: narrow coastal plain; El Beqaa (Bekaa Valley) separates Lebanon and Anti-Lebanon Mountains
Elevation extremes:
lowest point: Mediterranean Sea 0 m
highest point: Qurnat as Sawda' 3,088 m
Natural resources: limestone, iron ore, salt, water-surplus state in a water-deficit region, arable land
Land use:
arable land: 16.62%
permanent crops: 13.98%
other: 69.4% (2001)
Irrigated land: 1,200 sq km (1998 est.)
Natural hazards: dust storms, sandstorms

Environment - current issues: deforestation; soil erosion; desertification; air pollution in Beirut from vehicular traffic and the burning of industrial wastes; pollution of coastal waters from raw sewage and oil spills
Environment - international agreements:
party to: Biodiversity, Climate Change, Desertification, Hazardous Wastes, Law of the Sea, Ozone Layer Protection, Ship Pollution, Wetlands
signed, but not ratified: Environmental Modification, Marine Life Conservation
Geography - note: Nahr el Litani only major river in Near East not crossing an international boundary; rugged terrain historically helped isolate, protect, and develop numerous factional groups based on religion, clan, and ethnicity

PEOPLE

Population: 3,826,018 (July 2005 est.)
Age structure:
0-14 years: 26.7% (male 520,270/female 499,609)
15-64 years: 66.4% (male 1,216,738/female 1,324,031)
65 years and over: 6.9% (male 120,176/female 145,194) (2005 est.)
Median age:
total: 27.34 years
male: 26.28 years
female: 28.43 years (2005 est.)
Population growth rate: 1.26% (2005 est.)
Birth rate: 18.88 births/1,000 population (2005 est.)
Death rate: 6.24 deaths/1,000 population (2005 est.)
Net migration rate: 0 migrant(s)/1,000 population (2005 est.)
Sex ratio:
at birth: 1.05 male(s)/female
under 15 years: 1.04 male(s)/female
15-64 years: 0.92 male(s)/female
65 years and over: 0.83 male(s)/female
total population: 0.94 male(s)/female (2005 est.)
Infant mortality rate:
total: 24.52 deaths/1,000 live births
male: 27.19 deaths/1,000 live births
female: 21.71 deaths/1,000 live births (2005 est.)
Life expectancy at birth:
total population: 72.63 years
male: 70.17 years
female: 75.21 years (2005 est.)
Total fertility rate: 1.92 children born/woman (2005 est.)
HIV/AIDS - adult prevalence rate: 0.1% (2001 est.)
HIV/AIDS - people living with HIV/AIDS: 2,800 (2003 est.)
HIV/AIDS - deaths: less than 200 (2003 est.)
Nationality:
noun: Lebanese (singular and plural)
adjective: Lebanese
Ethnic groups: Arab 95%, Armenian 4%, other 1%
Religions: Muslim 59.7% (Shi'a, Sunni, Druze, Isma'ilite, Alawite or Nusayri), Christian 39% (Maronite Catholic, Greek Orthodox, Melkite Catholic, Armenian Orthodox, Syrian Catholic, Armenian Catholic, Syrian Orthodox, Roman Catholic, Chaldean, Assyrian, Copt, Protestant), other 1.3%
note: seventeen religious sects recognized
Languages: Arabic (official), French, English, Armenian
Literacy:
definition: age 15 and over can read and write
total population: 87.4%
male: 93.1%
female: 82.2% (2003 est.)

GOVERNMENT

Country name:
conventional long form: Lebanese Republic
conventional short form: Lebanon
local long form: Al Jumhuriyah al Lubnaniyah
local short form: Lubnan
Government type: republic
Capital: Beirut
Administrative divisions: 6 governorates (mohafazat, singular - mohafazah); Beyrouth, Beqaa, Liban-Nord, Liban-Sud, Mont-Liban, Nabatiye
Independence: 22 November 1943 (from League of Nations mandate under French administration)
National holiday: Independence Day, 22 November (1943)
Constitution: 23 May 1926; amended a number of times, most recently Charter of Lebanese National Reconciliation (Ta'if Accord) of October 1989
Legal system: mixture of Ottoman law, canon law, Napoleonic code, and civil law; no judicial review of legislative acts; has not accepted compulsory ICJ jurisdiction
Suffrage: 21 years of age; compulsory for all males; authorized for women at age 21 with elementary education
Executive branch:
chief of state: President Emile LAHUD (since 24 November 1998)
head of government: Prime Minister Fuad SINIORA (since 30 June 2005); Deputy Prime Minister Elias MURR (since April 2005)
cabinet: Cabinet chosen by the prime minister in consultation with the president and members of the National Assembly
elections: president elected by the National Assembly for a six-year term; election last held 15 October 1998 (next election date NA); note - on 3 September 2004 the National Assembly voted 96 to 29 to extend Emile LAHUD's six-year term by three years; the prime minister and deputy prime minister appointed by the president in consultation with the National Assembly; by agreement, the president is a Maronite Christian, the prime minister is a Sunni Muslim, and the speaker of the legislature is a Shia Muslim
election results: for 15 October 1998 election: Emile LAHUD elected president; National Assembly vote - 118 votes in favor, 0 against, 10 abstentions
Legislative branch: unicameral National Assembly or Majlis Alnuwab (Arabic) or Assemblee Nationale (French) (128 seats; members elected by popular vote on the basis of sectarian proportional representation to serve four-year terms)
elections: last held in four rounds on 29 May, 5, 12, 19 June 2005 (next to be held 2009)
election results: percent of vote by group - NA; seats by group - Future Movement Bloc 36; Democratic Gathering 15; Development and Resistance Bloc 15; Loyalty to the Resistance 14; Free Patriotic Movement 14; Lebanese Forces 6; Qornet Shewan 5; Popular Bloc 4; Tripoli Independent Bloc 3; Syrian National Socialist Party 2; Kataeb Reform Movement 2; Tachnaq Party 2; Democratic Renewal Movement 1; Democratic Left 1; Nasserite Popular Movement 1; Ba'th Party 1; Kataeb Party 1; independent 5
Judicial branch: four Courts of Cassation (three courts for civil and commercial cases and one court for criminal cases); Constitutional Council (called for in Ta'if Accord - rules on constitutionality of laws); Supreme Council (hears charges against the president and prime minister as needed)
Political parties and leaders: Ba'th Party [leader NA]; Democratic Gathering [Walid JUNBLATT]; Democratic Left [Ilyas ATALLAH]; Democratic Renewal Movement [Nassib LAHUD]; Development and Resistance Bloc [Nabih BERRI, Amal Movement leader/Speaker of the National Assembly]; Free Patriotic Movement [Michel AWN]; Future Movement Bloc [Sa'ad HARIRI]; Kataeb Party [Karim PAKRADONI]; Kataeb Reform Movement [Amine GEMAYAL]; Lebanese Forces [Samir JA'JA]; Loyalty to the Resistance [Mohammad RA'AD]; Metn Bloc [Michel MURR]; Nasserite Popular Movement [Ussama SAAD]; National Bloc [Carlos EDDE]; Popular Bloc [Elias SKAFF]; Qornet Shewan Gathering [a grouping with no individual leader]; Syrian National Socialist Party

[Ali QANSU]; Tripoli Independent Bloc [a grouping with no individual leader]
Political pressure groups and leaders: 05-Al-Mujtama' Al-Madani or 05-AMAM [leader NA]
International organization participation: ABEDA, ACCT, AFESD, AMF, FAO, G-24, G-77, IAEA, IBRD, ICAO, ICC, ICFTU, ICRM, IDA, IDB, IFAD, IFC, IFRCS, ILO, IMF, IMO, Interpol, IOC, ISO (correspondent), ITU, LAS, MIGA, NAM, OAS (observer), OIC, PCA, UN, UNCTAD, UNESCO, UNHCR, UNIDO, UNRWA, UPU, WCO, WFTU, WHO, WIPO, WMO, WToO, WTO (observer)
Diplomatic representation in the US:
chief of mission: Ambassador Dr. Farid ABBOUD
chancery: 2560 28th Street NW, Washington, DC 20008
telephone: [1] (202) 939-6300
FAX: [1] (202) 939-6324
consulate(s) general: Detroit, New York, and Los Angeles
Diplomatic representation from the US:
chief of mission: Ambassador Jeffrey D. FELTMAN
embassy: Awkar, Lebanon
mailing address: P. O. Box 70-840, Antelias, Lebanon; PSC 815, Box 2, FPO AE 09836-0002; from US: Embassy Beirut, 6070 Beirut Place, Washington, DC 20521-6070
telephone: [961] (4) 542600, 543600
FAX: [961] (4) 544136
Flag description: three horizontal bands consisting of red (top), white (middle, double width), and red (bottom) with a green cedar tree centered in the white band

ECONOMY

Economy - overview: The 1975-91 civil war seriously damaged Lebanon's economic infrastructure, cut national output by half, and all but ended Lebanon's position as a Middle Eastern entrepot and banking hub. In the years since, Lebanon has rebuilt much of its war-torn physical and financial infrastructure by borrowing heavily - mostly from domestic banks. In an attempt to reduce the ballooning national debt, the HARIRI government began an austerity program, reining in government expenditures, increasing revenue collection, and privatizing state enterprises. In November 2002, the government met with international donors at the Paris II conference to seek bilateral assistance in restructuring its massive domestic debt at lower rates of interest. Substantial receipts from donor nations stabilized government finances in 2003, but did little to reduce the debt, which stands at nearly 200% of GDP. In 2004 the HARIRI government issued Eurobonds in an effort to manage maturing debt, and the KARAMI government has continued this practice. The downturn in economic activity that followed the assassination of Rafiq al-HARIRI has eased, but has yet to be reversed. Tourism remains below the level of 2004. The new Prime Minister, Fuad SINIORA, has pledged to push ahead with economic reform, including privatization and more efficient government.
GDP (purchasing power parity): $19.49 billion (2005 est.)
GDP (official exchange rate): $20.7 billion (2005 est.)
GDP - real growth rate: 0.5% (2005 est.)
GDP - per capita: purchasing power parity - $5,100 (2005 est.)
GDP - composition by sector:
agriculture: 12%
industry: 21%
services: 67% (2000)
Labor force: 2.6 million
note: in addition, there are as many as 1 million foreign workers (2001 est.)
Labor force - by occupation: agriculture NA, industry NA, services NA
Unemployment rate: 18% (1997 est.)
Population below poverty line: 28% (1999 est.)
Household income or consumption by percentage share:
lowest 10%: NA
highest 10%: NA
Inflation rate (consumer prices): 2.4% (2005 est.)
Investment (gross fixed): 25.5% of GDP (2005 est.)
Budget:
revenues: $4.953 billion
expenditures: $6.595 billion, including capital expenditures of NA (2005 est.)
Public debt: 200.7% of GDP (2005 est.)
Agriculture - products: citrus, grapes, tomatoes, apples, vegetables, potatoes, olives, tobacco; sheep, goats
Industries: banking, tourism, food processing, jewelry, cement, textiles, mineral and chemical products, wood and furniture products, oil refining, metal fabricating
Industrial production growth rate: NA
Electricity - production: 10.67 billion kWh (2003)
Electricity - production by source:
fossil fuel: 97.2%
hydro: 2.8%
nuclear: 0%
other: 0% (2001)
Electricity - consumption: 10.67 billion kWh (2003)
Electricity - exports: 0 kWh (2003)
Electricity - imports: 750 million kWh (2003)
Oil - production: 0 bbl/day (2003 est.)
Oil - consumption: 102,000 bbl/day (2003 est.)
Oil - exports: NA (2001)
Oil - imports: NA (2001)
Current account balance: $-4.09 billion (2005 est.)
Exports: $1.782 billion f.o.b. (2005 est.)
Exports - partners: Syria 24.9%, UAE 10%, Turkey 6.9%, Switzerland 6.7%, Saudi Arabia 5.3% (2004)
Imports: $8.855 billion f.o.b. (2005 est.)
Imports - partners: Italy 11.2%, France 10.3%, Syria 9.8%, Germany 8.6%, China 5.8%, US 5.5%, UK 4.6% (2004)
Reserves of foreign exchange and gold: $15.34 billion (2005 est.)
Debt - external: $25.92 billion (2005 est.)
Economic aid — recipient: $2.2 billion received (2003), out of the $4.2 billion in soft loans pledged at the November 2002 Paris II Aid Conference
Currency (code): Lebanese pound (LBP)
Currency code: LBP
Exchange rates: Lebanese pounds per US dollar - 1,507.5 (2005), 1,507.5 (2004), 1,507.5 (2003), 1,507.5 (2002), 1,507.5 (2001)
Fiscal year: calendar year

COMMUNICATIONS

Telephones - main lines in use: 678,800 (2002)
Telephones - mobile cellular: 775,100 (2002)
Telephone system:
general assessment: telecommunications system severely damaged by civil war; rebuilding well underway
domestic: primarily microwave radio relay and cable
international: country code - 961; satellite earth stations - 2 Intelsat (1 Indian Ocean and 1 Atlantic Ocean) (erratic operations); coaxial cable to Syria; microwave radio relay to Syria but inoperable beyond Syria to Jordan; 3 submarine coaxial cables
Radio broadcast stations: AM 20, FM 22, shortwave 4 (1998)
Radios: 2.85 million (1997)
Television broadcast stations: 15 (plus 5 repeaters) (1995)
Televisions: 1.18 million (1997)
Internet country code: .lb
Internet hosts: 6,998 (2004)
Internet Service Providers (ISPs): 22 (2000)
Internet users: 400,000 (2002)

TRANSPORTATION

Airports: 8 (2004 est.)
Airports - with paved runways:
total: 5
over 3,047 m: 1
2,438 to 3,047 m: 2

under 914 m: 2 (2005 est.)
Airports - with unpaved runways:
total: 2
914 to 1,523 m: 2 (2005 est.)
Pipelines: oil 209 km (2004)
Railways:
total: 401 km
standard gauge: 319 km 1.435-m
narrow gauge: 82 km 1.050-m
note: rail system became unusable because of damage during the civil war in the 1980s; short sections are operable (2004)
Roadways:
total: 7,300 km
paved: 6,198 km
unpaved: 1,102 km (1999)
Merchant marine:
total: 44 ships (1,000 GRT or over) 198,602 GRT/248,313 DWT
by type: bulk carrier 4, cargo 26, livestock carrier 8, refrigerated cargo 1, roll on/roll off 2, vehicle carrier 3
foreign-owned: 6 (Austria 1, Greece 5)
registered in other countries: 40 (2005)
Ports and terminals: Beirut, Chekka, Jounie, Tripoli

MILITARY

Military branches: Lebanese Armed Forces (LAF): Army, Navy, and Air Force
Military service age and obligation: 18-30 years of age for compulsory and voluntary military service; conscript service obligation - 12 months (2004)
Manpower available for military service: *males age 18-49:* 974,363 (2005 est.)
Manpower fit for military service: *males age 18-49:* 821,762 (2005 est.)
Military expenditures - dollar figure: $540.6 million (2002) (2004)
Military expenditures - percent of GDP: 3.1% (FY99) (2004)

TRANSNATIONAL ISSUES

Disputes - international: intense international pressure prompts the removal of Syrian troops and intelligence personnel from Lebanon; Lebanese Government claims Shab'a Farms area of Israeli-occupied Golan Heights; the roughly 2,000-strong UN Interim Force in Lebanon (UNIFIL) has been in place since 1978
Refugees and internally displaced persons: *refugees (country of origin):* 394,532 (Palestinian Refugees (UNRWA))
IDPs: 300,000 (1975-90 civil war, Israeli invasions) (2004)
Illicit drugs: cannabis cultivation dramatically reduced to 2,500 hectares in 2002; opium poppy cultivation minimal; small amounts of Latin American cocaine and Southwest Asian heroin transit country on way to European markets and for Middle Eastern consumption

LESOTHO

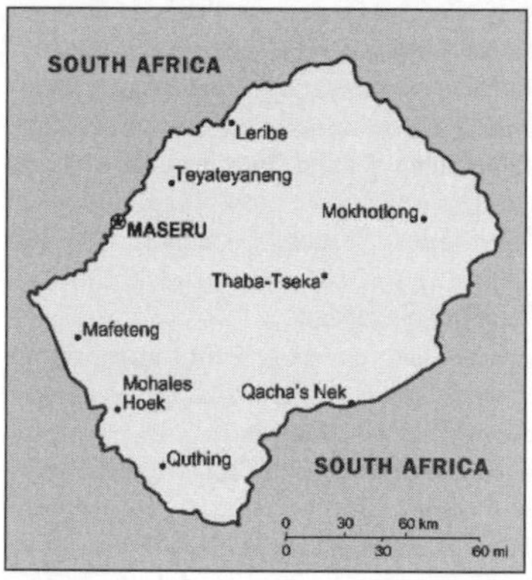

INTRODUCTION

Background: Basutoland was renamed the Kingdom of Lesotho upon independence from the UK in 1966. King MOSHOESHOE was exiled in 1990, but returned to Lesotho in 1992 and reinstated in 1995. Constitutional government was restored in 1993 after 23 years of military rule. In 1998, violent protests and a military mutiny following a contentious election prompted a brief but bloody intervention by South African and Botswanan military forces under the aegis of the Southern African Development Community. Constitutional reforms have since restored political stability; peaceful parliamentary elections were held in 2002.

GEOGRAPHY

Location: Southern Africa, an enclave of South Africa
Geographic coordinates: 29 30 S, 28 30 E
Map references: Africa
Area:
total: 30,355 sq km
land: 30,355 sq km
water: 0 sq km
Area - comparative: slightly smaller than Maryland
Land boundaries:
total: 909 km
border countries: South Africa 909 km
Coastline: 0 km (landlocked)
Maritime claims: none (landlocked)
Climate: temperate; cool to cold, dry winters; hot, wet summers
Terrain: mostly highland with plateaus, hills, and mountains
Elevation extremes:
lowest point: junction of the Orange and Makhaleng Rivers 1,400 m
highest point: Thabana Ntlenyana 3,482 m
Natural resources: water, agricultural and grazing land, diamonds, sand, clay, building stone
Land use:
arable land: 10.87%
permanent crops: 0.13%
other: 89% (2001)
Irrigated land: 10 sq km (1998 est.)
Natural hazards: periodic droughts
Environment - current issues: population pressure forcing settlement in marginal areas results in overgrazing, severe soil erosion, and soil exhaustion; desertification; Highlands Water Project controls, stores, and redirects water to South Africa
Environment - international agreements:
party to: Biodiversity, Climate Change, Climate Change-Kyoto Protocol, Desertification, Endangered Species, Hazardous Wastes, Marine Life Conservation, Ozone Layer Protection
signed, but not ratified: Law of the Sea
Geography - note: landlocked, completely surrounded by South Africa; mountainous, more than 80% of the country is 1,800 meters above sea level

PEOPLE

Population: 1,867,035
note: estimates for this country explicitly take into account the effects of excess mortality due to AIDS; this can result in lower life expectancy, higher infant mortality and death rates, lower population and growth rates, and changes in the distribution of population by age and sex than would otherwise be expected (July 2005 est.)
Age structure:
0-14 years: 36.9% (male 346,930/female 342,459)
15-64 years: 57.6% (male 526,642/female 548,096)
65 years and over: 5.5% (male 42,003/female 60,905) (2005 est.)
Median age:
total: 20.19 years
male: 19.68 years
female: 20.74 years (2005 est.)
Population growth rate: 0.08% (2005 est.)
Birth rate: 26.53 births/1,000 population (2005 est.)
Death rate: 25.03 deaths/1,000 population (2005 est.)

Net migration rate: -0.74 migrant(s)/1,000 population (2005 est.)
Sex ratio:
at birth: 1.03 male(s)/female
under 15 years: 1.01 male(s)/female
15-64 years: 0.96 male(s)/female
65 years and over: 0.69 male(s)/female
total population: 0.96 male(s)/female (2005 est.)
Infant mortality rate:
total: 84.23 deaths/1,000 live births
male: 89.11 deaths/1,000 live births
female: 79.21 deaths/1,000 live births (2005 est.)
Life expectancy at birth:
total population: 34.47 years
male: 35.49 years
female: 33.42 years (2005 est.)
Total fertility rate: 3.35 children born/woman (2005 est.)
HIV/AIDS - adult prevalence rate: 28.9% (2003 est.)
HIV/AIDS - people living with HIV/AIDS: 320,000 (2003 est.)
HIV/AIDS - deaths: 29,000 (2003 est.)
Nationality:
noun: Mosotho (singular), Basotho (plural)
adjective: Basotho
Ethnic groups: Sotho 99.7%, Europeans, Asians, and other 0.3%,
Religions: Christian 80%, indigenous beliefs 20%
Languages: Sesotho (southern Sotho), English (official), Zulu, Xhosa
Literacy:
definition: age 15 and over can read and write
total population: 84.8%
male: 74.5%
female: 94.5% (2003 est.)

GOVERNMENT

Country name:
conventional long form: Kingdom of Lesotho
conventional short form: Lesotho
former: Basutoland
Government type: parliamentary constitutional monarchy
Capital: Maseru
Administrative divisions: 10 districts; Berea, Butha-Buthe, Leribe, Mafeteng, Maseru, Mohale's Hoek, Mokhotlong, Qacha's Nek, Quthing, Thaba-Tseka
Independence: 4 October 1966 (from UK)
National holiday: Independence Day, 4 October (1966)
Constitution: 2 April 1993
Legal system: based on English common law and Roman-Dutch law; judicial review of legislative acts in High Court and Court of Appeal; has not accepted compulsory ICJ jurisdiction
Suffrage: 18 years of age; universal
Executive branch:
chief of state: King LETSIE III (since 7 February 1996); note - King LETSIE III formerly occupied the throne from November 1990 to February 1995, while his father was in exile
head of government: Prime Minister Pakalitha MOSISILI (since 23 May 1998)
cabinet: Cabinet
elections: none; according to the constitution, the leader of the majority party in the Assembly automatically becomes prime minister; the monarch is hereditary, but, under the terms of the constitution, which came into effect after the March 1993 election, the monarch is a "living symbol of national unity" with no executive or legislative powers; under traditional law the college of chiefs has the power to determine who is next in the line of succession, who shall serve as regent in the event that the successor is not of mature age, and may even depose the monarch
Legislative branch: bicameral Parliament consists of the Senate (33 members - 22 principal chiefs and 11 other members appointed by the ruling party) and the Assembly (120 seats, 80 by direct popular vote and 40 by proportional vote; members elected by popular vote for five-year terms); note - number of seats in the Assembly rose from 80 to 120 in the May 2002 election
elections: last held 25 May 2002 (next to be held May 2007)
election results: percent of vote by party - LCD 54%, BNP 21%, LPC 7%, other 18%; seats by party - LCD 76, BNP 21, LPC 5, other 18
Judicial branch: High Court (chief justice appointed by the monarch acting on the advice of the Prime Minister); Court of Appeal; Magistrate's Court; customary or traditional court
Political parties and leaders: Basotholand African Congress or BAC [Khauhelo RALITAPOLE]; Basotholand Congress Party or BCP [Ntsukunyane MPHANYA]; Basotho National Party or BNP [Maj. Gen. Justine Metsing LEKHANYA]; Lesotho Congress for Democracy or LCD [Pakalitha MOSISILI] - the governing party; Lesotho People's Congress or LPC [Kelebone MAOPE]; Lesotho Workers Party of LWP [Macaefa BILLY]; Marematlou Freedom Party or MFP [Vincent MALEBO]; National Independent Party or NIP [Anthony MANYELI]; National Progressive Party or NPP [Chief Peete Nkoebe PEETE]; Popular Front for Democracy or PFD [Lekhetho RAKUOANE]; Sefate Democratic Party or SDP [Bofihla NKUEBE]
Political pressure groups and leaders: NA
International organization participation: ACP, AfDB, AU, C, FAO, G-77, IBRD, ICAO, ICCt, ICRM, IDA, IFAD, IFC, IFRCS, ILO, IMF, Interpol, IOC, ISO (subscriber), ITU, MIGA, NAM, OPCW, SACU, SADC, UN, UNCTAD, UNESCO, UNHCR, UNIDO, UPU, WCO, WFTU, WHO, WIPO, WMO, WToO, WTO
Diplomatic representation in the US:
chief of mission: Ambassador Molelekeng E. RAPOLAKI
chancery: 2511 Massachusetts Avenue NW, Washington, DC 20008
telephone: [1] (202) 797-5533 through 5536
FAX: [1] (202) 234-6815
Diplomatic representation from the US:
chief of mission: Ambassador June Carter PERRY
embassy: 254 Kingsway, Maseru West (Consular Section)
mailing address: P. O. Box 333, Maseru 100, Lesotho
telephone: [266] 22 312666
FAX: [266] 22 310116
Flag description: divided diagonally from the lower hoist side corner; the upper half is white, bearing the brown silhouette of a large shield with crossed spear and club; the lower half is a diagonal blue band with a green triangle in the corner

ECONOMY

Economy - overview: Small, landlocked, and mountainous, Lesotho relies on remittances from miners employed in South Africa and customs duties from the Southern Africa Customs Union for the majority of government revenue, but the government has strengthened its tax system to reduce dependency on customs duties. Completion of a major hydropower facility in January 1998 now permits the sale of water to South Africa, also generating royalties for Lesotho. As the number of mineworkers has declined steadily over the past several years, a small manufacturing base has developed based on farm products that support the milling, canning, leather, and jute industries and a rapidly growing apparel-assembly sector. The garment industry has grown significantly, mainly due to Lesotho qualifying for the trade benefits contained in the Africa Growth and Opportunity Act. The economy is still primarily based on subsistence agriculture, especially livestock, although drought has decreased agricultural activity. The extreme inequality in the distribution of income remains a major drawback. Lesotho has signed an Interim Poverty Reduction and Growth Facility with the IMF.

GDP (purchasing power parity): $6.123 billion (2005 est.)
GDP (official exchange rate): $1.405 billion (2005 est.)
GDP - real growth rate: 2% (2005 est.)
GDP - per capita: purchasing power parity - $3,300 (2005 est.)
GDP - composition by sector:
agriculture: 15.4%
industry: 44.2%
services: 40.4% (2005 est.)
Labor force: 838,000 (2000)
Labor force - by occupation: 86% of resident population engaged in subsistence agriculture; roughly 35% of the active male wage earners work in South Africa
Unemployment rate: 45% (2002)
Population below poverty line: 49% (1999)
Household income or consumption by percentage share:
lowest 10%: 0.9%
highest 10%: 43.4%
Distribution of family income - Gini index: 63.2 (1995)
Inflation rate (consumer prices): 4.7% (2005 est.)
Investment (gross fixed): 29.5% of GDP (2005 est.)
Budget:
revenues: $738.5 million
expenditures: $792.1 million, including capital expenditures of $15 million (2005 est.)
Agriculture - products: corn, wheat, pulses, sorghum, barley; livestock
Industries: food, beverages, textiles, apparel assembly, handicrafts; construction; tourism
Industrial production growth rate: 15.5% (1999)
Electricity - production: 350 million kWh; note - electricity supplied by South Africa (2003)
Electricity - consumption: 363.5 million kWh (2003)
Electricity - exports: 0 kWh (2003)
Electricity - imports: 38 million kWh; note - electricity supplied by South Africa (2003)
Oil - production: 0 bbl/day (2003 est.)
Oil - consumption: 1,400 bbl/day (2003)
Oil - exports: NA (2001)
Oil - imports: NA (2001)
Current account balance: $-152.1 million (2005 est.)
Exports: $602.8 million f.o.b. (2005 est.)
Exports - partners: US 97%, Canada 2.1%, UK 0.3% (2004)
Imports: $1.166 billion f.o.b. (2005 est.)
Imports - partners: Hong Kong 43%, China 23.4%, India 5.5%, South Korea 5.1%, Germany 4.4% (2004)
Reserves of foreign exchange and gold: $411 million (2005 est.)
Debt - external: $735 million (2002)
Economic aid - donor: ODA $4.4 million
Economic aid - recipient: $41.5 million (2000)
Currency (code): loti (LSL); South African rand (ZAR)
Currency code: LSL; ZAR
Exchange rates: maloti per US dollar - 6.2 (2005), 6.4597 (2004), 7.5648 (2003), 10.5407 (2002), 8.6092 (2001)
Fiscal year: 1 April - 31 March

COMMUNICATIONS

Telephones - main lines in use: 28,600 (2002)
Telephones - mobile cellular: 92,000 (2002)
Telephone system:
general assessment: rudimentary system
domestic: consists of a modest but growing number of landlines, a small microwave radio relay system, and a minor radiotelephone communication system; a cellular mobile telephone system is growing
international: country code - 266; satellite earth station - 1 Intelsat (Atlantic Ocean)
Radio broadcast stations: AM 1, FM 2, shortwave 1 (1998)
Radios: NA (2002)
Television broadcast stations: 1 (2000)
Televisions: NA
Internet country code: .ls
Internet hosts: 119 (2003)
Internet Service Providers (ISPs): 1 (2000)
Internet users: 21,000 (2002)

TRANSPORTATION

Airports: 28 (2004 est.)
Airports - with paved runways:
total: 3
over 3,047 m: 1
914 to 1,523 m: 1
under 914 m: 1 (2005 est.)
Airports - with unpaved runways:
total: 25
914 to 1,523 m: 4
under 914 m: 21 (2005 est.)
Roadways:
total: 5,940 km
paved: 1,087 km
unpaved: 4,853 km (1999)

MILITARY

Military branches: Lesotho Defense Force (LDF): Army and Air Wing
Military service age and obligation: 18 years of age (est.); no conscription (2001)
Manpower available for military service:
males age 18-49: 400,457 (2005 est.)
Manpower fit for military service: *males age 18-49:* 162,857 (2005 est.)
Military expenditures - dollar figure: $32.3 million (2004)
Military expenditures - percent of GDP: 2.3% (2004)
Military - note: the Lesotho Government in 1999 began an open debate on the future structure, size, and role of the armed forces, especially considering the Lesotho Defense Force's (LDF) history of intervening in political affairs

TRANSNATIONAL ISSUES

Disputes - international: none

LIBERIA

INTRODUCTION

Background: In August 2003, a comprehensive peace agreement ended 14 years of civil war and prompted the resignation of former president Charles TAYLOR, who was exiled to Nigeria. After two years of rule by a transitional government, democratic elections in late 2005 brought President Ellen JOHNSON-SIRLEAF to power. The legislative and presidential polls were broadly deemed free and fair despite fraud allegations from JOHNSON-SIRLEAF's rival George WEAH. The United Nations Mission in Liberia (UNMIL), which maintains a strong presence throughout the country, completed a disarmament program for former combatants in late 2004, but the security situation is still volatile and the process of rebuilding the social and economic structure of this war-torn country remains sluggish.

GEOGRAPHY

Location: Western Africa, bordering the North Atlantic Ocean, between Cote d'Ivoire and Sierra Leone
Geographic coordinates: 6 30 N, 9 30 W
Map references: Africa
Area:
total: 111,370 sq km
land: 96,320 sq km
water: 15,050 sq km
Area - comparative: slightly larger than Tennessee
Land boundaries:
total: 1,585 km
border countries: Guinea 563 km, Cote d'Ivoire 716 km, Sierra Leone 306 km
Coastline: 579 km
Maritime claims: *territorial sea:* 200 nm

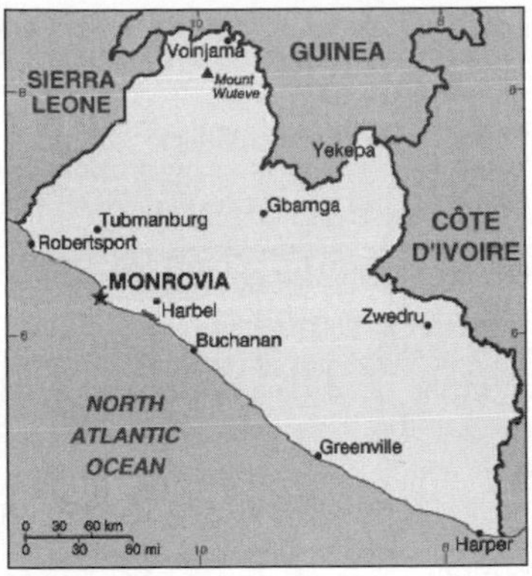

Climate: tropical; hot, humid; dry winters with hot days and cool to cold nights; wet, cloudy summers with frequent heavy showers
Terrain: mostly flat to rolling coastal plains rising to rolling plateau and low mountains in northeast
Elevation extremes:
lowest point: Atlantic Ocean 0 m
highest point: Mount Wuteve 1,380 m
Natural resources: iron ore, timber, diamonds, gold, hydropower
Land use:
arable land: 3.95%
permanent crops: 2.28%
other: 93.77% (2001)
Irrigated land: 30 sq km (1998 est.)
Natural hazards: dust-laden harmattan winds blow from the Sahara (December to March)
Environment - current issues: tropical rain forest deforestation; soil erosion; loss of biodiversity; pollution of coastal waters from oil residue and raw sewage
Environment - international agreements:
party to: Biodiversity, Climate Change, Climate Change-Kyoto Protocol, Desertification, Endangered Species, Ozone Layer Protection, Ship Pollution, Tropical Timber 83, Tropical Timber 94
signed, but not ratified: Environmental Modification, Law of the Sea, Marine Life Conservation
Geography - note: facing the Atlantic Ocean, the coastline is characterized by lagoons, mangrove swamps, and river-deposited sandbars; the inland grassy plateau supports limited agriculture

PEOPLE

Population: 3,482,211 (July 2005 est.)
Age structure:
0-14 years: 43.6% (male 765,662/female 751,134)
15-64 years: 52.8% (male 896,206/female 940,985)
65 years and over: 3.7% (male 64,547/female 63,677) (2005 est.)
Median age:
total: 18.06 years
male: 17.69 years
female: 18.42 years (2005 est.)
Population growth rate: 2.64% (2005 est.)
Birth rate: 44.22 births/1,000 population (2005 est.)
Death rate: 17.87 deaths/1,000 population (2005 est.)
Net migration rate: 0 migrant(s)/1,000 population
note: at least 200,000 Liberian refugees are in surrounding countries; the uncertain security situation has hindered their ability to return (2005 est.)
Sex ratio:
at birth: 1.03 male(s)/female
under 15 years: 1.02 male(s)/female
15-64 years: 0.95 male(s)/female
65 years and over: 1.01 male(s)/female
total population: 0.98 male(s)/female (2005 est.)
Infant mortality rate:
total: 128.87 deaths/1,000 live births
male: 135.64 deaths/1,000 live births
female: 121.9 deaths/1,000 live births (2005 est.)
Life expectancy at birth:
total population: 38.89 years
male: 37.03 years
female: 40.81 years (2005 est.)
Total fertility rate: 6.09 children born/woman (2005 est.)
HIV/AIDS - adult prevalence rate: 5.9% (2003 est.)
HIV/AIDS - people living with HIV/AIDS: 100,000 (2003 est.)
HIV/AIDS - deaths: 7,200 (2003 est.)
Major infectious diseases:
degree of risk: very high
food or waterborne diseases: bacterial and protozoal diarrhea, hepatitis A, and typhoid fever
vectorborne diseases: malaria and yellow fever are high risks in some locations
water contact disease: schistosomiasis
aerosolized dust or soil contact disease: Lassa fever (2004)
Nationality:
noun: Liberian(s)
adjective: Liberian
Ethnic groups: indigenous African tribes 95% (including Kpelle, Bassa, Gio, Kru, Grebo, Mano, Krahn, Gola, Gbandi, Loma, Kissi, Vai, Dei, Bella, Mandingo, and Mende), Americo-Liberians 2.5% (descendants of immigrants from the US who had been slaves), Congo People 2.5% (descendants of immigrants from the Caribbean who had been slaves)
Religions: indigenous beliefs 40%, Christian 40%, Muslim 20%
Languages: English 20% (official), some 20 ethnic group languages, of which a few can be written and are used in correspondence
Literacy:
definition: age 15 and over can read and write
total population: 57.5%
male: 73.3%
female: 41.6% (2003 est.)

GOVERNMENT

Country name:
conventional long form: Republic of Liberia
conventional short form: Liberia
Government type: republic
Capital: Monrovia
Administrative divisions: 15 counties; Bomi, Bong, Gbarpolu, Grand Bassa, Grand Cape Mount, Grand Gedeh, Grand Kru, Lofa, Margibi, Maryland, Montserrado, Nimba, River Cess, River Gee, Sinoe
Independence: 26 July 1847
National holiday: Independence Day, 26 July (1847)
Constitution: 6 January 1986
Legal system: dual system of statutory law based on Anglo-American common law for the modern sector and customary law based on unwritten tribal practices for indigenous sector
Suffrage: 18 years of age; universal
Executive branch:
chief of state: President Ellen JOHNSON-SIRLEAF (since 16 January 2006) note - the President is both the chief of state and head of government
head of government: President Ellen JOHNSON-SIRLEAF (since 6 January 2006); note - the President is both the chief of state and head of government
cabinet: Cabinet appointed by the president and confirmed by the Senate;
elections: president elected by popular vote for a six-year term (renewable); election last held 8 November 2005 (next to be held NA 2011)
election results: Ellen JOHNSON-SIRLEAF elected president; percent of vote (second round - Ellen JOHNSON-SIRLEAF (UP) 59.6%, George WEAH (CDC) 40.4%
note: a UN-brokered cease-fire among warring factions and the Liberian government resulted in the August 2003 resignation of former president Charles TAYLOR; a jointly agreed upon replacement, Chairman Gyude BRYANT, assumed office as head of the National Transitional Government on 14 October 2003; free elections were held 11 October 2005 with a runoff election between the two leading candidates on 8 November 2005
Legislative branch: bicameral National Assembly consists of the Senate (30 seats - number of seats changed in 11 October 2005 elections; members elected by pop-

ular vote to serve nine-year terms) and the House of Representatives (64 seats; members elected by popular vote to serve six-year terms)
elections: Senate - last held 11 October 2005 (next to be held NA 2014); House of Representatives - last held 11 October 2005 (next to be held NA 2011)
election results: Senate - percent of vote by party - NA%; seats by party - COTOL 7, NPP 4, CDC 3, LP 3, UP 3, APD 3; House of Representatives - percent of vote by party - NA%; seats by party - CDC 15, LP 9, UP 8, COTOL 8, APD 5, NPP 4
note: the current six-year term for junior senators - those who received the second most votes in the election - is mandated by the Liberian constitution to stagger Senate elections and ensure continuity of government
Judicial branch: Supreme Court
Political parties and leaders: Alliance for Peace and Democracy or APD [Togba-na TIPOTEH]; Congress for Democratic Change or CDC [George WEAH]; Liberian Action Party or LAP [H. Varney SHERMAN]; Liberty Party or LP [Charles BRUMSKINE]; National Patriotic Party or NPP [Cyril ALLEN]; Unity Party or UP [Charles CLARKE]
Political pressure groups and leaders: NA
International organization participation: ACP, AfDB, AU, ECOWAS, FAO, G-77, IAEA, IBRD, ICAO, ICCt, ICFTU, ICRM, IDA, IFAD, IFC, IFRCS, ILO, IMF, IMO, Interpol, IOC, IOM, ITU, NAM, OPCW (signatory), UN, UNCTAD, UNESCO, UNIDO, UPU, WCL, WCO, WFTU, WHO, WIPO, WMO
Diplomatic representation in the US:
chief of mission: Ambassador (vacant); Charge d'Affaires Aaron B. KOLLIE
chancery: 5201 16th Street NW, Washington, DC 20011
telephone: [1] (202) 723-0437
FAX: [1] (202) 723-0436
consulate(s) general: New York
Diplomatic representation from the US:
chief of mission: Ambassador Donald E. BOOTH
embassy: 111 United Nations Drive, P. O. Box 10-0098, Mamba Point, 1000 Monrovia, 10 Liberia
mailing address: use embassy street address
telephone: [231] 226-370 through 226-380
FAX: [231] 226-148
Flag description: 11 equal horizontal stripes of red (top and bottom) alternating with white; there is a white five-pointed star on a blue square in the upper hoist-side corner; the design was based on the US flag

ECONOMY

Economy - overview: Civil war and government mismanagement have destroyed much of Liberia's economy, especially the infrastructure in and around Monrovia, while continued international sanctions on diamonds and timber exports will limit growth prospects for the foreseeable future. Many businessmen have fled the country, taking capital and expertise with them. Some have returned, but many will not. Richly endowed with water, mineral resources, forests, and a climate favorable to agriculture, Liberia had been a producer and exporter of basic products - primarily raw timber and rubber. Local manufacturing, mainly foreign owned, had been small in scope. The departure of the former president, Charles TAYLOR, to Nigeria in August 2003, the establishment of the all-inclusive Transitional Government, and the arrival of a UN mission have helped diffuse the political crisis, but have done little to encourage economic development. Wealthy international donors, who are ready to assist reconstruction efforts, are withholding funding until Liberia's National Assembly signs onto a Governance and Economic Management Action Plan (GEMAP). The Plan was created in October 2005 by the International Contact Group for Liberia to help ensure transparent revenue collection and allocation - something that was lacking under the Transitional Government and that has limited Liberia's economic recovery. The reconstruction of infrastructure and the raising of incomes in this ravaged economy will largely depend on generous financial support and technical assistance from donor countries.
GDP (purchasing power parity): $2.593 billion (2005 est.)
GDP (official exchange rate): NA
GDP - real growth rate: 8% (2005 est.)
GDP - per capita: purchasing power parity - $700 (2005 est.)
GDP - composition by sector:
agriculture: 76.9%
industry: 5.4%
services: 17.7% (2002 est.)
Labor force - by occupation: agriculture 70%, industry 8%, services 22% (2000 est.)
Unemployment rate: 85% (2003 est.)
Population below poverty line: 80%
Household income or consumption by percentage share:
lowest 10%: NA
highest 10%: NA
Inflation rate (consumer prices): 15% (2003 est.)
Budget:
revenues: $85.4 million
expenditures: $90.5 million, including capital expenditures of NA (2000 est.)
Agriculture - products: rubber, coffee, cocoa, rice, cassava (tapioca), palm oil, sugarcane, bananas; sheep, goats; timber
Industries: rubber processing, palm oil processing, timber, diamonds
Industrial production growth rate: NA
Electricity - production: 509.4 million kWh (2003)
Electricity - production by source:
fossil fuel: 100%
hydro: 0%
nuclear: 0%
other: 0% (2001)
Electricity - consumption: 473.8 million kWh (2003)
Electricity - exports: 0 kWh (2003)
Electricity - imports: 0 kWh (2003)
Oil - production: 0 bbl/day (2003 est.)
Oil - consumption: 3,400 bbl/day (2003 est.)
Oil - imports: NA (2001)
Exports: $910 million f.o.b. (2004 est.)
Exports - partners: Denmark 28.1%, Germany 18%, Poland 13.6%, US 8.5%, Greece 7.6%, Thailand 4.8% (2004)
Imports: $4.839 billion f.o.b. (2004 est.)
Imports - partners: South Korea 38.8%, Japan 21.2%, Singapore 12.2%, Croatia 5.3%, Germany 4.2% (2004)
Debt - external: $3.2 billion (2005 est.)
Economic aid - recipient: $94 million (1999)
Currency (code): Liberian dollar (LRD)
Currency code: LRD
Exchange rates: Liberian dollars per US dollar - NA (2005), 54.906 (2004), 59.379 (2003), 61.754 (2002), 48.583 (2001)
Fiscal year: calendar year

COMMUNICATIONS

Telephones - main lines in use: 7,000 (2001)
Telephones - mobile cellular: 2,000 (2001)
Telephone system:
general assessment: the limited services available are found almost exclusively in the capital Monrovia
domestic: fully automatic system with very low density of .21 fixed mainlines per 100 persons; limited wireless service available
international: country code - 231; satellite earth station - 1 Intelsat (Atlantic Ocean)
Radio broadcast stations: AM 0, FM 7, shortwave 2 (2001)
Radios: 790,000 (1997)
Television broadcast stations: 1 (plus four low-power repeaters) (2001)
Televisions: 70,000 (1997)
Internet country code: .lr
Internet hosts: 14 (2004)
Internet Service Providers (ISPs): 2 (2001)
Internet users: 1,000 (2002)

TRANSPORTATION

Airports: 53 (2004 est.)
Airports - with paved runways:
total: 2
over 3,047 m: 1
1,524 to 2,437 m: 1 (2005 est.)
Airports - with unpaved runways:
total: 51
1,524 to 2,437 m: 5
914 to 1,523 m: 8
under 914 m: 38 (2005 est.)
Railways:
total: 490 km
standard gauge: 345 km 1.435-m gauge
narrow gauge: 145 km 1.067-m gauge
note: none of the railways are in operation because of the civil war (2004)
Roadways:
total: 10,600 km
paved: 657 km
unpaved: 9,943 km (1999)
Merchant marine:
total: 1,465 ships (1,000 GRT or over) 50,555,752 GRT/79,125,329 DWT
by type: barge carrier 3, bulk carrier 275, cargo 91, chemical tanker 173, combination ore/oil 22, container 388, liquefied gas 78, passenger 2, passenger/cargo 2, petroleum tanker 324, refrigerated cargo 57, roll on/roll off 6, specialized tanker 9, vehicle carrier 35
foreign-owned: 1,392 (Argentina 8, Australia 2, Austria 13, Bahamas 3, Brazil 6, British 1, Canada 2, Chile 1, China 36, Croatia 7, Cyprus 1, Denmark 5, France 3, Germany 511, Greece 149, Hong Kong 29, India 4, Indonesia 1, Isle of Man 5, Israel 7, Italy 12, Japan 106, Latvia 18, Monaco 10, Netherlands 18, Nigeria 1, Norway 57, Pakistan 1, Poland 14, Romania 1, Russia 63, Saudi Arabia 23, Singapore 29, Slovenia 1, South Korea 4, Sweden 12, Switzerland 10, Taiwan 54, Turkey 4, Ukraine 7, UAE 10, United Kingdom 56, United States 84, Uruguay 3) (2005)
Ports and terminals: Buchanan, Monrovia

MILITARY

Military branches: Armed Forces of Liberia (AFL): Army, Navy, Air Force
Military service age and obligation: 18 years of age for voluntary military service; no conscription (2001)
Manpower available for military service: *males age 18-49:* 659,795 (2005 est.)
Manpower fit for military service: *males age 18-49:* 360,373 (2005 est.)
Military expenditures - dollar figure: $1.5 million (2004)
Military expenditures - percent of GDP: 0.2% (2004)

TRANSNATIONAL ISSUES

Disputes - international: although Liberia's domestic fighting among disparate rebel groups, warlords, and youth gangs was declared over in 2003, civil unrest persists, and in 2004, 133,000 Liberian refugees remained in Guinea, 72,000 in Cote d'Ivoire, 67,000 in Sierra Leone, and 43,000 in Ghana; Liberia, in turn, shelters refugees fleeing turmoil in Cote d'Ivoire and Sierra Leone; since 2003, the UN Mission in Liberia (UNMIL) has maintained about 18,000 peacekeepers in Liberia; the Cote d'Ivoire Government accuses Liberia of supporting Ivoirian rebels; UN sanctions ban Liberia from exporting diamonds and timber
Refugees and internally displaced persons: *refugees (country of origin):* 13,941 (Sierra Leone) 38,325 (Cote d'Ivoire)
IDPs: 500,000 (civil war from 1990-2004; IDP resettlement began in November 2004) (2004)
Illicit drugs: transshipment point for Southeast and Southwest Asian heroin and South American cocaine for the European and US markets; corruption, criminal activity, arms-dealing, and diamond trade provide significant potential for money laundering, but the lack of well-developed financial system limits the country's utility as a major money-laundering center

LIBYA

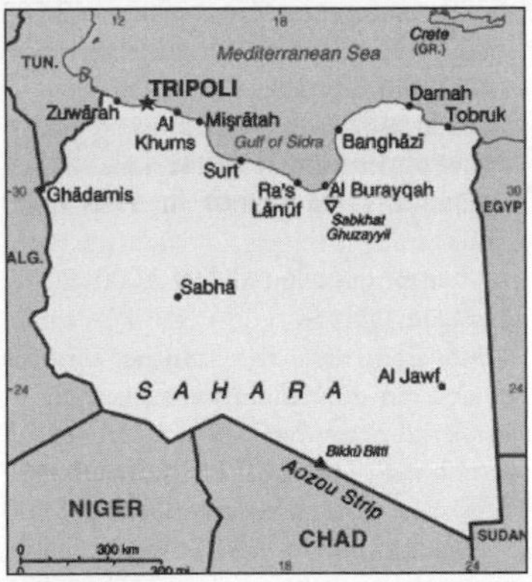

INTRODUCTION

Background: From the earliest days of his rule following his 1969 military coup, Col. Muammar Abu Minyar al-QADHAFI has espoused his own political system, the Third Universal Theory. The system is a combination of socialism and Islam derived in part from tribal practices and is supposed to be implemented by the Libyan people themselves in a unique form of "direct democracy." QADHAFI has always seen himself as a revolutionary and visionary leader. He used oil funds during the 1970s and 1980s to promote his ideology outside Libya, supporting subversives and terrorists abroad to hasten the end of Marxism and capitalism. In addition, beginning in 1973, he engaged in military operations in northern Chad's Aozou Strip - to gain access to minerals and to use as a base of influence in Chadian politics - but was forced to retreat in 1987. UN sanctions in 1992 isolated QADHAFI politically following the downing of Pan AM Flight 103 over Lockerbie, Scotland. Libyan support for terrorism appeared to have decreased after the imposition of sanctions. During the 1990s, QADHAFI also began to rebuild his relationships with Europe. UN sanctions were suspended in April 1999 and finally lifted in September 2003 after Libya resolved the Lockerbie case. In December 2003, Libya announced that it had agreed to reveal and end its programs to develop weapons of mass destruction, and QADHAFI has made significant strides in normalizing relations with western nations since then. He has received various Western European leaders as well as many working-level and commercial delegations, and made his first trip to Western Europe in 15 years when he traveled to Brussels in April 2004. QADHAFI also finally resolved in 2004 several outstanding cases against his government for terrorist activities in the 1980s by paying compensation to the families of victims of the UTA and La Belle disco bombings.

GEOGRAPHY

Location: Northern Africa, bordering the Mediterranean Sea, between Egypt and Tunisia
Geographic coordinates: 25 00 N, 17 00 E
Map references: Africa
Area:
total: 1,759,540 sq km
land: 1,759,540 sq km
water: 0 sq km
Area - comparative: slightly larger than Alaska
Land boundaries:
total: 4,348 km
border countries: Algeria 982 km, Chad 1,055 km, Egypt 1,115 km, Niger 354

km, Sudan 383 km, Tunisia 459 km
Coastline: 1,770 km
Maritime claims:
territorial sea: 12 nm
note: Gulf of Sidra closing line - 32 degrees, 30 minutes north
Climate: Mediterranean along coast; dry, extreme desert interior
Terrain: mostly barren, flat to undulating plains, plateaus, depressions
Elevation extremes:
lowest point: Sabkhat Ghuzayyil -47 m
highest point: Bikku Bitti 2,267 m
Natural resources: petroleum, natural gas, gypsum
Land use:
arable land: 1.03%
permanent crops: 0.19%
other: 98.78% (2001)
Irrigated land: 4,700 sq km (1998 est.)
Natural hazards: hot, dry, dust-laden ghibli is a southern wind lasting one to four days in spring and fall; dust storms, sandstorms
Environment - current issues: desertification; very limited natural fresh water resources; the Great Manmade River Project, the largest water development scheme in the world, is being built to bring water from large aquifers under the Sahara to coastal cities
Environment - international agreements:
party to: Biodiversity, Climate Change, Desertification, Endangered Species, Hazardous Wastes, Marine Dumping, Ozone Layer Protection
signed, but not ratified: Law of the Sea
Geography - note: more than 90% of the country is desert or semidesert

PEOPLE

Population: 5,765,563
note: includes 166,510 non-nationals (July 2005 est.)
Age structure:
0-14 years: 33.9% (male 997,364/female 955,272)
15-64 years: 62% (male 1,842,775/female 1,729,235)
65 years and over: 4.2% (male 117,967/female 122,950) (2005 est.)
Median age:
total: 22.68 years
male: 22.8 years
female: 22.56 years (2005 est.)
Population growth rate: 2.33% (2005 est.)
Birth rate: 26.82 births/1,000 population (2005 est.)
Death rate: 3.48 deaths/1,000 population (2005 est.)
Net migration rate: 0 migrant(s)/1,000 population (2005 est.)
Sex ratio:
at birth: 1.05 male(s)/female
under 15 years: 1.04 male(s)/female
15-64 years: 1.07 male(s)/female
65 years and over: 0.96 male(s)/female
total population: 1.05 male(s)/female (2005 est.)
Infant mortality rate:
total: 24.6 deaths/1,000 live births
male: 26.92 deaths/1,000 live births
female: 22.17 deaths/1,000 live births (2005 est.)
Life expectancy at birth:
total population: 76.5 years
male: 74.29 years
female: 78.82 years (2005 est.)
Total fertility rate: 3.34 children born/woman (2005 est.)
HIV/AIDS - adult prevalence rate: 0.3% (2001 est.)
HIV/AIDS - people living with HIV/AIDS: 10,000 (2001 est.)
HIV/AIDS - deaths: NA
Major infectious diseases:
degree of risk: intermediate
food or waterborne diseases: bacterial diarrhea, hepatitis A, and typhoid fever
vectorborne diseases: may be a significant risk in some locations during the transmission season (typically April through October) (2004)
Nationality:
noun: Libyan(s)
adjective: Libyan
Ethnic groups: Berber and Arab 97%, Greeks, Maltese, Italians, Egyptians, Pakistanis, Turks, Indians, Tunisians
Religions: Sunni Muslim 97%
Languages: Arabic, Italian, English, all are widely understood in the major cities
Literacy:
definition: age 15 and over can read and write
total population: 82.6%
male: 92.4%
female: 72% (2003 est.)

GOVERNMENT

Country name:
conventional long form: Great Socialist People's Libyan Arab Jamahiriya
conventional short form: Libya
local long form: Al Jumahiriyah al Arabiyah al Libiyah ash Shabiyah al Ishtirakiyah al Uzma
local short form: none
Government type: Jamahiriya (a state of the masses) in theory, governed by the populace through local councils; in fact, a military dictatorship
Capital: Tripoli
Administrative divisions: 25 municipalities (baladiyat, singular - baladiyah); Ajdabiya, Al 'Aziziyah, Al Fatih, Al Jabal al Akhdar, Al Jufrah, Al Khums, Al Kufrah, An Nuqat al Khams, Ash Shati', Awbari, Az Zawiyah, Banghazi, Darnah, Ghadamis, Gharyan, Misratah, Murzuq, Sabha, Sawfajjin, Surt, Tarabulus, Tarhunah, Tubruq, Yafran, Zlitan; note - the 25 municipalities may have been replaced by 13 regions
Independence: 24 December 1951 (from Italy)
National holiday: Revolution Day, 1 September (1969)
Constitution: 11 December 1969; amended 2 March 1977
Legal system: based on Italian civil law system and Islamic law; separate religious courts; no constitutional provision for judicial review of legislative acts; has not accepted compulsory ICJ jurisdiction
Suffrage: 18 years of age; universal and compulsory
Executive branch:
chief of state: Revolutionary Leader Col. Muammar Abu Minyar al-QADHAFI (since 1 September 1969); note - holds no official title, but is de facto chief of state
head of government: Secretary of the General People's Committee (Prime Minister) Shukri Muhammad GHANIM (since 14 June 2003)
cabinet: General People's Committee established by the General People's Congress
elections: national elections are indirect through a hierarchy of people's committees; head of government elected by the General People's Congress; election last held 2 March 2000 (next to be held NA)
election results: NA
Legislative branch: unicameral General People's Congress (NA seats; members elected indirectly through a hierarchy of people's committees)
Judicial branch: Supreme Court
Political parties and leaders: none
Political pressure groups and leaders: various Arab nationalist movements with almost negligible memberships may be functioning clandestinely, as well as some Islamic elements; an anti-QADHAFI Libyan exile movement exists, primarily based in London, but has little influence
International organization participation: ABEDA, AfDB, AFESD, AMF, AMU, AU, CAEU, COMESA, FAO, G-77, IAEA, IBRD, ICAO, ICRM, IDA, IDB, IFAD, IFC, IFRCS, ILO, IMF, IMO, Interpol, IOC, IOM, ISO, ITU, LAS, MIGA, NAM, OAPEC, OIC, OPCW, OPEC, PCA, UN, UNCTAD, UNESCO, UNIDO, UPU, WCL, WCO, WFTU, WHO, WIPO, WMO, WToO, WTO (observer)
Diplomatic representation in the US: Libya does not have an embassy in the US but maintains an interest section under the protective power of the United Arab Emirates Embassy in the US

Diplomatic representation from the US: the US suspended all embassy activities in Tripoli in May 1980, resumed embassy activities in February 2004 under the protective power of the US interests section of the Belgian Embassy in Tripoli, then opened a Liaison Office in Tripoli in June 2004
Flag description: plain green; green is the traditional color of Islam (the state religion)

ECONOMY

Economy - overview: The Libyan economy depends primarily upon revenues from the oil sector, which contribute practically all export earnings and about one-quarter of GDP. These oil revenues and a small population give Libya one of the highest per capita GDPs in Africa, but little of this income flows down to the lower orders of society. Libyan officials in the past four years have made progress on economic reforms as part of a broader campaign to reintegrate the country into the international fold. This effort picked up steam after UN sanctions were lifted in September 2003 and as Libya announced in December 2003 that it would abandon programs to build weapons of mass destruction. Almost all US unilateral sanctions against Libya were removed in April 2004, helping Libya attract more foreign direct investment. Libya faces a long road ahead in liberalizing the socialist-oriented economy, but initial steps - including applying for WTO membership, reducing some subsidies, and announcing plans for privatization - are laying the groundwork for a transition to a more market-based economy. The non-oil manufacturing and construction sectors, which account for about 20% of GDP, have expanded from processing mostly agricultural products to include the production of petrochemicals, iron, steel, and aluminum. Climatic conditions and poor soils severely limit agricultural output, and Libya imports about 75% of its food.
GDP (purchasing power parity): $48.19 billion (2005 est.)
GDP (official exchange rate): $34.31 billion (2005 est.)
GDP - real growth rate: 8.5% (2005 est.)
GDP - per capita: purchasing power parity - $8,400 (2005 est.)
GDP - composition by sector:
agriculture: 7.6%
industry: 49.9%
services: 42.5% (2005 est.)
Labor force: 1.64 million (2005 est.)
Labor force - by occupation: agriculture 17%, industry 29%, services 54% (1997 est.)
Unemployment rate: 30% (2004)
Population below poverty line: NA
Household income or consumption by percentage share:
lowest 10%: NA
highest 10%: NA
Inflation rate (consumer prices): -1% (2005 est.)
Investment (gross fixed): 11.4% of GDP (2005 est.)
Budget:
revenues: $25.34 billion
expenditures: $15.47 billion, including capital expenditures of $5.6 billion (2005 est.)
Public debt: 8% of GDP (2005 est.)
Agriculture - products: wheat, barley, olives, dates, citrus, vegetables, peanuts, soybeans; cattle
Industries: petroleum, iron and steel, food processing, textiles, handicrafts, cement
Industrial production growth rate: NA
Electricity - production: 14.4 billion kWh (2003)
Electricity - production by source:
fossil fuel: 100%
hydro: 0%
nuclear: 0%
other: 0% (2001)
Electricity - consumption: 13.39 billion kWh (2003)
Electricity - exports: 0 kWh (2003)
Electricity - imports: 0 kWh (2003)
Oil - production: 1.643 million bbl/day (2005 est.)
Oil - consumption: 236,000 bbl/day (2003 est.)
Oil - exports: NA (2001)
Oil - imports: NA (2001)
Oil - proved reserves: 40 billion bbl (2005 est.)
Natural gas - production: 6.18 billion cu m (2001 est.)
Natural gas - consumption: 5.41 billion cu m (2001 est.)
Natural gas - exports: 770 million cu m (2001 est.)
Natural gas - imports: 0 cu m (2001 est.)
Natural gas - proved reserves: 1.321 trillion cu m (2005)
Current account balance: $14.44 billion (2005 est.)
Exports: $30.79 billion f.o.b. (2005 est.)
Exports - partners: Italy 37%, Germany 16.6%, Spain 11.9%, Turkey 7.1%, France 6.2% (2004)
Imports: $10.82 billion f.o.b. (2005 est.)
Imports – partners: Italy 25.5%, Germany 11%, South Korea 6.1%, UK 5.4%, Tunisia 4.7%, Turkey 4.6% (2004)
Reserves of foreign exchange and gold: $32.31 billion (2005 est.)
Debt - external: $4.267 billion (2005 est.)
Economic aid - recipient: $4.4 million ODA (2002)
Currency (code): Libyan dinar (LYD)
Currency code: LYD
Exchange rates: Libyan dinars per US dollar - 1.3 (2005), 1.305 (2004), 1.2929 (2003), 1.2707 (2002), 0.6051 (2001)
Fiscal year: calendar year

COMMUNICATIONS

Telephones - main lines in use: 750,000 (2003)
Telephones - mobile cellular: 100,000 (2003)
Telephone system:
general assessment: telecommunications system is being modernized; mobile cellular telephone system became operational in 1996
domestic: microwave radio relay, coaxial cable, cellular, tropospheric scatter, and a domestic satellite system with 14 earth stations
international: country code - 218; satellite earth stations - 4 Intelsat, NA Arabsat, and NA Intersputnik; submarine cables to France and Italy; microwave radio relay to Tunisia and Egypt; tropospheric scatter to Greece; participant in Medarabtel (1999)
Radio broadcast stations: AM 16, FM 3, shortwave 3 (2002)
Radios: 1.35 million (1997)
Television broadcast stations: 12 (plus one low-power repeater) (1999)
Televisions: 730,000 (1997)
Internet country code: .ly
Internet hosts: 67 (2003)
Internet Service Providers (ISPs): 1 (2002)
Internet users: 160,000 (2003)

TRANSPORTATION

Airports: 139 (2004 est.)
Airports - with paved runways:
total: 59
over 3,047 m: 23
2,438 to 3,047 m: 6
1,524 to 2,437 m: 23
914 to 1,523 m: 5
under 914 m: 2 (2005 est.)
Airports - with unpaved runways:
total: 80
over 3,047 m: 5
2,438 to 3,047 m: 2
1,524 to 2,437 m: 14
914 to 1,523 m: 41
under 914 m: 18 (2005 est.)
Heliports: 2 (2005 est.)
Pipelines: condensate 225 km; gas 3,611 km; oil 7,252 km (2004)
Railways: 0 km
note: Libya is working on 7 lines totaling 2,757 km of 1.435-m gauge track; it hopes to have trains running by 2008 (2004)
Roadways:
total: 83,200 km
paved: 47,590 km

unpaved: 35,610 km (1999)
Merchant marine:
total: 17 ships (1,000 GRT or over) 129,627 GRT/105,110 DWT
by type: cargo 7, liquefied gas 3, passenger/cargo 2, petroleum tanker 1, roll on/roll off 4
foreign-owned: 1 (Algeria 1) (2005)
Ports and terminals: As Sidrah, Az Zuwaytinah, Marsa al Burayqah, Ra's Lanuf, Tripoli, Zawiyah

MILITARY

Military branches: Armed Peoples on Duty (Army), Navy, Air Force, Air Defense Command
Military service age and obligation: 17 years of age (2004)
Manpower available for military service: *males age 17-49:* 1,505,675 (2005 est.)
Manpower fit for military service: *males age 17-49:* 1,291,624 (2005 est.)
Manpower reaching military service age annually: *males:* 62,034 (2005 est.)
Military expenditures - dollar figure: $1.3 billion (FY99)
Military expenditures - percent of GDP: 3.9% (FY99)

TRANSNATIONAL ISSUES

Disputes - international: Libya has claimed more than 32,000 sq km in southeastern Algeria and about 25,000 sq km in Niger in currently dormant disputes; various Chadian rebels from the Aozou region reside in southern Libya

LIECHTENSTEIN

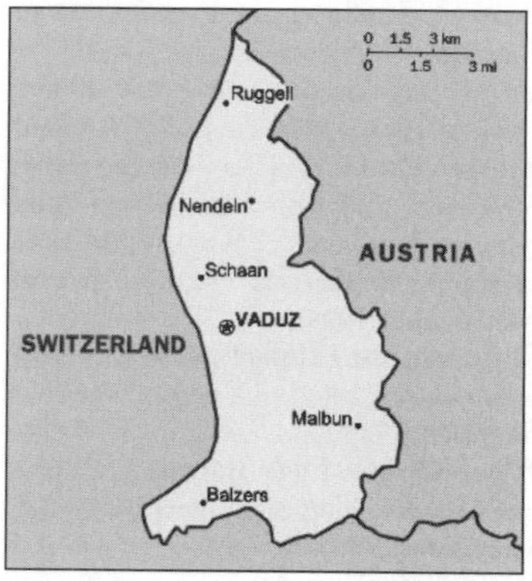

INTRODUCTION

Background: The Principality of Liechtenstein was established within the Holy Roman Empire in 1719; it became a sovereign state in 1806. Until the end of World War I, it was closely tied to Austria, but the economic devastation caused by that conflict forced Liechtenstein to enter into a customs and monetary union with Switzerland. Since World War II (in which Liechtenstein remained neutral), the country's low taxes have spurred outstanding economic growth. Shortcomings in banking regulatory oversight have resulted in concerns about the use of the financial institutions for money laundering. Liechtenstein has, however, implemented new anti-money-laundering legislation and recently concluded a Mutual Legal Assistance Treaty with the US.

GEOGRAPHY

Location: Central Europe, between Austria and Switzerland
Geographic coordinates: 47 16 N, 9 32 E
Map references: Europe
Area:
total: 160 sq km
land: 160 sq km
water: 0 sq km
Area - comparative: about 0.9 times the size of Washington, DC
Land boundaries:
total: 76 km
border countries: Austria 34.9 km, Switzerland 41.1 km
Coastline: 0 km (doubly landlocked)
Maritime claims: none (landlocked)
Climate: continental; cold, cloudy winters with frequent snow or rain; cool to moderately warm, cloudy, humid summers
Terrain: mostly mountainous (Alps) with Rhine Valley in western third
Elevation extremes:
lowest point: Ruggeller Riet 430 m
highest point: Grauspitz 2,599 m
Natural resources: hydroelectric potential, arable land
Land use:
arable land: 25%
permanent crops: 0%
other: 75% (2001)
Irrigated land: NA sq km
Natural hazards: NA
Environment - current issues: NA
Environment - international agreements:
party to: Air Pollution, Air Pollution-Nitrogen Oxides, Air Pollution-Persistent Organic Pollutants, Air Pollution-Sulfur 85, Air Pollution-Sulfur 94, Air Pollution-Volatile Organic Compounds, Biodiversity, Climate Change, Climate Change-Kyoto Protocol, Desertification, Endangered Species, Hazardous Wastes, Ozone Layer Protection, Wetlands
signed, but not ratified: Law of the Sea
Geography - note: along with Uzbekistan, one of only two doubly landlocked countries in the world; variety of microclimatic variations based on elevation

PEOPLE

Population: 33,717 (July 2005 est.)
Age structure:
0-14 years: 17.6% (male 2,938/female 3,009)
15-64 years: 70.4% (male 11,795/female 11,927)
65 years and over: 12% (male 1,685/female 2,363) (2005 est.)
Median age:
total: 39.22 years
male: 38.74 years
female: 39.68 years (2005 est.)
Population growth rate: 0.82% (2005 est.)
Birth rate: 10.41 births/1,000 population (2005 est.)
Death rate: 7.06 deaths/1,000 population (2005 est.)
Net migration rate: 4.8 migrant(s)/1,000 population (2005 est.)
Sex ratio:
at birth: 1.01 male(s)/female
under 15 years: 0.98 male(s)/female
15-64 years: 0.99 male(s)/female
65 years and over: 0.71 male(s)/female
total population: 0.95 male(s)/female (2005 est.)
Infant mortality rate:
total: 4.7 deaths/1,000 live births
male: 6.34 deaths/1,000 live births
female: 3.05 deaths/1,000 live births (2005 est.)
Life expectancy at birth:
total population: 79.55 years
male: 75.96 years
female: 83.16 years (2005 est.)
Total fertility rate: 1.51 children born/woman (2005 est.)
HIV/AIDS - adult prevalence rate: NA%
HIV/AIDS - people living with HIV/AIDS: NA
HIV/AIDS - deaths: NA
Nationality:
noun: Liechtensteiner(s)
adjective: Liechtenstein
Ethnic groups: Alemannic 86%, Italian, Turkish, and other 14%
Religions: Roman Catholic 76.2%, Protestant 7%, unknown 10.6%, other 6.2% (June 2002)
Languages: German (official), Alemannic dialect
Literacy:
definition: age 10 and over can read and write

total population: 100%
male: 100%
female: 100%

GOVERNMENT

Country name:
conventional long form: Principality of Liechtenstein
conventional short form: Liechtenstein
local long form: Fuerstentum Liechtenstein
local short form: Liechtenstein
Government type: hereditary constitutional monarchy on a democratic and parliamentary basis
Capital: Vaduz
Administrative divisions: 11 communes (Gemeinden, singular - Gemeinde); Balzers, Eschen, Gamprin, Mauren, Planken, Ruggell, Schaan, Schellenberg, Triesen, Triesenberg, Vaduz
Independence: 23 January 1719 (Principality of Liechtenstein established); 12 July 1806 (independence from the Holy Roman Empire)
National holiday: Assumption Day, 15 August
Constitution: 5 October 1921
Legal system: local civil and penal codes; accepts compulsory ICJ jurisdiction, with reservations
Suffrage: 18 years of age; universal
Executive branch:
chief of state: Prince HANS ADAM II (since 13 November 1989, assumed executive powers 26 August 1984); Heir Apparent Prince ALOIS, son of the monarch (born 11 June 1968); note - on 15 August 2004, HANS ADAM transferred the official duties of the ruling prince to ALOIS, but HANS ADAM retains status of chief of state
head of government: Head of Government Ottmar HASLER (since 5 April 2001) and Deputy Head of Government Rita KIEBER-BECK (since 5 April 2001)
cabinet: Cabinet elected by the parliament, confirmed by the monarch
elections: none; the monarch is hereditary; following legislative elections, the leader of the majority party in the Landtag is usually appointed the head of government by the monarch and the leader of the largest minority party in the Landtag is usually appointed the deputy head of government by the monarch
Legislative branch: unicameral Parliament or Landtag (25 seats; members are elected by direct, popular vote under proportional representation to serve four-year terms)
elections: last held 11 and 13 March 2005 (next to be held by NA 2009)
election results: percent of vote by party - FBP 48.7%, VU 38.2%, FL 13%; seats by party - FBP 12, VU 10, FL 3
Judicial branch: Supreme Court or Oberster Gerichtshof; Court of Appeal or Obergericht
Political parties and leaders: Patriotic Union (was Fatherland Union) or VU [Heinz FROMMELT]; Progressive Citizens' Party or FBP [Johannes MATT]; The Free List or FL [Dr. Pepo FRICK, Elisabeth TELLENBACH-FRICK, Adolf RITTER]
Political pressure groups and leaders: NA
International organization participation: CE, EBRD, EFTA, IAEA, ICCt, ICRM, IFRCS, Interpol, IOC, ITU, OPCW, OSCE, PCA, UN, UNCTAD, UPU, WCL, WIPO, WTO
Diplomatic representation in the US:
chief of mission: Ambassador Claudia FRITSCHE
chancery: 1300 Eye Street NW, Suite 550W, Washington, DC 20005
telephone: [1] (202) 216-0460
FAX: [1] (202) 216-0459
Diplomatic representation from the US: the US does not have an embassy in Liechtenstein, but the US Ambassador to Switzerland is also accredited to Liechtenstein
Flag description: two equal horizontal bands of blue (top) and red with a gold crown on the hoist side of the blue band

ECONOMY

Economy - overview: Despite its small size and limited natural resources, Liechtenstein has developed into a prosperous, highly industrialized, free-enterprise economy with a vital financial service sector and living standards on a par with its large European neighbors. The Liechtenstein economy is widely diversified with a large number of small businesses. Low business taxes - the maximum tax rate is 20% - and easy incorporation rules have induced many holding or so-called letter box companies to establish nominal offices in Liechtenstein, providing 30% of state revenues. The country participates in a customs union with Switzerland and uses the Swiss franc as its national currency. It imports more than 90% of its energy requirements. Liechtenstein has been a member of the European Economic Area (an organization serving as a bridge between the European Free Trade Association (EFTA) and the EU) since May 1995. The government is working to harmonize its economic policies with those of an integrated Europe.
GDP (purchasing power parity): $825 million (1999 est.)
GDP (official exchange rate): NA
GDP - real growth rate: 11% (1999 est.)
GDP - per capita: purchasing power parity - $25,000 (1999 est.)
GDP - composition by sector:
agriculture: NA%
industry: 40%
services: NA% (1999)
Labor force: 29,000 of whom 19,000 are foreigners; 13,000 commute from Austria, Switzerland, and Germany to work each day (31 December 2001)
Labor force - by occupation: agriculture 1.3%, industry 47.4%, services 51.3% (31 December 2001 est.)
Unemployment rate: 1.3% (September 2002)
Population below poverty line: NA
Household income or consumption by percentage share:
lowest 10%: NA%
highest 10%: NA%
Inflation rate (consumer prices): 1% (2001)
Budget:
revenues: $424.2 million
expenditures: $414.1 million, including capital expenditures of NA (1998 est.)
Agriculture - products: wheat, barley, corn, potatoes; livestock, dairy products
Industries: electronics, metal manufacturing, dental products, ceramics, pharmaceuticals, food products, precision instruments, tourism, optical instruments
Industrial production growth rate: NA%
Exports: $2.47 billion (1996)
Exports - partners: EU 62.6% (Germany 24.3%, Austria 9.5%, France 8.9%, Italy 6.6%, UK 4.6%), US 18.9%, Switzerland 15.7% (2004)
Imports: $917.3 million (1996)
Imports - partners: EU, Switzerland (2004)
Debt - external: $0 (2001)
Economic aid - recipient: none
Currency (code): Swiss franc (CHF)
Currency code: CHF
Exchange rates: Swiss francs per US dollar - NA (2005), 1.2435 (2004), 1.3467 (2003), 1.5586 (2002), 1.6876 (2001)
Fiscal year: calendar year

COMMUNICATIONS

Telephones - main lines in use: 19,900 (2002)
Telephones - mobile cellular: 11,400 (2002)
Telephone system:
general assessment: automatic telephone system
domestic: NA
international: country code - 423; linked to Swiss networks by cable and microwave radio relay
Radio broadcast stations: AM 0, FM 4, shortwave 0 (1998)
Radios: 21,000 (1997)
Television broadcast stations: NA (linked to Swiss networks) (1997)

Televisions: 12,000 (1997)
Internet country code: .li
Internet hosts: 3,727 (2004)
Internet Service Providers (ISPs): 44 (Liechtenstein and Switzerland) (2000)
Internet users: 20,000 (2002)

TRANSPORTATION

Airports: none (2004 est.)
Pipelines: gas 20 km (2004)
Waterways: 28 km (2004)
Ports and terminals: none

MILITARY

Military - note: defense is the responsibility of Switzerland

TRANSNATIONAL ISSUES

Disputes - international: in February 2005, the ICJ refused to rule on the restitution of Liechtenstein's land and property assets in the Czech Republic confiscated in 1945 as German property
Illicit drugs: has strengthened money-laundering controls, but money laundering remains a concern due to Liechtenstein sophisticated offshore financial services sector

LITHUANIA

INTRODUCTION

Background: Independent between the two World Wars, Lithuania was annexed by the USSR in 1940. On 11 March 1990, Lithuania became the first of the Soviet republics to declare its independence, but Moscow did not recognize this proclamation until September of 1991 (following the abortive coup in Moscow). The last Russian troops withdrew in 1993. Lithuania subsequently restructured its economy for integration into Western European institutions; it joined both NATO and the EU in the spring of 2004.

GEOGRAPHY

Location: Eastern Europe, bordering the Baltic Sea, between Latvia and Russia
Geographic coordinates: 56 00 N, 24 00 E
Map references: Europe
Area:
total: 65,200 sq km
land: NA sq km
water: NA sq km
Area - comparative: slightly larger than West Virginia
Land boundaries:
total: 1,273 km
border countries: Belarus 502 km, Latvia 453 km, Poland 91 km, Russia (Kaliningrad) 227 km
Coastline: 99 km
Maritime claims:
territorial sea: 12 nm
Climate: transitional, between maritime and continental; wet, moderate winters and summers
Terrain: lowland, many scattered small lakes, fertile soil
Elevation extremes:
lowest point: Baltic Sea 0 m
highest point: Juozapines/Kalnas 292 m
Natural resources: peat, arable land
Land use:
arable land: 45.22%
permanent crops: 0.91%
other: 53.87% (2001)
Irrigated land: 90 sq km (1998 est.)
Natural hazards: NA
Environment - current issues: contamination of soil and groundwater with petroleum products and chemicals at military bases
Environment - international agreements:
party to: Air Pollution, Biodiversity, Climate Change, Climate Change-Kyoto Protocol, Endangered Species, Hazardous Wastes, Law of the Sea, Ozone Layer Protection, Ship Pollution, Wetlands
signed, but not ratified: Air Pollution-Persistent Organic Pollutants
Geography - note: fertile central plains are separated by hilly uplands that are ancient glacial deposits

PEOPLE

Population: 3,596,617 (July 2005 est.)
Age structure:
0-14 years: 16.1% (male 297,271/female 282,269)
15-64 years: 68.7% (male 1,206,731/female 1,264,359)
65 years and over: 15.2% (male 186,979/female 359,008) (2005 est.)
Median age:
total: 37.83 years
male: 35.25 years
female: 40.46 years (2005 est.)
Population growth rate: -0.3% (2005 est.)
Birth rate: 8.62 births/1,000 population (2005 est.)
Death rate: 10.92 deaths/1,000 population (2005 est.)
Net migration rate: -0.71 migrant(s)/1,000 population (2005 est.)
Sex ratio:
at birth: 1.06 male(s)/female
under 15 years: 1.05 male(s)/female
15-64 years: 0.95 male(s)/female
65 years and over: 0.52 male(s)/female
total population: 0.89 male(s)/female (2005 est.)
Infant mortality rate:
total: 6.89 deaths/1,000 live births
male: 8.25 deaths/1,000 live births
female: 5.45 deaths/1,000 live births (2005 est.)
Life expectancy at birth:
total population: 73.97 years
male: 68.94 years
female: 79.28 years (2005 est.)
Total fertility rate: 1.19 children born/woman (2005 est.)
HIV/AIDS - adult prevalence rate: 0.1% (2001 est.)
HIV/AIDS - people living with HIV/AIDS: 1,300 (2003 est.)
HIV/AIDS - deaths: less than 200 (2003 est.)
Nationality:
noun: Lithuanian(s)
adjective: Lithuanian
Ethnic groups: Lithuanian 83.4%, Polish 6.7%, Russian 6.3%, other or unspecified 3.6% (2001 census)
Religions: Roman Catholic 79%, Russian Orthodox 4.1%, Protestant (including Lutheran and Evangelical Christian Baptist) 1.9%, other or unspecified 5.5%, none 9.5% (2001 census)
Languages: Lithuanian (official) 82%, Russian 8%, Polish 5.6%, other and unspecified 4.4% (2001 census)
Literacy:
definition: age 15 and over can read and write
total population: 99.6%
male: 99.7%
female: 99.6% (2003 est.)

GOVERNMENT

Country name:
conventional long form: Republic of Lithuania
conventional short form: Lithuania
local long form: Lietuvos Respublika
local short form: Lietuva
former: Lithuanian Soviet Socialist Republic

Government type: parliamentary democracy
Capital: Vilnius
Administrative divisions:
10 counties (apskritys, singular - apskritis); Alytaus, Kauno, Klaipedos, Marijampoles, Panevezio, Siauliu, Taurages, Telsiu, Utenos, Vilniaus
Independence: 11 March 1990 (independence declared from Soviet Union); 6 September 1991 (Soviet Union recognizes Lithuania's independence)
National holiday: Independence Day, 16 February (1918); note - 16 February 1918 is the date Lithuania declared its independence from Soviet Russia and established its statehood; 11 March 1990 is the date it declared its independence from the Soviet Union
Constitution: adopted 25 October 1992
Legal system: based on civil law system; legislative acts can be appealed to the constitutional court
Suffrage: 18 years of age; universal
Executive branch:
chief of state: President Valdas ADAMKUS (since 12 July 2004)
head of government: Premier Algirdas Mykolas BRAZAUSKAS (since 3 July 2001)
cabinet: Council of Ministers appointed by the president on the nomination of the premier
elections: president elected by popular vote for a five-year term; election last held 13 June 2004 and 27 June 2004 (next to be held June 2009); premier appointed by the president on the approval of the Parliament
election results: Valdas ADAMKUS elected president; percent of vote - Valdas ADAMKUS 52.2%, Kazimiera PRUNSKIENE 47.8%
Legislative branch: unicameral Parliament or Seimas (141 seats, 71 members are directly elected by popular vote, 70 are elected by proportional representation; members serve four-year terms)
elections: last held 10 and 24 October 2004 (next to be held October 2008)
election results: percent of vote by party - Labor 28.6%, Working for Lithuania (Social Democrats and Social Liberals) 20.7%, Homeland Union (Conservatives) 14.6%, For Order and Justice (Liberal Democrats and Lithuanian People's Union) 11.4%, Liberal and Center Union 9.1%, Union of Farmers and New Democracy 6.6%; seats by faction - Labor 39, Homeland Union 26, Social Democrats 22, Social Liberals 10, Liberal Political group 10, Union of Farmers and New Democracy Parties 11, Liberal Democrats 9, Liberal Center Political group 8, independents 6
Judicial branch: Constitutional Court; Supreme Court; Court of Appeal; judges for all courts appointed by the President
Political parties and leaders: Electoral Action of Lithuanian Poles [Valdemar TOMASZEVSKI, chairman]; Homeland Union/Conservative Party or TS [Andrius KUBILIUS, chairman]; Labor Party [Viktor USPASKICH, chairman]; Liberal Center Political group [Arturas ZUOKAS, chairman]; Liberal Democratic Party [Valentinas MAZURONIS, chairman]; Liberal Political group; Lithuanian Christian Democrats or LKD [Valentinas STUNDYS, chairman]; Lithuanian People's Union for a Fair Lithuania; Lithuanian Social Democratic Coalition [Algirdas BRAZAUSKAS, chairman] consists of the Lithuanian Democratic Labor Party or LDDP and the Lithuanian Social Democratic Party or LSDP; New Democracy and Farmer's Union or VNDPS [Kazimiera PRUNSKIENE, chairman]; Social Liberals (New Union) [Arturas PAULAUSKAS, chairman]; Social Union of Christian Conservatives [Gediminas VAGNORIUS, chairman]; Young Lithuania and New Nationalists
Political pressure groups and leaders: NA
International organization participation: ACCT (observer), Australia Group, BIS, CBSS, CE, EAPC, EBRD, EIB, EU (new member), FAO, IAEA, IBRD, ICAO, ICC, ICCt, ICFTU, ICRM, IFC, IFRCS, ILO, IMF, IMO, Interpol, IOC, IOM, ISO (correspondent), ITU, MIGA, NATO, NIB, NSG, OPCW, OSCE, PCA, UN, UNCTAD, UNESCO, UNIDO, UPU, WCL, WCO, WEU (associate partner), WHO, WIPO, WMO, WToO, WTO
Diplomatic representation in the US:
chief of mission: Ambassador Vygaudas USACKAS
chancery: 2622 16th Street NW, Washington, DC 20009
telephone: [1] (202) 234-5860
FAX: [1] (202) 328-0466
consulate(s) general: Chicago and New York
Diplomatic representation from the US:
chief of mission: Ambassador Stephen D. MULL
embassy: 2600 Akmenu 6, Vilnius
mailing address: American Embassy, Almeny gatve 6, Vilnius LT-03106
telephone: [370] (5) 266 5500
FAX: [370] (5) 266 5510
Flag description: three equal horizontal bands of yellow (top), green, and red

ECONOMY

Economy - overview: Lithuania, the Baltic state that has conducted the most trade with Russia, has slowly rebounded from the 1998 Russian financial crisis. Unemployment dropped from 11% in 2003 to 5.3% in 2005. Growing domestic consumption and increased investment have furthered recovery. Trade has been increasingly oriented toward the West. Lithuania has gained membership in the World Trade Organization and joined the EU in May 2004. Privatization of the large, state-owned utilities, particularly in the energy sector, is nearing completion. Overall, more than 80% of enterprises have been privatized. Foreign government and business support have helped in the transition from the old command economy to a market economy.
GDP (purchasing power parity): $49.38 billion (2005 est.)
GDP (official exchange rate): $24.01 billion (2005 est.)
GDP - real growth rate: 6.4% (2005 est.)
GDP - per capita: purchasing power parity - $13,700 (2005 est.)
GDP - composition by sector:
agriculture: 5.7%
industry: 32.4%
services: 62% (2005 est.)
Labor force: 1.61 million (2005 est.)
Labor force - by occupation: agriculture 20%, industry 30%, services 50% (1997 est.)
Unemployment rate: 5.3% (2005 est.)
Population below poverty line: NA
Household income or consumption by percentage share:
lowest 10%: 3.1%
highest 10%: 25.6% (1996)
Distribution of family income - Gini index: 31.9 (2000)
Inflation rate (consumer prices): 2.6% (2005 est.)
Investment (gross fixed): 22.1% of GDP (2005 est.)
Budget:
revenues: $8.429 billion
expenditures: $9.103 billion, including capital expenditures of NA (2005 est.)
Public debt: 21.4% of GDP (2005 est.)
Agriculture - products: grain, potatoes, sugar beets, flax, vegetables; beef, milk, eggs; fish
Industries: metal-cutting machine tools, electric motors, television sets, refrigerators and freezers, petroleum refining, shipbuilding (small ships), furniture making, textiles, food processing, fertilizers, agricultural machinery, optical equipment, electronic components, computers, amber
Industrial production growth rate: 6% (2005 est.)
Electricity - production: 18.64 billion kWh (2003)
Electricity - production by source:
fossil fuel: 16.5%
hydro: 5.7%
nuclear: 77.7%

other: 0% (2001)
Electricity - consumption: 9.109 billion kWh (2003)
Electricity - exports: 12.37 billion kWh (2003)
Electricity - imports: 4.144 billion kWh (2003)
Oil - production: 12,360 bbl/day (2003 est.)
Oil - consumption: 89,000 bbl/day (2003 est.)
Oil - exports: NA (2001)
Oil - imports: NA (2001)
Natural gas - production: 0 cu m (2001 est.)
Natural gas - consumption: 2.76 billion cu m (2001 est.)
Natural gas - exports: 0 cu m (2001 est.)
Natural gas - imports: 2.76 billion cu m (2001 est.)
Current account balance: $-1.87 billion (2005 est.)
Exports: $10.95 billion f.o.b. (2005 est.)
Exports - partners: Germany 10.2%, Latvia 10.2%, Russia 9.3%, France 6.3%, UK 5.3%, Sweden 5.1%, Estonia 5%, Poland 4.8%, Netherlands 4.8%, Denmark 4.8%, US 4.7%, Switzerland 4.6% (2004)
Imports: $13.33 billion f.o.b. (2005 est.)
Imports - partners: Russia 23.1%, Germany 16.7%, Poland 7.7%, Netherlands 4% (2004)
Reserves of foreign exchange and gold: $3.785 billion (2005 est.)
Debt - external: $10.47 billion (31 December 2004 est.)
Economic aid - recipient: $228.5 million (1995)
Currency (code): litas (LTL)
Currency code: LTL
Exchange rates: litai per US dollar - 2.75 (2005), 2.7806 (2004), 3.0609 (2003), 3.677 (2002), 4 (2001)
Fiscal year: calendar year

COMMUNICATIONS

Telephones - main lines in use: 824,200 (2003)
Telephones - mobile cellular: 2,169,900 (2003)
Telephone system:
general assessment: inadequate, but is being modernized to provide an improved international capability and better residential access
domestic: a national, fiber-optic cable, interurban, trunk system is nearing completion; rural exchanges are being improved and expanded; mobile cellular systems are being installed; access to the Internet is available; still many unsatisfied telephone subscriber applications
international: country code - 370; landline connections to Latvia and Poland; major international connections to Denmark, Sweden, and Norway by submarine cable for further transmission by satellite
Radio broadcast stations: AM 29, FM 142, shortwave 1 (2001)
Radios: 1.9 million (1997)
Television broadcast stations: 27
note: Lithuania has approximately 27 broadcasting stations, but may have as many as 100 transmitters, including repeater stations (2001)
Televisions: 1.7 million (1997)
Internet country code: .lt
Internet hosts: 67,769 (2004)
Internet Service Providers (ISPs): 32 (2001)
Internet users: 695,700 (2003)

TRANSPORTATION

Airports: 102 (2004 est.)
Airports - with paved runways:
total: 33
over 3,047 m: 4
2,438 to 3,047 m: 1
1,524 to 2,437 m: 7
914 to 1,523 m: 2
under 914 m: 19 (2005 est.)
Airports - with unpaved runways:
total: 62
1,524 to 2,437 m: 2
914 to 1,523 m: 4
under 914 m: 56 (2005 est.)
Pipelines: gas 1,696 km; oil 331 km; refined products 109 km (2004)
Railways:
total: 1,998 km
broad gauge: 1,807 km 1.524-m gauge (122 km electrified)
standard gauge: 22 km 1.435-m gauge
narrow gauge: 169 km 0.750-m gauge (2004)
Roadways:
total: 78,893 km
paved: 21,617 km (including 417 km of expressways)
unpaved: 57,276 km (2003)
Waterways: 600 km (2004)
Merchant marine:
total: 54 ships (1,000 GRT or over) 296,856 GRT/317,731 DWT
by type: bulk carrier 8, cargo 24, chemical tanker 1, passenger/cargo 6, petroleum tanker 1, refrigerated cargo 13, roll on/roll off 1
foreign-owned: 12 (Denmark 12)
registered in other countries: 16 (2005)
Ports and terminals: Klaipeda

MILITARY

Military branches: Ground Forces, Navy, Lithuanian Military Air Forces, National Defense Volunteer Forces (SKAT) (2005)
Military service age and obligation: 19-45 years of age for compulsory military service, conscript service obligation - 12 months; 18 years of age for volunteers (2004)
Manpower available for military service: *males age 19-49:* 830,368 (2005 est.)
Manpower fit for military service: *males age 19-49:* 590,606 (2005 est.)
Manpower reaching military service age annually: *males:* 29,689 (2005 est.)
Military expenditures - dollar figure: $230.8 million (FY01)
Military expenditures - percent of GDP: 1.9% (FY01)

TRANSNATIONAL ISSUES

Disputes - international: in 2003, the Lithuania-Russia land and maritime boundary treaty was ratified and a transit regime established through Lithuania linking Russia and its Kaliningrad coastal exclave, leaving only improvements to the border demarcation in 2005; by 2004, a third of the Belarus-Lithuania boundary had been demarcated; the Latvian parliament has not ratified its 1998 maritime boundary treaty with Lithuania, primarily due to concerns over oil; as a member state that forms part of the EU's external border, Lithuania must implement the strict Schengen border rules
Illicit drugs: transshipment point for opiates and other illicit drugs from Southwest Asia, Latin America, and Western Europe to Western Europe and Scandinavia; limited production of methamphetamine and ecstasy; susceptible to money laundering despite changes to banking legislation

LUXEMBOURG

INTRODUCTION

Background: Founded in 963, Luxembourg became a grand duchy in 1815 and an independent state under the Netherlands. It lost more than half of its territory to Belgium in 1839, but gained a larger measure of autonomy. Full independence was attained in 1867. Overrun by Germany in both World Wars, it ended its neutrality in 1948 when it entered into the Benelux Customs Union and when it joined NATO the following year. In 1957, Luxembourg became one of the six founding countries of the European Economic Community (later the European Union), and in 1999 it joined the euro currency area.

GEOGRAPHY

Location: Western Europe, between France and Germany
Geographic coordinates: 49 45 N, 6 10 E
Map references: Europe
Area:
total: 2,586 sq km
land: 2,586 sq km
water: 0 sq km
Area - comparative: slightly smaller than Rhode Island
Land boundaries:
total: 359 km
border countries: Belgium 148 km, France 73 km, Germany 138 km
Coastline: 0 km (landlocked)
Maritime claims: none (landlocked)
Climate: modified continental with mild winters, cool summers
Terrain: mostly gently rolling uplands with broad, shallow valleys; uplands to slightly mountainous in the north; steep slope down to Moselle flood plain in the southeast
Elevation extremes:
lowest point: Moselle River 133 m
highest point: Buurgplaatz 559 m
Natural resources: iron ore (no longer exploited), arable land
Land use:
arable land: 23.28%
permanent crops: 0.4%
other: 76.32% (includes Belgium) (2001)
Irrigated land: 40 sq km (includes Belgium) (1998 est.)
Natural hazards: NA
Environment - current issues: air and water pollution in urban areas, soil pollution of farmland
Environment - international agreements:
party to: Air Pollution, Air Pollution-Nitrogen Oxides, Air Pollution-Persistent Organic Pollutants, Air Pollution-Sulfur 85, Air Pollution-Sulfur 94, Air Pollution-Volatile Organic Compounds, Biodiversity, Climate Change, Climate Change-Kyoto Protocol, Desertification, Endangered Species, Hazardous Wastes, Law of the Sea, Marine Dumping, Ozone Layer Protection, Ship Pollution, Tropical Timber 83, Tropical Timber 94, Wetlands
signed, but not ratified: Environmental Modification
Geography - note: landlocked; the only Grand Duchy in the world

PEOPLE

Population: 468,571 (July 2005 est.)
Age structure:
0-14 years: 18.9% (male 45,768/female 42,980)
15-64 years: 66.5% (male 157,453/female 153,927)
65 years and over: 14.6% (male 27,573/female 40,870) (2005 est.)
Median age:
total: 38.51 years
male: 37.56 years
female: 39.48 years (2005 est.)
Population growth rate: 1.25% (2005 est.)
Birth rate: 12.06 births/1,000 population (2005 est.)
Death rate: 8.41 deaths/1,000 population (2005 est.)
Net migration rate: 8.86 migrant(s)/1,000 population (2005 est.)
Sex ratio:
at birth: 1.07 male(s)/female
under 15 years: 1.06 male(s)/female
15-64 years: 1.02 male(s)/female
65 years and over: 0.68 male(s)/female
total population: 0.97 male(s)/female (2005 est.)
Infant mortality rate:
total: 4.81 deaths/1,000 live births
male: 4.79 deaths/1,000 live births
female: 4.83 deaths/1,000 live births (2005 est.)
Life expectancy at birth:
total population: 78.74 years
male: 75.45 years
female: 82.24 years (2005 est.)
Total fertility rate: 1.79 children born/woman (2005 est.)
HIV/AIDS - adult prevalence rate: 0.2% (2001 est.)
HIV/AIDS - people living with HIV/AIDS: less than 500 (2003 est.)
HIV/AIDS - deaths: less than 100 (2003 est.)
Nationality:
noun: Luxembourger(s)
adjective: Luxembourg
Ethnic groups: Celtic base (with French and German blend), Portuguese, Italian, Slavs (from Montenegro, Albania, and Kosovo) and European (guest and resident workers)
Religions: 87% Roman Catholic, 13% Protestants, Jews, and Muslims (2000)
Languages: Luxembourgish (national language), German (administrative language), French (administrative language)
Literacy:
definition: age 15 and over can read and write
total population: 100%
male: 100%
female: 100% (2000 est.)

GOVERNMENT

Country name:
conventional long form: Grand Duchy of Luxembourg
conventional short form: Luxembourg
local long form: Grand Duche de Luxembourg
local short form: Luxembourg
Government type: constitutional monarchy
Capital: Luxembourg
Administrative divisions: 3 districts; Diekirch, Grevenmacher, Luxembourg
Independence: 1839 (from the Netherlands)
National holiday: National Day (Birthday of Grand Duchess Charlotte) 23 June
Constitution: 17 October 1868; occasional revisions
Legal system: based on civil law system; accepts compulsory ICJ jurisdiction
Suffrage: 18 years of age; universal and compulsory
Executive branch:
chief of state: Grand Duke HENRI (since 7 October 2000); Heir Apparent Prince GUILLAUME (son of the monarch, born 11 November 1981)
head of government: Prime Minister Jean-Claude JUNCKER (since 1 January 1995) and Vice Prime Minister Jean ASSELBORN (since 31 July 2004)

cabinet: Council of Ministers recommended by the prime minister and appointed by the monarch
elections: none; the monarch is hereditary; following popular elections to the Chamber of Deputies, the leader of the majority party or the leader of the majority coalition is usually appointed prime minister by the monarch; the deputy prime minister is appointed by the monarch; they are responsible to the Chamber of Deputies
note: government coalition - CSV and LSAP
Legislative branch: unicameral Chamber of Deputies or Chambre des Deputes (60 seats; members are elected by direct popular vote to serve five-year terms)
elections: last held 13 June 2004 (next to be held by June 2009)
election results: percent of vote by party - CSV 36.1%, LSAP 23.4%, DP 16.1%, Green Party 11.6%, ADR 10%; seats by party - CSV 24, LSAP 14, DP 10, Green Party 7, ADR 5
note: there is also a Council of State that serves as an advisory body to the Chamber of Deputies; the Council of State has 21 members appointed by the Grand Duke on the advice of the prime minister
Judicial branch: judicial courts and tribunals (3 Justices of the Peace, 2 district courts, and 1 Supreme Court of Appeals); administrative courts and tribunals (State Prosecutor's Office, administrative courts and tribunals, and the Constitutional Court); judges for all courts are appointed for life by the monarch
Political parties and leaders: Action Committee for Democracy and Justice or ADR [Gast GIBERYEN]; Christian Social People's Party or CSV (known also as Christian Social Party or PCS) [Francois BILTGEN]; Democratic Party or DP [Claude MEISCH]; Green Party [Francois BAUSCH]; Luxembourg Socialist Workers' Party or LSAP [Alex BODRY]; Marxist and Reformed Communist Party dei Lenk/la Gauche (the Left) [no formal leadership]; other minor parties
Political pressure groups and leaders: ABBL (bankers' association); ALEBA (financial sector trade union); Centrale Paysanne (federation of agricultural producers); CEP (professional sector chamber); CGFP (trade union representing civil service); Chambre de Commerce (Chamber of Commerce); Chambre des Metiers (Chamber of Artisans); FEDIL (federation of industrialists); LCGP (center-right trade union); OGBL (center-left trade union)
International organization participation: ACCT, AsDB, Australia Group, Benelux, CE, EAPC, EBRD, EIB, EMU, ESA, EU, FAO, IAEA, IBRD, ICAO, ICC, ICCt, ICFTU, ICRM, IDA, IEA, IFAD, IFC, IFRCS, ILO, IMF, IMO, Interpol, IOC, IOM, ISO, ITU, MIGA, NATO, NEA, NSG, OAS (observer), OECD, OPCW, OSCE, PCA, UN, UNCTAD, UNESCO, UNIDO, UPU, WCL, WCO, WEU, WHO, WIPO, WMO, WTO, ZC
Diplomatic representation in the US:
chief of mission: Ambassador Arlette CONZEMIUS-PACCOURD
chancery: 2200 Massachusetts Avenue NW, Washington, DC 20008
telephone: [1] (202) 265-4171
FAX: [1] (202) 328-8270
consulate(s) general: New York and San Francisco
Diplomatic representation from the US:
chief of mission: Ambassador Ann WAGNER
embassy: 22 Boulevard Emmanuel Servais, L-2535 Luxembourg City
mailing address: American Embassy Luxembourg, Unit 1410, APO AE 09126-1410 (official mail); American Embassy Luxembourg, PSC 9, Box 9500, APO AE 09123 (personal mail)
telephone: [352] 46 01 23
FAX: [352] 46 14 01
Flag description: three equal horizontal bands of red (top), white, and light blue; similar to the flag of the Netherlands, which uses a darker blue and is shorter; design was based on the flag of France

ECONOMY

Economy - overview: This stable, high-income economy - in between France, Belgium, and Germany - features solid growth, low inflation, and low unemployment. The industrial sector, initially dominated by steel, has become increasingly diversified to include chemicals, rubber, and other products. Growth in the financial sector, which now accounts for about 22% of GDP, has more than compensated for the decline in steel. Most banks are foreign-owned and have extensive foreign dealings. Agriculture is based on small family-owned farms. The economy depends on foreign and cross-border workers for more than 30% of its labor force. Although Luxembourg, like all EU members, has suffered from the global economic slump, the country enjoys an extraordinarily high standard of living - GDP per capita ranks first in the world.
GDP (purchasing power parity): $29.37 billion (2005 est.)
GDP (official exchange rate): $32.76 billion (2005 est.)
GDP - real growth rate: 3.5% (2005 est.)
GDP - per capita: purchasing power parity - $62,700 (2005 est.)
GDP - composition by sector:
agriculture: 0.5%
industry: 16.3%
services: 83.1% (2004 est.)
Labor force: 200,000 (of whom 105,000 are foreign cross-border workers commuting primarily from France, Belgium, and Germany) (2005 est.)
Labor force - by occupation: agriculture 1%, industry 13%, services 86% (2004 est.)
Unemployment rate: 3.7% (2005 est.)
Population below poverty line: NA
Household income or consumption by percentage share:
lowest 10%: NA%
highest 10%: NA%
Inflation rate (consumer prices): 2.6% (2005 est.)
Investment (gross fixed): 19.7% of GDP (2005 est.)
Budget:
revenues: $15.13 billion
expenditures: $15.82 billion, including capital expenditures of $760 million (2005 est.)
Agriculture - products: barley, oats, potatoes, wheat, fruits, wine grapes; livestock products
Industries: banking, iron and steel, food processing, chemicals, metal products, engineering, tires, glass, aluminum, information technology, tourism and banking
Industrial production growth rate: 4.4% (2005 est.)
Electricity - production: 2.808 billion kWh (2003)
Electricity - production by source:
fossil fuel: 57.3%
hydro: 25.2%
nuclear: 0%
other: 17.5% (2001)
Electricity - consumption: 6.112 billion kWh (2003)
Electricity - exports: 3 billion kWh (2003)
Electricity - imports: 6.5 billion kWh (2003)
Oil - production: 0 bbl/day (2003 est.)
Oil - consumption: 55,700 bbl/day (2003 est.)
Oil - exports: 634 bbl/day (2001)
Oil - imports: 50,700 bbl/day (2001)
Natural gas - production: 0 cu m (2001 est.)
Natural gas - consumption: 865 million cu m (2001 est.)
Natural gas - exports: 0 cu m (2001 est.)
Natural gas - imports: 867 million cu m (2001 est.)
Exports: $13.39 billion f.o.b. (2005 est.)
Exports - partners: Germany 22.2%, France 19.8%, Belgium 10%, UK 8.5%, Italy 7.3%, Spain 6%, Netherlands 4.3% (2004)
Imports: $18.74 billion c.i.f. (2005 est.)

Imports - partners: Belgium 29.8%, Germany 22.6%, China 12.6%, France 12%, Netherlands 4.2% (2004)
Reserves of foreign exchange and gold: $330.8 million (2004 est.)
Debt - external: $NA
Economic aid - donor: ODA, $147 million (2002)
Currency (code): euro (EUR)
note: on 1 January 1999, the European Monetary Union introduced the euro as a common currency to be used by financial institutions of member countries; on 1 January 2002, the euro became the sole currency for everyday transactions within the member countries
Currency code: EUR
Exchange rates: euros per US dollar - 0.79697 (2005), 0.8054 (2004), 0.886 (2003), 1.0626 (2002), 1.1175 (2001)
Fiscal year: calendar year

COMMUNICATIONS

Telephones - main lines in use: 355,400 (2002)
Telephones - mobile cellular: 473,000 (2002)
Telephone system:
general assessment: highly developed, completely automated and efficient system, mainly buried cables
domestic: nationwide cellular telephone system; buried cable
international: country code - 352; 3 channels leased on TAT-6 coaxial submarine cable (Europe to North America)
Radio broadcast stations: AM 2, FM 9, shortwave 2 (1999)
Radios: 285,000 (1997)
Television broadcast stations: 5 (1999)
Televisions: 285,000 (1998 est.)
Internet country code: .lu
Internet hosts: 28,214 (2003)
Internet Service Providers (ISPs): 8 (2000)
Internet users: 165,000 (2002)

TRANSPORTATION

Airports: 2 (2004 est.)
Airports - with paved runways:
total: 1
over 3,047 m: 1 (2005 est.)
Airports - with unpaved runways:
total: 1
under 914 m: 1 (2005 est.)
Heliports: 1 (2005 est.)
Pipelines: gas 155 km (2004)
Railways:
total: 274 km
standard gauge: 274 km 1.435-m gauge (242 km electrified) (2004)
Roadways:
total: 5,210 km
paved: 5,210 km (including 147 km of expressways) (2002)
Waterways: 37 km (on Moselle River) (2003)
Merchant marine:
total: 40 ships (1,000 GRT or over) 652,454 GRT/805,101 DWT
by type: chemical tanker 16, container 6, liquefied gas 2, passenger 3, petroleum tanker 6, roll on/roll off 6, vehicle carrier 1
foreign-owned: 40 (Belgium 12, Finland 3, France 8, Germany 10, Netherlands 4, United States 3) (2005)
Ports and terminals: Mertert

MILITARY

Military branches: Army
Military service age and obligation: a 1967 law made the Army an all-volunteer force; 17 years of age for voluntary military service; soldiers under 18 are not deployed into combat or with peacekeeping missions (2004)
Manpower available for military service: *males age 17-49:* 110,867 (2005 est.)
Manpower fit for military service: *males age 17-49:* 90,279 (2005 est.)
Manpower reaching military service age annually: *males:* 2,775 (2005 est.)
Military expenditures - dollar figure: $231.6 million (2003)
Military expenditures - percent of GDP: 0.9% (2003)

TRANSNATIONAL ISSUES

Disputes - international: none

M

MACAU

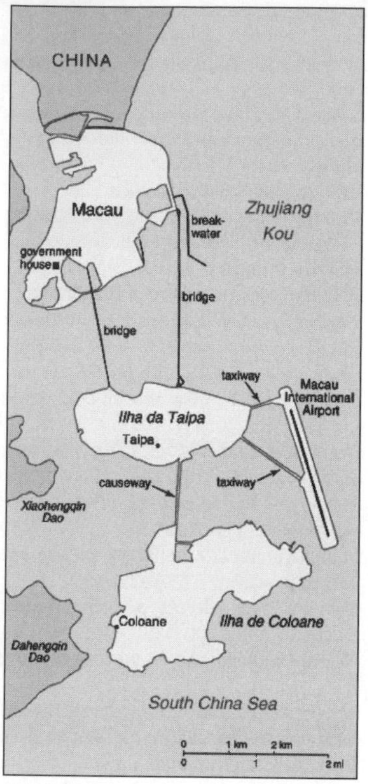

INTRODUCTION

Background: Colonized by the Portuguese in the 16th century, Macau was the first European settlement in the Far East. Pursuant to an agreement signed by China and Portugal on 13 April 1987, Macau became the Macau Special Administrative Region (SAR) of China on 20 December 1999. China has promised that, under its "one country, two systems" formula, China's socialist economic system will not be practiced in Macau, and that Macau will enjoy a high degree of autonomy in all matters except foreign and defense affairs for the next 50 years.

GEOGRAPHY

Location: Eastern Asia, bordering the South China Sea and China
Geographic coordinates: 22 10 N, 113 33 E
Map references: Southeast Asia
Area:
total: 25.4 sq km
land: 25.4 sq km
water: 0 sq km
Area - comparative: about 0.1 times the size of Washington, DC
Land boundaries:
total: 0.34 km
regional border: China 0.34 km
Coastline: 41 km
Maritime claims: not specified
Climate: subtropical; marine with cool winters, warm summers
Terrain: generally flat
Elevation extremes:
lowest point: South China Sea 0 m
highest point: Coloane Alto 172.4 m
Natural resources: NEGL
Land use:
arable land: 0%
permanent crops: 0%
other: 100%
note: "green areas" represent 22.4% (2001)
Irrigated land: NA sq km
Natural hazards: typhoons
Environment - current issues: NA
Geography - note: essentially urban; one causeway and two bridges connect the two islands of Coloane and Taipa to the peninsula on mainland

PEOPLE

Population: 449,198 (July 2005 est.)
Age structure:
0-14 years: 17% (male 39,564/female 36,947)
15-64 years: 75.1% (male 160,957/female 176,386)
65 years and over: 7.9% (male 14,713/female 20,631) (2005 est.)
Median age:
total: 35.2 years
male: 34.9 years
female: 35.4 years (2005 est.)
Population growth rate: 0.87% (2005 est.)
Birth rate: 8.04 births/1,000 population (2005 est.)
Death rate: 4.23 deaths/1,000 population (2005 est.)
Net migration rate: 4.86 migrant(s)/1,000 population (2005 est.)
Sex ratio:
at birth: 1.07 male(s)/female
under 15 years: 1.07 male(s)/female
15-64 years: 0.91 male(s)/female
65 years and over: 0.71 male(s)/female
total population: 0.92 male(s)/female (2005 est.)
Infant mortality rate:
total: 4.39 deaths/1,000 live births
male: 4.59 deaths/1,000 live births
female: 4.19 deaths/1,000 live births (2005 est.)
Life expectancy at birth:
total population: 82.12 years
male: 79.29 years
female: 85.09 years (2005 est.)
Total fertility rate: 0.93 children born/woman (2005 est.)
HIV/AIDS - adult prevalence rate: NA
HIV/AIDS - people living with HIV/AIDS: NA
HIV/AIDS - deaths: NA
Nationality:
noun: Chinese
adjective: Chinese
Ethnic groups: Chinese 95.7%, Macanese (mixed Portuguese and Asian ancestry) 1%, other 3.3% (2001 census)
Religions: Buddhist 50%, Roman Catholic 15%, none and other 35% (1997 est.)
Languages: Cantonese 87.9%, Hokkien 4.4%, Mandarin 1.6%, other Chinese dialects 3.1%, other 3% (2001 census)
Literacy:
definition: age 15 and over can read and write
total population: 94.5%
male: 97.2%
female: 92% (2003 est.)

GOVERNMENT

Country name:
conventional long form: Macau Special Administrative Region
conventional short form: Macau
local long form: Aomen Tebie Xingzhengqu (Chinese); Regiao Administrativa Especial de Macau (Portuguese)
local short form: Aomen (Chinese); Macau (Portuguese)
Dependency status: special administrative region of China
Government type: limited democracy
Administrative divisions: none (special administrative region of China)
Independence: none (special administrative region of China)
National holiday: National Day (Anniversary of the Founding of the People's Republic of China), 1 October (1949); note - 20 December 1999 is celebrated as Macau Special Administrative Region Establishment Day
Constitution: Basic Law, approved in March 1993 by China's National People's Congress, is Macau's "mini-constitution"
Legal system: based on Portuguese civil law system
Suffrage: direct election 18 years of age, universal for permanent residents living in Macau for the past seven years; indirect election limited to organizations registered as "corporate voters" (257 are currently registered) and a 300-member Election Committee drawn from broad regional groupings, municipal organizations, and central government bodies
Executive branch:
chief of state: President of China HU Jintao (since 15 March 2003)
head of government: Chief Executive Edmund HO Hau-wah (since 20 December 1999)
cabinet: Executive Council consists of one government secretary, four legislators,

four businessmen, and one pro-Beijing unionist
elections: chief executive chosen by a 300-member Election Committee for up to two five-year terms
election results: Edmund HO Hau-wah reelected on 29 August 2004; received 296 votes in Election Committee out of 300 possible; 3 members submitted blank ballots; 1 member was absent
Legislative branch: unicameral Legislative Council or LEGCO (29 seats; 12 elected by popular vote, 10 by indirect vote, and seven appointed by the chief executive; members serve four-year terms)
elections: last held 26 September 2005 (next in September 2009)
election results: percent of vote - Development Union 12.8%, Macau Development Alliance 9%, Macau United Citizens' Association 16%, New Democratic Macau Association 18.2%, others na; seats by political group - Development Union 2, Macau Development Alliance 1, Macau United Citizens' Association 2, New Democratic Macau Association 2, New Hope 1, Union Forces 2, others 2; 10 seats filled by professional and business groups; seven members appointed by chief executive
Judicial branch: Court of Final Appeal in Macau Special Administrative Region
Political parties and leaders: Civil Service Union [Jose Maria Pereira COUTINHO]; Development Union [KWAN Tsui-hang]; Macau Development Alliance [Angela LEONG On-kei]; Macau United Citizens' Association [CHAN Meng-kam]; New Democratic Macau Association [Antonio NG Kuok-cheong]; United Forces [leader NA]
Political pressure groups and leaders: NA
International organization participation: IHO, IMF, IMO (associate), ISO (correspondent), UNESCO (associate), UPU, WCO, WMO, WToO (associate), WTO
Diplomatic representation in the US: none (special administrative region of China)
Diplomatic representation from the US: the US has no offices in Macau; US interests are monitored by the US Consulate General in Hong Kong
Flag description: light green with a lotus flower above a stylized bridge and water in white, beneath an arc of five gold, five-pointed stars: one large in center of arc and four smaller

ECONOMY

Economy - overview: Macau's well-to-do economy has remained one of the most open in the world since its reversion to China in 1999. Apparel exports and tourism are mainstays of the economy. Although the territory was hit hard by the 1997-1998 Asian financial crisis and the global downturn in 2001, its economy grew 9.5% in 2002 and 15.6% in 2003. During the first three quarters of 2004, Macau registered year-on-year GDP increases of more than 20 percent. A rapid rise in the number of mainland visitors because of China's easing of restrictions on travel, increased public works expenditures, and significant investment inflows associated with the liberalization of Macau's gaming industry drove the recovery. The budget also returned to surplus in 2002 because of the surge in visitors from China and a hike in taxes on gambling profits, which generated about 70% of government revenue. The three companies awarded gambling licenses have pledged to invest $2.2 billion in the territory, which will boost GDP growth. Much of Macau's textile industry may move to the mainland as the Multi-Fiber Agreement is phased out. The territory may have to rely more on gambling and trade-related services to generate growth. Two new casinos were opened by new foreign gambling licensees in 2004; development of new infrastructure and facilities in preparation for Macau's hosting of the 2005 East Asian Games led the construction sector. The Closer Economic Partnership Agreement (CEPA) between Macau and mainland China that came into effect on 1 January 2004 offers many Macau-made products tariff-free access to the mainland, and the range of products covered by CEPA was expanded on 1 January 2005.
GDP (purchasing power parity): $9.1 billion (2003)
GDP (official exchange rate):$10.05 billion (2004)
GDP - real growth rate: 8.2% (2nd Quarter 2005)
GDP - per capita: purchasing power parity - $19,400 (2003)
GDP - composition by sector:
agriculture: 0.1%
industry: 7.2%
services: 92.7% (2002 est.)
Labor force: 231,500 (3rd Quarter, 2004)
Labor force - by occupation: manufacturing 18.3%, construction 8%, transport and communications 7%, wholesale and retail trade 16.2%, restaurants and hotels 10.9%, gambling 11.6%, public sector 8.8%, other services and agriculture 19.2% (2003 est.)
Unemployment rate: 4.8% (2004)
Population below poverty line: NA
Household income or consumption by percentage share:
lowest 10%: NA
highest 10%: NA
Inflation rate (consumer prices): 3.8% (2nd quarter, 2005)
Budget:
revenues: $2.44 billion
expenditures: $1.67 billion, including capital expenditures of NA (2004)
Agriculture - products: only 2% of land area is cultivated, mainly by vegetable growers; fishing, mostly for crustaceans, is important, some of the catch is exported to Hong Kong; most food requirements are met by imports, primarily from China
Industries: tourism, gambling, clothing, textiles, electronics, footwear, toys
Industrial production growth rate: NA
Electricity - production: 1.616 billion kWh (2003)
Electricity - production by source:
fossil fuel: 100%
hydro: 0%
nuclear: 0%
other: 0% (2001)
Electricity - consumption: 1.682 billion kWh (2003)
Electricity - exports: 1 million kWh (2003)
Electricity - imports: 180 million kWh (2003)
Oil - production: 0 bbl/day (2003 est.)
Oil - consumption:12,000 bbl/day (2003 est.)
Oil - exports: NA (2001)
Oil - imports: NA (2001)
Exports: $3.465 billion f.o.b., including reexports (2004)
Exports - partners: US 48.7%, China 13.9%, Germany 8.3%, Hong Kong 7.6%, UK 4.4% (2004)
Imports: $3.478 billion c.i.f. (2004)
Imports - partners: China 44.4%, Hong Kong 10.6%, Japan 9.6%, Taiwan 4.9%, Singapore 4.1%, US 4.1% (2004)
Debt - external: $2.7 billion (2003)
Economic aid - recipient: NA
Currency (code): pataca (MOP)
Currency code: MOP
Exchange rates: patacas per US dollar - 8.01 (2005), 8.022 (2004), 8.021 (2003), 8.033 (2002), 8.034 (2001)
Fiscal year: calendar year

COMMUNICATIONS

Telephones - main lines in use: 174,600 (2003)
Telephones - mobile cellular: 364,000 (2003)
Telephone system:
general assessment: fairly modern communication facilities maintained for domestic and international services
domestic: NA
international: country code - 853; HF radiotelephone communication facility; access to international communications carriers provided via Hong Kong and China; satellite earth station - 1 Intelsat

(Indian Ocean)
Radio broadcast stations: AM 0, FM 2, shortwave 0 (1998)
Radios: 160,000 (1997)
Television broadcast stations: 1 (2003)
Televisions: 49,000 (1997)
Internet country code: .mo
Internet hosts: 89 (2003)
Internet Service Providers (ISPs): 1 (2000)
Internet users: 120,000 (2003)

TRANSPORTATION

Airports: 1 (2004 est.)
Airports - with paved runways:
total: 1
over 3,047 m: 1 (2005 est.)
Roadways:
total: 345 km
paved: 345 km (2003)
Ports and terminals: Macau

MILITARY

Military branches: China's People's Revolutionary Army (PLA) constitutes the only armed force in Macau; several police forces constitute the Security Forces of Macau (SFM) that are subordinate to the General Secretariat of Security, a body comparable to a ministry of interior (2004)
Manpower available for military service: *males age 18-49:* 112,744 (2005 est.)
Manpower fit for military service: *males age 18-49:* 91,299 (2005 est.)

TRANSNATIONAL ISSUES

Disputes - international: none

MACEDONIA

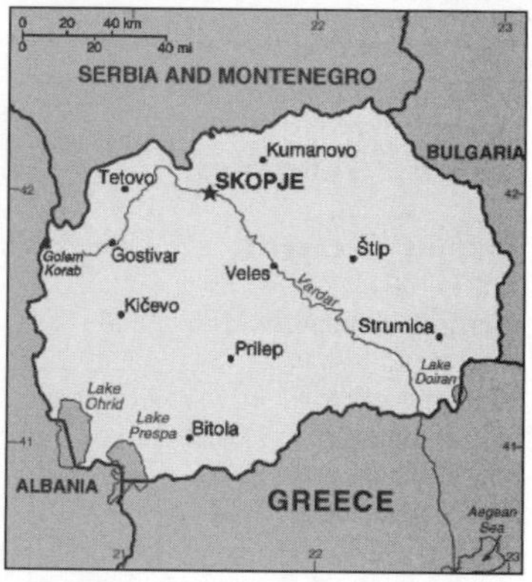

INTRODUCTION

Background: Macedonia gained its independence peacefully from Yugoslavia in 1991, but Greece's objection to the new state's use of what it considered a Hellenic name and symbols delayed international recognition, which occurred under the temporary moniker of the "Former Yugoslav Republic of Macedonia." In 1995, Greece lifted a 20-month trade embargo and the two countries agreed to normalize relations, although differences over Macedonia's name remain. The undetermined status of neighboring Kosovo, implementation of the Framework Agreement - which ended the 2001 ethnic Albanian armed insurgency - and a weak economy continue to be challenges for Macedonia

GEOGRAPHY

Location: Southeastern Europe, north of Greece
Geographic coordinates: 41 50 N, 22 00 E
Map references: Europe
Area:
total: 25,333 sq km
land: 24,856 sq km
water: 477 sq km
Area - comparative: slightly larger than Vermont
Land boundaries:
total: 766 km
border countries: Albania 151 km, Bulgaria 148 km, Greece 246 km, Serbia and Montenegro 221 km
Coastline: 0 km (landlocked)
Maritime claims: none (landlocked)
Climate: warm, dry summers and autumns and relatively cold winters with heavy snowfall
Terrain: mountainous territory covered with deep basins and valleys; three large lakes, each divided by a frontier line; country bisected by the Vardar River
Elevation extremes:
lowest point: Vardar River 50 m
highest point: Golem Korab (Maja e Korabit) 2,764 m
Natural resources: low-grade iron ore, copper, lead, zinc, chromite, manganese, nickel, tungsten, gold, silver, asbestos, gypsum, timber, arable land
Land use:
arable land: 22.26%
permanent crops: 1.81%
other: 75.93% (2001)
Irrigated land: 550 sq km (1998 est.)
Natural hazards: high seismic risks
Environment - current issues: air pollution from metallurgical plants
Environment - international agreements:
party to: Air Pollution, Biodiversity, Climate Change, Climate Change-Kyoto Protocol, Endangered Species, Hazardous Wastes, Law of the Sea, Ozone Layer Protection, Wetlands
signed, but not ratified: none of the selected agreements
Geography - note: landlocked; major transportation corridor from Western and Central Europe to Aegean Sea and Southern Europe to Western Europe

PEOPLE

Population: 2,045,262 (July 2005 est.)
Age structure:
0-14 years: 20.5% (male 217,057/female 202,465)
15-64 years: 68.7% (male 707,489/female 697,150)
65 years and over: 10.8% (male 97,117/female 123,984) (2005 est.)
Median age:
total: 32.8 years
male: 31.7 years
female: 33.9 years (2005 est.)
Population growth rate: 0.26% (2005 est.)
Birth rate: 12 births/1,000 population (2005 est.)
Death rate: 8.73 deaths/1,000 population (2005 est.)
Net migration rate: -0.7 migrant(s)/1,000 population (2005 est.)
Sex ratio:
at birth: 1.08 male(s)/female
under 15 years: 1.07 male(s)/female
15-64 years: 1.02 male(s)/female
65 years and over: 0.78 male(s)/female
total population: 1 male(s)/female (2005 est.)
Infant mortality rate:
total: 10.09 deaths/1,000 live births
male: 10.2 deaths/1,000 live births
female: 9.97 deaths/1,000 live births (2005 est.)
Life expectancy at birth:
total population: 73.73 years
male: 71.28 years
female: 76.37 years (2005 est.)
Total fertility rate: 1.57 children born/woman (2005 est.)
HIV/AIDS - adult prevalence rate: less than 0.1% (2001 est.)
HIV/AIDS - people living with HIV/AIDS: less than 200 (2003 est.)
HIV/AIDS - deaths: less than 100 (2003 est.)
Nationality:
noun: Macedonian(s)
adjective: Macedonian
Ethnic groups: Macedonian 64.2%, Albanian 25.2%, Turkish 3.9%, Roma 2.7%, Serb 1.8%, other 2.2% (2002 census)
Religions: Macedonian Orthodox 32.4%,

other Christian 0.2%, Muslim 16.9%, other and unspecified 50.5% (2002 census)
Languages: Macedonian 66.5%, Albanian 25.1%, Turkish 3.5%, Roma 1.9%, Serbian 1.2%, other 1.8% (2002 census)
Literacy:
definition: age 15 and over can read and write
total population: 96.1%
male: 98.2%
female: 94.1% (2002 est.)

GOVERNMENT

Country name:
conventional long form: Republic of Macedonia
conventional short form: Macedonia; note - the provisional designation used by the UN, EU, and NATO is Former Yugoslav Republic of Macedonia (FYROM)
local long form: Republika Makedonija
local short form: Makedonija
former: People's Republic of Macedonia, Socialist Republic of Macedonia
Government type: parliamentary democracy
Capital: Skopje
Administrative divisions: 85 municipalities (opstini, singular - opstina); Aerodrom (Skopje), Aracinovo, Berovo, Bitola, Bogdanci, Bogovinje, Bosilovo, Brvenica, Butel (Skopje), Cair (Skopje), Caska, Centar (Skopje), Centar Zupa, Cesinovo, Cucer-Sandevo, Debar, Debartsa, Delcevo, Demir Hisar, Demir Kapija, Dojran, Dolneni, Drugovo, Gazi Baba (Skopje), Gevgelija, Gjorce Petrov (Skopje), Gostivar, Gradsko, Ilinden, Jegunovce, Karbinci, Karpos (Skopje), Kavadarci, Kicevo, Kisela Voda (Skopje), Kocani, Konce, Kratovo, Kriva Palanka, Krivogastani, Krusevo, Kumanovo, Lipkovo, Lozovo, Makedonska Kamenica, Makedonski Brod, Mavrovo i Rastusa, Mogila, Negotino, Novaci, Novo Selo, Ohrid, Oslomej, Pehcevo, Petrovec, Plasnica, Prilep, Probistip, Radovis, Rankovce, Resen, Rosoman, Saraj (Skopje), Skopje, Sopiste, Staro Nagoricane, Stip, Struga, Strumica, Studenicani, Suto Orizari (Skopje), Sveti Nikole, Tearce, Tetovo, Valandovo, Vasilevo, Veles, Vevcani, Vinica, Vranestica, Vrapciste, Zajas, Zelenikovo, Zelino, Zrnovci
note: the ten municipalities followed by Skopje in parentheses collectively constitute "greater Skopje"
Independence: 8 September 1991 (referendum by registered voters endorsing independence from Yugoslavia)
National holiday: Uprising Day, 2 August (1903); note - also known as Saint Elijah's Day and Ilinden
Constitution: adopted 17 November 1991, effective 20 November 1991; amended November 2001 by a series of new constitutional amendments strengthening minority rights
Legal system: based on civil law system; judicial review of legislative acts
Suffrage: 18 years of age; universal
Executive branch:
chief of state: President Branko CRVENKOVSKI (since 12 May 2004)
head of government: Prime Minister Vlado BUCKOVSKI (since 17 December 2004)
cabinet: Council of Ministers elected by the majority vote of all the deputies in the Assembly; note - current cabinet formed by the government coalition parties SDSM, LDP, BDI, and several small ethnic parties
elections: president elected by popular vote for a five-year term; two-round election last held 14 April and 28 April 2004 (next to be held April 2009); prime minister elected by the Assembly; Assembly election last held 1 November 2002 (next to be held in summer or fall 2006)
election results: Branko CRVENKOVSKI elected president on second-round ballot; percent of vote - Branko CRVENKOVSKI 62.7%, Sasko KEDEV 37.3%; Vlado BUCKOVSKI elected prime minister by the Assembly
Legislative branch: unicameral Assembly or Sobranie (120 seats – members elected by popular vote from party lists based on the percentage of the overall vote the parties gain in each of six electoral districts; all serve four-year terms)
elections: last held 15 September 2002 (next to be held NA 2006)
election results: percent of vote by party - NA%; seats by party -Together for Macedonia coalition 60 (SDSM 43, LDP 12, others 5), VMRO-DPMNE 33 (VMRO 28 and LDT 5), Democratic Union for Integration 16, Democratic Party of Albanians 7, Party for Democratic Prosperity 2, National Democratic Party 1, Socialist Party of Macedonia 1
Judicial branch: Supreme Court - the Assembly appoints the judges; Constitutional Court - the Assembly appoints the judges; Republican Judicial Council - the Assembly appoints the judges
Political parties and leaders: Democratic Alliance [Pavle TRAJANOV]; Democratic Alternative or DA [Vasil TUPURKOVSKI, president]; Democratic League of the Bosniaks [Rafet MUMINOVIC]; Democratic Party of Albanians or PDSH/DPA [Arben XHAFERI, president]; Democratic Party of Serbs [Ivan STOILJKOVIC]; Democratic Party of Turks [Kenan HASIPI]; Democratic Renewal of Macedonia [Liljana POPOVSKA]; Democratic Republican Union of Macedonia or DRUM [Goran RAFAJLOVSKI]; Democratic Union of Vlachs for Macedonia [leader NA]; Democratic Union for Integration or BDI/DUI [Ali AHMETI]; Internal Macedonian Revolutionary Organization-Agrarian Party or VMRO-Agrarian Party [Marjan GJORCEV]; Internal Macedonian Revolutionary Organization-Democratic Party for Macedonian National Unity or VMRO-DPMNE [Nikola GRUEVSKI]; Internal Macedonian Revolutionary Organization-True Macedonian Option or VMRO-Vistinska [Boris ZMEJKOVSKI]; Internal Macedonian Revolutionary Organization-Macedonian [Boris STOJMENOV]; Internal Macedonian Revolutionary Organization-People's Party or VMRO-Narodna [Vesna JANEVSKA]; League for Democracy [Gjorgi MARJANOVIC]; Liberal Democratic Party or LDP [Risto PENOV]; Liberal Party [Stojan ANDOV]; National Alliance [Harun ALIU]; National Democratic Party or PDK [Basri HALITI]; National Farmers' Party [Vejljo TANTAROV]; New Democratic Forces [Hysni SHAQIRI]; New Social Democratic Party [Tito PETKOVSKI]; Party for Democratic Prosperity or PPD/PDP [Abduljhadi VEJSELI]; Social Democratic Alliance of Macedonia or SDSM [Vlado BUCKOVSKI, president]; Socialist Party of Macedonia or SP [Ljubisav IVANOV, president]; Together for Macedonia coalition (including the SDSM and LDP) [Vlado BUCKOVSI]; United Party for Emancipation or OPE [Nezdet MUSTAFA]
Political pressure groups and leaders: Civic Movement of Macedonia [Gordana SILJANOVSKA]; World Macedonian Congress [Todor PETROV]
International organization participation: ACCT (associate), BIS, CE, CEI, EAPC, EBRD, FAO, IAEA, IBRD, ICAO, ICCt, ICRM, IDA, IFAD, IFC, IFRCS, ILO, IMF, IMO, Interpol, IOC, IOM (observer), ISO, ITU, MIGA, OPCW, OSCE, PCA, PFP, UN, UNCTAD, UNESCO, UNIDO, UPU, WCL, WCO, WHO, WIPO, WMO, WToO, WTO
Diplomatic representation in the US:
chief of mission: Ambassador Nikola DIMITROV
chancery: 2129 Wyoming Avenue NW, Washington, DC 20008

telephone: [1] (202) 667-0501
FAX: [1] (202) 667-2131
consulate(s) general: Southfield (Michigan)
Diplomatic representation from the US:
chief of mission: Ambassador Gillian A. MILOVANOVIC
embassy: Bul. Ilindenska bb, 1000 Skopje
mailing address: American Embassy Skopje, Department of State, 7120 Skopje Place, Washington, DC 20521-7120 (pouch)
telephone: [389] 2 311-6180
FAX: [389] 2 311-7103
Flag description: a yellow sun with eight broadening rays extending to the edges of the red field

ECONOMY

Economy - overview: At independence in September 1991, Macedonia was the least developed of the Yugoslav republics, producing a mere 5% of the total federal output of goods and services. The collapse of Yugoslavia ended transfer payments from the center and eliminated advantages from inclusion in a de facto free trade area. An absence of infrastructure, UN sanctions on the down-sized Yugoslavia, one of its largest markets, and a Greek economic embargo over a dispute about the country's constitutional name and flag hindered economic growth until 1996. GDP subsequently rose each year through 2000. However, the leadership's commitment to economic reform, free trade, and regional integration was undermined by the ethnic Albanian insurgency of 2001. The economy shrank 4.5% because of decreased trade, intermittent border closures, increased deficit spending on security needs, and investor uncertainty. Growth barely recovered in 2002 to 0.9%, then rose by 3.4% in 2003, 2.9% in 2004, and about 4% in 2005. Macedonia has lagged the region in attracting foreign investment and job growth has been anemic. Macedonia has an extensive grey market, estimated to be more than 20 percent of GDP, that falls outside official statistics.
GDP (purchasing power parity): $15.55 billion (2005 est.)
GDP (official exchange rate): $5.397 billion (2005 est.)
GDP - real growth rate: 4% (2005 est.)
GDP - per capita: purchasing power parity - $7,400 (2005 est.)
GDP - composition by sector:
agriculture: 11.7%
industry: 32.1%
services: 56.2% (2005 est.)
Labor force: 855,000 (2004 est.)
Labor force - by occupation: agriculture NA%, industry NA%, services NA%
Unemployment rate: 38% (2005 est.)
Population below poverty line: 30.2% (2003 est.)
Household income or consumption by percentage share:
lowest 10%: NA%
highest 10%: NA%
Inflation rate (consumer prices):1% (2005 est.)
Investment (gross fixed):18% of GDP (2005 est.)
Budget:
revenues: $2.169 billion
expenditures: $2.253 billion, including capital expenditures of $114 million (2005 est.)
Public debt: 32.6% of GDP (2005 est.)
Agriculture - products: wheat, grapes, rice, tobacco, corn, millet, cotton, sesame, mulberry leaves, citrus, vegetables; beef, pork, poultry, mutton
Industries: coal, metallic chromium, lead, zinc, ferronickel, textiles, wood products, tobacco, food processing, buses, steel
Industrial production growth rate: 5.5% (2005 est.)
Electricity - production: 5.566 billion kWh (2003)
Electricity - production by source:
fossil fuel: 83.7%
hydro: 16.3%
nuclear: 0%
other: 0% (2001)
Electricity - consumption: 5.289 billion kWh (2003)
Electricity - exports: 0 kWh (2003)
Electricity - imports: 112 million kWh (2003)
Oil - production: 0 bbl/day (2003 est.)
Oil - consumption: 21,000 bbl/day (2003 est.)
Oil - exports: NA (2003)
Oil - imports: NA (2003)
Current account balance: $-303 million (2005 est.)
Exports: $2.047 billion f.o.b. (2005 est.)
Exports - partners: Serbia and Montenegro 31.4%, Germany 19.9%, Greece 9%, Croatia 6.9%, US 4.9% (2004)
Imports: $3.196 billion f.o.b. (2005 est.)
Imports - partners: Greece 15.5%, Germany 13.1%, Serbia and Montenegro 10.4%, Slovenia 8.6%, Bulgaria 8.1%, Turkey 6%, Romania 4.7% (2004)
Reserves of foreign exchange and gold: $1.17 billion (2005 est.)
Debt - external: $2.207 billion (2005 est.)
Economic aid - recipient: $250 million (2003 est.)
Currency (code): Macedonian denar (MKD)
Currency code: MKD
Exchange rates: Macedonian denars per US dollar - 48.92 (2005), 49.41 (2004), 54.322 (2003), 64.35 (2002), 68.037 (2001)
Fiscal year: calendar year

COMMUNICATIONS

Telephones - main lines in use: 560,000 (2002)
Telephones - mobile cellular: 830,000 (2005)
Telephone system:
general assessment: NA
domestic: NA
international: country code - 389
Radio broadcast stations: AM 29, FM 20, shortwave 0 (1998)
Radios: 410,000 (1997)
Television broadcast stations: 31 (plus 166 repeaters) (1995)
Televisions: 510,000 (1997)
Internet country code: .mk
Internet hosts: 3,738 (2004)
Internet Service Providers (ISPs): 6 (2000)
Internet users: 100,000 (2002)

TRANSPORTATION

Airports: 17 (2004 est.)
Airports - with paved runways:
total: 10
2,438 to 3,047 m: 2
under 914 m: 8 (2005 est.)
Airports - with unpaved runways:
total: 7
914 to 1,523 m: 3
under 914 m: 4 (2005 est.)
Pipelines: gas 268 km; oil 120 km (2004)
Railways:
total: 699 km
standard gauge: 699 km 1.435-m gauge (233 km electrified) (2004)
Roadways:
total: 8,684 km
paved: 5,540 km
unpaved: 3,144 km (1999)

MILITARY

Military branches: Army of the Republic of Macedonia (ARM; includes Air and Air Defense Command)
Military service age and obligation: conscription to be phased out by 2007; current tour of conscript duty is 6 months; 18 years of age for voluntary military service (January 2005)
Manpower available for military service: *males age 18-49:* 498,259 (2005 est.)
Manpower fit for military service: *males age 18-49:* 411,156 (2005 est.)
Manpower reaching military service age annually: *males:* 16,686 (2005 est.)
Military expenditures - dollar figure: $200 million (FY01/02 est.)
Military expenditures - percent of GDP: 6% (FY01/02 est.)

TRANSNATIONAL ISSUES

Disputes - international: ethnic Albanians in Kosovo object to demarcation of the boundary with Macedonia in accordance with the 2000 Macedonia-Serbia and Montenegro delimitation agreement; Greece continues to reject the use of the name Macedonia or Republic of Macedonia

Refugees and internally displaced persons: *IDPs:* 2,678 (ethnic conflict in 2001; most IDPs have returned) (2004)

Illicit drugs: major transshipment point for Southwest Asian heroin and hashish; minor transit point for South American cocaine destined for Europe; although most criminal activity is thought to be domestic and not a financial center, money laundering is a problem due to a mostly cash-based economy and weak enforcement (no arrests or prosecutions for money laundering to date)

MADAGASCAR

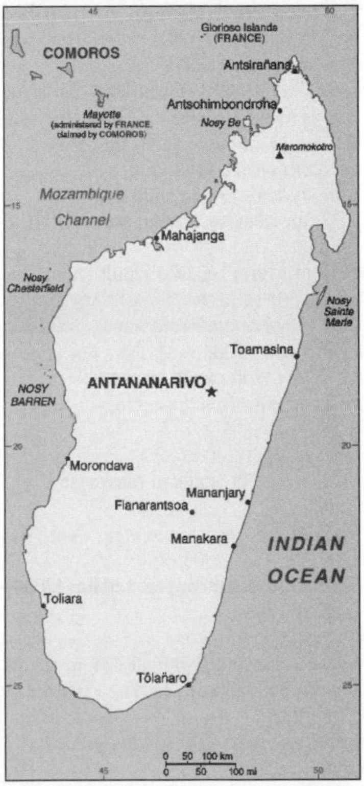

INTRODUCTION

Background: Formerly an independent kingdom, Madagascar became a French colony in 1896, but regained its independence in 1960. During 1992-93, free presidential and National Assembly elections were held, ending 17 years of single-party rule. In 1997, in the second presidential race, Didier RATSIRAKA, the leader during the 1970s and 1980s, was returned to the presidency. The 2001 presidential election was contested between the followers of Didier RATSIRAKA and Marc RAVALOMANANA, nearly causing secession of half of the country. In April 2002, the High Constitutional Court announced RAVALOMANANA the winner.

GEOGRAPHY

Location: Southern Africa, island in the Indian Ocean, east of Mozambique

Geographic coordinates: 20 00 S, 47 00 E

Map references: Africa

Area:
total: 587,040 sq km
land: 581,540 sq km
water: 5,500 sq km

Area - comparative: slightly less than twice the size of Arizona

Land boundaries: 0 km

Coastline: 4,828 km

Maritime claims:
territorial sea: 12 nm
contiguous zone: 24 nm
exclusive economic zone: 200 nm
continental shelf: 200 nm or 100 nm from the 2,500-m deep isobath

Climate: tropical along coast, temperate inland, arid in south

Terrain: narrow coastal plain, high plateau and mountains in center

Elevation extremes:
lowest point: Indian Ocean 0 m
highest point: Maromokotro 2,876 m

Natural resources: graphite, chromite, coal, bauxite, salt, quartz, tar sands, semi-precious stones, mica, fish, hydropower

Land use:
arable land: 5.07%
permanent crops: 1.03%
other: 93.91% (2001)

Irrigated land: 10,900 sq km (2000 est.)

Natural hazards: periodic cyclones, drought, and locust infestation

Environment - current issues: soil erosion results from deforestation and overgrazing; desertification; surface water contaminated with raw sewage and other organic wastes; several species of flora and fauna unique to the island are endangered

Environment - international agreements:
party to: Biodiversity, Climate Change, Climate Change-Kyoto Protocol, Desertification, Endangered Species, Hazardous Wastes, Law of the Sea, Marine Life Conservation, Ozone Layer Protection, Wetlands
signed, but not ratified: none of the selected agreements

Geography - note: world's fourth-largest island; strategic location along Mozambique Channel

PEOPLE

Population: 18,040,341 (July 2005 est.)

Age structure:
0-14 years: 44.8% (male 4,051,832/female 4,038,837)
15-64 years: 52.1% (male 4,657,346/female 4,745,971)
65 years and over: 3% (male 247,146/female 299,209) (2005 est.)

Median age:
total: 17.46 years
male: 17.24 years
female: 17.67 years (2005 est.)

Population growth rate: 3.03% (2005 est.)

Birth rate: 41.66 births/1,000 population (2005 est.)

Death rate: 11.35 deaths/1,000 population (2005 est.)

Net migration rate: 0 migrant(s)/1,000 population (2005 est.)

Sex ratio:
at birth: 1.03 male(s)/female
under 15 years: 1 male(s)/female
15-64 years: 0.98 male(s)/female
65 years and over: 0.83 male(s)/female
total population: 0.99 male(s)/female (2005 est.)

Infant mortality rate:
total: 76.83 deaths/1,000 live births
male: 85.05 deaths/1,000 live births
female: 68.36 deaths/1,000 live births (2005 est.)

Life expectancy at birth:
total population: 56.95 years
male: 54.57 years
female: 59.4 years (2005 est.)

Total fertility rate: 5.66 children born/woman (2005 est.)

HIV/AIDS - adult prevalence rate: 1.7% (2003 est.)

HIV/AIDS - people living with HIV/AIDS: 140,000 (2003 est.)

HIV/AIDS - deaths: 7,500 (2003 est.)

Major infectious diseases:
degree of risk: high
food or waterborne diseases: bacterial and protozoal diarrhea, hepatitis A, and typhoid fever
vectorborne diseases: malaria and plague are high risks in some locations
water contact disease: schistosomiasis (2004)

Nationality:
noun: Malagasy (singular and plural)
adjective: Malagasy

Ethnic groups: Malayo-Indonesian (Merina and related Betsileo), Cotiers (mixed African, Malayo-Indonesian, and Arab ancestry - Betsimisaraka,

Tsimihety, Antaisaka, Sakalava), French, Indian, Creole, Comoran
Religions: indigenous beliefs 52%, Christian 41%, Muslim 7%
Languages: French (official), Malagasy (official)
Literacy:
definition: age 15 and over can read and write
total population: 68.9%
male: 75.5%
female: 62.5% (2003 est.)

GOVERNMENT

Country name:
conventional long form: Republic of Madagascar
conventional short form: Madagascar
local long form: Republique de Madagascar
local short form: Madagascar
former: Malagasy Republic
Government type: republic
Capital: Antananarivo
Administrative divisions: 6 provinces (faritany); Antananarivo, Antsiranana, Fianarantsoa, Mahajanga, Toamasina, Toliara
Independence: 26 June 1960 (from France)
National holiday: Independence Day, 26 June (1960)
Constitution: 19 August 1992 by national referendum
Legal system: based on French civil law system and traditional Malagasy law; has not accepted compulsory ICJ jurisdiction
Suffrage:18 years of age; universal
Executive branch:
chief of state: President Marc RAVALOMANANA (since 6 May 2002)
head of government: Prime Minister Jacques SYLLA (27 May 2002)
cabinet: Council of Ministers appointed by the prime minister
elections: president elected by popular vote for a five-year term; election last held 16 December 2001 (next to be held November 2006); prime minister appointed by the president
election results: percent of vote - Didier RATSIRAKA (AREMA) 37.7%, Marc RAVALOMANANA (TIM) 50.5%
Legislative branch: bicameral legislature consists of a National Assembly or Assemblee Nationale (160 seats; members are directly elected by popular vote to serve four-year terms) and a Senate or Senat (100 seats; two-thirds of the seats filled by regional assemblies whose members will be elected by popular vote; the remaining one-third of the seats appointed by the president; all members will serve four-year terms)
elections: National Assembly - last held 15 December 2002 (next to be held NA 2006)
election results: National Assembly - percent of vote by party - NA%; seats by party - TIM 103, FP 22, AREMA 3, LEADER/Fanilo 2, RPSD 5, others 3, independents 22
Judicial branch: Supreme Court or Cour Supreme; High Constitutional Court or Haute Cour Constitutionnelle
Political parties and leaders: Association for the Rebirth of Madagascar or AREMA [Pierrot RAJAONARIVO]; Economic Liberalism and Democratic Action for National Recovery or LEADER/Fanilo [Herizo RAZAFIMAHALEO]; Fihaonana Party or FP [Guy-Willy RAZANAMASY]; I Love Madagascar or TIM [Marc RAVALOMANANA]; Renewal of the Social Democratic Party or RPSD [Evariste MARSON]
Political pressure groups and leaders: Committee for the Defense of Truth and Justice or KMMR; Committee for National Reconciliation or CRN [Albert Zafy]; National Council of Christian Churches or FFKM
International organization participation: ACCT, ACP, AfDB, AU, COMESA, FAO, G-77, IAEA, IBRD, ICAO, ICC, ICCt (signatory), ICFTU, ICRM, IDA, IFAD, IFC, IFRCS, ILO, IMF, IMO, InOC, Interpol, IOC, IOM, ISO (correspondent), ITU, MIGA, NAM, OPCW, SADC, UN, UNCTAD, UNESCO, UNHCR, UNIDO, UPU, WCL, WCO, WFTU, WHO, WIPO, WMO, WToO, WTO
Diplomatic representation in the US:
chief of mission: Ambassador Rajaonarivony NARISOA
chancery: 2374 Massachusetts Avenue NW, Washington, DC 20008
telephone: [1] (202) 265-5525, 5526
FAX: [1] (202) 483-7603
consulate(s) general: New York
Diplomatic representation from the US:
chief of mission: Ambassador Wanda L. NESBITT
embassy: 14-16 Rue Rainitovo, Antsahavola, Antananarivo 101
mailing address: B. P. 620, Antsahavola, Antananarivo
telephone: [261] (20) 22-212-57, 22-212-73, 22-209-56
FAX: [261] (20) 22-345-39
Flag description: two equal horizontal bands of red (top) and green with a vertical white band of the same width on

ECONOMY

Economy - overview: Having discarded past socialist economic policies, Madagascar has since the mid 1990s followed a World Bank and IMF led policy of privatization and liberalization. This strategy placed the country on a slow and steady growth path from an extremely low level. Agriculture, including fishing and forestry, is a mainstay of the economy, accounting for more than one-fourth of GDP and employing 80% of the population. Exports of apparel have boomed in recent years primarily due to duty-free access to the United States. Deforestation and erosion, aggravated by the use of firewood as the primary source of fuel are serious concerns. President RAVALOMANANA has worked aggressively to revive the economy following the 2002 political crisis, which triggered a 12% drop in GDP that year. Poverty reduction and combating corruption will be the centerpieces of economic policy for the next few years.
GDP (purchasing power parity): $15.82 billion (2005 est.)
GDP (official exchange rate): $4.705 billion (2005 est.)
GDP - real growth rate: 6.5% (2005 est.)
GDP - per capita: purchasing power parity - $900 (2005 est.)
GDP - composition by sector:
agriculture: 28.7%
industry: 16.5%
services: 54.8% (2005 est.)
Labor force: 7.3 million (2000)
Population below poverty line: 50% (2004 est.)
Household income or consumption by percentage share:
lowest 10%: 3%
highest 10%: 29% (1999)
Distribution of family income - Gini index: 47.5 (2001)
Inflation rate (consumer prices):10% (2005 est.)
Investment (gross fixed): 26.8% of GDP (2005 est.)
Budget:
revenues: $703.6 million
expenditures: $853 million, including capital expenditures of $331 million (2005 est.)
Agriculture - products: coffee, vanilla, sugarcane, cloves, cocoa, rice, cassava (tapioca), beans, bananas, peanuts; livestock products
Industries: meat processing, soap, breweries, tanneries, sugar, textiles, glassware, cement, automobile assembly plant, paper, petroleum, tourism
Industrial production growth rate: 3% (2000 est.)
Electricity - production: 825.4 million kWh (2003)
Electricity - production by source:
fossil fuel: 36.1%
hydro: 63.9%
nuclear: 0%
other: 0% (2001)
Electricity - consumption: 767.7 million kWh (2003)

Electricity - exports: 0 kWh (2003)
Electricity – imports: 0 kWh (2003)
Oil - production: 89.27 bbl/day (2003 est.)
Oil - consumption: 15,000 bbl/day (2003 est.)
Oil - exports: NA (2001)
Oil - imports: NA (2001)
Oil - proved reserves: 0 bbl (1 January 2002)
Natural gas - proved reserves: 0 cu m (1 January 2002)
Current account balance: $-292 million (2005 est.)
Exports: $951 million f.o.b. (2005 est.)
Exports - partners: US 35.8%, France 30.8%, Germany 7.7% (2004)
Imports: $1.4 billion f.o.b. (2005 est.)
Imports - partners: France 17.2%, China 9.7%, Hong Kong 6.6%, Iran 6.4%, Mauritius 6.2%, South Africa 5.6% (2004)
Reserves of foreign exchange and gold: $539 million (2005 est.)
Debt - external: $4.6 billion (2002)
Economic aid - recipient: $354 million (2001)
Currency (code): Madagascar ariary (MGA)
Currency code: MGF
Exchange rates: Malagasy francs per US dollar - 1,960 (2005), 1,868.9 (2004), 1,238.3 (2003), 1,366.4 (2002), 1,317.7 (2001)
Fiscal year: calendar year

COMMUNICATIONS

Telephones - main lines in use: 59,600 (2003)
Telephones - mobile cellular: 279,500 (2003)
Telephone system:
general assessment: system is above average for the region
domestic: open-wire lines, coaxial cables, microwave radio relay, and tropospheric scatter links connect regions
international: country code - 261; submarine cable to Bahrain; satellite earth stations - 1 Intelsat (Indian Ocean) and 1 Intersputnik (Atlantic Ocean region)
Radio broadcast stations: AM 2 (plus a number of repeater stations), FM 9, shortwave 6 (2001)
Radios: 3.05 million (1997)
Television broadcast stations: 1 (plus 36 repeaters) (2001)
Televisions: 325,000 (1997)
Internet country code: .mg
Internet hosts: 773 (2003)
Internet Service Providers (ISPs): 2 (2000)
Internet users: 70,500 (2003)

TRANSPORTATION

Airports: 116 (2004 est.)
Airports - with paved runways:
total: 29
over 3,047 m: 1
2,438 to 3,047 m: 2
1,524 to 2,437 m: 4
914 to 1,523 m: 20
under 914 m: 2 (2005 est.)
Airports - with unpaved runways:
total: 87
1,524 to 2,437 m: 2
914 to 1,523 m: 42
under 914 m: 43 (2005 est.)
Railways:
total: 732 km
narrow gauge: 732 km 1.000-m gauge (2004)
Roadways:
total: 49,827 km
paved: 5,780 km
unpaved: 44,047 km (1999)
Waterways: 600 km (2004)
Merchant marine:
total: 9 ships (1,000 GRT or over) 14,865 GRT/17,936 DWT
by type: cargo 5, passenger/cargo 2, petroleum tanker 2
registered in other countries: 1 (2005)
Ports and terminals: Antsiranana, Mahajanga, Toamasina, Toliara

MILITARY

Military branches: People's Armed Forces: Intervention Force, Development Force, and Aeronaval (Navy and Air) Force; National Gendarmerie
Military service age and obligation: 18 years of age (est.); conscript service obligation - 18 months (2004)
Manpower available for military service: *males age 18-49:* 3,542,797 (2005 est.)
Manpower fit for military service: *males age 18-49:* 2,218,662 (2005 est.)
Manpower reaching military service age annually: *males:* 187,000 (2005 est.)
Military expenditures - dollar figure: $44.6 million (2004)
Military expenditures - percent of GDP: 1.2% (2004)

TRANSNATIONAL ISSUES

Disputes - international: claims Bassas da India, Europa Island, Glorioso Islands, and Juan de Nova Island (all administered by France)
Illicit drugs: illicit producer of cannabis (cultivated and wild varieties) used mostly for domestic consumption; transshipment point for heroin

MALAWI

INTRODUCTION

Background: Established in 1891, the British protectorate of Nyasaland became the independent nation of Malawi in 1964. After three decades of one-party rule under President Hastings Kamuzu BANDA the country held multiparty elections in 1994, under a provisional constitution, which came into full effect the following year. Current President Bingu wa MUTHARIKA, elected in May 2004 after the previous president failed to amend the constitution to permit another term, has struggled to assert his authority against his predecessor, who still leads their shared political party. MATHARIKA's anti-corruption efforts have led to several high-level arrests and one prominent conviction. Increasing corruption, population growth, increasing pressure on agricultural lands, and HIV/AIDS pose major problems for the country.

GEOGRAPHY

Location: Southern Africa, east of Zambia
Geographic coordinates: 13 30 S, 34 00 E
Map references: Africa
Area:
total: 118,480 sq km
land: 94,080 sq km
water: 24,400 sq km
Area - comparative: slightly smaller than Pennsylvania
Land boundaries:
total: 2,881 km
border countries: Mozambique 1,569 km, Tanzania 475 km, Zambia 837 km
Coastline: 0 km (landlocked)
Maritime claims: none (landlocked)
Climate: sub-tropical; rainy season (November to May); dry season (May to November)
Terrain: narrow elongated plateau with rolling plains, rounded hills, some mountains
Elevation extremes:
lowest point: junction of the Shire River and international boundary with Mozambique 37 m
highest point: Sapitwa (Mount Mlanje) 3,002 m
Natural resources: limestone, arable land, hydropower, unexploited deposits of uranium, coal, and bauxite
Land use:
arable land: 23.38%
permanent crops: 1.49%
other: 75.13% (2001)
Irrigated land: 280 sq km (1998 est.)

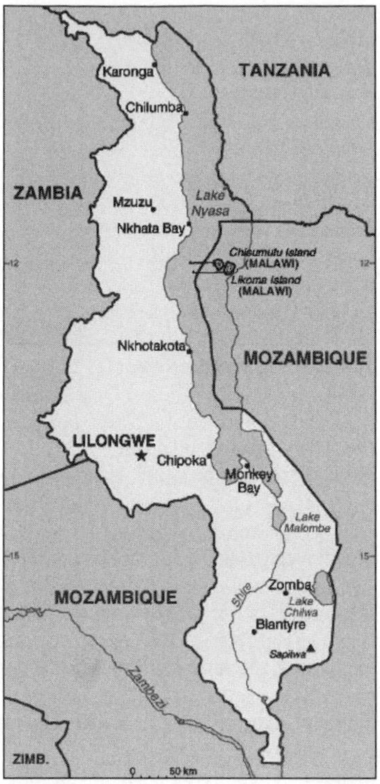

Natural hazards: NA

Environment - current issues: deforestation; land degradation; water pollution from agricultural runoff, sewage, industrial wastes; siltation of spawning grounds endangers fish populations

Environment - international agreements:
party to: Biodiversity, Climate Change, Climate Change-Kyoto Protocol, Desertification, Endangered Species, Environmental Modification, Hazardous Wastes, Marine Life Conservation, Ozone Layer Protection, Ship Pollution, Wetlands
signed, but not ratified: Law of the Sea

Geography - note: landlocked; Lake Nyasa, some 580 km long, is the country's most prominent physical feature

PEOPLE

Population: 12,158,924
note: estimates for this country explicitly take into account the effects of excess mortality due to AIDS; this can result in lower life expectancy, higher infant mortality and death rates, lower population and growth rates, and changes in the distribution of population by age and sex than would otherwise be expected (July 2005 est.)

Age structure:
0-14 years: 46.9% (male 2,877,568/female 2,823,296)
15-64 years: 50.4% (male 3,041,352/female 3,081,762)
65 years and over: 2.8% (male 132,175/female 202,771) (2005 est.)

Median age:
total: 16.34 years
male: 16.04 years
female: 16.65 years (2005 est.)

Population growth rate: 2.06% (2005 est.)

Birth rate: 43.95 births/1,000 population (2005 est.)

Death rate: 23.39 deaths/1,000 population (2005 est.)

Net migration rate: 0 migrant(s)/1,000 population (2005 est.)

Sex ratio:
at birth: 1.03 male(s)/female
under 15 years: 1.02 male(s)/female
15-64 years: 0.99 male(s)/female
65 years and over: 0.65 male(s)/female
total population: 0.99 male(s)/female (2005 est.)

Infant mortality rate:
total: 103.32 deaths/1,000 live births
male: 107.44 deaths/1,000 live births
female: 99.07 deaths/1,000 live births (2005 est.)

Life expectancy at birth:
total population: 41.43 years
male: 41.66 years
female: 41.2 years (2005 est.)

Total fertility rate: 5.98 children born/woman (2005 est.)

HIV/AIDS - adult prevalence rate: 14.2% (2003 est.)

HIV/AIDS - people living with HIV/AIDS: 900,000 (2003 est.)

HIV/AIDS - deaths: 84,000 (2003 est.)

Major infectious diseases:
degree of risk: very high
food or waterborne diseases: bacterial and protozoal diarrhea, hepatitis A, and typhoid fever
vectorborne diseases: malaria and plague are high risks in some locations
water contact disease: schistosomiasis (2004)

Nationality:
noun: Malawian(s)
adjective: Malawian

Ethnic groups: Chewa, Nyanja, Tumbuka, Yao, Lomwe, Sena, Tonga, Ngoni, Ngonde, Asian, European

Religions: Christian 79.9%, Muslim 12.8%, other 3%, none 4.3% (1998 census)

Languages: Chichewa 57.2% (official), Chinyanja 12.8%, Chiyao 10.1%, Chitumbuka 9.5%, Chisena 2.7%, Chilomwe 2.4%, Chitonga 1.7%, other 3.6% (1998 census)

Literacy:
definition: age 15 and over can read and write
total population: 62.7%
male: 76.1%
female: 49.8% (2003 est.)

GOVERNMENT

Country name:
conventional long form: Republic of Malawi
conventional short form: Malawi
former: British Central African Protectorate, Nyasaland Protectorate, Nyasaland

Government type: multiparty democracy

Capital: Lilongwe

Administrative divisions: 27 districts; Balaka, Blantyre, Chikwawa, Chiradzulu, Chitipa, Dedza, Dowa, Karonga, Kasungu, Likoma, Lilongwe, Machinga (Kasupe), Mangochi, Mchinji, Mulanje, Mwanza, Mzimba, Ntcheu, Nkhata Bay, Nkhotakota, Nsanje, Ntchisi, Phalombe, Rumphi, Salima, Thyolo, Zomba

Independence: 6 July 1964 (from UK)

National holiday: Independence Day (Republic Day), 6 July (1964)

Constitution: 18 May 1994

Legal system: based on English common law and customary law; judicial review of legislative acts in the Supreme Court of Appeal; has not accepted compulsory ICJ jurisdiction

Suffrage: 18 years of age; universal

Executive branch:
chief of state: President Bingu wa MUTHARIKA (since 24 May 2004); note - the president is both the chief of state and head of government
head of government: President Bingu wa MUTHARIKA (since 24 May 2004); note - the president is both the chief of state and head of government
cabinet: 46-member Cabinet named by the president
elections: president elected by popular vote for a five-year term; election last held 20 May 2004 (next to be held May 2009)
election results: Bingu wa MUTHARIKA elected president; percent of vote - Bingu wa MUTHARIKA (UDF) 35.9%, John TEMBO (MCP) 27.1%, Gwandaguluwe CHAKUAMBA (MC) 25.7%, Brown MPINGANJIRA (NDA) 8.7%, Justin MALEWEZI (independent) 2.5%

Legislative branch: unicameral National Assembly (193 seats; members elected by popular vote to serve five-year terms)
elections: last held 20 May 2004 (next to be held May 2009)
election results: percent of vote by party - NA%; seats by party - UDF 74, MCP 60, Independents 24, RP 16, others 18, vacancies 1

Judicial branch: Supreme Court of Appeal; High Court (chief justice appointed by the president, puisne judges appointed on the advice of the Judicial Service Commission); magistrate's courts

Political parties and leaders: Alliance for Democracy or AFORD [Chakufwa

CHIHANA]; Malawi Congress Party or MCP [John TEMBO]; Malawi Democratic Party or MDP [Kampelo KALUA]; Malawi Forum for Unity and Development or MAFUNDE [George MNESA]; Mgwirizano Coalition or MC (coalition of MAFUNDE, MDP, MGODE, NUP, PETRA, PPM, RP) [Gwandaguluwe CHAKUAMBA]; Movement for Genuine Democratic Change or MGODE [Sam Kandodo BANDA]; National Democratic Alliance or NDA [Brown MPINGANJIRA]; National Unity Party or NUP [Harry CHIUME]; New Congress for Democracy or NCD [Hetherwick NTABA]; People's Progressive Movement or PPM [Aleke BANDA]; People's Transformation Movement or PETRA [Kamuzu CHIBAMBO]; Republican Party or RP [Gwandaguluwe CHAKUAMBA]; United Democratic Front or UDF [Bingu wa MUTHARIKA] - governing party

Political pressure groups and leaders: NA

International organization participation: ACP, AfDB, AU, C, COMESA, FAO, G-77, IBRD, ICAO, ICCt, ICFTU, ICRM, IDA, IFAD, IFC, IFRCS, ILO, IMF, IMO, Interpol, IOC, ISO (correspondent), ITU, MIGA, MONUC, NAM, ONUB, OPCW, SADC, UN, UNCTAD, UNESCO, UNIDO, UNMIL, UNMIS, UPU, WCL, WCO, WFTU, WHO, WIPO, WMO, WToO, WTO

Diplomatic representation in the US:
chief of mission: Ambassador Bernard Herbert SANDE
chancery: 1156 15th Street, NW, Suite 320, Washington, DC 20005
telephone: [1] (202) 721-0270
FAX: [1] (202) 721-0288

Diplomatic representation from the US:
chief of mission: Ambassador (vacant); Charge d'Affaires David GILMOUR
embassy: Area 40, Plot 24, Kenyatta Road
mailing address: P. O. Box 30016, Lilongwe 3, Malawi
telephone: [265] (1) 773 166
FAX: [265] (1) 770 471

Flag description: three equal horizontal bands of black (top), red, and green with a radiant, rising, red sun centered in the black band

Government - note: the executive exerts considerable influence over the legislature

ECONOMY

Economy - overview: Landlocked Malawi ranks among the world's least developed countries. The economy is predominately agricultural, with about 90% of the population living in rural areas. Agriculture accounted for nearly 36% of GDP and 80% of export revenues in 2005. The performance of the tobacco sector is key to short-term growth as tobacco accounts for over 50% of exports. The economy depends on substantial inflows of economic assistance from the IMF, the World Bank, and individual donor nations. In late 2000, Malawi was approved for relief under the Heavily Indebted Poor Countries (HIPC) program. The government faces strong challenges, including developing a market economy, improving educational facilities, facing up to environmental problems, dealing with the rapidly growing problem of HIV/AIDS, and satisfying foreign donors that fiscal discipline is being tightened. In 2005, President MUTHARIKA championed an anti-corruption campaign. Malawi's recent fiscal policy performance has been very strong, but a serious drought in 2005 and 2006 will heighten pressure on the government to increase spending.

GDP (purchasing power parity): $7.629 billion (2005 est.)

GDP (official exchange rate): $1.957 billion (2005 est.)

GDP - real growth rate: 1% (2005 est.)

GDP - per capita: purchasing power parity - $600 (2005 est.)

GDP - composition by sector:
agriculture: 35.9%
industry: 14.5%
services: 49.6% (2005 est.)

Labor force: 4.5 million (2001 est.)

Labor force - by occupation: agriculture 90% (2003 est.)

Unemployment rate: NA (2003 est.)

Population below poverty line: 55% (2004 est.)

Household income or consumption by percentage share:
lowest 10%: NA
highest 10%: NA

Inflation rate (consumer prices): 15.4% (2005 est.)

Investment (gross fixed): 9.5% of GDP (2005 est.)

Budget:
revenues: $844.6 million
expenditures: $913.9 million, including capital expenditures of NA (2005 est.)

Public debt: 208.6% of GDP (2005 est.)

Agriculture - products: tobacco, sugarcane, cotton, tea, corn, potatoes, cassava (tapioca), sorghum, pulses; groundnuts, Macadamia nuts; cattle, goats

Industries: tobacco, tea, sugar, sawmill products, cement, consumer goods

Industrial production growth rate: -1.6% (2005 est.)

Electricity - production: 1.296 billion kWh (2003)

Electricity - production by source:
fossil fuel: 3.3%
hydro: 96.7%
nuclear: 0%
other: 0% (2001)

Electricity - consumption: 1.206 billion kWh (2003)

Electricity – exports: 0 kWh (2003)

Electricity - imports: 0 kWh (2003)

Oil - production: 0 bbl/day (2003 est.)

Oil - consumption: 5,450 bbl/day (2003 est.)

Oil - exports: NA (2001)

Oil - imports: NA (2001)

Current account balance: $-217 million (2005 est.)

Exports: $364 million f.o.b. (2005 est.)

Exports - partners: South Africa 13.4%, US 11.9%, Germany 11.5%, Egypt 8.4%, UK 6.6%, Mozambique 4.5% (2004)

Imports: $645 million f.o.b. (2005 est.)

Imports - partners: South Africa 35.5%, India 7.7%, Mozambique 7.3%, Zimbabwe 6.8%, Zambia 6.3%, Tanzania 4.3% (2004)

Reserves of foreign exchange and gold: $146 million (2005 est.)

Debt - external: $3.284 billion (2005 est.)

Economic aid - recipient: $401.5 million (2001)

Currency (code): Malawian kwacha (MWK)

Currency code: MWK

Exchange rates: Malawian kwachas per US dollar - 120.21 (2005), 108.894 (2004), 97.433 (2003), 76.687 (2002), 72.197 (2001)

Fiscal year: 1 July - 30 June

COMMUNICATIONS

Telephones - main lines in use: 85,000 (2003)

Telephones - mobile cellular: 135,100 (2003)

Telephone system:
general assessment: NA
domestic: system employs open-wire lines, microwave radio relay links, and radiotelephone communications stations
international: country code - 265; satellite earth stations - 2 Intelsat (1 Indian Ocean and 1 Atlantic Ocean)

Radio broadcast stations: AM 9, FM 5 (plus 15 repeater stations), shortwave 2 (plus a third station held in standby status) (2001)

Radios: 2.6 million (1997)

Television broadcast stations: 1 (2001)

Televisions: NA

Internet country code: .mw

Internet hosts: 18 (2003)

Internet Service Providers (ISPs): 3 (2002)

Internet users: 36,000 (2003)

TRANSPORTATION

Airports: 42 (2004 est.)

Airports - with paved runways:
total: 6
over 3,047 m: 1
1,524 to 2,437 m: 1
914 to 1,523 m: 4 (2005 est.)
Airports - with unpaved runways:
total: 36
1,524 to 2,437 m: 1
914 to 1,523 m: 15
under 914 m: 20 (2005 est.)
Railways:
total: 797 km
narrow gauge: 797 km 1.067-m gauge (2004)
Roadways:
total: 28,400 km
paved: 5,254 km
unpaved: 23,146 km (1999)
Waterways: 700 km
note: on Lake Nyasa (Lake Malawi) and Shire River (2003)
Ports and terminals: Chipoka, Monkey Bay, Nkhata Bay, Nkhotakota, Chilumba

MILITARY

Military branches: Malawi Armed Forces: Army (includes Air Wing and Naval Detachment), Police (includes Mobile Force Unit)
Military service age and obligation: 18 years of age for voluntary military service; no conscription (2001)
Manpower available for military service: *males age 18-49:* 2,320,190 (2005 est.)
Manpower fit for military service: *males age 18-49:* 995,084 (2005 est.)
Military expenditures - dollar figure: $11.1 million (2004)
Military expenditures - percent of GDP: 0.7% (2004)

TRANSNATIONAL ISSUES

Disputes - international: disputes with Tanzania over the boundary in Lake Nyasa (Lake Malawi) and the meandering Songwe River remain dormant

MALAYSIA

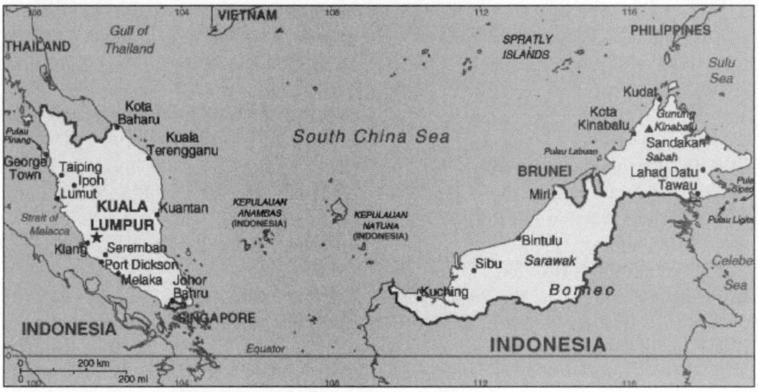

INTRODUCTION

Background: During the late 18th and 19th centuries, Great Britain established colonies and protectorates in the area of current Malaysia; these were occupied by Japan from 1942 to 1945. In 1948, the British-ruled territories on the Malay Peninsula formed the Federation of Malaya, which became independent in 1957. Malaysia was formed in 1963 when the former British colonies of Singapore and the East Malaysian states of Sabah and Sarawak on the northern coast of Borneo joined the Federation. The first several years of the country's history were marred by Indonesian efforts to control Malaysia, Philippine claims to Sabah, and Singapore's secession from the Federation in 1965.

GEOGRAPHY

Location: Southeastern Asia, peninsula bordering Thailand and northern one-third of the island of Borneo, bordering Indonesia, Brunei, and the South China Sea, south of Vietnam
Geographic coordinates: 2 30 N, 112 30 E
Map references: Southeast Asia
Area:
total: 329,750 sq km
land: 328,550 sq km
water: 1,200 sq km
Area - comparative: slightly larger than New Mexico
Land boundaries:
total: 2,669 km
border countries: Brunei 381 km, Indonesia 1,782 km, Thailand 506 km
Coastline: 4,675 km (Peninsular Malaysia 2,068 km, East Malaysia 2,607 km)
Maritime claims:
territorial sea: 12 nm
exclusive economic zone: 200 nm
continental shelf: 200-m depth or to the depth of exploitation; specified boundary in the South China Sea
Climate: tropical; annual southwest (April to October) and northeast (October to February) monsoons
Terrain: coastal plains rising to hills and mountains
Elevation extremes:
lowest point: Indian Ocean 0 m
highest point: Gunung Kinabalu 4,100 m
Natural resources: tin, petroleum, timber, copper, iron ore, natural gas, bauxite
Land use:
arable land: 5.48%
permanent crops: 17.61%
other: 76.91% (2001)
Irrigated land: 3,650 sq km (1998 est.)
Natural hazards: flooding, landslides, forest fires
Environment - current issues: air pollution from industrial and vehicular emissions; water pollution from raw sewage; deforestation; smoke/haze from Indonesian forest fires
Environment - international agreements:
party to: Biodiversity, Climate Change, Climate Change-Kyoto Protocol, Desertification, Endangered Species, Hazardous Wastes, Law of the Sea, Marine Life Conservation, Ozone Layer Protection, Ship Pollution, Tropical Timber 83, Tropical Timber 94, Wetlands
Geography - note: strategic location along Strait of Malacca and southern South China Sea

PEOPLE

Population: 23,953,136 (July 2005 est.)
Age structure:
0-14 years: 33% (male 4,067,006/female 3,837,758)
15-64 years: 62.4% (male 7,488,367/female 7,447,047)
65 years and over: 4.6% (male 490,334/female 622,624) (2005 est.)
Median age:
total: 23.92 years
male: 23.32 years
female: 24.54 years (2005 est.)
Population growth rate: 1.8% (2005 est.)
Birth rate: 23.07 births/1,000 population (2005 est.)
Death rate: 5.06 deaths/1,000 population (2005 est.)
Net migration rate: 0 migrant(s)/1,000 population
note: does not reflect net flow of an unknown number of illegal immigrants from other countries in the region (2005 est.)
Sex ratio:
at birth: 1.07 male(s)/female
under 15 years: 1.06 male(s)/female

15-64 years: 1.01 male(s)/female
65 years and over: 0.79 male(s)/female
total population: 1.01 male(s)/female (2005 est.)

Infant mortality rate:
total: 17.7 deaths/1,000 live births
male: 20.49 deaths/1,000 live births
female: 14.71 deaths/1,000 live births (2005 est.)

Life expectancy at birth:
total population: 72.24 years
male: 69.56 years
female: 75.11 years (2005 est.)

Total fertility rate: 3.07 children born/woman (2005 est.)

HIV/AIDS - adult prevalence rate: 0.4% (2003 est.)

HIV/AIDS - people living with HIV/AIDS: 52,000 (2003 est.)

HIV/AIDS - deaths: 2,000 (2003 est.)

Major infectious diseases:
degree of risk: high
food or waterborne diseases: bacterial diarrhea, hepatitis A, and typhoid fever
vectorborne diseases: dengue fever and malaria are high risks in some locations (2004)

Nationality:
noun: Malaysian(s)
adjective: Malaysian

Ethnic groups: Malay 50.4%, Chinese 23.7%, Indigenous 11%, Indian 7.1%, others 7.8% (2004 est.)

Religions: Muslim, Buddhist, Daoist, Hindu, Christian, Sikh; note – in addition, Shamanism is practiced in East Malaysia

Languages: Bahasa Melayu (official), English, Chinese (Cantonese, Mandarin, Hokkien, Hakka, Hainan, Foochow), Tamil, Telugu, Malayalam, Panjabi, Thai note: in addition, in East Malaysia several indigenous languages are spoken, the largest are Iban and Kadazan

Literacy:
definition: age 15 and over can read and write
total population: 88.7%
male: 92%
female: 85.4% (2002)

GOVERNMENT

Country name:
conventional long form: none
conventional short form: Malaysia
former: Federation of Malaysia

Government type: constitutional monarchy note: nominally headed by paramount ruler and a bicameral Parliament consisting of a nonelected upper house and an elected lower house; all Peninsular Malaysian states have hereditary rulers except Melaka and Pulau Pinang (Penang); those two states along with Sabah and Sarawak in East Malaysia have governors appointed by government; powers of state governments are limited by federal constitution; under terms of federation, Sabah and Sarawak retain certain constitutional prerogatives (e.g., right to maintain their own immigration controls); Sabah - holds 25 seats in House of Representatives; Sarawak holds 28 seats in House of Representatives

Capital: Kuala Lumpurnote: Putrajaya is referred to as administrative center not capital; Parliament meets in Kuala Lumpur

Administrative divisions: 13 states (negeri-negeri, singular - negeri) Johor, Kedah, Kelantan, Melaka, Negeri Sembilan, Pahang, Perak, Perlis, Pulau Pinang, Sabah, Sarawak, Selangor, and Terengganu; and one federal territory (wilayah persekutuan) with three components, city of Kuala Lumpur, Labuan, and Putrajaya

Independence: 31 August 1957 (from UK)

National holiday: Independence Day/Malaysia Day, 31 August (1957)

Constitution: 31 August 1957; amended 16 September 1963

Legal system: based on English common law; judicial review of legislative acts in the Supreme Court at request of supreme head of the federation; has not accepted compulsory ICJ jurisdiction

Suffrage: 21 years of age; universal

Executive branch:
chief of state: Paramount Ruler Tuanku SYED SIRAJUDDIN ibni Almarhum Tuanku Syed Putra Jamalullail, the Raja of Perlis (since 12 December 2001)
head of government: Prime Minister ABDULLAH bin Ahmad Badawi (since 31 October 2003); Deputy Prime Minister Mohamed NAJIB bin Abdul Razak (since 7 January 2004)
cabinet: Cabinet appointed by the prime minister from among the members of Parliament with consent of the paramount ruler
elections: paramount ruler elected by and from the hereditary rulers of nine of the states for five-year terms; election last held 12 December 2001 (next to be held in 2006); prime minister designated from among the members of the House of Representatives; following legislative elections, the leader of the party that wins a plurality of seats in the House of Representatives becomes prime minister
election results: Tuanku SYED SIRAJUDDIN ibni Almarhum Tuanku Syed Putra Jamalullail elected paramount ruler

Legislative branch: bicameral Parliament or Parlimen consists of the Senate or Dewan Negara (70 seats; 44 appointed by the paramount ruler, 26 appointed by the state legislatures) and the House of Representatives or Dewan Rakyat (219 seats; members elected by popular vote to serve five-year terms)
elections: House of Representatives - last held 21 March 2004 (next must be held by 2009)
election results: House of Representatives - percent of vote by party – BN 91%, DAP 5%, PAS 3%, other 1%; seats by party - BN 199, DAP 12, PAS 6, PKR 1, independent 1

Judicial branch: Federal Court (judges appointed by the paramount ruler on the advice of the prime minister)

Political parties and leaders: ruling-coalition National Front (Barisan Nasional) or BN, consisting of the following parties: Gerakan Rakyat Malaysia Party or PGRM [LIM Keng Yaik]; Liberal Democratic Party (Parti Liberal Demokratik - Sabah) or LDP [CHONG Kah Kiat]; Malaysian Chinese Association (Persatuan China Malaysia) or MCA [ONG Ka Ting]; Malaysian Indian Congress (Kongresi India Malaysia) or MIC [S. Samy VELLU]; Parti Bersatu Pakyat Sabah or PBRS [Joseph KURUP]; Parti Bersatu Sabah or PBS [Joseph PAIRIN Kitingan]; Parti Pesaka Bumiputra Bersatu or PBB [Patinggi Haji Abdul TAIB Mahmud]; Parti Rakyat Sarawak or PRS [James MASING]; Sabah Progressive Party (Parti Progresif Sabah) or SAPP [YONG Teck Lee]; Sarawak United People's Party (Parti Bersatu Rakyat Sarawak) or SUPP [George CHAN Hong Nam]; United Malays National Organization or UMNO [ABDULLAH bin Ahmad Badawi]; United Pasokmomogun Kadazandusun Murut Organization (Pertubuhan Pasko Momogun Kadazan Dusun Bersatu) or UPKO [Bernard DOMPOK]; People's Progressive Party (Parti Progresif Penduduk Malaysia) or PPP [M.Keyveas]; Sarawak Progressive Democratic Party or SPDP [William MAWANI]; opposition parties: Democratic Action Party (Parti Tindakan Demokratik) or DAP [KARPAL Singh]; Islamic Party of Malaysia (Parti Islam se Malaysia) or PAS [Abdul HADI Awang]; People's Justice Party (Parti Keadilan Rakyat) or PKR [WAN AZIZAH Wan Ismael]; Sarawak National Party or SNAP [Edwin DANDUNG]; opposition coalition Alternative Front (Barisan Alternatif) or BA consists of PAS and PKR

Political pressure groups and leaders: NA

International organization participation: APEC, APT, ARF, AsDB, ASEAN, BIS, C, CP, EAS, FAO, G-15, G-77,

IAEA, IBRD, ICAO, ICC, ICFTU, ICRM, IDA, IDB, IFAD, IFC, IFRCS, IHO, ILO, IMF, IMO, Interpol, IOC, ISO, ITU, MIGA,MINURSO, MINUSTAH, MONUC, NAM, OIC, ONUB, OPCW, PCA, PIF (partner), UN,UNAMSIL, UNCTAD, UNESCO, UNIDO, UNMEE, UNMIL, UNMIS, UPU, WCL, WCO, WFTU, WHO, WIPO, WMO, WToO, WTO
Diplomatic representation in the US:
chief of mission: Ambassador GHAZZALI bin Sheikh Abdul Khalid
chancery: 3516 International Court NW, Washington, DC 20008
telephone: [1] (202) 572-9700
FAX: [1] (202) 572-9882
consulate(s) general: Los Angeles and New York
Diplomatic representation from the US:
chief of mission: Ambassador Christopher J. LAFLEUR
embassy: 376 Jalan Tun Razak, 50400 Kuala Lumpur
mailing address: P. O. Box No. 10035, 50400 Kuala Lumpur; American Embassy Kuala Lumpur, APO AP 96535-8152
telephone: [60] (3) 2168-5000
FAX: [60] (3) 2142-2207
Flag description: 14 equal horizontal stripes of red (top) alternating with white (bottom); there is a blue rectangle in the upper hoist-side corner bearing a yellow crescent and a yellow 14-pointed star; the crescent and the star are traditional symbols of Islam; the design was based on the flag of the US

ECONOMY

Economy - overview: Malaysia, a middle-income country, transformed itself from 1971 through the late 1990's from a producer of raw materials into an emerging multi-sector economy. Growth was almost exclusively driven by exports - particularly of electronics. As a result, Malaysia was hard hit by the global economic downturn and the slump in the information technology (IT) sector in 2001 and 2002. GDP in 2001 grew only 0.5% because of an estimated 11% contraction in exports, but a substantial fiscal stimulus package equal to US $1.9 billion mitigated the worst of the recession, and the economy rebounded in 2002 with a 4.1% increase. The economy grew 4.9% in 2003, notwithstanding a difficult first half, when external pressures from SARS and the Iraq War led to caution in the business community. Growth topped 7% in 2004 and 5% in 2005. Healthy foreign exchange reserves, low inflation, and a small external debt are all strengths that make it unlikely that Malaysia will experience a financial crisis over the near term similar to the one in 1997. The economy remains dependent on continued growth in the US, China, and Japan, top export destinations and key sources of foreign investment.
GDP (purchasing power parity): $248 billion (2005 est.)
GDP (official exchange rate): $124.1 billion (2005 est.)
GDP - real growth rate: 5.1% (2005 est.)
GDP - per capita: purchasing power parity - $10,400 (2005 est.)
GDP - composition by sector:
agriculture: 7.2%
industry: 33.3%
services: 59.5% (2005 est.)
Labor force: 10.67 million (2005 est.)
Labor force - by occupation: agriculture 14.5%, industry 36%, services 49.5% (2000 est.)
Unemployment rate: 3.6% (2005 est.)
Population below poverty line: 8% (1998 est.)
Household income or consumption by percentage share:
lowest 10%: 1.4%
highest 10%: 39.2% (2003 est.)
Distribution of family income - Gini index: 49.2 (1997)
Inflation rate (consumer prices): 2.9% (2005 est.)
Investment (gross fixed): 20.3% of GDP (2005 est.)
Budget:
revenues: $30.57 billion
expenditures: $34.62 billion, including capital expenditures of $9.4 billion (2005 est.)
Public debt: 48.3% of GDP (2005 est.)
Agriculture - products: Peninsular Malaysia - rubber, palm oil, cocoa, rice; Sabah - subsistence crops, rubber, timber, coconuts, rice; Sarawak - rubber, pepper, timber
Industries: Peninsular Malaysia - rubber and oil palm processing and manufacturing, light manufacturing industry, electronics, tin mining and smelting, logging and processing timber; Sabah - logging, petroleum production; Sarawak - agriculture processing, petroleum production and refining, logging
Industrial production growth rate: 4.8% (2005 est.)
Electricity - production: 79.28 billion kWh (2003)
Electricity - production by source:
fossil fuel: 89.5%
hydro: 10.5%
nuclear: 0%
other: 0% (2001)
Electricity - consumption: 73.63 billion kWh (2003)
Electricity - exports: 100 million kWh (2003)
Electricity - imports: 0 kWh (2003)
Oil - production: 770,000 bbl/day (2005 est.)
Oil - consumption: 510,000 bbl/day (2003 est.)
Oil - exports: 230,200 bbl/day (2003)
Oil - imports: NA (2003)
Oil - proved reserves: 3.1 billion bbl (2005 est.)
Natural gas - production: 53.66 billion cu m (2001 est.)
Natural gas - consumption: 31.25 billion cu m (2001 est.)
Natural gas - exports: 22.41 billion cu m (2001 est.)
Natural gas - imports: 0 cu m (2001 est.)
Natural gas - proved reserves: 2.23 trillion cu m (2005)
Current account balance: $15.35 billion (2005 est.)
Exports: $147.1 billion f.o.b. (2005 est.)
Exports - partners: US 18.8%, Singapore 15%, Japan 10.1%, China 6.7%, Hong Kong 6%, Thailand 4.8% (2004)
Imports: $118.7 billion f.o.b. (2005 est.)
Imports - partners: Japan 16.1%, US 14.6%, Singapore 11.2%, China 9.9%, Thailand 5.6%, Taiwan 5.5%, South Korea 5%, Germany 4.5%, Indonesia 4% (2004)
Reserves of foreign exchange and gold: $78.9 billion (2005 est.)
Debt - external: $56.72 billion (30 June 2005 est.)
Currency (code): ringgit (MYR)
Currency code: MYR
Exchange rates: ringgits per US dollar - 3.78 (2005), 3.8 (2004), 3.8 (2003), 3.8 (2002), 3.8 (2001)
Fiscal year: calendar year

COMMUNICATIONS

Telephones - main lines in use: 4,571,600 (2003)
Telephones - mobile cellular: 11,124,100 (2003)
Telephone system:
general assessment: modern system; international service excellent
domestic: good intercity service provided on Peninsular Malaysia mainly by microwave radio relay; adequate intercity microwave radio relay network between Sabah and Sarawak via Brunei; domestic satellite system with 2 earth stations
international: country code - 60; submarine cables to India, Hong Kong, and Singapore; satellite earth stations - 2 Intelsat (1 Indian Ocean and 1 Pacific Ocean) (2001)
Radio broadcast stations: AM 35, FM 391, shortwave 15 (2001)
Radios: 10.9 million (1999)
Television broadcast stations: 1 (plus 15 high-power repeaters) (2001)
Televisions: 10.8 million (1999)
Internet country code: .my
Internet hosts: 107,971 (2003)

Internet Service Providers (ISPs): 7 (2000)
Internet users: 8,692,100 (2003)

TRANSPORTATION

Airports: 117 (2004 est.)
Airports - with paved runways: total: 37
over 3,047 m: 5
2,438 to 3,047 m: 7
1,524 to 2,437 m: 10
914 to 1,523 m: 8
under 914 m: 7 (2005 est.)
Airports - with unpaved runways:
total: 80
1,524 to 2,437 m: 1
914 to 1,523 m: 7
under 914 m: 72 (2005 est.)
Heliports: 1 (2005 est.)
Pipelines: condensate 279 km; gas 5,047 km; oil 1,841 km; refined products 114 km (2004)
Railways:
total: 1,890 km (207 km electrified)
standard gauge: 57 km 1.435-m gauge (57 km electrified)
narrow gauge: 1,833 km 1.000-m gauge (150 km electrified) (2004)
Roadways:
total: 65,877 km
paved: 51,318 km
unpaved: 14,559 km (2001)
Waterways: 7,200 km
note: Peninsular Malaysia 3,200 km, Sabah 1,500 km, Sarawak 2,500 km (2004)
Merchant marine:
total: 346 ships (1,000 GRT or over) 5,389,397 GRT/7,539,178 DWT
by type: bulk carrier 45, cargo 109, chemical tanker 38, container 47, liquefied gas 26, livestock carrier 1, passenger 1, passenger/cargo 6, petroleum tanker 62, roll on/roll off 6, vehicle carrier 5
foreign-owned: 77 (China 1, Hong Kong 12, Japan 3, Singapore 61)
registered in other countries: 59 (2005)
Ports and terminals: Bintulu, Johor, Labuan, Lahad Datu, Lumut, Miri, George Town (Penang), Port Kelang, Tanjung Pelepas

MILITARY

Military branches: Malaysian Army (Tentera Darat Malaysia), Royal Malaysian Navy (Tentera Laut Diraja Malaysia, TLDM), Royal Malaysian Air Force (Tentera Udara Diraja Malaysia, TUDM) (2005)
Military service age and obligation: 18 years of age for voluntary military service (2005)
Manpower available for military service:
males age 18-49: 5,584,231 (2005 est.)
Manpower fit for military service: *males age 18-49:* 4,574,854 (2005 est.)
Manpower reaching military service age annually: *males:* 244,418 (2005 est.)
Military expenditures - dollar figure: $1.69 billion (FY00 est.)
Military expenditures - percent of GDP: 2.03% (FY00)

TRANSNATIONAL ISSUES

Disputes - international: Malaysia has asserted sovereignty over the Spratly Islands together with China, Philippines, Taiwan, Vietnam, and possibly Brunei; while the 2002 "Declaration on the Conduct of Parties in the South China Sea" has eased tensions over the Spratly Islands, it is not the legally binding "code of conduct" sought by some parties; Malaysia was not party to the March 2005 joint accord among the national oil companies of China, the Philippines, and Vietnam on conducting marine seismic activities in the Spratly Islands; disputes continue over deliveries of fresh water to Singapore, Singapore's land reclamation, bridge construction, maritime boundaries, and Pedra Branca Island/Pulau Batu Putih - but parties agree to ICJ arbitration on island dispute within three years; ICJ awarded Ligitan and Sipadan islands, also claimed by Indonesia and Philippines, to Malaysia but left maritime boundary in the hydrocarbon-rich Celebes Sea in dispute, culminating in hostile confrontations in March 2005 over concessions to the Ambalat oil block; separatist violence in Thailand's predominantly Muslim southern provinces prompts measures to close and monitor border with Malaysia to stem terrorist activities; Philippines retains a now dormant claim to Malaysia's Sabah State in northern Borneo; in 2003, Brunei and Malaysia ceased gas and oil exploration in their disputed offshore and deepwater seabeds and negotiations have stalemated prompting consideration of international adjudication; Malaysia's land boundary with Brunei around Limbang is in dispute; piracy remains a problem in the Malacca Strait
Illicit drugs: transit point for some illicit drugs; drug trafficking prosecuted vigorously and carries severe penalties

MALDIVES

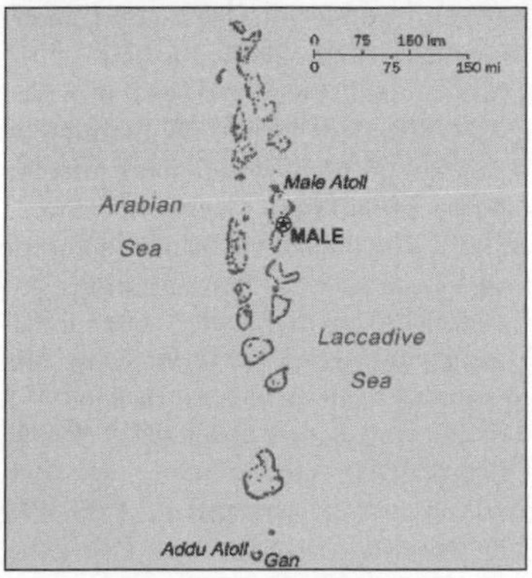

INTRODUCTION

Background: The Maldives was long a sultanate, first under Dutch and then under British protection. It became a republic in 1968, three years after independence. Since 1978, President Maumoon Abdul GAYOOM - currently in his sixth term in office - has dominated the islands' political scene. Following riots in the capital Male in August 2004, the president and his government have pledged to embark upon democratic reforms, including a more representative political system and expanded political freedoms. Tourism and fishing are being developed on the archipelago.

GEOGRAPHY

Location: Southern Asia, group of atolls in the Indian Ocean, south-southwest of India
Geographic coordinates: 3 15 N, 73 00 E
Map references: Asia
Area:
total: 300 sq km
land: 300 sq km
water: 0 sq km
Area - comparative: about 1.7 times the size of Washington, DC
Land boundaries: 0 km
Coastline: 644 km
Maritime claims: measured from claimed archipelagic straight baselines
territorial sea: 12 nm
contiguous zone: 24 nm
exclusive economic zone: 200 nm
Climate: tropical; hot, humid; dry, northeast monsoon (November to March); rainy, southwest monsoon (June to August)
Terrain: flat, with white sandy beaches
Elevation extremes:
lowest point: Indian Ocean 0 m
highest point: unnamed location on Wilingili island in the Addu Atoll 2.4m
Natural resources: fish

Land use:
arable land: 13.33%
permanent crops: 16.67%
other: 70% (2001)
Irrigated land: NA sq km
Natural hazards: low level of islands makes them very sensitive to sea level rise
Environment - current issues: depletion of freshwater aquifers threatens water supplies; global warming and sea level rise; coral reef bleaching
Environment - international agreements:
party to: Biodiversity, Climate Change, Climate Change-Kyoto Protocol, Hazardous Wastes, Law of the Sea, Ozone Layer Protection
signed, but not ratified: none of the selected agreements
Geography - note: 1,190 coral islands grouped into 26 atolls (200 inhabited islands, plus 80 islands with tourist resorts); archipelago with strategic location astride and along major sea lanes in Indian Ocean

PEOPLE

Population: 349,106 (July 2005 est.)
Age structure:
0-14 years: 43.9% (male 78,794/female 74,505)
15-64 years: 53% (male 94,488/female 90,624)
65 years and over: 3.1% (male 5,339/female 5,356) (2005 est.)
Median age:
total: 17.69 years
male: 17.58 years
female: 17.8 years (2005 est.)
Population growth rate: 2.82% (2005 est.)
Birth rate: 35.43 births/1,000 population (2005 est.)
Death rate: 7.24 deaths/1,000 population (2005 est.)
Net migration rate: 0 migrant(s)/1,000 population (2005 est.)
Sex ratio:
at birth: 1.05 male(s)/female
under 15 years: 1.06 male(s)/female
15-64 years: 1.04 male(s)/female
65 years and over: 1 male(s)/female
total population: 1.05 male(s)/female (2005 est.)
Infant mortality rate:
total: 56.52 deaths/1,000 live births
male: 55.63 deaths/1,000 live births
female: 57.45 deaths/1,000 live births (2005 est.)
Life expectancy at birth:
total population: 64.06 years
male: 62.76 years
female: 65.42 years (2005 est.)
Total fertility rate: 5.02 children born/woman (2005 est.)
HIV/AIDS - adult prevalence rate: 0.1% (2001 est.)
HIV/AIDS - people living with HIV/AIDS: less than 100 (2001 est.)
HIV/AIDS - deaths: NA
Nationality:
noun: Maldivian(s)
adjective: Maldivian
Ethnic groups: South Indians, Sinhalese, Arabs
Religions: Sunni Muslim
Languages: Maldivian Dhivehi (dialect of Sinhala, script derived from Arabic), English spoken by most government officials
Literacy:
definition: age 15 and over can read and write
total population: 97.2%
male: 97.1%
female: 97.3% (2003 est.)

GOVERNMENT

Country name:
conventional long form: Republic of Maldives
conventional short form: Maldives
local long form: Dhivehi Raajjeyge Jumhooriyyaa
local short form: Dhivehi Raajje
Government type: republic
Capital: Male
Administrative divisions: 19 atolls (atholhu, singular and plural) and the capital city*; Alifu, Baa, Dhaalu, Faafu, Gaafu Alifu, Gaafu Dhaalu, Gnaviyani, Haa Alifu, Haa Dhaalu, Kaafu, Laamu, Lhaviyani, Maale* (Male), Meemu, Noonu, Raa, Seenu, Shaviyani, Thaa, Vaavu
Independence: 26 July 1965 (from UK)
National holiday: Independence Day, 26 July (1965)
Constitution: adopted 1 January 1998
Legal system: based on Islamic law with admixtures of English common law primarily in commercial matters; has not accepted compulsory ICJ jurisdiction
Suffrage: 21 years of age; universal
Executive branch:
chief of state: President Maumoon Abdul GAYOOM (since 11 November 1978); note - the president is both the chief of state and head of government
head of government: President Maumoon Abdul GAYOOM (since 11 November 1978); note - the president is both the chief of state and head of government
cabinet: Cabinet of Ministers appointed by the president
elections: president nominated by the Majlis and then the nomination must be ratified by a national referendum (at least a 51% approval margin is required); president elected for a five-year term; election last held 17 October 2003 (next to be held NA 2008)
election results: President Maumoon Abdul GAYOOM reelected in referendum held 17 October 2003; percent of popular vote - Maumoon Abdul GAYOOM 90.3%
Legislative branch: unicameral People's Council or Majlis (50 seats; 42 elected by popular vote, 8 appointed by the president; members serve five-year terms)
elections: last held 22 January 2005 (next to be held NA 2010)
election results: percent of vote - NA%; seats - independents 50
Judicial branch: High Court
Political parties and leaders: political parties were allowed to register in June 2005; the first entrants are: Adhaalath (Justice) Party or AP [Abdul Majeed Abdul BARI]; Dhivehi Rayyithunge Party (Maldivian People's Party) or DRP [Maumoon Abdul GAYOOM]; Islamic Democratic Party or IDP [Omar NASEER]; Maldivian Democratic Party or MDP [Mohamed NASHEED]
Political pressure groups and leaders: various unregistered political parties
International organization participation: AsDB, C, CP, FAO, G-77, IBRD, ICAO, IDA, IDB, IFAD, IFC, IMF, IMO, Interpol, IOC, ITU, NAM, OIC, OPCW, SAARC, SACEP, UN, UNCTAD, UNESCO, UNIDO, UPU, WCO, WHO, WIPO, WMO, WToO, WTO
Diplomatic representation in the US:
chief of mission: Ambassador Dr. Mohamed LATHEEF
chancery: 800 2nd Avenue, Suite 400E, New York, NY 10017
telephone: [1] (212) 599-6195
FAX: [1] (212) 661-6405
Diplomatic representation from the US: the US does not have an embassy in Maldives; the US Ambassador to Sri Lanka is accredited to Maldives and makes periodic visits there
Flag description: red with a large green rectangle in the center bearing a vertical white crescent; the closed side of the crescent is on the hoist side of the flag

ECONOMY

Economy - overview: Tourism, Maldives' largest industry, accounts for 20% of GDP and more than 60% of the Maldives' foreign exchange receipts. Over 90% of government tax revenue comes from import duties and tourism-related taxes. Fishing is a second leading sector. The Maldivian Government began an economic reform program in 1989 initially by lifting import quotas and opening some exports to the private sector. Subsequently, it has liberalized regulations to allow more foreign investment. Agriculture and manufacturing continue to play a lesser role in the economy, constrained by the limited availability of cul-

tivable land and the shortage of domestic labor. Most staple foods must be imported. Industry, which consists mainly of garment production, boat building, and handicrafts, accounts for about 18% of GDP. Maldivian authorities worry about the impact of erosion and possible global warming on their low-lying country; 80% of the area is one meter or less above sea level. In late December 2004, a major tsunami left more than 100 dead, 12,000 displaced, and property damage exceeding $300 million.
GDP (purchasing power parity): $1.25 billion (2002 est.)
GDP (official exchange rate): NA
GDP - real growth rate: 2.3% (2002 est.)
GDP - per capita: purchasing power parity - $3,900 (2002 est.)
GDP - composition by sector:
agriculture: 20%
industry: 18%
services: 62% (2000 est.)
Labor force: 88,000 (2000)
Labor force - by occupation: agriculture 22%, industry 18%, services 60% (1995)
Unemployment rate: NEGL% (2003 est.)
Population below poverty line: NA
Household income or consumption by percentage share:
lowest 10%: NA
highest 10%: NA
Inflation rate (consumer prices): 1% (2002 est.)
Budget:
revenues: $224 million (excluding foreign grants)
expenditures: $282 million, including capital expenditures of $80 million (2002 est.)
Agriculture - products: coconuts, corn, sweet potatoes; fish
Industries: fish processing, tourism, shipping, boat building, coconut processing, garments, woven mats, rope, handicrafts, coral and sand mining
Industrial production growth rate: 4.4% (1996 est.)
Electricity - production: 135 million kWh (2003)
Electricity - production by source:
fossil fuel: 100%
hydro: 0%
nuclear: 0%
other: 0% (2001)
Electricity - consumption: 125.6 million kWh (2003)
Electricity - exports: 0 kWh (2003)
Electricity – imports: 0 kWh (2003)
Oil - production: 0 bbl/day (2003 est.)
Oil - consumption: 4,000 bbl/day (2003 est.)
Oil - exports: NA (2001)
Oil - imports: NA (2001)
Exports: $123 million f.o.b. (2004 est.)
Exports - partners: US 26.5%, Thailand 23.5%, Sri Lanka 12.3%, Japan 11.7%, UK 9.8%, Germany 4.9% (2004)
Imports: $645 million f.o.b. (2004 est.)
Imports - partners: Singapore 24.9%, Sri Lanka 10.6%, UAE 10.3%, India 10.2%, Malaysia 7.6%, Bahrain 5.4% (2004)
Debt - external: $281 million (2003 est.)
Economic aid - recipient: NA (1995)
Currency (code): rufiyaa (MVR)
Currency code: MVR
Exchange rates: rufiyaa per US dollar - NA (2005), 12.8 (2004), 12.8 (2003), 12.8 (2002), 12.24 (2001)
Fiscal year: calendar year

COMMUNICATIONS

Telephones - main lines in use: 28,700 (2002)
Telephones - mobile cellular: 41,900 (2002)
Telephone system:
general assessment: minimal domestic and international facilities
domestic: interatoll communication through microwave links; all inhabited islands are connected with telephone and fax service
international: country code - 960; satellite earth station - 3 Intelsat (Indian Ocean)
Radio broadcast stations: AM 1, FM 1, shortwave 1 (1998)
Radios: 35,000 (1999)
Television broadcast stations: 1 (1997)
Televisions: 10,000 (1999)
Internet country code: .mv
Internet hosts: 532 (2003)
Internet Service Providers (ISPs): 1 (2000)
Internet users: 15,000 (2002)

TRANSPORTATION

Airports: 5 (2004 est.)
Airports - with paved runways:
total: 2
over 3,047 m: 1
2,438 to 3,047 m: 1 (2005 est.)
Airports - with unpaved runways:
total: 3
914 to 1,523 m: 3 (2005 est.)
Roadways:
total: NA km
paved: NA km
unpaved: NA km
Merchant marine:
total: 16 ships (1,000 GRT or over) 57,118 GRT/72,831 DWT
by type: cargo 12, passenger/cargo 1, petroleum tanker 2, refrigerated cargo 1
registered in other countries: 1 (2005)
Ports and terminals: Male

MILITARY

Military branches: National Security Service includes Security Branch (ground forces), Air Element, Coast Guard
Military service age and obligation: 18 years of age (est.) (2004)
Manpower available for military service: *males age 18-49:* 71,774 (2005 est.)
Manpower fit for military service: *males age 18-49:* 56,687 (2005 est.)
Military expenditures - dollar figure: $41.1 million (2004)
Military expenditures - percent of GDP: 5.5% (2004)

TRANSNATIONAL ISSUES

Disputes - international: none
Refugees and internally displaced persons:
IDPs: 12,000 (26 December 2004 tsunami victims) (2005)

MALI

INTRODUCTION

Background: The Sudanese Republic and Senegal became independent of France in 1960 as the Mali Federation. When Senegal withdrew after only a few months, what formerly made up the Sudanese Republic was renamed Mali. Rule by dictatorship was brought to a close in 1991 by a coup that ushered in democratic government. President Alpha KONARE won Mali's first democratic presidential election in 1992 and was reelected in 1997. In keeping with Mali's two-term constitutional limit, KONARE stepped down in 2002 and was succeeded by Amadou TOURE.

GEOGRAPHY

Location: Western Africa, southwest of Algeria
Geographic coordinates: 17 00 N, 4 00 W
Map references: Africa
Area:
total: 1.24 million sq km
land: 1.22 million sq km
water: 20,000 sq km
Area - comparative: slightly less than twice the size of Texas
Land boundaries:
total: 7,243 km
border countries: Algeria 1,376 km, Burkina Faso 1,000 km, Guinea 858 km, Cote d'Ivoire 532 km, Mauritania 2,237 km, Niger 821 km, Senegal 419 km
Coastline: 0 km (landlocked)
Maritime claims: none (landlocked)
Climate: subtropical to arid; hot and dry

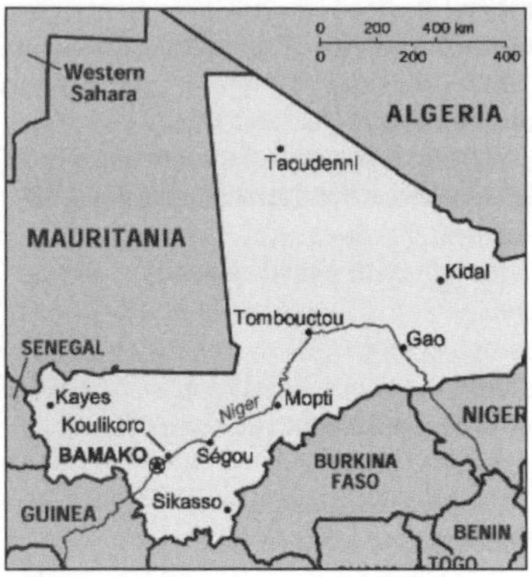

February to June; rainy, humid, and mild June to November; cool and dry November to February
Terrain: mostly flat to rolling northern plains covered by sand; savanna in south, rugged hills in northeast
Elevation extremes:
lowest point: Senegal River 23 m
highest point: Hombori Tondo 1,155 m
Natural resources: gold, phosphates, kaolin, salt, limestone, uranium, gypsum, granite, hydropower
note: bauxite, iron ore, manganese, tin, and copper deposits are known but not exploited
Land use:
arable land: 3.82%
permanent crops: 0.03%
other: 96.15% (2001)
Irrigated land: 1,380 sq km (1998 est.)
Natural hazards: hot, dust-laden harmattan haze common during dry seasons; recurring droughts; occasional Niger River flooding
Environment - current issues: deforestation; soil erosion; desertification; inadequate supplies of potable water; poaching
Environment - international agreements:
party to: Biodiversity, Climate Change, Climate Change-Kyoto Protocol, Desertification, Endangered Species, Hazardous Wastes, Law of the Sea, Ozone Layer Protection, Wetlands
signed, but not ratified: none of the selected agreements
Geography - note: landlocked; divided into three natural zones: the southern, cultivated Sudanese; the central, semiarid Sahelian; and the northern, arid Saharan

PEOPLE

Population: 12,291,529 (July 2005 est.)
Age structure:
0-14 years: 47.1% (male 2,910,944/female 2,876,010)
15-64 years: 50% (male 2,955,496/female 3,185,666)
65 years and over: 3% (male 165,867/female 197,546) (2005 est.)
Median age:
total: 16.35 years
male: 15.79 years
female: 16.92 years (2005 est.)
Population growth rate: 2.74% (2005 est.)
Birth rate: 46.77 births/1,000 population (2005 est.)
Death rate: 19.05 deaths/1,000 population (2005 est.)
Net migration rate: -0.33 migrant(s)/1,000 population (2005 est.)
Sex ratio:
at birth: 1.03 male(s)/female
under 15 years: 1.01 male(s)/female
15-64 years: 0.93 male(s)/female
65 years and over: 0.84 male(s)/female
total population: 0.96 male(s)/female (2005 est.)
Infant mortality rate
total: 116.79 deaths/1,000 live births
male: 123.32 deaths/1,000 live births
female: 110.07 deaths/1,000 live births (2005 est.)
Life expectancy at birth:
total population: 48.64 years
male: 46.68 years
female: 50.66 years (2005 est.)
Total fertility rate: 6.5 children born/woman (2005 est.)
HIV/AIDS - adult prevalence rate: 1.9% (2003 est.)
HIV/AIDS - people living with HIV/AIDS: 140,000 (2003 est.)
HIV/AIDS - deaths: 12,000 (2003 est.)
Major infectious diseases:
degree of risk: very high
food or waterborne diseases: bacterial and protozoal diarrhea, hepatitis A, and typhoid fever
vectorborne disease: malaria is a high risk in some locations
water contact disease: schistosomiasis
respiratory disease: meningococcal meningitis (2004)
Nationality:
noun: Malian(s)
adjective: Malian
Ethnic groups: Mande 50% (Bambara, Malinke, Soninke), Peul 17%, Voltaic 12%, Songhai 6%, Tuareg and Moor 10%, other 5%
Religions: Muslim 90%, indigenous beliefs 9%, Christian 1%
Languages: French (official), Bambara 80%, numerous African languages
Literacy:
definition: age 15 and over can read and write
total population: 46.4%
male: 53.5%
female: 39.6% (2003 est.)

GOVERNMENT

Country name:
conventional long form: Republic of Mali
conventional short form: Mali
local long form: Republique de Mali
local short form: Mali
former: French Sudan and Sudanese Republic
Government type: republic
Capital: Bamako
Administrative divisions: 8 regions (regions, singular - region); Gao, Kayes, Kidal, Koulikoro, Mopti, Segou, Sikasso, Tombouctou
Independence: 22 September 1960 (from France)
National holiday: Independence Day, 22 September (1960)
Constitution: adopted 12 January 1992
Legal system: based on French civil law system and customary law; judicial review of legislative acts in Constitutional Court (which was formally established on 9 March 1994); has not accepted compulsory ICJ jurisdiction
Suffrage: 18 years of age; universal
Executive branch:
chief of state: President Amadou Toumani TOURE (since 8 June 2002)
head of government: Prime Minister Ousmane Issoufi MAIGA (since 30 April 2004)
cabinet: Council of Ministers appointed by the prime minister
elections: president elected by popular vote for a five-year term (two-term limit); election last held 12 May 2002 (next to be held May 2007); prime minister appointed by the president
election results: Amadou Toumani TOURE elected president; percent of vote - Amadou Toumani TOURE 64.4%, Soumaila CISSE 35.6%
Legislative branch: unicameral National Assembly or Assemblee Nationale (147 seats; members are elected by popular vote to serve five-year terms)
elections: last held 14 July and 28 July 2002 (next to be held July 2007)
election results: percent of vote by party - NA%; seats by party – Hope 2002 coalition 66, ADEMA 51, other 30
Judicial branch: Supreme Court or Cour Supreme
Political parties and leaders: Alliance for Democracy or ADEMA [Diounconda TRAORE, party chairman]; National Congress for Democratic Initiative or CNID [Mountaga TALL, chairman]; Party for Democracy and Progress or PDP [Me Idrissa TRAORE]; Party for National Renewal or PARENA [Tiebile DRAME, secretary general]; Patriotic Movement for Renewal or MPR [Choguel MAIGA]; Rally for Mali or RPM [Ibrahim Boubacar KEITA, chairman]; Sudanese Union/African Democratic Rally or US/RDA

[Mamadou Bamou TOURE, secretary general]; Union for Democracy and Development or UDD [Moussa Balla COULIBALY]; Union for Republic and Democracy or URD [Soumaila CISSE]
Political pressure groups and leaders: Patriotic Movement of the Ghanda Koye or MPGK; United Movement and Fronts of Azawad or MFUA
International organization participation: ACCT, ACP, AfDB, AU, CEMAC, ECOWAS, FAO, FZ, G-77, IAEA, IBRD, ICAO, ICCt, ICFTU, ICRM, IDA, IDB, IFAD, IFC, IFRCS, ILO, IMF, Interpol, IOC, IOM, ISO (correspondent), ITU, MIGA, MONUC, NAM, OIC, ONUB, OPCW, UN, UNCTAD, UNESCO, UNIDO, UNMIL, UPU, WADB (regional), WAEMU, WCO, WFTU, WHO, WIPO, WMO, WToO, WTO
Diplomatic representation in the US:
chief of mission: Ambassador Abdoulaye DIOP
chancery: 2130 R Street NW, Washington, DC 20008
telephone: [1] (202) 332-2249, 939-8950
FAX: [1] (202) 332-6603
Diplomatic representation from the US:
chief of mission: Ambassador Vicki HUDDLESTONE
embassy: Rue Rochester NY and Rue Mohamed V, Bamako
mailing address: B. P. 34, Bamako
telephone: [223] (2) 223-833
FAX: [223] (2) 223-712
Flag description: three equal vertical bands of green (hoist side), yellow, and red; uses the popular pan-African colors of Ethiopia

ECONOMY

Economy - overview: Mali is among the poorest countries in the world, with 65% of its land area desert or semidesert and with a highly unequal distribution of income. Economic activity is largely confined to the riverine area irrigated by the Niger. About 10% of the population is nomadic and some 80% of the labor force is engaged in farming and fishing. Industrial activity is concentrated on processing farm commodities. Mali is heavily dependent on foreign aid and vulnerable to fluctuations in world prices for cotton, its main export, along with gold. The government has continued its successful implementation of an IMF-recommended structural adjustment program that is helping the economy grow, diversify, and attract foreign investment. Mali's adherence to economic reform and the 50% devaluation of the CFA franc in January 1994 have pushed up economic growth to a sturdy 5% average in 1996-2005. Worker remittances and external trade routes for the landlocked country have been jeopardized by continued unrest in neighboring Cote d'Ivoire.
GDP (purchasing power parity): $11.83 billion (2005 est.)
GDP (official exchange rate): $5.569 billion (2005 est.)
GDP - real growth rate: 5.5% (2005 est.)
GDP - per capita: purchasing power parity - $1,000 (2005 est.)
GDP - composition by sector:
agriculture: 45%
industry: 17%
services: 38% (2001 est.)
Labor force: 3.93 million (2001 est.)
Labor force - by occupation: agriculture and fishing 80% (2001 est.)
Unemployment rate: 14.6% NA (2001 est.)
Population below poverty line: 64% average; 30% of the total population living in urban areas; 70% of the total population living in rural areas) (2001 est.)
Household income or consumption by percentage share:
lowest 10%: 1.8%
highest 10%: 40.4% (1994)
Distribution of family income - Gini index: 50.5 (1994)
Inflation rate (consumer prices): 4.5% (2002 est.)
Budget:
revenues: $764 million
expenditures: $828 million, including capital expenditures of NA (2002 est.)
Agriculture - products: cotton, millet, rice, corn, vegetables, peanuts; cattle, sheep, goats
Industries: food processing; construction; phosphate and gold mining
Industrial production growth rate: NA (FY96/97)
Electricity - production: 820 million kWh (2003)
Electricity - production by source:
fossil fuel: 41.7%
hydro: 58.3%
nuclear: 0%
other: 0% (2001)
Electricity - consumption: 762.6 million kWh (2003)
Electricity - exports: 0 kWh; note - recent hydropower developments may be providing electricity to Senegal and Mauritania (2003)
Electricity - imports: 0 kWh (2003)
Oil - production: 0 bbl/day (2003 est.)
Oil - consumption: 4,250 bbl/day (2003 est.)
Oil - exports: NA (2001)
Oil - imports: NA (2001)
Exports: $323 million f.o.b. (2004 est.)
Exports - partners: China 31.2%, Pakistan 9.9%, Thailand 6.9%, Italy 6.9%, Germany 5.1%, India 4.7%, Bangladesh 4.4% (2004)
Imports: $1.858 billion f.o.b. (2004 est.)
Imports - partners: France 14.5%, Senegal 9.8%, Cote d"Ivoire 7.6% (2004)
Debt - external: $2.8 billion (2002)
Economic aid - recipient: $472.1 million (2002)
Currency (code): Communaute Financiere Africaine franc (XOF); note - responsible authority is the Central Bank of the West African States
Currency code: XOF
Exchange rates: Communaute Financiere Africaine francs (XOF) per US dollar - 528.28 (2005), 528.29 (2004), 581.2 (2003), 696.99 (2002), 733.04 (2001)
Fiscal year: calendar year

COMMUNICATIONS

Telephones - main lines in use: 56,600 (2002)
Telephones - mobile cellular: 250,000 (2003)
Telephone system:
general assessment: domestic system unreliable but improving; provides only minimal service
domestic: network consists of microwave radio relay, open-wire, and radiotelephone communications stations; expansion of microwave radio relay in progress
international: country code - 223; satellite earth stations - 2 Intelsat (1 Atlantic Ocean and 1 Indian Ocean)
Radio broadcast stations: AM 1, FM 28, shortwave 1
note: the shortwave station in Bamako has seven frequencies and five transmitters and relays broadcasts for China Radio International (2001)
Radios: 570,000 (1997)
Television broadcast stations: 1 (plus repeaters) (2001)
Televisions: 45,000 (1997)
Internet country code: .ml
Internet hosts: 187 (2003)
Internet Service Providers (ISPs): 13 (2001)
Internet users: 25,000 (2002)

TRANSPORTATION

Airports: 28 (2004 est.)
Airports - with paved runways:
total: 9
2,438 to 3,047 m: 4
1,524 to 2,437 m: 4
914 to 1,523 m: 1 (2005 est.)
Airports - with unpaved runways:
total: 19
2,438 to 3,047 m: 1
1,524 to 2,437 m: 5
914 to 1,523 m: 5
under 914 m: 8 (2005 est.)
Railways:
total: 729 km
narrow gauge: 729 km 1.000-m gauge (2004)

Roadways:
total: 15,100 km
paved: 1,827 km
unpaved: 13,273 km (1999 est.)
Waterways: 1,815 km (2004)
Ports and terminals: Koulikoro

MILITARY

Military branches: Army, Air Force, National Guard
Military service age and obligation: 18 years of age for compulsory and voluntary military service; conscript service obligation - 2 years (2004)
Manpower available for military service:
males age 18-49: 2,206,728 (2005 est.)
Manpower fit for military service: *males age 18-49:* 1,231,930 (2005 est.)
Military expenditures - dollar figure: $22.4 million (2004)
Military expenditures - percent of GDP: 0.4% (2004)

TRANSNATIONAL ISSUES

Disputes - international: none

MALTA

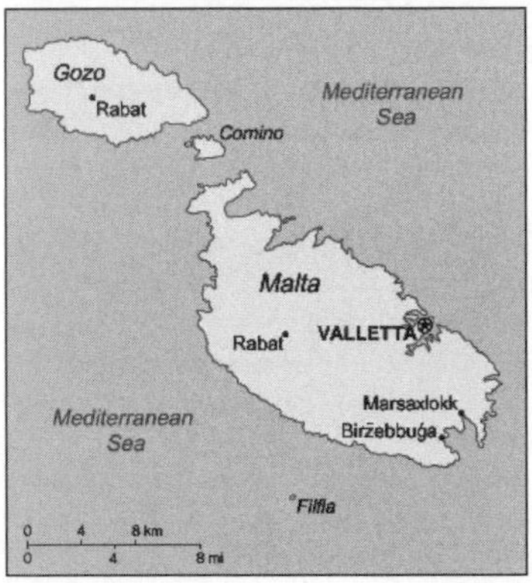

INTRODUCTION

Background: Great Britain formally acquired possession of Malta in 1814. The island staunchly supported the UK through both World Wars and remained in the Commonwealth when it became independent in 1964. A decade later Malta became a republic. Since about the mid-1980s, the island has transformed itself into a freight transshipment point, a financial center, and a tourist destination. Malta became an EU member in May of 2004.

GEOGRAPHY

Location: Southern Europe, islands in the Mediterranean Sea, south of Sicily (Italy)
Geographic coordinates: 35 50 N, 14 35 E
Map references: Europe
Area:
total: 316 sq km
land: 316 sq km
water: 0 sq km
Area - comparative: slightly less than twice the size of Washington, DC
Land boundaries: 0 km
Coastline:196.8 km (does not include 56.01 km for the island of Gozo)
Maritime claims:
territorial sea: 12 nm
contiguous zone: 24 nm
continental shelf: 200-m depth or to the depth of exploitation
exclusive fishing zone: 25 nm
Climate: Mediterranean with mild, rainy winters and hot, dry summers
Terrain: mostly low, rocky, flat to dissected plains; many coastal cliffs
Elevation extremes:
lowest point: Mediterranean Sea 0 m
highest point: Ta'Dmejrek 253 m (near Dingli)
Natural resources: limestone, salt, arable land
Land use:
arable land: 28.13%
permanent crops: 3.13%
other: 68.74% (2001)
Irrigated land: 20 sq km (1998 est.)
Natural hazards: NA
Environment - current issues: very limited natural fresh water resources; increasing reliance on desalination
Environment - international agreements:
party to: Air Pollution, Biodiversity, Climate Change, Climate Change-Kyoto Protocol, Desertification, Endangered Species, Hazardous Wastes, Law of the Sea, Marine Dumping, Ozone Layer Protection, Ship Pollution, Wetlands
signed, but not ratified: none of the selected agreements
Geography - note: the country comprises an archipelago, with only the three largest islands (Malta, Ghawdex or Gozo, and Kemmuna or Comino) being inhabited; numerous bays provide good harbors; Malta and Tunisia are discussing the commercial exploitation of the continental shelf between their countries, particularly for oil exploration

PEOPLE

Population: 398,534 (July 2005 est.)
Age structure:
0-14 years: 17.6% (male 36,056/female 34,097)
15-64 years: 68.8% (male 138,537/female 135,666)
65 years and over: 13.6% (male 23,184/female 30,994) (2005 est.)
Median age:
total: 38.36 years
male: 36.91 years
female: 39.84 years (2005 est.)
Population growth rate: 0.42% (2005 est.)
Birth rate: 10.17 births/1,000 population (2005 est.)
Death rate: 8 deaths/1,000 population (2005 est.)
Net migration rate: 2.06 migrant(s)/1,000 population (2005 est.)
Sex ratio:
at birth: 1.06 male(s)/female
under 15 years: 1.06 male(s)/female
15-64 years: 1.02 male(s)/female
65 years and over: 0.75 male(s)/female
total population: 0.99 male(s)/female (2005 est.)
Infant mortality rate:
total: 3.89 deaths/1,000 live births
male: 4.38 deaths/1,000 live births
female: 3.37 deaths/1,000 live births (2005 est.)
Life expectancy at birth:
total population: 78.86 years
male: 76.7 years
female: 81.15 years (2005 est.)
Total fertility rate: 1.5 children born/woman (2005 est.)
HIV/AIDS - adult prevalence rate: 0.2% (2001 est.)
HIV/AIDS - people living with HIV/AIDS: less than 500 (2003 est.)
HIV/AIDS - deaths: less than 100 (2003 est.)
Nationality:
noun: Maltese (singular and plural)
adjective: Maltese
Ethnic groups: Maltese (descendants of ancient Carthaginians and Phoenicians, with strong elements of Italian and other Mediterranean stock)
Religions: Roman Catholic 98%
Languages: Maltese (official), English (official)
Literacy:
definition: age 10 and over can read and write
total population: 92.8%
male: 92%
female: 93.6% (2003 est.)

GOVERNMENT

Country name:
conventional long form: Republic of Malta
conventional short form: Malta
local long form: Repubblika ta' Malta
local short form: Malta
Government type: republic
Capital: Valletta

Administrative divisions: none (administered directly from Valletta); note - Local Councils carry out administrative orders
Independence: 21 September 1964 (from UK)
National holiday: Independence Day, 21 September (1964)
Constitution: 1964 constitution; amended many times
Legal system: based on English common law and Roman civil law; accepts compulsory ICJ jurisdiction, with reservations
Suffrage: 18 years of age; universal
Executive branch:
chief of state: President Eddie FENECH ADAMI (since 4 April 2004)
head of government: Prime Minister Lawrence GONZI (since 23 March 2004)
cabinet: Cabinet appointed by the president on the advice of the prime minister
elections: president elected by the House of Representatives for a five-year term; election last held 29 March 2004 (next to be held by April 2009); following legislative elections, the leader of the majority party or leader of a majority coalition is usually appointed prime minister by the president for a five-year term; the deputy prime minister is appointed by the president on the advice of the prime minister
election results: Eddie FENECH ADAMI elected president; percent of House of Representatives vote - 33 out of 65 votes
Legislative branch: unicameral House of Representatives (usually 65 seats; note - additional seats are given to the party with the largest popular vote to ensure a legislative majority; members are elected by popular vote on the basis of proportional representation to serve five-year terms)
elections: last held 12 April 2003 (next to be held by April 2008)
election results: percent of vote by party - PN 51.7%, MLP 47.6%, AD 0.7%; seats by party - PN 34, MLP 31
Judicial branch: Constitutional Court; Court of Appeal; judges for both courts are appointed by the president on the advice of the prime minister
Political parties and leaders: Alternativa Demokratika/Alliance for Social Justice or AD [Harry VASSALLO]; Malta Labor Party or MLP [Alfred SANT]; Nationalist Party or PN [Lawrence GONZI]
Political pressure groups and leaders: NA
International organization participation: Australia Group, C, CE, EBRD, EIB, EU (new member), FAO, IAEA, IBRD, ICAO, ICCt, ICFTU, ICRM, IFAD, IFC, IFRCS, ILO, IMF, IMO, Interpol, IOC, IOM, ISO, ITU, MIGA, NAM, NSG, OPCW, OSCE, PCA, UN, UNCTAD, UNESCO, UNIDO, UPU, WCL, WCO, WHO, WIPO, WMO, WToO, WTO
Diplomatic representation in the US:
chief of mission: Ambassador John LOWELL
chancery: 2017 Connecticut Avenue NW, Washington, DC 20008
telephone: [1] (202) 462-3611, 3612
FAX: [1] (202) 387-5470
consulate(s): New York
Diplomatic representation from the US:
chief of mission: Ambassador Molly BORDONARO
embassy: 3rd Floor, Development House, Saint Anne Street, Floriana, Malta VLT 01
mailing address: P. O. Box 535, Valletta, Malta, CMR01
telephone: [356] 2561 4000
FAX: [356] 21 243229
Flag description: two equal vertical bands of white (hoist side) and red; in the upper hoist-side corner is a representation of the George Cross, edged in red

ECONOMY

Economy - overview: Major resources are limestone, a favorable geographic location, and a productive labor force. Malta produces only about 20% of its food needs, has limited fresh water supplies, and has no domestic energy sources. The economy is dependent on foreign trade, manufacturing (especially electronics and textiles), and tourism. Continued sluggishness in the European economy is holding back exports, tourism, and overall growth.
GDP (purchasing power parity): $7.485 billion (2005 est.)
GDP (official exchange rate): $5.027 billion (2005 est.)
GDP - real growth rate: 1.4% (2005 est.)
GDP - per capita: purchasing power parity - $18,800 (2005 est.)
GDP - composition by sector:
agriculture: 3%
industry: 23%
services: 74% (2003 est.)
Labor force:160,000 (2002 est.)
Labor force - by occupation: agriculture 5%, industry 24%, services 71% (1999 est.)
Unemployment rate: 7% (2003 est.)
Population below poverty line: NA
Household income or consumption by percentage share:
lowest 10%: NA%
highest 10%: NA%
Inflation rate (consumer prices): 2.8% (2005 est.)
Investment (gross fixed): 26.1% of GDP (2005 est.)
Budget:
revenues: $2.503 billion
expenditures: $2.703 billion, including capital expenditures of NA (2005 est.)
Agriculture - products: potatoes, cauliflower, grapes, wheat, barley, tomatoes, citrus, cut flowers, green peppers; pork, milk, poultry, eggs
Industries: tourism; electronics, ship building and repair, construction; food and beverages, textiles, footwear, clothing, tobacco
Industrial production growth rate: NA%
Electricity - production: 2.082 billion kWh (2003)
Electricity - production by source:
fossil fuel: 100%
hydro: 0%
nuclear: 0%
other: 0% (2001)
Electricity - consumption: 1.936 billion kWh (2003)
Electricity - exports: 0 kWh (2003)
Electricity - imports: 0 kWh (2003)
Oil - production: 0 bbl/day (2003 est.)
Oil - consumption: 18,000 bbl/day (2003 est.)
Oil - exports: NA (2001)
Oil - imports: NA (2001)
Current account balance: $-593 million (2005 est.)
Exports: $2.744 billion f.o.b. (2005 est.)
Exports - partners: US 15.7%, France 15.5%, Singapore 14.5%, UK 11.2%, Germany 10.8% (2004)
Imports: $3.859 billion f.o.b. (2005 est.)
Imports - partners: Italy 25.4%, France 13.1%, UK 12%, Germany 8.9%, US 5.2%, Singapore 4.1% (2004)
Reserves of foreign exchange and gold: $3.42 billion (2005 est.)
Debt - external: $130 million (1997)
Economic aid - recipient: NA
Currency (code): Maltese lira (MTL)
Currency code: MTL
Exchange rates: Maltese liri per US dollar - 0.37 (2005), 0.34436 (2004), 0.37725 (2003), 0.43365 (2002), 0.45007 (2001)
Fiscal year: 1 April - 31 March

COMMUNICATIONS

Telephones - main lines in use: 208,300 (2003)
Telephones - mobile cellular: 290,000 (2003)
Telephone system:
general assessment: automatic system satisfies normal requirements
domestic: submarine cable and microwave radio relay between islands
international: country code - 356; 2 submarine cables; satellite earth station - 1 Intelsat (Atlantic Ocean)
Radio broadcast stations: AM 1, FM 18, shortwave 6 (1999)
Radios: 255,000 (1997)
Television broadcast stations: 6 (2000)
Televisions: 280,000 (1997)
Internet country code: .mt
Internet hosts: 7,156 (2004)
Internet Service Providers (ISPs): 6 (2002)
Internet users: 120,000 (2002)

TRANSPORTATION

Airports: 1 (2004 est.)
Airports - with paved runways:
total: 1
over 3,047 m: 1 (2005 est.)
Roadways:
total: 2,222 km
paved: 2,000 km
unpaved: 222 km (2002)
Merchant marine:
total: 1,140 ships (1,000 GRT or over) 25,102,401 GRT/41,176,791 DWT
by type: barge carrier 1, bulk carrier 438, cargo 303, chemical tanker 70, combination ore/oil 2, container 54, liquefied gas 8, livestock carrier 1, passenger 5, passenger/cargo 13, petroleum tanker 162, refrigerated cargo 43, roll on/roll off 26, specialized tanker 1, vehicle carrier 13
foreign-owned: 1,080 (Austria 3, Azerbaijan 1, Bangladesh 3, Belgium 12, British 1, Bulgaria 18, Canada 9, China 15, Croatia 10, Cyprus 2, Czech Republic 2, Estonia 2, Finland 1, France 5, Germany 51, Greece 527, Hong Kong 1, Iceland 7, Iran 4, Israel 26, Italy 17, Japan 2, Latvia 30, Lebanon 6, Madagascar 1, Monaco 3, Netherlands 3, Norway 42, Pakistan 2, Poland 24, Portugal 4, Romania 5, Russia 64, Slovenia 3, South Korea 4, Sweden 3, Switzerland 32, Syria 6, Taiwan 1, Turkey 87, Ukraine 25, UAE 5, United Kingdom 8, United States 3)
registered in other countries: 3 (2005)
Ports and terminals: Marsaxlokk, Valletta

MILITARY

Military branches: Armed Forces of Malta (AFM; includes air and maritime elements) (2005)
Military service age and obligation: 18 years of age for voluntary military service; no conscription (2001)
Manpower available for military service: *males age 18-49:* 90,651 (2005 est.)
Manpower fit for military service: *males age 18-49:* 74,525 (2005 est.)
Military expenditures - dollar figure: $31.1 million (2004)
Military expenditures - percent of GDP: 0.7% (2004)

TRANSNATIONAL ISSUES

Disputes - international: none
Illicit drugs: minor transshipment point for hashish from North Africa to Western Europe

MARSHALL ISLANDS

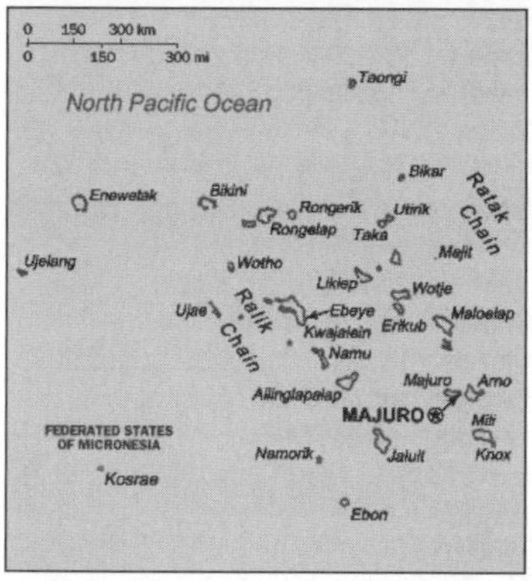

INTRODUCTION

Background: After almost four decades under US administration as the easternmost part of the UN Trust Territory of the Pacific Islands, the Marshall Islands attained independence in 1986 under a Compact of Free Association. Compensation claims continue as a result of US nuclear testing on some of the atolls between 1947 and 1962. The Marshall Islands hosts the US Army Kwajalein Atoll (USAKA) Reagan Missile Test Site, a key installation in the US missile defense network.

GEOGRAPHY

Location: Oceania, group of atolls and reefs in the North Pacific Ocean, about one-half of the way from Hawaii to Australia
Geographic coordinates: 9 00 N, 168 00 E
Map references: Oceania
Area:
total: 181.3 sq km
land: 181.3 sq km
water: 0 sq km
note: includes the atolls of Bikini, Enewetak, Kwajalein, Majuro, Rongelap, and Utirik
Area - comparative: about the size of Washington, DC
Land boundaries: 0 km
Coastline: 370.4 km
Maritime claims:
territorial sea: 12 nm
contiguous zone: 24 nm
exclusive economic zone: 200 nm
Climate: tropical; hot and humid; wet season from May to November; islands border typhoon belt
Terrain: low coral limestone and sand islands
Elevation extremes:
lowest point: Pacific Ocean 0 m
highest point: unnamed location on Likiep 10 m
Natural resources: coconut products, marine products, deep seabed minerals
Land use:
arable land: 16.67%
permanent crops: 38.89%
other: 44.44% (2001)
Irrigated land: 0 sq km
Natural hazards: infrequent typhoons
Environment - current issues: inadequate supplies of potable water; pollution of Majuro lagoon from household waste and discharges from fishing vessels
Environment - international agreements:
party to: Biodiversity, Climate Change, Climate Change-Kyoto Protocol, Desertification, Hazardous Wastes, Law of the Sea, Ozone Layer Protection, Ship Pollution
signed, but not ratified: none of the selected agreements
Geography - note: two archipelagic island chains of 30 atolls and 1,152 islands; Bikini and Enewetak are former US nuclear test sites; Kwajalein, the famous World War II battleground, is now used as a US missile test range

PEOPLE

Population: 59,071 (July 2005 est.)
Age structure:
0-14 years: 38.2% (male 11,488/female 11,071)
15-64 years: 59.1% (male 17,887/female 17,023)
65 years and over: 2.7% (male 771/female 831) (2005 est.)
Median age:
total: 19.95 years
male: 19.98 years
female: 19.92 years (2005 est.)
Population growth rate: 2.27% (2005 est.)
Birth rate: 33.52 births/1,000 population (2005 est.)
Death rate: 4.88 deaths/1,000 population (2005 est.)
Net migration rate: -5.91 migrant(s)/1,000 population (2005 est.)
Sex ratio:
at birth: 1.05 male(s)/female
under 15 years: 1.04 male(s)/female
15-64 years: 1.05 male(s)/female
65 years and over: 0.93 male(s)/female
total population: 1.04 male(s)/female (2005 est.)
Infant mortality rate:
total: 29.45 deaths/1,000 live births
male: 33.05 deaths/1,000 live births
female: 25.67 deaths/1,000 live births (2005 est.)

Life expectancy at birth:
total population: 70.01 years
male: 68.05 years
female: 72.06 years (2005 est.)
Total fertility rate: 3.93 children born/woman (2005 est.)
HIV/AIDS - adult prevalence rate: NA
HIV/AIDS - people living with HIV/AIDS: NA
HIV/AIDS - deaths: NA
Nationality:
noun: Marshallese (singular and plural)
adjective: Marshallese
Ethnic groups: Micronesian
Religions: Protestant 54.8%, Assembly of God 25.8%, Roman Catholic 8.4%, Bukot nan Jesus 2.8%, Mormon 2.1%, other Christian 3.6%, other 1%, none 1.5% (1999 census)
Languages: Marshallese 98.2%, other languages 1.8% (1999 census) note: English widely spoken as a second language; both Marshallese and English are official languages
Literacy:
definition: age 15 and over can read and write
total population: 93.7%
male: 93.6%
female: 93.7% (1999)

GOVERNMENT

Country name:
conventional long form: Republic of the Marshall Islands
conventional short form: Marshall Islands
former: Marshall Islands District (Trust Territory of the Pacific Islands)
Government type: constitutional government in free association with the US; the Compact of Free Association entered into force 21 October 1986 and the Amended Compact entered into force in May 2004
Capital: Majuro
Administrative divisions: 33 municipalities; Ailinginae, Ailinglaplap, Ailuk, Arno, Aur, Bikar, Bikini, Bokak, Ebon, Enewetak, Erikub, Jabat, Jaluit, Jemo, Kili, Kwajalein, Lae, Lib, Likiep, Majuro, Maloelap, Mejit, Mili, Namorik, Namu, Rongelap, Rongrik, Toke, Ujae, Ujelang, Utirik, Wotho, Wotje
Independence: 21 October 1986 (from the US-administered UN trusteeship)
National holiday: Constitution Day, 1 May (1979)
Constitution: 1 May 1979
Legal system: based on adapted Trust Territory laws, acts of the legislature, municipal, common, and customary laws
Suffrage: 18 years of age; universal
Executive branch:
chief of state: President Kessai Hesa NOTE (since 5 January 2004); note - the president is both the chief of state and head of government
head of government: President Kessai Hesa NOTE (since 5 January 2004); note - the president is both the chief of state and head of government
cabinet: Cabinet selected by the president from among the members of Parliament
elections: president elected by Parliament from among its own members for a four-year term; election last held 17 November 2003 (next to be held November 2007)
election results: Kessai Hesa NOTE elected president; percent of Parliament vote - 100%
Legislative branch: unicameral Parliament or Nitijela (33 seats; members elected by popular vote to serve four-year terms)
elections: last held 17 November 2003 (next to be held not later than November 2007)
election results: percent of vote by party - NA%; seats by party – NA note: the Council of Chiefs is a 12-member body that advises on matters affecting customary law and practice
Judicial branch: Supreme Court; High Court
Political parties and leaders: traditionally there have been no formally organized political parties; what has existed more closely resembles factions or interest groups because they do not have party headquarters, formal platforms, or party structures; the following two "groupings" have competed in legislative balloting in recent years - Kabua Party [Imata KABUA] and United Democratic Party or UDP [Litokwa TOMEING]
Political pressure groups and leaders: NA
International organization participation: ACP, AsDB, FAO, G-77, IAEA, IBRD, ICAO, ICCt, IDA, IFC, IMF, IMO, Interpol, ITU, OPCW, PIF, Sparteca, SPC, UN, UNCTAD, UNESCO, WHO
Diplomatic representation in the US:
chief of mission: Ambassador Banny DE BRUM
chancery: 2433 Massachusetts Avenue NW, Washington, DC 20008
telephone: [1] (202) 234-5414
FAX: [1] (202) 232-3236
consulate(s) general: Honolulu
Diplomatic representation from the US:
chief of mission: Ambassador Greta N. MORRIS
embassy: Oceanside, Mejen Weto, Long Island, Majuro
mailing address: P. O. Box 1379, Majuro, Republic of the Marshall Islands 96960-1379
telephone: [692] 247-4011
FAX: [692] 247-4012
Flag description: blue with two stripes radiating from the lower hoist-side corner - orange (top) and white; there is a white star with four large rays and 20 small rays on the hoist side above the two stripes

ECONOMY

Economy - overview: US Government assistance is the mainstay of this tiny island economy. Agricultural production, primarily subsistence, is concentrated on small farms; the most important commercial crops are coconuts and breadfruit. Small-scale industry is limited to handicrafts, tuna processing, and copra. The tourist industry, now a small source of foreign exchange employing less than 10% of the labor force, remains the best hope for future added income. The islands have few natural resources, and imports far exceed exports. Under the terms of the Amended Compact of Free Association, the US will provide millions of dollars per year to the Marshall Islands (RMI) through 2023, at which time a Trust Fund made up of US and RMI contributions will begin perpetual annual payouts. Government downsizing, drought, a drop in construction, the decline in tourism and foreign investment due to the Asian financial difficulties, and less income from the renewal of fishing vessel licenses have held GDP growth to an average of 1% over the past decade.
GDP (purchasing power parity): $115 million (2001 est.)
GDP (official exchange rate): NA
GDP - real growth rate: 1% (2001 est.)
GDP - per capita: purchasing power parity - $1,600 (2001 est.)
GDP - composition by sector:
agriculture: 14%
industry: 16%
services: 70% (2000 est.)
Labor force: 28,700 (1996 est.)
Labor force - by occupation: agriculture 21.4%, industry 20.9%, services 57.7%
Unemployment rate: 30.9% (1999 est.)
Population below poverty line: NA
Household income or consumption by percentage share:
lowest 10%: NA
highest 10%: NA
Inflation rate (consumer prices): 2% (2001 est.)
Budget:
revenues: $42 million
expenditures: $40 million, including capital expenditures of NA (1999)
Agriculture - products: coconuts, tomatoes, melons, taro, breadfruit, fruits; pigs, chickens
Industries: copra, tuna processing, tourism, craft items from shell, wood, and pearls

Industrial production growth rate: NA
Electricity - production by source:
fossil fuel: 99%
hydro: 0%
nuclear: 0%
other: 1% (solar)
Exports: $9 million f.o.b. (2000)
Exports - partners: US, Japan, Australia, China (2004)
Imports: $54 million f.o.b. (2000)
Imports - partners: US, Japan, Australia, NZ, Singapore, Fiji, China, Philippines (2004)
Debt - external: $86.5 million (FY99/00 est.)
Economic aid — recipient: more than $1 billion from the US, 1986-2002
Currency (code): US dollar (USD)
Currency code: USD
Exchange rates: the US dollar is the legal tender
Fiscal year: 1 October - 30 September

COMMUNICATIONS

Telephones - main lines in use: 4,500 (2003)
Telephones - mobile cellular: 600 (2002)
Telephone system:
general assessment: digital switching equipment; modern services include telex, cellular, internet, international calling, caller ID, and leased data circuits
domestic: Majuro Atoll and Ebeye and Kwajalein islands have regular, seven-digit, direct-dial telephones; other islands interconnected by shortwave radiotelephone (used mostly for government purposes)
international: country code - 692; satellite earth stations - 2 Intelsat (Pacific Ocean); US Government satellite communications system on Kwajalein (2001)
Radio broadcast stations: AM 2, FM 1, shortwave 0 note: additionally, the US Armed Forces Radio and Television Services (Central Pacific Network) operate one FM and one AM station on Kwajalein (2002)
Radios: NA
Television broadcast stations: 2 (both are US military stations) (2002)
Televisions: NA
Internet country code: .mh
Internet hosts: 6 (2003)
Internet Service Providers (ISPs): 1 (2002)
Internet users: 1,400 (2003)

TRANSPORTATION

Airports: 15 (2004 est.)
Airports - with paved runways:
total: 4
1,524 to 2,437 m: 3
914 to 1,523 m: 1 (2005 est.)
Airports - with unpaved runways:
total: 11
914 to 1,523 m: 10
under 914 m: 1 (2005 est.)
Roadways:
total: 64.5 km
paved: 64.5 km
unpaved: NA km
note: paved roads on major islands (Majuro, Kwajalein), otherwise stone-, coral-, or laterite-surfaced roads and tracks (2002)
Merchant marine:
total: 540 ships (1,000 GRT or over) 16,954,092 GRT/28,176,762 DWT
by type: barge carrier 2, bulk carrier 83, cargo 47, chemical tanker 77, combination ore/oil 12, container 88, liquefied gas 16, passenger 8, petroleum tanker 192, refrigerated cargo 4, roll on/roll off 6, vehicle carrier 5
foreign-owned: 462 (Australia 1, Bahamas 1, Bermuda 1, Canada 4, Chile 2, Croatia 2, Cyprus 7, Denmark 2, Georgia 1, Germany 124, Greece 106, Hong Kong 7, India 1, Italy 1, Japan 5, Latvia 6, Monaco 9, Netherlands 4, New Zealand 1, Norway 21, Philippines 1, Russia 1, Saudi Arabia 1, Singapore 2, Slovenia 2, Spain 1, Switzerland 5, Taiwan 1, Turkey 11, Ukraine 1, UAE 3, United Kingdom 15, United States 112) (2005)
Ports and terminals: Majuro

MILITARY

Military branches: no regular military forces; Marshall Islands Police
Military expenditures - dollar figure: NA
Military expenditures - percent of GDP: NA
Military - note: defense is the responsibility of the US

TRANSNATIONAL ISSUES

Disputes - international: claims US territory of Wake Island

MARTINIQUE

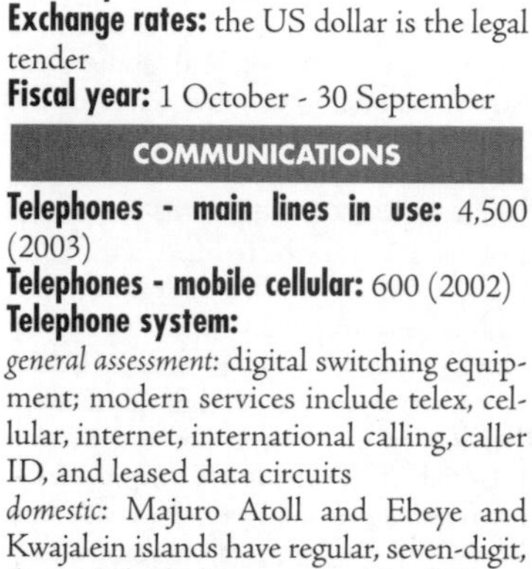

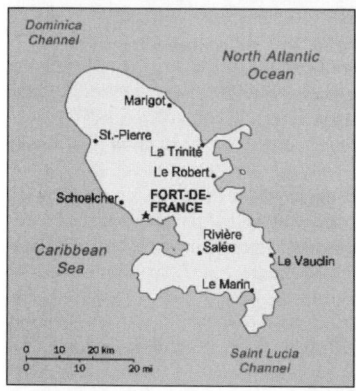

INTRODUCTION

Background: Colonized by France in 1635, the island has subsequently remained a French possession except for three brief periods of foreign occupation.

GEOGRAPHY

Location: Caribbean, island between the Caribbean Sea and North Atlantic Ocean, north of Trinidad and Tobago
Geographic coordinates: 14 40 N, 61 00 W
Map references: Central America and the Caribbean
Area:
total: 1,100 sq km
land: 1,060 sq km
water: 40 sq km
Area - comparative: slightly more than six times the size of Washington, DC
Land boundaries: 0 km
Coastline: 350 km
Maritime claims:
territorial sea: 12 nm
exclusive economic zone: 200 nm
Climate: tropical; moderated by trade winds; rainy season (June to October); vulnerable to devastating cyclones (hurricanes) every eight years on average; average temperature 17.3 degrees C; humid
Terrain: mountainous with indented coastline; dormant volcano
Elevation extremes:
lowest point: Caribbean Sea 0 m
highest point: Montagne Pelee 1,397 m
Natural resources: coastal scenery and beaches, cultivable land
Land use:
arable land: 10.38%
permanent crops: 9.43%
other: 80.19% (2001)
Irrigated land: 30 sq km (1998 est.)
Natural hazards: hurricanes, flooding, and volcanic activity (an average of one major natural disaster every five years)
Environment - current issues: NA
Geography - note: the island is dominated by Mount Pelee, which on 8 May 1902 erupted and completely destroyed the city of Saint Pierre, killing 30,000 inhabitants

PEOPLE

Population: 432,900 (July 2005 est.)
Age structure:
0-14 years: 22.4% (male 49,112/female 47,697)
15-64 years: 67.2% (male 145,531/female 145,250)
65 years and over: 10.5% (male

20,423/female 24,887) (2005 est.)
Median age:
total: 33.61 years
male: 32.95 years
female: 34.28 years (2005 est.)
Population growth rate: 0.76% (2005 est.)
Birth rate: 14.14 births/1,000 population (2005 est.)
Death rate: 6.44 deaths/1,000 population (2005 est.)
Net migration rate: -0.04 migrant(s)/ 1,000 population (2005 est.)
Sex ratio:
at birth: 1.02 male(s)/female
under 15 years: 1.03 male(s)/female
15-64 years: 1 male(s)/female
65 years and over: 0.82 male(s)/female
total population: 0.99 male(s)/female (2005 est.)
Infant mortality rate:
total: 7.09 deaths/1,000 live births
male: 4.73 deaths/1,000 live births
female: 9.51 deaths/1,000 live births (2005 est.)
Life expectancy at birth:
total population: 79.04 years
male: 79.43 years
female: 78.64 years (2005 est.)
Total fertility rate: 1.79 children born/ woman (2005 est.)
HIV/AIDS - adult prevalence rate: NA%
HIV/AIDS - people living with HIV/AIDS: NA
HIV/AIDS - deaths: NA
Nationality:
noun: Martiniquais (singular and plural)
adjective: Martiniquais
Ethnic groups: African and African-white-Indian mixture 90%, white 5%, East Indian, Chinese less than 5%
Religions: Roman Catholic 85%, Protestant 10.5%, Muslim 0.5%, Hindu 0.5%, other 3.5% (1997)
Languages: French, Creole patois
Literacy:
definition: age 15 and over can read and write
total population: 97.7%
male: 97.4%
female: 98.1% (2003 est.)

GOVERNMENT

Country name:
conventional long form: Department of Martinique
conventional short form: Martinique
local long form: Departement de la Martinique
local short form: Martinique
Dependency status: overseas department of France
Government type: NA
Capital: Fort-de-France
Administrative divisions: none (overseas department of France)
Independence: none (overseas department of France)
National holiday: Bastille Day, 14 July (1789)
Constitution: 4 October 1958 (French Constitution)
Legal system: French legal system
Suffrage:18 years of age; universal
Executive branch:
chief of state: President Jacques CHIRAC of France (since 17 May 1995); Prefect Yves DASSONVILLE (since 14 January 2004); note - took office 8 February 2004
head of government: President of the General Council Claude LISE (since 22 March 1992); President of the Regional Council Alfred MARIE-JEANNE (since NA March 1998)
cabinet: NA
elections: French president elected by popular vote for a five-year term; prefect appointed by the French president on the advice of the French Ministry of Interior; the presidents of the General and Regional Councils are elected by the members of those councils
Legislative branch: unicameral General Council or Conseil General (45 seats; members are elected by popular vote to serve six-year terms) and a unicameral Regional Assembly or Conseil Regional (41 seats; members are elected by popular vote to serve six-year terms)
elections: General Council - last held NA March 2000 (next to be held NA 2006); Regional Assembly - last held on 28 March 2004 (next to be held by March 2010)
election results: General Council - percent of vote by party - NA%; seats by party - left-wing candidates 13, PPM 11, RPR 6, right-wing candidates 5, PCM 3, UDF 3, PMS 2, independents 2; note - the PPM won a plurality; Regional Assembly (second round) - percent of vote by party - MIM 53.8%, PPM 30.6%; seats by party - MIM 28, PPM 9, other 4 note: Martinique elects 2 seats to the French Senate; elections last held NA September 2001 (next to be held September 2004); results - percent of vote by party - NA%; seats by party - PPM 2; Martinique also elects 4 seats to the French National Assembly; elections last held, first round - 9 June 2002, second round - 16 June 2002 (next to be held not later than June 2007); results - percent of vote by party - NA%; seats by party - UMP-RPR 1, PS 1, MIM 1, left-wing candidate 1 (candidacy of the left-wing candidate was found invalid by the Constitutional Council; new elections will be called)
Judicial branch: Court of Appeal or Cour d'Appel
Political parties and leaders: Martinique Communist Party or PCM [Georges ERICHOT]; Martinique Independence Movement or MIM [Alfred MARIE-JEANNE]; Martinique Progressive Party or PPM [Pierre SUEDILE]; Martinique Socialist Party or PMS [Ernest WAN-AJOUHU]; Movement of Democrats and Ecologists for a Sovereign Martinique or Modemas [Garcin MALSA]; Rally for the Republic or RPR [Michel CHARLONE]; Socialist Revolution Group or GRS [Philippe PIERRE-CHARLES]; Union for French Democracy or UDF [Jean MAREN]
Political pressure groups and leaders: Caribbean Revolutionary Alliance or ARC; Central Union for Martinique Workers or CSTM [Marc PULVAR]; Frantz Fanon Circle; League of Workers and Peasants; Proletarian Action Group or GAP
International organization participation: UPU, WCL, WFTU
Diplomatic representation in the US: none (overseas department of France)
Diplomatic representation from the US: none (overseas department of France)
Flag description: a light blue background is divided into four quadrants by a white cross; in the center of each rectangle is a white snake; the flag of France is used for official occasions

ECONOMY

Economy - overview: The economy is based on sugarcane, bananas, tourism, and light industry. Agriculture accounts for about 6% of GDP and the small industrial sector for 11%. Sugar production has declined, with most of the sugarcane now used for the production of rum. Banana exports are increasing, going mostly to France. The bulk of meat, vegetable, and grain requirements must be imported, contributing to a chronic trade deficit that requires large annual transfers of aid from France. Tourism, which employs more than 11,000 people, has become more important than agricultural exports as a source of foreign exchange.
GDP (purchasing power parity): $6.117 billion (2003 est.)
GDP (official exchange rate): NA
GDP - real growth rate: NA%
GDP - per capita: purchasing power parity - $14,400 (2003 est.)
GDP - composition by sector:
agriculture: 6%
industry: 11%
services: 83% (1997 est.)
Labor force: 165,900 (1998)
Labor force - by occupation: agriculture

10%, industry 17%, services 73% (1997)
Unemployment rate: 27.2% (1998)
Population below poverty line: NA
Household income or consumption by percentage share:
lowest 10%: NA%
highest 10%: NA%
Inflation rate (consumer prices): 3.9% (1990)
Budget:
revenues: $900 million
expenditures: $2.5 billion, including capital expenditures of $140 million (1996)
Agriculture - products: pineapples, avocados, bananas, flowers, vegetables, sugarcane
Industries: construction, rum, cement, oil refining, sugar, tourism
Industrial production growth rate: NA%
Electricity - production: 1.205 billion kWh (2003)
Electricity - production by source:
fossil fuel: 100%
hydro: 0%
nuclear: 0%
other: 0% (2001)
Electricity - consumption: 1.12 billion kWh (2003)
Electricity - exports: 0 kWh (2003)
Electricity - imports: 0 kWh (2003)
Oil - production: 0 bbl/day (2003 est.)
Oil - consumption: 13,800 bbl/day (2003 est.)
Oil - exports: NA (2001)
Oil - imports: NA (2001)
Exports: $250 million f.o.b. (1997)
Exports - partners: France 45%, Guadeloupe 28% (2004)
Imports: $2 billion c.i.f. (1997)
Imports - partners: France 62%, Venezuela 6%, Germany 4%, Italy 4%, US 3% (2004)
Debt - external: $180 million (1994)
Economic aid - recipient: NA; note - substantial annual aid from France (1998)
Currency (code): euro (EUR)
Currency code: EUR
Exchange rates: euros per US dollar - 0.79697 (2005), 0.8054 (2004), 0.886 (2003), 1.0626 (2002), 1.1175 (2001)
Fiscal year: calendar year

COMMUNICATIONS

Telephones - main lines in use: 172,000 est (2001)
Telephones - mobile cellular: 319,900 (2002)
Telephone system:
general assessment: domestic facilities are adequate
domestic: NA
international: country code - 596; microwave radio relay to Guadeloupe, Dominica, and Saint Lucia; satellite earth stations - 2 Intelsat (Atlantic Ocean)
Radio broadcast stations: AM 0, FM 14, shortwave 0 (1998)
Radios: 82,000 (1997)
Television broadcast stations: 11 (plus nine repeaters) (1997)
Televisions: 66,000 (1997)
Internet country code: .mq
Internet Service Providers (ISPs): 2 (2000)
Internet users: 40,000 (2002)

TRANSPORTATION

Airports: 2 (2004 est.)
Airports - with paved runways:
total: 1
over 3,047 m: 1 (2005 est.)
Airports - with unpaved runways:
total: 1
under 914 m: 1 (2005 est.)
Roadways:
total: 2,105 km (2000)
Ports and terminals: Fort-de-France, La Trinite, Marin

MILITARY

Military branches: no regular military forces; Gendarmerie Military - note: defense is the responsibility of France

TRANSNATIONAL ISSUES

Disputes - international: none
Illicit drugs: transshipment point for cocaine and marijuana bound for the US and Europe

MAURITANIA

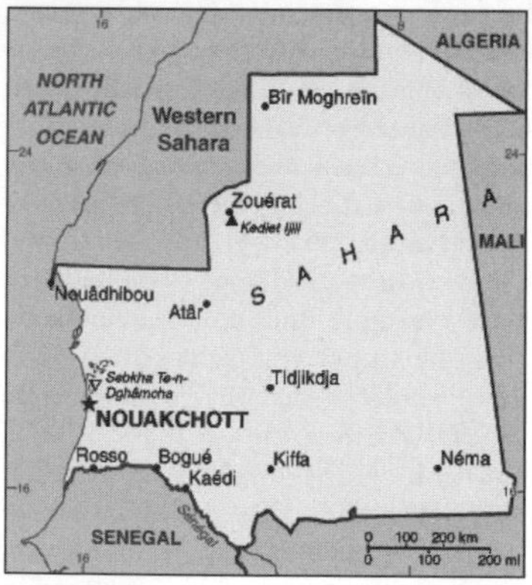

INTRODUCTION

Background: Independent from France in 1960, Mauritania annexed the southern third of the former Spanish Sahara (now Western Sahara) in 1976, but relinquished it after three years of raids by the Polisario guerrilla front seeking independence for the territory. Maaouya Ould Sid Ahmed TAYA seized power in a coup in 1984. Opposition parties were legalized and a new constitution approved in 1991. Two multiparty presidential municipal elections were generally free and open. A bloodless coup in August 2005 deposed President TAYA and ushered in a military council headed by Col. Ely Ould Mohamed VALL, which declared it would remain in power for up to two years while it created conditions for genuine democratic institutions and organized elections. For now, however, Mauritania remains an autocratic state, and the country continues to experience ethnic tensions among its black population and different Moor (Arab-Berber) communities.

GEOGRAPHY

Location: Northern Africa, bordering the North Atlantic Ocean, between Senegal and Western Sahara
Geographic coordinates: 20 00 N, 12 00 W
Map references: Africa
Area:
total: 1,030,700 sq km
land: 1,030,400 sq km
water: 300 sq km
Area - comparative: slightly larger than three times the size of New Mexico
Land boundaries:
total: 5,074 km
border countries: Algeria 463 km, Mali 2,237 km, Senegal 813 km, Western Sahara 1,561 km
Coastline: 754 km
Maritime claims:
territorial sea: 12 nm
contiguous zone: 24 nm
exclusive economic zone: 200 nm
continental shelf: 200 nm or to the edge of the continental margin
Climate: desert; constantly hot, dry, dusty
Terrain: mostly barren, flat plains of the Sahara; some central hills
Elevation extremes:
lowest point: Sebkhet Te-n-Dghamcha -5 m
highest point: Kediet Ijill 915 m
Natural resources: iron ore, gypsum, copper, phosphate, diamonds, gold, oil, fish
Land use:
arable land: 0.48%
permanent crops: 0.01%
other: 99.51% (2001)
Irrigated land: 490 sq km (1998 est.)
Natural hazards: hot, dry, dust/sand-laden sirocco wind blows primarily in March and April; periodic droughts

Environment - current issues: overgrazing, deforestation, and soil erosion aggravated by drought are contributing to desertification; very limited natural fresh water resources away from the Senegal, which is the only perennial river; locust infestation

Environment - international agreements:
party to: Biodiversity, Climate Change, Desertification, Endangered Species, Hazardous Wastes, Law of the Sea, Ozone Layer Protection, Ship Pollution, Wetlands
signed, but not ratified: none of the selected agreements

Geography - note: most of the population concentrated in the cities of Nouakchott and Nouadhibou and along the Senegal River in the southern part of the country

PEOPLE

Population: 3,086,859 (July 2005 est.)

Age structure:
0-14 years: 45.8% (male 707,728/female 704,616)
15-64 years: 52% (male 792,589/female 813,763)
65 years and over: 2.2% (male 27,560/female 40,603) (2005 est.)

Median age:
total: 16.98 years
male: 16.71 years
female: 17.24 years (2005 est.)

Population growth rate: 2.9% (2005 est.)

Birth rate: 41.43 births/1,000 population (2005 est.)

Death rate: 12.44 deaths/1,000 population (2005 est.)

Net migration rate: 0 migrant(s)/1,000 population (2005 est.)

Sex ratio:
at birth: 1.03 male(s)/female
under 15 years: 1 male(s)/female
15-64 years: 0.97 male(s)/female
65 years and over: 0.68 male(s)/female
total population: 0.98 male(s)/female (2005 est.)

Infant mortality rate: total: 70.89 deaths/1,000 live births
male: 73.81 deaths/1,000 live births
female: 67.89 deaths/1,000 live births (2005 est.)

Life expectancy at birth:
total population: 52.73 years
male: 50.52 years
female: 55 years (2005 est.)

Total fertility rate: 5.94 children born/woman (2005 est.)

HIV/AIDS - adult prevalence rate: 0.6% (2003 est.)

HIV/AIDS - people living with HIV/AIDS: 9,500 (2003 est.)

HIV/AIDS - deaths: less than 500 (2003 est.)

Major infectious diseases:
degree of risk: very high
food or waterborne diseases: bacterial and protozoal diarrhea, hepatitis A, and typhoid fever
vectorborne diseases: malaria and Rift Valley fever are high risks in some locations
respiratory disease: meningococcal meningitis (2004)

Nationality:
noun: Mauritanian(s)
adjective: Mauritanian

Ethnic groups: mixed Maur/black 40%, Moor 30%, black 30%

Religions: Muslim 100%

Languages: Arabic (official), Pulaar, Soninke, French, Hassaniya, Wolof

Literacy:
definition: age 15 and over can read and write
total population: 41.7%
male: 51.8%
female: 31.9% (2003 est.)

GOVERNMENT

Country name:
conventional long form: Islamic Republic of Mauritania
conventional short form: Mauritania
local long form: Al Jumhuriyah al Islamiyah al Muritaniyah
local short form: Muritaniyah

Government type: republic

Capital: Nouakchott

Administrative divisions: 12 regions (regions, singular - region) and 1 capital district*; Adrar, Assaba, Brakna, Dakhlet Nouadhibou, Gorgol, Guidimaka, Hodh Ech Chargui, Hodh El Gharbi, Inchiri, Nouakchott*, Tagant, Tiris Zemmour, Trarza

Independence: 28 November 1960 (from France)

National holiday: Independence Day, 28 November (1960)

Constitution: 12 July 1991

Legal system: a combination of Shari'a (Islamic law) and French civil law

Suffrage: 18 years of age; universal

Executive branch:
chief of state: Col. Ely Ould Mohamed VALL, whose Military Council for Justice and Democracy deposed longtime President Maaouya Ould Sid Ahmed TAYA in a coup on 3 August 2005
head of government: Prime Minister Sidi Mohamed Ould BOUBAKAR (since 8 August 2005)
cabinet: Council of Ministers
elections: president elected by popular vote for a six-year term; last held 7 November 2003 (next to be held in March 2007); prime minister appointed by the president
election results: President Maaouya Ould Sid Ahmed TAYA reelected for a third term with 60.8% of the vote

Legislative branch: bicameral legislature consists of the Senate or Majlis al-Shuyukh (56 seats; a portion of seats up for election every two years; members elected by municipal leaders to serve six-year terms) and the National Assembly or Majlis al-Watani (81 seats; members elected by popular vote to serve five-year terms)
elections: Senate - last held 9 and 16 April 2004 (next to be held January 2007); National Assembly - last held 19 and 26 October 2001 (next to be held November 2006)
election results: Senate - percent of vote by party - NA%; seats by party - NA; National Assembly - percent of vote by party - PRDS 79%, RDU 3.5%, UDP 3.5%, AC 5%, UFP 3.5%, FP 1.5%; seats by party - PRDS 64, UDP 3, RDU 3, AC 4, RFD 3, UFP 3, and FP 1

Judicial branch: Supreme Court or Cour Supreme; Court of Appeals; lower courts

Political parties and leaders: Action for Change or AC (no longer active) [Messoud Ould BOULKHEIR], Alliance for Justice and Democracy or AJD [Cisse Amadou CHEIKHOU]; National Union for Democracy and Development or UNDD [Tidjane KOITA]; Party for Liberty, Equality and Justice or PLEJ [Ba Mamdou ALASSANE]; Party of Democratic Convergence or PCD [Cheikh Ould HORMA]; Popular Front or FP [Ch'bih Ould CHEIKH MALAININE]; Popular Progressive Alliance or APP [Messoud Ould BOULKHEIR]; Progress Force Union or UFP (no longer active) [Mohamed Ould MAOULOUD]; Rally of Democratic Forces or RFD [Ahmed Ould DADDAH]; Rally for Democracy and Unity or RDU [Ahmed Ould SIDI BABA]; Republican Party for Democracy and Renewal or PRDR (formerly ruling Democratic and Social Republican Party or PRDS [Boullah Ould MOGUEYA]; Right Way or SAWAB [Cheikh Ould Sidi Ould HANANA]; Union for Democracy and Progress or UDP [Naha Mint MOUKNASS]; Union of Forces of Progress or UFP [Mohamed Ould MAOULOUD]
note: the Party of Democratic Convergence was banned in October 2005 because it was regarded as Islamist and therefore in breach of Mauritanian law

Political pressure groups and leaders: Arab nationalists; Ba'thists; General Confederation of Mauritanian Workers or CGTM [Abdallahi Ould MOHAMED, secretary general]; Independent Confederation of Mauritanian Workers or CLTM

[Samory Ould BEYE]; Islamists; Mauritanian Workers Union or UTM [Mohamed Ely Ould BRAHIM, secretary general]

International organization participation: ABEDA, ACCT, ACP, AfDB, AFESD, AMF, AMU, AU, CAEU, FAO, G-77, IAEA, IBRD, ICAO, ICFTU, ICRM, IDA, IDB, IFAD, IFC, IFRCS, ILO, IMF, IMO, Interpol, IOC, IOM, ITU, LAS, MIGA, NAM, OIC, OPCW, UN, UNCTAD, UNESCO, UNIDO, UPU, WCL, WCO, WHO, WIPO, WMO, WToO, WTO

Diplomatic representation in the US:
chief of mission: Ambassador Tijani Ould KERIM
chancery: 2129 Leroy Place NW, Washington, DC 20008
telephone: [1] (202) 232-5700, 5701
FAX: [1] (202) 319-2623

Diplomatic representation from the US:
chief of mission: Ambassador Joseph E. LEBARON
embassy: 288 Rue Abdallaye (between Presidency building and Spanish Embassy), Nouakchott
mailing address: BP 222, Nouakchott
telephone: [222] 525-2660/525-2663
FAX: [222] 525-1592

Flag description: green with a yellow five-pointed star above a yellow, horizontal crescent; the closed side of the crescent is down; the crescent, star, and color green are traditional symbols of Islam

ECONOMY

Economy - overview: Half the population still depends on agriculture and livestock for a livelihood, even though many of the nomads and subsistence farmers were forced into the cities by recurrent droughts in the 1970s and 1980s. Mauritania has extensive deposits of iron ore, which account for nearly 40% of total exports. The decline in world demand for this ore, however, has led to cutbacks in production. The nation's coastal waters are among the richest fishing areas in the world, but overexploitation by foreigners threatens this key source of revenue. The country's first deepwater port opened near Nouakchott in 1986. In the past, drought and economic mismanagement resulted in a buildup of foreign debt which now stands at more than three times the level of annual exports. In February 2000, Mauritania qualified for debt relief under the Heavily Indebted Poor Countries (HIPC) initiative and in December 2001 received strong support from donor and lending countries at a triennial Consultative Group review. A new investment code approved in December 2001 improved the opportunities for direct foreign investment. Ongoing negotiations with the IMF involve problems of economic reforms and fiscal discipline. In 2001, exploratory oil wells in tracts 80 km offshore indicated potential extraction at current world oil prices. Mauritania has an estimated 1 billion barrels of proved reserves. Substantial oil production and exports are scheduled to begin in early 2006 and may average 75,000 barrels per day for that year. Meantime the government emphasizes reduction of poverty, improvement of health and education, and promoting privatization of the economy.

GDP (purchasing power parity): $6.185 billion (2005 est.)

GDP (official exchange rate): $1.39 billion (2005 est.)

GDP - real growth rate: 5.5% (2005 est.)

GDP - per capita: purchasing power parity - $2,000 (2005 est.)

GDP - composition by sector:
agriculture: 25%
industry: 29%
services: 46% (2001 est.)

Labor force: 786,000 (2001)

Labor force - by occupation: agriculture 50%, industry 10%, services 40% (2001 est.)

Unemployment rate: 20% (2004 est.)

Population below poverty line: 40% (2004 est.)

Household income or consumption by percentage share:
lowest 10%: 2.5%
highest 10%: 30.2% (2000)

Distribution of family income - Gini index: 39 (2000)

Inflation rate (consumer prices): 7% (2003 est.)

Budget:
revenues: $421 million
expenditures: $378 million, including capital expenditures of $154 million (2002 est.)

Agriculture - products: dates, millet, sorghum, rice, corn, dates; cattle, sheep

Industries: fish processing, mining of iron ore and gypsum

Industrial production growth rate: 2% (2000 est.)

Electricity - production: 185.6 million kWh (2003)

Electricity - production by source:
fossil fuel: 85.9%
hydro: 14.1%
nuclear: 0%
other: 0% (2001)

Electricity - consumption: 172.6 million kWh (2003)

Electricity - exports: 0 kWh (2003)

Electricity - imports: 0 kWh (2003)

Oil - production: 0 bbl/day (2005 est.)

Oil - consumption: 24,000 bbl/day (2003 est.)

Oil - exports: NA (2001)

Oil - imports: NA (2001)

Oil - proved reserves: 1 billion bbl (2005)

Exports: $784 million f.o.b. (2004 est.)

Exports - partners: Japan 13.1%, France 11%, Spain 9.7%, Germany 9.7%, Italy 9.6%, Belgium 7.5%, China 6.1%, Russia 4.6%, Cote d'Ivoire 4.1% (2004)

Imports: $1.124 billion f.o.b. (2004 est.)

Imports - partners: France 14.1%, US 7.6%, China 6.4%, Spain 5.8%, UK 4.6%, Germany 4.3%, Belgium 4.2% (2004)

Debt - external: $2.5 billion (2000)

Economic aid - recipient: $305.7 million (2002)

Currency (code): ouguiya (MRO)

Currency code: MRO

Exchange rates: ouguiyas per US dollar - NA (2005), NA (2004), 263.03 (2003), 271.74 (2002), 255.63 (2001)

Fiscal year: calendar year

COMMUNICATIONS

Telephones - main lines in use: 31,500 (2002)

Telephones - mobile cellular: 300,000 (2003)

Telephone system:
general assessment: limited system of cable and open-wire lines, minor microwave radio relay links, and radiotelephone communications stations (improvements being made)
domestic: mostly cable and open-wire lines; a recently completed domestic satellite telecommunications system links Nouakchott with regional capitals
international: country code - 222; satellite earth stations - 1 Intelsat (Atlantic Ocean) and 2 Arabsat

Radio broadcast stations: AM 1, FM 14, shortwave 1 (2001)

Radios: 410,000 (2001)

Television broadcast stations: 1 (2002)

Televisions: 98,000 (2001)

Internet country code: .mr

Internet hosts: 25 (2003)

Internet Service Providers (ISPs): 5 (2001)

Internet users: 10,000 (2002)

TRANSPORTATION

Airports: 24 (2004 est.)

Airports - with paved runways:
total: 8
2,438 to 3,047 m: 3
1,524 to 2,437 m: 5 (2005 est.)

Airports - with unpaved runways:
total: 16
1,524 to 2,437 m: 9
914 to 1,523 m: 6
under 914 m: 1 (2005 est.)

Railways: 717 km
standard gauge: 717 km 1.435-m gauge (2004)

Roadways:
total: 7,660 km
paved: 866 km

unpaved: 6,794 km (1999 est.)
Waterways: some ferry traffic on Senegal River (2004)
Ports and terminals: Nouadhibou, Nouakchott

MILITARY

Military branches: Mauritanian Armed Forces: Army, Navy (Marine Mauritanienne; includes Naval Infantry), Air Force (Force Aerienne Islamique de Mauritanie, FAIM) (2005)
Military service age and obligation: 18 years of age (est.); conscript service obligation - 2 years; majority of servicemen believed to be volunteers; service in Air Force and Navy is voluntary (April 2005)
Manpower available for military service: *males age 18-49:* 606,463 (2005 est.)
Manpower fit for military service: *males age 18-49:* 370,513 (2005 est.)
Military expenditures - dollar figure: $20.8 million (2004)
Military expenditures - percent of GDP: 1.7% (2004)

TRANSNATIONAL ISSUES

Disputes - international: Mauritanian claims to Western Sahara have been dormant in recent years

MAURITIUS

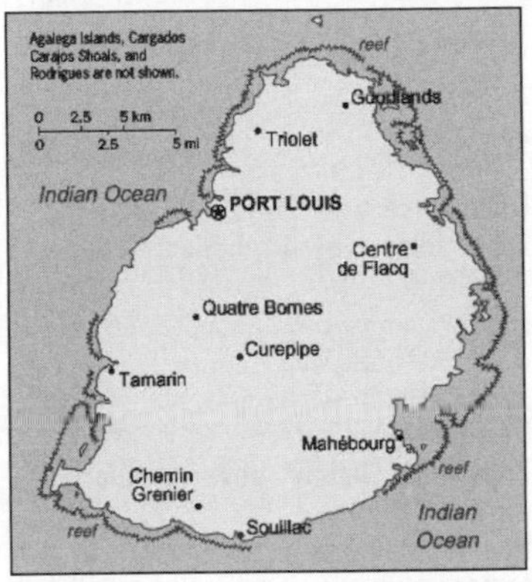

INTRODUCTION

Background: Discovered by the Portuguese in 1505, Mauritius was subsequently held by the Dutch, French, and British before independence was attained in 1968. A stable democracy with regular free elections and a positive human rights record, the country has attracted considerable foreign investment and has earned one of Africa's highest per capita incomes. Recent poor weather and declining sugar prices have slowed economic growth, leading to some protests over standards of living in the Creole community.

GEOGRAPHY

Location: Southern Africa, island in the Indian Ocean, east of Madagascar
Geographic coordinates: 20 17 S, 57 33 E
Map references: Political Map of the World
Area:
total: 2,040 sq km
land: 2,030 sq km
water: 10 sq km
note: includes Agalega Islands, Cargados Carajos Shoals (Saint Brandon), and Rodrigues
Area - comparative: almost 11 times the size of Washington, DC
Land boundaries: 0 km
Coastline: 177 km
Maritime claims:
territorial sea: 12 nm
exclusive economic zone: 200 nm
continental shelf: 200 nm or to the edge of the continental margin
Climate: tropical, modified by southeast trade winds; warm, dry winter (May to November); hot, wet, humid summer (November to May)
Terrain: small coastal plain rising to discontinuous mountains encircling central plateau
Elevation extremes:
lowest point: Indian Ocean 0 m
highest point: Mont Piton 828 m
Natural resources: arable land, fish
Land use:
arable land: 49.26%
permanent crops: 2.96%
other: 47.78% (2001)
Irrigated land: 200 sq km (2000 est.)
Natural hazards: cyclones (November to April); almost completely surrounded by reefs that may pose maritime hazards
Environment - current issues: water pollution, degradation of coral reefs
Environment - international agreements:
party to: Biodiversity, Climate Change, Climate Change-Kyoto Protocol, Desertification, Endangered Species, Environmental Modification, Hazardous Wastes, Law of the Sea, Marine Life Conservation, Ozone Layer Protection, Ship Pollution, Wetlands
signed, but not ratified: none of the selected agreements
Geography - note: the main island, from which the country derives its name, is of volcanic origin and is almost entirely surrounded by coral reefs

PEOPLE

Population: 1,230,602 (July 2005 est.)
Age structure:
0-14 years: 24.4% (male 151,043/female 148,847)
15-64 years: 69.1% (male 424,472/female 425,974)
65 years and over: 6.5% (male 31,506/female 48,760) (2005 est.)
Median age:
total: 30.5 years
male: 29.65 years
female: 31.46 years (2005 est.)
Population growth rate: 0.84% (2005 est.)
Birth rate: 15.62 births/1,000 population (2005 est.)
Death rate: 6.83 deaths/1,000 population (2005 est.)
Net migration rate: -0.41 migrant(s)/1,000 population (2005 est.)
Sex ratio:
at birth: 1.02 male(s)/female
under 15 years: 1.02 male(s)/female
15-64 years: 1 male(s)/female
65 years and over: 0.65 male(s)/female
total population: 0.97 male(s)/female (2005 est.)
Infant mortality rate:
total: 15.03 deaths/1,000 live births
male: 17.74 deaths/1,000 live births
female: 12.27 deaths/1,000 live births (2005 est.)
Life expectancy at birth:
total population: 72.38 years
male: 68.4 years
female: 76.41 years (2005 est.)
Total fertility rate: 1.96 children born/woman (2005 est.)
HIV/AIDS - adult prevalence rate: 0.1% (2001 est.)
HIV/AIDS - people living with HIV/AIDS: 700 (2001 est.)
HIV/AIDS - deaths: less than 100 (2001 est.)
Nationality:
noun: Mauritian(s)
adjective: Mauritian
Ethnic groups: Indo-Mauritian 68%, Creole 27%, Sino-Mauritian 3%, Franco-Mauritian 2%
Religions: Hindu 48%, Roman Catholic 23.6%, other Christian 8.6%, Muslim 16.6%, other 2.5%, unspecified 0.3%, none 0.4% (2000 census)
Languages: Creole 80.5%, Bhojpuri 12.1%, French 3.4% (official), other 3.7%, unspecified 0.3% (2000 census)
Literacy:
definition: age 15 and over can read and write

total population: 85.6%
male: 88.6%
female: 82.7% (2003 est.)

GOVERNMENT

Country name:
conventional long form: Republic of Mauritius
conventional short form: Mauritius
Government type: parliamentary democracy
Capital: Port Louis
Administrative divisions: 9 districts and 3 dependencies*; Agalega Islands*, Black River, Cargados Carajos Shoals*, Flacq, Grand Port, Moka, Pamplemousses, Plaines Wilhems, Port Louis, Riviere du Rempart, Rodrigues*, Savanne
Independence: 12 March 1968 (from UK)
National holiday: Independence Day, 12 March (1968)
Constitution: 12 March 1968; amended 12 March 1992
Legal system: based on French civil law system with elements of English common law in certain areas
Suffrage: 18 years of age; universal
Executive branch:
chief of state: President Sir Anerood JUGNAUTH (since 7 October 2003) and Vice President Abdool Raouf BUNDHUN (since 25 February 2002)
head of government: Prime Minister Navinchandra RAMGOOLAM (since 5 July 2005)
cabinet: Council of Ministers appointed by the president on the recommendation of the prime minister
elections: president and vice president elected by the National Assembly for five-year terms; election last held 25 February 2002 (next to be held NA 2007); prime minister and deputy prime minister appointed by the president, responsible to the National Assembly
election results: Karl OFFMANN elected president and Raouf BUNDHUN elected vice president; percent of vote by the National Assembly - NA%; note - Karl OFFMANN stepped down on 30 September 2003
Legislative branch: unicameral National Assembly (70 seats; 62 elected by popular vote, 8 appointed by the election commission to give representation to various ethnic minorities; members serve five-year terms)
elections: last held on 3 July 2005 (next to be held NA 2010)
election results: percent of vote by party - NA; seats by party - AS 38, MSM/MMM 22, OPR 2; appointed seats - AS 4, MASM/MMM 2. OPR 2
Judicial branch: Supreme Court
Political parties and leaders:
Alliance Sociale or AS [leader NA]; Hizbullah [Cehl Mohamed FAKEEMEEAH]; Mauritian Labor Party or MLP [Navinchandra RAMGOOLAM]; Mauritian Militant Movement or MMM [Paul BERENGER] - in coalition with MSM; Mauritian Social Democrat Party or PMSD [Charles Xavier-Luc DUVAL]; Militant Socialist Movement or MSM [Pravind JUGNAUTH] - governing party; Rodrigues Movement or MR [Joseph (Nicholas) Von MALLY]; Rodrigues Peoples Organization or OPR [Serge CLAIR]
Political pressure groups and leaders: various labor unions
International organization participation: ACCT, ACP, AfDB, AU, C, COMESA, FAO, G-77, IAEA, IBRD, ICAO, ICCt, ICFTU, ICRM, IDA, IFAD, IFC, IFRCS, IHO, ILO, IMF, IMO, InOC, Interpol, IOC, ISO, ITU, MIGA, NAM, OPCW, PCA, SADC, UN, UNCTAD, UNESCO, UNIDO, UPU, WCL, WCO, WFTU, WHO, WIPO, WMO, WToO, WTO
Diplomatic representation in the US:
chief of mission: Ambassador Usha JEETAH
chancery: 4301 Connecticut Avenue NW, Suite 441, Washington, DC 20008
telephone: [1] (202) 244-1491, 1492
FAX: [1] (202) 966-0983
Diplomatic representation from the US:
chief of mission: Ambassador John PRICE
embassy: 4th Floor, Rogers House, John Kennedy Street, Port Louis
mailing address: international mail: P. O. Box 544, Port Louis; US mail: American Embassy, Port Louis, Department of State, Washington, DC 20521-2450
telephone: [230] 202-4400
FAX: [230] 208-9534
Flag description: four equal horizontal bands of red (top), blue, yellow, and green

ECONOMY

Economy - overview: Since independence in 1968, Mauritius has developed from a low-income, agriculturally based economy to a middle-income diversified economy with growing industrial, financial, and tourist sectors. For most of the period, annual growth has been in the order of 5% to 6%. This remarkable achievement has been reflected in more equitable income distribution, increased life expectancy, lowered infant mortality, and a much-improved infrastructure. Sugarcane is grown on about 90% of the cultivated land area and accounts for 25% of export earnings. The government's development strategy centers on expanding local financial institutions and building a domestic information telecommunications industry. Mauritius has attracted more than 9,000 offshore entities, many aimed at commerce in India and South Africa, and investment in the banking sector alone has reached over $1 billion. Mauritius, with its strong textile sector, has been well poised to take advantage of the Africa Growth and Opportunity Act (AGOA).
GDP (purchasing power parity): $16.36 billion (2005 est.)
GDP (official exchange rate): $6.45 billion (2005 est.)
GDP - real growth rate: 3.8% (2005 est.)
GDP - per capita: purchasing power parity - $13,300 (2005 est.)
GDP - composition by sector:
agriculture: 6.1%
industry: 29.9%
services: 64% (2005 est.)
Labor force: 570,000 (2005 est.)
Labor force - by occupation: agriculture and fishing 14%, construction and industry 36%, transportation and communication 7%, trade, restaurants, hotels 16%, finance 3%, other services 24% (1995)
Unemployment rate: 10.5% (2005 est.)
Population below poverty line: 10% (2001 est.)
Household income or consumption by percentage share:
lowest 10%: NA
highest 10%: NA
Distribution of family income - Gini index: 37 (1987 est.)
Inflation rate (consumer prices): 5.6% (2005 est.)
Investment (gross fixed): 21.9% of GDP (2005 est.)
Budget:
revenues: $1.377 billion
expenditures: $1.77 billion, including capital expenditures of NA (2005 est.)
Public debt: 26.2% of GDP (2005 est.)
Agriculture - products: sugarcane, tea, corn, potatoes, bananas, pulses; cattle, goats; fish
Industries: food processing (largely sugar milling), textiles, clothing; chemicals, metal products, transport equipment, nonelectrical machinery; tourism
Industrial production growth rate: 8% (2000 est.)
Electricity - production: 1.941 billion kWh (2003)
Electricity - production by source:
fossil fuel: 90.8%
hydro: 9.2%
nuclear: 0%
other: 0% (2001)
Electricity - consumption: 1.805 billion kWh (2003)
Electricity - exports: 0 kWh (2003)
Electricity - imports: 0 kWh (2003)
Oil - production: 0 bbl/day (2003 est.)

Oil - consumption: 21,000 bbl/day (2003 est.)
Oil - exports: NA (2001)
Oil - imports: NA (2001)
Current account balance: $151 million (2005 est.)
Exports: $1.949 billion f.o.b. (2005 est.)
Exports - partners: UK 33.1%, France 20.4%, US 14.8%, Madagascar 5.1%, Italy 4.1% (2004)
Imports: $2.507 billion f.o.b. (2005 est.)
Imports - partners: South Africa 11.3%, China 9.4%, India 9.3%, France 9.2%, Bahrain 5.3%, Japan 4.1% (2004)
Reserves of foreign exchange and gold: $1.605 billion (2005 est.)
Debt - external: $2.958 billion (2005 est.)
Economic aid - recipient: $42 million (1997)
Currency (code): Mauritian rupee (MUR)
Currency code: MUR
Exchange rates: Mauritian rupees per US dollar - 29.14 (2005), 27.499 (2004), 27.902 (2003), 29.962 (2002), 29.129 (2001)
Fiscal year: 1 July - 30 June

COMMUNICATIONS

Telephones - main lines in use: 348,200 (2003)
Telephones - mobile cellular: 462,400 (2003)
Telephone system:
general assessment: small system with good service
domestic: primarily microwave radio relay trunk system
international: country code - 230; satellite earth station - 1 Intelsat (Indian Ocean); new microwave link to Reunion; HF radiotelephone links to several countries; fiber optic submarine cable (SAT-3/WASC/SAFE) provides connectivity to Europe and Asia
Radio broadcast stations: AM 4, FM 9, shortwave 0 (2002)
Radios: 420,000 (1997)
Television broadcast stations: 2 (plus several repeaters) (1997)
Televisions: 258,000 (1997)
Internet country code: .mu
Internet hosts: 3,985 (2003)
Internet Service Providers (ISPs): 2 (2000)
Internet users: 150,000 (2003)

TRANSPORTATION

Airports: 6 (2004 est.)
Airports - with paved runways:
total: 2
over 3,047 m: 1
914 to 1,523 m: 1 (2005 est.)
Airports - with unpaved runways:
total: 4
914 to 1,523 m: 3
under 914 m: 1 (2005 est.)
Roadways:
total: 2,000 km
paved: 1,960 km (including 60 km of expressways)
unpaved: 40 km (2002)
Merchant marine:
total: 8 ships (1,000 GRT or over) 22,946 GRT/27,102 DWT
by type: bulk carrier 4, passenger/cargo 2, refrigerated cargo 2
foreign-owned: 6 (India 4, Switzerland 2) (2005)
Ports and terminals: Port Louis

MILITARY

Military branches: National Police Force (includes the paramilitary Special Mobile Force or SMF and National Coast Guard)
Manpower available for military service: *males age 18-49:* 313,271 (2005 est.)
Manpower fit for military service: *males age 18-49:* 248,659 (2005 est.)
Military expenditures - dollar figure: $12.5 million (2004)
Military expenditures - percent of GDP: 0.2% (2004)

TRANSNATIONAL ISSUES

Disputes - international: Mauritius claims the Chagos Archipelago (UK-administered British Indian Ocean Territory), and its former inhabitants, who reside chiefly in Mauritius, were granted UK citizenship but no right to patriation in the UK; claims French-administered Tromelin Island
Illicit drugs: minor consumer and transshipment point for heroin from South Asia; small amounts of cannabis produced and consumed locally; significant offshore financial industry creates potential for money laundering, but corruption levels are relatively low and the government appears generally to be committed to regulating its banking industry

MAYOTTE

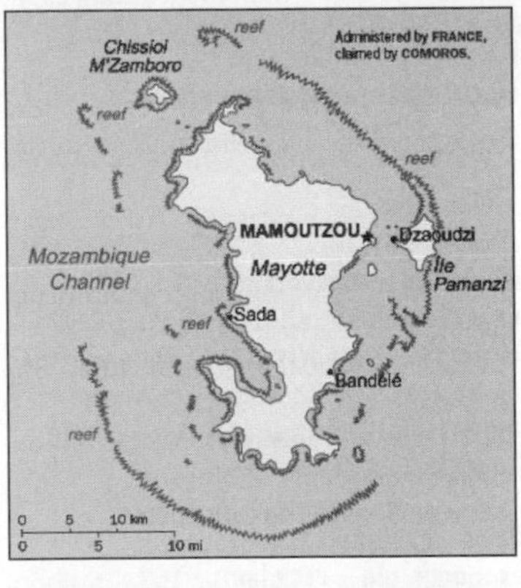

INTRODUCTION

Background: Mayotte was ceded to France along with the other islands of the Comoros group in 1843. It was the only island in the archipelago that voted in 1974 to retain its link with France and forego independence.

GEOGRAPHY

Location: Southern Africa, island in the Mozambique Channel, about one-half of the way from northern Madagascar to northern Mozambique
Geographic coordinates: 12 50 S, 45 10 E
Map references: Africa
Area:
total: 374 sq km
land: 374 sq km
water: 0 sq km
Area - comparative: slightly more than twice the size of Washington, DC
Land boundaries: 0 km
Coastline: 185.2 km
Maritime claims:
territorial sea: 12 nm
exclusive economic zone: 200 nm
Climate: tropical; marine; hot, humid, rainy season during northeastern monsoon (November to May); dry season is cooler (May to November)
Terrain: generally undulating, with deep ravines and ancient volcanic peaks
Elevation extremes:
lowest point: Indian Ocean 0 m
highest point: Benara 660 m
Natural resources: NEGL
Land use:
arable land: NA%
permanent crops: NA%
other: NA%
Irrigated land: NA sq km
Natural hazards: cyclones during rainy season
Environment - current issues: NA
Geography - note: part of Comoro Archipelago; 18 islands

PEOPLE

Population: 193,633 (July 2005 est.)
Age structure:
0-14 years: 46.2% (male 44,926/female 44,521)

15-64 years: 52.1% (male 54,713/female 46,156)
65 years and over: 1.7% (male 1,666/female 1,651) (2005 est.)
Median age:
total: 16.96 years
male: 18.04 years
female: 15.87 years (2005 est.)
Population growth rate: 3.93% (2005 est.)
Birth rate: 41.58 births/1,000 population (2005 est.)
Death rate: 7.9 deaths/1,000 population (2005 est.)
Net migration rate: 5.62 migrant(s)/1,000 population (2005 est.)
Sex ratio:
at birth: 1.03 male(s)/female
under 15 years: 1.01 male(s)/female
15-64 years: 1.18 male(s)/female
65 years and over: 1.01 male(s)/female
total population: 1.1 male(s)/female (2005 est.)
Infant mortality rate:
total: 62.4 deaths/1,000 live births
male: 68.51 deaths/1,000 live births
female: 56.11 deaths/1,000 live births (2005 est.)
Life expectancy at birth:
total population: 61.39 years
male: 59.22 years
female: 63.62 years (2005 est.)
Total fertility rate: 5.89 children born/woman (2005 est.)
HIV/AIDS - adult prevalence rate: NA%
HIV/AIDS - people living with HIV/AIDS: NA
HIV/AIDS - deaths: NA
Nationality:
noun: Mahorais (singular and plural)
adjective: Mahoran
Ethnic groups: NA
Religions: Muslim 97%, Christian (mostly Roman Catholic)
Languages: Mahorian (a Swahili dialect), French (official language) spoken by 35% of the population
Literacy:
definition: NA
total population: NA%
male: NA%
female: NA%

GOVERNMENT

Country name:
conventional long form: Territorial Collectivity of Mayotte
conventional short form: Mayotte
Dependency status: territorial collectivity of France
Government type: NA
Capital: Mamoutzou
Administrative divisions: none (territorial collectivity of France)
Independence: none (territorial collectivity of France)
National holiday: Bastille Day, 14 July (1789)
Constitution: 4 October 1958 (French Constitution)
Legal system: French law
Suffrage: 18 years of age; universal
Executive branch:
chief of state: President Jacques CHIRAC of France (since 17 May 1995), represented by Prefect Jean-Paul KIHL (since 17 January 2005)
head of government: President of the General Council Said Omar OILI (since NA 2004)
cabinet: NA
elections: French president elected by popular vote for a five-year term; prefect appointed by the French president on the advice of the French Ministry of the Interior; president of the General Council elected by the members of the General Council for a six-year term
Legislative branch: unicameral General Council or Conseil General (19 seats; members are elected by popular vote to serve three-year terms)
elections: last held 21 and 28 March 2004 (next to be held NA 2007)
election results: percent of vote by party - MDM 23.3%, UMP 22.8%, PS 10.2%, MRC 8.9%, FRAP 6.5%, MPM 1.2%; seats by party - MDM 6, UMP 9, MRC 2, MPM 1, diverse left 1
note: Mayotte elects one member of the French Senate; elections last held 24 September 2001 (next to be held September 2007); results - percent of vote by party - NA%; seats by party - NA; Mayotte also elects one member to the French National Assembly; elections last held 16 June 2002 (next to be held as a special election in June 2005); results - percent of vote by party - UMP-RPR 55.08%, UDF 44.92%; seats by party - UMP-RPR 1
Judicial branch: Supreme Court or Tribunal Superieur d'Appel
Political parties and leaders: Democratic Front or FD [Youssouf MOUSSA]; Mahoran Popular Movement or MPM [Ahmed MADI]; FARC [leader NA]; Federation of Mahorans or RPR (UMP) [Mansour KAMARDINE]; Movement for Department Status Mayotte or MDM [Mouhoutar SALIM]; Renewed Communist Party of Mayotte or MRC [Omar SIMBA]; Socialist Party or PS (local branch of French Parti Socialiste) [Ibrahim ABUBACAR]; Union for French Democracy or UDF [Henri JEAN-BAPTISTE]
Political pressure groups and leaders: NA
International organization participation: UPU
Diplomatic representation in the US: none (territorial collectivity of France)
Diplomatic representation from the US: none (territorial collectivity of France)
Flag description: the flag of France is used

ECONOMY

Economy - overview: Economic activity is based primarily on the agricultural sector, including fishing and livestock raising. Mayotte is not self-sufficient and must import a large portion of its food requirements, mainly from France. The economy and future development of the island are heavily dependent on French financial assistance, an important supplement to GDP. Mayotte's remote location is an obstacle to the development of tourism.
GDP (purchasing power parity): $466.8 million (2003 est.)
GDP (official exchange rate): NA
GDP - real growth rate: NA%
GDP - per capita: purchasing power parity - $2,600 (2003 est.)
GDP - composition by sector:
agriculture: NA%
industry: NA%
services: NA%
Labor force: 48,800 (2000)
Unemployment rate: 38% (1999)
Population below poverty line: NA
Household income or consumption by percentage share:
lowest 10%: NA%
highest 10%: NA%
Inflation rate (consumer prices): NA%
Budget:
revenues: NA
expenditures: $73 million, including capital expenditures of NA (1991 est.)
Agriculture - products: vanilla, ylang-ylang (perfume essence), coffee, copra
Industries: newly created lobster and shrimp industry, construction
Industrial production growth rate: NA%
Electricity - production: NA kWh
Electricity - production by source:
fossil fuel: 0%
hydro: 0%
nuclear: 0%
other: 0%
Electricity - consumption: NA kWh
Exports: $3.44 million f.o.b. (1997)
Exports - partners: France 80%, Comoros 15%, Reunion (2004)
Imports: $141.3 million f.o.b. (1997)
Imports - partners: France 66%, Africa 14%, Southeast Asia 11% (2004)
Debt - external: $NA
Economic aid - recipient: $107.7 million; note - extensive French financial assistance (1995)
Currency (code): euro (EUR)
Currency code: EUR
Exchange rates: euros per US dollar - 0.79697 (2005), 0.8054 (2004), 0.886 (2003), 1.0626 (2002), 1.1175 (2001)

Fiscal year: calendar year

COMMUNICATIONS

Telephones - main lines in use: 10,000 (2001)
Telephones - mobile cellular: 21,700 (2002)
Telephone system:
general assessment: small system administered by French Department of Posts and Telecommunications
domestic: NA
international: country code - 269; microwave radio relay and HF radiotelephone communications to Comoros (2001)
Radio broadcast stations: AM 1, FM 5, shortwave 0 (2001)
Radios: NA
Television broadcast stations: 3 (2001)
Televisions: 3,500 (1994)
Internet country code: .yt
Internet Service Providers (ISPs): NA
Internet users: NA

TRANSPORTATION

Airports: 1 (2004 est.)
Airports - with paved runways:
total: 1
1,524 to 2,437 m: 1 (2005 est.)
Roadways:
total: 93 km
paved: 72 km
unpaved: 21 km
Ports and terminals: Dzaoudzi

MILITARY

Military - note: defense is the responsibility of France; small contingent of French forces stationed on the island

TRANSNATIONAL ISSUES

Disputes - international: claimed by Comoros

MEXICO

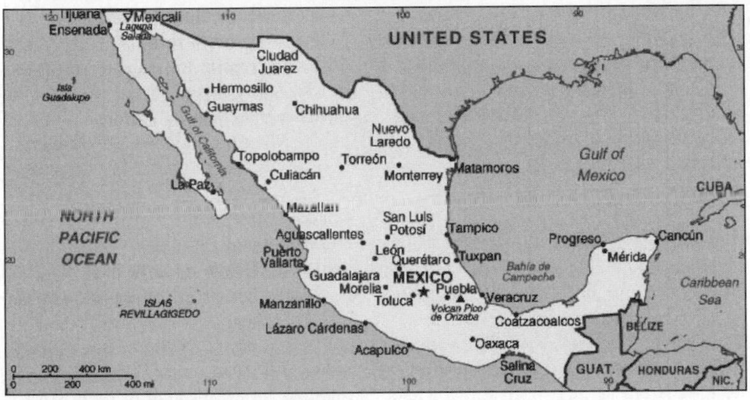

INTRODUCTION

Background: The site of advanced Amerindian civilizations, Mexico came under Spanish rule for three centuries before achieving independence early in the 19th century. A devaluation of the peso in late 1994 threw Mexico into economic turmoil, triggering the worst recession in over half a century. The nation continues to make an impressive recovery. Ongoing economic and social concerns include low real wages, underemployment for a large segment of the population, inequitable income distribution, and few advancement opportunities for the largely Amerindian population in the impoverished southern states. Elections held in July 2000 marked the first time since the 1910 Mexican Revolution that the opposition defeated the party in government, the Institutional Revolutionary Party (PRI). Vicente FOX of the National Action Party (PAN) was sworn in on 1 December 2000 as the first chief executive elected in free and fair elections.

GEOGRAPHY

Location: Middle America, bordering the Caribbean Sea and the Gulf of Mexico, between Belize and the US and bordering the North Pacific Ocean, between Guatemala and the US
Geographic coordinates: 23 00 N, 102 00 W
Map references: North America
Area:
total: 1,972,550 sq km
land: 1,923,040 sq km
water: 49,510 sq km
Area - comparative: slightly less than three times the size of Texas
Land boundaries:
total: 4,353 km
border countries: Belize 250 km, Guatemala 962 km, US 3,141 km
Coastline: 9,330 km
Maritime claims:
territorial sea: 12 nm
contiguous zone: 24 nm
exclusive economic zone: 200 nm
continental shelf: 200 nm or to the edge of the continental margin
Climate: varies from tropical to desert
Terrain: high, rugged mountains; low coastal plains; high plateaus; desert
Elevation extremes:
lowest point: Laguna Salada -10 m
highest point: Volcan Pico de Orizaba 5,700 m
Natural resources: petroleum, silver, copper, gold, lead, zinc, natural gas, timber
Land use:
arable land: 12.99%
permanent crops: 1.31%
other: 85.7% (2001)
Irrigated land: 65,000 sq km (1998 est.)
Natural hazards: tsunamis along the Pacific coast, volcanoes and destructive earthquakes in the center and south, and hurricanes on the Pacific, Gulf of Mexico, and Caribbean coasts
Environment - current issues: scarcity of hazardous waste disposal facilities; rural to urban migration; natural fresh water resources scarce and polluted in north, inaccessible and poor quality in center and extreme southeast; raw sewage and industrial effluents polluting rivers in urban areas; deforestation; widespread erosion; desertification; deteriorating agricultural lands; serious air and water pollution in the national capital and urban centers along US-Mexico border; land subsidence in Valley of Mexico caused by groundwater depletion
note: the government considers the lack of clean water and deforestation national security issues
Environment - international agreements:
party to: Biodiversity, Climate Change, Climate Change-Kyoto Protocol, Desertification, Endangered Species, Hazardous Wastes, Law of the Sea, Marine Dumping, Marine Life Conservation, Ozone Layer Protection, Ship Pollution, Wetlands, Whaling
signed, but not ratified: none of the selected agreements
Geography - note: strategic location on southern border of US; corn (maize), one of the world's major grain crops, is thought to have originated in Mexico

PEOPLE

Population: 106,202,903 (July 2005 est.)
Age structure:
0-14 years: 31.1% (male 16,844,400/ female 16,159,511)

15-64 years: 63.3% (male 32,521,043/ female 34,704,093)
65 years and over: 5.6% (male 2,715,010/female 3,258,846) (2005 est.)
Median age:
total: 24.93 years
male: 24.04 years
female: 25.85 years (2005 est.)
Population growth rate: 1.17% (2005 est.)
Birth rate: 21.01 births/1,000 population (2005 est.)
Death rate: 4.73 deaths/1,000 population (2005 est.)
Net migration rate: -4.57 migrant(s)/ 1,000 population (2005 est.)
Sex ratio:
at birth: 1.05 male(s)/female
under 15 years: 1.04 male(s)/female
15-64 years: 0.94 male(s)/female
65 years and over: 0.83 male(s)/female
total population: 0.96 male(s)/female (2005 est.)
Infant mortality rate:
total: 20.91 deaths/1,000 live births
male: 22.85 deaths/1,000 live births
female: 18.88 deaths/1,000 live births (2005 est.)
Life expectancy at birth:
total population: 75.19 years
male: 72.42 years
female: 78.1 years (2005 est.)
Total fertility rate: 2.45 children born/ woman (2005 est.)
HIV/AIDS - adult prevalence rate: 0.3% (2003 est.)
HIV/AIDS - people living with HIV/AIDS: 160,000 (2003 est.)
HIV/AIDS - deaths: 5,000 (2003 est.)
Nationality:
noun: Mexican(s)
adjective: Mexican
Ethnic groups: mestizo (Amerindian-Spanish) 60%, Amerindian or predominantly Amerindian 30%, white 9%, other 1%
Religions: nominally Roman Catholic 89%, Protestant 6%, other 5%
Languages: Spanish, various Mayan, Nahuatl, and other regional indigenous languages
Literacy:
definition: age 15 and over can read and write
total population: 92.2%
male: 94%
female: 90.5% (2003 est.)

GOVERNMENT

Country name:
conventional long form: United Mexican States
conventional short form: Mexico
local long form: Estados Unidos Mexicanos
local short form: Mexico
Government type: federal republic
Capital: Mexico (Distrito Federal)
Administrative divisions: 31 states (estados, singular - estado) and 1 federal district* (distrito federal); Aguascalientes, Baja California, Baja California Sur, Campeche, Chiapas, Chihuahua, Coahuila de Zaragoza, Colima, Distrito Federal*, Durango, Guanajuato, Guerrero, Hidalgo, Jalisco, Mexico, Michoacan de Ocampo, Morelos, Nayarit, Nuevo Leon, Oaxaca, Puebla, Queretaro de Arteaga, Quintana Roo, San Luis Potosi, Sinaloa, Sonora, Tabasco, Tamaulipas, Tlaxcala, Veracruz-Llave, Yucatan, Zacatecas
Independence: 16 September 1810 (from Spain)
National holiday: Independence Day, 16 September (1810)
Constitution: 5 February 1917
Legal system: mixture of US constitutional theory and civil law system; judicial review of legislative acts; accepts compulsory ICJ jurisdiction, with reservations
Suffrage: 18 years of age; universal and compulsory (but not enforced)
Executive branch:
chief of state: President Vicente FOX Quesada (since 1 December 2000); note - the president is both the chief of state and head of government
head of government: President Vicente FOX Quesada (since 1 December 2000); note - the president is both the chief of state and head of government
cabinet: Cabinet appointed by the president; note - appointment of attorney general requires consent of the Senate
elections: president elected by popular vote for a six-year term; election last held 2 July 2000 (next to be held 2 July 2006)
election results: Vicente FOX Quesada elected president; percent of vote - Vicente FOX Quesada (PAN) 42.52%, Francisco LABASTIDA Ochoa (PRI) 36.1%, Cuauhtemoc CARDENAS Solorzano (PRD) 16.64%, other 4.74%
Legislative branch: bicameral National Congress or Congreso de la Union consists of the Senate or Camara de Senadores (128 seats; 96 are elected by popular vote to serve six-year terms, and 32 are allocated on the basis of each party's popular vote) and the Federal Chamber of Deputies or Camara Federal de Diputados (500 seats; 300 members are directly elected by popular vote to serve three-year terms; remaining 200 members are allocated on the basis of each party's popular vote, also for three-year terms)
elections: Senate - last held 2 July 2000 for all of the seats (next to be held 2 July 2006); Chamber of Deputies - last held 6 July 2003 (next to be held 2 July 2006)
election results: Senate - percent of vote by party - NA%; seats by party - PRI 60, PAN 46, PRD 16, PVEM 5, unassigned 1; Chamber of Deputies - percent of vote by party - NA%; seats by party - PRI 222, PAN 151, PRD 95, PVEM 17, PT 6, CD 5, unassigned 4; note - special elections were held in December 2003; the PRI and the PRD each won one seat and were each assigned one additional proportional representation seat
Judicial branch: Supreme Court of Justice or Suprema Corte de Justicia Nacional (justices or ministros are appointed by the president with consent of the Senate)
Political parties and leaders: Convergence for Democracy or CD [Dante DELGADO Ranauro]; Institutional Revolutionary Party or PRI [Mariano PALACIOS Alcocer]; Mexican Green Ecological Party or PVEM [Jorge Emilio GONZALEZ Martinez]; National Action Party or PAN [Manuel ESPINO Barrientos]; Party of the Democratic Revolution or PRD [Leonel COTA Montano]; Workers Party or PT [Alberto ANAYA Gutierrez]
Political pressure groups and leaders: Confederation of Employers of the Mexican Republic or COPARMEX; Confederation of Industrial Chambers or CONCAMIN; Confederation of Mexican Workers or CTM; Confederation of National Chambers of Commerce or CONCANACO; Coordinator for Foreign Trade Business Organizations or COECE; Federation of Unions Providing Goods and Services or FESEBES; National Chamber of Transformation Industries or CANACINTRA; National Peasant Confederation or CNC; National Union of Workers or UNT; Regional Confederation of Mexican Workers or CROM; Revolutionary Confederation of Workers and Peasants or CROC; Roman Catholic Church
International organization participation: APEC, BCIE, BIS, CDB, CE (observer), EBRD, FAO, G-3, G-6, G-15, G-24, IADB, IAEA, IBRD, ICAO, ICC, ICCt (signatory), ICFTU, ICRM, IDA, IFAD, IFC, IFRCS, IHO, ILO, IMF, IMO, Interpol, IOC, IOM, ISO, ITU, LAES, LAIA, NAFTA, NAM (observer), NEA, OAS, OECD, OPANAL, OPCW, PCA, RG, UN, UNCTAD, UNESCO, UNHCR, UNIDO, UNITAR, UNMOVIC, UPU, WCL, WCO, WFTU, WHO, WIPO, WMO, WToO, WTO
Diplomatic representation in the US:
chief of mission: Ambassador-designate Carlos Alberto de ICAZA Gonzalez

chancery: 1911 Pennsylvania Avenue NW, Washington, DC 20006
telephone: [1] (202) 728-1600
FAX: [1] (202) 728-1698
consulate(s) general: Atlanta, Austin, Boston, Chicago, Dallas, Denver, El Paso, Houston, Laredo (Texas), Los Angeles, Miami, New Orleans, New York, Nogales (Arizona), Phoenix, Sacramento, San Antonio, San Diego, San Francisco, San Jose, San Juan (Puerto Rico)
consulate(s): Albuquerque, Brownsville (Texas), Calexico (California), Corpus Christi (Texas), Del Rio (Texas), Detroit, Douglas (Arizona), Eagle Pass (Texas), Fresno (California), Indianapolis (Indiana), Kansas City (Missouri), Las Vegas, McAllen (Texas), Midland (Texas), Omaha, Orlando, Oxnard (California), Philadelphia, Portland (Oregon), Presidio (Texas), Raleigh, Salt Lake City, San Bernardino, Santa Ana (California), Seattle, Tucson, Yuma (Arizona)
Diplomatic representation from the US:
chief of mission: Ambassador Antonio O. GARZA
embassy: Paseo de la Reforma 305, Colonia Cuauhtemoc, 06500 Mexico, Distrito Federal
mailing address: P. O. Box 9000, Brownsville, TX 78520-0900
telephone: [52] (55) 5080-2000
FAX: [52] (55) 5511-9980
consulate(s) general: Ciudad Juarez, Guadalajara, Monterrey, Tijuana
consulate(s): Hermosillo, Matamoros, Merida, Nogales, Nuevo Laredo
Flag description: three equal vertical bands of green (hoist side), white, and red; the coat of arms (an eagle perched on a cactus with a snake in its beak) is centered in the white band

ECONOMY

Economy - overview: Mexico has a free market economy that recently entered the trillion dollar class. It contains a mixture of modern and outmoded industry and agriculture, increasingly dominated by the private sector. Recent administrations have expanded competition in seaports, railroads, telecommunications, electricity generation, natural gas distribution, and airports. Per capita income is one-fourth that of the US; income distribution remains highly unequal. Trade with the US and Canada has tripled since the implementation of NAFTA in 1994. Mexico has 12 free trade agreements with over 40 countries including, Guatemala, Honduras, El Salvador, the European Free Trade Area, and Japan, putting more than 90% of trade under free trade agreements. The Fox administration is cognizant of the need to upgrade infrastructure, modernize the tax system and labor laws, and allow private investment in the energy sector, but has been unable to win the support of the opposition-led Congress. The next government that takes office in December 2006 will confront the same challenges of boosting economic growth, improving Mexico's international competitiveness, and reducing poverty.
GDP (purchasing power parity): $1.066 trillion (2005 est.)
GDP (official exchange rate): $717 billion (2005 est.)
GDP - real growth rate: 3% (2005 est.)
GDP - per capita: purchasing power parity - $10,000 (2005 est.)
GDP - composition by sector:
agriculture: 4%
industry: 26.5%
services: 69.5% (2005 est.)
Labor force: 37.38 million (2005 est.)
Labor force - by occupation: agriculture 18%, industry 24%, services 58% (2003)
Unemployment rate: 3.6% plus underemployment of perhaps 25% (2005 est.)
Population below poverty line: 40% (2003 est.)
Household income or consumption by percentage share:
lowest 10%: 1.6%
highest 10%: 35.6% (2002)
Distribution of family income - Gini index: 54.6 (2000)
Inflation rate (consumer prices): 4.1% (2005 est.)
Investment (gross fixed): 21.1% of GDP (2005 est.)
Budget:
revenues: $173.2 billion
expenditures: $175.4 billion, including capital expenditures of NA (2005 est.)
Public debt: 21.2% of GDP (2005 est.)
Agriculture - products: corn, wheat, soybeans, rice, beans, cotton, coffee, fruit, tomatoes; beef, poultry, dairy products; wood products
Industries: food and beverages, tobacco, chemicals, iron and steel, petroleum, mining, textiles, clothing, motor vehicles, consumer durables, tourism
Industrial production growth rate: 2.5% (2005 est.)
Electricity - production: 209.2 billion kWh (2003)
Electricity - production by source:
fossil fuel: 78.7%
hydro: 14.2%
nuclear: 4.2%
other: 2.9% (2001)
Electricity - consumption: 193.9 billion kWh (2003)
Electricity - exports: 1.07 billion kWh (2003)
Electricity - imports: 390.2 million kWh (2003)
Oil - production: 3.42 million bbl/day (2005 est.)
Oil - consumption: 1.752 million bbl/day (2004 est.)
Oil - exports: 1.863 million bbl/day (2004)
Oil - imports: 205,000 bbl/day (2004)
Oil - proved reserves: 46.79 billion bbl (2005 est.)
Natural gas - production: 47.3 billion cu m (2004 est.)
Natural gas - consumption: 55.1 billion cu m (2004 est.)
Natural gas - exports: 0 cu m (2004 est.)
Natural gas - imports: 7.85 billion cu m (2004 est.)
Natural gas - proved reserves: 420 billion cu m (2005)
Current account balance: $-8.97 billion (2005 est.)
Exports: $213.7 billion f.o.b. (2005 est.)
Exports - partners: US 87.6%, Canada 1.8%, Spain 1.1% (2004)
Imports: $223.7 billion f.o.b. (2005 est.)
Imports - partners: US 55.1%, China 7.1%, Japan 5.3% (2004)
Reserves of foreign exchange and gold: $66.6 billion (2005 est.)
Debt - external: $174.3 billion (30 June 2005 est.)
Economic aid - recipient: $1.166 billion (1995)
Currency (code): Mexican peso (MXN)
Currency code: MXN
Exchange rates: Mexican pesos per US dollar - 10.97 (2005), 11.286 (2004), 10.789 (2003), 9.656 (2002), 9.342 (2001)
Fiscal year: calendar year

COMMUNICATIONS

Telephones - main lines in use: 15,958,700 (2003)
Telephones - mobile cellular: 28.125 million (2003)
Telephone system:
general assessment: low telephone density with about 15.2 main lines per 100 persons; privatized in December 1990; the opening to competition in January 1997 improved prospects for development, but Telmex remains dominant
domestic: adequate telephone service for business and government, but the population is poorly served; mobile subscribers far outnumber fixed-line subscribers; domestic satellite system with 120 earth stations; extensive microwave radio relay network; considerable use of fiber-optic cable and coaxial cable
international: country code - 52; satellite earth stations - 32 Intelsat, 2 Solidaridad (giving Mexico improved

access to South America, Central America, and much of the US as well as enhancing domestic communications), numerous Inmarsat mobile earth stations; linked to Central American Microwave System of trunk connections; high capacity Columbus-2 fiber-optic submarine cable with access to the US, Virgin Islands, Canary Islands, Morocco, Spain, and Italy (1997)
Radio broadcast stations: AM 850, FM 545, shortwave 15 (2003)
Radios: 31 million (1997)
Television broadcast stations: 236 (plus repeaters) (1997)
Televisions: 25.6 million (1997)
Internet country code: .mx
Internet hosts: 1,333,406 (2003)
Internet Service Providers (ISPs): 51 (2000)
Internet users: 10.033 million (2002)

TRANSPORTATION

Airports: 1,833 (2004 est.)
Airports - with paved runways:
total: 227
over 3,047 m: 12
2,438 to 3,047 m: 28
1,524 to 2,437 m: 81
914 to 1,523 m: 77
under 914 m: 29 (2005 est.)
Airports - with unpaved runways:
total: 1,605
over 3,047 m: 1
2,438 to 3,047 m: 1
1,524 to 2,437 m: 69
914 to 1,523 m: 457
under 914 m: 1,077 (2005 est.)
Heliports: 1 (2005 est.)
Pipelines: crude oil 28,200 km; petroleum products 10,150 km; natural gas 13,254 km; petrochemical 1,400 km (2003)
Railways:
total: 17,634 km
standard gauge: 17,634 km 1.435-m gauge (2004)
Roadways:
total: 329,532 km
paved: 108,087 km (including 6,429 km of expressways)
unpaved: 221,445 km (1999 est.)
Waterways: 2,900 km
note: navigable rivers and coastal canals (2004)
Merchant marine:
total: 57 ships (1,000 GRT or over) 649,389 GRT/942,766 DWT
by type: bulk carrier 2, cargo 6, chemical tanker 5, liquefied gas 5, passenger/cargo 9, petroleum tanker 26, roll on/roll off 4
foreign-owned: 4 (Denmark 1, Germany 1, UAE 1, United States 1)
registered in other countries: 6 (2005)
Ports and terminals: Altamira, Manzanillo, Morro Redondo, Salina Cruz, Tampico, Topolobampo, Veracruz

MILITARY

Military branches: *Secretariat of National Defense (Sedena):* Army and Air Force (FAM)
Secretariat of the Navy (Semar): Naval Air and Marines (2004)
Military service age and obligation: 18 years of age for compulsory military service, conscript service obligation - 12 months; 16 years of age with consent for voluntary enlistment (2004)
Manpower available for military service: *males age 18-49:* 24,488,008 (2005 est.)
Manpower fit for military service: *males age 18-49:* 19,058,337 (2005 est.)
Manpower reaching military service age annually: *males:* 1,063,233 (2005 est.)
Military expenditures - dollar figure: $6.043 billion (2004)
Military expenditures - percent of GDP: 0.9% (2004)

TRANSNATIONAL ISSUES

Disputes - international: prolonged drought, population growth, and outmoded practices and infrastructure in the border region have strained water-sharing arrangements with the US; the US has stepped up efforts to stem nationals from Mexico, Central America, and other parts of the world from illegally crossing the border with Mexico
Refugees and internally displaced persons: *IDPs:* 12,000 (government's quashing of Zapatista uprising in 1994 in eastern Chiapas Region) (2004)
Illicit drugs: illicit cultivation of opium poppy (cultivation in 2001 - 4,400 hectares; potential heroin production - 7 metric tons) and of cannabis (in 2001 - 4,100 hectares); government eradication efforts have been key in keeping illicit crop levels low; major supplier of heroin and largest foreign supplier of marijuana and methamphetamine to the US market; continues as the primary transshipment country for US-bound cocaine from South America, accounting for about 70 percent of estimated annual cocaine movement to the US; major drug syndicates control majority of drug trafficking throughout the country; producer and distributor of ecstasy; significant money-laundering center

MICRONESIA, FEDERATED STATES OF

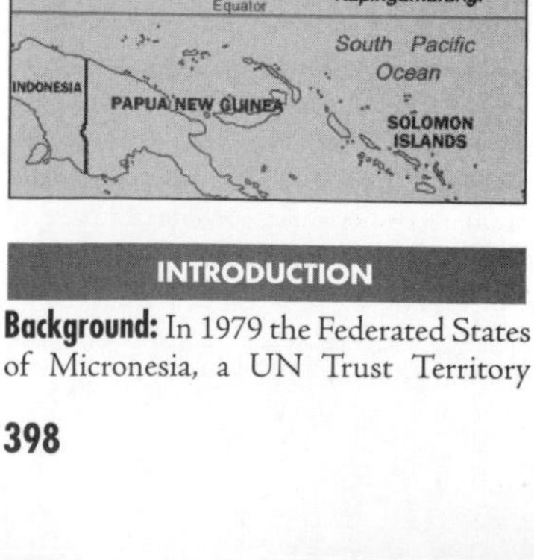

INTRODUCTION

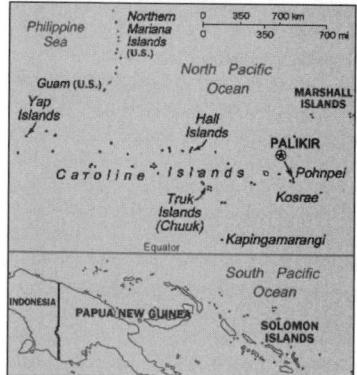

Background: In 1979 the Federated States of Micronesia, a UN Trust Territory under US administration, adopted a constitution. In 1986 independence was attained under a Compact of Free Association with the US, which was amended and renewed in 2004. Present concerns include large-scale unemployment, overfishing, and overdependence on US aid.

GEOGRAPHY

Location: Oceania, island group in the North Pacific Ocean, about three-quarters of the way from Hawaii to Indonesia
Geographic coordinates: 6 55 N, 158 15 E
Map references: Oceania
Area:
total: 702 sq km
land: 702 sq km
water: 0 sq km (fresh water only)
note: includes Pohnpei (Ponape), Chuuk (Truk) Islands, Yap Islands, and Kosrae (Kosaie)
Area - comparative: four times the size of Washington, DC (land area only)
Land boundaries: 0 km
Coastline: 6,112 km
Maritime claims:
territorial sea: 12 nm
exclusive economic zone: 200 nm
Climate: tropical; heavy year-round rainfall, especially in the eastern islands; located on southern edge of the typhoon belt with occasionally severe damage
Terrain: islands vary geologically from high mountainous islands to low, coral atolls; volcanic outcroppings on Pohnpei, Kosrae, and Chuuk
Elevation extremes:
lowest point: Pacific Ocean 0 m
highest point: Dolohmwar (Totolom) 791 m

Natural resources: forests, marine products, deep-seabed minerals, phosphate
Land use:
arable land: 5.71%
permanent crops: 45.71%
other: 48.58% (2001)
Irrigated land: NA
Natural hazards: typhoons (June to December)
Environment - current issues: overfishing, climate change, pollution
Environment - international agreements:
party to: Biodiversity, Climate Change, Climate Change-Kyoto Protocol, Desertification, Hazardous Wastes, Law of the Sea, Ozone Layer Protection
signed, but not ratified: none of the selected agreements
Geography - note: four major island groups totaling 607 islands

PEOPLE

Population: 108,105 (July 2005 est.)
Age structure:
0-14 years: 37.1% (male 20,439/female 19,674)
15-64 years: 59.8% (male 32,382/female 32,313)
65 years and over: 3% (male 1,461/female 1,836) (2005 est.)
Median age:
total: 18.9 years
male: NA
female: NA (2000)
Population growth rate: -0.08% (2005 est.)
Birth rate: 25.11 births/1,000 population (2005 est.)
Death rate: 4.87 deaths/1,000 population (2005 est.)
Net migration rate: -21.01 migrant(s)/1,000 population (2005 est.)
Sex ratio: NA
Infant mortality rate:
total: 30.21 deaths/1,000 live births
male: 33.3 deaths/1,000 live births
female: 26.97 deaths/1,000 live births (2005 est.)
Life expectancy at birth:
total population: 69.75 years
male: 67.96 years
female: 71.62 years (2005 est.)
Total fertility rate: 3.25 children born/woman (2005 est.)
HIV/AIDS - adult prevalence rate: NA
HIV/AIDS - people living with HIV/AIDS: NA
HIV/AIDS - deaths: NA
Nationality:
noun: Micronesian(s)
adjective: Micronesian; Chuukese, Kosraen(s), Pohnpeian(s), Yapese
Ethnic groups: nine ethnic Micronesian and Polynesian groups
Religions: Roman Catholic 50%, Protestant 47%
Languages: English (official and common language), Trukese, Pohnpeian, Yapese, Kosrean, Ulithian, Woleaian, Nukuoro, Kapingamarangi
Literacy:
definition: age 15 and over can read and write
total population: 89%
male: 91%
female: 88% (1980 est.)

GOVERNMENT

Country name:
conventional long form: Federated States of Micronesia
conventional short form: none
former: Ponape, Truk, and Yap Districts (Trust Territory of the Pacific Islands)
abbreviation: FSM
Government type: constitutional government in free association with the US; the Compact of Free Association entered into force 3 November 1986 and the Amended Compact entered into force May 2004
Capital: Palikir
Administrative divisions: 4 states; Chuuk (Truk), Kosrae (Kosaie), Pohnpei (Ponape), Yap
Independence: 3 November 1986 (from the US-administered UN Trusteeship)
National holiday: Constitution Day, 10 May (1979)
Constitution: 10 May 1979
Legal system: based on adapted Trust Territory laws, acts of the legislature, municipal, common, and customary laws
Suffrage: 18 years of age; universal
Executive branch:
chief of state: President Joseph J. URUSEMAL (since 11 May 2003); Vice President Redley KILLION (11 May 2003); note - the president is both the chief of state and head of government
head of government: President Joseph J. URUSEMAL (since 11 May 2003); Vice President Redley KILLION (11 May 2003); note - the president is both the chief of state and head of government
cabinet: Cabinet
elections: president and vice president elected by Congress from among the four senators at large for four-year terms; election last held 11 May 2003 (next to be held May 2007); note - a proposed constitutional amendment to establish popular elections for president and vice president failed
election results: Joseph J. URUSEMAL elected president; percent of Congress vote - NA%; Redley KILLION elected vice president; percent of Congress vote - NA%
Legislative branch: unicameral Congress (14 seats; four - one elected from each state to serve four-year terms and 10 - elected from single-member districts delineated by population to serve two-year terms; members elected by popular vote)
elections: elections for four-year term seats last held 4 March 2003 (next to be held March 2007); elections for two-year term seats last held 8 March 2005 (next to be held March 2007)
election results: percent of vote - NA%; seats - independents 14
Judicial branch: Supreme Court
Political parties and leaders: no formal parties
International organization participation: ACP, AsDB, FAO, G-77, IBRD, ICAO, ICRM, IDA, IFC, IFRCS, IMF, IOC, ITU, MIGA, OPCW, PIF, Sparteca, SPC, UN, UNCTAD, UNESCO, WHO, WMO
Diplomatic representation in the US:
chief of mission: Ambassador Jesse Bibiano MAREHALAU
chancery: 1725 N Street NW, Washington, DC 20036
telephone: [1] (202) 223-4383
FAX: [1] (202) 223-4391
consulate(s) general: Honolulu and Tamuning (Guam)
Diplomatic representation from the US:
chief of mission: Ambassador Suzanne K. HALE
embassy: 101 Upper Pics Road, Kolonia
mailing address: P. O. Box 1286, Kolonia, Pohnpei, Federated States of Micronesia 96941
telephone: [691] 320-2187
FAX: [691] 320-2186
Flag description: light blue with four white five-pointed stars centered; the stars are arranged in a diamond pattern

ECONOMY

Economy - overview: Economic activity consists primarily of subsistence farming and fishing. The islands have few mineral deposits worth exploiting, except for high-grade phosphate. The potential for a tourist industry exists, but the remote location, a lack of adequate facilities, and limited air connections hinder development. The Amended Compact of Free Association with the US guarantees the Federated States of Micronesia (FSM) millions of dollars in annual aid through 2023, and establishes a Trust Fund into which the US and the FSM make annual contributions in order to provide annual payouts to the FSM in perpetuity after 2023. The country's medium-term economic outlook appears fragile due not only to the reduction in US assistance but also to the slow growth of the private sector. Geographical isolation and a poorly developed infrastructure remain major impediments to long-term growth.

GDP (purchasing power parity): $277 million
note: GDP is supplemented by grant aid, averaging perhaps $100 million annually (2002 est.)
GDP (official exchange rate): NA
GDP - real growth rate: 1% (2002 est.)
GDP - per capita: purchasing power parity - $2,000 (2002 est.)
GDP - composition by sector:
agriculture: 50%
industry: 4%
services: 46% (2000 est.)
Labor force: NA
Labor force - by occupation: two-thirds are government employees
Unemployment rate: 16% (1999 est.)
Population below poverty line: 26.7%
Household income or consumption by percentage share:
lowest 10%: NA
highest 10%: NA
Inflation rate (consumer prices): 1% (2002 est.)
Budget:
revenues: $161 million ($69 million less grants)
expenditures: $160 million, including capital expenditures of NA (1998 est.)
Agriculture - products: black pepper, tropical fruits and vegetables, coconuts, cassava (tapioca), betel nuts, sweet potatoes; pigs, chickens
Industries: tourism, construction, fish processing, specialized aquaculture, craft items from shell, wood, and pearls
Industrial production growth rate: NA
Electricity - production: 192 million kWh (2002)
Electricity - production by source: NA
Electricity - consumption: 178.6 million kWh (2002)
Electricity - exports: 0 kWh (2002)
Electricity - imports: 0 kWh (2002)
Exports: $22 million (f.o.b.) (FY99/00 est.)
Exports - partners: Japan, US, Guam (2004)
Imports: $149 million f.o.b. (FY99/00 est.)
Imports - partners: US, Australia, Japan (2004)
Debt - external: $53.1 million (FY02/03 est.)
Economic aid - recipient: under terms of the Compact of Free Association, the US pledged $1.3 billion in grant aid during the period 1986-2001; the level of aid has been subsequently reduced
Currency (code): US dollar (USD)
Currency code: USD
Exchange rates: the US dollar is used
Fiscal year: 1 October - 30 September

COMMUNICATIONS

Telephones - main lines in use: 10,100 (2001)
Telephones - mobile cellular: 1,800 (2002)
Telephone system:
general assessment: adequate system
domestic: islands interconnected by shortwave radiotelephone (used mostly for government purposes), satellite (Intelsat) ground stations, and some coaxial and fiber-optic cable; cellular service available on Kosrae, Pohnpei, and Yap
international: country code - 691; satellite earth stations - 5 Intelsat (Pacific Ocean) (2002)
Radio broadcast stations: AM 5, FM 1, shortwave 0 (2004)
Radios: 9,400 (1996)
Television broadcast stations: 3; note - cable TV also available (2004)
Televisions: 2,800 (1999)
Internet country code: .fm
Internet Service Providers (ISPs): 1 (2000)
Internet users: 6,000 (2002)

TRANSPORTATION

Airports: 6 (2004 est.)
Airports - with paved runways:
total: 6
1,524 to 2,437 m: 4
914 to 1,523 m: 2 (2005 est.)
Roadways:
total: 240 km
paved: 42 km
unpaved: 198 km (1999 est.)
Merchant marine:
total: 2 ships (1,000 GRT or over) 2,423 GRT/1,551 DWT
by type: cargo 1, passenger/cargo 1
foreign-owned: 2 (United States 2) (2005)
Ports and terminals: Tomil Harbor

MILITARY

Military branches: no ministry of defense and no standing armed forces; the paramilitary Maritime Wing, a small maritime law enforcement unit, is responsible to the Division of Maritime Surveillance within the Office of the Attorney General (2003)
Military - note: Federated States of Micronesia (FSM) is a sovereign, self-governing state in free association with the US; FSM is totally dependent on the US for its defense

TRANSNATIONAL ISSUES

Disputes - international: none

MIDWAY ISLANDS

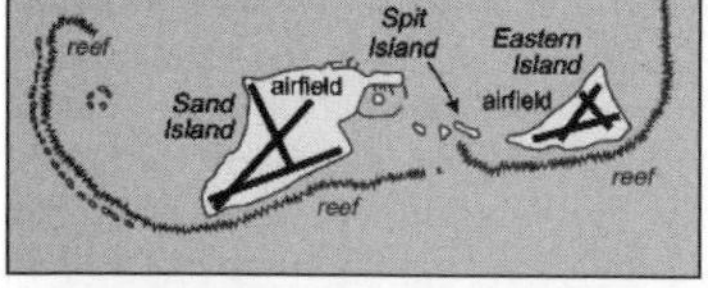

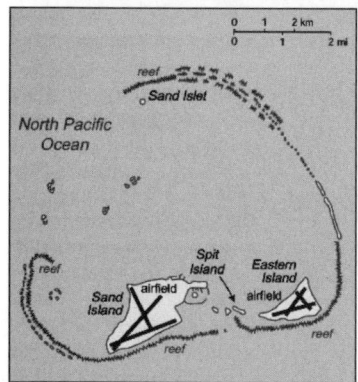

INTRODUCTION

Background: The US took formal possession of the islands in 1867. The laying of the trans-Pacific cable, which passed through the islands, brought the first residents in 1903. Between 1935 and 1947, Midway was used as a refueling stop for trans-Pacific flights. The US naval victory over a Japanese fleet off Midway in 1942 was one of the turning points of World War II. The islands continued to serve as a naval station until closed in 1993. Today the islands are a national wildlife refuge. From 1996 to 2001 the refuge was open to the public; it is now temporarily closed.

GEOGRAPHY

Location: Oceania, atoll in the North Pacific Ocean, about one-third of the way from Honolulu to Tokyo
Geographic coordinates: 28 12 N, 177 22 W
Map references: Oceania
Area:
total: 6.2 sq km
land: 6.2 sq km
water: 0 sq km
note: includes Eastern Island, Sand Island, and Spit Island
Area - comparative: about nine times the size of The Mall in Washington, DC
Land boundaries: 0 km
Coastline: 15 km
Maritime claims:
territorial sea: 12 nm
exclusive economic zone: 200 nm
Climate: subtropical; moderated by prevailing easterly winds
Terrain: low, nearly level
Elevation extremes:
lowest point: Pacific Ocean 0 m
highest point: unnamed location 13 m
Natural resources: wildlife, terrestrial and aquatic
Land use:
arable land: 0%

permanent crops: 0%
other: 100% (2001)
Irrigated land: 0 sq km (1998 est.)
Natural hazards: NA
Environment - current issues: NA
Geography - note: a coral atoll managed as a national wildlife refuge and open to the public for wildlife-related recreation in the form of wildlife observation and photography, sport fishing, snorkeling, and scuba diving; the refuge is temporarily closed for reorganization at present (2004)

PEOPLE

Population: no indigenous inhabitants; approximately 40 people make up the staff of US Fish and Wildlife Service and their services contractor living at the atoll (July 2005 est.)

GOVERNMENT

Country name:
conventional long form: none
conventional short form: Midway Islands
Dependency status: unincorporated territory of the US; formerly administered from Washington, DC, by the US Navy; on 31 October 1996, through a presidential executive order, the jurisdiction and control of the atoll was transferred to the Fish and Wildlife Service of the US Department of the Interior as part of the National Wildlife Refuge system
Legal system: the laws of the US, where applicable, apply
Flag description: the flag of the US is used

ECONOMY

Economy - overview: The economy is based on providing support services for the national wildlife refuge activities located on the islands. All food and manufactured goods must be imported.

TRANSPORTATION

Airports: 3 (2004 est.)
Airports - with paved runways:
total: 2
1,524 to 2,437 m: 2 (2005 est.)
Airports - with unpaved runways:
total: 1
914 to 1,523 m: 1 (2005 est.)
Roadways:
total: NA km
paved: NA km
unpaved: NA km
Ports and terminals: Sand Island
Transportation - note: airfield serves as an emergency landing site for commercial aircraft crossing the Pacific Ocean

MILITARY

Military - note: defense is the responsibility of the US

TRANSNATIONAL ISSUES

Disputes - international: none

MOLDOVA

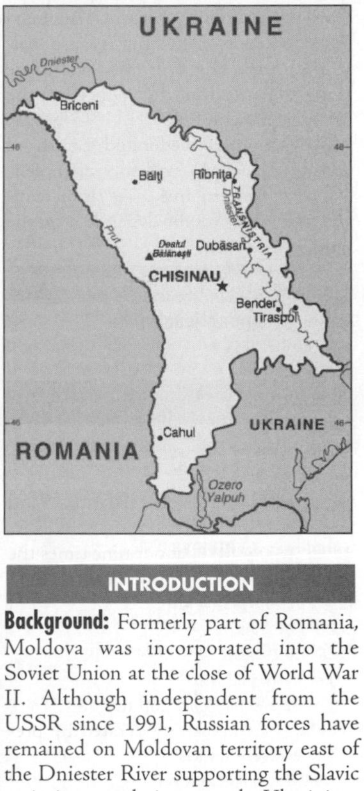

INTRODUCTION

Background: Formerly part of Romania, Moldova was incorporated into the Soviet Union at the close of World War II. Although independent from the USSR since 1991, Russian forces have remained on Moldovan territory east of the Dniester River supporting the Slavic majority population, mostly Ukrainians and Russians, who have proclaimed a "Transnistria" republic. The poorest nation in Europe, Moldova became the first former Soviet state to elect a Communist as its president in 2001.

GEOGRAPHY

Location: Eastern Europe, northeast of Romania
Geographic coordinates: 47 00 N, 29 00 E
Map references: Europe
Area:
total: 33,843 sq km
land: 33,371 sq km
water: 472 sq km
Area - comparative: slightly larger than Maryland
Land boundaries:
total: 1,389 km
border countries: Romania 450 km, Ukraine 939 km
Coastline: 0 km (landlocked)
Maritime claims: none (landlocked)
Climate: moderate winters, warm summers
Terrain: rolling steppe, gradual slope south to Black Sea
Elevation extremes:
lowest point: Dniester River 2 m
highest point: Dealul Balanesti 430 m
Natural resources: lignite, phosphorites, gypsum, arable land, limestone
Land use:
arable land: 55.3%
permanent crops: 10.79%
other: 33.91% (2001)
Irrigated land: 3,070 sq km (1998 est.)
Natural hazards: landslides (57 cases in 1998)
Environment - current issues: heavy use of agricultural chemicals, including banned pesticides such as DDT, has contaminated soil and groundwater; extensive soil erosion from poor farming methods
Environment - international agreements:
party to: Air Pollution, Air Pollution-Persistent Organic Pollutants, Biodiversity, Climate Change, Climate Change-Kyoto Protocol, Desertification, Endangered Species, Hazardous Wastes, Ozone Layer Protection
signed, but not ratified: none of the selected agreements
Geography - note: landlocked; well endowed with various sedimentary rocks and minerals including sand, gravel, gypsum, and limestone

PEOPLE

Population: 4,455,421 (July 2005 est.)
Age structure:
0-14 years: 20.2% (male 459,452/female 442,725)
15-64 years: 69.5% (male 1,489,813/female 1,606,202)
65 years and over: 10.3% (male 169,038/female 288,191) (2005 est.)
Median age:
total: 32.22 years
male: 30.14 years
female: 34.27 years (2005 est.)
Population growth rate: 0.22% (2005 est.)
Birth rate: 15.27 births/1,000 population (2005 est.)
Death rate: 12.79 deaths/1,000 population (2005 est.)
Net migration rate: -0.25 migrant(s)/1,000 population (2005 est.)
Sex ratio:
at birth: 1.05 male(s)/female
under 15 years: 1.04 male(s)/female
15-64 years: 0.93 male(s)/female

65 years and over: 0.59 male(s)/female
total population: 0.91 male(s)/female (2005 est.)
Infant mortality rate:
total: 40.42 deaths/1,000 live births
male: 43.11 deaths/1,000 live births
female: 37.58 deaths/1,000 live births (2005 est.)
Life expectancy at birth:
total population: 65.18 years
male: 61.12 years
female: 69.43 years (2005 est.)
Total fertility rate: 1.81 children born/woman (2005 est.)
HIV/AIDS - adult prevalence rate: 0.2% (2001 est.)
HIV/AIDS - people living with HIV/AIDS: 5,500 (2001 est.)
HIV/AIDS - deaths: less than 300 (2001 est.)
Nationality:
noun: Moldovan(s)
adjective: Moldovan
Ethnic groups: Moldovan/Romanian 78.2%, Ukrainian 8.4%, Russian 5.8%, Gagauz 4.4%, Bulgarian 1.9%, other 1.3% (2004 census)
note: internal disputes with ethnic Slavs in the Transnistrian region
Religions: Eastern Orthodox 98%, Jewish 1.5%, Baptist and other 0.5% (2000)
Languages: Moldovan (official, virtually the same as the Romanian language), Russian, Gagauz (a Turkish dialect)
Literacy:
definition: age 15 and over can read and write
total population: 99.1%
male: 99.6%
female: 98.7% (2003 est.)

GOVERNMENT

Country name:
conventional long form: Republic of Moldova
conventional short form: Moldova
local long form: Republica Moldova
local short form: none
former: Moldavian Soviet Socialist Republic; Moldovan Soviet Socialist Republic
Government type: republic
Capital: Chisinau
Administrative divisions: 32 raions (raioane, singular - raionul), 3 municipalities (municipiul), 1 autonomous territorial unit (unitatea teritoriala autonoma), and 1 territorial unit (unitatea teritoriala)
: counties: Anenii Noi, Basarabeasca, Briceni, Cahul, Cantemir, Calarasi, Causeni, Cimislia, Criuleni, Donduseni, Drochia, Dubasari, Edinet, Falesti, Floresti, Glodeni, Hincesti, Ialoveni, Leova, Nisporeni, Ocnita, Orhei, Rezina, Riscani, Singerei, Soldanesti, Soroca, Stefan-Voda, Straseni, Taraclia, Telenesti, Ungheni
: municipalities: Balti, Bender, Chisinau
: autonomous territorial unit: Gagauzia
: territorial unit: Stinga Nistrului
Independence: 27 August 1991 (from Soviet Union)
National holiday: Independence Day, 27 August (1991)
Constitution: new constitution adopted 29 July 1994, effective 27 August 1994; replaced old Soviet constitution of 1979
Legal system: based on civil law system; Constitutional Court reviews legality of legislative acts and governmental decisions of resolution; it is unclear if Moldova accepts compulsory ICJ jurisdiction but accepts many UN and Organization for Security and Cooperation in Europe (OSCE) documents
Suffrage: 18 years of age; universal
Executive branch:
chief of state: President Vladimir VORONIN (since 4 April 2001)
head of government: Prime Minister Vasile TARLEV (since 15 April 2001), First Deputy Prime Minister Zinaida GRECIANII (since 10 October 2005)
cabinet: selected by president, subject to approval of Parliament
elections: president elected by Parliament for a four-year term; election last held 4 April 2005 (next to be held NA 2009); note - prime minister designated by the president, upon consultation with Parliament; within 15 days from designation, the prime minister-designate must request a vote of confidence from the Parliament regarding his/her work program and entire cabinet; prime minister designated 15 April 2001, cabinet received a vote of confidence 19 April 2001
election results: Vladimir VORONIN reelected president; parliamentary votes - Vladimir VORONIN 75, Gheorghe DUCA 1; Vasile TARLEV designated prime minister; parliamentary votes of confidence - 75 of 101
Legislative branch: unicameral Parliament or Parlamentul (101 seats; parties and electoral blocs elected by popular vote to serve four-year terms)
elections: last held 6 March 2005 (next to be held NA 2009)
election results: percent of vote by party - PCRM 46.1%, Democratic Moldova Bloc 28.4%, PPCD 9.1%, other parties 16.4%; seats by party - PCRM 56, Democratic Moldova Bloc 34, PPCD 11
Judicial branch: Supreme Court; Constitutional Court (the sole authority for constitutional judicature)
Political parties and leaders: Braghis Faction [Dumitru BRAGHIS]; Christian Democratic Popular Party or PPCD [Iurie ROSCA]; Communist Party of the Republic of Moldova or PCRM [Vladimir VORONIN, first chairman]; Democratic Party [Dumitru DIACOV]; Our Moldova Alliance or AMN [Serafim URECHEANU]; Social Liberal Party or PSL [Oleg SEREBRIAN]
Political pressure groups and leaders: NA
International organization participation: ACCT, BSEC, CE, CEI, CIS, EAPC, EBRD, FAO, GUAM, IAEA, IBRD, ICAO, ICCt (signatory), ICFTU, IDA, IFAD, IFC, IFRCS, ILO, IMF, IMO, Interpol, IOC, IOM, ISO (correspondent), ITU, MIGA, OPCW, OSCE, PFP, UN, UNCTAD, UNESCO, UNIDO, UNMIL, UNMIS, UNOCI, UPU, WCO, WHO, WIPO, WMO, WToO, WTO
Diplomatic representation in the US:
chief of mission: Ambassador Mihail MANOLI
chancery: 2101 S Street NW, Washington, DC 20008
telephone: [1] (202) 667-1130
FAX: [1] (202) 667-1204
Diplomatic representation from the US:
chief of mission: Ambassador Heather M. HODGES
embassy: 103 Mateevici Street, Chisinau MD-2009
mailing address: use embassy street address
telephone: [373] (22) 408-300
FAX: [373] (22) 23-30-44
Flag description: same color scheme as Romania - three equal vertical bands of blue (hoist side), yellow, and red; emblem in center of flag is of a Roman eagle of gold outlined in black with a red beak and talons carrying a yellow cross in its beak and a green olive branch in its right talons and a yellow scepter in its left talons; on its breast is a shield divided horizontally red over blue with a stylized ox head, star, rose, and crescent all in black-outlined yellow

ECONOMY

Economy - overview: Moldova remains one of the poorest countries in Europe despite recent progress from its small economic base. It enjoys a favorable climate and good farmland but has no major mineral deposits. As a result, the economy depends heavily on agriculture, featuring fruits, vegetables, wine, and tobacco. Moldova must import almost all of its energy supplies. Energy shortages contributed to sharp production declines after the breakup of the Soviet Union in December 1991. As part of an ambitious reform effort after independence, Moldova introduced a convertible currency, freed prices, stopped issuing preferential credits to state enterprises, backed steady land privatization, removed export controls, and freed interest rates. The government entered into agreements with the World Bank and the IMF to promote growth and reduce poverty. The economy returned to positive growth in 2000, and has remained at or above 6% every year since. Further reforms will come slowly because of strong political forces backing government controls. The economy remains vulnerable to higher fuel prices, poor agricultural weather, and the skepticism of foreign investors.

GDP (purchasing power parity): $9.367 billion (2005 est.)
GDP (official exchange rate): $2.547 billion (2005 est.)
GDP - real growth rate: 6% (2005 est.)
GDP - per capita: purchasing power parity - $2,100 (2005 est.)
GDP - composition by sector:
agriculture: 20.5%
industry: 23.9%
services: 55.6% (2005 est.)
Labor force: 1.34 million (2005 est.)
Labor force - by occupation: agriculture 40%, industry 14%, services 46% (1998)
Unemployment rate: 8% (roughly 25% of working age Moldovans are employed abroad) (2002 est.)
Population below poverty line: 80% (2001 est.)
Household income or consumption by percentage share:
lowest 10%: 2.2%
highest 10%: 30.7% (1997)
Distribution of family income - Gini index: 36.2 (2001)
Inflation rate (consumer prices): 12% (2005 est.)
Investment (gross fixed): 21% of GDP (2005 est.)
Budget:
revenues: $1.069 billion
expenditures: $1.065 billion, including capital expenditures of NA (2005 est.)
Public debt: 72.9% of GDP (2005 est.)
Agriculture - products: vegetables, fruits, wine, grain, sugar beets, sunflower seed, tobacco; beef, milk
Industries: food processing, agricultural machinery, foundry equipment, refrigerators and freezers, washing machines, hosiery, sugar, vegetable oil, shoes, textiles
Industrial production growth rate: 17% (2003 est.)
Electricity - production: 2.942 billion kWh (2003)
Electricity - production by source:
fossil fuel: 90.6%
hydro: 9.4%
nuclear: 0%
other: 0% (2001)
Electricity - consumption: 3.036 billion kWh (2003)
Electricity - exports: 300 million kWh (2003)
Electricity - imports: 600 million kWh (2003)
Oil - production: 0 bbl/day (2003 est.)
Oil - consumption: 37,000 bbl/day (2003 est.)
Oil - exports: NA (2001)
Oil - imports: NA (2001)
Natural gas - production: 0 cu m (2001 est.)
Natural gas - consumption: 2.05 billion cu m (2001 est.)
Natural gas - exports: 0 cu m (2001 est.)
Natural gas - imports: 2.05 billion cu m (2001 est.)
Current account balance: $-178 million (2005 est.)
Exports: $1.04 billion f.o.b. (2005 est.)
Exports - partners: Russia 35.8%, Italy 13.9%, Romania 10%, Germany 7.3%, Ukraine 6.6%, Belarus 6%, US 4.6% (2004)
Imports: $2.23 billion f.o.b. (2005 est.)
Imports - partners: Ukraine 24.6%, Russia 12.2%, Romania 9.3%, Germany 8.5%, Italy 7.4% (2004)
Reserves of foreign exchange and gold: $520 million (2005 est.)
Debt - external: $1.926 billion (2005 est.)
Economic aid - recipient: $100 million (2000)
Currency (code): Moldovan leu (MDL)
Currency code: MDL
Exchange rates: lei per US dollar - 12.56 (2005), 12.33 (2004), 13.945 (2003), 13.571 (2002), 12.865 (2001)
Fiscal year: calendar year

COMMUNICATIONS

Telephones - main lines in use: 706,900 (2002)
Telephones - mobile cellular: 338,200 (2002)
Telephone system:
general assessment: inadequate, outmoded, poor service outside Chisinau; some effort to modernize is under way
domestic: new subscribers face long wait for service; mobile cellular telephone service being introduced
international: country code - 373; service through Romania and Russia via landline; satellite earth stations - Intelsat, Eutelsat, and Intersputnik
Radio broadcast stations: AM 7, FM 50, shortwave 3 (1998)
Radios: 3.22 million (1997)
Television broadcast stations: 1 (plus 30 repeaters) (1995)
Televisions: 1.26 million (1997)
Internet country code: .md
Internet hosts: 11,984 (2003)
Internet Service Providers (ISPs): 2 (1999)
Internet users: 150,000 (2002)

TRANSPORTATION

Airports: 23 (2004 est.)
Airports - with paved runways:
total: 6
over 3,047 m: 1
2,438 to 3,047 m: 2
1,524 to 2,437 m: 2
under 914 m: 1 (2005 est.)
Airports - with unpaved runways:
total: 9
1,524 to 2,437 m: 1
914 to 1,523 m: 4
under 914 m: 4 (2005 est.)
Pipelines: gas 606 km (2004)
Railways:
total: 1,138 km
broad gauge: 1,124 km 1.520-m gauge
standard gauge: 14 km 1.435-m gauge (2004)
Roadways:
total: 12,719 km
paved: 10,977 km
unpaved: 1,742 km (2002)
Waterways: 424 km (2004)
Merchant marine:
total: 2 ships (1,000 GRT or over) 1,636 GRT/1,088 DWT
by type: cargo 2 (2005)

MILITARY

Military branches: National Army: Ground Forces, Air Force
Military service age and obligation: 18 years of age for compulsory military service; national service obligation - 12 months (2004)
Manpower available for military service:
males age 18-49: 1,066,459 (2005 est.)
Manpower fit for military service: *males age 18-49:* 693,913 (2005 est.)
Manpower reaching military service age annually: *males:* 43,729 (2005 est.)
Military expenditures - dollar figure: $8.7 million (2004)
Military expenditures - percent of GDP: 0.4% (FY02)

TRANSNATIONAL ISSUES

Disputes - international: Moldova and Ukraine have established joint customs posts to monitor transit through Moldova's break-away Transnistria Region which remains under OSCE supervision
Refugees and internally displaced persons:
IDPs: 1,000 (internal secessionist uprising in Transdniestrian region in 1991) (2004)
Illicit drugs: limited cultivation of opium poppy and cannabis, mostly for CIS consumption; transshipment point for illicit drugs from Southwest Asia via Central Asia to Russia, Western Europe, and possibly the US; widespread crime and underground economic activity

MONACO

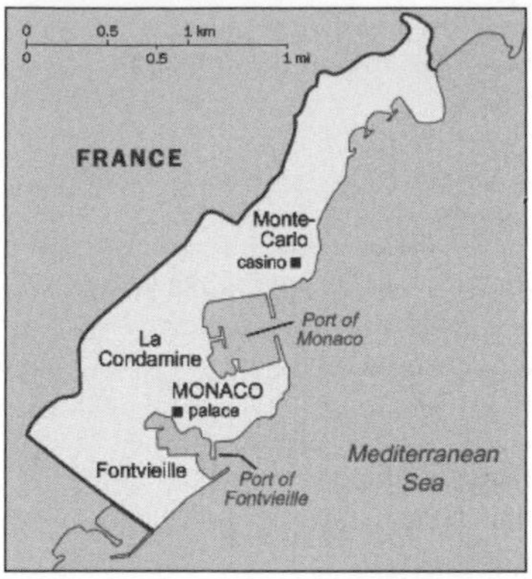

INTRODUCTION

Background: Economic development was spurred in the late 19th century with a railroad linkup to France and the opening of a casino. Since then, the principality's mild climate, splendid scenery, and gambling facilities have made Monaco world famous as a tourist and recreation center.

GEOGRAPHY

Location: Western Europe, bordering the Mediterranean Sea on the southern coast of France, near the border with Italy
Geographic coordinates: 43 44 N, 7 24 E
Map references: Europe
Area:
total: 1.95 sq km
land: 1.95 sq km
water: 0 sq km
Area - comparative: about three times the size of The Mall in Washington, DC
Land boundaries:
total: 4.4 km
border countries: France 4.4 km
Coastline: 4.1 km
Maritime claims:
territorial sea: 12 nm
Climate: Mediterranean with mild, wet winters and hot, dry summers
Terrain: hilly, rugged, rocky
Elevation extremes:
lowest point: Mediterranean Sea 0 m
highest point: Mont Agel 140 m
Natural resources: none
Land use:
arable land: 0%
permanent crops: 0%
other: 100% (urban area) (2001)
Irrigated land: NA sq km
Natural hazards: NA
Environment - current issues: NA
Environment - international agreements:
party to: Air Pollution, Air Pollution-Volatile Organic Compounds, Biodiversity, Climate Change, Desertification, Endangered Species, Hazardous Wastes, Law of the Sea, Marine Dumping, Ozone Layer Protection, Ship Pollution, Wetlands, Whaling
signed, but not ratified: Climate Change-Kyoto Protocol
Geography - note: second-smallest independent state in the world (after Holy See); almost entirely urban

PEOPLE

Population: 32,409 (July 2005 est.)
Age structure:
0-14 years: 15.5% (male 2,563/female 2,445)
15-64 years: 62.1% (male 9,909/female 10,217)
65 years and over: 22.4% (male 2,972/female 4,303) (2005 est.)
Median age:
total: 45.25 years
male: 43.27 years
female: 47.19 years (2005 est.)
Population growth rate: 0.43% (2005 est.)
Birth rate: 9.26 births/1,000 population (2005 est.)
Death rate: 12.71 deaths/1,000 population (2005 est.)
Net migration rate: 7.71 migrant(s)/1,000 population (2005 est.)
Sex ratio:
at birth: 1.05 male(s)/female
under 15 years: 1.05 male(s)/female
15-64 years: 0.97 male(s)/female
65 years and over: 0.69 male(s)/female
total population: 0.91 male(s)/female (2005 est.)
Infant mortality rate:
total: 5.43 deaths/1,000 live births
male: 6.29 deaths/1,000 live births
female: 4.53 deaths/1,000 live births (2005 est.)
Life expectancy at birth:
total population: 79.57 years
male: 75.7 years
female: 83.63 years (2005 est.)
Total fertility rate: 1.76 children born/woman (2005 est.)
HIV/AIDS - adult prevalence rate: NA%
HIV/AIDS - people living with HIV/AIDS: NA
HIV/AIDS - deaths: NA
Nationality:
noun: Monegasque(s) or Monacan(s)
adjective: Monegasque or Monacan
Ethnic groups: French 47%, Monegasque 16%, Italian 16%, other 21%
Religions: Roman Catholic 90%
Languages: French (official), English, Italian, Monegasque
Literacy:
definition: NA
total population: 99%
male: NA%
female: NA%

GOVERNMENT

Country name:
conventional long form: Principality of Monaco
conventional short form: Monaco
local long form: Principaute de Monaco
local short form: Monaco
Government type: constitutional monarchy
Capital: Monaco
Administrative divisions: none; there are no first-order administrative divisions as defined by the US Government, but there are four quarters (quartiers, singular - quartier); Fontvieille, La Condamine, Monaco-Ville, Monte-Carlo
Independence: 1419 (beginning of the rule by the House of Grimaldi)
National holiday: National Day (Prince of Monaco Holiday), 19 November
Constitution: 17 December 1962
Legal system: based on French law; has not accepted compulsory ICJ jurisdiction
Suffrage: 21 years of age; universal
Executive branch:
chief of state: Prince ALBERT II (since 6 April 2005)
head of government: Minister of State Jean-Paul PROUST (since 1 June 2005)
cabinet: Council of Government is under the authority of the monarch
elections: none; the monarchy is hereditary; minister of state appointed by the monarch from a list of three French national candidates presented by the French Government
Legislative branch: unicameral National Council or Conseil National (24 seats; 16 members elected by list majority system, 8 by proportional representation; to serve five-year terms)
elections: last held 9 February 2003 (next to be held February 2008)
election results: percent of vote by party - NA%; seats by party - UNAM 21, UND 3
Judicial branch: Supreme Court or Tribunal Supreme (judges appointed by the monarch on the basis of nominations by the National Council)
Political parties and leaders: National and Democratic Union or UND [Jean-Louis CAMPORA]; Union for Monaco or UPM (including National Union for the Future of Monaco or UNAM) [leader NA]
Political pressure groups and leaders: NA
International organization participation: ACCT, CE, FAO, IAEA, ICAO, ICC, ICCt (signatory), ICRM, IFRCS, IHO, IMO, Interpol, IOC, ITU, OPCW, OSCE, UN, UNCTAD, UNESCO, UNIDO, UNITAR, UPU, WHO, WIPO, WMO, WToO

Diplomatic representation in the US: Monaco does not have an embassy in the US
consulate(s) general: New York
Diplomatic representation from the US: the US does not have an embassy in Monaco; the US Consul General in Marseille (France) is accredited to Monaco
Flag description: two equal horizontal bands of red (top) and white; similar to the flag of Indonesia which is longer and the flag of Poland which is white (top) and red

ECONOMY

Economy - overview: Monaco, bordering France on the Mediterranean coast, is a popular resort, attracting tourists to its casino and pleasant climate. In 2001, a major construction project extended the pier used by cruise ships in the main harbor. The principality has successfully sought to diversify into services and small, high-value-added, nonpolluting industries. The state has no income tax and low business taxes and thrives as a tax haven both for individuals who have established residence and for foreign companies that have set up businesses and offices. The state retains monopolies in a number of sectors, including tobacco, the telephone network, and the postal service. Living standards are high, roughly comparable to those in prosperous French metropolitan areas. Monaco does not publish national income figures; the estimates below are extremely rough.
GDP (purchasing power parity): $870 million (2000 est.)
GDP (official exchange rate): NA
GDP - real growth rate: 0.9% (2000 est.)
GDP - per capita: purchasing power parity - $27,000 (2000 est.)
GDP - composition by sector:
agriculture: 17%
industry: NA%
services: NA% (2001 est.)
Labor force: 30,540 (January 1994)
Unemployment rate: 22% (1999)
Population below poverty line: NA
Household income or consumption by percentage share:
lowest 10%: NA%
highest 10%: NA%
Inflation rate (consumer prices): 1.9% (2000)
Budget:
revenues: $518 million
expenditures: $531 million, including capital expenditures of NA (1995)
Agriculture - products: none
Industries: tourism, construction, small-scale industrial and consumer products
Industrial production growth rate: NA%
Electricity - consumption: NA kWh
Electricity - imports: NA kWh
note: electricity supplied by France
Exports: $NA; full customs integration with France, which collects and rebates Monegasque trade duties; also participates in EU market system through customs union with France
Imports: $NA; full customs integration with France, which collects and rebates Monegasque trade duties; also participates in EU market system through customs union with France
Debt - external: $18 billion (2000 est.)
Economic aid - recipient: NA
Currency (code): euro (EUR)
Currency code: EUR
Exchange rates: euros per US dollar - 0.79697 (2005), 0.8054 (2004), 0.886 (2003), 1.0626 (2002), 1.1175 (2001)
Fiscal year: calendar year

COMMUNICATIONS

Telephones - main lines in use: 33,700 (2002)
Telephones - mobile cellular: 19,300 (2002)
Telephone system:
general assessment: modern automatic telephone system
domestic: NA
international: country code - 377; no satellite earth stations; connected by cable into the French communications system
Radio broadcast stations: AM 1, FM NA, shortwave 8 (1998)
Radios: 34,000 (1997)
Television broadcast stations: 5 (1998)
Televisions: 25,000 (1997)
Internet country code: .mc
Internet hosts: 533 (2004)
Internet Service Providers (ISPs): 2 (2000)
Internet users: 16,000 (2002)

TRANSPORTATION

Airports: none; linked to the airport at Nice, France by helicopter service (2004 est.)
Heliports: 1 (shuttle service between the international airport at Nice, France, and Monaco's heliport at Fontvieille) (2004 est.)
Roadways:
total: 50 km
paved: 50 km
unpaved: 0 km (1999 est.)
Merchant marine:
registered in other countries: 54 (2005)
Ports and terminals: Monaco

MILITARY

Military - note: defense is the responsibility of France; the Palace Guard performs ceremonial duties (2003)

TRANSNATIONAL ISSUES

Disputes - international: none

MONGOLIA

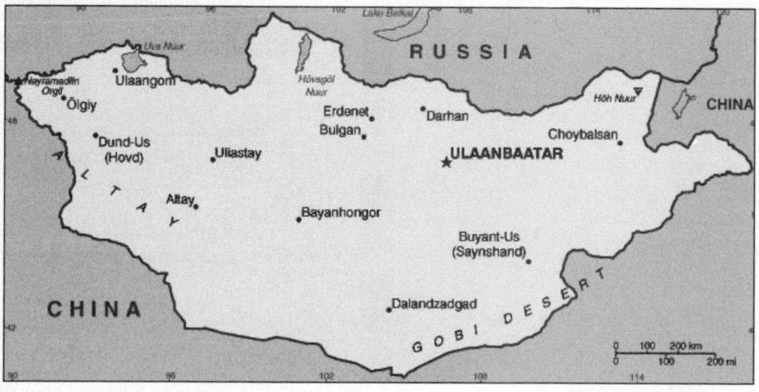

INTRODUCTION

Background: The Mongols gained fame in the 13th century when under Chinggis KHAN they conquered a huge Eurasian empire. After his death the empire was divided into several powerful Mongol states, but these broke apart in the 14th century. The Mongols eventually retired to their original steppe homelands and later came under Chinese rule. Mongolia won its independence in 1921 with Soviet backing. A Communist regime was installed in 1924. During the early 1990s, the ex-Communist Mongolian People's Revolutionary Party (MPRP) gradually yielded its monopoly on power to the Democratic Union Coalition (DUC), which defeated the MPRP in a national election in 1996. Since then, parliamentary elections returned the MPRP overwhelmingly to power in 2000 and produced a coalition government in 2004.

GEOGRAPHY

Location: Northern Asia, between China and Russia
Geographic coordinates: 46 00 N, 105 00 E
Map references: Asia
Area:
total: 1,564,116 sq km
Area - comparative: slightly smaller than Alaska
Land boundaries:
total: 8,220 km
border countries: China 4,677 km, Russia 3,543 km
Coastline: 0 km (landlocked)
Maritime claims: none (landlocked)
Climate: desert; continental (large daily and seasonal temperature ranges)
Terrain: vast semidesert and desert plains, grassy steppe, mountains in west and southwest; Gobi Desert in south-central
Elevation extremes:
lowest point: Hoh Nuur 518 m
highest point: Nayramadlin Orgil (Huyten Orgil) 4,374 m
Natural resources: oil, coal, copper, molybdenum, tungsten, phosphates, tin, nickel, zinc, fluorspar, gold, silver, iron
Land use:
arable land: 0.77%
permanent crops: 0%
other: 99.23% (2001)
Irrigated land: 840 sq km (1998 est.)
Natural hazards: dust storms, grassland and forest fires, drought, and "zud," which is harsh winter conditions
Environment - current issues: limited natural fresh water resources in some areas; the policies of former Communist regimes promoted rapid urbanization and industrial growth that had negative effects on the environment; the burning of soft coal in power plants and the lack of enforcement of environmental laws severely polluted the air in Ulaanbaatar; deforestation, overgrazing, and the converting of virgin land to agricultural production increased soil erosion from wind and rain; desertification and mining activities had a deleterious effect on the environment
Environment - international agreements:
party to: Biodiversity, Climate Change, Climate Change-Kyoto Protocol, Desertification, Endangered Species, Environmental Modification, Hazardous Wastes, Law of the Sea, Ozone Layer Protection, Wetlands
signed, but not ratified: none of the selected agreements
Geography - note: landlocked; strategic location between China and Russia

PEOPLE

Population: 2,791,272 (July 2005 est.)
Age structure:
0-14 years: 28.7% (male 407,547/female 392,440)
15-64 years: 67.7% (male 943,418/female 945,063)
65 years and over: 3.7% (male 44,413/female 58,391) (2005 est.)
Median age:
total: 24.28 years
male: 23.93 years
female: 24.64 years (2005 est.)
Population growth rate: 1.45% (2005 est.)
Birth rate: 21.52 births/1,000 population (2005 est.)
Death rate: 7.03 deaths/1,000 population (2005 est.)
Net migration rate: 0 migrant(s)/1,000 population (2005 est.)
Sex ratio:
at birth: 1.05 male(s)/female
under 15 years: 1.04 male(s)/female
15-64 years: 1 male(s)/female
65 years and over: 0.76 male(s)/female
total population: 1 male(s)/female (2005 est.)
Infant mortality rate:
total: 53.79 deaths/1,000 live births
male: 57.25 deaths/1,000 live births
female: 50.16 deaths/1,000 live births (2005 est.)
Life expectancy at birth:
total population: 64.52 years
male: 62.3 years
female: 66.86 years (2005 est.)
Total fertility rate: 2.26 children born/woman (2005 est.)
HIV/AIDS - adult prevalence rate: less than 0.1% (2003 est.)
HIV/AIDS - people living with HIV/AIDS: less than 500 (2003 est)
HIV/AIDS - deaths: less than 200 (2003 est.)
Nationality:
noun: Mongolian(s)
adjective: Mongolian
Ethnic groups: Mongol (mostly Khalkha) 94.9%, Turkic (mostly Kazakh) 5%, other (including Chinese and Russian) 0.1% (2000)
Religions: Buddhist Lamaist 50%, none 40%, Shamanist and Christian 6%, Muslim 4% (2004)
Languages: Khalkha Mongol 90%, Turkic, Russian (1999)
Literacy:
definition: age 15 and over can read and write
total population: 97.8%
male: 98%
female: 97.5% (2002)

GOVERNMENT

Country name:
conventional long form: none
conventional short form: Mongolia
local long form: none
local short form: Mongol Uls
former: Outer Mongolia
Government type: mixed parliamentary/presidential
Capital: Ulaanbaatar
Administrative divisions: 21 provinces (aymguud, singular - aymag) and 1 municipality* (singular - hot); Arhangay, Bayanhongor, Bayan-Olgiy, Bulgan, Darhan Uul, Dornod, Dornogovi, Dundgovi, Dzavhan, Govi-Altay, Govi-Sumber, Hentiy, Hovd, Hovsgol, Omnogovi, Orhon, Ovorhangay, Selenge, Suhbaatar, Tov, Ulaanbaatar*, Uvs
Independence: 11 July 1921 (from China)
National holiday: Independence Day/Revolution Day, 11 July (1921)
Constitution: 12 February 1992
Legal system: blend of Soviet, German, and US systems that combine "continental" or "civil" code and case-precedent; constitution ambiguous on judicial review of legislative acts; has not accepted compulsory ICJ jurisdiction
Suffrage: 18 years of age; universal
Executive branch:
chief of state: President Nambaryn ENKHBAYAR (since 24 June 2005)
head of government: Prime Minister Tsakhia ELBEGDORJ (since 20 August 2004); Deputy Prime Minister Chultem ULAAN (since 28 September 2004)
cabinet: Cabinet appointed by the State Great Hural (parliament) in consultation with the president
elections: presidential candidates nominated by political parties represented in State Great Hural and elected by popular vote for a four-year term; presidential tenure limited to two four-year terms; election last held 22 May 2005 (next to be held in May 2009); following legislative elections, leader of majority party or majority coalition is usually elected prime minister by State Great Hural
election results: Nambaryn ENKHBAYAR elected president; percent of vote - Nambaryn ENKHBAYAR (MPRP) 53.44%, Mendsaikhanin ENKHSAIKHAN (DP) 20.05%, Bazarsadyn JARGALSAIKHAN (MRP) 13.92%, Badarchyn ERDENEBAT (M-MNSDP) 12.59%; Tsakhi ELBEGDORJ elected prime minister by the State Great Hural 74 to 0
Legislative branch: unicameral State Great Hural 76 seats; members elected by popular vote to serve four-year terms
elections: last held 27 June 2004 (next to

be held in June 2008)
election results: percent of vote by party - MPRP 48.78%, MDC 44.8%, independents 3.5%, Republican Party 1.5%, others 1.42%; seats by party - MPRP 36, MDC 34, others 4; note - following June 2004 election MDC collapsed; as of 1 December 2005 composition of legislature was MPRP 37, DP 26, M-MNSDP 7, CWRP 2, MRP 1, independents 3
Judicial branch: Supreme Court (serves as appeals court for people's and provincial courts but rarely overturns verdicts of lower courts; judges are nominated by the General Council of Courts and approved by the president)
Political parties and leaders: Citizens' Will Republican Party or CWRP (also called Civil Courage Republican Party or CCRP) [Sanjaasurengiin OYUN]; Democratic Party or DP [R. GONCHIKDORJ]; Motherland-Mongolian New Socialist Democratic Party or M-MNSDP [Badarchyn ERDENEBAT]; Mongolian People's Revolutionary Party or MPRP [Nambaryn ENKHBAYAR], Mongolian Republican Party or MRP [Bazarsadyn JARGALSAIKHAN]
note: DP and M-MNSDP formed Motherland-Democracy Coalition (MDC) in 2003 and with CWRP contested June 2004 elections as single party; MDC's leadership dissolved coalition in December 2004
Political pressure groups and leaders: NA
International organization participation: ARF, AsDB, CP, EBRD, FAO, G-77, IAEA, IBRD, ICAO, ICCt, ICFTU, ICRM, IDA, IFAD, IFC, IFRCS, ILO, IMF, IMO, Interpol, IOC, ISO, ITU, MIGA, MINURSO, MONUC, NAM, OPCW, OSCE (partner), SCO (observer), UN, UNCTAD, UNESCO, UNIDO, UNMIS, UPU, WCO, WHO, WIPO, WMO, WToO, WTO
Diplomatic representation in the US:
chief of mission: Ambassador Ravdangiyn BOLD
chancery: 2833 M Street NW, Washington, DC 20007
telephone: [1] (202) 333-7117
FAX: [1] (202) 298-9227
consulate(s) general: New York
Diplomatic representation from the US:
chief of mission: Ambassador Pamela J. SLUTZ
embassy: Micro Region 11, Big Ring Road, C.P.O. 1021, Ulaanbaatar 13
mailing address: PSC 461, Box 300, FPO AP 96521-0002
telephone: [976] (11) 329095
FAX: [976] (11) 320776
Flag description: three equal, vertical bands of red (hoist side), blue, and red; centered on the hoist-side red band in yellow is the national emblem ("soyombo" - a columnar arrangement of abstract and geometric representation for fire, sun, moon, earth, water, and the yin-yang symbol)

ECONOMY

Economy - overview: Economic activity in Mongolia has traditionally been based on herding and agriculture. Mongolia has extensive mineral deposits. Copper, coal, molybdenum, tin, tungsten and gold account for a large part of industrial production. Soviet assistance, at its height one-third of GDP, disappeared almost overnight in 1990 and 1991 at the time of the dismantlement of the USSR. The following decade saw Mongolia endure both deep recession due to political inaction and natural disasters, as well as economic growth because of reform-embracing, free-market economics and extensive privatization of the formerly state-run economy. Severe winters and summer droughts in 2000, 2001, and 2002 resulted in massive livestock die-off and zero or negative GDP growth. This was compounded by falling prices for Mongolia's primary sector exports and widespread opposition to privatization. Growth averaged about 5% from 2002 to 2005, largely because of high copper prices and new gold production. Mongolia's economy continues to be heavily impacted by its neighbors. For example, Mongolia purchases 80% of its petroleum products and a substantial amount of electric power from Russia, leaving it vulnerable to price increases. China is Mongolia's chief export partner and a main source of the "shadow" or "grey" economy. The World Bank and other international financial institutions estimate the grey economy to be at least equal to that of the official economy. The actual size of this grey - largely cash - economy is difficult to calculate since the money does not pass through the hands of tax authorities or the banking sector. Remittances from Mongolians working abroad both legally and illegally constitute a sizeable portion. Money laundering is growing as an accompanying concern. Mongolia settled its $11 billion debt with Russia at the end of 2003 on favorable terms. Mongolia, which joined the World Trade Organization in 1997, seeks to expand its participation and integration into Asian regional economic and trade regimes.
GDP (purchasing power parity): $6.01 billion (2005 est.)
GDP (official exchange rate): $1.428 billion (2005 est.)
GDP - real growth rate: 5.5% according to official estimate (2005 est.)
GDP - per capita: purchasing power parity - $2,200 (2005 est.)
GDP - composition by sector:
agriculture: 20.6%
industry: 21.4%
services: 58% (2003 est.)
Labor force: 1.488 million (2003)
Labor force - by occupation: herding/agriculture 42%, mining 4%, manufacturing 6%, trade 14%, services 29%, public sector 5%, other 3.7% (2003)
Unemployment rate: 6.7% (2003)
Population below poverty line: 36.1% (2004 est.)
Household income or consumption by percentage share:
lowest 10%: 2.1%
highest 10%: 37% (1995)
Distribution of family income - Gini index: 44 (1998)
Inflation rate (consumer prices): 11% (2004 est.)
Budget:
revenues: $582 million
expenditures: $602 million, including capital expenditures of NA (2004)
Agriculture - products: wheat, barley, vegetables, forage crops, sheep, goats, cattle, camels, horses
Industries: construction and construction materials; mining (coal, copper, molybdenum, fluorspar, and gold); oil; food and beverages; processing of animal products, cashmere and natural fiber manufacturing
Industrial production growth rate: 4.1% (2002 est.)
Electricity - production: 2.692 billion kWh (2004 est.)
Electricity - production by source:
fossil fuel: 100%
hydro: 0%
nuclear: 0%
other: 0% (2001)
Electricity - consumption: 2.908 billion kWh (2004 est.)
Electricity - exports: 8.2 million kWh (2004 est.)
Electricity - imports: 130.5 million kWh (2004 est.)
Oil - production: 541.5 bbl/day (2004 est.)
Oil - consumption: 11,000 bbl/day (2004 est.)
Oil - exports: 497 bbl/day (2004 est.)
Oil - imports: 11,000 bbl/day (2004 est.)
Exports: $852 million f.o.b. (2004 est.)
Exports - partners: China 47.8%, US 17.9%, UK 15.7% (2004)
Imports: $1.011 billion c.i.f. (2004 est.)
Imports - partners: Russia 33.3%, China 23.6%, Japan 7.4%, South Korea 6%, US 4.6% (2004)
Debt - external: $1.36 billion (2004)
Economic aid - recipient: $215 million

(2003)
Currency (code): togrog/tugrik (MNT)
Currency code: MNT
Exchange rates: togrogs/tugriks per US dollar - 1,187.17 (2005), 1,185.3 (2004), 1,146.5 (2003), 1,110.3 (2002), 1,097.7 (2001)
Fiscal year: calendar year

COMMUNICATIONS

Telephones - main lines in use: 142,300 (2004)
Telephones - mobile cellular: 404,400 (2004)
Telephone system:
general assessment: network is improving with international direct dialing available in many areas
domestic: very low density of about 6.5 telephones for each thousand persons; two wireless providers cover all but two provinces
international: country code - 976; satellite earth station - 1 Intersputnik (Indian Ocean Region)
Radio broadcast stations: AM 7, FM 62, shortwave 3 (2004)
Radios: 155,900 (1999)
Television broadcast stations: 52 (plus 21 provincial repeaters and many low power repeaters) (2004)
Televisions: 168,800 (1999)
Internet country code: .mn
Internet hosts: 1,000 (2004)
Internet Service Providers (ISPs): 5 (2001)
Internet users: 220,000 (2004)

TRANSPORTATION

Airports: 46 (2004 est.)
Airports - with paved runways:
total: 14
over 3,047 m: 1
2,438 to 3,047 m: 12
1,524 to 2,437 m: 1 (2005 est.)
Airports - with unpaved runways:
total: 34
over 3,047 m: 3
2,438 to 3,047 m: 4
1,524 to 2,437 m: 24
914 to 1,523 m: 2
under 914 m: 1 (2005 est.)
Heliports: 2 (2005 est.)
Railways:
total: 1,810 km
broad gauge: 1,810 km 1.524-m gauge (2004)
Roadways:
total: 49,256 km
paved: 8,874 km
unpaved: 40,376 km (2002)
Waterways: 580 km
note: only waterway in operation is Lake Hovsgol (135 km); Selenge River (270 km) and Orhon River (175 km) are navigable but carry little traffic; lakes and rivers freeze in winter, are open from May to September (2004)
Merchant marine:
total: 65 ships (1,000 GRT or over) 339,423 GRT/533,853 DWT
by type: bulk carrier 6, cargo 54, liquefied gas 2, passenger/cargo 1, refrigerated cargo 1, roll on/roll off 1
foreign-owned: 38 (China 2, Lebanon 1, Philippines 1, Russia 10, Singapore 10, South Korea 1, Syria 1, Thailand 1, Ukraine 1, UAE 4, Vietnam 6) (2005)

MILITARY

Military branches: Mongolian Armed Forces: Mongolian People's Army (MPA), Mongolian People's Air Force (MPAF) (2005)
Military service age and obligation: 18-25 years of age for compulsory military service; conscript service obligation - 12 months (2004)
Manpower available for military service: *males age 18-49:* 736,182 (2005 est.)
Manpower fit for military service: *males age 18-49:* 570,435 (2005 est.)
Manpower reaching military service age annually: *males:* 34,674 (2005 est.)
Military expenditures - dollar figure: $23.1 million (FY02)
Military expenditures - percent of GDP: 2.2% (FY02)

TRANSNATIONAL ISSUES

Disputes - international: none

MONTSERRAT

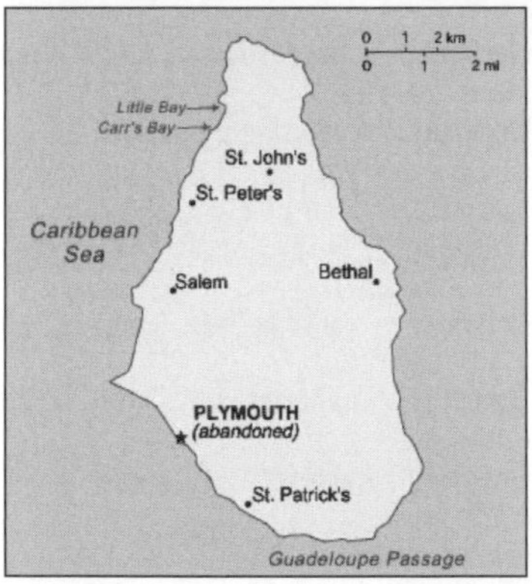

INTRODUCTION

Background: Much of this island was devastated and two-thirds of the population fled abroad because of the eruption of the Soufriere Hills Volcano that began on 18 July 1995. Montserrat has endured volcanic activity since, with the last eruption occurring in July 2003.

GEOGRAPHY

Location: Caribbean, island in the Caribbean Sea, southeast of Puerto Rico
Geographic coordinates: 16 45 N, 62 12 W
Map references: Central America and the Caribbean
Area:
total: 102 sq km
land: 102 sq km
water: 0 sq km
Area - comparative: about 0.6 times the size of Washington, DC
Land boundaries: 0 km
Coastline: 40 km
Maritime claims:
territorial sea: 3 nm
exclusive fishing zone: 200 nm
Climate: tropical; little daily or seasonal temperature variation
Terrain: volcanic island, mostly mountainous, with small coastal lowland
Elevation extremes:
lowest point: Caribbean Sea 0 m
highest point: Chances Peak (in the Soufriere Hills volcanic complex) 914 m
Natural resources: NEGL
Land use:
arable land: 20%
permanent crops: 0%
other: 80% (2001)
Irrigated land: NA sq km
Natural hazards: severe hurricanes (June to November); volcanic eruptions (Soufriere Hills volcano has erupted continuously since 1995)
Environment - current issues: land erosion occurs on slopes that have been cleared for cultivation
Geography - note: the island is entirely volcanic in origin and contains seven active volcanoes

PEOPLE

Population: 9,341
note: an estimated 8,000 refugees left the island following the resumption of volcanic activity in July 1995; some have returned (July 2005 est.)
Age structure:
0-14 years: 23.3% (male 1,109/female 1,072)
15-64 years: 65.6% (male 2,923/female 3,201)

65 years and over: 11.1% (male 536/female 500) (2005 est.)
Median age:
total: 28.56 years
male: 28.29 years
female: 28.79 years (2005 est.)
Population growth rate: 1.04% (2005 est.)
Birth rate: 17.56 births/1,000 population (2005 est.)
Death rate: 7.17 deaths/1,000 population (2005 est.)
Net migration rate: 0 migrant(s)/1,000 population (2005 est.)
Sex ratio:
at birth: 1.05 male(s)/female
under 15 years: 1.04 male(s)/female
15-64 years: 0.91 male(s)/female
65 years and over: 1.07 male(s)/female
total population: 0.96 male(s)/female (2005 est.)
Infant mortality rate:
total: 7.35 deaths/1,000 live births
male: 8.55 deaths/1,000 live births
female: 6.1 deaths/1,000 live births (2005 est.)
Life expectancy at birth:
total population: 78.71 years
male: 76.54 years
female: 80.98 years (2005 est.)
Total fertility rate: 1.78 children born/woman (2005 est.)
HIV/AIDS - adult prevalence rate: NA
HIV/AIDS - people living with HIV/AIDS: NA
HIV/AIDS - deaths: NA
Nationality:
noun: Montserratian(s)
adjective: Montserratian
Ethnic groups: black, white
Religions: Anglican, Methodist, Roman Catholic, Pentecostal, Seventh-Day Adventist, other Christian denominations
Languages: English
Literacy:
definition: age 15 and over has ever attended school
total population: 97%
male: 97%
female: 97% (1970 est.)

GOVERNMENT

Country name:
conventional long form: none
conventional short form: Montserrat
Dependency status: overseas territory of the UK
Government type: NA
Capital: Plymouth (abandoned in 1997 due to volcanic activity; interim government buildings have been built at Brades Estate, in the Carr's Bay/Little Bay vicinity at the northwest end of Montserrat)
Administrative divisions: 3 parishes; Saint Anthony, Saint Georges, Saint Peter
Independence: none (overseas territory of the UK)
National holiday: Birthday of Queen ELIZABETH II, second Saturday in June (1926)
Constitution: effective 19 December 1989
Legal system: English common law and statutory law
Suffrage: 18 years of age; universal
Executive branch:
chief of state: Queen ELIZABETH II (since 6 February 1952), represented by Governor Deborah BARNES-JONES (since 10 May 2004)
head of government: Chief Minister John OSBORNE (since 5 April 2001)
cabinet: Executive Council consists of the governor, the chief minister, three other ministers, the attorney general, and the finance secretary
elections: the monarch is hereditary; governor appointed by the monarch; following legislative elections, the leader of the majority party usually becomes chief minister
Legislative branch: unicameral Legislative Council (11 seats, 9 popularly elected; members serve five-year terms)
note: expanded in 2001 from 7 to 9 elected members with attorney general and financial secretary sitting as ex-officio members
elections: last held April 2001 (next to be held by November 2006)
election results: percent of vote by party - NA%; seats by party - NPLM 7, NPP 2
note: in 2001, the Elections Commission instituted a single constituency/voter-at-large system whereby all eligible voters cast ballots for all nine seats of the Legislative Council
Judicial branch: Eastern Caribbean Supreme Court (based in Saint Lucia, one judge of the Supreme Court is a resident of the islands and presides over the High Court)
Political parties and leaders: National Progressive Party or NPP [Reuben T. MEADE]; New People's Liberation Movement or NPLM [John A. OSBORNE]
Political pressure groups and leaders: NA
International organization participation: Caricom, CDB, ICFTU, Interpol (subbureau), OECS, UPU
Diplomatic representation in the US: none (overseas territory of the UK)
Diplomatic representation from the US: none (overseas territory of the UK)
Flag description: blue, with the flag of the UK in the upper hoist-side quadrant and the Montserratian coat of arms centered in the outer half of the flag; the coat of arms features a woman standing beside a yellow harp with her arm around a black cross

ECONOMY

Economy - overview: Severe volcanic activity, which began in July 1995, has put a damper on this small, open economy. A catastrophic eruption in June 1997 closed the airports and seaports, causing further economic and social dislocation. Two-thirds of the 12,000 inhabitants fled the island. Some began to return in 1998, but lack of housing limited the number. The agriculture sector continued to be affected by the lack of suitable land for farming and the destruction of crops. Prospects for the economy depend largely on developments in relation to the volcano and on public sector construction activity. The UK has launched a three-year $122.8 million aid program to help reconstruct the economy. Half of the island is expected to remain uninhabitable for another decade.
GDP (purchasing power parity): $29 million (2002 est.)
GDP (official exchange rate): NA
GDP - real growth rate: -1% (2002 est.)
GDP - per capita: purchasing power parity - $3,400 (2002 est.)
GDP - composition by sector:
agriculture: 5.4%
industry: 13.6%
services: 81% (1996 est.)
Labor force: 4,521 (lowered by flight of people from volcanic activity) (2000 est.)
Labor force - by occupation: agriculture NA%, industry NA%, services NA%
Unemployment rate: 6% (1998 est.)
Population below poverty line: NA
Household income or consumption by percentage share:
lowest 10%: NA
highest 10%: NA
Inflation rate (consumer prices): 2.6% (2002 est.)
Budget:
revenues: $31.4 million
expenditures: $31.6 million, including capital expenditures of $8.4 million (1997 est.)
Agriculture - products: cabbages, carrots, cucumbers, tomatoes, onions, peppers, livestock products
Industries: tourism, rum, textiles, electronic appliances
Industrial production growth rate: NA%
Electricity - production: 2 million kWh (2003)
Electricity - production by source:
fossil fuel: 100%
hydro: 0%
nuclear: 0%
other: 0% (2001)
Electricity - consumption: 1.86 million kWh (2003)
Electricity - exports: 0 kWh (2003)
Electricity - imports: 0 kWh (2003)
Oil - production: 0 bbl/day (2003 est.)
Oil - consumption: 380 bbl/day (2003 est.)
Oil - exports: NA (2001)

Oil - imports: NA (2001)
Exports: $700,000 (2001)
Exports - partners: US, Antigua and Barbuda (2004)
Imports: $17 million (2001)
Imports - partners: US, UK, Trinidad and Tobago, Japan, Canada (2004)
Debt - external: $8.9 million (1997)
Economic aid - recipient: Country Policy Plan (2001) is a three-year program for spending $122.8 million in British budgetary assistance (2002 est.)
Currency (code): East Caribbean dollar (XCD)
Currency code: XCD
Exchange rates: East Caribbean dollars per US dollar - NA (2005), 2.7 (2004), 2.7 (2003), 2.7 (2002), 2.7 (2001)
note: fixed rate since 1976
Fiscal year: 1 April - 31 March

COMMUNICATIONS

Telephones - main lines in use: NA
Telephones - mobile cellular: 70 (1994)
Telephone system:
general assessment: modern and fully digitalized
domestic: NA
international: country code - 1-664
Radio broadcast stations: AM 1, FM 2, shortwave 0 (1998)
Radios: 7,000 (1997)
Television broadcast stations: 1 (1997)
Televisions: 3,000 (1997)
Internet country code: .ms
Internet Service Providers (ISPs): 17 (2000)
Internet users: NA

TRANSPORTATION

Airports: 1 (2004 est.)
Airports - with paved runways:
total: 1
under 914 m: 1 (2005 est.)
Roadways:
total: 227 km
paved: NA km
unpaved: NA km
note: volcanic eruptions beginning in 1995 destroyed most of the road system (2003)
Ports and terminals: Plymouth

MILITARY

Military branches: no regular military forces; Royal Montserrat Police Force (2005)
Military - note: defense is the responsibility of the UK

TRANSNATIONAL ISSUES

Disputes - international: none
Illicit drugs: transshipment point for South American narcotics destined for the US and Europe

MOROCCO

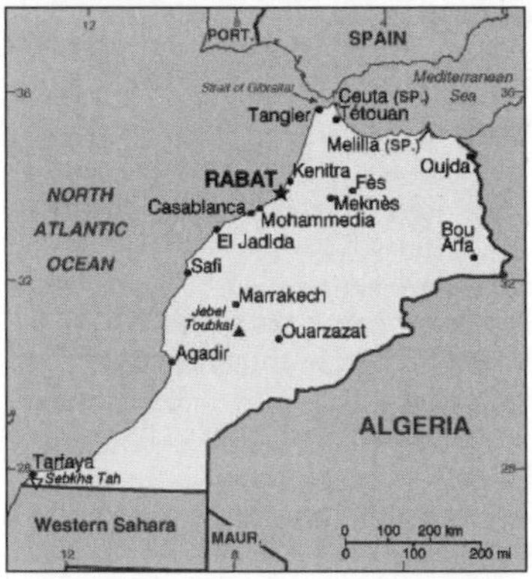

INTRODUCTION

Background: In 788, about a century after the Arab conquest of North Africa, successive Moorish dynasties began to rule in Morocco. In the 16th century, the Sa'adi monarchy, particularly under Ahmad AL-MANSUR (1578-1603), repelled foreign invaders and inaugurated a golden age. In 1860, Spain occupied northern Morocco and ushered in a half century of trade rivalry among European powers that saw Morocco's sovereignty steadily eroded; in 1912, the French imposed a protectorate over the country. A protracted independence struggle with France ended successfully in 1956. The internationalized city of Tangier and most Spanish possessions were turned over to the new country that same year. Morocco virtually annexed Western Sahara during the late 1970s, but final resolution on the status of the territory remains unresolved. Gradual political reforms in the 1990s resulted in the establishment of a bicameral legislature in 1997. Parliamentary elections were held for the second time in September 2002 and municipal elections were held in September 2003.

GEOGRAPHY

Location: Northern Africa, bordering the North Atlantic Ocean and the Mediterranean Sea, between Algeria and Western Sahara
Geographic coordinates: 32 00 N, 5 00 W
Map references: Africa
Area:
total: 446,550 sq km
land: 446,300 sq km
water: 250 sq km
Area - comparative: slightly larger than California
Land boundaries:
total: 2,017.9 km
border countries: Algeria 1,559 km, Western Sahara 443 km, Spain (Ceuta) 6.3 km, Spain (Melilla) 9.6 km
Coastline: 1,835 km
Maritime claims:
territorial sea: 12 nm
contiguous zone: 24 nm
exclusive economic zone: 200 nm
continental shelf: 200-m depth or to the depth of exploitation
Climate: Mediterranean, becoming more extreme in the interior
Terrain: northern coast and interior are mountainous with large areas of bordering plateaus, intermontane valleys, and rich coastal plains
Elevation extremes:
lowest point: Sebkha Tah -55 m
highest point: Jebel Toubkal 4,165 m
Natural resources: phosphates, iron ore, manganese, lead, zinc, fish, salt
Land use:
arable land: 19.61%
permanent crops: 2.17%
other: 78.22% (2001)
Irrigated land: 12,910 sq km (1998 est.)
Natural hazards: northern mountains geologically unstable and subject to earthquakes; periodic droughts
Environment - current issues: land degradation/desertification (soil erosion resulting from farming of marginal areas, overgrazing, destruction of vegetation); water supplies contaminated by raw sewage; siltation of reservoirs; oil pollution of coastal waters
Environment - international agreements:
party to: Biodiversity, Climate Change, Climate Change-Kyoto Protocol, Desertification, Endangered Species, Hazardous Wastes, Marine Dumping, Ozone Layer Protection, Ship Pollution, Wetlands, Whaling
signed, but not ratified: Environmental Modification, Law of the Sea
Geography - note: strategic location along Strait of Gibraltar

PEOPLE

Population: 32,725,847 (July 2005 est.)
Age structure:
0-14 years: 32.1% (male 5,349,247/female 5,150,497)
15-64 years: 63% (male 10,259,808/female 10,346,608)

65 years and over: 4.9% (male 708,921/ female 910,766) (2005 est.)
Median age:
total: 23.61 years
male: 23.11 years
female: 24.13 years (2005 est.)
Population growth rate: 1.57% (2005 est.)
Birth rate: 22.29 births/1,000 population (2005 est.)
Death rate: 5.64 deaths/1,000 population (2005 est.)
Net migration rate: -0.92 migrant(s)/ 1,000 population (2005 est.)
Sex ratio:
at birth: 1.05 male(s)/female
under 15 years: 1.04 male(s)/female
15-64 years: 0.99 male(s)/female
65 years and over: 0.78 male(s)/female
total population: 1 male(s)/female (2005 est.)
Infant mortality rate:
total: 41.62 deaths/1,000 live births
male: 45.42 deaths/1,000 live births
female: 37.63 deaths/1,000 live births (2005 est.)
Life expectancy at birth:
total population: 70.66 years
male: 68.35 years
female: 73.07 years (2005 est.)
Total fertility rate: 2.73 children born/ woman (2005 est.)
HIV/AIDS - adult prevalence rate: 0.1% (2001 est.)
HIV/AIDS - people living with HIV/AIDS: 15,000 (2001 est.)
HIV/AIDS - deaths: NA
Major infectious diseases:
degree of risk: intermediate
food or waterborne diseases: bacterial diarrhea, and hepatitis A
vectorborne diseases: may be a significant risk in some locations during the transmission season (typically April through November) (2004)
Nationality:
noun: Moroccan(s)
adjective: Moroccan
Ethnic groups: Arab-Berber 99.1%, other 0.7%, Jewish 0.2%
Religions: Muslim 98.7%, Christian 1.1%, Jewish 0.2%
Languages: Arabic (official), Berber dialects, French often the language of business, government, and diplomacy
Literacy:
definition: age 15 and over can read and write
total population: 51.7%
male: 64.1%
female: 39.4% (2003 est.)

GOVERNMENT

Country name:
conventional long form: Kingdom of Morocco
conventional short form: Morocco
local long form: Al Mamlakah al Maghribiyah
local short form: Al Maghrib
Government type: constitutional monarchy
Capital: Rabat
Administrative divisions: 14 regions: Grand Casablanca, Chaouia-Ouardigha, Doukkala-Abda, Fes-Boulemane, Gharb-Chrarda-Beni Hssen, Guelmim-Es Smara, Marrakech-Tensift-Al Haouz, Meknes-Tafilalet, Oriental, Rabat-Sale-Zemmour-Zaer, Souss-Massa-Draa, Tadla-Azilal, Tanger-Tetouan, Taza-Al Hoceima-Taounate
note: Morocco claims the territory of Western Sahara, the political status of which is considered undetermined by the United States Government; one additional region, Oued Eddahab-Lagouira, falls entirely within Western Sahara; another region, Laayoune-Boujdour-Sahia El Hamra, falls mostly within Western Sahara; a small portion of this region, in the southwestern part of the country, falls within Moroccan-administered territory as recognized by the United States; the province of Guelmim-Es Smara lies in both entities
Independence: 2 March 1956 (from France)
National holiday: Throne Day (accession of King MOHAMED VI to the throne), 30 July (1999)
Constitution: 10 March 1972; revised 4 September 1992, amended (to create bicameral legislature) September 1996
Legal system: based on Islamic law and French and Spanish civil law system; judicial review of legislative acts in Constitutional Chamber of Supreme Court
Suffrage: 18 years of age; universal (as of January 2003)
Executive branch:
chief of state: King MOHAMED VI (since 30 July 1999)
head of government: Prime Minister Driss JETTOU (since 9 October 2002)
cabinet: Council of Ministers appointed by the monarch
elections: none; the monarch is hereditary; prime minister appointed by the monarch following legislative elections
Legislative branch: bicameral Parliament consists of an upper house or Chamber of Counselors (270 seats; members elected indirectly by local councils, professional organizations, and labor syndicates for nine-year terms; one-third of the members are renewed every three years) and a lower house or Chamber of Representatives (325 seats; 295 by multi-seat constituencies and 30 from national lists of women; members elected by popular vote for five-year terms)
elections: Chamber of Counselors - last held 6 October 2003 (next to be held NA 2006); Chamber of Representatives - last held 27 September 2002 (next to be held NA 2007)
election results: Chamber of Counselors - percent of vote by party - NA%; seats by party - RNI 42, MDS 33, UC 28, MP 27, PND 21, PI 21, USFP 16, MNP 15, PA 13, FFD 12, other 42; Chamber of Representatives - percent of vote by party - NA%; seats by party - USFP 50, PI 48, PJD 42, RNI 41, MP 27, MNP 18, UC 16, PND 12, PPS 11, UD 10, other 50
Judicial branch: Supreme Court (judges are appointed on the recommendation of the Supreme Council of the Judiciary, presided over by the monarch)
Political parties and leaders: Action Party or PA [Muhammad EL IDRISSI]; Alliance of Liberties or ADL [Ali BELHAJ]; Annahj Addimocrati or Annahj [Abdellah EL HARIF]; Avant Garde Social Democratic Party or PADS [Ahmed BENJELLOUN]; Citizen Forces or FC [Abderrahman LAHJOUJI]; Citizen's Initiatives for Development [Mohamed BENHAMOU]; Constitutional Union or UC [Mohamed ABIED (interim)]; Democratic and Independence Party or PDI [Abdelwahed MAACH]; Democratic and Social Movement or MDS [Mahmoud ARCHANE]; Democratic Socialist Party or PSD [Aissa OUARDIGHI]; Democratic Union or UD [Bouazza IKKEN]; Environment and Development Party or PED [Ahmed EL ALAMI]; Front of Democratic Forces or FFD [Thami EL KHYARI]; Istiqlal Party (Independence Party) or PI [Abbas El FASSI]; Justice and Development Party or PJD [Saad Eddine OTHMANI]; Moroccan Liberal Party or PML [Mohamed ZIANE]; National Democratic Party or PND [Abdallah KADIRI]; National Ittihadi Congress Party or CNI [Abdelmajid BOUZOUBAA]; National Popular Movement or MNP [Mahjoubi AHERDANE]; National Rally of Independents or RNI [Ahmed OSMAN]; National Union of Popular Forces or UNFP [Abdellah IBRAHIM]; Parti Al Ahd or Al Ahd [Najib EL OUAZZANI, chairman]; Party of Progress and Socialism or PPS [Ismail ALAOUI]; Party of Renewal and Equity or PRE [Chakir ACHABAR]; Party of the Unified Socialist Left or GSU [Mohamed Ben Said AIT IDDER]; Popular Movement or MP [Mohamed LAENSER]; Reform and Development Party or PRD [Abderrahmane EL KOUHEN]; Social

Center Party or PSC [Lahcen MADIH]; Socialist Union of Popular Forces or USFP [Mohammed El-YAZGHI]
Political pressure groups and leaders: Democratic Confederation of Labor or CDT [Noubir AMAOUI]; General Union of Moroccan Workers or UGTM [Abderrazzak AFILAL]; Moroccan Employers Association or CGEM [Hassan CHAMI]; National Labor Union of Morocco or UNMT [Abdelslam MAATI]; Union of Moroccan Workers or UMT [Mahjoub BENSEDDIK]
International organization participation: ABEDA, ACCT, AfDB, AFESD, AMF, AMU, EBRD, FAO, G-77, IAEA, IBRD, ICAO, ICC, ICCt (signatory), ICFTU, ICRM, IDA, IDB, IFAD, IFC, IFRCS, IHO, ILO, IMF, IMO, Interpol, IOC, IOM, ISO, ITU, LAS, MIGA, MINUSTAH, MONUC, NAM, OAS (observer), OIC, OPCW, OSCE (partner), PCA, UN, UNCTAD, UNESCO, UNHCR, UNIDO, UNITAR, UNOCI, UPU, WCL, WCO, WHO, WIPO, WMO, WToO, WTO
Diplomatic representation in the US:
chief of mission: Ambassador Aziz MEKOUAR
chancery: 1601 21st Street NW, Washington, DC 20009
telephone: [1] (202) 462-7979 through 7982
FAX: [1] (202) 265-0161
consulate(s) general: New York
Diplomatic representation from the US:
chief of mission: Ambassador Thomas T. RILEY
embassy: 2 Avenue de Mohamed El Fassi, Rabat
mailing address: PSC 74, Box 021, APO AE 09718
telephone: [212] (37) 76 22 65
FAX: [212] (37) 76 56 61
consulate(s) general: Casablanca
Flag description: red with a green pentacle (five-pointed, linear star) known as Sulayman's (Solomon's) seal in the center of the flag; red and green are traditional colors in Arab flags, although the use of red is more commonly associated with the Arab states of the Persian gulf; design dates to 1912

ECONOMY

Economy - overview: Morocco faces problems typical for developing countries: restraining government spending, reducing constraints on private activity and foreign trade, and achieving sustainable growth. Despite structural adjustment programs supported by the IMF, the World Bank, and the Paris Club, the dirham is only fully convertible for current account transactions. In 2004 Moroccan authorities instituted measures to boost foreign direct investment and trade by signing a free trade agreement with the US and selling government shares in the state telecommunications company and in the largest state-owned bank. Favorable rainfall over the past two years has boosted agricultural output and GDP growth passed 4% in 2004. In 2005 GDP growth slipped to 1.8% and the budget deficit rose sharply - to 7.5% of GDP - because of substantial increases in wages and oil subsidies. Long-term challenges include preparing the economy for freer trade with the US and European Union, improving education and job prospects for Morocco's youth, and raising living standards.
GDP (purchasing power parity): $139.5 billion (2005 est.)
GDP (official exchange rate): $52.7 billion (2005 est.)
GDP - real growth rate: 1.8% (2005 est.)
GDP - per capita: purchasing power parity - $4,300 (2005 est.)
GDP - composition by sector:
agriculture: 21.7%
industry: 35.7%
services: 42.6% (2004 est.)
Labor force: 11.19 million (2005 est.)
Labor force - by occupation: agriculture 40%, industry 15%, services 45% (2003 est.)
Unemployment rate: 10.5% (2005 est.)
Population below poverty line: 19% (1999 est.)
Household income or consumption by percentage share:
lowest 10%: 2.6%
highest 10%: 30.9% (1998-99)
Distribution of family income - Gini index: 39.5 (1998-99)
Inflation rate (consumer prices): 2.1% (2005 est.)
Investment (gross fixed): 23.5% of GDP (2005 est.)
Budget:
revenues: $12.94 billion
expenditures: $16.77 billion, including capital expenditures of $2.19 billion (2005 est.)
Public debt: 72.3% of GDP (2005 est.)
Agriculture - products: barley, wheat, citrus, wine, vegetables, olives; livestock
Industries: phosphate rock mining and processing, food processing, leather goods, textiles, construction, tourism
Industrial production growth rate: NA
Electricity - production: 17.35 billion kWh (2003)
Electricity - production by source:
fossil fuel: 95.4%
hydro: 4.6%
nuclear: 0%
other: 0% (2001)
Electricity - consumption: 17.58 billion kWh (2003)
Electricity - exports: 0 kWh (2003)
Electricity - imports: 1.45 billion kWh (2003)
Oil - production: 300 bbl/day (2005 est.)
Oil - consumption: 158,000 bbl/day (2003 est.)
Oil - exports: NA (2001)
Oil - imports: NA (2001)
Oil - proved reserves: 100 million bbl (2005 est.)
Natural gas - production: 50 million cu m (2001 est.)
Natural gas - consumption: 50 million cu m (2001 est.)
Natural gas - exports: 0 cu m (2001 est.)
Natural gas - imports: 0 cu m (2001 est.)
Natural gas - proved reserves: 665.4 million cu m (2005)
Current account balance: $-607.5 million (2005 est.)
Exports: $9.472 billion f.o.b. (2005 est.)
Exports - partners: France 33.6%, Spain 17.4%, UK 7.7%, Italy 4.7%, US 4.1% (2004)
Imports: $18.15 billion f.o.b. (2005 est.)
Imports - partners: France 18.2%, Spain 12.1%, Italy 6.6%, Germany 6%, Russia 5.7%, Saudi Arabia 5.4%, China 4.2%, US 4.1% (2004)
Reserves of foreign exchange and gold: $16.2 billion (2005 est.)
Debt - external: $15.6 billion (2005 est.)
Economic aid - recipient: ODA $218 million (2002)
Currency (code): Moroccan dirham (MAD)
Currency code: MAD
Exchange rates: Moroccan dirhams per US dollar - 8.78 (2005), 8.868 (2004), 9.574 (2003), 11.021 (2002), 11.303 (2001)
Fiscal year: calendar year

COMMUNICATIONS

Telephones - main lines in use: 1,219,200 (2003)
Telephones - mobile cellular: 7,332,800 (2003)
Telephone system:
general assessment: modern system with all important capabilities; however, density is low with only 4.6 main lines available for each 100 persons
domestic: good system composed of open-wire lines, cables, and microwave radio relay links; Internet available but expensive; principal switching centers are Casablanca and Rabat; national network nearly 100% digital using fiber-optic links; improved rural service employs microwave radio relay
international: country code - 212; 7 submarine cables; satellite earth stations - 2

Intelsat (Atlantic Ocean) and 1 Arabsat; microwave radio relay to Gibraltar, Spain, and Western Sahara; coaxial cable and microwave radio relay to Algeria; participant in Medarabtel; fiber-optic cable link from Agadir to Algeria and Tunisia (1998)
Radio broadcast stations: AM 27, FM 25, shortwave 6 (1998)
Radios: 6.64 million (1997)
Television broadcast stations: 35 (plus 66 repeaters) (1995)
Televisions: 3.1 million (1997)
Internet country code: .ma
Internet hosts: 3,627 (2004)
Internet Service Providers (ISPs): 8 (2000)
Internet users: 800,000 (2003)

TRANSPORTATION

Airports: 63 (2004 est.)
Airports - with paved runways:
total: 25
over 3,047 m: 11
2,438 to 3,047 m: 4
1,524 to 2,437 m: 8
914 to 1,523 m: 1
under 914 m: 1 (2005 est.)
Airports - with unpaved runways:
total: 35
2,438 to 3,047 m: 2
1,524 to 2,437 m: 9
914 to 1,523 m: 13
under 914 m: 11 (2005 est.)
Heliports: 1 (2005 est.)
Pipelines: gas 695 km; oil 285 km (2004)
Railways:
total: 1,907 km
standard gauge: 1,907 km 1.435-m gauge (1,003 km electrified) (2004)
Roadways:
total: 57,694 km
paved: 32,551 km (including 481 km of expressways)
unpaved: 25,143 km (2002)
Merchant marine:
total: 41 ships (1,000 GRT or over) 236,131 GRT/252,367 DWT
by type: cargo 6, chemical tanker 6, container 8, passenger/cargo 13, petroleum tanker 1, refrigerated cargo 2, roll on/roll off 5
foreign-owned: 6 (France 1, Germany 2, Switzerland 2, United Kingdom 1) (2005)
Ports and terminals: Agadir, Casablanca, Mohammedia, Nador, Safi, Tangier

MILITARY

Military branches: Royal Armed Forces: Army, Navy, Air Force (Force Aerienne Royale Marocaine)
Military service age and obligation: 18 years of age for compulsory and voluntary military service; conscript service obligation - 18 months (2004)
Manpower available for military service: *males age 18-49:* 7,908,864 (2005 est.)
Manpower fit for military service: *males age 18-49:* 6,484,787 (2005 est.)
Manpower reaching military service age annually: *males:* 353,377 (2005 est.)
Military expenditures - dollar figure: $2,305.6 million (2003)
Military expenditures - percent of GDP: 5% (2004)

TRANSNATIONAL ISSUES

Disputes - international: claims and administers Western Sahara whose sovereignty remains unresolved - UN-administered cease-fire has remained in effect since September 1991, but attempts to hold a referendum have failed and parties thus far have rejected all brokered proposals; Morocco protests Spain's control over the coastal enclaves of Ceuta, Melilla, and Penon de Velez de la Gomera, the islands of Penon de Alhucemas and Islas Chafarinas, and surrounding waters; discussions have not progressed on a comprehensive maritime delimitation setting limits on exploration and refugee interdiction since Morocco's 2002 rejection of Spain's unilateral designation of a median line from the Canary Islands; Morocco serves as one of the primary launching areas of illegal migration into Spain from North Africa
Illicit drugs: illicit producer of hashish; shipments of hashish mostly directed to Western Europe; transit point for cocaine from South America destined for Western Europe

MOZAMBIQUE

INTRODUCTION

Background: Almost five centuries as a Portuguese colony came to a close with independence in 1975. Large-scale emigration by whites, economic dependence on South Africa, a severe drought, and a prolonged civil war hindered the country's development. The ruling Front for the Liberation of Mozambique (FRELIMO) party formally abandoned Marxism in 1989, and a new constitution the following year provided for multiparty elections and a free market economy. A UN-negotiated peace agreement between FRELIMO and rebel Mozambique National Resistance (RENAMO) forces ended the fighting in 1992. In December 2004, Mozambique underwent a delicate transition as Joaquim CHISSANO stepped down after 18 years in office. His newly elected successor, Armando Emilio GUEBUZA, has promised to continue the sound economic policies that have encouraged foreign investment.

GEOGRAPHY

Location: South-eastern Africa, bordering the Mozambique Channel, between South Africa and Tanzania
Geographic coordinates: 18 15 S, 35 00 E
Map references: Africa
Area:
total: 801,590 sq km
land: 784,090 sq km
water: 17,500 sq km
Area - comparative: slightly less than twice the size of California
Land boundaries:
total: 4,571 km
border countries: Malawi 1,569 km, South Africa 491 km, Swaziland 105 km, Tanzania 756 km, Zambia 419 km, Zimbabwe 1,231 km
Coastline: 2,470 km
Maritime claims:
territorial sea: 12 nm
exclusive economic zone: 200 nm
Climate: tropical to subtropical
Terrain: mostly coastal lowlands, uplands in center, high plateaus in northwest, mountains in west
Elevation extremes:
lowest point: Indian Ocean 0 m
highest point: Monte Binga 2,436 m
Natural resources: coal, titanium, natural gas, hydropower, tantalum, graphite
Land use:
arable land: 5.1%
permanent crops: 0.3%
other: 94.6% (2001)
Irrigated land: 1,070 sq km (1998 est.)
Natural hazards: severe droughts; devastating cyclones and floods in central and southern provinces
Environment - current issues: a long civil war and recurrent drought in the hinterlands have resulted in increased migration of the population to urban and coastal areas with adverse environmental consequences; desertification; pollution of surface and coastal waters; elephant poaching for ivory is a problem
Environment - international agreements:
party to: Biodiversity, Climate Change, Climate Change-Kyoto Protocol, Desertification, Endangered Species,

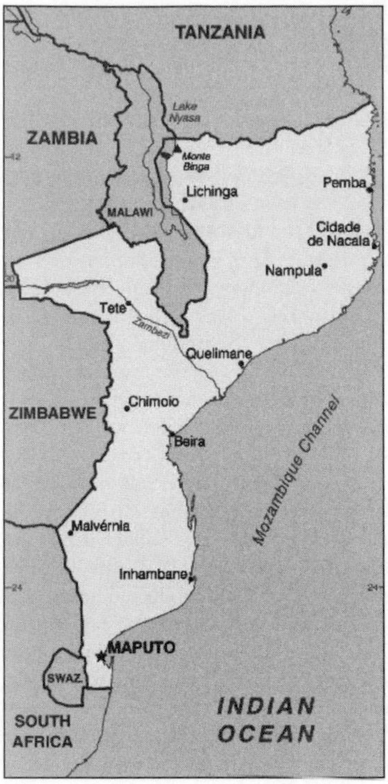

Hazardous Wastes, Law of the Sea, Ozone Layer Protection
signed, but not ratified: none of the selected agreements
Geography - note: the Zambezi flows through the north-central and most fertile part of the country

PEOPLE

Population: 19,406,703
note: estimates for this country explicitly take into account the effects of excess mortality due to AIDS; this can result in lower life expectancy, higher infant mortality and death rates, lower population and growth rates, and changes in the distribution of population by age and sex than would otherwise be expected; the 1997 Mozambican census reported a population of 16,099,246 (July 2005 est.)
Age structure:
0-14 years: 43.1% (male 4,206,654/female 4,157,898)
15-64 years: 54.1% (male 5,088,250/female 5,416,573)
65 years and over: 2.8% (male 224,682/female 312,646) (2005 est.)
Median age:
total: 18.29 years
male: 17.74 years
female: 18.83 years (2005 est.)
Population growth rate: 1.48% (2005 est.)
Birth rate: 35.79 births/1,000 population (2005 est.)
Death rate: 20.99 deaths/1,000 population (2005 est.)
Net migration rate: 0 migrant(s)/1,000 population (2005 est.)
Sex ratio:
at birth: 1.03 male(s)/female
under 15 years: 1.01 male(s)/female
15-64 years: 0.94 male(s)/female
65 years and over: 0.72 male(s)/female
total population: 0.96 male(s)/female (2005 est.)
Infant mortality rate:
total: 130.79 deaths/1,000 live births
male: 135.91 deaths/1,000 live births
female: 125.51 deaths/1,000 live births (2005 est.)
Life expectancy at birth:
total population: 40.32 years
male: 39.9 years
female: 40.75 years (2005 est.)
Total fertility rate: 4.7 children born/woman (2005 est.)
HIV/AIDS - adult prevalence rate: 12.2% (2003 est.)
HIV/AIDS - people living with HIV/AIDS: 1.3 million (2003 est.)
HIV/AIDS - deaths: 110,000 (2003 est.)
Major infectious diseases:
degree of risk: very high
food or waterborne diseases: bacterial and protozoal diarrhea, hepatitis A, and typhoid fever
vectorborne diseases: malaria and plague are high risks in some locations
water contact disease: schistosomiasis (2004)
Nationality:
noun: Mozambican(s)
adjective: Mozambican
Ethnic groups: indigenous tribal groups 99.66% (Makhuwa, Tsonga, Lomwe, Sena, and others), Europeans 0.06%, Euro-Africans 0.2%, Indians 0.08%
Religions: Catholic 23.8%, Zionist Christian 17.5%, Muslim 17.8%, other 17.8%, none 23.1% (1997 census)
Languages: Emakhuwa 26.1%, Xichangana 11.3%, Portuguese 8.8% (official; spoken by 27% of population as a second language), Elomwe 7.6%, Cisena 6.8%, Echuwabo 5.8%, other Mozambican languages 32%, other foreign languages 0.3%, unspecified 1.3% (1997 census)
Literacy:
definition: age 15 and over can read and write
total population: 47.8%
male: 63.5%
female: 32.7% (2003 est.)

GOVERNMENT

Country name:
conventional long form: Republic of Mozambique
conventional short form: Mozambique
local long form: Republica de Mocambique
local short form: Mocambique
former: Portuguese East Africa
Government type: republic
Capital: Maputo
Administrative divisions: 10 provinces (provincias, singular - provincia), 1 city (cidade)*; Cabo Delgado, Gaza, Inhambane, Manica, Maputo, Cidade de Maputo*, Nampula, Niassa, Sofala, Tete, Zambezia
Independence: 25 June 1975 (from Portugal)
National holiday: Independence Day, 25 June (1975)
Constitution: 30 November 1990
Legal system: based on Portuguese civil law system and customary law
Suffrage: 18 years of age; universal
Executive branch:
chief of state: President Armando GUEBUZA (since 2 February 2005)
head of government: Prime Minister Luisa DIOGO (since 17 February 2004)
cabinet: Cabinet
elections: president elected by popular vote for a five-year term; election last held 1-2 December 2004 (next to be held December 2009); prime minister appointed by the president
election results: Armando GUEBUZA elected president; percent of vote - Armando GUEBUZA 63.7%, Afonso DHLAKAMA 31.7%
Legislative branch: unicameral Assembly of the Republic or Assembleia da Republica (250 seats; members are directly elected by popular vote on a secret ballot to serve five-year terms)
elections: last held 1-2 December 2004 (next to be held December 2009)
election results: percent of vote by party - Frelimo 62%, Renamo 29.7%; seats by party - Frelimo 160, Renamo 90
Judicial branch: Supreme Court (the court of final appeal; some of its professional judges are appointed by the president and some are elected by the Assembly); other courts include an Administrative Court, customs courts, maritime courts, courts marshal, labor courts
note: although the constitution provides for a separate Constitutional Court, one has never been established; in its absence the Supreme Court reviews constitutional cases
Political parties and leaders: Front for the Liberation of Mozambique (Frente de Liberatacao de Mocambique) or FRELIMO [Armando Emilio GUEBUZA, president]; Mozambique National Resistance-Electoral Union (Resistencia Nacional Mocambicana-Uniao Eleitoral) or RENAMO-UE [Afonso DHLAKAMA, president]

Political pressure groups and leaders: Institute for Peace and Democracy (Instituto para Paz e Democracia) or IPADE [Raul DOMINGOS, president]; Etica [Abdul CARIMO Issa, chairman]; Movement for Peace and Citizenship (Movimento para Paz e Cidadania); Mozambican League of Human Rights (Liga Mocambicana dos Direitos Humanos) or LDH [Alice MABOTE, president]; Human Rights and Development (Direitos Humanos e Desenvolvimento) or DHD [Artemisia FRANCO, secretary general]
International organization participation: ACP, AfDB, AU, C, FAO, G-77, IBRD, ICAO, ICCt (signatory), ICFTU, ICRM, IDA, IDB, IFAD, IFC, IFRCS, IHO, ILO, IMF, IMO, Interpol, IOC, IOM (observer), ISO (correspondent), ITU, MIGA, MONUC, NAM, OIC, ONUB, OPCW, SADC, UN, UNCTAD, UNESCO, UNHCR, UNIDO, UNMIS, UPU, WCO, WFTU, WHO, WIPO, WMO, WToO, WTO
Diplomatic representation in the US:
chief of mission: Ambassador Armando PANGUENE
chancery: 1990 M Street NW, Suite 570, Washington, DC 20036
telephone: [1] (202) 293-7146
FAX: [1] (202) 835-0245
Diplomatic representation from the US:
chief of mission: Ambassador Helen LA LIME
embassy: Avenida Kenneth Kuanda 193, Maputo
mailing address: P. O. Box 783, Maputo
telephone: [258] (1) 492797
FAX: [258] (1) 490448
Flag description: three equal horizontal bands of green (top), black, and yellow with a red isosceles triangle based on the hoist side; the black band is edged in white; centered in the triangle is a yellow five-pointed star bearing a crossed rifle and hoe in black superimposed on an open white book

ECONOMY

Economy - overview: At independence in 1975, Mozambique was one of the world's poorest countries. Socialist mismanagement and a brutal civil war from 1977-92 exacerbated the situation. In 1987, the government embarked on a series of macroeconomic reforms designed to stabilize the economy. These steps, combined with donor assistance and with political stability since the multi-party elections in 1994, have led to dramatic improvements in the country's growth rate. Inflation was reduced to single digits during the late 1990s although it returned to double digits in 2000-03. Fiscal reforms, including the introduction of a value-added tax and reform of the customs service, have improved the government's revenue collection abilities. In spite of these gains, Mozambique remains dependent upon foreign assistance for much of its annual budget, and the majority of the population remains below the poverty line. Subsistence agriculture continues to employ the vast majority of the country's workforce. A substantial trade imbalance persists although the opening of the MOZAL aluminum smelter, the country's largest foreign investment project to date, has increased export earnings. In late 2005, and after years of negotiations, the government signed an agreement to gain Portugal's majority share of the Cahora Bassa Hydroelectricity (HCB) company, a dam that was not transferred to Mozambique at independence because of the ensuing civil war and unpaid debts. More power is needed for additional investment projects in titanium extraction and processing and garment manufacturing that could further close the import/export gap. Mozambique's once substantial foreign debt has been reduced through forgiveness and rescheduling under the IMF's Heavily Indebted Poor Countries (HIPC) and Enhanced HIPC initiatives, and is now at a manageable level.
GDP (purchasing power parity): $25.59 billion (2005 est.)
GDP (official exchange rate): $5.924 billion (2005 est.)
GDP - real growth rate: 7% (2005 est.)
GDP - per capita: purchasing power parity - $1,300 (2005 est.)
GDP - composition by sector:
agriculture: 24.2%
industry: 41.2%
services: 34.6% (2005 est.)
Labor force: 9.2 million (2000 est.)
Labor force - by occupation: agriculture 81%, industry 6%, services 13% (1997 est.)
Unemployment rate: 21% (1997 est.)
Population below poverty line: 70% (2001 est.)
Household income or consumption by percentage share:
lowest 10%: 2.5%
highest 10%: 31.7% (1997)
Distribution of family income - Gini index: 39.6 (1996-97)
Inflation rate (consumer prices): 7.8% (2005 est.)
Investment (gross fixed): 44.8% of GDP (2005 est.)
Budget:
revenues: $1.031 billion
expenditures: $1.93 billion (2005 est.)
Agriculture - products: cotton, cashew nuts, sugarcane, tea, cassava (tapioca), corn, coconuts, sisal, citrus and tropical fruits, potatoes, sunflowers; beef, poultry
Industries: food, beverages, chemicals (fertilizer, soap, paints), aluminum, petroleum products, textiles, cement, glass, asbestos, tobacco
Industrial production growth rate: 3.4% (2000)
Electricity - production: 15.14 billion kWh (2003)
Electricity - production by source:
fossil fuel: 2.9%
hydro: 97.1%
nuclear: 0%
other: 0% (2001)
Electricity - consumption: 10.46 billion kWh (2003)
Electricity - exports: 9.5 billion kWh (2003)
Electricity - imports: 5.875 billion kWh (2003)
Oil - production: 0 bbl/day (2003 est.)
Oil - consumption: 11,000 bbl/day (2003 est.)
Oil - exports: NA (2001)
Oil - imports: NA (2001)
Oil - proved reserves: 0 bbl (1 January 2002)
Natural gas - production: 60 million cu m (2001 est.)
Natural gas - consumption: 60 million cu m (2001 est.)
Natural gas - exports: 0 cu m (2001 est.)
Natural gas - imports: 0 cu m (2001 est.)
Natural gas - proved reserves: 63.71 billion cu m (1 January 2002)
Current account balance: $-530.9 million (2005 est.)
Exports: $1.69 billion f.o.b. (2005 est.)
Exports - partners: Netherlands 60.9%, South Africa 12.9%, Malawi 3.3% (2004)
Imports: $2.041 billion f.o.b. (2005 est.)
Imports - partners: South Africa 41.4%, Netherlands 11%, Portugal 3.3% (2004)
Reserves of foreign exchange and gold: $1.227 billion (2005 est.)
Debt - external: $966 million (2002 est.)
Economic aid - recipient: $632.8 million (2001)
Currency (code): metical (MZM)
Currency code: MZM
Exchange rates: meticais per US dollar - 19,445 (2005), 22,581 (2004), 23,782 (2003), 23,678 (2002), 20,704 (2001)
note: effective October 2000, the exchange rate is determined as the weighted average of buying and selling exchange rates of all transactions of commercial banks and stock exchanges with the public
Fiscal year: calendar year

COMMUNICATIONS

Telephones - main lines in use: 83,700 (2002)
Telephones - mobile cellular: 428,900 (2003)

Telephone system:
general assessment: fair system but not available generally (telephone density is only 16 telephones for each 1,000 persons)
domestic: the system consists of open-wire lines and trunk connection by microwave radio relay and tropospheric scatter
international: country code - 258; satellite earth stations - 5 Intelsat (2 Atlantic Ocean and 3 Indian Ocean)
Radio broadcast stations: AM 13, FM 17, shortwave 11 (2001)
Radios: 730,000 (1997)
Television broadcast stations: 1 (2001)
Televisions: 67,600 (2000)
Internet country code: .mz
Internet hosts: 3,249 (2003)
Internet Service Providers (ISPs): 11 (2002)
Internet users: 50,000 (2002)

TRANSPORTATION

Airports: 158 (2004 est.)
Airports - with paved runways:
total: 22
over 3,047 m: 1
2,438 to 3,047 m: 3
1,524 to 2,437 m: 10
914 to 1,523 m: 3
under 914 m: 5 (2005 est.)
Airports - with unpaved runways:
total: 136
2,438 to 3,047 m: 1
1,524 to 2,437 m: 14
914 to 1,523 m: 34
under 914 m: 87 (2005 est.)
Pipelines: gas 649 km; refined products 292 km (2004)
Railways:
total: 3,123 km
narrow gauge: 2,983 km 1.067-m gauge; 140 km 0.762-m gauge (2004)
Roadways:
total: 30,400 km
paved: 5,685 km
unpaved: 24,715 km (1999 est.)
Waterways: 460 km (Zambezi River navigable to Tete and along Cahora Bassa Lake) (2004)
Merchant marine:
total: 2 ships (1,000 GRT or over) 4,125 GRT/7,024 DWT
by type: cargo 2
foreign-owned: 2 (Belgium 2) (2005)
Ports and terminals: Beira, Maputo, Nacala

MILITARY

Military branches: Mozambique Armed Defense Forces (FADM): Army Command, Navy (Marinha Mocambique, MM), Air and Air Defense Forces (Forca Aerea de Mocambique, FAM) (2004)
Manpower available for military service: *males age 18-49:* 3,793,373 (2005 est.)
Manpower fit for military service: *males age 18-49:* 1,751,223 (2005 est.)
Military expenditures - dollar figure: $117.3 million (2004)
Military expenditures - percent of GDP: 2.2% (2004)

TRANSNATIONAL ISSUES

Disputes - international: none
Illicit drugs: Southern African transit point for South Asian hashish and heroin, and South American cocaine probably destined for the European and South African markets; producer of cannabis (for local consumption) and methaqualone (for export to South Africa); corruption and poor regulatory capability makes the banking system vulnerable to money laundering, but the lack of a well-developed financial infrastructure limits the country's utility as a money-laundering center

NAMIBIA

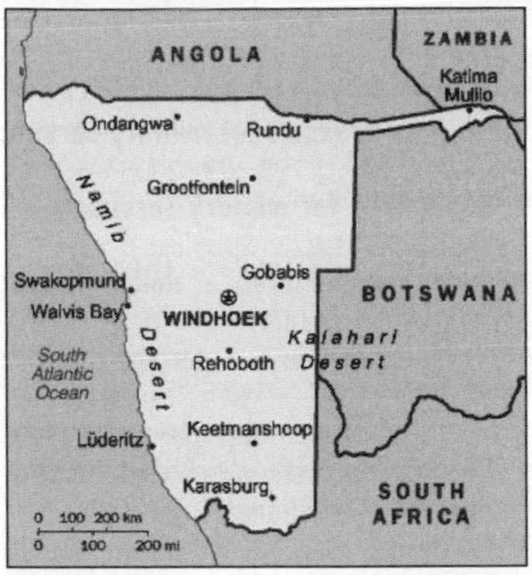

INTRODUCTION

Background: South Africa occupied the German colony of South-West Africa during World War I and administered it as a mandate until after World War II, when it annexed the territory. In 1966 the Marxist South-West Africa People's Organization (SWAPO) guerrilla group launched a war of independence for the area that was soon named Namibia, but it was not until 1988 that South Africa agreed to end its administration in accordance with a UN peace plan for the entire region. Namibia won its independence in 1990 and has been governed by SWAPO since. Hifikepunye POHAMBA was elected president in November 2004 in a landslide victory replacing Sam NUJOMA who led the country during its first 14 years of self rule.

GEOGRAPHY

Location: Southern Africa, bordering the South Atlantic Ocean, between Angola and South Africa
Geographic coordinates: 22 00 S, 17 00 E
Map references: Africa
Area:
total: 825,418 sq km
land: 825,418 sq km
water: 0 sq km
Area - comparative: slightly more than half the size of Alaska
Land boundaries:
total: 3,936 km
border countries: Angola 1,376 km, Botswana 1,360 km, South Africa 967 km, Zambia 233 km
Coastline: 1,572 km
Maritime claims:
territorial sea: 12 nm
contiguous zone: 24 nm
exclusive economic zone: 200 nm
Climate: desert; hot, dry; rainfall sparse and erratic
Terrain: mostly high plateau; Namib Desert along coast; Kalahari Desert in east
Elevation extremes:
lowest point: Atlantic Ocean 0 m
highest point: Konigstein 2,606 m
Natural resources: diamonds, copper, uranium, gold, lead, tin, lithium, cadmium, zinc, salt, hydropower, fish
note: suspected deposits of oil, coal, and iron ore
Land use:
arable land: 0.99%
permanent crops: 0%
other: 99.01% (2001)
Irrigated land: 70 sq km (1998 est.)
Natural hazards: prolonged periods of drought
Environment - current issues: very limited natural fresh water resources; desertification; wildlife poaching; land degradation has led to few conservation areas
Environment - international agreements:
party to: Antarctic-Marine Living Resources, Biodiversity, Climate Change, Climate Change-Kyoto Protocol, Desertification, Endangered Species, Hazardous Wastes, Law of the Sea, Ozone Layer Protection, Wetlands
signed, but not ratified: none of the selected agreements
Geography - note: first country in the world to incorporate the protection of the environment into its constitution; some 14% of the land is protected, including virtually the entire Namib Desert coastal strip

PEOPLE

Population: 2,030,692
note: estimates for this country explicitly take into account the effects of excess mortality due to AIDS; this can result in lower life expectancy, higher infant mortality and death rates, lower population and growth rates, and changes in the distribution of population by age and sex than would otherwise be expected (July 2005 est.)
Age structure:
0-14 years: 38.7% (male 396,247/female 389,543)
15-64 years: 57.7% (male 586,900/female 584,779)
65 years and over: 3.6% (male 33,524/female 39,699) (2005 est.)
Median age:
total: 19.79 years
male: 19.63 years
female: 19.94 years (2005 est.)
Population growth rate: 0.73% (2005 est.)
Birth rate: 25.16 births/1,000 population (2005 est.)
Death rate: 18.36 deaths/1,000 population (2005 est.)
Net migration rate: 0.52 migrant(s)/1,000 population (2005 est.)
Sex ratio:
at birth: 1.03 male(s)/female
under 15 years: 1.02 male(s)/female
15-64 years: 1 male(s)/female
65 years and over: 0.84 male(s)/female
total population: 1 male(s)/female (2005 est.)
Infant mortality rate:
total: 48.98 deaths/1,000 live births
male: 53 deaths/1,000 live births
female: 44.84 deaths/1,000 live births (2005 est.)
Life expectancy at birth:
total population: 43.93 years
male: 44.71 years
female: 43.13 years (2005 est.)
Total fertility rate: 3.18 children born/woman (2005 est.)
HIV/AIDS - adult prevalence rate: 21.3% (2003 est.)
HIV/AIDS - people living with HIV/AIDS: 210,000 (2001 est.)
HIV/AIDS - deaths: 16,000 (2003 est.)
Major infectious diseases:
degree of risk: high
food or waterborne diseases: bacterial diarrhea, hepatitis A, and typhoid fever
vectorborne disease: malaria
water contact disease: schistosomiasis (2004)
Nationality:
noun: Namibian(s)
adjective: Namibian
Ethnic groups: black 87.5%, white 6%, mixed 6.5%
note: about 50% of the population belong to the Ovambo tribe and 9% to the Kavangos tribe; other ethnic groups are: Herero 7%, Damara 7%, Nama 5%, Caprivian 4%, Bushmen 3%, Baster 2%, Tswana 0.5%
Religions: Christian 80% to 90% (Lutheran 50% at least), indigenous beliefs 10% to 20%
Languages: Oshivambo, Herero, Nama
Literacy:
definition: age 15 and over can read and write
total population: 84%
male: 84.4%
female: 83.7% (2003 est.)

GOVERNMENT

Country name:
conventional long form: Republic of Namibia
conventional short form: Namibia
former: German Southwest Africa, South-West Africa
Government type: republic
Capital: Windhoek
Administrative divisions: 13 regions;

Caprivi, Erongo, Hardap, Karas, Khomas, Kunene, Ohangwena, Okavango, Omaheke, Omusati, Oshana, Oshikoto, Otjozondjupa
Independence: 21 March 1990 (from South African mandate)
National holiday: Independence Day, 21 March (1990)
Constitution: ratified 9 February 1990, effective 12 March 1990
Legal system: based on Roman-Dutch law and 1990 constitution
Suffrage: 18 years of age, universal
Executive branch:
chief of state: President Hifikepunye POHAMBA (since 15 November 2004)
head of government: Prime Minister Nahas ANGULA (since 21 March 2005)
cabinet: Cabinet appointed by the president from among the members of the National Assembly
elections: president elected by popular vote for a five-year term; election last held 15 November 2004 (next to be held November 2009)
election results: Hifikepunye POHAMBA elected president; percent of vote - NA%
Legislative branch: bicameral legislature consists of the National Council (26 seats; two members are chosen from each regional council to serve six-year terms) and the National Assembly (72 seats; members are elected by popular vote to serve five-year terms)
elections: National Council - elections for regional councils, to determine members of the National Council, held 15-16 November 2004 (next to be held November 2009); National Assembly - last held 15-16 November 2004 (next to be held November 2009)
election results: National Council - percent of vote by party - NA%; seats by party - NA; National Assembly - percent of vote by party - NA%; seats by party - SWAPO 55, COD 5, DTA 4, UDF 3, MAG 1, other 4
note: the National Council is primarily an advisory body
Judicial branch: Supreme Court (judges appointed by the president on the recommendation of the Judicial Service Commission)
Political parties and leaders: Congress of Democrats or COD [Ben ULENGA]; Democratic Turnhalle Alliance of Namibia or DTA [Katuutire KAURA, president]; Monitor Action Group or MAG [Kosie PRETORIUS]; South West Africa People's Organization or SWAPO [Sam Shafishuna NUJOMA]; United Democratic Front or UDF [Justus GAROEB]
Political pressure groups and leaders: NA
International organization participation: ACP, AfDB, AU, C, FAO, G-77, IAEA, IBRD, ICAO, ICCt, ICFTU, ICRM, IFAD, IFC, IFRCS, ILO, IMF, IMO, Interpol, IOC, IOM (observer), ISO (correspondent), ITU, MIGA, NAM, ONUB, OPCW, SACU, SADC, UN, UNCTAD, UNESCO, UNHCR, UNIDO, UNMEE, UNMIL, UNMIS, UNOCI, UPU, WCL, WCO, WHO, WIPO, WMO, WToO, WTO
Diplomatic representation in the US:
chief of mission: Ambassador Leonard Nangolo IIPUMBU
chancery: 1605 New Hampshire Avenue NW, Washington, DC 20009
telephone: [1] (202) 986-0540
FAX: [1] (202) 986-0443
Diplomatic representation from the US:
chief of mission: Ambassador Joyce BARR
embassy: Ausplan Building, 14 Lossen Street, Windhoek
mailing address: Private Bag 12029 Ausspannplatz, Windhoek
telephone: [264] (61) 221601
FAX: [264] (61) 229792
Flag description: a large blue triangle with a yellow sunburst fills the upper left section and an equal green triangle (solid) fills the lower right section; the triangles are separated by a red stripe that is contrasted by two narrow white-edge borders

ECONOMY

Economy - overview: The economy is heavily dependent on the extraction and processing of minerals for export. Mining accounts for 20% of GDP. Rich alluvial diamond deposits make Namibia a primary source for gem-quality diamonds. Namibia is the fourth-largest exporter of nonfuel minerals in Africa, the world's fifth-largest producer of uranium, and the producer of large quantities of lead, zinc, tin, silver, and tungsten. The mining sector employs only about 3% of the population while about half of the population depends on subsistence agriculture for its livelihood. Namibia normally imports about 50% of its cereal requirements; in drought years food shortages are a major problem in rural areas. A high per capita GDP, relative to the region, hides the great inequality of income distribution; nearly one-third of Namibians had annual incomes of less than $1,400 in constant 1994 dollars, according to a 1993 study. The Namibian economy is closely linked to South Africa with the Namibian dollar pegged to the South African rand. Privatization of several enterprises in coming years may stimulate long-run foreign investment. Mining of zinc, copper, and silver and increased fish production led growth in 2003-05.
GDP (purchasing power parity): $15.78 billion (2005 est.)
GDP (official exchange rate): $5.076 billion (2005 est.)
GDP - real growth rate: 4.2% (2005 est.)
GDP - per capita: purchasing power parity - $7,800 (2005 est.)
GDP - composition by sector:
agriculture: 9.3%
industry: 27.8%
services: 62.9% (2005 est.)
Labor force: 820,000 (2005 est.)
Labor force - by occupation: agriculture 47%, industry 20%, services 33% (1999 est.)
Unemployment rate: 35% (1998)
Population below poverty line: 50% (2002 est.)
Household income or consumption by percentage share:
lowest 10%: NA
highest 10%: NA
Distribution of family income - Gini index: 70 (2003)
Inflation rate (consumer prices): 2.7% (2005 est.)
Investment (gross fixed): 21.2% of GDP (2005 est.)
Budget:
revenues: $1.945 billion
expenditures: $2.039 billion, including capital expenditures of NA (2005 est.)
Public debt: 39.6% of GDP (2005 est.)
Agriculture - products: millet, sorghum, peanuts; livestock; fish
Industries: meatpacking, fish processing, dairy products; mining (diamond, lead, zinc, tin, silver, tungsten, uranium, copper)
Industrial production growth rate: NA
Electricity - production: 1.464 billion kWh (2003)
Electricity - production by source: NA
Electricity - consumption: 2.372 billion kWh (2003)
Electricity - exports: 55 million kWh (2003)
Electricity - imports: 1.065 billion kWh; note - electricity supplied by South Africa (2003)
Oil - production: 0 bbl/day (2003 est.)
Oil - consumption: 16,000 bbl/day (2003 est.)
Oil - exports: NA (2001)
Oil - imports: NA (2001)
Oil - proved reserves: 0 bbl (1 January 2002)
Natural gas - proved reserves: 31.15 billion cu m (1 January 2002)
Current account balance: $579 million (2005 est.)
Exports: $2.04 billion f.o.b. (2005 est.)
Exports - partners: EU 79%, US 4% (2004)
Imports: $2.35 billion f.o.b. (2005 est.)
Imports - partners: US 50%, EU 31% (2004)

Reserves of foreign exchange and gold: $365 million (2005 est.)
Debt - external: $1.164 billion (2005 est.)
Economic aid - recipient: ODA $160 million (2000 est.)
Currency (code): Namibian dollar (NAD); South African rand (ZAR)
Currency code: NAD; ZAR
Exchange rates: Namibian dollars per US dollar - 6.35 (2005), 6.4597 (2004), 7.5648 (2003), 10.5407 (2002), 8.6092 (2001)
Fiscal year: 1 April - 31 March

COMMUNICATIONS

Telephones - main lines in use: 127,400 (2003)
Telephones - mobile cellular: 223,700 (2003)
Telephone system:
general assessment: good system; about 6 telephones for each 100 persons
domestic: good urban services; fair rural service; microwave radio relay links major towns; connections to other populated places are by open wire; 100% digital
international: country code - 264; fiber-optic cable to South Africa, microwave radio relay link to Botswana, direct links to other neighboring countries; connected to Africa ONE and South African Far East (SAFE) submarine cables through South Africa; satellite earth stations - 4 Intelsat (2002)
Radio broadcast stations: AM 2, FM 39, shortwave 4 (2001)
Radios: 232,000 (1997)
Television broadcast stations: 8 (plus about 20 low-power repeaters) (1997)
Televisions: 60,000 (1997)
Internet country code: .na
Internet hosts: 3,164 (2003)
Internet Service Providers (ISPs): 2 (2000)
Internet users: 65,000 (2003)

TRANSPORTATION

Airports: 136 (2004 est.)
Airports - with paved runways:
total: 21
over 3,047 m: 3
2,438 to 3,047 m: 2
1,524 to 2,437 m: 13
914 to 1,523 m: 3 (2005 est.)
Airports - with unpaved runways:
total: 115
2,438 to 3,047 m: 2
1,524 to 2,437 m: 22
914 to 1,523 m: 71
under 914 m: 20 (2005 est.)
Railways:
total: 2,382 km
narrow gauge: 2,382 km 1.067-m gauge (2004)
Roadways:
total: 42,237 km
paved: 5,406 km
unpaved: 36,831 km (2002)
Merchant marine:
total: 1 ship (1,000 GRT or over) 2,265 GRT/3,605 DWT
by type: cargo 1 (2005)
Ports and terminals: Luderitz, Walvis Bay

MILITARY

Military branches: Namibian Defense Force: Army (includes Air Wing), Navy, Police
Military service age and obligation: 18 years of age for voluntary military service (2001)
Manpower available for military service: *males age 18-49:* 441,293 (2005 est.)
Manpower fit for military service: *males age 18-49:* 217,118 (2005 est.)
Military expenditures - dollar figure: $168.4 million (2004)
Military expenditures - percent of GDP: 3.1% (2004)

TRANSNATIONAL ISSUES

Disputes - international: border commission has yet to resolve small residual disputes with Botswana along the Caprivi Strip, including the Situngu marshlands along the Linyanti River; Botswana residents protest Namibia's planned construction of the Okavango hydroelectric dam on Popa Falls; managed dispute with South Africa over the location of the boundary in the Orange River; Namibia has supported and in 2004 Zimbabwe dropped objections to plans between Botswana and Zambia to build a bridge over the Zambezi River, thereby de facto recognizing a short, but not clearly delimited Botswana-Zambia, boundary in the river

NAURU

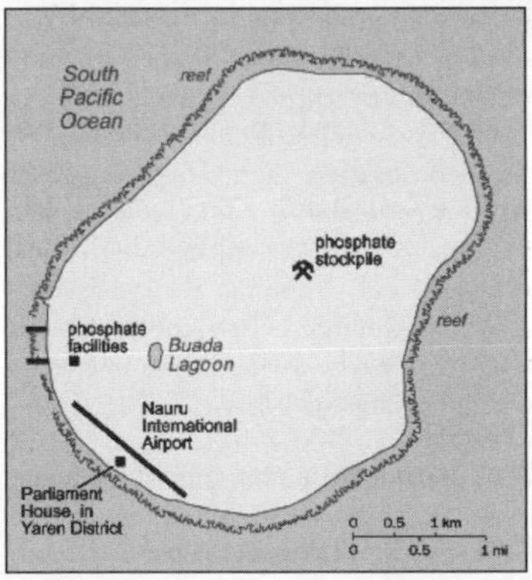

INTRODUCTION

Background: Nauru's phosphate deposits began to be mined early in the 20th century by a German-British consortium; the island was occupied by Australian forces in World War I. Nauru achieved independence in 1968 and joined the UN in 1999. Nauru is the world's smallest independent republic.

GEOGRAPHY

Location: Oceania, island in the South Pacific Ocean, south of the Marshall Islands
Geographic coordinates: 0 32 S, 166 55 E
Map references: Oceania
Area:
total: 21 sq km
land: 21 sq km
water: 0 sq km
Area - comparative: about 0.1 times the size of Washington, DC
Land boundaries: 0 km
Coastline: 30 km
Maritime claims:
territorial sea: 12 nm
contiguous zone: 24 nm
exclusive economic zone: 200 nm
Climate: tropical with a monsoonal pattern; rainy season (November to February)
Terrain: sandy beach rises to fertile ring around raised coral reefs with phosphate plateau in center
Elevation extremes:
lowest point: Pacific Ocean 0 m
highest point: unnamed location along plateau rim 61 m
Natural resources: phosphates, fish
Land use:
arable land: 0%
permanent crops: 0%
other: 100% (2001)
Irrigated land: NA
Natural hazards: periodic droughts
Environment - current issues: limited natural fresh water resources, roof storage tanks collect rainwater, but mostly dependent on a single, aging desalination plant; intensive phosphate mining during the past 90 years - mainly by a UK, Australia, and NZ consortium - has left the central 90% of Nauru a wasteland and threatens limited remaining land resources
Environment - international agreements:
party to: Biodiversity, Climate Change, Climate Change-Kyoto Protocol,

Desertification, Hazardous Wastes, Law of the Sea, Marine Dumping, Ozone Layer Protection
signed, but not ratified: none of the selected agreements
Geography - note: Nauru is one of the three great phosphate rock islands in the Pacific Ocean - the others are Banaba (Ocean Island) in Kiribati and Makatea in French Polynesia; only 53 km south of Equator

PEOPLE

Population: 13,048 (July 2005 est.)
Age structure:
0-14 years: 37.5% (male 2,511/female 2,379)
15-64 years: 60.6% (male 3,895/female 4,012)
65 years and over: 1.9% (male 132/female 119) (2005 est.)
Median age:
total: 20.24 years
male: 19.76 years
female: 20.78 years (2005 est.)
Population growth rate: 1.83% (2005 est.)
Birth rate: 25.14 births/1,000 population (2005 est.)
Death rate: 6.82 deaths/1,000 population (2005 est.)
Net migration rate: 0 migrant(s)/1,000 population (2005 est.)
Sex ratio:
at birth: 1.05 male(s)/female
under 15 years: 1.06 male(s)/female
15-64 years: 0.97 male(s)/female
65 years and over: 1.11 male(s)/female
total population: 1 male(s)/female (2005 est.)
Infant mortality rate:
total: 9.95 deaths/1,000 live births
male: 12.51 deaths/1,000 live births
female: 7.26 deaths/1,000 live births (2005 est.)
Life expectancy at birth:
total population: 62.73 years
male: 59.16 years
female: 66.48 years (2005 est.)
Total fertility rate: 3.19 children born/woman (2005 est.)
HIV/AIDS - adult prevalence rate: NA
HIV/AIDS - people living with HIV/AIDS: NA
HIV/AIDS - deaths: NA
Nationality:
noun: Nauruan(s)
adjective: Nauruan
Ethnic groups: Nauruan 58%, other Pacific Islander 26%, Chinese 8%, European 8%
Religions: Christian (two-thirds Protestant, one-third Roman Catholic)
Languages: Nauruan (official, a distinct Pacific Island language), English widely understood, spoken, and used for most government and commercial purposes
Literacy:
definition: NA
total population: NA%
male: NA%
female: NA%

GOVERNMENT

Country name:
conventional long form: Republic of Nauru
conventional short form: Nauru
former: Pleasant Island
Government type: republic
Capital: no official capital; government offices in Yaren District
Administrative divisions: 14 districts; Aiwo, Anabar, Anetan, Anibare, Baiti, Boe, Buada, Denigomodu, Ewa, Ijuw, Meneng, Nibok, Uaboe, Yaren
Independence: 31 January 1968 (from the Australia-, NZ-, and UK-administered UN trusteeship)
National holiday: Independence Day, 31 January (1968)
Constitution: 29 January 1968; amended 17 May 1968 (Constitution Day)
Legal system: acts of the Nauru Parliament and British common law
Suffrage: 20 years of age; universal and compulsory
Executive branch:
chief of state: President Ludwig SCOTTY (since 26 October 2004); note - the president is both the chief of state and head of government
head of government: President Ludwig SCOTTY (since 26 October 2004); note - the president is both the chief of state and head of government
cabinet: Cabinet appointed by the president from among the members of Parliament
elections: president elected by Parliament for a three-year term; election last held 23 October 2004 (next to be held NA 2007)
election results: Ludwig SCOTTY was unopposed in the parliamentary elections for president
Legislative branch: unicameral Parliament (18 seats; members elected by popular vote to serve three-year terms)
elections: last held 3 May 2003 (next to be held not later than May 2006)
election results: percent of vote - NA%; seats - Nauru First Party 3, independents 15
Judicial branch: Supreme Court
Political parties and leaders: loose multi-party system; Democratic Party [Kennan ADEANG]; Nauru Party (informal) [leader NA]; Naoero Amo (Nauru First) Party [leader NA]
Political pressure groups and leaders: NA
International organization participation: ACP, AsDB, C, FAO, ICAO, ICCt, Interpol, IOC, ITU, OPCW, PIF, Sparteca, SPC, UN, UNCTAD, UNESCO, UPU, WHO
Diplomatic representation in the US: Nauru does not have an embassy in the US, but does have a UN office at 800 2nd Avenue, Suite 400 D, New York, New York 10017; telephone: (212) 937-0074
consulate(s): Agana (Guam)
Diplomatic representation from the US: the US does not have an embassy in Nauru; the US Ambassador to Fiji is accredited to Nauru
Flag description: blue with a narrow, horizontal, yellow stripe across the center and a large white 12-pointed star below the stripe on the hoist side; the star indicates the country's location in relation to the Equator (the yellow stripe) and the 12 points symbolize the 12 original tribes of Nauru

ECONOMY

Economy - overview: Revenues of this tiny island have traditionally come from exports of phosphates, but reserves are now depleted. Few other resources exist with most necessities being imported, mainly from Australia, its former occupier and later major source of support. The rehabilitation of mined land and the replacement of income from phosphates are serious long-term problems. In anticipation of the exhaustion of Nauru's phosphate deposits, substantial amounts of phosphate income have been invested in trust funds to help cushion the transition and provide for Nauru's economic future. As a result of heavy spending from the trust funds, the government faces virtual bankruptcy. To cut costs the government has called for a freeze on wages, a reduction of over-staffed public service departments, privatization of numerous government agencies, and closure of some overseas consulates. In 2005 the deterioration in housing, hospitals, and other capital plant continued, and the cost to Australia of keeping the government and economy afloat has substantially mounted. Few comprehensive statistics on the Nauru economy exist, with estimates of Nauru's GDP varying widely.
GDP (purchasing power parity): $60 million (2001 est.)
GDP (official exchange rate): NA
GDP - real growth rate: NA
GDP - per capita: purchasing power parity - $5,000 (2001 est.)
GDP - composition by sector:
agriculture: NA
industry: NA
services: NA
Labor force - by occupation: employed in mining phosphates, public administration, education, and transportation

Unemployment rate: 90% (2004 est.)
Population below poverty line: NA
Household income or consumption by percentage share:
lowest 10%: NA
highest 10%: NA
Inflation rate (consumer prices): -3.6% (1993)
Investment (gross fixed): 17.1% of GDP (2005 est.)
Budget:
revenues: $23.4 million
expenditures: $64.8 million, including capital expenditures of NA (FY95/96)
Agriculture - products: coconuts
Industries: phosphate mining, offshore banking, coconut products
Industrial production growth rate: NA
Electricity - production: 23 million kWh (2003)
Electricity - production by source:
fossil fuel: 100%
hydro: 0%
nuclear: 0%
other: 0% (2001)
Electricity - consumption: 21.39 million kWh (2003)
Electricity - exports: 0 kWh (2003)
Electricity - imports: 0 kWh (2003)
Oil - production: 0 bbl/day (2003 est.)
Oil - consumption: 1,000 bbl/day (2003 est.)
Oil - exports: NA (2001)
Oil - imports: NA (2001)
Exports: $17 million f.o.b. (2004 est.)
Exports - partners: South Africa 43.4%, Germany 20.7%, India 11.8%, Japan 7.2%, Poland 4% (2004)
Imports: $20 million c.i.f. (2004 est.)
Imports - partners: Australia 65.6%, Indonesia 5.4%, Germany 5.3%, UK 4.4% (2004)
Debt - external: $33.3 million (2002)
Economic aid - recipient: $2.25 million from Australia (FY96/97 est.)
Currency (code): Australian dollar (AUD)
Currency code: AUD
Exchange rates: Australian dollars per US dollar - 1.31 (2005), 1.3598 (2004), 1.5419 (2003), 1.8406 (2002), 1.9334 (2001)
Fiscal year: 1 July - 30 June

COMMUNICATIONS

Telephones - main lines in use: 1,900 (2002)
Telephones - mobile cellular: 1,500 (2002)
Telephone system:
general assessment: adequate local and international radiotelephone communication provided via Australian facilities
domestic: NA
international: country code - 674; satellite earth station - 1 Intelsat (Pacific Ocean)
Radio broadcast stations: AM 1, FM 0, shortwave 0 (1998)
Radios: 7,000 (1997)
Television broadcast stations: 1 (1997)
Televisions: 500 (1997)
Internet country code: .nr
Internet Service Providers (ISPs): 1 (2000)
Internet users: 300 (2002)

TRANSPORTATION

Airports: 1 (2004 est.)
Airports - with paved runways:
1,524 to 2,437 m: 1 (2005 est.)
Roadways:
total: 30 km
paved: 24 km
unpaved: 6 km (1999 est.)
Ports and terminals: Nauru

MILITARY

Military branches: no regular military forces; Nauru Police Force
Manpower available for military service: *males age 18-49:* 2,874 (2005 est.)
Manpower fit for military service: *males age 18-49:* 1,963 (2005 est.)
Military expenditures - dollar figure: NA
Military expenditures - percent of GDP: NA
Military - note: Nauru maintains no defense forces; under an informal agreement, defense is the responsibility of Australia

TRANSNATIONAL ISSUES

Disputes - international: none
Illicit drugs: offshore banking recently stopped, remains on Financial Action Task Force Non-Cooperative Countries and Territories List for continued failure to address deficiencies in money-laundering control regime

NAVASSA ISLAND

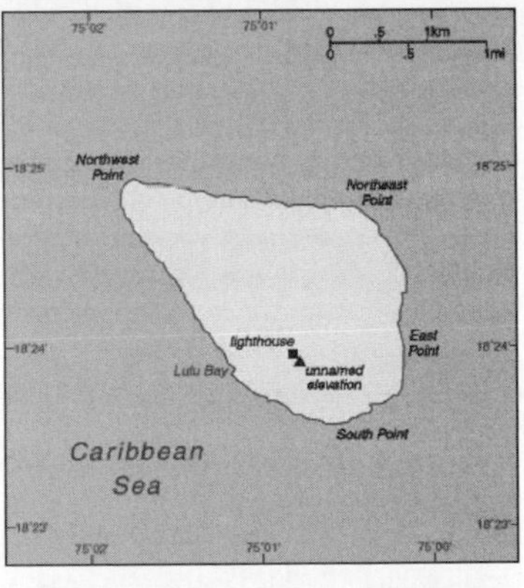

INTRODUCTION

Background: This uninhabited island was claimed by the US in 1857 for its guano. Mining took place between 1865 and 1898. The lighthouse, built in 1917, was shut down in 1996 and administration of Navassa Island transferred from the Coast Guard to the Department of the Interior. A 1998 scientific expedition to the island described it as a unique preserve of Caribbean biodiversity; the following year it became a National Wildlife Refuge and annual scientific expeditions have continued.

GEOGRAPHY

Location: Caribbean, island in the Caribbean Sea, 35 miles west of Tiburon Peninsula of Haiti
Geographic coordinates: 18 25 N, 75 02 W
Map references: Central America and the Caribbean
Area:
total: 5.4 sq km
land: 5.4 sq km
water: 0 sq km
Area - comparative: about nine times the size of The Mall in Washington, DC
Land boundaries: 0 km
Coastline: 8 km
Maritime claims:
territorial sea: 12 nm
exclusive economic zone: 200 nm
Climate: marine, tropical
Terrain: raised coral and limestone plateau, flat to undulating; ringed by vertical white cliffs (9 to 15 m high)
Elevation extremes:
lowest point: Caribbean Sea 0 m
highest point: unnamed location on southwest side 77 m
Natural resources: guano
Land use:
arable land: 0%
permanent crops: 0%
other: 100% (2001)
Irrigated land: 0 sq km (1998 est.)
Natural hazards: NA
Environment - current issues: NA
Geography - note: strategic location 160 km south of the US Naval Base at Guantanamo Bay, Cuba; mostly exposed rock but with enough grassland to support goat herds; dense stands of fig-like trees, scattered cactus

PEOPLE

Population: Uninhabited

note: transient Haitian fishermen and others camp on the island (July 2005 est.)

GOVERNMENT

Country name:
conventional long form: none
conventional short form: Navassa Island
Dependency status: unincorporated territory of the US; administered by the Fish and Wildlife Service, US Department of the Interior, from the Caribbean Islands National Wildlife Refuge in Boqueron, Puerto Rico; in September 1996, the Coast Guard ceased operations and maintenance of Navassa Island Light, a 46-meter-tall lighthouse on the southern side of the island; there has also been a private claim advanced against the island
Legal system: the laws of the US, where applicable, apply
Flag description: the flag of the US is used

ECONOMY

Economy - overview: subsistence fishing and commercial trawling activities within refuge waters

TRANSPORTATION

Ports and terminals: none; offshore anchorage only

MILITARY

Military - note: defense is the responsibility of the US

TRANSNATIONAL ISSUES

Disputes - international: claimed by Haiti, source of subsistence fishing

NEPAL

INTRODUCTION

Background: In 1951, the Nepalese monarch ended the century-old system of rule by hereditary premiers and instituted a cabinet system of government. Reforms in 1990 established a multiparty democracy within the framework of a constitutional monarchy. A Maoist insurgency, launched in 1996, has gained traction and is threatening to bring down the regime, especially after a negotiated cease-fire between the Maoists and government forces broke down in August 2003. In 2001, the crown prince massacred ten members of the royal family, including the king and queen, and then took his own life. In October 2002, the new king dismissed the prime minister and his cabinet for "incompetence" after they dissolved the parliament and were subsequently unable to hold elections because of the ongoing insurgency. While stopping short of reestablishing parliament, the king in June 2004 reinstated the most recently elected prime minister who formed a four-party coalition government. Citing dissatisfaction with the government's lack of progress in addressing the Maoist insurgency, the king in February 2005 dissolved the government, declared a state of emergency, imprisoned party leaders, and assumed power.

GEOGRAPHY

Location: Southern Asia, between China and India
Geographic coordinates: 28 00 N, 84 00 E
Map references: Asia
Area:
total: 140,800 sq km
land: 136,800 sq km
water: 4,000 sq km
Area - comparative: slightly larger than Arkansas
Land boundaries:
total: 2,926 km
border countries: China 1,236 km, India 1,690 km
Coastline: 0 km (landlocked)
Maritime claims: none (landlocked)
Climate: varies from cool summers and severe winters in north to subtropical summers and mild winters in south
Terrain: Tarai or flat river plain of the Ganges in south, central hill region, rugged Himalayas in north
Elevation extremes:
lowest point: Kanchan Kalan 70 m
highest point: Mount Everest 8,850 m
Natural resources: quartz, water, timber, hydropower, scenic beauty, small deposits of lignite, copper, cobalt, iron ore
Land use:
arable land: 21.68%
permanent crops: 0.64%
other: 77.68% (2001)
Irrigated land: 11,350 sq km (1998 est.)
Natural hazards: severe thunderstorms, flooding, landslides, drought, and famine depending on the timing, intensity, and duration of the summer monsoons
Environment - current issues: deforestation (overuse of wood for fuel and lack of alternatives); contaminated water (with human and animal wastes, agricultural runoff, and industrial effluents); wildlife conservation; vehicular emissions
Environment - international agreements:
party to: Biodiversity, Climate Change, Desertification, Endangered Species, Hazardous Wastes, Law of the Sea, Ozone Layer Protection, Tropical Timber 83, Tropical Timber 94, Wetlands
signed, but not ratified: Marine Life Conservation
Geography - note: landlocked; strategic location between China and India; contains eight of world's 10 highest peaks, including Mount Everest - the world's tallest - on the border with China

PEOPLE

Population: 27,676,547 (July 2005 est.)
Age structure:
0-14 years: 39% (male 5,575,157/female 5,221,794)
15-64 years: 57.3% (male 8,137,410/female 7,720,691)
65 years and over: 3.7% (male 499,039/female 522,456) (2005 est.)
Median age:
total: 20.07 years
male: 19.91 years
female: 20.24 years (2005 est.)
Population growth rate: 2.2% (2005 est.)
Birth rate: 31.45 births/1,000 population (2005 est.)
Death rate: 9.47 deaths/1,000 population (2005 est.)

Net migration rate: 0 migrant(s)/1,000 population (2005 est.)

Sex ratio:
at birth: 1.05 male(s)/female
under 15 years: 1.07 male(s)/female
15-64 years: 1.05 male(s)/female
65 years and over: 0.96 male(s)/female
total population: 1.06 male(s)/female (2005 est.)

Infant mortality rate:
total: 66.98 deaths/1,000 live births
male: 65.25 deaths/1,000 live births
female: 68.79 deaths/1,000 live births (2005 est.)

Life expectancy at birth:
total population: 59.8 years
male: 60.09 years
female: 59.5 years (2005 est.)

Total fertility rate: 4.19 children born/woman (2005 est.)

HIV/AIDS - adult prevalence rate: 0.5% (2001 est.)

HIV/AIDS - people living with HIV/AIDS: 61,000 (2001 est.)

HIV/AIDS - deaths: 3,100 (2003 est.)

Nationality:
noun: Nepalese (singular and plural)
adjective: Nepalese

Ethnic groups: Chhettri 15.5%, Brahman-Hill 12.5%, Magar 7%, Tharu 6.6%, Tamang 5.5%, Newar 5.4%, Muslim 4.2%, Kami 3.9%, Yadav 3.9%, other 32.7%, unspecified 2.8% (2001 census)

Religions: Hindu 80.6%, Buddhist 10.7%, Muslim 4.2%, Kirant 3.6%, other 0.9% (2001 census)
note: only official Hindu state in the world

Languages: Nepali 47.8%, Maithali 12.1%, Bhojpuri 7.4%, Tharu (Dagaura/Rana) 5.8%, Tamang 5.1%, Newar 3.6%, Magar 3.3%, Awadhi 2.4%, other 10%, unspecified 2.5% (2001 census)
note: many in government and business also speak English

Literacy:
definition: age 15 and over can read and write
total population: 45.2%
male: 62.7%
female: 27.6% (2003 est.)

GOVERNMENT

Country name:
conventional long form: Kingdom of Nepal
conventional short form: Nepal

Government type: parliamentary democracy and constitutional monarchy (since 1 February 2005 parliament has remained suspended and power rests with the palace)

Capital: Kathmandu

Administrative divisions: 14 zones (anchal, singular and plural); Bagmati, Bheri, Dhawalagiri, Gandaki, Janakpur, Karnali, Kosi, Lumbini, Mahakali, Mechi, Narayani, Rapti, Sagarmatha, Seti

Independence: 1768 (unified by Prithvi Narayan Shah)

National holiday: Birthday of King GYANENDRA, 7 July (1946)

Constitution: 9 November 1990

Legal system: based on Hindu legal concepts and English common law; has not accepted compulsory ICJ jurisdiction

Suffrage: 18 years of age, universal

Executive branch:
chief of state: King GYANENDRA Bir Bikram Shah (succeeded to the throne 4 June 2001 following the death of his nephew, King DIPENDRA Bir Bikram Shah)
head of government: King GYANENDRA Bir Bikram Shah; note - in Februrary 2005, the King sacked Sher Bahadur DEUBA, the last Prime Minister
cabinet: Cabinet appointed by the monarch on the recommendation of the prime minister; note - in February 2005 the King dissolved the Cabinet and set up a Council of Ministers, which he chairs
elections: none; the monarch is hereditary; following legislative elections, the leader of the majority party or leader of a majority coalition is usually appointed prime minister by the monarch
note: King BIRENDRA Bir Bikram Shah Dev died in a bloody shooting at the royal palace on 1 June 2001 that also claimed the lives of most of the royal family; King BIRENDRA's son, Crown Price DIPENDRA, is believed to have been responsible for the shootings before fatally wounding himself; immediately following the shootings and while still clinging to life, DIPENDRA was crowned king; he died three days later and was succeeded by his uncle

Legislative branch: bicameral Parliament consists of the National Council (60 seats; 35 appointed by the House of Representatives, 10 by the king, and 15 elected by an electoral college; one-third of the members elected every two years to serve six-year terms) and the House of Representatives (205 seats; members elected by popular vote to serve five-year terms)
elections: House of Representatives - last held 3 and 17 May 1999 (next election NA); note - Nepal's Parliament was dissolved on 22 May 2002
election results: House of Representatives (for 2002 parliament) - percent of vote by party - NC 37.3%, CPN/UML 31.6%, NDP 10.4%, NSP 3.2%, Rastriya Jana Morcha 1.4%, Samyukta Janmorcha Nepal 0.8%, NWPP 0.5%, others 14.8%; seats by party - NC 113, CPN/UML 69, NDP 11, NSP 5, Rastriya Jana Morcha 5, Samyukta Janmorcha Nepal 1, NWPP 1

Judicial branch: Supreme Court or Sarbochha Adalat (chief justice is appointed by the monarch on recommendation of the Constitutional Council; the other judges are appointed by the monarch on the recommendation of the Judicial Council)

Political parties and leaders: Communist Party of Nepal/United Marxist-Leninist or CPN/UML [Madhav Kumar NEPAL, general secretary]; National Democratic Party or NDP (also called Rastriya Prajantra Party or RPP) [Surya Bahadur THAPA, chairman]; People's Front Nepal (Rastriya Jana Morcha) [Chitra BAHADUR, chairman]; Nepali Congress-Democratic [Sher Bahadur DEUBA, president]; Nepali Congress or NC [Girija Prasad KOIRALA, party president; Sushil KOIRALA, general secretary]; Nepal Sadbhavana (Goodwill) Party or NSP [Bhadri Prasad MANDAL, acting party president]; Nepal Workers and Peasants Party or NWPP [Narayan Man BIJUKCHHE, party chairman]; Samyukta Janmorcha Nepal [leader NA]

Political pressure groups and leaders: Maoist guerrilla-based insurgency [Pushpa Kamal DAHAL, also known as PRAHANDA, chairman; Dr. Baburam BHATTARAI]; numerous small, left-leaning student groups in the capital; several small, radical Nepalese antimonarchist groups

International organization participation: AsDB, CP, FAO, G-77, IBRD, ICAO, ICC, ICFTU, ICRM, IDA, IFAD, IFC, IFRCS, ILO, IMF, IMO, Interpol, IOC, IOM (observer), ISO (correspondent), ITU, MIGA, MINUSTAH, MONUC, NAM, ONUB, OPCW, SAARC, SACEP, UN, UNAMSIL, UNCTAD, UNDOF, UNESCO, UNIDO, UNMEE, UNMIL, UNMIS, UNOCI, UNTSO, UPU, WCL, WCO, WFTU, WHO, WIPO, WMO, WToO, WTO

Diplomatic representation in the US:
chief of mission: Ambassador Kedar Bhakta SHRESTHA
chancery: 2131 Leroy Place NW, Washington, DC 20008
telephone: [1] (202) 667-4550
FAX: [1] (202) 667-5534
consulate(s) general: New York

Diplomatic representation from the US:
chief of mission: Ambassador James F. MORIARTY
embassy: Pani Pokhari, Kathmandu
mailing address: use embassy street address
telephone: [977] (1) 411-1179
FAX: [977] (1) 441-9963

Flag description: red with a blue border around the unique shape of two overlapping right triangles; the smaller, upper triangle bears a white stylized moon and the larger, lower triangle bears a white 12-pointed sun

ECONOMY

Economy - overview: Nepal is among the poorest and least developed countries in the world with 40% of its population living below the poverty line. Agriculture is the mainstay of the economy, providing a livelihood for over 80% of the population and accounting for 40% of GDP. Industrial activity mainly involves the processing of agricultural produce including jute, sugarcane, tobacco, and grain. Security concerns in the wake of the Maoist conflict have led to a decrease in tourism, a key source of foreign exchange. Nepal has considerable scope for exploiting its potential in hydropower and tourism, areas of recent foreign investment interest. Prospects for foreign trade or investment in other sectors will remain poor, however, because of the small size of the economy, its technological backwardness, its remoteness, its landlocked geographic location, its civil strife, and its susceptibility to natural disaster.
GDP (purchasing power parity): $42.17 billion (2005 est.)
GDP (official exchange rate): $6.792 billion (2005 est.)
GDP - real growth rate: 2.5% (2005 est.)
GDP - per capita: purchasing power parity - $1,500 (2005 est.)
GDP - composition by sector:
agriculture: 40%
industry: 20%
services: 40% (2002 est.)
Labor force: 10 million
note: severe lack of skilled labor (1996 est.)
Labor force - by occupation: agriculture 81%, industry 3%, services 16%
Unemployment rate: 47% (2001 est.)
Population below poverty line: 42% (1995-96)
Household income or consumption by percentage share:
lowest 10%: 3.2%
highest 10%: 29.8% (1995-96)
Distribution of family income - Gini index: 36.7 (FY95/96)
Inflation rate (consumer prices): 2.9% (2002 est.)
Budget:
revenues: $665 million
expenditures: $1.1 billion, including capital expenditures of NA (FY99/00 est.)
Agriculture - products: rice, corn, wheat, sugarcane, root crops; milk, water buffalo meat
Industries: tourism, carpet, textile; small rice, jute, sugar, and oilseed mills; cigarette; cement and brick production
Industrial production growth rate: 8.7% (FY99/00)
Electricity - production: 2.512 billion kWh (2003)
Electricity - production by source:
fossil fuel: 8.5%
hydro: 91.5%
nuclear: 0%
other: 0% (2001)
Electricity - consumption: 2.299 billion kWh (2003)
Electricity - exports: 186 million kWh (2003)
Electricity - imports: 149 million kWh (2003)
Oil - production: 0 bbl/day (2003 est.)
Oil - consumption: 15,400 bbl/day (2003 est.)
Oil - exports: NA (2001)
Oil - imports: NA (2001)
Exports: $626 million f.o.b., but does not include unrecorded border trade with India (2004 est.)
Exports - partners: India 47.4%, US 22.7%, Germany 8.4% (2004)
Imports: $1.696 billion f.o.b. (2004 est.)
Imports - partners: India 46.3%, China 10.8%, UAE 9.3%, Saudi Arabia 4.1% (2004)
Debt - external: $2.7 billion (2001)
Economic aid - recipient: $424 million (FY00/01)
Currency (code): Nepalese rupee (NPR)
Currency code: NPR
Exchange rates: Nepalese rupees per US dollar - NA (2005), 73.674 (2004), 76.141 (2003), 77.877 (2002), 74.949 (2001)
Fiscal year: 16 July - 15 July

COMMUNICATIONS

Telephones - main lines in use: 371,800 (2003)
Telephones - mobile cellular: 50,400 (2003)
Telephone system:
general assessment: poor telephone and telegraph service; fair radiotelephone communication service and mobile cellular telephone network
domestic: NA
international: country code - 977; radiotelephone communications; microwave landline to India; satellite earth station - 1 Intelsat (Indian Ocean)
Radio broadcast stations: AM 6, FM 5, shortwave 1 (January 2000)
Radios: 840,000 (1997)
Television broadcast stations: 1 (plus 9 repeaters) (1998)
Televisions: 130,000 (1997)
Internet country code: .np
Internet hosts: 917 (2003)
Internet Service Providers (ISPs): 6 (2000)
Internet users: 80,000 (2002)

TRANSPORTATION

Airports: 46 (2004 est.)
Airports - with paved runways:
total: 10
over 3,047 m: 1
914 to 1,523 m: 7
under 914 m: 2 (2005 est.)
Airports - with unpaved runways:
total: 38
1,524 to 2,437 m: 1
914 to 1,523 m: 8
under 914 m: 29 (2005 est.)
Railways:
total: 59 km
narrow gauge: 59 km 0.762-m gauge (2004)
Roadways:
total: 13,223 km
paved: 4,073 km
unpaved: 9,150 km (1999 est.)

MILITARY

Military branches: Royal Nepalese Army (includes Royal Nepalese Army Air Service), Nepalese Police Force
Military service age and obligation: 18 years of age for voluntary military service (2001)
Manpower available for military service: *males age 18-49:* 6,107,091 (2005 est.)
Manpower fit for military service: *males age 18-49:* 4.193 million (2005 est.)
Manpower reaching military service age annually: *males:* 308,031 (2005 est.)
Military expenditures - dollar figure: $99.2 million (2004)
Military expenditures - percent of GDP: 1.5% (2004)

TRANSNATIONAL ISSUES

Disputes - international: joint border commission continues to work on small disputed sections of boundary with India; India has instituted a stricter border regime to restrict transit of Maoist insurgents and illegal cross-border activities
Refugees and internally displaced persons:
refugees (country of origin): 104,235 (Bhutan)
IDPs: 100,000-200,000 (ongoing conflict between government forces and Maoist rebels; displacement spread across the country) (2004)
Illicit drugs: illicit producer of cannabis and hashish for the domestic and international drug markets; transit point for opiates from Southeast Asia to the West

NETHERLANDS ANTILLES

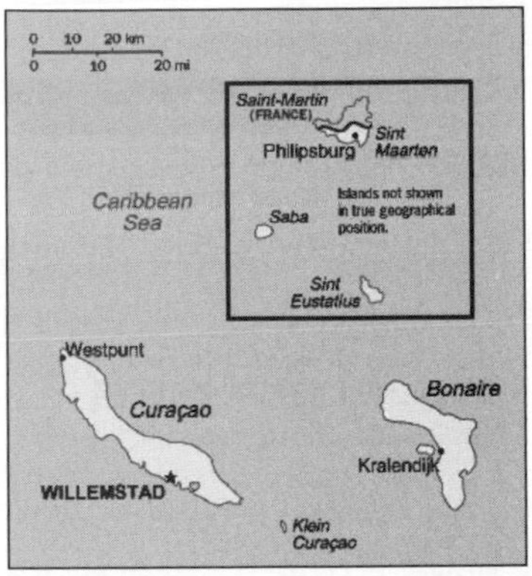

INTRODUCTION

Background: Once the center of the Caribbean slave trade, the island of Curacao was hard hit by the abolition of slavery in 1863. Its prosperity (and that of neighboring Aruba) was restored in the early 20th century with the construction of oil refineries to service the newly discovered Venezuelan oil fields. The island of Saint Martin is shared with France; its southern portion is named Sint Maarten and is part of the Netherlands Antilles; its northern portion is called Saint-Martin and is part of Guadeloupe (France).

GEOGRAPHY

Location: Caribbean, two island groups in the Caribbean Sea - composed of five islands, Curacao and Bonaire located off the coast of Venezuela, and St. Maarten, Saba, and St. Eustatius lie east of the US Virgin Islands
Geographic coordinates: 12 15 N, 68 45 W
Map references: Central America and the Caribbean
Area:
total: 960 sq km
land: 960 sq km
water: 0 sq km
note: includes Bonaire, Curacao, Saba, Sint Eustatius, and Sint Maarten (Dutch part of the island of Saint Martin)
Area - comparative: more than five times the size of Washington, DC
Land boundaries:
total: 10.2 km
border countries: Guadeloupe (Saint-Martin) 10.2 km
Coastline: 364 km
Maritime claims:
territorial sea: 12 nm
exclusive fishing zone: 12 nm
Climate: tropical; ameliorated by northeast trade winds
Terrain: generally hilly, volcanic interiors
Elevation extremes:
lowest point: Caribbean Sea 0 m
highest point: Mount Scenery 862 m
Natural resources: phosphates (Curacao only), salt (Bonaire only)
Land use:
arable land: 10%
permanent crops: 0%
other: 90% (2001)
Irrigated land: NA sq km
Natural hazards: Curacao and Bonaire are south of Caribbean hurricane belt and are rarely threatened; Sint Maarten, Saba, and Sint Eustatius are subject to hurricanes from July to October
Environment - current issues: NA
Geography - note: the five islands of the Netherlands Antilles are divided geographically into the Leeward Islands (northern) group (Saba, Sint Eustatius, and Sint Maarten) and the Windward Islands (southern) group (Bonaire and Curacao)

PEOPLE

Population: 219,958 (July 2005 est.)
Age structure:
0-14 years: 24.2% (male 27,302/female 26,002)
15-64 years: 67.3% (male 70,838/female 77,148)
65 years and over: 8.5% (male 7,673/female 10,995) (2005 est.)
Median age:
total: 32.46 years
male: 30.86 years
female: 34.01 years (2005 est.)
Population growth rate: 0.82% (2005 est.)
Birth rate: 15 births/1,000 population (2005 est.)
Death rate: 6.41 deaths/1,000 population (2005 est.)
Net migration rate: -0.4 migrant(s)/1,000 population (2005 est.)
Sex ratio:
at birth: 1.05 male(s)/female
under 15 years: 1.05 male(s)/female
15-64 years: 0.92 male(s)/female
65 years and over: 0.7 male(s)/female
total population: 0.93 male(s)/female (2005 est.)
Infant mortality rate:
total: 10.03 deaths/1,000 live births
male: 10.82 deaths/1,000 live births
female: 9.19 deaths/1,000 live births (2005 est.)
Life expectancy at birth:
total population: 75.83 years
male: 73.58 years
female: 78.2 years (2005 est.)
Total fertility rate: 2 children born/woman (2005 est.)
HIV/AIDS - adult prevalence rate: NA
HIV/AIDS - people living with HIV/AIDS: NA
HIV/AIDS - deaths: NA
Nationality:
noun: Dutch Antillean(s)
adjective: Dutch Antillean
Ethnic groups: mixed black 85%, Carib Amerindian, white, East Asian
Religions: Roman Catholic 72%, Pentecostal 4.9%, Protestant 3.5%, Seventh-Day Adventist 3.1%, Methodist 2.9%, Jehovah's Witnesses 1.7%, other Christian 4.2%, Jewish 1.3%, other or unspecified 1.2%, none 5.2% (2001 census)
Languages: Papiamento 65.4% (a Spanish-Portuguese-Dutch-English dialect), English 15.9% (widely spoken), Dutch 7.3% (official), Spanish 6.1%, Creole 1.6%, other 1.9%, unspecified 1.8% (2001 census)
Literacy:
definition: age 15 and over can read and write
total population: 96.7%
male: 96.7%
female: 96.8% (2003 est.)

GOVERNMENT

Country name:
conventional long form: none
conventional short form: Netherlands Antilles
local long form: none
local short form: Nederlandse Antillen
former: Curacao and Dependencies
Dependency status: an autonomous country within the Kingdom of the Netherlands; full autonomy in internal affairs granted in 1954; Dutch Government responsible for defense and foreign affairs
Government type: parliamentary
Capital: Willemstad; note - located on Curacao, the largest of the islands
Administrative divisions: none (part of the Kingdom of the Netherlands)
note: each island has its own government
Independence: none (part of the Kingdom of the Netherlands)
National holiday: Queen's Day (Birthday of Queen-Mother JULIANA in 1909 and accession to the throne of her oldest daughter BEATRIX in 1980), 30 April
Constitution: 29 December 1954, Statute of the Realm of the Netherlands, as amended
Legal system: based on Dutch civil law system with some English common law influence
Suffrage: 18 years of age, universal
Executive branch:
chief of state: Queen BEATRIX of the Netherlands (since 30 April 1980), represented by Governor General Frits GOEDGEDRAG (since 1 July 2002)

head of government: Prime Minister Etienne YS (since 3 June 2004)
cabinet: Council of Ministers elected by the Staten (legislature)
elections: the monarch is hereditary; governor general appointed by the monarch for a six-year term; following legislative elections, the leader of the majority party is usually elected prime minister by the Staten; election last held 18 January 2002 (next to be held by NA 2006)
note: government coalition - PAR, PNP, PLKP, DP St. Maarten, UP Bonaire, WIPM Saba, DP Statia
Legislative branch: unicameral States or Staten (22 seats - Curacao 14, Bonaire 3, St. Maarten 3, St. Eustatius 1, Saba 1; members are elected by popular vote to serve four-year terms)
elections: last held 18 January 2002 (next to be held in 2006)
election results: percent of vote by party - NA%; seats by party - PAR 4, PNP 3, PLKP 2, DP St. M 2, UP Bonaire 2, WIPM 1, DP
note: the government of Prime Minister Etienne YS is a coalition of several parties; current government formed after collapse of FOL led government on 4 April 2004
Judicial branch: Joint High Court of Justice (judges appointed by the monarch)
Political parties and leaders: Antillean Restructuring Party or PAR [Etienne YS]; C 93 [Stanley BROWN]; Democratic Party of Bonaire or PDB [Jopi ABRAHAM]; Democratic Party of Curacao or DP [Errol HERNANDEZ]; Democratic Party of Sint Eustatius or DP-St. E [Julian WOODLEY]; Democratic Party of Sint Maarten or DP-St. M [Sarah WESCOTT-WILLIAMS]; Foundation Energetic Management Anti-Narcotics or FAME [Eric LODEWIJKS]; Labor Party People's Crusade or PLKP [Errol COVA]; National Alliance [William MARLIN]; National People's Party or PNP [Susanne F. C. CAMELIA-ROMER]; New Antilles Movement or MAN [Kenneth GIJSBERTHA]; Patriotic Union of Bonaire or UP Bonaire [Ramonsito BOOI]; Patriotic Movement of Sint Maarten or SPA [Vance JAMES, Jr.]; People's Party or PAPU [Richard HODI]; Pro Curacao Party or PPK [Winston LOURENS]; Saba Democratic Labor Movement [Steve HASSELL]; Saba Unity Party [Carmen SIMMONDS]; St. Eustatius Alliance or SEA [Kenneth VAN PUTTEN]; Serious Alternative People's Party or Sapp [Julian ROLLOCKS]; Social Action Cause or KAS [Benny DEMEI]; Windward Islands People's Movement or WIPM [Will JOHNSTON]; Workers' Liberation Front or FOL [Anthony GODETT, Rignald LAK, Editha WRIGHT]
note: political parties are indigenous to each island
Political pressure groups and leaders: NA
International organization participation: ILO, IMF, Interpol, IOC, UNESCO (associate), UPU, WCL, WCO, WMO, WToO (associate)
Diplomatic representation in the US: none (represented by the Kingdom of the Netherlands)
Diplomatic representation from the US:
chief of mission: Consul General Robert E. SORENSON
consulate(s) general: J. B. Gorsiraweg #1, Willemstad AN, Curacao Robert E. SORENSON
mailing address: P. O. Box 158, Willemstad, Curacao
telephone: [599] (9) 4613066
FAX: [599] (9) 4616489
Flag description: white, with a horizontal blue stripe in the center superimposed on a vertical red band, also centered; five white, five-pointed stars are arranged in an oval pattern in the center of the blue band; the five stars represent the five main islands of Bonaire, Curacao, Saba, Sint Eustatius, and Sint Maarten

ECONOMY

Economy - overview: Tourism, petroleum refining, and offshore finance are the mainstays of this small economy, which is closely tied to the outside world. Although GDP has declined or grown slightly in each of the past eight years, the islands enjoy a high per capita income and a well-developed infrastructure compared with other countries in the region. Almost all consumer and capital goods are imported, the US and Mexico being the major suppliers. Poor soils and inadequate water supplies hamper the development of agriculture. Budgetary problems hamper reform of the health and pension systems of an aging population.
GDP (purchasing power parity): $2.45 billion (2003 est.)
GDP (official exchange rate): NA
GDP - real growth rate: 0.5% (2003 est.)
GDP - per capita: purchasing power parity - $11,400 (2003 est.)
GDP - composition by sector:
agriculture: 1%
industry: 15%
services: 84% (2000 est.)
Labor force: 89,000 (2000)
Labor force - by occupation: agriculture 1%, industry 13%, services 86% (2000 est.)
Unemployment rate: 15.6% (2002 est.)
Population below poverty line: NA
Household income or consumption by percentage share:
lowest 10%: NA
highest 10%: NA
Inflation rate (consumer prices): 2.1% (2003 est.)
Budget:
revenues: $710.8 million
expenditures: $741.6 million, including capital expenditures of NA (1997 est.)
Agriculture - products: aloes, sorghum, peanuts, vegetables, tropical fruit
Industries: tourism (Curacao, Sint Maarten, and Bonaire), petroleum refining (Curacao), petroleum transshipment facilities (Curacao and Bonaire), light manufacturing (Curacao)
Industrial production growth rate: NA%
Electricity - production: 1.017 billion kWh (2003)
Electricity - production by source:
fossil fuel: 100%
hydro: 0%
nuclear: 0%
other: 0% (2001)
Electricity - consumption: 945.8 million kWh (2003)
Electricity - exports: 0 kWh (2003)
Electricity - imports: 0 kWh (2003)
Oil - production: 0 bbl/day (2003 est.)
Oil - consumption: 72,500 bbl/day (2003 est.)
Oil - exports: NA (2001)
Oil - imports: NA (2001)
Exports: $2.076 billion f.o.b. (2004 est.)
Exports - partners: US 20.4%, Panama 11.2%, Guatemala 8.8%, Haiti 7.1%, Bahamas, The 5.6%, Honduras 4.2% (2004)
Imports: $4.383 billion f.o.b. (2004 est.)
Imports - partners: Venezuela 51.1%, US 21.9%, Netherlands 5% (2004)
Debt - external: $1.35 billion (1996)
Economic aid - recipient: IMF provided $61 million in 2000, and the Netherlands continued its support with $40 million (2000)
Currency (code): Netherlands Antillean guilder (ANG)
Currency code: ANG
Exchange rates: Netherlands Antillean guilders per US dollar - NA (2005), 1.79 (2004), 1.79 (2003), 1.79 (2002), 1.79 (2001)
Fiscal year: calendar year

COMMUNICATIONS

Telephones - main lines in use: 81,000 (2001)
Telephones - mobile cellular: 81,000 (2001)
Telephone system:
general assessment: generally adequate facilities
domestic: extensive interisland microwave radio relay links
international: country code - 599; subma-

rine cables - 2; satellite earth stations - 2 Intelsat (Atlantic Ocean)
Radio broadcast stations: AM 8, FM 19, shortwave 0 (2004)
Radios: 217,000 (1997)
Television broadcast stations: 3 (there is also a cable service, which supplies programs received from various US satellite networks and two Venezuelan channels) (2004)
Televisions: 69,000 (1997)
Internet country code: .an
Internet hosts: 119 (2001)
Internet Service Providers (ISPs): 6
Internet users: 2,000 (2000)

TRANSPORTATION

Airports: 5 (2004 est.)
Airports - with paved runways:
over 3,047 m: 1
2,438 to 3,047 m: 1
1,524 to 2,437 m: 1
914 to 1,523 m: 1
under 914 m: 1 (2005 est.)
Roadways:
total: 600 km
paved: 300 km
unpaved: 300 km
Merchant marine:
total: 168 ships (1,000 GRT or over) 1,317,007 GRT/1,668,499 DWT
by type: barge carrier 3, bulk carrier 23, cargo 72, chemical tanker 2, container 21, liquefied gas 6, passenger 2, petroleum tanker 3, refrigerated cargo 30, roll on/roll off 4, specialized tanker 2
foreign-owned: 158 (Belgium 5, Cyprus 1, Denmark 1, Germany 57, Hong Kong 3, Netherlands 71, Peru 1, Sweden 9, Turkey 7, United Kingdom 2, United States 1) (2005)
Ports and terminals: Bopec Terminal, Fuik Bay, Kralendijk, Willemstad

MILITARY

Military branches: no regular military forces; National Guard, Police Force (2005)
Military service age and obligation: 16 years of age for National Guard recruitment; no conscription (2002)
Manpower available for military service: *males age 16-49:* 54,200 (2005 est.)
Manpower fit for military service: *males age 16-49:* 45,273 (2005 est.)
Manpower reaching military service age annually: *males:* 1,720 (2005 est.)
Military - note: defense is the responsibility of the Kingdom of the Netherlands

TRANSNATIONAL ISSUES

Disputes - international: none
Illicit drugs: transshipment point for South American drugs bound for the US and Europe; money-laundering center

NETHERLANDS

INTRODUCTION

Background: The Kingdom of the Netherlands was formed in 1815. In 1830 Belgium seceded and formed a separate kingdom. The Netherlands remained neutral in World War I, but suffered invasion and occupation by Germany in World War II. A modern, industrialized nation, the Netherlands is also a large exporter of agricultural products. The country was a founding member of NATO and the EEC (now the EU), and participated in the introduction of the euro in 1999.

GEOGRAPHY

Location: Western Europe, bordering the North Sea, between Belgium and Germany
Geographic coordinates: 52 30 N, 5 45 E
Map references: Europe
Area:
total: 41,526 sq km
land: 33,883 sq km
water: 7,643 sq km
Area - comparative: slightly less than twice the size of New Jersey
Land boundaries:
total: 1,027 km
border countries: Belgium 450 km, Germany 577 km
Coastline: 451 km
Maritime claims:
territorial sea: 12 nm
exclusive fishing zone: 200 nm
Climate: temperate; marine; cool summers and mild winters
Terrain: mostly coastal lowland and reclaimed land (polders); some hills in southeast
Elevation extremes:
lowest point: Zuidplaspolder -7 m
highest point: Vaalserberg 322 m
Natural resources: natural gas, petroleum, peat, limestone, salt, sand and gravel, arable land
Land use:
arable land: 26.71%
permanent crops: 0.97%
other: 72.32% (2001)
Irrigated land: 5,650 sq km (1998 est.)
Natural hazards: flooding
Environment - current issues: water pollution in the form of heavy metals, organic compounds, and nutrients such as nitrates and phosphates; air pollution from vehicles and refining activities; acid rain
Environment - international agreements:
party to: Air Pollution, Air Pollution-Nitrogen Oxides, Air Pollution-Persistent Organic Pollutants, Air Pollution-Sulfur 85, Air Pollution-Sulfur 94, Air Pollution-Volatile Organic Compounds, Antarctic-Environmental Protocol, Antarctic-Marine Living Resources, Antarctic Treaty, Biodiversity, Climate Change, Climate Change-Kyoto Protocol, Desertification, Endangered Species, Environmental Modification, Hazardous Wastes, Kyoto Protocol, Law of the Sea, Marine Dumping, Marine Life Conservation, Ozone Layer Protection, Ship Pollution, Tropical Timber 83, Tropical Timber 94, Wetlands, Whaling
Geography - note: located at mouths of three major European rivers (Rhine, Maas or Meuse, and Schelde)

PEOPLE

Population: 16,407,491 (July 2005 est.)
Age structure:
0-14 years: 18.1% (male 1,523,316/female 1,453,232)
15-64 years: 67.8% (male 5,627,007/female 5,491,802)
65 years and over: 14.1% (male 974,037/female 1,338,097) (2005 est.)
Median age:
total: 39.04 years
male: 38.22 years
female: 39.9 years (2005 est.)
Population growth rate: 0.53% (2005 est.)
Birth rate: 11.14 births/1,000 population (2005 est.)
Death rate: 8.68 deaths/1,000 population (2005 est.)
Net migration rate: 2.8 migrant(s)/1,000 population (2005 est.)

Sex ratio:
at birth: 1.05 male(s)/female
under 15 years: 1.05 male(s)/female
15-64 years: 1.03 male(s)/female
65 years and over: 0.73 male(s)/female
total population: 0.98 male(s)/female (2005 est.)
Infant mortality rate:
total: 5.04 deaths/1,000 live births
male: 5.62 deaths/1,000 live births
female: 4.44 deaths/1,000 live births (2005 est.)
Life expectancy at birth:
total population: 78.81 years
male: 76.25 years
female: 81.51 years (2005 est.)
Total fertility rate: 1.66 children born/woman (2005 est.)
HIV/AIDS - adult prevalence rate: 0.2% (2001 est.)
HIV/AIDS - people living with HIV/AIDS: 19,000 (2001 est.)
HIV/AIDS - deaths: less than 100 (2003 est.)
Nationality:
noun: Dutchman (men), Dutchwoman (women)
adjective: Dutch
Ethnic groups: Dutch 83%, other 17% (of which 9% are non-Western origin mainly Turks, Moroccans, Antilleans, Surinamese, and Indonesians) (1999 est.)
Religions: Roman Catholic 31%, Dutch Reformed 13%, Calvinist 7%, Muslim 5.5%, other 2.5%, none 41% (2002)
Languages: Dutch (official), Frisian (official)
Literacy:
definition: age 15 and over can read and write
total population: 99% (2000 est.)
male: NA%
female: NA%

GOVERNMENT

Country name:
conventional long form: Kingdom of the Netherlands
conventional short form: Netherlands
local long form: Koninkrijk der Nederlanden
local short form: Nederland
Government type: constitutional monarchy
Capital: Amsterdam; The Hague is the seat of government
Administrative divisions: 12 provinces (provincies, singular - provincie); Drenthe, Flevoland, Friesland (Fryslan), Gelderland, Groningen, Limburg, Noord-Brabant, Noord-Holland, Overijssel, Utrecht, Zeeland, Zuid-Holland
Dependent areas: Aruba, Netherlands Antilles
Independence: 23 January 1579 (the northern provinces of the Low Countries conclude the Union of Utrecht breaking with Spain; it was not until 1648 that Spain recognized their independence)
National holiday: Queen's Day (Birthday of Queen-Mother JULIANA in 1909 and accession to the throne of her oldest daughter BEATRIX in 1980), 30 April
Constitution: adopted 1815; amended many times, last time 2002
Legal system: civil law system incorporating French penal theory; constitution does not permit judicial review of acts of the States General; accepts compulsory ICJ jurisdiction, with reservations
Suffrage: 18 years of age, universal
Executive branch:
chief of state: Queen BEATRIX (since 30 April 1980); Heir Apparent WILLEM-ALEXANDER (born 27 April 1967), son of the monarch
head of government: Prime Minister Jan Peter BALKENENDE (since 22 July 2002) and Deputy Prime Ministers Gerrit ZALM (since 27 May 2003) and Laurens Jan BRINKHORST (since 31 March 2005)
cabinet: Council of Ministers appointed by the monarch
elections: none; the monarchy is hereditary; following Second Chamber elections, the leader of the majority party or leader of a majority coalition is usually appointed prime minister by the monarch; vice prime ministers appointed by the monarch
note: there is also a Council of State composed of the monarch, heir apparent, and councilors that provides consultations to the cabinet on legislative and administrative policy
Legislative branch: bicameral States General or Staten Generaal consists of the First Chamber or Eerste Kamer (75 seats; members indirectly elected by the country's 12 provincial councils for four-year terms) and the Second Chamber or Tweede Kamer (150 seats; members directly elected by popular vote to serve four-year terms)
elections: First Chamber - last held 25 May 2003 (next to be held May 2007); Second Chamber - last held 22 January 2003 (next to be held May 2007)
election results: First Chamber - percent of vote by party - NA%; seats by party - CDA 23, PvdA 19, VVD 15, Green Party 5, Socialist Party 4, D66 3, other 6; Second Chamber - percent of vote by party - CDA 28.6%, PvdA 27.3%, VVD 12.9%, Socialist Party 6.3%, List Pim Fortuyn 5.7%, Green Party 5.1%, D66 4.1%; seats by party - CDA 44, PvdA 42, VVD 28, Socialist Party 9, List Pim Fortuyn 8, Green Party 8, D66 6, other 5
Judicial branch: Supreme Court or Hoge Raad (justices are nominated for life by the monarch)
Political parties and leaders: Christian Democratic Appeal or CDA [Maxime Jacques Marcel VERHAGEN]; Christian Union Party [Andre ROUVOET]; Democrats 66 or D66 [Boris DITTRICH]; Green Party [Femke HALSEMA]; Labor Party or PvdA [Wouter BOS]; List Pim Fortuyn [Gerard van AS]; People's Party for Freedom and Democracy (Liberal) or VVD [Jozias VAN AARTSEN]; Socialist Party [Jan MARIJNISSEN]; plus a few minor parties
Political pressure groups and leaders: Netherlands Trade Union Federation (FNV) (consisting of a merger of Socialist and Catholic trade unions); Christian Trade Union Federation (CNV); Trade Union Federation of Middle and High Personnel (MHP); Federation of Catholic and Protestant Employers Associations; Interchurch Peace Council or IKV; large multinational firms; the nondenominational Federation of Netherlands Enterprises
International organization participation: AfDB, AsDB, Australia Group, Benelux, BIS, CBSS (observer), CE, CERN, EAPC, EBRD, EIB, EMU, ESA, EU, FAO, G-10, IADB, IAEA, IBRD, ICAO, ICC, ICCt, ICFTU, ICRM, IDA, IEA, IFAD, IFC, IFRCS, IHO, ILO, IMF, IMO, Interpol, IOC, IOM, ISO, ITU, MIGA, MONUC, NAM (guest), NATO, NEA, NSG, OAS (observer), OECD, ONUB, OPCW, OSCE, Paris Club, PCA, UN, UNCTAD, UNESCO, UNHCR, UNIDO, UNTSO, UPU, WCL, WCO, WEU, WHO, WIPO, WMO, WToO, WTO, ZC
Diplomatic representation in the US:
chief of mission: Ambassador Boudewijn J. VAN EENENNAAM
chancery: 4200 Linnean Avenue NW, Washington, DC 20008
telephone: [1] (202) 244-5300
FAX: [1] (202) 362-3430
consulate(s) general: Chicago, Houston, Los Angeles, Miami, New York
consulate(s): Boston
Diplomatic representation from the US:
chief of mission: Ambassador (vacant); Charge d'Affaires Chat BLAKEMAN
embassy: Lange Voorhout 102, 2514 EJ, The Hague
mailing address: PSC 71, Box 1000, APO AE 09715
telephone: [31] (70) 310-9209
FAX: [31] (70) 361-4688
consulate(s) general: Amsterdam
Flag description: three equal horizontal

bands of red (top), white, and blue; similar to the flag of Luxembourg, which uses a lighter blue and is longer; one of the oldest flags in constant use, originating with WILLIAM I, Prince of Orange, in the latter half of the 16th century

ECONOMY

Economy - overview: The Netherlands has a prosperous and open economy, which depends heavily on foreign trade. The economy is noted for stable industrial relations, moderate unemployment and inflation, a sizable current account surplus, and an important role as a European transportation hub. Industrial activity is predominantly in food processing, chemicals, petroleum refining, and electrical machinery. A highly mechanized agricultural sector employs no more than 4% of the labor force but provides large surpluses for the food-processing industry and for exports. The Netherlands, along with 11 of its EU partners, began circulating the euro currency on 1 January 2002. The country continues to be one of the leading European nations for attracting foreign direct investment. Economic growth slowed considerably in 2001-05, as part of the global economic slowdown, but for the four years before that, annual growth averaged nearly 4%, well above the EU average.
GDP (purchasing power parity): $500 billion (2005 est.)
GDP (official exchange rate): $600.8 billion (2005 est.)
GDP - real growth rate: 0.6% (2005 est.)
GDP - per capita: purchasing power parity - $30,500 (2005 est.)
GDP - composition by sector:
agriculture: 2.1%
industry: 24.4%
services: 73.5% (2005 est.)
Labor force: 7.53 million (2005 est.)
Labor force - by occupation: agriculture 4%, industry 23%, services 73% (1998 est.)
Unemployment rate: 6.7% (2005 est.)
Population below poverty line: NA
Household income or consumption by percentage share:
lowest 10%: 2.8%
highest 10%: 25.1% (1994)
Distribution of family income - Gini index: 32.6 (1994)
Inflation rate (consumer prices): 1.6% (2005 est.)
Investment (gross fixed): 19.3% of GDP (2005 est.)
Budget:
revenues: $291.8 billion
expenditures: $303.7 billion, including capital expenditures of NA (2005 est.)
Public debt: 56.2% of GDP (2005 est.)
Agriculture - products: grains, potatoes, sugar beets, fruits, vegetables; livestock
Industries: agroindustries, metal and engineering products, electrical machinery and equipment, chemicals, petroleum, construction, microelectronics, fishing
Industrial production growth rate: 2.2% (2005 est.)
Electricity - production: 91 billion kWh (2003)
Electricity - production by source:
fossil fuel: 89.9%
hydro: 0.1%
nuclear: 4.3%
other: 5.7% (2001)
Electricity - consumption: 101.6 billion kWh (2003)
Electricity - exports: 3.8 billion kWh (2003)
Electricity - imports: 20.8 billion kWh (2003)
Oil - production: 94,870 bbl/day (2003)
Oil - consumption: 920,000 bbl/day (2003 est.)
Oil - exports: 1.418 million bbl/day (2001)
Oil - imports: 2.284 million bbl/day (2001)
Oil - proved reserves: 88.06 million bbl (1 January 2002)
Natural gas - production: 77.75 billion cu m (2001 est.)
Natural gas - consumption: 49.72 billion cu m (2001 est.)
Natural gas - exports: 49.28 billion cu m (2001 est.)
Natural gas - imports: 20.78 billion cu m (2001 est.)
Natural gas - proved reserves: 1.693 trillion cu m (1 January 2002)
Current account balance: $17.94 billion (2005 est.)
Exports: $365.1 billion f.o.b. (2005 est.)
Exports - partners: Germany 25%, Belgium 12.4%, UK 10.1%, France 9.9%, Italy 6%, US 4.3% (2004)
Imports: $326.6 billion f.o.b. (2005 est.)
Imports - partners: Germany 17.9%, Belgium 9.9%, US 7.9%, China 7.4%, UK 6.4%, France 4.8% (2004)
Reserves of foreign exchange and gold: $21.05 billion (2004 est.)
Debt - external: $1.645 trillion (30 June 2005)
Economic aid - donor: ODA, $4 billion (2003 est.)
Currency (code): euro (EUR)
note: on 1 January 1999, the European Monetary Union introduced the euro as a common currency to be used by financial institutions of member countries; on 1 January 2002, the euro became the sole currency for everyday transactions within the member countries
Currency code: EUR
Exchange rates: euros per US dollar - 0.79697 (2005), 0.8054 (2004), 0.886 (2003), 1.0626 (2002), 1.1175 (2001)
Fiscal year: calendar year

COMMUNICATIONS

Telephones - main lines in use: 10.004 million (2002)
Telephones - mobile cellular: 12.5 million (2003)
Telephone system:
general assessment: highly developed and well maintained
domestic: extensive fixed-line fiber-optic network; cellular telephone system is one of the largest in Europe with five major network operators utilizing the third generation of the Global System for Mobile Communications (GSM)
international: country code - 31; 9 submarine cables; satellite earth stations - 3 Intelsat (1 Indian Ocean and 2 Atlantic Ocean), 1 Eutelsat, and 1 Inmarsat (Atlantic and Indian Ocean regions) (2004)
Radio broadcast stations: AM 4, FM 246, shortwave 3 (2004)
Radios: 15.3 million (1996)
Television broadcast stations: 21 (plus 26 repeaters) (1995)
Televisions: 8.1 million (1997)
Internet country code: .nl
Internet hosts: 4,518,226 (2004)
Internet Service Providers (ISPs): 52 (2000)
Internet users: 8.5 million (2003)

TRANSPORTATION

Airports: 27 (2004 est.)
Airports - with paved runways:
total: 20
over 3,047 m: 2
2,438 to 3,047 m: 9
1,524 to 2,437 m: 3
914 to 1,523 m: 4
under 914 m: 2 (2005 est.)
Airports - with unpaved runways:
total: 7
914 to 1,523 m: 3
under 914 m: 4 (2005 est.)
Heliports: 1 (2005 est.)
Pipelines: condensate 325 km; gas 6,998 km; oil 590 km; refined products 716 km (2004)
Railways:
total: 2,808 km
standard gauge: 2,808 km 1.435-m gauge (2,061 km electrified) (2004)
Roadways:
total: 116,500 km
paved: 104,850 km (including 2,235 km of expressways)
unpaved: 11,650 km (1999)
Waterways: 5,046 km (navigable for

ships of 50 tons) (2004)
Merchant marine:
total: 558 ships (1,000 GRT or over) 4,796,460 GRT/5,212,557 DWT
by type: bulk carrier 14, cargo 361, chemical tanker 32, container 48, liquefied gas 13, passenger 11, passenger/cargo 14, petroleum tanker 14, refrigerated cargo 32, roll on/roll off 15, specialized tanker 4
foreign-owned: 139 (Bahamas 5, Belgium 2, Canada 1, Denmark 4, Finland 7, Germany 62, Ireland 13, Norway 9, Sweden 19, United Kingdom 6, United States 11)
registered in other countries: 223 (2005)
Ports and terminals: Amsterdam, Groningen, Ijmuiden, Rotterdam, Terneuzen, Vlissingen, Zaanstad

MILITARY

Military branches: Royal Netherlands Army, Royal Netherlands Navy (includes Naval Air Service and Marine Corps), Royal Netherlands Air Force (Koninklijke Luchtmacht, KLu), Royal Constabulary, Defense Interservice Command (DICO) (2004)
Military service age and obligation: 20 years of age for an all-volunteer force (2004)
Manpower available for military service: *males age 20-49:* 3,557,918 (2005 est.)
Manpower fit for military service: *males age 20-49:* 2,856,691 (2005 est.)
Manpower reaching military service age annually: *males:* 99,934 (2005 est.)
Military expenditures - dollar figure: $9.408 billion (2004)
Military expenditures - percent of GDP: 1.6% (2004)

TRANSNATIONAL ISSUES

Disputes - international: none
Illicit drugs: major European producer of ecstasy, illicit amphetamines, and other synthetic drugs; important gateway for cocaine, heroin, and hashish entering Europe; major source of US-bound ecstasy; large financial sector vulnerable to money laundering

NEW CALEDONIA

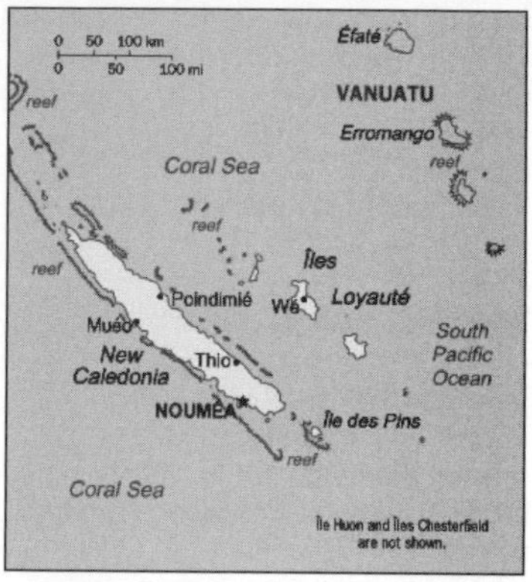

INTRODUCTION

Background: Settled by both Britain and France during the first half of the 19th century, the island was made a French possession in 1853. It served as a penal colony for four decades after 1864. Agitation for independence during the 1980s and early 1990s ended in the 1998 Noumea Accord, which over a period of 15 to 20 years will transfer an increasing amount of governing responsibility from France to New Caledonia. The agreement also commits France to conduct as many as three referenda between 2013 and 2018, to decide whether New Caledonia should assume full sovereignty and independence.

GEOGRAPHY

Location: Oceania, islands in the South Pacific Ocean, east of Australia
Geographic coordinates: 21 30 S, 165 30 E
Map references: Oceania
Area:
total: 19,060 sq km
land: 18,575 sq km
water: 485 sq km
Area - comparative: slightly smaller than New Jersey
Land boundaries: 0 km
Coastline: 2,254 km
Maritime claims:
territorial sea: 12 nm
exclusive economic zone: 200 nm
Climate: tropical; modified by southeast trade winds; hot, humid
Terrain: coastal plains with interior mountains
Elevation extremes:
lowest point: Pacific Ocean 0 m
highest point: Mont Panie 1,628 m
Natural resources: nickel, chrome, iron, cobalt, manganese, silver, gold, lead, copper
Land use:
arable land: 0.38%
permanent crops: 0.33%
other: 99.29% (2001)
Irrigated land: 160 sq km (1991)
Natural hazards: cyclones, most frequent from November to March
Environment - current issues: erosion caused by mining exploitation and forest fires
Geography - note: consists of the main island of New Caledonia (one of the largest in the Pacific Ocean), the archipelago of Iles Loyaute, and numerous small, sparsely populated islands and atolls

PEOPLE

Population: 216,494 (July 2005 est.)
Age structure:
0-14 years: 29% (male 32,030/female 30,714)
15-64 years: 64.6% (male 70,294/female 69,506)
65 years and over: 6.4% (male 6,513/female 7,437) (2005 est.)
Median age:
total: 27.5 years
male: 27.16 years
female: 27.84 years (2005 est.)
Population growth rate: 1.28% (2005 est.)
Birth rate: 18.49 births/1,000 population (2005 est.)
Death rate: 5.65 deaths/1,000 population (2005 est.)
Net migration rate: 0 migrant(s)/1,000 population (2005 est.)
Sex ratio:
at birth: 1.05 male(s)/female
under 15 years: 1.04 male(s)/female
15-64 years: 1.01 male(s)/female
65 years and over: 0.88 male(s)/female
total population: 1.01 male(s)/female (2005 est.)
Infant mortality rate:
total: 7.72 deaths/1,000 live births
male: 8.42 deaths/1,000 live births
female: 6.97 deaths/1,000 live births (2005 est.)
Life expectancy at birth:
total population: 74.04 years
male: 71.07 years
female: 77.16 years (2005 est.)
Total fertility rate: 2.31 children born/woman (2005 est.)
HIV/AIDS - adult prevalence rate: NA%
HIV/AIDS - people living with HIV/AIDS: NA
HIV/AIDS - deaths: NA
Nationality:
noun: New Caledonian(s)
adjective: New Caledonian
Ethnic groups: Melanesian 42.5%, European 37.1%, Wallisian 8.4%, Polynesian 3.8%, Indonesian 3.6%, Vietnamese 1.6%, other 3%
Religions: Roman Catholic 60%, Protestant 30%, other 10%
Languages: French (official), 33 Melanesian-Polynesian dialects

Literacy:
definition: age 15 and over can read and write
total population: 91%
male: 92%
female: 90% (1976 est.)

GOVERNMENT

Country name:
conventional long form: Territory of New Caledonia and Dependencies
conventional short form: New Caledonia
local long form: Territoire des Nouvelle-Caledonie et Dependances
local short form: Nouvelle-Caledonie
Dependency status: overseas territory of France since 1956
Government type: NA
Capital: Noumea
Administrative divisions: none (overseas territory of France); there are no first-order administrative divisions as defined by the US Government, but there are 3 provinces named Iles Loyaute, Nord, and Sud
Independence: none (overseas territory of France); note - a referendum on independence was held in 1998 but did not pass; a new referendum is scheduled for 2014
National holiday: Bastille Day, 14 July (1789)
Constitution: 4 October 1958 (French Constitution)
Legal system: the 1988 Matignon Accords grant substantial autonomy to the islands; formerly under French law
Suffrage: 18 years of age, universal
Executive branch:
chief of state: President of France Jacques CHIRAC (since 17 May 1995), represented by High Commissioner Michel MATHIEU (since 15 July 2005)
head of government: President of the Government Marie-Noelle THEMEREAU (since 10 June 2004)
cabinet: Consultative Committee
elections: French president elected by popular vote for a five-year term; high commissioner appointed by the French president on the advice of the French Ministry of Interior; president of the government elected by the members of the Territorial Congress; note - last election held 29 June 2004 when Marie-Noelle THEMEREAU was elected on the third vote with 8 votes for and 3 abstentions
Legislative branch: unicameral Territorial Congress or Congres Territorial (54 seats; members belong to the three Provincial Assemblies or Assemblees Provinciales elected by popular vote to serve five-year terms)
elections: last held 9 May 2004 (next to be held NA 2009)
election results: percent of vote by party - NA%; seats by party - RPCR-UMP 16, AE 16, UNI-FLNKS 8, UC 7, FN 4, others 3
note: New Caledonia currently holds 1 seat in the French Senate; elections last held 24 September 2001 (next to be held not later than September 2007; between now and 2010 New Caledonia will gain a second seat in the French Senate); results - percent of vote by party - NA%; seats by party - NA; New Caledonia also elects 2 seats to the French National Assembly; elections last held 9 and 16 June 2002 (next to be held by June 2007); results - percent of vote by party - NA%; seats by party - UMP 2
Judicial branch: Court of Appeal or Cour d'Appel; County Courts; Joint Commerce Tribunal Court; Children's Court
Political parties and leaders: Alliance pour la Caledonie or APLC [Didier LE ROUX]; Caleonian Union or UC [leader NA]; Federation des Comites de Coordination des Independantistes or FCCI [Francois BURCK]; Front National or FN [Guy GEORGE]; Front Uni de Liberation Kanak or FULK [Ernest UNE]; Kanak Socialist Front for National Liberation or FLNKS [leader NA] (includes PALIKA, UNI, UC, and UPM); Parti de Liberation Kanak or PALIKA [Paul NEAOUTYINE and Elie POIGOUNE]; Rally for Caledonia in the Republic (anti independent) or RPCR-UMP [Jacques LAFLEUR]; The Future Together or AE [Harold MARTIN]; Union Nationale pour l'Independance or UNI [Paul NEAOUTYINE]; note - may no longer exist, but Paul NEAOUTYINE has since become a president of Parti de Liberation Kanak or PALIKA; Union Progressiste Melanesienne or UPM [Victor TUTUGORO]
Political pressure groups and leaders: NA
International organization participation: ICFTU, PIF (observer), SPC, UPU, WFTU, WMO
Diplomatic representation in the US: none (overseas territory of France)
Diplomatic representation from the US: none (overseas territory of France)
Flag description: the flag of France is used

ECONOMY

Economy - overview: New Caledonia has about 25% of the world's known nickel resources. Only a small amount of the land is suitable for cultivation, and food accounts for about 20% of imports. In addition to nickel, substantial financial support from France - equal to more than one-fourth of GDP - and tourism are keys to the health of the economy. Substantial new investment in the nickel industry, combined with the recovery of global nickel prices, brightens the economic outlook for the next several years.
GDP (purchasing power parity): $3.158 billion (2003 est.)
GDP (official exchange rate): NA
GDP - real growth rate: NA%
GDP - per capita: purchasing power parity - $15,000 (2003 est.)
GDP - composition by sector:
agriculture: 5%
industry: 30%
services: 65% (1997 est.)
Labor force: 79,400 (including 15,018 unemployed) (1996)
Labor force - by occupation: agriculture 7%, industry 23%, services 70% (1999 est.)
Unemployment rate: 19% (1996)
Population below poverty line: NA
Household income or consumption by percentage share:
lowest 10%: NA%
highest 10%: NA%
Inflation rate (consumer prices): -0.6% (2000 est.)
Budget:
revenues: $861.3 million
expenditures: $735.3 million, including capital expenditures of $52 million (1996 est.)
Agriculture - products: vegetables; beef, deer, other livestock products
Industries: nickel mining and smelting
Industrial production growth rate: -0.6% (1996)
Electricity - production: 1.581 billion kWh (2003)
Electricity - production by source:
fossil fuel: 76.3%
hydro: 23.7%
nuclear: 0%
other: 0% (2001)
Electricity - consumption: 1.47 billion kWh (2003)
Electricity - exports: 0 kWh (2003)
Electricity - imports: 0 kWh (2003)
Oil - production: 0 bbl/day (2003 est.)
Oil - consumption: 10,000 bbl/day (2003 est.)
Oil - exports: NA (2001)
Oil - imports: NA (2001)
Exports: $999 million f.o.b. (2004 est.)
Exports - partners: Japan 22%, France 16.5%, Taiwan 12.3%, South Korea 12%, Spain 6.3%, Australia 6.1%, China 4.8%, South Africa 4.5% (2004)
Imports: $1.636 billion f.o.b. (2004 est.)
Imports - partners: France 40.3%, Singapore 10.9%, Australia 9.1%, New Zealand 4.9% (2004)
Debt - external: $79 million (1998 est.)
Economic aid - recipient: $880 million annual subsidy from France (1998)
Currency (code): Comptoirs Francais du Pacifique franc (XPF)
Currency code: XPF
Exchange rates: Comptoirs Francais du Pacifique francs (XPF) per US dollar -

NA (2005), 96.04 (2004), 105.66 (2003), 126.71 (2002), 133.26 (2001)
Fiscal year: calendar year

COMMUNICATIONS

Telephones - main lines in use: 52,000 (2002)
Telephones - mobile cellular: 80,000 (2002)
Telephone system:
general assessment: NA
domestic: NA
international: country code - 687; satellite earth station - 1 Intelsat (Pacific Ocean)
Radio broadcast stations: AM 1, FM 5, shortwave 0 (1998)
Radios: 107,000 (1997)
Television broadcast stations: 6 (plus 25 low-power repeaters) (1997)
Televisions: 52,000 (1997)
Internet country code: .nc
Internet hosts: 4,449 (2003)
Internet Service Providers (ISPs): 1 (2000)
Internet users: 60,000 (2003)

TRANSPORTATION

Airports: 25 (2004 est.)
Airports - with paved runways:
total: 11
over 3,047 m: 1
914 to 1,523 m: 8
under 914 m: 2 (2005 est.)
Airports - with unpaved runways:
total: 14
914 to 1,523 m: 8
under 914 m: 6 (2005 est.)
Heliports: 6 (2005 est.)
Roadways:
total: 5,432 km (2000)
Merchant marine:
total: 2 ships (1,000 GRT or over) 1,261 GRT/1,600 DWT
by type: cargo 1, passenger/cargo 1 (2005)
Ports and terminals: Noumea

MILITARY

Military branches: no regular indigenous military forces; French Armed Forces (includes Army, Navy, Air Force, Gendarmerie); Police Force
Military expenditures - dollar figure: $NA
Military expenditures - percent of GDP: NA
Military - note: defense is the responsibility of France

TRANSNATIONAL ISSUES

Disputes - international: Matthew and Hunter Islands east of New Caledonia claimed by France and Vanuatu

NEW ZEALAND

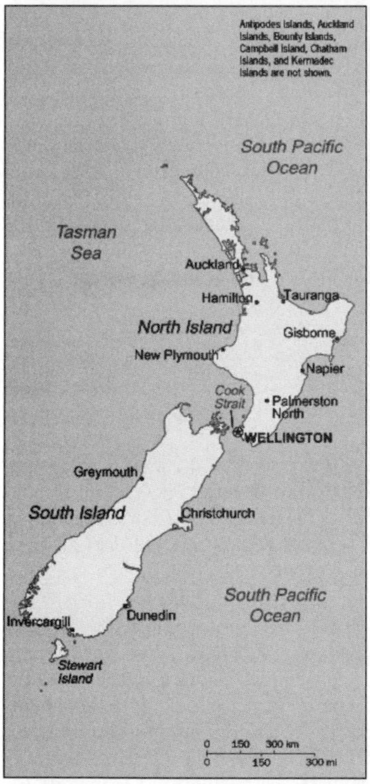

INTRODUCTION

Background: The Polynesian Maori reached New Zealand in about A.D. 800. In 1840, their chieftains entered into a compact with Britain, the Treaty of Waitangi, in which they ceded sovereignty to Queen Victoria while retaining territorial rights. In that same year, the British began the first organized colonial settlement. A series of land wars between 1843 and 1872 ended with the defeat of the native peoples. The British colony of New Zealand became an independent dominion in 1907 and supported the UK militarily in both World Wars. New Zealand's full participation in a number of defense alliances lapsed by the 1980s. In recent years, the government has sought to address longstanding Maori grievances.

GEOGRAPHY

Location: Oceania, islands in the South Pacific Ocean, southeast of Australia
Geographic coordinates: 41 00 S, 174 00 E
Map references: Oceania
Area:
total: 268,680 sq km
land: 268,021 sq km
water: NA
note: includes Antipodes Islands, Auckland Islands, Bounty Islands, Campbell Island, Chatham Islands, and Kermadec Islands
Area - comparative: about the size of Colorado
Land boundaries: 0 km
Coastline: 15,134 km
Maritime claims:
territorial sea: 12 nm
exclusive economic zone: 200 nm
continental shelf: 200 nm or to the edge of the continental margin
Climate: temperate with sharp regional contrasts
Terrain: predominately mountainous with some large coastal plains
Elevation extremes:
lowest point: Pacific Ocean 0 m
highest point: Aoraki-Mount Cook 3,754 m
Natural resources: natural gas, iron ore, sand, coal, timber, hydropower, gold, limestone
Land use:
arable land: 5.6%
permanent crops: 6.99%
other: 87.41% (2001)
Irrigated land: 2,850 sq km (1998 est.)
Natural hazards: earthquakes are common, though usually not severe; volcanic activity
Environment - current issues: deforestation; soil erosion; native flora and fauna hard-hit by species introduced from outside
Environment - international agreements:
party to: Antarctic-Environmental Protocol, Antarctic-Marine Living Resources, Antarctic Treaty, Biodiversity, Climate Change, Climate Change-Kyoto Protocol, Desertification, Endangered Species, Environmental Modification, Hazardous Wastes, Law of the Sea, Marine Dumping, Ozone Layer Protection, Ship Pollution, Tropical Timber 83, Tropical Timber 94, Wetlands, Whaling
signed, but not ratified: Antarctic Seals, Marine Life Conservation
Geography - note: about 80% of the population lives in cities; Wellington is the southernmost national capital in the world

PEOPLE

Population: 4,035,461 (July 2005 est.)
Age structure:
0-14 years: 21.4% (male 441,836/female 421,065)
15-64 years: 66.9% (male 1,356,095/female 1,343,728)
65 years and over: 11.7% (male 206,650/female 266,087) (2005 est.)

Median age:
total: 33.65 years
male: 32.92 years
female: 34.4 years (2005 est.)
Population growth rate: 1.02% (2005 est.)
Birth rate: 13.9 births/1,000 population (2005 est.)
Death rate: 7.53 deaths/1,000 population (2005 est.)
Net migration rate: 3.83 migrant(s)/1,000 population (2005 est.)
Sex ratio:
at birth: 1.04 male(s)/female
under 15 years: 1.05 male(s)/female
15-64 years: 1.01 male(s)/female
65 years and over: 0.78 male(s)/female
total population: 0.99 male(s)/female (2005 est.)
Infant mortality rate:
total: 5.85 deaths/1,000 live births
male: 6.7 deaths/1,000 live births
female: 4.96 deaths/1,000 live births (2005 est.)
Life expectancy at birth:
total population: 78.66 years
male: 75.67 years
female: 81.78 years (2005 est.)
Total fertility rate: 1.79 children born/woman (2005 est.)
HIV/AIDS - adult prevalence rate: 0.1% (2003 est.)
HIV/AIDS - people living with HIV/AIDS: 1,400 (2003 est.)
HIV/AIDS - deaths: less than 200 (2003 est.)
Nationality:
noun: New Zealander(s)
adjective: New Zealand
Ethnic groups: European 69.8%, Maori 7.9%, Asian 5.7%, Pacific islander 4.4%, other 0.5%, mixed 7.8%, unspecified 3.8% (2001 census)
Religions: Anglican 14.9%, Roman Catholic 12.4%, Presbyterian 10.9%, Methodist 2.9%, Pentecostal 1.7%, Baptist 1.3%, other Christian 9.4%, other 3.3%, unspecified 17.2%, none 26% (2001 census)
Languages: English (official), Maori (official)
Literacy:
definition: age 15 and over can read and write
total population: 99% (1980 est.)
male: NA%
female: NA%

GOVERNMENT

Country name:
conventional long form: none
conventional short form: New Zealand
abbreviation: NZ
Government type: parliamentary democracy
Capital: Wellington
Administrative divisions: 16 regions and 1 territory*; Auckland, Bay of Plenty, Canterbury, Chatham Islands*, Gisborne, Hawke's Bay, Manawatu-Wanganui, Marlborough, Nelson, Northland, Otago, Southland, Taranaki, Tasman, Waikato, Wellington, West Coast
Dependent areas: Cook Islands, Niue, Tokelau
Independence: 26 September 1907 (from UK)
National holiday: Waitangi Day (Treaty of Waitangi established British sovereignty over New Zealand), 6 February (1840)
Constitution: consists of a series of legal documents, including certain acts of the UK and New Zealand Parliaments, as well as The Constitution Act 1986, which is the principal formal charter; adopted 1 January 1987, effective 1 January 1987
Legal system: based on English law, with special land legislation and land courts for the Maori; accepts compulsory ICJ jurisdiction with reservations
Suffrage: 18 years of age; universal
Executive branch:
chief of state: Queen ELIZABETH II (since 6 February 1952), represented by Governor General Dame Silvia CARTWRIGHT (since 4 April 2001)
head of government: Prime Minister Helen CLARK (since 10 December 1999) and Deputy Prime Minister Michael CULLEN (since NA July 2002)
cabinet: Executive Council appointed by the governor general on the recommendation of the prime minister
elections: none; the monarch is hereditary; governor general appointed by the monarch; following legislative elections, the leader of the majority party or the leader of a majority coalition is usually appointed prime minister by the governor general; deputy prime minister appointed by the governor general
Legislative branch: unicameral House of Representatives - commonly called Parliament (120 seats; 69 members elected by popular vote in single-member constituencies including 7 Maori constituencies, and 51 proportional seats chosen from party lists, all to serve three-year terms)
elections: last held 17 September 2005 (next to be held not later than 15 November 2008)
election results: percent of vote by party - NZLP 41.1%, NP 39.1%, NZFP 5.72%, Green Party 5.3%, Maori 2.12%, UF 2.67%, ACT New Zealand 1.51%, Progressive 1.16%; seats by party - NZLP 50, NP 48, NZFP 7, Green Party 6, Maori 4, UF 3, ACT New Zealand 2, Progressive 1
note: results of 2005 election saw the total number of seats increase to 121 because the Maori Party won one more electorate seat than its entitlement under the party vote
Judicial branch: Supreme Court; Court of Appeal; High Court; note - Judges appointed by the Governor-General
Political parties and leaders: ACT New Zealand [Rodney HIDE]; Green Party [Jeanette FITZSIMONS]; Maori Party [Whatarangi WINIATA]; National Party or NP [Don BRASH]; New Zealand First Party or NZFP [Winston PETERS]; New Zealand Labor Party or NZLP [Helen CLARK]; Progressive Party [James (Jim) ANDERTON]; United Future or UF [Peter DUNNE]
Political pressure groups and leaders: NA
International organization participation: ANZUS (US suspended security obligations to NZ on 11 August 1986), APEC, ARF, AsDB, ASEAN (dialogue partner), Australia Group, BIS, C, CP, EAS, EBRD, FAO, IAEA, IBRD, ICAO, ICC, ICCt, ICFTU, ICRM, IDA, IEA, IFAD, IFC, IFRCS, IHO, ILO, IMF, IMO, Interpol, IOC, IOM, ISO, ITU, NAM (guest), NSG, OECD, OPCW, PCA, PIF, Sparteca, SPC, UN, UNCTAD, UNESCO, UNHCR, UNIDO, UNTSO, UPU, WCO, WFTU, WHO, WIPO, WMO, WTO
Diplomatic representation in the US:
chief of mission: Ambassador L. John WOOD
chancery: 37 Observatory Circle NW, Washington, DC 20008
telephone: [1] (202) 328-4800
FAX: [1] (202) 667-5227
consulate(s) general: Los Angeles, New York
Diplomatic representation from the US:
chief of mission: Ambassador William P. McCORMICK
embassy: 29 Fitzherbert Terrace, Thorndon, Wellington
mailing address: P. O. Box 1190, Wellington; PSC 467, Box 1, APO AP 96531-1034
telephone: [64] (4) 462-6000
FAX: [64] (4) 499-0490
consulate(s) general: Auckland
Flag description: blue with the flag of the UK in the upper hoist-side quadrant with four red five-pointed stars edged in white centered in the outer half of the flag; the stars represent the Southern Cross constellation

ECONOMY

Economy - overview: Over the past 20 years the government has transformed New Zealand from an agrarian economy dependent on concessionary British market access to a more industrialized, free market economy that can compete global-

ly. This dynamic growth has boosted real incomes (but left behind many at the bottom of the ladder), broadened and deepened the technological capabilities of the industrial sector, and contained inflationary pressures. Per capita income has risen for six consecutive years and is now more than $24,000 in purchasing power parity terms. New Zealand is heavily dependent on trade - particularly in agricultural products - to drive growth. Exports are equal to about 20% of GDP. Thus far the economy has been resilient, and the Labor Government promises that expenditures on health, education, and pensions will increase proportionately to output.
GDP (purchasing power parity): $97.39 billion (2005 est.)
GDP (official exchange rate): $99.97 billion (2005 est.)
GDP - real growth rate: 2.5% (2005 est.)
GDP - per capita: purchasing power parity - $24,100 (2005 est.)
GDP - composition by sector:
agriculture: 4.7%
industry: 27.8%
services: 67.6% (2005 est.)
Labor force: 2.13 million (2005 est.)
Labor force - by occupation: agriculture 10%, industry 25%, services 65% (1995)
Unemployment rate: 4% (2005 est.)
Population below poverty line: NA
Household income or consumption by percentage share:
lowest 10%: 0.3%
highest 10%: 29.8% (1991 est.)
Inflation rate (consumer prices): 3% (2005 est.)
Investment (gross fixed): 23.6% of GDP (2005 est.)
Budget:
revenues: $43.1 billion
expenditures: $37.57 billion, including capital expenditures of NA (2005 est.)
Public debt: 21.4% of GDP (2005 est.)
Agriculture - products: wheat, barley, potatoes, pulses, fruits, vegetables; wool, beef, lamb and mutton, dairy products; fish
Industries: food processing, wood and paper products, textiles, machinery, transportation equipment, banking and insurance, tourism, mining
Industrial production growth rate: 0.8% (2005 est.)
Electricity - production: 39.82 billion kWh (2003)
Electricity - production by source:
fossil fuel: 31.6%
hydro: 57.8%
nuclear: 0%
other: 10.7% (2001)
Electricity - consumption: 37.03 billion kWh (2003)
Electricity - exports: 0 kWh (2003)
Electricity - imports: 0 kWh (2003)
Oil - production: 31,740 bbl/day (2003 est.)
Oil - consumption: 151,900 bbl/day (2003 est.)
Oil - exports: 30,220 bbl/day (2001)
Oil - imports: 119,700 bbl/day (2001)
Oil - proved reserves: 89.62 million bbl (1 January 2002)
Natural gas - production: 6.504 billion cu m (2001 est.)
Natural gas - consumption: 6.504 billion cu m (2001 est.)
Natural gas - exports: 0 cu m (2001 est.)
Natural gas - imports: 0 cu m (2001 est.)
Natural gas - proved reserves: 58.94 billion cu m (1 January 2002)
Current account balance: $-8.137 billion (2005 est.)
Exports: $22.21 billion (2005 est.)
Exports - partners: Australia 21%, US 14.4%, Japan 11.3%, China 5.7%, UK 4.7% (2004)
Imports: $24.57 billion (2005 est.)
Imports - partners: Australia 22.4%, US 11.3%, Japan 11.2%, China 9.7%, Germany 5.2% (2004)
Reserves of foreign exchange and gold: $5.498 billion (2005 est.)
Debt - external: $57.67 billion (2005 est.)
Economic aid - donor: ODA, $99.7 million)
Currency (code): New Zealand dollar (NZD)
Currency code: NZD
Exchange rates: New Zealand dollars per US dollar - 1.43 (2005), 1.5087 (2004), 1.7221 (2003), 2.1622 (2002), 2.3788 (2001)
Fiscal year: 1 July - 30 June

COMMUNICATIONS

Telephones - main lines in use: 1.765 million (2002)
Telephones - mobile cellular: 2.599 million (2003)
Telephone system:
general assessment: excellent domestic and international systems
domestic: NA
international: country code - 64; submarine cables to Australia and Fiji; 8 satellite earth stations - 1 InMarSat (Pacific Ocean), 7 other
Radio broadcast stations: AM 124, FM 290, shortwave 4 (1998)
Radios: 3.75 million (1997)
Television broadcast stations: 41 (plus 52 medium-power repeaters and over 650 low-power repeaters) (1997)
Televisions: 1.926 million (1997)
Internet country code: .nz
Internet hosts: 474,395 (2003)
Internet Service Providers (ISPs): 36 (2000)
Internet users: 2.11 million (2003)

TRANSPORTATION

Airports: 116 (2004 est.)
Airports - with paved runways:
total: 46
over 3,047 m: 2
2,438 to 3,047 m: 1
1,524 to 2,437 m: 11
914 to 1,523 m: 27
under 914 m: 5 (2005 est.)
Airports - with unpaved runways:
total: 71
1,524 to 2,437 m: 2
914 to 1,523 m: 30
under 914 m: 39 (2005 est.)
Pipelines: gas 2,213 km; liquid petroleum gas 79 km; oil 160 km; refined products 304 km (2004)
Railways:
total: 3,898 km
narrow gauge: 3,898 km 1.067-m gauge (506 km electrified) (2004)
Roadways:
total: 92,382 km
paved: 59,124 km (including at least 169 km of expressways)
unpaved: 33,258 km (2002)
Merchant marine:
total: 13 ships (1,000 GRT or over) 77,523 GRT/108,352 DWT
by type: cargo 3, passenger/cargo 4, petroleum tanker 2, roll on/roll off 1, bulk carrier 3
foreign-owned: 2 (Germany 1, Isle of Man 1)
registered in other countries: 5 (2005)
Ports and terminals: Auckland, Lyttelton, Tauranga, Wellington, Whangarei

MILITARY

Military branches: New Zealand Army, Royal New Zealand Navy, Royal New Zealand Air Force
Military service age and obligation: 17 years of age for voluntary military service; soldiers cannot be deployed until the age of 18 (2001)
Manpower available for military service: *males age 17-49:* 984,700 (2005 est.)
Manpower fit for military service: *males age 17-49:* 809,519 (2005 est.)
Manpower reaching military service age annually: *males:* 29,738 (2005 est.)
Military expenditures - dollar figure: $1.147 billion (FY03/04)
Military expenditures - percent of GDP: 1% (FY02)

TRANSNATIONAL ISSUES

Disputes - international: asserts a territorial claim in Antarctica (Ross Dependency) [see Antarctica]

NICARAGUA

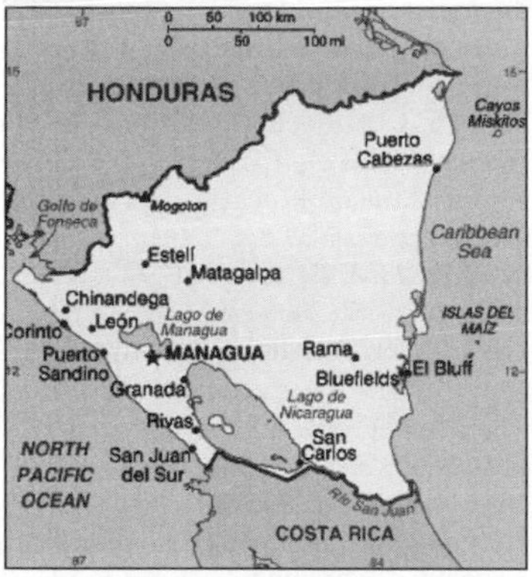

INTRODUCTION

Background: The Pacific Coast of Nicaragua was settled as a Spanish colony from Panama in the early 16th century. Independence from Spain was declared in 1821 and the country became an independent republic in 1838. Britain occupied the Caribbean Coast in the first half of the 19th century, but gradually ceded control of the region in subsequent decades. Violent opposition to governmental manipulation and corruption spread to all classes by 1978 and resulted in a short-lived civil war that brought the Marxist Sandinista guerrillas to power in 1979. Nicaraguan aid to leftist rebels in El Salvador caused the US to sponsor anti-Sandinista contra guerrillas through much of the 1980s. Free elections in 1990, 1996, and again in 2001 saw the Sandinistas defeated. The country has slowly rebuilt its economy during the 1990s, but was hard hit by Hurricane Mitch in 1998.

GEOGRAPHY

Location: Central America, bordering both the Caribbean Sea and the North Pacific Ocean, between Costa Rica and Honduras
Geographic coordinates: 13 00 N, 85 00 W
Map references: Central America and the Caribbean
Area:
total: 129,494 sq km
land: 120,254 sq km
water: 9,240 sq km
Area - comparative: slightly smaller than the state of New York
Land boundaries:
total: 1,231 km
border countries: Costa Rica 309 km, Honduras 922 km
Coastline: 910 km
Maritime claims:
territorial sea: 200 nm
continental shelf: natural prolongation
Climate: tropical in lowlands, cooler in highlands
Terrain: extensive Atlantic coastal plains rising to central interior mountains; narrow Pacific coastal plain interrupted by volcanoes
Elevation extremes:
lowest point: Pacific Ocean 0 m
highest point: Mogoton 2,438 m
Natural resources: gold, silver, copper, tungsten, lead, zinc, timber, fish
Land use:
arable land: 15.94%
permanent crops: 1.94%
other: 82.12% (2001)
Irrigated land: 880 sq km (1998 est.)
Natural hazards: destructive earthquakes, volcanoes, landslides; extremely susceptible to hurricanes
Environment - current issues: deforestation; soil erosion; water pollution
Environment - international agreements:
party to: Biodiversity, Climate Change, Climate Change-Kyoto Protocol, Desertification, Endangered Species, Hazardous Wastes, Law of the Sea, Ozone Layer Protection, Ship Pollution, Wetlands
signed, but not ratified: Environmental Modification
Geography - note: largest country in Central America; contains the largest freshwater body in Central America, Lago de Nicaragua

PEOPLE

Population: 5,465,100 (July 2005 est.)
Age structure:
0-14 years: 37.2% (male 1,036,487/female 999,226)
15-64 years: 59.7% (male 1,623,065/female 1,638,017)
65 years and over: 3.1% (male 73,935/female 94,370) (2005 est.)
Median age:
total: 20.56 years
male: 20.15 years
female: 20.98 years (2005 est.)
Population growth rate: 1.92% (2005 est.)
Birth rate: 24.88 births/1,000 population (2005 est.)
Death rate: 4.49 deaths/1,000 population (2005 est.)
Net migration rate: -1.19 migrant(s)/1,000 population (2005 est.)
Sex ratio:
at birth: 1.05 male(s)/female
under 15 years: 1.04 male(s)/female
15-64 years: 0.99 male(s)/female
65 years and over: 0.78 male(s)/female
total population: 1 male(s)/female (2005 est.)
Infant mortality rate:
total: 29.11 deaths/1,000 live births
male: 32.6 deaths/1,000 live births
female: 25.44 deaths/1,000 live births (2005 est.)
Life expectancy at birth:
total population: 70.33 years
male: 68.27 years
female: 72.49 years (2005 est.)
Total fertility rate: 2.81 children born/woman (2005 est.)
HIV/AIDS - adult prevalence rate: 0.2% (2003 est.)
HIV/AIDS - people living with HIV/AIDS: 6,400 (2003 est.)
HIV/AIDS - deaths: less than 500 (2003 est.)
Nationality:
noun: Nicaraguan(s)
adjective: Nicaraguan
Ethnic groups: mestizo (mixed Amerindian and white) 69%, white 17%, black 9%, Amerindian 5%
Religions: Roman Catholic 72.9%, Evangelical 15.1%, Moravian 1.5%, Episcopal 0.1%, other 1.9%, none 8.5% (1995 census)
Languages: Spanish 97.5% (official), Miskito 1.7%, other 0.8% (1995 census)
note: English and indigenous languages on Atlantic coast
Literacy:
definition: age 15 and over can read and write
total population: 67.5%
male: 67.2%
female: 67.8% (2003 est.)

GOVERNMENT

Country name:
conventional long form: Republic of Nicaragua
conventional short form: Nicaragua
local long form: Republica de Nicaragua
local short form: Nicaragua
Government type: republic
Capital: Managua
Administrative divisions: 15 departments (departamentos, singular - departamento) and 2 autonomous regions* (regiones autonomistas, singular - region autonomista); Atlantico Norte*, Atlantico Sur*, Boaco, Carazo, Chinandega, Chontales, Esteli, Granada, Jinotega, Leon, Madriz, Managua, Masaya, Matagalpa, Nueva Segovia, Rio San Juan, Rivas
Independence: 15 September 1821 (from Spain)
National holiday: Independence Day, 15 September (1821)
Constitution: 9 January 1987; reforms in 1995 and 2000
Legal system: civil law system; Supreme Court may review administrative acts

Suffrage: 16 years of age, universal
Executive branch:
chief of state: President Enrique BOLANOS Geyer (since 10 January 2002); Vice President Alfredo GOMEZ Urcuyo (since 10 October 2005); note - the president is both chief of state and head of government
head of government: President Enrique BOLANOS Geyer (since 10 January 2002); Vice President Alfredo GOMEZ Urcuyo (since 10 October 2005); note - the president is both chief of state and head of government
cabinet: Council of Ministers appointed by the president
elections: president and vice president elected on the same ticket by popular vote for a five-year term; election last held 4 November 2001 (next to be held by November 2006)
election results: Enrique BOLANOS Geyer (PLC) elected president - 56.3%, Daniel ORTEGA Saavedra (FSLN) 42.3%, Alberto SABORIO (PCN) 1.4%; Jose RIZO Castellon elected vice president
Legislative branch: unicameral National Assembly or Asamblea Nacional (92 seats; members are elected by proportional representation and party lists to serve five-year terms; one seat for previous President, one seat for runner-up in previous Presidential election); note - current Assembly has only 91 seats
elections: last held 4 November 2001 (next to be held by November 2006)
election results: percent of vote by party - Liberal Alliance (ruling party - includes PCCN, PLC, PALI, PLIUN, and PUCA) 46.03%, FSLN 36.55%, PCN 2.12%; seats by party - Liberal Alliance 53, FSLN 38, PCN 1
Judicial branch: Supreme Court or Corte Suprema (16 judges elected for five-year terms by the National Assembly)
Political parties and leaders: Alliance for the Republic or APRE [Miguel LOPEZ Baldizon]; Central American Unionist Party or PUCA [Blanca ROJAS]; Christian Alternative Party or AC [Orlando TARDENCILLA Espinoza]; Conservative Party or PC [Mario Sebastian RAPPACCIOLI]; Independent Liberal Party or PLI [Anibal MARTINEZ Nunez, Pedro REYES Vallejos]; Independent Liberal Party for National Unity or PLIUN [Carlos GUERRA Gallardo]; Liberal Constitutional Party or PLC [Jorge CASTILLO Quant]; Liberal Salvation Movement or MSL [Eliseo NUNEZ Hernandez]; New Liberal Party or PALI [Adolfo GARCIA Esquivel]; Nicaraguan Party of the Christian Path or CCN [Guillermo OSORNO Molina]; Nicaraguan Resistance Party or PRN [Salvador TALAVERA]; Sandinista National Liberation Front or FSLN [Daniel ORTEGA Saavedra]; Sandinista Renovation Movement or MRS [Dora Maria TELLEZ]; Unity Alliance or AU [leader NA]
Political pressure groups and leaders: National Workers Front or FNT is a Sandinista umbrella group of eight labor unions including - Farm Workers Association or ATC, Health Workers Federation or FETASALUD, Heroes and Martyrs Confederation of Professional Associations or CONAPRO, National Association of Educators of Nicaragua or ANDEN, National Union of Employees or UNE, National Union of Farmers and Ranchers or UNAG, Sandinista Workers Central or CST, and Union of Journalists of Nicaragua or UPN; Permanent Congress of Workers or CPT is an umbrella group of four non-Sandinista labor unions including - Autonomous Nicaraguan Workers Central or CTN-A, Confederation of Labor Unification or CUS, Independent General Confederation of Labor or CGT-I, and Labor Action and Unity Central or CAUS; Nicaraguan Workers' Central or CTN is an independent labor union; Superior Council of Private Enterprise or COSEP is a confederation of business groups
International organization participation: BCIE, CACM, FAO, G-77, IADB, IAEA, IBRD, ICAO, ICFTU, ICRM, IDA, IFAD, IFC, IFRCS, ILO, IMF, IMO, Interpol, IOC, IOM, ISO (correspondent), ITU, LAES, LAIA (observer), MIGA, NAM, OAS, OPANAL, OPCW, PCA, RG, UN, UNCTAD, UNESCO, UNHCR, UNIDO, UPU, WCL, WCO, WHO, WIPO, WMO, WToO, WTO
Diplomatic representation in the US:
chief of mission: Ambassador Salvador STADTHAGEN (since 5 December 2003)
chancery: 1627 New Hampshire Avenue NW, Washington, DC 20009
telephone: [1] (202) 939-6570, [1] (202) 939-6573
FAX: [1] (202) 939-6545
consulate(s) general: Houston, Los Angeles, Miami, New York, San Francisco
Diplomatic representation from the US:
chief of mission: Ambassador Paul A. TRIVELLI
embassy: Kilometer 4.5 Carretera Sur, Managua
mailing address: APO AA 34021
telephone: [505] 266-6010
FAX: [505] 266-3861
Flag description: three equal horizontal bands of blue (top), white, and blue with the national coat of arms centered in the white band; the coat of arms features a triangle encircled by the words REPUBLICA DE NICARAGUA on the top and AMERICA CENTRAL on the bottom; similar to the flag of El Salvador, which features a round emblem encircled by the words REPUBLICA DE EL SALVADOR EN LA AMERICA CENTRAL centered in the white band; also similar to the flag of Honduras, which has five blue stars arranged in an X pattern centered in the white band

ECONOMY

Economy - overview: Nicaragua, one of the hemisphere's poorest countries, faces low per capita income, widespread underemployment, and a heavy external debt burden. Distribution of income is one of the most unequal on the globe. While the country has progressed toward macroeconomic stability in the past few years, GDP annual growth has been far too low to meet the country's needs, forcing the country to rely on international economic assistance to meet fiscal and debt financing obligations. Nicaragua qualified in early 2004 for some $4 billion in foreign debt reduction under the Heavily Indebted Poor Countries (HIPC) initiative because of its earlier successful performance under its International Monetary Fund policy program and other efforts. In October 2005 Nicaragua ratified the US-Central America Free Trade Agreement (CAFTA), which will provide an opportunity for Nicaragua to attract investment, create jobs, and deepen economic development. High oil prices helped drive inflation to 10% in 2005, leading to a fall in real GDP growth to 3.5% from over 5% in 2004.
GDP (purchasing power parity): $16.05 billion (2005 est.)
GDP (official exchange rate): $5.03 billion (2005 est.)
GDP - real growth rate: 3.5% (2005 est.)
GDP - per capita: purchasing power parity - $2,800 (2005 est.)
GDP - composition by sector:
agriculture: 16.8%
industry: 27.6%
services: 55.6% (2005 est.)
Labor force: 2.17 million (2005 est.)
Labor force - by occupation: agriculture 30.5%, industry 17.3%, services 52.2% (2003 est.)
Unemployment rate: 6.4% plus underemployment of 46.5% (2005 est.)
Population below poverty line: 50% (2001 est.)

Household income or consumption by percentage share:
lowest 10%: 1.2%
highest 10%: 45% (2001)
Distribution of family income - Gini index: 55.1 (2001
Inflation rate (consumer prices): 10.1% (2005 est.)
Investment (gross fixed): 27.1% of GDP (2005 est.)
Budget:
revenues: $1.134 billion
expenditures: $1.358 billion, including capital expenditures of NA (2005 est.)
Public debt: 100.3% of GDP (2005 est.)
Agriculture - products: coffee, bananas, sugarcane, cotton, rice, corn, tobacco, sesame, soya, beans; beef, veal, pork, poultry, dairy products
Industries: food processing, chemicals, machinery and metal products, textiles, clothing, petroleum refining and distribution, beverages, footwear, wood
Industrial production growth rate: 4.4% (2000 est.)
Electricity - production: 2.503 billion kWh (2003)
Electricity - production by source:
fossil fuel: 83.9%
hydro: 7.7%
nuclear: 0%
other: 8.4% (2001)
Electricity - consumption: 2.343 billion kWh (2003)
Electricity - exports: 6.8 million kWh (2003)
Electricity - imports: 15 million kWh (2003)
Oil - production: 14,300 bbl/day (2005 est.)
Oil - consumption: 25,200 bbl/day (2005 est.)
Oil - exports: 737.5 bbl/day (2003)
Oil - imports: 27,950 bbl/day (2003)
Current account balance: $-984 million (2005 est.)
Exports: $1.55 billion f.o.b. (2005 est.)
Exports - partners: US 64.8%, El Salvador 7%, Mexico 3.6% (2004)
Imports: $2.952 billion f.o.b. (2005 est.)
Imports - partners: US 22.6%, Costa Rica 8.5%, Venezuela 8.4%, Guatemala 6.8%, Mexico 5.8%, El Salvador 4.9%, South Korea 4.5% (2004)
Reserves of foreign exchange and gold: $638 million (2005 est.)
Debt - external: $4.054 billion (2005 est.)
Economic aid - recipient: $541.8 million (2003)
Currency (code): gold cordoba (NIO)
Currency code: NIO
Exchange rates: gold cordobas per US dollar - 16.75 (2005), 15.937 (2004), 15.105 (2003), 14.251 (2002), 13.372 (2001)
Fiscal year: calendar year

COMMUNICATIONS

Telephones - main lines in use: 171,600 (2002)
Telephones - mobile cellular: 202,800 (2002)
Telephone system:
general assessment: inadequate system being upgraded by foreign investment
domestic: low-capacity microwave radio relay and wire system being expanded; connected to Central American Microwave System
international: country code - 505; satellite earth stations - 1 Intersputnik (Atlantic Ocean region) and 1 Intelsat (Atlantic Ocean)
Radio broadcast stations: AM 63, FM 32, shortwave 1 (1998)
Radios: 1.24 million (1997)
Television broadcast stations: 3 (plus seven low-power repeaters) (1997)
Televisions: 320,000 (1997)
Internet country code: .ni
Internet hosts: 7,094 (2003)
Internet Service Providers (ISPs): 3 (2000)
Internet users: 90,000 (2002)

TRANSPORTATION

Airports: 176 (2004 est.)
Airports - with paved runways:
total: 11
2,438 to 3,047 m: 3
1,524 to 2,437 m: 2
914 to 1,523 m: 3
under 914 m: 3 (2005 est.)
Airports - with unpaved runways:
total: 165
1,524 to 2,437 m: 1
914 to 1,523 m: 23
under 914 m: 141 (2005 est.)
Pipelines: oil 54 km (2004)
Railways:
total: 6 km
narrow gauge: 6 km 1.067-m gauge (2004)
Roadways:
total: 18,712 km
paved: 2,126 km
unpaved: 16,586 km (2002)
Waterways: 2,220 km (including lakes Managua and Nicaragua) (1997)
Ports and terminals: Bluefields, Corinto, El Bluff

MILITARY

Military branches: Army (includes Navy, Air Force)
Military service age and obligation: 17 years of age for voluntary military service (2001)
Manpower available for military service: *males age 17-49:* 1,309,970 (2005 est.)
Manpower fit for military service: *males age 17-49:* 1,051,425 (2005 est.)
Manpower reaching military service age annually: *males:* 65,170 (2005 est.)
Military expenditures - dollar figure: $32.8 million (2004)
Military expenditures - percent of GDP: 0.7% (2004)

TRANSNATIONAL ISSUES

Disputes - international: Nicaragua filed a claim against Honduras in 1999 and against Colombia in 2001 at the ICJ over disputed maritime boundary involving 50,000 sq km in the Caribbean Sea, including the Archipelago de San Andres y Providencia and Quita Sueno Bank; the 1992 ICJ ruling for El Salvador and Honduras advised a tripartite resolution to establish a maritime boundary in the Gulf of Fonseca, which considers Honduran access to the Pacific; legal dispute over navigational rights of San Juan River on border with Costa Rica
Illicit drugs: transshipment point for cocaine destined for the US and transshipment point for arms-for-drugs dealing

NIGER

INTRODUCTION

Background: Niger became independent from France in 1960 and experienced single-party and military rule until 1991, when Col. Ali SAIBOU was forced by public pressure to allow multiparty elections, which resulted in a democratic government in 1993. Political infighting brought the government to a standstill and in 1996 led to a coup by Col. Ibrahim BARE. In 1999 BARE was killed in a coup by military officers who promptly restored democratic rule and held elections that brought Mamadou TANDJA to power in December of that year. TANDJA was reelected in 2004. Niger is one of the poorest countries in the world with minimal government services and insufficient funds to develop its resource base. The largely agrarian and subsistence-based economy is frequently disrupted by extended droughts common to the Sahel region of Africa.

GEOGRAPHY

Location: Western Africa, southeast of Algeria
Geographic coordinates: 16 00 N, 8 00 E
Map references: Africa

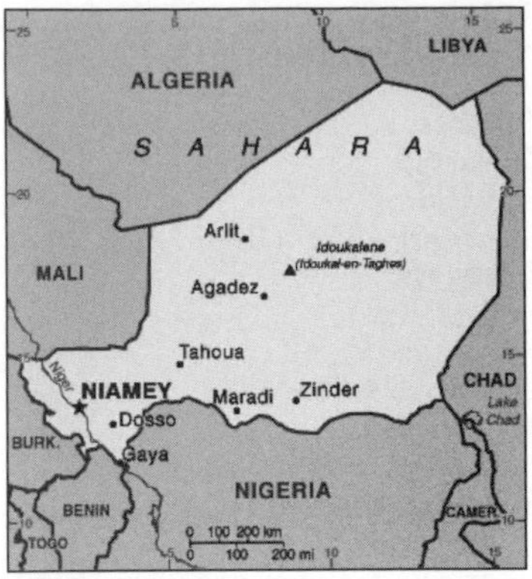

Area:
total: 1.267 million sq km
land: 1,266,700 sq km
water: 300 sq km
Area - comparative: slightly less than twice the size of Texas
Land boundaries:
total: 5,697 km
border countries: Algeria 956 km, Benin 266 km, Burkina Faso 628 km, Chad 1,175 km, Libya 354 km, Mali 821 km, Nigeria 1,497 km
Coastline: 0 km (landlocked)
Maritime claims: none (landlocked)
Climate: desert; mostly hot, dry, dusty; tropical in extreme south
Terrain: predominately desert plains and sand dunes; flat to rolling plains in south; hills in north
Elevation extremes:
lowest point: Niger River 200 m
highest point: Mont Bagzane 2,022 m
Natural resources: uranium, coal, iron ore, tin, phosphates, gold, molybdenum, gypsum, salt, petroleum
Land use:
arable land: 3.54%
permanent crops: 0.01%
other: 96.45% (2001)
Irrigated land: 660 sq km (1998 est.)
Natural hazards: recurring droughts
Environment - current issues: overgrazing; soil erosion; deforestation; desertification; wildlife populations (such as elephant, hippopotamus, giraffe, and lion) threatened because of poaching and habitat destruction
Environment - international agreements:
party to: Biodiversity, Climate Change, Climate Change-Kyoto Protocol, Desertification, Endangered Species, Environmental Modification, Hazardous Wastes, Ozone Layer Protection, Wetlands
signed, but not ratified: Law of the Sea
Geography - note: landlocked; one of the hottest countries in the world: northern four-fifths is desert, southern one-fifth is savanna, suitable for livestock and limited agriculture

PEOPLE

Population: 11,665,937 (July 2005 est.)
Age structure:
0-14 years: 47.3% (male 2,811,539/female 2,704,498)
15-64 years: 50.6% (male 2,890,119/ female 3,009,281)
65 years and over: 2.1% (male 130,953/ female 119,547) (2005 est.)
Median age:
total: 16.25 years
male: 15.8 years
female: 16.72 years (2005 est.)
Population growth rate: 2.63% (2005 est.)
Birth rate: 48.3 births/1,000 population (2005 est.)
Death rate: 21.33 deaths/1,000 population (2005 est.)
Net migration rate: -0.65 migrant(s)/ 1,000 population (2005 est.)
Sex ratio:
at birth: 1.03 male(s)/female
under 15 years: 1.04 male(s)/female
15-64 years: 0.96 male(s)/female
65 years and over: 1.1 male(s)/female
total population: 1 male(s)/female (2005 est.)
Infant mortality rate:
total: 121.69 deaths/1,000 live births
male: 125.93 deaths/1,000 live births
female: 117.33 deaths/1,000 live births (2005 est.)
Life expectancy at birth:
total population: 43.5 years
male: 43.54 years
female: 43.45 years (2005 est.)
Total fertility rate: 6.75 children born/woman (2005 est.)
HIV/AIDS - adult prevalence rate: 1.2% (2003 est.)
HIV/AIDS - people living with HIV/AIDS: 70,000 (2003 est.)
HIV/AIDS - deaths: 4,800 (2003 est.)
Major infectious diseases:
degree of risk: very high
food or waterborne diseases: bacterial and protozoal diarrhea, hepatitis A, and typhoid fever
vectorborne disease: malaria is a high risk in some locations respiratory disease: meningococcal meningitis (2004)
Nationality:
noun: Nigerien(s)
adjective: Nigerien
Ethnic groups: Hausa 56%, Djerma 22%, Fula 8.5%, Tuareg 8%, Beri Beri (Kanouri) 4.3%, Arab, Toubou, and Gourmantche 1.2%, about 1,200 French expatriates
Religions: Muslim 80%, remainder indigenous beliefs and Christian
Languages: French (official), Hausa, Djerma
Literacy:
definition: age 15 and over can read and write
total population: 17.6%
male: 25.8%
female: 9.7% (2003 est.)

GOVERNMENT

Country name:
conventional long form: Republic of Niger
conventional short form: Niger
local long form: Republique du Niger
local short form: Niger
Government type: republic
Capital: Niamey
Administrative divisions: 8 regions (regions, singular - region) includes 1 capital district* (commune urbaine); Agadez, Diffa, Dosso, Maradi, Niamey*, Tahoua, Tillaberi, Zinder
Independence: 3 August 1960 (from France)
National holiday: Republic Day, 18 December (1958)
Constitution: new constitution adopted 18 July 1999
Legal system: based on French civil law system and customary law; has not accepted compulsory ICJ jurisdiction
Suffrage: 18 years of age, universal
Executive branch:
chief of state: President Mamadou TANDJA (since 22 December 1999); note - the president is both chief of state and head of government
head of government: President Mamadou TANDJA (since 22 December 1999); note - the president is both chief of state and head of government; Prime Minister Hama AMADOU (since 31 December 1999) was appointed by the president and shares some executive responsibilities with the president
cabinet: 27-member Cabinet appointed by the president
elections: president elected by popular vote for a five-year term; second round last held 4 December 2004 (next to be held December 2009); prime minister appointed by the president
election results: Mamadou TANDJA reelected president; percent of vote - Mamadou TANDJA 65.5%, Mahamadou ISSOUFOU 34.5%
Legislative branch: unicameral National Assembly (113 seats; note - expanded from 83 seats; members elected by popular vote for five-year terms)
elections: last held 4 December 2004 (next to be held December 2009)
election results: percent of vote by party - NA%; seats by party - MNSD 47, CDS 22, PNDS 17, RSD 7, RDP 6, ANDP 5, Party for Socialism and Democracy in Niger 1, other 8
Judicial branch: State Court or Cour d'Etat; Court of Appeal or Cour d'Appel
Political parties and leaders: Democratic

and Social Convention-Rahama or CDS-Rahama [Mahamane OUSMANE]; National Movement for a Developing Society-Nassara or MNSD-Nassara [Hama AMADOU]; Nigerien Alliance for Democracy and Social Progress-Zaman Lahiya or ANDPS-Zaman Lahiya [Moumouni DJERMAKOYE]; Nigerien Party for Autonomy or PNA-Alouma'a [Sanousi JACKOU]; Nigerien Party for Democracy and Socialism or PNDS-Tarrayya [Issifou MAHAMADOU]; Nigerien Progressive Party or PPN-RDA [Abdoulaye DIORI]; Rally for Democracy and Progress or RDP-jama'a [Hamid ALGABID]; Social and Democratic Rally or RSD-Gaskiyya [Cheiffou AMADOU]

Political pressure groups and leaders: Coalition Against a High Cost of Living [Nouhou ARZIKA]

International organization participation: ACCT, ACP, AfDB, AU, CEMAC, ECOWAS, Entente, FAO, FZ, G-77, IAEA, IBRD, ICAO, ICCt, ICFTU, ICRM, IDA, IDB, IFAD, IFC, IFRCS, ILO, IMF, Interpol, IOC, IOM, ISO (correspondent), ITU, MONUC, NAM, OIC, ONUB, OPCW, UN, UNCTAD, UNESCO, UNIDO, UNMIL, UNOCI, UPU, WADB (regional), WAEMU, WCL, WCO, WFTU, WHO, WIPO, WMO, WToO, WTO

Diplomatic representation in the US:
chief of mission: Ambassador Joseph DIATTA
chancery: 2204 R Street NW, Washington, DC 20008
telephone: [1] (202) 483-4224 through 4227
FAX: [1] (202) 483-3169

Diplomatic representation from the US:
chief of mission: Ambassador Gail Dennise Thomas MATHIEU
embassy: Rue Des Ambassades, Niamey
mailing address: B. P. 11201, Niamey
telephone: [227] 72 26 61 through 72 26 64
FAX: [227] 73 31 67, 72-31-46

Flag description: three equal horizontal bands of orange (top), white, and green with a small orange disk (representing the sun) centered in the white band; similar to the flag of India, which has a blue spoked wheel centered in the white band

ECONOMY

Economy - overview: Niger is one of the poorest countries in the world, a landlocked Sub-Saharan nation, whose economy centers on subsistence crops, livestock, and some of the world's largest uranium deposits. Drought cycles, desertification, a 3.3% population growth rate, and the drop in world demand for uranium have undercut the economy. Niger shares a common currency, the CFA franc, and a common central bank, the Central Bank of West African States (BCEAO), with seven other members of the West African Monetary Union. In December 2000, Niger qualified for enhanced debt relief under the International Monetary Fund program for Highly Indebted Poor Countries (HIPC) and concluded an agreement with the Fund on a Poverty Reduction and Growth Facility (PRGF). Debt relief provided under the enhanced HIPC initiative significantly reduces Niger's annual debt service obligations, freeing funds for expenditures on basic health care, primary education, HIV/AIDS prevention, rural infrastructure, and other programs geared at poverty reduction. Nearly half of the government's budget is derived from foreign donor resources. Future growth may be sustained by exploitation of oil, gold, coal, and other mineral resources. A drought and locust infestation in 2005 led to food shortages for as many as 2.5 million Nigeriens.

GDP (purchasing power parity): $10.2 billion (2005 est.)

GDP (official exchange rate): $3.513 billion (2005 est.)

GDP - real growth rate: 3.8% (2005 est.)

GDP - per capita: purchasing power parity - $900 (2005 est.)

GDP - composition by sector:
agriculture: 39%
industry: 17%
services: 44% (2001)

Labor force: 70,000 receive regular wages or salaries (2002 est.)

Labor force - by occupation: agriculture 90%, industry and commerce 6%, government 4%

Unemployment rate: NA

Population below poverty line: 63% (1993 est.)

Household income or consumption by percentage share:
lowest 10%: 0.8%
highest 10%: 35.4% (1995)

Distribution of family income - Gini index: 50.5 (1995)

Inflation rate (consumer prices): 0.2% (2004 est.)

Budget:
revenues: $320 million - including $134 million from foreign sources
expenditures: $320 million, including capital expenditures of $178 million (2002 est.)

Agriculture - products: cowpeas, cotton, peanuts, millet, sorghum, cassava (tapioca), rice; cattle, sheep, goats, camels, donkeys, horses, poultry

Industries: uranium mining, cement, brick, soap, textiles, food processing, chemicals, slaughterhouses

Industrial production growth rate: 5.1% (2003 est.)

Electricity - production: 230 million kWh (2003)

Electricity - production by source:
fossil fuel: 100%
hydro: 0%
nuclear: 0%
other: 0% (2001)

Electricity - consumption: 263.9 million kWh (2003)

Electricity - exports: 0 kWh (2003)

Electricity - imports: 50 million kWh (2003)

Oil - production: 0 bbl/day (2003 est.)

Oil - consumption: 5,400 bbl/day (2003 est.)

Oil - exports: NA (2001)

Oil - imports: NA (2001)

Exports: $222 million f.o.b. (2004 est.)

Exports - partners: France 41%, Nigeria 22.4%, Japan 15.3%, Switzerland 6%, Spain 4.1%, Ghana 4% (2004)

Imports: $588 million f.o.b. (2004 est.)

Imports - partners: France 14.4%, US 10.3%, French Polynesia 9.4%, Nigeria 7.8%, Cote d"Ivoire 7.5%, Japan 5.2%, China 5.1%, Thailand 4.1% (2004)

Debt - external: $2.1 billion (2003 est.)

Economic aid - recipient: $453.3 million (2003)

Currency (code): Communaute Financiere Africaine franc (XOF); note - responsible authority is the Central Bank of the West African States

Currency code: XOF

Exchange rates: Communaute Financiere Africaine francs (XOF) per US dollar - 528.28 (2005), 528.29 (2004), 581.2 (2003), 696.99 (2002), 733.04 (2001)

Fiscal year: calendar year

COMMUNICATIONS

Telephones - main lines in use: 22,400 (2002)

Telephones - mobile cellular: 24,000 (2003)

Telephone system:
general assessment: small system of wire, radio telephone communications, and microwave radio relay links concentrated in the southwestern area of Niger
domestic: wire, radiotelephone communications, and microwave radio relay; domestic satellite system with 3 earth stations and 1 planned
international: country code - 227; satellite earth stations - 2 Intelsat (1 Atlantic Ocean and 1 Indian Ocean)

Radio broadcast stations: AM 5, FM 6, shortwave 4 (2001)

Radios: 680,000 (1997)

Television broadcast stations: 3 (plus seven low-power repeaters) (2002)

Televisions: 125,000 (1997)
Internet country code: .ne
Internet hosts: 134 (2003)
Internet Service Providers (ISPs): 1 (2002)
Internet users: 15,000 (2002)

TRANSPORTATION

Airports: 27 (2004 est.)
Airports - with paved runways:
total: 9
2,438 to 3,047 m: 3
1,524 to 2,437 m: 5
under 914 m: 1 (2005 est.)
Airports - with unpaved runways:
total: 18
1,524 to 2,437 m: 2
914 to 1,523 m: 14
under 914 m: 2 (2005 est.)
Roadways:
total: 10,100 km
paved: 798 km
unpaved: 9,302 km (1999 est.)
Waterways: 300 km
note: Niger River is navigable to Gaya between September and March (2004)
Ports and terminals: none

MILITARY

Military branches: Niger Armed Forces (Forces Armees Nigeriennes, FAN): Army, National Air Force (2005)
Military service age and obligation: 18 years of age for compulsory military service; conscript service obligation - 2 years (2004)
Manpower available for military service: *males age 18-49:* 2,135,680 (2005 est.)
Manpower fit for military service: *males age 18-49:* 1,180,027 (2005 est.)
Manpower reaching military service age annually: *males:* 126,719 (2005 est.)
Military expenditures - dollar figure: $33.3 million (2004)
Military expenditures - percent of GDP: 1.1% (2004)

TRANSNATIONAL ISSUES

Disputes - international: Libya claims about 25,000 sq km in a currently dormant dispute; much of Benin-Niger boundary, including tripoint with Nigeria, remains undemarcated, and states expect a ruling in 2005 from the ICJ over the disputed Niger and Mekrou River islands; only Nigeria and Cameroon have heeded the Lake Chad Commission's admonition to ratify the delimitation treaty which also includes Chad and Niger

NIGERIA

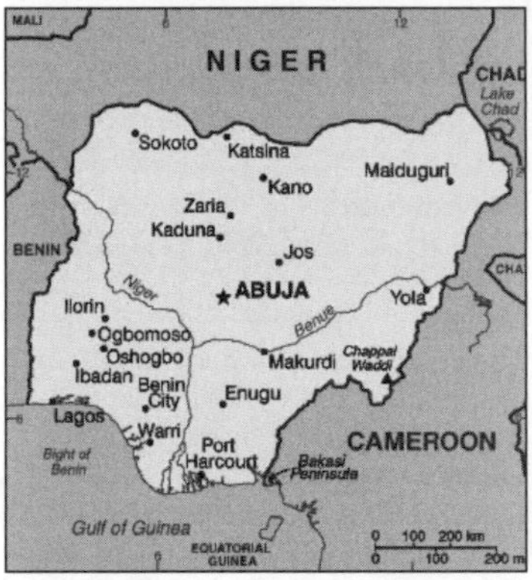

INTRODUCTION

Background: Following nearly 16 years of military rule, a new constitution was adopted in 1999, and a peaceful transition to civilian government was completed. The president faces the daunting task of reforming a petroleum-based economy, whose revenues have been squandered through corruption and mismanagement, and institutionalizing democracy. In addition, the OBASANJO administration must defuse longstanding ethnic and religious tensions, if it is to build a sound foundation for economic growth and political stability. Although the April 2003 elections were marred by some irregularities, Nigeria is currently experiencing its longest period of civilian rule since independence.

GEOGRAPHY

Location: Western Africa, bordering the Gulf of Guinea, between Benin and Cameroon
Geographic coordinates: 10 00 N, 8 00 E
Map references: Africa
Area:
total: 923,768 sq km
land: 910,768 sq km
water: 13,000 sq km
Area - comparative: slightly more than twice the size of California
Land boundaries:
total: 4,047 km
border countries: Benin 773 km, Cameroon 1,690 km, Chad 87 km, Niger 1,497 km
Coastline: 853 km
Maritime claims:
territorial sea: 12 nm
exclusive economic zone: 200 nm
continental shelf: 200-m depth or to the depth of exploitation
Climate: varies; equatorial in south, tropical in center, arid in north
Terrain: southern lowlands merge into central hills and plateaus; mountains in southeast, plains in north
Elevation extremes:
lowest point: Atlantic Ocean 0 m
highest point: Chappal Waddi 2,419 m
Natural resources: natural gas, petroleum, tin, iron ore, coal, limestone, niobium, lead, zinc, arable land
Land use:
arable land: 31.29%
permanent crops: 2.96%
other: 65.75% (2001)
Irrigated land: 2,330 sq km (1998 est.)
Natural hazards: periodic droughts; flooding
Environment - current issues: soil degradation; rapid deforestation; urban air and water pollution; desertification; oil pollution - water, air, and soil; has suffered serious damage from oil spills; loss of arable land; rapid urbanization
Environment - international agreements:
party to: Biodiversity, Climate Change, Climate Change-Kyoto Protocol, Desertification, Endangered Species, Hazardous Wastes, Law of the Sea, Marine Dumping, Marine Life Conservation, Ozone Layer Protection, Wetlands
signed, but not ratified: none of the selected agreements
Geography - note: the Niger enters the country in the northwest and flows southward through tropical rain forests and swamps to its delta in the Gulf of Guinea

PEOPLE

Population: 128,771,988
note: estimates for this country explicitly take into account the effects of excess mortality due to AIDS; this can result in lower life expectancy, higher infant mortality and death rates, lower population and growth rates, and changes in the distribution of population by age and sex than would otherwise be expected (July 2005 est.)
Age structure:
0-14 years: 42.3% (male 27,466,766/female 27,045,092)
15-64 years: 54.6% (male 35,770,593/female 34,559,414)
65 years and over: 3.1% (male 1,874,157/female 2,055,966) (2005 est.)
Median age:
total: 18.63 years
male: 18.71 years
female: 18.55 years (2005 est.)
Population growth rate: 2.37% (2005 est.)
Birth rate: 40.65 births/1,000 population (2005 est.)
Death rate: 17.18 deaths/1,000 popula-

tion (2005 est.)
Net migration rate: 0.27 migrant(s)/1,000 population (2005 est.)
Sex ratio:
at birth: 1.03 male(s)/female
under 15 years: 1.02 male(s)/female
15-64 years: 1.04 male(s)/female
65 years and over: 0.91 male(s)/female
total population: 1.02 male(s)/female (2005 est.)
Infant mortality rate:
total: 98.8 deaths/1,000 live births
male: 105.69 deaths/1,000 live births
female: 91.7 deaths/1,000 live births (2005 est.)
Life expectancy at birth:
total population: 46.74 years
male: 46.21 years
female: 47.29 years (2005 est.)
Total fertility rate: 5.53 children born/woman (2005 est.)
HIV/AIDS - adult prevalence rate: 5.4% (2003 est.)
HIV/AIDS - people living with HIV/AIDS: 3.6 million (2003 est.)
HIV/AIDS - deaths: 310,000 (2003 est.)
Major infectious diseases:
degree of risk: very high
food or waterborne diseases: bacterial and protozoal diarrhea, hepatitis A, and typhoid fever *vectorborne disease:* malaria
respiratory disease: meningococcal meningitis
aerosolized dust or soil contact disease: one of the most highly endemic areas for Lassa fever (2004)
Nationality:
noun: Nigerian(s)
adjective: Nigerian
Ethnic groups: Nigeria, Africa's most populous country, is composed of more than 250 ethnic groups; the following are the most populous and politically influential: Hausa and Fulani 29%, Yoruba 21%, Igbo (Ibo) 18%, Ijaw 10%, Kanuri 4%, Ibibio 3.5%, Tiv 2.5%
Religions: Muslim 50%, Christian 40%, indigenous beliefs 10%
Languages: English (official), Hausa, Yoruba, Igbo (Ibo), Fulani
Literacy:
definition: age 15 and over can read and write
total population: 68%
male: 75.7%
female: 60.6% (2003 est.)

GOVERNMENT

Country name:
conventional long form: Federal Republic of Nigeria
conventional short form: Nigeria
Government type: federal republic
Capital: Abuja; note - on 12 December 1991 the capital was officially transferred from Lagos to Abuja; most federal government offices have now moved to Abuja
Administrative divisions: 36 states and 1 territory*; Abia, Adamawa, Akwa Ibom, Anambra, Bauchi, Bayelsa, Benue, Borno, Cross River, Delta, Ebonyi, Edo, Ekiti, Enugu, Federal Capital Territory*, Gombe, Imo, Jigawa, Kaduna, Kano, Katsina, Kebbi, Kogi, Kwara, Lagos, Nassarawa, Niger, Ogun, Ondo, Osun, Oyo, Plateau, Rivers, Sokoto, Taraba, Yobe, Zamfara
Independence: 1 October 1960 (from UK)
National holiday: Independence Day (National Day), 1 October (1960)
Constitution: new constitution adopted May 1999
Legal system: based on English common law, Islamic Shariah law (in 12 northern states), and traditional law
Suffrage: 18 years of age, universal
Executive branch:
chief of state: President Olusegun OBASANJO (since 29 May 1999); note - the president is both the chief of state and head of government
head of government: President Olusegun OBASANJO (since 29 May 1999); note - the president is both the chief of state and head of government
cabinet: Federal Executive Council
elections: president is elected by popular vote for no more than two four-year terms; election last held 19 April 2003 (next to be held NA 2007)
election results: Olusegun OBASANJO elected president; percent of vote - Olusegun OBASANJO (PDP) 61.9%, Muhammadu BUHARI (ANPP) 31.2%, Chukwuemeka Odumegwu OJUKWU (APGA) 3.3%, other 3.6%
Legislative branch: bicameral National Assembly consists of Senate (109 seats - 3 from each state plus one from Abuja, members elected by popular vote to serve four-year terms) and House of Representatives (346 seats, members elected by popular vote to serve four-year terms)
elections: Senate - last held 12 April 2003 (next to be held NA 2007); House of Representatives - last held 12 April 2003 (next to be held NA 2007)
election results: Senate - percent of vote by party - PDP 53.7%, ANPP 27.9%, AD 9.7%; seats by party - PDP 76, ANPP 27, AD 6; House of Representatives - percent of vote by party - PDP 54.5%, ANPP 27.4%, AD 8.8%, other 9.3%; seats by party - PDP 223, ANPP 96, AD 34, other 6; note - one seat is vacant
Judicial branch: Supreme Court (judges appointed by the President); Federal Court of Appeal (judges are appointed by the federal government on the advice of the Advisory Judicial Committee)
Political parties and leaders: Alliance for Democracy or AD [Mojisoluwa AKINFENWA]; All Nigeria Peoples' Party or ANPP [Don ETIEBET]; All Progressives Grand Alliance or APGA [disputed leadership]; National Democratic Party or NDP [Aliyu Habu FARI]; Peoples Democratic Party or PDP [Dr. Ahmadu ALI]; Peoples Redemption Party or PRP [Abdulkadir Balarabe MUSA]; Peoples Salvation Party or PSP [Lawal MAITURARE]; United Nigeria Peoples Party or UNPP [disputed leadership]
Political pressure groups and leaders: NA
International organization participation: ACP, AfDB, AU, C, ECOWAS, FAO, G-15, G-24, G-77, IAEA, IBRD, ICAO, ICC, ICCt, ICFTU, ICRM, IDA, IFAD, IFC, IFRCS, IHO, ILO, IMF, IMO, Interpol, IOC, IOM, ISO, ITU, MIGA, MINURSO, MONUC, NAM, OAS (observer), OIC, ONUB, OPCW, OPEC, PCA, UN, UNAMSIL, UNCTAD, UNESCO, UNHCR, UNIDO, UNITAR, UNMEE, UNMIL, UNMIS, UNMOVIC, UNOCI, UPU, WCO, WFTU, WHO, WIPO, WMO, WToO, WTO
Diplomatic representation in the US:
chief of mission: Ambassador Professor George A. OBIOZOR
chancery: 3519 International Court NW, Washington, DC 20008
telephone: [1] (202) 986-8400
FAX: [1] (202) 775-1385
consulate(s) general: Atlanta and New York
Diplomatic representation from the US:
chief of mission: Ambassador John CAMPBELL
embassy: 7 Mambilla Drive, Abuja
mailing address: P. O. Box 554, Lagos
telephone: [234] (9) 523-0916/0906/5857/2235/2205
FAX: [234] (9) 523-0353
Flag description: three equal vertical bands of green (hoist side), white, and green

ECONOMY

Economy - overview: Oil-rich Nigeria, long hobbled by political instability, corruption, inadequate infrastructure, and poor macroeconomic management, is undertaking some reforms under a new reform-minded administration. Nigeria's former military rulers failed to diversify the economy away from its overdependence on the capital-intensive oil sector, which provides 20% of GDP, 95% of foreign exchange earnings, and about 65% of budgetary revenues. The largely subsistence agricultural sector has failed to keep up with rapid population growth - Nigeria is Africa's most populous country - and the country, once a large net exporter of food, now must import food. Following the signing of an IMF stand-by agreement in August 2000, Nigeria received a debt-restructuring deal from the Paris Club and a $1 billion credit from the IMF, both contingent on economic reforms. Nigeria pulled out of its IMF program in April 2002, after failing to meet spending and exchange rate targets, making it ineligible for additional debt forgiveness from the Paris Club. In the last year the government has begun showing the political will to implement the market-oriented reforms urged by the IMF, such as to modernize the banking system, to curb inflation by blocking excessive wage demands, and to resolve regional disputes over the distribution of earnings from the oil industry. In 2003 the government began deregulating fuel prices, announced the privatization of the country's four oil refineries, and instituted the National Economic Empowerment Development Strategy, a domestically designed and run program modeled on the IMF's Poverty Reduction and Growth Facility for fiscal and monetary management. GDP rose strongly in 2005, based largely on increased oil exports and high global crude prices. In November 2005, Abuja won Paris Club approval for an historic debt relief deal that by March 2006 should eliminate $30 billion worth of Nigeria's total $36 billion external debt. The deal first requires that Nigeria repay roughly $12 billion in arrears to its bilateral creditors. Nigeria would then be allowed to buyback its remaining debt stock at a discount. The deal commits Nigeria more intensified IMF reviews.

GDP (purchasing power parity): $132.1 billion (2005 est.)

GDP (official exchange rate): $78.08 billion (2005 est.)

GDP - real growth rate: 5.2% (2005 est.)

GDP - per capita: purchasing power parity - $1,000 (2005 est.)

GDP - composition by sector:
agriculture: 26.8%
industry: 48.8%
services: 24.4% (2005 est.)

Labor force: 57.21 million (2005 est.)

Labor force - by occupation: agriculture 70%, industry 10%, services 20% (1999 est.)

Unemployment rate: 2.9% NA (2005 est.)

Population below poverty line: 60% (2000 est.)

Household income or consumption by percentage share:
lowest 10%: 1.6%
highest 10%: 40.8% (1996-97)

Distribution of family income - Gini index: 50.6 (1996-97)

Inflation rate (consumer prices): 15.6% (2005 est.)

Investment (gross fixed): 23.1% of GDP (2005 est.)

Budget:
revenues: $12.86 billion
expenditures: $13.54 billion, including capital expenditures of NA (2005 est.)

Public debt: 11.2% of GDP (2005 est.)

Agriculture - products: cocoa, peanuts, palm oil, corn, rice, sorghum, millet, cassava (tapioca), yams, rubber; cattle, sheep, goats, pigs; timber; fish

Industries: crude oil, coal, tin, columbite, palm oil, peanuts, cotton, rubber, wood, hides and skins, textiles, cement and other construction materials, food products, footwear, chemicals, fertilizer, printing, ceramics, steel, small commercial ship construction and repair

Industrial production growth rate: 2.4% (2005 est.)

Electricity - production: 15.59 billion kWh (2003)

Electricity - production by source:
fossil fuel: 61.9%
hydro: 38.1%
nuclear: 0%
other: 0% (2001)

Electricity - consumption: 14.46 billion kWh (2003)

Electricity - exports: 40 million kWh (2003)

Electricity - imports: 0 kWh (2003)

Oil - production: 2.451 million bbl/day (2005 est.)

Oil - consumption: 310,000 bbl/day (2003 est.)

Oil - exports: NA (2001)

Oil - imports: NA (2001)

Oil - proved reserves: 36 billion bbl (2005 est.)

Natural gas - production: 15.68 billion cu m (2001 est.)

Natural gas - consumption: 7.85 billion cu m (2001 est.)

Natural gas - exports: 7.83 billion cu m (2001 est.)

Natural gas - imports: 0 cu m (2001 est.)

Natural gas - proved reserves: 4.007 trillion cu m (2005)

Current account balance: $9.622 billion (2005 est.)

Exports: $52.16 billion f.o.b. (2005 est.)

Exports - partners: US 47.4%, Brazil 10.7%, Spain 7.1% (2004)

Imports: $25.95 billion f.o.b. (2005 est.)

Imports - partners: China 9.4%, US 8.4%, UK 7.8%, Netherlands 5.9%, France 5.4%, Germany 4.8%, Italy 4% (2004)

Reserves of foreign exchange and gold: $30.16 billion (2005 est.)

Debt - external: $37.49 billion (2005 est.)

Economic aid - recipient: IMF $250 million (1998)

Currency (code): naira (NGN)

Currency code: NGN

Exchange rates: nairas per US dollar - 132.59 (2005), 132.89 (2004), 129.22 (2003), 120.58 (2002), 111.23 (2001)

Fiscal year: calendar year

COMMUNICATIONS

Telephones - main lines in use: 853,100 (2003)

Telephones - mobile cellular: 3,149,500 (2003)

Telephone system:
general assessment: an inadequate system, further limited by poor maintenance; major expansion is required and a start has been made
domestic: intercity traffic is carried by coaxial cable, microwave radio relay, a domestic communications satellite system with 19 earth stations, and a coastal submarine cable; mobile cellular facilities and the Internet are available
international: country code - 234; satellite earth stations - 3 Intelsat (2 Atlantic Ocean and 1 Indian Ocean); fiber optic submarine cable (SAT-3/WASC) provides connectivity to Europe and Asia

Radio broadcast stations: AM 83, FM 36, shortwave 11 (2001)

Radios: 23.5 million (1997)

Television broadcast stations: 3 (the government controls 2 of the broadcasting stations and 15 repeater stations) (2002)

Televisions: 6.9 million (1997)

Internet country code: .ng

Internet hosts: 1,142 (2004)

Internet Service Providers (ISPs): 11 (2000)

Internet users: 750,000 (2003)

TRANSPORTATION

Airports: 70 (2004 est.)

Airports - with paved runways:
total: 36
over 3,047 m: 6
2,438 to 3,047 m: 12
1,524 to 2,437 m: 9
914 to 1,523 m: 6
under 914 m: 3 (2005 est.)

Airports - with unpaved runways:
total: 34
1,524 to 2,437 m: 3
914 to 1,523 m: 13
under 914 m: 18 (2005 est.)

Heliports: 1 (2005 est.)

Pipelines: condensate 105 km; gas 1,896 km; oil 3,638 km; refined products 3,626 km (2004)

Railways:
total: 3,557 km
narrow gauge: 3,505 km 1.067-m gauge

standard gauge: 52 km 1.435-m gauge (2004)
Roadways:
total: 194,394 km
paved: 60,068 km (including 1,194 km of expressways)
unpaved: 134,326 km (1999 est.)
Waterways: 8,600 km (Niger and Benue rivers and smaller rivers and creeks) (2004)
Merchant marine:
total: 46 ships (1,000 GRT or over) 327,808 GRT/608,076 DWT
by type: cargo 5, chemical tanker 6, combination ore/oil 1, liquefied gas 1, passenger/cargo 1, petroleum tanker 31, refrigerated cargo 1
foreign-owned: 3 (Norway 2, Pakistan 1)
registered in other countries: 25 (2005)
Ports and terminals: Bonny Inshore Terminal, Calabar, Lagos, Port Harcourt

MILITARY

Military branches: Army, Navy, Air Force
Military service age and obligation: 18 years of age for voluntary military service (2001)
Manpower available for military service: *males age 18-49:* 26,804,314 (2005 est.)
Manpower fit for military service: *males age 18-49:* 15,053,936 (2005 est.)
Manpower reaching military service age annually: *males:* 1,353,161 (2005 est.)
Military expenditures - dollar figure: $544.6 million (2004)
Military expenditures - percent of GDP: 0.8% (2004)

TRANSNATIONAL ISSUES

Disputes - international: ICJ ruled in 2002 on the entire Cameroon-Nigeria land and maritime boundary but the parties formed a Joint Border Commission to resolve differences bilaterally and have commenced with demarcation in less-contested sections of the boundary, starting in Lake Chad in the north; Nigeria initially rejected cession of the Bakassi Peninsula, then agreed, but has yet to withdraw its forces while much of the indigenous population opposes cession; in 2004, some 17,000 Nigerian refugees fleeing ethnic conflicts between pastoralists and farmers in 2002 still reside in Cameroon; the ICJ ruled on an equidistance settlement of Cameroon-Equatorial Guinea-Nigeria maritime boundary in the Gulf of Guinea, but imprecisely defined coordinates in the ICJ decision, the unresolved Bakasi allocation, and a sovereignty dispute between Equatorial Guinea and Cameroon over an island at the mouth of the Ntem River all contribute to the delay in implementation; a joint task force was established in 2004 that resolved disputes over and redrew the maritime and the 870-km land boundary with Benin on the Okpara River; only Nigeria and Cameroon have heeded the Lake Chad Commission's admonition to ratify the delimitation treaty which also includes Chad and Niger
Refugees and internally displaced persons: *IDPs:* 250,000 (communal violence between Christians and Muslims since President OBASANJO's election in 999) (2004)
Illicit drugs: a transit point for heroin and cocaine intended for European, East Asian, and North American markets; safehaven for Nigerian narcotraffickers operating worldwide; major money-laundering center; massive corruption and criminal activity; remains on Financial Action Task Force Non-Cooperative Countries and Territories List for continued failure to address deficiencies in money-laundering control regime

NIUE

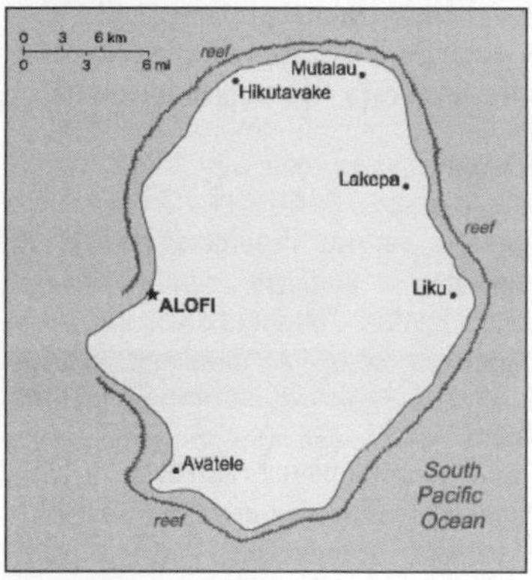

INTRODUCTION

Background: Niue's remoteness, as well as cultural and linguistic differences between its Polynesian inhabitants and those of the rest of the Cook Islands, have caused it to be separately administered. The population of the island continues to drop (from a peak of 5,200 in 1966 to about 2,150 in 2005), with substantial emigration to New Zealand, 2,400 km to the southwest.

GEOGRAPHY

Location: Oceania, island in the South Pacific Ocean, east of Tonga
Geographic coordinates: 19 02 S, 169 52 W
Map references: Oceania
Area:
total: 260 sq km
land: 260 sq km
water: 0 sq km
Area - comparative: 1.5 times the size of Washington, DC
Land boundaries: 0 km
Coastline: 64 km
Maritime claims:
territorial sea: 12 nm
exclusive economic zone: 200 nm
Climate: tropical; modified by southeast trade winds
Terrain: steep limestone cliffs along coast, central plateau
Elevation extremes:
lowest point: Pacific Ocean 0 m
highest point: unnamed location near Mutalau settlement 68 m
Natural resources: fish, arable land
Land use:
arable land: 15.38%
permanent crops: 11.54%
other: 73.08% (2001)
Irrigated land: NA
Natural hazards: typhoons
Environment - current issues: increasing attention to conservationist practices to counter loss of soil fertility from traditional slash and burn agriculture
Environment - international agreements:
party to: Biodiversity, Climate Change, Climate Change-Kyoto Protocol, Desertification
signed, but not ratified: Law of the Sea
Geography - note: one of world's largest coral islands

PEOPLE

Population: 2,166 (July 2005 est.)
Age structure:
0-14 years: NA
15-64 years: NA
65 years and over: NA
Population growth rate: 0% (2005 est.)
Birth rate: NA births/1,000 population
Death rate: NA deaths/1,000 population
Net migration rate: NA migrant(s)/1,000 population
Sex ratio: NA
Infant mortality rate:
total: NA
male: NA
female: NA
Life expectancy at birth:
total population: NA
male: NA
female: NA
Total fertility rate: NA

HIV/AIDS - adult prevalence rate: NA
HIV/AIDS - people living with HIV/AIDS: NA
HIV/AIDS - deaths: NA
Nationality:
noun: Niuean(s)
adjective: Niuean
Ethnic groups: Niuen 78.2%, Pacific islander 10.2%, European 4.5%, mixed 3.9%, Asian 0.2%, unspecified 3% (2001 census)
Religions: Ekalesia Niue (Niuean Church - a Protestant church related to the London Missionary Society) 61.1%, Latter-Day Saints 8.8%, Roman Catholic 7.2%, Jehovah's Witnesses 2.4%, Seventh-Day Adventist 1.4%, other 8.4%, unspecified 8.7%, none 1.9% (2001 census)
Languages: Niuean, a Polynesian language closely related to Tongan and Samoan; English
Literacy:
definition: NA
total population: 95%
male: NA%
female: NA%

GOVERNMENT

Country name:
conventional long form: none
conventional short form: Niue
former: Savage Island
Dependency status: self-governing in free association with New Zealand since 1974; Niue fully responsible for internal affairs; New Zealand retains responsibility for external affairs and defense; however, these responsibilities confer no rights of control and are only exercised at the request of the Government of Niue
Government type: self-governing parliamentary democracy
Capital: Alofi
Administrative divisions: none; note - there are no first-order administrative divisions as defined by the US Government, but there are 14 villages at the second order
Independence: on 19 October 1974, Niue became a self-governing parliamentary government in free association with New Zealand
National holiday: Waitangi Day (Treaty of Waitangi established British sovereignty over New Zealand), 6 February (1840)
Constitution: 19 October 1974 (Niue Constitution Act)
Legal system: English common law
note: Niue is self-governing, with the power to make its own laws
Suffrage: 18 years of age, universal
Executive branch:
chief of state: Queen ELIZABETH II (since 6 February 1952); the UK and New Zealand are represented by New Zealand High Commissioner John BRYAN (since NA May 2000)
head of government: Premier Young VIVIAN (since 1 May 2002)
cabinet: Cabinet consists of the premier and three ministers
elections: the monarch is hereditary; premier elected by the Legislative Assembly for a three-year term; election last held 12 May 2005 (next to be held May 2008)
election results: Young VIVIAN reelected premier; percent of Legislative Assembly vote - Young VIVIAN (NPP) 85%, O'Love JACOBSEN (independent) 15%
Legislative branch: unicameral Legislative Assembly (20 seats; members elected by popular vote to serve three-year terms; six elected from a common roll and 14 are village representatives)
elections: last held 30 April 2005 (next to be held April 2008)
election results: percent of vote by party - NA%; seats by party - NA
Judicial branch: Supreme Court of New Zealand; High Court of Niue
Political parties and leaders: Niue People's Action Party or NPP [Young VIVIAN]; Alliance of Independents or AI [leader NA]
Political pressure groups and leaders: NA
International organization participation: ACP, FAO, OPCW, PIF, Sparteca, SPC, UNESCO, UPU, WHO, WMO
Diplomatic representation in the US: none (self-governing territory in free association with New Zealand)
Diplomatic representation from the US: none (self-governing territory in free association with New Zealand)
Flag description: yellow with the flag of the UK in the upper hoist-side quadrant; the flag of the UK bears five yellow five-pointed stars - a large one on a blue disk in the center and a smaller one on each arm of the bold red cross

ECONOMY

Economy - overview: The economy suffers from the typical Pacific island problems of geographic isolation, few resources, and a small population. Government expenditures regularly exceed revenues, and the shortfall is made up by critically needed grants from New Zealand that are used to pay wages to public employees. Niue has cut government expenditures by reducing the public service by almost half. The agricultural sector consists mainly of subsistence gardening, although some cash crops are grown for export. Industry consists primarily of small factories to process passion fruit, lime oil, honey, and coconut cream. The sale of postage stamps to foreign collectors is an important source of revenue. The island in recent years has suffered a serious loss of population because of migration of Niueans to New Zealand. Efforts to increase GDP include the promotion of tourism and a financial services industry, although former Premier LAKATANI announced in February 2002 that Niue will shut down the offshore banking industry. Economic aid from New Zealand in 2002 was about $2.6 million. Niue suffered a devastating hurricane in January 2004, which decimated nascent economic programs. While in the process of rebuilding, Niue has been dependent on foreign aid.
GDP (purchasing power parity): $7.6 million (2000 est.)
GDP (official exchange rate): NA
GDP - real growth rate: -0.3% (2000 est.)
GDP - per capita: purchasing power parity - $3,600 (2000 est.)
GDP - composition by sector:
agriculture: NA
industry: NA
services: 55%
Labor force: NA
Labor force - by occupation: most work on family plantations; paid work exists only in government service, small industry, and the Niue Development Board
Unemployment rate: NA
Population below poverty line: NA
Household income or consumption by percentage share:
lowest 10%: NA
highest 10%: NA
Inflation rate (consumer prices): 1% (1995)
Budget:
revenues: NA
expenditures: NA
Agriculture - products: coconuts, passion fruit, honey, limes, taro, yams, cassava (tapioca), sweet potatoes; pigs, poultry, beef cattle
Industries: tourism, handicrafts, food processing
Industrial production growth rate: NA
Electricity - production: 3 million kWh (2003)
Electricity - production by source:
fossil fuel: 100%
hydro: 0%
nuclear: 0%
other: 0% (2001)
Electricity - consumption: 2.79 million kWh (2003)
Electricity - exports: 0 kWh (2003)
Electricity - imports: 0 kWh (2003)
Oil - production: 0 bbl/day (2003 est.)
Oil - consumption: 20 bbl/day (2003 est.)
Oil - exports: NA (2001)
Oil - imports: NA (2001)
Exports: $137,200 (1999)
Exports - partners: New Zealand main-

ly, Fiji, Cook Islands, Australia (2004)
Imports: $2.38 million (1999)
Imports - partners: New Zealand mainly, Fiji, Japan, Samoa, Australia, US (2004)
Debt - external: $418,000 (2002 est.)
Economic aid - recipient: $2.6 million from New Zealand (2002)
Currency (code): New Zealand dollar (NZD)
Currency code: NZD
Exchange rates: New Zealand dollars per US dollar - 1.31 (2005), 1.5087 (2004), 1.7221 (2003), 2.1622 (2002), 2.3788 (2001)
Fiscal year: 1 April - 31 March

COMMUNICATIONS

Telephones - main lines in use: 1,100 est (2002)
Telephones - mobile cellular: 400 (2002)
Telephone system:
domestic: single-line telephone system connects all villages on island
international: country code - 683
Radio broadcast stations: AM 1, FM 1, shortwave 0 (1998)
Radios: 1,000 (1997)
Television broadcast stations: 1 (1997)
Televisions: NA
Internet country code: .nu
Internet Service Providers (ISPs): 1 (2000)
Internet users: NA

TRANSPORTATION

Airports: 1 (2004 est.)
Airports - with paved runways:
total: 1
1,524 to 2,437 m: 1 (2005 est.)
Roadways:
total: 234 km
paved: 86 km
unpaved: 148 km (2001)
Ports and terminals: none; offshore anchorage only

MILITARY

Military branches: no regular indigenous military forces; Police Force
Military - note: defense is the responsibility of New Zealand

TRANSNATIONAL ISSUES

Disputes - international: none

NORFOLK ISLAND

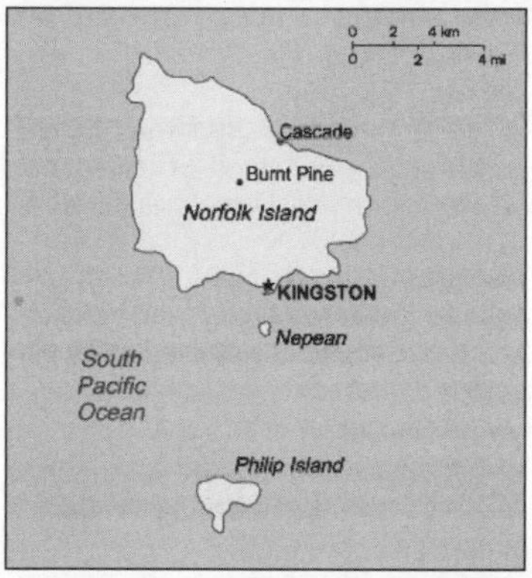

INTRODUCTION

Background: Two British attempts at establishing the island as a penal colony (1788-1814 and 1825-55) were ultimately abandoned. In 1856, the island was resettled by Pitcairn Islanders, descendants of the Bounty mutineers and their Tahitian companions.

GEOGRAPHY

Location: Oceania, island in the South Pacific Ocean, east of Australia
Geographic coordinates: 29 02 S, 167 57 E
Map references: Oceania
Area:
total: 34.6 sq km
land: 34.6 sq km
water: 0 sq km
Area - comparative: about 0.2 times the size of Washington, DC
Land boundaries: 0 km
Coastline: 32 km
Maritime claims:
territorial sea: 12 nm
exclusive fishing zone: 200 nm
Climate: subtropical; mild, little seasonal temperature variation
Terrain: volcanic formation with mostly rolling plains
Elevation extremes:
lowest point: Pacific Ocean 0 m
highest point: Mount Bates 319 m
Natural resources: fish
Land use:
arable land: 0%
permanent crops: 0%
other: 100% (2001)
Irrigated land: NA
Natural hazards: typhoons (especially May to July)
Environment - current issues: NA
Geography - note: most of the 32-km coastline consists of almost inaccessible cliffs, but the land slopes down to the sea in one small southern area on Sydney Bay, where the capital of Kingston is situated

PEOPLE

Population: 1,828 (July 2005 est.)
Age structure:
0-14 years: 20.2%
15-64 years: 63.9%
65 years and over: 15.9% (2005 est.)
Population growth rate: -0.01% (2005 est.)
Birth rate: NA
Death rate: NA
Net migration rate: NA
Sex ratio: NA
Infant mortality rate:
total: NA
male: NA
female: NA
Life expectancy at birth:
total population: NA
male: NA
female: NA
Total fertility rate: NA
HIV/AIDS - adult prevalence rate: NA
HIV/AIDS - people living with HIV/AIDS: NA
HIV/AIDS - deaths: NA
Nationality:
noun: Norfolk Islander(s)
adjective: Norfolk Islander(s)
Ethnic groups: descendants of the Bounty mutineers, Australian, New Zealander, Polynesians
Religions: Anglican 34.9%, Roman Catholic 11.7%, Uniting Church in Australia 11.2%, Seventh-Day Adventist 2.8%, Australian Christian 2.4%, Jehovah's Witness 0.9%, other 2.7%, unspecified 15.3%, none 18.1% (2001 census)
Languages: English (official), Norfolk a mixture of 18th century English and ancient Tahitian
Literacy: NA

GOVERNMENT

Country name:
conventional long form: Territory of Norfolk Island
conventional short form: Norfolk Island
Dependency status: territory of Australia; Canberra administers Commonwealth responsibilities on Norfolk Island through the Department of Environment, Sport, and Territories
Government type: NA
Capital: Kingston
Administrative divisions: none (territory of Australia)
Independence: none (territory of Australia)
National holiday: Bounty Day (commemorates the arrival of Pitcairn Islanders), 8 June (1856)
Constitution: Norfolk Island Act of 1979
Legal system: based on the laws of

Australia, local ordinances and acts; English common law applies in matters not covered by either Australian or Norfolk Island law
Suffrage: 18 years of age, universal
Executive branch:
chief of state: Queen ELIZABETH II (since 6 February 1952); the UK and Australia are represented by Administrator Grant TAMBLING (since 1 November 2003)
head of government: Assembly President and Chief Minister Geoffrey Robert GARDNER (since 5 December 2001)
cabinet: Executive Council is made up of four of the nine members of the Legislative Assembly; the council devises government policy and acts as an advisor to the administrator
elections: the monarch is hereditary; administrator appointed by the governor general of Australia; chief minister elected by the Legislative Assembly for a term of not more than three years; election last held 20 October 2004 (next to be held by December 2007)
election results: Geoffrey Robert GARDNER elected chief minister; percent of Legislative Assembly vote - 17.2%
Legislative branch: unicameral Legislative Assembly (9 seats; members elected by electors who have nine equal votes each but only four votes can be given to any one candidate; members serve three-year terms)
elections: last held 20 October 2004 (next to be held by December 2007)
election results: percent of vote - NA%; seats - independents 9 (note - no political parties)
Judicial branch: Supreme Court; Court of Petty Sessions
Political parties and leaders: none
Political pressure groups and leaders: none
International organization participation: UPU
Diplomatic representation in the US: none (territory of Australia)
Diplomatic representation from the US: none (territory of Australia)
Flag description: three vertical bands of green (hoist side), white, and green with a large green Norfolk Island pine tree centered in the slightly wider white band

ECONOMY

Economy - overview: Tourism, the primary economic activity, has steadily increased over the years and has brought a level of prosperity unusual among inhabitants of the Pacific islands. The agricultural sector has become self-sufficient in the production of beef, poultry, and eggs.
GDP (purchasing power parity): NA
GDP (official exchange rate): NA
GDP - real growth rate: NA
GDP - per capita: purchasing power parity - NA
GDP - composition by sector:
agriculture: NA
industry: NA
services: NA
Labor force: 1,345
Labor force - by occupation: tourism 90%, subsistence agriculture 10%
Unemployment rate: 0%
Population below poverty line: NA
Household income or consumption by percentage share:
lowest 10%: NA
highest 10%: NA
Inflation rate (consumer prices): NA
Budget:
revenues: $4.6 million
expenditures: $4.8 million, including capital expenditures of $2 million (FY99/00)
Agriculture - products: Norfolk Island pine seed, Kentia palm seed, cereals, vegetables, fruit; cattle, poultry
Industries: tourism, light industry, ready mixed concrete
Industrial production growth rate: NA
Electricity - production: NA kWh
Electricity - production by source:
fossil fuel: 0%
hydro: 0%
nuclear: 0%
other: 0% (2002)
Electricity - consumption: NA kWh
Exports: $1.5 million f.o.b. (FY91/92)
Exports - partners: Australia, other Pacific island countries, NZ, Asia, Europe (2004)
Imports: $17.9 million c.i.f. (FY91/92)
Imports - partners: Australia, other Pacific island countries, NZ, Asia, Europe (2004)
Debt - external: NA
Economic aid - recipient: NA
Currency (code): Australian dollar (AUD)
Currency code: AUD
Exchange rates: Australian dollars per US dollar - 1.31 (2005), 1.3598 (2004), 1.5419 (2003), 1.8406 (2002), 1.9334 (2001)
Fiscal year: 1 July - 30 June

COMMUNICATIONS

Telephones - main lines in use: 2,532; note - a mix of analog (2500) and digital (32) circuits (2004)
Telephones - mobile cellular: 0 (proposed cellular service disallowed in August 2002 island referendum) (2002)
Telephone system:
general assessment: adequate
domestic: free local calls
international: country code - 672; undersea coaxial cable links with Australia, New Zealand, and Canada; satellite earth station
Radio broadcast stations: AM 1, FM 3, shortwave 0 (2005)
Radios: 2,500 (1996)
Television broadcast stations: 1 (local programming station plus two repeaters that bring in Australian programs by satellite) (2005)
Televisions: 1,200 (1996)
Internet country code: .nf
Internet Service Providers (ISPs): 2 (2000)
Internet users: 700

TRANSPORTATION

Airports: 1 (2004 est.)
Airports - with paved runways:
total: 1
1,524 to 2,437 m: 1 (2005 est.)
Roadways:
total: 80 km
paved: 53 km
unpaved: 27 km (2001)
Ports and terminals: none; loading jetties at Kingston and Cascade

MILITARY

Military - note: defense is the responsibility of Australia

TRANSNATIONAL ISSUES

Disputes - international: none

NORTHERN MARIANA ISLANDS

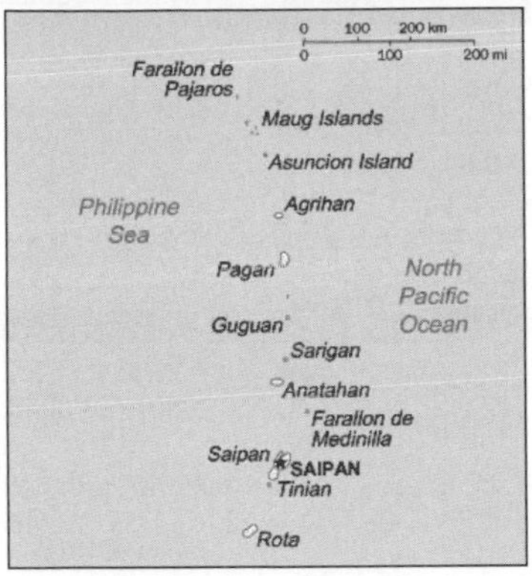

INTRODUCTION

Background: Under US administration as part of the UN Trust Territory of the Pacific, the people of the Northern Mariana Islands decided in the 1970s not to seek independence but instead to forge closer links with the US. Negotiations for territorial status began in 1972. A covenant to establish a commonwealth in political union with the US was approved in 1975. A new government and constitution went into effect in 1978.

GEOGRAPHY

Location: Oceania, islands in the North Pacific Ocean, about three-quarters of the way from Hawaii to the Philippines
Geographic coordinates: 15 12 N, 145 45 E
Map references: Oceania
Area:
total: 477 sq km
land: 477 sq km
water: 0 sq km
note: includes 14 islands including Saipan, Rota, and Tinian
Area - comparative: 2.5 times the size of Washington, DC
Land boundaries: 0 km
Coastline: 1,482 km
Maritime claims:
territorial sea: 12 nm
exclusive economic zone: 200 nm
Climate: tropical marine; moderated by northeast trade winds, little seasonal temperature variation; dry season December to June, rainy season July to October
Terrain: southern islands are limestone with level terraces and fringing coral reefs; northern islands are volcanic
Elevation extremes:
lowest point: Pacific Ocean 0 m
highest point: unnamed location on Agrihan 965 m
Natural resources: arable land, fish
Land use:
arable land: 13.04%
permanent crops: 4.35%
other: 82.61% (2001)
Irrigated land: NA
Natural hazards: active volcanoes on Pagan and Agrihan; typhoons (especially August to November)
Environment - current issues: contamination of groundwater on Saipan may contribute to disease; clean-up of landfill; protection of endangered species conflicts with development
Geography - note: strategic location in the North Pacific Ocean

PEOPLE

Population: 80,362 (July 2005 est.)
Age structure:
0-14 years: 19.9% (male 8,332/female 7,646)
15-64 years: 78.5% (male 26,121/female 36,982)
65 years and over: 1.6% (male 646/female 635) (2005 est.)
Median age:
total: 29.33 years
male: 31.54 years
female: 28.33 years (2005 est.)
Population growth rate: 2.61% (2005 est.)
Birth rate: 19.51 births/1,000 population (2005 est.)
Death rate: 2.3 deaths/1,000 population (2005 est.)
Net migration rate: 8.92 migrant(s)/ 1,000 population (2005 est.)
Sex ratio:
at birth: 1.06 male(s)/female
under 15 years: 1.09 male(s)/female
15-64 years: 0.71 male(s)/female
65 years and over: 1.02 male(s)/female
total population: 0.78 male(s)/female (2005 est.)
Infant mortality rate:
total: 7.11 deaths/1,000 live births
male: 7.05 deaths/1,000 live births
female: 7.17 deaths/1,000 live births (2005 est.)
Life expectancy at birth:
total population: 75.88 years
male: 73.31 years
female: 78.61 years (2005 est.)
Total fertility rate: 1.27 children born/ woman (2005 est.)
HIV/AIDS - adult prevalence rate: NA
HIV/AIDS - people living with HIV/AIDS: NA
HIV/AIDS - deaths: NA
Nationality:
noun: NA
adjective: NA
Ethnic groups: Asian 56.3%, Pacific islander 36.3%, Caucasian 1.8%, other 0.8%, mixed 4.8% (2000 census)
Religions: Christian (Roman Catholic majority, although traditional beliefs and taboos may still be found)
Languages: Philippine languages 24.4%, Chinese 23.4%, Chamorro 22.4%, English 10.8%, other Pacific island languages 9.5%, other 9.6% (2000 census)
Literacy:
definition: age 15 and over can read and write
total population: 97%
male: 97%
female: 96% (1980 est.)

GOVERNMENT

Country name:
conventional long form: Commonwealth of the Northern Mariana Islands
conventional short form: Northern Mariana Islands
former: Mariana Islands District (Trust Territory of the Pacific Islands)
Dependency status: commonwealth in political union with the US; federal funds to the Commonwealth administered by the US Department of the Interior, Office of Insular Affairs
Government type: commonwealth; self-governing with locally elected governor, lieutenant governor, and legislature
Capital: Saipan
Administrative divisions: none (commonwealth in political union with the US); there are no first-order administrative divisions as defined by the US Government, but there are four municipalities at the second order: Northern Islands, Rota, Saipan, Tinian
Independence: none (commonwealth in political union with the US)
National holiday: Commonwealth Day, 8 January (1978)
Constitution: Constitution of the Commonwealth of the Northern Mariana Islands effective 1 January 1978; Covenant Agreement effective 4 November 1986
Legal system: based on US system, except for customs, wages, immigration laws, and taxation
Suffrage: 18 years of age; universal; indigenous inhabitants are US citizens but do not vote in US presidential elections
Executive branch:
chief of state: President George W. BUSH of the US (since 20 January 2001); Vice President Richard B. CHENEY (since 20 January 2001)
head of government: Governor Juan N. BABAUTA (since 14 January 2002); Lieutenant Governor Diego T. BENAVENTE (since 14 January 2002)
cabinet: NA

elections: US president and vice president elected on the same ticket for four-year terms; governor and lieutenant governor elected on the same ticket by popular vote for four-year terms; election last held 5 November 2005 (next to be held November 2009)
election results: Benigno R. FITIAL elected governor in a four-way race; percent of vote - Benigno R. FITIAL (Covenant Party) 28.07%, Heinz HOFSCHNEIDER (Independent) 27.34%, Juan BABAUTA (Republican) 26.6%, Froilan TENORIO (Democrat) 17.99%; governor-elect takes office on 9 January 2006
Legislative branch: bicameral Legislature consists of the Senate (9 seats; members are elected by popular vote to serve four-year staggered terms) and the House of Representatives (18 seats; members are elected by popular vote to serve two-year terms)
elections: Senate - last held 5 November 2005 (next to be held November 2009); House of Representatives - last held 5 November 2005 (next to be held November 2007)
election results: Senate - percent of vote by party - NA%; seats by party - Covenant Party 3, Republican Party 3, Democratic Party 2, independent 1; House of Representatives - percent of vote by party - NA%; seats by party - Covenant Party 7, Republican Party 7, Democratic Party 2, independent 2
note: the Northern Mariana Islands does not have a nonvoting delegate in the US Congress; instead, it has an elected official or "resident representative" located in Washington, DC; seats by party - Republican Party 1 (Pedro A. TENORIO)
Judicial branch: Commonwealth Supreme Court; Superior Court; Federal District Court
Political parties and leaders: Democratic Party [Dr. Carlos S. CAMACHO]; Republican Party [NA]; Covenant Party [Benigno R. FITIAL]
Political pressure groups and leaders: NA
International organization participation: Interpol (subbureau), SPC
Flag description: blue, with a white, five-pointed star superimposed on the gray silhouette of a latte stone (a traditional foundation stone used in building) in the center, surrounded by a wreath

ECONOMY

Economy - overview: The economy benefits substantially from financial assistance from the US. The rate of funding has declined as locally generated government revenues have grown. The key tourist industry employs about 50% of the work force and accounts for roughly one-fourth of GDP. Japanese tourists predominate. Annual tourist entries have exceeded one-half million in recent years, but financial difficulties in Japan have caused a temporary slowdown. The agricultural sector is made up of cattle ranches and small farms producing coconuts, breadfruit, tomatoes, and melons. Garment production is by far the most important industry with employment of 17,500 mostly Chinese workers and sizable shipments to the US under duty and quota exemptions.
GDP (purchasing power parity): $900 million
note: GDP estimate includes US subsidy (2000 est.)
GDP (official exchange rate): NA
GDP - real growth rate: NA
GDP - per capita: purchasing power parity - $12,500 (2000 est.)
GDP - composition by sector:
agriculture: NA
industry: NA
services: NA
Labor force: 6,006 total indigenous labor force; 2,699 unemployed; 28,717 foreign workers (June 1995)
Labor force - by occupation: NA
Unemployment rate: NA
Population below poverty line: NA
Household income or consumption by percentage share:
lowest 10%: NA
highest 10%: NA
Inflation rate (consumer prices): 1.2% (1997 est.)
Budget:
revenues: $193 million
expenditures: $223 million, including capital expenditures of NA (FY01/02 est.)
Agriculture - products: coconuts, fruits, vegetables; cattle
Industries: tourism, construction, garments, handicrafts
Industrial production growth rate: NA
Electricity - production: NA kWh
Electricity - consumption: NA kWh
Electricity - exports: 0 kWh
Electricity - imports: 0 kWh
Exports: NA
Exports - partners: US (2004)
Imports: NA
Imports - partners: US, Japan (2004)
Debt - external: NA
Economic aid - recipient: extensive funding from US
Currency (code): US dollar (USD)
Currency code: USD
Exchange rates: the US dollar is used
Fiscal year: 1 October - 30 September

COMMUNICATIONS

Telephones - main lines in use: 21,000 (2000)
Telephones - mobile cellular: 3,000 (2000)
Telephone system:
general assessment: NA
domestic: NA
international: country code - 1-670; satellite earth stations - 2 Intelsat (Pacific Ocean)
Radio broadcast stations: AM 2, FM 3, shortwave 1 (2005)
Radios: NA
Television broadcast stations: 1 (on Saipan and one station planned for Rota; in addition, two cable services on Saipan provide varied programming from satellite networks) (1997)
Televisions: NA
Internet country code: .mp
Internet Service Providers (ISPs): 1 (2001)
Internet users: NA

TRANSPORTATION

Airports: 5 (2004 est.)
Airports - with paved runways:
total: 3
2,438 to 3,047 m: 2
1,524 to 2,437 m: 1 (2005 est.)
Airports - with unpaved runways:
total: 2
2,438 to 3,047 m: 1
under 914 m: 1 (2005 est.)
Heliports: 1 (2005 est.)
Roadways:
total: 362 km
paved: NA km
unpaved: NA km (1991)
Ports and terminals: Saipan, Tinian

MILITARY

Military - note: defense is the responsibility of the US

TRANSNATIONAL ISSUES

Disputes - international: none

NORWAY

INTRODUCTION

Background: Two centuries of Viking raids into Europe tapered off following the adoption of Christianity by King Olav TRYGGVASON in 994. Conversion of the Norwegian kingdom occurred over the next several decades. In 1397, Norway was absorbed into a union with Denmark that was to last for more than four centuries. In 1814, Norwegians resisted the cession of their country to Sweden and adopted a new constitution. Sweden then invaded Norway but agreed to let Norway keep its constitution in return for accepting the union under a Swedish king. Rising nationalism throughout the 19th century led to a 1905 referendum granting Norway independence. Although Norway remained neutral in World War I, it suffered heavy losses to its shipping. Norway proclaimed its neutrality at the outset of World War II, but was nonetheless occupied for five years by Nazi Germany (1940-45). In 1949, neutrality was abandoned and Norway became a member of NATO. Discovery of oil and gas in adjacent waters in the late 1960s boosted Norway's economic fortunes. The current focus is on containing spending on the extensive welfare system and planning for the time when petroleum reserves are depleted. In referenda held in 1972 and 1994, Norway rejected joining the EU.

GEOGRAPHY

Location: Northern Europe, bordering the North Sea and the North Atlantic Ocean, west of Sweden
Geographic coordinates: 62 00 N, 10 00 E
Map references: Europe
Area:
total: 324,220 sq km
land: 307,860 sq km
water: 16,360 sq km
Area - comparative: slightly larger than New Mexico
Land boundaries:
total: 2,542 km
border countries: Finland 727 km, Sweden 1,619 km, Russia 196 km
Coastline: 25,148 km (includes mainland 2,650 km, as well as long fjords, numerous small islands, and minor indentations 22,498 km; length of island coastlines 58,133 km)
Maritime claims:
territorial sea: 12 nm
contiguous zone: 10 nm
exclusive economic zone: 200 nm
continental shelf: 200 nm
Climate: temperate along coast, modified by North Atlantic Current; colder interior with increased precipitation and colder summers; rainy year-round on west coast
Terrain: glaciated; mostly high plateaus and rugged mountains broken by fertile valleys; small, scattered plains; coastline deeply indented by fjords; arctic tundra in north
Elevation extremes:
lowest point: Norwegian Sea 0 m
highest point: Galdhopiggen 2,469 m
Natural resources: petroleum, natural gas, iron ore, copper, lead, zinc, titanium, pyrites, nickel, fish, timber, hydropower
Land use:
arable land: 2.87%
permanent crops: 0%
other: 97.13% (2001)
Irrigated land: 1,270 sq km (1998 est.)
Natural hazards: rockslides, avalanches
Environment - current issues: water pollution; acid rain damaging forests and adversely affecting lakes, threatening fish stocks; air pollution from vehicle emissions
Environment - international agreements:
party to: Air Pollution, Air Pollution-Nitrogen Oxides, Air Pollution-Persistent Organic Pollutants, Air Pollution-Sulfur 85, Air Pollution-Sulfur 94, Air Pollution-Volatile Organic Compounds, Antarctic-Environmental Protocol, Antarctic-Marine Living Resources, Antarctic Seals, Antarctic Treaty, Biodiversity, Climate Change, Climate Change-Kyoto Protocol, Desertification, Endangered Species, Environmental Modification, Hazardous Wastes, Law of the Sea, Marine Dumping, Ozone Layer Protection, Ship Pollution, Tropical Timber 83, Tropical Timber 94, Wetlands, Whaling
signed, but not ratified: none of the selected agreements
Geography - note: about two-thirds mountains; some 50,000 islands off its much indented coastline; strategic location adjacent to sea lanes and air routes in North Atlantic; one of most rugged and longest coastlines in world

PEOPLE

Population: 4,593,041 (July 2005 est.)
Age structure:
0-14 years: 19.5% (male 459,418/female 437,734)
15-64 years: 65.7% (male 1,531,249/female 1,484,656)
65 years and over: 14.8% (male 286,343/female 393,641) (2005 est.)
Median age:
total: 38.17 years
male: 37.29 years
female: 39.07 years (2005 est.)
Population growth rate: 0.4% (2005 est.)
Birth rate: 11.67 births/1,000 population (2005 est.)
Death rate: 9.45 deaths/1,000 population (2005 est.)
Net migration rate: 1.73 migrant(s)/1,000 population (2005 est.)
Sex ratio:
at birth: 1.05 male(s)/female
under 15 years: 1.05 male(s)/female
15-64 years: 1.03 male(s)/female
65 years and over: 0.73 male(s)/female
total population: 0.98 male(s)/female (2005 est.)
Infant mortality rate:
total: 3.7 deaths/1,000 live births
male: 4.07 deaths/1,000 live births
female: 3.32 deaths/1,000 live births (2005 est.)
Life expectancy at birth:
total population: 79.4 years
male: 76.78 years
female: 82.17 years (2005 est.)
Total fertility rate: 1.78 children born/woman (2005 est.)
HIV/AIDS - adult prevalence rate: 0.1% (2001 est.)
HIV/AIDS - people living with HIV/AIDS: 2,100 (2001 est.)
HIV/AIDS - deaths: less than 100 (2003 est.)
Nationality:
noun: Norwegian(s)
adjective: Norwegian

Ethnic groups: Norwegian, Sami 20,000
Religions: Church of Norway 85.7%, Pentecostal 1%, Roman Catholic 1%, other Christian 2.4%, Muslim 1.8%, other 8.1% (2004)
Languages: Bokmal Norwegian (official), Nynorsk Norwegian (official), small Sami- and Finnish-speaking minorities
Literacy:
definition: age 15 and over can read and write
total population: 100%
male: 100%
female: 100%

GOVERNMENT

Country name:
conventional long form: Kingdom of Norway
conventional short form: Norway
local long form: Kongeriket Norge
local short form: Norge
Government type: constitutional monarchy
Capital: Oslo
Administrative divisions: 19 counties (fylker, singular - fylke); Akershus, Aust-Agder, Buskerud, Finnmark, Hedmark, Hordaland, More og Romsdal, Nordland, Nord-Trondelag, Oppland, Oslo, Ostfold, Rogaland, Sogn og Fjordane, Sor-Trondelag, Telemark, Troms, Vest-Agder, Vestfold
Dependent areas: Bouvet Island, Jan Mayen, Svalbard
Independence: 7 June 1905 (Norway declared the union with Sweden dissolved); 26 October 1905 (Sweden agreed to the repeal of the union)
National holiday: Constitution Day, 17 May (1814)
Constitution: 17 May 1814; amended many times
Legal system: mixture of customary law, civil law system, and common law traditions; Supreme Court renders advisory opinions to legislature when asked; accepts compulsory ICJ jurisdiction, with reservations
Suffrage: 18 years of age, universal
Executive branch:
chief of state: King HARALD V (since 17 January 1991); Heir Apparent Crown Prince HAAKON MAGNUS, son of the monarch (born 20 July 1973)
head of government: Prime Minister Jens STOLTENBERG (since 17 October 2005)
cabinet: State Council appointed by the monarch with the approval of parliament
elections: none; the monarch is hereditary; following parliamentary elections, the leader of the majority party or the leader of the majority coalition is usually appointed prime minister by the monarch with the approval of the parliament
Legislative branch: modified unicameral Parliament or Storting (169 seats; members are elected by popular vote by proportional representation to serve four-year terms)
elections: last held 12 September 2005 (next to be held September 2009)
election results: percent of vote by party - Labor Party 32.7%, Progress Party 22.1%, Conservative Party 14.1%, Socialist Left Party 8.8%, Christian People's Party 6.8%, Center Party 6.5%, Liberal Party 5.9%, Red Electoral Alliance 1.2%, other 1.9%; seats by party - Labor Party 61, Progress Party 38, Conservative Party 23, Socialist Left Party 15, Christian People's Party 11, Center Party 11, Liberal Party 10
note: for certain purposes, the parliament divides itself into two chambers and elects one-fourth of its membership to an upper house or Lagting
Judicial branch: Supreme Court or Hoyesterett (justices appointed by the monarch)
Political parties and leaders: Center Party [Aslaug Marie HAGA]; Christian People's Party [Dagfinn HOYBRATEN]; Coastal Party [Roy WAAGE]; Conservative Party [Erna SOLBERG]; Labor Party [Jens STOLTENBERG]; Liberal Party [Lars SPONHEIM]; Progress Party [Carl I. HAGEN]; Socialist Left Party [Kristin HALVORSEN]
Political pressure groups and leaders: NA
International organization participation: AfDB, AsDB, Australia Group, BIS, CBSS, CE, CERN, EAPC, EBRD, EFTA, ESA, FAO, IADB, IAEA, IBRD, ICAO, ICC, ICCt, ICFTU, ICRM, IDA, IEA, IFAD, IFC, IFRCS, IHO, ILO, IMF, IMO, Interpol, IOC, IOM, ISO, ITU, MIGA, NAM (guest), NATO, NC, NEA, NIB, NSG, OAS (observer), OECD, OPCW, OSCE, Paris Club, PCA, UN, UNCTAD, UNESCO, UNHCR, UNIDO, UNMEE, UNMIS, UNTSO, UPU, WCO, WEU (associate), WHO, WIPO, WMO, WTO, ZC
Diplomatic representation in the US:
chief of mission: Ambassador Knut VOLLEBAEK
chancery: 2720 34th Street NW, Washington, DC 20008
telephone: [1] (202) 333-6000
FAX: [1] (202) 337-0870
consulate(s) general: Houston, Minneapolis, New York, and San Francisco
Diplomatic representation from the US:
chief of mission: Ambassador Ben K. WHITNEY
embassy: Drammensveien 18, 0244 Oslo; note - the embassy will move to Huseby in the near future
mailing address: PSC 69, Box 1000, APO AE 09707
telephone: [47] (22) 44 85 50
FAX: [47] (22) 44 33 63
Flag description: red with a blue cross outlined in white that extends to he edges of the flag; the vertical part of the cross is shifted to the hoist side in the style of the Dannebrog (Danish flag)

ECONOMY

Economy - overview: The Norwegian economy is a prosperous bastion of welfare capitalism, featuring a combination of free market activity and government intervention. The government controls key areas, such as the vital petroleum sector (through large-scale state enterprises). The country is richly endowed with natural resources - petroleum, hydropower, fish, forests, and minerals - and is highly dependent on its oil production and international oil prices, with oil and gas accounting for one-third of exports. Only Saudi Arabia and Russia export more oil than Norway. Norway opted to stay out of the EU during a referendum in November 1994; nonetheless, it contributes sizably to the EU budget. The government has moved ahead with privatization. Norwegians worry about that time in the next two decades when the oil and gas will begin to run out; accordingly, Norway has been saving its oil-boosted budget surpluses in a Government Petroleum Fund, which is invested abroad and now is valued at more than $150 billion. After lackluster growth of 1% in 2002 and 0.5% in 2003, GDP growth picked up to 3.3% in 2004 and to 3.8% in 2005.
GDP (purchasing power parity): $194.7 billion (2005 est.)
GDP (official exchange rate): $264.6 billion (2005 est.)
GDP - real growth rate: 3.8% (2005 est.)
GDP - per capita: purchasing power parity - $42,400 (2005 est.)
GDP - composition by sector:
agriculture: 2.2%
industry: 37.2%
services: 60.6% (2005 est.)
Labor force: 2.4 million (2005 est.)
Labor force - by occupation: agriculture, forestry, and fishing 4%, industry 22%, services 74% (1995)
Unemployment rate: 4.2% (2005 est.)
Population below poverty line: NA
Household income or consumption by percentage share:
lowest 10%: 4.1%
highest 10%: 21.8% (1995)

Distribution of family income - Gini index: 25.8 (2000)
Inflation rate (consumer prices): 2.1% (2005 est.)
Investment (gross fixed): 18.6% of GDP (2005 est.)
Budget:
revenues: $176.1 billion
expenditures: $131.3 billion, including capital expenditures of NA (2005 est.)
Public debt: 36% of GDP (2005 est.)
Agriculture - products: barley, wheat, potatoes; pork, beef, veal, milk; fish
Industries: petroleum and gas, food processing, shipbuilding, pulp and paper products, metals, chemicals, timber, mining, textiles, fishing
Industrial production growth rate: 2.9% (2005 est.)
Electricity - production: 105.6 billion kWh (2003)
Electricity - production by source:
fossil fuel: 0.4%
hydro: 99.3%
nuclear: 0%
other: 0.4% (2001)
Electricity - consumption: 106.1 billion kWh (2003)
Electricity - exports: 5.6 billion kWh (2003)
Electricity - imports: 13.5 billion kWh (2003)
Oil - production: 3.22 million bbl/day (2005 est.)
Oil - consumption: 257,200 bbl/day (2003 est.)
Oil - exports: 3.466 million bbl/day (2001)
Oil - imports: 88,870 bbl/day (2001)
Oil - proved reserves: 9.859 billion bbl (1 January 2002)
Natural gas - production: 54.6 billion cu m (2001 est.)
Natural gas - consumption: 4.1 billion cu m (2001 est.)
Natural gas - exports: 50.5 billion cu m (2001 est.)
Natural gas - imports: 0 cu m (2001 est.)
Natural gas - proved reserves: 1.716 trillion cu m (1 January 2002)
Current account balance: $51.5 billion (2005 est.)
Exports: $111.2 billion f.o.b. (2005 est.)
Exports - partners: UK 22.4%, Germany 12.9%, Netherlands 9.9%, France 9.6%, US 8.4%, Sweden 6.7% (2004)
Imports: $58.12 billion f.o.b. (2005 est.)
Imports - partners: Sweden 15.7%, Germany 13.6%, Denmark 7.3%, UK 6.5%, China 5%, US 4.9%, Netherlands 4.4%, France 4.3%, Finland 4.1% (2004)
Reserves of foreign exchange and gold: $43.94 billion (2004 est.)
Debt - external: $281 billion (Norway is a net external creditor) (30 June 2005)
Economic aid - donor: ODA, $1.4 billion (1998)
Currency (code): Norwegian krone (NOK)
Currency code: NOK
Exchange rates: Norwegian kroner per US dollar - 6.33 (2005), 6.7408 (2004), 7.0802 (2003), 7.9838 (2002), 8.9917 (2001)
Fiscal year: calendar year

COMMUNICATIONS

Telephones - main lines in use: 3.343 million (2002)
Telephones - mobile cellular: 4,163,400 (2003)
Telephone system:
general assessment: modern in all respects; one of the most advanced telecommunications networks in Europe
domestic: Norway has a domestic satellite system; moreover, the prevalence of rural areas encourages the wide use of cellular mobile systems instead of fixed-wire systems
international: country code - 47; 2 buried coaxial cable systems; 4 coaxial submarine cables; satellite earth stations - NA Eutelsat, NA Intelsat (Atlantic Ocean), and 1 Inmarsat (Atlantic and Indian Ocean regions); note - Norway shares the Inmarsat earth station with the other Nordic countries (Denmark, Finland, Iceland, and Sweden) (1999)
Radio broadcast stations: AM 5, FM at least 650, shortwave 1 (1998)
Radios: 4.03 million (1997)
Television broadcast stations: 360 (plus 2,729 repeaters) (1995)
Televisions: 2.03 million (1997)
Internet country code: .no
Internet hosts: 593,850 (2004)
Internet Service Providers (ISPs): 13 (2000)
Internet users: 2.288 million (2002)

TRANSPORTATION

Airports: 101 (2004 est.)
Airports - with paved runways:
total: 67
2,438 to 3,047 m: 13
1,524 to 2,437 m: 12
914 to 1,523 m: 13
under 914 m: 29 (2005 est.)
Airports - with unpaved runways:
total: 33
914 to 1,523 m: 6
under 914 m: 27 (2005 est.)
Heliports: 1 (2005 est.)
Pipelines: condensate 411 km; gas 6,199 km; oil 2,213 km; oil/gas/water 746 km; unknown (oil/water) 38 km (2004)
Railways:
total: 4,077 km
standard gauge: 4,077 km 1.435-m gauge (2,518 km electrified) (2004)
Roadways:
total: 91,852 km
paved: 71,185 km (including 178 km of expressways)
unpaved: 20,667 km (2002)
Merchant marine:
total: 740 ships (1,000 GRT or over) 18,820,495 GRT/27,449,456 DWT
by type: bulk carrier 51, cargo 168, chemical tanker 142, combination ore/oil 20, container 3, liquefied gas 81, passenger 5, passenger/cargo 113, petroleum tanker 79, refrigerated cargo 6, roll on/roll off 30, vehicle carrier 42
foreign-owned: 174 (Belgium 1, China 3, Cyprus 5, Denmark 28, Estonia 2, Finland 5, Germany 4, Hong Kong 52, Iceland 3, Italy 3, Japan 3, Lithuania 1, Monaco 1, Netherlands 4, Poland 2, Saudi Arabia 7, Singapore 10, Sweden 24, United States 16)
registered in other countries: 1,117 (2005)
Ports and terminals: Borg Havn, Bergen, Mo i Rana, Molde, Mongstad, Narvik, Oslo, Sture

MILITARY

Military branches: Norwegian Army, Royal Norwegian Navy (includes Coastal Rangers and Coast Guard (Kystvakt)), Royal Norwegian Air Force (Kongelige Norske Luftforsvaret, RNoAF), Home Guard
Military service age and obligation: 18 years of age for compulsory military service; 16 years of age in wartime; 17 years of age for male volunteers; 18 years of age for women; 16 years of age for volunteers to the Home Guard; conscript service obligation - 12 months (2004)
Manpower available for military service: *males age 18-49:* 1,014,592 (2005 est.)
Manpower fit for military service: *males age 18-49:* 827,016 (2005 est.)
Manpower reaching military service age annually: *males:* 29,179 (2005 est.)
Military expenditures - dollar figure: $4,033.5 million (2003)
Military expenditures - percent of GDP: 1.9% (2003)

TRANSNATIONAL ISSUES

Disputes - international: Norway asserts a territorial claim in Antarctica (Queen Maud Land and its continental shelf); despite recent discussions, Russia and Norway continue to dispute their maritime limits in the Barents Sea and Russia's fishing rights beyond Svalbard's territorial limits within the Svalbard Treaty zone

OMAN

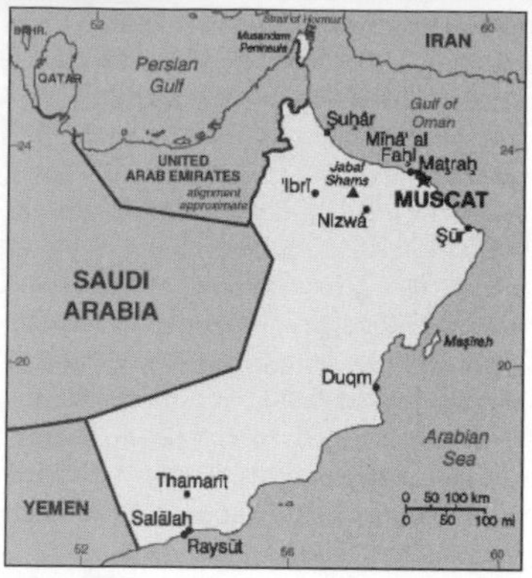

INTRODUCTION

Background: In 1970, QABOOS bin Said Al Said ousted his father and has ruled as sultan ever since. His extensive modernization program has opened the country to the outside world and has preserved a long-standing political and military relationship with the UK. Oman's moderate, independent foreign policy has sought to maintain good relations with all Middle Eastern countries.

GEOGRAPHY

Location: Middle East, bordering the Arabian Sea, Gulf of Oman, and Persian Gulf, between Yemen and UAE
Geographic coordinates: 21 00 N, 57 00 E
Map references: Middle East
Area:
total: 212,460 sq km
land: 212,460 sq km
water: 0 sq km
Area - comparative: slightly smaller than Kansas
Land boundaries:
total: 1,374 km
border countries: Saudi Arabia 676 km, UAE 410 km, Yemen 288 km
Coastline: 2,092 km
Maritime claims:
territorial sea: 12 nm
contiguous zone: 24 nm
exclusive economic zone: 200 nm
Climate: dry desert; hot, humid along coast; hot, dry interior; strong southwest summer monsoon (May to September) in far south
Terrain: central desert plain, rugged mountains in north and south
Elevation extremes:
lowest point: Arabian Sea 0 m
highest point: Jabal Shams 2,980 m
Natural resources: petroleum, copper, asbestos, some marble, limestone, chromium, gypsum, natural gas
Land use:
arable land: 0.12%
permanent crops: 0.14%
other: 99.74% (2001)
Irrigated land: 620 sq km (1998 est.)
Natural hazards: summer winds often raise large sandstorms and dust storms in interior; periodic droughts
Environment - current issues: rising soil salinity; beach pollution from oil spills; very limited natural fresh water resources
Environment - international agreements:
party to: Biodiversity, Climate Change, Climate Change-Kyoto Protocol, Desertification, Hazardous Wastes, Law of the Sea, Marine Dumping, Ozone Layer Protection, Ship Pollution, Whaling
signed, but not ratified: none of the selected agreements
Geography - note: strategic location on Musandam Peninsula adjacent to Strait of Hormuz, a vital transit point for world crude oil

PEOPLE

Population: 3,001,583
note: includes 577,293 non-nationals (July 2005 est.)
Age structure:
0-14 years: 42.6% (male 652,028/female 626,698)
15-64 years: 54.9% (male 978,183/female 668,814)
65 years and over: 2.5% (male 41,366/female 34,494) (2005 est.)
Median age:
total: 19.13 years
male: 21.88 years
female: 16.45 years (2005 est.)
Population growth rate: 3.32% (2005 est.)
Birth rate: 36.73 births/1,000 population (2005 est.)
Death rate: 3.86 deaths/1,000 population (2005 est.)
Net migration rate: 0.31 migrant(s)/1,000 population (2005 est.)
Sex ratio:
at birth: 1.05 male(s)/female
under 15 years: 1.04 male(s)/female
15-64 years: 1.46 male(s)/female
65 years and over: 1.2 male(s)/female
total population: 1.26 male(s)/female (2005 est.)
Infant mortality rate:
total: 19.51 deaths/1,000 live births
male: 22.35 deaths/1,000 live births
female: 16.53 deaths/1,000 live births (2005 est.)
Life expectancy at birth:
total population: 73.13 years
male: 70.92 years
female: 75.46 years (2005 est.)
Total fertility rate: 5.84 children born/woman (2005 est.)
HIV/AIDS - adult prevalence rate: 0.1% (2001 est.)
HIV/AIDS - people living with HIV/AIDS: 1,300 (2001 est.)
HIV/AIDS - deaths: less than 200 (2003 est.)
Nationality:
noun: Omani(s)
adjective: Omani
Ethnic groups: Arab, Baluchi, South Asian (Indian, Pakistani, Sri Lankan, Bangladeshi), African
Religions: Ibadhi Muslim 75%, Sunni Muslim, Shi'a Muslim, Hindu
Languages: Arabic (official), English, Baluchi, Urdu, Indian dialects
Literacy:
definition: NA
total population: 75.8%
male: 83.1%
female: 67.2% (2003 est.)

GOVERNMENT

Country name:
conventional long form: Sultanate of Oman
conventional short form: Oman
local long form: Saltanat Uman
local short form: Uman
former: Muscat and Oman
Government type: monarchy
Capital: Muscat
Administrative divisions: 5 regions (manaatiq, singular - mintaqat) and 3 governorates* (muhaafazaat, singular - muhaafaza) Ad Dakhiliyah, Al Batinah, Al Wusta, Ash Sharqiyah, Az Zahirah, Masqat*, Musandam*, Zufar (Dhofar)*
Independence: 1650 (expulsion of the Portuguese)
National holiday: Birthday of Sultan QABOOS, 18 November (1940)
Constitution: none; note - on 6 November 1996, Sultan QABOOS issued a royal decree promulgating a basic law considered by the government to be a constitution which, among other things, clarifies the royal succession, provides for a prime minister, bars ministers from holding interests in companies doing business with the government, establishes a bicameral legislature, and guarantees basic civil liberties for Omani citizens
Legal system: based on English common law and Islamic law; ultimate appeal to the monarch; has not accepted compulsory ICJ jurisdiction
Suffrage: in Oman's most recent Majlis al-Shura elections in 2003, suffrage was universal for all Omanis over age 21 except for members of the military and security forces; the next Majlis al-Shura elections are scheduled for 2007

Executive branch:
chief of state: Sultan and Prime Minister QABOOS bin Said al-Said (sultan since 23 July 1970 and prime minister since 23 July 1972); note - the monarch is both the chief of state and head of government
head of government: Sultan and Prime Minister QABOOS bin Said al-Said (sultan since 23 July 1970 and prime minister since 23 July 1972); note - the monarch is both the chief of state and head of government
cabinet: Cabinet appointed by the monarch
elections: none; the monarch is hereditary
Legislative branch: bicameral Majlis Oman consists of an upper chamber or Majlis al-Dawla (58 seats; members appointed by the monarch; has advisory powers only) and a lower chamber or Majlis al-Shura (83 seats; members elected by universal suffrage for four-year term; body has some limited power to propose legislation, but otherwise has only advisory powers)
elections: last held 4 October 2003 (next to be held NA 2007)
election results: NA
Judicial branch: Supreme Court
note: the nascent civil court system, administered by region, has judges who practice secular and Sharia (Islamic) law
Political parties and leaders: none
Political pressure groups and leaders: none
International organization participation: ABEDA, AFESD, AMF, FAO, G-77, GCC, IBRD, ICAO, ICCt (signatory), IDA, IDB, IFAD, IFC, IHO, ILO, IMF, IMO, Interpol, IOC, ISO, ITU, LAS, MIGA, NAM, OIC, OPCW, UN, UNCTAD, UNESCO, UNIDO, UPU, WCO, WFTU, WHO, WIPO, WMO, WTO, WToO
Diplomatic representation in the US:
chief of mission: Ambassador Hunaina bint Sultan bin Ahmad al-MUGHAIRI
chancery: 2535 Belmont Road, NW, Washington, DC 20008
telephone: [1] (202) 387-1980 through 1981, 1988
FAX: [1] (202) 745-4933
Diplomatic representation from the US:
chief of mission: Ambassador Richard Lewis BALTIMORE III
embassy: Jameat A'Duwal Al Arabiya Street, Al Khuwair area, Muscat
mailing address: P. O. Box 202, P.C. 115, Madinat Al-Sultan Qaboos, Muscat
telephone: [968] 24-698989
FAX: [968] 24-699771
Flag description: three horizontal bands of white, red, and green of equal width with a broad, vertical, red band on the hoist side; the national emblem (a khanjar dagger in its sheath superimposed on two crossed swords in scabbards) in white is centered near the top of the vertical band

ECONOMY

Economy - overview: Oman is a middle-income economy in the Middle East with notable oil and gas resources, a substantial trade surplus, and low inflation. Work on a new liquefied natural gas (LNG) facility progressed in 2005 and will contribute to slightly higher oil and gas exports in 2006. Oman continues to liberalize its markets and joined the World Trade Organization (WTO) in November 2000. To reduce unemployment and limit dependence on foreign labor, the government is encouraging the replacement of foreign expatriate workers with local workers, i.e., Omanization. Training in information technology, business management, and English support this objective. Industrial development plans focus on gas resources, metal manufacturing, petrochemicals, and international transshipment ports. In 2005 Oman signed agreements with several foreign investors to boost oil reserves, build and operate a power plant, and develop a second mobile phone network in the country.
GDP (purchasing power parity): $40.14 billion (2005 est.)
GDP (official exchange rate): $26.05 billion (2005 est.)
GDP - real growth rate: 1.9% (2005 est.)
GDP - per capita: purchasing power parity - $13,400 (2005 est.)
GDP - composition by sector:
agriculture: 2.8%
industry: 40%
services: 57.1% (2005 est.)
Labor force: 920,000 (2002 est.)
Labor force - by occupation: agriculture NA, industry NA, services NA
Unemployment rate: 15% (2004 est.)
Population below poverty line: NA
Household income or consumption by percentage share:
lowest 10%: NA
highest 10%: NA
Inflation rate (consumer prices): 0.4% (2005 est.)
Investment (gross fixed): 17% of GDP (2005 est.)
Budget:
revenues: $14.36 billion
expenditures: $10.61 billion, including capital expenditures of NA (2005 est.)
Public debt: 7.5% of GDP (2005 est.)
Agriculture - products: dates, limes, bananas, alfalfa, vegetables; camels, cattle; fish
Industries: crude oil production and refining, natural and liquefied natural gas (LNG) production, construction, cement, copper, steel, chemicals, optic fiber
Industrial production growth rate: 0.9% (2005 est.)
Electricity - production: 10.3 billion kWh (2003)
Electricity - production by source:
fossil fuel: 100%
hydro: 0%
nuclear: 0%
other: 0% (2001)
Electricity - consumption: 9.582 billion kWh (2003)
Electricity - exports: 0 kWh (2003)
Electricity - imports: 0 kWh (2003)
Oil - production: 769,000 bbl/day (2005 est.)
Oil - consumption: 62,000 bbl/day (2003 est.)
Oil - exports: 721,000 bbl/day (2004)
Oil - imports: NA
Oil - proved reserves: 6.1 billion bbl (2005 est.)
Natural gas - production: 13.77 billion cu m (2001 est.)
Natural gas - consumption: 6.34 billion cu m (2001 est.)
Natural gas - exports: 7.43 billion cu m (2001 est.)
Natural gas - imports: 0 cu m (2001 est.)
Natural gas - proved reserves: 829.7 billion cu m (2005)
Current account balance: $4.459 billion (2005 est.)
Exports: $19.01 billion f.o.b. (2005 est.)
Exports - partners: China 29.5%, South Korea 17.5%, Japan 11.5%, Thailand 10.6%, UAE 7.2% (2004)
Imports: $8.709 billion f.o.b. (2005 est.)
Imports - partners: UAE 21.2%, Japan 16.6%, UK 8.4%, Italy 6%, Germany 5.1%, US 4.7% (2004)
Reserves of foreign exchange and gold: $4.747 billion (2005 est.)
Debt - external: $4.586 billion (2005 est.)
Economic aid - recipient: $76.4 million (1995)
Currency (code): Omani rial (OMR)
Currency code: OMR
Exchange rates: Omani rials per US dollar - 0.39 (2005), 0.3845 (2004), 0.3845 (2003), 0.3845 (2002), 0.3845 (2001)
Fiscal year: calendar year

COMMUNICATIONS

Telephones - main lines in use: 233,900 (2002)
Telephones - mobile cellular: 464,900 (2002)
Telephone system:
general assessment: modern system consisting of open-wire, microwave, and radiotelephone communication stations; limited coaxial cable
domestic: open-wire, microwave, radiotelephone communications, and a domestic satellite system with 8 earth stations
international: country code - 968; satellite earth stations - 2 Intelsat (Indian Ocean) and 1 Arabsat

Radio broadcast stations: AM 3, FM 9, shortwave 2 (1999)
Radios: 1.4 million (1997)
Television broadcast stations: 13 (plus 25 low-power repeaters) (1999)
Televisions: 1.6 million (1997)
Internet country code: .om
Internet hosts: 726 (2003)
Internet Service Providers (ISPs): 1 (2000)
Internet users: 180,000 (2002)

TRANSPORTATION

Airports: 136 (2004 est.)
Airports - with paved runways:
total: 6
over 3,047 m: 4
2,438 to 3,047 m: 1
914 to 1,523 m: 1 (2005 est.)
Airports - with unpaved runways:
total: 131
over 3,047 m: 2
2,438 to 3,047 m: 7
1,524 to 2,437 m: 52
914 to 1,523 m: 35
under 914 m: 35 (2005 est.)
Heliports: 1 (2005 est.)
Pipelines: gas 3,754 km; oil 3,212 km (2004)
Roadways:
total: 34,965 km
paved: 9,673 km (including 550 km of expressways)
unpaved: 25,292 km (2001)
Merchant marine:
total: 1 ships (1,000 GRT or over) 15,430 GRT/6,360 DWT
by type: passenger 1 (2005)
Ports and terminals: Mina' Qabus, Salalah

MILITARY

Military branches: Royal Omani Armed Forces: Royal Army of Oman, Royal Navy of Oman, Royal Air Force of Oman (RAFO) (2005)
Military service age and obligation: 18 years of age for voluntary military service (2001)
Manpower available for military service: *males age 18-49:* 719,871 (2005 est.)
Manpower fit for military service: *males age 18-49:* 581,444 (2005 est.)
Manpower reaching military service age annually: *males:* 26,391 (2005 est.)
Military expenditures - dollar figure: $252.99 million (2004)
Military expenditures - percent of GDP: 11.4% (2003)

TRANSNATIONAL ISSUES

Disputes - international: boundary agreement reportedly signed and ratified with UAE in 2003 for entire border, including Oman's Musandam Peninsula and Al Madhah exclave, but details have not been made public

PACIFIC OCEAN

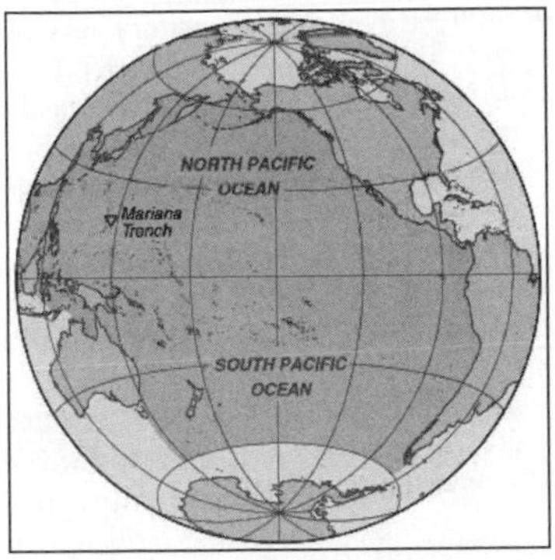

INTRODUCTION

Background: The Pacific Ocean is the largest of the world's five oceans (followed by the Atlantic Ocean, Indian Ocean, Southern Ocean, and Arctic Ocean). Strategically important access waterways include the La Perouse, Tsugaru, Tsushima, Taiwan, Singapore, and Torres Straits. The decision by the International Hydrographic Organization in the spring of 2000 to delimit a fifth ocean, the Southern Ocean, removed the portion of the Pacific Ocean south of 60 degrees south.

GEOGRAPHY

Location: body of water between the Southern Ocean, Asia, Australia, and the Western Hemisphere
Geographic coordinates: 0 00 N, 160 00 W
Map references: Political Map of the World
Area:
total: 155.557 million sq km
note: includes Bali Sea, Bering Sea, Bering Strait, Coral Sea, East China Sea, Gulf of Alaska, Gulf of Tonkin, Philippine Sea, Sea of Japan, Sea of Okhotsk, South China Sea, Tasman Sea, and other tributary water bodies
Area - comparative: about 15 times the size of the US; covers about 28% of the global surface; larger than the total land area of the world
Coastline: 135,663 km
Climate: planetary air pressure systems and resultant wind patterns exhibit remarkable uniformity in the south and east; trade winds and westerly winds are well-developed patterns, modified by seasonal fluctuations; tropical cyclones (hurricanes) may form south of Mexico from June to October and affect Mexico and Central America; continental influences cause climatic uniformity to be much less pronounced in the eastern and western regions at the same latitude in the North Pacific Ocean; the western Pacific is monsoonal - a rainy season occurs during the summer months, when moisture-laden winds blow from the ocean over the land, and a dry season during the winter months, when dry winds blow from the Asian landmass back to the ocean; tropical cyclones (typhoons) may strike southeast and east Asia from May to December
Terrain: surface currents in the northern Pacific are dominated by a clockwise, warm-water gyre (broad circular system of currents) and in the southern Pacific by a counterclockwise, cool-water gyre; in the northern Pacific, sea ice forms in the Bering Sea and Sea of Okhotsk in winter; in the southern Pacific, sea ice from Antarctica reaches its northernmost extent in October; the ocean floor in the eastern Pacific is dominated by the East Pacific Rise, while the western Pacific is dissected by deep trenches, including the Mariana Trench, which is the world's deepest
Elevation extremes:
lowest point: Challenger Deep in the Mariana Trench -10,924 m
highest point: sea level 0 m
Natural resources: oil and gas fields, polymetallic nodules, sand and gravel aggregates, placer deposits, fish
Natural hazards: surrounded by a zone of violent volcanic and earthquake activity sometimes referred to as the "Pacific Ring of Fire"; subject to tropical cyclones (typhoons) in southeast and east Asia from May to December (most frequent from July to October); tropical cyclones (hurricanes) may form south of Mexico and strike Central America and Mexico from June to October (most common in August and September); cyclical El Nino/La Nina phenomenon occurs in the equatorial Pacific, influencing weather in the Western Hemisphere and the western Pacific; ships subject to superstructure icing in extreme north from October to May; persistent fog in the northern Pacific can be a maritime hazard from June to December
Environment - current issues: endangered marine species include the dugong, sea lion, sea otter, seals, turtles, and whales; oil pollution in Philippine Sea and South China Sea
Geography - note: the major chokepoints are the Bering Strait, Panama Canal, Luzon Strait, and the Singapore Strait; the Equator divides the Pacific Ocean into the North Pacific Ocean and the South Pacific Ocean; dotted with low coral islands and rugged volcanic islands in the southwestern Pacific Ocean

ECONOMY

Economy - overview: The Pacific Ocean is a major contributor to the world economy and particularly to those nations its waters directly touch. It provides low-cost sea transportation between East and West, extensive fishing grounds, offshore oil and gas fields, minerals, and sand and gravel for the construction industry. In 1996, over 60% of the world's fish catch came from the Pacific Ocean. Exploitation of offshore oil and gas reserves is playing an ever-increasing role in the energy supplies of the US, Australia, NZ, China, and Peru. The high cost of recovering offshore oil and gas, combined with the wide swings in world prices for oil since 1985, has led to fluctuations in new drillings.

TRANSPORTATION

Ports and terminals: Bangkok (Thailand), Hong Kong (China), Kaohsiung (Taiwan), Los Angeles (US), Manila (Philippines), Pusan (South Korea), San Francisco (US), Seattle (US), Shanghai (China), Singapore, Sydney (Australia), Vladivostok (Russia), Wellington (NZ), Yokohama (Japan)
Transportation - note: Inside Passage offers protected waters from southeast Alaska to Puget Sound (Washington state)

TRANSNATIONAL ISSUES

Disputes - international: some maritime disputes (see littoral states)

PAKISTAN

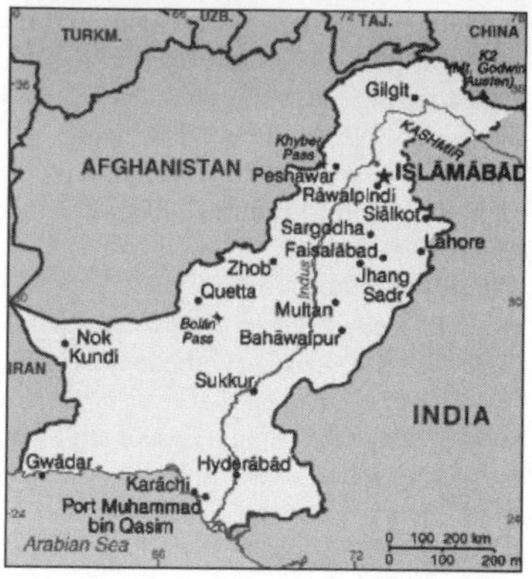

INTRODUCTION

Background: The separation in 1947 of British India into the Muslim state of Pakistan (with two sections West and East) and largely Hindu India was never satisfactorily resolved, and India and Pakistan fought two wars - in 1947-48 and 1965 - over the disputed Kashmir territory. A third war between these countries in 1971 - in which India capitalized on Islamabad's marginalization of Bengalis in Pakistani politics - resulted in East Pakistan becoming the separate nation of Bangladesh. In response to Indian nuclear weapons testing, Pakistan conducted its own tests in 1998. The dispute over the state of Kashmir is ongoing, but discussions and confidence-building measures have led to decreased tensions since 2002.

GEOGRAPHY

Location: Southern Asia, bordering the Arabian Sea, between India on the east and Iran and Afghanistan on the west and China in the north

Geographic coordinates: 30 00 N, 70 00 E

Map references: Asia

Area:
total: 803,940 sq km
land: 778,720 sq km
water: 25,220 sq km

Area - comparative: slightly less than twice the size of California

Land boundaries:
total: 6,774 km
border countries: Afghanistan 2,430 km, China 523 km, India 2,912 km, Iran 909 km

Coastline: 1,046 km

Maritime claims:
territorial sea: 12 nm
contiguous zone: 24 nm
exclusive economic zone: 200 nm
continental shelf: 200 nm or to the edge of the continental margin

Climate: mostly hot, dry desert; temperate in northwest; arctic in north

Terrain: flat Indus plain in east; mountains in north and northwest; Balochistan plateau in west

Elevation extremes:
lowest point: Indian Ocean 0 m
highest point: K2 (Mt. Godwin-Austen) 8,611 m

Natural resources: land, extensive natural gas reserves, limited petroleum, poor quality coal, iron ore, copper, salt, limestone

Land use:
arable land: 27.87%
permanent crops: 0.87%
other: 71.26% (2001)

Irrigated land: 180,000 sq km (1998 est.)

Natural hazards: frequent earthquakes, occasionally severe especially in north and west; flooding along the Indus after heavy rains (July and August)

Environment - current issues: water pollution from raw sewage, industrial wastes, and agricultural runoff; limited natural fresh water resources; a majority of the population does not have access to potable water; deforestation; soil erosion; desertification

Environment - international agreements:
party to: Biodiversity, Climate Change, Climate Change-Kyoto Protocol, Desertification, Endangered Species, Environmental Modification, Hazardous Wastes, Law of the Sea, Marine Dumping, Ozone Layer Protection, Ship Pollution, Wetlands
signed, but not ratified: Marine Life Conservation

Geography - note: controls Khyber Pass and Bolan Pass, traditional invasion routes between Central Asia and the Indian Subcontinent

PEOPLE

Population: 162,419,946 (July 2005 est.)

Age structure:
0-14 years: 39.6% (male 33,104,311/female 31,244,297)
15-64 years: 56.3% (male 46,759,333/female 44,685,828)
65 years and over: 4.1% (male 3,189,122/female 3,437,055) (2005 est.)

Median age:
total: 19.58 years
male: 19.44 years
female: 19.74 years (2005 est.)

Population growth rate: 2.03% (2005 est.)

Birth rate: 30.42 births/1,000 population (2005 est.)

Death rate: 8.45 deaths/1,000 population (2005 est.)

Net migration rate: -1.67 migrant(s)/1,000 population (2005 est.)

Sex ratio:
at birth: 1.05 male(s)/female
under 15 years: 1.06 male(s)/female
15-64 years: 1.05 male(s)/female
65 years and over: 0.93 male(s)/female
total population: 1.05 male(s)/female (2005 est.)

Infant mortality rate:
total: 72.44 deaths/1,000 live births
male: 72.84 deaths/1,000 live births
female: 72.03 deaths/1,000 live births (2005 est.)

Life expectancy at birth:
total population: 63 years
male: 62.04 years
female: 64.01 years (2005 est.)

Total fertility rate: 4.14 children born/woman (2005 est.)

HIV/AIDS - adult prevalence rate: 0.1% (2001 est.)

HIV/AIDS - people living with HIV/AIDS: 74,000 (2001 est.)

HIV/AIDS - deaths: 4,900 (2003 est.)

Major infectious diseases:
degree of risk: high
food or waterborne diseases: bacterial diarrhea, hepatitis A and E, and typhoid fever
vectorborne diseases: dengue fever, malaria, and cutaneous leishmaniasis are high risks depending on location
animal contact disease: rabies (2004)

Nationality:
noun: Pakistani(s)
adjective: Pakistani

Ethnic groups: Punjabi, Sindhi, Pashtun (Pathan), Baloch, Muhajir (immigrants from India at the time of partition and their descendants)

Religions: Muslim 97% (Sunni 77%, Shi'a 20%), Christian, Hindu, and other 3%

Languages: Punjabi 48%, Sindhi 12%, Siraiki (a Punjabi variant) 10%, Pashtu 8%, Urdu (official) 8%, Balochi 3%, Hindko 2%, Brahui 1%, English (official and lingua franca of Pakistani elite and most government ministries), Burushaski, and other 8%

Literacy:
definition: age 15 and over can read and write
total population: 48.7%
male: 61.7%
female: 35.2% (2004 est.)

GOVERNMENT

Country name:
conventional long form: Islamic Republic of Pakistan
conventional short form: Pakistan
former: West Pakistan

Government type: federal republic

Capital: Islamabad

Administrative divisions: 4 provinces, 1

territory*, and 1 capital territory**; Balochistan, Federally Administered Tribal Areas*, Islamabad Capital Territory**, North-West Frontier Province, Punjab, Sindh
note: the Pakistani-administered portion of the disputed Jammu and Kashmir region consist of two administrative entities: Azad Kashmir and Northern Areas
Independence: 14 August 1947 (from UK)
National holiday: Republic Day, 23 March (1956)
Constitution: 12 April 1973; suspended 5 July 1977, restored with amendments 30 December 1985; suspended 15 October 1999, restored 31 December 2002; amended 31 December 2003
Legal system: based on English common law with provisions to accommodate Pakistan's status as an Islamic state; accepts compulsory ICJ jurisdiction, with reservations
Suffrage: 18 years of age; universal; joint electorates and reserved parliamentary seats for women and non-Muslims
Executive branch:
note: following a military takeover on 12 October 1999, Chief of Army Staff and Chairman of the Joint Chiefs of Staff Committee, General Pervez MUSHARRAF, suspended Pakistan's constitution and assumed the additional title of Chief Executive; on 12 May 2000, Pakistan's Supreme Court unanimously validated the October 1999 coup and granted MUSHARRAF executive and legislative authority for three years from the coup date; on 20 June 2001, MUSHARRAF named himself as president and was sworn in, replacing Mohammad Rafiq TARAR; in a referendum held on 30 April 2002, MUSHARRAF's presidency was extended by five more years; on 1 January 2004, MUSHARRAF won a vote of confidence in the Senate, National Assembly, and four provincial assemblies
chief of state: President General Pervez MUSHARRAF (since 20 June 2001)
head of government: Prime Minister Shaukat AZIZ (since 28 August 2004)
cabinet: Cabinet appointed by the prime minister
elections: the president is elected by Parliament for a five-year term; note - in a referendum held on 30 April 2002, MUSHARRAF's presidency was extended by five more years (next to be held NA 2007); the prime minister is selected by the National Assembly for a five-year term (next to be held NA 2007)
election results: AZIZ elected by the National Assembly on 27 August 2004 with 191 of the votes
Legislative branch: bicameral Parliament or Majlis-e-Shoora consists of the Senate (100 seats - formerly 87; members indirectly elected by provincial assemblies to serve four-year terms; and the National Assembly (342 seats - formerly 217; 60 seats represent women; 10 seats represent minorities; members elected by popular vote to serve four-year terms)
elections: Senate - last held 24 and 27 February 2003 (next to be held March 2006); National Assembly - last held 10 October 2002 (next to be held by October 2006)
election results: Senate results - percent of vote by party - NA%; seats by party - PML/Q 40, PPPP 11, MMA 21, MQM/A 6, PML/N 4, NA 3, PML/F 1, PkMAP 2, ANP 2, PPP/S 2, JWP 1, BNP-Awami 1, BNP-Mengal 1, BNM/H 1, independents 4; National Assembly results - percent of votes by party - NA%; seats by party - PML/Q 126, PPPP 81, MMA 63, PML/N 19, MQM/A 17, NA 16, PML/F 5, PML/J 3, PPP/S 2, BNP 1, JWP 1, PAT 1, PML/Z 1, PTI 1, MQM/H 1, PkMAP 1, independents 3
Judicial branch: Supreme Court (justices appointed by the president); Federal Islamic or Shari'a Court
Political parties and leaders: Awami National Party or ANP [Wali KHAN]; Balochistan National Movement/Hayee Group or BNM/H [Dr. Hayee BALUCH]; Baluch National Party/Awami or BNP/Awami [Moheem Khan BALOCH]; Baluch National Party-Mengal or BNP/M [Sardar Ataullah MENGAL]; Jamhoori Watan Party or JWP [Akbar Khan BUGTI]; Jamiat-al-Hadith or JAH [Sajid MIR]; Jamiat-i-Islami or JI [Qazi Hussain AHMED]; Jamiat Ulema-i-Islam, Fazlur Rehman faction or JUI/F [Fazlur REHMAN]; Jamiat Ulema-i-Islam, Sami ul-HAQ faction or JUI/S [Sami ul-HAQ]; Jamiat Ulema-i-Pakistan or JUP [Shah Faridul HAQ]; Muttahida Majlis-e-Amal Pakistan or MMA [Qazi Hussain AHMED]; Muttahida Qaumi Movement, Altaf faction or MQM/A [Altaf HUSSAIN]; Muttahida Quami Movement, Haqiqi faction or MQM/H [Afaq AHMAD]; National People's Party or NPP [Ghulam Mustapha JATOI]; Pakhtun Khwa Milli Awami Party or PkMAP [Mahmood Khan ACHAKZAI]; Pakhtun Quami Party or PQP [Mohammed Afzal KHAN]; Pakistan Awami Tehrik or PAT [Tahir ul QADRI]; Pakistan Democratic Party or PDP [Mehbooba Mufti SAYEED]; Pakistan Muslim League, Functional Group or PML/F [Pir PAGARO]; Pakistan Muslim League, Nawaz Sharif faction or PML/N [Nawaz SHARIF]; Pakistan Muslim League or PML [Chaudhry Shujaat HUSSAIN]; note - as of May 2004, the PML/Q changed its name to PML and absorbed the PML/J, PML/Z, and NA; Pakistan National Party or PNP [Hasil BIZENJO]; Pakistan People's Party or PPP [Aftab Ahmed Khan SHERPAO]; Pakistan People's Party Parliamentarians or PPPP [Benazir BHUTTO]; Pakistan Tehrik-e-Insaaf or PTI [Imran KHAN]; Tehrik-i-Islami [Allama Sajid NAQVI]
note: political alliances in Pakistan can shift frequently
Political pressure groups and leaders: military remains most important political force; ulema (clergy), landowners, industrialists, and small merchants also influential
International organization participation: ARF, AsDB, C (reinstated 2004), CP, ECO, FAO, G-24, G-77, IAEA, IBRD, ICAO, ICC, ICFTU, ICRM, IDA, IDB, IFAD, IFC, IFRCS, IHO, ILO, IMF, IMO, Interpol, IOC, IOM, ISO, ITU, MIGA, MINURSO, MONUC, NAM, OAS (observer), OIC, ONUB, OPCW, PCA, SAARC, SACEP, SCO (observer), UN, UNAMSIL, UNCTAD, UNESCO, UNHCR, UNIDO, UNITAR, UNMIL, UNMIS, UNOCI, UNOMIG, UPU, WCL, WCO, WFTU, WHO, WIPO, WMO, WToO, WTO
Diplomatic representation in the US:
chief of mission: Ambassador Jehangir KARAMAT
chancery: 3517 International Court, Washington, DC 20008
telephone: [1] (202) 243-6500
FAX: [1] (202) 686-1534
consulate(s) general: Los Angeles, New York, Sunnyvale (California)
consulate(s): Chicago, Houston
Diplomatic representation from the US:
chief of mission: Ambassador Ryan CROCKER
embassy: Diplomatic Enclave, Ramna 5, Islamabad
mailing address: P. O. Box 1048, Unit 62200, APO AE 09812-2200
telephone: [92] (51) 2080-0000
FAX: [92] (51) 2276427
consulate(s): Karachi, Lahore, Peshawar
Flag description: green with a vertical white band (symbolizing the role of religious minorities) on the hoist side; a large white crescent and star are centered in the green field; the crescent, star, and color green are traditional symbols of Islam

ECONOMY

Economy - overview: Pakistan, an impoverished and underdeveloped country, has suffered from decades of internal political disputes, low levels of foreign investment, and a costly, ongoing confrontation with neighboring India. However, IMF-approved government policies, bolstered by generous foreign assistance and renewed access to global markets since 2001, have generated solid macroeconomic recovery the last four years. The government has made substantial macroeconomic reforms since 2000, although progress on more politically sensitive reforms has slowed. For example, in the budget for fiscal year 2006, Islamabad did not impose taxes on the agriculture or real estate sectors, despite Pakistan's chronically low tax-to-GDP ratio. While long-term prospects remain uncertain, given Pakistan's low level of development, medium-term prospects for job creation and poverty reduction are the best in more than a decade. Islamabad has raised development spending from about 2% of GDP in the 1990s to 4% in 2003, a necessary step towards reversing the broad underdevelopment of its social sector. GDP growth, spurred by double-digit gains in industrial production over the past year, has become less dependent on agriculture, and remained above 7% in 2004 and 2005. Inflation remains the biggest threat to the economy, jumping to more than 9% in 2005. The World Bank and Asian Development Bank announced that they would provide US $1 billion each in aid to help Pakistan rebuild areas hit by the October 2005 earthquake in Kashmir. Foreign exchange reserves continued to reach new levels in 2005, supported by steady worker remittances.

GDP (purchasing power parity): $385.2 billion (2005 est.)

GDP (official exchange rate): $92.2 billion (2005 est.)

GDP - real growth rate: 8.4% (2005 est.)

GDP - per capita: purchasing power parity - $2,400 (2005 est.)

GDP - composition by sector:
agriculture: 21.6%
industry: 25.1%
services: 53.3% (2005 est.)

Labor force: 46.84 million
note: extensive export of labor, mostly to the Middle East, and use of child labor (2005 est.)

Labor force - by occupation: agriculture 42%, industry 20%, services 38% (2004 est.)

Unemployment rate: 6.6% plus substantial underemployment (2005 est.)

Population below poverty line: 32% (FY00/01 est.)

Household income or consumption by percentage share:
lowest 10%: 4.1%
highest 10%: 27.6% (FY96/97)

Distribution of family income - Gini index: 41 (FY98/99)

Inflation rate (consumer prices): 9.2% (2005 est.)

Investment (gross fixed): 15.3% of GDP (2005 est.)

Budget:
revenues: $15.45 billion
expenditures: $18.42 billion, including capital expenditures of NA (2005 est.)

Public debt: 54.3% of GDP (2005 est.)

Agriculture - products: cotton, wheat, rice, sugarcane, fruits, vegetables; milk, beef, mutton, eggs

Industries: textiles and apparel, food processing, pharmaceuticals, construction materials, paper products, fertilizer, shrimp

Industrial production growth rate: 10.7% (2005 est.)

Electricity - production: 76.92 billion kWh (2003)

Electricity - production by source:
fossil fuel: 68.8%
hydro: 28.2%
nuclear: 3%
other: 0% (2001)

Electricity - consumption: 71.54 billion kWh (2003)

Electricity - exports: 0 kWh (2003)

Electricity - imports: 0 kWh (2003)

Oil - production: 63,000 bbl/day (2005 est.)

Oil - consumption: 365,000 bbl/day (2004 est.)

Oil - exports: NA (2004)

Oil - imports: NA (2004)

Oil - proved reserves: 341.8 million bbl (2005 est.)

Natural gas - production: 23.4 billion cu m (2001 est.)

Natural gas - consumption: 23.4 billion cu m (2001 est.)

Natural gas - exports: 0 cu m (2001 est.)

Natural gas - imports: 0 cu m (2001 est.)

Natural gas - proved reserves: 695.6 billion cu m (2005)

Current account balance: $-1.43 billion (2005 est.)

Exports: $14.85 billion f.o.b. (2005 est.)

Exports - partners: US 23.5%, UAE 7.4%, UK 7.3%, Germany 5%, Hong Kong 4.4% (2004)

Imports: $21.26 billion f.o.b. (2005 est.)

Imports - partners: Saudi Arabia 11.6%, UAE 10%, US 9.7%, China 8.4%, Japan 6.5%, Kuwait 5.6% (2004)

Reserves of foreign exchange and gold: $11.71 billion (2005 est.)

Debt - external: $39.94 billion (2005 est.)

Economic aid - recipient: $2.4 billion (FY01/02)

Currency (code): Pakistani rupee (PKR)

Currency code: PKR

Exchange rates: Pakistani rupees per US dollar - 59.6 (2005), 58.258 (2004), 57.752 (2003), 59.724 (2002), 61.927 (2001)

Fiscal year: 1 July - 30 June

COMMUNICATIONS

Telephones - main lines in use: 3,982,800 (2003)

Telephones - mobile cellular: 2,624,800 (2003)

Telephone system:
general assessment: the domestic system is mediocre, but improving; service is adequate for government and business use, in part because major businesses have established their own private systems; since 1988, the government has promoted investment in the national telecommunications system on a priority basis, significantly increasing network capacity; despite major improvements in trunk and urban systems, telecommunication services are still not readily available to the majority of the rural population
domestic: microwave radio relay, coaxial cable, fiber-optic cable, cellular, and satellite networks
international: country code - 92; satellite earth stations - 3 Intelsat (1 Atlantic Ocean and 2 Indian Ocean); 3 operational international gateway exchanges (1 at Karachi and 2 at Islamabad); microwave radio relay to neighboring countries (1999)

Radio broadcast stations: AM 27, FM 1, shortwave 21 (1998)

Radios: 13.5 million (1997)

Television broadcast stations: 22 (plus seven low-power repeaters) (1997)

Televisions: 3.1 million (1997)

Internet country code: .pk

Internet hosts: 15,124 (2003)

Internet Service Providers (ISPs): 30 (2000)

Internet users: 1.5 million (2002)

TRANSPORTATION

Airports: 131 (2004 est.)

Airports - with paved runways:
total: 91
over 3,047 m: 13
2,438 to 3,047 m: 22
1,524 to 2,437 m: 32
914 to 1,523 m: 16
under 914 m: 8 (2005 est.)

Airports - with unpaved runways:
total: 43
over 3,047 m: 1
1,524 to 2,437 m: 9
914 to 1,523 m: 12
under 914 m: 21 (2005 est.)

Heliports: 18 (2005 est.)

Pipelines: gas 9,945 km; oil 1,821 km (2004)

Railways:
total: 8,163 km
broad gauge: 7,718 km 1.676-m gauge (293 km electrified)
narrow gauge: 445 km 1.000-m gauge (2004)

Roadways:
total: 257,683 km
paved: 152,033 km (including 339 km of expressways)
unpaved: 105,650 km (2001)
Merchant marine:
total: 13 ships (1,000 GRT or over) 329,486 GRT/512,506 DWT
by type: cargo 10, petroleum tanker 3
registered in other countries: 14 (2005)
Ports and terminals: Karachi, Port Muhammad bin Qasim

MILITARY

Military branches: Army, Navy, Air Force
Military service age and obligation: 16 years of age for voluntary military service; soldiers cannot be deployed for combat until age of 18 (2001)
Manpower available for military service:
males age 16-49: 39,028,014 (2005 est.)
Manpower fit for military service: *males age 16-49:* 29,428,747 (2005 est.)
Manpower reaching military service age annually: *males:* 1,969,055 (2005 est.)
Military expenditures - dollar figure: $3.848 billion (2004)
Military expenditures - percent of GDP: 4.9% (2004)

TRANSNATIONAL ISSUES

Disputes - international: recent talks and confidence-building measures have begun to defuse tensions over Kashmir, site of the world's largest and most militarized territorial dispute with portions under the de facto administration of China (Aksai Chin), India (Jammu and Kashmir), and Pakistan (Azad Kashmir and Northern Areas); UN Military Observer Group in India and Pakistan (UNMOGIP) has maintained a small group of peacekeepers since 1949; India does not recognize Pakistan's ceding historic Kashmir lands to China in 1964; in 2004, India and Pakistan instituted a cease fire in the Kashmir, and in 2005 restored bus service across the highly militarized Line of Control; Pakistan has taken its dispute on the impact and benefits of India's building the Baglihar dam on the Chenab River in Jammu and Kashmir to the World Bank for arbitration and in general the two states still dispute Indus River water sharing; to defuse tensions and prepare for discussions on a maritime boundary, India and Pakistan resurveyed a portion of the disputed Sir Creek estuary at the mouth of the Rann of Kutch in 2004; Pakistani maps continue to show Junagadh in India's Gujarat State; by 2005, Pakistan with UN assistance had repatriated 2.3 million Afghan refugees and has undertaken a census to count the remaining million or more, many of whom remain at their own choosing; Pakistan maintains troops in remote tribal areas to control the border with Afghanistan and root out organized terrorist and other illegal cross-border activities; regular meetings with Afghan and Coalition allies aim to resolve periodic claims of boundary encroachments
Refugees and internally displaced persons:
refugees (country of origin): 1,064,230 (Afghanistan)
IDPs: undetermined (government strikes on Islamic militants in South Waziristan) (2004)
Illicit drugs: opium poppy in Federally Administered Tribal Areas, North-West Frontier Province, and Balochistan Province has rebounded since it was nearly eliminated in 2001; key transit point for Afghan drugs, including heroin, opium, morphine, and hashish, bound for Western markets, the Gulf States, and Africa; financial crimes related to drug trafficking, terrorism, corruption, and smuggling remain problems

PALAU

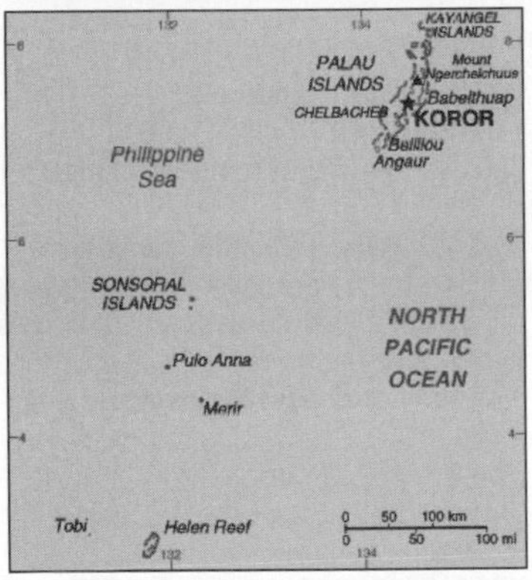

INTRODUCTION

Background: After three decades as part of the UN Trust Territory of the Pacific under US administration, this westernmost cluster of the Caroline Islands opted for independence in 1978 rather than join the Federated States of Micronesia. A Compact of Free Association with the US was approved in 1986, but not ratified until 1993. It entered into force the following year, when the islands gained independence.

GEOGRAPHY

Location: Oceania, group of islands in the North Pacific Ocean, southeast of the Philippines
Geographic coordinates: 7 30 N, 134 30 E
Map references: Oceania
Area:
total: 458 sq km
land: 458 sq km
water: 0 sq km
Area - comparative: slightly more than 2.5 times the size of Washington, DC
Land boundaries: 0 km
Coastline: 1,519 km
Maritime claims:
territorial sea: 3 nm
exclusive fishing zone: 200 nm
Climate: tropical; hot and humid; wet season May to November
Terrain: varying geologically from the high, mountainous main island of Babelthuap to low, coral islands usually fringed by large barrier reefs
Elevation extremes:
lowest point: Pacific Ocean 0 m
highest point: Mount Ngerchelchuus 242 m
Natural resources: forests, minerals (especially gold), marine products, deep-seabed minerals
Land use:
arable land: 8.7%
permanent crops: 4.35%
other: 86.95% (2001)
Irrigated land: NA
Natural hazards: typhoons (June to December)
Environment - current issues: inadequate facilities for disposal of solid waste; threats to the marine ecosystem from sand and coral dredging, illegal fishing practices, and overfishing
Environment - international agreements:
party to: Biodiversity, Climate Change, Climate Change-Kyoto Protocol, Desertification, Law of the Sea, Ozone Layer Protection
signed, but not ratified: none of the selected agreements
Geography - note: westernmost archipelago in the Caroline chain, consists of six island groups totaling more than 300 islands; includes World War II battleground of Beliliou (Peleliu) and world-famous rock islands

PEOPLE

Population: 20,303 (July 2005 est.)
Age structure:
0-14 years: 26.4% (male 2,768/female 2,601)

15-64 years: 69% (male 7,565/female 6,436)
65 years and over: 4.6% (male 443/female 490) (2005 est.)
Median age:
total: 31.43 years
male: 32.4 years
female: 30.36 years (2005 est.)
Population growth rate: 1.39% (2005 est.)
Birth rate: 18.37 births/1,000 population (2005 est.)
Death rate: 6.85 deaths/1,000 population (2005 est.)
Net migration rate: 2.36 migrant(s)/1,000 population (2005 est.)
Sex ratio:
at birth: 1.06 male(s)/female
under 15 years: 1.06 male(s)/female
15-64 years: 1.18 male(s)/female
65 years and over: 0.9 male(s)/female
total population: 1.13 male(s)/female (2005 est.)
Infant mortality rate:
total: 14.84 deaths/1,000 live births
male: 16.6 deaths/1,000 live births
female: 12.99 deaths/1,000 live births (2005 est.)
Life expectancy at birth:
total population: 70.14 years
male: 66.98 years
female: 73.48 years (2005 est.)
Total fertility rate: 2.46 children born/woman (2005 est.)
HIV/AIDS - adult prevalence rate: NA
HIV/AIDS - people living with HIV/AIDS: NA
HIV/AIDS - deaths: NA
Nationality:
noun: Palauan(s)
adjective: Palauan
Ethnic groups: Palauan (Micronesian with Malayan and Melanesian admixtures) 69.9%, Carolinian 1.4%, other Micronesian 1.1%, Filipino 15.3%, Chinese 4.9%, other Asian 2.4%, white 1.9%, other or unspecified 3.2% (2000 census)
Religions: Roman Catholic 41.6%, Protestant 23.3%, Modekngei 8.8% (indigenous to Palau), Seventh-Day Adventist 5.3%, Jehovah's Witness 0.9%, Latter-Day Saints 0.6%, other religion 3.1%, unspecified or none 16.4% (2000 census)
Languages: Palauan 64.7% official in all islands except Sonsoral (Sonsoralese and English are official), Tobi (Tobi and English are official), and Angaur (Angaur, Japanese, and English are official), Filipino 13.5%, English 9.4%, Chinese 5.7%, Carolinian 1.5%, Japanese 1.5%, other Asian 2.3%, other languages 1.5% (2000 census)
Literacy:
definition: age 15 and over can read and write
total population: 92%
male: 93%
female: 90% (1980 est.)

GOVERNMENT

Country name:
conventional long form: Republic of Palau
conventional short form: Palau
local long form: Beluu er a Belau
local short form: Belau
former: Palau District (Trust Territory of the Pacific Islands)
Government type: constitutional government in free association with the US; the Compact of Free Association entered into force 1 October 1994
Capital: Koror; note - a new capital is being built about 20 km northeast of Koror
Administrative divisions: 16 states; Aimeliik, Airai, Angaur, Hatohobei, Kayangel, Koror, Melekeok, Ngaraard, Ngarchelong, Ngardmau, Ngatpang, Ngchesar, Ngeremlengui, Ngiwal, Peleliu, Sonsorol
Independence: 1 October 1994 (from the US-administered UN Trusteeship)
National holiday: Constitution Day, 9 July (1979)
Constitution: 1 January 1981
Legal system: based on Trust Territory laws, acts of the legislature, municipal, common, and customary laws
Suffrage: 18 years of age; universal
Executive branch:
chief of state: President Tommy Esang REMENGESAU, Jr. (since 19 January 2001) and Vice President Camsek CHIN (since 1 January 2005); note - the president is both the chief of state and head of government
head of government: President Tommy Esang REMENGESAU, Jr. (since 19 January 2001) and Vice President Camsek CHIN (since 1 January 2005); note - the president is both the chief of state and head of government
cabinet: Cabinet
elections: president and vice president elected on separate tickets by popular vote for four-year terms; election last held 2 November 2004 (next to be held November 2008)
election results: Tommy Esang REMENGESAU, Jr. reelected president; percent of vote - Tommy Esang REMENGESAU, Jr. 64%, Polycarp BASILIUS 33%; Elias Camsek CHIN elected vice president; percent of vote - Elias Camsek CHIN 70%, Sandra PIERANTOZZI 29%
Legislative branch: bicameral Parliament or Olbiil Era Kelulau (OEK) consists of the Senate (9 seats; members elected by popular vote on a population basis to serve four-year terms) and the House of Delegates (16 seats; members elected by popular vote to serve four-year terms)
elections: Senate - last held 2 November 2004 (next to be held November 2008); House of Delegates - last held 2 November 2004 (next to be held November 2008)
election results: Senate - percent of vote - NA%; seats - independents 9 (four new members elected); House of Delegates - percent of vote - NA%; seats - independents 16 (one new member elected)
Judicial branch: Supreme Court; National Court; Court of Common Pleas
Political parties and leaders: none
Political pressure groups and leaders: NA
International organization participation: ACP, AsDB, FAO, G-77, IBRD, ICAO, ICRM, IDA, IFC, IFRCS, IMF, IOC, MIGA, OPCW, PIF, Sparteca, SPC, UN, UNCTAD, UNESCO, WHO
Diplomatic representation in the US:
chief of mission: Ambassador Hersey KYOTA
chancery: 1800 K Street NW, Suite 714, Washington, DC 20006
telephone: [1] (202) 452-6814
FAX: [1] (202) 452-6281
consulate(s): Tamuning (Guam)
Diplomatic representation from the US:
chief of mission: US ambassador to the Philippines is accredited to Palau
embassy: Koror (no street address)
mailing address: P. O. Box 6028, Republic of Palau 96940
telephone: [680] 488-2920, 2990
FAX: [680] 488-2911
Flag description: light blue with a large yellow disk (representing the moon) shifted slightly to the hoist side

ECONOMY

Economy - overview: The economy consists primarily of tourism, subsistence agriculture, and fishing. The government is the major employer of the work force, relying heavily on financial assistance from the US. Business and tourist arrivals numbered 63,000 in 2003. The population enjoys a per capita income twice that of the Philippines and much of Micronesia. Long-run prospects for the key tourist sector have been greatly bolstered by the expansion of air travel in the Pacific, the rising prosperity of leading East Asian countries, and the willingness of foreigners to finance infrastructure development.
GDP (purchasing power parity): $174 million
note: GDP estimate includes US subsidy (2001 est.)
GDP (official exchange rate): NA
GDP - real growth rate: 1% (2001 est.)
GDP - per capita: purchasing power parity - $9,000 (2001 est.)

GDP - composition by sector:
agriculture: NA
industry: NA
services: NA
Labor force: 9,845 (2000)
Labor force - by occupation: agriculture 20%, industry NA, services NA (1990)
Unemployment rate: 2.3% (2000 est.)
Population below poverty line: NA
Household income or consumption by percentage share:
lowest 10%: NA
highest 10%: NA
Inflation rate (consumer prices): 3.4% (2000 est.)
Budget:
revenues: $57.7 million
expenditures: $80.8 million, including capital expenditures of $17.1 million (FY98/99 est.)
Agriculture - products: coconuts, copra, cassava (tapioca), sweet potatoes
Industries: tourism, craft items (from shell, wood, pearls), construction, garment making
Industrial production growth rate: NA
Electricity - production by source: NA
Exports: $18 million f.o.b. (2001 est.)
Exports - partners: US, Japan, Singapore (2004)
Imports: $99 million f.o.b. (2001 est.)
Imports - partners: US, Guam, Japan, Singapore, South Korea (2004)
Debt - external: $0 (FY99/00)
Economic aid - recipient: $155.8 million; note - the Compact of Free Association with the US, entered into after the end of the UN trusteeship on 1 October 1994, provides Palau with up to $700 million in US aid over 15 years in return for furnishing military facilities
Currency (code): US dollar (USD)
Currency code: USD
Exchange rates: the US dollar is used
Fiscal year: 1 October - 30 September

COMMUNICATIONS

Telephones - main lines in use: 6,700 (2002)
Telephones - mobile cellular: 1,000 (2002)
Telephone system:
general assessment: NA
domestic: NA
international: country code - 680; satellite earth station - 1 Intelsat (Pacific Ocean)
Radio broadcast stations: AM 1, FM 4, shortwave 1 (2002)
Radios: 12,000 (1997)
Television broadcast stations: 1 (cable) (2005)
Televisions: 11,000 (1997)
Internet country code: .pw
Internet Service Providers (ISPs): 1 (2002)

TRANSPORTATION

Airports: 3 (2004 est.)
Airports - with paved runways:
total: 1
1,524 to 2,437 m: 1 (2005 est.)
Airports - with unpaved runways:
total: 2
1,524 to 2,437 m: 2 (2005 est.)
Roadways:
total: 61 km
paved: 36 km
unpaved: 25 km
Ports and terminals: Koror

MILITARY

Military branches: no regular military forces; Police Force
Military expenditures - dollar figure: NA
Military expenditures - percent of GDP: NA
Military - note: defense is the responsibility of the US; under a Compact of Free Association between Palau and the US, the US military is granted access to the islands for 50 years

TRANSNATIONAL ISSUES

Disputes - international: border delineation disputes being negotiated with Philippines, Indonesia

PALMYRA ATOLL

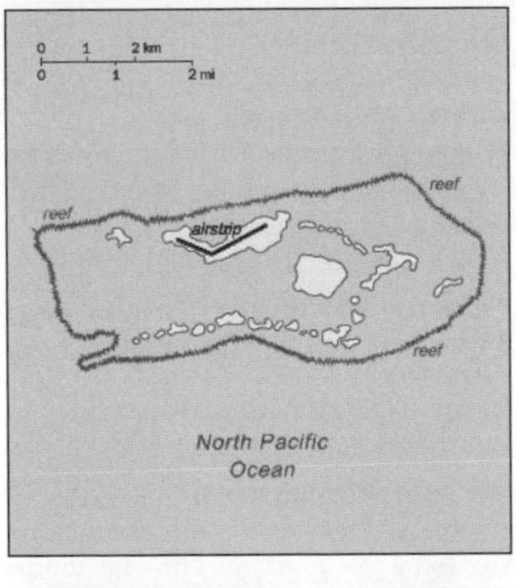

INTRODUCTION

Background: The Kingdom of Hawaii claimed the atoll in 1862, and the US included it among the Hawaiian Islands when it annexed the archipelago in 1898. The Hawaii Statehood Act of 1959 did not include Palmyra Atoll, which is now privately owned by the Nature Conservancy. This organization is managing the atoll as a nature preserve. The lagoons and surrounding waters within the 12 nautical mile US territorial seas were transferred to the US Fish and Wildlife Service and were designated a National Wildlife Refuge in January 2001.

GEOGRAPHY

Location: Oceania, atoll in the North Pacific Ocean, about half way between Hawaii and American Samoa
Geographic coordinates: 5 53 N, 162 05 W
Map references: Oceania
Area:
total: 11.9 sq km
land: 11.9 sq km
water: 0 sq km
Area - comparative: about 20 times the size of The Mall in Washington, DC
Land boundaries: 0 km
Coastline: 14.5 km
Maritime claims:
territorial sea: 12 nm
exclusive economic zone: 200 nm
Climate: equatorial, hot, and very rainy
Terrain: very low
Elevation extremes:
lowest point: Pacific Ocean 0 m
highest point: unnamed location 2 m
Natural resources: terrestrial and aquatic wildlife
Land use:
arable land: 0%
permanent crops: 0%
other: 100% (forests and woodlands) (2005)
Irrigated land: 0 sq km (1998 est.)
Natural hazards: NA
Environment - current issues: NA
Geography - note: about 50 islets covered with dense vegetation, coconut trees, and balsa-like trees up to 30 meters tall

PEOPLE

Population: no indigenous inhabitants; 4 to 20 Nature Conservancy staff, US Fish and Wildlife staff (July 2005 est.)

GOVERNMENT

Country name:
conventional long form: none
conventional short form: Palmyra Atoll
Dependency status: incorporated territory of the US; privately owned, but administered from Washington, DC, by the Fish and Wildlife Service of the US Department of the Interior; the Office of Insular Affairs of the US Department of the Interior continues to administer nine excluded areas comprising certain tidal

and submerged lands within the 12 nm territorial sea or within the lagoon
Legal system: the laws of the US, where applicable, apply
Flag description: the flag of the US is used

ECONOMY

Economy - overview: no economic activity

TRANSPORTATION

Airports: 1 (2004 est.)
Airports - with unpaved runways:
total: 1
1,524 to 2,437 m: 1 (2005 est.)
Roadways: most of the roads and many causeways built during World War II are unserviceable and overgrown (2001)
Ports and terminals: West Lagoon

MILITARY

Military - note: defense is the responsibility of the US

TRANSNATIONAL ISSUES

Disputes - international: none

PANAMA

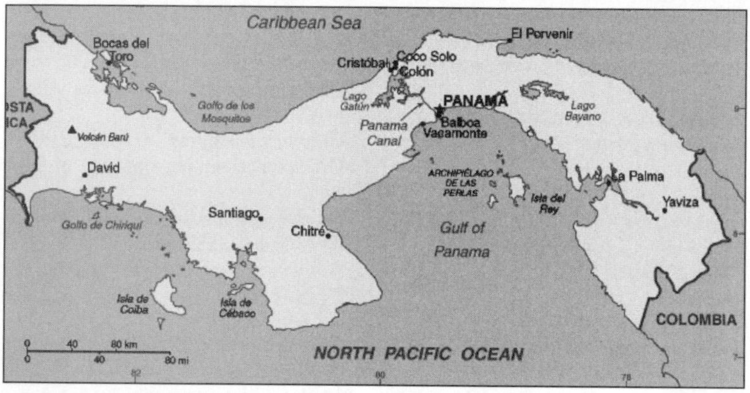

INTRODUCTION

Background: With US backing, Panama seceded from Colombia in 1903 and promptly signed a treaty with the US allowing for the construction of a canal and US sovereignty over a strip of land on either side of the structure (the Panama Canal Zone). The Panama Canal was built by the US Army Corps of Engineers between 1904 and 1914. On 7 September 1977, an agreement was signed for the complete transfer of the Canal from the US to Panama by the end of 1999. Certain portions of the Zone and increasing responsibility over the Canal were turned over in the intervening years. With US help, dictator Manuel NORIEGA was deposed in 1989. The entire Panama Canal, the area supporting the Canal, and remaining US military bases were turned over to Panama by or on 31 December 1999.

GEOGRAPHY

Location: Central America, bordering both the Caribbean Sea and the North Pacific Ocean, between Colombia and Costa Rica
Geographic coordinates: 9 00 N, 80 00 W
Map references: Central America and the Caribbean
Area:
total: 78,200 sq km
land: 75,990 sq km
water: 2,210 sq km
Area - comparative: slightly smaller than South Carolina
Land boundaries:
total: 555 km
border countries: Colombia 225 km, Costa Rica 330 km
Coastline: 2,490 km
Maritime claims:
territorial sea: 12 nm
contiguous zone: 24 nm
exclusive economic zone: 200 nm
Climate: tropical maritime; hot, humid, cloudy; prolonged rainy season (May to January), short dry season (January to May)
Terrain: interior mostly steep, rugged mountains and dissected, upland plains; coastal areas largely plains and rolling hills
Elevation extremes:
lowest point: Pacific Ocean 0 m
highest point: Volcan de Chiriqui 3,475 m
Natural resources: copper, mahogany forests, shrimp, hydropower
Land use:
arable land: 7.36%
permanent crops: 1.98%
other: 90.66% (2001)
Irrigated land: 320 sq km (1998 est.)
Natural hazards: occasional severe storms and forest fires in the Darien area
Environment - current issues: water pollution from agricultural runoff threatens fishery resources; deforestation of tropical rain forest; land degradation and soil erosion threatens siltation of Panama Canal; air pollution in urban areas; mining threatens natural resources
Environment - international agreements:
party to: Biodiversity, Climate Change, Climate Change-Kyoto Protocol, Desertification, Endangered Species, Hazardous Wastes, Law of the Sea, Marine Dumping, Ozone Layer Protection, Ship Pollution, Tropical Timber 83, Tropical Timber 94, Wetlands, Whaling
signed, but not ratified: Marine Life Conservation
Geography - note: strategic location on eastern end of isthmus forming land bridge connecting North and South America; controls Panama Canal that links North Atlantic Ocean via Caribbean Sea with North Pacific Ocean

PEOPLE

Population: 3,039,150 (July 2005 est.)
Age structure:
0-14 years: 29.8% (male 460,840/female 443,359)
15-64 years: 63.9% (male 984,558/female 956,748)
65 years and over: 6.4% (male 91,383/female 102,262) (2005 est.)
Median age:
total: 26.18 years
male: 25.89 years
female: 26.48 years (2005 est.)
Population growth rate: 1.26% (2005 est.)
Birth rate: 19.96 births/1,000 population (2005 est.)
Death rate: 6.54 deaths/1,000 population (2005 est.)
Net migration rate: -0.86 migrant(s)/1,000 population (2005 est.)
Sex ratio:
at birth: 1.04 male(s)/female
under 15 years: 1.04 male(s)/female
15-64 years: 1.03 male(s)/female
65 years and over: 0.89 male(s)/female
total population: 1.02 male(s)/female (2005 est.)
Infant mortality rate:
total: 20.47 deaths/1,000 live births
male: 22.59 deaths/1,000 live births
female: 18.26 deaths/1,000 live births (2005 est.)
Life expectancy at birth:
total population: 75.25 years

male: 72.68 years
female: 77.93 years (2005 est.)
Total fertility rate: 2.45 children born/ woman (2005 est.)
HIV/AIDS - adult prevalence rate: 0.9% (2003 est.)
HIV/AIDS - people living with HIV/AIDS: 16,000 (2003 est.)
HIV/AIDS - deaths: less than 500 (2003 est.)
Nationality:
noun: Panamanian(s)
adjective: Panamanian
Ethnic groups: mestizo (mixed Amerindian and white) 70%, Amerindian and mixed (West Indian) 14%, white 10%, Amerindian 6%
Religions: Roman Catholic 85%, Protestant 15%
Languages: Spanish (official), English 14%; note - many Panamanians bilingual
Literacy:
definition: age 15 and over can read and write
total population: 92.6%
male: 93.2%
female: 91.9% (2003 est.)

GOVERNMENT

Country name:
conventional long form: Republic of Panama
conventional short form: Panama
local long form: Republica de Panama
local short form: Panama
Government type: constitutional democracy
Capital: Panama
Administrative divisions: 9 provinces (provincias, singular - provincia) and 1 territory* (comarca); Bocas del Toro, Chiriqui, Cocle, Colon, Darien, Herrera, Los Santos, Panama, San Blas*(Kuna Yala), and Veraguas
Independence: 3 November 1903 (from Colombia; became independent from Spain 28 November 1821)
National holiday: Independence Day, 3 November (1903)
Constitution: 11 October 1972; major reforms adopted 1978, 1983, 1994, and 2004
Legal system: based on civil law system; judicial review of legislative acts in the Supreme Court of Justice; accepts compulsory ICJ jurisdiction, with reservations
Suffrage: 18 years of age; universal and compulsory
Executive branch:
chief of state: President Martin TORRIJOS Espino (since 1 September 2004); First Vice President Samuel LEWIS Navarro (since 1 September 2004); Second Vice President Ruben AROSEMENA Valdes (since 1 September 2004); note - the president is both the chief of state and head of government
head of government: President Martin TORRIJOS Espino (since 1 September 2004); First Vice President Samuel LEWIS Navarro (since 1 September 2004); Second Vice President Ruben AROSEMENA Valdes (since 1 September 2004); note - the president is both the chief of state and head of government
cabinet: Cabinet appointed by the president
elections: president and vice presidents elected on the same ticket by popular vote for five-year terms; election last held 2 May 2004 (next to be held 3 May 2009); note - beginning in 2009, Panama will have only one vice president.
election results: Martin TORRIJOS Espino elected president; percent of vote - Martin TORRIJOS Espino 47.5%, Guillermo ENDARA Galimany 30.6%, Jose Miguel ALEMAN 17%, Ricardo MARTINELLI 4.9%
note: government coalition - PRD (Democratic Revolutionary Party), PP (Popular Party)
Legislative branch: unicameral National Assembly (formerly called Legislative Assembly) or Asamblea Nacional (78 seats; members are elected by popular vote to serve five-year terms; note - in 2009, the number of seats will change to 71)
elections: last held 2 May 2004 (next to be held 3 May 2009)
election results: percent of vote by party - NA%; seats by party - PRD 40, PA 17, PS 8, MOLIRENA 3, CD 2, PP 2, PLN 1, other 5
note: legislators from outlying rural districts are chosen on a plurality basis while districts located in more populous towns and cities elect multiple legislators by means of a proportion-based formula
Judicial branch: Supreme Court of Justice or Corte Suprema de Justicia (nine judges appointed for 10-year terms); five superior courts; three courts of appeal
Political parties and leaders: Democratic Change or CD [Ricardo MARTINELLI]; Democratic Revolutionary Party or PRD [Hugo GUIRAUD]; National Liberal Party or PLN [Anibal GALINDO]; Nationalist Republican Liberal Movement or MOLIRENA [Jesus ROSAS]; Panamenista Party or PA (formerly the Arnulfista Party) [Marco AMEGLIO]; Popular Party or PP (formerly Christian Democratic Party or PDC) [Ricardo ARIAS Calderon]; Solidarity Party or PS [Jose Raul MULINO]
Political pressure groups and leaders: Chamber of Commerce; National Civic Crusade; National Council of Organized Workers or CONATO; National Council of Private Enterprise or CONEP; National Union of Construction and Similar Workers (SUNTRACS); Panamanian Association of Business Executives or APEDE; Panamanian Industrialists Society or SIP; Workers Confederation of the Republic of Panama or CTRP
International organization participation: FAO, G-77, IADB, IAEA, IBRD, ICAO, ICC, ICCt, ICFTU, ICRM, IDA, IFAD, IFC, IFRCS, ILO, IMF, IMO, Interpol, IOC, IOM, ISO, ITU, LAES, LAIA (observer), MIGA, NAM, OAS, OPANAL, OPCW, PCA, RG, UN, UNCTAD, UNESCO, UNIDO, UPU, WCL, WCO, WFTU, WHO, WIPO, WMO, WToO, WTO
Diplomatic representation in the US:
chief of mission: Ambassador Federico HUMBERT Arias
chancery: 2862 McGill Terrace NW, Washington, DC 20008
telephone: [1] (202) 483-1407
FAX: [1] (202) 483-8416
consulate(s) general: Atlanta, Houston, Miami, New Orleans, New York, Philadelphia, San Francisco, San Juan (Puerto Rico), Tampa
Diplomatic representation from the US:
chief of mission: Ambassador William A. EATON
embassy: Avenida Balboa and Calle 37, Apartado Postal 0816-02561, Zona 5, Panama City 5
mailing address: American Embassy Panama, Unit 0945, APO AA 34002
telephone: [507] 207-7000
FAX: [507] 227-1964
Flag description: divided into four, equal rectangles; the top quadrants are white (hoist side) with a blue five-pointed star in the center and plain red; the bottom quadrants are plain blue (hoist side) and white with a red five-pointed star in the center

ECONOMY

Economy - overview: Panama's dollarised economy rests primarily on a well-developed services sector that accounts for four-fifths of GDP. Services include operating the Panama Canal, banking, the Colon Free Zone, insurance, container ports, flagship registry, and tourism. A slump in Colon Free Zone and agricultural exports, the global slowdown, and the withdrawal of US military forces held back economic growth in 2000-03; growth picked up in 2004 and 2005 led by export-oriented services and a construction boom stimulated by tax incentives. The government has been backing tax reforms, reform of the social security program, new regional trade agreements, and development of tourism. Unemployment remains high.

GDP (purchasing power parity): $22.16 billion (2005 est.)
GDP (official exchange rate): $15.4 billion (2005 est.)
GDP - real growth rate: 4.3% (2005 est.)
GDP - per capita: purchasing power parity - $7,300 (2005 est.)
GDP - composition by sector:
agriculture: 7.6%
industry: 17.9%
services: 74.5% (2005 est.)
Labor force: 1.39 million
note: shortage of skilled labor, but an oversupply of unskilled labor (2005 est.)
Labor force - by occupation: agriculture 20.8%, industry 18%, services 61.2% (1995 est.)
Unemployment rate: 8.7% (2005 est.)
Population below poverty line: 37% (1999 est.)
Household income or consumption by percentage share:
lowest 10%: 1.2%
highest 10%: 35.7% (1997)
Distribution of family income - Gini index: 56.4 (2000)
Inflation rate (consumer prices): 2.5% (2005 est.)
Investment (gross fixed): 17.8% of GDP (2005 est.)
Budget:
revenues: $3.426 billion
expenditures: $3.959 billion, including capital expenditures of $471 million (2005 est.)
Public debt: 73.2% of GDP (2005 est.)
Agriculture - products: bananas, rice, corn, coffee, sugarcane, vegetables; livestock; shrimp
Industries: construction, brewing, cement and other construction materials, sugar milling
Industrial production growth rate: 3.5% (2005 est.)
Electricity - production: 5.398 billion kWh (2003)
Electricity - production by source:
fossil fuel: 37%
hydro: 61.3%
nuclear: 0%
other: 1.7% (2001)
Electricity - consumption: 4.87 billion kWh (2003)
Electricity - exports: 175 million kWh (2003)
Electricity - imports: 25 million kWh (2003)
Oil - production: 0 bbl/day (2004 est.)
Oil - consumption: 78,000 bbl/day (2003 est.)
Oil - exports: NA (2001)
Oil - imports: NA (2001)
Current account balance: $-559 million (2005 est.)
Exports: $7.481 billion f.o.b. (includes the Colon Free Zone) (2005 est.)
Exports - partners: US 50.5%, Sweden 6.6%, Spain 5.1%, Netherlands 4.4%, Costa Rica 4.2% (2004)
Imports: $8.734 billion f.o.b. (includes the Colon Free Zone) (2005 est.)
Imports - partners: US 33.3%, Netherlands Antilles 8.1%, Japan 6%, Costa Rica 5.7%, Mexico 4.6%, Colombia 4.2% (2004)
Reserves of foreign exchange and gold: $981 million (2005 est.)
Debt - external: $9.859 billion (2005 est.)
Economic aid - recipient: $197.1 million (1995)
Currency (code): balboa (PAB); US dollar (USD)
Currency code: PAB; USD
Exchange rates: balboas per US dollar - 1 (2005), 1 (2004), 1 (2003), 1 (2002), 1 (2001)
Fiscal year: calendar year

COMMUNICATIONS

Telephones - main lines in use: 386,900 (2002)
Telephones - mobile cellular: 834,000 (2003)
Telephone system:
general assessment: domestic and international facilities well developed
domestic: NA
international: country code - 507; 1 coaxial submarine cable; satellite earth stations - 2 Intelsat (Atlantic Ocean); connected to the Central American Microwave System
Radio broadcast stations: AM 101, FM 134, shortwave 0 (1998)
Radios: 815,000 (1997)
Television broadcast stations: 38 (including repeaters) (1998)
Televisions: 510,000 (1997)
Internet country code: .pa
Internet hosts: 7,129 (2003)
Internet Service Providers (ISPs): 6 (2000)
Internet users: 120,000 (2002)

TRANSPORTATION

Airports: 105 (2004 est.)
Airports - with paved runways:
total: 47
over 3,047 m: 1
2,438 to 3,047 m: 1
1,524 to 2,437 m: 5
914 to 1,523 m: 17
under 914 m: 23 (2005 est.)
Airports - with unpaved runways:
total: 62
914 to 1,523 m: 10
under 914 m: 52 (2005 est.)
Railways:
total: 355 km
standard gauge: 76 km 1.435-m gauge
narrow gauge: 279 km 0.914-m gauge (2004)
Roadways:
total: 11,643 km
paved: 4,028 km (including 30 km of expressways)
unpaved: 7,615 km (2000 est.)
Waterways: 800 km (includes 82 km Panama Canal) (2004)
Merchant marine:
total: 5,005 ships (1,000 GRT or over) 122,960,929 GRT/183,615,337 DWT
by type: barge carrier 1, bulk carrier 1,548, cargo 886, chemical tanker 465, combination ore/oil 13, container 605, liquefied gas 183, livestock carrier 8, passenger 42, passenger/cargo 77, petroleum tanker 521, refrigerated cargo 298, roll on/roll off 97, specialized tanker 5, vehicle carrier 256
foreign-owned: 4,388 (Andorra 1, Argentina 9, Australia 3, Bahamas 1, Belgium 14, Brazil 1, Canada 1, Chile 14, China 310, Colombia 5, Croatia 1, Cuba 9, Cyprus 7, Denmark 13, Egypt 15, France 7, Germany 23, Greece 546, Hong Kong 159, India 8, Indonesia 46, Ireland 1, Isle of Man 2, Israel 3, Italy 8, Japan 1814, Jordan 9, Latvia 2, Lithuania 5, Malaysia 11, Maldives 1, Malta 1, Mexico 4, Monaco 8, Netherlands 22, New Zealand 1, Nigeria 6, Norway 66, Pakistan 1, Peru 13, Philippines 15, Poland 19, Portugal 8, Romania 13, Russia 4, Saudi Arabia 4, Singapore 54, South Africa 3, South Korea 292, Spain 41, Sri Lanka 1, Sudan 1, Sweden 4, Switzerland 188, Syria 7, Taiwan 301, Thailand 10, Trinidad & Tobago 1, Tunisia 1, Turkey 18, Ukraine 9, UAE 83, United Kingdom 29, United States 88, Venezuela 20, Vietnam 2, Yemen 1) (2005)
Ports and terminals: Balboa, Colon, Cristobal

MILITARY

Military branches: an amendment to the Constitution abolished the armed forces, but there are security forces (Panamanian Public Forces or PPF includes the Panamanian National Police, National Maritime Service, and National Air Service)
Manpower available for military service: *males age 18-49:* 733,031 (2005 est.)
Manpower fit for military service: *males age 18-49:* 511,905 (2005 est.)
Military expenditures - dollar figure: $147 million (2004)
Military expenditures - percent of GDP: 1.1% (2004)
Military - note: on 10 February 1990, the government of then President ENDARA abolished Panama's military and reformed the security apparatus by creating the Panamanian Public Forces; in October 1994, Panama's Legislative Assembly approved a constitutional amendment

prohibiting the creation of a standing military force, but allowing the temporary establishment of special police units to counter acts of "external aggression"

TRANSNATIONAL ISSUES

Disputes - international: organized illegal narcotics operations in Colombia operate within the border region with Panama
Illicit drugs: major cocaine transshipment point and primary money-laundering center for narcotics revenue; money-laundering activity is especially heavy in the Colon Free Zone; offshore financial center; negligible signs of coca cultivation; monitoring of financial transactions is improving; official corruption remains a major problem

PAPUA NEW GUINEA

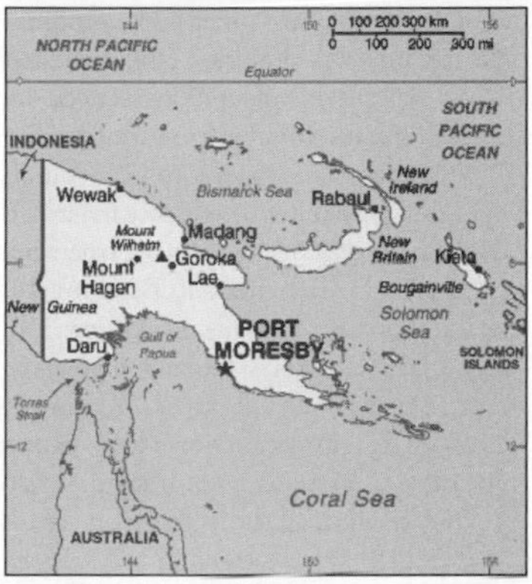

INTRODUCTION

Background: The eastern half of the island of New Guinea - second largest in the world - was divided between Germany (north) and the UK (south) in 1885. The latter area was transferred to Australia in 1902, which occupied the northern portion during World War I and continued to administer the combined areas until independence in 1975. A nine-year secessionist revolt on the island of Bougainville ended in 1997 after claiming some 20,000 lives.

GEOGRAPHY

Location: Oceania, group of islands including the eastern half of the island of New Guinea between the Coral Sea and the South Pacific Ocean, east of Indonesia
Geographic coordinates: 6 00 S, 147 00 E
Map references: Oceania
Area:
total: 462,840 sq km
land: 452,860 sq km
water: 9,980 sq km
Area - comparative: slightly larger than California
Land boundaries:
total: 820 km
border countries: Indonesia 820 km
Coastline: 5,152 km
Maritime claims: measured from claimed archipelagic baselines
territorial sea: 12 nm
continental shelf: 200-m depth or to the depth of exploitation
exclusive fishing zone: 200 nm
Climate: tropical; northwest monsoon (December to March), southeast monsoon (May to October); slight seasonal temperature variation
Terrain: mostly mountains with coastal lowlands and rolling foothills
Elevation extremes:
lowest point: Pacific Ocean 0 m
highest point: Mount Wilhelm 4,509 m
Natural resources: gold, copper, silver, natural gas, timber, oil, fisheries
Land use:
arable land: 0.46%
permanent crops: 1.44%
other: 98.1% (2001)
Irrigated land: NA sq km
Natural hazards: active volcanism; situated along the Pacific "Ring of Fire"; the country is subject to frequent and sometimes severe earthquakes; mud slides; tsunamis
Environment - current issues: rain forest subject to deforestation as a result of growing commercial demand for tropical timber; pollution from mining projects; severe drought
Environment - international agreements:
party to: Antarctic Treaty, Biodiversity, Climate Change, Climate Change-Kyoto Protocol, Desertification, Endangered Species, Environmental Modification, Hazardous Wastes, Law of the Sea, Marine Dumping, Ozone Layer Protection, Ship Pollution, Tropical Timber 83, Tropical Timber 94, Wetlands
signed, but not ratified: none of the selected agreements
Geography - note: shares island of New Guinea with Indonesia; one of world's largest swamps along southwest coast

PEOPLE

Population: 5,545,268 (July 2005 est.)
Age structure:
0-14 years: 38.1% (male 1,072,910/female 1,037,635)
15-64 years: 58.1% (male 1,662,166/ female 1,559,685)
65 years and over: 3.8% (male 99,777/ female 113,095) (2005 est.)
Median age:
total: 21.09 years
male: 21.25 years
female: 20.93 years (2005 est.)
Population growth rate: 2.26% (2005 est.)
Birth rate: 29.95 births/1,000 population (2005 est.)
Death rate: 7.37 deaths/1,000 population (2005 est.)
Net migration rate: 0 migrant(s)/1,000 population (2005 est.)
Sex ratio:
at birth: 1.05 male(s)/female
under 15 years: 1.03 male(s)/female
15-64 years: 1.07 male(s)/female
65 years and over: 0.88 male(s)/female
total population: 1.05 male(s)/female (2005 est.)
Infant mortality rate:
total: 51.45 deaths/1,000 live births
male: 55.63 deaths/1,000 live births
female: 47.07 deaths/1,000 live births (2005 est.)
Life expectancy at birth:
total population: 64.93 years
male: 62.76 years
female: 67.21 years (2005 est.)
Total fertility rate: 3.96 children born/woman (2005 est.)
HIV/AIDS - adult prevalence rate: 0.6% (2003 est.)
HIV/AIDS - people living with HIV/AIDS: 16,000 (2003 est.)
HIV/AIDS - deaths: 600 (2003 est.)
Major infectious diseases:
degree of risk: very high
food or waterborne diseases: bacterial and protozoal diarrhea, hepatitis A, and typhoid fever
vectorborne diseases: dengue fever and malaria are high risks in some locations (2004)
Nationality:
noun: Papua New Guinean(s)
adjective: Papua New Guinean
Ethnic groups: Melanesian, Papuan, Negrito, Micronesian, Polynesian
Religions: Roman Catholic 22%, Lutheran 16%, Presbyterian/Methodist/ London Missionary Society 8%, Anglican 5%, Evangelical Alliance 4%, Seventh-Day Adventist 1%, other Protestant 10%, indigenous beliefs 34%
Languages: Melanesian Pidgin serves as the lingua franca, English spoken by 1%-2%, Motu spoken in Papua region
note: 715 indigenous languages - many unrelated

Literacy:
definition: age 15 and over can read and write
total population: 64.6%
male: 71.1%
female: 57.7% (2002)

GOVERNMENT

Country name:
conventional long form: Independent State of Papua New Guinea
conventional short form: Papua New Guinea
former: Territory of Papua and New Guinea
abbreviation: PNG
Government type: constitutional monarchy with parliamentary democracy
Capital: Port Moresby
Administrative divisions: 20 provinces; Bougainville, Central, Chimbu, Eastern Highlands, East New Britain, East Sepik, Enga, Gulf, Madang, Manus, Milne Bay, Morobe, National Capital, New Ireland, Northern, Sandaun, Southern Highlands, Western, Western Highlands, West New Britain
Independence: 16 September 1975 (from the Australian-administered UN trusteeship)
National holiday: Independence Day, 16 September (1975)
Constitution: 16 September 1975
Legal system: based on English common law
Suffrage: 18 years of age; universal
Executive branch:
chief of state: Queen ELIZABETH II (since 6 February 1952), represented by governor general Sir Paulius MATANE (since 29 June 2004)
head of government: Prime Minister Sir Michael SOMARE (since 2 August 2002); deputy prime minister (vacant)
cabinet: National Executive Council appointed by the governor general on the recommendation of the prime minister
elections: none; the monarch is hereditary; governor general appointed by the National Executive Council; following legislative elections, the leader of the majority party or the leader of the majority coalition usually is appointed prime minister by the governor general
Legislative branch: unicameral National Parliament - sometimes referred to as the House of Assembly (109 seats, 89 elected from open electorates and 20 from provincial electorates; members elected by popular vote to serve five-year terms)
elections: last held 15-29 June 2002 and April and May 2003; completed in May 2003 (voting in the Southern Highlands was not completed during the June 2002 election period); next to be held not later than June 2007
election results: percent of vote by party - National Alliance 18%, URP 13%, PDM 12%, PPP 8%, Pangu 6%, PAP 5%, PLP 4%, others 34%; seats by party - National Alliance 19, URP 14, PDM 13, PPP 8, PANGU 6, PAP 5, PLP 4, others 40; note - association with political parties is fluid (2003)
Judicial branch: Supreme Court (the chief justice is appointed by the governor general on the proposal of the National Executive Council after consultation with the minister responsible for justice; other judges are appointed by the Judicial and Legal Services Commission)
Political parties and leaders: Christian Democratic Party [Dr. Banare BUN, party leader]; Melanesian Alliance Party or MAP [Sir Moi AVEL, party leader]; National Alliance Party or NA [Michael SOMARE, party leader; George MANOA, party president]; National Party [Melchior PEP, party leader]; Papua and Niugini Union Party or PANGU [Chris HAIVETA, party leader]; Papua New Guinea First Party [Cecilking DORUBA, party leader]; Papua New Guinea Labor Party [Bob DANAYA, party leader]; Papua New Guinea Party (was People's Democratic Movement or PDM) [Sir Mekere MORAUTA, party leader]; People's Action Party or PAP [Moses MALADINA, party leader]; People's Labor Party or PLP [Ekis ROPENU, party leader]; People's National Congress or PNC [Peter O'NEILL, party leader]; People's Progressive Party or PPP [Andrew BAING, party leader]; Pipol First Party [Luther WENGE, party leader]; Rural People's Party [Peter NAMUS, party leader]; United Party [Bire KIMASOPA, party leader]; United Resources Party or URP [Tim NEVILLE, party leader] (2004)
Political pressure groups and leaders: NA
International organization participation: ACP, APEC, ARF, AsDB, ASEAN (associate member), C, CP, FAO, G-77, IBRD, ICAO, ICFTU, ICRM, IDA, IFAD, IFC, IFRCS, IHO, ILO, IMF, IMO, Interpol, IOC, IOM (observer), ISO (correspondent), ITU, MIGA, NAM, OPCW, PIF, Sparteca, SPC, UN, UNCTAD, UNESCO, UNIDO, UPU, WCO, WFTU, WHO, WIPO, WMO, WTO
Diplomatic representation in the US:
chief of mission: Ambassador Evan Jeremy PAKI
chancery: 1779 Massachusetts Avenue NW, Suite 805, Washington, DC 20036
telephone: [1] (202) 745-3680
FAX: [1] (202) 745-3679
Diplomatic representation from the US:
chief of mission: Ambassador Robert W. FITTS
embassy: Douglas Street, Port Moresby
mailing address: 4240 Port Moresby PI, US Department of State, Washington DC 20521-4240
telephone: [675] 321-1455
FAX: [675] 321-3423
Flag description: divided diagonally from upper hoist-side corner; the upper triangle is red with a soaring yellow bird of paradise centered; the lower triangle is black with five, white, five-pointed stars of the Southern Cross constellation centered

ECONOMY

Economy - overview: Papua New Guinea is richly endowed with natural resources, but exploitation has been hampered by rugged terrain and the high cost of developing infrastructure. Agriculture provides a subsistence livelihood for 85% of the population. Mineral deposits, including oil, copper, and gold, account for nearly two-thirds of export earnings. The economy has improved over the past three years, following a prolonged period of instability. Former Prime Minister Mekere MORAUTA had tried to restore integrity to state institutions, to stabilize the kina, restore stability to the national budget, to privatize public enterprises where appropriate, and to ensure peace on Bougainville. Australia annually supplies $240 million in aid, which accounts for 20% of the national budget. Challenges face Prime Minister Michael SOMARE, including gaining further investor confidence, continuing efforts to privatize government assets, maintaining the support of members of Parliament, dealing with widespread crime and corruption, and balancing relations with Australia, the former colonial ruler.
GDP (purchasing power parity): $13.32 billion (2005 est.)
GDP (official exchange rate): $4.199 billion (2005 est.)
GDP - real growth rate: 1.1% (2005 est.)
GDP - per capita: purchasing power parity - $2,400 (2005 est.)
GDP - composition by sector:
agriculture: 35.2%
industry: 38.3%
services: 26.4% (2005 est.)
Labor force: 3.4 million (2005 est.)
Labor force - by occupation: agriculture 85%, industry NA, services NA
Unemployment rate: NA
Population below poverty line: 37% (2002 est.)
Household income or consumption by percentage share:
lowest 10%: 1.7%
highest 10%: 40.5% (1996)

Distribution of family income - Gini index: 50.9 (1996)
Inflation rate (consumer prices): 1.7% (2005 est.)
Investment (gross fixed): 20.4% of GDP (2005 est.)
Budget:
revenues: $1.368 billion
expenditures: $1.354 billion, including capital expenditures of $344 million (2005 est.)
Public debt: 47.1% of GDP (2005 est.)
Agriculture - products: coffee, cocoa, coconuts, palm kernels, tea, rubber, sweet potatoes, fruit, vegetables, poultry, pork
Industries: copra crushing, palm oil processing, plywood production, wood chip production; mining of gold, silver, and copper; crude oil production; construction, tourism
Industrial production growth rate: NA
Electricity - production: 1.592 billion kWh (2003)
Electricity - production by source:
fossil fuel: 54.1%
hydro: 45.9%
nuclear: 0%
other: 0% (2001)
Electricity - consumption: 1.481 billion kWh (2003)
Electricity - exports: 0 kWh (2003)
Electricity - imports: 0 kWh (2003)
Oil - production: 40,400 bbl/day (2005 est.)
Oil - consumption: 15,000 bbl/day (2003 est.)
Oil - exports: NA (2001)
Oil - imports: NA (2001)
Oil - proved reserves: 170 million bbl (2005 est.)
Natural gas - production: 110 million cu m (2001 est.)
Natural gas - consumption: 110 million cu m (2001 est.)
Natural gas - exports: 0 cu m (2001 est.)
Natural gas - imports: 0 cu m (2001 est.)
Natural gas - proved reserves: 385.5 billion cu m (2005)
Current account balance: $113 million (2005 est.)
Exports: $2.833 billion f.o.b. (2005 est.)
Exports - partners: Australia 28%, Japan 5.8%, Germany 4.7%, China 4.6% (2004)
Imports: $1.651 billion f.o.b. (2005 est.)
Imports - partners: Australia 46.4%, Singapore 21.6%, Japan 4.3%, New Zealand 4.2% (2004)
Reserves of foreign exchange and gold: $663 million (2005 est.)
Debt - external: $1.978 billion (2005 est.)
Economic aid - recipient: $400 million (1999 est.)
Currency (code): kina (PGK)
Currency code: PGK
Exchange rates: kina per US dollar - 3.08 (2005), 3.2225 (2004), 3.5635 (2003), 3.8952 (2002), 3.3887 (2001)
Fiscal year: calendar year

COMMUNICATIONS

Telephones - main lines in use: 62,000 (2002)
Telephones - mobile cellular: 15,000 (2002)
Telephone system:
general assessment: services are adequate; facilities provide radiotelephone and telegraph, coastal radio, aeronautical radio, and international radio communication services
domestic: mostly radiotelephone
international: country code - 675; submarine cables to Australia and Guam; satellite earth station - 1 Intelsat (Pacific Ocean); international radio communication service
Radio broadcast stations: AM 8, FM 19, shortwave 28 (1998)
Radios: 410,000 (1997)
Television broadcast stations: 3 (all in the Port Moresby area)
note: additional stations at Mt. Hagen, Goroka, Lae, and Rabaul are planned (2004)
Televisions: 59,841 (1999)
Internet country code: .pg
Internet hosts: 389 (2003)
Internet Service Providers (ISPs): 3 (2000)
Internet users: 75,000 (2002)

TRANSPORTATION

Airports: 571 (2004 est.)
Airports - with paved runways:
total: 21
2,438 to 3,047 m: 2
1,524 to 2,437 m: 14
914 to 1,523 m: 4
under 914 m: 1 (2005 est.)
Airports - with unpaved runways:
total: 551
1,524 to 2,437 m: 10
914 to 1,523 m: 62
under 914 m: 479 (2005 est.)
Heliports: 2 (2005 est.)
Pipelines: oil 264 km (2004)
Roadways:
total: 19,600 km
paved: 686 km
unpaved: 18,914 km (1999 est.)
Waterways: 10,940 km (2003)
Merchant marine:
total: 22 ships (1,000 GRT or over) 47,586 GRT/60,934 DWT
by type: bulk carrier 2, cargo 17, chemical tanker 1, petroleum tanker 2
foreign-owned: 8 (Singapore 2, United Kingdom 6) (2005)
Ports and terminals: Kimbe, Lae, Rabaul

MILITARY

Military branches: Papua New Guinea Defense Force (includes Maritime Operations Element, Air Operations Element)
Military service age and obligation: 18 years of age (est.); no conscription (2001)
Manpower available for military service:
males age 18-49: 1,264,728 (2005 est.)
Manpower fit for military service: *males age 18-49:* 902,432 (2005 est.)
Military expenditures - dollar figure: $16.9 million (2003)
Military expenditures - percent of GDP: 1.4% (FY02)

TRANSNATIONAL ISSUES

Disputes - international: relies on assistance from Australia to keep out illegal cross-border activities from primarily Indonesia, including goods smuggling, illegal narcotics trafficking, and squatters and secessionists

PARACEL ISLANDS

INTRODUCTION

Background: The Paracel Islands are surrounded by productive fishing grounds and by potential oil and gas reserves. In 1932, French Indochina annexed the islands and set up a weather station on Pattle Island; maintenance was continued by its successor, Vietnam. China has occupied the Paracel Islands since 1974, when its troops seized a South Vietnamese garrison occupying the western islands. The islands are claimed by Taiwan and Vietnam.

GEOGRAPHY

Location: Southeastern Asia, group of small islands and reefs in the South China Sea, about one-third of the way from central Vietnam to the northern Philippines
Geographic coordinates: 16 30 N, 112 00 E
Map references: Southeast Asia
Area:
total: NA sq km
land: NA sq km
water: 0 sq km
Area - comparative: NA
Land boundaries: 0 km
Coastline: 518 km
Maritime claims: NA

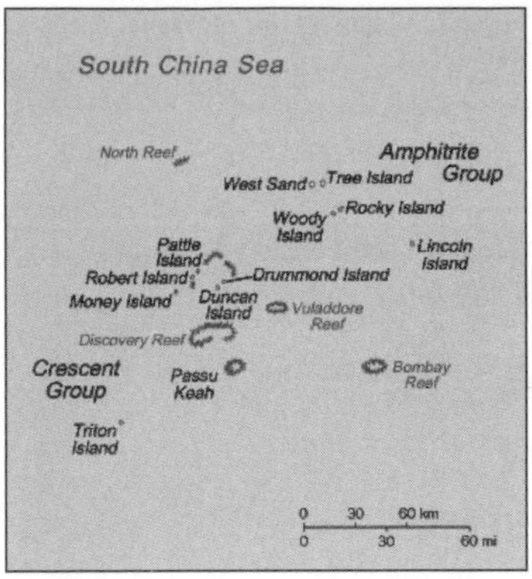

Climate: tropical
Terrain: mostly low and flat
Elevation extremes:
lowest point: South China Sea 0 m
highest point: unnamed location on Rocky Island 14 m
Natural resources: none
Land use:
arable land: 0%
permanent crops: 0%
other: 100% (2001)
Irrigated land: 0 sq km (1998 est.)
Natural hazards: typhoons
Environment - current issues: NA
Geography - note: composed of 130 small coral islands and reefs divided into the northeast Amphitrite Group and the western Crescent Group

PEOPLE

Population: no indigenous inhabitants
note: there are scattered Chinese garrisons

GOVERNMENT

Country name:
conventional long form: none
conventional short form: Paracel Islands

ECONOMY

Economy - overview: China announced plans in 1997 to open the islands for tourism.

TRANSPORTATION

Airports: 1 (2004 est.)
Airports - with paved runways:
total: 1
1,524 to 2,437 m: 1 (2005 est.)
Ports and terminals: small Chinese port facilities on Woody Island and Duncan Island being expanded

MILITARY

Military - note: occupied by China

TRANSNATIONAL ISSUES

Disputes - international: occupied by China, also claimed by Taiwan and Vietnam

PARAGUAY

INTRODUCTION

Background: In the disastrous War of the Triple Alliance (1865-70), Paraguay lost two-thirds of all adult males and much of its territory. It stagnated economically for the next half century. In the Chaco War of 1932-35, large, economically important areas were won from Bolivia. The 35-year military dictatorship of Alfredo STROESSNER was overthrown in 1989, and, despite a marked increase in political infighting in recent years, relatively free and regular presidential elections have been held since then.

GEOGRAPHY

Location: Central South America, northeast of Argentina
Geographic coordinates: 23 00 S, 58 00 W
Map references: South America
Area:
total: 406,750 sq km
land: 397,300 sq km
water: 9,450 sq km
Area - comparative: slightly smaller than California
Land boundaries:
total: 3,920 km
border countries: Argentina 1,880 km, Bolivia 750 km, Brazil 1,290 km
Coastline: 0 km (landlocked)
Maritime claims: none (landlocked)
Climate: subtropical to temperate; substantial rainfall in the eastern portions, becoming semiarid in the far west
Terrain: grassy plains and wooded hills east of Rio Paraguay; Gran Chaco region west of Rio Paraguay mostly low, marshy plain near the river, and dry forest and thorny scrub elsewhere
Elevation extremes:
lowest point: junction of Rio Paraguay and Rio Parana 46 m
highest point: Cerro Pero (Cerro Tres Kandu) 842 m
Natural resources: hydropower, timber, iron ore, manganese, limestone
Land use:
arable land: 7.6%
permanent crops: 0.23%
other: 92.17% (2001)
Irrigated land: 670 sq km (1998 est.)
Natural hazards: local flooding in southeast (early September to June); poorly drained plains may become boggy (early October to June)
Environment - current issues: deforestation; water pollution; inadequate means for waste disposal pose health risks for many urban residents; loss of wetlands
Environment - international agreements:
party to: Biodiversity, Climate Change, Climate Change-Kyoto Protocol, Desertification, Endangered Species, Hazardous Wastes, Law of the Sea, Ozone Layer Protection, Wetlands
signed, but not ratified: none of the selected agreements
Geography - note: landlocked; lies between Argentina, Bolivia, and Brazil; population concentrated in southern part of country

PEOPLE

Population: 6,347,884 (July 2005 est.)
Age structure:
0-14 years: 37.9% (male 1,223,479/female 1,184,134)
15-64 years: 57.3% (male 1,825,473/female 1,809,810)
65 years and over: 4.8% (male 140,935/female 164,053) (2005 est.)
Median age:
total: 21.2 years
male: 20.94 years
female: 21.46 years (2005 est.)
Population growth rate: 2.48% (2005 est.)
Birth rate: 29.43 births/1,000 population (2005 est.)
Death rate: 4.53 deaths/1,000 population (2005 est.)
Net migration rate: -0.08 migrant(s)/1,000 population (2005 est.)
Sex ratio:
at birth: 1.05 male(s)/female
under 15 years: 1.03 male(s)/female
15-64 years: 1.01 male(s)/female
65 years and over: 0.86 male(s)/female
total population: 1.01 male(s)/female (2005 est.)

Infant mortality rate:
total: 25.63 deaths/1,000 live births
male: 30.37 deaths/1,000 live births
female: 20.66 deaths/1,000 live births (2005 est.)
Life expectancy at birth:
total population: 74.89 years
male: 72.35 years
female: 77.55 years (2005 est.)
Total fertility rate: 3.93 children born/woman (2005 est.)
HIV/AIDS - adult prevalence rate: 0.5% (2003 est.)
HIV/AIDS - people living with HIV/AIDS: 15,000 (1999 est.)
HIV/AIDS - deaths: 600 (2003 est.)
Nationality:
noun: Paraguayan(s)
adjective: Paraguayan
Ethnic groups: mestizo (mixed Spanish and Amerindian) 95%, other 5%
Religions: Roman Catholic 90%, Mennonite and other Protestant 10%
Languages: Spanish (official), Guarani (official)
Literacy:
definition: age 15 and over can read and write
total population: 94%
male: 94.9%
female: 93% (2003 est.)

GOVERNMENT

Country name:
conventional long form: Republic of Paraguay
conventional short form: Paraguay
local long form: Republica del Paraguay
local short form: Paraguay
Government type: constitutional republic
Capital: Asuncion
Administrative divisions: 17 departments (departamentos, singular - departamento) and 1 capital city*; Alto Paraguay, Alto Parana, Amambay, Asuncion*, Boqueron, Caaguazu, Caazapa, Canindeyu, Central, Concepcion, Cordillera, Guaira, Itapua, Misiones, Neembucu, Paraguari, Presidente Hayes, San Pedro
Independence: 14 May 1811 (from Spain)
National holiday: Independence Day, 14 May 1811 (observed 15 May annually)
Constitution: promulgated 20 June 1992
Legal system: based on Argentine codes, Roman law, and French codes; judicial review of legislative acts in Supreme Court of Justice
Suffrage: 18 years of age; universal and compulsory up to age 75
Executive branch:
chief of state: President Nicanor DUARTE Frutos (since 15 August 2003); Vice President Luis CASTIGLIONI Joria (since 15 August 2003); note - the president is both the chief of state and head of government
head of government: President Nicanor DUARTE Frutos (since 15 August 2003); Vice President Luis CASTIGLIONI Joria (since 15 August 2003); note - the president is both the chief of state and head of government
cabinet: Council of Ministers nominated by the president
elections: president and vice president elected on the same ticket by popular vote for five-year terms; election last held 27 April 2003 (next to be held April 2008)
election results: Nicanor DUARTE Frutos elected president; percent of vote - Nicanor DUARTE Frutos 37.1%, Julio Cesar Ramon FRANCO Gomez 23.9%, Pedro Nicolas Maraa FADUL Niella 21.3%, Guillermo SANCHEZ Guffanti 13.5%, other 4.2%
Legislative branch: bicameral Congress or Congreso consists of the Chamber of Senators or Camara de Senadores (45 seats; members are elected by popular vote to serve five-year terms) and the Chamber of Deputies or Camara de Diputados (80 seats; members are elected by popular vote to serve five-year terms)
elections: Chamber of Senators - last held 27 April 2003 (next to be held April 2008); Chamber of Deputies - last held 27 April 2003 (next to be held April 2008)
election results: Chamber of Senators - percent of vote by party - NA%; seats by party - ANR 16, PLRA 12, UNACE 7, PQ 7, PPS 2, PEN 1; Chamber of Deputies - percent of vote by party - NA%; seats by party - ANR 37, PLRA 21, UNACE 10, PQ 10, PPS 2
Judicial branch: Supreme Court of Justice or Corte Suprema de Justicia (judges appointed on the proposal of the Council of Magistrates or Consejo de la Magistratura)
Political parties and leaders: Asociacion Nacional Republicana - Colorado Party or ANR [Herminio CACERES, interim president]; Movimiento Union Nacional de Ciudadanos Eticos or UNACE [Enrique GONZALEZ Quintana, acting chairman]; Patria Querida (Beloved Fatherland Party) or PQ [Pedro Nicolas Maraa FADUL Niella]; Partido Encuentro Nacional or PEN [Luis TORALES Kennedy]; Partido Liberal Radical Autentico or PLRA [Blas LLANO]; Partido Pais Solidario or PPS [Carlos Alberto FILIZZOLA Pallares]
note: Nicanor DUARTE Frutos on leave as party leader of the Colorado Party or ANR while serving as President of Paraguay; Lino Cesar OVIEDO Silva, leader of UNACE, is currently serving a ten-year prison term
Political pressure groups and leaders: Ahorristas Estafados or AE; Coordinating Table of National Campesino Organizations or MCNOC; National Federation of Campesinos or FNC; National Workers Central or CNT; Paraguayan Workers Confederation or CPT; Roman Catholic Church; Unitary Workers Central or CUT
International organization participation: CSN, FAO, G-77, IADB, IAEA, IBRD, ICAO, ICCt, ICFTU, ICRM, IDA, IFAD, IFC, IFRCS, ILO, IMF, IMO, Interpol, IOC, IOM, ISO (correspondent), ITU, LAES, LAIA, Mercosur, MIGA, MINUSTAH, MONUC, NAM (observer), OAS, ONUB, OPANAL, OPCW, PCA, RG, UN, UNCTAD, UNESCO, UNIDO, UNMEE, UNMIL, UNMIS, UNOCI, UPU, WCL, WCO, WHO, WIPO, WMO, WToO, WTO
Diplomatic representation in the US:
chief of mission: Ambassador James SPALDING Hellmers
chancery: 2400 Massachusetts Avenue NW, Washington, DC 20008
telephone: [1] (202) 483-6960 through 6962
FAX: [1] (202) 234-4508
consulate(s) general: Kansas City, Los Angeles, Miami, New York
Diplomatic representation from the US:
Ambassador James C. CASON
embassy: 1776 Avenida Mariscal Lopez, Casilla Postal 402, Asuncion
mailing address: Unit 4711, APO AA 34036-0001
telephone: [595] (21) 213-715
FAX: [595] (21) 213-728
Flag description: three equal, horizontal bands of red (top), white, and blue with an emblem centered in the white band; unusual flag in that the emblem is different on each side; the obverse (hoist side at the left) bears the national coat of arms (a yellow five-pointed star within a green wreath capped by the words REPUBLICA DEL PARAGUAY, all within two circles); the reverse (hoist side at the right) bears the seal of the treasury (a yellow lion below a red Cap of Liberty and the words Paz y Justicia (Peace and Justice) capped by the words REPUBLICA DEL PARAGUAY, all within two circles)

ECONOMY

Economy - overview: Landlocked Paraguay has a market economy marked by a large informal sector. This sector features both reexport of imported consumer goods to neighboring countries as well as the activities of thousands of microenterprises and urban street vendors. Because of the importance of the informal sector, accurate economic measures are difficult to obtain. A large percentage of the population derives their living from agricultural activity, often on a subsistence basis. The formal economy grew by an average of about 3% annually in 1995-97, but averaged near-zero growth in 1998-2001 and contracted by 2.3 percent in 2002, in response to regional contagion and an outbreak of hoof-and-mouth disease. On a per capita basis, real income has stagnated at 1980 levels. Most observers attribute Paraguay's poor economic performance to political uncertainty, corruption, lack of progress on structural reform, substantial internal and external debt, and deficient infrastructure. Aided by a firmer exchange rate and perhaps a greater confidence in the economic policy of the Duarte FRUTOS administration, the economy rebounded from 2003 to 2005, posting modest growth each year.

GDP (purchasing power parity): $30.9 billion (2005 est.)

GDP (official exchange rate): $7.586 billion (2005 est.)

GDP - real growth rate: 3.3% (2005 est.)

GDP - per capita: purchasing power parity - $4,900 (2005 est.)

GDP - composition by sector:
agriculture: 27.5%
industry: 24%
services: 48.5% (2005 est.)

Labor force: 2.68 million (2005 est.)

Labor force - by occupation: agriculture 45%

Unemployment rate: 16% (2005 est.)

Population below poverty line: 32% (2005 est.)

Household income or consumption by percentage share:
lowest 10%: 0.5%
highest 10%: 43.8% (1998)

Distribution of family income - Gini index: 56.8 (1999)

Inflation rate (consumer prices): 7.5% (2005 est.)

Investment (gross fixed): 20.1% of GDP (2005 est.)

Budget:
revenues: $1.334 billion
expenditures: $1.37 billion, including capital expenditures of $700 million (2005 est.)

Public debt: 36.1% of GDP (2005 est.)

Agriculture - products: cotton, sugarcane, soybeans, corn, wheat, tobacco, cassava (tapioca), fruits, vegetables; beef, pork, eggs, milk; timber

Industries: sugar, cement, textiles, beverages, wood products, steel, metallurgic, electric power

Industrial production growth rate: 0% (2000 est.)

Electricity - production: 51.29 billion kWh (2003)

Electricity - production by source:
fossil fuel: 0%
hydro: 99.9%
nuclear: 0%
other: 0.1% (2001)

Electricity - consumption: 3.528 billion kWh (2003)

Electricity - exports: 44.17 billion kWh (2003)

Electricity - imports: 0 kWh (2003)

Oil - production: 0 bbl/day (2003 est.)

Oil - consumption: 25,000 bbl/day (2003 est.)

Oil - exports: NA (2001)

Oil - imports: NA (2001)

Current account balance: $-170 million (2005 est.)

Exports: $3.13 billion f.o.b. (2005 est.)

Exports - partners: Uruguay 27.8%, Brazil 19.2%, Argentina 6.3%, Switzerland 4.1% (2004)

Imports: $3.832 billion f.o.b. (2005 est.)

Imports - partners: Brazil 30.9%, Argentina 23.3%, China 16.6%, US 4% (2004)

Reserves of foreign exchange and gold: $1.293 billion (2005 est.)

Debt - external: $3.535 billion (2005 est.)

Economic aid - recipient: NA

Currency (code): guarani (PYG)

Currency code: PYG

Exchange rates: guarani per US dollar - 6,158.47 (2005), 5,974.6 (2004), 6,424.3 (2003), 5,716.3 (2002), 4,105.9 (2001)

Fiscal year: calendar year

COMMUNICATIONS

Telephones - main lines in use: 273,200 (2002)

Telephones - mobile cellular: 1,770,300 (2003)

Telephone system:
general assessment: meager telephone service; principal switching center is Asuncion
domestic: fair microwave radio relay network
international: country code - 595; satellite earth station - 1 Intelsat (Atlantic Ocean)

Radio broadcast stations: AM 46, FM 27, shortwave 6 (three inactive) (1998)

Radios: 925,000 (1997)

Television broadcast stations: 5 (2003)

Televisions: 990,000 (2001)

Internet country code: .py

Internet hosts: 9,243 (2003)

Internet Service Providers (ISPs): 4 (2000)

Internet users: 120,000 (2003)

TRANSPORTATION

Airports: 878 (2004 est.)

Airports - with paved runways:
total: 12
over 3,047 m: 3
1,524 to 2,437 m: 5
914 to 1,523 m: 4 (2005 est.)

Airports - with unpaved runways:
total: 868
1,524 to 2,437 m: 26
914 to 1,523 m: 324
under 914 m: 518 (2005 est.)

Railways:
total: 441 km
standard gauge: 441 km 1.435-m gauge (2004)

Roadways:
total: 29,500 km
paved: 14,986 km
unpaved: 14,514 km (1999 est)

Waterways: 3,100 km (2004)

Merchant marine:
total: 21 ships (1,000 GRT or over) 31,667 GRT/30,826 DWT
by type: cargo 15, livestock carrier 1, passenger 1, petroleum tanker 2, roll on/roll off 2
foreign-owned: 2 (Argentina 2)
registered in other countries: 1 (2005)

Ports and terminals: Asuncion, Villeta, San Antonio, Encarnacion

MILITARY

Military branches: Army, Navy (includes Naval Aviation, River Defense Corps, Coast Guard), Air Force

Military service age and obligation: 18 years of age for compulsory and voluntary military service; conscript service obligation - 12 months for Army, 24 months for Navy (2004)

Manpower available for military service: *males age 18-49:* 1,345,022 (2005 est.)

Manpower fit for military service: *males age 18-49:* 1,109,166 (2005 est.)

Manpower reaching military service age annually: *males:* 63,058 (2005 est.)

Military expenditures - dollar figure: $53.1 million (2004)

Military expenditures - percent of GDP: 0.9% (2003)

TRANSNATIONAL ISSUES

Disputes - international: unruly region at convergence of Argentina-Brazil-Paraguay borders is locus of money laundering, smuggling, arms and illegal narcotics trafficking, and fundraising for extremist organizations

Illicit drugs: major illicit producer of cannabis, most or all of which is consumed in Brazil, Argentina, and Chile; transshipment country for Andean cocaine headed for Brazil, other Southern Cone markets, Europe, and US; corruption and some money-laundering activity, especially in the Tri-Border Area

PERU

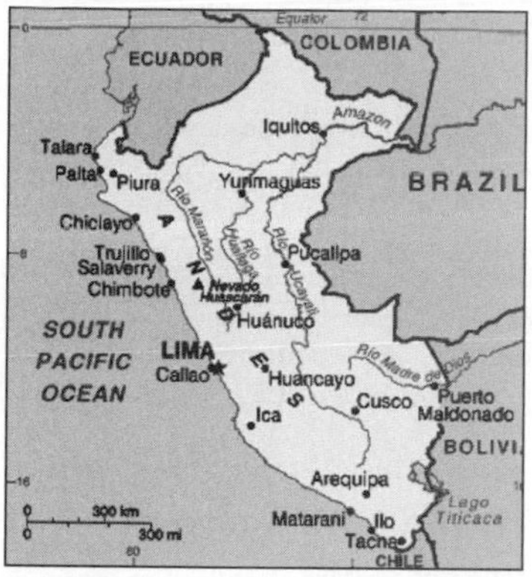

INTRODUCTION

Background: Ancient Peru was the seat of several prominent Andean civilizations, most notably that of the Incas whose empire was captured by the Spanish conquistadors in 1533. Peruvian independence was declared in 1821, and remaining Spanish forces defeated in 1824. After a dozen years of military rule, Peru returned to democratic leadership in 1980, but experienced economic problems and the growth of a violent insurgency. President Alberto FUJIMORI's election in 1990 ushered in a decade that saw a dramatic turnaround in the economy and significant progress in curtailing guerrilla activity. Nevertheless, the president's increasing reliance on authoritarian measures and an economic slump in the late 1990s generated mounting dissatisfaction with his regime. FUJIMORI won reelection to a third term in the spring of 2000, but international pressure and corruption scandals led to his ouster by Congress in November of that year. A caretaker government oversaw new elections in the spring of 2001, which ushered in Alejandro TOLEDO as the new head of government; his presidency has been hampered by allegations of corruption.

GEOGRAPHY

Location: Western South America, bordering the South Pacific Ocean, between Chile and Ecuador
Geographic coordinates: 10 00 S, 76 00 W
Map references: South America
Area:
total: 1,285,220 sq km
land: 1.28 million sq km
water: 5,220 sq km
Area - comparative: slightly smaller than Alaska
Land boundaries:
total: 5,536 km
border countries: Bolivia 900 km, Brazil 1,560 km, Chile 160 km, Colombia 1,496 km (est.), Ecuador 1,420 km
Coastline: 2,414 km
Maritime claims:
territorial sea: 200 nm
continental shelf: 200 nm
Climate: varies from tropical in east to dry desert in west; temperate to frigid in Andes
Terrain: western coastal plain (costa), high and rugged Andes in center (sierra), eastern lowland jungle of Amazon Basin (selva)
Elevation extremes:
lowest point: Pacific Ocean 0 m
highest point: Nevado Huascaran 6,768 m
Natural resources: copper, silver, gold, petroleum, timber, fish, iron ore, coal, phosphate, potash, hydropower, natural gas
Land use:
arable land: 2.89%
permanent crops: 0.4%
other: 96.71% (2001)
Irrigated land: 11,950 sq km (1998 est.)
Natural hazards: earthquakes, tsunamis, flooding, landslides, mild volcanic activity
Environment - current issues: deforestation (some the result of illegal logging); overgrazing of the slopes of the costa and sierra leading to soil erosion; desertification; air pollution in Lima; pollution of rivers and coastal waters from municipal and mining wastes
Environment - international agreements:
party to: Antarctic-Environmental Protocol, Antarctic-Marine Living Resources, Antarctic Treaty, Biodiversity, Climate Change, Climate Change-Kyoto Protocol, Desertification, Endangered Species, Hazardous Wastes, Marine Dumping, Ozone Layer Protection, Ship Pollution, Tropical Timber 83, Tropical Timber 94, Wetlands, Whaling
signed, but not ratified: none of the selected agreements
Geography - note: shares control of Lago Titicaca, world's highest navigable lake, with Bolivia; a remote slope of Nevado Mismi, a 5,316 m peak, is the ultimate source of the Amazon River

PEOPLE

Population: 27,925,628 (July 2005 est.)
Age structure:
0-14 years: 31.5% (male 4,479,278/female 4,323,356)
15-64 years: 63.3% (male 8,891,785/female 8,776,343)
65 years and over: 5.2% (male 685,179/female 769,687) (2005 est.)
Median age:
total: 24.95 years
male: 24.69 years
female: 25.21 years (2005 est.)
Population growth rate: 1.36% (2005 est.)
Birth rate: 20.87 births/1,000 population (2005 est.)
Death rate: 6.26 deaths/1,000 population (2005 est.)
Net migration rate: -1.03 migrant(s)/1,000 population (2005 est.)
Sex ratio:
at birth: 1.05 male(s)/female
under 15 years: 1.04 male(s)/female
15-64 years: 1.01 male(s)/female
65 years and over: 0.89 male(s)/female
total population: 1.01 male(s)/female (2005 est.)
Infant mortality rate:
total: 31.94 deaths/1,000 live births
male: 34.53 deaths/1,000 live births
female: 29.24 deaths/1,000 live births (2005 est.)
Life expectancy at birth:
total population: 69.53 years
male: 67.77 years
female: 71.37 years (2005 est.)
Total fertility rate: 2.56 children born/woman (2005 est.)
HIV/AIDS - adult prevalence rate: 0.5% (2003 est.)
HIV/AIDS - people living with HIV/AIDS: 82,000 (2003 est.)
HIV/AIDS - deaths: 4,200 (2003 est.)
Nationality:
noun: Peruvian(s)
adjective: Peruvian
Ethnic groups: Amerindian 45%, mestizo (mixed Amerindian and white) 37%, white 15%, black, Japanese, Chinese, and other 3%
Religions: Roman Catholic 81%, Seventh Day Adventist 1.4%, other Christian 0.7%, other 0.6%, unspecified or none 16.3% (2003 est.)
Languages: Spanish (official), Quechua (official), Aymara, and a large number of minor Amazonian languages
Literacy:
definition: age 15 and over can read and write
total population: 87.7%
male: 93.5%
female: 82.1% (2004 est.)

GOVERNMENT

Country name:
conventional long form: Republic of Peru
conventional short form: Peru
local long form: Republica del Peru
local short form: Peru
Government type: constitutional republic
Capital: Lima
Administrative divisions: 25 regions (regiones, singular - region) and 1 province* (provincia); Amazonas, Ancash, Apurimac, Arequipa, Ayacucho, Cajamarca, Callao, Cusco, Huancavelica,

Huanuco, Ica, Junin, La Libertad, Lambayeque, Lima, Lima*, Loreto, Madre de Dios, Moquegua, Pasco, Piura, Puno, San Martin, Tacna, Tumbes, Ucayali
Independence: 28 July 1821 (from Spain)
National holiday: Independence Day, 28 July (1821)
Constitution: 31 December 1993
Legal system: based on civil law system; has not accepted compulsory ICJ jurisdiction
Suffrage: 18 years of age; universal and compulsory until the age of 70; note - members of the military and national police may not vote
Executive branch:
chief of state: President Alejandro TOLEDO Manrique (since 28 July 2001); note - the president is both the chief of state and head of government; additionally, the constitution provides for two vice presidents, First Vice President (vacant) and Second Vice President David WAISMAN Rjavinsthi (since 28 July 2001)
head of government: President Alejandro TOLEDO Manrique (since 28 July 2001); note - the president is both the chief of state and head of government; additionally, the constitution provides for two vice presidents, First Vice President (vacant) and Second Vice President David WAISMAN Rjavinsthi (since 28 July 2001)
note: Prime Minister Pedro Pablo KUCZYNSKI (since 25 August 2005) does not exercise executive power; this power is in the hands of the president
cabinet: Council of Ministers appointed by the president
elections: president elected by popular vote for a five-year term; special presidential and congressional elections held 8 April 2001, with runoff election held 3 June 2001; next to be held 9 April 2006
election results: President Alejandro TOLEDO Manrique elected president in runoff election; percent of vote - Alejandro TOLEDO Manrique 53.1%, Alan GARCIA 46.9%
Legislative branch: unicameral Congress of the Republic of Peru or Congreso de la Republica del Peru (120 seats; members are elected by popular vote to serve five-year terms)
elections: last held 8 April 2001 (next to be held 9 April 2006)
election results: percent of vote by party - PP 26.3%, APRA 19.7%, UN 13.8%, FIM 11.0%, others 29.2%; seats by party - PP 47, APRA 28, UN 17, FIM 11, others 17
Judicial branch: Supreme Court of Justice or Corte Suprema de Justicia (judges are appointed by the National Council of the Judiciary)
Political parties and leaders: Independent Moralizing Front or FIM [Fernando OLIVERA Vega]; National Unity (Unidad Nacional) or UN [Lourdes FLORES Nano]; Peru Posible or PP [David WAISMAN]; Peruvian Aprista Party or PAP (also referred to by its original name Alianza Popular Revolucionaria Americana or APRA) [Alan GARCIA]; Popular Action or AP [Javier DIAZ Orihuela]; Solucion Popular [Carlos BOLANA]; Somos Peru or SP [Alberto ANDRADE]; Union for Peru or UPP [Roger GUERRA Garcia]
Political pressure groups and leaders: leftist guerrilla groups include Shining Path [Abimael GUZMAN Reynoso (imprisoned), Gabriel MACARIO (top leader at-large)]; Tupac Amaru Revolutionary Movement or MRTA [Victor POLAY (imprisoned), Hugo AVALLENEDA Valdez (top leader at-large)]
International organization participation: APEC, CAN, CSN, FAO, G-15, G-24, G-77, IADB, IAEA, IBRD, ICAO, ICC, ICCt, ICFTU, ICRM, IDA, IFAD, IFC, IFRCS, IHO, ILO, IMF, IMO, Interpol, IOC, IOM, ISO (correspondent), ITU, LAES, LAIA, Mercosur (associate), MIGA, MINUSTAH, MONUC, NAM, OAS, ONUB, OPANAL, OPCW, PCA, RG, UN, UNCTAD, UNESCO, UNIDO, UNMEE, UNMIL, UNMIS, UNOCI, UPU, WCL, WCO, WFTU, WHO, WIPO, WMO, WToO, WTO
Diplomatic representation in the US:
chief of mission: Ambassador Eduardo FERRERO Costa
chancery: 1700 Massachusetts Avenue NW, Washington, DC 20036
telephone: [1] (202) 833-9860 through 9869
FAX: [1] (202) 659-8124
consulate(s) general: Boston, Chicago, Denver, Hartford, Houston, Los Angeles, Miami, New York, Paterson (New Jersey), San Francisco, Washington, DC
Diplomatic representation from the US:
chief of mission: Ambassador J. Curtis STRUBLE
embassy: Avenida La Encalada, Cuadra 17s/n, Surco, Lima 33
mailing address: P. O. Box 1995, Lima 1; American Embassy (Lima), APO AA 34031-5000
telephone: [51] (1) 434-3000
FAX: [51] (1) 618-2397
Flag description: three equal, vertical bands of red (hoist side), white, and red with the coat of arms centered in the white band; the coat of arms features a shield bearing a vicuna, cinchona tree (the source of quinine), and a yellow cornucopia spilling out gold coins, all framed by a green wreath

ECONOMY

Economy - overview: Peru's economy reflects its varied geography - an arid coastal region, the Andes further inland, and tropical lands bordering Colombia and Brazil. Abundant mineral resources are found in the mountainous areas, and Peru's coastal waters provide excellent fishing grounds. However, overdependence on minerals and metals subjects the economy to fluctuations in world prices, and a lack of infrastructure deters trade and investment. After several years of inconsistent economic performance, the Peruvian economy grew by more than 4 percent per year during the period 2002-2005, with a stable exchange rate and low inflation. Risk premiums on Peruvian bonds on secondary markets reached historically low levels in late 2004, reflecting investor optimism regarding the government's prudent fiscal policies and openness to trade and investment. Despite the strong macroeconomic performance, the TOLEDO administration remained unpopular in 2005, and unemployment and poverty have stayed persistently high. Economic growth will be driven by the Camisea natural gas megaproject and by exports of minerals, textiles, and agricultural products. Peru is expected to sign a free-trade agreement with the United States in early 2006.
GDP (purchasing power parity): $168.9 billion (2005 est.)
GDP (official exchange rate): $73.3 billion (2005 est.)
GDP - real growth rate: 5.6% (2005 est.)
GDP - per capita: purchasing power parity - $6,000 (2005 est.)
GDP - composition by sector:
agriculture: 8%
industry: 27%
services: 65% (2003 est.)
Labor force: 9.06 million (2005 est.)
Labor force - by occupation: agriculture 9%, industry 18%, services 73% (2001)
Unemployment rate: 8.7% in metropolitan Lima; widespread underemployment (2005 est.)
Population below poverty line: 54% (2003 est.)
Household income or consumption by percentage share:
lowest 10%: 0.8%
highest 10%: 37.2% (2000)
Distribution of family income - Gini index: 49.8 (2000)
Inflation rate (consumer prices): 1.6% (2005 est.)
Investment (gross fixed): 18.6% of GDP (2005 est.)
Budget:
revenues: $21.87 billion

expenditures: $22.47 billion, including capital expenditures of $1.8 billion, for general government, excluding private enterprises (2005 est.)
Public debt: 41.8% of GDP (2005 est.)
Agriculture - products: coffee, cotton, sugarcane, rice, potatoes, corn, plantains, grapes, oranges, coca; poultry, beef, dairy products; fish
Industries: mining and refining of minerals and metals, petroleum extraction and refining, natural gas, fishing and fish processing, textiles, clothing, food processing, steel, metal fabrication
Industrial production growth rate: 6.6% (2005 est.)
Electricity - production: 22.68 billion kWh (2003 est.)
Electricity - production by source:
fossil fuel: 14.5%
hydro: 84.7%
nuclear: 0%
other: 0.8% (2001)
Electricity - consumption: 21.09 billion kWh (2003)
Electricity - exports: 0 kWh (2003)
Electricity - imports: 0 kWh (2003)
Oil - production: 120,000 bbl/day (2005 est.)
Oil - consumption: 157,000 bbl/day (2003 est.)
Oil - exports: 49,000 bbl/day (2004 est.)
Oil - imports: NA
Oil - proved reserves: 370 million bbl (2005 est.)
Natural gas - production: 910 million cu m (2004 est.)
Natural gas - consumption: 910 million cu m (2004 est.)
Natural gas - exports: 0 cu m (2004 est.)
Natural gas - imports: 0 cu m (2004 est.)
Natural gas - proved reserves: 245.1 billion cu m (2005)
Current account balance: $241 million (2005 est.)
Exports: $15.95 billion f.o.b. (2005 est.)
Exports - partners: US 29.5%, China 9.9%, UK 9%, Chile 5.1%, Japan 4.4% (2004)
Imports: $12.15 billion f.o.b. (2005 est.)
Imports - partners: US 30.3%, Spain 11.5%, Chile 7.2%, Brazil 5.4%, Colombia 5.2% (2004)
Reserves of foreign exchange and gold: $15.34 billion (2005 est.)
Debt - external: $30.18 billion (30 June 2005 est.)
Economic aid - recipient: $491 million (2002)
Currency (code): nuevo sol (PEN)
Currency code: PEN
Exchange rates: nuevo sol per US dollar - 3.29 (2005), 3.4132 (2004), 3.4785 (2003), 3.5165 (2002), 3.5068 (2001)
Fiscal year: calendar year

COMMUNICATIONS

Telephones - main lines in use: 1,839,200 (2003)
Telephones - mobile cellular: 2,908,800 (2003)
Telephone system:
general assessment: adequate for most requirements
domestic: nationwide microwave radio relay system and a domestic satellite system with 12 earth stations
international: country code - 51; satellite earth stations - 2 Intelsat (Atlantic Ocean); Pan American submarine cable
Radio broadcast stations: AM 472, FM 198, shortwave 189 (1999)
Radios: 6.65 million (1997)
Television broadcast stations: 13 (plus 112 repeaters) (1997)
Televisions: 3.06 million (1997)
Internet country code: .pe
Internet hosts: 65,868 (2003)
Internet Service Providers (ISPs): 10 (2000)
Internet users: 2.85 million (2003)

TRANSPORTATION

Airports: 234 (2004 est.)
Airports - with paved runways:
total: 54
over 3,047 m: 6
2,438 to 3,047 m: 20
1,524 to 2,437 m: 14
914 to 1,523 m: 11
under 914 m: 3 (2005 est.)
Airports - with unpaved runways:
total: 192
1,524 to 2,437 m: 22
914 to 1,523 m: 59
under 914 m: 111 (2005 est.)
Heliports: 1 (2005 est.)
Pipelines: gas 388 km; oil 1,557 km; refined products 13 km (2004)
Railways:
total: 3,462 km
standard gauge: 2,962 km 1.435-m gauge
narrow gauge: 500 km 0.914-m gauge (2004)
Roadways:
total: 78,230 km
paved: 10,452 km
unpaved: 67,778 km (2001)
Waterways: 8,808 km
note: 8,600 km of navigable tributaries of Amazon system and 208 km of Lago Titicaca (2004)
Merchant marine:
total: 4 ships (1,000 GRT or over) 13,666 GRT/17,611 DWT
by type: cargo 3, petroleum tanker 1
foreign-owned: 1 (United States 1)
registered in other countries: 14 (2005)
Ports and terminals: Callao, Iquitos, Matarani, Pucallpa, Yurimaguas
note: Iquitos, Pucallpa, and Yurimaguas are on the upper reaches of the Amazon and its tributaries

MILITARY

Military branches: Army (Ejercito Peruano), Navy (Marina de Guerra del Peru; includes Naval Air, Naval Infantry, and Coast Guard), Air Force (Fuerza Aerea del Peru; FAP)
Military service age and obligation: 18 years of age for compulsory military service (1999)
Manpower available for military service:
males age 18-49: 6,647,874 (2005 est.)
Manpower fit for military service: *males age 18-49:* 4,938,417 (2005 est.)
Manpower reaching military service age annually: *males:* 277,105 (2005 est.)
Military expenditures - dollar figure: $829.3 million (2003)
Military expenditures - percent of GDP: 1.4% (2004)

TRANSNATIONAL ISSUES

Disputes - international: Peru proposes changing its latitudinal maritime boundary with Chile to an equidistance line with a southwestern axis; organized illegal narcotics operations in Colombia have penetrated Peru's shared border; Peru does not support Bolivia's claim to restore maritime access through a sovereign corridor through Chile along the Peruvian border
Refugees and internally displaced persons: *IDPs:* 60,000 (civil war from 1980-2000; most IDPs are indigenous peasants in Andean and Amazonian regions) (2004)
Illicit drugs: until 1996 the world's largest coca leaf producer; emerging opium producer; cultivation of coca in Peru fell 15 percent to 31,150 hectares between 2002 and the end of 2003; much of the cocaine base is shipped to neighboring Colombia for processing into cocaine, while finished cocaine is shipped out from Pacific ports to the international drug market; increasing amounts of base and finished cocaine, however, are being moved to Brazil and Bolivia for use in the Southern Cone or transshipped to Europe and Africa

PHILIPPINES

INTRODUCTION

Background: The Philippine Islands became a Spanish colony during the 16th century; they were ceded to the US in 1898 following the Spanish-American War. In 1935 the Philippines became a self-governing commonwealth. Manuel QUEZON was elected President and was tasked with preparing the country for independence after a 10-year transition. In 1942 the islands fell under Japanese occupation during WWII, and US forces and Filipinos fought together during 1944-45 to regain control. On 4 July 1946 the Philippines attained their independence. The 21-year rule of Ferdinand MARCOS ended in 1986, when a widespread popular rebellion forced him into exile and installed Corazon AQUINO as president. Her presidency was hampered by several coup attempts, which prevented a return to full political stability and economic development. Fidel RAMOS was elected president in 1992 and his administration was marked by greater stability and progress on economic reforms. In 1992, the US closed its last military bases on the islands. Joseph ESTRADA was elected president in 1998, but was succeeded by his vice-president, Gloria MACAPAGAL-ARROYO, in January 2001 after ESTRADA's stormy impeachment trial on corruption charges broke down and widespread demonstrations led to his ouster. MACAPAGAL-ARROYO was elected to a six-year term in May 2004. The Philippine Government faces threats from armed communist insurgencies and from Muslim separatists in the south.

GEOGRAPHY

Location: Southeastern Asia, archipelago between the Philippine Sea and the South China Sea, east of Vietnam
Geographic coordinates: 13 00 N, 122 00 E
Map references: Southeast Asia
Area:
total: 300,000 sq km
land: 298,170 sq km
water: 1,830 sq km
Area - comparative: slightly larger than Arizona
Land boundaries: 0 km
Coastline: 36,289 km
Maritime claims:
territorial sea: irregular polygon extending up to 100 nm from coastline as defined by 1898 treaty; since late 1970s has also claimed polygonal-shaped area in South China Sea up to 285 nm in breadth
exclusive economic zone: 200 nm
continental shelf: to depth of exploitation
Climate: tropical marine; northeast monsoon (November to April); southwest monsoon (May to October)
Terrain: mostly mountains with narrow to extensive coastal lowlands
Elevation extremes:
lowest point: Philippine Sea 0 m
highest point: Mount Apo 2,954 m
Natural resources: timber, petroleum, nickel, cobalt, silver, gold, salt, copper
Land use:
arable land: 18.95%
permanent crops: 16.77%
other: 64.28% (2001)
Irrigated land: 15,500 sq km (1998 est.)
Natural hazards: astride typhoon belt, usually affected by 15 and struck by five to six cyclonic storms per year; landslides; active volcanoes; destructive earthquakes; tsunamis
Environment - current issues: uncontrolled deforestation especially in watershed areas; soil erosion; air and water pollution in major urban centers; coral reef degradation; increasing pollution of coastal mangrove swamps that are important fish breeding grounds
Environment - international agreements:
party to: Biodiversity, Climate Change, Climate Change-Kyoto Protocol, Desertification, Endangered Species, Hazardous Wastes, Law of the Sea, Marine Dumping, Ozone Layer Protection, Ship Pollution, Tropical Timber 83, Tropical Timber 94, Wetlands, Whaling
signed, but not ratified: Air Pollution-Persistent Organic Pollutants
Geography - note: the Philippine archipelago is made up of 7,107 islands; favorably located in relation to many of Southeast Asia's main water bodies: the South China Sea, Philippine Sea, Sulu Sea, Celebes Sea, and Luzon Strait

PEOPLE

Population: 87,857,473 (July 2005 est.)
Age structure:
0-14 years: 35.4% (male 15,869,636/female 15,255,588)
15-64 years: 60.6% (male 26,503,785/female 26,722,511)
65 years and over: 4% (male 1,523,213/female 1,982,740) (2005 est.)
Median age:
total: 22.27 years
male: 21.77 years
female: 22.8 years (2005 est.)
Population growth rate: 1.84% (2005 est.)
Birth rate: 25.31 births/1,000 population (2005 est.)
Death rate: 5.47 deaths/1,000 population (2005 est.)
Net migration rate: -1.49 migrant(s)/1,000 population (2005 est.)
Sex ratio:
at birth: 1.05 male(s)/female
under 15 years: 1.04 male(s)/female
15-64 years: 0.99 male(s)/female
65 years and over: 0.77 male(s)/female
total population: 1 male(s)/female (2005 est.)
Infant mortality rate:
total: 23.51 deaths/1,000 live births
male: 26.34 deaths/1,000 live births
female: 20.54 deaths/1,000 live births (2005 est.)
Life expectancy at birth:
total population: 69.91 years
male: 67.03 years
female: 72.92 years (2005 est.)
Total fertility rate: 3.16 children born/woman (2005 est.)
HIV/AIDS - adult prevalence rate: less than 0.1% (2003 est.)
HIV/AIDS - people living with HIV/AIDS: 9,000 (2003 est.)
HIV/AIDS - deaths: less than 500 (2003 est.)
Major infectious diseases:
degree of risk: high
food or waterborne diseases: bacterial diarrhea, hepatitis A, and typhoid fever
vectorborne diseases: dengue fever and malaria are high risks in some locations

animal contact disease: rabies (2004)

Nationality:
noun: Filipino(s)
adjective: Philippine

Ethnic groups: Tagalog 28.1%, Cebuano 13.1%, Ilocano 9%, Bisaya/Binisaya 7.6%, Hiligaynon Ilonggo 7.5%, Bikol 6%, Waray 3.4%, other 25.3% (2000 census)

Religions: Roman Catholic 80.9%, Evangelical 2.8%, Iglesia ni Kristo 2.3%, Aglipayan 2%, other Christian 4.5%, Muslim 5%, other 1.8%, unspecified 0.6%, none 0.1% (2000 census)

Languages: two official languages - Filipino (based on Tagalog) and English; eight major dialects - Tagalog, Cebuano, Ilocano, Hiligaynon or Ilonggo, Bicol, Waray, Pampango, and Pangasinan

Literacy:
definition: age 15 and over can read and write
total population: 92.6%
male: 92.5%
female: 92.7% (2002)

GOVERNMENT

Country name:
conventional long form: Republic of the Philippines
conventional short form: Philippines
local long form: Republika ng Pilipinas
local short form: Pilipinas

Government type: republic

Capital: Manila

Administrative divisions: 79 provinces and 117 chartered cities
: provinces: Abra, Agusan del Norte, Agusan del Sur, Aklan, Albay, Antique, Apayao, Aurora, Basilan, Bataan, Batanes, Batangas, Biliran, Benguet, Bohol, Bukidnon, Bulacan, Cagayan, Camarines Norte, Camarines Sur, Camiguin, Capiz, Catanduanes, Cavite, Cebu, Compostela, Davao del Norte, Davao del Sur, Davao Oriental, Eastern Samar, Guimaras, Ifugao, Ilocos Norte, Ilocos Sur, Iloilo, Isabela, Kalinga, Laguna, Lanao del Norte, Lanao del Sur, La Union, Leyte, Maguindanao, Marinduque, Masbate, Mindoro Occidental, Mindoro Oriental, Misamis Occidental, Misamis Oriental, Mountain Province, Negros Occidental, Negros Oriental, North Cotabato, Northern Samar, Nueva Ecija, Nueva Vizcaya, Palawan, Pampanga, Pangasinan, Quezon, Quirino, Rizal, Romblon, Samar, Sarangani, Siquijor, Sorsogon, South Cotabato, Southern Leyte, Sultan Kudarat, Sulu, Surigao del Norte, Surigao del Sur, Tarlac, Tawi-Tawi, Zambales, Zamboanga del Norte, Zamboanga del Sur, Zamboanga Sibugay
: chartered cities: Alaminos, Angeles, Antipolo, Bacolod, Bago, Baguio, Bais, Balanga, Batangas, Bayawan, Bislig, Butuan, Cabanatuan, Cadiz, Cagayan de Oro, Calamba, Calapan, Calbayog, Candon, Canlaon, Cauayan, Cavite, Cebu, Cotabato, Dagupan, Danao, Dapitan, Davao, Digos, Dipolog, Dumaguete, Escalante, Gapan, General Santos, Gingoog, Himamaylan, Iligan, Iloilo, Isabela, Iriga, Kabankalan, Kalookan, Kidapawan, Koronadal, La Carlota, Laoag, Lapu-Lapu, Las Pinas, Legazpi, Ligao, Lipa, Lucena, Maasin, Makati, Malabon, Malaybalay, Malolos, Mandaluyong, Mandaue, Manila, Marawi, Markina, Masbate, Muntinlupa, Munoz, Naga, Olongapo, Ormoc, Oroquieta, Ozamis, Pagadian, Palayan, Panabo, Paranaque, Pasay, Pasig, Passi, Puerto Princesa, Quezon, Roxas, Sagay, Samal, San Carlos (in Negros Occidental), San Carlos (in Pangasinan), San Fernando (in La Union), San Fernando (in Pampanga), San Jose, San Jose del Monte, San Pablo, Santa Rosa, Santiago, Silay, Sipalay, Sorsogon, Surigao, Tabaco, Tacloban, Tacurong, Tagaytay, Tagbilaran, Taguig, Tagum, Talisay (in Cebu), Talisay (in Negros Oriental), Tanauan, Tangub, Tanjay, Tarlac, Toledo, Tuguegarao, Trece Martires, Urdaneta, Valencia, Valenzuela, Victorias, Vigan, Zamboanga

Independence: 12 June 1898 (from Spain)

National holiday: Independence Day, 12 June (1898)
note: 12 June 1898 was date of declaration of independence from Spain; 4 July 1946 was date of independence from US

Constitution: 2 February 1987, effective 11 February 1987

Legal system: based on Spanish and Anglo-American law; accepts compulsory ICJ jurisdiction, with reservations

Suffrage: 18 years of age; universal

Executive branch:
chief of state: President Gloria MACAPAGAL-ARROYO (since 20 January 2001); note - president is both chief of state and head of government
head of government: President Gloria MACAPAGAL-ARROYO (since 20 January 2001)
cabinet: Cabinet appointed by the president with consent of Commission of Appointments
elections: president and vice president (Manuel "Noli" DE CASTRO) elected on separate tickets by popular vote for six-year terms; election last held 10 May 2004 (next to be held in May 2010)
election results: results of the election - Gloria MACAPAGAL-ARROYO elected president; percent of vote - Gloria MACAPAGAL-ARROYO 40%, Fernando POE 37%, three others 23%

Legislative branch: bicameral Congress or Kongreso consists of the Senate or Senado (24 seats - one-half elected every three years; members elected at large by popular vote to serve six-year terms) and the House of Representatives or Kapulungan Ng Mga Kinatawan (212 members representing districts plus 24 sectoral party-list members; members elected by popular vote to serve three-year terms; note - the Constitution prohibits the House of Representatives from having more than 250 members)
elections: Senate - last held 10 May 2004 (next to be held in May 2007); House of Representatives - elections last held 10 May 2004 (next to be held in May 2007)
election results: Senate - percent of vote by party - Lakas 30%, LP 13%, KNP 13%, independents 17%, others 27%; seats by party - Lakas 7, LP 3, KNP (coalition) 3, independents 4, others 6; note - there are 23 rather than 24 sitting senators because one senator was elected Vice President; House of Representatives - percent of vote by party - NA%; seats by party - Lakas 93, NPC 53, LP 34, LDP 11, others 20; party-listers 24 (2005)

Judicial branch: Supreme Court (15 justices are appointed by the president on the recommendation of the Judicial and Bar Council and serve until 70 years of age); Court of Appeals; Sandigan-bayan (special court for hearing corruption cases of government officials)

Political parties and leaders: Kabalikat Ng Malayang Pilipino (Kampi) [Ronaldo PUNO, president]; Laban Ng Demokratikong Pilipino (Struggle of Filipino Democrats) or LDP [Edgardo ANGARA, president]; Lakas Ng Edsa (National Union of Christian Democrats) or Lakas [Jose DE VENECIA, president; Gloria MACAPAGAL-ARROYO, chairperson]; Liberal Party or LP [Franklin DRILON, president; Jose ATIENZA, JR., chairman]; Nacionalista [Manuel VILLAR, president]; National People's Coalition or NPC [Eduardo COJUANGCO, chairman emeritus; Frisco SAN JUAN, president]; PDP-Laban [Aquilino PIMENTEL, president]; People's Reform Party [Miriam Defensor SANTIAGO, president]; PROMDI [Emilio OSMENA, president]; Pwersa ng Masang Pilipino (Party of the Philippine Masses) or PMP [Joseph ESTRADA, president; Juan Ponce ENRILE, chairman]; Reporma [Renato DE VILLA, chairman]

Political pressure groups and leaders: AKBAYAN [Reps. Etta ROSALES, Mario AGUJA, and Risa HON-

TIVEROS-BARAQUIEL]; ANAKPAWIS [Reps. Crispin BELTRAN and Rafael MARIANO]; Association of Philippine Electric Cooperatives (APEC) [Reps. Edgar VALDEZ, Ernesto PABLO, and Sunny Rose MADAMBA]; Bayan Muna [Reps. Satur OCAMPO, Joel VIRADOR, and Teodoro CASINO, Jr.]; BUHAY [Reps. Rene VELARDE and Hans Christian SENERES]; BUTIL [Rep. Benjamin CRUZ]; CIBAC [Rep. Emmanuel Joel VILLANUEVA]; GABRIELA [Rep. Liza MAZA]; PARTIDO NG MANGGAGAWA [Rep. Renato MAGTUBO] (2003)

International organization participation: APEC, APT, ARF, AsDB, ASEAN, BIS, CP, EAS, FAO, G-24, G-77, IAEA, IBRD, ICAO, ICC, ICCt (signatory), ICFTU, ICRM, IDA, IFAD, IFC, IFRCS, IHO, ILO, IMF, IMO, Interpol, IOC, IOM, ISO, ITU, MIGA, MINUSTAH, NAM, OAS (observer), ONUB, OPCW, PIF (partner), UN, UN Security Council (temporary), UNCTAD, UNESCO, UNHCR, UNIDO, UNMIL, UNOCI, UPU, WCL, WCO, WFTU, WHO, WIPO, WMO, WToO, WTO

Diplomatic representation in the US:
chief of mission: Ambassador Albert DEL ROSARIO
chancery: 1600 Massachusetts Avenue NW, Washington, DC 20036
telephone: [1] (202) 467-9300
FAX: [1] (202) 328-7614
consulate(s) general: Chicago, Honolulu, Los Angeles, New York, San Francisco, San Jose (Northern Mariana Islands), Tamuning (Guam)

Diplomatic representation from the US:
chief of mission: Charge d'Affaires Paul W. JONES
embassy: 1201 Roxas Boulevard, Ermita 1000, Manila
mailing address: PSC 500, FPO AP 96515-1000
telephone: [63] (2) 528-6300
FAX: [63] (2) 522-4361

Flag description: two equal horizontal bands of blue (top; representing peace and justice) and red (representing courage); a white equilateral triangle based on the hoist side represents equality; the center of the triangle displays a yellow sun with eight primary rays, each representing one of the first eight provinces that sought independence from Spain; each corner of the triangle contains a small, yellow, five-pointed star representing the three major geographical divisions of the country: Luzon, Visayas, and Mindanao; the design of the flag dates to 1897; in wartime the flag is flown upside down with the red band at the top

ECONOMY

Economy - overview: The Philippines was less severely affected by the Asian financial crisis of 1998 than its neighbors, aided in part by its high level of annual remittances from overseas workers, and no sustained runup in asset prices or foreign borrowing prior to the crisis. From a 0.6% decline in 1998, GDP expanded by 2.4% in 1999, and 4.4% in 2000, but slowed to 3.2% in 2001 in the context of a global economic slowdown, an export slump, and political and security concerns. GDP growth accelerated to about 5% between 2002 and 2005 reflecting the continued resilience of the service sector, and improved exports and agricultural output. Nonetheless, it will take a higher, sustained growth path to make appreciable progress in the alleviation of poverty given the Philippines' high annual population growth rate and unequal distribution of income. The Philippines also faces higher oil prices, higher interest rates on its dollar borrowings, and higher inflation. Fiscal constraints limit Manila's ability to finance infrastructure and social spending. The Philippines' consistently large budget deficit has produced a high debt level. This has forced Manila to spend a large portion of the national government budget on debt service. Large unprofitable public enterprises, especially in the energy sector, contribute to the government's debt because of slow progress on privatization. Credit rating agencies have expressed concern about the Philippines' ability to service the debt. Legislative progress on new revenue measures will weigh heavily on credit rating decisions.

GDP (purchasing power parity): $451.3 billion (2005 est.)
GDP (official exchange rate): $90.3 billion (2005 est.)
GDP - real growth rate: 4.7% (2005 est.)
GDP - per capita: purchasing power parity - $5,100 (2005 est.)
GDP - composition by sector:
agriculture: 14.8%
industry: 31.7%
services: 53.5% (2005 est.)
Labor force: 36.73 million (2005 est.)
Labor force - by occupation: agriculture 36%, industry 16%, services 48% (2004 est.)
Unemployment rate: 12.2% (2005 est.)
Population below poverty line: 40% (2001 est.)
Household income or consumption by percentage share:
lowest 10%: 2.3%
highest 10%: 31.9% (2003)
Distribution of family income - Gini index: 46.6 (2003)
Inflation rate (consumer prices): 7.9% (2005 est.)
Investment (gross fixed): 16.3% of GDP (2005 est.)
Budget:
revenues: $12.38 billion
expenditures: $15.77 billion, including capital expenditures of $2.4 million (2005 est.)
Public debt: 77.4% of GDP (2005 est.)
Agriculture - products: sugarcane, coconuts, rice, corn, bananas, casavas, pineapples, fish, mangoes, pork, eggs, beef
Industries: electronics assembly, garments, footwear, pharmaceuticals, chemicals, wood products, food processing, petroleum refining, fishing
Industrial production growth rate: 0.5% (2005 est.)
Electricity - production: 47.82 billion kWh (2003)
Electricity - production by source:
fossil fuel: 55.6%
hydro: 17.5%
nuclear: 0%
other: 26.9% (2001)
Electricity - consumption: 44.48 billion kWh (2003)
Electricity - exports: 0 kWh (2003)
Electricity - imports: 0 kWh (2003)
Oil - production: 14,360 bbl/day (2003 est.)
Oil - consumption: 335,000 bbl/day (2003 est.)
Oil - exports: 0 bbl/day (2001)
Oil - imports: 312,000 bbl/day (2003)
Oil - proved reserves: 152 million bbl (1 January 2004)
Natural gas - production: 2.5 million cu m (2004 est.)
Natural gas - consumption: 25 million cu m (2004 est.)
Natural gas - exports: 0 cu m (2004 est.)
Natural gas - imports: 0 cu m (2004 est.)
Natural gas - proved reserves: 107.6 billion cu m (1 January 2004)
Current account balance: $3.872 billion (2005 est.)
Exports: $41.25 billion f.o.b. (2005 est.)
Exports - partners: Japan 20.1%, US 18.2%, Netherlands 9%, Hong Kong 7.9%, China 6.7%, Singapore 6.6%, Taiwan 5.6%, Malaysia 5.2% (2004)
Imports: $42.66 billion f.o.b. (2005 est.)
Imports - partners: US 18.8%, Japan 17.4%, Singapore 7.8%, Taiwan 7.3%, South Korea 6.2%, China 6%, Malaysia 4.5% (2004)
Reserves of foreign exchange and gold: $18.09 billion (November 2005)
Debt - external: $67.62 billion (2005 est.)
Economic aid - recipient: ODA commitments, $2 billion (2004)
Currency (code): Philippine peso (PHP)
Currency code: PHP

Exchange rates: Philippine pesos per US dollar - 55.1 (2005), 56.04 (2004), 54.203 (2003), 51.604 (2002), 50.993 (2001)
Fiscal year: calendar year

COMMUNICATIONS

Telephones - main lines in use: 3,310,900 (2002)
Telephones - mobile cellular: 15.201 million (2002)
Telephone system:
general assessment: good international radiotelephone and submarine cable services; domestic and inter-island service adequate
domestic: domestic satellite system with 11 earth stations
international: country code - 63; 9 international gateways; satellite earth stations - 3 Intelsat (1 Indian Ocean and 2 Pacific Ocean); submarine cables to Hong Kong, Guam, Singapore, Taiwan, and Japan
Radio broadcast stations: AM 369, FM 583, shortwave 5
note: each shortwave station operates on multiple frequencies in the language of the target audience (2004)
Radios: 11.5 million (1997)
Television broadcast stations: 225; note - 1373 CATV networks (2004)
Televisions: 3.7 million (1997)
Internet country code: .ph
Internet hosts: 38,440 (2002)
Internet Service Providers (ISPs): 33 (2000)
Internet users: 3.5 million (2002)

TRANSPORTATION

Airports: 255 (2004 est.)
Airports - with paved runways:
total: 83
over 3,047 m: 4
2,438 to 3,047 m: 7
1,524 to 2,437 m: 26
914 to 1,523 m: 36
under 914 m: 10 (2005 est.)
Airports - with unpaved runways:
total: 173
1,524 to 2,437 m: 5
914 to 1,523 m: 68
under 914 m: 100 (2005 est.)
Heliports: 2 (2005 est.)
Pipelines: gas 565 km; oil 135 km; refined products 100 km (2004)
Railways:
total: 897 km
narrow gauge: 897 km 1.067-m gauge (492 km are in operation) (2004)
Roadways:
total: 202,124 km
paved: 19,202 km
unpaved: 182,922 km (2002)
Waterways: 3,219 km
note: limited to vessels with draft less than 1.5 m (2004)
Merchant marine:
total: 419 ships (1,000 GRT or over) 4,524,259 GRT/6,437,171 DWT
by type: bulk carrier 85, cargo 109, chemical tanker 13, container 5, liquefied gas 7, livestock carrier 15, passenger 11, passenger/cargo 73, petroleum tanker 47, refrigerated cargo 23, roll on/roll off 17, vehicle carrier 14
foreign-owned: 69 (Canada 1, China 2, Germany 2, Greece 5, Hong Kong 2, Japan 31, Malaysia 2, Netherlands 20, Norway 1, UAE 1, United States 2)
registered in other countries: 40 (2005)
Ports and terminals: Cagayan de Oro, Cebu, Davao, Iligan, Iloilo, Manila, Surigao

MILITARY

Military branches: Armed Forces of the Philippines (AFP): Army, Navy (includes Coast Guard, Marine Corps), Air Force
Military service age and obligation: 18 years of age for compulsory and voluntary military service (2001)
Manpower available for military service:
males age 18-49: 20,131,179 (2005 est.)
Manpower fit for military service: *males age 18-49:* 15,170,096 (2005 est.)
Manpower reaching military service age annually: *males:* 907,542 (2005 est.)
Military expenditures - dollar figure: $805.5 million (2004)
Military expenditures - percent of GDP: 1% (2004)

TRANSNATIONAL ISSUES

Disputes - international: The Philippines claims sovereignty over certain of the Spratly Islands, known locally as the Kalayaan (Freedom) Islands, also claimed by China, Malaysia, Taiwan, and Vietnam; the 2002 "Declaration on the Conduct of Parties in the South China Sea," has eased tensions in the Spratly Islands but falls short of a legally binding "code of conduct" desired by several of the disputants; in March 2005, the national oil companies of China, the Philippines, and Vietnam signed a joint accord to conduct marine seismic activities in the Spratly Islands; Philippines retains a dormant claim to Malaysia's Sabah State in northern Borneo based on the Sultanate of Sulu's granting the Philippines Government power of attorney to pursue a sovereignty claim on his behalf
Refugees and internally displaced persons: *IDPs:* 150,000 (fighting between government troops and MILF and Abu Sayyaf groups) (2004)
Illicit drugs: exports locally-produced marijuana and hashish to East Asia, the US, and other Western markets; serves as a transit point for heroin and crystal methamphetamine; domestic methamphetamine production is a growing problem; remains on Financial Action Task Force Non-Cooperative Countries and Territories List for continued failure to address deficiencies in money-laundering control regime

PITCAIRN ISLANDS

INTRODUCTION

Background: Pitcairn Island was discovered in 1767 by the British and settled in 1790 by the Bounty mutineers and their Tahitian companions. Pitcairn was the first Pacific island to become a British colony (in 1838) and today remains the last vestige of that empire in the South Pacific. Outmigration, primarily to New Zealand, has thinned the population from a peak of 233 in 1937 to less than 50 today.

GEOGRAPHY

Location: Oceania, islands in the South Pacific Ocean, about midway between Peru and New Zealand
Geographic coordinates: 25 04 S, 130 06 W
Map references: Oceania
Area:
total: 47 sq km
land: 47 sq km
water: 0 sq km
Area - comparative: about 0.3 times the size of Washington, DC
Land boundaries: 0 km
Coastline: 51 km
Maritime claims:
territorial sea: 3 nm
exclusive economic zone: 200 nm
Climate: tropical; hot and humid; modified by southeast trade winds; rainy season (November to March)
Terrain: rugged volcanic formation; rocky coastline with cliffs
Elevation extremes:
lowest point: Pacific Ocean 0 m
highest point: Pawala Valley Ridge 347 m
Natural resources: miro trees (used for handicrafts), fish
note: manganese, iron, copper, gold, silver, and zinc have been discovered offshore
Land use:
arable land: NA%

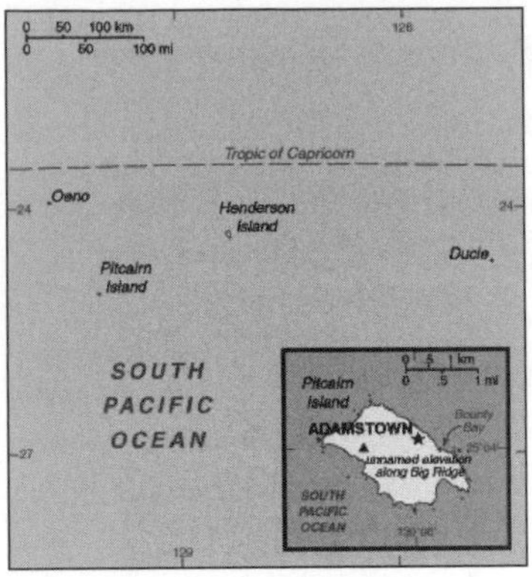

permanent crops: NA%
other: NA%
Irrigated land: NA
Natural hazards: typhoons (especially November to March)
Environment - current issues: deforestation (only a small portion of the original forest remains because of burning and clearing for settlement)
Geography - note: Britain's most isolated dependency; only the larger island of Pitcairn is inhabited but it has no port or natural harbor; supplies must be transported by rowed longboat from larger ships stationed offshore

PEOPLE

Population: 46 (July 2005 est.)
Age structure:
0-14 years: NA
15-64 years: NA
65 years and over: NA
Population growth rate: -0.01% (2005 est.)
Birth rate: NA
Death rate: NA
Net migration rate: NA
Sex ratio: NA
Infant mortality rate:
total: NA
male: NA
female: NA
Life expectancy at birth:
total population: NA
male: NA
female: NA
Total fertility rate: NA
HIV/AIDS - adult prevalence rate: NA
HIV/AIDS - people living with HIV/AIDS: NA
HIV/AIDS - deaths: NA
Nationality:
noun: Pitcairn Islander(s)
adjective: Pitcairn Islander
Ethnic groups: descendants of the Bounty mutineers and their Tahitian wives
Religions: Seventh-Day Adventist 100%
Languages: English (official), Pitcairnese (mixture of an 18th century English dialect and a Tahitian dialect)
Literacy: NA

GOVERNMENT

Country name:
conventional long form: Pitcairn, Henderson, Ducie, and Oeno Islands
conventional short form: Pitcairn Islands
Dependency status: overseas territory of the UK
Government type: NA
Capital: Adamstown
Administrative divisions: none (overseas territory of the UK)
Independence: none (overseas territory of the UK)
National holiday: Birthday of Queen ELIZABETH II, second Saturday in June (1926)
Constitution: 30 November 1838; reformed 1904 with additional reforms in 1940; further refined by the Local Government Ordinance of 1964
Legal system: local island by-laws
Suffrage: 18 years of age; universal with three years residency
Executive branch:
chief of state: Queen ELIZABETH II (since 6 February 1952), represented by UK High Commissioner to New Zealand and Governor (nonresident) of the Pitcairn Islands Richard FELL (since NA December 2001); Commissioner (nonresident) Leslie JAQUES (since September 2003); serves as liaison between the governor and the Island Council
head of government: Governor Richard FELL; mayor and chairman of the Island Council Jay WARREN (since 15 December 2004)
cabinet: NA
elections: the monarchy is hereditary; high commissioner and commissioner appointed by the monarch; island mayor elected by popular vote for a three-year term; election last held December 2004 (next to be held December 2007)
election results: Jay WARREN elected mayor and chairman of the Island Council
Legislative branch: unicameral Island Council (10 seats - 5 elected by popular vote, 1 nominated by the 5 elected members, 2 appointed by the governor including 1 seat for the Island Secretary, the Island Mayor, and a commissioner liaising between the governor and council; elected members serve one-year terms)
elections: last held 15 December 2004 (next to be held December 2005)
election results: percent of vote - NA%; seats - all independents
Judicial branch: Magistrate's Court; Supreme Court; Court of Appeal; Judicial Officers are appointed by the Governor
Political parties and leaders: none
Political pressure groups and leaders: none
International organization participation: SPC, UPU
Diplomatic representation in the US: none (overseas territory of the UK)
Diplomatic representation from the US: none (overseas territory of the UK)
Flag description: blue with the flag of the UK in the upper hoist-side quadrant and the Pitcairn Islander coat of arms centered on the outer half of the flag; the coat of arms is yellow, green, and light blue with a shield featuring a yellow anchor

ECONOMY

Economy - overview: The inhabitants of this tiny isolated economy exist on fishing, subsistence farming, handicrafts, and postage stamps. The fertile soil of the valleys produces a wide variety of fruits and vegetables, including citrus, sugarcane, watermelons, bananas, yams, and beans. Bartering is an important part of the economy. The major sources of revenue are the sale of postage stamps to collectors and the sale of handicrafts to passing ships. In October 2004, more than one-quarter of Pitcairn's labor force was arrested, putting the economy in a bind, since their services were required as lighter crew to load or unload passing ships.
GDP (purchasing power parity): NA
GDP (official exchange rate): NA
GDP - real growth rate: NA
GDP - per capita: purchasing power parity - NA
GDP - composition by sector:
agriculture: NA%
industry: NA%
services: NA%
Labor force: 15 able-bodied men (2004)
Labor force - by occupation: no business community in the usual sense; some public works; subsistence farming and fishing
Unemployment rate: NA
Population below poverty line: NA
Household income or consumption by percentage share:
lowest 10%: NA
highest 10%: NA
Inflation rate (consumer prices): NA
Budget:
revenues: $746,000
expenditures: $1.028 million, including capital expenditures of NA (FY04/05 est.)
Agriculture - products: wide variety of fruits and vegetables, goats, chickens
Industries: postage stamps, handicrafts, beekeeping, honey
Industrial production growth rate: NA
Electricity - production: NA kWh; note - electric power is provided by a small diesel-powered generator
Electricity - consumption: NA kWh

Exports: NA
Exports - partners: NA (2004)
Imports: NA
Imports - partners: NA (2004)
Debt - external: NA
Economic aid - recipient: $3.465 million (2004)
Currency (code): New Zealand dollar (NZD)
Currency code: NZD
Exchange rates: New Zealand dollars per US dollar - 1.43 (2005), 1.5087 (2004), 1.7221 (2003), 2.1622 (2002), 2.3788 (2001)
Fiscal year: 1 April - 31 March

COMMUNICATIONS

Telephones - main lines in use: 1 (there are 17 telephones on one party line); (2004)
Telephone system:
general assessment: satellite phone services
domestic: domestic communication via radio (CB)
international: country code - 872; satellite earth station (Inmarsat)
Radio broadcast stations: AM 1, FM 0, shortwave 0, note - 15 Ham radio operators (VP6) (2004)
Radios: NA
Televisions: NA
Internet country code: .pn
Internet Service Providers (ISPs): NA
Internet users: NA

TRANSPORTATION

Airports: none (2004 est.)
Roadways:
total: 6.4 km
paved: 0 km
unpaved: 6.4 km
Ports and terminals: Adamstown (on Bounty Bay)

MILITARY

Military - note: defense is the responsibility of the UK

TRANSNATIONAL ISSUES

Disputes - international: none

POLAND

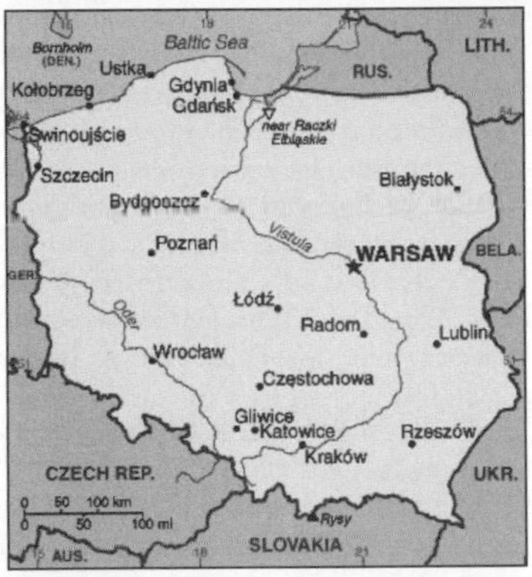

INTRODUCTION

Background: Poland is an ancient nation that was conceived near the middle of the 10th century. Its golden age occurred in the 16th century. During the following century, the strengthening of the gentry and internal disorders weakened the nation. In a series of agreements between 1772 and 1795, Russia, Prussia, and Austria partitioned Poland amongst themselves. Poland regained its independence in 1918 only to be overrun by Germany and the Soviet Union in World War II. It became a Soviet satellite state following the war, but its government was comparatively tolerant and progressive. Labor turmoil in 1980 led to the formation of the independent trade union "Solidarity" that over time became a political force and by 1990 had swept parliamentary elections and the presidency. A "shock therapy" program during the early 1990s enabled the country to transform its economy into one of the most robust in Central Europe, but Poland still faces the lingering challenges of high unemployment, underdeveloped and dilapidated infrastructure, and a poor rural underclass. Solidarity suffered a major defeat in the 2001 parliamentary elections when it failed to elect a single deputy to the lower house of Parliament, and the new leaders of the Solidarity Trade Union subsequently pledged to reduce the Trade Union's political role. Poland joined NATO in 1999 and the European Union in 2004. With its transformation to a democratic, market-oriented country largely completed, Poland is an increasingly active member of European organizations.

GEOGRAPHY

Location: Central Europe, east of Germany
Geographic coordinates: 52 00 N, 20 00 E
Map references: Europe
Area:
total: 312,685 sq km
land: 304,465 sq km
water: 8,220 sq km
Area - comparative: slightly smaller than New Mexico
Land boundaries:
total: 2,788 km
border countries: Belarus 407 km, Czech Republic 658 km, Germany 456 km, Lithuania 91 km, Russia (Kaliningrad Oblast) 206 km, Slovakia 444 km, Ukraine 526 km
Coastline: 491 km
Maritime claims:
territorial sea: 12 nm
exclusive economic zone: defined by international treaties
Climate: temperate with cold, cloudy, moderately severe winters with frequent precipitation; mild summers with frequent showers and thundershowers
Terrain: mostly flat plain; mountains along southern border
Elevation extremes:
lowest point: near Raczki Elblaskie -2 m
highest point: Rysy 2,499 m
Natural resources: coal, sulfur, copper, natural gas, silver, lead, salt, amber, arable land
Land use:
arable land: 45.91%
permanent crops: 1.12%
other: 52.97% (2001)
Irrigated land: 1,000 sq km (1998 est.)
Natural hazards: flooding
Environment - current issues: situation has improved since 1989 due to decline in heavy industry and increased environmental concern by post-Communist governments; air pollution nonetheless remains serious because of sulfur dioxide emissions from coal-fired power plants, and the resulting acid rain has caused forest damage; water pollution from industrial and municipal sources is also a problem, as is disposal of hazardous wastes; pollution levels should continue to decrease as industrial establishments bring their facilities up to European Union code, but at substantial cost to business and the government
Environment - international agreements:
party to: Air Pollution, Antarctic-Environmental Protocol, Antarctic-Marine Living Resources, Antarctic Seals, Antarctic Treaty, Biodiversity, Climate Change, Climate Change-Kyoto Protocol, Desertification, Endangered Species, Environmental Modification, Hazardous Wastes, Kyoto Protocol, Law of the Sea, Marine Dumping, Ozone Layer Protection, Ship Pollution, Wetlands
signed, but not ratified: Air Pollution-Nitrogen Oxides, Air Pollution-Persistent Organic Pollutants, Air Pollution-Sulfur 94
Geography - note: historically, an area of conflict because of flat terrain and the

lack of natural barriers on the North European Plain

PEOPLE

Population: 38,635,144 (July 2005 est.)
Age structure:
0-14 years: 16.7% (male 3,319,176/female 3,150,859)
15-64 years: 70.3% (male 13,506,153/ female 13,638,265)
65 years and over: 13% (male 1,912,431/ female 3,108,260) (2005 est.)
Median age:
total: 36.43 years
male: 34.52 years
female: 38.49 years (2005 est.)
Population growth rate: 0.03% (2005 est.)
Birth rate: 10.78 births/1,000 population (2005 est.)
Death rate: 10.01 deaths/1,000 population (2005 est.)
Net migration rate: -0.49 migrant(s)/ 1,000 population (2005 est.)
Sex ratio:
at birth: 1.06 male(s)/female
under 15 years: 1.05 male(s)/female
15-64 years: 0.99 male(s)/female
65 years and over: 0.62 male(s)/female
total population: 0.94 male(s)/female (2005 est.)
Infant mortality rate:
total: 8.51 deaths/1,000 live births
male: 9.59 deaths/1,000 live births
female: 7.37 deaths/1,000 live births (2005 est.)
Life expectancy at birth:
total population: 74.74 years
male: 70.71 years
female: 79.03 years (2005 est.)
Total fertility rate: 1.39 children born/woman (2005 est.)
HIV/AIDS - adult prevalence rate: 0.1% ; note - no country specific models provided (2001 est.)
HIV/AIDS - people living with HIV/AIDS: 14,000 (2003 est.)
HIV/AIDS - deaths: 100 (2001 est.)
Nationality:
noun: Pole(s)
adjective: Polish
Ethnic groups: Polish 96.7%, German 0.4%, Belarusian 0.1%, Ukrainian 0.1%, other and unspecified 2.7% (2002 census)
Religions: Roman Catholic 89.8% (about 75% practicing), Eastern Orthodox 1.3%, Protestant 0.3%, other 0.3%, unspecified 8.3% (2002)
Languages: Polish 97.8%, other and unspecified 2.2% (2002 census)
Literacy:
definition: age 15 and over can read and write
total population: 99.8%
male: 99.8%
female: 99.7% (2003 est.)

GOVERNMENT

Country name:
conventional long form: Republic of Poland
conventional short form: Poland
local long form: Rzeczpospolita Polska
local short form: Polska
Government type: republic
Capital: Warsaw
Administrative divisions: 16 provinces (wojewodztwa, singular - wojewodztwo); Dolnoslaskie, Kujawsko-Pomorskie, Lodzkie, Lubelskie, Lubuskie, Malopolskie, Mazowieckie, Opolskie, Podkarpackie, Podlaskie, Pomorskie, Slaskie, Swietokrzyskie, Warminsko-Mazurskie, Wielkopolskie, Zachodniopomorskie
Independence: 11 November 1918 (independent republic proclaimed)
National holiday: Constitution Day, 3 May (1791)
Constitution: adopted by the National Assembly 2 April 1997, passed by national referendum 25 May 1997, effective 17 October 1997
Legal system: mixture of Continental (Napoleonic) civil law and holdover Communist legal theory; changes being gradually introduced as part of broader democratization process; limited judicial review of legislative acts, but rulings of the Constitutional Tribunal are final; court decisions can be appealed to the European Court of Justice in Strasbourg
Suffrage: 18 years of age; universal
Executive branch:
chief of state: President Lech KACZYNSKI (since 23 December 2005)
head of government: Prime Minister Kazimierz MARCINKIEWICZ (since 31 October 2005); Deputy Prime Ministers Ludwik DORN (since 23 November 2005) and Zyta GILOWSKA (since 7 January 2006)
cabinet: Council of Ministers responsible to the prime minister and the Sejm; the prime minister proposes, the president appoints, and the Sejm approves the Council of Ministers
elections: president elected by popular vote for a five-year term; election last held 9 and 23 October 2005 (next to be held October 2010); prime minister and deputy prime ministers appointed by the president and confirmed by the Sejm
election results: Lech KACZYNSKI elected president; percent of popular vote - Lech KACZYNSKI 54%, Donald Tusk 46%
Legislative branch: bicameral legislature consisting of an upper house, the Senate or Senat (100 seats; members are elected by a majority vote on a provincial basis to serve four-year terms), and a lower house, the Sejm (460 seats; members are elected under a complex system of proportional representation to serve four-year terms); the designation of National Assembly or Zgromadzenie Narodowe is only used on those rare occasions when the two houses meet jointly
elections: Senate - last held 25 September 2005 (next to be held by September 2009); Sejm elections last held September 25 2005 (next to be held by September 2009)
election results: Senate - percent of vote by party - NA%; seats by party - PiS 49, PO 34, LPR 7, SO 3, PSL 2, independents 5; Sejm - percent of vote by party - PiS 27%, PO 24.1%, SO 11.4%, SLD 11.3%, LPR 8%, PSL 7%, other 11.2%; seats by party - PiS 155, PO 133, SO 56, SLD 55, LPR 34, PSL 25, German minorities 2
note: two seats are assigned to ethnic minority parties in the Sejm only
Judicial branch: Supreme Court (judges are appointed by the president on the recommendation of the National Council of the Judiciary for an indefinite period); Constitutional Tribunal (judges are chosen by the Sejm for nine-year terms)
Political parties and leaders: Catholic-National Movement or RKN [Antoni MACIEREWICZ]; Civic Platform or PO [Donald TUSK]; Conservative Peasants Party or SKL [Artur BALAZS]; Democratic Left Alliance or SLD [Wojciech OLEJNICZAK]; Democratic Party or PD [Wladyslaw FRASYNIUK]; Dom Ojczysty (Fatherland Home); German Minority of Lower Silesia or MNSO [Henryk KROLL]; Law and Justice or PiS [Jaroslaw KACZYNSKI]; League of Polish Families or LPR [Marek KOTLINOWSKI]; Peasant-Democratic Party or PLD [Roman JAGIELINSKI]; Polish Accord or PP [Jan LOPUSZANSKI]; Polish Peasant Party or PSL [Waldemar PAWLAK]; Ruch Patriotyczny or RP [Jan OLSZEWSKI]; Samoobrona or SO [Andrzej LEPPER]; Social Democratic Party of Poland or SDPL [Marek BOROWSKI]; Social Movement or RS [Krzysztof PIESIEWICZ]; Union of Labor or UP [Izabela JARUGA-NOWACKA]
Political pressure groups and leaders: All Poland Trade Union Alliance or OPZZ (trade union) [Jan GUZ]; Roman Catholic Church [Cardinal Jozef GLEMP]; Solidarity Trade Union [Janusz SNIADEK]
International organization participation: ACCT (observer), Australia Group, BIS, BSEC (observer), CBSS, CE, CEI, CERN, EAPC, EBRD, EIB, EU, FAO, IAEA, IBRD, ICAO, ICC, ICCt, ICFTU, ICRM, IDA, IFC, IFRCS, IHO, ILO, IMF, IMO, Interpol, IOC,

IOM, ISO, ITU, MIGA, MINURSO, MONUC, NAM (guest), NATO, NSG, OAS (observer), OECD, OPCW, OSCE, PCA, UN, UNCTAD, UNDOF, UNESCO, UNHCR, UNIDO, UNIFIL, UNMEE, UNMIL, UNMIS, UNOCI, UNOMIG, UPU, WCL, WCO, WEU (associate), WFTU, WHO, WIPO, WMO, WToO, WTO, ZC

Diplomatic representation in the US:
chief of mission: Ambassador Janusz REITER
chancery: 2640 16th Street NW, Washington, DC 20009
telephone: [1] (202) 234-3800 through 3802
FAX: [1] (202) 328-6270
consulate(s) general: Chicago, Los Angeles, and New York

Diplomatic representation from the US:
chief of mission: Ambassador Victor ASHE
embassy: Aleje Ujazdowskie 29/31 00-540 Warsaw
mailing address: American Embassy Warsaw, US Department of State, 5010 Warsaw Place, Washington, DC 20521-5010 (pouch)
telephone: [48] (22) 504-2000
FAX: [48] (22) 504-2688
consulate(s) general: Krakow

Flag description: two equal horizontal bands of white (top) and red; similar to the flags of Indonesia and Monaco which are red (top) and white

ECONOMY

Economy - overview: Poland has steadfastly pursued a policy of economic liberalization throughout the 1990s and today stands out as a success story among transition economies. Even so, much remains to be done, especially in bringing down the unemployment rate-currently the highest in the EU. The privatization of small and medium-sized state-owned companies and a liberal law on establishing new firms has encouraged the development of the private business sector, but legal and bureaucratic obstacles alongside persistent corruption are hampering its further development. Poland's agricultural sector remains handicapped by surplus labor, inefficient small farms, and lack of investment. Restructuring and privatization of "sensitive sectors" (e.g., coal, steel, railroads, and energy), while recently initiated, have stalled. Reforms in health care, education, the pension system, and state administration have resulted in larger-than-expected fiscal pressures. Further progress in public finance depends mainly on reducing losses in Polish state enterprises, restraining entitlements, and overhauling the tax code to incorporate the growing gray economy and farmers, most of whom pay no tax. The previous Socialist-led government introduced a package of social and administrative spending cuts to reduce public spending by about $17 billion through 2007, but full implementation of the plan was trumped by election-year politics in 2005. The right-wing Law and Justice party won parliamentary elections in September, and Lech KACZYNSKI won the presidential election in October, running on a state-interventionist fiscal and monetary platform. Poland joined the EU in May 2004, and surging exports to the EU contributed to Poland's strong growth in 2004, though its competitiveness could be threatened by the zloty's appreciation. GDP per capita roughly equals that of the three Baltic states. Poland stands to benefit from nearly $23.2 billion in EU funds, available through 2006. Farmers have already begun to reap the rewards of membership via booming exports, higher food prices, and EU agricultural subsidies.

GDP (purchasing power parity): $489.3 billion (2005 est.)
GDP (official exchange rate): $249 billion (2005 est.)
GDP - real growth rate: 3.3% (2005 est.)
GDP - per capita: purchasing power parity - $12,700 (2005 est.)
GDP - composition by sector:
agriculture: 2.8%
industry: 31.7%
services: 65.5% (2005 est.)
Labor force: 17.1 million (2005 est.)
Labor force - by occupation: agriculture 16.1%, industry 29%, services 54.9% (2002)
Unemployment rate: 18.3% (2005 est.)
Population below poverty line: 17% (2003 est.)
Household income or consumption by percentage share:
lowest 10%: 3.1%
highest 10%: 26.7% (2002)
Distribution of family income - Gini index: 34.1 (2002)
Inflation rate (consumer prices): 2.1% (2005 est.)
Investment (gross fixed): 18.5% of GDP (2005 est.)
Budget:
revenues: $52.73 billion
expenditures: $63.22 billion, including capital expenditures of NA (2005 est.)
Public debt: 47.3% of GDP (2005 est.)
Agriculture - products: potatoes, fruits, vegetables, wheat; poultry, eggs, pork, dairy
Industries: machine building, iron and steel, coal mining, chemicals, shipbuilding, food processing, glass, beverages, textiles
Industrial production growth rate: 8.5% (2005 est.)
Electricity - production: 150.8 billion kWh (2004)
Electricity - production by source:
fossil fuel: 98.1%
hydro: 1.5%
nuclear: 0%
other: 0.4% (2001)
Electricity - consumption: 121.3 billion kWh (2004)
Electricity - exports: 15.2 billion kWh (2004)
Electricity - imports: 5 billion kWh (2004)
Oil - production: 24,530 bbl/day (2003 est.)
Oil - consumption: 476,200 bbl/day (2003 est.)
Oil - exports: 53,000 bbl/day (2001)
Oil - imports: 413,700 bbl/day (2001)
Oil - proved reserves: 116.4 million bbl (1 January 2002)
Natural gas - production: 2.1 billion cu m (2003)
Natural gas - consumption: 11.5 billion cu m (2003)
Natural gas - exports: 44 million cu m (2003)
Natural gas - imports: 8.7 billion cu m (2003)
Natural gas - proved reserves: 154.4 billion cu m (1 January 2002)
Current account balance: $-4.159 billion (2005 est.)
Exports: $92.72 billion f.o.b. (2005 est.)
Exports - partners: Germany 30%, Italy 6.1%, France 6%, UK 5.4%, Czech Republic 4.3%, Netherlands 4.3% (2004)
Imports: $95.67 billion f.o.b. (2005 est.)
Imports - partners: Germany 24.4%, Italy 7.9%, Russia 7.3%, France 6.7%, China 4.6% (2004)
Reserves of foreign exchange and gold: $41.63 billion (2005 est.)
Debt - external: $123.4 billion (30 June 2005 est.)
Economic aid - recipient: $13.9 billion in available EU structural adjustment and cohesion funds (2004-06)
Currency (code): zloty (PLN)
Currency code: PLN
Exchange rates: zlotych per US dollar - 3.19 (2005), 3.6576 (2004), 3.8891 (2003), 4.08 (2002), 4.0939 (2001)
note: zlotych is the plural form of zloty
Fiscal year: calendar year

COMMUNICATIONS

Telephones - main lines in use: 12.3 million (2003)
Telephones - mobile cellular: 17.401 million (2003)
Telephone system:
general assessment: underdeveloped and outmoded system in the process of being

overhauled; partial privatization of the state-owned telephone monopoly is underway; the long waiting list for main line telephone service has resulted in a boom in mobile cellular telephone use
domestic: cable, open-wire, and microwave radio relay; 3 cellular networks; local exchanges 56.6% digital
international: country code - 48; satellite earth stations - 2 Intelsat, NA Eutelsat, 2 Inmarsat (Atlantic and Indian Ocean regions), and 1 Intersputnik (Atlantic Ocean region)
Radio broadcast stations: AM 14, FM 777, shortwave 1 (1998)
Radios: 20.2 million (1997)
Television broadcast stations: 179 (plus 256 repeaters) (September 1995)
Televisions: 13.05 million (1997)
Internet country code: .pl
Internet hosts: 804,915 (2004)
Internet Service Providers (ISPs): 19 (2000)
Internet users: 8.97 million (2003)

TRANSPORTATION

Airports: 23 (2004 est.)
Airports - with paved runways:
total: 84
over 3,047 m: 4
2,438 to 3,047 m: 29
1,524 to 2,437 m: 41
914 to 1,523 m: 7
under 914 m: 3 (2005 est.)
Airports - with unpaved runways:
total: 39
2,438 to 3,047 m: 1
1,524 to 2,437 m: 4
914 to 1,523 m: 13
under 914 m: 21 (2005 est.)
Heliports: 2 (2005 est.)
Pipelines: gas 13,552 km; oil 1,772 km (2004)
Railways:
total: 23,852 km
broad gauge: 629 km 1.524-m gauge
standard gauge: 23,223 km 1.435-m gauge (20,555 km operational) (11,962 km electrified) (2004)
Roadways:
total: 364,697 km
paved: 249,088 km (including 399 km of expressways)
unpaved: 115,609 km (2001)
Waterways: 3,997 km (navigable rivers and canals) (2003)
Merchant marine:
total: 7 ships (1,000 GRT or over) 154,710 GRT/228,132 DWT
by type: cargo 3, chemical tanker 2, passenger/cargo 1, roll on/roll off 1
registered in other countries: 107 (2005)
Ports and terminals: Gdansk, Gdynia, Swinoujscie, Szczecin

MILITARY

Military branches: Land Forces, Navy, Polish Air Force (PSP)
Military service age and obligation: 17 years of age for compulsory military service after January 1st of the year of 18th birthday; 17 years of age for voluntary military service; in 2005 Poland plans to shorten the length of conscript service obligation from 12 to 9 months; by 2008, plans call for at least 60% of military personnel to be volunteers; only soldiers who have completed their conscript service are allowed to volunteer for professional service; as of April 2004 women are only allowed to serve as officers and non-commissioned officers (April 2004)
Manpower available for military service:
males age 17-49: 9,673,712 (2005 est.)
Manpower fit for military service: *males age 17-49:* 7,740,164 (2005 est.)
Manpower reaching military service age annually: *males:* 275,521 (2005 est.)
Military expenditures - dollar figure: $3.5 billion (2002)
Military expenditures - percent of GDP: 1.71% (2002)

TRANSNATIONAL ISSUES

Disputes - international: as a member state that forms part of the EU's external border, Poland must implement the strict Schengen border rules
Illicit drugs: major illicit producer of synthetic drugs for the international market; minor transshipment point for Asian and Latin American illicit drugs to Western Europe

PORTUGAL

INTRODUCTION

Background: Following its heyday as a world power during the 15th and 16th centuries, Portugal lost much of its wealth and status with the destruction of Lisbon in a 1755 earthquake, occupation during the Napoleonic Wars, and the independence in 1822 of Brazil as a colony. A 1910 revolution deposed the monarchy; for most of the next six decades, repressive governments ran the country. In 1974, a left-wing military coup installed broad democratic reforms. The following year, Portugal granted independence to all of its African colonies. Portugal is a founding member of NATO and entered the EC (now the EU) in 1986.

GEOGRAPHY

Location: Southwestern Europe, bordering the North Atlantic Ocean, west of Spain
Geographic coordinates: 39 30 N, 8 00 W
Map references: Europe
Area:
total: 92,391 sq km
land: 91,951 sq km
water: 440 sq km
note: includes Azores and Madeira Islands
Area - comparative: slightly smaller than Indiana
Land boundaries:
total: 1,214 km
border countries: Spain 1,214 km
Coastline: 1,793 km
Maritime claims:
territorial sea: 12 nm
contiguous zone: 24 nm
exclusive economic zone: 200 nm
continental shelf: 200-m depth or to the depth of exploitation
Climate: maritime temperate; cool and rainy in north, warmer and drier in south
Terrain: mountainous north of the Tagus River, rolling plains in south
Elevation extremes:
lowest point: Atlantic Ocean 0 m
highest point: Ponta do Pico (Pico or Pico Alto) on Ilha do Pico in the Azores 2,351 m
Natural resources: fish, forests (cork), iron ore, copper, zinc, tin, tungsten, silver, gold, uranium, marble, clay, gypsum, salt, arable land, hydropower
Land use:
arable land: 21.75%
permanent crops: 7.81%
other: 70.44% (2001)
Irrigated land: 6,320 sq km (1998 est.)
Natural hazards: Azores subject to severe earthquakes
Environment - current issues: soil erosion; air pollution caused by industrial and vehicle emissions; water pollution, especially in coastal areas
Environment - international agreements:
party to: Air Pollution, Biodiversity, Climate Change, Climate Change-Kyoto Protocol, Desertification, Endangered Species, Hazardous Wastes, Law of the Sea, Marine Dumping, Marine Life Conservation, Ozone Layer Protection, Ship Pollution, Tropical Timber 83, Tropical Timber 94, Wetlands
signed, but not ratified: Air Pollution-Persistent Organic Pollutants, Air Pollution-Volatile Organic Compounds, Environmental Modification

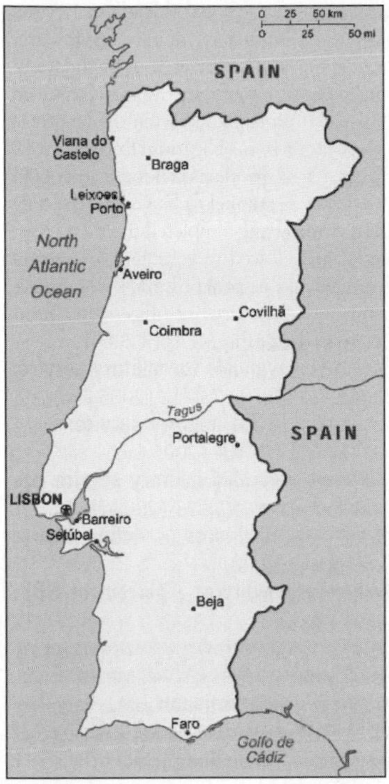

Geography - note: Azores and Madeira Islands occupy strategic locations along western sea approaches to Strait of Gibraltar

PEOPLE

Population: 10,566,212 (July 2005 est.)
Age structure:
0-14 years: 16.6% (male 916,234/female 839,935)
15-64 years: 66.3% (male 3,468,844/ female 3,538,779)
65 years and over: 17.1% (male 744,787/ female 1,057,633) (2005 est.)
Median age:
total: 38.2 years
male: 36.06 years
female: 40.33 years (2005 est.)
Population growth rate: 0.39% (2005 est.)
Birth rate: 10.82 births/1,000 population (2005 est.)
Death rate: 10.43 deaths/1,000 population (2005 est.)
Net migration rate: 3.49 migrant(s)/ 1,000 population (2005 est.)
Sex ratio:
at birth: 1.07 male(s)/female
under 15 years: 1.09 male(s)/female
15-64 years: 0.98 male(s)/female
65 years and over: 0.7 male(s)/female
total population: 0.94 male(s)/female (2005 est.)
Infant mortality rate:
total: 5.05 deaths/1,000 live births
male: 5.53 deaths/1,000 live births
female: 4.55 deaths/1,000 live births (2005 est.)
Life expectancy at birth:
total population: 77.53 years
male: 74.25 years
female: 81.03 years (2005 est.)
Total fertility rate: 1.47 children born/ woman (2005 est.)
HIV/AIDS - adult prevalence rate: 0.4% (2001 est.)
HIV/AIDS - people living with HIV/AIDS: 22,000 (2001 est.)
HIV/AIDS - deaths: less than 1,000 (2003 est.)
Nationality:
noun: Portuguese (singular and plural)
adjective: Portuguese
Ethnic groups: homogeneous Mediterranean stock; citizens of black African descent who immigrated to mainland during decolonization number less than 100,000; since 1990 East Europeans have entered Portugal
Religions: Roman Catholic 94%, Protestant (1995)
Languages: Portuguese (official), Mirandese (official - but locally used)
Literacy:
definition: age 15 and over can read and write
total population: 93.3%
male: 95.5%
female: 91.3% (2003 est.)

GOVERNMENT

Country name:
conventional long form: Portuguese Republic
conventional short form: Portugal
local long form: Republica Portuguesa
local short form: Portugal
Government type: parliamentary democracy
Capital: Lisbon
Administrative divisions: 18 districts (distritos, singular - distrito) and 2 autonomous regions* (regioes autonomas, singular - regiao autonoma); Aveiro, Acores (Azores)*, Beja, Braga, Braganca, Castelo Branco, Coimbra, Evora, Faro, Guarda, Leiria, Lisboa, Madeira*, Portalegre, Porto, Santarem, Setubal, Viana do Castelo, Vila Real, Viseu
Independence: 1143 (Kingdom of Portugal recognized); 5 October 1910 (independent republic proclaimed)
National holiday: Portugal Day (Day of Portugal), 10 June (1580); note - also called Camoes Day, the day that revered national poet Luis de Camoes (1524-80) died
Constitution: 25 April 1976; revised many times
Legal system: civil law system; the Constitutional Tribunal reviews the constitutionality of legislation; accepts compulsory ICJ jurisdiction, with reservations
Suffrage: 18 years of age; universal
Executive branch:
chief of state: President Jorge SAMPAIO (since 9 March 1996)
head of government: Prime Minister Jose SOCRATES (since 12 March 2005)
cabinet: Council of Ministers appointed by the president on the recommendation of the prime minister
note: there is also a Council of State that acts as a consultative body to the president
elections: president elected by popular vote for a five-year term; election last held 14 January 2001 (next to be held January 2006); following legislative elections, the leader of the majority party or leader of a majority coalition is usually appointed prime minister by the president
election results: Jorge SAMPAIO reelected president; percent of vote - Jorge SAMPAIO (Socialist) 55.8%, Joaquim FERREIRA Do Amaral (Social Democrat) 34.5%, Antonio ABREU (Communist) 5.1%
Legislative branch: unicameral Assembly of the Republic or Assembleia da Republica (230 seats; members are elected by popular vote to serve four-year terms)
elections: last held 20 February 2005 (next to be held February 2009); note - President SAMPAIO called for early elections after dissolving parliament on 10 December 2004 because he lacked confidence in the four-month center-right government
election results: percent of vote by party - PS 45.1%, PSD 28.7%, CDU 7.6%, PP 7.3%, BE 6.4%; seats by party - PS 121, PSD 75, CDU 14, PP 12, BE 8
Judicial branch: Supreme Court or Supremo Tribunal de Justica (judges appointed for life by the Conselho Superior da Magistratura)
Political parties and leaders: Green Ecologist Party or PEV [Heloisa APOLONIA]; Popular Party or PP [Jose Ribeiro e CASTRO]; Portuguese Communist Party or PCP [Jeronimo de SOUSA]; Portuguese Socialist Party or PS [Jose SOCRATES Carvalho Pinto de Sousa]; Social Democratic Party or PSD [Luis Marques MENDES]; The Left Bloc or BE [Franciso Anacleto LOUCA]; Unitarian Democratic Coalition or CDU [Jeronimo de SOUSA]; includes PEV and PCP
Political pressure groups and leaders: NA
International organization participation: AfDB, AsDB, Australia Group, BIS, CE, CERN, EAPC, EBRD, EIB, EMU, ESA, EU, FAO, IADB, IAEA, IBRD, ICAO, ICC, ICCt, ICFTU, ICRM, IDA, IEA, IFAD, IFC, IFRCS, IHO, ILO, IMF, IMO, Interpol, IOC, IOM, ISO, ITU, LAIA (observer), MIGA, NATO, NEA, NSG, OAS (observer), OECD, ONUB, OPCW, OSCE, PCA, UN,

UNCTAD, UNESCO, UNIDO, UPU, WCL, WCO, WEU, WFTU, WHO, WIPO, WMO, WToO, WTO, ZC
Diplomatic representation in the US:
chief of mission: Ambassador Pedro Manuel Dos Reis Alves CATARINO
chancery: 2125 Kalorama Road NW, Washington, DC 20008
telephone: [1] (202) 328-8610
FAX: [1] (202) 462-3726
consulate(s) general: Boston, New York, Newark (New Jersey), and San Francisco
consulate(s): New Bedford (Massachusetts), Providence (Rhode Island)
Diplomatic representation from the US:
chief of mission: Ambassador Alfred HOFFMAN
embassy: Avenida das Forcas Armadas, 1600-081 Lisbon
mailing address: Apartado 43033, 1601-301 Lisboa; PSC 83, APO AE 09726
telephone: [351] (21) 727-3300
FAX: [351] (21) 726-9109
consulate(s): Ponta Delgada (Azores)
Flag description: two vertical bands of green (hoist side, two-fifths) and red (three-fifths) with the Portuguese coat of arms centered on the dividing line

ECONOMY

Economy - overview: Portugal has become a diversified and increasingly service-based economy since joining the European Community in 1986. Over the past decade, successive governments have privatized many state-controlled firms and liberalized key areas of the economy, including the financial and telecommunications sectors. The country qualified for the European Monetary Union (EMU) in 1998 and began circulating the euro on 1 January 2002 along with 11 other EU member economies. Economic growth had been above the EU average for much of the past decade, but fell back in 2001-05. GDP per capita stands at two-thirds that of the Big Four EU economies. A poor educational system, in particular, has been an obstacle to greater productivity and growth. Portugal has been increasingly overshadowed by lower-cost producers in Central Europe and Asia as a target for foreign direct investment. The government faces tough choices in its attempts to boost Portugal's economic competitiveness while keeping the budget deficit within the eurozone's 3%-of-GDP ceiling.
GDP (purchasing power parity): $194.8 billion (2005 est.)
GDP (official exchange rate): $173.1 billion (2005 est.)
GDP - real growth rate: 0.7% (2005 est.)
GDP - per capita:
purchasing power parity - $18,400 (2005 est.)
GDP - composition by sector:
agriculture: 5.2%
industry: 28.9%
services: 65.9% (2005 est.)
Labor force: 5.52 million (2005 est.)
Labor force - by occupation: agriculture 10%, industry 30%, services 60% (1999 est.)
Unemployment rate: 7.3% (2005 est.)
Population below poverty line: NA
Household income or consumption by percentage share:
lowest 10%: 3.1%
highest 10%: 28.4% (1995 est.)
Distribution of family income - Gini index: 38.5 (1997)
Inflation rate (consumer prices): 2.4% (2005 est.)
Investment (gross fixed): 21.7% of GDP (2005 est.)
Budget:
revenues: $78.84 billion
expenditures: $90.27 billion, including capital expenditures of NA (2005 est.)
Public debt: 69.4% of GDP (2005 est.)
Agriculture - products: grain, potatoes, tomatoes, olives, grapes; sheep, cattle, goats, swine, poultry, fish, dairy products
Industries: textiles and footwear; wood pulp, paper, and cork; metals and metalworking; oil refining; chemicals; fish canning; rubber and plastic products; ceramics; electronics and communications equipment; rail transportation equipment; aerospace equipment; ship construction and refurbishment; wine; tourism
Industrial production growth rate: -0.1% (2005 est.)
Electricity - production: 44.32 billion kWh (2003)
Electricity - production by source:
fossil fuel: 64.5%
hydro: 31.3%
nuclear: 0%
other: 4.1% (2001)
Electricity - consumption: 44.01 billion kWh (2003)
Electricity - exports: 3.1 billion kWh (2003)
Electricity - imports: 5.9 billion kWh (2003)
Oil - production: 3,745 bbl/day (2003 est.)
Oil - consumption: 326,500 bbl/day (2003 est.)
Oil - exports: 28,830 bbl/day (2001)
Oil - imports: 357,300 bbl/day (2001)
Natural gas - production: 0 cu m (2001 est.)
Natural gas - consumption: 2.542 billion cu m (2001 est.)
Natural gas - exports: 0 cu m (2001 est.)
Natural gas - imports: 2.553 billion cu m (2001 est.)
Current account balance: $-15 billion (2005 est.)
Exports: $38.8 billion f.o.b. (2005 est.)
Exports - partners: Spain 25%, France 14%, Germany 13.5%, UK 9.6%, US 6%, Italy 4.3%, Netherlands 4% (2004)
Imports: $60.35 billion f.o.b. (2005 est.)
Imports - partners: Spain 29.3%, Germany 14.3%, France 9.3%, Italy 6.1%, UK 4.6%, Netherlands 4.6% (2004)
Reserves of foreign exchange and gold: $11 billion (2005 est.)
Debt - external: $298.7 billion (30 June 2005 est.)
Economic aid - donor: ODA, $271 million (1995)
Currency (code): euro (EUR)
note: on 1 January 1999, the European Monetary Union introduced the euro as a common currency to be used by financial institutions of member countries; on 1 January 2002, the euro became the sole currency for everyday transactions within the member countries
Currency code: EUR
Exchange rates: euros per US dollar - 0.79697 (2005), 0.8054 (2004), 0.886 (2003), 1.0626 (2002), 1.1175 (2001)
Fiscal year: calendar year

COMMUNICATIONS

Telephones - main lines in use: 4,278,800 (2003)
Telephones - mobile cellular: 9,341,400 (2003)
Telephone system:
general assessment: Portugal's telephone system has achieved a state-of-the-art network with broadband, high-speed capabilities and a main line telephone density of 53%
domestic: integrated network of coaxial cables, open-wire, microwave radio relay, and domestic satellite earth stations
international: country code - 351; 6 submarine cables; satellite earth stations - 3 Intelsat (2 Atlantic Ocean and 1 Indian Ocean), NA Eutelsat; tropospheric scatter to Azores; note - an earth station for Inmarsat (Atlantic Ocean region) is planned
Radio broadcast stations: AM 47, FM 172 (many are repeaters), shortwave 2 (1998)
Radios: 3.02 million (1997)
Television broadcast stations: 62 (plus 166 repeaters)
note: includes Azores and Madeira Islands (1995)
Televisions: 3.31 million (1997)
Internet country code: .pt
Internet hosts: 346,078 (2004)
Internet Service Providers (ISPs): 16 (2000)
Internet users: 3.6 million (2002)

TRANSPORTATION

Airports: 65 (2004 est.)
Airports - with paved runways:
total: 42

over 3,047 m: 5
2,438 to 3,047 m: 9
1,524 to 2,437 m: 4
914 to 1,523 m: 14
under 914 m: 10 (2005 est.)
Airports - with unpaved runways:
total: 24
914 to 1,523 m: 1
under 914 m: 23 (2005 est.)
Pipelines: gas 1,099 km; oil 8 km; refined products 174 km (2004)
Railways:
total: 2,850 km
broad gauge: 2,576 km 1.668-m gauge (623 km electrified)
narrow gauge: 274 km 1.000-m gauge (2004)
Roadways:
total: 17,135 km
paved: 14,736 km (including 1,659 km of expressways)
unpaved: 2,399 km (2002)
Waterways: 210 km (on Douro River from Porto) (2003)
Merchant marine:
total: 114 ships (1,000 GRT or over) 872,557 GRT/1,236,025 DWT
by type: bulk carrier 10, cargo 38, chemical tanker 14, container 7, liquefied gas 9, passenger 8, passenger/cargo 7, petroleum tanker 9, roll on/roll off 4, vehicle carrier 8
foreign-owned: 97 (Australia 1, Belgium 6, Denmark 5, Germany 18, Greece 4, Iceland 1, Italy 11, Japan 8, Lebanon 1, Malta 1, Norway 4, Spain 19, Switzerland 4)
registered in other countries: 28 (2005)
Ports and terminals: Leixoes, Lisbon, Setubal, Sines

MILITARY

Military branches: Army, Navy (Marinha Portuguesa; includes Marine Corps), Air Force (Forca Aerea Portuguesa, FAP), National Republican Guard (Guarda Nacional Republicana) (2005)
Military service age and obligation: 18 years of age for voluntary military service; compulsory military service was ended in 2004 (January 2005)
Manpower available for military service: *males age 18-49:* 2,435,042 (2005 est.)
Manpower fit for military service: *males age 18-49:* 1,952,819 (2005 est.)
Manpower reaching military service age annually: *males:* 67,189 (2005 est.)
Military expenditures - dollar figure: $3,497.8 million (2003)
Military expenditures - percent of GDP: 2.3% (2003)

TRANSNATIONAL ISSUES

Disputes - international: none
Illicit drugs: gateway country for Latin American cocaine and Southwest Asian heroin entering the European market (especially from Brazil); transshipment point for hashish from North Africa to Europe; consumer of Southwest Asian heroin

PUERTO RICO

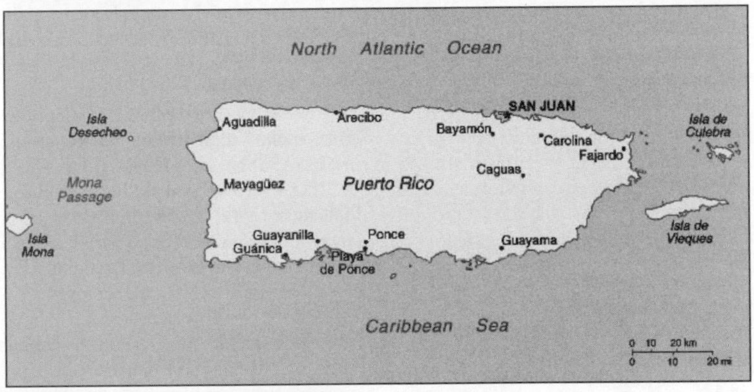

INTRODUCTION

Background: Populated for centuries by aboriginal peoples, the island was claimed by the Spanish Crown in 1493 following Columbus' second voyage to the Americas. In 1898, after 400 years of colonial rule that saw the indigenous population nearly exterminated and African slave labor introduced, Puerto Rico was ceded to the US as a result of the Spanish-American War. Puerto Ricans were granted US citizenship in 1917. Popularly-elected governors have served since 1948. In 1952, a constitution was enacted providing for internal self government. In plebiscites held in 1967, 1993, and 1998, voters chose to retain commonwealth status.

GEOGRAPHY

Location: Caribbean, island between the Caribbean Sea and the North Atlantic Ocean, east of the Dominican Republic
Geographic coordinates: 18 15 N, 66 30 W
Map references: Central America and the Caribbean
Area:
total: 9,104 sq km
land: 8,959 sq km
water: 145 sq km
Area - comparative: slightly less than three times the size of Rhode Island
Land boundaries: 0 km
Coastline: 501 km
Maritime claims:
territorial sea: 12 nm
exclusive economic zone: 200 nm
Climate: tropical marine, mild; little seasonal temperature variation
Terrain: mostly mountains with coastal plain belt in north; mountains precipitous to sea on west coast; sandy beaches along most coastal areas
Elevation extremes:
lowest point: Caribbean Sea 0 m
highest point: Cerro de Punta 1,338 m
Natural resources: some copper and nickel; potential for onshore and offshore oil
Land use:
arable land: 3.95%
permanent crops: 5.52%
other: 90.53% (2001)
Irrigated land: 400 sq km (1998 est.)
Natural hazards: periodic droughts; hurricanes
Environment - current issues: erosion; occasional drought causing water shortages
Geography - note: important location along the Mona Passage - a key shipping lane to the Panama Canal; San Juan is one of the biggest and best natural harbors in the Caribbean; many small rivers and high central mountains ensure land is well watered; south coast relatively dry; fertile coastal plain belt in north

PEOPLE

Population: 3,916,632 (July 2005 est.)
Age structure:
0-14 years: 22% (male 441,594/female 421,986)
15-64 years: 65.5% (male 1,228,583/female 1,337,066)
65 years and over: 12.4% (male 211,283/female 276,120) (2005 est.)
Median age:
total: 34.23 years
male: 32.5 years
female: 35.87 years (2005 est.)
Population growth rate: 0.47% (2005 est.)

Birth rate: 13.93 births/1,000 population (2005 est.)
Death rate: 7.86 deaths/1,000 population (2005 est.)
Net migration rate: -1.38 migrant(s)/1,000 population (2005 est.)
Sex ratio:
at birth: 1.05 male(s)/female
under 15 years: 1.05 male(s)/female
15-64 years: 0.92 male(s)/female
65 years and over: 0.76 male(s)/female
total population: 0.92 male(s)/female (2005 est.)
Infant mortality rate:
total: 8.24 deaths/1,000 live births
male: 9.52 deaths/1,000 live births
female: 6.9 deaths/1,000 live births (2005 est.)
Life expectancy at birth:
total population: 78.29 years
male: 74.35 years
female: 82.43 years (2005 est.)
Total fertility rate: 1.91 children born/woman (2005 est.)
HIV/AIDS - adult prevalence rate: NA
HIV/AIDS - people living with HIV/AIDS: 7,397 (1997)
HIV/AIDS - deaths: NA
Nationality:
noun: Puerto Rican(s) (US citizens)
adjective: Puerto Rican
Ethnic groups: white (mostly Spanish origin) 80.5%, black 8%, Amerindian 0.4%, Asian 0.2%, mixed and other 10.9%
Religions: Roman Catholic 85%, Protestant and other 15%
Languages: Spanish, English
Literacy:
definition: age 15 and over can read and write
total population: 94.1%
male: 93.9%
female: 94.4% (2002 est.)

GOVERNMENT

Country name:
conventional long form: Commonwealth of Puerto Rico
conventional short form: Puerto Rico
Dependency status: commonwealth associated with the US
Government type: commonwealth
Capital: San Juan
Administrative divisions: none (commonwealth associated with the US); there are no first-order administrative divisions as defined by the US Government, but there are 78 municipalities (municipios, singular - municipio) at the second order; Adjuntas, Aguada, Aguadilla, Aguas Buenas, Aibonito, Anasco, Arecibo, Arroyo, Barceloneta, Barranquitas, Bayamon, Cabo Rojo, Caguas, Camuy, Canovanas, Carolina, Catano, Cayey, Ceiba, Ciales, Cidra, Coamo, Comerio, Corozal, Culebra, Dorado, Fajardo, Florida, Guanica, Guayama, Guayanilla, Guaynabo, Gurabo, Hatillo, Hormigueros, Humacao, Isabela, Jayuya, Juana Diaz, Juncos, Lajas, Lares, Las Marias, Las Piedras, Loiza, Luquillo, Manati, Maricao, Maunabo, Mayaguez, Moca, Morovis, Naguabo, Naranjito, Orocovis, Patillas, Penuelas, Ponce, Quebradillas, Rincon, Rio Grande, Sabana Grande, Salinas, San German, San Juan, San Lorenzo, San Sebastian, Santa Isabel, Toa Alta, Toa Baja, Trujillo Alto, Utuado, Vega Alta, Vega Baja, Vieques, Villalba, Yabucoa, Yauco
Independence: none (commonwealth associated with the US)
National holiday: US Independence Day, 4 July (1776); Puerto Rico Constitution Day, 25 July (1952)
Constitution: ratified 3 March 1952, approved by US Congress 3 July 1952, effective 25 July 1952
Legal system: based on Spanish civil code and within the US Federal system of justice
Suffrage: 18 years of age; universal; island residents are US citizens but do not vote in US presidential elections
Executive branch:
chief of state: President George W. BUSH of the US (since 20 January 2001)
head of government: Governor Anibal ACEVEDO-VILA (since 2 January 2005)
cabinet: Cabinet appointed by the governor with the consent of the legislature
elections: US president and vice president elected on the same ticket for four-year terms; governor elected by popular vote for a four-year term; election last held 2 November 2004 (next to be held November 2008)
election results: Anibal ACEVEDO-VILA (PPD) elected governor; percent of vote - 48.4%
Legislative branch: bicameral Legislative Assembly consists of the Senate (at least 27 seats - currently 29; members are directly elected by popular vote to serve four-year terms) and the House of Representatives (51 seats; members are directly elected by popular vote to serve four-year terms)
elections: Senate - last held 2 November 2004 (next to be held November 2008); House of Representatives - last held 2 November 2004 (next to be held November 2008)
election results: Senate - percent of vote by party - PNP 43.4%, PPD 40.3%, PIP 9.4%; seats by party - PNP 17, PPD 9, PIP 1; House of Representatives - percent of vote by party - PNP 46.3%, PPD 43.1%, PIP 9.7%; seats by party - PNP 32, PPD 18, PIP 1
note: Puerto Rico elects, by popular vote, a resident commissioner to serve a four-year term as a nonvoting representative in the US House of Representatives; aside from not voting on the House floor, he enjoys all the rights of a member of Congress; elections last held 2 November 2004 (next to be held November 2008); results - percent of vote by party - PNP 48.6%; seats by party - PNP 1; Luis FORTUNO elected resident commissioner
Judicial branch: Supreme Court; Appellate Court; Court of First Instance composed of two sections: a Superior Court and a Municipal Court (justices for all these courts appointed by the governor with the consent of the Senate)
Political parties and leaders: National Democratic Party [Celeste BENITEZ]; National Republican Party of Puerto Rico [Dr. Tiody FERRE]; New Progressive Party or PNP (pro-US statehood) [Pedro ROSSELLO]; Popular Democratic Party or PPD (pro-commonwealth) [Anibal ACEVEDO-VILA]; Puerto Rican Independence Party or PIP (pro-independence) [Ruben BERRIOS Martinez]
Political pressure groups and leaders: Armed Forces for National Liberation or FALN; Armed Forces of Popular Resistance; Boricua Popular Army (also known as the Macheteros); Volunteers of the Puerto Rican Revolution
International organization participation: Interpol (subbureau), IOC, UPU, WCL, WFTU, WToO (associate)
Diplomatic representation in the US: none (commonwealth associated with the US)
Diplomatic representation from the US: none (commonwealth associated with the US)
Flag description: five equal horizontal bands of red (top and bottom) alternating with white; a blue isosceles triangle based on the hoist side bears a large, white, five-pointed star in the center; design initially influenced by the US flag, but similar to the Cuban flag, with the colors of the bands and triangle reversed

ECONOMY

Economy - overview: Puerto Rico has one of the most dynamic economies in the Caribbean region. A diverse industrial sector has far surpassed agriculture as the primary locus of economic activity and income. Encouraged by duty-free access to the US and by tax incentives, US firms have invested heavily in Puerto Rico since the 1950s. US minimum wage laws apply. Sugar production has lost out to dairy production and other livestock products as the main source of income in the agricultural sector. Tourism has traditionally been an important source of income, with

estimated arrivals of nearly 5 million tourists in 1999. Growth fell off in 2001-03, largely due to the slowdown in the US economy, and has recovered in 2004-2005.
GDP (purchasing power parity): $72.37 billion (2005 est.)
GDP (official exchange rate): NA
GDP - real growth rate: 2.5% (2005 est.)
GDP - per capita: purchasing power parity - $18,500 (2005 est.)
GDP - composition by sector:
agriculture: 1%
industry: 45%
services: 54% (2002 est.)
Labor force: 1.3 million (2000)
Labor force - by occupation: agriculture 3%, industry 20%, services 77% (2000 est.)
Unemployment rate: 12% (2002)
Population below poverty line: NA
Household income or consumption by percentage share:
lowest 10%: NA
highest 10%: NA
Inflation rate (consumer prices): 6.5% (2003 est.)
Budget:
revenues: $6.7 billion
expenditures: $9.6 billion, including capital expenditures of NA (FY99/00)
Agriculture - products: sugarcane, coffee, pineapples, plantains, bananas, livestock products, chickens
Industries: pharmaceuticals, electronics, apparel, food products, tourism
Industrial production growth rate: NA%
Electricity - production: 23.03 billion kWh (2003)
Electricity - production by source:
fossil fuel: 99.2%
hydro: 0.8%
nuclear: 0%
other: 0% (2001)
Electricity - consumption: 21.42 billion kWh (2003)
Electricity - exports: 0 kWh (2003)
Electricity - imports: 0 kWh (2003)
Oil - production: 436.1 bbl/day (2003 est.)
Oil - consumption: 218,000 bbl/day (2003 est.)
Oil - exports: NA (2001)
Oil - imports: NA (2001)
Natural gas - production: 0 cu m (2001 est.)
Natural gas - consumption: 630 million cu m (2001 est.)
Natural gas - exports: 0 cu m (2001 est.)
Natural gas - imports: 630 million cu m (2001 est.)
Exports: $46.9 billion f.o.b. (2001)
Exports - partners: US 90.3%, UK 1.6%, Netherlands 1.4%, Dominican Republic 1.4% (2004)
Imports: $29.1 billion c.i.f. (2001)
Imports - partners: US 55.0%, Ireland 23.7%, Japan 5.4% (2004)
Debt - external: NA
Economic aid - recipient: NA (2001)
Currency (code): US dollar (USD)
Currency code: USD
Exchange rates: the US dollar is used
Fiscal year: 1 July - 30 June

COMMUNICATIONS

Telephones - main lines in use: 1,329,500 (2002)
Telephones - mobile cellular: 1,211,111 (2001)
Telephone system:
general assessment: modern system integrated with that of the US by high-capacity submarine cable and Intelsat with high-speed data capability
domestic: digital telephone system; cellular telephone service
international: country code - 1-787, 939; satellite earth station - 1 Intelsat; submarine cable to US
Radio broadcast stations: AM 72, FM 17, shortwave 0 (1998)
Radios: 2.7 million (1997)
Television broadcast stations: 26 (2004)
Televisions: 1.021 million (1997)
Internet country code: .pr
Internet Service Providers (ISPs): 76 (2000)
Internet users: 600,000 (2002)

TRANSPORTATION

Airports: 30 (2004 est.)
Airports - with paved runways:
total: 17
over 3,047 m: 3
1,524 to 2,437 m: 2
914 to 1,523 m: 7
under 914 m: 5 (2005 est.)
Airports - with unpaved runways:
total: 13
1,524 to 2,437 m: 1
914 to 1,523 m: 2
under 914 m: 10 (2005 est.)
Railways:
total: 96 km
narrow gauge: 96 km 1.000-m gauge (2004)
Roadways:
total: 25,328 km
paved: 23,665 km (including 426 km of expressways)
unpaved: 1,363 km (2004)
Merchant marine:
total: 2 ships (1,000 GRT or over) 36,728 GRT/37,048 DWT
by type: roll on/roll off 2
foreign-owned: 2 (United States 2)
registered in other countries: 1 (2005)
Ports and terminals: Las Mareas, Mayaguez, San Juan

MILITARY

Military branches: no regular indigenous military forces; paramilitary National Guard, Police Force
Military - note: defense is the responsibility of the US

TRANSNATIONAL ISSUES

Disputes - international: increasing numbers of illegal migrants from the Dominican Republic cross the Mona Passage to Puerto Rico each year looking for work

QATAR

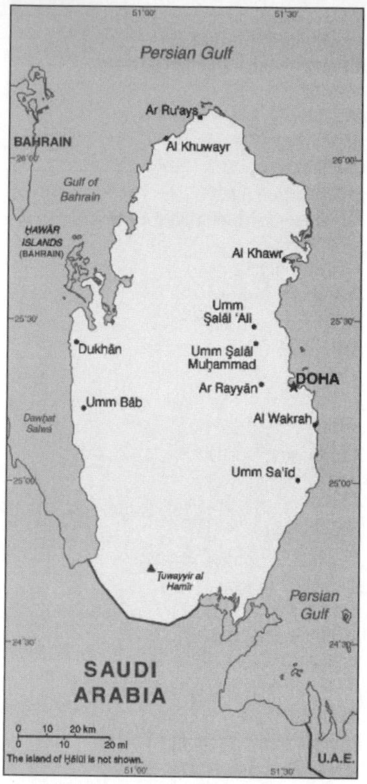

INTRODUCTION

Background: Ruled by the Al Thani family since the mid-1800s, Qatar transformed itself from a poor British protectorate noted mainly for pearling into an independent state with significant oil and natural gas revenues. During the late 1980s and early 1990s, the Qatari economy was crippled by a continuous siphoning off of petroleum revenues by the amir, who had ruled the country since 1972. His son, the current Amir HAMAD bin Khalifa Al Thani, overthrew him in a bloodless coup in 1995. In 2001, Qatar resolved its longstanding border disputes with both Bahrain and Saudi Arabia. Oil and natural gas revenues enable Qatar to have one of the highest per capita incomes in the world.

GEOGRAPHY

Location: Middle East, peninsula bordering the Persian Gulf and Saudi Arabia
Geographic coordinates: 25 30 N, 51 15 E
Map references: Middle East
Area:
total: 11,437 sq km
land: 11,437 sq km
water: 0 sq km
Area - comparative: slightly smaller than Connecticut
Land boundaries:
total: 60 km
border countries: Saudi Arabia 60 km
Coastline: 563 km
Maritime claims:
territorial sea: 12 nm
contiguous zone: 24 nm
exclusive economic zone: as determined by bilateral agreements or the median line
Climate: arid; mild, pleasant winters; very hot, humid summers
Terrain: mostly flat and barren desert covered with loose sand and gravel
Elevation extremes:
lowest point: Persian Gulf 0 m
highest point: Qurayn Abu al Bawl 103 m
Natural resources: petroleum, natural gas, fish
Land use:
arable land: 1.64%
permanent crops: 0.27%
other: 98.09% (2001)
Irrigated land: 130 sq km (1998 est.)
Natural hazards: haze, dust storms, sandstorms common
Environment - current issues: limited natural fresh water resources are increasing dependence on large-scale desalination facilities
Environment - international agreements:
party to: Biodiversity, Climate Change, Climate Change-Kyoto Protocol, Desertification, Endangered Species, Hazardous Wastes, Law of the Sea, Ozone Layer Protection
signed, but not ratified: none of the selected agreements
Geography - note: strategic location in central Persian Gulf near major petroleum deposits

PEOPLE

Population: 863,051 (July 2005 est.)
Age structure:
0-14 years: 23.7% (male 104,453/female 100,295)
15-64 years: 72.9% (male 437,118/female 191,830)
65 years and over: 3.4% (male 21,599/female 7,756) (2005 est.)
Median age:
total: 31.57 years
male: 36.87 years
female: 22.33 years (2005 est.)
Population growth rate: 2.61% (2005 est.)
Birth rate: 15.54 births/1,000 population (2005 est.)
Death rate: 4.61 deaths/1,000 population (2005 est.)
Net migration rate: 15.17 migrant(s)/1,000 population (2005 est.)
Sex ratio:
at birth: 1.05 male(s)/female
under 15 years: 1.04 male(s)/female
15-64 years: 2.28 male(s)/female
65 years and over: 2.78 male(s)/female
total population: 1.88 male(s)/female (2005 est.)
Infant mortality rate:
total: 18.61 deaths/1,000 live births
male: 21.95 deaths/1,000 live births
female: 15.11 deaths/1,000 live births (2005 est.)
Life expectancy at birth:
total population: 73.67 years
male: 71.15 years
female: 76.32 years (2005 est.)
Total fertility rate: 2.87 children born/woman (2005 est.)
HIV/AIDS - adult prevalence rate: 0.09% (2001 est.)
HIV/AIDS - people living with HIV/AIDS: NA
HIV/AIDS - deaths: NA
Nationality:
noun: Qatari(s)
adjective: Qatari
Ethnic groups: Arab 40%, Pakistani 18%, Indian 18%, Iranian 10%, other 14%
Religions: Muslim 95%
Languages: Arabic (official), English commonly used as a second language
Literacy:
definition: age 15 and over can read and write
total population: 89%
male: 89.1%
female: 88.6% (2004 est.)

GOVERNMENT

Country name:
conventional long form: State of Qatar
conventional short form: Qatar
local long form: Dawlat Qatar
local short form: Qatar
note: closest approximation of the native pronunciation falls between cutter and gutter, but not like guitar
Government type: traditional monarchy
Capital: Doha
Administrative divisions: 10 municipalities (baladiyat, singular - baladiyah); Ad Dawhah, Al Ghuwayriyah, Al Jumayliyah, Al Khawr, Al Wakrah, Ar Rayyan, Jarayan al Batinah, Madinat ash Shamal, Umm Sa'id, Umm Salal
Independence: 3 September 1971 (from UK)
National holiday: Independence Day, 3 September (1971)
Constitution: ratified by public referendum on 29 April 2003, endorsed by the Emir on 8 June 2004, effective on 9 June 2005
Legal system: discretionary system of law controlled by the amir, although civil codes are being implemented; Islamic law

dominates family and personal matters
Suffrage: 18 years of age; universal
Executive branch:
chief of state: Amir HAMAD bin Khalifa al-Thani (since 27 June 1995 when, as crown prince, he ousted his father, Amir KHALIFA bin Hamad al-Thani, in a bloodless coup); Crown Prince TAMIM bin Hamad bin Khalifa al-Thani, third son of the monarch (selected Heir Apparent by the monarch on 5 August 2003); note - Amir HAMAD also holds the positions of Minister of Defense and Commander-in-chief of the Armed Forces
head of government: Prime Minister ABDALLAH bin Khalifa al-Thani, brother of the monarch (since 30 October 1996); Deputy Prime Minister MUHAMMAD bin Khalifa al-Thani, brother of the monarch (since 20 January 1998); First Deputy Prime Minister HAMAD bin JASIM bin JABIR al-Thani (since 16 September 2003; also Foreign Minister since 1992); Second Deputy Prime Minister Abdallah bin Hamad al-ATTIYAH (since 16 September 2003; also Energy Minister since NA 1992)
cabinet: Council of Ministers appointed by the monarch
elections: none; the monarch is hereditary
note: in April 2003, Qatar held nationwide elections for a 29-member Central Municipal Council (CMC), which has consultative powers aimed at improving the provision of municipal services; the first election for the CMC was held in March 1999
Legislative branch: unicameral Advisory Council or Majlis al-Shura (35 seats; members appointed)
note: no legislative elections have been held since 1970 when there were partial elections to the body; Council members have had their terms extended every four years since; the new constitution, which came into force on 9 June 2005, provides for a 45-member Consultative Council, or Majlis al-Shura; the public would elect two-thirds of the Majlis al-Shura; the amir would appoint the remaining members; preparations are underway to conduct elections to the Majlis al-Shura in early 2007
Judicial branch: Court of Appeal
note: under the new judiciary law issued in 2003, the former two court systems, civil and Islamic law, were merged under a higher court, the Court of Cassation, established for appeals
Political parties and leaders: none
Political pressure groups and leaders: none
International organization participation: ABEDA, AFESD, AMF, FAO, G-77, GCC, IAEA, IBRD, ICAO, ICC, ICRM, IDB, IFAD, IFRCS, ILO, IMF, IMO, Interpol, IOC, ISO, ITU, LAS, MIGA, NAM, OAPEC, OAS (observer), OIC, OPCW, OPEC, UN, UNCTAD, UNESCO, UNIDO, UPU, WCO, WHO, WIPO, WMO, WToO, WTO
Diplomatic representation in the US:
chief of mission: Ambassador Nasir bin Hamad bin Mubarak al-KHALIFA
chancery: 2555 M Street NW, Washington, DC 20037
telephone: [1] (202) 274-1600 and 274-1603
FAX: [1] (202) 237-0059
consulate(s) general: Houston
Diplomatic representation from the US:
chief of mission: Ambassador Chase UNTERMEYER
embassy: Al-Luqta District, 22 February Road, Doha
mailing address: P. O. Box 2399, Doha
telephone: [974] 488 4101
FAX: [974] 488 4176
Flag description: maroon with a broad white serrated band (nine white points) on the hoist side

ECONOMY

Economy - overview: Oil and gas account for more than 60% of GDP, roughly 85% of export earnings, and 70% of government revenues. Oil and gas have given Qatar a per capita GDP about 80% of that of the leading West European industrial countries. Proved oil reserves of 16 billion barrels should ensure continued output at current levels for 23 years. Qatar's proved reserves of natural gas exceed 14 trillion cubic meters, more than 5% of the world total and third largest in the world. Qatar has permitted substantial foreign investment in the development of its gas fields during the last decade and is expected to become the world's top liquefied natural gas (LNG) exporter by 2007. In recent years, Qatar has consistently posted trade surpluses largely because of high oil prices and increased natural gas exports, becoming one of the world's fastest growing and highest per-capita income countries.
GDP (purchasing power parity): $22.47 billion (2005 est.)
GDP (official exchange rate): $30.17 billion (2005 est.)
GDP - real growth rate: 8.8% (2005 est.)
GDP - per capita: purchasing power parity - $26,000 (2005 est.)
GDP - composition by sector:
agriculture: 0.2%
industry: 81%
services: 18.8% (2005 est.)
Labor force: 440,000 (2005 est.)
Unemployment rate: 2.7% (2001)
Population below poverty line: NA
Household income or consumption by percentage share:
lowest 10%: NA
highest 10%: NA
Inflation rate (consumer prices): 7.8% (2005 est.)
Investment (gross fixed): 20.9% of GDP (2005 est.)
Budget:
revenues: $17.31 billion
expenditures: $11.31 billion, including capital expenditures of $2.2 billion (2005 est.)
Public debt: 36.7% of GDP NA (2005 est.)
Agriculture - products: fruits, vegetables; poultry, dairy products, beef; fish
Industries: crude oil production and refining, ammonia, fertilizers, petrochemicals, steel reinforcing bars, cement, commercial ship repair
Industrial production growth rate: 10% (2003 est.)
Electricity - production: 9.735 billion kWh (2003)
Electricity - production by source:
fossil fuel: 100%
hydro: 0%
nuclear: 0%
other: 0% (2001)
Electricity - consumption: 9.053 billion kWh (2003)
Electricity - exports: 0 kWh (2003)
Electricity - imports: 0 kWh (2003)
Oil - production: 790,500 bbl/day (2005 est.)
Oil - consumption: 33,000 bbl/day (2003 est.)
Oil - exports: NA
Oil - imports: NA
Oil - proved reserves: 16 billion bbl (2005 est.)
Natural gas - production: 32.4 billion cu m (2001 est.)
Natural gas - consumption: 15.86 billion cu m (2001 est.)
Natural gas - exports: 18.2 billion cu m (2004 est.)
Natural gas - imports: 0 cu m (2001 est.)
Natural gas - proved reserves: 14.41 trillion cu m (2005)
Current account balance: $10.53 billion (2005 est.)
Exports: $24.9 billion f.o.b. (2005 est.)
Exports - partners: Japan 41.9%, South Korea 15.8%, Singapore 9.1%, India 5.4% (2004)
Imports: $6.706 billion f.o.b. (2005 est.)
Imports - partners: France 26.6%, US 9.5%, Saudi Arabia 9.4%, UAE 6.3%, Germany 5.2%, Japan 5.2%, UK 5.1% (2004)
Reserves of foreign exchange and gold: $4.754 billion (2005 est.)
Debt - external: $20.63 billion (2005 est.)
Economic aid - recipient: NA
Currency (code): Qatari rial (QAR)
Currency code: QAR
Exchange rates: Qatari rials per US dol-

lar - 3.64 (2005), 3.64 (2004), 3.64 (2003), 3.64 (2002), 3.64 (2001)
Fiscal year: 1 April - 31 March

COMMUNICATIONS

Telephones - main lines in use: 184,500 (2003)
Telephones - mobile cellular: 376,500 (2003)
Telephone system:
general assessment: modern system centered in Doha
domestic: NA
international: country code - 974; tropospheric scatter to Bahrain; microwave radio relay to Saudi Arabia and UAE; submarine cable to Bahrain and UAE; satellite earth stations - 2 Intelsat (1 Atlantic Ocean and 1 Indian Ocean) and 1 Arabsat
Radio broadcast stations: AM 6, FM 5, shortwave 1 (1998)
Radios: 256,000 (1997)
Television broadcast stations: 1 (plus three repeaters) (2001)
Televisions: 230,000 (1997)
Internet country code: .qa
Internet hosts: 221 (2004)
Internet Service Providers (ISPs): 1 (2000)
Internet users: 126,000 (2003)

TRANSPORTATION

Airports: 4 (2004 est.)
Airports - with paved runways:
total: 3
over 3,047 m: 2
1,524 to 2,437 m: 1 (2005 est.)
Airports - with unpaved runways:
total: 2
914 to 1,523 m: 1
under 914 m: 1 (2005 est.)
Heliports: 1 (2005 est.)
Pipelines: condensate 319 km; condensate/gas 209 km; gas 1,024 km; liquid petroleum gas 87 km; oil 702 km; oil/gas/water 41 km (2004)
Roadways:
total: 1,230 km
paved: 1,107 km
unpaved: 123 km (1999 est.)
Merchant marine:
total: 22 ships (1,000 GRT or over) 525,051 GRT/772,635 DWT
by type: cargo 3, chemical tanker 5, container 8, liquefied gas 2, petroleum tanker 3, roll on/roll off 1
foreign-owned: 6 (Kuwait 6) (2005)
Ports and terminals: Doha

MILITARY

Military branches: Qatari Amiri Land Force (QALF), Qatari Amiri Navy (QAN), Qatari Amiri Air Force (QAAF)
Military service age and obligation: 18 years of age for voluntary military service; Land Force's enlisted personnel are largely nonprofessional foreign nationals (2005)
Manpower available for military service:
males age 18-49: 302,873
note: includes non-nationals (2005 est.)
Manpower fit for military service: *males age 18-49:* 238,566 (2005 est.)
Manpower reaching military service age annually: *males:* 7,851 (2005 est.)
Military expenditures - dollar figure: $723 million (FY00)
Military expenditures - percent of GDP: 10% (FY00)

TRANSNATIONAL ISSUES

Disputes - international: none

REUNION

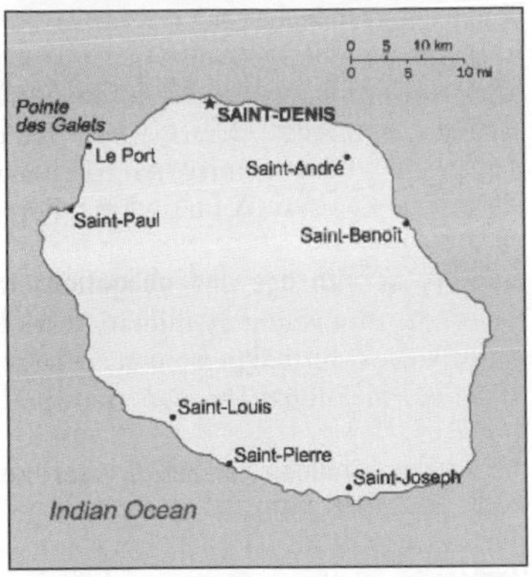

INTRODUCTION

Background: The Portuguese discovered the uninhabited island in 1513. From the 17th to the 19th centuries, French immigration, supplemented by influxes of Africans, Chinese, Malays, and Malabar Indians, gave the island its ethnic mix. The opening of the Suez Canal in 1869 cost the island its importance as a stopover on the East Indies trade route.

GEOGRAPHY

Location: Southern Africa, island in the Indian Ocean, east of Madagascar
Geographic coordinates: 21 06 S, 55 36 E
Map references: World
Area:
total: 2,517 sq km
land: 2,507 sq km
water: 10 sq km
Area - comparative: slightly smaller than Rhode Island
Land boundaries: 0 km
Coastline: 207 km
Maritime claims:
territorial sea: 12 nm
exclusive economic zone: 200 nm
Climate: tropical, but temperature moderates with elevation; cool and dry from May to November, hot and rainy from November to April
Terrain: mostly rugged and mountainous; fertile lowlands along coast
Elevation extremes:
lowest point: Indian Ocean 0 m
highest point: Piton des Neiges 3,069 m
Natural resources: fish, arable land, hydropower
Land use:
arable land: 13.6%
permanent crops: 1.2%
other: 85.2% (2001)
Irrigated land: 120 sq km (1998 est.)
Natural hazards: periodic, devastating cyclones (December to April); Piton de la Fournaise on the southeastern coast is an active volcano
Environment - current issues: NA
Geography - note: this mountainous, volcanic island has an active volcano, Piton de la Fournaise; there is a tropical cyclone center at Saint-Denis, which is the monitoring station for the whole of the Indian Ocean

PEOPLE

Population: 776,948 (July 2005 est.)
Age structure:
0-14 years: 30.4% (male 120,698/female 115,108)
15-64 years: 63.6% (male 243,668/female 250,143)
65 years and over: 6.1% (male 19,234/female 28,097) (2005 est.)
Median age:
total: 26.72 years
male: 25.53 years
female: 27.92 years (2005 est.)
Population growth rate: 1.38% (2005 est.)
Birth rate: 19.26 births/1,000 population (2005 est.)
Death rate: 5.48 deaths/1,000 population (2005 est.)
Net migration rate: 0 migrant(s)/1,000 population (2005 est.)
Sex ratio:
at birth: 1.05 male(s)/female
under 15 years: 1.05 male(s)/female
15-64 years: 0.97 male(s)/female
65 years and over: 0.68 male(s)/female
total population: 0.98 male(s)/female (2005 est.)
Infant mortality rate:
total: 7.78 deaths/1,000 live births
male: 8.52 deaths/1,000 live births
female: 6.99 deaths/1,000 live births (2005 est.)
Life expectancy at birth:
total population: 73.95 years
male: 70.55 years
female: 77.52 years (2005 est.)
Total fertility rate: 2.47 children born/woman (2005 est.)
HIV/AIDS - adult prevalence rate: NA%
HIV/AIDS - people living with HIV/AIDS: NA
HIV/AIDS - deaths: NA
Nationality:
noun: Reunionese (singular and plural)
adjective: Reunionese
Ethnic groups: French, African, Malagasy, Chinese, Pakistani, Indian
Religions: Roman Catholic 86%, Hindu, Muslim, Buddhist (1995)
Languages: French (official), Creole widely used
Literacy:
definition: age 15 and over can read and write
total population: 88.9%
male: 87%
female: 90.8% (2003 est.)

GOVERNMENT

Country name:
conventional long form: Department of Reunion
conventional short form: Reunion
local long form: none
local short form: Ile de la Reunion
former: Bourbon Island
Dependency status: overseas department of France
Government type: NA
Capital: Saint-Denis
Administrative divisions: none (overseas department of France); there are no first-order administrative divisions as defined by the US Government, but there are 4 arrondissements, 24 communes, and 47 cantons
Independence: none (overseas department of France)
National holiday: Bastille Day, 14 July (1789)
Constitution: 4 October 1958 (French Constitution)
Legal system: French law
Suffrage: 18 years of age; universal
Executive branch:
chief of state: President Jacques CHIRAC of France (since 17 May 1995), represented by Prefect Laurent CAYREL (since 16 July 2005)
head of government: President of the General Council Nassimah DINDAR (since NA March 2004) and President of the Regional Council Paul VERGES (since NA March 1993)
cabinet: NA
elections: French president elected by popular vote for a five-year term; prefect appointed by the French president on the advice of the French Ministry of the Interior; the presidents of the General and Regional Councils are elected by the members of those councils
Legislative branch: unicameral General Council (49 seats; members are elected by direct, popular vote to serve six-year terms) and a unicameral Regional Council (45 seats; members are elected by direct, popular vote to serve six-year terms)
elections: General Council - last held 15 and 22 March 1998 (next to be held NA); Regional Council - last held 28 March 2004 (next to be held NA 2010)
election results: General Council - percent of vote by party - NA%; seats by party - various right-wing candidates 13, PCR 10, PS 10, UDF 8, RPR 6, other left-wing candidates 2; Regional Council

(second round) - percent of vote by party - PCR 44.9%, UMP 32.8%, PS-Greens 22.3%; seats by party - PCR 27, UMP 11, PS-Greens 7
note: Reunion elects three representatives to the French Senate; elections last held NA 2001 (next to be held NA 2006); results - percent of vote by party - NA%; seats by party - NA; Reunion also elects five deputies to the French National Assembly; elections last held 9 June-16 June 2002 (next to be held NA 2007); results - percent of vote by party - NA%; seats by party - UMP-RPR 1, UMP 1, PCR 1
Judicial branch: Court of Appeals or Cour d'Appel
Political parties and leaders: Communist Party of Reunion or PCR [Paul VERGES]; Rally for the Republic or RPR [Andre Maurice PIHOUEE]; Socialist Party or PS [Jean-Claude FRUTEAU]; Union for French Democracy or UDF [Gilbert GERARD]; Union for a Popular Movement or UMP [leader NA]
Political pressure groups and leaders: NA
International organization participation: InOC, UPU, WFTU
Diplomatic representation in the US: none (overseas department of France)
Diplomatic representation from the US: none (overseas department of France)
Flag description: the flag of France is used

ECONOMY

Economy - overview: The economy has traditionally been based on agriculture, but services now dominate. Sugarcane has been the primary crop for more than a century, and in some years it accounts for 85% of exports. The government has been pushing the development of a tourist industry to relieve high unemployment, which amounts to one-third of the labor force. The gap in Reunion between the well-off and the poor is extraordinary and accounts for the persistent social tensions. The white and Indian communities are substantially better off than other segments of the population, often approaching European standards, whereas minority groups suffer the poverty and unemployment typical of the poorer nations of the African continent. The outbreak of severe rioting in February 1991 illustrates the seriousness of socioeconomic tensions. The economic well-being of Reunion depends heavily on continued financial assistance from France.
GDP (purchasing power parity): $4.802 billion (2005 est.)
GDP (official exchange rate): NA
GDP - real growth rate: 2.5% (2005 est.)
GDP - per capita: purchasing power parity - $6,200 (2005 est.)
GDP - composition by sector:
agriculture: 8%
industry: 19%
services: 73% (2000 est.)
Labor force: 309,900 (2000)
Labor force - by occupation: agriculture 13%, industry 12%, services 75% (2000)
Unemployment rate: 36% (1999 est.)
Population below poverty line: NA
Household income or consumption by percentage share:
lowest 10%: NA%
highest 10%: NA%
Inflation rate (consumer prices): NA%
Budget:
revenues: $1.26 billion
expenditures: $2.62 billion, including capital expenditures of NA (1998)
Agriculture - products: sugarcane, vanilla, tobacco, tropical fruits, vegetables, corn
Industries: sugar, rum, cigarettes, handicraft items, flower oil extraction
Industrial production growth rate: NA%
Electricity - production: 1.19 billion kWh (2003)
Electricity - production by source:
fossil fuel: 55.5%
hydro: 44.5%
nuclear: 0%
other: 0% (2001)
Electricity - consumption: 1.107 billion kWh (2003)
Electricity - exports: 0 kWh (2003)
Electricity - imports: 0 kWh (2003)
Oil - production: 0 bbl/day (2003 est.)
Oil - consumption: 18,500 bbl/day (2003 est.)
Oil - exports: NA (2001)
Oil - imports: NA (2001)
Exports: $214 million f.o.b. (1997)
Exports - partners: France 74%, Japan 6%, Comoros 4% (2004)
Imports: $2.5 billion c.i.f. (1997)
Imports - partners: France 64%, Bahrain 3%, Germany 3%, Italy 3% (2004)
Debt - external: $NA
Economic aid - recipient: NA; note - substantial annual subsidies from France (2001 est.)
Currency (code): euro (EUR)
Currency code: EUR
Exchange rates: euros per US dollar - 0.79697 (2005), 0.8054 (2004), 0.886 (2003), 1.0626 (2002), 1.1175 (2001)
Fiscal year: calendar year

COMMUNICATIONS

Telephones - main lines in use: 300,000 est (2001)
Telephones - mobile cellular: 489,800 (2002)
Telephone system:
general assessment: adequate system; principal center is Saint-Denis
domestic: modern open-wire and microwave radio relay network
international: country code - 262; radiotelephone communication to Comoros, France, Madagascar; new microwave route to Mauritius; satellite earth station - 1 Intelsat (Indian Ocean); fiber optic submarine cable (SAT-3/WASC/SAFE) provides connectivity to Europe and Asia
Radio broadcast stations: AM 2, FM 55, shortwave 0 (2001)
Radios: 173,000 (1997)
Television broadcast stations: 35 (plus 18 low-power repeaters) (2001)
Televisions: 127,000 (1997)
Internet country code: .re
Internet Service Providers (ISPs): 1 (2000)
Internet users: 150,000 (2002)

TRANSPORTATION

Airports: 2 (2004 est.)
Airports - with paved runways:
total: 2
2,438 to 3,047 m: 1
914 to 1,523 m: 1 (2005 est.)
Roadways:
total: 1,214 km (including 88 km of four-lane roads) (2001)
Merchant marine:
total: 1 ships (1,000 GRT or over) 28,264 GRT/44,885 DWT
by type: chemical tanker 1
foreign-owned: 1 (France 1)
registered in other countries: 1 (2005)
Ports and terminals: Le Port

MILITARY

Military branches: no regular indigenous military forces; French forces (includes Army, Navy, Air Force, and Gendarmerie) (2005)
Military service age and obligation: 18 years of age (2004)
Manpower available for military service:
males age 18-49: 183,421 (2005 est.)
Manpower fit for military service: *males age 18-49:* 142,578 (2005 est.)
Manpower reaching military service age annually: *males:* 7,339 (2005 est.)
Military - note: defense is the responsibility of France

TRANSNATIONAL ISSUES

Disputes - international: none

ROMANIA

INTRODUCTION

Background: The principalities of Wallachia and Moldavia - for centuries under the suzerainty of the Turkish Ottoman Empire - secured their autonomy in 1856; they united in 1859 and a few years later adopted the new name of Romania. The country gained recognition of its independence in 1878. It joined the Allied Powers in World War I and acquired new territories following the conflict. In 1940, it allied with the Axis powers and participated in the 1941 German invasion of the USSR. Three years later, overrun by the Soviets, Romania signed an armistice. The post-war Soviet occupation led to the formation of a Communist "people's republic" in 1947 and the abdication of the king. The decades-long rule of dictator Nicolae CEAUSESCU, who took power in 1965, and his Securitate police state became increasingly oppressive and draconian through the 1980s. CEAUSESCU was overthrown and executed in late 1989. Former Communists dominated the government until 1996, when they were swept from power by a fractious coalition of centrist parties. In 2000, the center-left Social Democratic Party (PSD) became Romania's leading party, governing with the support of the Democratic Union of Hungarians in Romania (UDMR). The opposition center-right alliance formed by the National Liberal Party (PNL) and the Democratic Party (PD) scored a surprise victory over the ruling PSD in December 2004 presidential elections. The PNL-PD alliance maintains a parliamentary majority with the support of the UDMR, the Humanist Party (PUR), and various ethnic minority groups. Although Romania completed accession talks with the European Union (EU) in December 2004, it must continue to address rampant corruption - while invigorating lagging economic and democratic reforms - before it can achieve its hope of joining the EU, tentatively set for 2007. Romania joined NATO in March of 2004.

GEOGRAPHY

Location: Southeastern Europe, bordering the Black Sea, between Bulgaria and Ukraine
Geographic coordinates: 46 00 N, 25 00 E
Map references: Europe
Area:
total: 237,500 sq km
land: 230,340 sq km
water: 7,160 sq km
Area - comparative: slightly smaller than Oregon
Land boundaries:
total: 2,508 km
border countries: Bulgaria 608 km, Hungary 443 km, Moldova 450 km, Serbia and Montenegro 476 km, Ukraine (north) 362 km, Ukraine (east) 169 km
Coastline: 225 km
Maritime claims:
territorial sea: 12 nm
contiguous zone: 24 nm
exclusive economic zone: 200 nm
continental shelf: 200-m depth or to the depth of exploitation
Climate: temperate; cold, cloudy winters with frequent snow and fog; sunny summers with frequent showers and thunderstorms
Terrain: central Transylvanian Basin is separated from the Plain of Moldavia on the east by the Carpathian Mountains and separated from the Walachian Plain on the south by the Transylvanian Alps
Elevation extremes:
lowest point: Black Sea 0 m
highest point: Moldoveanu 2,544 m
Natural resources: petroleum (reserves declining), timber, natural gas, coal, iron ore, salt, arable land, hydropower
Land use:
arable land: 40.82%
permanent crops: 2.25%
other: 56.93% (2001)
Irrigated land: 28,800 sq km (1998 est.)
Natural hazards: earthquakes, most severe in south and southwest; geologic structure and climate promote landslides
Environment - current issues: soil erosion and degradation; water pollution; air pollution in south from industrial effluents; contamination of Danube delta wetlands
Environment - international agreements:
party to: Air Pollution, Air Pollution-Persistent Organic Pollutants, Antarctic Treaty, Biodiversity, Climate Change, Climate Change-Kyoto Protocol, Desertification, Endangered Species, Environmental Modification, Hazardous Wastes, Law of the Sea, Ozone Layer Protection, Ship Pollution, Wetlands
signed, but not ratified: none of the selected agreements
Geography - note: controls most easily traversable land route between the Balkans, Moldova, and Ukraine

PEOPLE

Population: 22,329,977 (July 2005 est.)
Age structure:
0-14 years: 15.9% (male 1,818,488/female 1,727,598)
15-64 years: 69.5% (male 7,726,903/female 7,801,441)
65 years and over: 14.6% (male 1,342,827/female 1,912,720) (2005 est.)
Median age:
total: 36.39 years
male: 35.04 years
female: 37.77 years (2005 est.)
Population growth rate: -0.12% (2005 est.)
Birth rate: 10.7 births/1,000 population (2005 est.)
Death rate: 11.74 deaths/1,000 population (2005 est.)
Net migration rate: -0.13 migrant(s)/1,000 population (2005 est.)
Sex ratio:
at birth: 1.06 male(s)/female
under 15 years: 1.05 male(s)/female
15-64 years: 0.99 male(s)/female
65 years and over: 0.7 male(s)/female
total population: 0.95 male(s)/female (2005 est.)
Infant mortality rate:
total: 26.43 deaths/1,000 live births
male: 29.6 deaths/1,000 live births
female: 23.06 deaths/1,000 live births (2005 est.)
Life expectancy at birth:
total population: 71.35 years
male: 67.86 years
female: 75.06 years (2005 est.)
Total fertility rate: 1.36 children born/woman (2005 est.)
HIV/AIDS - adult prevalence rate: less than 0.1% (2001 est.)
HIV/AIDS - people living with HIV/AIDS: 6,500 (2001 est.)
HIV/AIDS - deaths: 350 (2001 est.)
Nationality:
noun: Romanian(s)
adjective: Romanian
Ethnic groups: Romanian 89.5%, Hungarian 6.6%, Roma 2.5%, Ukrainian 0.3%, German 0.3%, Russian 0.2%, Turkish 0.2%, other 0.4% (2002 census)
Religions: Eastern Orthodox (including all sub-denominations) 86.8%, Protestant (various denominations including Reformate and Pentecostal)

7.5%, Roman Catholic 4.7%, other (mostly Muslim) and unspecified 0.9%, none 0.1% (2002 census)
Languages: Romanian (official), Hungarian, German
Literacy:
definition: age 15 and over can read and write
total population: 98.4%
male: 99.1%
female: 97.7% (2003 est.)

GOVERNMENT

Country name:
conventional long form: none
conventional short form: Romania
local long form: none
local short form: Romania
Government type: republic
Capital: Bucharest
Administrative divisions: 41 counties (judete, singular - judet) and 1 municipality* (municipiu); Alba, Arad, Arges, Bacau, Bihor, Bistrita-Nasaud, Botosani, Braila, Brasov, Bucuresti (Bucharest)*, Buzau, Calarasi, Caras-Severin, Cluj, Constanta, Covasna, Dimbovita, Dolj, Galati, Gorj, Giurgiu, Harghita, Hunedoara, Ialomita, Iasi, Ilfov, Maramures, Mehedinti, Mures, Neamt, Olt, Prahova, Salaj, Satu Mare, Sibiu, Suceava, Teleorman, Timis, Tulcea, Vaslui, Vilcea, Vrancea
Independence: 9 May 1877 (independence proclaimed from the Ottoman Empire; independence recognized 13 July 1878 by the Treaty of Berlin; kingdom proclaimed 26 March 1881); 30 December 1947 (republic proclaimed)
National holiday: Unification Day (of Romania and Transylvania), 1 December (1918)
Constitution: 8 December 1991; revision effective 29 October 2003
Legal system: former mixture of civil law system and communist legal theory; is now based on the constitution of France's Fifth Republic
Suffrage: 18 years of age; universal
Executive branch:
chief of state: President Traian BASESCU (since 20 December 2004)
head of government: Prime Minister Calin Popescu-TARICEANU (since 29 December 2004)
cabinet: Council of Ministers appointed by the prime minister
elections: president elected by popular vote for a five-year term; election last held 28 November 2004, with runoff between the top two candidates held 12 December 2004 (next to be held 28 November 2009 and 12 December 2009); prime minister appointed by the president
election results: percent of vote - Traian BASESCU 51.23%, Adrian NASTASE 48.77%
Legislative branch: bicameral Parliament or Parlament consists of the Senate or Senat (137 seats; members are elected by direct, popular vote on a proportional representation basis to serve four-year terms) and the Chamber of Deputies or Adunarea Deputatilor (332 seats; members are elected by direct, popular vote on a proportional representation basis to serve four-year terms)
elections: Senate - last held 28 November 2004 (next to be held 28 November 2008); Chamber of Deputies - last held 28 November 2004 (next to be held 28 November 2008)
election results: Senate - percent of vote by alliance/party - PSD-PUR 37.1%, PNL-PD 31.8%, PRM 13.6%, UDMR 6.2%; seats by party - PSD 44, PNL 30, PD 20, PRM 20, PC 11, UMDR 10, independents 2; Chamber of Deputies - percent of vote by alliance/party - PSD-PUR 36.6%, PNL-PD 31.3%%, PRM 12.9%, UDMR 6.2%; seats by party - PSD 111, PNL 66, PD 45, PRM 34, ex-PRM (Ciontu Group) 12, UDMR 22, PC 20, PIN (GUSA Group) 3, independent 1, ethnic minorities 18
Judicial branch: Supreme Court of Justice (judges are appointed by the president on the recommendation of the Superior Council of Magistrates, a board of eleven judges and six prosecutors elected by parliament)
Political parties and leaders: Conservative Party or PC [Dan VOICULESCU], formerly Humanist Party or PUR; Democratic Party or PD [Emil BOC]; Democratic Union of Hungarians in Romania or UDMR [Bela MARKO]; National Liberal Party or PNL [Calin Popescu TARICEANU]; Romania Mare Party (Greater Romanian Party) or PRM [Corneliu Vadim TUDOR]; Social Democratic Party or PSD [Mircea Dan GEOANA], formerly Party of Social Democracy in Romania or PDSR
Political pressure groups and leaders: various human rights and professional associations
International organization participation: ACCT, Australia Group, BIS, BSEC, CE, CEI, EAPC, EBRD, EU (applicant), FAO, G- 9, G-77, IAEA, IBRD, ICAO, ICC, ICCt, ICFTU, ICRM, IFAD, IFC, IFRCS, ILO, IMF, IMO, Interpol, IOC, IOM, ISO, ITU, LAIA (observer), MIGA, MONUC, NAM (guest), NATO, NSG, OAS (observer), ONUB, OPCW, OSCE, PCA, UN, UN Security Council (temporary), UNCTAD, UNESCO, UNHCR, UNIDO, UNMEE, UNMIL, UNMIS, UNOCI, UNOMIG, UPU, WCL, WCO, WEU (associate partner), WFTU, WHO, WIPO, WMO, WToO, WTO, ZC
Diplomatic representation in the US:
chief of mission: Ambassador Sorin Dumitru DUCARU
chancery: 1607 23rd Street NW, Washington, DC 20008
telephone: [1] (202) 332-4846, 4848, 4851
FAX: [1] (202) 232-4748
consulate(s) general: Chicago, Los Angeles, and New York
Diplomatic representation from the US:
chief of mission: Ambassador Nicholas F. TAUBMAN
embassy: Strada Tudor Arghezi 7-9, Bucharest
mailing address: American Embassy Bucharest, Department of State, 5260 Bucharest Place, Washington, DC 20521-5260 (pouch)
telephone: [40] (21) 316-4052
FAX: [40] (21) 316-0395
branch office(s): Cluj-Napoca
Flag description: three equal vertical bands of blue (hoist side), yellow, and red; the national coat of arms that used to be centered in the yellow band has been removed; now similar to the flag of Chad, also resembles the flags of Andorra and Moldova

ECONOMY

Economy - overview: Romania began the transition from Communism in 1989 with a largely obsolete industrial base and a pattern of output unsuited to the country's needs. The country emerged in 2000 from a punishing three-year recession thanks to strong demand in EU export markets. Despite the global slowdown in 2001-02, strong domestic activity in construction, agriculture, and consumption have kept growth above 4%. An IMF standby agreement, signed in 2001, has been accompanied by slow but palpable gains in privatization, deficit reduction, and the curbing of inflation. The IMF Board approved Romania's completion of the standby agreement in October 2003, the first time Romania has successfully concluded an IMF agreement since the 1989 revolution. In July 2004, the executive board of the IMF approved a 24-month standby agreement for $367 million. Wayward economic policies led to a breakdown of this agreement in 2005, and the IMF has issued harsh criticisms of the government's fiscal, wage, and monetary policies. Meanwhile, recent macroeconomic gains have done little to address Romania's widespread poverty, while corruption and red tape continue to handicap the business environment.

GDP (purchasing power parity): $186.4 billion (2005 est.)
GDP (official exchange rate): $73.96 billion (2005 est.)
GDP - real growth rate: 5.2% (2005 est.)
GDP - per capita: purchasing power parity - $8,300 (2005 est.)
GDP - composition by sector:
agriculture: 13.1%
industry: 33.7%
services: 53.2% (2004 est.)
Labor force: 9.31 million (2005 est.)
Labor force - by occupation: agriculture 31.6%, industry 30.7%, services 37.7% (2004)
Unemployment rate: 6.5% (2005 est.)
Population below poverty line: 28.9% (2002)
Household income or consumption by percentage share:
lowest 10%: 2.4%
highest 10%: 27.6% (2003)
Distribution of family income - Gini index: 28.8 (2003)
Inflation rate (consumer prices): 8.9% (2005 est.)
Investment (gross fixed): 23.5% of GDP (2005 est.)
Budget:
revenues: $29.97 billion
expenditures: $31.37 billion, including capital expenditures of $2.2 billion (2005 est.)
Public debt: 21.1% of GDP (2005 est.)
Agriculture - products: wheat, corn, barley, sugar beets, sunflower seed, potatoes, grapes; eggs, sheep
Industries: textiles and footwear, light machinery and auto assembly, mining, timber, construction materials, metallurgy, chemicals, food processing, petroleum refining
Industrial production growth rate: 2.5% (2005 est.)
Electricity - production: 51.7 billion kWh (2003)
Electricity - production by source:
fossil fuel: 62.5%
hydro: 27.6%
nuclear: 9.9%
other: 0% (2001)
Electricity - consumption: 45.16 billion kWh (2003)
Electricity - exports: 3.3 billion kWh (2003)
Electricity - imports: 380 million kWh (2003)
Oil - production: 119,000 bbl/day (2005 est.)
Oil - consumption: 235,000 bbl/day (2003 est.)
Oil - exports: NA (2001)
Oil - imports: NA (2001)
Oil - proved reserves: 1.055 billion bbl (1 January 2002)
Natural gas - production: 12.6 billion cu m (2003 est.)
Natural gas - consumption: 18.5 billion cu m (2003 est.)
Natural gas - exports: 0 cu m (2001 est.)
Natural gas - imports: 5.4 billion cu m (2001 est.)
Natural gas - proved reserves: 111.1 billion cu m (1 January 2002)
Current account balance: $-9.541 billion (2005 est.)
Exports: $27.72 billion f.o.b. (2005 est.)
Exports - partners: Italy 21.4%, Germany 15%, France 8.5%, Turkey 7%, UK 6.6% (2004)
Imports: $38.15 billion f.o.b. (2005 est.)
Imports - partners: Italy 17.2%, Germany 14.9%, France 7.1%, Russia 6.8%, Turkey 4.2% (2004)
Reserves of foreign exchange and gold: $22.77 billion (2005 est.)
Debt - external: $29.47 billion (2005 est.)
Currency (code): leu (ROL)
Currency code: ROL
Exchange rates: lei per US dollar - 2.88 (2005), 32,637 (2004), 33,200 (2003), 33,055 (2002), 29,061 (2001)
Fiscal year: calendar year

COMMUNICATIONS

Telephones - main lines in use: 4.3 million (2003)
Telephones - mobile cellular: 6.9 million (2003)
Telephone system:
general assessment: poor domestic service, but improving
domestic: 90% of telephone network is automatic; trunk network is mostly microwave radio relay, with some fiber-optic cable; about one-third of exchange capacity is digital; roughly 3,300 villages have no service
international: country code - 40; satellite earth station - 1 Intelsat; new digital, international, direct-dial exchanges operate in Bucharest; note - Romania is an active participant in several international telecommunication network projects (1999)
Radio broadcast stations: AM 40, FM 202, shortwave 3 (1998)
Radios: 7.2 million (1997)
Television broadcast stations: 48 (plus 392 repeaters) (1995)
Televisions: 5.25 million (1997)
Internet country code: .ro
Internet hosts: 50,807 (2004)
Internet Service Providers (ISPs): 38 (2000)
Internet users: 4 million (2003)

TRANSPORTATION

Airports: 61 (2004 est.)
Airports - with paved runways:
total: 25
over 3,047 m: 4
2,438 to 3,047 m: 9
1,524 to 2,437 m: 12 (2005 est.)
Airports - with unpaved runways:
total: 36
1,524 to 2,437 m: 2
914 to 1,523 m: 11
under 914 m: 23 (2005 est.)
Heliports: 1 (2005 est.)
Pipelines: gas 3,508 km; oil 2,427 km (2004)
Railways:
total: 11,385 km (3,888 km electrified)
standard gauge: 10,898 km 1.435-m gauge
broad gauge: 60 km 1.524-m gauge
narrow gauge: 427 km 0.760-m gauge (2004)
Roadways:
total: 198,755 km
paved: 100,173 km (including 113 km of expressways)
unpaved: 98,582 km (2002)
Waterways: 1,731 km (2004)
Merchant marine:
total: 34 ships (1,000 GRT or over) 395,350 GRT/510,232 DWT
by type: bulk carrier 5, cargo 20, passenger 1, passenger/cargo 2, petroleum tanker 2, roll on/roll off 4
foreign-owned: 2 (Italy 2)
registered in other countries: 39 (2005)
Ports and terminals: Braila, Constanta, Galati, Tulcea

MILITARY

Military branches: Land Forces, Naval Forces, Air and Air Defense Forces (AMR), Special Operations, Civil Defense (2005)
Military service age and obligation: 20 years of age for compulsory military service, 18 in wartime; conscript service obligation - 12 months; 18 years of age for voluntary military service (2004)
Manpower available for military service:
males age 20-49: 5,061,984 (2005 est.)
Manpower fit for military service: *males age 20-49:* 3,932,579 (2005 est.)
Manpower reaching military service age annually: *males:* 172,093 (2005 est.)
Military expenditures - dollar figure: $985 million (2002)
Military expenditures - percent of GDP: 2.47% (2002)

TRANSNATIONAL ISSUES

Disputes - international: Romania and Ukraine have taken their dispute over Ukrainian-administered Zmiyinyy (Snake) Island and Black Sea maritime boundary to the ICJ for adjudication; Romania also opposes Ukraine's reopening of a navigation canal from the Danube border through Ukraine to the Black Sea; Hungary amended the status law extending special social and cultural benefits to ethnic Hungarians in Romania, to which

Romania had objected
Illicit drugs: major transshipment point for Southwest Asian heroin transiting the Balkan route and small amounts of Latin American cocaine bound for Western Europe; although not a significant financial center, role as a narcotics conduit leaves it vulnerable to laundering which occurs via the banking system, currency exchange houses, and casinos

RUSSIA

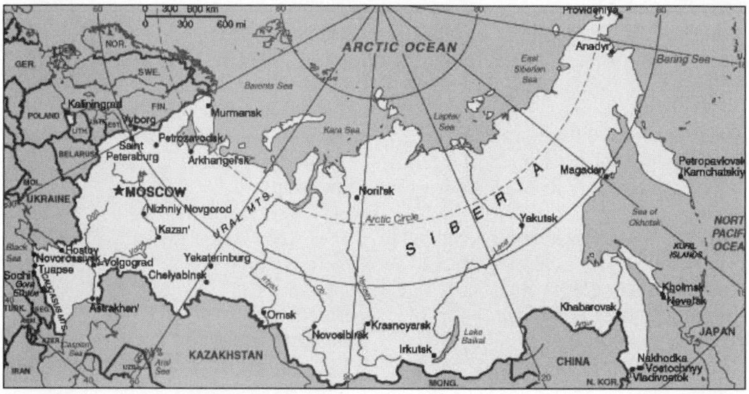

INTRODUCTION

Background: Founded in the 12th century, the Principality of Muscovy, was able to emerge from over 200 years of Mongol domination (13th-15th centuries) and to gradually conquer and absorb surrounding principalities. In the early 17th century, a new Romanov Dynasty continued this policy of expansion across Siberia to the Pacific. Under PETER I (ruled 1682-1725), hegemony was extended to the Baltic Sea and the country was renamed the Russian Empire. During the 19th century, more territorial acquisitions were made in Europe and Asia. Repeated devastating defeats of the Russian army in World War I led to widespread rioting in the major cities of the Russian Empire and to the overthrow in 1917 of the imperial household. The Communists under Vladimir LENIN seized power soon after and formed the USSR. The brutal rule of and threatens to destabilize the North Caucasus region. Iosif STALIN (1928-53) strengthened Russian dominance of the Soviet Union at a cost of tens of millions of lives. The Soviet economy and society stagnated in the following decades until General Secretary Mikhail GORBACHEV (1985-91) introduced glasnost (openness) and perestroika (restructuring) in an attempt to modernize Communism, but his initiatives inadvertently released forces that by December 1991 splintered the USSR into 15 independent republics. Since then, Russia has struggled in its efforts to build a democratic political system and market economy to replace the strict social, political, and economic controls of the Communist period. While some progress has been made on the economic front, recent years have seen a recentralization of power under Vladimir PUTIN and an erosion in nascent democratic institutions. A determined guerrilla conflict still plagues Russia in Chechnya and threatens to destabilize the North Caucasus region.

GEOGRAPHY

Location: Northern Asia (that part west of the Urals is included with Europe), bordering the Arctic Ocean, between Europe and the North Pacific Ocean
Geographic coordinates: 60 00 N, 100 00 E
Map references: Asia
Area:
total: 17,075,200 sq km
land: 16,995,800 sq km
water: 79,400 sq km
Area - comparative: approximately 1.8 times the size of the US
Land boundaries:
total: 20,017 km
border countries: Azerbaijan 284 km, Belarus 959 km, China (southeast) 3,605 km, China (south) 40 km, Estonia 294 km, Finland 1,340 km, Georgia 723 km, Kazakhstan 6,846 km, North Korea 19 km, Latvia 217 km, Lithuania (Kaliningrad Oblast) 227 km, Mongolia 3,485 km, Norway 196 km, Poland (Kaliningrad Oblast) 206 km, Ukraine 1,576 km
Coastline: 37,653 km
Maritime claims:
territorial sea: 12 nm
exclusive economic zone: 200 nm
continental shelf: 200-m depth or to the depth of exploitation
Climate: ranges from steppes in the south through humid continental in much of European Russia; subarctic in Siberia to tundra climate in the polar north; winters vary from cool along Black Sea coast to frigid in Siberia; summers vary from warm in the steppes to cool along Arctic coast
Terrain: broad plain with low hills west of Urals; vast coniferous forest and tundra in Siberia; uplands and mountains along southern border regions
Elevation extremes:
lowest point: Caspian Sea -28 m
highest point: Gora El'brus 5,633 m
Natural resources: wide natural resource base including major deposits of oil, natural gas, coal, and many strategic minerals, timber
note: formidable obstacles of climate, terrain, and distance hinder exploitation of natural resources
Land use:
arable land: 7.33%
permanent crops: 0.11%
other: 92.56% (2001)
Irrigated land: 46,630 sq km (1998 est.)
Natural hazards: permafrost over much of Siberia is a major impediment to development; volcanic activity in the Kuril Islands; volcanoes and earthquakes on the Kamchatka Peninsula; spring floods and summer/autumn forest fires throughout Siberia and parts of European Russia
Environment - current issues: air pollution from heavy industry, emissions of coal-fired electric plants, and transportation in major cities; industrial, municipal, and agricultural pollution of inland waterways and seacoasts; deforestation; soil erosion; soil contamination from improper application of agricultural chemicals; scattered areas of sometimes intense radioactive contamination; groundwater contamination from toxic waste; urban solid waste management; abandoned stocks of obsolete pesticides
Environment - international agreements:
party to: Air Pollution, Air Pollution-Nitrogen Oxides, Air Pollution-Sulfur 85, Antarctic-Environmental Protocol, Antarctic-Marine Living Resources, Antarctic Seals, Antarctic Treaty, Biodiversity, Climate Change, Climate Change-Kyoto Protocol, Endangered Species, Environmental Modification, Hazardous Wastes, Law of the Sea, Marine Dumping, Ozone Layer

Protection, Ship Pollution, Tropical Timber 83, Wetlands, Whaling
signed, but not ratified: Air Pollution-Sulfur 94
Geography - note: largest country in the world in terms of area but unfavorably located in relation to major sea lanes of the world; despite its size, much of the country lacks proper soils and climates (either too cold or too dry) for agriculture; Mount El'brus is Europe's tallest peak

PEOPLE

Population: 143,420,309 (July 2005 est.)
Age structure:
0-14 years: 14.6% (male 10,704,617/female 10,173,313)
15-64 years: 71.3% (male 49,429,716/female 52,799,740)
65 years and over: 14.2% (male 6,405,027/female 13,907,896) (2005 est.)
Median age:
total: 38.15 years
male: 34.99 years
female: 41.03 years (2005 est.)
Population growth rate: -0.37% (2005 est.)
Birth rate: 9.8 births/1,000 population (2005 est.)
Death rate: 14.52 deaths/1,000 population (2005 est.)
Net migration rate: 1.03 migrant(s)/1,000 population (2005 est.)
Sex ratio:
at birth: 1.06 male(s)/female
under 15 years: 1.05 male(s)/female
15-64 years: 0.94 male(s)/female
65 years and over: 0.46 male(s)/female
total population: 0.86 male(s)/female (2005 est.)
Infant mortality rate:
total: 15.39 deaths/1,000 live births
male: 17.7 deaths/1,000 live births
female: 12.94 deaths/1,000 live births (2005 est.)
Life expectancy at birth:
total population: 67.1 years
male: 60.55 years
female: 74.04 years (2005 est.)
Total fertility rate: 1.27 children born/woman (2005 est.)
HIV/AIDS - adult prevalence rate: 1.1% (2001 est.)
HIV/AIDS - people living with HIV/AIDS: 860,000 (2001 est.)
HIV/AIDS - deaths: 9,000 (2001 est.)
Nationality:
noun: Russian(s)
adjective: Russian
Ethnic groups: Russian 79.8%, Tatar 3.8%, Ukrainian 2%, Bashkir 1.2%, Chuvash 1.1%, other or unspecified 12.1% (2002 census)
Religions: Russian Orthodox, Muslim, other
Languages: Russian, many minority languages
Literacy:
definition: age 15 and over can read and write
total population: 99.6%
male: 99.7%
female: 99.5% (2003 est.)

GOVERNMENT

Country name:
conventional long form: Russian Federation
conventional short form: Russia
local long form: Rossiyskaya Federatsiya
local short form: Rossiya
former: Russian Empire, Russian Soviet Federative Socialist Republic
Government type: federation
Capital: Moscow
Administrative divisions: 48 oblasts (oblastey, singular - oblast), 21 republics (respublik, singular - respublika), 9 autonomous okrugs (avtonomnykh okrugov, singular - avtonomnyy okrug), 7 krays (krayev, singular - kray), 2 federal cities (singular - gorod), and 1 autonomous oblast (avtonomnaya oblast')
: oblasts: Amur (Blagoveshchensk), Arkhangel'sk, Astrakhan', Belgorod, Bryansk, Chelyabinsk, Chita, Irkutsk, Ivanovo, Kaliningrad, Kaluga, Kamchatka (Petropavlovsk-Kamchatskiy), Kemerovo, Kirov, Kostroma, Kurgan, Kursk, Leningrad, Lipetsk, Magadan, Moscow, Murmansk, Nizhniy Novgorod, Novgorod, Novosibirsk, Omsk, Orenburg, Orel, Penza, Pskov, Rostov, Ryazan', Sakhalin (Yuzhno-Sakhalinsk), Samara, Saratov, Smolensk, Sverdlovsk (Yekaterinburg), Tambov, Tomsk, Tula, Tver', Tyumen', Ul'yanovsk, Vladimir, Volgograd, Vologda, Voronezh, Yaroslavl'
: republics: Adygeya (Maykop), Altay (Gorno-Altaysk), Bashkortostan (Ufa), Buryatiya (Ulan-Ude), Chechnya (Groznyy), Chuvashiya (Cheboksary), Dagestan (Makhachkala), Ingushetiya (Magas), Kabardino-Balkariya (Nal'chik), Kalmykiya (Elista), Karachayevo-Cherkesiya (Cherkessk), Kareliya (Petrozavodsk), Khakasiya (Abakan), Komi (Syktyvkar), Mariy-El (Yoshkar-Ola), Mordoviya (Saransk), Sakha [Yakutiya] (Yakutsk), North Ossetia (Vladikavkaz), Tatarstan (Kazan'), Tyva (Kyzyl), Udmurtiya (Izhevsk)
: autonomous okrugs: Aga Buryat (Aginskoye), Chukotka (Anadyr'), Evenk (Tura), Khanty-Mansi, Koryak (Palana), Nenets (Nar'yan-Mar), Taymyr [Dolgano-Nenets] (Dudinka), Ust'-Orda Buryat (Ust'-Ordynskiy), Yamalo-Nenets (Salekhard)
: krays: Altay (Barnaul), Khabarovsk, Krasnodar, Krasnoyarsk, Permskiy, Primorskiy (Vladivostok), Stavropol'
: federal cities: Moscow (Moskva), Saint Petersburg (Sankt-Peterburg)
: autonomous oblast: Yevrey [Jewish] (Birobidzhan)
note: administrative divisions have the same names as their administrative centers (exceptions have the administrative center name following in parentheses)
Independence: 24 August 1991 (from Soviet Union)
National holiday: Russia Day, 12 June (1990)
Constitution: adopted 12 December 1993
Legal system: based on civil law system; judicial review of legislative acts
Suffrage: 18 years of age; universal
Executive branch:
chief of state: President Vladimir Vladimirovich PUTIN (acting president 31 December 1999 - 6 May 2000, president since 7 May 2000)
head of government: Premier Mikhail Yefimovich FRADKOV (since 5 March 2004); First Deputy Premier Dmitriy Anatolyevich MEDVEDEV (since 14 November 2005), Deputy Premiers Aleksandr Dmitriyevich ZHUKOV (since 9 March 2004) and Sergey Borisovich IVANOV (since 14 November 2005)
cabinet: Ministries of the Government or "Government" composed of the premier and his deputies, ministers, and selected other individuals; all are appointed by the president
note: there is also a Presidential Administration (PA) that provides staff and policy support to the president, drafts presidential decrees, and coordinates policy among government agencies; a Security Council also reports directly to the president
elections: president elected by popular vote for a four-year term; election last held 14 March 2004 (next to be held March 2008); note - no vice president; if the president dies in office, cannot exercise his powers because of ill health, is impeached, or resigns, the premier serves as acting president until a new presidential election is held, which must be within three months; premier appointed by the president with the approval of the Duma
election results: Vladimir Vladimirovich PUTIN reelected president; percent of vote - Vladimir Vladimirovich PUTIN 71.2%, Nikolay KHARITONOV 13.7%, other (no candidate above 5%) 15.1%
Legislative branch: bicameral Federal Assembly or Federalnoye Sobraniye consists of the Federation Council or Sovet Federatsii (178 seats; as of July 2000, members appointed by the top executive and legislative officials in each of the 88 federal administrative units - oblasts, krays, republics, autonomous okrugs and

oblasts, and the federal cities of Moscow and Saint Petersburg; members serve four-year terms) and the State Duma or Gosudarstvennaya Duma (450 seats; currently elected by proportional representation from party lists winning at least 7% of the vote; members are elected by direct, popular vote to serve four-year terms)
elections: State Duma - last held 7 December 2003 (next to be held NA December 2007)
election results: State Duma - percent of vote received by parties clearing the 5% threshold entitling them to a proportional share of the 225 party list seats - United Russia 37.1%, CPRF 12.7%, LDPR 11.6%, Motherland 9.1%; seats by party - United Russia 222, CPRF 53, LDPR 38, Motherland 37, People's Party 19, Yabloko 4, SPS 2, other 7, independents 65, repeat election required 3
Judicial branch: Constitutional Court; Supreme Court; Superior Court of Arbitration; judges for all courts are appointed for life by the Federation Council on the recommendation of the president
Political parties and leaders: Communist Party of the Russian Federation or CPRF [Gennadiy Andreyevich ZYUGANOV]; Liberal Democratic Party of Russia or LDPR [Vladimir Volfovich ZHIRINOVSKIY]; Motherland Bloc (Rodina) [Dmitriy ROGOZIN]; Union of Right Forces or SPS [Nikita BELYKH]; United Russia [Boris Vyacheslavovich GRYZLOV]; Yabloko Party [Grigoriy Alekseyevich YAVLINSKIY]
Political pressure groups and leaders: NA
International organization participation: APEC, ARF, ASEAN (dialogue partner), BIS, BSEC, CBSS, CE, CERN (observer), CIS, EAPC, EBRD, G- 8, IAEA, IBRD, ICAO, ICC, ICCt (signatory), ICFTU, ICRM, IDA, IFC, IFRCS, IHO, ILO, IMF, IMO, Interpol, IOC, IOM (observer), ISO, ITU, LAIA (observer), MIGA, MINURSO, MONUC, NAM (guest), NSG, OAS (observer), OIC (observer), ONUB, OPCW, OSCE, Paris Club, PCA, PFP, SCO, UN, UN Security Council, UNAMSIL, UNCTAD, UNESCO, UNHCR, UNIDO, UNITAR, UNMEE, UNMIL, UNMIS, UNMOVIC, UNOCI, UNOMIG, UNTSO, UPU, WCO, WFTU, WHO, WIPO, WMO, WToO, WTO (observer), ZC
Diplomatic representation in the US:
chief of mission: Ambassador Yuriy Viktorovich USHAKOV
chancery: 2650 Wisconsin Avenue NW, Washington, DC 20007
telephone: [1] (202) 298-5700, 5701, 5704, 5708
FAX: [1] (202) 298-5735
consulate(s) general: Houston, New York, San Francisco, and Seattle
Diplomatic representation from the US:
chief of mission: Ambassador William J. BURNS
embassy: Bolshoy Devyatinskiy Pereulok No. 8, 121099 Moscow
mailing address: PSC-77, APO AE 09721
telephone: [7] (095) 728-5000
FAX: [7] (095) 728-5090
consulate(s) general: Saint Petersburg, Vladivostok, Yekaterinburg
Flag description: three equal horizontal bands of white (top), blue, and red

ECONOMY

Economy - overview: Russia ended 2005 with its seventh straight year of growth, averaging 6.4% annually since the financial crisis of 1998. Although high oil prices and a relatively cheap ruble are important drivers of this economic rebound, since 2000 investment and consumer-driven demand have played a noticeably increasing role. Real fixed capital investments have averaged gains greater than 10% over the last five years, and real personal incomes have realized average increases over 12%. Russia has also improved its international financial position since the 1998 financial crisis, with its foreign debt declining from 90% of GDP to around 36%. Strong oil export earnings have allowed Russia to increase its foreign reserves from only $12 billion to some $180 billion at yearend 2005. These achievements, along with a renewed government effort to advance structural reforms, have raised business and investor confidence in Russia's economic prospects. Nevertheless, serious problems persist. Economic growth slowed to 5.9% for 2005 while unemployment and inflation remain high. Oil, natural gas, metals, and timber account for more than 80% of exports, leaving the country vulnerable to swings in world prices. Russia's manufacturing base is dilapidated and must be replaced or modernized if the country is to achieve broad-based economic growth. Other problems include a weak banking system, a poor business climate that discourages both domestic and foreign investors, corruption, and widespread lack of trust in institutions. In addition, a string of investigations launched against a major Russian oil company, culminating with the arrest of its CEO in the fall of 2003, have raised concerns by some observers that President PUTIN is granting more influence to forces within his government that desire to reassert state control over the economy.
GDP (purchasing power parity): $1.535 trillion (2005 est.)
GDP (official exchange rate): $740.7 billion (2005 est.)
GDP - real growth rate: 5.9% (2005 est.)
GDP - per capita: purchasing power parity - $10,700 (2005 est.)
GDP - composition by sector:
agriculture: 5%
industry: 35%
services: 60% (2005 est.)
Labor force: 74.22 million (2005 est.)
Labor force - by occupation: agriculture 10.3%, industry 21.4%, services 68.3% (2004 est.)
Unemployment rate: 7.6% plus considerable underemployment (2005 est.)
Population below poverty line: 17.8% (2004 est.)
Household income or consumption by percentage share:
lowest 10%: 1.7%
highest 10%: 38.7% (1998)
Distribution of family income - Gini index: 40 (2002)
Inflation rate (consumer prices): 12.9% (2005 est.)
Investment (gross fixed): 17.5% of GDP (2005 est.)
Budget:
revenues: $176.7 billion
expenditures: $125.6 billion, including capital expenditures of NA (2005 est.)
Public debt: 15.6% of GDP (2005 est.)
Agriculture - products: grain, sugar beets, sunflower seed, vegetables, fruits; beef, milk
Industries: complete range of mining and extractive industries producing coal, oil, gas, chemicals, and metals; all forms of machine building from rolling mills to high-performance aircraft and space vehicles; defense industries including radar, missile production, and advanced electronic components, shipbuilding; road and rail transportation equipment; communications equipment; agricultural machinery, tractors, and construction equipment; electric power generating and transmitting equipment; medical and scientific instruments; consumer durables, textiles, foodstuffs, handicrafts
Industrial production growth rate: 4% (2005 est.)
Electricity - production: 931 billion kWh (2004)
Electricity - production by source:
fossil fuel: 66.3%
hydro: 17.2%
nuclear: 16.4%
other: 0.1% (2003)
Electricity - consumption: 811.5 billion kWh (2004)
Electricity - exports: 24 billion kWh (2003)
Electricity - imports: 14 billion kWh (2002)

Oil - production: 9.15 million bbl/day (2005 est.)
Oil - consumption: 2.8 million bbl/day (2005 est.)
Oil - exports: 5.15 million bbl/day (2004)
Oil - imports: 75,000 bbl/day NA (2004)
Oil - proved reserves: 69 billion bbl (2003 est.)
Natural gas - production: 587 billion cu m (2005 est.)
Natural gas - consumption: 402.1 billion cu m (2004 est.)
Natural gas - exports: 157.2 billion cu m (2004 est.)
Natural gas - imports: 12 billion cu m (2004 est.)
Natural gas - proved reserves: 47 trillion cu m (2003)
Current account balance: $89.31 billion (2005 est.)
Exports: $245 billion (2005 est.)
Exports - partners: Netherlands 9.1%, Germany 8%, Ukraine 6.4%, Italy 6.2%, China 6%, US 5%, Switzerland 4.7%, Turkey 4.3% (2004)
Imports: $125 billion (2005 est.)
Imports - partners: Germany 15.3%, Ukraine 8.8%, China 6.9%, Japan 5.7%, Kazakhstan 5%, US 4.6%, Italy 4.6%, France 4.4% (2004)
Reserves of foreign exchange and gold: $181.3 billion (2005 est.)
Debt - external: $230.3 billion (30 June 2005 est.)
Economic aid - recipient: in FY01 from US, $979 million (including $750 million in non-proliferation subsidies); in 2001 from EU, $200 million (2000 est.)
Currency (code): Russian ruble (RUR)
Currency code: RUR
Exchange rates: Russian rubles per US dollar - 28.17 (2005), 28.814 (2004), 30.692 (2003), 31.349 (2002), 29.169 (2001)
Fiscal year: calendar year

COMMUNICATIONS

Telephones - main lines in use: 35.5 million (2002)
Telephones - mobile cellular: 17,608,800 (2002)
Telephone system:
general assessment: the telephone system underwent significant changes in the 1990s; there are more than 1,000 companies licensed to offer communication services; access to digital lines has improved, particularly in urban centers; Internet and e-mail services are improving; Russia has made progress toward building the telecommunications infrastructure necessary for a market economy; however, a large demand for main line service remains unsatisfied
domestic: cross-country digital trunk lines run from Saint Petersburg to Khabarovsk, and from Moscow to Novorossiysk; the telephone systems in 60 regional capitals have modern digital infrastructures; cellular services, both analog and digital, are available in many areas; in rural areas, the telephone services are still outdated, inadequate, and low density
international: country code - 7; Russia is connected internationally by three undersea fiber-optic cables; digital switches in several cities provide more than 50,000 lines for international calls; satellite earth stations provide access to Intelsat, Intersputnik, Eutelsat, Inmarsat, and Orbita systems
Radio broadcast stations: AM 323, FM 1,500 est., shortwave 62 (2004)
Radios: 61.5 million (1997)
Television broadcast stations: 7,306 (1998)
Televisions: 60.5 million (1997)
Internet country code: .ru; Russia also has responsibility for a legacy domain ".su" that was allocated to the Soviet Union, and whose legal status and ownership are contested by the Russian Government, ICANN, and several Russian commercial entities
Internet hosts: 560,874 (2004)
Internet Service Providers (ISPs): 300 (June 2000)
Internet users: 6 million (2002)

TRANSPORTATION

Airports: 2,586 (2004 est.)
Airports - with paved runways:
total: 640
over 3,047 m: 51
2,438 to 3,047 m: 199
1,524 to 2,437 m: 129
914 to 1,523 m: 109
under 914 m: 152 (2005 est.)
Airports - with unpaved runways:
total: 1,092
over 3,047 m: 16
2,438 to 3,047 m: 30
1,524 to 2,437 m: 88
914 to 1,523 m: 135
under 914 m: 821 (2005 est.)
Heliports: 42 (2005 est.)
Pipelines: condensate 122 km; gas 150,007 km; oil 75,539 km; refined products 13,771 km (2004)
Railways:
total: 87,157 km
broad gauge: 86,200 km 1.520-m gauge (40,300 km electrified)
narrow gauge: 957 km 1.067-m gauge (on Sakhalin Island)
note: an additional 30,000 km of non-common carrier lines serve industries (2004)
Roadways:
total: 537,289 km
paved: 362,133 km
unpaved: 175,156 km (2001)
Waterways: 96,000 km
note: 72,000 km system in European Russia links Baltic Sea, White Sea, Caspian Sea, Sea of Azov, and Black Sea (2004)
Merchant marine:
total: 1,194 ships (1,000 GRT or over) 4,521,472 GRT/5,505,118 DWT
by type: barge carrier 1, bulk carrier 45, cargo 767, chemical tanker 20, combination ore/oil 48, container 21, passenger 11, passenger/cargo 8, petroleum tanker 213, refrigerated cargo 46, roll on/roll off 12, specialized tanker 2
foreign-owned: 56 (Belgium 2, Cyprus 1, Estonia 2, Germany 1, Hong Kong 1, Latvia 3, Norway 1, Sweden 1, Turkey 28, Ukraine 10, United Kingdom 2, United States 4)
registered in other countries: 326 (2005)
Ports and terminals: Anapa, Kaliningrad, Murmansk, Nakhodka, Novorossiysk, Rostov-na-Donu, Saint Petersburg, Taganrog, Vanino, Vostochnyy

MILITARY

Military branches: Ground Forces (SV), Navy (VMF), Air Forces (VVS); Airborne Troops (VDV), Strategic Rocket Troops (RVSN), and Space Troops (KV) are independent "combat arms," not subordinate to any of the three branches
Military service age and obligation: Russia has adopted a mixed conscript-contract force; service age is 18-27 years of age; males are registered for the draft at 17 years of age; length of compulsory military service is 2 years; plans as of November 2005 call for reduction in mandatory service to 1 year by 2008; 30% of Russian army personnel were contract servicemen at the end of 2005; planning calls for volunteer servicemen to compose 70% of armed forces by 2010, with the remaining servicemen consisting of conscripts; at the end of 2005, the Army had 40 all-volunteer permanent-readiness units to be formed in 2006; 88 MOD units have been designated as permanent-readiness units and are expected to become all-volunteer by the end of 2007; these include most air force, naval, and nuclear arms units, as well as all airborne and naval infantry units, most motorized rifle brigades, and all special forces detachments (2005)
Manpower available for military service: *males age 18-49:* 35,247,049 (2005 est.)
Manpower fit for military service: *males age 18-49:* 21,049,651 (2005 est.)

Manpower reaching military service age annually: *males:* 1,286,069 (2005 est.)
Military expenditures - dollar figure: NA
Military expenditures - percent of GDP: NA

TRANSNATIONAL ISSUES

Disputes - international: in 2004, China and Russia divided up the islands in the Amur, Ussuri, and Argun Rivers, ending a century-old border dispute; the sovereignty dispute over the islands of Etorofu, Kunashiri, Shikotan, and the Habomai group, known in Japan as the "Northern Territories" and in Russia as the "Southern Kurils," occupied by the Soviet Union in 1945, now administered by Russia, and claimed by Japan, remains the primary sticking point to signing a peace treaty formally ending World War II hostilities; Russia and Georgia agree on delimiting 80% of their common border, leaving certain small, strategic segments and the maritime boundary unresolved; OSCE observers monitor volatile areas such as the Pankisi Gorge in the Akhmeti region and the Kodori Gorge in Abkhazia; equidistant seabed treaties were signed and ratified with Azerbaijan and Kazakhstan in the Caspian Sea but no consensus exists on dividing the water column among the littoral states; Russia and Norway dispute their maritime limits in the Barents Sea and Russia's fishing rights beyond Svalbard's territorial limits within the Svalbard Treaty zone; various groups in Finland advocate restoration of Karelia and other areas ceded to the Soviet Union following the Second World War but the Finnish Government asserts no territorial demands; in 1996, the Estonia-Russia technical border agreement was initialed but both have been hesitant to sign and ratify it, with Russia asserting that Estonia needs to better assimilate Russian-speakers and Estonian groups advocating realignment of the boundary based more closely on the 1920 Tartu Peace Treaty that would bring the now divided ethnic Setu people and parts of the Narva region within Estonia; the Latvian-Russian boundary treaty of 1997 remains unsigned and unratified with Russia linking it to better Latvian treatment of ethnic Russians and Latvian politicians demanding Russian agreement to a declaration that admits Soviet aggression during the Second World War and other issues; in 2003, the Lithuania-Russia land and maritime boundary treaty was ratified and a transit regime established through Lithuania linking Russia and its Kaliningrad coastal exclave, leaving only improvements to the border demarcation in 2005; delimitation of land boundary with Ukraine is complete, but states have agreed to defer demarcation; Russia and Ukraine continue talks but still dispute the alignment of a maritime boundary through the Kerch Strait and Sea of Azov; Kazakhstan and Russia continue demarcation of their long border; Russian Duma has not yet ratified 1990 Maritime Boundary Agreement with the US in the Bering Sea
Refugees and internally displaced persons: *IDPs:* 368,000 (displacement from Chechnya and North Ossetia) (2004)
Illicit drugs: limited cultivation of illicit cannabis and opium poppy and producer of methamphetamine, mostly for domestic consumption; government has active illicit crop eradication program; used as transshipment point for Asian opiates, cannabis, and Latin American cocaine bound for growing domestic markets, to a lesser extent Western and Central Europe, and occasionally to the US; major source of heroin precursor chemicals; corruption and organized crime are key concerns; heroin increasingly popular in domestic market

RWANDA

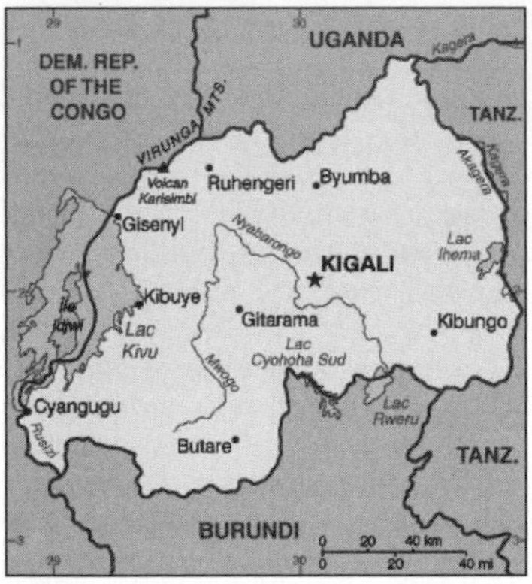

INTRODUCTION

Background: In 1959, three years before independence from Belgium, the majority ethnic group, the Hutus, overthrew the ruling Tutsi king. Over the next several years, thousands of Tutsis were killed, and some 150,000 driven into exile in neighboring countries. The children of these exiles later formed a rebel group, the Rwandan Patriotic Front (RPF), and began a civil war in 1990. The war, along with several political and economic upheavals, exacerbated ethnic tensions, culminating in April 1994 in the genocide of roughly 800,000 Tutsis and moderate Hutus. The Tutsi rebels defeated the Hutu regime and ended the killing in July 1994, but approximately 2 million Hutu refugees - many fearing Tutsi retribution - fled to neighboring Burundi, Tanzania, Uganda, and the former Zaire. Since then, most of the refugees have returned to Rwanda, but about 10,000 remain in neighboring Democratic Republic of the Congo and have formed an extremist insurgency bent on retaking Rwanda, much as the RPF tried in 1990. Despite substantial international assistance and political reforms - including Rwanda's first local elections in March 1999 and its first post-genocide presidential and legislative elections in August and September 2003, respectively - the country continues to struggle to boost investment and agricultural output, and ethnic reconciliation is complicated by the real and perceived Tutsi political dominance. Kigali's increasing centralization and intolerance of dissent, the nagging Hutu extremist insurgency across the border, and Rwandan involvement in two wars in recent years in the neighboring Democratic Republic of the Congo continue to hinder Rwanda's efforts to escape its bloody legacy.

GEOGRAPHY

Location: Central Africa, east of Democratic Republic of the Congo
Geographic coordinates: 2 00 S, 30 00 E
Map references: Africa
Area:
total: 26,338 sq km
land: 24,948 sq km
water: 1,390 sq km
Area - comparative: slightly smaller than Maryland
Land boundaries:
total: 893 km
border countries: Burundi 290 km, Democratic Republic of the Congo 217 km, Tanzania 217 km, Uganda 169 km
Coastline: 0 km (landlocked)
Maritime claims: none (landlocked)
Climate: temperate; two rainy seasons (February to April, November to January); mild in mountains with frost and snow possible
Terrain: mostly grassy uplands and hills; relief is mountainous with altitude declining from west to east
Elevation extremes:
lowest point: Rusizi River 950 m
highest point: Volcan Karisimbi 4,519 m
Natural resources: gold, cassiterite (tin

ore), wolframite (tungsten ore), methane, hydropower, arable land

Land use:
arable land: 40.54%
permanent crops: 12.16%
other: 47.3% (2001)

Irrigated land: 40 sq km (1998 est.)

Natural hazards: periodic droughts; the volcanic Virunga mountains are in the northwest along the border with Democratic Republic of the Congo

Environment - current issues: deforestation results from uncontrolled cutting of trees for fuel; overgrazing; soil exhaustion; soil erosion; widespread poaching

Environment - international agreements:
party to: Biodiversity, Climate Change, Climate Change-Kyoto Protocol, Desertification, Endangered Species, Hazardous Wastes, Ozone Layer Protection
signed, but not ratified: Law of the Sea

Geography - note: landlocked; most of the country is savanna grassland with the population predominantly rural

PEOPLE

Population: 8,440,820
note: estimates for this country explicitly take into account the effects of excess mortality due to AIDS; this can result in lower life expectancy, higher infant mortality and death rates, lower population and growth rates, and changes in the distribution of population by age and sex than would otherwise be expected (July 2005 est.)

Age structure:
0-14 years: 41.9% (male 1,777,178/female 1,762,252)
15-64 years: 55.5% (male 2,328,686/female 2,356,572)
65 years and over: 2.6% (male 87,155/female 128,977) (2005 est.)

Median age:
total: 18.48 years
male: 18.26 years
female: 18.7 years (2005 est.)

Population growth rate: 2.43% (2005 est.)

Birth rate: 40.6 births/1,000 population (2005 est.)

Death rate: 16.32 deaths/1,000 population (2005 est.)

Net migration rate: 0 migrant(s)/1,000 population (2005 est.)

Sex ratio:
at birth: 1.03 male(s)/female
under 15 years: 1.01 male(s)/female
15-64 years: 0.99 male(s)/female
65 years and over: 0.68 male(s)/female
total population: 0.99 male(s)/female (2005 est.)

Infant mortality rate:
total: 91.23 deaths/1,000 live births
male: 96.37 deaths/1,000 live births
female: 85.93 deaths/1,000 live births (2005 est.)

Life expectancy at birth:
total population: 46.96 years
male: 45.92 years
female: 48.03 years (2005 est.)

Total fertility rate: 5.49 children born/woman (2005 est.)

HIV/AIDS - adult prevalence rate: 5.1% (2003 est.)

HIV/AIDS - people living with HIV/AIDS: 250,000 (2003 est.)

HIV/AIDS - deaths: 22,000 (2003 est.)

Major infectious diseases:
degree of risk: very high
food or waterborne diseases: bacterial diarrhea, hepatitis A, and typhoid fever
vectorborne disease: malaria (2004)

Nationality:
noun: Rwandan(s)
adjective: Rwandan

Ethnic groups: Hutu 84%, Tutsi 15%, Twa (Pygmoid) 1%

Religions: Roman Catholic 56.5%, Protestant 26%, Adventist 11.1%, Muslim 4.6%, indigenous beliefs 0.1%, none 1.7% (2001)

Languages: Kinyarwanda (official) universal Bantu vernacular, French (official), English (official), Kiswahili (Swahili) used in commercial centers

Literacy:
definition: age 15 and over can read and write
total population: 70.4%
male: 76.3%
female: 64.7% (2003 est.)

People - note: Rwanda is the most densely populated country in Africa

GOVERNMENT

Country name:
conventional long form: Republic of Rwanda
conventional short form: Rwanda
local long form: Republika y'u Rwanda
local short form: Rwanda
former: Ruanda

Government type: republic; presidential, multiparty system

Capital: Kigali

Administrative divisions: 12 provinces (in French - provinces, singular - province; in Kinyarwanda - prefigintara for singular and plural); Butare, Byumba, Cyangugu, Gikongoro, Gisenyi, Gitarama, Kibungo, Kibuye, Kigali Rurale, Kigali-ville, Umutara, Ruhengeri

Independence: 1 July 1962 (from Belgium-administered UN trusteeship)

National holiday: Independence Day, 1 July (1962)

Constitution: new constitution adopted 4 June 2003

Legal system: based on German and Belgian civil law systems and customary law; judicial review of legislative acts in the Supreme Court; has not accepted compulsory ICJ jurisdiction

Suffrage: 18 years of age; universal adult

Executive branch:
chief of state: President Paul KAGAME (since 22 April 2000)
head of government: Prime Minister Bernard MAKUZA (since 8 March 2000)
cabinet: Council of Ministers appointed by the president
elections: last held 25 August 2003 (next to be held NA 2008)
election results: Paul KAGAME elected president in first direct popular vote; Paul KAGAME 95.05%, Faustin TWAGIRAMUNGU 3.62%, Jean-Nepomuscene NAYINZIRA 1.33%

Legislative branch: unicameral National Assembly or Assemblee Nationale (53 seats; members elected by direct vote)
elections: last held 29 September 2003 (next to be held Chamber of Deputies - NA 2008; Senate - NA 2011)
election results: seats by party under the 2003 Constitution - RPF 40, PSD 7, PL 6

Judicial branch: Supreme Court; High Courts of the Republic; Provincial Courts; District Courts; mediation committees

Political parties and leaders: Centrist Democratic Party or PDC [Alfred MUKEZAMFURA]; Democratic Popular Union of Rwanda or UDPR [Adrien RANGIRA]; Democratic Republican Movement or MDR (officially banned) [Celestin KABANDA]; Islamic Democratic Party or PDI [Andre BUMAYA]; Liberal Party or PL [Prosper HIGIRO]; Party for Democratic Renewal (officially banned) [NA]; Rwandan Patriotic Front or RPF [Paul KAGAME]; Social Democratic Party or PSD [Vincent BIRUTA]

Political pressure groups and leaders: IBUKA - association of genocide survivors

International organization participation: ACCT, ACP, AfDB, AU, CEPGL, COMESA, FAO, G-77, IBRD, ICAO, ICFTU, ICRM, IDA, IFAD, IFC, IFRCS, ILO, IMF, Interpol, IOC, IOM, ISO (correspondent), ITU, MIGA, NAM, OPCW, UN, UNCTAD, UNESCO, UNIDO, UNMIS, UPU, WCL, WCO, WHO, WIPO, WMO, WToO, WTO

Diplomatic representation in the US:
chief of mission: Ambassador Zac NSENGA
chancery: 1714 New Hampshire Ave. NW, Washington, DC 20009
telephone: [1] (202) 232-2882
FAX: [1] (202) 232-4544

Diplomatic representation from the US:
chief of mission: Ambassador Michael

ARIETTI
embassy: 337 Boulevard de la Revolution, Kigali
mailing address: B. P. 28, Kigali
telephone: [250] 50 56 01 through 03
FAX: [250] 57 2128
Flag description: three horizontal bands of sky blue (top, double width), yellow, and green, with a golden sun with 24 rays near the fly end of the blue band

ECONOMY

Economy - overview: Rwanda is a poor rural country with about 90% of the population engaged in (mainly subsistence) agriculture. It is the most densely populated country in Africa and is landlocked with few natural resources and minimal industry. Primary foreign exchange earners are coffee and tea. The 1994 genocide decimated Rwanda's fragile economic base, severely impoverished the population, particularly women, and eroded the country's ability to attract private and external investment. However, Rwanda has made substantial progress in stabilizing and rehabilitating its economy to pre-1994 levels, although poverty levels are higher now. GDP has rebounded and inflation has been curbed. Despite Rwanda's fertile ecosystem, food production often does not keep pace with population growth, requiring food imports. Rwanda continues to receive substantial aid money and received IMF-World Bank Heavily Indebted Poor Country (HIPC) initiative debt relief in 2005. Kigali's high defense expenditures have caused tension between the government and international donors and lending agencies. An energy shortage and instability in neighboring states may slow growth in 2006, while the lack of adequate transportation linkages to other countries continues to handicap export growth.
GDP (purchasing power parity): $11.24 billion (2005 est.)
GDP (official exchange rate): $1.892 billion (2005 est.)
GDP - real growth rate: 4.8% (2005 est.)
GDP - per capita: purchasing power parity - $1,300 (2005 est.)
GDP - composition by sector:
agriculture: 37.6%
industry: 22.8%
services: 39.6% (2005 est.)
Labor force: 4.6 million (2000)
Labor force - by occupation: agriculture 90%
Unemployment rate: NA
Population below poverty line: 60% (2001 est.)
Household income or consumption by percentage share:
lowest 10%: 4.2%
highest 10%: 24.2% (1985)
Distribution of family income - Gini index: 28.9 (1985)
Inflation rate (consumer prices): 8% (2005 est.)
Investment (gross fixed): 18.6% of GDP (2005 est.)
Budget:
revenues: $509.9 million
expenditures: $584.6 million, including capital expenditures of NA (2005 est.)
Agriculture - products: coffee, tea, pyrethrum (insecticide made from chrysanthemums), bananas, beans, sorghum, potatoes; livestock
Industries: cement, agricultural products, small-scale beverages, soap, furniture, shoes, plastic goods, textiles, cigarettes
Industrial production growth rate: 7% (2001 est.)
Electricity - production: 98 million kWh (2003)
Electricity - production by source:
fossil fuel: 2.3%
hydro: 97.7%
nuclear: 0%
other: 0% (2001)
Electricity - consumption: 121.1 million kWh (2003)
Electricity - exports: 0 kWh (2003)
Electricity - imports: 30 million kWh (2003)
Oil - production: 0 bbl/day (2003 est.)
Oil - consumption: 6,000 bbl/day (2003 est.)
Oil - exports: NA (2001)
Oil - imports: NA (2001)
Oil - proved reserves: 0 bbl (1 January 2002)
Natural gas - proved reserves: 28.32 billion cu m (1 January 2002)
Current account balance: $-79 million (2005 est.)
Exports: $98 million f.o.b. (2005 est.)
Exports - partners: Indonesia 64.2%, China 3.6%, Germany 2.7% (2004)
Imports: $243 million f.o.b. (2005 est.)
Imports - partners: Kenya 24.4%, Germany 7.4%, Belgium 6.6%, Uganda 6.3%, France 5.1% (2004)
Reserves of foreign exchange and gold: $300 million (2005 est.)
Debt - external: $1.4 billion (2004 est.)
Economic aid - recipient: $425 million (2003)
Currency (code): Rwandan franc (RWF)
Currency code: RWF
Exchange rates: Rwandan francs per US dollar - 610 (2005), 574.62 (2004), 537.66 (2003), 476.33 (2002), 442.8 (2001)
Fiscal year: calendar year

COMMUNICATIONS

Telephones - main lines in use: 23,200 (2002)
Telephones - mobile cellular: 134,000
note: Rwanda has mobile cellular service between Kigali and several provincial capitals (2003)
Telephone system:
general assessment: telephone system primarily serves business and government
domestic: the capital, Kigali, is connected to the centers of the provinces by microwave radio relay and, recently, by cellular telephone service; much of the network depends on wire and HF radiotelephone
international: country code - 250; international connections employ microwave radio relay to neighboring countries and satellite communications to more distant countries; satellite earth stations - 1 Intelsat (Indian Ocean) in Kigali (includes telex and telefax service)
Radio broadcast stations: AM 0, FM 8 (two main FM programs are broadcast through a system of repeaters, three international FM programs include the BBC, VOA, and Deutchewelle), shortwave 1 (2005)
Radios: 601,000 (1997)
Television broadcast stations: 2 (2004)
Televisions: NA; probably less than 1,000 (1997)
Internet country code: .rw
Internet hosts: 1,495 (2003)
Internet Service Providers (ISPs): 2 (2002)
Internet users: 25,000 (2002)

TRANSPORTATION

Airports: 9 (2004 est.)
Airports - with paved runways:
total: 4
over 3,047 m: 1
914 to 1,523 m: 2
under 914 m: 1 (2005 est.)
Airports - with unpaved runways:
total: 5
914 to 1,523 m: 2
under 914 m: 3 (2005 est.)
Roadways:
total: 12,000 km
paved: 996 km
unpaved: 11,004 km (1999 est.)
Waterways: Lac Kivu navigable by shallow-draft barges and native craft (2004)
Ports and terminals: Cyangugu, Gisenyi, Kibuye

MILITARY

Military branches: Rwandan Defense Forces: Army, Air Force
Military service age and obligation: 16 years of age for voluntary military service; no conscription (2001)
Manpower available for military service: *males age 16-49:* 2,004,750 (2005 est.)
Manpower fit for military service: *males age 16-49:* 1,103,823 (2005 est.)
Military expenditures - dollar figure:

$50.1 million (2004)
Military expenditures - percent of GDP: 3.2% (2004)

TRANSNATIONAL ISSUES

Disputes - international: Tutsi, Hutu, Hema, Lendu, and other conflicting ethnic groups, associated political rebels, armed gangs, and various government forces continue fighting in Great Lakes region, transcending the boundaries of Burundi, Democratic Republic of the Congo, Rwanda, and Uganda to gain control over populated areas and natural resources - government heads pledge to end conflicts, but localized violence continues despite UN peacekeeping efforts; DROC and Rwanda established a border verification mechanism in 2005 to address accusations of Rwandan military supporting Congolese rebels and the Congo providing rebel Rwandan "Interhamwe" forces the means and bases to attack Rwandan forces; as of 2004, Rwandan refugees lived in the Democratic Republic of the Congo, Uganda, and Zambia
Refugees and internally displaced persons: *refugees (country of origin):* 37,691 (Democratic Republic of the Congo)
IDPs: 4,158 (incursions by Hutu rebels from Democratic Republic of the Congo, 1997-99; most IDPs in northwest) (2004)

SAINT HELENA

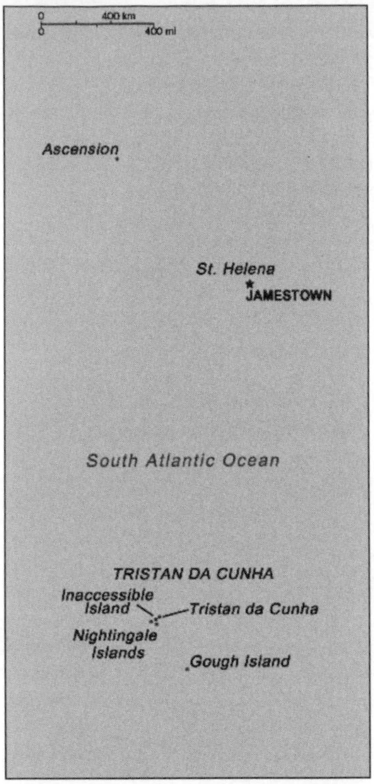

INTRODUCTION

Background: Uninhabited when first discovered by the Portuguese in 1502, Saint Helena was garrisoned by the British during the 17th century. It acquired fame as the place of Napoleon BONAPARTE's exile, from 1815 until his death in 1821, but its importance as a port of call declined after the opening of the Suez Canal in 1869. Ascension Island is the site of a US Air Force auxiliary airfield; Gough Island has a meteorological station.

GEOGRAPHY

Location: islands in the South Atlantic Ocean, about midway between South America and Africa
Geographic coordinates: 15 56 S, 5 42 W
Map references: Africa
Area:
total: 410 sq km
land: 410 sq km
water: 0 sq km
note: includes Saint Helena Island, Ascension, and the island group of Tristan da Cunha, which consists of Tristan da Cunha Island, Gough Island, Inaccessible Island, and the three Nightingale Islands
Area - comparative: slightly more than twice the size of Washington, DC
Land boundaries: 0 km
Coastline: 60 km
Maritime claims:
territorial sea: 12 nm
exclusive fishing zone: 200 nm
Climate: Saint Helena - tropical; marine; mild, tempered by trade winds; Tristan da Cunha - temperate; marine, mild, tempered by trade winds (tends to be cooler than Saint Helena)
Terrain: Saint Helena - rugged, volcanic; small scattered plateaus and plains
note: the other islands of the group have a volcanic origin
Elevation extremes:
lowest point: Atlantic Ocean 0 m
highest point: Queen Mary's Peak on Tristan da Cunha 2,060 m
Natural resources: fish
Land use:
arable land: 12.9%
permanent crops: 0%
other: 87.1% (2001)
Irrigated land: NA sq km
Natural hazards: active volcanism on Tristan da Cunha
Environment - current issues: NA
Geography - note: harbors at least 40 species of plants unknown anywhere else in the world; Ascension is a breeding ground for sea turtles and sooty terns

PEOPLE

Population: 7,460 (July 2005 est.)
Age structure:
0-14 years: 18.8% (male 715/female 691)
15-64 years: 71.3% (male 2,745/female 2,575)
65 years and over: 9.8% (male 330/female 404) (2005 est.)
Median age:
total: 35.4 years
male: 35.61 years
female: 35.21 years (2005 est.)
Population growth rate: 0.59% (2005 est.)
Birth rate: 12.33 births/1,000 population (2005 est.)
Death rate: 6.43 deaths/1,000 population (2005 est.)
Net migration rate: 0 migrant(s)/1,000 population (2005 est.)
Sex ratio:
at birth: 1.04 male(s)/female
under 15 years: 1.04 male(s)/female
15-64 years: 1.07 male(s)/female
65 years and over: 0.82 male(s)/female
total population: 1.03 male(s)/female (2005 est.)
Infant mortality rate:
total: 19 deaths/1,000 live births
male: 22.74 deaths/1,000 live births
female: 15.08 deaths/1,000 live births (2005 est.)
Life expectancy at birth:
total population: 77.76 years
male: 74.86 years
female: 80.81 years (2005 est.)
Total fertility rate: 1.54 children born/woman (2005 est.)
HIV/AIDS - adult prevalence rate: NA
HIV/AIDS - people living with HIV/AIDS: NA
HIV/AIDS - deaths: NA
Nationality:
noun: Saint Helenian(s)
adjective: Saint Helenian
Ethnic groups: African descent 50%, white 25%, Chinese 25%
Religions: Anglican (majority), Baptist, Seventh-Day Adventist, Roman Catholic
Languages: English
Literacy:
definition: age 20 and over can read and write
total population: 97%
male: 97%
female: 98% (1987 est.)

GOVERNMENT

Country name:
conventional long form: none
conventional short form: Saint Helena
Dependency status: overseas territory of the UK
Government type: NA
Capital: Jamestown
Administrative divisions: 1 administrative area and 2 dependencies*; Ascension*, Saint Helena, Tristan da Cunha*
Independence: none (overseas territory of the UK)
National holiday: Birthday of Queen ELIZABETH II, second Saturday in June (1926)
Constitution: 1 January 1989
Legal system: NA
Suffrage: NA years of age
Executive branch:
chief of state: Queen ELIZABETH II (since 6 February 1952)
head of government: Governor and Commander in Chief Michael CLANCY (since 15 October 2004)
cabinet: Executive Council consists of the governor, two ex officio officers, and six elected members of the Legislative Council
elections: none; the monarch is hereditary; governor is appointed by the monarch
Legislative branch: unicameral Legislative Council (16 seats, including the speaker, 3 ex officio and 12 elected members; members are elected by popular vote to serve four-year terms)
elections: last held 31 August 2005 (next to be held NA 2009)
election results: percent of vote - NA%;

seats - independents 15
Judicial branch: Supreme Court; Magistrate's Court; Small Debts Court; Juvenile Court
Political parties and leaders: none
Political pressure groups and leaders: none
International organization participation: ICFTU, UPU
Diplomatic representation in the US: none (overseas territory of the UK)
Diplomatic representation from the US: none (overseas territory of the UK)
Flag description: blue with the flag of the UK in the upper hoist-side quadrant and the Saint Helenian shield centered on the outer half of the flag; the shield features a rocky coastline and three-masted sailing ship

ECONOMY

Economy - overview: The economy depends largely on financial assistance from the UK, which amounted to about $5 million in 1997 or almost one-half of annual budgetary revenues. The local population earns income from fishing, raising livestock, and sales of handicrafts. Because there are few jobs, 25% of the work force has left to seek employment on Ascension Island, on the Falklands, and in the UK.
GDP (purchasing power parity): $18 million (1998 est.)
GDP (official exchange rate): NA
GDP - real growth rate: NA
GDP - per capita: purchasing power parity - $2,500 (1998 est.)
GDP - composition by sector:
agriculture: NA
industry: NA
services: NA
Labor force: 3,500
note: 1,200 work offshore (1998 est.)
Labor force - by occupation: agriculture and fishing 6%, industry (mainly construction) 48%, services 46% (1987 est.)
Unemployment rate: 14% (1998 est.)
Population below poverty line: NA
Household income or consumption by percentage share:
lowest 10%: NA
highest 10%: NA
Inflation rate (consumer prices): 3.2% (1997 est.)
Budget:
revenues: $11.2 million
expenditures: $11 million, including capital expenditures of NA (FY92/93)
Agriculture - products: corn, potatoes, vegetables; timber; fish, crawfish (on Tristan da Cunha)
Industries: construction, crafts (furniture, lacework, fancy woodwork), fishing
Industrial production growth rate: NA
Electricity - production: 5 million kWh (2003)
Electricity - production by source:
fossil fuel: 100%
hydro: 0%
nuclear: 0%
other: 0% (2001)
Electricity - consumption: 4.65 million kWh (2003)
Electricity - exports: 0 kWh (2003)
Electricity - imports: 0 kWh (2003)
Oil - production: 0 bbl/day (2003 est.)
Oil - consumption: 100 bbl/day (2003 est.)
Oil - exports: NA (2001)
Oil - imports: NA (2001)
Exports: $19 million f.o.b. (2004 est.)
Exports - partners: Tanzania 30.3%, US 23.8%, Japan 10.4%, UK 7.1%, Spain 6.3% (2004)
Imports: $45 million c.i.f. (2004 est.)
Imports - partners: UK 35.6%, US 17.5%, South Africa 17.5%, Tanzania 10.4%, Australia 5.5%, Spain 4.1% (2004)
Debt - external: NA (1996)
Economic aid - recipient: $12.6 million (1995); note - $5.3 million from UK (1997)
Currency (code): Saint Helenian pound (SHP)
Currency code: SHP
Exchange rates: Saint Helenian pounds per US dollar - NA (2005), 0.5462 (2004), 0.6125 (2003), 0.6672 (2002), 0.6947 (2001)
note: the Saint Helenian pound is on par with the British pound
Fiscal year: 1 April - 31 March

COMMUNICATIONS

Telephones - main lines in use: 2,200 (2002)
Telephones - mobile cellular: 0 (1997)
Telephone system:
general assessment: can communicate worldwide
domestic: automatic network
international: country code - 290; HF radiotelephone from Saint Helena to Ascension Island, which is a major coaxial submarine cable relay point between South Africa, Portugal, and UK; satellite earth stations - 5 (Ascension Island - 4, Saint Helena - 1)
Radio broadcast stations: AM 1, FM 0, shortwave 0 (1998)
Radios: 3,000 (1997)
Television broadcast stations: 0
note: television programs are received in Saint Helena via satellite and distributed by cable (2002)
Televisions: 2,000 (1997)
Internet country code: .sh
Internet Service Providers (ISPs): 1 (2000)
Internet users: 500 (2002)
Communications - note: Gough Island has a meteorological station

TRANSPORTATION

Airports: 1 (2004 est.)
Airports - with paved runways:
total: 1
over 3,047 m: 1 (2005 est.)
Roadways:
total: 198 km (Saint Helena 138 km, Ascension 40 km, Tristan da Cunha 20 km)
paved: 168 km (Saint Helena 118km, Ascension 40 km, Tristan da Cunha 10 km)
unpaved: 30 km (Saint Helena 20 km, Ascension 0 km, Tristan da Cunha 10 km) (2000)
Ports and terminals: Georgetown (on Ascension), Jamestown

MILITARY

Military - note: defense is the responsibility of the UK

TRANSNATIONAL ISSUES

Disputes - international: none

SAINT KITTS AND NEVIS

INTRODUCTION

Background: First settled by the British in 1623, the islands became an associated state with full internal autonomy in 1967. The island of Anguilla rebelled and was allowed to secede in 1971. Saint Kitts and Nevis achieved independence in 1983. In 1998, a vote in Nevis on a referendum to separate from Saint Kitts fell short of the two-thirds majority needed. Nevis is once more trying to separate from the Saint Kitts.

GEOGRAPHY

Location: Caribbean, islands in the Caribbean Sea, about one-third of the way from Puerto Rico to Trinidad and Tobago
Geographic coordinates: 17 20 N, 62 45 W
Map references: Central America and the Caribbean
Area:
total: 261 sq km (Saint Kitts 168 sq km; Nevis 93 sq km)
land: 261 sq km
water: 0 sq km
Area - comparative: 1.5 times the size of Washington, DC
Land boundaries: 0 km

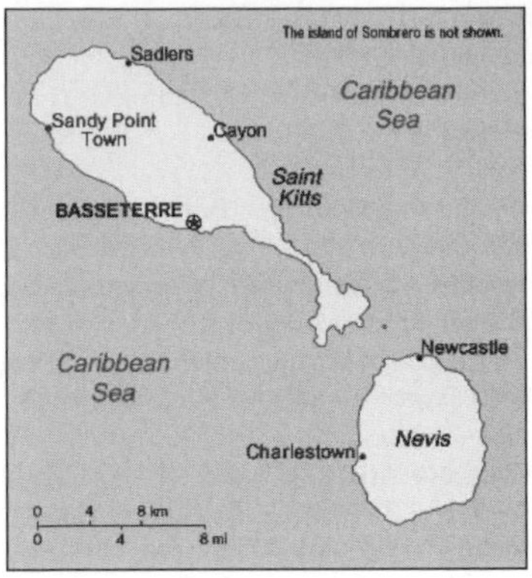

Coastline: 135 km
Maritime claims:
territorial sea: 12 nm
contiguous zone: 24 nm
exclusive economic zone: 200 nm
continental shelf: 200 nm or to the edge of the continental margin
Climate: tropical tempered by constant sea breezes; little seasonal temperature variation; rainy season (May to November)
Terrain: volcanic with mountainous interiors
Elevation extremes:
lowest point: Caribbean Sea 0 m
highest point: Mount Liamuiga 1,156 m
Natural resources: arable land
Land use:
arable land: 19.44%
permanent crops: 2.78%
other: 77.78% (2001)
Irrigated land: NA sq km
Natural hazards: hurricanes (July to October)
Environment - current issues: NA
Environment - international agreements:
party to: Biodiversity, Climate Change, Desertification, Endangered Species, Hazardous Wastes, Law of the Sea, Ozone Layer Protection, Ship Pollution, Whaling
signed, but not ratified: none of the selected agreements
Geography - note: with coastlines in the shape of a baseball bat and ball, the two volcanic islands are separated by a three-km-wide channel called The Narrows; on the southern tip of long, baseball bat-shaped Saint Kitts lies the Great Salt Pond; Nevis Peak sits in the center of its almost circular namesake island and its ball shape complements that of its sister island

PEOPLE

Population: 38,958 (July 2005 est.)
Age structure:
0-14 years: 28% (male 5,586/female 5,330)
15-64 years: 63.7% (male 12,424/female 12,403)
65 years and over: 8.3% (male 1,328/female 1,887) (2005 est.)
Median age:
total: 27.6 years
male: 26.78 years
female: 28.38 years (2005 est.)
Population growth rate: 0.38% (2005 est.)
Birth rate: 18.12 births/1,000 population (2005 est.)
Death rate: 8.47 deaths/1,000 population (2005 est.)
Net migration rate: -5.9 migrant(s)/1,000 population (2005 est.)
Sex ratio:
at birth: 1.06 male(s)/female
under 15 years: 1.05 male(s)/female
15-64 years: 1 male(s)/female
65 years and over: 0.7 male(s)/female
total population: 0.99 male(s)/female (2005 est.)
Infant mortality rate:
total: 14.49 deaths/1,000 live births
male: 16.25 deaths/1,000 live births
female: 12.63 deaths/1,000 live births (2005 est.)
Life expectancy at birth:
total population: 72.15 years
male: 69.31 years
female: 75.16 years (2005 est.)
Total fertility rate: 2.33 children born/woman (2005 est.)
HIV/AIDS - adult prevalence rate: NA
HIV/AIDS - people living with HIV/AIDS: NA
HIV/AIDS - deaths: NA
Nationality:
noun: Kittitian(s), Nevisian(s)
adjective: Kittitian, Nevisian
Ethnic groups: predominantly black; some British, Portuguese, and Lebanese
Religions: Anglican, other Protestant, Roman Catholic
Languages: English
Literacy:
definition: age 15 and over has ever attended school
total population: 97%
male: 97%
female: 98% (1980 est.)

GOVERNMENT

Country name:
conventional long form: Federation of Saint Kitts and Nevis
conventional short form: Saint Kitts and Nevis
former: Federation of Saint Christopher and Nevis
Government type: constitutional monarchy with Westminster-style parliament
Capital: Basseterre
Administrative divisions: 14 parishes; Christ Church Nichola Town, Saint Anne Sandy Point, Saint George Basseterre, Saint George Gingerland, Saint James Windward, Saint John Capesterre, Saint John Figtree, Saint Mary Cayon, Saint Paul Capesterre, Saint Paul Charlestown, Saint Peter Basseterre, Saint Thomas Lowland, Saint Thomas Middle Island, Trinity Palmetto Point
Independence: 19 September 1983 (from UK)
National holiday: Independence Day, 19 September (1983)
Constitution: 19 September 1983
Legal system: based on English common law
Suffrage: 18 years of age; universal
Executive branch:
chief of state: Queen ELIZABETH II (since 6 February 1952), represented by Governor General Cuthbert Montraville SEBASTIAN (since 1 January 1996)
head of government: Prime Minister Dr. Denzil DOUGLAS (since 6 July 1995) and Deputy Prime Minister Sam CONDOR (since 6 July 1995)
cabinet: Cabinet appointed by the governor general in consultation with the prime minister
elections: none; the monarch is hereditary; the governor general is appointed by the monarch; following legislative elections, the leader of the majority party or leader of a majority coalition is usually appointed prime minister by the governor general; deputy prime minister appointed by the governor general
Legislative branch: unicameral National Assembly (14 seats, 3 appointed and 11 popularly elected from single-member constituencies; members serve five-year terms)
elections: last held 25 October 2004 (next to be held by 2009)
election results: percent of vote by party - NA%; seats by party - SKNLP 7, CCM 2, NRP 1, PAM 1
Judicial branch: Eastern Caribbean Supreme Court (based on Saint Lucia; one judge of the Supreme Court resides in Saint Kitts and Nevis)
Political parties and leaders: Concerned Citizens Movement or CCM [Vance AMORY]; Nevis Reformation Party or NRP [Joseph PARRY]; People's Action Movement or PAM [Lindsey GRANT]; Saint Kitts and Nevis Labor Party or SKNLP [Dr. Denzil DOUGLAS]
Political pressure groups and leaders: NA
International organization participation: ACP, C, Caricom, CDB, FAO, G-77, IBRD, ICAO, ICFTU, ICRM, IDA, IFAD, IFC, IFRCS, ILO, IMF, IMO, Interpol, IOC, MIGA, OAS, OECS,

OPANAL, OPCW, UN, UNCTAD, UNESCO, UNIDO, UPU, WHO, WIPO, WTO

Diplomatic representation in the US:
chief of mission: Ambassador Dr. Izben Cordinal WILLIAMS
chancery: 3216 New Mexico Avenue NW, Washington, DC 20016
telephone: [1] (202) 686-2636
FAX: [1] (202) 686-5740
consulate(s) general: New York

Diplomatic representation from the US: the US does not have an embassy in Saint Kitts and Nevis; the US Ambassador to Barbados is accredited to Saint Kitts and Nevis

Flag description: divided diagonally from the lower hoist side by a broad black band bearing two white, five-pointed stars; the black band is edged in yellow; the upper triangle is green, the lower triangle is red

ECONOMY

Economy - overview: Sugar was the traditional mainstay of the Saint Kitts economy until the 1970s. Although the crop still dominates the agricultural sector, activities such as tourism, export-oriented manufacturing, and offshore banking have assumed larger roles in the economy. Tourism revenues are now the chief source of the islands' foreign exchange. The opening of a 470-room resort in February 2003 was expected to bring in much-needed revenue.

GDP (purchasing power parity): $339 million (2002 est.)

GDP (official exchange rate): NA

GDP - real growth rate: -1.9% (2002 est.)

GDP - per capita: purchasing power parity - $8,800 (2002 est.)

GDP - composition by sector:
agriculture: 3.5%
industry: 25.8%
services: 70.7% (2001)

Labor force: 18,170 (June 1995)

Labor force - by occupation: NA

Unemployment rate: 4.5% (1997)

Population below poverty line: NA

Household income or consumption by percentage share:
lowest 10%: NA
highest 10%: NA

Inflation rate (consumer prices): 1.7% (2001 est.)

Budget:
revenues: $89.7 million
expenditures: $128.2 million, including capital expenditures of $19.5 million (2003 est.)

Agriculture - products: sugarcane, rice, yams, vegetables, bananas; fish

Industries: sugar processing, tourism, cotton, salt, copra, clothing, footwear, beverages

Industrial production growth rate: NA%

Electricity - production: 111.7 million kWh (2003)

Electricity - production by source:
fossil fuel: 100%
hydro: 0%
nuclear: 0%
other: 0% (2001)

Electricity - consumption: 103.9 million kWh (2003)

Electricity - exports: 0 kWh (2003)

Electricity - imports: 0 kWh (2003)

Oil - production: 0 bbl/day (2003 est.)

Oil - consumption: 700 bbl/day (2003 est.)

Oil - exports: NA (2001)

Oil - imports: NA (2001)

Exports: $70 million (2004 est.)

Exports - partners: US 57.5%, Canada 9%, Portugal 8.3%, UK 6.7% (2004)

Imports: $405 million (2004 est.)

Imports - partners: Ukraine 44.7%, US 22.1%, Trinidad and Tobago 8.8%, UK 6.2% (2004)

Debt - external: $171 million (2001)

Economic aid - recipient: $8 million (2001)

Currency (code): East Caribbean dollar (XCD)

Currency code: XCD

Exchange rates: East Caribbean dollars per US dollar - NA (2005), 2.7 (2004), 2.7 (2003), 2.7 (2002), 2.7 (2001)

Fiscal year: calendar year

COMMUNICATIONS

Telephones - main lines in use: 23,500 (2002)

Telephones - mobile cellular: 5,000 (2002)

Telephone system:
general assessment: good interisland and international connections
domestic: inter-island links via Eastern Caribbean Fiber Optic cable; construction of enhanced wireless infrastructure launched in November 2004
international: country code - 1-869; international calls are carried by submarine cable or Intelsat

Radio broadcast stations: AM 3, FM 3, shortwave 0 (2004)

Radios: 28,000 (1997)

Television broadcast stations: 1 (plus three repeaters) (2004)

Televisions: 10,000 (1997)

Internet country code: .kn

Internet hosts: 51 (2003)

Internet Service Providers (ISPs): 16 (2000)

Internet users: 10,000 (2002)

TRANSPORTATION

Airports: 2 (2004 est.)

Airports - with paved runways:
total: 2
1,524 to 2,437 m: 1
914 to 1,523 m: 1 (2005 est.)

Railways:
total: 50 km
narrow gauge: 50 km 0.762-m gauge on Saint Kitts to serve sugarcane plantations during harvest season (2003)

Roadways:
total: 320 km
paved: 136 km
unpaved: 184 km (1999 est)

Ports and terminals: Basseterre, Charlestown

MILITARY

Military branches: Saint Kitts and Nevis Defense Force (includes Coast Guard), Royal Saint Kitts and Nevis Police Force

Military service age and obligation: 18 years of age (est.) (2004)

Military expenditures - dollar figure: NA

Military expenditures - percent of GDP: NA

TRANSNATIONAL ISSUES

Disputes - international: joins other Caribbean states to counter Venezuela's claim that Aves Island sustains human habitation, a criterion under UNCLOS, which permits Venezuela to extend its EEZ/continental shelf over a large portion of the Caribbean Sea

Illicit drugs: transshipment point for South American drugs destined for the US and Europe; some money-laundering activity

SAINT LUCIA

INTRODUCTION

Background: The island, with its fine natural harbor at Castries, was contested between England and France throughout the 17th and early 18th centuries (changing possession 14 times); it was finally ceded to the UK in 1814. Self-government was granted in 1967 and independence in 1979.

GEOGRAPHY

Location: Caribbean, island between the Caribbean Sea and North Atlantic Ocean, north of Trinidad and Tobago

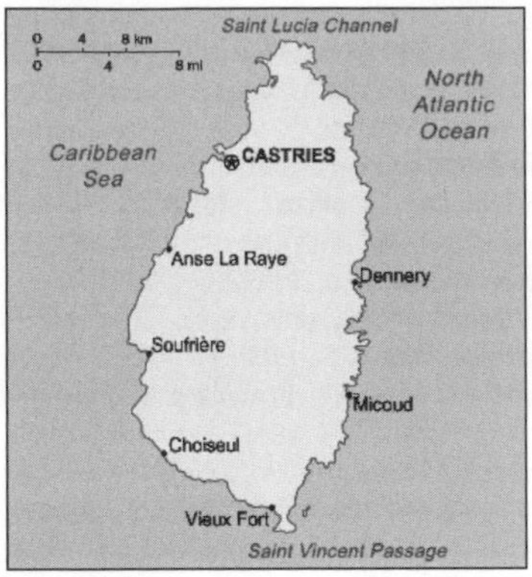

Geographic coordinates: 13 53 N, 60 68 W
Map references: Central America and the Caribbean
Area:
total: 616 sq km
land: 606 sq km
water: 10 sq km
Area - comparative: 3.5 times the size of Washington, DC
Land boundaries: 0 km
Coastline: 158 km
Maritime claims:
territorial sea: 12 nm
contiguous zone: 24 nm
exclusive economic zone: 200 nm
continental shelf: 200 nm or to the edge of the continental margin
Climate: tropical, moderated by northeast trade winds; dry season from January to April, rainy season from May to August
Terrain: volcanic and mountainous with some broad, fertile valleys
Elevation extremes:
lowest point: Caribbean Sea 0 m
highest point: Mount Gimie 950 m
Natural resources: forests, sandy beaches, minerals (pumice), mineral springs, geothermal potential
Land use:
arable land: 6.56%
permanent crops: 22.95%
other: 70.49% (2001)
Irrigated land: 30 sq km (1998 est.)
Natural hazards: hurricanes and volcanic activity
Environment - current issues: deforestation; soil erosion, particularly in the northern region
Environment - international agreements:
party to: Biodiversity, Climate Change, Climate Change-Kyoto Protocol, Desertification, Endangered Species, Environmental Modification, Hazardous Wastes, Law of the Sea, Marine Dumping, Ozone Layer Protection, Ship Pollution, Whaling
signed, but not ratified: none of the selected agreements
Geography - note: the twin Pitons (Gros Piton and Petit Piton), striking cone-shaped peaks south of Soufriere, are one of the scenic natural highlights of the Caribbean

PEOPLE

Population: 166,312 (July 2005 est.)
Age structure:
0-14 years: 30.3% (male 25,937/female 24,391)
15-64 years: 64.6% (male 52,813/female 54,544)
65 years and over: 5.2% (male 3,172/female 5,455) (2005 est.)
Median age:
total: 24.81 years
male: 24.03 years
female: 25.66 years (2005 est.)
Population growth rate: 1.28% (2005 est.)
Birth rate: 20.05 births/1,000 population (2005 est.)
Death rate: 5.12 deaths/1,000 population (2005 est.)
Net migration rate: -2.19 migrant(s)/1,000 population (2005 est.)
Sex ratio:
at birth: 1.07 male(s)/female
under 15 years: 1.06 male(s)/female
15-64 years: 0.97 male(s)/female
65 years and over: 0.58 male(s)/female
total population: 0.97 male(s)/female (2005 est.)
Infant mortality rate:
total: 13.53 deaths/1,000 live births
male: 14.66 deaths/1,000 live births
female: 12.32 deaths/1,000 live births (2005 est.)
Life expectancy at birth:
total population: 73.61 years
male: 70.05 years
female: 77.42 years (2005 est.)
Total fertility rate: 2.21 children born/woman (2005 est.)
HIV/AIDS - adult prevalence rate: NA
HIV/AIDS - people living with HIV/AIDS: NA
HIV/AIDS - deaths: NA
Nationality:
noun: Saint Lucian(s)
adjective: Saint Lucian
Ethnic groups: black 90%, mixed 6%, East Indian 3%, white 1%
Religions: Roman Catholic 67.5%, Seventh Day Adventist 8.5%, Pentecostal 5.7%, Anglican 2%, Evangelical 2%, other Christian 5.1%, Rastafarian 2.1%, other 1.1%, unspecified 1.5%, none 4.5% (2001 census)
Languages: English (official), French patois
Literacy:
definition: age 15 and over has ever attended school
total population: 90.1%
male: 89.5%
female: 90.6% (2001 est.)

GOVERNMENT

Country name:
conventional long form: none
conventional short form: Saint Lucia
Government type: Westminster-style parliamentary democracy
Capital: Castries
Administrative divisions: 11 quarters; Anse-la-Raye, Castries, Choiseul, Dauphin, Dennery, Gros-Islet, Laborie, Micoud, Praslin, Soufriere, Vieux-Fort
Independence: 22 February 1979 (from UK)
National holiday: Independence Day, 22 February (1979)
Constitution: 22 February 1979
Legal system: based on English common law
Suffrage: 18 years of age; universal
Executive branch:
chief of state: Queen ELIZABETH II (since 6 February 1952), represented by Governor General Dame Pearlette LOUISY (since September 1997)
head of government: Prime Minister Kenneth Davis ANTHONY (since 24 May 1997) and Deputy Prime Minister Mario MICHEL (since 24 May 1997)
cabinet: Cabinet appointed by the governor general on the advice of the prime minister
elections: none; the monarch is hereditary; the governor general is appointed by the monarch; following legislative elections, the leader of the majority party or the leader of a majority coalition is usually appointed prime minister by the governor general; deputy prime minister appointed by the governor general
Legislative branch: bicameral Parliament consists of the Senate (11 seats; six members appointed on the advice of the prime minister, three on the advice of the leader of the opposition, and two after consultation with religious, economic, and social groups) and the House of Assembly (17 seats; members are elected by popular vote from single-member constituencies to serve five-year terms)
elections: House of Assembly - last held 3 December 2001 (next to be held in December 2006)
election results: House of Assembly - percent of vote by party - SLP 55%, UWP 37%, NA 3.5%; seats by party - SLP 14, UWP 3
Judicial branch: Eastern Caribbean Supreme Court (jurisdiction extends to Anguilla, Antigua and Barbuda, the British Virgin Islands, Dominica, Grenada, Montserrat, Saint Kitts and Nevis, Saint Lucia, and Saint Vincent and the Grenadines)

Political parties and leaders: National Alliance or NA [George ODLUM]; Saint Lucia Freedom Party or SFP [Martinus FRANCOIS]; Saint Lucia Labor Party or SLP [Kenneth ANTHONY]; Sou Tout Apwe Fete Fini or STAFF [Christopher HUNTE]; United Workers Party or UWP [Dr. Morella JOSEPH]
Political pressure groups and leaders: NA
International organization participation: ACCT, ACP, C, Caricom, CDB, FAO, G-77, IBRD, ICAO, ICCt (signatory), ICFTU, ICRM, IDA, IFAD, IFC, IFRCS, ILO, IMF, IMO, Interpol, IOC, ISO, ITU, MIGA, NAM, OAS, OECS, OPANAL, OPCW, UN, UNCTAD, UNESCO, UNIDO, UPU, WCL, WCO, WFTU, WHO, WIPO, WMO, WTO
Diplomatic representation in the US:
chief of mission: Ambassador Sonia Merlyn JOHNNY
chancery: 3216 New Mexico Avenue NW, Washington, DC 20016
telephone: [1] (202) 364-6792 through 6795
FAX: [1] (202) 364-6723
consulate(s) general: Miami and New York
Diplomatic representation from the US: the US does not have an embassy in Saint Lucia; the US Ambassador to Barbados is accredited to Saint Lucia
Flag description: blue, with a gold isosceles triangle below a black arrowhead; the upper edges of the arrowhead have a white border

ECONOMY

Economy - overview: Changes in the EU import preference regime and the increased competition from Latin American bananas have made economic diversification increasingly important in Saint Lucia. The island nation has been able to attract foreign business and investment, especially in its offshore banking and tourism industries. The manufacturing sector is the most diverse in the Eastern Caribbean area, and the government is trying to revitalize the banana industry. Economic fundamentals remain solid, even though unemployment needs to be cut.
GDP (purchasing power parity): $866 million (2002 est.)
GDP (official exchange rate): NA
GDP - real growth rate: 3.3% (2002 est.)
GDP - per capita: purchasing power parity - $5,400 (2002 est.)
GDP - composition by sector:
agriculture: 7%
industry: 20%
services: 73% (2002 est.)
Labor force: 43,800 (2001 est.)
Labor force - by occupation: agriculture 21.7%, industry, commerce, and manufacturing 24.7%, services 53.6% (2002 est.)
Unemployment rate: 20% (2003 est.)
Population below poverty line: NA
Household income or consumption by percentage share:
lowest 10%: NA
highest 10%: NA
Inflation rate (consumer prices): 3% (2001 est.)
Budget:
revenues: $141.2 million
expenditures: $146.7 million, including capital expenditures of $25.1 million (2000 est.)
Agriculture - products: bananas, coconuts, vegetables, citrus, root crops, cocoa
Industries: clothing, assembly of electronic components, beverages, corrugated cardboard boxes, tourism, lime processing, coconut processing
Industrial production growth rate: -8.9% (1997 est.)
Electricity - production: 281 million kWh (2003)
Electricity - production by source:
fossil fuel: 100%
hydro: 0%
nuclear: 0%
other: 0% (2001)
Electricity - consumption: 261.4 million kWh (2003)
Electricity - exports: 0 kWh (2003)
Electricity - imports: 0 kWh (2003)
Oil - production: 0 bbl/day (2003 est.)
Oil - consumption: 2,520 bbl/day (2003 est.)
Oil - exports: NA (2001)
Oil - imports: NA (2001)
Exports: $82 million (2004 est.)
Exports - partners: UK 41.4%, US 16.5%, Brazil 11.6%, Barbados 5.8%, Antigua and Barbuda 4.6%, Dominica 4.5% (2004)
Imports: $410 million (2004 est.)
Imports - partners: US 27.8%, Trinidad and Tobago 20.4%, UK 8%, Venezuela 7.6%, Finland 7% (2004)
Debt - external: $214 million (2000)
Economic aid - recipient: $51.8 million (1995)
Currency (code): East Caribbean dollar (XCD)
Currency code: XCD
Exchange rates: East Caribbean dollars per US dollar - NA (2005), 2.7 (2004), 2.7 (2003), 2.7 (2002), 2.7 (2001)
Fiscal year: 1 April - 31 March

COMMUNICATIONS

Telephones - main lines in use: 51,100 (2002)
Telephones - mobile cellular: 14,300 (2002)
Telephone system:
general assessment: adequate system
domestic: system is automatically switched
international: country code - 1-758; direct microwave radio relay link with Martinique and Saint Vincent and the Grenadines; tropospheric scatter to Barbados; international calls beyond these countries are carried by Intelsat from Martinique
Radio broadcast stations: AM 2, FM 7, shortwave 0 (2004)
Radios: 111,000 (1997)
Television broadcast stations: 2 (of which one is a commercial broadcast station and one is a community antenna television or CATV channel) (2004)
Televisions: 32,000 (1997)
Internet country code: .lc
Internet hosts: 41 (2003)
Internet Service Providers (ISPs): 15 (2000)
Internet users: 13,000 (2002)

TRANSPORTATION

Airports: 2 (2004 est.)
Airports - with paved runways:
total: 2
2,438 to 3,047 m: 1
1,524 to 2,437 m: 1 (2005 est.)
Roadways:
total: 1,210 km
paved: 63 km
unpaved: 1,147 km (1999 est.)
Ports and terminals: Castries, Cul-de-Sac, Vieux-Fort

MILITARY

Military branches: no regular military forces; Royal Saint Lucia Police Force (includes Special Service Unit, Coast Guard) (2003)
Military expenditures - dollar figure: NA
Military expenditures - percent of GDP: NA

TRANSNATIONAL ISSUES

Disputes - international: joins other Caribbean states to counter Venezuela's claim that Aves Island sustains human habitation, a criterion under UNCLOS, which permits Venezuela to extend its EEZ/continental shelf over a large portion of the Caribbean Sea
Illicit drugs: transit point for South American drugs destined for the US and Europe

SAINT PIERRE AND MIQUELON

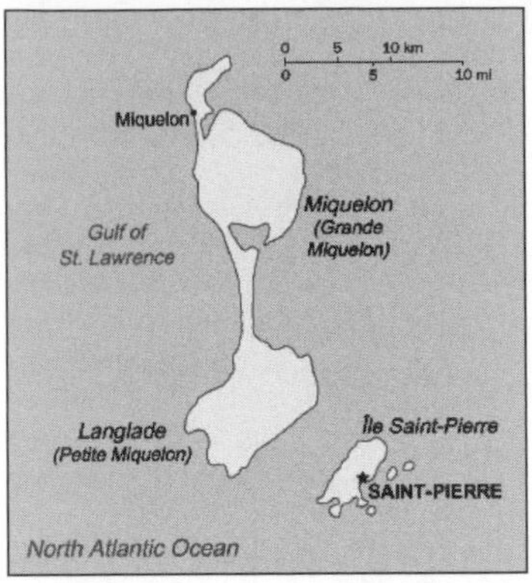

INTRODUCTION

Background: First settled by the French in the early 17th century, the islands represent the sole remaining vestige of France's once vast North American possessions.

GEOGRAPHY

Location: Northern North America, islands in the North Atlantic Ocean, south of Newfoundland (Canada)
Geographic coordinates: 46 50 N, 56 20 W
Map references: North America
Area:
total: 242 sq km
land: 242 sq km
water: 0 sq km
note: includes eight small islands in the Saint Pierre and the Miquelon groups
Area - comparative: 1.5 times the size of Washington, DC
Land boundaries: 0 km
Coastline: 120 km
Maritime claims:
territorial sea: 12 nm
exclusive economic zone: 200 nm
Climate: cold and wet, with much mist and fog; spring and autumn are windy
Terrain: mostly barren rock
Elevation extremes:
lowest point: Atlantic Ocean 0 m
highest point: Morne de la Grande Montagne 240 m
Natural resources: fish, deepwater ports
Land use:
arable land: 13.04%
permanent crops: 0%
other: 86.96% (2001)
Irrigated land: NA sq km
Natural hazards: persistent fog throughout the year can be a maritime hazard
Environment - current issues: recent test drilling for oil in waters around Saint Pierre and Miquelon may bring future development that would impact the environment
Geography - note: vegetation scanty

PEOPLE

Population: 7,012 (July 2005 est.)
Age structure:
0-14 years: 24% (male 861/female 825)
15-64 years: 65.3% (male 2,330/female 2,251)
65 years and over: 10.6% (male 335/female 410) (2005 est.)
Median age:
total: 33.7 years
male: 33.39 years
female: 33.96 years (2005 est.)
Population growth rate: 0.21% (2005 est.)
Birth rate: 13.83 births/1,000 population (2005 est.)
Death rate: 6.7 deaths/1,000 population (2005 est.)
Net migration rate: -4.99 migrant(s)/1,000 population (2005 est.)
Sex ratio:
at birth: 1.06 male(s)/female
under 15 years: 1.04 male(s)/female
15-64 years: 1.04 male(s)/female
65 years and over: 0.82 male(s)/female
total population: 1.01 male(s)/female (2005 est.)
Infant mortality rate:
total: 7.54 deaths/1,000 live births
male: 8.66 deaths/1,000 live births
female: 6.38 deaths/1,000 live births (2005 est.)
Life expectancy at birth:
total population: 78.46 years
male: 76.13 years
female: 80.9 years (2005 est.)
Total fertility rate: 2.03 children born/woman (2005 est.)
HIV/AIDS - adult prevalence rate: NA%
HIV/AIDS - people living with HIV/AIDS: NA
HIV/AIDS - deaths: NA
Nationality:
noun: Frenchman(men), Frenchwoman (women)
adjective: French
Ethnic groups: Basques and Bretons (French fishermen)
Religions: Roman Catholic 99%
Languages: French (official)
Literacy:
definition: age 15 and over can read and write
total population: 99%
male: 99%
female: 99% (1982 est.)

GOVERNMENT

Country name:
conventional long form: Territorial Collectivity of Saint Pierre and Miquelon
conventional short form: Saint Pierre and Miquelon
local long form: Departement de Saint-Pierre et Miquelon
local short form: Saint-Pierre et Miquelon
Dependency status: self-governing territorial collectivity of France
Government type: NA
Capital: Saint-Pierre
Administrative divisions: none (territorial collectivity of France); note - there are no first-order administrative divisions as defined by the US Government, but there are two communes - Saint Pierre, Miquelon at the second order
Independence: none (territorial collectivity of France; has been under French control since 1763)
National holiday: Bastille Day, 14 July (1789)
Constitution: 4 October 1958 (French Constitution)
Legal system: French law with special adaptations for local conditions, such as housing and taxation
Suffrage: 18 years of age; universal
Executive branch:
chief of state: President Jacques CHIRAC of France (since 17 May 1995), represented by Prefect Albert DUPUY (since 10 January 2005)
head of government: President of the General Council Marc PLANTAGENEST (since NA)
cabinet: NA
elections: French president elected by popular vote for a five-year term; election last held, first round - 21 April 2002, second round - 5 May 2002 (next to be held NA 2007); prefect appointed by the French president on the advice of the French Ministry of Interior; president of the General Council is elected by the members of the council
Legislative branch: unicameral General Council or Conseil General (19 seats - 15 from Saint Pierre and 4 from Miquelon; members are elected by popular vote to serve six-year terms)
elections: elections last held 19 and 26 March 2000 (next to be held NA April 2006)
election results: percent of vote by party - NA%; seats by party - PS 12, PRG 2, UDF-RPR 5
note: Saint Pierre and Miquelon elect 1 seat to the French Senate; elections last held NA September 1995 (next to be held NA September 2004); results - percent of vote by party - NA%; seats by party - RPR 1; Saint Pierre and Miquelon also elects 1 seat to the French National Assembly; elections last held, first round - 9 June 2002, second round - 16 June 2002 (next to be held NA 2007);

results - percent of vote by party - NA%; seats by party - UDF 1
Judicial branch: Superior Tribunal of Appeals or Tribunal Superieur d'Appel
Political parties and leaders: Left Radical Party or PRG [leader NA]; Rassemblement pour la Republique or RPR (now UMP) [leader NA]; Socialist Party or PS [leader NA]; Union pour la Democratie Francaise or UDF [leader NA]
Political pressure groups and leaders: NA
International organization participation: UPU, WFTU
Diplomatic representation in the US: none (territorial collectivity of France)
Diplomatic representation from the US: none (territorial collectivity of France)
Flag description: a yellow sailing ship facing the hoist side rides on a dark blue background with yellow wavy lines under the ship; on the hoist side, a vertical band is divided into three parts: the top part (called ikkurina) is red with a green diagonal cross extending to the corners overlaid by a white cross dividing the rectangle into four sections; the middle part has a white background with an ermine pattern; the third part has a red background with two stylized yellow lions outlined in black, one above the other; these three heraldic arms represent settlement by colonists from the Basque Country (top), Brittany, and Normandy; the flag of France is used for official occasions

ECONOMY

Economy - overview: The inhabitants have traditionally earned their livelihood by fishing and by servicing fishing fleets operating off the coast of Newfoundland. The economy has been declining, however, because of disputes with Canada over fishing quotas and a steady decline in the number of ships stopping at Saint Pierre. In 1992, an arbitration panel awarded the islands an exclusive economic zone of 12,348 sq km to settle a longstanding territorial dispute with Canada, although it represents only 25% of what France had sought. The islands are heavily subsidized by France to the great betterment of living standards. The government hopes an expansion of tourism will boost economic prospects. Recent test drilling for oil may pave the way for development of the energy sector.
GDP (purchasing power parity): $48.3 million - supplemented by annual payments from France of about $60 million (2003 est.)
GDP (official exchange rate): NA
GDP - real growth rate: NA%
GDP - per capita: purchasing power parity - $7,000 (2001 est.)
GDP - composition by sector:
agriculture: NA%
industry: NA%
services: NA%
Labor force: 3,261 (1999)
Labor force - by occupation: fishing 18%, industry (mainly fish-processing) 41%, services 41% (1996 est.)
Unemployment rate: 9.8% (1997)
Population below poverty line: NA
Household income or consumption by percentage share:
lowest 10%: NA%
highest 10%: NA%
Inflation rate (consumer prices): 2.1% (1991-96 average)
Budget:
revenues: $70 million
expenditures: $60 million, including capital expenditures of $24 million (1996 est.)
Agriculture - products: vegetables; poultry, cattle, sheep, pigs; fish
Industries: fish processing and supply base for fishing fleets; tourism
Industrial production growth rate: NA%
Electricity - production: 44.15 million kWh (2003)
Electricity - production by source:
fossil fuel: 100%
hydro: 0%
nuclear: 0%
other: 0% (2001)
Electricity - consumption: 41.06 million kWh (2003)
Electricity - exports: 0 kWh (2003)
Electricity - imports: 0 kWh (2003)
Oil - production: 0 bbl/day (2003 est.)
Oil - consumption: 480 bbl/day (2003 est.)
Oil - exports: NA (2001)
Oil - imports: NA (2001)
Exports: $7 million f.o.b. (2004 est.)
Exports - partners: Belgium 41.3%, US 19.9%, Spain 14.9%, France 10%, Germany 4.1% (2004)
Imports: $70 million f.o.b. (2004 est.)
Imports - partners: France 37.6%, Canada 25.3%, Ireland 25.2%, Italy 5.1% (2004)
Debt - external: $NA
Economic aid - recipient: approximately $60 million in annual grants from France
Currency (code): euro (EUR)
Currency code: EUR
Exchange rates: euros per US dollar - 0.79697 (2005), 0.8054 (2004), 0.886 (2003), 1.0626 (2002), 1.1175 (2001)
Fiscal year: calendar year

COMMUNICATIONS

Telephones - main lines in use: 4,800 (2002)
Telephones - mobile cellular: 0 (1994)
Telephone system:
general assessment: adequate
domestic: NA
international: country code - 508; radiotelephone communication with most countries in the world; 1 earth station in French domestic satellite system
Radio broadcast stations: AM 1, FM 4, shortwave 0 (1998)
Radios: 4,000 (1997)
Television broadcast stations: 0 (there are, however, two repeaters which rebroadcast programs from France, Canada, and the US) (1997)
Televisions: 4,000 (1997)
Internet country code: .pm
Internet Service Providers (ISPs): 1 (2000)
Internet users: NA

TRANSPORTATION

Airports: 2 (2004 est.)
Airports - with paved runways:
total: 2
1,524 to 2,437 m: 1
914 to 1,523 m: 1 (2005 est.)
Roadways:
total: 114 km
paved: 69 km
unpaved: 45 km
Ports and terminals: Saint-Pierre

MILITARY

Military - note: defense is the responsibility of France

TRANSNATIONAL ISSUES

Disputes - international: none

SAINT VINCENT AND THE GRENADINES

INTRODUCTION

Background: Disputed between France and the United Kingdom in the 18th century, Saint Vincent was ceded to the latter in 1783. Autonomy was granted in 1969 and independence in 1979.

GEOGRAPHY

Location: Caribbean, islands between the Caribbean Sea and North Atlantic Ocean, north of Trinidad and Tobago
Geographic coordinates: 13 15 N, 61 12 W
Map references: Central America and the Caribbean
Area:
total: 389 sq km (Saint Vincent 344 sq km)
land: 389 sq km

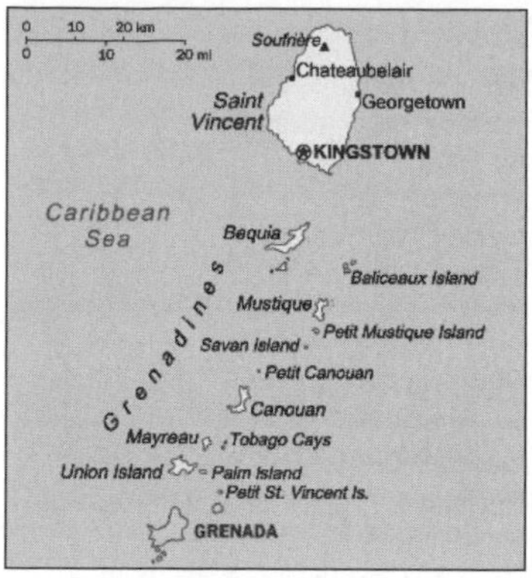

water: 0 sq km
Area - comparative: twice the size of Washington, DC
Land boundaries: 0 km
Coastline: 84 km
Maritime claims:
territorial sea: 12 nm
contiguous zone: 24 nm
exclusive economic zone: 200 nm
continental shelf: 200 nm
Climate: tropical; little seasonal temperature variation; rainy season (May to November)
Terrain: volcanic, mountainous
Elevation extremes:
lowest point: Caribbean Sea 0 m
highest point: Soufriere 1,234 m
Natural resources: hydropower, cropland
Land use:
arable land: 17.95%
permanent crops: 17.95%
other: 64.1% (2001)
Irrigated land: 10 sq km (1998 est.)
Natural hazards: hurricanes; Soufriere volcano on the island of Saint Vincent is a constant threat
Environment - current issues: pollution of coastal waters and shorelines from discharges by pleasure yachts and other effluents; in some areas, pollution is severe enough to make swimming prohibitive
Environment - international agreements:
party to: Biodiversity, Climate Change, Climate Change-Kyoto Protocol, Desertification, Endangered Species, Environmental Modification, Hazardous Wastes, Law of the Sea, Marine Dumping, Ozone Layer Protection, Ship Pollution, Whaling
signed, but not ratified: none of the selected agreements
Geography - note: the administration of the islands of the Grenadines group is divided between Saint Vincent and the Grenadines and Grenada; Saint Vincent and the Grenadines is comprised of 32 islands and cays

PEOPLE

Population: 117,534 (July 2005 est.)
Age structure:
0-14 years: 27.1% (male 16,208/female 15,621)
15-64 years: 66.5% (male 40,287/female 37,883)
65 years and over: 6.4% (male 3,280/female 4,255) (2005 est.)
Median age:
total: 26.36 years
male: 26.21 years
female: 26.53 years (2005 est.)
Population growth rate: 0.27% (2005 est.)
Birth rate: 16.34 births/1,000 population (2005 est.)
Death rate: 6 deaths/1,000 population (2005 est.)
Net migration rate: -7.61 migrant(s)/1,000 population (2005 est.)
Sex ratio:
at birth: 1.03 male(s)/female
under 15 years: 1.04 male(s)/female
15-64 years: 1.06 male(s)/female
65 years and over: 0.77 male(s)/female
total population: 1.04 male(s)/female (2005 est.)
Infant mortality rate:
total: 14.78 deaths/1,000 live births
male: 16.09 deaths/1,000 live births
female: 13.44 deaths/1,000 live births (2005 est.)
Life expectancy at birth:
total population: 73.62 years
male: 71.78 years
female: 75.51 years (2005 est.)
Total fertility rate: 1.85 children born/woman (2005 est.)
HIV/AIDS - adult prevalence rate: NA
HIV/AIDS - people living with HIV/AIDS: NA
HIV/AIDS - deaths: NA
Nationality:
noun: Saint Vincentian(s) or Vincentian(s)
adjective: Saint Vincentian or Vincentian
Ethnic groups: black 66%, mixed 19%, East Indian 6%, Carib Amerindian 2%, other 7%
Religions: Anglican 47%, Methodist 28%, Roman Catholic 13%, Hindu, Seventh-Day Adventist, other Protestant
Languages: English, French patois
Literacy:
definition: age 15 and over has ever attended school
total population: 96%
male: 96%
female: 96% (1970 est.)

GOVERNMENT

Country name:
conventional long form: none
conventional short form: Saint Vincent and the Grenadines
Government type: parliamentary democracy; independent sovereign state within the Commonwealth
Capital: Kingstown
Administrative divisions: 6 parishes; Charlotte, Grenadines, Saint Andrew, Saint David, Saint George, Saint Patrick
Independence: 27 October 1979 (from UK)
National holiday: Independence Day, 27 October (1979)
Constitution: 27 October 1979
Legal system: based on English common law
Suffrage: 18 years of age; universal
Executive branch:
chief of state: Queen ELIZABETH II (since 6 February 1952), represented by Governor General Sir Fredrick Nathaniel BALLANTYNE (since 2 September 2002)
head of government: Prime Minister Ralph E. GONSALVES (since 29 March 2001)
cabinet: Cabinet appointed by the governor general on the advice of the prime minister
elections: none; the monarch is hereditary; the governor general is appointed by the monarch; following legislative elections, the leader of the majority party is usually appointed prime minister by the governor general; deputy prime minister appointed by the governor general on the advice of the prime minister
Legislative branch: unicameral House of Assembly (21 seats, 15 elected representatives and 6 appointed senators; representatives are elected by popular vote from single-member constituencies to serve five-year terms)
elections: last held 7 December 2005 (next to be held 2010)
election results: percent of vote by party - ULP 55.26%, NDP 44.68%; seats by party - ULP 12, NDP 3
Judicial branch: Eastern Caribbean Supreme Court (based on Saint Lucia; one judge of the Supreme Court resides in Saint Vincent and the Grenadines)
Political parties and leaders: National Reform Party or NRP [Joel MIGUEL]; New Democratic Party or NDP [Arnhim EUSTACE]; People's Progressive Movement or PPM [Ken BOYEA]; Progressive Labor Party or PLP [leader NA]; United People's Movement or UPM [Adrian SAUNDERS]; Unity Labor Party or ULP [Ralph GONSALVES] (formed by the coalition of Saint Vincent Labor Party or SVLP and the Movement for National Unity or MNU)
Political pressure groups and leaders: NA
International organization participation: ACP, C, Caricom, CDB, FAO, G-77, IBRD, ICAO, ICCt, ICFTU, ICRM, IDA, IFAD, IFRCS, ILO, IMF, IMO, Interpol, IOC, ISO (subscriber), ITU, MIGA, OAS, OECS, OPANAL, OPCW, UN, UNCTAD, UNESCO, UNIDO, UPU, WCL, WFTU, WHO, WIPO, WTO

Diplomatic representation in the US:
chief of mission: Ambassador Ellsworth I. A. JOHN
chancery: 3216 New Mexico Avenue NW, Washington, DC 20016
telephone: [1] (202) 364-6730
FAX: [1] (202) 364-6736
consulate(s) general: New York
Diplomatic representation from the US: the US does not have an embassy in Saint Vincent and the Grenadines; the US Ambassador to Barbados is accredited to Saint Vincent and the Grenadines
Flag description: three vertical bands of blue (hoist side), gold (double width), and green; the gold band bears three green diamonds arranged in a V pattern

ECONOMY

Economy - overview: Economic growth in this lower-middle-income country hinges upon seasonal variations in the agricultural and tourism sectors. Tropical storms wiped out substantial portions of crops in 1994, 1995, and 2002, and tourism in the Eastern Caribbean has suffered low arrivals following 11 September 2001. Saint Vincent is home to a small offshore banking sector and has moved to adopt international regulatory standards. Saint Vincent is also a large producer of marijuana and is being used as a transshipment point for illegal narcotics from South America.
GDP (purchasing power parity): $342 million (2002 est.)
GDP (official exchange rate): NA
GDP - real growth rate: 0.7% (2002 est.)
GDP - per capita: purchasing power parity - $2,900 (2002 est.)
GDP - composition by sector:
agriculture: 10%
industry: 26%
services: 64% (2001 est.)
Labor force: 67,000 (1984 est.)
Labor force - by occupation: agriculture 26%, industry 17%, services 57% (1980 est.)
Unemployment rate: 15% (2001 est.)
Population below poverty line: NA
Household income or consumption by percentage share:
lowest 10%: NA
highest 10%: NA
Inflation rate (consumer prices): -0.4% (2001 est.)
Budget:
revenues: $94.6 million
expenditures: $85.8 million, including capital expenditures of NA (2000 est.)
Agriculture - products: bananas, coconuts, sweet potatoes, spices, small numbers of cattle, sheep, pigs, goats, fish
Industries: food processing, cement, furniture, clothing, starch
Industrial production growth rate: -0.9% (1997 est.)
Electricity - production: 95 million kWh (2003)
Electricity - production by source:
fossil fuel: 69.3%
hydro: 30.7%
nuclear: 0%
other: 0% (2001)
Electricity - consumption: 88.35 million kWh (2003)
Electricity - exports: 0 kWh (2003)
Electricity - imports: 0 kWh (2003)
Oil - production: 0 bbl/day (2003 est.)
Oil - consumption: 1,300 bbl/day (2003 est.)
Oil - exports: NA (2001)
Oil - imports: NA (2001)
Exports: $37 million (2004 est.)
Exports - partners: UK 33.5%, Barbados 13.1%, Saint Lucia 11.5%, Trinidad and Tobago 9.9%, Antigua and Barbuda 8.3%, US 5.3%, Grenada 5.3%, Dominica 4.1% (2004)
Imports: $225 million (2004 est.)
Imports - partners: US 37.5%, Trinidad and Tobago 21.3%, UK 10.5% (2004)
Debt - external: $167.2 million (2000)
Economic aid - recipient: $47.5 million (1995); note - EU $34.5 million (1998)
Currency (code): East Caribbean dollar (XCD)
Currency code: XCD
Exchange rates: East Caribbean dollars per US dollar - NA (2005), 2.7 (2004), 2.7 (2003), 2.7 (2002), 2.7 (2001)
Fiscal year: calendar year

COMMUNICATIONS

Telephones - main lines in use: 27,300 (2002)
Telephones - mobile cellular: 10,000 (2002)
Telephone system:
general assessment: adequate system
domestic: islandwide, fully automatic telephone system; VHF/UHF radiotelephone from Saint Vincent to the other islands of the Grenadines
international: country code - 1-784; VHF/UHF radiotelephone from Saint Vincent to Barbados; new SHF radiotelephone to Grenada and to Saint Lucia; access to Intelsat earth station in Martinique through Saint Lucia
Radio broadcast stations: AM 1, FM 6, shortwave 0 (2004)
Radios: 77,000 (1997)
Television broadcast stations: 1 (plus three repeaters) (2004)
Televisions: 18,000 (1997)
Internet country code: .vc
Internet hosts: 4 (2003)
Internet Service Providers (ISPs): 15 (2000)
Internet users: 7,000 (2002)

TRANSPORTATION

Airports: 6 (2004 est.)
Airports - with paved runways:
total: 5
914 to 1,523 m: 4
under 914 m: 1 (2005 est.)
Airports - with unpaved runways:
total: 1
under 914 m: 1 (2005 est.)
Roadways:
total: 829 km
paved: 580 km
unpaved: 249 km (2002)
Merchant marine:
total: 657 ships (1,000 GRT or over) 5,967,418 GRT/9,041,023 DWT
by type: bulk carrier 112, cargo 366, chemical tanker 18, combination ore/oil 1, container 24, liquefied gas 4, livestock carrier 6, passenger 5, passenger/cargo 19, petroleum tanker 29, refrigerated cargo 48, roll on/roll off 22, specialized tanker 2, vehicle carrier 1
foreign-owned: 554 (Australia 2, Bangladesh 5, Barbados 1, Belgium 1, British 5, Bulgaria 17, China 115, Congo 1, Croatia 7, Cuba 1, Czech Republic 1, Denmark 12, Egypt 2, Estonia 19, France 12, Germany 8, Greece 99, Guyana 3, Hong Kong 10, Iceland 11, India 6, Iran 1, Ireland 1, Israel 3, Italy 18, Kenya 4, Latvia 9, Lebanon 6, Lithuania 3, Monaco 4, Netherlands 7, Nigeria 3, Norway 19, Pakistan 4, Poland 1, Puerto Rico 1, Romania 1, Russia 20, Saudi Arabia 3, Serbia & Montenegro 1, Singapore 2, Slovenia 6, South Korea 3, Spain 2, Sweden 1, Switzerland 7, Syria 6, Trinidad & Tobago 1, Tunisia 2, Turkey 16, Ukraine 6, UAE 21, United Kingdom 10, United States 24) (2005)
Ports and terminals: Kingstown

MILITARY

Military branches: no regular military forces; Royal Saint Vincent and the Grenadines Police Force (includes Special Service Unit), Coast Guard
Military expenditures - dollar figure: NA
Military expenditures - percent of GDP: NA

TRANSNATIONAL ISSUES

Disputes - international: joins other Caribbean states to counter Venezuela's claim that Aves Island sustains human habitation, a criterion under UNCLOS, which permits Venezuela to extend its EEZ/continental shelf over a large portion of the Caribbean Sea
Illicit drugs: transshipment point for South American drugs destined for the US and Europe; small-scale cannabis cultivation

SAMOA

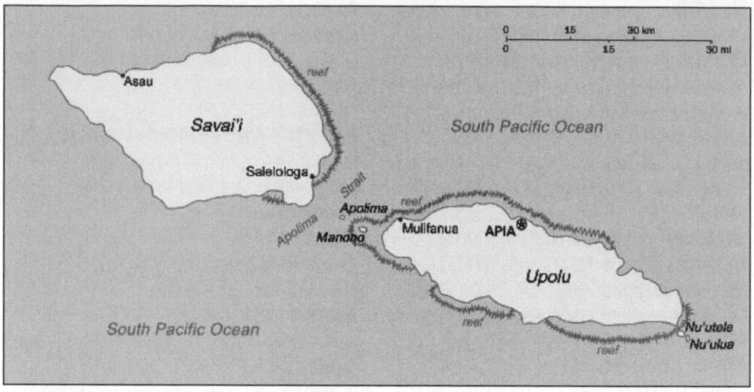

INTRODUCTION

Background: New Zealand occupied the German protectorate of Western Samoa at the outbreak of World War I in 1914. It continued to administer the islands as a mandate and then as a trust territory until 1962, when the islands became the first Polynesian nation to reestablish independence in the 20th century. The country dropped the "Western" from its name in 1997.

GEOGRAPHY

Location: Oceania, group of islands in the South Pacific Ocean, about one-half of the way from Hawaii to New Zealand
Geographic coordinates: 13 35 S, 172 20 W
Map references: Oceania
Area:
total: 2,944 sq km
land: 2,934 sq km
water: 10 sq km
Area - comparative: slightly smaller than Rhode Island
Land boundaries: 0 km
Coastline: 403 km
Maritime claims:
territorial sea: 12 nm
exclusive economic zone: 200 nm
Climate: tropical; rainy season (November to April), dry season (May to October)
Terrain: two main islands (Savaii, Upolu) and several smaller islands and uninhabited islets; narrow coastal plain with volcanic, rocky, rugged mountains in interior
Elevation extremes:
lowest point: Pacific Ocean 0 m
highest point: Mauga Silisili (Savaii) 1,857 m
Natural resources: hardwood forests, fish, hydropower
Land use:
arable land: 21.2%
permanent crops: 24.38%
other: 54.42% (2001)
Irrigated land: NA
Natural hazards: occasional typhoons; active volcanism
Environment - current issues: soil erosion, deforestation, invasive species, overfishing
Environment - international agreements:
party to: Biodiversity, Climate Change, Climate Change-Kyoto Protocol, Desertification, Hazardous Wastes, Law of the Sea, Ozone Layer Protection
signed, but not ratified: none of the selected agreements
Geography - note: occupies an almost central position within Polynesia

PEOPLE

Population: 177,287 (July 2005 est.)
Age structure:
0-14 years: 27.2% (male 24,517/female 23,660)
15-64 years: 66.4% (male 73,495/female 44,208)
65 years and over: 6.4% (male 5,204/female 6,203) (2005 est.)
Median age:
total: 24.59 years
male: 27.42 years
female: 21.42 years (2005 est.)
Population growth rate: -0.23% (2005 est.)
Birth rate: 15.95 births/1,000 population (2005 est.)
Death rate: 6.54 deaths/1,000 population (2005 est.)
Net migration rate: -11.73 migrant(s)/1,000 population (2005 est.)
Sex ratio:
at birth: 1.05 male(s)/female
under 15 years: 1.04 male(s)/female
15-64 years: 1.66 male(s)/female
65 years and over: 0.84 male(s)/female
total population: 1.39 male(s)/female (2005 est.)
Infant mortality rate:
total: 27.71 deaths/1,000 live births
male: 32.68 deaths/1,000 live births
female: 22.48 deaths/1,000 live births (2005 est.)
Life expectancy at birth:
total population: 70.72 years
male: 67.93 years
female: 73.65 years (2005 est.)
Total fertility rate: 3.01 children born/woman (2005 est.)
HIV/AIDS - adult prevalence rate: NA
HIV/AIDS - people living with HIV/AIDS: 12
HIV/AIDS - deaths: 3
Nationality:
noun: Samoan(s)
adjective: Samoan
Ethnic groups: Samoan 92.6%, Euronesians 7% (persons of European and Polynesian blood), Europeans 0.4%
Religions: Congregationalist 34.8%, Roman Catholic 19.6%, Methodist 15%, Latter-Day Saints 12.7%, Assembly of God 6.6%, Seventh-Day Adventist 3.5%, other Christian 4.5%, Worship Centre 1.3%, other 1.7%, unspecified 0.1% (2001 census)
Languages: Samoan (Polynesian), English
Literacy:
definition: age 15 and over can read and write
total population: 99.7%
male: 99.6%
female: 99.7% (2003 est.)

GOVERNMENT

Country name:
conventional long form: Independent State of Samoa
conventional short form: Samoa
former: Western Samoa
Government type: mix of parliamentary democracy and constitutional monarchy
Capital: Apia
Administrative divisions: 11 districts; A'ana, Aiga-i-le-Tai, Atua, Fa'asaleleaga, Gaga'emauga, Gagaifomauga, Palauli, Satupa'itea, Tuamasaga, Va'a-o-Fonoti, Vaisigano
Independence: 1 January 1962 (from New Zealand-administered UN trusteeship)
National holiday: Independence Day Celebration, 1 June (1962); note - 1 January 1962 is the date of independence from the New Zealand-administered UN trusteeship, 1 June 1962 is the date that independence is celebrated
Constitution: 1 January 1962
Legal system: based on English common law and local customs; judicial review of legislative acts with respect to fundamental rights of the citizen; has not accepted compulsory ICJ jurisdiction
Suffrage: 21 years of age; universal
Executive branch:
chief of state: Chief Tanumafili II MALIETOA (cochief of state from 1 January 1962 until becoming sole chief of state 5 April 1963)
head of government: Prime Minister Sailele Malielegaoi TUILA'EPA (since 1996);

note - TUILA'EPA served as deputy prime minister from 1992 and assumed the duties of acting prime minister in 1996, when former Prime Minister TOFILAU Eti Alesana resigned in poor health; TUILA'EPA was confirmed as prime minister (November 1998) after TOFILAU died; Deputy Prime Minister MISA Telefoni (since 2001)
cabinet: Cabinet consists of 12 members, appointed by the chief of state on the prime minister's advice
elections: upon the death of Chief Tanumafili II MALIETOA, a new chief of state will be elected by the Legislative Assembly to serve a five-year term; following legislative elections, the leader of the majority party is usually appointed prime minister by the chief of state with the approval of the Legislative Assembly
Legislative branch: unicameral Legislative Assembly or Fono (49 seats - 47 elected by voters affiliated with traditional village-based electoral districts, 2 elected by independent, mostly non-Samoan or part-Samoan, voters who cannot, (or choose not to) establish a village affiliation; only chiefs (matai) may stand for election to the Fono from the 47 village-based electorates; members serve five-year terms)
elections: election last held 3 March 2001 (next election to be held not later than March 2006)
election results: percent of vote by party - NA%; seats by party - HRPP 30, SNDP 13, independents 6
Judicial branch: Court of Appeal; Supreme Court; District Court; Land and Titles Court
Political parties and leaders: Christian Democratic Party [leader NA]; Human Rights Protection Party or HRPP [Sailele Malielegaoi TUILA'EPA, chairman]; Samoan Democratic United Party or SDUP [LE MAMEA Ropati, chairman] (opposition)
Political pressure groups and leaders: NA
International organization participation: ACP, AsDB, C, FAO, G-77, IBRD, ICAO, ICCt, ICFTU, ICRM, IDA, IFAD, IFC, IFRCS, ILO, IMF, IMO, IOC, ITU, MIGA, OPCW, PIF, Sparteca, SPC, UN, UNCTAD, UNESCO, UPU, WCO, WHO, WIPO, WMO, WTO (observer)
Diplomatic representation in the US:
chief of mission: Ambassador Aliioaiga Feturi ELISAIA
chancery: 800 Second Avenue, Suite 400D, New York, NY 10017
telephone: [1] (212) 599-6196, 6197
FAX: [1] (212) 599-0797
Diplomatic representation from the US:
chief of mission: US Ambassador to New Zealand is accredited to Samoa
embassy: Accident Compensation Board (ACB) Building, 5th Floor, Apia
mailing address: P. O. Box 3430, Apia
telephone: [685] 21631/22696
FAX: [685] 22030
Flag description: red with a blue rectangle in the upper hoist-side quadrant bearing five white five-pointed stars representing the Southern Cross constellation

ECONOMY

Economy - overview: The economy of Samoa has traditionally been dependent on development aid, family remittances from overseas, agriculture, and fishing. The country is vulnerable to devastating storms. Agriculture employs two-thirds of the labor force, and furnishes 90% of exports, featuring coconut cream, coconut oil, and copra. The manufacturing sector mainly processes agricultural products. The decline of fish stocks in the area is a continuing problem. Tourism is an expanding sector, accounting for 25% of GDP; about 88,000 tourists visited the islands in 2001. One factory in the Foreign Trade Zone employs 3,000 people to make automobile electrical harnesses for an assembly plant in Australia. The Samoan Government has called for deregulation of the financial sector, encouragement of investment, and continued fiscal discipline, meantime protecting the environment. Observers point to the flexibility of the labor market as a basic strength for future economic advances. Foreign reserves are in a relatively healthy state, the external debt is stable, and inflation is low.
GDP (purchasing power parity): $1 billion (2002 est.)
GDP (official exchange rate): NA
GDP - real growth rate: 5% (2002 est.)
GDP - per capita: purchasing power parity - $5,600 (2002 est.)
GDP - composition by sector:
agriculture: 14%
industry: 23%
services: 63% (2001 est.)
Labor force: 90,000 (2000 est.)
Labor force - by occupation: NA
Unemployment rate: NA; note - substantial underemployment
Population below poverty line: NA
Household income or consumption by percentage share:
lowest 10%: NA
highest 10%: NA
Inflation rate (consumer prices): 4% (2001 est.)
Budget:
revenues: $105 million
expenditures: $119 million, including capital expenditures of NA (2001-02)
Agriculture - products: coconuts, bananas, taro, yams, coffee, cocoa
Industries: food processing, building materials, auto parts
Industrial production growth rate: 2.8% (2000)
Electricity - production: 116 million kWh (2003)
Electricity - production by source:
fossil fuel: 58%
hydro: 42%
nuclear: 0%
other: 0% (2001)
Electricity - consumption: 107.9 million kWh (2003)
Electricity - exports: 0 kWh (2003)
Electricity - imports: 0 kWh (2003)
Oil - production: 0 bbl/day (2003 est.)
Oil - consumption: 1,000 bbl/day (2003 est.)
Oil - exports: NA (2001)
Oil - imports: NA (2001)
Exports: $94 million f.o.b. (2004 est.)
Exports - partners: Australia 67.2%, US 5.7%, Indonesia 5.3% (2004)
Imports: $285 million f.o.b. (2004 est.)
Imports - partners: New Zealand 25.1%, Fiji 21.5%, Taiwan 9.1%, Australia 8.9%, Singapore 8.5%, Japan 7.5%, US 4.7% (2004)
Debt - external: $197 million (2000)
Economic aid - recipient: $42.9 million (1995)
Currency (code): tala (SAT)
Currency code: SAT (former WST code is still in wide use)
Exchange rates: tala per US dollar - NA (2005), 2.7807 (2004), 2.9732 (2003), 3.3763 (2002), 3.478 (2001)
Fiscal year: June 1 - May 31

COMMUNICATIONS

Telephones - main lines in use: 11,800 (2002)
Telephones - mobile cellular: 2,700 (2002)
Telephone system:
general assessment: adequate
domestic: NA
international: country code - 685; satellite earth station - 1 Intelsat (Pacific Ocean)
Radio broadcast stations: AM 2, FM 5, shortwave 0 (2004)
Radios: 174,849 (1997)
Television broadcast stations: 2 (2002)
Televisions: 8,634 (1999)
Internet country code: .ws
Internet hosts: 8,225 (2003)
Internet Service Providers (ISPs): 2 (2000)
Internet users: 4,000 (2002)

TRANSPORTATION

Airports: 4 (2004 est.)
Airports - with paved runways:
total: 3

2,438 to 3,047 m: 1
under 914 m: 2 (2005 est.)
Airports - with unpaved runways:
total: 1
under 914 m: 1 (2005 est.)
Roadways:
total: 790 km
paved: 332 km
unpaved: 458 km (1999 est.)
Merchant marine:
total: 1 ships (1,000 GRT or over) 7,091 GRT/8,127 DWT
by type: cargo 1
foreign-owned: 1 (Germany 1) (2005)
Ports and terminals: Apia

MILITARY

Military branches: no regular armed services; Samoa Police Force
Military expenditures - dollar figure: NA
Military expenditures - percent of GDP: NA
Military - note: Samoa has no formal defense structure or regular armed forces; informal defense ties exist with NZ, which is required to consider any Samoan request for assistance under the 1962 Treaty of Friendship

TRANSNATIONAL ISSUES

Disputes - international: none

SAN MARINO

INTRODUCTION

Background: The third smallest state in Europe (after the Holy See and Monaco) also claims to be the world's oldest republic. According to tradition, it was founded by a Christian stonemason named Marino in 301 A.D. San Marino's foreign policy is aligned with that of Italy. Social and political trends in the republic also track closely with those of its larger neighbor.

GEOGRAPHY

Location: Southern Europe, an enclave in central Italy
Geographic coordinates: 43 46 N, 12 25 E
Map references: Europe
Area:
total: 61.2 sq km
land: 61.2 sq km
water: 0 sq km
Area - comparative: about 0.3 times the size of Washington, DC
Land boundaries:
total: 39 km
border countries: Italy 39 km
Coastline: 0 km (landlocked)
Maritime claims: none (landlocked)
Climate: Mediterranean; mild to cool winters; warm, sunny summers
Terrain: rugged mountains
Elevation extremes:
lowest point: Torrente Ausa 55 m
highest point: Monte Titano 755 m
Natural resources: building stone
Land use:
arable land: 16.67%
permanent crops: 0%
other: 83.33% (2001)
Irrigated land: NA sq km
Natural hazards: NA
Environment - current issues: NA
Environment - international agreements:
party to: Biodiversity, Climate Change, Desertification
signed, but not ratified: Air Pollution
Geography - note: landlocked; smallest independent state in Europe after the Holy See and Monaco; dominated by the Apennines

PEOPLE

Population: 28,880 (July 2005 est.)
Age structure:
0-14 years: 16.7% (male 2,482/female 2,328)
15-64 years: 66.5% (male 9,255/female 9,943)
65 years and over: 16.9% (male 2,106/female 2,766) (2005 est.)
Median age:
total: 40.29 years
male: 39.91 years
female: 40.65 years (2005 est.)
Population growth rate: 1.3% (2005 est.)
Birth rate: 10.18 births/1,000 population (2005 est.)
Death rate: 8.07 deaths/1,000 population (2005 est.)
Net migration rate: 10.84 migrant(s)/1,000 population (2005 est.)
Sex ratio:
at birth: 1.09 male(s)/female
under 15 years: 1.07 male(s)/female
15-64 years: 0.93 male(s)/female
65 years and over: 0.76 male(s)/female
total population: 0.92 male(s)/female (2005 est.)
Infant mortality rate:
total: 5.73 deaths/1,000 live births
male: 6.16 deaths/1,000 live births
female: 5.26 deaths/1,000 live births (2005 est.)
Life expectancy at birth:
total population: 81.62 years
male: 78.13 years
female: 85.43 years (2005 est.)
Total fertility rate: 1.33 children born/woman (2005 est.)
HIV/AIDS - adult prevalence rate: NA%
HIV/AIDS - people living with HIV/AIDS: NA
HIV/AIDS - deaths: NA
Nationality:
noun: Sammarinese (singular and plural)
adjective: Sammarinese
Ethnic groups: Sammarinese, Italian
Religions: Roman Catholic
Languages: Italian
Literacy:
definition: age 10 and over can read and write
total population: 96%
male: 97%
female: 95% (1976 est.)

GOVERNMENT

Country name:
conventional long form: Republic of San Marino
conventional short form: San Marino
local long form: Repubblica di San Marino
local short form: San Marino
Government type: independent republic
Capital: San Marino
Administrative divisions: 9 municipalities (castelli, singular - castello); Acquaviva, Borgo Maggiore, Chiesanuova, Domagnano, Faetano, Fiorentino, Montegiardino, San Marino Citta, Serravalle
Independence: 3 September 301
National holiday: Founding of the Republic, 3 September (301)
Constitution: 8 October 1600; electoral law of 1926 serves some of the functions of a constitution
Legal system: based on civil law system with Italian law influences; has not accepted compulsory ICJ jurisdiction
Suffrage: 18 years of age; universal
Executive branch:
chief of state: cochiefs of state Captain Regent Claudio MUCCIOLI and Captain Regent Antonello BACCIOCHI (for the period 1 October 2005 - 31 March 2006)
head of government: Secretary of State for Foreign and Political Affairs Fabio

BERARDI (15 December 2003)
cabinet: Congress of State elected by the Great and General Council for a five-year term
elections: cochiefs of state (captains regent) elected by the Great and General Council for a six-month term; election last held NA September 2005 (next to be held March 2006); secretary of state for foreign and political affairs elected by the Great and General Council for a five-year term; election last held 13 December 2003 (next to be held June 2006 when general elections are scheduled)
election results: Claudio MUCCIOLI and Antonello BACCIOCHI elected captains regent; percent of legislative vote - NA%; Fabio BERARDI elected secretary of state for foreign and political affairs; percent of legislative vote - NA%
note: the popularly elected parliament (Grand and General Council) selects two of its members to serve as the Captains Regent (cochiefs of state) for a six-month period; they preside over meetings of the Grand and General Council and its cabinet (Congress of State), which has 10 other members, all selected by the Grand and General Council; assisting the captains regent are 10 secretaries of state; the secretary of state for Foreign Affairs has assumed some of the prerogatives of a prime minister
Legislative branch: unicameral Grand and General Council or Consiglio Grande e Generale (60 seats; members are elected by direct, popular vote to serve five-year terms)
elections: last held 10 June 2001 (next to be held by June 2006)
election results: percent of vote by party - PDCS 41.4%, PSS 24.2%, PD 20.8%, APDS 8.2%, RC 3.4%, AN 1.9%; seats by party - PDCS 25, PSS 15, PD 12, APDS 5, RC 2, AN 1
Judicial branch: Council of Twelve or Consiglio dei XII
Political parties and leaders: Communist Refoundation or RC [Ivan FOSHI]; Ideas in Movement or IM [Alessandro ROSSI]; National Alliance or AN [leader NA]; Party of Democrats or PD [Claudio FELICI]; San Marino Christian Democratic Party or PDCS [Giovanni LONFERNINI]; San Marino Popular Alliance of Democrats or APDS [Roberto GIORGETTI]; San Marino Socialist Party or PSS [Alberto CECCHETTI]; Socialists for Reform or SR [Renzo GIARDI]
Political pressure groups and leaders: NA
International organization participation: CE, FAO, IBRD, ICAO, ICCt, ICFTU, ICRM, IFRCS, ILO, IMF, IMO, IOC, IOM (observer), ITU, NAM (guest), OPCW, OSCE, UN, UNCTAD, UNESCO, UPU, WHO, WIPO, WToO
Diplomatic representation in the US: San Marino does not have an embassy in the US
honorary consulate(s) general: Washington, DC and New York
honorary consulate(s): Detroit and Honolulu
Diplomatic representation from the US: the US does not have an embassy in San Marino; the US Consul General in Florence (Italy) is accredited to San Marino
Flag description: two equal horizontal bands of white (top) and light blue with the national coat of arms superimposed in the center; the coat of arms has a shield (featuring three towers on three peaks) flanked by a wreath, below a crown and above a scroll bearing the word LIBERTAS (Liberty)

ECONOMY

Economy overview: The tourist sector contributes over 50% of GDP. In 2000 more than 3 million tourists visited San Marino. The key industries are banking, wearing apparel, electronics, and ceramics. Main agricultural products are wine and cheeses. The per capita level of output and standard of living are comparable to those of the most prosperous regions of Italy, which supplies much of its food.
GDP (purchasing power parity): $940 million (2001 est.)
GDP (official exchange rate): NA
GDP - real growth rate: 7.5% (2001 est.)
GDP - per capita: purchasing power parity - $34,600 (2001 est.)
GDP - composition by sector:
agriculture: NA%
industry: NA%
services: NA%
Labor force: 18,500 (1999)
Labor force - by occupation: agriculture 1%, industry 42%, services 57% (2000 est.)
Unemployment rate: 2.6% (2001)
Population below poverty line: NA
Household income or consumption by percentage share:
lowest 10%: NA%
highest 10%: NA%
Inflation rate (consumer prices): 3.3% (2001)
Budget:
revenues: $400 million
expenditures: $400 million, including capital expenditures of NA (2000 est.)
Agriculture - products: wheat, grapes, corn, olives; cattle, pigs, horses, beef, cheese, hides
Industries: tourism, banking, textiles, electronics, ceramics, cement, wine
Industrial production growth rate: 6% (1997 est.)
Exports: trade data are included with the statistics for Italy
Imports: trade data are included with the statistics for Italy
Debt - external: $NA
Economic aid - recipient: $NA
Currency (code): euro (EUR)
Currency code: EUR
Exchange rates: euros per US dollar - 0.79697 (2005), 0.8054 (2004), 0.886 (2003), 1.0626 (2002), 1.1175 (2001)
Fiscal year: calendar year

COMMUNICATIONS

Telephones - main lines in use: 20,600 (2002)
Telephones - mobile cellular: 16,800 (2002)
Telephone system:
general assessment: adequate connections
domestic: automatic telephone system completely integrated into Italian system
international: country code - 378; connected to Italian international network
Radio broadcast stations: AM 0, FM 3, shortwave 0 (1998)
Radios: 16,000 (1997)
Television broadcast stations: 1 (San Marino residents also receive broadcasts from Italy) (1997)
Televisions: 9,000 (1997)
Internet country code: .sm
Internet hosts: 1,763 (2004)
Internet Service Providers (ISPs): 2 (2000)
Internet users: 14,300 (2002)

TRANSPORTATION

Airports: none (2004 est.)
Roadways:
total: 220 km
paved: 220 km
unpaved: 0 km (2001)

MILITARY

Military branches: no regular military forces; Voluntary Military Force (Corpi Militari Voluntar) performs ceremonial duties and limited police assistance
Military expenditures - dollar figure: $700,000 (FY00/01)
Military expenditures - percent of GDP: NA
Military - note: defense is the responsibility of Italy

TRANSNATIONAL ISSUES

Disputes - international: none

SAO TOME AND PRINCIPE

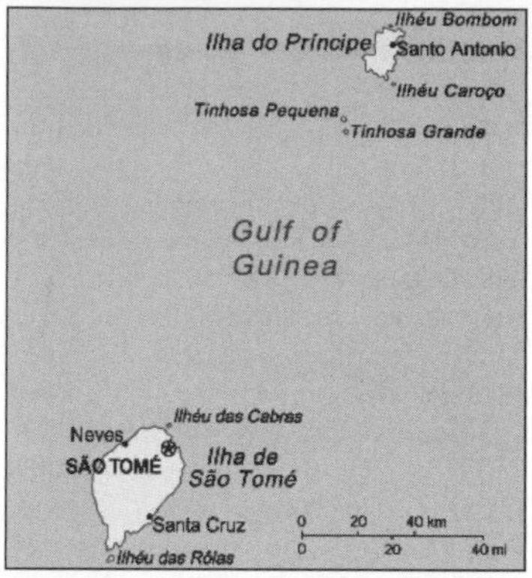

INTRODUCTION

Background: Discovered and claimed by Portugal in the late 15th century, the islands' sugar-based economy gave way to coffee and cocoa in the 19th century - all grown with plantation slave labor, a form of which lingered into the 20th century. Although independence was achieved in 1975, democratic reforms were not instituted until the late 1980s. Though the first free elections were held in 1991, the political environment has been one of continued instability with frequent changes in leadership and coup attempts in 1995 and 2003. The recent discovery of oil in the Gulf of Guinea is likely to have a significant impact on the country's economy.

GEOGRAPHY

Location: Western Africa, islands in the Gulf of Guinea, straddling the Equator, west of Gabon
Geographic coordinates: 1 00 N, 7 00 E
Map references: Africa
Area:
total: 1,001 sq km
land: 1,001 sq km
water: 0 sq km
Area - comparative: more than five times the size of Washington, DC
Land boundaries: 0 km
Coastline: 209 km
Maritime claims:
measured from claimed archipelagic baselines
territorial sea: 12 nm
exclusive economic zone: 200 nm
Climate: tropical; hot, humid; one rainy season (October to May)
Terrain: volcanic, mountainous
Elevation extremes:
lowest point: Atlantic Ocean 0 m
highest point: Pico de Sao Tome 2,024 m
Natural resources: fish, hydropower
Land use:
arable land: 6.25%
permanent crops: 48.96%
other: 44.79% (2001)
Irrigated land: 100 sq km (1998 est.)
Natural hazards: NA
Environment - current issues: deforestation; soil erosion and exhaustion
Environment - international agreements:
party to: Biodiversity, Climate Change, Desertification, Endangered Species, Environmental Modification, Law of the Sea, Ozone Layer Protection, Ship Pollution
signed, but not ratified: none of the selected agreements
Geography - note: the smallest country in Africa; the two main islands form part of a chain of extinct volcanoes and both are fairly mountainous

PEOPLE

Population: 187,410 (July 2005 est.)
Age structure:
0-14 years: 47.6% (male 45,145/female 44,007)
15-64 years: 48.6% (male 43,996/female 47,011)
65 years and over: 3.9% (male 3,333/female 3,918) (2005 est.)
Median age:
total: 16.12 years
male: 15.53 years
female: 16.71 years (2005 est.)
Population growth rate: 3.16% (2005 est.)
Birth rate: 40.8 births/1,000 population (2005 est.)
Death rate: 6.68 deaths/1,000 population (2005 est.)
Net migration rate: -2.51 migrant(s)/1,000 population (2005 est.)
Sex ratio:
at birth: 1.03 male(s)/female
under 15 years: 1.03 male(s)/female
15-64 years: 0.94 male(s)/female
65 years and over: 0.85 male(s)/female
total population: 0.97 male(s)/female (2005 est.)
Infant mortality rate:
total: 43.11 deaths/1,000 live births
male: 45.06 deaths/1,000 live births
female: 41.11 deaths/1,000 live births (2005 est.)
Life expectancy at birth:
total population: 66.99 years
male: 65.43 years
female: 68.59 years (2005 est.)
Total fertility rate: 5.71 children born/woman (2005 est.)
HIV/AIDS - adult prevalence rate: NA
HIV/AIDS - people living with HIV/AIDS: NA
HIV/AIDS - deaths: NA
Major infectious diseases:
degree of risk: high
food or waterborne diseases: bacterial diarrhea, hepatitis A, and typhoid fever
vectorborne disease: malaria (2004)
Nationality:
noun: Sao Tomean(s)
adjective: Sao Tomean
Ethnic groups: mestico, angolares (descendants of Angolan slaves), forros (descendants of freed slaves), servicais (contract laborers from Angola, Mozambique, and Cape Verde), tongas (children of servicais born on the islands), Europeans (primarily Portuguese)
Religions: Catholic 70.3%, Evangelical 3.4%, New Apostolic 2%, Adventist 1.8%, other 3.1%, none 19.4% (2001 census)
Languages: Portuguese (official)
Literacy:
definition: age 15 and over can read and write
total population: 79.3%
male: 85%
female: 62% (1991 est.)

GOVERNMENT

Country name:
conventional long form: Democratic Republic of Sao Tome and Principe
conventional short form: Sao Tome and Principe
local long form: Republica Democratica de Sao Tome e Principe
local short form: Sao Tome e Principe
Government type: republic
Capital: Sao Tome
Administrative divisions: 2 provinces; Principe, Sao Tome
note: Principe has had self-government since 29 April 1995
Independence: 12 July 1975 (from Portugal)
National holiday: Independence Day, 12 July (1975)
Constitution: approved March 1990, effective 10 September 1990
Legal system: based on Portuguese legal system and customary law; has not accepted compulsory ICJ jurisdiction
Suffrage: 18 years of age; universal
Executive branch:
chief of state: President Fradique DE MENEZES (since 3 September 2001)
head of government: Prime Minister Maria do Carmo SILVEIRA (since 7 June 2005);
cabinet: Council of Ministers appointed by the president on the proposal of the prime minister
elections: president elected by popular vote for a five-year term; election last held 29 July 2001 (next to be held July 2006); prime minister chosen by the National

Assembly and approved by the president
election results: Fradique DE MENEZES elected president in Sao Tome's third multiparty presidential election; percent of vote - NA%
Legislative branch: unicameral National Assembly or Assembleia Nacional (55 seats; members are elected by direct, popular vote to serve four-year terms)
elections: last held 3 March 2002 (next to be held March 2006)
election results: percent of vote by party - MLSTP 39.6%, Force for Change Democratic Movement 39.4%, Ue-Kedadji coalition 16.2%; seats by party - MLSTP 24, Force for Change Democratic Movement 23, Ue-Kedadji coalition 8
Judicial branch: Supreme Court (judges are appointed by the National Assembly)
Political parties and leaders: Democratic Renovation Party [Armindo GRACA]; Force for Change Democratic Movement [leader NA]; Independent Democratic Action or ADI [Carlos NEVES]; Movement for the Liberation of Sao Tome and Principe-Social Democratic Party or MLSTP-PSD [Manuel Pinto Da COSTA]; Party for Democratic Convergence or PCD [Aldo BANDEIRA]; Ue-Kedadji coalition [leader NA]; other small parties
Political pressure groups and leaders: NA
International organization participation: ACCT, ACP, AfDB, AU, FAO, G-77, IBRD, ICAO, ICCt (signatory), ICFTU, ICRM, IDA, IFAD, IFRCS, ILO, IMF, IMO, Interpol, IOC, IOM (observer), ITU, NAM, OPCW, UN, UNCTAD, UNESCO, UNIDO, UPU, WCL, WHO, WIPO, WMO, WToO, WTO (observer)
Diplomatic representation in the US: Sao Tome and Principe does not have an embassy in the US, but does have a Permanent Mission to the UN, headed by First Secretary Domingos Augusto FERREIRA, located at 400 Park Avenue, 7th Floor, New York, NY 10022, telephone [1] (212) 317-0580
Diplomatic representation from the US: the US does not have an embassy in Sao Tome and Principe; the Ambassador to Gabon is accredited to Sao Tome and Principe on a nonresident basis and makes periodic visits to the islands
Flag description: three horizontal bands of green (top), yellow (double width), and green with two black five-pointed stars placed side by side in the center of the yellow band and a red isosceles triangle based on the hoist side; uses the popular pan-African colors of Ethiopia

ECONOMY

Economy - overview: This small poor island economy has become increasingly dependent on cocoa since independence in 1975. Cocoa production has substantially declined in recent years because of drought and mismanagement, but strengthening prices helped boost export earnings in 2003. Sao Tome has to import all fuels, most manufactured goods, consumer goods, and a substantial amount of food. Over the years, it has had difficulty servicing its external debt and has relied heavily on concessional aid and debt rescheduling. Sao Tome benefited from $200 million in debt relief in December 2000 under the Highly Indebted Poor Countries (HIPC) program, and is expected to benefit from an additional round of HIPC debt relief in early 2006, to help bring down the country's $300 million debt burden. In August 2005, Sao Tome signed on to a new 3-year IMF PRGF program worth $4.3 million. Considerable potential exists for development of a tourist industry, and the government has taken steps to expand facilities in recent years. The government also has attempted to reduce price controls and subsidies. Sao Tome is optimistic about the development of petroleum resources in its territorial waters in the oil-rich Gulf of Guinea that is being jointly developed in a 60-40 split with Nigeria. The first production licenses were sold in 2004, though a dispute over licensing with Nigeria delayed Sao Tome's receipt of more than $20 million in signing bonuses for almost a year. Real GDP growth reached 6% in 2004 and also probably in 2005 as a result of increases in public expenditures and oil-related capital investment.
GDP (purchasing power parity): $214 million (2003 est.)
GDP (official exchange rate): NA
GDP - real growth rate: 6% (2004 est.)
GDP - per capita: purchasing power parity - $1,200 (2003 est.)
GDP - composition by sector:
agriculture: 16.7%
industry: 14.8%
services: 68.4% (2005 est.)
Labor force: NA
Labor force - by occupation: population mainly engaged in subsistence agriculture and fishing
note: shortages of skilled workers
Unemployment rate: NA
Population below poverty line: 54% (2004 est.)
Household income or consumption by percentage share:
lowest 10%: NA
highest 10%: NA
Inflation rate (consumer prices): 15.1% (2005 est.)
Investment (gross fixed): 31.2% of GDP (2005 est.)
Budget:
revenues: $26.39 million
expenditures: $59.48 million, including capital expenditures of $54 million (2005 est.)
Agriculture - products: cocoa, coconuts, palm kernels, copra, cinnamon, pepper, coffee, bananas, papayas, beans; poultry; fish
Industries: light construction, textiles, soap, beer; fish processing; timber
Industrial production growth rate: NA
Electricity - production: 15 million kWh (2003)
Electricity - production by source:
fossil fuel: 41.2%
hydro: 58.8%
nuclear: 0%
other: 0% (2001)
Electricity - consumption: 13.95 million kWh (2003)
Electricity - exports: 0 kWh (2003)
Electricity - imports: 0 kWh (2003)
Oil - production: 0 bbl/day (2003 est.)
Oil - consumption: 650 bbl/day (2003 est.)
Oil - exports: NA (2001)
Oil - imports: NA (2001)
Current account balance: $-19 million (2005 est.)
Exports: $8 million f.o.b. (2005 est.)
Exports - partners: Netherlands 37.3%, China 12.8%, Belgium 7.6%, Germany 6.6%, Poland 5.3%, France 5%, Brazil 4.1% (2004)
Imports: $38 million f.o.b. (2005 est.)
Imports - partners: Portugal 52.3%, Germany 9.5%, US 6%, Netherlands 4.8%, South Africa 4.3%, Belgium 4.1% (2004)
Reserves of foreign exchange and gold: $20 million (2005 est.)
Debt - external: $318 million (2002)
Economic aid - recipient: $200 million in December 2000 under the HIPC program
Currency (code): dobra (STD)
Currency code: STD
Exchange rates: dobras per US dollar - 10,414.2 (2005), 9,900.4 (2004), 9,347.6 (2003), 9,088.3 (2002), 8,842.1 (2001)
Fiscal year: calendar year

COMMUNICATIONS

Telephones - main lines in use: 7,000 (2003)
Telephones - mobile cellular: 4,800 (2003)
Telephone system:
general assessment: adequate facilities
domestic: minimal system
international: country code - 239; satellite earth station - 1 Intelsat (Atlantic Ocean)
Radio broadcast stations: AM 1, FM 5, shortwave 1 (2002)

Radios: 38,000 (1997)
Television broadcast stations: 2 (2002)
Televisions: 23,000 (1997)
Internet country code: .st
Internet hosts: 1,069 (2003)
Internet Service Providers (ISPs): 1 (2002)
Internet users: 15,000 (2003)

TRANSPORTATION

Airports: 2 (2004 est.)
Airports - with paved runways:
total: 2
1,524 to 2,437 m: 1
914 to 1,523 m: 1 (2005 est.)
Roadways:
total: 320 km
paved: 218 km
unpaved: 102 km (1999 est.)
Merchant marine:
total: 15 ships (1,000 GRT or over) 79,490 GRT/97,077 DWT
by type: bulk carrier 2, cargo 11, chemical tanker 2
foreign-owned: 2 (Egypt 1, Greece 1) (2005)
Ports and terminals: Sao Tome

MILITARY

Military branches: Armed Forces of Sao Tome and Principe (FASTP): Army, Coast Guard, Presidential Guard (2004)
Military service age and obligation: 18 years of age (est.) (2004)
Manpower available for military service: *males age 18-49:* 33,438 (2005 est.)
Manpower fit for military service: *males age 18-49:* 25,950 (2005 est.)
Military expenditures - dollar figure: $700,000 (2004)
Military expenditures - percent of GDP: 0.8% (2004)
Military - note: Sao Tome and Principe's army is a tiny force with almost no resources at its disposal and would be wholly ineffective operating unilaterally; infantry equipment is considered simple to operate and maintain but may require refurbishment or replacement after 25 years in tropical climates; poor pay and conditions have been a problem in the past, as has alleged nepotism in the promotion of officers, as reflected in the 1995 and 2003 coups; these issues are being addressed with foreign assistance as initial steps towards the improvement of the army and its focus on realistic security concerns; command is exercised from the president, through the Minister of Defense, to the Chief of the Armed Forces staff (2005)

TRANSNATIONAL ISSUES

Disputes - international: none

SAUDI ARABIA

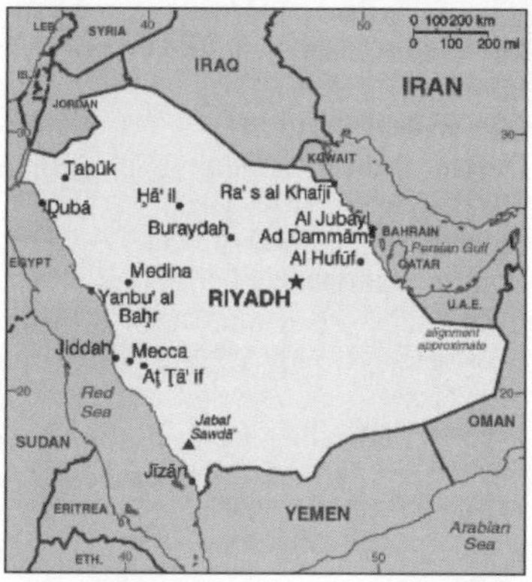

INTRODUCTION

Background: In 1902, ABD AL-AZIZ bin Abd al-Rahman Al Saud captured Riyadh and set out on a 30-year campaign to unify the Arabian Peninsula. A son of ABD AL-AZIZ rules the country today, and the country's Basic Law stipulates that the throne shall remain in the hands of the aging sons and grandsons of the kingdom's founder. Following Iraq's invasion of Kuwait in 1990, Saudi Arabia accepted the Kuwaiti royal family and 400,000 refugees while allowing Western and Arab troops to deploy on its soil for the liberation of Kuwait the following year. The continuing presence of foreign troops on Saudi soil after Operation Desert Storm remained a source of tension between the royal family and the public until the US military's near-complete withdrawal to neighboring Qatar in 2003. The first major terrorist attacks in Saudi Arabia in several years, which occurred in May and November 2003, prompted renewed efforts on the part of the Saudi government to counter domestic terrorism and extremism, which also coincided with a slight upsurge in media freedom and announcement of government plans to phase in partial political representation. As part of this effort, the government permitted elections - held nationwide from February through April 2005 - for half the members of 179 municipal councils. A burgeoning population, aquifer depletion, and an economy largely dependent on petroleum output and prices are all ongoing governmental concerns.

GEOGRAPHY

Location: Middle East, bordering the Persian Gulf and the Red Sea, north of Yemen
Geographic coordinates: 25 00 N, 45 00 E
Map references: Middle East
Area:
total: 1,960,582 sq km
land: 1,960,582 sq km
water: 0 sq km
Area - comparative: slightly more than one-fifth the size of the US
Land boundaries:
total: 4,431 km
border countries: Iraq 814 km, Jordan 744 km, Kuwait 222 km, Oman 676 km, Qatar 60 km, UAE 457 km, Yemen 1,458 km
Coastline: 2,640 km
Maritime claims:
territorial sea: 12 nm
contiguous zone: 18 nm
continental shelf: not specified
Climate: harsh, dry desert with great temperature extremes
Terrain: mostly uninhabited, sandy desert
Elevation extremes:
lowest point: Persian Gulf 0 m
highest point: Jabal Sawda' 3,133 m
Natural resources: petroleum, natural gas, iron ore, gold, copper
Land use:
arable land: 1.67%
permanent crops: 0.09%
other: 98.24% (2001)
Irrigated land: 16,200 sq km (1998 est.)
Natural hazards: frequent sand and dust storms
Environment - current issues: desertification; depletion of underground water resources; the lack of perennial rivers or permanent water bodies has prompted the development of extensive seawater desalination facilities; coastal pollution from oil spills
Environment - international agreements:
party to: Biodiversity, Climate Change, Climate Change-Kyoto Protocol, Desertification, Endangered Species, Hazardous Wastes, Law of the Sea, Ozone Layer Protection
signed, but not ratified: none of the selected agreements
Geography - note: extensive coastlines on Persian Gulf and Red Sea provide great leverage on shipping (especially crude oil) through Persian Gulf and Suez Canal

PEOPLE

Population: 26,417,599
note: includes 5,576,076 non-nationals (July 2005 est.)

Age structure:
0-14 years: 38.2% (male 5,149,960/female 4,952,138)
15-64 years: 59.4% (male 8,992,348/female 6,698,633)
65 years and over: 2.4% (male 334,694/female 289,826) (2005 est.)
Median age:
total: 21.28 years
male: 22.84 years
female: 19.28 years (2005 est.)
Population growth rate: 2.31% (2005 est.)
Birth rate: 29.56 births/1,000 population (2005 est.)
Death rate: 2.62 deaths/1,000 population (2005 est.)
Net migration rate: -3.85 migrant(s)/1,000 population (2005 est.)
Sex ratio:
at birth: 1.05 male(s)/female
under 15 years: 1.04 male(s)/female
15-64 years: 1.34 male(s)/female
65 years and over: 1.16 male(s)/female
total population: 1.21 male(s)/female (2005 est.)
Infant mortality rate:
total: 13.24 deaths/1,000 live births
male: 15.19 deaths/1,000 live births
female: 11.18 deaths/1,000 live births (2005 est.)
Life expectancy at birth:
total population: 75.46 years
male: 73.46 years
female: 77.55 years (2005 est.)
Total fertility rate: 4.05 children born/woman (2005 est.)
HIV/AIDS - adult prevalence rate: 0.01% (2001 est.)
HIV/AIDS - people living with HIV/AIDS: NA
HIV/AIDS - deaths: NA
Nationality:
noun: Saudi(s)
adjective: Saudi or Saudi Arabian
Ethnic groups: Arab 90%, Afro-Asian 10%
Religions: Muslim 100%
Languages: Arabic
Literacy:
definition: age 15 and over can read and write
total population: 78.8%
male: 84.7%
female: 70.8% (2003 est.)

GOVERNMENT

Country name:
conventional long form: Kingdom of Saudi Arabia
conventional short form: Saudi Arabia
local long form: Al Mamlakah al Arabiyah as Suudiyah
local short form: Al Arabiyah as Suudiyah
Government type: monarchy
Capital: Riyadh
Administrative divisions: 13 provinces (mintaqat, singular - mintaqah); Al Bahah, Al Hudud ash Shamaliyah, Al Jawf, Al Madinah, Al Qasim, Ar Riyad, Ash Sharqiyah (Eastern Province), 'Asir, Ha'il, Jizan, Makkah, Najran, Tabuk
Independence: 23 September 1932 (unification of the kingdom)
National holiday: Unification of the Kingdom, 23 September (1932)
Constitution: governed according to Shari'a (Islamic law); the Basic Law that articulates the government's rights and responsibilities was introduced in 1993
Legal system: based on Islamic law, several secular codes have been introduced; commercial disputes handled by special committees; has not accepted compulsory ICJ jurisdiction
Suffrage: adult male citizens age 21 or older
note: voter registration began in November 2004 for partial municipal council elections held nationwide from February through April 2005
Executive branch:
chief of state: King and Prime Minister ABDALLAH bin Abd al-Aziz Al Saud (since 1 August 2005); Heir Apparent Crown Prince SULTAN bin Abd al-Aziz Al Saud (half brother of the monarch, born 5 January 1928) note - the monarch is both the chief of state and head of government
head of government: King and Prime Minister ABDALLAH bin Abd al-Aziz Al Saud (since 1 August 2005); Heir Apparent Crown Prince SULTAN bin Abd al- Aziz Al Saud (half brother of the monarch, born 5 January 1928) note - the monarch is both the chief of state and head of government
cabinet: Council of Ministers is appointed by the monarch and includes many royal family members
elections: note - in October 2003, Council of Ministers announced its intent to introduce elections for half of the members of local and provincial assemblies and a third of the members of the national Consultative Council or Majlis al-Shura, incrementally over a period of four to five years; in November 2004, the Ministry of Municipal and Rural Affairs initiated voter registration for partial municipal council elections held nationwide from February through April 2005
Legislative branch: Consultative Council or Majlis al-Shura (120 members and a chairman appointed by the monarch for four-year terms)
Judicial branch: Supreme Council of Justice
Political parties and leaders: none
Political pressure groups and leaders: none
International organization participation: ABEDA, AfDB, AFESD, AMF, BIS, FAO, G-77, GCC, IAEA, IBRD, ICAO, ICC, ICRM, IDA, IDB, IFAD, IFC, IFRCS, ILO, IMF, IMO, Interpol, IOC, ISO, ITU, LAS, MIGA, NAM, OAPEC, OAS (observer), OIC, OPCW, OPEC, PCA, UN, UNCTAD, UNESCO, UNIDO, UPU, WCO, WFTU, WHO, WIPO, WMO, WToO, WTO (observer)
Diplomatic representation in the US:
chief of mission: Ambassador Turki al-Faysal bin Abd al-Aziz Al Saud
chancery: 601 New Hampshire Avenue NW, Washington, DC 20037
telephone: [1] (202) 342-3800
consulate(s) general: Houston, Los Angeles, and New York
Diplomatic representation from the US:
chief of mission: Ambassador James Curtis OBERWETTER
embassy: Collector Road M, Diplomatic Quarter, Riyadh
mailing address: American Embassy Riyadh, Unit 61307, APO AE 09803-1307; International Mail: P. O. Box 94309, Riyadh 11693
telephone: [966] (1) 488-3800
FAX: [966] (1) 488-3989
consulate(s) general: Dhahran, Jiddah (Jeddah)
Flag description: green, a traditional color in Islamic flags, with the Shahada or Muslim creed in large white Arabic script (translated as "There is no god but God; Muhammad is the Messenger of God") above a white horizontal saber (the tip points to the hoist side); design dates to the early twentieth century and is closely associated with the Al Saud family which established the kingdom in 1932

ECONOMY

Economy - overview: This is an oil-based economy with strong government controls over major economic activities. Saudi Arabia possesses 25% of the world's proven petroleum reserves, ranks as the largest exporter of petroleum, and plays a leading role in OPEC. The petroleum sector accounts for roughly 75% of budget revenues, 45% of GDP, and 90% of export earnings. About 40% of GDP comes from the private sector. Roughly five and a half million foreign workers play an important role in the Saudi economy, for example, in the oil and service sectors. The government is encouraging private sector growth to lessen the kingdom's dependence on oil and increase employment opportunities for the swelling Saudi population. The government has begun to permit private sector and foreign investor participation in the power generation and telecom sectors. As part of its effort to attract foreign investment and diversify the economy, Saudi Arabia this year acceded to the WTO after many years of negotiations. With high oil revenues enabling the government to post large budget surpluses, Riyadh has been able to substantially boost spending on job training and education, infrastructure development, and government salaries.

GDP (purchasing power parity): $340.5 billion (2005 est.)
GDP (official exchange rate): $281.2 billion (2005 est.)
GDP - real growth rate: 6.4% (2005 est.)
GDP - per capita: purchasing power parity - $12,900 (2005 est.)
GDP - composition by sector:
agriculture: 3.3%
industry: 74.7%
services: 21.9% (2005 est.)
Labor force: 6.76 million
note: more than 35% of the population in the 15-64 age group is non-national (2005 est.)
Labor force - by occupation: agriculture 12%, industry 25%, services 63% (1999 est.)
Unemployment rate: 13% male only (local bank estimate; some estimates range as high as 25%) (2004 est.)
Population below poverty line: NA
Household income or consumption by percentage share:
lowest 10%: NA
highest 10%: NA
Inflation rate (consumer prices): 0.6% (2005 est.)
Investment (gross fixed): 16.3% of GDP (2005 est.)
Budget:
revenues: $143.7 billion
expenditures: $89.65 billion, including capital expenditures of NA (2005 est.)
Public debt: 56.7% of GDP (2005 est.)
Agriculture - products: wheat, barley, tomatoes, melons, dates, citrus; mutton, chickens, eggs, milk
Industries: crude oil production, petroleum refining, basic petrochemicals, ammonia, industrial gases, sodium hydroxide (caustic soda), cement, construction, fertilizer, plastics, commercial ship repair, commercial aircraft repair
Industrial production growth rate: 2.8% (2005 est.)
Electricity - production: 145.1 billion kWh (2003)
Electricity - production by source:
fossil fuel: 100%
hydro: 0%
nuclear: 0%
other: 0% (2001)
Electricity - consumption: 134.9 billion kWh (2003)
Electricity - exports: 0 kWh (2003)
Electricity - imports: 0 kWh (2003)
Oil - production: 9.475 million bbl/day (2005 est.)
Oil - consumption: 1.775 million bbl/day (2003)
Oil - exports: 7.92 million bbl/day (2003)
Oil - imports: 0 bbl/day (2003)
Oil - proved reserves: 262.7 billion bbl (2005 est.)
Natural gas - production: 56.4 billion cu m (2002)
Natural gas - consumption: 56.4 billion cu m (2002)
Natural gas - exports: 0 cu m (2002)
Natural gas - imports: 0 cu m (2002)
Natural gas - proved reserves: 6.339 trillion cu m (2005)
Current account balance: $84.14 billion (2005 est.)
Exports: $165 billion f.o.b. (2005 est.)
Exports - partners: US 18.2%, Japan 14.9%, South Korea 9.5%, China 6.1%, Taiwan 4.5%, Singapore 4.1% (2004)
Imports: $44.93 billion f.o.b. (2005 est.)
Imports - partners: US 15.3%, Japan 9.8%, Germany 8.1%, China 6.6%, UK 5.7% (2004)
Reserves of foreign exchange and gold: $30.55 billion (2005 est.)
Debt - external: $34.55 billion (2005 est.)
Economic aid - donor: pledged $100 million in 1993 to fund reconstruction of Lebanon; since 2000, Saudi Arabia has committed $307 million for assistance to the Palestinians; pledged $240 million to development in Afghanistan; pledged $1 billion in export guarantees and soft loans to Iraq
Currency (code): Saudi riyal (SAR)
Currency code: SAR
Exchange rates: Saudi riyals per US dollar - 3.75 (2005), 3.745 (2004), 3.745 (2003), 3.745 (2002), 3.745 (2001)
Fiscal year: 1 March - 28 February

COMMUNICATIONS

Telephones - main lines in use: 3,502,600 (2003)
Telephones - mobile cellular: 7,238,200 (2003)
Telephone system:
general assessment: modern system
domestic: extensive microwave radio relay, coaxial cable, and fiber-optic cable systems
international: country code - 966; microwave radio relay to Bahrain, Jordan, Kuwait, Qatar, UAE, Yemen, and Sudan; coaxial cable to Kuwait and Jordan; submarine cable to Djibouti, Egypt and Bahrain; satellite earth stations - 5 Intelsat (3 Atlantic Ocean and 2 Indian Ocean), 1 Arabsat, and 1 Inmarsat (Indian Ocean region)
Radio broadcast stations: AM 43, FM 31, shortwave 2 (1998)
Radios: 6.25 million (1997)
Television broadcast stations: 117 (1997)
Televisions: 5.1 million (1997)
Internet country code: .sa
Internet hosts: 15,931 (2004)
Internet Service Providers (ISPs): 22 (2003)
Internet users: 1.5 million (2003)

TRANSPORTATION

Airports: 201 (2004 est.)
Airports - with paved runways:
total: 73
over 3,047 m: 32
2,438 to 3,047 m: 13
1,524 to 2,437 m: 24
914 to 1,523 m: 2
under 914 m: 2 (2005 est.)
Airports - with unpaved runways:
total: 129
over 3,047 m: 1
2,438 to 3,047 m: 5
1,524 to 2,437 m: 72
914 to 1,523 m: 39
under 914 m: 12 (2005 est.)
Heliports: 6 (2005 est.)
Pipelines: condensate 212 km; gas 1,780 km; liquid petroleum gas 1,191 km; oil 5,068 km; refined products 1,162 km (2004)
Railways:
total: 1,392 km
standard gauge: 1,392 km 1.435-m gauge (with branch lines and sidings) (2004)
Roadways:
total: 152,044 km
paved: 45,461 km
unpaved: 106,583 km (2000)
Merchant marine:
total: 64 ships (1,000 GRT or over) 1,306,706 GRT/1,963,191 DWT
by type: cargo 5, chemical tanker 12, container 4, passenger/cargo 8, petroleum tanker 23, refrigerated cargo 3, roll on/roll off 9
foreign-owned: 14 (Egypt 2, Hong Kong 1, Kuwait 5, Singapore 1, Sudan 1, UAE 1, United Kingdom 3)
registered in other countries: 54 (2005)
Ports and terminals: Ad Dammam, Al Jubayl, Jiddah, Yanbu' al Sinaiyah

MILITARY

Military branches: Land Forces (Army), Navy, Air Force, Air Defense Force, National Guard, Ministry of Interior Forces (paramilitary)
Military service age and obligation: 18 years of age (est.); no conscription (2004)
Manpower available for military service:
males age 18-49: 7,648,999 (2005 est.)
Manpower fit for military service: *males age 18-49:* 6,592,709 (2005 est.)

Manpower reaching military service age annually: *males:* 247,334 (2005 est.)
Military expenditures - dollar figure: $18 billion (2002)
Military expenditures - percent of GDP: 10% (2002)

TRANSNATIONAL ISSUES

Disputes - international: despite resistance from nomadic groups, the demarcation of the Saudi Arabia-Yemen boundary established under the 2000 Jeddah Treaty is almost complete; Yemen protests Saudi erection of a concrete-filled pipe as a security barrier in 2004 to stem illegal cross-border activities in sections of the boundary; Kuwait and Saudi Arabia continue discussions on a maritime boundary with Iran; because the treaties have not been made public, the exact alignment of the boundary with the UAE is still unknown
Refugees and internally displaced persons: *refugees (country of origin):* 240,000 (Palestinian Territories) (2004)
Illicit drugs: death penalty for traffickers; increasing consumption of heroin, cocaine, and hashish; not a major money-laundering center, improving anti-money-laundering legislation

SENEGAL

INTRODUCTION

Background: Independent from France in 1960, Senegal was ruled by the Socialist Party for forty years until current President Abdoulaye WADE was elected in 2000. Senegal joined with The Gambia to form the nominal confederation of Senegambia in 1982, but the envisaged integration of the two countries was never carried out, and the union was dissolved in 1989. A southern separatist group sporadically has clashed with government forces since 1982, but Senegal remains one of the most stable democracies in Africa. Senegal has a long history of participating in international peacekeeping.

GEOGRAPHY

Location: Western Africa, bordering the North Atlantic Ocean, between Guinea-Bissau and Mauritania
Geographic coordinates: 14 00 N, 14 00 W
Map references: Africa
Area:
total: 196,190 sq km
land: 192,000 sq km
water: 4,190 sq km
Area - comparative: slightly smaller than South Dakota
Land boundaries:
total: 2,640 km
border countries: The Gambia 740 km, Guinea 330 km, Guinea-Bissau 338 km, Mali 419 km, Mauritania 813 km
Coastline: 531 km
Maritime claims:
territorial sea: 12 nm
contiguous zone: 24 nm
exclusive economic zone: 200 nm
continental shelf: 200 nm or to the edge of the continental margin
Climate: tropical; hot, humid; rainy season (May to November) has strong southeast winds; dry season (December to April) dominated by hot, dry, harmattan wind
Terrain: generally low, rolling, plains rising to foothills in southeast
Elevation extremes:
lowest point: Atlantic Ocean 0 m
highest point: unnamed feature near Nepen Diakha 581 m
Natural resources: fish, phosphates, iron ore
Land use:
arable land: 12.78%
permanent crops: 0.21%
other: 87.01% (2001)
Irrigated land: 710 sq km (1998 est.)
Natural hazards: lowlands seasonally flooded; periodic droughts
Environment - current issues: wildlife populations threatened by poaching; deforestation; overgrazing; soil erosion; desertification; overfishing
Environment - international agreements:
party to: Biodiversity, Climate Change, Climate Change-Kyoto Protocol, Desertification, Endangered Species, Hazardous Wastes, Law of the Sea, Marine Life Conservation, Ozone Layer Protection, Ship Pollution, Wetlands, Whaling
Geography - note: westernmost country on the African continent; The Gambia is almost an enclave within Senegal

PEOPLE

Population: 11,126,832 (July 2005 est.)
Age structure:
0-14 years: 42.8% (male 2,404,461/female 2,360,167)
15-64 years: 54.1% (male 2,901,689/female 3,122,854)
65 years and over: 3% (male 161,173/female 176,488) (2005 est.)
Median age:
total: 18.15 years
male: 17.6 years
female: 18.7 years (2005 est.)
Population growth rate: 2.48% (2005 est.)
Birth rate: 35.21 births/1,000 population (2005 est.)
Death rate: 10.6 deaths/1,000 population (2005 est.)
Net migration rate: 0.2 migrant(s)/1,000 population (2005 est.)
Sex ratio:
at birth: 1.03 male(s)/female
under 15 years: 1.02 male(s)/female
15-64 years: 0.93 male(s)/female
65 years and over: 0.91 male(s)/female
total population: 0.97 male(s)/female (2005 est.)
Infant mortality rate:
total: 55.51 deaths/1,000 live births
male: 59.17 deaths/1,000 live births
female: 51.75 deaths/1,000 live births (2005 est.)
Life expectancy at birth:
total population: 58.9 years
male: 57.37 years
female: 60.47 years (2005 est.)
Total fertility rate: 4.75 children born/woman (2005 est.)
HIV/AIDS - adult prevalence rate: 0.8% (2003 est.)
HIV/AIDS - people living with HIV/AIDS: 44,000 (2003 est.)
HIV/AIDS - deaths: 3,500 (2003 est.)
Major infectious diseases:
degree of risk: very high
food or waterborne diseases: bacterial and protozoal diarrhea, hepatitis A, and typhoid fever
vectorborne diseases: dengue fever, malaria, yellow fever, Crimean-Congo hemorrhagic fever, and Rift Valley fever are high risks in some locations
water contact disease: schistosomiasis
respiratory disease: meningococcal meningitis (2004)
Nationality:
noun: Senegalese (singular and plural)
adjective: Senegalese
Ethnic groups: Wolof 43.3%, Pular 23.8%, Serer 14.7%, Jola 3.7%, Mandinka 3%,

Soninke 1.1%, European and Lebanese 1%, other 9.4%
Religions: Muslim 94%, indigenous beliefs 1%, Christian 5% (mostly Roman Catholic)
Languages: French (official), Wolof, Pulaar, Jola, Mandinka
Literacy:
definition: age 15 and over can read and write
total population: 40.2%
male: 50%
female: 30.7% (2003 est.)

GOVERNMENT

Country name:
conventional long form: Republic of Senegal
conventional short form: Senegal
local long form: Republique du Senegal
local short form: Senegal
Government type: republic under multiparty democratic rule
Capital: Dakar
Administrative divisions: 11 regions (regions, singular - region); Dakar, Diourbel, Fatick, Kaolack, Kolda, Louga, Matam, Saint-Louis, Tambacounda, Thies, Ziguinchor
Independence: 4 April 1960 (from France); note - complete independence was achieved upon dissolution of federation with Mali on 20 August 1960
National holiday: Independence Day, 4 April (1960)
Constitution: new constitution adopted 7 January 2001
Legal system: based on French civil law system; judicial review of legislative acts in Constitutional Court; the Council of State audits the government's accounting office; has not accepted compulsory ICJ jurisdiction
Suffrage: 18 years of age; universal
Executive branch:
chief of state: President Abdoulaye WADE (since 1 April 2000)
head of government: Prime Minister Macky SALL (since 21 April 2004)
cabinet: Council of Ministers appointed by the prime minister in consultation with the president
elections: president elected by popular vote for a five-year term under new constitution; election last held under prior constitution (seven-year terms) 27 February and 19 March 2000 (next to be held February 2007); prime minister appointed by the president
election results: Abdoulaye WADE elected president; percent of vote in the second round of voting - Abdoulaye WADE (PDS) 58.49%, Abdou DIOUF (PS) 41.51%
Legislative branch: unicameral National Assembly or Assemblee Nationale (120 seats; members are elected by direct, popular vote to serve five-year terms)
note: the former National Assembly, dissolved in the spring of 2001, had 140 seats
elections: last held 29 April 2001 (next to be held NA 2007) note - the National Assembly in December 2005 voted to postpone legislative elections originally scheduled for 2006, they will now coincide with presidential elections in 2007
election results: percent of vote by party - NA%; seats by party - SOPI Coalition 89, AFP 11, PS 10, other 10
Judicial branch: Constitutional Court; Council of State; Court of Final Appeals or Cour de Cassation; Court of Appeals; note - the judicial system was reformed in 1992
Political parties and leaders: African Party for Democracy and Socialism or And Jef (also known as PADS/AJ) [Landing SAVANE, secretary general]; African Party of Independence [Majhemout DIOP]; Alliance of Forces of Progress or AFP [Moustapha NIASSE]; Democratic and Patriotic Convention or CDP (also known as Garab-Gi) [Dr. Iba Der THIAM]; Democratic League-Labor Party Movement or LD-MPT [Dr. Abdoulaye BATHILY]; Front for Socialism and Democracy or FSD [Cheikh Abdoulaye DIEYE]; Gainde Centrist Bloc or BGC [Jean-Paul DIAS]; Independence and Labor Party or PIT [Amath DANSOKHO]; National Democratic Rally or RND [Madier DIOUF]; Senegalese Democratic Party or PDS [Abdoulaye WADE]; Socialist Party or PS [Ousmane Tanor DIENG]; SOPI Coalition (a coalition led by the PDS) [Abdoulaye WADE]; Union for Democratic Renewal or URD [Djibo Leyti KA]; other small parties
Political pressure groups and leaders: labor; Muslim brotherhoods; students; teachers
International organization participation: ACCT, ACP, AfDB, AU, CEMAC, ECOWAS, FAO, FZ, G-15, G-77, IAEA, IBRD, ICAO, ICC, ICCt, ICFTU, ICRM, IDA, IDB, IFAD, IFC, IFRCS, ILO, IMF, IMO, Interpol, IOC, IOM, ISO (correspondent), ITU, MIGA, MONUC, NAM, OIC, ONUB, OPCW, PCA, UN, UNCTAD, UNESCO, UNIDO, UNMIL, UNMOVIC, UNOCI, UPU, WADB (regional), WAEMU, WCL, WCO, WFTU, WHO, WIPO, WMO, WToO, WTO
Diplomatic representation in the US:
chief of mission: Ambassador Amadou Lamine BA
chancery: 2112 Wyoming Avenue NW, Washington, DC 20008
telephone: [1] (202) 234-0540
FAX: [1] (202) 332-6315
consulate(s) general: New York
Diplomatic representation from the US:
chief of mission: Ambassador (vacant)
embassy: Avenue Jean XXIII at the corner of Rue Kleber, Dakar
mailing address: B. P. 49, Dakar
telephone: [221] 823-4296
FAX: [221] 822-2991
Flag description: three equal vertical bands of green (hoist side), yellow, and red with a small green five-pointed star centered in the yellow band; uses the popular pan-African colors of Ethiopia

ECONOMY

Economy - overview: In January 1994, Senegal undertook a bold and ambitious economic reform program with the support of the international donor community. This reform began with a 50% devaluation of Senegal's currency, the CFA franc, which was linked at a fixed rate to the French franc. Government price controls and subsidies have been steadily dismantled. After seeing its economy contract by 2.1% in 1993, Senegal made an important turnaround, thanks to the reform program, with real growth in GDP averaging over 5% annually during 1995-2004. Annual inflation had been pushed down to the low single digits. As a member of the West African Economic and Monetary Union (WAEMU), Senegal is working toward greater regional integration with a unified external tariff and a more stable monetary policy. Senegal still relies heavily upon outside donor assistance, however. Under the IMF's Highly Indebted Poor Countries debt relief program, Senegal will benefit from eradication of two-thirds of its bilateral, multilateral, and private sector debt.
GDP (purchasing power parity): $20.56 billion (2005 est.)
GDP (official exchange rate): $8.281 billion (2005 est.)
GDP - real growth rate: 6.1% (2005 est.)
GDP - per capita: purchasing power parity - $1,800 (2005 est.)
GDP - composition by sector:
agriculture: 16.1%
industry: 21.4%
services: 62.5% (2005 est.)
Labor force: 4.82 million (2005 est.)
Labor force - by occupation: agriculture 77% (1990 est.)
Unemployment rate: 48% (urban youth 40%) (2001 est.)
Population below poverty line: 54% (2001 est.)
Household income or consumption by percentage share:
lowest 10%: 2.6%

highest 10%: 33.5% (1995)
Distribution of family income - Gini index: 41.3 (1995)
Inflation rate (consumer prices): 1.7% (2005 est.)
Investment (gross fixed): 22.4% of GDP (2005 est.)
Budget:
revenues: $1.657 billion
expenditures: $1.926 billion, including capital expenditures of $357 million (2005 est.)
Public debt: 46.5% of GDP (2005 est.)
Agriculture - products: peanuts, millet, corn, sorghum, rice, cotton, tomatoes, green vegetables; cattle, poultry, pigs; fish
Industries: agricultural and fish processing, phosphate mining, fertilizer production, petroleum refining, construction materials, ship construction and repair
Industrial production growth rate: 2% (2005 est.)
Electricity - production: 1.332 billion kWh (2003)
Electricity - production by source:
fossil fuel: 100%
hydro: 0%
nuclear: 0%
other: 0% (2001)
Electricity - consumption: 1.239 billion kWh (2003)
Electricity - exports: 0 kWh (2003)
Electricity - imports: 0 kWh (2003)
Oil - production: 0 bbl/day (2003 est.)
Oil - consumption: 31,000 bbl/day (2003 est.)
Oil - exports: NA
Oil - imports: NA
Natural gas - production: 50 million cu m (2001 est.)
Natural gas - consumption: 50 million cu m (2001 est.)
Natural gas - exports: 0 cu m (2001 est.)
Natural gas - imports: 0 cu m (2001 est.)
Current account balance: $-638 million (2005 est.)
Exports: $1.526 billion f.o.b. (2005 est.)
Exports - partners: India 14.4%, Mali 13.1%, France 9.8%, Italy 7.3%, Spain 6.6%, Guinea-Bissau 5.6%, Gambia, The 4.8% (2004)
Imports: $2.405 billion f.o.b. (2005 est.)
Imports - partners: France 24.8%, Nigeria 11.9%, Thailand 6.1% (2004)
Reserves of foreign exchange and gold: $1.324 billion (2005 est.)
Debt - external: $3.61 billion (2003 est.)
Economic aid - recipient: $449.6 million (2003 est.)
Currency (code): Communaute Financiere Africaine franc (XOF); note - responsible authority is the Central Bank of the West African States
Currency code: XOF
Exchange rates: Communaute Financiere Africaine francs (XOF) per US dollar - 522.78 (2005), 528.29 (2004), 581.2 (2003), 696.99 (2002), 733.04 (2001)
Fiscal year: calendar year

COMMUNICATIONS

Telephones - main lines in use: 228,800 (2003)
Telephones - mobile cellular: 575,900 (2003)
Telephone system:
general assessment: good system
domestic: above-average urban system; microwave radio relay, coaxial cable and fiber-optic cable in trunk system
international: country code - 221; 4 submarine cables; satellite earth station - 1 Intelsat (Atlantic Ocean)
Radio broadcast stations: AM 8, FM 20, shortwave 1 (2001)
Radios: 1.24 million (1997)
Television broadcast stations: 1 (1997)
Televisions: 361,000 (1997)
Internet country code: .sn
Internet hosts: 672 (2003)
Internet Service Providers (ISPs): 1 (2002)
Internet users: 225,000 (2003)

TRANSPORTATION

Airports: 20 (2004 est.)
Airports - with paved runways:
total: 9
over 3,047 m: 1
1,524 to 2,437 m: 6
914 to 1,523 m: 2 (2005 est.)
Airports - with unpaved runways:
total: 11
1,524 to 2,437 m: 6
914 to 1,523 m: 4
under 914 m: 1 (2005 est.)
Pipelines: gas 564 km (2004)
Railways:
total: 906 km
narrow gauge: 906 km 1.000-meter gauge (2004)
Roadways:
total: 14,576 km
paved: 4,271 km including 7 km of expressways
unpaved: 10,305 km (2000)
Waterways: 1,000 km (primarily on Senegal, Saloum, and Casamance rivers) (2003)
Ports and terminals: Dakar

MILITARY

Military branches: Army, Navy (Marine Senegalaise), Air Force (2005)
Military service age and obligation: 18 years of age for compulsory and voluntary military service; conscript service obligation - 2 years (2004)
Manpower available for military service: *males age 18-49*: 2,183,343 (2005 est.)
Manpower fit for military service: *males age 18-49*: 1,300,502 (2005 est.)
Manpower reaching military service age annually: *males*: 124,096 (2005 est.)
Military expenditures - dollar figure: $107.3 million (2004)
Military expenditures - percent of GDP: 1.5% (2004)

TRANSNATIONAL ISSUES

Disputes - international: The Gambia and Guinea-Bissau attempt to stem Senegalese citizens from the Casamance region fleeing separatist violence, cross border raids, and arms smuggling
Refugees and internally displaced persons: *IDPs*: 17,000 (clashes between government troops and separatists in Casamance region) (2004)
Illicit drugs: transshipment point for Southwest and Southeast Asian heroin and South American cocaine moving to Europe and North America; illicit cultivator of cannabis

SERBIA AND MONTENEGRO

INTRODUCTION

Background: The Kingdom of Serbs, Croats, and Slovenes was formed in 1918; its name was changed to Yugoslavia in 1929. Occupation by Nazi Germany in 1941 was resisted by various paramilitary bands that fought each other as well as the invaders. The group headed by Josip TITO took full control of Yugoslavia upon German expulsion in 1945. Although Communist, his new government and its successors (he died in 1980) managed to steer their own path between the Warsaw Pact nations and the West for the next four and a half decades. In the early 1990s, post-TITO Yugoslavia began to unravel along ethnic lines: Slovenia, Croatia, Macedonia, and Bosnia and Herzegovina were recognized as independent states in 1992. The remaining republics of Serbia and Montenegro declared a new "Federal Republic of Yugoslavia" (FRY) in April 1992 and, under President Slobodan MILOSEVIC, Serbia led various military intervention efforts to unite ethnic Serbs in neighboring republics into a "Greater Serbia." These actions led to Yugoslavia being ousted from the UN in

1992, but Serbia continued its campaign until signing the Dayton Peace Accords in 1995. In 1998-99, massive expulsions by FRY forces and Serb paramilitaries of ethnic Albanians living in Kosovo provoked an international response, including the NATO bombing of Belgrade and the stationing of a NATO-led force (KFOR), in Kosovo. Federal elections in the fall of 2000, brought about the ouster of MILOSEVIC and installed Vojislav KOSTUNICA as president. The arrest of MILOSEVIC in 2001 allowed for his subsequent transfer to the International Criminal Tribunal for the Former Yugoslavia in The Hague to be tried for crimes against humanity. In 2001, the country's suspension from the UN was lifted, and it was once more accepted into UN organizations under the name of the Federal Republic of Yugoslavia. Kosovo has been governed by the UN Interim Administration Mission in Kosovo (UNMIK) since June 1999, under the authority of UN Security Council Resolution 1244, pending a determination by the international community of its future status. In 2002, the Serbian and Montenegrin components of Yugoslavia began negotiations to forge a looser relationship. In February 2003 lawmakers restructured the country into a loose federation of two republics called Serbia and Montenegro. The Constitutional Charter of Serbia and Montenegro includes a provision that allows either republic to hold a referendum after three years that would allow for their independence from the state union. In 2003 Svetozar MAROVIC was elected president of Serbia and Montenegro.

GEOGRAPHY

Location: Southeastern Europe, bordering the Adriatic Sea, between Albania and Bosnia and Herzegovina
Geographic coordinates: 44 00 N, 21 00 E
Map references: Europe
Area:
total: 102,350 sq km
land: 102,136 sq km
water: 214 sq km
Area - comparative: slightly smaller than Kentucky
Land boundaries:
total: 2,246 km
border countries: Albania 287 km, Bosnia and Herzegovina 527 km, Bulgaria 318 km, Croatia (north) 241 km, Croatia (south) 25 km, Hungary 151 km, Macedonia 221 km, Romania 476 km
Coastline: 199 km
Maritime claims: NA
Climate: in the north, continental climate (cold winters and hot, humid summers with well distributed rainfall); central portion, continental and Mediterranean climate; to the south, Adriatic climate along the coast, hot, dry summers and autumns and relatively cold winters with heavy snowfall inland
Terrain: extremely varied; to the north, rich fertile plains; to the east, limestone ranges and basins; to the southeast, ancient mountains and hills; to the southwest, extremely high shoreline with no islands off the coast
Elevation extremes:
lowest point: Adriatic Sea 0 m
highest point: Daravica 2,656 m
Natural resources: oil, gas, coal, iron ore, bauxite, copper, lead, zinc, antimony, chromite, nickel, gold, silver, magnesium, pyrite, limestone, marble, salt, hydropower, arable land
Land use:
arable land: 33.35%
permanent crops: 3.2%
other: 63.45% (2001)
Irrigated land: 570 sq km
Natural hazards: destructive earthquakes
Environment - current issues: pollution of coastal waters from sewage outlets, especially in tourist-related areas such as Kotor; air pollution around Belgrade and other industrial cities; water pollution from industrial wastes dumped into the Sava which flows into the Danube
Environment - international agreements:
party to: Air Pollution, Biodiversity, Climate Change, Endangered Species, Hazardous Wastes, Law of the Sea, Marine Dumping, Marine Life Conservation, Ozone Layer Protection, Ship Pollution, Wetlands
signed, but not ratified: none of the selected agreements
Geography - note: controls one of the major land routes from Western Europe to Turkey and the Near East; strategic location along the Adriatic coast

PEOPLE

Population: 10,829,175 (July 2005 est.)
Age structure:
0-14 years: 18.1% (male 1,014,443/female 943,702)
15-64 years: 66.9% (male 3,610,646/female 3,632,365)
65 years and over: 15% (male 699,446/female 928,573) (2005 est.)
Median age:
total: 36.79 years
male: 35.3 years
female: 38.29 years (2005 est.)
Population growth rate: 0.03% (2005 est.)
Birth rate: 12.12 births/1,000 population (2005 est.)
Death rate: 10.49 deaths/1,000 population (2005 est.)
Net migration rate: -1.3 migrant(s)/1,000 population (2005 est.)
Sex ratio:
at birth: 1.08 male(s)/female
under 15 years: 1.08 male(s)/female
15-64 years: 0.99 male(s)/female
65 years and over: 0.75 male(s)/female
total population: 0.97 male(s)/female (2005 est.)
Infant mortality rate:
total: 12.89 deaths/1,000 live births
male: 14.54 deaths/1,000 live births
female: 11.1 deaths/1,000 live births (2005 est.)
Life expectancy at birth:
total population: 74.73 years
male: 72.15 years
female: 77.51 years (2005 est.)
Total fertility rate: 1.67 children born/woman (2005 est.)
HIV/AIDS - adult prevalence rate: 0.2% (2001 est.)
HIV/AIDS - people living with HIV/AIDS: 10,000 (2001 est.)
HIV/AIDS - deaths: less than 100 (2003 est.)
Nationality:
noun: Serb(s); Montenegrin(s)
adjective: Serbian; Montenegrin
Ethnic groups: Serb 62.6%, Albanian 16.5%, Montenegrin 5%, Hungarian 3.3%, other 12.6% (1991)
Religions: Orthodox 65%, Muslim 19%, Roman Catholic 4%, Protestant 1%, other 11%
Languages: Serbian 95%, Albanian 5%
Literacy:
definition: age 15 and over can read and write
total population: 96.4%
male: 98.9%
female: 94.1% (2002 est.)

GOVERNMENT

Country name:
conventional long form: Serbia and Montenegro

conventional short form: none
local long form: Srbija i Crna Gora
local short form: none
former: Federal Republic of Yugoslavia
abbreviation: SCG
Government type: republic
Capital: Belgrade
Administrative divisions: 2 republics (republike, singular - republika); and 2 nominally autonomous provinces (both in the republic of Serbia)* (autonomn pokrajine, singular - autonomna pokrajina); Kosovo* (temporarily under UN administration, per UN Security Council Resolution 1244), Montenegro, Serbia, Vojvodina*
Independence: 27 April 1992 (Federal Republic of Yugoslavia or FRY - now Serbia and Montenegro - formed as self-proclaimed successor to the Socialist Federal Republic of Yugoslavia or SFRY)
National holiday: National Day, 27 April
Constitution: 4 February 2003
Legal system: based on civil law system
Suffrage: 16 years of age, if employed; 18 years of age, universal
Executive branch:
chief of state: President Svetozar MAROVIC (since 7 March 2003); note - the president is both the chief of state and head of government
head of government: President Svetozar MAROVIC (since 7 March 2003); note - the president is both the chief of state and head of government
cabinet: Federal Ministries act as Cabinet
elections: president elected by the parliament for a four-year term; election last held 7 March 2003 (next to be held 2007)
election results: Svetozar MAROVIC elected president by the parliament; vote was Svetozar MAROVIC 65, other 47
Legislative branch: unicameral Parliament (126 seats - 91 Serbian, 35 Montenegrin - filled by nominees of the two state parliaments for the first two years, after which the Constitutional Charter calls for direct elections
elections: last held 25 February 2003 (next to be held 2006 in Montenegro and 2007 in Serbia)
election results: percent of vote by party - NA%; seats by party - Serbian parties: SRS 30, DSS 20, DS 13, G17 Plus 12, SPO-NS 8, SPS 8; Montenegrin parties: DPS 15, SNP 9, SDP 4, DSS 3, NS 2, LSCG 2
Judicial branch: The Court of Serbia and Montenegro; judges are elected by the Serbia and Montenegro Parliament for six-year terms
note: since the promulgation of the 2003 Constitution, the Federal Court has constitutional and administrative functions; it has an equal number of judges from each republic
Political parties and leaders: Democratic Party or DS [Boris TADIC]; Democratic Party of Serbia or DSS [Vojislav KOSTUNICA]; Democratic Party of Socialists of Montenegro or DPS [Milo DJUKANOVIC]; Democratic Serbian Party of Montenegro or DSS [Bozidar BOJOVIC]; G17 Plus [Miroljub LABUS]; New Serbia or NS [Velimir ILIC]; Liberal Party of Montenegro or LSCG [Miodrag ZIVKOVIC]; People's Party of Montenegro or NS [Predrag POPOVIC]; Power of Serbia Movement or PSS [Bogoljub KARIC]; Serbian Peoples' Party of Montenegro or SNS [Andrija MANDIC]; Serbian Radical Party or SRS [Tomislav NIKOLIC]; Serbian Renewal Movement or SPO [Vuk DRASKOVIC]; Serbian Socialist Party or SPS (former Communist Party and party of Slobodan MILOSEVIC) [Ivica DACIC, president of Main Board]; Social Democratic Party of Montenegro or SDP [Ranko KRIVOKAPIC]; Socialist People's Party of Montenegro or SNP [Predrag BULATOVIC]
note: the following political parties participate in elections and institutions only in Kosovo, which has been governed by the UN under UNSCR 1244 since 1999: Albanian Christian Democratic Party or PSHDK [Mark KRASNIQI]; Alliance for the Future of Kosovo or AAK [Ramush HARADINAJ]; Citizens' Initiative of Gora or GIG [leader NA]; Democratic Ashkali Party of Kosovo or PDAK [Sabit RRAHMANI]; Democratic League of Kosovo or LDK [Ibrahim RUGOVA]; Democratic Party of Kosovo or PDK [Hashim THACI]; Justice Party or PD [Sylejman CERKEZI]; Kosovo Democratic Turkish Party of KDTP [Mahir YAGCILAR]; Liberal Party of Kosovo or PLK [Gjergj DEDAJ]; Ora [Veton SURROI]; New Democratic Initiative of Kosovo or IRDK [Bislim HOTI]; Party of Democratic Action or SDA [Numan BALIC]; Popular Movement of Kosovo or LPK [Emrush XHEMAJLI]; Prizren-Dragas Initiative or PDI [Ismajl KARADOLAMI]; Serb Democratic Party or SDS [Slavisa PETKOVIC]; Serb List for Kosovo and Metohija or SLKM [Oliver IVANOVIC]; United Roma Party of Kosovo or PREBK [Haxhi Zylfi MERXHA]; Vakat [leader NA]
Political pressure groups and leaders: Political Council for Presevo, Medvedja and Bujanovac or PCPMB [leader NA]; Group for Changes of Montenegro or GZP [Nebojsa MEDOJEVIC]
International organization participation: BIS, BSEC, CE, CEI, EBRD, FAO, G-9, IAEA, IBRD, ICAO, ICC, ICCt, ICFTU, ICRM, IDA, IFAD, IFC, IFRCS, IHO, ILO, IMF, IMO, Interpol, IOC, IOM, ISO, ITU, MIGA, MONUC, NAM, OAS (observer), ONUB, OPCW, OSCE, PCA, UN, UNCTAD, UNESCO, UNHCR, UNIDO, UNMIL, UNOCI, UPU, WCL, WCO, WHO, WIPO, WMO, WToO, WTO (observer)
Diplomatic representation in the US:
chief of mission: Ambassador Ivan VUJACIC
chancery: 2134 Kalorama Road NW, Washington, DC 20008
telephone: [1] (202) 332-0333
FAX: [1] (202) 332-3933
consulate(s) general: Chicago
Diplomatic representation from the US:
chief of mission: Ambassador Michael C. POLT
embassy: Kneza Milosa 50, 11000 Belgrade
mailing address: 5070 Belgrade Place, Washington, DC 20521-5070
telephone: [381] (11) 361-9344
FAX: [381] (11) 361-8230
consulate(s): Podgorica
note: there is a branch office in Pristina at 30 Nazim Hikmet 38000 Pristina, Kosovo; telephone: [381](38)549-516; FAX: [381](38)549-890
Flag description: three equal horizontal bands of blue (top), white, and red

ECONOMY

Economy - overview: MILOSEVIC-era mismanagement of the economy, an extended period of economic sanctions, and the damage to Yugoslavia's infrastructure and industry during the NATO airstrikes in 1999 left the economy only half the size it was in 1990. After the ousting of former Federal Yugoslav President MILOSEVIC in October 2000, the Democratic Opposition of Serbia (DOS) coalition government implemented stabilization measures and embarked on an aggressive market reform program. After renewing its membership in the IMF in December 2000, a down-sized Yugoslavia continued to reintegrate into the international community by rejoining the World Bank (IBRD) and the European Bank for Reconstruction and Development (EBRD). A World Bank-European Commission sponsored Donors' Conference held in June 2001 raised $1.3 billion for economic restructuring. An agreement rescheduling the country's $4.5 billion Paris Club government debts was concluded in November 2001 - it wrote off 66% of the debt - and the London Club of private creditors forgave $1.7 billion of

debt, just over half the total owed, in July 2004. The smaller republic of Montenegro severed its economy from federal control and from Serbia during the MILOSEVIC era and continues to maintain its own central bank, uses the euro instead of the Yugoslav dinar as official currency, collects customs tariffs, and manages its own budget. Kosovo's economy continues to transition to a market-based system, and is largely dependent on the international community and the diaspora for financial and technical assistance. The euro and the Yugoslav dinar are both accepted currencies in Kosovo. While maintaining ultimate oversight, UNMIK continues to work with the European Union and Kosovo's local provisional government to accelerate economic growth, lower unemployment, and attract foreign investment to help Kosovo integrate into regional economic structures. The complexity of Serbia and Montenegro political relationships, slow progress in privatization, legal uncertainty over property rights, scarcity of foreign-investment and a substantial foreign trade deficit are holding back the economy. Arrangements with the IMF, especially requirements for fiscal discipline, are an important element in policy formation. Severe unemployment remains a key political economic problem for this entire region.
GDP (purchasing power parity): $28.37 billion (2005 est.)
GDP (official exchange rate): $25.46 billion (2005 est.)
GDP - real growth rate: 4% (2005 est.)
GDP - per capita: purchasing power parity - $2,600 (2005 est.)
GDP - composition by sector:
agriculture: 16.6%
industry: 25.5%
services: 57.9% (2005 est.)
Labor force: 3.22 million (2005 est.)
Labor force - by occupation: agriculture NA, industry NA, services NA
Unemployment rate: 31.6%
note: unemployment is approximately 50% in Kosovo (2005 est.)
Population below poverty line: 30% (1999 est.)
Household income or consumption by percentage share:
lowest 10%: NA%
highest 10%: NA%
Inflation rate (consumer prices): 15.5% (2005 est.)
Investment (gross fixed): 14.2% of GDP (2005 est.)
Budget:
revenues: $11.45 billion
expenditures: $11.12 billion, including capital expenditures of NA (2005 est.)
Public debt: 53.1% of GDP (2005 est.)
Agriculture - products: cereals, fruits, vegetables, tobacco, olives; cattle, sheep, goats
Industries: machine building (aircraft, trucks, and automobiles; tanks and weapons; electrical equipment; agricultural machinery); metallurgy (steel, aluminum, copper, lead, zinc, chromium, antimony, bismuth, cadmium); mining (coal, bauxite, nonferrous ore, iron ore, limestone); consumer goods (textiles, footwear, foodstuffs, appliances); electronics, petroleum products, chemicals, and pharmaceuticals
Industrial production growth rate: 1.7% (2002 est.)
Electricity - production: 36.04 billion kWh (2003)
Electricity - production by source:
fossil fuel: 62.9%
hydro: 37.1%
nuclear: 0%
other: 0% (2001)
Electricity - consumption: 36.62 billion kWh (2003)
Electricity - exports: 400 million kWh (2003)
Electricity - imports: 3.5 billion kWh (2003)
Oil - production: 14,660 bbl/day (2003)
Oil - consumption: 85,000 bbl/day (2003 est.)
Oil - exports: NA (2001)
Oil - imports: NA (2001)
Oil - proved reserves: 38.75 million bbl (1 January 2002)
Natural gas - production: 602 million cu m (2001 est.)
Natural gas - consumption: 602 million cu m (2001 est.)
Natural gas - exports: 0 cu m (2001 est.)
Natural gas - imports: 0 cu m (2001 est.)
Natural gas - proved reserves: 24.07 billion cu m (1 January 2002)
Current account balance: $-2.451 billion (2005 est.)
Exports: $5.485 billion f.o.b. (2005 est.)
Exports - partners: Italy 29%, Germany 16.6%, Austria 7%, Greece 6.7%, France 4.9%, Slovenia 4.1% (2004)
Imports: $11.94 billion f.o.b. (2005 est.)
Imports - partners: Germany 18.5%, Italy 16.5%, Austria 8.3%, Slovenia 6.7%, Bulgaria 4.7%, France 4.5% (2004)
Reserves of foreign exchange and gold: $5.35 billion (2005 est.)
Debt - external: $15.43 billion (2005 est.)
Economic aid - recipient: $2 billion pledged in 2001 (disbursements to follow for several years)
Currency (code): new Yugoslav dinar (YUM); note - in Montenegro the euro is legal tender; in Kosovo both the euro and the Yugoslav dinar are legal
Currency code: CSD, EUR
Exchange rates: new Yugoslav dinars per US dollar - 66.57 (official rate: 65) (2002)
Fiscal year: calendar year

COMMUNICATIONS

Telephones - main lines in use: 2,611,700 (2003)
Telephones - mobile cellular: 3,634,600 (2003)
Telephone system:
general assessment: NA
domestic: NA
international: country code - 381; satellite earth station - 1 Intelsat (Atlantic Ocean)
Radio broadcast stations: AM 113, FM 194, shortwave 2 (1998)
Radios: 3.15 million (1997)
Television broadcast stations: more than 771 (including 86 strong stations and 685 low-power stations, plus 20 repeaters in the principal networks; also numerous local or private stations in Serbia and Vojvodina) (1997)
Televisions: 2.75 million (1997)
Internet country code: .cs
Internet hosts: 20,207 (2004)
Internet Service Providers (ISPs): 9 (2000)
Internet users: 847,000 (2003)

TRANSPORTATION

Airports: 44 (2004 est.)
Airports - with paved runways:
total: 19
over 3,047 m: 2
2,438 to 3,047 m: 5
1,524 to 2,437 m: 6
914 to 1,523 m: 2
under 914 m: 4 (2005 est.)
Airports - with unpaved runways:
total: 25
1,524 to 2,437 m: 2
914 to 1,523 m: 10
under 914 m: 13 (2005 est.)
Heliports: 4 (2005 est.)
Pipelines: gas 3,177 km; oil 393 km (2004)
Railways:
total: 4,380 km
standard gauge: 4,380 km 1.435-m gauge (1,364 km electrified) (2004)
Roadways:
total: 45,290 km
paved: 28,261 km (including 374 km of expressways)
unpaved: 17,029 km (2002)
Waterways: 587 km
note: Danube River traffic delayed by pontoon bridge at Novi Sad; plan to replace by summer of 2005 (2004)
Merchant marine:
total: 2
by type: cargo 1, chemical tanker 1
foreign-owned: 2 (Finland 1, Turkey 1)

registered in other countries: 3 (2005)
Ports and terminals: Bar

MILITARY

Military branches: Serbian and Montenegrin Armed Forces (Vojska Srbije i Crne Gore, VSCG): Ground Forces, Air and Air Defense Forces, Naval Forces (2005)
Military service age and obligation: 19 years of age (nine months compulsory service) (2004)
Manpower available for military service: *males age 19-49:* 2,389,729 (2005 est.)
Manpower fit for military service: *males age 19-49:* 1,959,166 (2005 est.)
Manpower reaching military service age annually: *males:* 81,033 (2005 est.)
Military expenditures - dollar figure: $654 million (2002)
Military expenditures - percent of GDP: NA

TRANSNATIONAL ISSUES

Disputes - international: Kosovo remains unresolved administered by several thousand peacekeepers from the UN Interim Administration Mission in Kosovo (UNMIK) since 1999, with Kosovar Albanians overwhelmingly supporting and Serbian officials opposing Kosovo independence; the international community had agreed to begin a process to determine final status but contingency of solidifying multi-ethnic democracy in Kosovo has not been satisfied; ethnic Albanians in Kosovo refuse demarcation of the boundary with Macedonia in accordance with the 2000 Macedonia-Serbia and Montenegro delimitation agreement; Serbia and Montenegro have delimited about half of the boundary with Bosnia and Herzegovina, but sections along the Drina River remain in dispute
Refugees and internally displaced persons: *refugees (country of origin):* 99,170 (Bosnia) 188,656 (Croatia)
IDPs: 225,000 (mostly ethnic Serbs and Roma who fled Kosovo in 1999) (2004)
Illicit drugs: transshipment point for Southwest Asian heroin moving to Western Europe on the Balkan route; economy vulnerable to money laundering

SEYCHELLES

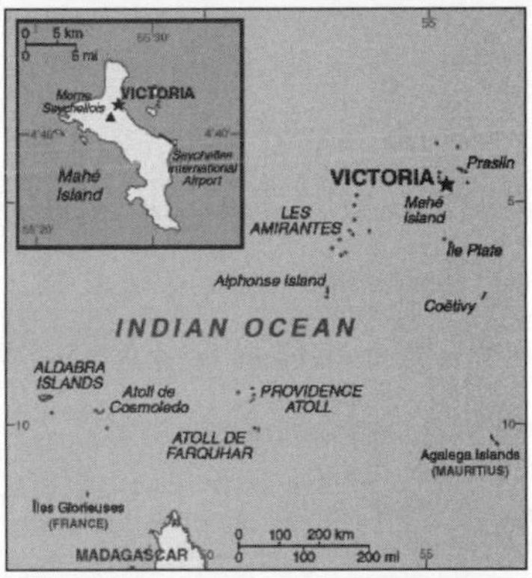

INTRODUCTION

Background: A lengthy struggle between France and Great Britain for the islands ended in 1814, when they were ceded to the latter. Independence came in 1976. Socialist rule was brought to a close with a new constitution and free elections in 1993. The most recent presidential elections were held in 2001; President RENE, who had served since 1977, was re-elected. In April 2004 RENE stepped down and Vice President James MICHEL was sworn in as president.

GEOGRAPHY

Location: archipelago in the Indian Ocean, northeast of Madagascar
Geographic coordinates: 4 35 S, 55 40 E
Map references: Africa
Area:
total: 455 sq km
land: 455 sq km
water: 0 sq km
Area - comparative: 2.5 times the size of Washington, DC
Land boundaries: 0 km
Coastline: 491 km
Maritime claims:
territorial sea: 12 nm
contiguous zone: 24 nm
exclusive economic zone: 200 nm
continental shelf: 200 nm or to the edge of the continental margin
Climate: tropical marine; humid; cooler season during southeast monsoon (late May to September); warmer season during northwest monsoon (March to May)
Terrain: Mahe Group is granitic, narrow coastal strip, rocky, hilly; others are coral, flat, elevated reefs
Elevation extremes:
lowest point: Indian Ocean 0 m
highest point: Morne Seychellois 905 m
Natural resources: fish, copra, cinnamon trees
Land use:
arable land: 2.22%
permanent crops: 13.33%
other: 84.45% (2001)
Irrigated land: NA sq km
Natural hazards: lies outside the cyclone belt, so severe storms are rare; short droughts possible
Environment - current issues: water supply depends on catchments to collect rainwater
Environment - international agreements:
party to: Biodiversity, Climate Change, Climate Change-Kyoto Protocol, Desertification, Endangered Species, Hazardous Wastes, Law of the Sea, Marine Dumping, Ozone Layer Protection, Ship Pollution
signed, but not ratified: none of the selected agreements
Geography - note: 41 granitic and about 75 coralline islands

PEOPLE

Population: 81,188 (July 2005 est.)
Age structure:
0-14 years: 26.4% (male 10,839/female 10,601)
15-64 years: 67.4% (male 26,709/female 28,025)
65 years and over: 6.2% (male 1,622/female 3,392) (2005 est.)
Median age:
total: 27.7 years
male: 26.62 years
female: 28.76 years (2005 est.)
Population growth rate: 0.43% (2005 est.)
Birth rate: 16.22 births/1,000 population (2005 est.)
Death rate: 6.34 deaths/1,000 population (2005 est.)
Net migration rate: -5.54 migrant(s)/1,000 population (2005 est.)
Sex ratio:
at birth: 1.03 male(s)/female
under 15 years: 1.02 male(s)/female
15-64 years: 0.95 male(s)/female
65 years and over: 0.48 male(s)/female
total population: 0.93 male(s)/female (2005 est.)
Infant mortality rate:
total: 15.53 deaths/1,000 live births
male: 19.65 deaths/1,000 live births
female: 11.28 deaths/1,000 live births (2005 est.)
Life expectancy at birth:
total population: 71.82 years
male: 66.41 years
female: 77.4 years (2005 est.)
Total fertility rate: 1.75 children born/woman (2005 est.)
HIV/AIDS - adult prevalence rate: NA
HIV/AIDS - people living with HIV/AIDS: NA
HIV/AIDS - deaths: NA

Nationality:
noun: Seychellois (singular and plural)
adjective: Seychellois
Ethnic groups: mixed French, African, Indian, Chinese, and Arab
Religions: Roman Catholic 82.3%, Anglican 6.4%, Seventh Day Adventist 1.1%, other Christian 3.4%, Hindu 2.1%, Muslim 1.1%, other non-Christian 1.5%, unspecified 1.5%, none 0.6% (2002 census)
Languages: Creole 91.8%, English 4.9% (official), other 3.1%, unspecified 0.2% (2002 census)
Literacy:
definition: age 15 and over can read and write
total population: 91.9%
male: 91.4%
female: 92.3% (2003 est.)

GOVERNMENT

Country name:
conventional long form: Republic of Seychelles
conventional short form: Seychelles
Government type: republic
Capital: Victoria
Administrative divisions: 23 administrative districts; Anse aux Pins, Anse Boileau, Anse Etoile, Anse Louis, Anse Royale, Baie Lazare, Baie Sainte Anne, Beau Vallon, Bel Air, Bel Ombre, Cascade, Glacis, Grand' Anse (on Mahe), Grand' Anse (on Praslin), La Digue, La Riviere Anglaise, Mont Buxton, Mont Fleuri, Plaisance, Pointe La Rue, Port Glaud, Saint Louis, Takamaka
Independence: 29 June 1976 (from UK)
National holiday: Constitution Day (National Day), 18 June (1993)
Constitution: 18 June 1993
Legal system: based on English common law, French civil law, and customary law
Suffrage: 17 years of age; universal
Executive branch:
chief of state: President James MICHEL (since 14 April 2004); note - the president is both the chief of state and head of government
head of government: President James MICHEL (since 14 April 2004); note - the president is both the chief of state and head of government
cabinet: Council of Ministers appointed by the president
elections: president elected by popular vote for a five-year term; election last held 31 August-2 September 2001 (next to be held August 2006)
election results: France Albert RENE reelected president; percent of vote - France Albert RENE (SPPF) 54.19%, Wavel RAMKALAWAN (UO) 44.95%, Philippe BOULLE 0.86%; note - the first time that presidential elections have been held separately from legislative elections; France Albert RENE stepped down 14 April 2004 and Vice President James MICHEL was sworn in as president
Legislative branch: unicameral National Assembly or Assemblee Nationale (34 seats - 25 elected by popular vote, 9 allocated on a proportional basis to parties winning at least 10% of the vote; members serve five-year terms)
elections: last held 4-6 December 2002 (next to be held by 2007)
election results: percent of vote by party - SPPF 54.3%, SNP 42.6%, DP 3.1%; seats by party - SPPF 23, SNP 11
note: the 9 awarded seats are apportioned according to the percentage that each party won of the total vote
Judicial branch: Court of Appeal; Supreme Court; judges for both courts are appointed by the president
Political parties and leaders: Democratic Party or DP [James MANCHAM, Daniel BELLE]; Mouvement Seychellois pour la Democratie [Jacques HODOUL]; Seychelles National Party or SNP (formerly the United Opposition or UO) [Wavel RAMKALAWAN]; Seychelles People's Progressive Front or SPPF [France Albert RENE, James MICHEL] - the governing party
Political pressure groups and leaders: Roman Catholic Church; trade unions
International organization participation: ACCT, ACP, AfDB, AU, C, COMESA, FAO, G-77, IAEA, IBRD, ICAO, ICCt (signatory), ICFTU, ICRM, IFAD, IFC, IFRCS, ILO, IMF, IMO, InOC, Interpol, IOC, ISO (correspondent), ITU, MIGA, NAM, OPCW, UN, UNCTAD, UNESCO, UNIDO, UPU, WCO, WHO, WIPO, WMO, WToO, WTO (observer)
Diplomatic representation in the US:
chief of mission: Ambassador Jeremie BONNELAME
chancery: 800 Second Avenue, Suite 400C, New York, NY 10017
telephone: [1] (212) 972-1785
FAX: [1] (212) 972-1786
Diplomatic representation from the US: the US does not have an embassy in Seychelles; the ambassador to Mauritius is accredited to the Seychelles
Flag description: five oblique bands of blue (hoist side), yellow, red, white, and green (bottom) radiating from the bottom of the hoist side

ECONOMY

Economy - overview: Since independence in 1976, per capita output in this Indian Ocean archipelago has expanded to roughly seven times the old near-subsistence level. Growth has been led by the tourist sector, which employs about 30% of the labor force and provides more than 70% of hard currency earnings, and by tuna fishing. In recent years the government has encouraged foreign investment in order to upgrade hotels and other services. At the same time, the government has moved to reduce the dependence on tourism by promoting the development of farming, fishing, and small-scale manufacturing. A sharp drop illustrated the vulnerability of the tourist sector in 1991-92 due largely to the Gulf war, and once again following the 11 September 2001 terrorist attacks on the US. Growth slowed in 1998-2002, and fell in 2003, due to sluggish tourist and tuna sectors, but resumed in 2004, erasing a persistent budget deficit. Growth turned negative again in 2005. Tight controls on exchange rates and the scarcity of foreign exchange have impaired short-term economic prospects. The black market value of the Seychelles rupee is half the official exchange rate; without a devaluation of the currency the tourist sector may remain sluggish as vacationers seek cheaper destinations such as Comoros, Mauritius, and Madagascar.
GDP (purchasing power parity): $626 million (2002 est.)
GDP (official exchange rate): $722 million (2005 est.)
GDP - real growth rate: -3% (2005 est.)
GDP - per capita: purchasing power parity - $7,800 (2002 est.)
GDP - composition by sector:
agriculture: 3.2%
industry: 30.4%
services: 66.4% (2005 est.)
Labor force: 30,900 (1996)
Labor force - by occupation: agriculture 10%, industry 19%, services 71% (1989)
Unemployment rate: NA
Population below poverty line: NA
Household income or consumption by percentage share:
lowest 10%: NA
highest 10%: NA
Inflation rate (consumer prices): 4.4% (2005 est.)
Investment (gross fixed): 41.5% of GDP (2005 est.)
Budget:
revenues: $343.3 million
expenditures: $332.2 million, including capital expenditures of NA (2005 est.)
Public debt: 129.7% of GDP (2005 est.)
Agriculture - products: coconuts, cinnamon, vanilla, sweet potatoes, cassava (tapioca), bananas; broiler chickens; tuna fish
Industries: fishing; tourism; processing of coconuts and vanilla, coir (coconut fiber) rope, boat building, printing, furniture; beverages

Industrial production growth rate: NA
Electricity - production: 241.3 million kWh (2003)
Electricity - production by source:
fossil fuel: 100%
hydro: 0%
nuclear: 0%
other: 0% (2001)
Electricity - consumption: 224.4 million kWh (2003)
Electricity - exports: 0 kWh (2003)
Electricity - imports: 0 kWh (2003)
Oil - production: 0 bbl/day (2003 est.)
Oil - consumption: 7,600 bbl/day (2003 est.)
Oil - exports: NA (2001)
Oil - imports: NA (2001)
Current account balance: $-16.66 million (2005 est.)
Exports: $312.1 million f.o.b. (2005 est.)
Exports - partners: UK 27.7%, France 15.8%, Spain 12.6%, Japan 8.6%, Italy 7.5%, Germany 5.6% (2004)
Imports: $459.9 million f.o.b. (2005 est.)
Imports - partners: Saudi Arabia 15.5%, Spain 13.3%, France 10.3%, Singapore 7%, South Africa 6.8%, Italy 6.7%, UK 4.7% (2004)
Reserves of foreign exchange and gold: $29.16 million (2005 est.)
Debt - external: $276.8 million (2005 est.)
Economic aid - recipient: $16.4 million (1995)
Currency (code): Seychelles rupee (SCR)
Currency code: SCR
Exchange rates: Seychelles rupees per US dollar - 5.5 (2005), 5.5 (2004), 5.4007 (2003), 5.48 (2002), 5.8575 (2001)
Fiscal year: calendar year

COMMUNICATIONS

Telephones - main lines in use: 21,700 (2002)
Telephones - mobile cellular: 54,500 (2003)
Telephone system:
general assessment: effective system
domestic: radiotelephone communications between islands in the archipelago
international: country code - 248; direct radiotelephone communications with adjacent island countries and African coastal countries; satellite earth station - 1 Intelsat (Indian Ocean)
Radio broadcast stations: AM 1, FM 1, shortwave 2 (1998)
Radios: 42,000 (1997)
Television broadcast stations: 2 (plus 9 repeaters) (1997)
Televisions: 11,000 (1997)
Internet country code: .sc
Internet hosts: 264 (2003)
Internet Service Providers (ISPs): 1 (2000)
Internet users: 11,700 (2002)

TRANSPORTATION

Airports: 15 (2004 est.)
Airports - with paved runways:
total: 8
2,438 to 3,047 m: 1
914 to 1,523 m: 4
under 914 m: 3 (2005 est.)
Airports - with unpaved runways:
total: 7
914 to 1,523 m: 3
under 914 m: 4 (2005 est.)
Roadways:
total: 373 km
paved: 315 km
unpaved: 58 km (1997 est.)
Merchant marine:
total: 5 ships (1,000 GRT or over) 42,223 GRT/63,538 DWT
by type: cargo 1, chemical tanker 3, refrigerated cargo 1
foreign-owned: 1 (Nigeria 1) (2005)
Ports and terminals: Victoria

MILITARY

Military branches: Seychelles Defense Force: Army, Coast Guard (includes Navy Wing, Air Wing), National Guard (2005)
Military service age and obligation: 18 years of age (est.); no conscription (2001)
Manpower available for military service: *males age 18-49:* 21,612 (2005 est.)
Manpower fit for military service: *males age 18-49:* 16,122 (2005 est.)
Military expenditures - dollar figure: $12.3 million (2004)
Military expenditures - percent of GDP: 1.8% (2004)

TRANSNATIONAL ISSUES

Disputes - international: together with Mauritius, Seychelles claims the Chagos Archipelago (UK-administered British Indian Ocean Territory)

SIERRA LEONE

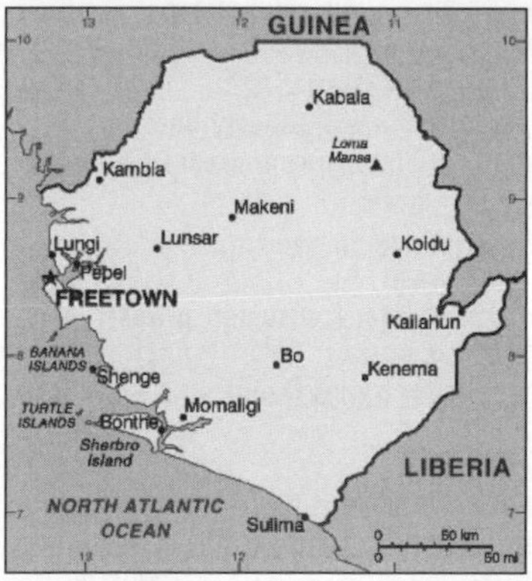

INTRODUCTION

Background: The government is slowly reestablishing its authority after the 1991 to 2002 civil war that resulted in tens of thousands of deaths and the displacement of more than 2 million people (about one-third of the population).. The last UN peacekeepers withdrew in December 2005, leaving full responsibility for security with domestic forces, but a new civilian UN office remains to support the government. Mounting tensions related to planned 2007 elections, deteriorating political and economic conditions in Guinea, and the tenuous security situation in neighboring Liberia may present challenges to continuing progress in Sierra Leone's stability.

GEOGRAPHY

Location: Western Africa, bordering the North Atlantic Ocean, between Guinea and Liberia
Geographic coordinates: 8 30 N, 11 30 W
Map references: Africa
Area:
total: 71,740 sq km
land: 71,620 sq km
water: 120 sq km
Area - comparative: slightly smaller than South Carolina
Land boundaries:
total: 958 km
border countries: Guinea 652 km, Liberia 306 km
Coastline: 402 km
Maritime claims:
territorial sea: 12 nm
contiguous zone: 24 nm
exclusive economic zone: 200 nm
continental shelf: 200 nm
Climate: tropical; hot, humid; summer rainy season (May to December); winter dry season (December to April)
Terrain: coastal belt of mangrove swamps, wooded hill country, upland plateau, mountains in east
Elevation extremes:
lowest point: Atlantic Ocean 0 m
highest point: Loma Mansa (Bintimani) 1,948 m
Natural resources: diamonds, titanium ore, bauxite, iron ore, gold, chromite
Land use:
arable land: 6.98%

permanent crops: 0.89%
other: 92.13% (2001)
Irrigated land: 290 sq km (1998 est.)
Natural hazards: dry, sand-laden harmattan winds blow from the Sahara (December to February); sandstorms, dust storms
Environment - current issues: rapid population growth pressuring the environment; overharvesting of timber, expansion of cattle grazing, and slash-and-burn agriculture have resulted in deforestation and soil exhaustion; civil war depleting natural resources; overfishing
Environment - international agreements:
party to: Biodiversity, Climate Change, Desertification, Endangered Species, Law of the Sea, Marine Life Conservation, Ozone Layer Protection, Ship Pollution, Wetlands
signed, but not ratified: Environmental Modification
Geography - note: rainfall along the coast can reach 495 cm (195 inches) a year, making it one of the wettest places along coastal, western Africa

PEOPLE

Population: 6,017,643 (July 2005 est.)
Age structure:
0-14 years: 44.7% (male 1,318,508/female 1,371,164)
15-64 years: 52% (male 1,494,068/female 1,637,276)
65 years and over: 3.3% (male 93,047/female 103,580) (2005 est.)
Median age:
total: 17.53 years
male: 17.2 years
female: 17.84 years (2005 est.)
Population growth rate: 2.22% (2005 est.)
Birth rate: 42.84 births/1,000 population (2005 est.)
Death rate: 20.61 deaths/1,000 population (2005 est.)
Net migration rate: 0 migrant(s)/1,000 population
note: refugees currently in surrounding countries are slowly returning (2005 est.)
Sex ratio:
at birth: 1.03 male(s)/female
under 15 years: 0.96 male(s)/female
15-64 years: 0.91 male(s)/female
65 years and over: 0.9 male(s)/female
total population: 0.93 male(s)/female (2005 est.)
Infant mortality rate:
total: 143.64 deaths/1,000 live births
male: 161.06 deaths/1,000 live births
female: 125.69 deaths/1,000 live births (2005 est.)
Life expectancy at birth:
total population: 39.87 years
male: 37.74 years
female: 42.06 years (2005 est.)
Total fertility rate: 5.72 children born/woman (2005 est.)
HIV/AIDS - adult prevalence rate: 7% (2001 est.)
HIV/AIDS - people living with HIV/AIDS: 170,000 (2001 est.)
HIV/AIDS - deaths: 11,000 (2001 est.)
Major infectious diseases:
degree of risk: very high
food or waterborne diseases: bacterial and protozoal diarrhea, hepatitis A, and typhoid fever
vectorborne diseases: malaria and yellow fever are high risks in some locations
water contact disease: schistosomiasis
aerosolized dust or soil contact disease: Lassa fever (2004)
Nationality:
noun: Sierra Leonean(s)
adjective: Sierra Leonean
Ethnic groups: 20 native African tribes 90% (Temne 30%, Mende 30%, other 30%), Creole (Krio) 10% (descendants of freed Jamaican slaves who were settled in the Freetown area in the late-18th century), refugees from Liberia's recent civil war, small numbers of Europeans, Lebanese, Pakistanis, and Indians
Religions: Muslim 60%, indigenous beliefs 30%, Christian 10%
Languages: English (official, regular use limited to literate minority), Mende (principal vernacular in the south), Temne (principal vernacular in the north), Krio (English-based Creole, spoken by the descendants of freed Jamaican slaves who were settled in the Freetown area, a lingua franca and a first language for 10% of the population but understood by 95%)
Literacy:
definition: age 15 and over can read and write English, Mende, Temne, or Arabic
total population: 29.6%
male: 39.8%
female: 20.5% (2000 est.)

GOVERNMENT

Country name:
conventional long form: Republic of Sierra Leone
conventional short form: Sierra Leone
Government type: constitutional democracy
Capital: Freetown
Administrative divisions: 3 provinces and 1 area*; Eastern, Northern, Southern, Western*
Independence: 27 April 1961 (from UK)
National holiday: Independence Day, 27 April (1961)
Constitution: 1 October 1991; subsequently amended several times
Legal system: based on English law and customary laws indigenous to local tribes; has not accepted compulsory ICJ jurisdiction
Suffrage: 18 years of age; universal
Executive branch:
chief of state: President Ahmad Tejan KABBAH (since 29 March 1996, reinstated 10 March 1998); note - the president is both the chief of state and head of government
head of government: President Ahmad Tejan KABBAH (since 29 March 1996, reinstated 10 March 1998); note - the president is both the chief of state and head of government
cabinet: Ministers of State appointed by the president with the approval of the House of Representatives; the cabinet is responsible to the president
elections: president elected by popular vote for a five-year term; election last held 14 May 2002 (next to be held May 2007); note - president's tenure of office is limited to two five-year terms
election results: Ahmad Tejan KABBAH reelected president; percent of vote - Ahmad Tejan KABBAH (SLPP) 70.6%, Ernest KOROMA (APC) 22.4%
Legislative branch: unicameral Parliament (124 seats - 112 elected by popular vote, 12 filled by paramount chiefs elected in separate elections; members serve five-year terms)
elections: last held 14 May 2002 (next to be held May 2007)
election results: percent of vote by party - SLPP 70.06%, APC 22.35%, PLP 3%, others 4.59%; seats by party - SLPP 83, APC 27, PLP 2
Judicial branch: Supreme Court; Appeals Court; High Court
Political parties and leaders: All People's Congress or APC [Ben KANU]; Peace and Liberation Party or PLP [Darlington MORRISON, interim chairman]; Sierra Leone People's Party or SLPP [Sama BANYA]; numerous others
Political pressure groups and leaders: trade unions and student unions
International organization participation: ACP, AfDB, AU, C, ECOWAS, FAO, G-77, IAEA, IBRD, ICAO, ICCt, ICFTU, ICRM, IDA, IDB, IFAD, IFC, IFRCS, ILO, IMF, IMO, Interpol, IOC, IOM, ITU, MIGA, NAM, OIC, OPCW, UN, UNCTAD, UNESCO, UNIDO, UPU, WCL, WCO, WFTU, WHO, WIPO, WMO, WToO, WTO
Diplomatic representation in the US:
chief of mission: Ambassador Ibrahim M. KAMARA
chancery: 1701 19th Street NW, Washington, DC 20009
telephone: [1] (202) 939-9261 through 9263
FAX: [1] (202) 483-1793

Diplomatic representation from the US:
chief of mission: Ambassador Thomas N. HULL
embassy: Corner of Walpole and Siaka Stevens Streets, Freetown
mailing address: use embassy street address
telephone: [232] (22) 226481 through 226485
FAX: [232] (22) 225471
Flag description: three equal horizontal bands of light green (top), white, and light blue

ECONOMY

Economy - overview: Sierra Leone is an extremely poor African nation with tremendous inequality in income distribution. While it possesses substantial mineral, agricultural, and fishery resources, its economic and social infrastructure is not well developed, and serious social disorders continue to hamper economic development. About two-thirds of the working-age population engages in subsistence agriculture. Manufacturing consists mainly of the processing of raw materials and of light manufacturing for the domestic market. Alluvial diamond mining remains the major source of hard currency earnings, accounting for nearly half of Sierra Leone's exports. The fate of the economy depends upon the maintenance of domestic peace and the continued receipt of substantial aid from abroad, which is essential to offset the severe trade imbalance and supplement government revenues. The IMF has completed a Poverty Reduction and Growth Facility program that helped stabilize economic growth and reduce inflation. A recent increase in political stability has led to a revival of economic activity, such as the rehabilitation of bauxite mining.
GDP (purchasing power parity): $5.012 billion (2005 est.)
GDP (official exchange rate): $1.135 billion (2005 est.)
GDP - real growth rate: 5.5% (2005 est.)
GDP - per capita: purchasing power parity - $800 (2005 est.)
GDP - composition by sector:
agriculture: 49%
industry: 31%
services: 21% (2001 est.)
Labor force: 1.369 million (1981 est.)
Labor force - by occupation: agriculture NA, industry NA, services NA
Unemployment rate: NA
Population below poverty line: 68% (1989 est.)
Household income or consumption by percentage share:
lowest 10%: 0.5%
highest 10%: 43.6% (1989)
Distribution of family income - Gini index: 62.9 (1989)
Inflation rate (consumer prices): 1% (2002 est.)
Budget:
revenues: $96 million
expenditures: $351 million, including capital expenditures of NA (2000 est.)
Agriculture - products: rice, coffee, cocoa, palm kernels, palm oil, peanuts; poultry, cattle, sheep, pigs; fish
Industries: diamonds mining; small-scale manufacturing (beverages, textiles, cigarettes, footwear); petroleum refining, small commercial ship repair
Industrial production growth rate: NA
Electricity - production: 260.6 million kWh (2003)
Electricity - production by source:
fossil fuel: 100%
hydro: 0%
nuclear: 0%
other: 0% (2001)
Electricity - consumption: 242.4 million kWh (2003)
Electricity - exports: 0 kWh (2003)
Electricity - imports: 0 kWh (2003)
Oil - production: 0.84 bbl/day (2003 est.)
Oil - consumption: 6,510 bbl/day (2003 est.)
Oil - exports: NA
Oil - imports: NA
Exports: $185 million f.o.b. (2004 est.)
Exports - partners: Belgium 61.6%, Germany 11.8%, US 5.4% (2004)
Imports: $531 million f.o.b. (2004 est.)
Imports - partners: Germany 14%, Cote d"Ivoire 10.7%, UK 9.1%, US 8.4%, China 5.6%, Netherlands 5%, South Africa 4.1% (2004)
Debt - external: $1.61 billion (2003 est.)
Economic aid - recipient: $297.4 million (2003 est.)
Currency (code): leone (SLL)
Currency code: SLL
Exchange rates: leones per US dollar - 2,452.91 (2005), 2,701.3 (2004), 2,347.9 (2003), 2,099 (2002), 1,986.2 (2001)
Fiscal year: calendar year

COMMUNICATIONS

Telephones - main lines in use: 24,000 (2002)
Telephones - mobile cellular: 67,000 (2002)
Telephone system:
general assessment: marginal telephone and telegraph service
domestic: the national microwave radio relay trunk system connects Freetown to Bo and Kenema
international: country code - 232; satellite earth station - 1 Intelsat (Atlantic Ocean)
Radio broadcast stations: AM 1, FM 9, shortwave 1 (1999)
Radios: 1.12 million (1997)
Television broadcast stations: 2 (1999)
Televisions: 53,000 (1997)
Internet country code: .sl
Internet hosts: 277 (2004)
Internet Service Providers (ISPs): 1 (2001)
Internet users: 8,000 (2002)

TRANSPORTATION

Airports: 10 (2004 est.)
Airports - with paved runways:
total: 1
over 3,047 m: 1 (2005 est.)
Airports - with unpaved runways:
total: 9
914 to 1,523 m: 7
under 914 m: 2 (2005 est.)
Heliports: 2 (2005 est.)
Roadways:
total: 11,300 km
paved: 904 km
unpaved: 10,396 km (2002)
Waterways: 800 km (2003)
Merchant marine:
total: 2 ships (1,000 GRT or over) 7,435 GRT/8,750 DWT
by type: petroleum tanker 2 (2005)
Ports and terminals: Freetown, Pepel, Sherbro Islands

MILITARY

Military branches: Republic of Sierra Leone Armed Forces (RSLAF): Army (includes Air Wing, Maritime Wing)
Military service age and obligation: 18 years of age (est.); no conscription (2001)
Manpower available for military service:
males age 18-49: 1,110,077 (2005 est.)
Manpower fit for military service: *males age 18-49:* 552,785 (2005 est.)
Military expenditures - dollar figure: $13.2 million (2004)
Military expenditures - percent of GDP: 1.7% (2004)

TRANSNATIONAL ISSUES

Disputes - international: domestic fighting among disparate rebel groups, warlords, and youth gangs in Cote d'Ivoire, Guinea, Liberia, and Sierra Leone perpetuate insurgencies, street violence, looting, arms trafficking, ethnic conflicts, and refugees in border areas; UN Mission in Sierra Leone (UNAMSIL) has maintained over 4,000 peacekeepers in Sierra Leone since 1999; Sierra Leone pressures Guinea to remove its forces from the town of Yenga occupied since 1998
Refugees and internally displaced persons:
refugees (country of origin): 67,000 (Liberia) (2004)

SINGAPORE

INTRODUCTION

Background: Singapore was founded as a British trading colony in 1819. It joined the Malaysian Federation in 1963 but separated two years later and became independent. It subsequently became one of the world's most prosperous countries with strong international trading links (its port is one of the world's busiest in terms of tonnage handled) and with per capita GDP equal to that of the leading nations of Western Europe.

GEOGRAPHY

Location: Southeastern Asia, islands between Malaysia and Indonesia
Geographic coordinates: 1 22 N, 103 48 E
Map references: Southeast Asia
Area:
total: 692.7 sq km
land: 682.7 sq km
water: 10 sq km
Area - comparative: slightly more than 3.5 times the size of Washington, DC
Land boundaries: 0 km
Coastline: 193 km
Maritime claims:
territorial sea: 3 nm
exclusive fishing zone: within and beyond territorial sea, as defined in treaties and practice
Climate: tropical; hot, humid, rainy; two distinct monsoon seasons - Northeastern monsoon from December to March and Southwestern monsoon from June to September; inter-monsoon - frequent afternoon and early evening thunderstorms
Terrain: lowland; gently undulating central plateau contains water catchment area and nature preserve
Elevation extremes:
lowest point: Singapore Strait 0 m
highest point: Bukit Timah 166 m
Natural resources: fish, deepwater ports
Land use:
arable land: 1.64%
permanent crops: 0%
other: 98.36% (2001)
Irrigated land: NA sq km
Natural hazards: NA
Environment - current issues: industrial pollution; limited natural fresh water resources; limited land availability presents waste disposal problems; seasonal smoke/haze resulting from forest fires in Indonesia
Environment - international agreements:
party to: Biodiversity, Climate Change, Desertification, Endangered Species, Hazardous Wastes, Law of the Sea, Ozone Layer Protection, Ship Pollution
signed, but not ratified: none of the selected agreements
Geography - note: focal point for Southeast Asian sea routes

PEOPLE

Population: 4,425,720 (July 2005 est.)
Age structure:
0-14 years: 16% (male 366,971/female 342,295)
15-64 years: 75.9% (male 1,639,842/female 1,719,829)
65 years and over: 8.1% (male 157,636/female 199,147) (2005 est.)
Median age:
total: 36.76 years
male: 36.4 years
female: 37.07 years (2005 est.)
Population growth rate: 1.56% (2005 est.)
Birth rate: 9.49 births/1,000 population (2005 est.)
Death rate: 4.16 deaths/1,000 population (2005 est.)
Net migration rate: 10.3 migrant(s)/1,000 population (2005 est.)
Sex ratio:
at birth: 1.08 male(s)/female
under 15 years: 1.07 male(s)/female
15-64 years: 0.95 male(s)/female
65 years and over: 0.79 male(s)/female
total population: 0.96 male(s)/female (2005 est.)
Infant mortality rate:
total: 2.29 deaths/1,000 live births
male: 2.5 deaths/1,000 live births
female: 2.06 deaths/1,000 live births (2005 est.)
Life expectancy at birth:
total population: 81.62 years
male: 79.05 years
female: 84.39 years (2005 est.)
Total fertility rate: 1.05 children born/woman (2005 est.)
HIV/AIDS - adult prevalence rate: 0.2% (2003 est.)
HIV/AIDS - people living with HIV/AIDS: 4,100 (2003 est.)
HIV/AIDS - deaths: less than 200 (2003 est.)
Nationality:
noun: Singaporean(s)
adjective: Singapore
Ethnic groups: Chinese 76.8%, Malay 13.9%, Indian 7.9%, other 1.4% (2000 census)
Religions: Buddhist 42.5%, Muslim 14.9%, Taoist 8.5%, Hindu 4%, Catholic 4.8%, other Christian 9.8%, other 0.7%, none 14.8% (2000 census)
Languages: Mandarin 35%, English 23%, Malay 14.1%, Hokkien 11.4%, Cantonese 5.7%, Teochew 4.9%, Tamil 3.2%, other Chinese dialects 1.8%, other 0.9% (2000 census)
Literacy:
definition: age 15 and over can read and write
total population: 92.5%
male: 96.6%
female: 88.6% (2002)

GOVERNMENT

Country name:
conventional long form: Republic of Singapore
conventional short form: Singapore
Government type: parliamentary republic
Capital: Singapore
Administrative divisions: none
Independence: 9 August 1965 (from Malaysian Federation)
National holiday: National Day, 9 August (1965)
Constitution: 3 June 1959; amended 1965 (based on preindependence State of Singapore Constitution)
Legal system: based on English common law; has not accepted compulsory ICJ jurisdiction
Suffrage: 21 years of age; universal and compulsory
Executive branch:
chief of state: President Sellapan Rama (S. R.) NATHAN (since 1 September 1999)
head of government: Prime Minister LEE Hsien Loong (since 12 August 2004); Senior Minister GOH Chok Tong (since 12 August 2004); Minister Mentor LEE Kuan Yew (since 12 August 2004); Deputy Prime Ministers Shunmugan JAYAKUMAR (since 12 August 2004) and WONG Kan Seng (since 1 September 2005)
cabinet: Cabinet appointed by president, responsible to Parliament
elections: president elected by popular vote for six-year term; last appointed 17 August 2005 (next election to be held by

August 2011); following legislative elections, leader of majority party or leader of majority coalition is usually appointed prime minister by president; deputy prime ministers appointed by president
election results: Sellapan Rama (S. R.) NATHAN appointed president in August 2005 after Presidential Elections Committee disqualified three other would-be candidates
Legislative branch: unicameral Parliament (84 seats; members elected by popular vote to serve five-year terms); note - in addition, there are up to nine nominated members; the losing opposition candidate who came closest to winning a seat may be appointed as a "nonconstituency" member
elections: last held 3 November 2001 (next to be held not later than 25 June 2007)
election results: percent of vote by party - PAP 75.3% (in contested constituencies), other 24.7%; seats by party - PAP 82, WP 1, SPP 1
Judicial branch: Supreme Court (chief justice is appointed by the president with the advice of the prime minister, other judges are appointed by the president with the advice of the chief justice); Court of Appeals
Political parties and leaders: governing party: People's Action Party or PAP [LEE Hsien Loong]; opposition parties: Democratic Progressive Party or DPP [LING How Dong]; National Solidarity Party or NSP [YIP Yew Weng] (SDA group); Singapore Democratic Alliance or SDA [CHIAM See Tong] (includes SPP, PKMS, NSP, SJP); Singapore Democratic Party or SDP [CHEE Soon Juan]; Singapore Justice Party or SJP [Desmond LIM] (SDA group); Singapore National Malay Organization or PKMS [Malik ISMAIL] (SDA group); Singapore People's Party or SPP [CHIAM See Tong] (SDA group); Workers' Party or WP [Sylvia Lim Swee LIAN]
Political pressure groups and leaders: NA
International organization participation: APEC, APT, ARF, AsDB, ASEAN, BIS, C, CP, EAS, G-77, IAEA, IBRD, ICAO, ICC, ICFTU, ICRM, IDA, IFC, IFRCS, IHO, ILO, IMF, IMO, Interpol, IOC, ISO, ITU, MIGA, NAM, OPCW, PCA, UN, UNCTAD, UPU, WCL, WCO, WHO, WIPO, WMO, WTO
Diplomatic representation in the US:
chief of mission: Ambassador CHAN Heng Chee
chancery: 3501 International Place NW, Washington, DC 20008
telephone: [1] (202) 537-3100
FAX: [1] (202) 537-0876
consulate(s) general: San Francisco
consulate(s): New York
Diplomatic representation from the US:
chief of mission: Ambassador Patricia L. HERBOLD
embassy: 27 Napier Road, Singapore 258508
mailing address: FPO AP 96507-0001
telephone: [65] 6476-9100
FAX: [65] 6476-9340
Flag description: two equal horizontal bands of red (top) and white; near the hoist side of the red band, there is a vertical, white crescent (closed portion is toward the hoist side) partially enclosing five white five-pointed stars arranged in a circle

ECONOMY

Economy - overview: Singapore, a highly-developed and successful free-market economy, enjoys a remarkably open and corruption-free environment, stable prices, and a per capita GDP equal to that of the Big 4 West European countries. The economy depends heavily on exports, particularly in electronics and manufacturing. It was hard hit in 2001-03 by the global recession, by the slump in the technology sector, and by an outbreak of Severe Acute Respiratory Syndrome in 2003, which curbed tourism and consumer spending. The government hopes to establish a new growth path that will be less vulnerable to the external business cycle and will continue efforts to establish Singapore as Southeast Asia's financial and high-tech hub. Fiscal stimulus, low interest rates, a surge in exports, and internal flexibility led to vigorous growth in 2004, with real GDP rising by 8% by far the economy's best performance since 2000, but growth slowed to 4.5% in 2005.
GDP (purchasing power parity): $131.3 billion (2005 est.)
GDP (official exchange rate): $113.6 billion (2005 est.)
GDP - real growth rate: 4.5% (2005 est.)
GDP - per capita: purchasing power parity - $29,700 (2005 est.)
GDP - composition by sector:
agriculture: 0% negligible
industry: 33.6%
services: 66.4% (2005 est.)
Labor force: 2.19 million (2005 est.)
Labor force - by occupation: manufacturing 18%, construction 6%, transportation and communication 11%, financial, business, and other services 49%, other 16% (2003)
Unemployment rate: 3.4% (2005 est.)
Population below poverty line: NA
Household income or consumption by percentage share:
lowest 10%: NA
highest 10%: NA
Inflation rate (consumer prices): 0.3% (2005 est.)
Investment (gross fixed): 23% of GDP (2005 est.)
Budget:
revenues: $18.67 billion
expenditures: $18.21 billion, including capital expenditures of $5.8 billion (2005 est.)
Public debt: 102% of GDP (2005 est.)
Agriculture - products: rubber, copra, fruit, orchids, vegetables, poultry, eggs, fish, ornamental fish
Industries: electronics, chemicals, financial services, oil drilling equipment, petroleum refining, rubber processing and rubber products, processed food and beverages, ship repair, offshore platform construction, life sciences, entrepot trade
Industrial production growth rate: 4.8% (2005 est.)
Electricity - production: 33.21 billion kWh (2003)
Electricity - production by source:
fossil fuel: 100%
hydro: 0%
nuclear: 0%
other: 0% (2001)
Electricity - consumption: 30.89 billion kWh (2003)
Electricity - exports: 0 kWh (2003)
Electricity - imports: 0 kWh (2003)
Oil - production: 8,290 bbl/day (2003 est.)
Oil - consumption: 705,000 bbl/day (2003 est.)
Oil - exports: NA (2001)
Oil - imports: NA (2001)
Natural gas - production: 0 cu m (2001 est.)
Natural gas - consumption: 2.5 billion cu m (2001 est.)
Natural gas - exports: 0 cu m (2001 est.)
Natural gas - imports: 2.5 billion cu m
note: from Indonesia and Malaysia (2001 est.)
Current account balance: $25.24 billion (2005 est.)
Exports: $212.4 billion f.o.b. (2005 est.)
Exports - partners: Malaysia 15.2%, US 13%, Hong Kong 9.8%, China 8.6%, Japan 6.4%, Taiwan 4.6%, Thailand 4.3%, South Korea 4.1% (2004)
Imports: $187.5 billion (2005 est.)
Imports - partners: Malaysia 15.3%, US 12.7%, Japan 11.7%, China 9.9%, Taiwan 5.7%, South Korea 4.3%, Thailand 4.1% (2004)
Reserves of foreign exchange and gold: $123.5 billion (2005 est.)
Debt - external: $24.67 billion (2005 est.)
Economic aid - recipient: NA
Currency (code): Singapore dollar (SGD)
Currency code: SGD
Exchange rates: Singapore dollars per US dollar - 1.65 (2005), 1.6902 (2004), 1.7422 (2003), 1.7906 (2002), 1.7917 (2001)
Fiscal year: 1 April - 31 March

COMMUNICATIONS

Telephones - main lines in use: 1,896,100 (2004)
Telephones - mobile cellular: 3,521,800 (2004)
Telephone system:
general assessment: excellent service
domestic: excellent domestic facilities
international: country code - 65; submarine cables to Malaysia (Sabah and Peninsular Malaysia), Indonesia, and the Philippines; satellite earth stations - 2 Intelsat (1 Indian Ocean and 1 Pacific Ocean), and 1 Inmarsat (Pacific Ocean region)
Radio broadcast stations: AM 0, FM 17, shortwave 2 (2003)
Radios: 2.6 million (2000)
Television broadcast stations: 7 (2003)
Televisions: 1.33 million (1997)
Internet country code: .sg
Internet hosts: 484,825 (2003)
Internet Service Providers (ISPs): 9 (2000)
Internet users: 2.31 million (2002)

TRANSPORTATION

Airports: 10 (2004 est.)
Airports - with paved runways:
total: 9
over 3,047 m: 2
2,438 to 3,047 m: 1
1,524 to 2,437 m: 4
914 to 1,523 m: 1
under 914 m: 1 (2005 est.)
Pipelines: gas 139 km (2004)
Roadways:
total: 3,130 km
paved: 3,130 km (including 150 km of expressways)
unpaved: 0 km (2002)
Merchant marine:
total: 923 ships (1,000 GRT or over) 23,065,290 GRT/36,393,317 DWT
by type: bulk carrier 138, cargo 86, chemical tanker 115, combination ore/oil 5, container 180, liquefied gas 42, livestock carrier 1, passenger/cargo 1, petroleum tanker 316, refrigerated cargo 3, vehicle carrier 36
foreign-owned: 487 (Australia 5, Bangladesh 1, Belgium 10, China 15, Denmark 34, Germany 7, Greece 5, Hong Kong 43, India 3, Indonesia 54, Japan 83, Malaysia 31, Norway 83, Philippines 3, Russia 1, Slovenia 1, South Korea 12, Sweden 12, Taiwan 44, Thailand 17, UAE 6, United Kingdom 12, United States 5)
registered in other countries: 276 (2005)
Ports and terminals: Singapore

MILITARY

Military branches: Singapore Armed Forces: Army, Navy, Air Force, Air Defense (2005)
Military service age and obligation: 18 years of age for compulsory military service; 16 years of age for volunteers; conscript service obligation reduced to 24 months beginning December 2004 (December 2004)
Manpower available for military service:
males age 18-49: 1,215,568 (2005 est.)
Manpower fit for military service: *males age 18-49:* 982,368 (2005 est.)
Military expenditures - dollar figure: $4.47 billion (FY01 est.)
Military expenditures - percent of GDP: 4.9% (FY01)

TRANSNATIONAL ISSUES

Disputes - international: disputes persist with Malaysia over deliveries of fresh water to Singapore, Singapore's extensive land reclamation works, bridge construction, maritime boundaries, and Pedra Branca Island/Pulau Batu Putih - parties agree to ICJ arbitration on island dispute within three years; Indonesia and Singapore pledged in 2005 to finalize their 1973 maritime boundary agreement by defining unresolved areas north of Batam Island; piracy remains a problem in the Malacca Strait
Illicit drugs: as a transportation and financial services hub, Singapore is vulnerable, despite strict laws and enforcement, to be used as a transit point for Golden Triangle heroin and as a venue for money laundering

SLOVAKIA

INTRODUCTION

Background: In 1918 the Slovaks joined the closely related Czechs to form Czechoslovakia. Following the chaos of World War II, Czechoslovakia became a Communist nation within Soviet-ruled Eastern Europe. Soviet influence collapsed in 1989 and Czechoslovakia once more became free. The Slovaks and the Czechs agreed to separate peacefully on 1 January 1993. Slovakia joined both NATO and the EU in the spring of 2004.

GEOGRAPHY

Location: Central Europe, south of Poland
Geographic coordinates: 48 40 N, 19 30 E
Map references: Europe
Area:
total: 48,845 sq km
land: 48,800 sq km
water: 45 sq km
Area - comparative: about twice the size of New Hampshire
Land boundaries:
total: 1,524 km
border countries: Austria 91 km, Czech Republic 215 km, Hungary 677 km, Poland 444 km, Ukraine 97 km
Coastline: 0 km (landlocked)
Maritime claims: none (landlocked)
Climate: temperate; cool summers; cold, cloudy, humid winters
Terrain: rugged mountains in the central and northern part and lowlands in the south
Elevation extremes:
lowest point: Bodrok River 94 m
highest point: Gerlachovsky Stit 2,655 m
Natural resources: brown coal and lignite; small amounts of iron ore, copper and manganese ore; salt; arable land
Land use:
arable land: 30.16%
permanent crops: 2.62%
other: 67.22% (2001)
Irrigated land: 1,740 sq km (1998 est.)

Natural hazards: NA
Environment - current issues: air pollution from metallurgical plants presents human health risks; acid rain damaging forests
Environment - international agreements:
party to: Air Pollution, Air Pollution-Nitrogen Oxides, Air Pollution-Persistent Organic Pollutants, Air Pollution-Sulfur 85, Air Pollution-Sulfur 94, Air Pollution-Volatile Organic Compounds, Antarctic Treaty, Biodiversity, Climate Change, Climate Change-Kyoto Protocol, Desertification, Endangered Species, Environmental Modification, Hazardous Wastes, Law of the Sea, Ozone Layer Protection, Ship Pollution, Wetlands
signed, but not ratified: none of the selected agreements
Geography - note: landlocked; most of the country is rugged and mountainous; the Tatra Mountains in the north are interspersed with many scenic lakes and valleys

PEOPLE

Population: 5,431,363 (July 2005 est.)
Age structure:
0-14 years: 17.1% (male 475,263/female 453,340)
15-64 years: 71% (male 1,919,222/female 1,939,097)
65 years and over: 11.9% (male 241,610/female 402,831) (2005 est.)
Median age:
total: 35.43 years
male: 33.85 years
female: 37.25 years (2005 est.)
Population growth rate: 0.15% (2005 est.)
Birth rate: 10.62 births/1,000 population (2005 est.)
Death rate: 9.43 deaths/1,000 population (2005 est.)
Net migration rate: 0.3 migrant(s)/1,000 population (2005 est.)
Sex ratio:
at birth: 1.05 male(s)/female
under 15 years: 1.05 male(s)/female
15-64 years: 0.99 male(s)/female
65 years and over: 0.6 male(s)/female
total population: 0.94 male(s)/female (2005 est.)
Infant mortality rate:
total: 7.41 deaths/1,000 live births
male: 8.65 deaths/1,000 live births
female: 6.1 deaths/1,000 live births (2005 est.)
Life expectancy at birth:
total population: 74.5 years
male: 70.52 years
female: 78.68 years (2005 est.)
Total fertility rate: 1.32 children born/woman (2005 est.)
HIV/AIDS - adult prevalence rate: less than 0.1% (2001 est.)
HIV/AIDS - people living with HIV/AIDS: less than 200 (2003 est.)
HIV/AIDS - deaths: less than 100 (2001 est.)
Nationality:
noun: Slovak(s)
adjective: Slovak
Ethnic groups: Slovak 85.8%, Hungarian 9.7%, Roma 1.7%, Ruthenian/Ukrainian 1%, other and unspecified 1.8% (2001 census)
Religions: Roman Catholic 68.9%, Protestant 10.8%, Greek Catholic 4.1%, other or unspecified 3.2%, none 13% (2001 census)
Languages: Slovak (official) 83.9%, Hungarian 10.7%, Roma 1.8%, Ukrainian 1%, other or unspecified 2.6% (2001 census)
Literacy:
definition: age 15 and over can read and write
total population: 99.6%
male: 99.7%
female: 99.6% (2001 est.)

GOVERNMENT

Country name:
conventional long form: Slovak Republic
conventional short form: Slovakia
local long form: Slovenska Republika
local short form: Slovensko
Government type: parliamentary democracy
Capital: Bratislava
Administrative divisions: 8 regions (kraje, singular - kraj); Banskobystricky, Bratislavsky, Kosicky, Nitriansky, Presovsky, Trenciansky, Trnavsky, Zilinsky
Independence: 1 January 1993 (Czechoslovakia split into the Czech Republic and Slovakia)
National holiday: Constitution Day, 1 September (1992)
Constitution: ratified 1 September 1992, effective 1 January 1993; changed in September 1998 to allow direct election of the president; amended February 2001 to allow Slovakia to apply for NATO and EU membership
Legal system: civil law system based on Austro-Hungarian codes; has not accepted compulsory ICJ jurisdiction; legal code modified to comply with the obligations of Organization on Security and Cooperation in Europe (OSCE) and to expunge Marxist-Leninist legal theory
Suffrage: 18 years of age; universal
Executive branch:
chief of state: President Ivan GASPAROVIC (since 15 June 2004)
head of government: Prime Minister Mikulas DZURINDA (since 30 October 1998); Deputy Prime Minister Ivan MIKLOS (since 30 October 1998); Deputy Prime Minister Pal CSAKY (since 30 October 1998); Deputy Prime Minister Pavol RUSKO (since May 2004)
cabinet: Cabinet appointed by the president on the recommendation of the prime minister
elections: president elected by direct, popular vote for a five-year term; election last held 3 April and 17 April 2004 (next to be held April 2009); following National Council elections, the leader of the majority party or the leader of a majority coalition is usually appointed prime minister by the president
election results: Ivan GASPAROVIC elected president in runoff; percent of vote - Ivan GASPAROVIC 59.9%, Vladimir MECIAR 40.1%; Mikulas DZURINDA reelected prime minister October 2002
note: government coalition - SDKU, SMK, KDH, ANO
Legislative branch: unicameral National Council of the Slovak Republic or Narodna Rada Slovenskej Republiky (150 seats; members are elected on the basis of proportional representation to serve four-year terms)
elections: last held 20-21 September 2002 (next to be held September 2006)
election results: percent of vote by party - HZDS-LS 19.5%, SDKU 15.1%, Smer 13.5%, SMK 11.2%, KDH 8.3%, ANO 8%, KSS 6.3%; seats by party - governing coalition 69 (SDKU 22, SMK 20, KDH 15, ANO 12), opposition 81 (HZDS 26, Smer 25, KSS 9, Free Forum 6, People's Union 5, and independents 10)
Judicial branch: Supreme Court (judges are elected by the National Council); Constitutional Court (judges appointed by president from group of nominees approved by the National Council)
Political parties and leaders: Christian Democratic Movement or KDH [Pavol HRUSOVSKY]; Direction (Smer) [Robert FICO]; Free Forum [Zuzana MARTINAKOVA]; Movement for Democracy or HZD [Jozef GRAPA]; Movement for a Democratic Slovakia-People's Party or HZDS-LS [Vladimir MECIAR]; New Citizens Alliance or ANO [Pavol RUSKO]; Party of the Hungarian Coalition or SMK [Bela BUGAR]; People's Union or LU [Gustav KRAJCI]; Slovak Communist Party or KSS [Jozef SEVC]; Slovak Democratic and Christian Union or SDKU [Mikulas DZURINDA]; Slovak National Party or SNS [Peter SULOVSKY]
Political pressure groups and leaders: Association of Employers of Slovakia; Association of Towns and Villages or ZMOS; Confederation of Trade Unions or KOZ; Metal Workers Unions or

KOVO and METALURG
International organization participation: ACCT (observer), Australia Group, BIS, BSEC (observer), CE, CEI, CERN, EAPC, EBRD, EIB, EU (new member), FAO, IAEA, IBRD, ICAO, ICC, ICCt, ICFTU, ICRM, IDA, IEA, IFC, IFRCS, ILO, IMF, IMO, Interpol, IOC, IOM, ISO, ITU, MIGA, NAM (guest), NATO, NEA, NSG, OAS (observer), OECD, OPCW, OSCE, PCA, UN, UNAMSIL, UNCTAD, UNDOF, UNESCO, UNFICYP, UNIDO, UNTSO, UPU, WCL, WCO, WEU (associate partner), WFTU, WHO, WIPO, WMO, WToO, WTO, ZC
Diplomatic representation in the US:
chief of mission: Ambassador Rastislav KACER
chancery: 3523 International Court NW, Washington, DC 20008
telephone: [1] (202) 237-1054
FAX: [1] (202) 237-6438
consulate(s) general: Los Angeles and New York
Diplomatic representation from the US:
chief of mission: Ambassador Rodolphe "Skip" M. VALLEE
embassy: Hviezdoslavovo Namestie 4, 81102 Bratislava
mailing address: P.O. Box 309, 814 99 Bratislava
telephone: [421] (2) 5443-3338
FAX: [421] (2) 5443-0096
Flag description: three equal horizontal bands of white (top), blue, and red superimposed with the Slovak cross in a shield centered on the hoist side; the cross is white centered on a background of red and blue

ECONOMY

Economy - overview: Slovakia has mastered much of the difficult transition from a centrally planned economy to a modern market economy. The DZURINDA government made excellent progress during 2001-04 in macroeconomic stabilization and structural reform. Major privatizations are nearly complete, the banking sector is almost completely in foreign hands, and the government has helped facilitate a foreign investment boom with business-friendly policies, such as labor market liberalization and a 19% flat tax. Foreign investment in the automotive sector has been strong. Slovakia's economic growth exceeded expectations in 2001-05, despite the general European slowdown. Unemployment, at an unacceptable 15% in 2003-04, dropped to 11.5% in 2005, but remains the economy's Achilles heel. Slovakia joined the EU on 1 May 2004.
GDP (purchasing power parity): $85.14 billion (2005 est.)
GDP (official exchange rate): $43.69 billion (2005 est.)
GDP - real growth rate: 5.1% (2005 est.)
GDP - per capita: purchasing power parity - $15,700 (2005 est.)
GDP - composition by sector:
agriculture: 3.6%
industry: 29.7%
services: 66.7% (2005 est.)
Labor force: 2.62 million (2005 est.)
Labor force - by occupation: agriculture 5.8%, industry 29.3%, construction 9%, services 55.9% (2003)
Unemployment rate: 11.5% (2005 est.)
Population below poverty line: NA
Household income or consumption by percentage share:
lowest 10%: 5.1%
highest 10%: 18.2% (1992)
Distribution of family income - Gini index: 25.8 (1996)
Inflation rate (consumer prices): 2.8% (2005 est.)
Investment (gross fixed): 25.8% of GDP (2005 est.)
Budget:
revenues: $21.49 billion
expenditures: $23.15 billion, including capital expenditures of NA (2005 est.)
Public debt: 16.9% of GDP (2005 est.)
Agriculture - products: grains, potatoes, sugar beets, hops, fruit; pigs, cattle, poultry; forest products
Industries: metal and metal products; food and beverages; electricity, gas, coke, oil, nuclear fuel; chemicals and manmade fibers; machinery; paper and printing; earthenware and ceramics; transport vehicles; textiles; electrical and optical apparatus; rubber products
Industrial production growth rate: 9.3% (2005 est.)
Electricity - production: 29.71 billion kWh (2003)
Electricity - production by source:
fossil fuel: 30.3%
hydro: 16%
nuclear: 53.6%
other: 0% (2001)
Electricity - consumption: 25.23 billion kWh (2003)
Electricity - exports: 8.9 billion kWh (2003)
Electricity - imports: 6.5 billion kWh (2003)
Oil - production: 3,808 bbl/day (2003 est.)
Oil - consumption: 71,400 bbl/day (2003 est.)
Oil - exports: NA (2001)
Oil - imports: NA (2001)
Oil - proved reserves: 4.5 million bbl (1 January 2002)
Natural gas - production: 190 million cu m (2003 est.)
Natural gas - consumption: 6.8 billion cu m (2003 est.)
Natural gas - exports: 0 cu m (2003 est.)
Natural gas - imports: 6.6 billion cu m (2003 est.)
Natural gas - proved reserves: 7.504 billion cu m (1 January 2002)
Current account balance: $-2.881 billion (2005 est.)
Exports: $32.39 billion f.o.b. (2005 est.)
Exports - partners: Germany 34.4%, Czech Republic 14.6%, Austria 8.2%, Italy 5.8%, Poland 5.3%, US 4.5%, Hungary 4.3% (2004)
Imports: $34.48 billion f.o.b. (2005 est.)
Imports - partners: Germany 26%, Czech Republic 21.3%, Russia 9.1%, Austria 6.6%, Poland 4.9%, Italy 4.9% (2004)
Reserves of foreign exchange and gold: $16.25 billion (2005 est.)
Debt - external: $25.81 billion (2005 est.)
Economic aid - recipient: $2.2 billion in available EU structural adjustment and cohesion funds (2004-06)
Currency (code): Slovak koruna (SKK)
Currency code: SKK
Exchange rates: koruny per US dollar - 30 (2005), 32.257 (2004), 36.773 (2003), 45.327 (2002), 48.355 (2001)
Fiscal year: calendar year

COMMUNICATIONS

Telephones - main lines in use: 1,294,700 (2003)
Telephones - mobile cellular: 3,678,800 (2003)
Telephone system:
general assessment: a modernization and privatization program is increasing accessibility to telephone service, reducing the waiting time for new subscribers, and generally improving service quality
domestic: predominantly an analog system that is now receiving digital equipment and is being enlarged with fiber-optic cable, especially in the larger cities; mobile cellular capability has been added
international: country code - 421; three international exchanges (one in Bratislava and two in Banska Bystrica) are available; Slovakia is participating in several international telecommunications projects that will increase the availability of external services
Radio broadcast stations: AM 15, FM 78, shortwave 2 (1998)
Radios: 3.12 million (1997)
Television broadcast stations: 6 national broadcasting, 7 regional, 67 local (2004)
Televisions: 2.62 million (1997)
Internet country code: .sk
Internet hosts: 89,592 (2004)
Internet Service Providers (ISPs): 6 (2000)
Internet users: 1,375,800 (2003)

TRANSPORTATION

Airports: 34 (2004 est.)
Airports - with paved runways:
total: 17
over 3,047 m: 2
2,438 to 3,047 m: 2
1,524 to 2,437 m: 3
914 to 1,523 m: 3
under 914 m: 7 (2005 est.)
Airports - with unpaved runways:
total: 17
2,438 to 3,047 m: 1
914 to 1,523 m: 9
under 914 m: 7 (2005 est.)
Heliports: 1 (2005 est.)
Pipelines: gas 6,769 km; oil 449 km (2004)
Railways:
total: 3,662 km
broad gauge: 100 km 1.520-m gauge
standard gauge: 3,512 km 1.435-m gauge (1,588 km electrified)
narrow gauge: 50 km (1.000-m or 0.750-m gauge) (2004)
Roadways:
total: 42,970 km
paved: 37,698 km (including 302 km of expressways)
unpaved: 5,272 km (2002)
Waterways: 172 km (on Danube River) (2004)
Merchant marine:
total: 24 ships (1,000 GRT or over) 41,891 GRT/63,185 DWT
by type: bulk carrier 5, cargo 18, chemical tanker 1
foreign-owned: 18 (Bulgaria 8, Estonia 1, Greece 1, Syria 1, Turkey 6, United Kingdom 1) (2005)
Ports and terminals: Bratislava, Komarno

MILITARY

Military branches: Armed Forces of the Slovak Republic (Ozbrojene Sily Slovenskej Republiky): Land Forces (Pozemne Sily), Air Forces (Vozdushne Sily), Training and Support Forces (Vycviku a Podpory Sily) (2005)
Military service age and obligation: complete transition to an all-volunteer professional force is planned for 1 January 2007; 82% of Slovak armed forces were volunteers as of January 2005; volunteers include women, with minimum age of 17 years, 18 years of age for compulsory military service (January 2005)
Manpower available for military service: *males age 18-49:* 1,351,848 (2005 est.)
Manpower fit for military service: *males age 18-49:* 1,089,645 (2005 est.)
Manpower reaching military service age annually: *males:* 41,544 (2005 cst.)
Military expenditures - dollar figure: $406 million (2002)
Military expenditures - percent of GDP: 1.87% FY05 (2005)

TRANSNATIONAL ISSUES

Disputes - international: Hungary amended its status law extending special social and cultural benefits to ethnic Hungarians in Slovakia, to which Slovakia had protested; consultations continue between Slovakia and Hungary over Hungary's completion of its portion of the Gabcikovo-Nagymaros hydroelectric dam project along the Danube; as a member state that forms part of the EU's external border, Slovakia must implement the strict Schengen border rules
Illicit drugs: transshipment point for Southwest Asian heroin bound for Western Europe; producer of synthetic drugs for regional market

SLOVENIA

INTRODUCTION

Background: The Slovene lands were part of the Holy Roman Empire and Austria until 1918 when the Slovenes joined the Serbs and Croats in forming a new multinational state, renamed Yugoslavia in 1929. After World War II, Slovenia became a republic of the renewed Yugoslavia, which though Communist, distanced itself from Moscow's rule. Dissatisfied with the exercise of power by the majority Serbs, the Slovenes succeeded in establishing their independence in 1991 after a short 10-day war. Historical ties to Western Europe, a strong economy, and a stable democracy have assisted in Slovenia's transformation to a modern state. Slovenia acceded to both NATO and the EU in the spring of 2004.

GEOGRAPHY

Location: Central Europe, eastern Alps bordering the Adriatic Sea, between Austria and Croatia
Geographic coordinates: 46 07 N, 14 49 E
Map references: Europe
Area:
total: 20,273 sq km
land: 20,151 sq km
water: 122 sq km
Area - comparative: slightly smaller than New Jersey
Land boundaries:
total: 1,334 km
border countries: Austria 330 km, Croatia 670 km, Italy 232 km, Hungary 102 km
Coastline: 46.6 km
Maritime claims: NA
Climate: Mediterranean climate on the coast, continental climate with mild to hot summers and cold winters in the plateaus and valleys to the east
Terrain: a short coastal strip on the Adriatic, an alpine mountain region adjacent to Italy and Austria, mixed mountains and valleys with numerous rivers to the east
Elevation extremes:
lowest point: Adriatic Sea 0 m
highest point: Triglav 2,864 m
Natural resources: lignite coal, lead, zinc, mercury, uranium, silver, hydropower, forests
Land use:
arable land: 8.6%
permanent crops: 1.49%
other: 89.91% (2001)
Irrigated land: 20 sq km (1998 est.)
Natural hazards: flooding and earthquakes
Environment - current issues: Sava River polluted with domestic and industrial waste; pollution of coastal waters with heavy metals and toxic chemicals; forest damage near Koper from air pollution (originating at metallurgical and chemical plants) and resulting acid rain
Environment - international agreements:
party to: Air Pollution, Air Pollution-Sulfur 94, Biodiversity, Climate Change, Climate Change-Kyoto Protocol, Desertification, Endangered Species, Hazardous Wastes, Law of the Sea, Marine Dumping, Ozone Layer Protection, Ship Pollution, Wetlands
signed, but not ratified: Air Pollution-Persistent Organic Pollutants
Geography - note: despite its small size, this eastern Alpine country controls some of Europe's major transit routes

PEOPLE

Population: 2,011,070 (July 2005 est.)
Age structure:
0-14 years: 14% (male 145,016/female 137,012)
15-64 years: 70.6% (male 715,629/female 704,079)
65 years and over: 15.4% (male 118,298/female 191,036) (2005 est.)
Median age:
total: 40.23 years
male: 38.65 years
female: 41.75 years (2005 est.)
Population growth rate: -0.03% (2005 est.)
Birth rate: 8.95 births/1,000 population (2005 est.)
Death rate: 10.22 deaths/1,000 population (2005 est.)
Net migration rate: 1 migrant(s)/1,000 population (2005 est.)
Sex ratio:
at birth: 1.07 male(s)/female
under 15 years: 1.06 male(s)/female
15-64 years: 1.02 male(s)/female
65 years and over: 0.62 male(s)/female
total population: 0.95 male(s)/female (2005 est.)
Infant mortality rate:
total: 4.45 deaths/1,000 live births
male: 5.05 deaths/1,000 live births
female: 3.8 deaths/1,000 live births (2005 est.)
Life expectancy at birth:
total population: 76.14 years
male: 72.42 years
female: 80.1 years (2005 est.)
Total fertility rate: 1.24 children born/woman (2005 est.)
HIV/AIDS - adult prevalence rate: less than 0.1% (2001 est.)
HIV/AIDS - people living with HIV/AIDS: 280 (2001 est.)
HIV/AIDS - deaths: less than 100 (2003 est.)
Nationality:
noun: Slovene(s)
adjective: Slovenian
Ethnic groups: Slovene 83.1%, Serb 2%, Croat 1.8%, Bosniak 1.1%, other or unspecified 12% (2002 census)
Religions: Catholic 57.8%, Orthodox 2.3%, other Christian 0.9%, Muslim 2.4%, unaffiliated 3.5%, other or unspecified 23%, none 10.1% (2002 census)
Languages: Slovenian 91.1%, Serbo-Croatian 4.5%, other or unspecified 4.4% (2002 census)
Literacy:
definition: NA
total population: 99.7%
male: 99.7%
female: 99.6% (2003 est.)

GOVERNMENT

Country name:
conventional long form: Republic of Slovenia
conventional short form: Slovenia
local long form: Republika Slovenija
local short form: Slovenija
former: People's Republic of Slovenia, Socialist Republic of Slovenia
Government type: parliamentary democratic republic
Capital: Ljubljana
Administrative divisions: 182 municipalities (obcine, singular - obcina) and 11 urban municipalities* (mestne obcine , singular - mestna obcina) Ajdovscina, Beltinci, Benedikt, Bistrica ob Sotli, Bled, Bloke, Bohinj, Borovnica, Bovec, Braslovce, Brda, Brezice, Brezovica, Cankova, Celje*, Cerklje na Gorenjskem, Cerknica, Cerkno, Cerkvenjak, Crensovci, Crna na Koroskem, Crnomelj, Destrnik, Divaca, Dobje, Dobrepolje, Dobrna, Dobrova-Horjul-Polhov Gradec, Dobrovnik-Dobronak, Dolenjske Toplice, Dol pri Ljubljani, Domzale, Dornava, Dravograd, Duplek, Gorenja Vas-Poljane, Gorisnica, Gornja Radgona, Gornji Grad, Gornji Petrovci, Grad, Grosuplje, Hajdina, Hoce-Slivnica, Hodos-Hodos, Horjul, Hrastnik, Hrpelje-Kozina, Idrija, Ig, Ilirska Bistrica, Ivancna Gorica, Izola-Isola, Jesenice, Jezersko, Jursinci, Kamnik, Kanal, Kidricevo, Kobarid, Kobilje, Kocevje, Komen, Komenda, Koper-Capodistria*, Kostel, Kozje, Kranj*, Kranjska Gora, Krizevci, Krsko, Kungota, Kuzma, Lasko, Lenart, Lendava-Lendva, Litija, Ljubljana*, Ljubno, Ljutomer, Logatec, Loska Dolina, Loski Potok, Lovrenc na Pohorju, Luce, Lukovica, Majsperk, Maribor*, Markovci, Medvode, Menges, Metlika, Mezica, Miklavz na Dravskem Polju, Miren-Kostanjevica, Mirna Pec, Mislinja, Moravce, Moravske Toplice, Mozirje, Murska Sobota*, Muta, Naklo, Nazarje, Nova Gorica*, Novo Mesto*, Odranci, Oplotnica, Ormoz, Osilnica, Pesnica, Piran-Pirano, Pivka, Podcetrtek, Podlehnik, Podvelka, Polzela, Postojna, Prebold, Preddvor, Prevalje, Ptuj*, Puconci, Race-Fram, Radece, Radenci, Radlje ob Dravi, Radovljica, Ravne na Koroskem, Razkrizje, Ribnica, Ribnica na Pohorju, Rogasovci, Rogaska Slatina, Rogatec, Ruse, Salovci, Selnica ob Dravi, Semic, Sempeter-Vrtojba, Sencur, Sentilj, Sentjernej, Sentjur pri Celju, Sevnica, Sezana, Skocjan, Skofja Loka,Skofljica, Slovenj Gradec*, Slovenska Bistrica, Slovenske Konjice, Smarje pri Jelsah, Smartno ob Paki, Smartno pri Litiji, Sodrazica, Solcava, Sostanj, Starse, Store, Sveta Ana, Sveti Andraz v Slovenskih Goricah, Sveti Jurij, Tabor, Tisina, Tolmin, Trbovlje, Trebnje, Trnovska Vas, Trzic, Trzin, Turnisce, Velenje*, Velika Polana, Velike Lasce, Verzej, Videm, Vipava, Vitanje, Vodice, Vojnik, Vransko, Vrhnika, Vuzenica, Zagorje ob Savi, Zalec, Zavrc, Zelezniki, Zetale, Ziri, Zirovnica, Zuzemberk, Zrece
note: there may be 45 more municipalities
Independence: 25 June 1991 (from Yugoslavia)
National holiday: Independence Day/Statehood Day, 25 June (1991)
Constitution: adopted 23 December 1991, effective 23 December 1991
Legal system: based on civil law system
Suffrage: 18 years of age; universal (16 years of age, if employed)
Executive branch:
chief of state: President Janez DRNOVSEK (since 22 December 2002)
head of government: Prime Minister Janez JANSA (since 9 November 2004)
cabinet: Council of Ministers nominated by the prime minister and elected by the National Assembly
elections: president elected by popular vote for a five-year term; election last held 10 November and 1 December 2002 (next to be held in the fall of 2007); following National Assembly elections, the leader of the majority party or the leader of a majority coalition is usually nominated to become prime minister by the president and elected by the National Assembly; election last held 9 November 2004 (next National Assembly elections to be held October 2008)
election results: Janez DRNOVSEK elected president; percent of vote - Janez DRNOVSEK 56.5%, Barbara BREZIGAR 43.5%; Janez JANSA elected prime minister; National Assembly vote - 57 to 27
Legislative branch: bicameral Parliament consisting of a National Assembly or Drzavni Zbor (90 seats; 40 are directly elected and 50 are selected on a proportional basis; note - the numbers of directly elected and proportionally elected seats varies with each election; members are elected by popular vote to serve four-year terms) and the National Council or Drzavni Svet (this is primarily an advisory body organized on corporatist principles with limited legislative powers; it may propose laws, ask to review any National Assembly decisions, and call national referenda; members are indirectly elected to five-year terms by an electoral college)
elections: National Assembly - last held 3 October 2004 (next to be held October 2008)
election results: percent of vote by party - SDS 29.1%, LDS 22.8%, ZLSD 10.2%, NSi 9%, SLS 6.8%, SNS 6.3%, DeSUS 4.1%, other 11.7%; seats by party - SDS 29, LDS 23, ZLSD 10, NSi 9, SLS 7,

SNS 6, DeSUS 4, Hungarian and Italian minorities 1 each
Judicial branch: Supreme Court (judges are elected by the National Assembly on the recommendation of the Judicial Council); Constitutional Court (judges elected for nine-year terms by the National Assembly and nominated by the president)
Political parties and leaders: Democratic Party of Retired (Persons) of Slovenia or DeSUS [Karl ERJAVEC]; Liberal Democratic Party or LDS [Jelko KACIN]; New Slovenia or NSi [Andrej BAJUK]; Slovene Democratic Party or SDS [Janez JANSA]; Slovene National Party or SNS [Zmago JELINCIC]; Slovene People's Party or SLS [Janez PODOBNIK]; Slovene Youth Party or SMS [Darko KRANJC]; United List of Social Democrats or ZLSD [Borut PAHOR]
Political pressure groups and leaders: NA
International organization participation: ACCT (observer), Australia Group, BIS, CE, CEI, EAPC, EBRD, EIB, EU (new member), FAO, IADB, IAEA, IBRD, ICAO, ICC, ICCt, ICRM, IDA, IFC, IFRCS, IHO, ILO, IMF, IMO, Interpol, IOC, IOM, ISO, ITU, MIGA, NAM (guest), NATO, NSG, OAS (observer), OPCW, OSCE, PCA, UN, UNCTAD, UNESCO, UNIDO, UNTSO, UPU, WCO, WEU (associate partner), WHO, WIPO, WMO, WToO, WTO, ZC
Diplomatic representation in the US:
chief of mission: Ambassador Samuel ZBOGAR
chancery: 1525 New Hampshire Avenue NW, Washington, DC 20036
telephone: [1] (202) 667-5363
FAX: [1] (202) 667-4563
consulate(s) general: New York and Cleveland
Diplomatic representation from the US:
chief of mission: Ambassador Thomas B. ROBERTSON
embassy: Presernova 31, 1000 Ljubljana
mailing address: American Embassy Ljubljana, Department of State, 7140 Ljubljana Place, Washington, DC 20521-7140
telephone: [386] (1) 200-5500
FAX: [386] (1) 200-5555
Flag description: three equal horizontal bands of white (top), blue, and red, with the Slovenian seal (a shield with the image of Triglav, Slovenia's highest peak, in white against a blue background at the center; beneath it are two wavy blue lines depicting seas and rivers, and above it are three six-pointed stars arranged in an inverted triangle, which are taken from the coat of arms of the Counts of Celje, the great Slovene dynastic house of the late 14th and early 15th centuries); the seal is located in the upper hoist side of the flag centered in the white and blue bands

ECONOMY

Economy - overview: Slovenia, with its historical ties to Western Europe, enjoys a GDP per capita substantially higher than that of the other transitioning economies of Central Europe. In March 2004, Slovenia became the first transition country to graduate from borrower status to donor partner at the World Bank. Privatization of the economy proceeded at an accelerated pace in 2002-05. Despite lackluster performance in Europe in 2001-05, Slovenia maintained moderate growth. Structural reforms to improve the business environment have allowed for greater foreign participation in Slovenia's economy and have helped to lower unemployment. Further measures to curb inflation are still needed. Corruption and the high degree of coordination between government, business, and central bank policy were issues of concern in the run-up to Slovenia's 1 May 2004 accession to the European Union. In mid-2004 Slovenia agreed to adopt the euro by 2007 and, therefore, must keep its debt levels, budget deficits, interest rates, and inflation levels within the EU's Maastrict criteria.
GDP (purchasing power parity): $42.09 billion (2005 est.)
GDP (official exchange rate): $35.72 billion (2005 est.)
GDP - real growth rate: 3.8% (2005 est.)
GDP - per capita: purchasing power parity - $20,900 (2005 est.)
GDP - composition by sector:
agriculture: 2.8%
industry: 36.9%
services: 60.3% (2005 est.)
Labor force: 920,000 (2005 est.)
Labor force - by occupation: agriculture 6%, industry 40%, services 55% (2002)
Unemployment rate: 9.8% (2005 est.)
Population below poverty line: NA
Household income or consumption by percentage share:
lowest 10%: 3.9%
highest 10%: 23% (1998)
Distribution of family income - Gini index: 28.4 (1998)
Inflation rate (consumer prices): 2.4% (2005 est.)
Investment (gross fixed): 24.8% of GDP (2005 est.)
Budget:
revenues: $16.02 billion
expenditures: $16.73 billion, including capital expenditures of NA (2005 est.)
Public debt: 29.9% of GDP (2005 est.)
Agriculture - products: potatoes, hops, wheat, sugar beets, corn, grapes; cattle, sheep, poultry
Industries: ferrous metallurgy and aluminum products, lead and zinc smelting, electronics (including military electronics), trucks, electric power equipment, wood products, textiles, chemicals, machine tools
Industrial production growth rate: 2.9% (2005 est.)
Electricity - production: 13.23 billion kWh (2003)
Electricity - production by source:
fossil fuel: 35.2%
hydro: 27.3%
nuclear: 36.8%
other: 0.7% (2001)
Electricity - consumption: 12.47 billion kWh (2003)
Electricity - exports: 5.811 billion kWh (2003)
Electricity - imports: 5.975 billion kWh (2003)
Oil - production: 11.05 bbl/day (2003 est.)
Oil - consumption: 52,000 bbl/day (2003 est.)
Oil - exports: NA (2001)
Oil - imports: NA (2001)
Natural gas - production: 0 cu m (2001 est.)
Natural gas - consumption: 1.04 billion cu m (2001 est.)
Natural gas - exports: 0 cu m (2001 est.)
Natural gas - imports: 1.04 billion cu m (2001 est.)
Current account balance: $-202 million (2005 est.)
Exports: $18.53 billion f.o.b. (2005 est.)
Exports - partners: Germany 18.3%, Italy 11.6%, Austria 11.5%, France 7.4%, Croatia 7.3%, Bosnia and Herzegovina 4.8% (2004)
Imports: $19.62 billion f.o.b. (2005 est.)
Imports - partners: Germany 19.9%, Italy 17%, Austria 14.9%, France 10.2% (2004)
Reserves of foreign exchange and gold: $8.805 billion (2005 est.)
Debt - external: $20.57 billion (30 June 2005 est.)
Economic aid - recipient: ODA, $62 million (2000 est.)
Currency (code): tolar (SIT)
Currency code: SIT
Exchange rates: tolars per US dollar - 187.42 (2005), 192.38 (2004), 207.11 (2003), 240.25 (2002), 242.75 (2001)
Fiscal year: calendar year

COMMUNICATIONS

Telephones - main lines in use: 812,300 (2003)
Telephones - mobile cellular: 1,739,100 (2003)
Telephone system:
general assessment: NA
domestic: 100% digital (2000)
international: country code - 386

Radio broadcast stations: AM 17, FM 160, shortwave 0 (1998)
Radios: 805,000 (1997)
Television broadcast stations: 48 (2001)
Televisions: 710,000 (1997)
Internet country code: .si
Internet hosts: 45,491 (2004)
Internet Service Providers (ISPs): 11 (2000)
Internet users: 750,000 (2002)

TRANSPORTATION

Airports: 14 (2004 est.)
Airports - with paved runways:
total: 6
over 3,047 m: 1
2,438 to 3,047 m: 1
1,524 to 2,437 m: 1
914 to 1,523 m: 2
under 914 m: 1 (2005 est.)
Airports - with unpaved runways:
total: 8
1,524 to 2,437 m: 2
914 to 1,523 m: 2
under 914 m: 4 (2005 est.)
Pipelines: gas 2,526 km; oil 11 km (2004)
Railways:
total: total: 1,201 km
standard gauge: 1,201 km 1.435-m gauge (499 km electrified) (2004)
Roadways:
total: 20,250 km
paved: 20,250 km (including 456 km of expressways)
unpaved: 0 km (2002)
Merchant marine:
registered in other countries: 23
Ports and terminals: Koper

MILITARY

Military branches: Slovenian Army (includes Air and Naval Forces)
Military service age and obligation: 17 years of age for voluntary military service; conscription abolished in 2003 (2004)
Manpower available for military service: males age 17-49: 496,929 (2005 est.)
Manpower fit for military service: males age 17-49: 405,593 (2005 est.)
Manpower reaching military service age annually: males: 12,816 (2005 est.)
Military expenditures - dollar figure: $370 million (FY00)
Military expenditures - percent of GDP: 1.7% (FY00)

TRANSNATIONAL ISSUES

Disputes - international: the Croatia-Slovenia land and maritime boundary agreement, which would have ceded most of Piran Bay and maritime access to Slovenia and several villages to Croatia, remains unratified and in dispute; as a member state that forms part of the EU's external border, Slovenia must implement the strict Schengen border rules to curb illegal migration and commerce through southeastern Europe while encouraging close cross-border ties with Croatia
Illicit drugs: minor transit point for cocaine and Southwest Asian heroin bound for Western Europe, and for precursor chemicals

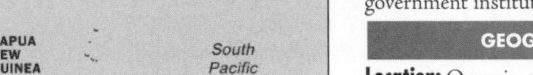

SOLOMON ISLANDS

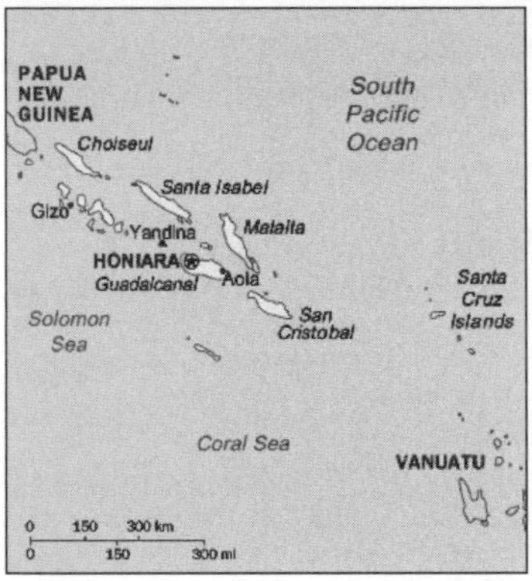

INTRODUCTION

Background: The UK established a protectorate over the Solomon Islands in the 1890s. Some of the bitterest fighting of World War II occurred on these islands. Self-government was achieved in 1976 and independence two years later. Ethnic violence, government malfeasance, and endemic crime have undermined stability and civil society. In June 2003, Prime Minister Sir Allen KEMAKEZA sought the assistance of Australia in reestablishing law and order; the following month, an Australian-led multinational force arrived to restore peace and disarm ethnic militias. The Regional Assistance Mission to the Solomon Islands (RAMSI) has been very effective in restoring law and order and rebuilding government institutions.

GEOGRAPHY

Location: Oceania, group of islands in the South Pacific Ocean, east of Papua New Guinea
Geographic coordinates: 8 00 S, 159 00 E
Map references: Oceania
Area:
total: 28,450 sq km
land: 27,540 sq km
water: 910 sq km
Area - comparative: slightly smaller than Maryland
Land boundaries: 0 km
Coastline: 5,313 km
Maritime claims: measured from claimed archipelagic baselines
territorial sea: 12 nm
exclusive economic zone: 200 nm
continental shelf: 200 nm
Climate: tropical monsoon; few extremes of temperature and weather
Terrain: mostly rugged mountains with some low coral atolls
Elevation extremes:
lowest point: Pacific Ocean 0 m
highest point: Mount Makarakomburu 2,447 m
Natural resources: fish, forests, gold, bauxite, phosphates, lead, zinc, nickel
Land use:
arable land: 0.64%
permanent crops: 2%
other: 97.36% (2001)
Irrigated land: NA
Natural hazards: typhoons, but rarely destructive; geologically active region with frequent earth tremors; volcanic activity
Environment - current issues: deforestation; soil erosion; many of the surrounding coral reefs are dead or dying
Environment - international agreements:
party to: Biodiversity, Climate Change, Climate Change-Kyoto Protocol, Desertification, Environmental Modification, Law of the Sea, Marine Dumping, Marine Life Conservation, Ozone Layer Protection, Whaling
signed, but not ratified: none of the selected agreements
Geography - note: strategic location on sea routes between the South Pacific Ocean, the Solomon Sea, and the Coral Sea

PEOPLE

Population: 538,032 (July 2005 est.)
Age structure:
0-14 years: 41.9% (male 114,860/female 110,404)
15-64 years: 54.9% (male 149,400/female 145,970)
65 years and over: 3.2% (male 8,371/female 9,027) (2005 est.)
Median age:
total: 18.63 years
male: 18.5 years
female: 18.76 years (2005 est.)
Population growth rate: 2.68% (2005 est.)
Birth rate: 30.74 births/1,000 population (2005 est.)

Death rate: 3.98 deaths/1,000 population (2005 est.)
Net migration rate: 0 migrant(s)/1,000 population (2005 est.)
Sex ratio:
at birth: 1.05 male(s)/female
under 15 years: 1.04 male(s)/female
15-64 years: 1.02 male(s)/female
65 years and over: 0.93 male(s)/female
total population: 1.03 male(s)/female (2005 est.)
Infant mortality rate:
total: 21.29 deaths/1,000 live births
male: 24.27 deaths/1,000 live births
female: 18.17 deaths/1,000 live births (2005 est.)
Life expectancy at birth:
total population: 72.66 years
male: 70.16 years
female: 75.28 years (2005 est.)
Total fertility rate: 4.04 children born/woman (2005 est.)
HIV/AIDS - adult prevalence rate: NA
HIV/AIDS - people living with HIV/AIDS: NA
HIV/AIDS - deaths: NA
Nationality:
noun: Solomon Islander(s)
adjective: Solomon Islander
Ethnic groups: Melanesian 94.5%, Polynesian 3%, Micronesian 1.2%, other 1.1%, unspecified 0.2% (1999 census)
Religions: Church of Melanesia 32.8%, Roman Catholic 19%, South Seas Evangelical 17%, Seventh-Day Adventist 11.2%, United Church 10.3%, Christian Fellowship Church 2.4%, other Christian 4.4%, other 2.4%, unspecified 0.3%, none 0.2% (1999 census)
Languages: Melanesian pidgin in much of the country is lingua franca; English is official but spoken by only 1%-2% of the population
note: 120 indigenous languages
Literacy:
definition: NA
total population: NA%
male: NA%
female: NA%

GOVERNMENT

Country name:
conventional long form: none
conventional short form: Solomon Islands
former: British Solomon Islands
Government type: parliamentary democracy
Capital: Honiara
Administrative divisions: 9 provinces and 1 capital territory*; Central, Choiseul, Guadalcanal, Honiara*, Isabel, Makira, Malaita, Rennell and Bellona, Temotu, Western
Independence: 7 July 1978 (from UK)
National holiday: Independence Day, 7 July (1978)
Constitution: 7 July 1978
Legal system: English common law, which is widely disregarded
Suffrage: 21 years of age; universal
Executive branch:
chief of state: Queen ELIZABETH II (since 6 February 1952), represented by Governor General Nathaniel WAENA (since 7 July 2004)
head of government: Prime Minister Sir Allan KEMAKEZA (since 17 December 2001); Deputy Prime Minister Snyder RINI (since 17 December 2001)
cabinet: Cabinet consists of 20 members appointed by the governor general on the advice of the prime minister from among the members of Parliament
elections: none; the monarch is hereditary; governor general appointed by the monarch on the advice of Parliament for up to five years; following legislative elections, the leader of the majority party or the leader of a majority coalition is usually elected prime minister by Parliament; deputy prime minister appointed by the governor general on the advice of the prime minister from among the members of Parliament
Legislative branch: unicameral National Parliament (50 seats; members elected from single-member constituencies by popular vote to serve four-year terms)
elections: last held 5 December 2001 (next to be held not later than December 2005)
election results: percent of vote by party - PAP 40%, SIACC 40%, PPP 20%; seats by party - PAP 16, SIACC 13, PPP 2, SILP 1, independents 18
Judicial branch: Court of Appeal
Political parties and leaders: Association of Independents [Snyder RINI]; People's Alliance Party or PAP [Allan KEMAKEZA]; People's Progressive Party or PPP [Mannaseh Damukana SOGAVARE]; Solomon Islands Alliance for Change Coalition or SIACC [Bartholomew ULUFA'ALU]; Solomon Islands Labor Party or SILP [Joses TUHANUKU]
note: in general, Solomon Islands politics is characterized by fluid coalitions
Political pressure groups and leaders: NA
International organization participation: ACP, AsDB, C, ESCAP, FAO, G-77, IBRD, ICAO, ICCt (signatory), ICRM, IDA, IFAD, IFC, IFRCS, ILO, IMF, IMO, IOC, ITU, MIGA, OPCW, PIF, Sparteca, SPC, UN, UNCTAD, UNESCO, UPU, WFTU, WHO, WMO, WTO
Diplomatic representation in the US:
chief of mission: Ambassador Collin David BECK
chancery: 800 Second Avenue, Suite 400L, New York, NY 10017
telephone: [1] (212) 599-6192, 6193
FAX: [1] (212) 661-8925
Diplomatic representation from the US: the US does not have an embassy in Solomon Islands (embassy closed July 1993); the ambassador to Papua New Guinea is accredited to the Solomon Islands
Flag description: divided diagonally by a thin yellow stripe from the lower hoist-side corner; the upper triangle (hoist side) is blue with five white five-pointed stars arranged in an X pattern; the lower triangle is green
Government - note: June 2003 Prime Minister Sir Allan KEMAKEZA sought the intervention of Australia to aid in restoring order; parliament approved the request for intervention in July 2003; troops from Australia, New Zealand, Fiji, Papua New Guinea, and Tonga arrived 24 July 2003. By the end of 2004 the Regional Assistance Mission to the Solomon Islands (RAMSI) had been scaled back to 302 police officers and 120 military in addition to civilian technical advisors.

ECONOMY

Economy - overview: The bulk of the population depends on agriculture, fishing, and forestry for at least part of their livelihood. Most manufactured goods and petroleum products must be imported. The islands are rich in undeveloped mineral resources such as lead, zinc, nickel, and gold. Prior to the arrival of the Regional Assistance Mission to the Solomon Islands (RAMSI), severe ethnic violence, the closing of key businesses, and an empty government treasury culminated in economic collapse. RAMSI has enabled a return to law and order, a new period of economic stability, and modest growth as the economy rebuilds.
GDP (purchasing power parity): $800 million (2002 est.)
GDP (official exchange rate): NA
GDP - real growth rate: 5.8% (2003 est.)
GDP - per capita: purchasing power parity - $1,700 (2002 est.)
GDP - composition by sector:
agriculture: 42%
industry: 11%
services: 47% (2000 est.)
Labor force: 26,840 (1999)
Labor force - by occupation: agriculture 75%, industry 5%, services 20% (2000 est.)
Unemployment rate: NA%
Population below poverty line: NA
Household income or consumption by percentage share:
lowest 10%: NA
highest 10%: NA
Inflation rate (consumer prices): 10% (2003 est.)

Budget:
revenues: $49.7 million
expenditures: $75.1 million, including capital expenditures of $0 (2003)
Agriculture - products: cocoa beans, coconuts, palm kernels, rice, potatoes, vegetables, fruit; cattle, pigs; timber; fish
Industries: fish (tuna), mining, timber
Industrial production growth rate: NA
Electricity - production: 55 million kWh (2003)
Electricity - production by source:
fossil fuel: 100%
hydro: 0%
nuclear: 0%
other: 0% (2001)
Electricity - consumption: 51.15 million kWh (2003)
Electricity - exports: 0 kWh (2003)
Electricity - imports: 0 kWh (2003)
Oil - production: 0 bbl/day (2003 est.)
Oil - consumption: 1,270 bbl/day (2003 est.)
Oil - exports: NA (2001)
Oil - imports: NA (2001)
Exports: $171 million f.o.b. (2004 est.)
Exports - partners: China 27.8%, South Korea 17%, Thailand 15.8%, Japan 9.7%, Philippines 4.8% (2004)
Imports: $159 million f.o.b. (2004 est.)
Imports - partners: Australia 24.6%, Singapore 23.1%, New Zealand 7.7%, Fiji 4.8%, Papua New Guinea 4.7% (2004)
Debt - external: $180.4 million (2002)
Economic aid - recipient: $28 million annually, mainly from Australia (2003 est.)
Currency (code): Solomon Islands dollar (SBD)
Currency code: SBD
Exchange rates: Solomon Islands dollars per US dollar - NA (2005), 7.4847 (2004), 7.5059 (2003), 6.7488 (2002), 5.278 (2001)
Fiscal year: calendar year

COMMUNICATIONS

Telephones - main lines in use: 6,600 (2002)
Telephones - mobile cellular: 1,000 (2002)
Telephone system:
general assessment: NA
domestic: NA
international: country code - 677; satellite earth station - 1 Intelsat (Pacific Ocean)
Radio broadcast stations: AM 1, FM 1, shortwave 1 (2004)
Radios: 57,000 (1997)
Televisions: 3,000 (1997)
Internet country code: .sb
Internet hosts: 398 (2003)
Internet Service Providers (ISPs): 1 (2000)
Internet users: 2,200 (2002)

TRANSPORTATION

Airports: 33 (2004 est.)
Airports - with paved runways:
total: 2
1,524 to 2,437 m: 1
914 to 1,523 m: 1 (2005 est.)
Airports - with unpaved runways:
total: 32
1,524 to 2,437 m: 1
914 to 1,523 m: 9
under 914 m: 22 (2005 est.)
Roadways:
total: 1,360 km
paved: 34 km
unpaved: 1,326 km (1999 est.)
Ports and terminals: Honiara, Malloco Bay, Shortland Harbor, Viru Harbor, Yandina

MILITARY

Military branches: no regular military forces; Royal Solomon Islands Police (RSIP)
Military expenditures - dollar figure: NA
Military expenditures - percent of GDP: NA

TRANSNATIONAL ISSUES

Disputes - international: Australian Defense Force leads the Regional Assistance Mission to the Solomon Islands (RAMSI) at the invitation of the Solomon Islands' Government to maintain civil and political order and reinforce regional security

SOMALIA

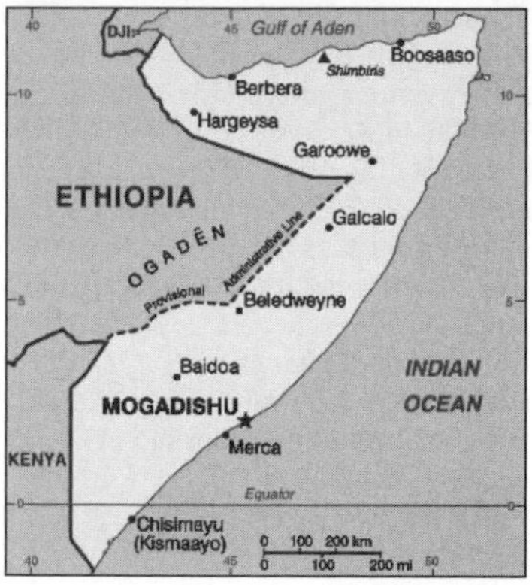

INTRODUCTION

Background: The regime of Mohamed SIAD Barre was ousted in January 1991; turmoil, factional fighting, and anarchy have followed in the years since. In May of 1991, northern clans declared an independent Republic of Somaliland that now includes the administrative regions of Awdal, Woqooyi Galbeed, Togdheer, Sanaag, and Sool. Although not recognized by any government, this entity has maintained a stable existence, aided by the overwhelming dominance of a ruling clan and economic infrastructure left behind by British, Russian, and American military assistance programs. The regions of Bari and Nugaal and northern Mudug comprise a neighboring self-declared autonomous state of Puntland, which has been self-governing since 1998, but does not aim at independence; it has also made strides towards reconstructing a legitimate, representative government, but has suffered some civil strife. Puntland disputes its border with Somaliland as it also claims portions of eastern Sool and Sanaag. Beginning in 1993, a two-year UN humanitarian effort (primarily in the south) was able to alleviate famine conditions, but when the UN withdrew in 1995, having suffered significant casualties, order still had not been restored. The mandate of the Transitional National Government (TNG), created in August 2000 in Arta, Djibouti, expired in August 2003. New Somali President Abdullahi YUSUF Ahmed has formed a new Transitional Federal Government (TFG) consisting of a 275-member parliament. Discussions regarding moving the new government from Jawhar to Mogadishu are ongoing. Numerous warlords and factions are still fighting for control of the capital city as well as for other southern regions. Suspicion of Somali links with global terrorism further complicates the picture.

GEOGRAPHY

Location: Eastern Africa, bordering the Gulf of Aden and the Indian Ocean, east of Ethiopia
Geographic coordinates: 10 00 N, 49 00 E
Map references: Africa
Area:
total: 637,657 sq km
land: 627,337 sq km
water: 10,320 sq km
Area - comparative: slightly smaller than Texas
Land boundaries:
total: 2,340 km
border countries: Djibouti 58 km, Ethiopia 1,600 km, Kenya 682 km
Coastline: 3,025 km
Maritime claims:
territorial sea: 200 nm
Climate: principally desert; December to

February - northeast monsoon, moderate temperatures in north and very hot in south; May to October - southwest monsoon, torrid in the north and hot in the south, irregular rainfall, hot and humid periods (tangambili) between monsoons
Terrain: mostly flat to undulating plateau rising to hills in north
Elevation extremes:
lowest point: Indian Ocean 0 m
highest point: Shimbiris 2,416 m
Natural resources: uranium and largely unexploited reserves of iron ore, tin, gypsum, bauxite, copper, salt, natural gas, likely oil reserves
Land use:
arable land: 1.67%
permanent crops: 0.04%
other: 98.29% (2001)
Irrigated land: 2,000 sq km (1998 est.)
Natural hazards: recurring droughts; frequent dust storms over eastern plains in summer; floods during rainy season
Environment - current issues: famine; use of contaminated water contributes to human health problems; deforestation; overgrazing; soil erosion; desertification
Environment - international agreements:
party to: Endangered Species, Law of the Sea, Ozone Layer Protection
Geography - note: strategic location on Horn of Africa along southern approaches to Bab el Mandeb and route through Red Sea and Suez Canal

PEOPLE

Population: 8,591,629
note: this estimate was derived from an official census taken in 1975 by the Somali Government; population counting in Somalia is complicated by the large number of nomads and by refugee movements in response to famine and clan warfare (July 2005 est.)
Age structure:
0-14 years: 44.5% (male 1,918,209/female 1,905,974)
15-64 years: 52.9% (male 2,278,406/female 2,263,602)
65 years and over: 2.6% (male 96,256/female 129,182) (2005 est.)
Median age:
total: 17.59 years
male: 17.53 years
female: 17.65 years (2005 est.)
Population growth rate: 3.38% (2005 est.)
Birth rate: 45.62 births/1,000 population (2005 est.)
Death rate: 16.97 deaths/1,000 population (2005 est.)
Net migration rate: 5.19 migrant(s)/1,000 population (2005 est.)
Sex ratio:
at birth: 1.03 male(s)/female
under 15 years: 1.01 male(s)/female
15-64 years: 1.01 male(s)/female
65 years and over: 0.74 male(s)/female
total population: 1 male(s)/female (2005 est.)
Infant mortality rate:
total: 116.7 deaths/1,000 live births
male: 126.06 deaths/1,000 live births
female: 107.06 deaths/1,000 live births (2005 est.)
Life expectancy at birth:
total population: 48.09 years
male: 46.36 years
female: 49.87 years (2005 est.)
Total fertility rate: 6.84 children born/woman (2005 est.)
HIV/AIDS - adult prevalence rate: 1% (2001 est.)
HIV/AIDS - people living with HIV/AIDS: 43,000 (2001 est.)
HIV/AIDS - deaths: NA
Major infectious diseases:
degree of risk: very high
food or waterborne diseases: bacterial and protozoal diarrhea, hepatitis A and E, and typhoid fever
vectorborne diseases: malaria and dengue fever are high risks in some locations
water contact disease: schistosomiasis
animal contact disease: rabies (2004)
Nationality:
noun: Somali(s)
adjective: Somali
Ethnic groups: Somali 85%, Bantu and other non-Somali 15% (including Arabs 30,000)
Religions: Sunni Muslim
Languages: Somali (official), Arabic, Italian, English
Literacy:
definition: age 15 and over can read and write
total population: 37.8%
male: 49.7%
female: 25.8% (2001 est.)

GOVERNMENT

Country name:
conventional long form: none
conventional short form: Somalia
former: Somali Republic, Somali Democratic Republic
Government type: no permanent national government; transitional, parliamentary federal government
Capital: Mogadishu
Administrative divisions: 18 regions (plural - NA, singular - gobolka); Awdal, Bakool, Banaadir, Bari, Bay, Galguduud, Gedo, Hiiraan, Jubbada Dhexe, Jubbada Hoose, Mudug, Nugaal, Sanaag, Shabeellaha Dhexe, Shabeellaha Hoose, Sool, Togdheer, Woqooyi Galbeed
Independence: 1 July 1960 (from a merger of British Somaliland, which became independent from the UK on 26 June 1960, and Italian Somaliland, which became independent from the Italian-administered UN trusteeship on 1 July 1960, to form the Somali Republic)
National holiday: Foundation of the Somali Republic, 1 July (1960); note - 26 June (1960) in Somaliland
Constitution: 25 August 1979, presidential approval 23 September 1979
note: the formation of transitional governing institutions, known as the Transitional Federal Government, is currently ongoing
Legal system: no national system; Shari'a and secular courts are in some localities
Suffrage: 18 years of age, universal
Executive branch:
chief of state: Abdullahi YUSUF Ahmed (since 14 October 2004); note - a new Transitional Federal Government consisting of a 275-member parliament was established in October 2004; the TFG moved from Kenya to Jowhar, Somalia in June 2004 but is struggling to establish effective governance in the country
head of government: Prime Minister Ali Muhammad GHEDI (since 24 December 2004)
cabinet: Cabinet appointed by the prime minister and approved by the Transitional Federal Assembly
election results: Abdullahi YUSUF Ahmed, the leader of the Puntland region of Somalia, was elected president by the Transitional Federal Assembly
Legislative branch: unicameral National Assembly
note: fledgling parliament; a 275-member Transitional Federal Assembly; the new parliament consists of 61 seats assigned to each of four large clan groups (Darod, Digil-Mirifle, Dir, and Hawiye) with the remaining 31 seats divided between minority clans
Judicial branch: following the breakdown of the central government, most regions have reverted to local forms of conflict resolution, either secular, traditional clan-based arbitration, or Islamic (Shari'a) law with a provision for appeal of all sentences
Political parties and leaders: none
Political pressure groups and leaders: numerous clan and subclan factions are currently vying for power
International organization participation: ACP, AfDB, AFESD, AMF, AU, CAEU, FAO, G-77, IBRD, ICAO, ICRM, IDA, IDB, IFAD, IFC, IFRCS, IGAD, ILO, IMF, IMO, Interpol, IOC, IOM (observer), ITU, LAS, NAM, OIC, UN, UNCTAD, UNESCO, UNHCR, UNIDO, UPU, WFTU, WHO, WIPO, WMO
Diplomatic representation in the US: Somalia does not have an embassy in the US (ceased operations on 8 May 1991);

note - the TFG and other factions have representatives in Washington and at the United Nations
Diplomatic representation from the US: the US does not have an embassy in Somalia; US interests are represented by the US Embassy in Nairobi, Kenya at United Nations Avenue, Gigira, Nairobi; mailing address: Unit 64100, Nairobi; APO AE 09831; telephone: [254] (20) 363-6000; FAX [254] (20) 363-6157
Flag description: light blue with a large white five-pointed star in the center; blue field influenced by the flag of the UN
Government - note: although an interim government was created in 2004 other governing bodies continue to exist and control various cities and regions of the country, including the self-declared Republic of Somaliland, and traditional clan and faction strongholds

ECONOMY

Economy - overview: Somalia's economic fortunes are driven by its deep political divisions. The northwestern area has declared its independence as the "Republic of Somaliland"; the northeastern region of Puntland is a semi-autonomous state; and the remaining southern portion is riddled with the struggles of rival factions. Economic life continues, in part because much activity is local and relatively easily protected. Agriculture is the most important sector, with livestock normally accounting for about 40% of GDP and about 65% of export earnings, but Saudi Arabia's recent ban on Somali livestock, because of Rift Valley Fever concerns, has severely hampered the sector. Nomads and semi-nomads, who are dependent upon livestock for their livelihood, make up a large portion of the population. Livestock, hides, fish, charcoal, and bananas are Somalia's principal exports, while sugar, sorghum, corn, qat, and machined goods are the principal imports. Somalia's small industrial sector, based on the processing of agricultural products, has largely been looted and sold as scrap metal. Despite the seeming anarchy, Somalia's service sector has managed to survive and grow. Telecommunication firms provide wireless services in most major cities and offer the lowest international call rates on the continent. In the absence of a formal banking sector, money exchange services have sprouted throughout the country, handling between $500 million and $1 billion in remittances annually. Mogadishu's main market offers a variety of goods from food to the newest electronic gadgets. Hotels continue to operate, and militias provide security. The ongoing civil disturbances and clan rivalries, however, have interfered with any broad-based economic development and international aid arrangements. In 2004 and 2005 Somalia's overdue financial obligations to the IMF continued to grow. Statistics on Somalia's GDP, growth, per capita income, and inflation should be viewed skeptically. In late December 2004, a major tsunami took an estimated 150 lives and caused destruction of property in coastal areas.
GDP (purchasing power parity): $4.825 billion (2005 est.)
GDP (official exchange rate): NA
GDP - real growth rate: 2.4% (2005 est.)
GDP - per capita: purchasing power parity - $600 (2005 est.)
GDP - composition by sector:
agriculture: 65%
industry: 10%
services: 25% (2000 est.)
Labor force: 3.7 million (very few are skilled laborers)
Labor force - by occupation: agriculture (mostly pastoral nomadism) 71%, industry and services 29%
Unemployment rate: NA
Population below poverty line: NA
Household income or consumption by percentage share:
lowest 10%: NA
highest 10%: NA
Inflation rate (consumer prices): note - businesses print their own money, so inflation rates cannot be sensibly determined (2004 est.)
Budget:
revenues: NA
expenditures: NA, including capital expenditures of NA
Agriculture - products: cattle, sheep, goats; bananas, sorghum, corn, coconuts, rice, sugarcane, mangoes, sesame seeds, beans; fish
Industries: a few light industries, including sugar refining, textiles, wireless communication
Industrial production growth rate: NA
Electricity - production: 235.6 million kWh (2003)
Electricity - production by source:
fossil fuel: 100%
hydro: 0%
nuclear: 0%
other: 0% (2001)
Electricity - consumption: 219.1 million kWh (2003)
Electricity - exports: 0 kWh (2003)
Electricity - imports: 0 kWh (2003)
Oil - production: 0 bbl/day (2003 est.)
Oil - consumption: 5,000 bbl/day (2003 est.)
Oil - exports: NA (2001)
Oil - imports: NA (2001)
Oil - proved reserves: 0 bbl (1 January 2002)
Natural gas - proved reserves: 2.832 billion cu m (1 January 2002)
Exports: $241 million f.o.b. (2004 est.)
Exports - partners: UAE 50.3%, Yemen 15.6%, Oman 6% (2004)
Imports: $576 million f.o.b. (2004 est.)
Imports - partners: Djibouti 30.1%, Kenya 13.7%, India 8.6%, Brazil 8.5%, Oman 4.4%, UAE 4.2% (2004)
Debt - external: $3 billion (2001 est.)
Economic aid - recipient: $60 million (1999 est.)
Currency (code): Somali shilling (SOS)
Currency code: SOS
Exchange rates: Somali shillings per US dollar - 11,000 (November 2000), 2,620 (January 1999), 7,500 (November 1997 est.), 7,000 (January 1996 est.), 5,000 (1 January 1995)
note: the Republic of Somaliland, a self-declared independent country not recognized by any foreign government, issues its own currency, the Somaliland shilling
Fiscal year: NA

COMMUNICATIONS

Telephones - main lines in use: 100,000 (2002 est.)
Telephones - mobile cellular: 35,000 (2002)
Telephone system:
general assessment: the public telecommunications system was almost completely destroyed or dismantled by the civil war factions; private wireless companies offer service in most major cities and charge the lowest international rates on the continent
domestic: local cellular telephone systems have been established in Mogadishu and in several other population centers
international: country code - 252; international connections are available from Mogadishu by satellite
Radio broadcast stations: AM 0, FM 11, shortwave 1 in Mogadishu; 1 FM in Puntland, 1 FM in Somaliland (2001)
Radios: 470,000 (1997)
Television broadcast stations: 4
note: two in Mogadishu; two in Hargeisa (2001)
Televisions: 135,000 (1997)
Internet country code: .so
Internet hosts: 4 (2004)
Internet Service Providers (ISPs): 3 (one each in Boosaaso, Hargeisa, and Mogadishu) (2000)
Internet users: 89,000 (2002)

TRANSPORTATION

Airports: 60 (2004 est.)
Airports - with paved runways:
total: 6
over 3,047 m: 4

2,438 to 3,047 m: 1
1,524 to 2,437 m: 1 (2005 est.)
Airports - with unpaved runways:
total: 58
2,438 to 3,047 m: 4
1,524 to 2,437 m: 19
914 to 1,523 m: 29
under 914 m: 6 (2005 est.)
Roadways:
total: 22,100 km
paved: 2,608 km
unpaved: 19,492 km (1999 est.)
Ports and terminals: Boosaaso, Berbera, Chisimayu (Kismaayo), Merca, Mogadishu

MILITARY

Military branches: A Somali National Army was attempted under the interim government; numerous factions and clans maintain independent militias, and the Somaliland and Puntland regional governments maintain their own security and police forces
Military service age and obligation: 18 years of age (est.) (2001)
Manpower available for military service:
males age 18-49: 1,787,727 (2005 est.)
Manpower fit for military service: *males age 18-49:* 1,022,360 (2005 est.)
Military expenditures - dollar figure: $18.9 million (2003)
Military expenditures - percent of GDP: 0.9% (2003)

TRANSNATIONAL ISSUES

Disputes - international: "Somaliland" secessionists provide port facilities to land-locked Ethiopia and establish commercial ties with regional states; "Puntland" and "Somaliland" "governments" seek support from neighboring states in their secessionist aspirations and in conflicts with each other; Ethiopia has only an administrative line with the Oromo region of southern Somalia and maintains alliances with local Somali clans opposed to the unrecognized Somali Interim Government, which plans eventual relocation from Kenya to Mogadishu; rival militia and clan fighting in southern Somalia periodically spills over into Kenya; most of the remaining 23,000 Somali refugees in Ethiopia are expected to be repatriated in 2005
Refugees and internally displaced persons: *IDPs:* 375,000 (civil war since 1988, clan-based competition for resources) (2004)

SOUTH AFRICA

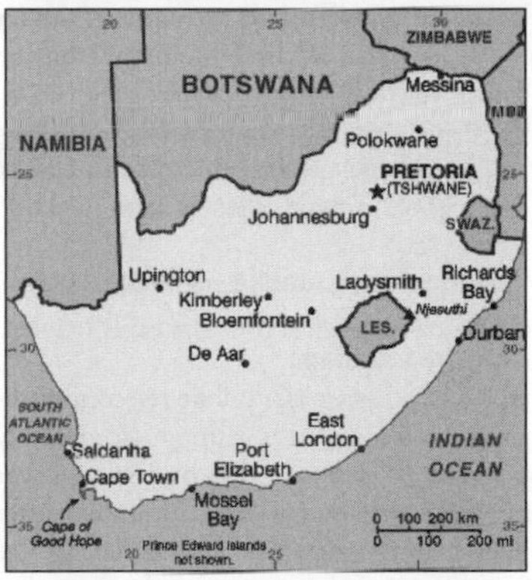

INTRODUCTION

Background: After the British seized the Cape of Good Hope area in 1806, many of the Dutch settlers (the Boers) trekked north to found their own republics. The discovery of diamonds (1867) and gold (1886) spurred wealth and immigration and intensified the subjugation of the native inhabitants. The Boers resisted British encroachments, but were defeated in the Boer War (1899-1902). The resulting Union of South Africa operated under a policy of apartheid - the separate development of the races. The 1990s brought an end to apartheid politically and ushered in black majority rule.

GEOGRAPHY

Location: Southern Africa, at the southern tip of the continent of Africa
Geographic coordinates: 29 00 S, 24 00 E
Map references: Africa
Area:
total: 1,219,912 sq km
land: 1,219,912 sq km
water: 0 sq km
note: includes Prince Edward Islands (Marion Island and Prince Edward Island)
Area - comparative: slightly less than twice the size of Texas
Land boundaries:
total: 4,862 km
border countries: Botswana 1,840 km, Lesotho 909 km, Mozambique 491 km, Namibia 967 km, Swaziland 430 km, Zimbabwe 225 km
Coastline: 2,798 km
Maritime claims:
territorial sea: 12 nm
contiguous zone: 24 nm
exclusive economic zone: 200 nm
continental shelf: 200 nm or to edge of the continental margin
Climate: mostly semiarid; subtropical along east coast; sunny days, cool nights
Terrain: vast interior plateau rimmed by rugged hills and narrow coastal plain
Elevation extremes:
lowest point: Atlantic Ocean 0 m
highest point: Njesuthi 3,408 m
Natural resources: gold, chromium, antimony, coal, iron ore, manganese, nickel, phosphates, tin, uranium, gem diamonds, platinum, copper, vanadium, salt, natural gas
Land use:
arable land: 12.08%
permanent crops: 0.79%
other: 87.13% (2001)
Irrigated land: 13,500 sq km (1998 est.)
Natural hazards: prolonged droughts
Environment - current issues: lack of important arterial rivers or lakes requires extensive water conservation and control measures; growth in water usage outpacing supply; pollution of rivers from agricultural runoff and urban discharge; air pollution resulting in acid rain; soil erosion; desertification
Environment - international agreements:
party to: Antarctic-Environmental Protocol, Antarctic-Marine Living Resources, Antarctic Seals, Antarctic Treaty, Biodiversity, Climate Change, Climate Change-Kyoto Protocol, Desertification, Endangered Species, Hazardous Wastes, Law of the Sea, Marine Dumping, Marine Life Conservation, Ozone Layer Protection, Ship Pollution, Wetlands, Whaling
signed, but not ratified: none of the selected agreements
Geography - note: South Africa completely surrounds Lesotho and almost completely surrounds Swaziland

PEOPLE

Population: 44,344,136
note: estimates for this country explicitly take into account the effects of excess mortality due to AIDS; this can result in lower life expectancy, higher infant mortality and death rates, lower population and growth rates, and changes in the distribution of population by age and sex than would otherwise be expected (July 2005 est.)
Age structure:
0-14 years: 30.3% (male 6,760,137/female 6,682,013)
15-64 years: 64.5% (male 13,860,727/female 14,750,496)
65 years and over: 5.2% (male 893,360/female 1,397,403) (2005 est.)
Median age:
total: 23.98 years
male: 23.12 years
female: 24.86 years (2005 est.)
Population growth rate: -0.31% (2005 est.)

Birth rate: 18.48 births/1,000 population (2005 est.)
Death rate: 21.32 deaths/1,000 population (2005 est.)
Net migration rate: -0.22 migrant(s)/ 1,000 population (2005 est.)
Sex ratio:
at birth: 1.02 male(s)/female
under 15 years: 1.01 male(s)/female
15-64 years: 0.94 male(s)/female
65 years and over: 0.64 male(s)/female
total population: 0.94 male(s)/female (2005 est.)
Infant mortality rate:
total: 61.81 deaths/1,000 live births
male: 65.6 deaths/1,000 live births
female: 57.93 deaths/1,000 live births (2005 est.)
Life expectancy at birth:
total population: 43.27 years
male: 43.47 years
female: 43.06 years (2005 est.)
Total fertility rate: 2.24 children born/woman (2005 est.)
HIV/AIDS - adult prevalence rate: 21.5% (2003 est.)
HIV/AIDS - people living with HIV/AIDS: 5.3 million (2003 est.)
HIV/AIDS - deaths: 370,000 (2003 est.)
Nationality:
noun: South African(s)
adjective: South African
Ethnic groups: black African 79%, white 9.6%, colored 8.9%, Indian/Asian 2.5% (2001 census)
Religions: Zion Christian 11.1%, Pentecostal/Charismatic 8.2%, Catholic 7.1%, Methodist 6.8%, Dutch Reformed 6.7%, Anglican 3.8%, other Christian 36%, Islam 1.5%, other 2.3%, unspecified 1.4%, none 15.1% (2001 census)
Languages: IsiZulu 23.8%, IsiXhosa 17.6%, Afrikaans 13.3%, Sepedi 9.4%, English 8.2%, Setswana 8.2%, Sesotho 7.9%, Xitsonga 4.4%, other 7.2% (2001 census)
Literacy:
definition: age 15 and over can read and write
total population: 86.4%
male: 87%
female: 85.7% (2003 est.)

GOVERNMENT

Country name:
conventional long form: Republic of South Africa
conventional short form: South Africa
former: Union of South Africa
abbreviation: RSA
Government type: republic
Capital: Pretoria; note - Cape Town is the legislative center and Bloemfontein the judicial center
Administrative divisions: 9 provinces; Eastern Cape, Free State, Gauteng, KwaZulu-Natal, Limpopo, Mpumalanga, North-West, Northern Cape, Western Cape
Independence: 31 May 1910 (from UK); note - South Africa became a republic in 1961 following an October 1960 referendum
National holiday: Freedom Day, 27 April (1994)
Constitution: 10 December 1996; this new constitution was certified by the Constitutional Court on 4 December 1996, was signed by then President MANDELA on 10 December 1996, and entered into effect on 3 February 1997; it is being implemented in phases
Legal system: based on Roman-Dutch law and English common law; accepts compulsory ICJ jurisdiction, with reservations
Suffrage: 18 years of age, universal
Executive branch:
chief of state: President Thabo MBEKI (since 16 June 1999); Executive Deputy President Phumzile MLAMBO-NGCUKA (since 23 June 2005); note - the president is both the chief of state and head of government
head of government: President Thabo MBEKI (since 16 June 1999); Executive Deputy President Phumzile MLAMBO-NGCUKA (since 23 June 2005); note - the president is both the chief of state and head of government
cabinet: Cabinet appointed by the president
elections: president elected by the National Assembly for a five-year term; election last held 24 April 2004 (next to be held April 2009)
election results: Thabo MBEKI elected president; percent of National Assembly vote - 100% (by acclamation)
note: ANC-IFP is the governing coalition
Legislative branch: bicameral Parliament consisting of the National Assembly (400 seats; members are elected by popular vote under a system of proportional representation to serve five-year terms) and the National Council of Provinces (90 seats, 10 members elected by each of the nine provincial legislatures for five-year terms; has special powers to protect regional interests, including the safeguarding of cultural and linguistic traditions among ethnic minorities); note - following the implementation of the new constitution on 3 February 1997 the former Senate was disbanded and replaced by the National Council of Provinces with essentially no change in membership and party affiliations, although the new institution's responsibilities have been changed somewhat by the new constitution
elections: National Assembly and National Council of Provinces - last held 14 April 2004 (next to be held NA 2009)
election results: National Assembly - percent of vote by party - ANC 69.7%, DA 12.4%, IFP 7%, UDM 2.3%, NNP 1.7%, ACDP 1.6%, other 5.3%; seats by party - ANC 279, DA 50, IFP 28, UDM 9, NNP 7, ACDP 6, other 21; National Council of Provinces - percent of vote by party - NA%; seats by party - NA
Judicial branch: Constitutional Court; Supreme Court of Appeals; High Courts; Magistrate Courts
Political parties and leaders: African Christian Democratic Party or ACDP [Kenneth MESHOE, president]; African National Congress or ANC [Thabo MBEKI, president]; Democratic Alliance or DA (formed from the merger of the Democratic Party or DP and the Freedom Alliance or FA) [Anthony LEON]; Inkatha Freedom Party or IFP [Mangosuthu BUTHELEZI, president]; Pan-Africanist Congress or PAC [Stanley MOGOBA, president]; United Democratic Movement or UDM [Bantu HOLOMISA]
Political pressure groups and leaders: Congress of South African Trade Unions or COSATU [Zwelinzima VAVI, general secretary]; South African Communist Party or SACP [Blade NZIMANDE, general secretary]; South African National Civics Organization or SANCO [Mlungisi HLONGWANE, national president]; note - COSATU and SACP are in a formal alliance with the ANC
International organization participation: ACP, AfDB, AU, BIS, C, FAO, G-24, G-77, IAEA, IBRD, ICAO, ICC, ICCt, ICFTU, ICRM, IDA, IFAD, IFC, IFRCS, IHO, ILO, IMF, IMO, Interpol, IOC, IOM, ISO, ITU, MIGA, MONUC, NAM, NSG, ONUB, OPCW, PCA, SACU, SADC, UN, UNCTAD, UNESCO, UNHCR, UNIDO, UNITAR, UNMEE, UNMIL, UPU, WCL, WCO, WFTU, WHO, WIPO, WMO, WToO, WTO, ZC
Diplomatic representation in the US:
chief of mission: Ambassador Barbara Joyce Mosima MASEKELA
chancery: 3051 Massachusetts Avenue NW, Washington, DC 20008
telephone: [1] (202) 232-4400
FAX: [1] (202) 265-1607
consulate(s) general: Chicago, Los Angeles, and New York
Diplomatic representation from the US:
chief of mission: Ambassador Jendayi E. FRAZER
embassy: 877 Pretorius Street, Pretoria
mailing address: P. O. Box 9536, Pretoria 0001
telephone: [27] (12) 342-1048
FAX: [27] (12) 342-2244

consulate(s) general: Cape Town, Durban, Johannesburg
Flag description: two equal width horizontal bands of red (top) and blue separated by a central green band which splits into a horizontal Y, the arms of which end at the corners of the hoist side; the Y embraces a black isosceles triangle from which the arms are separated by narrow yellow bands; the red and blue bands are separated from the green band and its arms by narrow white stripes

ECONOMY

Economy - overview: South Africa is a middle-income, emerging market with an abundant supply of natural resources; well-developed financial, legal, communications, energy, and transport sectors; a stock exchange that ranks among the 10 largest in the world; and a modern infrastructure supporting an efficient distribution of goods to major urban centers throughout the region. However, growth has not been strong enough to lower South Africa's high unemployment rate; and daunting economic problems remain from the apartheid era, especially poverty and lack of economic empowerment among the disadvantaged groups. South African economic policy is fiscally conservative, but pragmatic, focusing on targeting inflation and liberalizing trade as means to increase job growth and household income.
GDP (purchasing power parity): $527.4 billion (2005 est.)
GDP (official exchange rate): $191.3 billion (2005 est.)
GDP - real growth rate: 4.5% (2005 est.)
GDP - per capita: purchasing power parity - $11,900 (2005 est.)
GDP - composition by sector:
agriculture: 3.4%
industry: 31.6%
services: 65.1% (2005 est.)
Labor force: 15.23 million economically active (2005 est.)
Labor force - by occupation: agriculture 30%, industry 25%, services 45% (1999 est.)
Unemployment rate: 25.2% (2005 est.)
Population below poverty line: 50% (2000 est.)
Household income or consumption by percentage share:
lowest 10%: 1.1%
highest 10%: 45.9% (1994)
Distribution of family income - Gini index: 59.3 (1995)
Inflation rate (consumer prices): 4.6% (2005 est.)
Investment (gross fixed): 17.9% of GDP (2005 est.)
Budget:
revenues: $65.91 billion
expenditures: $70.62 billion, including capital expenditures of NA (2005 est.)
Public debt: 37.7% of GDP (2005 est.)
Agriculture - products: corn, wheat, sugarcane, fruits, vegetables; beef, poultry, mutton, wool, dairy products
Industries: mining (world's largest producer of platinum, gold, chromium), automobile assembly, metalworking, machinery, textile, iron and steel, chemicals, fertilizer, foodstuffs, commercial ship repair
Industrial production growth rate: 4.5% (2005 est.)
Electricity - production: 215.9 billion kWh (2003)
Electricity - production by source:
fossil fuel: 93.5%
hydro: 1.1%
nuclear: 5.5%
other: 0% (2001)
Electricity - consumption: 197.4 billion kWh (2003)
Electricity - exports: 10.14 billion kWh (2003)
Electricity - imports: 6.739 billion kWh (2003)
Oil - production: 216,700 bbl/day (2003 est.)
Oil - consumption: 484,000 bbl/day (2003 est.)
Oil - exports: NA (2001)
Oil - imports: NA (2001)
Oil - proved reserves: 7.84 million bbl (1 January 2002)
Natural gas - production: 1.8 billion cu m (2001 est.)
Natural gas - consumption: 1.8 billion cu m (2001 est.)
Natural gas - exports: 0 cu m (2001 est.)
Natural gas - imports: 0 cu m (2001 est.)
Natural gas - proved reserves: 14.16 billion cu m (1 January 2002)
Current account balance: $-9.584 billion (2005 est.)
Exports: $50.91 billion f.o.b. (2005 est.)
Exports - partners: US 10.2%, UK 9.2%, Japan 9%, Germany 7.1%, Netherlands 4% (2004)
Imports: $52.97 billion f.o.b. (2005 est.)
Imports - partners: Germany 14.2%, US 8.5%, China 7.5%, Japan 6.9%, UK 6.9%, France 6%, Saudi Arabia 5.6%, Iran 5% (2004)
Reserves of foreign exchange and gold: $20.16 billion (2005 est.)
Debt - external: $44.33 billion (30 June 2005 est.)
Economic aid - recipient: $487.5 million (2000)
Currency (code): rand (ZAR)
Currency code: ZAR
Exchange rates: rand per US dollar - 6.19 (2005), 6.4597 (2004), 7.5648 (2003), 10.5407 (2002), 8.6092 (2001)
Fiscal year: 1 April - 31 March

COMMUNICATIONS

Telephones - main lines in use: 4.844 million (2002)
Telephones - mobile cellular: 16.86 million (2003)
Telephone system:
general assessment: the system is the best developed and most modern in Africa
domestic: consists of carrier-equipped open-wire lines, coaxial cables, microwave radio relay links, fiber-optic cable, radiotelephone communication stations, and wireless local loops; key centers are Bloemfontein, Cape Town, Durban, Johannesburg, Port Elizabeth, and Pretoria
international: country code - 27; 2 submarine cables; satellite earth stations - 3 Intelsat (1 Indian Ocean and 2 Atlantic Ocean)
Radio broadcast stations: AM 14, FM 347 (plus 243 repeaters), shortwave 1 (1998)
Radios: 17 million (2001)
Television broadcast stations: 556 (plus 144 network repeaters) (1997)
Televisions: 6 million (2000)
Internet country code: .za
Internet hosts: 288,633 (2003)
Internet Service Providers (ISPs): 150 (2001)
Internet users: 3.1 million (2002)

TRANSPORTATION

Airports: 728 (2004 est.)
Airports - with paved runways:
total: 146
over 3,047 m: 10
2,438 to 3,047 m: 5
1,524 to 2,437 m: 51
914 to 1,523 m: 67
under 914 m: 13 (2005 est.)
Airports - with unpaved runways:
total: 582
1,524 to 2,437 m: 34
914 to 1,523 m: 300
under 914 m: 248 (2005 est.)
Pipelines: condensate 100 km; gas 1,052 km; oil 847 km; refined products 1,354 km (2004)
Railways:
total: 20,872 km
narrow gauge: 20,436 km 1.065-m gauge (10,436 km electrified); 436 km 0.610-m gauge
note: includes a 1,210 km commuter rail system (2004)
Roadways:
total: 275,971 km
paved: 57,568 km (including 2,032 km of expressways)
unpaved: 218,403 km (2002)
Merchant marine:
total: 2 ships (1,000 GRT or over) 31,505 GRT/37,091 DWT

by type: container 1, petroleum tanker 1
foreign-owned: 1 (Denmark 1)
registered in other countries: 7 (2005)
Ports and terminals: Cape Town, Durban, East London, Port Elizabeth, Richards Bay, Saldanha Bay

MILITARY

Military branches: South African National Defense Force (SANDF): Army, Navy, Air Force, Joint Operations, Joint Support, Military Intelligence, Military Health Service (2004)
Military service age and obligation: 18 years of age for voluntary military service; women have a long history of military service in non-combat roles - dating back to World War I (2004)
Manpower available for military service: *males age 18-49:* 10,354,769 (2005 est.)
Manpower fit for military service: *males age 18-49:* 4,927,757 (2005 est.)
Manpower reaching military service age annually: *males:* 512,407 (2005 est.)
Military expenditures - dollar figure: $3.172 billion (2004)
Military expenditures - percent of GDP: 1.5% (2004)
Military - note: with the end of apartheid and the establishment of majority rule, former military, black homelands forces, and ex-opposition forces were integrated into the South African National Defense Force (SANDF); as of 2003 the integration process was considered complete

TRANSNATIONAL ISSUES

Disputes - international: South Africa has placed military along the border to stem the thousands of Zimbabweans fleeing to find work and escape political persecution; managed dispute with Namibia over the location of the boundary in the Orange River
Illicit drugs: transshipment center for heroin, hashish, marijuana, and cocaine; cocaine consumption on the rise; world's largest market for illicit methaqualone, usually imported illegally from India through various east African countries; illicit cultivation of marijuana; attractive venue for money launderers given the increasing level of organized criminal and narcotics activity in the region

SOUTH GEORGIA AND THE SOUTH SANDWICH ISLANDS

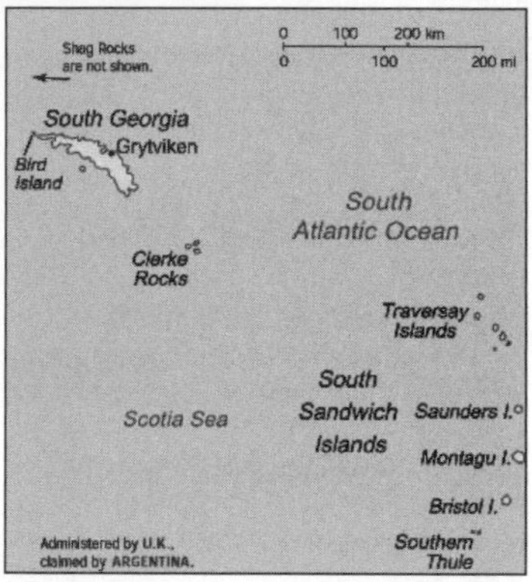

INTRODUCTION

Background: The islands lie approximately 1,000 km east of the Falkland Islands and have been under British administration since 1908, except for a brief period in 1982 when Argentina occupied them. Grytviken, on South Georgia, was a 19th and early 20th century whaling station. Famed explorer Ernest SHACKLETON stopped there in 1914 en route to his ill-fated attempt to cross Antarctica on foot. He returned some 20 months later with a few companions in a small boat and arranged a successful rescue for the rest of his crew, stranded off the Antarctic Peninsula. He died in 1922 on a subsequent expedition and is buried in Grytviken. Today, the station houses scientists from the British Antarctic Survey. The islands have large bird and seal populations, and, recognizing the importance of preserving the marine stocks in adjacent waters, the UK, in 1993, extended the exclusive fishing zone from 12 nm to 200 nm around each island.

GEOGRAPHY

Location: Southern South America, islands in the South Atlantic Ocean, east of the tip of South America
Geographic coordinates: 54 30 S, 37 00 W
Map references: Antarctic Region
Area:
total: 3,903 sq km
land: 3,903 sq km
water: 0 sq km
note: includes Shag Rocks, Black Rock, Clerke Rocks, South Georgia Island, Bird Island, and the South Sandwich Islands, which consist of some nine islands
Area - comparative: slightly larger than Rhode Island
Land boundaries: 0 km
Coastline: NA km
Maritime claims:
territorial sea: 12 nm
exclusive fishing zone: 200 nm
Climate: variable, with mostly westerly winds throughout the year interspersed with periods of calm; nearly all precipitation falls as snow
Terrain: most of the islands, rising steeply from the sea, are rugged and mountainous; South Georgia is largely barren and has steep, glacier-covered mountains; the South Sandwich Islands are of volcanic origin with some active volcanoes
Elevation extremes:
lowest point: Atlantic Ocean 0 m
highest point: Mount Paget (South Georgia) 2,934 m
Natural resources: fish
Land use:
arable land: 0%
permanent crops: 0%
other: 100% (largely covered by permanent ice and snow with some sparse vegetation consisting of grass, moss, and lichen) (2001)
Irrigated land: 0 sq km (1998 est.)
Natural hazards: the South Sandwich Islands have prevailing weather conditions that generally make them difficult to approach by ship; they are also subject to active volcanism
Environment - current issues: NA
Geography - note: the north coast of South Georgia has several large bays, which provide good anchorage; reindeer, introduced early in the 20th century, live on South Georgia

PEOPLE

Population: no indigenous inhabitants
note: the small military garrison on South Georgia withdrew in March 2001, to be replaced by a permanent group of scientists of the British Antarctic Survey, which also has a biological station on Bird Island; the South Sandwich Islands are uninhabited (July 2005 est.)

GOVERNMENT

Country name:
conventional long form: South Georgia and the South Sandwich Islands
conventional short form: none
Dependency status: overseas territory of the UK, also claimed by Argentina; administered from the Falkland Islands by a commissioner, who is concurrently governor of the Falkland Islands, representing Queen ELIZABETH II; Grytviken, formerly a whaling station on South Georgia, is a scientific base
Legal system: the laws of the UK, where applicable, apply; the senior magistrate from the Falkland Islands presides over

the Magistrates Court
Diplomatic representation in the US: none (overseas territory of the UK, also claimed by Argentina)
Diplomatic representation from the US: none (overseas territory of the UK, also claimed by Argentina)
Flag description: blue, with the flag of the UK in the upper hoist-side quadrant and the South Georgia and the South Sandwich Islands coat of arms centered on the outer half of the flag; the coat of arms features a shield with a golden lion centered; the shield is supported by a fur seal on the left and a penguin on the right; a reindeer appears above the shield, and below it on a scroll is the motto LEO TERRAM PROPRIAM PROTEGAT (Let the Lion Protect its Own Land)

ECONOMY

Economy - overview: Some fishing takes place in adjacent waters. There is a potential source of income from harvesting finfish and krill. The islands receive income from postage stamps produced in the UK, sale of fishing licenses, and harbor and landing fees from tourist vessels. Tourism from specialized cruise ships is increasing rapidly.

COMMUNICATIONS

Telephone system:
general assessment: NA
domestic: NA
international: coastal radiotelephone station at Grytviken
Radio broadcast stations: 0 (2003)
Television broadcast stations: 0 (2003)
Internet country code: .gs

TRANSPORTATION

Airports: none (2004 est.)
Ports and terminals: Grytviken

MILITARY

Military - note: defense is the responsibility of the UK

TRANSNATIONAL ISSUES

Disputes - international: Argentina, which claims the islands in its constitution and briefly occupied the islands by force in 1982, agreed in 1995 to no longer seek settlement by force

SOUTHERN OCEAN

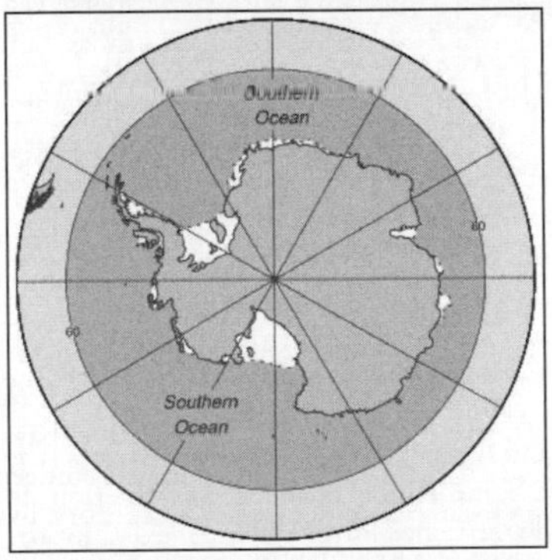

INTRODUCTION

Background: A large body of recent oceanographic research has shown that the Antarctic Circumpolar Current (ACC), an ocean current that flows from west to east around Antarctica, plays a crucial role in global ocean circulation. The region where the cold waters of the ACC meet and mingle with the warmer waters of the north defines a distinct border - the Antarctic Convergence - which fluctuates with the seasons, but which encompasses a discrete body of water and a unique ecologic region. The Convergence concentrates nutrients, which promotes marine plant life, and which in turn allows for a greater abundance of animal life. In the spring of 2000, the International Hydrographic Organization decided to delimit the waters within the Convergence as a fifth world ocean - the Southern Ocean - by combining the southern portions of the Atlantic Ocean, Indian Ocean, and Pacific Ocean. The Southern Ocean extends from the coast of Antarctica north to 60 degrees south latitude, which coincides with the Antarctic Treaty Limit and which approximates the extent of the Antarctic Convergence. As such, the Southern Ocean is now the fourth largest of the world's five oceans (after the Pacific Ocean, Atlantic Ocean, and Indian Ocean, but larger than the Arctic Ocean). It should be noted that inclusion of the Southern Ocean does not imply recognition of this feature as one of the world's primary oceans by the US Government.

GEOGRAPHY

Location: body of water between 60 degrees south latitude and Antarctica
Geographic coordinates: 60 00 S, 90 00 E (nominally), but the Southern Ocean has the unique distinction of being a large circumpolar body of water totally encircling the continent of Antarctica; this ring of water lies between 60 degrees south latitude and the coast of Antarctica and encompasses 360 degrees of longitude
Map references: Antarctic Region
Area:
total: 20.327 million sq km
note: includes Amundsen Sea, Bellingshausen Sea, part of the Drake Passage, Ross Sea, a small part of the Scotia Sea, Weddell Sea, and other tributary water bodies
Area - comparative: slightly more than twice the size of the US
Coastline: 17,968 km
Climate: sea temperatures vary from about 10 degrees Celsius to -2 degrees Celsius; cyclonic storms travel eastward around the continent and frequently are intense because of the temperature contrast between ice and open ocean; the ocean area from about latitude 40 south to the Antarctic Circle has the strongest average winds found anywhere on Earth; in winter the ocean freezes outward to 65 degrees south latitude in the Pacific sector and 55 degrees south latitude in the Atlantic sector, lowering surface temperatures well below 0 degrees Celsius; at some coastal points intense persistent drainage winds from the interior keep the shoreline ice-free throughout the winter
Terrain: the Southern Ocean is deep, 4,000 to 5,000 meters over most of its extent with only limited areas of shallow water; the Antarctic continental shelf is generally narrow and unusually deep, its edge lying at depths of 400 to 800 meters (the global mean is 133 meters); the Antarctic icepack grows from an average minimum of 2.6 million square kilometers in March to about 18.8 million square kilometers in September, better than a sixfold increase in area; the Antarctic Circumpolar Current (21,000 km in length) moves perpetually eastward; it is the world's largest ocean current, transporting 130 million cubic meters of water per second - 100 times the flow of all the world's rivers
Elevation extremes:
lowest point: -7,235 m at the southern end of the South Sandwich Trench
highest point: sea level 0 m
Natural resources: probable large and possible giant oil and gas fields on the continental margin, manganese nodules, possible placer deposits, sand and gravel, fresh water as icebergs; squid, whales, and seals - none exploited; krill, fishes
Natural hazards: huge icebergs with drafts up to several hundred meters; smaller bergs and iceberg fragments; sea

ice (generally 0.5 to 1 meter thick) with sometimes dynamic short-term variations and with large annual and interannual variations; deep continental shelf floored by glacial deposits varying widely over short distances; high winds and large waves much of the year; ship icing, especially May-October; most of region is remote from sources of search and rescue
Environment - current issues: increased solar ultraviolet radiation resulting from the Antarctic ozone hole in recent years, reducing marine primary productivity (phytoplankton) by as much as 15% and damaging the DNA of some fish; illegal, unreported, and unregulated fishing in recent years, especially the landing of an estimated five to six times more Patagonian toothfish than the regulated fishery, which is likely to affect the sustainability of the stock; large amount of incidental mortality of seabirds resulting from long-line fishing for toothfish
note: the now-protected fur seal population is making a strong comeback after severe overexploitation in the 18th and 19th centuries
Environment - international agreements: the Southern Ocean is subject to all international agreements regarding the world's oceans; in addition, it is subject to these agreements specific to the Antarctic region: International Whaling Commission (prohibits commercial whaling south of 40 degrees south [south of 60 degrees south between 50 degrees and 130 degrees west]); Convention on the Conservation of Antarctic Seals (limits sealing); Convention on the Conservation of Antarctic Marine Living Resources (regulates fishing)
note: many nations (including the US) prohibit mineral resource exploration and exploitation south of the fluctuating Polar Front (Antarctic Convergence) which is in the middle of the Antarctic Circumpolar Current and serves as the dividing line between the very cold polar surface waters to the south and the warmer waters to the north
Geography - note: the major chokepoint is the Drake Passage between South America and Antarctica; the Polar Front (Antarctic Convergence) is the best natural definition of the northern extent of the Southern Ocean; it is a distinct region at the middle of the Antarctic Circumpolar Current that separates the very cold polar surface waters to the south from the warmer waters to the north; the Front and the Current extend entirely around Antarctica, reaching south of 60 degrees south near New Zealand and near 48 degrees south in the far South Atlantic coinciding with the path of the maximum westerly winds

ECONOMY

Economy - overview: Fisheries in 2000-01 (1 July to 30 June) landed 112,934 metric tons, of which 87% was krill and 11% Patagonian toothfish. International agreements were adopted in late 1999 to reduce illegal, unreported, and unregulated fishing, which in the 2000-01 season landed, by one estimate, 8,376 metric tons of Patagonian and antarctic toothfish. In the 2000-01 antarctic summer 12,248 tourists, most of them seaborne, visited the Southern Ocean and Antarctica, compared to 14,762 the previous year.

TRANSPORTATION

Ports and terminals: McMurdo, Palmer, and offshore anchorages in Antarctica
note: few ports or harbors exist on the southern side of the Southern Ocean; ice conditions limit use of most of them to short periods in midsummer; even then some cannot be entered without icebreaker escort; most antarctic ports are operated by government research stations and, except in an emergency, are not open to commercial or private vessels; vessels in any port south of 60 degrees south are subject to inspection by Antarctic Treaty observers (see Article 7)
Transportation - note: Drake Passage offers alternative to transit through the Panama Canal

TRANSNATIONAL ISSUES

Disputes - international: Antarctic Treaty defers claims (see Antarctica entry), but Argentina, Australia, Chile, France, NZ, Norway, and UK assert claims (some overlapping), including the continental shelf in the Southern Ocean; several states have expressed an interest in extending those continental shelf claims under the United Nations Convention on the Law of the Sea (UNCLOS) to include undersea ridges; the US and most other states do not recognize the land or maritime claims of other states and have made no claims themselves (the US and Russia have reserved the right to do so); no formal claims exist in the waters in the sector between 90 degrees west and 150 degrees west

SPAIN

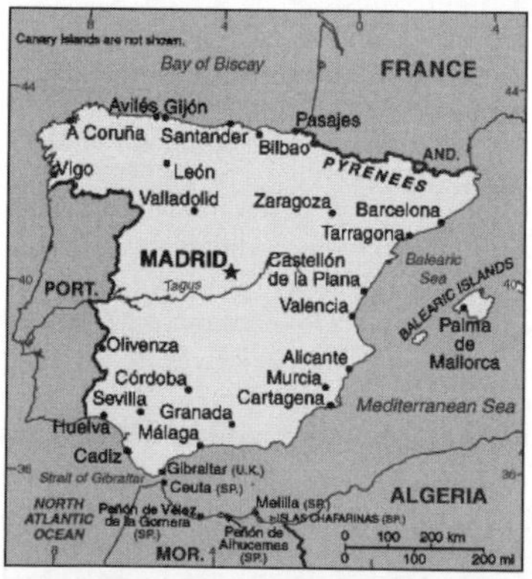

INTRODUCTION

Background: Spain's powerful world empire of the 16th and 17th centuries ultimately yielded command of the seas to England. Subsequent failure to embrace the mercantile and industrial revolutions caused the country to fall behind Britain, France, and Germany in economic and political power. Spain remained neutral in World Wars I and II, but suffered through a devastating civil war (1936-39). In the second half of the 20th century, Spain has played a catch-up role in the western international community; it joined the EU in 1986. Continuing challenges include Basque Fatherland and Liberty (ETA) terrorism and further reductions in unemployment.

GEOGRAPHY

Location: Southwestern Europe, bordering the Bay of Biscay, Mediterranean Sea, North Atlantic Ocean, and Pyrenees Mountains, southwest of France
Geographic coordinates: 40 00 N, 4 00 W
Map references: Europe
Area:
total: 504,782 sq km
land: 499,542 sq km
water: 5,240 sq km
note: there are 2 autonomous cities - Ceuta and Melilla - and 17 autonomous communities including Balearic Islands and Canary Islands, and three small Spanish possessions off the coast of Morocco - Islas Chafarinas, Penon de Alhucemas, and Penon de Velez de la Gomera
Area - comparative: slightly more than twice the size of Oregon
Land boundaries:
total: 1,917.8 km
border countries: Andorra 63.7 km, France

623 km, Gibraltar 1.2 km, Portugal 1,214 km, Morocco (Ceuta) 6.3 km, Morocco (Melilla) 9.6 km
Coastline: 4,964 km
Maritime claims:
territorial sea: 12 nm
contiguous zone: 24 nm
exclusive economic zone: 200 nm (applies only to the Atlantic Ocean)
Climate: temperate; clear, hot summers in interior, more moderate and cloudy along coast; cloudy, cold winters in interior, partly cloudy and cool along coast
Terrain: large, flat to dissected plateau surrounded by rugged hills; Pyrenees in north
Elevation extremes:
lowest point: Atlantic Ocean 0 m
highest point: Pico de Teide (Tenerife) on Canary Islands 3,718 m
Natural resources: coal, lignite, iron ore, copper, lead, zinc, uranium, tungsten, mercury, pyrites, magnesite, fluorspar, gypsum, sepiolite, kaolin, potash, hydropower, arable land
Land use:
arable land: 26.07%
permanent crops: 9.87%
other: 64.06% (2001)
Irrigated land: 36,400 sq km (1998 est.)
Natural hazards: periodic droughts g
Environment - current issues: pollution of the Mediterranean Sea from raw sewage and effluents from the offshore production of oil and gas; water quality and quantity nationwide; air pollution; deforestation; desertification
Environment - international agreements:
party to: Air Pollution, Air Pollution-Nitrogen Oxides, Air Pollution-Sulfur 94, Air Pollution-Volatile Organic Compounds, Antarctic-Environmental Protocol, Antarctic-Marine Living Resources, Antarctic Treaty, Biodiversity, Climate Change, Climate Change-Kyoto Protocol, Desertification, Endangered Species, Environmental Modification, Hazardous Wastes, Law of the Sea, Marine Dumping, Marine Life Conservation, Ozone Layer Protection, Ship Pollution, Tropical Timber 83, Tropical Timber 94, Wetlands, Whaling
signed, but not ratified: Air Pollution-Persistent Organic Pollutants
Geography - note: strategic location along approaches to Strait of Gibraltar

PEOPLE

Population: 40,341,462 (July 2005 est.)
Age structure:
0-14 years: 14.4% (male 2,994,124/female 2,815,456)
15-64 years: 68% (male 13,762,281/female 13,664,762)
65 years and over: 17.6% (male 2,965,859/female 4,138,980) (2005 est.)
Median age:
total: 39.51 years
male: 38.18 years
female: 40.93 years (2005 est.)
Population growth rate: 0.15% (2005 est.)
Birth rate: 10.1 births/1,000 population (2005 est.)
Death rate: 9.63 deaths/1,000 population (2005 est.)
Net migration rate: 0.99 migrant(s)/1,000 population (2005 est.)
Sex ratio:
at birth: 1.07 male(s)/female
under 15 years: 1.06 male(s)/female
15-64 years: 1.01 male(s)/female
65 years and over: 0.72 male(s)/female
total population: 0.96 male(s)/female (2005 est.)
Infant mortality rate:
total: 4.42 deaths/1,000 live births
male: 4.82 deaths/1,000 live births
female: 4 deaths/1,000 live births (2005 est.)
Life expectancy at birth:
total population: 79.52 years
male: 76.18 years
female: 83.08 years (2005 est.
Total fertility rate: 1.28 children born/woman (2005 est.)
HIV/AIDS - adult prevalence rate: 0.7% (2001 est.)
HIV/AIDS - people living with HIV/AIDS: 140,000 (2001 est.)
HIV/AIDS - deaths: less than 1,000 (2003 est.)
Nationality:
noun: Spaniard(s)
adjective: Spanish
Ethnic groups: composite of Mediterranean and Nordic types
Religions: Roman Catholic 94%, other 6%
Languages: Castilian Spanish 74%, Catalan 17%, Galician 7%, Basque 2%; note - Castilian is the official language nationwide; the other languages are official regionally
Literacy:
definition: age 15 and over can read and write
total population: 97.9%
male: 98.7%
female: 97.2% (2003 est.)

GOVERNMENT

Country name:
conventional long form: Kingdom of Spain
conventional short form: Spain
local short form: Espana
Government type: parliamentary monarchy
Capital: Madrid
Administrative divisions: 17 autonomous communities (comunidades autonomas, singular - comunidad autonoma)and 2 autonomous cities* (ciudades autonomas, singular - ciudad autonoma); Andalucia, Aragon, Asturias, Baleares (Balearic Islands), Ceuta*, Canarias (Canary Islands), Cantabria, Castilla-La Mancha, Castilla y Leon, Cataluna, Comunidad Valenciana, Extremadura, Galicia, La Rioja, Madrid, Melilla*, Murcia, Navarra, Pais Vasco (Basque Country)
note: the autonomous cities of Ceuta and Melilla plus three small islands of Islas Chafarinas, Penon de Alhucemas, and Penon de Velez de la Gomera, administered directly by the Spanish central government, are all located along the coast of Morocco and are collectively referred to as Places of Sovereignty (Plazas de Soberania)
Independence: the Iberian peninsula was characterized by a variety of independent kingdoms prior to the Moslem occupation that began in the early 8th century A. D. and lasted nearly seven centuries; the small Christian redoubts of the north began the reconquest almost immediately, culminating in the seizure of Granada in 1492; this event completed the unification of several kingdoms and is traditionally considered the forging of present-day Spain
National holiday: National Day, 12 October
Constitution: 6 December 1978, effective 29 December 1978
Legal system: civil law system, with regional applications; has not accepted compulsory ICJ jurisdiction
Suffrage: 18 years of age, universal
Executive branch:
chief of state: King JUAN CARLOS I (since 22 November 1975); Heir Apparent Prince FELIPE, son of the monarch, born 30 January 1968
head of government: President of the Government and Prime Minister Jose Luis RODRIGUEZ ZAPATERO (since 17 April 2004); First Vice President and Deputy Prime Minister (and Minister of the Presidency) Maria Teresa FERNANDEZ DE LA VEGA (since 18 April 2004) and Second Vice President (and Minister of Economy and Finance) Pedro SOLBES (since 18 April 2004)
cabinet: Council of Ministers designated by the president
note: there is also a Council of State that is the supreme consultative organ of the government, but its recommendations are non-binding
elections: the monarchy is hereditary; following legislative elections, the leader of the majority party or the leader of the majority coalition is usually proposed president by the monarch and elected by the National Assembly; election last held 14 March 2004 (next to be held March 2008); vice presidents appointed by the monarch on the proposal of the president

election results: Jose Luis RODRIGUEZ ZAPATERO (PSOE) elected president; percent of National Assembly vote - 52.29%
Legislative branch: bicameral; General Courts or National Assembly or Las Cortes Generales consists of the Senate or Senado (259 seats - 208 members directly elected by popular vote and the other 51 appointed by the regional legislatures to serve four-year terms) and the Congress of Deputies or Congreso de los Diputados (350 seats; members are elected by popular vote on block lists by proportional representation to serve four-year terms)
elections: Senate - last held 14 March 2004 (next to be held March 2008); Congress of Deputies - last held 14 March 2004 (next to be held March 2008)
election results: Senate - percent of vote by party - PP 49%, PSOE 38.9%, Entesa Catalona de Progress 5.7%, CiU 1.99%, PNV 2.8%, CC 1.4%; seats by party - PP 102, PSOE 81, Entesa Catalona de Progress 12, CiU 4, PNV 6, CC 3; Congress of Deputies - percent of vote by party - PSOE 43.3%, PP 37.8%, CiU 3.2%, ERC 2.5%, PNV 1.6%, IU 3.2%, CC 0.9%; seats by party - PSOE 164, PP 148, CiU 10, ERC 8, PNV 7, IU 2, CC 3, other 8
Judicial branch: Supreme Court or Tribunal Supremo
Political parties and leaders: Basque Nationalist Party or PNV [Josu Jon IMAZ]; Canarian Coalition or CC (a coalition of five parties) [Paulino RIVERO Baute]; Convergence and Union or CiU [Artur MAS i Gavarro] (a coalition of the Democratic Convergence of Catalonia or CDC [Artur MAS i Gavarro] and the Democratic Union of Catalonia or UDC [Josep Antoni DURAN y LLEIDA]); Entesa Catalonia de Progress (a Senate coalition grouping four Catalan parties - PSC, ERC, ICV, EUA) [leader NA]; Galician Nationalist Bloc or BNG [Anxo Manuel QUINTANA]; Party of Independents from Lanzarote or PIL [Dimas MARTIN Martin]; Popular Party or PP [Mariano RAJOY]; Republican Left of Catalonia or ERC [Josep-Lluis CAROD-ROVIRA]; Spanish Socialist Workers Party or PSOE [Jose Luis RODRIGUEZ ZAPATERO]; United Left or IU (a coalition of parties including the PCE and other small parties) [Gaspar LLAMAZARES]
Political pressure groups and leaders: business and landowning interests; Catholic Church; free labor unions (authorized in April 1977); Socialist General Union of Workers or UGT and the smaller independent Workers Syndical Union or USO; university students; Trade Union Confederation of Workers' Commissions or CC.OO.; Nunca Mas (Galician for "Never Again"; formed in response to the oil tanker Prestige oil spill)
International organization participation: AfDB, AsDB, Australia Group, BCIE, BIS, CE, CERN, EAPC, EBRD, EIB, EMU, ESA, EU, FAO, IADB, IAEA, IBRD, ICAO, ICC, ICCt, ICFTU, ICRM, IDA, IEA, IFAD, IFC, IFRCS, IHO, ILO, IMF, IMO, Interpol, IOC, IOM (observer), ISO, ITU, LAIA (observer), MIGA, MINUSTAH, MONUC, NAM (guest), NATO, NEA, NSG, OAS (observer), OECD, ONUB, OPCW, OSCE, Paris Club, PCA, UN, UNCTAD, UNESCO, UNHCR, UNIDO, UNMEE, UNMIS, UPU, WCL, WCO, WEU, WHO, WIPO, WMO, WToO, WTO, ZC
Diplomatic representation in the US:
chief of mission: Ambassador Carlos WESTENDORP
chancery: 2375 Pennsylvania Avenue NW, Washington, DC 20037
telephone: [1] (202) 452-0100, 728-2340
FAX: [1] (202) 833-5670
consulate(s) general: Boston, Chicago, Houston, Los Angeles, Miami, New Orleans, New York, San Francisco, and San Juan (Puerto Rico)
Diplomatic representation from the US:
chief of mission: Ambassador Eduardo AGUIRRE, Jr.
embassy: Serrano 75, 28006 Madrid
mailing address: PSC 61, APO AE 09642
telephone: [34] (91) 587-2200
FAX: [34] (91) 587-2303
consulate(s) general: Barcelona
Flag description: three horizontal bands of red (top), yellow (double width), and red with the national coat of arms on the hoist side of the yellow band; the coat of arms includes the royal seal framed by the Pillars of Hercules, which are the two promontories (Gibraltar and Ceuta) on either side of the eastern end of the Strait of Gibraltar

ECONOMY

Economy - overview: The Spanish economy boomed from 1986 to 1990, averaging five percent annual growth. After a European-wide recession in the early 1990s, the Spanish economy resumed moderate growth starting in 1994. Spain's mixed capitalist economy supports a GDP that on a per capita basis is 80% that of the four leading West European economies. The center-right government of former President AZNAR successfully worked to gain admission to the first group of countries launching the European single currency (the euro) on 1 January 1999. The AZNAR administration continued to advocate liberalization, privatization, and deregulation of the economy and introduced some tax reforms to that end. Unemployment fell steadily under the AZNAR administration but remains high at 10.1%. Growth of 2.5% in 2003, 2.6% in 2004, and 3.3% in 2005 was satisfactory given the background of a faltering European economy. The socialist president, RODRIGUEZ ZAPATERO, has initiated economic and social reforms that are generally popular among the masses of people but that are anathema to religious and other conservative elements. Adjusting to the monetary and other economic policies of an integrated Europe, reducing unemployment, and absorbing widespread social changes will pose challenges to Spain over the next few years.
GDP (purchasing power parity): $1.014 trillion (2005 est.)
GDP (official exchange rate): $1.046 trillion (2005 est.)
GDP - real growth rate: 3.3% (2005 est.)
GDP - per capita: purchasing power parity - $25,100 (2005 est.)
GDP - composition by sector:
agriculture: 3.4%
industry: 28.7%
services: 67.9% (2005 est.)
Labor force: 20.67 million (2005 est.)
Labor force - by occupation: agriculture 5.3%, manufacturing, mining, and construction 30.1%, services 64.6% (2004 est.)
Unemployment rate: 10.1% (2005 est.)
Population below poverty line: NA
Household income or consumption by percentage share:
lowest 10%: 2.8%
highest 10%: 25.2% (1990)
Distribution of family income - Gini index: 32.5 (1990)
Inflation rate (consumer prices): 3.4% (2005 est.)
Investment (gross fixed): 28.1% of GDP (2005 est.)
Budget:
revenues: $440.9 billion
expenditures: $448.4 billion, including capital expenditures of $12.8 billion (2005 est.)
Public debt: 48.5% of GDP (2005 est.)
Agriculture - products: grain, vegetables, olives, wine grapes, sugar beets, citrus; beef, pork, poultry, dairy products; fish
Industries: textiles and apparel (including footwear), food and beverages, metals and metal manufactures, chemicals, shipbuilding, automobiles, machine tools, tourism, clay and refractory products, footwear, pharmaceuticals, medical equipment

Industrial production growth rate: 1.6% (2005 est.)
Electricity - production: 247.3 billion kWh (2003)
Electricity - production by source:
fossil fuel: 50.4%
hydro: 18.2%
nuclear: 27.2%
other: 4.1% (2001)
Electricity - consumption: 231.2 billion kWh (2003)
Electricity - exports: 7.5 billion kWh (2003)
Electricity - imports: 8.7 billion kWh (2003)
Oil - production: 24,540 bbl/day (2003 est.)
Oil - consumption: 1.544 million bbl/day (2003 est.)
Oil - exports: 135,100 bbl/day (2001)
Oil - imports: 1.582 million bbl/day (2001)
Oil - proved reserves: 10.5 million bbl (1 January 2002)
Natural gas - production: 516 million cu m (2001 est.)
Natural gas - consumption: 17.96 billion cu m (2001 est.)
Natural gas - exports: :0 cu m (2001 est.)
Natural gas - imports: 17.26 billion cu m (2001 est.)
Natural gas - proved reserves: 254.9 million cu m (1 January 2002)
Current account balance: $-64.62 billion (2005 est.)
Exports: $194.3 billion f.o.b. (2005 est.)
Exports - partners: France 19.3%, Germany 11.7%, Portugal 9.6%, UK 9%, Italy 9%, US 4% (2004)
Imports: $271.8 billion f.o.b. (2005 est.)
Imports - partners: Germany 16.6%, France 15.8%, Italy 8.9%, UK 6.3%, Netherlands 4.8% (2004)
Reserves of foreign exchange and gold: $18.5 billion (2005 est.)
Debt - external: $1.249 trillion (30 June 2005 est.)
Economic aid - donor: ODA, $1.33 billion (1999)
Currency (code): euro (EUR)
note: on 1 January 1999, the European Monetary Union introduced the euro as a common currency to be used by financial institutions of member countries; on 1 January 2002, the euro became the sole currency for everyday transactions within the member countries
Currency code: EUR
Exchange rates: euros per US dollar - 0.79697 (2005), 0.8054 (2004), 0.886 (2003), 1.0626 (2002), 1.1175 (2001)
Fiscal year: calendar year

COMMUNICATIONS

Telephones - main lines in use: 17,567,500 (2003)
Telephones - mobile cellular: 37,506,700 (2003)
Telephone system:
general assessment: generally adequate, modern facilities; teledensity is 44 main lines for each 100 persons
domestic: NA
international: country code - 34; 22 coaxial submarine cables; satellite earth stations - 2 Intelsat (1 Atlantic Ocean and 1 Indian Ocean), NA Eutelsat; tropospheric scatter to adjacent countries
Radio broadcast stations: AM 208, FM 715, shortwave 1 (1998)
Radios: 13.1 million (1997)
Television broadcast stations: 224 (plus 2,105 repeaters)
note: these figures include 11 television broadcast stations and 88 repeaters in the Canary Islands (1995)
Televisions: 16.2 million (1997)
Internet country code: .es
Internet hosts: 1,056,950 (2004)
Internet Service Providers (ISPs): 56 (2000)
Internet users: 9.789 million (2003)

TRANSPORTATION

Airports: 156 (2004 est.)
Airports - with paved runways:
total: 95
over 3,047 m: 15
2,438 to 3,047 m: 10
1,524 to 2,437 m: 19
914 to 1,523 m: 25
under 914 m: 26 (2005 est.)
Airports - with unpaved runways:
total: 62
over 3,047 m: 1
1,524 to 2,437 m: 2
914 to 1,523 m: 15
under 914 m: 44 (2005 est.)
Heliports: 8 (2005 est.)
Pipelines: gas 7,306 km; oil 730 km; refined products 3,512 km (2004)
Railways:
total: 14,781 km (7,718 km electrified)
broad gauge: 11,829 km 1.668-m gauge (6,950 km electrified)
standard gauge: 998 km 1.435-m gauge (998 km electrified)
narrow gauge: 1,926 km 1.000-m gauge (815 km electrified); 28 km 0.914-m gauge (28 km electrified) (2004)
Roadways:
total: 664,852 km
paved: 658,203 km (including 11,152 km of expressways)
unpaved: 6,649 km (2001)
Waterways: 1,045 km (2003)
Merchant marine:
total: 182 ships (1,000 GRT or over) 1,740,974 GRT/2,157,551 DWT
by type: bulk carrier 10, cargo 22, chemical tanker 16, container 19, liquefied gas 8, passenger 2, passenger/cargo 47, petroleum tanker 20, refrigerated cargo 6, roll on/roll off 25, vehicle carrier 7
foreign-owned: 29 (Cuba 2, Denmark 1, Germany 9, Italy 2, Norway 6, United States 7, Uruguay 2)
registered in other countries: 192 (2005)
Ports and terminals: Algeciras, Barcelona, Cartagena, Gijon, Huelva, La Coruna, Tarragona, Valencia

MILITARY

Military branches: Army, Navy, Air Force (Ejercito del Aire, EdA), Naval Infantry
Military service age and obligation: 20 years of age (2004)
Manpower available for military service: *males age 20-49:* 9,366,588 (2005 est.)
Manpower fit for military service: *males age 20-49:* 7,623,356 (2005 est.)
Manpower reaching military service age annually: *males:* 233,384 (2005 est.)
Military expenditures - dollar figure: $9,906.5 million (2003)
Military expenditures - percent of GDP: 1.2% (2003)

TRANSNATIONAL ISSUES

Disputes - international: in 2003, Gibraltar residents voted overwhelmingly by referendum to remain a British colony and against a "total shared sovereignty" arrangement while demanding participation in talks between the UK and Spain; Spain disapproves of UK plans to grant Gibraltar greater autonomy; Morocco protests Spain's control over the coastal enclaves of Ceuta, Melilla, and the islands of Penon de Velez de la Gomera, Penon de Alhucemas and Islas Chafarinas, and surrounding waters; Morocco serves as the primary launching site of illegal migration into Spain from North Africa
Illicit drugs: key European gateway country and consumer for Latin American cocaine and North African hashish entering the European market; destination and minor transshipment point for Southwest Asian heroin; money-laundering site for European earnings of Colombian narcotics trafficking organizations

SPRATLY ISLANDS

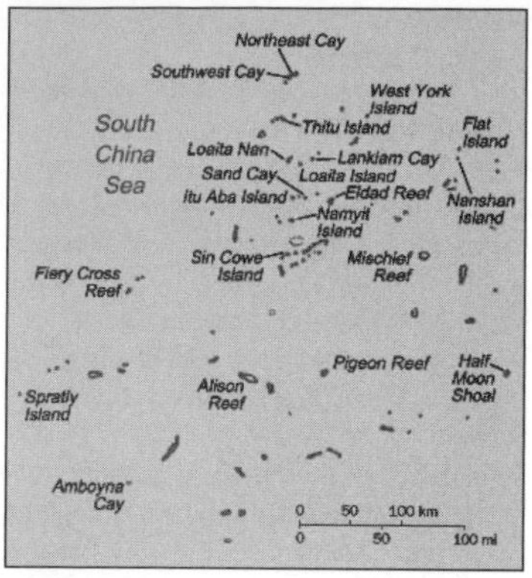

INTRODUCTION

Background: The Spratly Islands consist of more than 100 small islands or reefs. They are surrounded by rich fishing grounds and potentially by gas and oil deposits. They are claimed in their entirety by China, Taiwan, and Vietnam, while portions are claimed by Malaysia and the Philippines. About 45 islands are occupied by relatively small numbers of military forces from China, Malaysia, the Philippines, Taiwan, and Vietnam. Brunei has established a fishing zone that overlaps a southern reef, but has not made any formal claim.

GEOGRAPHY

Location: Southeastern Asia, group of reefs and islands in the South China Sea, about two-thirds of the way from southern Vietnam to the southern Philippines
Geographic coordinates: 8 38 N, 111 55 E
Map references: Southeast Asia
Area:
total: less than 5 sq km
land: less than 5 sq km
water: 0 sq km
note: includes 100 or so islets, coral reefs, and sea mounts scattered over an area of nearly 410,000 sq km of the central South China Sea
Area - comparative: NA
Land boundaries: 0 km
Coastline: 926 km
Maritime claims: NA
Climate: tropical
Terrain: flat
Elevation extremes:
lowest point: South China Sea 0 m
highest point: unnamed location on Southwest Cay 4 m
Natural resources: fish, guano, undetermined oil and natural gas potential
Land use:
arable land: 0%
permanent crops: 0%
other: 100% (2001)
Irrigated land: 0 sq km (1998 est.)
Natural hazards: typhoons; serious maritime hazard because of numerous reefs and shoals
Environment - current issues: NA
Geography - note: strategically located near several primary shipping lanes in the central South China Sea; includes numerous small islands, atolls, shoals, and coral reefs

PEOPLE

Population: no indigenous inhabitants
note: there are scattered garrisons occupied by personnel of several claimant states (2004)

GOVERNMENT

Country name:
conventional long form: none
conventional short form: Spratly Islands

ECONOMY

Economy - overview: Economic activity is limited to commercial fishing. The proximity to nearby oil- and gas-producing sedimentary basins suggests the potential for oil and gas deposits, but the region is largely unexplored. There are no reliable estimates of potential reserves. Commercial exploitation has yet to be developed.

TRANSPORTATION

Airports: 3 (2004 est.)
Airports - with paved runways:
total: 2
914 to 1,523 m: 1
under 914 m: 1 (2005 est.)
Airports - with unpaved runways:
total: 1
914 to 1,523 m: 1 (2005 est.)
Ports and terminals: none; offshore anchorage only

MILITARY

Military - note: Spratly Islands consist of more than 100 small islands or reefs, of which about 45 are claimed and occupied by China, Malaysia, the Philippines, Taiwan, and Vietnam

TRANSNATIONAL ISSUES

Disputes - international: all of the Spratly Islands are claimed by China, Taiwan, and Vietnam; parts of them are claimed by Malaysia and the Philippines; in 1984, Brunei established an exclusive fishing zone that encompasses Louisa Reef in the southern Spratly Islands but has not publicly claimed the reef; claimants in November 2002 signed the "Declaration on the Conduct of Parties in the South China Sea," which has eased tensions but falls short of a legally binding "code of conduct"; in March 2005, the national oil companies of China, the Philippines, and Vietnam signed a joint accord to conduct marine seismic activities in the Spratlys

SRI LANKA

INTRODUCTION

Background: The Sinhalese arrived in Sri Lanka late in the 6th century B.C., probably from northern India. Buddhism was introduced beginning in about the mid-third century B.C., and a great civilization developed at the cities of Anuradhapura (kingdom from circa 200 B.C. to circa A.D. 1000) and Polonnaruwa (from about 1070 to 1200). In the 14th century, a south Indian dynasty seized power in the north and established a Tamil kingdom. Occupied by the Portuguese in the 16th century and by the Dutch in the 17th century, the island was ceded to the British in 1796, became a crown colony in 1802, and was united under British rule by 1815. As Ceylon, it became independent in 1948; its name was changed to Sri Lanka in 1972. Tensions between the Sinhalese majority and Tamil separatists erupted into war in 1983. Tens of thousands have died in an ethnic conflict that continues to fester. After two decades of fighting, the government and Liberation Tigers of Tamil Eelam formalized a cease-fire in February 2002, with Norway brokering peace negotiations.

GEOGRAPHY

Location: Southern Asia, island in the Indian Ocean, south of India
Geographic coordinates: 7 00 N, 81 00 E
Map references: Asia
Area:
total: 65,610 sq km
land: 64,740 sq km
water: 870 sq km
Area - comparative: slightly larger than West Virginia
Land boundaries: 0 km
Coastline: 1,340 km

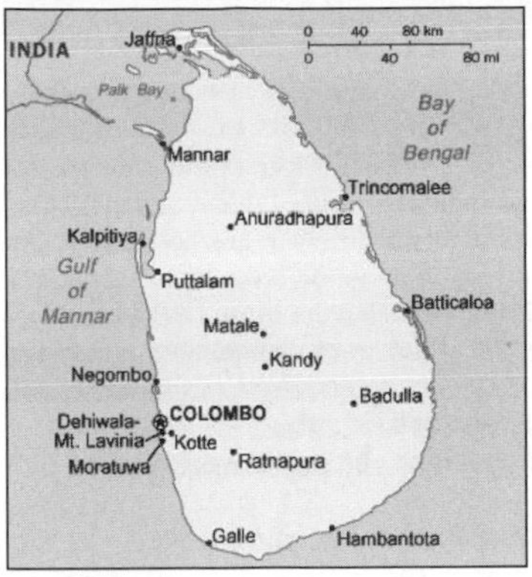

Maritime claims:
territorial sea: 12 nm
contiguous zone: 24 nm
exclusive economic zone: 200 nm
continental shelf: 200 nm or to the edge of the continental margin
Climate: tropical monsoon; northeast monsoon (December to March); southwest monsoon (June to October)
Terrain: mostly low, flat to rolling plain; mountains in south-central interior
Elevation extremes:
lowest point: Indian Ocean 0 m
highest point: Pidurutalagala 2,524 m
Natural resources: limestone, graphite, mineral sands, gems, phosphates, clay, hydropower
Land use:
arable land: 13.86%
permanent crops: 15.7%
other: 70.44% (2001)
Irrigated land: 6,510 sq km (1998 est.)
Natural hazards: occasional cyclones and tornadoes
Environment - current issues: deforestation; soil erosion; wildlife populations threatened by poaching and urbanization; coastal degradation from mining activities and increased pollution; freshwater resources being polluted by industrial wastes and sewage runoff; waste disposal; air pollution in Colombo
Environment - international agreements:
party to: Biodiversity, Climate Change, Climate Change-Kyoto Protocol, Desertification, Endangered Species, Environmental Modification, Hazardous Wastes, Law of the Sea, Ozone Layer Protection, Ship Pollution, Wetlands
signed, but not ratified: Marine Life Conservation
Geography - note: strategic location near major Indian Ocean sea lanes

PEOPLE

Population: 20,064,776
note: since the outbreak of hostilities between the government and armed Tamil separatists in the mid-1980s, several hundred thousand Tamil civilians have fled the island and more than 200,000 Tamils have sought refuge in the West (July 2005 est.)
Age structure:
0-14 years: 24.5% (male 2,508,384/female 2,397,986)
15-64 years: 68.4% (male 6,658,765/female 7,059,468)
65 years and over: 7.2% (male 670,813/female 769,360) (2005 est.)
Median age:
total: 29.44 years
male: 28.38 years
female: 30.51 years (2005 est.)
Population growth rate: 0.79% (2005 est.)
Birth rate: 15.63 births/1,000 population (2005 est.)
Death rate: 6.49 deaths/1,000 population (2005 est.)
Net migration rate: -1.27 migrant(s)/1,000 population (2005 est.)
Sex ratio:
at birth: 1.05 male(s)/female
under 15 years: 1.05 male(s)/female
15-64 years: 0.94 male(s)/female
65 years and over: 0.87 male(s)/female
total population: 0.96 male(s)/female (2005 est.)
Infant mortality rate:
total: 14.35 deaths/1,000 live births
male: 15.57 deaths/1,000 live births
female: 13.07 deaths/1,000 live births (2005 est.)
Life expectancy at birth:
total population: 73.17 years
male: 70.6 years
female: 75.86 years (2005 est.)
Total fertility rate: 1.85 children born/woman (2005 est.)
HIV/AIDS - adult prevalence rate: less than 0.1% (2001 est.)
HIV/AIDS - people living with HIV/AIDS: 3,500 (2001 est.)
HIV/AIDS - deaths: less than 200 (2003 est.)
Nationality:
noun: Sri Lankan(s)
adjective: Sri Lankan
Ethnic groups: Sinhalese 73.8%, Sri Lankan Moors 7.2%, Indian Tamil 4.6%, Sri Lankan Tamil 3.9%, other 0.5%, unspecified 10% (2001 census provisional data)
Religions: Buddhist 69.1%, Muslim 7.6%, Hindu 7.1%, Christian 6.2%, unspecified 10% (2001 census provisional data)
Languages: Sinhala (official and national language) 74%, Tamil (national language) 18%, other 8%
note: English is commonly used in government and is spoken competently by about 10% of the population
Literacy:
definition: age 15 and over can read and write
total population: 92.3%
male: 94.8%
female: 90% (2003 est.)

GOVERNMENT

Country name:
conventional long form: Democratic Socialist Republic of Sri Lanka
conventional short form: Sri Lanka
former: Serendib, Ceylon
Government type: republic
Capital: Colombo; note - Sri Jayewardenepura Kotte is the legislative capital
Administrative divisions: 8 provinces; Central, North Central, North Eastern, North Western, Sabaragamuwa, Southern, Uva, Western; note - North Eastern province may have been divided in two - Northern and Eastern
Independence: 4 February 1948 (from UK)
National holiday: Independence Day, 4 February (1948)
Constitution: adopted 16 August 1978, certified 31 August 1978
Legal system: a highly complex mixture of English common law, Roman-Dutch, Muslim, Sinhalese, and customary law; has not accepted compulsory ICJ jurisdiction
Suffrage: 18 years of age, universal
Executive branch:
chief of state: President Mahinda RAJAPAKSE (since 19 November 2005); note - Ratnasiri WICKREMANAYAKE (since 21 November 2005) is the prime minister; the president is considered both the chief of state and head of government
head of government: President Mahinda RAJAPAKSE (since 19 November 2005); note - Ratnasiri WICKREMANAYAKE (since 21 November 2005) is the prime minister; the president is considered both the chief of state and head of government
cabinet: Cabinet appointed by the president in consultation with the prime minister
elections: president elected by popular vote for a six-year term; election last held 17 November 2005 (next to be held 2011)
election results: Mahinda RAJAPAKSE elected president; percent of vote - Mahinda RAJAPAKSE 50.3%, Ranil WICKREMESINGHE 48.4%, other 1.3%
Legislative branch: unicameral Parliament (225 seats; members elected by popular vote on the basis of a modified proportional representation system by district to serve six-year terms)
elections: last held 2 April 2004 (next to be held by 2010)
election results: percent of vote by party or electoral alliance - SLFP and JVP 45.6%,

UNP 37.83%, TNA 6.84%, JHU 5.97%, SLMC 2.02%, UPF 0.54%, EPDP 0.27%, others 0.93%; seats by party or electoral alliance - SLFP and JVP 105, UNP 82, TNA 22, JHU 9, SLMC 5, UPF 1, EPDP 1

Judicial branch: Supreme Court; Court of Appeals; judges for both courts are appointed by the president

Political parties and leaders: All Ceylon Tamil Congress or ACTC [KUMARGURUPARAM]; Ceylon Workers Congress or CWC [Arumugam THONDAMAN]; Communist Party or CP [D. GUNASEKERA]; Democratic United National (Lalith) Front or DUNLF [Shrimani ATULATHMUDALI]; Eelam People's Democratic Party or EPDP [Douglas DEVANANDA]; Eelam People's Revolutionary Liberation Front or EPRLF [Suresh PREMACHANDRAN]; Janatha Vimukthi Perumuna or JVP [Somawansa AMARASINGHE]; National Heritage Party or JHU [Tilak KARUNARATNE]; National Unity Alliance or NUA [Ferial ASHRAFF]; People's Liberation Organization of Tamil Eelam or PLOTE [leader NA]; Sihala Urumaya or SU [leader NA]; Sri Lanka Freedom Party or SLFP [Chandrika Bandaranaike KUMARATUNGA]; Sri Lanka Muslim Congress or SLMC [Rauff HAKEEM]; Sri Lanka Progressive Front or SLPF [P. Nelson PERERA]; Tamil Eelam Liberation Organization or TELO [SABARATNAM]; Tamil National Alliance or TNA [R. SAMPANTHAN]; Tamil United Liberation Front or TULF [V. ANANDASANGAREE]; United National Party or UNP [Ranil WICKREMASINGHE]; Up-country People's Front or UPF [P. CHANDRASEKARAN]; several ethnic Tamil and Muslim parties, represented in either Parliament or provincial councils

Political pressure groups and leaders: Buddhist clergy; labor unions; Liberation Tigers of Tamil Eelam or LTTE [Velupillai PRABHAKARAN](insurgent group fighting for a separate state); radical chauvinist Sinhalese groups such as the National Movement Against Terrorism; Sinhalese Buddhist lay groups

International organization participation: AsDB, C, CP, FAO, G-15, G-24, G-77, IAEA, IBRD, ICAO, ICC, ICFTU, ICRM, IDA, IFAD, IFC, IFRCS, IHO, ILO, IMF, IMO, Interpol, IOC, IOM, ISO, ITU, MIGA, MINURSO, MINUSTAH, MONUC, NAM, OAS (observer), ONUB, OPCW, PCA, SAARC, SACEP, UN, UNCTAD, UNESCO, UNIDO, UPU, WCL, WCO, WFTU, WHO, WIPO, WMO, WToO, WTO

Diplomatic representation in the US:
chief of mission: Ambassador Bernard GOONETILLEKE
chancery: 2148 Wyoming Avenue NW, Washington, DC 20008
telephone: [1] (202) 483-4025 (through 4028)
FAX: [1] (202) 232-7181
consulate(s) general: Los Angeles
consulate(s): New York

Diplomatic representation from the US:
chief of mission: Ambassador Jeffrey J. LUNSTEAD
embassy: 210 Galle Road, Colombo 3
mailing address: P. O. Box 106, Colombo
telephone: [94] (11) 244-8007
FAX: [94] (11) 243-7345

Flag description: yellow with two panels; the smaller hoist-side panel has two equal vertical bands of green (hoist side) and orange; the other panel is a large dark red rectangle with a yellow lion holding a sword, and there is a yellow bo leaf in each corner; the yellow field appears as a border around the entire flag and extends between the two panels

ECONOMY

Economy - overview: In 1977, Colombo abandoned statist economic policies and its import substitution trade policy for market-oriented policies and export-oriented trade. Sri Lanka's most dynamic sectors now are food processing, textiles and apparel, food and beverages, telecommunications, and insurance and banking. In 2003, plantation crops made up only 15% of exports (compared with 93% in 1970), while textiles and garments accounted for 63%. GDP grew at an average annual rate of about 5.5% in the 1990s, but 2001 saw the first contraction in the country's history -1.4%, due to a combination of power shortages, severe budgetary problems, the global slowdown, and continuing civil strife. Growth recovered to 5% between 2002 and 2005. About 800,000 Sri Lankans work abroad, 90% in the Middle East. They send home about $1 billion a year. The struggle by the Tamil Tigers of the north and east for a largely independent homeland continues to cast a shadow over the economy. In late December 2004, a major tsunami took about 31,000 lives, left more than 6,300 missing and 443,000 displaced, and destroyed an estimated $1.5 billion worth of property.

GDP (purchasing power parity): $86.72 billion (2005 est.)

GDP (official exchange rate): $21.98 billion (2005 est.)

GDP - real growth rate: 4.7% (2005 est.)

GDP - per capita: purchasing power parity - $4,300 (2005 est.)

GDP - composition by sector:
agriculture: 17.7%
industry: 27.1%
services: 55.2% (2005 est.)

Labor force: 8.08 million (2005 est.)

Labor force - by occupation: agriculture 38%, industry 17%, services 45% (1998 est.)

Unemployment rate: 8.4% (2005 est.)

Population below poverty line: 22% (1997 est.)

Household income or consumption by percentage share:
lowest 10%: 3.5%
highest 10%: 28% (1995)

Distribution of family income - Gini index: 34.4 (1995)

Inflation rate (consumer prices): 11.2% (2005 est.)

Investment (gross fixed): 27% of GDP (2005 est.)

Budget:
revenues: $3.804 billion
expenditures: $5.469 billion, including capital expenditures of NA (2005 est.)

Public debt: 98.5% of GDP (2005 est.)

Agriculture - products: rice, sugarcane, grains, pulses, oilseed, spices, tea, rubber, coconuts; milk, eggs, hides, beef

Industries: rubber processing, tea, coconuts, and other agricultural commodities; telecommunications, insurance, and banking; clothing, cement, petroleum refining, textiles, tobacco

Industrial production growth rate: 6.1% (2005 est.)

Electricity - production: 7.308 billion kWh (2003)

Electricity - production by source:
fossil fuel: 51.7%
hydro: 48.3%
nuclear: 0%
other: 0% (2001)

Electricity - consumption: 6.796 billion kWh (2003)

Electricity - exports: 0 kWh (2003)

Electricity - imports: 0 kWh (2003)

Oil - production: 0 bbl/day (2003 est.)

Oil - consumption: 79,000 bbl/day (2003 est.)

Oil - exports: NA (2001)

Oil - imports: NA (2001)

Current account balance: $-388 million (2005 est.)

Exports: $6.442 billion f.o.b. (2005 est.)

Exports - partners: US 32.4%, UK 13.5%, India 6.8%, Germany 4.8% (2004)

Imports: $8.37 billion f.o.b. (2005 est.)

Imports - partners: India 18%, Singapore 8.7%, Hong Kong 7.7%, China 5.7%, Iran 5.2%, Japan 5.1%, Malaysia 4.1% (2004)

Reserves of foreign exchange and gold: $2.384 billion (2005 est.)

Debt - external: $11.59 billion (2005 est.)
Economic aid - recipient: $577 million (1998)
Currency (code): Sri Lankan rupee (LKR)
Currency code: LKR
Exchange rates: Sri Lankan rupees per US dollar - 100.19 (2005), 101.194 (2004), 96.521 (2003), 95.662 (2002), 89.383 (2001)
Fiscal year: calendar year

COMMUNICATIONS

Telephones - main lines in use: 881,400 (2002)
Telephones - mobile cellular: 931,600 (2002)
Telephone system:
general assessment: very inadequate domestic service, particularly in rural areas; likely improvement with privatization of national telephone company and encouragement to private investment; good international service (1999)
domestic: national trunk network consists mostly of digital microwave radio relay; fiber-optic links now in use in Colombo area and two fixed wireless local loops have been installed; competition is strong in mobile cellular systems; telephone density remains low at 2.6 main lines per 100 persons (1999)
international: country code - 94; submarine cables to Indonesia and Djibouti; satellite earth stations - 2 Intelsat (Indian Ocean) (1999)
Radio broadcast stations: AM 26, FM 45, shortwave 1 (1998)
Radios: 3.85 million (1997)
Television broadcast stations: 21 (1997)
Televisions: 1.53 million (1997)
Internet country code: .lk
Internet hosts: 1,882 (2003)
Internet Service Providers (ISPs): 5 (2000)
Internet users: 200,000 (2002)

TRANSPORTATION

Airports: 14 (2004 est.)
Airports - with paved runways:
total: 14
over 3,047 m: 1
1,524 to 2,437 m: 6
914 to 1,523 m: 7 (2005 est.)
Airports - with unpaved runways:
total: 2
under 914 m: 2 (2005 est.)
Railways:
total: 1,449 km
broad gauge: 1,449 km 1.676-m gauge (2004)
Roadways:
total: 11,650 km
paved: 11,068 km
unpaved: 582 km (2002)
Waterways: 160 km (primarily on rivers in southwest) (2004)
Merchant marine:
total: 23 ships (1,000 GRT or over) 120,924 GRT/173,604 DWT
by type: cargo 18, container 2, passenger 1, petroleum tanker 2
foreign-owned: 10 (Germany 10)
registered in other countries: 1 (2005)
Ports and terminals: Colombo, Galle

MILITARY

Military branches: Army, Navy, Air Force, Police Force
Military service age and obligation: 18 years of age for voluntary military service (2001)
Manpower available for military service: *males age 18-49:* 4,933,217 (2005 est.)
Manpower fit for military service: *males age 18-49:* 3,789,627 (2005 est.)
Manpower reaching military service age annually: *males:* 174,049 (2005 est.)
Military expenditures - dollar figure: $514.8 million (2004)
Military expenditures - percent of GDP: 2.6% (2004)

TRANSNATIONAL ISSUES

Disputes - international: none
Refugees and internally displaced persons:
IDPs: 362,000 (both Tamils and non-Tamils displaced due to Tamil conflict); 555,000 (resulting from 26 December 2004 tsunami) (2004)

SUDAN

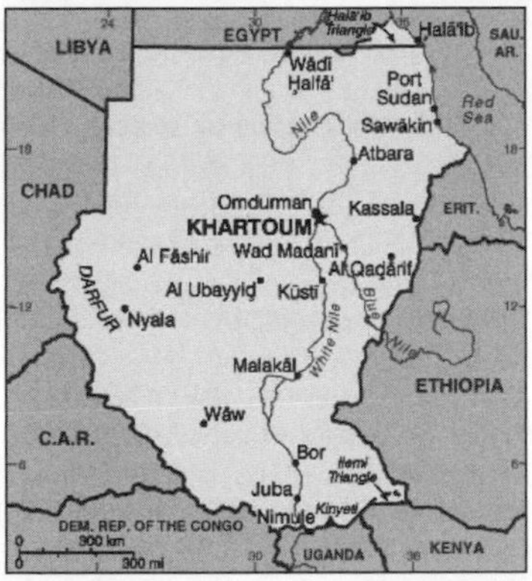

INTRODUCTION

Background: Military regimes favoring Islamic-oriented governments have dominated national politics since independence from the UK in 1956. Sudan was embroiled in two prolonged civil wars during most of the remainder of the 20th century. These conflicts were rooted in northern economic, political, and social domination of largely non-Muslim, non-Arab southern Sudanese. The first civil war ended in 1972, but broke out again in 1983. The second war and famine-related effects resulted in more than 4 million people displaced and, according to rebel estimates, more than 2 million deaths over a period of two decades. Peace talks gained momentum in 2002-04 with the signing of several accords; a final Naivasha peace treaty of January 2005 granted the southern rebels autonomy for six years, after which a referendum for independence is scheduled to be held. A separate conflict that broke out in the western region of Darfur in 2003 has resulted in tens of thousands of deaths and nearly 2 million displaced; as of late 2005, peacekeeping troops were struggling to stabilize the situation. Sudan also has faced large refugee influxes from neighboring countries, primarily Ethiopia and Chad, and armed conflict, poor transport infrastructure, and lack of government support have chronically obstructed the provision of humanitarian assistance to affected populations.

GEOGRAPHY

Location: Northern Africa, bordering the Red Sea, between Egypt and Eritrea
Geographic coordinates: 15 00 N, 30 00 E
Map references: Africa
Area:
total: 2,505,810 sq km
land: 2.376 million sq km
water: 129,810 sq km
Area - comparative: slightly more than one-quarter the size of the US
Land boundaries:
total: 7,687 km
border countries: Central African Republic 1,165 km, Chad 1,360 km, Democratic Republic of the Congo 628 km, Egypt 1,273 km, Eritrea 605 km, Ethiopia 1,606 km, Kenya 232 km, Libya 383 km, Uganda 435 km
Coastline: 853 km
Maritime claims:
territorial sea: 12 nm
contiguous zone: 18 nm
continental shelf: 200-m depth or to the depth of exploitation
Climate: tropical in south; arid desert in

north; rainy season varies by region (April to November)
Terrain: generally flat, featureless plain; mountains in far south, northeast and west; desert dominates the north
Elevation extremes:
lowest point: Red Sea 0 m
highest point: Kinyeti 3,187 m
Natural resources: petroleum; small reserves of iron ore, copper, chromium ore, zinc, tungsten, mica, silver, gold, hydropower
Land use:
arable land: 6.83%
permanent crops: 0.18%
other: 92.99% (2001)
Irrigated land: 19,500 sq km (1998 est.)
Natural hazards: dust storms and periodic persistent droughts
Environment - current issues: inadequate supplies of potable water; wildlife populations threatened by excessive hunting; soil erosion; desertification; periodic drought
Environment - international agreements:
party to: Biodiversity, Climate Change, Climate Change-Kyoto Protocol, Desertification, Endangered Species, Law of the Sea, Ozone Layer Protection
signed, but not ratified: none of the selected agreements
Geography - note: largest country in Africa; dominated by the Nile and its tributaries

PEOPLE

Population: 40,187,486 (July 2005 est.)
Age structure:
0-14 years: 43.2% (male 8,865,331/female 8,488,982)
15-64 years: 54.5% (male 10,952,566/ female 10,930,218)
65 years and over: 2.4% (male 513,679/ female 436,710) (2005 est.)
Median age:
total: 18.07 years
male: 17.86 years
female: 18.29 years (2005 est.)
Population growth rate: 2.6% (2005 est.)
Birth rate: 35.17 births/1,000 population (2005 est.)
Death rate: 9.16 deaths/1,000 population (2005 est.)
Net migration rate: -0.02 migrant(s)/ 1,000 population (2005 est.)
Sex ratio:
at birth: 1.05 male(s)/female
under 15 years: 1.04 male(s)/female
15-64 years: 1 male(s)/female
65 years and over: 1.18 male(s)/female
total population: 1.02 male(s)/female (2005 est.)
Infant mortality rate:
total: 62.5 deaths/1,000 live births
male: 63.29 deaths/1,000 live births
female: 61.67 deaths/1,000 live births (2005 est.)
Life expectancy at birth:
total population: 58.54 years
male: 57.33 years
female: 59.8 years (2005 est.)
Total fertility rate: 4.85 children born/woman (2005 est.)
HIV/AIDS - adult prevalence rate: 2.3% (2001 est.)
HIV/AIDS - people living with HIV/AIDS: 400,000 (2001 est.)
HIV/AIDS - deaths: 23,000 (2003 est.)
Major infectious diseases:
degree of risk: very high
food or waterborne diseases: bacterial and protozoal diarrhea, hepatitis A, and typhoid fever
vectorborne diseases: malaria, dengue fever, African trypanosomiasis (sleeping sickness) are high risks in some locations
water contact disease: schistosomiasis
respiratory disease: meningococcal meningitis (2004)
Nationality:
noun: Sudanese (singular and plural)
adjective: Sudanese
Ethnic groups: black 52%, Arab 39%, Beja 6%, foreigners 2%, other 1%
Religions: Sunni Muslim 70% (in north), indigenous beliefs 25%, Christian 5% (mostly in south and Khartoum)
Languages: Arabic (official), Nubian, Ta Bedawie, diverse dialects of Nilotic, Nilo-Hamitic, Sudanic languages, English
note: program of "Arabization" in process
Literacy:
definition: age 15 and over can read and write
total population: 61.1%
male: 71.8%
female: 50.5% (2003 est.)

GOVERNMENT

Country name:
conventional long form: Republic of the Sudan
conventional short form: Sudan
local long form: Jumhuriyat as-Sudan
local short form: As-Sudan
former: Anglo-Egyptian Sudan
Government type: coalition government run by an alliance of the National Congress Party (NCP) and the Sudan People's Liberation Movement (SPLM)
Capital: Khartoum
Administrative divisions: 26 states (wilayat, singular - wilayah); A'ali an Nil (Upper Nile), Al Bahr al Ahmar (Red Sea), Al Buhayrat (Lakes), Al Jazirah (El Gezira), Al Khartum (Khartoum), Al Qadarif (Gedaref), Al Wahdah (Unity), An Nil al Abyad (White Nile), An Nil al Azraq (Blue Nile), Ash Shamaliyah (Northern), Bahr al Jabal (Bahr al Jabal), Gharb al Istiwa'iyah (Western Equatoria), Gharb Bahr al Ghazal (Western Bahr al Ghazal), Gharb Darfur (Western Darfur), Gharb Kurdufan (Western Kordofan), Janub Darfur (Southern Darfur), Janub Kurdufan (Southern Kordofan), Junqali (Jonglei), Kassala (Kassala), Nahr an Nil (Nile), Shamal Bahr al Ghazal (Northern Bahr al Ghazal), Shamal Darfur (Northern Darfur), Shamal Kurdufan (Northern Kordofan), Sharq al Istiwa'iyah (Eastern Equatoria), Sinnar (Sinnar), Warab (Warab)
Independence: 1 January 1956 (from Egypt and UK)
National holiday: Independence Day, 1 January (1956)
Constitution: 12 April 1973; suspended following coup of 6 April 1985; interim constitution of 10 October 1985 suspended following coup of 30 June 1989; new constitution implemented on 30 June 1998 partially suspended 12 December 1999 by President BASHIR; coalition government constitution adopted 9 July 2005.
Legal system: based on English common law and Islamic law; as of 20 January 1991, the now defunct Revolutionary Command Council imposed Islamic law in the northern states; Islamic law applies to all residents of the northern states regardless of their religion; some separate religious courts; accepts compulsory ICJ jurisdiction, with reservations
Suffrage: 17 years of age; universal, but noncompulsory
Executive branch:
chief of state: President Field Marshal Umar Hassan Ahmad al-BASHIR (since 16 October 1993); First Vice President Salva KIIR (since 4 August 2005), Second Vice President Ali Osman TAHA (since 20 September 2005); note - the president is both the chief of state and head of government
head of government: President Field Marshal Umar Hassan Ahmad al-BASHIR (since 16 October 1993); First Vice President Salva KIIR (since 4 August 2005), Second Vice President Ali Osman TAHA (since 20 September 2005); note - the president is both the chief of state and head of government
cabinet: Council of Ministers appointed by the president; note - the National Congress Party or NCP (formerly the National Islamic Front or NIF) dominates al-BASHIR's cabinet
elections: president elected by popular vote for a five-year term; election last held 13-23 December 2000 (next to be held 2009)
election results: Field Marshall Umar

Hassan Ahmad al-BASHIR reelected president; percent of vote - Umar Hassan Ahmad al-BASHIR 86.5%, Ja'afar Muhammed NUMAYRI 9.6%, three other candidates received a combined vote of 3.9%; election widely viewed as rigged; all popular opposition parties boycotted elections because of a lack of guarantees for a free and fair election
note: al-BASHIR assumed power as chairman of Sudan's Revolutionary Command Council for National Salvation (RCC) in June 1989 and served concurrently as chief of state, chairman of the RCC, prime minister, and minister of defense until mid-October 1993 when he was appointed president by the RCC; he was elected president by popular vote for the first time in March 1996
Legislative branch: bicameral body consisting of the National Assembly (450 seats; members appointed from within the National Congress Party (NCP) 52%, Sudan People's Liberation Movement (SPLM) 28%, northern opposition 14% and southern opposition 6%; members serve four-year terms) and the Council of States (52 seats; members appointed from within the National Congress Party (NCP) 52%, Sudan People's Liberation Movement (SPLM) 28%, northern opposition 14%, and southern opposition 6%; members serve four-year terms)
elections: last held 13-22 December 2000 (next to be held 2009)
election results: NCP 355, others 5
Judicial branch: Supreme Court; Special Revolutionary Courts
Political parties and leaders: to obtain government approval parties must accept the constitution and refrain from advocating or using violence against the regime; approved parties include the National Congress Party or NCP [Ibrahim Ahmed UMAR], the Sudan People's Liberation Movement or SPLM [Salva KIIR]; Popular National Congress or PNC [Hassan al-TURABI], and over 20 minor, pro-government parties
Political pressure groups and leaders: Democratic Unionist Party [Muhammed Uthman AL-MIRGHANI]; National Democratic Alliance [Muhammed Uthman AL-MIRGHANI, chairman]; Sudan People's Liberation Movement/Army [Salva KIIR]; Umma Party [Sadiq al-MAHDI]
International organization participation: ABEDA, ACP, AfDB, AFESD, AMF, AU, CAEU, COMESA, FAO, G-77, IAEA, IBRD, ICAO, ICCt (signatory), ICRM, IDA, IDB, IFAD, IFC, IFRCS, IGAD, ILO, IMF, IMO, Interpol, IOC, IOM, ISO, ITU, LAS, MIGA, NAM, OIC, OPCW, PCA, UN, UNCTAD, UNESCO, UNHCR, UNIDO, UPU, WCO, WFTU, WHO, WIPO, WMO, WToO, WTO (observer)
Diplomatic representation in the US:
chief of mission: Ambassador (vacant); Charge d'Affaires, Ad Interim Khidir Haroun AHMED (since April 2001)
chancery: 2210 Massachusetts Avenue NW, Washington, DC 20008
telephone: [1] (202) 338-8565
FAX: [1] (202) 667-2406
Diplomatic representation from the US:
chief of mission: Ambassador (vacant); Charge d'Affaires Cameron HUME
embassy: Sharia Ali Abdul Latif Avenue, Khartoum
mailing address: P. O. Box 699, Khartoum; APO AE 09829
telephone: [249] (11) 774611 or 774700
FAX: [249] (11) 774137
note: US Consul in Cairo is providing backup service for Khartoum
Flag description: three equal horizontal bands of red (top), white, and black with a green isosceles triangle based on the hoist side

ECONOMY

Economy - overview: Sudan has turned around a struggling economy with sound economic policies and infrastructure investments, but it still faces formidable economic problems, starting from its low level of per capita output. From 1997 to date, Sudan has been implementing IMF macroeconomic reforms. In 1999, Sudan began exporting crude oil and in the last quarter of 1999 recorded its first trade surplus, which, along with monetary policy, has stabilized the exchange rate. Increased oil production, revived light industry, and expanded export processing zones helped sustain GDP growth at 8.6% in 2004. Agriculture production remains Sudan's most important sector, employing 80% of the work force, contributing 39% of GDP, and accounting for most of GDP growth, but most farms remain rain-fed and susceptible to drought. Chronic instability - resulting from the long-standing civil war between the Muslim north and the Christian/pagan south, adverse weather, and weak world agricultural prices - ensure that much of the population will remain at or below the poverty line for years.
GDP (purchasing power parity): $85.46 billion (2005 est.)
GDP (official exchange rate): $23.02 billion (2005 est.)
GDP - real growth rate: 8.6% (2005 est.)
GDP - per capita: purchasing power parity - $2,100 (2005 est.)
GDP - composition by sector:
agriculture: 38.7%
industry: 20.3%
services: 41% (2003 est.)
Labor force: 11 million (1996 est.)
Labor force - by occupation: agriculture 80%, industry and commerce 7%, government 13% (1998 est.)
Unemployment rate: 18.7% (2002 est.)
Population below poverty line: 40% (2004 est.)
Household income or consumption by percentage share:
lowest 10%: NA
highest 10%: NA
Inflation rate (consumer prices): 11% (2005 est.)
Investment (gross fixed): 15.4% of GDP (2005 est.)
Budget:
revenues: $6.182 billion
expenditures: $5.753 billion, including capital expenditures of $304
Public debt: 79% of GDP (2005 est.)
Agriculture - products: cotton, groundnuts (peanuts), sorghum, millet, wheat, gum arabic, sugarcane, cassava (tapioca), mangos, papaya, bananas, sweet potatoes, sesame; sheep, livestock
Industries: oil, cotton ginning, textiles, cement, edible oils, sugar, soap distilling, shoes, petroleum refining, pharmaceuticals, armaments, automobile/light truck assembly
Industrial production growth rate: 8.5% (1999 est.)
Electricity - production: 3.165 billion kWh (2003)
Electricity - production by source:
fossil fuel: 52.1%
hydro: 47.9%
nuclear: 0%
other: 0% (2001)
Electricity - consumption: 2.943 billion kWh (2003)
Electricity - exports: 0 kWh (2003)
Electricity - imports: 0 kWh (2003)
Oil - production: 401,300 bbl/day (2005 est.)
Oil - consumption: 70,000 bbl/day (2004 est.)
Oil - exports: 275,000 bbl/day (2004)
Oil - imports: 0 bbl/day (2004)
Oil - proved reserves: 1.6 billion bbl (2005 est.)
Natural gas - proved reserves: 99.11 billion cu m (2005)
Current account balance: $-658 million (2005 est.)
Exports: $6.989 billion f.o.b. (2005 est.)
Exports - partners: China 66.9%, Japan 10.7%, Saudi Arabia 4.4% (2004)
Imports: $5.028 billion f.o.b. (2005 est.)
Imports - partners: China 13%, Saudi Arabia 11.5%, UAE 5.9%, Egypt 5.1%, India 4.8%, Germany 4.5%, Australia 4.1%, Japan 4% (2004)

Reserves of foreign exchange and gold: $2.52 billion (2005 est.)
Debt - external: $18.15 billion (2005 est.)
Economic aid - recipient: $172 million (2001)
Currency (code): Sudanese dinar (SDD)
Currency code: SDD
Exchange rates: Sudanese dinars per US dollar - 247.17 (2005), 257.91 (2004), 260.98 (2003), 263.31 (2002), 258.7 (2001)
Fiscal year: calendar year

COMMUNICATIONS

Telephones - main lines in use: 900,000 (2003)
Telephones - mobile cellular: 650,000 (2003)
Telephone system:
general assessment: large, well-equipped system by regional standards and being upgraded; cellular communications started in 1996 and have expanded substantially
domestic: consists of microwave radio relay, cable, radiotelephone communications, tropospheric scatter, and a domestic satellite system with 14 earth stations
international: country code - 249; satellite earth stations - 1 Intelsat (Atlantic Ocean) and 1 Arabsat (2000)
Radio broadcast stations: AM 12, FM 1, shortwave 1 (1998)
Radios: 7.55 million (1997)
Television broadcast stations: 3 (1997)
Televisions: 2.38 million (1997)
Internet country code: .sd
Internet hosts: NA
Internet Service Providers (ISPs): 2 (2002)
Internet users: 300,000 (2003)

TRANSPORTATION

Airports: 75 (2004 est.)
Airports - with paved runways:
total: 14
over 3,047 m: 1
2,438 to 3,047 m: 9
1,524 to 2,437 m: 4 (2005 est.)
Airports - with unpaved runways:
total: 72
over 3,047 m: 1
1,524 to 2,437 m: 18
914 to 1,523 m: 37
under 914 m: 16 (2005 est.)
Heliports: 1 (2005 est.)
Pipelines: gas 156 km; oil 2,365 km; refined products 810 km (2004)
Railways:
total: 5,995 km
narrow gauge: 4,595 km 1.067-m gauge; 1,400 km .600-m gauge for cotton plantations (2004)
Roadways:
total: 11,900 km
paved: 4,320 km
unpaved: 7,580 km (1999 est.)
Waterways: 4,068 km (1,723 km open year round on White and Blue Nile rivers) (2004)
Merchant marine:
total: 2 ships (1,000 GRT or over) 20,466 GRT/26,973 DWT
by type: cargo 1, livestock carrier 1
registered in other countries: 2 (2005)
Ports and terminals: Port Sudan

MILITARY

Military branches: Sudanese People's Armed Forces (SPAF): Army, Navy, Air Force, Popular Defense Force
Military service age and obligation: 18-30 years of age for compulsory military service; conscript service obligation - 3 years (August 2004)
Manpower available for military service:
males age 18-49: 8,291,695 (2005 est.)
Manpower fit for military service: *males age 18-49:* 5,427,474 (2005 est.)
Manpower reaching military service age annually: *males:* 442,915 (2005 est.)
Military expenditures - dollar figure: $587 million (2001 est.) (2004)
Military expenditures - percent of GDP: 3% (1999) (2004)

TRANSNATIONAL ISSUES

Disputes - international: the effects of Sudan's almost constant ethnic and rebel militia fighting since the mid-twentieth century have penetrated all of its border states who provide shelter for fleeing refugees and cover to disparate domestic and foreign conflicting elements; since 2003, Janjawid armed militia and Sudanese military have driven about 200,000 Darfur region refugees into eastern Chad; large numbers of Sudanese refugees have also fled to Uganda, Ethiopia, Kenya, the Central African Republic, and the Democratic Republic of the Congo; southern Sudan provides shelter to Ugandans seeking periodic protection from soldiers of the Lord's Resistance Army; Sudan accuses Eritrea of supporting Sudanese rebel groups; efforts to demarcate the porous boundary with Ethiopia have been delayed by civil and ethnic fighting in Sudan; Kenya's administrative boundary extends into the southern Sudan, creating the "Ilemi Triangle"; Egypt and Sudan retain claims to administer triangular areas that extend north and south of the 1899 Treaty boundary along the 22nd Parallel, but have withdrawn their military presence; Egypt is economically developing the "Hala'ib Triangle" north of the Treaty Line; periodic violent skirmishes with Sudanese residents over water and grazing rights persist among related pastoral populations from the Central African Republic along the border
Refugees and internally displaced persons:
refugees (country of origin): 108,251 (Eritrea) 5,023 (Chad) 7,983 (Uganda)
IDPs: 4.367 million (internal conflict since 1980s; ongoing genocide) (2004)

SURINAME

INTRODUCTION

Background: Independence from the Netherlands was granted in 1975. Five years later the civilian government was replaced by a military regime that soon declared a socialist republic. It continued to rule through a succession of nominally civilian administrations until 1987, when international pressure finally forced a democratic election. In 1989, the military overthrew the civilian government, but a democratically-elected government returned to power in 1991.

GEOGRAPHY

Location: Northern South America, bordering the North Atlantic Ocean, between French Guiana and Guyana
Geographic coordinates: 4 00 N, 56 00 W
Map references: South America
Area:
total: 163,270 sq km
land: 161,470 sq km
water: 1,800 sq km
Area - comparative: slightly larger than Georgia
Land boundaries:
total: 1,707 km
border countries: Brazil 597 km, French Guiana 510 km, Guyana 600 km
Coastline: 386 km
Maritime claims:
territorial sea: 12 nm
exclusive economic zone: 200 nm
Climate: tropical; moderated by trade winds
Terrain: mostly rolling hills; narrow coastal plain with swamps
Elevation extremes:
lowest point: unnamed location in the coastal plain -2 m
highest point: Juliana Top 1,230 m
Natural resources: timber, hydropower,

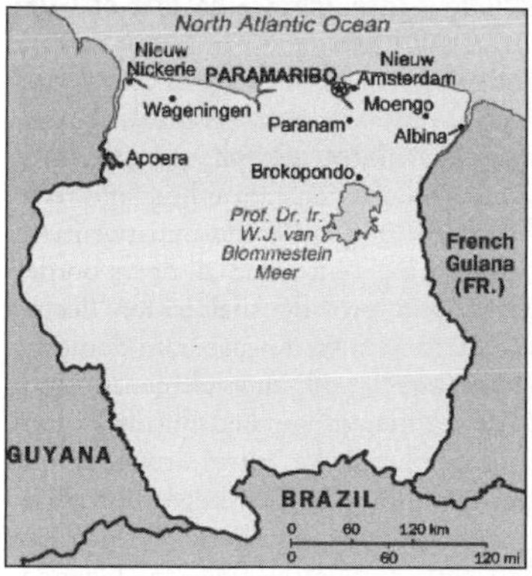

fish, kaolin, shrimp, bauxite, gold, and small amounts of nickel, copper, platinum, iron ore

Land use:
arable land: 0.37%
permanent crops: 0.06%
other: 99.57% (2001)

Irrigated land: 490 sq km (1998 est.)

Natural hazards: NA

Environment - current issues: deforestation as timber is cut for export; pollution of inland waterways by small-scale mining activities

Environment - international agreements:
party to: Biodiversity, Climate Change, Desertification, Endangered Species, Law of the Sea, Marine Dumping, Ozone Layer Protection, Ship Pollution, Tropical Timber 94, Wetlands
signed, but not ratified: none of the selected agreements

Geography - note: smallest independent country on South American continent; mostly tropical rain forest; great diversity of flora and fauna that, for the most part, is increasingly threatened by new development; relatively small population, mostly along the coast

PEOPLE

Population: 438,144 (July 2005 est.)

Age structure:
0-14 years: 29.6% (male 66,537/female 63,182)
15-64 years: 64.2% (male 144,285/female 136,942)
65 years and over: 6.2% (male 12,092/female 15,106) (2005 est.)

Median age:
total: 26.13 years
male: 25.72 years
female: 26.58 years (2005 est.)

Population growth rate: 0.25% (2005 est.)

Birth rate: 18.39 births/1,000 population (2005 est.)

Death rate: 7.16 deaths/1,000 population (2005 est.)

Net migration rate: -8.78 migrant(s)/1,000 population (2005 est.)

Sex ratio:
at birth: 1.05 male(s)/female
under 15 years: 1.05 male(s)/female
15-64 years: 1.05 male(s)/female
65 years and over: 0.8 male(s)/female
total population: 1.04 male(s)/female (2005 est.)

Infant mortality rate:
total: 23.57 deaths/1,000 live births
male: 27.57 deaths/1,000 live births
female: 19.37 deaths/1,000 live births (2005 est.)

Life expectancy at birth:
total population: 68.96 years
male: 66.75 years
female: 71.27 years (2005 est.)

Total fertility rate: 2.34 children born/woman (2005 est.)

HIV/AIDS - adult prevalence rate: 1.7% (2001 est.)

HIV/AIDS - people living with HIV/AIDS: 5,200 (2001 est.)

HIV/AIDS - deaths: less than 500 (2003 est.)

Nationality:
noun: Surinamer(s)
adjective: Surinamese

Ethnic groups: Hindustani (also known locally as "East Indians"; their ancestors emigrated from northern India in the latter part of the 19th century) 37%, Creole (mixed white and black) 31%, Javanese 15%, "Maroons" (their African ancestors were brought to the country in the 17th and 18th centuries as slaves and escaped to the interior) 10%, Amerindian 2%, Chinese 2%, white 1%, other 2%

Religions: Hindu 27.4%, Protestant 25.2% (predominantly Moravian), Roman Catholic 22.8%, Muslim 19.6%, indigenous beliefs 5%

Languages: Dutch (official), English (widely spoken), Sranang Tongo (Surinamese, sometimes called Taki-Taki, is native language of Creoles and much of the younger population and is lingua franca among others), Hindustani (a dialect of Hindi), Javanese

Literacy:
definition: age 15 and over can read and write
total population: 88%
male: 92.3%
female: 84.1% (2000 est.)

GOVERNMENT

Country name:
conventional long form: Republic of Suriname
conventional short form: Suriname
local long form: Republiek Suriname
local short form: Suriname
former: Netherlands Guiana, Dutch Guiana

Government type: constitutional democracy

Capital: Paramaribo

Administrative divisions: 10 districts (distrikten, singular - distrikt); Brokopondo, Commewijne, Coronie, Marowijne, Nickerie, Para, Paramaribo, Saramacca, Sipaliwini, Wanica

Independence: 25 November 1975 (from Netherlands)

National holiday: Independence Day, 25 November (1975)

Constitution: ratified 30 September 1987

Legal system: based on Dutch legal system incorporating French penal theory

Suffrage: 18 years of age, universal

Executive branch:
chief of state: President Runaldo Ronald VENETIAAN (since 12 August 2000); Vice President Jules Rattankoemar AJODHIA (since 12 August 2000); note - the president is both the chief of state and head of government
head of government: President Runaldo Ronald VENETIAAN (since 12 August 2000); Vice President Jules Rattankoemar AJODHIA (since 12 August 2000); note - the president is both the chief of state and head of government
cabinet: Cabinet of Ministers appointed by the president from among the members of the National Assembly
elections: president and vice president elected by the National Assembly or, if no presidential or vice presidential candidate receives a two-thirds constitutional majority in the National Assembly after two votes, by a simple majority in the larger People's United Assembly (869 representatives from the national, local, and regional councils), for five-year terms; election last held 25 May 2005 (next to be held 25 May 2010)

Legislative branch: unicameral National Assembly or Nationale Assemblee (51 seats; members are elected by popular vote to serve five-year terms)
elections: last held 25 May 2005 (next to be held May 2010)
election results: percent of vote by party - NF 41.2%, NDP 23.1%, VVV 14.5%, A-Com 7.3%, A1 6.2%, other 5.9%; seats by party - NF 23, NDP 15, VVV 5, A-Com 5, A1 3

Judicial branch: Cantonal Courts and a Court of Justice as an appellate court (justices are nominated for life)

Political parties and leaders: Alternative-1 or A-1 (a coalition of Democrats of the 21st Century or D-21 [Soewarto MOESTADJA], Nieuw Suriname or NS [Radjen Nanan PANDAY], Political Wing of the FAL or PVF [Jiwan SITAL], Trefpunt 2000 or T-2000 [Arti JESSURUN]); General Interior Development Party or ABOP [Ronnie BRUNSWIJK]; National Democratic Party or NDP [Desire BOUTERSE];

New Front for Democracy and Development or NF (a coalition which includes Democratic Alternative 1991 or DA-91 which split from the A-1 combination before the elections of May 2005 and are an independent, business-oriented party [Winston JESSURUN], National Party Suriname or NPS (Ronald VENETIAAN], United Reform Party or VHP [Ram SARDJOE], Pertjaja Luhur or PL [Salam Paul SOMOHARDJO], Surinamese Labor Party or SPA [Siegfried GILDS]); Party for Democracy and Development in Unity or DOE [Marten Schalkwijk]; People's Alliance for Progress or VVV (a coalition of Democratic National Platform 2000 or DNP-2000 [Jules WIJDENBOSCH], Grassroots Party for Renewal and Democracy or BVD [Tjan GOBARDHAN], Party for National Unity and Solidarity of the Highest Order or KTPI [Willy SOEMITA], Party for Progression, Justice, and Perserverance or PPRS [Renee KAIMAN], Pendawalima or PL [Raymond SAPOEN]); Progressive Laborers and Farmers Union or PALU [Jim HOK]; Seeka [Paul ABENA]; Union of Progressive Surinamers or UPS [Sheoradj PANDAY]

Political pressure groups and leaders: Association of Indigenous Village Chiefs [Ricardo PANE]; Association of Saramaccan Authorities or Maroon [Head Captain WASE]; Women's Parliament Forum or PVF [Iris GILLIAD]

International organization participation: ACP, Caricom, CSN, FAO, G-77, IADB, IBRD, ICAO, ICFTU, ICRM, IDB, IFAD, IFRCS, IHO, ILO, IMF, IMO, Interpol, IOC, ITU, LAES, MIGA, NAM, OAS, OIC, OPANAL, OPCW, PCA, UN, UNCTAD, UNESCO, UNIDO, UPU, WCL, WHO, WIPO, WMO, WTO

Diplomatic representation in the US:
chief of mission: Ambassador Henry Lothar ILLES
chancery: Suite 460, 4301 Connecticut Avenue NW, Washington, DC 20008
telephone: [1] (202) 244-7488
FAX: [1] (202) 244-5878
consulate(s) general: Miami

Diplomatic representation from the US:
chief of mission: Ambassador Marsha E. BARNES
embassy: Dr. Sophie Redmondstraat 129, Paramaribo
mailing address: Department of State, 3390 Paramaribo Place, Washington, DC, 20521-3390
telephone: [597] 472-900
FAX: [597] 425-690

Flag description: five horizontal bands of green (top, double width), white, red (quadruple width), white, and green (double width); there is a large, yellow, five-pointed star centered in the red band

ECONOMY

Economy - overview: The economy is dominated by the alumina industry, which accounts for more than 15% of GDP and 70% of export earnings. Suriname's economic prospects for the medium term will depend on continued commitment to responsible monetary and fiscal policies and to the introduction of structural reforms to liberalize markets and promote competition. The government of Ronald VENETIAAN has begun an austerity program, raised taxes, and attempted to control spending. While - in 2002 - President VENETIAAN agreed to a large pay raise for civil servants, threatening his earlier gains in stabilizing the economy, he did not repeat this promise in the run-up to the May 2005 elections, which he won. Economic policies are likely to remain the same during VENETIAAN's second term. The Dutch Government has agreed to restart the aid flow, which will allow Suriname to access international development financing, but plans to phase out funds over the next five years. The short-term economic outlook depends on the government's ability to control inflation and on the development of projects in the bauxite and gold mining sectors. The opening of the Gross Rosbel gold mine is expected to boost exports and GDP growth. Prospects for local onshore oil production are good, as a drilling program is underway. Offshore oil drilling was given a boost in 2004 when the State Oil Company (Staatsolie) signed exploration agreements with Repsol and Mearsk.

GDP (purchasing power parity): $2.077 billion (2005 est.)

GDP (official exchange rate): $1.389 billion (2005 est.)

GDP - real growth rate: 4% (2005 est.)

GDP - per capita: purchasing power parity - $4,700 (2005 est.)

GDP - composition by sector:
agriculture: 13%
industry: 22%
services: 65% (2001 est.)

Labor force: 104,000 (2003)

Labor force - by occupation: agriculture NA%, industry NA%, services NA%

Unemployment rate: 17% (2000)

Population below poverty line: 70% (2002 est.)

Household income or consumption by percentage share:
lowest 10%: NA%
highest 10%: NA%

Inflation rate (consumer prices): 23% (2003 est.)

Budget:
revenues: $400 million
expenditures: $440 million, including capital expenditures of $34 million (2003 est.)

Agriculture - products: paddy rice, bananas, palm kernels, coconuts, plantains, peanuts; beef, chickens; forest products; shrimp

Industries: bauxite and gold mining, alumina production, oil, lumbering, food processing, fishing

Industrial production growth rate: 6.5% (1994 est.)

Electricity - production: 2.014 billion kWh (2003)

Electricity - production by source:
fossil fuel: 25.2%
hydro: 74.8%
nuclear: 0%
other: 0% (2001)

Electricity - consumption: 1.873 billion kWh (2003)

Electricity - exports: 0 kWh (2003)

Electricity - imports: 0 kWh (2003)

Oil - production: 12,000 bbl/day (2004 est.)

Oil - consumption: 14,000 bbl/day (2004 est.)

Oil - exports: 1,370 bbl/day (2003)

Oil - imports: 1,644 bbl/day (2003)

Oil - proved reserves: 99 million bbl (2004)

Natural gas - proved reserves: 0 cu m (2004)

Exports: $881 million f.o.b. (2004 est.)

Exports - partners: Norway 29.4%, US 15.2%, Canada 12.5%, Belgium 10.3%, France 8.4%, UAE 6.2% (2004)

Imports: $750 million f.o.b. (2004 est.)

Imports - partners: US 26.2%, Netherlands 19.3%, Trinidad and Tobago 13.5%, Japan 6.6%, China 4.6%, Brazil 4.2% (2004)

Debt - external: $321 million (2002 est.)

Economic aid - recipient: Netherlands provided $37 million for project and program assistance, European Development Fund $4 million, Belgium $2 million (1998)

Currency (code): Surinam dollar (SRD)

Currency code: SRG

Exchange rates: Surinamese dollars per US dollar - 2.7 (2005), Surinamese guilders per US dollar - 2.7336 (2004), 2.6013 (2003), 2.3468 (2002), 2.1785 (2001)
note: during 1998, the exchange rate splintered into four distinct rates; in January 1999 the government floated the guilder, but subsequently fixed it when the black-market rate plunged; in January 2004, the government introduced the Surinamese dollar as replacement for the guilder, tied to a US dollar-dominated currency basket

Fiscal year: calendar year

COMMUNICATIONS

Telephones - main lines in use: 79,800 (2003)
Telephones - mobile cellular: 168,100 (2003)
Telephone system:
general assessment: international facilities are good
domestic: microwave radio relay network
international: country code - 597; satellite earth stations - 2 Intelsat (Atlantic Ocean)
Radio broadcast stations: AM 4, FM 13, shortwave 1 (1998)
Radios: 300,000 (1997)
Television broadcast stations: 3 (plus seven repeaters) (2000)
Televisions: 63,000 (1997)
Internet country code: .sr
Internet hosts: 18 (2003)
Internet Service Providers (ISPs): 2 (2000)
Internet users: 20,000 (2002)

TRANSPORTATION

Airports: 46 (2004 est.)
Airports - with paved runways:
total: 5
over 3,047 m: 1
under 914 m: 4 (2005 est.)
Airports - with unpaved runways:
total: 42
1,524 to 2,437 m: 1
914 to 1,523 m: 5
under 914 m: 36 (2005 est.)
Pipelines: oil 51 km (2004)
Roadways:
total: 4,492 km
paved: 1,168 km
unpaved: 3,324 km (2002)
Waterways: 1,200 km (most navigable by ships with drafts up to 7 m) (2003)
Merchant marine:
total: 1 ships (1,000 GRT or over) 1,078 GRT/1,214 DWT
by type: cargo 1 (2005)
Ports and terminals: Paramaribo

MILITARY

Military branches: National Army (includes small Navy and Air Force elements)
Military service age and obligation: 18 years of age (est.); no conscription
Manpower available for military service:
males age 18-49: 111,582 (2005 est.)
Manpower fit for military service: *males age 18-49:* 77,793 (2005 est.)
Military expenditures - dollar figure: $7.5 million (2003)
Military expenditures - percent of GDP: 0.7% (2003)

TRANSNATIONAL ISSUES

Disputes - international: area claimed by French Guiana between Riviere Litani and Riviere Marouini (both headwaters of the Lawa); Suriname claims a triangle of land between the New and Kutari/Koetari rivers in a historic dispute over the headwaters of the Courantyne; Guyana seeks UNCLOS arbitration to resolve the long-standing dispute with Suriname over the axis of the territorial sea boundary in potentially oil-rich waters
Illicit drugs: growing transshipment point for South American drugs destined for Europe and Brazil; transshipment point for arms-for-drugs dealing

SVALBARD

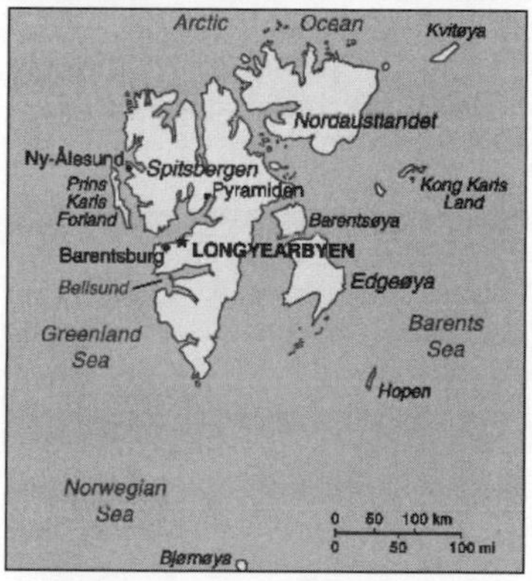

INTRODUCTION

Background: First discovered by the Norwegians in the 12th century, the islands served as an international whaling base during the 17th and 18th centuries. Norway's sovereignty was recognized in 1920; five years later it officially took over the territory.

GEOGRAPHY

Location: Northern Europe, islands between the Arctic Ocean, Barents Sea, Greenland Sea, and Norwegian Sea, north of Norway
Geographic coordinates: 78 00 N, 20 00 E
Map references: Arctic Region
Area:
total: 62,049 sq km
land: 62,049 sq km
water: 7 0 sq km
note: includes Spitsbergen and Bjornoya (Bear Island)
Area - comparative: slightly smaller than West Virginia
Land boundaries: 0 km
Coastline: 3,587 km
Maritime claims:
territorial sea: 4 nm
exclusive fishing zone: 200 nm unilaterally claimed by Norway but not recognized by Russia
Climate: arctic, tempered by warm North Atlantic Current; cool summers, cold winters; North Atlantic Current flows along west and north coasts of Spitsbergen, keeping water open and navigable most of the year
Terrain: wild, rugged mountains; much of high land ice covered; west coast clear of ice about one-half of the year; fjords along west and north coasts
Elevation extremes:
lowest point: Arctic Ocean 0 m
highest point: Newtontoppen 1,717 m
Natural resources: coal, iron ore, copper, zinc, phosphate, wildlife, fish
Land use:
arable land: 0%
permanent crops: 0%
other: 100% (no trees, and the only bushes are crowberry and cloudberry) (2001)
Irrigated land: NA sq km
Natural hazards: ice floes often block the entrance to Bellsund (a transit point for coal export) on the west coast and occasionally make parts of the northeastern coast inaccessible to maritime traffic
Environment - current issues: NA
Geography - note: northernmost part of the Kingdom of Norway; consists of nine main islands; glaciers and snowfields cover 60% of the total area

PEOPLE

Population: 2,701 (July 2005 est.)
Age structure:
0-14 years: NA
15-64 years: NA
65 years and over: NA
Population growth rate: -0.02% (2005 est.)
Birth rate: NA births/1,000 population
Death rate: NA deaths/1,000 population
Net migration rate: NA migrant(s)/1,000 population
Sex ratio: NA%
Infant mortality rate:
total: NA
male: NA
female: NA
Life expectancy at birth:
total population: NA years
male: NA years
female: NA years
Total fertility rate: NA children born/woman
HIV/AIDS - adult prevalence rate: 0% (2001)

HIV/AIDS - people living with HIV/AIDS: 0 (2001)
HIV/AIDS - deaths: 0 (2001)
Ethnic groups: Norwegian 55.4%, Russian and Ukrainian 44.3%, other 0.3% (1998)
Languages: Norwegian, Russian
Literacy: NA

GOVERNMENT

Country name:
conventional long form: none
conventional short form: Svalbard (sometimes referred to as Spitzbergen)
Dependency status: territory of Norway; administered by the Polar Department of the Ministry of Justice, through a governor (sysselmann) residing in Longyearbyen, Spitsbergen; by treaty (9 February 1920) sovereignty was awarded to Norway
Government type: NA
Capital: Longyearbyen
Independence: none (territory of Norway)
National holiday: NA
Legal system: NA
Executive branch:
chief of state: King HARALD V of Norway (since 17 January 1991)
head of government: Governor Odd Olsen INGERO (since 8 June 2001) and Assistant Governor Rune Baard HANSEN (since NA)
elections: none; the monarch is hereditary; governor and assistant governor responsible to the Polar Department of the Ministry of Justice
International organization participation: none
Flag description: the flag of Norway is used

ECONOMY

Economy - overview: Coal mining is the major economic activity on Svalbard. The treaty of 9 February 1920 gives the 41 signatories equal rights to exploit mineral deposits, subject to Norwegian regulation. Although US, UK, Dutch, and Swedish coal companies have mined in the past, the only companies still mining are Norwegian and Russian. The settlements on Svalbard are essentially company towns. The Norwegian state-owned coal company employs nearly 60% of the Norwegian population on the island, runs many of the local services, and provides most of the local infrastructure. There is also some hunting of seal, reindeer, and fox.
GDP (purchasing power parity): $NA
GDP (official exchange rate): NA
GDP - real growth rate: NA%
Labor force: NA
Budget:
revenues: $11.5 million
expenditures: $11.5 million, including capital expenditures of NA (1998 est.)
Electricity - production by source:
fossil fuel: 57.9984%
hydro: 42.0016%
nuclear: 0%
other: 0%
Exports: $NA
Imports: $NA
Economic aid - recipient: $8.2 million from Norway (1998)
Currency (code): Norwegian krone (NOK)
Currency code: NOK
Exchange rates: Norwegian kroner per US dollar - NA (2005), 6.7408 (2004), 7.0802 (2003), 7.9838 (2002), 8.9917 (2001)

COMMUNICATIONS

Telephones - main lines in use: NA
Telephones - mobile cellular: NA
Telephone system:
general assessment: probably adequate
domestic: local telephone service
international: country code - 47-790; satellite earth station - 1 of unknown type (for communication with Norwegian mainland only)
Radio broadcast stations: AM 1, FM 1 (plus 2 repeaters), shortwave 0 (1998)
Radios: NA
Television broadcast stations: NA
Televisions: NA
Internet country code: .sj
Internet Service Providers (ISPs): 13 (Svalbard and Jan Mayen) (2000)
Internet users: NA

TRANSPORTATION

Airports: 4 (2004 est.)
Airports - with paved runways:
total: 2
1,524 to 2,437 m: 1
914 to 1,523 m: 1 (2005 est.)
Airports - with unpaved runways:
total: 2
under 914 m: 2 (2005 est.)
Roadways:
total: NA km
paved: NA km
unpaved: NA km
Ports and terminals: Barentsburg, Longyearbyen, Ny-Alesund, Pyramiden

MILITARY

Military - note: demilitarized by treaty on 9 February 1920

TRANSNATIONAL ISSUES

Disputes - international: despite recent discussions, Russia and Norway dispute their maritime limits in the Barents Sea and Russia's fishing rights beyond Svalbard's territorial limits within the Svalbard Treaty zone

SWAZILAND

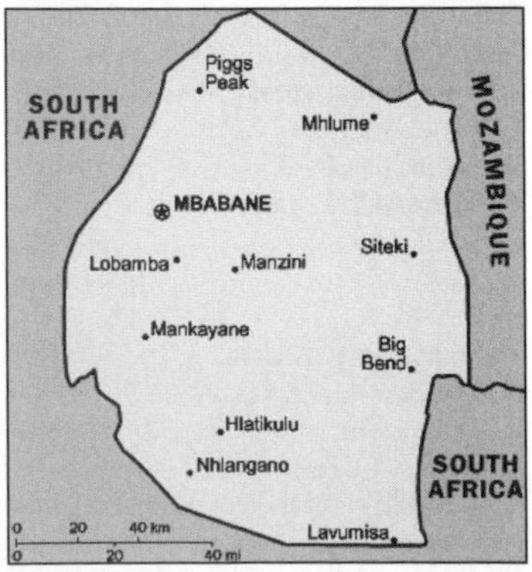

INTRODUCTION

Background: Autonomy for the Swazis of southern Africa was guaranteed by the British in the late 19th century; independence was granted in 1968. Student and labor unrest during the 1990s pressured the monarchy (one of the oldest on the continent) to grudgingly allow political reform and greater democracy. Swaziland recently surpassed Botswana as the country with the world's highest known rates of HIV/AIDS infection

GEOGRAPHY

Location: Southern Africa, between Mozambique and South Africa
Geographic coordinates: 26 30 S, 31 30 E
Map references: Africa
Area:
total: 17,363 sq km
land: 17,203 sq km
water: 160 sq km
Area - comparative: slightly smaller than New Jersey
Land boundaries:
total: total: 535 km
border countries: Mozambique 105 km, South Africa 430 km
Coastline: 0 km (landlocked)
Maritime claims: none (landlocked)

Climate: varies from tropical to near temperate
Terrain: mostly mountains and hills; some moderately sloping plains
Elevation extremes:
lowest point: Great Usutu River 21 m
highest point: Emlembe 1,862 m
Natural resources: asbestos, coal, clay, cassiterite, hydropower, forests, small gold and diamond deposits, quarry stone, and talc
Land use:
arable land: 10.35%
permanent crops: 0.7%
other: 88.95% (2001)
Irrigated land: 690 sq km (1998 est.)
Natural hazards: drought
Environment - current issues: limited supplies of potable water; wildlife populations being depleted because of excessive hunting; overgrazing; soil degradation; soil erosion
Environment - international agreements:
party to: Biodiversity, Climate Change, Desertification, Endangered Species, Ozone Layer Protection
signed, but not ratified: Law of the Sea
Geography - note: landlocked; almost completely surrounded by South Africa

PEOPLE

Population: 1,173,900
note: estimates for this country explicitly take into account the effects of excess mortality due to AIDS; this can result in lower life expectancy, higher infant mortality and death rates, lower population and growth rates, and changes in the distribution of population by age and sex than would otherwise be expected (July 2005 est.)
Age structure:
0-14 years: 40.6% (male 240,643/female 235,895)
15-64 years: 55.6% (male 327,661/female 325,400)
65 years and over: 3.8% (male 19,273/female 25,028) (2005 est.)
Median age:
total: 18.72 years
male: 18.53 years
female: 18.92 years (2005 est.)
Population growth rate: 0.25% (2005 est.)
Birth rate: 27.72 births/1,000 population (2005 est.)
Death rate: 25.26 deaths/1,000 population (2005 est.)
Net migration rate: 0 migrant(s)/1,000 population (2005 est.)
Sex ratio:
at birth: 1.03 male(s)/female
under 15 years: 1.02 male(s)/female
15-64 years: 1.01 male(s)/female
65 years and over: 0.77 male(s)/female
total population: 1 male(s)/female (2005 est.)
Infant mortality rate:
total: 69.27 deaths/1,000 live births
male: 72.51 deaths/1,000 live births
female: 65.94 deaths/1,000 live births (2005 est.)
Life expectancy at birth:
total population: 33.22 years
male: 32.49 years
female: 33.98 years (2005 est.)
Total fertility rate: 3.7 children born/woman (2005 est.)
HIV/AIDS - adult prevalence rate: 38.8% (2003 est.)
HIV/AIDS - people living with HIV/AIDS: 220,000 (2003 est.)
HIV/AIDS - deaths: 17,000 (2003 est.)
Nationality:
noun: Swazi(s)
adjective: Swazi
Ethnic groups: African 97%, European 3%
Religions: Zionist (a blend of Christianity and indigenous ancestral worship) 40%, Roman Catholic 20%, Muslim 10%, Anglican, Bahai, Methodist, Mormon, Jewish and other 30%
Languages: English (official, government business conducted in English), siSwati (official)
Literacy:
definition: age 15 and over can read and write
total population: 81.6%
male: 82.6%
female: 80.8% (2003 est.)

GOVERNMENT

Country name:
conventional long form: Kingdom of Swaziland
conventional short form: Swaziland
Government type: monarchy; independent member of Commonwealth
Capital: Mbabane; note - Lobamba is the royal and legislative capital
Administrative divisions: 4 districts; Hhohho, Lubombo, Manzini, Shiselweni
Independence: 6 September 1968 (from UK)
National holiday: Independence Day, 6 September (1968)
Constitution: the first constitution was signed into law in July 2005 and is scheduled to be implemented in early 2006
Legal system: based on South African Roman-Dutch law in statutory courts and Swazi traditional law and custom in traditional courts; has not accepted compulsory ICJ jurisdiction
Suffrage: 18 years of age
Executive branch:
chief of state: King MSWATI III (since 25 April 1986)
head of government: Prime Minister Absolom Themba DLAMINI (since 14 November 2003)
cabinet: Cabinet recommended by the prime minister and confirmed by the monarch
elections: none; the monarch is hereditary; prime minister appointed by the monarch
Legislative branch: bicameral Parliament or Libandla, an advisory body, consists of the Senate (30 seats - 10 appointed by the House of Assembly and 20 appointed by the monarch; members serve five-year terms) and the House of Assembly (65 seats - 10 appointed by the monarch and 55 elected by popular vote; members serve five-year terms)
elections: House of Assembly - last held 18 October 2003 (next to be held October 2008)
election results: House of Assembly - balloting is done on a nonparty basis; candidates for election are nominated by the local council of each constituency and for each constituency the three candidates with the most votes in the first round of voting are narrowed to a single winner by a second round
Judicial branch: High Court; Court of Appeal; judges for both courts are appointed by the monarch
Political parties and leaders: political parties are banned by the government - the following are considered political associations; Imbokodvo National Movement or INM [leader NA]; Ngwane National Liberatory Congress or NNLC [Obed DLAMINI, president]; People's United Democratic Movement or PUDEMO [Mario MASUKU, president]
Political pressure groups and leaders: NA
International organization participation: ACP, AfDB, AU, C, COMESA, FAO, G-77, IBRD, ICAO, ICFTU, ICRM, IDA, IFAD, IFC, IFRCS, ILO, IMF, Interpol, IOC, ISO (correspondent), ITU, MIGA, NAM, OPCW, PCA, SACU, SADC, UN, UNCTAD, UNESCO, UNIDO, UPU, WCO, WHO, WIPO, WMO, WToO, WTO
Diplomatic representation in the US:
chief of mission: Ambassador Mary Madzandza KANYA
chancery: 1712 New Hampshire Avenue, NW, Washington, DC 20009
telephone: [1] (202) 234-5002
FAX: [1] (202) 234-8254
Diplomatic representation from the US:
chief of mission: Ambassador Lewis LUCKE
embassy: Central Bank Building, Warner Street, Mbabane
mailing address: P. O. Box 199, Mbabane
telephone: [268] 404-6441 through 404-6445
FAX: [268] 404-5959

Flag description: three horizontal bands of blue (top), red (triple width), and blue; the red band is edged in yellow; centered in the red band is a large black and white shield covering two spears and a staff decorated with feather tassels, all placed horizontally

ECONOMY

Economy - overview: In this small, landlocked economy, subsistence agriculture occupies more than 80% of the population. The manufacturing sector has diversified since the mid-1980s. Sugar and wood pulp remain important foreign exchange earners. Mining has declined in importance in recent years with only coal and quarry stone mines remaining active. Surrounded by South Africa, except for a short border with Mozambique, Swaziland is heavily dependent on South Africa from which it receives about nine-tenths of its imports and to which it sends nearly three-quarters of its exports. Customs duties from the Southern African Customs Union and worker remittances from South Africa substantially supplement domestically earned income. The government is trying to improve the atmosphere for foreign investment. Overgrazing, soil depletion, drought, and sometimes floods persist as problems for the future. More than one-fourth of the population needed emergency food aid in 2004-05 because of drought, and more than one-third of the adult population was infected by HIV/AIDS.
GDP (purchasing power parity): $6.239 billion (2005 est.)
GDP (official exchange rate): $2.095 billion (2005 est.)
GDP - real growth rate: 1.8% (2005 est.)
GDP - per capita: purchasing power parity - $5,300 (2005 est.)
GDP - composition by sector:
agriculture: 15.1%
industry: 49.7%
services: 35.3% (2005 est.)
Labor force: 155,700 (2003)
Labor force - by occupation: NA
Unemployment rate: 40% (2004 est.)
Population below poverty line: 66% (2004)
Household income or consumption by percentage share:
lowest 10%: 1%
highest 10%: 50.2% (1995)
Inflation rate (consumer prices): 4% (2005 est.)
Investment (gross fixed): 10.4% of GDP (2005 est.)
Budget:
revenues: $805.6 million
expenditures: $957.1 million, including capital expenditures of $147 million (2005 est.)
Agriculture - products: sugarcane, cotton, corn, tobacco, rice, citrus, pineapples, sorghum, peanuts; cattle, goats, sheep
Industries: mining (coal, raw asbestos), wood pulp, sugar, soft drink concentrates, textile and apparel
Industrial production growth rate: 3.7% (FY95/96)
Electricity - production: 392 million kWh (2003)
Electricity - production by source:
fossil fuel: 58%
hydro: 42%
nuclear: 0%
other: 0% (2001)
Electricity - consumption: 1.161 billion kWh (2003)
Electricity - exports: 0 kWh (2004)
Electricity - imports: 821.4 million kWh; note - electricity supplied by South Africa (2004)
Oil - production: 0 bbl/day (2004 est.)
Oil - consumption: 3,500 bbl/day (2003 est.)
Oil - exports: NA (2004)
Oil - imports: NA (2004)
Current account balance: $-142.4 million (2005 est.)
Exports: $1.991 billion f.o.b. (2005 est.)
Exports - partners: South Africa 59.7%, EU 8.8%, US 8.8%, Mozambique 6.2% (2004)
Imports: $2.149 billion f.o.b. (2005 est.)
Imports - partners: South Africa 95.6%, EU 0.9%, Japan 0.9%, Singapore 0.3% (2004)
Reserves of foreign exchange and gold: $357.2 million (2005 est.)
Debt - external: $357 million (2003 est.)
Economic aid - recipient: $104 million (2001)
Currency (code): lilangeni (SZL)
Currency code: SZL
Exchange rates: emalangeni per US dollar - 6.2 (2005), 6.4597 (2004), 7.5648 (2003), 10.5407 (2002), 8.6092 (2001)
Fiscal year: 1 April - 31 March

COMMUNICATIONS

Telephones - main lines in use: 46,200 (2003)
Telephones - mobile cellular: 88,000 (2003)
Telephone system:
general assessment: a somewhat modern but not an advanced system
domestic: system consists of carrier-equipped, open-wire lines and low-capacity, microwave radio relay
international: country code - 268; satellite earth station - 1 Intelsat (Atlantic Ocean)
Radio broadcast stations: AM 3, FM 2 plus 4 repeaters, shortwave 3 (2004)
Radios: 170,000 (1999)
Television broadcast stations: 5 plus 7 relay stations (2004)
Televisions: 23,000 (2000)
Internet country code: .sz
Internet hosts: 1,401 (2003)
Internet Service Providers (ISPs): 5 (2002)
Internet users: 27,000 (2003)

TRANSPORTATION

Airports: 18 (2004 est.)
Airports - with paved runways:
total: 1
2,438 to 3,047 m: 1 (2005 est.)
Airports - with unpaved runways:
total: 17
914 to 1,523 m: 7
under 914 m: 10 (2005 est.)
Railways:
total: 301 km
narrow gauge: 301 km 1.067-m gauge (2004)
Roadways:
total: 3,107 km
paved: NA
unpaved: NA (2000)

MILITARY

Military branches: Umbutfo Swaziland Defense Force (USDF): Ground Force (includes Air Wing), Royal Swaziland Police Force (RSPF) (2005)
Military service age and obligation: 18 years of age for voluntary military service; both sexes are eligible for military service (2005)
Manpower available for military service: *males age 18-49:* 248,676 (2005 est.)
Manpower fit for military service: *males age 18-49:* 98,530 (2005 est.)
Military expenditures - dollar figure: $40.5 million (2004)
Military expenditures - percent of GDP: 1.4% (2004)

TRANSNATIONAL ISSUES

Disputes - international: none

SWEDEN

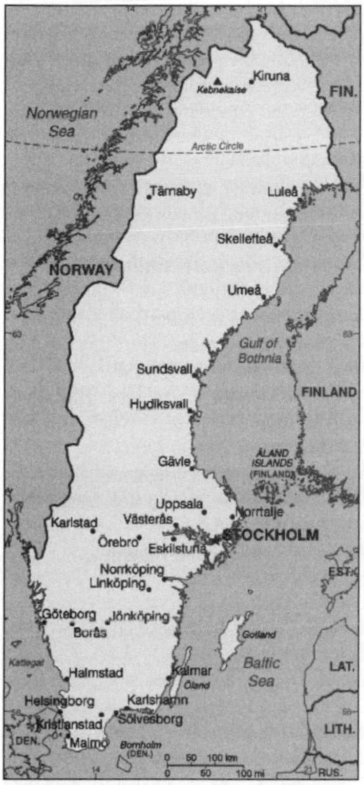

INTRODUCTION

Background: A military power during the 17th century, Sweden has not participated in any war in almost two centuries. An armed neutrality was preserved in both World Wars. Sweden's long-successful economic formula of a capitalist system interlarded with substantial welfare elements was challenged in the 1990s by high unemployment and in 2000-02 by the global economic downturn, but fiscal discipline over the past several years has allowed the country to weather economic vagaries. Indecision over the country's role in the political and economic integration of Europe delayed Sweden's entry into the EU until 1995, and waived the introduction of the euro in 1999.

GEOGRAPHY

Location: Northern Europe, bordering the Baltic Sea, Gulf of Bothnia, Kattegat, and Skagerrak, between Finland and Norway
Geographic coordinates: 62 00 N, 15 00 E
Map references: Europe
Area:
total: 449,964 sq km
land: 410,934 sq km
water: 39,030 sq km
Area - comparative: slightly larger than California
Land boundaries:
total: 2,233 km
border countries: Finland 614 km, Norway 1,619 km
Coastline: 3,218 km
Maritime claims:
territorial sea: 12 nm (adjustments made to return a portion of straits to high seas)
exclusive economic zone: agreed boundaries or midlines
continental shelf: 200-m depth or to the depth of exploitation
Climate: temperate in south with cold, cloudy winters and cool, partly cloudy summers; subarctic in north
Terrain: mostly flat or gently rolling lowlands; mountains in west
Elevation extremes:
lowest point: reclaimed bay of Lake Hammarsjon, near Kristianstad -2.41 m
highest point: Kebnekaise 2,111 m
Natural resources: iron ore, copper, lead, zinc, gold, silver, tungsten, uranium, arsenic, feldspar, timber, hydropower
Land use:
arable land: 6.54%
permanent crops: 0.01%
other: 93.45% (2001)
Irrigated land: 1,150 sq km (1998 est.)
Natural hazards: ice floes in the surrounding waters, especially in the Gulf of Bothnia, can interfere with maritime traffic
Environment - current issues: acid rain damage to soils and lakes; pollution of the North Sea and the Baltic Sea
Environment - international agreements:
party to: Air Pollution, Air Pollution-Nitrogen Oxides, Air Pollution-Persistent Organic Pollutants, Air Pollution-Sulfur 85, Air Pollution-Sulfur 94, Air Pollution-Volatile Organic Compounds, Antarctic-Environmental Protocol, Antarctic-Marine Living Resources, Antarctic Treaty, Biodiversity, Climate Change, Climate Change-Kyoto Protocol, Desertification, Endangered Species, Environmental Modification, Hazardous Wastes, Law of the Sea, Marine Dumping, Ozone Layer Protection, Ship Pollution, Tropical Timber 83, Tropical Timber 94, Wetlands, Whaling
signed, but not ratified: none of the selected agreements
Geography - note: strategic location along Danish Straits linking Baltic and North Seas

PEOPLE

Population: 9,001,774 (July 2005 est.)
Age structure:
0-14 years: 17.1% (male 791,215/female 747,621)
15-64 years: 65.5% (male 2,990,436/female 2,904,873)
65 years and over: 17.4% (male 677,161/female 890,468) (2005 est.)
Median age:
total: 40.6 years
male: 39.49 years
female: 41.75 years (2005 est.)
Population growth rate: 0.17% (2005 est.)
Birth rate: 10.36 births/1,000 population (2005 est.)
Death rate: 10.36 deaths/1,000 population (2005 est.)
Net migration rate: 1.67 migrant(s)/1,000 population (2005 est.)
Sex ratio:
at birth: 1.06 male(s)/female
under 15 years: 1.06 male(s)/female
15-64 years: 1.03 male(s)/female
65 years and over: 0.76 male(s)/female
total population: 0.98 male(s)/female (2005 est.)
Infant mortality rate:
total: 2.77 deaths/1,000 live births
male: 2.93 deaths/1,000 live births
female: 2.59 deaths/1,000 live births (2005 est.)
Life expectancy at birth:
total population: 80.4 years
male: 78.19 years
female: 82.74 years (2005 est.)
Total fertility rate: 1.66 children born/woman (2005 est.)
HIV/AIDS - adult prevalence rate: 0.1% (2001 est.)
HIV/AIDS - people living with HIV/AIDS: 3,600 (2001 est.)
HIV/AIDS - deaths: less than 100 (2003 est.)
Nationality:
noun: Swede(s)
adjective: Swedish
Ethnic groups: indigenous population: Swedes and Finnish and Sami minorities; foreign-born or first-generation immigrants: Finns, Yugoslavs, Danes, Norwegians, Greeks, Turks
Religions: Lutheran 87%, Roman Catholic, Orthodox, Baptist, Muslim, Jewish, Buddhist
Languages: Swedish, small Sami- and Finnish-speaking minorities
Literacy:
definition: age 15 and over can read and write
total population: 99% (1979 est.)
male: NA%
female: NA%

GOVERNMENT

Country name:
conventional long form: Kingdom of Sweden
conventional short form: Sweden

local long form: Konungariket Sverige
local short form: Sverige
Government type: constitutional monarchy
Capital: Stockholm
Administrative divisions: 21 counties (lan, singular and plural); Blekinge, Dalarnas, Gavleborgs, Gotlands, Hallands, Jamtlands, Jonkopings, Kalmar, Kronobergs, Norrbottens, Orebro, Ostergotlands, Skane, Sodermanlands, Stockholms, Uppsala, Varmlands, Vasterbottens, Vasternorrlands, Vastmanlands, Vastra Gotalands
Independence: 6 June 1523 (Gustav VASA elected king)
National holiday: Flag Day, 6 June
Constitution: 1 January 1975
Legal system: civil law system influenced by customary law; accepts compulsory ICJ jurisdiction, with reservations
Suffrage: 18 years of age, universal
Executive branch:
chief of state: King CARL XVI GUSTAF (since 19 September 1973); Heir Apparent Princess VICTORIA Ingrid Alice Desiree, daughter of the monarch (born 14 July 1977)
head of government: Prime Minister Goran PERSSON (since 21 March 1996)
cabinet: Cabinet appointed by the prime minister
elections: the monarchy is hereditary; following legislative elections, the prime minister is elected by the parliament; election last held 15 September 2002 (next to be held NA September 2006)
election results: Goran PERSSON reelected prime minister with 131 out of 349 votes
Legislative branch: unicameral Parliament or Riksdag (349 seats; members are elected by popular vote on a proportional representation basis to serve four-year terms)
elections: last held 15 September 2002 (next to be held September 2006)
election results: percent of vote by party - Social Democrats 39.8%, Moderates 15.2%, Liberal Party 13.3%, Christian Democrats 9.1%, Left Party 8.3%, Center Party 6.1%, Greens 4.6%; seats by party - Social Democrats 144, Moderates 55, Liberal Party 48, Christian Democrats 33, Left Party 30, Center Party 22, Greens 17
Judicial branch: Supreme Court or Hogsta Domstolen (judges are appointed by the prime minister and the cabinet)
Political parties and leaders: Center Party [Maud OLOFSSON]; Christian Democratic Party [Goran HAGGLUND]; Green Party [no formal leader but party spokespersons are Maria WETTERSTRAND and Peter ERIKSSON]; Left Party or V (formerly Communist) [Lars OHLY]; Liberal People's Party [Lars LEIJONBORG]; Moderate Party (conservative) [Fredrik REINFELDT]; Social Democratic Party [Goran PERSSON]
Political pressure groups and leaders: NA
International organization participation: AfDB, AsDB, Australia Group, BIS, CBSS, CE, CERN, EAPC, EBRD, EIB, ESA, EU, FAO, G-6, G-9, G-10, IADB, IAEA, IBRD, ICAO, ICC, ICCt, ICFTU, ICRM, IDA, IEA, IFAD, IFC, IFRCS, IHO, ILO, IMF, IMO, Interpol, IOC, IOM, ISO, ITU, MIGA, MONUC, NAM (guest), NC, NEA, NIB, NSG, OAS (observer), OECD, OPCW, OSCE, Paris Club, PCA, PFP, UN, UNAMSIL, UNCTAD, UNESCO, UNHCR, UNIDO, UNMEE, UNMIL, UNMIS, UNMOGIP, UNOMIG, UNTSO, UPU, WCO, WEU (observer), WFTU, WHO, WIPO, WMO, WTO, ZC
Diplomatic representation in the US:
chief of mission: Ambassador Gunnar LUND
chancery: 1501 M Street NW, Washington, DC 20005-1702
telephone: [1] (202) 467-2600
FAX: [1] (202) 467-2699
consulate(s) general: Los Angeles and New York
Diplomatic representation from the US:
chief of mission: Ambassador M. Teel BIVINS
embassy: Dag Hammarskjolds VAG 31, SE-11589 Stockholm
mailing address: American Embassy Stockholm, Department of State, 5750 Stockholm Place, Washington, DC 20521-5750 (pouch)
telephone: [46] (08) 783 53 00
FAX: [46] (08) 661 19 64
Flag description: blue with a golden yellow cross extending to the edges of the flag; the vertical part of the cross is shifted to the hoist side in the style of the Dannebrog (Danish flag)

ECONOMY

Economy - overview: Aided by peace and neutrality for the whole 20th century, Sweden has achieved an enviable standard of living under a mixed system of high-tech capitalism and extensive welfare benefits. It has a modern distribution system, excellent internal and external communications, and a skilled labor force. Timber, hydropower, and iron ore constitute the resource base of an economy heavily oriented toward foreign trade. Privately owned firms account for about 90% of industrial output, of which the engineering sector accounts for 50% of output and exports. Agriculture accounts for only 2% of GDP and of jobs. The government's commitment to fiscal discipline resulted in a substantial budgetary surplus in 2001, which was cut by more than half in 2002, due to the global economic slowdown, declining revenue, and increased spending. The Swedish central bank (the Riksbank) focuses on price stability with its inflation target of 2%. Growth remained sluggish in 2003, but picked up in 2004 and 2005. Presumably because of generous sicktime benefits, Swedish workers report in sick more often than other Europeans. On 14 September 2003, Swedish voters turned down entry into the euro system, concerned about the impact on democracy and sovereignty.
GDP (purchasing power parity): $266.5 billion (2005 est.)
GDP (official exchange rate): $362.1 billion (2005 est.)
GDP - real growth rate: 2.4% (2005 est.)
GDP - per capita: purchasing power parity - $29,600 (2005 est.)
GDP - composition by sector:
agriculture: 1.8%
industry: 28.6%
services: 69.7% (2005 est.)
Labor force: 4.49 million (2005 est.)
Labor force - by occupation: agriculture 2%, industry 24%, services 74% (2000 est.)
Unemployment rate: 6% (2005 est.)
Population below poverty line: NA
Household income or consumption by percentage share:
lowest 10%: 3.7%
highest 10%: 20.1% (1992)
Distribution of family income - Gini index: 25 (2000)
Inflation rate (consumer prices): 0.5% (2005 est.)
Investment (gross fixed): 17.3% of GDP (2005 est.)
Budget:
revenues: $210.5 billion
expenditures: $205.9 billion, including capital expenditures of NA (2005 est.)
Public debt: 50.3% of GDP (2005 est.)
Agriculture - products: barley, wheat, sugar beets; meat, milk
Industries: iron and steel, precision equipment (bearings, radio and telephone parts, armaments), wood pulp and paper products, processed foods, motor vehicles
Industrial production growth rate: 3.3% (2005 est.)
Electricity - production: 127.9 billion kWh (2003)
Electricity - production by source:
fossil fuel: 4%
hydro: 50.8%
nuclear: 43%
other: 2.3% (2001)
Electricity - consumption: 131.8 billion kWh (2003)

Electricity - exports: 11.5 billion kWh (2003)
Electricity - imports: 24.3 billion kWh (2003)
Oil - production: 2,441 bbl/day (2003 est.)
Oil - consumption: 346,100 bbl/day (2003 est.)
Oil - exports: 203,700 bbl/day (2001)
Oil - imports: 553,100 bbl/day (2001)
Natural gas - production: 0 cu m (2001 est.)
Natural gas - consumption: 949 million cu m (2001 est.)
Natural gas - exports: 0 cu m (2001 est.)
Natural gas - imports: 968 million cu m (2001 est.)
Current account balance: $25.68 billion (2005 est.)
Exports: $126.6 billion f.o.b. (2005 est.)
Exports - partners: US 10.7%, Germany 10.2%, Norway 8.6%, UK 7.8%, Denmark 6.7%, Finland 5.7%, France 4.8%, Netherlands 4.8%, Belgium 4.5% (2004)
Imports: $104.4 billion f.o.b. (2005 est.)
Imports - partners: Germany 18.7%, Denmark 9.2%, Norway 7.6%, UK 7.5%, Netherlands 6.8%, Finland 6.4%, France 5.5%, Belgium 4% (2004)
Reserves of foreign exchange and gold: $22.45 billion (2004 est.)
Debt - external: $516.1 billion (30 June 2005)
Economic aid - donor: ODA, $1.7 billion (1997)
Currency (code): Swedish krona (SEK)
Currency code: SEK
Exchange rates: Swedish kronor per US dollar - 7.32 (2005), 7.3489 (2004), 8.0863 (2003), 9.7371 (2002), 10.3291 (2001)
Fiscal year: calendar year

COMMUNICATIONS

Telephones - main lines in use: 6,579,200 (2002)
Telephones - mobile cellular: 7.949 million (2002)
Telephone system:
general assessment: excellent domestic and international facilities; automatic system
domestic: coaxial and multiconductor cables carry most of the voice traffic; parallel microwave radio relay systems carry some additional telephone channels
international: country code - 46; 5 submarine coaxial cables; satellite earth stations - 1 Intelsat (Atlantic Ocean), 1 Eutelsat, and 1 Inmarsat (Atlantic and Indian Ocean regions); note - Sweden shares the Inmarsat earth station with the other Nordic countries (Denmark, Finland, Iceland, and Norway)
Radio broadcast stations: AM 1, FM 265, shortwave 1 (1998)
Radios: 8.25 million (1997)
Television broadcast stations: 169 (plus 1,299 repeaters) (1995)
Televisions: 4.6 million (1997)
Internet country code: .se
Internet hosts: 945,221 (2004)
Internet Service Providers (ISPs): 29 (2000)
Internet users: 5.125 million (2002)

TRANSPORTATION

Airports: 254 (2004 est.)
Airports - with paved runways:
total: 155
over 3,047 m: 3
2,438 to 3,047 m: 13
1,524 to 2,437 m: 80
914 to 1,523 m: 23
under 914 m: 36 (2005 est.)
Airports - with unpaved runways:
total: 100
914 to 1,523 m: 9
under 914 m: 91 (2005 est.)
Heliports: 2 (2005 est.)
Pipelines: gas 798 km (2004)
Railways:
total: 11,481 km
standard gauge: 11,481 km 1.435-m gauge (9,400 km electrified) (2004)
Roadways:
total: 213,237 km
paved: 167,604 km (including 1,542 km of expressways)
unpaved: 45,633 km (2002)
Merchant marine:
total: 205 ships (1,000 GRT or over) 2,702,763 GRT/1,884,570 DWT
by type: bulk carrier 6, cargo 33, chemical tanker 51, passenger 4, passenger/cargo 37, petroleum tanker 14, roll on/roll off 37, specialized tanker 1, vehicle carrier 22
foreign-owned: 42 (Belgium 2, Denmark 4, Finland 11, Germany 6, Italy 7, Japan 2, Netherlands 1, Norway 9)
registered in other countries: 155 (2005)
Ports and terminals: Goteborg, Helsingborg, Karlshamn, Lulea, Malmo, Oxelosund, Stenungsund, Stockholm, Trelleborg

MILITARY

Military branches: Army, Royal Swedish Navy (RSwN), Air Force (Flygvapnet)
Military service age and obligation: 19 years of age for compulsory military service; conscript service obligation is 7 to 17 months depending on conscript role; after completing initial service, soldiers have a reserve commitment until the age of 47 (2004)
Manpower available for military service: *males age 19-49:* 1,838,427 (2005 est.)
Manpower fit for military service: *males age 19-49:* 1,493,668 (2005 est.)
Manpower reaching military service age annually: *males:* 58,724 (2005 est.)
Military expenditures - dollar figure: $5.729 billion (2004)
Military expenditures - percent of GDP: 1.7% (2004)

TRANSNATIONAL ISSUES

Disputes - international: none

SWITZERLAND

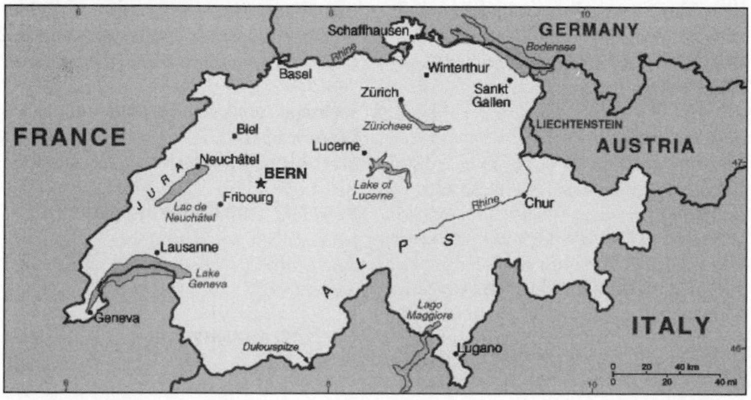

INTRODUCTION

Background: The Swiss Confederation was founded in 1291 as a defensive alliance among three cantons. In succeeding years, other localities joined the original three. The Swiss Confederation secured its independence from the Holy Roman Empire in 1499. Switzerland's sovereignty and neutrality have long been honored by the major European powers, and the country was not involved in either of the two World Wars. The political and economic integration of Europe over the past half century, as well as

Switzerland's role in many UN and international organizations, has strengthened Switzerland's ties with its neighbors. However, the country did not officially become a UN member until 2002. Switzerland remains active in many UN and international organizations, but retains a strong commitment to neutrality.

GEOGRAPHY

Location: Central Europe, east of France, north of Italy
Geographic coordinates: 47 00 N, 8 00 E
Map references: Europe
Area:
total: 41,290 sq km
land: 39,770 sq km
water: 1,520 sq km
Area - comparative: slightly less than twice the size of New Jersey
Land boundaries:
total: 1,852 km
border countries: Austria 164 km, France 573 km, Italy 740 km, Liechtenstein 41 km, Germany 334 km
Coastline: 0 km (landlocked)
Maritime claims: none (landlocked)
Climate: temperate, but varies with altitude; cold, cloudy, rainy/snowy winters; cool to warm, cloudy, humid summers with occasional showers
Terrain: mostly mountains (Alps in south, Jura in northwest) with a central plateau of rolling hills, plains, and large lakes
Elevation extremes:
lowest point: Lake Maggiore 195 m
highest point: Dufourspitze 4,634 m
Natural resources: hydropower potential, timber, salt
Land use:
arable land: 10.42%
permanent crops: 0.61%
other: 88.97% (2001)
Irrigated land: 250 sq km (1998 est.)
Natural hazards: avalanches, landslides, flash floods
Environment - current issues: air pollution from vehicle emissions and open-air burning; acid rain; water pollution from increased use of agricultural fertilizers; loss of biodiversity
Environment - international agreements:
party to: Air Pollution, Air Pollution-Nitrogen Oxides, Air Pollution-Persistent Organic Pollutants, Air Pollution-Sulfur 85, Air Pollution-Sulfur 94, Air Pollution-Volatile Organic Compounds, Antarctic Treaty, Biodiversity, Climate Change, Climate Change-Kyoto Protocol, Desertification, Endangered Species, Environmental Modification, Hazardous Wastes, Marine Dumping, Marine Life Conservation, Ozone Layer Protection, Ship Pollution, Tropical Timber 83, Tropical Timber 94, Wetlands, Whaling
signed, but not ratified: Law of the Sea
Geography - note: landlocked; crossroads of northern and southern Europe; along with southeastern France, northern Italy, and southwestern Austria, has the highest elevations in the Alps

PEOPLE

Population: 7,489,370 (July 2005 est.)
Age structure:
0-14 years: 16.6% (male 643,497/female 597,565)
15-64 years: 68% (male 2,570,544/female 2,522,365)
65 years and over: 15.4% (male 472,769/female 682,630) (2005 est.)
Median age:
total: 39.77 years
male: 38.75 years
female: 40.81 years (2005 est.)
Population growth rate: 0.49% (2005 est.)
Birth rate: 9.77 births/1,000 population (2005 est.)
Death rate: 8.48 deaths/1,000 population (2005 est.)
Net migration rate: 3.58 migrant(s)/1,000 population (2005 est.)
Sex ratio:
at birth: 1.05 male(s)/female
under 15 years: 1.08 male(s)/female
15-64 years: 1.02 male(s)/female
65 years and over: 0.69 male(s)/female
total population: 0.97 male(s)/female (2005 est.)
Infant mortality rate:
total: 4.39 deaths/1,000 live births
male: 4.9 deaths/1,000 live births
female: 3.86 deaths/1,000 live births (2005 est.)
Life expectancy at birth:
total population: 80.39 years
male: 77.58 years
female: 83.36 years (2005 est.)
Total fertility rate: 1.42 children born/woman (2005 est.)
HIV/AIDS - adult prevalence rate: 0.4% (2001 est.)
HIV/AIDS - people living with HIV/AIDS: 13,000 (2001 est.)
HIV/AIDS - deaths: less than 100 (2003 est.)
Nationality:
noun: Swiss (singular and plural)
adjective: Swiss
Ethnic groups: German 65%, French 18%, Italian 10%, Romansch 1%, other 6%
Religions: Roman Catholic 41.8%, Protestant 35.3%, Orthodox 1.8%, other Christian 0.4%, Muslim 4.3%, other 1%, unspecified 4.3%, none 11.1% (2000 census)
Languages: German (official) 63.7%, French (official) 20.4%, Italian (official) 6.5%, Serbo-Croatian 1.5%, Albanian 1.3%, Portuguese 1.2%, Spanish 1.1%, English 1%, Romansch 0.5%, other 2.8% (2000 census)
note: German, French, Italian, and Romansch are all national languages, but only the first three are official languages
Literacy:
definition: age 15 and over can read and write
total population: 99% (1980 est.)
male: NA%
female: NA%

GOVERNMENT

Country name:
conventional long form: Swiss Confederation
conventional short form: Switzerland
local long form: Schweizerische Eidgenossenschaft (German), Confederation Suisse (French), Confederazione Svizzera (Italian)
local short form: Schweiz (German), Suisse (French), Svizzera (Italian)
Government type: formally a confederation, but similar in structure to a federal republic
Capital: Bern
Administrative divisions: 26 cantons (cantons, singular - canton in French; cantoni, singular - cantone in Italian; kantone, singular - kanton in German); Aargau, Appenzell Ausser-Rhoden, Appenzell Inner-Rhoden, Basel-Landschaft, Basel-Stadt, Bern, Fribourg, Geneve, Glarus, Graubunden, Jura, Luzern, Neuchatel, Nidwalden, Obwalden, Sankt Gallen, Schaffhausen, Schwyz, Solothurn, Thurgau, Ticino, Uri, Valais, Vaud, Zug, Zurich
Independence: 1 August 1291 (founding of the Swiss Confederation)
National holiday: Founding of the Swiss Confederation, 1 August (1291)
Constitution: revision of Constitution of 1874 approved by the Federal Parliament 18 December 1998, adopted by referendum 18 April 1999, officially entered into force 1 January 2000
Legal system: civil law system influenced by customary law; judicial review of legislative acts, except with respect to federal decrees of general obligatory character; accepts compulsory ICJ jurisdiction, with reservations
Suffrage: 18 years of age, universal
Executive branch:
chief of state: President Moritz LEUENBERGER (since 8 January 2006); Vice President Micheline CALMY-REY (since 8 January 2006); note - the president is both the chief of state and head of government
head of government: President Moritz LEUENBERGER (since 8 January 2006); Vice President Micheline

CALMY-REY (since 8 January 2006); note - the president is both the chief of state and head of government
cabinet: Federal Council or Bundesrat (in German), Conseil Federal (in French), Consiglio Federale (in Italian) elected by the Federal Assembly usually from among its own members for a four-year term
elections: president and vice president elected by the Federal Assembly from among the members of the Federal Council for one-year terms that run concurrently; election last held 8 December 2004 (next to be held December 2005))
election results: Moritz LUENBERGER elected president; percent of Federal Assembly vote - NA%; Micheline CALMY-REY elected vice president; percent of legislative vote - NA%
Legislative branch: bicameral Federal Assembly or Bundesversammlung (in German), Assemblee Federale (in French), Assemblea Federale (in Italian) consists of the Council of States or Standerat (in German), Conseil des Etats (in French), Consiglio degli Stati (in Italian) (46 seats - members serve four-year terms) and the National Council or Nationalrat (in German), Conseil National (in French), Consiglio Nazionale (in Italian) (200 seats - members are elected by popular vote on the basis of proportional representation to serve four-year terms)
elections: Council of States - last held in most cantons 19 October 2003 (each canton determines when the next election will be held); National Council - last held 19 October 2003 (next to be held October 2007)
election results: Council of States - percent of vote by party - NA%; seats by party - CVP 15, FDP 14, SVP 8, SPS 6, other 3; National Council - percent of vote by party - SVP 26.6%, SPS 23.3%, FDP 17.3%, CVP 14.4%, Greens 7.4%, other small parties all under 5%; seats by party - SVP 55, SPS 54, FDP 36, CVP 28, Green Party 13, other small parties 14
Judicial branch: Federal Supreme Court (judges elected for six-year terms by the Federal Assembly)
Political parties and leaders: Green Party (Grune Partei der Schweiz or Grune, Parti Ecologiste Suisse or Les Verts, Partito Ecologista Svizzero or I Verdi, Partida Ecologica Svizra or La Verda) [Ruth GENNER]; Christian Democratic People's Party (Christichdemokratische Volkspartei der Schweiz or CVP, Parti Democrate-Chretien Suisse or PDC, Partito Democratico-Cristiano Popolare Svizzero or PDC, Partida Cristiandemocratica dalla Svizra or PCD) [Doris LEUTHARD, president]; Radical Free Democratic Party (Freisinnig-Demokratische Partei der Schweiz or FDP, Parti Radical-Democratique Suisse or PRD, Partitio Liberal-Radicale Svizzero or PLR) [Marianne KLEINER-SCHLAEPFER, president]; Social Democratic Party (Sozialdemokratische Partei der Schweiz or SPS, Parti Socialist Suisse or PSS, Partito Socialista Svizzero or PSS, Partida Socialdemocratica de la Svizra or PSS) [Hans-Juerg FEHR, president]; Swiss People's Party (Schweizerische Volkspartei or SVP, Union Democratique du Centre or UDC, Unione Democratica de Centro or UDC, Uniun Democratica dal Center or UDC) [Ueli MAURER, president]; and other minor parties
Political pressure groups and leaders: NA
International organization participation: ACCT, AfDB, AsDB, Australia Group, BIS, CE, CERN, EAPC, EBRD, EFTA, ESA, FAO, G-10, IADB, IAEA, IBRD, ICAO, ICC, ICCt, ICFTU, ICRM, IDA, IEA, IFAD, IFC, IFRCS, ILO, IMF, IMO, Interpol, IOC, IOM, ISO, ITU, LAIA (observer), MIGA, MONUC, NAM (guest), NEA, NSG, OAS (observer), OECD, OPCW, OSCE, Paris Club, PCA, PFP, UN, UNCTAD, UNESCO, UNHCR, UNIDO, UNITAR, UNMEE, UNMIS, UNOMIG, UNTSO, UPU, WCL, WCO, WHO, WIPO, WMO, WToO, WTO, ZC
Diplomatic representation in the US:
chief of mission: Ambassador Christian BLICKENSTORFER
chancery: 2900 Cathedral Avenue NW, Washington, DC 20008
telephone: [1] (202) 745-7900
FAX: [1] (202) 387-2564
consulate(s) general: Atlanta, Chicago, Houston, Los Angeles, New York, and San Francisco
consulate(s): Boston
Diplomatic representation from the US:
chief of mission: Ambassador Pamela P. WILLEFORD
embassy: Jubilaumsstrasse 93, CH-3005 Bern
mailing address: use embassy street address
telephone: [41] (031) 357 70 11
FAX: [41] (031) 357 73 44
Flag description: red square with a bold, equilateral white cross in the center that does not extend to the edges of the flag

ECONOMY

Economy - overview: Switzerland is a peaceful, prosperous, and stable modern market economy with low unemployment, a highly skilled labor force, and a per capita GDP larger than that of the big Western European economies. The Swiss in recent years have brought their economic practices largely into conformity with the EU's to enhance their international competitiveness. Switzerland remains a safe haven for investors, because it has maintained a degree of bank secrecy and has kept up the franc's long-term external value. Reflecting the anemic economic conditions of Europe, GDP growth dropped in 2001 to about 0.8%, to 0.2% in 2002, and to -0.3% in 2003, with a small rise to 1.8% in 2004, and 1.2% in 2005. Even so, unemployment has remained at less than half the EU average.
GDP (purchasing power parity): $262.1 billion (2005 est.)
GDP (official exchange rate): $374 billion (2005 est.)
GDP - real growth rate: 1.2% (2005 est.)
GDP - per capita: purchasing power parity - $35,000 (2005 est.)
GDP - composition by sector:
agriculture: 1.5%
industry: 34%
services: 64.5% (2003 est.)
Labor force: 3.8 million (2005 est.)
Labor force - by occupation: agriculture 4.6%, industry 26.3%, services 69.1% (1998)
Unemployment rate: 3.8% (2005 est.)
Population below poverty line: NA
Household income or consumption by percentage share:
lowest 10%: 2.6%
highest 10%: 25.2% (1992)
Distribution of family income - Gini index: 33.1 (1992)
Inflation rate (consumer prices): 1.2% (2005 est.)
Investment (gross fixed): 21.2% of GDP (2005 est.)
Budget:
revenues: $138.1 billion
expenditures: $143.6 billion, including capital expenditures of NA (2005 est.)
Public debt: 53.3% of GDP (2005 est.)
Agriculture - products: grains, fruits, vegetables; meat, eggs
Industries: machinery, chemicals, watches, textiles, precision instruments
Industrial production growth rate: 3.9% (2005 est.)
Electricity - production: 63.4 billion kWh (2003)
Electricity - production by source:
fossil fuel: 1.3%
hydro: 59.5%
nuclear: 37.1%
other: 2% (2001)
Electricity - consumption: 55.86 billion kWh (2003)
Electricity - exports: 33.2 billion kWh (2003)

Electricity - imports: 30.1 billion kWh (2003)
Oil - production: 1,950 bbl/day (2003 est.)
Oil - consumption: 258,900 bbl/day (2003 est.)
Oil - exports: 10,420 bbl/day (2001)
Oil - imports: 289,500 bbl/day (2001)
Natural gas - production: 0 cu m (2001 est.)
Natural gas - consumption: 3.093 billion cu m (2001 est.)
Natural gas - exports: 0 cu m (2001 est.)
Natural gas - imports: 3.093 billion cu m (2001 est.)
Current account balance: $49.66 billion (2005 est.)
Exports: $148.6 billion f.o.b. (2005 est.)
Exports - partners: Germany 20.2%, US 10.5%, France 8.7%, Italy 8.3%, UK 5.1%, Spain 4% (2004)
Imports: $135 billion f.o.b. (2005 est.)
Imports - partners: Germany 32.8%, Italy 11.3%, France 9.9%, US 5.2%, Netherlands 5%, Austria 4.3% (2004)
Reserves of foreign exchange and gold: $74.62 billion (2004 est.)
Debt - external: $856 billion (30 June 2005)
Economic aid - donor: ODA, $1.1 billion (1995)
Currency (code): Swiss franc (CHF)
Currency code: CHF
Exchange rates: Swiss francs per US dollar - 1.23 (2005), 1.2435 (2004), 1.3467 (2003), 1.5586 (2002), 1.6876 (2001)
Fiscal year: calendar year

COMMUNICATIONS

Telephones - main lines in use: 5.419 million (2002)
Telephones - mobile cellular: 6.172 million (2003)
Telephone system:
general assessment: excellent domestic and international services
domestic: extensive cable and microwave radio relay networks
international: country code - 41; satellite earth stations - 2 Intelsat (Atlantic Ocean and Indian Ocean)
Radio broadcast stations: AM 4, FM 113 (plus many low power stations), shortwave 2 (1998)
Radios: 7.1 million (1997)
Television broadcast stations: 115 (plus 1,919 repeaters) (1995)
Televisions: 3.31 million (1997)
Internet country code: .ch
Internet hosts: 667,275 (2004)
Internet Service Providers (ISPs): 44 (Switzerland and Liechtenstein) (2000)
Internet users: 2.556 million (2002)

TRANSPORTATION

Airports: 65 (2004 est.)
Airports - with paved runways:
total: 42
over 3,047 m: 3
2,438 to 3,047 m: 4
1,524 to 2,437 m: 11
914 to 1,523 m: 8
under 914 m: 16 (2005 est.)
Airports - with unpaved runways:
total: 23
under 914 m: 23 (2005 est.)
Heliports: 2 (2005 est.)
Pipelines: gas 1,831 km; oil 94 km; refined products 7 km (2004)
Railways:
total: 4,527 km
standard gauge: 3,232 km 1.435-m gauge (3,211 km electrified)
narrow gauge: 1,285 km 1.000-m gauge (1,273 km electrified); 10 km 0.800-m gauge (10 km electrified) (2004)
Roadways:
total: 71,212 km
paved: 71,212 km (including 1,706 of expressways)
unpaved: 0 km (2002)
Waterways: 65 km
note: Rhine River between Basel-Rheinfelden and Schaffhausen-Bodensee, some canals, and 12 navigable lakes (2003)
Merchant marine:
total: 23 ships (1,000 GRT or over) 604,843 GRT/1,050,914 DWT
by type: bulk carrier 12, cargo 6, chemical tanker 2, container 3
foreign-owned: 6 (United Kingdom 6)
registered in other countries: 291 (2005)
Ports and terminals: Basel

MILITARY

Military branches: Land Forces, Swiss Air Force (Schweizer Luftwaffe)
Military service age and obligation: the Swiss Confederation states that "every Swiss male is obligated to do military service"; every Swiss male has to serve for at least 260 days in the armed forces; 19 years of age for compulsory military service; 17 years of age for voluntary military service; conscripts receive 15 weeks of compulsory training, followed by 10 intermittent recalls for training over the next 22 years; women are accepted on a voluntary basis, but are not drafted (2005)
Manpower available for military service: *males age 19-49:* 1,707,694 (2005 est.)
Manpower fit for military service: *males age 19-49:* 1,375,889 (2005 est.)
Manpower reaching military service age annually: *males:* 46,319 (2005 est.)
Military expenditures - dollar figure: $2.548 billion (FY01)
Military expenditures - percent of GDP: 1% (FY01))

TRANSNATIONAL ISSUES

Disputes - international: none
Illicit drugs: a major international financial center vulnerable to the layering and integration stages of money laundering; despite significant legislation and reporting requirements, secrecy rules persist and nonresidents are permitted to conduct business through offshore entities and various intermediaries; transit country for and consumer of South American cocaine and Southwest Asian heroin

SYRIA

INTRODUCTION

Background: Following the breakup of the Ottoman Empire during World War I, France administered Syria until its independence in 1946. The country lacked political stability, however, and experienced a series of military coups during its first decades. Syria united with Egypt in February 1958 to form the United Arab Republic, but in September 1961 the two entities separated and the Syrian Arab Republic was reestablished. In November 1970, Hafiz al-ASAD, a member of the Socialist Ba'th Party and the minority Alawite sect, seized power in a bloodless coup and brought political stability to the country. In the 1967 Arab-Israeli War, Syria lost the Golan Heights to Israel, and over the past decade Syria and Israel have held occasional peace talks over its return. Following the death of President al-ASAD in July 2000, his son, Bashar al-ASAD, was approved as president by popular referendum. Syrian troops - stationed in Lebanon since 1976 in an ostensible peacekeeping role - were withdrawn in April of 2005.

GEOGRAPHY

Location: Middle East, bordering the Mediterranean Sea, between Lebanon and Turkey
Geographic coordinates: 35 00 N, 38 00 E
Map references: Middle East
Area:
total: 185,180 sq km
land: 184,050 sq km
water: 1,130 sq km
note: includes 1,295 sq km of Israeli-occupied territory
Area - comparative: slightly larger than

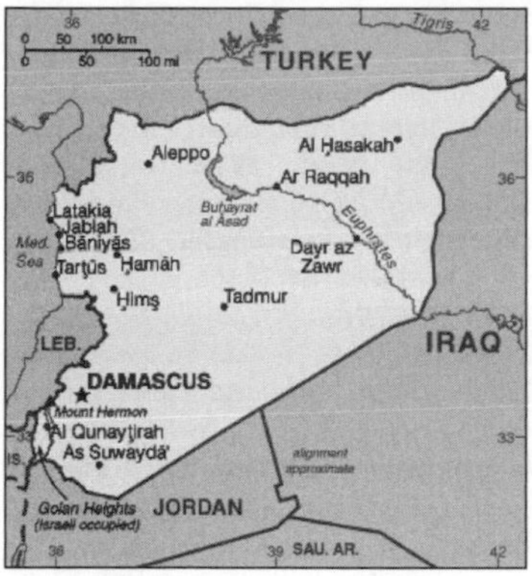

North Dakota

Land boundaries:
total: 2,253 km
border countries: Iraq 605 km, Israel 76 km, Jordan 375 km, Lebanon 375 km, Turkey 822 km

Coastline: 193 km

Maritime claims:
territorial sea: 12 nm
contiguous zone: 41 nm

Climate: mostly desert; hot, dry, sunny summers (June to August) and mild, rainy winters (December to February) along coast; cold weather with snow or sleet periodically in Damascus

Terrain: primarily semiarid and desert plateau; narrow coastal plain; mountains in west

Elevation extremes:
lowest point: unnamed location near Lake Tiberias -200 m
highest point: Mount Hermon 2,814 m

Natural resources: petroleum, phosphates, chrome and manganese ores, asphalt, iron ore, rock salt, marble, gypsum, hydropower

Land use:
arable land: 25.22%
permanent crops: 4.43%
other: 70.35% (2001)

Irrigated land: 12,130 sq km (1998 est.)

Natural hazards: dust storms, sandstorms

Environment - current issues: deforestation; overgrazing; soil erosion; desertification; water pollution from raw sewage and petroleum refining wastes; inadequate potable water

Environment - international agreements:
party to: Biodiversity, Climate Change, Desertification, Endangered Species, Hazardous Wastes, Ozone Layer Protection, Ship Pollution, Wetlands
signed, but not ratified: Environmental Modification

Geography - note: there are 42 Israeli settlements and civilian land use sites in the Israeli-occupied Golan Heights (February 2002 est.)

PEOPLE

Population: 18,448,752
note: in addition, about 40,000 people live in the Israeli-occupied Golan Heights - 20,000 Arabs (18,000 Druze and 2,000 Alawites) and about 20,000 Israeli settlers (July 2005 est.)

Age structure:
0-14 years: 37.4% (male 3,556,795/female 3,350,267)
15-64 years: 59.3% (male 5,601,971/female 5,333,799)
65 years and over: 3.3% (male 288,868/female 317,052) (2005 est.)

Median age:
total: 20.37 years
male: 20.24 years
female: 20.51 years (2005 est.)

Population growth rate: 2.34% (2005 est.)

Birth rate: 28.29 births/1,000 population (2005 est.)

Death rate: 4.88 deaths/1,000 population (2005 est.)

Net migration rate: 0 migrant(s)/1,000 population (2005 est.)

Sex ratio:
at birth: 1.06 male(s)/female
under 15 years: 1.06 male(s)/female
15-64 years: 1.05 male(s)/female
65 years and over: 0.91 male(s)/female
total population: 1.05 male(s)/female (2005 est.)

Infant mortality rate:
total: 29.53 deaths/1,000 live births
male: 29.76 deaths/1,000 live births
female: 29.28 deaths/1,000 live births (2005 est.)

Life expectancy at birth:
total population: 70.03 years
male: 68.75 years
female: 71.38 years (2005 est.)

Total fertility rate: 3.5 children born/woman (2005 est.)

HIV/AIDS - adult prevalence rate: less than 0.1% (2001 est.)

HIV/AIDS - people living with HIV/AIDS: less than 500 (2003 est.)

HIV/AIDS - deaths: less than 200 (2003 est.)

Nationality:
noun: Syrian(s)
adjective: Syrian

Ethnic groups: Arab 90.3%, Kurds, Armenians, and other 9.7%

Religions: Sunni Muslim 74%, Alawite, Druze, and other Muslim sects 16%, Christian (various sects) 10%, Jewish (tiny communities in Damascus, Al Qamishli, and Aleppo)

Languages: Arabic (official); Kurdish, Armenian, Aramaic, Circassian widely understood; French, English somewhat understood

Literacy:
definition: age 15 and over can read and write
total population: 76.9%
male: 89.7%
female: 64% (2003 est.)

GOVERNMENT

Country name:
conventional long form: Syrian Arab Republic
conventional short form: Syria
local long form: Al Jumhuriyah al Arabiyah as Suriyah
local short form: Suriyah
former: United Arab Republic (with Egypt)

Government type: republic under an authoritarian, military-dominated regime since March 1963

Capital: Damascus

Administrative divisions: 14 provinces (muhafazat, singular - muhafazah); Al Hasakah, Al Ladhiqiyah, Al Qunaytirah, Ar Raqqah, As Suwayda', Dar'a, Dayr az Zawr, Dimashq, Halab, Hamah, Hims, Idlib, Rif Dimashq, Tartus

Independence: 17 April 1946 (from League of Nations mandate under French administration)

National holiday: Independence Day, 17 April (1946)

Constitution: 13 March 1973

Legal system: based on a combination of French and Ottoman civil law; religious law is used in the family court system; has not accepted compulsory ICJ jurisdiction

Suffrage: 18 years of age, universal

Executive branch:
chief of state: President Bashar al-ASAD (since 17 July 2000); Vice Presidency vacant since June 2005
head of government: Prime Minister Muhammad Naji al-UTRI (since 10 September 2003); Deputy Prime Minister Abdallah al-DARDARI (since 14 June 2005)
cabinet: Council of Ministers appointed by the president
elections: president approved by popular referendum for a seven-year term; referendum last held 10 July 2000 - after the death of President Hafiz al-ASAD, father of Bashar al-ASAD - (next to be held 2007); vice presidents appointed by the president; prime minister and deputy prime ministers appointed by the president
election results: Bashar al-ASAD approved as president; percent of vote - Bashar al-ASAD 97.29%
note: Hafiz al-ASAD died on 10 June 2000; on 20 June, the Ba'th Party nominated Bashar al-ASAD for president and presented his name to the People's Council on 25 June; he was approved by a popular referendum on 10 July

Legislative branch: unicameral People's Council or Majlis al-Shaab (250 seats;

members elected by popular vote to serve four-year terms)
elections: last held 2-3 March 2003 (next to be held NA 2007)
election results: percent of vote by party - NPF 67%, independents 33%; seats by party - NPF 167, independents 83; note - the constitution guarantees that the Ba'th Party (part of the NPF alliance) receives one-half of the seats
Judicial branch: Supreme Constitutional Court (adjudicates electoral disputes and rules on constitutionality of laws and decrees; justices appointed for four-year terms by the President); High Judicial Council (appoints and dismisses judges; headed by the President); Court of Cassation (national level); State Security Courts (hear cases related to national security); Personal Status Courts (religious; hear cases related to marriage and divorce); Courts of First Instance (local level; include magistrate, summary, and peace courts)
Political parties and leaders: Arab Socialist Unionist Movement [Ahmed al-AHMED]; National Progressive Front or NPF (includes Arab Socialist Renaissance (Ba'th) Party; the governing party) [President Bashar al-ASAD, secretary general]; Socialist Unionist Democratic Party [Fadlallal Nasr Al-DIN]; Syrian Arab Socialist Party or ASP [Safwan QUDSI]; Syrian Communist Party (two branches) [Wissal Farha BAKDASH, Yuusuf Rashid FAYSAL]; Syrian Social National Party [Jubran URAYJI]; Unionist Socialist Party [Fayez ISMAIL]
Political pressure groups and leaders: Kurdish Democratic Alliance (includes several groups but has no designated leader); Kurdish Democratic Front (includes several groups but has no designated leader); Muslim Brotherhood (operates in exile in London) [Sadr al-Din al-BAYANUNI]; National Democratic Front [Hassan Abd al-AZIM]
International organization participation: ABEDA, AFESD, AMF, CAEU, FAO, G-24, G-77, IAEA, IBRD, ICAO, ICC, ICCt (signatory), ICRM, IDA, IDB, IFAD, IFC, IFRCS, IHO, ILO, IMF, IMO, Interpol, IOC, ISO, ITU, LAS, MIGA, NAM, OAPEC, OIC, UN, UNCTAD, UNESCO, UNIDO, UNRWA, UPU, WCO, WFTU, WHO, WIPO, WMO, WToO
Diplomatic representation in the US:
chief of mission: Ambassador Imad MUSTAFA
chancery: 2215 Wyoming Avenue NW, Washington, DC 20008
telephone: [1] (202) 232-6313
FAX: [1] (202) 234-9548
Diplomatic representation from the US:
chief of mission: Ambassador Margaret SCOBEY
embassy: Abou Roumaneh, Al-Mansur Street, No. 2, Damascus *mailing address:* PSC 120, Box 1000, APO AE 09265
mailing address: P. O. Box 29, Damascus
telephone: [963] (11) 333-1342
FAX: [963] (11) 224-7938
Flag description: three equal horizontal bands of red (top), white, and black, colors associated with the Arab Liberation flag; two small green five-pointed stars in a horizontal line centered in the white band; former flag of the United Arab Republic where the two stars represented the constituent states of Syria and Egypt; similar to the flag of Yemen, which has a plain white band, Iraq, which has three green stars (plus an Arabic inscription) in a horizontal line centered in the white band, and that of Egypt, which has a gold Eagle of Saladin centered in the white band; the current design dates to 1980

ECONOMY

Economy - overview: Real GDP growth slowed to 1.4 percent in 2005, a slight decrease from an average annual growth of 2.3 percent for the last eight years. The assassination in February of former Lebanese Prime Minister Rafiq al-HARIRI diverted attention from economic policymaking and raised the specter of international sanctions. Oil output and exports declined. Buoyant world oil prices, however, narrowed the budget deficit and widened the current account surplus. The Government of Syria has implemented modest economic reforms in the last few years, including cutting interest rates, opening private banks, consolidating some of the multiple exchange rates, and raising prices on some subsidized foodstuffs. Nevertheless, the economy remains highly controlled by the government. Long run economic constraints include declining oil production and exports and pressure on water supplies caused by rapid population growth, industrial expansion, and increased water pollution.
GDP (purchasing power parity): $63.86 billion (2005 est.)
GDP (official exchange rate): $25.68 billion (2005 est.)
GDP - real growth rate: 1.4% (2005 est.)
GDP - per capita: purchasing power parity - $3,500 (2005 est.)
GDP - composition by sector:
agriculture: 25%
industry: 31%
services: 44% (2003 est.)
Labor force: 5.12 million (2004 est.)
Labor force - by occupation: agriculture 30%, industry 27%, services 43% (2002 est.)
Unemployment rate: 20% (2002 est.)
Population below poverty line: 20% (2004 est.)
Household income or consumption by percentage share:
lowest 10%: NA
highest 10%: NA
Inflation rate (consumer prices): 2.6% (2005 est.)
Investment (gross fixed): 21.1% of GDP (2005 est.)
Budget:
revenues: $5.685 billion
expenditures: $6.521 billion, including capital expenditures of $4.67 billion (2005 est.)
Public debt: 45% of GDP (2005 est.)
Agriculture - products: wheat, barley, cotton, lentils, chickpeas, olives, sugar beets; beef, mutton, eggs, poultry, milk
Industries: petroleum, textiles, food processing, beverages, tobacco, phosphate rock mining
Industrial production growth rate: 7% (2002 est.)
Electricity - production: 27.18 billion kWh (2003)
Electricity - production by source:
fossil fuel: 57.6%
hydro: 42.4%
nuclear: 0%
other: 0% (2001)
Electricity - consumption: 25.28 billion kWh (2003)
Electricity - exports: 0 kWh (2003)
Electricity - imports: 0 kWh (2003)
Oil - production: 403,800 bbl/day (2005 est.)
Oil - consumption: 240,000 bbl/day (2004 est.)
Oil - exports: 285,000 bbl/day (2004)
Oil - imports: NA
Oil - proved reserves: 2.5 billion bbl (2005 est.)
Natural gas - production: 5.84 billion cu m (2001 est.)
Natural gas - consumption: 5.84 billion cu m (2001 est.)
Natural gas - exports: 0 cu m (2001 est.)
Natural gas - imports: 0 cu m (2001 est.)
Natural gas - proved reserves: 240.7 billion cu m (2005)
Current account balance: $980 million (2005 est.)
Exports: $6.344 billion f.o.b. (2005 est.)
Exports - partners: Italy 22.7%, France 18%, Turkey 12.9%, Iraq 9%, Saudi Arabia 6.2% (2004)
Imports: $5.973 billion f.o.b. (2005 est.)
Imports - partners: Turkey 9.4%, Ukraine 8.7%, China 7.8%, Russia 5.4%, Saudi Arabia 5.2%, US 4.7%, South Korea 4.6%, Italy 4.3% (2004)

Reserves of foreign exchange and gold: $4.104 billion (2005 est.)
Debt - external: $8.59 billion (excludes military debt and debt to Russia) (2005 est.)
Economic aid - recipient: $180 million (2002 est.)
Currency (code): Syrian pound (SYP)
Currency code: SYP
Exchange rates: Syrian pounds per US dollar - (official rate): NA (2005), 48.5 (2004), 46.5 (2003), 52.4 (2002), 50.4 (2001), (parallel market rate in Amman and Beirut) NA (2005), NA (2004), 52.8 (2003), 52.4 (2002), 50.4 (2001), (Official rate for repaying loans): 11.225 (2004)
Fiscal year: calendar year

COMMUNICATIONS

Telephones - main lines in use: 2,099,300 (2002)
Telephones - mobile cellular: 400,000 (2002)
Telephone system:
general assessment: fair system currently undergoing significant improvement and digital upgrades, including fiber-optic technology
domestic: coaxial cable and microwave radio relay network
international: country code - 963; satellite earth stations - 1 Intelsat (Indian Ocean) and 1 Intersputnik (Atlantic Ocean region); 1 submarine cable; coaxial cable and microwave radio relay to Iraq, Jordan, Lebanon, and Turkey; participant in Medarabtel
Radio broadcast stations: AM 14, FM 2, shortwave 1 (1998)
Radios: 4.15 million (1997)
Television broadcast stations: 44 (plus 17 repeaters) (1995)
Televisions: 1.05 million (1997)
Internet country code: .sy
Internet hosts: 11 (2004)
Internet Service Providers (ISPs): 1 (2000)
Internet users: 220,000 (2002)

TRANSPORTATION

Airports: 92 (2004 est.)
Airports - with paved runways:
total: 26
over 3,047 m: 6
2,438 to 3,047 m: 15
914 to 1,523 m: 3
under 914 m: 2 (2005 est.)
Airports - with unpaved runways:
total: 66
1,524 to 2,437 m: 2
914 to 1,523 m: 10
under 914 m: 54 (2005 est.)
Heliports: 7 (2005 est.)
Pipelines: gas 2,300 km; oil 2,183 km (2004)
Railways:
total: 2,711 km
standard gauge: 2,460 km 1.435-m gauge
narrow gauge: 251 km 1.050-m gauge (2004)
Roadways:
total: 45,697 km
paved: 6,489 km (including 1,001 km of expressways)
unpaved: 39,208 km (2002)
Waterways: 900 km (not economically significant) (2002)
Merchant marine:
total: 120 ships (1,000 GRT or over) 446,981 GRT/636,620 DWT
by type: bulk carrier 8, cargo 105, container 1, livestock carrier 4, petroleum tanker 1, roll on/roll off 1
foreign-owned: 12 (Egypt 1, Greece 1, Jordan 2, Lebanon 7, Romania 1)
registered in other countries: 73 (2005)
Ports and terminals: Baniyas, Latakia

MILITARY

Military branches: Syrian Arab Army, Syrian Arab Navy, Syrian Arab Air Force (includes Air Defense Command), Police and Security Force
Military service age and obligation: 18 years of age for compulsory military service; conscript service obligation - 30 months (2004)
Manpower available for military service: *males age 18-49:* 4,356,413 (2005 est.)
Manpower fit for military service: *males age 18-49:* 3,453,888 (2005 est.)
Manpower reaching military service age annually: *males:* 225,113 (2005 est.)
Military expenditures - dollar figure: $858 million (FY00 est.); note - based on official budget data that may understate actual spending
Military expenditures - percent of GDP: 5.9% (FY00)

TRANSNATIONAL ISSUES

Disputes - international: Golan Heights is Israeli-occupied with the almost 1,000-strong UN Disengagement Observer Force (UNDOF) patrolling a buffer zone since 1964; Lebanon claims Shaba'a farms in Golan Heights; international pressure prompts the removal of Syrian troops and intelligence personnel stationed in Lebanon since October 1976; Syria protests Turkish hydrological projects regulating upper Euphrates waters; 2004 Agreement and pending demarcation settles border dispute with Jordan
Refugees and internally displaced persons:
refugees (country of origin): 413,827 (Palestinian Refugees (UNRWA))
IDPs: 170,000 (most displaced from Golan Heights during 1967 Arab-Israeli War) (2004)
Illicit drugs: a transit point for opiates and hashish bound for regional and Western markets; weak anti-money-laundering controls, bank privatization may leave it vulnerable to money-laundering

TAIWAN

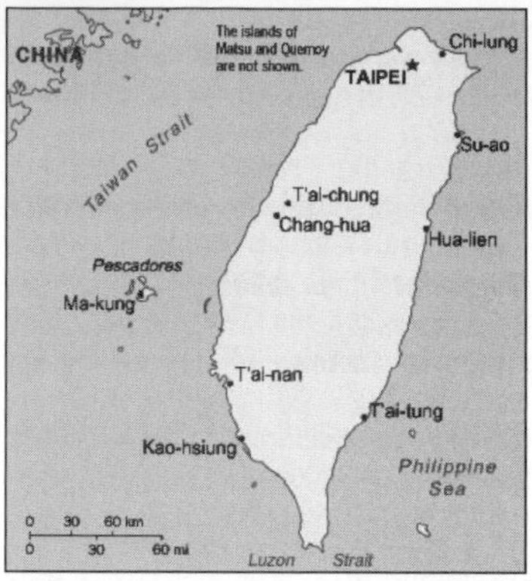

INTRODUCTION

Background: In 1895, military defeat forced China to cede Taiwan to Japan. Taiwan reverted to Chinese control after World War II. Following the Communist victory on the mainland in 1949, 2 million Nationalists fled to Taiwan and established a government using the 1946 constitution drawn up for all of China. Over the next five decades, the ruling authorities gradually democratized and incorporated the native population within the governing structure. In 2000, Taiwan underwent its first peaceful transfer of power from the Nationalist to the Democratic Progressive Party. Throughout this period, the island prospered and became one of East Asia's economic "Tigers." The dominant political issues continue to be the relationship between Taiwan and China - specifically the question of eventual unification - as well as domestic political and economic reform.

GEOGRAPHY

Location: Eastern Asia, islands bordering the East China Sea, Philippine Sea, South China Sea, and Taiwan Strait, north of the Philippines, off the southeastern coast of China
Geographic coordinates: 23 30 N, 121 00 E
Map references: Southeast Asia
Area:
total: 35,980 sq km
land: 32,260 sq km
water: 3,720 sq km
note: includes the Pescadores, Matsu, and Quemoy
Area - comparative: slightly smaller than Maryland and Delaware combined
Land boundaries: 0 km
Coastline: 1,566.3 km
Maritime claims:
territorial sea: 12 nm
exclusive economic zone: 200 nm
Climate: tropical; marine; rainy season during southwest monsoon (June to August); cloudiness is persistent and extensive all year
Terrain: eastern two-thirds mostly rugged mountains; flat to gently rolling plains in west
Elevation extremes:
lowest point: South China Sea 0 m
highest point: Yu Shan 3,952 m
Natural resources: small deposits of coal, natural gas, limestone, marble, and asbestos
Land use:
arable land: 24%
permanent crops: 1%
other: 75% (2001)
Irrigated land: NA sq km
Natural hazards: earthquakes and typhoons
Environment - current issues: air pollution; water pollution from industrial emissions, raw sewage; contamination of drinking water supplies; trade in endangered species; low-level radioactive waste disposal
Environment - international agreements:
party to: none of the selected agreements because of Taiwan's international status
signed, but not ratified: none of the selected agreements because of Taiwan's international status
Geography - note: strategic location adjacent to both the Taiwan Strait and the Luzon Strait

PEOPLE

Population: 22,894,384 (July 2005 est.)
Age structure:
0-14 years: 19.7% (male 2,349,077/ female 2,156,755)
15-64 years: 70.7% (male 8,205,933/ female 7,980,056)
65 years and over: 9.6% (male 1,107,708/ female 1,094,855) (2005 est.)
Median age:
total: 34.14 years
male: 33.71 years
female: 34.57 years (2005 est.)
Population growth rate: 0.63% (2005 est.)
Birth rate: 12.64 births/1,000 population (2005 est.)
Death rate: 6.38 deaths/1,000 population (2005 est.)
Net migration rate: 0 migrant(s)/ 1,000 population (2005 est.)
Sex ratio:
at birth: 1.1 male(s)/female
under 15 years: 1.09 male(s)/ female
15-64 years: 1.03 male(s)/female
65 years and over: 1.01 male(s)/ female
total population: 1.04 male(s)/ female (2005 est.)
Infant mortality rate:
total: 6.4 deaths/1,000 live births
male: 7.09 deaths/1,000 live births
female: 5.65 deaths/1,000 live births (2005 est.)
Life expectancy at birth:
total population: 77.26 years
male: 74.49 years
female: 80.28 years (2005 est.)
Total fertility rate: 1.57 children born/ woman (2005 est.)
HIV/AIDS - adult prevalence rate: NA
HIV/AIDS - people living with HIV/AIDS: NA
HIV/AIDS - deaths: NA
Nationality:
noun: Taiwan (singular and plural)
note: example: he or she is from Taiwan; they are from Taiwan
adjective: Taiwan
Ethnic groups: Taiwanese (including Hakka) 84%, mainland Chinese 14%, aborigine 2%
Religions: mixture of Buddhist, Confucian, and Taoist 93%, Christian 4.5%, other 2.5%
Languages: Mandarin Chinese (official), Taiwanese (Min), Hakka dialects
Literacy:
definition: age 15 and over can read and write
total population: 96.1% (2003)

GOVERNMENT

Country name:
conventional long form: none
conventional short form: Taiwan
local long form: none
local short form: T'ai-wan
former: Formosa
Government type: multiparty democratic regime headed by popularly-elected president and unicameral legislature
Capital: Taipei
Administrative divisions: includes central island of Taiwan plus numerous smaller islands near central island and off coast of China's Fujian Province; Taiwan is divided into 18 counties (hsien, singular and plural), 5 municipalities (shih, singular and plural), and 2 special municipalities (chuan-shih, singular and plural)
: counties: Chang-hua, Chia-i, Hsin-chu, Hua-lien, I-lan, Kao-hsiung county, Kinmen, Lien-chiang, Miao-li, Nan-t'ou, P'eng-hu, P'ing-tung, T'ai-chung, T'ai-nan, T'ai-pei county, T'ai-tung, T'ao-yuan, and Yun-lin
: municipalities: Chia-i, Chi-lung, Hsin-chu, T'ai-chung, T'ai-nan
: special municipalities: Kao-hsiung city, T'ai-pei city
note: Taiwan generally uses Wade-Giles system for romanization; special munici-

pality of Taipei adopted standard pinyin romanization for street and place names within city boundaries, other local authorities have selected a variety of romanization systems

National holiday: Republic Day (Anniversary of the Chinese Revolution), 10 October (1911)

Constitution: 25 December 1946; amended in 1992, 1994, 1997, 1999, and 2000

Legal system: based on civil law system; accepts compulsory ICJ jurisdiction, with reservations

Suffrage: 20 years of age; universal

Executive branch:

chief of state: President CHEN Shui-bian (since 20 May 2000) and Vice President Annette LU (LU Hsiu-lien) (since 20 May 2000)

head of government: Premier (President of the Executive Yuan) Frank HSIEH (since 1 February 2005) and Vice Premier (Vice President of the Executive Yuan) - WU Rong-i) (since 18 February 2005)

cabinet: Executive Yuan appointed by the president

elections: president and vice president elected on the same ticket by popular vote for four-year terms; election last held 20 March 2004 (next to be held in March 2008); premier appointed by the president; vice premiers appointed by the president on the recommendation of the premier

election results: CHEN Shui-bian re-elected president; percent of vote - CHEN Shui-bian (DPP) 50.1%, LIEN Chan (KMT) 49.9%

Legislative branch: unicameral Legislative Yuan (225 seats - 168 elected by popular vote, 41 elected on basis of proportion of islandwide votes received by participating political parties, 8 elected from overseas Chinese constituencies on basis of proportion of island-wide votes received by participating political parties, 8 elected by popular vote among aboriginal populations; members serve three-year terms) and unicameral National Assembly (300 seat nonstanding body; delegates nominated by parties and elected by proportional representation six to nine months after Legislative Yuan calls to amend Constitution, impeach president, or change national borders)

note: as a result of constitutional amendments approved by the National Assembly on 7 June 2005, the number of seats in the legislature will be reduced from 225 to 113 beginning with the election in 2007; the amendments also eliminate the National Assembly, thus giving Taiwan a unicameral legislature

elections: Legislative Yuan - last held 11 December 2004 (next to be held in December 2007); National Assembly - last held 14 May 2005

election results: Legislative Yuan - percent of vote by party - DPP 38%, KMT 35%, PFP 15%, TSU 8%, other parties and independents 4%; seats by party - DPP 89, KMT 79, PFP 34, TSU 12, other parties 7, independents 4; National Assembly - percent of vote by party - DPP 42.5%, KMT 38.9%, TSU 7%, PFP 6%, others 6.6%; seats by party - DPP 127, KMT 117, TSU 21, PFP 18, others 17 (2005)

Judicial branch: Judicial Yuan (justices appointed by the president with consent of the Legislative Yuan)

Political parties and leaders: Democratic Progressive Party or DPP [Annette LU, acting chairwoman]; Kuomintang or KMT (Nationalist Party) [MA Ying-jeou, chairman]; People First Party or PFP [James SOONG (SOONG Chu-yu), chairman]; Taiwan Solidarity Union or TSU [SU Chin-chiang, chairman]; other minor parties including the Chinese New Party or CNP

Political pressure groups and leaders: Taiwan independence movement, various business and environmental groups

note: debate on Taiwan independence has become acceptable within the mainstream of domestic politics on Taiwan; political liberalization and the increased representation of opposition parties in Taiwan's legislature have opened public debate on the island's national identity; a broad popular consensus has developed that Taiwan currently enjoys de facto independence and - whatever the ultimate outcome regarding reunification or independence - that Taiwan's people must have the deciding voice; advocates of Taiwan independence oppose the stand that the island will eventually unify with mainland China; goals of the Taiwan independence movement include establishing a sovereign nation on Taiwan and entering the UN; other organizations supporting Taiwan independence include the World United Formosans for Independence and the Organization for Taiwan Nation Building

International organization participation: APEC, AsDB, ICC, ICFTU, ICRM, IFRCS, IOC, WCL, WTO

Diplomatic representation in the US: none; unofficial commercial and cultural relations with the people of the US are maintained through an unofficial instrumentality, the Taipei Economic and Cultural Representative Office (TECRO) in the US with headquarters in Taipei and field offices in Washington and 12 other US cities

Diplomatic representation from the US: none; unofficial commercial and cultural relations with the people on Taiwan are maintained through an unofficial instrumentality - the American Institute in Taiwan (AIT) - which has offices in the US and Taiwan; US office at 1700 N. Moore St., Suite 1700, Arlington, VA 22209-1996, telephone: [1] (703) 525-8474, FAX: [1] (703) 841-1385); Taiwan offices at #7 Lane 134, Hsin Yi Road, Section 3, Taipei, Taiwan, telephone: [886] (2) 2162-2000, FAX: [886] (2) 2162-2251; #2 Chung Cheng 3rd Road, 5th Floor, Kao-hsiung, Taiwan, telephone: [886] (7) 238-7744, FAX: [886] (7) 238-5237; and the American Trade Center, Room 3208 International Trade Building, Taipei World Trade Center, 333 Keelung Road Section 1, Taipei, Taiwan 10548, telephone: [886] (2) 2720-1550, FAX: [886] (2) 2757-7162

Flag description: red with a dark blue rectangle in the upper hoist-side corner bearing a white sun with 12 triangular rays

ECONOMY

Economy - overview: Taiwan has a dynamic capitalist economy with gradually decreasing guidance of investment and foreign trade by government authorities. In keeping with this trend, some large government-owned banks and industrial firms are being privatized. Exports have provided the primary impetus for industrialization. The trade surplus is substantial, and foreign reserves are the world's third largest. Agriculture contributes less than 2% to GDP, down from 32% in 1952. Taiwan is a major investor throughout Southeast Asia. China has overtaken the US to become Taiwan's largest export market. Because of its conservative financial approach and its entrepreneurial strengths, Taiwan suffered little compared with many of its neighbors from the Asian financial crisis in 1998. The global economic downturn, combined with problems in policy coordination by the administration and bad debts in the banking system, pushed Taiwan into recession in 2001, the first year of negative growth ever recorded. Unemployment also reached record levels. Output recovered moderately in 2002 in the face of continued global slowdown, fragile consumer confidence, and bad bank loans. The essentially vibrant economy pushed ahead in 2003-05. Growing economic ties with China are a dominant long-term factor, e.g., exports to China of parts and equipment for the assembly of goods for export to developed countries.

GDP (purchasing power parity): $610.8 billion (2005 est.)
GDP (official exchange rate): $334.4 billion (2005 est.)
GDP - real growth rate: 3.6% (2005 est.)
GDP - per capita: purchasing power parity - $26,700 (2005 est.)
GDP - composition by sector:
agriculture: 1.6%
industry: 29.3%
services: 69% (2005 est.)
Labor force: 10.31 million (2005 est.)
Labor force - by occupation: agriculture 6%, industry 35.8%, services 58.2% (2005 est.)
Unemployment rate: 4.2% (2005 est.)
Population below poverty line: 0.9% (2005)
Household income or consumption by percentage share:
lowest 10%: 6.7%
highest 10%: 41.1% (2002 est.)
Inflation rate (consumer prices): 1.8% (2005 est.)
Investment (gross fixed): 20.8% of GDP (2005 est.)
Budget:
revenues: $70.93 billion
expenditures: $80.14 billion, including capital expenditures of $14.4 billion (2005 est.)
Public debt: 33.3% of GDP (2005 est.)
Agriculture - products: rice, corn, vegetables, fruit, tea; pigs, poultry, beef, milk; fish
Industries: electronics, petroleum refining, armaments, chemicals, textiles, iron and steel, machinery, cement, food processing, vehicles, consumer products, pharmaceuticals
Industrial production growth rate: 3% (2005 est.)
Electricity - production: 218.3 billion kWh (2004)
Electricity - production by source:
fossil fuel: 71.4%
hydro: 6%
nuclear: 22.6%
other: 0% (2001)
Electricity - consumption: 206.1 billion kWh (2004)
Electricity - exports: 0 kWh (2004)
Electricity - imports: 0 kWh (2004)
Oil - production: 8,354 bbl/day (2003 est.)
Oil - consumption: 915,000 bbl/day (2003 est.)
Oil - exports: NA (2001)
Oil - imports: NA (2001)
Oil - proved reserves: 2.9 million bbl (2005 est.)
Natural gas - production: 962.8 million cu m (2005 est.)
Natural gas - consumption: 8.32 billion cu m (2005 est.)
Natural gas - exports: 410 million cu m (2001 est.)
Natural gas - imports: 7.48 billion cu m (2005 est.)
Natural gas - proved reserves: 38.23 billion cu m (2005)
Current account balance: $15.03 billion (2005 est.)
Exports: $185.1 billion f.o.b. (2005 est.)
Exports - partners: China, including Hong Kong 37%, US 15.3%, Japan 7.7% (2005)
Imports: $172.9 billion f.o.b. (2005 est.)
Imports - partners: Japan 26%, US 12%, China, including Hong Kong 12%, South Korea 7% (2005)
Reserves of foreign exchange and gold: $269.7 billion (2005 est.)
Debt - external: $81.64 billion (2005 est.)
Currency (code): new Taiwan dollar (TWD)
Currency code: TWD
Exchange rates: new Taiwan dollars per US dollar - 31.71 (2005), 33.422 (2004), 34.418 (2003), 34.575 (2002), 33.8 (2001)
Fiscal year: 1 July - 30 June (up to FY98/99); 1 July 1999 - 31 December 2000 for FY00; calendar year (after FY00)

COMMUNICATIONS

Telephones - main lines in use: 13.355 million (2003)
Telephones - mobile cellular: 25,089,600 (2003)
Telephone system:
general assessment: provides telecommunications service for every business and private need
domestic: thoroughly modern; completely digitalized
international: country code - 886; satellite earth stations - 2 Intelsat (1 Pacific Ocean and 1 Indian Ocean); submarine cables to Japan (Okinawa), Philippines, Guam, Singapore, Hong Kong, Indonesia, Australia, Middle East, and Western Europe (1999)
Radio broadcast stations: AM 218, FM 333, shortwave 50 (1999)
Radios: 16 million (1994)
Television broadcast stations: 29 (plus two repeaters) (1997)
Televisions: 8.8 million (1998)
Internet country code: .tw
Internet hosts: 2,777,085 (2003)
Internet Service Providers (ISPs): 8 (2000)
Internet users: 13.8 million (2005)

TRANSPORTATION

Airports: 40 (2004 est.)
Airports - with paved runways:
total: 38
over 3,047 m: 8
2,438 to 3,047 m: 8
1,524 to 2,437 m: 12
914 to 1,523 m: 8
under 914 m: 2 (2005 est.)
Airports - with unpaved runways:
total: 4
1,524 to 2,437 m: 1
under 914 m: 3 (2005 est.)
Heliports: 3 (2005 est.)
Pipelines: condensate 25 km; gas 435 km (2004)
Railways:
total: 2,497 km
narrow gauge: 1,097 km 1.067-m gauge (685 km electrified)
note: 1,400 km .762-m gauge (belonging to the Taiwan Sugar Corporation and to the Taiwan Forestry Bureau used to haul products and limited numbers of passengers (2004)
Roadways:
total: 37,299 km
paved: 35,621 km (including 608 km of expressways)
unpaved: 1,678 km (2002)
Merchant marine:
total: 126 ships (1,000 GRT or over) 3,417,768 GRT/5,617,318 DWT
by type: bulk carrier 36, cargo 23, chemical tanker 2, container 37, passenger/cargo 3, petroleum tanker 15, refrigerated cargo 9, roll on/roll off 1
foreign-owned: 3 (Hong Kong 3)
registered in other countries: 432 (2005)
Ports and terminals: Chi-lung (Keelung), Hua-lien, Kao-hsiung, Su-ao, T'ai-chung

MILITARY

Military branches: Army, Navy (includes Marine Corps), Air Force, Coast Guard Administration, Armed Forces Reserve Command, Combined Service Forces Command, Armed Forces Police Command
Military service age and obligation: 19-35 years of age for military service; service obligation 16 months (to be shortened to 12 months in 2008); women in Air Force service are restricted to noncombat roles (2005)
Manpower available for military service: *males age 19-49:* 5,883,828 (2005 est.)
Manpower fit for military service: *males age 19-49:* 4,749,537 (2005 est.)
Manpower reaching military service age annually: *males:* 174,173 (2005 est.)
Military expenditures - dollar figure: $7.574 billion (2003)
Military expenditures - percent of GDP: 2.6% (2004)

TRANSNATIONAL ISSUES

Disputes - international: involved in complex dispute with China, Malaysia, Philippines, Vietnam, and possibly Brunei over the Spratly Islands; the 2002 "Declaration on the Conduct of Parties in the South China Sea" has eased tensions but falls short of a legally binding "code of conduct" desired by several of the disputants; Paracel Islands are occupied by China, but claimed by Taiwan and Vietnam; in 2003, China and Taiwan became more vocal in rejecting both Japan's claims to the uninhabited islands of the Senkaku-shoto (Diaoyu Tai) and Japan's unilaterally declared exclusive economic zone in the East China Sea where all parties engage in hydrocarbon prospecting

Illicit drugs: regional transit point for heroin and methamphetamine; major problem with domestic consumption of methamphetamine and heroin; renewal of domestic methamphetamine production is a problem

TAJIKISTAN

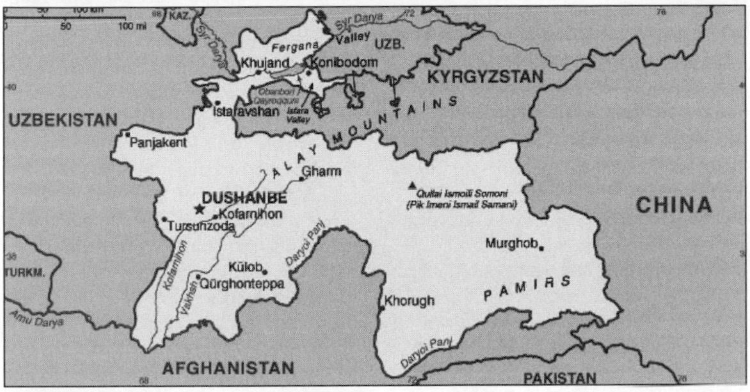

INTRODUCTION

Background: The Tajik people came under Russian rule in the 1860s and 1870s, but Russia's hold on Central Asia weakened following the Revolution of 1917. Bolshevik control of the area was fiercely contested and not fully reestablished until 1925. Tajikistan became independent in 1991 following the breakup of the Soviet Union and has now completed its transition from the civil war that plagued the country from 1992 to 1997. There have been no major security incidents in recent years, although the country remains the poorest in the former Soviet sphere. Attention by the international community in the wake of the war in Afghanistan has brought increased economic development assistance, which could create jobs and increase stability in the long term. Tajikistan is in the early stages of seeking World Trade Organization membership and has joined NATO's Partnership for Peace.

GEOGRAPHY

Location: Central Asia, west of China
Geographic coordinates: 39 00 N, 71 00 E
Map references: Asia
Area:
total: 143,100 sq km
land: 142,700 sq km
water: 400 sq km
Area - comparative: slightly smaller than Wisconsin
Land boundaries:
total: 3,651 km
border countries: Afghanistan 1,206 km, China 414 km, Kyrgyzstan 870 km, Uzbekistan 1,161 km
Coastline: 0 km (landlocked)
Maritime claims: none (landlocked)
Climate: midlatitude continental, hot summers, mild winters; semiarid to polar in Pamir Mountains
Terrain: Pamir and Alay Mountains dominate landscape; western Fergana Valley in north, Kofarnihon and Vakhsh Valleys in southwest
Elevation extremes:
lowest point: Syr Darya (Sirdaryo) 300 m
highest point: Qullai Ismoili Somoni 7,495 m
Natural resources: hydropower, some petroleum, uranium, mercury, brown coal, lead, zinc, antimony, tungsten, silver, gold
Land use:
arable land: 6.61%
permanent crops: 0.92%
other: 92.47% (2001)
Irrigated land: 7,200 sq km (1998 est.)
Natural hazards: earthquakes and floods
Environment - current issues: inadequate sanitation facilities; increasing levels of soil salinity; industrial pollution; excessive pesticides
Environment - international agreements:
party to: Biodiversity, Climate Change, Desertification, Environmental Modification, Ozone Layer Protection, Wetlands
signed, but not ratified: none of the selected agreements
Geography - note: landlocked; mountainous region dominated by the Trans-Alay Range in the north and the Pamirs in the southeast; highest point, Qullai Ismoili Somoni (formerly Communism Peak), was the tallest mountain in the former USSR

PEOPLE

Population: 7,163,506 (July 2005 est.)
Age structure:
0-14 years: 38.5% (male 1,390,220/female 1,368,268)
15-64 years: 56.7% (male 2,022,764/female 2,040,524)
65 years and over: 4.8% (male 150,372/female 191,358) (2005 est.)
Median age:
total: 19.73 years
male: 19.45 years
female: 20.02 years (2005 est.)
Population growth rate: 2.15% (2005 est.)
Birth rate: 32.58 births/1,000 population (2005 est.)
Death rate: 8.39 deaths/1,000 population (2005 est.)
Net migration rate: -2.67 migrant(s)/1,000 population (2005 est.)
Sex ratio:
at birth: 1.05 male(s)/female
under 15 years: 1.02 male(s)/female
15-64 years: 0.99 male(s)/female
65 years and over: 0.79 male(s)/ female
total population: 0.99 male(s)/ female (2005 est.)
Infant mortality rate:
total: 110.76 deaths/1,000 live births
male: 122.35 deaths/1,000 live births
female: 98.6 deaths/1,000 live births (2005 est.)
Life expectancy at birth:
total population: 64.56 years
male: 61.68 years
female: 67.59 years (2005 est.)
Total fertility rate: 4.05 children born/woman (2005 est.)
HIV/AIDS - adult prevalence rate: less than 0.1% (2001 est.)
HIV/AIDS - people living with HIV/AIDS: less than 200 (2003 est.)
HIV/AIDS - deaths: less than 100 (2001 est.)
Nationality:
noun: Tajikistani(s)
adjective: Tajikistani
Ethnic groups: Tajik 79.9%, Uzbek 15.3%, Russian 1.1%, Kyrgyz 1.1%, other 2.6% (2000 census)
Religions: Sunni Muslim 85%, Shi'a Muslim 5%, other 10% (2003 est.)

Languages: Tajik (official), Russian widely used in government and business
Literacy:
definition: age 15 and over can read and write
total population: 99.4%
male: 99.6%
female: 99.1% (2003 est.)

GOVERNMENT

Country name:
conventional long form: Republic of Tajikistan
conventional short form: Tajikistan
local long form: Jumhurii Tojikiston
local short form: Tojikiston
former: Tajik Soviet Socialist Republic
Government type: republic
Capital: Dushanbe
Administrative divisions: 2 provinces (viloyatho, singular - viloyat) and 1 autonomous province* (viloyati mukhtor); Viloyati Mukhtori Kuhistoni Badakhshon* [Gorno-Badakhshan] (Khorugh), Viloyati Khatlon (Qurghonteppa), Viloyati Sughd (Khujand)
note: the administrative center name follows in parentheses
Independence: 9 September 1991 (from Soviet Union)
National holiday: Independence Day (or National Day), 9 September (1991)
Constitution: 6 November 1994
Legal system: based on civil law system; no judicial review of legislative acts
Suffrage: 18 years of age; universal
Executive branch:
chief of state: President Emomali RAHMONOV (since 6 November 1994; head of state and Supreme Assembly chairman since 19 November 1992)
head of government: Prime Minister Oqil OQILOV (since 20 January 1999)
cabinet: Council of Ministers appointed by the president, approved by the Supreme Assembly
elections: president elected by popular vote for a seven-year term; election last held 6 November 1999 (next to be held November 2006); prime minister appointed by the president; Tajikistan held a constitutional referendum on 22 June 2003 that, among other things, set a limit of two seven-year terms for the president
election results: Emomali RAHMONOV elected president; percent of vote - Emomali RAHMONOV 97%, Davlat USMON 2%
Legislative branch: bicameral Supreme Assembly or Majlisi Oli consists of the Assembly of Representatives (lower chamber) or Majlisi Namoyandagon (63 seats; members are elected by popular vote to serve five-year terms) and the National Assembly (upper chamber) or Majlisi Milliy (33 seats; members are indirectly elected, 25 selected by local deputies, 8 appointed by the president; all serve five-year terms)
elections: last held 27 February and 13 March 2005 for the Assembly of Representatives (next to be held NA 2010) and 25 March 2005 for the National Assembly (next to be held NA 2010)
election results: Assembly of Representatives - percent of vote by party - PDPT 74.9%, CPT 13.6%, Islamic Revival Party 8.9%, other 2.5%; seats by party - PDPT 51, CPT 5, Islamic Revival Party 2, independents 5; National Assembly - percent of vote by party - NA%; seats by party - NA
Judicial branch: Supreme Court (judges are appointed by the president)
Political parties and leaders: Agrarian Party of Tajikistan or APT [Amir KARAKULOV]; Democratic Party or DPT [Mahmadruzi ISKANDAROV]; Islamic Revival Party [Said Abdullo NURI]; Party of Economic Reform or PER [Olimzhon BOBOYEV]; People's Democratic Party of Tajikistan or PDPT [Emomali RAHMONOV]; Social Democratic Party or SDPT [Rahmatullo ZOIROV]; Socialist Party or SPT [Mirhuseyn NAZRIYEV]; Tajik Communist Party or CPT [Shodi SHABDOLOV]
Political pressure groups and leaders: there are two unregistered political parties: Progressive Party [Sulton QUVVATOV]; Unity Party [Hikmatullo SAIDOV]
International organization participation: AsDB, CIS, EAPC, EBRD, ECO, FAO, IAEA, IBRD, ICAO, ICCt, ICRM, IDA, IDB, IFAD, IFC, IFRCS, ILO, IMF, Interpol, IOC, IOM, ISO (subscriber), ITU, MIGA, OIC, OPCW, OSCE, PFP, SCO, UN, UNCTAD, UNESCO, UNIDO, UPU, WCO, WFTU, WHO, WIPO, WMO, WTO (observer)
Diplomatic representation in the US:
chief of mission: Ambassador Hamrohon ZARIPOV
chancery: 1725 K Street NW, Suite 409, Washington, DC 20006
telephone: [1] (202) 223-6090
FAX: [1] (202) 223-6091
Diplomatic representation from the US:
chief of mission: Ambassador Richard E. HOAGLAND
embassy: 10 Pavlova Street, Dushanbe, Tajikistan 734003
mailing address: 7090 Dushanbe Place, Dulles, VA 20189
telephone: [992] (372) 21-03-48, 21-03-52, 24-15-60
FAX: [992] (372) 21-03-62, 51-00-29
Flag description: three horizontal stripes of red (top), a wider stripe of white, and green; a gold crown surmounted by seven gold, five-pointed stars is located in the center of the white stripe

ECONOMY

Economy - overview: Tajikistan has one of the lowest per capita GDPs among the 15 former Soviet republics. Only 5% to 6% of the land area is arable. Cotton is the most important crop. Mineral resources, varied but limited in amount, include silver, gold, uranium, and tungsten. Industry consists only of a large aluminum plant, hydropower facilities, and small obsolete factories mostly in light industry and food processing. The civil war (1992-97) severely damaged the already weak economic infrastructure and caused a sharp decline in industrial and agricultural production. Even though 60% of its people continue to live in abject poverty, Tajikistan has experienced steady economic growth since 1997. Continued privatization of medium and large state-owned enterprises would further increase productivity. Tajikistan's economic situation, however, remains fragile due to uneven implementation of structural reforms, weak governance, widespread unemployment, and the external debt burden. A debt restructuring agreement was reached with Russia in December 2002, including an interest rate of 4%, a 3-year grace period, and a US $49.8 million credit to the Central Bank of Tajikistan. Tajikistan ranks third in the world in terms of water resources per head. A proposed investment to finish the hydropower dams Rogun and Sangtuda would substantially add to electricity production. If finished, Rogun will be the world's tallest dam.
GDP (purchasing power parity): $8.808 billion (2005 est.)
GDP (official exchange rate): $1.991 billion (2005 est.)
GDP - real growth rate: 8% (2005 est.)
GDP - per capita: purchasing power parity - $1,200 (2005 est.)
GDP - composition by sector:
agriculture: 24%
industry: 28.4%
services: 47.7% (2005 est.)
Labor force: 3.7 million (2003)
Labor force - by occupation: agriculture 67.2%, industry 7.5%, services 25.3% (2000 est.)
Unemployment rate: 50% (2003 est.)
Population below poverty line: 60% (2004 est.)
Household income or consumption by percentage share:
lowest 10%: 3.2%
highest 10%: 25.2% (1998)

Distribution of family income - Gini index: 34.7 (1998)
Inflation rate (consumer prices): 8% (2005 est.)
Investment (gross fixed): 19.1% of GDP (2005 est.)
Budget:
revenues: $442.3 million
expenditures: $542.6 million, including capital expenditures of $86 million (2005 est.)
Agriculture - products: cotton, grain, fruits, grapes, vegetables; cattle, sheep, goats
Industries: aluminum, zinc, lead, chemicals and fertilizers, cement, vegetable oil, metal-cutting machine tools, refrigerators and freezers
Industrial production growth rate: 8.2% (2002 est.)
Electricity - production: 15.41 billion kWh (2003)
Electricity - production by source:
fossil fuel: 1.9%
hydro: 98.1%
nuclear: 0%
other: 0% (2001)
Electricity - consumption: 15.05 billion kWh (2003)
Electricity - exports: 3.874 billion kWh (2003)
Electricity - imports: 4.6 billion kWh (2003)
Oil - production: 354.8 bbl/day (2003 est.)
Oil - consumption: 25,000 bbl/day (2003 est.)
Oil - exports: NA (2001)
Oil - imports: NA (2001)
Natural gas - production: 30 million cu m (2004 est.)
Natural gas - consumption: 1.4 billion cu m (2004 est.)
Natural gas - exports: 0 cu m (2004 est.)
Natural gas - imports: 1.4 billion cu m (2004 est.)
Current account balance: $-92 million (2005 est.)
Exports: $950 million f.o.b. (2005 est.)
Exports - partners: Netherlands 41.4%, Turkey 15.3%, Uzbekistan 7.2%, Latvia 7.1%, Switzerland 6.9%, Russia 6.6% (2004)
Imports: $1.25 billion f.o.b. (2005 est.)
Imports - partners: Russia 20.2%, Uzbekistan 14.2%, Kazakhstan 12.8%, Azerbaijan 7.2%, US 6.7%, China 4.8%, Ukraine 4.5% (2004)
Reserves of foreign exchange and gold: $195 million (2005 est.)
Debt - external: $888 million (2004 est.)
Economic aid - recipient: $60.7 million from US (2001)
Currency (code): somoni
Currency code: TJS
Exchange rates: Tajikistani somoni per US dollar - 3.12 (2005), 2.9705 (2004), 3.0614 (2003), 2.7641 (2002), 2.3722 (2001)
note: the new unit of exchange was introduced on 30 October 2000, with one somoni equal to 1,000 of the old Tajikistani rubles
Fiscal year: calendar year

COMMUNICATIONS

Telephones - main lines in use: 242,100 (2003)
Telephones - mobile cellular: 47,600 (2003)
Telephone system:
general assessment: poorly developed and not well maintained; many towns are not linked to the national network
domestic: cable and microwave radio relay
international: country code - 992; linked by cable and microwave radio relay to other CIS republics and by leased connections to the Moscow international gateway switch; Dushanbe linked by Intelsat to international gateway switch in Ankara (Turkey); satellite earth stations - 1 Orbita and 2 Intelsat
Radio broadcast stations: AM 8, FM 10, shortwave 2 (2002)
Radios: 1.291 million (1991)
Television broadcast stations: 13 (2001)
Televisions: 820,000 (1997)
Internet country code: .tj
Internet hosts: 69 (2004)
Internet Service Providers (ISPs): 4 (2002)
Internet users: 4,100 (2003)

TRANSPORTATION

Airports: 55 (2004 est.)
Airports - with paved runways:
total: 17
over 3,047 m: 2
2,438 to 3,047 m: 4
1,524 to 2,437 m: 5
914 to 1,523 m: 3
under 914 m: 3 (2005 est.)
Airports - with unpaved runways:
total: 28
1,524 to 2,437 m: 1
914 to 1,523 m: 1
under 914 m: 26 (2005 est.)
Pipelines: gas 541 km; oil 38 km (2004)
Railways:
total: 482 km
broad gauge: 482 km 1.520-m gauge (2004)
Roadways:
total: 27,767 km
paved: NA
unpaved: NA (2000)
Waterways: 200 km (along Vakhsh River) (2003)

MILITARY

Military branches: Ground Troops, Air and Air Defense Force, Mobile Troops (2005)
Military service age and obligation: 18 years of age for compulsory military service; conscript service obligation - 2 years (2004)
Manpower available for military service: *males age 18-49:* 1,556,415 (2005 est.)
Manpower fit for military service: *males age 18-49:* 1,244,941 (2005 est.)
Manpower reaching military service age annually: *males:* 87,846 (2005 est.)
Military expenditures - dollar figure: $35.4 million (FY01)
Military expenditures - percent of GDP: 3.9% (FY01)

TRANSNATIONAL ISSUES

Disputes - international: boundary agreements signed in 2002 cede 1,000 sq km of Pamir Mountain range to China in return for China relinquishing claims to 28,000 sq km of Tajikistani lands but neither state has published maps of ceded areas and demarcation has not yet commenced; talks continue with Uzbekistan to delimit border and remove minefields; disputes in Isfara Valley delay delimitation with Kyrgyzstan
Illicit drugs: major transit country for Afghan narcotics bound for Russian and, to a lesser extent, Western European markets; limited illicit cultivation of opium poppy for domestic consumption; Tajikistan seizes roughly 80 percent of all drugs captured in Central Asia and stands third worldwide in seizures of opiates (heroin and raw opium)

TANZANIA

INTRODUCTION

Background: Shortly after independence, Tanganyika and Zanzibar merged to form the nation of Tanzania in 1964. One-party rule came to an end in 1995 with the first democratic elections held in the country since the 1970s. Zanzibar's semi-autonomous status and popular opposition have led to two contentious elections since 1995, which the ruling party won despite international observers' claims of voting irregularities.

GEOGRAPHY

Location: Eastern Africa, bordering the Indian Ocean, between Kenya and Mozambique

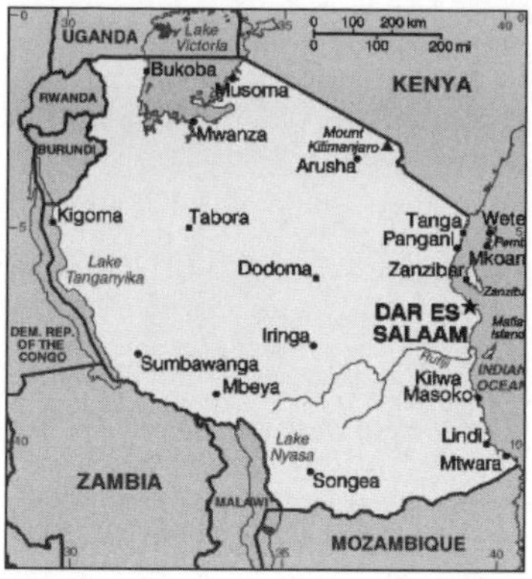

Geographic coordinates: 6 00 S, 35 00 E
Map references: Africa
Area:
total: 945,087 sq km
land: 886,037 sq km
water: 59,050 sq km
note: includes the islands of Mafia, Pemba, and Zanzibar
Area - comparative: slightly larger than twice the size of California
Land boundaries:
total: 3,861 km
border countries: Burundi 451 km, Democratic Republic of the Congo 459 km, Kenya 769 km, Malawi 475 km, Mozambique 756 km, Rwanda 217 km, Uganda 396 km, Zambia 338 km
Coastline: 1,424 km
Maritime claims:
territorial sea: 12 nm
exclusive economic zone: 200 nm
Climate: varies from tropical along coast to temperate in highlands
Terrain: plains along coast; central plateau; highlands in north, south
Elevation extremes:
lowest point: Indian Ocean 0 m
highest point: Kilimanjaro 5,895 m
Natural resources: hydropower, tin, phosphates, iron ore, coal, diamonds, gemstones, gold, natural gas, nickel
Land use:
arable land: 4.52%
permanent crops: 1.08%
other: 94.4% (2001)
Irrigated land: 1,550 sq km (1998 est.)
Natural hazards: flooding on the central plateau during the rainy season; drought
Environment - current issues: soil degradation; deforestation; desertification; destruction of coral reefs threatens marine habitats; recent droughts affected marginal agriculture; wildlife threatened by illegal hunting and trade, especially for ivory
Environment - international agreements:
party to: Biodiversity, Climate Change, Climate Change-Kyoto Protocol, Desertification, Endangered Species, Hazardous Wastes, Law of the Sea, Ozone Layer Protection, Wetlands
signed, but not ratified: none of the selected agreements
Geography - note: Kilimanjaro is highest point in Africa; bordered by three of the largest lakes on the continent: Lake Victoria (the world's second-largest freshwater lake) in the north, Lake Tanganyika (the world's second deepest) in the west, and Lake Nyasa in the southwest

PEOPLE

Population: 36,766,356
note: estimates for this country explicitly take into account the effects of excess mortality due to AIDS; this can result in lower life expectancy, higher infant mortality and death rates, lower population and growth rates, and changes in the distribution of population by age and sex than would otherwise be expected (July 2005 est.)
Age structure:
0-14 years: 44% (male 8,100,216/ female 8,074,171)
15-64 years: 53.4% (male 9,665,957/ female 9,963,772)
65 years and over: 2.6% (male 418,080/female 544,160) (2005 est.)
Median age:
total: 17.62 years
male: 17.36 years
female: 17.89 years (2005 est.)
Population growth rate: 1.83% (2005 est.)
Birth rate: 38.16 births/1,000 population (2005 est.)
Death rate: 16.71 deaths/1,000 population (2005 est.)
Net migration rate: -3.11 migrant(s)/ 1,000 population (2005 est.)
Sex ratio:
at birth: 1.03 male(s)/female
under 15 years: 1 male(s)/female
15-64 years: 0.97 male(s)/female
65 years and over: 0.77 male(s)/female
total population: 0.98 male(s)/ female (2005 est.)
Infant mortality rate:
total: 98.54 deaths/1,000 live births
male: 107.85 deaths/1,000 live births
female: 88.95 deaths/1,000 live births (2005 est.)
Life expectancy at birth:
total population: 45.24 years
male: 44.56 years
female: 45.94 years (2005 est.)
Total fertility rate: 5.06 children born/ woman (2005 est.)
HIV/AIDS - adult prevalence rate: 8.8% (2003 est.)
HIV/AIDS - people living with HIV/AIDS: 1.6 million (2003 est.)
HIV/AIDS - deaths: 160,000 (2003 est.)
Major infectious diseases:
degree of risk: very high
food or waterborne diseases: bacterial diarrhea, hepatitis A, and typhoid fever
vectorborne diseases: malaria, Rift Valley fever and plague are high risks in some locations
water contact disease: schistosomiasis (2004)
Nationality:
noun: Tanzanian(s)
adjective: Tanzanian
Ethnic groups: mainland - native African 99% (of which 95% are Bantu consisting of more than 130 tribes), other 1% (consisting of Asian, European, and Arab); Zanzibar - Arab, native African, mixed Arab and native African
Religions: mainland - Christian 30%, Muslim 35%, indigenous beliefs 35%; Zanzibar - more than 99% Muslim
Languages: Kiswahili or Swahili (official), Kiunguja (name for Swahili in Zanzibar), English (official, primary language of commerce, administration, and higher education), Arabic (widely spoken in Zanzibar), many local languages
note: Kiswahili (Swahili) is the mother tongue of the Bantu people living in Zanzibar and nearby coastal Tanzania; although Kiswahili is Bantu in structure and origin, its vocabulary draws on a variety of sources, including Arabic and English, and it has become the lingua franca of central and eastern Africa; the first language of most people is one of the local languages
Literacy:
definition: age 15 and over can read and write Kiswahili (Swahili), English, or Arabic
total population: 78.2%
male: 85.9%
female: 70.7% (2003 est.)

GOVERNMENT

Country name:
conventional long form: United Republic of Tanzania
conventional short form: Tanzania
former: United Republic of Tanganyika and Zanzibar
Government type: republic
Capital: Dar es Salaam; note - legislative offices have been transferred to Dodoma, which is planned as the new national capital; the National Assembly now meets there on regular basis
Administrative divisions: 26 regions; Arusha, Dar es Salaam, Dodoma, Iringa, Kagera, Kigoma, Kilimanjaro, Lindi, Manyara, Mara, Mbeya, Morogoro, Mtwara, Mwanza, Pemba North, Pemba South, Pwani, Rukwa, Ruvuma, Shinyanga, Singida, Tabora, Tanga, Zanzibar Central/South, Zanzibar North, Zanzibar Urban/West

Independence: 26 April 1964; Tanganyika became independent 9 December 1961 (from UK-administered UN trusteeship); Zanzibar became independent 19 December 1963 (from UK); Tanganyika united with Zanzibar 26 April 1964 to form the United Republic of Tanganyika and Zanzibar; renamed United Republic of Tanzania 29 October 1964
National holiday: Union Day (Tanganyika and Zanzibar), 26 April (1964)
Constitution: 25 April 1977; major revisions October 1984
Legal system: based on English common law; judicial review of legislative acts limited to matters of interpretation; has not accepted compulsory ICJ jurisdiction
Suffrage: 18 years of age; universal
Executive branch:
chief of state: President Jakaya KIKWETE (since 21 December 2005); Vice President Dr. Ali Mohammed SHEIN (since 5 July 2001); note - the president is both chief of state and head of government
head of government: President Jakaya KIKWETE (since 21 December 2005); Vice President Dr. Ali Mohammed SHEIN (since 5 July 2001); note - the president is both chief of state and head of government
note: Zanzibar elects a president who is head of government for matters internal to Zanzibar; Amani Abeid KARUME was elected to that reelected to that office on 30 October 2005
cabinet: Cabinet ministers, including the prime minister, are appointed by the president from among the members of the National Assembly
elections: president and vice president elected on the same ballot by popular vote for five-year terms; election last held 14 December 2005(next to be held NA December 2010); prime minister appointed by the president
election results: Jakaya KIKWETE elected president; percent of vote - Jakaya KIKWETE 80.3%, Ibrahim LIPUMBA 11.7%, Freeman MBOWE 5.9%
Legislative branch: unicameral National Assembly or Bunge (274 seats - 232 elected by popular vote, 37 allocated to women nominated by the president, five to members of the Zanzibar House of Representatives; members serve five-year terms); note - in addition to enacting laws that apply to the entire United Republic of Tanzania, the Assembly enacts laws that apply only to the mainland; Zanzibar has its own House of Representatives to make laws especially for Zanzibar (the Zanzibar House of Representatives has 50 seats, directly elected by universal suffrage to serve five-year terms)
elections: last held 14 December 2005 (next to be held NA December 2010)
election results: National Assembly - percent of vote by party - NA%; seats by party - CCM 206, CUF 19, CHADEMA 5, other 2, and 37 women appointed by the president, and Zanzibar representatives 5; Zanzibar House of Representatives - percent of vote by party - NA%; seats by party - CCM 30, CUF 19; 1 seat was nullified with a rerun to take place soon
Judicial branch: Permanent Commission of Enquiry (official ombudsman); Court of Appeal (consists of a chief justice and four judges); High Court (consists of a Jaji Kiongozi and 29 judges appointed by the president; holds regular sessions in all regions); District Courts; Primary Courts (limited jurisdiction and appeals can be made to the higher courts)
Political parties and leaders: Chama Cha Demokrasia na Maendeleo (Party of Democracy and Development) or CHADEMA [Bob MAKANI]; Chama Cha Mapinduzi or CCM (Revolutionary Party) [Benjamin William MKAPA]; Civic United Front or CUF [Ibrahim LIPUMBA]; Democratic Party (unregistered) [Christopher MTIKLA]; Tanzania Labor Party or TLP [Augustine Lyatonga MREME]; United Democratic Party or UDP [John CHEYO]
Political pressure groups and leaders: NA
International organization participation: ACP, AfDB, AU, C, EADB, FAO, G- 6, G-77, IAEA, IBRD, ICAO, ICC, ICCt, ICFTU, ICRM, IDA, IFAD, IFC, IFRCS, ILO, IMF, IMO, Interpol, IOC, IOM, ISO, ITU, MIGA, NAM, OPCW, SADC, UN, UN Security Council (temporary), UNAMSIL, UNCTAD, UNESCO, UNHCR, UNIDO, UNMEE, UPU, WCO, WFTU, WHO, WIPO, WMO, WToO, WTO
Diplomatic representation in the US:
chief of mission: Ambassador Andrew Mhando DARAJA
chancery: 2139 R Street NW, Washington, DC 20008
telephone: [1] (202) 939-6125
FAX: [1] (202) 797-7408
Diplomatic representation from the US:
chief of mission: Ambassador Robert V. ROYALL
embassy: 140 Msese Road, Kinondoni District, Dar es Salaam
mailing address: P. O. Box 9123, Dar es Salaam
telephone: [255] (22) 2666-010 through 2666-015
FAX: [255] (22) 2666-701, 2668-501
Flag description: divided diagonally by a yellow-edged black band from the lower hoist-side corner; the upper triangle (hoist side) is green and the lower triangle is blue

ECONOMY

Economy - overview: Tanzania is one of the poorest countries in the world. The economy depends heavily on agriculture, which accounts for almost half of GDP, provides 85% of exports, and employs 80% of the work force. Topography and climatic conditions, however, limit cultivated crops to only 4% of the land area. Industry traditionally featured the processing of agricultural products and light consumer goods. The World Bank, the International Monetary Fund, and bilateral donors have provided funds to rehabilitate Tanzania's out-of-date economic infrastructure and to alleviate poverty. Long-term growth through 2005 featured a pickup in industrial production and a substantial increase in output of minerals, led by gold. Recent banking reforms have helped increase private sector growth and investment. Continued donor assistance and solid macroeconomic policies supported real GDP growth of more than 6% in 2005.
GDP (purchasing power parity): $26.62 billion (2005 est.)
GDP (official exchange rate): $11.83 billion (2005 est.)
GDP - real growth rate: 6.1% (2005 est.)
GDP - per capita: purchasing power parity - $700 (2005 est.)
GDP - composition by sector:
agriculture: 43.2%
industry: 17.2%
services: 39.6% (2004 est.)
Labor force: 19.22 million (2005 est.)
Labor force - by occupation: agriculture 80%, industry and services 20% (2002 est.)
Unemployment rate: NA
Population below poverty line: 36% (2002 est.)
Household income or consumption by percentage share:
lowest 10%: 2.8%
highest 10%: 30.1% (1993)
Distribution of family income - Gini index: 38.2 (1993)
Inflation rate (consumer prices): 4% (2005 est.)
Investment (gross fixed): 19.5% of GDP (2005 est.)
Budget:
revenues: $2.235 billion
expenditures: $2.669 billion, including capital expenditures of NA (2005 est.)
Public debt: 5% of GDP (2005 est.)
Agriculture - products: coffee, sisal, tea, cotton, pyrethrum (insecticide made from chrysanthemums), cashew nuts, tobacco, cloves, corn, wheat, cassava (tapioca), bananas, fruits, vegetables; cattle, sheep, goats

Industries: agricultural processing (sugar, beer, cigarettes, sisal twine), diamond, gold and iron mining, soda ash, oil refining, shoes, cement, apparel, wood products, fertilizer, salt
Industrial production growth rate: 8.4% (1999 est.)
Electricity - production: 3.152 billion kWh (2003)
Electricity - production by source:
fossil fuel: 18.9%
hydro: 81.1%
nuclear: 0%
other: 0% (2001)
Electricity - consumption: 2.959 billion kWh (2003)
Electricity - exports: 0 kWh (2003)
Electricity - imports: 28 million kWh (2003)
Oil - production: 0 bbl/day (2003 est.)
Oil - consumption: 22,000 bbl/day (2003 est.)
Oil - exports: NA (2001)
Oil - imports: NA (2001)
Oil - proved reserves: 0 bbl (1 January 2002)
Natural gas - proved reserves: 11.33 billion cu m (1 January 2002)
Current account balance: $-508 million (2005 est.)
Exports: $1.581 billion f.o.b. (2005 est.)
Exports - partners: India 8.9%, Spain 8.2%, Netherlands 6.3%, Japan 5.7%, UK 4.9%, China 4.7%, Kenya 4.7% (2004)
Imports: $2.391 billion f.o.b. (2005 est.)
Imports - partners: South Africa 12.7%, China 7.8%, India 6.4%, Kenya 5.4%, UAE 5.3%, US 4.8%, UK 4.6%, Zambia 4% (2004)
Reserves of foreign exchange and gold: $2.335 billion (2005 est.)
Debt - external: $7.95 billion (2005 est.)
Economic aid - recipient: $1.2 billion (2001)
Currency (code): Tanzanian shilling (TZS)
Currency code: TZS
Exchange rates: Tanzanian shillings per US dollar - 1,123.2 (2005), 1,089.33 (2004), 1,038.42 (2003), 966.58 (2002), 876.41 (2001)
Fiscal year: 1 July - 30 June

COMMUNICATIONS

Telephones - main lines in use: 149,100 (2003)
Telephones - mobile cellular: 891,200 (2003)
Telephone system:
general assessment: fair system operating below capacity and being modernized for better service; VSAT (very small aperture terminal) system under construction
domestic: trunk service provided by open-wire, microwave radio relay, tropospheric scatter, and fiber-optic cable; some links being made digital
international: country code - 255; satellite earth stations - 2 Intelsat (1 Indian Ocean and 1 Atlantic Ocean)
Radio broadcast stations: AM 12, FM 11, shortwave 2 (1998)
Radios: 8.8 million (1997)
Television broadcast stations: 3 (1999)
Televisions: 103,000 (1997)
Internet country code: .tz
Internet hosts: 5,534 (2003)
Internet Service Providers (ISPs): 6 (2000)
Internet users: 250,000 (2003)

TRANSPORTATION

Airports: 123 (2004 est.)
Airports - with paved runways:
total: 11
over 3,047 m: 2
2,438 to 3,047 m: 2
1,524 to 2,437 m: 5
914 to 1,523 m: 1
under 914 m: 1 (2005 est.)
Airports - with unpaved runways:
total: 112
1,524 to 2,437 m: 18
914 to 1,523 m: 61
under 914 m: 33 (2005 est.)
Pipelines: gas 29 km; oil 866 km (2004)
Railways:
total: 3,690 km
narrow gauge: 969 km 1.067-m gauge; 2,721 km 1.000-m gauge (2004)
Roadways:
total: 88,200 km
paved: 3,704 km
unpaved: 84,496 km (1999 est.)
Waterways: Lake Tanganyika, Lake Victoria, and Lake Nyasa principal avenues of commerce with neighboring countries; rivers not navigable (2004)
Merchant marine:
total: 11 ships (1,000 GRT or over) 25,481 GRT/31,011 DWT
by type: cargo 2, passenger/cargo 5, petroleum tanker 4
registered in other countries: 1 (2005)
Ports and terminals: Dar es Salaam, Mtwara, Zanzibar City

MILITARY

Military branches: Tanzanian People's Defense Force (JWTZ): Army, Naval Wing, Air Defense Command (includes Air Wing), National Service
Military service age and obligation: 15 years of age for voluntary military service; 18 years of age for compulsory military service upon graduation from secondary school; conscript service obligation - 2 years (2004)
Manpower available for military service: *males age 18-49:* 7,422,869 (2005 est.)
Manpower fit for military service: *males age 18-49:* 3,879,630 (2005 est.)
Military expenditures - dollar figure: $20.6 million (2004)
Military expenditures - percent of GDP: 0.2% (2004)

TRANSNATIONAL ISSUES

Disputes - international: disputes with Malawi over the boundary in Lake Nyasa (Lake Malawi) and the meandering Songwe River remain dormant
Refugees and internally displaced persons: *refugees (country of origin):* 447,877 (Burundi) 153,155 (Democratic Republic of the Congo) 3,036 (Somalia) (2004)
Illicit drugs: growing role in transshipment of Southwest and Southeast Asian heroin and South American cocaine destined for South African, European, and US markets and of South Asian methaqualone bound for southern Africa; money laundering remains a problem

THAILAND

INTRODUCTION

Background: A unified Thai kingdom was established in the mid-14th century. Known as Siam until 1939, Thailand is the only Southeast Asian country never to have been taken over by a European power. A bloodless revolution in 1932 led to a constitutional monarchy. In alliance with Japan during World War II, Thailand became a US ally following the conflict. Thailand is currently facing armed violence in its three Muslim-majority southernmost provinces.

GEOGRAPHY

Location: Southeastern Asia, bordering the Andaman Sea and the Gulf of Thailand, southeast of Burma
Geographic coordinates: 15 00 N, 100 00 E
Map references: Southeast Asia
Area:
total: 514,000 sq km
land: 511,770 sq km
water: 2,230 sq km
Area - comparative: slightly more than twice the size of Wyoming

Land boundaries:
total: 4,863 km
border countries: Burma 1,800 km, Cambodia 803 km, Laos 1,754 km, Malaysia 506 km
Coastline: 3,219 km
Maritime claims:
territorial sea: 12 nm
exclusive economic zone: 200 nm
continental shelf: 200-m depth or to the depth of exploitation
Climate: tropical; rainy, warm, cloudy southwest monsoon (mid-May to September); dry, cool northeast monsoon (November to mid-March); southern isthmus always hot and humid
Terrain: central plain; Khorat Plateau in the east; mountains elsewhere
Elevation extremes:
lowest point: Gulf of Thailand 0 m
highest point: Doi Inthanon 2,576 m
Natural resources: tin, rubber, natural gas, tungsten, tantalum, timber, lead, fish, gypsum, lignite, fluorite, arable land
Land use:
arable land: 29.36%
permanent crops: 6.46%
other: 64.18% (2001)
Irrigated land: 47,490 sq km (1998 est.)
Natural hazards: land subsidence in Bangkok area resulting from the depletion of the water table; droughts
Environment - current issues: air pollution from vehicle emissions; water pollution from organic and factory wastes; deforestation; soil erosion; wildlife populations threatened by illegal hunting
Environment - international agreements:
party to: Biodiversity, Climate Change, Climate Change-Kyoto Protocol, Desertification, Endangered Species, Hazardous Wastes, Marine Life Conservation, Ozone Layer Protection, Tropical Timber 83, Tropical Timber 94, Wetlands
signed, but not ratified: Law of the Sea
Geography - note: controls only land route from Asia to Malaysia and Singapore

PEOPLE

Population: 65,444,371
note: estimates for this country explicitly take into account the effects of excess mortality due to AIDS; this can result in lower life expectancy, higher infant mortality and death rates, lower population and growth rates, and changes in the distribution of population by age and sex than would otherwise be expected (July 2005 est.)
Age structure:
0-14 years: 23.9% (male 7,988,529/female 7,633,405)
15-64 years: 68.6% (male 22,195,625/ female 22,731,767)
65 years and over: 7.5% (male 2,251,112/ female 2,643,933) (2005 est.)
Median age:
total: 30.88 years
male: 30.11 years
female: 31.66 years (2005 est.)
Population growth rate: 0.87% (2005 est.)
Birth rate: 15.7 births/1,000 population (2005 est.)
Death rate: 7.02 deaths/1,000 population (2005 est.)
Net migration rate: 0 migrant(s)/ 1,000 population (2005 est.)
Sex ratio:
at birth: 1.05 male(s)/female
under 15 years: 1.05 male(s)/ female
15-64 years: 0.98 male(s)/female
65 years and over: 0.85 male(s)/ female
total population: 0.98 male(s)/female (2005 est.)
Infant mortality rate:
total: 20.48 deaths/1,000 live births
male: 21.83 deaths/1,000 live births
female: 19.06 deaths/1,000 live births (2005 est.)
Life expectancy at birth:
total population: 71.95 years
male: 69.65 years
female: 74.37 years (2005 est.)
Total fertility rate: 1.88 children born/woman (2005 est.)
HIV/AIDS - adult prevalence rate: 1.5% (2003 est.)
HIV/AIDS - people living with HIV/AIDS: 570,000 (2003 est.)
HIV/AIDS - deaths: 58,000 (2003 est.)
Major infectious diseases:
degree of risk: high
food or waterborne diseases: bacterial diarrhea and hepatitis A
vectorborne diseases: dengue fever, malaria, Japanese encephalitis, and plague are high risks in some locations
animal contact disease: rabies
water contact disease: leptospirosis
note: at present, H5N1 avian influenza poses a minimal risk; during outbreaks among birds, rare cases could occur among US personnel who have close contact with infected birds or poultry (2005)
Nationality:
noun: Thai (singular and plural)
adjective: Thai
Ethnic groups: Thai 75%, Chinese 14%, other 11%
Religions: Buddhist 94.6%, Muslim 4.6%, Christian 0.7%, other 0.1% (2000 census)
Languages: Thai, English (secondary language of the elite), ethnic and regional dialects
Literacy:
definition: age 15 and over can read and write
total population: 92.6%
male: 94.9%
female: 90.5% (2002)

GOVERNMENT

Country name:
conventional long form: Kingdom of Thailand
conventional short form: Thailand
former: Siam
Government type: constitutional monarchy
Capital: Bangkok
Administrative divisions: 76 provinces (changwat, singular and plural); Amnat Charoen, Ang Thong, Buriram, Chachoengsao, Chai Nat, Chaiyaphum, Chanthaburi, Chiang Mai, Chiang Rai, Chon Buri, Chumphon, Kalasin, Kamphaeng Phet, Kanchanaburi, Khon Kaen, Krabi, Krung Thep Mahanakhon (Bangkok), Lampang, Lamphun, Loei, Lop Buri, Mae Hong Son, Maha Sarakham, Mukdahan, Nakhon Nayok, Nakhon Pathom, Nakhon Phanom, Nakhon Ratchasima, Nakhon Sawan, Nakhon Si Thammarat, Nan, Narathiwat, Nong Bua Lamphu, Nong Khai, Nonthaburi, Pathum Thani, Pattani, Phangnga, Phatthalung, Phayao, Phetchabun, Phetchaburi, Phichit, Phitsanulok, Phra Nakhon Si Ayutthaya, Phrae, Phuket, Prachin Buri, Prachuap Khiri Khan, Ranong, Ratchaburi,

Rayong, Roi Et, Sa Kaeo, Sakon Nakhon, Samut Prakan, Samut Sakhon, Samut Songkhram, Sara Buri, Satun, Sing Buri, Sisaket, Songkhla, Sukhothai, Suphan Buri, Surat Thani, Surin, Tak, Trang, Trat, Ubon Ratchathani, Udon Thani, Uthai Thani, Uttaradit, Yala, Yasothon
Independence: 1238 (traditional founding date; never colonized)
National holiday: Birthday of King PHUMIPHON, 5 December (1927)
Constitution: new constitution signed by King PHUMIPHON on 11 October 1997
Legal system: based on civil law system, with influences of common law; has not accepted compulsory ICJ jurisdiction
Suffrage: 18 years of age; universal and compulsory
Executive branch:
chief of state: King PHUMIPHON Adunyadet (since 9 June 1946)
head of government: Prime Minister THAKSIN Chinnawat (since 9 February 2001) and Deputy Prime Ministers CHITCHAI Wannasathi (since 11 March 2005), SOMKHIT Chatusiphithak (since 11 March 2005), SUCHAI Charoenrattanakhun (since 31 October 2005), SURAKIAT Sathianthai (since 11 March 2005); SURIYA Chungrungruankit (since 2 August 2005), SUWAT Liptapanlop (since 2 August 2005), WISANU Kruangam (since 3 November 2002)
cabinet: Council of Ministers
note: there is also a Privy Council
elections: none; the monarch is hereditary; prime minister is designated from among the members of the House of Representatives; following national elections for the House of Representatives, the leader of the party that can organize a majority coalition usually is appointed prime minister by the king
Legislative branch: bicameral National Assembly or Rathasapha consists of the Senate or Wuthisapha (200 seats; members elected by popular vote to serve six-year terms) and the House of Representatives or Sapha Phuthaen Ratsadon (500 seats; members elected by popular vote to serve four-year terms)
elections: Senate - last held 4 March, 29 April, 4 June, 9 July, and 22 July 2000 (next to be held by March 2006); House of Representatives - last held 6 February 2005 (next to be held in February 2009)
election results: Senate - percent of vote by party - NA; seats by party - NA; House of Representatives - percent of vote by party - NA; seats by party - TRT 376, DP 97, TNP 25, PP 2
Judicial branch: Supreme Court or Sandika (judges appointed by the monarch)
Political parties and leaders: Democrat Party or DP (Prachathipat Party) [ABHISIT Wetchachiwa]; People's Party or PP (Mahachon Party) [ANEK Laothamatas]; Thai Nation Party or TNP (Chat Thai Party) [BARNHARN SILPA-ARCHA]; Thai Rak Thai Party or TRT [THAKSIN Chinnawat]
Political pressure groups and leaders: NA
International organization participation: APEC, APT, ARF, AsDB, ASEAN, BIS, CP, EAS, FAO, G-77, IAEA, IBRD, ICAO, ICC, ICCt (signatory), ICFTU, ICRM, IDA, IFAD, IFC, IFRCS, IHO, ILO, IMF, IMO, Interpol, IOC, IOM, ISO, ITU, MIGA, NAM, OAS (observer), OIC (observer), ONUB, OPCW, OSCE (partner), PCA, UN, UNAMSIL, UNCTAD, UNESCO, UNHCR, UNIDO, UPU, WCL, WCO, WFTU, WHO, WIPO, WMO, WToO, WTO
Diplomatic representation in the US:
chief of mission: KASIT Piromya
chancery: 1024 Wisconsin Avenue NW, Suite 401, Washington, DC 20007-3681
telephone: [1] (202) 944-3600
FAX: [1] (202) 944-3611
consulate(s) general: Chicago, Los Angeles, and New York
Diplomatic representation from the US:
chief of mission: Ambassador Ralph L. BOYCE
embassy: 120-122 Wireless Road, Bangkok 10330
mailing address: APO AP 96546
telephone: [66] (2) 205-4000
FAX: [66] (2) 254-2990, 205-4131
consulate(s) general: Chiang Mai
Flag description: five horizontal bands of red (top), white, blue (double width), white, and red

ECONOMY

Economy - overview: With a well-developed infrastructure, a free-enterprise economy, and pro-investment policies, Thailand appears to have fully recovered from the 1997-98 Asian Financial Crisis. The country was one of East Asia's best performers in 2002-04. Boosted by increased consumption, high investment spending, and strong export growth the Thai economy grew 6.9% in 2003 and 6.1% in 2004 despite a sluggish global economy. Bangkok has pursued preferential trade agreements with a variety of partners in an effort to boost exports and to maintain high growth. In 2004 Thailand and the United States began negotiations on a Free Trade Agreement. In late December 2004, a major tsunami took 8,500 lives in Thailand and caused massive destruction of property in the southern provinces of Krabi, Phangnga, and Phuket. Growth slowed to 4.6% in 2005. The downturn can be attributed to high oil prices, weaker demand from Western markets, severe drought in rural regions, tsunami-related declines in tourism, and lower consumer confidence. Moreover, the THAKSIN administration's expansionist economic policies, including multi-billion-dollar mega-projects in infrastructure and social development, has raised concerns about fiscal discipline and the health of financial institutions. On the positive side, the Thai economy performed well beginning in the third quarter of 2005. Export-oriented manufacturing - in particular automobile production - and farm output are driving these gains. In 2006 the economy should benefit from an influx of investment and stronger private consumption, however, a possible avian flu epidemic could significantly harm economic prospects throughout the region.
GDP (purchasing power parity): $545.8 billion (2005 est.)
GDP (official exchange rate): $180.9 billion (2005 est.)
GDP - real growth rate: 4.6% (2005 est.)
GDP - per capita: purchasing power parity - $8,300 (2005 est.)
GDP - composition by sector:
agriculture: 9.3%
industry: 45.1%
services: 45.6% (2005 est.)
Labor force: 35.36 million (2005 est.)
Labor force - by occupation: agriculture 49%, industry 14%, services 37% (2000 est.)
Unemployment rate: 1.4% (September 2005)
Population below poverty line: 10% (2004 est.)
Household income or consumption by percentage share:
lowest 10%: 2.8%
highest 10%: 32.4% (1998)
Distribution of family income - Gini index: 51.1 (2002)
Inflation rate (consumer prices): 4.8% (2005 est.)
Investment (gross fixed): 31.7% of GDP (2005 est.)
Budget: *revenues:* $30.64 billion
expenditures: $31.76 billion, including capital expenditures of $5 billion (2005 est.)
Public debt: 35.9% of GDP (2005 est.)
Agriculture - products: rice, cassava (tapioca), rubber, corn, sugarcane, coconuts, soybeans
Industries: tourism, textiles and garments, agricultural processing, beverages, tobacco, cement, light manufacturing such as jewelry, electric appliances and components, computers and parts, inte-

grated circuits, furniture, plastics, automobiles and automotive parts, world's second-largest tungsten producer, and third-largest tin producer
Industrial production growth rate: 8.2% (2005 est.)
Electricity - production: 114.7 billion kWh (2003)
Electricity - production by source:
fossil fuel: 91.3%
hydro: 6.4%
nuclear: 0%
other: 2.4% (2001)
Electricity - consumption: 107.3 billion kWh (2003)
Electricity - exports: 315 million kWh (2003)
Electricity - imports: 980 million kWh (2003)
Oil - production: 230,000 bbl/day (2005 est.)
Oil - consumption: 851,000 bbl/day (2004 est.)
Oil - exports: NA (2001)
Oil - imports: NA (2001)
Oil - proved reserves: 583 million bbl (November 2003)
Natural gas - production: 19.4 billion cu m (2002 est.)
Natural gas - consumption: 25.6 billion cu m (2002 est.)
Natural gas - exports: 0 cu m (2001 est.)
Natural gas - imports: 5.2 billion cu m (2001 est.)
Natural gas - proved reserves: 376.7 billion cu m (November 2003)
Current account balance: $-5.901 billion (2005 est.)
Exports: $105.8 billion f.o.b. (2005 est.)
Exports - partners: US 16.1%, Japan 14%, China 7.4%, Singapore 7.3%, Malaysia 5.5%, Hong Kong 5.1% (2004)
Imports: $107 billion f.o.b. (2005 est.)
Imports - partners: Japan 23.6%, China 8.6%, US 7.7%, Malaysia 5.8%, Singapore 4.4%, Taiwan 4.1%, UAE 4% (2004)
Reserves of foreign exchange and gold: $51.9 billion (December 2005)
Debt - external: $50.63 billion (30 June 2005 est.)
Economic aid - recipient: $72 million (2002)
Currency (code): baht (THB)
Currency code: THB
Exchange rates: baht per US dollar - 40.95 (2005), 40.222 (2004), 41.485 (2003), 42.96 (2002), 44.432 (2001)
Fiscal year: 1 October - 30 September

COMMUNICATIONS

Telephones - main lines in use: 6,617,400 (2003)
Telephones - mobile cellular: 26.5 million (2005)
Telephone system:
general assessment: high quality system, especially in urban areas like Bangkok; WTO requirement for privatization of telecom sector is planned to be complete by 2006
domestic: fixed line system provided by both a government owned and commercial provider; wireless service expanding rapidly and outpacing fixed lines
international: country code - 66; satellite earth stations - 2 Intelsat (1 Indian Ocean and 1 Pacific Ocean); landing country for APCN submarine cable
Radio broadcast stations: AM 204, FM 334, shortwave 6 (1999)
Radios: 13.96 million (1997)
Television broadcast stations: 5 (all in Bangkok; plus 131 repeaters) (1997)
Televisions: 15.19 million (1997)
Internet country code: .th
Internet hosts: 103,700 (2003)
Internet Service Providers (ISPs): 15 (2000)
Internet users: 6,971,500 (2003)

TRANSPORTATION

Airports: 109 (2004 est.)
Airports - with paved runways:
total: 65
over 3,047 m: 7
2,438 to 3,047 m: 10
1,524 to 2,437 m: 24
914 to 1,523 m: 19
under 914 m: 5 (2005 est.)
Airports - with unpaved runways:
total: 43
over 3,047 m: 1
1,524 to 2,437 m: 1
914 to 1,523 m: 15
under 914 m: 26 (2005 est.)
Heliports: 3 (2005 est.)
Pipelines: gas 3,112 km; refined products 265 km (2004)
Railways:
total: 4,071 km
narrow gauge: 4,071 km 1.000-m gauge (2004)
Roadways:
total: 57,403 km
paved: 56,542 km
unpaved: 861 km (2000 est.)
Waterways: 4,000 km
note: 3,701 km navigable by boats with drafts up to 0.9 m (2003)
Merchant marine:
total: 386 ships (1,000 GRT or over) 2,038,597 GRT/3,104,712 DWT
by type: bulk carrier 57, cargo 142, chemical tanker 12, combination ore/oil 1, container 21, liquefied gas 25, passenger 3, passenger/cargo 4, petroleum tanker 89, refrigerated cargo 30, roll on/roll off 1, specialized tanker 1
foreign-owned: 55 (Indonesia 1, Japan 3, Norway 45, Singapore 6)
registered in other countries: 35 (2005)
Ports and terminals: Bangkok, Laem Chabang, Prachuap Port, Si Racha

MILITARY

Military branches: Royal Thai Army, Royal Thai Navy (includes Royal Thai Marine Corps), Royal Thai Air Force
Military service age and obligation: 21 years of age for compulsory military service; males are registered at 18 years of age; conscript service obligation - 2 years; 18 years of age for voluntary military service (2004)
Manpower available for military service: *males age 21-49:* 14.984 million (2005 est.)
Manpower fit for military service: *males age 21-49:* 10,342,337 (2005 est.)
Manpower reaching military service age annually: *males:* 530,493 (2005 est.)
Military expenditures - dollar figure: $1.775 billion (FY00)
Military expenditures - percent of GDP: 1.8% (2003)

TRANSNATIONAL ISSUES

Disputes - international: separatist violence in Thailand's predominantly Muslim southern provinces prompt border closures and controls with Malaysia to stem terrorist activities; southeast Asian states have enhanced border surveillance to check the spread of avian flu; Laos and Thailand pledge to complete demarcation of their boundary in 2005; despite continuing border committee talks, significant differences remain with Burma over boundary alignment and the handling of ethnic rebels, refugees, and illegal cross-border activities; Cambodia and Thailand dispute sections of boundary with missing boundary markers; Cambodia claims Thai encroachments into Cambodian territory and obstructing access to Preah Vihear temple ruins awarded to Cambodia by ICJ decision in 1962; ethnic Karens from Burma flee into Thailand to escape fighting between Karen rebels and Burmese troops resulting in Thailand sheltering about 118,000 Burmese refugees in 2004; Karens also protest Thai support for a Burmese hydroelectric dam construction on the Salween River near the border; environmentalists in Burma and Thailand remain concerned about China's construction of hydroelectric dams upstream on the Nujiang/Salween River in Yunnan Province
Refugees and internally displaced persons:
refugees (country of origin): 118,407 (Burma) (2004)
Illicit drugs: a minor producer of opium, heroin, and marijuana; illicit transit point for heroin en route to the international

drug market from Burma and Laos; eradication efforts have reduced the area of cannabis cultivation and shifted some production to neighboring countries; opium poppy cultivation has been reduced by eradication efforts; also a drug money-laundering center; minor role in amphetamine production for regional consumption; increasing indigenous abuse of methamphetamine

TOGO

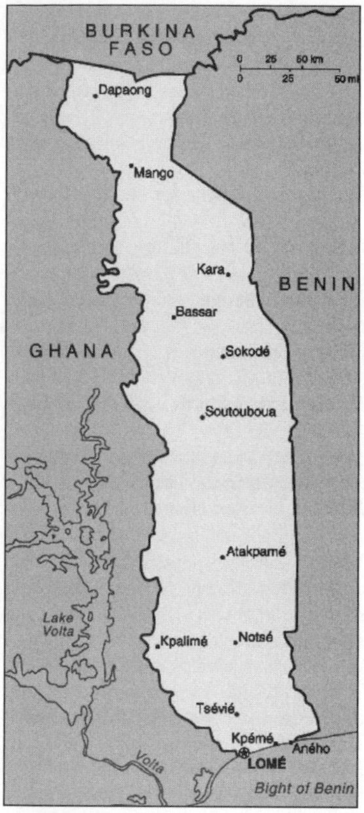

INTRODUCTION

Background: French Togoland became Togo in 1960. Gen. Gnassingbe EYADEMA, installed as military ruler in 1967, continued to rule well into the 21st century. Despite the facade of multiparty elections instituted in the early 1990s, the government continued to be dominated by President EYADEMA, whose Rally of the Togolese People (RPT) party maintained power almost continually since 1967. Togo has come under fire from international organizations for human rights abuses and is plagued by political unrest. While most bilateral and multilateral aid to Togo remains frozen, the European Union initiated a partial resumption of cooperation and development aid to Togo in late 2004 based upon commitments by Togo to expand opportunities for political opposition and liberalize portions of the economy. Upon his death in February 2005, President EYADEMA was succeeded by his son Faure GNASSINGBE. The succession, supported by the military and in contravention of the nation's constitution, was challenged by popular protest and a threat of sanctions from regional leaders. GNASSINGBE succumbed to pressure and agreed to hold elections in late April 2005.

GEOGRAPHY

Location: Western Africa, bordering the Bight of Benin, between Benin and Ghana
Geographic coordinates: 8 00 N, 1 10 E
Map references: Africa
Area:
total: 56,785 sq km
land: 54,385 sq km
water: 2,400 sq km
Area - comparative: slightly smaller than West Virginia
Land boundaries:
total: 1,647 km
border countries: Benin 644 km, Burkina Faso 126 km, Ghana 877 km
Coastline: 56 km
Maritime claims:
territorial sea: 30 nm
exclusive economic zone: 200 nm
Climate: tropical; hot, humid in south; semiarid in north
Terrain: gently rolling savanna in north; central hills; southern plateau; low coastal plain with extensive lagoons and marshes
Elevation extremes:
lowest point: Atlantic Ocean 0 m
highest point: Mont Agou 986 m
Natural resources: phosphates, limestone, marble, arable land
Land use:
arable land: 46.15%
permanent crops: 2.21%
other: 51.64% (2001)
Irrigated land: 70 sq km (1998 est.)
Natural hazards: hot, dry harmattan wind can reduce visibility in north during winter; periodic droughts
Environment - current issues: deforestation attributable to slash-and-burn agriculture and the use of wood for fuel; water pollution presents health hazards and hinders the fishing industry; air pollution increasing in urban areas
Environment - international agreements:
party to: Biodiversity, Climate Change, Climate Change-Kyoto Protocol, Desertification, Endangered Species, Law of the Sea, Ozone Layer Protection, Ship Pollution, Tropical Timber 83, Tropical Timber 94, Wetlands
signed, but not ratified: none of the selected agreements
Geography - note: the country's length allows it to stretch through six distinct geographic regions; climate varies from tropical to savanna

PEOPLE

Population: 5,681,519
note: estimates for this country explicitly take into account the effects of excess mortality due to AIDS; this can result in lower life expectancy, higher infant mortality and death rates, lower population and growth rates, and changes in the distribution of population by age and sex than would otherwise be expected (July 2005 est.)
Age structure:
0-14 years: 43.2% (male 1,232,759/female 1,224,060)
15-64 years: 54.2% (male 1,505,737/ female 1,571,201)
65 years and over: 2.6% (male 60,799/female 86,963) (2005 est.)
Median age:
total: 17.78 years
male: 17.42 years
female: 18.14 years (2005 est.)
Population growth rate: 2.17% (2005 est.)
Birth rate: 33.48 births/1,000 population (2005 est.)
Death rate: 11.8 deaths/1,000 population (2005 est.)
Net migration rate: 0 migrant(s)/ 1,000 population (2005 est.)
Sex ratio:
at birth: 1.03 male(s)/female
under 15 years: 1.01 male(s)/ female
15-64 years: 0.96 male(s)/female
65 years and over: 0.7 male(s)/ female
total population: 0.97 male(s)/ female (2005 est.)
Infant mortality rate:
total: 66.61 deaths/1,000 live births
male: 74.24 deaths/1,000 live births
female: 58.76 deaths/1,000 live births (2005 est.)
Life expectancy at birth:
total population: 57.01 years
male: 55.02 years
female: 59.06 years (2005 est.)
Total fertility rate: 4.61 children born/woman (2005 est.)

HIV/AIDS - adult prevalence rate: 4.1% (2003 est.)
HIV/AIDS - people living with HIV/AIDS: 110,000 (2003 est.)
HIV/AIDS - deaths: 10,000 (2003 est.)
Major infectious diseases:
degree of risk: very high
food or waterborne diseases: bacterial and protozoal diarrhea, hepatitis A, and typhoid fever
vectorborne diseases: malaria and yellow fever are high risks in some locations
water contact disease: schistosomiasis
respiratory disease: meningococcal meningitis (2004)
Nationality:
noun: Togolese (singular and plural)
adjective: Togolese
Ethnic groups: native African (37 tribes; largest and most important are Ewe, Mina, and Kabre) 99%, European and Syrian-Lebanese less than 1%
Religions: indigenous beliefs 51%, Christian 29%, Muslim 20%
Languages: French (official and the language of commerce), Ewe and Mina (the two major African languages in the south), Kabye (sometimes spelled Kabiye) and Dagomba (the two major African languages in the north)
Literacy:
definition: age 15 and over can read and write
total population: 60.9%
male: 75.4%
female: 46.9% (2003 est.)

GOVERNMENT

Country name:
conventional long form: Togolese Republic
conventional short form: Togo
local long form: Republique Togolaise
local short form: none
former: French Togoland
Government type: republic under transition to multiparty democratic rule
Capital: Lome
Administrative divisions: 5 regions (regions, singular - region); Kara, Plateaux, Savanes, Centrale, Maritime
Independence: 27 April 1960 (from French-administered UN trusteeship)
National holiday: Independence Day, 27 April (1960)
Constitution: multiparty draft constitution approved by High Council of the Republic 1 July 1992, adopted by public referendum 27 September 1992
Legal system: French-based court system
Suffrage: NA years of age; universal adult
Executive branch:
chief of state: President Faure GNASSINGBE (since 6 February 2005); note - Gnassingbe EYADEMA died on 5 February 2005 and was succeeded by his son, Faure GNASSINGBE; popular elections in April 2005 validated the succession
head of government: Prime Minister Edem KODJO (since 8 June 2005)
cabinet: Council of Ministers appointed by the president and the prime minister
elections: president elected by popular vote for a five-year term; election last held 24 April 2005 (next to be held NA); prime minister appointed by the president
election results: Faure GNASSINGBE elected president; percent of vote - Faure GNASSINGBE 60.2%, Emmanuel Akitani BOB 38.3%, Nicolas LAWSON 1.0%, Harry OLYMPIO 0.6%
Legislative branch: unicameral National Assembly (81 seats; members are elected by popular vote to serve five-year terms)
elections: last held 27 October 2002 (next to be held NA 2007)
election results: percent of vote by party - NA%; seats by party - RPT 72, RSDD 3, UDPS 2, Juvento 2, MOCEP 1, independents 1
note: two opposition parties boycotted the election, the Union of the Forces for Change, and the Action Committee for Renewal
Judicial branch: Court of Appeal or Cour d'Appel; Supreme Court or Cour Supreme
Political parties and leaders: Juvento [Monsilia DJATO]; Movement of the Believers of Peace and Equality or MOCEP [leader NA]; Rally for the Support for Development and Democracy or RSDD [Harry OLYMPIO]; Rally of the Togolese People or RPT [Faure GNASSINGBE]; Union for Democracy and Social Progress or UDPS [Gagou KOKOU]
note: Rally of the Togolese People or RPT, led by President GNASSINGBE, was the only party until the formation of multiple parties was legalized 12 April 1991
Political pressure groups and leaders: NA
International organization participation: ABEDA, ACCT, ACP, AfDB, AU, CEMAC, ECOWAS, Entente, FAO, FZ, G-77, IBRD, ICAO, ICC, ICFTU, ICRM, IDA, IDB, IFAD, IFC, IFRCS, ILO, IMF, IMO, Interpol, IOC, ISO (correspondent), ITU, MIGA, NAM, OIC, ONUB, OPCW, PCA, UN, UNCTAD, UNESCO, UNIDO, UNMIL, UNOCI, UPU, WADB (regional), WAEMU, WCL, WCO, WFTU, WHO, WIPO, WMO, WToO, WTO
Diplomatic representation in the US:
chief of mission: Ambassador Akoussoulelou BODJONA
chancery: 2208 Massachusetts Avenue NW, Washington, DC 20008
telephone: [1] (202) 234-4212
FAX: [1] (202) 232-3190
Diplomatic representation from the US:
chief of mission: Ambassador Gregory ENGLE
embassy: Angle Rue Kouenou and Rue 15 Beniglato, Lome
mailing address: B. P. 852, Lome
telephone: [228] 221 29 91 through 221 29 94
FAX: [228] 221 79 52
Flag description: five equal horizontal bands of green (top and bottom) alternating with yellow; there is a white five-pointed star on a red square in the upper hoist-side corner; uses the popular pan-African colors of Ethiopia

ECONOMY

Economy - overview: This small sub-Saharan economy is heavily dependent on both commercial and subsistence agriculture, which provides employment for 65% of the labor force. Some basic foodstuffs must still be imported. Cocoa, coffee, and cotton generate about 40% of export earnings, with cotton being the most important cash crop. Togo is the world's fourth-largest producer of phosphate. The government's decade-long effort, supported by the World Bank and the IMF, to implement economic reform measures, encourage foreign investment, and bring revenues in line with expenditures has moved slowly. Progress depends on following through on privatization, increased openness in government financial operations, progress toward legislative elections, and continued support from foreign donors. Togo is working with donors to write a PRGF that could eventually lead to a debt reduction plan.
GDP (purchasing power parity): $9.018 billion (2005 est.)
GDP (official exchange rate): $2.076 billion (2005 est.)
GDP - real growth rate: 2.8% (2005 est.)
GDP - per capita: purchasing power parity - $1,600 (2005 est.)
GDP - composition by sector:
agriculture: 39.5%
industry: 20.4%
services: 40.1% (2003 est.)
Labor force: 1.74 million (1996)
Labor force - by occupation: agriculture 65%, industry 5%, services 30% (1998 est.)
Unemployment rate: NA (2003 est.)
Population below poverty line: 32% (1989 est.)
Household income or consumption by percentage share:
lowest 10%: NA
highest 10%: NA

Inflation rate (consumer prices): 5.5% (2005 est.)
Investment (gross fixed): 21.9% of GDP (2005 est.)
Budget:
revenues: $251.3 million
expenditures: $292.9 million, including capital expenditures of NA (2005 est.)
Agriculture - products: coffee, cocoa, cotton, yams, cassava (tapioca), corn, beans, rice, millet, sorghum; livestock; fish
Industries: phosphate mining, agricultural processing, cement; handicrafts, textiles, beverages
Industrial production growth rate: NA
Electricity - production: 165.9 million kWh (2003)
Electricity - production by source:
fossil fuel: 98.7%
hydro: 1.3%
nuclear: 0%
other: 0% (2001)
Electricity - consumption: 654.3 million kWh (2003)
Electricity - exports: 0 kWh (2003)
Electricity - imports: 500 million kWh; note - electricity supplied by Ghana (2003)
Oil - production: 0 bbl/day (2003 est.)
Oil - consumption: 8,500 bbl/day (2003 est.)
Oil - exports: NA (2001)
Oil - imports: NA (2001)
Current account balance: $-223 million (2005 est.)
Exports: $768 million f.o.b. (2005 est.)
Exports - partners: Burkina Faso 16.3%, Ghana 15%, Benin 9.4%, Mali 7.6%, China 7.4%, India 5.6% (2004)
Imports: $1.047 billion f.o.b. (2005 est.)
Imports - partners: China 25.5%, India 13.3%, France 11.5% (2004)
Reserves of foreign exchange and gold: $331 million (2005 est.)
Debt - external: $2 billion (2005)
Economic aid - recipient: ODA $80 million (2000 est.)
Currency (code): Communaute Financiere Africaine franc (XOF); note - responsible authority is the Central Bank of the West African States
Currency code: XOF
Exchange rates: Communaute Financiere Africaine francs (XOF) per US dollar - 521.74 (2005), 528.29 (2004), 581.2 (2003), 696.99 (2002), 733.04 (2001)
Fiscal year: calendar year

COMMUNICATIONS

Telephones - main lines in use: 60,600 (2003)
Telephones - mobile cellular: 220,000 (2003)
Telephone system:
general assessment: fair system based on a network of microwave radio relay routes supplemented by open-wire lines and a mobile cellular system
domestic: microwave radio relay and open-wire lines for conventional system; cellular system has capacity of 10,000 telephones
international: country code - 228; satellite earth stations - 1 Intelsat (Atlantic Ocean) and 1 Symphonie
Radio broadcast stations: AM 2, FM 9, shortwave 4 (1998)
Radios: 940,000 (1997)
Television broadcast stations: 3 (plus two repeaters) (1997)
Televisions: 73,000 (1997)
Internet country code: .tg
Internet hosts: 82 (2003)
Internet Service Providers (ISPs): 3 (2001)
Internet users: 210,000 (2003)

TRANSPORTATION

Airports: 9 (2004 est.)
Airports - with paved runways:
total: 2
2,438 to 3,047 m: 2 (2005 est.)
Airports - with unpaved runways:
total: 7
914 to 1,523 m: 5
under 914 m: 2 (2005 est.)
Railways:
total: 568 km
narrow gauge: 568 km 1.000-m gauge (2004)
Roadways:
total: 7,520 km
paved: 2,376 km
unpaved: 5,144 km (1999 est.)
Waterways: 50 km (seasonally on Mono River depending on rainfall) (2003)
Merchant marine:
total: 2 ships (1,000 GRT or over) 3,918 GRT/3,852 DWT
by type: cargo 1, refrigerated cargo 1 (2005)
Ports and terminals: Kpeme, Lome

MILITARY

Military branches: Togolese Armed Forces (FAT): Army, Navy, Air Force, Gendarmerie (2005)
Military service age and obligation: 18 years of age for voluntary and compulsory military service (2001)
Manpower available for military service: *males age 18-49:* 1,148,890 (2005 est.)
Manpower fit for military service: *males age 18-49:* 629,933 (2005 est.)
Military expenditures - dollar figure: $35.5 million (2004)
Military expenditures - percent of GDP: 1.9% (2004)

TRANSNATIONAL ISSUES

Disputes - international: in 2001 Benin claimed Togo moved boundary monuments - joint commission continues to resurvey the boundary
Illicit drugs: transit hub for Nigerian heroin and cocaine traffickers; money laundering not a significant problem

TOKELAU

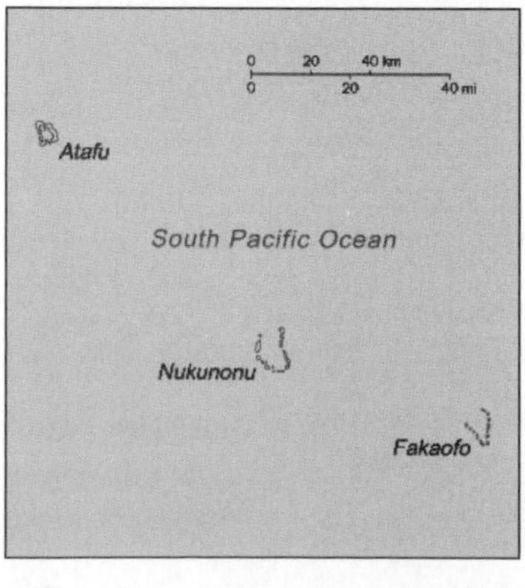

INTRODUCTION

Background: Originally settled by Polynesian emigrants from surrounding island groups, the Tokelau Islands were made a British protectorate in 1889. They were transferred to New Zealand administration in 1925.

GEOGRAPHY

Location: Oceania, group of three atolls in the South Pacific Ocean, about one-half of the way from Hawaii to New Zealand
Geographic coordinates: 9 00 S, 172 00 W
Map references: Oceania
Area:
total: 10 sq km
land: 10 sq km
water: 0 sq km
Area - comparative: about 17 times the size of The Mall in Washington, DC
Land boundaries: 0 km
Coastline: 101 km
Maritime claims:
territorial sea: 12 nm
exclusive economic zone: 200 nm
Climate: tropical; moderated by trade winds (April to November)
Terrain: low-lying coral atolls enclosing large lagoons

Elevation extremes:
lowest point: Pacific Ocean 0 m
highest point: unnamed location 5 m
Natural resources: NEGL
Land use:
arable land: 0% (soil is thin and infertile)
permanent crops: 0%
other: 100% (2001)
Irrigated land: NA sq km
Natural hazards: lies in Pacific typhoon belt
Environment - current issues: very limited natural resources and overcrowding are contributing to emigration to New Zealand
Geography - note: consists of three atolls, each with a lagoon surrounded by a number of reef-bound islets of varying length and rising to over three meters above sea level

PEOPLE

Population: 1,405 (July 2005 est.)
Age structure:
0-14 years: 42%
15-64 years: 53%
65 years and over: 5% (2005 est.)
Population growth rate: -0.01% (2005 est.)
Birth rate: NA
Death rate: NA
Net migration rate: NA
Sex ratio: NA
Infant mortality rate:
total: NA
male: NA
female: NA
Life expectancy at birth:
total population: NA
male: -9 years
female: -9 years (2005 est.)
Total fertility rate: NA
HIV/AIDS - adult prevalence rate: NA
HIV/AIDS - people living with HIV/AIDS: NA
HIV/AIDS - deaths: NA
Nationality:
noun: Tokelauan(s)
adjective: Tokelauan
Ethnic groups: Polynesian
Religions: Congregational Christian Church 70%, Roman Catholic 28%, other 2%
note: on Atafu, all Congregational Christian Church of Samoa; on Nukunonu, all Roman Catholic; on Fakaofo, both denominations, with the Congregational Christian Church predominant
Languages: Tokelauan (a Polynesian language), English
Literacy: NA

GOVERNMENT

Country name:
conventional long form: none
conventional short form: Tokelau
Dependency status: self-administering territory of New Zealand; note - Tokelauans are drafting a constitution and developing institutions and patterns of self-government as Tokelau moves toward free association with New Zealand
Government type: NA
Capital: none; each atoll has its own administrative center
Administrative divisions: none (territory of New Zealand)
Independence: none (territory of New Zealand)
National holiday: Waitangi Day (Treaty of Waitangi established British sovereignty over New Zealand), 6 February (1840)
Constitution: administered under the Tokelau Islands Act of 1948; amended in 1970
Legal system: New Zealand and local statutes
Suffrage: 21 years of age; universal
Executive branch:
chief of state: Queen ELIZABETH II (since 6 February 1952), represented by Governor General of New Zealand Dame Silvia CARTWRIGHT (since 4 April 2001); New Zealand is represented by Administrator Neil WALTER (since 1 March 2003)
head of government: Pio TUIA (since February 2005); note - position rotates annually among the three Faipule (village leaders)
cabinet: the Council for the Ongoing Government of Tokelau, consisting of three Faipule (village leaders) and three Pulenuku (village mayors) functions as a cabinet
elections: none; the monarch is hereditary; administrator appointed by the Minister of Foreign Affairs and Trade in New Zealand; the head of government is chosen from the Council of Faipule and serves a one-year term
Legislative branch: unicameral General Fono (21 seats; based upon proportional representation from the three islands elected by popular vote to serve three-year terms; Nukunonu has 6 seats, Fakaofo has 7 seats, Atafu has 8 seats); note - the Tokelau Amendment Act of 1996 confers limited legislative power on the General Fono
elections: last held January 2002 (next to be held January 2005)
Judicial branch: Supreme Court in New Zealand exercises civil and criminal jurisdiction in Tokelau
Political parties and leaders: none
Political pressure groups and leaders: none
International organization participation: PIF, SPC, UNESCO (associate), UPU
Diplomatic representation in the US: none (territory of New Zealand)
Diplomatic representation from the US: none (territory of New Zealand)
Flag description: the flag of New Zealand is used

ECONOMY

Economy - overview: Tokelau's small size (three villages), isolation, and lack of resources greatly restrain economic development and confine agriculture to the subsistence level. The people rely heavily on aid from New Zealand - about $4 million annually - to maintain public services, with annual aid being substantially greater than GDP. The principal sources of revenue come from sales of copra, postage stamps, souvenir coins, and handicrafts. Money is also remitted to families from relatives in New Zealand.
GDP (purchasing power parity): $1.5 million (1993 est.)
GDP (official exchange rate): NA
GDP - real growth rate: NA
GDP - per capita: purchasing power parity - $1,000 (1993 est.)
GDP - composition by sector:
agriculture: NA%
industry: NA%
services: NA%
Labor force: NA
Unemployment rate: NA%
Population below poverty line: NA
Household income or consumption by percentage share:
lowest 10%: NA
highest 10%: NA
Inflation rate (consumer prices): NA%
Budget:
revenues: $430,800
expenditures: $2.8 million, including capital expenditures of $37,300 (1987 est.)
Agriculture - products: coconuts, copra, breadfruit, papayas, bananas; pigs, poultry, goats
Industries: small-scale enterprises for copra production, woodworking, plaited craft goods; stamps, coins; fishing
Industrial production growth rate: NA%
Electricity - production: NA kWh
Electricity - production by source:
fossil fuel: 100%
hydro: 0%
nuclear: 0%
other: 0% (2001)
Electricity - consumption: NA kWh
Exports: $98,000 f.o.b. (1983)
Exports - partners: New Zealand (2004)
Imports: $323,000 c.i.f. (1983)
Imports - partners: New Zealand (2004)
Debt - external: $0
Economic aid - recipient: from New Zealand about $4 million annually

Currency (code): New Zealand dollar (NZD)
Currency code: NZD
Exchange rates: New Zealand dollars per US dollar - 1.43 (2005), 1.5087 (2004), 1.7221 (2003), 2.1622 (2002), 2.3788 (2001)
Fiscal year: 1 April - 31 March

COMMUNICATIONS

Telephones - main lines in use: 300 (2002)
Telephones - mobile cellular: 0 (2001)
Telephone system:
general assessment: modern satellite-based communications system;
domestic: radiotelephone service between islands
international: country code - 690; radiotelephone service to Samoa; government-regulated telephone service (TeleTok), with 3 satellite earth stations, established in 1997
Radio broadcast stations: AM NA, FM NA, shortwave NA
note: 1 radio station provides service to all islands (2002)
Radios: 1,000 (1997)
Internet country code: .tk
Internet Service Providers (ISPs): 1 (2000)
Internet users: NA

TRANSPORTATION

Airports: none; lagoon landings are possible by amphibious aircraft (2004 est.)
Roadways:
total: NA
paved: NA
unpaved: NA
Ports and terminals: none; offshore anchorage only

MILITARY

Military - note: defense is the responsibility of New Zealand

TRANSNATIONAL ISSUES

Disputes - international: none

TONGA

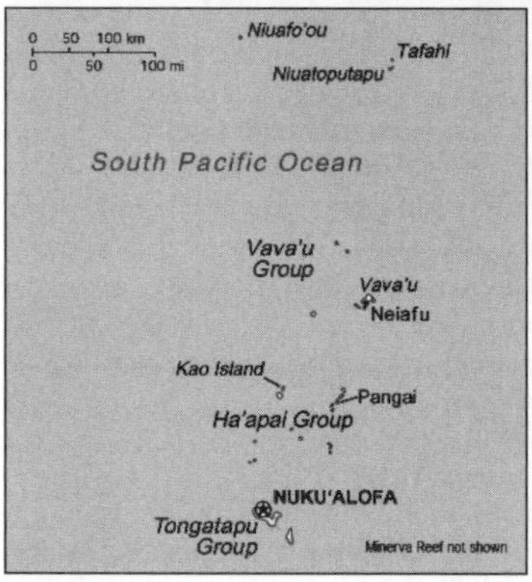

INTRODUCTION

Background: The archipelago of "The Friendly Islands" was united into a Polynesian kingdom in 1845. It became a constitutional monarchy in 1875 and a British protectorate in 1900. Tonga acquired its independence in 1970 and became a member of the Commonwealth of Nations. It remains the only monarchy in the Pacific.

GEOGRAPHY

Location: Oceania, archipelago in the South Pacific Ocean, about two-thirds of the way from Hawaii to New Zealand
Geographic coordinates: 20 00 S, 175 00 W
Map references: Oceania
Area:
total: 748 sq km
land: 718 sq km
water: 30 sq km
Area - comparative: four times the size of Washington, DC
Land boundaries: 0 km
Coastline: 419 km
Maritime claims:
territorial sea: 12 nm
exclusive economic zone: 200 nm
continental shelf: 200-m depth or to the depth of exploitation
Climate: tropical; modified by trade winds; warm season (December to May), cool season (May to December)
Terrain: most islands have limestone base formed from uplifted coral formation; others have limestone overlying volcanic base
Elevation extremes:
lowest point: Pacific Ocean 0 m
highest point: unnamed location on Kao Island 1,033 m
Natural resources: fish, fertile soil
Land use:
arable land: 23.61%
permanent crops: 43.06%
other: 33.33% (2001)
Irrigated land: NA
Natural hazards: cyclones (October to April); earthquakes and volcanic activity on Fonuafo'ou
Environment - current issues: deforestation results as more and more land is being cleared for agriculture and settlement; some damage to coral reefs from starfish and indiscriminate coral and shell collectors; overhunting threatens native sea turtle populations
Environment - international agreements:
party to: Biodiversity, Climate Change, Desertification, Law of the Sea, Marine Dumping, Marine Life Conservation, Ozone Layer Protection, Ship Pollution
signed, but not ratified: none of the selected agreements
Geography - note: archipelago of 169 islands (36 inhabited)

PEOPLE

Population: 112,422 (July 2005 est.)
Age structure:
0-14 years: 36.2% (male 20,738/ female 19,907)
15-64 years: 59.7% (male 33,226/ female 33,853)
65 years and over: 4.2% (male 2,031/ female 2,667) (2005 est.)
Median age:
total: 20.46 years
male: 19.93 years
female: 21.02 years (2005 est.)
Population growth rate: 1.98% (2005 est.)
Birth rate: 25.18 births/1,000 population (2005 est.)
Death rate: 5.35 deaths/1,000 population (2005 est.)
Net migration rate: 0 migrant(s)/ 1,000 population (2005 est.)
Sex ratio:
at birth: 1.05 male(s)/female
under 15 years: 1.04 male(s)/ female
15-64 years: 0.98 male(s)/female
65 years and over: 0.76 male(s)/ female
total population: 0.99 male(s)/ female (2005 est.)
Infant mortality rate:
total: 12.62 deaths/1,000 live births
male: 13.97 deaths/1,000 live births
female: 11.2 deaths/1,000 live births (2005 est.)
Life expectancy at birth:
total population: 69.53 years
male: 67.05 years
female: 72.14 years (2005 est.)
Total fertility rate: 3 children born/ woman (2005 est.)
HIV/AIDS - adult prevalence rate: NA
HIV/AIDS - people living with HIV/AIDS: NA
HIV/AIDS - deaths: NA
Nationality:
noun: Tongan(s)
adjective: Tongan
Ethnic groups: Polynesian, Europeans about 300
Religions: Christian (Free Wesleyan Church claims over 30,000 adherents)

Languages: Tongan, English
Literacy:
definition: can read and write Tongan and/or English
total population: 98.9%
male: 98.8%
female: 99% (1996 est.)

GOVERNMENT

Country name:
conventional long form: Kingdom of Tonga
conventional short form: Tonga
former: Friendly Islands
Government type: hereditary constitutional monarchy
Capital: Nuku'alofa
Administrative divisions: 3 island groups; Ha'apai, Tongatapu, Vava'u
Independence: 4 June 1970 (from UK protectorate)
National holiday: Emancipation Day, 4 June (1970)
Constitution: 4 November 1875; revised 1 January 1967
Legal system: based on English law
Suffrage: 21 years of age; universal
Executive branch:
chief of state: King Taufa'ahau TUPOU IV (since 16 December 1965)
head of government: Prime Minister Prince Lavaka ata ULUKALALA (since 3 January 2000) and Deputy Prime Minister James C. COCKER (since NA January 2001)
cabinet: cabinet consists of 16 members, 12 appointed by the monarch for life; 4 appointed from among the elected members of the Legislative Assembly including 2 each from the Nobles and Peoples representatives serving three year terms
note: there is also a Privy Council that consists of the monarch, the Cabinet, and two governors
elections: none; the monarch is hereditary; prime minister and deputy prime minister appointed for life by the monarch
Legislative branch: unicameral Legislative Assembly or Fale Alea (30 seats - 12 reserved for cabinet ministers sitting ex officio, nine for nobles selected by the country's 33 nobles, and nine elected by popular vote; members serve three-year terms)
elections: last held 21 March 2005 (next to be held in 2008)
election results: Peoples Representatives: percent of vote - HRDMT 70%; seats - HRDMT 7, independents 2
Judicial branch: Supreme Court (judges are appointed by the monarch); Court of Appeal (consists of the Privy Council with the addition of the chief justice of the Supreme Court)
Political parties and leaders: there are no political parties
Political pressure groups and leaders: Human Rights and Democracy Movement Tonga or HRDMT [Rev. Simote VEA, chairman]
International organization participation: ACP, AsDB, C, FAO, G-77, IBRD, ICAO, ICFTU, ICRM, IDA, IFAD, IFC, IFRCS, IHO, IMF, IMO, Interpol, IOC, ITU, OPCW, PIF, Sparteca, SPC, UN, UNCTAD, UNESCO, UNIDO, UPU, WCO, WHO, WIPO, WMO, WTO (observer)
Diplomatic representation in the US:
chief of mission: Ambassador Fekitamoeloa 'UTOIKAMANU
chancery: 250 East 51st Street, New York, NY 10022
telephone: [1] (917) 369-1025
FAX: [1] (917) 369-1024
consulate(s) general: San Francisco
Diplomatic representation from the US: the US does not have an embassy in Tonga; the ambassador to Fiji is accredited to Tonga
Flag description: red with a bold red cross on a white rectangle in the upper hoist-side corner

ECONOMY

Economy - overview: Tonga, a small, open, South Pacific island economy, has a narrow export base in agricultural goods. Squash, coconuts, bananas, and vanilla beans are the main crops, and agricultural exports make up two-thirds of total exports. The country must import a high proportion of its food, mainly from New Zealand. Tourism is the second largest source of hard currency earnings following remittances. The country remains dependent on external aid and remittances from Tongan communities overseas to offset its trade deficit. The government is emphasizing the development of the private sector, especially the encouragement of investment, and is committing increased funds for health and education. Tonga has a reasonably sound basic infrastructure and well-developed social services. High unemployment among the young, a continuing upturn in inflation, pressures for democratic reform, and rising civil service expenditures are major issues facing the government.
GDP (purchasing power parity): $244 million (2002 est.)
GDP (official exchange rate): NA
GDP - real growth rate: 1.5% (2002 est.)
GDP - per capita: purchasing power parity - $2,300 (2002 est.)
GDP - composition by sector:
agriculture: 23%
industry: 13%
services: 64% (2002 est.)
Labor force: 33,910 (1996)
Labor force - by occupation: agriculture 65% (1997 est.)
Unemployment rate: 13.3% (1996 est.)
Population below poverty line: NA
Household income or consumption by percentage share:
lowest 10%: NA
highest 10%: NA
Inflation rate (consumer prices): 10.3% (2002 est.)
Budget:
revenues: $39.9 million
expenditures: $52.4 million, including capital expenditures of $1.9 million (FY99/00 est.)
Agriculture - products: squash, coconuts, copra, bananas, vanilla beans, cocoa, coffee, ginger, black pepper; fish
Industries: tourism, fishing
Industrial production growth rate: 8.6% (FY98/99)
Electricity - production: 34 million kWh (2003)
Electricity - production by source:
fossil fuel: 100%
hydro: 0%
nuclear: 0%
other: 0% (2001)
Electricity - consumption: 31.62 million kWh (2003)
Electricity - exports: 0 kWh (2003)
Electricity - imports: 0 kWh (2003)
Oil - production: 0 bbl/day (2003 est.)
Oil - consumption: 800 bbl/day (2003 est.)
Oil - exports: NA (2001)
Oil - imports: NA (2001)
Exports: $34 million f.o.b. (2004 est.)
Exports - partners: Japan 37.1%, China 18.7%, US 17.7%, Taiwan 8.7%, New Zealand 7.4% (2004)
Imports: $122 million f.o.b. (2004 est.)
Imports - partners: New Zealand 37.1%, Fiji 24.3%, Australia 9.1%, China 8.9%, US 6.3% (2004)
Debt - external: $63.4 million (2001)
Economic aid - recipient: Australia $5.5 million, New Zealand $2.3 million (FY01/02)
Currency (code): pa'anga (TOP)
Currency code: TOP
Exchange rates: pa'anga per US dollar - NA (2005), 1.9716 (2004), 2.142 (2003), 2.1952 (2002), 2.1236 (2001)
Fiscal year: 1 July - 30 June

COMMUNICATIONS

Telephones - main lines in use: 11,200 (2002)
Telephones - mobile cellular: 9,000 (2004)
Telephone system:
general assessment: competition between Tonga Telecommunications Corporation (TCC) and Shoreline Communications Tonga (SCT) is accelerating expansion of telecommunications; SCT recently granted

authority to develop high-speed digital service for telephone, Internet, and television
domestic: fully automatic switched network
international: country code - 676; satellite earth station - 1 Intelsat (Pacific Ocean) (2004)
Radio broadcast stations: AM 1, FM 4, shortwave 1 (2004)
Radios: 61,000 (1997)
Television broadcast stations: 3 (2004)
Televisions: 2,000 (1997)
Internet country code: .to
Internet hosts: 18,906 (2003)
Internet Service Providers (ISPs): 2 (2000)
Internet users: 2,900 (2002)

TRANSPORTATION

Airports: 6 (2004 est.)
Airports - with paved runways:
total: 1
2,438 to 3,047 m: 1 (2005 est.)
Airports - with unpaved runways:
total: 5
1,524 to 2,437 m: 1
914 to 1,523 m: 3
under 914 m: 1 (2005 est.)
Roadways:
total: 680 km
paved: 184 km
unpaved: 496 km (1999 est.)
Merchant marine:
total: 29 ships (1,000 GRT or over) 136,977 GRT/200,751 DWT
by type: cargo 21, chemical tanker 1, liquefied gas 2, passenger/cargo 1, petroleum tanker 1, refrigerated cargo 1, roll on/roll off 1, vehicle carrier 1
foreign-owned: 7 (Cyprus 1, France 1, Greece 1, Norway 1, Romania 2, United Kingdom 1) (2005)
Ports and terminals: Nuku'alofa

MILITARY

Military branches: Tonga Defense Services: Ground Forces (Royal Marines, Royal Guard), Maritime Force (includes Air Wing)
Military service age and obligation: 18 years of age (est.) (2004)
Military expenditures - dollar figure: NA
Military expenditures - percent of GDP: NA

TRANSNATIONAL ISSUES

Disputes - international: none

TRINIDAD AND TOBAGO

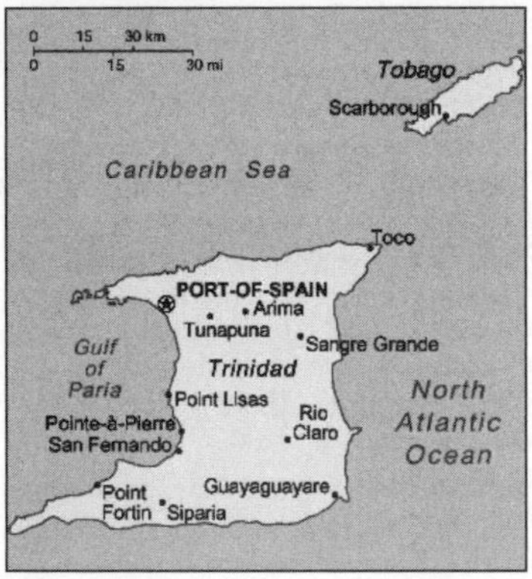

INTRODUCTION

Background: The islands came under British control in the 19th century; independence was granted in 1962. The country is one of the most prosperous in the Caribbean thanks largely to petroleum and natural gas production and processing. Tourism, mostly in Tobago, is targeted for expansion and is growing.

GEOGRAPHY

Location: Caribbean, islands between the Caribbean Sea and the North Atlantic Ocean, northeast of Venezuela
Geographic coordinates: 11 00 N, 61 00 W
Map references: Central America and the Caribbean
Area:
total: 5,128 sq km
land: 5,128 sq km
water: 0 sq km
Area - comparative: slightly smaller than Delaware
Land boundaries: 0 km
Coastline: 362 km
Maritime claims:measured from claimed archipelagic baselines
territorial sea: 12 nm
contiguous zone: 24 nm
exclusive economic zone: 200 nm
continental shelf: 200 nm or to the outer edge of the continental margin
Climate: tropical; rainy season (June to December)
Terrain: mostly plains with some hills and low mountains
Elevation extremes:
lowest point: Caribbean Sea 0 m
highest point: El Cerro del Aripo 940 m
Natural resources: petroleum, natural gas, asphalt
Land use:
arable land: 14.62%
permanent crops: 9.16%
other: 76.22% (2001)
Irrigated land: 30 sq km (1998 est.)
Natural hazards: outside usual path of hurricanes and other tropical storms
Environment - current issues: water pollution from agricultural chemicals, industrial wastes, and raw sewage; oil pollution of beaches; deforestation; soil erosion
Environment - international agreements:
party to: Biodiversity, Climate Change, Climate Change-Kyoto Protocol, Desertification, Endangered Species, Hazardous Wastes, Law of the Sea, Marine Life Conservation, Ozone Layer Protection, Ship Pollution, Tropical Timber 83, Tropical Timber 94, Wetlands
signed, but not ratified: none of the selected agreements
Geography - note: Pitch Lake, on Trinidad's southwestern coast, is the world's largest natural reservoir of asphalt

PEOPLE

Population: 1,088,644 (July 2005 est.)
Age structure:
0-14 years: 20.7% (male 115,594/ female 109,665)
15-64 years: 71% (male 403,301/ female 369,664)
65 years and over: 8.3% (male 40,638/female 49,782) (2005 est.)
Median age:
total: 30.91 years
male: 30.46 years
female: 31.44 years (2005 est.)
Population growth rate: -0.74% (2005 est.)
Birth rate: 12.81 births/1,000 population (2005 est.)
Death rate: 9.37 deaths/1,000 population (2005 est.)
Net migration rate: -10.87 migrant(s)/ 1,000 population (2005 est.)
Sex ratio:
at birth: 1.05 male(s)/female
under 15 years: 1.05 male(s)/ female
15-64 years: 1.09 male(s)/female
65 years and over: 0.82 male(s)/ female
total population: 1.06 male(s)/ female (2005 est.)
Infant mortality rate:
total: 24.31 deaths/1,000 live births
male: 26.23 deaths/1,000 live births
female: 22.31 deaths/1,000 live births (2005 est.)
Life expectancy at birth:
total population: 66.73 years
male: 65.6 years
female: 67.91 years (2005 est.)
Total fertility rate: 1.75 children born/woman (2005 est.)
HIV/AIDS - adult prevalence rate: 3.2% (2003 est.)

HIV/AIDS - people living with HIV/AIDS: 29,000 (2003 est.)
HIV/AIDS - deaths: 1,900 (2003 est.)
Nationality:
noun: Trinidadian(s), Tobagonian(s)
adjective: Trinidadian, Tobagonian
Ethnic groups: Indian (South Asian) 40%, African 37.5%, mixed 20.5%, other 1.2%, unspecified 0.8% (2000 census)
Religions: Roman Catholic 26%, Hindu 22.5%, Anglican 7.8%, Baptist 7.2%, Pentecostal 6.8%, Seventh Day Adventist 4%, other Christian 5.8%, Muslim 5.8%, other 10.8%, unspecified 1.4%, none 1.9% (2000 census)
Languages: English (official), Hindi, French, Spanish, Chinese
Literacy:
definition: age 15 and over can read and write
total population: 98.6%
male: 99.1%
female: 98% (2003 est.)

GOVERNMENT

Country name:
conventional long form: Republic of Trinidad and Tobago
conventional short form: Trinidad and Tobago
Government type: parliamentary democracy
Capital: Port-of-Spain
Administrative divisions: 9 regional corporations, 2 city corporations, 3 borough corporations, and 1 ward
regional corporations: Couva/Tabaquite/Talparo, Diego Martin, Mayaro/Rio Claro, Penal/Debe, Princes Town, Sangre Grande, San Juan/Laventille, Siparia, Tunapuna/Piarco
city corporations: Port-of-Spain, San Fernando
borough corporations: Arima, Point Fortin, Chaguanas
ward: Tobago
Independence: 31 August 1962 (from UK)
National holiday: Independence Day, 31 August (1962)
Constitution: 1 August 1976
Legal system: based on English common law; judicial review of legislative acts in the Supreme Court; has not accepted compulsory ICJ jurisdiction
Suffrage: 18 years of age; universal
Executive branch:
chief of state: President George Maxwell RICHARDS (since 17 March 2003)
head of government: Prime Minister Patrick MANNING (since 24 December 2001)
cabinet: Cabinet appointed from among the members of Parliament
elections: president elected by an electoral college, which consists of the members of the Senate and House of Representatives, for a five-year term; election last held 14 February 2003 (next to be held in 2008); the president usually appoints as prime minister the leader of the majority party in the House of Representatives
election results: George Maxwell RICHARDS elected president; percent of electoral college vote - 43%
Legislative branch: bicameral Parliament consists of the Senate (31 seats; 16 members appointed by the ruling party, 9 by the President, 6 by the opposition party for a maximum term of five years) and the House of Representatives (36 seats; members are elected by popular vote to serve five-year terms)
elections: House of Representatives - last held 7 October 2002 (next to be held by October 2007)
election results: House of Representatives - percent of vote - PNM 55.5%, UNC 44.5%; seats by party - PNM 20, UNC 16
note: Tobago has a unicameral House of Assembly with 12 members serving four-year terms
Judicial branch: Supreme Court of Judicature (comprised of the High Court of Justice and the Court of Appeals; the chief justice is appointed by the president after consultation with the prime minister and the leader of the opposition; other justices are appointed by the president on the advice of the Judicial and Legal Service Commission); High Court of Justice; Court of Appeals; the highest court of appeal is the Privy Council in London
Political parties and leaders: National Alliance for Reconstruction or NAR [Lennox SANKERSINGH]; People's National Movement or PNM [Patrick MANNING]; Team Unity or TU [Ramesh MAHARAJ]; United National Congress or UNC [Basdeo PANDAY]; Democratic Action Committee or DAC [Hochoy CHARLES], note - only active in Tobago
Political pressure groups and leaders: Jamaat-al Muslimeen [Yasin BAKR]
International organization participation: ACP, C, Caricom, CDB, FAO, G-24, G-77, IADB, IBRD, ICAO, ICCt, ICFTU, ICRM, IDA, IFAD, IFC, IFRCS, IHO, ILO, IMF, IMO, Interpol, IOC, ISO, ITU, LAES, MIGA, NAM, OAS, OPANAL, OPCW, UN, UNCTAD, UNESCO, UNIDO, UPU, WCL, WCO, WFTU, WHO, WIPO, WMO, WTO
Diplomatic representation in the US:
chief of mission: Ambassador Marina Annette VALERE
chancery: 1708 Massachusetts Avenue NW, Washington, DC 20036
telephone: [1] (202) 467-6490
FAX: [1] (202) 785-3130
consulate(s) general: Miami and New York
Diplomatic representation from the US:
chief of mission: Ambassador Roy L. AUSTIN
embassy: 15 Queen's Park West, Port-of-Spain
mailing address: P. O. Box 752, Port-of-Spain
telephone: [1] (868) 622-6371 through 6376
FAX: [1] (868) 628-5462
Flag description: red with a white-edged black diagonal band from the upper hoist side to the lower fly side

ECONOMY

Economy - overview: Trinidad and Tobago, the leading Caribbean producer of oil and gas, has earned a reputation as an excellent investment site for international businesses. Tourism is a growing sector, although not proportionately as important as in many other Caribbean islands. The economy benefits from low inflation and a growing trade surplus. Prospects for growth in 2006 are good as prices for oil, petrochemicals, and liquefied natural gas are expected to remain high, and foreign direct investment continues to grow to support expanded capacity in the energy sector. The government is coping with a rise in violent crime.
GDP (purchasing power parity): $13.79 billion (2005 est.)
GDP (official exchange rate): $13.73 billion (2005 est.)
GDP - real growth rate: 6.5% (2005 est.)
GDP - per capita: purchasing power parity - $12,700 (2005 est.)
GDP - composition by sector:
agriculture: 0.7%
industry: 57%
services: 42.3% (2005 est.)
Labor force: 620,000 (2005 est.)
Labor force - by occupation: agriculture 9.5%, manufacturing, mining, and quarrying 14%, construction and utilities 12.4%, services 64.1% (1997 est.)
Unemployment rate: 8% (2005 est.)
Population below poverty line: 21% (1992 est.)
Household income or consumption by percentage share:
lowest 10%: NA
highest 10%: NA
Inflation rate (consumer prices): 6.8% (2005 est.)
Investment (gross fixed): 19% of GDP (2005 est.)
Budget:
revenues: $4.5 billion
expenditures: $4.06 billion, including capital expenditures of $117.3 million (2005 est.)

Public debt: 41.4% of GDP (2005 est.)
Agriculture - products: cocoa, rice, citrus, coffee, vegetables; poultry
Industries: petroleum, chemicals, tourism, food processing, cement, beverage, cotton textiles
Industrial production growth rate: 9% (2005 est.)
Electricity - production: 6.076 billion kWh (2003)
Electricity - production by source:
fossil fuel: 99.8%
hydro: 0%
nuclear: 0%
other: 0.2% (2001)
Electricity - consumption: 5.651 billion kWh (2003)
Electricity - exports: 0 kWh (2003)
Electricity - imports: 0 kWh (2003)
Oil - production: 150,000 bbl/day (2005 est.)
Oil - consumption: 29,000 bbl/day (2003 est.)
Oil - exports: NA (2001)
Oil - imports: NA (2001)
Oil - proved reserves: 990 million bbl (1 January 2004)
Natural gas - production: 25 billion cu m (2003 est.)
Natural gas - consumption: 13.76 billion cu m (2003 est.)
Natural gas - exports: 11.79 billion cu m (2003 est.)
Natural gas - imports: 0 cu m (2001 est.)
Natural gas - proved reserves: 589 billion cu m (1 January 2004)
Current account balance: $3.27 billion (2005 est.)
Exports: $9.161 billion f.o.b. (2005 est.)
Exports - partners: US 67.1%, Jamaica 5.7%, France 3.5% (2004)
Imports: $6.011 billion f.o.b. (2005 est.)
Imports - partners: US 23.9%, Venezuela 11.5%, Germany 11.2%, Brazil 10.7%, Spain 6.4%, Italy 5.1% (2004)
Reserves of foreign exchange and gold: $4.045 billion (2005 est.)
Debt - external: $2.986 billion (2005 est.)
Economic aid - recipient: $24 million (1999 est.)
Currency (code): Trinidad and Tobago dollar (TTD)
Currency code: TTD
Exchange rates: Trinidad and Tobago dollars per US dollar - 6.27 (2005), 6.299 (2004), 6.2951 (2003), 6.2487 (2002), 6.2332 (2001)
Fiscal year: 1 October - 30 September

COMMUNICATIONS

Telephones - main lines in use: 325,100 (2002)
Telephones - mobile cellular: 361,900 (2002)
Telephone system:
general assessment: excellent international service; good local service
domestic: NA
international: country code - 1-868; satellite earth station - 1 Intelsat (Atlantic Ocean); tropospheric scatter to Barbados and Guyana
Radio broadcast stations: AM 4, FM 18, shortwave 0 (2004)
Radios: 680,000 (1997)
Television broadcast stations: 4 (2004)
Televisions: 425,000 (1997)
Internet country code: .tt
Internet hosts: 8,003 (2003)
Internet Service Providers (ISPs): 17 (2000)
Internet users: 138,000 (2002)

TRANSPORTATION

Airports: 6 (2004 est.)
Airports - with paved runways:
total: 3
over 3,047 m: 1
2,438 to 3,047 m: 1
1,524 to 2,437 m: 1 (2005 est.)
Airports - with unpaved runways:
total: 3
914 to 1,523 m: 1
under 914 m: 2 (2005 est.)
Pipelines: condensate 253 km; gas 1,117 km; oil 478 km (2004)
Roadways:
total: 8,320 km
paved: 4,252 km
unpaved: 4,068 km (1999 est.)
Merchant marine:
total: 6 ships (1,000 GRT or over) 7,178 GRT/3,633 DWT
by type: passenger 2, passenger/ cargo 3, petroleum tanker 1
foreign-owned: 1 (United States 1)
registered in other countries: 4 (2005)
Ports and terminals:
Pointe-a-Pierre, Point Lisas, Port-of-Spain

MILITARY

Military branches: Trinidad and Tobago Defense Force: Ground Force, Coast Guard (includes Air Wing) (2004)
Military service age and obligation: 18 years of age for voluntary military service; no conscription (2001)
Manpower available for military service: *males age 18-49:* 293,094 (2005 est.)
Manpower fit for military service: *males age 18-49:* 203,531 (2005 est.)
Military expenditures - dollar figure: $66.7 million (2003)
Military expenditures - percent of GDP: 0.6% (2003)

TRANSNATIONAL ISSUES

Disputes - international: Barbados will assert its claim before UNCLOS that the northern limit of Trinidad and Tobago's maritime boundary with Venezuela extends into its waters; Guyana has also expressed its intention to challenge this boundary as it may extend into its waters as well
Illicit drugs: transshipment point for South American drugs destined for the US and Europe; producer of cannabis

TROMELIN ISLAND

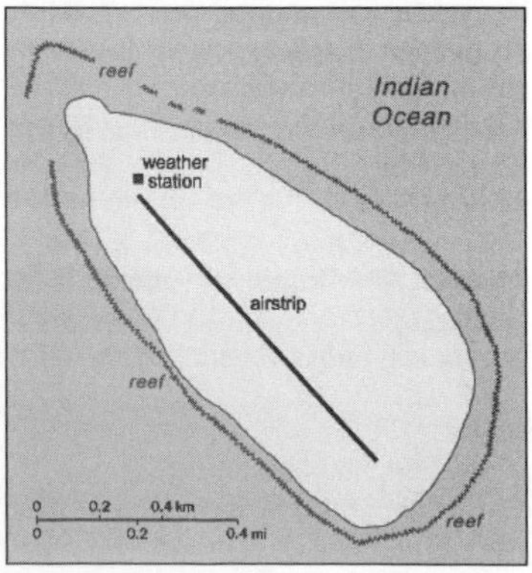

INTRODUCTION

Background: First explored by the French in 1776, the island came under the jurisdiction of Reunion in 1814. At present, it serves as a sea turtle sanctuary and is the site of an important meteorological station.

GEOGRAPHY

Location: Southern Africa, island in the Indian Ocean, east of Madagascar
Geographic coordinates: 15 52 S, 54 25 E
Map references: Africa
Area:
total: 1 sq km
land: 1 sq km
water: 0 sq km
Area - comparative: about 1.7 times the size of The Mall in Washington, DC
Land boundaries: 0 km
Coastline: 3.7 km
Maritime claims:
territorial sea: 12 nm
exclusive economic zone: 200 nm
continental shelf: 200-m depth or to the depth of exploitation
Climate: tropical
Terrain: low, flat, and sandy; likely volcanic

Elevation extremes:
lowest point: Indian Ocean 0 m
highest point: unnamed location 7 m
Natural resources: fish
Land use:
arable land: 0%
permanent crops: 0%
other: 100% (grasses; scattered bushes) (2001)
Irrigated land: 0 sq km (1998 est.)
Natural hazards: NA
Environment - current issues: NA
Geography - note: climatologically important location for forecasting cyclones; wildlife sanctuary (seabirds, tortoises)

PEOPLE

Population: uninhabited, except for visits by scientists (July 2005 est.)

GOVERNMENT

Country name:
conventional long form: none
conventional short form: Tromelin Island
local long form: none
local short form: Ile Tromelin
Dependency status: possession of France; administered by the Administrateur Superieur of the French Southern and Antarctic Lands
Legal system: the laws of France, where applicable, apply
Flag description: the flag of France is used

ECONOMY

Economy - overview: no economic activity

COMMUNICATIONS

Communications - note: important meteorological station

TRANSPORTATION

Airports: 1 (2004 est.)
Airports - with unpaved runways:
total: 1
under 914 m: 1 (2005 est.)
Ports and terminals: none; offshore anchorage only

MILITARY

Military - note: defense is the responsibility of France

TRANSNATIONAL ISSUES

Disputes - international: claimed by Mauritius

TUNISIA

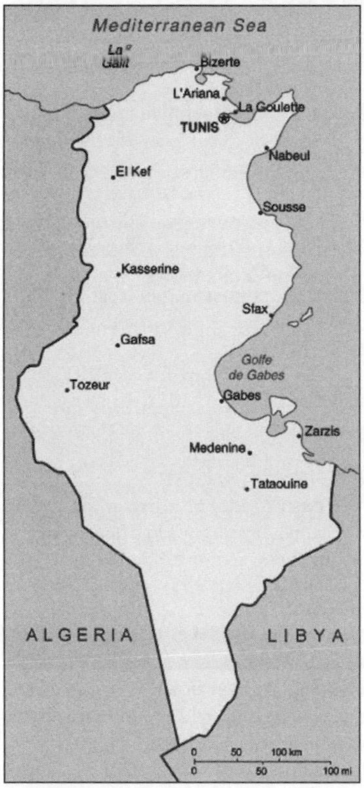

INTRODUCTION

Background: Following independence from France in 1956, President Habib BOURGUIBA established a strict one-party state. He dominated the country for 31 years, repressing Islamic fundamentalism and establishing rights for women unmatched by any other Arab nation. In recent years, Tunisia has taken a moderate, non-aligned stance in its foreign relations. Domestically, it has sought to defuse rising pressure for a more open political society.

GEOGRAPHY

Location: Northern Africa, bordering the Mediterranean Sea, between Algeria and Libya
Geographic coordinates: 34 00 N, 9 00 E
Map references: Africa
Area:
total: 163,610 sq km
land: 155,360 sq km
water: 8,250 sq km
Area - comparative: slightly larger than Georgia
Land boundaries:
total: 1,424 km
border countries: Algeria 965 km, Libya 459 km
Coastline: 1,148 km
Maritime claims:
territorial sea: 12 nm
contiguous zone: 24 nm
Climate: temperate in north with mild, rainy winters and hot, dry summers; desert in south
Terrain: mountains in north; hot, dry central plain; semiarid south merges into the Sahara
Elevation extremes:
lowest point: Shatt al Gharsah -17 m
highest point: Jebel ech Chambi 1,544 m
Natural resources: petroleum, phosphates, iron ore, lead, zinc, salt
Land use:
arable land: 17.86%
permanent crops: 13.74%
other: 68.4% (2001)
Irrigated land: 3,800 sq km (1998 est.)
Natural hazards: NA
Environment - current issues: toxic and hazardous waste disposal is ineffective and poses health risks; water pollution from raw sewage; limited natural fresh water resources; deforestation; overgrazing; soil erosion; desertification
Environment - international agreements:
party to: Biodiversity, Climate Change, Climate Change-Kyoto Protocol, Desertification, Endangered Species, Environmental Modification, Hazardous Wastes, Law of the Sea, Marine Dumping, Ozone Layer Protection, Ship Pollution, Wetlands
signed, but not ratified: Marine Life Conservation
Geography - note: strategic location in central Mediterranean; Malta and Tunisia are discussing the commercial exploitation of the continental shelf between their countries, particularly for oil exploration

PEOPLE

Population: 10,074,951 (July 2005 est.)
Age structure:
0-14 years: 25.3% (male 1,316,308/female 1,234,309)
15-64 years: 68.1% (male 3,437,880/female 3,418,591)
65 years and over: 6.6% (male 321,287/female 346,576) (2005 est.)
Median age:
total: 27.29 years
male: 26.78 years
female: 27.82 years (2005 est.)
Population growth rate: 0.99% (2005 est.)
Birth rate: 15.5 births/1,000 population (2005 est.)
Death rate: 5.09 deaths/1,000 population (2005 est.)

Net migration rate: -0.54 migrant(s)/ 1,000 population (2005 est.)
Sex ratio:
at birth: 1.07 male(s)/female
under 15 years: 1.07 male(s)/ female
15-64 years: 1.01 male(s)/female
65 years and over: 0.93 male(s)/ female
total population: 1.02 male(s)/ female (2005 est.)
Infant mortality rate:
total: 24.77 deaths/1,000 live births
male: 27.68 deaths/1,000 live births
female: 21.65 deaths/1,000 live births (2005 est.)
Life expectancy at birth:
total population: 74.89 years
male: 73.2 years
female: 76.71 years (2005 est.)
Total fertility rate: 1.75 children born/woman (2005 est.)
HIV/AIDS - adult prevalence rate: less than 0.1% (2005 est.)
HIV/AIDS - people living with HIV/AIDS: 1,000 (2003 est.)
HIV/AIDS - deaths: less than 200 (2003 est.)
Major infectious diseases:
degree of risk: intermediate
food or waterborne diseases: bacterial diarrhea, and hepatitis A
vectorborne diseases: may be a significant risk in some locations during the transmission season (typically April through November) (2004)
Nationality:
noun: Tunisian(s)
adjective: Tunisian
Ethnic groups: Arab 98%, European 1%, Jewish and other 1%
Religions: Muslim 98%, Christian 1%, Jewish and other 1%
Languages: Arabic (official and one of the languages of commerce), French (commerce)
Literacy:
definition: age 15 and over can read and write
total population: 74.3%
male: 83.4%
female: 65.3% (2004 est.)

GOVERNMENT

Country name:
conventional long form: Tunisian Republic
conventional short form: Tunisia
local long form: Al Jumhuriyah at Tunisiyah
local short form: Tunis
Government type: republic
Capital: Tunis
Administrative divisions: 24 governorates; Ariana (Aryanah), Beja (Bajah), Ben Arous (Bin 'Arus), Bizerte (Banzart), Gabes (Qabis), Gafsa (Qafsah), Jendouba (Jundubah), Kairouan (Al Qayrawan), Kasserine (Al Qasrayn), Kebili (Qibili), Kef (Al Kaf), Mahdia (Al Mahdiyah), Manouba (Manubah), Medenine (Madanin), Monastir (Al Munastir), Nabeul (Nabul), Sfax (Safaqis), Sidi Bou Zid (Sidi Bu Zayd), Siliana (Silyanah), Sousse (Susah), Tataouine (Tatawin), Tozeur (Tawzar), Tunis, Zaghouan (Zaghwan)
Independence: 20 March 1956 (from France)
National holiday: Independence Day, 20 March (1956)
Constitution: 1 June 1959; amended 1988, 2002
Legal system: based on French civil law system and Islamic law; some judicial review of legislative acts in the Supreme Court in joint session
Suffrage: 20 years of age; universal
Executive branch:
chief of state: President Zine El Abidine BEN ALI (since 7 November 1987)
head of government: Prime Minister Mohamed GHANNOUCHI (since 17 November 1999)
cabinet: Council of Ministers appointed by the president
elections: president elected by popular vote for a five-year term; election last held 24 October 2004 (next to be held October 2009); prime minister appointed by the president
election results: President Zine El Abidine BEN ALI reelected for a fourth term; percent of vote - Zine El Abidine BEN ALI 94.5%, Mohamed BOUCHIHA 3.8%, Mohamed Ali HALOUANI 1%
Legislative branch: unicameral bicameral system consists of the Chamber of Deputies or Majlis al-Nuwaab (189 seats; members elected by popular vote to serve five-year terms) and the Chamber of Advisors (126 seats; 85 members elected by municipal counselors, deputies, mayors, and professional associations and trade unions; 41 members are presidential appointees; members serve six-year terms)
elections: Chamber of Deputies - last held 24 October 2004 (next to be held October 2009); Chamber of Advisors - last held 3 July 2005 (next to be held July 2011)
election results: Chamber of Deputies - percent of vote by party - NA; seats by party - RCD 152, MDS 14, PUP 11, UDU 7, Al-Tajdid 3, PSL 2; Chamber of Advisors - percent of vote by party - NA; seats by party - RCD 71 (41 presidential appointees and 14 trade union seats remain undecided)
Judicial branch: Court of Cassation or Cour de Cassation
Political parties and leaders: Al-Tajdid Movement [Ali HALOUANI]; Constitutional Democratic Rally Party (Rassemblement Constitutionnel Democratique) or RCD [President Zine El Abidine BEN ALI (official ruling party)]; Liberal Social Party or PSL [Mounir BEJI]; Movement of Socialist Democrats or MDS [Ismail BOULAHYA]; Popular Unity Party or PUP [Mohamed BOUCHIHA]; Progressive Democratic Party [Nejib CHEBBI]; Unionist Democratic Union or UDU [Abderrahmane TLILI]
Political pressure groups and leaders: the Islamic fundamentalist party, Al Nahda (Renaissance), is outlawed
International organization participation: ABEDA, ACCT, AfDB, AFESD, AMF, AMU, AU, BSEC (observer), FAO, G-77, IAEA, IBRD, ICAO, ICC, ICFTU, ICRM, IDA, IDB, IFAD, IFC, IFRCS, IHO, ILO, IMF, IMO, Interpol, IOC, IOM, ISO, ITU, LAS, MIGA, MONUC, NAM, OAPEC (suspended), OAS (observer), OIC, ONUB, OPCW, OSCE (partner), UN, UNCTAD, UNESCO, UNHCR, UNIDO, UNMEE, UNOCI, UPU, WCO, WFTU, WHO, WIPO, WMO, WToO, WTO
Diplomatic representation in the US:
chief of mission: Ambassador Mohamed Nejib HACHANA
chancery: 1515 Massachusetts Avenue NW, Washington, DC 20005
telephone: [1] (202) 862-1850
FAX: [1] (202) 862-1858
Diplomatic representation from the US:
chief of mission: Ambassador William J. HUDSON
embassy: Zone Nord-Est des Berges du Lac Nord de Tunis 1053, Tunisia
mailing address: use embassy street address
telephone: [216] 71 107-000
FAX: [216] 71 107-090
Flag description: red with a white disk in the center bearing a red crescent nearly encircling a red five-pointed star; the crescent and star are traditional symbols of Islam

ECONOMY

Economy - overview: Tunisia has a diverse economy, with important agricultural, mining, energy, tourism, and manufacturing sectors. Governmental control of economic affairs while still heavy has gradually lessened over the past decade with increasing privatization, simplification of the tax structure, and a prudent approach to debt. Progressive social policies also have helped raise living conditions in Tunisia relative to the region. Real growth slowed to a 15-year low of 1.9% in 2002 because of agricultural drought and lackluster tourism. Better rains in 2003 through 2005, however,

helped push GDP growth above 5% for these years. Tourism also recovered after the end of combat operations in Iraq. Tunisia is gradually removing barriers to trade with the European Union. Broader privatization, further liberalization of the investment code to increase foreign investment, improvements in government efficiency, and reduction of the trade deficit are among the challenges ahead.
GDP (purchasing power parity): $76.91 billion (2005 est.)
GDP (official exchange rate): $31.74 billion (2005 est.)
GDP - real growth rate: 4.9% (2005 est.)
GDP - per capita: purchasing power parity - $7,600 (2005 est.)
GDP - composition by sector:
agriculture: 13.8%
industry: 30.7%
services: 55.6% (2005 est.)
Labor force: 3.41 million
note: shortage of skilled labor (2005 est.)
Labor force - by occupation: services 55%, industry 23%, agriculture 22% (1995 est.)
Unemployment rate: 13.5% (2005 est.)
Population below poverty line: 7.6% (2001 est.)
Household income or consumption by percentage share:
lowest 10%: 2.3%
highest 10%: 31.8% (1995)
Distribution of family income - Gini index: 39.8 (2000)
Inflation rate (consumer prices): 2% (2005 est.)
Investment (gross fixed): 21.8% of GDP (2005 est.)
Budget:
revenues: $7.322 billion
expenditures: $8.304 billion, including capital expenditures of $1.6 billion (2005 est.)
Public debt: 58.7% of GDP (2005 est.)
Agriculture - products: olives, olive oil, grain, dairy products, tomatoes, citrus fruit, beef, sugar beets, dates, almonds
Industries: petroleum, mining (particularly phosphate and iron ore), tourism, textiles, footwear, agribusiness, beverages
Industrial production growth rate: 3.8% (2005 est.)
Electricity - production: 11.56 billion kWh (2003)
Electricity - production by source:
fossil fuel: 99.5%
hydro: 0.5%
nuclear: 0%
other: 0% (2001)
Electricity - consumption: 10.76 billion kWh (2003)
Electricity - exports: 10 million kWh (2003)
Electricity - imports: 5 million kWh (2003)
Oil - production: 77,650 bbl/day (2003 est.)
Oil - consumption: 90,000 bbl/day (2003 est.)
Oil - exports: NA (2001)
Oil - imports: NA (2001)
Oil - proved reserves: 1.7 billion bbl (2005 est.)
Natural gas - production: 2.25 billion cu m (2001 est.)
Natural gas - consumption: 3.83 billion cu m (2001 est.)
Natural gas - exports: 0 cu m (2001 est.)
Natural gas - imports: 1.58 billion cu m (2001 est.)
Natural gas - proved reserves: 77.16 billion cu m (2005)
Current account balance: $-492 million (2005 est.)
Exports: $10.3 billion f.o.b. (2005 est.)
Exports - partners: France 33.1%, Italy 25.3%, Germany 9.2%, Spain 6.1% (2004)
Imports: $12.86 billion f.o.b. (2005 est.)
Imports - partners: France 25.1%, Italy 19%, Germany 8.5%, Spain 5.3% (2004)
Reserves of foreign exchange and gold: $4.333 billion (2005 est.)
Debt - external: $18.91 billion (30 June 2005 est.)
Economic aid - recipient: $114.6 million (2002)
Currency (code): Tunisian dinar (TND)
Currency code: TND
Exchange rates: Tunisian dinars per US dollar - 1.28 (2005), 1.2455 (2004), 1.2885 (2003), 1.4217 (2002), 1.4387 (2001)
Fiscal year: calendar year

COMMUNICATIONS

Telephones - main lines in use: 1,163,800 (2003)
Telephones - mobile cellular: 1,899,900 (2003)
Telephone system:
general assessment: above the African average and continuing to be upgraded; key centers are Sfax, Sousse, Bizerte, and Tunis; Internet access available
domestic: trunk facilities consist of open-wire lines, coaxial cable, and microwave radio relay
international: country code - 216; 5 submarine cables; satellite earth stations - 1 Intelsat (Atlantic Ocean) and 1 Arabsat; coaxial cable and microwave radio relay to Algeria and Libya; participant in Medarabtel; two international gateway digital switches
Radio broadcast stations: AM 7, FM 20, shortwave 2 (1998)
Radios: 2.06 million (1997)
Television broadcast stations: 26 (plus 76 repeaters) (1995)
Televisions: 920,000 (1997)
Internet country code: .tn
Internet hosts: 281 (2004)
Internet Service Providers (ISPs): 1 (2000)
Internet users: 630,000 (2003)

TRANSPORTATION

Airports: 30 (2004 est.)
Airports - with paved runways:
total: 14
over 3,047 m: 3
2,438 to 3,047 m: 6
1,524 to 2,437 m: 2
914 to 1,523 m: 3 (2005 est.)
Airports - with unpaved runways:
total: 16
1,524 to 2,437 m: 2
914 to 1,523 m: 7
under 914 m: 7 (2005 est.)
Pipelines: gas 3,059 km; oil 1,203 km; refined products 345 km (2004)
Railways:
total: 2,152 km
standard gauge: 468 km 1.435-m gauge
narrow gauge: 1,674 km 1.000-m gauge (65 km electrified)
dual gauge: 10 km 1.435 m and 1.000-m gauges (three rails) (2004)
Roadways:
total: 18,997 km
paved: 12,424 km (including 142 km of expressways)
unpaved: 6,573 km (2001)
Merchant marine:
total: 12 ships (1,000 GRT or over) 124,733 GRT/122,664 DWT
by type: bulk carrier 1, cargo 1, chemical tanker 5, passenger/cargo 4, petroleum tanker 1
registered in other countries: 3 (2005)
Ports and terminals: Bizerte, Gabes, La Goulette, Skhira

MILITARY

Military branches: Army, Navy, Air Force (2003)
Military service age and obligation: 20 years of age for compulsory military service; conscript service obligation - 12 months; 18 years of age for voluntary military service (2004)
Manpower available for military service: *males age 20-49:* 2,441,741 (2005 est.)
Manpower fit for military service: *males age 20-49:* 2,035,431 (2005 est.)
Manpower reaching military service age annually: *males:* 108,817 (2005 est.)
Military expenditures - dollar figure: $356 million (FY99)
Military expenditures - percent of GDP: 1.5% (FY99)

TRANSNATIONAL ISSUES

Disputes - international: none

TURKEY

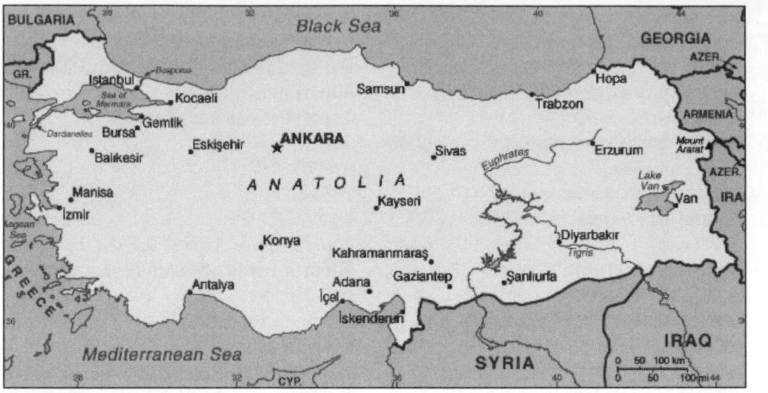

INTRODUCTION

Background: Modern Turkey was founded in 1923 from the Anatolian remnants of the defeated Ottoman Empire by national hero Mustafa KEMAL, who was later honored with the title Ataturk, or "Father of the Turks." Under his authoritarian leadership, the country adopted wide-ranging social, legal, and political reforms. After a period of one-party rule, an experiment with multi-party politics led to the 1950 election victory of the opposition Democratic Party and the peaceful transfer of power. Since then, Turkish political parties have multiplied, but democracy has been fractured by periods of instability and intermittent military coups (1960, 1971, 1980), which in each case eventually resulted in a return of political power to civilians. In 1997, the military again helped engineer the ouster - popularly dubbed a "post-modern coup" - of the then Islamic-oriented government. Turkey intervened militarily on Cyprus in 1974 to prevent a Greek takeover of the island and has since acted as patron state to the "Turkish Republic of Northern Cyprus," which only Turkey recognizes. A separatist insurgency begun in 1984 by the Kurdistan Workers' Party (PKK) - now known as the People's Congress of Kurdistan or Kongra-Gel (KGK) - has dominated the Turkish military's attention and claimed more than 30,000 lives, but after the capture of the group's leader in 1999, the insurgents largely withdrew from Turkey, mainly to northern Iraq. In 2004, KGK announced an end to its ceasefire and attacks attributed to the KGK increased. Turkey joined the UN in 1945 and in 1952 it became a member of NATO. In 1964, Turkey became an associate member of the European Community; over the past decade, it has undertaken many reforms to strengthen its democracy and economy, enabling it to begin accession membership talks with the European Union.

GEOGRAPHY

Location: southeastern Europe and southwestern Asia (that portion of Turkey west of the Bosporus is geographically part of Europe), bordering the Black Sea, between Bulgaria and Georgia, and bordering the Aegean Sea and the Mediterranean Sea, between Greece and Syria

Geographic coordinates: 39 00 N, 35 00 E

Map references: Middle East

Area:
total: 780,580 sq km
land: 770,760 sq km
water: 9,820 sq km

Area - comparative: slightly larger than Texas

Land boundaries:
total: 2,648 km
border countries: Armenia 268 km, Azerbaijan 9 km, Bulgaria 240 km, Georgia 252 km, Greece 206 km, Iran 499 km, Iraq 352 km, Syria 822 km

Coastline: 7,200 km

Maritime claims:
territorial sea: 6 nm in the Aegean Sea; 12 nm in Black Sea and in Mediterranean Sea
exclusive economic zone: in Black Sea only: to the maritime boundary agreed upon with the former USSR

Climate: temperate; hot, dry summers with mild, wet winters; harsher in interior

Terrain: high central plateau (Anatolia); narrow coastal plain; several mountain ranges

Elevation extremes:
lowest point: Mediterranean Sea 0 m
highest point: Mount Ararat 5,166 m

Natural resources: coal, iron ore, copper, chromium, antimony, mercury, gold, barite, borate, celestite (strontium), emery, feldspar, limestone, magnesite, marble, perlite, pumice, pyrites (sulfur), clay, arable land, hydropower

Land use:
arable land: 30.93%
permanent crops: 3.31%
other: 65.76% (2001)

Irrigated land: 42,000 sq km (1998 est.)

Natural hazards: very severe earthquakes, especially in northern Turkey, along an arc extending from the Sea of Marmara to Lake Van

Environment - current issues: water pollution from dumping of chemicals and detergents; air pollution, particularly in urban areas; deforestation; concern for oil spills from increasing Bosporus ship traffic

Environment - international agreements:
party to: Air Pollution, Antarctic Treaty, Biodiversity, Climate Change, Desertification, Endangered Species, Hazardous Wastes, Ozone Layer Protection, Ship Pollution, Wetlands
signed, but not ratified: Environmental Modification

Geography - note: strategic location controlling the Turkish Straits (Bosporus, Sea of Marmara, Dardanelles) that link Black and Aegean Seas; Mount Ararat, the legendary landing place of Noah's Ark, is in the far eastern portion of the country

PEOPLE

Population: 69,660,559 (July 2005 est.)

Age structure:
0-14 years: 26% (male 9,232,439/ female 8,897,135)
15-64 years: 67.3% (male 23,806,367/ female 23,053,536)
65 years and over: 6.7% (male 2,140,242/ female 2,530,840) (2005 est.)

Median age:
total: 27.7 years
male: 27.52 years
female: 27.89 years (2005 est.)

Population growth rate: 1.09% (2005 est.)

Birth rate: 16.83 births/1,000 population (2005 est.)

Death rate: 5.96 deaths/1,000 population (2005 est.)

Net migration rate: 0 migrant(s)/ 1,000 population (2005 est.)

Sex ratio:
at birth: 1.05 male(s)/female
under 15 years: 1.04 male(s)/ female
15-64 years: 1.03 male(s)/female
65 years and over: 0.85 male(s)/ female
total population: 1.02 male(s)/ female (2005 est.)

Infant mortality rate:
total: 41.04 deaths/1,000 live births
male: 44.68 deaths/1,000 live births
female: 37.22 deaths/1,000 live births (2005 est.)

Life expectancy at birth:
total population: 72.36 years
male: 69.94 years
female: 74.91 years (2005 est.)
Total fertility rate: 1.94 children born/woman (2005 est.)
HIV/AIDS - adult prevalence rate: less than 0.1% - note - no country specific models provided (2001 est.)
HIV/AIDS - people living with HIV/AIDS: NA
HIV/AIDS - deaths: NA
Nationality:
noun: Turk(s)
adjective: Turkish
Ethnic groups: Turkish 80%, Kurdish 20% (estimated)
Religions: Muslim 99.8% (mostly Sunni), other 0.2% (mostly Christians and Jews)
Languages: Turkish (official), Kurdish, Arabic, Armenian, Greek
Literacy:
definition: age 15 and over can read and write
total population: 86.5%
male: 94.3%
female: 78.7% (2003 est.)

GOVERNMENT

Country name:
conventional long form: Republic of Turkey
conventional short form: Turkey
local long form: Turkiye Cumhuriyeti
local short form: Turkiye
Government type: republican parliamentary democracy
Capital: Ankara
Administrative divisions: 81 provinces (iller, singular - il); Adana, Adiyaman, Afyonkarahisar, Agri, Aksaray, Amasya, Ankara, Antalya, Ardahan, Artvin, Aydin, Balikesir, Bartin, Batman, Bayburt, Bilecik, Bingol, Bitlis, Bolu, Burdur, Bursa, Canakkale, Cankiri, Corum, Denizli, Diyarbakir, Duzce, Edirne, Elazig, Erzincan, Erzurum, Eskisehir, Gaziantep, Giresun, Gumushane, Hakkari, Hatay, Igdir, Isparta, Istanbul, Izmir, Kahramanmaras, Karabuk, Karaman, Kars, Kastamonu, Kayseri, Kilis, Kirikkale, Kirklareli, Kirsehir, Kocaeli, Konya, Kutahya, Malatya, Manisa, Mardin, Mersin, Mugla, Mus, Nevsehir, Nigde, Ordu, Osmaniye, Rize, Sakarya, Samsun, Sanliurfa, Siirt, Sinop, Sirnak, Sivas, Tekirdag, Tokat, Trabzon, Tunceli, Usak, Van, Yalova, Yozgat, Zonguldak
Independence: 29 October 1923 (successor state to the Ottoman Empire)
National holiday: Republic Day, 29 October (1923)
Constitution: 7 November 1982
Legal system: civil law system derived from various European continental legal systems; accepts compulsory ICJ jurisdiction, with reservations; note - member of the European Court of Human Rights (ECHR), although Turkey claims limited derogations on the ratified European Convention on Human Rights
Suffrage: 18 years of age; universal
Executive branch:
chief of state: President Ahmet Necdet SEZER (since 16 May 2000)
head of government: Prime Minister Recep Tayyip ERDOGAN (14 March 2003)
cabinet: Council of Ministers appointed by the president on the nomination of the prime minister
elections: president elected by the National Assembly for a seven-year term; election last held 5 May 2000 (next to be held May 2007); prime minister appointed by the president from among members of parliament
election results: Ahmed Necdet SEZER elected president on the third ballot; percent of National Assembly vote - 60%
note: president must have a two-thirds majority of the National Assembly on the first two ballots and a simple majority on the third ballot
Legislative branch: unicameral Grand National Assembly of Turkey or Turkiye Buyuk Millet Meclisi (550 seats; members are elected by popular vote to serve five-year terms)
elections: last held 3 November 2002 (next to be held NA 2007); note - a special rerun of the General Election in the province of Siirt on 9 March 2003 resulted in the election of Recep Tayyip ERDOGAN to a seat in parliament, a prerequisite for becoming prime minister, on 14 March 2003
election results: percent of vote by party - AKP 34.3%, CHP 19.4%, DYP 9.6%, MHP 8.3%, Anavatan 5.1%, DSP 1.1%, and others; seats by party - AKP 363, CHP 178, independents 9; note - parties surpassing the 10% threshold are entitled to parliamentary seats; seats by party as of 1 December 2005 - AKP 357, CHP 154, ANAVATAN 22, DYP 4, SHP 4, HYP 1, independents 4, vacant 4
Judicial branch: Constitutional Court; High Court of Appeals (Yargitay); Council of State (Danistay); Court of Accounts (Sayistay); Military High Court of Appeals; Military High Administrative Court
Political parties and leaders: Anavatan Partisi (once was Motherland Party) or ANAVATAN [Erkan MUMCU]; Democratic Left Party or DSP [Mehmet Zeki SEZER]; Democratic People's Party or DEHAP [Tuncer BAKIRHAN]; Felicity Party (sometimes translated as Contentment Party) or SP [Necmettin ERBAKAN]; Justice and Development Party or AKP [Recep Tayyip ERDOGAN]; Liberal Democratic Party or LDP [Emin SIRIN]; Nationalist Action Party or MHP [Devlet BAHCELI]; People's Rise Party (Halkin Yukselisi Partisi) or HYP [Yasr Nuri OZTURK]; Republican People's Party or CHP [Deniz BAYKAL]; Social Democratic People's Party or SHP [Murat KARAYALCIN]; True Path Party (sometimes translated as Correct Way Party) or DYP [Mehmet AGAR]
note: the parties listed above are some of the more significant of the 49 parties that Turkey had on 1 December 2004
Political pressure groups and leaders: Confederation of Public Sector Unions or KESK [Sami EVREN]; Confederation of Revolutionary Workers Unions or DISK [Suleyman CELEBI]; Independent Industrialists' and Businessmen's Association or MUSIAD [Omer BOLAT]; Moral Rights Workers Union or Hak-Is [Salim USLU]; Turkish Industrialists' and Businessmen's Association or TUSIAD [Omer SABANCI]; Turkish Confederation of Employers' Unions or TISK [Refik BAYDUR]; Turkish Confederation of Labor or Turk-Is [Salih KILIC]; Turkish Confederation of Tradesmen and Craftsmen or TESK [Dervis GUNDAY]; Turkish Union of Chambers of Commerce and Commodity Exchanges or TOBB [M. Rifat HISARCIKLIOGLU]
International organization participation: AsDB, Australia Group, BIS, BSEC, CE, CERN (observer), EAPC, EBRD, ECO, EU (applicant), FAO, IAEA, IBRD, ICAO, ICC, ICFTU, ICRM, IDA, IDB, IEA, IFAD, IFC, IFRCS, IHO, ILO, IMF, IMO, Interpol, IOC, IOM, ISO, ITU, MIGA, NATO, NEA, NSG, OAS (observer), OECD, OIC, OPCW, OSCE, PCA, UN, UNCTAD, UNESCO, UNHCR, UNIDO, UNMIS, UNOMIG, UNRWA, UPU, WCO, WEU (associate), WFTU, WHO, WIPO, WMO, WToO, WTO, ZC
Diplomatic representation in the US:
chief of mission: Ambassador Dr. Osman Faruk LOGOGLU
chancery: 2525 Massachusetts Avenue NW, Washington, DC 20008
telephone: [1] (202) 612-6700
FAX: [1] (202) 612-6744
consulate(s) general: Chicago, Houston, Los Angeles, and New York
Diplomatic representation from the US:
chief of mission: Ambassador Ross WILSON
embassy: 110 Ataturk Boulevard, Kavaklidere, 06100 Ankara

mailing address: PSC 93, Box 5000, APO AE 09823
telephone: [90] (312) 455-5555
FAX: [90] (312) 467-0019
consulate(s) general: Istanbul
consulate(s): Adana; note - there is a Consular Agent in Izmir
Flag description: red with a vertical white crescent (the closed portion is toward the hoist side) and white five-pointed star centered just outside the crescent opening

ECONOMY

Economy - overview: Turkey's dynamic economy is a complex mix of modern industry and commerce along with a traditional agriculture sector that in 2004 still accounted for more than 34% of employment. It has a strong and rapidly growing private sector, yet the state still plays a major role in basic industry, banking, transport, and communication. The largest industrial sector is textiles and clothing, which accounts for one-third of industrial employment; it faces stiff competition in international markets with the end of the global quota system. However, other sectors, notably the automotive and electronics industries, are rising in importance within Turkey's export mix. Real GNP growth has exceeded 6% in many years, but this strong expansion has been interrupted by sharp declines in output in 1994, 1999, and 2001. The economy is turning around with the implementation of economic reforms, and 2004 GDP growth reached 9%. Inflation fell to 7.7% in 2005 - a 30-year low. Despite these strong economic gains in 2002-05, which were largely due to renewed investor interest in emerging markets, IMF backing, and tighter fiscal policy, the economy is still burdened by a high current account deficit and high debt. The public sector fiscal deficit exceeds 6% of GDP - due in large part to high interest payments, which accounted for about 37% of central government spending in 2004. Prior to 2005, foreign direct investment (FDI) in Turkey averaged less than $1 billion annually, but further economic and judicial reforms and prospective EU membership are expected to boost FDI. Privatization sales are currently approaching $21 billion.
GDP (purchasing power parity): $551.6 billion (2005 est.)
GDP (official exchange rate): $344.8 billion (2005 est.)
GDP - real growth rate: 5.1% (2005 est.)
GDP - per capita: purchasing power parity - $7,900 (2005 est.)
GDP - composition by sector:
agriculture: 11.7%
industry: 29.8%
services: 58.5% (2005 est.)
Labor force: 24.7 million
note: about 1.2 million Turks work abroad (2005 est.)
Labor force - by occupation: agriculture 35.9%, industry 22.8%, services 41.2% (3rd quarter, 2004)
Unemployment rate: 10% (plus underemployment of 4.0%) (2005 est.)
Population below poverty line: 20% (2002)
Household income or consumption by percentage share:
lowest 10%: 2.3%
highest 10%: 30.7% (2000)
Distribution of family income - Gini index: 42 (2003)
Inflation rate (consumer prices): 7.7% (2005 est.)
Investment (gross fixed): 19.3% of GDP (2005 est.)
Budget:
revenues: $93.58 billion
expenditures: $115.3 billion, including capital expenditures of NA (2005 est.)
Public debt: 67.5% of GDP (2005 est.)
Agriculture - products: tobacco, cotton, grain, olives, sugar beets, pulse, citrus; livestock
Industries: textiles, food processing, autos, mining (coal, chromite, copper, boron), steel, petroleum, construction, lumber, paper
Industrial production growth rate: 5.5% (2005 est.)
Electricity - production: 133.6 billion kWh (2003)
Electricity - production by source:
fossil fuel: 79.3%
hydro: 20.4%
nuclear: 0%
other: 0.3% (2001)
Electricity - consumption: 140.3 billion kWh (2005)
Electricity - exports: 600 million kWh (2002)
Electricity - imports: 1.2 billion kWh (2002)
Oil - production: 50,000 bbl/day (2005 est.)
Oil - consumption: 715,100 bbl/day (2005 est.)
Oil - exports: 46,110 bbl/day (2001)
Oil - imports: 616,500 bbl/day (2001)
Oil - proved reserves: 288.4 million bbl (1 January 2002)
Natural gas - production: 561 million cu m (2003 est.)
Natural gas - consumption: 22.6 billion cu m (2005 est.)
Natural gas - exports: 0 cu m (2001 est.)
Natural gas - imports: 15.75 billion cu m (2001 est.)
Natural gas - proved reserves: 8.685 billion cu m (1 January 2002)
Current account balance: $-22 billion (2005 est.)
Exports: $72.49 billion f.o.b. (2005 est.)
Exports - partners: Germany 13.9%, UK 8.8%, US 7.7%, Italy 7.4%, France 5.8%, Spain 4.2% (2004)
Imports: $101.2 billion f.o.b. (2005 est.)
Imports - partners: Germany 12.9%, Russia 9.3%, Italy 7.1%, France 6.4%, US 4.8%, China 4.6%, UK 4.4% (2004)
Reserves of foreign exchange and gold: $46.5 billion (2005 est.)
Debt - external: $161.8 billion (30 June 2005 est.)
Economic aid - recipient: ODA, $635.8 million (2002)
Currency (code): Turkish lira (TRL), New Turkish lira (YTL) after 1 January 2005
Currency code: TRL, YTL
Exchange rates: Turkish liras per US dollar - 1.36 (2005), 1,425,500 (2004), 1,500,900 (2003), 1,507,200 (2002), 1,225,600 (2001)
note: on 1 January 2005 the old Turkish Lira (TRL)was converted to New Turkish Lira (YTL) at a rate of 1,000,000 old to 1 New Turkish Lira
Fiscal year: calendar year

COMMUNICATIONS

Telephones - main lines in use: 18,916,700 (2003)
Telephones - mobile cellular: 27,887,500 (2003)
Telephone system:
general assessment: undergoing rapid modernization and expansion, especially with cellular telephones
domestic: additional digital exchanges are permitting a rapid increase in subscribers; the construction of a network of technologically advanced intercity trunk lines, using both fiber-optic cable and digital microwave radio relay is facilitating communication between urban centers; remote areas are reached by a domestic satellite system; the number of subscribers to mobile cellular telephone service is growing rapidly
international: country code - 90; international service is provided by three submarine fiber-optic cables in the Mediterranean and Black Seas, linking Turkey with Italy, Greece, Israel, Bulgaria, Romania, and Russia; also by 12 Intelsat earth stations, and by 328 mobile satellite terminals in the Inmarsat and Eutelsat systems (2002)
Radio broadcast stations: AM 16, FM 107, shortwave 6 (2001)
Radios: 11.3 million (1997)
Television broadcast stations: 635 (plus 2,934 repeaters) (1995)
Televisions: 20.9 million (1997)
Internet country code: .tr
Internet hosts: 355,215 (2004)

Internet Service Providers (ISPs): 50 (2001)
Internet users: 5.5 million (2003)

TRANSPORTATION

Airports: 119 (2004 est.)
Airports - with paved runways:
total: 88
over 3,047 m: 15
2,438 to 3,047 m: 32
1,524 to 2,437 m: 19
914 to 1,523 m: 18
under 914 m: 4 (2005 est.)
Airports - with unpaved runways:
total: 32
over 3,047 m: 1
2,438 to 3,047 m: 1
1,524 to 2,437 m: 2
914 to 1,523 m: 8
under 914 m: 20 (2005 est.)
Heliports: 16 (2005 est.)
Pipelines: gas 3,177 km; oil 3,562 km (2004)
Railways:
total: 8,697 km
standard gauge: 8,697 km 1.435-m gauge (2,122 km electrified) (2004)
Roadways:
total: 354,421 km
paved: 147,404 km (including 1,851 km of expressways)
unpaved: 207,017 km (2002)
Waterways: 1,200 km (2003)
Merchant marine:
total: 526 ships (1,000 GRT or over) 4,666,895 GRT/7,311,504 DWT
by type: bulk carrier 108, cargo 228, chemical tanker 45, combination ore/oil 1, container 25, liquefied gas 6, passenger 5, passenger/cargo 50, petroleum tanker 33, refrigerated cargo 2, roll on/roll off 22, specialized tanker 1
foreign-owned: 8 (Cyprus 3, Denmark 2, Greece 1, Italy 1, Switzerland 1)
registered in other countries: 231 (2005)
Ports and terminals: Aliaga, Ambarli, Eregli, Haydarpasa, Istanbul, Kocaeli (Izmit), Skhira, Toros

MILITARY

Military branches: Turkish Armed Forces (TSK): Land Forces, Naval Forces (includes Naval Air and Naval Infantry), Air Force
Military service age and obligation: 20 years of age (2004)
Manpower available for military service:
males age 20-49: 16,756,323 (2005 est.)
Manpower fit for military service: *males age 20-49:* 13,905,901 (2005 est.)
Manpower reaching military service age annually: *males:* 679,734 (2005 est.)
Military expenditures - dollar figure: $12.155 billion (2003)
Military expenditures - percent of GDP: 5.3% (2003)
Military - note: in the early 1990s, the Turkish Land Force was a large but badly equipped infantry force; there were 14 infantry divisions, but only one was mechanized, and out of 16 infantry brigades, only six were mechanized; the overhaul that has taken place since has produced highly mobile forces with greatly enhanced firepower in accordance with NATO's new strategic concept (2005)

TRANSNATIONAL ISSUES

Disputes - international: complex maritime, air, and territorial disputes with Greece in the Aegean Sea; status of north Cyprus question remains; Syria and Iraq protest Turkish hydrological projects to control upper Euphrates waters; Turkey has expressed concern over the status of Kurds in Iraq; border with Armenia remains closed over Nagorno-Karabakh
Refugees and internally displaced persons:
IDPs: 350,000-1,000,000 (fighting from 1984-99 between Kurdish PKK and Turkish military; most IDPs in southeastern provinces) (2004)
Illicit drugs: key transit route for Southwest Asian heroin to Western Europe and - to a far lesser extent the US - via air, land, and sea routes; major Turkish, Iranian, and other international trafficking organizations operate out of Istanbul; laboratories to convert imported morphine base into heroin are in remote regions of Turkey as well as near Istanbul; government maintains strict controls over areas of legal opium poppy cultivation and output of poppy straw concentrate

TURKMENISTAN

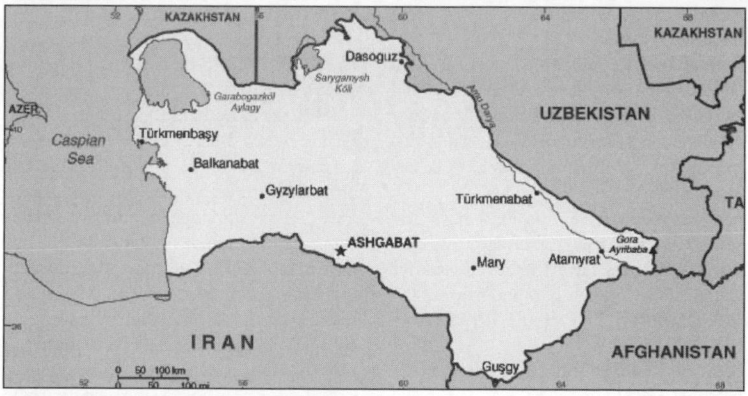

INTRODUCTION

Background: Annexed by Russia between 1865 and 1885, Turkmenistan became a Soviet republic in 1924. It achieved its independence upon the dissolution of the USSR in 1991. President NIYAZOV retains absolute control over the country and opposition is not tolerated. Extensive hydrocarbon/natural gas reserves could prove a boon to this underdeveloped country if extraction and delivery projects were to be expanded. The Turkmenistan Government is actively seeking to develop alternative petroleum transportation routes in order to break Russia's pipeline monopoly.

GEOGRAPHY

Location: Central Asia, bordering the Caspian Sea, between Iran and Kazakhstan
Geographic coordinates: 40 00 N, 60 00 E
Map references: Asia
Area:
total: 488,100 sq km
land: 488,100 sq km
water: negl.
Area - comparative: slightly larger than California
Land boundaries:
total: 3,736 km
border countries: Afghanistan 744 km, Iran 992 km, Kazakhstan 379 km, Uzbekistan 1,621 km
Coastline: 0 km; note - Turkmenistan borders the Caspian Sea (1,768 km)
Maritime claims: none (landlocked)
Climate: subtropical desert
Terrain: flat-to-rolling sandy desert with dunes rising to mountains in the south; low mountains along border with Iran; borders Caspian Sea in west
Elevation extremes:
lowest point: Vpadina Akchanaya -81 m; note - Sarygamysh Koli is a lake in northern Turkmenistan with a water level that

fluctuates above and below the elevation of Vpadina Akchanaya (the lake has dropped as low as -110 m)
highest point: Gora Ayribaba 3,139 m
Natural resources: petroleum, natural gas, sulfur, salt
Land use:
arable land: 3.72%
permanent crops: 0.14%
other: 96.14% (2001)
Irrigated land: 17,500 sq km (2003 est.)
Natural hazards: NA
Environment - current issues: contamination of soil and groundwater with agricultural chemicals, pesticides; salination, water-logging of soil due to poor irrigation methods; Caspian Sea pollution; diversion of a large share of the flow of the Amu Darya into irrigation contributes to that river's inability to replenish the Aral Sea; desertification
Environment - international agreements:
party to: Biodiversity, Climate Change, Climate Change-Kyoto Protocol, Desertification, Hazardous Wastes, Ozone Layer Protection
signed, but not ratified: none of the selected agreements
Geography - note: landlocked; the western and central low-lying, desolate portions of the country make up the great Garagum (Kara-Kum) desert, which occupies over 80% of the country; eastern part is plateau

PEOPLE

Population: 4,952,081 (July 2005 est.)
Age structure:
0-14 years: 35.7% (male 909,113/ female 860,128)
15-64 years: 60.2% (male 1,462,198/ female 1,516,836)
65 years and over: 4.1% (male 78,119/ female 125,687) (2005 est.)
Median age:
total: 21.56 years
male: 20.68 years
female: 22.44 years (2005 est.)
Population growth rate: 1.81% (2005 est.)
Birth rate: 27.68 births/1,000 population (2005 est.)
Death rate: 8.78 deaths/1,000 population (2005 est.)
Net migration rate: -0.81 migrant(s)/ 1,000 population (2005 est.)
Sex ratio:
at birth: 1.05 male(s)/female
under 15 years: 1.06 male(s)/ female
15-64 years: 0.96 male(s)/female
65 years and over: 0.62 male(s)/ female
total population: 0.98 male(s)/ female (2005 est.)
Infant mortality rate:
total: 73.08 deaths/1,000 live births
male: 76.9 deaths/1,000 live births
female: 69.07 deaths/1,000 live births (2005 est.)
Life expectancy at birth:
total population: 61.39 years
male: 58.02 years
female: 64.93 years (2005 est.)
Total fertility rate: 3.41 children born/woman (2005 est.)
HIV/AIDS - adult prevalence rate: less than 0.1% (2004 est.)
HIV/AIDS - people living with HIV/AIDS: less than 200 (2003 est.)
HIV/AIDS - deaths: less than 100 (2004 est.)
Nationality:
noun: Turkmen(s)
adjective: Turkmen
Ethnic groups: Turkmen 85%, Uzbek 5%, Russian 4%, other 6% (2003)
Religions: Muslim 89%, Eastern Orthodox 9%, unknown 2%
Languages: Turkmen 72%, Russian 12%, Uzbek 9%, other 7%
Literacy:
definition: age 15 and over can read and write
total population: 98.8%
male: 99.3%
female: 98.3% (1995 est.)

GOVERNMENT

Country name:
conventional long form: none
conventional short form: Turkmenistan
local long form: none
local short form: Turkmenistan
former: Turkmen Soviet Socialist Republic
Government type: republic; authoritarian presidential rule, with little power outside the executive branch
Capital: Ashgabat
Administrative divisions: 5 provinces (welayatlar, singular - welayat): Ahal Welayaty (Ashgabat), Balkan Welayaty (Balkanabat), Dashoguz Welayaty, Lebap Welayaty (Turkmenabat), Mary Welayaty
note: administrative divisions have the same names as their administrative centers (exceptions have the administrative center name following in parentheses)
Independence: 27 October 1991 (from the Soviet Union)
National holiday: Independence Day, 27 October (1991)
Constitution: adopted 18 May 1992
Legal system: based on civil law system
Suffrage: 18 years of age; universal
Executive branch:
chief of state: President and Chairman of the Cabinet of Ministers Saparmurat NIYAZOV (since 27 October 1990, when the first direct presidential election occurred); note - the president is both the chief of state and head of government
head of government: President and Chairman of the Cabinet of Ministers Saparmurat NIYAZOV (since 27 October 1990, when the first direct presidential election occurred); note - the president is both the chief of state and head of government
cabinet: Cabinet of Ministers appointed by the president
note: NIYAZOV's term in office was extended indefinitely on 28 December 1999 during a session of the People's Council (Halk Maslahaty); in November 2005 the People's Council voted down Niyazov's suggestion to hold presidential elections in 2009
elections: president elected by popular vote for a five-year term; election last held 21 June 1992; note - President NIYAZOV was unanimously approved as president for life by the People's Council on 28 December 1999; deputy chairmen of the cabinet of ministers are appointed by the president
election results: Saparmurat NIYAZOV elected president without opposition; percent of vote - Saparmurat NIYAZOV 99.5%
Legislative branch: under the 1992 constitution, there are two parliamentary bodies, a unicameral People's Council or Halk Maslahaty (supreme legislative body of up to 2,500 delegates, some of whom are elected by popular vote and some of whom are appointed; meets at least yearly) and a unicameral Parliament or Mejlis (50 seats; members are elected by popular vote to serve five-year terms); membership is scheduled to be increased to 65 seats
elections: People's Council - last held in April 2003 (next to be held December 2008); Mejlis - last held 19 December 2004 (next to be held December 2008)
election results: Mejlis - DPT 100%; seats by party - DPT 50; note - all 50 elected officials are members of the Democratic Party of Turkmenistan and are preapproved by President NIYAZOV
note: in late 2003, a new law was adopted, reducing the powers of the Mejlis and making the Halk Maslahaty the supreme legislative organ; the Halk Maslahaty can now legally dissolve the Mejlis, and the president is now able to participate in the Mejlis as its supreme leader; the Mejlis can no longer adopt or amend the constitution, or announce referendums or its elections; since the president is both the "Chairman for Life" of the Halk Maslahaty and the supreme leader of the Mejlis, the 2003 law has the effect of making him the sole authority of both the executive and legislative branches of government

Judicial branch: Supreme Court (judges are appointed by the president)
Political parties and leaders: Democratic Party of Turkmenistan or DPT [Saparmurat NIYAZOV]
note: formal opposition parties are outlawed; unofficial, small opposition movements exist underground or in foreign countries; the two most prominent opposition groups-in-exile have been National Democratic Movement of Turkmenistan (NDMT) and the United Democratic Party of Turkmenistan (UDPT); NDMT was led by former Foreign Minister Boris SHIKHMURADOV until his arrest and imprisonment in the wake of the 25 November 2002 assassination attempt on President NIYAZOV; UDPT is led by former Foreign Minister Abdy KULIEV and is based out of Moscow
Political pressure groups and leaders: NA
International organization participation: AsDB, CIS (associate), EAPC, EBRD, ECO, FAO, G-77, IBRD, ICAO, ICRM, IDB, IFC, IFRCS, ILO, IMF, IMO, Interpol, IOC, IOM (observer), ISO (correspondent), ITU, MIGA, NAM, OIC, OPCW, OSCE, PFP, UN, UNCTAD, UNESCO, UNIDO, UPU, WCO, WFTU, WHO, WIPO, WMO, WToO
Diplomatic representation in the US:
chief of mission: Ambassador Mered Bairamovich ORAZOV
chancery: 2207 Massachusetts Avenue NW, Washington, DC 20008
telephone: [1] (202) 588-1500
FAX: [1] (202) 588-0697
Diplomatic representation from the US:
chief of mission: Ambassador Tracey A. JACOBSON
embassy: No. 9 1984 Street (formerly Pushkin Street), Ashgabat, Turkmenistan 774000
mailing address: 7070 Ashgabat Place, Washington, D.C. 20521-7070
telephone: [9] (9312) 35-00-45
FAX: [9] (9312) 39-26-14
Flag description: green field with a vertical red stripe near the hoist side, containing five tribal guls (designs used in producing carpets) stacked above two crossed olive branches similar to the olive branches on the UN flag; a white crescent moon representing Islam with five white stars representing the regions or velayats of Turkmenistan appear in the upper corner of the field just to the fly side of the red stripe

ECONOMY

Economy - overview: Turkmenistan is a largely desert country with intensive agriculture in irrigated oases and large gas and oil resources. One-half of its irrigated land is planted in cotton; formerly it was the world's tenth-largest producer. Poor harvests in recent years have led to an almost 50% decline in cotton exports. With an authoritarian ex-Communist regime in power and a tribally based social structure, Turkmenistan has taken a cautious approach to economic reform, hoping to use gas and cotton sales to sustain its inefficient economy. Privatization goals remain limited. In 1998-2005, Turkmenistan suffered from the continued lack of adequate export routes for natural gas and from obligations on extensive short-term external debt. At the same time, however, total exports rose by 20% to 30% per year in 2003-2005, largely because of higher international oil and gas prices. In 2005 Ashgabat sought to raise natural gas export prices to its main customers, Russia and Ukraine, from $44 per thousand cubic meters (tcm) to $66 per tcm. Overall prospects in the near future are discouraging because of widespread internal poverty, the burden of foreign debt, the government's irrational use of oil and gas revenues, and its unwillingness to adopt market-oriented reforms. Turkmenistan's economic statistics are state secrets, and GDP and other figures are subject to wide margins of error. In particular, the rate of GDP growth is uncertain.
GDP (purchasing power parity): $29.38 billion (2005 est.)
GDP (official exchange rate): $13.97 billion (2005 est.)
GDP - real growth rate: IMF estimate: 7%
note: official government statistics show 21.4% growth, but these estimates are notoriously unreliable (2005 est.)
GDP - per capita: purchasing power parity - $5,900 (2005 est.)
GDP - composition by sector:
agriculture: 26.9%
industry: 39.5%
services: 33.6% (2005 est.)
Labor force: 2.32 million (2003 est.)
Labor force - by occupation: agriculture 48.2%, industry 13.8%, services 37% (2003 est.)
Unemployment rate: 60% (2004 est.)
Population below poverty line: 58% (2003 est.)
Household income or consumption by percentage share:
lowest 10%: 2.6%
highest 10%: 31.7% (1998)
Distribution of family income - Gini index: 40.8 (1998)
Inflation rate (consumer prices): 10% (2005 est.)
Investment (gross fixed): 25.6% of GDP (2005 est.)
Budget:
revenues: $1.401 billion
expenditures: $1.542 billion, including capital expenditures of NA (2005 est.)
Agriculture - products: cotton, grain; livestock
Industries: natural gas, oil, petroleum products, textiles, food processing
Industrial production growth rate: official government estimate: 22% (2003 est.)
Electricity - production: 11.41 billion kWh (2004 est.)
Electricity - production by source:
fossil fuel: 99.9%
hydro: 0.1%
nuclear: 0%
other: 0% (2001)
Electricity - consumption: 8.847 billion kWh (2002)
Electricity - exports: 1.136 billion kWh (2004)
Electricity - imports: 0 kWh (2002)
Oil - production: 203,400 bbl/day (2003 est.)
Oil - consumption: 80,000 bbl/day (2003 est.)
Oil - exports: NA (2001)
Oil - imports: NA (2001)
Oil - proved reserves: 273 million bbl (1 January 2002)
Natural gas - production: 54.6 billion cu m (2004 est.)
Natural gas - consumption: 15.5 billion cu m (2004 est.)
Natural gas - exports: 38.6 billion cu m (2004 est.)
Natural gas - imports: 0 cu m (2004 est.)
Natural gas - proved reserves: 2.9 trillion cu m (1 January 2002)
Current account balance: $-204.3 million (2005 est.)
Exports: $4.7 billion f.o.b. (2005 est.)
Exports - partners: Ukraine 46.6%, Iran 17.3%, Turkey 4.2%, Italy 4.1% (2004)
Imports: $4.175 billion f.o.b. (2005 est.)
Imports - partners: US 11.8%, Russia 9.7%, UAE 9.2%, Ukraine 9%, Turkey 8.6%, Germany 8%, France 5%, Georgia 4.6%, Iran 4.5% (2004)
Reserves of foreign exchange and gold: $3.358 billion (2005 est.)
Debt - external: $2.4 billion to $5 billion (2001 est.)
Economic aid - recipient: $16 million from the US (2001)
Currency (code): Turkmen manat (TMM)
Currency code: TMM
Exchange rates: in recent years the unofficial rate has hovered around 24,000 to 25,000 Turkmen manats to the dollar. The official rate has consistently been 5,200 Manat to the dollar.
Fiscal year: calendar year

COMMUNICATIONS

Telephones - main lines in use: 374,000 (2002)

Telephones - mobile cellular: 52,000 (2004)
Telephone system:
general assessment: poorly developed
domestic: NA
international: country code - 993; linked by cable and microwave radio relay to other CIS republics and to other countries by leased connections to the Moscow international gateway switch; a new telephone link from Ashgabat to Iran has been established; a new exchange in Ashgabat switches international traffic through Turkey via Intelsat; satellite earth stations - 1 Orbita and 1 Intelsat
Radio broadcast stations: AM 16, FM 8, shortwave 2 (1998)
Radios: 1.225 million (1997)
Television broadcast stations: 4 (government owned and programmed) (2004)
Televisions: 820,000 (1997)
Internet country code: .tm
Internet hosts: 524 (2004)
Internet Service Providers (ISPs): 1
Internet users: 8,000 (2002)

TRANSPORTATION

Airports: 53 (2004 est.)
Airports - with paved runways:
total: 22
over 3,047 m: 1
2,438 to 3,047 m: 10
1,524 to 2,437 m: 9
914 to 1,523 m: 2 (2005 est.)
Airports - with unpaved runways:
total: 17
1,524 to 2,437 m: 2
914 to 1,523 m: 1
under 914 m: 14 (2005 est.)
Heliports: 1 (2005 est.)
Pipelines: gas 6,549 km; oil 1,395 km (2004)
Railways:
total: 2,440 km
broad gauge: 2,440 km 1.520-m gauge (2004)
Roadways:
total: 24,000 km
paved: 19,488 km
unpaved: 4,512 km (1999 est.)
Waterways: 1,300 km (Amu Darya and Kara Kum canal important inland waterways) (2003)
Merchant marine:
total: 7 ships (1,000 GRT or over) 6,873 GRT/8,345 DWT
by type: cargo 3, combination ore/oil 1, petroleum tanker 2, refrigerated cargo 1 (2005)
Ports and terminals: Turkmenbasy

MILITARY

Military branches: Ground Forces, Air and Air Defense Forces (2004)
Military service age and obligation: 18 years of age for compulsory military service; conscript service obligation - 2 years (2004)
Manpower available for military service: *males age 18-49:* 1,132,833 (2005 est.)
Manpower fit for military service: *males age 18-49:* 759,978 (2005 est.)
Manpower reaching military service age annually: *males:* 56,532 (2005 est.)
Military expenditures - dollar figure: $90 million (FY99)
Military expenditures - percent of GDP: 3.4% (FY99)

TRANSNATIONAL ISSUES

Disputes - international: cotton monoculture in Uzbekistan and Turkmenistan creates water-sharing difficulties for Amu Darya river states; bilateral talks continue with Azerbaijan on dividing the seabed and contested oilfields in the middle of the Caspian; demarcation of land boundary with Kazakhstan has started but Caspian seabed delimitation remains stalled
Illicit drugs: transit country for Afghan narcotics bound for Russian and Western European markets; transit point for heroin precursor chemicals bound for Afghanistan

TURKS AND CAICOS ISLANDS

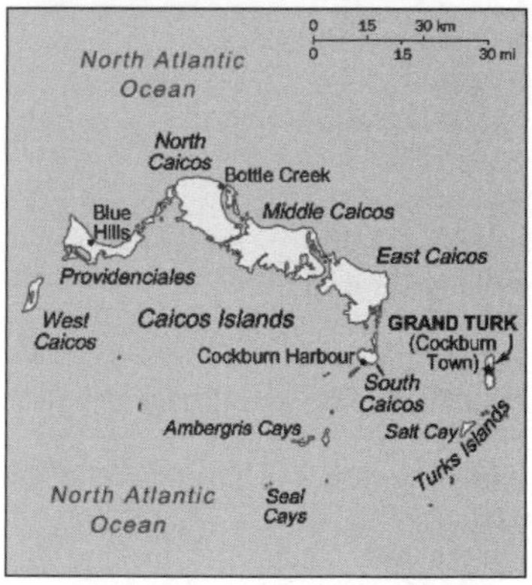

INTRODUCTION

Background: The islands were part of the UK's Jamaican colony until 1962, when they assumed the status of a separate crown colony upon Jamaica's independence. The governor of The Bahamas oversaw affairs from 1965 to 1973. With Bahamian independence, the islands received a separate governor in 1973. Although independence was agreed upon for 1982, the policy was reversed and the islands remain a British overseas territory.

GEOGRAPHY

Location: Caribbean, two island groups in the North Atlantic Ocean, southeast of The Bahamas, north of Haiti
Geographic coordinates: 21 45 N, 71 35 W
Map references: Central America and the Caribbean
Area:
total: 430 sq km
land: 430 sq km
water: 0 sq km
Area - comparative: 2.5 times the size of Washington, DC
Land boundaries: 0 km
Coastline: 389 km
Maritime claims:
territorial sea: 12 nm
exclusive fishing zone: 200 nm
Climate: tropical; marine; moderated by trade winds; sunny and relatively dry
Terrain: low, flat limestone; extensive marshes and mangrove swamps
Elevation extremes:
lowest point: Caribbean Sea 0 m
highest point: Blue Hills 49 m
Natural resources: spiny lobster, conch
Land use:
arable land: 2.33%
permanent crops: 0%
other: 97.67% (2001)
Irrigated land: NA sq km
Natural hazards: frequent hurricanes
Environment - current issues: limited natural fresh water resources, private cisterns collect rainwater
Geography - note: about 40 islands (eight inhabited)

PEOPLE

Population: 20,556 (July 2005 est.)
Age structure:
0-14 years: 32.5% (male 3,396/ female 3,277)
15-64 years: 63.8% (male 6,900/ female 6,220)
65 years and over: 3.7% (male 342/female 421) (2005 est.)
Median age:
total: 27.35 years
male: 28.08 years
female: 26.62 years (2005 est.)
Population growth rate: 2.9% (2005 est.)
Birth rate: 22.23 births/1,000 population (2005 est.)
Death rate: 4.28 deaths/1,000 population (2005 est.)
Net migration rate: 11.09 migrant(s)/

1,000 population (2005 est.)
Sex ratio:
at birth: 1.05 male(s)/female
under 15 years: 1.04 male(s)/ female
15-64 years: 1.11 male(s)/female
65 years and over: 0.81 male(s)/ female
total population: 1.07 male(s)/ female (2005 est.)
Infant mortality rate:
total: 15.67 deaths/1,000 live births
male: 18.11 deaths/1,000 live births
female: 13.11 deaths/1,000 live births (2005 est.)
Life expectancy at birth:
total population: 74.51 years
male: 72.28 years
female: 76.84 years (2005 est.)
Total fertility rate: 3.08 children born/woman (2005 est.)
HIV/AIDS - adult prevalence rate: NA
HIV/AIDS - people living with HIV/AIDS: NA
HIV/AIDS - deaths: NA
Nationality:
noun: none
adjective: none
Ethnic groups: black 90%, mixed, European, or North American 10%
Religions: Baptist 40%, Methodist 16%, Anglican 18%, Church of God 12%, other 14% (1990)
Languages: English (official)
Literacy:
definition: age 15 and over has ever attended school
total population: 98%
male: 99%
female: 98% (1970 est.)
People - note: destination and transit point for illegal Haitian immigrants bound for the Turks and Caicos Islands, Bahamas, and US

GOVERNMENT

Country name:
conventional long form: none
conventional short form: Turks and Caicos Islands
Dependency status: overseas territory of the UK
Government type: NA
Capital: Grand Turk
Administrative divisions: none (overseas territory of the UK)
Independence: none (overseas territory of the UK)
National holiday: Constitution Day, 30 August (1976)
Constitution: introduced 30 August 1976; suspended in 1986; restored and revised 5 March 1988
Legal system: based on laws of England and Wales, with a few adopted from Jamaica and The Bahamas
Suffrage: 18 years of age; universal
Executive branch:
chief of state: Queen ELIZABETH II (since 6 February 1953), represented by Governor Richard TAUWHARE (since 11 July 2005)
head of government: Chief Minister Michael Eugene MISICK (since 15 August 2003)
cabinet: Executive Council consists of three ex officio members and five appointed by the governor from among the members of the Legislative Council
elections: none; the monarch is hereditary; governor appointed by the monarch; following legislative elections, the leader of the majority party is appointed chief minister by the governor
Legislative branch: unicameral Legislative Council (19 seats of which 13 are popularly elected; members serve four-year terms)
elections: last held 24 April 2003 (next to be held in 2007)
election results: percent of vote by party - PDM 53.8%, PNP 46.2%; seats by party - PDM 7, PNP 6; note - in by-elections held 7 August 2003, the PNP gained two seats for a majority of 8 seats; PDM now has 5
Judicial branch: Supreme Court
Political parties and leaders: People's Democratic Movement or PDM [Derek H. TAYLOR]; Progressive National Party or PNP [Michael Eugene MISICK]
Political pressure groups and leaders: NA
International organization participation: Caricom (associate), CDB, Interpol (subbureau), UPU
Diplomatic representation in the US: none (overseas territory of the UK)
Diplomatic representation from the US: none (overseas territory of the UK)
Flag description: blue, with the flag of the UK in the upper hoist-side quadrant and the colonial shield centered on the outer half of the flag; the shield is yellow and contains a conch shell, lobster, and cactus

ECONOMY

Economy - overview: The Turks and Caicos economy is based on tourism, fishing, and offshore financial services. Most capital goods and food for domestic consumption are imported. The US is the leading source of tourists, accounting for more than half of the annual 93,000 visitors in the late 1990s. Major sources of government revenue also include fees from offshore financial activities and customs receipts.
GDP (purchasing power parity): $216 million (2002 est.)
GDP (official exchange rate): NA
GDP - real growth rate: 4.9% (2000 est.)
GDP - per capita: purchasing power parity - $11,500 (2002 est.)
GDP - composition by sector:
agriculture: NA%
industry: NA%
services: NA%
Labor force: 4,848 (1990 est.)
Labor force - by occupation: about 33% in government and 20% in agriculture and fishing; significant numbers in tourism, financial, and other services
Unemployment rate: 10% (1997 est.)
Population below poverty line: NA
Household income or consumption by percentage share:
lowest 10%: NA
highest 10%: NA
Inflation rate (consumer prices): 4% (1995)
Budget:
revenues: $47 million
expenditures: $33.6 million, including capital expenditures of NA (1997-98 est.)
Agriculture - products: corn, beans, cassava (tapioca), citrus fruits; fish
Industries: tourism, offshore financial services
Industrial production growth rate: NA%
Electricity - production: 5 million kWh (2003)
Electricity - production by source:
fossil fuel: 100%
hydro: 0%
nuclear: 0%
other: 0% (2001)
Electricity - consumption: 4.65 million kWh (2003)
Electricity - exports: 0 kWh (2003)
Electricity - imports: 0 kWh (2003)
Oil - production: 0 bbl/day (2003 est.)
Oil - consumption: 80 bbl/day (2003 est.)
Oil - exports: NA (2001)
Oil - imports: NA (2001)
Exports: $169.2 million (2000)
Exports - partners: US, UK (2004)
Imports: $175.6 million (2000)
Imports - partners: US, UK (2004)
Debt - external: NA
Economic aid - recipient: $4.1 million (1997)
Currency (code): US dollar (USD)
Currency code: USD
Exchange rates: the US dollar is used
Fiscal year: calendar year

COMMUNICATIONS

Telephones - main lines in use: 5,700 (2002)
Telephones - mobile cellular: 1,700 (1999)
Telephone system:
general assessment: fully digital system with international direct dialing
domestic: full range of services available
international: country code - 1-649; 2 submarine cables; satellite earth station - 1 Intelsat (Atlantic Ocean)

Radio broadcast stations: AM 2, FM 7, shortwave 0 (2004)
Radios: 8,000 (1997)
Television broadcast stations: 0 (broadcasts from The Bahamas are received; 2 cable television networks) (2004)
Televisions: NA
Internet country code: .tc
Internet Service Providers (ISPs): 14 (2000)
Internet users: NA

TRANSPORTATION

Airports: 8 (2004 est.)
Airports - with paved runways:
total: 6
1,524 to 2,437 m: 3
914 to 1,523 m: 1
under 914 m: 2 (2005 est.)
Airports - with unpaved runways:
total: 2
under 914 m: 2 (2005 est.)
Roadways:
total: 121 km
paved: 24 km
unpaved: 97 km (2000)
Ports and terminals: Grand Turk, Providenciales

MILITARY

Military - note: defense is the responsibility of the UK

TRANSNATIONAL ISSUES

Disputes - international: have received Haitians fleeing economic and civil disorder
Illicit drugs: transshipment point for South American narcotics destined for the US and Europe

TUVALU

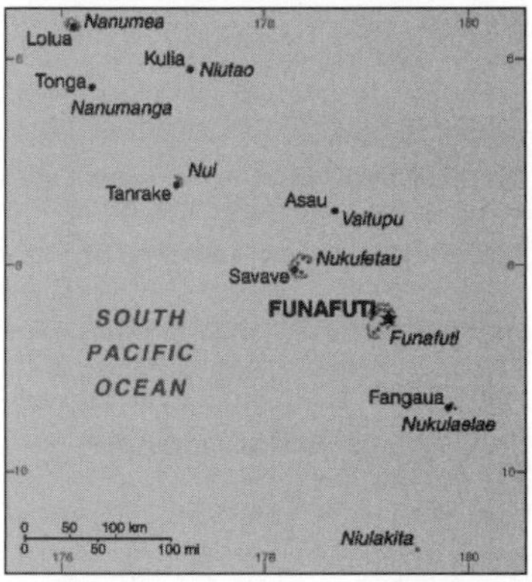

INTRODUCTION

Background: In 1974, ethnic differences within the British colony of the Gilbert and Ellice Islands caused the Polynesians of the Ellice Islands to vote for separation from the Micronesians of the Gilbert Islands. The following year, the Ellice Islands became the separate British colony of Tuvalu. Independence was granted in 1978. In 2000, Tuvalu negotiated a contract leasing its Internet domain name ".tv" for $50 million in royalties over the next dozen years.

GEOGRAPHY

Location: Oceania, island group consisting of nine coral atolls in the South Pacific Ocean, about one-half of the way from Hawaii to Australia
Geographic coordinates: 8 00 S, 178 00 E
Map references: Oceania
Area:
total: 26 sq km
land: 26 sq km
water: 0 sq km
Area - comparative: 0.1 times the size of Washington, DC
Land boundaries: 0 km
Coastline: 24 km
Maritime claims:
territorial sea: 12 nm
contiguous zone: 24 nm
exclusive economic zone: 200 nm
Climate: tropical; moderated by easterly trade winds (March to November); westerly gales and heavy rain (November to March)
Terrain: very low-lying and narrow coral atolls
Elevation extremes:
lowest point: Pacific Ocean 0 m
highest point: unnamed location 5 m
Natural resources: fish
Land use:
arable land: 0%
permanent crops: 0%
other: 100% (2001)
Irrigated land: NA
Natural hazards: severe tropical storms are usually rare, but, in 1997, there were three cyclones; low level of islands make them very sensitive to changes in sea level
Environment - current issues: since there are no streams or rivers and groundwater is not potable, most water needs must be met by catchment systems with storage facilities (the Japanese Government has built one desalination plant and plans to build one other); beachhead erosion because of the use of sand for building materials; excessive clearance of forest undergrowth for use as fuel; damage to coral reefs from the spread of the Crown of Thorns starfish; Tuvalu is very concerned about global increases in greenhouse gas emissions and their effect on rising sea levels, which threaten the country's underground water table; in 2000, the government appealed to Australia and New Zealand to take in Tuvaluans if rising sea levels should make evacuation necessary
Environment - international agreements:
party to: Biodiversity, Climate Change, Climate Change-Kyoto Protocol, Desertification, Law of the Sea, Ozone Layer Protection, Ship Pollution
signed, but not ratified: none of the selected agreements
Geography - note: one of the smallest and most remote countries on Earth; six of the coral atolls - Nanumea, Nui, Vaitupu, Nukufetau, Funafuti, and Nukulaelae - have lagoons open to the ocean; Nanumaya and Niutao have landlocked lagoons; Niulakita does not have a lagoon

PEOPLE

Population: 11,636 (July 2005 est.)
Age structure:
0-14 years: 30.8% (male 1,823/ female 1,756)
15-64 years: 64.2% (male 3,620/ female 3,847)
65 years and over: 5.1% (male 229/female 361) (2005 est.)
Median age:
total: 24.45 years
male: 23.36 years
female: 25.85 years (2005 est.)
Population growth rate: 1.47% (2005 est.)
Birth rate: 21.91 births/1,000 population (2005 est.)
Death rate: 7.22 deaths/1,000 population (2005 est.)
Net migration rate: 0 migrant(s)/ 1,000 population (2005 est.)
Sex ratio:
at birth: 1.06 male(s)/female
under 15 years: 1.04 male(s)/ female
15-64 years: 0.94 male(s)/female
65 years and over: 0.63 male(s)/ female
total population: 0.95 male(s)/ female (2005 est.)
Infant mortality rate:
total: 20.03 deaths/1,000 live births
male: 22.9 deaths/1,000 live births
female: 17.02 deaths/1,000 live births (2005 est.)
Life expectancy at birth:
total population: 68.01 years
male: 65.79 years
female: 70.33 years (2005 est.)

Total fertility rate: 3 children born/woman (2005 est.)
HIV/AIDS - adult prevalence rate: NA
HIV/AIDS - people living with HIV/AIDS: NA
HIV/AIDS - deaths: NA
Nationality:
noun: Tuvaluan(s)
adjective: Tuvaluan
Ethnic groups: Polynesian 96%, Micronesian 4%
Religions: Church of Tuvalu (Congregationalist) 97%, Seventh-Day Adventist 1.4%, Baha'i 1%, other 0.6%
Languages: Tuvaluan, English, Samoan, Kiribati (on the island of Nui)
Literacy:
definition: NA
total population: NA%
male: NA%
female: NA%

GOVERNMENT

Country name:
conventional long form: none
conventional short form: Tuvalu
former: Ellice Islands
note: "Tuvalu" means "group of eight," referring to the country's eight traditionally inhabited islands
Government type: constitutional monarchy with a parliamentary democracy; began debating republic status in 1992
Capital: Funafuti; note - administrative offices are located in Vaiaku Village on Fongafale Islet
Administrative divisions: none
Independence: 1 October 1978 (from UK)
National holiday: Independence Day, 1 October (1978)
Constitution: 1 October 1978
Legal system: NA
Suffrage: 18 years of age; universal
Executive branch:
chief of state: Queen ELIZABETH II (since 6 February 1952), represented by Governor General Filoimea TELITO (since 15 April 2005)
head of government: Prime Minister Maatia TOAFA (since 11 October 2004)
cabinet: Cabinet appointed by the governor general on the recommendation of the prime minister
elections: the monarch is hereditary; governor general appointed by the monarch on the recommendation of the prime minister; prime minister and deputy prime minister elected by and from the members of Parliament; election last held 11 October 2004 (next to be held following parliamentary elections in 2006)
election results: Saufatu SOPOANGA resigned parliamentary seat on 27 August 2004 following no-confidence vote on 25 August 2004; succeeded by Deputy Prime Minister Maatia TOAFA in an acting capacity on 27 August 2004; Maatia TOAFA confirmed Prime Minister in a Parliamentary election (8-7 vote) on 11 October 2004
Legislative branch: unicameral Parliament or Fale I Fono, also called House of Assembly (15 seats; members elected by popular vote to serve four-year terms)
elections: last held 25 July 2002 (next to be held NA 2006)
election results: percent of vote - NA%; seats - independents 15
Judicial branch: High Court (a chief justice visits twice a year to preside over its sessions; its rulings can be appealed to the Court of Appeal in Fiji); eight Island Courts (with limited jurisdiction)
Political parties and leaders: there are no political parties but members of Parliament usually align themselves in informal groupings
Political pressure groups and leaders: none
International organization participation: ACP, AsDB, C, FAO, IFRCS (observer), IMO, ITU, OPCW, PIF, Sparteca, SPC, UN, UNCTAD, UNESCO, UPU, WHO
Diplomatic representation in the US: Tuvalu does not have an embassy in the US - the country's only diplomatic post is in Fiji - Tuvalu does, however, have a UN office located at 800 2nd Avenue, Suite 400D, New York, New York 10017, telephone: [1] (212) 490-0534
Diplomatic representation from the US: the US does not have an embassy in Tuvalu; the US ambassador to Fiji is accredited to Tuvalu
Flag description: light blue with the flag of the UK in the upper hoist-side quadrant; the outer half of the flag represents a map of the country with nine yellow five-pointed stars symbolizing the nine islands

ECONOMY

Economy - overview: Tuvalu consists of a densely populated, scattered group of nine coral atolls with poor soil. The country has no known mineral resources and few exports. Subsistence farming and fishing are the primary economic activities. Fewer than 1,000 tourists, on average, visit Tuvalu annually. Government revenues largely come from the sale of stamps and coins and worker remittances. About 1,000 Tuvaluans work in Nauru in the phosphate mining industry. Nauru has begun repatriating Tuvaluans, however, as phosphate resources decline. Substantial income is received annually from an international trust fund established in 1987 by Australia, NZ, and the UK and supported also by Japan and South Korea. Thanks to wise investments and conservative withdrawals, this fund has grown from an initial $17 million to over $35 million in 1999. The US government is also a major revenue source for Tuvalu because of payments from a 1988 treaty on fisheries. In an effort to reduce its dependence on foreign aid, the government is pursuing public sector reforms, including privatization of some government functions and personnel cuts of up to 7%. In 1998, Tuvalu began deriving revenue from use of its area code for "900" lines and in 2000, from the lease of its ".tv" Internet domain name. Royalties from these new technology sources could increase substantially over the next decade. With merchandise exports only a fraction of merchandise imports, continued reliance must be placed on fishing and telecommunications license fees, remittances from overseas workers, official transfers, and income from overseas investments.
GDP (purchasing power parity): $12.2 million (2000 est.)
GDP (official exchange rate): NA
GDP - real growth rate: 3% (2000 est.)
GDP - per capita: purchasing power parity - $1,100 (2000 est.)
GDP - composition by sector:
agriculture: NA%
industry: NA%
services: NA%
Labor force: 7,000 (2001 est.)
Labor force - by occupation: people make a living mainly through exploitation of the sea, reefs, and atolls and from wages sent home by those abroad (mostly workers in the phosphate industry and sailors)
Unemployment rate: NA%
Population below poverty line: NA
Household income or consumption by percentage share:
lowest 10%: NA
highest 10%: NA
Inflation rate (consumer prices): 5% (2000 est.)
Budget:
revenues: $22.5 million
expenditures: $11.2 million, including capital expenditures of $4.2 million (2000 est.)
Agriculture - products: coconuts; fish
Industries: fishing, tourism, copra
Industrial production growth rate: NA%
Electricity - production by source:
fossil fuel: NA
hydro: NA
nuclear: NA
other: NA
Exports: $1 million f.o.b. (2004 est.)

Exports - partners: Germany 56.5%, Fiji 14.3%, Italy 10.9%, UK 7.7%, Poland 4.9% (2004)
Imports: $31 million c.i.f. (2004 est.)
Imports - partners: Fiji 50.2%, Japan 18.1%, Australia 9.6%, China 8%, New Zealand 5.5% (2004)
Debt - external: NA
Economic aid - recipient: $13 million; note - major donors are Australia, Japan, and the US (1999 est.)
Currency (code): Australian dollar (AUD); note - there is also a Tuvaluan dollar
Currency code: AUD
Exchange rates: Tuvaluan dollars or Australian dollars per US dollar - 1.31 (2005), 1.3598 (2004), 1.5419 (2003), 1.8406 (2002), 1.9334 (2001)
Fiscal year: calendar year

COMMUNICATIONS

Telephones - main lines in use: 700 (2002)
Telephones - mobile cellular: 0 (2004)
Telephone system:
general assessment: serves particular needs for internal communications
domestic: radiotelephone communications between islands
international: country code - 688; international calls can be made by satellite
Radio broadcast stations: AM 1, FM 1, shortwave 0 (2004)
Radios: 4,000 (1997)
Television broadcast stations: 0 (2004)
Televisions: 800
Internet country code: .tv
Internet Service Providers (ISPs): 1 (2000)
Internet users: 1,300 (2002)

TRANSPORTATION

Airports: 1 (2004 est.)
Airports - with unpaved runways:
total: 1
1,524 to 2,437 m: 1 (2005 est.)
Roadways:
total: 8 km
paved: 0 km
unpaved: 8 km (1999 est.)
Merchant marine:
total: 23 ships (1,000 GRT or over) 54,993 GRT/86,048 DWT
by type: cargo 20, passenger/cargo 1, petroleum tanker 2
foreign-owned: 16 (China 9, Germany 2, Hong Kong 4, Thailand 1) (2005)
Ports and terminals: Funafuti

MILITARY

Military branches: no regular military forces; national police force
Military expenditures - dollar figure: NA
Military expenditures - percent of GDP: NA

TRANSNATIONAL ISSUES

Disputes - international: none

UGANDA

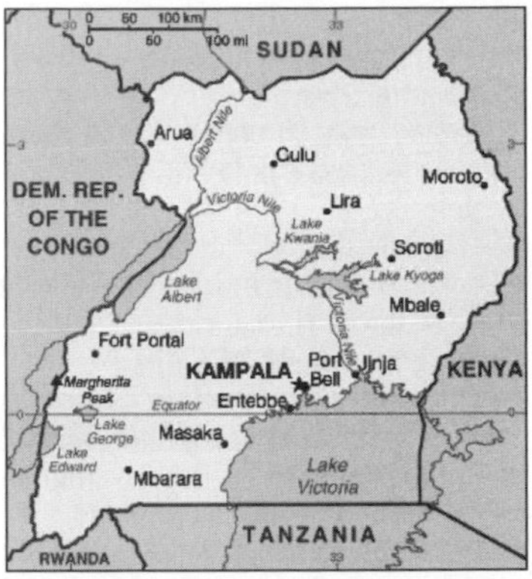

INTRODUCTION

Background: Uganda achieved independence from the UK in 1962. The dictatorial regime of Idi AMIN (1971-79) was responsible for the deaths of some 300,000 opponents; guerrilla war and human rights abuses under Milton OBOTE (1980-85) claimed at least another 100,000 lives. During the 1990s, the government promulgated non-party presidential and legislative elections.

GEOGRAPHY

Location: Eastern Africa, west of Kenya
Geographic coordinates: 1 00 N, 32 00 E
Map references: Africa
Area:
total: 236,040 sq km
land: 199,710 sq km
water: 36,330 sq km
Area - comparative: slightly smaller than Oregon
Land boundaries:
total: 2,698 km
border countries: Democratic Republic of the Congo 765 km, Kenya 933 km, Rwanda 169 km, Sudan 435 km, Tanzania 396 km
Coastline: 0 km (landlocked)
Maritime claims: none (landlocked)
Climate: tropical; generally rainy with two dry seasons (December to February, June to August); semiarid in northeast
Terrain: mostly plateau with rim of mountains
Elevation extremes:
lowest point: Lake Albert 621 m
highest point: Margherita Peak on Mount Stanley 5,110 m
Natural resources: copper, cobalt, hydropower, limestone, salt, arable land
Land use:
arable land: 25.88%
permanent crops: 10.65%
other: 63.47% (2001)
Irrigated land: 90 sq km (1998 est.)
Natural hazards: NA
Environment - current issues: draining of wetlands for agricultural use; deforestation; overgrazing; soil erosion; water hyacinth infestation in Lake Victoria; poaching is widespread
Environment - international agreements:
party to: Biodiversity, Climate Change, Climate Change-Kyoto Protocol, Desertification, Endangered Species, Hazardous Wastes, Law of the Sea, Marine Life Conservation, Ozone Layer Protection, Wetlands
signed, but not ratified: Environmental Modification
Geography - note: landlocked; fertile, well-watered country with many lakes and rivers

PEOPLE

Population: 27,269,482
note: estimates for this country explicitly take into account the effects of excess mortality due to AIDS; this can result in lower life expectancy, higher infant mortality and death rates, lower population and growth rates, and changes in the distribution of population by age and sex than would otherwise be expected (July 2005 est.)
Age structure:
0-14 years: 50.1% (male 6,875,663/female 6,784,378)
15-64 years: 47.7% (male 6,511,867/female 6,494,859)
65 years and over: 2.2% (male 263,790/female 338,925) (2005 est.)
Median age:
total: 14.97 years
male: 14.87 years
female: 15.08 years (2005 est.)
Population growth rate: 3.31% (2005 est.)
Birth rate: 47.39 births/1,000 population (2005 est.)
Death rate: 12.8 deaths/1,000 population (2005 est.)
Net migration rate: -1.49 migrant(s)/1,000 population (2005 est.)
Sex ratio:
at birth: 1.03 male(s)/female
under 15 years: 1.01 male(s)/female
15-64 years: 1 male(s)/female
65 years and over: 0.78 male(s)/female
total population: 1 male(s)/female (2005 est.)
Infant mortality rate:
total: 67.83 deaths/1,000 live births
male: 71.18 deaths/1,000 live births
female: 64.37 deaths/1,000 live births (2005 est.)
Life expectancy at birth:
total population: 51.59 years
male: 50.74 years
female: 52.46 years (2005 est.)
Total fertility rate: 6.74 children born/woman (2005 est.)
HIV/AIDS - adult prevalence rate: 4.1% (2003 est.)
HIV/AIDS - people living with HIV/AIDS: 530,000 (2001 est.)
HIV/AIDS - deaths: 78,000 (2003 est.)
Major infectious diseases:
degree of risk: very high
food or waterborne diseases: bacterial diarrhea, hepatitis A, and typhoid fever
vectorborne diseases: malaria and African trypanosomiasis (sleeping sickness) are high risks in some locations
water contact disease: schistosomiasis (2004)
Nationality:
noun: Ugandan(s)
adjective: Ugandan
Ethnic groups: Baganda 17%, Ankole 8%, Basoga 8%, Iteso 8%, Bakiga 7%, Langi 6%, Rwanda 6%, Bagisu 5%, Acholi 4%, Lugbara 4%, Batoro 3%, Bunyoro 3%, Alur 2%, Bagwere 2%, Bakonjo 2%, Jopodhola 2%, Karamojong 2%, Rundi 2%, non-African (European, Asian, Arab) 1%, other 8%
Religions: Roman Catholic 33%, Protestant 33%, Muslim 16%, indigenous beliefs 18%
Languages: English (official national language, taught in grade schools, used in courts of law and by most newspapers and some radio broadcasts), Ganda or Luganda (most widely used of the Niger-Congo languages, preferred for native language publications in the capital and may be taught in school), other Niger-Congo languages, Nilo-Saharan languages, Swahili, Arabic
Literacy:
definition: age 15 and over can read and write
total population: 69.9%
male: 79.5%
female: 60.4% (2003 est.)

GOVERNMENT

Country name:
conventional long form: Republic of Uganda
conventional short form: Uganda
Government type: republic
Capital: Kampala
Administrative divisions: 56 districts; Adjumani, Apac, Arua, Bugiri, Bundibugyo, Bushenyi, Busia, Gulu, Hoima, Iganga, Jinja, Kabale, Kabarole, Kaberamaido, Kalangala, Kampala, Kamuli, Kamwenge, Kanungu, Kapchorwa, Kasese, Katakwi, Kayunga, Kibale, Kiboga, Kisoro, Kitgum, Kotido, Kumi, Kyenjojo, Lira, Luwero, Masaka, Masindi, Mayuge, Mbale, Mbarara,

Moroto, Moyo, Mpigi, Mubende, Mukono, Nakapiripirit, Nakasongola, Nebbi, Ntungamo, Pader, Pallisa, Rakai, Rukungiri, Sembabule, Sironko, Soroti, Tororo, Wakiso, Yumbe
Independence: 9 October 1962 (from UK)
National holiday: Independence Day, 9 October (1962)
Constitution: 8 October 1995
Legal system: in 1995, the government restored the legal system to one based on English common law and customary law; accepts compulsory ICJ jurisdiction, with reservations
Suffrage: 18 years of age, universal
Executive branch:
chief of state: President Lt. Gen. Yoweri Kaguta MUSEVENI (since seizing power 26 January 1986); note - the president is both chief of state and head of government
head of government: President Lt. Gen. Yoweri Kaguta MUSEVENI (since seizing power 29 January 1986); Prime Minister Apollo NSIBAMBI (since 5 April 1999); note - the president is both chief of state and head of government; the prime minister assists the president in the supervision of the cabinet
cabinet: Cabinet appointed by the president from among elected legislators
elections: president reelected by popular vote for a five-year term; election last held 12 March 2001 (next to be held 23 February 2006); note - first popular election for president since independence in 1962 was held in 1996; prime minister appointed by the president
election results: Lt. Gen. Yoweri Kaguta MUSEVENI elected president; percent of vote - Lt. Gen. Yoweri Kaguta MUSEVENI 69.3%, Kizza BESIGYE 27.8%
Legislative branch: unicameral National Assembly (303 members - 214 directly elected by popular vote, 81 nominated by legally established special interest groups [women 56, army 10, disabled 5, youth 5, labor 5], 8 ex officio members; members serve five-year terms)
elections: last held 26 June 2001 (next to be held by 23 February 2006)
election results: percent of vote by party - NA%; seats by party - NA; note - election campaigning by party was not permitted
Judicial branch: Court of Appeal (judges are appointed by the president and approved by the legislature); High Court (judges are appointed by the president)
Political parties and leaders: Conservative Party or CP [Ken LUKYAMUZI]; Democratic Party or DP [Kizito SSEBAANA]; Forum for Democratic Change or FDC [Kizza BESIGYE]; Justice Forum or JEEMA [Muhammad Kibirige MAYANJA]; National Democrats Forum [Chapaa KARUHANGA]; National Resistance Movement or NRM [Yoweri MUSEVENI]; Ugandan People's Congress or UPC [Miria OBOTE]
note: a national referendum in July 2005 opened the way for Uganda's transition to a multi-party political system
Political pressure groups and leaders: Popular Resistance Against a Life President or PRALP
International organization participation: ACP, AfDB, AU, C, COMESA, EADB, FAO, G-77, IAEA, IBRD, ICAO, ICCt, ICFTU, ICRM, IDA, IDB, IFAD, IFC, IFRCS, IGAD, ILO, IMF, Interpol, IOC, IOM, ISO (correspondent), ITU, MIGA, NAM, OIC, OPCW, PCA, UN, UNCTAD, UNESCO, UNHCR, UNIDO, UNMIS, UNOCI, UPU, WCO, WFTU, WHO, WIPO, WMO, WToO, WTO
Diplomatic representation in the US:
chief of mission: Ambassador Francis BUTAGIRA
chancery: 5911 16th Street NW, Washington, DC 20011
telephone: [1] (202) 726-7100 through 7102, 0416
FAX: [1] (202) 726-1727
Diplomatic representation from the US:
chief of mission: Ambassador (vacant); Charge d'Affaires William FITZGERALD
embassy: 1577 Ggaba Rd., Kampala
mailing address: P. O. Box 7007, Kampala
telephone: [256] (41) 234-142
FAX: [256] (41) 258-451
Flag description: six equal horizontal bands of black (top), yellow, red, black, yellow, and red; a white disk is superimposed at the center and depicts a red-crested crane (the national symbol) facing the hoist side

ECONOMY

Economy - overview: Uganda has substantial natural resources, including fertile soils, regular rainfall, and sizable mineral deposits of copper and cobalt. Agriculture is the most important sector of the economy, employing over 80% of the work force. Coffee accounts for the bulk of export revenues. Since 1986, the government - with the support of foreign countries and international agencies - has acted to rehabilitate and stabilize the economy by undertaking currency reform, raising producer prices on export crops, increasing prices of petroleum products, and improving civil service wages. The policy changes are especially aimed at dampening inflation and boosting production and export earnings. During 1990-2001, the economy turned in a solid performance based on continued investment in the rehabilitation of infrastructure, improved incentives for production and exports, reduced inflation, gradually improved domestic security, and the return of exiled Indian-Ugandan entrepreneurs. Corruption within the government and slippage in the government's determination to press reforms raise doubts about the continuation of strong growth. In 2000, Uganda qualified for enhanced Highly Indebted Poor Countries (HIPC) debt relief worth $1.3 billion and Paris Club debt relief worth $145 million. These amounts combined with the original HIPC debt relief added up to about $2 billion. Growth for 2001-02 was solid despite continued decline in the price of coffee, Uganda's principal export. Growth in 2003-05 reflected an upturn in Uganda's export markets.
GDP (purchasing power parity): $45.97 billion (2005 est.)
GDP (official exchange rate): $8.489 billion (2005 est.)
GDP - real growth rate: 9% (2005 est.)
GDP - per capita: purchasing power parity - $1,700 (2005 est.)
GDP - composition by sector:
agriculture: 31.1%
industry: 22.2%
services: 46.9% (2004 est.)
Labor force: 13.17 million (2005 est.)
Labor force - by occupation: agriculture 82%, industry 5%, services 13% (1999 est.)
Unemployment rate: NA (2002 est.)
Population below poverty line: 35% (2001 est.)
Household income or consumption by percentage share:
lowest 10%: 4%
highest 10%: 21% (2000)
Distribution of family income - Gini index: 43 (1999)
Inflation rate (consumer prices): 9.7% (2005 est.)
Investment (gross fixed): 23.4% of GDP (2005 est.)
Budget:
revenues: $1.845 billion
expenditures: $1.904 billion, including capital expenditures of NA (2005 est.)
Public debt: 62.8% of GDP (2005 est.)
Agriculture - products: coffee, tea, cotton, tobacco, cassava (tapioca), potatoes, corn, millet, pulses; beef, goat meat, milk, poultry, cut flowers
Industries: sugar, brewing, tobacco, cotton textiles, cement, steel production
Industrial production growth rate: 9% (2005 est.)
Electricity - production: 1.729 billion kWh (2003)

Electricity - production by source:
fossil fuel: 0.9%
hydro: 99.1%
nuclear: 0%
other: 0% (2001)
Electricity - consumption: 1.448 billion kWh (2003)
Electricity - exports: 160 million kWh (2003)
Electricity - imports: 0 kWh (2003)
Oil - production: 0 bbl/day (2003 est.)
Oil - consumption: 10,000 bbl/day (2003 est.)
Oil - exports: NA (2001)
Oil - imports: NA (2001)
Current account balance: $-339 million (2005 est.)
Exports: $768 million f.o.b. (2005 est.)
Exports - partners: Kenya 15.4%, Netherlands 11%, Belgium 9.3%, France 4.5%, Germany 4.5%, Rwanda 4.1%, US 4% (2004)
Imports: $1.608 billion f.o.b. (2005 est.)
Imports - partners: Kenya 32.3%, UAE 7.3%, South Africa 6.5%, India 5.8%, China 5.6%, UK 5.1%, US 4.8%, Japan 4.8% (2004)
Reserves of foreign exchange and gold: $1.45 billion (2005 est.)
Debt - external: $4.949 billion (2005 est.)
Economic aid - recipient: $959 million (2003)
Currency (code): Ugandan shilling (UGX)
Currency code: UGX
Exchange rates: Ugandan shillings per US dollar - 1,776.68 (2005), 1,810.3 (2004), 1,963.7 (2003), 1,797.6 (2002), 1,755.7 (2001)
Fiscal year: 1 July - 30 June

COMMUNICATIONS

Telephones - main lines in use: 61,000 (2003)
Telephones - mobile cellular: 776,200 (2003)
Telephone system:
general assessment: seriously inadequate; two cellular systems have been introduced, but a sharp increase in the number of main lines is essential; e-mail and Internet services are available
domestic: intercity traffic by wire, microwave radio relay, and radiotelephone communication stations, fixed and mobile cellular systems for short-range traffic
international: country code - 256; satellite earth stations - 1 Intelsat (Atlantic Ocean) and 1 Inmarsat; analog links to Kenya and Tanzania
Radio broadcast stations: AM 7, FM 33, shortwave 2 (2001)
Radios: 5 million (2001)
Television broadcast stations: 8 (plus one low-power repeater) (2001)
Televisions: 500,000 (2001)
Internet country code: .ug
Internet hosts: 2,692 (2004)
Internet Service Providers (ISPs): 2 (2000)
Internet users: 125,000 (2003)

TRANSPORTATION

Airports: 29 (2004 est.)
Airports - with paved runways:
total: 4
over 3,047 m: 3
1,524 to 2,437 m: 1 (2005 est.)
Airports - with unpaved runways:
total: 24
2,438 to 3,047 m: 1
1,524 to 2,437 m: 6
914 to 1,523 m: 10
under 914 m: 7 (2005 est.)
Railways:
total: 1,241 km
narrow gauge: 1,241 km 1.000-m gauge (2004)
Roadways:
total: 27,000 km
paved: 1,809 km
unpaved: 25,191 km (1999 est.)
Waterways: 300 km (on Lake Victoria, 200 km on Lake Albert, Lake Kyoga, and parts of Albert Nile) (2004 est.)
Ports and terminals: Entebbe, Jinja, Port Bell

MILITARY

Military branches: Ugandan Peoples' Defense Force (UPDF): Army, Marine Unit, Air Wing
Military service age and obligation: 18 years of age for compulsory and voluntary military duty; the government has stated that recruitment below that age could occur with proper consent and that "no person under the apparent age of 13 years shall be enrolled in the armed forces"
Manpower available for military service: *males age 18-49:* 5,012,620 (2005 est.)
Manpower fit for military service: *males age 18-49:* 2,889,808 (2005 est.)
Military expenditures - dollar figure: $170.3 million (2004)
Military expenditures - percent of GDP: 2.2% (2004)

TRANSNATIONAL ISSUES

Disputes - international: Uganda is subject to armed fighting among hostile ethnic groups, rebels, armed gangs, militias, and various government forces; Ugandan refugees have fled the Lord's Resistance Army (LRA) into the southern Sudan and the Democratic Republic of the Congo; LRA forces have also attacked Kenyan villages across the border
Refugees and internally displaced persons:
refugees (country of origin): 184,731 (Sudan) 18,000 (Rwanda)
IDPs: 1.4 million; note - ongoing Lord's Resistance Army (LRA) rebellion, mainly in the north; LRA frequently attacks IDP camps (2004)

UKRAINE

INTRODUCTION

Background: Ukraine was the center of the first Slavic state, Kievan Rus, which during the 10th and 11th centuries was the largest and most powerful state in Europe. Weakened by internecine quarrels and Mongol invasions, Kievan Rus was incorporated into the Grand Duchy of Lithuania and eventually into the Polish-Lithuanian Commonwealth. The cultural and religious legacy of Kievan Rus laid the foundation for Ukrainian nationalism through subsequent centuries. A new Ukrainian state, the Cossack Hetmanate, was established during the mid-17th century after an uprising against the Poles. Despite continuous Muscovite pressure, the Hetmanate managed to remain autonomous for well over 100 years. During the latter part of the 18th century, most Ukrainian ethnographic territory was absorbed by the Russian Empire. Following the collapse of czarist Russia in 1917, Ukraine was able to bring about a short-lived period of independence (1917-20), but was reconquered and forced to endure a brutal Soviet rule that engineered two artificial famines (1921-22 and 1932-33) in which over 8 million died. In World War II, German and Soviet armies were responsible for some 7 to 8 million more deaths. Although final independence for Ukraine was achieved in 1991 with the dissolution of the USSR, democracy remained elusive as the legacy of state control and endemic corruption stalled efforts at economic reform, privatization, and civil liberties. A peaceful mass protest "Orange Revolution" in the closing months of 2004 forced the authorities to overturn a rigged presidential election and to allow a new internationally monitored vote that swept into power a reformist slate under Viktor YUSHCHENKO. The new government presents its citizens with hope that the country may at last attain true freedom and prosperity.

GEOGRAPHY

Location: Eastern Europe, bordering the Black Sea, between Poland, Romania, and Moldova in the west and Russia in the east

Geographic coordinates: 49 00 N, 32 00 E

Map references: Asia, Europe

Area:
total: 603,700 sq km
land: 603,700 sq km
water: 0 sq km

Area - comparative: slightly smaller than Texas

Land boundaries:
total: 4,663 km
border countries: Belarus 891 km, Hungary 103 km, Moldova 939 km, Poland 526 km, Romania (south) 169 km, Romania (west) 362 km, Russia 1,576 km, Slovakia 97 km

Coastline: 2,782 km

Maritime claims:
territorial sea: 12 nm
exclusive economic zone: 200 nm
continental shelf: 200-m or to the depth of exploitation

Climate: temperate continental; Mediterranean only on the southern Crimean coast; precipitation disproportionately distributed, highest in west and north, lesser in east and southeast; winters vary from cool along the Black Sea to cold farther inland; summers are warm across the greater part of the country, hot in the south

Terrain: most of Ukraine consists of fertile plains (steppes) and plateaus, mountains being found only in the west (the Carpathians), and in the Crimean Peninsula in the extreme south

Elevation extremes:
lowest point: Black Sea 0 m
highest point: Hora Hoverla 2,061 m

Natural resources: iron ore, coal, manganese, natural gas, oil, salt, sulfur, graphite, titanium, magnesium, kaolin, nickel, mercury, timber, arable land

Land use:
arable land: 56.21%
permanent crops: 1.61%
other: 42.18% (2001)

Irrigated land: 24,540 sq km (1998 est.)

Natural hazards: NA

Environment - current issues: inadequate supplies of potable water; air and water pollution; deforestation; radiation contamination in the northeast from 1986 accident at Chornobyl' Nuclear Power Plant

Environment - international agreements:
party to: Air Pollution, Air Pollution-Nitrogen Oxides, Air Pollution-Sulfur 85, Antarctic-Environmental Protocol, Antarctic-Marine Living Resources, Antarctic Treaty, Biodiversity, Climate Change, Climate Change-Kyoto Protocol, Endangered Species, Environmental Modification, Hazardous Wastes, Law of the Sea, Marine Dumping, Ozone Layer Protection, Ship Pollution, Wetlands
signed, but not ratified: Air Pollution-Persistent Organic Pollutants, Air Pollution-Sulfur 94, Air Pollution-Volatile Organic Compounds

Geography - note: strategic position at the crossroads between Europe and Asia; second-largest country in Europe

PEOPLE

Population: 47,425,336 (July 2005 est.)

Age structure:
0-14 years: 15.6% (male 3,783,725/female 3,619,754)
15-64 years: 68.8% (male 15,619,989/female 16,992,628)
65 years and over: 15.6% (male 2,497,851/female 4,911,389) (2005 est.)

Median age:
total: 38.22 years
male: 34.91 years
female: 41.21 years (2005 est.)

Population growth rate: -0.63% (2005 est.)

Birth rate: 10.49 births/1,000 population (2005 est.)

Death rate: 16.42 deaths/1,000 population (2005 est.)

Net migration rate: -0.38 migrant(s)/1,000 population (2005 est.)

Sex ratio:
at birth: 1.05 male(s)/female
under 15 years: 1.05 male(s)/female
15-64 years: 0.92 male(s)/female
65 years and over: 0.51 male(s)/female
total population: 0.86 male(s)/female (2005 est.)

Infant mortality rate:
total: 20.34 deaths/1,000 live births
male: 21.55 deaths/1,000 live births
female: 19.07 deaths/1,000 live births (2005 est.)

Life expectancy at birth:
total population: 69.68 years
male: 64.39 years
female: 75.31 years (2005 est.)

Total fertility rate: 1.4 children born/woman (2005 est.)

HIV/AIDS - adult prevalence rate: 1.4% (2003 est.)

HIV/AIDS - people living with HIV/AIDS: 360,000 (2001 est.)

HIV/AIDS - deaths: 20,000 (2003 est.)

Nationality:
noun: Ukrainian(s)
adjective: Ukrainian

Ethnic groups: Ukrainian 77.8%, Russian 17.3%, Belarusian 0.6%, Moldovan 0.5%, Crimean Tatar 0.5%, Bulgarian 0.4%, Hungarian 0.3%, Romanian 0.3%, Polish 0.3%, Jewish 0.2%, other 1.8% (2001 census)

Religions: Ukrainian Orthodox - Kiev Patriarchate 19%, Orthodox (no particular jurisdiction) 16%, Ukrainian Orthodox - Moscow Patriarchate 9%, Ukrainian Greek Catholic 6%, Ukrainian Autocephalous Orthodox 1.7%, Protestant, Jewish, none 38% (2004 est.)

Languages: Ukrainian (official) 67%, Russian 24%; small Romanian-, Polish-, and Hungarian-speaking minorities

Literacy:
definition: age 15 and over can read and write
total population: 99.7%
male: 99.8%
female: 99.6% (2003 est.)

People - note: the sex trafficking of Ukrainian women is a serious problem that has only recently been addressed

GOVERNMENT

Country name:
conventional long form: none
conventional short form: Ukraine
local long form: none
local short form: Ukrayina
former: Ukrainian National Republic, Ukrainian State, Ukrainian Soviet Socialist Republic

Government type: republic

Capital: Kiev (Kyyiv)

Administrative divisions: 24 provinces (oblasti, singular - oblast'), 1 autonomous republic* (avtonomna respublika), and 2 municipalities (mista, singular - misto) with oblast status**; Cherkasy, Chernihiv, Chernivtsi, Crimea or Avtonomna Respublika Krym* (Simferopol'), Dnipropetrovs'k, Donets'k, Ivano-Frankivs'k, Kharkiv, Kherson, Khmel'nyts'kyy, Kirovohrad, Kiev (Kyyiv)**, Kyyiv, Luhans'k, L'viv, Mykolayiv, Odesa, Poltava, Rivne, Sevastopol'**, Sumy, Ternopil', Vinnytsya, Volyn' (Luts'k), Zakarpattya (Uzhhorod), Zaporizhzhya, Zhytomyr
note: administrative divisions have the same names as their administrative centers (exceptions have the administrative center name following in parentheses)

Independence: 24 August 1991 (from the Soviet Union)

National holiday: Independence Day, 24 August (1991); the date of 22 January (1918), the day Ukraine first declared its independence (from Soviet Russia), is now celebrated as Unity Day

Constitution: adopted 28 June 1996

Legal system: based on civil law system; judicial review of legislative acts

Suffrage: 18 years of age, universal

Executive branch:
chief of state: President Viktor A. YUSHCHENKO (since 23 January 2005)
head of government: Prime Minister Yuriy YEKHANUROV (since 22 September 2005); First Deputy Prime Minister - Stanislav STASHEVSKYY (since 27 September 2005)
cabinet: Cabinet of Ministers appointed by the president and approved by the Supreme Council
note: there is also a National Security and Defense Council or NSDC originally created in 1992 as the National Security Council; the NSDC staff is tasked with developing national security policy on domestic and international matters and advising the president; a Presidential Secretariat helps draft presidential edicts and provides policy support to the president
elections: president elected by popular vote for a five-year term; note - a special repeat runoff presidential election between Viktor YUSHCHENKO and Viktor YANUKOVYCH took place on 26 December 2004 after the earlier 21 November 2004 contest - won by Mr. YANUKOVYCH - was invalidated by the Ukrainian Supreme Court because of widespread and significant violations; prime minister and deputy prime ministers appointed by the president and approved by the Supreme Council
election results: Viktor YUSHCHENKO elected president; percent of vote - Viktor YUSHCHENKO 51.99%, Viktor YANUKOVYCH 44.2%

Legislative branch: unicameral Supreme Council or Verkhovna Rada (450 seats; under recent amendments to Ukraine's election law, the Rada's seats are allocated on a proportional basis to those parties that gain 3% or more of the national electoral vote; members serve five-year terms beginning with the next election in 2006)
elections: last held 31 March 2002 (next to be held March 2006)
election results: percent of vote by party/bloc in 2002 - Our Ukraine 24%, CPU 20%, United Ukraine 12%, SPU 7%, Yuliya Tymoshenko Bloc 7%, United Social Democratic Party 6%, other 24%; seats by party/bloc - Our Ukraine 101, Regions of Ukraine 61, CPU 59, Working Ukraine 14, United Social Democratic Party 33, Agrarian Party 22, SPU 20, Yuliya Tymoshenko Bloc 19, United Ukraine 19, People's Democratic Party-Party of Industrialists and Entrepreneurs 16, Center Group 15, Democratic Initiatives 14, unaffiliated 57 (December 2004)
note: since the "Orange Revolution," bloc allegiances and faction names have undergone significant shifts, so the current composition of the Rada is altered

Judicial branch: Supreme Court; Constitutional Court

Political parties and leaders: Communist Party of Ukraine or CPU [Petro SYMONENKO]; Lytyvn People's Bloc group [Ihor SHAROV]; Party of Industrialists and Entrepreneurs [Anatoliy KINAKH]; People's Movement of Ukraine [Borys TARASYUK]; People's Party [Volodymyr LYTVYN]; People's Trust group [Anton KISSE]; People's Union Our Ukraine [Viktor YUSHCHENKO]; Reforms and Order Party [Viktor PYNZENYK]; Regions of Ukraine [Viktor YANUKOVYCH]; Republican Party [Yuriy Boyko]; Socialist Party of Ukraine or SPU [Oleksandr MOROZ, chairman]; Ukrainian People's Party [Yuriy KOSTENKO]; United Social Democratic Party [Viktor MEDVEDCHUK]; United Ukraine [Bohdan HUBSKYY]; Yuliya Tymoshenko Bloc [Yuliya TYMOSHENKO]

Political pressure groups and leaders: Pora (It's Time!) youth movement [Vladyslav KASKIV]; Committee of Voters of Ukraine [Ihor POPOV]

International organization participation: Australia Group, BSEC, CBSS (observer), CE, CEI, CIS, EAPC, EBRD, FAO, GUAM, IAEA, IBRD, ICAO, ICC, ICCt (signatory), ICFTU, ICRM, IDA, IFC, IFRCS, IHO, ILO, IMF, IMO, Interpol, IOC, IOM, ISO, ITU, MIGA, MONUC, NAM (observer), NSG, OAS (observer), OPCW, OSCE, PCA, PFP, UN, UNAMSIL, UNCTAD, UNESCO, UNIDO, UNIFIL, UNMEE, UNMIL, UNMOVIC, UNOMIG, UPU, WCL, WCO, WFTU, WHO, WIPO, WMO, WToO, WTO (observer), ZC

Diplomatic representation in the US:
chief of mission: Ambassador Mykhailo B. REZNIK
chancery: 3350 M Street NW, Washington, DC 20007
telephone: [1] (202) 349-2920
FAX: [1] (202) 333-0817
consulate(s) general: Chicago, New York, San Francisco

Diplomatic representation from the US:
chief of mission: Ambassador John E. HERBST
embassy: 10 Yuriia Kotsiubynskoho, 04053 Kiev
mailing address: 5850 Kiev Place, Washington, DC 20521-5850
telephone: [380] (44) 490-4000
FAX: [380] (44) 490-4085

Flag description: two equal horizontal bands of azure (top) and golden yellow represent grainfields under a blue sky

ECONOMY

Economy - overview: After Russia, the Ukrainian republic was far and away the most important economic component of the former Soviet Union, producing about four times the output of the next-ranking republic. Its fertile black soil generated more than one-fourth of Soviet agricultural output, and its farms provided substantial quantities of meat, milk, grain, and vegetables to other republics. Likewise, its diversified heavy industry supplied the unique equipment (for example, large diameter pipes) and raw materials to industrial and mining sites (vertical drilling apparatus) in other regions of the former USSR. Ukraine depends on imports of energy, especially natural gas, to meet some 85% of its annual energy requirements. Shortly after independence in December 1991, the Ukrainian Government liberalized most prices and erected a legal framework for privatization, but widespread resistance to reform within the government and the legislature soon stalled reform efforts and led to some backtracking. Output by 1999 had fallen to less than 40% of the 1991 level. Loose monetary policies pushed inflation to hyperinflationary levels in late 1993. Ukraine's dependence on Russia for energy supplies and the lack of significant structural reform have made the Ukrainian economy vulnerable to external shocks. Ukrainian government officials have taken some steps to reform the country's Byzantine tax code, such as the implementation of lower tax rates aimed at bringing more economic activity out of Ukraine's large shadow economy, but more improvements are needed, including closing tax loopholes and eliminating tax privileges and exemptions. Reforms in the more politically sensitive areas of structural reform and land privatization are still lagging. Outside institutions - particularly the IMF - have encouraged Ukraine to quicken the pace and scope of reforms. Growth was 4.4% in 2005, underpinned by strong domestic demand, and solid consumer and investor confidence. The current account surplus reached a record high in 2005.

GDP (purchasing power parity): $321.2 billion (2005 est.)
GDP (official exchange rate): $67.65 billion (2005 est.)
GDP - real growth rate: 4.4% (2005 est.)
GDP - per capita: purchasing power parity - $6,800 (2005 est.)
GDP - composition by sector:
agriculture: 18.5%
industry: 44.7%
services: 36.8% (2005 est.)
Labor force: 20.46 million (2005 est.)
Labor force - by occupation: agriculture 24%, industry 32%, services 44% (1996)
Unemployment rate: 3.8% officially registered; large number of unregistered or underemployed workers; the International Labor Organization calculates that Ukraine's real unemployment level is around 9-10 percent (2005 est.)
Population below poverty line: 29% (2003 est.)
Household income or consumption by percentage share:
lowest 10%: 3.7%
highest 10%: 23.2% (1999)
Distribution of family income - Gini index: 29 (1999)
Inflation rate (consumer prices): 13.9% (2005 est.)
Investment (gross fixed): 18.5% of GDP (2005 est.)
Budget:
revenues: $22.95 billion
expenditures: $24.48 billion, including capital expenditures of NA; note - these estimates probably do not include the government's doubling of pensions in September of 2004 (2005 est.)
Public debt: 20.5% of GDP (2005 est.)
Agriculture - products: grain, sugar beets, sunflower seeds, vegetables; beef, milk
Industries: coal, electric power, ferrous and nonferrous metals, machinery and transport equipment, chemicals, food processing (especially sugar)
Industrial production growth rate: 1% (2005 est.)
Electricity - production: 169.9 billion kWh (2003)
Electricity - production by source:
fossil fuel: 48.6%
hydro: 7.9%
nuclear: 43.5%
other: 0% (2001)
Electricity - consumption: 153.1 billion kWh (2003)
Electricity - exports: 5.5 billion kWh (2003)
Electricity - imports: 600 million kWh (2003)
Oil - production: 86,540 bbl/day (2003 est.)
Oil - consumption: 401,000 bbl/day (2003 est.)
Oil - exports: NA (2001)
Oil - imports: NA (2001)
Oil - proved reserves: 395 million bbl (9 November 2004)
Natural gas - production: 19.6 billion cu m (2003 est.)
Natural gas - consumption: 79.86 billion cu m (2003 est.)
Natural gas - exports: 5.8 billion cu m (2003 est.)
Natural gas - imports: 60.4 billion cu m (2003 est.)
Natural gas - proved reserves: 560.7 billion cu m (9 November 2004)
Current account balance: $4.338 billion (2005 est.)
Exports: $38.22 billion (2005 est.)
Exports - partners: Russia 18%, Germany 5.8%, Turkey 5.7%, Italy 5%, US 4.6% (2004)
Imports: $37.18 billion (2005 est.)
Imports - partners: Russia 41.8%, Germany 9.6%, Turkmenistan 6.7% (2004)
Reserves of foreign exchange and gold: $14.64 billion (2005 est.)
Debt - external: $33.93 billion (30 June 2005 est.)
Economic aid - recipient: $637.7 million (1995); IMF Extended Funds Facility $2.2 billion (1998)
Currency (code): hryvnia (UAH)
Currency code: UAH
Exchange rates: hryvnia per US dollar - 5.13 (2005), 5.3192 (2004), 5.3327 (2003), 5.3266 (2002), 5.3722 (2001)
Fiscal year: calendar year

COMMUNICATIONS

Telephones - main lines in use: 10,833,300 (2002)
Telephones - mobile cellular: 4.2 million (2002)
Telephone system:
general assessment: Ukraine's telecommunication development plan, running through 2005, emphasizes improving domestic trunk lines, international connections, and the mobile cellular system
domestic: at independence in December 1991, Ukraine inherited a telephone system that was antiquated, inefficient, and in disrepair; more than 3.5 million applications for telephones could not be satisfied; telephone density is now rising slowly and the domestic trunk system is being improved; the mobile cellular telephone system is expanding at a high rate
international: country code - 380; two new domestic trunk lines are a part of the fiber-optic Trans-Asia-Europe (TAE) system and three Ukrainian links have been installed in the fiber-optic Trans-European Lines (TEL) project that connects 18 countries; additional international service is provided by the Italy-Turkey-Ukraine-Russia (ITUR) fiber-optic submarine cable and by earth stations in the Intelsat, Inmarsat, and Intersputnik satellite systems
Radio broadcast stations: AM 134, FM 289, shortwave 4 (1998)
Radios: 45.05 million (1997)
Television broadcast stations: at least 33 (plus 21 repeaters that relay broadcasts from Russia) (1997)
Televisions: 18.05 million (1997)
Internet country code: .ua
Internet hosts: 94,345 (2004)
Internet Service Providers (ISPs): 260 (2001)
Internet users: 3.8 million (2003)

TRANSPORTATION

Airports: 656 (2004 est.)
Airports - with paved runways:
total: 199
over 3,047 m: 13
2,438 to 3,047 m: 57
1,524 to 2,437 m: 30
914 to 1,523 m: 5
under 914 m: 94 (2005 est.)
Airports - with unpaved runways:
total: 338
over 3,047 m: 2
2,438 to 3,047 m: 3
1,524 to 2,437 m: 13
914 to 1,523 m: 22
under 914 m: 298 (2005 est.)
Heliports: 10 (2005 est.)
Pipelines: gas 20,069 km; oil 4,540 km; refined products 4,169 km (2004)
Railways:
total: 22,473 km
broad gauge: 22,473 km 1.524-m gauge (9,250 km electrified) (2004)
Roadways:
total: 169,679 km
paved: 164,249 km
unpaved: 5,430 km (2002)
Waterways: 1,672 km (most on Dnieper River) (2004)

Merchant marine:
total: 201 ships (1,000 GRT or over) 675,904 GRT/709,802 DWT
by type: bulk carrier 6, cargo 148, container 4, passenger 7, passenger/cargo 6, petroleum tanker 10, refrigerated cargo 11, roll on/roll off 7, specialized tanker 2
foreign-owned: 1 (Russia 1)
registered in other countries: 113 (2005)
Ports and terminals: Feodosiya, Kerch, Kherson, Mariupol', Mykolayiv, Odesa, Reni, Yuzhnyy

MILITARY

Military branches: Ground Forces, Naval Forces, Air Forces (Viyskovo-Povitryani Syly), Air Defense Forces (2002)
Military service age and obligation: 18-27 years of age for compulsory and voluntary military service; conscript service obligation - 18 months for Army and Air Force, 24 months for Navy (2004)
Manpower available for military service: *males age 18-49:* 11,067,239 (2005 est.)
Manpower fit for military service: *males age 18-49:* 7,114,337 (2005 est.)
Manpower reaching military service age annually: *males:* 378,176 (2005 est.)
Military expenditures - dollar figure: $617.9 million (FY02)
Military expenditures - percent of GDP: 1.4% (FY02)

TRANSNATIONAL ISSUES

Disputes - international: 1997 boundary treaty with Belarus remains un-ratified due to unresolved financial claims, stalling demarcation and reducing border security; delimitation of land boundary with Russia is complete but the parties have agreed to defer demarcation; maritime boundary through the Sea of Azov and Kerch Strait remains unresolved despite a December 2003 framework agreement and on-going expert-level discussions; Moldova and Ukraine have established joint customs posts to monitor transit through Moldova's break-away Transnistria Region which remains under OSCE supervision; Ukraine and Romania have taken their dispute over Ukrainian-administered Zmiyinyy (Snake) Island and Black Sea maritime boundary to the ICJ for adjudication; Romania opposes Ukraine's reopening of a navigation canal from the Danube border through the Ukraine to the Black Sea
Illicit drugs: limited cultivation of cannabis and opium poppy, mostly for CIS consumption; some synthetic drug production for export to the West; limited government eradication program; used as transshipment point for opiates and other illicit drugs from Africa, Latin America, and Turkey to Europe and Russia; Ukraine has improved anti-money-laundering controls, resulting in its removal from the Financial Action Task Force's (FATF's) Noncooperative Countries and Territories List in February 2004; Ukraine's anti-money-laundering regime continues to be monitored by FATF

UNITED ARAB EMIRATES

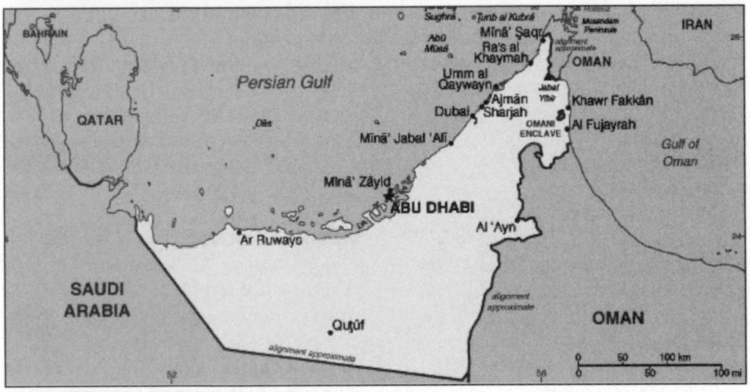

INTRODUCTION

Background: The Trucial States of the Persian Gulf coast granted the UK control of their defense and foreign affairs in 19th century treaties. In 1971, six of these states - Abu Zaby, 'Ajman, Al Fujayrah, Ash Shariqah, Dubayy, and Umm al Qaywayn - merged to form the United Arab Emirates (UAE). They were joined in 1972 by Ra's al Khaymah. The UAE's per capita GDP is on par with those of leading West European nations. Its generosity with oil revenues and its moderate foreign policy stance have allowed the UAE to play a vital role in the affairs of the region.

GEOGRAPHY

Location: Middle East, bordering the Gulf of Oman and the Persian Gulf, between Oman and Saudi Arabia
Geographic coordinates: 24 00 N, 54 00 E
Map references: Middle East
Area:
total: 82,880 sq km
land: 82,880 sq km
water: 0 sq km
Area - comparative: slightly smaller than Maine
Land boundaries:
total: 867 km
border countries: Oman 410 km, Saudi Arabia 457 km
Coastline: 1,318 km
Maritime claims:
territorial sea: 12 nm
contiguous zone: 24 nm
exclusive economic zone: 200 nm
continental shelf: 200 nm or to the edge of the continental margin
Climate: desert; cooler in eastern mountains
Terrain: flat, barren coastal plain merging into rolling sand dunes of vast desert wasteland; mountains in east
Elevation extremes:
lowest point: Persian Gulf 0 m
highest point: Jabal Yibir 1,527 m
Natural resources: petroleum, natural gas
Land use:
arable land: 0.6%
permanent crops: 2.25%
other: 97.15% (2001)
Irrigated land: 720 sq km (1998 est.)
Natural hazards: frequent sand and dust storms
Environment - current issues: lack of natural freshwater resources compensated by desalination plants; desertification; beach pollution from oil spills
Environment - international agreements:
party to: Biodiversity, Climate Change, Climate Change-Kyoto Protocol, Desertification, Endangered Species, Hazardous Wastes, Marine Dumping, Ozone Layer Protection
signed, but not ratified: Law of the Sea
Geography - note: strategic location along southern approaches to Strait of Hormuz, a vital transit point for world crude oil

PEOPLE

Population: 2,563,212
note: includes an estimated 1,606,079 non-nationals; the 17 December 1995

census presents a total population figure of 2,377,453, and there are estimates of 3.44 million for 2002 (July 2005 est.)
Age structure:
0-14 years: 25.3% (male 331,269; female 317,977)
15-64 years: 71.1% (male 1,115,826; female 707,058)
65 years and over: 3.6% (male 66,404; female 24,678) (2005 est.)
Median age:
total: 27.9 years
male: 35.2 years
female: 22.9 years (2005 est.)
Population growth rate: 1.54% (2005 est.)
Birth rate: 18.78 births/1,000 population (2005 est.)
Death rate: 4.26 deaths/1,000 population (2005 est.)
Net migration rate: 0.84 migrant(s)/1,000 population (2005 est.)
Sex ratio:
at birth: 1.05 male(s)/female
under 15 years: 1.05 male(s)/female
15-64 years: 1.58 male(s)/female
65 years and over: 2.691 male(s)/female
total population: 1.442 male(s)/female (2005 est.)
Infant mortality rate:
total: 14.51 deaths/1,000 live births
male: 17.05 deaths/1,000 live births
female: 11.84 deaths/1,000 live births (2005 est.)
Life expectancy at birth:
total population: 75.24 years
male: 72.73 years
female: 77.87 years (2005 est.)
Total fertility rate: 2.94 children born/woman (2005 est.)
HIV/AIDS - adult prevalence rate: 0.18% (2001 est.)
HIV/AIDS - people living with HIV/AIDS: NA
HIV/AIDS - deaths: NA
Nationality:
noun: Emirati(s)
adjective: Emirati
Ethnic groups: Emirati 19%, other Arab and Iranian 23%, South Asian 50%, other expatriates (includes Westerners and East Asians) 8% (1982)
note: less than 20% are UAE citizens (1982)
Religions: Muslim 96% (Shi'a 16%), Christian, Hindu, and other 4%
Languages: Arabic (official), Persian, English, Hindi, Urdu
Literacy:
definition: age 15 and over can read and write
total population: 77.9%
male: 76.1%
female: 81.7% (2003 est.)

GOVERNMENT

Country name:
conventional long form: United Arab Emirates
conventional short form: none
local long form: Al Imarat al Arabiyah al Muttahidah
local short form: none
former: Trucial Oman, Trucial States
abbreviation: UAE
Government type: federation with specified powers delegated to the UAE federal government and other powers reserved to member emirates
Capital: Abu Dhabi
Administrative divisions: 7 emirates (imarat, singular - imarah); Abu Zaby (Abu Dhabi), 'Ajman, Al Fujayrah, Ash Shariqah (Sharjah), Dubayy (Dubai), Ra's al Khaymah, Umm al Qaywayn
Independence: 2 December 1971 (from UK)
National holiday: Independence Day, 2 December (1971)
Constitution: 2 December 1971 (made permanent in 1996)
Legal system: federal court system introduced in 1971; applies to all emirates except Dubayy (Dubai) and Ra's al Khaymah, which are not fully integrated into the federal judicial system; all emirates have secular courts to adjudicate criminal, civil, and commercial matters and Islamic courts to review family and religious disputes
Suffrage: none
Executive branch:
chief of state: President KHALIFA bin Zayid al-Nuhayyan (since 3 November 2004), ruler of Abu Zaby (Abu Dhabi) (since 4 November 2004); Vice President MUHAMMAD bin Rashid al-Maktum (since 5 January 2006)
head of government: Prime Minister MUHAMMAD bin Rashid al-Maktum (since 5 January 2006); Deputy Prime Minister SULTAN bin Zayid al-Nuhayyan (since 20 November 1990); Deputy Prime Minister HAMDAN bin Zayid al-Nuhayyan (since 20 October 2003)
cabinet: Council of Ministers appointed by the president
note: there is also a Federal Supreme Council (FSC) composed of the seven emirate rulers; the FSC is the highest constitutional authority in the UAE; establishes general policies and sanctions federal legislation; meets four times a year; Abu Zaby (Abu Dhabi) and Dubayy (Dubai) rulers have effective veto power
elections: president and vice president elected by the Federal Supreme Council (composed of rulers of the seven emirates) for five-year terms; election last held 3 November 2004 upon the death of the UAE's Founding Father and first President ZAYID bin Sultan Al Nuhayyan (next to be held 2009); prime minister and deputy prime minister appointed by the president
election results: KHALIFA bin Zayid Al Nuhayyan elected president by a unanimous vote of the FSC; MAKTUM bin Rashid al-Maktum unanimously reaffirmed vice president
Legislative branch: unicameral Federal National Council (FNC) or Majlis al-Ittihad al-Watani (40 seats; members appointed by the rulers of the constituent states to serve two-year terms)
elections: President Khalifa in December 2005 announced that indirect elections would be held in early 2006 for half of the seats in the FNC; the other half would be filled by appointment
note: reviews legislation, but cannot change or veto
Judicial branch: Union Supreme Court (judges are appointed by the president)
Political parties and leaders: none
Political pressure groups and leaders: NA
International organization participation: ABEDA, AFESD, AMF, FAO, G-77, GCC, IAEA, IBRD, ICAO, ICC, ICCt (signatory), ICRM, IDA, IDB, IFAD, IFC, IFRCS, IHO, ILO, IMF, IMO, Interpol, IOC, ISO, ITU, LAS, MIGA, NAM, OAPEC, OIC, OPCW, OPEC, UN, UNCTAD, UNESCO, UNIDO, UPU, WCO, WHO, WIPO, WMO, WTO
Diplomatic representation in the US:
chief of mission: Ambassador Asri Said Ahmad al-DHAHIRI
chancery: 3522 International Court NW, Suite 400, Washington, DC 20008
telephone: [1] (202) 243-2400
FAX: [1] (202) 243-2432
note: consulates in New York and Houston
Diplomatic representation from the US:
chief of mission: Ambassador Michele J. SISON
embassy: Embassies District, Plot 38 Sector W59-02, Street No. 4, Abu Dhabi
mailing address: P. O. Box 4009, Abu Dhabi
telephone: [971] (2) 414-2200
FAX: [971] (2) 414-2469
consulate(s) general: Dubai
Flag description: three equal horizontal bands of green (top), white, and black with a wider vertical red band on the hoist side

ECONOMY

Economy - overview: The UAE has an open economy with a high per capita

income and a sizable annual trade surplus. Its wealth is based on oil and gas output (about 30% of GDP), and the fortunes of the economy fluctuate with the prices of those commodities. Since the discovery of oil in the UAE more than 30 years ago, the UAE has undergone a profound transformation from an impoverished region of small desert principalities to a modern state with a high standard of living. At present levels of production, oil and gas reserves should last for more than 100 years. The government has increased spending on job creation and infrastructure expansion and is opening up its utilities to greater private sector involvement. Higher oil revenue, strong liquidity, and cheap credit in 2005 led to a surge in asset prices (shares and real estate) and consumer inflation. Any sharp correction to the UAE's equity markets could damage investor and consumer sentiment and affect bank asset quality. In April 2004, the UAE signed a Trade and Investment Framework Agreement (TIFA) with Washington and in November 2004 agreed to undertake negotiations toward a Free Trade Agreement (FTA) with the US.
GDP (purchasing power parity): $74.51 billion (2005 est.)
GDP (official exchange rate): $104.2 billion (2005 est.)
GDP - real growth rate: 6.7% (2005 est.)
GDP - per capita: purchasing power parity - $29,100 (2005 est.)
GDP - composition by sector:
agriculture: 4%
industry: 58.5%
services: 37.5% (2002 est.)
Labor force: 2.8 million
note: 73.9% of the population in the 15-64 age group is non-national (2005 est.)
Labor force - by occupation: agriculture 7%, industry 15%, services 78% (2000 est.)
Unemployment rate: 2.4% (2001)
Population below poverty line: NA
Household income or consumption by percentage share:
lowest 10%: NA
highest 10%: NA
Inflation rate (consumer prices): 4.5% (2005 est.)
Investment (gross fixed): 20.7% of GDP (2005 est.)
Budget:
revenues: $34.93 billion
expenditures: $29.41 billion, including capital expenditures of $3.4 billion (2005 est.)
Public debt: 17.5% of GDP (2005 est.)
Agriculture - products: dates, vegetables, watermelons; poultry, eggs, dairy products; fish
Industries: petroleum, fishing, aluminum, cement, fertilizers, commercial ship repair, petrochemicals, construction materials, some boat building, handicrafts, textiles
Industrial production growth rate: 4% (2000)
Electricity - production: 45.12 billion kWh (2004)
Electricity - production by source:
fossil fuel: 100%
hydro: 0%
nuclear: 0%
other: 0% (2001)
Electricity - consumption: 38.32 billion kWh (2002)
Electricity - exports: 0 kWh (2004)
Electricity - imports: 0 kWh (2004)
Oil - production: 2.396 million bbl/day (2005 est.)
Oil - consumption: 310,000 bbl/day (2004 est.)
Oil - exports: 2.5 million bbl/day (2004 est.)
Oil - imports: 0 bbl/day (2004)
Oil - proved reserves: 97.8 billion bbl (2005 est.)
Natural gas - production: 44.4 billion cu m (2003 est.)
Natural gas - consumption: 33.7 billion cu m (2003 est.)
Natural gas - exports: 7.19 billion cu m (2003 est.)
Natural gas - imports: 0 cu m (2003 est.)
Natural gas - proved reserves: 6.06 trillion cu m (2005)
Current account balance: $25.66 billion (2005 est.)
Exports: $103.1 billion f.o.b. (2005 est.)
Exports - partners: Japan 24.8%, South Korea 9.9%, India 5.4%, Thailand 5.2% (2004)
Imports: $60.15 billion f.o.b. (2005 est.)
Imports - partners: China 10%, India 9.8%, Japan 6.8%, Germany 6.5%, UK 6.2%, France 6.1%, US 6% (2004)
Reserves of foreign exchange and gold: $23.53 billion (2005 est.)
Debt - external: $30.21 billion (2005 est.)
Economic aid - donor: since its founding in 1971, the Abu Dhabi Fund for Development has given about $5.2 billion in aid to 56 countries (2004)
Currency (code): Emirati dirham (AED)
Currency code: AED
Exchange rates: Emirati dirhams per US dollar - 3.67 (2005), 3.6725 (2004), 3.6725 (2003), 3.6725 (2002), 3.6725 (2001)
note: officially pegged to the US dollar since February 2002
Fiscal year: calendar year

COMMUNICATIONS

Telephones - main lines in use: 1,135,800 (2003)
Telephones - mobile cellular: 2,972,300 (2003)
Telephone system:
general assessment: modern fiber-optic integrated services; digital network with rapidly growing use of mobile cellular telephones; key centers are Abu Dhabi and Dubai
domestic: microwave radio relay, fiber optic and coaxial cable
international: country code - 971; satellite earth stations - 3 Intelsat (1 Atlantic Ocean and 2 Indian Ocean) and 1 Arabsat; submarine cables to Qatar, Bahrain, India, and Pakistan; tropospheric scatter to Bahrain; microwave radio relay to Saudi Arabia
Radio broadcast stations: AM 13, FM 8, shortwave 2 (2004)
Radios: 820,000 (1997)
Television broadcast stations: 15 (2004)
Televisions: 310,000 (1997)
Internet country code: .ae
Internet hosts: 56,283 (2004)
Internet Service Providers (ISPs): 1 (2000)
Internet users: 1,110,200 (2003)

TRANSPORTATION

Airports: 35 (2004 est.)
Airports - with paved runways:
total: 22
over 3,047 m: 9
2,438 to 3,047 m: 2
1,524 to 2,437 m: 4
914 to 1,523 m: 4
under 914 m: 3 (2005 est.)
Airports - with unpaved runways:
total: 13
over 3,047 m: 1
2,438 to 3,047 m: 2
1,524 to 2,437 m: 3
914 to 1,523 m: 3
under 914 m: 4 (2005 est.)
Heliports: 2 (2005 est.)
Pipelines: condensate 469 km; gas 2,655 km; liquid petroleum gas 300 km; oil 2,936 km; oil/gas/water 5 km (2004)
Roadways:
total: 1,088 km
paved: 1,088 km (including 253 km of expressways)
unpaved: 0 km (1999 est.)
Merchant marine:
total: 56 ships (1,000 GRT or over) 578,477 GRT/739,823 DWT
by type: bulk carrier 1, cargo 11, chemical tanker 5, container 6, liquefied gas 1, passenger/cargo 4, petroleum tanker 21, roll on/roll off 7
foreign-owned: 14 (Greece 2, Kuwait 6)
registered in other countries: 200 (2005)
Ports and terminals: Al Fujayrah, Khawr Fakkan, Mina' Jabal 'Ali, Mina' Rashid, Mina' Saqr, Mina' Zayid, Sharjan

MILITARY

Military branches: Army, Navy (includes Marines and Coast Guard), Air and Air Defense Force, paramilitary forces (includes Federal Police Force)
Military service age and obligation: 18 years of age (est.); no conscription (2001)
Manpower available for military service:
males age 18-49: 653,181
note: includes non-nationals (2005 est.)
Manpower fit for military service: *males age 18-49*: 526,671 (2005 est.)
Manpower reaching military service age annually: *males*: 30,706 (2005
Military expenditures - dollar figure: $1.6 billion (FY00)
Military expenditures - percent of GDP: 3.1% (FY00)

TRANSNATIONAL ISSUES

Disputes - international: because the treaties have not been made public, the exact alignment of the boundary with Saudi Arabia is still unknown; boundary agreement was signed and ratified with Oman in 2003 for entire border, including Oman's Musandam Peninsula and Al Madhah enclaves, but contents of the agreement and maps showing the alignment have not been published; UAE engage in direct talks and solicit Arab League support to resolve disputes over Iran's occupation of Lesser and Greater Tunb Islands and Abu Musa Island
Illicit drugs: the UAE is a drug transshipment point for traffickers given its proximity to Southwest Asian drug producing countries; the UAE's position as a major financial center makes it vulnerable to money laundering; anti-money-laundering controls improving

UNITED KINGDOM

INTRODUCTION

Background: Great Britain, the dominant industrial and maritime power of the 19th century, played a leading role in developing parliamentary democracy and in advancing literature and science. At its zenith, the British Empire stretched over one-fourth of the earth's surface. The first half of the 20th century saw the UK's strength seriously depleted in two World Wars. The second half witnessed the dismantling of the Empire and the UK rebuilding itself into a modern and prosperous European nation. As one of five permanent members of the UN Security Council, a founding member of NATO, and of the Commonwealth, the UK pursues a global approach to foreign policy; it currently is weighing the degree of its integration with continental Europe. A member of the EU, it chose to remain outside the Economic and Monetary Union for the time being. Constitutional reform is also a significant issue in the UK. The Scottish Parliament, the National Assembly for Wales, and the Northern Ireland Assembly were established in 1999, but the latter is suspended due to wrangling over the peace process.

GEOGRAPHY

Location: Western Europe, islands including the northern one-sixth of the island of Ireland between the North Atlantic Ocean and the North Sea, northwest of France
Geographic coordinates: 54 00 N, 2 00 W
Map references: Europe
Area:
total: 244,820 sq km
land: 241,590 sq km
water: 3,230 sq km
note: includes Rockall and Shetland Islands
Area - comparative: slightly smaller than Oregon
Land boundaries:
total: 360 km
border countries: Ireland 360 km
Coastline: 12,429 km
Maritime claims:
territorial sea: 12 nm
exclusive fishing zone: 200 nm
continental shelf: as defined in continental shelf orders or in accordance with agreed upon boundaries
Climate: temperate; moderated by prevailing southwest winds over the North Atlantic Current; more than one-half of the days are overcast
Terrain: mostly rugged hills and low mountains; level to rolling plains in east and southeast
Elevation extremes:
lowest point: The Fens -4 m
highest point: Ben Nevis 1,343 m
Natural resources: coal, petroleum, natural gas, iron ore, lead, zinc, gold, tin, limestone, salt, clay, chalk, gypsum, potash, silica sand, slate, arable land
Land use:
arable land: 23.46%
permanent crops: 0.21%
other: 76.33% (2001)
Irrigated land: 1,080 sq km (1998 est.)
Natural hazards: winter windstorms; floods
Environment - current issues: continues to reduce greenhouse gas emissions (has met Kyoto Protocol target of a 12.5% reduction from 1990 levels and intends to meet the legally binding target and move towards a domestic goal of a 20% cut in emissions by 2010); by 2005 the government aims to reduce the amount of industrial and commercial waste disposed of in landfill sites to 85% of 1998 levels and to recycle or compost at least 25% of household waste, increasing to 33% by 2015; between 1998-99 and 1999-2000, household recycling increased from 8.8% to 10.3%
Environment - international agreements:
party to: Air Pollution, Air Pollution-Nitrogen Oxides, Air Pollution-Sulfur 94, Air Pollution-Volatile Organic Compounds, Antarctic-Environmental Protocol, Antarctic-Marine Living Resources, Antarctic Seals, Antarctic Treaty, Biodiversity, Climate Change, Climate Change-Kyoto Protocol, Desertification, Endangered Species, Environmental Modification, Hazardous Wastes, Law of the Sea, Marine Dumping, Marine Life Conservation, Ozone Layer Protection, Ship Pollution, Tropical Timber 83, Tropical Timber 94,

Wetlands, Whaling
signed, but not ratified: Air Pollution-Persistent Organic Pollutants
Geography - note: lies near vital North Atlantic sea lanes; only 35 km from France and now linked by tunnel under the English Channel; because of heavily indented coastline, no location is more than 125 km from tidal waters

PEOPLE

Population: 60,441,457 (July 2005 est.)
Age structure:
0-14 years: 17.7% (male 5,490,592/female 5,229,691)
15-64 years: 66.5% (male 20,329,272/female 19,855,862)
65 years and over: 15.8% (male 4,063,357/female 5,472,683) (2005 est.)
Median age:
total: 38.99 years
male: 37.89 years
female: 40.13 years (2005 est.)
Population growth rate: 0.28% (2005 est.)
Birth rate: 10.78 births/1,000 population (2005 est.)
Death rate: 10.18 deaths/1,000 population (2005 est.)
Net migration rate: 2.18 migrant(s)/1,000 population (2005 est.)
Sex ratio:
at birth: 1.05 male(s)/female
under 15 years: 1.05 male(s)/female
15-64 years: 1.02 male(s)/female
65 years and over: 0.74 male(s)/female
total population: 0.98 male(s)/female (2005 est.)
Infant mortality rate:
total: 5.16 deaths/1,000 live births
male: 5.76 deaths/1,000 live births
female: 4.53 deaths/1,000 live births (2005 est.)
Life expectancy at birth:
total population: 78.38 years
male: 75.94 years
female: 80.96 years (2005 est.)
Total fertility rate: 1.66 children born/woman (2005 est.)
HIV/AIDS - adult prevalence rate: 0.2% (2001 est.)
HIV/AIDS - people living with HIV/AIDS: 51,000 (2001 est.)
HIV/AIDS - deaths: less than 500 (2003 est.)
Nationality:
noun: Briton(s), British (collective plural)
adjective: British
Ethnic groups: white (English 83.6%, Scottish 8.6%, Welsh 4.9%, Northern Irish 2.9%) 92.1%, black 2%, Indian 1.8%, Pakistani 1.3%, mixed 1.2%, other 1.6% (2001 census)
Religions: Christian (Anglican, Roman Catholic, Presbyterian, Methodist) 71.6%, Muslim 2.7%, Hindu 1%, other 1.6%, unspecified or none 23.1% (2001 census)
Languages: English, Welsh (about 26% of the population of Wales), Scottish form of Gaelic (about 60,000 in Scotland)
Literacy:
definition: age 15 and over has completed five or more years of schooling
total population: 99% (2000 est.)
male: NA%
female: NA%

GOVERNMENT

Country name:
conventional long form: United Kingdom of Great Britain and Northern Ireland; note - Great Britain includes England, Scotland, and Wales
conventional short form: United Kingdom
abbreviation: UK
Government type: constitutional monarchy
Capital: London
Administrative divisions:
England - 47 boroughs, 36 counties, 29 London boroughs, 12 cities and boroughs, 10 districts, 12 cities, 3 royal boroughs
boroughs: Barnsley, Blackburn with Darwen, Blackpool, Bolton, Bournemouth, Bracknell Forest, Brighton and Hove, Bury, Calderdale, Darlington, Doncaster, Dudley, Gateshead, Halton, Hartlepool, Kirklees, Knowsley, Luton, Medway, Middlesbrough, Milton Keynes, North Tyneside, Oldham, Poole, Reading, Redcar and Cleveland, Rochdale, Rotherham, Sandwell, Sefton, Slough, Solihull, Southend-on-Sea, South Tyneside, St. Helens, Stockport, Stockton-on-Tees, Swindon, Tameside, Thurrock, Torbay, Trafford, Walsall, Warrington, Wigan, Wirral, Wolverhampton
counties: Bedfordshire, Buckinghamshire, Cambridgeshire, Cheshire, Cornwall, Cumbria, Derbyshire, Devon, Dorset, Durham, East Sussex, Essex, Gloucestershire, Hampshire, Herefordshire, Hertfordshire, Isle of Wight, Kent, Lancashire, Leicestershire, Lincolnshire, Norfolk, Northamptonshire, Northumberland, North Yorkshire, Nottinghamshire, Oxfordshire, Shropshire, Somerset, Staffordshire, Suffolk, Surrey, Warwickshire, West Sussex, Wiltshire, Worcestershire
London boroughs: Barking and Dagenham, Barnet, Bexley, Brent, Bromley, Camden, Croydon, Ealing, Enfield, Greenwich, Hackney, Hammersmith and Fulham, Haringey, Harrow, Havering, Hillingdon, Hounslow, Islington, Lambeth, Lewisham, Merton, Newham, Redbridge, Richmond upon Thames, Southwark, Sutton, Tower Hamlets, Waltham Forest, Wandsworth
cities and boroughs: Birmingham, Bradford, Coventry, Leeds, Liverpool, Manchester, Newcastle upon Tyne, Salford, Sheffield, Sunderland, Wakefield, Westminster
districts: Bath and North East Somerset, East Riding of Yorkshire, North East Lincolnshire, North Lincolnshire, North Somerset, Rutland, South Gloucestershire, Telford and Wrekin, West Berkshire, Wokingham
cities: City of Bristol, Derby, City of Kingston upon Hull, Leicester, City of London, Nottingham, Peterborough, Plymouth, Portsmouth, Southampton, Stoke-on-Trent, York
royal boroughs: Kensington and Chelsea, Kingston upon Thames, Windsor and Maidenhead
Northern Ireland - 24 districts, 2 cities, 6 counties
districts: Antrim, Ards, Armagh, Ballymena, Ballymoney, Banbridge, Carrickfergus, Castlereagh, Coleraine, Cookstown, Craigavon, Down, Dungannon, Fermanagh, Larne, Limavady, Lisburn, Magherafelt, Moyle, Newry and Mourne, Newtownabbey, North Down, Omagh, Strabane
cities: Belfast, Derry
counties: County Antrim, County Armagh, County Down, County Fermanagh, County Londonderry, County Tyrone
Scotland - 32 council areas: Aberdeen City, Aberdeenshire, Angus, Argyll and Bute, The Scottish Borders, Clackmannanshire, Dumfries and Galloway, Dundee City, East Ayrshire, East Dunbartonshire, East Lothian, East Renfrewshire, City of Edinburgh, Falkirk, Fife, Glasgow City, Highland, Inverclyde, Midlothian, Moray, North Ayrshire, North Lanarkshire, Orkney Islands, Perth and Kinross, Renfrewshire, Shetland Islands, South Ayrshire, South Lanarkshire, Stirling, West Dunbartonshire, Eilean Siar (Western Isles), West Lothian;
Wales - 11 county boroughs, 9 counties, 2 cities and counties
county boroughs: Blaenau Gwent, Bridgend, Caerphilly, Conwy, Gwynedd, Merthyr Tydfil, Neath Port Talbot, Newport, Rhondda Cynon Taff, Torfaen, Wrexham
counties: Isle of Anglesey, Ceredigion, Carmarthenshire, Denbighshire, Flintshire, Monmouthshire, Pembrokeshire, Powys, The Vale of Glamorgan
cities and counties: Cardiff, Swansea
Dependent areas: Anguilla, Bermuda, British Indian Ocean Territory, British Virgin Islands, Cayman Islands, Falkland Islands, Gibraltar, Guernsey, Jersey, Isle of Man, Montserrat, Pitcairn Islands, Saint Helena and Ascension, South Georgia and the South Sandwich Islands, Turks and Caicos Islands

Independence: England has existed as a unified entity since the 10th century; the union between England and Wales, begun in 1284 with the Statute of Rhuddlan, was not formalized until 1536 with an Act of Union; in another Act of Union in 1707, England and Scotland agreed to permanently join as Great Britain; the legislative union of Great Britain and Ireland was implemented in 1801, with the adoption of the name the United Kingdom of Great Britain and Ireland; the Anglo-Irish treaty of 1921 formalized a partition of Ireland; six northern Irish counties remained part of the United Kingdom as Northern Ireland and the current name of the country, the United Kingdom of Great Britain and Northern Ireland, was adopted in 1927

National holiday: the UK does not celebrate one particular national holiday

Constitution: unwritten; partly statutes, partly common law and practice

Legal system: common law tradition with early Roman and modern continental influences; has nonbinding judicial review of Acts of Parliament under the Human Rights Act of 1998; accepts compulsory ICJ jurisdiction, with reservations

Suffrage: 18 years of age, universal

Executive branch:
chief of state: Queen ELIZABETH II (since 6 February 1952); Heir Apparent Prince CHARLES (son of the queen, born 14 November 1948)
head of government: Prime Minister Anthony (Tony) BLAIR (since 2 May 1997)
cabinet: Cabinet of Ministers appointed by the prime minister
elections: none; the monarchy is hereditary; following legislative elections, the leader of the majority party or the leader of the majority coalition is usually the prime minister

Legislative branch: bicameral Parliament comprised of House of Lords (consists of approximately 500 life peers, 92 hereditary peers and 26 clergy) and House of Commons (646 seats since 2005 elections; members are elected by popular vote to serve five-year terms unless the House is dissolved earlier)
elections: House of Lords - no elections (note - in 1999, as provided by the House of Lords Act, elections were held in the House of Lords to determine the 92 hereditary peers who would remain there; pending further reforms, elections are held only as vacancies in the hereditary peerage arise); House of Commons - last held 5 May 2005 (next to be held by May 2010)
election results: House of Commons - percent of vote by party - Labor 35.2%, Conservative 32.3%, Liberal Democrats 22%, other 10.5%; seats by party - Labor 356, Conservative 197, Liberal Democrat 62, other 31; note - as of 30 September 2005 the seats by party - Labor 354, Conservative 196, Liberal Democrat 62, other 34
note: in 1998 elections were held for a Northern Ireland Assembly (because of unresolved disputes among existing parties, the transfer of power from London to Northern Ireland came only at the end of 1999 and has been suspended four times the latest occurring in October 2002); in 1999 there were elections for a new Scottish Parliament and a new Welsh Assembly

Judicial branch: House of Lords (highest court of appeal; several Lords of Appeal in Ordinary are appointed by the monarch for life); Supreme Courts of England, Wales, and Northern Ireland (comprising the Courts of Appeal, the High Courts of Justice, and the Crown Courts); Scotland's Court of Session and Court of the Justiciary

Political parties and leaders: Conservative and Unionist Party [David CAMERON]; Democratic Unionist Party (Northern Ireland) [Rev. Ian PAISLEY]; Labor Party [Anthony (Tony) BLAIR]; Liberal Democrats [Charles KENNEDY]; Party of Wales (Plaid Cymru) [Dafydd IWAN]; Scottish National Party or SNP [Alex SALMOND]; Sinn Fein (Northern Ireland) [Gerry ADAMS]; Social Democratic and Labor Party or SDLP (Northern Ireland) [Mark DURKAN]; Ulster Unionist Party (Northern Ireland) [Sir Reg EMPEY]

Political pressure groups and leaders: Campaign for Nuclear Disarmament; Confederation of British Industry; National Farmers' Union; Trades Union Congress

International organization participation: AfDB, AsDB, Australia Group, BIS, C, CBSS (observer), CDB, CE, CERN, EAPC, EBRD, EIB, ESA, EU, FAO, G-5, G- 7, G- 8, G-10, IADB, IAEA, IBRD, ICAO, ICC, ICCt, ICFTU, ICRM, IDA, IEA, IFAD, IFC, IFRCS, IHO, ILO, IMF, IMO, Interpol, IOC, IOM, ISO, ITU, MIGA, MONUC, NAM (guest), NATO, NEA, NSG, OAS (observer), OECD, OPCW, OSCE, Paris Club, PCA, PIF (partner), UN, UN Security Council, UNAMSIL, UNCTAD, UNESCO, UNFICYP, UNHCR, UNIDO, UNMIL, UNMIS, UNMOVIC, UNOMIG, UNRWA, UPU, WCO, WEU, WHO, WIPO, WMO, WTO, ZC

Diplomatic representation in the US:
chief of mission: Ambassador David G. MANNING
chancery: 3100 Massachusetts Avenue NW, Washington, DC 20008
telephone: [1] (202) 588-6500
FAX: [1] (202) 588-7870
consulate(s) general: Atlanta, Boston, Chicago, Houston, Los Angeles, New York, and San Francisco
consulate(s): Dallas, Denver, Miami, and Seattle

Diplomatic representation from the US:
chief of mission: Ambassador Robert Holmes TUTTLE
embassy: 24/31 Grosvenor Square, London, W1A 1AE
mailing address: PSC 801, Box 40, FPO AE 09498-4040
telephone: [44] (0) 20 7499-9000
FAX: [44] (0) 20 7629-9124
consulate(s) general: Belfast, Edinburgh

Flag description: blue field with the red cross of Saint George (patron saint of England) edged in white superimposed on the diagonal red cross of Saint Patrick (patron saint of Ireland), which is superimposed on the diagonal white cross of Saint Andrew (patron saint of Scotland); properly known as the Union Flag, but commonly called the Union Jack; the design and colors (especially the Blue Ensign) have been the basis for a number of other flags including other Commonwealth countries and their constituent states or provinces, as well as British overseas territories

ECONOMY

Economy - overview: The UK, a leading trading power and financial center, is one of the quintet of trillion dollar economies of Western Europe. Over the past two decades the government has greatly reduced public ownership and contained the growth of social welfare programs. Agriculture is intensive, highly mechanized, and efficient by European standards, producing about 60% of food needs with less than 2% of the labor force. The UK has large coal, natural gas, and oil reserves; primary energy production accounts for 10% of GDP, one of the highest shares of any industrial nation. Services, particularly banking, insurance, and business services, account by far for the largest proportion of GDP while industry continues to decline in importance. GDP growth slipped in 2001-03 as the global downturn, the high value of the pound, and the bursting of the "new economy" bubble hurt manufacturing and exports. Output recovered in 2004, to 3.2% growth, but fell in 2005, to 1.8%. Despite slower growth, the economy is one of the strongest in Europe; inflation, interest rates, and unemployment remain low. The relatively good economic performance has complicated the BLAIR government's efforts to make a case for Britain to join the European Economic and Monetary Union (EMU). Critics point out that the economy is doing well outside of EMU, and they cite public opinion polls that continue to show a majority of Britons opposed to the euro. Meantime, the government has been speeding up the improvement of education, transport, and health services, at a cost in higher taxes and a widening public deficit.

GDP (purchasing power parity): $1.867 trillion (2005 est.)
GDP (official exchange rate): $2.275 trillion (2005 est.)
GDP - real growth rate: 1.8% (2005 est.)
GDP - per capita: purchasing power parity - $30,900 (2005 est.)
GDP - composition by sector:
agriculture: 1.1%
industry: 26%
services: 72.9% (2005 est.)
Labor force: 30.07 million (2005 est.)
Labor force - by occupation: agriculture 1.5%, industry 19.1%, services 79.5% (2004)
Unemployment rate: 4.7% (2005 est.)
Population below poverty line: 17% (2002 est.)
Household income or consumption by percentage share:
lowest 10%: 2.1%
highest 10%: 28.5% (1999)
Distribution of family income - Gini index: 36.8 (1999)
Inflation rate (consumer prices): 2.2% (2005 est.)
Investment (gross fixed): 16.3% of GDP (2005 est.)
Budget:
revenues: $881.4 billion
expenditures: $951 billion, including capital expenditures of NA (2005 est.)
Public debt: 42.2% of GDP (2005 est.)
Agriculture - products: cereals, oilseed, potatoes, vegetables; cattle, sheep, poultry; fish
Industries: machine tools, electric power equipment, automation equipment, railroad equipment, shipbuilding, aircraft, motor vehicles and parts, electronics and communications equipment, metals, chemicals, coal, petroleum, paper and paper products, food processing, textiles, clothing, and other consumer goods
Industrial production growth rate: -0.9% (2005 est.)
Electricity - production: 369.9 billion kWh (2003)
Electricity - production by source:
fossil fuel: 73.8%
hydro: 0.9%
nuclear: 23.7%
other: 1.6% (2001)
Electricity - consumption: 346.1 billion kWh (2003)
Electricity - exports: 3 billion kWh (2003)
Electricity - imports: 5.1 billion kWh (2003)
Oil - production: 2.393 million bbl/day (2003 est.)
Oil - consumption: 1.722 million bbl/day (2003 est.)
Oil - exports: 1.498 million bbl/day (2001)
Oil - imports: 1.084 million bbl/day (2003)
Oil - proved reserves: 4.5 billion bbl (31 December 2004)
Natural gas - production: 105.9 billion cu m (2001 est.)
Natural gas - consumption: 92.85 billion cu m (2001 est.)
Natural gas - exports: 15.75 billion cu m (2001 est.)
Natural gas - imports: 2.7 billion cu m (2001 est.)
Natural gas - proved reserves: 714.9 billion cu m (31 December 2004)
Current account balance: $-38.4 billion (2005 est.)
Exports: $372.7 billion f.o.b. (2005 est.)
Exports - partners: US 15.3%, Germany 10.8%, France 9.2%, Ireland 6.8%, Netherlands 6%, Belgium 5.1%, Spain 4.5%, Italy 4.2% (2004)
Imports: $483.7 billion f.o.b. (2005 est.)
Imports - partners: Germany 13%, US 9.3%, France 7.4%, Netherlands 6.6%, Belgium 4.9%, China 4.3%, Italy 4.3% (2004)
Reserves of foreign exchange and gold: $48.73 billion (2004)
Debt - external: $7.107 trillion (30 June 2005)
Economic aid - donor: ODA, $7.9 billion (2004)
Currency (code): British pound (GBP)
Currency code: GBP
Exchange rates: British pounds per US dollar - 0.54 (2005), 0.5462 (2004), 0.6125 (2003), 0.6672 (2002), 0.6947 (2001)
Fiscal year: 6 April - 5 April

COMMUNICATIONS

Telephones - main lines in use: 34.898 million (2002)
Telephones - mobile cellular: 49.677 million (2002)
Telephone system:
general assessment: technologically advanced domestic and international system
domestic: equal mix of buried cables, microwave radio relay, and fiber-optic systems
international: country code - 44; 40 coaxial submarine cables; satellite earth stations - 10 Intelsat (7 Atlantic Ocean and 3 Indian Ocean), 1 Inmarsat (Atlantic Ocean region), and 1 Eutelsat; at least 8 large international switching centers
Radio broadcast stations: AM 219, FM 431, shortwave 3 (1998)
Radios: 84.5 million (1997)
Television broadcast stations: 228 (plus 3,523 repeaters) (1995)
Televisions: 30.5 million (1997)
Internet country code: .uk
Internet hosts: 3,398,708 (2004))
Internet Service Providers (ISPs): more than 400 (2000)
Internet users: 25 million (2002)

TRANSPORTATION

Airports: 471 (2004 est.)
Airports - with paved runways:
total: 334
over 3,047 m: 8
2,438 to 3,047 m: 33
1,524 to 2,437 m: 149
914 to 1,523 m: 85
under 914 m: 59 (2005 est.)
Airports - with unpaved runways:
total: 137
2,438 to 3,047 m: 1
1,524 to 2,437 m: 1
914 to 1,523 m: 23
under 914 m: 112 (2005 est.)
Heliports: 11 (2005 est.)
Pipelines: condensate 370 km; gas 21,446 km; liquid petroleum gas 59 km; oil 6,420 km; oil/gas/water 63 km; refined products 4,474 km (2004)
Railways:
total: 17,274 km
standard gauge: 16,814 km 1.435-m gauge (5,296 km electrified)
broad gauge: 460 km 1.600-m gauge (in Northern Ireland) (2004)
Roadways:
total: 392,931 km
paved: 392,931 km (including 3,431 km of expressways)
unpaved: 0 km (2003)
Waterways: 3,200 km (620 km used for commerce) (2004)
Merchant marine:
total: 429 ships (1,000 GRT or over) 9,181,284 GRT/9,566,275 DWT
by type: bulk carrier 18, cargo 55, chemical tanker 48, container 134, liquefied gas 11, passenger 12, passenger/cargo 64, petroleum tanker 40, refrigerated cargo 19, roll on/roll off 25, vehicle carrier 3
foreign-owned: 202 (Australia 3, Canada 15, Denmark 38, Finland 2, Germany 56, Greece 4, Ireland 1, Italy 9, Netherlands 12, Norway 28, South Africa 4, Sweden 15, Taiwan 7, United States 8)
registered in other countries: 446 (2005)

Ports and terminals: Hound Point, Immingham, Milford Haven, Liverpool, London, Southampton, Sullom Voe, Teesport

MILITARY

Military branches: Army, Royal Navy (includes Royal Marines), Royal Air Force
Military service age and obligation: 16 years of age for voluntary military service (January 2004)
Manpower available for military service: *males age 16-49:* 14,607,724 (2005 est.)
Manpower fit for military service: *males age 16-49:* 12,046,268 (2005 est.)
Military expenditures - dollar figure: $42,836.5 million (2003)
Military expenditures - percent of GDP: 2.4% (2003)

TRANSNATIONAL ISSUES

Disputes - international: in 2003, Gibraltar residents voted overwhelmingly by referendum to remain a British colony and against a "total shared sovereignty" arrangement while demanding participation in talks between the UK and Spain; Spain disapproves of UK plans to grant Gibraltar greater autonomy; Mauritius and Seychelles claim the Chagos Archipelago (British Indian Ocean Territory), and its former inhabitants since their eviction in 1965; most Chagosians reside in Mauritius, and in 2001 were granted UK citizenship but no right to patriation in the UK; UK rejects sovereignty talks requested by Argentina, which still claims the Falkland Islands (Islas Malvinas) and South Georgia and the South Sandwich Islands; territorial claim in Antarctica (British Antarctic Territory) overlaps Argentine claim and partially overlaps Chilean claim; Iceland, the UK, and Ireland dispute Denmark's claim that the Faroe Islands' continental shelf extends beyond 200 nm
Illicit drugs: producer of limited amounts of synthetic drugs and synthetic precursor chemicals; major consumer of Southwest Asian heroin, Latin American cocaine, and synthetic drugs; money-laundering center

UNITED STATES

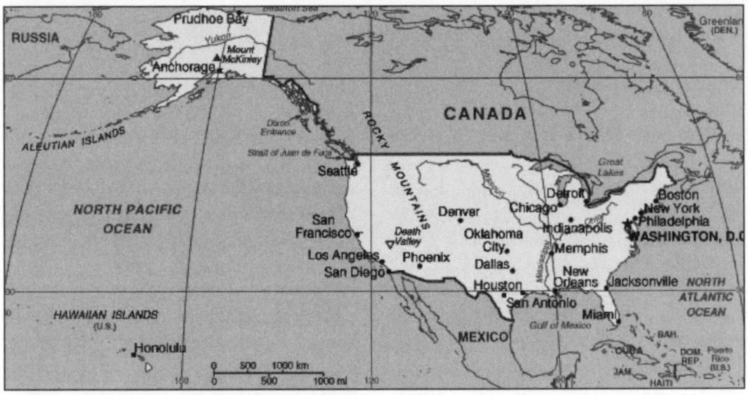

INTRODUCTION

Background: Britain's American colonies broke with the mother country in 1776 and were recognized as the new nation of the United States of America following the Treaty of Paris in 1783. During the 19th and 20th centuries, 37 new states were added to the original 13 as the nation expanded across the North American continent and acquired a number of overseas possessions. The two most traumatic experiences in the nation's history were the Civil War (1861-65) and the Great Depression of the 1930s. Buoyed by victories in World Wars I and II and the end of the Cold War in 1991, the US remains the world's most powerful nation state. The economy is marked by steady growth, low unemployment and inflation, and rapid advances in technology.

GEOGRAPHY

Location: North America, bordering both the North Atlantic Ocean and the North Pacific Ocean, between Canada and Mexico
Geographic coordinates: 38 00 N, 97 00 W
Map references: North America
Area:
total: 9,631,418 sq km
land: 9,161,923 sq km
water: 469,495 sq km
note: includes only the 50 states and District of Columbia
Area - comparative: about half the size of Russia; about three-tenths the size of Africa; about half the size of South America (or slightly larger than Brazil); slightly larger than China; almost two and a half times the size of the European Union
Land boundaries:
total: 12,034 km
border countries: Canada 8,893 km (including 2,477 km with Alaska), Mexico 3,141 km
note: US Naval Base at Guantanamo Bay, Cuba is leased by the US and is part of Cuba; the base boundary is 29 km
Coastline: 19,924 km
Maritime claims:
territorial sea: 12 nm
contiguous zone: 24 nm
exclusive economic zone: 200 nm
continental shelf: not specified
Climate: mostly temperate, but tropical in Hawaii and Florida, arctic in Alaska, semiarid in the great plains west of the Mississippi River, and arid in the Great Basin of the southwest; low winter temperatures in the northwest are ameliorated occasionally in January and February by warm chinook winds from the eastern slopes of the Rocky Mountains
Terrain: vast central plain, mountains in west, hills and low mountains in east; rugged mountains and broad river valleys in Alaska; rugged, volcanic topography in Hawaii
Elevation extremes:
lowest point: Death Valley -86 m
highest point: Mount McKinley 6,194 m
Natural resources: coal, copper, lead, molybdenum, phosphates, uranium, bauxite, gold, iron, mercury, nickel, potash, silver, tungsten, zinc, petroleum, natural gas, timber
Land use:
arable land: 19.13%
permanent crops: 0.22%
other: 80.65% (2001
Irrigated land: 214,000 sq km (1998 est.)
Natural hazards: tsunamis, volcanoes, and earthquake activity around Pacific Basin; hurricanes along the Atlantic and Gulf of Mexico coasts; tornadoes in the midwest and southeast; mud slides in California; forest fires in the west; flooding; permafrost in northern Alaska, a major impediment to development
Environment - current issues: air pollution resulting in acid rain in both the US and Canada; the US is the largest single emitter of carbon dioxide from the burning of fossil fuels; water pollution from

runoff of pesticides and fertilizers; limited natural fresh water resources in much of the western part of the country require careful management; desertification

Environment - international agreements:
party to: Air Pollution, Air Pollution-Nitrogen Oxides, Antarctic-Environmental Protocol, Antarctic-Marine Living Resources, Antarctic Seals, Antarctic Treaty, Climate Change, Desertification, Endangered Species, Environmental Modification, Marine Dumping, Marine Life Conservation, Ozone Layer Protection, Ship Pollution, Tropical Timber 83, Tropical Timber 94, Wetlands, Whaling
signed, but not ratified: Air Pollution-Persistent Organic Pollutants, Air Pollution-Volatile Organic Compounds, Biodiversity, Climate Change-Kyoto Protocol, Hazardous Wastes

Geography - note: world's third-largest country by size (after Russia and Canada) and by population (after China and India); Mt. McKinley is highest point in North America and Death Valley the lowest point on the continent

PEOPLE

Population: 295,734,134 (July 2005 est.)

Age structure:
0-14 years: 20.6% (male 31,095,725/ female 29,703,997)
15-64 years: 67% (male 98,914,382/female 99,324,126)
65 years and over: 12.4% (male 15,298,676/ female 21,397,228) (2005 est.)

Median age:
total: 36.27 years
male: 34.94 years
female: 37.6 years (2005 est.)

Population growth rate: 0.92% (2005 est.)

Birth rate: 14.14 births/1,000 population (2005 est.)

Death rate: 8.25 deaths/1,000 population (2005 est.)

Net migration rate: 3.31 migrant(s)/ 1,000 population (2005 est.)

Sex ratio:
at birth: 1.05 male(s)/female
under 15 years: 1.05 male(s)/female
15-64 years: 1 male(s)/female
65 years and over: 0.72 male(s)/female
total population: 0.97 male(s)/female (2005 est.)

Infant mortality rate:
total: 6.5 deaths/1,000 live births
male: 7.17 deaths/1,000 live births
female: 5.8 deaths/1,000 live births (2005 est.)

Life expectancy at birth:
total population: 77.71 years
male: 74.89 years
female: 80.67 years (2005 est.)

Total fertility rate: 2.08 children born/woman (2005 est.)

HIV/AIDS - adult prevalence rate: 0.6% (2003 est.)

HIV/AIDS - people living with HIV/AIDS: 950,000 (2003 est.)

HIV/AIDS - deaths: 14,000 (2003 est.)

Nationality:
noun: American(s)
adjective: American

Ethnic groups: white 81.7%, black 12.9%, Asian 4.2%, Amerindian and Alaska native 1%, native Hawaiian and other Pacific islander 0.2% (2003 est.)
note: a separate listing for Hispanic is not included because the US Census Bureau considers Hispanic to mean a person of Latin American descent (including persons of Cuban, Mexican, or Puerto Rican origin) living in the US who may be of any race or ethnic group (white, black, Asian, etc.)

Religions: Protestant 52%, Roman Catholic 24%, Mormon 2%, Jewish 1%, Muslim 1%, other 10%, none 10% (2002 est.)

Languages: English 82.1%, Spanish 10.7%, other Indo-European 3.8%, Asian and Pacific island 2.7%, other 0.7% (2000 census)

Literacy:
definition: age 15 and over can read and write
total population: 97%
male: 97%
female: 97% (1999 est.)

GOVERNMENT

Country name:
conventional long form: United States of America
conventional short form: United States
abbreviation: US or USA

Government type: Constitution-based federal republic; strong democratic tradition

Capital: Washington, DC

Administrative divisions: 50 states and 1 district*; Alabama, Alaska, Arizona, Arkansas, California, Colorado, Connecticut, Delaware, District of Columbia*, Florida, Georgia, Hawaii, Idaho, Illinois, Indiana, Iowa, Kansas, Kentucky, Louisiana, Maine, Maryland, Massachusetts, Michigan, Minnesota, Mississippi, Missouri, Montana, Nebraska, Nevada, New Hampshire, New Jersey, New Mexico, New York, North Carolina, North Dakota, Ohio, Oklahoma, Oregon, Pennsylvania, Rhode Island, South Carolina, South Dakota, Tennessee, Texas, Utah, Vermont, Virginia, Washington, West Virginia, Wisconsin, Wyoming

Dependent areas: American Samoa, Baker Island, Guam, Howland Island, Jarvis Island, Johnston Atoll, Kingman Reef, Midway Islands, Navassa Island, Northern Mariana Islands, Palmyra Atoll, Puerto Rico, Virgin Islands, Wake Island
note: from 18 July 1947 until 1 October 1994, the US administered the Trust Territory of the Pacific Islands; it entered into a political relationship with all four political units: the Northern Mariana Islands is a commonwealth in political union with the US (effective 3 November 1986); the Republic of the Marshall Islands signed a Compact of Free Association with the US (effective 21 October 1986); the Federated States of Micronesia signed a Compact of Free Association with the US (effective 3 November 1986); Palau concluded a Compact of Free Association with the US (effective 1 October 1994)

Independence: 4 July 1776 (from Great Britain)

National holiday: Independence Day, 4 July (1776)

Constitution: 17 September 1787, effective 4 March 1789

Legal system: federal court system based on English common law; each state has its own unique legal system, of which all but one (Louisiana's) is based on English common law; judicial review of legislative acts; accepts compulsory ICJ jurisdiction with reservations

Suffrage: 18 years of age, universal

Executive branch:
chief of state: President George W. BUSH (since 20 January 2001); note - the president is both the chief of state and head of government
head of government: President George W. BUSH (since 20 January 2001); note - the president is both the chief of state and head of government
cabinet: Cabinet appointed by the president with Senate approval
elections: president and vice president elected on the same ticket by a college of representatives who are elected directly from each state; president and vice president serve four-year terms; election last held 2 November 2004 (next to be held November 2008)
election results: George W. BUSH reelected president; percent of popular vote - George W. BUSH (Republican Party) 50.9%, John KERRY (Democratic Party) 48.1%, other 1.0%

Legislative branch: bicameral Congress consists of the Senate (100 seats, one-third are renewed every two years; two members are elected from each state by popular vote to serve six-year terms) and the House of Representatives (435 seats; members are directly elected by popular vote to serve two-year terms)
elections: Senate - last held 2 November 2004 (next to be held November 2006); House of Representatives - last held 2 November 2004 (next to be held November 2006)
election results: Senate - percent of vote by party - NA%; seats by party - Republican

Party 55, Democratic Party 44, independent 1; House of Representatives - percent of vote by party - NA%; seats by party - Republican Party 231, Democratic Party 200, undecided 4
Judicial branch: Supreme Court (its nine justices are appointed for life on condition of good behavior by the president with confirmation by the Senate); United States Courts of Appeal; United States District Courts; State and County Courts
Political parties and leaders: Democratic Party [Howard DEAN]; Green Party [leader NA]; Libertarian Party [Steve DAMERELL]; Republican Party [Ken MEHLMAN]
Political pressure groups and leaders: NA
International organization participation: AfDB, ANZUS, APEC, ARF, AsDB, ASEAN (dialogue partner), Australia Group, BIS, CBSS (observer), CE (observer), CERN (observer), CP, EAPC, EBRD, FAO, G-5, G-7, G- 8, G-10, IADB, IAEA, IBRD, ICAO, ICC, ICFTU, ICRM, IDA, IEA, IFAD, IFC, IFRCS, IHO, ILO, IMF, IMO, Interpol, IOC, IOM, ISO, ITU, MIGA, MINUSTAH, NAFTA, NAM (guest), NATO, NEA, NSG, OAS, OECD, OPCW, OSCE, Paris Club, PCA, PIF (partner), SPC, UN, UN Security Council, UNCTAD, UNESCO, UNHCR, UNITAR, UNMEE, UNMIL, UNMOVIC, UNOMIG, UNRWA, UNTSO, UPU, WCL, WCO, WHO, WIPO, WMO, WTO, ZC
Flag description: 13 equal horizontal stripes of red (top and bottom) alternating with white; there is a blue rectangle in the upper hoist-side corner bearing 50 small, white, five-pointed stars arranged in nine offset horizontal rows of six stars (top and bottom) alternating with rows of five stars; the 50 stars represent the 50 states, the 13 stripes represent the 13 original colonies; known as Old Glory; the design and colors have been the basis for a number of other flags, including Chile, Liberia, Malaysia, and Puerto Rico

ECONOMY

Economy - overview: The US has the largest and most technologically powerful economy in the world, with a per capita GDP of $41,800. In this market-oriented economy, private individuals and business firms make most of the decisions, and the federal and state governments buy needed goods and services predominantly in the private marketplace. US business firms enjoy considerably greater flexibility than their counterparts in Western Europe and Japan in decisions to expand capital plant, to lay off surplus workers, and to develop new products. At the same time, they face higher barriers to entry in their rivals' home markets than the barriers to entry of foreign firms in US markets. US firms are at or near the forefront in technological advances, especially in computers and in medical, aerospace, and military equipment; their advantage has narrowed since the end of World War II. The onrush of technology largely explains the gradual development of a "two-tier labor market" in which those at the bottom lack the education and the professional/technical skills of those at the top and, more and more, fail to get comparable pay raises, health insurance coverage, and other benefits. Since 1975, practically all the gains in household income have gone to the top 20% of households. The response to the terrorist attacks of 11 September 2001 showed the remarkable resilience of the economy. The war in March/April 2003 between a US-led coalition and Iraq, and the subsequent occupation of Iraq, required major shifts in national resources to the military. The rise in GDP in 2004 and 2005 was undergirded by substantial gains in labor productivity. The economy suffered from a sharp increase in energy prices in mid-2005, but by late in the year those prices dropped back to earlier levels. Hurricane Katrina caused extensive damage in the Gulf Coast region, but had a small impact on overall GDP growth for the year. Long-term problems include inadequate investment in economic infrastructure, rapidly rising medical and pension costs of an aging population, sizable trade and budget deficits, and stagnation of family income in the lower economic groups.
GDP (purchasing power parity): $12.37 trillion (2005 est.)
GDP (official exchange rate): $12.77 trillion (2005 est.)
GDP - real growth rate: 3.5% (2005 est.)
GDP - per capita: purchasing power parity - $41,800 (2005 est.)
GDP - composition by sector:
agriculture: 1%
industry: 20.7%
services: 78.3% (2005 est.)
Labor force: 149.3 million (includes unemployed) (2005)
Labor force - by occupation: farming, forestry, and fishing 0.7%, manufacturing, extraction, transportation, and crafts 22.9%, managerial, professional, and technical 34.7%, sales and office 25.4%, other services 16.3%
note: figures exclude the unemployed (2005)
Unemployment rate: 5.1% (2005)
Population below poverty line: 12% (2004 est.)
Household income or consumption by percentage share:
lowest 10%: 1.8%
highest 10%: 30.5% (1997)
Distribution of family income - Gini index: 45 (2004)
Inflation rate (consumer prices): 3.2% (2005 est.)
Investment (gross fixed): 16.8% of GDP (2005 est.)
Budget:
revenues: $2.119 trillion
expenditures: $2.466 trillion, including capital expenditures of NA (2005 est.)
Public debt: 64.7% of GDP (2005 est.)
Agriculture - products: wheat, corn, other grains, fruits, vegetables, cotton; beef, pork, poultry, dairy products; forest products; fish
Industries: leading industrial power in the world, highly diversified and technologically advanced; petroleum, steel, motor vehicles, aerospace, telecommunications, chemicals, electronics, food processing, consumer goods, lumber, mining
Industrial production growth rate: 3.2% (2005 est.)
Electricity - production: 3.892 trillion kWh (2003)
Electricity - production by source:
fossil fuel: 71.4%
hydro: 5.6%
nuclear: 20.7%
other: 2.3% (2001)
Electricity - consumption: 3.656 trillion kWh (2003)
Electricity - exports: 23.97 billion kWh (2003)
Electricity - imports: 30.39 billion kWh (2003)
Oil - production: 7.61 million bbl/day (2005 est.)
Oil - consumption: 20.03 million bbl/day (2003 est.)
Oil - exports: NA (2001)
Oil - imports: NA (2001)
Oil - proved reserves: 22.45 billion bbl (1 January 2002)
Natural gas - production: 548.1 billion cu m (2001 est.)
Natural gas - consumption: 640.9 billion cu m (2001 est.)
Natural gas - exports: 11.16 billion cu m (2001 est.)
Natural gas - imports: 114.1 billion cu m (2001 est.)
Natural gas - proved reserves: 5.195 trillion cu m (1 January 2002)
Current account balance: $-829.1 billion (2005 est.)
Exports: $927.5 billion f.o.b. (2005 est.)
Exports - partners: Canada 23%, Mexico 13.6%, Japan 6.7%, UK 4.4%, China 4.3% (2004)
Imports: $1.727 trillion f.o.b. (2005 est.)

Imports - partners: Canada 17%, China 13.8%, Mexico 10.3%, Japan 8.7%, Germany 5.2% (2004)
Reserves of foreign exchange and gold: $86.94 billion (2004 est.)
Debt - external: $8.837 trillion (30 June 2005 est.)
Economic aid - donor: ODA, $6.9 billion (1997)
Currency (code): US dollar (USD)
Currency code: USD
Exchange rates: 1 British pounds per US dollar - 0.5457 (2004), 0.6139 (2003), 0.6661 (2002), 0.6944 (2001), 0.6596 (2000); Canadian dollars per US dollar - 1.3014 (2004), 1.4045 (2003), 1.5693 (2002), 1.5488 (2001), 1.4851 (2000); Japanese yen per US dollar - 108.13 (2004), 116.08 (2003), 125.39 (2002), 121.53 (2001), 107.77 (2000); euros per US dollar - 0.8048 (2004), 0.8866 (2003), 1.0626 (2002), 1.1175 (2001), 1.08540 (2000)
Fiscal year: 1 October - 30 September

COMMUNICATIONS

Telephones - main lines in use: 181,599,900 (2003)
Telephones - mobile cellular: 158.722 million (2003)
Telephone system:
general assessment: a large, technologically advanced, multipurpose communications system
domestic: a large system of fiber-optic cable, microwave radio relay, coaxial cable, and domestic satellites carries every form of telephone traffic; a rapidly growing cellular system carries mobile telephone traffic throughout the country
international: country code - 1; 24 ocean cable systems in use; satellite earth stations - 61 Intelsat (45 Atlantic Ocean and 16 Pacific Ocean), 5 Intersputnik (Atlantic Ocean region), and 4 Inmarsat (Pacific and Atlantic Ocean regions) (2000)
Radio broadcast stations: AM 4,854, FM 8,950, shortwave 18 (2004)
Radios: 575 million (1997)
Television broadcast stations: 1,740 (2004)
Televisions: 219 million (1997)
Internet country code: .us
Internet hosts: 115,311,958 (2002)
Internet Service Providers (ISPs): 7,000 (2002 est.)
Internet users: 159 million (2002)

TRANSPORTATION

Airports: 14,857 (2004 est.)
Airports - with paved runways:
total: 5,120
over 3,047 m: 191
2,438 to 3,047 m: 223
1,524 to 2,437 m: 1,402
914 to 1,523 m: 2,355
under 914 m: 949 (2005 est.)
Airports - with unpaved runways:
total: 9,773
over 3,047 m: 1
2,438 to 3,047 m: 7
1,524 to 2,437 m: 156
914 to 1,523 m: 1,736
under 914 m: 7,873 (2005 est.)
Heliports: 153 (2005 est.)
Pipelines: petroleum products 244,620 km; natural gas 548,665 km (2003)
Railways:
total: 227,736 km
standard gauge: 227,736 km 1.435-m gauge (2003)
Roadways:
total: 6,393,603 km
paved: 4,180,053 km (including 74,406 km of expressways)
unpaved: 2,213,550 km (2003)
Waterways: 41,009 km (19,312 km used for commerce)

Saint Lawrence Seaway of 3,769 km, including the Saint Lawrence River of 3,058 km, shared with Canada (2004)
Merchant marine:
total: 486 ships (1,000 GRT or over) 12,436,658 GRT/14,630,116 DWT
by type: barge carrier 7, bulk carrier 19, cargo 152, chemical tanker 19, container 92, passenger 17, passenger/cargo 57, petroleum tanker 79, refrigerated cargo 2, roll on/roll off 28, vehicle carrier 14
foreign-owned: 49 (Australia 2, Canada 8, China 1, Denmark 20, Malaysia 2, Netherlands 1, Norway 2, Singapore 11, Sweden 1, United Kingdom 1)
registered in other countries: 680 (2005)
Ports and terminals: Corpus Christi, Duluth, Hampton Roads, Houston, Long Beach, Los Angeles, New Orleans, New York, Philadelphia, Tampa, Texas City
note: 13 ports north of New Orleans (South Louisiana Ports) on the Mississippi River handle 290,000,000 tons of cargo annually.

MILITARY

Military branches: Army, Navy and Marine Corps, Air Force, and Coast Guard (Coast Guard administered in peacetime by the Department of Homeland Security, but in wartime reports to the Department of the Navy)
Military service age and obligation: 18 years of age (2004)
Manpower available for military service:
males age 18-49: 67,742,879
females age 18-49: 67,070,144 (2005 est.)
Manpower fit for military service:
males age 18-49: 54,609,050
females age 18-49: 54,696,706 (2005 est.)
Manpower reaching military service age annually:
males: 2,143,873
females: 2,036,201 (2005 est.)
Military expenditures - dollar figure: $370.7 billion (FY04 est.) (March 2003)
Military expenditures - percent of GDP: 3.3% (FY03 est.) (February 2004)

TRANSNATIONAL ISSUES

Disputes - international: prolonged drought, population growth, and outmoded practices and infrastructure in the border region strains water-sharing arrangements with Mexico; the US has stepped up efforts to stem nationals from Mexico, Central America, and other parts of the world from crossing illegally into the United States from Mexico; illegal immigrants from the Caribbean, notably Haiti and the Dominican Republic, attempt to enter the US through Florida by sea; 1990 Maritime Boundary Agreement in the Bering Sea still awaits Russian Duma ratification; managed maritime boundary disputes with Canada at Dixon Entrance, Beaufort Sea, Strait of Juan de Fuca, and around the disputed Machias Seal Island and North Rock; US and Canada seek greater cooperation in monitoring people and commodities crossing the border; The Bahamas and US have not been able to agree on a maritime boundary; US Naval Base at Guantanamo Bay is leased from Cuba and only mutual agreement or US abandonment of the area can terminate the lease; Haiti claims US-administered Navassa Island; US has made no territorial claim in Antarctica (but has reserved the right to do so) and does not recognize the claims of any other state; Marshall Islands claims Wake Island
Refugees and internally displaced persons:
refugees (country of origin): the United States admitted 52,868 refugees during FY03/04 including: 13,331 (Somalia), 6,000 (Laos), 3,482 (Ukraine), 2,959 (Cuba), 1,787 (Iran); note - 27,239 refugees have been admitted as of 31 May 2005
Illicit drugs: consumer of cocaine shipped from Colombia through Mexico and the Caribbean; consumer of heroin, marijuana, and increasingly methamphetamine from Mexico; consumer of high-quality Southeast Asian heroin; illicit producer of cannabis, marijuana, depressants, stimulants, hallucinogens, and methamphetamine; money-laundering center

URUGUAY

INTRODUCTION

Background: Montevideo, founded by the Spanish in 1726 as a military stronghold, soon took advantage of its natural harbor to became an important commercial center. Annexed by Brazil as a separate province in 1821, Uruguay declared its independence four years later and secured its freedom in 1828 after a three-year struggle. The administrations of President BATLLE in the early 20th century established widespread political, social, and economic reforms. A violent Marxist urban guerrilla movement named the Tupamaros, launched in the late 1960s, led Uruguay's president to agree to military control of his administration in 1973. By yearend, the rebels had been crushed, but the military continued to expand its hold throughout the government. Civilian rule was not restored until 1985. Uruguay's political and labor conditions are among the freest on the continent.

GEOGRAPHY

Location: Southern South America, bordering the South Atlantic Ocean, between Argentina and Brazil
Geographic coordinates: 33 00 S, 56 00 W
Map references: South America
Area:
total: 176,220 sq km
land: 173,620 sq km
water: 2,600 sq km
Area - comparative: slightly smaller than the state of Washington
Land boundaries:
total: 1,564 km
border countries: Argentina 579 km, Brazil 985 km
Coastline: 660 km
Maritime claims:
territorial sea: 12 nm
contiguous zone: 24 nm
exclusive economic zone: 200 nm
continental shelf: 200-m depth or to the depth of exploitation
Climate: warm temperate; freezing temperatures almost unknown
Terrain: mostly rolling plains and low hills; fertile coastal lowland
Elevation extremes:
lowest point: Atlantic Ocean 0 m
highest point: Cerro Catedral 514 m
Natural resources: arable land, hydropower, minor minerals, fisheries
Land use:
arable land: 7.43%
permanent crops: 0.23%
other: 92.34% (2001)
Irrigated land: 1,800 sq km (1998 est.)
Natural hazards: seasonally high winds (the pampero is a chilly and occasional violent wind which blows north from the Argentine pampas), droughts, floods; because of the absence of mountains, which act as weather barriers, all locations are particularly vulnerable to rapid changes from weather fronts
Environment - current issues: water pollution from meat packing/tannery industry; inadequate solid/hazardous waste disposal
Environment - international agreements:
party to: Antarctic-Environmental Protocol, Antarctic-Marine Living Resources, Antarctic Treaty, Biodiversity, Climate Change, Climate Change-Kyoto Protocol, Desertification, Endangered Species, Environmental Modification, Hazardous Wastes, Law of the Sea, Ozone Layer Protection, Ship Pollution, Tropical Timber 94, Wetlands
signed, but not ratified: Marine Dumping, Marine Life Conservation
Geography - note: second-smallest South American country (after Suriname); most of the low-lying landscape (three-quarters of the country) is grassland, ideal for cattle and sheep raising

PEOPLE

Population: 3,415,920 (July 2005 est.)
Age structure:
0-14 years: 23.2% (male 403,041/female 389,427)
15-64 years: 63.6% (male 1,076,960/female 1,095,833)
65 years and over: 13.2% (male 183,877/female 266,782) (2005 est.)
Median age:
total: 32.46 years
male: 31.02 years
female: 33.95 years (2005 est.)
Population growth rate: 0.47% (2005 est.)
Birth rate: 14.09 births/1,000 population (2005 est.)
Death rate: 9.06 deaths/1,000 population (2005 est.)
Net migration rate: -0.28 migrant(s)/1,000 population (2005 est.)
Sex ratio:
at birth: 1.04 male(s)/female
under 15 years: 1.04 male(s)/female
15-64 years: 0.98 male(s)/female
65 years and over: 0.69 male(s)/female
total population: 0.95 male(s)/female (2005 est.)
Infant mortality rate:
total: 11.95 deaths/1,000 live births
male: 13.27 deaths/1,000 live births
female: 10.58 deaths/1,000 live births (2005 est.)
Life expectancy at birth:
total population: 76.13 years
male: 72.92 years
female: 79.45 years (2005 est.)
Total fertility rate: 1.91 children born/woman (2005 est.)
HIV/AIDS - adult prevalence rate: 0.3% (2001 est.)
HIV/AIDS - people living with HIV/AIDS: 6,000 (2001 est.)
HIV/AIDS - deaths: less than 500 (2003 est.)
Nationality:
noun: Uruguayan(s)
adjective: Uruguayan
Ethnic groups: white 88%, mestizo 8%, black 4%, Amerindian (practically nonexistent)
Religions: Roman Catholic 66% (less than half of the adult population attends church regularly), Protestant 2%, Jewish 1%, nonprofessing or other 31%
Languages: Spanish, Portunol, or Brazilero (Portuguese-Spanish mix on the Brazilian frontier)
Literacy:
definition: age 15 and over can read and write
total population: 98%
male: 97.6%
female: 98.4% (2003 est.)

GOVERNMENT

Country name:
conventional long form: Oriental Republic of Uruguay
conventional short form: Uruguay
local long form: Republica Oriental del Uruguay
local short form: Uruguay
former: Banda Oriental, Cisplatine Province
Government type: constitutional republic
Capital: Montevideo
Administrative divisions: 19 departments (departamentos, singular - departamento); Artigas, Canelones, Cerro Largo, Colonia, Durazno, Flores, Florida, Lavalleja, Maldonado, Montevideo, Paysandu, Rio Negro, Rivera, Rocha, Salto, San Jose, Soriano, Tacuarembo, Treinta y Tres

Independence: 25 August 1825 (from Brazil)
National holiday: Independence Day, 25 August (1825)
Constitution: 27 November 1966, effective February 1967; suspended 27 June 1973, new constitution rejected by referendum 30 November 1980; two constitutional reforms approved by plebiscite 26 November 1989 and 7 January 1997
Legal system: based on Spanish civil law system; accepts compulsory ICJ jurisdiction
Suffrage: 18 years of age, universal and compulsory
Executive branch:
chief of state: President Tabare VAZQUEZ (since 1 March 2005) and Vice President Rodolfo NIN Novoa (since 1 March 2005); note - the president is both the chief of state and head of government
head of government: President Tabare VAZQUEZ (since 1 March 2005) and Vice President Rodolfo NIN Novoa (since 1 March 2005); note - the president is both the chief of state and head of government
cabinet: Council of Ministers appointed by the president with parliamentary approval
elections: president and vice president elected on the same ticket by popular vote for five-year terms; election last held 31 October 2004 (next to be held October 2009)
election results: Tabare VAZQUEZ elected president; percent of vote - Tabare VAZQUEZ 50.5%, Jorge LARRANAGA 35.1%, Guillermo STIRLING 10.3%
Legislative branch: bicameral General Assembly or Asamblea General consists of Chamber of Senators or Camara de Senadores (30 seats; members are elected by popular vote to serve five-year terms) and Chamber of Representatives or Camara de Representantes (99 seats; members are elected by popular vote to serve five-year terms)
elections: Chamber of Senators - last held 31 October 2004 (next to be held October 2009); Chamber of Representatives - last held 31 October 2004 (next to be held October 2009)
election results: Chamber of Senators - percent of vote by party - NA%; seats by party - EP-FA 16, Blanco 11, Colorado Party 3; Chamber of Representatives - percent of vote by party - NA%; seats by party - EP-FA 52, Blanco 36, Colorado Party 10, Independent Party 1
Judicial branch: Supreme Court (judges are nominated by the president and elected for 10-year terms by the General Assembly)
Political parties and leaders: Colorado Party [Jorge BATLLE Ibanez]; Independent Party (Partido Independiente) [Pablo MIERES]; Movement of Popular Participation or MPP [Jose MUJICA]; National Party or Blanco [Luis Alberto LACALLE Herrera]; New Sector/Space Coalition (Nuevo Espacio) [Rafael MICHELINI]; Progressive Encounter/Broad Front Coalition (Encuentro Progresista/Frente Amplio) or EP-FA [Tabare VAZQUEZ]; Socialist Party of Uruguay or Socialists [Reinaldo GARGANO]; Uruguayan Assembly or Asamblea Uruguay [Danilo ASTORI]
Political pressure groups and leaders: PIT-CNT (umbrella union of state and private employees), Agrupacion UTE (state worker's union), Rural Association of Uruguay (rancher's association), Uruguayan Construction League, Chamber of Uruguayan Industries (manufacturer's association), Chemist and Pharmaceutical Association (professional organization), Architects Society of Uruguay (professional organization), the Catholic Church, students
International organization participation: CSN, FAO, G-77, IADB, IAEA, IBRD, ICAO, ICC, ICCt, ICRM, IFAD, IFC, IFRCS, IHO, ILO, IMF, IMO, Interpol, IOC, IOM, ISO, ITU, LAES, LAIA, Mercosur, MIGA, MINURSO, MINUSTAH, MONUC, NAM (observer), OAS, ONUB, OPANAL, OPCW, PCA, RG, UN, UNAMSIL, UNCTAD, UNESCO, UNFICYP, UNIDO, UNMEE, UNMOGIP, UNOCI, UNOMIG, UPU, WCL, WCO, WFTU, WHO, WIPO, WMO, WToO, WTO
Diplomatic representation in the US:
chief of mission: Ambassador Carlos GIANELLI Derois
chancery: 1913 I Street NW, Washington, DC 20006
telephone: [1] (202) 331-1313 through 1316
FAX: [1] (202) 331-8142
consulate(s) general: Chicago, Los Angeles, Miami, and New York
consulate(s): San Juan (Puerto Rico)
Diplomatic representation from the US:
chief of mission: Charge d'Affaires James D. NEALON
embassy: Lauro Muller 1776, Montevideo 11200
mailing address: APO AA 34035
telephone: [598] (2) 418-7777
FAX: [598] (2) 418-8611
Flag description: nine equal horizontal stripes of white (top and bottom) alternating with blue; there is a white square in the upper hoist-side corner with a yellow sun bearing a human face known as the Sun of May and 16 rays alternately triangular and wavy

ECONOMY

Economy - overview: Uruguay's well-to-do economy is characterized by an export-oriented agricultural sector, a well-educated workforce, and high levels of social spending. After averaging growth of 5% annually during 1996-98, in 1999-2002 the economy suffered a major downturn, stemming largely from the spillover effects of the economic problems of its large neighbors, Argentina and Brazil. For instance, in 2001-02 massive withdrawals by Argentina of dollars deposited in Uruguayan banks led to a plunge in the Uruguyan peso and a massive rise in unemployment. Total GDP in these four years dropped by nearly 20%, with 2002 the worst year due to the serious banking crisis. Unemployment rose to nearly 20% in 2002, inflation surged, and the burden of external debt doubled. Cooperation with the IMF limited the damage. The debt swap with private creditors carried out in 2003, which extended the maturity dates on nearly half of Uruguay's $14 billion in public debt, substantially alleviated the country's amortization burden in the coming years and restored public confidence. The economy grew about 10% in 2004 as a result of high commodity prices for Uruguayan exports, the weakness of the dollar against the euro, growth in the region, low international interest rates, and greater export competitiveness, but slowed to a 6.2% pace in 2005.
GDP (purchasing power parity): $32.92 billion (2005 est.)
GDP (official exchange rate): $17.03 billion (2005 est.)
GDP - real growth rate: 6.2% (2005 est.)
GDP - per capita: purchasing power parity - $10,000 (2005 est.)
GDP - composition by sector:
agriculture: 7.1%
industry: 27.7%
services: 65.2% (2005 est.)
Labor force: 1.52 million (2005 est.)
Labor force - by occupation: agriculture 14%, industry 16%, services 70%
Unemployment rate: 12% (2005 est.)
Population below poverty line: 21% of households (2003)
Household income or consumption by percentage share:
lowest 10%: 3.7%
highest 10%: 25.8% (1997)
Distribution of family income - Gini index: 44.6 (2000)
Inflation rate (consumer prices): 4.9% (2005 est.)
Investment (gross fixed): 12.2% of GDP

(2005 est.)
Budget:
revenues: $4.468 billion
expenditures: $4.845 billion, including capital expenditures of $193 million (2005 est.)
Public debt: 82.1% of GDP (2005 est.)
Agriculture - products: rice, wheat, corn, barley; livestock; fish
Industries: food processing, electrical machinery, transportation equipment, petroleum products, textiles, chemicals, beverages
Industrial production growth rate: 5.1% (2005 est.)
Electricity - production: 8.611 billion kWh (2003)
Electricity - production by source:
fossil fuel: 0.7%
hydro: 99.1%
nuclear: 0%
other: 0.3% (2001)
Electricity - consumption: 7.762 billion kWh (2003)
Electricity - exports: 900 million kWh (2003)
Electricity - imports: 654 million kWh (2003)
Oil - production: 435 bbl/day (2003 est.)
Oil - consumption: 38,000 bbl/day (2003 est.)
Oil - exports: NA (2001)
Oil - imports: NA (2001)
Natural gas - production: 0 cu m (2003 est.)
Natural gas - consumption: 64.5 million cu m (2003 est.)
Natural gas - exports: 0 cu m (2003 est.)
Natural gas - imports: 65 million cu m (2003 est.)
Current account balance: $-19 million (2005 est.)
Exports: $3.55 billion f.o.b. (2005 est.)
Exports - partners: US 17.4%, Brazil 16.1%, Germany 6.3%, Argentina 6.2%, Mexico 4.2% (2004)
Imports: $3.54 billion f.o.b. (2005 est.)
Imports - partners: Argentina 19.5%, Brazil 19%, Paraguay 12.9%, US 9.2%, China 6% (2004)
Reserves of foreign exchange and gold: $2.654 billion (2005 est.)
Debt - external: $9.931 billion (30 June 2005 est.)
Economic aid - recipient: NA
Currency (code): Uruguayan peso (UYU)
Currency code: UYU
Exchange rates: Uruguayan pesos per US dollar - 24.86 (2005), 28.704 (2004), 28.209 (2003), 21.257 (2002), 13.319 (2001)
Fiscal year: calendar year

COMMUNICATIONS

Telephones - main lines in use: 946,500 (2002)
Telephones - mobile cellular: 652,000 (2002)
Telephone system:
general assessment: fully digitalized
domestic: most modern facilities concentrated in Montevideo; new nationwide microwave radio relay network
international: country code - 598; satellite earth stations - 2 Intelsat (Atlantic Ocean) (2002)
Radio broadcast stations: AM 91, FM 149, shortwave 7 (2001)
Radios: 1.97 million (1997)
Television broadcast stations: 23 (2002)
Televisions: 782,000 (1997)
Internet country code: .uy
Internet hosts: 87,630 (2003)
Internet Service Providers (ISPs): 14 (2001)
Internet users: 400,000 (2002)

TRANSPORTATION

Airports: 64 (2004 est.)
Airports - with paved runways:
total: 9
over 3,047 m: 1
1,524 to 2,437 m: 4
914 to 1,523 m: 2
under 914 m: 2 (2005 est.)
Airports - with unpaved runways:
total: 55
1,524 to 2,437 m: 3
914 to 1,523 m: 21
under 914 m: 31 (2005 est.)
Pipelines: gas 192 km (2004)
Railways:
total: total: 2,073 km
standard gauge: 2,073 km 1.435-m gauge
note: 461 km have been taken out of service and 460 km are in partial use (2004)
Roadways:
total: 8,983 km
paved: 8,081 km
unpaved: 902 km (1999 est.)
Waterways: 1,600 km (2002)
Merchant marine:
total: 11 ships (1,000 GRT or over) 10,918 GRT/10,342 DWT
by type: cargo 1, chemical tanker 1, passenger/cargo 6, petroleum tanker 2, roll on/roll off 1
foreign-owned: 4 (Argentina 3, Greece 1)
registered in other countries: 8 (2005)
Ports and terminals: Montevideo

MILITARY

Military branches: Army, Navy (includes Naval Air Arm, Marines, Maritime Prefecture in wartime), Air Force
Military service age and obligation: 18 years of age for voluntary and compulsory military service (2001)
Manpower available for military service: *males age 18-49:* 764,408 (2005 est.)
Manpower fit for military service: *males age 18-49:* 637,445 (2005 est.)
Military expenditures - dollar figure: $257.5 million (2004)
Military expenditures - percent of GDP: 2% (2004)

TRANSNATIONAL ISSUES

Disputes - international: uncontested dispute with Brazil over certain islands in the Quarai/Cuareim and Invernada streams and the resulting tripoint with Argentina

UZBEKISTAN

INTRODUCTION

Background: Russia conquered Uzbekistan in the late 19th century. Stiff resistance to the Red Army after World War I was eventually suppressed and a socialist republic set up in 1924. During the Soviet era, intensive production of "white gold" (cotton) and grain led to overuse of agrochemicals and the depletion of water supplies, which have left the land poisoned and the Aral Sea and certain rivers half dry. Independent since 1991, the country seeks to gradually lessen its dependence on agriculture while developing its mineral and petroleum reserves. Current concerns include terrorism by Islamic militants, economic stagnation, and the curtailment of human rights and democratization.

GEOGRAPHY

Location: Central Asia, north of Afghanistan
Geographic coordinates: 41 00 N, 64 00 E
Map references: Asia
Area:
total: 447,400 sq km
land: 425,400 sq km
water: 22,000 sq km
Area - comparative: slightly larger than California
Land boundaries:
total: 6,221 km
border countries: Afghanistan 137 km, Kazakhstan 2,203 km, Kyrgyzstan 1,099 km, Tajikistan 1,161 km, Turkmenistan 1,621 km
Coastline: 0 km (doubly landlocked); note - Uzbekistan includes the southern portion of the Aral Sea with a 420 km shoreline
Maritime claims: none (doubly landlocked)
Climate: mostly midlatitude desert, long,

hot summers, mild winters; semiarid grassland in east
Terrain: mostly flat-to-rolling sandy desert with dunes; broad, flat intensely irrigated river valleys along course of Amu Darya, Syr Darya (Sirdaryo), and Zarafshon; Fergana Valley in east surrounded by mountainous Tajikistan and Kyrgyzstan; shrinking Aral Sea in west
Elevation extremes:
lowest point: Sariqarnish Kuli -12 m
highest point: Adelunga Toghi 4,301 m
Natural resources: natural gas, petroleum, coal, gold, uranium, silver, copper, lead and zinc, tungsten, molybdenum
Land use:
arable land: 10.83%
permanent crops: 0.83%
other: 88.34% (2001)
Irrigated land: 42,810 sq km (1998 est.)
Natural hazards: NA
Environment - current issues: shrinkage of the Aral Sea is resulting in growing concentrations of chemical pesticides and natural salts; these substances are then blown from the increasingly exposed lake bed and contribute to desertification; water pollution from industrial wastes and the heavy use of fertilizers and pesticides is the cause of many human health disorders; increasing soil salination; soil contamination from buried nuclear processing and agricultural chemicals, including DDT
Environment - international agreements:
party to: Biodiversity, Climate Change, Climate Change-Kyoto Protocol, Desertification, Endangered Species, Environmental Modification, Hazardous Wastes, Ozone Layer Protection, Wetlands
signed, but not ratified: none of the selected agreements
Geography - note: along with Liechtenstein, one of the only two doubly landlocked countries in the world

PEOPLE

Population: 26,851,195 (July 2005 est.)
Age structure:
0-14 years: 33.5% (male 4,575,443/female 4,408,146)
15-64 years: 61.7% (male 8,201,993/female 8,371,933)
65 years and over: 4.8% (male 528,334/female 765,346) (2005 est.)
Median age:
total: 22.36 years
male: 21.74 years
female: 23 years (2005 est.)
Population growth rate: 1.67% (2005 est.)
Birth rate: 26.22 births/1,000 population (2005 est.)
Death rate: 7.95 deaths/1,000 population (2005 est.)
Net migration rate: -1.61 migrant(s)/1,000 population (2005 est.)
Sex ratio:
at birth: 1.05 male(s)/female
under 15 years: 1.04 male(s)/female
15-64 years: 0.98 male(s)/female
65 years and over: 0.69 male(s)/female
total population: 0.98 male(s)/female (2005 est.)
Infant mortality rate:
total: 71.1 deaths/1,000 live births
male: 74.78 deaths/1,000 live births
female: 67.22 deaths/1,000 live births (2005 est.)
Life expectancy at birth:
total population: 64.19 years
male: 60.82 years
female: 67.73 years (2005 est.)
Total fertility rate: 2.94 children born/woman (2005 est.)
HIV/AIDS - adult prevalence rate: less than 0.1% (2001 est.)
HIV/AIDS - people living with HIV/AIDS: 11,000 (2003 est.)
HIV/AIDS - deaths: less than 500 (2003 est.)
Nationality:
noun: Uzbekistani
adjective: Uzbekistani
Ethnic groups: Uzbek 80%, Russian 5.5%, Tajik 5%, Kazakh 3%, Karakalpak 2.5%, Tatar 1.5%, other 2.5% (1996 est.)
Religions: Muslim 88% (mostly Sunnis), Eastern Orthodox 9%, other 3%
Languages: Uzbek 74.3%, Russian 14.2%, Tajik 4.4%, other 7.1%
Literacy:
definition: age 15 and over can read and write
total population: 99.3%
male: 99.6%
female: 99% (2003 est.)

GOVERNMENT

Country name:
conventional long form: Republic of Uzbekistan
conventional short form: Uzbekistan
local long form: Ozbekiston Respublikasi
local short form: Ozbekiston
former: Uzbek Soviet Socialist Republic
Government type: republic; authoritarian presidential rule, with little power outside the executive branch
Capital: Tashkent (Toshkent)
Administrative divisions: 12 provinces (viloyatlar, singular - viloyat), 1 autonomous republic* (respublika), and 1 city** (shahar): Andijon Viloyati, Buxoro Viloyati, Farg'ona Viloyati, Jizzax Viloyati, Namangan Viloyati, Navoiy Viloyati, Qashqadaryo Viloyati (Qarshi), Qoraqalpog'iston Respublikasi* (Nukus), Samarqand Viloyati, Sirdaryo Viloyati (Guliston), Surxondaryo Viloyati (Termiz), Toshkent Shahri**, Toshkent Viloyati, Xorazm Viloyati (Urganch)
note: administrative divisions have the same names as their administrative centers (exceptions have the administrative center name following in parentheses)
Independence: 1 September 1991 (from Soviet Union)
National holiday: Independence Day, 1 September (1991)
Constitution: new constitution adopted 8 December 1992
Legal system: evolution of Soviet civil law; still lacks independent judicial system
Suffrage: 18 years of age, universal
Executive branch:
chief of state: President Islom KARIMOV (since 24 March 1990, when he was elected president by the then Supreme Soviet)
head of government: Prime Minister Shavkat MIRZIYAYEV (since 11 December 2003)
cabinet: Cabinet of Ministers appointed by the president with approval of the Supreme Assembly
elections: president elected by popular vote for a seven-year term (previously was a five-year term, extended by constitutional amendment in 2002); election last held 9 January 2000 (next to be held NA 2007); prime minister and deputy ministers appointed by the president
election results: Islom KARIMOV reelect-

ed president; percent of vote - Islom KARIMOV 91.9%, Abdulkhafiz JALALOV 4.2%
Legislative branch: bicameral Supreme Assembly or Oliy Majlis consists of an Upper House or Senate (100 seats; 84 members are elected by regional governing councils to serve five-year terms and 16 are appointed by the president) and a Lower House or Legislative Chamber (120 seats; elected by popular vote to serve five-year terms)
elections: last held 26 December 2004 and 9 January 2005 (next to be held December 2009)
election results: Senate - percent of vote by party - NA%; seats by party - NA; Legislative Chamber - percent of vote by party - NA%; seats by party - LDPU 41, NDP 32, Fidokorlar 17, MTP 11, Adolat 9, unaffiliated 10
note: all parties in the Supreme Assembly support President KARIMOV
Judicial branch: Supreme Court (judges are nominated by the president and confirmed by the Supreme Assembly)
Political parties and leaders: Adolat (Justice) Social Democratic Party [Dilorom TOSHMUHAMMADOVA, chairman]; Democratic National Rebirth Party (Milly Tiklanish) or MTP [Xurshid DOSTMUHAMMADOV, chief]; Liberal Democratic Party of Uzbekistan or LDPU [Adham SHODMONOV, chairman]; People's Democratic Party or NDP (formerly Communist Party) [Asliddin RUSTAMOV, first secretary]; Self-Sacrificers Party or Fidokorlar National Democratic Party [Ahtam TURSUNOV, chief]; note - Fatherland Progress Party merged with Self-Sacrificers Party
Political pressure groups and leaders: Agrarian and Entrepreneurs' Party [Marat ZAHIDOV]; Birlik (Unity) Movement [Abdurakhim POLAT, chairman]; Erk (Freedom) Democratic Party [Muhammad SOLIH, chairman] was banned 9 December 1992; Ezgulik Human Rights Society [Vasilia INOYATOVA]; Free Farmers' Party or Ozod Dehqonlar [Nigara KHIDOYATOVA]; Human Rights Society of Uzbekistan [Tolib YAKUBOV, chairman]; Independent Human Rights Society of Uzbekistan [Mikhail ARDZINOV, chairman]; Mazlum [leader NA]
International organization participation: AsDB, CIS, EAPC, EBRD, ECO, FAO, IAEA, IBRD, ICAO, ICCt (signatory), ICRM, IDA, IDB, IFC, IFRCS, ILO, IMF, Interpol, IOC, ISO, ITU, MIGA, NAM, OIC, OPCW, OSCE, PFP, SCO, UN, UNCTAD, UNESCO, UNIDO, UPU, WCO, WFTU, WHO, WIPO, WMO, WToO, WTO (observer)
Diplomatic representation in the US:
chief of mission: Ambassador Abdulaziz KAMILOV
chancery: 1746 Massachusetts Avenue NW, Washington, DC 20036
telephone: [1] (202) 293-6803
FAX: [1] (202) 293-6804
consulate(s) general: New York
Diplomatic representation from the US:
chief of mission: Ambassador Jon PURNELL
embassy: 82 Chilanzarskaya, Tashkent 700115
mailing address: use embassy street address
telephone: [998] (71) 120-5450
FAX: [998] (71) 120-6335
Flag description: three equal horizontal bands of blue (top), white, and green separated by red fimbriations with a white crescent moon and 12 white stars in the upper hoist-side quadrant

ECONOMY

Economy - overview: Uzbekistan is a dry, landlocked country of which 11% consists of intensely cultivated, irrigated river valleys. More than 60% of its population lives in densely populated rural communities. Uzbekistan is now the world's second-largest cotton exporter, and fifth largest producer; it relies heavily on cotton production as the major source of export earnings. Other major export earners include gold and oil. Following independence in December 1991, the government sought to prop up its Soviet-style command economy with subsidies and tight controls on production and prices. Uzbekistan responded to the negative external conditions generated by the Asian and Russian financial crises by emphasizing import substitute industrialization and by tightening export and currency controls within its already largely closed economy. The government, while aware of the need to improve the investment climate, sponsors measures that often increase, not decrease, the government's control over business decisions. A sharp increase in the inequality of income distribution has hurt the lower ranks of society since independence. In 2003, the government accepted the obligations of Article VIII under the International Monetary Fund (IMF), providing for full currency convertibility. However, strict currency controls and tightening of borders have lessened the effects of convertibility and have also led to some shortages that have further stifled economic activity. Potential investment by Russia and China in Uzbekistan's gas and oil industry would increase economic growth prospects.
GDP (purchasing power parity): $52.21 billion (2005 est.)
GDP (official exchange rate): $10.24 billion (2005 est.)
GDP - real growth rate: 5.4% (2005 est.)
GDP - per capita: purchasing power parity - $1,900 (2005 est.)
GDP - composition by sector:
agriculture: 38%
industry: 26.3%
services: 35.7% (2003 est.)
Labor force: 14.26 million (2005 est.)
Labor force - by occupation: agriculture 44%, industry 20%, services 36% (1995)
Unemployment rate: 0.7% officially, plus another 20% underemployed (2005 est.)
Population below poverty line: 28% (2004 est.)
Household income or consumption by percentage share:
lowest 10%: 3.6%
highest 10%: 22% (2000)
Distribution of family income - Gini index: 26.8 (2000)
Inflation rate (consumer prices): 7.1% (2005 est.)
Budget:
revenues: $2.815 billion
expenditures: $2.917 billion, including capital expenditures of NA (2005 est.)
Public debt: 39% of GDP (2005 est.)
Agriculture - products: cotton, vegetables, fruits, grain; livestock
Industries: textiles, food processing, machine building, metallurgy, gold petroleum, natural gas, chemicals
Industrial production growth rate: 9.4% (2004 est.)
Electricity - production: 46.52 billion kWh (2003)
Electricity - production by source:
fossil fuel: 88.2%
hydro: 11.8%
nuclear: 0%
other: 0% (2001)
Electricity - consumption: 48.45 billion kWh (2003)
Electricity - exports: 5.36 billion kWh (2003)
Electricity - imports: 10.55 billion kWh (2003)
Oil - production: 152,000 bbl/day (2004)
Oil - consumption: 120,000 bbl/day (2004)
Oil - exports: NA (2004)
Oil - imports: NA (2004)
Oil - proved reserves: 600 million bbl (1 January 2005)
Natural gas - production: 55.8 billion cu m (2004)
Natural gas - consumption: 49.3 billion cu m (2004)
Natural gas - exports: 6.5 billion cu m (2004)
Natural gas - imports: 0 cu m (2004)
Natural gas - proved reserves: 1.86 trillion cu m (1 January 2005)
Current account balance: $882 million

(2005 est.)
Exports: $5.36 billion f.o.b. (2005 est.)
Exports - partners: Russia 22%, China 14.7%, Turkey 6.4%, Tajikistan 6.1%, Kazakhstan 4.2%, Bangladesh 4% (2004)
Imports: $4.14 billion f.o.b. (2005 est.)
Imports - partners: Russia 26.8%, South Korea 12.6%, US 8%, Germany 7.7%, Kazakhstan 6.3%, China 5.8%, Turkey 5.1%, Ukraine 4.5% (2004)
Reserves of foreign exchange and gold: $2.123 billion (2005 est.)
Debt - external: $5.184 billion (2005 est.)
Economic aid - recipient: $87.4 million from the US (2003)
Currency (code): Uzbekistani soum (UZS)
Currency code: UZS
Exchange rates: Uzbekistani soum per US dollar - 1,114.17 (2005), 1,020 (2004), 771.03 (2002), 423.832 (2002), 423.832 (2001)
Fiscal year: calendar year

COMMUNICATIONS

Telephones - main lines in use: 1,717,100 (2003)
Telephones - mobile cellular: 320,800 (2003)
Telephone system:
general assessment: antiquated and inadequate; in serious need of modernization
domestic: the domestic telephone system is being expanded and technologically improved, particularly in Tashkent (Toshkent) and Samarqand, under contracts with prominent companies in industrialized countries; moreover, by 1998, six cellular networks had been placed in operation - four of the GSM type (Global System for Mobile Communication), one D-AMPS type (Digital Advanced Mobile Phone System), and one AMPS type (Advanced Mobile Phone System)
international: country code - 998; linked by landline or microwave radio relay with CIS member states and to other countries by leased connection via the Moscow international gateway switch; after the completion of the Uzbek link to the Trans-Asia-Europe (TAE) fiber-optic cable, Uzbekistan will be independent of Russian facilities for international communications; Inmarsat also provides an international connection, albeit an expensive one; satellite earth stations - NA (1998)
Radio broadcast stations: AM 20, FM 7, shortwave 10 (1998)
Radios: 10.8 million (1997)
Television broadcast stations: 4 (plus two repeaters that relay Russian programs), 1 cable rebroadcaster in Tashkent; approximately 20 stations in regional capitals (2003)
Televisions: 6.4 million (1997)
Internet country code: .uz
Internet hosts: 1,040 (2003)
Internet Service Providers (ISPs): 42 (2000)
Internet users: 492,000 (2003)

TRANSPORTATION

Airports: 226 (2004 est.)
Airports - with paved runways:
total: 33
over 3,047 m: 6
2,438 to 3,047 m: 13
1,524 to 2,437 m: 5
914 to 1,523 m: 5
under 914 m: 4 (2005 est.)
Airports - with unpaved runways:
total: 46
2,438 to 3,047 m: 2
1,524 to 2,437 m: 2
under 914 m: 42 (2005 est.)
Pipelines: gas 9,149 km; oil 869 km; refined products 33 km (2004)
Railways:
total: 3,950 km
broad gauge: 3,950 km 1.520-m gauge (620 km electrified) (2004)
Roadways:
total: 81,600 km
paved: 71,237 km
unpaved: 10,363 km (1999 est.)
Waterways: 1,100 km (2004)
Ports and terminals: Termiz (Amu Darya)

MILITARY

Military branches: Army, Air and Air Defense Forces, National Guard
Military service age and obligation: 18 years of age for compulsory military service; conscript service obligation - 12 months (2004)
Manpower available for military service: *males age 18-49:* 6,340,220 (2005 est.)
Manpower fit for military service: *males age 18-49:* 4,609,621 (2005 est.)
Manpower reaching military service age annually: *males:* 324,722 (2005 est.)
Military expenditures - dollar figure: $200 million (FY97)
Military expenditures - percent of GDP: 2% (FY97)

TRANSNATIONAL ISSUES

Disputes - international: cotton monoculture in Uzbekistan and Turkmenistan creates water-sharing difficulties for Amu Darya river states; delimitation with Kazakhstan complete with demarcation underway; delimitation is underway with Kyrgyzstan but serious disputes around enclaves and elsewhere continue to mar progress for some 130 km of border; talks continue with Tajikistan to delimit border and remove minefields
Refugees and internally displaced persons: *IDPs:* 3,000 (forced population transfers by government from villages near Tajikistan border) (2004)
Illicit drugs: transit country for Afghan narcotics bound for Russian and, to a lesser extent, Western European markets; limited illicit cultivation of cannabis and small amounts of opium poppy for domestic consumption; poppy cultivation almost wiped out by government crop eradication program; transit point for heroin precursor chemicals bound for Afghanistan

VANUATU

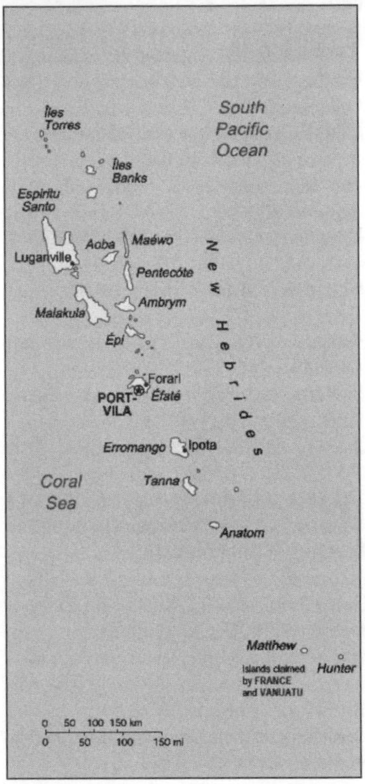

INTRODUCTION

Background: The British and French, who settled the New Hebrides in the 9th century, agreed in 1906 to an Anglo-French Condominium, which administered the islands until independence in 1980.

GEOGRAPHY

Location: Oceania, group of islands in the South Pacific Ocean, about three-quarters of the way from Hawaii to Australia
Geographic coordinates: 16 00 S, 167 00 E
Map references: Oceania
Area:
total: 12,200 sq km
land: 12,200 sq km
water: 0 sq km
note: includes more than 80 islands, about 65 of which are inhabited
Area - comparative: slightly larger than Connecticut
Land boundaries: 0 km
Coastline: 2,528 km
Maritime claims: measured from claimed archipelagic baselines
territorial sea: 12 nm
contiguous zone: 24 nm
exclusive economic zone: 200 nm
continental shelf: 200 nm or to the edge of the continental margin
Climate: tropical; moderated by southeast trade winds from May to October; moderate rainfall from November to April; may be affected by cyclones from December to April
Terrain: mostly mountainous islands of volcanic origin; narrow coastal plains
Elevation extremes:
lowest point: Pacific Ocean 0 m
highest point: Tabwemasana 1,877 m
Natural resources: manganese, hardwood forests, fish
Land use:
arable land: 2.46%
permanent crops: 7.38%
other: 90.16% (2001)
Irrigated land: NA
Natural hazards: tropical cyclones or typhoons (January to April); volcanic eruption on Aoba (Ambae) island began 27 November 2005, volcanism also causes minor earthquakes; tsunamis
Environment - current issues: a majority of the population does not have access to a reliable supply of potable water; deforestation
Environment - international agreements:
party to: Antarctic-Marine Living Resources, Biodiversity, Climate Change, Climate Change-Kyoto Protocol, Desertification, Endangered Species, Law of the Sea, Marine Dumping, Ozone Layer Protection, Ship Pollution, Tropical Timber 94
signed, but not ratified: none of the selected agreements
Geography - note: a Y-shaped chain of four main islands and 80 smaller islands; several of the islands have active volcanoes

PEOPLE

Population: 205,754 (July 2005 est.)
Age structure:
0-14 years: 33.3% (male 35,039/female 33,553)
15-64 years: 63.1% (male 66,311/female 63,502)
65 years and over: 3.6% (male 3,878/female 3,471) (2005 est.)
Median age:
total: 22.64 years
male: 22.68 years
female: 22.59 years (2005 est.)
Population growth rate: 1.52% (2005 est.)
Birth rate: 23.06 births/1,000 population (2005 est.)
Death rate: 7.9 deaths/1,000 population (2005 est.)
Net migration rate: 0 migrant(s)/1,000 population (2005 est.)
Sex ratio:
at birth: 1.05 male(s)/female
under 15 years: 1.04 male(s)/female
15-64 years: 1.04 male(s)/female
65 years and over: 1.12 male(s)/female
total population: 1.05 male(s)/female (2005 est.)
Infant mortality rate:
total: 55.16 deaths/1,000 live birth
male: 57.73 deaths/1,000 live births
female: 52.45 deaths/1,000 live births (2005 est.)
Life expectancy at birth:
total population: 62.49 years
male: 61 years
female: 64.05 years (2005 est.)
Total fertility rate: 2.77 children born/woman (2005 est.)
HIV/AIDS - adult prevalence rate: NA
HIV/AIDS - people living with HIV/AIDS: NA
HIV/AIDS - deaths: NA
Nationality:
noun: Ni-Vanuatu (singular and plural)
adjective: Ni-Vanuatu
Ethnic groups: Ni-Vanuatu 98.5%, other 1.5% (1999 Census)
Religions: Presbyterian 31.4%, Anglican 13.4%, Roman Catholic 13.1%, Seventh-Day Adventist 10.8%, other Christian 13.8%, indigenous beliefs 5.6% (including Jon Frum cargo cult), other 9.6%, none 1%, unspecified 1.3% (1999 Census)
Languages: local languages (more than 100) 72.6%, pidgin (known as Bislama or Bichelama) 23.1%, English 1.9%, French 1.4%, other 0.3%, unspecified 0.7% (1999 Census)
Literacy:
definition: age 15 and over can read and write
total population: 74%
male: NA%
female: NA% (1999 est.)

GOVERNMENT

Country name:
conventional long form: Republic of Vanuatu
conventional short form: Vanuatu
former: New Hebrides
Government type: parliamentary republic
Capital: Port-Vila (Efate)
Administrative divisions: 6 provinces; Malampa, Penama, Sanma, Shefa, Tafea, Torba
Independence: 30 July 1980 (from France and UK)
National holiday: Independence Day, 30 July (1980)
Constitution: 30 July 1980
Legal system: unified system being created from former dual French and British systems
Suffrage: 18 years of age, universal
Executive branch:
chief of state: President Kalkot Matas

KELEKELE (since 16 August 2004)
head of government: Prime Minister Ham LINI (since 11 December 2004); Deputy Prime Minister Sato KILMAN (since 11 December 2004); Prime Minister Serge VOHOR ousted in no-confidence vote on 11 December 2004
cabinet: Council of Ministers appointed by the prime minister, responsible to Parliament
elections: president elected for a five-year term by an electoral college consisting of Parliament and the presidents of the regional councils; election for president last held 16 August 2004 (next to be held in 2009); following legislative elections, the leader of the majority party or majority coalition is usually elected prime minister by Parliament from among its members; election for prime minister last held 29 July 2004 (next to be held following general elections in 2008)
election results: Kalkot Matas KELEKELE elected president, with 49 votes out of 56, after several ballots on 16 August 2004
Legislative branch: unicameral Parliament (52 seats; members elected by popular vote to serve four-year terms)
elections: last held 6 July 2004 (next to be held 2008)
election results: percent of vote by party - NA%; seats by party - UMP 8, VP 8, NUP 10, VRP 4, MPP 3, VGP 3, other and independent 16; note - political party associations are fluid
note: the National Council of Chiefs advises on matters of culture and language
Judicial branch: Supreme Court (chief justice is appointed by the president after consultation with the prime minister and the leader of the opposition, three other justices are appointed by the president on the advice of the Judicial Service Commission)
Political parties and leaders: Jon Frum Movement [Song KEASPAI]; Melanesian Progressive Party or MPP [Barak SOPE]; National United Party or NUP [leader NA]; Union of Moderate Parties or UMP [Serge VOHOR]; Vanua'aku Pati (Our Land Party) or VP [Edward NATAPEI]; Vanuatu Republican Party or VRP [Maxime Carlot KORMAN]; Vanuatu Greens Party or VGP [Moana CARCASSES]
Political pressure groups and leaders: NA
International organization participation: ACCT, ACP, AsDB, C, FAO, G-77, IBRD, ICAO, ICFTU, ICRM, IDA, IFC, IFRCS, ILO, IMF, IMO, IOC, ITU, MIGA, NAM, OPCW, PIF, Sparteca, SPC, UN, UNCTAD, UNESCO, UNIDO, UPU, WFTU, WHO, WMO, WTO (observer)
Diplomatic representation in the US: Vanuatu does not have an embassy in the US; it does, however, have a Permanent Mission to the UN
Diplomatic representation from the US: the US does not have an embassy in Vanuatu; the ambassador to Papua New Guinea is accredited to Vanuatu
Flag description: two equal horizontal bands of red (top) and green with a black isosceles triangle (based on the hoist side) all separated by a black-edged yellow stripe in the shape of a horizontal Y (the two points of the Y face the hoist side and enclose the triangle); centered in the triangle is a boar's tusk encircling two crossed namele leaves, all in yellow

ECONOMY

Economy - overview: This South Pacific island economy is based primarily on small-scale agriculture, which provides a living for 65% of the population. Fishing, offshore financial services, and tourism, with about 50,000 visitors in 2004, are other mainstays of the economy. Mineral deposits are negligible; the country has no known petroleum deposits. A small light industry sector caters to the local market. Tax revenues come mainly from import duties. Economic development is hindered by dependence on relatively few commodity exports, vulnerability to natural disasters, and long distances from main markets and between constituent islands. GDP growth rose less than 3% on average in the 1990s. In response to foreign concerns, the government has promised to tighten regulation of its offshore financial center. In mid-2002 the government stepped up efforts to boost tourism. Agriculture, especially livestock farming, is a second target for growth. Australia and New Zealand are the main suppliers of tourists and foreign aid.
GDP (purchasing power parity): $580 million (2003 est.)
GDP (official exchange rate): NA
GDP - real growth rate: 1.1% (2003 est.)
GDP - per capita: purchasing power parity - $2,900 (2003 est.)
GDP - composition by sector:
agriculture: 26%
industry: 12%
services: 62% (2000 est.)
Labor force: NA
Labor force - by occupation: agriculture 65%, industry 5%, services 30% (2000 est.)
Unemployment rate: NA%
Population below poverty line: NA
Household income or consumption by percentage share:
lowest 10%: NA
highest 10%: NA
Inflation rate (consumer prices): 3.1% (2003 est.)
Budget:
revenues: $52.6 million
expenditures: $54.3 million, including capital expenditures of $700,000 (2003 est.)
Agriculture - products: copra, coconuts, cocoa, coffee, taro, yams, coconuts, fruits, vegetables; fish, beef
Industries: food and fish freezing, wood processing, meat canning
Industrial production growth rate: 1% (1997 est.)
Electricity - production: 41 million kWh (2003)
Electricity - production by source:
fossil fuel: 100%
hydro: 0%
nuclear: 0%
other: 0% (2001)
Electricity - consumption: 38.13 million kWh (2003)
Electricity - exports: 0 kWh (2003)
Electricity - imports: 0 kWh (2003)
Oil - production: 0 bbl/day (2003 est.)
Oil - consumption: 620 bbl/day (2003 est.)
Oil - exports: NA (2001)
Oil - imports: NA (2001)
Exports: $205 million f.o.b. (2004 est.)
Exports - partners: Thailand 47%, Malaysia 18.4%, Japan 7.5%, Belgium 5.4%, China 4.9% (2004)
Imports: $233 million c.i.f. (2004 est.)
Imports - partners: Taiwan 24%, Australia 16.5%, Japan 11.4%, Singapore 8.5%, New Zealand 7.2%, Fiji 6.3%, US 4.4% (2004)
Debt - external: $83.7 million (2002)
Economic aid - recipient: $27.5 million (2002)
Currency (code): vatu (VUV)
Currency code: VUV
Exchange rates: vatu per US dollar - NA (2005), 111.79 (2004), 122.19 (2003), 139.2 (2002), 145.31 (2001)
Fiscal year: calendar year

COMMUNICATIONS

Telephones - main lines in use: 6,500 (2003)
Telephones - mobile cellular: 7,800 (2003)
Telephone system:
general assessment: NA
domestic: NA
international: country code - 678; satellite earth station - 1 Intelsat (Pacific Ocean)
Radio broadcast stations: AM 2, FM 4, shortwave 1 (2004)
Radios: 67,000 (1997)
Television broadcast stations: 1 (2004)
Televisions: 2,300 (1999)
Internet country code: .vu
Internet hosts: 512 (2003)
Internet Service Providers (ISPs): 1 (2000)
Internet users: 7,500 (2003)

TRANSPORTATION

Airports: 30 (2004 est.)
Airports - with paved runways:
total: 3
2,438 to 3,047 m: 1
1,524 to 2,437 m: 1
914 to 1,523 m: 1 (2005 est.)
Airports - with unpaved runways:
total: 28
914 to 1,523 m: 10
under 914 m: 18 (2005 est.)
Roadways:
total: 1,070 km
paved: 256 km
unpaved: 814 km (1999 est.)
Merchant marine:
total: total: 52 ships (1,000 GRT or over) 1,192,474 GRT/1,560,828 DWT
by type: bulk carrier 22, cargo 16, container 1, liquefied gas 2, refrigerated cargo 4, roll on/roll off 2, vehicle carrier 5
foreign-owned: 52 (Australia 2, Canada 5, Estonia 1, Greece 1, Israel 1, Japan 25, New Zealand 1, Poland 11, Russia 1, Switzerland 2, Thailand 1, United States 1)
registered in other countries: 1 (2005)
Ports and terminals: Forari, Port-Vila, Santo (Espiritu Santo)

MILITARY

Military branches: no regular military forces; security forces comprise the Vanuatu Police Force (VPF) and paramilitary Vanuatu Mobile Force (VMF), which includes Vanuatu's naval force, known as the Police Maritime Wing (PMW); border security in Vanuatu is the joint responsibility of the Customs and Inland Revenue Service, VPF, VMF, and PMW (2003)
Military expenditures - dollar figure: NA
Military expenditures - percent of GDP: NA

TRANSNATIONAL ISSUES

Disputes - international: Matthew and Hunter Islands east of New Caledonia claimed by Vanuatu and France

VENEZUELA

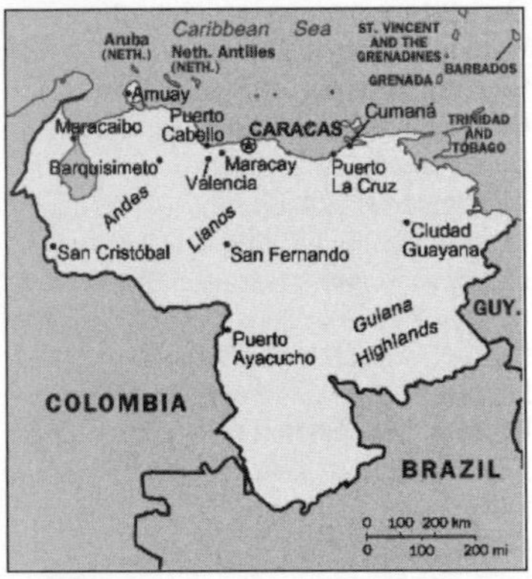

INTRODUCTION

Background: Venezuela was one of three countries that emerged from the collapse of Gran Colombia in 1830 (the others being Colombia and Ecuador). For most of the first half of the 20th century, Venezuela was ruled by generally benevolent military strongmen, who promoted the oil industry and allowed for some social reforms. Democratically elected governments have held sway since 1959. Current concerns include: a weakening of democratic institutions, political polarization, a politicized military, drug-related violence along the Colombian border, increasing internal drug consumption, overdependence on the petroleum industry with its price fluctuations, and irresponsible mining operations that are endangering the rain forest and indigenous peoples.

GEOGRAPHY

Location: Northern South America, bordering the Caribbean Sea and the North Atlantic Ocean, between Colombia and Guyana
Geographic coordinates: 8 00 N, 66 00 W
Map references: South America
Area:
total: 912,050 sq km
land: 882,050 sq km
water: 30,000 sq km
Area - comparative: slightly more than twice the size of California
Land boundaries:
total: 4,993 km
border countries: Brazil 2,200 km, Colombia 2,050 km, Guyana 743 km
Coastline: 2,800 km
Maritime claims:
territorial sea: 12 nm
contiguous zone: 15 nm
exclusive economic zone: 200 nm
continental shelf: 200-m depth or to the depth of exploitation
Climate: tropical; hot, humid; more moderate in highlands
Terrain: Andes Mountains and Maracaibo Lowlands in northwest; central plains (llanos); Guiana Highlands in southeast
Elevation extremes:
lowest point: Caribbean Sea 0 m
highest point: Pico Bolivar (La Columna) 5,007 m
Natural resources: petroleum, natural gas, iron ore, gold, bauxite, other minerals, hydropower, diamonds
Land use:
arable land: 2.95%
permanent crops: 0.92%
other: 96.13% (2001
Irrigated land: 540 sq km (1998 est.)
Natural hazards: subject to floods, rockslides, mudslides; periodic droughts
Environment - current issues: sewage pollution of Lago de Valencia; oil and urban pollution of Lago de Maracaibo; deforestation; soil degradation; urban and industrial pollution, especially along the Caribbean coast; threat to the rainforest ecosystem from irresponsible mining operations
Environment - international agreements:
party to: Antarctic Treaty, Biodiversity, Climate Change, Climate Change-Kyoto Protocol, Desertification, Endangered Species, Hazardous Wastes, Marine Life Conservation, Ozone Layer Protection, Ship Pollution, Tropical Timber 83, Tropical Timber 94, Wetlands
signed, but not ratified: none of the selected agreements
Geography - note: on major sea and air routes linking North and South America; Angel Falls in the Guiana Highlands is the world's highest waterfall

PEOPLE

Population: 25,375,281 (July 2005 est.)
Age structure:
0-14 years: 29.9% (male 3,909,876/female 3,667,958)
15-64 years: 65% (male 8,287,255/female 8,209,599)
65 years and over: 5.1% (male 590,236/female 710,357) (2005 est.)
Median age:
total: 25.6 years
male: 24.98 years
female: 26.24 years (2005 est.)
Population growth rate: 1.4% (2005 est.)
Birth rate: 18.91 births/1,000 population (2005 est.)
Death rate: 4.9 deaths/1,000 population (2005 est.)
Net migration rate: 0 migrant(s)/1,000 population (2005 est.)
Sex ratio:
at birth: 1.07 male(s)/female
under 15 years: 1.07 male(s)/female
15-64 years: 1.01 male(s)/female
65 years and over: 0.83 male(s)/female
total population: 1.02 male(s)/female (2005 est.)
Infant mortality rate:
total: 22.2 deaths/1,000 live births
male: 25.31 deaths/1,000 live births

female: 18.85 deaths/1,000 live births (2005 est.)
Life expectancy at birth:
total population: 74.31 years
male: 71.27 years
female: 77.58 years (2005 est.)
Total fertility rate: 2.26 children born/woman (2005 est.)
HIV/AIDS - adult prevalence rate: 0.7% - note - no country specific models provided (2001 est.)
HIV/AIDS - people living with HIV/AIDS: 110,000 (1999 est.)
HIV/AIDS - deaths: 4,100 (2003 est.)
Nationality:
noun: Venezuelan(s)
adjective: Venezuelan
Ethnic groups: Spanish, Italian, Portuguese, Arab, German, African, indigenous people
Religions: nominally Roman Catholic 96%, Protestant 2%, other 2%
Languages: Spanish (official), numerous indigenous dialects
Literacy:
definition: age 15 and over can read and write
total population: 93.4%
male: 93.8%
female: 93.1% (2003 est.)

GOVERNMENT

Country name:
conventional long form: Bolivarian Republic of Venezuela
conventional short form: Venezuela
local long form: Republica Bolivariana de Venezuela
local short form: Venezuela
Government type: federal republic
Capital: Caracas
Administrative divisions: 23 states (estados, singular - estado), 1 federal district* (distrito federal), and 1 federal dependency** (dependencia federal); Amazonas, Anzoategui, Apure, Aragua, Barinas, Bolivar, Carabobo, Cojedes, Delta Amacuro, Dependencias Federales**, Distrito Federal*, Falcon, Guarico, Lara, Merida, Miranda, Monagas, Nueva Esparta, Portuguesa, Sucre, Tachira, Trujillo, Vargas, Yaracuy, Zulia
note: the federal dependency consists of 11 federally controlled island groups with a total of 72 individual islands
Independence: 5 July 1811 (from Spain)
National holiday: Independence Day, 5 July (1811)
Constitution: 30 December 1999
Legal system: open, adversarial court system
Suffrage: 18 years of age, universal
Executive branch:
chief of state: President Hugo CHAVEZ Frias (since 3 February 1999); Vice President Jose Vicente RANGEL Vale (since 28 April 2002); note - the president is both the chief of state and head of government
head of government: President Hugo CHAVEZ Frias (since 3 February 1999); Vice President Jose Vicente RANGEL Vale (since 28 April 2002); note - the president is both the chief of state and head of government
cabinet: Council of Ministers appointed by the president
elections: president elected by popular vote for a six-year term; election last held 30 July 2000 (next to be held NA 2006)
election results: Hugo CHAVEZ Frias reelected president; percent of vote - 60%
note: a special presidential recall vote on 15 August 2004 resulted in a victory for CHAVEZ; percent of vote - 58% in favor of CHAVEZ fulfilling the remaining two years of his term, 42% in favor of terminating his presidency immediately
Legislative branch: unicameral National Assembly or Asamblea Nacional (167 seats; members elected by popular vote to serve five-year terms; three seats reserved for the indigenous peoples of Venezuela)
elections: last held 4 December 2005 (next to be held NA 2010)
election results: percent of vote by party - NA%; seats by party - pro-government 167 (MVR 114, PODEMOS 15, PPT 11, indigenous 2, other 25), opposition 0
Judicial branch: Supreme Tribunal of Justice or Tribuna Suprema de Justicia (magistrates are elected by the National Assembly for a single 12-year term)
Political parties and leaders: Christian Democrats or COPEI [Eduardo FERNANDEZ]; Democratic Action or AD [Jesus MENDEZ Quijada]; Fifth Republic Movement or MVR [Hugo CHAVEZ]; Homeland for All or PPT [Jose ALBORNOZ]; Justice First [Julio BORGES]; Movement Toward Socialism or MAS [Hector MUJICA]; Venezuela Project or PV [Henrique SALAS Romer]; We Can or PODEMOS [Ismael GARCIA]
Political pressure groups and leaders: FEDECAMARAS, a conservative business group; VECINOS groups; Venezuelan Confederation of Workers or CTV (labor organization dominated by the Democratic Action)
International organization participation: CAN, CDB, CSN, FAO, G-3, G-15, G-24, G-77, IADB, IAEA, IBRD, ICAO, ICC, ICCt, ICFTU, ICRM, IFAD, IFC, IFRCS, IHO, ILO, IMF, IMO, Interpol, IOC, IOM, ISO, ITU, LAES, LAIA, Mercosur (associate), MIGA, NAM, OAS, OPANAL, OPCW, OPEC, PCA, RG, UN, UNCTAD, UNESCO, UNHCR, UNIDO, UPU, WCL, WCO, WFTU, WHO, WIPO, WMO, WToO, WTO
Diplomatic representation in the US:
chief of mission: Ambassador Bernardo ALVAREZ Herrera
chancery: 1099 30th Street NW, Washington, DC 20007
telephone: [1] (202) 342-2214
FAX: [1] (202) 342-6820
consulate(s) general: Boston, Chicago, Houston, Miami, New Orleans, New York, San Francisco, and San Juan (Puerto Rico)
Diplomatic representation from the US:
chief of mission: Ambassador William R. BROWNFIELD
embassy: Calle F con Calle Suapure, Urbanizacion Colinas de Valle Arriba, Caracas 1080
mailing address: P. O. Box 62291, Caracas 1060-A; APO AA 34037
telephone: [58] (212) 975-9234, 975-6411
FAX: [58] (212) 975-8991
Flag description: three equal horizontal bands of yellow (top), blue, and red with the coat of arms on the hoist side of the yellow band and an arc of seven white five-pointed stars centered in the blue band

ECONOMY

Economy - overview: Venezuela continues to be highly dependent on the petroleum sector, accounting for roughly one-third of GDP, around 80% of export earnings, and over half of government operating revenues. Government revenue has also been bolstered by increased tax collection, which has surpassed its 2005 collection goal by almost 50%. Tax revenue is the primary source of non-oil revenue, which accounts for 53% of the 2006 budget. A disastrous two-month national oil strike from December 2002 to February 2003, temporarily halted economic activity. The economy remained in depression in 2003, declining by 9.2% after an 8.9% fall in 2002. Output recovered strongly in 2004-2005, aided by high oil prices and strong consumption growth. Venezuela continues to be an important source of crude oil for the US market. Both inflation and unemployment remain fundamental problems.
GDP (purchasing power parity): $161.7 billion (2005 est.)
GDP (official exchange rate): $118.3 billion (2005 est.)
GDP - real growth rate: 8.3% (2005 est.)
GDP - per capita: purchasing power parity - $6,400 (2005 est.)
GDP - composition by sector:
agriculture: 4.6%
industry: 48.2%
services: 47.2% (2005 est.)
Labor force: 12.31 million (2005 est.)

Labor force - by occupation: agriculture 13%, industry 23%, services 64% (1997 est.)
Unemployment rate: 12.3% (2005 est.)
Population below poverty line: 47% (1998 est.)
Household income or consumption by percentage share:
lowest 10%: 0.8%
highest 10%: 36.5% (1998)
Distribution of family income - Gini index: 49.1 (1998)
Inflation rate (consumer prices): 15.7% (2005 est.)
Investment (gross fixed): 23.8% of GDP (2005 est.)
Budget:
revenues: $39.63 billion
expenditures: $41.27 billion, including capital expenditures of $2.6 billion (2005 est.)
Public debt: 32% of GDP (2005 est.)
Agriculture - products: corn, sorghum, sugarcane, rice, bananas, vegetables, coffee; beef, pork, milk, eggs; fish
Industries: petroleum, iron ore mining, construction materials, food processing, textiles, steel, aluminum, motor vehicle assembly
Industrial production growth rate: 3.4% (2005 est.)
Electricity - production: 87.44 billion kWh (2003)
Electricity - production by source:
fossil fuel: 31.7%
hydro: 68.3%
nuclear: 0%
other: 0% (2001)
Electricity - consumption: 81.32 billion kWh (2003)
Electricity - exports: 0 kWh (2003)
Electricity - imports: 0 kWh (2003)
Oil - production: 3.081 million bbl/day (2005 est.)
Oil - consumption: 530,000 bbl/day (2003 est.)
Oil - exports: 2.1 million bbl/day (2004 est.)
Oil - imports: NA (2004 est.)
Oil - proved reserves: 75.59 billion bbl (2005 est.)
Natural gas - production: 29.4 billion cu m (2003 est.)
Natural gas - consumption: 29.4 billion cu m (2003 est.)
Natural gas - exports: 0 cu m (2004 est.)
Natural gas - imports: 0 cu m (2004 est.)
Natural gas - proved reserves: 4.19 trillion cu m (2005)
Current account balance: $20.3 billion (2005 est.)
Exports: $52.73 billion f.o.b. (2005 est.)
Exports - partners: US 55.6%, Netherlands Antilles 4.7%, Dominican Republic 2.8% (2004)
Imports: $24.63 billion f.o.b. (2005 est.)
Imports - partners: US 28.8%, Colombia 9.9%, Brazil 7%, Mexico 4.1% (2004)
Reserves of foreign exchange and gold: $30.74 billion (2005 est.)
Debt - external: $39.79 billion (2005 est.)
Economic aid - recipient: $74 million (2000)
Currency (code): bolivar (VEB)
Currency code: VEB
Exchange rates: bolivares per US dollar - 2,090.75 (2005), 1,891.3 (2004), 1,607 (2003), 1,161 (2002), 723.7 (2001)
Fiscal year: calendar year

COMMUNICATIONS

Telephones - main lines in use: 2,841,800 (2002)
Telephones - mobile cellular: 6,463,600 (2002)
Telephone system:
general assessment: modern and expanding
domestic: domestic satellite system with 3 earth stations; recent substantial improvement in telephone service in rural areas; substantial increase in digitalization of exchanges and trunk lines; installation of a national interurban fiber-optic network capable of digital multimedia services
international: country code - 58; 3 submarine coaxial cables; satellite earth stations - 1 Intelsat (Atlantic Ocean) and 1 PanAmSat; participating with Colombia, Ecuador, Peru, and Bolivia in the construction of an international fiber-optic network
Radio broadcast stations: AM 201, FM NA (20 in Caracas), shortwave 11 (1998)
Radios: 10.75 million (1997)
Television broadcast stations: 66 (plus 45 repeaters) (1997)
Televisions: 4.1 million (1997)
Internet country code: .ve
Internet hosts: 35,301 (2003)
Internet Service Providers (ISPs): 16 (2000)
Internet users: 1,274,400 (2002)

TRANSPORTATION

Airports: 369 (2004 est.)
Airports - with paved runways:
total: 128
over 3,047 m: 5
2,438 to 3,047 m: 11
1,524 to 2,437 m: 33
914 to 1,523 m: 60
under 914 m: 19 (2005 est.)
Airports - with unpaved runways:
total: 242
1,524 to 2,437 m: 9
914 to 1,523 m: 89
under 914 m: 144 (2005 est.)
Heliports: 1 (2005 est.)
Pipelines: extra heavy crude 992 km; gas 5,262 km; oil 7,360 km; refined products 1,681 km; unknown (oil/water) 141 km (2004)
Railways:
total: 682 km
standard gauge: 682 km 1.435-m gauge (2004)
Roadways:
total: 96,155 km
paved: 32,308 km
unpaved: 63,847 km (1999 est.)
Waterways: 7,100 km
note: Orinoco River and Lake de Maracaibo navigable by oceangoing vessels, Orinoco for 400 km (2004)
Merchant marine:
total: 56 ships (1,000 GRT or over) 740,919 GRT/1,191,483 DWT
by type: bulk carrier 4, cargo 16, chemical tanker 1, container 1, liquefied gas 5, passenger/cargo 9, petroleum tanker 19, roll on/roll off 1
foreign-owned: 9 (Denmark 2, Greece 1, Hong Kong 2, Mexico 1, Russia 2, Spain 1)
registered in other countries: 20 (2005)
Ports and terminals: Amuay, La Guaira, Maracaibo, Puerto Cabello, Punta Cardon

MILITARY

Military branches: National Armed Forces (Fuerzas Armadas Nacionales, FAN): Ground Forces or Army (Fuerzas Terrestres or Ejercito), Naval Forces (Fuerzas Navales or Armada - includes Marines, Coast Guard), Air Force (Fuerzas Aereas or Aviacion), Armed Forces of Cooperation or National Guard (Fuerzas Armadas de Cooperacion or Guardia Nacional)
Military service age and obligation: 18 years of age for compulsory and voluntary military service; conscript service obligation - 30 months (2004)
Manpower available for military service: *males age 18-49:* 6,236,012 (2005 est.)
Manpower fit for military service: *males age 18-49:* 4,907,947 (2005 est.)
Manpower reaching military service age annually: *males:* 252,396 (2005 est.)
Military expenditures - dollar figure: $1.687 billion (2004)
Military expenditures - percent of GDP: 1.5% (2004)

TRANSNATIONAL ISSUES

Disputes - international: claims all of the area west of the Essequibo River in Guyana, preventing any discussion of a maritime boundary; Guyana has expressed its intention to join Barbados in asserting claims before UNCLOS that the Trinidad and Tobago's maritime boundary with Venezuela extends into their waters; dispute with Colombia over Los Monjes islands and maritime boundary near the Gulf of Venezuela; Colombian-organized illegal narcotics

and paramilitary activities penetrate Venezuela's shared border region resulting in several thousand residents migrating away from the border; US, France and the Netherlands recognize Venezuela's claim to give full effect to Aves Island, which creates a Venezuelan EEZ/continental shelf extending over a large portion of the Caribbean Sea; Dominica, Saint Kitts and Nevis, Saint Lucia, and Saint Vincent and the Grenadines protest Venezuela's claim that Aves Island sustains human habitation and other states' recognition of it
Illicit drugs: small-scale illicit producer of opium and coca for the processing of opiates and coca derivatives; however, large quantities of cocaine, heroin, and marijuana transit the country from Colombia bound for US and Europe; significant narcotics-related money-laundering activity, especially along the border with Colombia and on Margarita Island; active eradication program primarily targeting opium; increasing signs of drug-related activities by Colombian insurgents on border

VIETNAM

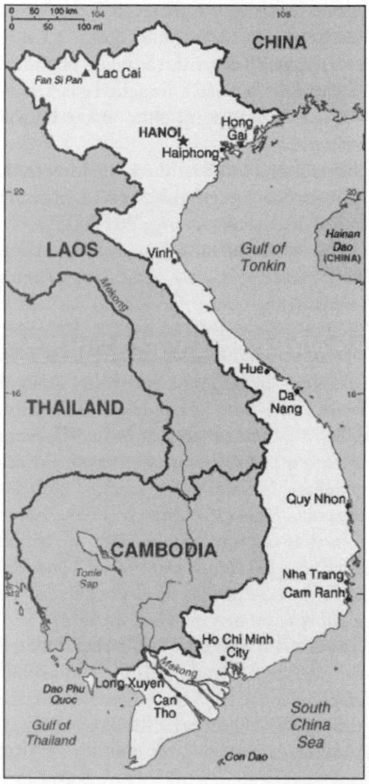

INTRODUCTION

Background: The conquest of Vietnam by France began in 1858 and was completed by 1884. It became part of French Indochina in 1887. Vietnam declared independence after World War II, but France continued to rule until its 1954 defeat by Communist forces under Ho Chi MINH. Under the Geneva Accords of 1954, Vietnam was divided into the Communist North and anti-Communist South. US economic and military aid to South Vietnam grew through the 1960s in an attempt to bolster the government, but US armed forces were withdrawn following a cease-fire agreement in 1973. Two years later, North Vietnamese forces overran the South reuniting the country under Communist rule. Despite the return of peace, for over two decades the country experienced little economic growth because of conservative leadership policies. Since 2001, Vietnamese authorities have committed to increased economic liberalization and enacted structural reforms needed to modernize the economy and to produce more competitive, export-driven industries. The country continues to experience protests from various groups such as the Protestant Montagnard ethnic minority population of the Central Highlands and the Hoa Hao Buddhists in southern Vietnam over religious persecution. Montagnard grievances also include the loss of land to Vietnamese settlers.

GEOGRAPHY

Location: Southeastern Asia, bordering the Gulf of Thailand, Gulf of Tonkin, and South China Sea, alongside China, Laos, and Cambodia
Geographic coordinates: 16 00 N, 106 00 E
Map references: Southeast Asia
Area:
total: 329,560 sq km
land: 325,360 sq km
water: 4,200 sq km
Area - comparative: slightly larger than New Mexico
Land boundaries:
total: 4,639 km
border countries: Cambodia 1,228 km, China 1,281 km, Laos 2,130 km
Coastline: 3,444 km (excludes islands)
Maritime claims:
territorial sea: 12 nm
contiguous zone: 12 nm
exclusive economic zone: 200 nm
continental shelf: 200 nm or to the edge of the continental margin
Climate: tropical in south; monsoonal in north with hot, rainy season (mid-May to mid-September) and warm, dry season (mid-October to mid-March)
Terrain: low, flat delta in south and north; central highlands; hilly, mountainous in far north and northwest
Elevation extremes:
lowest point: South China Sea 0 m
highest point: Fan Si Pan 3,144 m
Natural resources: phosphates, coal, manganese, bauxite, chromate, offshore oil and gas deposits, forests, hydropower
Land use:
arable land: 19.97%
permanent crops: 5.95%
other: 74.08% (2001)
Irrigated land: 30,000 sq km (1998 est.)
Natural hazards: occasional typhoons (May to January) with extensive flooding, especially in the Mekong River delta
Environment - current issues: logging and slash-and-burn agricultural practices contribute to deforestation and soil degradation; water pollution and overfishing threaten marine life populations; groundwater contamination limits potable water supply; growing urban industrialization and population migration are rapidly degrading environment in Hanoi and Ho Chi Minh City
Environment - international agreements:
party to: Biodiversity, Climate Change, Climate Change-Kyoto Protocol, Desertification, Endangered Species, Environmental Modification, Hazardous Wastes, Law of the Sea, Ozone Layer Protection, Ship Pollution, Wetlands
signed, but not ratified: none of the selected agreements
Geography - note: extending 1,650 km north to south, the country is only 50 km across at its narrowest point

PEOPLE

Population: 83,535,576 (July 2005 est.)
Age structure:
0-14 years: 27.9% (male 12,065,777/ female 11,212,299)
15-64 years: 66.4% (male 27,406,456/ female 28,024,250)
65 years and over: 5.8% (male 1,889,585/ female 2,937,209) (2005 est.)
Median age:
total: 25.51 years
male: 24.47 year
female: 26.68 years (2005 est.)
Population growth rate: 1.04% (2005 est.)
Birth rate: 17.07 births/1,000 population (2005 est.)
Death rate: 6.2 deaths/1,000 population (2005 est.)
Net migration rate: -0.43 migrant(s)/ 1,000 population (2005 est.)

Sex ratio:
at birth: 1.08 male(s)/female
under 15 years: 1.08 male(s)/female
15-64 years: 0.98 male(s)/female
65 years and over: 0.64 male(s)/female
total population: 0.98 male(s)/female (2005 est.)
Infant mortality rate:
total: 25.95 deaths/1,000 live births
male: 26.35 deaths/1,000 live births
female: 25.52 deaths/1,000 live births (2005 est.)
Life expectancy at birth:
total population: 70.61 years
male: 67.82 year
female: 73.6 years (2005 est.)
Total fertility rate: 1.94 children born/woman (2005 est.)
HIV/AIDS - adult prevalence rate: 0.4% (2003 est.)
HIV/AIDS - people living with HIV/AIDS: 220,000 (2003 est.)
HIV/AIDS - deaths: 9,000 (2003 est.)
Major infectious diseases:
degree of risk: high
food or waterborne diseases: bacterial diarrhea, hepatitis A, and typhoid fever
vectorborne diseases: dengue fever, malaria, Japanese encephalitis, and plague are high risks in some locations
animal contact disease: rabies
water contact disease: leptospirosis
note: at present, H5N1 avian influenza poses a minimal risk; during outbreaks among birds, rare cases could occur among US personnel who have close contact with infected birds or poultry (2005)
Nationality:
noun: Vietnamese (singular and plural)
adjective: Vietnamese
Ethnic groups: Kinh (Viet) 86.2%, Tay 1.9%, Thai 1.7%, Muong 1.5%, Khome 1.4%, Hoa 1.1%, Nun 1.1%, Hmong 1%, others 4.1% (1999 census)
Religions: Buddhist 9.3%, Catholic 6.7%, Hoa Hao 1.5%, Cao Dai 1.1%, Protestant 0.5%, Muslim 0.1%, none 80.8% (1999 census)
Languages: Vietnamese (official), English (increasingly favored as a second language), some French, Chinese, and Khmer; mountain area languages (Mon-Khmer and Malayo-Polynesian)
Literacy:
definition: age 15 and over can read and write
total population: 90.3%
male: 93.9%
female: 86.9% (2002)

GOVERNMENT

Country name:
conventional long form: Socialist Republic of Vietnam
conventional short form: Vietnam
local long form: Cong Hoa Xa Hoi Chu Nghia Viet Nam
local short form: Viet Nam
abbreviation: SRV
Government type: Communist state
Capital: Hanoi
Administrative divisions: 59 provinces (tinh, singular and plural) and 5 municipalities (thu do, singular and plural)
provinces: An Giang, Bac Giang, Bac Kan, Bac Lieu, Bac Ninh, Ba Ria-Vung Tau, Ben Tre, Binh Dinh, Binh Duong, Binh Phuoc, Binh Thuan, Ca Mau, Cao Bang, Dac Lak, Dac Nong, Dien Bien, Dong Nai, Dong Thap, Gia Lai, Ha Giang, Hai Duong, Ha Nam, Ha Tay, Ha Tinh, Hau Giang, Hoa Binh, Hung Yen, Khanh Hoa, Kien Giang, Kon Tum, Lai Chau, Lam Dong, Lang Son, Lao Cai, Long An, Nam Dinh, Nghe An, Ninh Binh, Ninh Thuan, Phu Tho, Phu Yen, Quang Binh, Quang Nam, Quang Ngai, Quang Ninh, Quang Tri, Soc Trang, Son La, Tay Ninh, Thai Binh, Thai Nguyen, Thanh Hoa, Thua Thien-Hue, Tien Giang, Tra Vinh, Tuyen Quang, Vinh Long, Vinh Phuc, Yen Bai
municipalities: Can Tho, Da Nang, Hai Phong, Hanoi, Ho Chi Minh
Independence: 2 September 1945 (from France)
National holiday: Independence Day, 2 September (1945)
Constitution: 15 April 1992
Legal system: based on communist legal theory and French civil law system
Suffrage: 18 years of age, universal
Executive branch:
chief of state: President Tran Duc LUONG (since 24 September 1997)
head of government: Prime Minister Phan Van KHAI (since 25 September 1997); First Deputy Prime Minister Nguyen Tan DUNG (since 29 September 1997); Deputy Prime Ministers Vu KHOAN (8 August 2002) and Pham Gia KHIEM (since 29 September 1997)
cabinet: Cabinet appointed by president based on proposal of prime minister and ratification of National Assembly
elections: president elected by the National Assembly from among its members for a five-year term; election last held 25 July 2002 (next to be held when National Assembly meets following legislative elections in 2007); prime minister appointed by the president from among the members of the National Assembly; deputy prime ministers appointed by the prime minister
election results: Tran Duc LUONG elected president; percent of National Assembly vote - NA%
Legislative branch: unicameral National Assembly or Quoc-Hoi (498 seats; members elected by popular vote to serve five-year terms)
elections: last held 19 May 2002 (next to be held 2007)
election results: percent of vote by party - CPV 90%, other 10% (the 10% are not CPV members but are approved by the CPV to stand for election); seats by party - CPV 447, CPV-approved 51
Judicial branch: Supreme People's Court (chief justice is elected for a five-year term by the National Assembly on the recommendation of the president)
Political parties and leaders: only party - Communist Party of Vietnam or CPV [Nong Duc MANH, general secretary]
Political pressure groups and leaders: none
International organization participation: ACCT (observer), APEC, APT, ARF, AsDB, ASEAN, CP, EAS, FAO, G-77, IAEA, IBRD, ICAO, ICRM, IDA, IFAD, IFC, IFRCS, ILO, IMF, IMO, Interpol, IOC, IOM (observer), ISO, ITU, MIGA, NAM, OPCW, UN, UNCTAD, UNESCO, UNIDO, UPU, WCL, WCO, WFTU, WHO, WIPO, WMO, WToO, WTO (observer)
Diplomatic representation in the US:
chief of mission: Ambassador Nguyen Tam CHIEN
chancery: 1233 20th Street NW, Suite 400, Washington, DC 20036
telephone: [1] (202) 861-0737
FAX: [1] (202) 861-0917
consulate(s) general: San Francisco
Diplomatic representation from the US:
chief of mission: Ambassador Michael W. MARINE
embassy: 7 Lang Ha Street, Ba Dinh District, Hanoi
mailing address: PSC 461, Box 400, FPO AP 96521-0002
telephone: [84] (4) 772-1500
FAX: [84] (4) 772-1510
consulate(s) general: Ho Chi Minh City
Flag description: red with a large yellow five-pointed star in the center

ECONOMY

Economy - overview: Vietnam is a densely-populated, developing country that in the last 30 years has had to recover from the ravages of war, the loss of financial support from the old Soviet Bloc, and the rigidities of a centrally-planned economy. Substantial progress was achieved from 1986 to 1997 in moving forward from an extremely low level of development and significantly reducing poverty. Growth averaged around 9% per year from 1993 to 1997. The 1997 Asian financial crisis highlighted the problems in the Vietnamese economy and temporarily allowed opponents of reform to slow progress towards a market-oriented economy. GDP growth of 8.5% in 1997 fell to 6% in 1998 and 5% in 1999. Growth then rose to 7% in 2000-05 even against the background of global recession. Since 2001, however, Vietnamese authorities have reaffirmed their commitment to economic liberalization and international integration. They have moved to implement the structural reforms needed to modernize the economy and to produce more competitive, export-driven industries. However, equitization of state-owned enterprises and reduction in the proportion of non-performing loans has fallen behind schedule. Vietnam's membership in the ASEAN Free Trade Area (AFTA) and entry into force of the US-Vietnam Bilateral Trade in December 2001 have led to even more rapid changes in Vietnam's trade and economic regime. Vietnam's exports to the US doubled in 2002 and again in 2003. Vietnam became a member of the WTO in 2005. Among other benefits, accession allows Vietnam to take advantage of the phase out of the Agreement on Textiles and Clothing, which eliminated quotas on textiles and clothing for WTO partners on 1 January 2005. Vietnam is working to promote job creation to keep up with the country's high population growth rate. However, high levels of inflation have prompted Vietnamese authorities to tighten monetary and fiscal policies.

GDP (purchasing power parity): $251.8 billion (2005 est.)

GDP (official exchange rate): $45.61 billion (2005 est.)

GDP - real growth rate: 7.6% (2005 est.)

GDP - per capita: purchasing power parity - $3,000 (2005 est.)

GDP - composition by sector:
agriculture: 21%
industry: 40.9%
services: 38.1% (2005 est.)

Labor force: 44.03 million (2005 est.)

Labor force - by occupation: agriculture 63%, industry and services 37% (2000 est.)

Unemployment rate: 2.4% (2005 est.)

Population below poverty line: 28.9% (2002 est.)

Household income or consumption by percentage share:
lowest 10%: 3.6%
highest 10%: 29.9% (1998)

Distribution of family income - Gini index: 36.1 (1998)

Inflation rate (consumer prices): 8% (2005 est.)

Investment (gross fixed): 35.8% of GDP (2005 est.)

Budget:
revenues: $11.64 billion
expenditures: $12.95 billion, including capital expenditures of $1.8 billion (2005 est.)

Public debt: 75.5% of GDP (2005 est.)

Agriculture - products: paddy rice, coffee, fish and seafood, rubber, cotton, tea, pepper, soybeans, cashews, sugar cane, peanuts, bananas, poultry

Industries: food processing, garments, shoes, machine-building, mining, cement, chemical fertilizer, glass, tires, oil, coal, steel, paper

Industrial production growth rate: 15.2% (2005 est.)

Electricity - production: 39.7 billion kWh (2003)

Electricity - production by source:
fossil fuel: 43.7%
hydro: 56.3%
nuclear: 0%
other: 0% (2001)

Electricity - consumption: 36.92 billion kWh (2003)

Electricity - exports: 0 kWh (2003)

Electricity - imports: 0 kWh (2003)

Oil - production: 400,000 bbl/day (2005 est.)

Oil - consumption: 216,000 bbl/day (2003 est.)

Oil - exports: NA (2001)

Oil - imports: NA (2001)

Oil - proved reserves: 2.5 billion bbl (2005 est.)

Natural gas - production: 1.3 billion cu m (2001 est.)

Natural gas - consumption: 1.3 billion cu m (2001 est.)

Natural gas - exports: 0 cu m (2001 est.)

Natural gas - imports: 0 cu m (2001 est.)

Natural gas - proved reserves: 192.6 billion cu m (2005)

Current account balance: $-1.695 billion (2005 est.)

Exports: $31.34 billion f.o.b. (2005 est.)

Exports - partners: US 20.2%, Japan 13.6%, China 9%, Australia 7%, Germany 5.9%, Singapore 4.8%, UK 4.6% (2004)

Imports: $34.44 billion f.o.b. (2005 est.)

Imports - partners: China 13.7%, Taiwan 11.3%, South Korea 10.8%, Japan 10.5%, Singapore 10.5%, Thailand 6.2%, Hong Kong 4% (2004)

Reserves of foreign exchange and gold: $7.503 billion (2005 est.)

Debt - external: $19.17 billion (2005 est.)

Economic aid - recipient: $2.8 billion in credits and grants pledged by international donors for 2000 (2004)

Currency (code): dong (VND)

Currency code: VND

Exchange rates: dong per US dollar - 15,855 (2005), 15,746 (2004), 15,510 (2003), 15,280 (2002), 14,725 (2001)

Fiscal year: calendar year

COMMUNICATIONS

Telephones - main lines in use: 4.402 million (2003)

Telephones - mobile cellular: 2.742 million (2003)

Telephone system:
general assessment: Vietnam is putting considerable effort into modernization and expansion of its telecommunication system, but its performance continues to lag behind that of its more modern neighbors
domestic: all provincial exchanges are digitalized and connected to Hanoi, Da Nang, and Ho Chi Minh City by fiber-optic cable or microwave radio relay networks; main lines have been substantially increased, and the use of mobile telephones is growing rapidly
international: country code - 84; satellite earth stations - 2 Intersputnik (Indian Ocean region)

Radio broadcast stations: AM 65, FM 7, shortwave 29 (1999)

Radios: 8.2 million (1997)

Television broadcast stations: at least 7 (plus 13 repeaters) (1998)

Televisions: 3.57 million (1997)

Internet country code: .vn

Internet hosts: 340 (2003)

Internet Service Providers (ISPs): 5 (2000)

Internet users: 3.5 million (2003)

TRANSPORTATION

Airports: 24 (2004 est.)

Airports - with paved runways:
total: 23
over 3,047 m: 7
2,438 to 3,047 m: 5
1,524 to 2,437 m: 10
914 to 1,523 m: 1 (2005 est.)

Airports - with unpaved runways:
total: 5
1,524 to 2,437 m: 1
914 to 1,523 m: 2
under 914 m: 2 (2005 est.)

Pipelines: condensate/gas 432 km; gas 210 km; oil 3 km; refined products 206 km (2004)

Railways:
total: 2,600 km
standard gauge: 178 km 1.435-m gauge
narrow gauge: 2,169 km 1.000-m gauge
dual gauge: 253 km three-rail track combining 1.435-m and 1.000-m gauges (2004)

Roadways:
total: 93,300 km
paved: 23,418 km
unpaved: 69,882 km (1999 est.)

Waterways: 17,702 km (5,000 km navigable by vessels up to 1.8 m draft) (2004)

Merchant marine:
total: 194 ships (1,000 GRT or over)

1,170,621 GRT/1,798,376 DWT
by type: bulk carrier 18, cargo 142, chemical tanker 3, container 2, liquefied gas 4, petroleum tanker 22, refrigerated cargo 2, roll on/roll off 1
registered in other countries: 11 (2005)
Ports and terminals: Hai Phong, Ho Chi Minh City

MILITARY

Military branches: People's Army of Vietnam: Ground Forces, People's Navy Command (includes Naval Infantry), Air and Air Defense Force, Coast Guard
Military service age and obligation: 18 years of age for compulsory military service; conscript service obligation - 2 years (2004)
Manpower available for military service: *males age 18-49:* 21,341,813 (2005 est.)
Manpower fit for military service: *males age 18-49:* 16,032,358 (2005 est.)
Manpower reaching military service age annually: *males:* 915,572 (2005 est.)
Military expenditures - dollar figure: $650 million (FY98)
Military expenditures - percent of GDP: 2.5% (FY98)

TRANSNATIONAL ISSUES

Disputes - international: southeast Asian states have enhanced border surveillance to check the spread of avian flu; Cambodia and Laos protest Vietnamese squatters and armed encroachments along border; in 2004 Laotian-Vietnamese boundary commission agrees to erect missing markers in two adjoining provinces; demarcation of the China-Vietnam boundary proceeds slowly and although the maritime boundary delimitation and fisheries agreements were ratified in June 2004, implementation has been delayed; China occupies Paracel Islands also claimed by Vietnam and Taiwan; involved in complex dispute with China, Malaysia, Philippines, Taiwan, and possibly Brunei over the Spratly Islands; the 2002 "Declaration on the Conduct of Parties in the South China Sea" has eased tensions but falls short of a legally binding "code of conduct" desired by several of the disputants; Vietnam continues to expand construction of facilities in the Spratly Islands; in March 2005, the national oil companies of China, the Philippines, and Vietnam signed a joint accord to conduct marine seismic activities in the Spratly Islands
Illicit drugs: minor producer of opium poppy; probable minor transit point for Southeast Asian heroin; domestic opium/heroin/methamphetamine addiction problems

VIRGIN ISLANDS

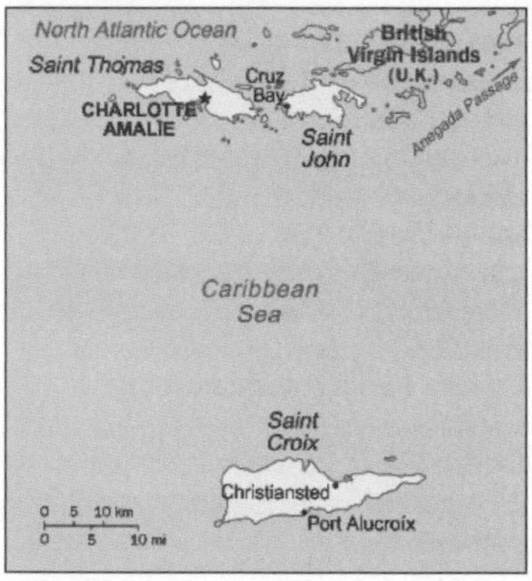

INTRODUCTION

Background: During the 17th century, the archipelago was divided into two territorial units, one English and the other Danish. Sugarcane, produced by slave labor, drove the islands' economy during the 18th and early 19th centuries. In 1917, the US purchased the Danish portion, which had been in economic decline since the abolition of slavery in 1848.

GEOGRAPHY

Location: Caribbean, islands between the Caribbean Sea and the North Atlantic Ocean, east of Puerto Rico
Geographic coordinates: 18 20 N, 64 50 W
Map references: Central America and the Caribbean
Area:
total: 352 sq km
land: 349 sq km
water: 3 sq km
Area - comparative: twice the size of Washington, DC
Land boundaries: 0 km
Coastline: 188 km
Maritime claims:
territorial sea: 12 nm
exclusive economic zone: 200 nm
Climate: subtropical, tempered by easterly trade winds, relatively low humidity, little seasonal temperature variation; rainy season September to November
Terrain: mostly hilly to rugged and mountainous with little level land
Elevation extremes:
lowest point: Caribbean Sea 0 m
highest point: Crown Mountain 474 m
Natural resources: sun, sand, sea, surf
Land use:
arable land: 11.76%
permanent crops: 2.94%
other: 85.3% (2001)
Irrigated land: NA
Natural hazards: several hurricanes in recent years; frequent and severe droughts and floods; occasional earthquakes
Environment - current issues: lack of natural freshwater resources
Geography - note: important location along the Anegada Passage - a key shipping lane for the Panama Canal; Saint Thomas has one of the best natural deepwater harbors in the Caribbean

PEOPLE

Population: 108,708 (July 2005 est.)
Age structure:
0-14 years: 23.1% (male 12,676/female 12,421)
15-64 years: 66.2% (male 34,069/female 37,918)
65 years and over: 10.7% (male 5,125/female 6,499) (2005 est.)
Median age:
total: 36.52 years
male: 35.6 years
female: 37.33 years (2005 est.)
Population growth rate: -0.07% (2005 est.)
Birth rate: 14.2 births/1,000 population (2005 est.)
Death rate: 6.26 deaths/1,000 population (2005 est.)
Net migration rate: -8.64 migrant(s)/1,000 population (2005 est.)
Sex ratio:
at birth: 1.06 male(s)/female
under 15 years: 1.02 male(s)/female
15-64 years: 0.9 male(s)/female
65 years and over: 0.79 male(s)/female
total population: 0.91 male(s)/female (2005 est.)
Infant mortality rate:
total: 8.03 deaths/1,000 live births
male: 9.11 deaths/1,000 live births
female: 6.88 deaths/1,000 live births (2005 est.)
Life expectancy at birth:
total population: 78.91 years
male: 75.08 years
female: 82.96 years (2005 est.)
Total fertility rate: 2.19 children born/woman (2005 est.)
HIV/AIDS - adult prevalence rate: NA
HIV/AIDS - people living with HIV/AIDS: NA
HIV/AIDS - deaths: NA
Nationality:
noun: Virgin Islander(s)

adjective: Virgin Islander
Ethnic groups: black 76.2%, white 13.1%, Asian 1.1%, other 6.1%, mixed 3.5% (2000 census)
Religions: Baptist 42%, Roman Catholic 34%, Episcopalian 17%, other 7%
Languages: English 74.7%, Spanish or Spanish Creole 16.8%, French or French Creole 6.6%, other 1.9% (2000 census)
Literacy:
definition: NA
total population: NA%
male: NA%
female: NA%

GOVERNMENT

Country name:
conventional long form: United States Virgin Islands
conventional short form: Virgin Islands
former: Danish West Indies
Dependency status: organized, unincorporated territory of the US with policy relations between the Virgin Islands and the US under the jurisdiction of the Office of Insular Affairs, US Department of the Interior
Government type: NA
Capital: Charlotte Amalie
Administrative divisions: none (territory of the US); there are no first-order administrative divisions as defined by the US Government, but there are three islands at the second order; Saint Croix, Saint John, Saint Thomas
National holiday: Transfer Day (from Denmark to the US), 27 March (1917)
Constitution: Revised Organic Act of 22 July 1954
Legal system: based on US laws
Suffrage: 18 years of age; universal; note - island residents are US citizens but do not vote in US presidential elections
Executive branch:
chief of state: President George W. BUSH of the US (since 20 January 2001)
head of government: Governor Dr. Charles Wesley TURNBULL (since 5 January 1999)
cabinet: NA
elections: US president and vice president elected on the same ticket for four-year terms; governor and lieutenant governor elected on the same ticket by popular vote for four-year terms; election last held 5 November 2002 (next to be held November 2006)
election results: Dr. Charles Wesley TURNBULL reelected governor; percent of vote - Dr. Charles Wesley TURNBULL (Democrat) 50.5%, John de JONGH 24.4%
Legislative branch: unicameral Senate (15 seats; members are elected by popular vote to serve two-year terms)
elections: last held 6 November 2002 (next to be held 2 November 2004)
election results: percent of vote by party - NA%; seats by party - Democratic Party 10, ICM 2, independent 3
note: the Virgin Islands elects one nonvoting representative to the US House of Representatives; election last held 6 November 2002 (next to be held 2 November 2004); results - Donna M. CHRISTIAN-CHRISTENSON (Democrat) reelected
Judicial branch: US District Court of the Virgin Islands (under Third Circuit jurisdiction); Territorial Court (judges appointed by the governor for 10-year terms)
Political parties and leaders: Democratic Party [Arturo WATLINGTON]; Independent Citizens' Movement or ICM [Usie RICHARDS]; Republican Party [Gary SPRAUVE]
Political pressure groups and leaders: NA
International organization participation: IOC, UPU
Diplomatic representation in the US: none (territory of the US)
Diplomatic representation from the US: none (territory of the US)
Flag description: white, with a modified US coat of arms in the center between the large blue initials V and I; the coat of arms shows a yellow eagle holding an olive branch in one talon and three arrows in the other with a superimposed shield of vertical red and white stripes below a blue panel

ECONOMY

Economy - overview: Tourism is the primary economic activity, accounting for 80% of GDP and employment. The islands normally host 2 million visitors a year. The manufacturing sector consists of petroleum refining, textiles, electronics, pharmaceuticals, and watch assembly. The agricultural sector is small, with most food being imported. International business and financial services are a small but growing component of the economy. One of the world's largest petroleum refineries is at Saint Croix. The islands are subject to substantial damage from storms. The government is working to improve fiscal discipline, to support construction projects in the private sector, to expand tourist facilities, to reduce crime, and to protect the environment.
GDP (purchasing power parity): $2.5 billion (2002 est.)
GDP (official exchange rate): NA
GDP - real growth rate: 2% (2002 est.)
GDP - per capita: purchasing power parity - $17,200 (2002 est.)
GDP - composition by sector:
agriculture: 1%
industry: 19%
services: 80% (2003 est.)
Labor force: 48,900 (2003 est.)
Labor force - by occupation: agriculture 1%, industry 19%, services 80% (2003 est.)
Unemployment rate: 9.3% (2003 est.)
Population below poverty line: NA
Household income or consumption by percentage share:
lowest 10%: NA
highest 10%: NA
Inflation rate (consumer prices): 2.2% (2003)
Budget:
revenues: $559.7
expenditures: NA (2003)
Agriculture - products: fruit, vegetables, sorghum; Senepol cattle
Industries: tourism, petroleum refining, watch assembly, rum distilling, construction, pharmaceuticals, textiles, electronics
Industrial production growth rate: NA%
Electricity - production: 1.04 billion kWh (2003)
Electricity - production by source:
fossil fuel: 100%
hydro: 0%
nuclear: 0%
other: 0% (2001)
Electricity - consumption: 967.3 million kWh (2003)
Electricity - exports: 0 kWh (2003)
Electricity - imports: 0 kWh (2003)
Oil - production: 14,650 bbl/day (2003 est.)
Oil - consumption: 105,000 bbl/day (2003 est.)
Oil - exports: NA (2001)
Oil - imports: NA (2001)
Exports: NA
Exports - partners: US, Puerto Rico (2004)
Imports: NA
Imports - partners: US, Puerto Rico (2004)
Debt - external: NA
Economic aid - recipient: NA
Currency (code): US dollar (USD)
Currency code: USD
Exchange rates: the US dollar is used
Fiscal year: 1 October - 30 September

COMMUNICATIONS

Telephones - main lines in use: 69,400 (2002)
Telephones - mobile cellular: 41,000 (2002)
Telephone system:
general assessment: modern system with total digital switching, uses fiber-optic cable and microwave radio relay
domestic: full range of services available
international: country code - 1-340; 2 submarine cable connections (Taino Carib,

Americas-1); satellite earth stations - NA
Radio broadcast stations: AM 6, FM 17, shortwave 0 (2004)
Radios: 107,000 (1997)
Television broadcast stations: 16 (2004)
Televisions: 68,000 (1997)
Internet country code: .vi
Internet Service Providers (ISPs): 50 (2000)
Internet users: 30,000 (2002)

TRANSPORTATION

Airports: 2 (2004 est.)
Airports - with paved runways:
total: 2
1,524 to 2,437 m: 2 (2005 est.)
Roadways:
total: 1,257 km
paved: 1,192 km
unpaved: 65 km
note: the only US possession where driving on the left side of the road is practiced (2003)
Ports and terminals: Charlotte Amalie, Limetree Bay

MILITARY

Military - note: defense is the responsibility of the US

TRANSNATIONAL ISSUES

Disputes - international: none

WAKE ISLAND

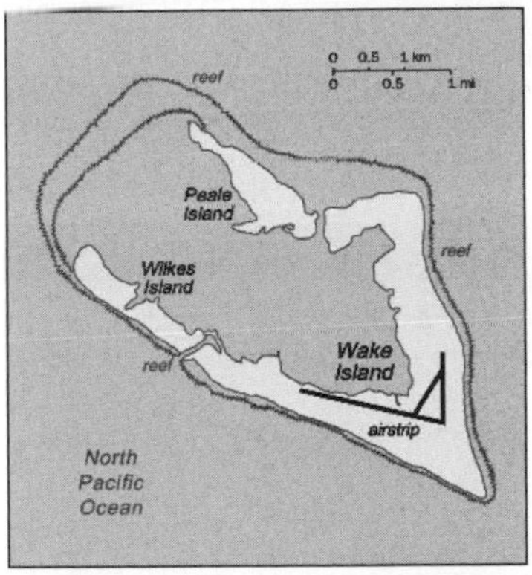

INTRODUCTION

Background: The US annexed Wake Island in 1899 for a cable station. An important air and naval base was constructed in 1940-41. In December 1941, the island was captured by the Japanese and held until the end of World War II. In subsequent years, Wake was developed as a stopover and refueling site for military and commercial aircraft transiting the Pacific. Since 1974, the island's airstrip has been used by the US military and some commercial cargo planes, as well as for emergency landings. There are over 700 landings a year on the island.

GEOGRAPHY

Location: Oceania, atoll in the North Pacific Ocean, about two-thirds of the way from Hawaii to the Northern Mariana Islands
Geographic coordinates: 19 17 N, 166 36 E
Map references: Oceania
Area:
total: 6.5 sq km
land: 6.5 sq km
water: 0 sq km
Area - comparative: about 11 times the size of The Mall in Washington, DC
Land boundaries: 0 km
Coastline: 19.3 km
Maritime claims:
territorial sea: 12 nm
exclusive economic zone: 200 nm
Climate: tropical
Terrain: atoll of three coral islands built up on an underwater volcano; central lagoon is former crater, islands are part of the rim
Elevation extremes:
lowest point: Pacific Ocean 0 m
highest point: unnamed location 6 m
Natural resources: none
Land use:
arable land: 0%
permanent crops: 0%
other: 100% (2001)
Irrigated land: 0 sq km (1998 est.)
Natural hazards: occasional typhoons
Environment - current issues: NA
Geography - note: strategic location in the North Pacific Ocean; emergency landing location for transpacific flights

PEOPLE

Population: no indigenous inhabitants
note: US military personnel have left the island, but contractor personnel remain; as of October 2001, 200 contractor personnel were present (July 2005 est.)

GOVERNMENT

Country name:
conventional long form: none
conventional short form: Wake Island
Dependency status: unincorporated territory of the US; administered from Washington, DC, by the Department of the Interior; activities on the island are conducted by the US Air Force
Legal system: the laws of the US, where applicable, apply
Flag description: the flag of the US is used

ECONOMY

Economy - overview: Economic activity is limited to providing services to contractors located on the island. All food and manufactured goods must be imported.
Electricity - production: NA

COMMUNICATIONS

Telephone system:
general assessment: satellite communications; 1 DSN circuit off the Overseas Telephone System (OTS)
domestic: NA
international: NA
Radio broadcast stations: AM 0, FM NA, shortwave NA
note: Armed Forces Radio/Television Service (AFRTS) radio service provided by satellite (1998)
Television broadcast stations: 0 (1997)

TRANSPORTATION

Airports: 1 (2004 est.)
Airports - with paved runways:
total: 1
2,438 to 3,047 m: 1 (2005 est.)
Ports and terminals: none; two offshore anchorages for large ships
Transportation - note: formerly an important commercial aviation base, now used by US military, some commercial cargo planes, and for emergency landings

MILITARY

Military - note: defense is the responsibility of the US; launch support facility is part of the Ronald Reagan Ballistic Missile Defense Test Site (RTS) administered by US Army Space and Missile Defense Command (SMDC)

TRANSNATIONAL ISSUES

Disputes - international: claimed by Marshall Islands

WALLIS AND FUTUNA

INTRODUCTION

Background: Although discovered by the Dutch and the British in the 17th and 18th centuries, it was the French who declared a protectorate over the islands in 1842. In 1959, the inhabitants of the islands voted to become a French overseas territory.

GEOGRAPHY

Location: Oceania, islands in the South Pacific Ocean, about two-thirds of the way from Hawaii to New Zealand
Geographic coordinates: 13 18 S, 176 12 W
Map references: Oceania
Area:
total: 274 sq km
land: 274 sq km
water: 0 sq km
note: includes Ile Uvea (Wallis Island), Ile Futuna (Futuna Island), Ile Alofi, and 20 islets
Area - comparative: 1.5 times the size of Washington, DC
Land boundaries: 0 km
Coastline: 129 km
Maritime claims:
territorial sea: 12 nm
exclusive economic zone: 200 nm
Climate: tropical; hot, rainy season (November to April); cool, dry season (May to October); rains 2,500-3,000 mm per year (80% humidity); average temperature 26.6 degrees C
Terrain: volcanic origin; low hills
Elevation extremes:
lowest point: Pacific Ocean 0 m

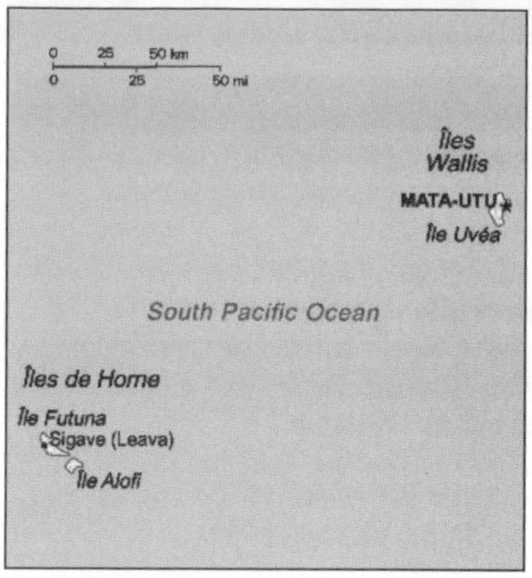

highest point: Mont Singavi 765 m
Natural resources: NEGL
Land use:
arable land: 5%
permanent crops: 25%
other: 70% (2001)
Irrigated land: NA sq km
Natural hazards: NA
Environment - current issues: deforestation (only small portions of the original forests remain) largely as a result of the continued use of wood as the main fuel source; as a consequence of cutting down the forests, the mountainous terrain of Futuna is particularly prone to erosion; there are no permanent settlements on Alofi because of the lack of natural fresh water resources
Geography - note: both island groups have fringing reefs

PEOPLE

Population: 16,025 (July 2005 est.)
Age structure:
0-14 years: NA
15-64 years: NA
65 years and over: NA
Population growth rate: NA%
Birth rate: NA births/1,000 population
Death rate: NA deaths/1,000 population
Net migration rate: NA migrant(s)/1,000 population
note: there has been steady emigration from Wallis and Futuna to New Caledonia (2005 est.)
Infant mortality rate:
total: NA
male: NA
female: NA
Life expectancy at birth:
total population: NA years
male: NA years
female: NA years
Total fertility rate: NA children born/woman
HIV/AIDS - adult prevalence rate: NA%
HIV/AIDS - people living with HIV/AIDS: NA
HIV/AIDS - deaths: NA
Nationality:
noun: Wallisian(s), Futunan(s), or Wallis and Futuna Islanders
adjective: Wallisian, Futunan, or Wallis and Futuna Islander
Ethnic groups: Polynesian
Religions: Roman Catholic 99%, other 1%
Languages: Wallisian 58.9% (indigenous Polynesian language), Futunian 30.1%, French 10.8%, other 0.2% (2003 census)
Literacy:
definition: age 15 and over can read and write
total population: 50%
male: 50%
female: 50% (1969 est.)

GOVERNMENT

Country name:
conventional long form: Territory of the Wallis and Futuna Islands
conventional short form: Wallis and Futuna
local long form: Territoire des Iles Wallis et Futuna
local short form: Wallis et Futuna
Dependency status: overseas territory of France
Government type: NA
Capital: Mata-Utu (on Ile Uvea)
Administrative divisions: none (overseas territory of France); there are no first-order administrative divisions as defined by the US Government, but there are three kingdoms at the second order named Alo, Sigave, Wallis
Independence: none (overseas territory of France)
National holiday: Bastille Day, 14 July (1789)
Constitution: 4 October 1958 (French Constitution)
Legal system: French legal system
Suffrage: 18 years of age, universal
Executive branch:
chief of state: President Jacques CHIRAC of France (since 17 May 1995), represented by High Administrator Xavier DE FURST (since 18 January 2005)
head of government: President of the Territorial Assembly Patalione KANIMOA (since NA January 2001)
cabinet: Council of the Territory consists of three kings and three members appointed by the high administrator on the advice of the Territorial Assembly
note: there are three traditional kings with limited powers
elections: French president elected by popular vote for a five-year term; high administrator appointed by the French president on the advice of the French Ministry of the Interior; the presidents of the Territorial Government and the Territorial Assembly are elected by the members of the assembly
Legislative branch: unicameral Territorial Assembly or Assemblee Territoriale (20 seats; members are elected by popular vote to serve five-year terms)
elections: last held 11 March 2002 (next to be held March 2007)
election results: percent of vote by party - NA%; seats by party - RPR and affiliates 13, Socialists and affiliates 7
note: Wallis and Futuna elects one senator to the French Senate and one deputy to the French National Assembly; French Senate - elections last held 27 September 1998 (next to be held by September 2007); results - percent of vote by party - NA%; seats - RPR (now UMP) 1; French National Assembly - elections last held 16 June 2002 (next to be held by NA 2007); results - percent of vote by party - NA%; seats - RPR (UMP) 1
Judicial branch: none; justice generally administered under French law by the high administrator, but the three traditional kings administer customary law and there is a magistrate in Mata-Utu
Political parties and leaders: Lua Kae Tahi (Giscardians) [leader NA]; Mouvement des Radicaux de Gauche or MRG [leader NA]; Rally for the Republic or RPR [Clovis LOGOLOGOFOLAU]; Taumu'a Lelei [Soane Muni UHILA]; Union Populaire Locale or UPL [Falakiko GATA]; Union Pour la Democratie Francaise or UDF [leader NA]
Political pressure groups and leaders: NA
International organization participation: SPC, UPU
Diplomatic representation in the US: none (overseas territory of France)
Diplomatic representation from the US: none (overseas territory of France)
Flag description: a large white modified Maltese cross - shifted a little off center toward the fly and slightly downward - on a red background; the flag of France outlined in white on two sides is in the upper hoist quadrant; the flag of France is used for official occasions

ECONOMY

Economy - overview: The economy is limited to traditional subsistence agriculture, with about 80% labor force earnings from agriculture (coconuts and vegetables), livestock (mostly pigs), and fishing. About 4% of the population is employed in government. Revenues come from French Government subsidies, licensing of fishing rights to Japan and South Korea, import taxes, and remittances from expatriate workers in New Caledonia.
GDP (purchasing power parity): $60 million (2004 est.)
GDP (official exchange rate): NA
GDP - real growth rate: NA%

GDP - per capita: purchasing power parity - $3,800 (2004 est.)
GDP - composition by sector:
agriculture: NA%
industry: NA%
services: NA%
Labor force: NA
Labor force - by occupation: agriculture, livestock, and fishing 80%, government 4% (2001 est.)
Unemployment rate: NA%
Population below poverty line: NA
Household income or consumption by percentage share:
lowest 10%: NA%
highest 10%: NA%
Inflation rate (consumer prices): NA%
Budget:
revenues: $20 million
expenditures: $17 million, including capital expenditures of NA (1998 est.)
Agriculture - products: breadfruit, yams, taro, bananas; pigs, goats
Industries: copra, handicrafts, fishing, lumber
Industrial production growth rate: NA%
Electricity - production: NA kWh
Electricity - production by source:
fossil fuel: 0%
hydro: 0%
nuclear: 0%
other: 0%
Electricity - consumption: NA kWh
Electricity - exports: 0 kWh (2002)
Electricity - imports: 0 kWh (2002)
Exports: $250,000 f.o.b. (1999)
Exports - partners: Italy 40%, Croatia 15%, US 14%, Denmark 13% (2004)
Imports: $300,000 f.o.b. (1999)
Imports - partners: France 97%, Australia 2%, New Zealand 1% (2004)
Debt - external: $NA
Economic aid - recipient: assistance from France
Currency (code): Comptoirs Francais du Pacifique franc (XPF)
Currency code: XPF
Exchange rates: Comptoirs Francais du Pacifique francs (XPF) per US dollar - NA (2005), 96.04 (2004), 105.66 (2003), 126.71 (2002), 133.26 (2001)
Fiscal year: calendar year

COMMUNICATIONS

Telephones - main lines in use: 1,900 (2002)
Telephones - mobile cellular: 0 (1994)
Telephone system:
general assessment: NA
domestic: NA
international: country code - 681
Radio broadcast stations: AM 1, FM 0, shortwave 0 (2000)
Radios: NA
Television broadcast stations: 2 (2000)
Televisions: NA
Internet country code: .wf
Internet Service Providers (ISPs): 1 (2000)
Internet users: 900 (2002)

TRANSPORTATION

Airports: 2 (2004 est.)
Airports - with paved runways:
total: 1
1,524 to 2,437 m: 1 (2005 est.)
Airports - with unpaved runways:
total: 1
914 to 1,523 m: 1 (2005 est.)
Roadways:
total: 120 km (Ile Uvea 100 km, Ile Futuna 20 km)
paved: 16 km (all on Ile Uvea)
unpaved: 104 km (Ile Uvea 84 km, Ile Futuna 20 km)
Merchant marine:
total: 4 ships (1,000 GRT or over) 74,754 GRT/1,187 DWT
by type: passenger 4
foreign-owned: 4 (France 3, United States 1) (2005)
Ports and terminals: Leava, Mata-Utu

MILITARY

Military - note: defense is the responsibility of France

TRANSNATIONAL ISSUES

Disputes - international: none

WEST BANK

INTRODUCTION

Background: The Israel-PLO Declaration of Principles on Interim Self-Government Arrangements (the DOP), signed in Washington on 13 September 1993, provided for a transitional period not exceeding five years of Palestinian interim self-government in the Gaza Strip and the West Bank. Under the DOP, Israel agreed to transfer certain powers and responsibilities to the Palestinian Authority (PA) as part of the interim self-governing arrangements in the West Bank and Gaza Strip. A transfer of powers and responsibilities for the Gaza Strip and Jericho took place pursuant to the Israel-PLO 4 May 1994 Cairo Agreement on the Gaza Strip and the Jericho Area and in additional areas of the West Bank pursuant to the Israel-PLO 28 September 1995 Interim Agreement, the Israel-PLO 15 January 1997 Protocol Concerning Redeployment in Hebron, the Israel-PLO 23 October 1998 Wye River Memorandum, and the 4 September 1999 Sharm el-Sheikh Agreement. The DOP provided that Israel would retain responsibility during the transitional period for external and internal security and for public order of settlements and Israeli citizens. Direct negotiations to determine the permanent status of Gaza and West Bank began in September 1999 after a three-year hiatus, but were derailed by a second intifada that broke out in September 2000. In June 2003 the Quartet (US, European Union, United Nations, and Russia) presented a roadmap to a final settlement of the conflict by 2005 based on reciprocal steps by the two parties leading to two states, Israel and a democratic Palestine. The proposed date for a permanent status agreement has been postponed indefinitely due to violence and accusations that both sides have not followed through on their commitments. Longtime Palestinian leader Yasir ARAFAT died in November 2004 and Mahmud ABBAS was elected PA President in January 2005, bringing hope of a turning point in the conflict. Israel and the PA agreed in February 2005 to the Sharm el-Sheikh Commitments, focused on security issues, in an effort to move the peace process forward. Progress has been slow because of different interpretations of the verbal agreement by the two sides.

GEOGRAPHY

Location: Middle East, west of Jordan
Geographic coordinates: 32 00 N, 35 15 E
Map references: Middle East
Area:
total: 5,860 sq km
land: 5,640 sq km
water: 220 sq km
note: includes West Bank, Latrun Salient, and the northwest quarter of the Dead Sea, but excludes Mt. Scopus; East Jerusalem and Jerusalem No Man's Land are also included only as a means of depicting the entire area occupied by Israel in 1967
Area - comparative: slightly smaller than Delaware
Land boundaries:
total: 404 km

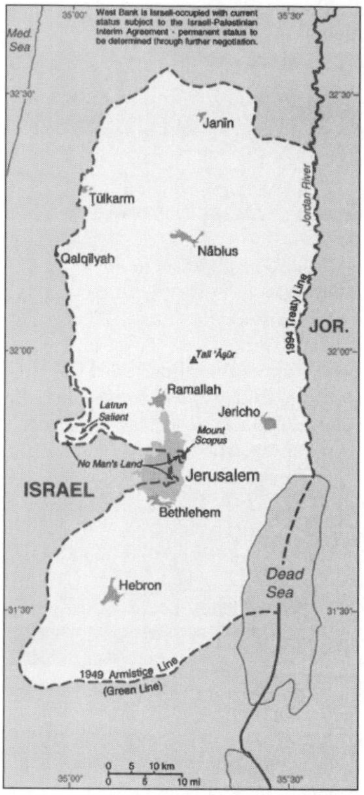

border countries: Israel 307 km, Jordan 97 km
Coastline: 0 km (landlocked)
Maritime claims: none (landlocked)
Climate: temperate; temperature and precipitation vary with altitude, warm to hot summers, cool to mild winters
Terrain: mostly rugged dissected upland, some vegetation in west, but barren in east
Elevation extremes:
lowest point: Dead Sea -408 m
highest point: Tall Asur 1,022 m
Natural resources: arable land
Land use:
arable land: 16.9%
permanent crops: 18.97%
other: 64.13% (2001)
Irrigated land: NA sq km
Natural hazards: droughts
Environment - current issues: adequacy of fresh water supply; sewage treatment
Geography - note: landlocked; highlands are main recharge area for Israel's coastal aquifers; there are 244 West Bank settlements and 29 East Jerusalem settlements in addition to at least 20 occupied outposts (August 2003 est.)

PEOPLE

Population: 2,385,615
note: in addition, there are about 187,000 Israeli settlers in the West Bank and fewer than 177,000 in East Jerusalem (July 2004 est.)
Age structure:
0-14 years: 43.4% (male 530,197/female 504,794)
15-64 years: 53.2% (male 649,610/female 619,335)
65 years and over: 3.4% (male 34,803/female 46,876) (2005 est.)
Median age:
total: 18.14 years
male: 17.99 years
female: 18.3 years (2005 est.)
Population growth rate: 3.13% (2005 est.)
Birth rate: 32.37 births/1,000 population (2005 est.)
Death rate: 3.99 deaths/1,000 population (2005 est.)
Net migration rate: 2.88 migrant(s)/1,000 population (2005 est.)
Sex ratio:
at birth: 1.06 male(s)/female
under 15 years: 1.05 male(s)/female
15-64 years: 1.05 male(s)/female
65 years and over: 0.74 male(s)/female
total population: 1.04 male(s)/female (2005 est.)
Infant mortality rate:
total: 19.62 deaths/1,000 live births
male: 21.66 deaths/1,000 live births
female: 17.45 deaths/1,000 live births (2005 est.)
Life expectancy at birth:
total population: 73.08 years
male: 71.33 years
female: 74.95 years (2005 est.)
Total fertility rate: 4.4 children born/woman (2005 est.)
HIV/AIDS - adult prevalence rate: NA
HIV/AIDS - people living with HIV/AIDS: NA
HIV/AIDS - deaths: NA
Nationality:
noun: NA
adjective: NA
Ethnic groups: Palestinian Arab and other 83%, Jewish 17%
Religions: Muslim 75% (predominantly Sunni), Jewish 17%, Christian and other 8%
Languages: Arabic, Hebrew (spoken by Israeli settlers and many Palestinians), English (widely understood)
Literacy:
definition: age 15 and over can read and write
total population: 91.9%
male: 96.3%
female: 87.4% (2003 est.)

GOVERNMENT

Country name:
conventional long form: none
conventional short form: West Bank

ECONOMY

Economy - overview: The West Bank - the larger of the two areas under the Palestinian Authority (PA) - has experienced a general decline in economic growth and a degradation in economic conditions made worse since the second intifadah began in September 2000. The downturn has been largely the result of the Israeli closure policies - the imposition of border closures in response to security incidents in Israel - which disrupted labor and commodity market relationships. In 2001, and even more severely in 2002, Israeli military measures in PA areas resulted in the destruction of much capital plant, the disruption of administrative structure, and widespread business closures. Including the Gaza Strip, the UN estimates that more than 100,000 Palestinians out of the 125,000 who used to work in Israeli settlements, or in joint industrial zones, have lost their jobs. International aid of $2 billion to the West Bank and Gaza strip in 2004 prevented the complete collapse of the economy and allowed some reforms in the government's financial operations. In 2005 high unemployment and limited trade opportunities, due to continued closures both within the West Bank and externally, have stymied growth.
GDP (purchasing power parity): $1.8 billion (2003 est.)
GDP (official exchange rate): NA
GDP - real growth rate: 6.2% (2004 est.)
GDP - per capita: purchasing power parity - $1,100 (2003 est.)
GDP - composition by sector:
agriculture: 9%
industry: 28%
services: 63%
note: includes Gaza Strip (2002 est.)
Labor force: 614,000 (April-June 2005)
Labor force - by occupation: agriculture 18.4%, industry 24%, services 57.6% (April-June 2005)
Unemployment rate: 19.9% (includes Gaza Strip) (January-September 2005)
Population below poverty line: 46% including Gaza Strip (2004 est.)
Household income or consumption by percentage share:
lowest 10%: NA
highest 10%: NA
Inflation rate (consumer prices): 2.2% (includes Gaza Strip) (2001 est.)
Budget:
revenues: $964 million
expenditures: $1.34 billion, including capital expenditures of NA; note - these budget data include Gaza Strip (2004)
Agriculture - products: olives, citrus, vegetables; beef, dairy products
Industries: generally small family businesses that produce cement, textiles, soap, olive-wood carvings, and mother-of-pearl souvenirs; the Israelis have established

some small-scale, modern industries in the settlements and industrial centers
Industrial production growth rate: NA
Electricity - production: NA kWh; note - most electricity imported from Israel; East Jerusalem Electric Company buys and distributes electricity to Palestinians in East Jerusalem and its concession in the West Bank; the Israel Electric Company directly supplies electricity to most Jewish residents and military facilities; some Palestinian municipalities, such as Nablus and Janin, generate their own electricity from small power plants
Electricity - production by source:
fossil fuel: 100%
hydro: 0%
nuclear: 0%
other: 0% (2001)
Electricity - consumption: NA kWh
Electricity - imports: NA kWh
Exports: $270 million f.o.b., includes Gaza Strip (2003)
Exports - partners: Israel, Jordan, Gaza Strip (2004)
Imports: $1.952 billion c.i.f., includes Gaza Strip (2003)
Imports - partners: Israel, Jordan, Gaza Strip (2004)
Debt - external: $0 (includes Gaza Strip) (2002)
Economic aid - recipient: $2 billion (includes Gaza Strip) (2004 est.)
Currency (code): new Israeli shekel (ILS); Jordanian dinar (JOD)
Currency code: ILS; JOD
Exchange rates: new Israeli shekels per US dollar - 4.35 (2005), 4.482 (2004), 4.5541 (2003), 4.7378 (2002), 4.2057 (2001)
Fiscal year: calendar year (since 1 January 1992)

COMMUNICATIONS

Telephones - main lines in use: 301,600 (total for West Bank and Gaza Strip) (2002)
Telephones - mobile cellular: 480,000 (cellular subscribers in both West Bank and Gaza Strip) (2003)
Telephone system:
general assessment: NA
domestic: NA
international: NA
note: Israeli company BEZEK and the Palestinian company PALTEL are responsible for communication services in the West Bank
Radio broadcast stations: AM 1, FM 20, shortwave 0
note: the Palestinian Broadcasting Corporation broadcasts from an AM station in Ramallah on 675 kHz; numerous local, private stations are reported to be in operation (2005)
Radios: NA; note - most Palestinian households have radios (1999)
Television broadcast stations: NA
Televisions: NA; note - many Palestinian households have televisions (1999)
Internet country code: .ps
Internet Service Providers (ISPs): 8 (1999)
Internet users: 145,000 (includes Gaza Strip) (2003)

TRANSPORTATION

Airports: 3 (2004 est.)
Airports - with paved runways:
total: 3
2,438 to 3,047 m: 1
1,524 to 2,437 m: 1
under 914 m: 1 (2005 est.)
Roadways:
total: 4,500 km
paved: 2,700 km
unpaved: 1,800 km
note: Israelis have developed many highways to service Jewish settlements (1997 est.)

MILITARY

Military expenditures - dollar figure: NA
Military expenditures - percent of GDP: NA

TRANSNATIONAL ISSUES

Disputes - international: West Bank and Gaza Strip are Israeli-occupied with current status subject to the Israeli-Palestinian Interim Agreement - permanent status to be determined through further negotiation; Israel continues construction of a "seam line" separation barrier along parts of the Green Line and within the West Bank; Israel announced its intention to pull out settlers and withdraw from four settlements in the northern West Bank in 2005; since 1948, about 350 peacekeepers from the UN Truce Supervision Organization (UNTSO), headquartered in Jerusalem, monitor ceasefires, supervise armistice agreements, prevent isolated incidents from escalating, and assist other UN personnel in the region
Refugees and internally displaced persons:
refugees (country of origin): 665,246 (Palestinian Refugees (UNRWA)) (2004)

WESTERN SAHARA

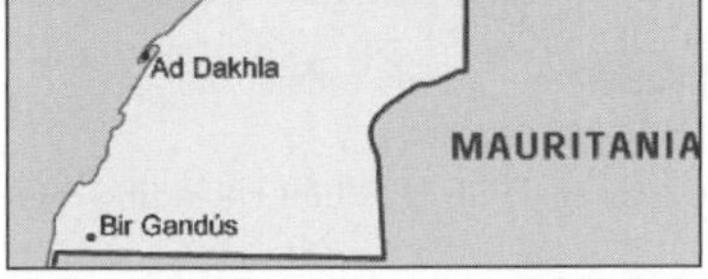

INTRODUCTION

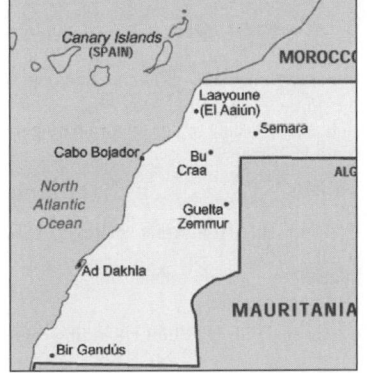

Background: Morocco virtually annexed the northern two-thirds of Western Sahara (formerly Spanish Sahara) in 1976, and the rest of the territory in 1979, following Mauritania's withdrawal. A guerrilla war with the Polisario Front contesting Rabat's sovereignty ended in a 1991 UN-brokered cease-fire; a UN-organized referendum on final status has been repeatedly postponed.

GEOGRAPHY

Location: Northern Africa, bordering the North Atlantic Ocean, between Mauritania and Morocco
Geographic coordinates: 24 30 N, 13 00 W
Map references: Africa
Area:
total: 266,000 sq km
land: 266,000 sq km
water: 0 sq km
Area - comparative: about the size of Colorado
Land boundaries:
total: 2,046 km
border countries: Algeria 42 km, Mauritania 1,561 km, Morocco 443 km
Coastline: 1,110 km
Maritime claims: contingent upon resolution of sovereignty issue
Climate: hot, dry desert; rain is rare; cold offshore air currents produce fog and heavy dew
Terrain: mostly low, flat desert with large areas of rocky or sandy surfaces rising to small mountains in south and northeast
Elevation extremes:
lowest point: Sebjet Tah -55 m
highest point: unnamed location 463 m
Natural resources: phosphates, iron ore
Land use:
arable land: 0.02%
permanent crops: 0%
other: 99.98% (2001)
Irrigated land: NA sq km
Natural hazards: hot, dry, dust/sand-laden sirocco wind can occur during winter and spring; widespread harmattan

haze exists 60% of time, often severely restricting visibility
Environment - current issues: sparse water and lack of arable land
Environment - international agreements:
party to: none of the selected agreements
signed, but not ratified: none of the selected agreements
Geography - note: the waters off the coast are particularly rich fishing areas

PEOPLE

Population: 273,008 (July 2005 est.)
Age structure:
0-14 years: NA
15-64 years: NA
65 years and over: NA
Population growth rate: NA
Birth rate: NA births/1,000 population
Death rate: NA births/1,000 population
Sex ratio: NA
Infant mortality rate:
total: NA
male: NA
female: NA
Life expectancy at birth:
total population: NA years
male: NA years
female: NA years
Total fertility rate: NA children born/woman
HIV/AIDS - adult prevalence rate: NA
HIV/AIDS - people living with HIV/AIDS: NA
HIV/AIDS - deaths: NA
Major infectious diseases:
degree of risk: intermediate
food or waterborne diseases: bacterial and protozoal diarrhea, hepatitis A, and typhoid fever
vectorborne diseases: may be a significant risk in some locations during the transmission season (typically April through November) (2004)
Nationality:
noun: Sahrawi(s), Sahraoui(s)
adjective: Sahrawi, Sahrawian, Sahraouian
Ethnic groups: Arab, Berber
Religions: Muslim
Languages: Hassaniya Arabic, Moroccan Arabic
Literacy:
definition: NA
total population: NA%
male: NA%
female: NA%

GOVERNMENT

Country name:
conventional long form: none
conventional short form: Western Sahara
former: Spanish Sahara
Government type: legal status of territory and issue of sovereignty unresolved; territory contested by Morocco and Polisario Front (Popular Front for the Liberation of the Saguia el Hamra and Rio de Oro), which in February 1976 formally proclaimed a government-in-exile of the Sahrawi Arab Democratic Republic (SADR), led by President Mohamed ABDELAZIZ; territory partitioned between Morocco and Mauritania in April 1976, with Morocco acquiring northern two-thirds; Mauritania, under pressure from Polisario guerrillas, abandoned all claims to its portion in August 1979; Morocco moved to occupy that sector shortly thereafter and has since asserted administrative control; the Polisario's government-in-exile was seated as an OAU member in 1984; guerrilla activities continued sporadically, until a UN-monitored cease-fire was implemented 6 September 1991
Capital: none
Administrative divisions: none (under de facto control of Morocco)
Suffrage: none; a UN-sponsored voter identification campaign not yet completed
Executive branch: none
Political pressure groups and leaders: none
International organization participation: none
Diplomatic representation in the US: none
Diplomatic representation from the US: none

ECONOMY

Economy - overview: Western Sahara depends on pastoral nomadism, fishing, and phosphate mining as the principal sources of income for the population. The territory lacks sufficient rainfall for sustainable agricultural production, and most of the food for the urban population must be imported. All trade and other economic activities are controlled by the Moroccan Government. Moroccan energy interests in 2001 signed contracts to explore for oil off the coast of Western Sahara, which has angered the Polisario. Incomes and standards of living in Western Sahara are substantially below the Moroccan level.
GDP (purchasing power parity): NA
GDP (official exchange rate): NA
GDP - real growth rate: NA
GDP - per capita: NA
GDP - composition by sector:
agriculture: NA
industry: NA
services: 40% (1996 est.)
Labor force: 12,000
Labor force - by occupation: animal husbandry and subsistence farming 50%
Unemployment rate: NA
Population below poverty line: NA
Household income or consumption by percentage share:
lowest 10%: NA
highest 10%: NA
Inflation rate (consumer prices): NA
Budget:
revenues: NA
expenditures: NA, including capital expenditures of NA
Public debt: 68.1% of GDP (2005 est.)
Agriculture - products: fruits and vegetables (grown in the few oases); camels, sheep, goats (kept by nomads)
Industries: phosphate mining, handicrafts
Industrial production growth rate: NA
Electricity - production: 85 million kWh (2003)
Electricity - production by source:
fossil fuel: 100%
hydro: 0%
nuclear: 0%
other: 0%
Electricity - consumption: 83.7 million kWh (2003)
Electricity - exports: 0 kWh (2003)
Electricity - imports: 0 kWh (2003)
Oil - production: 0 bbl/day (2003 est.)
Oil - consumption: 1,750 bbl/day (2003 est.)
Oil - exports: NA (2001)
Oil - imports: NA (2001)
Exports: NA
Exports - partners: Morocco claims and administers Western Sahara, so trade partners are included in overall Moroccan accounts (2004)
Imports: NA
Imports - partners: Morocco claims and administers Western Sahara, so trade partners are included in overall Moroccan accounts (2004)
Debt - external: NA
Economic aid - recipient: NA
Currency (code): Moroccan dirham (MAD)
Currency code: MAD
Exchange rates: Moroccan dirhams per US dollar - NA (2005), 8.868 (2004), 9.5744 (2003), 11.0206 (2002), 11.303 (2001)
Fiscal year: calendar year

COMMUNICATIONS

Telephones - main lines in use: about 2,000 (1999 est.)
Telephones - mobile cellular: 0 (1999)
Telephone system:
general assessment: sparse and limited system
domestic: NA
international: country code - 212; tied into Morocco's system by microwave radio relay, tropospheric scatter, and satellite; satellite earth stations - 2 Intelsat (Atlantic Ocean) linked to Rabat, Morocco
Radio broadcast stations: AM 2, FM 0, shortwave 0 (1998)

Radios: 56,000 (1997)
Television broadcast stations: NA
Televisions: 6,000 (1997)
Internet country code: .eh
Internet Service Providers (ISPs): 1 (2000)
Internet users: NA

TRANSPORTATION

Airports: 11 (2004 est.)
Airports - with paved runways:
total: 3
2,438 to 3,047 m: 3 (2005 est.)
Airports - with unpaved runways:
total: 8
1,524 to 2,437 m: 1
914 to 1,523 m: 4
under 914 m: 3 (2005 est.)
Roadways:
total: 6,200 km
paved: 1,350 km
unpaved: 4,850 km (1991 est)
Ports and terminals: Ad Dakhla, Cabo Bojador, Laayoune (El Aaiun)

TRANSNATIONAL ISSUES

Disputes - international: Morocco claims and administers Western Sahara, whose sovereignty remains unresolved - UN-administered cease-fire has remained in effect since September 1991, administered by the UN Mission for the Referendum in Western Sahara (MINURSO), but attempts to hold a referendum have failed and parties thus far have rejected all brokered proposals

WORLD

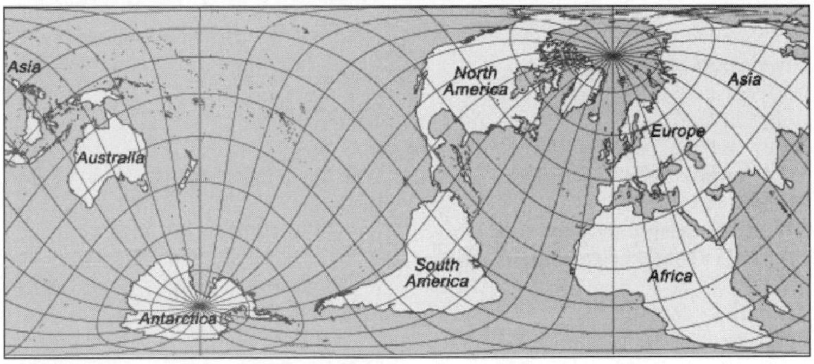

INTRODUCTION

Background: Globally, the 20th century was marked by: (a) two devastating world wars; (b) the Great Depression of the 1930s; (c) the end of vast colonial empires; (d) rapid advances in science and technology, from the first airplane flight at Kitty Hawk, North Carolina (US) to the landing on the moon; (e) the Cold War between the Western alliance and the Warsaw Pact nations; (f) a sharp rise in living standards in North America, Europe, and Japan; (g) increased concerns about the environment, including loss of forests, shortages of energy and water, the decline in biological diversity, and air pollution; (h) the onset of the AIDS epidemic; and (i) the ultimate emergence of the US as the only world superpower. The planet's population continues to explode: from 1 billion in 1820, to 2 billion in 1930, 3 billion in 1960, 4 billion in 1974, 5 billion in 1988, and 6 billion in 2000. For the 21st century, the continued exponential growth in science and technology raises both hopes (e.g., advances in medicine) and fears (e.g., development of even more lethal weapons of war).

GEOGRAPHY

Map references: Physical Map of the World, Political Map of the World, Standard Time Zones of the World
Area:
total: 510.072 million sq km
land: 148.94 million sq km
water: 361.132 million sq km
note: 70.8% of the world's surface is water, 29.2% is land
Area - comparative: land area about 16 times the size of the US
Land boundaries: the land boundaries in the world total 250,472 km (not counting shared boundaries twice); two nations, China and Russia, each border 14 other countries
note: 43 nations and other areas are landlocked, these include: Afghanistan, Andorra, Armenia, Austria, Azerbaijan, Belarus, Bhutan, Bolivia, Botswana, Burkina Faso, Burundi, Central African Republic, Chad, Czech Republic, Ethiopia, Holy See (Vatican City), Hungary, Kazakhstan, Kyrgyzstan, Laos, Lesotho, Liechtenstein, Luxembourg, Macedonia, Malawi, Mali, Moldova, Mongolia, Nepal, Niger, Paraguay, Rwanda, San Marino, Slovakia, Swaziland, Switzerland, Tajikistan, Turkmenistan, Uganda, Uzbekistan, West Bank, Zambia, Zimbabwe; two of these, Liechtenstein and Uzbekistan, are doubly landlocked
Coastline: 356,000 km
note: 98 nations and other entities are islands that border no other countries, they include: American Samoa, Anguilla, Antigua and Barbuda, Aruba, Ashmore and Cartier Islands, The Bahamas, Bahrain, Baker Island, Barbados, Bassas da India, Bermuda, Bouvet Island, British Indian Ocean Territory, British Virgin Islands, Cape Verde, Cayman Islands, Christmas Island, Clipperton Island, Cocos (Keeling) Islands, Comoros, Cook Islands, Coral Sea Islands, Cuba, Cyprus, Dominica, Europa Island, Falkland Islands (Islas Malvinas), Faroe Islands, Fiji, French Polynesia, French Southern and Antarctic Lands, Glorioso Islands, Greenland, Grenada, Guam, Guernsey, Heard Island and McDonald Islands, Howland Island, Iceland, Jamaica, Jan Mayen, Japan, Jarvis Island, Jersey, Johnston Atoll, Juan de Nova Island, Kingman Reef, Kiribati, Madagascar, Maldives, Malta, Isle of Man, Marshall Islands, Martinique, Mauritius, Mayotte, Federated States of Micronesia, Midway Islands, Montserrat, Nauru, Navassa Island, New Caledonia, New Zealand, Niue, Norfolk Island, Northern Mariana Islands, Palau, Palmyra Atoll, Paracel Islands, Philippines, Pitcairn Islands, Puerto Rico, Reunion, Saint Helena, Saint Kitts and Nevis, Saint Lucia, Saint Pierre and Miquelon, Saint Vincent and the Grenadines, Samoa, Sao Tome and Principe, Seychelles, Singapore, Solomon Islands, South Georgia and the South Sandwich Islands, Spratly Islands, Sri Lanka, Svalbard, Tokelau, Tonga, Trinidad and Tobago, Tromelin Island, Turks and Caicos Islands, Tuvalu, Vanuatu, Virgin Islands, Wake Island, Wallis and Futuna, Taiwan
Maritime claims: a variety of situations exist, but in general, most countries make the following claims measured from the mean low-tide baseline as described in the 1982 UN Convention on the Law of the Sea: territorial sea - 12 nm, contiguous zone - 24 nm, and exclusive economic zone - 200 nm; additional zones provide for exploitation of continental shelf resources and an exclusive fishing zone; boundary situations with neighboring

states prevent many countries from extending their fishing or economic zones to a full 200 nm
Climate: two large areas of polar climates separated by two rather narrow temperate zones form a wide equatorial band of tropical to subtropical climates
Terrain: the greatest ocean depth is the Mariana Trench at 10,924 m in the Pacific Ocean
Elevation extremes:
lowest point: Bentley Subglacial Trench -2,540 m
note: in the oceanic realm, Challenger Deep in the Mariana Trench is the lowest point, lying -10,924 m below the surface of the Pacific Ocean
highest point: Mount Everest 8,850 m
Natural resources: the rapid depletion of nonrenewable mineral resources, the depletion of forest areas and wetlands, the extinction of animal and plant species, and the deterioration in air and water quality (especially in Eastern Europe, the former USSR, and China) pose serious long-term problems that governments and peoples are only beginning to address
Land use:
arable land: 10.73%
permanent crops: 1%
other: 88.27% (2001)
Irrigated land: 2,714,320 sq km (1998 est.)
Natural hazards: large areas subject to severe weather (tropical cyclones), natural disasters (earthquakes, landslides, tsunamis, volcanic eruptions)
Environment - current issues: large areas subject to overpopulation, industrial disasters, pollution (air, water, acid rain, toxic substances), loss of vegetation (overgrazing, deforestation, desertification), loss of wildlife, soil degradation, soil depletion, erosion
Geography - note: the world is now thought to be about 4.55 billion years old, just about one-third of the 13-billion-year age estimated for the universe

PEOPLE

Population: 6,446,131,400 (July 2005 est.)
Age structure:
0-14 years: 27.8% (male 919,726,623; female 870,468,158)
15-64 years: 64.9% (male 2,117,230,183; female 2,066,864,970)
65 years and over: 7.3% (male 207,903,775; female 263,627,270)
note: some countries do not maintain age structure information, thus a slight discrepancy exists between the total world population and the total for world age structure (2005 est.)
Median age:
total: 27.6 years
male: 27 years
female: 28.2 years (2005 est.)
Population growth rate: 1.14% (2005 est.)
Birth rate: 20.15 births/1,000 population (2005 est.)
Death rate: 8.78 deaths/1,000 population (2005 est.)
Sex ratio:
at birth: 1.06 male(s)/female
under 15 years: 1.06 male(s)/female
15-64 years: 1.03 male(s)/female
65 years and over: 0.79 male(s)/female
total population: 1.01 male(s)/female (2005 est.)
Infant mortality rate:
total: 50.11 deaths/1,000 live births
male: 52.1 deaths/1,000 live births
female: 48.01 deaths/1,000 live births (2005 est.)
Life expectancy at birth:
total population: 64.33 years
male: 62.73 years
female: 66.04 years (2005 est.)
Total fertility rate: 2.6 children born/woman (2005 est.)
HIV/AIDS - adult prevalence rate: NA%
HIV/AIDS - people living with HIV/AIDS: NA
HIV/AIDS - deaths: NA
Religions: Christians 33.03% (of which Roman Catholics 17.33%, Protestants 5.8%, Orthodox 3.42%, Anglicans 1.23%), Muslims 20.12%, Hindus 13.34%, Buddhists 5.89%, Sikhs 0.39%, Jews 0.23%, other religions 12.61%, non-religious 12.03%, atheists 2.36% (2004 est.)
Languages: Chinese, Mandarin 13.69%, Spanish 5.05%, English 4.84%, Hindi 2.82%, Portuguese 2.77%, Bengali 2.68%, Russian 2.27%, Japanese 1.99%, German, Standard 1.49%, Chinese, Wu 1.21% (2004 est.)
note: percents are for "first language" speakers only
Literacy:
definition: age 15 and over can read and write
total population: 82%
male: 87%
female: 77%
note: over two-thirds of the world's 785 million illiterate adults are found in only eight countries (India, China, Bangladesh, Pakistan, Nigeria, Ethiopia, Indonesia, and Egypt); of all the illiterate adults in the world, two-thirds are women; extremely low literacy rates are concentrated in three regions, South and West Asia, Sub-Saharan Africa, and the Arab states, where around one-third of the men and half of all women are illiterate (2005 est.)

GOVERNMENT

Administrative divisions: 271 nations, dependent areas, and other entities
Legal system: all members of the UN are parties to the statute that established the International Court of Justice (ICJ) or World Court

ECONOMY

Economy - overview: Global output rose by 4.9% in 2004, led by China (9.1%), Russia (6.7%), and India (6.2%). The other 14 successor nations of the USSR and the other old Warsaw Pact nations again experienced widely divergent growth rates; the three Baltic nations continued as strong performers, in the 7% range of growth. Growth results posted by the major industrial countries varied from a small gain in Italy (1.3%) to a strong gain by the United States (4.4%). The developing nations also varied in their growth results, with many countries facing population increases that erode gains in output. Externally, the nation-state, as a bedrock economic-political institution, is steadily losing control over international flows of people, goods, funds, and technology. Internally, the central government often finds its control over resources slipping as separatist regional movements - typically based on ethnicity - gain momentum, e.g., in many of the successor states of the former Soviet Union, in the former Yugoslavia, in India, in Iraq, in Indonesia, and in Canada. Externally, the central government is losing decisionmaking powers to international bodies, notably the European Union. In Western Europe, governments face the difficult political problem of channeling resources away from welfare programs in order to increase investment and strengthen incentives to seek employment. The addition of 75 million people each year to an already overcrowded globe is exacerbating the problems of pollution, desertification, underemployment, epidemics, and famine. Because of their own internal problems and priorities, the industrialized countries devote insufficient resources to deal effectively with the poorer areas of the world, which, at least from an economic point of view, are becoming further marginalized. The introduction of the euro as the common currency of much of Western Europe in January 1999, while paving the way for an integrated economic powerhouse, poses economic risks because of varying levels of income and cultural and political differences among the participating nations. The terrorist attacks on the US on 11 September 2001 accentuate a further growing risk to global prosperity, illustrated, for example, by the reallocation of resources away from investment to anti-

terrorist programs. The opening of war in March 2003 between a US-led coalition and Iraq added new uncertainties to global economic prospects. After the coalition victory, the complex political difficulties and the high economic cost of establishing domestic order in Iraq became major global problems that continued into 2005.
GDP (purchasing power parity): GWP (gross world product) - purchasing power parity - $59.38 trillion (2005 est.)
GDP (official exchange rate): $43.92 trillion (2005 est.)
GDP - real growth rate: 4.3% (2005 est.)
GDP - per capita: purchasing power parity - $9,300 (2005 est.)
GDP - composition by sector:
agriculture: 4%
industry: 32%
services: 64% (2004 est.)
Labor force: NA
Labor force - by occupation: agriculture NA%, industry NA%, services NA%
Unemployment rate: 30% combined unemployment and underemployment in many non-industrialized countries; developed countries typically 4%-12% unemployment
Household income or consumption by percentage share:
lowest 10%: NA %
highest 10%: NA %
Inflation rate (consumer prices): developed countries 1% to 4% typically; developing countries 5% to 60% typically; national inflation rates vary widely in individual cases, from declining prices in Japan to hyperinflation in several Third World countries (2004 est.)
Industries: dominated by the onrush of technology, especially in computers, robotics, telecommunications, and medicines and medical equipment; most of these advances take place in OECD nations; only a small portion of non-OECD countries have succeeded in rapidly adjusting to these technological forces; the accelerated development of new industrial (and agricultural) technology is complicating already grim environmental problems
Industrial production growth rate: 3% (2003 est.)
Electricity - production: 15.85 trillion kWh (2003 est.)
Electricity - production by source:
fossil fuel: NA
hydro: NA
nuclear: NA
other: NA (2001)
Electricity - consumption: 14.28 trillion kWh (2003 est.)
Electricity - exports: 536 billion kWh (2003)
Electricity - imports: 530.2 billion kWh (2003)
Oil - production: 79.65 million bbl/day (2003 est.)
Oil - consumption: 80.1 million bbl/day (2003 est.)
Oil - proved reserves: 1.025 trillion bbl (1 January 2002 est.)
Natural gas - production: 2.64 trillion cu m (2001 est.)
Natural gas - consumption: 2.619 trillion cu m (2001 est.)
Natural gas - exports: 659.5 billion cu m (2001 est.)
Natural gas - imports: 694.2 billion cu m (2001 est.)
Natural gas - proved reserves: 161.2 trillion cu m (1 January 2002)
Exports: $9.099 trillion f.o.b. (2004 est.)
Exports - partners: US 15.7%, Germany 7.7%, China 5.4%, France 5.1%, UK 5.1%, Japan 4.5% (2004)
Imports: $9.47 trillion f.o.b. (2004 est.)
Imports - partners: Germany 9.4%, US 9.3%, China 8.5%, Japan 6.5%, France 4.5% (2004)
Debt - external: $12.7 trillion (2004 est.)
Economic aid - recipient: $154 billion official development assistance (ODA) (2004)

COMMUNICATIONS

Telephones - main lines in use: 843,923,500 (2003)
Telephones - mobile cellular: NA
Telephone system:
general assessment: NA
domestic: NA
international: NA
Radio broadcast stations: AM NA, FM NA, shortwave NA
Radios: NA
Television broadcast stations: NA
Televisions: NA
Internet Service Providers (ISPs): 10,350 (2000 est.)
Internet users: 604,111,719 (2002 est.)

TRANSPORTATION

Airports: 49,973 (2004)
Railways:
total: 1,115,205 km
broad gauge: 257,481 km
standard gauge: 671,413 km
narrow gauge: 186,311 km (2003)
Roadways:
total: 32,345,165 km
paved: 19,403,061 km
unpaved: 12,942,104 km (2002)
Waterways: 671,886 km (2004):
Merchant marine:
total ships: 30,936 (2005)

MILITARY

Military expenditures - dollar figure: aggregate real expenditure on arms worldwide in 1999 remained at approximately the 1998 level, about three-quarters of a trillion dollars (1999 est.)
Military expenditures - percent of GDP: roughly 2% of gross world product (1999 est.)

TRANSNATIONAL ISSUES

Disputes - international: stretching over 250,000 km, the world's 325 international land boundaries separate the 192 independent states and 73 dependencies, areas of special sovereignty, and other miscellaneous entities; ethnicity, culture, race, religion, and language have divided states into separate political entities as much as history, physical terrain, political fiat, or conquest, resulting in sometimes arbitrary and imposed boundaries; maritime states have claimed limits and have so far established over 130 maritime boundaries and joint development zones to allocate ocean resources and to provide for national security at sea; boundary, borderland/resource, and territorial disputes vary in intensity from managed or dormant to violent or militarized; most disputes over the alignment of political boundaries are confined to short segments and are today less common and less hostile than borderland, resource, and territorial disputes; undemarcated, indefinite, porous, and unmanaged boundaries, however, encourage illegal cross-border activities, uncontrolled migration, and confrontation; territorial disputes may evolve from historical and/or cultural claims, or they may be brought on by resource competition; ethnic clashes continue to be responsible for much of the territorial fragmentation around the world; disputes over islands at sea or in rivers frequently form the source of territorial and boundary conflict; other sources of contention include access to water and mineral (especially petroleum) resources, fisheries, and arable land; nonetheless, most nations cooperate to clarify their international boundaries and to resolve territorial and resource disputes peacefully; regional discord directly affects the sustenance and welfare of local populations, often leaving the world community to cope with resultant refugees, hunger, disease, impoverishment, deforestation, and desertification
Refugees and internally displaced persons: the United Nations High Commissioner for Refugees (UNHCR) estimated that in December 2003 there was a global population of 9.7 million refugees and as many as 25 million IDPs
Illicit drugs:
cocaine: worldwide, coca is grown on an estimated 173,450 hectares - almost exclusively in South America with 70%

in Colombia; potential cocaine production during 2003 is estimated at 728 metric tons (or 835 metric tons of export quality cocaine); coca eradication programs continue in Bolivia, Colombia, and Peru; 376 metric tons of export quality cocaine are documented to have been seized in 2003, and 26 metric tons disrupted (jettisoned or destroyed); consumption of export quality cocaine is estimated to have been 800 metric tons
opiates: cultivation of opium poppy occurred on an estimated 137,944 hectares in 2003 - mostly in Southwest and Southeast Asia - with 44% in Afghanistan, potentially produced 3,775 metric tons of opium, which conceivably could be converted to the equivalent of 429 metric tons of pure heroin; opium eradication programs have been undertaken in Afghanistan, Burma, Colombia, Mexico, Pakistan, Thailand, and Vietnam

YEMEN

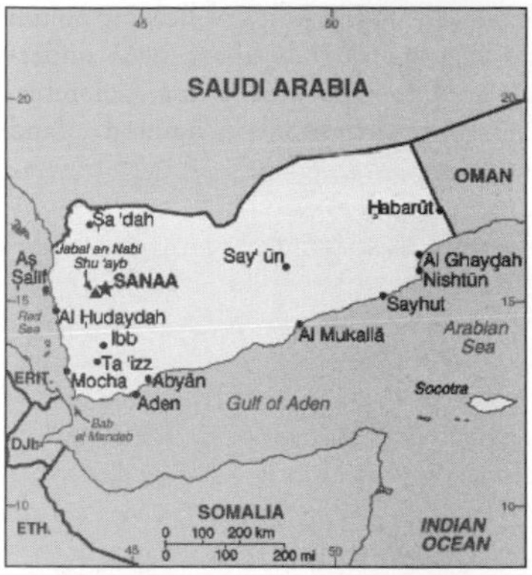

INTRODUCTION

Background: North Yemen became independent of the Ottoman Empire in 1918. The British, who had set up a protectorate area around the southern port of Aden in the 19th century, withdrew in 1967 from what became South Yemen. Three years later, the southern government adopted a Marxist orientation. The massive exodus of hundreds of thousands of Yemenis from the south to the north contributed to two decades of hostility between the states. The two countries were formally unified as the Republic of Yemen in 1990. A southern secessionist movement in 1994 was quickly subdued. In 2000, Saudi Arabia and Yemen agreed to a delimitation of their border.

GEOGRAPHY

Location: Middle East, bordering the Arabian Sea, Gulf of Aden, and Red Sea, between Oman and Saudi Arabia
Geographic coordinates: 15 00 N, 48 00 E
Map references: Middle East
Area:
total: 527,970 sq km
land: 527,970 sq km
water: 0 sq km
note: includes Perim, Socotra, the former Yemen Arab Republic (YAR or North Yemen), and the former People's Democratic Republic of Yemen (PDRY or South Yemen)
Area - comparative: slightly larger than twice the size of Wyoming
Land boundaries:
total: 1,746 km
border countries: Oman 288 km, Saudi Arabia 1,458 km
Coastline: 1,906 km
Maritime claims:
territorial sea: 12 nm
contiguous zone: 24 nm
exclusive economic zone: 200 nm
continental shelf: 200 nm or to the edge of the continental margin
Climate: mostly desert; hot and humid along west coast; temperate in western mountains affected by seasonal monsoon; extraordinarily hot, dry, harsh desert in east
Terrain: narrow coastal plain backed by flat-topped hills and rugged mountains; dissected upland desert plains in center slope into the desert interior of the Arabian Peninsula
Elevation extremes:
lowest point: Arabian Sea 0 m
highest point: Jabal an Nabi Shu'ayb 3,760 m
Natural resources: petroleum, fish, rock salt, marble, small deposits of coal, gold, lead, nickel, and copper, fertile soil in west
Land use:
arable land: 2.78%
permanent crops: 0.24%
other: 96.98% (2001
Irrigated land: 4,900 sq km (1998 est.)
Natural hazards: sandstorms and dust storms in summer
Environment - current issues: very limited natural fresh water resources; inadequate supplies of potable water; overgrazing; soil erosion; desertification
Environment - international agreements:
party to: Biodiversity, Climate Change, Climate Change-Kyoto Protocol, Desertification, Endangered Species, Environmental Modification, Hazardous Wastes, Law of the Sea, Ozone Layer Protection
signed, but not ratified: none of the selected agreements
Geography - note: strategic location on Bab el Mandeb, the strait linking the Red Sea and the Gulf of Aden, one of world's most active shipping lanes

PEOPLE

Population: 20,727,063 (July 2005 est.)
Age structure:
0-14 years: 46.5% (male 4,905,831/female 4,727,177)
15-64 years: 50.8% (male 5,364,711/female 5,172,811)
65 years and over: 2.7% (male 274,166/female 282,367) (2005 est.)
Median age:
total: 16.54 years
male: 16.53 years
female: 16.56 years (2005 est.)
Population growth rate: 3.45% (2005 est.)
Birth rate: 43.07 births/1,000 population (2005 est.)
Death rate: 8.53 deaths/1,000 population (2005 est.)
Net migration rate: 0 migrant(s)/1,000 population (2005 est.)
Sex ratio:
at birth: 1.05 male(s)/female
under 15 years: 1.04 male(s)/female
15-64 years: 1.04 male(s)/female
65 years and over: 0.97 male(s)/female
total population: 1.04 male(s)/female (2005 est.)
Infant mortality rate:
total: 61.5 deaths/1,000 live births
male: 66.26 deaths/1,000 live births
female: 56.49 deaths/1,000 live births (2005 est.)
Life expectancy at birth:
total population: 61.75 years
male: 59.89 years
female: 63.71 years (2005 est.)
Total fertility rate: 6.67 children born/woman (2005 est.)
HIV/AIDS - adult prevalence rate: 0.1% (2001 est.)
HIV/AIDS - people living with HIV/AIDS: 12,000 (2001 est.)
HIV/AIDS - deaths: NA
Nationality:
noun: Yemeni(s)
adjective: Yemeni
Ethnic groups: predominantly Arab; but also Afro-Arab, South Asians, Europeans
Religions: Muslim including Shaf'i (Sunni) and Zaydi (Shi'a), small numbers of Jewish, Christian, and Hindu
Languages: Arabic
Literacy:
definition: age 15 and over can read and write
total population: 50.2%
male: 70.5%
female: 30% (2003 est.)

GOVERNMENT

Country name:
conventional long form: Republic of Yemen
conventional short form: Yemen
local long form: Al Jumhuriyah al Yamaniyah
local short form: Al Yaman
former: Yemen Arab Republic [Yemen (Sanaa) or North Yemen] and People's Democratic Republic of Yemen [Yemen (Aden) or South Yemen]
Government type: republic
Capital: Sanaa
Administrative divisions: 19 governorates (muhafazat, singular - muhafazah); Abyan, 'Adan, Ad Dali', Al Bayda', Al Hudaydah, Al Jawf, Al Mahrah, Al Mahwit, 'Amran, Dhamar, Hadramawt, Hajjah, Ibb, Lahij, Ma'rib, Sa'dah, San'a', Shabwah, Ta'izz
note: for electoral and administrative purposes, the capital city of Sanaa is treated as an additional governorate
Independence: 22 May 1990 (Republic of

Yemen established with the merger of the Yemen Arab Republic [Yemen (Sanaa) or North Yemen] and the Marxist-dominated People's Democratic Republic of Yemen [Yemen (Aden) or South Yemen]); note - previously North Yemen had become independent in November of 1918 (from the Ottoman Empire) and South Yemen had become independent on 30 November 1967 (from the UK)
National holiday: Unification Day, 22 May (1990)
Constitution: 16 May 1991; amended 29 September 1994 and February 2001
Legal system: based on Islamic law, Turkish law, English common law, and local tribal customary law; has not accepted compulsory ICJ jurisdiction
Suffrage: 18 years of age; universal
Executive branch:
chief of state: President Ali Abdallah SALIH (since 22 May 1990, the former president of North Yemen, assumed office upon the merger of North and South Yemen); Vice President Maj. Gen. Abd al-Rab Mansur al-HADI (since 3 October 1994)
head of government: Prime Minister Abd al-Qadir BA JAMAL (since 4 April 2001)
cabinet: Council of Ministers appointed by the president on the advice of the prime minister
elections: president elected by direct, popular vote for a seven-year term (recently extended from a five-year term by constitutional amendment); election last held 23 September 1999 (next to be held September 2006); vice president appointed by the president; prime minister and deputy prime ministers appointed by the president
election results: Ali Abdallah SALIH elected president; percent of vote - Ali Abdallah SALIH 96.3%, Najib Qahtan AL-SHAABI 3.7%; note - elections for governate and district councils were held for the first time in February 2001 (next to be held September 2006)
Legislative branch: a new constitutional amendment ratified on 20 February 2001 created a bicameral legislature consisting of a Shura Council (111 seats; members appointed by the president) and a House of Representatives (301 seats; members elected by popular vote to serve six-year terms)
elections: last held 27 April 2003 (next to be held NA April 2009)
election results: percent of vote by party - NA%; seats by party - GPC 228, Islah 47, YSP 7, Nasserite Unionist Party 3, National Arab Socialist Ba'th Party 2, independents 14
Judicial branch: Supreme Court
Political parties and leaders: there are more than 12 political parties active in Yemen, some of the more prominent are: General People's Congress or GPC [President Ali Abdallah SALIH]; Islamic Reform Grouping or Islah [Shaykh Abdallah bin Husayn al-AHMAR]; Nasserite Unionist Party [Abdel Malik al-MAKHLAFI]; National Arab Socialist Ba'th Party [Dr. Qassim SALAAM]; Yemeni Socialist Party or YSP [Ali Salih MUQBIL]
note: President SALIH's General People's Congress or GPC won a landslide victory in the April 1997 legislative election and no longer governs in coalition with Shaykh Abdallah bin Husayn al-AHMAR's Islamic Reform Grouping or Islah - the two parties had been in coalition since the end of the civil war in 1994; the YSP, a loyal opposition party, represents the remnants of the former South Yemeni leadership; leaders of the 1994 secessionist movement have been pardoned by President SALIH and some are now returning to Yemen from exile
Political pressure groups and leaders: NA
International organization participation: AFESD, AMF, CAEU, FAO, G-77, IAEA, IBRD, ICAO, ICCt (signatory), ICFTU, ICRM, IDA, IDB, IFAD, IFC, IFRCS, ILO, IMF, IMO, Interpol, IOC, IOM, ISO (correspondent), ITU, LAS, MIGA, MINUSTAH, NAM, OAS (observer), OIC, ONUB, OPCW, UN, UNCTAD, UNESCO, UNHCR, UNIDO, UNMIS, UNOCI, UPU, WCO, WFTU, WHO, WIPO, WMO, WToO, WTO (observer)
Diplomatic representation in the US:
chief of mission: Ambassador Abd al-Wahab Abdallah al-HAJRI
chancery: 2319 Wyoming Avenue NW, Washington, DC 20008
telephone: [1] (202) 965-4760
FAX: [1] (202) 337-2017
Diplomatic representation from the US:
chief of mission: Ambassador Thomas C. KRAJESKI
embassy: Sa'awan Street, Sanaa
mailing address: P. O. Box 22347, Sanaa
telephone: [967] (1) 755-2000 ext. 2153 or 2266
FAX: [967] (1) 303-182
Flag description: three equal horizontal bands of red (top), white, and black; similar to the flag of Syria, which has two green stars and of Iraq which has three green stars (plus an Arabic inscription) in a horizontal line centered in the white band; also similar to the flag of Egypt, which has a heraldic eagle centered in the white band

ECONOMY

Economy - overview: Yemen, one of the poorest countries in the Arab world, has reported meager growth since 2000. Its economic fortunes depend mostly on oil. In 2005 oil revenues increased due to higher prices. Yemen was on an IMF-supported structural adjustment program designed to modernize and streamline the economy, which led to substantial foreign debt relief and restructuring. However government dedication to the program waned in 2001 for political reasons. Yemen is struggling to control excessive spending and rampant corruption. The population has grown increasingly upset over the economic situation. In July 2005 a reduction in fuel subsidies sparked riots in which over 20 Yemenis were killed and hundreds were injured.
GDP (purchasing power parity): $17.2 billion (2005 est.)
GDP (official exchange rate): $14.1 billion (2005 est.)
GDP - real growth rate: 2.5% (2005 est.)
GDP - per capita: purchasing power parity - $800 (2005 est.)
GDP - composition by sector:
agriculture: 13.3%
industry: 47.9%
services: 38.8% (2005 est.)
Labor force: 5.83 million (2005 est.)
Labor force - by occupation: most people are employed in agriculture and herding; services, construction, industry, and commerce account for less than one-fourth of the labor force
Unemployment rate: 35% (2003 est.)
Population below poverty line: 45.2% (2003)
Household income or consumption by percentage share:
lowest 10%: 3%
highest 10%: 25.9% (2003)
Distribution of family income - Gini index: 33.4 (1998)
Inflation rate (consumer prices): 9.6% (2005 est.)
Investment (gross fixed): 14.3% of GDP (2005 est.)
Budget:
revenues: $5.616 billion
expenditures: $5.719 billion, including capital expenditures of NA (2005 est.)
Public debt: 35.9% of GDP (2005 est.)
Agriculture - products: grain, fruits, vegetables, pulses, qat (mildly narcotic shrub), coffee, cotton; dairy products, livestock (sheep, goats, cattle, camels), poultry; fish
Industries: crude oil production and petroleum refining; small-scale production of cotton textiles and leather goods; food processing; handicrafts; small alu-

minum products factory; cement; commercial ship repair
Industrial production growth rate: 3% (2003 est.)
Electricity - production: 3.848 billion kWh (2003 est.)
Electricity - production by source:
fossil fuel: 100%
hydro: 0%
nuclear: 0%
other: 0% (2001)
Electricity - consumption: 2.827 billion kWh (2003 est.)
Electricity - exports: 0 kWh (2003)
Electricity - imports: 0 kWh (2003)
Oil - production: 387,500 bbl/day (2005 est.)
Oil - consumption: 80,000 bbl/day (2003 est.)
Oil - exports: 370,300 bbl/day (2003)
Oil - imports: NA (2001)
Oil - proved reserves: 4.37 billion bbl (2005 est.)
Natural gas - production: 0 cu m (2003 est.)
Natural gas - consumption: 0 cu m (2003 est.)
Natural gas - exports: 0 cu m (2003 est.)
Natural gas - imports: 0 cu m (2003 est.)
Natural gas - proved reserves: 480 billion cu m (2005)
Current account balance: $1.282 billion (2005 est.)
Exports: $6.387 billion f.o.b. (2005 est.)
Exports - partners: Thailand 33.8%, China 30.3%, Singapore 7.8% (2004)
Imports: $4.19 billion f.o.b. (2005 est.)
Imports - partners: UAE 12.2%, Saudi Arabia 9.7%, China 8.8%, France 7.3%, India 4.4%, US 4.4%, Kuwait 4.2% (2004)
Reserves of foreign exchange and gold: $5.858 billion (2005 est.)
Debt - external: $5.689 billion (2005 est.)
Economic aid - recipient: $2.3 billion (2003-07 disbursements) (2003-07 disbursements)
Currency (code): Yemeni rial (YER)
Currency code: YER
Exchange rates: Yemeni rials per US dollar - 192.67 (2005), 184.78 (2004), 183.45 (2003), 175.63 (2002), 168.67 (2001)
Fiscal year: calendar year

COMMUNICATIONS

Telephones - main lines in use: 542,200 (2002)
Telephones - mobile cellular: 411,100 (2002)
Telephone system:
general assessment: since unification in 1990, efforts have been made to create a national telecommunications network
domestic: the national network consists of microwave radio relay, cable, tropospheric scatter, and GSM cellular mobile telephone systems
international: country code - 967; satellite earth stations - 3 Intelsat (2 Indian Ocean and 1 Atlantic Ocean), 1 Intersputnik (Atlantic Ocean region), and 2 Arabsat; microwave radio relay to Saudi Arabia and Djibouti
Radio broadcast stations: AM 6, FM 1, shortwave 2 (1998)
Radios: 1.05 million (1997)
Television broadcast stations: 7 (plus several low-power repeaters) (1997)
Televisions: 470,000 (1997)
Internet country code: .ye
Internet hosts: 138 (2004)
Internet Service Providers (ISPs): 1 (2000)
Internet users: 100,000 (2002)

TRANSPORTATION

Airports: 44 (2004 est.)
Airports - with paved runways:
total: 16
over 3,047 m: 4
2,438 to 3,047 m: 8
1,524 to 2,437 m: 2
914 to 1,523 m: 1
under 914 m: 1 (2005 est.)
Airports - with unpaved runways:
total: 29
over 3,047 m: 3
2,438 to 3,047 m: 7
1,524 to 2,437 m: 4
914 to 1,523 m: 11
under 914 m: 4 (2005 est.)
Pipelines: gas 88 km; oil 1,174 km (2004)
Roadways:
total: 67,000 km
paved: 7,705 km
unpaved: 59,295 km (1999 est.)
Merchant marine:
total: 5 ships (1,000 GRT or over) 19,766 GRT/24,794 DWT
by type: cargo 1, chemical tanker 1, petroleum tanker 2, roll on/roll off 1
registered in other countries: 2 (2005)
Ports and terminals: Aden, Nishtun

MILITARY

Military branches: Army (includes Special Forces), Naval Forces and Coastal Defenses (includes Marines), Air Force (includes Air Defense Forces), Republican Guard (2002)
Military service age and obligation: 18 years of age for compulsory military service; conscript service obligation - 2 years (2004)
Manpower available for military service: *males age 18-49:* 4,058,223 (2005 est.)
Manpower fit for military service: *males age 18-49:* 2,790,705 (2005 est.)
Manpower reaching military service age annually: *males:* 236,517 (2005 est.)
Military expenditures - dollar figure: $885.5 million (2003)
Military expenditures - percent of GDP: 7.8% (2003)
Military - note: a Coast Guard was established in 2002

TRANSNATIONAL ISSUES

Disputes - international: Yemen protests Eritrea fishing around the Hanish Islands awarded to Yemen by the ICJ in 1999; despite resistance from nomadic groups, the demarcation of the Saudi Arabia-Yemen boundary established under the 2000 Jeddah Treaty is almost complete; Yemen protests Saudi erection of a concrete-filled pipe as a security barrier in 2004 to stem illegal cross-border activities in sections of the boundary
Refugees and internally displaced persons:
refugees (country of origin): 60,901 (Somalia) (2004)

Z

ZAMBIA

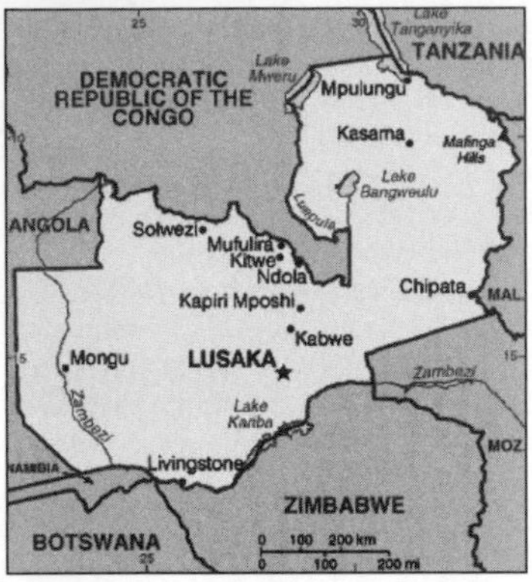

INTRODUCTION

Background: The territory of Northern Rhodesia was administered by the South Africa Company from 1891 until it was taken over by the UK in 1923. During the 1920s and 1930s, advances in mining spurred development and immigration. The name was changed to Zambia upon independence in 1964. In the 1980s and 1990s, declining copper prices and a prolonged drought hurt the economy. Elections in 1991 brought an end to one-party rule, but the subsequent vote in 1996 saw blatant harassment of opposition parties. The election in 2001 was marked by administrative problems with three parties filing a legal petition challenging the election of ruling party candidate Levy MWANAWASA. The new president launched a far-reaching anti-corruption campaign in 2002, which resulted in the prosecution of former President Frederick CHILUBA and many of his supporters in late 2003. Opposition parties currently hold a majority of seats in the National Assembly.

GEOGRAPHY

Location: Southern Africa, east of Angola
Geographic coordinates: 15 00 S, 30 00 E
Map references: Africa
Area:
total: 752,614 sq km
land: 740,724 sq km
water: 11,890 sq km
Area - comparative: slightly larger than Texas
Land boundaries:
total: 5,664 km
border countries: Angola 1,110 km, Democratic Republic of the Congo 1,930 km, Malawi 837 km, Mozambique 419 km, Namibia 233 km, Tanzania 338 km, Zimbabwe 797 km
Coastline: 0 km (landlocked)
Maritime claims: none (landlocked)
Climate: tropical; modified by altitude; rainy season (October to April)
Terrain: mostly high plateau with some hills and mountains
Elevation extremes:
lowest point: Zambezi river 329 m
highest point: unnamed location in Mafinga Hills 2,301 m
Natural resources: copper, cobalt, zinc, lead, coal, emeralds, gold, silver, uranium, hydropower
Land use:
arable land: 7.08%
permanent crops: 0.03%
other: 92.9% (2001)
Irrigated land: 460 sq km (1998 est.)
Natural hazards: periodic drought, tropical storms (November to April)
Environment - current issues: air pollution and resulting acid rain in the mineral extraction and refining region; chemical runoff into watersheds; poaching seriously threatens rhinoceros, elephant, antelope, and large cat populations; deforestation; soil erosion; desertification; lack of adequate water treatment presents human health risks
Environment - international agreements:
party to: Biodiversity, Climate Change, Desertification, Endangered Species, Hazardous Wastes, Law of the Sea, Ozone Layer Protection, Wetlands
signed, but not ratified: Climate Change-Kyoto Protocol
Geography - note: landlocked; the Zambezi forms a natural riverine boundary with Zimbabwe

PEOPLE

Population: 11,261,795
note: estimates for this country explicitly take into account the effects of excess mortality due to AIDS; this can result in lower life expectancy, higher infant mortality and death rates, lower population and growth rates, and changes in the distribution of population by age and sex than would otherwise be expected (July 2005 est.)
Age structure:
0-14 years: 46.5% (male 2,626,911/female 2,609,857)
15-64 years: 51.1% (male 2,848,402/female 2,904,376)
65 years and over: 2.4% (male 118,043/female 154,206) (2005 est.)
Median age:
total: 16.46 years
male: 16.26 years
female: 16.67 years (2005 est.)
Population growth rate: 2.12% (2005 est.)
Birth rate: 41.38 births/1,000 population (2005 est.)
Death rate: 20.23 deaths/1,000 population (2005 est.)
Net migration rate: 0 migrant(s)/1,000 population (2005 est.)
Sex ratio:
at birth: 1.03 male(s)/female
under 15 years: 1.01 male(s)/female
15-64 years: 0.98 male(s)/female
65 years and over: 0.76 male(s)/female
total population: 0.99 male(s)/female (2005 est.)
Infant mortality rate:
total: 88.29 deaths/1,000 live births
male: 95.63 deaths/1,000 live births
female: 80.72 deaths/1,000 live births (2005 est.)
Life expectancy at birth:
total population: 39.7 years
male: 39.43 years
female: 39.98 years (2005 est.)
Total fertility rate: 5.47 children born/woman (2005 est.)
HIV/AIDS - adult prevalence rate: 16.5% (2003 est.)
HIV/AIDS - people living with HIV/AIDS: 920,000 (2003 est.)
HIV/AIDS - deaths: 89,000 (2003 est.)
Major infectious diseases:
degree of risk: very high
food or waterborne diseases: bacterial diarrhea, hepatitis A, and typhoid fever
vectorborne diseases: malaria and plague are high risks in some locations
water contact disease: schistosomiasis (2004)
Nationality:
noun: Zambian(s)
adjective: Zambian
Ethnic groups: African 98.7%, European 1.1%, other 0.2%
Religions: Christian 50%-75%, Muslim and Hindu 24%-49%, indigenous beliefs 1%
Languages: English (official), major vernaculars - Bemba, Kaonda, Lozi, Lunda, Luvale, Nyanja, Tonga, and about 70 other indigenous languages
Literacy:
definition: age 15 and over can read and write English
total population: 80.6%
male: 86.8%
female: 74.8% (2003 est.)

GOVERNMENT

Country name:
conventional long form: Republic of Zambia
conventional short form: Zambia
former: Northern Rhodesia
Government type: republic
Capital: Lusaka
Administrative divisions: 9 provinces; Central, Copperbelt, Eastern, Luapula,

Lusaka, Northern, North-Western, Southern, Western
Independence: 24 October 1964 (from UK)
National holiday: Independence Day, 24 October (1964)
Constitution: 24 August 1991
Legal system: based on English common law and customary law; judicial review of legislative acts in an ad hoc constitutional council; has not accepted compulsory ICJ jurisdiction
Suffrage: 18 years of age, universal
Executive branch:
chief of state: President Levy MWANAWASA (since 2 January 2002); Vice President Lupando MWAPE (since 4 October 2004); note - the president is both the chief of state and head of government
head of government: President Levy MWANAWASA (since 2 January 2002); Vice President Lupando MWAPE (since 4 October 2004); note - the president is both the chief of state and head of government
cabinet: Cabinet appointed by the president from among the members of the National Assembly
elections: president elected by popular vote for a five-year term; election last held 27 December 2001 (next to be held December 2006); vice president appointed by the president
election results: Levy MWANAWASA elected president; percent of vote - Levy MWANAWASA 29%, Anderson MAZOKA 27%, Christon TEMBO 13%, Tilyenji KAUNDA 10%, Godfrey MIYANDA 8%, Benjamin MWILA 5%, Michael SATA 3%, other 5%
Legislative branch: unicameral National Assembly (150 seats; members are elected by popular vote to serve five-year terms)
elections: last held 27 December 2001 (next to be held December 2006)
election results: percent of vote by party - MMD 45.9%, UPND 32.4%, UNIP 8.8%, FDD 8.1%, HP 2.7%, PF 0.7%, ZRP 0.7%, independents 0.7%; seats by party - MMD 68, UPND 48, UNIP 13, FDD 12, HP 4, PF 1, ZRP 1, independents 1; seats not determined 2
Judicial branch: Supreme Court (the final court of appeal; justices are appointed by the president); High Court (has unlimited jurisdiction to hear civil and criminal cases)
Political parties and leaders: Agenda for Zambia or AZ [Inonge MBIKUSITA-LEWANIKA]; Forum for Democracy and Development or FDD [Christon TEMBO]; Heritage Party or HP [Godfrey MIYANDA]; Liberal Progressive Front or LPF [Roger CHONGWE, president]; Movement for Multiparty Democracy or MMD [Levy MWANAWASA, acting president]; National Leadership for Development or NLD [Yobert SHAMAPANDE]; National Party or NP [Dr. Sam CHIPUNGU]; Patriotic Front or PF [Michael SATA]; Zambian Republican Party or ZRP [Benjamin MWILA]; Social Democratic Party or SDP [Gwendoline KONIE]; United National Independence Party or UNIP [Francis NKHOMA, president]; United Party for National Development or UPND [Anderson MAZOKA]
Political pressure groups and leaders: NA
International organization participation: ACP, AfDB, AU, C, COMESA, FAO, G-77, IAEA, IBRD, ICAO, ICCt, ICFTU, ICRM, IDA, IFAD, IFC, IFRCS, ILO, IMF, Interpol, IOC, IOM, ISO (correspondent), ITU, MIGA, MONUC, NAM, ONUB, OPCW, PCA, SADC, UN, UNAMSIL, UNCTAD, UNESCO, UNHCR, UNIDO, UNMEE, UNMIL, UNMIS, UNOCI, UPU, WCL, WCO, WHO, WIPO, WMO, WToO, WTO
Diplomatic representation in the US:
chief of mission: Ambassador Inonge MBIKUSITA-LEWANIKA
chancery: 2419 Massachusetts Avenue NW, Washington, DC 20008
telephone: [1] (202) 265-9717 through 9719
FAX: [1] (202) 332-0826
Diplomatic representation from the US:
chief of mission: Ambassador Martin George BRENNAN
embassy: corner of Independence and United Nations Avenues
mailing address: P. O. Box 31617, Lusaka
telephone: [260] (1) 250-955
FAX: [260] (1) 252-225
Flag description: green with a panel of three vertical bands of red (hoist side), black, and orange below a soaring orange eagle, on the outer edge of the flag

ECONOMY

Economy - overview: Despite progress in privatization and budgetary reform, Zambia's economic growth remains somewhat below the 6% to 7% needed to reduce poverty significantly. Privatization of government-owned copper mines relieved the government from covering mammoth losses generated by the industry and greatly improved the chances for copper mining to return to profitability and spur economic growth. Copper output has increased steadily since 2004, due to higher copper prices and the opening of new mines. The maize harvest was again good in 2005, helping boost GDP and agricultural exports. Cooperation continues with international bodies on programs to reduce poverty, including a new lending arrangement with the IMF in the second quarter, 2004. A tighter monetary policy will help cut inflation, but Zambia still has a serious problem with high public debt.
GDP (purchasing power parity): $10.28 billion (2005 est.)
GDP (official exchange rate): $5.701 billion (2005 est.)
GDP - real growth rate: 5.8% (2005 est.)
GDP - per capita: purchasing power parity - $900 (2005 est.)
GDP - composition by sector:
agriculture: 21.7%
industry: 29.5%
services: 48.8% (2005 est.)
Labor force: 4.8 million (2005 est.)
Labor force - by occupation: agriculture 85%, industry 6%, services 9%
Unemployment rate: 50% (2000 est.)
Population below poverty line: 86% (1993)
Household income or consumption by percentage share:
lowest 10%: 1.1%
highest 10%: 41% (1998)
Distribution of family income - Gini index: 52.6 (1998)
Inflation rate (consumer prices): 19% (2005 est.)
Investment (gross fixed): 25.9% of GDP (2005 est.)
Budget:
revenues: $1.688 billion
expenditures: $1.866 billion, including capital expenditures of NA (2005 est.)
Public debt: 104.2% of GDP (2005 est.)
Agriculture - products: corn, sorghum, rice, peanuts, sunflower seed, vegetables, flowers, tobacco, cotton, sugarcane, cassava (tapioca); cattle, goats, pigs, poultry, milk, eggs, hides; coffee
Industries: copper mining and processing, construction, foodstuffs, beverages, chemicals, textiles, fertilizer, horticulture
Industrial production growth rate: 9.8% (2005 est.)
Electricity - production: 8.347 billion kWh (2003)
Electricity - production by source:
fossil fuel: 0.5%
hydro: 99.5%
nuclear: 0%
other: 0% (2001)
Electricity - consumption: 5.345 billion kWh (2003)
Electricity - exports: 2 billion kWh (2003)
Electricity - imports: 0 kWh (2003)
Oil - production: 130.2 bbl/day (2003 est.)
Oil - consumption: 12,250 bbl/day (2003 est.)

Oil - exports: NA (2001)
Oil - imports: NA (2001)
Current account balance: $-327 million (2005 est.)
Exports: $1.947 billion f.o.b. (2005 est.)
Exports - partners: South Africa 25.6%, UK 17%, Switzerland 16%, Tanzania 7.4%, Democratic Republic of the Congo 7%, Zimbabwe 5.8% (2004)
Imports: $1.934 billion f.o.b. (2005 est.)
Imports - partners: South Africa 46.2%, UK 14.2%, UAE 7.1%, Zimbabwe 6% (2004)
Reserves of foreign exchange and gold: $500 million (2005 est.)
Debt - external: $5.866 billion (2005 est.)
Economic aid - recipient: $640.6 million (2002)
Currency (code): Zambian kwacha (ZMK)
Currency code: ZMK
Exchange rates: Zambian kwacha per US dollar - 4,549.58 (2005), 4,778.9 (2004), 4,733.3 (2003), 4,398.6 (2002), 3,610.9 (2001)
Fiscal year: calendar year

COMMUNICATIONS

Telephones - main lines in use: 88,400 (2003)
Telephones - mobile cellular: 241,000 (2003)
Telephone system:
general assessment: facilities are aging but still among the best in Sub-Saharan Africa
domestic: high-capacity microwave radio relay connects most larger towns and cities; several cellular telephone services in operation; Internet service is widely available; very small aperture terminal (VSAT) networks are operated by private firms
international: country code - 260; satellite earth stations - 2 Intelsat (1 Indian Ocean and 1 Atlantic Ocean)
Radio broadcast stations: AM 19, FM 5, shortwave 4 (2001)
Radios: 1.2 million (2001)
Television broadcast stations: 9 (2002)
Televisions: 277,000 (1997)
Internet country code: .zm
Internet hosts: 1,880 (2003)
Internet Service Providers (ISPs): 5 (2001)
Internet users: 68,200 (2003)

TRANSPORTATION

Airports: 109 (2004 est.)
Airports - with paved runways:
total: 10
over 3,047 m: 1
2,438 to 3,047 m: 3
1,524 to 2,437 m: 4
914 to 1,523 m: 2 (2005 est.)
Airports - with unpaved runways:
total: 99
2,438 to 3,047 m: 1
1,524 to 2,437 m: 4
914 to 1,523 m: 62
under 914 m: 32 (2005 est.)
Pipelines: oil 771 km (2004)
Railways:
total: 2,173 km
narrow gauge: 2,173 km 1.067-m gauge
note: includes 891 km of the Tanzania-Zambia Railway Authority (TAZARA) (2004)
Roadways:
total: 91,440 km
paved: 20,117 km
unpaved: 71,323 km (2001)
Waterways: 2,250 km
note: includes Lake Tanganyika and the Zambezi and Luapula rivers (2003)
Ports and terminals: Mpulungu

MILITARY

Military branches: Zambian National Defense Force (ZNDF): Army, Air Force, Police, National Service
Military service age and obligation: 18 years of age (est.) (2004)
Manpower available for military service: *males age 18-49:* 2,219,739 (2005 est.)
Manpower fit for military service: *males age 18-49:* 1,043,702 (2005 est.)
Military expenditures - dollar figure: $106.8 million (2004)
Military expenditures - percent of GDP: 1.8% (2004)

TRANSNATIONAL ISSUES

Disputes - international: in 2004 Zimbabwe dropped objections and joined Namibia in supporting plans between Botswana and Zambia to build a bridge over the Zambezi River, thereby de facto recognizing a short, but not clearly delimited Botswana-Zambia boundary in the river; 90,000 Angolan refugees were repatriated from Zambia by 2004, the remaining 160,000 are expected to return in 2005
Refugees and internally displaced persons: *refugees (country of origin):* 158,894 (Angola) 58,405 (Democratic Republic of the Congo) 5,767 (Rwanda) (2004)
Illicit drugs: transshipment point for moderate amounts of methaqualone, small amounts of heroin, and cocaine bound for Southern Africa and possibly Europe; a poorly developed financial infrastructure coupled with a government commitment to combating money laundering make it an unattractive venue for money launderers

ZIMBABWE

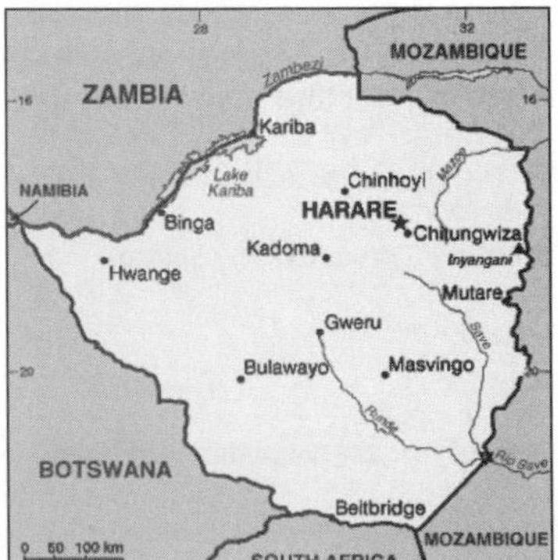

INTRODUCTION

Background: The UK annexed Southern Rhodesia from the South Africa Company in 1923. A 1961 constitution was formulated that favored whites in power. In 1965 the government unilaterally declared its independence, but the UK did not recognize the act and demanded more complete voting rights for the black African majority in the country (then called Rhodesia). UN sanctions and a guerrilla uprising finally led to free elections in 1979 and independence (as Zimbabwe) in 1980. Robert MUGABE, the nation's first prime minister, has been the country's only ruler (as president since 1987) and has dominated the country's political system since independence. His chaotic land redistribution campaign begun in 2000 caused an exodus of white farmers, crippled the economy, and ushered in widespread shortages of basic commodities. Ignoring international condemnation, MUGABE rigged the 2002 presidential election to ensure his reelection. Opposition and labor groups launched general strikes in 2003 to pressure MUGABE to retire early; security forces continued their brutal repression of regime opponents.

GEOGRAPHY

Location: Southern Africa, between South Africa and Zambia

Geographic coordinates: 20 00 S, 30 00 E
Map references: Africa
Area:
total: 390,580 sq km
land: 386,670 sq km
water: 3,910 sq km
Area - comparative: slightly larger than Montana
Land boundaries:
total: 3,066 km
border countries: Botswana 813 km, Mozambique 1,231 km, South Africa 225 km, Zambia 797 km
Coastline: 0 km (landlocked)
Maritime claims: none (landlocked)
Climate: tropical; moderated by altitude; rainy season (November to March)
Terrain: mostly high plateau with higher central plateau (high veld); mountains in east
Elevation extremes:
lowest point: junction of the Runde and Save rivers 162 m
highest point: Inyangani 2,592 m
Natural resources: coal, chromium ore, asbestos, gold, nickel, copper, iron ore, vanadium, lithium, tin, platinum group metals
Land use:
arable land: 8.32%
permanent crops: 0.34%
other: 91.34% (2001)
Irrigated land: 1,170 sq km (1998 est.)
Natural hazards: recurring droughts; floods and severe storms are rare
Environment - current issues: deforestation; soil erosion; land degradation; air and water pollution; the black rhinoceros herd - once the largest concentration of the species in the world - has been significantly reduced by poaching; poor mining practices have led to toxic waste and heavy metal pollution
Environment - international agreements:
party to: Biodiversity, Climate Change, Desertification, Endangered Species, Law of the Sea, Ozone Layer Protection
signed, but not ratified: none of the selected agreements
Geography - note: landlocked; the Zambezi forms a natural riverine boundary with Zambia; in full flood (February-April) the massive Victoria Falls on the river forms the world's largest curtain of falling water

PEOPLE

Population: 12,746,990
note: estimates for this country explicitly take into account the effects of excess mortality due to AIDS; this can result in lower life expectancy, higher infant mortality and death rates, lower population and growth rates, and changes in the distribution of population by age and sex than would otherwise be expected (July 2005 est.)
Age structure:
0-14 years: 39.2% (male 2,522,609/female 2,474,131)
15-64 years: 57.1% (male 3,686,354/female 3,592,662)
65 years and over: 3.7% (male 235,478/female 235,756) (2005 est.)
Median age:
total: 19.26 years
male: 19.28 years
female: 19.24 years (2005 est.)
Population growth rate: 0.51% (2005 est.)
Birth rate: 29.74 births/1,000 population (2005 est.)
Death rate: 24.66 deaths/1,000 population (2005 est.)
Net migration rate: 0 migrant(s)/1,000 population negligible migrant(s)/1,000 population
note: there is an increasing flow of Zimbabweans into South Africa and Botswana in search of better economic opportunities (2005 est.)
Sex ratio:
at birth: 1.03 male(s)/female
under 15 years: 1.02 male(s)/female
15-64 years: 1.03 male(s)/female
65 years and over: 1 male(s)/female
total population: 1.02 male(s)/female (2005 est.)
Infant mortality rate:
total: 67.69 deaths/1,000 live births
male: 70.32 deaths/1,000 live births
female: 64.98 deaths/1,000 live births (2005 est.)
Life expectancy at birth:
total population: 39.13 years
male: 40.2 years
female: 38.03 years (2005 est.)
Total fertility rate: 3.54 children born/woman (2005 est.)
HIV/AIDS - adult prevalence rate: 24.6% (2001 est.)
HIV/AIDS - people living with HIV/AIDS: 1.8 million (2001 est.)
HIV/AIDS - deaths: 170,000 (2003 est.)
Major infectious diseases:
degree of risk: high
food or waterborne diseases: bacterial diarrhea, hepatitis A, and typhoid
vectorborne disease: malaria
water contact disease: schistosomiasis (2004)
Nationality:
noun: Zimbabwean(s)
adjective: Zimbabwean
Ethnic groups: African 98% (Shona 82%, Ndebele 14%, other 2%), mixed and Asian 1%, white less than 1%
Religions: syncretic (part Christian, part indigenous beliefs) 50%, Christian 25%, indigenous beliefs 24%, Muslim and other 1%
Languages: English (official), Shona, Sindebele (the language of the Ndebele, sometimes called Ndebele), numerous but minor tribal dialects
Literacy:
definition: age 15 and over can read and write
total population: 90.7%
male: 94.2%
female: 87.2% (2003 est.)

GOVERNMENT

Country name:
conventional long form: Republic of Zimbabwe
conventional short form: Zimbabwe
former: Southern Rhodesia, Rhodesia
Government type: parliamentary democracy
Capital: Harare
Administrative divisions: 8 provinces and 2 cities* with provincial status; Bulawayo*, Harare*, Manicaland, Mashonaland Central, Mashonaland East, Mashonaland West, Masvingo, Matabeleland North, Matabeleland South, Midlands
Independence: 18 April 1980 (from UK)
National holiday: Independence Day, 18 April (1980)
Constitution: 21 December 1979
Legal system: mixture of Roman-Dutch and English common law
Suffrage: 18 years of age, universal
Executive branch:
chief of state: Executive President Robert Gabriel MUGABE (since 31 December 1987); Vice President Joyce MUJURU (since 6 December 2004); note - the president is both the chief of state and head of government
head of government: Executive President Robert Gabriel MUGABE (since 31 December 1987); Vice President Joyce MUJURU (since 6 December 2004); note - the president is both the chief of state and head of government
cabinet: Cabinet appointed by the president; responsible to the House of Assembly
elections: presidential candidates nominated with a nomination paper signed by at least 10 registered voters (at least one from each province) and elected by popular vote for a 6-year term; election last held 9-11 March 2002 (next to be held March 2008); co-vice presidents appointed by the president
election results: Robert Gabriel MUGABE reelected president; percent of vote - Robert Gabriel MUGABE 56.2%, Morgan TSVANGIRAI 41.9%
Legislative branch: unicameral House of Assembly (150 seats - 120 elected by popular vote for five-year terms, 12 nominated by the president, 10 occupied by

traditional chiefs chosen by their peers, and 8 occupied by provincial governors appointed by the president)
elections: last held 31 March 2005 (next to be held NA 2010)
election results: percent of vote by party - ZANU-PF 59.6%, MDC 39.5%, other 0.9%; seats by party - ZANU-PF 78, MDC 41, Independents 1
Judicial branch: Supreme Court; High Court
Political parties and leaders: Movement for Democratic Change or MDC [Morgan TSVANGIRAI]; National Alliance for Good Governance or NAGG [Shakespeare MAYA]; United Parties [Abel MUZOREWA]; Zimbabwe African National Union-Ndonga or ZANU-Ndonga [Wilson KUMBULA]; Zimbabwe African National Union-Patriotic Front or ZANU-PF [Robert Gabriel MUGABE]; Zimbabwe African Peoples Union or ZAPU [Agrippa MADLELA]
Political pressure groups and leaders: National Constitutional Assembly or NCA [Lovemore MADHUKU]; Crisis in Zimbabwe Coalition [Brian KAGORO]; Zimbabwe Congress of Trade Unions or ZCTU [Lovemore MATOMBO]
International organization participation: ACP, AfDB, AU, COMESA, FAO, G-15, G-77, IAEA, IBRD, ICAO, ICCt (signatory), ICFTU, ICRM, IDA, IFAD, IFC, IFRCS, ILO, IMF, IMO, Interpol, IOC, IOM, ISO, ITU, MIGA, NAM, OPCW, PCA, SADC, UN, UNCTAD, UNESCO, UNIDO, UNMIS, UPU, WCL, WCO, WFTU, WHO, WIPO, WMO, WToO, WTO
Diplomatic representation in the US:
chief of mission: Ambassador Simbi Veke MUBAKO
chancery: 1608 New Hampshire Avenue NW, Washington, DC 20009
telephone: [1] (202) 332-7100
FAX: [1] (202) 483-9326
Diplomatic representation from the US:
chief of mission: Ambassador Joseph G. SULLIVAN
embassy: 172 Herbert Chitepo Avenue, Harar
mailing address: P. O. Box 3340, Harare
telephone: [263] (4) 250-593 and 250-594
FAX: [263] (4) 796488
Flag description: seven equal horizontal bands of green, yellow, red, black, red, yellow, and green with a white isosceles triangle edged in black with its base on the hoist side; a yellow Zimbabwe bird representing the long history of the country is superimposed on a red five-pointed star in the center of the triangle, which symbolizes peace; green symbolizes agriculture, yellow - mineral wealth, red - blood shed to achieve independence, and black stands for the native people

ECONOMY

Economy - overview: The government of Zimbabwe faces a wide variety of difficult economic problems as it struggles with an unsustainable fiscal deficit, an overvalued exchange rate, soaring inflation, and bare shelves. Its 1998-2002 involvement in the war in the Democratic Republic of the Congo, for example, drained hundreds of millions of dollars from the economy. Badly needed support from the IMF has been suspended because of the country's failure to meet budgetary goals. Inflation rose from an annual rate of 32% in 1998 to 133% at the end of 2004 and 246.7% in 2005, while the exchange rate fell from 24 Zimbabwean dollars per US dollar to 15,200 in the same time period. The government's land reform program, characterized by chaos and violence, has badly damaged the commercial farming sector, the traditional source of exports and foreign exchange and the provider of 400,000 jobs.
GDP (purchasing power parity): $23.98 billion (2005 est.)
GDP (official exchange rate): $5.817 billion (2005 est.)
GDP - real growth rate: -4% (2005 est.)
GDP - per capita: purchasing power parity - $1,900 (2005 est.)
GDP - composition by sector:
agriculture: 17.9%
industry: 24.3%
services: 57.9% (2005 est.)
Labor force: 3.94 million (2005 est.)
Labor force - by occupation: agriculture 66%, industry 10%, services 24% (1996)
Unemployment rate: 60% (2004 est.)
Population below poverty line: 80% (2004 est.)
Household income or consumption by percentage share:
lowest 10%: 1.97%
highest 10%: 40.42% (1995)
Distribution of family income - Gini index: 56.8 (2003)
Inflation rate (consumer prices): 246.7% (2005 est.)
Investment (gross fixed): 7.9% of GDP (2005 est.)
Budget:
revenues: $1.409 billion
expenditures: $1.905 billion, including capital expenditures of NA (2005 est.)
Public debt: 30.1% of GDP (2005 est.)
Agriculture - products: corn, cotton, tobacco, wheat, coffee, sugarcane, peanuts; sheep, goats, pigs
Industries: mining (coal, gold, platinum, copper, nickel, tin, clay, numerous metallic and nonmetallic ores), steel, wood products, cement, chemicals, fertilizer, clothing and footwear, foodstuffs, beverages
Industrial production growth rate: -1.7% (2005 est.)
Electricity - production: 8.877 billion kWh (2003)
Electricity - production by source:
fossil fuel: 47%
hydro: 53%
nuclear: 0%
other: 0% (2001)
Electricity - consumption: 11.22 billion kWh (2003)
Electricity - exports: 0 kWh (2003)
Electricity - imports: 3.3 billion kWh (2003)
Oil - production: 0 bbl/day (2003 est.)
Oil - consumption: 22,500 bbl/day (2003 est.)
Oil - exports: 0 bbl/day NA (2004 est.)
Oil - imports: 23,000 bbl/day NA (2004 est.)
Current account balance: $-517 million (2005 est.)
Exports: $1.644 billion f.o.b. (2005 est.)
Exports - partners: South Africa 31.5%, Switzerland 7.4%, UK 7.3%, China 6.1%, Germany 4.3% (2004)
Imports: $2.059 billion f.o.b. (2005 est.)
Imports - partners: South Africa 46.9%, Botswana 3.6%, UK 3.4% (2004)
Reserves of foreign exchange and gold: $160 million (2005 est.)
Debt - external: $5.17 billion (2005 est.)
Economic aid - recipient: $178 million; note - the EU and the US provide food aid on humanitarian grounds (2000 est.)
Currency (code): Zimbabwean dollar (ZWD)
Currency code: ZWD
Exchange rates: Zimbabwean dollars per US dollar - 15,190.8 (2005), 4,303.28 (2004), 697.424 (2003), 55.036 (2002), 55.052 (2001)
note: these are official exchange rates, non-official rates vary significantly
Fiscal year: calendar year

COMMUNICATIONS

Telephones - main lines in use: 300,900 (2003)
Telephones - mobile cellular: 379,100 (2003)
Telephone system:
general assessment: system was once one of the best in Africa, but now suffers from poor maintenance; more than 100,000 outstanding requests for connection despite an equally large number of installed but unused main lines
domestic: consists of microwave radio relay links, open-wire lines, radiotelephone communication stations, fixed wireless local loop installations, and a substantial mobile cellular network; Internet connection is available in Harare and planned for all major towns and for some of the smaller ones

international: country code - 263; satellite earth stations - 2 Intelsat; two international digital gateway exchanges (in Harare and Gweru)
Radio broadcast stations: AM 7, FM 20 (plus 17 repeater stations), shortwave 1 (1998)
Radios: 1.14 million (1997)
Television broadcast stations: 16 (1997)
Televisions: 370,000 (1997)
Internet country code: .zw
Internet hosts: 4,501 (2003)
Internet Service Providers (ISPs): 6 (2000)
Internet users: 500,000 (2002)

TRANSPORTATION

Airports: 404 (2004 est.)
Airports - with paved runways:
total: 17
over 3,047 m: 3
2,438 to 3,047 m: 2
1,524 to 2,437 m: 4
914 to 1,523 m: 8 (2005 est.)
Airports - with unpaved runways:
total: 387
1,524 to 2,437 m: 5
914 to 1,523 m: 186
under 914 m: 196 (2005 est.)
Pipelines: refined products 261 km (2004)
Railways:
total: 3,077 km
narrow gauge: 3,077 km 1.067-m gauge (313 km electrified) (2004)
Roadways:
total: 18,338 km
paved: 8,692 km
unpaved: 9,646 km (1999 est.)
Waterways: on Lake Kariba, length small (2003)
Ports and terminals: Binga, Kariba

MILITARY

Military branches: Zimbabwe Defense Forces (ZDF): Zimbabwe National Army, Air Force of Zimbabwe (AFZ), Zimbabwe Republic Police (2005)
Military service age and obligation: 18 years of age (est.) (2004)
Manpower available for military service:
males age 18-49: 2,840,053 (2005 est.)
Manpower fit for military service: *males age 18-49:* 1,148,590 (2005 est.)
Military expenditures - dollar figure: $217 million (2004)
Military expenditures - percent of GDP: 4.3% (2004)

TRANSNATIONAL ISSUES

Disputes - international: Botswana has built electric fences and South Africa has placed military along the border to stem the flow of thousands of Zimbabweans fleeing to find work and escape political persecution; Namibia has supported and in 2004 Zimbabwe dropped objections to plans between Botswana and Zambia to build a bridge over the Zambezi River, thereby de facto recognizing a short, but not clearly delimited Botswana-Zambia boundary in the river
Refugees and internally displaced persons: *IDPs:* 100,000-150,000 (MUGABE-led political violence, human rights violations, land reform, and economic collapse) (2004)
Illicit drugs: transit point for African cannabis and South Asian heroin, mandrax, and methamphetamines destined for the South African and European markets

APPENDIX A

ABBREVIATIONS

ABEDA	Arab Bank for Economic Development in Africa
ACCT	Agency for the French-Speaking Community
ACP Group	African, Caribbean, and Pacific Group of States
AfDB	African Development Bank
AFESD	Arab Fund for Economic and Social Development
Air Pollution	Convention on Long-Range Transboundary Air Pollution
Air Pollution-Nitrogen Oxides	Protocol to the 1979 Convention on Long-Range Transboundary Air Pollution Concerning the Control of Emissions of Nitrogen Oxides or Their Transboundary Fluxes
Air Pollution-Persistent Organic Pollutants	Protocol to the 1979 Convention on Long-Range Transboundary Air Pollution on Persistent Organic Pollutants
Air Pollution-Sulphur 85	Protocol to the 1979 Convention on Long-Range Transboundary Air Pollution on the Reduction of Sulphur Emissions or Their Transboundary Fluxes by at Least 30%
Air Pollution-Sulphur 94	Protocol to the 1979 Convention on Long-Range Transboundary Air Pollution on Further Reduction of Sulphur Emissions
Air Pollution-Volatile Organic Compounds	Protocol to the 1979 Convention on Long-Range Transboundary Air Pollution Concerning the Control of Emissions of Volatile Organic Compounds or Their Transboundary Fluxes
AMF	Arab Monetary Fund
AMU	Arab Maghreb Union
Antarctic-Environmental Protocol	Protocol on Environmental Protection to the Antarctic Treaty
Antarctic Marine Living Resources	Convention on the Conservation of Antarctic Marine Living Resources
Antarctic Seals	Convention for the Conservation of Antarctic Seals
ANZUS	Australia-New Zealand-United States Security Treaty
APEC	Asia-Pacific Economic Cooperation
Arabsat	Arab Satellite Communications Organization
ARF	ASEAN Regional Forum
AsDB	Asian Development Bank
ASEAN	Association of Southeast Asian Nations
AU	African Union
Autodin	Automatic Digital Network
BA	Baltic Assembly
bbl/day	barrels per day
BCIE	Central American Bank for Economic Integration
BDEAC	Central African States Development Bank
Benelux	Benelux Economic Union
BIMSTEC	Bay of Bengal Iniative for Multisectoral Technical and Economic Cooperation
Biodiversity	Convention on Biological Diversity
BGN	United States Board on Geographic Names
BIS	Bank for International Settlements
BSEC	Black Sea Economic Cooperation Zone
C	Commonwealth
c.i.f.	cost, insurance, and freight
CACM	Central American Common Market
CAEU	Council of Arab Economic Unity

CAN	Andean Community of Nations
Caricom	Caribbean Community and Common Market
CB	citizen's band mobile radio communications
CBSS	Council of the Baltic Sea States
CCC	Customs Cooperation Council
CDB	Caribbean Development Bank
CE	Council of Europe
CEI	Central European Initiative
CEMAC	Monetary and Economic Community of Central Africa
CEPGL	Economic Community of the Great Lakes Countries
CERN	European Organization for Nuclear Research
CEPT	Conference Europeanne des Poste et Telecommunications
CIS	Commonwealth of Independent States
CITES	see Endangered Species
Climate Change	United Nations Framework Convention on Climate Change
Climate Change-Kyoto Protocol	Kyoto Protocol to the United Nations Framework Convention on Climate Change
COCOM	Coordinating Committee on Export Controls
Comsat	Communications Satellite Corporation
COMESA	Common Market for Eastern and Southern Africa
CP	Colombo Plan
CY	calendar year
DC	developed country
Desertification	United Nations Convention to Combat Desertification in Those Countries Experiencing Serious Drought and/or Desertification, Particularly in Africa
DDT	dichloro-diphenyl-trichloro-ethane
DIA	United States Defense Intelligence Agency
DSN	Defense Switched Network
DWT	deadweight ton
EADB	East African Development Bank
EAPC	Euro-Atlantic Partnership Council
EBRD	European Bank for Reconstruction and Development
EC	European Community
ECA	Economic Commission for Africa
ECE	Economic Commission for Europe
ECLAC	Economic Commission for Latin America and the Caribbean
ECO	Economic Cooperation Organization
ECOSOC	Economic and Social Council
ECOWAS	Economic Community of West African States
ECSC	European Coal and Steel Community
EEC	European Economic Community
EFTA	European Free Trade Association
EEZ	exclusive economic zone
EIB	European Investment Bank
EMU	European Monetary Union
Endangered Species	Convention on the International Trade in Endangered Species of Wild Flora and Fauna (CITES)
Entente	Council of the Entente
Environmental Modification	Convention on the Prohibition of Military or Any Other Hostile Use of Environmental Modification Techniques
ESA	European Space Agency

ESCAP	Economic and Social Commission for Asia and the Pacific
ESCWA	Economic and Social Commission for Western Asia
est.	estimate
EU	European Union
Euratom	European Atomic Energy Community
Eutelsat	European Telecommunications Satellite Organization
Ex-Im	Export-Import Bank of the United States
f.o.b.	free on board
FAO	Food and Agriculture Organization
FAX	facsimile
FLS	Front Line States
FOC	flags of convenience
FSU	former Soviet Union
FY	fiscal year
FZ	Franc Zone
G-2	Group of 2
G-3	Group of 3
G-5	Group of 5
G-6	Group of 6
G-7	Group of 7
G-8	Group of 8
G-9	Group of 9
G-10	Group of 10
G-15	Group of 15
G-11	Group of 11
G-24	Group of 24
G-77	Group of 77
GATT	General Agreement on Tariffs and Trade; now WTO
GCC	Gulf Cooperation Council
GDP	gross domestic product
GNP	gross national product
GRT	gross register ton
GSM	global system for mobile cellular communications
GUAM	acronym for member states - Georgia, Ukraine, Azerbaijan, Moldova
GWP	gross world product
Hazardous Wastes	Basel Convention on the Control of Transboundary Movements of Hazardous Wastes and Their Disposal
HF	high-frequency
HIV/AIDS	human immunodeficiency virus/acquired immune deficiency syndrome
IADB	Inter-American Development Bank
IAEA	International Atomic Energy Agency
IANA	Internet Assigned Numbers Authority
IBRD	International Bank for Reconstruction and Development (World Bank)
ICAO	International Civil Aviation Organization
ICC	International Chamber of Commerce
ICCt	International Criminal Court
ICFTU	International Confederation of Free Trade Unions
ICJ	International Court of Justice (World Court)
ICRC	International Committee of the Red Cross
ICRM	International Red Cross and Red Crescent Movement
ICSID	International Center for Secretariat of Investment Disputes

ICTR	International Criminal Tribunal for Rwanda
ICTY	International Criminal Tribunal for the former Yugoslavia
IDA	International Development Association
IDB	Islamic Development Bank
IDP	internally displaced person
IEA	International Energy Agency
IFAD	International Fund for Agricultural Development
IFC	International Finance Corporation
IFRCS	International Federation of Red Cross and Red Crescent Societies
IGAD	Inter-Governmental Authority on Development
IHO	International Hydrographic Organization
ILO	International Labor Organization
IMF	International Monetary Fund
IMO	International Maritime Organization
Inmarsat	International Maritime Satellite Organization
InOC	Indian Ocean Commission
INSTRAW	International Research and Training Institute for the Advancement of Women
Intelsat	International Telecommunications Satellite Organization
Interpol	International Criminal Police Organization
Intersputnik	International Organization of Space Communications
IOC	International Olympic Committee
IOM	International Organization for Migration
IPU	Inter-parliamentary Union
ISO	International Organization for Standardization
ISP	Internet Service Provider
ITU	International Telecommunication Union
kHz	kilohertz
km	kilometer
kW	kilowatt
kWh	kilowatt-hour
LAES	Latin American Economic System
LAIA	Latin American Integration Association
LAS	League of Arab States
Law of the Sea	United Nations Convention on the Law of the Sea (LOS)
LDC	less developed country
LLDC	least developed country
London Convention	see Marine Dumping
LOS	see Law of the Sea
m	meter
Marecs	Maritime European Communications Satellite
Marine Dumping	Convention on the Prevention of Marine Pollution by Dumping Wastes and Other Matter
Marine Life Conservation	Convention on Fishing and Conservation of Living Resources of the High Seas
MARPOL	see Ship Pollution
Medarabtel	Middle East Telecommunications Project of the International Telecommunications Union
Mercosur	Southern Cone Common Market
MHz	megahertz
MICAH	International Civilian Support Mission in Haiti
MINURSO	United Nations Mission for the Referendum in Western Sahara
MIGA	Multilateral Investment Geographic Agency

MINUSTAH	United Nations Stabilization Mission in Haiti
MONUC	United Nations Organization Mission in the Democratic Republic of the Congo
NA	not available
NAFTA	North American Free Trade Agreement
NAM	Nonaligned Movement
NATO	North Atlantic Treaty Organization
NC	Nordic Council
NEA	Nuclear Energy Agency
NEGL	negligible
NGA	National Geospatial-Intelligence Agency
NIB	Nordic Investment Bank
NIC	newly industrializing country
NIE	newly industrializing economy
NIS	new independent states
nm	nautical mile
NMT	Nordic Mobile Telephone
NSG	Nuclear Suppliers Group
Nuclear Test Ban	Treaty Banning Nuclear Weapons Tests in the Atmosphere, in Outer Space, and Under Water
NZ	New Zealand
OAPEC	Organization of Arab Petroleum Exporting Countries
OAS	Organization of American States
OAU	Organization of African Unity; see African Union
ODA	official development assistance
OECD	Organization for Economic Cooperation and Development
OECS	Organization of Eastern Caribbean States
OHCHR	Office of the United Nations High Commissioner for Human Rights
OIC	Organization of the Islamic Conference
OIF	International Francophone Organization
ONUB	United Nations Operation in Burundi
OOF	other official flows
OPANAL	Agency for the Prohibition of Nuclear Weapons in Latin America and the Caribbean
OPCW	Organization for the Prohibition of Chemical Weapons
OPEC	Organization of Petroleum Exporting Countries
OSCE	Organization for Security and Cooperation in Europe
Ozone Layer Protection	Montreal Protocol on Substances That Deplete the Ozone Layer
PCA	Permanent Court of Arbitration
PFP	Partnership for Peace
PIF	Pacific Islands Forum
PPP	purchasing power parity
Ramsar	see Wetlands
RG	Rio Group
SAARC	South Asian Association for Regional Cooperation
SACU	Southern African Customs Union
SACEP	South Asia Co-opeative Environment Programme
SADC	Southern African Development Community
SCO	Shanghai Cooperative Organization
SAFE	South African Far East Cable
SECI	Southeast European Cooperative Initiative
SHF	super-high-frequency

Ship Pollution	Protocol of 1978 Relating to the International Convention for the Prevention of Pollution From Ships, 1973 (MARPOL)
Sparteca	South Pacific Regional Trade and Economic Cooperation Agreement
SPC	Secretariat of the Pacific Communities
SPF	South Pacific Forum
sq km	square kilometer
sq mi	square mile
TAT	Trans-Atlantic Telephone
Tropical Timber 83	International Tropical Timber Agreement, 1983
Tropical Timber 94	International Tropical Timber Agreement, 1994
UAE	United Arab Emirates
UDEAC	Central African Customs and Economic Union
UHF	ultra-high-frequency
UK	United Kingdom
UN	United Nations
UNAMSIL	United Nations Mission in Sierra Leone
UNCLOS	United Nations Convention on the Law of the Sea, also know as LOS
UNCTAD	United Nations Conference on Trade and Development
UNDCP	United Nations Drug Control Program
UNDOF	United Nations Disengagement Observer Force
UNDP	United Nations Development Program
UNEP	United Nations Environment Program
UNESCO	United Nations Educational, Scientific, and Cultural Organization
UNFICYP	United Nations Peace-keeping Force in Cyprus
UNFPA	United Nations Population Fund
UNHCR	United Nations High Commissioner for Refugees
UNICEF	United Nations Children's Fund
UNICRI	United Nations Interregional Crime and Justice Research Institute
UNIDIR	United Nations Institute for Disarmament Research
UNIDO	United Nations Industrial Development Organization
UNIFIL	United Nations Interim Force in Lebanon
UNITAR	United Nations Institute for Training and Research
UNMEE	United Nations Mission in Ethiopia and Eritrea
UNMIK	United Nations Interim Administration Mission in Kosovo
UNMIL	United Nations Mission in Liberia
UNMOGIP	United Nations Military Observer Group in India and Pakistan
UNMOVIC	United Nations Monitoring, Verification, and Inspection Commission
UNOCI	United Nations Operation in Cote d'Ivoire
UNOMIG	United Nations Observer Mission in Georgia
UNOPS	United Nations Office of Project Services
UNRISD	United Nations Research Institute for Social Development
UNRWA	United Nations Relief and Works Agency for Palestine Refugees in the Near East
UNSC	United Nations Security Council
UNSSC	Untied Nations System Staff College
UNTSO	United Nations Truce Supervision Organization
UNU	United Nations University
UPU	Universal Postal Union
US	United States
USSR	Union of Soviet Socialist Republics (Soviet Union); used for information dated before 25 December 1991
UV	ultra violet

VHF	very-high-frequency
VSAT	very small aperture terminal
WADB	West African Development Bank
WAEMU	West African Economic and Monetary Union
WCL	World Confederation of Labor
WCO	World Customs Organization
Wetlands	Convention on Wetlands of International Importance Especially As Waterfowl Habitat
WEU	Western European Union
WFP	World Food Program
WFTU	World Federation of Trade Unions
Whaling	International Convention for the Regulation of Whaling
WHO	World Health Organization
WIPO	World Intellectual Property Organization
WMO	World Meteorological Organization
WP	Warsaw Pact
WTO	World Trade Organization note - see WToO for World Tourism Organization
WToO	World Tourism Organization
ZC	Zangger Committee

APPENDIX B

INTERNATIONAL ORGANIZATIONS AND GROUPS

ASEAN Regional Forum (ARF)

established - 25 July 1994
aim - to foster constructive dialogue and consultation on political and security issues of common interest and concern
members - (25) Australia, Brunei, Burma, Cambodia, Canada, China, East Timor, EU, India, Indonesia, Japan, North Korea, South Korea, Laos, Malaysia, Mongolia, NZ, Pakistan, Papua New Guinea, Philippines, Russia, Singapore, Thailand, US, Vietnam

African Development Bank (AfDB)

note - its predecessor was Organization of African Unity (OAU)
established - 9 September 1999
aim - to promote economic and social development
regional members - (53) Algeria, Angola, Benin, Botswana, Burkina Faso, Burundi, Cameroon, Cape Verde, Central African Republic, Chad, Comoros, Democratic Republic of the Congo, Republic of the Congo, Cote d'Ivoire, Djibouti, Egypt, Equatorial Guinea, Eritrea, Ethiopia, Gabon, The Gambia, Ghana, Guinea, Guinea-Bissau, Kenya, Lesotho, Liberia, Libya, Madagascar, Malawi, Mali, Mauritania, Mauritius, Morocco, Mozambique, Namibia, Niger, Nigeria, Rwanda, Sao Tome and Principe, Senegal, Seychelles, Sierra Leone, Somalia, South Africa, Sudan, Swaziland, Tanzania, Togo, Tunisia, Uganda, Zambia, Zimbabwe
nonregional members - (24) Argentina, Austria, Belgium, Brazil, Canada, China, Denmark, Finland, France, Germany, India, Italy, Japan, South Korea, Kuwait, Netherlands, Norway, Portugal, Saudi Arabia, Spain, Sweden, Switzerland, UK, US

African Union (AU)

note - replaces Organization of African Unity (OAU)
established - 8 July 2001
aim - to achieve greater unity among African States; to defend states' integrity and independence; to accelerate political, social, and economic integration; to encourage international cooperation; to promote democratic principles and institutions
members - (53) Algeria, Angola, Benin, Botswana, Burkina Faso, Burundi, Cameroon, Cape Verde, Central African Republic, Chad, Comoros, Democratic Republic of the Congo, Republic of the Congo, Cote d'Ivoire, Djibouti, Egypt, Equatorial Guinea, Eritrea, Ethiopia, Gabon, The Gambia, Ghana, Guinea, Guinea-Bissau, Kenya, Lesotho, Liberia, Libya, Madagascar, Malawi, Mali, Mauritania, Mauritius, Mozambique, Namibia, Niger, Nigeria, Rwanda, Sahrawi Arab Democratic Republic (Western Sahara), Sao Tome and Principe, Senegal, Seychelles, Sierra Leone, Somalia, South Africa, Sudan, Swaziland, Tanzania, Togo, Tunisia, Uganda, Zambia, Zimbabwe

African, Caribbean, and Pacific Group of States (ACP Group)

established - 6 June 1975
aim - to manage their preferential economic and aid relationship with the EU
members - (79) Angola, Antigua and Barbuda, The Bahamas, Barbados, Belize, Benin, Botswana, Burkina Faso, Burundi, Cameroon, Cape Verde, Central African Republic, Chad, Comoros, Democratic Republic of the Congo, Republic of the Congo, Cook Islands, Cote d'Ivoire, Cuba, Djibouti,

Dominica, Dominican Republic, East Timor, Equatorial Guinea, Eritrea, Ethiopia, Fiji, Gabon, The Gambia, Ghana, Grenada, Guinea, Guinea-Bissau, Guyana, Haiti, Jamaica, Kenya, Kiribati, Lesotho, Liberia, Madagascar, Malawi, Mali, Marshall Islands, Mauritania, Mauritius, Federated States of Micronesia, Mozambique, Namibia, Nauru, Niger, Nigeria, Niue, Palau, Papua New Guinea, Rwanda, Saint Kitts and Nevis, Saint Lucia, Saint Vincent and the Grenadines, Samoa, Sao Tome and Principe, Senegal, Seychelles, Sierra Leone, Solomon Islands, Somalia, South Africa, Sudan, Suriname, Swaziland, Tanzania, Togo, Tonga, Trinidad and Tobago, Tuvalu, Uganda, Vanuatu, Zambia, Zimbabwe

Agency for the French-Speaking Community (ACCT)

note - formerly Agency for Cultural and Technical Cooperation
established - 20 March 1970; name changed 1996
aim - to promote cultural and technical cooperation among French-speaking countries
members - (49) Belgium, Benin, Bulgaria, Burkina Faso, Burundi, Cambodia, Cameroon, Canada, Cape Verde, Central African Republic, Chad, Comoros, Democratic Republic of the Congo, Republic of the Congo, Cote d'Ivoire, Djibouti, Dominica, Egypt, Equatorial Guinea, France, French Community of Belgium, Gabon, Guinea, Guinea-Bissau, Haiti, Laos, Lebanon, Luxembourg, Madagascar, Mali, Mauritania, Mauritius, Moldova, Monaco, Morocco, New Brunswick (Canada), Niger, Quebec (Canada), Romania, Rwanda, Saint Lucia, Sao Tome and Principe, Senegal, Seychelles, Switzerland, Togo, Tunisia, Vanuatu, Vietnam
associates - (4) Albania, Andorra, Greece, Macedonia
observers

Agency for the Prohibition of Nuclear Weapons in Latin America and the Caribbean (OPANAL)

note - acronym from Organismo para la Proscripcion de las Armas Nucleares en la America Latina y el Caribe (OPANAL)
established - 14 February 1967 under the Treaty of Tlatelolco; effective - 25 April 1969 on the 11th ratification
aim - to encourage the peaceful uses of atomic energy and prohibit nuclear weapons
members - (33) Antigua and Barbuda, Argentina, The Bahamas, Barbados, Belize, Bolivia, Brazil, Chile, Colombia, Costa Rica, Cuba, Dominica, Dominican Republic, Ecuador, El Salvador, Grenada, Guatemala, Guyana, Haiti, Honduras, Jamaica, Mexico, Nicaragua, Panama, Paraguay, Peru, Saint Kitts and Nevis, Saint Lucia, Saint Vincent and the Grenadines, Suriname, Trinidad and Tobago, Uruguay, Venezuela

Andean Community of Nations (CAN)

note - formerly known as the Andean Group (AG), the Andean Parliament, and most recently as the Andean Common Market (Ancom)
established - 26 May 1969; present name established 1 October 1992; effective - 16 October 1969
aim - to promote harmonious development through economic integration
members - (5) Bolivia, Colombia, Ecuador, Peru, Venezuela

Arab Bank for Economic Development in Africa (ABEDA)

note - also known as Banque Arabe de Developpement Economique en Afrique (BADEA)
established - 18 February 1974; effective - 16 September 1974
aim - to promote economic development

members - (17 plus the Palestine Liberation Organization) Algeria, Bahrain, Egypt, Iraq, Jordan, Kuwait, Lebanon, Libya, Mauritania, Morocco, Oman, Qatar, Saudi Arabia, Sudan, Syria, Tunisia, UAE, Palestine Liberation Organization; note - these are all the members of the Arab League excluding Comoros, Djibouti, Somalia, Yemen

Arab Fund for Economic and Social Development (AFESD)

established - 16 May 1968
aim - to promote economic and social development
members - (20 plus the Palestine Liberation Organization) Algeria, Bahrain, Djibouti, Egypt, Iraq (suspended 1993), Jordan, Kuwait, Lebanon, Libya, Mauritania, Morocco, Oman, Qatar, Saudi Arabia, Somalia (suspended 1993), Sudan, Syria, Tunisia, UAE, Yemen, Palestine Liberation Organization

Arab Maghreb Union (AMU)

established - 17 February 1989
aim - to promote cooperation and integration among the Arab states of northern Africa
members - (5) Algeria, Libya, Mauritania, Morocco, Tunisia

Arab Monetary Fund (AMF)

established - 27 April 1976; effective - 2 February 1977
aim - to promote Arab cooperation, development, and integration in monetary and economic affairs
members - (21 plus the Palestine Liberation Organization) Algeria, Bahrain, Comoros, Djibouti, Egypt, Iraq, Jordan, Kuwait, Lebanon, Libya, Mauritania, Morocco, Oman, Qatar, Saudi Arabia, Somalia, Sudan, Syria, Tunisia, UAE, Yemen, Palestine Liberation Organization

Arctic Council

established - 18 September 1996
aim - to address the common concerns and challenges faced by Arctic governments and the people of the Arctic; to protect the Arctic environment
members - (8) Canada, Denmark (Greenland, Faroe Islands), Finland, Iceland, Norway, Russia, Sweden, US
permanent participants - (6) Aleut International Association, Arctic Athabaskan Council, Gurch'in Council International, Inuit Circumpolar Conference, Russian Association of Indigenous People of the North, Saami Council
observers - (5) France, Germany, Netherlands, Poland, UK

Asia-Pacific Economic Cooperation (APEC)

established - 7 November 1989
aim - to promote trade and investment in the Pacific basin
members - (21) Australia, Brunei, Canada, Chile, China, Hong Kong, Indonesia, Japan, South Korea, Malaysia, Mexico, NZ, Papua New Guinea, Peru, Philippines, Russia, Singapore, Taiwan, Thailand, US, Vietnam
observers - (3) Association of Southeast Asian Nations, Pacific Economic Cooperation Council, Pacific Islands Forum Secretariat

Asian Development Bank (AsDB)

established - 19 December 1966
aim - to promote regional economic cooperation
members - (46) Afghanistan, Armenia, Australia, Azerbaijan, Bangladesh, Bhutan, Burma, Cambodia, China, Cook Islands, East Timor, Fiji, Hong Kong, India, Indonesia, Japan, Kazakhstan, Kiribati, South Korea, Kyrgyzstan, Laos, Malaysia, Maldives, Marshall Islands, Federated States of Micronesia,

Mongolia, Nauru, Nepal, NZ, Pakistan, Palau, Papua New Guinea, Philippines, Samoa, Singapore, Solomon Islands, Sri Lanka, Taiwan, Tajikistan, Thailand, Tonga, Turkmenistan, Tuvalu, Uzbekistan, Vanuatu, Vietnam
nonregional members - (18) Austria, Belgium, Canada, Denmark, Finland, France, Germany, Italy, Luxembourg, Netherlands, Norway, Portugal, Spain, Sweden, Switzerland, Turkey, UK, US

Association of Southeast Asian Nations (ASEAN)

established - 8 August 1967
aim - to encourage regional economic, social, and cultural cooperation among the non-Communist countries of Southeast Asia
members - (10) Brunei, Burma, Cambodia, Indonesia, Laos, Malaysia, Philippines, Singapore, Thailand, Vietnam
associate member - (1) Papua New Guinea
dialogue partners - (12) Australia, Canada, China, EU, India, Japan, South Korea, NZ, Pakistan, Russia, US, UNDP

Australia Group

established - June 1985
aim - to consult on and coordinate export controls related to chemical and biological weapons
members - (40) Argentina, Australia, Austria, Belgium, Bulgaria, Canada, Cyprus, Czech Republic, Denmark, Estonia, European Commission, Finland, France, Germany, Greece, Hungary, Iceland, Ireland, Italy, Japan, South Korea, Latvia, Lithuania, Luxembourg, Malta, Netherlands, NZ, Norway, Poland, Portugal, Romania, Slovakia, Slovenia, Spain, Sweden, Switzerland, Turkey, Ukraine, UK, US

Australia-New Zealand-United States Security Treaty (ANZUS)

established - 1 September 1951; effective - 29 April 1952
aim - to implement a trilateral mutual security agreement, although the US suspended security obligations to NZ on 11 August 1986; Australia and the US continue to hold annual meetings
members - (3) Australia, NZ, US

Baltic Assembly (BA)

established - 12 May 1990
aim - to thoroughly discuss various cooperation issues between Baltic states
members - (3) Estonia, Latvia, Lithuania

Bank for International Settlements (BIS)

established - 20 January 1930; effective - 17 March 1930
aim - to promote cooperation among central banks in international financial settlements
members - (55) Algeria, Argentina, Australia, Austria, Belgium, Bosnia and Herzegovina, Brazil, Bulgaria, Canada, Chile, China, Croatia, Czech Republic, Denmark, Estonia, European Central Bank, Finland, France, Germany, Greece, Hong Kong, Hungary, Iceland, India, Indonesia, Ireland, Israel, Italy, Japan, South Korea, Latvia, Lithuania, Macedonia, Malaysia, Mexico, Netherlands, NZ, Norway, Philippines, Poland, Portugal, Romania, Russia, Saudi Arabia, Serbia and Montenegro, Singapore, Slovakia, Slovenia, South Africa, Spain, Sweden, Switzerland, Thailand, Turkey, UK, US; note - Serbia and Montenegro have separate central banks; their links with BIS are currently under review

Bay of Bengal Iniative for

established - June 1997

Multisectoral Technical and Economic Coopertion (BIMSTEC)

aim - to foster socio-economic cooperation among members
members - (7) Bangladesh, Bhutan, Burma, India, Nepal, Sri Lanka, Thailand

Benelux Economic Union (Benelux)

note - acronym from Belgium, Netherlands, and Luxembourg
established - 3 February 1958; effective - 1 November 1960
aim - to develop closer economic cooperation and integration
members - (3) Belgium, Luxembourg, Netherlands

Big Seven

note - membership is the same as the Group of 7
established - 1975
aim - to discuss and coordinate major economic policies
members - (7) Big Six (Canada, France, Germany, Italy, Japan, UK) plus the US

Big Six

note - not to be confused with the Group of 6
established - 1967
aim - to foster economic cooperation
members - (6) Canada, France, Germany, Italy, Japan, UK

Black Sea Economic Cooperation Zone (BSEC)

established - 25 June 1992
aim - to enhance regional stability through economic cooperation
members - (12) Albania, Armenia, Azerbaijan, Bulgaria, Georgia, Greece, Moldova, Romania, Russia, Serbia and Montenegro, Turkey, Ukraine; note - Macedonia is in the process of joining
observers - (9) Austria, Egypt, France, Germany, Israel, Italy, Poland, Slovakia, Tunisia; note - Bosnia and Herzegovina, Croatia, and Slovenia have applied for observer status

Caribbean Community and Common Market (Caricom)

established - 4 July 1973; effective - 1 August 1973
aim - to promote economic integration and development, especially among the less developed countries
members - (15) Antigua and Barbuda, The Bahamas, Barbados, Belize, Dominica, Grenada, Guyana, Haiti, Jamaica, Montserrat, Saint Kitts and Nevis, Saint Lucia, Saint Vincent and the Grenadines, Suriname, Trinidad and Tobago
associate members - (5) Anguilla, Bermuda, British Virgin Islands, Cayman Islands, Turks and Caicos Islands

Caribbean Development Bank (CDB)

established - 18 October 1969; effective - 26 January 1970
aim - to promote economic development and cooperation
regional members - (20) Anguilla, Antigua and Barbuda, The Bahamas, Barbados, Belize, British Virgin Islands, Cayman Islands, Colombia, Dominica, Grenada, Guyana, Jamaica, Mexico, Montserrat, Saint Kitts and Nevis, Saint Lucia, Saint Vincent and the Grenadines, Trinidad and Tobago, Turks and Caicos Islands, Venezuela
nonregional members - (5) Canada, China, Germany, Italy, UK

Central African Customs and Economic Union (UDEAC)

see Monetary and Economic Community of Central Africa (CEMAC)

Central African States Development Bank (BDEAC)

note - acronym from Banque de Developpement des Etats de l'Afrique Centrale
established - 3 December 1975
aim - to provide loans for economic development
members - (10) African Development Bank (AfDB), Cameroon, Central African States Bank (BEAC), Central African Republic, Chad, Republic of the Congo, Equatorial Guinea, France, Gabon, Kuwait

Central American Bank for Economic Integration (BCIE)

note - acronym from Banco Centroamericano de Integracion Economico
established - 13 December 1960 signature of Articles of Agreement; 31 May 1961 began operations
aim - to promote economic integration and development
members - (5) Costa Rica, El Salvador, Guatemala, Honduras, Nicaragua
nonregional members - (5) Argentina, China, Colombia, Mexico, Spain

Central American Common Market (CACM)

established - 13 December 1960, collapsed in 1969, reinstated in 1991
aim - to promote establishment of a Central American Common Market
members - (5) Costa Rica, El Salvador, Guatemala, Honduras, Nicaragua; note - Panama, although not a member, pursues full regional cooperation

Central European Initiative (CEI)

note - evolved from the Quadrilateral Initiative and the Hexagonal Initiative
established - 11 November 1989 as the Quadrilateral Initiative, 27 July 1991 became the Hexagonal Initiative, July 1992 its present name was adopted
aim - to form an economic and political cooperation group for the region between the Adriatic and the Baltic Seas
members - (17) Albania, Austria, Belarus, Bosnia and Herzegovina, Bulgaria, Croatia, Czech Republic, Hungary, Italy, Macedonia, Moldova, Poland, Romania, Serbia and Montenegro, Slovakia, Slovenia, Ukraine

Colombo Plan (CP)

established - May 1950 proposal was adopted; 1 July 1951 commenced full operations
aim - to promote economic and social development in Asia and the Pacific
members - (25) Afghanistan, Australia, Bangladesh, Bhutan, Burma, Fiji, India, Indonesia, Iran, Japan, South Korea, Laos, Malaysia, Maldives, Mongolia, Nepal, NZ, Pakistan, Papua New Guinea, Philippines, Singapore, Sri Lanka, Thailand, US, Vietnam

Common Market for Eastern and Southern Africa (COMESA)

note - formerly known as Preferential Trade Area for Eastern and Southern Africa (PTA)
established - 5 November 1993
aim - recognizing, promoting and protecting fundamental human rights, commitment to the principles of liberty and rule of law, maintaining peace and stability through the promotion and strengthening of good neighborliness, commitment to peaceful settlement of disputes among member states
members - (20) Angola, Burundi, Comoros, Democratic Republic of the Congo, Djibouti, Egypt, Eritrea, Ethiopia, Kenya, Libya, Madagascar, Malawi, Mauritius, Rwanda, Seychelles, Sudan, Swaziland, Uganda, Zambia, Zimbabwe

Commonwealth (C)

note - also known as Commonwealth of Nations
established - 31 December 1931
aim - to foster multinational cooperation and assistance, as a voluntary asso-

ciation that evolved from the British Empire
members - (53) Antigua and Barbuda, Australia, The Bahamas, Bangladesh, Barbados, Belize, Botswana, Brunei, Cameroon, Canada, Cyprus, Dominica, Fiji, The Gambia, Ghana, Grenada, Guyana, India, Jamaica, Kenya, Kiribati, Lesotho, Malawi, Malaysia, Maldives, Malta, Mauritius, Mozambique, Namibia, Nauru, NZ, Nigeria, Pakistan (suspended), Papua New Guinea, Saint Kitts and Nevis, Saint Lucia, Saint Vincent and the Grenadines, Samoa, Seychelles, Sierra Leone, Singapore, Solomon Islands, South Africa, Sri Lanka, Swaziland, Tanzania, Tonga, Trinidad and Tobago, Tuvalu, Uganda, UK, Vanuatu, Zambia; note - on 7 December 2003 Zimbabwe withdrew its membership from the Commonwealth

Commonwealth of Independent States (CIS)

established - 8 December 1991; effective - 21 December 1991
aim - to coordinate intercommonwealth relations and to provide a mechanism for the orderly dissolution of the USSR
members - (11) Armenia, Azerbaijan, Belarus, Georgia, Kazakhstan, Kyrgyzstan, Moldova, Russia, Tajikistan, Ukraine, Uzbekistan
associates - (1) Turkmenistan

Communist countries

traditionally the Marxist-Leninist states with authoritarian governments and command economies based on the Soviet model; most of the original and the successor states are no longer Communist; see centrally planned economies

Coordinating Committee on Export Controls (COCOM)

established in 1949 to control the export of strategic products and technical data from member countries to proscribed destinations; members were: Australia, Belgium, Canada, Denmark, France, Germany, Greece, Italy, Japan, Luxembourg, Netherlands, Norway, Portugal, Spain, Turkey, UK, US; abolished 31 March 1994; COCOM members established a new organization, the Wassenaar Arrangement, with expanded membership on 12 July 1996 that focuses on nonproliferation export controls as opposed to East-West control of advanced technology

Council for Mutual Economic Assistance (CEMA)

note - also known as CMEA or Comecon
established 25 January 1949 to promote the development of socialist economies and abolished 1 January 1991; members included Afghanistan (observer), Albania (had not participated since 1961 break with USSR), Angola (observer), Bulgaria, Cuba, Czechoslovakia, Ethiopia (observer), GDR, Hungary, Laos (observer), Mongolia, Mozambique (observer), Nicaragua (observer), Poland, Romania, USSR, Vietnam, Yemen (observer), Yugoslavia (associate)

Council of Arab Economic Unity (CAEU)

established - 3 June 1957; effective - 30 May 1964
aim - to promote economic integration among Arab nations
members - (10 plus the Palestine Liberation Organization) Egypt, Iraq, Jordan, Kuwait, Libya, Mauritania, Somalia, Sudan, Syria, Yemen, Palestine Liberation Organization

Council of Europe (CE)

established - 5 May 1949; effective - 3 August 1949
aim - to promote increased unity and quality of life in Europe
members - (46) Albania, Andorra, Armenia, Austria, Azerbaijan, Belgium,

Bosnia and Herzegovina, Bulgaria, Croatia, Cyprus, Czech Republic, Denmark, Estonia, Finland, France, Georgia, Germany, Greece, Hungary, Iceland, Ireland, Italy, Latvia, Liechtenstein, Lithuania, Luxembourg, Macedonia, Malta, Moldova, Monaco, Netherlands, Norway, Poland, Portugal, Romania, Russia, San Marino, Serbia and Montenegro, Slovakia, Slovenia, Spain, Sweden, Switzerland, Turkey, Ukraine, UK
observers - (6) Canada, Holy See, Israel, Japan, Mexico, US

Council of the Baltic Sea States (CBSS)

established - 6 March 1992
aim - to promote cooperation among the Baltic Sea states in the areas of aid to new democratic institutions, economic development, humanitarian aid, energy and the environment, cultural programs and education, and transportation and communication
members - (12) Denmark, Estonia, EC, Finland, Germany, Iceland, Latvia, Lithuania, Norway, Poland, Russia, Sweden
observers - (7) France, Italy, Netherlands, Slovakia, Ukraine, UK, US

Council of the Entente (Entente)

established - 29 May 1959
aim - to promote economic, social, and political coordination
members - (5) Benin, Burkina Faso, Cote d'Ivoire, Niger, Togo

Customs Cooperation Council (CCC)

note - see World Customs Organization (WCO)

East African Development Bank (EADB)

established - 6 June 1967; effective - 1 December 1967
aim - to promote economic development
members - (3) Kenya, Tanzania, Uganda

East Asia Summit (EAS)

established - 14 December 2005
aim - to promote cooperation in political and security issues; to promote development, financial stability, energy security, economic integration and growth; to eradicate poverty and narrow the development gap in East Asia, and to promote deeper cultural understanding
members - (16) Australia, Brunei, Burma, Cambodia, China, India, Indonesia, Japan, South Korea, Laos, Malaysia, NZ, Philippines, Singapore, Thailand, Vietnam

Economic Community of West African States (ECOWAS)

established - 28 May 1975
aim - to promote regional economic cooperation
members - (15) Benin, Burkina Faso, Cape Verde, Cote d'Ivoire, The Gambia, Ghana, Guinea, Guinea-Bissau, Liberia, Mali, Niger, Nigeria, Senegal, Sierra Leone, Togo

Economic Community of the Great Lakes Countries (CEPGL)

note - acronym from Communaute Economique des Pays des Grands Lacs
established - 20 September 1976
aim - to promote regional economic cooperation and integration
members - (3) Burundi, Democratic Republic of the Congo, Rwanda

Economic Cooperation Organization (ECO)

established - 27-29 January 1985
aim - to promote regional cooperation in trade, transportation, communications, tourism, cultural affairs, and economic development
members - (10) Afghanistan, Azerbaijan, Iran, Kazakhstan, Kyrgyzstan, Pakistan, Tajikistan, Turkey, Turkmenistan, Uzbekistan

Economic and Monetary Union (EMU)

note - an integral part of the European Union; also known as the European Economic and Monetary Union
established - 1-2 December 1969 (proposed at summit conference of heads of government; 7 February 1992 (Maastricht Treaty signed)
aim - to promote a single market by creating a single currency, the euro; timetable - 2 May 1998: European exchange rates fixed for 1 January 1999; 1 January 1999: all banks and stock exchanges begin using euros; 1 January 2002: the euro goes into circulation; 1 July 2002 local currencies no longer accepted
members - (12) Austria, Belgium, Finland, France, Germany, Greece, Ireland, Italy, Luxembourg, Netherlands, Portugal, Spain

Economic and Social Council (ECOSOC)

established - 26 June 1945; effective - 24 October 1945
aim - to coordinate the economic and social work of the UN; includes five regional commissions (Economic Commission for Africa, Economic Commission for Europe, Economic Commission for Latin America and the Caribbean, Economic and Social Commission for Asia and the Pacific, Economic and Social Commission for Western Asia) and nine functional commissions (Commission for Social Development, Commission on Human Rights, Commission on Narcotic Drugs, Commission on the Status of Women, Commission on Population and Development, Statistical Commission, Commission on Science and Technology for Development, Commission on Sustainable Development, and Commission on Crime Prevention and Criminal Justice)
members - (54) selected on a rotating basis from all regions

Euro-Atlantic Partnership Council (EAPC)

note - began as the North Atlantic Cooperation Council (NACC); an extension of NATO
established - 8 November 1991; effective - 20 December 1991
aim - to discuss cooperation on mutual political and security issues
members - (46) Albania, Armenia, Austria, Azerbaijan, Belarus, Belgium, Bulgaria, Canada, Croatia, Czech Republic, Denmark, Estonia, Finland, France, Georgia, Germany, Greece, Hungary, Iceland, Ireland, Italy, Kazakhstan, Kyrgyzstan, Latvia, Lithuania, Luxembourg, Macedonia, Moldova, Netherlands, Norway, Poland, Portugal, Romania, Russia, Slovakia, Slovenia, Spain, Sweden, Switzerland, Tajikistan, Turkey, Turkmenistan, Ukraine, UK, US, Uzbekistan

European Bank for Reconstruction and Development (EBRD)

established - 8-9 January 1990 (proposals made); 15 April 1991 (bank inaugurated)
aim - to facilitate the transition of seven centrally planned economies in Europe (Bulgaria, former Czechoslovakia, Hungary, Poland, Romania, former USSR, and former Yugoslavia) to market economies by committing 60% of its loans to privatization
members - (62) Albania, Armenia, Australia, Austria, Azerbaijan, Belarus, Belgium, Bosnia and Herzegovina, Bulgaria, Canada, Croatia, Cyprus, Czech Republic, Denmark, Egypt, EU, European Investment Bank (EIB), Estonia, Finland, France, Georgia, Germany, Greece, Hungary, Iceland, Ireland, Israel, Italy, Japan, Kazakhstan, South Korea, Kyrgyzstan, Latvia, Liechtenstein, Lithuania, Luxembourg, Macedonia, Malta, Mexico, Moldova, Mongolia, Morocco, Netherlands, NZ, Norway, Poland, Portugal, Romania, Russia,

Serbia and Montenegro, Slovakia, Slovenia, Spain, Sweden, Switzerland, Tajikistan, Turkey, Turkmenistan, Ukraine, UK, US, Uzbekistan

European Community (or European Communities, EC)

established 8 April 1965 to integrate the European Atomic Energy Community (Euratom), the European Coal and Steel Community (ECSC), the European Economic Community (EEC or Common Market), and to establish a completely integrated common market and an eventual federation of Europe; merged into the European Union (EU) on 7 February 1992; member states at the time of merger were Belgium, Denmark, France, Germany, Greece, Ireland, Italy, Luxembourg, Netherlands, Portugal, Spain, UK

European Free Trade Association (EFTA)

established - 4 January 1960; effective - 3 May 1960
aim - to promote expansion of free trade
members - (4) Iceland, Liechtenstein, Norway, Switzerland

European Investment Bank (EIB)

established - 25 March 1957; effective - 1 January 1958
aim - to promote economic development of the EU and its predecessors, the EEC and the EC
members - (25) Austria, Belgium, Cyprus, Czech Republic, Denmark, Estonia, Finland, France, Germany, Greece, Hungary, Ireland, Italy, Latvia, Lithuania, Luxembourg, Malta, Netherlands, Poland, Portugal, Slovakia, Slovenia, Spain, Sweden, UK

European Organization for Nuclear Research (CERN)

note - acronym retained from the predecessor organization Conseil Europeenne pour la Recherche Nucleaire
established - 1 July 1953; effective - 29 September 1954
aim - to foster nuclear research for peaceful purposes only
members - (20) Austria, Belgium, Bulgaria, Czech Republic, Denmark, Finland, France, Germany, Greece, Hungary, Italy, Netherlands, Norway, Poland, Portugal, Slovakia, Spain, Sweden, Switzerland, UK
observers - (8) European Commission, India, Israel, Japan, Russia, Turkey, United Nations Educational, Scientific, and Cultural Organization (UNESCO), US

European Space Agency (ESA)

established - 31 May 1975
aim - to promote peaceful cooperation in space research and technology
members - (17) Austria, Belgium, Denmark, Finland, France, Germany, Greece, Ireland, Italy, Luxembourg, Netherlands, Norway, Portugal, Spain, Sweden, Switzerland, UK
cooperating states - (3) Canada, Czech Republic, Hungary

European Union (EU)

note - see European Union entry at the end of the "country" listings

First World

another term for countries with advanced, industrialized economies; this term is fading from use; see developed countries (DCs)

Food and Agriculture Organization (FAO)

established - 16 October 1945
aim - to raise living standards and increase availability of agricultural products; a UN specialized agency
members - (187) includes all UN member countries except Andorra, Belarus, Brunei, Liechtenstein, Russia, and Singapore (185 total); plus Cook Islands and Niue

Four Dragons

the four small Asian less developed countries (LDCs) that have experienced unusually rapid economic growth; also known as the Four Tigers; this group consists of Hong Kong, South Korea, Singapore, Taiwan; these countries are included in the IMF's "advanced economies" group

Franc Zone (FZ)

note - also known as Conference des Ministres des Finances des Pays de la Zone Franc
established - 1964
aim - to form a monetary union among countries whose currencies were linked to the French franc
members - (16) Benin, Burkina Faso, Cameroon, Central African Republic, Chad, Comoros, Republic of the Congo, Cote d'Ivoire, Equatorial Guinea, France, Gabon, Guinea-Bissau, Mali, Niger, Senegal, Togo

Front Line States (FLS)

established to achieve black majority rule in South Africa; has since gone out of existence; members included Angola, Botswana, Mozambique, Namibia, Tanzania, Zambia, Zimbabwe

GUAM

note-acronym standing for the member countries, Georgia, Ukraine, Azerbaijan, Moldova; formerly known as GUUAM before Uzbekistan with drew in 5 May 2005
established - 7 June 2001
aim - commits the countries to cooperation and assistance in social and economic development, the strengthening and broadening of trade and economic relations, and the development and effective use of transport and communications, highways, and related infrastructure crossing the boundaries of the member states
members - (4) Azerbaijan, Georgia, Moldova, Ukraine

General Agreement on Tariffs and Trade (GATT)

see the World Trade Organization (WTO)

Group of 10 (G-10)

note - also known as the Paris Club; includes the wealthiest members of the IMF who provide most of the money to be loaned and act as the informal steering committee; name persists despite increased membership
established - October 1962
aim - to coordinate credit policy
members - (11) Belgium, Canada, France, Germany, Italy, Japan, Netherlands, Sweden, Switzerland, UK, US
nonstate participants - (4) BIS, EU, IMF, OECD

Group of 11 (G-11)

note - also known as the Cartagena Group
established in 21-22 June 1984, in Cartagena, Colombia, aim was to provide a forum for largest debtor nations in Latin America; members were: Argentina, Bolivia, Brazil, Chile, Colombia, Dominican Republic, Ecuador, Mexico, Peru, Uruguay, Venezuela

Group of 15 (G-15)

note - byproduct of the Nonaligned Movement; name persists despite increased membership
established - September 1989
aim - to promote economic cooperation among developing nations; to act as

the main political organ for the Nonaligned Movement
members - (19) Algeria, Argentina, Brazil, Chile, Colombia, Egypt, India, Indonesia, Iran, Jamaica, Kenya, Malaysia, Mexico, Nigeria, Peru, Senegal, Sri Lanka, Venezuela, Zimbabwe

Group of 2 (G-2)

informal term that came into use about 1986; to facilitate bilateral economic cooperation between the two most powerful economic giants; members were Japan, US

Group of 24 (G-24)

established - 1 August 1989
aim - to promote the interests of developing countries in Africa, Asia, and Latin America within the IMF
members - (24) Algeria, Argentina, Brazil, Colombia, Democratic Republic of the Congo, Cote d'Ivoire, Egypt, Ethiopia, Gabon, Ghana, Guatemala, India, Iran, Lebanon, Mexico, Nigeria, Pakistan, Peru, Philippines, South Africa, Sri Lanka, Syria, Trinidad and Tobago, Venezuela

Group of 3 (G-3)

established - September 1990
aim - mechanism for policy coordination
members - (3) Colombia, Mexico, Venezuela

Group of 5 (G-5)

established - 22 September 1985
aim - to coordinate the economic policies of five major noncommunist economic powers
members - (5) France, Germany, Japan, UK, US

Group of 6 (G-6)

note - also known as Groupe des Six Sur le Desarmement; not to be confused with the Big Six
established - 22 May 1984
aim - to achieve nuclear disarmament
members - (6) Argentina, Greece, India, Mexico, Sweden, Tanzania

Group of 7 (G-7)

note - membership is the same as the Big Seven
established - 22 September 1985
aim - to facilitate economic cooperation among the seven major noncommunist economic powers
members - (7) Group of 5 (France, Germany, Japan, UK, US) plus Canada and Italy

Group of 77 (G-77)

established - 15 June1964; October 1967 first ministerial meeting
aim - to promote economic cooperation among developing countries; name persists in spite of increased membership
members - (131 plus the Palestine Liberation Organization) Afghanistan, Algeria, Angola, Antigua and Barbuda, Argentina, The Bahamas, Bahrain, Bangladesh, Barbados, Belize, Benin, Bhutan, Bolivia, Bosnia and Herzegovina, Botswana, Brazil, Brunei, Burkina Faso, Burma, Burundi, Cambodia, Cameroon, Cape Verde, Central African Republic, Chad, Chile, China, Colombia, Comoros, Democratic Republic of the Congo, Republic of the Congo, Costa Rica, Cote d'Ivoire, Cuba, Djibouti, Dominica, Dominican Republic, East Timor, Ecuador, Egypt, El Salvador, Equatorial Guinea, Eritrea, Ethiopia, Fiji, Gabon, The Gambia, Ghana, Grenada, Guatemala,

Guinea, Guinea-Bissau, Guyana, Haiti, Honduras, India, Indonesia, Iran, Iraq, Jamaica, Jordan, Kenya, North Korea, Kuwait, Laos, Lebanon, Lesotho, Liberia, Libya, Madagascar, Malawi, Malaysia, Maldives, Mali, Marshall Islands, Mauritania, Mauritius, Federated States of Micronesia, Mongolia, Morocco, Mozambique, Namibia, Nepal, Nicaragua, Niger, Nigeria, Oman, Pakistan, Palau, Panama, Papua New Guinea, Paraguay, Peru, Philippines, Qatar, Romania, Rwanda, Saint Kitts and Nevis, Saint Lucia, Saint Vincent and the Grenadines, Samoa, Sao Tome and Principe, Saudi Arabia, Senegal, Seychelles, Sierra Leone, Singapore, Solomon Islands, Somalia, South Africa, Sri Lanka, Sudan, Suriname, Swaziland, Syria, Tanzania, Thailand, Togo, Tonga, Trinidad and Tobago, Tunisia, Turkmenistan, Uganda, UAE, Uruguay, Vanuatu, Venezuela, Vietnam, Yemen, Zambia, Zimbabwe, Palestine Liberation Organization

Group of 8 (G-8)

established - October 1975
aim - to facilitate economic cooperation among the developed countries (DCs) that participated in the Conference on International Economic Cooperation (CIEC), held in several sessions between December 1975 and 3 June 1977
members - (8) Canada, France, Germany, Italy, Japan, Russia, UK, US

Group of 9 (G-9)

established - NA
aim - to discuss matters of mutual interest on an informal basis
members - (9) Austria, Belgium, Bulgaria, Denmark, Finland, Hungary, Romania, Serbia and Montenegro, Sweden

Gulf Cooperation Council (GCC)

note - also known as the Cooperation Council for the Arab States of the Gulf
established - 25 May 1981
aim - to promote regional cooperation in economic, social, political, and military affairs
members - (6) Bahrain, Kuwait, Oman, Qatar, Saudi Arabia, UAE

Indian Ocean Commission (InOC)

established - 21 December 1982
aim - to organize and promote regional cooperation in all sectors, especially economic
members - (5) Comoros, France (for Reunion), Madagascar, Mauritius, Seychelles

Inter-American Development Bank (IADB)

note - also known as Banco Interamericano de Desarrollo (BID)
established - 8 April 1959; effective - 30 December 1959
aim - to promote economic and social development in Latin America
members - (46) Argentina, Austria, The Bahamas, Barbados, Belgium, Belize, Bolivia, Brazil, Canada, Chile, Colombia, Costa Rica, Croatia, Denmark, Dominican Republic, Ecuador, El Salvador, Finland, France, Germany, Guatemala, Guyana, Haiti, Honduras, Israel, Italy, Jamaica, Japan, Mexico, Netherlands, Nicaragua, Norway, Panama, Paraguay, Peru, Portugal, Slovenia, Spain, Suriname, Sweden, Switzerland, Trinidad and Tobago, UK, US, Uruguay, Venezuela

Inter-Governmental Authority on Development (IGAD)

note - formerly known as Inter-Governmental Authority on Drought and Development (IGADD)

established - 15-16 January 1986 as the Inter-Governmental Authority on Drought and Development; revitalized - 21 March 1996 as the Inter-Governmental Authority on Development
aim - to promote a social, economic, and scientific community among its members
members - (7) Djibouti, Eritrea, Ethiopia, Kenya, Somalia, Sudan, Uganda

Inter-Parliamentary Union (IPU)

established - 1889
aim - fosters contacts among parliamentarians, considers and expresses views of international interest and concern with the purpose of bringing about action by parliaments and parliamentarians, contributes to the defense and promotion of human rights, contributes to better knowledge of representative institutions
members - (143) Albania, Algeria, Andorra, Angola, Argentina, Armenia, Australia, Austria, Azerbaijan, Bahrain, Bangladesh, Belarus, Belgium, Benin, Bolivia, Bosnia and Herzegovina, Botswana, Brazil, Bulgaria, Burkina Faso, Burundi, Cambodia, Cameroon, Canada, Cape Verde, Chile, China, Colombia, Democratic Republic of the Congo, Republic of the Congo, Costa Rica, Cote d'Ivoire, Croatia, Cuba, Cyprus, Czech Republic, Denmark, Djibouti, Dominican Republic, Ecuador, Egypt, El Salvador, Estonia, Ethiopia, Fiji, Finland, France, Gabon, Georgia, Germany, Ghana, Greece, Guatemala, Guinea, Hungary, Iceland, India, Indonesia, Iran, Ireland, Israel, Italy, Japan, Jordan, Kazahstan, Kenya, North Korea, South Korea, Kuwait, Kyrgyzstan, Laos, Latvia, Lebanon, Liberia, Libya, Lichtenstein, Lithuania, Luxembourg, Macedonia, Madagascar, Malaysia, Maldives, Mali, Malta, Mauritius, Mexico, Moldova, Monaco, Mongolia, Morocco, Mozambique, Namibia, Nepal, Netherlands, NZ, Nicaragua, Niger, Nigeria, Norway, Pakistan, Panama, Papua New Guinea, Peru, Philippines, Poland, Portugal, Romania, Russia, Rwanda, Samoa, San Marino, Sao Tome and Principe, Saudi Arabia, Senegal, Serbia and Montenegro, Singapore, Slovakia, Slovenia, South Africa, Spain, Sri Lanka, Sudan, Suriname, Sweden, Switzerland, Syria, Tanzania, Tajikistan, Thailand, Togo, Tunisia, Turkey, Uganda, Ukraine, UAE, UK, Uruguay, Uzbekistan, Venezuela, Vietnam, Yemen, Zambia, Zimbabwe
associate members - (7) Andean Parliament, Central American Parliament, Community Parliament of the Economic Community of West African States, East African Legislative Assembly, European Parliament, Latin American Parliament, Parliamentary Assembly of the Council of Europe

International Atomic Energy Agency (IAEA)

established - 26 October 1956; effective - 29 July 1957
aim - to promote peaceful uses of atomic energy
members - (140) Afghanistan, Albania, Algeria, Angola, Argentina, Armenia, Australia, Austria, Azerbaijan, Bangladesh, Belarus, Belgium, Benin, Bolivia, Bosnia and Herzegovina, Botswana, Brazil, Bulgaria, Burkina Faso, Burma, Cameroon, Canada, Central African Republic, Chad, Chile, China, Colombia, Democratic Republic of the Congo, Costa Rica, Cote d'Ivoire, Croatia, Cuba, Cyprus, Czech Republic, Denmark, Dominican Republic, Ecuador, Egypt, El Salvador, Eritrea, Estonia, Ethiopia, Finland, France, Gabon, Georgia, Germany, Ghana, Greece, Guatemala, Haiti, Holy See, Honduras, Hungary, Iceland, India, Indonesia, Iran, Iraq, Ireland, Israel, Italy, Jamaica, Japan, Jordan, Kazakhstan, Kenya, South Korea, Kuwait,

Kyrgyzstan, Latvia, Lebanon, Liberia, Libya, Liechtenstein, Lithuania, Luxembourg, Macedonia, Madagascar, Malaysia, Mali, Malta, Marshall Islands, Mauritania, Mauritius, Mexico, Moldova, Monaco, Mongolia, Morocco, Namibia, Netherlands, NZ, Nicaragua, Niger, Nigeria, Norway, Pakistan, Panama, Paraguay, Peru, Philippines, Poland, Portugal, Qatar, Romania, Russia, Saudi Arabia, Senegal, Serbia and Montenegro, Seychelles, Sierra Leone, Singapore, Slovakia, Slovenia, South Africa, Spain, Sri Lanka, Sudan, Sweden, Switzerland, Syria, Tajikistan, Tanzania, Thailand, Togo, Tunisia, Turkey, Uganda, Ukraine, UAE, UK, US, Uruguay, Uzbekistan, Venezuela, Vietnam, Yemen, Zambia, Zimbabwe

International Bank for Reconstruction and Development (IBRD)

note - also known as the World Bank
established - 22 July 1944; effective - 27 December 1945
aim - to provide economic development loans; a UN specialized agency
members - (184) includes all UN member countries except Andorra, Cuba, North Korea, Liechtenstein, Monaco, Nauru, and Tuvalu

International Chamber of Commerce (ICC)

established - 1919
aim - to promote free trade and private enterprise and to represent business interests at national and international levels
members - (91 national committees) Algeria, Argentina, Australia, Austria, Bahrain, Bangladesh, Belgium, Brazil, Burkina Faso, Cameroon, Canada, Caribbean, Chile, China, Colombia, Costa Rica, Croatia, Cuba, Cyprus, Czech Republic, Denmark, Dominican Republic, Ecuador, Egypt, El Salvador, Finland, France, Georgia, Germany, Ghana, Greece, Guatemala, Hong Kong, Hungary, Iceland, India, Indonesia, Iran, Ireland, Israel, Italy, Japan, Jordan, South Korea, Kuwait, Lebanon, Lithuania, Luxembourg, Madagascar, Malaysia, Mexico, Monaco, Morocco, Nepal, Netherlands, NZ, Nigeria, Norway, Pakistan, Panama, Peru, Philippines, Poland, Portugal, Qatar, Romania, Russia, Saudi Arabia, Senegal, Serbia and Montenegro, Singapore, Slovakia, Slovenia, South Africa, Spain, Sri Lanka, Sweden, Switzerland, Syria, Taiwan, Tanzania, Thailand, Togo, Tunisia, Turkey, Ukraine, UAE, UK, US, Uruguay, Venezuela

International Civil Aviation Organization (ICAO)

established - 7 December 1944; effective - 4 April 1947
aim - to promote international cooperation in civil aviation; a UN specialized agency
members - (189) includes all UN member countries except Dominica, Liechtenstein, and Tuvalu (188 total); plus Cook Islands

International Civilian Support Mission in Haiti (MICAH)

established 17 December 1999 to promote respect for human rights; members included Argentina, Benin, Canada, France, India, Mali, Niger, Senegal, Togo, Tunisia, US; closed 2001

International Committee of the Red Cross (ICRC)

established - 17 February 1863
aim - to provide humanitarian aid in wartime
members - (25 individuals) all Swiss nationals

International Confederation of Free Trade Unions (ICFTU)

established - December 1949
aim - to promote the trade union movement
members - (233 affiliated organizations in the following 153 countries plus

the Palestine Liberation Organization) Albania, Algeria, Angola, Antigua and Barbuda, Argentina, Australia, Austria, Azerbaijan, The Bahamas, Bahrain, Bangladesh, Barbados, Belarus, Belgium, Belize, Benin, Bermuda, Bosnia and Herzegovina, Botswana, Brazil, Bulgaria, Burkina Faso, Burundi, Cameroon, Canada, Cape Verde, Central African Republic, Chad, Chile, Colombia, Democratic Republic of the Congo, Republic of the Congo, Cook Islands, Costa Rica, Cote d'Ivoire, Croatia, Curacao, Cyprus, Czech Republic, Denmark, Djibouti, Dominica, Dominican Republic, Ecuador, El Salvador, Eritrea, Estonia, Ethiopia, Fiji, Finland, France, French Polynesia, Gabon, The Gambia, Georgia, Germany, Ghana, Greece, Grenada, Guatemala, Guinea, Guinea-Bissau, Guyana, Honduras, Hong Kong, Hungary, Iceland, India, Indonesia, Israel, Italy, Jamaica, Japan, Jordan, Kenya, Kiribati, South Korea, Kosovo, Latvia, Lebanon, Liberia, Lithuania, Luxembourg, Madagascar, Malawi, Malaysia, Mali, Malta, Mauritania, Mauritius, Mexico, Moldova, Mongolia, Montserrat, Morocco, Mozambique, Namibia, Nepal, Netherlands, New Caledonia, NZ, Nicaragua, Niger, Nigeria, Norway, Pakistan, Panama, Papua New Guinea, Paraguay, Peru, Philippines, Poland, Portugal, Romania, Russia, Rwanda, Saint Helena, Saint Kitts and Nevis, Saint Lucia, Saint Vincent and the Grenadines, Samoa, San Marino, Sao Tome and Principe, Senegal, Serbia and Montenegro, Seychelles, Sierra Leone, Singapore, Slovakia, South Africa, Spain, Sri Lanka, Suriname, Swaziland, Sweden, Switzerland, Taiwan, Tanzania, Thailand, Togo, Tonga, Trinidad and Tobago, Tunisia, Turkey, Uganda, Ukraine, UK, US, Vanuatu, Venezuela, Yemen, Zambia, Zimbabwe, Palestine Liberation Organization

International Court of Justice (ICJ)

note - also known as the World Court
established - 3 February 1946 superseded Permanent Court of International Justice
aim - primary judicial organ of the UN
members - (15 judges) elected by the UN General Assembly and Security Council to represent all principal legal systems

International Criminal Court (ICCt)

established - 11 April 2002
aim - to hold all individuals and countries accountable to international laws of conduct; to specify international standards of conduct; to provide an important mechanism for implementing these standards; to ensure that perpetrators are brought to justice
members (countries that have ratified the treaty) - (99) Afghanistan, Albania, Andorra, Antigua and Barbuda, Argentina, Australia, Austria, Barbados, Belgium, Belize, Benin, Bolivia, Bosnia and Herzegovina, Botswana, Brazil, Bulgaria, Burkina Faso, Burundi, Cambodia, Canada, Central African Republic, Colombia, Democratic Republic of the Congo, Republic of the Congo, Costa Rica, Croatia, Cyprus, Denmark, Djibouti, Dominica, Dominican Republic, East Timor, Ecuador, Estonia, Fiji, Finland, France, Gabon, The Gambia, Georgia, Germany, Ghana, Greece, Guinea, Guyana, Honduras, Hungary, Iceland, Ireland, Italy, Jordan, Kenya, South Korea, Latvia, Lesotho, Liberia, Liechtenstein, Lithuania, Luxembourg, Macedonia, Malawi, Mali, Malta, Marshall Islands, Mauritius, Mongolia, Namibia, Nauru, Netherlands, NZ, Niger, Nigeria, Norway, Panama, Paraguay, Peru, Poland, Portugal, Romania, Saint Vincent and the Grenadines, Samoa, San

Marino, Senegal, Serbia and Montenegro, Sierra Leone, Slovakia, Slovenia, South Africa, Spain, Sweden, Switzerland, Tajikistan, Tanzania, Trinidad and Tobago, Uganda, UK, Uruguay, Venezuela, Zambia
signatory states (countries that have signed, but not ratified, the treaty) - (43) Algeria, Angola, Armenia, The Bahamas, Bahrain, Bangladesh, Cameroon, Cape Verde, Chad, Chile, Comoros, Cote d'Ivoire, Czech Republic, Egypt, Eritrea, Guinea-Bissau, Haiti, Iran, Israel, Jamaica, Kuwait, Kyrgyzstan, Madagascar, Mexico, Moldova, Monaco, Morocco, Mozambique, Oman, Philippines, Russia, Saint Lucia, Sao Tome and Principe, Seychelles, Solomon Islands, Sudan, Syria, Thailand, Ukraine, UAE, Uzbekistan, Yemen, Zimbabwe

International Criminal Police Organization (Interpol)

established - September 1923 set up as the International Criminal Police Commission; 13 June 1956 constitution modified and present name adopted
aim - to promote international cooperation among police authorities in fighting crime
members - (184) Afghanistan, Albania, Algeria, Andorra, Angola, Antigua and Barbuda, Argentina, Armenia, Aruba, Australia, Austria, Azerbaijan, The Bahamas, Bahrain, Bangladesh, Barbados, Belarus, Belgium, Belize, Benin, Bhutan, Bolivia, Bosnia and Herzegovina, Botswana, Brazil, Brunei, Bulgaria, Burkina Faso, Burma, Burundi, Cambodia, Cameroon, Canada, Cape Verde, Central African Republic, Chad, Chile, China, Colombia, Comoros, Democratic Republic of the Congo, Republic of the Congo, Costa Rica, Cote d'Ivoire, Croatia, Cuba, Cyprus, Czech Republic, Denmark, Djibouti, Dominica, Dominican Republic, East Timor, Ecuador, Egypt, El Salvador, Equatorial Guinea, Eritrea, Estonia, Ethiopia, Fiji, Finland, France, Gabon, The Gambia, Georgia, Germany, Ghana, Greece, Grenada, Guatemala, Guinea, Guinea-Bissau, Guyana, Haiti, Honduras, Hungary, Iceland, India, Indonesia, Iran, Iraq, Ireland, Israel, Italy, Jamaica, Japan, Jordan, Kazakhstan, Kenya, South Korea, Kuwait, Kyrgyzstan, Laos, Latvia, Lebanon, Lesotho, Liberia, Libya, Liechtenstein, Lithuania, Luxembourg, Macedonia, Madagascar, Malawi, Malaysia, Maldives, Mali, Malta, Marshall Islands, Mauritania, Mauritius, Mexico, Moldova, Monaco, Mongolia, Morocco, Mozambique, Namibia, Nauru, Nepal, Netherlands, Netherlands Antilles, NZ, Nicaragua, Niger, Nigeria, Norway, Oman, Pakistan, Panama, Papua New Guinea, Paraguay, Peru, Philippines, Poland, Portugal, Qatar, Romania, Russia, Rwanda, Saint Kitts and Nevis, Saint Lucia, Saint Vincent and the Grenadines, Sao Tome and Principe, Saudi Arabia, Senegal, Serbia and Montenegro, Seychelles, Sierra Leone, Singapore, Slovakia, Slovenia, Somalia, South Africa, Spain, Sri Lanka, Sudan, Suriname, Swaziland, Sweden, Switzerland, Syria, Tajikistan, Tanzania, Thailand, Togo, Tonga, Trinidad and Tobago, Tunisia, Turkey, Turkmenistan, Uganda, Ukraine, UAE, UK, US, Uruguay, Uzbekistan, Venezuela, Vietnam, Yemen, Zambia, Zimbabwe
subbureaus - (10) American Samoa, Anguilla, Bermuda, British Virgin Islands, Cayman Islands, Eastern Africa, Gibraltar, Montserrat, Puerto Rico, Turks and Caicos Islands

International Development Association (IDA)

established - 26 January 1960; effective - 24 September 1960
aim - to provide economic loans for low-income countries; UN specialized agency and IBRD affiliate
members - (166)

Part I - (27 developed countries) Australia, Austria, Belgium, Canada, Denmark, EU, Finland, France, Germany, Iceland, Ireland, Italy, Japan, Kuwait, Luxembourg, Netherlands, NZ, Norway, Portugal, Russia, South Africa, Spain, Sweden, Switzerland, UAE, UK, US
Part II - (139 less developed countries) Afghanistan, Albania, Algeria, Angola, Argentina, Armenia, Azerbaijan, Bangladesh, Barbados, Belize, Benin, Bhutan, Bolivia, Bosnia and Herzegovina, Botswana, Brazil, Burkina Faso, Burma, Burundi, Cambodia, Cameroon, Cape Verde, Central African Republic, Chad, Chile, China, Colombia, Comoros, Democratic Republic of the Congo, Republic of the Congo, Costa Rica, Cote d'Ivoire, Croatia, Cyprus, Czech Republic, Djibouti, Dominica, Dominican Republic, East Timor, Ecuador, Egypt, El Salvador, Equatorial Guinea, Eritrea, Ethiopia, Fiji, Gabon, The Gambia, Georgia, Ghana, Greece, Grenada, Guatemala, Guinea, Guinea-Bissau, Guyana, Haiti, Honduras, Hungary, India, Indonesia, Iran, Iraq, Israel, Jordan, Kazakhstan, Kenya, Kiribati, South Korea, Kyrgyzstan, Laos, Latvia, Lebanon, Lesotho, Liberia, Libya, Macedonia, Madagascar, Malawi, Malaysia, Maldives, Mali, Marshall Islands, Mauritania, Mauritius, Mexico, Federated States of Micronesia, Moldova, Mongolia, Morocco, Mozambique, Nepal, Nicaragua, Niger, Nigeria, Oman, Pakistan, Palau, Panama, Papua New Guinea, Paraguay, Peru, Philippines, Poland, Rwanda, Saint Kitts and Nevis, Saint Lucia, Saint Vincent and the Grenadines, Samoa, Sao Tome and Principe, Saudi Arabia, Senegal, Serbia and Montenegro, Sierra Leone, Singapore, Slovakia, Slovenia, Solomon Islands, Somalia, Sri Lanka, Sudan, Swaziland, Syria, Tajikistan, Tanzania, Thailand, Togo, Tonga, Trinidad and Tobago, Tunisia, Turkey, Uganda, Ukraine, Uzbekistan, Vanuatu, Vietnam, Yemen, Zambia, Zimbabwe

International Energy Agency (IEA)

established - 15 November 1974
aim - to promote cooperation on energy matters, especially emergency oil sharing and relations between oil consumers and oil producers; established by the OECD
members - (27) Australia, Austria, Belgium, Canada, Czech Republic, Denmark, Finland, France, Germany, Greece, Hungary, Ireland, Italy, Japan, South Korea, Luxembourg, Netherlands, NZ, Norway, Portugal, Slovakia, Spain, Sweden, Switzerland, Turkey, UK, US

International Federation of Red Cross and Red Crescent Societies (IFRCS)

note - formerly known as League of Red Cross and Red Crescent Societies (LORCS)
established - 5 May 1919
aim - to organize, coordinate, and direct international relief actions; to promote humanitarian activities; to represent and encourage the development of National Societies; to bring help to victims of armed conflicts, refugees, and displaced people; to reduce the vulnerability of people through development programs
members - (182) Afghanistan, Albania, Algeria, Andorra, Angola, Antigua and Barbuda, Argentina, Armenia, Australia, Austria, Azerbaijan, The Bahamas, Bahrain, Bangladesh, Barbados, Belarus, Belgium, Belize, Benin, Bolivia, Bosnia and Herzegovina, Botswana, Brazil, Brunei, Bulgaria, Burkina Faso, Burma, Burundi, Cambodia, Cameroon, Canada, Cape Verde, Central African Republic, Chad, Chile, China, Colombia, Democratic Republic of the Congo, Republic of the Congo, Cook Islands, Costa Rica,

Cote d'Ivoire, Croatia, Cuba, Czech Republic, Denmark, Djibouti, Dominica, Dominican Republic, Ecuador, Egypt, El Salvador, Equatorial Guinea, Estonia, Ethiopia, Fiji, Finland, France, Gabon, The Gambia, Georgia, Germany, Ghana, Greece, Grenada, Guatemala, Guinea, Guinea-Bissau, Guyana, Haiti, Honduras, Hungary, Iceland, India, Indonesia, Iran, Iraq, Ireland, Italy, Jamaica, Japan, Jordan, Kazakhstan, Kenya, Kiribati, North Korea, South Korea, Kuwait, Kyrgyzstan, Laos, Latvia, Lebanon, Lesotho, Liberia, Libya, Liechtenstein, Lithuania, Luxembourg, Macedonia, Madagascar, Malawi, Malaysia, Mali, Malta, Mauritania, Mauritius, Mexico, Federated States of Micronesia, Moldova, Monaco, Mongolia, Morocco, Mozambique, Namibia, Nepal, Netherlands, NZ, Nicaragua, Niger, Nigeria, Norway, Pakistan, Palau, Panama, Papua New Guinea, Paraguay, Peru, Philippines, Poland, Portugal, Qatar, Romania, Russia, Rwanda, Saint Kitts and Nevis, Saint Lucia, Saint Vincent and the Grenadines, Samoa, San Marino, Sao Tome and Principe, Saudi Arabia, Senegal, Serbia and Montenegro, Seychelles, Sierra Leone, Singapore, Slovakia, Slovenia, Solomon Islands, Somalia, South Africa, Spain, Sri Lanka, Sudan, Suriname, Swaziland, Sweden, Switzerland, Syria, Taiwan, Tajikistan, Tanzania, Thailand, Togo, Tonga, Trinidad and Tobago, Tunisia, Turkey, Turkmenistan, Uganda, Ukraine, UAE, UK, US, Uruguay, Uzbekistan, Vanuatu, Venezuela, Vietnam, Yemen, Zambia, Zimbabwe
observers - (5 plus the Palestine Liberation Organization) Comoros, East Timor, Eritrea, Israel, Tuvalu, Palestine Liberation Organization

International Finance Corporation (IFC)

established - 25 May 1955; effective - 24 July 1956
aim - to support private enterprise in international economic development; a UN specialized agency and IBRD affiliate
members - (178) includes all UN member countries except Andorra, Brunei, Cuba, North Korea, Liechtenstein, Monaco, Nauru, Qatar, Saint Vincent and the Grenadines, San Marino, Sao Tome and Principe, Suriname, Tuvalu

International Francophone Organization (OIF)

established - 20 March 1970
aim - founded around a common language to promote and spread the cultures of its members and to reinforce cultural and technical cooperation between them
members - (53) Albania, Andorra, Belgium, Benin, Bulgaria, Burkina Faso, Burundi, Cambodia, Cameroon, Canada, Canada - New Brunswick, Canada - Quebec, Cape Verde, Central African Republic, Chad, Comoros, Democratic Republic of Congo, Republic of Congo, Cote d'Ivoire, Djibouti, Dominican Republic, Egypt, Equatorial Guinea, France, French Community of Belgium, Gabon, Greece, Guinea, Guinea-Bissau, Haiti, Laos, Lebanon, Luxembourg, Macedonia, Madagascar, Mali, Mauritania, Mauritius, Moldova, Monaco, Morocco, Niger, Romania, Rwanda, Saint Lucia, Sao Tome and Principe, Senegal, Seychelles, Switzerland, Togo, Tunisia, Vanuatu, Vietnam
observers - (10) Armenia, Austria, Croatia, Czech Republic, Georgia, Hungary, Lithuania, Poland, Slovakia, Slovenia

International Fund for Agricultural Development (IFAD)

established - November 1974
aim - to promote agricultural development; a UN specialized agency
members - (164)

Category I - (23 industrialized aid contributors) Australia, Austria, Belgium, Canada, Denmark, Finland, France, Germany, Greece, Iceland, Ireland, Italy, Japan, Luxembourg, Netherlands, NZ, Norway, Portugal, Spain, Sweden, Switzerland, UK, US
Category II - (12 petroleum-exporting aid contributors) Algeria, Gabon, Indonesia, Iran, Iraq, Kuwait, Libya, Nigeria, Qatar, Saudi Arabia, UAE, Venezuela
Category III - (129 aid recipients) Afghanistan, Albania, Angola, Antigua and Barbuda, Argentina, Armenia, Azerbaijan, Bangladesh, Barbados, Belize, Benin, Bhutan, Bolivia, Bosnia and Herzegovina, Botswana, Brazil, Burkina Faso, Burma, Burundi, Cambodia, Cameroon, Cape Verde, Central African Republic, Chad, Chile, China, Colombia, Comoros, Democratic Republic of the Congo, Republic of the Congo, Cook Islands, Costa Rica, Cote d'Ivoire, Croatia, Cuba, Cyprus, Djibouti, Dominica, Dominican Republic, East Timor, Ecuador, Egypt, El Salvador, Equatorial Guinea, Eritrea, Ethiopia, Fiji, The Gambia, Georgia, Ghana, Grenada, Guatemala, Guinea, Guinea-Bissau, Guyana, Haiti, Honduras, India, Israel, Jamaica, Jordan, Kazakhstan, Kenya, Kiribati, North Korea, South Korea, Kyrgyzstan, Laos, Lebanon, Lesotho, Liberia, Macedonia, Madagascar, Malawi, Malaysia, Maldives, Mali, Malta, Mauritania, Mauritius, Mexico, Moldova, Mongolia, Morocco, Mozambique, Namibia, Nepal, Nicaragua, Niger, Oman, Pakistan, Panama, Papua New Guinea, Paraguay, Peru, Philippines, Romania, Rwanda, Saint Kitts and Nevis, Saint Lucia, Saint Vincent and the Grenadines, Samoa, Sao Tome and Principe, Senegal, Serbia and Montenegro, Seychelles, Sierra Leone, Solomon Islands, Somalia, South Africa, Sri Lanka, Sudan, Suriname, Swaziland, Syria, Tajikistan, Tanzania, Thailand, Togo, Tonga, Trinidad and Tobago, Tunisia, Turkey, Uganda, Uruguay, Vietnam, Yemen, Zambia, Zimbabwe

International Hydrographic Organization (IHO)

note - name changed from International Hydrographic Bureau on 22 September 1970
established - June 1919; effective - June 1921
aim - to train hydrographic surveyors and nautical cartographers to achieve standardization in nautical charts and electronic chart displays; to provide advice on nautical cartography and hydrography; to develop the sciences in the field of hydrography and techniques used for descriptive oceanogrannphy
members - (76) Algeria, Argentina, Australia, Bahrain, Bangladesh, Belgium, Brazil, Burma, Canada, Chile, China (including Hong Kong and Macau), Colombia, Democratic Republic of the Congo, Croatia, Cuba, Cyprus, Denmark, Dominican Republic, Ecuador, Egypt, Estonia, Fiji, Finland, France, Germany, Greece, Guatemala, Iceland, India, Indonesia, Iran, Italy, Jamaica, Japan, North Korea, South Korea, Kuwait, Latvia, Malaysia, Mauritius, Mexico, Monaco, Morocco, Mozambique, Netherlands, NZ, Nigeria, Norway, Oman, Pakistan, Papua New Guinea, Peru, Philippines, Poland, Portugal, Russia, Serbia and Montenegro, Singapore, Slovenia, South Africa, Spain, Sri Lanka, Suriname, Sweden, Syria, Thailand, Tonga, Trinidad and Tobago, Tunisia, Turkey, Ukraine, UAE, UK, US, Uruguay, Venezuela

International Labor Organization (ILO)

established - 28 June 1919 set up as part of Treaty of Versailles; 11 April 1919 became operative; 14 December 1946 affiliated with the UN

aim - to deal with world labor issues; a UN specialized agency
members - (178) includes all UN member countries except Andorra, Bhutan, Brunei, North Korea, Liechtenstein, Maldives, Marshall Islands, Federated States of Micronesia, Monaco, Nauru, Palau, Tonga and Tuvalu; note - includes the following dependencies: Netherlands (Netherlands Antilles and Aruba)

International Maritime Organization (IMO)

note - name changed from Intergovernmental Maritime Consultative Organization (IMCO) on 22 May 1982
established - 6 March 1948 set up as the Inter-Governmental Maritime Consultative Organization; effective - 17 March 1958
aim - to deal with international maritime affairs; a UN specialized agency
members - (167) includes all UN member countries except Afghanistan, Andorra, Armenia, Belarus, Bhutan, Botswana, Burkina Faso, Burundi, Central African Republic, Chad, Kyrgyzstan, Laos, Lesotho, Liechtenstein, Mali, Federated States of Micronesia, Nauru, Niger, Palau, Rwanda, Tajikistan, Uganda, Uzbekistan, Zambia
associate members - (3) Faroe Islands, Hong Kong, Macau

International Monetary Fund (IMF)

established - 22 July 1944; effective - 27 December 1945
aim - to promote world monetary stability and economic development; a UN specialized agency
members - (184) includes all UN member countries except Andorra, Cuba, North Korea, Liechtenstein, Monaco, Nauru, Tuvalu; note - includes the following dependencies or areas of special interest: China (Hong Kong and Macau), Netherlands (Netherlands Antilles and Aruba)

International Olympic Committee (IOC)

established - 23 June 1894
aim - to promote the Olympic ideals and administer the Olympic games: 2006 Winter Olympics in Turin, Italy; 2008 Summer Olympics in Beijing, China; 2010 Winter Olympics in Vancouver, Canada; 2012 Summer Olympics in London, UK
National Olympic Committees - (201 and the Palestine Liberation Organization) Afghanistan, Albania, Algeria, American Samoa, Andorra, Angola, Antigua and Barbuda, Argentina, Armenia, Aruba, Australia, Austria, Azerbaijan, The Bahamas, Bahrain, Bangladesh, Barbados, Belarus, Belgium, Belize, Benin, Bermuda, Bhutan, Bolivia, Bosnia and Herzegovina, Botswana, Brazil, British Virgin Islands, Brunei, Bulgaria, Burkina Faso, Burma, Burundi, Cambodia, Cameroon, Canada, Cape Verde, Cayman Islands, Central African Republic, Chad, Chile, China, Colombia, Comoros, Democratic Republic of the Congo, Republic of the Congo, Cook Islands, Costa Rica, Cote d'Ivoire, Croatia, Cuba, Cyprus, Czech Republic, Denmark, Djibouti, Dominica, Dominican Republic, East Timor, Ecuador, Egypt, El Salvador, Equatorial Guinea, Eritrea, Estonia, Ethiopia, Fiji, Finland, France, Gabon, The Gambia, Georgia, Germany, Ghana, Greece, Grenada, Guam, Guatemala, Guinea, Guinea-Bissau, Guyana, Haiti, Honduras, Hong Kong, Hungary, Iceland, India, Indonesia, Iran, Iraq, Ireland, Israel, Italy, Jamaica, Japan, Jordan, Kazakhstan, Kenya, Kiribati, North Korea, South Korea, Kuwait, Kyrgyzstan, Laos, Latvia, Lebanon, Lesotho, Liberia, Libya, Liechtenstein, Lithuania, Luxembourg, Macedonia, Madagascar, Malawi, Malaysia, Maldives, Mali, Malta, Marshall Islands, Mauritania, Mauritius,

Mexico, Federated States of Micronesia, Moldova, Monaco, Mongolia, Morocco, Mozambique, Namibia, Nauru, Nepal, Netherlands, Netherlands Antilles, NZ, Nicaragua, Niger, Nigeria, Norway, Oman, Pakistan, Palau, Panama, Papua New Guinea, Paraguay, Peru, Philippines, Poland, Portugal, Puerto Rico, Qatar, Romania, Russia, Rwanda, Saint Kitts and Nevis, Saint Lucia, Saint Vincent and the Grenadines, Samoa, San Marino, Sao Tome and Principe, Saudi Arabia, Senegal, Serbia and Montenegro, Seychelles, Sierra Leone, Singapore, Slovakia, Slovenia, Solomon Islands, Somalia, South Africa, Spain, Sri Lanka, Sudan, Suriname, Swaziland, Sweden, Switzerland, Syria, Taiwan, Tajikistan, Tanzania, Thailand, Togo, Tonga, Trinidad and Tobago, Tunisia, Turkey, Turkmenistan, Uganda, Ukraine, UAE, UK, US, Uruguay, Uzbekistan, Vanuatu, Venezuela, Vietnam, Virgin Islands, Yemen, Zambia, Zimbabwe, Palestine Liberation Organization

International Organization for Migration (IOM)

note - established as Provisional Intergovernmental Committee for the Movement of Migrants from Europe; renamed Intergovernmental Committee for European Migration (ICEM) on 15 November 1952; renamed Intergovernmental Committee for Migration (ICM) in November 1980; current name adopted 14 November 1989
established - 5 December 1951
aim - to facilitate orderly international emigration and immigration
members - (116) Afghanistan, Albania, Algeria, Angola, Argentina, Armenia, Australia, Austria, Azerbaijan, The Bahamas, Bangladesh, Belarus, Belgium, Belize, Benin, Bolivia, Bosnia and Herzegovina, Brazil, Bulgaria, Burkina Faso, Cambodia, Cameroon, Canada, Cape Verde, Chile, Colombia, Democratic Republic of the Congo, Republic of the Congo, Costa Rica, Cote d'Ivoire, Croatia, Cyprus, Czech Republic, Denmark, Dominican Republic, Ecuador, Egypt, El Salvador, Estonia, Finland, France, Gabon, The Gambia, Georgia, Germany, Ghana, Greece, Guatemala, Guinea, Guinea-Bissau, Haiti, Honduras, Hungary, Iran, Ireland, Israel, Italy, Jamaica, Japan, Jordan, Kazakhstan, Kenya, South Korea, Kyrgyzstan, Latvia, Liberia, Libya, Lithuania, Luxembourg, Madagascar, Mali, Malta, Mauritania, Mexico, Moldova, Morocco, Netherlands, NZ, Nicaragua, Niger, Nigeria, Norway, Pakistan, Panama, Paraguay, Peru, Philippines, Poland, Portugal, Romania, Rwanda, Senegal, Serbia and Montenegro, Sierra Leone, Slovakia, Slovenia, South Africa, Sri Lanka, Sudan, Sweden, Switzerland, Tajikistan, Tanzania, Thailand, Togo, Tunisia, Turkey, Uganda, Ukraine, UK, US, Uruguay, Venezuela, Yemen, Zambia, Zimbabwe
observers - (21) Bhutan, Burundi, China, Cuba, Ethiopia, Guyana, Holy See, India, Indonesia, Macedonia, Mozambique, Namibia, Nepal, Papua New Guinea, Russia, San Marino, Sao Tome and Principe, Somalia, Spain, Turkmenistan, Vietnam

International Organization for Standardization (ISO)

established - February 1947
aim - to promote the development of international standards with a view to facilitating international exchange of goods and services and to developing cooperation in the sphere of intellectual, scientific, technological and economic activity
members - (100 national standards organizations) Algeria, Argentina, Armenia, Australia, Austria, Azerbaijan, Bahrain, Bangladesh, Barbados, Belarus, Belgium, Bosnia and Herzegovina, Botswana, Brazil, Bulgaria,

Canada, Chile, China, Colombia, Costa Rica, Cote d'Ivoire, Croatia, Cuba, Cyprus, Czech Republic, Denmark, Ecuador, Egypt, Ethiopia, Finland, France, Germany, Ghana, Greece, Hungary, Iceland, India, Indonesia, Iran, Iraq, Ireland, Israel, Italy, Jamaica, Japan, Jordan, Kazakhstan, Kenya, North Korea, South Korea, Kuwait, Libya, Luxembourg, Macedonia, Malaysia, Malta, Mauritius, Mexico, Mongolia, Morocco, Netherlands, NZ, Nigeria, Norway, Oman, Pakistan, Panama, Philippines, Poland, Portugal, Qatar, Romania, Russia, Saint Lucia, Saudi Arabia, Serbia and Montenegro, Singapore, Slovakia, Slovenia, South Africa, Spain, Sri Lanka, Sudan, Sweden, Switzerland, Syria, Tanzania, Thailand, Trinidad and Tobago, Tunisia, Turkey, Ukraine, UAE, UK, US, Uruguay, Uzbekistan, Venezuela, Vietnam, Zimbabwe
correspondent members - (45 plus the Palestine Liberation Organization) Afghanistan, Albania, Angola, Benin, Bhutan, Bolivia, Brunei, Burkina Faso, Burma, Democratic Republic of the Congo, Dominican Republic, El Salvador, Eritrea, Estonia, Fiji, Guatemala, Guinea, Guinea-Bissau, Hong Kong, Kyrgyzstan, Latvia, Lebanon, Lithuania, Macau, Madagascar, Malawi, Mali, Moldova, Mozambique, Namibia, Nepal, Nicaragua, Niger, Papua New Guinea, Paraguay, Peru, Rwanda, Senegal, Seychelles, Swaziland, Togo, Turkmenistan, Uganda, Yemen, Zambia, Palestine Liberation Organization
subscriber members - (10) Antigua and Barbuda, Burundi, Cambodia, Dominica, Grenada, Guyana, Honduras, Lesotho, Saint Vincent and the Grenadines, Tajikistan

International Red Cross and Red Crescent Movement (ICRM)

established - 1928
aim - to promote worldwide humanitarian aid through the International Committee of the Red Cross (ICRC) in wartime, and International Federation of Red Cross and Red Crescent Societies (IFRCS; formerly League of Red Cross and Red Crescent Societies or LORCS) in peacetime
National Societies - (182 countries); note - same as membership for International Federation of Red Cross and Red Crescent Societies (IFRCS)

International Telecommunication Union (ITU)

established - 17 May 1865 set up as the International Telegraph Union; 9 December 1932 adopted present name; effective - 1 January 1934; affiliated with the UN - 15 November 1947
aim - to deal with world telecommunications issues; a UN specialized agency
members - (189) includes all UN member countries except East Timor, Palau, Saint Kitts and Nevis (188 total); plus Holy See

Islamic Development Bank (IDB)

established - 15 December 1973 by declaration of intent; effective - 12 August 1974
aim - to promote Islamic economic aid and social development
members - (54 plus the Palestine Liberation Organization) Afghanistan, Albania, Algeria, Azerbaijan, Bahrain, Bangladesh, Benin, Brunei, Burkina Faso, Cameroon, Chad, Comoros, Cote d'Ivoire, Djibouti, Egypt, Gabon, The Gambia, Guinea, Guinea-Bissau, Indonesia, Iran, Iraq, Jordan, Kazakhstan, Kuwait, Kyrgyzstan, Lebanon, Libya, Malaysia, Maldives, Mali, Mauritania, Morocco, Mozambique, Niger, Oman, Pakistan, Qatar, Saudi Arabia, Senegal, Sierra Leone, Somalia, Sudan, Suriname, Syria, Tajikistan, Togo, Tunisia, Turkey, Turkmenistan, Uganda, UAE, Uzbekistan, Yemen, Palestine Liberation Organization

Latin American Economic System (LAES)

note - also known as Sistema Economico Latinoamericana (SELA)
established - 17 October 1975
aim - to promote economic and social development through regional cooperation
members - (26) Argentina, The Bahamas, Barbados, Belize, Bolivia, Brazil, Chile, Colombia, Costa Rica, Cuba, Dominican Republic, Ecuador, Guatemala, Guyana, Haiti, Honduras, Jamaica, Mexico, Nicaragua, Panama, Paraguay, Peru, Suriname, Trinidad and Tobago, Uruguay, Venezuela

Latin American Integration Association (LAIA)

note - also known as Asociacion Latinoamericana de Integracion (ALADI)
established - 12 August 1980; effective - 18 March 1981
aim - to promote freer regional trade
members - (12) Argentina, Bolivia, Brazil, Chile, Colombia, Cuba, Ecuador, Mexico, Paraguay, Peru, Uruguay, Venezuela
observers - (25) China, Corporacion Andina de Fomento, Costa Rica, Dominican Republic, EC, El Salvador, Guatemala, Honduras, Inter-American Development Bank, Inter-American Institute for Cooperation on Agriculture, Italy, Japan, South Korea, Latin America Economic System, Nicaragua, Organization of American States, Panama, Pan-American Health Organization, Portugal, Romania, Russia, Spain, Switzerland, United Nations Development Program, United Nations Economic Commission for Latin America and the Caribbean

League of Arab States (LAS)

note - also known as Arab League (AL)
established - 22 March 1945
aim - aim - to promote economic, social, political, and military cooperation
members - (21 plus the Palestine Liberation Organization) Algeria, Bahrain, Comoros, Djibouti, Egypt, Iraq, Jordan, Kuwait, Lebanon, Libya, Mauritania, Morocco, Oman, Qatar, Saudi Arabia, Somalia, Sudan, Syria, Tunisia, UAE, Yemen, Palestine Liberation Organization

Monetary and Economic Community of Central Africa (CEMAC)

note - was formerly the Central African Customs and Economic Union (UDEAC)
established - 8 December 1964; effective - 1 January 1966
aim - to promote the establishment of a Central African Common Market
members - (14) Benin, Burkina Faso, Cote d'Ivoire, Cameroon, Central African Republic, Chad, Republic of the Congo, Equatorial Guinea, Gabon, Guinea-Bissau, Mali, Niger, Senegal, Togo

Multilateral Investment Guarantee Agency (MIGA)

established - 12 April 1988
aim - encourages flow of foreign direct investment among member countries by offering investment insurance, consultation, and negotiation on conditions for foreign investment and technical assistance; a UN specialized agency
members - (166) includes all UN member countries except Andorra, Bhutan, Brunei, Burma, Comoros, Cuba, Djibouti, Guinea-Bissau, Iraq, Kirabati, North Korea, Liberia, Liechtenstein, Maldives, Marshall Islands, Mexico, Monaco, Nauru, NZ, Niger, San Marino, Sao Tome and Principe, Somalia, Tonga, Tuvalu

Near Abroad

Russian term for the 14 non-Russian successor states of the USSR, in which 25 million ethnic Russians live and in which Moscow has expressed a strong national security interest; the 14 countries are Armenia, Azerbaijan, Belarus, Estonia, Georgia, Kazakhstan, Kyrgyzstan, Latvia, Lithuania, Moldova, Tajikistan, Turkmenistan, Ukraine, Uzbekistan

Nonaligned Movement (NAM)

established - 1-6 September 1961
aim - to establish political and military cooperation apart from the traditional East or West blocs
members - (114 plus the Palestine Liberation Organization) Afghanistan, Algeria, Angola, The Bahamas, Bahrain, Bangladesh, Barbados, Belarus, Belize, Benin, Bhutan, Bolivia, Botswana, Brunei, Burkina Faso, Burma, Burundi, Cambodia, Cameroon, Cape Verde, Central African Republic, Chad, Chile, Colombia, Comoros, Democratic Republic of the Congo, Republic of the Congo, Cote d'Ivoire, Cuba, Cyprus, Djibouti, Dominican Republic, Ecuador, Egypt, Equatorial Guinea, Eritrea, Ethiopia, Gabon, The Gambia, Ghana, Grenada, Guatemala, Guinea, Guinea-Bissau, Guyana, Honduras, India, Indonesia, Iran, Iraq, Jamaica, Jordan, Kenya, North Korea, Kuwait, Laos, Lebanon, Lesotho, Liberia, Libya, Madagascar, Malawi, Malaysia, Maldives, Mali, Malta, Mauritania, Mauritius, Mongolia, Morocco, Mozambique, Namibia, Nepal, Nicaragua, Niger, Nigeria, Oman, Pakistan, Panama, Papua New Guinea, Peru, Philippines, Qatar, Rwanda, Saint Lucia, Sao Tome and Principe, Saudi Arabia, Senegal, Serbia and Montenegro, Seychelles, Sierra Leone, Singapore, Somalia, South Africa, Sri Lanka, Sudan, Suriname, Swaziland, Syria, Tanzania, Thailand, Togo, Trinidad and Tobago, Tunisia, Turkmenistan, Uganda, UAE, Uzbekistan, Vanuatu, Venezuela, Vietnam, Yemen, Zambia, Zimbabwe, Palestine Liberation Organization
observers - (15) Antigua and Barbuda, Armenia, Azerbaijan, Brazil, China, Costa Rica, Croatia, Dominica, El Salvadore, Kazakhstan, Kyrgyzstan, Mexico, Paraguay, Ukraine, Uruguay
guests - (28) Australia, Austria, Bosnia and Herzegovina, Bulgaria, Canada, Czech Republic, Finland, Germany, Greece, Holy See, Hungary, Italy, Japan, South Korea, Netherlands, NZ, Norway, Poland, Romania, Russia, San Marino, Slovakia, Slovenia, Spain, Sweden, Switzerland, UK, US

Nordic Council (NC)

established - 16 March 1952; effective - 12 February 1953
aim - to promote regional economic, cultural, and environmental cooperation
members - (5) Denmark (including Faroe Islands and Greenland), Finland (including Aland Islands), Iceland, Norway, Sweden
observers - (3) the Sami (Lapp) local parliaments of Finland, Norway, and Sweden

Nordic Investment Bank (NIB)

established - 4 December 1975; effective - 1 June 1976
aim - to promote economic cooperation and development
members - (8) Denmark (including Faroe Islands and Greenland), Estonia, Finland (including Aland Islands), Iceland, Latvia, Lithuania, Norway, Sweden

North

a popular term for the rich industrialized countries generally located in the northern portion of the Northern Hemisphere; the counterpart of the South; see developed countries (DCs)

North American Free Trade Agreement (NAFTA)

established - 17 December 1992
aim - to eliminate trade barriers, promote fair competition, increase investment opportunities, provide protection of intellectual property rights, and create procedures to settle disputes
members - (3) Canada, Mexico, US

North Atlantic Treaty Organization (NATO)

established - 4 April 1949
aim - to promote mutual defense and cooperation
members - (26) Belgium, Bulgaria, Canada, Czech Republic, Denmark, Estonia, France, Germany, Greece, Hungary, Iceland, Italy, Latvia, Lithuania, Luxembourg, Netherlands, Norway, Poland, Portugal, Romania, Slovakia, Slovenia, Spain, Turkey, UK, US

Nuclear Energy Agency (NEA)

note - also known as OECD Nuclear Energy Agency
established - 1 February 1958
aim - to promote the peaceful uses of nuclear energy; associated with OECD
members - (28) Australia, Austria, Belgium, Canada, Czech Republic, Denmark, Finland, France, Germany, Greece, Hungary, Iceland, Ireland, Italy, Japan, South Korea, Luxembourg, Mexico, Netherlands, Norway, Portugal, Slovakia, Spain, Sweden, Switzerland, Turkey, UK, US

Nuclear Suppliers Group (NSG)

note - also known as the London Suppliers Group or the London Group
established - 1974; effective - 1975
aim - to establish guidelines for exports of nuclear materials, processing equipment for uranium enrichment, and technical information to countries of proliferation concern and regions of conflict and instability
members - (44) Argentina, Australia, Austria, Belarus, Belgium, Brazil, Bulgaria, Canada, China, Cyprus, Czech Republic, Denmark, Estonia, Finland, France, Germany, Greece, Hungary, Ireland, Italy, Japan, Kazakhstan, South Korea, Latvia, Lithuania, Luxembourg, Malta, Netherlands, NZ, Norway, Poland, Portugal, Romania, Russia, Slovakia, Slovenia, South Africa, Spain, Sweden, Switzerland, Turkey, Ukraine, UK, US
observer - (1) European Commission (a policy-planning body for the EU)

Organization for Economic Cooperation and Development (OECD)

established - 14 December 1960; effective - 30 September 1961
aim - to promote economic cooperation and development
members - (30) Australia, Austria, Belgium, Canada, Czech Republic, Denmark, Finland, France, Germany, Greece, Hungary, Iceland, Ireland, Italy, Japan, South Korea, Luxembourg, Mexico, Netherlands, NZ, Norway, Poland, Portugal, Slovakia, Spain, Sweden, Switzerland, Turkey, UK, US
special member - (1) EU

Organization for Security and Cooperation in Europe (OSCE)

note - formerly the Conference on Security and Cooperation in Europe (CSCE) established 3 July 1975
established - 1 January 1995
aim - to foster the implementation of human rights, fundamental freedoms, democracy, and the rule of law; to act as an instrument of early warning, conflict prevention, and crisis management; and to serve as a framework for conventional arms control and confidence building measures
members - (55) Albania, Andorra, Armenia, Austria, Azerbaijan, Belarus, Belgium, Bosnia and Herzegovina, Bulgaria, Canada, Croatia, Cyprus, Czech

Republic, Denmark, Estonia, Finland, France, Georgia, Germany, Greece, Holy See, Hungary, Iceland, Ireland, Italy, Kazakhstan, Kyrgyzstan, Latvia, Liechtenstein, Lithuania, Luxembourg, Macedonia, Malta, Moldova, Monaco, Netherlands, Norway, Poland, Portugal, Romania, Russia, San Marino, Serbia and Montenegro, Slovakia, Slovenia, Spain, Sweden, Switzerland, Tajikistan, Turkey, Turkmenistan, Ukraine, UK, US, Uzbekistan
partners for cooperation - (11) Afghanistan, Algeria, Egypt, Israel, Japan, Jordan, South Korea, Mongolia, Morocco, Thailand, Tunisia

Organization for the Prohibition of Chemical Weapons (OPCW)

established - 29 April 1997
aim - to enforce the Convention on the Prohibition of the Development, Production, Stockpiling, and Use of Chemical Weapons and on Their Destruction; to provide a forum for consultation and cooperation among the signatories of the Convention
members (countries that have ratified the Convention) - (175) Afghanistan, Albania, Algeria, Andorra, Antigua and Barbuda, Argentina, Armenia, Australia, Austria, Azerbaijan, Bahrain, Bangladesh, Belarus, Belgium, Belize, Benin, Bhutan, Bolivia, Bosnia and Herzegovina, Botswana, Brazil, Brunei, Bulgaria, Burkina Faso, Burundi, Cambodia, Cameroon, Canada, Cape Verde, Chad, Chile, China, Colombia, Democratic Republic of the Congo, Cook Islands, Costa Rica, Cote d'Ivoire, Croatia, Cuba, Cyprus, Czech Republic, Denmark, Dominica, East Timor, Ecuador, El Salvador, Equatorial Guinea, Eritrea, Estonia, Ethiopia, Fiji, Finland, France, Gabon, The Gambia, Georgia, Germany, Ghana, Greece, Grenada, Guatemala, Guinea, Guyana, Holy See, Honduras, Hungary, Iceland, India, Indonesia, Iran, Ireland, Italy, Jamaica, Japan, Jordan, Kazakhstan, Kenya, Kiribati, South Korea, Kuwait, Kyrgyzstan, Laos, Latvia, Lesotho, Libya, Liechtenstein, Lithuania, Luxembourg, Macedonia, Madagascar, Malawi, Malaysia, Maldives, Mali, Malta, Marshall Islands, Mauritania, Mauritius, Mexico, Federated States of Micronesia, Moldova, Monaco, Mongolia, Morocco, Mozambique, Namibia, Nauru, Nepal, Netherlands, NZ, Nicaragua, Niger, Nigeria, Niue, Norway, Oman, Pakistan, Palau, Panama, Papua New Guinea, Paraguay, Peru, Philippines, Poland, Portugal, Qatar, Romania, Russia, Rwanda, Saint Kitts and Nevis, Saint Lucia, Saint Vincent and the Grenadines, Samoa, San Marino, Sao Tome and Principe, Saudi Arabia, Senegal, Serbia and Montenegro, Seychelles, Sierra Leone, Singapore, Slovakia, Slovenia, Solomon Islands, South Africa, Spain, Sri Lanka, Sudan, Suriname, Swaziland, Sweden, Switzerland, Tajikistan, Tanzania, Thailand, Togo, Tonga, Trinidad and Tobago, Tunisia, Turkey, Turkmenistan, Tuvalu, Uganda, Ukraine, UAE, UK, US, Uruguay, Uzbekistan, Vanuatu, Venezuela, Vietnam, Yemen, Zambia, Zimbabwe
signatory states (countries that have signed, but not ratified, the Convention) - (11) The Bahamas, Burma, Cambodia, Central African Republic, Comoros, Republic of the Congo, Djibouti, Dominican Republic, Guinea-Bissau, Haiti, Israel, Liberia

Organization of African Unity (OAU)

see African Union

Organization of American States (OAS)

established - 14 April 1890 as the International Union of American Republics; 30 April 1948 adopted present charter; effective - 13 December 1951

aim - to promote regional peace and security as well as economic and social development
members - (35) Antigua and Barbuda, Argentina, The Bahamas, Barbados, Belize, Bolivia, Brazil, Canada, Chile, Colombia, Costa Rica, Cuba (excluded from formal participation since 1962), Dominica, Dominican Republic, Ecuador, El Salvador, Grenada, Guatemala, Guyana, Haiti, Honduras, Jamaica, Mexico, Nicaragua, Panama, Paraguay, Peru, Saint Kitts and Nevis, Saint Lucia, Saint Vincent and the Grenadines, Suriname, Trinidad and Tobago, US, Uruguay, Venezuela
observers - (60) Algeria, Angola, Armenia, Austria, Azerbaijan, Belgium, Bosnia and Herzegovina, Bulgaria, China, Croatia, Cyprus, Czech Republic, Denmark, Egypt, Equatorial Guinea, Estonia, EU, Finland, France, Georgia, Germany, Ghana, Greece, Holy See, Hungary, India, Ireland, Israel, Italy, Japan, Kazakhstan, South Korea, Latvia, Lebanon, Luxembourg, Morocco, Netherlands, Nigeria, Norway, Pakistan, Philippines, Poland, Portugal, Qatar, Romania, Russia, Saudi Arabia, Serbia and Montenegro, Slovakia, Slovenia, Spain, Sri Lanka, Sweden, Switzerland, Thailand, Tunisia, Turkey, Ukraine, UK, Yemen

Organization of Arab Petroleum Exporting Countries (OAPEC)

established - 9 January 1968
aim - to promote cooperation in the petroleum industry
members - (11) Algeria, Bahrain, Egypt, Iraq, Kuwait, Libya, Qatar, Saudi Arabia, Syria, Tunisia (suspended), UAE

Organization of Eastern Caribbean States (OECS)

established - 18 June 1981; effective - 4 July 1981
aim - to promote political, economic, and defense cooperation
members - (7) Antigua and Barbuda, Dominica, Grenada, Montserrat, Saint Kitts and Nevis, Saint Lucia, Saint Vincent and the Grenadines
associate member - (2) Anguilla, British Virgin Islands

Organization of Petroleum Exporting Countries (OPEC)

established - 14 September 1960
aim - to coordinate petroleum policies
members - (11) Algeria, Indonesia, Iran, Iraq, Kuwait, Libya, Nigeria, Qatar, Saudi Arabia, UAE, Venezuela

Organization of the Islamic Conference (OIC)

established - 22-25 September 1969
aim - to promote Islamic solidarity in economic, social, cultural, and political affairs
members - (56 plus the Palestine Liberation Organization) Afghanistan, Albania, Algeria, Azerbaijan, Bahrain, Bangladesh, Benin, Brunei, Burkina Faso, Cameroon, Chad, Comoros, Cote d'Ivoire, Djibouti, Egypt, Gabon, The Gambia, Guinea, Guinea-Bissau, Guyana, Indonesia, Iran, Iraq, Jordan, Kazakhstan, Kuwait, Kyrgyzstan, Lebanon, Libya, Malaysia, Maldives, Mali, Mauritania, Morocco, Mozambique, Niger, Nigeria, Oman, Pakistan, Qatar, Saudi Arabia, Senegal, Sierra Leone, Somalia, Sudan, Suriname, Syria, Tajikistan, Togo, Tunisia, Turkey, Turkmenistan, Uganda, UAE, Uzbekistan, Yemen, Palestine Liberation Organization
observers - (11) AU, Bosnia and Herzegovina, Central African Republic, ECO, LAS, Moro National Liberation Front, NAM, Russia, Thailand, Turkish Muslim Community of Kibris, UN

Pacific Community (SPC)

note - formerly known as the South Pacific Commission (SPC)

established - 6 February 1947; effective - 29 July 1948
aim - to promote regional cooperation in economic and social matters
members - (27) American Samoa, Australia, Cook Islands, Fiji, France, French Polynesia, Guam, Kiribati, Marshall Islands, Federated States of Micronesia, Nauru, New Caledonia, NZ, Niue, Northern Mariana Islands, Palau, Papua New Guinea, Pitcairn Islands, Samoa, Solomon Islands, Tokelau, Tonga, Tuvalu, UK, US, Vanuatu, Wallis and Futuna

Pacific Islands Forum (PIF)

note - formerly known as South Pacific Forum (SPF)
established - 5 August 1971
aim - to promote regional cooperation in political matters
members - (16) Australia, Cook Islands, Fiji, Kiribati, Marshall Islands, Federated States of Micronesia, Nauru, NZ, Niue, Palau, Papua New Guinea, Samoa, Solomon Islands, Tonga, Tuvalu, Vanuatu
observers - (3) East Timor, French Polynesia, New Caledonia

Paris Club

established - 1956
aim - to provide a forum for debtor countries to negotiate rescheduling of debt service payments or loans extended by governments or official agencies of participating countries; to help restore normal trade and project finance to debtor countries
members - (19) Australia, Austria, Belgium, Canada, Denmark, Finland, France, Germany, Ireland, Italy, Japan, Netherlands, Norway, Russia, Spain, Sweden, Switzerland, UK, US

Partnership for Peace (PFP)

established - 10-11 January 1994
aim - to expand and intensify political and military cooperation throughout Europe, increase stability, diminish threats to peace, and build relationships by promoting the spirit of practical cooperation and commitment to democratic principles that underpin NATO; program under the auspices of NATO
members - (20) Albania, Armenia, Austria, Azerbaijan, Belarus, Croatia, Finland, Georgia, Ireland, Kazakhstan, Kyrgyzstan, Macedonia, Moldova, Russia, Sweden, Switzerland, Tajikistan, Turkmenistan, Ukraine, Uzbekistan; note - a nation that becomes a member of NATO is no longer a member of PFP

Permanent Court of Arbitration (PCA)

established - 29 July 1899
aim - to facilitate the settlement of international disputes
members - (103) Argentina, Australia, Austria, Belarus, Belgium, Belize, Bolivia, Brazil, Bulgaria, Burkina Faso, Cambodia, Cameroon, Canada, Chile, China, Colombia, Democratic Republic of the Congo, Costa Rica, Croatia, Cuba, Cyprus, Czech Republic, Denmark, Dominican Republic, Ecuador, Egypt, El Salvador, Eritrea, Estonia, Ethiopia, Fiji, Finland, France, Germany, Greece, Guatemala, Guyana, Haiti, Honduras, Hungary, Iceland, India, Iran, Iraq, Ireland, Israel, Italy, Japan, Jordan, South Korea, Kuwait, Kyrgyzstan, Laos, Latvia, Lebanon, Libya, Liechtenstein, Lithuania, Luxembourg, Macedonia, Malaysia, Malta, Mauritius, Mexico, Morocco, Netherlands, NZ, Nicaragua, Nigeria, Norway, Pakistan, Panama, Paraguay, Peru, Poland, Portugal, Romania, Russia, Saudi Arabia, Senegal, Serbia and Montenegro, Singapore, Slovakia, Slovenia, South Africa, Spain, Sri Lanka,

Sudan, Suriname, Swaziland, Sweden, Switzerland, Thailand, Togo, Turkey, Uganda, Ukraine, UK, US, Uruguay, Venezuela, Zambia, Zimbabwe

Rio Group (RG)

note - formerly known as Grupo de los Ocho, established NA December 1986; composed of the Contadora Group and the Lima Group
established - 1988
aim - to consult on regional Latin American issues
members - (18) Argentina, Bolivia, Brazil, CARICOM, Chile, Colombia, Costa Rica, Dominican Republic, Ecuador, El Salvador, Honduras, Mexico, Nicaragua, Panama, Paraguay, Peru, Uruguay, Venezuela

Second World

another term for the traditionally Marxist-Leninist states of the USSR and Eastern Europe, with authoritarian governments and command economies based on the Soviet model; the term is fading from use; see centrally planned economies

Secretariat of the Pacific Communities (SPC)

established - 6 February 1947
aim - to serve island development in 22 Pacific countries; to develop technical assistance and professional, scientific, and research support; to build planning and management capability
members - (26) America Samoa, Australia, Cook Islands, Fiji, France, French Polynesia, Guam, Kiribati, Marshall Islands, Federated States of Micronesia, Nauru, New Caledonia, Niue, Northern Mariana Islands, NZ, Palau, Papua New Guinea, Pitcairn Islands, Samoa, Solomon Islands, Tokelau, Tonga, Tuvalu, Vanuatu, US, Wallis and Futuna

Shanghai Cooperative Organization (SCO)

established - 15 June 1901
aim - to combat terrorism, extremism, and separatism; to safeguard regional security through mutual trust, disarmament, and cooperative security; and to increase cooperation in political, trade, economic, scientific and technological, cultural, and educational fields
members - (6) China, Kazakhstan, Kyrgyzstan, Russia, Tajikistan, Uzbekistan
observer - (4) India, Iran, Mongolia, Pakistan

South

a popular term for the poorer, less industrialized countries generally located south of the developed countries; the counterpart of the North; see less developed countries (LDCs)

South American Community of Nations (CSN)

established - 9 December 2004
aim - to coordinate common policies regarding multilateral organizations, to integrate physical infrastructure, and to consolidate the merger of CAN and Mercosur
members - (12) Argentina, Bolivia, Brazil, Chile, Colombia, Ecuador, Guyana, Paraguay, Peru, Surinam, Uruguay, Venezuela

South Asia Co-operative Environment Program (SACEP)

established - January 1983
aim - to promote regional cooperation in South Asia in the field of environment, both natural and human, and on issues of economic and social development; to support conservation and management of natural resources of the region
members - (8) Afghanistan, Bangladesh, Bhutan, India, Maldives, Nepal, Pakistan, Sri Lanka

South Asian Association for Regional Cooperation (SAARC)

established - 8 December 1985
aim - to promote economic, social, and cultural cooperation
members - (8) Afghanistan, Bangladesh, Bhutan, India, Maldives, Nepal, Pakistan, Sri Lanka
observers - (2) China, Japan

South Pacific Forum (SPF)

note - see Pacific Island Forum

South Pacific Regional Trade and Economic Cooperation Agreement (Sparteca)

established - 1981
aim - to redress unequal trade relationships of Australia and New Zealand with small island economies in the Pacific region
members - (16) Australia, Cook Islands, Fiji, Kiribati, Marshall Islands, Federated States of Micronesia, Nauru, NZ, Niue, Palau, Papua New Guinea, Samoa, Solomon Islands, Tonga, Tuvalu, Vanuatu

Southeast European Cooperative Initiative (SECI)

established - 6 December 1996
aim - to encourage cooperation among participating states and to facilitate their integration into European structures
members - (12) Albania, Bosnia and Herzegovina, Bulgaria, Croatia, Greece, Hungary, Macedonia, Moldova, Romania, Serbia and Montenegro, Slovenia, Turkey

Southern African Customs Union (SACU)

established - 11 December 1969
aim - to promote free trade and cooperation in customs matters
members - (5) Botswana, Lesotho, Namibia, South Africa, Swaziland

Southern African Development Community (SADC)

note - evolved from the Southern African Development Coordination Conference (SADCC)
established - 17 August 1992
aim - to promote regional economic development and integration
members - (14) Angola, Botswana, Democratic Republic of the Congo, Lesotho, Madagascar, Malawi, Mauritius, Mozambique, Namibia, South Africa, Swaziland, Tanzania, Zambia, Zimbabwe

Southern Cone Common Market (Mercosur) or Southern Common Market

note - also known as Mercado Comun del Cono Sur (Mercosur)
established - 26 March 1991
aim - to increase regional economic cooperation
members - (4) Argentina, Brazil, Paraguay, Uruguay
associate members - (6) Bolivia, Chile, Colombia, Ecuador, Peru, Venezuela

Third World

another term for the less developed countries; the term is obsolescent; see less developed countries (LDCs)

United Nations (UN)

established - 26 June 1945; effective - 24 October 1945
aim - to maintain international peace and security and to promote cooperation involving economic, social, cultural, and humanitarian problems
constituent organizations - the UN is composed of six principal organs and numerous subordinate agencies and bodies as follows:
1) Secretariat
2) General Assembly: Joint United Nations Program on HIV/AIDS (UN AIDS), International Research and Training Institute for the Advancement

of Women (INSTRAW), Office of the United Nations High Commissioner for Human Rights (OHCHR), United Nations Center for Human Settlements (UN-Habitat), United Nations Children's Fund (UNICEF), United Nations Conference on Trade and Development (UNCTAD), United Nations Development Program (UNDP), United Nations Drug Control Program (UNDCP), United Nations Environment Program (UNEP), United Nations High Commissioner for Refugees (UNHCR), United Nations Institute for Disarmament Research (UNIDIR), United Nations Institute for Training and Research (UNITAR), United Nations Interregional Crime and Justice Research Institute (UNICRI), United Nations Population Fund (UNFPA), United Nations Office of Project Services (UNOPS), United Nations Relief and Works Agency for Palestine Refugees in the Near East (UNRWA), United Nations Research Institute for Social Development (UNRISD), United Nations System Staff College (UNSSC), United Nations University (UNU), World Food Program (WFP)

3) *Security Council:* International Criminal Tribunal for the Former Yugoslavia (ICTY), International Criminal Tribunal for Rwanda (ICTR), United Nations Compensation Commission, United Nations Disengagement Observer Force (UNDOF), United Nations Interim Administration Mission in Kosovo (UNMIK), United Nations Interim Force in Lebanon (UNIFIL), United Nations Mission in Liberia (UNMIL), United Nations Military Observer Group in India and Pakistan (UNMOGIP), United Nations Operation in Burundi (ONUB), United Nations Operation in Cote d'Ivoire (UNOCI), United Nations Mission for the Referendum in Western Sahara (MINURSO), United Nations Mission in Ethiopia and Eritrea (UNMEE), United Nations Mission in Sierra Leone (UNAMSIL), United Nations Mission in the Sudan (UNMIS), United Nations Monitoring and Verification Commission (UNMOVIC), United Nations Observer Mission in Georgia (UNOMIG), United Nations Organization Mission in the Democratic Republic of the Congo (MONUC), United Nations Peace-Keeping Force in Cyprus (UNFICYP), United Nations Stabilization Mission in Haiti (MINUSTAH), and United Nations Truce Supervision Organization (UNTSO)

4) *Economic and Social Council (ECOSOC):* Commission for Social Development, Commission on Crime Prevention and Criminal Justice, Commission on Human Rights, Commission on Narcotics Drugs, Commission on Population and Development, Commission on Science and Technology for Development, Commission on Sustainable Development, Commission on the Status of Women, Economic and Social Commission for Asia and the Pacific (ESCAP), Economic and Social Commission for Western Asia (ESCWA), Economic Commission for Africa (ECA), Economic Commission for Europe (ECE), Economic Commission for Latin America and the Caribbean (ECLAC), Food and Agriculture Organization of the United Nations (FAO), International Atomic Energy Agency (IAEA), International Bank for Reconstruction and Development (IBRD), International Center for Secretariat of Investment Disputes (ICSID), International Civil Aviation Organization (ICAO), International Development Association (IDA), International Finance Corporation (IFC), International Fund for Agricultural Development (IFAD), International Labor Organization (ILO), International Maritime Organization (IMO),

International Monetary Fund (IMF), International Telecommunication Union (ITU), Multilateral Investment Geographic Agency (MIGA), Statistical Commission, United Nations Educational, Scientific, and Cultural Organization (UNESCO), United Nations Forum on Forests, United Nations Industrial Development Organization (UNIDO), Universal Postal Union (UPU), World Health Organization (WHO), World Intellectual Property Organization (WIPO), World Meteorological Organization (WMO), World Tourism Organization (WToO), and World Trade Organization (WTO)
5) *Trusteeship Council* (inactive; no trusteeships at this time)
6) *International Court of Justice (ICJ)*

United Nations Children's Fund (UNICEF)

note - acronym retained from the predecessor organization, UN International Children's Emergency Fund
established - 11 December 1946
aim - to help establish child health and welfare services
members - (37) selected on a rotating basis from all regions

United Nations Conference on Trade and Development (UNCTAD)

established - 30 December 1964
aim - to promote international trade
members - (192) all UN members plus Holy See

United Nations Development Program (UNDP)

established - 22 November 1965
aim - to provide technical assistance to stimulate economic and social development
members (executive board) - (36) selected on a rotating basis from all regions

United Nations Disengagement Observer Force (UNDOF)

established - 31 May 1974
aim - to observe the 1973 Arab-Israeli cease-fire; established by the UN Security Council
members - (6) Austria, Canada, Japan, Nepal, Poland, Slovakia

United Nations Educational, Scientific, and Cultural Organization (UNESCO)

established - 16 November 1945; effective - 4 November 1946
aim - to promote cooperation in education, science, and culture
members - (190) includes all UN member countries except Brunei, Liechtenstein, and Singapore (188 total); plus Cook Islands and Niue
associate members - (6) Aruba, British Virgin Islands, Cayman Islands, Macau, Netherlands Antilles, Tokelau

United Nations Environment Program (UNEP)

established - 15 December 1972
aim - to promote international cooperation on all environmental matters
members - (58) selected on a rotating basis from all regions

United Nations General Assembly

established - 26 June 1945; effective - 24 October 1945
aim - to function as the primary deliberative organ of the UN
members - (191) all UN members are represented in the General Assembly

United Nations High Commissioner for Refugees (UNHCR)

established - 3 December 1949; effective - 1 January 1951
aim - to ensure the humanitarian treatment of refugees and find permanent solutions to refugee problems
members (executive committee) - (68) Algeria, Argentina, Australia, Austria,

Bangladesh, Belgium, Brazil, Canada, Chile, China, Colombia, Democratic Republic of the Congo, Cote d'Ivoire, Cyprus, Denmark, Ecuador, Egypt, Ethiopia, Finland, France, Germany, Ghana, Greece, Guinea, Holy See, Hungary, India, Iran, Ireland, Israel, Italy, Japan, Kenya, South Korea, Lebanon, Lesotho, Madagascar, Mexico, Morocco, Mozambique, Namibia, Netherlands, NZ, Nicaragua, Nigeria, Norway, Pakistan, Philippines, Poland, Romania, Russia, Serbia and Montenegro, Somalia, South Africa, Spain, Sudan, Sweden, Switzerland, Tanzania, Thailand, Tunisia, Turkey, Uganda, UK, US, Venezuela, Yemen, Zambia

United Nations Industrial Development Organization (UNIDO)

established - 17 November 1966; effective - 1 January 1967
aim - UN specialized agency that promotes industrial development especially among the members
members - (171) includes all UN member countries except Andorra, Antigua and Barbuda, Australia, Brunei, Canada, Estonia, Iceland, Kiribati, Latvia, Liechtenstein, Marshall Islands, Federated States of Micronesia, Nauru, Palau, Samoa, San Marino, Singapore, Solomon Islands, Tuvalu, US

United Nations Institute for Training and Research (UNITAR)

established - 11 December 1963 adoption of the resolution establishing the Institute; effective - 24 March 1965
aim - to help the UN become more effective through training and research
members (Board of Trustees) - (18) Belgium, Brazil, China, Czech Republic, Egypt, France, Ghana, Japan, Kuwait, Mexico, Monaco, Morocco, Nigeria, Pakistan, Russia, South Africa, Switzerland, US; note - the UN Secretary General can appoint up to 30 members

United Nations Interim Administration Mission in Kosovo (UNMIK)

established - 10 June 1999
aim - to promote the establishment of substantial autonomy and self-government in Kosovo; to perform basic civilian administrative functions; to support the reconstruction of key infrastructure and humanitarian and disaster relief
note - gives civilian support only; works closely with UFOR

United Nations Interim Force in Lebanon (UNIFIL)

established - 19 March 1978
aim - to confirm the withdrawal of Israeli forces, and assist in reestablishing Lebanese authority in southern Lebanon; established by the UN Security Council
members - (7) France, Ghana, India, Ireland, Italy, Poland, Ukraine

United Nations Military Observer Group in India and Pakistan (UNMOGIP)

established - 24 January 1949
aim - to observe the 1949 India-Pakistan cease-fire; established by the UN Security Council
members - (9) Belgium, Chile, Croatia, Denmark, Finland, Italy, South Korea, Sweden, Uruguay

United Nations Mission for the Referendum in Western Sahara (MINURSO)

established - 29 April 1991
aim - to supervise the cease-fire and conduct a referendum in Western Sahara; established by the UN Security Council
members - (25) Argentina, Austria, Bangladesh, China, Croatia, Egypt, El Salvador, France, Ghana, Greece, Guinea, Honduras, Hungary, Ireland, Italy, Kenya, South Korea, Malaysia, Mongolia, Nigeria, Pakistan, Poland, Russia, Sri Lanka, Uruguay

United Nations Mission in Ethiopia and Eritrea (UNMEE)

established - 31 July 2000
aim - to monitor the cessation of hostilities
members - (40) Algeria, Austria, Bangladesh, Bosnia and Herzegovina, Bulgaria, China, Croatia, Czech Republic, Denmark, Finland, France, The Gambia, Germany, Ghana, Greece, India, Iran, Italy, Jordan, Kenya, Malaysia, Namibia, Nepal, Nigeria, Norway, Paraguay, Peru, Poland, Romania, Russia, South Africa, Spain, Sweden, Switzerland, Tanzania, Tunisia, Ukraine, US, Uruguay, Zambia

United Nations Mission in Liberia (UNMIL)

established - 19 September 2003
aim - to support the cease-fire agreement and peace process, protect UN facilities and people, support humanitarian activities, and assist in national security reform
members - (48) Bangladesh, Benin, Bolivia, Brazil, Bulgaria, China, Croatia, Czech Republic, Denmark, Ecuador, Egypt, El Salvador, Ethiopia, Finland, France, The Gambia, Germany, Ghana, Indonesia, Ireland, Jordan, Kenya, South Korea, Kyrgyzstan, Malawi, Malaysia, Mali, Moldova, Namibia, Nepal, Niger, Nigeria, Pakistan, Paraguay, Peru, Philippines, Poland, Romania, Russia, Senegal, Serbia and Montenegro, Sierra Leone, Sweden, Togo, Ukraine, UK, US, Zambia

United Nations Mission in Sierra Leone (UNAMSIL)

established - 22 October 1999
aim - to cooperate with the Government of Sierra Leone and the other parties to the Peace Agreement in the implementation of the agreement; to monitor the military and security situation in Sierra Leone; to monitor the disarmament and demobilization of combatants and members of the Civil Defense Forces (CFD); to assist in monitoring respect for international humanitarian law
members - (27) Bangladesh, Bolivia, China, Croatia, Czech Republic, Egypt, The Gambia, Germany, Ghana, Guinea, Indonesia, Jordan, Kenya, Kyrgyzstan, Malaysia, Nepal, Nigeria, Pakistan, Russia, Slovakia, Sweden, Tanzania, Thailand, Ukraine, UK, Uruguay, Zambia

United Nations Mission in the Sudan (UNMIS)

established - March 2005
aim - to support implementation of the comprehensive Peace Agreement by Monitoring and verifying the implementation of the Cease Fire Agreement, by observing and monitoring movements of armed groups, and by helping disarm, demobilizing and reintegrating armed bands
members - (48) Australia, Austria, Bangladesh, Benin, Brazil, Cambodia, Canada, China, Croatia, Denmark, Egypt, El Salvador, Fiji, Finland, Germany, Greece, Guatemala, India, Indonesia, Italy, Jordan, Kenya, Kyrgyzstan, Malawi, Malaysia, Moldova, Mongolia, Mozambique, Namibia, Nepal, Nigeria, Norway, Pakistan, Paraguay, Peru, Poland, Romania, Russia, Rwanda, Spain, Sweden, Switzerland, Turkey, Uganda, UK, Yemen, Zambia, Zimbabwwe

United Nations Mission of Support in East Timor (UNMISET)

established - 17 May 2002
aim - to provide assistance to structures critical to political stability; to provide law enforcement and public security and to assist in the development of law enforcement agencies; to contribute to external security

established on 17 May 2002 to provide assistance to structures critical to public security and to assist in the development of law enforcement agencies; to contribute to extenal security; members were Australia, Bangladesh, Bolivia, Brazil, Denmark, Fiji, Jordan, Malaysia, Mozambique, Nepal, NZ, Pakistan, Philippines, Portugal, Russia, Sweden; completed its mandate 20 May 2005

United Nations Monitoring, Verification, and Inspection Commission (UNMOVIC)

note - formerly known as United Nations Special Commission for the Elimination of Iraq's Weapons of Mass Destruction (UNSCOM)
established - December 1999
aim - to identify, account for, and eliminate Iraq's weapons of mass destruction and the capacity to produce them
commissioners - (16) Argentina, Brazil, Canada, China, France, Germany, India, Ireland, Japan, Mexico, Nigeria, Russia, Senegal, Ukraine, UK, US; note - the organization's mandate has been extended up to early 2006

United Nations Observer Mission in Georgia (UNOMIG)

established - 24 August 1993
aim - to verify compliance with the cease-fire agreement, to monitor weapons exclusion zone, and to supervise CIS peacekeeping force for Abkhazia; established by the UN Security Council
members - (25) Albania, Austria, Bangladesh, Croatia, Czech Republic, Denmark, Egypt, France, Germany, Greece, Hungary, Indonesia, Jordan, South Korea, Pakistan, Poland, Romania, Russia, Sweden, Switzerland, Turkey, Ukraine, UK, US, Uruguay

United Nations Operation in Burundi (ONUB)

established - 21 May 2004
aim - to support and help implement the efforts undertaken by Burundians to restore lasting peace and bring about national reconciliation
members - (47) Algeria, Bangladesh, Belgium, Benin, Bolivia, Burkina Faso, Chad, China, Egypt, Ethiopia, Gabon, The Gambia, Ghana, Guatemala, Guinea, India, Jordan, Kenya, South Korea, Kyrgyzstan, Malawi, Malaysia, Mali, Mozambique, Nambia, Nepal, Netherlands, Niger, Nigeria, Pakistan, Paraguay, Peru, Philippines, Portugal, Romania, Russia, Senegal, Serbia and Montenegro, South Africa, Spain, Sri Lanka, Thailand, Togo, Tunisia, Uruguay, Yemen, Zambia

United Nations Operation in Cote d'Ivoire (UNOCI)

established - 27 February 2004
aim - to facilitate the implementation by the Ivorian parties of the peace agreement signed by them in January 2003
members - (41) Bangladesh, Benin, Bolivia, Brazil, Chad, China, Republic of the Congo, Croatia, Dominican Republic, Ecuador, El Salvador, France, The Gambia, Ghana, Guatemala, Guinea, India, Ireland, Jordan, Kenya, Moldova, Morocco, Namibia, Nepal, Niger, Nigeria, Pakistan, Paraguay, Peru, Philippines, Poland, Romania, Russia, Senegal, Serbia and Montenegro, Togo, Tunisia, Uganda, Uruguay, Yemen, Zambia

United Nations Organization Mission in the Democratic Republic of the Congo (MONUC)

established - 30 November 1999
aim - to establish contacts with the signatories to the cease-fire agreement and to plan for the observation of the cease-fire and disengagement of forces
members - (49) Algeria, Bangladesh, Belgium, Benin, Bolivia, Bosnia and Herzegovina, Burkina Faso, Cameroon, Canada, China, Czech Republic, Denmark, Egypt, France, Ghana, Guatemala, India, Indonesia, Ireland,

Jordan, Kenya, Malawi, Malaysia, Mali, Mongolia, Morocco, Mozambique, Nepal, Netherlands, Niger, Nigeria, Pakistan, Paraguay, Peru, Poland, Romania, Russia, Senegal, Serbia and Montenegro, South Africa, Spain, Sri Lanka, Sweden, Switzerland, Tunisia, Ukraine, UK, Uruguay, Zambia

United Nations Peace-keeping Force in Cyprus (UNFICYP)

established - 4 March 1964
aim - to serve as a peacekeeping force between Greek Cypriots and Turkish Cypriots in Cyprus; established by the UN Security Council
members - (9) Argentina, Austria, Canada, Croatia, Finland, Hungary, Slovakia, UK, Uruguay

United Nations Population Fund (UNFPA)

note - acronym retained from predecessor organization UN Fund for Population Activities
established - July 1967
aim - to assist both developed and developing countries to deal with their population problems
members (executive board) - (36) selected on a rotating basis from all regions

United Nations Relief and Works Agency for Palestine Refugees in the Near East (UNRWA)

established - 8 December 1949
aim - to provide assistance to Palestinian refugees
members (advisory commission) - (10) Belgium, Egypt, France, Japan, Jordan, Lebanon, Syria, Turkey, UK, US

United Nations Research Institute for Social Development (UNRISD)

established - 1963
aim - to conduct research into the problems of economic development during different phases of economic growth
members - no country members, but a Board of Directors consisting of a chairman appointed by the UN secretary general and 7 individual members

United Nations Secretariat

established - 26 June 1945; effective - 24 October 1945
aim - to serve as the primary administrative organ of the UN; a Secretary General is appointed for a five-year term by the General Assembly on the recommendation of the Security Council
members - the UN Secretary General and staff

United Nations Security Council (UNSC)

established - 26 June 1945; effective - 24 October 1945
aim - to maintain international peace and security
permanent members - (5) China, France, Russia, UK, US
nonpermanent members - (10) elected for two-year terms by the UN General Assembly; Argentina (2005-06), Republic of the Congo (2006-07), Denmark (2005-06), Ghana (2006-07), Greece (2005-06), Japan (2005-06), Peru (2006-07), Qatar (2006-07), Slovakia (2006-07), Tanzania (2005-06)

United Nations Stabilization Mission in Haiti (MINUSTAH)

established - 30 April 2004
aim - to stabilize Haiti in many areas for at least six months
members - (22) Argentina, Benin, Bolivia, Brazil, Canada, Chile, Croatia, Ecuador, France, Guatemala, Jordan, Malaysia, Morocco, Nepal, Paraguay, Peru, Philippines, Spain, Sri Lanka, US, Uruguay, Yemen

United Nations Truce Supervision Organization (UNTSO)

established - June 1948
aim - to supervise the 1948 Arab-Israeli cease-fire; currently supports timely

deployment of reinforcements to other peacekeeping operations in the region as needed; initially established by the UN Security Council
members - (23) Argentina, Australia, Austria, Belgium, Canada, Chile, China, Denmark, Estonia, Finland, France, Ireland, Italy, Nepal, Netherlands, NZ, Norway, Russia, Slovakia, Slovenia, Sweden, Switzerland, US

United Nations Trusteeship Council

established on 26 June 1945, effective on 24 October 1945, to supervise the administration of the 11 UN trust territories; members were China, France, Russia, UK, US; it formally suspended operations 1 November 1995 after the Trust Territory of the Pacific Islands (Palau) became the Republic of Palau, a constitutional government in free association with the US; the Trusteeship Council was not dissolved

United Nations University (UNU)

established - 3 December 1973
aim - to conduct research in development, welfare, and human survival and to train scholars
members - (24 members of UNU Council and the Rector are appointed by the Secretary General of the United Nations and the Director General of UNESCO)

Universal Postal Union (UPU)

established - 9 October 1874, affiliated with the UN 15 November 1947; effective - 1 July 1948
aim - to promote international postal cooperation; a UN specialized agency
members - (188) includes all UN member countries except Andorra, Marshall Islands, Federated States of Micronesia, and Palau (187 total); plus Holy See; note - includes the following dependencies or areas of special interest: Australia (Norfolk Island), China (Hong Kong, Macau), Denmark (Faroe Islands, Greenland), France (French Guiana, French Polynesia, Martinique, Mayotte, New Caledonia, Reunion, Saint Pierre and Miquelon, Wallis and Futuna), Netherlands (Aruba, Netherlands Antilles), NZ (Cook Island, Niue, Tokelau), UK (Guernsey, Isle of Man, Jersey; Anguilla, Bermuda, British Virgin Islands, Cayman Islands, Falkland Islands, Gibraltar, Montserrat, Pitcairn, Saint Helena, Turks and Caicos), US (American Samoa, Guam, Puerto Rico, Virgin Islands)

Warsaw Pact (WP)

established 14 May 1955 to promote mutual defense; members met 1 July 1991 to dissolve the alliance; member states at the time of dissolution were: Bulgaria, Czechoslovakia, Hungary, Poland, Romania, and the USSR; earlier members included German Democratic Republic (GDR) and Albania

West African Development Bank (WADB)

note - also known as Banque Ouest-Africaine de Developpement (BOAD); is a financial institution of WAEMU
established - 14 November 1973
aim - to promote regional economic development and integration
regional members - (9) Central Bank of West African States, Benin, Burkina Faso, Cote d'Ivoire, Guinea-Bissau, Mali, Niger, Senegal, Togo
international/nonregional members - (5) African Development Bank, Belgium, European Investment Bank, France, Germany

West African Economic and Monetary Union (WAEMU)

note - also known as Union Economique et Monetaire Ouest Africaine (UEMOA)

established - 1 August 1994
aim - to increase competitiveness of members' economic markets; to create a common market
members - (8) Benin, Burkina Faso, Cote d'Ivoire, Guinea-Bissau, Mali, Niger, Senegal, Togo

Western European Union (WEU)

established - 23 October 1954; effective - 6 May 1955
aim - to provide mutual defense and to move toward political unification
members - (10) Belgium, France, Germany, Greece, Italy, Luxembourg, Netherlands, Portugal, Spain, UK
associate members - (6) Czech Republic, Hungary, Iceland, Norway, Poland, Turkey
associate partners - (7) Bulgaria, Estonia, Latvia, Lithuania, Romania, Slovakia, Slovenia
observers - (5) Austria, Denmark, Finland, Ireland, Sweden

World Bank Group

includes International Bank for Reconstruction and Development (IBRD), International Development Association (IDA), International Finance Corporation (IFC), and Multilateral Investment Guarantee Agency (MIGA)

World Confederation of Labor (WCL)

established - 19 June 1920 as the International Federation of Christian Trade Unions (IFCTU), renamed 4 October 1968
aim - to promote the trade union movement
members - (105 national organizations) Antigua and Barbuda, Argentina, Aruba, Austria, Bangladesh, Belgium, Belize, Benin, Bolivia, Brazil, Bulgaria, Burkina Faso, Cameroon, Canada, Central African Republic, Chad, Chile, Colombia, Democratic Republic of the Congo, Republic of the Congo, Costa Rica, Cote d'Ivoire, Cuba, Cyprus, Czech Republic, Denmark, Dominica, Dominican Republic, Ecuador, El Salvador, France, French Guiana, Gabon, The Gambia, Ghana, Guadeloupe, Guatemala, Guinea, Guyana, Haiti, Honduras, Hong Kong, Hungary, India, Indonesia, Iran, Italy, Japan, Kazakhstan, South Korea, Liberia, Libya, Liechtenstein, Lithuania, Luxembourg, Macedonia, Madagascar, Malawi, Malaysia, Malta, Martinique, Mauritania, Mauritius, Mexico, Morocco, Namibia, Nepal, Netherlands, Netherlands Antilles, Nicaragua, Niger, Pakistan, Panama, Paraguay, Peru, Philippines, Poland, Portugal, Puerto Rico, Romania, Rwanda, Saint Lucia, Saint Vincent and the Grenadines, Sao Tome and Principe, Senegal, Serbia and Montenegro, Sierra Leone, Singapore, Slovakia, South Africa, Spain, Sri Lanka, Suriname, Switzerland, Taiwan, Thailand, Togo, Trinidad and Tobago, Ukraine, US, Uruguay, Venezuela, Vietnam, Zambia, Zimbabwe

World Customs Organization (WCO)

note - began as the Customs Cooperation Council (CCC)
established - 15 December 1950
aim - to promote international cooperation in customs matters
members - (168) Afghanistan, Albania, Algeria, Andorra, Angola, Argentina, Armenia, Australia, Austria, Azerbaijan, The Bahamas, Bahrain, Bangladesh, Barbados, Belarus, Belgium, Benin, Bermuda, Bhutan, Bolivia, Botswana, Brazil, Brunei, Bulgaria, Burkina Faso, Burma, Burundi, Cambodia, Cameroon, Canada, Cape Verde, Central African Republic, Chad, Chile, China, Colombia, Comoros, Democratic Republic of the Congo, Republic of

the Congo, Costa Rica, Cote d?Ivoire, Croatia, Cuba, Cyprus, Czech Republic, Denmark, Dominican Republic, East Timor, Ecuador, Egypt, El Salvador, Eritrea, Estonia, Ethiopia, Fiji, Finland, France, Gabon, The Gambia, Georgia, Germany, Ghana, Greece, Guatemala, Guinea, Guyana, Haiti, Hong Kong, Hungary, Iceland, India, Indonesia, Iran, Iraq, Ireland, Israel, Italy, Jamaica, Japan, Jordan, Kazakhstan, Kenya, South Korea, Kuwait, Kyrgyzstan, Latvia, Lebanon, Lesotho, Liberia, Libya, Lithuania, Luxembourg, Macau, Macedonia, Madagascar, Malawi, Malaysia, Maldives, Mali, Malta, Mauritania, Mauritius, Mexico, Moldova, Mongolia, Morocco, Mozambique, Namibia, Nepal, Netherlands, Netherlands Antilles, NZ, Nicaragua, Niger, Nigeria, Norway, Oman, Pakistan, Panama, Papua New Guinea, Paraguay, Peru, Philippines, Poland, Portugal, Qatar, Romania, Russia, Rwanda, Saint Lucia, Samoa, Saudi Arabia, Senegal, Serbia and Montenegro, Seychelles, Sierra Leone, Singapore, Slovakia, Slovenia, South Africa, Spain, Sri Lanka, Sudan, Swaziland, Sweden, Switzerland, Syria, Tajikistan, Tanzania, Thailand, Togo, Tonga, Trinidad and Tobago, Tunisia, Turkey, Turkmenistan, Uganda, Ukraine, UAE, UK, US, Uruguay, Uzbekistan, Venezuela, Vietnam, Yemen, Zambia, Zimbabwe

World Federation of Trade Unions (WFTU)

established - 3 October 1945
aim - to promote the trade union movement
members - (125 and the Palestine Liberation Organization) Afghanistan, Albania, Angola, Antigua and Barbuda, Argentina, Armenia, Australia, Austria, Azerbaijan, Bahrain, Bangladesh, Barbados, Belarus, Benin, Bolivia, Botswana, Brazil, Bulgaria, Burkina Faso, Cambodia, Cameroon, Canada, Chile, Colombia, Democratic Republic of the Congo, Republic of the Congo, Costa Rica, Cote d'Ivoire, Cuba, Cyprus, Czech Republic, Djibouti, Dominican Republic, Ecuador, Egypt, El Salvador, Eritrea, Ethiopia, Fiji, Finland, France, French Guiana, The Gambia, Ghana, Greece, Guadeloupe, Guatemala, Guinea, Guinea-Bissau, Guyana, Haiti, Honduras, Hungary, India, Indonesia, Iran, Iraq, Jamaica, Japan, Jordan, Kazakhstan, North Korea, Kuwait, Kyrgyzstan, Laos, Lebanon, Lesotho, Liberia, Libya, Madagascar, Malawi, Malaysia, Mali, Martinique, Mauritius, Mexico, Mozambique, Nepal, New Caledonia, NZ, Niger, Nigeria, Oman, Pakistan, Panama, Papua New Guinea, Peru, Philippines, Poland, Portugal, Puerto Rico, Reunion, Romania, Russia, Saint Lucia, Saint Pierre and Miquelon, Saint Vincent and the Grenadines, Saudi Arabia, Senegal, Sierra Leone, Slovakia, Solomon Islands, Somalia, South Africa, Sri Lanka, Sudan, Sweden, Syria, Tajikistan, Tanzania, Thailand, Togo, Trinidad and Tobago, Tunisia, Turkey, Turkmenistan, Uganda, Ukraine, Uruguay, Uzbekistan, Vanuatu, Venezuela, Vietnam, Yemen, Zimbabwe, Palestine Liberation Organization

World Food Program (WFP)

established - 24 November 1961
aim - to provide food aid in support of economic development or disaster relief; an ECOSOC organization
members - (36) selected on a rotating basis from all regions

World Health Organization (WHO)

established - 22 July 1946; effective - 7 April 1948
aim - to deal with health matters worldwide; a UN specialized agency
members - (192) includes all UN member countries except Liechtenstein (190 total); plus Cook Islands and Niue

World Intellectual Property Organization (WIPO)

established - 14 July 1967; effective - 26 April 1970
aim - to furnish protection for literary, artistic, and scientific works; a UN specialized agency
members - (183) includes all UN member countries except East Timor, Kiribati, Marshall Islands, Federated States of Micronesia, Nauru, Palau, Solomon Islands, Tuvalu, Vanuatu (182 total); plus Holy See

World Meteorological Organization (WMO)

established - 11 October 1947; effective - 4 April 1951
aim - to sponsor meteorological cooperation; a UN specialized agency
members - (189) includes all UN member countries except Andorra, East Timor, Equatorial Guinea, Liechtenstein, Marshall Islands, Nauru, Palau, Saint Kitts and Nevis, Saint Vincent and the Grenadines, San Marino, Tuvalu (180 total); plus Aruba, British Caribbean Territories, Cook Islands, French Polynesia, Hong Kong, Macau, Netherlands Antilles, New Caledonia, and Niue

World Tourism Organization (WToO)

established - 2 January 1975
aim - to promote tourism as a means of contributing to economic development, international understanding, and peace
members - (146) Afghanistan, Albania, Algeria, Andorra, Angola, Argentina, Armenia, Australia, Austria, Azerbaijan, Bahrain, Bangladesh, Belarus, Benin, Bhutan, Bolivia, Bosnia and Herzegovina, Botswana, Brazil, Bulgaria, Burkina Faso, Burundi, Cambodia, Cameroon, Canada, Cape Verde, Central African Republic, Chad, Chile, China, Colombia, Democratic Republic of the Congo, Republic of the Congo, Costa Rica, Cote d'Ivoire, Croatia, Cuba, Cyprus, Czech Republic, Djibouti, Dominican Republic, Ecuador, Egypt, El Salvador, Equatorial Guinea, Eritrea, Ethiopia, Fiji, France, Gabon, The Gambia, Georgia, Germany, Ghana, Greece, Guatemala, Guinea, Guinea-Bissau, Haiti, Honduras, Hungary, India, Indonesia, Iran, Iraq, Israel, Italy, Jamaica, Japan, Jordan, Kazakhstan, Kenya, North Korea, South Korea, Kuwait, Kyrgyzstan, Laos, Latvia, Lebanon, Lesotho, Libya, Lithuania, Macedonia, Madagascar, Malawi, Malaysia, Maldives, Mali, Malta, Mauritania, Mauritius, Mexico, Moldova, Monaco, Mongolia, Morocco, Mozambique, Namibia, Nepal, Netherlands, Nicaragua, Niger, Nigeria, Oman, Pakistan, Panama, Paraguay, Peru, Philippines, Poland, Portugal, Qatar, Romania, Russia, Rwanda, San Marino, Sao Tome and Principe, Saudi Arabia, Senegal, Serbia and Montenegro, Seychelles, Sierra Leone, Slovakia, Slovenia, South Africa, Spain, Sri Lanka, Sudan, Swaziland, Switzerland, Syria, Tanzania, Thailand, Togo, Tunisia, Turkey, Turkmenistan, Uganda, Ukraine, Uruguay, Uzbekistan, Venezuela, Vietnam, Yemen, Zambia, Zimbabwe
associate members - (7) Aruba, Flanders, Hong Kong, Macau, Madeira Islands, Netherlands Antilles, Puerto Rico
observers - (1 plus Palestine Liberation Organization) Holy See, Palestine Liberation Organization

World Trade Organization (WTO)

note - succeeded General Agreement on Tariff and Trade (GATT)
established - 15 April 1994; effective - 1 January 1995
aim - to provide a forum to resolve trade conflicts between members and to carry on negotiations with the goal of further lowering and/or eliminating tariffs and other trade barriers
members - (149) Albania, Angola, Antigua and Barbuda, Argentina, Armenia,

Australia, Austria, Bahrain, Bangladesh, Barbados, Belgium, Belize, Benin, Bolivia, Botswana, Brazil, Brunei, Bulgaria, Burkina Faso, Burma, Burundi, Cambodia, Cameroon, Canada, Central African Republic, Chad, Chile, China, Colombia, Democratic Republic of the Congo, Republic of the Congo, Costa Rica, Cote d'Ivoire, Croatia, Cuba, Cyprus, Czech Republic, Denmark, Djibouti, Dominica, Dominican Republic, Ecuador, Egypt, El Salvador, Estonia, EC, Fiji, Finland, France, Gabon, The Gambia, Georgia, Germany, Ghana, Greece, Grenada, Guatemala, Guinea, Guinea-Bissau, Guyana, Haiti, Honduras, Hong Kong, Hungary, Iceland, India, Indonesia, Ireland, Israel, Italy, Jamaica, Japan, Jordan, Kenya, South Korea, Kuwait, Kyrgyzstan, Latvia, Lesotho, Liechtenstein, Lithuania, Luxembourg, Macau, Macedonia, Madagascar, Malawi, Malaysia, Maldives, Mali, Malta, Mauritania, Mauritius, Mexico, Moldova, Mongolia, Morocco, Mozambique, Namibia, Nepal, Netherlands, NZ, Nicaragua, Niger, Nigeria, Norway, Oman, Pakistan, Panama, Papua New Guinea, Paraguay, Peru, Philippines, Poland, Portugal, Qatar, Romania, Rwanda, Saint Kitts and Nevis, Saint Lucia, Saint Vincent and the Grenadines, Saudi Arabia, Senegal, Sierra Leone, Singapore, Slovakia, Slovenia, Solomon Islands, South Africa, Spain, Sri Lanka, Suriname, Swaziland, Sweden, Switzerland, Taiwan, Tanzania, Thailand, Togo, Trinidad and Tobago, Tunisia, Turkey, Uganda, UAE, UK, US, Uruguay, Venezuela, Zambia, Zimbabwe
observers - (32) Afghanistan, Algeria, Andorra, Azerbaijan, The Bahamas, Belarus, Bhutan, Bosnia and Herzegovina, Cape Verde, Equatorial Guinea, Ethiopia, Holy See, Iran, Iraq, Kazakhstan, Laos, Lebanon, Libya, Montenegro, Russia, Samoa, Sao Tome and Principe, Serbia, Seychelles, Sudan, Tajikistan, Tonga, Ukraine, Uzbekistan, Vanuatu, Vietnam, Yemen; note - with the exception of the Holy See, an observer must start accession negotiations within five years of becoming observers; Montenegro and Serbia each sent observers

Zangger Committee (ZC)

established - early 1970s
aim - to establish guidelines for the export control provisions of the Nonproliferation of Nuclear Weapons Treaty (NPT)
members - (35) Argentina, Australia, Austria, Belgium, Bulgaria, Canada, China, Czech Republic, Denmark, Finland, France, Germany, Greece, Hungary, Ireland, Italy, Japan, South Korea, Luxembourg, Netherlands, Norway, Poland, Portugal, Romania, Russia, Slovakia, Slovenia, South Africa, Spain, Sweden, Switzerland, Turkey, Ukraine, UK, US

advanced economies

a term used by the International Monetary FUND (IMF) for the top group in its hierarchy of advanced economies, countries in transition, and developing countries; it includes the following 28 advanced economies: Australia, Austria, Belgium, Canada, Denmark, Finland, France, Germany, Greece, Hong Kong, Iceland, Ireland, Israel, Italy, Japan, South Korea, Luxembourg, Netherlands, NZ, Norway, Portugal, Singapore, Spain, Sweden, Switzerland, Taiwan, UK, US; note - this group would presumably also cover the following seven smaller countries of Andorra, Bermuda, Faroe Islands, Holy See, Liechtenstein, Monaco, and San Marino that are included in the more comprehensive group of "developed countries"

centrally planned economies

a term applied mainly to the traditionally Communist states that looked to the former USSR for leadership; most are now evolving toward more democratic and market-oriented systems; also known formerly as the Second World or as as the Communist countries; through the 1980s, this group included Albania, Bulgaria, Cambodia, China, Cuba, Czechoslovakia, GDR, Hungary, North Korea, Laos, Mongolia, Poland, Romania, Serbia and Montenegro, USSR, Vietnam

countries in transition

a term used by the International Monetary Fund (IMF) for the middle group in its hierarchy of advanced economies, countries in transition, and developing countries; IMF statistics include the following 28 countries in transition: Albania, Armenia, Azerbaijan, Belarus, Bosnia and Herzegovina, Bulgaria, Croatia, Czech Republic, Estonia, Georgia, Hungary, Kazakhstan, Kyrgyzstan, Latvia, Lithuania, Macedonia, Moldova, Mongolia, Poland, Romania, Russia, Serbia and Montenegro, Slovakia, Slovenia, Tajikistan, Turkmenistan, Ukraine, Uzbekistan; note - this group is identical to the group traditionally referred to as the "former USSR/Eastern Europe" except for the addition of Mongolia

developed countries (DCs)

the top group in the hierarchy of developed countries (DCs), former USSR/Eastern Europe (former USSR/EE), and less developed countries (LDCs); includes the market-oriented economies of the mainly democratic nations in the Organization for Economic Cooperation and Development (OECD), Bermuda, Israel, South Africa, and the European ministates; also known as the First World, high-income countries, the North, industrial countries; generally have a per capita GDP in excess of $10,000 although four OECD countries and South Africa have figures well under $10,000 and two of the excluded OPEC countries have figures of more than $10,000; the 34 DCs are: Andorra, Australia, Austria, Belgium, Bermuda, Canada, Denmark, Faroe Islands, Finland, France, Germany, Greece, Holy See, Iceland, Ireland, Israel, Italy, Japan, Liechtenstein, Luxembourg, Malta, Monaco, Netherlands, NZ, Norway, Portugal, San Marino, South Africa, Spain, Sweden, Switzerland, Turkey, UK, US; note - similar to the new International Monetary Fund (IMF) term "advanced economies" that adds Hong Kong, South Korea, Singapore, and Taiwan but drops Malta, Mexico, South Africa, and Turkey

developing countries

a term used by the International Monetary Fund (IMF) for the bottom group in its hierarchy of advanced economies, countries in transition, and developing countries; IMF statistics include the following 126 developing countries: Afghanistan, Algeria, Angola, Antigua and Barbuda, Argentina, Aruba, The Bahamas, Bahrain, Bangladesh, Barbados, Belize, Benin, Bhutan, Bolivia, Botswana, Brazil, Burkina Faso, Burma, Burundi, Cambodia, Cameroon, Cape Verde, Central African Republic, Chad, Chile, China, Colombia, Comoros, Democratic Republic of the Congo, Republic of the Congo, Costa Rica, Cote d'Ivoire, Cyprus, Djibouti, Dominica, Dominican Republic, Ecuador, Egypt, El Salvador, Equatorial Guinea, Ethiopia, Fiji, Gabon, The Gambia, Ghana, Grenada, Guatemala, Guinea, Guinea-Bissau, Guyana, Haiti, Honduras, India, Indonesia, Iran, Iraq, Jamaica, Jordan, Kenya, Kiribati, Kuwait, Laos, Lebanon, Lesotho, Liberia, Libya, Madagascar, Malawi, Malaysia, Maldives, Mali, Malta, Marshall Islands, Mauritania, Mauritius, Mexico, Federated States of Micronesia, Morocco, Mozambique, Namibia, Nepal, Netherlands Antilles, Nicaragua, Niger, Nigeria, Oman, Pakistan, Panama, Papua New Guinea, Paraguay, Peru, Philippines, Qatar, Rwanda,

Saint Kitts and Nevis, Saint Lucia, Saint Vincent and the Grenadines, Samoa, Sao Tome and Principe, Saudi Arabia, Senegal, Seychelles, Sierra Leone, Solomon Islands, Somalia, South Africa, Sri Lanka, Sudan, Suriname, Swaziland, Syria, Tanzania, Thailand, Togo, Trinidad and Tobago, Tunisia, Turkey, UAE, Uganda, Uruguay, Vanuatu, Venezuela, Vietnam, Yemen, Zambia, Zimbabwe; note - this category would presumably also cover the following 46 other countries that are traditionally included in the more comprehensive group of "less developed countries": American Samoa, Anguilla, British Virgin Islands, Brunei, Cayman Islands, Christmas Island, Cocos Islands, Cook Islands, Cuba, Eritrea, Falkland Islands, French Guiana, French Polynesia, Gaza Strip, Gibraltar, Greenland, Grenada, Guadeloupe, Guam, Guernsey, Isle of Man, Jersey, North Korea, Macau, Martinique, Mayotte, Montserrat, Nauru, New Caledonia, Niue, Norfolk Island, Northern Mariana Islands, Palau, Pitcairn Islands, Puerto Rico, Reunion, Saint Helena, Saint Pierre and Miquelon, Tokelau, Tonga, Turks and Caicos Islands, Tuvalu, Virgin Islands, Wallis and Futuna, West Bank, Western Sahara

former Soviet Union (FSU)

former term often used to identify as a group the successor nations to the Soviet Union or USSR; this group of 15 countries consists of: Armenia, Azerbaijan, Belarus, Estonia, Georgia, Kazakhstan, Kyrgyzstan, Latvia, Lithuania, Moldova, Russia, Tajikistan, Turkmenistan, Ukraine, Uzbekistan

former USSR/Eastern Europe (former USSR/EE)

the middle group in the hierarchy of developed countries (DCs), former USSR/Eastern Europe (former USSR/EE), and less developed countries (LDCs); these countries are in political and economic transition and may well be grouped differently in the near future; this group of 27 countries consists of: Albania, Armenia, Azerbaijan, Belarus, Bosnia and Herzegovina, Bulgaria, Croatia, Czech Republic, Estonia, Georgia, Hungary, Kazakhstan, Kyrgyzstan, Latvia, Lithuania, Macedonia, Moldova, Poland, Romania, Russia, Slovakia, Slovenia, Tajikistan, Turkmenistan, Ukraine, Uzbekistan, Yugoslavia; this group is identical to the IMF group "countries in transition" except for the IMF's inclusion of Mongolia

high income countries

another term for the industrialized countries with high per capita GDPs; see developed countries (DCs)

industrial countries

another term for the developed countries; see developed countries (DCs)

least developed countries (LLDCs)

that subgroup of the less developed countries (LDCs) initially identified by the UN General Assembly in 1971 as having no significant economic growth, per capita GDPs normally less than $1,000, and low literacy rates; also known as the undeveloped countries; the 42 LLDCs are: Afghanistan, Bangladesh, Benin, Bhutan, Botswana, Burkina Faso, Burma, Burundi, Cape Verde, Central African Republic, Chad, Comoros, Djibouti, Equatorial Guinea, Eritrea, Ethiopia, The Gambia, Guinea, Guinea-Bissau, Haiti, Kiribati, Laos, Lesotho, Malawi, Maldives, Mali, Mauritania, Mozambique, Nepal, Niger, Rwanda, Samoa, Sao Tome and Principe, Sierra Leone, Somalia, Sudan, Tanzania, Togo, Tuvalu, Uganda, Vanuatu, Yemen

less developed countries (LDCs)

the bottom group in the hierarchy of developed countries (DCs), former USSR/Eastern Europe (former USSR/EE), and less developed countries

(LDCs); mainly countries and dependent areas with low levels of output, living standards, and technology; per capita GDPs are generally below $5,000 and often less than $1,500; however, the group also includes a number of countries with high per capita incomes, areas of advanced technology, and rapid rates of growth; includes the advanced developing countries, developing countries, Four Dragons (Four Tigers), least developed countries (LLDCs), low-income countries, middle-income countries, newly industrializing economies (NIEs), the South, Third World, underdeveloped countries, undeveloped countries; the 172 LDCs are: Afghanistan, Algeria, American Samoa, Angola, Anguilla, Antigua and Barbuda, Argentina, Aruba, The Bahamas, Bahrain, Bangladesh, Barbados, Belize, Benin, Bhutan, Bolivia, Botswana, Brazil, British Virgin Islands, Brunei, Burkina Faso, Burma, Burundi, Cambodia, Cameroon, Cape Verde, Cayman Islands, Central African Republic, Chad, Chile, China, Christmas Island, Cocos Islands, Colombia, Comoros, Democratic Republic of the Congo, Republic of the Congo, Cook Islands, Costa Rica, Cote d'Ivoire, Cuba, Cyprus, Djibouti, Dominica, Dominican Republic, Ecuador, Egypt, El Salvador, Equatorial Guinea, Eritrea, Ethiopia, Falkland Islands, Fiji, French Guiana, French Polynesia, Gabon, The Gambia, Gaza Strip, Ghana, Gibraltar, Greenland, Grenada, Guadeloupe, Guam, Guatemala, Guernsey, Guinea, Guinea-Bissau, Guyana, Haiti, Honduras, Hong Kong, India, Indonesia, Iran, Iraq, Isle of Man, Jamaica, Jersey, Jordan, Kenya, Kiribati, North Korea, South Korea, Kuwait, Laos, Lebanon, Lesotho, Liberia, Libya, Macau, Madagascar, Malawi, Malaysia, Maldives, Mali, Marshall Islands, Martinique, Mauritania, Mauritius, Mayotte, Federated States of Micronesia, Mongolia, Montserrat, Morocco, Mozambique, Namibia, Nauru, Nepal, Netherlands Antilles, New Caledonia, Nicaragua, Niger, Nigeria, Niue, Norfolk Island, Northern Mariana Islands, Oman, Palau, Pakistan, Panama, Papua New Guinea, Paraguay, Peru, Philippines, Pitcairn Islands, Puerto Rico, Qatar, Reunion, Rwanda, Saint Helena, Saint Kitts and Nevis, Saint Lucia, Saint Pierre and Miquelon, Saint Vincent and the Grenadines, Samoa, Sao Tome and Principe, Saudi Arabia, Senegal, Seychelles, Sierra Leone, Singapore, Solomon Islands, Somalia, Sri Lanka, Sudan, Suriname, Swaziland, Syria, Taiwan, Tanzania, Thailand, Togo, Tokelau, Tonga, Trinidad and Tobago, Tunisia, Turks and Caicos Islands, Tuvalu, UAE, Uganda, Uruguay, Vanuatu, Venezuela, Vietnam, Virgin Islands, Wallis and Futuna, West Bank, Western Sahara, Yemen, Zambia, Zimbabwe; note - similar to the new International Monetary Fund (IMF) term "developing countries" which adds Malta, Mexico, South Africa, and Turkey but omits in its recently published statistics American Samoa, Anguilla, British Virgin Islands, Brunei, Cayman Islands, Christmas Island, Cocos Islands, Cook Islands, Cuba, Eritrea, Falkland Islands, French Guiana, French Polynesia, Gaza Strip, Gibraltar, Greenland, Grenada, Guadeloupe, Guam, Guernsey, Isle of Man, Jersey, North Korea, Macau, Martinique, Mayotte, Montserrat, Nauru, New Caledonia, Niue, Norfolk Island, Northern Mariana Islands, Palau, Pitcairn Islands, Puerto Rico, Reunion, Saint Helena, Saint Pierre and Miquelon, Tokelau, Tonga, Turks and Caicos Islands, Tuvalu, Virgin Islands, Wallis and Futuna, West Bank, Western Sahara

low-income countries

another term for those less developed countries with below-average per capita GDPs; see less developed countries (LDCs)

middle-income countries another term for those less developed countries with above-average per capita GDPs; see less developed countries (LDCs)

new independent states (NIS) a term referring to all the countries of the FSU except the Baltic countries (Estonia, Latvia, Lithuania)

newly industrializing countries (NICs) former term for the newly industrializing economies; see newly industrializing economies (NIEs)

newly industrializing economies (NIEs) that subgroup of the less developed countries (LDCs) that has experienced particularly rapid industrialization of their economies; formerly known as the newly industrializing countries (NICs); also known as advanced developing countries; usually includes the Four Dragons (Hong Kong, South Korea, Singapore, Taiwan), and Brazil

socialist countries in general, countries in which the government owns and plans the use of the major factors of production; note - the term is sometimes used incorrectly as a synonym for Communist countries

underdeveloped countries refers to those less developed countries with the potential for above-average economic growth; see less developed countries (LDCs)

undeveloped countries refers to those extremely poor less developed countries (LDCs) with little prospect for economic growth; see least developed countries (LLDCs)
another term for those less developed countries (LDCs) with particularly rapid industrial development; see newly industrializing economies (NIEs)

APPENDIX C

SELECTED INTERNATIONAL ENVIRONMENTAL AGREEMENTS

Air Pollution

see Convention on Long-Range Transboundary Air Pollution

Air Pollution-Nitrogen Oxides

see Protocol to the 1979 Convention on Long-Range Transboundary Air Pollution Concerning the Control of Emissions of Nitrogen Oxides or Their Transboundary Fluxes

---

Air Pollution-Persistent Organic Pollutants

see Protocol to the 1979 Convention on Long-Range Transboundary Air Pollution on Persistent Organic Pollutants

---

Air Pollution-Sulphur 85

see Protocol to the 1979 Convention on Long-Range Transboundary Air Pollution on the Reduction of Sulphur Emissions or Their Transboundary Fluxes by at least 30%

Air Pollution-Sulphur 94

see Protocol to the 1979 Convention on Long-Range Transboundary Air Pollution on Further Reduction of Sulphur Emissions

---

Air Pollution-Volatile Organic Compounds

see Protocol to the 1979 Convention on Long-Range Transboundary Air Pollution Concerning the Control of Emissions of Volatile Organic Compounds or Their Transboundary Fluxes

---

Antarctic - Environmental Protocol

see Protocol on Environmental Protection to the Antarctic Treaty

---

Antarctic Treaty

opened for signature - 1 December 1959
entered into force - 23 June 1961
objective - to ensure that Antarctica is used for peaceful purposes only (such as international cooperation in scientific research); to defer the question of territorial claims asserted by some nations and not recognized by others; to provide an international forum for management of the region; applies to land and ice shelves south of 60 degrees south latitude
parties - (45) Argentina, Australia, Austria, Belgium, Brazil, Bulgaria, Canada, Chile, China, Colombia, Cuba, Czech Republic, Denmark, Ecuador, Estonia, Finland, France, Germany, Greece, Guatemala, Hungary, India, Italy, Japan, North Korea, South Korea, Netherlands, NZ, Norway, Papua New Guinea, Peru, Poland, Romania, Russia, Slovakia, South Africa, Spain, Sweden, Switzerland, Turkey, Ukraine, UK, US, Uruguay, Venezuela

---

Basel Convention on the Control of Transboundary Movements of Hazardous Wastes and Their Disposal

note - abbreviated as Hazardous Wastes
opened for signature - 22 March 1989
entered into force - 5 May 1992
objective - to reduce transboundary movements of wastes subject to the Convention to a minimum consistent with the environmentally sound and efficient management of such wastes; to minimize the amount and toxicity of wastes generated and ensure their environ-

mentally sound management as closely as possible to the source of generation; and to assist LDCs in environmentally sound management of the hazardous and other wastes they generate
parties - (149) Albania, Algeria, Andorra, Antigua and Barbuda, Argentina, Armenia, Australia, Austria, Azerbaijan, The Bahamas, Bahrain, Bangladesh, Barbados, Belarus, Belgium, Belize, Benin, Bolivia, Bosnia and Herzegovina, Botswana, Brazil, Bulgaria, Burkina Faso, Burundi, Cambodia, Cameroon, Canada, Cape Verde, Chile, China, Colombia, Comoros, Democratic Republic of the Congo, Costa Rica, Cote d'Ivoire, Croatia, Cuba, Cyprus, Czech Republic, Denmark, Dominica, Dominican Republic, Ecuador, Egypt, El Salvador, Estonia, Ethiopia, EU, Finland, France, The Gambia, Georgia, Germany, Greece, Guatemala, Guinea, Guyana, Honduras, Hungary, Iceland, India, Indonesia, Iran, Ireland, Israel, Italy, Japan, Jordan, Kenya, Kiribati, South Korea, Kuwait, Kyrgyzstan, Latvia, Lebanon, Lesotho, Libya, Liechtenstein, Lithuania, Luxembourg, Macedonia, Madagascar, Malawi, Malaysia, Maldives, Mali, Malta, Mauritania, Mauritius, Mexico, Federated States of Micronesia, Moldova, Monaco, Mongolia, Morocco, Mozambique, Namibia, Nauru, Nepal, Netherlands, NZ, Nicaragua, Niger, Nigeria, Norway, Oman, Pakistan, Panama, Papua New Guinea, Paraguay, Peru, Philippines, Poland, Portugal, Qatar, Romania, Russia, Saint Kitts and Nevis, Saint Lucia, Saint Vincent and the Grenadines, Saudi Arabia, Senegal, Serbia and Montenegro, Seychelles, Singapore, Slovakia, Slovenia, South Africa, Spain, Sri Lanka, Sweden, Switzerland, Syria, Tanzania, Thailand, Trinidad and Tobago, Tunisia, Turkey, Turkmenistan, Uganda, Ukraine, UAE, UK, Uruguay, Uzbekistan, Venezuela, Vietnam, Yemen, Zambia
countries that have signed, but not yet ratified - (3) Afghanistan, Haiti, US

Biodiversity

see Convention on Biological Diversity

Climate Change

see United Nations Framework Convention on Climate Change

Climate Change-Kyoto Protocol

see Kyoto Protocol to the United Nations Framework Convention on Climate Change

---

Convention for the Conservation of Antarctic Seals

note - abbreviated as Antarctic Seals
opened for signature - 1 June 1972
entered into force - 11 March 1978
objective - to promote and achieve the protection, scientific study, and rational use of Antarctic seals, and to maintain a satisfactory balance within the ecological system of Antarctica
parties - (16) Argentina, Australia, Belgium, Brazil, Canada, Chile, France, Germany, Italy, Japan, Norway, Poland, Russia, South Africa, UK, US
countries that have signed, but not yet ratified - (1) NZ

Convention on Biological Diversity

note - abbreviated as Biodiversity
opened for signature - 5 June 1992
entered into force - 29 December 1993

objective - to develop national strategies for the conservation and sustainable use of biological diversity
parties - (182) Albania, Algeria, Angola, Antigua and Barbuda, Argentina, Armenia, Australia, Austria, Azerbaijan, The Bahamas, Bahrain, Bangladesh, Barbados, Belarus, Belgium, Belize, Benin, Bhutan, Bolivia, Botswana, Brazil, Bulgaria, Burkina Faso, Burma, Burundi, Cambodia, Cameroon, Canada, Cape Verde, Central African Republic, Chad, Chile, China, Colombia, Comoros, Democratic Republic of the Congo, Republic of the Congo, Cook Islands, Costa Rica, Cote d'Ivoire, Croatia, Cuba, Cyprus, Czech Republic, Denmark, Djibouti, Dominica, Dominican Republic, Ecuador, Egypt, El Salvador, Equatorial Guinea, Eritrea, Estonia, Ethiopia, EU, Fiji, Finland, France, Gabon, The Gambia, Georgia, Germany, Ghana, Greece, Grenada, Guatemala, Guinea, Guinea-Bissau, Guyana, Haiti, Honduras, Hungary, Iceland, India, Indonesia, Iran, Ireland, Israel, Italy, Jamaica, Japan, Jordan, Kazakhstan, Kenya, Kiribati, North Korea, South Korea, Kyrgyzstan, Laos, Latvia, Lebanon, Lesotho, Liberia, Libya, Liechtenstein, Lithuania, Luxembourg, Macedonia, Madagascar, Malawi, Malaysia, Maldives, Mali, Malta, Marshall Islands, Mauritania, Mauritius, Mexico, Federated States of Micronesia, Moldova, Monaco, Mongolia, Morocco, Mozambique, Namibia, Nauru, Nepal, Netherlands, NZ, Nicaragua, Niger, Nigeria, Niue, Norway, Oman, Pakistan, Palau, Panama, Papua New Guinea, Paraguay, Peru, Philippines, Poland, Portugal, Qatar, Romania, Russia, Rwanda, Saint Kitts and Nevis, Saint Lucia, Saint Vincent and the Grenadines, Samoa, San Marino, Sao Tome and Principe, Saudi Arabia, Senegal, Seychelles, Sierra Leone, Singapore, Slovakia, Slovenia, Solomon Islands, South Africa, Spain, Sri Lanka, Sudan, Suriname, Swaziland, Sweden, Switzerland, Syria, Tajikistan, Tanzania, Togo, Tonga, Trinidad and Tobago, Tunisia, Turkey, Turkmenistan, Uganda, Ukraine, UAE, UK, Uruguay, Uzbekistan, Vanuatu, Venezuela, Vietnam, Yemen, Zambia, Zimbabwe
countries that have signed, but not yet ratified - (6) Afghanistan, Kuwait, Serbia and Montenegro, Thailand, Tuvalu, US

Convention on Fishing and Conservation of Living Resources of the High Seas

note - abbreviated as Marine Life Conservation
opened for signature - 29 April 1958
entered into force - 20 March 1966
objective - to solve through international cooperation the problems involved in the conservation of living resources of the high seas, considering that because of the development of modern technology some of these resources are in danger of being overexploited
parties - (37) Australia, Belgium, Bosnia and Herzegovina, Burkina Faso, Cambodia, Colombia, Denmark, Dominican Republic, Fiji, Finland, France, Haiti, Jamaica, Kenya, Lesotho, Madagascar, Malawi, Malaysia, Mauritius, Mexico, Netherlands, Nigeria, Portugal, Senegal, Serbia and Montenegro, Sierra Leone, Solomon Islands, South Africa, Spain, Switzerland, Thailand, Tonga, Trinidad and Tobago, Uganda, UK, US, Venezuela

countries that have signed, but not yet ratified - (21) Afghanistan, Argentina, Bolivia, Canada, Costa Rica, Cuba, Ghana, Iceland, Indonesia, Iran, Ireland, Israel, Lebanon, Liberia, Nepal, NZ, Pakistan, Panama, Sri Lanka, Tunisia, Uruguay

---

Convention on Long-Range Transboundary Air Pollution

note - abbreviated as Air Pollution
opened for signature - 13 November 1979
entered into force - 16 March 1983
objective - to protect the human environment against air pollution and to gradually reduce and prevent air pollution, including long-range transboundary air pollution
parties - (48) Armenia, Austria, Belarus, Belgium, Bosnia and Herzegovina, Bulgaria, Canada, Croatia, Cyprus, Czech Republic, Denmark, Estonia, EU, Finland, France, Georgia, Germany, Greece, Hungary, Iceland, Ireland, Italy, Kazakhstan, Kyrgyzstan, Latvia, Liechtenstein, Lithuania, Luxembourg, Macedonia, Malta, Moldova, Monaco, Netherlands, Norway, Poland, Portugal, Romania, Russia, Serbia and Montenegro, Slovakia, Slovenia, Spain, Sweden, Switzerland, Turkey, Ukraine, UK, US
countries that have signed, but not yet ratified - (2) Holy See, San Marino

---

Convention on Wetlands of International Importance Especially as Waterfowl Habitat (Ramsar)

note - abbreviated as Wetlands
opened for signature - 2 February 1971
entered into force - 21 December 1975
objective - to stem the progressive encroachment on and loss of wetlands now and in the future, recognizing the fundamental ecological functions of wetlands and their economic, cultural, scientific, and recreational value
parties - (125) Albania, Algeria, Argentina, Armenia, Australia, Austria, Azerbaijan, The Bahamas, Bahrain, Bangladesh, Belarus, Belgium, Belize, Benin, Bolivia, Bosnia and Herzegovina, Botswana, Brazil, Bulgaria, Burkina Faso, Cambodia, Canada, Chad, Chile, China, Colombia, Comoros, Democratic Republic of the Congo, Republic of the Congo, Costa Rica, Cote d'Ivoire, Croatia, Cuba, Czech Republic, Denmark, Ecuador, Egypt, El Salvador, Estonia, Finland, France, Gabon, The Gambia, Georgia, Germany, Ghana, Greece, Guatemala, Guinea, Guinea-Bissau, Honduras, Hungary, Iceland, India, Indonesia, Iran, Ireland, Israel, Italy, Jamaica, Japan, Jordan, Kenya, South Korea, Latvia, Lebanon, Liechtenstein, Lithuania, Luxembourg, Macedonia, Madagascar, Malawi, Malaysia, Mali, Malta, Mauritania, Mauritius, Mexico, Monaco, Mongolia, Morocco, Namibia, Nepal, Netherlands, NZ, Nicaragua, Niger, Norway, Pakistan, Panama, Papua New Guinea, Paraguay, Peru, Philippines, Poland, Portugal, Romania, Russia, Senegal, Serbia and Montenegro, Sierra Leone, Slovakia, Slovenia, South Africa, Spain, Sri Lanka, Suriname, Sweden, Switzerland, Syria, Tajikistan, Thailand, Togo, Trinidad and Tobago, Tunisia, Turkey, Uganda, Ukraine, UK, US, Uruguay, Uzbekistan, Venezuela, Vietnam, Zambia

Convention on the Conservation of Antarctic Marine Living Resources

note - abbreviated as Antarctic-Marine Living Resources
opened for signature - 5 May 1980
entered into force - 7 April 1982
objective - to safeguard the environment and protect the integrity of the ecosystem of the seas surrounding Antarctica, and to conserve Antarctic marine living resources
parties - (31) Argentina, Australia, Belgium, Brazil, Bulgaria, Canada, Chile, EU, Finland, France, Germany, Greece, India, Italy, Japan, South Korea, Namibia, Netherlands, NZ, Norway, Peru, Poland, Russia, South Africa, Spain, Sweden, Ukraine, UK, US, Uruguay, Vanuatu

---

Convention on the International Trade in Endangered Species of Wild Flora and Fauna (CITES)

note - abbreviated as Endangered Species
opened for signature - 3 March 1973
entered into force - 1 July 1975
objective - to protect certain endangered species from overexploitation by means of a system of import/export permits
parties - (156) Afghanistan, Algeria, Antigua and Barbuda, Argentina, Australia, Austria, Azerbaijan, The Bahamas, Bangladesh, Barbados, Belarus, Belgium, Belize, Benin, Bolivia, Botswana, Brazil, Brunei, Bulgaria, Burkina Faso, Burma, Burundi, Cambodia, Cameroon, Canada, Central African Republic, Chad, Chile, China, Colombia, Comoros, Democratic Republic of the Congo, Republic of the Congo, Costa Rica, Cote d'Ivoire, Croatia, Cuba, Cyprus, Czech Republic, Denmark, Djibouti, Dominica, Dominican Republic, Ecuador, Egypt, El Salvador, Equatorial Guinea, Eritrea, Estonia, Ethiopia, Fiji, Finland, France, Gabon, The Gambia, Georgia, Germany, Ghana, Greece, Grenada, Guatemala, Guinea, Guinea-Bissau, Guyana, Honduras, Hungary, Iceland, India, Indonesia, Iran, Israel, Italy, Jamaica, Japan, Jordan, Kazakhstan, Kenya, South Korea, Latvia, Liberia, Liechtenstein, Lithuania, Luxembourg, Macedonia, Madagascar, Malawi, Malaysia, Mali, Malta, Mauritania, Mauritius, Mexico, Moldova, Monaco, Mongolia, Morocco, Mozambique, Namibia, Nepal, Netherlands, NZ, Nicaragua, Niger, Nigeria, Norway, Pakistan, Panama, Papua New Guinea, Paraguay, Peru, Philippines, Poland, Portugal, Qatar, Romania, Russia, Rwanda, Saint Kitts and Nevis, Saint Lucia, Saint Vincent and the Grenadines, Sao Tome and Principe, Saudi Arabia, Senegal, Seychelles, Sierra Leone, Singapore, Slovakia, Slovenia, Somalia, South Africa, Spain, Sri Lanka, Sudan, Suriname, Swaziland, Sweden, Switzerland, Tanzania, Thailand, Togo, Trinidad and Tobago, Tunisia, Turkey, Uganda, Ukraine, UAE, UK, US, Uruguay, Uzbekistan, Vanuatu, Venezuela, Vietnam, Yemen, Zambia, Zimbabwe
countries that have signed, but not yet ratified - (3) Ireland, Kuwait, Lesotho

---

Convention on the Prevention of Marine Pollution by Dumping Wastes and Other Matter (London Convention)

note - abbreviated as Marine Dumping
opened for signature - 29 December 1972
entered into force - 30 August 1975
objective - to control pollution of the sea by dumping and to

encourage regional agreements supplementary to the Convention
parties - (78) Afghanistan, Antigua and Barbuda, Argentina, Australia, Azerbaijan, Barbados, Belarus, Belgium, Brazil, Canada, Cape Verde, Chile, China, Democratic Republic of the Congo, Costa Rica, Cote d'Ivoire, Croatia, Cuba, Cyprus, Denmark, Dominican Republic, Egypt, Finland, France, Gabon, Germany, Greece, Guatemala, Haiti, Honduras, Hong Kong (associate member), Hungary, Iceland, Iran, Ireland, Italy, Jamaica, Japan, Jordan, Kenya, Kiribati, South Korea, Libya, Luxembourg, Malta, Mexico, Monaco, Morocco, Nauru, Netherlands, NZ, Nigeria, Norway, Oman, Pakistan, Panama, Papua New Guinea, Philippines, Poland, Portugal, Russia, Saint Lucia, Serbia and Montenegro, Seychelles, Slovenia, Solomon Islands, South Africa, Spain, Suriname, Sweden, Switzerland, Tonga, Tunisia, Ukraine, UAE, UK, US, Vanuatu

---

Convention on the Prohibition of Military or Any Other Hostile Use of Environmental Modification Techniques

note - abbreviated as Environmental Modification
opened for signature - 10 December 1976
entered into force - 5 October 1978
objective - to prohibit the military or other hostile use of environmental modification techniques in order to further world peace and trust among nations
parties - (66) Afghanistan, Algeria, Antigua and Barbuda, Argentina, Australia, Austria, Bangladesh, Belarus, Belgium, Benin, Brazil, Bulgaria, Canada, Cape Verde, Chile, Costa Rica, Cuba, Cyprus, Czech Republic, Denmark, Dominica, Egypt, Finland, Germany, Ghana, Greece, Guatemala, Hungary, India, Ireland, Italy, Japan, North Korea, South Korea, Kuwait, Laos, Malawi, Mauritius, Mongolia, Netherlands, NZ, Niger, Norway, Pakistan, Papua New Guinea, Poland, Romania, Russia, Saint Lucia, Saint Vincent and the Grenadines, Sao Tome and Principe, Slovakia, Solomon Islands, Spain, Sri Lanka, Sweden, Switzerland, Tajikistan, Tunisia, Ukraine, UK, US, Uruguay, Uzbekistan, Vietnam, Yemen
countries that have signed, but not yet ratified - (17) Bolivia, Democratic Republic of the Congo, Ethiopia, Holy See, Iceland, Iran, Iraq, Lebanon, Liberia, Luxembourg, Morocco, Nicaragua, Portugal, Sierra Leone, Syria, Turkey, Uganda

---

Desertification

see United Nations Convention to Combat Desertification in those Countries Experiencing Serious Drought and/or Desertification, Particularly in Africa

---

Endangered Species

see Convention on the International Trade in Endangered Species of Wild Flora and Fauna (CITES)

Environmental Modification

see Convention on the Prohibition of Military or Any Other Hostile Use of Environmental Modification Techniques

---

Hazardous Wastes

see Basel Convention on the Control of Transboundary Movements of Hazardous Wastes and Their Disposal

International Convention for the Regulation of Whaling

note - abbreviated as Whaling
opened for signature - 2 December 1946
entered into force - 10 November 1948
objective - to protect all species of whales from overhunting; to establish a system of international regulation for the whale fisheries to ensure proper conservation and development of whale stocks; and to safeguard for future generations the great natural resources represented by whale stocks
parties - (42) Antigua and Barbuda, Argentina, Australia, Austria, Brazil, Chile, China, Costa Rica, Denmark, Dominica, Finland, France, Germany, Grenada, Guinea, India, Ireland, Italy, Japan, Kenya, South Korea, Mexico, Monaco, Morocco, Netherlands, NZ, Norway, Oman, Panama, Peru, Russia, Saint Kitts and Nevis, Saint Lucia, Saint Vincent and the Grenadines, Senegal, Solomon Islands, South Africa, Spain, Sweden, Switzerland, UK, US

International Tropical Timber Agreement, 1983

note - abbreviated as Tropical Timber 83
opened for signature - 18 November 1983
entered into force - 1 April 1985; this agreement expired when the International Tropical Timber Agreement, 1994, went into force
objective - to provide an effective framework for cooperation between tropical timber producers and consumers and to encourage the development of national policies aimed at sustainable utilization and conservation of tropical forests and their genetic resources
parties - (54) Australia, Austria, Belgium, Bolivia, Brazil, Burma, Cameroon, Canada, China, Colombia, Democratic Republic of the Congo, Republic of the Congo, Cote d'Ivoire, Denmark, Ecuador, Egypt, EU, Fiji, Finland, France, Gabon, Germany, Ghana, Greece, Guyana, Honduras, India, Indonesia, Ireland, Italy, Japan, South Korea, Liberia, Luxembourg, Malaysia, Nepal, Netherlands, NZ, Norway, Panama, Papua New Guinea, Peru, Philippines, Portugal, Russia, Spain, Sweden, Switzerland, Thailand, Togo, Trinidad and Tobago, UK, US, Venezuela

---

International Tropical Timber Agreement, 1994

note - abbreviated as Tropical Timber 94
opened for signature - 26 January 1994
entered into force - 1 January 1997
objective - to ensure that by the year 2000 exports of tropical timber originate from sustainably managed sources; to establish a fund to assist tropical timber producers in obtaining the resources necessary to reach this objective
parties - (58) Australia, Austria, Belgium, Bolivia, Brazil, Burma, Cambodia, Cameroon, Canada, Central African Republic, China, Colombia, Democratic Republic of the Congo, Republic of the Congo, Cote d'Ivoire, Denmark, Ecuador, Egypt, EU, Fiji, Finland, France, Gabon, Germany, Ghana, Greece, Guyana, Honduras, India, Indonesia, Ireland, Italy, Japan, South Korea, Liberia, Luxembourg, Malaysia, Nepal, Netherlands, NZ, Norway, Panama, Papua New Guinea, Peru, Philippines, Portugal, Spain, Suriname, Sweden, Switzerland, Thailand, Togo, Trinidad and

Tobago, UK, US, Uruguay, Vanuatu, Venezuela
countries that have signed, but not yet ratified - (1) Ireland

---

Kyoto Protocol to the United Nations Framework Convention on Climate Change

note - abbreviated as Climate Change-Kyoto Protocol
opened for signature - 16 March 1998
entered into force - 23 February 2005
objective - to further reduce greenhouse gas emissions by enhancing the national programs of developed countries aimed at this goal and by establishing percentage reduction targets for the developed countries
parties - (144) Algeria, Antigua and Barbuda, Argentina, Armenia, Austria, Azerbaijan, The Bahamas, Bangladesh, Barbados, Belgium, Belize, Benin, Bhutan, Bolivia, Botswana, Brazil, Bulgaria, Burma, Burundi, Cambodia, Cameroon, Canada, Chile, China, Colombia, Cook Island, Costa Rica, Cuba, Cyprus, Czech Republic, Denmark, Djibouti, Dominica, Dominican Republic, Ecuador, Egypt, El Salvador, Equatorial Guinea, Estonia, EU, Fiji, Finland, France, The Gambia, Georgia, Germany, Ghana, Greece, Grenada, Guatemala, Guinea, Guyana, Honduras, Hungary, Iceland, India, Indonesia, Ireland, Israel, Italy, Jamaica, Japan, Jordan, Kenya, Kiribati, South Korea, Kyrgyzstan, Laos, Latvia, Lesotho, Liberia, Liechtenstein, Lithuania, Luxembourg, Macedonia, Madagascar, Malawi, Malaysia, Maldives, Mali, Malta, Marshall Islands, Mauritius, Mexico, Federated States of Micronesia, Moldova, Mongolia, Morocco, Mozambique, Namibia, Nauru, Netherlands, NZ, Nicaragua, Niger, Nigeria, Niue, Norway, Oman, Pakistan, Palau, Panama, Papua New Guinea, Paraguay, Peru, Philippines, Poland, Portugal, Qatar, Romania, Russia, Rwanda, Saint Lucia, Saint Vincent and the Grenadines, Samoa, Saudi Arabia, Senegal, Seychelles, Slovakia, Slovenia, Solomon Islands, South Africa, Spain, Sri Lanka, Sudan, Sweden, Switzerland, Tanzania, Thailand, Togo, Trinidad and Tobago, Tunisia, Turkmenistan, Tuvalu, Uganda, Ukraine, UAE, UK, Uruguay, Uzbekistan, Vanuatu, Venezuela, Vietnam, Yemen
countries that have signed, but not yet ratified - (6) Australia, Croatia, Kazakhstan, Monaco, US, Zambia

---

Law of the Sea

see United Nations Convention on the Law of the Sea (LOS)

Marine Dumping

see Convention on the Prevention of Marine Pollution by Dumping Wastes and Other Matter (London Convention)

Marine Life Conservation

see Convention on Fishing and Conservation of Living Resources of the High Seas

---

Montreal Protocol on Substances That Deplete the Ozone Layer

note - abbreviated as Ozone Layer Protection
opened for signature - 16 September 1987
entered into force - 1 January 1989
objective - to protect the ozone layer by controlling emissions of substances that deplete it
parties - (183) Albania, Algeria, Angola, Antigua and Barbuda,

Argentina, Armenia, Australia, Austria, Azerbaijan, The Bahamas, Bahrain, Bangladesh, Barbados, Belarus, Belgium, Belize, Benin, Bolivia, Bosnia and Herzegovina, Botswana, Brazil, Brunei, Bulgaria, Burkina Faso, Burma, Burundi, Cambodia, Cameroon, Canada, Cape Verde, Central African Republic, Chad, Chile, China, Colombia, Comoros, Democratic Republic of the Congo, Republic of the Congo, Costa Rica, Cote d'Ivoire, Croatia, Cuba, Cyprus, Czech Republic, Denmark, Djibouti, Dominica, Dominican Republic, Ecuador, Egypt, El Salvador, Estonia, Ethiopia, EU, Fiji, Finland, France, Gabon, The Gambia, Georgia, Germany, Ghana, Greece, Grenada, Guatemala, Guinea, Guyana, Haiti, Honduras, Hungary, Iceland, India, Indonesia, Iran, Ireland, Israel, Italy, Jamaica, Japan, Jordan, Kazakhstan, Kenya, Kiribati, North Korea, South Korea, Kuwait, Kyrgyzstan, Laos, Latvia, Lebanon, Lesotho, Liberia, Libya, Liechtenstein, Lithuania, Luxembourg, Macedonia, Madagascar, Malawi, Malaysia, Maldives, Mali, Malta, Marshall Islands, Mauritania, Mauritius, Mexico, Federated States of Micronesia, Moldova, Monaco, Mongolia, Morocco, Mozambique, Namibia, Nauru, Nepal, Netherlands, NZ, Nicaragua, Niger, Nigeria, Norway, Oman, Pakistan, Palau, Panama, Papua New Guinea, Paraguay, Peru, Philippines, Poland, Portugal, Qatar, Romania, Russia, Rwanda, Saint Kitts and Nevis, Saint Lucia, Saint Vincent and the Grenadines, Samoa, Sao Tome and Principe, Saudi Arabia, Senegal, Serbia and Montenegro, Seychelles, Sierra Leone, Singapore, Slovakia, Slovenia, Solomon Islands, Somalia, South Africa, Spain, Sri Lanka, Sudan, Suriname, Swaziland, Sweden, Switzerland, Syria, Tajikistan, Tanzania, Thailand, Togo, Tonga, Trinidad and Tobago, Tunisia, Turkey, Turkmenistan, Tuvalu, Uganda, Ukraine, UAE, UK, US, Uruguay, Uzbekistan, Vanuatu, Venezuela, Vietnam, Yemen, Zambia, Zimbabwe

Nuclear Test Ban

see Treaty Banning Nuclear Weapons Tests in the Atmosphere, in Outer Space, and Under Water

Ozone Layer Protection

see Montreal Protocol on Substances That Deplete the Ozone Layer

Protocol of 1978 Relating to the International Convention for the Prevention of Pollution From Ships, 1973 (MARPOL)

note - abbreviated as Ship Pollution
opened for signature - 17 February 1978
entered into force - 2 October 1983
objective - to preserve the marine environment through the complete elimination of pollution by oil and other harmful substances and the minimization of accidental discharge of such substances
parties - (119) Algeria, Angola, Antigua and Barbuda, Argentina, Australia, Austria, The Bahamas, Barbados, Belarus, Belgium, Belize, Benin, Bolivia, Brazil, Brunei, Bulgaria, Burma, Cambodia, Canada, Chile, China, Colombia, Comoros, Cote d'Ivoire, Croatia, Cuba, Cyprus, Czech Republic, Denmark, Djibouti, Dominica, Dominican Republic, Ecuador, Egypt, Equatorial Guinea, Estonia, Finland, France, Gabon, The Gambia, Georgia, Germany, Ghana,

Greece, Guatemala, Guyana, Honduras, Hungary, Iceland, India, Indonesia, Ireland, Israel, Italy, Jamaica, Japan, Kazakhstan, Kenya, North Korea, South Korea, Latvia, Lebanon, Liberia, Lithuania, Luxembourg, Malawi, Malaysia, Malta, Marshall Islands, Mauritania, Mauritius, Mexico, Monaco, Morocco, Netherlands, NZ, Nicaragua, Norway, Oman, Pakistan, Panama, Papua New Guinea, Peru, Philippines, Poland, Portugal, Romania, Russia, Saint Kitts and Nevis, Saint Lucia, Saint Vincent and the Grenadines, Sao Tome and Principe, Senegal, Serbia and Montenegro, Seychelles, Sierra Leone, Singapore, Slovakia, Slovenia, South Africa, Spain, Sri Lanka, Suriname, Sweden, Switzerland, Syria, Togo, Tonga, Trinidad and Tobago, Tunisia, Turkey, Tuvalu, Ukraine, UK, US, Uruguay, Vanuatu, Venezuela, Vietnam

---

Protocol on Environmental Protection to the Antarctic Treaty

note - abbreviated as Antarctic-Environmental Protocol
opened for signature - 4 October 1991
entered into force - 14 January 1998
objective - to provide for comprehensive protection of the Antarctic environment and dependent and associated ecosystems; applies to the area covered by the Antarctic Treaty
consultative parties - (27) Argentina, Australia, Belgium, Brazil, Bulgaria, Chile, China, Ecuador, Finland, France, Germany, India, Italy, Japan, South Korea, Netherlands, NZ, Norway, Peru, Poland, Russia, South Africa, Spain, Sweden, UK, US, Uruguay
non consultative parties - (16) Austria, Canada, Colombia, Cuba, Czech Republic, Denmark, Greece, Guatemala, Hungary, North Korea, Papua New Guinea, Romania, Slovakia, Switzerland, Turkey, Ukraine

---

Protocol to the 1979 Convention on Long-Range Transboundary Air Pollution Concerning the Control of Emissions of Nitrogen Oxides or Their Transboundary Fluxes

note - abbreviated as Air Pollution-Nitrogen Oxides
opened for signature - 31 October 1988
entered into force - 14 February 1991
objective - to provide for the control or reduction of nitrogen oxides and their transboundary fluxes
parties - (28) Austria, Belarus, Belgium, Bulgaria, Canada, Czech Republic, Denmark, Estonia, EU, Finland, France, Germany, Greece, Hungary, Ireland, Italy, Liechtenstein, Luxembourg, Netherlands, Norway, Russia, Slovakia, Spain, Sweden, Switzerland, Ukraine, UK, US
countries that have signed, but not yet ratified - (1) Poland

---

Protocol to the 1979 Convention on Long-Range Transboundary Air Pollution Concerning the Control of Emissions of Volatile Organic Compounds or Their Transboundary Fluxes

note - abbreviated as Air Pollution-Volatile Organic Compounds
opened for signature - 18 November 1991
entered into force - 29 September 1997
objective - to provide for the control and reduction of emissions of volatile organic compounds in order to reduce their transboundary fluxes so as to protect human health and the environment from adverse effects
parties - (21) Austria, Belgium, Bulgaria, Czech Republic, Denmark, Estonia, Finland, France, Germany, Hungary, Italy,

Liechtenstein, Luxembourg, Monaco, Netherlands, Norway, Slovakia, Spain, Sweden, Switzerland, UK
countries that have signed, but not yet ratified - (6) Canada, EU, Greece, Portugal, Ukraine, US

Protocol to the 1979 Convention on Long-Range Transboundary Air Pollution on Further Reduction of Sulphur Emissions

note - abbreviated as Air Pollution-Sulphur 94
opened for signature - 14 June 1994
entered into force - 5 August 1998
objective - to provide for a further reduction in sulfur emissions or transboundary fluxes
parties - (23) Austria, Belgium, Canada, Croatia, Czech Republic, Denmark, EU, Finland, France, Germany, Greece, Ireland, Italy, Liechtenstein, Luxembourg, Netherlands, Norway, Slovakia, Slovenia, Spain, Sweden, Switzerland, UK
countries that have signed, but not yet ratified - (5) Bulgaria, Hungary, Poland, Russia, Ukraine

---

Protocol to the 1979 Convention on Long-Range Transboundary Air Pollution on Persistent Organic Pollutants

note - abbreviated as Air Pollution-Persistent Organic Pollutants
opened for signature - 24 June 1998
entered into force - 23 October 2003
objective - to provide for the control and reduction of emissions of persistent organic pollutants in order to reduce their transboundary fluxes so as to protect human health and the environment from adverse effects
parties - (22) Austria, Bulgaria, Canada, Cyprus, Czech Republic, Denmark, EU, Finland, France, Germany, Hungary, Iceland, Latvia, Liechtenstein, Luxembourg, Moldova, Netherlands, Norway, Romania, Slovakia, Sweden, Switzerland
countries that have signed, but not yet ratified - (14) Armenia, Belgium, Croatia, Greece, Ireland, Italy, Lithuania, Poland, Portugal, Slovenia, Spain, Ukraine, UK, US

Protocol to the 1979 Convention on Long-Range Transboundary Air Pollution on the Reduction of Sulphur Emissions or Their Transboundary Fluxes by at Least 30%

note - abbreviated as Air Pollution-Sulphur 85
opened for signature - 8 July 1985
entered into force - 2 September 1987
objective - to provide for a 30% reduction in sulfur emissions or transboundary fluxes by 1993
parties - (22) Austria, Belarus, Belgium, Bulgaria, Canada, Czech Republic, Denmark, Estonia, Finland, France, Germany, Hungary, Italy, Liechtenstein, Luxembourg, Netherlands, Norway, Russia, Slovakia, Sweden, Switzerland, Ukraine

---

Ship Pollution

see Protocol of 1978 Relating to the International Convention for the Prevention of Pollution From Ships, 1973 (MARPOL)

Treaty Banning Nuclear Weapon Tests in the Atmosphere, in Outer Space, and Under Water

note - abbreviated as Nuclear Test Ban
opened for signature - 5 August 1963
entered into force - 10 October 1963
objective - to obtain an agreement on general and complete disarmament under strict international control in accordance with the objectives of the United Nations; to put an end to the armaments

race and eliminate incentives for the production and testing of all kinds of weapons, including nuclear weapons
parties - (113) Afghanistan, Antigua and Barbuda, Argentina, Armenia, Australia, Austria, The Bahamas, Bangladesh, Belgium, Benin, Bhutan, Bolivia, Bosnia and Herzegovina, Botswana, Brazil, Bulgaria, Burma, Canada, Central African Republic, Chad, China, Colombia, Democratic Republic of the Congo, Costa Rica, Cote d'Ivoire, Croatia, Cyprus, Czech Republic, Denmark, Dominican Republic, Ecuador, Egypt, El Salvador, Fiji, Finland, Gabon, The Gambia, Germany, Ghana, Greece, Guatemala, Honduras, Hungary, Iceland, India, Indonesia, Iran, Iraq, Ireland, Israel, Italy, Jamaica, Japan, Jordan, Kenya, South Korea, Kuwait, Laos, Lebanon, Liberia, Luxembourg, Madagascar, Malawi, Malaysia, Malta, Mauritania, Mauritius, Mexico, Morocco, Nepal, Netherlands, NZ, Nicaragua, Niger, Nigeria, Norway, Panama, Papua New Guinea, Peru, Philippines, Poland, Romania, Russia, Rwanda, Samoa, San Marino, Senegal, Serbia and Montenegro, Seychelles, Sierra Leone, Singapore, Slovakia, Slovenia, South Africa, Spain, Sri Lanka, Sudan, Suriname, Swaziland, Sweden, Switzerland, Syria, Thailand, Togo, Tonga, Trinidad and Tobago, Tunisia, Turkey, Uganda, UK, US, Venezuela, Zambia
countries that have signed, but not yet ratified - (17) Algeria, Burkina Faso, Burundi, Cameroon, Chile, Ethiopia, Haiti, Libya, Mali, Pakistan, Paraguay, Portugal, Somalia, Tanzania, Uruguay, Vietnam, Yemen

Tropical Timber 83

see International Tropical Timber Agreement, 1983

Tropical Timber 94

see International Tropical Timber Agreement, 1994

United Nations Convention on the Law of the Sea (LOS)

note - abbreviated as Law of the Sea
opened for signature - 10 December 1982
entered into force - 16 November 1994
objective - to set up a comprehensive new legal regime for the sea and oceans; to include rules concerning environmental standards as well as enforcement provisions dealing with pollution of the marine environment
parties - (148) Albania, Algeria, Angola, Antigua and Barbuda, Argentina, Armenia, Australia, Austria, The Bahamas, Bahrain, Bangladesh, Barbados, Belgium, Belize, Benin, Bolivia, Bosnia and Herzegovina, Botswana, Brazil, Brunei, Bulgaria, Burkina Faso, Burma, Cameroon, Canada, Cape Verde, Chile, China, Comoros, Democratic Republic of the Congo, Cook Islands, Costa Rica, Cote d'Ivoire, Croatia, Cuba, Cyprus, Czech Republic, Denmark, Djibouti, Dominica, Egypt, Equatorial Guinea, EU, Fiji, Finland, France, Gabon, The Gambia, Georgia, Germany, Ghana, Greece, Grenada, Guatemala, Guinea, Guinea-Bissau, Guyana, Haiti, Honduras, Hungary, Iceland, India, Indonesia, Iraq, Ireland, Italy, Jamaica, Japan, Jordan, Kenya, Kiribati, South Korea, Kuwait, Laos, Latvia, Lebanon, Lithuania, Luxembourg, Macedonia, Madagascar, Malaysia, Maldives, Mali, Malta, Marshall Islands,

Mauritania, Mauritius, Mexico, Federated States of Micronesia, Monaco, Mongolia, Mozambique, Namibia, Nauru, Nepal, Netherlands, NZ, Nicaragua, Nigeria, Norway, Oman, Pakistan, Palau, Panama, Papua New Guinea, Paraguay, Philippines, Poland, Portugal, Qatar, Romania, Russia, Saint Kitts and Nevis, Saint Lucia, Saint Vincent and the Grenadines, Samoa, Sao Tome and Principe, Saudi Arabia, Senegal, Serbia and Montenegro, Seychelles, Sierra Leone, Singapore, Slovakia, Slovenia, Solomon Islands, Somalia, South Africa, Spain, Sri Lanka, Sudan, Suriname, Sweden, Tanzania, Togo, Tonga, Trinidad and Tobago, Tunisia, Tuvalu, Uganda, Ukraine, UK, Uruguay, Vanuatu, Vietnam, Yemen, Zambia, Zimbabwe
countries that have signed, but not yet ratified - (29) Afghanistan, Bangladesh, Belarus, Bhutan, Burundi, Cambodia, Central African Republic, Chad, Colombia, Republic of the Congo, Dominican Republic, El Salvador, Ethiopia, Iran, North Korea, Lesotho, Liberia, Libya, Liechtenstein, Madagascar, Malawi, Morocco, Niger, Niue, Rwanda, Swaziland, Switzerland, Thailand, UAE

United Nations Convention to Combat Desertification in Those Countries Experiencing Serious Drought and/or Desertification, Particularly in Africa

note - abbreviated as Desertification
opened for signature - 14 October 1994
entered into force - 26 December 1996
objective - to combat desertification and mitigate the effects of drought through national action programs that incorporate long-term strategies supported by international cooperation and partnership arrangements
parties - (178) Afghanistan, Albania, Algeria, Angola, Antigua and Barbuda, Argentina, Armenia, Australia, Austria, Azerbaijan, The Bahamas, Bahrain, Bangladesh, Barbados, Belarus, Belgium, Belize, Benin, Bolivia, Botswana, Brazil, Bulgaria, Burkina Faso, Burma, Burundi, Cambodia, Cameroon, Canada, Cape Verde, Central African Republic, Chad, Chile, China, Colombia, Comoros, Democratic Republic of the Congo, Republic of the Congo, Cook Islands, Costa Rica, Cote d'Ivoire, Croatia, Cuba, Cyprus, Czech Republic, Denmark, Djibouti, Dominica, Dominican Republic, Ecuador, Egypt, El Salvador, Equatorial Guinea, Eritrea, Ethiopia, EU, Fiji, Finland, France, Gabon, The Gambia, Georgia, Germany, Ghana, Greece, Grenada, Guatemala, Guinea, Guinea-Bissau, Guyana, Haiti, Honduras, Hungary, Iceland, India, Indonesia, Iran, Ireland, Israel, Italy, Jamaica, Japan, Jordan, Kazakhstan, Kenya, Kiribati, South Korea, Kuwait, Kyrgyzstan, Laos, Lebanon, Lesotho, Liberia, Libya, Liechtenstein, Luxembourg, Madagascar, Malawi, Malaysia, Mali, Malta, Marshall Islands, Mauritania, Mauritius, Mexico, Federated States of Micronesia, Moldova, Monaco, Mongolia, Morocco, Mozambique, Namibia, Nauru, Nepal, Netherlands, NZ, Nicaragua, Niger, Nigeria, Niue, Norway, Oman, Pakistan, Palau, Panama, Papua New Guinea, Paraguay, Peru, Philippines, Poland, Portugal, Qatar, Romania, Rwanda, Saint Kitts and Nevis, Saint Lucia, Saint Vincent and the Grenadines, Samoa, San Marino, Sao Tome and Principe, Saudi Arabia, Senegal, Seychelles, Sierra Leone, Singapore, Slovakia,

Slovenia, Solomon Islands, South Africa, Spain, Sri Lanka, Sudan, Suriname, Swaziland, Sweden, Switzerland, Syria, Thailand, Tajikistan, Tanzania, Togo, Tonga, Trinidad and Tobago, Tunisia, Turkey, Turkmenistan, Tuvalu, Uganda, UAE, UK, US, Uruguay, Uzbekistan, Vanuatu, Venezuela, Vietnam, Yemen, Zambia, Zimbabwe

United Nations Framework Convention on Climate Change

note - abbreviated as Climate Change
opened for signature - 9 May 1992
entered into force - 21 March 1994
objective - to achieve stabilization of greenhouse gas concentrations in the atmosphere at a low enough level to prevent dangerous anthropogenic interference with the climate system
parties - (189) Afghanistan, Albania, Algeria, Angola, Antigua and Barbuda, Argentina, Armenia, Australia, Austria, Azerbaijan, The Bahamas, Bahrain, Bangladesh, Barbados, Belarus, Belgium, Belize, Benin, Bhutan, Bolivia, Bosnia and Herzegovina, Botswana, Brazil, Brunei, Bulgaria, Burkina Faso, Burma, Burundi, Cambodia, Cameroon, Canada, Cape Verde, Central African Republic, Chad, Chile, China, Colombia, Comoros, Democratic Republic of the Congo, Republic of the Congo, Cook Islands, Costa Rica, Cote d'Ivoire, Croatia, Cuba, Cyprus, Czech Republic, Denmark, Djibouti, Dominica, Dominican Republic, Ecuador, Egypt, El Salvador, Equatorial Guinea, Eritrea, Estonia, Ethiopia, EU, Fiji, Finland, France, Gabon, The Gambia, Georgia, Germany, Ghana, Greece, Grenada, Guatemala, Guinea, Guinea-Bissau, Guyana, Haiti, Honduras, Hungary, Iceland, India, Indonesia, Iran, Ireland, Israel, Italy, Jamaica, Japan, Jordan, Kazakhstan, Kenya, Kiribati, North Korea, South Korea, Kuwait, Kyrgyzstan, Laos, Latvia, Lebanon, Lesotho, Liberia, Libya, Liechtenstein, Lithuania, Luxembourg, Macedonia, Madagascar, Malawi, Malaysia, Maldives, Mali, Malta, Marshall Islands, Mauritania, Mauritius, Mexico, Federated States of Micronesia, Moldova, Monaco, Mongolia, Morocco, Mozambique, Namibia, Nauru, Nepal, Netherlands, NZ, Nicaragua, Niger, Nigeria, Niue, Norway, Oman, Pakistan, Palau, Panama, Papua New Guinea, Paraguay, Peru, Philippines, Poland, Portugal, Qatar, Romania, Russia, Rwanda, Saint Kitts and Nevis, Saint Lucia, Saint Vincent and the Grenadines, Samoa, San Marino, Sao Tome and Principe, Saudi Arabia, Senegal, Serbia and Montenegro, Seychelles, Sierra Leone, Singapore, Slovakia, Slovenia, Solomon Islands, South Africa, Spain, Sri Lanka, Sudan, Suriname, Swaziland, Sweden, Switzerland, Syria, Tajikistan, Tanzania, Thailand, Togo, Tonga, Trinidad and Tobago, Tunisia, Turkey, Turkmenistan, Tuvalu, Uganda, Ukraine, UAE, UK, US, Uruguay, Uzbekistan, Vanuatu, Venezuela, Vietnam, Yemen, Zambia, Zimbabwe

Wetlands

see Convention on Wetlands of International Importance Especially As Waterfowl Habitat (Ramsar)

Whaling

see International Convention for the Regulation of Whaling

APPENDIX D

CROSS-REFERENCE LIST OF COUNTRY DATA CODES

FIPS 10: *Countries, Dependencies, Areas of Special Sovereignty, and Their Principal Administrative Divisions (FIPS 10)* is maintained by the Office of Targeting and Transnational Issues, National Geospatial-Intelligence Agency, and published by the National Institute of Standards and Technology (Department of Commerce). FIPS 10 codes are intended for general use throughout the US Government, especially in activities associated with the mission of the Department of State and national defense programs.

ISO 3166: *Codes for the Representation of Names of Countries (ISO 3166)* is prepared by the International Organization for Standardization. ISO 3166 includes two- and three-character alphabetic codes and three-digit numeric codes that may be needed for activities involving exchange of data with international organizations that have adopted that standard. Except for the numeric codes, ISO 3166 codes have been adopted in the US as FIPS 104-1: *American National Standard Codes for the Representation of Names of Countries, Dependencies, and Areas of Special Sovereignty for Information Interchange.*

Internet: The Internet country code is the two-letter digraph maintained by the International Organization for Standardization (ISO) in *the ISO 3166 Alpha-2 list* and used by the Internet Assigned Numbers Authority (IANA) to establish country-coded top-level domains (ccTLDs).

Entity	FIPS 10	ISO 3166			Internet	Comment
Afghanistan	AF	AF	AFG	004	.af	
Albania	AL	AL	ALB	008	.al	
Algeria	AG	DZ	DZA	012	.dz	
American Samoa	AQ	AS	ASM	016	.as	
Andorra	AN	AD	AND	020	.ad	
Angola	AO	AO	AGO	024	.ao	
Anguilla	AV	AI	AIA	660	.ai	
Antarctica	AY	AQ	ATA	010	.aq	ISO defines as the territory south of 60 degrees south latitude
Antigua and Barbuda	AC	AG	ATG	028	.ag	
Argentina	AR	AR	ARG	032	.ar	
Armenia	AM	AM	ARM	051	.am	
Aruba	AA	AW	ABW	533	.aw	
Ashmore and Cartier Islands	AT	-	-	-		ISO includes with Australia
Australia	AS	AU	AUS	036	.au	ISO includes Ashmore and Cartier Islands, Coral Sea Islands
Austria	AU	AT	AUT	040	.at	
Azerbaijan	AJ	AZ	AZE	031	.az	
Bahamas, The	BF	BS	BHS	044	.bs	
Bahrain	BA	BH	BHR	048	.bh	
Baker Island	FQ	-	-	-		ISO includes with the US Minor Outlying Islands
Bangladesh	BG	BD	BGD	050	.bd	
Barbados	BB	BB	BRB	052	.bb	
Bassas da India	BS	-	-	-	-	administered from Reunion; no ISO codes assigned
Belarus	BO	BY	BLR	112	.by	
Belgium	BE	BE	BEL	056	.be	

Entity	FIPS 10	ISO 3166			Internet	Comment
Belize	BH	BZ	BLZ	084	.bz	
Benin	BN	BJ	BEN	204	.bj	
Bermuda	BD	BM	BMU	060	.bm	
Bhutan	BT	BT	BTN	064	.bt	
Bolivia	BL	BO	BOL	068	.bo	
Bosnia and Herzegovina	BK	BA	BIH	070	.ba	
Botswana	BC	BW	BWA	072	.bw	
Bouvet Island	BV	BV	BVT	074	.bv	
Brazil	BR	BR	BRA	076	.br	
British Indian Ocean Territory	IO	IO	IOT	086	.io	
British Virgin Islands	VI	VG	VGB	092	.vg	
Brunei	BX	BN	BRN	096	.bn	
Bulgaria	BU	BG	BGR	100	.bg	
Burkina Faso	UV	BF	BFA	854	.bf	
Burma	BM	MM	MMR	104	.mm	ISO uses the name Myanmar
Burundi	BY	BI	BDI	108	.bi	
Cambodia	CB	KH	KHM	116	.kh	
Cameroon	CM	CM	CMR	120	.cm	
Canada	CA	CA	CAN	124	.ca	
Cape Verde	CV	CV	CPV	132	.cv	
Cayman Islands	CJ	KY	CYM	136	.ky	
Central African Republic	CT	CF	CAF	140	.cf	
Chad	CD	TD	TCD	148	.td	
Chile	CI	CL	CHL	152	.cl	
China	CH	CN	CHN	156	.cn	see also Taiwan
Christmas Island	KT	CX	CXR	162	.cx	
Clipperton Island	IP	-	-	-		ISO includes with French Polynesia
Cocos (Keeling) Islands	CK	CC	CCK	166	.cc	
Colombia	CO	CO	COL	170	.co	
Comoros	CN	KM	COM	174	.km	
Congo, Democratic Republic of the	CG	CD	COD	180	.cd	formerly Zaire
Congo, Republic of the	CF	CG	COG	178	.cg	
Cook Islands	CW	CK	COK	184	.ck	
Coral Sea Islands	CR	-	-	-		ISO includes with Australia
Costa Rica	CS	CR	CRI	188	.cr	
Cote d'Ivoire	IV	CI	CIV	384	.ci	
Croatia	HR	HR	HRV	191	.hr	
Cuba	CU	CU	CUB	192	.cu	
Cyprus	CY	CY	CYP	196	.cy	
Czech Republic	EZ	CZ	CZE	203	.cz	
Denmark	DA	DK	DNK	208	.dk	
Djibouti	DJ	DJ	DJI	262	.dj	
Dominica	DO	DM	DMA	212	.dm	
Dominican Republic	DR	DO	DOM	214	.do	
East Timor	TT	TL	TLS	626	.tl	
Ecuador	EC	EC	ECU	218	.ec	
Egypt	EG	EG	EGY	818	.eg	

Entity	FIPS 10	ISO 3166			Internet	Comment
El Salvador	ES	SV	SLV	222	.sv	
Equatorial Guinea	EK	GQ	GNQ	226	.gq	
Eritrea	ER	ER	ERI	232	.er	
Estonia	EN	EE	EST	233	.ee	
Ethiopia	ET	ET	ETH	231	.et	
Europa Island	EU	-	-	-	-	administered from Reunion; no ISO codes assigned
Falkland Islands (Islas Malvinas)	FK	FK	FLK	238	.fk	
Faroe Islands	FO	FO	FRO	234	.fo	
Fiji	FJ	FJ	FJI	242	.fj	
Finland	FI	FI	FIN	246	.fi	
France	FR	FR	FRA	250	.fr	
France, Metropolitan	-	FX	FXX	249	.fx	ISO limits to the European part of France, excluding French Guiana, French Polynesia, French Southern and Antarctic Lands, Guadeloupe, Martinique, Mayotte, New Caledonia, Reunion, Saint Pierre and Miquelon, Wallis and Futuna
French Guiana	FG	GF	GUF	254	.gf	
French Polynesia	FP	PF	PYF	258	.pf	ISO includes Clipperton Island
French Southern and Antarctic Lands	FS	TF	ATF	260	.tf	FIPS 10-4 does not include the French-claimed portion of Antarctica (Terre Adelie)
Gabon	GB	GA	GAB	266	.ga	
Gambia, The	GA	GM	GMB	270	.gm	
Gaza Strip	GZ	PS	PSE	275	.ps	ISO identifies as Occupied Palestinian Territory
Georgia	GG	GE	GEO	268	.ge	
Germany	GM	DE	DEU	276	.de	
Ghana	GH	GH	GHA	288	.gh	
Gibraltar	GI	GI	GIB	292	.gi	
Glorioso Islands	GO	-	-	-	-	administered from Reunion; no ISO codes assigned
Greece	GR	GR	GRC	300	.gr	
Greenland	GL	GL	GRL	304	.gl	
Grenada	GJ	GD	GRD	308	.gd	
Guadeloupe	GP	GP	GLP	312	.gp	
Guam	GQ	GU	GUM	316	.gu	
Guatemala	GT	GT	GTM	320	.gt	
Guernsey	GK	-	-		.gg	ISO includes with the UK
Guinea	GV	GN	GIN	324	.gn	
Guinea-Bissau	PU	GW	GNB	624	.gw	
Guyana	GY	GY	GUY	328	.gy	
Haiti	HA	HT	HTI	332	.ht	
Heard Island and McDonald Islands	HM	HM	HMD	334	.hm	
Holy See (Vatican City)	VT	VA	VAT	336	.va	
Honduras	HO	HN	HND	340	.hn	

Entity	FIPS 10	ISO 3166			Internet	Comment
Hong Kong	HK	HK	HKG	344	.hk	
Howland Island	HQ	-	-	-		ISO includes with the US Minor Outlying Islands
Hungary	HU	HU	HUN	348	.hu	
Iceland	IC	IS	ISL	352	.is	
India	IN	IN	IND	356	.in	
Indonesia	ID	ID	IDN	360	.id	
Iran	IR	IR	IRN	364	.ir	
Iraq	IZ	IQ	IRQ	368	.iq	
Ireland	EI	IE	IRL	372	.ie	
Israel	IS	IL	ISR	376	.il	
Italy	IT	IT	ITA	380	.it	
Jamaica	JM	JM	JAM	388	.jm	
Jan Mayen	JN	-	-	-		ISO includes with Svalbard
Japan	JA	JP	JPN	392	.jp	
Jarvis Island	DQ	-	-	-		ISO includes with the US Minor Outlying Islands
Jersey	JE	-	-	.je		ISO includes with the UK
Johnston Atoll	JQ	-	-	-		ISO includes with the US Minor Outlying Islands
Jordan	JO	JO	JOR	400	.jo	
Juan de Nova Island	JU	-	-	-	-	adminstered from Reunion; no ISO codes assigned
Kazakhstan	KZ	KZ	KAZ	398	.kz	
Kenya	KE	KE	KEN	404	.ke	
Kingman Reef	KQ	-	-		-	ISO includes with the US Minor Outlying Islands
Kiribati	KR	KI	KIR	296	.ki	
Korea, North	KN	KP	PRK	408	.kp	
Korea, South	KS	KR	KOR	410	.kr	
Kuwait	KU	KW	KWT	414	.kw	
Kyrgyzstan	KG	KG	KGZ	417	.kg	
Laos	LA	LA	LAO	418	.la	
Latvia	LG	LV	LVA	428	.lv	
Lebanon	LE	LB	LBN	422	.lb	
Lesotho	LT	LS	LSO	426	.ls	
Liberia	LI	LR	LBR	430	.lr	
Libya	LY	LY	LBY	434	.ly	
Liechtenstein	LS	LI	LIE	438	.li	
Lithuania	LH	LT	LTU	440	.lt	
Luxembourg	LU	LU	LUX	442	.lu	
Macau	MC	MO	MAC	446	.mo	
Macedonia	MK	MK	MKD	807	.mk	
Madagascar	MA	MG	MDG	450	.mg	
Malawi	MI	MW	MWI	454	.mw	
Malaysia	MY	MY	MYS	458	.my	
Maldives	MV	MV	MDV	462	.mv	
Mali	ML	ML	MLI	466	.ml	
Malta	MT	MT	MLT	470	.mt	
Man, Isle of	IM	-	-		.im	ISO includes with the UK

Entity	FIPS 10	ISO 3166			Internet	Comment
Marshall Islands	RM	MH	MHL	584	.mh	
Martinique	MB	MQ	MTQ	474	.mq	
Mauritania	MR	MR	MRT	478	.mr	
Mauritius	MP	MU	MUS	480	.mu	
Mayotte	MF	YT	MYT	175	.yt	
Mexico	MX	MX	MEX	484	.mx	
Micronesia, Federated States of	FM	FM	FSM	583	.fm	
Midway Islands	MQ	-	-		-	ISO includes with the US Minor Outlying Islands
Moldova	MD	MD	MDA	498	.md	
Monaco	MN	MC	MCO	492	.mc	
Mongolia	MG	MN	MNG	496	.mn	
Montserrat	MH	MS	MSR	500	.ms	
Morocco	MO	MA	MAR	504	.ma	
Mozambique	MZ	MZ	MOZ	508	.mz	
Myanmar	-	-	-		-	see Burma
Namibia	WA	NA	NAM	516	.na	
Nauru	NR	NR	NRU	520	.nr	
Navassa Island	BQ	-	-	-	-	ISO includes with the US Minor Outlying Islands
Nepal	NP	NP	NPL	524	.np	
Netherlands	NL	NL	NLD	528	.nl	
Netherlands Antilles	NT	AN	ANT	530	.an	
New Caledonia	NC	NC	NCL	540	.nc	
New Zealand	NZ	NZ	NZL	554	.nz	
Nicaragua	NU	NI	NIC	558	.ni	
Niger	NG	NE	NER	562	.ne	
Nigeria	NI	NG	NGA	566	.ng	
Niue	NE	NU	NIU	570	.nu	
Norfolk Island	NF	NF	NFK	574	.nf	
Northern Mariana Islands	CQ	MP	MNP	580	.mp	
Norway	NO	NO	NOR	578	.no	
Oman	MU	OM	OMN	512	.om	
Pakistan	PK	PK	PAK	586	.pk	
Palau	PS	PW	PLW	585	.pw	
Palmyra Atoll	LQ	-	-		-	ISO includes with the US Minor Outlying Islands
Panama	PM	PA	PAN	591	.pa	
Papua New Guinea	PP	PG	PNG	598	.pg	
Paracel Islands	PF	-	-	-		
Paraguay	PA	PY	PRY	600	.py	
Peru	PE	PE	PER	604	.pe	
Philippines	RP	PH	PHL	608	.ph	
Pitcairn Islands	PC	PN	PCN	612	.pn	
Poland	PL	PL	POL	616	.pl	
Portugal	PO	PT	PRT	620	.pt	
Puerto Rico	RQ	PR	PRI	630	.pr	
Qatar	QA	QA	QAT	634	.qa	

Entity	FIPS 10	ISO 3166			Internet	Comment
Reunion	RE	RE	REU	638	.re	
Romania	RO	RO	ROU	642	.ro	
Russia	RS	RU	RUS	643	.ru	
Rwanda	RW	RW	RWA	646	.rw	
Saint Helena	SH	SH	SHN	654	.sh	
Saint Kitts and Nevis	SC	KN	KNA	659	.kn	
Saint Lucia	ST	LC	LCA	662	.lc	
Saint Pierre and Miquelon	SB	PM	SPM	666	.pm	
Saint Vincent and the Grenadines	VC	VC	VCT	670	.vc	
Samoa	WS	WS	WSM	882	.ws	
San Marino	SM	SM	SMR	674	.sm	
Sao Tome and Principe	TP	ST	STP	678	.st	
Saudi Arabia	SA	SA	SAU	682	.sa	
Senegal	SG	SN	SEN	686	.sn	
Serbia and Montenegro	YI	CS	SCG	891	.cs	
Seychelles	SE	SC	SYC	690	.sc	
Sierra Leone	SL	SL	SLE	694	.sl	
Singapore	SN	SG	SGP	702	.sg	
Slovakia	LO	SK	SVK	703	.sk	
Slovenia	SI	SI	SVN	705	.si	
Solomon Islands	BP	SB	SLB	090	.sb	
Somalia	SO	SO	SOM	706	.so	
South Africa	SF	ZA	ZAF	710	.za	
South Georgia and the Islands	SX	GS	SGS	239	.gs	
Spain	SP	ES	ESP	724	.es	
Spratly Islands	PG	-	-	-		
Sri Lanka	CE	LK	LKA	144	.lk	
Sudan	SU	SD	SDN	736	.sd	
Suriname	NS	SR	SUR	740	.sr	
Svalbard	SV	SJ	SJM	744	.sj	ISO includes Jan Mayen
Swaziland	WZ	SZ	SWZ	748	.sz	
Sweden	SW	SE	SWE	752	.se	
Switzerland	SZ	CH	CHE	756	.ch	
Syria	SY	SY	SYR	760	.sy	
Taiwan	TW	TW	TWN	158	.tw	
Tajikistan	TI	TJ	TJK	762	.tj	
Tanzania	TZ	TZ	TZA	834	.tz	
Thailand	TH	TH	THA	764	.th	
Togo	TO	TG	TGO	768	.tg	
Tokelau	TL	TK	TKL	772	.tk	
Tonga	TN	TO	TON	776	.to	
Trinidad and Tobago	TD	TT	TTO	780	.tt	
Tromelin Island	TE	-	-	-	-	administered from Reunion; no ISO codes assigned
Tunisia	TS	TN	TUN	788	.tn	
Turkey	TU	TR	TUR	792	.tr	
Turkmenistan	TX	TM	TKM	795	.tm	

Entity	FIPS 10	ISO 3166			Internet	Comment
Turks and Caicos Islands	TK	TC	TCA	796	.tc	
Tuvalu	TV	TV	TUV	798	.tv	
Uganda	UG	UG	UGA	800	.ug	
Ukraine	UP	UA	UKR	804	.ua	
United Arab Emirates	AE	AE	ARE	784	.ae	
United Kingdom	UK	GB	GBR	826	.uk	ISO includes Guernsey, Isle of Man, Jersey
United States	US	US	USA	840	.us	
United States Minor Outlying Islands	-	UM	UMI	581	.um	ISO includes Baker Island, Howland Island, Jarvis Island, Johnston Atoll, Kingman Reef, Midway Islands, Navassa Island, Palmyra Atoll, Wake Island
Uruguay	UY	UY	URY	858	.uy	
Uzbekistan	UZ	UZ	UZB	860	.uz	
Vanuatu	NH	VU	VUT	548	.vu	
Venezuela	VE	VE	VEN	862	.ve	
Vietnam	VM	VN	VNM	704	.vn	
Virgin Islands	VQ	VI	VIR	850	.vi	
Virgin Islands (UK)	-	-	-		.vg	see British Virgin Islands
Virgin Islands (US)	-	-	-		.vi	see Virgin Islands
Wake Island	WQ	-	-	-	-	ISO includes with the US Minor Outlying Islands
Wallis and Futuna	WF	WF	WLF	876	.wf	
West Bank	WE	PS	PSE	275	.ps	ISO identifies as Occupied Palestinian Territory
Western Sahara	WI	EH	ESH	732	.eh	
Western Samoa	-	-	-		.ws	see Samoa
World	-	-	-		-	the *Factbook* uses the W data code from DIAM 65-18 Geopolitical Data Elements and Related Features, Data Standard No. 3, December 1994, published by the Defense Intelligence Agency
Yemen	YM	YE	YEM	887	.ye	
Zaire	-	-	-		-	see Democratic Republic of the Congo
Zambia	ZA	ZM	ZMB	894	.zm	
Zimbabwe	ZI	ZW	ZWE	716	.zw	

APPENDIX E

CROSS-REFERENCE LIST OF HYDROGRAPHIC DATA CODES

IHO 23-4th: *Limits of Oceans and Seas,* Special Publication 23, Draft 4th Edition 1986, published by the International Hydrographic Bureau of the International Hydrographic Organization

IHO 23-3rd: *Limits of Oceans and Seas,* Special Publication 23, 3rd Edition 1953, published by the International Hydrographic Organization

ACIC M 49-1: *Chart of Limits of Seas and Oceans,* revised January 1958, published by the Aeronautical Chart and Information Center (ACIC), United States Air Force; note - ACIC is now part of the National Imagery and Mapping Agency (NIMA)

DIAM 65-18: *Geopolitical Data Elements and Related Features,* Data Standard No. 4, Defense Intelligence Agency Manual 65-18, December 1994, published by the Defense Intelligence Agency

The US Government has not yet adopted a standard for hydrographic codes similar to the Federal Information Processing Standards (FIPS) 10-4 country codes. The names and limits of the following oceans and seas are not always directly comparable because of differences in the customers, needs, and requirements of the individual organizations. Even the number of principal water bodies varies from organization to organization. *Factbook* users, for example, find the Atlantic Ocean and Pacific Ocean entries useful, but none of the following standards include those oceans in their entirety. Nor is there any provision for combining codes or overcodes to aggregate water bodies. The recently delimited Southern Ocean is not included.

Principal Oceans and Seas of the World With Hydrographic Codes by Institution

	HO 23-4th	IHO 23-3rd*	ACIC M 49-1	DIAM 65-18
Arctic Ocean	9	17	A	5A
Atlantic Ocean	-	-	-	-
Baltic Sea	2	1	B26	7B
Eastern Mediterranean	3.1.2	28 B	-	8E
Indian Ocean	5	45	F	6A
Mediterranean Sea	3.1	28	B11	-
North Atlantic Ocean	1	23	B	1A
North Pacific Ocean	7	57	D	3A
Pacific Ocean	-	-	-	-
South Atlantic Ocean	4	32	C	2A
South China and Eastern Archipelagic Seas	6	49, 48	D18 plus others	3U plus others
South Pacific Ocean	8	61	E	4A
Western Mediterranean	3.1.1	28 A	-	8W

*The letters after the numbers are subdivisions, not footnotes.

APPENDIX F

CROSS-REFERENCE LIST OF GEOGRAPHIC NAMES

Name	Entry in *The World Factbook*	Latitude (deg min)	Longitude (deg min)
Abkhazia (region)	Georgia	43 00 N	41 00 E
Abidjan (capital)	Cote d'Ivoire	5 19 N	4 02 W
Abu Dhabi (capital)	United Arab Emirates	24 28 N	54 22 E
Abu Musa (island)	Iran	25 52 N	55 03 E
Abuja (capital)	Nigeria	9 12 N	7 11 E
Abyssinia (former name for Ethiopia)	Ethiopia	8 00 N	38 00 E
Acapulco (city)	Mexico	16 51 N	99 55 W
Accra (capital)	Ghana	5 33 N	0 13 W
Adamstown (capital)	Pitcairn Islands	25 04 S	130 05 W
Addis Ababa (capital)	Ethiopia	9 02 N	38 42 E
Adelie Land (claimed by France; also Terre Adelie)	Antarctica	66 30 S	139 00 E
Aden (city)	Yemen	12 46 N	45 01 E
Aden, Gulf of	Indian Ocean	12 30 N	48 00 E
Admiralty Island	United States (Alaska)	57 44 N	134 20 W
Admiralty Islands	Papua New Guinea	2 10 S	147 00 E
Adriatic Sea	Atlantic Ocean	42 30 N	16 00 E
Adygey (region)	Russia	44 30 N	40 10 E
Aegean Islands	Greece	38 00 N	25 00 E
Aegean Sea	Atlantic Ocean	38 30 N	25 00 E
Afars and Issas, French Territory of the (or FTAI; ormer name for Djibouti)	Djibouti	11 30 N	43 00 E
Afghanestan (local name for Afghanistan)	Afghanistan	33 00 N	65 00 E
Agalega Islands	Mauritius	10 25 S	56 40 E
Agana (city; former name for Hagatna)	Guam	13 28 N	144 45 E
Ajaccio (city)	France (Corsica)	41 55 N	8 44 E
Ajaria (region)	Georgia	41 45 N	42 10 E
Akmola (city; former name for Astana)	Kazakhstan	51 10 N	71 30 E
Aksai Chin (region)	China (de facto), India (claimed)	35 00 N	79 00 E
Al Arabiyah as Suudiyah (local name for Saudi Arabia)	Saudi Arabia	25 00 N	45 00 E
Al Bahrayn (local name for Bahrain)	Bahrain	26 00 N	50 33 E
Al Imarat al Arabiyah al Muttahidah (local name for the United Arab Emirates)	United Arab Emirates	24 00 N	54 00 E
Al Iraq (local name for Iraq)	Iraq	33 00 N	44 00 E

Name	Entry in *The World Factbook*	Latitude (deg min)	Longitude (deg min)
Al Jaza'ir (local name for Algeria)	Algeria	28 00 N	3 00 E
Al Kuwayt (local name for Kuwait)	Kuwait	29 30 N	45 45 E
Al Maghrib (local name for Morocco)	Morocco	32 00 N	5 00 W
Al Urdun (local name for Jordan)	Jordan	31 00 N	36 00 E
Al Yaman (local name for Yemen)	Yemen	15 00 N	48 00 E
Aland Islands	Finland	60 15 N	20 00 E
Alaska (state)	United States	65 00 N	153 00 W
Alaska, Gulf of	Pacific Ocean	58 00 N	145 00 W
Alboran Sea	Atlantic Ocean	36 00 N	2 30 W
Aldabra Islands (Groupe d'Aldabra)	Seychelles	9 25 S	46 22 E
Alderney (island)	Guernsey	49 43 N	2 12 W
Aleutian Islands	United States (Alaska)	52 00 N	176 00 W
Alexander Archipelago (island group)	United States (Alaska)	57 00 N	134 00 W
Alexander Island	Antarctica	71 00 S	70 00 W
Alexandretta (region; former name for Iskenderun)	Turkey	36 34 N	36 08 E
Alexandria (city)	Egypt	31 12 N	29 54 E
Algiers (capital)	Algeria	36 47 N	2 03 E
Alhucemas, Penon de (island group)	Spain	35 13 N	3 53 W
Alma-Ata (city; former name for Almaty)	Kazakhstan	43 15 N	76 57 E
Almaty (former capital)	Kazakhstan	43 15 N	76 57 E
Alofi (capital)	Niue	19 01 S	169 55 W
Alphonse Island	Seychelles	7 01 S	52 45 E
Alsace (region)	France	48 30 N	7 20 E
Amami Strait	Pacific Ocean	28 40 N	129 30 E
Amindivi Islands (former name for Laccadive Islands)	India	11 30 N	72 30 E
Amirante Isles (island group; also Les Amirantes)	Seychelles	6 00 S	53 10 E
Amman (capital)	Jordan	31 57 N	35 56 E
Amsterdam (capital)	Netherlands	52 23 N	4 54 E
Amsterdam Island (Ile Amsterdam)	French Southern and Antarctic Lands	37 52 S	77 32 E
Amundsen Sea	Southern Ocean	72 30 S	112 00 W
Amur River	China, Russia	52 56 N	141 10 E
Amurskiy Liman (strait)	Pacific Ocean	53 00 N	141 30 E
Anadyrskiy Zaliv (gulf)	Pacific Ocean	64 00 N	177 00 E
Anatolia (region)	Turkey	39 00 N	35 00 E
Andaman Islands	India	12 00 N	92 45 E
Andaman Sea	Indian Ocean	10 00 N	95 00 E
Andorra la Vella (capital)	Andorra	42 30 N	1 30 E

Name	Entry in *The World Factbook*	Latitude (deg min)	Longitude (deg min)
Andros (island)	Greece	37 45 N	24 42 E
Andros Island	The Bahamas	24 26 N	77 57 W
Anegada Passage	Atlantic Ocean	18 30 N	63 40 W
Angkor Wat (ruins)	Cambodia	13 26 N	103 50 E
Anglo-Egyptian Sudan (former name for Sudan)	Sudan	15 00 N	30 00 E
Anjouan (island)	Comoros	12 15 S	44 25 E
Ankara (capital)	Turkey	39 56 N	32 52 E
Annobon (island)	Equatorial Guinea	1 25 S	5 36 E
Antananarivo (capital)	Madagascar	18 52 S	47 30 E
Antigua (island)	Antigua and Barbuda	14 34 N	90 44 W
Antipodes Islands	New Zealand	49 41 S	178 43 E
Antwerp (city)	Belgium	51 13 N	4 25 E
Aomen (local Chinese short-form name for Macau)	Macau	22 10 N	113 33 E
Aozou Strip (region)	Chad	22 00 N	18 00 E
Apia (capital)	Samoa	13 50 S	171 45W
Aqaba, Gulf of	Indian Ocean	29 00 N	34 30 E
Arab, Shatt al (river)	Iran, Iraq	29 57 N	48 34 E
Arabian Sea	Indian Ocean	15 00 N	65 00 E
Arafura Sea	Pacific Ocean	9 00 S	133 00 E
Aral Sea	Kazakhstan, Uzbekistan	45 00 N	60 00 E
Argun River	China, Russia	53 20 N	121 28 E
Aru Sea	Pacific Ocean	6 15 S	135 00 E
As-Sudan (local name for Sudan)	Sudan	15 00 N	30 00 E
Ascension Island	Saint Helena	7 57 S	14 22 W
Ashgabat, Ashkhabad (capital)	Turkmenistan	37 57 N	58 23 E
Asmara, Asmera (capital)	Eritrea	15 20 N	38 53 E
Assumption Island	Seychelles	9 46 S	46 34 E
Astana (capital; formerly Akmola)	Kazakhstan	51 10 N	71 30 E
Asuncion (capital)	Paraguay	25 16 S	57 40 W
Asuncion Island	Northern Mariana Islands	19 40 N	145 24 E
Atacama (desert)	Chile	23 00 S	70 10 W
Atacama (region)	Chile	24 30 S	69 15 W
Athens (capital)	Greece	37 59 N	23 44 E
Attu Island	United States	52 55 N	172 57 E
Auckland Islands	New Zealand	51 00 S	166 30 E
Australes, Iles (island group; also Iles Tubuai)	French Polynesia	23 20 S	151 00 W
Avarua (capital)	Cook Islands	21 12 S	159 46 W
Axel Heiberg Island	Canada	79 30 N	90 00 W
Azad Kashmir (region)	Pakistan	34 30 N	74 00 E

Name	Entry in *The World Factbook*	Latitude (deg min)	Longitude (deg min)
Azarbaycan, Azerbaidzhan (local name for Azerbaijan)	Azerbaijan	40 30 N	47 30 E
Azores (islands)	Portugal	38 30 N	28 00 W
Azov, Sea of	Atlantic Ocean	49 00 N	36 00 E
Bab el Mandeb (strait)	Indian Ocean	12 40 N	43 20 E
Babuyan Channel	Pacific Ocean	18 44 N	121 40 E
Babuyan Islands	Philippines	19 10 N	121 40 E
Baffin Bay	Arctic Ocean	73 00 N	66 00 W
Baffin Island	Canada	68 00 N	70 00 W
Baghdad (capital)	Iraq	33 21 N	44 25 E
Baku (capital; also Baki, Baky)	Azerbaijan	40 23 N	49 51 E
Balabac Strait	Pacific Ocean	7 35 N	117 00 E
Balearic Islands	Spain	39 30 N	3 00 E
Balearic Sea (Iberian Sea)	Atlantic Ocean	40 30 N	2 00 E
Bali (island)	Indonesia	8 20 S	115 00 E
Bali Sea	Indian Ocean	7 45 S	115 30 E
Balintang Channel	Pacific Ocean	19 49 N	121 40 E
Balintang Islands	Philippines	19 55 N	122 10 E
Balkan Peninsula	Albania, Bosnia and Herzegovina, Bulgaria, Croatia, Greece, Macedonia, Romania, Serbia and Montenegro, Slovenia, Turkey (European part)	42 00 N	23 00 E
Balleny Islands	Antarctica	67 00 S	163 00 E
Balochistan (region)	Pakistan	28 00 N	63 00 E
Baltic Sea	Atlantic Ocean	57 00 N	19 00 E
Bamako (capital)	Mali	12 39 N	8 00 W
Banaba (Ocean Island)	Kiribati	0 52 S	169 35 E
Banat (region)	Hungary, Serbia and Montenegro, Romania	45 30 N	21 00 E
Banda Sea	Pacific Ocean	5 00 S	128 00 E
Bandar Seri Begawan (capital)	Brunei	4 52 S	114 55 E
Bangka (island)	Indonesia	2 30 S	106 00 E
Bangkok (capital)	Thailand	13 45 N	100 31 E
Bangui (capital)	Central African Republic	4 22 N	18 35 E
Banjul (capital)	The Gambia	13 28 N	16 39 W
Banks Island	Australia	10 12 S	142 16 E
Banks Island	Canada	75 15 N	121 30 W
Banks Islands (Iles Banks)	Vanuatu	14 00 S	167 30 E
Barbuda (island)	Antigua and Barbuda	17 38 N	61 48 W
Barents Sea	Arctic Ocean	74 00 N	36 00 E
Barranquilla (city)	Colombia	10 59 N	74 48 W

Name	Entry in *The World Factbook*	Latitude (deg min)	Longitude (deg min)
Bashi Channel	Pacific Ocean	22 00 N	121 00 E
Basilan Strait	Pacific Ocean	6 49 N	122 05 E
Basque Provinces	Spain	43 00 N	2 30 W
Bass Strait	Pacific Ocean	39 20 S	145 30 E
Basse-Terre (capital)	Guadeloupe	16 00 N	61 44 W
Basseterre (capital)	Saint Kitts and Nevis	17 18 N	62 43 W
Bastia (city)	France (Corsica)	42 42 N	9 27 E
Basutoland (former name for Lesotho)	Lesotho	29 30 S	28 30 E
Batan Islands	Philippines	20 30 N	121 50 E
Bavaria (region; also Bayern)	Germany	48 30 N	11 30 E
Beagle Channel	Atlantic Ocean	54 53 S	68 10 W
Bear Island (see Bjornoya)	Svalbard	74 26 N	19 05 E
Beaufort Sea	Arctic Ocean	73 00 N	140 00 W
Bechuanaland (former name for Botswana)	Botswana	22 00 S	24 00 E
Beijing (capital)	China	39 56 N	116 24 E
Beirut (capital)	Lebanon	33 53 N	35 30 E
Bekaa Valley	Lebanon	34 00 N	36 05 E
Belau (Palau Islands)	Palau	7 30 N	134 30 E
Belep Islands (Iles Belep)	New Caledonia	19 45 S	163 40 E
Belgian Congo (former name for Democratic Republic of the Congo)	Democratic Republic of the Congo	0 00 N	25 00 E
Belgie, Belgique (local name for Belgium)	Belgium	50 50 N	4 00 E
Belgrade (capital)	Serbia and Montenegro	44 50 N	20 30 E
Belize City	Belize	17 30 N	88 12 W
Belle Isle, Strait of	Atlantic Ocean	51 35 N	56 30 W
Bellingshausen Sea	Southern Ocean	71 00 S	85 00 W
Belmopan (capital)	Belize	17 15 N	88 46 W
Belorussia (former name for Belarus)	Belarus	53 00 N	28 00 E
Benadir (region; former name of Italian Somaliland)	Somalia	4 00 N	46 00 E
Bengal, Bay of	Indian Ocean	15 00 N	90 00 E
Berau, Gulf of	Pacific Ocean	2 30 S	132 30 E
Bering Island	Russia	55 00 N	166 30 E
Bering Sea	Pacific Ocean	60 00 N	175 00 W
Bering Strait	Pacific Ocean	65 30 N	169 00 W
Berkner Island	Antarctica	79 30 S	49 30 W
Berlin (capital)	Germany	52 31 N	13 24 E
Berlin, East (former name for eastern sector of Berlin)	Germany	52 30 N	13 33 E
Berlin, West (former name for western sector of Berlin)	Germany	52 30 N	13 20 E

Name	Entry in *The World Factbook*	Latitude (deg min)	Longitude (deg min)
Bern (capital)	Switzerland	46 57 N	7 26 E
Bessarabia (region)	Moldova, Romania, Ukraine	47 00 N	28 30 E
Bharat (local name for India)	India	20 00 N	77 00 E
Bhopal (city)	India	23 16 N	77 24 E
Biafra (region)	Nigeria	5 30 N	7 30 E
Big Diomede Island	Russia	65 46 N	169 06 W
Bijagos, Arquipelago dos (island group)	Guinea-Bissau	11 25 N	16 20 W
Bikini Atoll	Marshall Islands	11 35 N	165 23 E
Bilbao (city)	Spain	43 15 N	2 58 W
Bioko (island)	Equatorial Guinea	3 30 N	8 42 E
Biscay, Bay of	Atlantic Ocean	44 00 N	4 00 W
Bishkek (capital)	Kyrgyzstan	42 54 N	74 36 E
Bishop Rock	United Kingdom	49 52 N	6 27 W
Bismarck Archipelago (island group)	Papua New Guinea	5 00 S	150 00 E
Bismarck Sea	Pacific Ocean	4 00 S	148 00 E
Bissau (capital)	Guinea-Bissau	11 51 N	15 35 W
Bjornoya (Bear Island)	Svalbard	74 26 N	19 05 E
Black Forest (region)	Germany	48 00 N	8 15 E
Black Rock (island)	South Georgia and the South Sandwich Islands	53 39 S	41 48 W
Black Sea	Atlantic Ocean	43 00 N	35 00 E
Bloemfontein (judicial capital)	South Africa	29 12 S	26 07 E
Bo Hai (gulf)	Pacific Ocean	38 00 N	120 00 E
Boa Vista (island)	Cape Verde	16 05 N	22 50 W
Bogota (capital)	Colombia	4 36 N	74 05 W
Bohemia (region)	Czech Republic	50 00 N	14 30 E
Bombay (see Mumbai)	India	18 58 N	72 50 E
Bonaire (island)	Netherlands Antilles	12 10 N	68 15 W
Bonifacio, Strait of	Atlantic Ocean	41 01 N	14 00 E
Bonin Islands	Japan	27 00 N	142 10 E
Bonn (former capital)	Germany	50 44 N	7 05 E
Bophuthatswana (region; enclave)	South Africa	26 30 S	25 30 E
Bora-Bora (island)	French Polynesia	16 30 S	151 45 W
Bordeaux (city)	France	44 50 N	0 34 W
Borneo (island)	Brunei, Indonesia, Malaysia	0 30 N	114 00 E
Bornholm (island)	Denmark	55 10 N	15 00 E
Bosna i Hercegovina (local name for Bosnia and Herzegovina)	Bosnia and Herzegovina	44 00 N	18 00 E
Bosnia (political region)	Bosnia and Herzegovina	44 00 N	18 00 E
Bosporus (strait)	Atlantic Ocean	41 00 N	29 00 E
Bothnia, Gulf of	Atlantic Ocean	63 00 N	20 00 E

Name	Entry in *The World Factbook*	Latitude (deg min)	Longitude (deg min)
Bougainville (island)	Papua New Guinea	6 00 S	155 00 E
Bougainville Strait	Pacific Ocean	6 40 S	156 10 E
Bounty Islands	New Zealand	47 43 S	174 00 E
Bourbon Island (former name of Reunion)	Reunion	21 06 S	55 36 E
Brasilia (capital)	Brazil	15 47 S	47 55 W
Bratislava (capital)	Slovakia	48 09 N	17 07 E
Brazzaville (capital)	Republic of the Congo	4 16 S	15 17 E
Bridgetown (capital)	Barbados	13 06 N	59 37 W
Brisbane (city)	Australia	27 28 S	153 02 E
Bristol Bay	Pacific Ocean	57 00 N	160 00 W
Bristol Channel	Atlantic Ocean	51 18 N	3 30 W
Britain (see Great Britain)	United Kingdom	54 00 N	2 00 W
British Bechuanaland (region; former name for northwest South Africa)	South Africa	27 30 S	23 30 E
British Central African Protectorate (former name of Nyasaland)	Malawi	13 30 S	34 00 E
British East Africa (former name for British possessions in eastern Africa)	Kenya, Tanzania, Uganda	1 00 N	38 00 E
British Guiana (former name for Guyana)	Guyana	5 00 N	59 00 W
British Honduras (former name for Belize)	Belize	17 15 N	88 45 W
British Solomon Islands (former name for Solomon Islands)	Solomon Islands	8 00 S	159 00 E
British Somaliland (former name for northern Somalia)	Somalia	10 00 N	49 00 E
Brussels (capital)	Belgium	50 50 N	4 20 E
Bubiyan (island)	Kuwait	29 47 N	48 10 E
Bucharest (capital)	Romania	44 26 N	26 06 E
Budapest (capital)	Hungary	47 30 N	19 05 E
Buenos Aires (capital)	Argentina	34 36 S	58 27 W
Bujumbura (capital)	Burundi	3 23 S	29 22 E
Bukovina (region)	Romania, Ukraine	48 00 N	26 00 E
Byelarus (local name for Belarus)	Belarus	53 00 N	28 00 E
Byelorussia (former name for Belarus)	Belarus	53 00 N	28 00 E
Cabinda (province)	Angola	5 33 S	12 12 E
Cabo Verde (local name for Cape Verde)	Cape Verde	16 00 N	24 00 W
Cabot Strait	Atlantic Ocean	47 20 N	59 30 W
Caicos Islands	Turks and Caicos Islands	21 56 N	71 58 W
Cairo (capital)	Egypt	30 03 N	31 15 E
California, Gulf of	Pacific Ocean	28 00 N	112 00 W
Cameroun (local name for Cameroon)	Cameroon	6 00 N	12 00 E
Campbell Island	New Zealand	52 33 S	169 09 E

Name	Entry in *The World Factbook*	Latitude (deg min)	Longitude (deg min)
Campeche, Bay of	Atlantic Ocean	20 00 N	94 00 W
Canal Zone (former name for US possessions in Panama)	Panama	9 00 N	79 45 W
Canarias Sea	Atlantic Ocean	28 00 N	16 00 W
Canary Islands	Spain	28 00 N	15 30 W
Canberra (capital)	Australia	35 17 S	149 08 E
Cancun (city)	Mexico	21 10 N	86 50 W
Canton (city; now Guangzhou)	China	23 06 N	113 16 E
Canton Island (Kanton Island)	Kiribati	2 49 S	171 40 W
Cape Juby (region; former name for Southern Morocco)	Morocco	27 53 N	12 58 W
Cape Province (region; former name for Northern, Western, and Eastern Cape Provinces of South Africa)	South Africa	31 30 S	22 30 E
Cape Town (legislative capital)	South Africa	33 57 S	18 28 W
Cape of Good Hope (cape; also alternate name for Cape Province of South Africa)	South Africa	34 15 S	18 25 E
Caracas (capital)	Venezuela	10 30 N	66 56 W
Cargados Carajos Shoals	Mauritius	16 25 S	59 38 E
Caribbean Sea	Atlantic Ocean	15 00 N	73 00 W
Caroline Islands	Federated States of Micronesia, Palau	7 30 N	148 00 E
Carpatho-Ukraine (region; former name for Zakarpats'ka oblast')	Ukraine	48 22 N	23 32 E
Carpentaria, Gulf of	Pacific Ocean	14 00 S	139 00 E
Castries (capital)	Saint Lucia	14 01 N	61 00 W
Catalonia (region)	Spain	42 00 N	2 00 E
Cato Island	Australia	23 15 S	155 32 E
Caucasus (region)	Russia	42 00 N	45 00 E
Cayenne (capital)	French Guiana	4 56 N	52 20 W
Celebes (island)	Indonesia	2 00 S	121 00 E
Celebes Sea	Pacific Ocean	3 00 N	122 00 E
Celtic Sea	Atlantic Ocean	51 00 N	6 30 W
Central African Empire (former name for Central African Republic)	Central African Republic	7 00 N	21 00 E
Ceram (Seram) Sea	Pacific Ocean	2 30 S	129 30 E
Ceska Republika (local name for Czech Republic)	Czech Republic	49 45 N	15 30 E
Ceskoslovensko (former local name for Czechoslovakia)	Czech Republic, Slovakia	49 00 N	17 30 E
Ceuta (city)	Spain	35 53 N	5 19 W
Ceylon (former name for Sri Lanka)	Sri Lanka	7 00 N	81 00 E
Chafarinas, Islas (island)	Spain	35 12 N	2 26 W

Name	Entry in *The World Factbook*	Latitude (deg min)	Longitude (deg min)
Chagos Archipelago (Oil Islands)	British Indian Ocean Territory	6 00 S	71 30 E
Challenger Deep (Mariana Trench)	Pacific Ocean	11 22 N	142 36 E
Channel Islands	Guernsey, Jersey	49 20 N	2 20 W
Charlotte Amalie (capital)	Virgin Islands	18 21 N	64 56 W
Chatham Islands	New Zealand	44 00 S	176 30 W
Chechnya (region; also Chechnia)	Russia	43 15 N	45 40 E
Cheju Strait	Pacific Ocean	34 00 N	126 30 E
Cheju-do (island)	Korea, South	33 20 N	126 30 E
Chennai (city; also Madras)	India	13 04 N	80 16 E
Chesterfield Islands (Iles Chesterfield)	New Caledonia	19 52 S	158 15 E
Chihli, Gulf of (see Bo Hai)	Pacific Ocean	38 30 N	120 00 E
Chiloe (island)	Chile	42 50 S	74 00 W
China, People's Republic of	China	35 00 N	105 00 E
China, Republic of	Taiwan	23 30 N	121 00 E
Chisinau (capital)	Moldova	47 00 N	28 50 E
Choiseul (island)	Solomon Islands	7 05 S	121 00 E
Choson (local name for North Korea)	North Korea	40 00 N	127 00 E
Christmas Island (Indian Ocean)	Australia	10 25 S	105 39 E
Christmas Island (Pacific Ocean; also Kiritimati)	Kiribati	1 52 N	157 20 W
Chukchi Sea	Arctic Ocean	69 00 N	171 00 W
Chuuk Islands (Truk Islands)	Federated States of Micronesia	7 25 N	151 47 W
Cilicia (region)	Turkey	36 50 N	34 30 E
Ciskei (enclave)	South Africa	33 00 S	27 00 E
Citta del Vaticano (local name for Vatican City)	Holy See	41 54 N	12 27 E
Cochin China (region)	Vietnam	11 00 N	107 00 E
Coco, Isla del (island)	Costa Rica	5 32 N	87 04 W
Cocos Islands	Cocos (Keeling) Islands	12 30 S	96 50 E
Colombo (capital)	Sri Lanka	6 56 N	79 51 E
Colon, Archipielago de (Galapagos Islands)	Ecuador	0 00 N	90 30 W
Commander Islands (Komandorskiye Ostrova)	Russia	55 00 N	167 00 E
Comores (local name for Comoros)	Comoros	12 10 S	44 15 E
Con Son (islands)	Vietnam	8 43 N	106 36 E
Conakry (capital)	Guinea	9 31 N	13 43 W
Confederatio Helvetica (local name for Switzerland)	Switzerland	47 00 N	8 00 E
Congo (Brazzaville) (former name for Republic of the Congo)	Republic of the Congo	1 00 S	15 00 E
Congo (Leopoldville) (former name for the Democratic Republic of the Congo)	Democratic Republic of the Congo	0 00 N	25 00 E

Name	Entry in *The World Factbook*	Latitude (deg min)	Longitude (deg min)
Constantinople (city; former name for Istanbul)	Turkey	41 01 N	28 58 E
Cook Strait	Pacific Ocean	41 15 S	174 30 E
Copenhagen (capital)	Denmark	55 40 N	12 35 E
Coral Sea	Pacific Ocean	15 00 S	150 00 E
Corfu (island)	Greece	39 40 N	19 45 E
Corinth (region)	Greece	37 56 N	22 56 E
Corisco (island)	Equatorial Guinea	0 55 N	9 19 E
Corn Islands (Islas del Maiz)	Nicaragua	12 15 N	83 00 W
Corocoro Island	Guyana, Venezuela	3 38 N	66 50 W
Corsica (island; also Corse)	France	42 00 N	9 00 E
Cosmoledo Group (island group; also Atoll de Cosmoledo)	Seychelles	9 43 S	47 35 E
Cotonou (former capital)	Benin	6 21 N	2 26 E
Cotopaxi (volcano)	Ecuador	0 39 S	78 26 W
Courantyne River	Guyana, Suriname	5 57 N	57 06 W
Cozumel (island)	Mexico	20 30 N	86 55 W
Crete (island)	Greece	35 15 N	24 45 E
Crimea (region)	Ukraine	45 00 N	34 00 E
Crimean Peninsula	Ukraine	45 00 N	34 00 E
Crooked Island Passage	Atlantic Ocean	22 55 N	74 35 W
Crozet Islands (Iles Crozet)	French Southern and Antarctic Lands	46 30 S	51 00 E
Cyclades (island group)	Greece	37 00 N	25 10 E
Cyrenaica (region)	Libya	31 00 N	22 00 E
Czechoslovakia (former name for the entity that subsequently split into the Czech Republic and Slovakia)	Czech Republic, Slovakia	49 00 N	18 00 E
D'Entrecasteaux Islands	Papua New Guinea	9 30 S	150 40 E
Dagestan (region)	Russia	43 00 N	47 00 E
Dahomey (former name for Benin)	Benin	9 30 N	2 15 E
Daito Islands	Japan	43 00 N	17 00 E
Dakar (capital)	Senegal	14 40 N	17 26 W
Dalmatia (region)	Croatia	43 00 N	17 00 E
Daman (city; also Damao)	India	20 10 N	73 00 E
Damascus (capital)	Syria	33 30 N	36 18 E
Danger Islands (see Pukapuka Atoll)	Cook Islands	10 53 S	165 49 W
Danish Straits	Atlantic Ocean	58 00 N	11 00 E
Danish West Indies (former name for the Virgin Islands)	Virgin Islands	18 20 N	64 50 W
Danmark (local name)	Denmark	56 00 N	10 00 E
Danzig (city; former name for Gdansk)	Poland	54 23 N	18 40 E

Name	Entry in *The World Factbook*	Latitude (deg min)	Longitude (deg min)
Dao Bach Long Vi (island)	Vietnam	20 08 N	107 44 E
Dar es Salaam (capital)	Tanzania	6 48 S	39 17 E
Dardanelles (strait)	Atlantic Ocean	40 15 N	26 25 E
Davis Strait	Atlantic Ocean	67 00 N	57 00 W
Dead Sea	Israel, Jordan, West Bank	32 30 N	35 30 E
Deception Island	Antarctica	62 56 S	60 34 W
Denmark Strait	Atlantic Ocean	67 00 N	24 00 W
Desolation Islands (Isles Kerguelen)	French Southern and Antarctic Lands	49 30 S	69 30 E
Deutschland (local name for Germany)	Germany	51 00 N	9 00 E
Devils Island (Ile du Diable)	French Guiana	5 17 N	52 35 W
Devon Island	Canada	76 00 N	87 00 W
Dhaka (capital)	Bangladesh	23 43 N	90 25 E
Dhivehi Raajje (local name for Maldives)	Maldives	3 15 N	73 00 E
Dhofar (region)	Oman	17 00 N	54 10 E
Diego Garcia (island)	British Indian Ocean Territory	7 20 S	72 25 E
Diego Ramirez (islands)	Chile	56 30 S	68 43 W
Dili (capital)	East Timor	8 35 S	125 36 E
Dilmun (former name for Bahrain)	Bahrain	7 00 N	81 00 E
Diomede Islands	Russia (Big Diomede), United States (Little Diomede)	65 47 N	169 00 W
Diu (region)	India	20 42 N	70 59 E
Djibouti (capital)	Djibouti	11 30 N	43 15 E
Dnieper (river)	Belarus, Russia, Ukraine (Dnyapro, Dnepr, Dnipro)	46 30 N	32 18 E
Dniester (river)	Moldova, Ukraine (Nistru, Dnister)	46 18 N	30 17 E
Dobruja (region)	Bulgaria, Romania	43 30 N	28 00 E
Dodecanese (island group)	Greece	36 00 N	27 05 E
Dodoma (city)	Tanzania	6 11 S	35 45 E
Doha (capital)	Qatar	25 17 N	51 32 E
Donets Basin	Russia, Ukraine	48 15 N	38 30 E
Douala (city)	Cameroon	4 03 N	9 42 E
Douglas (capital)	Man, Isle of	54 09 N	4 28 W
Dover, Strait of	Atlantic Ocean	51 00 N	1 30 E
Drake Passage	Atlantic Ocean, Southern Ocean	60 00 S	60 00 W
Druk Yul (local name for Bhutan)	Bhutan	27 30 N	90 30 E
Dubai, Dubayy (city)	United Arab Emirates	25 18 N	55 18 E
Dublin (capital)	Ireland	53 20 N	6 15 W
Dushanbe (capital)	Tajikistan	38 35 N	68 48 E
Dutch Antilles (former name for the Netherlands Antilles)	Netherlands Antilles	12 10 N	68 30 W

Name	Entry in *The World Factbook*	Latitude (deg min)	Longitude (deg min)
Dutch East Indies (former name for Indonesia)	Indonesia	5 00 S	120 00 E
Dutch Guiana (former name for Suriname)	Suriname	4 00 N	56 00 W
Dutch West Indies (former name for the Netherlands Antilles)	Netherlands Antilles	12 10 N	68 30 W
Dzungarian Gate (valley)	China, Kazakhstan	45 25 N	82 25 E
East China Sea	Pacific Ocean	30 00 N	126 00 E
East Frisian Islands	Germany	53 44 N	7 25 E
East Germany (German Democratic Republic; former name for eastern portion of Germany)	Germany	52 00 N	13 00 E
East Korea Strait (Eastern Channel or Tsushima Strait)	Pacific Ocean	34 00 N	129 00 E
East Pakistan (former name for Bangladesh)	Bangladesh	24 00 N	90 00 E
East Siberian Sea	Arctic Ocean	74 00 N	166 00
Easter Island (Isla de Pascua)	Chile	27 07 S	109 22 W
Eastern Channel (East Korea Strait or Tsushima Strait)	Pacific Ocean	34 00 N	129 00 E
Eastern Samoa (former name for American Samoa)	American Samoa	14 20 S	170 00 W
Eesti (local name for Estonia)	Estonia	59 00 N	26 00 E
Eire (local name for Ireland)	Ireland	53 00 N	8 00 W
Elba (island)	Italy	42 46 N	10 17 E
Elemi Triangle (region)	Ethiopia (claimed), Kenya (de facto), Sudan (claimed)	5 00 N	35 30 E
Ellada, Ellas (local name for Greece)	Greece	39 00 N	22 00 E
Ellef Ringnes Island	Canada	78 00 N	103 00 W
Ellesmere Island	Canada	81 00 N	80 00 W
Ellice Islands	Tuvalu	8 00 S	178 00 E
Ellsworth Land (region)	Antarctica	75 00 S	92 00 W
Elobey, Islas de (island group)	Equatorial Guinea	0 59 N	9 33 E
Enderbury Island	Kiribati	3 08 S	171 05 W
Enewetak Atoll (Eniwetok Atoll)	Marshall Islands	11 30 N	162 15 E
England (region)	United Kingdom	52 30 N	1 30 W
English Channel	Atlantic Ocean	50 20 N	1 00 W
Eniwetok Atoll (see Enewetak Atoll)	Marshall Islands	11 30 N	162 15 E
Eolie, Isole (island group)	Italy	38 30 N	15 00 E
Epirus, Northern (region)	Albania, Greece	40 00 N	20 30 E
Episkopi Cantonment (capital)	Akrotiri, Dhekelia	34 40 N	32 51 E
Ertra (local name for Eritrea)	Eritrea	15 00 N	39 00 E

Name	Entry in *The World Factbook*	Latitude (deg min)	Longitude (deg min)
Espana	Spain	40 00 N	4 00 W
Essequibo (region; claimed by Venezuela)	Guyana	6 59 N	58 23 W
Etorofu (island; also Iturup)	Russia (de facto)	44 55 N	147 40 E
Farquhar Group (island group; also Atoll de Farquhar)	Seychelles	10 10 S	51 10 E
Fergana Valley	Kyrgyzstan, Tajikistan, Uzbekistan	41 00 N	72 00 E
Fernando Po (island; see Bioko)	Equatorial Guinea	3 30 N	8 42 E
Fernando de Noronha (island group)	Brazil	3 51 S	32 25 W
Filipinas (local name for the Philippines; also Pilipinas)	Philippines	13 00 N	122 00 E
Finland, Gulf of	Atlantic Ocean	60 00 N	27 00 E
Flores (island)	Indonesia	8 45 S	121 00 E
Flores Sea	Pacific Ocean	7 40 S	119 45 E
Florida, Straits of	Atlantic Ocean	25 00 N	79 45 W
Fongafale (capital)	Tuvalu	8 30 S	179 12 E
Former Soviet Union (FSU)	Armenia, Azerbaijan, Belarus, Estonia, Georgia, Kazakhstan, Kyrgyzstan, Latvia, Lithuania, Moldova, Russia, Tajikistan, Turkmenistan, Ukraine, Uzbekistan		
Formosa (island)	Taiwan	23 30 N	121 00 E
Formosa Strait (see Taiwan Strait)	Pacific Ocean	24 00 N	119 00 E
Foroyar (local name for Faroe Islands)	Faroe Islands	62 00 N	7 00 W
Fort-de-France (capital)	Martinique	14 36 N	61 05 W
Franz Josef Land (island group)	Russia	81 00 N	55 00 E
Freetown (capital)	Sierra Leone	8 30 N	13 15 W
French Cameroon (former name for Cameroon)	Cameroon	6 00 N	12 00 E
French Guinea (former name for Guinea)	Guinea	11 00 N	10 00 W
French Indochina (former name for French possessions in southeast Asia)	Cambodia, Laos, Vietnam	15 00 N	107 00 E
French Morocco (former name for Morocco)	Morocco	32 00 N	5 00 W
French Somaliland (former name for Djibouti)	Djibouti	11 30 N	43 00 E
French Sudan (former name for Mali)	Mali	17 00 N	4 00 W
French Territory of the Afars and Issas (or FTAI; former name for Djibouti)	Djibouti	11 30 N	43 00 E
French Togoland (former name for Togo)	Togo	8 00 N	1 10 E
French West Indies (former name for French possessions in the West Indies)	Guadeloupe, Martinique	16 30 N	62 00 W

Name	Entry in *The World Factbook*	Latitude (deg min)	Longitude (deg min)
Friendly Islands	Tonga	20 00 S	175 00 W
Frisian Islands	Denmark, Germany, Netherlands	53 35 N	6 40 E
Frunze (city; former name for Bishkek)	Kyrgyzstan	42 54 N	74 36 E
Funafuti (capital, former name for Fongafale)	Tuvalu	8 30 S	179 12 E
Fundy, Bay of	Atlantic Ocean	45 00 N	66 00 W
Futuna Islands (Hoorn Islands/Iles de Horne)	Wallis and Futuna	14 19 S	178 05 W
Fyn (island)	Denmark	55 20 N	10 25 E
Gaborone (capital)	Botswana	24 45 S	25 55 E
Galapagos Islands (Archipielago de Colon)	Ecuador	0 00 N	90 30 W
Galicia (region)	Poland, Ukraine	49 30 N	23 00 E
Galicia (region)	Spain	42 45 N	8 10 E
Galilee (region)	Israel	32 54 N	35 20 E
Galleons Passage	Atlantic Ocean	11 00 N	60 55 W
Gambier Islands (Iles Gambier)	French Polynesia	23 09 S	134 58 W
Gaspar Strait	Pacific Ocean	3 00 S	107 00 E
Gdansk (city; formerly Danzig)	Poland	54 23 N	18 40 E
Geneva (city)	Switzerland	46 12 N	6 10 E
Genoa (city)	Italy	44 25 N	8 57 E
George Town (capital)	Cayman Islands	19 20 N	81 23 W
George Town (city)	Malaysia	5 26 N	100 16 E
George Town (city)	The Bahamas	23 30 N	75 46 W
Georgetown (capital)	Guyana	6 48 N	58 10 W
Georgetown (city)	The Gambia	13 30 N	14 47 W
German Democratic Republic (East Germany; former name for eastern portion of Germany)	Germany	52 00 N	13 00 E
German Southwest Africa (former name for Namibia)	Namibia	22 00 S	17 00 E
Germany, Federal Republic of	Germany	51 00 N	9 00 E
Gibraltar (city, peninsula)	Gibraltar	36 11 N	5 22 W
Gibraltar, Strait of	Atlantic Ocean	35 57 N	5 36 W
Gidi Pass	Egypt	30 13 N	33 09 E
Gilbert Islands	Kiribati	1 25 N	173 00 E
Goa (state)	India	15 20 N	74 00 E
Gobi (desert)	China, Mongolia	42 30 N	107 00 E
Godthab (capital; also Nuuk)	Greenland	64 11 N	51 44 W
Golan Heights (region)	Syria	33 00 N	35 45 E
Gold Coast (former name for Ghana)	Ghana	8 00 N	2 00 W

Name	Entry in *The World Factbook*	Latitude (deg min)	Longitude (deg min)
Golfo San Jorge (gulf)	Atlantic Ocean	46 00 S	66 00 W
Golfo San Matias (gulf)	Atlantic Ocean	41 30 S	64 00 W
Good Hope, Cape of	South Africa	34 24 S	18 30 E
Goteborg (city)	Sweden	57 43 N	11 58 E
Gotland (island)	Sweden	57 30 N	18 33 E
Gough Island	Saint Helena	40 20 S	9 55 W
Graham Land (region)	Antarctica	65 00 S	64 00 W
Gran Chaco (region)	Argentina, Paraguay	24 00 S	60 00 W
Grand Bahama (island)	The Bahamas	26 40 N	78 35 W
Grand Banks (fishing ground)	Atlantic Ocean	47 06 N	55 48 W
Grand Cayman (island)	Cayman Islands	19 20 N	81 20 W
Grand Turk (capital; also Cockburn Town)	Turks and Caicos Islands	21 28 N	71 08 W
Great Australian Bight	Indian Ocean	35 00 S	130 00 E
Great Belt (strait; also Store Baelt)	Atlantic Ocean	55 30 N	11 00 E
Great Bitter Lake	Egypt	30 20 N	32 23 E
Great Britain (island)	United Kingdom	54 00 N	2 00 W
Great Channel	Indian Ocean	6 25 N	94 20 E
Great Inagua (island)	The Bahamas	21 00 N	73 20 W
Great Rift Valley	Ethiopia, Kenya	0 30 N	36 00 E
Greater Sunda Islands	Brunei, Indonesia, Malaysia	2 00 S	110 00 E
Green Islands	Papua New Guinea	4 30 S	154 10 E
Greenland Sea	Arctic Ocean	79 00 N	5 00 W
Grenadines, Northern (island group)	Saint Vincent and the Grenadines	13 15 N	61 12 W
Grenadines, Southern (island group)	Grenada	12 07 N	61 40 W
Grytviken (town; on South Georgia)	South Georgia and the South Sandwich Islands	54 15 S	36 45 W
Guadalcanal (island)	Solomon Islands	9 32 S	160 12 E
Guadalupe, Isla de (island)	Mexico	29 11 N	118 17 W
Guantanamo Bay (US Naval Base)	Cuba	20 00 N	75 08 W
Guatemala (capital)	Guatemala	14 38 N	90 31 W
Guine-Bissau (local name for Guinea-Bissau)	Guinea-Bissau	12 00 N	15 00 W
Guinea Ecuatorial (local name for Equatorial Guinea)	Equatorial Guinea	2 00 N	10 00 E
Guinea, Gulf of	Atlantic Ocean	3 00 N	2 30 E
Guinee (local name for Guinea)	Guinea	11 00 N	10 00 W
Guyane Francaise (local name for French Guiana)	French Guiana	4 00 N	53 00 W
Ha'apai Group (island group)	Tonga	19 42 S	174 29 W
Habomai Islands	Russia (de facto)	43 30 N	146 10 E
Hadhramaut (region)	Yemen	15 00 N	50 00 E

Name	Entry in *The World Factbook*	Latitude (deg min)	Longitude (deg min)
Hagatna (capital; formerly Agana)	Guam	13 28 N	144 45 E
Hague, The (seat of government)	Netherlands	52 05 N	4 18 E
Haifa (city)	Israel	32 50 N	35 00 E
Hainan Dao (island)	China	19 00 N	109 30 E
Haiphong (city)	Vietnam	20 52 N	106 41 E
Hala'ib Triangle (region)	Egypt (claimed), Sudan (de facto)	22 30 N	35 00 E
Halmahera (island)	Indonesia	1 00 N	128 00 E
Halmahera Sea	Pacific Ocean	0 30 S	129 00 E
Hamilton (capital)	Bermuda	32 17 N	64 46 W
Han-guk (local name for South Korea	South Korea	37 00 N	127 30 E
Hanoi (capital)	Vietnam	21 02 N	105 51 E
Harare (capital)	Zimbabwe	17 50 S	31 03 E
Harvey Islands (former name for Cook Islands)	Cook Islands	21 14 S	159 46 W
Hatay (province)	Turkey	36 30 N	36 15 E
Havana (capital)	Cuba	23 08 N	82 22 W
Hawaii (island)	United States	19 45 N	155 45 W
Hawaiian Islands	United States	21 00 N	157 45 W
Hawar (island)	Bahrain	25 40 N	50 47 E
Hayastan (local name for Armenia)	Armenia	40 00 N	45 00 E
Heard Island	Heard Island and McDonald Islands	53 06 S	73 30 E
Hejaz (region)	Saudi Arabia	24 30 N	38 30 E
Helsinki (capital)	Finland	60 10 N	24 58 E
Herzegovina (political region)	Bosnia and Herzegovina	44 00 N	18 00 E
Hiiumaa (island)	Estonia	58 50 N	22 30 E
Hispaniola (island)	Dominican Republic, Haiti	18 45 N	71 00 W
Ho Chi Minh City (Saigon)	Vietnam	10 45 N	106 40 E
Hokkaido (island)	Japan	44 00 N	143 00 E
Holland (region)	Netherlands	52 30 N	5 45 E
Hong Kong (special administrative region)	Hong Kong	22 15 N	114 10 E
Honiara (capital)	Solomon Islands	9 26 S	159 57 E
Honshu (island)	Japan	36 00 N	138 00 E
Hormuz, Strait of	Indian Ocean	26 34 N	56 15 E
Horn of Africa (region)	Djibouti, Eritrea, Ethiopia, Somalia	8 00 N	48 00 E
Horn, Cape (Cabo de Hornos)	Chile	55 59 S	67 16 W
Horne, Iles de (island group)	Wallis and Futuna	14 19 S	178 05 W
Hrvatska (local name for Croatia)	Croatia	45 10 N	15 30 E
Hudson Bay	Arctic Ocean	60 00 N	86 00 W
Hudson Strait	Arctic Ocean	62 00 N	71 00 W
Hunter Island	New Caledonia, Vanuatu	22 24 S	172 06 E

Name	Entry in *The World Factbook*	Latitude (deg min)	Longitude (deg min)
Iberian Peninsula	Portugal, Spain	40 00 N	5 00 W
Iceland Sea	Arctic Ocean	68 00 N	20 00 W
Ifni (region; former name of part of Spanish West Africa)	Morocco	29 22 N	10 09 W
Inaccessible Island	Saint Helena	37 17 S	12 40 W
Indochina (region)	Cambodia, Laos, Vietnam	15 00 N	107 00 E
Ingushetia (region)	Russia	43 15 N	45 00 E
Inhambane (region)	Mozambique	22 30 S	34 30 E
Inini (former name for French Guiana)	French Guiana	4 00 N	53 00 W
Inland Sea	Japan	34 20 N	133 30 E
Inner Hebrides (islands)	United Kingdom	56 30 N	6 20 W
Inner Mongolia (region; also Nei Mongol)	China	42 00 N	113 00 E
Ionian Islands	Greece	38 30 N	20 30 E
Ionian Sea	Atlantic Ocean	38 30 N	18 00 E
Irian Jaya (province)	Indonesia	5 00 S	138 00 E
Irish Sea	Atlantic Ocean	53 30 N	5 20 W
Iron Gate (river gorge)	Romania, Serbia and Montenegro	44 41 N	22 31 E
Iskenderun (region; formerly Alexandretta)	Turkey	36 34 N	36 08 E
Islamabad (capital)	Pakistan	33 42 N	73 10 E
Island (local name for Iceland)	Iceland	65 00 N	18 00 W
Islas Malvinas (island group)	Falkland Islands (Islas Malvinas)	51 45 S	59 00 W
Istanbul (city)	Turkey	41 01 N	28 58 E
Istrian Peninsula	Croatia, Slovenia	45 00 N	14 00 E
Italia (local name for Italy)	Italy	42 50 N	12 50 E
Italian East Africa (former name for Italian possessions in eastern Africa)	Eritrea, Ethiopia, Somalia	8 00 N	38 00 E
Italian Somaliland (former name for southern Somalia)	Somalia	10 00 N	49 00 E
Ittihad al-Imarat al-Arabiyah (local name for the United Arab Emirates)	United Arab Emirates	24 00 N	54 00 E
Iturup (island; see Etorofu)	Russia (de facto)	44 55 N	147 40 E
Ityop'iya (local name for Ethiopia)	Ethiopia	8 00 N	38 00 E
Ivory Coast (former name for Cote d'Ivoire)	Cote d'Ivoire	8 00 N	5 00 W
Iwo Jima (island)	Japan	24 47 N	141 20 E
Izmir (region)	Turkey	38 25 N	27 10 E
Jakarta (capital)	Indonesia	6 10 S	106 48 E
James Bay	Arctic Ocean	54 00 N	80 00 W
Jamestown (capital)	Saint Helena	15 56 S	5 44 W
Jammu (city)	India	32 42 N	74 52 E
Jammu and Kashmir (region)	India, Pakistan	34 00 N	76 00 E

Name	Entry in *The World Factbook*	Latitude (deg min)	Longitude (deg min)
Japan, Sea of	Pacific Ocean	40 00 N	135 00 E
Jars, Plain of	Laos	19 27 N	103 10 E
Java (island)	Indonesia	7 30 S	110 00 E
Java Sea	Pacific Ocean	5 00 S	110 00 E
Jerusalem (capital, proclaimed)	Israel, West Bank	31 47 N	35 14 E
Jiddah, Jeddah (city)	Saudi Arabia	21 30 N	39 12 E
Johannesburg (city)	South Africa	26 15 S	28 00 E
Joseph Bonaparte Gulf	Pacific Ocean	14 00 S	128 45 E
Juan Fernandez, Islas de (island group)	Chile	33 00 S	80 00 W
Juan de Fuca, Strait of	Pacific Ocean	48 18 N	124 00 W
Jubal, Strait of	Indian Ocean	27 40 N	33 55 E
Judaea (region)	Israel, West Bank	31 35 N	35 00 E
Jugoslavia, Jugoslavija (local names for Yugoslavia, a former Balkan federation)	Bosnia and Herzegovina, Croatia, Macedonia, Serbia and Montenegro, Slovenia	43 00 N	21 00 E
Jutland (region)	Denmark	56 00 N	9 15 E
Juventud, Isla de la (Isle of Youth)	Cuba	21 40 N	82 50 W
Kabardino-Balkaria (region)	Russia	43 30 N	43 30 E
Kabul (capital)	Afghanistan	34 31 N	69 12 E
Kaduna (city)	Nigeria	10 33 N	7 27 E
Kailas Range	China, India	30 00 N	82 00 E
Kalaallit Nunaat (local name for Greenland)	Greenland	72 00 N	40 00 W
Kalahari (desert)	Botswana, Namibia	24 30 S	21 00 E
Kalimantan (region)	Indonesia	0 00 N	115 00 E
Kaliningrad (region; formerly part of East Prussia)	Russia	54 30 N	21 00 E
Kamaran (island)	Yemen	15 21 N	42 34 E
Kamchatka Peninsula (Poluostrov Kamchatka)	Russia	56 00 N	160 00 E
Kampala (capital)	Uganda	0 19 N	32 25 E
Kampuchea (former name for Cambodia)	Cambodia	13 00 N	105 00 E
Kane Basin (portion of channel)	Arctic Ocean	79 30 N	68 00 W
Kanton Island	Kiribati	2 49 S	171 40 W
Kara Sea	Arctic Ocean	76 00 N	80 00 E
Karachevo-Cherkessia (region)	Russia	43 40 N	41 50 E
Karafuto (island; former name for southern Sakhalin Island)	Russia	50 00 N	143 00 E
Karakoram Pass	China, India	35 30 N	77 50 E
Karelia (region)	Finland, Russia	63 15 N	30 48 E
Karelian Isthmus	Russia	60 25 N	30 00 E
Karimata Strait	Pacific Ocean	2 05 S	108 40 E

Name	Entry in *The World Factbook*	Latitude (deg min)	Longitude (deg min)
Kashmir (region)	India, Pakistan	34 00 N	76 00 E
Katanga (region)	Democratic Republic of the Congo	10 00 S	26 00 E
Kathmandu (capital)	Nepal	27 43 N	85 19 E
Kattegat (strait)	Atlantic Ocean	57 00 N	11 00 E
Kauai Channel	Pacific Ocean	21 45 N	158 50 W
Kazakstan (former name for Kazakhstan)	Kazakhstan	48 00 N	68 00 E
Keeling Islands	Cocos (Keeling) Islands	12 30 S	96 50 E
Kerguelen, Iles (island group)	French Southern and Antarctic Lands	49 30 S	69 30 E
Kermadec Islands	New Zealand	29 50 S	178 15 W
Kerulen River	China, Mongolia	48 48 N	117 00 E
Khabarovsk (city)	Russia	48 27 N	135 06 E
Khanka, Lake	China, Russia	45 00 N	132 24 E
Khartoum (capital)	Sudan	15 36 N	32 32 E
Khios (island)	Greece	38 22 N	26 04 E
Khmer Republic (former name for Cambodia)	Cambodia	13 00 N	105 00 E
Khuriya Muriya Islands (Kuria Muria Islands)	Oman	17 30 N	56 00 E
Khyber Pass	Afghanistan, Pakistan	34 05 N	71 10 E
Kibris (Turkish local name for Cyprus)	Cyprus	35 00 N	33 00 E
Kiel Canal (Nord-Ostsee Kanal)	Atlantic Ocean	53 53 N	9 08 E
Kiev (capital)	Ukraine	50 26 N	30 31 E
Kigali (capital)	Rwanda	1 57 S	30 04 E
Kingston (capital)	Jamaica	18 00 N	76 48 W
Kingston (capital)	Norfolk Island	29 03 S	167 58 E
Kingstown (capital)	Saint Vincent and the Grenadines	13 09 N	61 14 W
Kinshasa (capital)	Democratic Republic of the Congo	4 18 S	15 18 E
Kipros (Greek local name for Cyprus)	Cyprus	35 00 N	33 00 E
Kirghiziya, Kirgizia (former name for Kyrgyzstan)	Kyrgyzstan	41 00 N	75 00 E
Kirguizstan (local name for Kyrgyzstan)	Kyrgyzstan	41 00 N	75 00 E
Kiritimati (Christmas Island)	Kiribati	1 52 N	157 20 W
Kishinev (see Chisinau)	Moldova	47 00 N	28 50 E
Kithira Strait	Atlantic Ocean	36 00 N	23 00 E
Kobe (city)	Japan	34 41 N	135 10 E
Kodiak Island	United States	57 49 N	152 23 W
Kola Peninsula (Kol'skiy Poluostrov)	Russia	67 20 N	37 00 E
Kolonia (town; former capital; changed to Palikir)	Federated States of Micronesia	6 58 N	158 13 E
Korea Bay	Pacific Ocean	39 00 N	124 00 E
Korea Strait	Pacific Ocean	34 00 N	129 00 E

Name	Entry in *The World Factbook*	Latitude (deg min)	Longitude (deg min)
Korea, Democratic People's Republic of	North Korea	40 00 N	127 00 E
Korea, Republic of	South Korea	37 00 N	127 30 E
Koror (capital)	Palau	7 20 N	134 29 E
Kosovo (region)	Serbia and Montenegro	42 30 N	21 00 E
Kosrae (island)	Federated States of Micronesia	5 20 N	163 00 E
Kowloon (city)	Hong Kong	22 18 N	114 10 E
Kra, Isthmus of	Burma, Thailand	10 20 N	99 00 E
Krakatoa (volcano)	Indonesia	6 07 S	105 24 E
Kuala Lumpur (capital)	Malaysia	3 10 N	101 42 E
Kunashiri (island; also Kunashir)	Russia (de facto)	44 20 N	146 00 E
Kunlun Mountains	China	36 00 N	84 00 E
Kuril Islands	Russia (de facto)	46 10 N	152 00 E
Kuwait (capital)	Kuwait	29 20 N	47 59 E
Kuznetsk Basin	Russia	54 00 N	86 00 E
Kwajalein Atoll	Marshall Islands	9 05 N	167 20 E
Kyiv, Kyyiv (see Kiev)	Ukraine	50 26 N	30 31 E
Kyushu (island)	Japan	33 00 N	131 00 E
La Paz (administrative capital)	Bolivia	16 30 S	68 09 W
La Perouse Strait	Pacific Ocean	45 45 N	142 00 E
Labrador (peninsula, region)	Canada	54 00 N	62 00 W
Labrador Sea	Atlantic Ocean	60 00 N	55 00 W
Laccadive Islands	India	10 00 N	73 00 E
Laccadive Sea	Indian Ocean	7 00 N	76 00 E
Lagos (former capital)	Nigeria	6 27 N	3 24 E
Lake Erie	Atlantic Ocean	42 30 N	81 00 W
Lake Huron	Atlantic Ocean	45 00 N	83 00 W
Lake Michigan	Atlantic Ocean	43 30 N	87 30 W
Lake Ontario	Atlantic Ocean	43 30 N	78 00 W
Lake Superior	Atlantic Ocean	48 00 N	88 00 W
Lakshadweep (Laccadive Islands)	India	10 00 N	73 00 E
Lantau Island	Hong Kong	22 15 N	113 55 E
Lao (local name for Laos)	Laos	18 00 N	105 00 E
Laptev Sea	Arctic Ocean	76 00 N	126 00 E
Las Palmas (city)	Spain (Canary Islands)	28 06 N	15 24 W
Latakia (region)	Syria	36 00 N	35 50 E
Latvija (local name for Latvia)	Latvia	57 00 N	25 00 E
Lau Group (island group)	Fiji	18 20 S	178 30 E
Lefkosa (see Nicosia)	Cyprus	35 10 N	33 22 E
Lemnos (island)	Greece	39 54 N	25 21 E
Leningrad (see Saint Petersburg)	Russia	59 55 N	30 15 E
Lesser Sunda Islands	Indonesia	9 00 S	120 00 E

Name	Entry in *The World Factbook*	Latitude (deg min)	Longitude (deg min)
Lesvos (island)	Greece	39 15 N	26 15 E
Leyte (island)	Philippines	10 50 N	124 50 E
Liancourt Rocks (claimed by Japan)	South Korea	37 15 N	131 50 E
Liaodong Wan (gulf)	Pacific Ocean	40 30 N	121 20 E
Liban (local name for Lebanon)	Lebanon	33 50 N	36 50 E
Libreville (capital)	Gabon	0 23 N	9 27 E
Lietuva (local name for Lithuania)	Lithuania	56 00 N	24 00 E
Ligurian Sea	Atlantic Ocean	43 30 N	9 00 E
Lilongwe (capital)	Malawi	13 59 S	33 44 E
Lima (capital)	Peru	12 03 S	77 03 W
Lincoln Sea	Arctic Ocean	83 00 N	56 00 W
Line Islands	Jarvis Island, Kingman Reef, Kiribati, Palmyra Atoll	0 05 N	157 00 W
Lion, Gulf of	Atlantic Ocean	43 20 N	4 00 E
Lisbon (capital)	Portugal	38 43 N	9 08 W
Little Belt (strait; also Lille Baelt)	Atlantic Ocean	55 05 N	9 55 E
Ljubljana (capital)	Slovenia	46 03 N	14 31 E
Llanos (region)	Venezuela	8 00 N	68 00 W
Lobamba (city)	Swaziland	26 27 S	31 12 E
Lombok (island)	Indonesia	8 28 S	116 40 E
Lombok Strait	Indian Ocean	8 30 S	115 50 E
Lome (capital)	Togo	6 08 N	1 13 E
London (capital)	United Kingdom	51 30 N	0 10 W
Longyearbyen (capital)	Svalbard	78 13 N	15 33 E
Lord Howe Island	Australia	31 30 S	159 00 E
Lorraine (region)	France	48 42 N	6 11 E
Louisiade Archipelago	Papua New Guinea	11 00 S	153 00 E
Lourenco Marques (city; former name for Maputo)	Mozambique	25 56 S	32 34 E
Loyalty Islands (Iles Loyaute)	New Caledonia	21 00 S	167 00 E
Luanda (capital)	Angola	8 48 S	13 14 E
Lubnan (local name for Lebanon)	Lebanon	33 50 N	36 50 E
Lubumbashi (city)	Democratic Republic of the Congo	11 40 S	27 28 E
Lusaka (capital)	Zambia	15 25 S	28 17 E
Luxembourg (capital)	Luxembourg	49 45 N	6 10 E
Luzon (island)	Philippines	16 00 N	121 00 E
Luzon Strait	Pacific Ocean	20 30 N	121 00 E
Lyakhov Islands	Russia	73 45 N	138 00 E
Macao	Macau	22 10 N	113 33 E
Macquarie Island	Australia	54 36 S	158 54 E
Madagasikara (local name for Madagascar)	Madagascar	20 00 S	47 00 E

Name	Entry in *The World Factbook*	Latitude (deg min)	Longitude (deg min)
Maddalena, Isola	Italy	41 13 N	09 24 E
Madeira Islands	Portugal	32 40 N	16 45 W
Madras (city; see Chennai)	India	13 04 N	80 16 E
Madrid (capital)	Spain	40 24 N	3 41 W
Magellan, Strait of	Atlantic Ocean	54 00 S	71 00 W
Maghreb (region)	Algeria, Libya, Mauritania, Morocco, Tunisia	34 00 N	3 00 E
Magreb (local name for Morocco)	Morocco	32 00 N	5 00 W
Magyarorszag (local name for Hungary)	Hungary	47 00 N	20 00 E
Mahe Island	Seychelles	4 41 S	55 30 E
Maiz, Islas del (Corn Islands)	Nicaragua	12 15 N	83 00 W
Majorca Island (Isla de Mallorca)	Spain	39 30 N	3 00 E
Majuro (capital)	Marshall Islands	7 05 N	171 08 E
Makassar Strait	Pacific Ocean	2 00 S	117 30 E
Makedonija (local name for Macedonia)	Macedonia	41 50 N	22 00 E
Malabo (capital)	Equatorial Guinea	3 45 N	8 47 E
Malacca, Strait of	Indian Ocean	2 30 N	101 20 E
Malagasy Republic	Madagascar	20 00 S	47 00 E
Malay Archipelago	Brunei, Indonesia, Malaysia, Papua New Guinea, Philippines	2 30 N	120 00 E
Malay Peninsula	Malaysia, Thailand	7 10 N	100 35 E
Male (capital)	Maldives	4 10 N	73 31 E
Mallorca, Isla de (island; also Majorca)	Spain	39 30 N	3 00 E
Malmady (region)	Belgium	50 26 N	6 02 E
Malpelo, Isla de (island)	Colombia	4 00 N	90 30 W
Malta Channel	Atlantic Ocean	56 44 N	26 53 E
Malvinas, Islas (island group)	Falkland Islands (Islas Malvinas)	51 45 S	59 00 W
Mamoutzou (capital)	Mayotte	12 47 S	45 14 E
Managua (capital)	Nicaragua	12 09 N	86 17 W
Manama (capital)	Bahrain	26 13 N	50 35 E
Manchukuo (former state)	China	44 00 N	124 00 E
Manchuria (region)	China	44 00 N	124 00 E
Manila (capital)	Philippines	14 35 N	121 00 E
Manipa Strait	Pacific Ocean	3 20 S	127 23 E
Mannar, Gulf of	Indian Ocean	8 30 N	79 00 E
Manua Islands	American Samoa	14 13 S	169 35 W
Maputo (capital)	Mozambique	25 58 S	32 35 E
Marcus Island (Minami-tori-shima)	Japan	24 16 N	154 00 E
Margarita, Isla (island)	Venezuela	10 00 N	64 00 W
Mariana Islands	Guam, Northern Mariana Islands	16 00 N	145 30 E

Name	Entry in *The World Factbook*	Latitude (deg min)	Longitude (deg min)
Marie Byrd Land (region)	Antarctica	77 00 S	130 00 W
Marion Island	South Africa	46 51 S	37 52 E
Marmara, Sea of	Atlantic Ocean	40 40 N	28 15 E
Marquesas Islands (Iles Marquises)	French Polynesia	9 00 S	139 30 W
Martin Vaz, Ilhas (island group)	Brazil	20 30 S	28 51 W
Mas a Tierra (Robinson Crusoe Island)	Chile	33 38 S	78 52 W
Mascarene Islands	Mauritius, Reunion	21 00 S	57 00 E
Maseru (capital)	Lesotho	29 28 S	27 30 E
Mata-Utu (capital)	Wallis and Futuna	13 57 S	171 56 W
Matsu (island)	Taiwan	26 13 N	119 56 E
Matthew Island	New Caledonia, Vanuatu	22 20 S	171 20 E
Mauritanie (local name for Mauritania)	Mauritania	20 00 N	12 00 W
Mazatlan (city)	Mexico	23 13 N	106 25 W
Mbabane (capital)	Swaziland	26 18 S	31 06 E
McDonald Islands	Heard Island and McDonald Islands	53 06 S	73 30 E
Mecca (city)	Saudi Arabia	21 27 N	39 49 E
Mediterranean Sea	Atlantic Ocean	36 00 N	15 00 E
Melilla (exclave)	Spain	35 19 N	2 58 W
Memel (region)	Lithuania	55 43 N	21 30 E
Mesopotamia (region)	Iraq	33 00 N	44 00 E
Messina, Strait of	Atlantic Ocean	38 15 N	15 35 E
Mexico City (capital)	Mexico	19 24 N	99 09 W
Mexico, Gulf of	Atlantic Ocean	25 00 N	90 00 W
Middle Congo (former name for Republic of the Congo)	Republic of the Congo	1 00 S	15 00 E
Milwaukee Deep (Puerto Rico Trench)	Atlantic Ocean	19 55 N	65 27 W
Minami-tori-shima (Marcus Island)	Japan	24 16 N	154 00 E
Mindanao (island)	Philippines	8 00 N	125 00 E
Mindanao Sea	Pacific Ocean	9 15 N	124 30 E
Mindoro (island)	Philippines	12 50 N	121 05 E
Mindoro Strait	Pacific Ocean	12 20 N	120 40 E
Mingrelia (region)	Georgia	42 30 N	41 52 E
Minicoy Island	India	8 17 N	73 02 E
Minorca Island (Isla de Menorca)	Spain	40 00 N	4 00 E
Minsk (capital)	Belarus	53 54 N	27 34 E
Misr (local name for Egypt)	Egypt	27 00 N	30 00 E
Mitla Pass	Egypt	30 02 N	32 54 E
Mocambique (local name for Mozambique)	Mozambique	18 15 S	35 00 E
Mogadishu (capital)	Somalia	2 04 N	45 22 E
Moldavia (region)	Moldova, Romania	47 00 N	29 00 E

Name	Entry in *The World Factbook*	Latitude (deg min)	Longitude (deg min)
Molucca Sea	Pacific Ocean	2 00 N	127 00 E
Moluccas (Spice Islands)	Indonesia	2 00 S	128 00 E
Mombasa (city)	Kenya	4 03 S	39 40 E
Mona Passage	Atlantic Ocean	18 30 N	67 45 W
Monaco (capital)	Monaco	43 44 N	7 25 E
Mongol Uls (local name for Mongolia)	Mongolia	46 00 N	105 00 E
Monrovia (capital)	Liberia	6 18 N	10 47 W
Montenegro (political region)	Serbia and Montenegro	42 30 N	19 00 E
Monterrey (city)	Mexico	25 40 N	100 19 W
Montevideo (capital)	Uruguay	34 53 S	56 11 W
Montreal (city)	Canada	45 31 N	73 34 W
Moravia (region)	Czech Republic	49 30 N	17 00 E
Moravian Gate (pass)	Czech Republic	49 35 N	17 50 E
Moroni (capital)	Comoros	11 41 S	43 16 E
Mortlock Islands (Nomoi Islands)	Federated States of Micronesia	5 30 N	153 40 E
Moscow (capital)	Russia	55 45 N	37 35 E
Mount Pinatubo (volcano)	Philippines	15 08 N	120 21 E
Mozambique Channel	Indian Ocean	19 00 S	41 00 E
Mumbai	India	18 58 N	72 49 E
Muritaniyah (local name for Mauritania)	Mauritania	20 00 N	12 00 W
Musandam Peninsula	Oman, United Arab Emirates	26 18 N	56 24 E
Muscat (capital)	Oman	23 37 N	58 35 E
Muscat and Oman (former name for Oman)	Oman	21 00 N	57 00 E
Myanma, Myanmar	Burma	22 00 N	98 00 E
N'Djamena (capital)	Chad	12 07 N	15 03 E
Nagorno-Karabakh (region)	Azerbaijan	40 00 N	46 40 E
Nairobi (capital)	Kenya	1 17 S	36 49 E
Namib (desert)	Namibia	24 00 S	15 00 E
Nampo-shoto (island group)	Japan	30 00 N	140 00 E
Nassau (capital)	The Bahamas	25 05 N	77 21 W
Natal (region)	South Africa	29 00 S	30 25 E
Natuna Besar Islands	Indonesia	3 30 N	102 30 E
Natuna Sea	Pacific Ocean	3 30 N	108 00 E
Naxcivan (region)	Azerbaijan	39 20 N	45 20 E
Naxos (island)	Greece	37 05 N	25 30 E
Nederland (local name for the Netherlands)	Netherlands	52 30 N	5 45 E
Nederlandse Antillen (local name for the Netherlands Antilles)	Netherlands Antilles	12 15 N	68 45 W

Name	Entry in *The World Factbook*	Latitude (deg min)	Longitude (deg min)
Negev (region)	Israel	30 30 N	34 55 E
Negros (island)	Philippines	10 00 N	123 00 E
Nejd (region)	Saudi Arabia	24 05 N	45 15 E
Netherlands East Indies (former name for Indonesia)	Indonesia	5 00 S	120 00 E
Netherlands Guiana (former name for Suriname)	Suriname	4 00 N	56 00 W
Nevis (island)	Saint Kitts and Nevis	17 09 N	62 35 W
New Britain (island)	Papua New Guinea	6 00 S	150 00 E
New Delhi (capital)	India	28 36 N	77 12 E
New Guinea (island)	Indonesia, Papua New Guinea	5 00 S	140 00 E
New Hebrides (island group)	Vanuatu	16 00 S	167 00 E
New Ireland (island)	Papua New Guinea	3 20 N	152 00 E
New Siberian Islands	Russia	75 00 N	142 00 E
New Territories (mainland region)	Hong Kong	22 24 N	114 10 E
Newfoundland (island, with mainland area, and a province)	Canada	52 00 N	56 00 W
Niamey (capital)	Niger	13 31 N	2 07 E
Nicobar Islands	India	8 00 N	93 30 E
Nicosia (capital)	Cyprus	35 10 N	33 22 E
Nightingale Island	Saint Helena	37 25 S	12 30 W
Nihon, Nippon (local name for Japan)	Japan	36 00 N	138 00 E
Nomoi Islands (Mortlock Islands)	Federated States of Micronesia	5 30 N	153 40 E
Norge (local name for Norway)	Norway	62 00 N	10 00 E
Norman Isles (Channel Islands)	Guernsey, Jersey	49 20 N	2 20 W
North Atlantic Ocean	Atlantic Ocean	30 00 N	45 00 W
North Channel	Atlantic Ocean	55 10 N	5 40 W
North Frisian Islands	Denmark, Germany	54 50 N	8 12 E
North Greenland Sea	Arctic Ocean	78 00 N	5 00 W
North Island	New Zealand	39 00 S	176 00 E
North Ossetia (region)	Russia	43 00 N	44 10 E
North Pacific Ocean	Pacific Ocean	30 00 N	165 00 W
North Sea	Atlantic Ocean	56 00 N	4 00 E
North Vietnam (former name for northern portion of Vietnam)	Vietnam	23 00 N	106 00 E
North Yemen (Yemen Arab Republic; now part of Yemen)	Yemen	15 00 N	44 00 E
Northeast Providence Channel	Atlantic Ocean	25 40 N	77 09 W
Northern Areas	Pakistan	36 0 N	75 0 E
Northern Cyprus (region)	Cyprus	35 15 N	33 44 E
Northern Epirus (region)	Albania, Greece	40 00 N	20 30 E
Northern Grenadines (political region)	Saint Vincent and the Grenadines	12 45 N	61 15 W

Name	Entry in *The World Factbook*	Latitude (deg min)	Longitude (deg min)
Northern Ireland	United Kingdom	54 40 N	6 45 W
Northern Rhodesia (former name for Zambia)	Zambia	15 00 S	30 00 E
Northwest Passages	Arctic Ocean	74 40 N	100 00 W
Norwegian Sea	Atlantic Ocean	66 00 N	6 00 E
Nouakchott (capital)	Mauritania	18 06 N	15 57 W
Noumea (capital)	New Caledonia	22 16 S	166 27 E
Nouvelle-Caledonie (local name for New Caledonia)	New Caledonia	21 30 S	165 30 E
Nouvelles Hebrides (former name for Vanuatu)	Vanuatu	16 00 S	167 00 E
Novaya Zemlya (islands)	Russia	74 00 N	57 00 E
Nubia (region)	Egypt, Sudan	20 30 N	33 00 E
Nuku'alofa (capital)	Tonga	21 08 S	175 12 W
Nunavut (region)	Canada	72 00 N	90 00 W
Nuuk (capital; also Godthab)	Greenland	64 11 N	51 44 W
Nyasaland (former name for Malawi)	Malawi	13 30 S	34 00 E
Nyassa (region)	Mozambique	13 30 S	37 00 E
Oahu (island)	United States (Hawaii)	21 30 N	158 00 W
Ocean Island (Banaba)	Kiribati	0 52 S	169 35 E
Ocean Island (Kure Island)	United States	28 25 N	178 20 W
Oesterreich (local name for Austria)	Austria	47 20 N	13 20 E
Ogaden (region)	Ethiopia, Somalia	7 00 N	46 00 E
Oil Islands (Chagos Archipelago)	British Indian Ocean Territory	6 00 S	71 30 E
Okhotsk, Sea of	Pacific Ocean	53 00 N	150 00 E
Okinawa (island group)	Japan	26 30 N	128 00 E
Oland (island)	Sweden	56 45 N	16 40 E
Oman, Gulf of	Indian Ocean	24 30 N	58 30 E
Ombai Strait	Pacific Ocean	8 30 S	125 00 E
Oran (city)	Algeria	35 43 N	0 43 W
Orange River Colony (region; former name of Free State Province of South Africa)	South Africa	28 20 S	26 40 E
Oranjestad (capital)	Aruba	12 33 N	70 06 W
Oresund (The Sound) (strait)	Atlantic Ocean	55 50 N	12 40 E
Orkney Islands	United Kingdom	59 00 N	3 00 W
Oslo (capital)	Norway	59 55 N	10 45 E
Osumi Strait (Van Diemen Strait)	Pacific Ocean	31 00 N	131 00 E
Otranto, Strait of	Atlantic Ocean	40 00 N	19 00 E
Ottawa (capital)	Canada	45 25 N	75 40 W
Ouagadougou (capital)	Burkina Faso	12 22 N	1 31 W
Outer Hebrides (islands)	United Kingdom	57 45 N	7 00 W

Name	Entry in *The World Factbook*	Latitude (deg min)	Longitude (deg min)
Outer Mongolia (region)	Mongolia	46 00 N	105 00 E
P'yongyang (capital)	North Korea	39 01 N	125 45 E
Pacific Islands, Trust Territory of the (former name of a large area of the western North Pacific Ocean)	Marshall Islands, Federated States of Micronesia, Northern Mariana Islands, Palau	10 00 N	155 00 E
Pagan (island)	Northern Mariana Islands	18 08 N	145 47 E
Pago Pago (capital)	American Samoa	14 16 S	170 42 W
Palawan (island)	Philippines	9 30 N	118 30 E
Palermo (city)	Italy	38 07 N	13 21 E
Palestine (region)	Israel, West Bank	32 00 N	35 15 E
Palikir (capital)	Federated States of Micronesia	6 55 N	158 08 E
Palk Strait	Indian Ocean	10 00 N	79 45 E
Pamirs (mountains)	China, Tajikistan	38 00 N	73 00 E
Pampas (region)	Argentina	35 00 S	63 00 W
Panama (capital)	Panama	8 58 N	79 32 W
Panama Canal	Panama	9 00 N	79 45 W
Panama, Gulf of	Pacific Ocean	8 00 N	79 30 W
Panay (island)	Philippines	11 15 N	122 30 E
Pantelleria, Isola di (island)	Italy	36 47 N	12 00 E
Papeete (capital)	French Polynesia	17 32 S	149 34 W
Paramaribo (capital)	Suriname	5 50 N	55 10 W
Parece Vela (island)	Japan	20 20 N	136 00 E
Paris (capital)	France	48 52 N	2 20 E
Pascua, Isla de (Easter Island)	Chile	27 07 S	109 22 W
Pashtunistan (region)	Afghanistan, Pakistan	32 00 N	69 00 E
Passion, Ile de la (island)	Clipperton Island	10 17 N	109 13 W
Patagonia (region)	Argentina	48 00 S	61 00 W
Peking (see Beijing)	China	39 56 N	116 24 E
Pelagian Islands (Isole Pelagie)	Italy	35 40 N	12 40 E
Peleliu (Beliliou) (island)	Palau	7 01 N	134 15 E
Peloponnese (peninsula)	Greece	37 30 N	22 25 E
Pemba Island	Tanzania	5 20 S	39 45 E
Penang Island	Malaysia	5 23 N	100 15 E
Pentland Firth (channel)	Atlantic Ocean	58 44 N	3 13 W
Perim (island)	Yemen	12 39 N	43 25 E
Perouse Strait, La	Pacific Ocean	44 45 N	142 00 E
Persia (former name for Iran)	Iran	32 00 N	53 00 E
Persian Gulf	Indian Ocean	27 00 N	51 00 E
Pescadores (islands)	Taiwan	23 30 N	119 30 E
Peter I Island	Antarctica	68 48 S	90 35 W
Philip Island	Norfolk Island	29 08 S	167 57 E
Philippine Sea	Pacific Ocean	20 00 N	134 00 E

Name	Entry in *The World Factbook*	Latitude (deg min)	Longitude (deg min)
Phnom Penh (capital)	Cambodia	11 33 N	104 55 E
Phoenix Islands	Kiribati	3 30 S	172 00 W
Pinatubo, Mount (volcano)	Philippines	15 08 N	120 21 E
Pines, Isle of (island; former name for Isla de la Juventud)	Cuba	21 40 N	82 50 W
Pleasant Island	Nauru	0 32 S	166 55 E
Plymouth (capital)	Montserrat	16 44 N	62 14 W
Polska (local name)	Poland	52 00 N	20 00 E
Polynesie Francaise (local name for French Polynesia)	French Polynesia	15 00 S	140 00 W
Pomerania (region)	Germany, Poland	53 40 N	15 35 E
Ponape (Pohnpei) (island)	Federated States of Micronesia	6 55 N	158 15 E
Port Louis (capital)	Mauritius	20 10 S	57 30 E
Port Moresby (capital)	Papua New Guinea	9 30 S	147 10 E
Port-Vila (capital)	Vanuatu	17 44 S	168 19 E
Port-au-Prince (capital)	Haiti	18 32 N	72 20 W
Port-of-Spain (capital)	Trinidad and Tobago	10 39 N	61 31 W
Porto-Novo (capital)	Benin	6 29 N	2 37 E
Portuguese East Africa (former name for Mozambique)	Mozambique	18 15 S	35 00 E
Portuguese Guinea (former name for Guinea-Bissau)	Guinea-Bissau	12 00 N	15 00 W
Portuguese Timor (former name for East Timor)	East Timor	9 00 S	126 00 E
Poznan (city)	Poland	52 25 N	16 55 E
Prague (capital)	Czech Republic	40 55 N	21 00 E
Praia (capital)	Cape Verde	14 55 N	23 31 W
Prathet Thai (local name for Thailand)	Thailand	15 00 N	100 00 E
Pretoria (administrative capital)	South Africa	25 45 S	28 10 E
Prevlaka peninsula	Croatia	42 24 N	18 31 E
Pribilof Islands	United States	57 00 N	170 00 W
Prince Edward Island	Canada	46 20 N	63 20 W
Prince Edward Islands	South Africa	46 35 S	38 00 E
Prince Patrick Island	Canada	76 30 N	119 00 W
Principe (island)	Sao Tome and Principe	1 38 N	7 25 E
Prussia (region)	Germany, Poland, Russia	53 00 N	14 00 E
Pukapuka Atoll	Cook Islands	10 53 S	165 49 W
Punjab (region)	India, Pakistan	30 50 N	73 30 E
Puntland (region)	Somalia	8 21 N	49 08 E
Qazaqstan (local name for Kazakhstan)	Kazakhstan	48 00 N	68 00 E
Qita Ghazzah (local name Gaza Strip)	Gaza Strip	31 25 N	34 20 E
Queen Charlotte Islands	Canada	53 00 N	132 00 W

Name	Entry in *The World Factbook*	Latitude (deg min)	Longitude (deg min)
Queen Elizabeth Islands	Canada	78 00 N	95 00 W
Queen Maud Land (claimed by Norway)	Antarctica	73 30 S	12 00 E
Quemoy (island)	Taiwan	24 27 N	118 23 E
Quito (capital)	Ecuador	0 13 S	78 30 W
Rabat (capital)	Morocco	34 02 N	6 51 W
Ralik Chain (island group)	Marshall Islands	8 00 N	167 00 E
Rangoon (capital; also Yangon)	Burma	16 47 N	96 10 E
Rapa Nui (Easter Island)	Chile	27 07 S	109 22 W
Ratak Chain (island group)	Marshall Islands	9 00 N	171 00 E
Red Sea	Indian Ocean	20 00 N	38 00 E
Redonda (island)	Antigua and Barbuda	16 55 N	62 19 W
Republica Dominicana (local name for Dominican Republic)	Dominican Republic	19 00 N	70 40 W
Republique Centrafricain (local name for Central African Republic)	Central African Republic	7 00 N	21 00 E
Republique Francaise (local name for France)	France	46 00 N	2 00 E
Republique Gabonaise (local name for Gabon)	Gabon	1 00 S	11 45 E
Republique Rwandaise (local name for Rwanda)	Rwanda	2 00 S	30 00 E
Republique Togolaise (local name for Togo)	Togo	8 00 N	1 10 E
Revillagigedo Island	United States (Alaska)	55 35 N	131 06 W
Revillagigedo Islands	Mexico	19 00 N	112 45 W
Reykjavik (capital)	Iceland	64 09 N	21 57 W
Rhodes (island)	Greece	36 10 N	28 00 E
Rhodesia, Northern (former name for Zambia)	Zambia	15 00 S	30 00 E
Rhodesia, Southern (former name for Zimbabwe)	Zimbabwe	20 00 S	30 00 E
Riga (capital)	Latvia	56 57 N	24 06 E
Riga, Gulf of	Atlantic Ocean	57 30 N	23 30 E
Rio Muni (mainland region)	Equatorial Guinea	1 30 N	10 00 E
Rio de Oro (region)	Western Sahara	23 45 N	15 45 W
Rio de la Plata (gulf)	Atlantic Ocean	35 00 S	59 00 W
Riyadh (capital)	Saudi Arabia	24 38 N	46 43 E
Road Town (capital)	British Virgin Islands	18 27 N	64 37 W
Robinson Crusoe Island (Mas a Tierra)	Chile	33 38 S	78 52 W
Rocas, Atol das (island)	Brazil	3 51 S	33 49 W
Rockall (island)	United Kingdom	57 35 N	13 48 W
Rodrigues (island)	Mauritius	19 42 S	63 25 E

Name	Entry in *The World Factbook*	Latitude (deg min)	Longitude (deg min)
Rome (capital)	Italy	41 54 N	12 29 E
Roncador Cay (island)	Colombia	13 32 N	80 03 W
Roosevelt Island	Antarctica	79 30 S	162 00 W
Roseau (capital)	Dominica	15 18 N	61 24 W
Ross Dependency (claimed by New Zealand)	Antarctica	80 00 S	180 00 E
Ross Island	Antarctica	81 30 S	175 00 W
Ross Sea	Antarctica, Southern Ocean	76 00 S	175 00 W
Rossiya (local name for Russia)	Russia	60 00 N	100 00 E
Rota (island)	Northern Mariana Islands	14 10 N	145 12 E
Rotuma (island)	Fiji	12 30 S	177 05 E
Ruanda (former name for Rwanda)	Rwanda	2 00 S	30 00 E
Rub al Khali (desert)	Saudi Arabia	19 30 N	49 00 E
Rumelia (region)	Albania, Bulgaria, Macedonia	42 00 N	22 30 E
Ruthenia (region; former name for Carpatho-Ukraine)	Ukraine	48 22 N	23 32 E
Ryukyu Islands	Japan	26 30 N	128 00 E
Saar (region)	Germany	49 25 N	7 00 E
Saaremaa (island)	Estonia	58 25 N	22 30 E
Saba (island)	Netherlands Antilles	17 38 N	63 10 W
Sabah (state)	Malaysia	5 20 N	117 10 E
Sable Island	Canada	43 55 N	59 50 W
Safety Islands (Iles du Salut)	French Guiana	5 20 N	52 37 W
Sahara Occidental (former name for Western Sahara)	Western Sahara	24 30 N	13 00 W
Sahel (region)	Burkina Faso, Chad, The Gambia, Guinea-Bissau, Mali, Mauritania, Niger, Senegal	15 00 N	8 00 W
Saigon (city; former name for Ho Chi Minh City)	Vietnam	10 45 N	106 40 E
Saint Barthelemy (island; also Saint Bart's)	Guadeloupe	17 55 N	62 52 W
Saint Brandon (Cargados Carajos Shoals)	Mauritius	16 25 S	59 38 E
Saint Christopher (island)	Saint Kitts and Nevis	17 20 N	62 45 W
Saint Christopher and Nevis	Saint Kitts and Nevis	17 20 N	62 45 W
Saint Eustatius (island)	Netherlands Antilles	17 30 N	63 00 W
Saint George's (capital)	Grenada	12 03 N	61 45 W
Saint George's Channel	Atlantic Ocean	52 00 N	6 00 W
Saint Helena Island	Saint Helena	15 57 S	5 42 W
Saint Helens, Mount (volcano)	United States	46 15 N	122 12 W
Saint Helier (capital)	Jersey	49 12 N	2 07 W
Saint John (city)	Canada (New Brunswick)	45 16 N	66 04 W

Name	Entry in *The World Factbook*	Latitude (deg min)	Longitude (deg min)
Saint John's (capital)	Antigua and Barbuda	17 06 N	61 51 W
Saint Lawrence Island	United States	49 30 N	67 00 W
Saint Lawrence Seaway	Atlantic Ocean	49 15 N	67 00 W
Saint Lawrence, Gulf of	Atlantic Ocean	48 00 N	62 00 W
Saint Paul Island	Canada	47 12 N	60 09 W
Saint Paul Island	United States	57 11 N	170 16 W
Saint Paul Island (Ile Saint-Paul)	French Southern and Antarctic Lands	38 43 S	77 29 E
Saint Peter Port (capital)	Guernsey	49 27 N	2 32 W
Saint Peter and Saint Paul Rocks (Penedos de Sao Pedro e Sao Paulo)	Brazil	0 23 N	29 23 W
Saint Petersburg (city; former capital)	Russia	59 55 N	30 15 E
Saint Thomas (island)	Virgin Islands	18 21 N	64 55 W
Saint Vincent Passage	Atlantic Ocean	13 30 N	61 00 W
Saint-Denis (capital)	Reunion	20 52 S	55 28 E
Saint-Martin (island; also Sint Maarten)	Guadeloupe	18 04 N	63 04 W
Saint-Pierre (capital)	Saint Pierre and Miquelon	46 46 N	56 11 W
Saipan (island)	Northern Mariana Islands	15 12 N	145 45 E
Sak'art'velo (local name for Georgia)	Georgia	42 00 N	43 30 E
Sakhalin Island (Ostrov Sakhalin)	Russia	51 00 N	143 00 E
Sakishima Islands	Japan	24 30 N	124 00 E
Sala y Gomez, Isla (island)	Chile	26 28 S	105 00 W
Salisbury (city; former name for Harare)	Zimbabwe	17 50 S	105 00 W
Salzburg (city)	Austria	47 48 N	13 02 E
Samar (island)	Philippines	12 00 N	125 00 E
Samaria (region)	West Bank	32 15 N	35 10 E
Samoa Islands	American Samoa, Samoa	14 00 S	171 00 W
Samos (island)	Greece	37 48 N	26 44 E
San Ambrosio, Isla (island)	Chile	26 21 S	79 52 W
San Andres y Providencia, Archipielago (island group)	Colombia	13 00 N	81 30 W
San Bernardino Strait	Pacific Ocean	12 32 N	124 10 E
San Felix, Isla (island)	Chile	26 17 S	80 05 W
San Jose (capital)	Costa Rica	9 56 N	84 05 W
San Juan (capital)	Puerto Rico	18 28 N	66 07 W
San Marino (capital)	San Marino	43 56 N	12 25 E
San Salvador (capital)	El Salvador	13 42 N	89 12 W
Sanaa (capital)	Yemen	15 21 N	44 12 E
Sandzak (region)	Serbia and Montenegro	43 05 N	19 45 E
Santa Cruz (city)	Bolivia	17 48 S	63 10 W
Santa Cruz Islands	Solomon Islands	11 00 S	166 15 E

Name	Entry in *The World Factbook*	Latitude (deg min)	Longitude (deg min)
Santa Sede (local name for the Holy See)	Holy See	41 54 N	12 27 E
Santiago (capital)	Chile	33 27 S	70 40 W
Santo Antao (island)	Cape Verde	17 05 N	25 10 W
Santo Domingo (capital)	Dominican Republic	18 28 N	69 54 W
Sao Pedro e Sao Paulo, Penedos de (rocks)	Brazil	0 23 N	29 23 W
Sao Tiago (island)	Cape Verde	15 05 N	23 40 W
Sao Tome (island)	Sao Tome and Principe	0 12 N	6 39 E
Sapudi Strait	Pacific Ocean	7 05 S	114 10 E
Sarajevo (capital)	Bosnia and Herzegovina	43 52 N	18 25 E
Sarawak (state)	Malaysia	2 30 N	113 30 E
Sardinia (island)	Italy	40 00 N	9 00 E
Sargasso Sea (region)	Atlantic Ocean	30 00 N	55 00 W
Sark (island)	Guernsey	49 26 N	2 21 W
Savage Island (former name for Niue)	Niue	19 02 S	169 52 W
Savu Sea	Pacific Ocean	9 30 S	122 00 E
Saxony (region)	Germany	51 00 N	13 00 E
Schleswig-Holstein (region)	Germany	54 31 N	9 33 E
Schweiz (local German name for Switzerland)	Switzerland	47 00 N	8 00 E
Scopus, Mount	Israel, West Bank	31 48 N	35 14 E
Scotia Sea	Atlantic Ocean, Southern Ocean	56 00 S	40 00 W
Scotland (region)	United Kingdom	57 00 N	4 00 W
Scott Island	Antarctica	67 24 S	179 55 W
Senegambia (region; former name of confederation of Senegal and The Gambia)	The Gambia, Senegal	13 50 N	15 25 W
Senyavin Islands	Federated States of Micronesia	6 55 N	158 00 E
Seoul (capital)	South Korea	37 34 N	127 00 E
Serendib (former name for Sri Lanka)	Sri Lanka	7 00 N	81 00 E
Serrana Bank (shoal)	Colombia	14 25 N	80 16 W
Serranilla Bank (shoal)	Colombia	15 51 N	79 46 W
Settlement, The (capital)	Christmas Island	18 44 N	64 19 W
Severnaya Zemlya (island group; also Northland)	Russia	79 30 N	98 00 E
Shaba (region)	Democratic Republic of the Congo	8 00 S	27 00 E
Shag Island	Heard Island and McDonald Islands	53 00 S	72 30 E
Shag Rocks	South Georgia and the South Sandwich Islands	53 33 S	42 02 W
Shetland Islands	United Kingdom	60 30 N	1 30 W

Name	Entry in *The World Factbook*	Latitude (deg min)	Longitude (deg min)
Shikoku (island)	Japan	33 45 N	133 30 E
Shikotan (island)	Russia (de facto)	43 47 N	146 45 E
Shqiperia (local name for Albania)	Albania	41 00 N	20 00 E
Siam (former name for Thailand)	Thailand	15 00 N	100 00 E
Siberia (region)	Russia	60 00 N	100 00 E
Sibutu Passage	Pacific Ocean	4 50 N	119 35 E
Sicily (island)	Italy	37 30 N	14 00 E
Sicily, Strait of	Atlantic Ocean	37 20 N	11 20 E
Sidra, Gulf of	Atlantic Ocean	31 30 N	18 00 E
Sikkim (state)	India	27 50 N	88 30 E
Silesia (region)	Czech Republic, Germany, Poland	51 00 N	17 00 E
Sinai Peninsula	Egypt	29 30 N	34 00 E
Singapore (capital)	Singapore	1 17 N	103 51 E
Singapore Strait	Pacific Ocean	1 15 N	104 00 E
Sinkiang (autonomous region; also Xinjiang)	China	42 00 N	86 00 E
Sint Eustatius (island)	Netherlands Antilles	17 29 N	62 58 W
Sint Maarten (island; also Saint-Martin)	Netherlands Antilles	18 04 N	63 04 W
Sjaelland (island)	Denmark	55 30 N	12 00 E
Skagerrak (strait)	Atlantic Ocean	57 45 N	9 00 E
Skopje (capital)	Macedonia	41 59 N	21 26 E
Slavonia (region)	Croatia	45 27 N	18 00 E
Slovenija (local name for Slovenia)	Slovenia	46 00 N	15 00 E
Slovensko (local name for Slovakia)	Slovakia	48 40 N	19 30 E
Smyrna (region; former name for Izmir)	Turkey	38 25 N	27 10 E
Society Islands (Iles de la Societe)	French Polynesia	17 00 S	150 00 W
Socotra (island)	Yemen	12 30 N	54 00 E
Sofia (capital)	Bulgaria	42 41 N	23 19 E
Solomon Islands, northern	Papua New Guinea	6 00 S	155 00 E
Solomon Islands, southern	Solomon Islands	8 00 S	159 00 E
Solomon Sea	Pacific Ocean	8 00 S	153 00 E
Somaliland (region)	Somalia	9 30 N	46 00 E
Somers Islands (former name for Bermuda)	Bermuda	32 20 N	64 45 W
Songkhla (city)	Thailand	7 12 N	100 36 E
Sound, The (strait; also Oresund)	Atlantic Ocean	55 50 N	12 40 E
South Atlantic Ocean	Atlantic Ocean	30 00 S	15 00 W
South China Sea	Pacific Ocean	10 00 N	113 00 E
South Georgia (island)	South Georgia and the South Sandwich Islands	54 15 S	36 45 W
South Island	New Zealand	43 00 S	171 00 E

Name	Entry in *The World Factbook*	Latitude (deg min)	Longitude (deg min)
South Korea	South Korea	37 00 N	127 30 E
South Orkney Islands	Antarctica	61 00 S	45 00 W
South Ossetia (region)	Georgia	42 20 N	44 00 E
South Pacific Ocean	Pacific Ocean	30 00 S	130 00 W
South Sandwich Islands	South Georgia and the South Sandwich Islands	57 45 S	26 30 W
South Shetland Islands	Antarctica	62 00 S	59 00 W
South Tyrol (region)	Italy	46 30 N	10 30 E
South Vietnam (former name for the southern portion of Vietnam)	Vietnam	12 00 N	108 00 E
South Yemen (People's Democratic Republic of Yemen; now part of Yemen)	Yemen	14 00 N	48 00 E
South-West Africa (former name for Namibia)	Namibia	22 00 S	17 00 E
Southern Grenadines (island group)	Grenada	12 20 N	61 30 W
Southern Rhodesia (former name for Zimbabwe)	Zimbabwe	20 00 S	30 00 E
Soviet Union (former name of a large Eurasian empire, roughly coequal with the former Russian Empire)	Armenia, Azerbaijan, Belarus, Estonia, Georgia, Kazakhstan, Kyrgyzstan, Latvia, Lithuania, Moldova, Russia, Tajikistan, Turkmenistan, Ukraine, Uzbekistan		
Spanish Guinea (former name for Equatorial Guinea)	Equatorial Guinea	2 00 N	10 00 E
Spanish Morocco (former name for northern Morocco)	Morocco	32 00 N	7 00 W
Spanish North Africa (exclaves)	Spain (Ceuta, Islas Chafarinas, Melilla, Penon de Alhucemas, Penon de Velez de la Gomera)	35 15 N	4 00 W
Spanish Sahara (former name)	Western Sahara	24 30 N	13 00 W
Spanish West Africa (former name for Ifni and Spanish Sahara)	Morocco, Western Sahara	25 00 N	13 00 W
Spice Islands (Moluccas)	Indonesia	2 00 S	28 00 E
Spitsbergen (island)	Svalbard	78 00 N	20 00 E
Srbija-Crna Gora (local name for Serbia and Montenegro)	Serbia and Montenegro	44 00 N	21 00 E
St. John's (city)	Canada (Newfoundland)	47 34 N	52 43 W
Stanley (capital)	Falkland Islands (Islas Malvinas)	51 42 S	57 41 W
Stockholm (capital)	Sweden	59 20 N	18 03 E
Stuttgart (city)	Germany	48 46 N	9 11 E

Name	Entry in *The World Factbook*	Latitude (deg min)	Longitude (deg min)
Sucre (constitutional capital)	Bolivia	19 02 S	65 17 W
Suez Canal	Egypt	29 55 N	32 33 E
Suez, Gulf of	Indian Ocean	28 10 N	33 27 E
Suisse (local French name for Switzerland)	Switzerland	47 00 N	8 00 E
Sulawesi (island; Celebes)	Indonesia	2 00 S	121 00 E
Sulawesi Sea	Pacific Ocean	3 00 N	122 00 E
Sulu Archipelago (island group)	Philippines	6 00 N	121 00 E
Sulu Sea	Pacific Ocean	8 00 N	120 00 E
Sumatra (island)	Indonesia	0 00 N	102 00 E
Sumba (island)	Indonesia	10 00 S	120 00 E
Sumba Strait	Pacific Ocean	9 10 S	120 00 E
Sumbawa (island)	Indonesia	8 30 S	118 00 E
Sunda Islands (Soenda Isles)	Indonesia, Malaysia	2 00 S	110 00 E
Sunda Strait	Indian Ocean	6 00 S	105 45 E
Suomi (local name for Finland)	Finland	64 00 N	26 00 E
Surigao Strait	Pacific Ocean	10 15 N	125 23 E
Surinam (former name for Suriname)	Suriname	4 00 N	56 00 W
Suriyah (local name for Syria)	Syria	35 00 N	38 00 E
Surtsey (volcanic island)	Iceland	63 17 N	20 40 W
Suva (capital)	Fiji	18 08 S	178 25 E
Sverdlovsk (city; also Yekaterinburg)	Russia	56 50 N	60 39 E
Sverige (local name for Sweden)	Sweden	62 00 N	15 00 E
Svizzera (local Italian name for Switzerland)	Switzerland	47 00 N	8 00 E
Swains Island	American Samoa	11 03 S	171 15 W
Swan Islands	Honduras	17 25 S	83 56 W
T'bilisi (capital)	Georgia	41 43 N	44 49 E
Tadzhikistan (former name for Tajikistan)	Tajikistan	39 00 N	71 00 E
Tahiti (island)	French Polynesia	17 37 S	149 27 W
Taipei (capital)	Taiwan	25 03 N	121 30 E
Taiwan Strait	Pacific Ocean	24 00 N	119 00 E
Tallinn (capital)	Estonia	59 25 N	24 45 E
Tanganyika (former name for the mainland portion of Tanzania)	Tanzania	6 00 S	35 00 E
Tangier (city)	Morocco	35 48 N	5 45 W
Tannu-Tuva (region)	Russia	51 25 N	94 45 E
Tarawa (island)	Kiribati	1 25 N	173 00 E
Tartary, Gulf of	Pacific Ocean	50 00 N	141 00 E
Tashkent (capital)	Uzbekistan	41 20 N	69 18 E
Tasman Sea	Pacific Ocean	4 30 S	168 00 E
Tasmania (island)	Australia	43 00 S	147 00 E

Name	Entry in *The World Factbook*	Latitude (deg min)	Longitude (deg min)
Tatar Strait	Pacific Ocean	50 00 N	141 00 E
Taymyr Peninsula (Poluostrov Taymyr)	Russia	76 00 N	104 00 E
Tchad (local name for Chad)	Chad	15 00 N	19 00 E
Tegucigalpa (capital)	Honduras	14 06 N	87 13 W
Tehran (capital)	Iran	35 40 N	51 26 E
Tel Aviv (capital, de facto)	Israel	32 05 N	34 48 E
Teluk Bone (gulf)	Pacific Ocean	4 00 S	120 45 E
Teluk Tomini (gulf)	Pacific Ocean	0 30 S	121 00 E
Terre Adelie (claimed by France; also Adelie Land)	Antarctica	66 30 S	139 00 E
Terres Australes et Antarctiques Francaises (local name for the French Southern and Antarctic Lands)	French Southern and Antarctic Lands	43 00 S	67 00 E
Thailand, Gulf of	Pacific Ocean	10 00 N	101 00 E
The Former Yugoslav Republic of Macedonia	Macedonia	41 50 N	22 00 E
Thimphu (capital)	Bhutan	27 28 N	89 39 E
Thuringia (region)	Germany	51 00 N	11 00 E
Thurston Island	Antarctica	72 20 S	99 00 W
Tiberias, Lake	Israel	32 48 N	35 35 E
Tibet (autonomous region; also Xizang)	China	32 00 N	90 00 E
Tibilisi (see T'bilisi)	Georgia	41 43 N	44 49 E
Tien Shan (mountains)	China, Kyrgyzstan	42 00 N	80 00 E
Tierra del Fuego (island, island group)	Argentina, Chile	54 00 S	69 00 W
Timor (island)	East Timor, Indonesia	9 00 S	125 00 E
Timor Sea	Pacific Ocean	11 00 S	128 00 E
Timor-Leste, Timor Lorosa'e (local names for East Timor)	East Timor	9 00 N	126 00 E
Tinian (island)	Northern Mariana Islands	15 00 N	145 38 E
Tiran, Strait of	Indian Ocean	28 00 N	34 27 E
Tirana, Tirane (capital)	Albania	41 20 N	19 50 E
Tirol, Tyrol (region)	Austria, Italy	47 00 N	11 00 E
Tobago (island)	Trinidad and Tobago	11 15 N	60 40 W
Tokyo (capital)	Japan	35 42 N	139 46 E
Tonkin, Gulf of	Pacific Ocean	20 00 N	108 00 E
Torres Strait	Pacific Ocean	10 25 S	142 10 E
Torshavn (capital)	Faroe Islands	62 01 N	6 46 W
Toshkent (see Tashkent)	Uzbekistan	41 20 N	69 18 E
Transcarpathia (region; alternate name for Carpatho-Ukraine)	Ukraine	48 22 N	23 32 E
Transjordan (former name for Jordan)	Jordan	31 00 N	36 00 E
Transkei (enclave)	South Africa	32 15 S	28 15 E

Name	Entry in *The World Factbook*	Latitude (deg min)	Longitude (deg min)
Transvaal (region; former name for northeastern South Africa)	South Africa	25 10 S	29 25 E
Transylvania (region)	Romania	46 30 N	24 00 E
Trindade, Ilha de (island)	Brazil	20 31 S	29 20 W
Trinidad (island)	Trinidad and Tobago	10 22 N	61 15 W
Tripoli (capital)	Libya	32 54 N	13 11 E
Tripoli (city)	Lebanon	34 26 N	35 51 E
Tripolitania (region)	Libya	31 00 N	14 00 E
Tristan da Cunha Group (island group)	Saint Helena	37 15 S	12 30 W
Trobriand Islands	Papua New Guinea	8 38 S	151 04 E
Trucial Coast (former name for the United Arab Emirates)	United Arab Emirates	24 00 N	54 00 E
Trucial Oman (former name for the United Arab Emirates)	United Arab Emirates	24 00 N	54 00 E
Trucial States (former name for the United Arab Emirates)	United Arab Emirates	24 00 N	54 00 E
Truk Islands (former name for the Chuuk Islands)	Federated States of Micronesia	7 25 N	151 47 E
Tsugaru Strait	Pacific Ocean	41 35 N	141 00 E
Tuamotu Islands (Iles Tuamotu)	French Polynesia	19 00 S	142 00 W
Tubuai Islands (Iles Tubuai)	French Polynesia	23 00 S	150 00 W
Tunb al Kubra (island)	Iran	26 14 N	55 19 E
Tunb as Sughra (island)	Iran	26 14 N	55 09 E
Tunis (capital)	Tunisia	36 48 N	10 11 E
Turin (city)	Italy	45 04 N	7 40 E
Turkish Straits (see Bosporus and Dardenelles)	Atlantic Ocean	40 40 N	28 00 E
Turkiye (local name for Turkey)	Turkey	39 00 N	35 00 E
Turkmenia, Turkmeniya (former name for Turkmenistan)	Turkmenistan	40 00 N	60 00 E
Turks Island Passage	Atlantic Ocean	21 40 N	71 00 W
Tuscany (region)	Italy	43 25 N	11 00 E
Tutuila (island)	American Samoa	14 18 S	170 42 W
Tyrrhenian Sea	Atlantic Ocean	40 00 N	12 00 E
Ubangi-Shari (former name for the Central African Republic	Central African Republic	6 38 N	20 33 E
Ukrayina (local name for Ukraine)	Ukraine	49 00 N	32 00 E
Ulaanbaatar (capital)	Mongolia	47 55 N	106 53 E
Ullung-do (island)	South Korea	37 29 N	130 52 E
Ulster (region)	Ireland, United Kingdom	54 35 N	7 00 W
Uman (local name for Oman)	Oman	21 00 N	57 00 E
Unimak Pass (strait)	Pacific Ocean	54 20 N	164 50 W

Name	Entry in *The World Factbook*	Latitude (deg min)	Longitude (deg min)
Union of Soviet Socialist Republics or USSR (former name of a large Eurasian empire, roughly coequal with the former Russian Empire)	Armenia, Azerbaijan, Belarus, Estonia, Georgia, Kazakhstan, Kyrgyzstan, Latvia, Lithuania, Moldova, Russia, Tajikistan, Turkmenistan, Ukraine, Uzbekistan		
United Arab Republic or UAR (former name for a federation between Egypt and Syria)	Egypt, Syria		
Upper Volta (former name for Burkina Faso)	Burkina Faso	13 00 N	2 00 W
Ural Mountains	Kazakhstan, Russia	60 00 N	60 00 E
Urdunn (local name for Jordan)	Jordan	31 00 N	36 00 E
Urundi (former name for Burundi)	Burundi	3 30 S	30 00 E
Ussuri River	China, Russia	48 28 N	135 02 E
Vaduz (capital)	Liechtenstein	47 09 N	9 31 E
Vakhan (Wakhan Corridor)	Afghanistan	37 00 N	73 00 E
Valletta (capital)	Malta	35 54 N	14 31 E
Valley, The (capital)	Anguilla	18 13 N	63 04 W
Van Diemen Strait (Osumi Strait)	Pacific Ocean	31 00 N	131 00 E
Vancouver Island	Canada	49 45 N	126 00 W
Vatican City (capital)	Holy See	41 54 N	12 27 E
Velez de la Gomera, Penon de (island)	Spain	35 11 N	4 18 W
Venda (enclave)	South Africa	23 00 S	31 00 E
Verde Island Passage	Pacific Ocean	13 34 N	120 51 E
Victoria (capital)	Seychelles	4 38 S	55 27 E
Victoria (island)	Canada	71 00 N	110 00 W
Victoria Land (region)	Antarctica	72 00 S	155 00 E
Vienna (capital)	Austria	48 12 N	16 22 E
Vientiane (capital)	Laos	17 58 N	102 36 E
Vilnius (capital)	Lithuania	54 41 N	25 19 E
Viti Levu (island)	Fiji	18 00 S	178 00 E
Vladivostok (city)	Russia	43 10 N	131 56 E
Vojvodina (region)	Serbia and Montenegro	45 35 N	20 00 E
Volcano Islands	Japan	25 00 N	141 00 E
Vostok Island	Kiribati	10 06 S	152 23 W
Wake Atoll	Wake Island	19 17 N	166 39 E
Wakhan Corridor (see Vakhan)	Afghanistan	37 00 N	73 00 E
Walachia (region)	Romania	44 45 N	26 05 E
Wales (region)	United Kingdom	52 30 N	3 30 W

Name	Entry in *The World Factbook*	Latitude (deg min)	Longitude (deg min)
Wallis Islands	Wallis and Futuna	13 17 S	176 10 W
Walvis Bay (city; former exclave)	Namibia	22 59 S	14 31 E
Warsaw (capital)	Poland	52 15 N	21 00 E
Washington, DC (capital)	United States	38 53 N	77 02 W
Weddell Sea	Southern Ocean	72 00 S	45 00 W
Wellington (capital)	New Zealand	41 28 S	174 51 E
West Frisian Islands	Netherlands	53 26 N	5 30 E
West Germany (Federal Republic of Germany; former name for western portion of Germany)	Germany	53 22 N	5 20 E
West Island (capital)	Cocos (Keeling) Islands	12 10 S	96 55 E
West Korea Strait (Western Channel)	Pacific Ocean	34 40 N	129 00 E
West Pakistan (former name for present-day Pakistan)	Pakistan	30 00 N	70 00 E
West Siberian Plain	Russia	60 00 N	75 00 E
Western Channel (West Korea Strait)	Pacific Ocean	34 40 N	129 00 E
Western Samoa (former name for Samoa)	Samoa	13 35 S	172 20 W
Wetar Strait	Pacific Ocean	8 20 S	126 30 E
White Sea	Arctic Ocean	65 30 N	38 00 E
Wilkes Land (region)	Antarctica	71 00 S	120 00 E
Willemstad (capital)	Netherlands Antilles	12 06 N	68 56 W
Windhoek (capital)	Namibia	22 34 S	17 06 E
Windward Passage	Atlantic Ocean	20 00 N	73 50 W
Wrangel Island (Ostrov Vrangelya)	Russia	71 14 N	179 36 W
Xianggang (local name for Hong Kong)	Hong Kong	22 15 N	114 10 E
Y'israel (local name for Israel)	Israel	31 30 N	34 45 E
Yaitopya (local name for Ethiopia)	Ethiopia	8 00 N	38 00 E
Yalu River	China, North Korea	39 55 N	124 20 E
Yamoussoukro (capital)	Cote d'Ivoire	6 49 N	5 17 W
Yangon (see Rangoon)	Burma	16 47 N	96 10 E
Yaounde (capital)	Cameroon	3 52 N	11 31 E
Yap Islands	Federated States of Micronesia	9 30 N	138 00 E
Yaren (governmental center)	Nauru	0 32 S	166 55 E
Yekaterinburg (city)	Russia	56 50 N	60 39 E
Yellow Sea	Pacific Ocean	36 00 N	123 00 E
Yemen Arab Republic (also Yemen (Sanaa); former name for northern portion of Yemen)	Yemen	15 00 N	44 00 E
Yemen, People's Democratic Republic of (also Yemen (Aden); former name for southern portion of Yemen)	Yemen	14 00 N	46 00 E

Name	Entry in *The World Factbook*	Latitude (deg min)	Longitude (deg min)
Yerevan (capital)	Armenia	40 11 N	44 30 E
Youth, Isle of (Isla de la Juventud)	Cuba	21 40 N	82 50 W
Yucatan Channel	Atlantic Ocean	21 45 N	85 45 W
Yucatan Peninsula	Mexico	19 30 N	89 00 W
Yugoslavia (former name for Serbia and Montenegro)	Serbia and Montenegro	43 00 N	21 00 E
Yugoslavia, Kingdom of (former name for a Balkan federation)	Bosnia and Herzegovina, Croatia, Macedonia, Serbia and Montenegro, Slovenia	43 00 N	19 00 E
Yugoslavia, Socialist Federal Republic of (former name for a Balkan federation)	Bosnia and Herzegovina, Croatia, Macedonia, Serbia and Montenegro, Slovenia	43 00 N	19 00 E
Zagreb (capital)	Croatia	45 48 N	15 58 E
Zaire (former name for the Democratic Republic of the Congo)	Democratic Republic of the Congo	15 00 S	30 00 E
Zakhalinskiy Zaliv (bay)	Pacific Ocean	54 00 N	142 00 E
Zaliv Shelikhova (bay)	Pacific Ocean	60 00 N	157 30 E
Zambezia (region)	Mozambique	16 00 S	37 00 E
Zanzibar (island)	Tanzania	6 10 S	39 11 E
Zhong Guo, Zhonghua (local name for China)	China	35 00 N	105 00 E
Zion, Mount (locale in Jerusalem)	Israel, West Bank	31 46 N	35 14 E
Zurich (city)	Switzerland	47 23 N	8 32 E

AFRICA

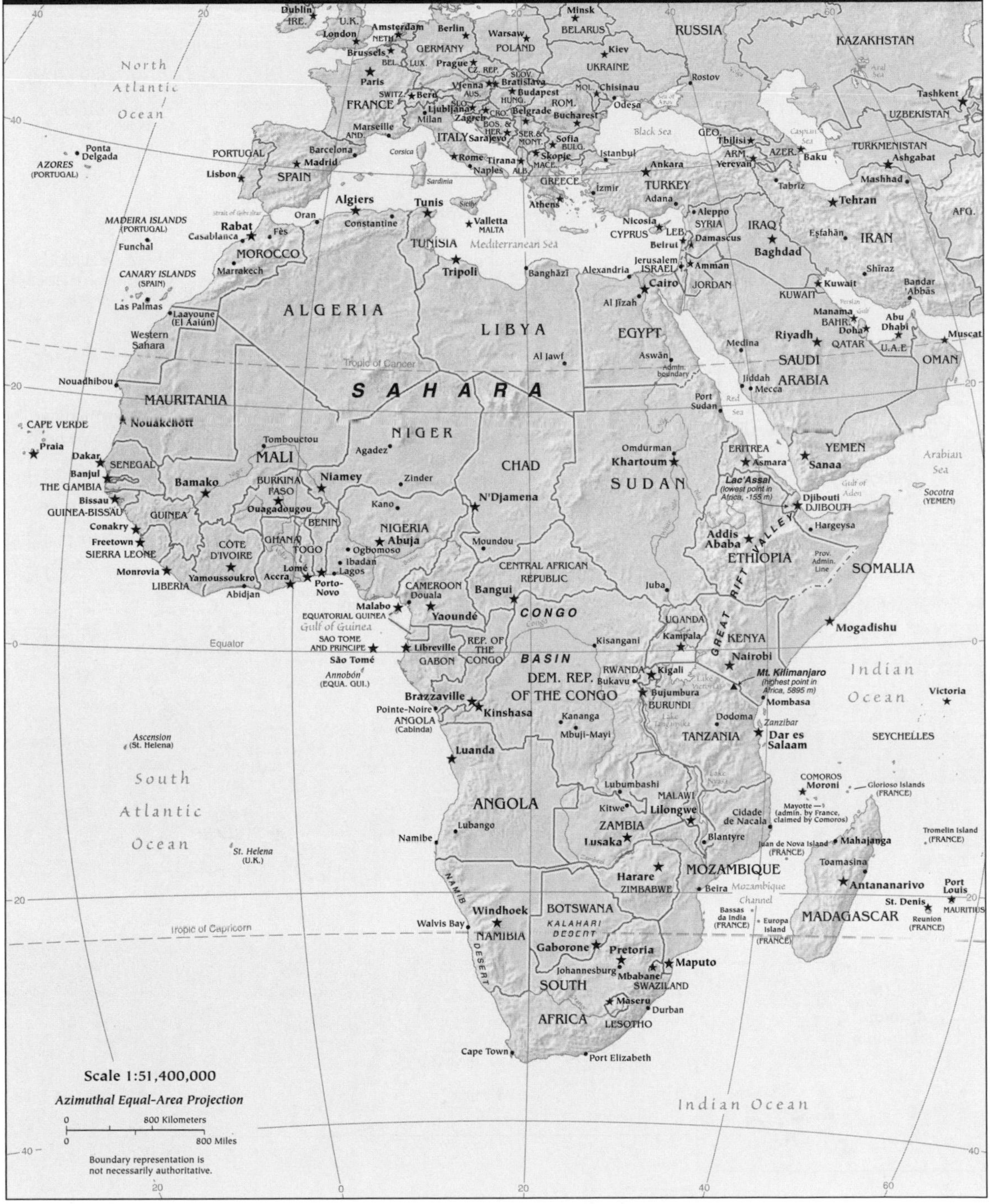
North Atlantic Ocean
AZORES (PORTUGAL)
Ponta Delgada
MADEIRA ISLANDS (PORTUGAL)
Funchal
CANARY ISLANDS (SPAIN)
Las Palmas
Dublin
IRE.
U.K.
London
Amsterdam
NETH.
Brussels
BEL.
LUX.
Paris
FRANCE
Berlin
GERMANY
Prague
CZ. REP.
Warsaw
POLAND
Minsk
BELARUS
RUSSIA
KAZAKHSTAN
Kiev
UKRAINE
SLOV.
Bratislava
Vienna
AUS.
Budapest
HUNG.
SWITZ.
Bern
Ljubljana
SLO.
Zagreb
CRO.
Belgrade
BOS. & HER.
Sarajevo
SER.& MONT.
Milan
Marseille
AND.
ITALY
Corsica
Sardinia
Sicily
Rome
Naples
Tirana
ALB.
Skopje
MACE.
Sofia
BULG.
ROM.
Bucharest
MOL.
Chisinau
Odesa
Black Sea
Rostov
Aral Sea
Tashkent
UZBEKISTAN
TURKMENISTAN
Ashgabat
GEO.
Tbilisi
ARM.
Yerevan
AZER.
Baku
Caspian Sea
Tabriz
Mashhad
Tehran
IRAN
AFG.
Esfahan
Shiraz
Bandar 'Abbas
PORTUGAL
Lisbon
Madrid
SPAIN
Barcelona
Istanbul
Ankara
TURKEY
Izmir
Adana
GREECE
Athens
Aleppo
SYRIA
Nicosia
CYPRUS
LEB.
Beirut
Damascus
IRAQ
Baghdad
Jerusalem
ISRAEL
Amman
JORDAN
Kuwait
KUWAIT
Manama
BAHR.
Doha
QATAR
Abu Dhabi
U.A.E.
Muscat
OMAN
Riyadh
SAUDI ARABIA
Medina
Jiddah
Mecca
YEMEN
Sanaa
Arabian Sea
Gulf of Aden
Socotra (YEMEN)
Algiers
Oran
Constantine
Tunis
TUNISIA
Valletta
MALTA
Mediterranean Sea
Rabat
Casablanca
Fès
MOROCCO
Marrakech
Tripoli
Banghazi
Alexandria
Cairo
Al Jīzah
EGYPT
Aswān
Admin. boundary
Red Sea
Laayoune (El Aaiún)
Western Sahara
ALGERIA
LIBYA
Al Jawf
Tropic of Cancer
SAHARA
Nouadhibou
MAURITANIA
Nouakchott
CAPE VERDE
Praia
Dakar
SENEGAL
Banjul
THE GAMBIA
Bissau
GUINEA-BISSAU
GUINEA
Conakry
Freetown
SIERRA LEONE
Monrovia
LIBERIA
Tombouctou
MALI
Bamako
NIGER
Agadez
Niamey
Zinder
BURKINA FASO
Ouagadougou
CÔTE D'IVOIRE
Yamoussoukro
Abidjan
GHANA
Accra
TOGO
Lomé
BENIN
Porto-Novo
Kano
NIGERIA
Abuja
Ogbomoso
Ibadan
Lagos
CHAD
N'Djamena
Moundou
Port Sudan
Omdurman
Khartoum
SUDAN
ERITREA
Asmara
Lac'Assal (lowest point in Africa, -155 m)
Djibouti
DJIBOUTI
Hargeysa
Addis Ababa
ETHIOPIA
Prov. Admin. Line
SOMALIA
GREAT RIFT VALLEY
CENTRAL AFRICAN REPUBLIC
Bangui
CAMEROON
Douala
Yaoundé
Malabo
EQUATORIAL GUINEA
Gulf of Guinea
SAO TOME AND PRINCIPE
São Tomé
Annobón (EQUA. GUI.)
Libreville
GABON
REP. OF THE CONGO
Equator
CONGO BASIN
Juba
UGANDA
Kampala
KENYA
Nairobi
Mogadishu
Kisangani
DEM. REP. OF THE CONGO
RWANDA
Kigali
Bukavu
Bujumbura
BURUNDI
Mt. Kilimanjaro (highest point in Africa, 5895 m)
Mombasa
Dodoma
Zanzibar
TANZANIA
Dar es Salaam
Indian Ocean
Victoria
SEYCHELLES
Brazzaville
Kinshasa
Pointe-Noire
ANGOLA (Cabinda)
Kananga
Mbuji-Mayi
Luanda
Ascension (St. Helena)
South Atlantic Ocean
St. Helena (U.K.)
ANGOLA
Lubango
Namibe
Lubumbashi
MALAWI
Kitwe
Lilongwe
ZAMBIA
Lusaka
Cidade de Nacala
COMOROS
Moroni
Glorioso Islands (FRANCE)
Mayotte (admin. by France, claimed by Comoros)
Juan de Nova Island (FRANCE)
Mahajanga
Tromelin Island (FRANCE)
Blantyre
Harare
ZIMBABWE
MOZAMBIQUE
Beira
Mozambique Channel
Toamasina
Antananarivo
MADAGASCAR
Port Louis
MAURITIUS
St. Denis
Reunion (FRANCE)
Bassas da India (FRANCE)
Europa Island (FRANCE)
NAMIB DESERT
Windhoek
NAMIBIA
Walvis Bay
BOTSWANA
KALAHARI DESERT
Gaborone
Pretoria
Johannesburg
Mbabane
Maputo
SWAZILAND
SOUTH AFRICA
Maseru
LESOTHO
Durban
Tropic of Capricorn
Cape Town
Port Elizabeth
Indian Ocean
Scale 1:51,400,000
Azimuthal Equal-Area Projection
0 800 Kilometers
0 800 Miles
Boundary representation is not necessarily authoritative.

ANTARCTIC REGION

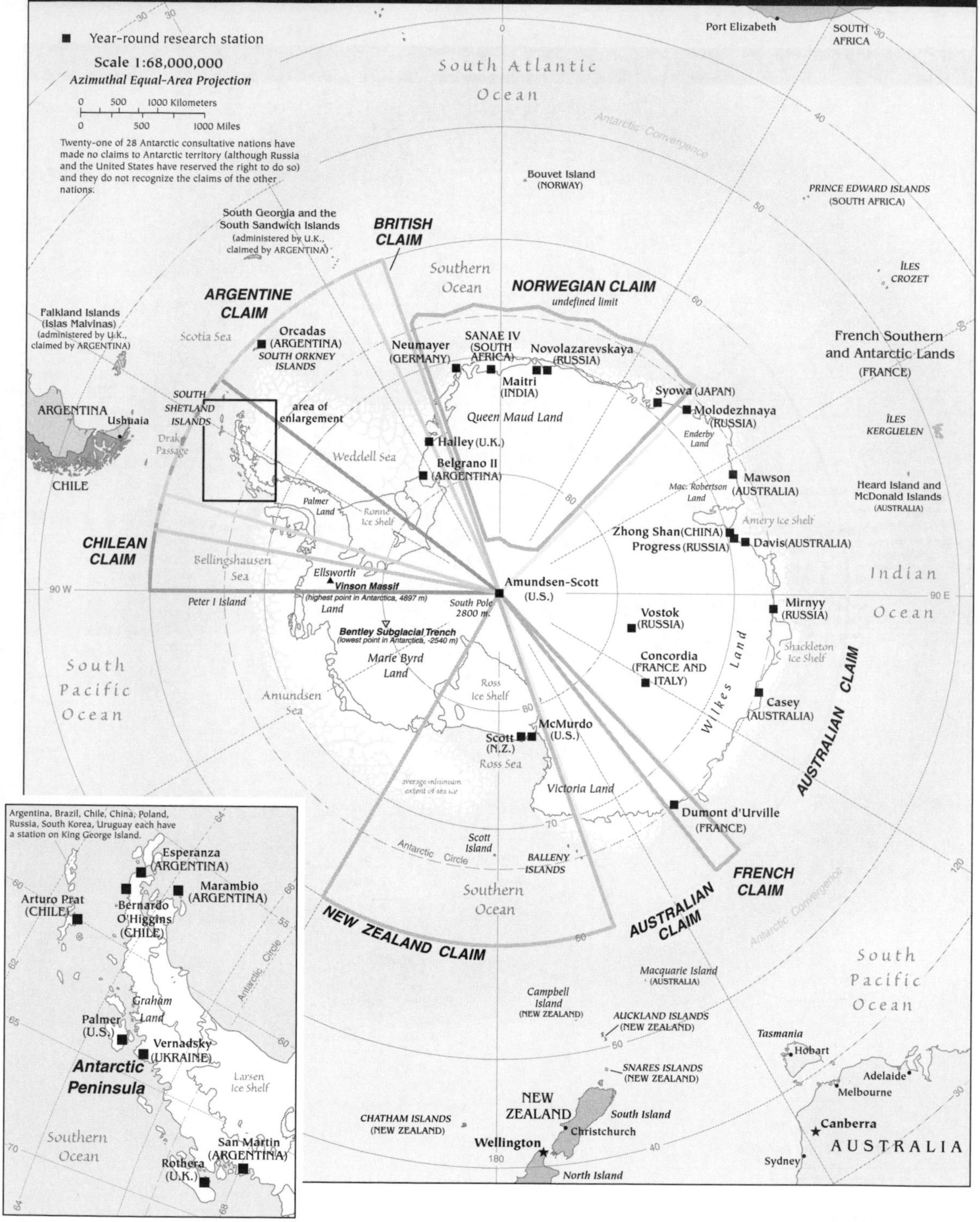
Year-round research station
Scale 1:68,000,000
Azimuthal Equal-Area Projection
0 500 1000 Kilometers
0 500 1000 Miles
Twenty-one of 28 Antarctic consultative nations have made no claims to Antarctic territory (although Russia and the United States have reserved the right to do so) and they do not recognize the claims of the other nations.
South Atlantic Ocean
Port Elizabeth
SOUTH AFRICA
Antarctic Convergence
Bouvet Island (NORWAY)
PRINCE EDWARD ISLANDS (SOUTH AFRICA)
ÎLES CROZET
French Southern and Antarctic Lands (FRANCE)
ÎLES KERGUELEN
Heard Island and McDonald Islands (AUSTRALIA)
South Georgia and the South Sandwich Islands (administered by U.K., claimed by ARGENTINA)
BRITISH CLAIM
Southern Ocean
NORWEGIAN CLAIM
undefined limit
ARGENTINE CLAIM
Falkland Islands (Islas Malvinas) (administered by U.K., claimed by ARGENTINA)
Scotia Sea
Orcadas (ARGENTINA)
SOUTH ORKNEY ISLANDS
Neumayer (GERMANY)
SANAE IV (SOUTH AFRICA)
Novolazarevskaya (RUSSIA)
Maitri (INDIA)
Syowa (JAPAN)
Molodezhnaya (RUSSIA)
Enderby Land
Queen Maud Land
ARGENTINA
Ushuaia
SOUTH SHETLAND ISLANDS
area of enlargement
Drake Passage
CHILE
Halley (U.K.)
Weddell Sea
Belgrano II (ARGENTINA)
Mawson (AUSTRALIA)
Mac. Robertson Land
Palmer Land
Ronne Ice Shelf
Amery Ice Shelf
Zhong Shan (CHINA)
Progress (RUSSIA)
Davis (AUSTRALIA)
CHILEAN CLAIM
Bellingshausen Sea
Ellsworth Land
Vinson Massif (highest point in Antarctica, 4897 m)
Amundsen-Scott (U.S.)
South Pole 2800 m.
90 W
90 E
Peter I Island
Indian Ocean
Mirnyy (RUSSIA)
Vostok (RUSSIA)
Bentley Subglacial Trench (lowest point in Antarctica, -2540 m)
Shackleton Ice Shelf
South Pacific Ocean
Marie Byrd Land
Concordia (FRANCE AND ITALY)
Wilkes Land
Ross Ice Shelf
Amundsen Sea
Casey (AUSTRALIA)
AUSTRALIAN CLAIM
McMurdo (U.S.)
Scott (N.Z.)
Ross Sea
average minimum extent of sea ice
Victoria Land
Dumont d'Urville (FRANCE)
Scott Island
BALLENY ISLANDS
Antarctic Circle
FRENCH CLAIM
AUSTRALIAN CLAIM
Southern Ocean
NEW ZEALAND CLAIM
Macquarie Island (AUSTRALIA)
Campbell Island (NEW ZEALAND)
AUCKLAND ISLANDS (NEW ZEALAND)
SNARES ISLANDS (NEW ZEALAND)
Tasmania
Hobart
Adelaide
Melbourne
South Pacific Ocean
CHATHAM ISLANDS (NEW ZEALAND)
NEW ZEALAND
South Island
Christchurch
Wellington
North Island
180
Canberra
AUSTRALIA
Sydney
Argentina, Brazil, Chile, China, Poland, Russia, South Korea, Uruguay each have a station on King George Island.
Esperanza (ARGENTINA)
Marambio (ARGENTINA)
Arturo Prat (CHILE)
Bernardo O'Higgins (CHILE)
Antarctic Circle
Graham Land
Palmer (U.S.)
Vernadsky (UKRAINE)
Antarctic Peninsula
Larsen Ice Shelf
Southern Ocean
San Martin (ARGENTINA)
Rothera (U.K.)

ARCTIC REGION

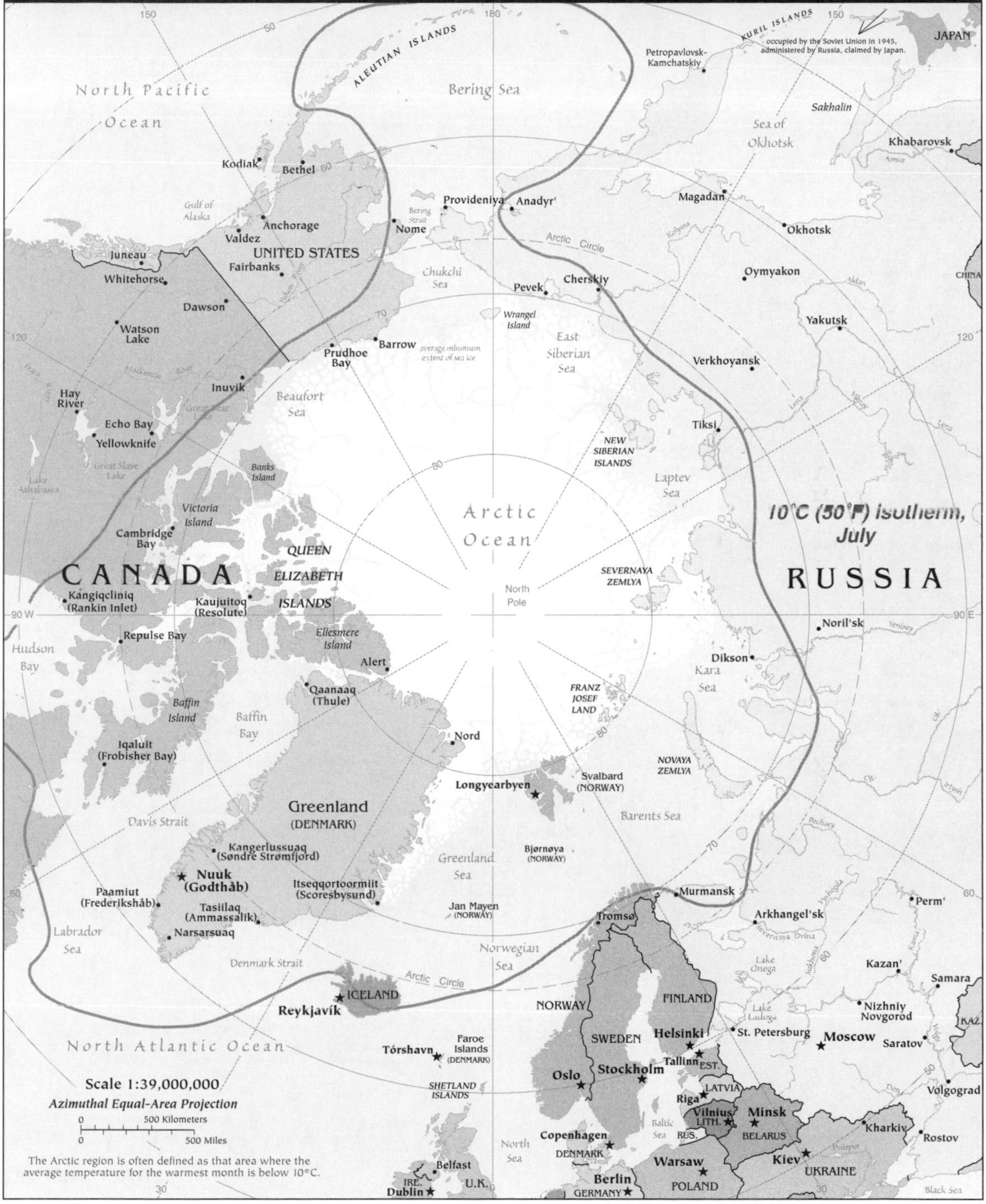

ASIA

Glasgow
U.K.
Norwegian Sea
Svalbard (NORWAY)
FRANZ JOSEF LAND
Arctic Ocean
Wrangel Island
U.S.
Provideniya
North Sea
NORWAY
Oslo
DEN.
Copenhagen
SWEDEN
Stockholm
FINLAND
Helsinki
Tallinn
EST.
Riga
LAT.
RUS.
POL.
LITH.
Vilnius
Warsaw
Minsk
BELA.
Kiev
UKR.
Kharkiv
Donets'k
Rostov
Barents Sea
NOVAYA ZEMLYA
Murmansk
St. Petersburg
Arkhangel'sk
Lake Ladoga
Lake Onega
Kara Sea
SEVERNAYA ZEMLYA
NEW SIBERIAN ISLANDS
East Siberian Sea
Laptev Sea
Anadyr'
Cherskiy
KOLYMSKOYE NAGOR'YE
Bering Sea
Tiksi
KHREBET CHERSKOGO
VERKHOYANSK KHREBET
Magadan
Petropavlovsk-Kamchatskiy
Noril'sk
Arctic Circle
URAL MOUNTAINS
SIBERIA
RUSSIA
Moscow
Nizhniy Novgorod
Voronezh
Kazan'
Perm'
Yekaterinburg
Saratov
Samara
Ufa
Chelyabinsk
Volgograd
Yakutsk
KHREBET DZHUGDZHUR
Sea of Okhotsk
KURIL ISLANDS
Occupied by the Soviet Union in 1945, administered by Russia, claimed by Japan.
Sakhalin
Black Sea
CAUCASUS MTS.
GEORGIA
Tbilisi
ARMENIA
Yerevan
AZERBAIJAN
Baku
Caspian Sea
Atyraū (Atyrau)
Aral Sea
Omsk
Krasnoyarsk
Novosibirsk
Astana
Qaraghandy (Karaganda)
KAZAKHSTAN
Lake Balkhash
Irkutsk
YABLONOVYY KHREBET
Khabarovsk
SIKHOTE-ALIN
Sapporo
Harbin
DA HINGGAN LING
MANCHURIAN PLAIN
Changchun
Vladivostok
Ulaanbaatar
MONGOLIA
ALTAY MTS.
GOBI DESERT
Shenyang
Sea of Japan
JAPAN
NORTH KOREA
Pyongyang
Tokyo
Yokohama
Nagoya
Osaka
Tabriz
QIZILQUM
UZBEKISTAN
TURKMENISTAN
Ashgabat
Tashkent
Bishkek
Almaty
KYRGYZSTAN
TIEN SHAN
Ürümqi
GARAGUM
Tehran
Mashhad
Dushanbe
TAJIKISTAN
Kashi
TAKLA MAKAN DESERT
Baotou
Beijing
Dalian
Seoul
SOUTH KOREA
Demarcation Line
Tianjin
Jinan
Taiyuan
Yellow Sea
Qingdao
Pusan
Fukuoka
Esfahān
ZAGROS MTS.
IRAN
Shīrāz
Kabul
AFGHANISTAN
1972 Line of Control
KUNLUN MOUNTAINS
Indian claim
Lanzhou
Zhengzhou
Xi'an
Nanjing
Shanghai
Bandar 'Abbās
Kandahār
Quetta
Islamabad
Line of Actual Control
Lahore
QING ZANG GAOYUAN
CHINA
Wuhan
Hangzhou
East China Sea
RYUKYU ISLANDS (JAPAN)
Okinawa
Persian Gulf
Abu Dhabi
U.A.E.
PAKISTAN
New Delhi
HIMALAYAS
Mt. Everest (highest point in the world, 8850 m)
Lhasa
HENGDUAN
Chengdu
Changsha
Chongqing
Nanchang
Muscat
SAUDI ARABIA
OMAN
Karāchi
Jaipur
NEPAL
Lucknow
Kānpur
Kathmandu
BHUTAN
Thimphu
Guiyang
Taipei
Tropic of Cancer
Taiwan
Ahmadābād
INDIA
Kunming
BANGLADESH
Dhaka
Guangzhou
Hong Kong S.A.R.
Macau S.A.R.
Nanning
Philippine Sea
Surat
Kolkata (Calcutta)
Nāgpur
Chittagong
Mandalay
Hanoi
Haiphong
Mumbai (Bombay)
Pune
DECCAN
Hyderābād
WESTERN GHATS
EASTERN GHATS
BURMA
LAOS
Vientiane
Hainan Dao
Luzon
Manila
Arabian Sea
Rangoon
THAILAND
Hue
South China Sea
PHILIPPINES
Bangalore
Chennai (Madras)
Bay of Bengal
Bangkok
VIETNAM
Cebu
LAKSHADWEEP (INDIA)
CAMBODIA
SPRATLY ISLANDS
Mindanao
Davao
Cochin
ANDAMAN ISLANDS (INDIA)
Andaman Sea
Phnom Penh
Ho Chi Minh City
Sulu Sea
Jaffna
SRI LANKA
Gulf of Thailand
Laccadive Sea
Colombo
NICOBAR ISLANDS (INDIA)
Bandar Seri Begawan
BRUNEI
Celebes Sea
MALDIVES
Male
MALAYSIA
Kuala Lumpur
Medan
Singapore
SINGAPORE
Borneo
Pontianak
Celebes
Equator
Banda Sea
Sumatra
Makassar
Scale 1:48,000,000
Azimuthal Equal-Area Projection
800 Kilometers
800 Miles
Palembang
INDONESIA
Java Sea
Dili
EAST TIMOR
Timor
Jakarta
Surabaya
Semarang
Bandung
Java
Timor Sea
Indian Ocean
Boundary representation is not necessarily authoritative.
AUSTRALIA

CENTRAL AMERICA AND THE CARIBBEAN

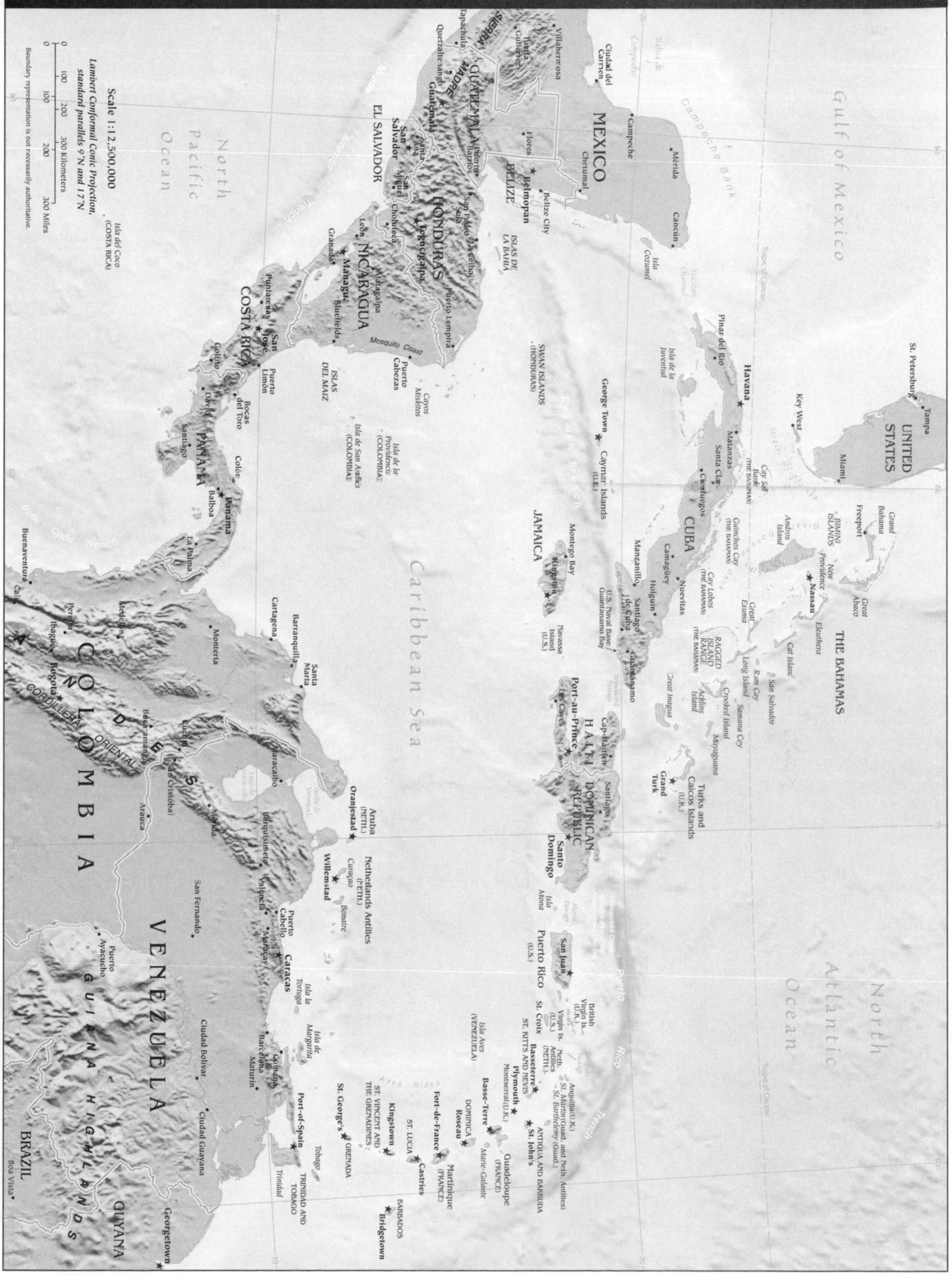

EUROPE

Greenland (DENMARK)
Jan Mayen (NORWAY)
Greenland Sea
Denmark Strait
Norwegian Sea
Arctic Circle
Barents Sea
Hammerfest
Tromsø
Murmansk
Kiruna
White Sea
Arkhangel'sk
Reykjavík
ICELAND
NORWAY
Luleå
Oulu
Umeå
FINLAND
Lake Onega
Trondheim
SWEDEN
Gulf of Bothnia
Tampere
Lake Ladoga
Tórshavn
Faroe Islands (DENMARK)
SHETLAND ISLANDS
Turku
Helsinki
Gävle
Gulf of Finland
St. Petersburg
Bergen
Oslo
ALAND ISLANDS
Tallinn
ESTONIA
RUSSIA
Rockall (U.K.)
ORKNEY ISLANDS
Stockholm
HEBRIDES
Stavanger
Moscow
North Atlantic Ocean
Aberdeen
Göteborg
Gotland
Riga
LATVIA
Skagerrak
Kattegat
Baltic Sea
Glasgow
Edinburgh
North Sea
Öland
LITHUANIA
Vitsyebsk
Smolensk
Vilnius
Mahilyow
DENMARK
Malmö
Minsk
Belfast
UNITED
Copenhagen
Kaliningrad
RUSSIA
Isle of Man (U.K.)
Bornholm
BELARUS
Dublin
Irish Sea
Leeds
Gdańsk
Hrodna
Manchester
Homyel'
IRELAND
Liverpool
Hamburg
KINGDOM
Warsaw
Brest
NETH.
Birmingham
Amsterdam
Bremen
Berlin
Poznań
POLAND
Kiev
Cardiff
Rotterdam
Łódź
Rivne
London
Essen
Leipzig
Wroclaw
Celtic Sea
Cologne
Brussels
English Channel
Lille
BEL.
Bonn
GERMANY
Prague
L'viv
UKRAINE
Frankfurt am Main
Kraków
Guernsey (U.K.)
Jersey (U.K.)
CZECH REPUBLIC
Chernivtsi
LUX.
Luxembourg
Brno
SLOVAKIA
CARPATHIAN MTS.
Mykolayiv
Paris
Stuttgart
Bratislava
Chisinau
Strasbourg
Munich
Vienna
Budapest
Iaşi
Odesa
Nantes
Cluj-Napoca
MOLDOVA
LIECH.
AUSTRIA
Zürich
Vaduz
HUNGARY
Bern
SWITZ.
ROMANIA
Bay of Biscay
FRANCE
ALPS
Geneva
Ljubljana
Constanţa
SLOVENIA
Zagreb
Bucharest
MASSIF CENTRAL
Lyon
Milan
Venice
Black Sea
Bordeaux
Turin
BOSNIA AND HERZEGOVINA
Belgrade
Varna
Genoa
SAN MARINO
CROATIA
DINARIC ALPS
Bilbao
Toulouse
MONACO
Sarajevo
SERBIA AND MONTENEGRO
BULGARIA
Andorra la Vella
Marseille
Ligurian Sea
Florence
Sofia
Porto
PYRENEES
Adriatic Sea
Istanbul
Zaragoza
ANDORRA
APENNINES
ITALY
Skopje
Corsica
MACEDONIA
Rome
Bursa
PORTUGAL
Madrid
Barcelona
VATICAN CITY
Tirana
Thessaloníki
ALB.
TURKEY
Lisbon
Naples
SPAIN
Valencia
Balearic Sea
Sardinia
Tyrrhenian Sea
GREECE
Izmir
Aegean Sea
BALEARIC ISLANDS
Athens
Sevilla
Cagliari
Ionian Sea
Palermo
Mediterranean Sea
Gibraltar (U.K.)
Málaga
Sicily
Rhodes
Strait of Gibraltar
Ceuta (SPAIN)
Alborán Sea
Algiers
Tunis
Crete
Melilla (SPAIN)
Oran
Rabat
Valletta
MALTA
Casablanca
TUNISIA
ALGERIA
MOROCCO
Scale 1: 19,500,000
Lambert Conformal Conic Projection, standard parallels 40°N and 56°N
300 Kilometers
300 Miles
Boundary representation is not necessarily authoritative.

MIDDLE EAST

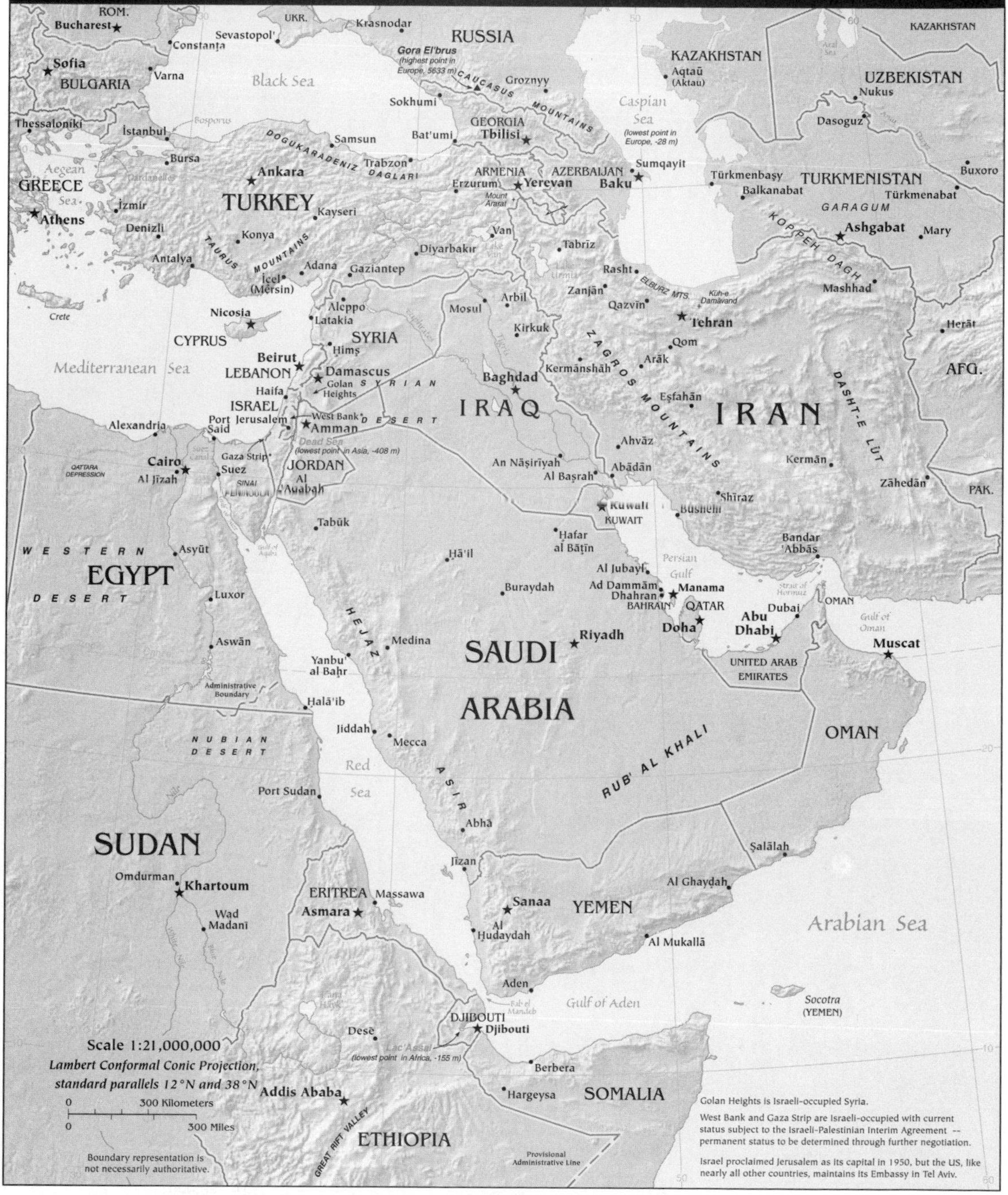
ROM.
Bucharest
Sofia
BULGARIA
Varna
Constanța
Sevastopol'
UKR.
Krasnodar
RUSSIA
Gora El'brus
(highest point in Europe, 5633 m)
CAUCASUS MOUNTAINS
Groznyy
Sokhumi
Black Sea
KAZAKHSTAN
Aqtaū
(Aktau)
Caspian Sea
(lowest point in Europe, -28 m)
KAZAKHSTAN
Aral Sea
UZBEKISTAN
Nukus
Dasoguz
Thessaloniki
İstanbul
Bosporus
Samsun
Bat'umi
GEORGIA
Tbilisi
DOGUKARADENIZ DAGLARI
Trabzon
Bursa
Dardanelles
Aegean Sea
GREECE
Athens
İzmir
Ankara
TURKEY
Kayseri
Denizli
Konya
Antalya
TAURUS MOUNTAINS
Adana
Gaziantep
İçel
(Mersin)
Crete
ARMENIA
Erzurum
Yerevan
Mount Ararat
AZERBAIJAN
Baku
Sumqayit
Van
Diyarbakır
Tabrīz
Türkmenbaşy
Balkanabat
TURKMENISTAN
Buxoro
Türkmenabat
GARAGUM
KOPPEH DAGH
Ashgabat
Mary
Mashhad
Rasht
ELBURZ MTS.
Kūh-e Damāvand
Zanjān
Qazvīn
Tehran
Qom
Arāk
Herāt
AFG.
Nicosia
CYPRUS
Aleppo
Latakia
SYRIA
Ḥimṣ
Mosul
Arbil
Kirkuk
Mediterranean Sea
Beirut
LEBANON
Damascus
Golan Heights
SYRIAN DESERT
Haifa
ISRAEL
Port Said
Jerusalem
West Bank
Amman
Baghdad
Kermānshāh
ZAGROS MOUNTAINS
Eṣfahān
IRAQ
IRAN
DASHT-E LŪT
Alexandria
Dead Sea
(lowest point in Asia, -408 m)
QATTARA DEPRESSION
Cairo
Al Jīzah
Gaza Strip
Suez
SINAI PENINSULA
JORDAN
Al 'Aqabah
An Nāṣirīyah
Al Baṣrah
Abādān
Ahvāz
Kermān
Zāhedān
PAK.
Shīrāz
Kuwait
KUWAIT
Bushehr
Tabūk
Ḥafar al Bāṭin
Bandar 'Abbās
WESTERN DESERT
Asyūt
EGYPT
Ḥā'il
Al Jubayl
Persian Gulf
Buraydah
Ad Dammām
Dhahran
Manama
BAHRAIN
QATAR
Strait of Hormuz
Dubai
OMAN
Gulf of Oman
Luxor
HEJAZ
Doha
Abu Dhabi
Riyadh
Muscat
Aswān
Medina
Yanbu' al Baḥr
SAUDI ARABIA
UNITED ARAB EMIRATES
Administrative Boundary
Ḥalā'ib
Jiddah
Mecca
NUBIAN DESERT
OMAN
RUB' AL KHALI
Red Sea
ASIR
Port Sudan
Abhā
SUDAN
Ṣalālah
Jīzān
Omdurman
Khartoum
ERITREA
Massawa
Asmara
Sanaa
YEMEN
Al Ghaydah
Wad Madanī
Al Ḥudaydah
Al Mukallā
Arabian Sea
Aden
Gulf of Aden
Bab el Mandeb
Socotra
(YEMEN)
DJIBOUTI
Djibouti
Dese
Lac 'Assal
(lowest point in Africa, -155 m)
Berbera
Scale 1:21,000,000
Lambert Conformal Conic Projection, standard parallels 12°N and 38°N
0 300 Kilometers
0 300 Miles
Addis Ababa
Hargeysa
SOMALIA
GREAT RIFT VALLEY
ETHIOPIA
Boundary representation is not necessarily authoritative.
Provisional Administrative Line
Golan Heights is Israeli-occupied Syria.
West Bank and Gaza Strip are Israeli-occupied with current status subject to the Israeli-Palestinian Interim Agreement -- permanent status to be determined through further negotiation.
Israel proclaimed Jerusalem as its capital in 1950, but the US, like nearly all other countries, maintains its Embassy in Tel Aviv.

NORTH AMERICA

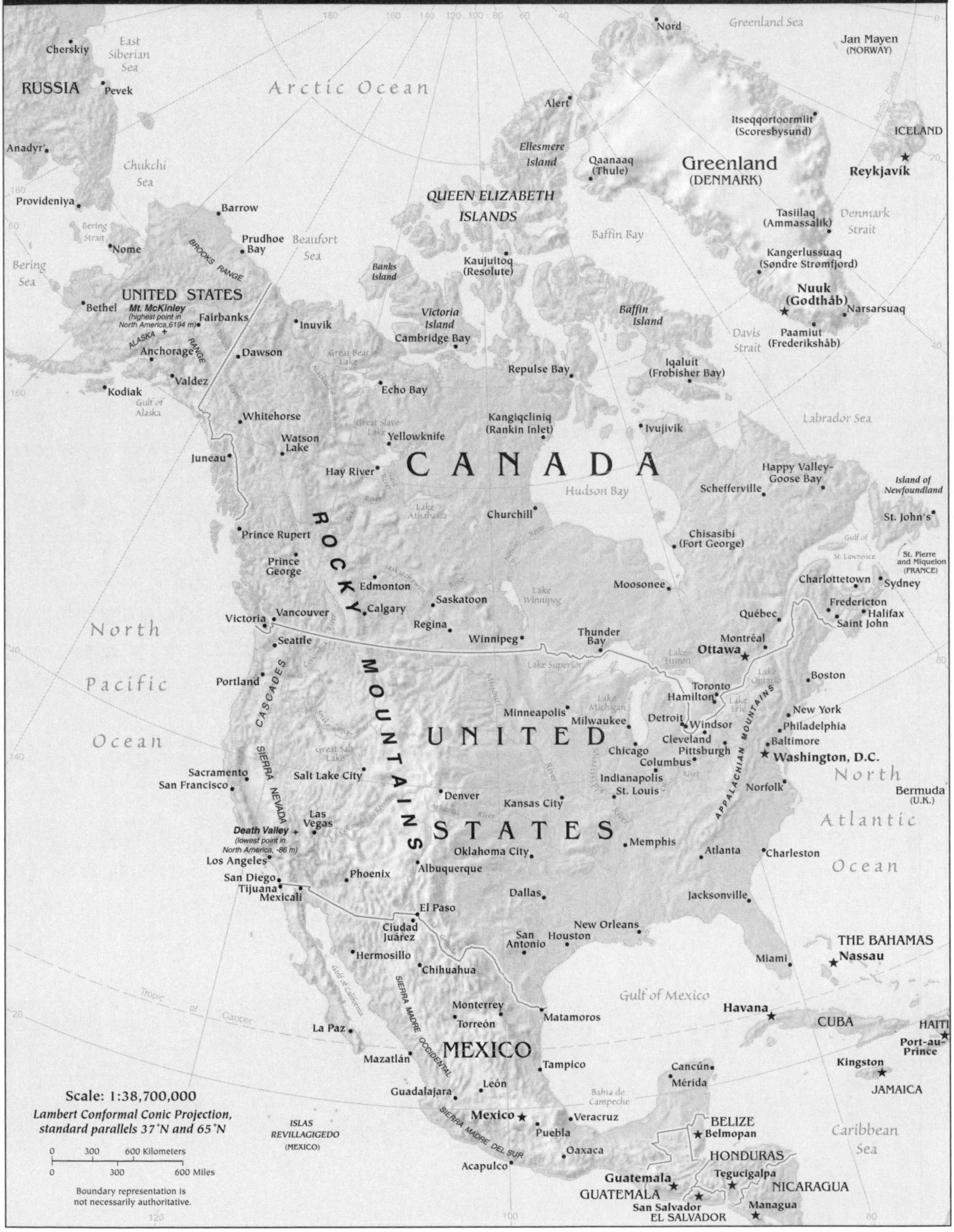

OCEANIA

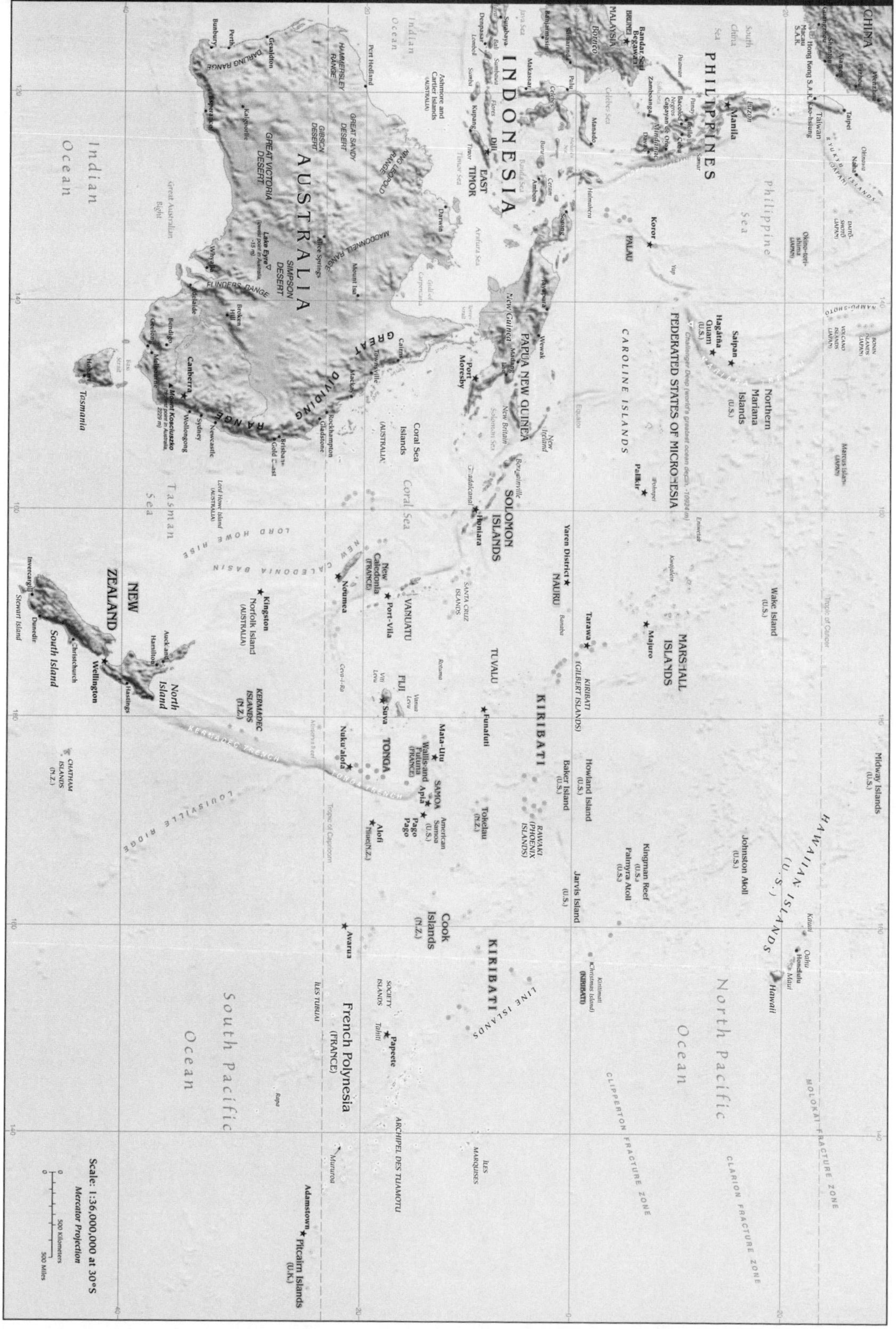
CHINA
Taiwan
Taipei
Hong Kong S.A.R.
Macau S.A.R.
PHILIPPINES
Manila
Philippine Sea
South China Sea
Celebes Sea
MALAYSIA
Bandar Seri Begawan
BRUNEI
Borneo
INDONESIA
Java Sea
Surabaya
Denpasar
Makassar
Kupang
Dili
EAST TIMOR
Timor Sea
Banda Sea
Ambon
Arafura Sea
Manado
PALAU
Koror
Yap
FEDERATED STATES OF MICRONESIA
CAROLINE ISLANDS
Northern Mariana Islands (U.S.)
Saipan
Hagåtña
Guam (U.S.)
Palikir
PAPUA NEW GUINEA
Port Moresby
Wewak
New Guinea
New Britain
New Ireland
Bougainville
SOLOMON ISLANDS
Honiara
Guadalcanal
Coral Sea
Coral Sea Islands (AUSTRALIA)
AUSTRALIA
Darwin
Cairns
Townsville
Mackay
Rockhampton
Gladstone
Brisbane
Gold Coast
Newcastle
Sydney
Wollongong
Canberra
Mount Kosciuszko
Melbourne
Geelong
Bendigo
Adelaide
Whyalla
Broken Hill
Perth
Bunbury
Geraldton
Kalgoorlie
Esperance
Port Hedland
Alice Springs
Mount Isa
Lake Eyre
GREAT SANDY DESERT
GIBSON DESERT
GREAT VICTORIA DESERT
SIMPSON DESERT
GREAT DIVIDING RANGE
FLINDERS RANGE
MACDONNELL RANGES
DARLING RANGE
HAMERSLEY RANGE
KING LEOPOLD RANGE
Great Australian Bight
Ashmore and Cartier Islands (AUSTRALIA)
Indian Ocean
Tasmania
Hobart
Tasman Sea
Lord Howe Island (AUSTRALIA)
LORD HOWE RISE
NEW CALEDONIA BASIN
NEW ZEALAND
North Island
South Island
Auckland
Hamilton
Wellington
Hastings
Christchurch
Dunedin
Invercargill
Stewart Island
Norfolk Island (AUSTRALIA)
Kingston
New Caledonia (FRANCE)
Nouméa
VANUATU
Port-Vila
SANTA CRUZ ISLANDS
NAURU
Yaren District
TUVALU
Funafuti
FIJI
Suva
Viti Levu
Vanua Levu
Rotuma
TONGA
Nuku'alofa
KERMADEC ISLANDS (N.Z.)
KERMADEC TRENCH
TONGA TRENCH
LOUISVILLE RIDGE
CHATHAM ISLANDS (N.Z.)
Wallis and Futuna (FRANCE)
Mata-Utu
SAMOA
Apia
American Samoa (U.S.)
Pago Pago
Tokelau (N.Z.)
Niue (N.Z.)
Alofi
KIRIBATI
Tarawa
KIRIBATI (GILBERT ISLANDS)
RAWAKI (PHOENIX ISLANDS)
MARSHALL ISLANDS
Majuro
Wake Island (U.S.)
Howland Island (U.S.)
Baker Island (U.S.)
Jarvis Island (U.S.)
Kingman Reef (U.S.)
Palmyra Atoll (U.S.)
Johnston Atoll (U.S.)
Midway Islands (U.S.)
HAWAIIAN ISLANDS (U.S.)
Hawaii
Honolulu
Kauai
Oahu
Maui
LINE ISLANDS
Cook Islands (N.Z.)
Avarua
French Polynesia (FRANCE)
Papeete
Tahiti
SOCIETY ISLANDS
ÎLES TUBUAI
ARCHIPEL DES TUAMOTU
ÎLES MARQUISES
Pitcairn Islands (U.K.)
Adamstown
North Pacific Ocean
South Pacific Ocean
Tropic of Cancer
Tropic of Capricorn
Equator
CLIPPERTON FRACTURE ZONE
CLARION FRACTURE ZONE
MOLOKAI FRACTURE ZONE
Scale: 1:36,000,000 at 30°S
Mercator Projection
500 Kilometers
500 Miles

PHYSICAL MAP OF THE WORLD

POLITICAL MAP OF THE WORLD

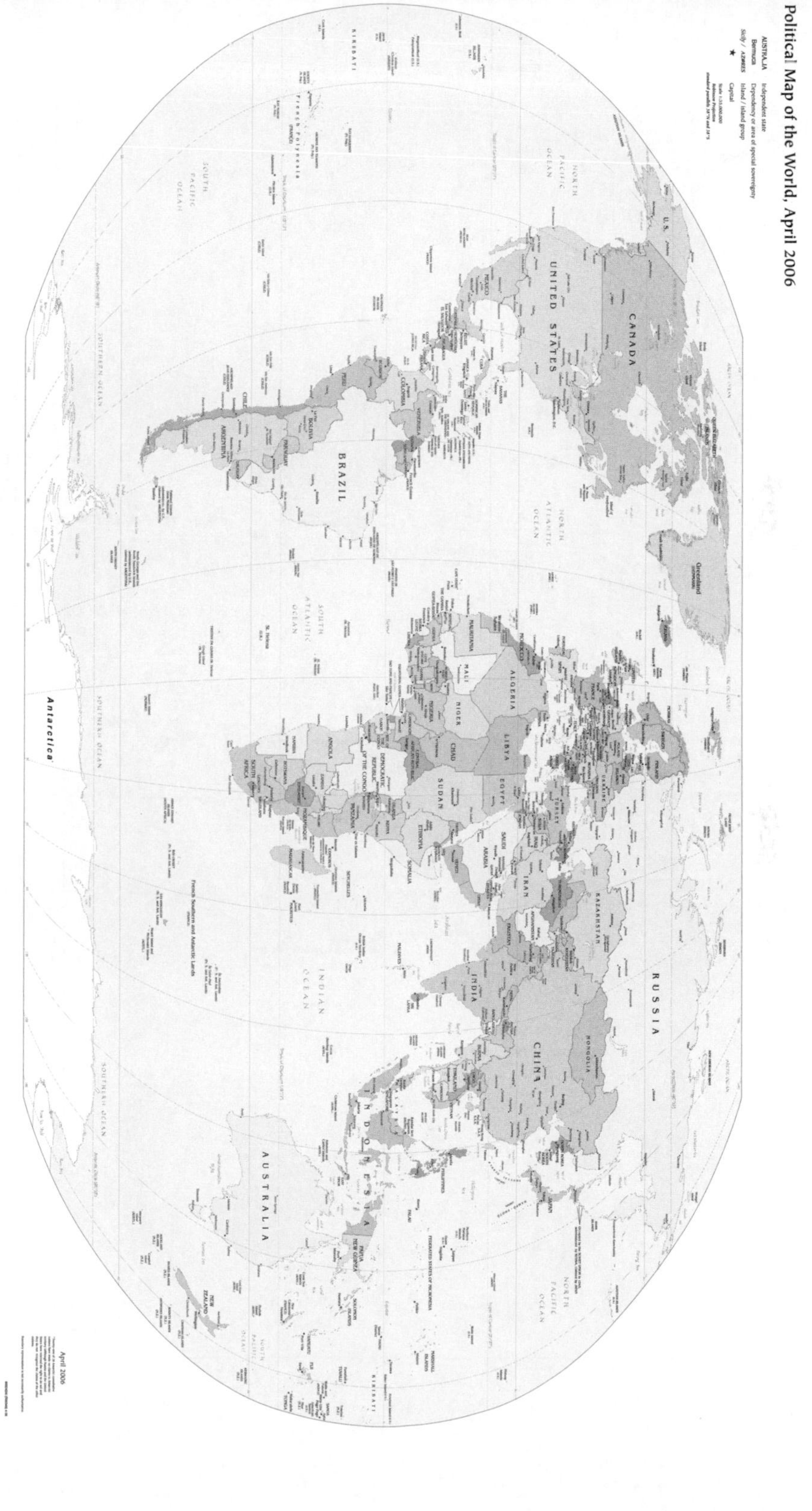

SOUTH AMERICA

Caribbean Sea
HONDURAS
Tegucigalpa
Isla de San Andrés (COLOMBIA)
NICARAGUA
Managua
San José
COSTA RICA
Panama
PANAMA
Aruba (NETH.)
Netherlands Antilles (NETH.)
Martinique (FRANCE)
ST. LUCIA
ST. VINCENT AND THE GRENADINES
GRENADA
BARBADOS
Barranquilla
Cartagena
Maracaibo
Caracas
Valencia
Barquisimeto
Port-of-Spain
TRINIDAD AND TOBAGO
Cúcuta
San Cristóbal
Ciudad Guayana
Río Orinoco
VENEZUELA
Georgetown
GUYANA
Paramaribo
Cayenne
SURINAME
French Guiana (FRANCE)
North Atlantic Ocean
Medellín
Bogotá
A N D E S
COLOMBIA
Cali
G U I A N A
H I G H L A N D S
Boa Vista
Isla de Malpelo (COLOMBIA)
Equator
Quito
ECUADOR
Guayaquil
Macapá
A M A Z O N
Río Negro
Amazon
Manaus
Santarém
Belém
São Luís
Fortaleza
Teresina
Iquitos
Piura
B A S I N
Rio Madeira
Xingu
Tocantins
Natal
Recife
Maceió
Trujillo
Huánuco
Rio Branco
Pôrto Velho
B R A Z I L
PERU
Lima
Cusco
Lake Titicaca
MATO GROSSO PLATEAU
B R A Z I L I A N
H I G H L A N D S
Salvador
South Pacific Ocean
Trinidad
La Paz
BOLIVIA
Cuiabá
Brasília
Goiânia
Arequipa
Cochabamba
Santa Cruz
ALTIPLANO
Sucre
Potosí
Arica
Uberlândia
Belo Horizonte
Campo Grande
Iquique
Vitória
ATACAMA DESERT
PARAGUAY
Rio de Janeiro
Antofagasta
Tropic of Capricorn
Salta
Asunción
São Paulo
Santos
San Miguel de Tucumán
Curitiba
Resistencia
Florianópolis
Isla San Ambrosio (CHILE)
Isla San Félix (CHILE)
CHILE
Pôrto Alegre
Cerro Aconcagua
(highest point in South America, 6962 m)
Córdoba
Santa Fe
Salto
Mendoza
Rosario
URUGUAY
Valparaíso
ARCHIPIÉLAGO JUAN FERNÁNDEZ (CHILE)
Santiago
P A M P A S
Buenos Aires
La Plata
Montevideo
South Atlantic Ocean
Concepción
ARGENTINA
Bahía Blanca
Mar del Plata
Puerto Montt
San Carlos de Bariloche
P A T A G O N I A
Comodoro Rivadavia
Laguna del Carbón
(lowest point in South America and the Western Hemisphere, -105 m)
Scale 1:35,000,000
Azimuthal Equal-Area Projection
0
500 Kilometers
0
500 Miles
Boundary representation is not necessarily authoritative.
Río Gallegos
Strait of Magellan
Stanley
Falkland Islands (Islas Malvinas)
(administered by U.K., claimed by ARGENTINA)
South Georgia and the South Sandwich Islands
(administered by U.K., claimed by ARGENTINA)
Punta Arenas
Ushuaia
Cape Horn
80
60
40
0
20
40
100
80
60
40
20

SOUTHEAST ASIA

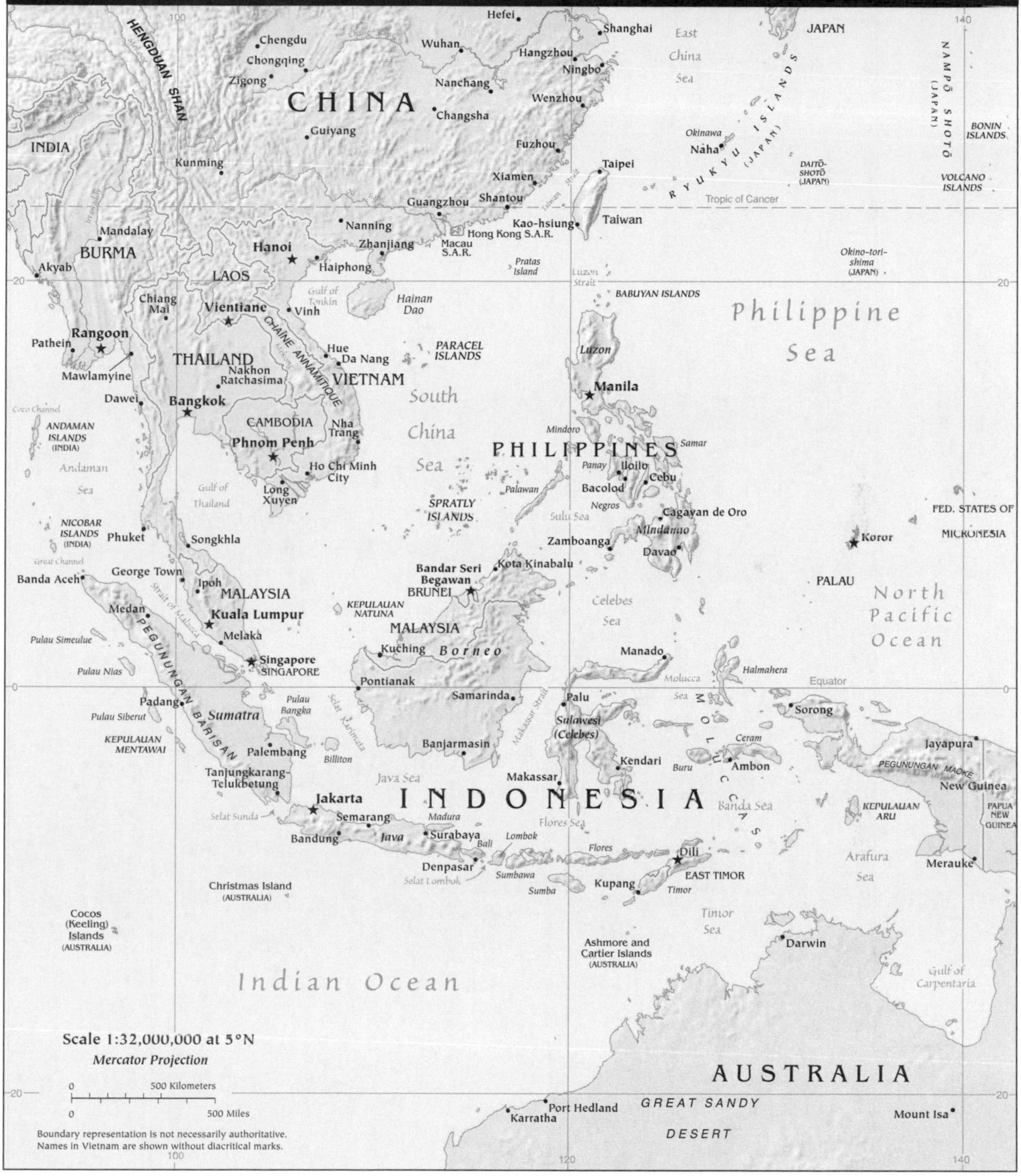

STANDARD TIME ZONES OF THE WORLD

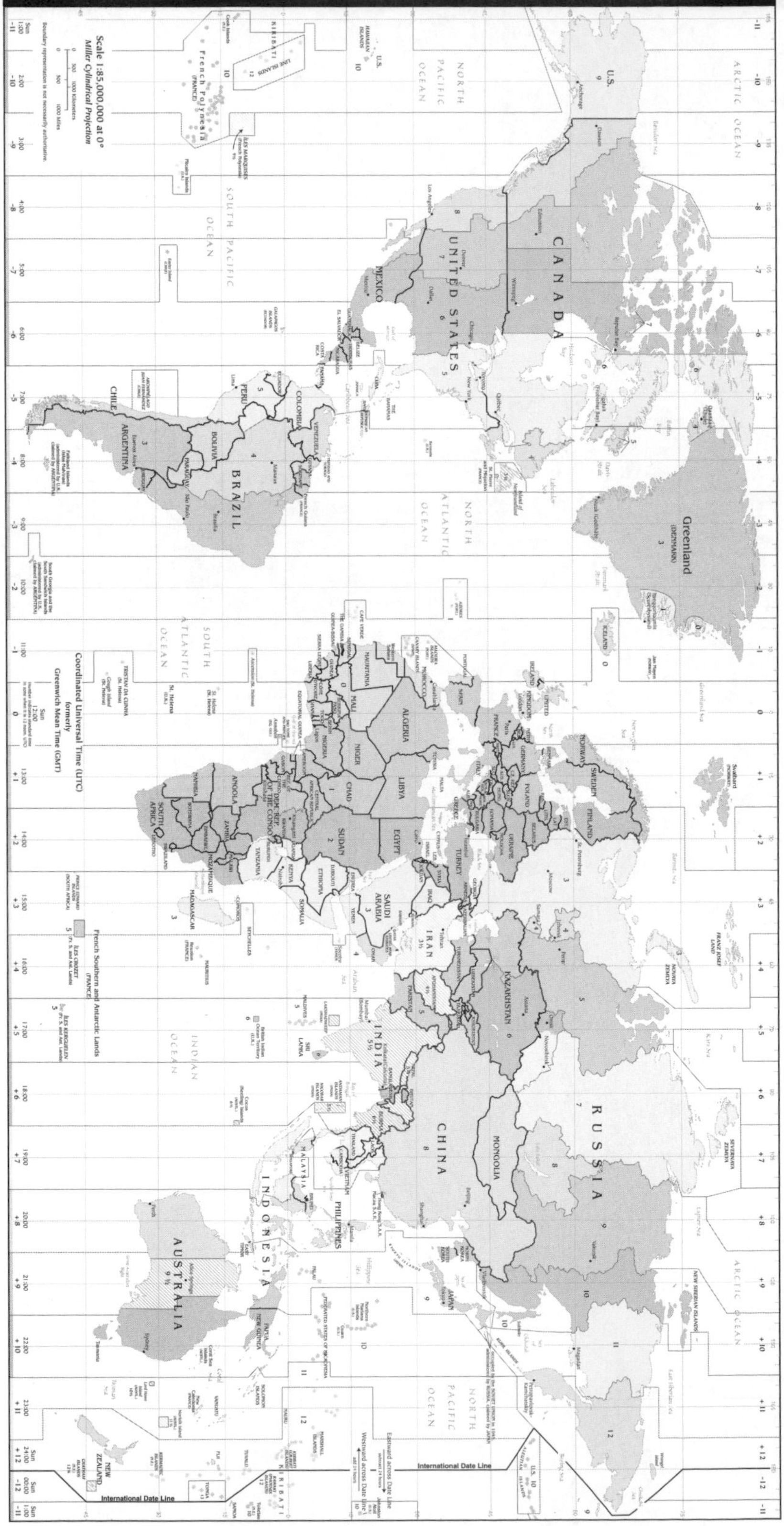

UNITED STATES

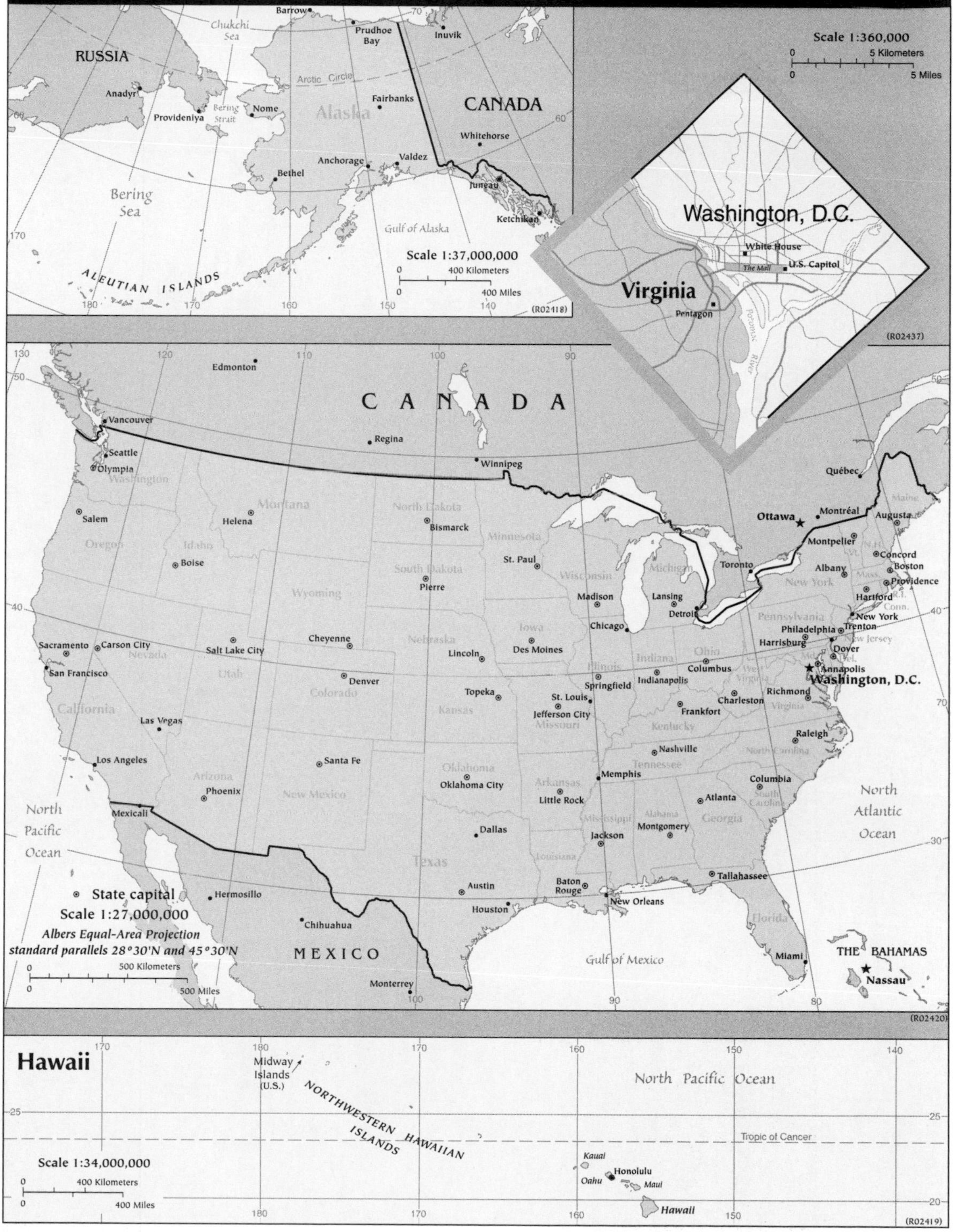